RAND McNALLY

GOODE'S
WORLD ATLAS

Howard Veregin, Ph.D., Editor

Editorial Advisory Board

Byron Augustin, D.A., Texas State University-San Marcos

Joshua Comenetz, Ph.D., University of Florida

Francis Galgano, Ph.D., United States Military Academy

Sallie A. Marston, Ph.D., University of Arizona

Virginia Thompson, Ph.D., Towson University

21ST Edition

CONTENTS

Goode's World Atlas

Copyright ©2005 by Rand McNally & Company; 2nd Printing, Revised

Copyright ©1922, 1923, 1932, 1933, 1937, 1939, 1943, 1946, 1949, 1954, 1957, 1960, 1964, 1970, 1974, 1978, 1982, 1986, 1990, 1995, 2000 by Rand McNally & Company. All rights reserved.

Formerly *Goode's School Atlas*

Made in U.S.A.

Library of Congress Catalog Card Number 99-38535

Cover Photo: Machu Picchu, Peru

The 21st Edition of *Goode's World Atlas*

Goode's World Atlas was first published by Rand McNally in 1923 as *Goode's School Atlas*, under the editorship of J. Paul Goode, a distinguished Professor of Geography at the University of Chicago. The atlas was designed for use in schools and universities, with the choice of topics and materials reflecting Goode's thirty years of experience as a geographic educator.

Many of the features of that first atlas continue to be relevant today, including its basic organization and layout, an emphasis on map accuracy and legibility, and the admixture of maps of different types and scales to facilitate interpretation of geographic phenomena. One of the more significant innovations of the 1923 edition was the introduction of an "interrupted" map of the world, which featured large discontinuities in oceanic areas in order to reduce map distortion of continental landmasses. Goode developed this map to allow geographic phenomena to be portrayed more accurately. This map, and its descendants, have given *Goode's World Atlas* a distinctive look for more than eighty years.

The 21st Edition boasts a number of innovative features of its own:

- The world, continental, and regional population density maps have been re-created using LandScan, a digital population database developed using satellite and computer-mapping technology.
- A number of new world thematic maps have been added, including HIV Infection, Military Power, Women's Rights, and Food Aid.
- A global telecommunications map has been added, showing the submarine fiber-optic network, and worldwide internet and telephone usage.
- The world cartogram series has been redrafted to make the cartograms easier to interpret.
- The United States demographic map series has been expanded from sixteen to twenty-four maps to provide additional coverage of key census variables.
- New graphs have been added to many of the maps, showing important statistical information, trends over time, and relationships between variables.

Other maps and graphs have been updated using the most current available data in accordance with the high standards and quality that have always been a defining feature of this atlas. This edition also retains many of the "classic" maps with which longtime users of the atlas will be familiar, including Natural Vegetation (A. W. Küchler), Landforms (Richard E. Murphy), Physiography (Erwin Raisz), Climatic Regions (Glenn T. Trewartha), Agricultural Regions (Derwent Whittlesey), and Languages (Bogdan Zaborski).

Putting together a complex atlas requires the dedication of a large and diverse team. The contributions of the following individuals helped make this 21st Edition a success:

Robert Argersinger, Gregory Babiak, Julie Bastian, Karen Cuiskelly, John Davies, Dave Duncan, Marzee Eckhoff, Justin Griffin, Felix Lopez, Nina Lusterman, Chuck MacDonald, Rob Merrill, Angela Mrotek, Darren Raffel, Pat Riley, Amy Ruggles, David Simmons, Andrew Skinner, Raymond Tobiaski, Tom Vitacco, Yanyan Zhang.

The 21st Edition benefited greatly from the creative efforts of Susan Hudson, head of Rand McNally's geographical research unit.

Important contributions were also made by the members of the Editorial Advisory Board:

Byron Augustin, D.A., Texas State University-San Marcos; Joshua Comenetz, Ph.D., University of Florida; Francis Galgano, Ph.D., United States Military Academy; Sallie A. Marston, Ph.D., University of Arizona; and Virginia Thompson, Ph.D., Towson University.

With the 21st Edition, *Goode's World Atlas* is well into its ninth consecutive decade of publication. While the atlas has changed with the times, it continues to be the same accurate and reliable educational resource that J. Paul Goode originally intended. We at Rand McNally remain committed to providing the most trusted tools to help you discover, map, and navigate your world.

Howard Veregin

Howard Veregin, Ph.D., Editor
Skokie, Illinois

Introduction

Basic Earth Properties

The subject matter of **geography** includes people, landforms, climate, and all the other physical and human phenomena that make up the earth's environments and give unique character to different places. Geographers construct maps to visualize the **spatial distributions** of these phenomena: that is, how the phenomena vary over geographic space. Maps help geographers understand and explain phenomena and their interactions.

To better understand how maps portray geographic distributions, it is helpful to have an understanding of the basic properties of the earth.

The earth is essentially **spherical** in shape. Two basic reference points — the **North and South Poles** — mark the locations of the earth's axis of rotation. Equidistant between the two poles and encircling the earth is the **equator**. The equator divides the earth into two halves, called the **northern and southern hemispheres**. (See the figures to the right.)

Latitude and longitude are used to identify the locations of features on the earth's surface. They are measured in degrees, minutes and seconds. There are 60 minutes in a degree and 60 seconds in a minute. Latitude is the angle north or south of the equator. The symbols °, ', and " represent degrees, minutes and seconds, respectively. The N means north of the equator. For latitudes south of the equator, S is used. For example, the Rand McNally head office in Skokie, Illinois, is located at 42°1'51" N. The minimum latitude of 0° occurs at the equator. The maximum latitudes of 90° N and 90° S occur at the North and South Poles.

A **line of latitude** is a line connecting all points on the earth having the same latitude. Lines of latitude are also called **parallels**, as they run parallel to each other. Two parallels of special importance are the **Tropic of Cancer** and the **Tropic of Capricorn**, at approximately 23°30' N and S respectively. This angle coincides with the inclination of the earth's axis relative to its orbital plane around the sun. These tropics are the lines of latitude where the noon sun is directly overhead on the solstices. (See figure on page 66.) Two other important parallels are the **Arctic Circle** and the **Antarctic Circle**, at approximately 66°30' N and S respectively. These lines mark the most northerly and southerly points at which the sun can be seen on the solstices.

While latitude measures locations in a north-south direction, longitude measures them east-west. Longitude is the angle east or west of the **Prime Meridian**. A **meridian** is a line of longitude, a straight line extending from the North Pole to the South Pole. The Prime Meridian is the meridian passing through the Royal Observatory in Greenwich, England. For this reason the Prime Meridian is sometimes referred to as the **Greenwich Meridian**. This location for the Prime Meridian was adopted at the International Meridian Conference in Washington, D.C., in 1884.

Like latitude, longitude is measured in degrees, minutes, and seconds. For example, the Rand McNally head office is located at 87°43'6" W. The qualifiers E and W indicate whether a location is east or west of the Greenwich Meridian. Longitude ranges from 0° at Greenwich to 180° E or W. The meridian at 180° E is the same as the meridian at 180° W. This meridian, together with the Greenwich Meridian, divides the earth into **eastern and western hemispheres**.

Any circle that divides the earth into equal hemispheres is called a **great circle**. The equator is an example. The shortest distance between any two points on the earth is along a great circle. Other circles, including all other lines of latitude, are called **small circles**. Small circles divide the earth into two unequal pieces.

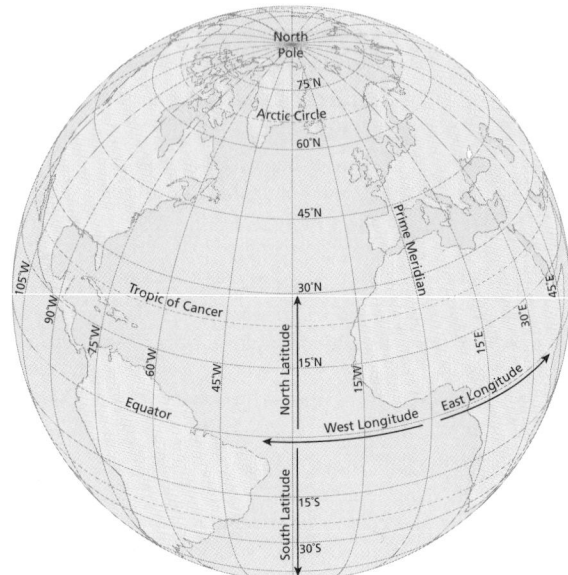

View of earth centered on 30° N, 30° W

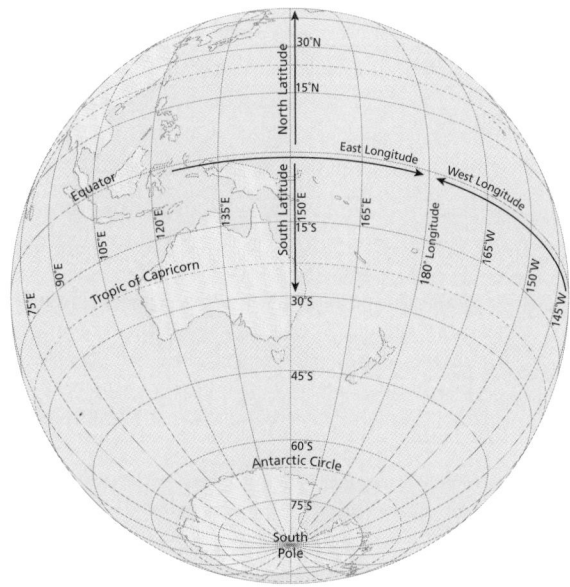

View of earth centered on 30° S, 150° E

The Geographic Grid

The grid of lines of latitude and longitude is known as the **geographic grid**. The following are some important characteristics of the grid.

All lines of longitude are equal in length and meet at the North and South Poles. These lines are called meridians.

All lines of latitude are parallel and equally spaced along meridians. These lines are called parallels.

The length of parallels increases with distance from the poles. For example, the length of the parallel at 60° latitude is one-half the length of the equator.

Meridians get closer together with increasing distance from the equator, and finally converge at the poles.

Parallels and meridians meet at right angles.

Map Scale

To use maps effectively it is important to have a basic understanding of map scale.

Map scale is defined as the ratio of distance on the map to distance on the earth's surface. For example, if a map shows two towns as separated by a distance of 1 inch, and these towns are actually 1 mile apart, then the scale of the map is 1 inch to 1 mile.

The statement "1 inch to 1 mile" is called a **verbal scale**. Verbal scales are simple and intuitive, but a drawback is that they are tied to the specific set of map and real-world units in the numerator and denominator of the ratio. This makes it difficult to compare the scales of different maps.

A more flexible way of expressing scale is as a **representative fraction**. In this case, both the numerator and denominator are converted to the same unit of measurement. For example, since there are 63,360 inches in a mile, the verbal scale "1 inch to 1 mile" can be expressed as the representative fraction 1:63,360. This means that 1 inch on the map represents 63,360 inches on the earth's surface. The advantage of the representative fraction is that it applies to any linear unit of measurement, including inches, feet, miles, meters, and kilometers.

Map scale can also be represented in graphical form. Many maps contain a **graphic scale** (or **bar scale**) showing real-world units such as miles or kilometers. The bar scale is usually subdivided to allow easy calculation of distance on the map.

Map scale has a significant effect on the amount of detail that can be portrayed on a map. This concept is illustrated here using a series of maps of the Washington, D.C., area. (See the figures to the right.) The scales of these maps range from 1:40,000,000 (top map) to 1:4,000,000 (center map) to 1:25,000 (bottom map). The top map has the **smallest scale** of the three maps, and the bottom map has the **largest scale**.

Note that as scale increases, the area of the earth's surface covered by the map decreases. The smallest-scale map covers thousands of square miles, while the largest-scale map covers only a few square miles within the city of Washington. This means that a given feature on the earth's surface will appear larger as map scale increases. On the smallest-scale map, Washington is represented by a small dot. As scale increases the dot becomes an orange shape representing the built-up area of Washington. At the largest scale Washington is so large that only a portion of it fits on the map.

Because small-scale maps cover such a large area, only the largest and most important features can be shown, such as large cities, major rivers and lakes, and international boundaries. In contrast, large-scale maps contain relatively small features, such as city streets, buildings, parks, and monuments.

Small-scale maps depict features in a more simplified manner than large-scale maps. As map scale decreases, the shapes of rivers and other features must be simplified to allow them to be depicted at a highly reduced size. This simplification process is known as **map generalization**.

Maps in *Goode's World Atlas* have a wide range of scales. The smallest scales are used for the world thematic map series, where scales range from approximately 1:200,000,000 to 1:75,000,000. Reference map scales range from a minimum of 1:100,000,000 for world maps to a maximum of 1:1,000,000 for city maps. Most reference maps are regional views with a scale of 1:4,000,000.

1:40,000,000 scale

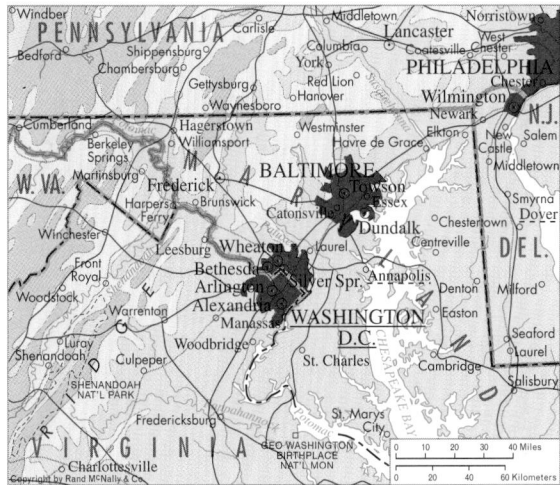

1:4,000,000 scale

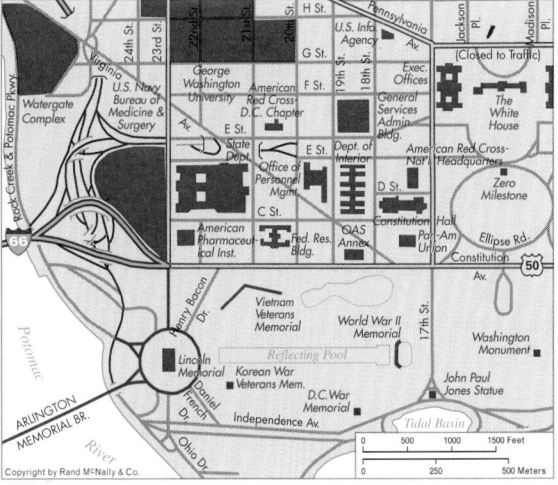

1:25,000 scale

Map Projections

Map projections influence the appearance of features on the map and the ability to interpret geographic phenomena.

A **map projection** is a geometric representation of the earth's surface on a flat or plane surface. Since the earth's surface is curved, a map projection is needed to produce any flat map, whether a page in this atlas or a computer-generated map of driving directions on www.randmcnally.com. Hundreds of projections have been developed since the dawn of mapmaking. A limitation of all projections is that they distort some geometric properties of the earth, such as shape, area, distance, or direction. However, certain properties are preserved on some projections.

If shape is preserved, the projection is called **conformal**. On conformal projections the shapes of features agree with the shapes these features have on the earth. A limitation of conformal projections is that they necessarily distort area, sometimes severely.

Equal-area projections preserve area. On equal area projections the areas of features correspond to their areas on the earth. To achieve this effect, equal-area projections distort shape.

Some projections preserve neither shape nor area, but instead balance shape and area distortion to create an aesthetically-pleasing result. These are often referred to as **compromise** projections.

Distance is preserved on **equidistant** projections, but this can only be achieved selectively, such as along specific meridians or parallels. No projection correctly preserves distance in all directions at all locations. As a result, the stated scale of a map may be accurate for only a limited set of locations. This problem is especially acute for small-scale maps covering large areas.

The projection selected for a particular map depends on the relative importance of different types of distortion, which often depends on the purpose of the map. For example, world maps showing phenomena that vary with area, such as population density or the distribution of agricultural crops, often use an equal-area projection to give an accurate depiction of the importance of each region.

Map projections are created using mathematical procedures. To illustrate the general principles of projections without using mathematics, we can view a projection as the geometric transfer of information from a globe to a flat projection surface, such as a sheet of paper. If we allow the paper to be rolled in different ways, we can derive three basic types of map projections: **cylindrical, conic,** and **azimuthal**. (See the figures to the right.)

For cylindrical projections, the sheet of paper is rolled into a tube and wrapped around the globe so that it is **tangent** (touching) along the equator. Information from the globe is transferred to the tube, and the tube is then unrolled to produce the final flat map.

Conic projections use a cone rather than a cylinder. The figure shows the cone tangent to the earth along a line of latitude with the apex of the cone over the pole. The line of tangency is called the **standard parallel** of the projection.

Azimuthal projections use a flat projection surface that is tangent to the globe at a single point, such as one of the poles.

The figures show the **normal orientation** of each type of surface relative to the globe. The **transverse orientation** is produced when the surface is rotated 90 degrees from normal. For azimuthal projections this orientation is usually called **equatorial** rather than transverse. An **oblique orientation** is created if the projection surface is oriented at an angle between normal and transverse. In general, map distortion increases with distance away from the point or line of tangency. This is why the normal orientations of the cylindrical, conic, and azimuthal projections are often used for mapping equatorial, mid-latitude, and polar regions, respectively.

The projection surface model is a visual tool useful for illustrating how information from the globe can be projected to the map. However, each of the three projection surfaces actually represents scores of individual projections. There are, for example, many projections with the term "cylindrical" in the name, each of which has the same basic rectangular shape, but different spacings of parallels and meridians. The projection surface model does not account for the numerous mathematical details that differentiate one cylindrical, conic, or azimuthal projection from another.

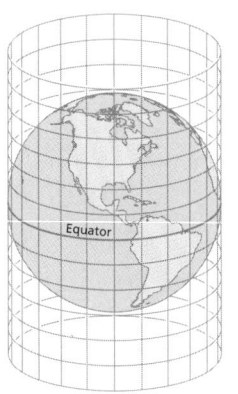
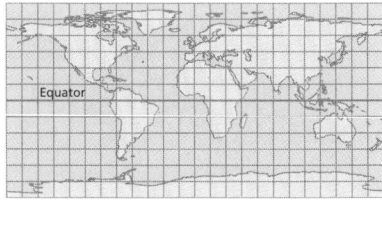

Cylindrical Projection

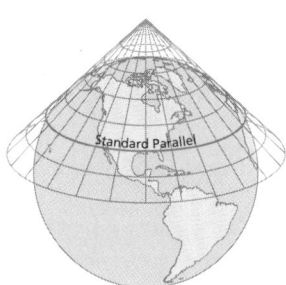
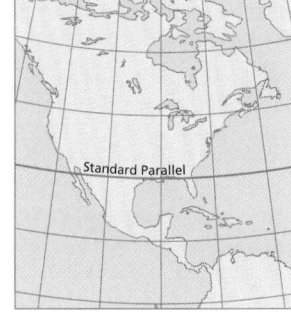

Conic Projection

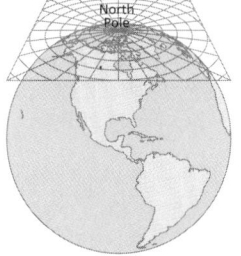

Azimuthal Projection

Map Projections Used in *Goode's World Atlas*

Of the hundreds of projections that have been developed, only a fraction are in everyday use. The main projections used in *Goode's World Atlas* are described below.

Simple Conic

Type: Conic   **Conformal:** No   **Equal-area:** No

Notes: Shape and area distortion on the Simple Conic projection are relatively low, even though the projection is neither conformal nor equal-area. The origins of the Simple Conic can be traced back nearly two thousand years, with the modern form of the projection dating to the 18th century.

Uses in *Goode's World Atlas*: Larger-scale reference maps of North America, Europe, Asia, and other regions.

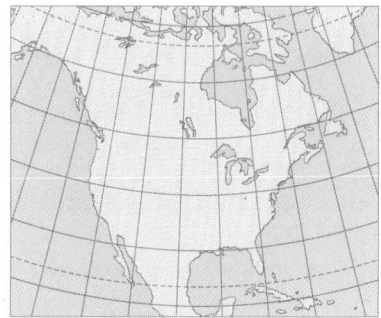

Simple Conic Projection

Lambert Conformal Conic

Type: Conic   **Conformal:** Yes   **Equal-area:** No

Notes: On the Lambert Conformal Conic projection, spacing between parallels increases with distance away from the standard parallel, which allows the property of shape to be preserved. The projection is named after Johann Lambert, an 18th century mathematician who developed some of the most important projections in use today. It became widely used in the United States in the 20th century following its adoption for many statewide mapping programs.

Uses in *Goode's World Atlas*: Thematic maps of the United States and Canada, and reference maps of parts of Asia.

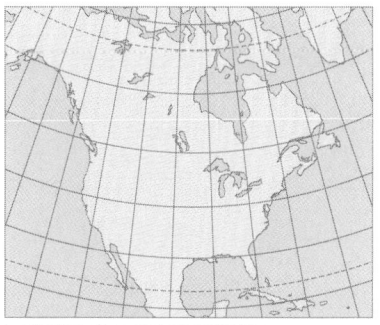

Lambert Conformal Conic Projection

Albers Equal-Area Conic

Type: Conic   **Conformal:** No   **Equal-area:** Yes

Notes: On the Albers Equal-Area Conic projection, spacing between parallels decreases with distance away from the standard parallel, which allows the property of area to be preserved. The projection is named after Heinrich Albers, who developed it in 1805. It became widely used in the 20th century, when the United States Coast and Geodetic Survey made it a standard for equal area maps of the United States.

Uses in *Goode's World Atlas*: Thematic maps of North America and Asia.

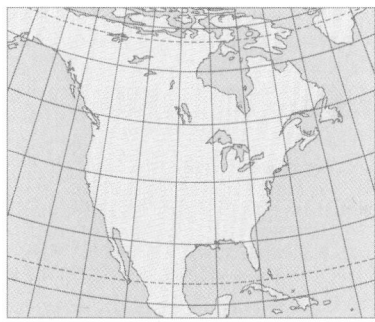

Albers Equal-Area Conic Projection

Polyconic

Type: Conic   **Conformal:** No   **Equal-area:** No

Notes: The term polyconic — literally "many-cones" — refers to the fact that this projection is an assemblage of different cones, each tangent at a different line of latitude. In contrast to many other conic projections, parallels are not concentric, and meridians are curved rather than straight. The Polyconic was first proposed by Ferdinand Hassler, who became Head of the United States Survey of the Coast (later renamed the Coast and Geodetic Survey) in 1807. The United States Geological Survey used this projection exclusively for large-scale topographic maps until the mid-20th century.

Uses in *Goode's World Atlas*: Reference maps of North America and Asia.

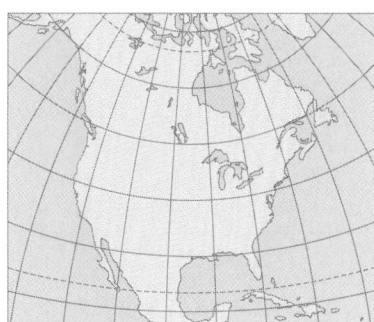

Polyconic Projection

Lambert Azimuthal Equal-Area

Type: Azimuthal   **Conformal:** No   **Equal-area:** Yes

Notes: This projection (another named after Johann Lambert) is useful for mapping large regions, as area is correctly preserved while shape distortion is relatively low. All orientations — polar, equatorial, and oblique — are common.

Uses in *Goode's World Atlas*: Thematic and reference maps of North and South America, Asia, Africa, Australia, and polar regions.

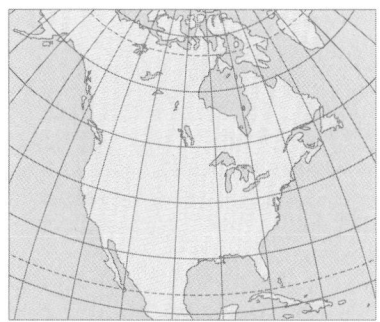

Lambert Azimuthal Equal-Area Projection

Miller Cylindrical

Type: Cylindrical   **Conformal:** No   **Equal-area:** No

Notes: This projection is useful for showing the entire earth in a simple rectangular form. However, polar areas exhibit significant exaggeration of area, a problem common to many cylindrical projections. The projection is named after Osborn Miller, Director of the American Geographical Society, who developed it in 1942 as a compromise projection that is neither conformal nor equal-area.

Uses in *Goode's World Atlas*: World climate and time zone maps.

Sinusoidal

Type: Pseudocylindrical   **Conformal:** No   **Equal-area:** Yes

Notes: The straight, evenly spaced parallels on this projection resemble the parallels on cylindrical projections. Unlike cylindrical projections, however, meridians are curved and converge at the poles. This causes significant shape distortion in polar regions. The Sinusoidal is the oldest-known pseudocylindrical projection, dating to the 16th century.

Uses in *Goode's World Atlas*: Reference maps of equatorial regions.

Mollweide

Type: Pseudocylindrical   **Conformal:** No   **Equal-area:** Yes

Notes: The Mollweide (or Homolographic) projection resembles the Sinusoidal but has less shape distortion in polar areas due to its elliptical (or oval) form. One of several pseudocylindrical projections developed in the 19th century, it is named after Karl Mollweide, an astronomer and mathematician.

Uses in *Goode's World Atlas*: Oceanic reference maps.

Goode's Interrupted Homolosine

Type: Pseudocylindrical   **Conformal:** No   **Equal-area:** Yes

Notes: This projection is a fusion of the Sinusoidal between 40°44'N and S, and the Mollweide between these parallels and the poles. The unique appearance of the projection is due to the introduction of discontinuities in oceanic regions, the goal of which is to reduce distortion for continental landmasses. A condensed version of the projection also exists in which the Atlantic Ocean is compressed in an east-west direction. This modification helps maximize the scale of the map on the page. The Interrupted Homolosine projection is named after J. Paul Goode of the University of Chicago, who developed it in 1923. Goode was an advocate of interrupted projections and, as editor of *Goode's School Atlas*, promoted their use in education.

Uses in *Goode's World Atlas*: Small-scale world thematic and reference maps. Both condensed and non-condensed forms are used. An uninterrupted example is used for the Pacific Ocean map.

Robinson

Type: Pseudocylindrical   **Conformal:** No   **Equal-area:** No

Notes: This projection resembles the Mollweide except that polar regions are flattened and stretched out. While it is neither conformal nor equal-area, both shape and area distortion are relatively low. The projection was developed in 1963 by Arthur Robinson of the University of Wisconsin, at the request of Rand McNally.

Uses in *Goode's World Atlas*: World maps where the interrupted nature of Goode's Homolosine would be inappropriate, such as the World Oceanic Environments map.

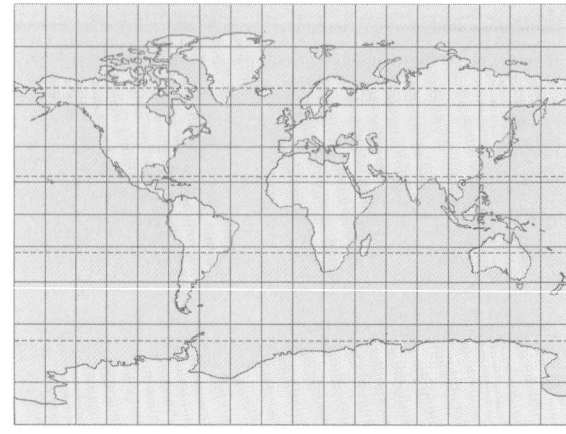

Miller Cylindrical Projection

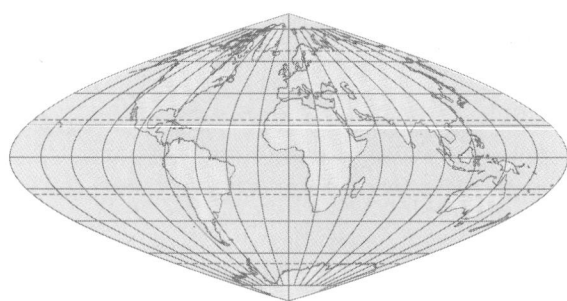

Sinusoidal Projection

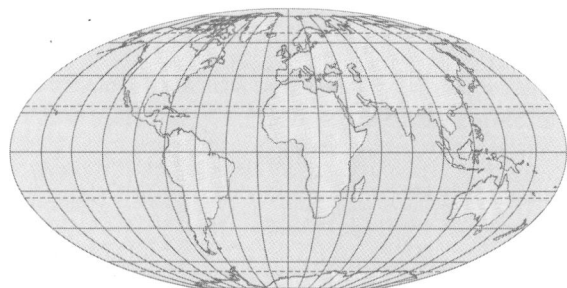

Mollweide Projection

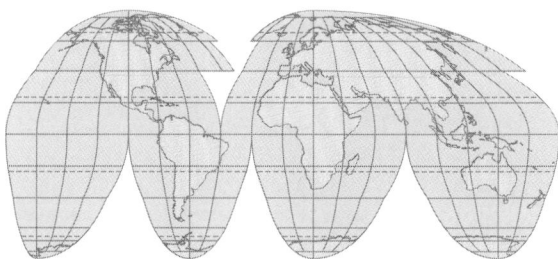

Goode's Interrupted Homolosine Projection

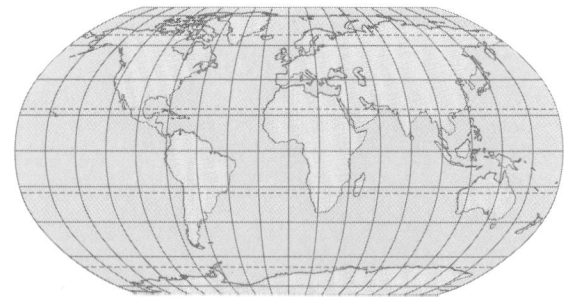

Robinson Projection

Thematic Maps in *Goode's World Atlas*

Thematic maps depict a single "theme" such as population density, agricultural productivity, or annual precipitation. The selected theme is presented on a base of locational information, such as coastlines, country boundaries, and major drainage features. The primary purpose of a thematic map is to convey an impression of the overall geographic distribution of the theme. It is usually not the intent of the map to provide exact numerical values. To obtain such information, the graphs and tables accompanying the map should be used.

Goode's World Atlas contains many different types of thematic maps. The characteristics of each are summarized below.

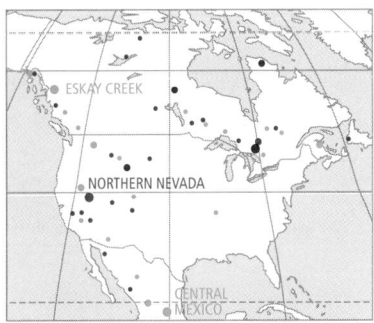
Point symbol map: Detail of Precious Metals (p. 55)

Point Symbol Maps

Point symbol maps are perhaps the simplest type of thematic map. They show features that occur at discrete locations. Examples include earthquakes, nuclear power plants, and minerals-producing areas. The Precious Metals map (p. 55) is an example of a point symbol map showing the locations of areas producing gold, silver, and platinum. A different color is used for each type of metal, while symbol size indicates relative importance.

Area Symbol Maps

Area symbol maps are useful for delineating regions of interest on the earth's surface. For example, the Tobacco and Fisheries map (p. 44) shows major tobacco-producing regions in one color and important fishing areas in another. On some area symbol maps, different shadings or colors are used to differentiate between major and minor areas.

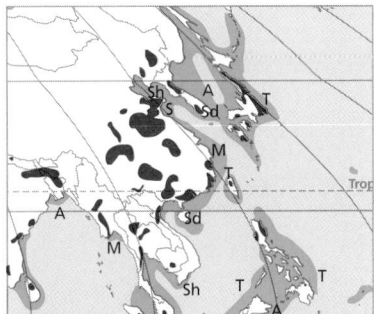
Area symbol map: Detail of Tobacco and Fisheries (p. 44)

Dot Maps

Dot maps show a distribution using a pattern of dots, where each dot represents a certain quantity or amount. For example, on the Sugar map (p. 43), each dot represents 20,000 metric tons of sugar produced. Different dot colors are used to distinguish cane sugar from beet sugar. Dot maps are an effective way of representing the variable density of geographic phenomena over the earth's surface. This type of map is used extensively in *Goode's World Atlas* to show the distribution of agricultural commodities.

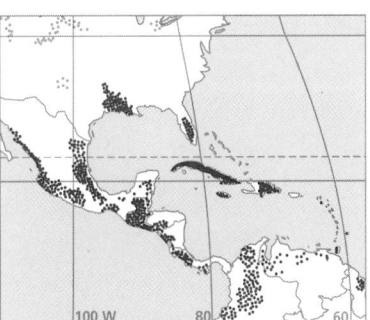
Dot map: Detail of Sugar (p. 43)

Area Class Maps

On area class maps, the earth's surface is divided into areas based on different classes or categories of a particular geographic phenomenon. For example, the Ecoregions map (pp. 28-29) differentiates natural landscape categories, such as Tundra, Savanna, and Prairie. Other examples of area class maps in *Goode's World Atlas* include Landforms (pp. 6-7), Climatic Regions (pp. 14-15), Natural Vegetation (pp. 24-25), Soils (pp. 26-27), Agricultural Areas (p. 38-39), Languages (p. 35) and Religions (p. 35).

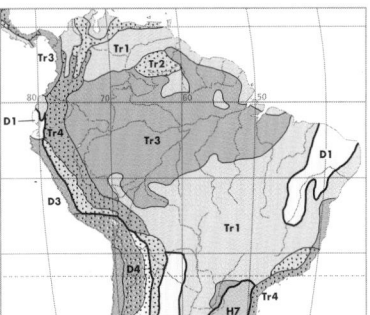
Area class map: Detail of Ecoregions (pp. 28-29)

Isoline Maps

Isoline maps are used to portray quantities that vary smoothly over the surface of the earth. These maps are frequently used for climatic variables such as precipitation and temperature, but a variety of other quantities — from crop yield to population density — can also be treated in this way.

An isoline is a line on the map that joins locations with the same value. For example, the Summer (May to October) Precipitation map (p. 19) contains isolines at 5, 10, 20, and 40 inches. On this map, any 10-inch isoline separates areas that have less than 10 inches of precipitation from areas that have more than 10 inches. Note that the areas between isolines are given different colors to assist in map interpretation.

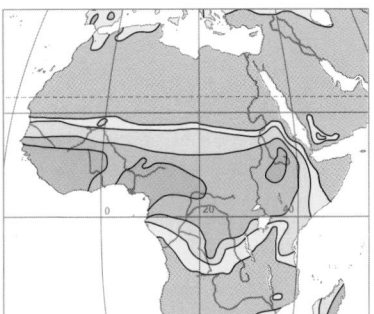
Isoline map: Detail of Precipitation (p. 19)

Proportional Symbol Maps

Proportional symbol maps portray numerical quantities, such as the total population of each state, the total value of agricultural goods produced in different regions, or the amount of hydroelectricity generated in different countries. The symbols on these maps — usually circles —- are drawn such that the size of each is proportional to the value at that location. For example the Exports map (p. 60) shows the value of goods exported by each country in the world, in millions of U.S. dollars.

Proportional symbols are frequently subdivided based on the percentage of individual components making up the total. The Exports map uses wedges of different color to show the percentages of various types of exports, such as manufactured articles and raw materials.

Flow Line Maps

Flow line maps show flows between locations. Usually, the thickness of the flow lines is proportional to flow volume. Flows may be physical commodities like petroleum, or less tangible quantities like information. The flow lines on the Mineral Fuels map (pp. 58-59) represent movement of petroleum measured in billions of U.S. dollars. Note that the locations of flow lines may not represent actual physical routes.

Choropleth Maps

Choropleth maps apply distinctive colors to predefined areas, such as counties or states, to represent different quantities in each area. The quantities shown are usually rates, percentages, or densities. For example, the Birth Rate map (p. 32) shows the annual number of births per one thousand people for each country.

Digital Images

Some maps are actually digital images, analogous to the pictures captured by digital cameras. These maps are created from a very fine grid of cells called **pixels**, each of which is assigned a color that corresponds to a specific value or range of values. The population density maps in this atlas (e.g., pp. 30-31) are examples of this type. The effect is much like an isoline map, but the isolines themselves are not shown and the resulting geographic patterns are more subtle and variable. This approach is increasingly being used to map environmental phenomena observable from remote sensing systems.

Cartograms

Cartograms deliberately distort map shapes to achieve specific effects. On **area cartograms**, the size of each area, such as a country, is made proportional to its population. Countries with large populations are therefore drawn larger than countries with smaller populations, regardless of the actual size of these countries on the earth.

The world cartogram series in this atlas depicts each country as a rectangle. This is a departure from cartograms in earlier editions of the atlas, which attempted to preserve some of the salient shape characteristics for each country. The advantage of the rectangle method is that it is easier to compare the area of countries when their shapes are consistent.

The cartogram series incorporates choropleth shading on top of the rectangular cartogram base. In this way map readers can make inferences about the relationship between population and another thematic variable, such as HIV-infection rates (p. 37).

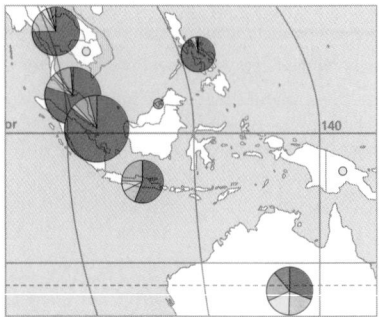
Proportional symbol map: Detail of Exports (p. 60)

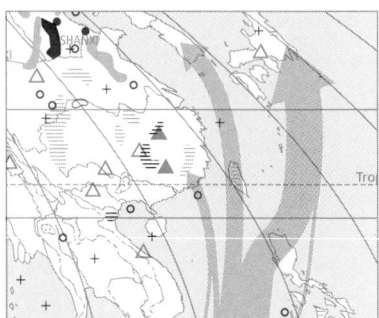
Flow line map: Detail of Mineral Fuels (pp. 58-59)

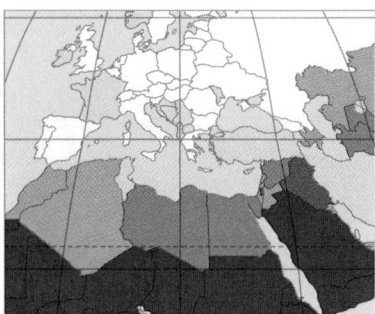
Choropleth map: Detail of Birth Rate (p. 32)

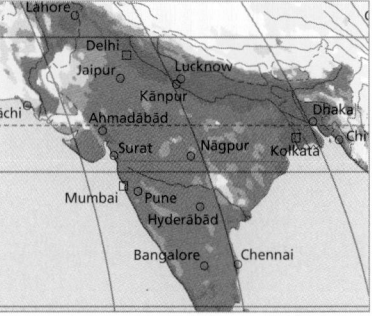
Digital image map: Detail of Population Density (pp. 30-31)

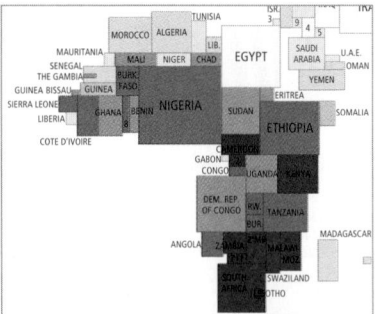
Cartogram: Detail of HIV Infection (p. 37)

Map Legend

Political Boundaries

Political maps	Physical maps	
▬ ▬▬	▬▬▬	International (Demarcated, Undemarcated, and Administrative)
▬ ▪▬	▬▬ ▪▬	Disputed de facto
▪▪▪▪	▪▪▪	Indefinite or Undefined
▬ ▪ ▬	▬▬▬	Secondary, State, Provincial, etc.
⬚		Parks, Indian Reservations
		City Limits
		Urbanized Areas

Transportation

Political maps	Physical maps	
▬▬▬	▬▬▬	Railroads
▬▬▬	▬▬▬	Railroad Ferries
	▬▬▬	Major Roads
	▬▬▬	Minor Roads
	··········	Caravan Routes
	✈	Airports

Cultural Features

- ⤙ Dams
- ·········· Pipelines
- ▲ Points of Interest
- ∴ Ruins

Populated Places

- ◉ 1,000,000 and over
- ◎ 250,000 to 1,000,000
- ⊙ 100,000 to 250,000
- • 25,000 to 100,000
- ○ Under 25,000
- ◻ Neighborhoods, Sections of Cities
- T̄OKYŌ National Capitals
- Boise Secondary Capitals

Note: On maps at 1:20,000,000 and smaller, symbols do not follow the population classification shown above. Some other maps use a slightly different classification, which is shown in a separate legend in the map margin. On all maps, type size indicates the relative importance of the city.

Land Features

- △ Peaks, Spot Heights
- ⤬ Passes
- Sand
- Contours

Elevation

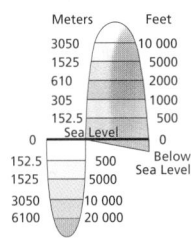

Meters	Feet
3050	10 000
1525	5000
610	2000
305	1000
152.5	500
0 Sea Level	0
152.5	500 Below Sea Level
1525	5000
3050	10 000
6100	20 000

Lakes and Reservoirs

- Fresh Water
- Fresh Water: Intermittent
- Salt Water
- Salt Water: Intermittent

Other Water Features

- Salt Basins, Flats
- Swamps
- Ice Caps and Glaciers
- Rivers
- Intermittent Rivers
- Aqueducts and Canals
- Ship Channels
- Falls
- Rapids
- Springs
- Water Depths
- Sand Bars
- Reefs
- → Warm Ocean Currents
- → Cold Ocean Currents

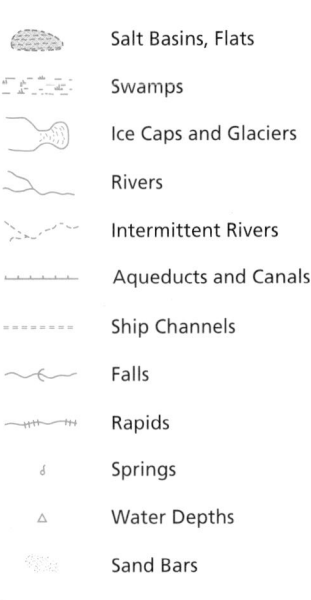

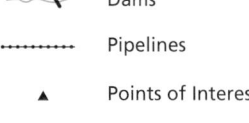

The legend above shows the symbols used for the political and physical reference maps in *Goode's World Atlas*.

To portray relative areas correctly, uniform map scales have been used wherever possible:

Continents – 1:40,000,000
Countries and regions – between 1:4,000,000 and 1:20,000,000
World, polar areas and oceans – between 1:50,000,000 and 1:100,000,000
Urbanized areas – 1:1,000,000

Elevations on the maps are shown using a combination of shaded relief and hypsometric tints. Shaded relief (or hill-shading) gives a three-dimensional impression of the landscape, while hypsometric tints show elevation ranges in different colors.

The choice of names for mapped features is complicated by the fact that a variety of languages and alphabets are used throughout the world. A local-names policy is used in *Goode's World Atlas* for populated places and local physical features. For some major features, an English form of the name is used with the local name given below in parentheses. Examples include Moscow (Moskva), Vienna (Wien) and Naples (Napoli). In countries where more than one official language is used, names are given in the dominant local language. For large physical features spanning international borders, the conventional English form of the name is used. In cases where a non-Roman alphabet is used, names have been transliterated according to accepted practice.

Selected features are also listed in the Index (pp. 262-370), which includes a pronunciation guide. A list of foreign geographic terms is provided in the Glossary (p. 260).

POLITICAL

Scale 1 : 100 000 000 (approximate)
One inch to 1,600 miles

```
0    500   1000   1500        2000 miles
0   500  1000  1500  2000  2500 Kilometers
```

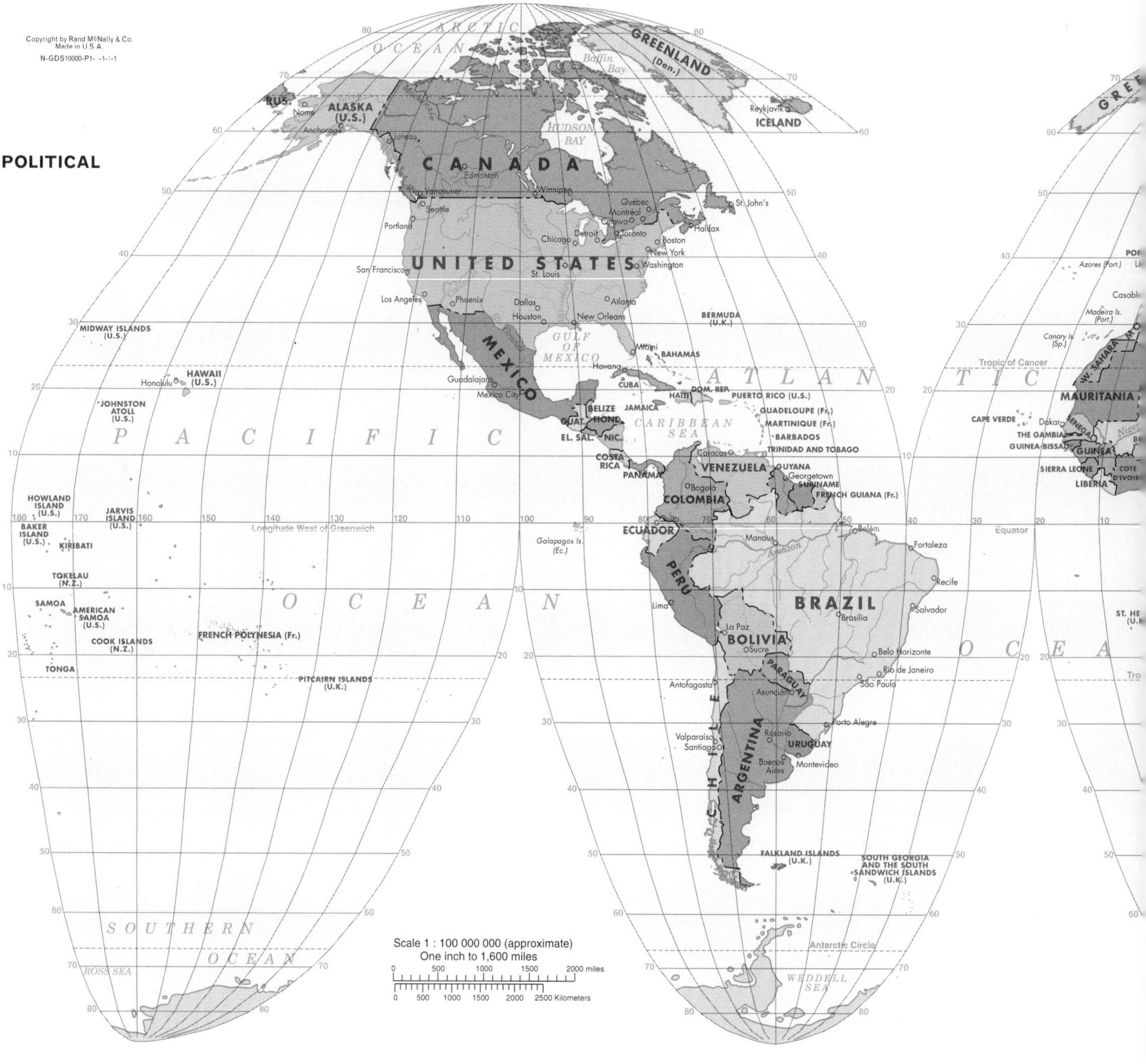

Comparative Land Areas (Land and inland water. Numbers indicate thousands of square miles.)

CHINA	INDIA	KAZAKHSTAN	SAUDI ARABIA	INDONESIA	IRAN	MONGOLIA	PAKISTAN	TURKEY	MYANMAR	OTHER ASIA	RUSSIA	UKRAINE	FRANCE	SPAIN	OTHER EUROPE	SUDAN	ALGERIA	D.R. OF CONGO	LIBYA	CHAD	NIGER	MALI	ANGOLA	S. AFRICA	ETHIOPIA	MAURITANIA	EGYPT	TANZANIA	NIGERIA
3,690	1,237	1,049	830	752	631	605	340	301	261	2,539	5,065	233	211	195	1,311	967	920	905	679	496	489	482	481	471	447	398	387	365	357

ASIA 17,300 — EUROPE 3,800 — AFRICA 11,700

Comparative Populations (Numbers indicate millions of people.) 1/1/04 estimate

CHINA	INDIA	INDONESIA	PAKISTAN	BANGLA-DESH	JAPAN	PHILIPPINES	VIETNAM
1,298.7	1,057.4	236.7	152.2	139.9	127.3	85.4	82.

ASIA 3,839.3

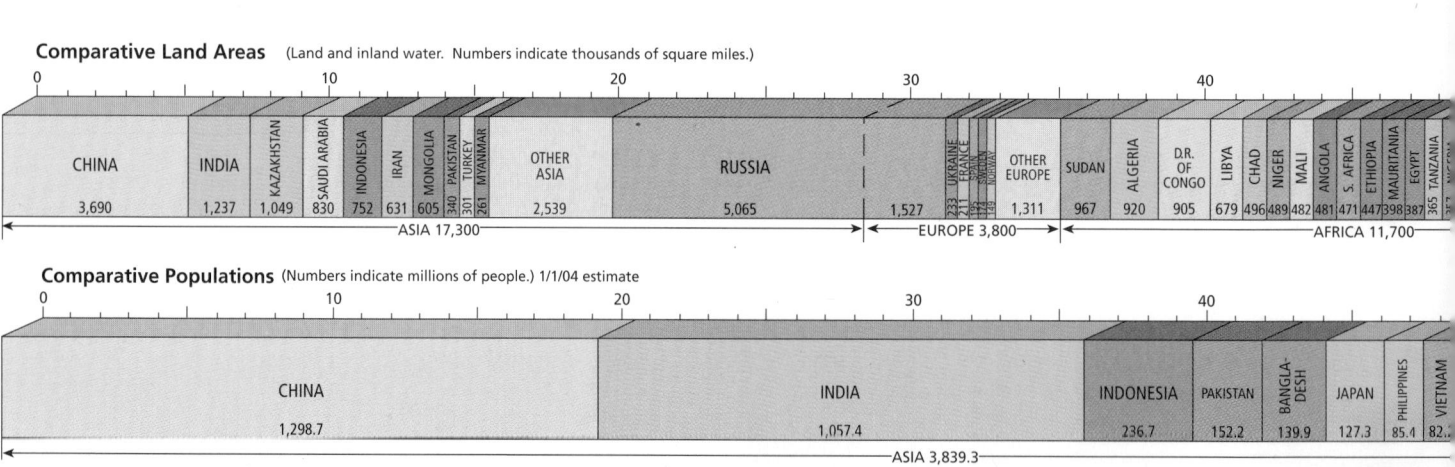

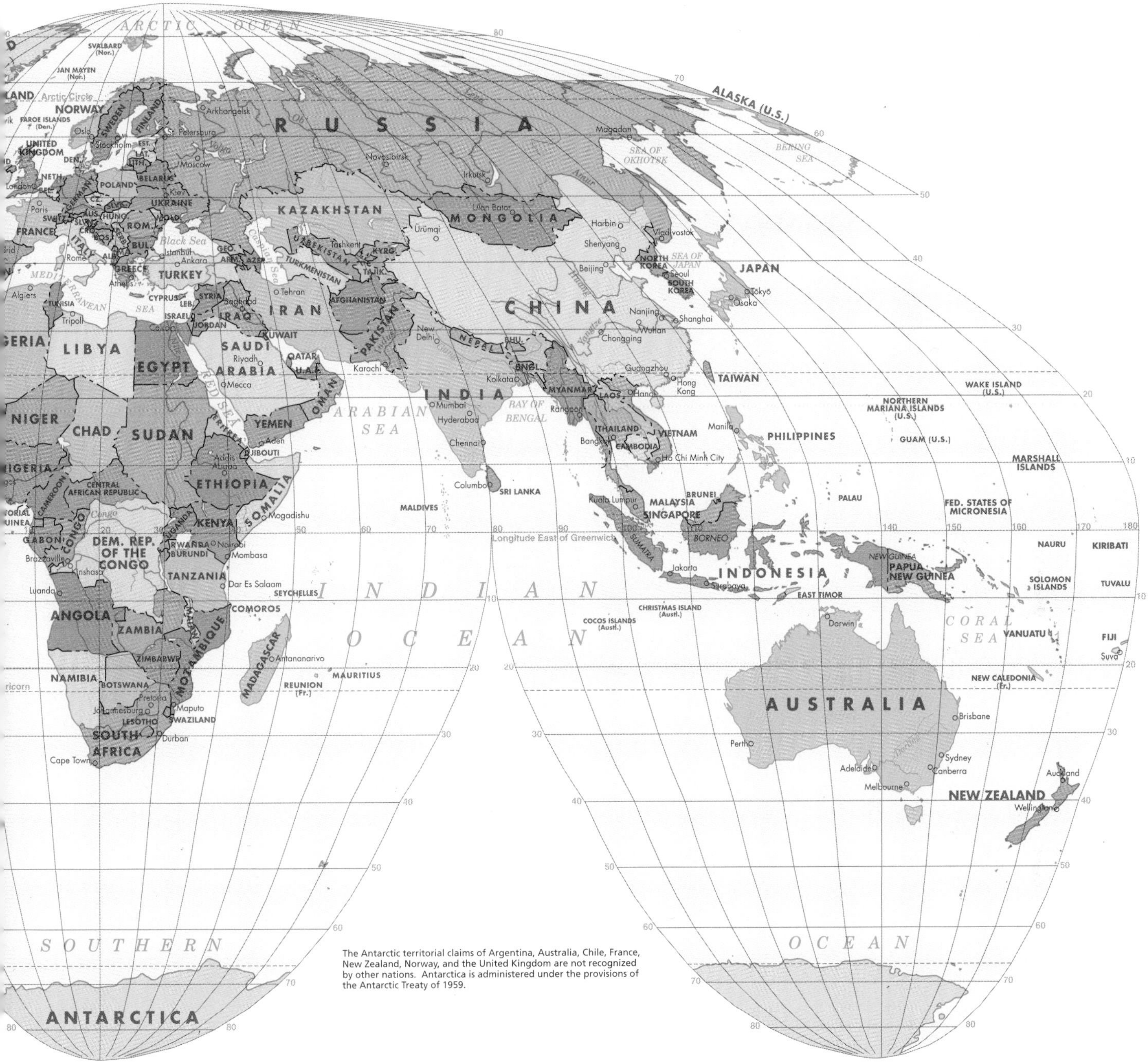

ARCTIC OCEAN

SVALBARD (Nor.)
JAN MAYEN (Nor.)
FAROE ISLANDS (Den.)
Arctic Circle
NORWAY
SWEDEN FINLAND
Arkhangelsk
ALASKA (U.S.)
BERING SEA
Magadan
SEA OF OKHOTSK

R U S S I A

St. Petersburg
Oslo Stockholm EST. LAT. LITH.
Moscow
UNITED KINGDOM DEN.
NETH.
Paris POLAND BELARUS
Kiev
FRANCE SWITZ. HUNG. UKRAINE
GOLD
ROM.
Rome BUL.
GREECE Istanbul Ankara AZER.
Athens TURKEY
CYPRUS LEB. SYRIA Baghdad
ISRAEL JORDAN IRAQ

KAZAKHSTAN
Tashkent KYRG.
UZBEKISTAN
TURKMENISTAN
Tehran
IRAN AFGHANISTAN
KUWAIT
QATAR
U.A.E.
SAUDI ARABIA
OMAN
YEMEN Aden
DJIBOUTI

MONGOLIA
Ulan Bator
Harbin
Shenyang Vladivostok
Beijing NORTH KOREA SEA OF JAPAN
SOUTH KOREA Seoul
JAPAN Tōkyō
Osaka
CHINA
Nanjing Shanghai
Chongqing Wuhan
Guangzhou
Hong Kong TAIWAN

New Delhi NEPAL BHU.
PAKISTAN
Karachi BNGL.
INDIA MYANMAR LAOS Hanoi
Mumbai Kolkata Rangoon THAILAND VIETNAM
Hyderabad BAY OF BENGAL Bangkok CAMBODIA
Chennai Ho Chi Minh City
Columbo SRI LANKA Manila PHILIPPINES
MALDIVES MALAYSIA BRUNEI
Kuala Lumpur SINGAPORE BORNEO

WAKE ISLAND (U.S.)
NORTHERN MARIANA ISLANDS (U.S.)
GUAM (U.S.)
MARSHALL ISLANDS
PALAU
FED. STATES OF MICRONESIA
NAURU KIRIBATI
NEW GUINEA PAPUA NEW GUINEA
SOLOMON ISLANDS TUVALU
EAST TIMOR VANUATU
FIJI Suva

ALGIERS
TUNISIA MEDITERRANEAN SEA
Tripoli RED SEA
LIBYA EGYPT Mecca
NIGER CHAD SUDAN Riyadh Mecca
NIGERIA ARABIAN SEA
CENTRAL AFRICAN REPUBLIC ETHIOPIA Addis Abeba
EQUATORIAL GUINEA UGANDA SOMALIA Mogadishu
GABON CONGO KENYA Nairobi
DEM. REP. OF THE CONGO RWANDA Mombasa
Kinshasa BURUNDI TANZANIA Dar Es Salaam
Luanda SEYCHELLES
ANGOLA ZAMBIA COMOROS
ZIMBABWE MOZAMBIQUE MADAGASCAR Antananarivo
NAMIBIA BOTSWANA MAURITIUS REUNION (Fr.)
Johannesburg Pretoria SWAZILAND
SOUTH AFRICA LESOTHO Maputo
Cape Town Durban

INDIAN OCEAN
Longitude East of Greenwich

Jakarta INDONESIA
Surabaya
CHRISTMAS ISLAND (Austl.)
COCOS ISLANDS (Austl.)
Darwin
CORAL SEA
NEW CALEDONIA (Fr.)

A U S T R A L I A
Perth Brisbane
Adelaide Sydney Canberra
Melbourne Auckland
NEW ZEALAND Wellington

SOUTHERN OCEAN

The Antarctic territorial claims of Argentina, Australia, Chile, France, New Zealand, Norway, and the United Kingdom are not recognized by other nations. Antarctica is administered under the provisions of the Antarctic Treaty of 1959.

A N T A R C T I C A

Goode's Homolosine Equal Area Projection

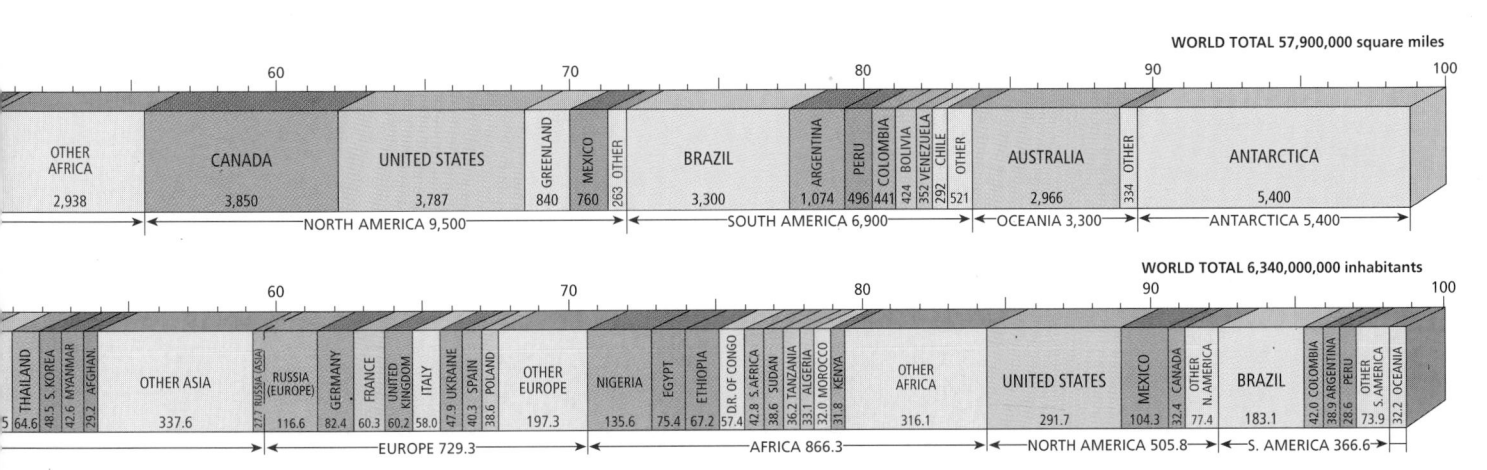

WORLD TOTAL 57,900,000 square miles

OTHER AFRICA 2,938 | CANADA 3,850 | UNITED STATES 3,787 | GREENLAND 840 | MEXICO 760 | OTHER 263 | BRAZIL 3,300 | ARGENTINA 1,074 | PERU 496 | COLOMBIA 441 | BOLIVIA 424 | VENEZUELA 352 | CHILE 292 | OTHER 521 | AUSTRALIA 2,966 | OTHER 334 | ANTARCTICA 5,400

NORTH AMERICA 9,500 — SOUTH AMERICA 6,900 — OCEANIA 3,300 — ANTARCTICA 5,400

WORLD TOTAL 6,340,000,000 inhabitants

THAILAND | S. KOREA 48.5 | MYANMAR 42.6 | AFGHAN 29.2 | OTHER ASIA 337.6 | RUSSIA (ASIA) 27.7 | RUSSIA (EUROPE) 116.6 | GERMANY 82.4 | FRANCE 60.3 | UNITED KINGDOM 60.2 | ITALY 58.0 | UKRAINE 47.9 | SPAIN 40.3 | POLAND 38.6 | OTHER EUROPE 197.3 | NIGERIA 135.6 | EGYPT 75.4 | ETHIOPIA 67.2 | D.R. OF CONGO 57.4 | S. AFRICA 42.8 | TANZANIA 38.6 | ALGERIA 36.2 | MOROCCO 33.1 | KENYA 31.8 | OTHER AFRICA 316.1 | UNITED STATES 291.7 | MEXICO 104.3 | CANADA 32.4 | OTHER N. AMERICA 77.4 | BRAZIL 183.1 | COLOMBIA 42.0 | ARGENTINA 38.9 | PERU 28.6 | OTHER S. AMERICA 73.9 | OCEANIA 32.2

EUROPE 729.3 — AFRICA 866.3 — NORTH AMERICA 505.8 — S. AMERICA 366.6

PHYSICAL

Scale 1 : 100 000 000 (approximate)
One inch to 1,600 miles

0 500 1000 1500 2000 miles

0 500 1000 1500 2000 2500 Kilometers

Meters	Feet	
3 050	10 000	
1 525	5 000	
610	2 000	
305	1 000	
0	SEA L.	
	BELOW SEA LEVEL	
152.5	500	
3 050	10 000	
6 100	20 000	

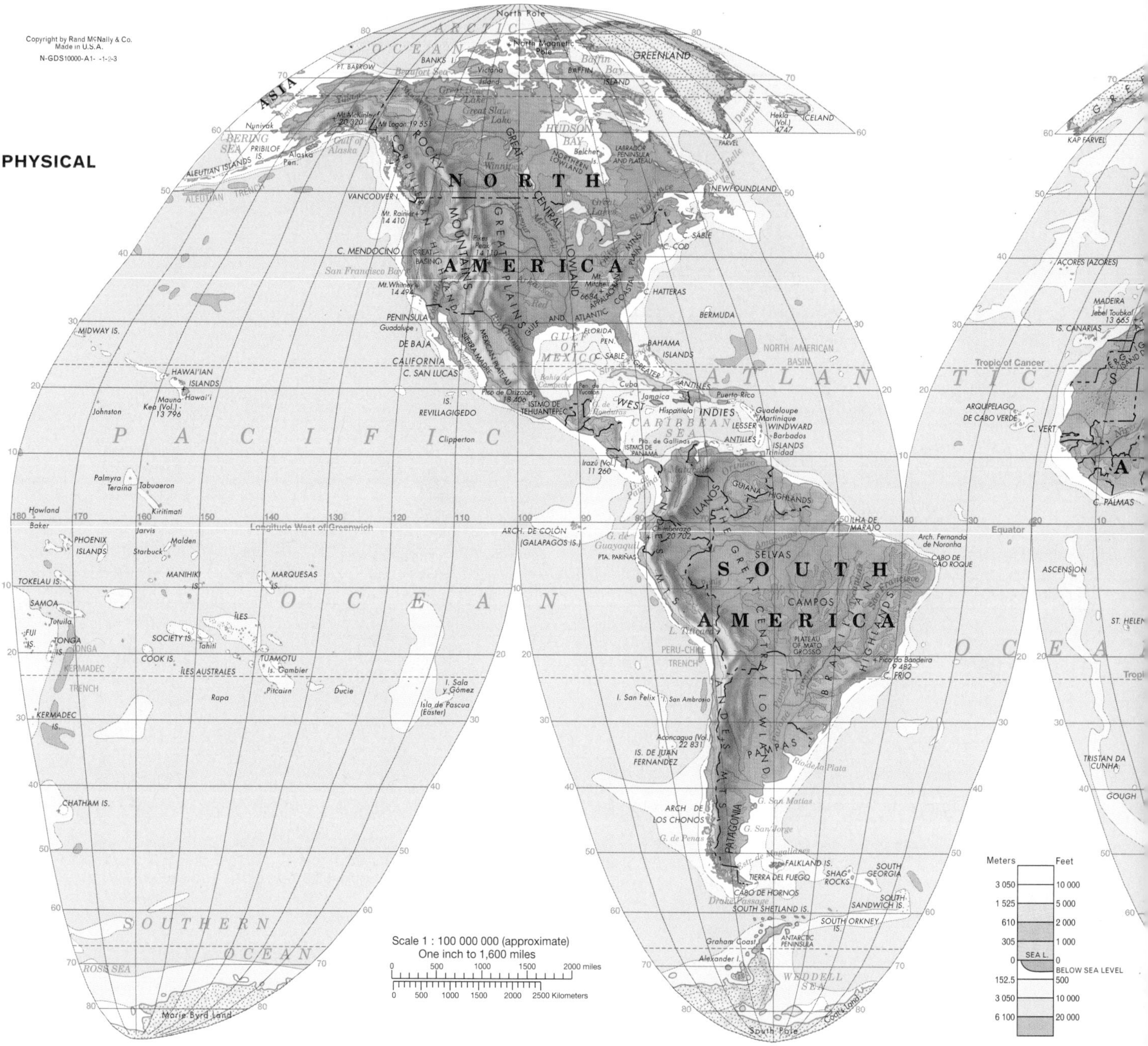

Land Elevations in Profile

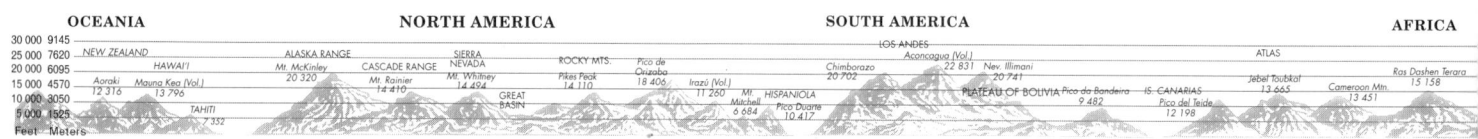

Ocean Depths in Profile

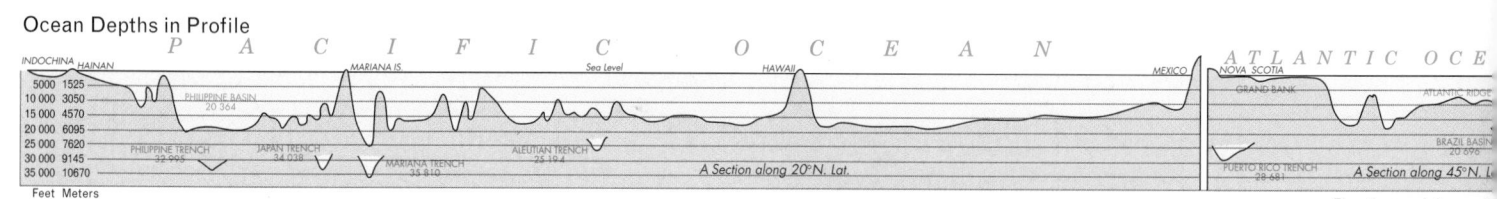

Elevations and depressi

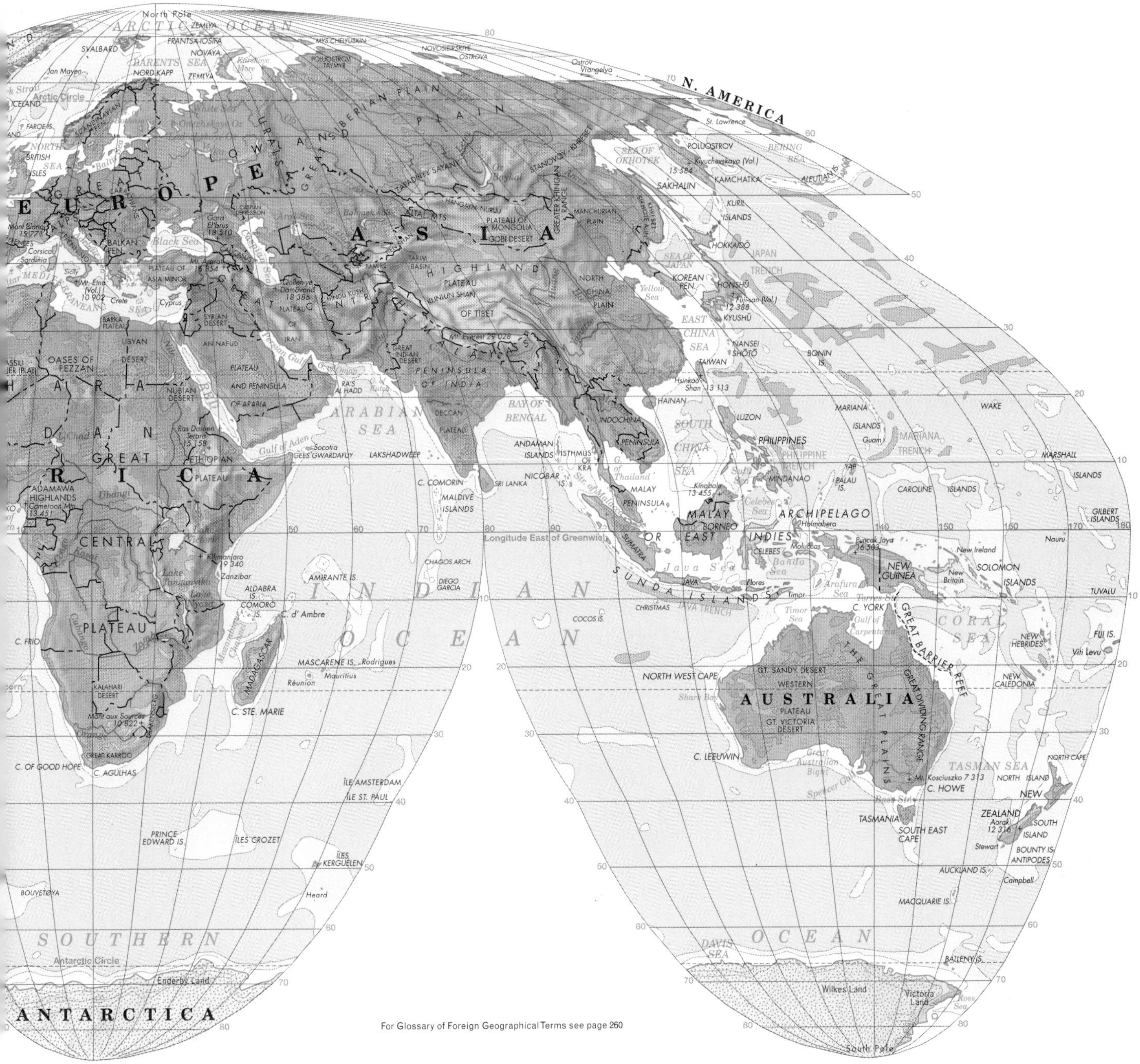

Map Labels

ARCTIC OCEAN

North Pole
SVALBARD · FRANTSA-IOSIFA · ZEMLYA · NOVAYA · ZEMLYA · MYS CHELYUSKIN · NOVOSIBIRSKIYE OSTROVA · Ostrov Vrangelya
Jan Mayen · BARENTS SEA · NORD KAPP · Kara Sea · POLUOSTROV TAYMYR
ICELAND · Arctic Circle · White Sea · Ob · GREAT SIBERIAN PLAIN · N. AMERICA
FAROES · NORTH SEA · BRITISH ISLES

EUROPE · ASIA

Mont Blanc 15 771 · Gora El'brus 18 510 · URALS · WEST SIBERIAN PLAIN · St. Lawrence
ALPS · Black Sea · TAVADNYY SAYANY · STANOVOY KHREBET · SEA OF OKHOTSK · Klyuchevskaya (Vol.) 15 584 · BERING SEA
Corsica · BALKAN PEN. · PLATEAU OF ASIA MINOR · Aral Sea · TIEN SHAN · PLATEAU OF MONGOLIA · GOBI DESERT · MANCHURIAN PLAIN · SAKHALIN · KAMCHATKA · ALEUTIAN IS.
Sardinia · Mt. Etna (Vol.) 10 902 · Crete · Cyprus · Gora Damávand 18 386 · HINDU KUSH · TARIM BASIN · KUNLUN SHAN · PLATEAU OF TIBET · KURIL ISLANDS · HOKKAIDO · JAPAN
SYRIAN DESERT · PLATEAU OF IRAN · HIMALAYAS · Mt. Everest 29 028 · KOREAN PEN. · SEA OF JAPAN · HONSHU · JAPAN TRENCH
LIBYAN DESERT · OASES OF FEZZAN · NUBIAN DESERT · AN NAFUD · PLATEAU AND PENINSULA OF ARABIA · GREAT INDIAN DESERT · NORTH CHINA PLAIN · Fujisan (Vol.) 12 388 · KYUSHU
SAHARA · RAS AL HADD · DECCAN PLATEAU · Yellow Sea · EAST CHINA SEA · NANSEI SHOTO · BONIN IS. · WAKE
Lake Chad · Ras Dashen Terara 15 158 · Gulf of Aden · Gulf of Oman · Hsinkao Shan 13 113 · TAIWAN · HAINAN · SOUTH CHINA SEA · LUZON · MARIANA ISLANDS · Guam · MARIANA TRENCH · MARSHALL ISLANDS
GREAT RIFT VALLEY · ETHIOPIAN PLATEAU · Socotra · GEES GWARDAFUY · LAKSHADWEEP · ANDAMAN ISLANDS · ISTHMUS OF KRA · Gulf of Thailand · PHILIPPINES · PHILIPPINE TRENCH · CAROLINE ISLANDS · GILBERT ISLANDS
ADAMAWA HIGHLANDS · Cameroon Mtn. 13 451 · C. COMORIN · SRI LANKA · NICOBAR IS. · MALAY PENINSULA · Kinabalu 13 455 · MINDANAO · PALAU IS. · Nauru
Ubangi · CENTRAL · Kilimanjaro 19 340 · Zanzibar · MALDIVE ISLANDS · Sulu Sea · Celebes Sea · MALAY ARCHIPELAGO OR EAST INDIES · Halmahera · MALDIVE ISLANDS
Lake Tanganyika · Lake Victoria · CHAGOS ARCH. · BORNEO · CELEBES · Moluccas · Puncak Jaya 16 503 · New Ireland · SOLOMON ISLANDS
PLATEAU · AMIRANTE IS. · DIEGO GARCIA · SUMATRA · Java Sea · Banda Sea · NEW GUINEA · New Britain
C. FRIO · ALDABRA IS. · COMORO IS. · C. d'Ambre · JAVA · Flores · Timor Sea · C. YORK · GREAT BARRIER REEF · CORAL SEA · NEW HEBRIDES · FIJI IS.
INDIAN OCEAN · COCOS IS. · CHRISTMAS · JAVA TRENCH · SUNDA ISLANDS · Arafura Sea · Gulf of Carpentaria · Viti Levu · NEW CALEDONIA
MASCARENE IS. · Rodrigues · MADAGASCAR · Réunion · Mauritius · NORTH WEST CAPE · GT. SANDY DESERT · THE GREAT DIVIDING RANGE
KALAHARI DESERT · C. STE. MARIE · Shark Bay · WESTERN PLATEAU · AUSTRALIA · GT. VICTORIA DESERT · THE GREAT PLAINS
Mont aux Sources 10 822 · GREAT KARROO · C. LEEUWIN · Great Australian Bight · Spencer Gulf · Mt. Kosciusko 7 313 · C. HOWE · NORTH CAPE
C. OF GOOD HOPE · C. AGULHAS · ÎLE AMSTERDAM · ÎLE ST. PAUL · TASMAN SEA · NEW ZEALAND · NORTH ISLAND
PRINCE EDWARD IS. · ÎLES CROZET · ÎLES KERGUELEN · TASMANIA · SOUTH EAST CAPE · Aoraki 12 316 · SOUTH ISLAND · BOUNTY IS. · ANTIPODES
BOUVETØYA · Heard · AUCKLAND IS. · Campbell
SOUTHERN · MACQUARIE IS. · OCEAN
Antarctic Circle · DAVIS SEA · BALLENY IS.
Enderby Land · Wilkes Land · Victoria Land · Ross Sea
ANTARCTICA · South Pole

AFRICA · GREAT RIFT VALLEY

Longitude East of Greenwich

For Glossary of Foreign Geographical Terms see page 260

Goode's Homolosine Equal Area Projection

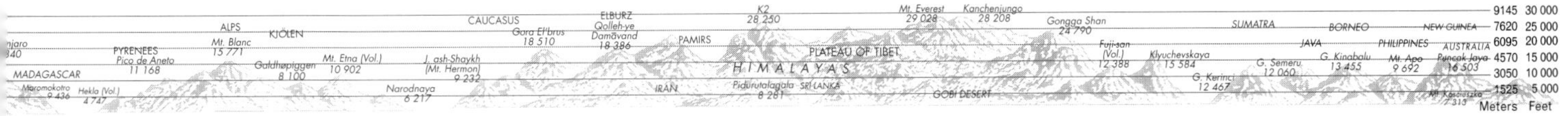

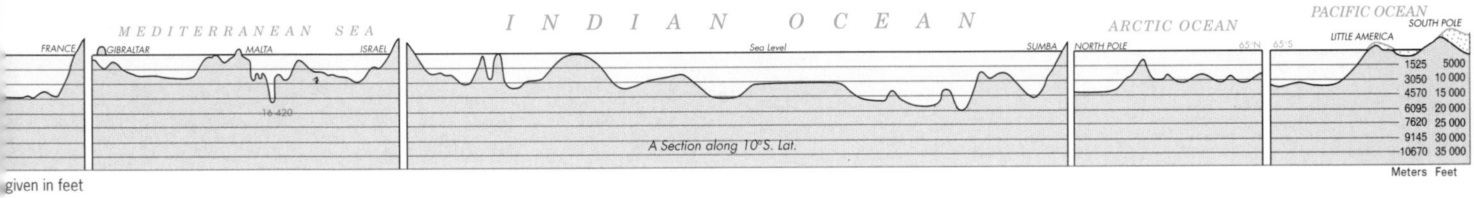

Profile — EUROPE / ASIA / OCEANIA

EUROPE · ASIA · OCEANIA

					9145	30 000

CAUCASUS · ELBURZ · K2 28 250 · Mt. Everest 29 028 · Kanchenjunga 28 208 · NEW GUINEA · 9145 · 30 000
ALPS · KJÖLEN · Gora El'brus 18 510 · Qolleh-ye Damávand 18 386 · PAMIRS · Gongga Shan 24 790 · SUMATRA · BORNEO · 7620 · 25 000
PYRENEES · Mt. Blanc 15 771 · Fujisan (Vol.) 12 388 · Klyuchevskaya 15 584 · JAVA · PHILIPPINES · AUSTRALIA · 6095 · 20 000
Pico de Aneto 11 168 · Mt. Etna (Vol.) 10 902 · J. ash Shaykh (Mt. Hermon) 9 232 · PLATEAU OF TIBET · G. Kinabalu 13 455 · Puncak Jaya 16 503 · 4570 · 15 000
MADAGASCAR · Galdhøpiggen 8 100 · HIMALAYAS · G. Semeru 12 060 · Mt. Apo 9 692 · 3050 · 10 000
Maromokotro 9 436 · Hekla (Vol.) 4 747 · Narodnaya 6 217 · IRAN · Pidurutalagala 8 281 · SRI LANKA · GOBI DESERT · G. Kerinci 12 467 · Mt. Kosciusko 7 313 · 1525 · 5 000
Meters · Feet

Profile — A Section along 10° S. Lat.

MEDITERRANEAN SEA · INDIAN OCEAN · ARCTIC OCEAN · PACIFIC OCEAN · SOUTH POLE

FRANCE · GIBRALTAR · MALTA · ISRAEL · Sea Level · SUMBA · NORTH POLE · 65°N · 65°S · LITTLE AMERICA
16 420

	1525	5000
	3050	10 000
	4570	15 000
	6095	20 000
	7620	25 000
	9145	30 000
	10670	35 000

Meters · Feet

A Section along 10° S. Lat.

given in feet

6

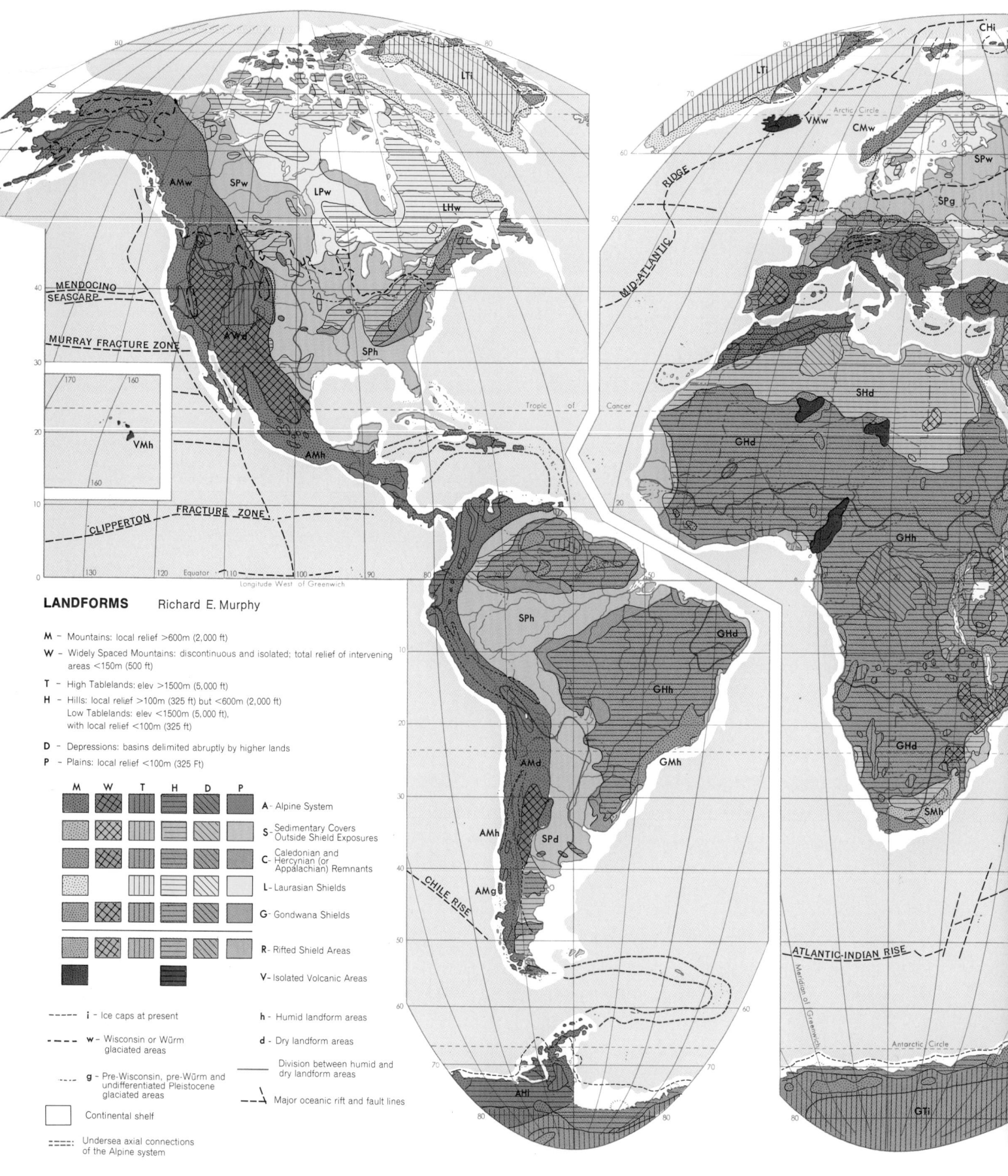

LANDFORMS   Richard E. Murphy

M – Mountains: local relief >600m (2,000 ft)

W – Widely Spaced Mountains: discontinuous and isolated; total relief of intervening areas <150m (500 ft)

T – High Tablelands: elev >1500m (5,000 ft)

H – Hills: local relief >100m (325 ft) but <600m (2,000 ft)
Low Tablelands: elev <1500m (5,000 ft), with local relief <100m (325 ft)

D – Depressions: basins delimited abruptly by higher lands

P – Plains: local relief <100m (325 Ft)

M   W   T   H   D   P

A - Alpine System

S - Sedimentary Covers Outside Shield Exposures

C - Caledonian and Hercynian (or Appalachian) Remnants

L - Laurasian Shields

G - Gondwana Shields

R - Rifted Shield Areas

V - Isolated Volcanic Areas

----- **i** - Ice caps at present

- - - **w** - Wisconsin or Würm glaciated areas

-··- **g** - Pre-Wisconsin, pre-Würm and undifferentiated Pleistocene glaciated areas

☐ Continental shelf

≡≡≡≡ Undersea axial connections of the Alpine system

h - Humid landform areas

d - Dry landform areas

Division between humid and dry landform areas

-··- Major oceanic rift and fault lines

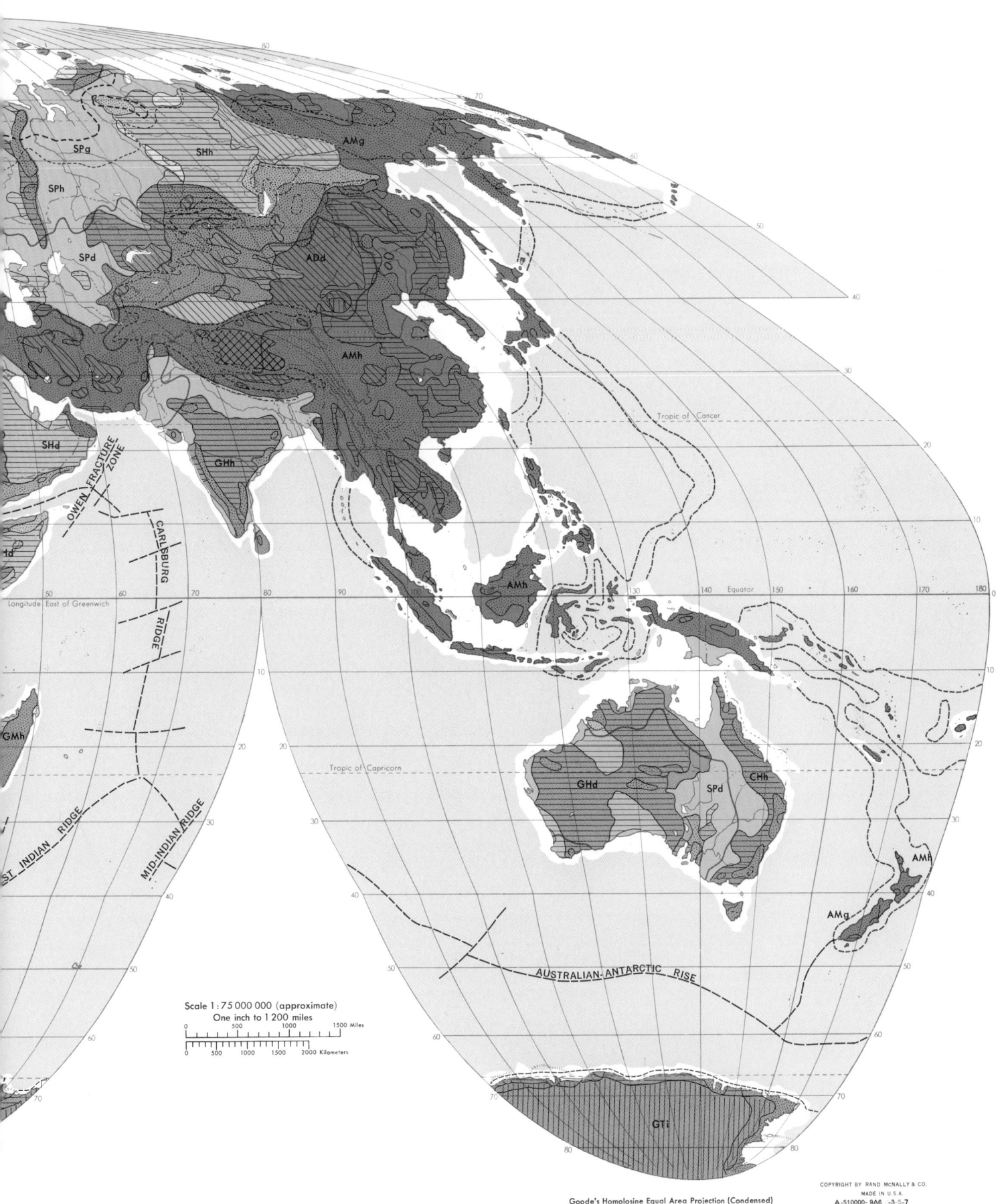

SPg

SHh

AMg

SPh

SPd

ADd

AMh

SHd

GHh

OWEN FRACTURE ZONE

CARLSBURG RIDGE

Id

Longitude East of Greenwich

Tropic of Cancer

Equator

AMh

GMh

Tropic of Capricorn

GHd

SPd

CHh

ST INDIAN RIDGE

MID-INDIAN RIDGE

AMh

AMg

AUSTRALIAN-ANTARCTIC RISE

GTi

Scale 1:75 000 000 (approximate)
One inch to 1 200 miles

0   500   1000   1500 Miles

0   500   1000   1500   2000 Kilometers

Goode's Homolosine Equal Area Projection (Condensed)

8

CONTINENTAL DRIFT

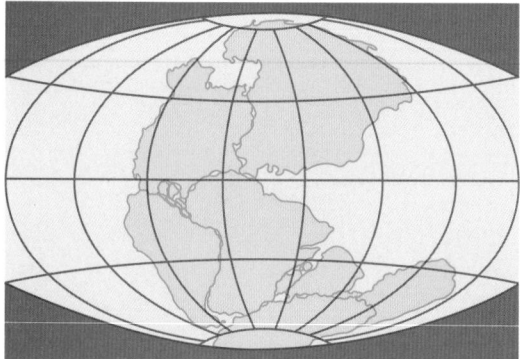

225 million years ago the supercontinent of Pangaea exists and Panthalassa forms the ancestral ocean. Tethys Sea separates Eurasia and Africa.

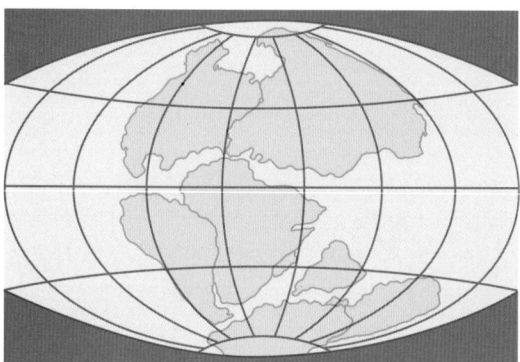

180 million years ago Pangaea splits, Laurasia drifts north. Gondwanaland breaks into South America/Africa, India, and Australia/Antarctica.

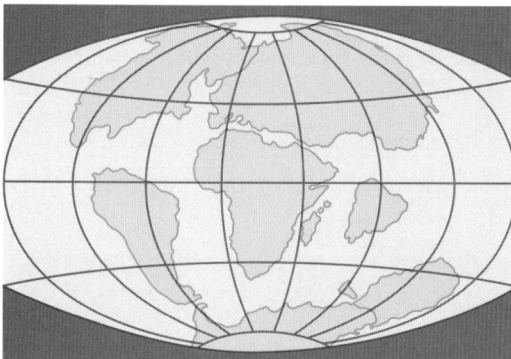

65 million years ago ocean basins take shape as South America and India move from Africa and the Tethys Sea closes to form the Mediterranean Sea.

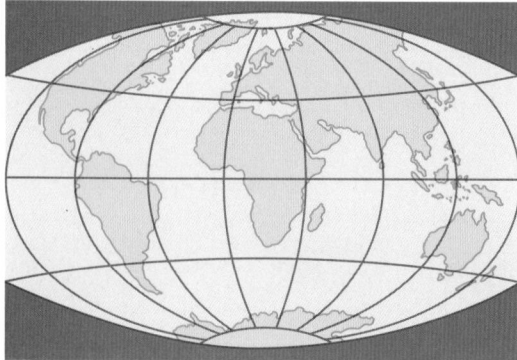

The present day: India has merged with Asia, Australia is free of Antarctica, and North America is free of Eurasia.

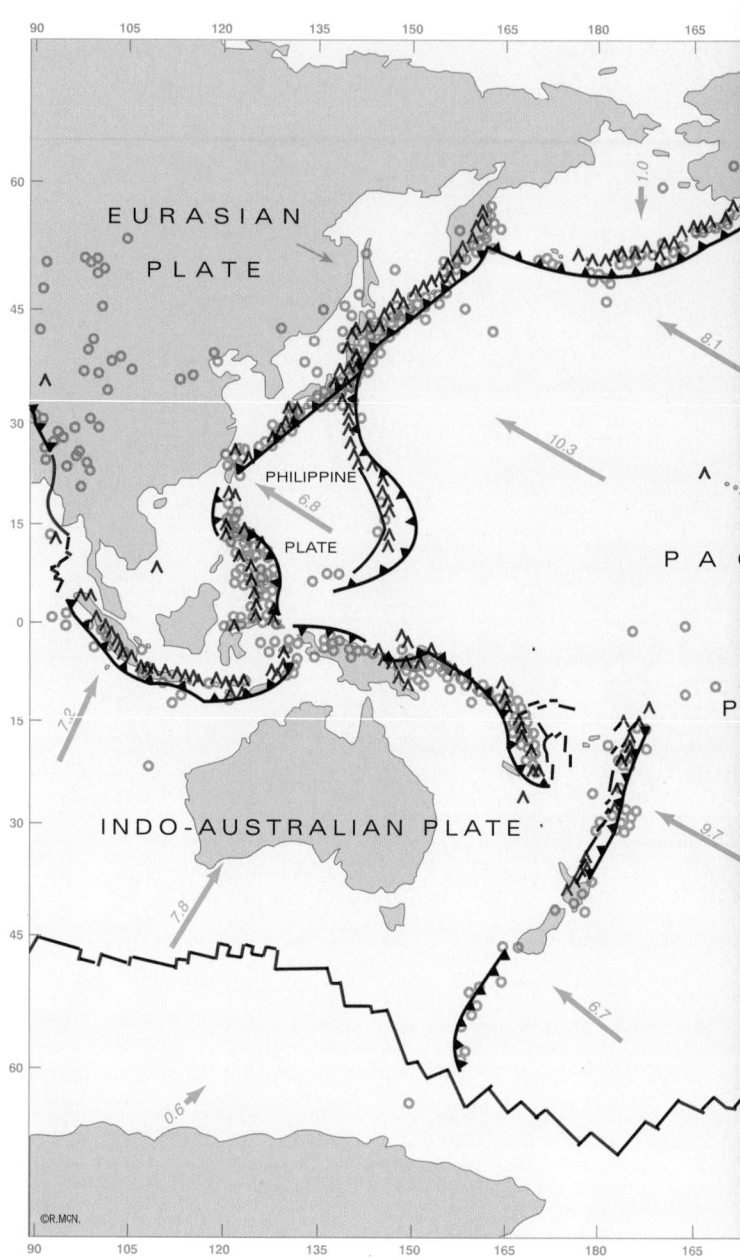

PLATE TECTONICS

Types of plate boundaries

▬▬▬ **Divergent:** magma emerges from the earth's mantle at the mid-ocean ridges forming new crust and forcing the plates to spread apart at the ridges.

▲▲▲▲ **Convergent:** plates collide at subduction zones where the denser plate is forced back into the earth's mantle forming deep ocean trenches.

▬▬▬ **Transform:** plates slide past one another producing faults and fracture zones.

Other map symbols

→ Direction of plate movement

6.7 → Length of arrow is proportional to the amount of plate movement (number indicates centimeters of movement per year)

○ Earthquake of magnitude 7.5 and above (from 10 A.D. to the present)

∧ Volcano (eruption since 1900)

✳ Selected hot spots

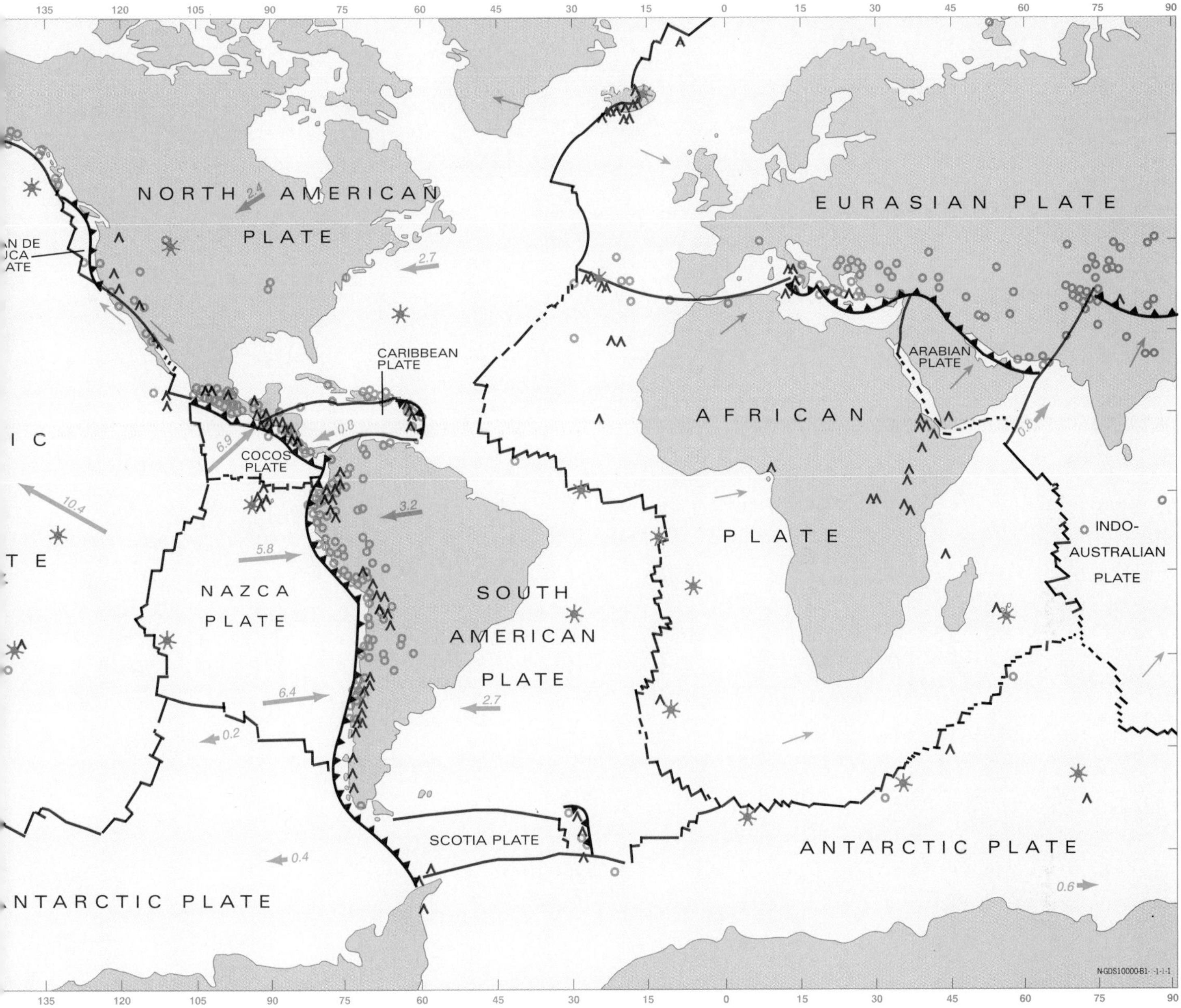

NORTH AMERICAN PLATE

EURASIAN PLATE

CARIBBEAN PLATE

ARABIAN PLATE

AFRICAN PLATE

COCOS PLATE

INDO-AUSTRALIAN PLATE

NAZCA PLATE

SOUTH AMERICAN PLATE

SCOTIA PLATE

ANTARCTIC PLATE

ANTARCTIC PLATE

N·GDS10000-B1· ·1·1·1

The plate tectonic theory describes the movement of the earth's surface and subsurface and explains why surface features are where they are.

Stated concisely, the theory presumes the lithosphere - the outside crust and uppermost mantle of the earth - is divided into about a dozen major rigid plates and several smaller platelets that move relative to one another. The position and names of the plates are shown on the map above.

The motor that drives the plates is found deep in the mantle. The theory states that because of temperature differences in the mantle, slow convection currents circulate there. Where two molten currents converge and move upward, they separate, causing the crustal plates to bulge and move apart in mid-ocean regions. Transverse fractures disrupt these broad regions. Lava wells up at these points to cause volcanic activity and to form ridges. The plates grow larger by accretion along these mid-ocean ridges, cause vast regions of the crust to move apart, and force the plates to collide with one another. As the plates do so, they are destroyed at subduction zones, where the plates are consumed downward, back into the earth's mantle, forming deep ocean trenches. The diagrams to the right illustrate the processes.

Most of the earth's volcanic and seismic activities

occur where plates slide past each other at transform boundaries or collide along subduction zones. The friction and heat caused by the grinding motion of the subducted plates causes rock to liquify and rise to the surface as volcanoes and eventually form vast mountain ranges. Strong and deep earthquakes are common here.

Volcanoes and earthquakes also occur at random locations around the earth known as "hot spots". Hot rock from deep in the mantle rises to the surface creating some of the earth's tallest mountains. As the lithospheric plates move slowly over these stationary plumes of magma, island chains (such as the Hawaiian Islands) are formed.

The overall result of tectonic movement is that the crustal plates move slowly and inexorably as relatively rigid entitles, carrying the continents along with them. The history of this continental drifting is illustrated in the four maps to the left. It began with a single landmass called the supercontinent of Pangaea and the ancestral sea, the Panthalassa Ocean. Pangaea first split into a northern landmass called Laurasia and a southern block called Gondwanaland and subsequently into the continents we map today. The map of the future will be significantly different as the continents continue to drift.

Subduction Zone

Ocean Ridge Zone

Scale 1:72 000 000 at 40° latitude

OBINSON PROJECTION

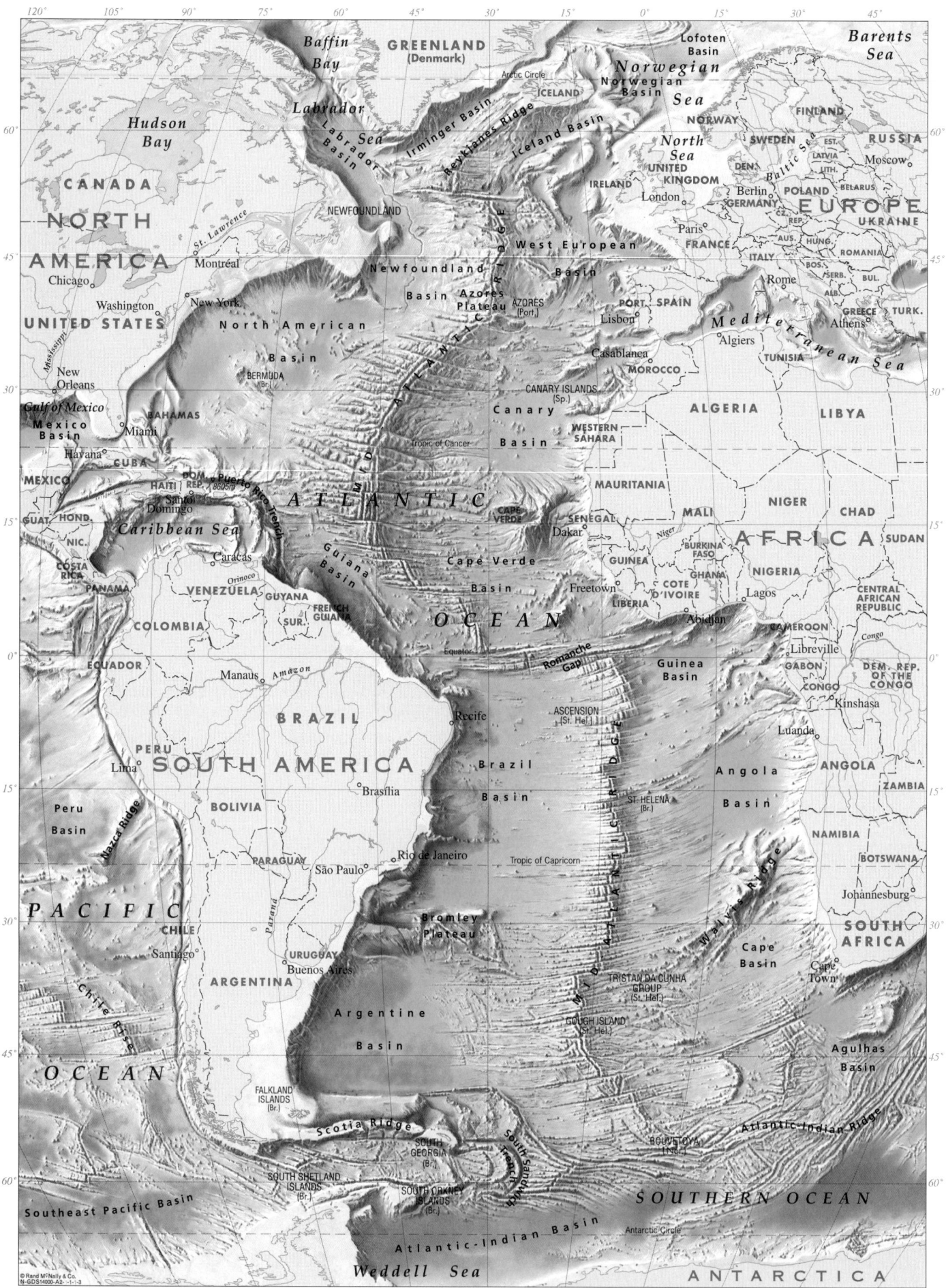

Scale 1:72 000 000 at 40° latitude. ROBINSON PROJECTION

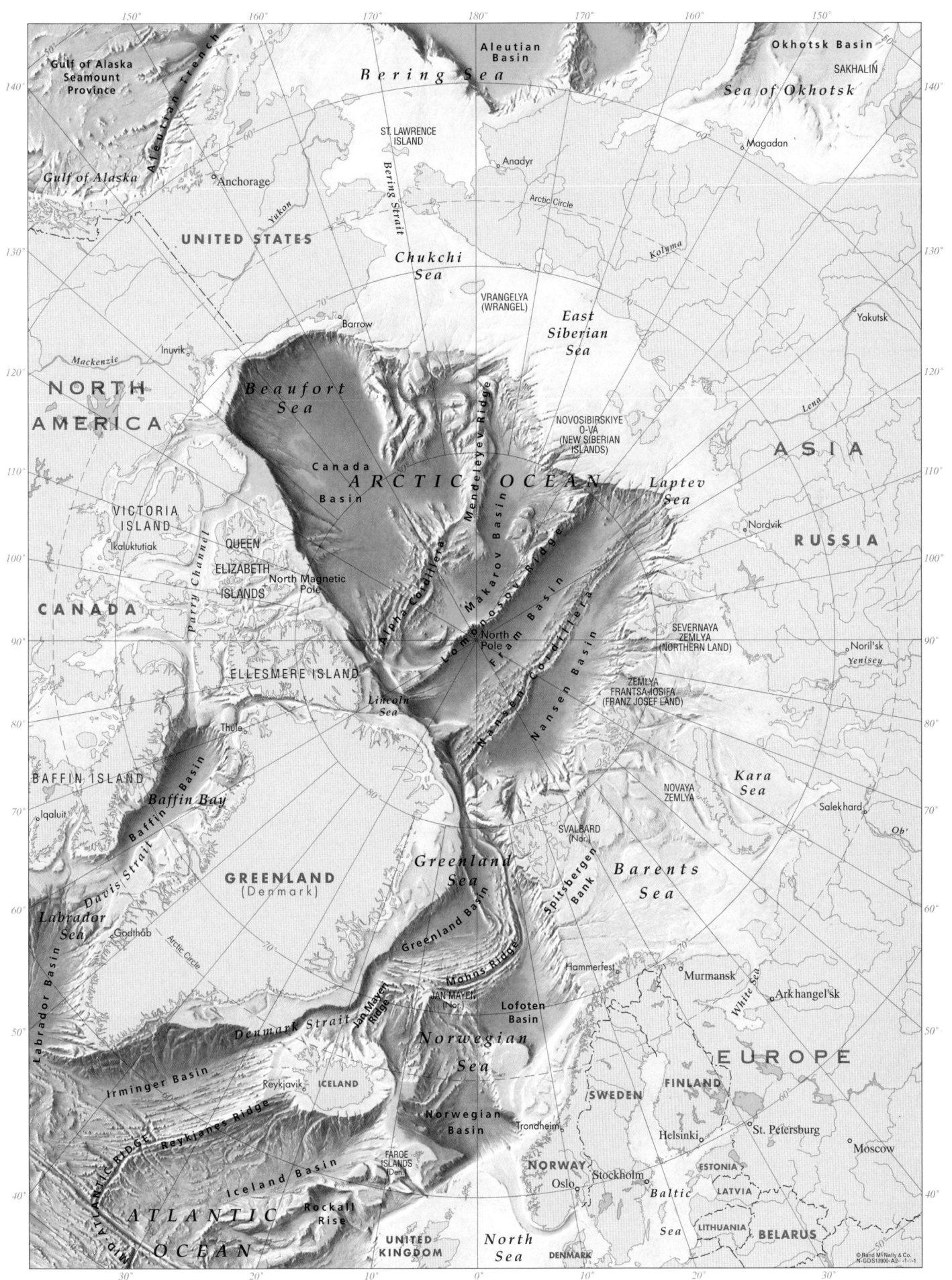

Scale 1:30 000 000. LAMBERT AZIMUTHAL EQUAL AREA PROJECTION

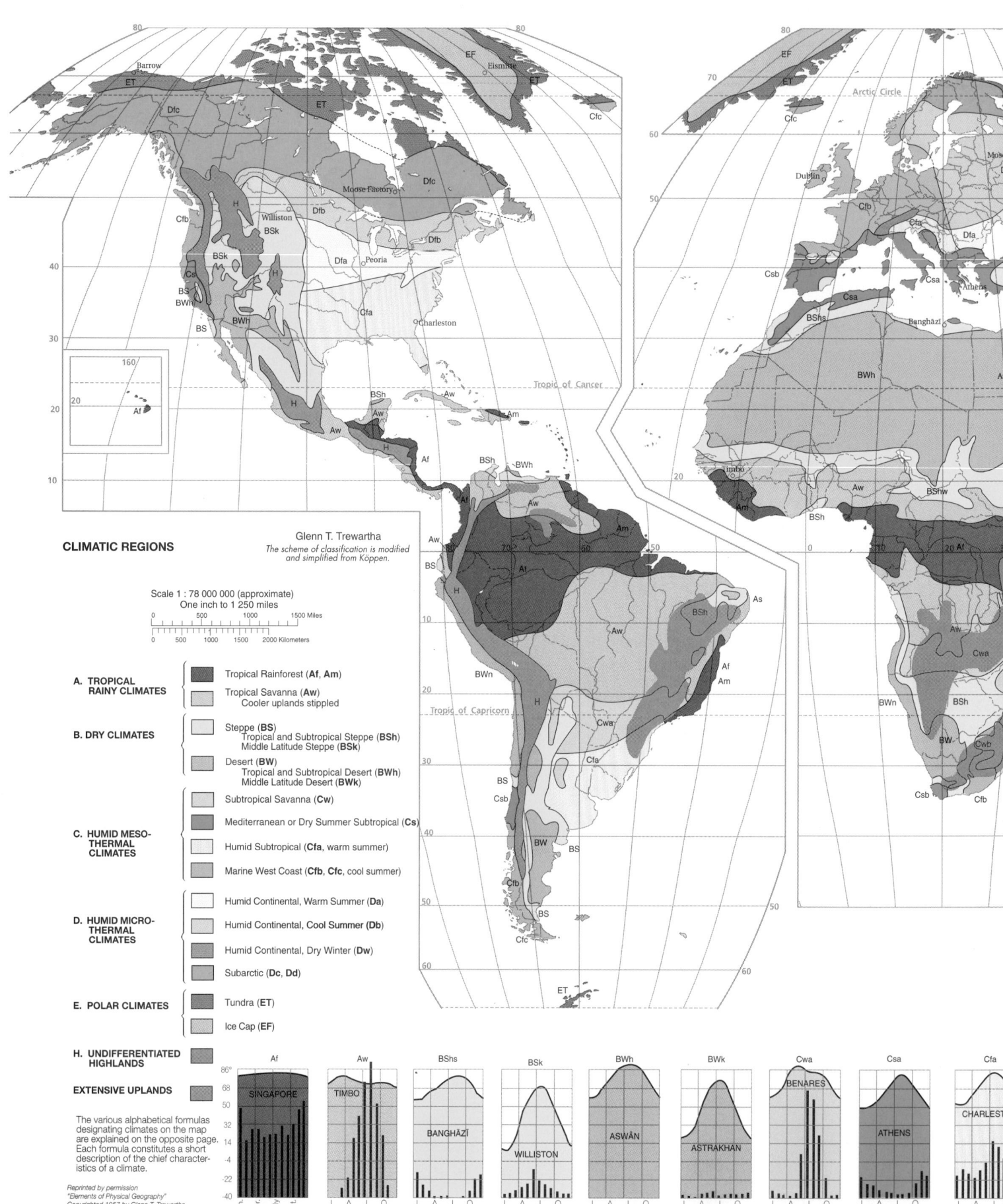

14

CLIMATIC REGIONS

Glenn T. Trewartha
The scheme of classification is modified and simplified from Köppen.

Scale 1 : 78 000 000 (approximate)
One inch to 1 250 miles

0	500	1000	1500 Miles	

0	500	1000	1500	2000 Kilometers

A. TROPICAL RAINY CLIMATES
Tropical Rainforest (**Af, Am**)
Tropical Savanna (**Aw**)
Cooler uplands stippled

B. DRY CLIMATES
Steppe (**BS**)
Tropical and Subtropical Steppe (**BSh**)
Middle Latitude Steppe (**BSk**)
Desert (**BW**)
Tropical and Subtropical Desert (**BWh**)
Middle Latitude Desert (**BWk**)

C. HUMID MESO-THERMAL CLIMATES
Subtropical Savanna (**Cw**)
Mediterranean or Dry Summer Subtropical (**Cs**)
Humid Subtropical (**Cfa**, warm summer)
Marine West Coast (**Cfb, Cfc**, cool summer)

D. HUMID MICRO-THERMAL CLIMATES
Humid Continental, Warm Summer (**Da**)
Humid Continental, Cool Summer (**Db**)
Humid Continental, Dry Winter (**Dw**)
Subarctic (**Dc, Dd**)

E. POLAR CLIMATES
Tundra (**ET**)
Ice Cap (**EF**)

H. UNDIFFERENTIATED HIGHLANDS

EXTENSIVE UPLANDS

The various alphabetical formulas designating climates on the map are explained on the opposite page. Each formula constitutes a short description of the chief characteristics of a climate.

*Reprinted by permission
"Elements of Physical Geography"
Copyrighted 1957 by Glenn T. Trewartha.
Published by the McGraw-Hill Book Company, Inc.*

Copyright by Rand McNally & Co.
Made in U.S.A.
N-GDS10000-C1- -2-2-4

Af	Aw	BShs	BSk	BWh	BWk	Cwa	Csa	Cfa
SINGAPORE	TIMBO	BANGHÄZÏ	WILLISTON	ASWÄN	ASTRAKHAN	BENARES	ATHENS	CHARLESTO

Tropical rain-forest climate | Tropical savanna climate; with wet and dry seasons | Tropical and sub-tropical steppe climate | Middle latitude steppe climate. | Tropical and sub-tropical desert climate | Middle latitude desert climate | Subtropical climate; winter drought and summer rain | Mild climate; sum-mer drought and winter rain | Moderate conti-tal forest climat mild winters

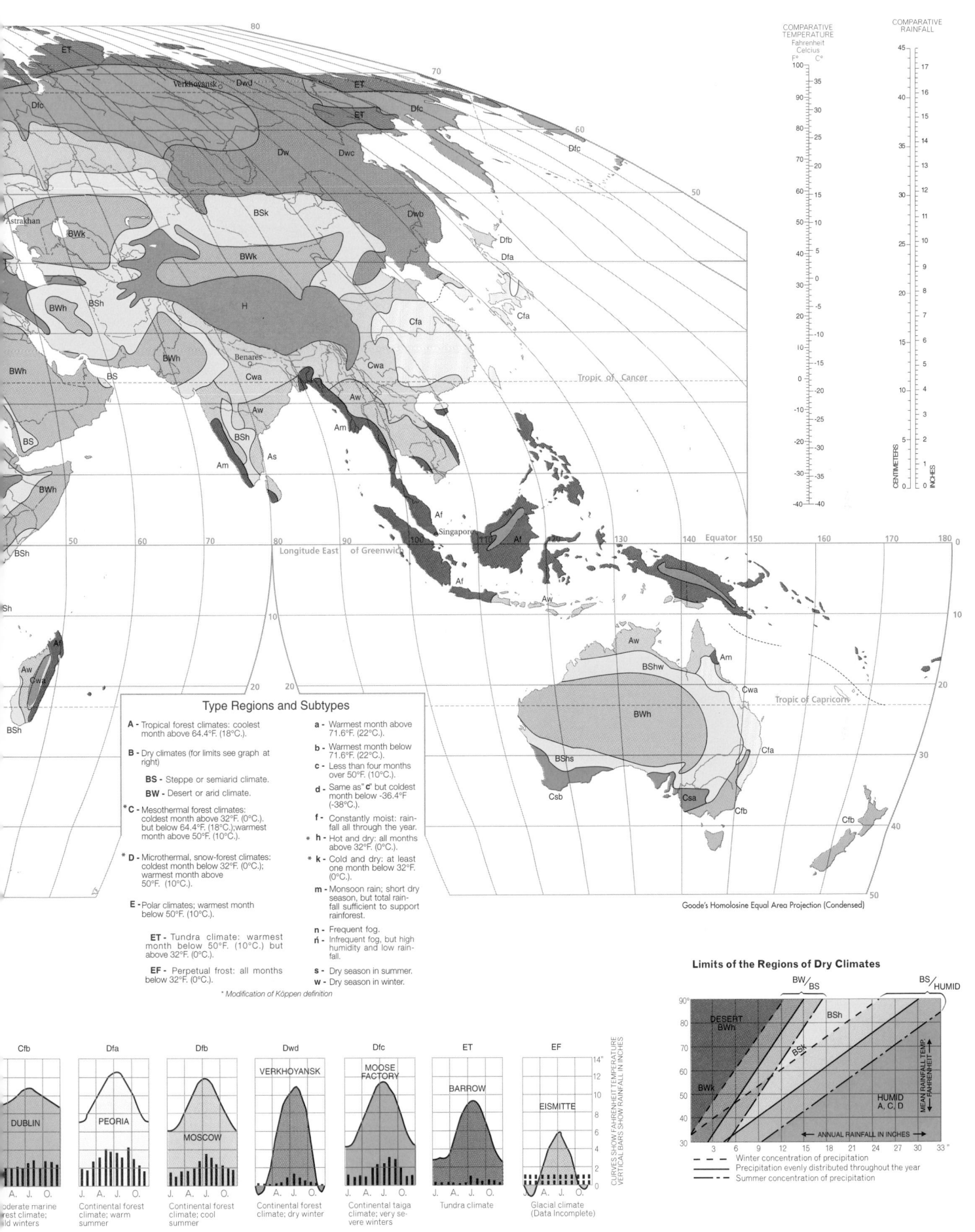

COMPARATIVE
TEMPERATURE
Fahrenheit
Celcius
F° C°

COMPARATIVE
RAINFALL

CENTIMETERS
INCHES

Tropic of Cancer

Equator

Tropic of Capricorn

Goode's Homolosine Equal Area Projection (Condensed)

Type Regions and Subtypes

A - Tropical forest climates: coolest month above 64.4°F. (18°C.).

B - Dry climates (for limits see graph at right)

  BS - Steppe or semiarid climate.

  BW - Desert or arid climate.

* **C** - Mesothermal forest climates: coldest month above 32°F. (0°C.). but below 64.4°F. (18°C.); warmest month above 50°F. (10°C.).

* **D** - Microthermal, snow-forest climates: coldest month below 32°F. (0°C.); warmest month above 50°F. (10°C.).

E - Polar climates; warmest month below 50°F. (10°C.).

  ET - Tundra climate: warmest month below 50°F. (10°C.) but above 32°F. (0°C.).

  EF - Perpetual frost: all months below 32°F. (0°C.).

* *Modification of Köppen definition*

a - Warmest month above 71.6°F. (22°C.).

b - Warmest month below 71.6°F. (22°C.).

c - Less than four months over 50°F. (10°C.).

d - Same as" c" but coldest month below -36.4°F (-38°C.).

f - Constantly moist: rainfall all through the year.

* **h** - Hot and dry: all months above 32°F. (0°C.).

* **k** - Cold and dry: at least one month below 32°F. (0°C.).

m - Monsoon rain; short dry season, but total rainfall sufficient to support rainforest.

n - Frequent fog.

ń - Infrequent fog, but high humidity and low rainfall.

s - Dry season in summer.

w - Dry season in winter.

Limits of the Regions of Dry Climates

BW/BS   BS/HUMID

DESERT BWh

BSh

BSk

BWk

HUMID A, C, D

ANNUAL RAINFALL IN INCHES

MEAN RAINFALL TEMP FAHRENHEIT

--- Winter concentration of precipitation
— Precipitation evenly distributed throughout the year
-·- Summer concentration of precipitation

CURVES SHOW FAHRENHEIT TEMPERATURE
VERTICAL BARS SHOW RAINFALL IN INCHES

Cfb
DUBLIN
J. A. J. O.
oderate marine rest climate; ild winters

Dfa
PEORIA
J. A. J. O.
Continental forest climate; warm summer

Dfb
MOSCOW
J. A. J. O.
Continental forest climate; cool summer

Dwd
VERKHOYANSK
J. A. J. O.
Continental forest climate; dry winter

Dfc
MOOSE FACTORY
J. A. J. O.
Continental taiga climate; very severe winters

ET
BARROW
J. A. J. O.
Tundra climate

EF
EISMITTE
A. J. O.
Glacial climate (Data Incomplete)

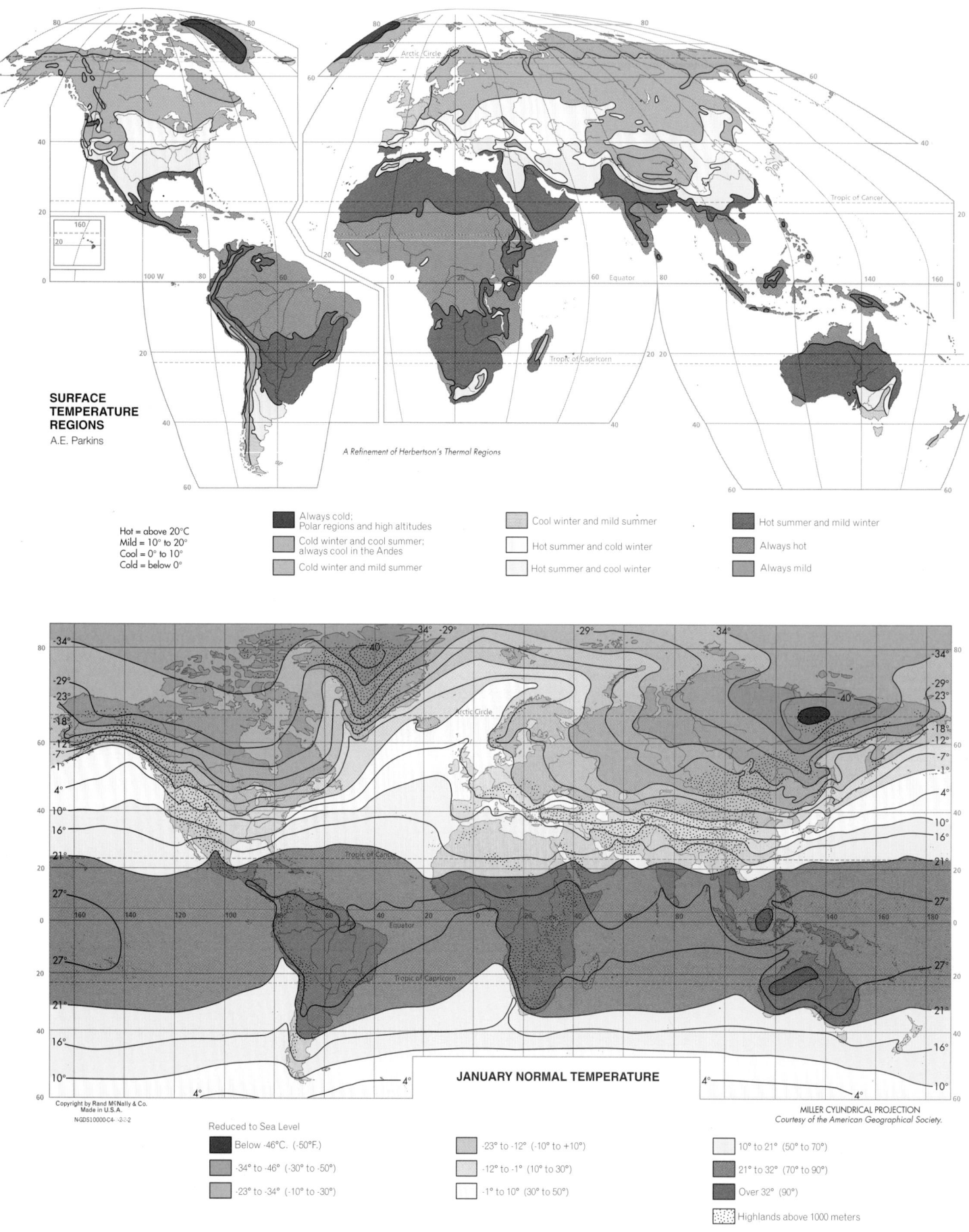

SURFACE TEMPERATURE REGIONS

A.E. Parkins

A Refinement of Herbertson's Thermal Regions

Hot = above 20°C
Mild = 10° to 20°
Cool = 0° to 10°
Cold = below 0°

Always cold; Polar regions and high altitudes

Cold winter and cool summer; always cool in the Andes

Cold winter and mild summer

Cool winter and mild summer

Hot summer and cold winter

Hot summer and cool winter

Hot summer and mild winter

Always hot

Always mild

JANUARY NORMAL TEMPERATURE

MILLER CYLINDRICAL PROJECTION
Courtesy of the American Geographical Society.

Copyright by Rand McNally & Co.
Made in U.S.A.

N-GDS10000-C4 -2-2-2

Reduced to Sea Level

Below -46°C. (-50°F.)

-34° to -46° (-30° to -50°)

-23° to -34° (-10° to -30°)

-23° to -12° (-10° to +10°)

-12° to -1° (10° to 30°)

-1° to 10° (30° to 50°)

10° to 21° (50° to 70°)

21° to 32° (70° to 90°)

Over 32° (90°)

Highlands above 1000 meters

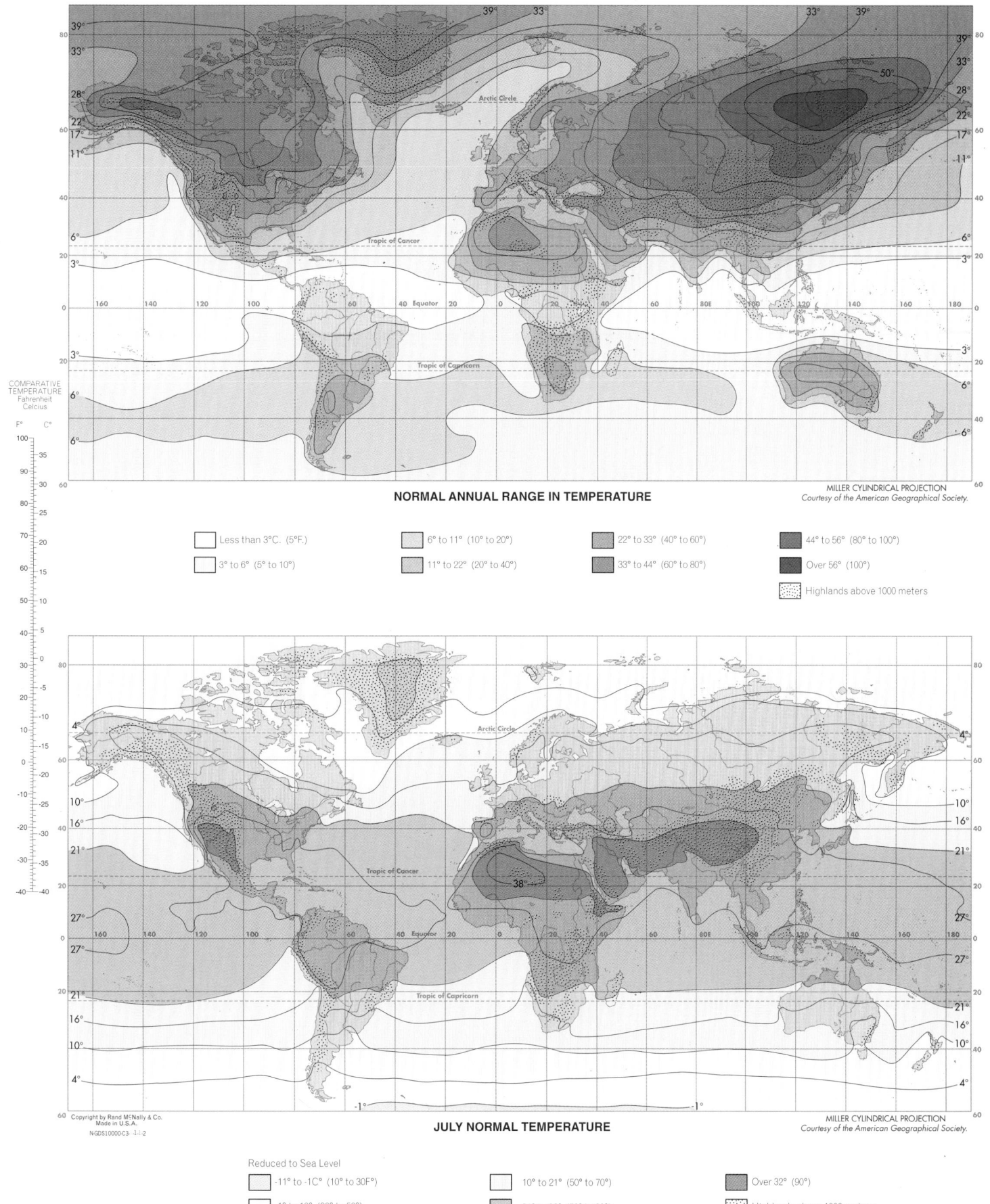

COMPARATIVE
TEMPERATURE
Fahrenheit
Celcius

NORMAL ANNUAL RANGE IN TEMPERATURE

MILLER CYLINDRICAL PROJECTION
Courtesy of the American Geographical Society.

Less than 3°C. (5°F.)

3° to 6° (5° to 10°)

6° to 11° (10° to 20°)

11° to 22° (20° to 40°)

22° to 33° (40° to 60°)

33° to 44° (60° to 80°)

44° to 56° (80° to 100°)

Over 56° (100°)

Highlands above 1000 meters

JULY NORMAL TEMPERATURE

Copyright by Rand McNally & Co.
Made in U.S.A.
NGDS10000-C3- -1-1-2

MILLER CYLINDRICAL PROJECTION
Courtesy of the American Geographical Society.

Reduced to Sea Level

-11° to -1C° (10° to 30F°)

-1° to 10° (30° to 50°)

10° to 21° (50° to 70°)

21° to 32° (70° to 90°)

Over 32° (90°)

Highlands above 1000 meters

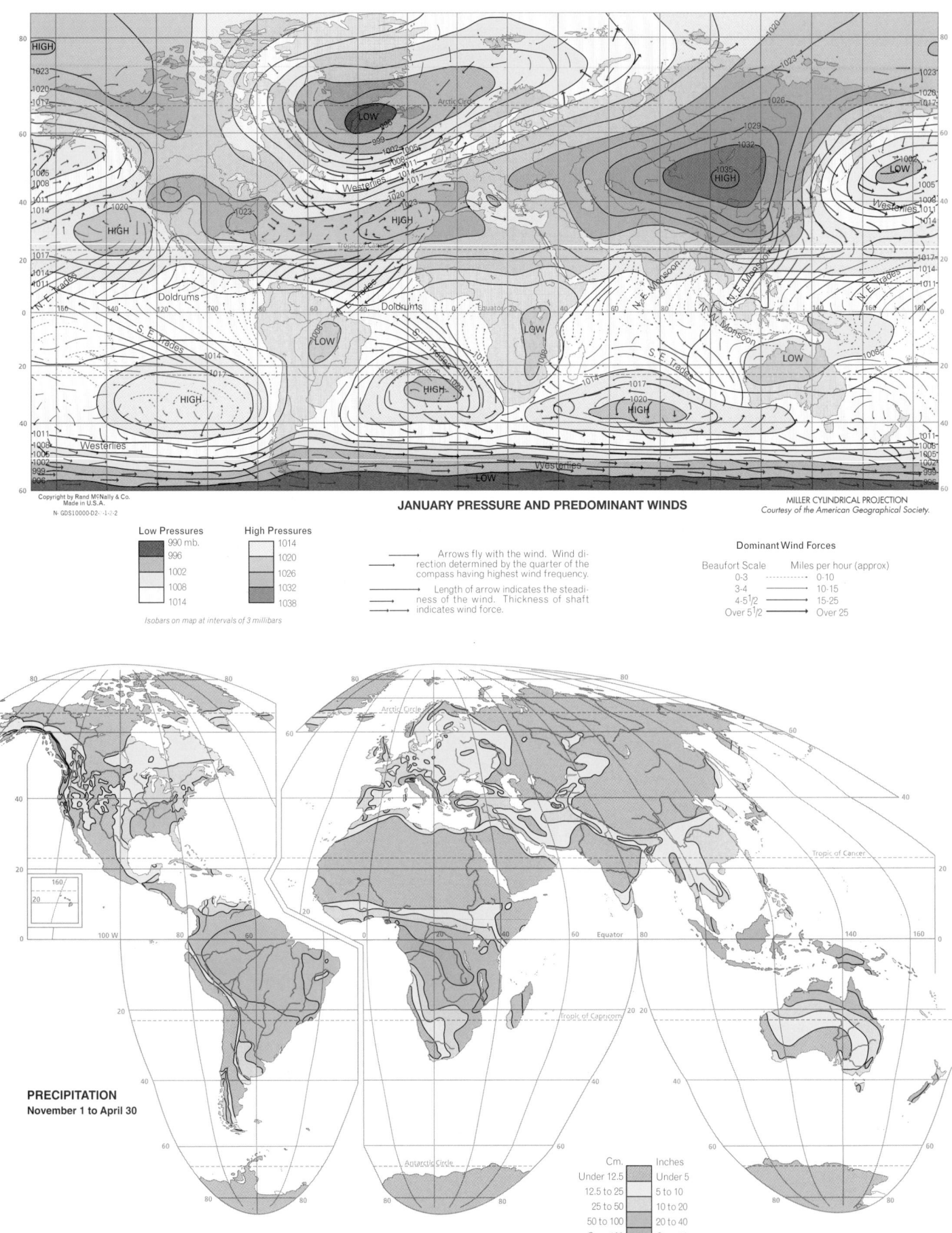

JANUARY PRESSURE AND PREDOMINANT WINDS

Copyright by Rand McNally & Co.
Made in U.S.A.
N- GDS10000-D2- -1-2-2

MILLER CYLINDRICAL PROJECTION
Courtesy of the American Geographical Society.

Low Pressures
990 mb.
996
1002
1008
1014

High Pressures
1014
1020
1026
1032
1038

Isobars on map at intervals of 3 millibars

Arrows fly with the wind. Wind direction determined by the quarter of the compass having highest wind frequency.

Length of arrow indicates the steadiness of the wind. Thickness of shaft indicates wind force.

Dominant Wind Forces

Beaufort Scale	Miles per hour (approx)
0-3	0-10
3-4	10-15
4-5½	15-25
Over 5½	Over 25

PRECIPITATION
November 1 to April 30

Cm.	Inches
Under 12.5	Under 5
12.5 to 25	5 to 10
25 to 50	10 to 20
50 to 100	20 to 40
Over 100	Over 40

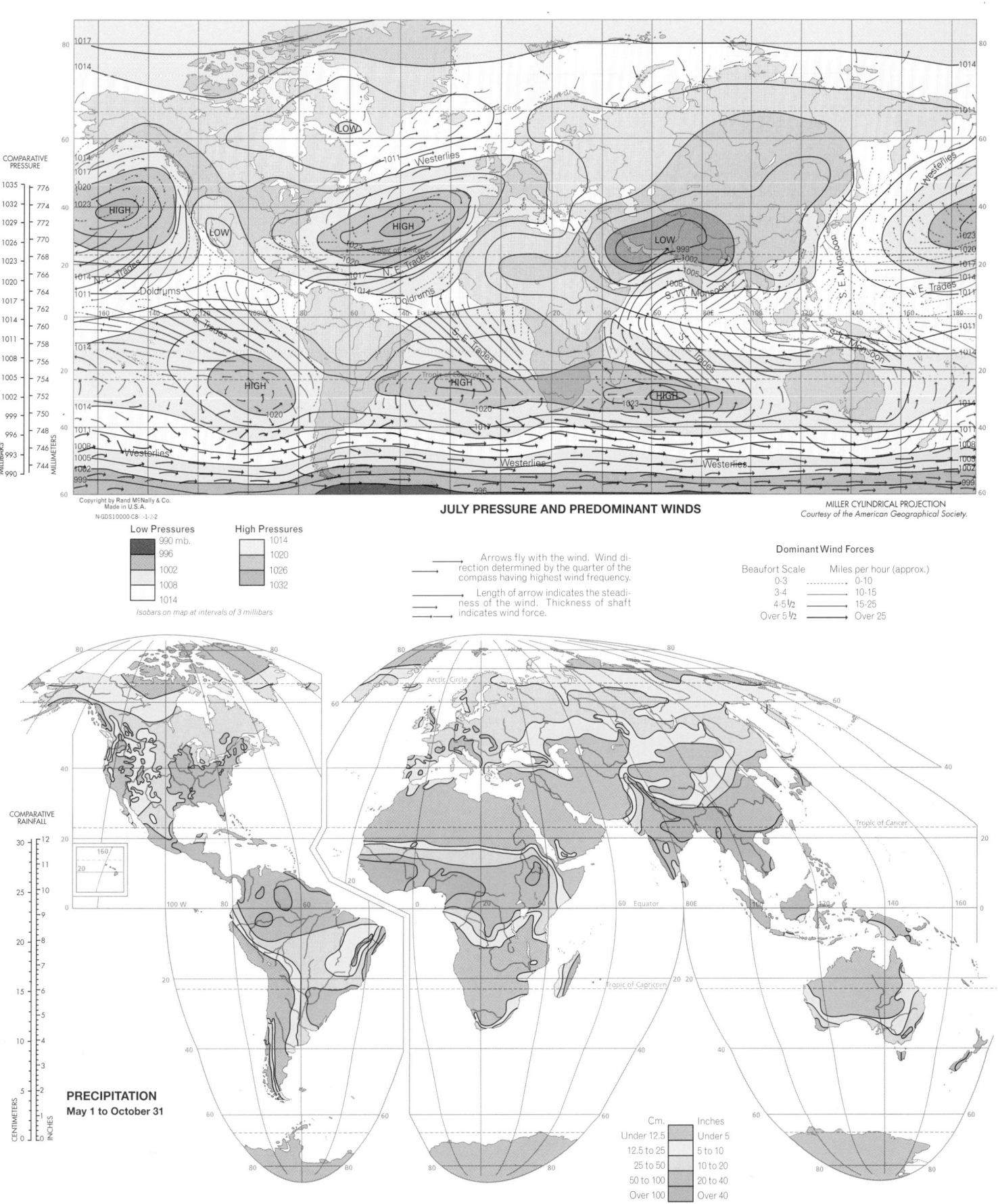

JULY PRESSURE AND PREDOMINANT WINDS

MILLER CYLINDRICAL PROJECTION
Courtesy of the American Geographical Society.

Copyright by Rand McNally & Co.
Made in U.S.A.
N-GDS10000-CB--1-2-2

COMPARATIVE
PRESSURE

1035	776
1032	774
1029	772
1026	770
1023	768
1020	766
1017	764
1014	762
1011	760
1008	758
1005	756
1002	754
999	752
996	750
993	748
990	746
	744

Low Pressures
990 mb.
996
1002
1008
1014

High Pressures
1014
1020
1026
1032

Isobars on map at intervals of 3 millibars

Arrows fly with the wind. Wind direction determined by the quarter of the compass having highest wind frequency.

Length of arrow indicates the steadiness of the wind. Thickness of shaft indicates wind force.

Dominant Wind Forces

Beaufort Scale   Miles per hour (approx.)
0-3 0-10
3-4 ———— 10-15
4-5½ ———— 15-25
Over 5½ ———— Over 25

COMPARATIVE
RAINFALL

PRECIPITATION
May 1 to October 31

Cm.   Inches
Under 12.5   Under 5
12.5 to 25   5 to 10
25 to 50   10 to 20
50 to 100   20 to 40
Over 100   Over 40

ANNUAL PRECIPITATON AND OCEAN CURRENTS

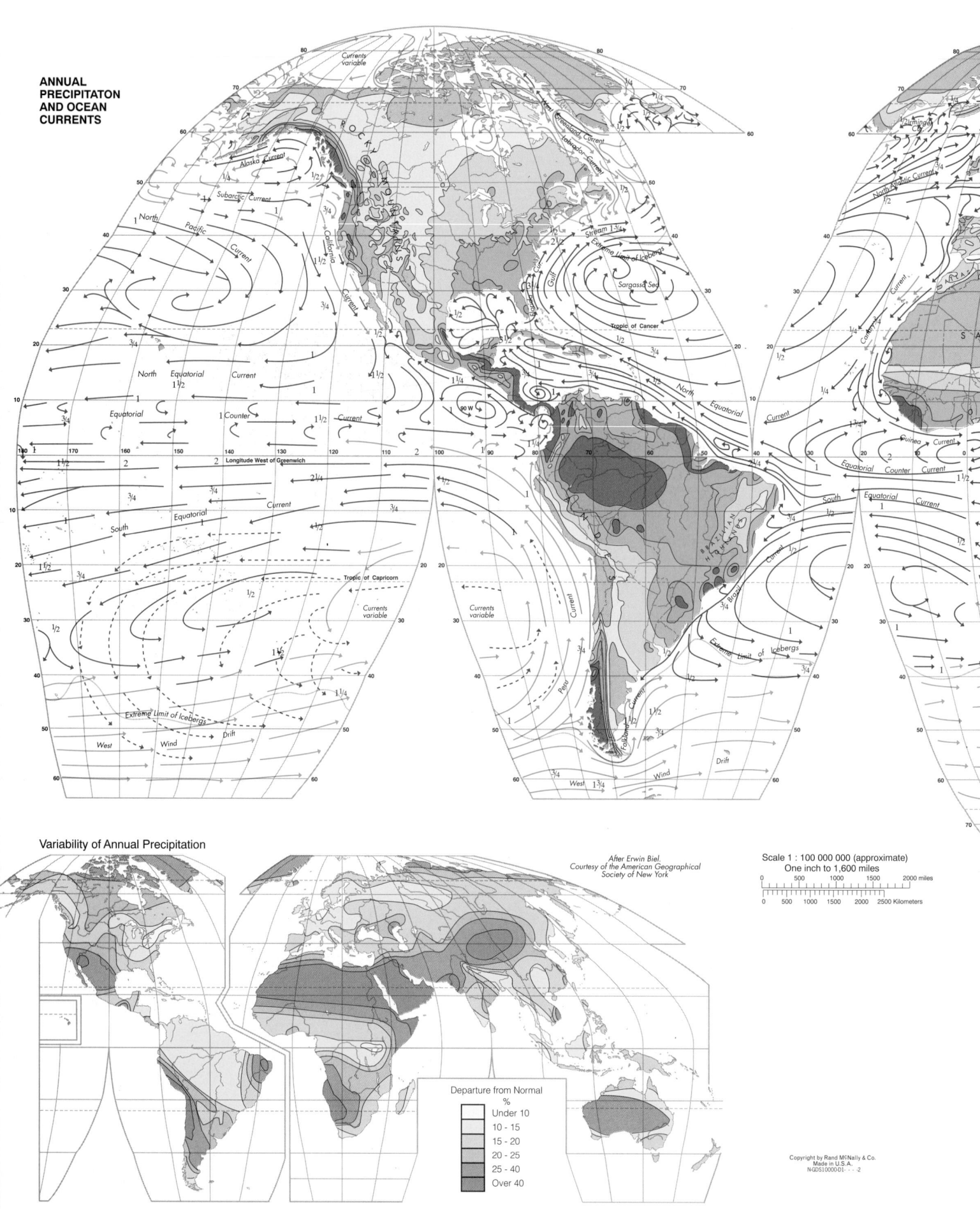

Currents variable

ROCKY MOUNTAINS

Alaska Current
Subarctic Current
North Pacific Current
California Current
North Equatorial Current
Equatorial Counter Current
Longitude West of Greenwich
South Equatorial Current
West Wind Drift
Extreme Limit of Icebergs

West Greenland Current
Labrador Current
Gulf Stream 1 3/4
Extreme Limit of Icebergs
Sargasso Sea
Tropic of Cancer
North Equatorial Current

Irminger
North Atlantic Current

Guinea Current
Equatorial Counter Current
South Equatorial Current

Tropic of Capricorn
Currents variable
Currents variable

BRAZILIAN HIGHLANDS
Brazil Current
Peru Current
Falkland Current
Extreme Limit of Icebergs
West Wind Drift

Variability of Annual Precipitation

After Erwin Biel.
Courtesy of the American Geographical Society of New York

Scale 1 : 100 000 000 (approximate)
One inch to 1,600 miles

0 500 1000 1500 2000 miles
0 500 1000 1500 2000 2500 Kilometers

Departure from Normal
%
Under 10
10 - 15
15 - 20
20 - 25
25 - 40
Over 40

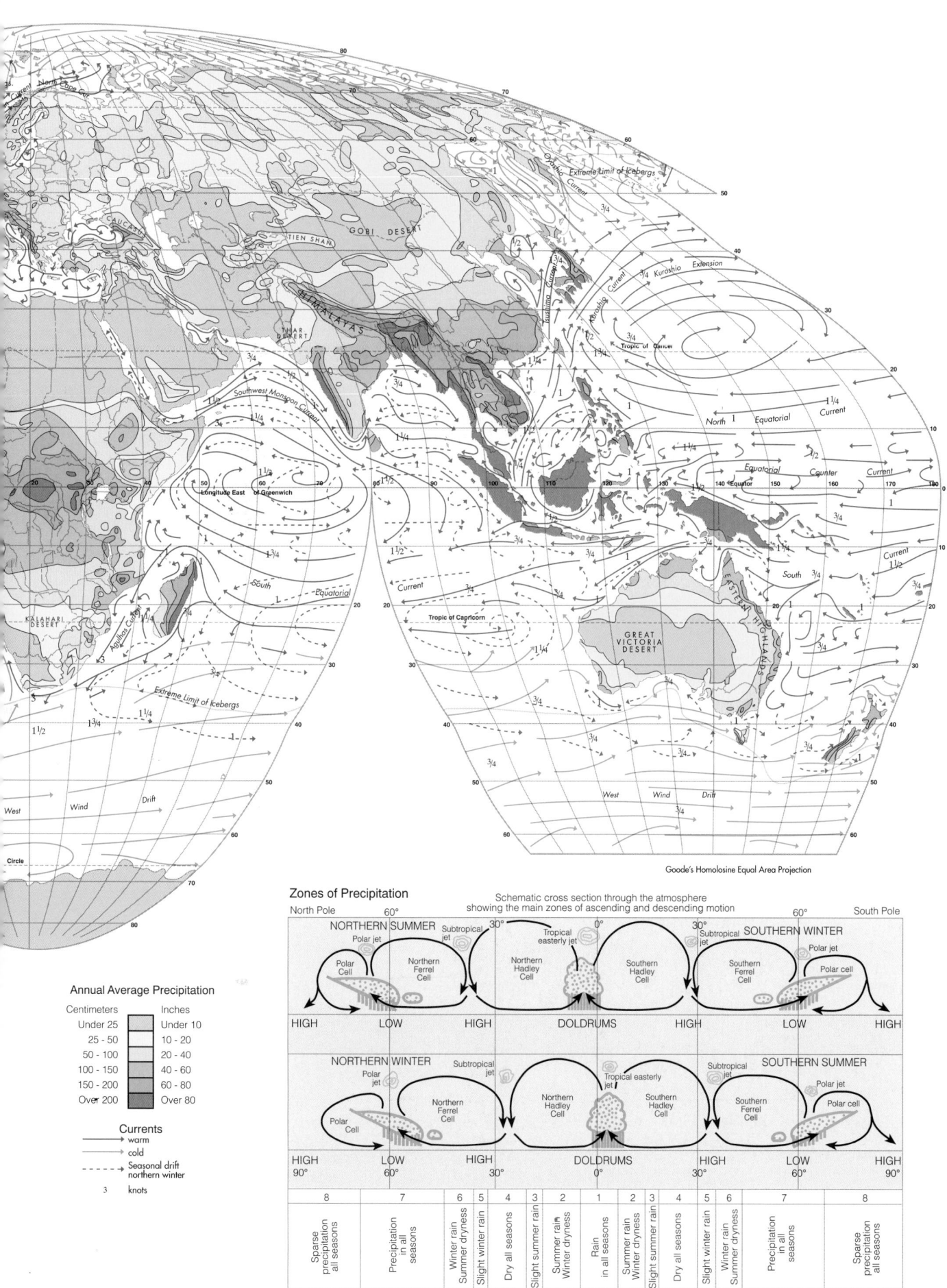

Goode's Homolosine Equal Area Projection

Zones of Precipitation

North Pole ... 60°

Schematic cross section through the atmosphere
showing the main zones of ascending and descending motion

60° ... South Pole

NORTHERN SUMMER

Polar jet — Subtropical jet — 30° — Tropical easterly jet — 0° — 30° — Subtropical jet — SOUTHERN WINTER

Polar Cell — Northern Ferrel Cell — Northern Hadley Cell — Southern Hadley Cell — Southern Ferrel Cell — Polar cell

HIGH — LOW — HIGH — DOLDRUMS — HIGH — LOW — HIGH

NORTHERN WINTER — Subtropical jet — Tropical easterly jet — Subtropical jet — SOUTHERN SUMMER

Polar jet — Polar Cell — Northern Ferrel Cell — Northern Hadley Cell — Southern Hadley Cell — Southern Ferrel Cell — Polar jet — Polar cell

HIGH — LOW — HIGH — DOLDRUMS — HIGH — LOW — HIGH
90° — 60° — 30° — 0° — 30° — 60° — 90°

8	7	6	5	4	3	2	1	2	3	4	5	6	7	8
Sparse precipitation all seasons	Precipitation in all seasons	Winter rain Summer dryness	Slight winter rain	Dry all seasons	Slight summer rain	Summer rain Winter dryness	Rain in all seasons	Summer rain Winter dryness	Slight summer rain	Dry all seasons	Slight winter rain	Winter rain Summer dryness	Precipitation in all seasons	Sparse precipitation all seasons

Annual Average Precipitation

Centimeters	Inches
Under 25	Under 10
25 - 50	10 - 20
50 - 100	20 - 40
100 - 150	40 - 60
150 - 200	60 - 80
Over 200	Over 80

Currents
→ warm
→ cold
- - - → Seasonal drift northern winter

3   knots

22

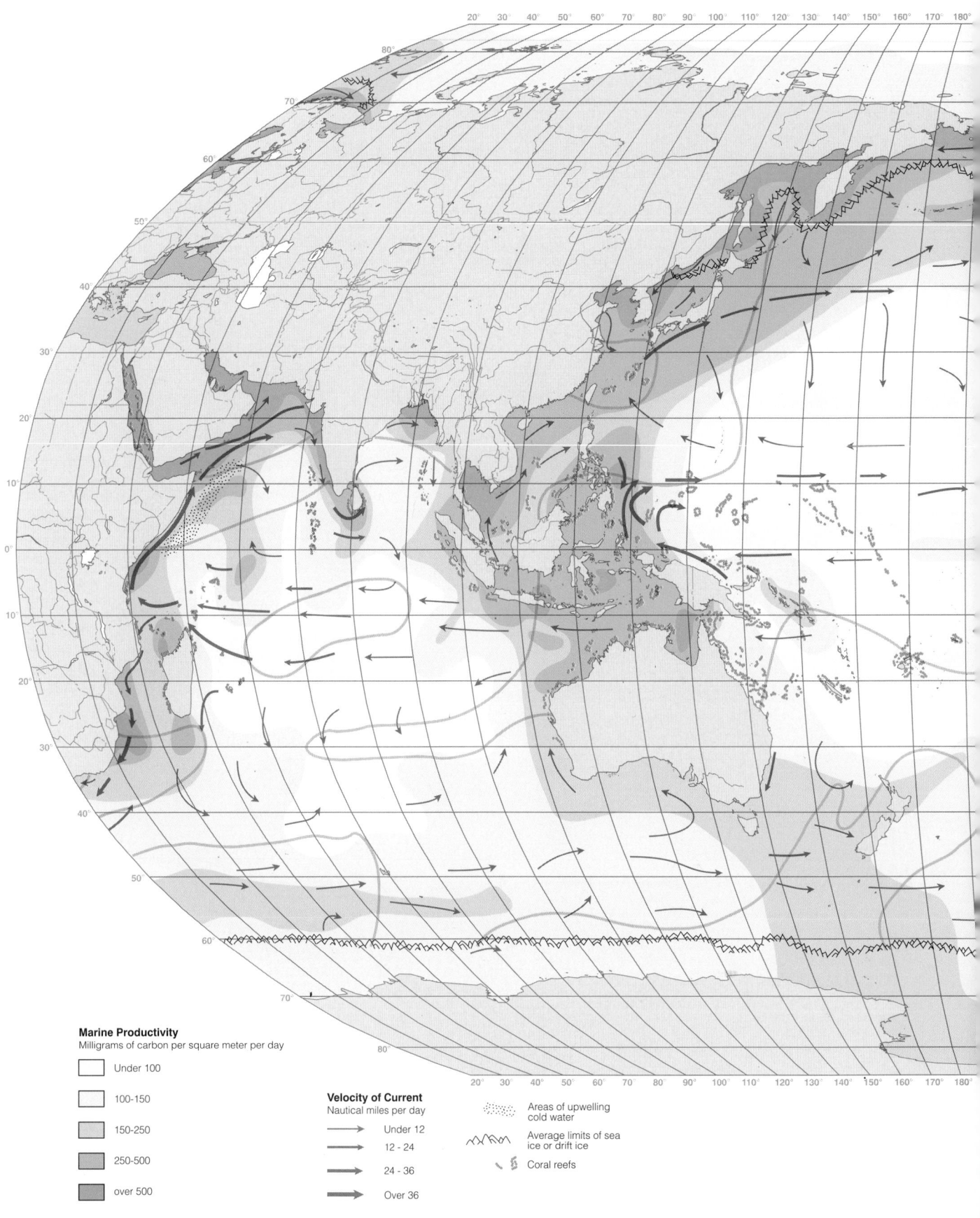

Marine Productivity
Milligrams of carbon per square meter per day

Under 100

100-150

150-250

250-500

over 500

Velocity of Current
Nautical miles per day

Under 12

12 - 24

24 - 36

Over 36

Areas of upwelling cold water

Average limits of sea ice or drift ice

Coral reefs

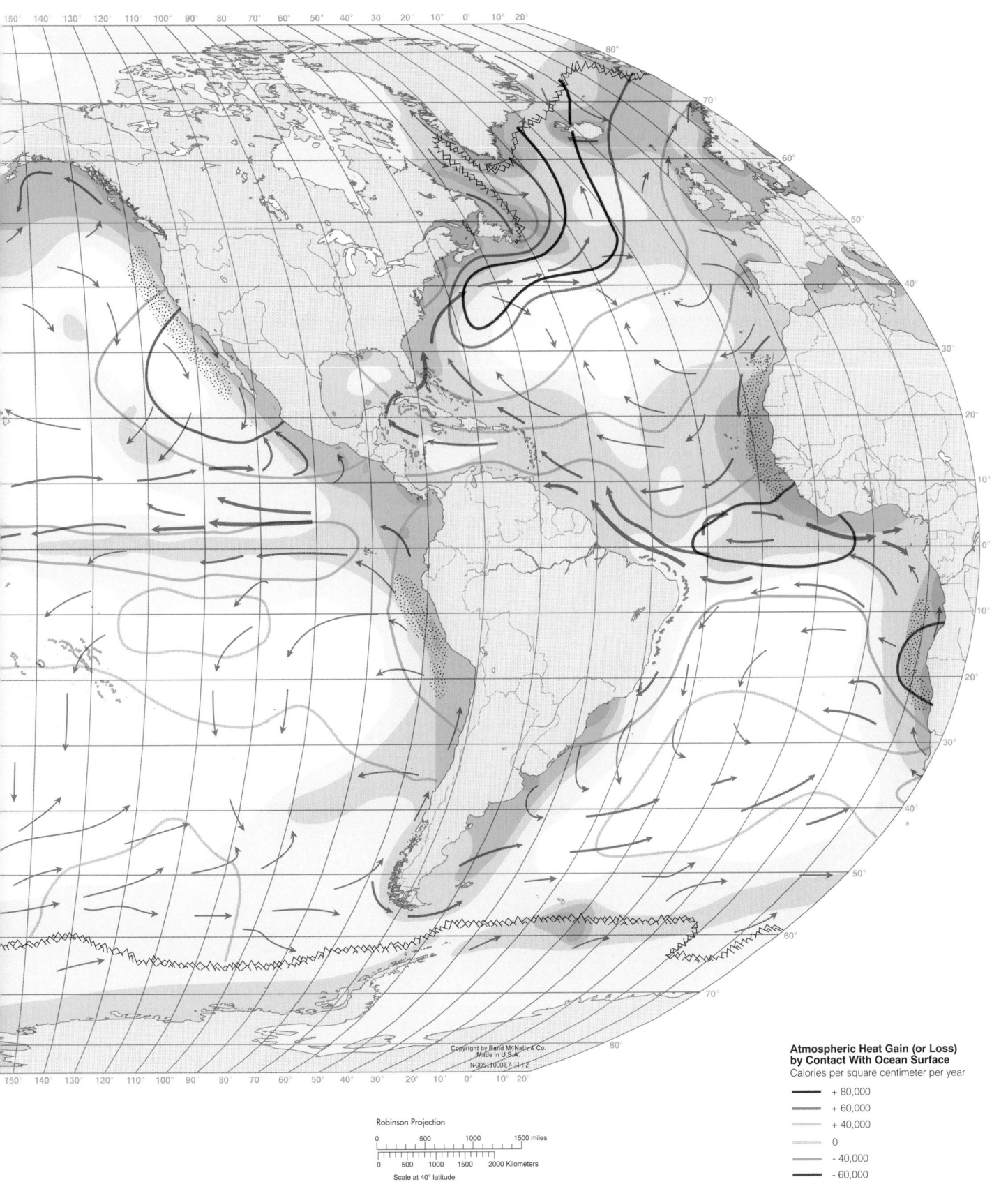

Atmospheric Heat Gain (or Loss) by Contact With Ocean Surface

Calories per square centimeter per year

———	+ 80,000
———	+ 60,000
———	+ 40,000
———	0
———	- 40,000
———	- 60,000

Robinson Projection

0   500   1000   1500 miles

0   500   1000   1500   2000 Kilometers

Scale at 40° latitude

Copyright by Rand McNally & Co.
Made in U.S.A.

N-GDSH1000E7 1-1-2

NATURAL VEGETATION

A.W. Küchler

Scale 1 : 78 000 000 (approximate)
One inch to 1 250 miles

0   500   1000   1500 Miles

0   500   1000   1500   2000 Kilometers

The various formulas are used to designate types of vegetation on this map. Each formula constitutes a short description of the chief characteristics of a vegetation. The classification is based on whether plants are woody or herbaceous, and if woody, whether they are broadleaf or needleleaf and evergreen or deciduous. The small letters are added to give more detail to the description. All capital letters other than **G** and **L** imply trees, unless accompanied by **s** or **z**. The small letters refer to the capital letter immediately preceding them. Thus, **DsG** means that the vegetation consists of broadleaf deciduous shrubs (**Ds**) and of grass (**G**); **GBp** represents grass (**G**) with patches of broadleaf evergreen trees (**Bp**).

B - Broadleaf evergreen

D - Broadleaf deciduous

E - Needleleaf evergreen

G - Grass

L - Herbaceous plants other than grass

M - Mixed broadleaf deciduous and needleleaf evergreen

N - Needleleaf deciduous

S - Semideciduous: broadleaf evergreen and broadleaf deciduous

b - Vegetation largely or entirely absent

i - Plants sufficiently far apart that they frequently do not touch

p - Growth singly or in groups or patches

s - Shrubform, minimum height 3 feet

z - Dwarf shrubform, maximum height 3 feet

B		Broadleaf evergreen trees
Bs		Broadleaf evergreen, shrubform, minimum height 3 feet
Bsp		Broadleaf evergreen, shrubform, minimum height 3 feet, growth singly or in groups or patches
Bzi, Bz		Broadleaf evergreen, dwarf shrubform, maximum height 3 feet, plants sufficiently far apart that they frequently do not touch
D		Broadleaf deciduous trees
Di		Broadleaf deciduous trees, plants sufficiently far apart that they frequently do not touch

TUNDRA

TAIGA

GOBI

TAKLA MAKAN

TERAI

Tropic of Cancer

Longitude East of Greenwich

Equator

Tropic of Capricorn

MALLEE

Goode's Homolosine Equal Area Projection (Condensed)

	Broadleaf deciduous, shrubform, minimum height 3 feet
	Broadleaf deciduous, shrubform, minimum height 3 feet, plants sufficiently far apart that they frequently do not touch
	Broadleaf deciduous, shrubform, minimum height 3 feet, growth singly or in groups or patches
	Broadleaf deciduous, dwarf shrubform, maximum height 3 feet, growth singly or in groups or patches
	Broadleaf deciduous, shrubform, minimum height 3 feet, Grass and other herbaceous plants
	Broadleaf deciduous trees, Grass and other herbaceous plants
	Broadleaf deciduous trees, Broadleaf evergreen, shrubform, minimum height 3 feet

E		Needleleaf evergreen trees
Ep		Needleleaf evergreen trees, growth singly or in groups or patches
G		Grass and other herbaceous plants
Gp		Grass and other herbaceous plants, growth singly or in groups or patches
GBp		Grass and other herbaceous plants, Broadleaf evergreen trees, growth singly or in groups or patches
GD		Grass and other herbaceous plants, Broadleaf deciduous trees
GDp		Grass and other herbaceous plants, Broadleaf deciduous trees, growth singly or in groups or patches

GDsp		Grass and other herbaceous plants, Broadleaf deciduous, shrubform, minimum height 3 feet, growth singly or in groups or patches
GSp		Grass and other herbaceous plants, Semideciduous: broadleaf evergreen and broadleaf deciduous trees, growth singly or in groups or patches
L		Herbaceous plants other than grass
M		Mixed: broadleaf deciduous and needleleaf evergreen trees
N		Needleleaf deciduous trees
ND		Needleleaf deciduous trees, Broadleaf deciduous trees

S		Semideciduous: broadleaf evergreen and broadleaf deciduous trees
Ss		Semideciduous: broadleaf evergreen and broadleaf deciduous, shrubform, minimum height 3 feet
SsG		Semideciduous: broadleaf evergreen and broadleaf deciduous, shrubform, minimum height 3 feet, Grass and other herbaceous plants
Szp		Semideciduous: broadleaf evergreen and broadleaf deciduous, dwarf shrubform, maximum height 3 feet, growth singly or in groups or patches
SE		Semideciduous: broadleaf evergreen and broadleaf deciduous, Needleleaf evergreen trees
b		Vegetation largely or entirely absent

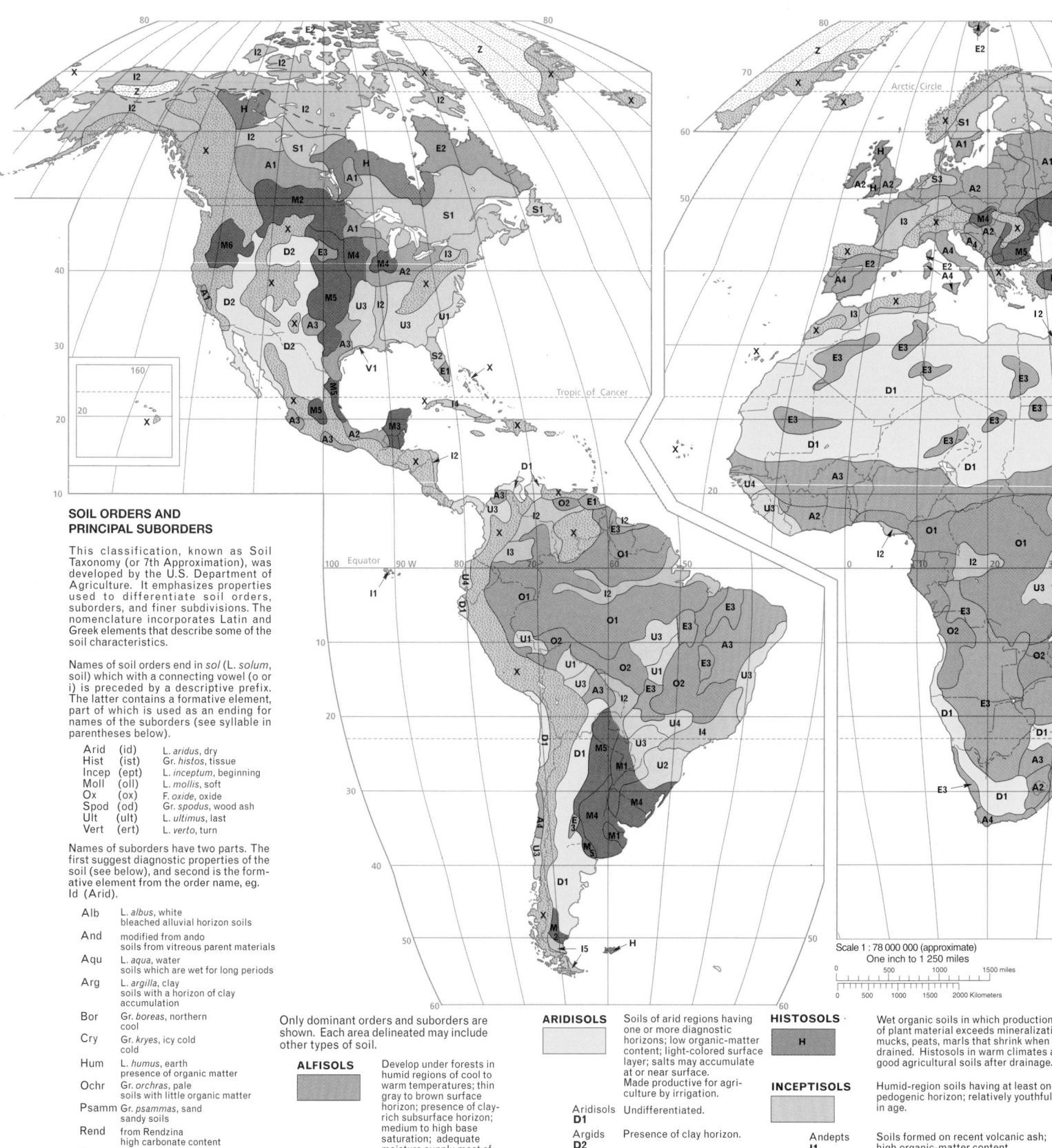

SOIL ORDERS AND PRINCIPAL SUBORDERS

This classification, known as Soil Taxonomy (or 7th Approximation), was developed by the U.S. Department of Agriculture. It emphasizes properties used to differentiate soil orders, suborders, and finer subdivisions. The nomenclature incorporates Latin and Greek elements that describe some of the soil characteristics.

Names of soil orders end in *sol* (L. *solum*, soil) which with a connecting vowel (o or i) is preceded by a descriptive prefix. The latter contains a formative element, part of which is used as an ending for names of the suborders (see syllable in parentheses below).

Arid	(id)	L. *aridus*, dry
Hist	(ist)	Gr. *histos*, tissue
Incep	(ept)	L. *inceptum*, beginning
Moll	(oll)	L. *mollis*, soft
Ox	(ox)	F. *oxide*, oxide
Spod	(od)	Gr. *spodus*, wood ash
Ult	(ult)	L. *ultimus*, last
Vert	(ert)	L. *verto*, turn

Names of suborders have two parts. The first suggest diagnostic properties of the soil (see below), and second is the formative element from the order name, eg. Id (Arid).

Alb	L. *albus*, white	bleached alluvial horizon soils
And	modified from ando	soils from vitreous parent materials
Aqu	L. *aqua*, water	soils which are wet for long periods
Arg	L. *argilla*, clay	soils with a horizon of clay accumulation
Bor	Gr. *boreas*, northern	cool
Cry	Gr. *kryes*, icy cold	cold
Hum	L. *humus*, earth	presence of organic matter
Ochr	Gr. *orchras*, pale	soils with little organic matter
Psamm	Gr. *psammos*, sand	sandy soils
Rend	from Rendzina	high carbonate content
Torr	L. *torridus*, hot and dry	soils of very dry climate
Ud	L. *udus*, humid	soils of humid climate
Umbr	L. *umbra*, shade	dark color reflecting relatively high organic matter
Ust	L. *ustus*, burnt	soils of dry climates with summer rains
Xer	Gr. *xeros*, dry	soils of dry climates with winter rains

Only dominant orders and suborders are shown. Each area delineated may include other types of soil.

ALFISOLS

Develop under forests in humid regions of cool to warm temperatures; thin gray to brown surface horizon; presence of clay-rich subsurface horizon; medium to high base saturation; adequate moisture supply most of year. Generally fertile agricultural soils.

Boralfs **A1**	Well-drained soils of boreal and subalpine forests.
Udalfs **A2**	Humid, well-drained, highly fertile soils of warm-summer climates.
Ustalfs **A3**	Reddish-brown forest and grassland soils of warm, subhumid to semiarid climates.
Xeralfs **A4**	Reddish soils lacking moisture during summer in Mediterranean climate zones.

ARIDISOLS

Soils of arid regions having one or more diagnostic horizons; low organic-matter content; light-colored surface layer; salts may accumulate at or near surface. Made productive for agriculture by irrigation.

Aridisols **D1**	Undifferentiated.
Argids **D2**	Presence of clay horizon.

ENTISOLS

Soils lacking pedogenic horizons; varied in nature.

Aquents **E1**	Seasonally or perenially wet; bluish or gray and mottled.
Orthents **E2**	Soils thinning due to erosion or where no sedimentation occurs.
Psamments **E3**	Sandy texture in all layers below surface; form on dune sands.

HISTOSOLS

Wet organic soils in which production of plant material exceeds mineralization mucks, peats, marls that shrink when drained. Histosols in warm climates are good agricultural soils after drainage.

INCEPTISOLS

Humid-region soils having at least one pedogenic horizon; relatively youthful in age.

Andepts **I1**	Soils formed on recent volcanic ash; high organic-matter content.
Aquepts **I2**	Humid region soils developed on river floodplains. Cryaquepts are tundra soils on permafrost.
Ochrepts **I3**	Thin, light-colored surface horizons; little organic-matter content.
Tropepts **I4**	Brownish or reddish soils of tropical environments.
Umbrepts **I5**	Dark-colored surface layer; high organic-matter content; hilly to mountainous topography.

Scale 1 : 78 000 000 (approximate)
One inch to 1 250 miles

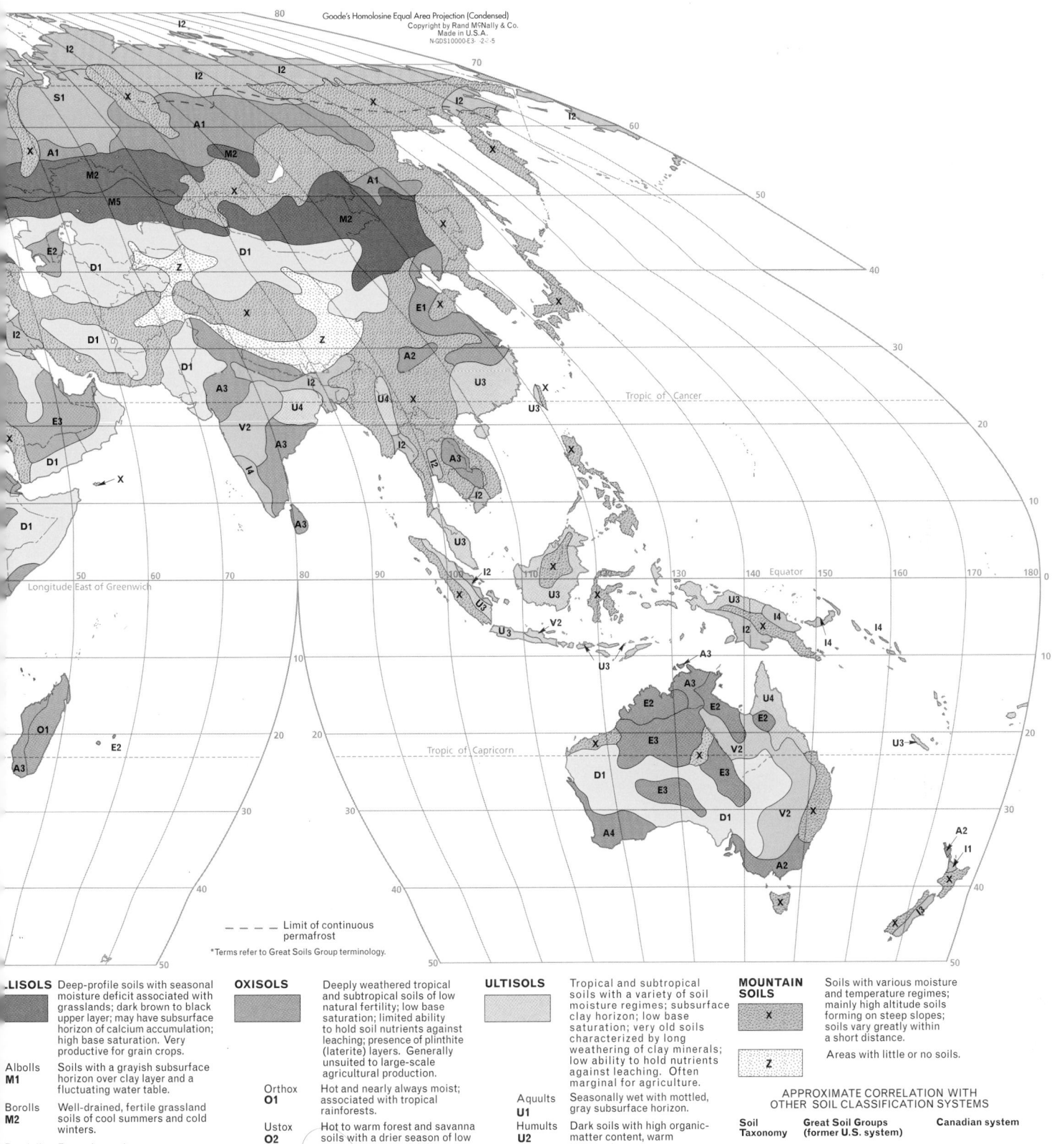

Goode's Homolosine Equal Area Projection (Condensed)
Copyright by Rand McNally & Co.
Made in U.S.A.
N-GDS10000-E3

– – – – Limit of continuous
permafrost

*Terms refer to Great Soils Group terminology.

LISOLS	Deep-profile soils with seasonal moisture deficit associated with grasslands; dark brown to black upper layer; may have subsurface horizon of calcium accumulation; high base saturation. Very productive for grain crops.	
Albolls **M1**	Soils with a grayish subsurface horizon over clay layer and a fluctuating water table.	
Borolls **M2**	Well-drained, fertile grassland soils of cool summers and cold winters.	
Rendolls **M3**	Formed on calcareous limestones.	
Udolls **M4**	Freely drained soils of humid regions with warm summers; excellent agricultural soils.	
Ustolls **M5**	Fertile agricultural soils of subhumid climates.	
Xerolls **M6**	Pronounced soil-moisture deficit during high-sun season; associated with Mediterranean climates.	

OXISOLS		Deeply weathered tropical and subtropical soils of low natural fertility; low base saturation; limited ability to hold soil nutrients against leaching; presence of plinthite (laterite) layers. Generally unsuited to large-scale agricultural production.
Orthox **O1**		Hot and nearly always moist; associated with tropical rainforests.
Ustox **O2**		Hot to warm forest and savanna soils with a drier season of low soil-moisture availability.
SPODOSOLS		Soils of moist climates ranging from subtropical to cold conditions; include a spodic subsurface horizon incorporating active organic matter beneath a light-colored, leached, sandy horizon. Generally marginal for agriculture.
Spodo-sols **S1**		Undifferentiated, mostly in high latitudes.
Aquods **S2**		Seasonally wet developed on sandy parent material.
Humods **S3**		Considerable organic matter present in subsurface horizon.
Orthods **S4**		Subsurface accumulations of iron, aluminum, and organic matter.

ULTISOLS		Tropical and subtropical soils with a variety of soil moisture regimes; subsurface clay horizon; low base saturation; very old soils characterized by long weathering of clay minerals; low ability to hold nutrients against leaching. Often marginal for agriculture.
Aquults **U1**		Seasonally wet with mottled, gray subsurface horizon.
Humults **U2**		Dark soils with high organic-matter content, warm temperatures.
Udults **U3**		Low organic-matter content and temperate to hot conditions.
Ustults **U4**		Seasonally dry, warm to hot conditions.
VERTISOLS		Dark tropical and subtropical soils developed on heavy clays; deep shrinkage cracks appear during dry season which become filled with loose surface materials that absorb moisture and swell during wet season. Generally fertile and well suited to crop production.
Uderts **V1**		Generally moist with limited period for shrinkage cracks to develop.
Usterts **V2**		Over three months of shrinkage-crack formation.

MOUNTAIN SOILS	Soils with various moisture and temperature regimes; mainly high altitude soils forming on steep slopes; soils vary greatly within a short distance.
X	
Z	Areas with little or no soils.

APPROXIMATE CORRELATION WITH OTHER SOIL CLASSIFICATION SYSTEMS

Soil Taxonomy	Great Soil Groups (former U.S. system)	Canadian system
Udalfs	Gray-brown Podzolic	Luvisolic Gray-Brown
Ustalfs	Reddish Chestnut; Red and Yellow Podzolic	
Aridisols	Desert and Reddish Desert Solonetz, Solonchak	
Entisols	Lithosols	Regosolic
Histosols	Bog	Organic
Inceptisol		Brunisolic
Orthents	Lithosols	
Aquepts	Humic Gley	Gleysolic
Cryaquept	Tundra	Cryosolic
Boralfs		Luvisolic Gray; Solonetzic
Borolls	Chernozem Chestnut Brown	Chernozemic, Solonetzic
Rendolls	Rendzina	
Udolls	Prairie	
Ustolls	Brown	
Oxisols	Latosols	
Humod		Humic Podzolic
Orthods	Podzols	Podzolic
Udults	Red and Yellow Podzolic Reddish Brown Lateritic	
Vertisols	Rendzina	

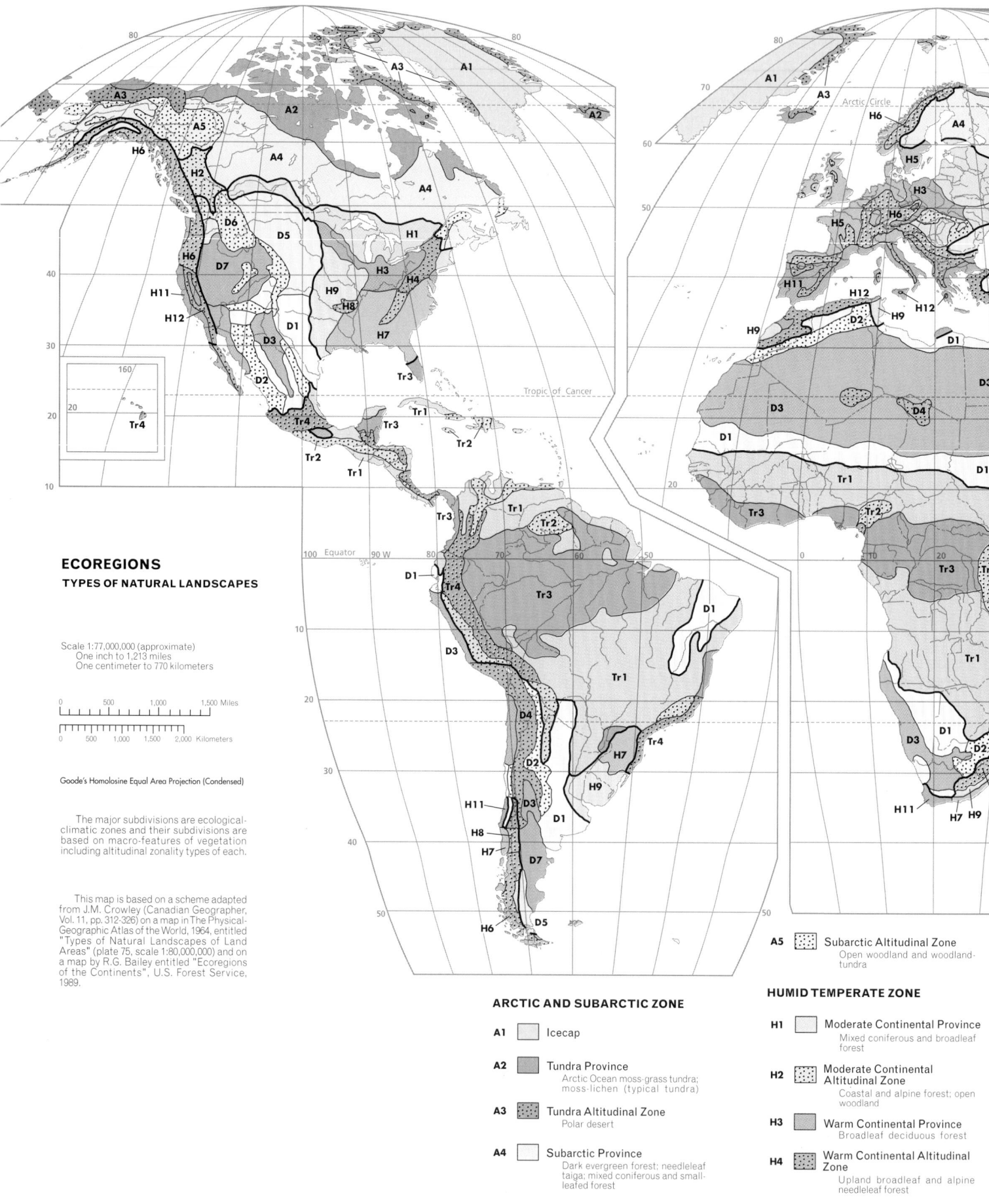

ECOREGIONS

TYPES OF NATURAL LANDSCAPES

Scale 1:77,000,000 (approximate)
One inch to 1,213 miles
One centimeter to 770 kilometers

| 0 | 500 | 1,000 | 1,500 Miles |

| 0 | 500 | 1,000 | 1,500 | 2,000 Kilometers |

Goode's Homolosine Equal Area Projection (Condensed)

The major subdivisions are ecological-climatic zones and their subdivisions are based on macro-features of vegetation including altitudinal zonality types of each.

This map is based on a scheme adapted from J.M. Crowley (Canadian Geographer, Vol. 11, pp. 312-326) on a map in The Physical-Geographic Atlas of the World, 1964, entitled "Types of Natural Landscapes of Land Areas" (plate 75, scale 1:80,000,000) and on a map by R.G. Bailey entitled "Ecoregions of the Continents", U.S. Forest Service, 1989.

ARCTIC AND SUBARCTIC ZONE

A1   Icecap

A2   Tundra Province
Arctic Ocean moss-grass tundra; moss-lichen (typical tundra)

A3   Tundra Altitudinal Zone
Polar desert

A4   Subarctic Province
Dark evergreen forest; needleleaf taiga; mixed coniferous and small-leafed forest

A5   Subarctic Altitudinal Zone
Open woodland and woodland-tundra

HUMID TEMPERATE ZONE

H1   Moderate Continental Province
Mixed coniferous and broadleaf forest

H2   Moderate Continental Altitudinal Zone
Coastal and alpine forest; open woodland

H3   Warm Continental Province
Broadleaf deciduous forest

H4   Warm Continental Altitudinal Zone
Upland broadleaf and alpine needleleaf forest

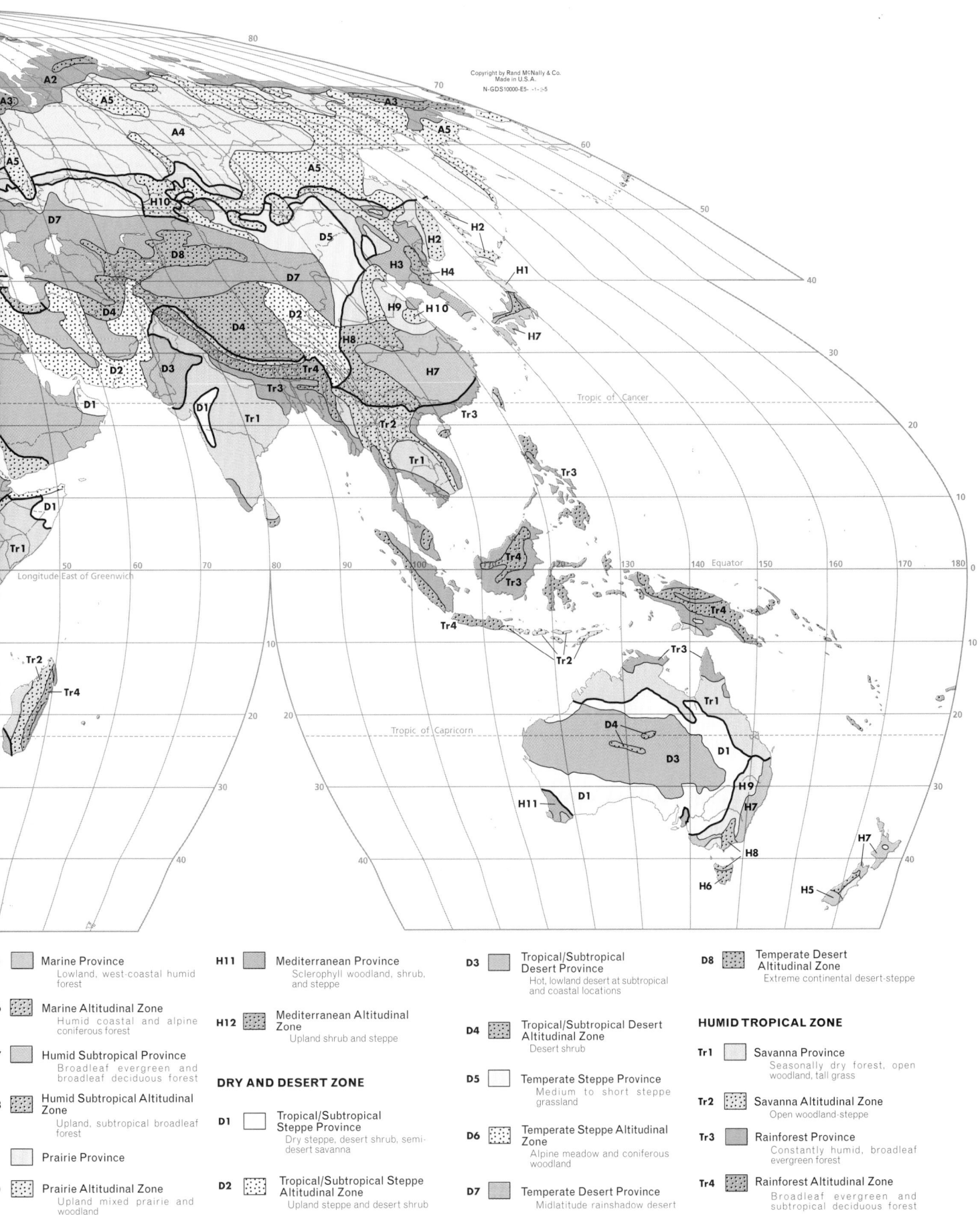

Copyright by Rand McNally & Co.
Made in U.S.A.
N-GDS10000-E5- -1- >-5

Longitude East of Greenwich

Tropic of Cancer

Equator

Tropic of Capricorn

	Marine Province					
	Lowland, west-coastal humid forest					

	Marine Altitudinal Zone
	Humid coastal and alpine coniferous forest

	Humid Subtropical Province
	Broadleaf evergreen and broadleaf deciduous forest

	Humid Subtropical Altitudinal Zone
	Upland, subtropical broadleaf forest

	Prairie Province

	Prairie Altitudinal Zone
	Upland mixed prairie and woodland

H11 Mediterranean Province
   Sclerophyll woodland, shrub, and steppe

H12 Mediterranean Altitudinal Zone
   Upland shrub and steppe

DRY AND DESERT ZONE

D1 Tropical/Subtropical Steppe Province
   Dry steppe, desert shrub, semi-desert savanna

D2 Tropical/Subtropical Steppe Altitudinal Zone
   Upland steppe and desert shrub

D3 Tropical/Subtropical Desert Province
   Hot, lowland desert at subtropical and coastal locations

D4 Tropical/Subtropical Desert Altitudinal Zone
   Desert shrub

D5 Temperate Steppe Province
   Medium to short steppe grassland

D6 Temperate Steppe Altitudinal Zone
   Alpine meadow and coniferous woodland

D7 Temperate Desert Province
   Midlatitude rainshadow desert

D8 Temperate Desert Altitudinal Zone
   Extreme continental desert-steppe

HUMID TROPICAL ZONE

Tr1 Savanna Province
   Seasonally dry forest, open woodland, tall grass

Tr2 Savanna Altitudinal Zone
   Open woodland-steppe

Tr3 Rainforest Province
   Constantly humid, broadleaf evergreen forest

Tr4 Rainforest Altitudinal Zone
   Broadleaf evergreen and subtropical deciduous forest

POPULATION DENSITY

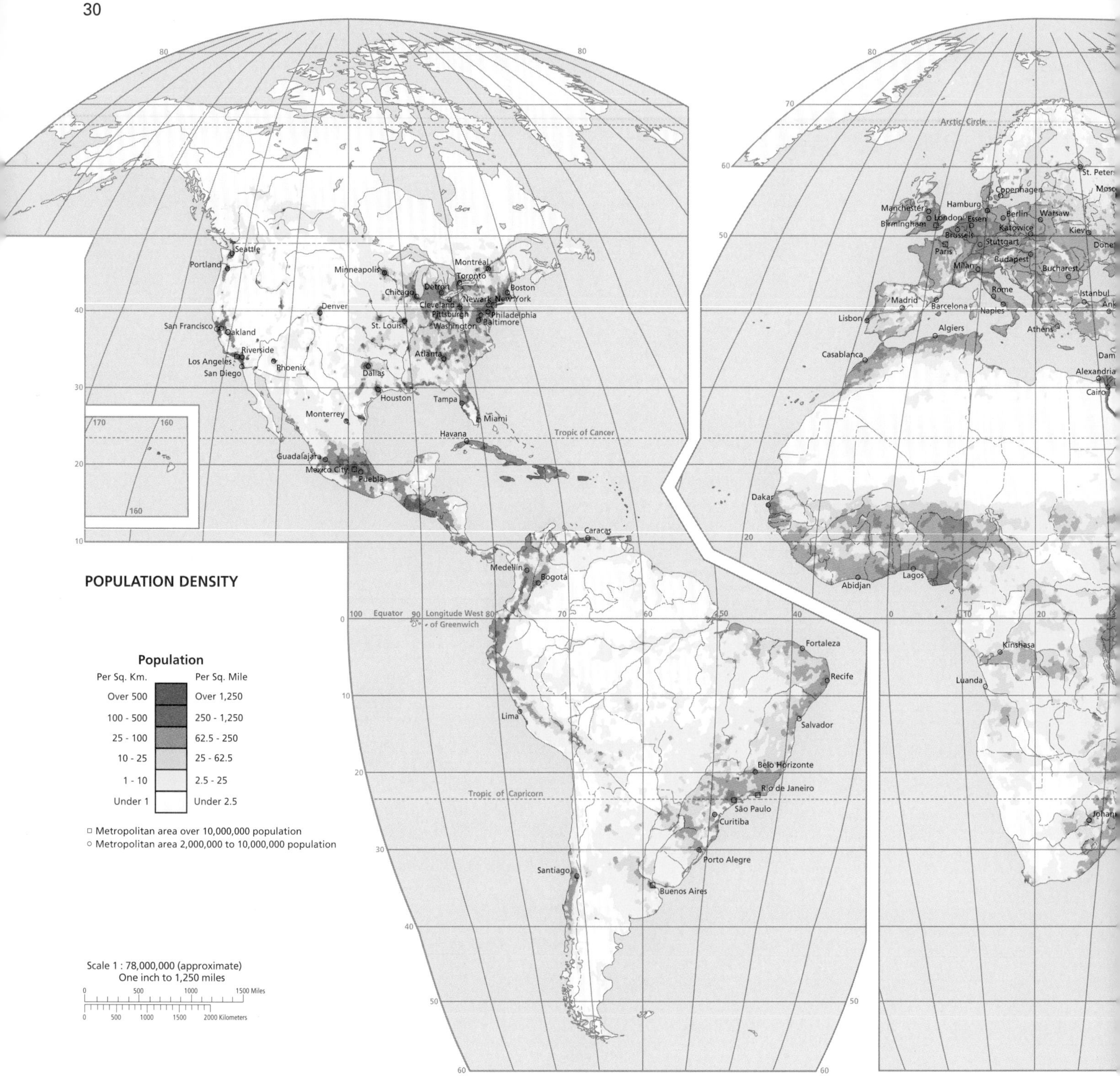

Population
Per Sq. Km. | Per Sq. Mile
Over 500 | Over 1,250
100 - 500 | 250 - 1,250
25 - 100 | 62.5 - 250
10 - 25 | 25 - 62.5
1 - 10 | 2.5 - 25
Under 1 | Under 2.5
□ Metropolitan area over 10,000,000 population
○ Metropolitan area 2,000,000 to 10,000,000 population
Scale 1 : 78,000,000 (approximate)
One inch to 1,250 miles
0 500 1000 1500 Miles
0 500 1000 1500 2000 Kilometers
Arctic Circle
Tropic of Cancer
Equator
Longitude West of Greenwich
Tropic of Capricorn
Seattle
Portland
Minneapolis
Montréal
Toronto
Boston
Detroit
Chicago
Cleveland
Newark
New York
Pittsburgh
Philadelphia
Washington
Baltimore
Denver
St. Louis
San Francisco
Oakland
Riverside
Los Angeles
San Diego
Phoenix
Dallas
Atlanta
Houston
Tampa
Miami
Monterrey
Havana
Guadalajara
Mexico City
Puebla
Caracas
Medellín
Bogotá
Lima
Fortaleza
Recife
Salvador
Belo Horizonte
Rio de Janeiro
São Paulo
Curitiba
Porto Alegre
Santiago
Buenos Aires
Manchester
Birmingham
London
Hamburg
Copenhagen
Essen
Berlin
Warsaw
Brussels
Katowice
Kiev
Paris
Stuttgart
Milan
Budapest
Bucharest
Madrid
Barcelona
Rome
Naples
Istanbul
Lisbon
Algiers
Athens
Casablanca
Alexandria
Cairo
Dakar
Abidjan
Lagos
Kinshasa
Luanda

Largest Countries of the World 1950, 2000, 2050

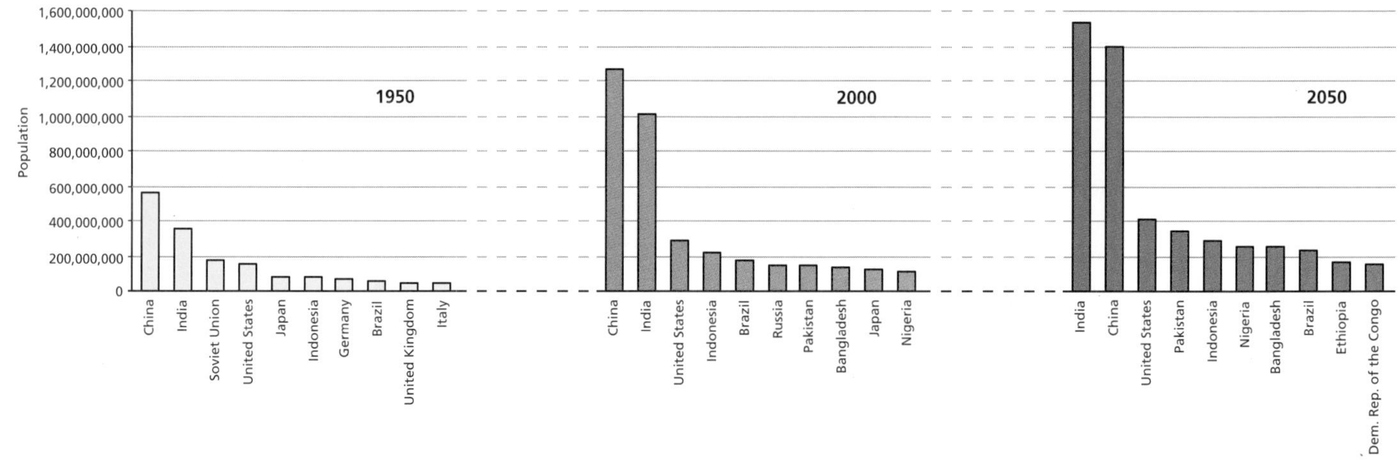

Population
1,600,000,000
1,400,000,000
1,200,000,000
1,000,000,000
800,000,000
600,000,000
400,000,000
200,000,000
0
1950
China
India
Soviet Union
United States
Japan
Indonesia
Germany
Brazil
United Kingdom
Italy
2000
China
India
United States
Indonesia
Brazil
Russia
Pakistan
Bangladesh
Japan
Nigeria
2050
India
China
United States
Pakistan
Indonesia
Nigeria
Bangladesh
Brazil
Ethiopia
Dem. Rep. of the Congo

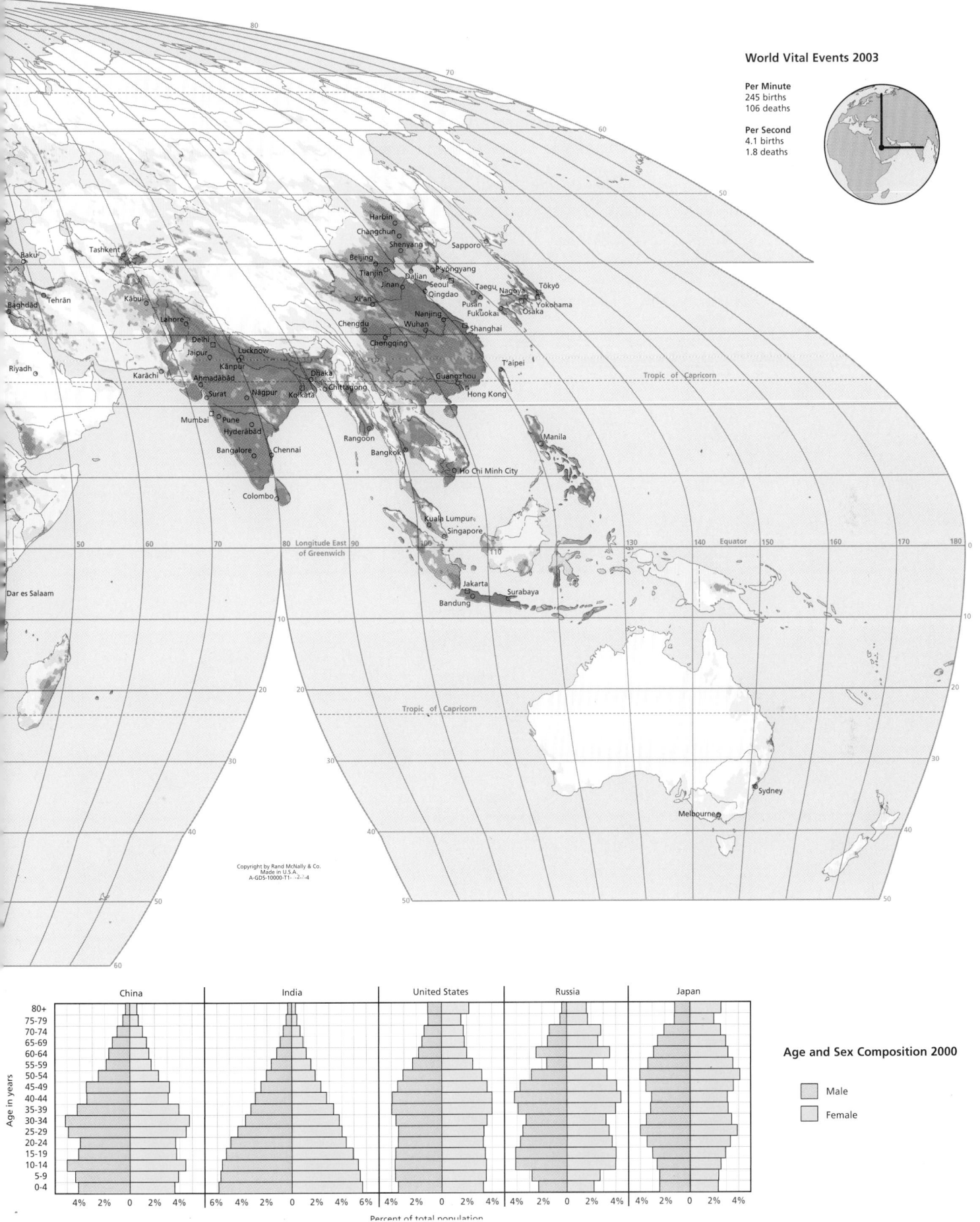

World Vital Events 2003

Per Minute
245 births
106 deaths

Per Second
4.1 births
1.8 deaths

Age and Sex Composition 2000

Male

Female

Copyright by Rand McNally & Co.
Made in U.S.A.
A-GD5-10000-T1-

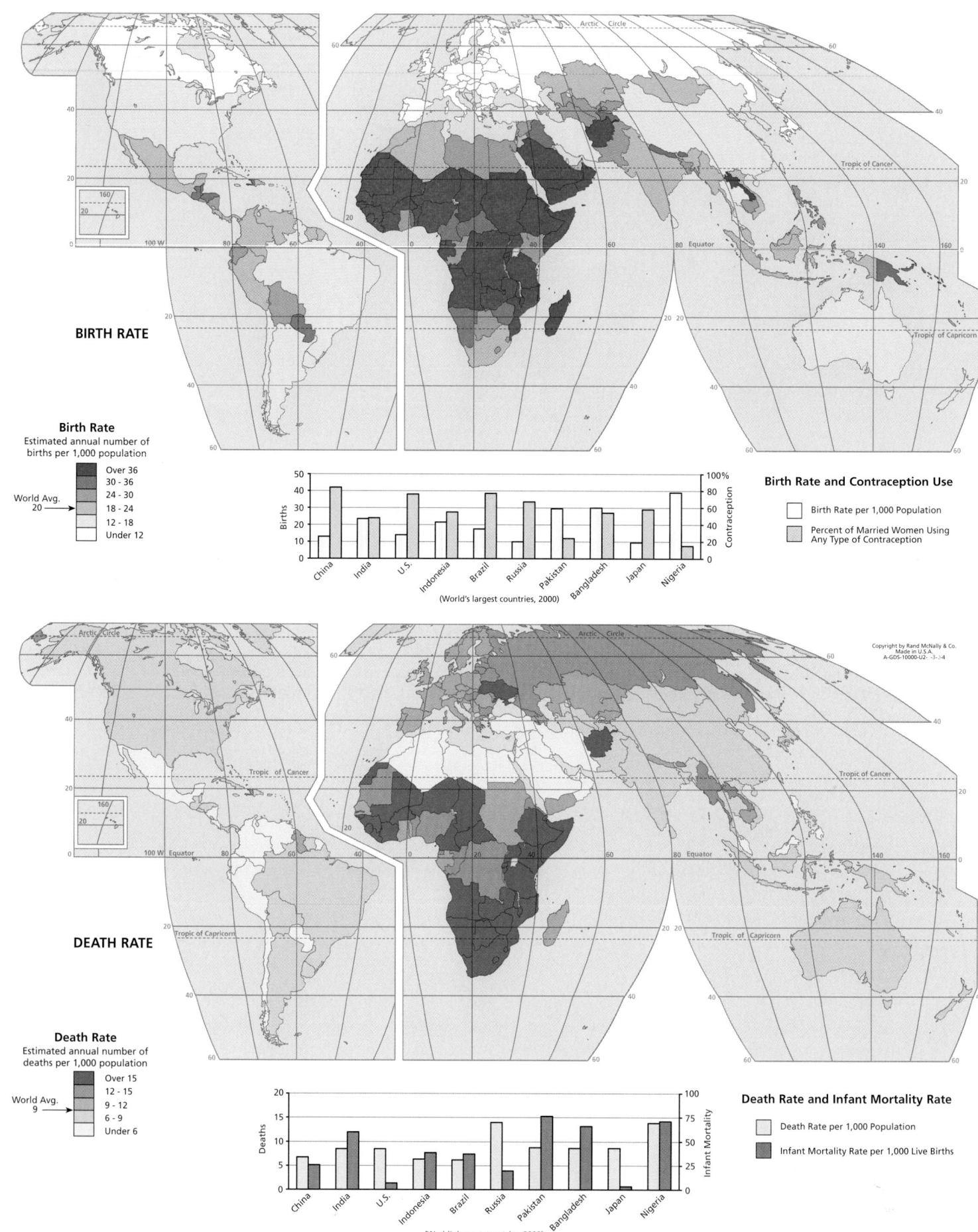

BIRTH RATE

Birth Rate
Estimated annual number of
births per 1,000 population

World Avg.
20 →

Over 36
30 - 36
24 - 30
18 - 24
12 - 18
Under 12

Birth Rate and Contraception Use

☐ Birth Rate per 1,000 Population

☐ Percent of Married Women Using
Any Type of Contraception

(World's largest countries, 2000)

DEATH RATE

Death Rate
Estimated annual number of
deaths per 1,000 population

World Avg.
9 →

Over 15
12 - 15
9 - 12
6 - 9
Under 6

Death Rate and Infant Mortality Rate

☐ Death Rate per 1,000 Population

☐ Infant Mortality Rate per 1,000 Live Births

(World's largest countries, 2000)

Copyright by Rand McNally & Co.
Made in U.S.A.
A-GDS-10000-U2- -3-2-4

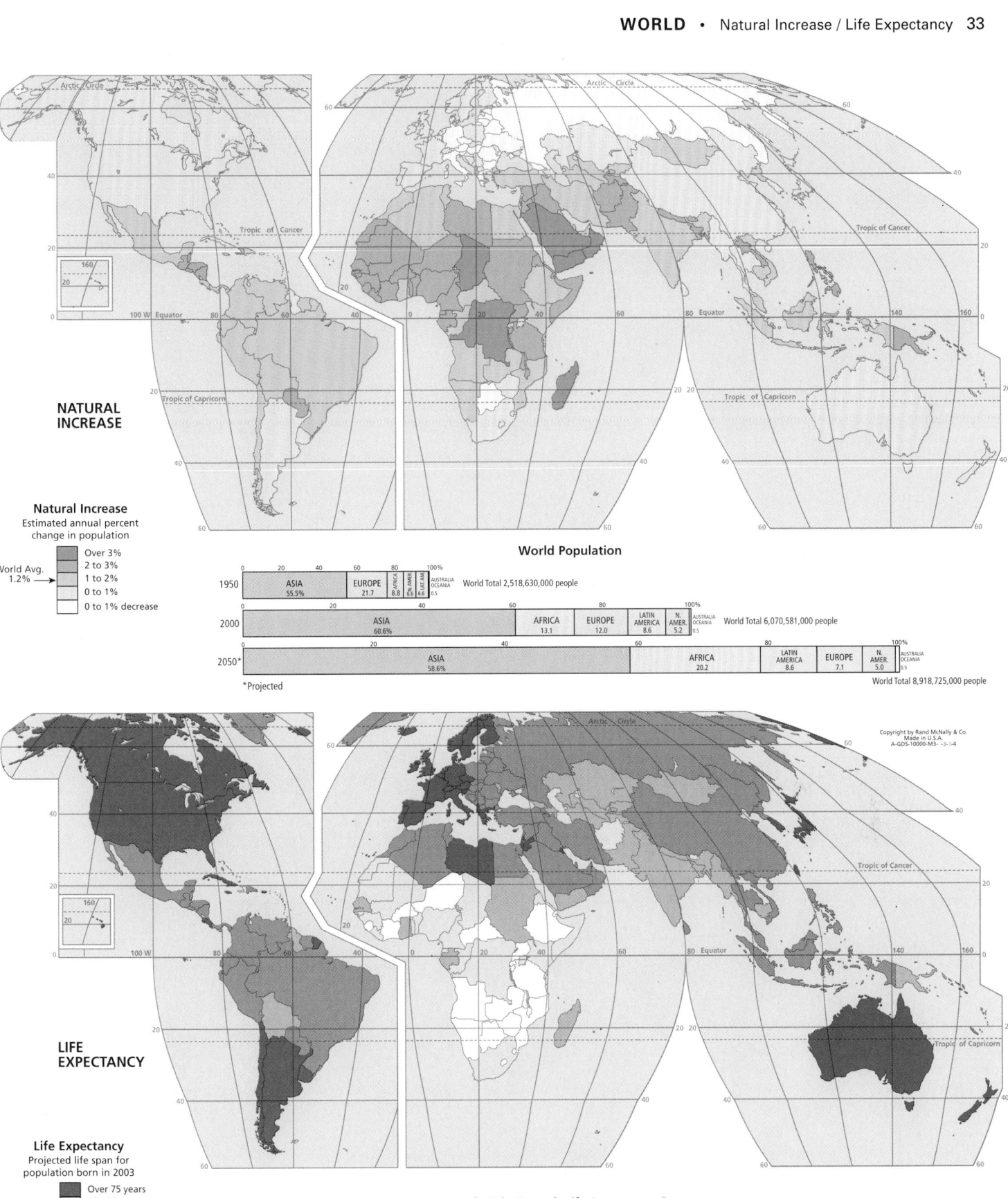

NATURAL INCREASE

Natural Increase
Estimated annual percent
change in population

World Avg. → Over 3%
1.2%   2 to 3%
            1 to 2%
            0 to 1%
            0 to 1% decrease

World Population

1950   ASIA 55.5%   EUROPE 21.7   AFRICA 8.8   N. AMER. 6.7   LAT. AM. 6.6   AUSTRALIA OCEANIA 0.5   World Total 2,518,630,000 people

2000   ASIA 60.6%   AFRICA 13.1   EUROPE 12.0   LATIN AMERICA 8.6   N. AMER. 5.2   AUSTRALIA OCEANIA 0.5   World Total 6,070,581,000 people

2050*   ASIA 58.6%   AFRICA 20.2   LATIN AMERICA 8.6   EUROPE 7.1   N. AMER. 5.0   AUSTRALIA OCEANIA 0.5   World Total 8,918,725,000 people

*Projected

Copyright by Rand McNally & Co.
Made in U.S.A.
A-GDS-10000-M3- -3-:-4

LIFE EXPECTANCY

Life Expectancy
Projected life span for
population born in 2003

World Avg. → Over 75 years
64   65 - 75
            55 - 65
            45 - 55
            Under 45

Percentage of Births in each Life Expectancy Category

Over 75	65 - 75	55 - 65	45 - 55	Under 45
9.7%	39.9%	32.3%	9.3%	8.8%

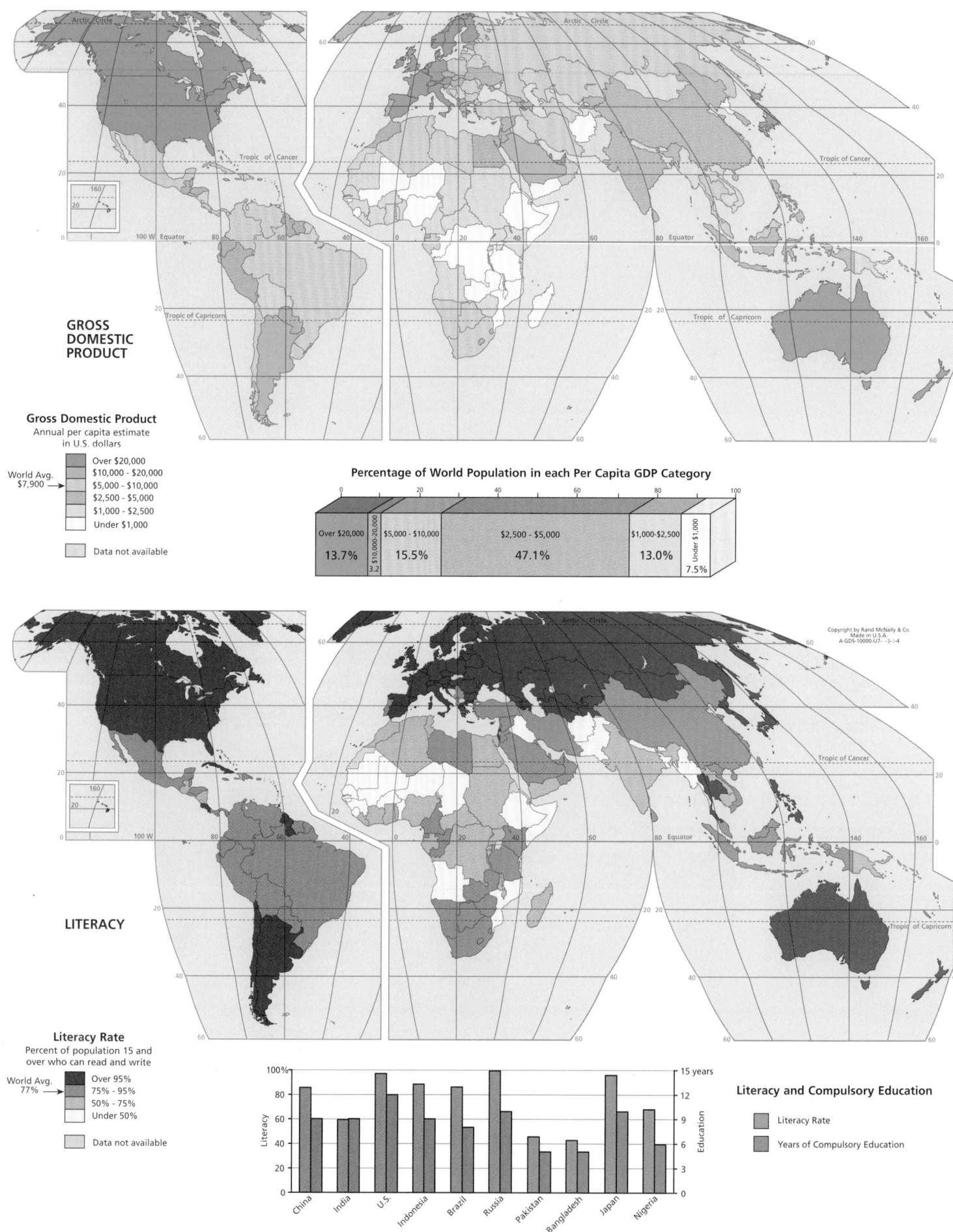

GROSS DOMESTIC PRODUCT

Gross Domestic Product
Annual per capita estimate
in U.S. dollars

World Avg. $7,900 →

- Over $20,000
- $10,000 - $20,000
- $5,000 - $10,000
- $2,500 - $5,000
- $1,000 - $2,500
- Under $1,000

- Data not available

Percentage of World Population in each Per Capita GDP Category

Over $20,000	$10,000-20,000	$5,000 - $10,000	$2,500 - $5,000	$1,000-$2,500	Under $1,000
13.7%	3.2	15.5%	47.1%	13.0%	7.5%

Copyright by Rand McNally & Co.
Made in U.S.A.
A-GDS-10000-U7- -3-3-4

LITERACY

Literacy Rate
Percent of population 15 and
over who can read and write

World Avg. 77% →

- Over 95%
- 75% - 95%
- 50% - 75%
- Under 50%

- Data not available

Literacy and Compulsory Education

- Literacy Rate
- Years of Compulsory Education

(World's largest countries, 2000)

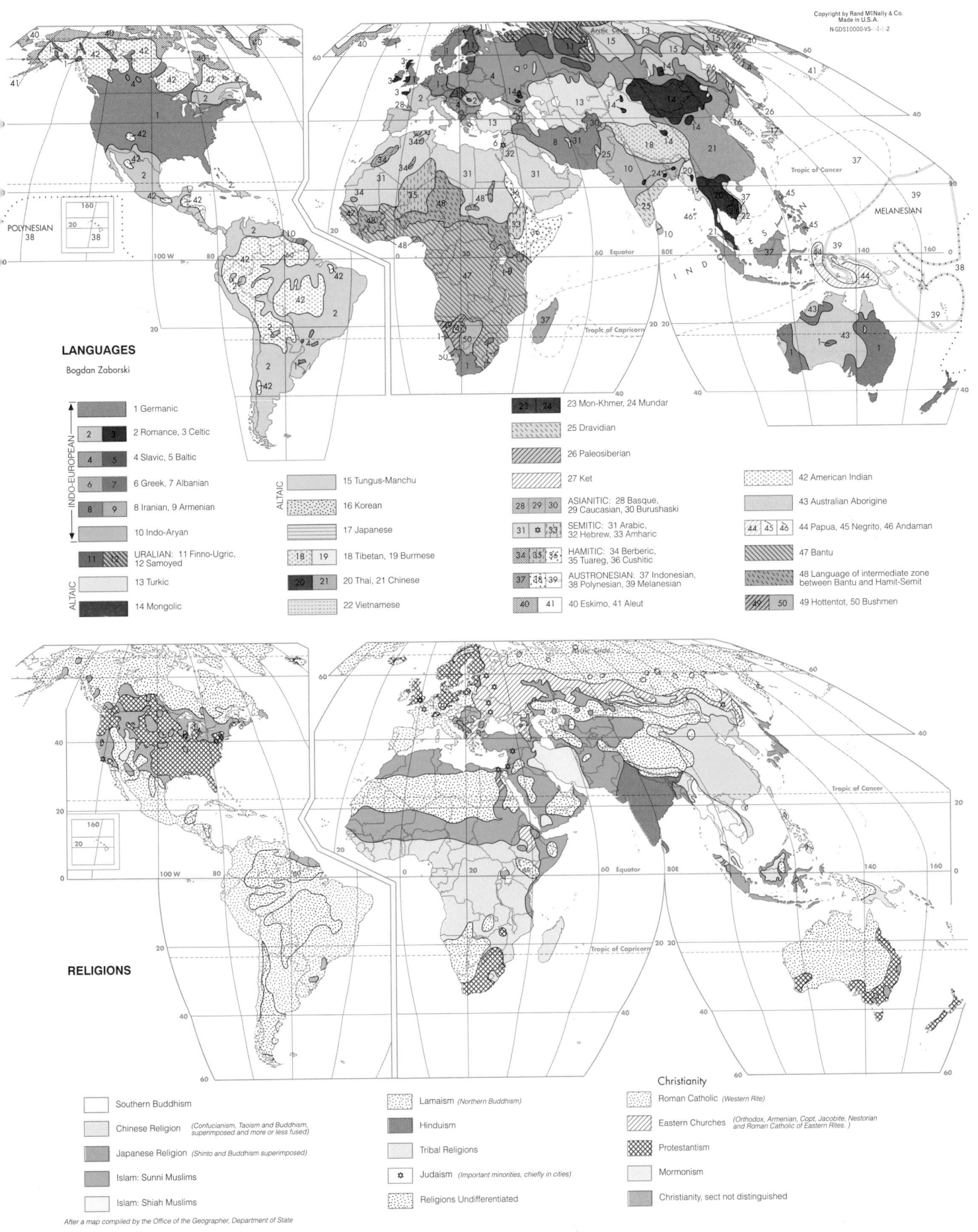

Copyright by Rand McNally & Co.
Made in U.S.A.
N-GDS10000-VS- -1-1--2

POLYNESIAN
38

LANGUAGES

Bogdan Zaborski

INDO-EUROPEAN

1 Germanic

2 Romance, 3 Celtic

4 Slavic, 5 Baltic

6 Greek, 7 Albanian

8 Iranian, 9 Armenian

10 Indo-Aryan

URALIAN: 11 Finno-Ugric, 12 Samoyed

ALTAIC

13 Turkic

14 Mongolic

15 Tungus-Manchu

16 Korean

17 Japanese

18 Tibetan, 19 Burmese

20 Thai, 21 Chinese

22 Vietnamese

23 Mon-Khmer, 24 Mundar

25 Dravidian

26 Paleosiberian

27 Ket

ASIANITIC: 28 Basque, 29 Caucasian, 30 Burushaski

SEMITIC: 31 Arabic, 32 Hebrew, 33 Amharic

HAMITIC: 34 Berberic, 35 Tuareg, 36 Cushitic

AUSTRONESIAN: 37 Indonesian, 38 Polynesian, 39 Melanesian

40 Eskimo, 41 Aleut

42 American Indian

43 Australian Aborigine

44 Papua, 45 Negrito, 46 Andaman

47 Bantu

48 Language of intermediate zone between Bantu and Hamit-Semit

49 Hottentot, 50 Bushmen

MELANESIAN

RELIGIONS

Southern Buddhism

Chinese Religion *(Confucianism, Taoism and Buddhism, superimposed and more or less fused)*

Japanese Religion *(Shinto and Buddhism superimposed)*

Islam: Sunni Muslims

Islam: Shiah Muslims

Lamaism *(Northern Buddhism)*

Hinduism

Tribal Religions

Judaism *(Important minorities, chiefly in cities)*

Religions Undifferentiated

Christianity

Roman Catholic *(Western Rite)*

Eastern Churches *(Orthodox, Armenian, Copt, Jacobite, Nestorian and Roman Catholic of Eastern Rites.)*

Protestantism

Mormonism

Christianity, sect not distinguished

After a map compiled by the Office of the Geographer, Department of State

URBANIZED POPULATION

**Percent of Population Living
in Urban Areas - 2001**

- Over 80%
- 60 - 80%
- 40 - 60%
- 20 - 40%
- Under 20%

Size of each country is proportional to its population.

☐ = 25,000,000 people

Countries with populations under
1,000,000 are not shown.

1 Botswana	6 Moldova
2 Central African Republic	7 Namibia
3 Gaza Strip	8 Togo
4 Jordan	9 West Bank
5 Kuwait	

NUTRITION

Protein Consumed
Grams Per Capita Per Day

Over 110 · 90 - 110 · 70 - 90 · 50 - 70 · Less than 50

Calories Consumed
Per Capita Per Day

- Over 3500
- 3,000 - 3,500
- 2,500 - 3,000
- 2,000 - 2,500
- Less than 2,000

☐ Data not available

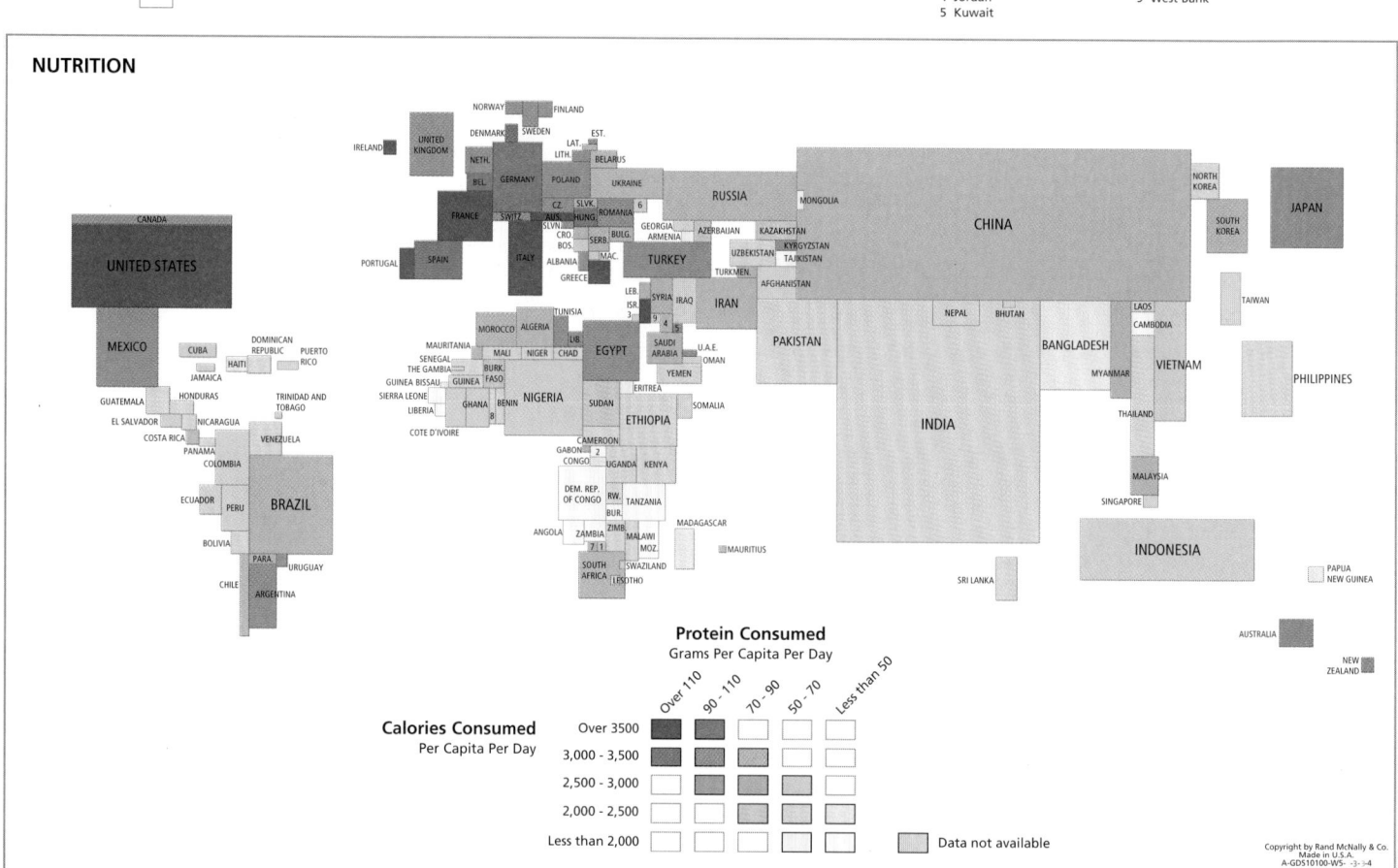

PHYSICIANS

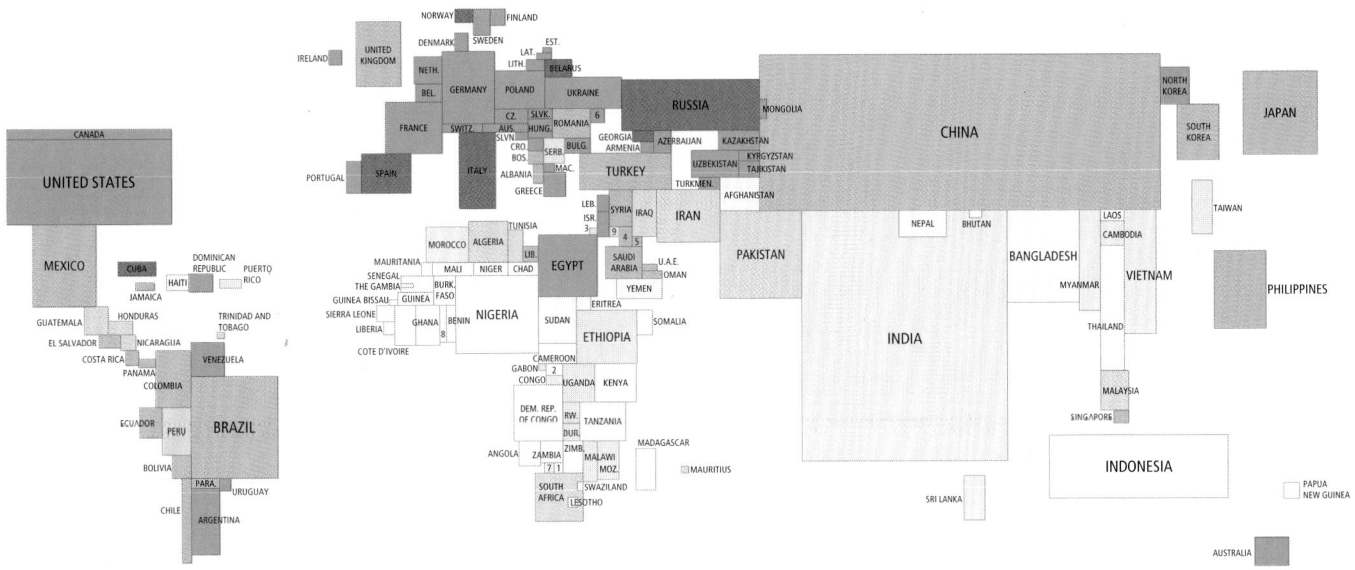

NORWAY FINLAND
IRELAND UNITED KINGDOM DENMARK SWEDEN LAT. EST. LITH. BELARUS
NETH. GERMANY POLAND UKRAINE RUSSIA MONGOLIA NORTH KOREA JAPAN
BEL. CZ. SLVK. ROMANIA 6 CHINA SOUTH KOREA
FRANCE SWITZ. AUS. HUNG. GEORGIA KAZAKHSTAN
SLVN. CRO. BOS. SERB. BULG. ARMENIA AZERBAIJAN UZBEKISTAN KYRGYZSTAN TAIWAN
PORTUGAL SPAIN ITALY ALBANIA MAC. TURKEY TURKMEN. TAJIKISTAN
GREECE AFGHANISTAN LAOS
TUNISIA LEB. SYRIA IRAQ IRAN NEPAL BHUTAN BANGLADESH
ISR. 3. 9 4 5 PAKISTAN CAMBODIA VIETNAM
CANADA MOROCCO ALGERIA U.A.E. MYANMAR PHILIPPINES
UNITED STATES MAURITANIA MALI NIGER CHAD EGYPT SAUDI ARABIA OMAN THAILAND
MEXICO CUBA DOMINICAN REPUBLIC PUERTO RICO SENEGAL YEMEN INDIA MALAYSIA
HAITI THE GAMBIA ERITREA SINGAPORE
JAMAICA GUINEA BISSAU GUINEA SUDAN SOMALIA
GUATEMALA HONDURAS TRINIDAD AND TOBAGO SIERRA LEONE GHANA BENIN NIGERIA ETHIOPIA SRI LANKA INDONESIA PAPUA NEW GUINEA
EL SALVADOR NICARAGUA LIBERIA 8 COTE D'IVOIRE CAMEROON
COSTA RICA PANAMA VENEZUELA GABON 2 UGANDA KENYA
COLOMBIA CONGO
ECUADOR PERU BRAZIL DEM. REP. OF CONGO RW. TANZANIA MADAGASCAR
BUR. AUSTRALIA
BOLIVIA ZIMB. MALAWI MAURITIUS NEW ZEALAND
PARA. ANGOLA ZAMBIA 7 1 MOZ.
CHILE URUGUAY SOUTH SWAZILAND
ARGENTINA AFRICA LESOTHO

Number of Physicians Per 100,000 People - 2001

	Over 400
	200 - 400
	100 - 200
	50 - 100
	25 - 50
	Under 25
	Data Not Available

Copyright by Rand McNally & Co.
Made in U.S.A.

Size of each country is proportional to its population.

☐ = 25,000,000 people

Countries with populations under 1,000,000 are not shown.

1	Botswana	6	Moldova
2	Central African Republic	7	Namibia
3	Gaza Strip	8	Togo
4	Jordan	9	West Bank
5	Kuwait		

HIV INFECTION

NORWAY FINLAND
IRELAND UNITED KINGDOM DENMARK SWEDEN LAT. EST. LITH. BELARUS
NETH. GERMANY POLAND UKRAINE RUSSIA MONGOLIA NORTH KOREA JAPAN
BEL. CZ. SLVK. ROMANIA 6 CHINA SOUTH KOREA
FRANCE SWITZ. AUS. HUNG. GEORGIA KAZAKHSTAN
CRO. BOS. SERB. BULG. ARMENIA AZERBAIJAN UZBEKISTAN KYRGYZSTAN TAIWAN
PORTUGAL SPAIN ITALY ALBANIA MAC. TURKEY TURKMEN. TAJIKISTAN
GREECE AFGHANISTAN LAOS
TUNISIA LEB. SYRIA IRAQ IRAN NEPAL BHUTAN BANGLADESH
ISR. 3. 9 4 5 PAKISTAN CAMBODIA VIETNAM
CANADA MOROCCO ALGERIA U.A.E. MYANMAR PHILIPPINES
UNITED STATES MAURITANIA MALI NIGER CHAD EGYPT SAUDI ARABIA OMAN THAILAND
MEXICO CUBA DOMINICAN REPUBLIC PUERTO RICO SENEGAL YEMEN INDIA MALAYSIA
HAITI BURK. THE GAMBIA ERITREA SINGAPORE
JAMAICA GUINEA BISSAU GUINEA FASO SUDAN SOMALIA
GUATEMALA HONDURAS TRINIDAD AND TOBAGO SIERRA LEONE GHANA BENIN NIGERIA ETHIOPIA SRI LANKA INDONESIA PAPUA NEW GUINEA
EL SALVADOR NICARAGUA LIBERIA 8 COTE D'IVOIRE CAMEROON
COSTA RICA PANAMA VENEZUELA GABON UGANDA KENYA
COLOMBIA CONGO
ECUADOR PERU BRAZIL DEM. REP. OF CONGO RW. TANZANIA MADAGASCAR
BUR. AUSTRALIA
BOLIVIA ZIMB. MALAWI MAURITIUS NEW ZEALAND
PARA. ANGOLA ZAMBIA 7 1 MOZ.
CHILE URUGUAY SOUTH SWAZILAND
ARGENTINA AFRICA LESOTHO

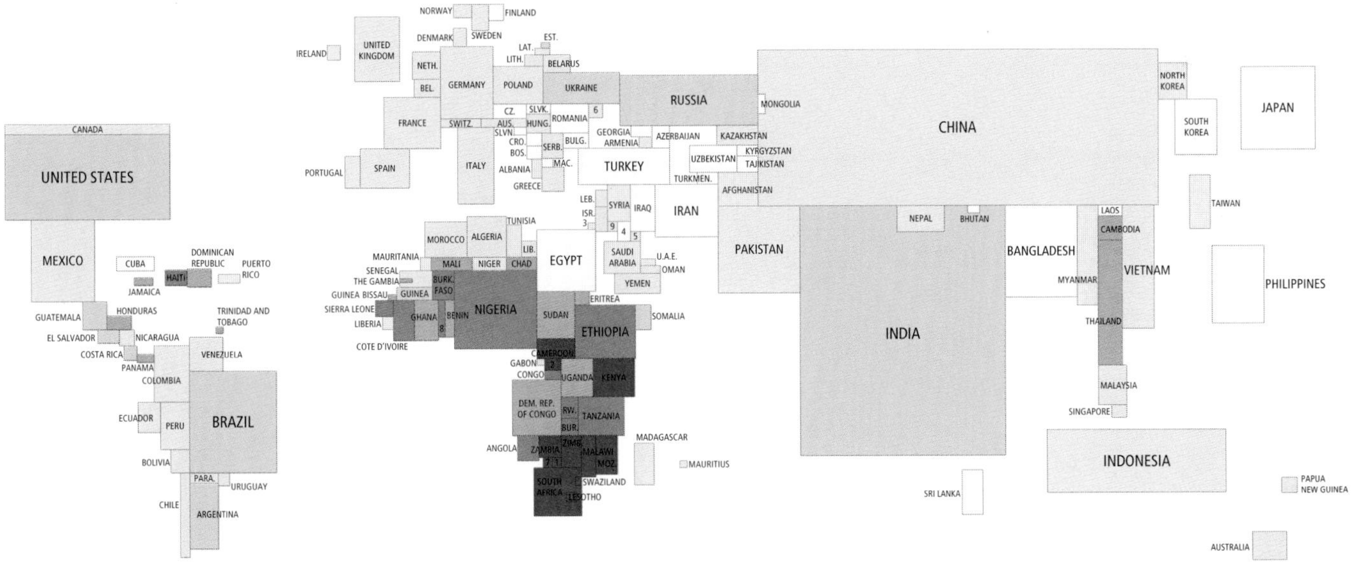

Percent of Adult Population Diagnosed HIV-Positive

	Over 10%
	5 - 10%
	1 - 5%
	0.5 - 1%
	0.1 - 0.5%
	Under 0.1%
	Data Not Available

Copyright by Rand McNally & Co.
Made in U.S.A.
A-GDS10100-W3- -3- -3-4

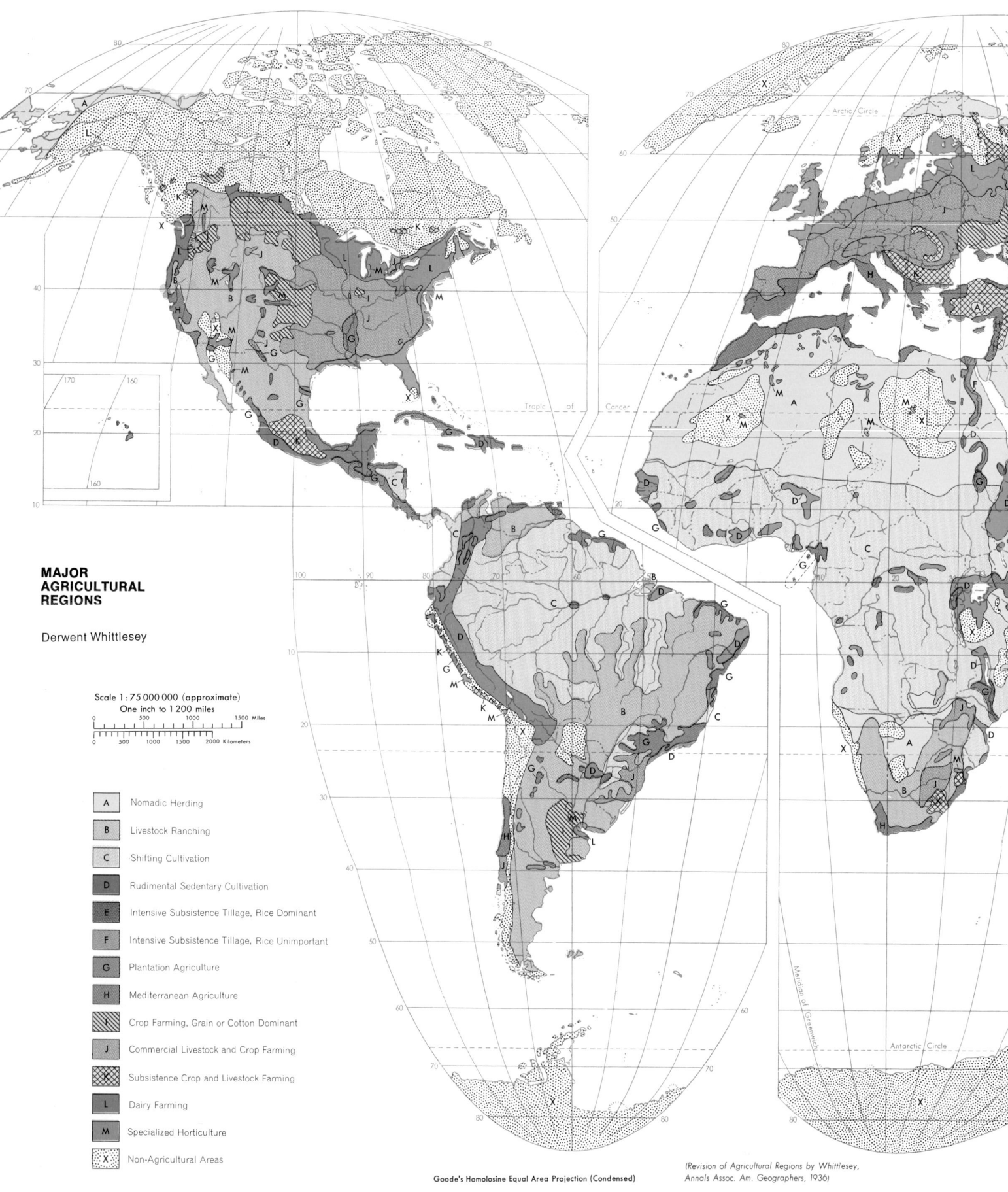

MAJOR AGRICULTURAL REGIONS

Derwent Whittlesey

Scale 1:75 000 000 (approximate)
One inch to 1 200 miles

0   500   1000   1500 Miles

0   500   1000   1500   2000 Kilometers

A	Nomadic Herding
B	Livestock Ranching
C	Shifting Cultivation
D	Rudimental Sedentary Cultivation
E	Intensive Subsistence Tillage, Rice Dominant
F	Intensive Subsistence Tillage, Rice Unimportant
G	Plantation Agriculture
H	Mediterranean Agriculture
I	Crop Farming, Grain or Cotton Dominant
J	Commercial Livestock and Crop Farming
K	Subsistence Crop and Livestock Farming
L	Dairy Farming
M	Specialized Horticulture
X	Non-Agricultural Areas

Goode's Homolosine Equal Area Projection (Condensed)

(Revision of Agricultural Regions by Whittlesey,
Annals Assoc. Am. Geographers, 1936)

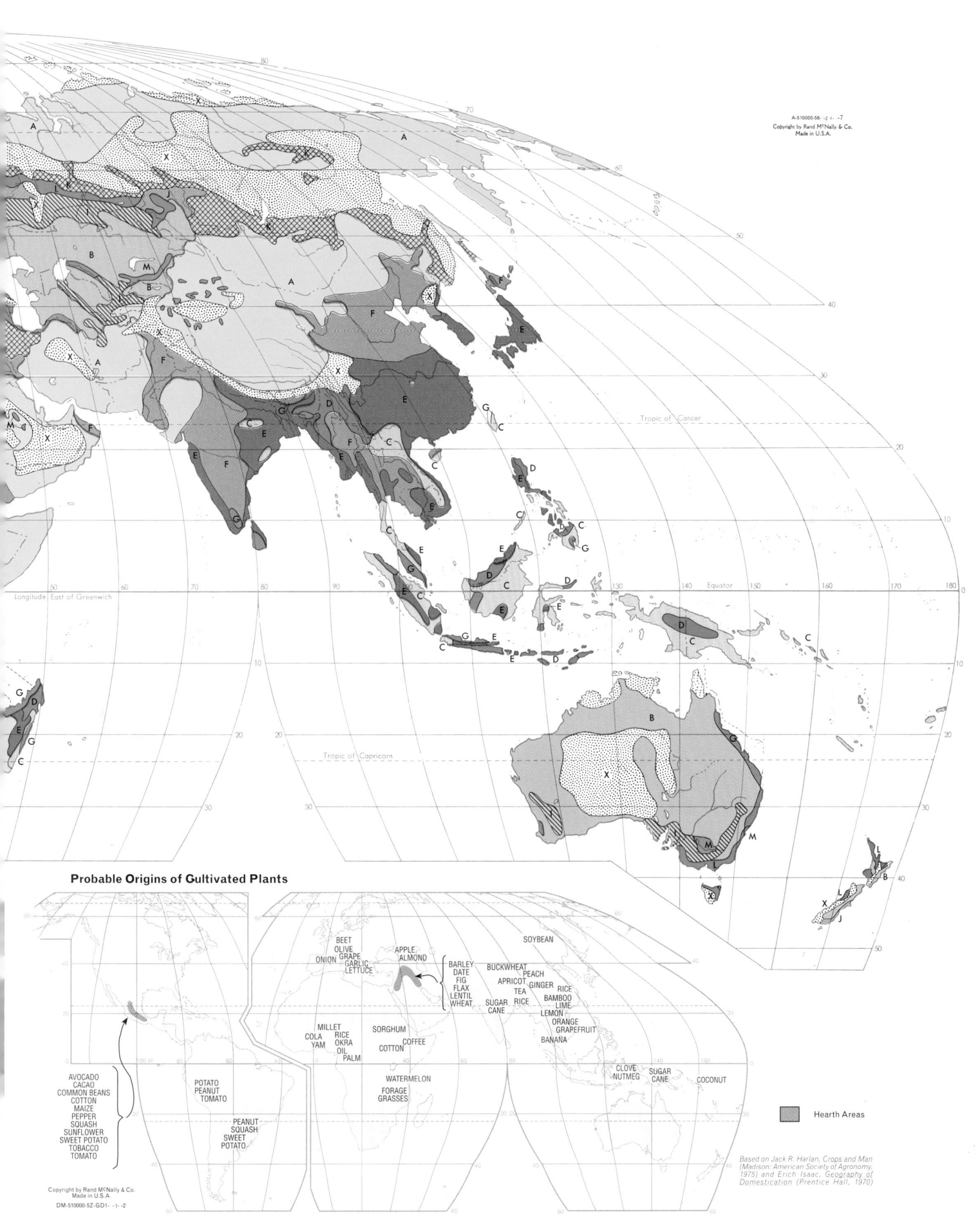

A-510000-56- -2 +- -7
Copyright by Rand McNally & Co.
Made in U.S.A.

Tropic of Cancer

Equator

Longitude East of Greenwich

Tropic of Capricorn

Probable Origins of Cultivated Plants

SOYBEAN

BEET
OLIVE
GRAPE   APPLE
ONION GARLIC   ALMOND
LETTUCE   BARLEY   BUCKWHEAT
            DATE   PEACH
            FIG   APRICOT GINGER RICE
            FLAX   TEA   BAMBOO
            LENTIL   SUGAR RICE   LIME
            WHEAT   CANE   LEMON
                                ORANGE
            MILLET RICE   SORGHUM   GRAPEFRUIT
            COLA   OKRA   BANANA
            YAM   OIL   COFFEE
                   PALM COTTON

AVOCADO
CACAO
COMMON BEANS   POTATO
COTTON   PEANUT   WATERMELON
MAIZE   TOMATO
PEPPER   FORAGE
SQUASH   GRASSES   CLOVE SUGAR
SUNFLOWER   NUTMEG CANE   COCONUT
SWEET POTATO   PEANUT
TOBACCO   SQUASH
TOMATO   SWEET
                  POTATO

Hearth Areas

*Based on Jack R. Harlan, Crops and Man
(Madison: American Society of Agronomy,
1975) and Erich Isaac, Geography of
Domestication (Prentice Hall, 1970)*

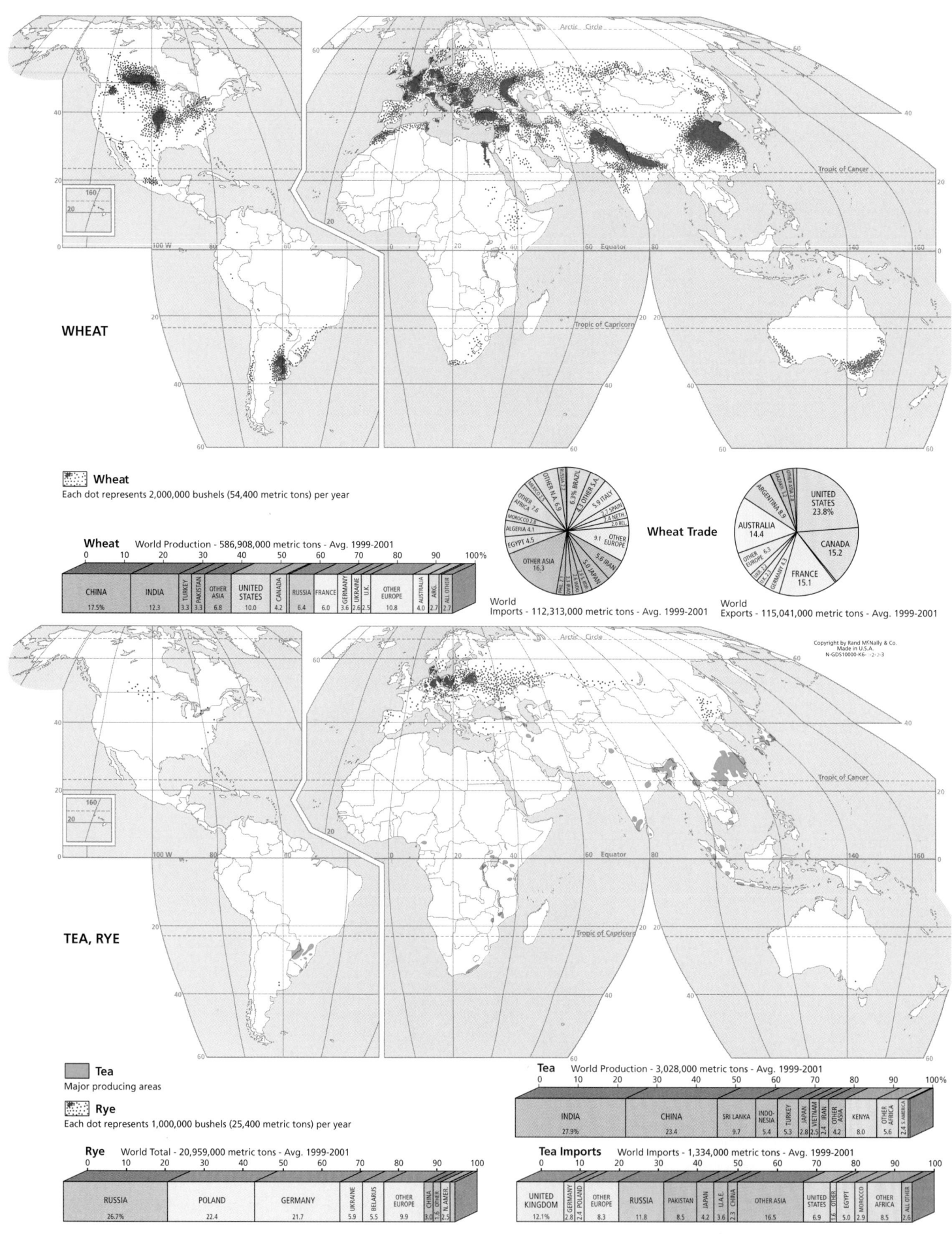

WHEAT

Wheat
Each dot represents 2,000,000 bushels (54,400 metric tons) per year

Wheat World Production - 586,908,000 metric tons - Avg. 1999-2001

0	10	20	30	40	50	60	70	80	90	100%

CHINA	INDIA	TURKEY	PAKISTAN	OTHER ASIA	UNITED STATES	CANADA	RUSSIA	FRANCE	GERMANY	UKRAINE	U.K.	OTHER EUROPE	AUSTRALIA	ARG.	ALL OTHER
17.5%	12.3	3.3	3.3	6.8	10.0	4.2	6.4	6.0	3.6	2.6	2.5	10.8	4.0	2.7	2.7

Wheat Trade

World
Imports - 112,313,000 metric tons - Avg. 1999-2001

Wheat Trade pie chart (imports): OTHER N.A. 6.3, MEXICO 7.6, MOROCCO 2.8, ALGERIA 4.1, EGYPT 4.5, OTHER ASIA 16.3, BRAZIL 6.3%, OTHER S.A., ITALY 5.9, SPAIN 2.1, NETH. 4.4, BEL. 2.0, OTHER EUROPE 9.1, IRAN 5.6, JAPAN 5.0

World
Exports - 115,041,000 metric tons - Avg. 1999-2001

Wheat Trade pie chart (exports): UNITED STATES 23.8%, CANADA 15.2, FRANCE 15.1, GERMANY 4.3, U.K. 3.3, OTHER EUROPE 6.3, AUSTRALIA 14.4, ARGENTINA 8.9, KAZAK. 1.2

Copyright by Rand McNally & Co.
Made in U.S.A.
N-GDS10000-K6- -2-:-3

TEA, RYE

Tea
Major producing areas

Rye
Each dot represents 1,000,000 bushels (25,400 metric tons) per year

Tea World Production - 3,028,000 metric tons - Avg. 1999-2001

0	10	20	30	40	50	60	70	80	90	100%

INDIA	CHINA	SRI LANKA	INDO-NESIA	TURKEY	JAPAN	VIETNAM	IRAN	OTHER ASIA	KENYA	OTHER AFRICA	S. AMERICA
27.9%	23.4	9.7	5.4	5.3	2.8	2.4	4.2	8.0	5.6	2.4	

Rye World Total - 20,959,000 metric tons - Avg. 1999-2001

0	10	20	30	40	50	60	70	80	90	100

RUSSIA	POLAND	GERMANY	UKRAINE	BELARUS	OTHER EUROPE	CHINA	OTHER	N. AMER.
26.7%	22.4	21.7	5.9	5.5	9.9	3.0	1.6	2.5

Tea Imports World Imports - 1,334,000 metric tons - Avg. 1999-2001

0	10	20	30	40	50	60	70	80	90	100

UNITED KINGDOM	GERMANY	POLAND	OTHER EUROPE	RUSSIA	PAKISTAN	JAPAN	U.A.E.	CHINA	OTHER ASIA	UNITED STATES	EGYPT	MOROCCO	OTHER AFRICA	ALL OTHER
12.1%	2.8	2.4	8.3	11.8	8.5	4.2	3.6	2.3	16.5	6.9	1.6	5.0	2.9	8.5	2.6

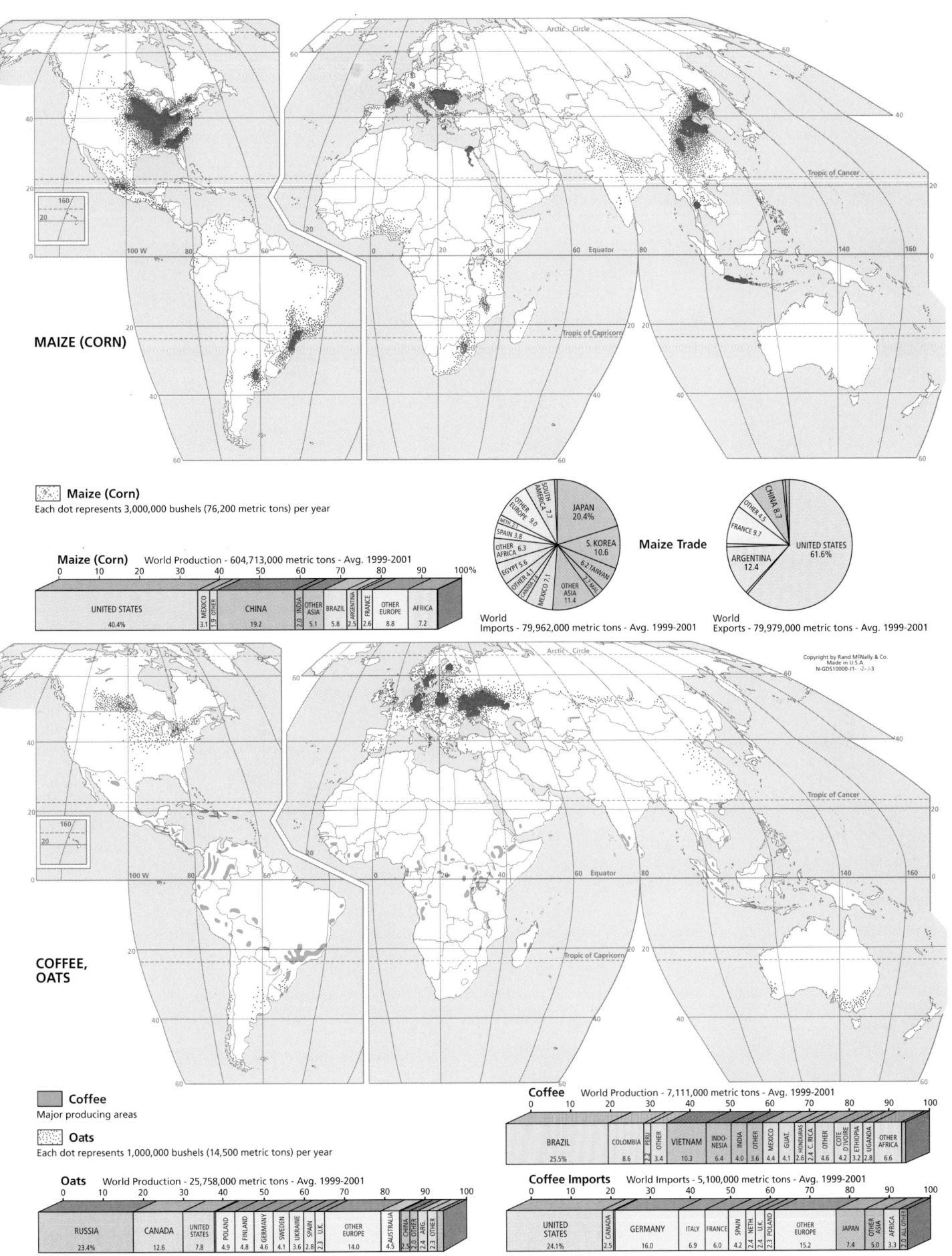

MAIZE (CORN)

Maize (Corn)
Each dot represents 3,000,000 bushels (76,200 metric tons) per year

Maize (Corn) World Production - 604,713,000 metric tons - Avg. 1999-2001

| UNITED STATES 40.4% | MEXICO 3.1 | 1.9 OTHER | CHINA 19.2 | INDIA 2.0 | OTHER ASIA 5.1 | BRAZIL 5.8 | ARGENTINA 2.5 | FRANCE 2.6 | OTHER EUROPE 8.8 | AFRICA 7.2 |

Maize Trade

World Imports - 79,962,000 metric tons - Avg. 1999-2001
(Pie: JAPAN 20.4%, S. KOREA 10.6, TAIWAN 6.2, MALI, OTHER ASIA 11.4, MEXICO 7.1, OTHER 4.1, EGYPT 5.6, OTHER AFRICA 6.3, SPAIN 3.8, METH 4.1, OTHER EUROPE, SOUTH AMERICA, JAPAN 9.0)

World Exports - 79,979,000 metric tons - Avg. 1999-2001
(Pie: UNITED STATES 61.6%, ARGENTINA 12.4, FRANCE 9.7, OTHER 4.5, CHINA 8.7)

Copyright by Rand McNally & Co.
Made in U.S.A.
N-GDS10000-J1- -2->3

COFFEE, OATS

Coffee
Major producing areas

Oats
Each dot represents 1,000,000 bushels (14,500 metric tons) per year

Coffee World Production - 7,111,000 metric tons - Avg. 1999-2001

| BRAZIL 25.5% | COLOMBIA 8.6 | PERU 2.2 | OTHER 3.4 | VIETNAM 10.3 | INDO-NESIA 6.4 | INDIA 4.0 | MEXICO 3.6 | GUAT. 4.1 | HONDURAS 2.6 | C. RICA 2.4 | OTHER 4.6 | COTE D'IVOIRE 4.2 | ETHIOPIA 3.2 | UGANDA 2.8 | OTHER AFRICA 6.6 |

Oats World Production - 25,758,000 metric tons - Avg. 1999-2001

| RUSSIA 23.4% | CANADA 12.6 | UNITED STATES 7.8 | POLAND 4.9 | FINLAND 4.8 | GERMANY 4.6 | SWEDEN 4.1 | UKRAINE 3.6 | SPAIN 2.8 | U.K. 2.3 | OTHER EUROPE 14.0 | AUSTRALIA 4.5 | CHINA 2.0 | OTHER 2.4 | ARG 2.3 | OTHER |

Coffee Imports World Imports - 5,100,000 metric tons - Avg. 1999-2001

| UNITED STATES 24.1% | CANADA 2.5 | GERMANY 16.0 | ITALY 6.9 | FRANCE 6.0 | SPAIN 4.2 | NETH. 2.4 | U.K. 2.3 | POLAND | OTHER EUROPE 15.2 | JAPAN 7.4 | OTHER ASIA 5.0 | AFRICA 3.3 | ALL OTHER |

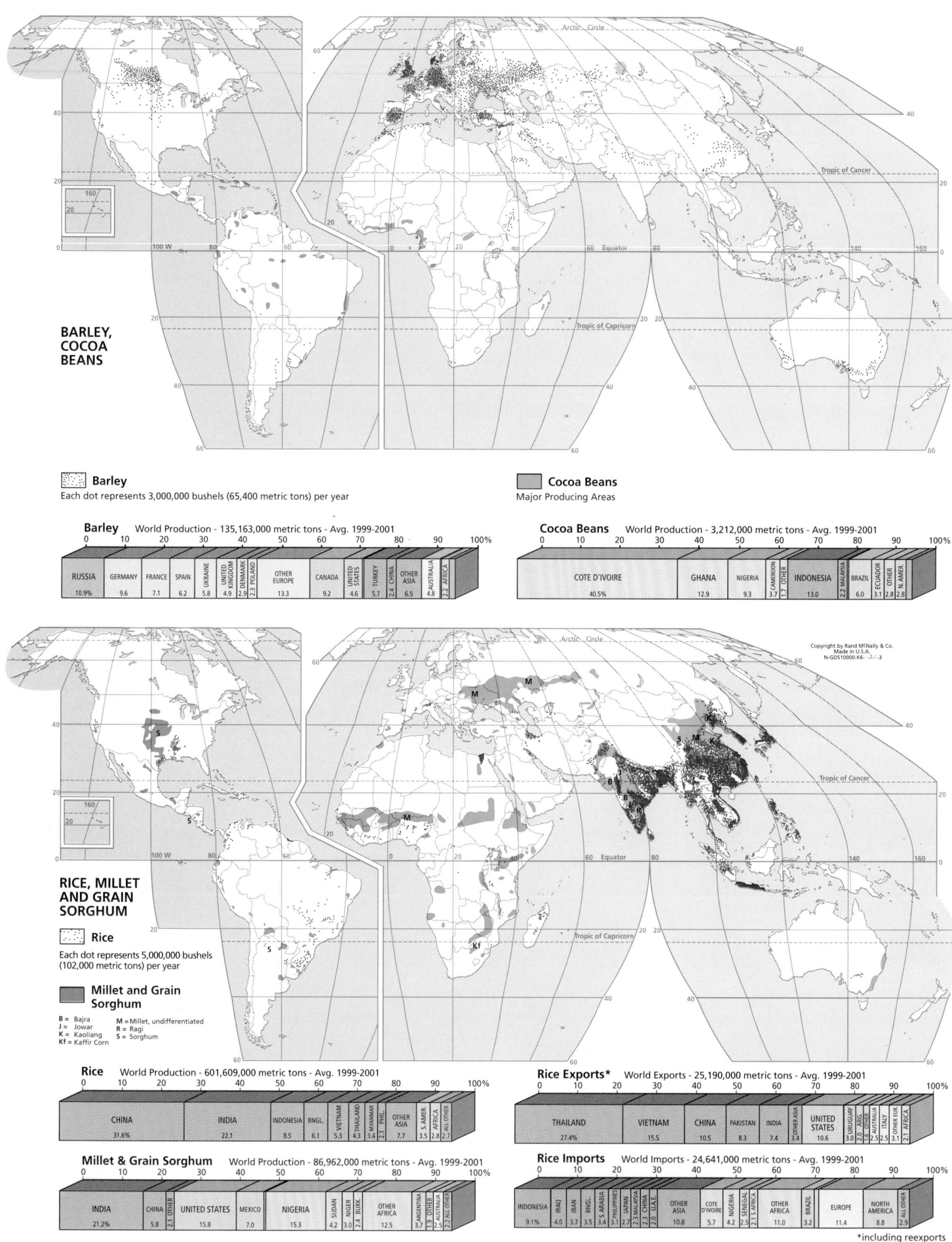

Barley
Each dot represents 3,000,000 bushels (65,400 metric tons) per year

Cocoa Beans
Major Producing Areas

Barley World Production - 135,163,000 metric tons - Avg. 1999-2001

	0	10	20	30	40	50	60	70	80	90	100%

RUSSIA	GERMANY	FRANCE	SPAIN	UKRAINE	UNITED KINGDOM	DENMARK	POLAND	OTHER EUROPE	CANADA	UNITED STATES	TURKEY	CHINA	OTHER ASIA	AUSTRALIA	AFRICA
10.9%	9.6	7.1	6.2	5.8	4.9	2.9	2.3	13.3	9.2	4.6	5.7	2.4	6.5	4.8	2.2

Cocoa Beans World Production - 3,212,000 metric tons - Avg. 1999-2001

	0	10	20	30	40	50	60	70	80	90	100%

COTE D'IVOIRE	GHANA	NIGERIA	CAMEROON	OTHER	INDONESIA	MALAYSIA	BRAZIL	ECUADOR	OTHER	N. AMER.
40.5%	12.9	9.3	3.7	1.7	13.0	2.2	6.0	3.1	2.8	2.8

Copyright by Rand McNally & Co.
Made in U.S.A.
N-GDS10000-K6- -2-7 -3

RICE, MILLET AND GRAIN SORGHUM

Rice
Each dot represents 5,000,000 bushels (102,000 metric tons) per year

Millet and Grain Sorghum

B = Bajra
J = Jowar
K = Kaoliang
Kf = Kaffir Corn
M = Millet, undifferentiated
R = Ragi
S = Sorghum

Rice World Production - 601,609,000 metric tons - Avg. 1999-2001

	0	10	20	30	40	50	60	70	80	90	100%

CHINA	INDIA	INDONESIA	BNGL.	VIETNAM	THAILAND	MYANMAR	PHIL.	OTHER ASIA	S. AMER.	AFRICA	ALL OTHER
31.6%	22.1	8.5	6.1	5.3	4.3	3.4	2.1	7.7	3.5	2.8	2.7

Rice Exports* World Exports - 25,190,000 metric tons - Avg. 1999-2001

	0	10	20	30	40	50	60	70	80	90	100%

THAILAND	VIETNAM	CHINA	PAKISTAN	INDIA	OTHER ASIA	UNITED STATES	URUGUAY	ARG.	OTHER	AUSTRALIA	ITALY	OTHER EUR.	AFRICA
27.4%	15.5	10.5	8.3	7.4	3.4	10.6	3.0	2.0	2.5	2.5	1.5	2.8	2.1

Millet & Grain Sorghum World Production - 86,962,000 metric tons - Avg. 1999-2001

	0	10	20	30	40	50	60	70	80	90	100%

INDIA	CHINA	OTHER	UNITED STATES	MEXICO	NIGERIA	SUDAN	NIGER	BURK.	OTHER AFRICA	ARGENTINA	OTHER	AUSTRALIA	ALL OTHER
21.2%	5.8	2.1	15.8	7.0	15.3	4.2	3.0	2.4	12.5	1.9	3.7	2.2	2.2

Rice Imports World Imports - 24,641,000 metric tons - Avg. 1999-2001

	0	10	20	30	40	50	60	70	80	90	100%

INDONESIA	IRAQ	IRAN	BNGL.	S. ARABIA	JAPAN	PHILIPPINES	MALAYSIA	CHINA	U.A.E.	OTHER ASIA	COTE D'IVOIRE	NIGERIA	S. AFRICA	OTHER AFRICA	BRAZIL	EUROPE	NORTH AMERICA	ALL OTHER
9.1%	4.0	3.7	3.5	3.4	3.1	2.3	2.3	2.0	2.0	10.8	5.7	4.2	2.5	11.0	3.2	11.4	8.8	2.9

*including reexports

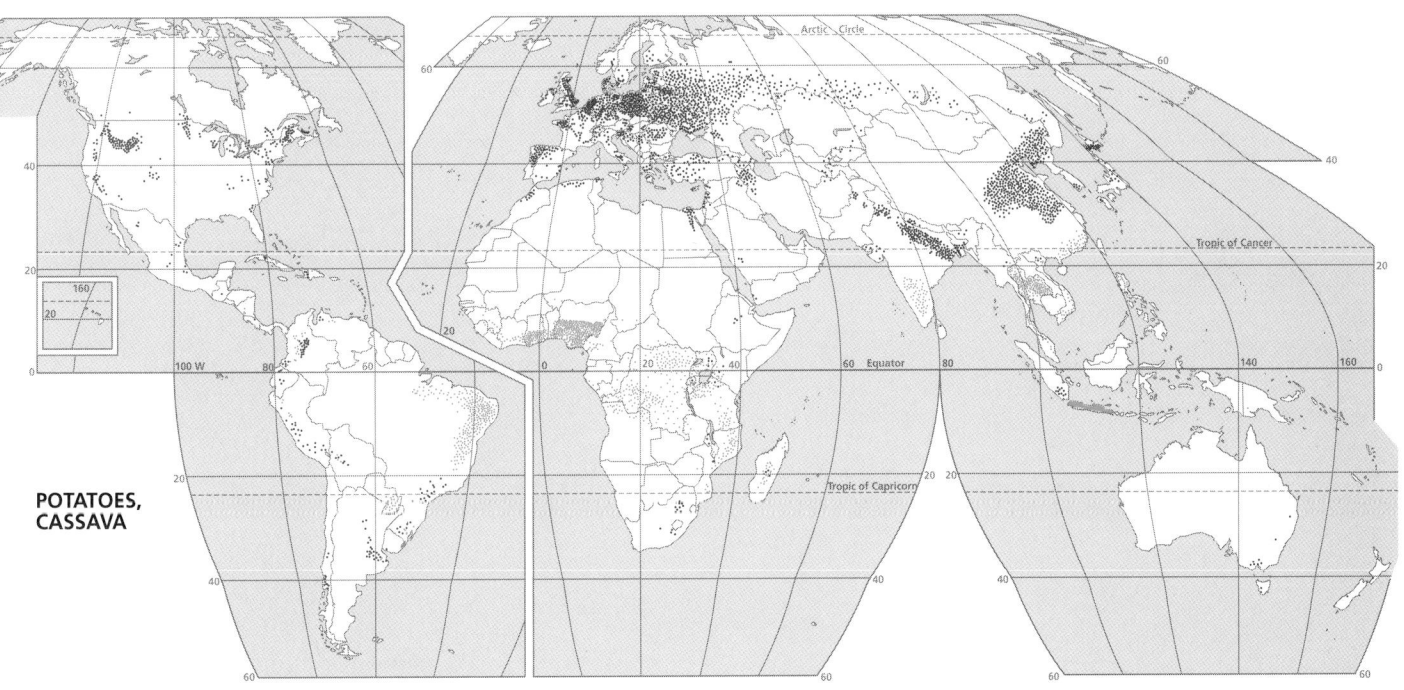

POTATOES, CASSAVA

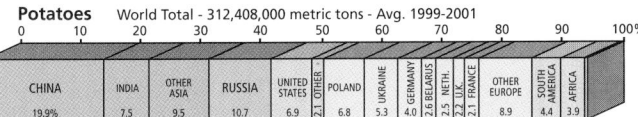

Potatoes
Each dot represents 100,000 metric tons average annual production

Potatoes   World Total - 312,408,000 metric tons - Avg. 1999-2001

| | 0 | 10 | 20 | 30 | 40 | 50 | 60 | 70 | 80 | 90 | 100% |

CHINA	INDIA	OTHER ASIA	RUSSIA	UNITED STATES	POLAND	UKRAINE	GERMANY	BELARUS	NETH.	U.K.	FRANCE	OTHER EUROPE	SOUTH AMERICA	AFRICA
19.9%	7.5	9.5	10.7	6.9	2.1	6.8	5.3	4.0	2.6	2.5	2.2	2.1	8.9	4.4	3.9

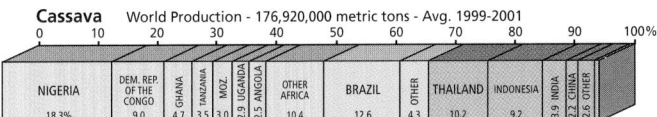

Cassava
Each dot represents 100,000 metric tons average annual production

Cassava   World Production - 176,920,000 metric tons - Avg. 1999-2001

| | 0 | 10 | 20 | 30 | 40 | 50 | 60 | 70 | 80 | 90 | 100% |

NIGERIA	DEM. REP. OF THE CONGO	GHANA	TANZANIA	MOZ.	UGANDA	ANGOLA	OTHER AFRICA	BRAZIL	OTHER	THAILAND	INDONESIA	INDIA	CHINA	OTHER
18.3%	9.0	4.7	3.5	3.0	2.9	2.5	10.4	12.6	4.3	10.2	9.2	3.9	2.2	2.6

Copyright by Rand McNally & Co.
Made in U.S.A.
N-GDS10000-J8- -2-:-3

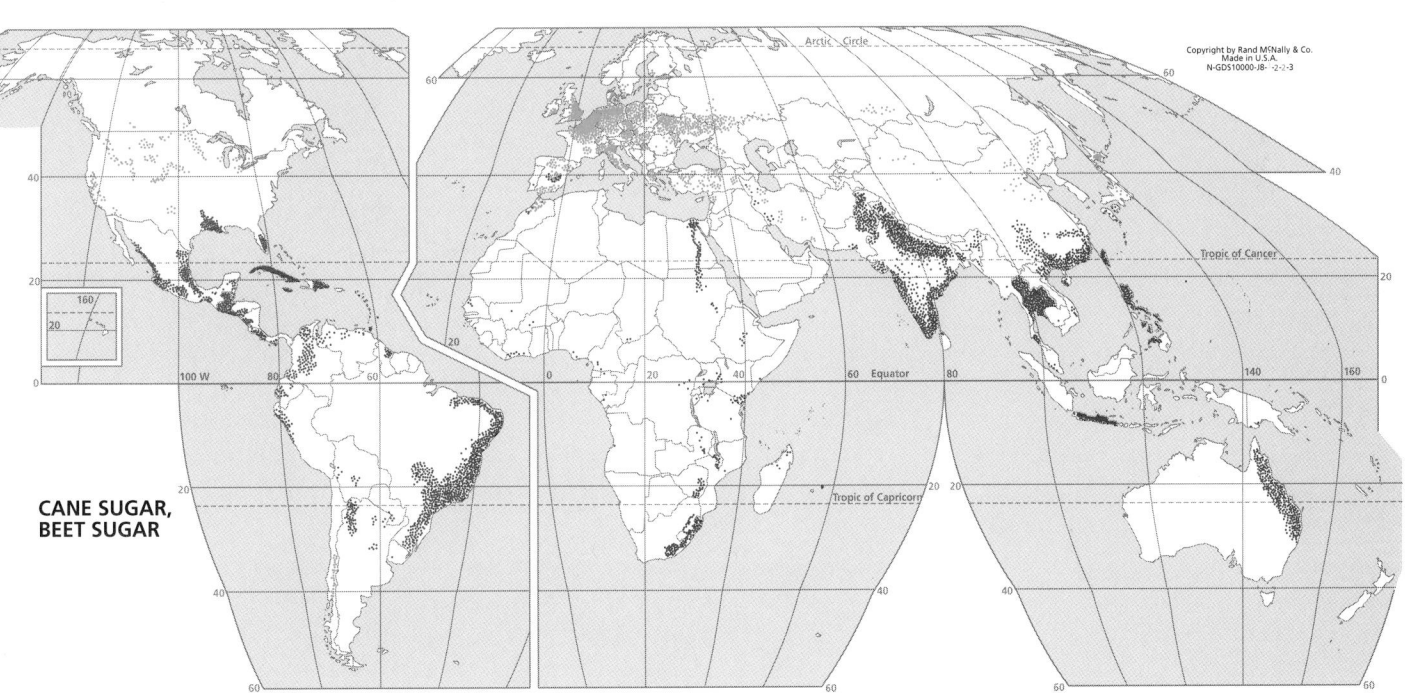

CANE SUGAR, BEET SUGAR

Cane Sugar
Each dot represents 20,000 metric tons average annual production

Cane Sugar   World Production - 98,587,000 metric tons - Avg. 1999-2001

| | 0 | 10 | 20 | 30 | 40 | 50 | 60 | 70 | 80 | 90 | 100% |

INDIA	CHINA	THAILAND	PAKISTAN	OTHER ASIA	BRAZIL	COL.	OTHER S.A.	MEXICO	CUBA	UNITED STATES	OTHER N.A.	AUSTRALIA	OTHER AFRICA
20.3%	7.0	6.0	2.9	5.8	19.5	2.4	4.3	5.2	3.9	3.7	4.6	5.0	2.5	6.4

Beet Sugar
Each dot represents 20,000 metric tons average annual production

Beet Sugar   World Production - 35,732,000 metric tons - Avg. 1999-2001

| | 0 | 10 | 20 | 30 | 40 | 50 | 60 | 70 | 80 | 90 | 100% |

GERMANY	FRANCE	POLAND	UKRAINE	ITALY	UNITED KINGDOM	SPAIN	NETH.	BELGIUM	OTHER EUROPE	UNITED STATES	TURKEY	CHINA	OTHER ASIA	RUSSIA	AFRICA	ALL OTHER
12.7%	12.6	5.4	4.9	4.6	4.2	3.2	3.2	2.9	12.7	11.6	6.3	2.6	4.4	4.8	2.2	

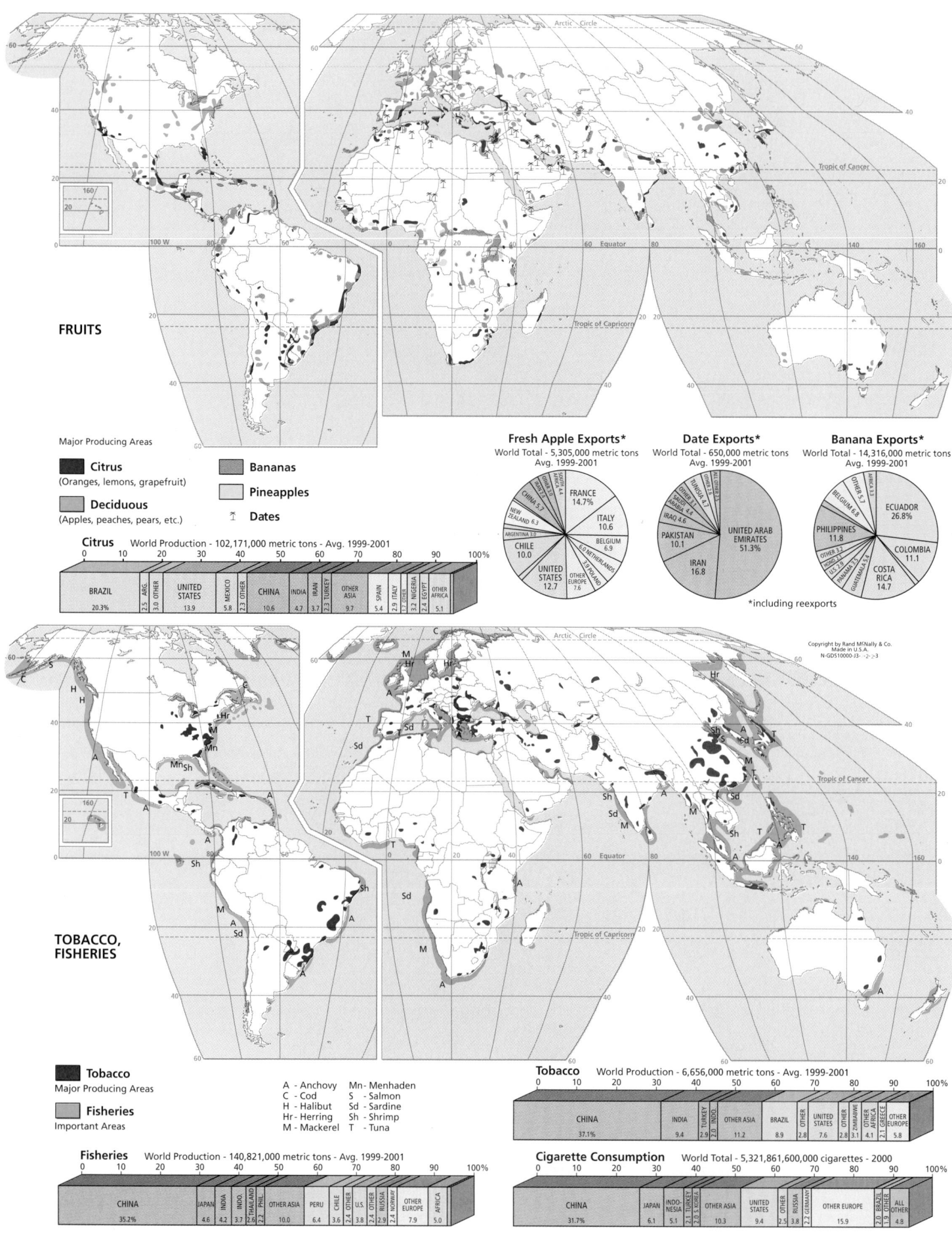

FRUITS

Major Producing Areas

Citrus
(Oranges, lemons, grapefruit)

Deciduous
(Apples, peaches, pears, etc.)

Bananas

Pineapples

🌴 **Dates**

Citrus World Production - 102,171,000 metric tons - Avg. 1999-2001

BRAZIL 20.3%	ARG. 2.5	OTHER 3.0	UNITED STATES 13.9	MEXICO 5.8	OTHER	CHINA 10.6	INDIA 4.7	IRAN 3.7	TURKEY 2.3	OTHER ASIA 9.7	SPAIN 5.4	ITALY 2.9	OTHER 1.7	NIGERIA 3.2	EGYPT 2.4	OTHER AFRICA 5.1

Fresh Apple Exports*
World Total - 5,305,000 metric tons
Avg. 1999-2001

- FRANCE 14.7%
- ITALY 10.6
- BELGIUM 6.9
- NETHERLANDS 6.0
- POLAND 5.9
- OTHER EUROPE 7.6
- UNITED STATES 12.7
- CHILE 10.0
- ARGENTINA 3.0
- NEW ZEALAND 6.3
- CHINA 5.7
- SOUTH AFRICA 4.4
- ALL OTHER 3.3

Date Exports*
World Total - 650,000 metric tons
Avg. 1999-2001

- UNITED ARAB EMIRATES 51.3%
- IRAN 16.8
- PAKISTAN 10.1
- IRAQ 4.6
- SAUDI ARABIA 4.6
- TUNISIA 4.7
- OTHER 1.9
- ALL OTHER 6.0

Banana Exports*
World Total - 14,316,000 metric tons
Avg. 1999-2001

- ECUADOR 26.8%
- COLOMBIA 11.1
- COSTA RICA 14.7
- GUATEMALA 5.7
- PANAMA 2.8
- U.S. 2.8
- HOND. 5.1
- OTHER 3.2
- PHILIPPINES 11.8
- BELGIUM 6.8
- OTHER 5.7
- AFRICA 3.3

*including reexports

TOBACCO, FISHERIES

Copyright by Rand McNally & Co.
Made in U.S.A.
N-GD510000-J3- -2- ≥3

Tobacco
Major Producing Areas

Fisheries
Important Areas

A - Anchovy   Mn - Menhaden
C - Cod   S - Salmon
H - Halibut   Sd - Sardine
Hr - Herring   Sh - Shrimp
M - Mackerel   T - Tuna

Tobacco World Production - 6,656,000 metric tons - Avg. 1999-2001

CHINA 37.1%	INDIA 9.4	TURKEY 2.9	INDO. 2.0	OTHER ASIA 11.2	BRAZIL 8.9	OTHER 2.8	UNITED STATES 7.6	OTHER 2.8	ZIMBABWE 3.1	OTHER AFRICA 4.1	GREECE 2.1	OTHER EUROPE 5.8

Fisheries World Production - 140,821,000 metric tons - Avg. 1999-2001

CHINA 35.2%	JAPAN 4.6	INDIA 4.2	INDO. 3.7	THAILAND 2.6	PHIL. 2.2	OTHER ASIA 10.0	PERU 6.4	CHILE 3.6	U.S. 2.4	RUSSIA 3.8	NORWAY 2.9	OTHER EUROPE 7.9	AFRICA 5.0

Cigarette Consumption World Total - 5,321,861,600,000 cigarettes - 2000

CHINA 31.7%	JAPAN 6.1	INDO-NESIA 5.1	TURKEY 2.0	S. KOREA 2.0	OTHER ASIA 10.3	UNITED STATES 9.4	OTHER 2.5	RUSSIA 3.8	GERMANY 2.2	OTHER EUROPE 15.9	BRAZIL 2.0	OTHER 1.9	ALL OTHER 4.8

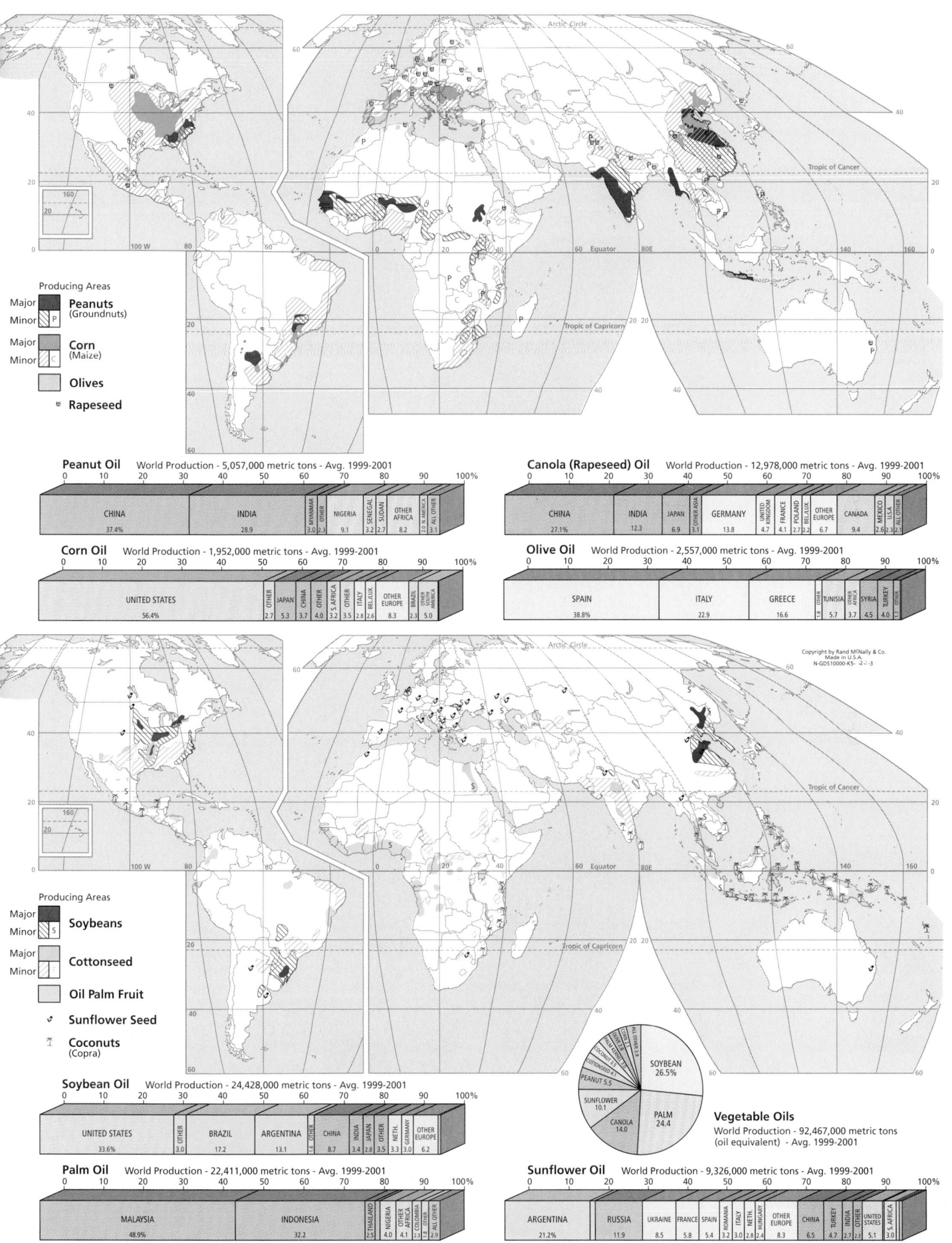

Producing Areas

| Major | | Peanuts |
| Minor | P | (Groundnuts) |

| Major | | Corn |
| Minor | C | (Maize) |

| | Olives |
| ᵚ | Rapeseed |

Peanut Oil World Production - 5,057,000 metric tons - Avg. 1999-2001

| 0 | 10 | 20 | 30 | 40 | 50 | 60 | 70 | 80 | 90 | 100% |

| CHINA 37.4% | INDIA 28.9 | MYANMAR 3.0 | OTHER 2.3 | NIGERIA 9.1 | SENEGAL 3.2 | SUDAN 2.7 | OTHER AFRICA 8.2 | N. AMERICA 2.0 | ALL OTHER 3.1 |

Corn Oil World Production - 1,952,000 metric tons - Avg. 1999-2001

| 0 | 10 | 20 | 30 | 40 | 50 | 60 | 70 | 80 | 90 | 100% |

| UNITED STATES 56.4% | OTHER 2.7 | JAPAN 5.3 | CHINA 3.7 | OTHER 4.0 | S. AFRICA 3.5 | OTHER 2.8 | ITALY BELJUX. 2.6 | OTHER EUROPE 8.3 | BRAZIL 2.3 | OTHER SOUTH AMERICA 5.0 |

Canola (Rapeseed) Oil World Production - 12,978,000 metric tons - Avg. 1999-2001

| 0 | 10 | 20 | 30 | 40 | 50 | 60 | 70 | 80 | 90 | 100% |

| CHINA 27.1% | INDIA 12.3 | JAPAN 6.9 | OTHER ASIA 3.1 | GERMANY 13.8 | UNITED KINGDOM 4.7 | FRANCE 4.1 | POLAND 2.7 | BELJUX. 2.2 | OTHER EUROPE 6.7 | CANADA 9.4 | MEXICO 2.6 | U.S.A. 4.0 | ALL OTHER 2.1 |

Olive Oil World Production - 2,557,000 metric tons - Avg. 1999-2001

| 0 | 10 | 20 | 30 | 40 | 50 | 60 | 70 | 80 | 90 | 100% |

| SPAIN 38.8% | ITALY 22.9 | GREECE 16.6 | OTHER 1.8 | TUNISIA 5.7 | OTHER AFRICA 3.7 | SYRIA 4.5 | TURKEY 4.0 | OTHER 1.5 |

Producing Areas

| Major | | Soybeans |
| Minor | S | |

| Major | | Cottonseed |
| Minor | T | |

	Oil Palm Fruit
ᶲ	Sunflower Seed
⊤	Coconuts (Copra)

Soybean Oil World Production - 24,428,000 metric tons - Avg. 1999-2001

| 0 | 10 | 20 | 30 | 40 | 50 | 60 | 70 | 80 | 90 | 100% |

| UNITED STATES 33.6% | OTHER 3.0 | BRAZIL 17.2 | ARGENTINA 13.1 | OTHER 1.6 | CHINA 8.7 | INDIA 3.4 | JAPAN 2.8 | NETH. 3.5 | GERMANY 3.0 | OTHER EUROPE 6.2 |

Palm Oil World Production - 22,411,000 metric tons - Avg. 1999-2001

| 0 | 10 | 20 | 30 | 40 | 50 | 60 | 70 | 80 | 90 | 100% |

| MALAYSIA 48.9% | INDONESIA 32.2 | THAILAND 2.5 | NIGERIA 4.0 | OTHER AFRICA 4.1 | COLOMBIA 2.3 | OTHER 1.8 | ALL OTHER 2.9 |

Vegetable Oils

World Production - 92,467,000 metric tons
(oil equivalent) - Avg. 1999-2001

Pie chart: SOYBEAN 26.5%, PALM 24.4, CANOLA 14.0, SUNFLOWER 10.1, PEANUT 5.5, COTTONSEED 4.1, COCONUT 3.5, PALM KERNEL 2.3, OTHER 9.6

Sunflower Oil World Production - 9,326,000 metric tons - Avg. 1999-2001

| 0 | 10 | 20 | 30 | 40 | 50 | 60 | 70 | 80 | 90 | 100% |

| ARGENTINA 21.2% | RUSSIA 11.9 | UKRAINE 8.5 | FRANCE 5.8 | SPAIN 5.4 | ROMANIA 3.2 | ITALY 3.0 | NETH. 2.8 | HUNGARY 2.4 | OTHER EUROPE 8.3 | CHINA 6.5 | TURKEY 4.7 | INDIA 2.7 | OTHER 2.3 | UNITED STATES 5.1 | S. AFRICA 3.0 |

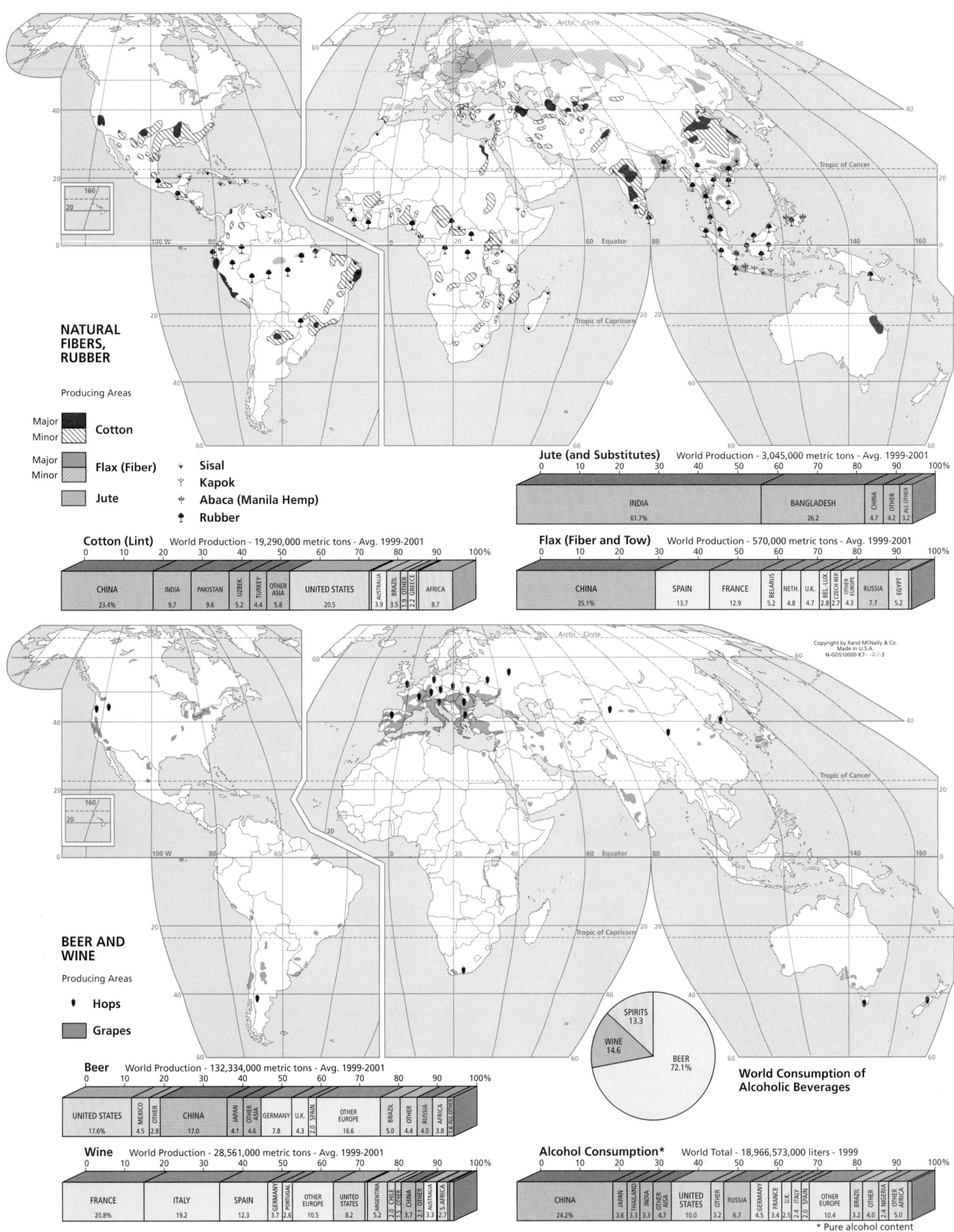

NATURAL FIBERS, RUBBER

Producing Areas

| Major | | Cotton |
| Minor | | |

| Major | | Flax (Fiber) |
| Minor | | |

| | Jute |

⚲ Sisal
☥ Kapok
⚹ Abaca (Manila Hemp)
♣ Rubber

Cotton (Lint)   World Production - 19,290,000 metric tons - Avg. 1999-2001

| 0 | 10 | 20 | 30 | 40 | 50 | 60 | 70 | 80 | 90 | 100% |

| CHINA 23.4% | INDIA 9.7 | PAKISTAN 9.6 | UZBEK. 5.2 | TURKEY 4.4 | OTHER ASIA 5.8 | UNITED STATES 20.5 | AUSTRALIA 3.9 | BRAZIL 3.5 | OTHER 1.9 | GREECE 2.2 | AFRICA 8.7 |

Jute (and Substitutes)   World Production - 3,045,000 metric tons - Avg. 1999-2001

| 0 | 10 | 20 | 30 | 40 | 50 | 60 | 70 | 80 | 90 | 100% |

| INDIA 61.7% | BANGLADESH 26.2 | CHINA 4.7 | OTHER 4.2 | ALL OTHER 3.2 |

Flax (Fiber and Tow)   World Production - 570,000 metric tons - Avg. 1999-2001

| 0 | 10 | 20 | 30 | 40 | 50 | 60 | 70 | 80 | 90 | 100% |

| CHINA 35.1% | SPAIN 13.7 | FRANCE 12.9 | BELARUS 5.2 | NETH. 4.8 | U.K. 4.7 | BEL.-LUX. 2.8 | CZECH REP. 2.7 | OTHER EUROPE 4.3 | RUSSIA 7.7 | EGYPT 5.2 |

BEER AND WINE

Producing Areas

⬥ Hops

▬ Grapes

World Consumption of Alcoholic Beverages

SPIRITS 13.3
WINE 14.6
BEER 72.1%

Beer   World Production - 132,334,000 metric tons - Avg. 1999-2001

| 0 | 10 | 20 | 30 | 40 | 50 | 60 | 70 | 80 | 90 | 100% |

| UNITED STATES 17.6% | MEXICO 4.5 | OTHER 2.8 | CHINA 17.0 | JAPAN 4.1 | OTHER ASIA 4.6 | GERMANY 7.8 | U.K. 4.3 | SPAIN 2.0 | OTHER EUROPE 16.6 | BRAZIL 5.0 | OTHER 4.4 | RUSSIA 4.0 | AFRICA 3.8 | ALL OTHER 1.6 |

Wine   World Production - 28,561,000 metric tons - Avg. 1999-2001

| 0 | 10 | 20 | 30 | 40 | 50 | 60 | 70 | 80 | 90 | 100% |

| FRANCE 20.8% | ITALY 19.2 | SPAIN 12.3 | GERMANY 3.7 | PORTUGAL 2.6 | OTHER EUROPE 10.5 | UNITED STATES 8.2 | ARGENTINA 5.2 | CHILE 2.0 | OTHER 1.5 | CHINA 3.7 | OTHER 2.1 | AUSTRALIA 3.3 | S. AFRICA 2.7 |

Alcohol Consumption*   World Total - 18,966,573,000 liters - 1999

| 0 | 10 | 20 | 30 | 40 | 50 | 60 | 70 | 80 | 90 | 100% |

| CHINA 24.2% | JAPAN 3.6 | THAILAND 3.3 | INDIA 3.3 | OTHER ASIA 4.7 | UNITED STATES 10.0 | OTHER 3.2 | RUSSIA 6.7 | FRANCE 4.5 | U.K. 3.4 | ITALY 2.5 | SPAIN 2.0 | OTHER EUROPE 10.4 | BRAZIL 4.5 | OTHER 2.4 | NIGERIA 2.4 | OTHER AFRICA 5.0 |

* Pure alcohol content

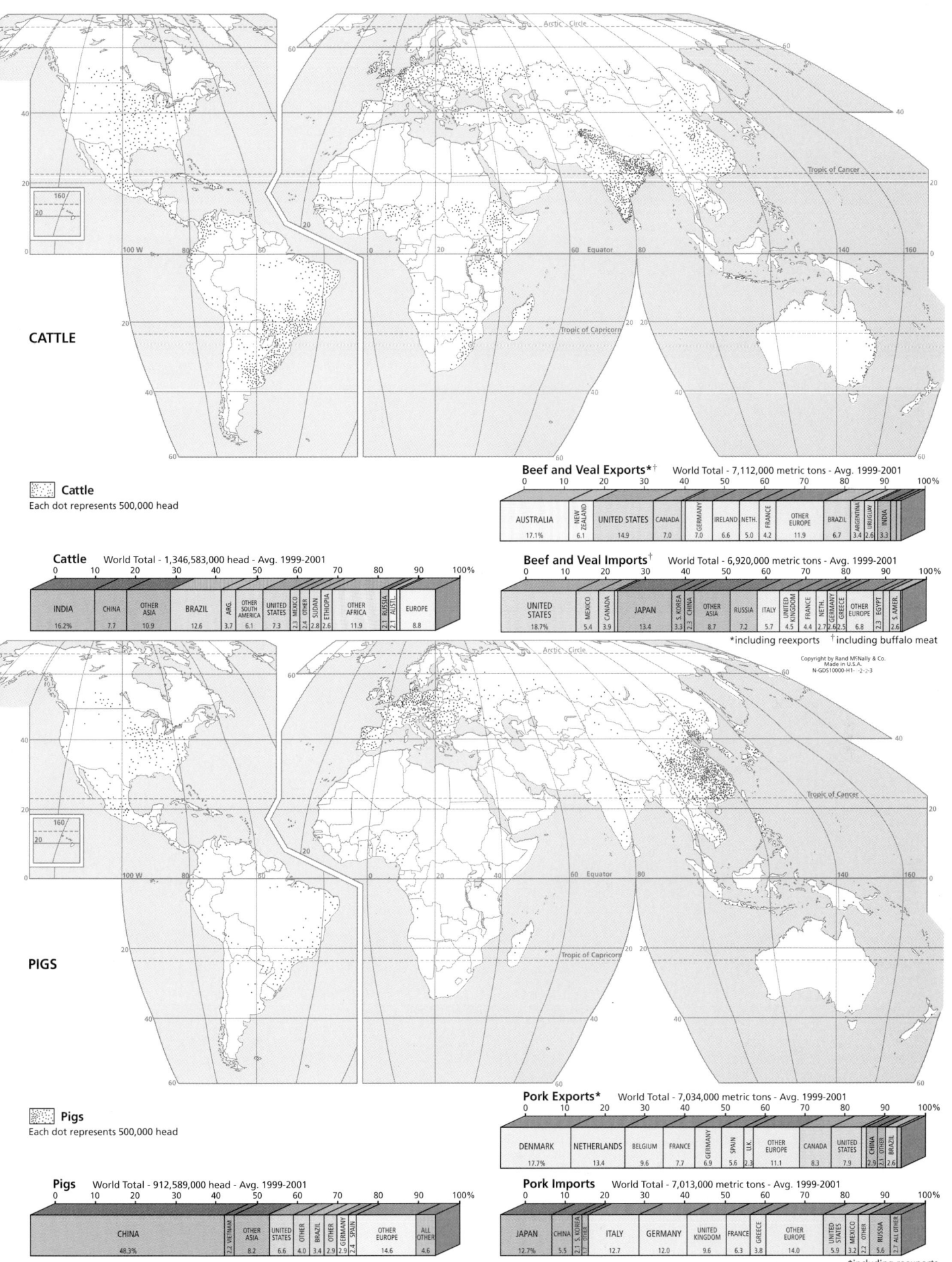

CATTLE

Cattle
Each dot represents 500,000 head

Beef and Veal Exports*† World Total - 7,112,000 metric tons - Avg. 1999-2001

0	10	20	30	40	50	60	70	80	90	100%

AUSTRALIA	NEW ZEALAND	UNITED STATES	CANADA	GERMANY	IRELAND	NETH.	FRANCE	OTHER EUROPE	BRAZIL	ARGENTINA	URUGUAY	INDIA	
17.1%	6.1	14.9	7.0	7.0	6.6	5.0	4.2	11.9	6.7	3.4	2.6	3.3	

Cattle World Total - 1,346,583,000 head - Avg. 1999-2001

0	10	20	30	40	50	60	70	80	90	100%

INDIA	CHINA	OTHER ASIA	BRAZIL	ARG.	OTHER SOUTH AMERICA	UNITED STATES	MEXICO	OTHER	SUDAN	ETHIOPIA	OTHER AFRICA	RUSSIA	AUSTL.	EUROPE
16.2%	7.7	10.9	12.6	3.7	6.1	7.3	2.3	2.4	2.8	2.6	11.9	2.1	2.1	8.8

Beef and Veal Imports† World Total - 6,920,000 metric tons - Avg. 1999-2001

0	10	20	30	40	50	60	70	80	90	100%

UNITED STATES	MEXICO	CANADA	JAPAN	S. KOREA	CHINA	OTHER ASIA	RUSSIA	ITALY	UNITED KINGDOM	FRANCE	NETH.	GERMANY	GREECE	OTHER EUROPE	EGYPT	S. AMER.
18.7%	5.4	3.9	13.4	3.3	2.3	8.7	7.2	5.7	4.5	4.4	2.7	2.6	2.5	6.8	2.3	2.6

*including reexports †including buffalo meat

PIGS

Pigs
Each dot represents 500,000 head

Pigs World Total - 912,589,000 head - Avg. 1999-2001

0	10	20	30	40	50	60	70	80	90	100%

CHINA	VIETNAM	OTHER ASIA	UNITED STATES	OTHER	BRAZIL	OTHER	SPAIN	OTHER EUROPE	ALL OTHER
48.3%	2.2	8.2	6.6	4.0	3.4	2.9	2.4	14.6	4.6

Pork Exports* World Total - 7,034,000 metric tons - Avg. 1999-2001

0	10	20	30	40	50	60	70	80	90	100%

DENMARK	NETHERLANDS	BELGIUM	FRANCE	GERMANY	SPAIN	U.K.	OTHER EUROPE	CANADA	UNITED STATES	CHINA	OTHER	BRAZIL
17.7%	13.4	9.6	7.7	6.9	5.6	2.3	11.1	8.3	7.9	2.9	2.1	2.6

Pork Imports World Total - 7,013,000 metric tons - Avg. 1999-2001

0	10	20	30	40	50	60	70	80	90	100%

JAPAN	CHINA	S. KOREA	OTHER	ITALY	GERMANY	UNITED KINGDOM	FRANCE	GREECE	OTHER EUROPE	UNITED STATES	MEXICO	RUSSIA	ALL OTHER
12.7%	5.5	2.1	1.7	12.7	12.0	9.6	6.3	3.8	14.0	5.9	3.2	5.6	2.7

*including reexports

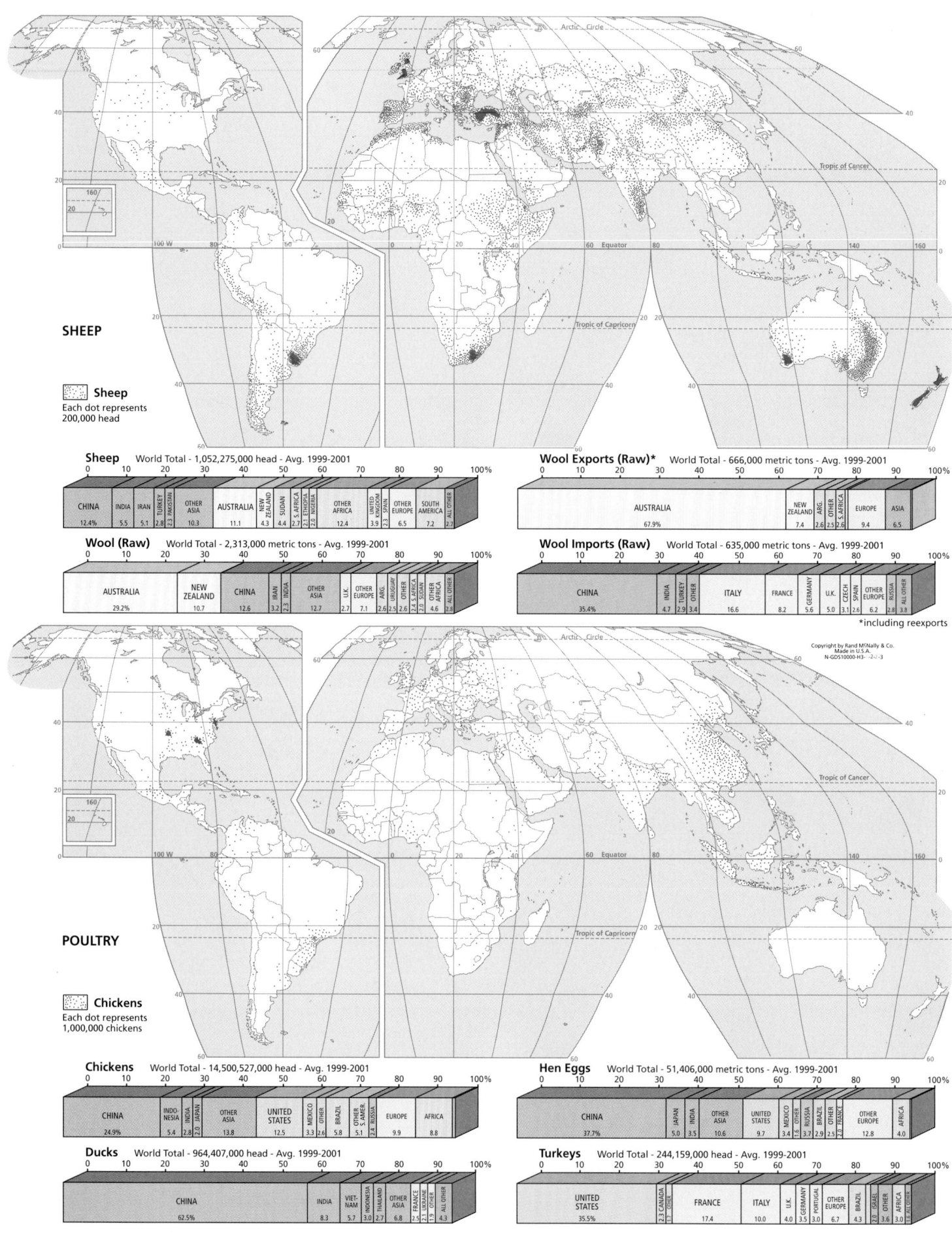

SHEEP

Sheep
Each dot represents
200,000 head

Sheep World Total - 1,052,275,000 head - Avg. 1999-2001

CHINA	INDIA	IRAN	TURKEY	PAKISTAN	OTHER ASIA	AUSTRALIA	NEW ZEALAND	SUDAN	S. AFRICA	ETHIOPIA	NIGERIA	OTHER AFRICA	UNITED KINGDOM	SPAIN	OTHER EUROPE	SOUTH AMERICA	ALL OTHER
12.4%	5.5	5.1	2.8	2.3	10.3	11.1	4.3	4.4	2.7	2.1	2.0	12.4	3.9	2.3	6.5	7.2	2.7

Wool (Raw) World Total - 2,313,000 metric tons - Avg. 1999-2001

AUSTRALIA	NEW ZEALAND	CHINA	IRAN	INDIA	OTHER ASIA	U.K.	OTHER EUROPE	ARG.	URUGUAY	OTHER	S. AFRICA	SUDAN	OTHER AFRICA	ALL OTHER
29.2%	10.7	12.6	3.2	2.3	12.7	2.7	7.1	2.6	2.5	2.6	2.4	2.0	4.6	2.8

Wool Exports (Raw)* World Total - 666,000 metric tons - Avg. 1999-2001

AUSTRALIA	NEW ZEALAND	ARG.	OTHER	S. AFRICA	EUROPE	ASIA
67.9%	7.4	2.6	2.5	2.6	9.4	6.5

Wool Imports (Raw) World Total - 635,000 metric tons - Avg. 1999-2001

CHINA	INDIA	TURKEY	OTHER	ITALY	FRANCE	GERMANY	U.K.	CZECH	SPAIN	OTHER EUROPE	RUSSIA	ALL OTHER
35.4%	4.7	2.9	3.4	16.6	8.2	5.6	5.0	3.1	2.5	6.2	2.8	3.8

*including reexports

Copyright by Rand McNally & Co.
Made in U.S.A.
N-GDS10000-H3- -2-/-3

POULTRY

Chickens
Each dot represents
1,000,000 chickens

Chickens World Total - 14,500,527,000 head - Avg. 1999-2001

CHINA	INDONESIA	INDIA	JAPAN	OTHER ASIA	UNITED STATES	MEXICO	OTHER	BRAZIL	S. AMER.	RUSSIA	EUROPE	AFRICA
24.9%	5.4	2.8	2.0	13.8	12.5	3.3	2.6	5.8	5.1	2.4	9.9	8.8

Hen Eggs World Total - 51,406,000 metric tons - Avg. 1999-2001

CHINA	JAPAN	INDIA	OTHER ASIA	UNITED STATES	MEXICO	OTHER	BRAZIL	OTHER	OTHER EUROPE	AFRICA
37.7%	5.0	3.5	10.6	9.7	3.4	1.6	2.9	2.5	12.8	4.0

Ducks World Total - 964,407,000 head - Avg. 1999-2001

CHINA	INDIA	VIET-NAM	THAILAND	OTHER ASIA	FRANCE	UKRAINE	ALL OTHER
62.5%	8.3	5.7	3.0	6.8	2.5	1.9	4.3

Turkeys World Total - 244,159,000 head - Avg. 1999-2001

UNITED STATES	CANADA	OTHER	FRANCE	ITALY	U.K.	GERMANY	PORTUGAL	OTHER EUROPE	BRAZIL	ISRAEL	AFRICA	ALL OTHER
35.5%	2.3	1.7	17.4	10.0	4.0	3.5	3.0	6.7	4.3	2.0	3.0	1.6

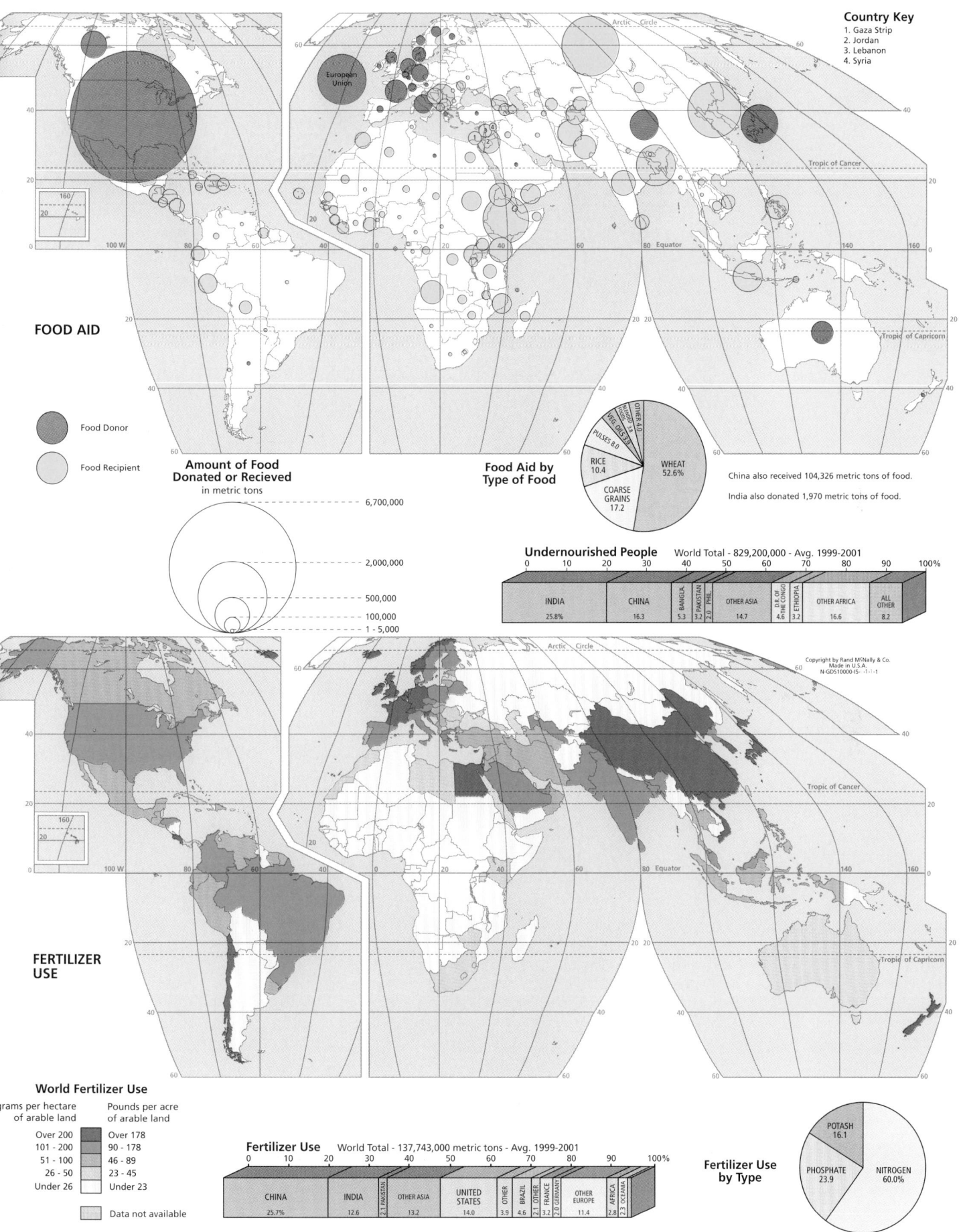

Copyright by Rand McNally & Co.
Made in U.S.A.
N-GDS10000-I5- -1-:-1

Country Key
1. Gaza Strip
2. Jordan
3. Lebanon
4. Syria

FOOD AID

European Union

Food Donor

Food Recipient

**Amount of Food
Donated or Recieved**
in metric tons

6,700,000

2,000,000

500,000

100,000

1 - 5,000

**Food Aid by
Type of Food**

OTHER 6.0
BUTTER OIL 1.4
VEG. OILS 3.1
PULSES 8.0
RICE 10.4
COARSE GRAINS 17.2
WHEAT 52.6%

China also received 104,326 metric tons of food.

India also donated 1,970 metric tons of food.

Undernourished People   World Total - 829,200,000 - Avg. 1999-2001

0	10	20	30	40	50	60	70	80	90	100%
INDIA 25.8%			CHINA 16.3		BANGLA. 5.3	PAKISTAN 3.2	PHIL. 2.0	OTHER ASIA 14.7	D.R. OF THE CONGO 4.6	ETHIOPIA 3.2	OTHER AFRICA 16.6		ALL OTHER 8.2

**FERTILIZER
USE**

World Fertilizer Use

grams per hectare of arable land | Pounds per acre of arable land
Over 200	Over 178
101 - 200	90 - 178
51 - 100	46 - 89
26 - 50	23 - 45
Under 26	Under 23

Data not available

Fertilizer Use   World Total - 137,743,000 metric tons - Avg. 1999-2001

0	10	20	30	40	50	60	70	80	90	100%
CHINA 25.7%		INDIA 12.6	PAKISTAN 2.1	OTHER ASIA 13.2		UNITED STATES 14.0		OTHER 3.9	BRAZIL 4.6	OTHER 2.1	FRANCE 3.2	GERMANY 2.0	OTHER EUROPE 11.4		AFRICA 2.8	OCEANIA 2.3

**Fertilizer Use
by Type**

POTASH 16.1
PHOSPHATE 23.9
NITROGEN 60.0%

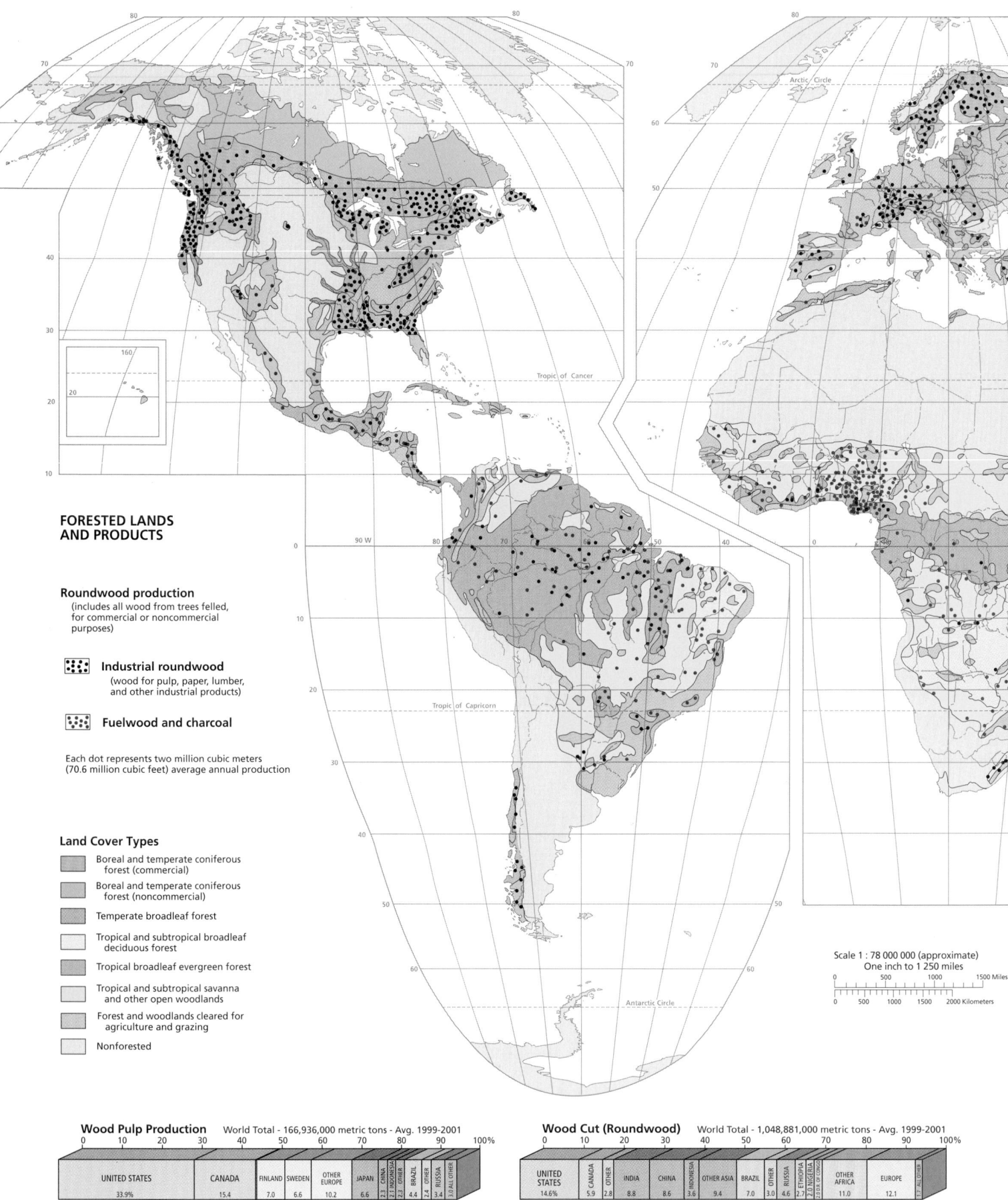

FORESTED LANDS AND PRODUCTS

Roundwood production
(includes all wood from trees felled, for commercial or noncommercial purposes)

Industrial roundwood
(wood for pulp, paper, lumber, and other industrial products)

Fuelwood and charcoal

Each dot represents two million cubic meters (70.6 million cubic feet) average annual production

Land Cover Types

- Boreal and temperate coniferous forest (commercial)
- Boreal and temperate coniferous forest (noncommercial)
- Temperate broadleaf forest
- Tropical and subtropical broadleaf deciduous forest
- Tropical broadleaf evergreen forest
- Tropical and subtropical savanna and other open woodlands
- Forest and woodlands cleared for agriculture and grazing
- Nonforested

Scale 1 : 78 000 000 (approximate)
One inch to 1 250 miles

0   500   1000   1500 Miles

0   500   1000   1500   2000 Kilometers

Wood Pulp Production
World Total - 166,936,000 metric tons - Avg. 1999-2001

UNITED STATES 33.9%	CANADA 15.4	FINLAND 7.0	SWEDEN 6.6	OTHER EUROPE 10.2	JAPAN 6.6	CHINA 2.3	INDONESIA 2.1	OTHER 2.3	BRAZIL 4.4	OTHER 2.4	RUSSIA 3.4	ALL OTHER 3.0

Wood Cut (Roundwood)
World Total - 1,048,881,000 metric tons - Avg. 1999-2001

UNITED STATES 14.6%	CANADA 5.9	OTHER 2.8	INDIA 8.8	CHINA 8.6	INDONESIA 3.6	OTHER ASIA 9.4	BRAZIL 7.0	OTHER 3.0	RUSSIA 4.6	ETHIOPIA 2.7	NIGERIA 2.0	DR OF CONGO	OTHER AFRICA 11.0	EUROPE 12.1	ALL OTHER

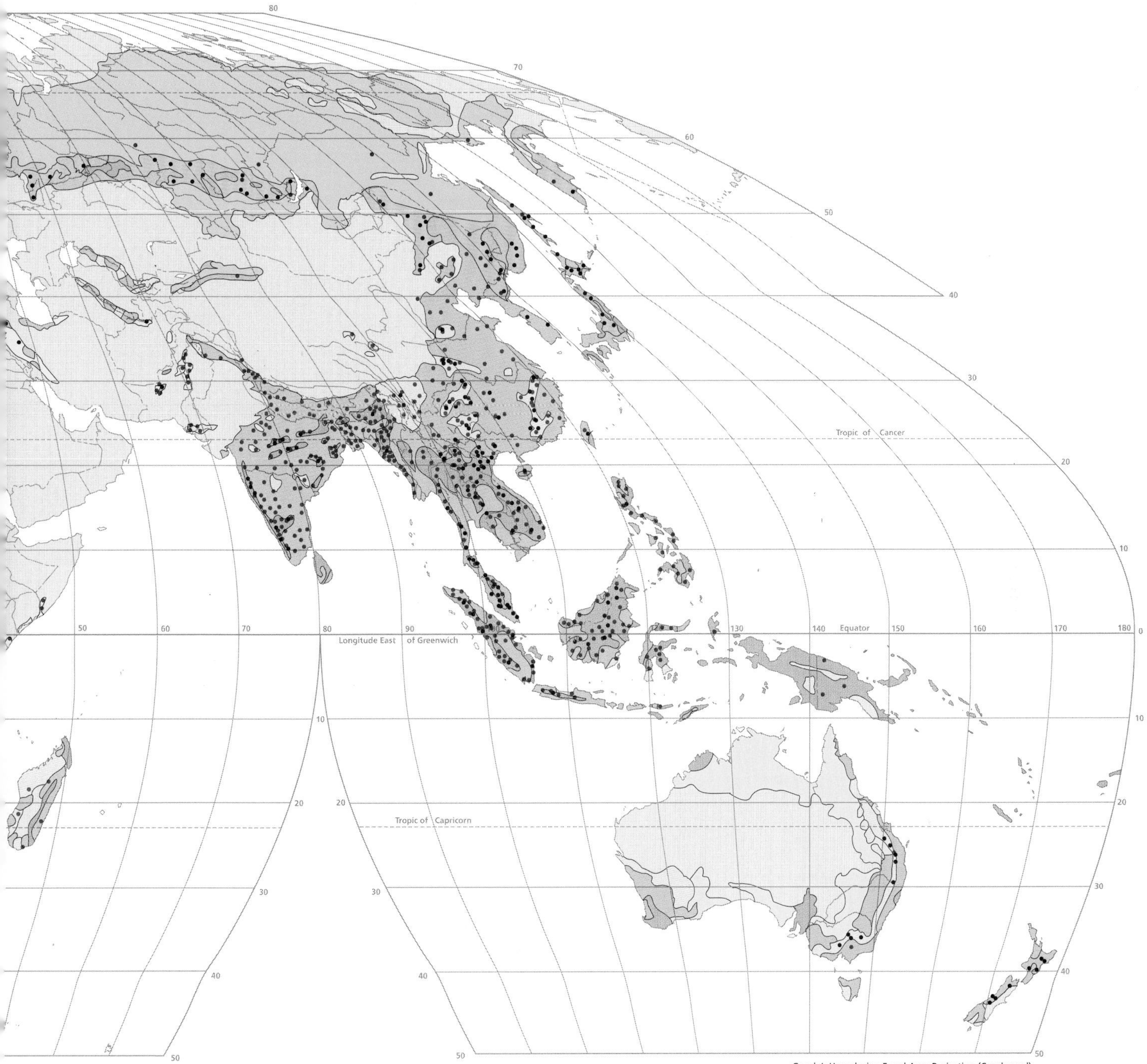

80
70
60
50
40
30
Tropic of Cancer
20
10
50
60
70
80
90
Longitude East of Greenwich
130
140
Equator
150
160
170
180
0
10
20
Tropic of Capricorn
30
40
50

Goode's Homolosine Equal Area Projection (Condensed)

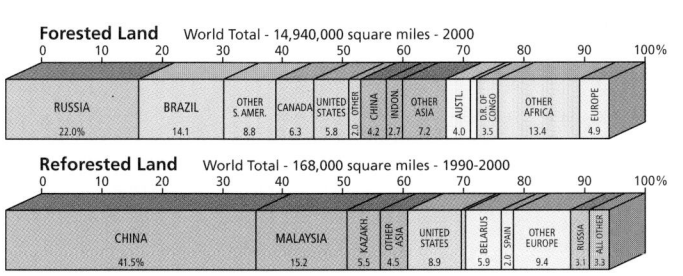

Forested Land World Total - 14,940,000 square miles - 2000

0
10
20
30
40
50
60
70
80
90
100%
RUSSIA 22.0%
BRAZIL 14.1
OTHER S. AMER. 8.8
CANADA 6.3
UNITED STATES 5.8
OTHER 2.0
CHINA 4.2
INDON. 2.7
OTHER ASIA 7.2
AUSTL. 4.0
D.R. OF CONGO 3.5
OTHER AFRICA 13.4
EUROPE 4.9

Reforested Land World Total - 168,000 square miles - 1990-2000

0
10
20
30
40
50
60
70
80
90
100%
CHINA 41.5%
MALAYSIA 15.2
KAZAKH. 5.5
OTHER ASIA 4.5
UNITED STATES 8.9
BELARUS 5.9
SPAIN 2.0
OTHER EUROPE 9.4
RUSSIA 3.1
ALL OTHER 3.3

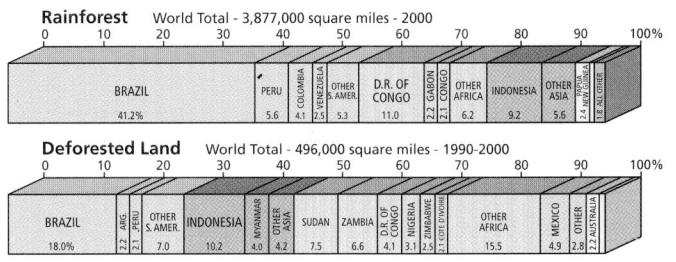

Rainforest World Total - 3,877,000 square miles - 2000

0
10
20
30
40
50
60
70
80
90
100%
BRAZIL 41.2%
PERU 5.6
COLOMBIA 4.1
VENEZUELA 2.5
OTHER S. AMER. 5.3
D.R. OF CONGO 11.0
GABON 2.2
CONGO 2.1
OTHER AFRICA 6.2
INDONESIA 9.2
OTHER ASIA 5.6
PAPUA NEW GUINEA 2.4
ALL OTHER 1.8

Deforested Land World Total - 496,000 square miles - 1990-2000

0
10
20
30
40
50
60
70
80
90
100%
BRAZIL 18.0%
ARG. 2.2
PERU 2.1
OTHER S. AMER. 7.0
INDONESIA 10.2
MYANMAR 4.0
OTHER ASIA 4.2
SUDAN 7.5
ZAMBIA 6.6
D.R. OF CONGO 4.1
NIGERIA 3.1
ZIMBABWE 2.5
COTE D'IVOIRE 2.1
OTHER AFRICA 15.5
MEXICO 4.9
OTHER 2.8
AUSTRALIA 2.2

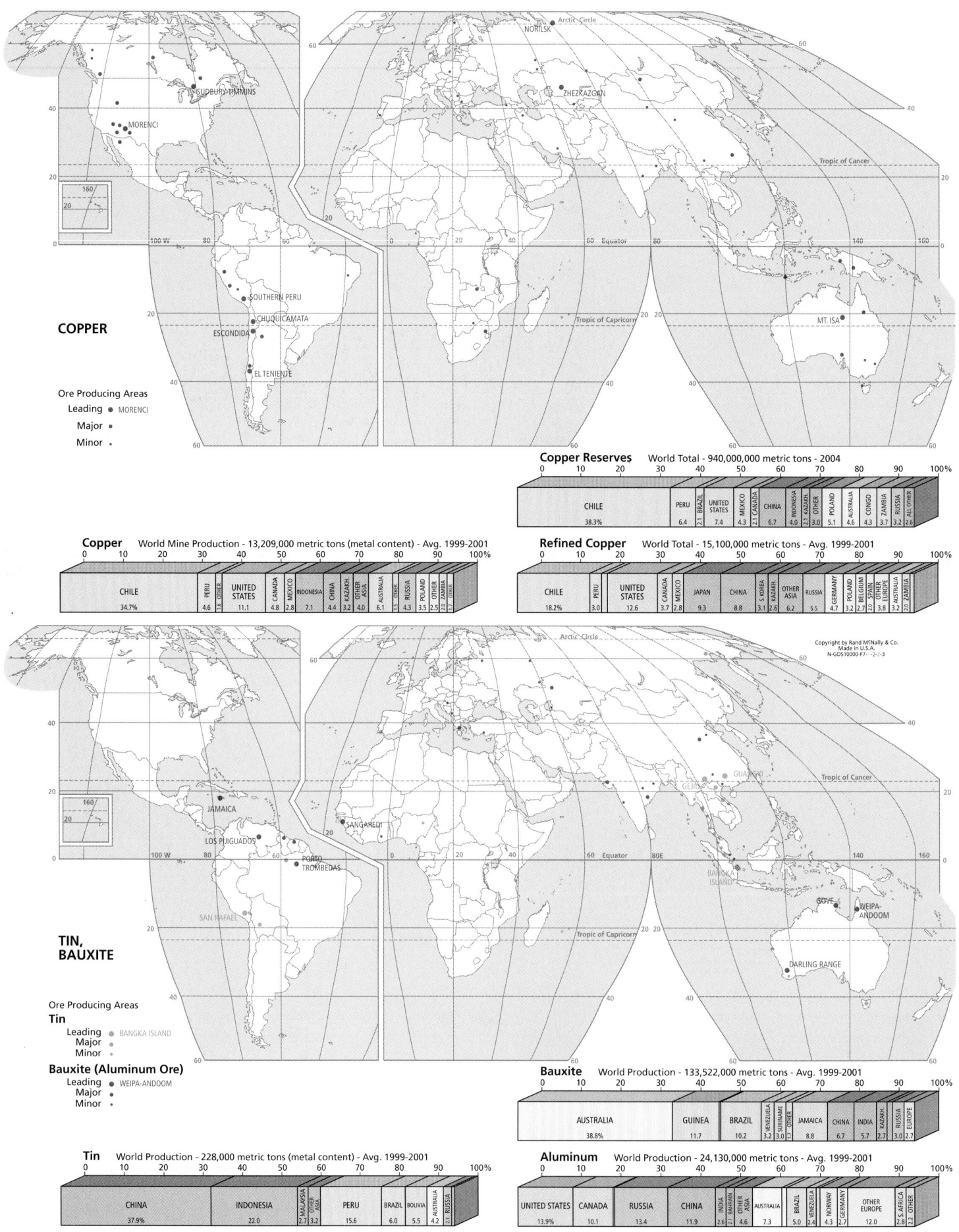

COPPER

Ore Producing Areas
Leading ● MORENCI
Major ●
Minor ·

Copper Reserves World Total - 940,000,000 metric tons - 2004

0	10	20	30	40	50	60	70	80	90	100%						

| CHILE 38.3% | PERU 6.4 | BRAZIL 2.1 | UNITED STATES 7.4 | MEXICO 4.3 | CANADA 2.1 | CHINA 6.7 | INDONESIA 4.0 | KAZAKH. 2.7 | OTHER 5.1 | POLAND 3.0 | AUSTRALIA 4.6 | CONGO 4.3 | ZAMBIA 3.7 | RUSSIA 3.2 | ALL OTHER 2.6 |

Copper World Mine Production - 13,209,000 metric tons (metal content) - Avg. 1999-2001

0	10	20	30	40	50	60	70	80	90	100%

| CHILE 34.7% | PERU 4.6 | OTHER 1.6 | UNITED STATES 11.1 | CANADA 4.8 | MEXICO 2.8 | INDONESIA 7.1 | CHINA 4.4 | KAZAKH. 3.2 | OTHER ASIA 4.0 | AUSTRALIA 6.1 | OTHER 1.1 | RUSSIA 4.3 | POLAND 3.5 | OTHER 2.0 | ZAMBIA 1.7 | OTHER |

Refined Copper World Total - 15,100,000 metric tons - Avg. 1999-2001

0	10	20	30	40	50	60	70	80	90	100%

| CHILE 18.2% | PERU 3.0 | UNITED STATES 12.6 | CANADA 3.7 | MEXICO 2.8 | JAPAN 9.3 | CHINA 8.8 | S. KOREA 3.1 | KAZAKH. 2.6 | OTHER ASIA 6.2 | RUSSIA 5.5 | GERMANY 4.7 | POLAND 3.2 | BELGIUM 2.0 | SPAIN OTHER EUROPE 3.8 | AUSTRALIA 3.2 | ZAMBIA 2.6 |

TIN, BAUXITE

Ore Producing Areas
Tin
Leading ● BANGKA ISLAND
Major ●
Minor ·

Bauxite (Aluminum Ore)
Leading ● WEIPA-ANDOOM
Major ●
Minor ·

Bauxite World Production - 133,522,000 metric tons - Avg. 1999-2001

0	10	20	30	40	50	60	70	80	90	100%

| AUSTRALIA 38.8% | GUINEA 11.7 | BRAZIL 10.2 | VENEZUELA 3.2 | SURINAME 3.0 | OTHER 1.7 | JAMAICA 8.8 | CHINA 6.7 | INDIA 5.7 | KAZAKH. 2.7 | RUSSIA 3.0 | EUROPE 2.7 |

Tin World Production - 228,000 metric tons (metal content) - Avg. 1999-2001

0	10	20	30	40	50	60	70	80	90	100%

| CHINA 37.9% | INDONESIA 22.0 | MALAYSIA 2.7 | OTHER ASIA 3.2 | PERU 15.6 | BRAZIL 6.0 | BOLIVIA 5.5 | AUSTRALIA 4.2 | RUSSIA 2.1 |

Aluminum World Production - 24,130,000 metric tons - Avg. 1999-2001

0	10	20	30	40	50	60	70	80	90	100%

| UNITED STATES 13.9% | CANADA 10.1 | RUSSIA 13.4 | CHINA 11.9 | INDIA 2.6 | BAHRAIN 2.1 | OTHER ASIA 4.6 | AUSTRALIA 7.3 | BRAZIL 5.0 | VENEZUELA 2.4 | NORWAY 4.3 | GERMANY 2.7 | OTHER EUROPE 12.0 | S. AFRICA 2.8 | OTHER 2.2 |

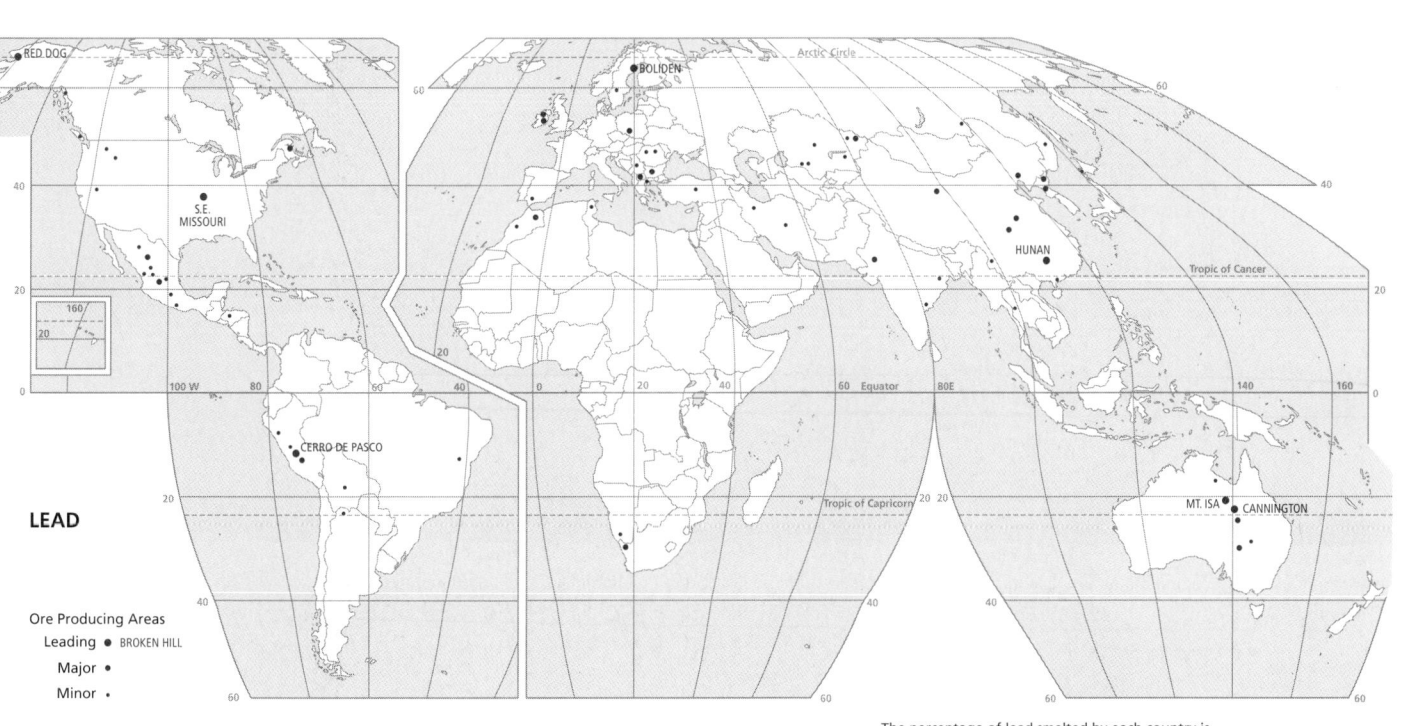

LEAD

Ore Producing Areas

Leading ● BROKEN HILL

Major ●

Minor ·

The percentage of lead smelted by each country is not necessarily identical to its percentage of lead ore production. Some countries, such as Australia, export large amounts of ore to other countries for smelting.

Lead World Mine Production - 3,124,000 metric tons (metal content) - Avg. 1999-2001

0	10	20	30	40	50	60	70	80	90	100%

AUSTRALIA	CHINA	N. KOREA	OTHER ASIA	UNITED STATES	CANADA	MEXICO	PERU	SWEDEN	POLAND	OTHER EUROPE	MOROCCO	S. AFRICA
22.8%	19.3	2.2	3.9	15.5	5.0	4.3	8.7	3.4	2.0	5.9	2.6	2.2

Lead Smelted* World Production - 6,417,000 metric tons - Avg. 1999-2001

0	10	20	30	40	50	60	70	80	90	100%

UNITED STATES	CANADA	ARUBA	MEXICO	CHINA	JAPAN	S. KOREA	KAZAKH.	OTHER ASIA	GERMANY	U.K.	FRANCE	ITALY	BELGIUM	SPAIN	OTHER EUROPE	PERU	ALL OTHER
22.4%	4.3	4.3	2.2	16.6	4.7	2.7	2.6	6.0	6.0	5.5	4.0	3.4	1.6	1.6	5.0	1.8	4.0

*includes recycled materials

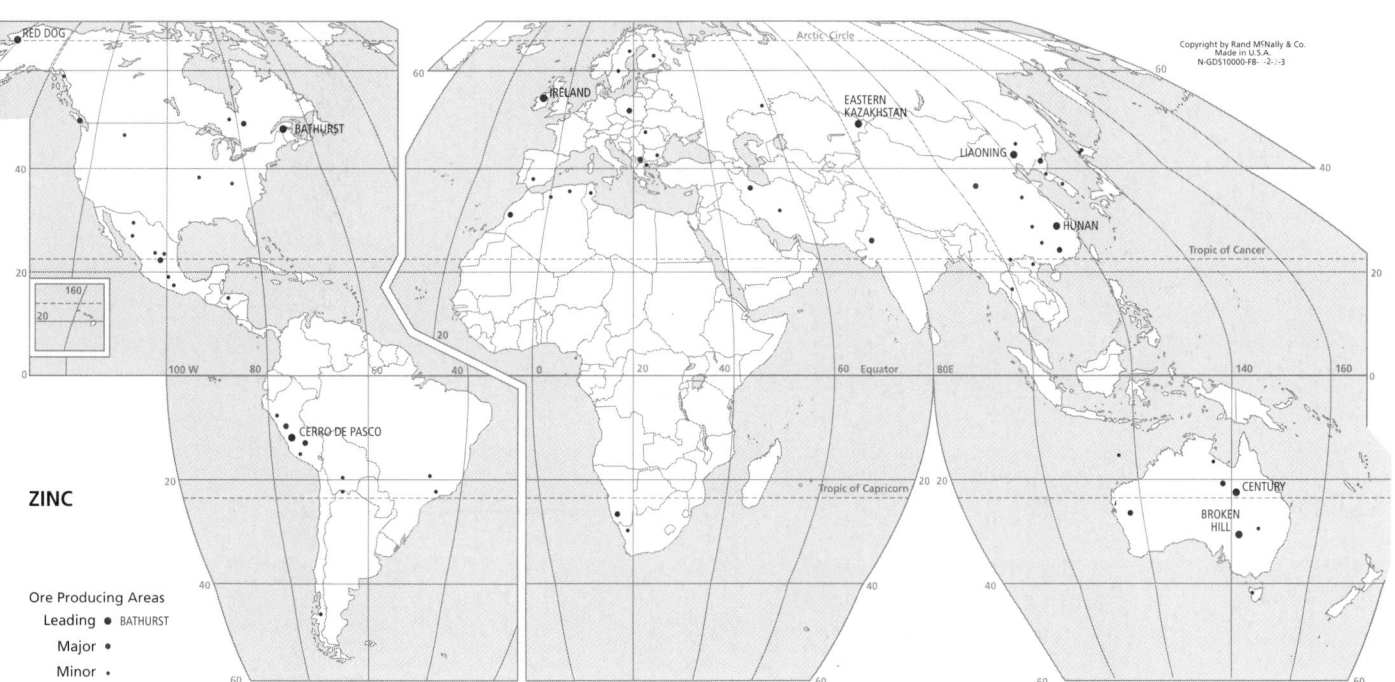

Copyright by Rand McNally & Co.
Made in U.S.A.
N-GDS10000-F8- -2-:-3

ZINC

Ore Producing Areas

Leading ● BATHURST

Major ●

Minor ·

The percentage of zinc smelted by each country is not necessarily identical to its percentage of zinc ore production. Some countries, such as Australia, export large amounts of ore to other countries for smelting.

Zinc World Mine Production - 8,559,000 metric tons (metal content) - Avg. 1999-2001

0	10	20	30	40	50	60	70	80	90	100%

CHINA	KAZAKHSTAN	N. KOREA	OTHER ASIA	AUSTRALIA	CANADA	UNITED STATES	MEXICO	PERU	OTHER S. AMERICA	IRELAND	OTHER EUROPE	ALL OTHER
18.9%	3.7	2.9	4.1	16.0	11.3	9.9	4.5	11.2	3.3	2.8	6.6	5.1

Zinc Smelted* World Production - 9,011,000, metric tons - Avg. 1999-2001

0	10	20	30	40	50	60	70	80	90	100%

CHINA	JAPAN	SOUTH KOREA	KAZAKHSTAN	INDIA	N. KOREA	CANADA	UNITED STATES	MEXICO	AUSTL.	SPAIN	GERMANY	FRANCE	BELGIUM	FINLAND	NETH.	OTHER EUROPE	RUSSIA	PERU	ALL OTHER
21.2%	7.7	5.1	2.9	2.3	2.1	8.7	3.9	2.6	5.2	4.1	3.9	3.8	2.7	2.6	2.4	8.5	2.5	2.2	1.6

*includes recycled materials

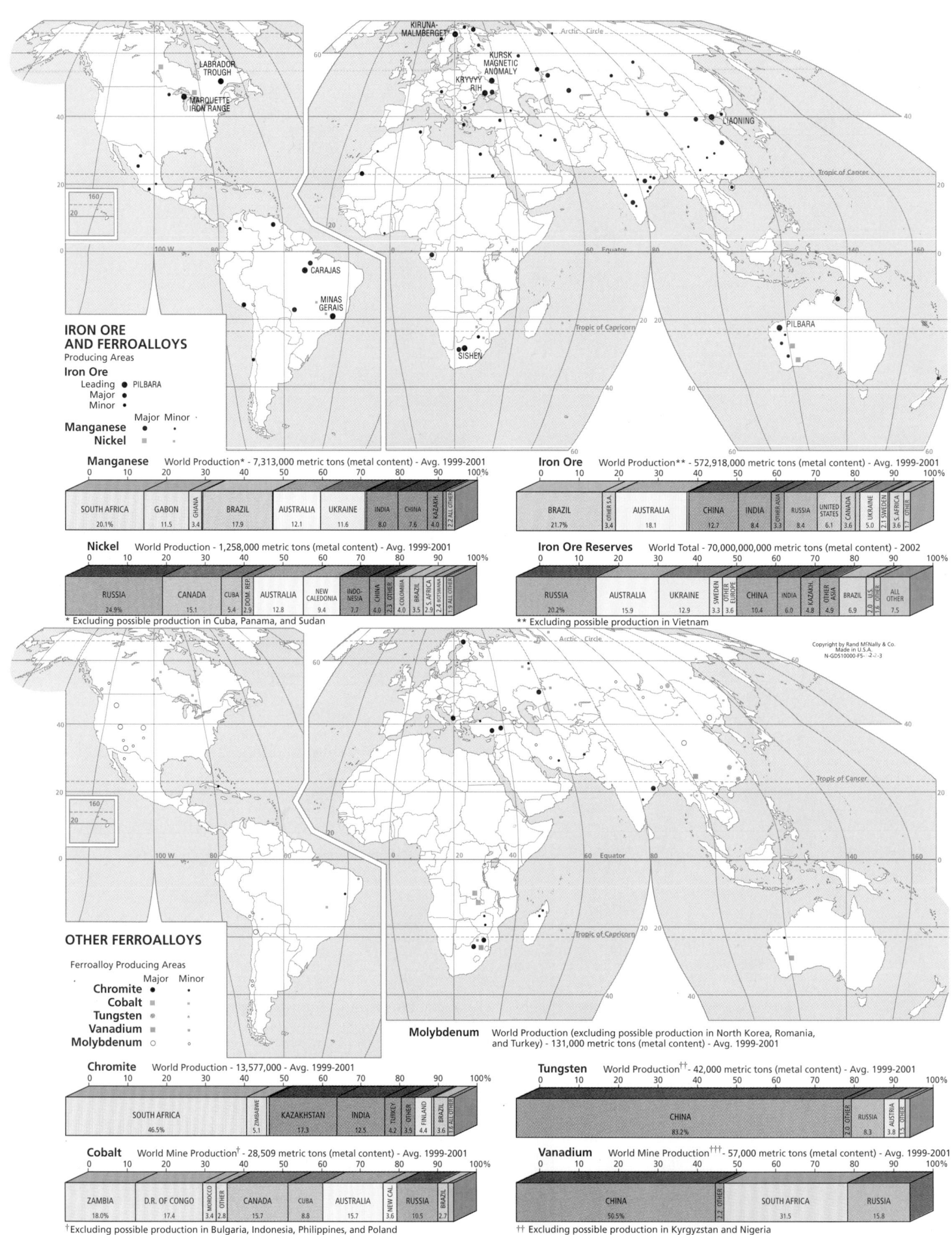

IRON ORE AND FERROALLOYS

Producing Areas

Iron Ore
Leading ● PILBARA
Major ●
Minor ●

Manganese Major ● Minor ●
Nickel ■ ■

Manganese World Production* - 7,313,000 metric tons (metal content) - Avg. 1999-2001

SOUTH AFRICA	GABON	GHANA	BRAZIL	AUSTRALIA	UKRAINE	INDIA	CHINA	KAZAKH.	ALL OTHER
20.1%	11.5	3.4	17.9	12.1	11.6	8.0	7.6	4.0	2.2

Nickel World Production - 1,258,000 metric tons (metal content) - Avg. 1999-2001

RUSSIA	CANADA	CUBA	DOM. REP.	AUSTRALIA	NEW CALEDONIA	INDO-NESIA	CHINA	OTHER	COLOMBIA	BRAZIL	S. AFRICA	ALL OTHER
24.9%	15.1	5.4	2.9	12.8	9.4	7.7	4.0	2.3	4.0	3.5	2.4	1.9

* Excluding possible production in Cuba, Panama, and Sudan

Iron Ore World Production** - 572,918,000 metric tons (metal content) - Avg. 1999-2001

BRAZIL	OTHER S.A.	AUSTRALIA	CHINA	INDIA	OTHER ASIA	RUSSIA	UNITED STATES	CANADA	UKRAINE	SWEDEN	S. AFRICA	OTHER
21.7%	3.4	18.1	12.7	8.4	3.3	8.4	6.1	3.6	5.0	2.1	3.6	1.7

Iron Ore Reserves World Total - 70,000,000,000 metric tons (metal content) - 2002

RUSSIA	AUSTRALIA	UKRAINE	SWEDEN OTHER EUROPE	CHINA	INDIA	KAZAKH.	OTHER ASIA	BRAZIL	U.S.	ALL OTHER
20.2%	15.9	12.9	3.3 / 3.6	10.4	6.0	4.8	4.9	6.9	2.0 / 1.6	7.5

** Excluding possible production in Vietnam

Copyright by Rand McNally & Co.
Made in U.S.A.
N-GDS10000-F5- -2--3

OTHER FERROALLOYS

Ferroalloy Producing Areas

	Major	Minor
Chromite	●	●
Cobalt	■	■
Tungsten	▪	▪
Vanadium	■	■
Molybdenum	○	○

Molybdenum World Production (excluding possible production in North Korea, Romania, and Turkey) - 131,000 metric tons (metal content) - Avg. 1999-2001

Chromite World Production - 13,577,000 - Avg. 1999-2001

SOUTH AFRICA	ZIMBABWE	KAZAKHSTAN	INDIA	TURKEY	OTHER	FINLAND	BRAZIL	ALL OTHER
46.5%	5.1	17.3	12.5	4.2	3.5	4.4	3.6	

Cobalt World Mine Production† - 28,509 metric tons (metal content) - Avg. 1999-2001

ZAMBIA	D.R. OF CONGO	MOROCCO	OTHER	CANADA	CUBA	AUSTRALIA	NEW CAL	RUSSIA	BRAZIL
18.0%	17.4	3.4	2.8	15.7	8.8	15.7	3.6	10.5	2.7

† Excluding possible production in Bulgaria, Indonesia, Philippines, and Poland

Tungsten World Production†† - 42,000 metric tons (metal content) - Avg. 1999-2001

CHINA	OTHER	RUSSIA	AUSTRIA	OTHER
83.2%	2.0	8.3	3.8	1.5

Vanadium World Mine Production††† - 57,000 metric tons (metal content) - Avg. 1999-2001

CHINA	OTHER	SOUTH AFRICA	RUSSIA
50.5%	2.2	31.5	15.8

†† Excluding possible production in Kyrgyzstan and Nigeria
††† Excluding possible production in Australia, Germany, and the United States

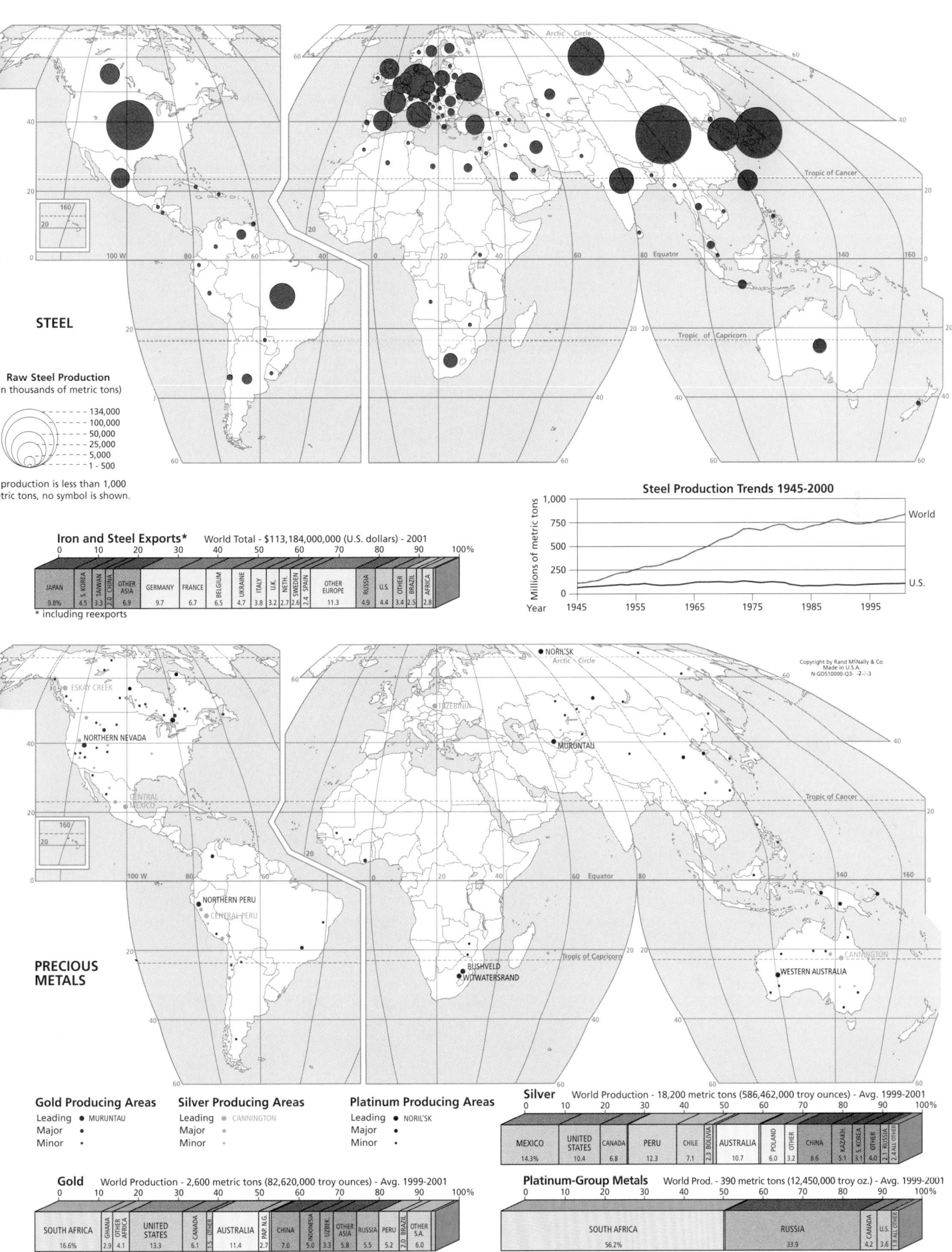

STEEL

Raw Steel Production
(in thousands of metric tons)

- 134,000
- 100,000
- 50,000
- 25,000
- 5,000
- 1 - 500

If production is less than 1,000 metric tons, no symbol is shown.

Iron and Steel Exports*
World Total - $113,184,000,000 (U.S. dollars) - 2001

0	10	20	30	40	50	60	70	80	90	100%

JAPAN	S. KOREA	TAIWAN	CHINA	OTHER ASIA	GERMANY	FRANCE	BELGIUM	UKRAINE	ITALY	U.K.	NETH.	SWEDEN	SPAIN	OTHER EUROPE	RUSSIA	U.S.	OTHER	BRAZIL	AFRICA
9.8%	4.5	3.3	2.0	6.9	9.7	6.7	6.5	4.7	3.8	3.2	2.7	2.4		11.3	4.9	4.4	3.4	2.5	2.8

* including reexports

Steel Production Trends 1945-2000

Millions of metric tons — Year: 1945, 1955, 1965, 1975, 1985, 1995

World / U.S.

PRECIOUS METALS

NORIL'SK
TAZEBINTA
MURUNTAU
ESKAY CREEK
NORTHERN NEVADA
CENTRAL MEXICO
NORTHERN PERU
CENTRAL PERU
BUSHVELD
WITWATERSRAND
CANNINGTON
WESTERN AUSTRALIA

Gold Producing Areas
- Leading ● MURUNTAU
- Major ●
- Minor ·

Silver Producing Areas
- Leading ● CANNINGTON
- Major ·
- Minor ·

Platinum Producing Areas
- Leading ● NORIL'SK
- Major ●
- Minor ·

Silver
World Production - 18,200 metric tons (586,462,000 troy ounces) - Avg. 1999-2001

0	10	20	30	40	50	60	70	80	90	100%

MEXICO	UNITED STATES	CANADA	PERU	CHILE	BOLIVIA	AUSTRALIA	POLAND	OTHER	CHINA	KAZAKH.	S. KOREA	RUSSIA	OTHER	ALL OTHER
14.3%	10.4	6.8	12.3	7.1	2.3	10.7	6.0	3.2	8.6	5.1	3.1	2.1	4.0	2.4

Gold
World Production - 2,600 metric tons (82,620,000 troy ounces) - Avg. 1999-2001

0	10	20	30	40	50	60	70	80	90	100%

SOUTH AFRICA	GHANA	OTHER AFRICA	UNITED STATES	CANADA	OTHER	AUSTRALIA	PAP. N.G.	CHINA	INDONESIA	UZBEK.	OTHER ASIA	RUSSIA	PERU	BRAZIL	OTHER S.A.
16.6%	2.9	4.1	13.3	6.1	1.5	11.4	2.7	7.0	5.0	3.3	5.8	5.5	2.0	2.0	6.0

Platinum-Group Metals
World Prod. - 390 metric tons (12,450,000 troy oz.) - Avg. 1999-2001

0	10	20	30	40	50	60	70	80	90	100%

SOUTH AFRICA	RUSSIA	CANADA	U.S.	ALL OTHER
56.2%	33.9	4.2	3.6	1.8

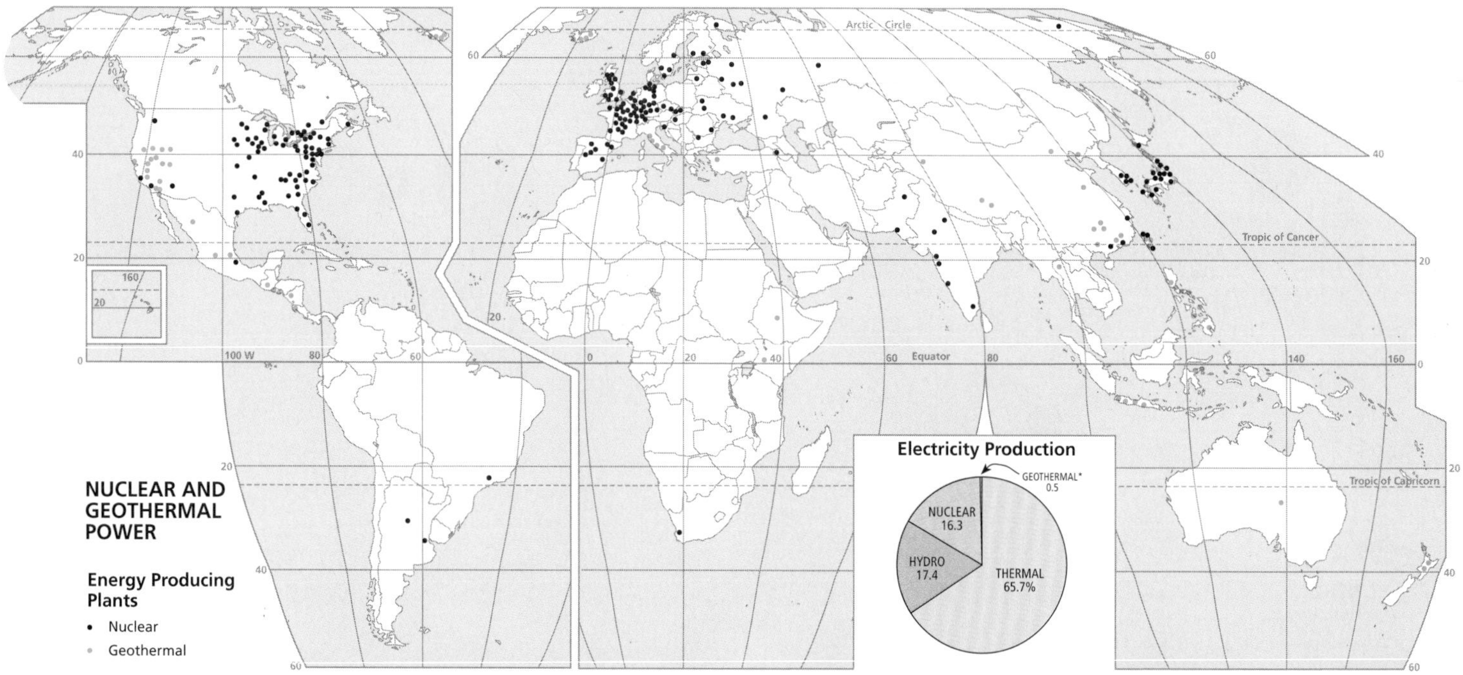

NUCLEAR AND GEOTHERMAL POWER

Energy Producing Plants

- Nuclear
- Geothermal

Electricity Production

- GEOTHERMAL* 0.5
- NUCLEAR 16.3
- HYDRO 17.4
- THERMAL 65.7%

Nuclear Energy — World Production - 2,547,000 gigawatt hours - 2000

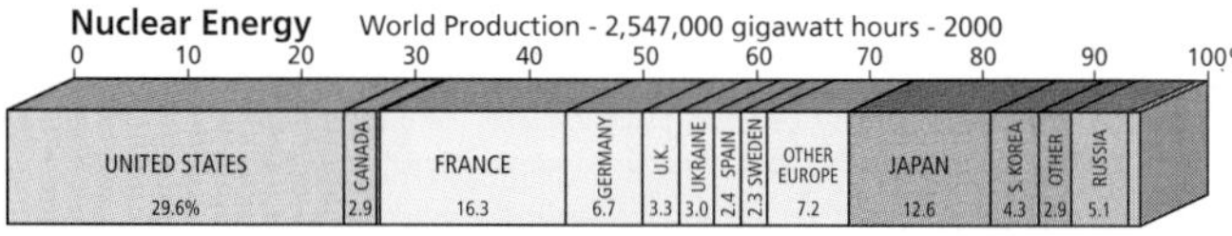

UNITED STATES 29.6%	CANADA 2.9	FRANCE 16.3	GERMANY 6.7	U.K. 3.3	UKRAINE 3.0	SPAIN 2.4	SWEDEN 2.3	OTHER EUROPE 7.2	JAPAN 12.6	S. KOREA 4.3	OTHER 2.9	RUSSIA 5.1

Thermal Electricity — World Production - 10,260,000 gigawatt hours - 2000

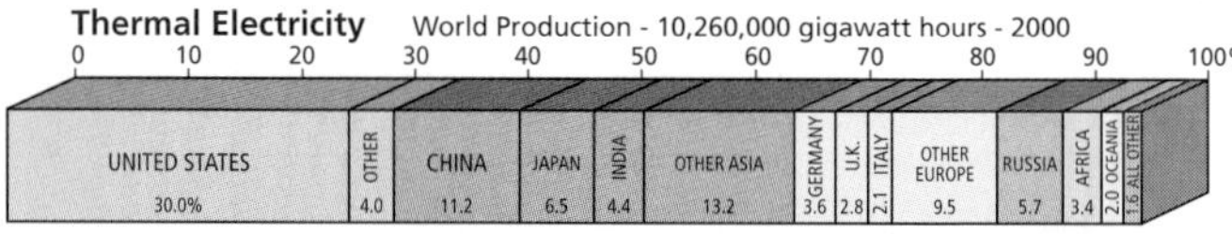

UNITED STATES 30.0%	OTHER 4.0	CHINA 11.2	JAPAN 6.5	INDIA 4.4	OTHER ASIA 13.2	GERMANY 3.6	U.K. 2.1	ITALY	OTHER EUROPE 9.5	RUSSIA 5.7	AFRICA 3.4 / OCEANIA 2.0 / ALL OTHER 1.6

Geothermal Electricity* — World Production - 85,000 gigawatt hours - 2000

UNITED STATES 28.3%	MEXICO 6.9	OTHER 3.2	PHILIPPINES 13.6	JAPAN 4.0	INDO. 3.1	OTHER 2.7	GERMANY 11.3	ITALY 6.2	SPAIN 5.5	DENMARK 5.3	OTHER EUROPE 5.9	N.Z. 3.4	

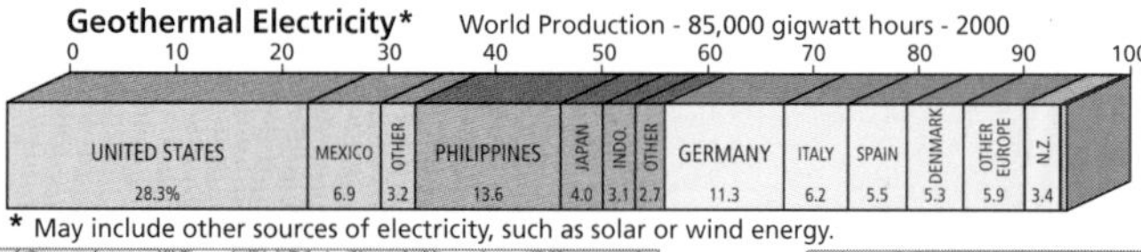

All Electricity — World Production - 15,614,000 gigawatt hours - 2000

UNITED STATES 26.4%	CANADA 3.8	OTHER 2.1	CHINA 8.9	JAPAN 7.0	INDIA 3.5	OTHER ASIA 11.1	RUSSIA 5.6	GERMANY 3.7	FRANCE 3.5	U.K. 2.4	OTHER EUROPE 13.0	BRAZIL 2.2 / OTHER 2.3 / AFRICA 2.8 / ALL OTHER 1.4

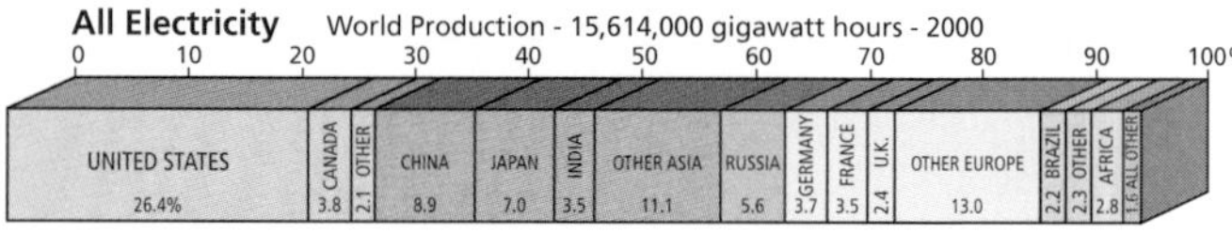

* May include other sources of electricity, such as solar or wind energy.

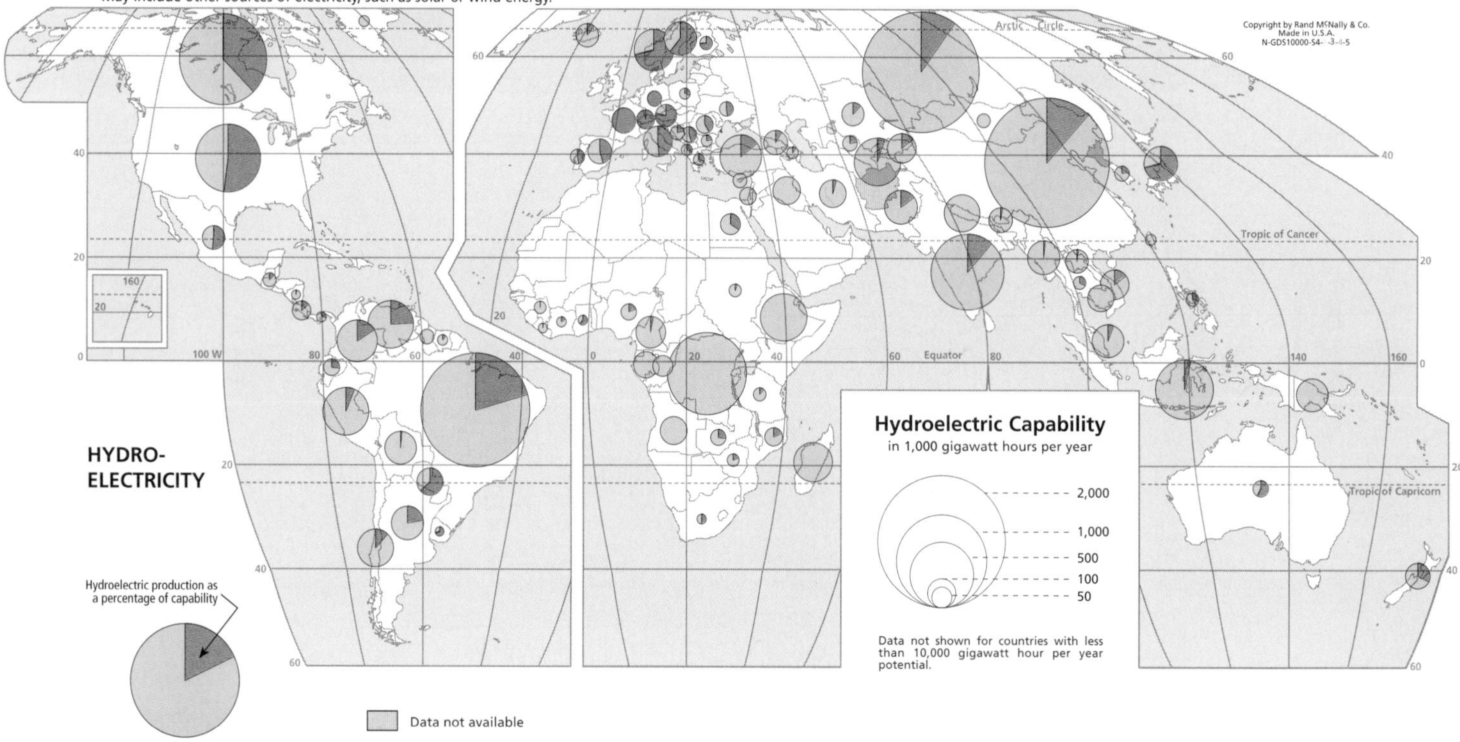

Copyright by Rand McNally & Co.
Made in U.S.A.
N-GD510000-54- -3-+-5

HYDRO-ELECTRICITY

Hydroelectric Capability
in 1,000 gigawatt hours per year

- 2,000
- 1,000
- 500
- 100
- 50

Data not shown for countries with less than 10,000 gigawatt hour per year potential.

Hydroelectric production as a percentage of capability

Data not available

Hydroelectric Capability* — World Total - 14,379,000 gigawatt hours/year - 2000

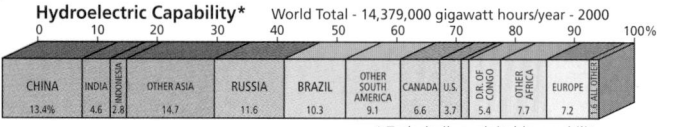

CHINA 13.4%	INDIA 4.6	INDONESIA 2.8	OTHER ASIA 14.7	RUSSIA 11.6	BRAZIL 10.3	OTHER SOUTH AMERICA 9.1	CANADA 6.6	U.S. 3.7	D.R. OF CONGO 5.4	OTHER AFRICA 7.7	EUROPE 7.2 / ALL OTHER 1.6

* Technically exploitable capability

Hydroelectricity — World Production - 2,722,000 gigawatt hours - 2000

CANADA 13.2%	UNITED STATES 10.1	OTHER 1.9	BRAZIL 11.2	VENEZ./PARA. 2.3	OTHER 2.0	CHINA 8.2	JAPAN 3.6	INDIA 2.7	OTHER ASIA 7.6	RUSSIA 6.1	NORWAY 5.2	SWEDEN 2.9	FRANCE 2.7	OTHER EUROPE 11.8	AFRICA 2.8 / ALL OTHER 1.6

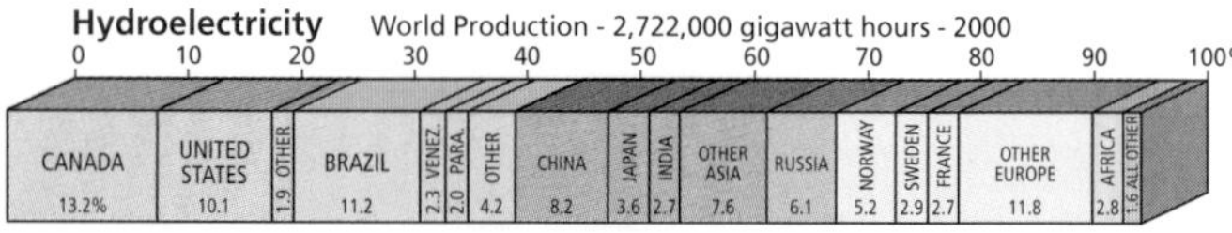

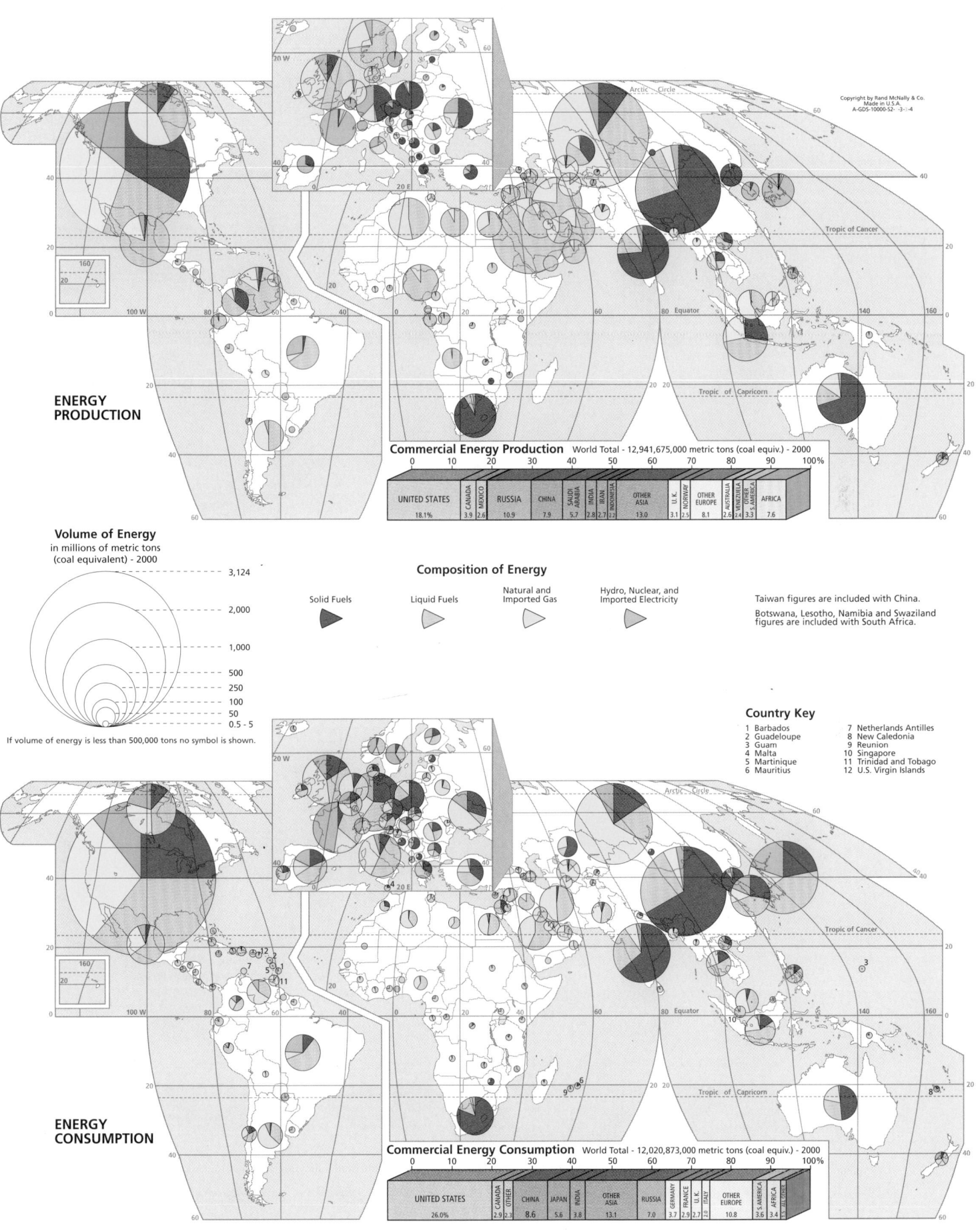

ENERGY PRODUCTION

Copyright by Rand McNally & Co.
Made in U.S.A.
A-GDS-10000-S2- -3- -4

Commercial Energy Production World Total - 12,941,675,000 metric tons (coal equiv.) - 2000

UNITED STATES	CANADA	MEXICO	RUSSIA	CHINA	SAUDI ARABIA	INDIA	IRAN	INDONESIA	OTHER ASIA	U.K.	NORWAY	OTHER EUROPE	AUSTRALIA	VENEZUELA	OTHER S. AMERICA	AFRICA
18.1%	3.9	2.6	10.9	7.9	5.7	2.8	2.7	2.2	13.0	3.1	2.5	8.1	2.6	2.4	3.3	7.6

Volume of Energy
in millions of metric tons
(coal equivalent) - 2000

- 3,124
- 2,000
- 1,000
- 500
- 250
- 100
- 50
- 0.5 - 5

If volume of energy is less than 500,000 tons no symbol is shown.

Composition of Energy

Solid Fuels   Liquid Fuels   Natural and Imported Gas   Hydro, Nuclear, and Imported Electricity

Taiwan figures are included with China.

Botswana, Lesotho, Namibia and Swaziland figures are included with South Africa.

Country Key

1 Barbados	7 Netherlands Antilles
2 Guadeloupe	8 New Caledonia
3 Guam	9 Reunion
4 Malta	10 Singapore
5 Martinique	11 Trinidad and Tobago
6 Mauritius	12 U.S. Virgin Islands

ENERGY CONSUMPTION

Commercial Energy Consumption World Total - 12,020,873,000 metric tons (coal equiv.) - 2000

UNITED STATES	CANADA	OTHER	CHINA	JAPAN	INDIA	OTHER ASIA	RUSSIA	GERMANY	FRANCE	U.K.	ITALY	OTHER EUROPE	S. AMERICA	AFRICA	OTHER
26.0%	2.9	2.3	8.6	5.6	3.8	13.1	7.0	3.7	2.9	2.7	2.0	10.8	3.6	3.4	

NORTH SLOPE

ALBERTA

INTERIOR

ANADARKD BASIN

APPALACHIAN

PERMIAN BASIN

NORTH SEA

SILESIA

MARACAIBO

MINERAL FUELS

Coal and Lignite

- Major bituminous coal deposit
- Minor bituminous coal deposit
- Lignite deposit
- Major anthracite deposit
- Minor anthracite deposit

Petroleum

Major producing field

○ Minor producing field

Natural Gas

+ Major field

Uranium

▲ Major deposits

△ Minor deposits

Scale 1 : 78,000,000 (approximate)
One inch to 1,250 miles

0 500 1000 1500 Miles

0 500 1000 1500 2000 Kilometers

Movement of Petroleum

Width of flow lines is proportional to value of trade.
Trades less than US$ 4,000,000,000 are not shown.
Flow lines do not indicate exact trade routes.

- - - US $128 Billion
- - - $64 Billion
- - - $32 Billion
- - - $8 Billion

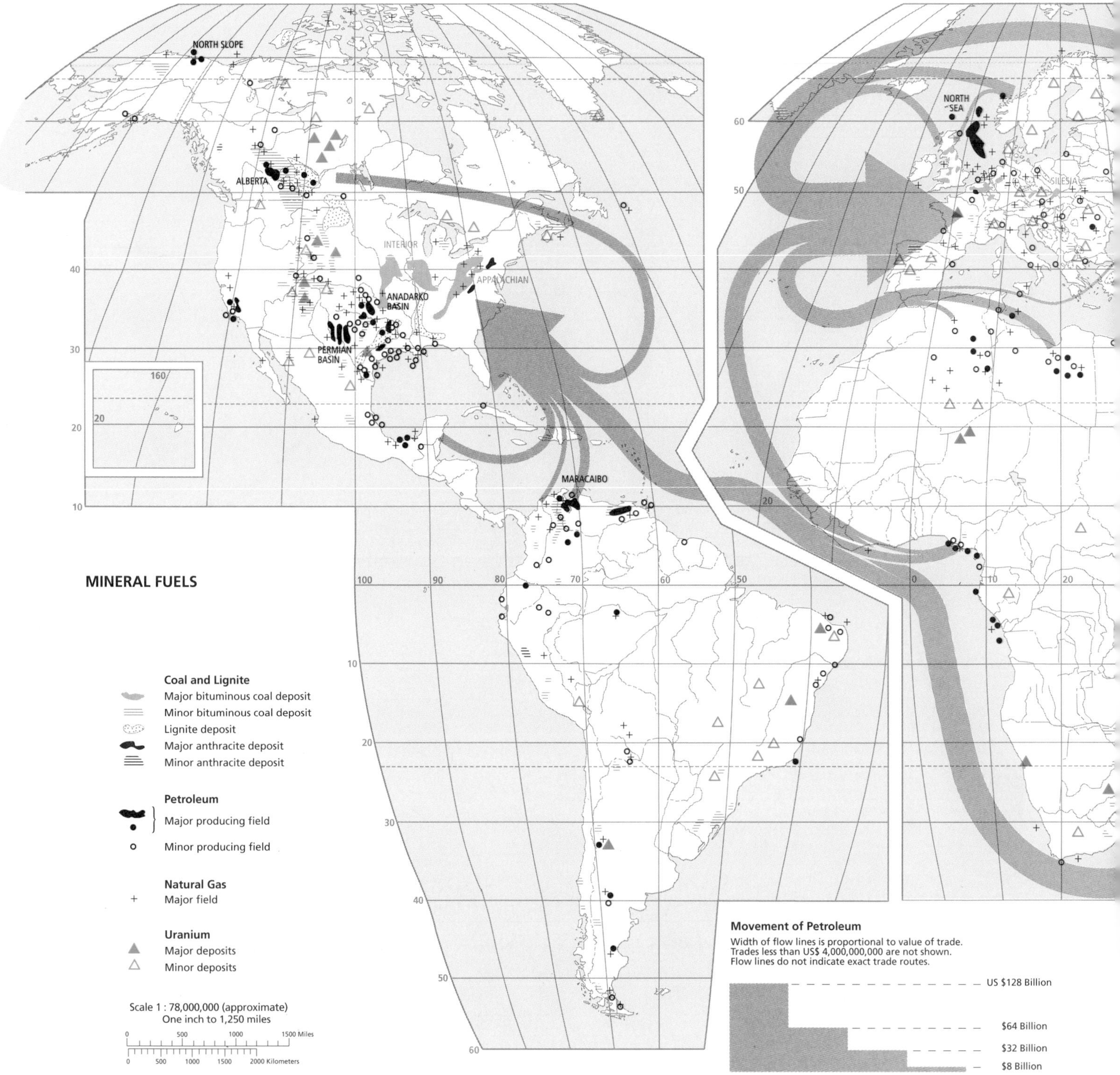

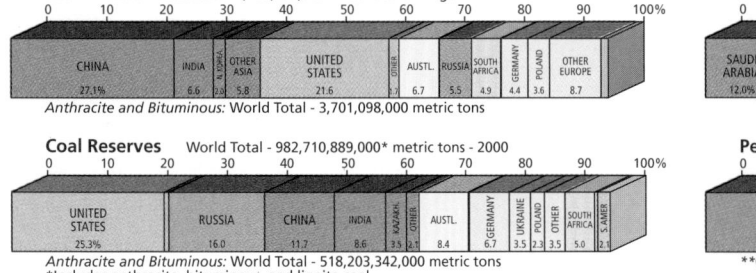

Coal World Production - 4,183,295,000* metric tons - Avg. 1999-2001

0	10	20	30	40	50	60	70	80	90	100%

CHINA	INDIA	A. KOREA	OTHER ASIA	UNITED STATES	OTHER	AUSTL.	RUSSIA	SOUTH AFRICA	GERMANY	POLAND	OTHER EUROPE
27.1%	6.6		5.8	21.6		6.7	5.5	4.9	4.4	3.6	8.7

Anthracite and Bituminous: World Total - 3,701,098,000 metric tons

Coal Reserves World Total - 982,710,889,000* metric tons - 2000

0	10	20	30	40	50	60	70	80	90	100%

UNITED STATES	RUSSIA	CHINA	INDIA	KAZAKH.	AUSTL.	GERMANY	UKRAINE	POLAND	SOUTH AFRICA	S. AMER.
25.3%	16.0	11.7	8.6	3.5	8.4	3.5	3.5	2.3	5.0	2.4

Anthracite and Bituminous: World Total - 518,203,342,000 metric tons
*Includes anthracite, bituminous, and lignite coal

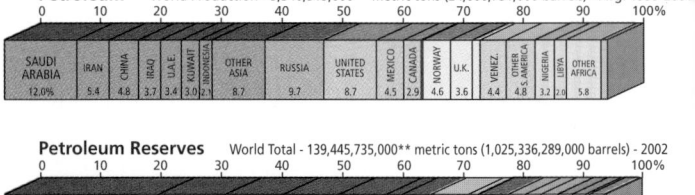

Petroleum World Production - 3,346,515,000** metric tons (24,606,731,000 barrels) - Avg. 1999-2001

0	10	20	30	40	50	60	70	80	90	100%

SAUDI ARABIA	IRAN	CHINA	IRAQ	U.A.E.	KUWAIT	INDONESIA	OTHER ASIA	RUSSIA	UNITED STATES	MEXICO	CANADA	NORWAY	U.K.	VENEZ.	OTHER S. AMERICA	NIGERIA	LIBYA	OTHER AFRICA
12.0%	5.4	4.8	3.7	3.4	3.0	2.1	8.7	9.7	8.7	4.5	2.9	4.6	3.6	4.4	4.8	3.2	2.0	5.8

Petroleum Reserves World Total - 139,445,735,000** metric tons (1,025,336,289,000 barrels) - 2002

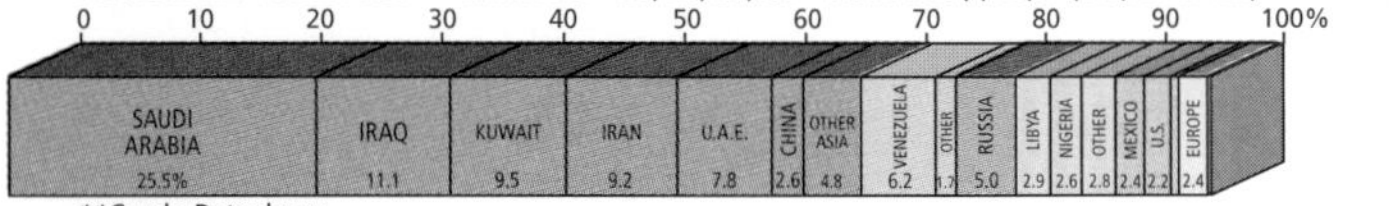

0	10	20	30	40	50	60	70	80	90	100%

SAUDI ARABIA	IRAQ	KUWAIT	IRAN	U.A.E.	OTHER ASIA	VENEZUELA	OTHER	RUSSIA	LIBYA	NIGERIA	MEXICO	U.S.	EUROPE
25.5%	11.1	9.5	9.2	7.8	2.6	4.8	6.2	5.0	2.9	2.8	2.4	2.2	2.4

**Crude Petroleum

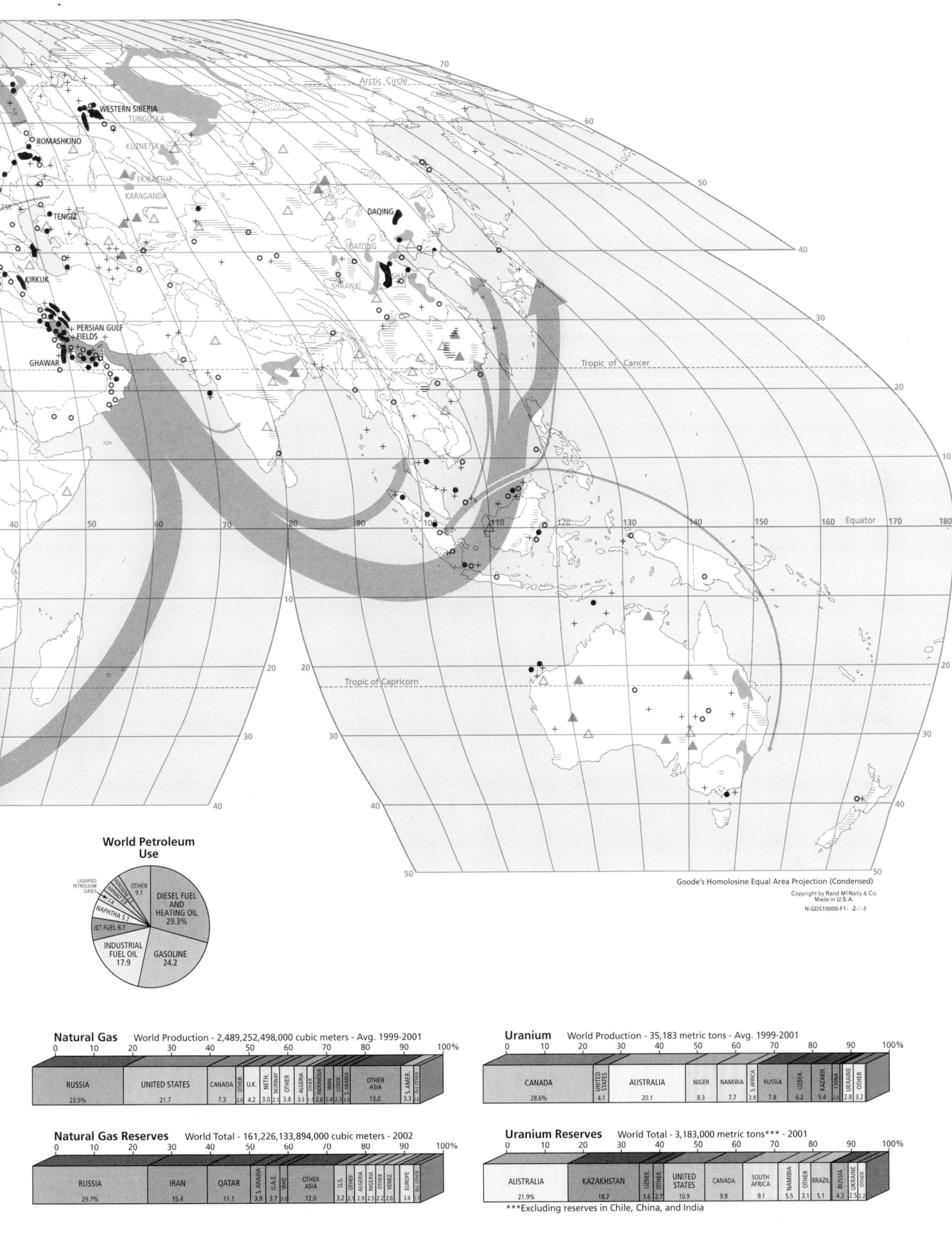

Arctic Circle

WESTERN SIBERIA
TUNGUSKA

ROMASHKINO

KUZNETSK

EKIBASTUZ

KARAGANDA

DAQING

DATONG

TENGIZ

SHAANXI

KIRKUK

PERSIAN GULF
FIELDS

GHAWAR

Tropic of Cancer

Equator

Tropic of Capricorn

Goode's Homolosine Equal Area Projection (Condensed)

Copyright by Rand McNally & Co.
Made in U.S.A.
N-GDS10000-F1- -2 - -3

World Petroleum Use

- LIQUIFIED PETROLEUM GASES
- KEROSENE 1.9
- ASPHALT 2.3
- OTHER 9.1
- DIESEL FUEL AND HEATING OIL 29.3%
- NAPHTHA 5.1
- JET FUEL 6.1
- INDUSTRIAL FUEL OIL 17.9
- GASOLINE 24.2

Natural Gas
World Production - 2,489,252,498,000 cubic meters - Avg. 1999-2001

RUSSIA	UNITED STATES	CANADA	OTHER	U.K.	NETH.	NORWAY	OTHER	ALGERIA	OTHER	INDONESIA	IRAN	UZBEK.	S. ARABIA	OTHER ASIA	OTHER	S. AMER.	ALL OTHER
23.5%	21.7	7.3	2.0	4.2	3.0	2.1	3.8	3.3	2.8	2.4	2.3	2.0	13.0	3.3

Natural Gas Reserves
World Total - 161,226,133,894,000 cubic meters - 2002

RUSSIA	IRAN	QATAR	S. ARABIA	U.A.E.	IRAQ	OTHER ASIA	U.S.	OTHER	ALGERIA	NIGERIA	OTHER	VENEZ.	EUROPE	ALL OTHER
29.7%	15.4	11.1	3.9	3.7	2.0	12.0	3.2	2.1	2.9	2.5	2.4	2.2	3.6

Uranium
World Production - 35,183 metric tons - Avg. 1999-2001

CANADA	UNITED STATES	AUSTRALIA	NIGER	NAMIBIA	S. AFRICA	RUSSIA	UZBEK.	KAZAKH.	CHINA	UKRAINE	OTHER
28.6%	4.1	20.1	8.3	7.7	2.8	7.8	6.2	5.4	2.6	2.8	3.2

Uranium Reserves
World Total - 3,183,000 metric tons*** - 2001

AUSTRALIA	KAZAKHSTAN	UZBEK.	OTHER	UNITED STATES	CANADA	SOUTH AFRICA	NAMIBIA	OTHER	BRAZIL	RUSSIA	UKRAINE	OTHER
21.9%	18.7	3.6	2.7	10.9	9.9	9.1	5.5	3.1	5.1	4.3	2.8	2.2

***Excluding reserves in Chile, China, and India

EXPORTS

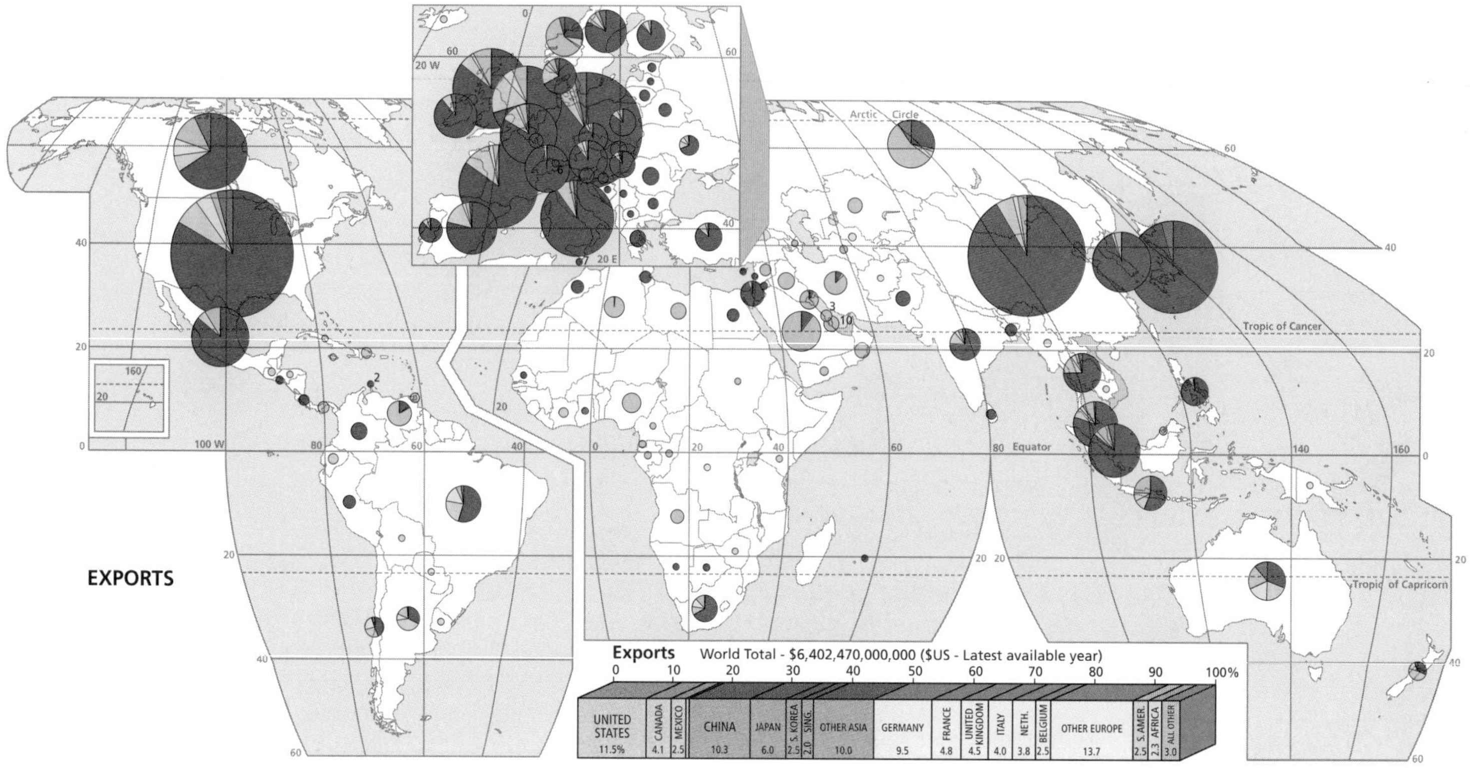

Exports World Total - $6,402,470,000,000 ($US - Latest available year)

0		10	20	30		40	50	60		70		80		90		100%

| UNITED STATES 11.5% | CANADA 4.1 | MEXICO 2.5 | CHINA 10.3 | JAPAN 6.0 | S. KOREA 2.5 | SING. 2.0 | OTHER ASIA 10.0 | GERMANY 9.5 | FRANCE 4.8 | UNITED KINGDOM 4.5 | ITALY 4.0 | NETH. 3.8 | BELGIUM 2.5 | OTHER EUROPE 13.7 | S. AMER. 2.5 | AFRICA 2.3 | ALL OTHER 3.0 |

Volume of Trade

in billions of U.S. dollars - latest available year

```
---- 1,200

---- 500

---- 200
---- 100
---- 50
---- 20
---- 10
---- 1 - 2
```

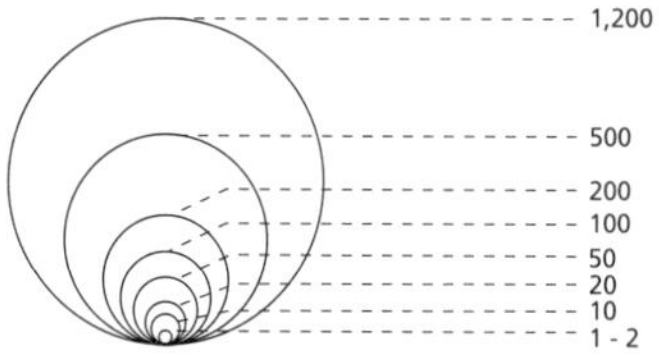

If volume of trade is less than 15 billion dollars, color indicates major class only. If no symbol is shown, volume of trade is less than 1 billion dollars.

Composition of Trade

Manufactured Articles

Food, Beverage & Tobacco

Raw Materials

Fuel & Related Products

All Other or Undifferentiated

Taiwan figures are included with China.

Puerto Rico figures are included with the United States.

Data not available

Country Key

1	Andorra	6	Liechtenstein
2	Aruba	7	Malta
3	Bahrain	8	Martinique
4	Gaza Strip and West Bank	9	Netherlands Antilles
5	Guadeloupe	10	Qatar

IMPORTS

Imports World Total - $6,388,329,000,000 ($US - Latest available year)

0		10	20	30		40	50	60		70		80		90		100%

| UNITED STATES 18.7% | CANADA 3.6 | MEXICO 2.6 | CHINA 9.7 | JAPAN 4.6 | S. KOREA 2.3 | OTHER ASIA 10.4 | GERMANY 7.6 | UNITED KINGDOM 5.2 | FRANCE 4.8 | ITALY 3.7 | NETH. 3.1 | SPAIN 2.5 | BELGIUM 2.4 | OTHER EUROPE 11.4 | AFRICA 2.2 | ALL OTHER 4.2 |

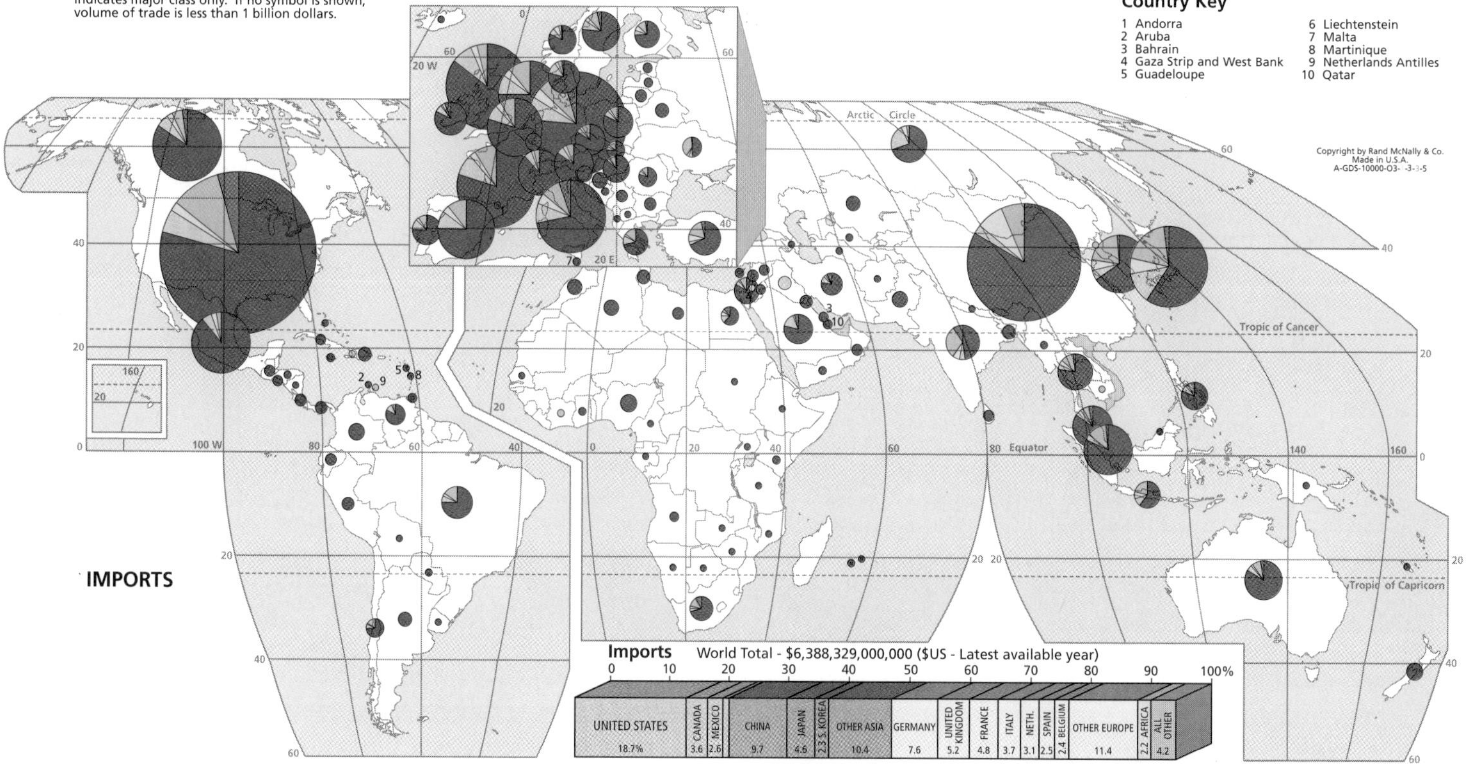

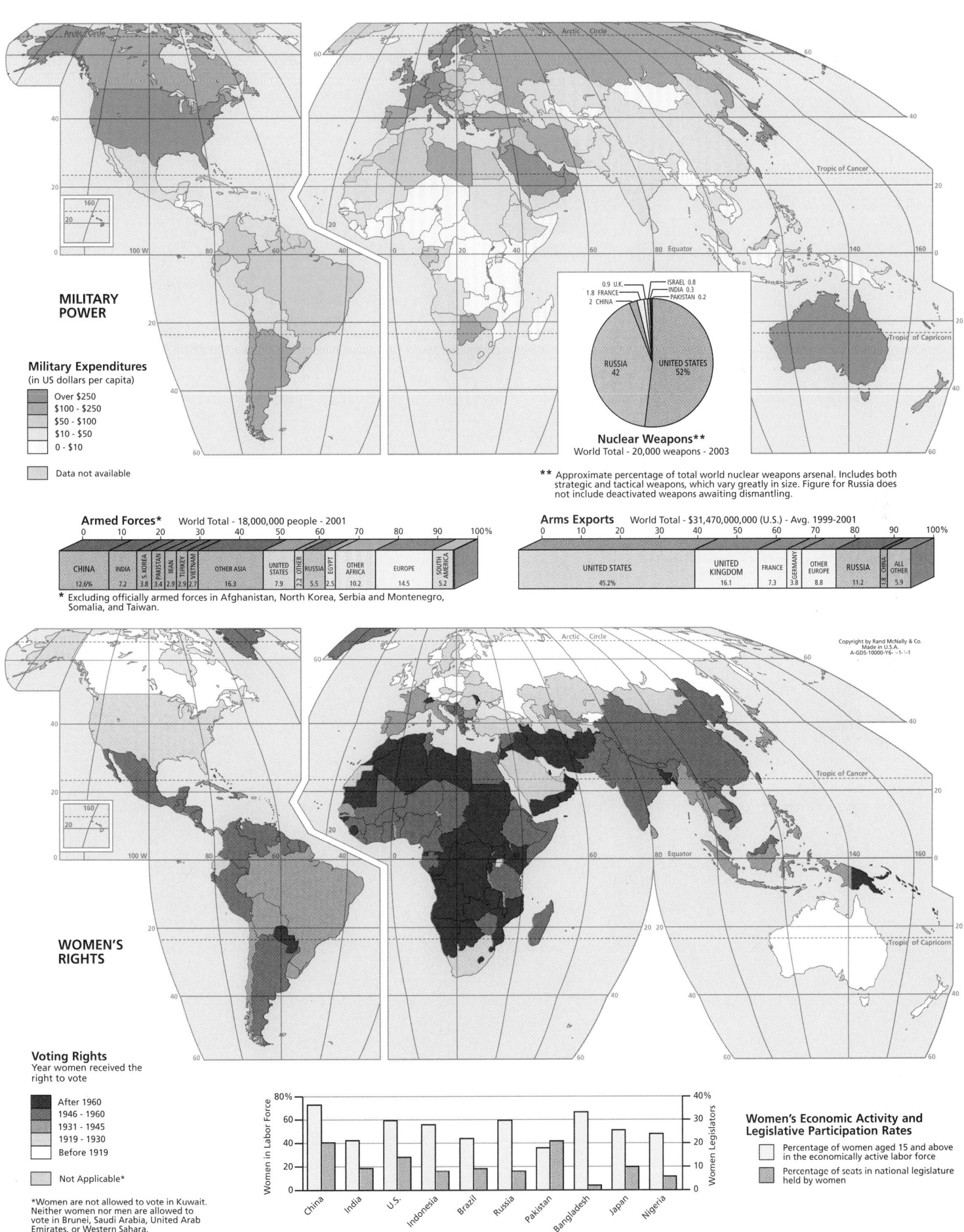

MILITARY POWER

Military Expenditures
(in US dollars per capita)

- Over $250
- $100 - $250
- $50 - $100
- $10 - $50
- 0 - $10

Data not available

Nuclear Weapons**
World Total - 20,000 weapons - 2003

0.9 U.K. — ISRAEL 0.8
1.8 FRANCE — INDIA 0.3
2 CHINA — PAKISTAN 0.2
RUSSIA 42
UNITED STATES 52%

** Approximate percentage of total world nuclear weapons arsenal. Includes both strategic and tactical weapons, which vary greatly in size. Figure for Russia does not include deactivated weapons awaiting dismantling.

Armed Forces*
World Total - 18,000,000 people - 2001

CHINA	INDIA	S. KOREA	PAKISTAN	IRAN	TURKEY	VIETNAM	OTHER ASIA	UNITED STATES	OTHER	RUSSIA	EGYPT	OTHER AFRICA	EUROPE	SOUTH AMERICA
12.6%	7.2	3.8	3.4	2.9	2.9	2.7	16.3	7.9	2.2	5.5	2.5	10.2	14.5	5.2

* Excluding officially armed forces in Afghanistan, North Korea, Serbia and Montenegro, Somalia, and Taiwan.

Arms Exports
World Total - $31,470,000,000 (U.S.) - Avg. 1999-2001

UNITED STATES	UNITED KINGDOM	FRANCE	GERMANY	OTHER EUROPE	RUSSIA	CHINA	ALL OTHER
45.2%	16.1	7.3	3.8	8.8	11.2	1.8	5.9

Copyright by Rand McNally & Co.
Made in U.S.A.
A-GDS-10000-Y6- -1-1-1

WOMEN'S RIGHTS

Voting Rights
Year women received the right to vote

- After 1960
- 1946 - 1960
- 1931 - 1945
- 1919 - 1930
- Before 1919

Not Applicable*

*Women are not allowed to vote in Kuwait. Neither women nor men are allowed to vote in Brunei, Saudi Arabia, United Arab Emirates, or Western Sahara.

Women's Economic Activity and Legislative Participation Rates

- Percentage of women aged 15 and above in the economically active labor force
- Percentage of seats in national legislature held by women

(World's largest countries, 2000)

China, India, U.S., Indonesia, Brazil, Russia, Pakistan, Bangladesh, Japan, Nigeria

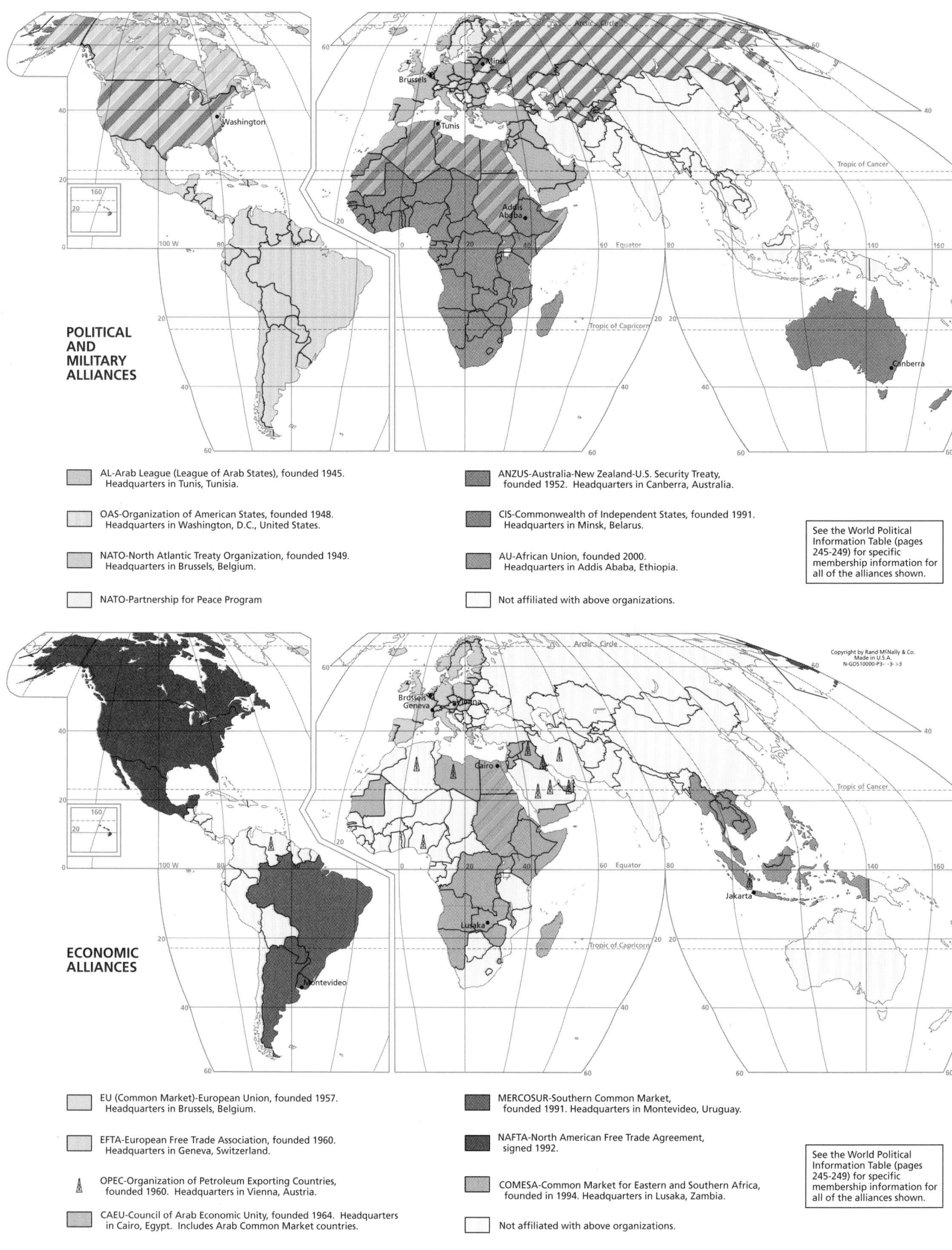

POLITICAL AND MILITARY ALLIANCES

AL-Arab League (League of Arab States), founded 1945. Headquarters in Tunis, Tunisia.

OAS-Organization of American States, founded 1948. Headquarters in Washington, D.C., United States.

NATO-North Atlantic Treaty Organization, founded 1949. Headquarters in Brussels, Belgium.

NATO-Partnership for Peace Program

ANZUS-Australia-New Zealand-U.S. Security Treaty, founded 1952. Headquarters in Canberra, Australia.

CIS-Commonwealth of Independent States, founded 1991. Headquarters in Minsk, Belarus.

AU-African Union, founded 2000. Headquarters in Addis Ababa, Ethiopia.

Not affiliated with above organizations.

See the World Political Information Table (pages 245-249) for specific membership information for all of the alliances shown.

ECONOMIC ALLIANCES

EU (Common Market)-European Union, founded 1957. Headquarters in Brussels, Belgium.

EFTA-European Free Trade Association, founded 1960. Headquarters in Geneva, Switzerland.

OPEC-Organization of Petroleum Exporting Countries, founded 1960. Headquarters in Vienna, Austria.

CAEU-Council of Arab Economic Unity, founded 1964. Headquarters in Cairo, Egypt. Includes Arab Common Market countries.

ASEAN-Association of Southeast Asian Nations, founded 1967. Headquarters in Jakarta, Indonesia.

MERCOSUR-Southern Common Market, founded 1991. Headquarters in Montevideo, Uruguay.

NAFTA-North American Free Trade Agreement, signed 1992.

COMESA-Common Market for Eastern and Southern Africa, founded in 1994. Headquarters in Lusaka, Zambia.

Not affiliated with above organizations.

See the World Political Information Table (pages 245-249) for specific membership information for all of the alliances shown.

Copyright by Rand McNally & Co.
Made in U.S.A.
N-GDS10000-P3- -3- ->3

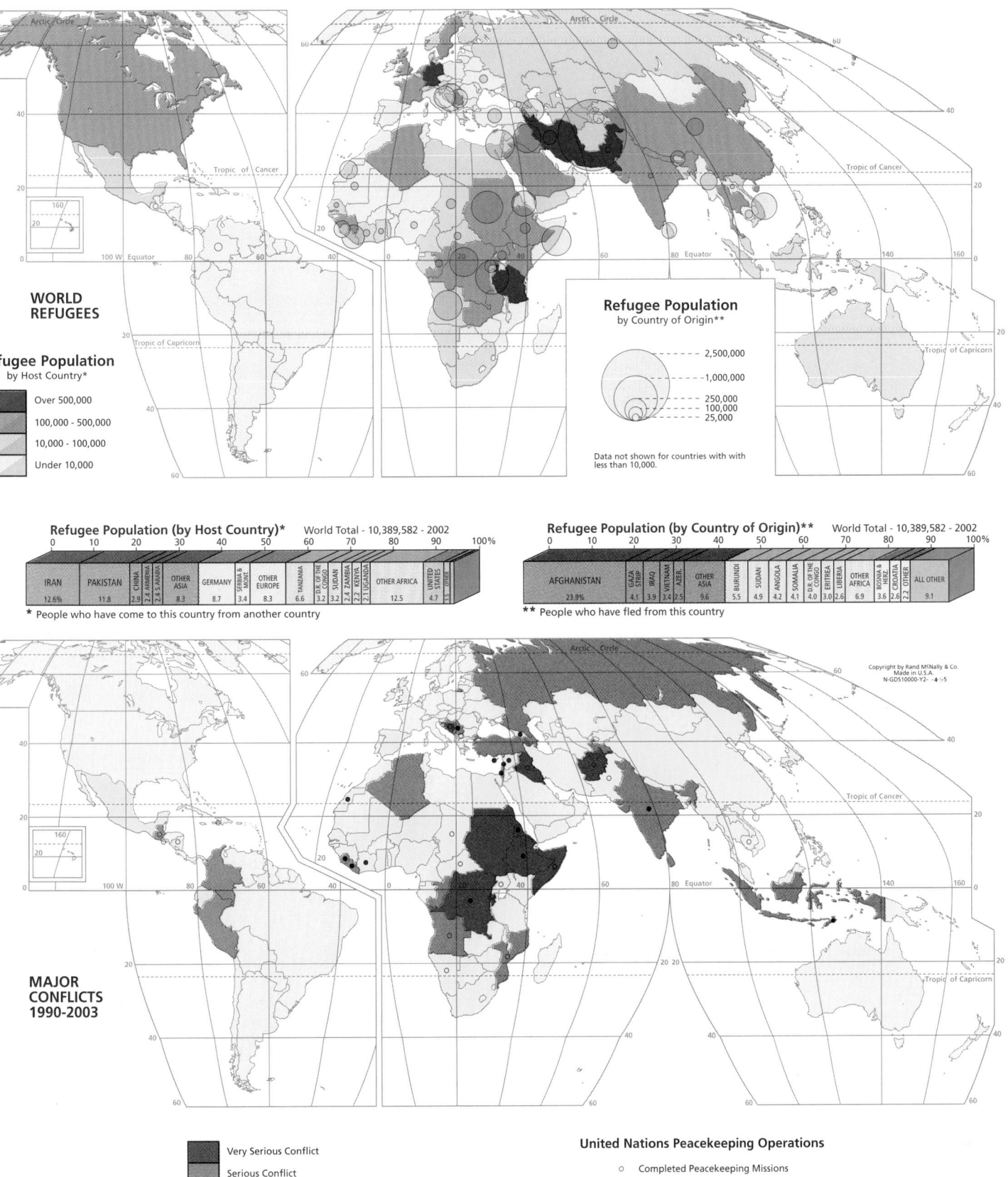

WORLD REFUGEES

Refugee Population
by Host Country*

- Over 500,000
- 100,000 - 500,000
- 10,000 - 100,000
- Under 10,000

Refugee Population
by Country of Origin**

- 2,500,000
- 1,000,000
- 250,000
- 100,000
- 25,000

Data not shown for countries with with less than 10,000.

Refugee Population (by Host Country)* — World Total - 10,389,582 - 2002

IRAN	PAKISTAN	CHINA	ARMENIA	S. ARABIA	OTHER ASIA	GERMANY	SERBIA & MONT.	OTHER EUROPE	TANZANIA	D.R. OF THE CONGO	SUDAN	ZAMBIA	KENYA	UGANDA	OTHER AFRICA	UNITED STATES	OTHER
12.6%	11.8	2.9	2.6	2.4	8.3	8.7	3.4	8.3	6.6	3.2	3.2	2.4	2.2	2.1	12.5	4.7	1.1

* People who have come to this country from another country

Refugee Population (by Country of Origin)** — World Total - 10,389,582 - 2002

AFGHANISTAN	GAZA STRIP	IRAQ	VIETNAM	AZER.	OTHER ASIA	BURUNDI	SUDAN	ANGOLA	SOMALIA	D.R. OF THE CONGO	ERITREA	LIBERIA	OTHER AFRICA	BOSNIA & HERZ.	CROATIA	OTHER	ALL OTHER
23.9%	4.1	3.9	3.4	2.5	9.6	5.5	4.9	4.2	4.1	4.0	3.0	2.6	6.9	3.6	2.6	2.2	9.1

** People who have fled from this country

MAJOR CONFLICTS 1990-2003

- Very Serious Conflict
- Serious Conflict
- Hot Spot

United Nations Peacekeeping Operations

- ○ Completed Peacekeeping Missions
- ● Ongoing Peacekeeping Missions

Copyright by Rand McNally & Co.
Made in U.S.A.
N-GDS10000-Y2- -4->5

TELECOMMUNICATIONS

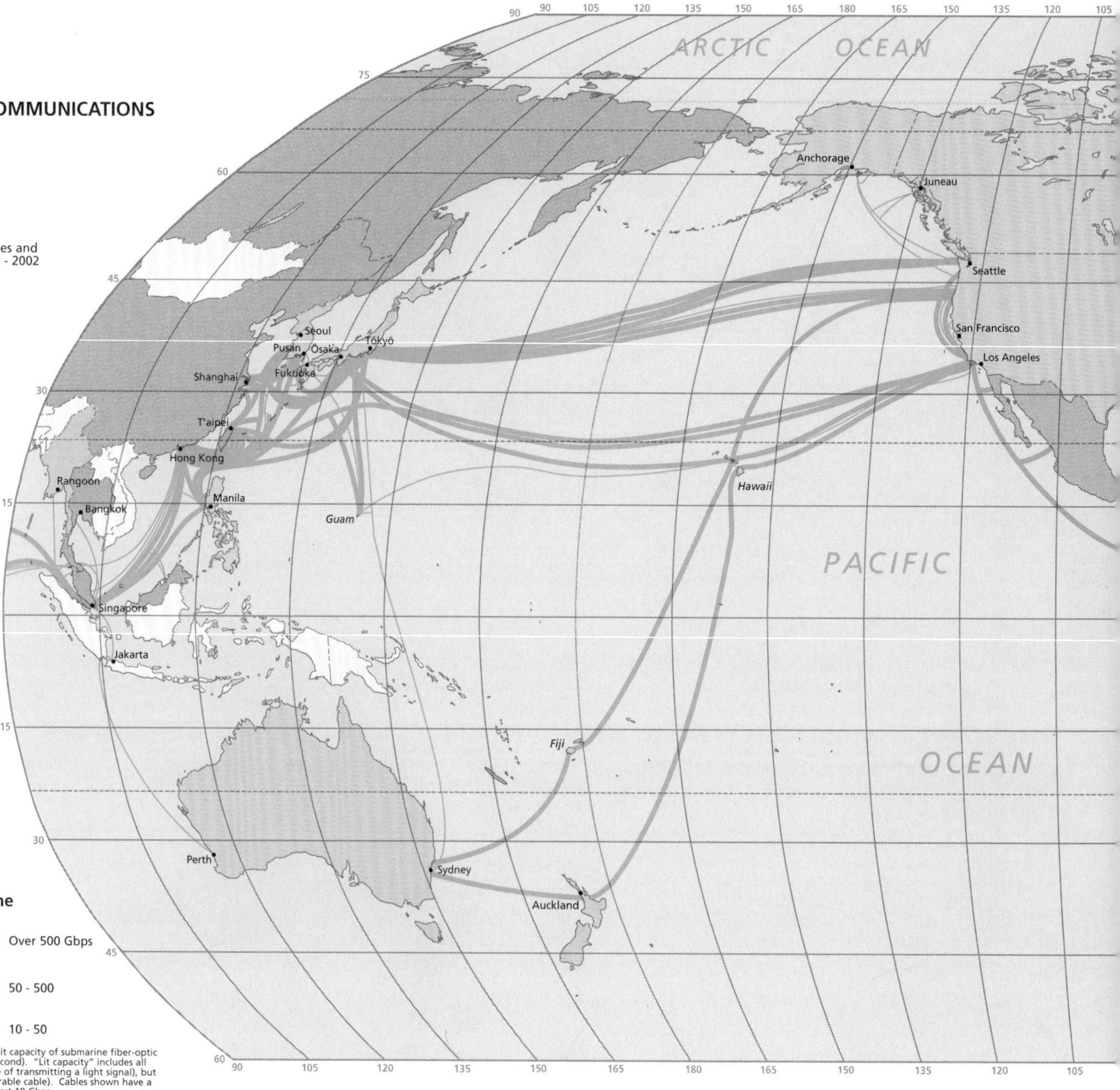

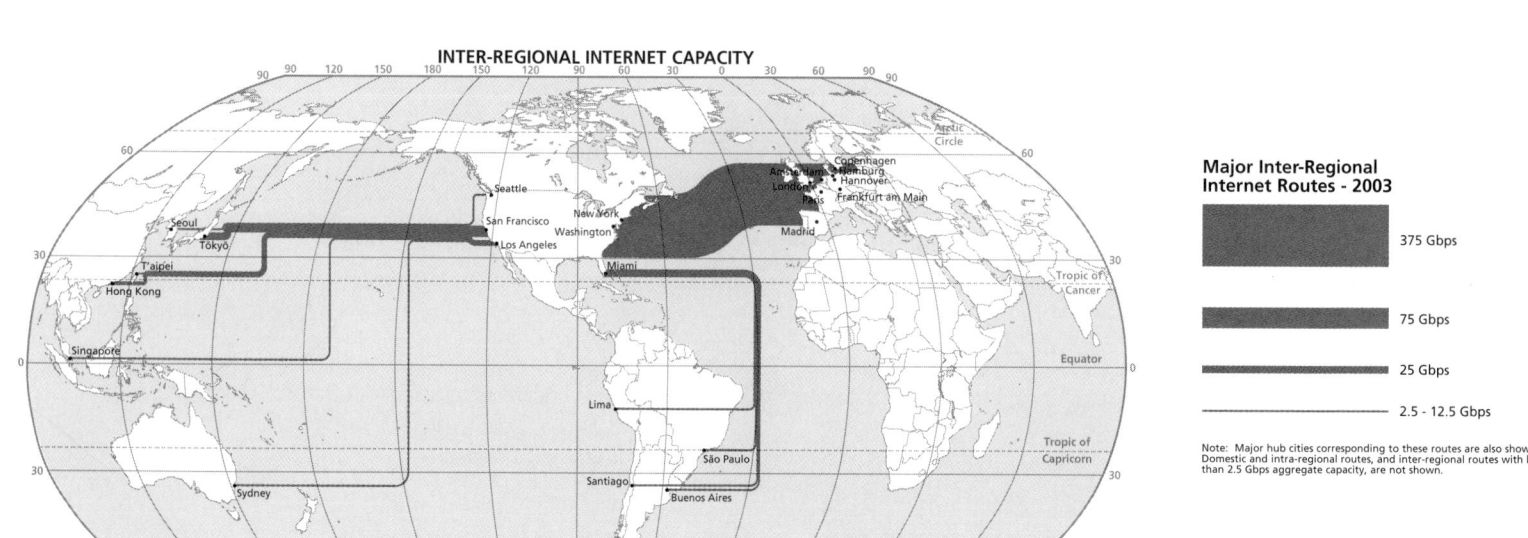

Teledensity
Number of fixed telephone lines and
mobile phones per 100 people - 2002

- Over 120
- 60 - 120
- 30 - 60
- 15 - 30
- Under 15

- No data available

**International Submarine
Cable Capacity - 2004**

- Over 500 Gbps
- 50 - 500
- 10 - 50

Note: Line thickness is proportional to lit capacity of submarine fiber-optic
cable measured in Gbps (Gigabits per second). "Lit capacity" includes all
cable that is "lit" (operable and capable of transmitting a light signal), but
excludes "dark fiber" (inactive or inoperable cable). Cables shown have a
maximum upgradeable capacity of at least 10 Gbps.

ARCTIC OCEAN

Anchorage
Juneau
Seattle
San Francisco
Los Angeles

Seoul
Pusan Osaka
Tōkyō
Shanghai
Fukuoka

Hawaii

T'aipei
Hong Kong

Rangoon
Bangkok
Manila
Guam

PACIFIC

Singapore
Jakarta

OCEAN

Fiji

Perth
Sydney
Auckland

INTER-REGIONAL INTERNET CAPACITY

Seattle
San Francisco
New York
Los Angeles
Washington
Miami

Seoul
Tōkyō
Taipei
Hong Kong

Copenhagen
Amsterdam Hamburg
London Hannover
Paris Frankfurt am Main
Madrid

Arctic
Circle

Singapore

Lima

Tropic of
Cancer

Equator

Sydney

São Paulo
Santiago
Buenos Aires

Tropic of
Capricorn

**Major Inter-Regional
Internet Routes - 2003**

- 375 Gbps
- 75 Gbps
- 25 Gbps
- 2.5 - 12.5 Gbps

Note: Major hub cities corresponding to these routes are also show
Domestic and intra-regional routes, and inter-regional routes with l
than 2.5 Gbps aggregate capacity, are not shown.

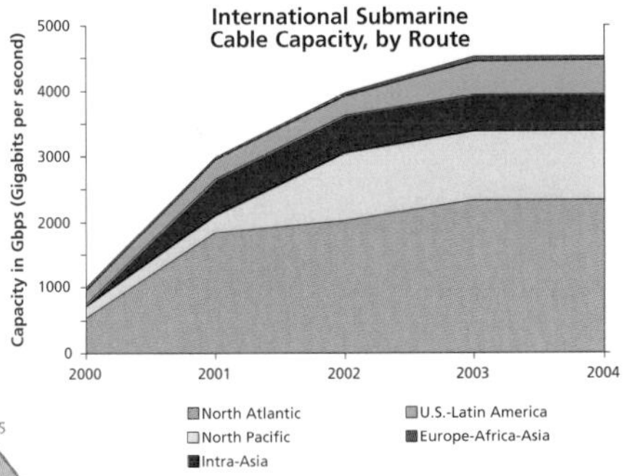

International Submarine Cable Capacity, by Route

Capacity in Gbps (Gigabits per second)

5000
4000
3000
2000
1000

2000   2001   2002   2003   2004

North Atlantic
North Pacific
Intra-Asia
U.S.-Latin America
Europe-Africa-Asia

Note: Figures denote lit capacity of submarine fiber-optic cable. Figures for the North Pacific exclude cables linking the United States to Australia and New Zealand. Figures for the North Atlantic exclude cables linking South America to Europe.

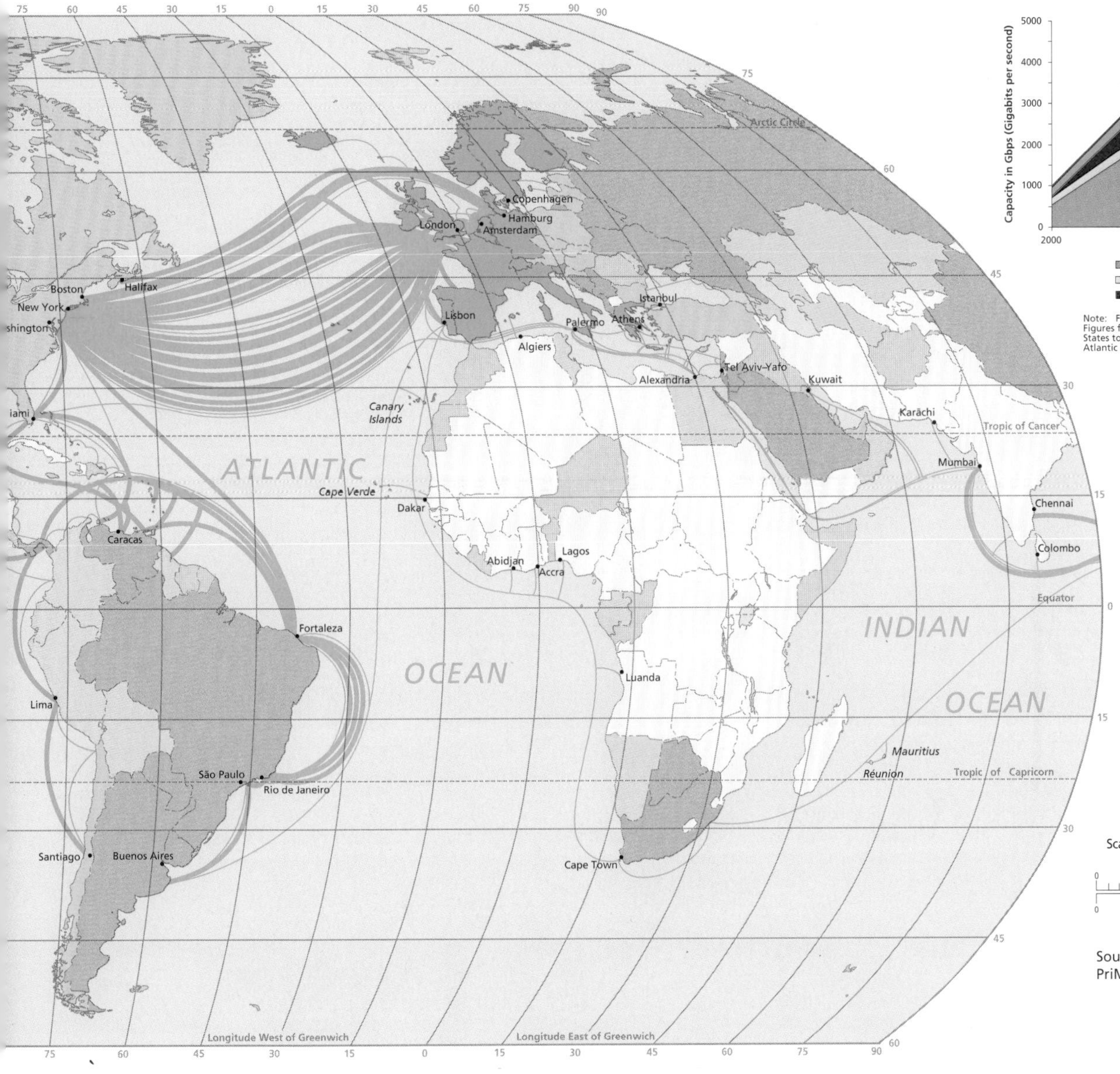

Robinson Projection

Scale 1 : 100,000,000 (approximate)
One inch to 1,600 miles

0   500   1000   1500   2000 Miles

0   500   1000   1500   2000   2500 Kilometers

Source: TeleGeography research,
PriMetrica, Inc. (www.primetrica.com)

ATLANTIC OCEAN

INDIAN OCEAN

Arctic Circle
Tropic of Cancer
Equator
Tropic of Capricorn

Longitude West of Greenwich   Longitude East of Greenwich

Copenhagen
Hamburg
Amsterdam
London
Lisbon
Palermo   Athens
Istanbul
Algiers
Tel Aviv-Yafo
Kuwait
Alexandria
Karachi
Mumbai
Chennai
Colombo
Boston
Halifax
New York
Washington
Miami
Canary Islands
Cape Verde
Dakar
Caracas
Abidjan   Accra
Lagos
Fortaleza
Luanda
Lima
Mauritius
Réunion
São Paulo
Rio de Janeiro
Santiago   Buenos Aires
Cape Town

INTER-REGIONAL INTERNET HUBS

Fifty Largest Inter-Regional Internet Hubs - 2003

Circle size is proportional to each metropolitan area's aggregate capacity connected across international borders.

270 Gbps
100
50
25
10
1

Note: Hubs for domestic and intra-regional routes are not shown. Internet bandwidth for domestic and intra-regional routes is excluded.

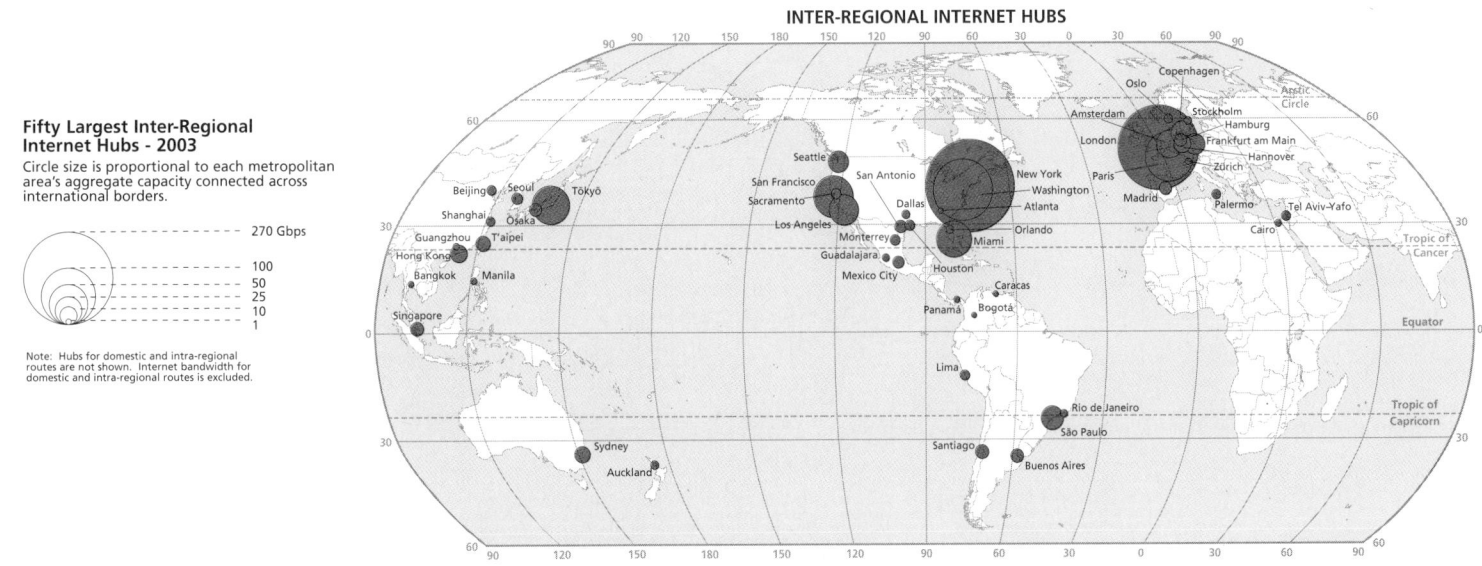

Oslo   Copenhagen
Amsterdam   Stockholm   Hamburg
London   Frankfurt am Main
Paris   Zürich   Hannover
Madrid   Palermo
Tel Aviv-Yafo
Cairo
Seattle
San Francisco   San Antonio
Sacramento   New York
Los Angeles   Washington
Dallas   Atlanta
Monterrey   Orlando
Guadalajara   Miami
Mexico City   Houston
Caracas
Panamá   Bogotá
Lima
Beijing   Seoul
Shanghai   Tōkyō
Guangzhou   Ōsaka
Hong Kong   T'aipei
Bangkok   Manila
Singapore
Rio de Janeiro
São Paulo
Santiago   Buenos Aires
Sydney
Auckland

Arctic Circle
Tropic of Cancer
Equator
Tropic of Capricorn

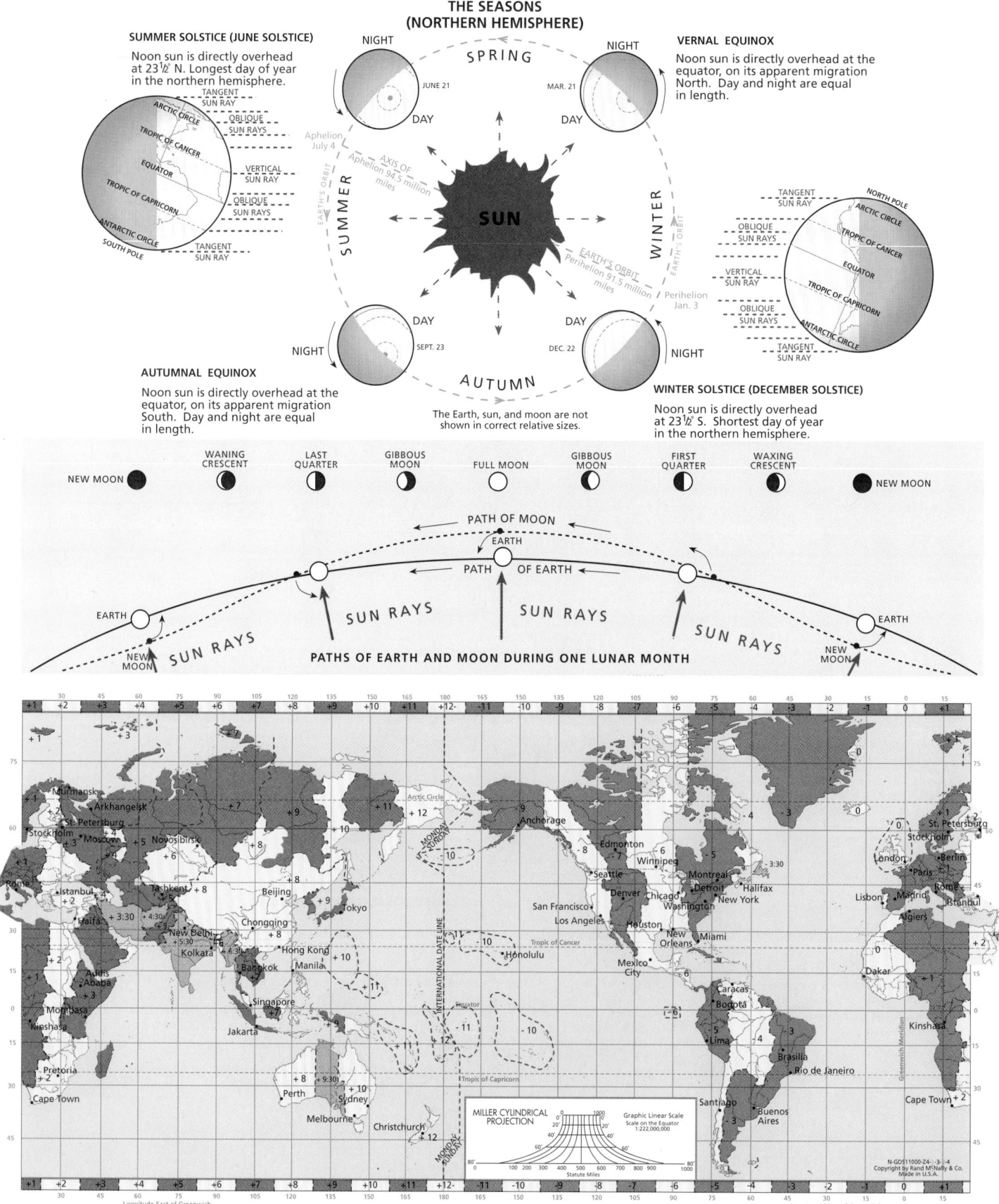

THE SEASONS (NORTHERN HEMISPHERE)

SUMMER SOLSTICE (JUNE SOLSTICE)
Noon sun is directly overhead at 23½° N. Longest day of year in the northern hemisphere.

VERNAL EQUINOX
Noon sun is directly overhead at the equator, on its apparent migration North. Day and night are equal in length.

AUTUMNAL EQUINOX
Noon sun is directly overhead at the equator, on its apparent migration South. Day and night are equal in length.

WINTER SOLSTICE (DECEMBER SOLSTICE)
Noon sun is directly overhead at 23½° S. Shortest day of year in the northern hemisphere.

The Earth, sun, and moon are not shown in correct relative sizes.

PATHS OF EARTH AND MOON DURING ONE LUNAR MONTH

MILLER CYLINDRICAL PROJECTION
Graphic Linear Scale
Scale on the Equator
1:222,000,000

N-GDS11000-Z4 -3- -4
Copyright by Rand McNally & Co.
Made in U.S.A.

Time Zones

The surface of the earth is divided into 24 time zones. Each zone represents 15° of longitude or one hour of time. The time of the initial, or zero, zone is based on the Greenwich Meridian and extends eastward and westward for a distance of 7½° of longitude. Each of the zones is designated by a number representing the hours (+ or -) by which its standard time differs from Greenwich mean time. These standard time zones are indicated by bands of orange and yellow. Areas which have a fractional deviation from standard time are shown in an intermediate color. The irregularities in the zones and the fractional deviations are due to political and economic factors.

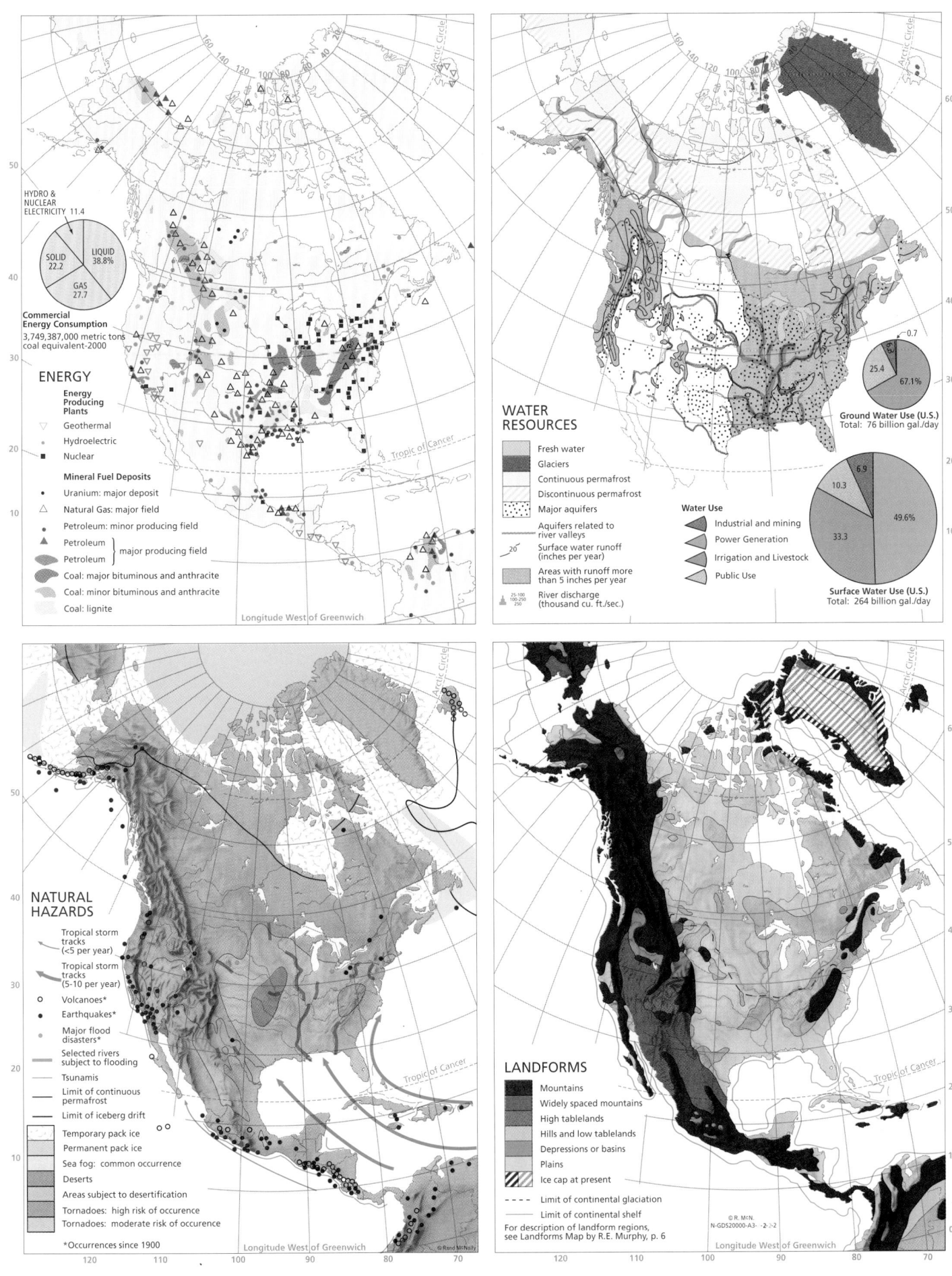

ENERGY

Energy Producing Plants
- ▽ Geothermal
- • Hydroelectric
- ■ Nuclear

Mineral Fuel Deposits
- • Uranium: major deposit
- △ Natural Gas: major field
- • Petroleum: minor producing field
- ▲ Petroleum } major producing field
- ⬮ Petroleum } major producing field
- Coal: major bituminous and anthracite
- Coal: minor bituminous and anthracite
- Coal: lignite

HYDRO & NUCLEAR ELECTRICITY 11.4

SOLID 22.2
LIQUID 38.8%
GAS 27.7

Commercial Energy Consumption
3,749,387,000 metric tons coal equivalent-2000

Longitude West of Greenwich

WATER RESOURCES

- Fresh water
- Glaciers
- Continuous permafrost
- Discontinuous permafrost
- Major aquifers
- Aquifers related to river valleys
- ⟍20⟍ Surface water runoff (inches per year)
- Areas with runoff more than 5 inches per year
- River discharge (thousand cu. ft./sec.) 25-100 100-250 250

Water Use
- Industrial and mining
- Power Generation
- Irrigation and Livestock
- Public Use

Ground Water Use (U.S.)
Total: 76 billion gal./day
0.7
25.4
67.1%

Surface Water Use (U.S.)
Total: 264 billion gal./day
6.9
10.3
33.3
49.6%

NATURAL HAZARDS

- Tropical storm tracks (<5 per year)
- Tropical storm tracks (5-10 per year)
- ○ Volcanoes*
- ● Earthquakes*
- ● Major flood disasters*
- Selected rivers subject to flooding
- Tsunamis
- Limit of continuous permafrost
- Limit of iceberg drift
- Temporary pack ice
- Permanent pack ice
- Sea fog: common occurrence
- Deserts
- Areas subject to desertification
- Tornadoes: high risk of occurence
- Tornadoes: moderate risk of occurence

*Occurrences since 1900

Tropic of Cancer

Longitude West of Greenwich

© Rand McNally

LANDFORMS

- Mountains
- Widely spaced mountains
- High tablelands
- Hills and low tablelands
- Depressions or basins
- Plains
- Ice cap at present
- Limit of continental glaciation
- Limit of continental shelf

For description of landform regions, see Landforms Map by R.E. Murphy, p. 6

© R. McN.
N-GDS20000-A3- -2-2-2

Tropic of Cancer

Longitude West of Greenwich

120 110 100 90 80 70

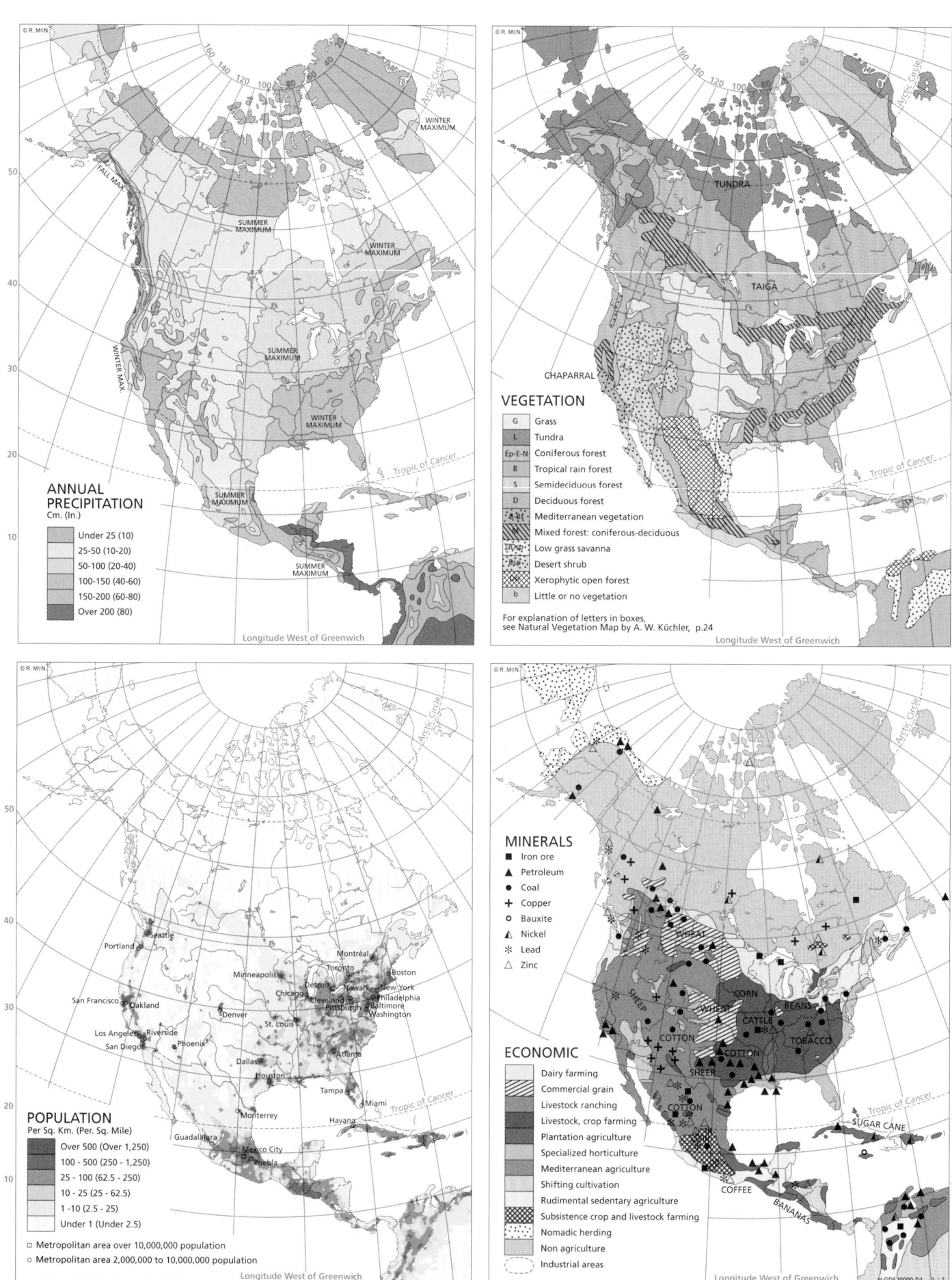

ANNUAL
PRECIPITATION
Cm. (In.)

- Under 25 (10)
- 25-50 (10-20)
- 50-100 (20-40)
- 100-150 (40-60)
- 150-200 (60-80)
- Over 200 (80)

Longitude West of Greenwich

VEGETATION

G	Grass
L	Tundra
Ep-E-N	Coniferous forest
B	Tropical rain forest
S	Semideciduous forest
D	Deciduous forest
m-Mp	Mediterranean vegetation
	Mixed forest: coniferous-deciduous
Gp-Sp	Low grass savanna
Bsp	Desert shrub
	Xerophytic open forest
b	Little or no vegetation

For explanation of letters in boxes,
see Natural Vegetation Map by A. W. Küchler, p.24

Longitude West of Greenwich

POPULATION
Per Sq. Km. (Per. Sq. Mile)

- Over 500 (Over 1,250)
- 100 - 500 (250 - 1,250)
- 25 - 100 (62.5 - 250)
- 10 - 25 (25 - 62.5)
- 1 - 10 (2.5 - 25)
- Under 1 (Under 2.5)

□ Metropolitan area over 10,000,000 population
○ Metropolitan area 2,000,000 to 10,000,000 population

Longitude West of Greenwich

MINERALS

- ■ Iron ore
- ▲ Petroleum
- ● Coal
- + Copper
- ○ Bauxite
- ◬ Nickel
- ✳ Lead
- △ Zinc

ECONOMIC

- Dairy farming
- Commercial grain
- Livestock ranching
- Livestock, crop farming
- Plantation agriculture
- Specialized horticulture
- Mediterranean agriculture
- Shifting cultivation
- Rudimental sedentary agriculture
- Subsistence crop and livestock farming
- Nomadic herding
- Non agriculture
- Industrial areas

Longitude West of Greenwich

N-GDS20000-D1- -2- 2

ALEUTIAN ISLANDS

Bering Sea

Nome Bering Strait

ARCTIC OCEAN

Beaufort Sea

ELLESMERE ISLAND

BROOKS RANGE

ALASKA RANGE

Anchorage

Fairbanks

Yukon

Juneau

Gulf of Alaska

PACIFIC OCEAN

Prince Rupert

Great Slave Lake

BANKS ISLAND

MELVILLE ISLAND

VICTORIA ISLAND

DEVON ISLAND

BAFFIN ISLAND

Baffin Bay

GREENLAND

Arctic Circle

Godthab

Vancouver

Seattle

Portland

ROCKY MOUNTAINS

Edmonton

Calgary

Regina

Peace

Winnipeg

Churchill

UNGAVA PENINSULA

Hudson Bay

Labrador Sea

SIERRA NEVADA

SAN FRANCISCO

Salt Lake City

GREAT BASIN

Billings

Bismarck

Rapid City

Minneapolis

Lake Superior

St. Lawrence

St. John's

LOS ANGELES

Colorado

Denver

Omaha

Missouri

Mississippi

Lake Michigan

Lake Huron

MONTRÉAL

TORONTO

Ont.

Halifax

Phoenix

Albuquerque

Kansas City

ST. LOUIS

CHICAGO

DETROIT

L. Erie

Ohio

Cincinnati

Pittsburgh

BOSTON

NEW YORK

PHILADELPHIA

WASHINGTON

APPALACHIAN MOUNTAINS

Gulf of California

La Paz

Mazatlán

SIERRA MADRE OCCIDENTAL

Chihuahua

Rio Grande

Monterrey

SIERRA MADRE ORIENTAL

Dallas

Houston

Mississippi

Nashville

Atlanta

New Orleans

Jacksonville

ATLANTIC OCEAN

Guadalajara

MEXICO CITY

SIERRA MADRE DEL SUR

Gulf of Mexico

Mérida

Havana

Miami

Nassau

BAHAMA ISLANDS

Tropic of Cancer

CUBA

OCEAN

San Salvador

Managua

San José

Panamá

PACIFIC OCEAN

Port-au-Prince

JAMAICA

Kingston

HISPANIOLA

San Juan

PUERTO RICO

Caribbean Sea

Maracaibo

CARACAS

TRINIDAD

Legend:

- Urban
- Cropland
- Cropland & Woodland
- Cropland & Grazing Land
- Grassland, Grazing Land
- Forest, Woodland
- Swamp, Marshland
- Tundra
- Shrub, Sparse Grass, Wasteland
- Barren Land

COPYRIGHT BY
RAND McNALLY & COMPANY
MADE IN U.S.A.

A-520000-36 -2-6

Scale 1:36,000,000; one inch to 570 miles. Lambert Azimuthal Equal-Area Projection

0 100 200 400 600 800 Miles

0 150 300 600 900 1200 Kilometers

PHYSIOGRAPHIC DIVISIONS

1 Pacific Mountain System
2 Intermontane Plateaus
3 Rocky Mountain System
4 Interior Plains
5 Ozark-Ouachita Highlands
6 Gulf-Atlantic Plain
7 Appalachian Highlands
8 Laurentian Upland (Canadian Shield)
9 Hudson Bay Lowland

0 25 50 75 100   200   300   400   500 Miles

0 50 100   200   400   600   800 Kilometers

Scale 1 : 12 000 000; One inch to 190 miles.   POLYCONIC PROJECTION

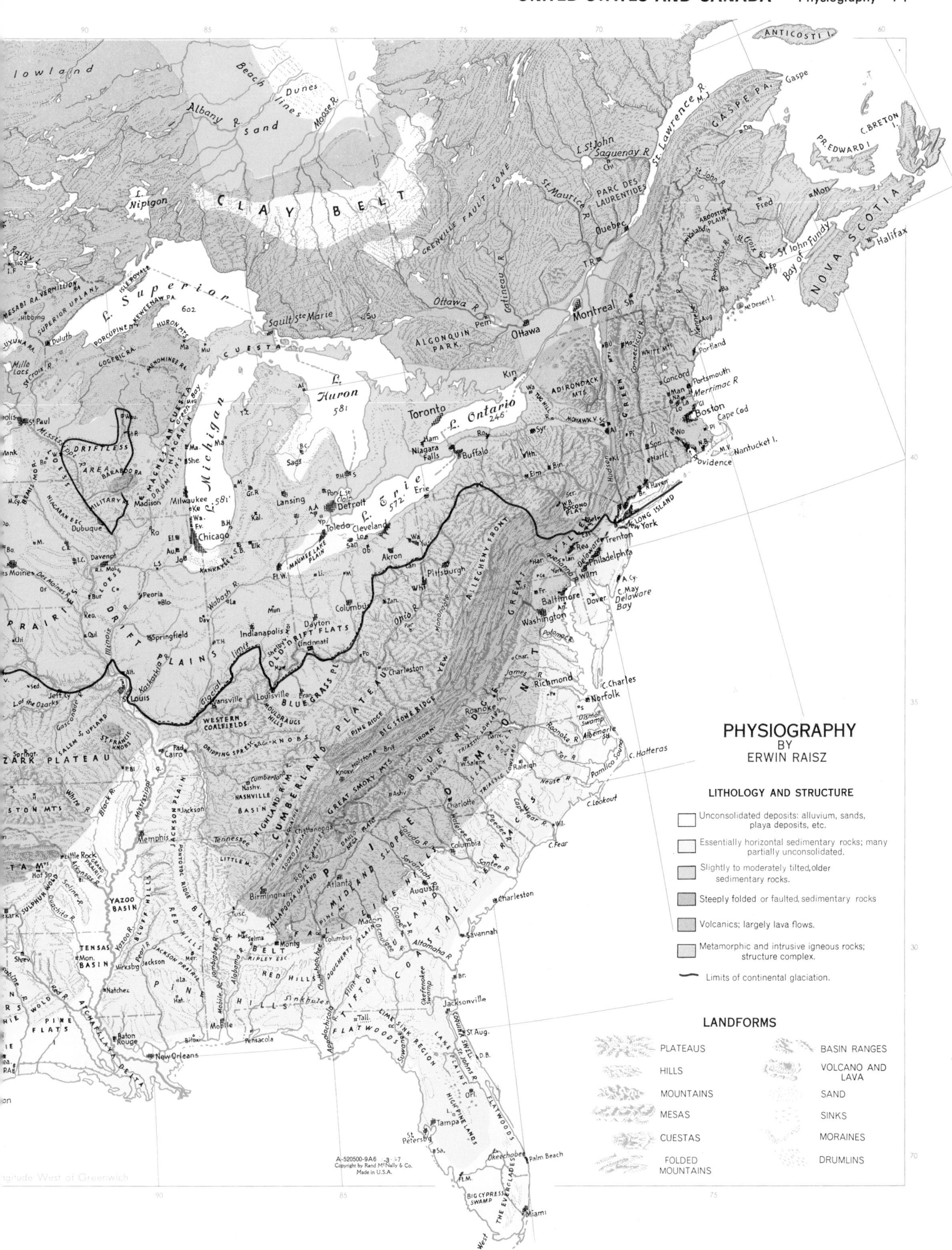

PHYSIOGRAPHY
BY
ERWIN RAISZ

LITHOLOGY AND STRUCTURE

Unconsolidated deposits: alluvium, sands, playa deposits, etc.

Essentially horizontal sedimentary rocks; many partially unconsolidated.

Slightly to moderately tilted, older sedimentary rocks.

Steeply folded or faulted, sedimentary rocks

Volcanics; largely lava flows.

Metamorphic and intrusive igneous rocks; structure complex.

Limits of continental glaciation.

LANDFORMS

PLATEAUS

HILLS

MOUNTAINS

MESAS

CUESTAS

FOLDED MOUNTAINS

BASIN RANGES

VOLCANO AND LAVA

SAND

SINKS

MORAINES

DRUMLINS

A-520500-9A6 -3 -7
Copyright by Rand McNally & Co.
Made in U.S.A.

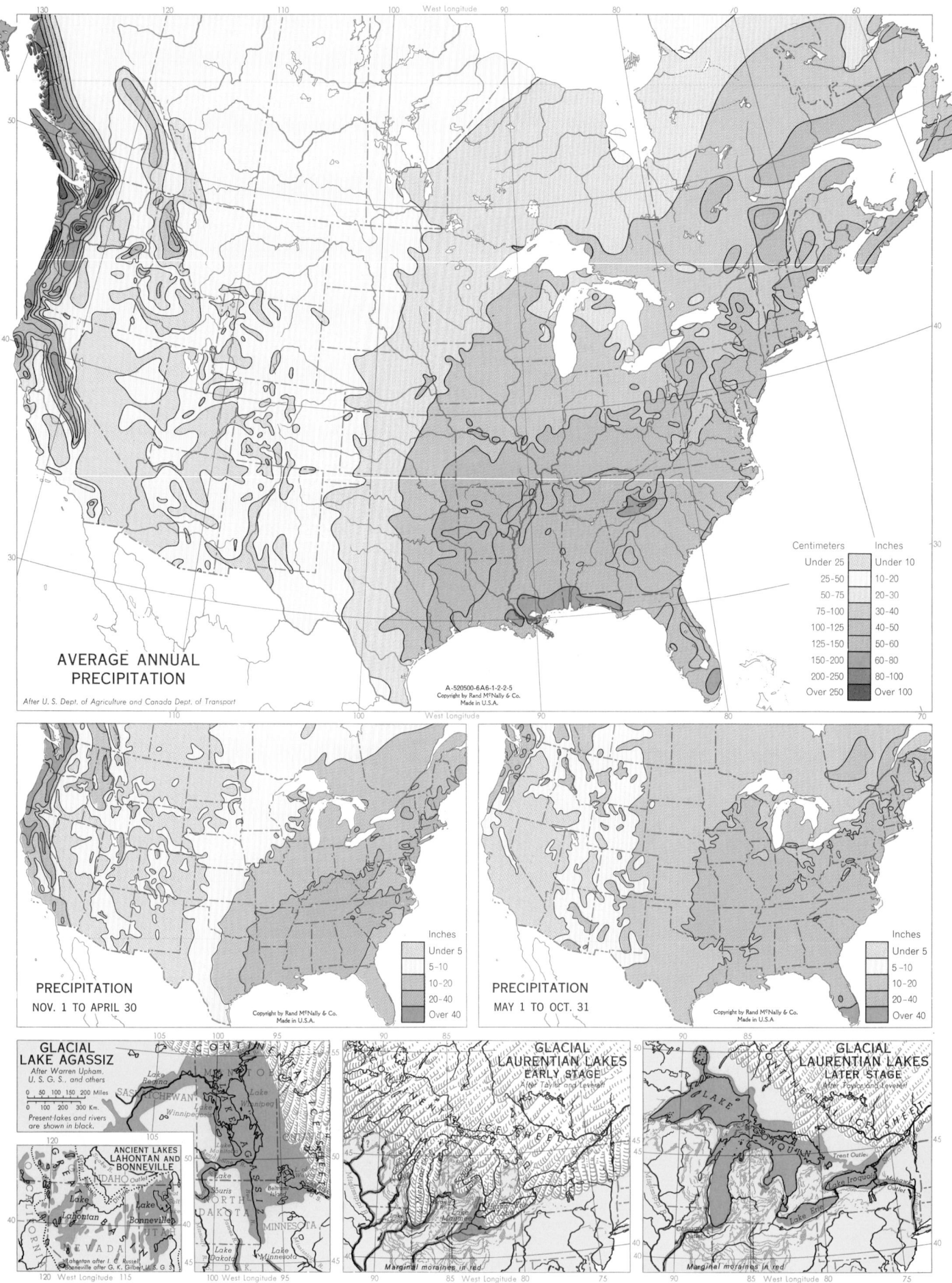

Centimeters / Inches

Centimeters	Inches
Under 25	Under 10
25–50	10–20
50–75	20–30
75–100	30–40
100–125	40–50
125–150	50–60
150–200	60–80
200–250	80–100
Over 250	Over 100

**AVERAGE ANNUAL
PRECIPITATION**

After U. S. Dept. of Agriculture and Canada Dept. of Transport

A-520500-6A6-1-2-2-5
Copyright by Rand McNally & Co.
Made in U.S.A.

PRECIPITATION

NOV. 1 TO APRIL 30

Inches
Under 5
5–10
10–20
20–40
Over 40

Copyright by Rand McNally & Co.
Made in U.S.A.

PRECIPITATION

MAY 1 TO OCT. 31

Inches
Under 5
5–10
10–20
20–40
Over 40

Copyright by Rand McNally & Co.
Made in U.S.A.

**GLACIAL
LAKE AGASSIZ**
After Warren Upham,
U. S. G. S., and others
0 50 100 150 200 Miles
0 100 200 300 Km.
Present lakes and rivers
are shown in black.

**ANCIENT LAKES
LAHONTAN AND
BONNEVILLE**

Lahontan after I. C. Russell
Bonneville after G. K. Gilbert, U. S. G. S.

**GLACIAL
LAURENTIAN LAKES
EARLY STAGE**
After Taylor and Leverett

Marginal moraines in red

**GLACIAL
LAURENTIAN LAKES
LATER STAGE**
After Taylor and Leverett

Marginal moraines in red

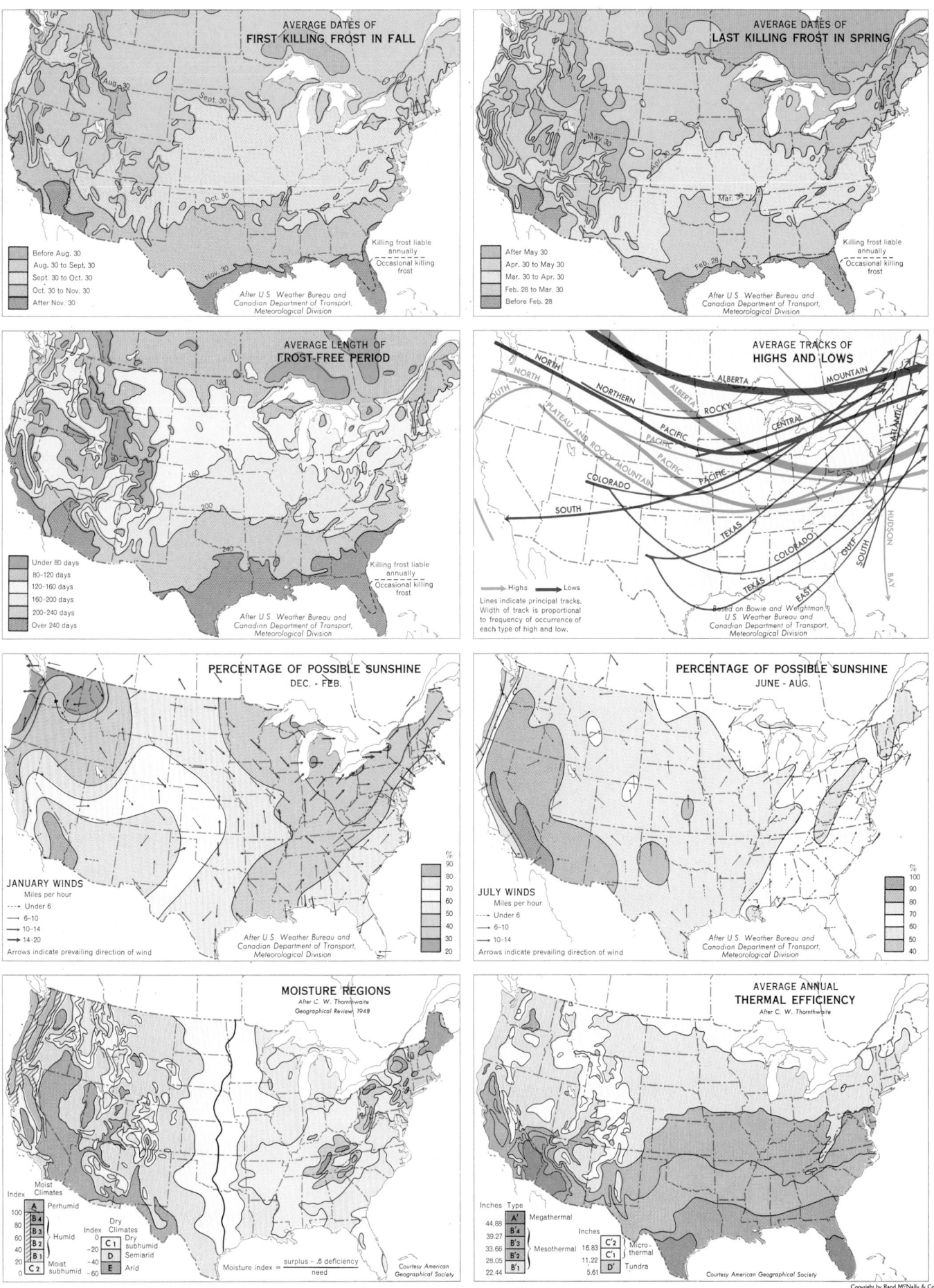

AVERAGE DATES OF
FIRST KILLING FROST IN FALL

Before Aug. 30
Aug. 30 to Sept. 30
Sept. 30 to Oct. 30
Oct. 30 to Nov. 30
After Nov. 30

Killing frost liable annually
Occasional killing frost

After U.S. Weather Bureau and
Canadian Department of Transport,
Meteorological Division

AVERAGE DATES OF
LAST KILLING FROST IN SPRING

After May 30
Apr. 30 to May 30
Mar. 30 to Apr. 30
Feb. 28 to Mar. 30
Before Feb. 28

Killing frost liable annually
Occasional killing frost

After U.S. Weather Bureau and
Canadian Department of Transport,
Meteorological Division

AVERAGE LENGTH OF
FROST-FREE PERIOD

Under 80 days
80–120 days
120–160 days
160–200 days
200–240 days
Over 240 days

Killing frost liable annually
Occasional killing frost

After U.S. Weather Bureau and
Canadian Department of Transport,
Meteorological Division

AVERAGE TRACKS OF
HIGHS AND LOWS

Highs
Lows

Lines indicate principal tracks.
Width of track is proportional
to frequency of occurrence of
each type of high and low.

Based on Bowie and Weightman,
U.S. Weather Bureau and
Canadian Department of Transport,
Meteorological Division

PERCENTAGE OF POSSIBLE SUNSHINE
DEC. - FEB.

JANUARY WINDS
Miles per hour
---- Under 6
→ 6–10
→ 10–14
→ 14–20
Arrows indicate prevailing direction of wind

%
90
80
70
60
50
40
30
20

After U.S. Weather Bureau and
Canadian Department of Transport,
Meteorological Division

PERCENTAGE OF POSSIBLE SUNSHINE
JUNE - AUG.

JULY WINDS
Miles per hour
---- Under 6
→ 6–10
→ 10–14
Arrows indicate prevailing direction of wind

%
100
90
80
70
60
50
40

After U.S. Weather Bureau and
Canadian Department of Transport,
Meteorological Division

MOISTURE REGIONS
After C. W. Thornthwaite
Geographical Review 1948

Moist
Climates
Index
100 A   Perhumid
80   B4
60   B3 Humid
40   B2
20   B1
0   C2 Moist subhumid

Dry
Climates
Index
0   C1 Dry subhumid
-20 D   Semiarid
-40 E   Arid
-60

Moisture index = surplus – .6 deficiency / need

Courtesy American Geographical Society

AVERAGE ANNUAL
THERMAL EFFICIENCY
After C. W. Thornthwaite

Inches Type
44.88   A'   Megathermal
39.27   B'4
33.66   B'3   Mesothermal
28.05   B'2
22.44   B'1

Inches
16.83   C'2   Microthermal
11.22   C'1
5.61   D'   Tundra

Courtesy American Geographical Society

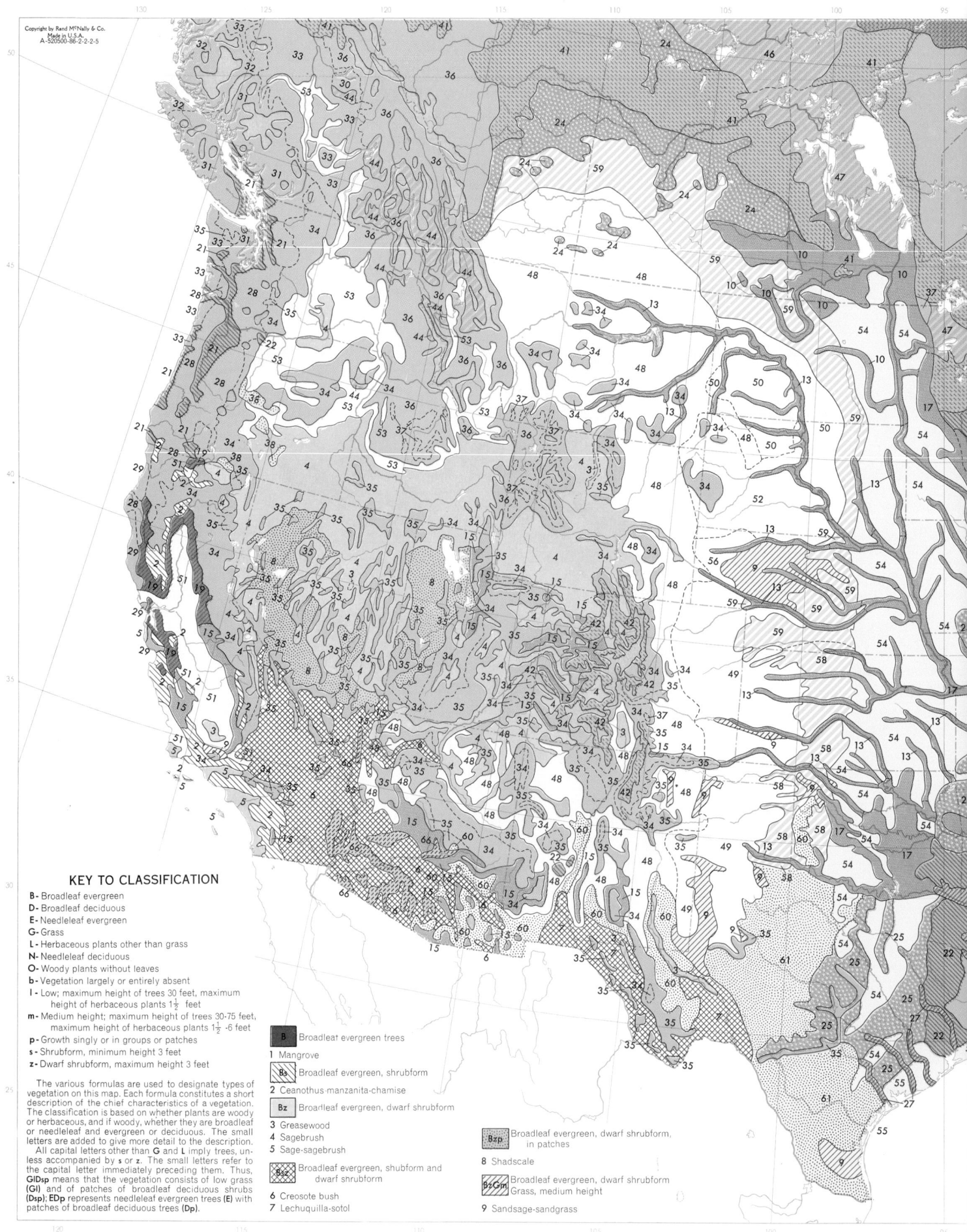

74

KEY TO CLASSIFICATION

B - Broadleaf evergreen
D - Broadleaf deciduous
E - Needleleaf evergreen
G - Grass
L - Herbaceous plants other than grass
N - Needleleaf deciduous
O - Woody plants without leaves
b - Vegetation largely or entirely absent
l - Low; maximum height of trees 30 feet, maximum
    height of herbaceous plants $1\frac{1}{2}$ feet
m - Medium height; maximum height of trees 30-75 feet,
    maximum height of herbaceous plants $1\frac{1}{2}$ -6 feet
p - Growth singly or in groups or patches
s - Shrubform, minimum height 3 feet
z - Dwarf shrubform, maximum height 3 feet

   The various formulas are used to designate types of
vegetation on this map. Each formula constitutes a short
description of the chief characteristics of a vegetation.
The classification is based on whether plants are woody
or herbaceous, and if woody, whether they are broadleaf
or needleleaf and evergreen or deciduous. The small
letters are added to give more detail to the description.
   All capital letters other than **G** and **L** imply trees, unless accompanied by **s** or **z**. The small letters refer to
the capital letter immediately preceding them. Thus,
GlDsp means that the vegetation consists of low grass
(**Gl**) and of patches of broadleaf deciduous shrubs
(**Dsp**); **EDp** represents needleleaf evergreen trees (**E**) with
patches of broadleaf deciduous trees (**Dp**).

B Broadleaf evergreen trees

1 Mangrove

Bs Broadleaf evergreen, shrubform

2 Ceanothus-manzanita-chamise

Bz Broadleaf evergreen, dwarf shrubform

3 Greasewood
4 Sagebrush
5 Sage-sagebrush

Bsz Broadleaf evergreen, shubform and
    dwarf snrubform

6 Creosote bush
7 Lechuquilla-sotol

Bzp Broadleaf evergreen, dwarf shrubform,
    in patches

8 Shadscale

BzGm Broadleaf evergreen, dwarf shrubform
    Grass, medium height

9 Sandsage-sandgrass

0 25 50 75 100   200   300   400   500 Miles

0 50 100 200   400   600   800 Kilometers

Scale 1: 14 000 000; One inch to 220 m

NATURAL VEGETATION

BY A. W. KÜCHLER

Based on "A Physiognomic Classification of Vegetation"
Annals of the Assoc. of American Geographers, Vol. 39, September, 1949

ERT CONFORMAL CONIC PROJECTION

D Broadleaf deciduous trees

10 Aspen-oak
11 Beech-maple
12 Beech-tulip tree-maple-basswood
13 Cottonwood-willow
14 Maple-basswood
15 Oak
16 Oak-ash-maple
17 Oak-hickory
18 Oak-tulip tree

DB Broadleaf deciduous trees
Broadleaf evergreen trees

19 Oak-madrone

DE Broadleaf deciduous trees
Needleleaf evergreen trees

20 Maple-yellow birch-hemlock-pine
21 Oak-Douglas fir
22 Oak-pine
23 Maple-beech-hemlock

D/Gmp Broadleaf deciduous trees
Grass, medium height, in patches

24 Aspen-needle grass-wheat grass
25 Oak-hickory-bluestem

DN Broadleaf deciduous trees
Needleleaf deciduous trees

26 Bay trees-bald cypress
27 Tupelo-gum-bald cypress

E Needleleaf evergreen trees

28 Douglas fir
29 Douglas fir-redwood
30 Hemlock-arbor vitae
31 Hemlock-arbor vitae-Douglas fir
32 Hemlock-arbor vitae-fir
33 Hemlock-spruce
34 Pine
35 Pine-juniper
36 Pine-spruce
37 Spruce-fir

Esp Needleleaf evergreen, shrubform, in patches

38 Juniper

EDp Needleleaf evergreen trees
Broadleaf deciduous trees, in patches

39 Douglas fir-pine-aspen
40 Pine-spruce-birch
41 Spruce-aspen
42 Spruce-fir-aspen
43 Spruce-poplar-birch

EN Needleleaf evergreen trees
Needleleaf deciduous trees

44 Hemlock-arbor vitae-Douglas fir-larch
45 Pine-bald cypress
46 Pine-spruce-larch
47 Spruce-larch

Gl Grass, low

48 Grama grass
49 Grama grass-buffalo grass
50 Grama grass-needle grass
51 Needle grass-blue grass
52 Wheat grass
53 Wheat grass-blue grass

Gm Grass, medium height

54 Bluestem
55 Broom grass-water grass
56 Marsh grass
57 Saw grass

Gml Grass, medium and low height

58 Bluestem-bunch grass
59 Needle grass-wheat grass

Gl/Dsp Grass, low
Broadleaf deciduous, shrubform, in patches

60 Bunch grass-oak

Gm/Dsp Grass, medium height
Broadleaf deciduous, shrubform, in patches

61 Mesquite grass-mesquite

L Herbaceous plants other than grass

62 Lichens, etc.

LEp Herbaceous plants other than grass
Needleleaf evergreen trees, in patches

63 Lichens-spruce

LEp/Np Herbaceous plants other than grass
Needleleaf evergreen trees, in patches
Needleleaf deciduous trees, in patches

64 Lichens-spruce-larch

N Needleleaf deciduous trees

65 Bald cypress

Op Woody plants without leaves, in patches

66 Palo verde-cacti-ocotillo

b Vegetation largely or entirely absent

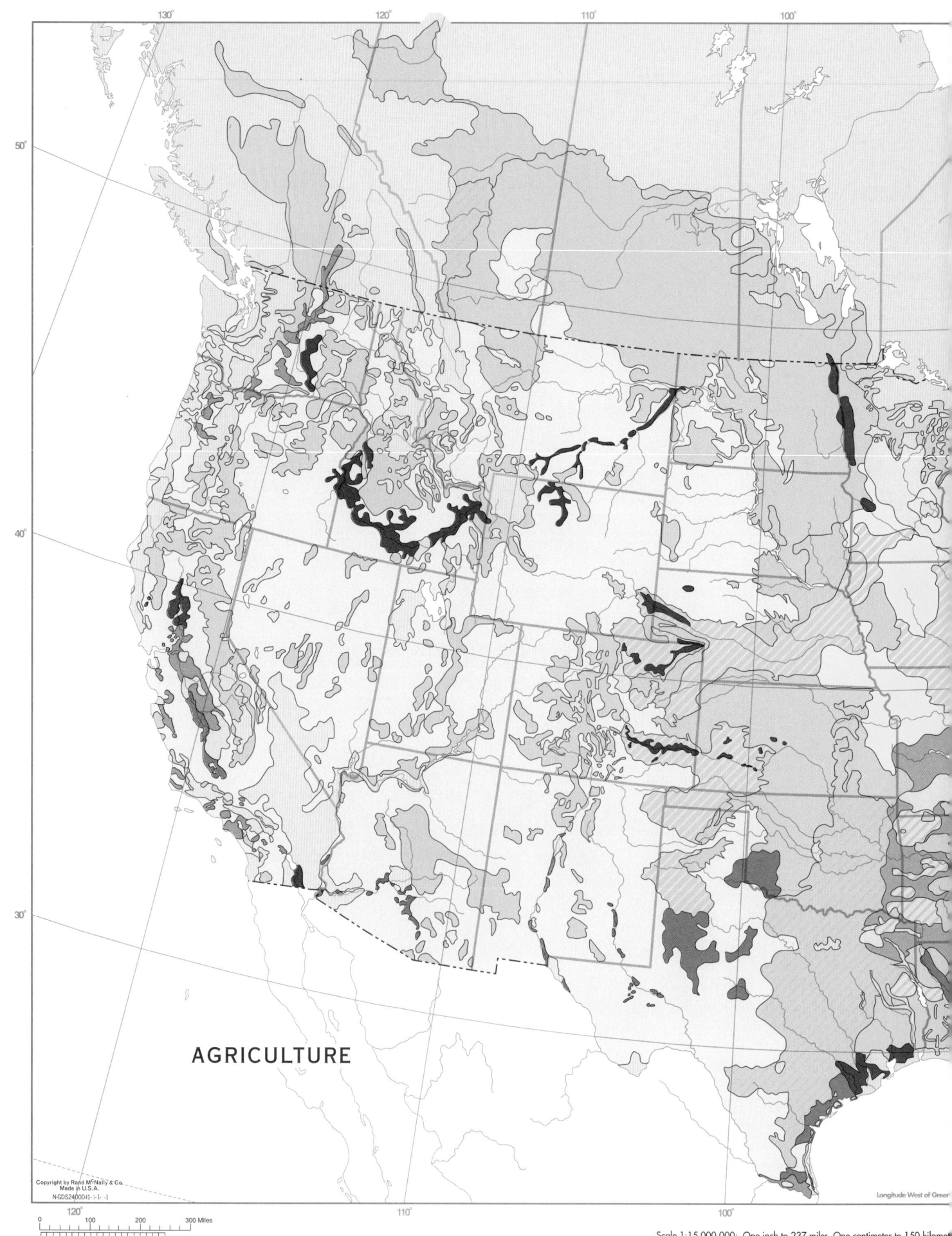

AGRICULTURE

130°

120°

110°

100°

50°

40°

30°

120°

110°

100°

Longitude West of Greenwich

0   100   200   300 Miles

0   100   200   300   400 Kilometers

Scale 1:15,000,000; One inch to 237 miles. One centimeter to 150 kilometers

Dairying

Fruits and Vegetables

Wheat, Barley, and Oilseeds

Cash Corn and Soybeans

Tobacco

Cotton

Livestock and Feed Grains: Beef

Livestock and Feed Grains: Hogs

Livestock and Feed Grains: Poultry

Livestock and Feed Grains: Mixed

Specialty Crops (Peanuts, Potatoes, Rice, Sugar)

Western Livestock Ranching

Western Feedlots

Agriculture and Forestry

Non-Agricultural Areas

Tropic of Cancer

ERS CONIC PROJECTION

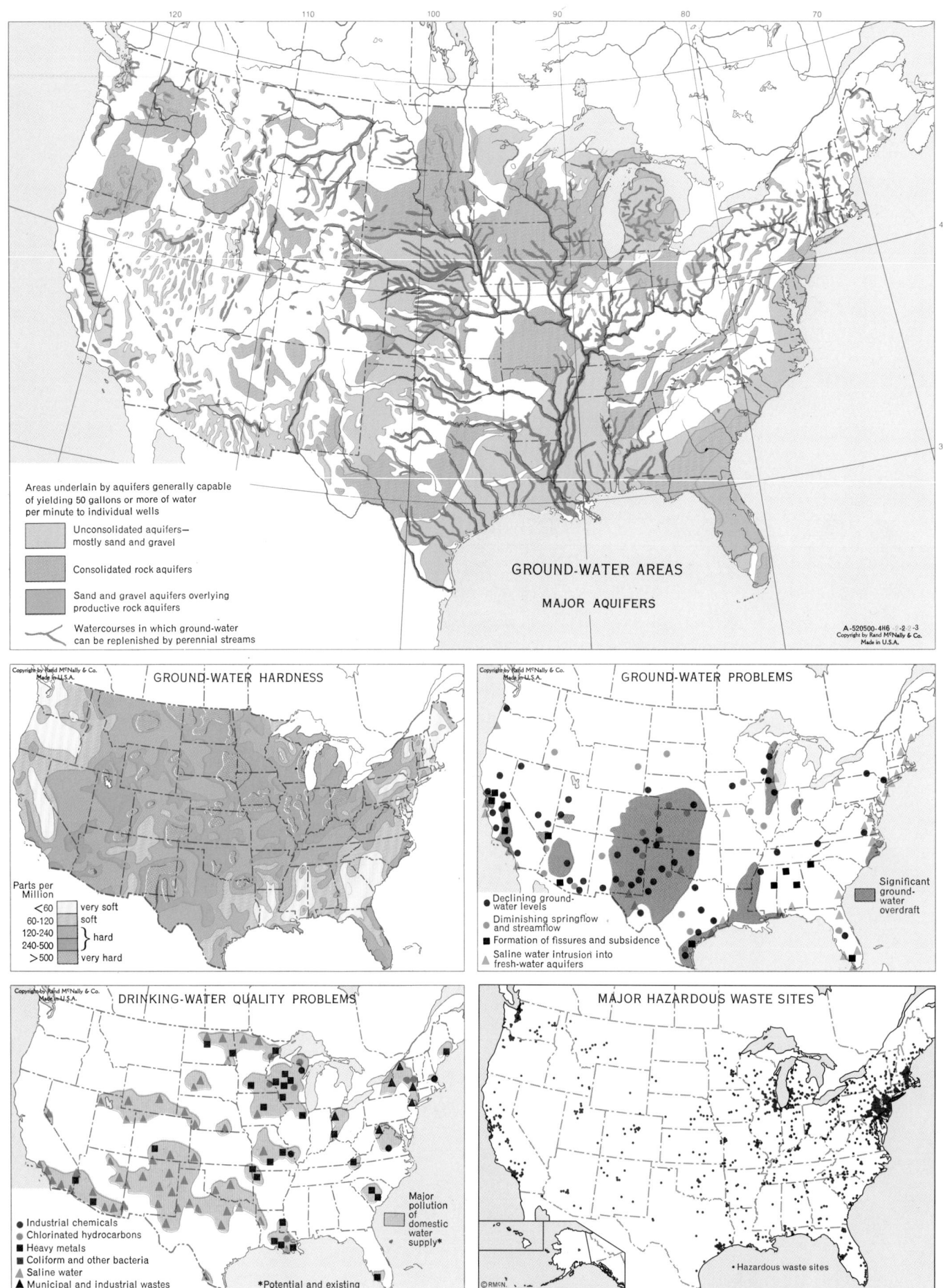

GROUND-WATER AREAS

MAJOR AQUIFERS

Areas underlain by aquifers generally capable
of yielding 50 gallons or more of water
per minute to individual wells

Unconsolidated aquifers—
mostly sand and gravel

Consolidated rock aquifers

Sand and gravel aquifers overlying
productive rock aquifers

Watercourses in which ground-water
can be replenished by perennial streams

A-520500-4H6 -2-2-3
Copyright by Rand McNally & Co.
Made in U.S.A.

GROUND-WATER HARDNESS

Parts per
Million
<60   very soft
60-120 soft
120-240 } hard
240-500
>500   very hard

GROUND-WATER PROBLEMS

● Declining ground-
   water levels
● Diminishing springflow
   and streamflow
■ Formation of fissures and subsidence
▲ Saline water intrusion into
   fresh-water aquifers

Significant
ground-
water
overdraft

DRINKING-WATER QUALITY PROBLEMS

● Industrial chemicals
● Chlorinated hydrocarbons
■ Heavy metals
■ Coliform and other bacteria
▲ Saline water
▲ Municipal and industrial wastes

Major
pollution
of
domestic
water
supply*

*Potential and existing

MAJOR HAZARDOUS WASTE SITES

• Hazardous waste sites

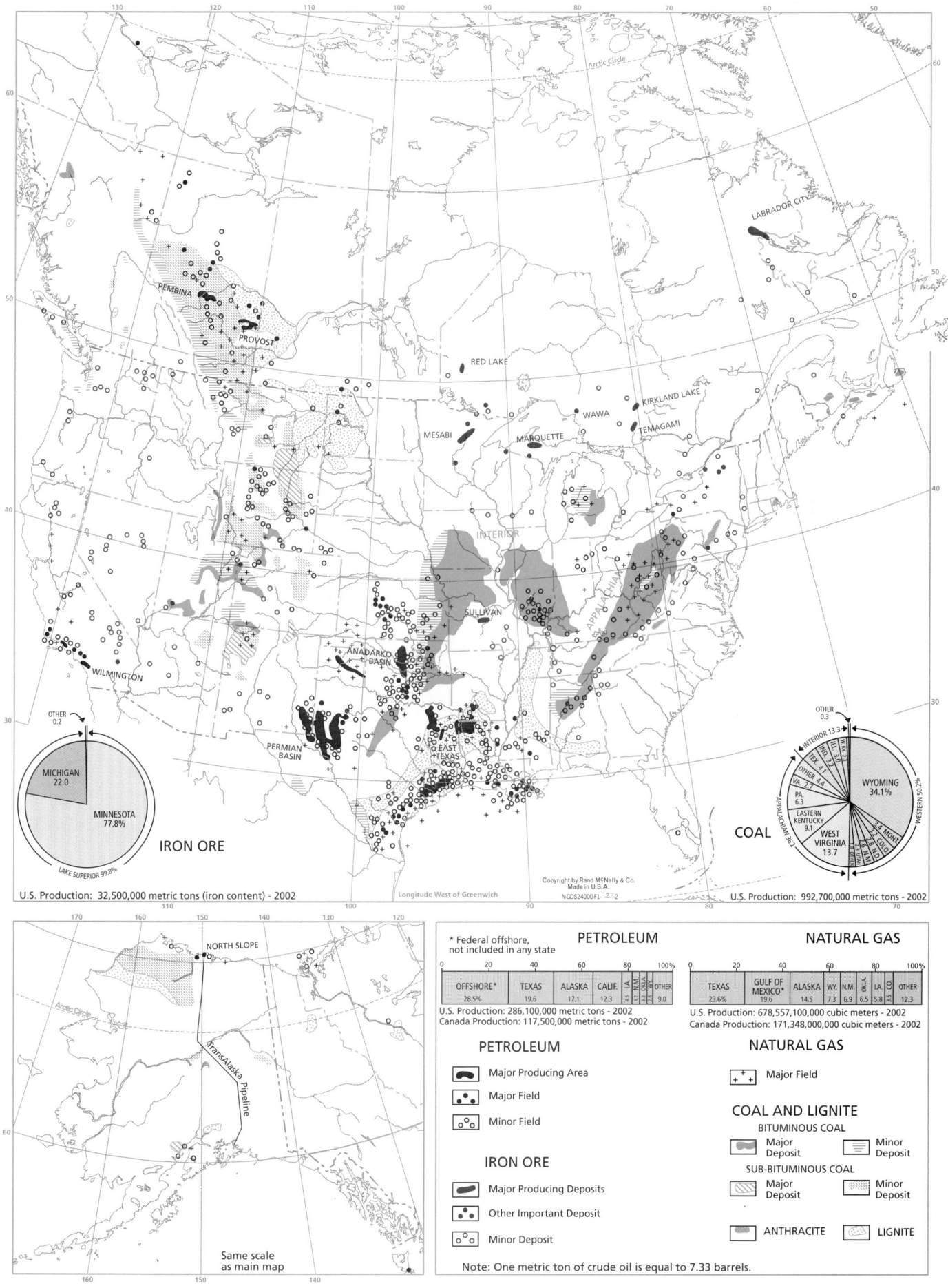

PEMBINA

PROVOST

RED LAKE

KIRKLAND LAKE

WAWA

MESABI

MARQUETTE

TEMAGAMI

LABRADOR CITY

INTERIOR

SULLIVAN

ANADARKO
BASIN

APPALACHIAN

WILMINGTON

PERMIAN
BASIN

EAST
TEXAS

IRON ORE

OTHER
0.2

MICHIGAN
22.0

MINNESOTA
77.8%

LAKE SUPERIOR 99.8%

U.S. Production: 32,500,000 metric tons (iron content) - 2002

COAL

OTHER
0.3

INTERIOR 13.3

ILL 3.0

IND. 2.7

TX. 4.1

OTHER 4.4

VA. 2.7

PA.
6.3

EASTERN
KENTUCKY
9.1

WEST
VIRGINIA
13.7

APPALACHIAN 36.1

WYOMING
34.1%

WESTERN 50.7%

U.S. Production: 992,700,000 metric tons - 2002

Copyright by Rand McNally & Co.
Made in U.S.A.
Longitude West of Greenwich
NGDS24000-F1- 2 2

NORTH SLOPE

Arctic Circle

Trans-Alaska Pipeline

Same scale
as main map

* Federal offshore,
not included in any state

PETROLEUM

OFFSHORE*	TEXAS	ALASKA	CALIF.	LA.	N.M.	OKLA.	WY.	OTHER
28.5%	19.6	17.1	12.3					9.0

U.S. Production: 286,100,000 metric tons - 2002
Canada Production: 117,500,000 metric tons - 2002

NATURAL GAS

TEXAS	GULF OF MEXICO*	ALASKA	WY.	N.M.	OKLA.	LA.	CO.	OTHER
23.6%	19.6	14.5	7.3	6.9	6.5	5.8		12.3

U.S. Production: 678,557,100,000 cubic meters - 2002
Canada Production: 171,348,000,000 cubic meters - 2002

PETROLEUM

⬛ Major Producing Area

⬬ Major Field

◦◦ Minor Field

IRON ORE

⬛ Major Producing Deposits

⬬ Other Important Deposit

◦◦ Minor Deposit

NATURAL GAS

+ Major Field

COAL AND LIGNITE

BITUMINOUS COAL

▨ Major Deposit ▤ Minor Deposit

SUB-BITUMINOUS COAL

▨ Major Deposit ▤ Minor Deposit

◼ ANTHRACITE ▦ LIGNITE

Note: One metric ton of crude oil is equal to 7.33 barrels.

Scale 1:29,000,000; One inch to 457 miles. ALBERS CONIC PROJECTION

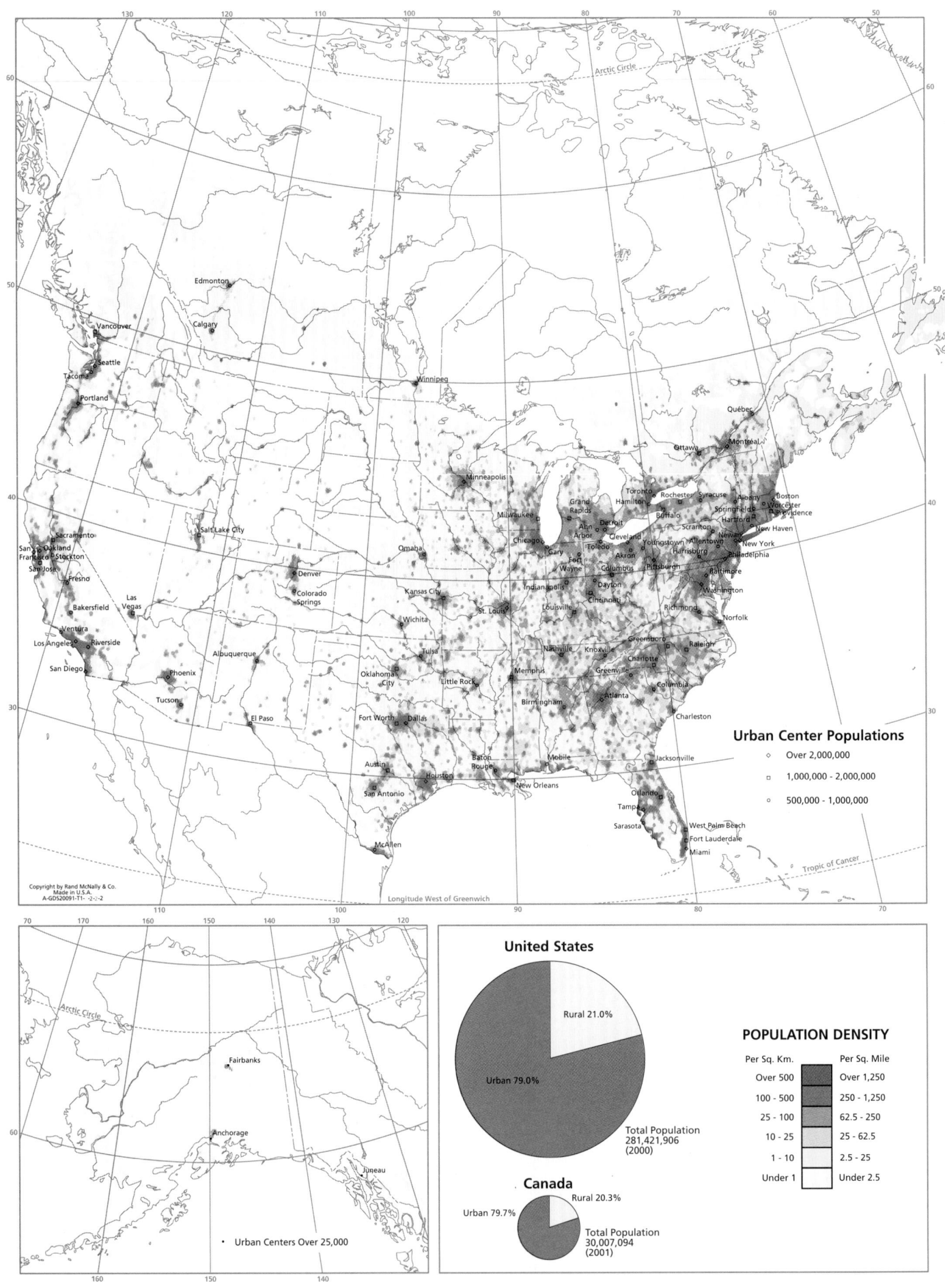

Urban Center Populations

◇ Over 2,000,000

▫ 1,000,000 - 2,000,000

◦ 500,000 - 1,000,000

Longitude West of Greenwich

• Urban Centers Over 25,000

United States

Rural 21.0%

Urban 79.0%

Total Population
281,421,906
(2000)

Canada

Rural 20.3%

Urban 79.7%

Total Population
30,007,094
(2001)

POPULATION DENSITY

Per Sq. Km.	Per Sq. Mile
Over 500	Over 1,250
100 - 500	250 - 1,250
25 - 100	62.5 - 250
10 - 25	25 - 62.5
1 - 10	2.5 - 25
Under 1	Under 2.5

WHITE POPULATION

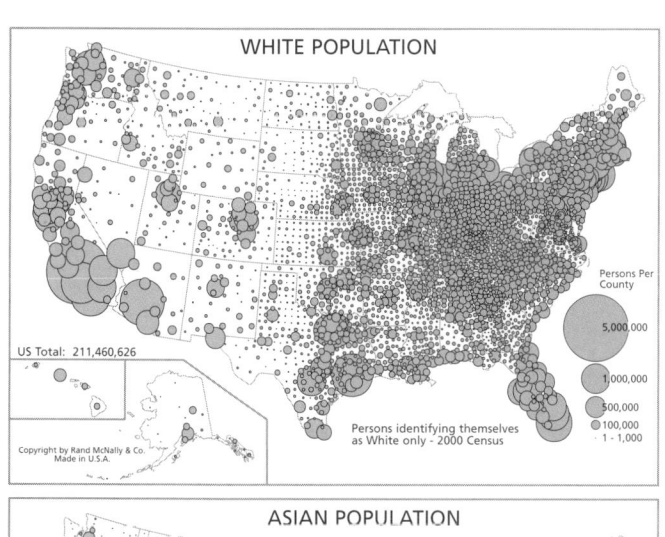

US Total: 211,460,626

Persons Per County

5,000,000
1,000,000
500,000
100,000
1 - 1,000

Persons identifying themselves as White only - 2000 Census

Copyright by Rand McNally & Co.
Made in U.S.A.

AFRICAN AMERICAN POPULATION

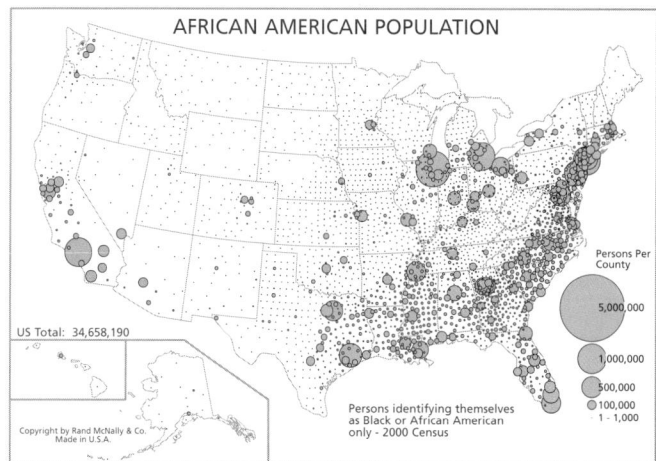

US Total: 34,658,190

Persons Per County

5,000,000
1,000,000
500,000
100,000
1 - 1,000

Persons identifying themselves as Black or African American only - 2000 Census

Copyright by Rand McNally & Co.
Made in U.S.A.

ASIAN POPULATION

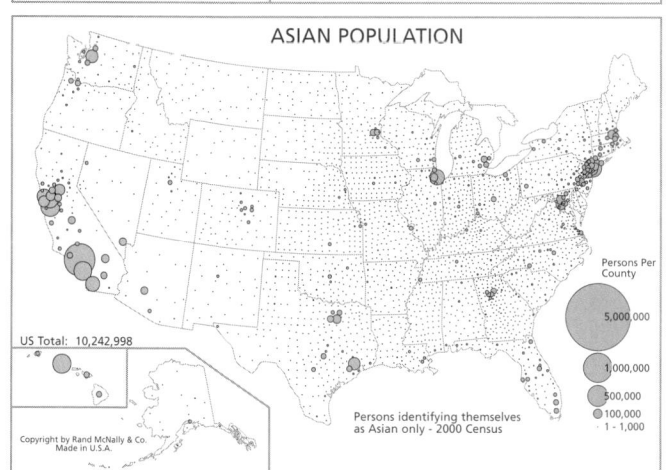

US Total: 10,242,998

Persons Per County

5,000,000
1,000,000
500,000
100,000
1 - 1,000

Persons identifying themselves as Asian only - 2000 Census

Copyright by Rand McNally & Co.
Made in U.S.A.

AMERICAN INDIAN AND ALASKA NATIVE POPULATION

US Total: 2,475,956

Persons Per County

5,000,000
1,000,000
500,000
100,000
1 - 1,000

Persons identifying themselves as American Indian or Alaska Native only - 2000 Census

Copyright by Rand McNally & Co.
Made in U.S.A.

NATIVE HAWAIIAN AND PACIFIC ISLANDER POPULATION

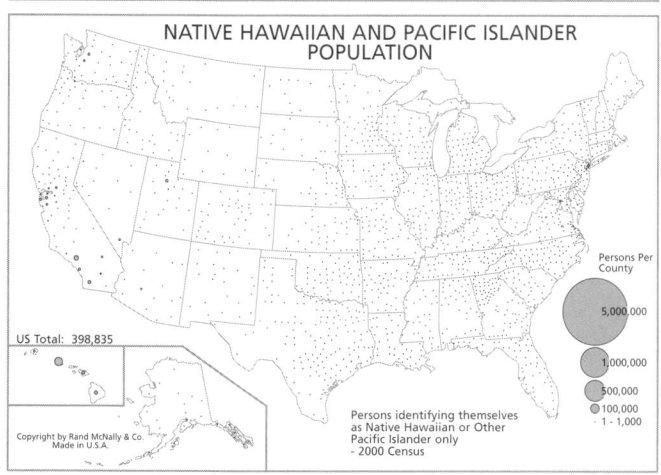

US Total: 398,835

Persons Per County

5,000,000
1,000,000
500,000
100,000
1 - 1,000

Persons identifying themselves as Native Hawaiian or Other Pacific Islander only - 2000 Census

Copyright by Rand McNally & Co.
Made in U.S.A.

SOME OTHER RACE

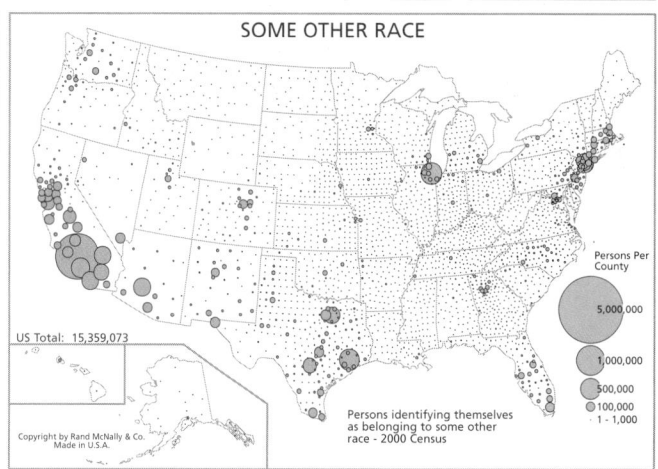

US Total: 15,359,073

Persons Per County

5,000,000
1,000,000
500,000
100,000
1 - 1,000

Persons identifying themselves as belonging to some other race - 2000 Census

Copyright by Rand McNally & Co.
Made in U.S.A.

TWO OR MORE RACES

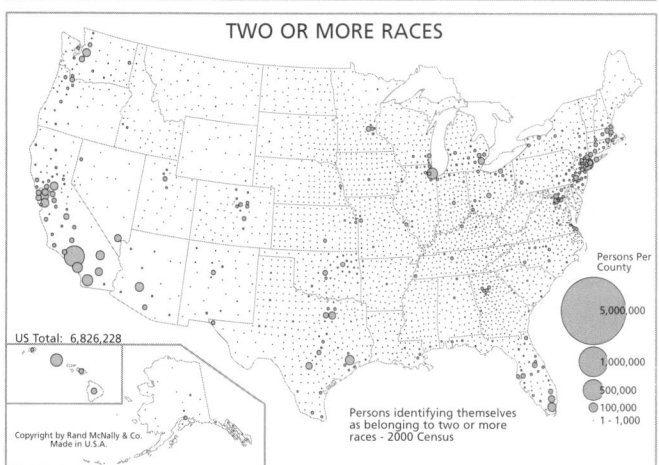

US Total: 6,826,228

Persons Per County

5,000,000
1,000,000
500,000
100,000
1 - 1,000

Persons identifying themselves as belonging to two or more races - 2000 Census

Copyright by Rand McNally & Co.
Made in U.S.A.

HISPANIC POPULATION (ANY RACE)

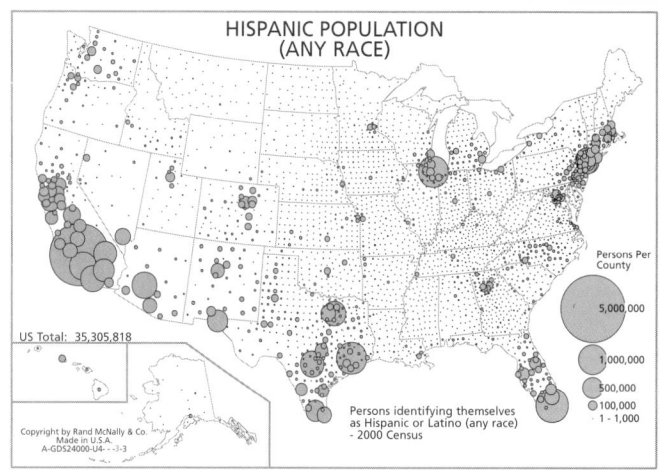

US Total: 35,305,818

Persons Per County

5,000,000
1,000,000
500,000
100,000
1 - 1,000

Persons identifying themselves as Hispanic or Latino (any race) - 2000 Census

Copyright by Rand McNally & Co.
Made in U.S.A.
A-GDS24000-U4- --3-3

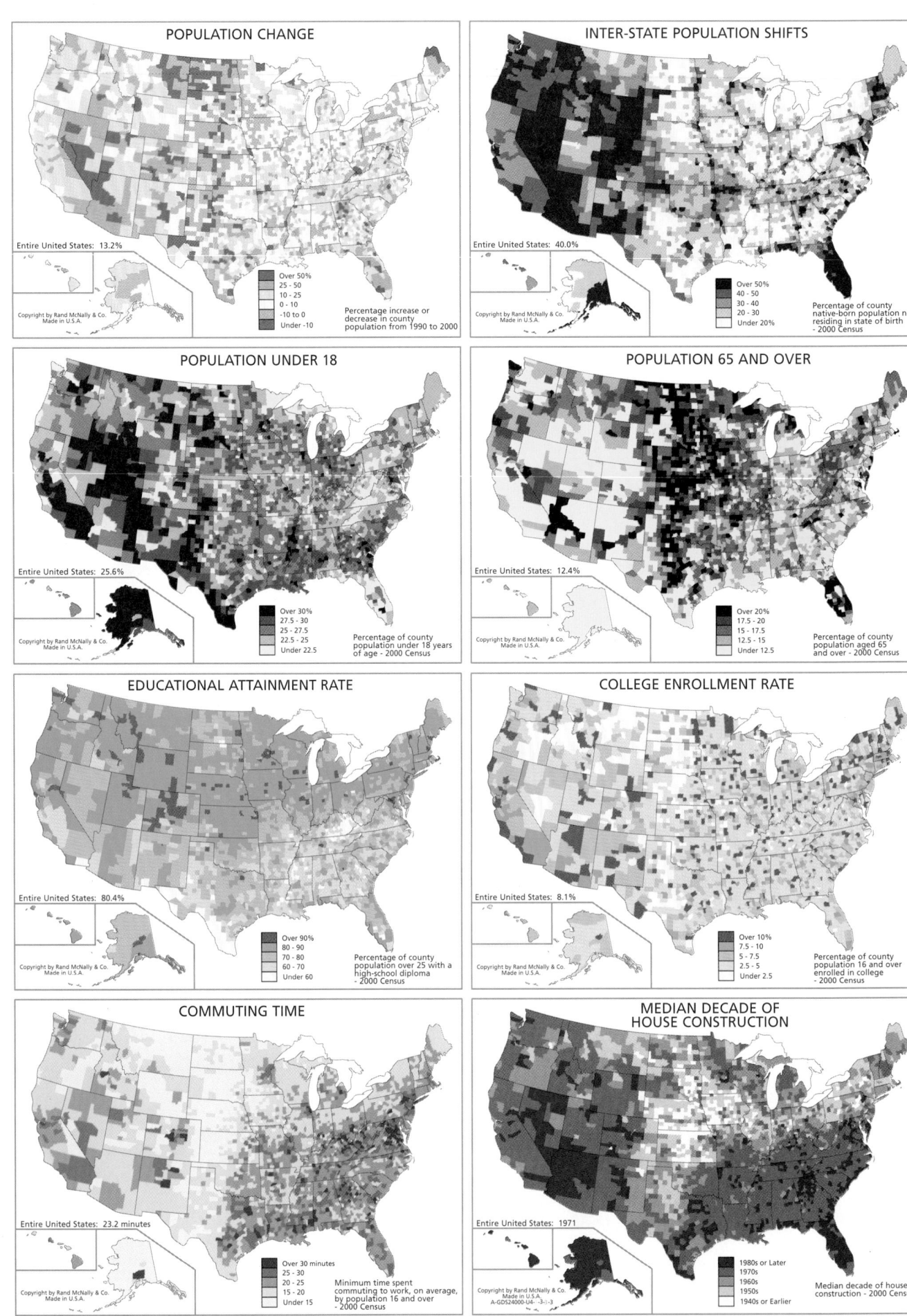

POPULATION CHANGE

Entire United States: 13.2%

Over 50%
25 - 50
10 - 25
0 - 10
-10 to 0
Under -10

Percentage increase or decrease in county population from 1990 to 2000

Copyright by Rand McNally & Co.
Made in U.S.A.

INTER-STATE POPULATION SHIFTS

Entire United States: 40.0%

Over 50%
40 - 50
30 - 40
20 - 30
Under 20%

Percentage of county native-born population not residing in state of birth - 2000 Census

Copyright by Rand McNally & Co.
Made in U.S.A.

POPULATION UNDER 18

Entire United States: 25.6%

Over 30%
27.5 - 30
25 - 27.5
22.5 - 25
Under 22.5

Percentage of county population under 18 years of age - 2000 Census

Copyright by Rand McNally & Co.
Made in U.S.A.

POPULATION 65 AND OVER

Entire United States: 12.4%

Over 20%
17.5 - 20
15 - 17.5
12.5 - 15
Under 12.5

Percentage of county population aged 65 and over - 2000 Census

Copyright by Rand McNally & Co.
Made in U.S.A.

EDUCATIONAL ATTAINMENT RATE

Entire United States: 80.4%

Over 90%
80 - 90
70 - 80
60 - 70
Under 60

Percentage of county population over 25 with a high-school diploma - 2000 Census

Copyright by Rand McNally & Co.
Made in U.S.A.

COLLEGE ENROLLMENT RATE

Entire United States: 8.1%

Over 10%
7.5 - 10
5 - 7.5
2.5 - 5
Under 2.5

Percentage of county population 16 and over enrolled in college - 2000 Census

Copyright by Rand McNally & Co.
Made in U.S.A.

COMMUTING TIME

Entire United States: 23.2 minutes

Over 30 minutes
25 - 30
20 - 25
15 - 20
Under 15

Minimum time spent commuting to work, on average, by population 16 and over - 2000 Census

Copyright by Rand McNally & Co.
Made in U.S.A.

MEDIAN DECADE OF HOUSE CONSTRUCTION

Entire United States: 1971

1980s or Later
1970s
1960s
1950s
1940s or Earlier

Median decade of house construction - 2000 Census

Copyright by Rand McNally & Co.
Made in U.S.A.
A-GDS24000-U4- -3-1-3

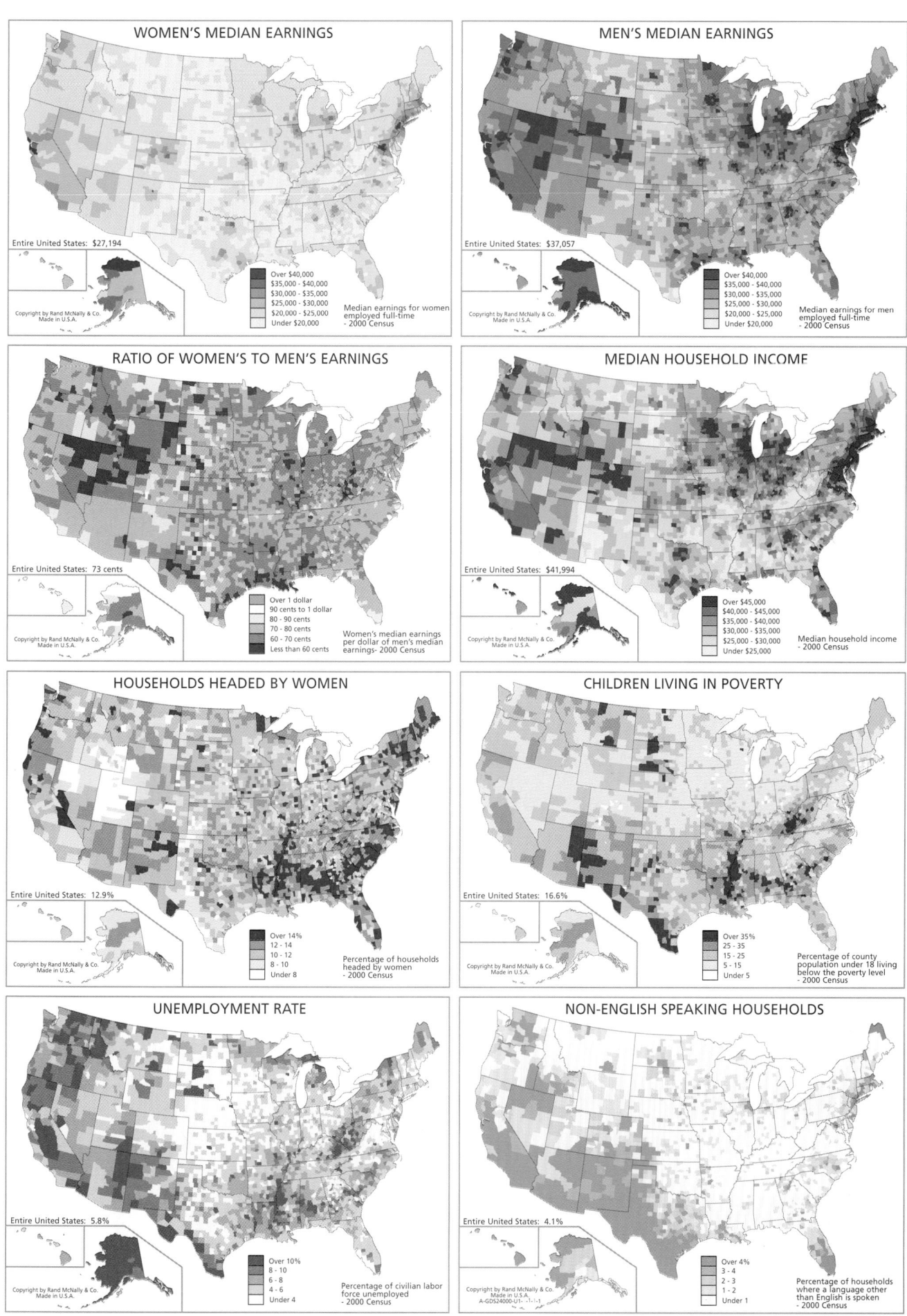

WOMEN'S MEDIAN EARNINGS

Entire United States: $27,194

Copyright by Rand McNally & Co.
Made in U.S.A.

Over $40,000
$35,000 - $40,000
$30,000 - $35,000
$25,000 - $30,000
$20,000 - $25,000
Under $20,000

Median earnings for women
employed full-time
- 2000 Census

MEN'S MEDIAN EARNINGS

Entire United States: $37,057

Copyright by Rand McNally & Co.
Made in U.S.A.

Over $40,000
$35,000 - $40,000
$30,000 - $35,000
$25,000 - $30,000
$20,000 - $25,000
Under $20,000

Median earnings for men
employed full-time
- 2000 Census

RATIO OF WOMEN'S TO MEN'S EARNINGS

Entire United States: 73 cents

Copyright by Rand McNally & Co.
Made in U.S.A.

Over 1 dollar
90 cents to 1 dollar
80 - 90 cents
70 - 80 cents
60 - 70 cents
Less than 60 cents

Women's median earnings
per dollar of men's median
earnings- 2000 Census

MEDIAN HOUSEHOLD INCOME

Entire United States: $41,994

Copyright by Rand McNally & Co.
Made in U.S.A.

Over $45,000
$40,000 - $45,000
$35,000 - $40,000
$30,000 - $35,000
$25,000 - $30,000
Under $25,000

Median household income
- 2000 Census

HOUSEHOLDS HEADED BY WOMEN

Entire United States: 12.9%

Copyright by Rand McNally & Co.
Made in U.S.A.

Over 14%
12 - 14
10 - 12
8 - 10
Under 8

Percentage of households
headed by women
- 2000 Census

CHILDREN LIVING IN POVERTY

Entire United States: 16.6%

Copyright by Rand McNally & Co.
Made in U.S.A.

Over 35%
25 - 35
15 - 25
5 - 15
Under 5

Percentage of county
population under 18 living
below the poverty level
- 2000 Census

UNEMPLOYMENT RATE

Entire United States: 5.8%

Copyright by Rand McNally & Co.
Made in U.S.A.

Over 10%
8 - 10
6 - 8
4 - 6
Under 4

Percentage of civilian labor
force unemployed
- 2000 Census

NON-ENGLISH SPEAKING HOUSEHOLDS

Entire United States: 4.1%

Copyright by Rand McNally & Co.
Made in U.S.A.
A-GDS24000-U1-.-1-1-1

Over 4%
3 - 4
2 - 3
1 - 2
Under 1

Percentage of households
where a language other
than English is spoken
- 2000 Census

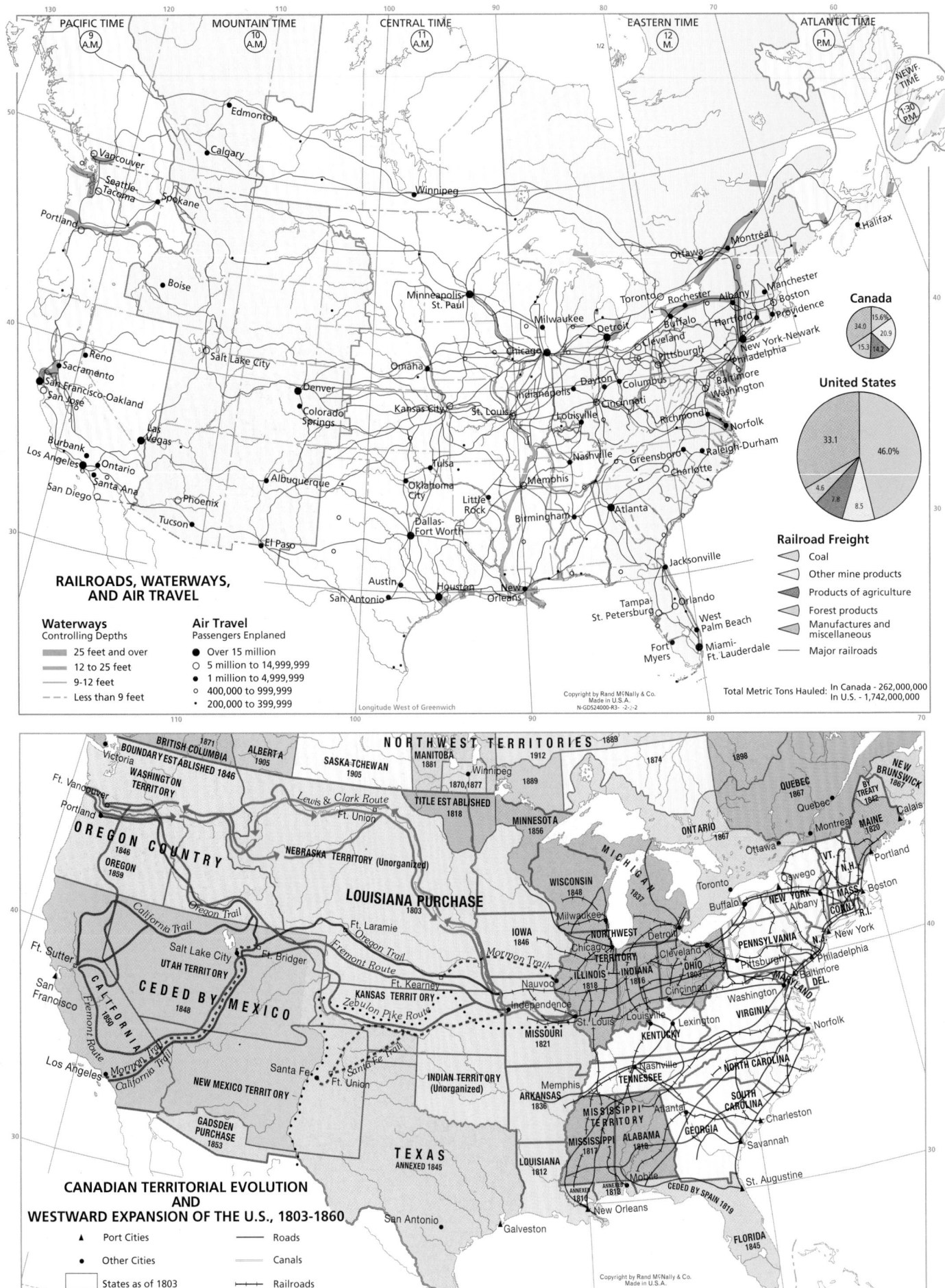

PACIFIC TIME
9 A.M.

MOUNTAIN TIME
10 A.M.

CENTRAL TIME
11 A.M.

EASTERN TIME
12 M.

ATLANTIC TIME
1 P.M.

NEWF. TIME
1:30 P.M.

RAILROADS, WATERWAYS, AND AIR TRAVEL

Waterways
Controlling Depths

▬▬▬	25 feet and over
▬▬	12 to 25 feet
——	9-12 feet
– – –	Less than 9 feet

Air Travel
Passengers Enplaned

● Over 15 million
○ 5 million to 14,999,999
● 1 million to 4,999,999
○ 400,000 to 999,999
· 200,000 to 399,999

Copyright by Rand McNally & Co.
Made in U.S.A.
N-GDS24000-R3- -2-2-2

Longitude West of Greenwich

Canada
15.6
34.0   20.9
15.3   14.2

United States
33.1   46.0%
4.6
7.8   8.5

Railroad Freight

◁ Coal
◁ Other mine products
◀ Products of agriculture
◁ Forest products
◁ Manufactures and miscellaneous
—— Major railroads

Total Metric Tons Hauled: In Canada - 262,000,000
In U.S. - 1,742,000,000

CANADIAN TERRITORIAL EVOLUTION AND WESTWARD EXPANSION OF THE U.S., 1803-1860

BRITISH COLUMBIA 1871
BOUNDARY ESTABLISHED 1846
ALBERTA 1905
SASKATCHEWAN 1905
MANITOBA 1881
NORTHWEST TERRITORIES 1889
1912
1874
1898
NEW BRUNSWICK 1867

WASHINGTON TERRITORY
Lewis & Clark Route
Ft. Union
TITLE ESTABLISHED 1818
1870,1877
1889
QUEBEC 1867
BY TREATY 1842
MAINE 1820

OREGON COUNTRY 1846
OREGON 1859
Oregon Trail
California Trail
NEBRASKA TERRITORY (Unorganized)
LOUISIANA PURCHASE 1803
MINNESOTA 1856
MICHIGAN 1837
ONTARIO 1867

Ft. Laramie
Oregon Trail
Fremont Route
Mormon Trail
WISCONSIN 1848
NORTHWEST TERRITORY
MICHIGAN

Salt Lake City
UTAH TERRITORY
Ft. Bridger
Ft. Kearney
IOWA 1846
ILLINOIS 1818
INDIANA 1816
OHIO 1803
PENNSYLVANIA
NEW YORK

CEDED BY MEXICO 1848
Zebulon Pike Route
KANSAS TERRITORY
Independence
MISSOURI 1821
KENTUCKY
VIRGINIA

CALIFORNIA 1850
Fremont Route
Mormon Trail
California Trail
Santa Fe
Ft. Union
Santa Fe Trail
INDIAN TERRITORY (Unorganized)
ARKANSAS 1836
TENNESSEE
NORTH CAROLINA
SOUTH CAROLINA

NEW MEXICO TERRITORY
GADSDEN PURCHASE 1853
TEXAS ANNEXED 1845
LOUISIANA 1812
MISSISSIPPI TERRITORY
MISSISSIPPI 1817
ALABAMA 1819
GEORGIA
CEDED BY SPAIN 1819
FLORIDA 1845

▲ Port Cities
● Other Cities
▭ States as of 1803
—— Roads
—— Canals
+−+−+ Railroads

Copyright by Rand McNally & Co.
Made in U.S.A.
H-GDS24000-B6- -1-1-2

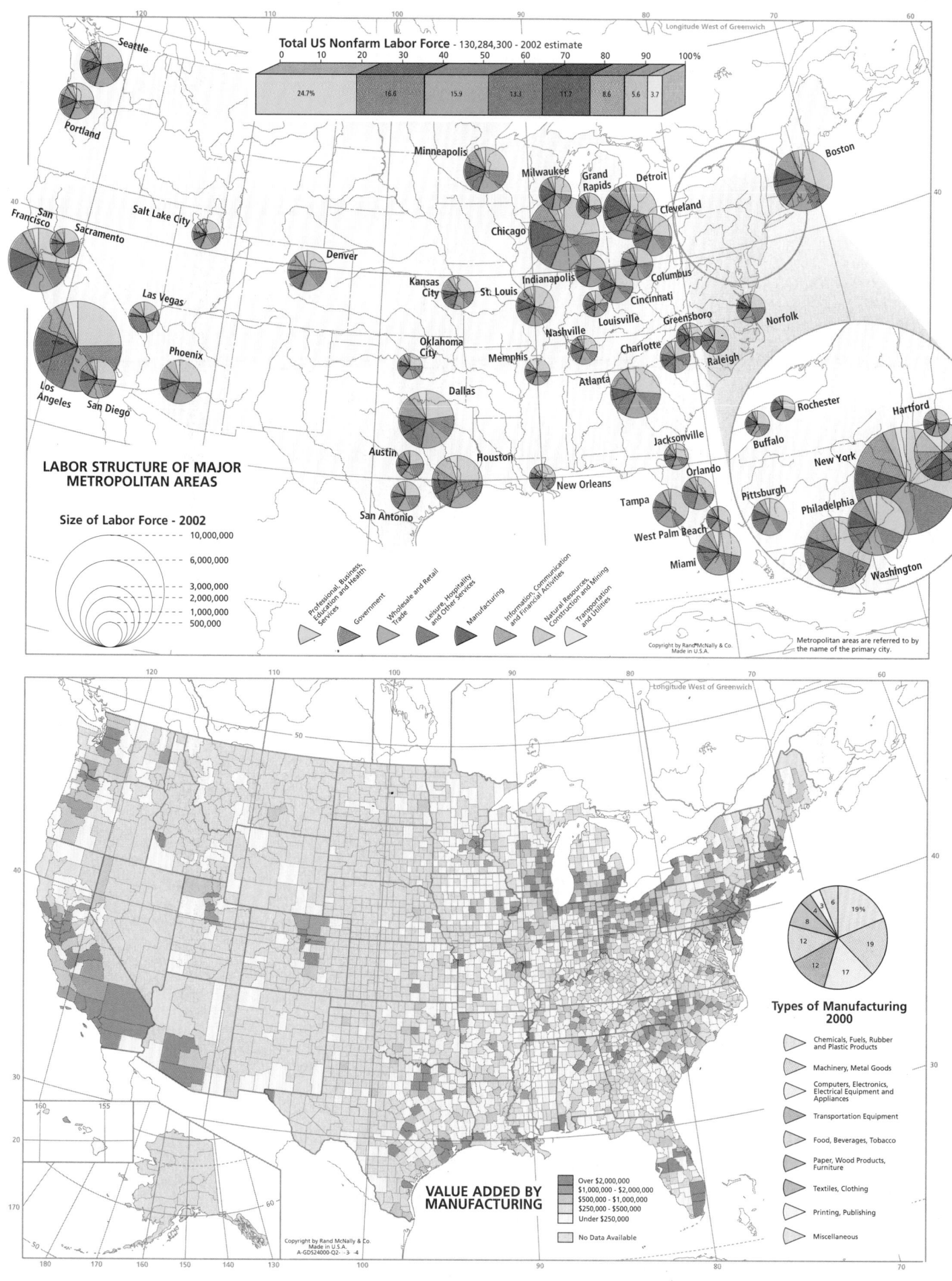

Total US Nonfarm Labor Force - 130,284,300 - 2002 estimate

24.7%	16.6	15.9	13.3	11.7	8.6	5.6	3.7

LABOR STRUCTURE OF MAJOR METROPOLITAN AREAS

Size of Labor Force - 2002

10,000,000
6,000,000
3,000,000
2,000,000
1,000,000
500,000

Professional, Business, Education and Health Services
Government
Wholesale and Retail Trade
Leisure, Hospitality and Other Services
Manufacturing
Information, Communication and Financial Activities
Natural Resources, Construction and Mining
Transportation and Utilities

Copyright by Rand McNally & Co.
Made in U.S.A.

Metropolitan areas are referred to by the name of the primary city.

Types of Manufacturing 2000

19%
19
17
12
12
8
6

Chemicals, Fuels, Rubber and Plastic Products
Machinery, Metal Goods
Computers, Electronics, Electrical Equipment and Appliances
Transportation Equipment
Food, Beverages, Tobacco
Paper, Wood Products, Furniture
Textiles, Clothing
Printing, Publishing
Miscellaneous

VALUE ADDED BY MANUFACTURING

Over $2,000,000
$1,000,000 - $2,000,000
$500,000 - $1,000,000
$250,000 - $500,000
Under $250,000

No Data Available

Copyright by Rand McNally & Co.
Made in U.S.A.
A-GD52400O-Q2- -3- -4

Scale 1:12,000,000.   One inch to 190 miles.   Albers Conic Projection
                         One centimeter to 120 kilometers.

0 50 100   200   300   400 Miles

0 50 100 150 200   300   400   500   600 Kilometers

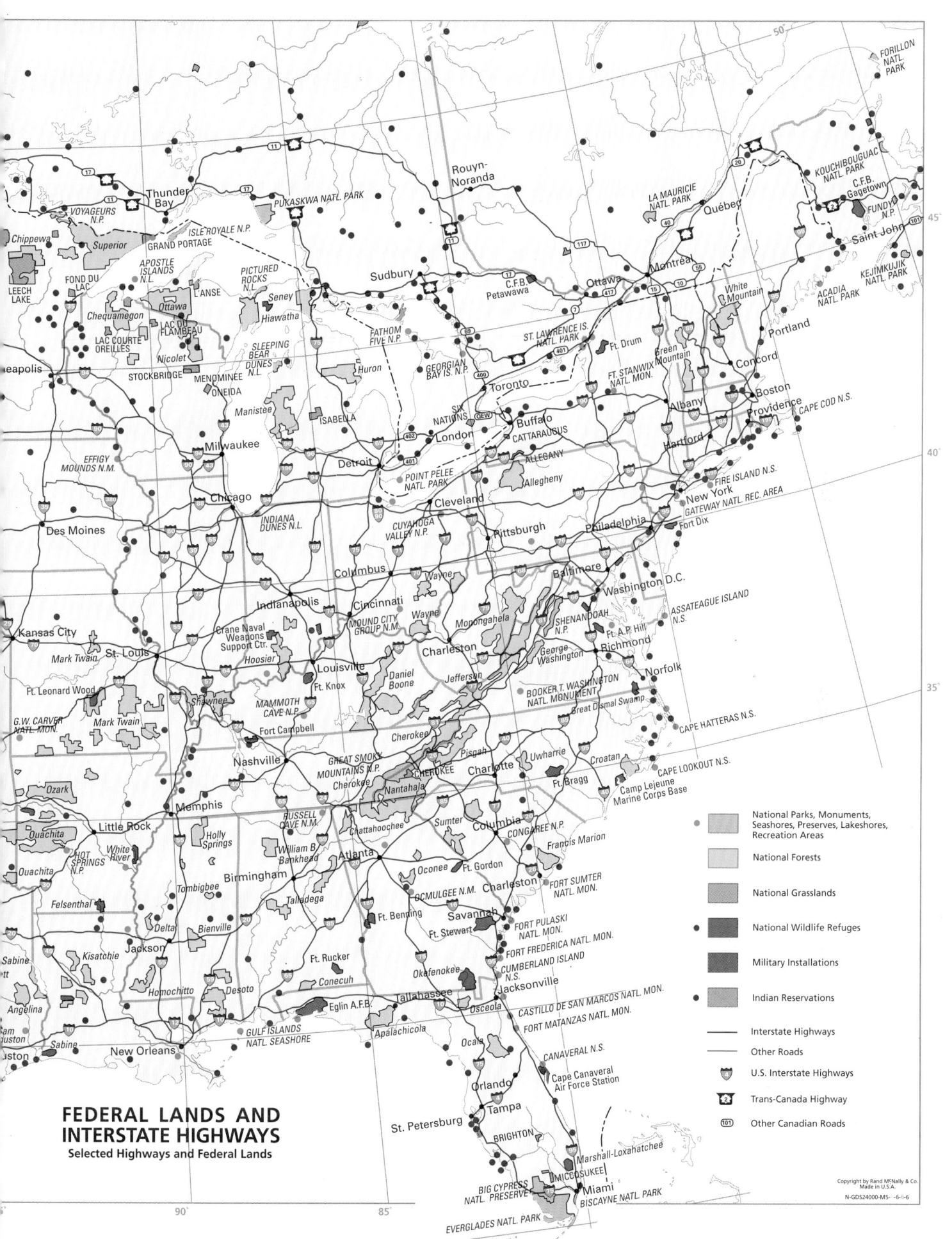

FEDERAL LANDS AND
INTERSTATE HIGHWAYS
Selected Highways and Federal Lands

National Parks, Monuments, Seashores, Preserves, Lakeshores, Recreation Areas

National Forests

National Grasslands

National Wildlife Refuges

Military Installations

Indian Reservations

Interstate Highways

Other Roads

U.S. Interstate Highways

Trans-Canada Highway

Other Canadian Roads

Copyright by Rand McNally & Co.
Made in U.S.A.
N-GDS24000-M5- -6-(-6

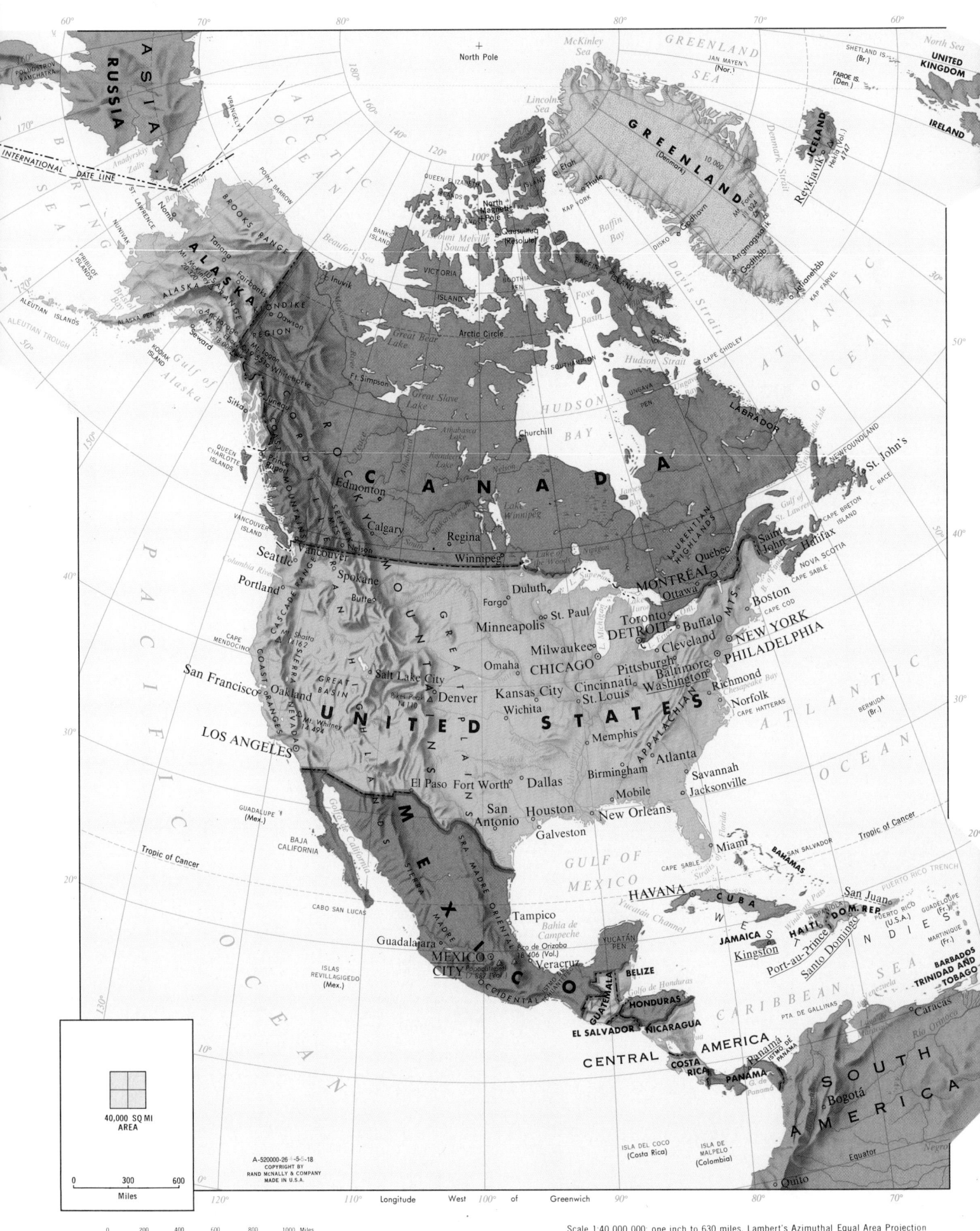

RUSSIA
ASIA
POLUOSTROV KAMCHATKA

North Pole
+

GREENLAND SEA

SHETLAND IS. (Br.)

UNITED KINGDOM

JAN MAYEN (Nor.)

FAROE IS. (Den.)

IRELAND

North Sea

INTERNATIONAL DATE LINE

Anadyrskiy Zaliv

ARCTIC OCEAN

McKinley Sea

GREENLAND (Denmark)

10,000

ICELAND
Reykjavik
Hekla (Vol.)
4147

BERING SEA

St. Lawrence I.
Nome
POINT BARROW
BROOKS RANGE
Fairbanks
Inuvik

Lincoln Sea

Mt. Forel 11,024

Angmagssalik

ATLANTIC OCEAN

NUNIVAK

ALASKA
MT. McKINLEY 20,320
ALASKA RANGE

Beaufort Sea

BANKS ISLAND

North Magnetic Pole

Godthåb

Mount Melville Sound

Etah

KAP YORK

Godhavn

Julianehåb

KAP FARVEL

PRIBILOF ISLANDS

Bristol Bay

KLONDIKE REGION
Dawson
MT. LOGAN 19,850
MT. ST. ELIAS 18,008
Whitehorse

VICTORIA ISLAND

BOOTHIA PEN.

QUEEN ELIZABETH ISLANDS

ELLESMERE I.

Thule
Qaanaaq
Resolute

Baffin Bay

DISKO

ALEUTIAN ISLANDS

Gulf of Alaska
Seward
Sitka
Juneau

Great Bear Lake

Arctic Circle

BAFFIN ISLAND

Davis Strait

ALEUTIAN TROUGH

KODIAK ISLAND

QUEEN CHARLOTTE ISLANDS

Prince Rupert

Ft. Simpson

Great Slave Lake

Reindeer Lake

Foxe Basin

SOUTHAMPTON

Denmark Strait

VANCOUVER ISLAND

COAST MOUNTAINS

Edmonton

Calgary

Athabasca Lake

C A N A D A

Churchill

HUDSON BAY

UNGAVA PEN.

Ungava Bay

LABRADOR

NEWFOUNDLAND

St. John's

C. RACE

PACIFIC OCEAN

CAPE MENDOCINO

Seattle
Vancouver
Portland
Spokane
Butte

Regina

Winnipeg

Lake Winnipeg

Lake of the Woods

Nelson

James Bay

Lake Nipigon

LAURENTIAN HIGHLANDS

Québec

Ottawa

MONTRÉAL

Saint John

Halifax

NOVA SCOTIA

CAPE BRETON ISLAND

CAPE SABLE

Gulf of St. Lawrence

San Francisco
Oakland

CASCADE RANGE
MT. SHASTA 14,162
SIERRA NEVADA

GREAT BASIN

Salt Lake City

Denver

PIKES PEAK 14,110

Fargo

Duluth

Minneapolis

St. Paul

Milwaukee

CHICAGO

Omaha

Kansas City

St. Louis

Cincinnati

Pittsburgh

Washington

Baltimore

Lake Superior

Toronto

DETROIT

Cleveland

Buffalo

NEW YORK

PHILADELPHIA

Richmond

Chesapeake Bay

CAPE COD

Boston

APPALACHIAN MTS.

COAST RANGES

LOS ANGELES

MT. WHITNEY 14,494

U N I T E D   S T A T E S

GREAT PLAINS

Wichita

Memphis

Norfolk

CAPE HATTERAS

ATLANTIC OCEAN

GUADALUPE I. (Mex.)

El Paso

Fort Worth

Dallas

Birmingham

Atlanta

Savannah

Jacksonville

BERMUDA (Br.)

Tropic of Cancer

BAJA CALIFORNIA

San Antonio

Houston

Galveston

New Orleans

Mobile

Florida

CAPE SABLE

Miami

Tropic of Cancer

CABO SAN LUCAS

Golfo de California

SIERRA MADRE OCCIDENTAL

SIERRA MADRE ORIENTAL

M E X I C O

Tampico

GULF OF MEXICO

Straits of Florida

HAVANA

CUBA

BAHAMAS

SAN SALVADOR

San Juan

PUERTO RICO (U.S.A.)

PUERTO RICO TRENCH

GUADELOUPE (Fr.)

ISLAS REVILLAGIGEDO (Mex.)

Guadalajara

MEXICO CITY
Popocatépetl (17,887 (Vol.))

Pico de Orizaba 18,406 (Vol.)

Bahía de Campeche

YUCATÁN PEN.

Yucatán Channel

JAMAICA

Kingston

HAITI

Port-au-Prince

DOM. REP.

Santo Domingo

MARTINIQUE (Fr.)

W E S T   I N D I E S

BARBADOS

TRINIDAD AND TOBAGO

Veracruz

BELIZE

Golfo de Honduras

GUATEMALA

HONDURAS

EL SALVADOR

NICARAGUA

COSTA RICA

PANAMÁ

CARIBBEAN SEA

PTA. DE GALLINAS

Caracas

Rio Orinoco

C E N T R A L   A M E R I C A

ISTMO DE PANAMÁ

G. de Panamá

S O U T H   A M E R I C A

Bogotá

ISLA DEL COCO (Costa Rica)

ISLA DE MALPELO (Colombia)

Rio Negro

Equator

Quito

Longitude   West   of   Greenwich

40,000 SQ MI AREA

0   300   600
Miles

A-520000-26-5-18
COPYRIGHT BY
RAND McNALLY & COMPANY
MADE IN U.S.A.

0   200   400   600   800   1000 Miles
0   400   800   1200   1600 Kilometers

Scale 1:40 000 000; one inch to 630 miles. Lambert's Azimuthal Equal Area Projection
Elevations and depressions are given in feet

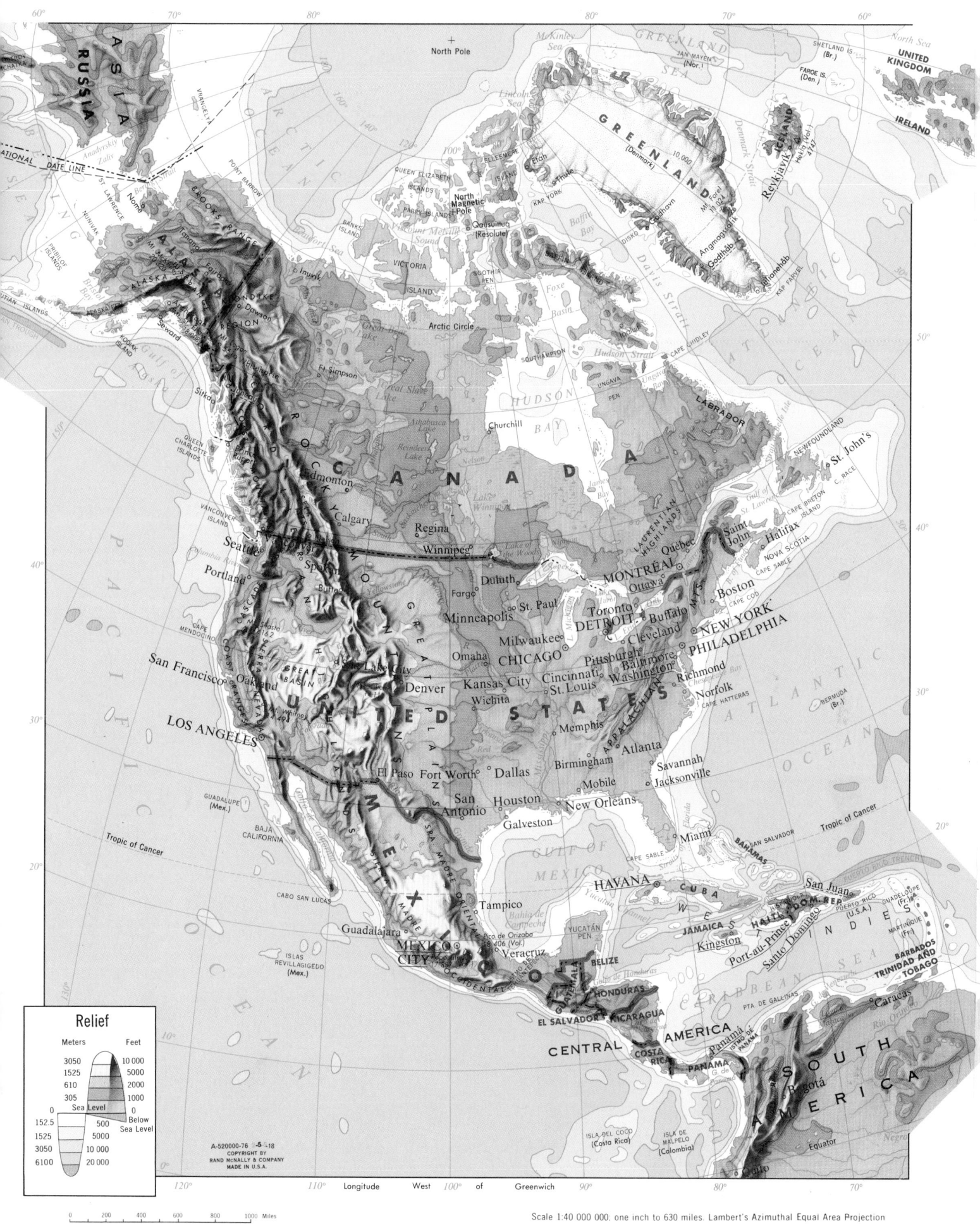

Relief

Meters		Feet
3050		10 000
1525		5000
610		2000
305		1000
0	Sea Level	0
152.5		500 Below
1525		5000 Sea Level
3050		10 000
6100		20 000

A-520000-76 -5-18
COPYRIGHT BY
RAND MCNALLY & COMPANY
MADE IN U.S.A.

0   200   400   600   800   1000 Miles
0   400   800   1200   1600 Kilometers

Scale 1:40 000 000: one inch to 630 miles. Lambert's Azimuthal Equal Area Projection
Elevations and depressions are given in feet

Continued on pages 104-105

Longitude West of Greenwich

Scale 1: 12 000 000; one inch to 190 miles. Conic Projection

Elevations and depressions are given in feet

Continued on pages 106-107

Longitude West of Greenwich

Scale 1: 12 000 000; one inch to 190 miles. Conic Projection

Elevations and depressions are given in feet

a

INSET MAP:

QUEBEC

Strait of Belle Isle

NEWFOUNDLAND
AND
LABRADOR

CAPE BAULD

Gulf of

St. Lawrence

LONG RANGE MTS.

C. ST. JOHN

GROS MORNE
NAT'L PARK

Deer Lake

Botwood

Twillingate

Windsor

Gander

Bonavista

Corner Brook

Grand Falls

TERRA NOVA
NAT'L PARK

Stephenville

Trinity

St.
George's

NEWFOUNDLAND

St. John's

CAPE RAY

Channel-Port-aux-Basques

Grand Bank

Burin

CAPE NORTH

Fortune Bay

Placentia Bay

CAPE BRETON
ISLAND

ST. PIERRE AND MIQUELON (Fr.)

ATLANTIC OCEAN

© RMCN

MAIN MAP LABELS:

Longitude West of Greenwich

Same scale as main map

BAFFIN
ISLAND
NAT'L PARK

BAFFIN

ISLAND

Arctic Circle

CUMBERLAND
PEN.

Cumberland Sound

MERCY

RESOLUTION

MELVILLE

PENINSULA

Foxe
Basin

PRINCE
CHARLES
ISLAND

Iqaluit

HALL
PEN.

EVERETT
MTS.

Frobisher Bay

Foxe
Channel

FOXE
PEN.

SALISBURY

Hudson

Strait

C. DE
NOUVELLE-
FRANCE

HOPES
ADVANCE

AKPATOK

KILLINIQ I.

TORNGAT
MTS.

Hebron

Roes Welcome Sound

SOUTHAMPTON
ISLAND

NOTTINGHAM
ISLAND

MANSEL

Wilnik

PENINSULE

D'UNGAVA

Payne

Ungava
Bay

Kuujjuaq

Nain

NEWFOUNDLAND

C. LOW

COATS

Povungnituk

Hopedale

Maktovik

Fisher Strait

BELL
PEN.

OTTAWA
ISLANDS

Minto

Rigolet

Cartwright

MEALY MTS.

Battle Harbour

HUDSON

BAY

All islands within bays and straits
lie within Nunavut.

BELCHER
ISLANDS

Lac
Bienville

Schefferville

Happy
Valley
Goose Bay

St. Anthony

LABRADOR

LONG RANGE MTS.

Ft. Severn

C. HENRIETTA MARIA

PTE. LOUIS-XIV

Grande
de la Baleine

Caniapiscau

Ashuanipi

Q U E B E C

GROS MORNE
NAT'L PARK

Corner Brook

Stephenville

St. George

James
Bay

Chisasibi

Eastmain

Nichicun

MTS.
OTISH

Manicouagan

Natashquan

ILE D'ANTICOSTI

AKIMISKI

Ft. Albany

Opinaca

Grand

Mistassini

Chibougamau

Sept-Îles

Clarke City

Gulf of

St. Lawrence

Moosonee

Nitchequon

Manouane

Réservoir Gouin

Baie-Comeau

Gaspé

CHIC-CHOCS
MTS.

St-Chandler

New Carlisle

ILES DE LA
MADELEINE

Coral Rapids

Fraserdale

St. Félicien

Dolbeau

Alma
Kenogami
Jonquière

Chicoutimi

Roberval
Chambord

La Malbaie

St. Paul

Matane

Mont-Joli

Rimouski

Rivière-du-Loup

Campbellton

Caraquet

P.E.I.

Summerside

New Waterford

Sydney Mines

Sydney

ONTARIO

Nakina

Armstrong Sta.

Hearst

Kapuskasing

La Sarre

Amos

Rouyn

Senneterre

Val-d'Or

Parent

La Tuque

Shawinigan

Grand-
Mère

Victoriaville

Edmundston

PRINCE EDWARD
ISLAND NAT'L PARK

Charlottetown

Amherst

Springhill

Truro

New Glasgow

Antigonish

Geraldton

Longlac

Cochrane

Iroquois Falls

Timmins

Malartic

Trois-
Rivières

Drummondville

NEW
BRUNSWICK

Richibucto

Moncton

Fredericton

FUNDY NAT'L PARK

N O V A

S C O T I A

Oba

Kirkland Lake

Joliette

St. Hyacinthe

Granby

St. Jérôme

Fredericton

St. George

Halifax

Dartmouth

Dryden

Nipigon

Chapleau

Ville-Marie

Témiscaming

MONTREAL

Sorel

Sherbrooke

MAINE

Saint John

Kentville

Lunenburg

Bridgewater

Liverpool

CAPE SABLE

Marathon

PUKASKWA
NAT'L PARK

Sudbury

Sturgeon
Falls

North
Bay

Mattawa

Laval

VERMONT

NEW
HAMPSHIRE

Augusta

Yarmouth

Digby

Shelburne

Lake of the Woods

Rainy

Lake Superior

MICHIPICOTEN

Sault Ste. Marie

Thessalon

Espanola

Pembroke

Renfrew

Ottawa

Hull

Smiths Falls

Cornwall

Concord

Portland

Thunder Bay

Blind River

Huntsville

Bancroft

Brockville

Ogdensburg

Alexandria
Bay

BOSTON

CAPE COD

Duluth

Superior

Marquette

Escanaba

MANITOULIN

Georgian
Bay

Parry Sound

Orillia

Peterborough

Kingston

Trenton

Cobourg

Rochester

Albany

MASS.

Hartford

Providence

R.I.

Relief

MINNE-
SOTA

WISCONSIN

MICHIGAN

Wiarton

Midland

Barrie

Lindsay

Whitby

Lake Ontario

Syracuse

CONN.

St. Paul

Sault Ste. Marie

Lake
Michigan

Lake Huron

Owen Sound

Kincardine

Oshawa

TORONTO

Hamilton

NEW YORK

NEW YORK

Meters   Feet

3050   10 000

Madison

MILWAUKEE

Green Bay

Saginaw

Flint

Lansing

Kitchener

London

St.
Catharines

Niagara Falls

BUFFALO

Scranton

1525   5000

610   2000

305   1000

152.5   500

Sea Level   0

MINNEAPOLIS

CHICAGO

ILL.

Grand
Rapids

Detroit

Windsor

Sarnia

St. Thomas

Chatham

Leamington

Lake Erie

OHIO

PENNSYLVANIA

N.J.

152.5   500
1525   5000
3050   10 000

Toledo

A-520200-76   -10.-23
COPYRIGHT BY
RAND McNALLY & COMPANY
MADE IN U.S.A.

0 25 50 75 100   200   300   400   500 Miles

0   100   200   400   600   800 Kilometers

ATLANTIC

OCEAN

134° 132° 130° 128° 126° 124°

PRINCE
OF
WALES
ISLAND
Mt. Reid
4592
REVILLAGIGEDO
ISLAND
PRINCE
Klawock
Hydaburg
Copper Mtn.
3916
Kerchikan
ANNETTE
ISLAND
Metlakatla
DALL
ISLAND
LADY
ISLAND

SKEENA
MOUNTAINS
Stedin Pk.
8750
Mt. Thomlinson
8050
OMINECA
MOUNTAINS
Williston
Lake
McLeod

UNITED STATES
CANADA

Alice Arm
Nass
Hazelton
Tchento
Lake
MOUNTAINS
Takla
Lake

DUNDAS
ISLAND

Dixon Entrance

Terrace
Smithers
Babine
Lake
Stuart
Lake
Fort
St. James
Nilkitkwa

54°

CAPE KNOX
Masset
PORCHER
ISLAND
Prince Rupert
Howson Pk.
9050
BULKLEY
MOUNTAINS
RANGES
Burns Lake
NECHAKO
Endako
Vanderhoof

QUEEN

QUEEN
CHARLOTTE
RANGES
GRAHAM ISLAND
Masset Inlet
Skidegate Inlet
PITT
ISLAND
BANKS
ISLAND
Kitimat
Kitimat
COAST
KITIMAT
RANGES
Francois Lake
Ootsa
Lake
Michel Pk.
7396
Nechako
Reservoir
PLATEAU
KENNEY DAM
NECHAKO
RANGE
BRITISH

CHARLOTTE

MORESBY ISLAND
Mount Kermode
3550
Hecate
Strait
Hartley Bay
PRINCESS
ROYAL
ISLAND
Whitesail
Lake
Eutsuk Lake
Tetachuck
Lake
West Road

ISLANDS
ESTEVAN
GROUP
Mt. Parry
3450
RODERICK
ISLAND
DOLEY
ISLAND
Labou
West

52°
ARISTAZABAL
ISLAND
SWINDLE
ISLAND
RANGES
COLUM
FRAS

CAPE ST. JAMES
Ocean Falls
Bella Coola
Charlotte
Lake
Redstone
Chilcotin

Bella Bella
Monarch Mtn
11590
MOUNTAINS

Queen
Namu
Rivers Inlet
Silverthrone Mtn.
9700
Razorback Mtn.
10432
PACIFIC
Chilko
PLA

Charlotte
CALVERT ISLAND
Mt. Waddington
13163
Mt. Queen Bess
10791
Mt. Tatlow
10058
Chilko
Lake

Sound
CAPE
CAUTION
Good Hope Mtn.
10615
Manmouth Mtn
10480

Bull Harbour
Queen Charlotte Strait
Fitz Hugh Sound
Mt. Gilbert
3109
Br

CAPE SCOTT
Port Hardy
GILFORD
ISLAND
Simood
Sound
RANGES

50°
Quatsino Sound
Port Alice
Kelsey Bay
REDONDA
ISLANDS
Mt. Gran
87

CAPE COOK
VANCOUVER
Victorio Pk.
7095
Bloedel
Campbell
River
Powell River

VANCOUVER
NOOTKA
ISLAND
Golden Hinde
7291
Courtenay
Comox
Vananda
TEXADA
ISLAND
Squamish

Nootka
Sound
ISLAND
Port Alberni
North Vancouver
Vancouver
Burnaby
New West

PACIFIC
Tofino
PACIFIC RIM
NATIONAL PARK
Nanaimo
Ladysmith
Mt. Whymper
5056
Lake Cowichan
SALTSPRING
ISLAND
Sidney

OCEAN
Barkley
Sound
CAPE BEALE
Duncan
Victoria

48°
CAPE FLATTERY
Strait of Juan de Fuca
Esquimalt
Vict

132°
OLYMPIC
NATIONAL
PARK
OLYMPIC
NATIONAL
PARK
Port Angeles

Relief

Meters		Feet
3050		10 000
1525		5000
610		2000
305		1000
152.5		500
0	Sea Level	0
152.5		500
1525		5000

A-520220-76 6-9
COPYRIGHT BY
RAND M^{c}NALLY & COMPANY
MADE IN U.S.A.

130° Continued on pages 114-115 128° Longitude West of Greenwich 126° 124°

Scale 1:4 000 000; one inch to 64 miles. Conic Projection
Elevations and depressions are given in feet.

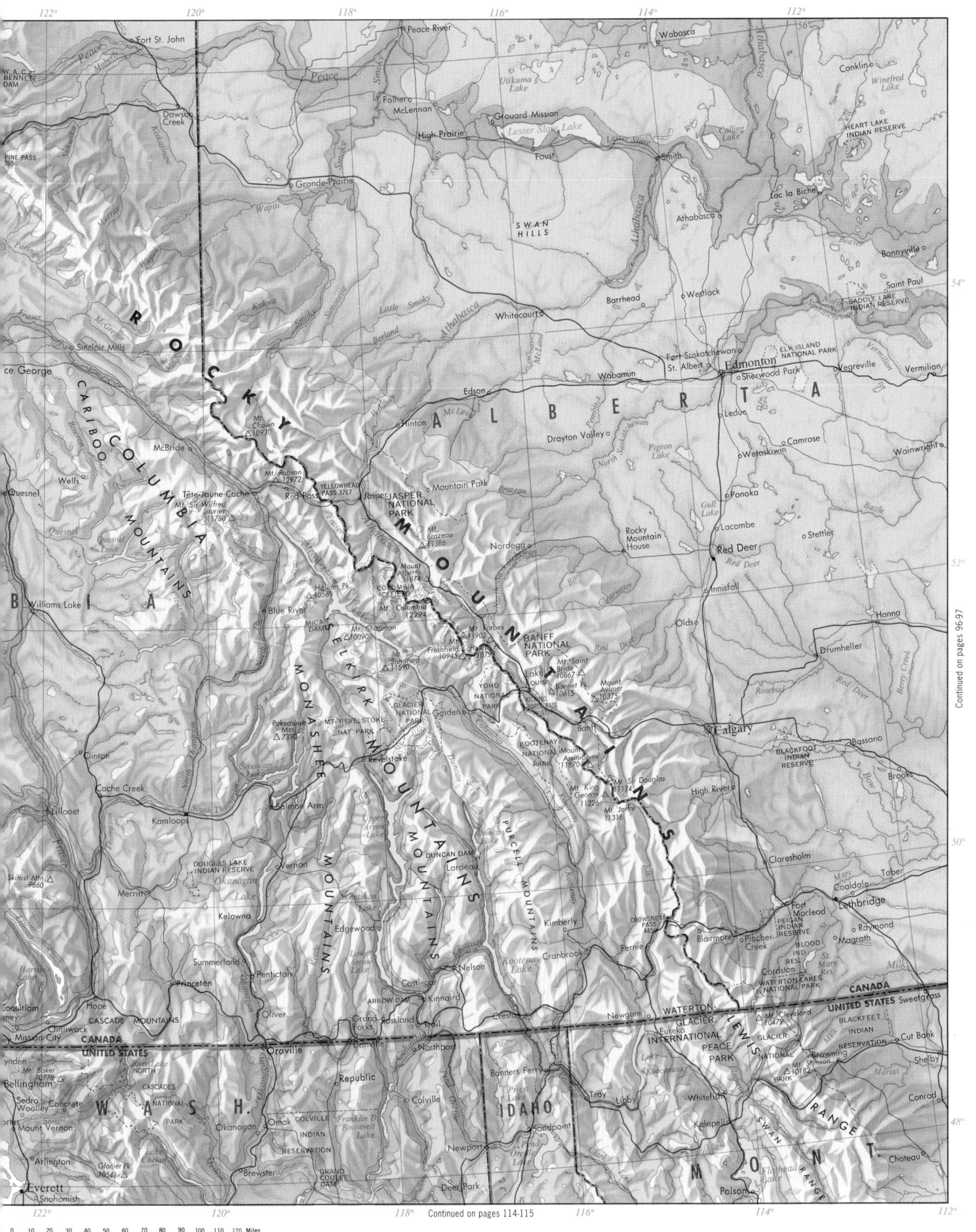

Continued on pages 96-97

Continued on pages 114-115

0 10 20 30 40 50 60 70 80 90 100 110 120 Miles

0 20 40 60 80 100 120 140 160 180 200 Kilometers

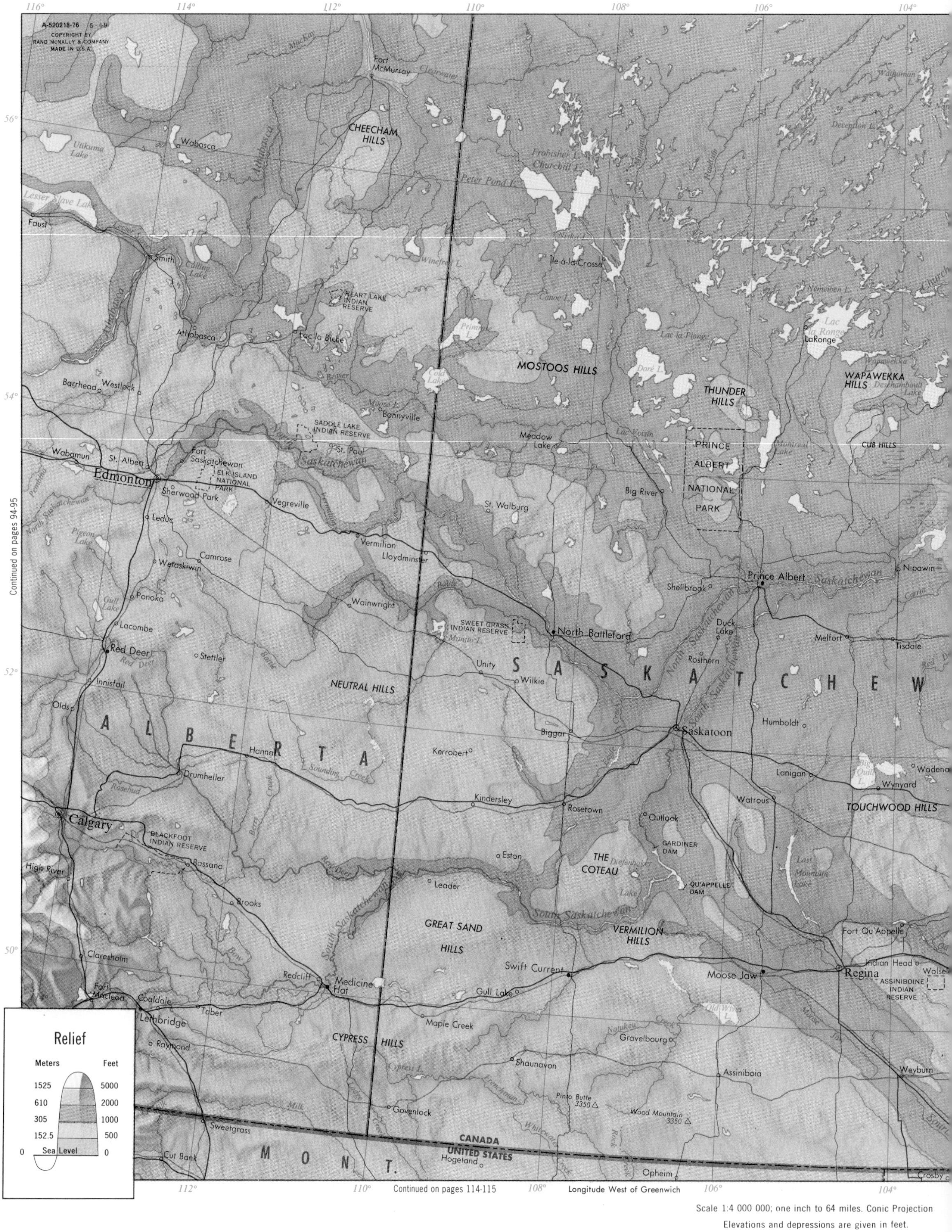

116° 114° 112° 110° 108° 106° 104°

A-520218-76 5-49
COPYRIGHT BY
RAND McNALLY & COMPANY
MADE IN U.S.A.

Fort McMurray
Clearwater

56°

CHEECHAM HILLS

Frobisher L.
Churchill L.

Ulikuma Lake
Wabasca

Peter Pond L.

Deception L.

Athabasca

Lesser Slave Lake

Ile-à-la-Crosse

Faust

Winefred L.

Canoe L.

Nemeiben L.

Smith
Calling Lake

HEART LAKE INDIAN RESERVE

Primrose L.

Lac la Plonge

Lac la Ronge
LaRonge

Athabasca

Lac la Biche

Doré L.

Deschambault Lake

Barrhead Westlock

Beaver

Moose L.

MOSTOOS HILLS

WAPAWEKKA HILLS

54°

Cold L.

Bonnyville

THUNDER HILLS

Wabamun St. Albert
Edmonton

SADDLE LAKE INDIAN RESERVE

St. Paul

North Saskatchewan

Meadow Lake

Lac Voisin

CUB HILLS

Fort Saskatchewan
ELK ISLAND NATIONAL PARK

PRINCE ALBERT NATIONAL PARK

Sherwood Park

Big River

Ledus

Vegreville

Vermilion

St. Walburg

Camrose

Vermilion
Lloydminster

Wetaskiwin

Shellbrook

Prince Albert

Saskatchewan

Nipawin

Pigeon Lake

Battle

Ponoka

Wainwright

SWEET GRASS INDIAN RESERVE

Rosthern

Melfort

Tisdale

Gull Lake

Manito L.

North Battleford

Duck Lake

Lacombe

Red Deer

Stettler

SASKATCHEWAN

52°

Innisfail

Unity
Wilkie

Humboldt

Olds

NEUTRAL HILLS

Biggar

Saskatoon

Hanna

Kerrobert

Lanigan

Wadena

ALBERTA

Drumheller

Sounding Creek

Kindersley

Watrous

Wynyard

Rosebud

Berry Creek

TOUCHWOOD HILLS

Calgary

BLACKFOOT INDIAN RESERVE

Rosetown

Outlook

GARDINER DAM

Last Mountain Lake

Bassano

Eston

THE COTEAU

QU'APPELLE DAM

High River

Red Deer

Leader

Diefenbaker Lake

Fort Qu'Appelle

Brooks

South Saskatchewan

VERMILION HILLS

50°

Claresholm

GREAT SAND HILLS

Swift Current

Moose Jaw

Regina

Walsh

Fort Macleod

Redcliff
Medicine Hat

Gull Lake

ASSINIBOINE INDIAN RESERVE

Coaldale Taber

Maple Creek

Indian Head

Lethbridge

CYPRESS HILLS

Gravelbourg

Raymond

Cypress L.

Shaunavon

Assiniboia

Weyburn

Milk

Govenlock

Pinto Butte 3350 △

Wood Mountain 3350 △

CANADA
UNITED STATES

Sweetgrass

Cut Bank

MONT.

Hogeland

Opheim

Crosby

112° 110° 108° 106° 104°

Continued on pages 94-95

Continued on pages 114-115

Longitude West of Greenwich

Relief

Meters		Feet
1525		5000
610		2000
305		1000
152.5		500
0	Sea Level	0

Scale 1:4 000 000; one inch to 64 miles. Conic Projection
Elevations and depressions are given in feet.

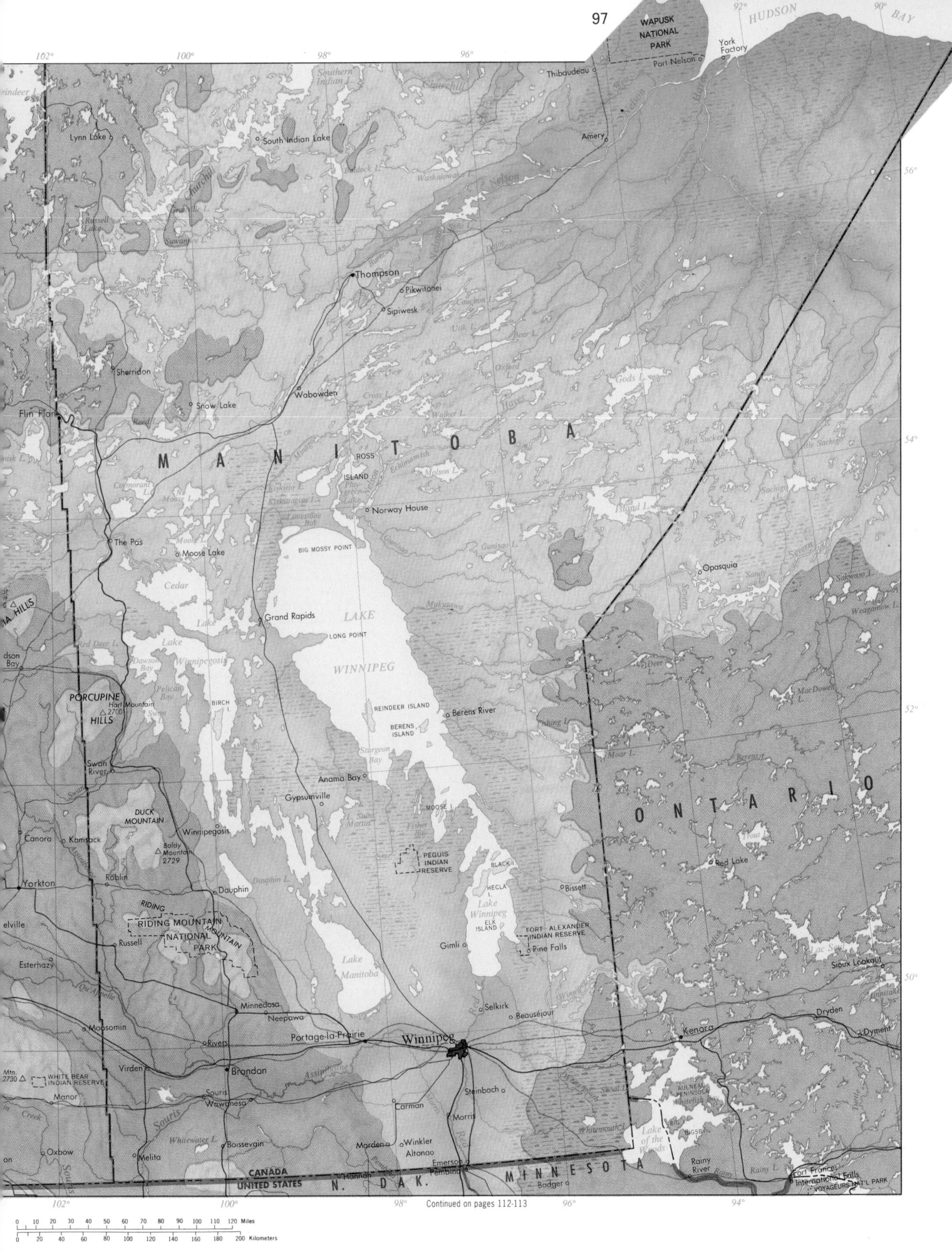

HUDSON BAY

WAPUSK NATIONAL PARK

York Factory

Thibadeau
Port Nelson

Amery

56°

Lynn Lake

South Indian Lake

Nelson

Thompson
Pikwitonei
Sipiwesk

Bear L.

Caughon

Oxford L.

Gods L.

54°

Sherridon

Wabowden
Snow Lake

Cross L.

Walker L.

Hayes

Red Sucker L.

Echimamish

M A N I T O B A

Flin Flon

ROSS ISLAND

Molson L.

Island L.

Norway House

Gods L.

O N T A R I O

The Pas

Moose Lake

BIG MOSSY POINT

Opasquia

Sandy

Cedar

Grand Rapids

LAKE

LONG POINT

Guniso L.

Mykumata

MacDowell L.

Winnipegosis

WINNIPEG

PORCUPINE HILLS

Hart Mountain
2700

Pelican Bay

BIRCH

REINDEER ISLAND

Berens River

Fishing L.

Berens I.

52°

Swan River

BERENS ISLAND

Moar L.

Sturgeon Bay

DUCK MOUNTAIN

Winnipegosis

Anama Bay

MOOSE I.

Trout L.

Canora
Kamsack

Baldy Mountain
2729

Gypsumville

Saint Martin

PEGUIS INDIAN RESERVE

Yorkton
Roblin

Dauphin L.

Dauphin

BLACK I.

Red Lake

Esterhazy

RIDING

RIDING MOUNTAIN
NATIONAL PARK

MOUNTAIN

HECLA I.

Lake Winnipeg

ELK ISLAND

Bissett

50°

Russell

Lake Manitoba

FORT ALEXANDER INDIAN RESERVE

Pine Falls

Sioux Lookout

Gimli

Minnedosa

Neepawa

Selkirk

Beauséjour

Dryden

Moosomin
Rivers

Portage-la-Prairie

Winnipeg

Kenora

Dyment

Virden

Brandon

Assiniboine

Mtn. 2730
WHITE BEAR INDIAN RESERVE

Steinbach

AULNEAU PENINSULA

Manor

Souris
Wawanesa

Carman

Lake of the Woods

Oxbow

Boissevain

Whitewater L.

Morden
Winkler
Altona

Whitemouth

Rainy River

Melita

Morris

CANADA
UNITED STATES

Emerson
Pembina

N. DAK.

Hannah

Badger

MINNESOTA

Rainy L.

Fort Frances
International Falls
VOYAGEURS NAT'L PARK

Continued on pages 112-113

102°   100°   98°   96°   94°

0 10 20 30 40 50 60 70 80 90 100 110 120 Miles
0 20 40 60 80 100 120 140 160 180 200 Kilometers

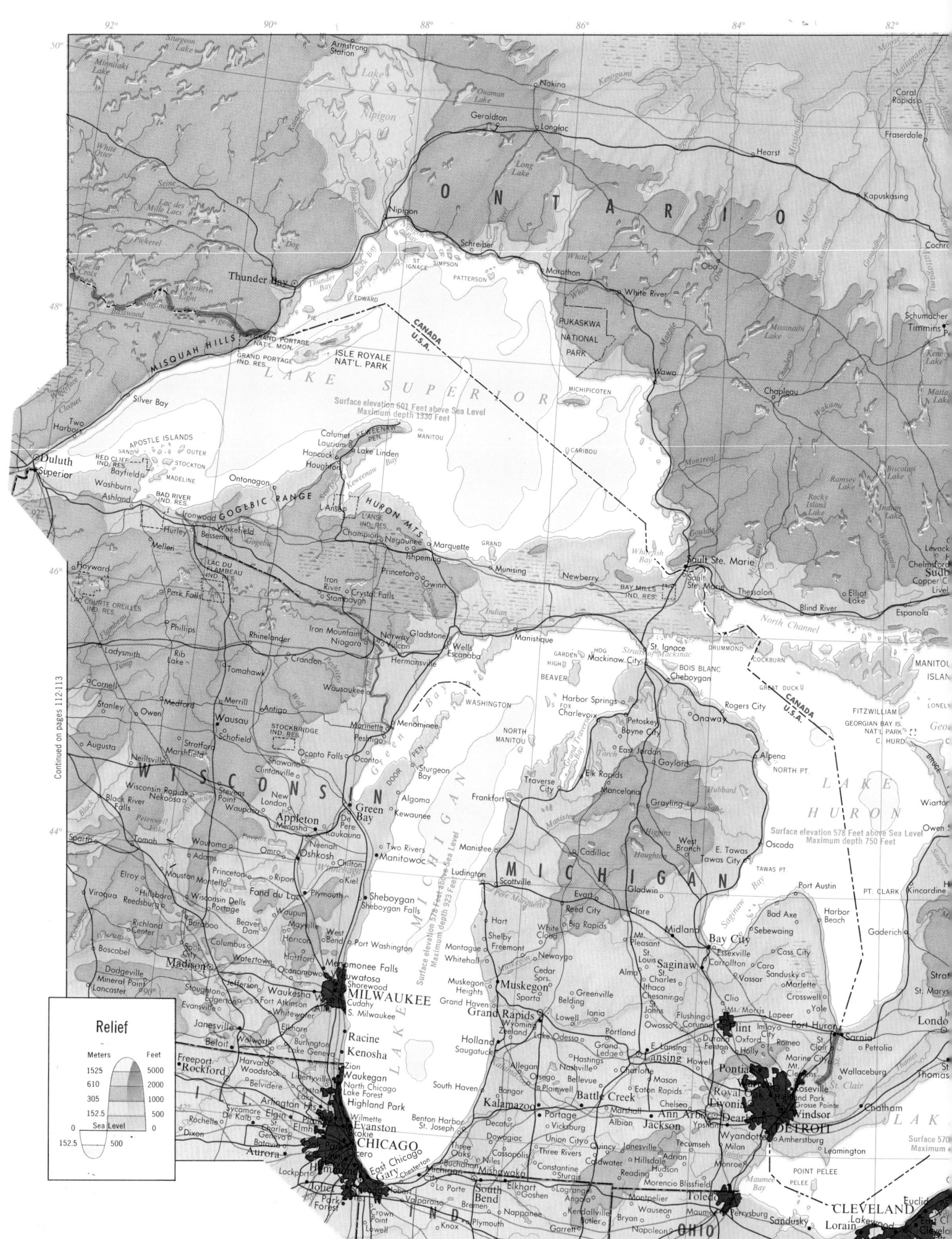

Continued on pages 112-113

Relief

Meters		Feet
1525		5000
610		2000
305		1000
152.5		500
0	Sea Level	0
152.5		500

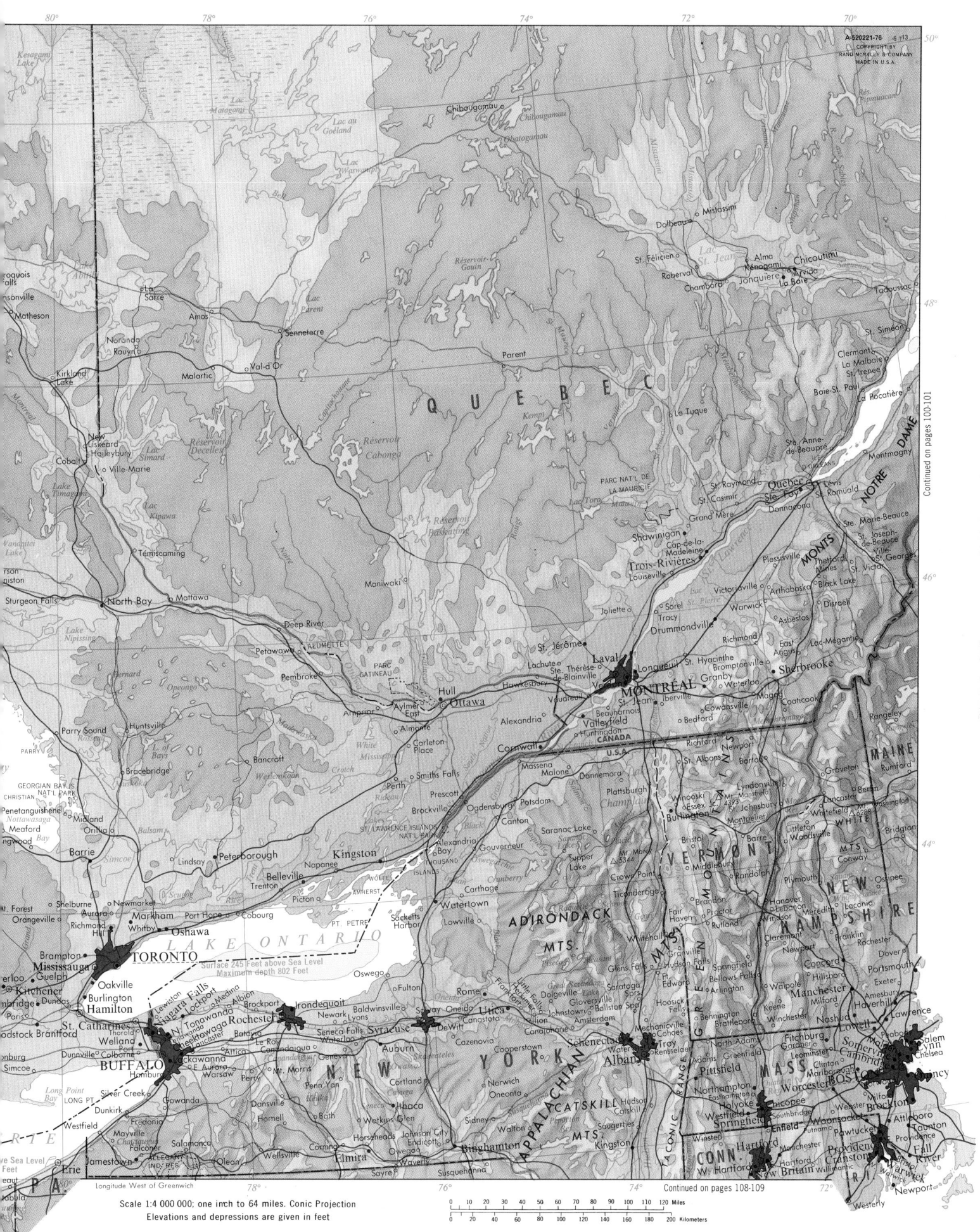

Scale 1:4 000 000; one inch to 64 miles. Conic Projection
Elevations and depressions are given in feet

Continued on pages 100-101

Continued on pages 108-109

Longitude West of Greenwich

Continued on pages 98-99

Continued on pages 108-109

Longitude West of Greenwich

Scale 1:4 000 000; one inch to 64 miles. Conic Projection
Elevations and depressions are given in feet.

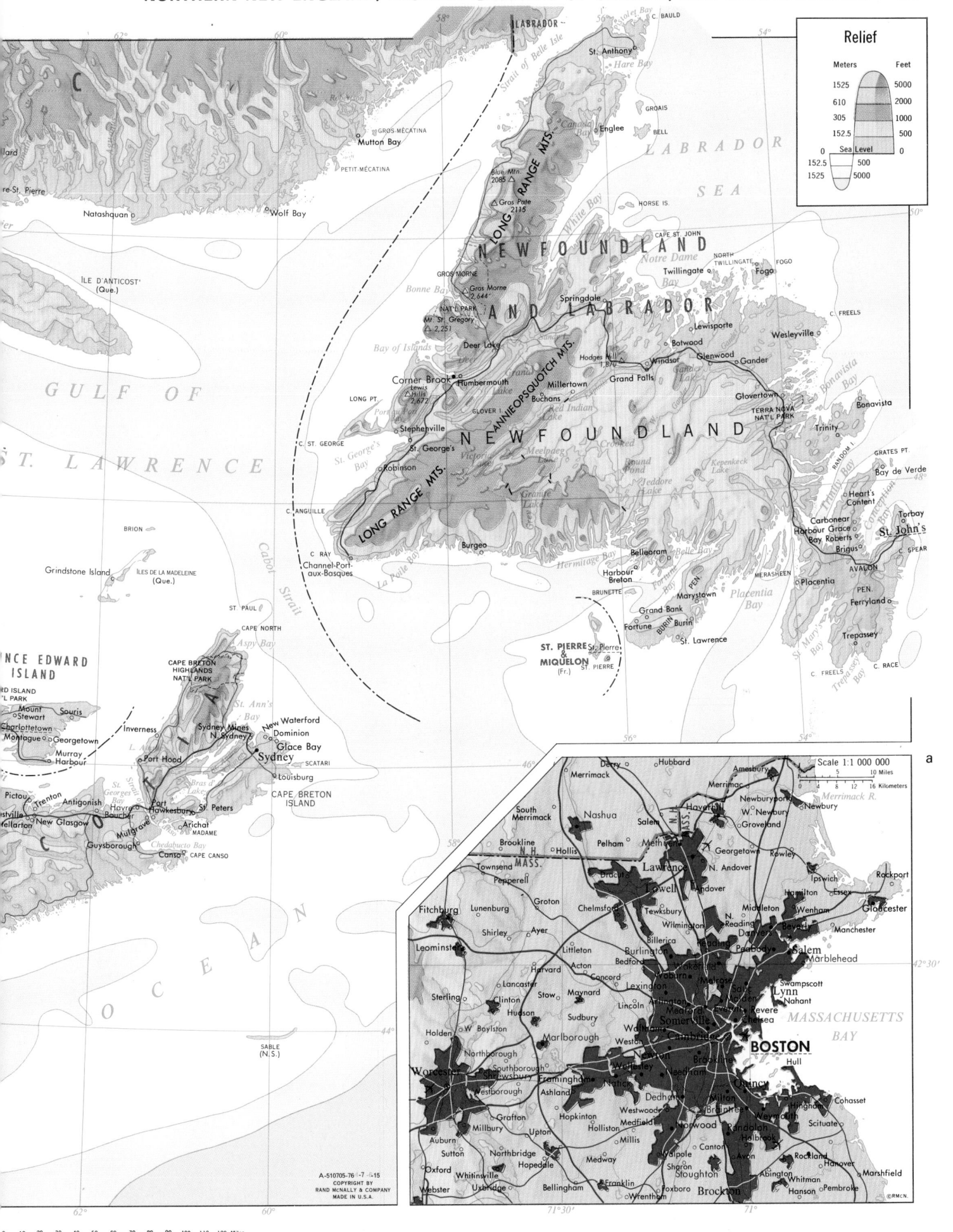

a — MONTRÉAL

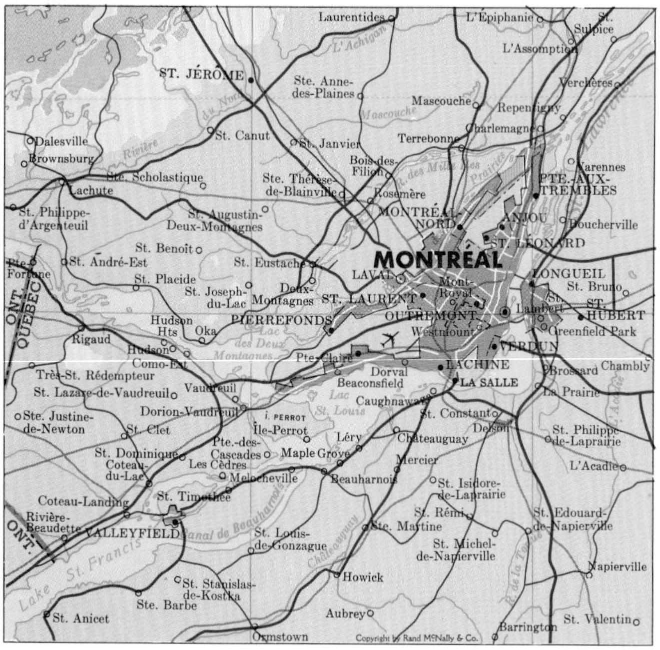

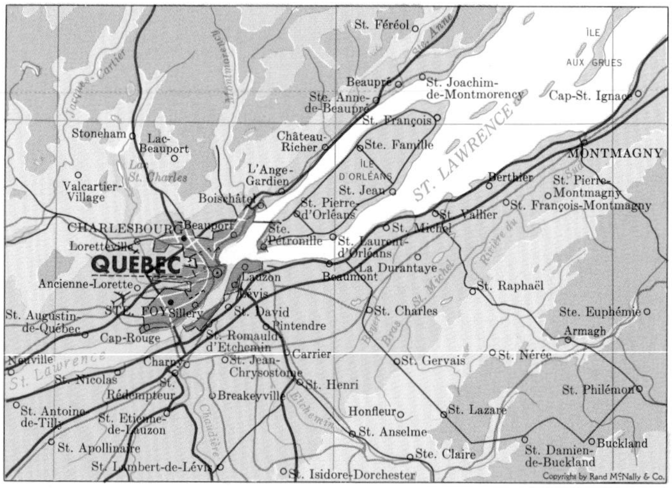

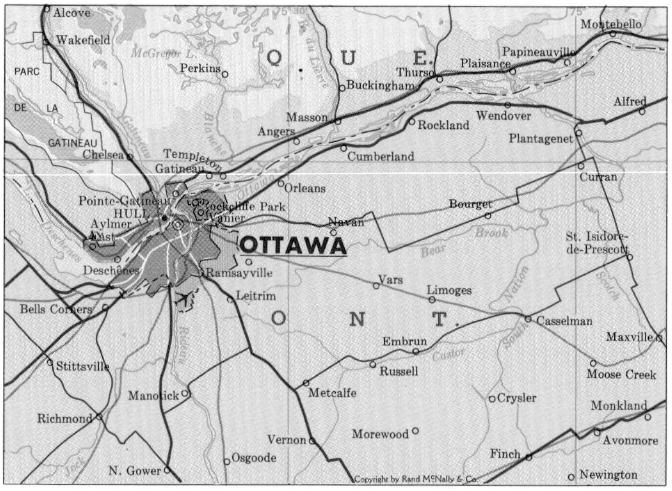

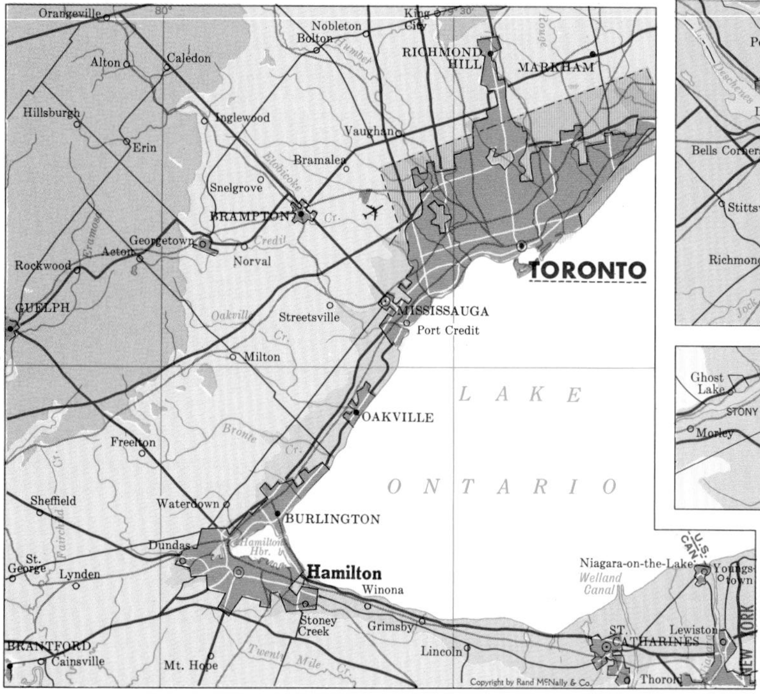

b — QUÉBEC

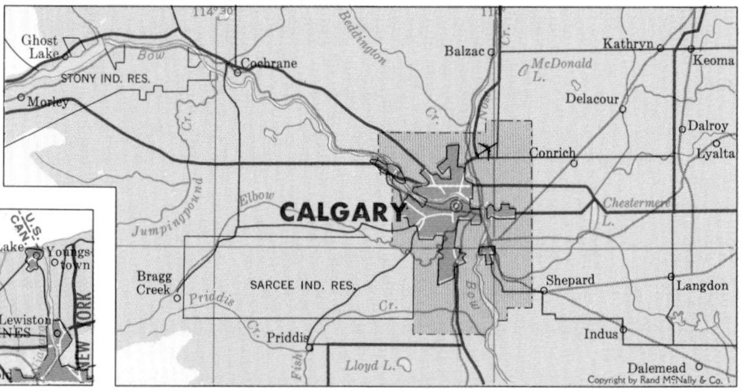

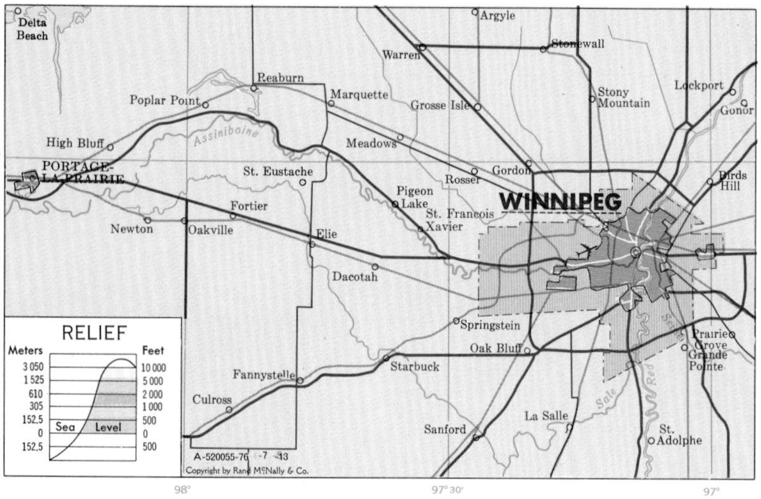

c — OTTAWA

d — TORONTO

e — CALGARY

f — WINNIPEG

g — EDMONTON

RELIEF

Meters		Feet
3 050		10 000
1 525		5 000
610		2 000
305		1 000
152.5		500
0	Sea Level	0
152.5		500

A-520055-76 -7 -43

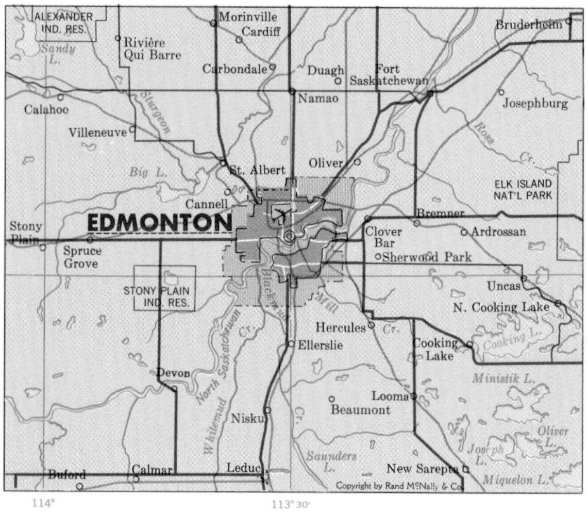

Scale 1:1 000 000; One inch to 16 miles.
Elevations and depressions are given in feet.

Miles: 0 2 4 6 8 10 12 14 16 18 20 22 24
Kilometers: 0 4 8 12 16 20 24 28 32 36 40

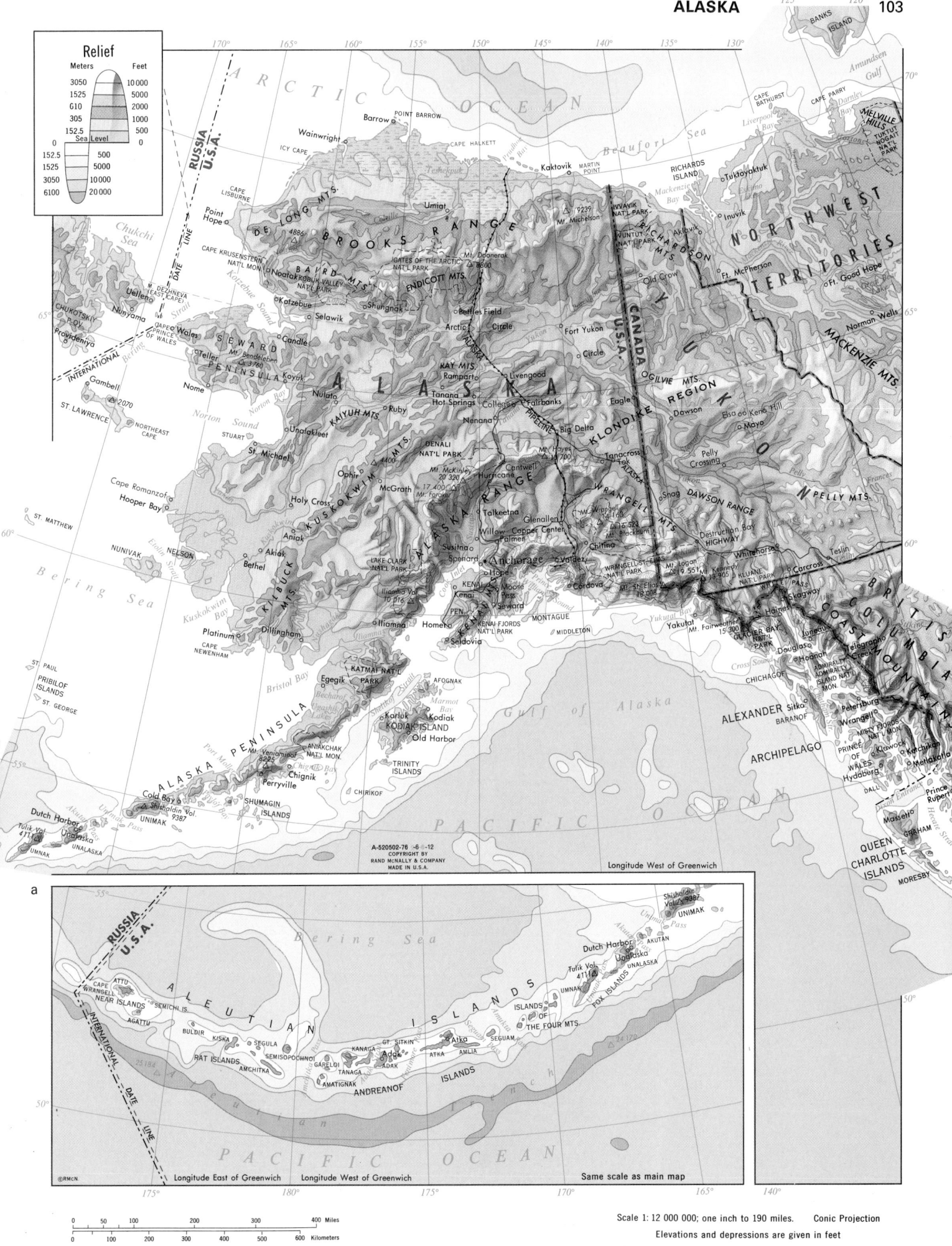

Relief

Meters	Feet
3050	10 000
1525	5000
610	2000
305	1000
152.5	500
Sea Level	0
152.5	500
1525	5000
3050	10 000
6100	20 000

ARCTIC OCEAN

Beaufort Sea

RUSSIA
U.S.A.

DATE LINE

Barrow
POINT BARROW
Wainwright
ICY CAPE
CAPE HALKETT
Kaktovik
MARTIN POINT
Prudhoe Bay
Umiat
Teshekpuk

CAPE LISBURNE
DE LONG MTS.
4886
BROOKS RANGE
Mt. Michelson 9239
IVVAVIK NAT'L PARK
RICHARDS ISLAND
CAPE BATHURST
CAPE PARRY
Darnley Bay
Amundsen Gulf

Point Hope
CAPE KRUSENSTERN NAT'L MON.
BAIRD MTS.
GATES OF THE ARCTIC NAT'L PARK
Mt. Doonerak 7760
Mt. Igikpak 8800
ENDICOTT MTS.
VUNTUT NAT'L PARK
RICHARDSON MTS.
AKLAVIK
Inuvik
Tuktoyaktuk
MELVILLE HILLS
TUKTUT NOGAIT NAT'L PARK

Chukchi Sea
M. DEZHNEVA
EAST CAPE
CHUKOTSKIY PEN.
Uelleno
Ninyama
Providenjya
NOATAK NAT'L PARK
KOBUK VALLEY NAT'L PARK
Shungnak
Bettles Field
Old Crow
Ft. McPherson
Ft. Good Hope
NORTHWEST TERRITORIES

Gambell
Wales
CAPE PRINCE OF WALES
Kotzebue
Selawik
Arctic
Circle
Fort Yukon
Circle
Eagle
Dawson
MACKENZIE MTS.
Norman Wells

ST. LAWRENCE
2070
NORTHEAST CAPE
SEWARD PENINSULA
Mt. Bendeleben 3786
Teller
Candle
Koyuk
Nome
ALASKA
Rampart
Livengood
OGILVIE MTS.
KLONDIKE REGION
Elsa Keno Hill
Mayo

INTERNATIONAL
Bering Strait
Nulato
Ruby
Tanana
Hot Springs
College Fairbanks
Big Delta
Pelly Crossing

ST. MATTHEW
Stuart
St. Michael
KAIYUH MTS.
Nenana
PIPELINE
Mt. Hayes 13 700
Tanacross
Tok
YUKON
DAWSON RANGE

Cape Romanzof
Hooper Bay
Unalakleet
Ophir
McGrath
DENALI NAT'L PARK
4400
Cantwell
Hurricane
Glennallen
Copper Center
Mt. Wrangell 14 163
Mt. Blackburn
Mt. Sanford
Snag
Destruction Bay
HIGHWAY
Whitehorse
Teslin

NUNIVAK
NELSON
Akiak
Bethel
Holy Cross
Anvik
ALASKA RANGE
Mt. McKinley 20 320
17 400
Mt. Foraker
Talkeetna
Willow
Palmer
Chitina
WRANGELL-ST. ELIAS NAT'L PARK
Mt. Logan 19 551
Mt. Kennedy 16 905
KLUANE NAT'L PARK
Carcross
Skagway

Bering Sea
Kuskokwim Bay
KILBUCK MTS.
LAKE CLARK NAT'L PARK
Iliamna Vol. 10 016
KUSKOKWIM MTS.
Susitna
Spenard
Anchorage
Hope
Valdez
Mt. St. Elias 18 008
Mt. Fairweather 15 300
Haines
GLACIER BAY NAT'L PARK
Juneau
Douglas
COAST MOUNTAINS
BRITISH COLUMBIA

ST. PAUL
PRIBILOF ISLANDS
ST. GEORGE
Platinum
CAPE NEWENHAM
Dillingham
Iliamna
KENAI NAT'L PARK
Kenai
Moose Pass
Seward
PEN.
KENAI FJORDS NAT'L PARK
Cordova
MONTAGUE
Yakutat
Hoonar
ADMIRALTY ISLAND NAT'L MON.
Sitka
BARANOF
Petersburg
MISTY FJORDS NAT'L MON.
Wrangell

Homer
Seldovia
Prince William Sound
MIDDLETON
Cross Sound
CHICHAGOF
ALEXANDER
ARCHIPELAGO
PRINCE OF WALES
Klawock
Hydaburg
Ketchikan
Metlakatla
Prince Rupert
Dixon Entrance

KATMAI NAT'L PARK
Egegik
AFOGNAK
Marmot Bay
Karluk
Kodiak
Old Harbor
Gulf of Alaska
DALL
Masset
GRAHAM
QUEEN CHARLOTTE ISLANDS
MORESBY

ALASKA PENINSULA
Mt. Veniaminof 8225
ANIAKCHAK NAT'L MON.
KODIAK ISLAND
TRINITY ISLANDS
CHIRIKOF

Cold Bay
Shishaldin Vol. 9387
UNIMAK
Perryville
Chignik
SHUMAGIN ISLANDS

Dutch Harbor
Unalaska
UNALASKA
Tulik Vol. 4111
UMNAK

PACIFIC OCEAN

Longitude West of Greenwich

a

RUSSIA
U.S.A.
Bering Sea
CAPE WRANGELL
ATTU
NEAR ISLANDS
SEMICHI IS.
AGATTU
ALEUTIAN ISLANDS
Shishaldin Vol. 9387
UNIMAK
Akutan
Dutch Harbor Unalaska
UNALASKA
Tulik Vol. 4111
UMNAK
FOX ISLANDS
Unimak Pass

INTERNATIONAL DATE LINE
25 184
BULDIR
KISKA
SEGULA
SEMISOPOCHNOI
RAT ISLANDS
AMCHITKA
GARELOI
TANAGA
AMATIGNAK
KANAGA
GT. SITKIN
Adak
ATKA
AMLIA
SEGUAM
ISLANDS OF THE FOUR MTS.
24 170
ANDREANOF ISLANDS
ISLANDS

PACIFIC OCEAN

Longitude East of Greenwich | Longitude West of Greenwich | Same scale as main map

0 50 100 200 300 400 Miles
0 100 200 300 400 500 600 Kilometers

Scale 1: 12 000 000; one inch to 190 miles.   Conic Projection

Elevations and depressions are given in feet

Continued on pages 90-91

a

ARCTIC OCEAN

RUSSIA

C. LISBURNE

Barrow

Umiat

Kotzebue

ST. LAWRENCE

Nome

BROOKS RANGE

Ft. Yukon

Inuvik

Circle

ALASKA

DENALI NAT'L PARK

Fairbanks

Dawson

NORTHWEST TERR.

CANADA

Ruby

Circle

McGrath

Mt. McKinley 20,320

Burwash Landing

YUKON

Watson Lake

Bethel

NUNIVAK

Anchorage

Cordova

Whitehorse

Skagway

BRITISH COLUMBIA

Dillingham

Seward

Juneau

Wrangell

KATMAI NAT'L PARK

GLACIER BAY NAT'L PARK

Sitka

Ketchikan

Kodiak

Prince Rupert

QUEEN CHARLOTTE IS.

PACIFIC OCEAN

Dutch Harbor

b

Scale 1: 36 000 000

ATTU

ALEUTIAN IS.

Dutch Harbor

UNALASKA

UMNAK

KISKA

ANDREANOF IS.

ATKA

Scale 1: 36 000 000

One inch to 570 miles

©RMCN.

c

Longitude West of Greenwich

NI'IHAU

KAUA'I

Lihue

HAWAIIAN IS.

O'AHU

Kailua

PACIFIC

Honolulu

MOLOKA'I

Wailuku

Kahului

LANA'I

KAHO'OLAWE

MAUI

OCEAN

HAWAII

HAWAI'I

Mauna Kea 13 796

Hilo

Mauna Loa 13 680

HAWAII VOLCANOES NAT'L PARK

Same scale as main map

d

Scale 1: 3 400 000

KAHUKU PT.

O'AHU

Kahuku

KA'ENA PT.

Wahiawā

Waipahu

Kailua

Honolulu

Pearl Harbor

©RMCN.

Scale 1:12 000 000; one inch to 190 miles. Polyconic Projection

Elevations and depressions are given in feet

Longitude West of Greenwich

Cities and Towns

0 to 50,000 ◦   500,000 to 1,000,000 ⦾

50,000 to 500,000 ⊙   1,000,000 and over

40,000 SQ MI AREA

0   100   200

Miles

Continued on pages 92-93

a

b Scale 1: 36 000 000

Scale 1: 36 000 000
One inch to 570 miles

c Longitude West of Greenwich

d Scale 1: 3 400 000

Same scale as main map

A-520500-76 -8 ·21
COPYRIGHT BY
RAND McNALLY & COMPANY
MADE IN U.S.A.

Longitude West of Greenwich

Scale 1:12 000 000; one inch to 190 miles. Polyconic Projection
Elevations and depressions are given in feet

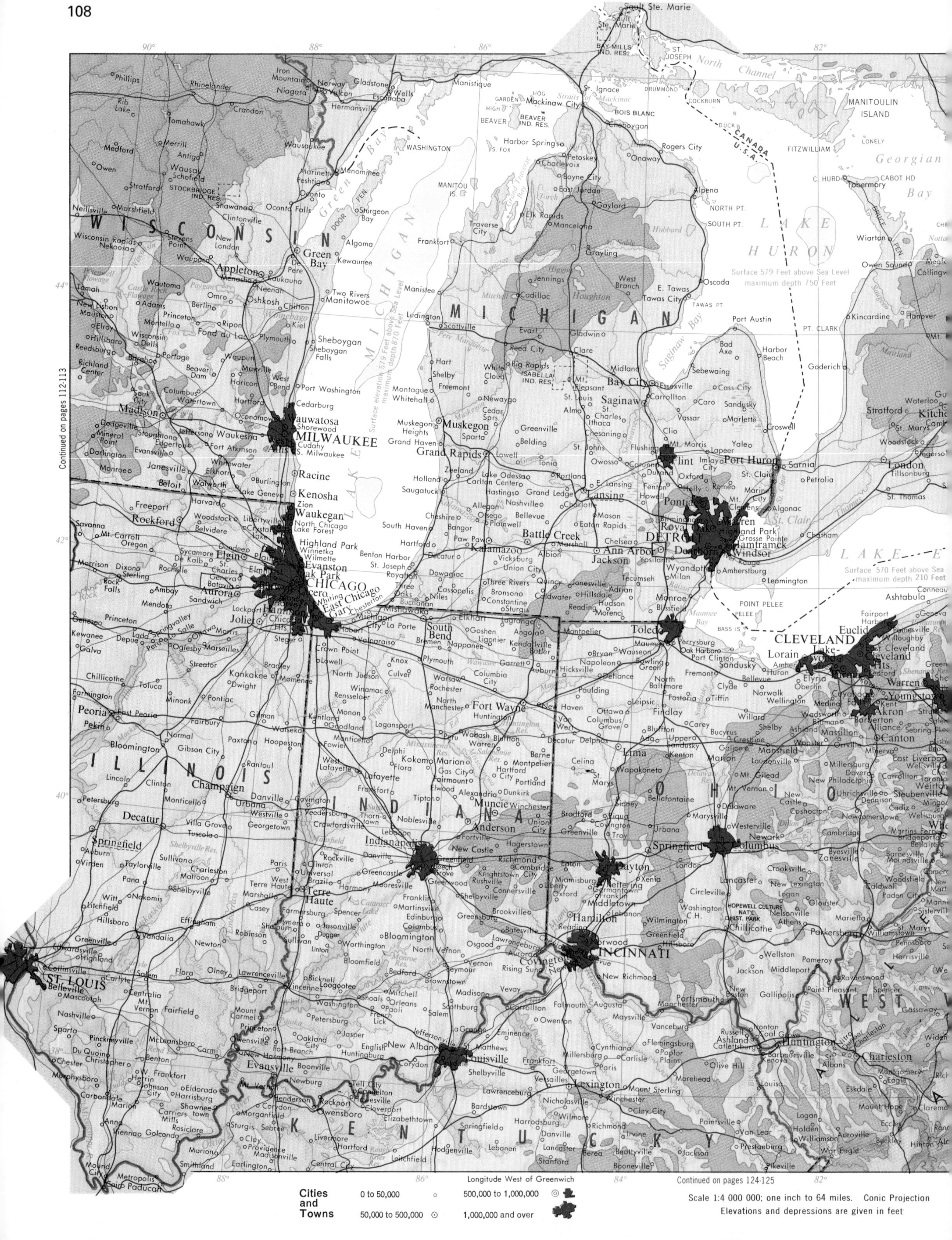

WISCONSIN
MICHIGAN
ILLINOIS
INDIANA
OHIO
KENTUCKY
WEST
LAKE MICHIGAN
Surface elevation 579 Feet above Sea Level maximum depth 870 Feet
LAKE HURON
Surface 579 Feet above Sea Level
maximum depth 750 Feet
LAKE ERIE
Surface 570 Feet above Sea
maximum depth 210 Feet
Georgian Bay
Saginaw Bay
Green Bay
North Channel
Straits of Mackinac
CANADA
U.S.A.
MANITOULIN ISLAND
Sault Ste. Marie
CHICAGO
MILWAUKEE
DETROIT
CLEVELAND
CINCINNATI
ST. LOUIS
Madison
Green Bay
Grand Rapids
Lansing
Flint
Toledo
Fort Wayne
Indianapolis
Columbus
Dayton
Louisville
Lexington
Evansville
Springfield
Peoria
Rockford
Kalamazoo
Saginaw
Bay City
Muskegon
South Bend
Gary
Akron
Youngstown
Canton
Windsor
London
Huntington
Charleston
Terre Haute
Champaign
Decatur
Muncie
Anderson
Racine
Kenosha
Waukegan
Evanston
Joliet
Aurora
Elgin
Appleton
Oshkosh
Sheboygan
Traverse City
Cadillac
Ann Arbor
Jackson
Battle Creek
Port Huron
Sarnia
Pontiac
Hamtramck
Lima
Mansfield
Hamilton
Covington
90°
88°
86°
84°
82°
44°
42°
40°
38°
Longitude West of Greenwich

Continued on pages 112-113

Continued on pages 124-125

Cities and Towns

0 to 50,000	○	500,000 to 1,000,000	◎
50,000 to 500,000	⊙	1,000,000 and over	

Scale 1:4 000 000; one inch to 64 miles. Conic Projection

Elevations and depressions are given in feet

Continued on pages 98-99

Relief

Meters		Feet
1525		5000
610		2000
305		1000
152.5		500
0	Sea Level	0
152.5		500
1525		5000
3050		10 000

A-520596-76- 5-13
COPYRIGHT BY
RAND McNALLY & COMPANY
MADE IN U.S.A.

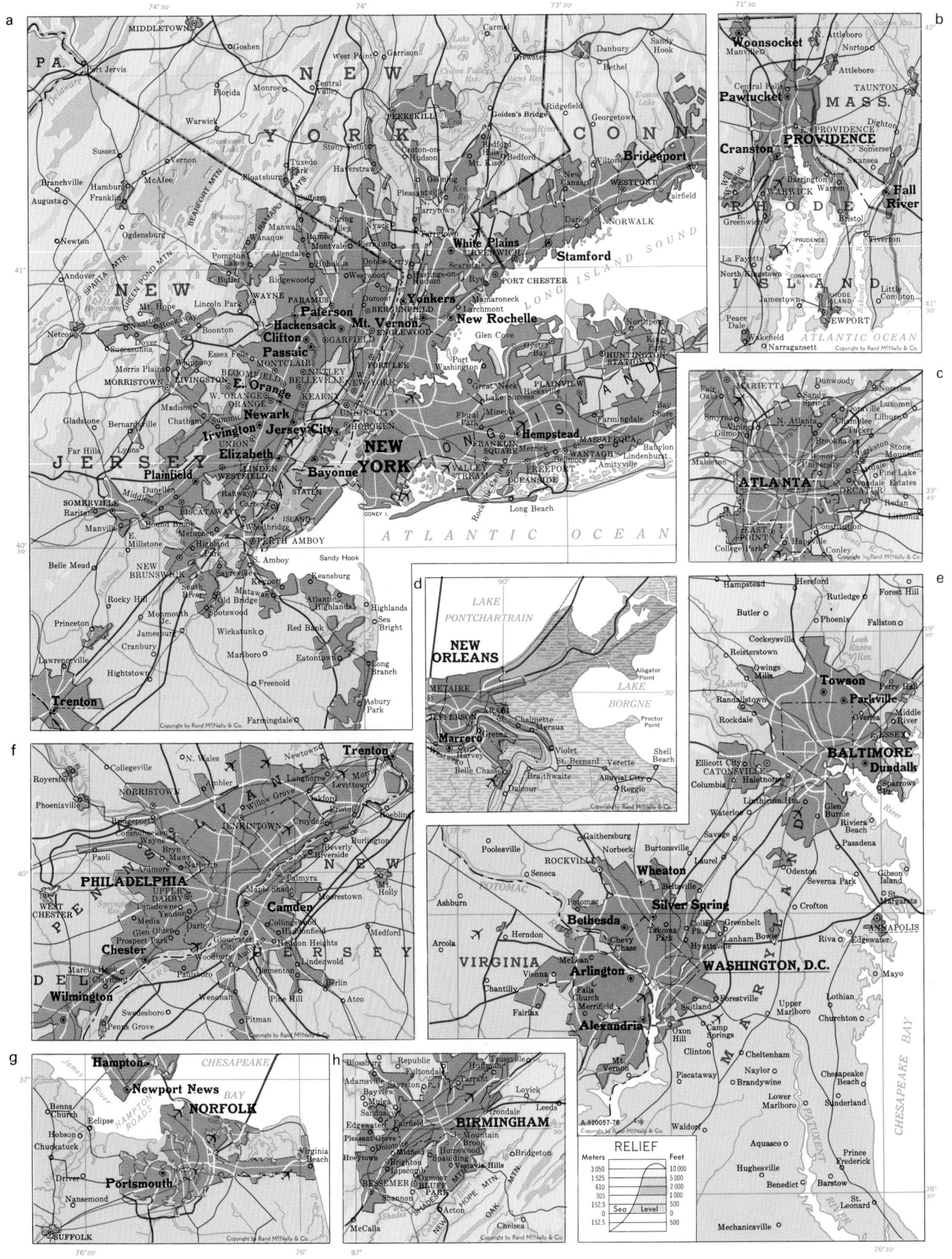

a

PA.

MIDDLETOWN

NEW YORK

Goshen
West Point
Garrison
Carmel
Danbury
Sandy
Hook
Bethel
CONN

Port Jervis
Florida
Monroe
Central
Valley
Brewster
Ridgefield
Georgetown

Warwick
Tuxedo
Park
PEEKSKILL
Golden's
Bridge
Wilton
Bridgeport

Sussex
Vernon
McAfee
Sloatsburg
Croton-on-Hudson
New Canaan
WESTPORT
Fairfield

Branchville
Hamburg
Franklin
Suffern
Spring
Valley
Ossining
Pleasantville
Tarrytown
Darien
NORWALK

Augusta
Ogdensburg
Pompton
Lakes
Nyack
White Plains
GREENWICH
Stamford

Newton
Andover
Pompton
Dobbs
Ferry
Scarsdale
PORT CHESTER

NEW
Butler
Ridgewood
Yonkers
Rye
LONG ISLAND SOUND

Paterson
PARAMUS
Mt. Vernon
New Rochelle
Northport

Hackensack
ENGLEWOOD
Glen Cove
Oyster
Bay

Clifton
GARFIELD
FORT LEE
Port
Washington
Great Neck
PLAINVIEW
Babylon

Passaic
NUTLEY
NEW YORK
Hicksville
Bay
Shore

MORRISTOWN
BLOOMFIELD
BELLEVILLE
Lake
Success
Farmingdale

E. Orange
KEARNY
Mineola
Hempstead
MASSAPEQUA

Newark
UNION CITY
HOBOKEN
Floral
Park
FRANKLIN
SQUARE
Merrick
WANTAGH
Lindenhurst

JERSEY
Irvington
Jersey City
LONG ISLAND
FREEPORT
Amityville

Union
Elizabeth
VALLEY
STREAM
OCEANSIDE

Plainfield
Bayonne
STATEN
ISLAND
Long Beach

SOMERVILLE
Rahway
CONEY I.
ATLANTIC OCEAN

NEW
BRUNSWICK
PERTH AMBOY
Sandy Hook

Princeton
Highlands
Sea
Bright

Trenton
Freehold
Long
Branch

Farmingdale
Asbury
Park

b

Woonsocket
Attleboro
Norton

Pawtucket
Central Falls
TAUNTON
MASS.

Cranston
PROVIDENCE
E. PROVIDENCE
Somerset
Fall
River

RHODE
WARWICK
Warren
Bristol
Tiverton

Jamestown
ISLAND
NEWPORT
Little
Compton

Narragansett
ATLANTIC OCEAN

c

MARIETTA
Dunwoody
Norcross

Smyrna
N. Atlanta
Chamblee
Tucker

Mableton
ATLANTA
DECATUR
Stone
Mountain

EAST
POINT
Conley
Lithonia

College Park

d

LAKE
PONTCHARTRAIN

NEW
ORLEANS

METAIRE
Alligator
Point

JEFFERSON
Chalmette
LAKE
BORGNE

Marrero
Meraux

Harvey
St. Bernard
Shell
Beach

Belle Chasse
Braithwaite

Daleour
Reggio

e

Hampstead
Hereford
Forest
Hill

Butler
Rutledge
Phoenix
Fallston

Cockeysville
Reisterstown
Owings
Mills
Towson
Parkville

Randallstown
BALTIMORE
Dundalk

Rockdale
Ellicott City
CATONSVILLE
Glen
Burnie
Essex

Columbia
Waterloo
Sparrows
Pt.

ANNAPOLIS

f

N. Wales
Newtown
Trenton

Royersford
Collegeville
Langhorne
Levittown

Phoenixville
NORRISTOWN
Ambler
Willow
Grove

Paoli
JENKINTOWN
Croydon
Burlington

PHILADELPHIA
UPPER
DARBY
Palmyra
Mt.
Holly

WEST
CHESTER
Camden
Maple Shade
Moorestown

Chester
Collingswood
Medford

Wilmington
Haddonfield
Berlin

Pitman

g

Hampton
CHESAPEAKE

Newport News
BAY

NORFOLK

Portsmouth
Virginia
Beach

SUFFOLK

h

Blossburg
Republic
Trussville

Adamsville
Fultondale
Huffman

BIRMINGHAM
Leeds

BESSEMER
Chelsea

McCalla

ROCKVILLE
Gaithersburg
Norbeck
Laurel

Poolesville
Wheaton
Beltsville

Seneca
Silver Spring
Greenbelt

POTOMAC
Bethesda
Takoma
Park
Lanham

Ashburn
Herndon
Chevy
Chase
Hyattsville

VIRGINIA
Arlington
WASHINGTON, D.C.

Fairfax
Falls
Church
Annandale

Alexandria
Oxon
Hill

Mt.
Vernon
Clinton
Waldorf

RELIEF

Meters		Feet
3 050		10 000
1 525		5 000
610		2 000
305		1 000
152.5		500
Sea	Level	0
152.5		500

Miles
0 2 4 6 8 10 12 14 16 18 20 22 24

Kilometers
0 4 8 12 16 20 24 28 32 36 40

Scale 1:1 000 000; One inch to 16 miles.
Elevations and depressions are given in feet.

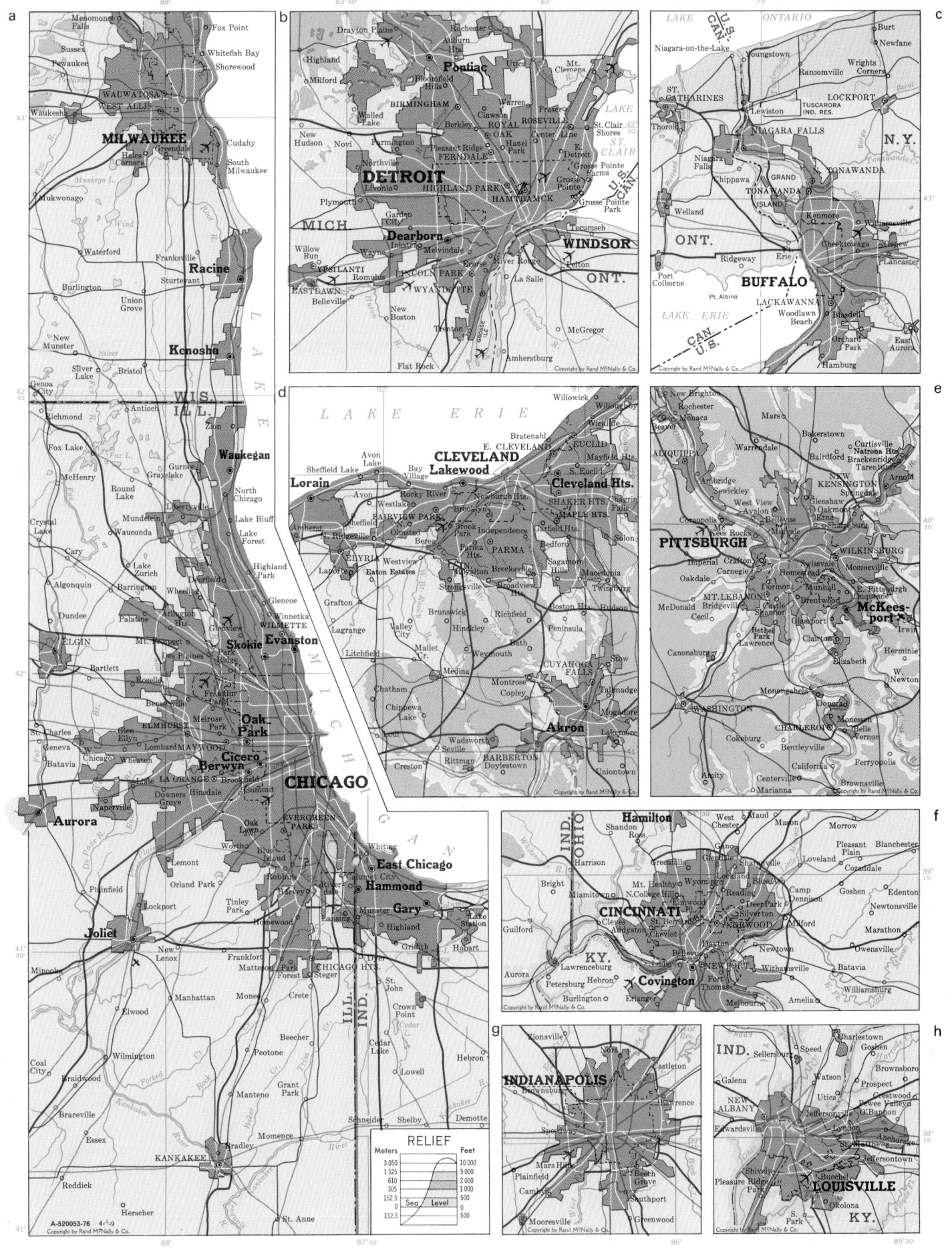

RELIEF

Meters		Feet
3 050		10 000
1 525		5 000
610		2 000
305		1 000
152.5		500
0	Sea Level	0
152.5		500

Scale 1:1 000 000; One inch to 16 miles.
Elevations and depressions are given in feet.

0 2 4 6 8 10 12 14 16 18 20 22 24 Miles
0 4 8 12 16 20 24 28 32 36 40 Kilometers

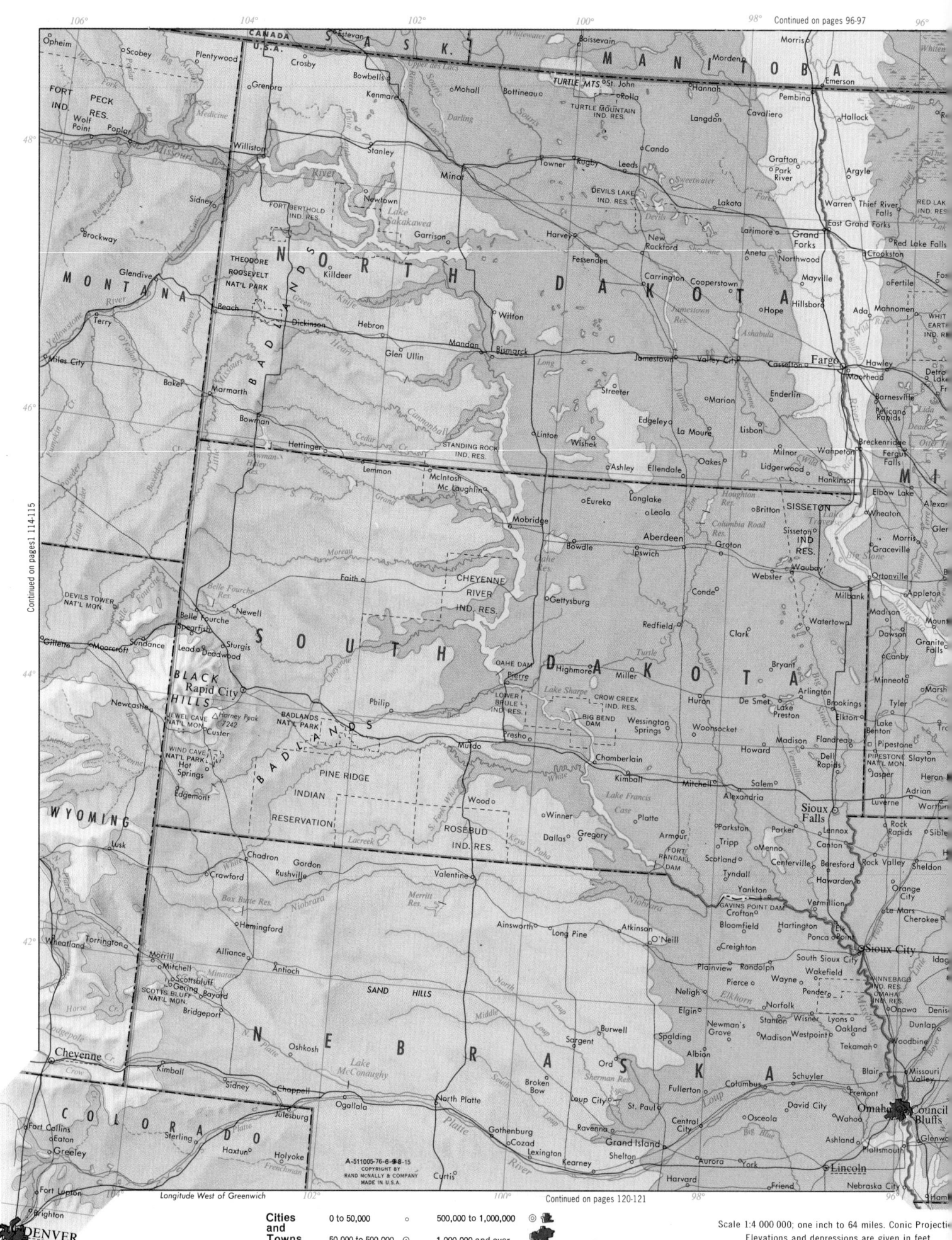

Continued on pages 96-97

Continued on pages 114-115

Continued on pages 120-121

106° 104° 102° 100° 98° 96°

CANADA
U.S.A.
S A S K. M A N I T O B A

M O N T A N A

N O R T H   D A K O T A

S O U T H   D A K O T A

W Y O M I N G

N E B R A S K A

C O L O R A D O

48° 46° 44° 42° 40°

Longitude West of Greenwich

A-511005-76-6-98-15
COPYRIGHT BY
RAND McNALLY & COMPANY
MADE IN U.S.A.

DENVER

Cities and Towns

| | 0 to 50,000 | ○ | 500,000 to 1,000,000 | ◉ |
| | 50,000 to 500,000 | ⊙ | 1,000,000 and over | |

Scale 1:4 000 000; one inch to 64 miles. Conic Projection
Elevations and depressions are given in feet

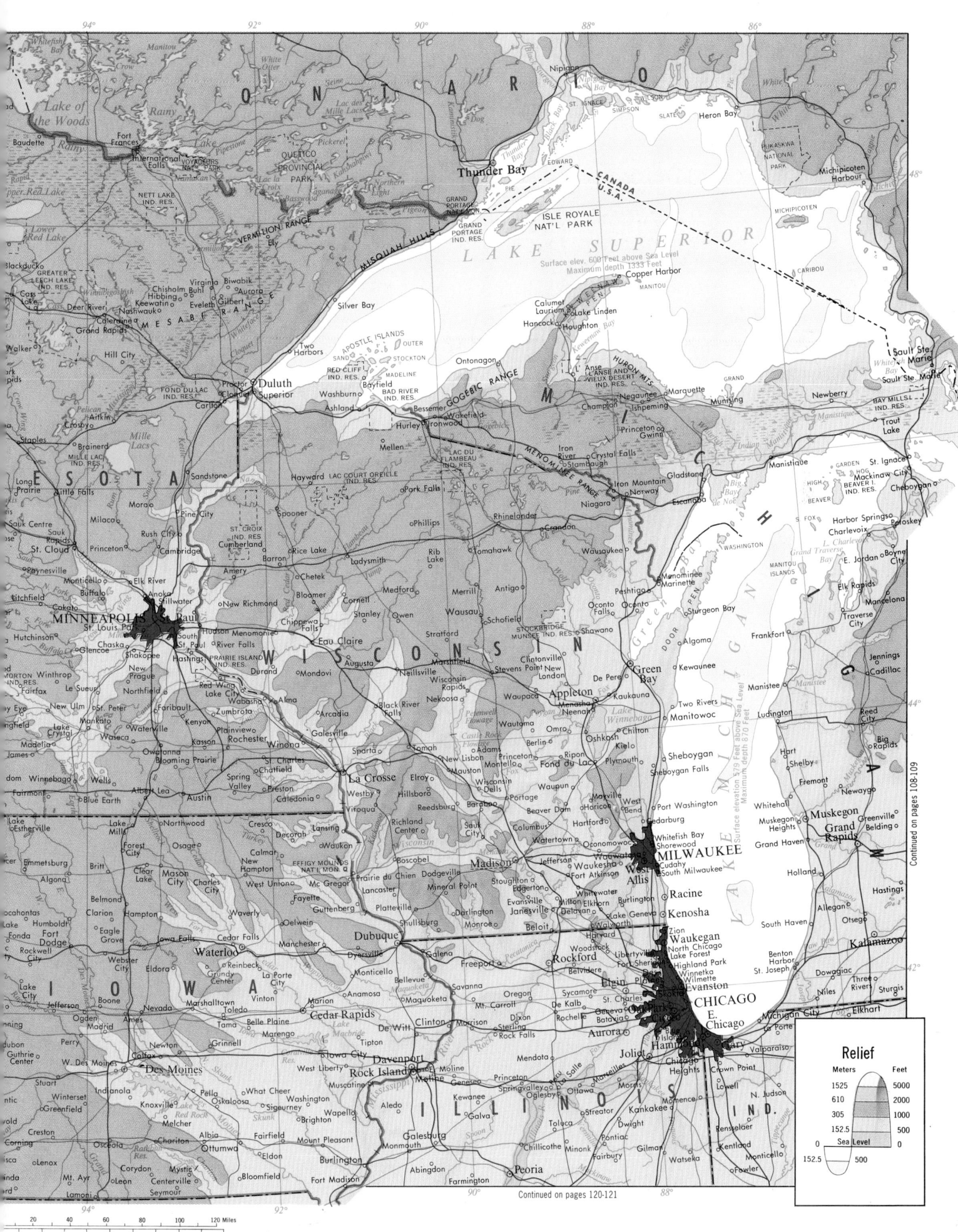

Continued on pages 108-109

Continued on pages 120-121

Relief

Meters		Feet
1525		5000
610		2000
305		1000
152.5		500
0	Sea Level	0
152.5		500

120° Continued on pages 94-95

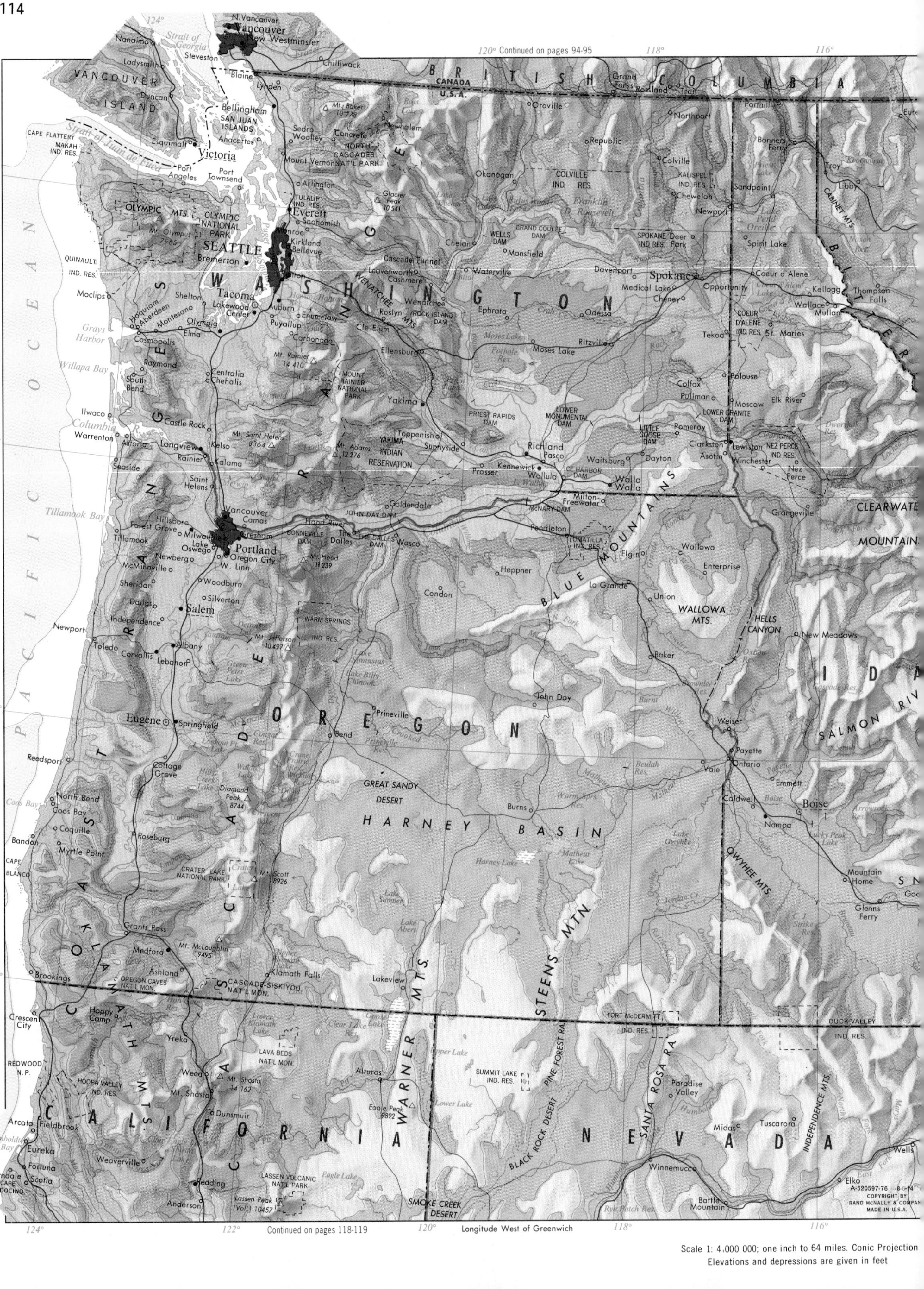

BRITISH COLUMBIA
CANADA
U.S.A.

VANCOUVER ISLAND

WASHINGTON

OREGON

CALIFORNIA   NEVADA   IDA

PACIFIC OCEAN

OLYMPIC NATIONAL PARK

NORTH CASCADES NAT'L PARK

MOUNT RAINIER NATIONAL PARK

YAKIMA INDIAN RESERVATION

BLUE MOUNTAINS

WALLOWA MTS.

HELLS CANYON

GREAT SANDY DESERT

HARNEY BASIN

STEENS MTN.

WARNER MTS.

KLAMATH MTS.

CRATER LAKE NATIONAL PARK

CASCADE-SISKIYOU NAT'L MON.

OREGON CAVES NAT'L MON.

LAVA BEDS NAT'L MON.

REDWOOD N.P.

LASSEN VOLCANIC NATIONAL PARK

BLACK ROCK DESERT

SMOKE CREEK DESERT

DUCK VALLEY IND. RES.

Longitude West of Greenwich

Scale 1: 4,000 000; one inch to 64 miles. Conic Projection
Elevations and depressions are given in feet

RAND McNALLY & COMPANY
COPYRIGHT BY
MADE IN U.S.A.
A-520597-76

ALBERTA SASKATCHEWAN
CANADA
U.S.A.

Continued on pages 96-97

114°   112°   110°   108°   106°

Plentywood

Morgan
Hogeland
Opheim
Scobey
Grenora

ERTON-GLACIER
INTERNATIONAL
PEACE PARK
BLACKFEET
IND. RES.
Cut
Bank
Sunburst
Chinook
Harlem
Malta
FORT PECK
IND. RES.
Williston

Browning
Shelby
Havre
Glasgow
Wolf Point
Poplar
Sidney
N.
DAK.

Valier
Conrad
Ft. Belknap
ROCKY BOYS
IND. RES.
FT. BELKNAP
IND.
RES.
Fort Peck
Lake

kalispell
NATIONAL
BISON RANGE
Choteau
Fort Benton
Missouri
Winifred
Brockway

SWAN RANGE
Ronan
R O C K Y
Great
Falls
Belt
Lewistown
Winnett
Glendive
Beach

Missoula
Lolo
LITTLE BELT MTS.
Neihart
M O N T A N A
Terry
Baker
Marmarth

Stevensville
Helena
East
Helena
White Sulphur
Spgs.
Harlowton
Roundup
Musselshell
Miles City

Hamilton
Philipsburg
Deer Lodge
Townsend
CRAZY
MTS.
Forsyth

Anaconda
Walkerville
Butte
Three Forks
Big Timber
Billings
Hardin
Colstrip

BIG HOLE NAT'L
BATTLEFIELD
Bozeman
Livingston
Columbus
Laurel
Huntley
Crow Agency
LITTLE
BIGHORN
BATTLEFIELD
NAT'L MON.
NORTHERN CHEYENNE
IND. RES.
Lame Deer

PIONEER
MTS.
Twin
Bridges
Red Lodge
Granite Peak
Bear
Creek
CROW IND. RES.

Homer
Youngs Peak
10 621
Dillon
Electric Peak
10 992
Gardiner
Mt. Washburn
10 243
Lovell
Powell
Sheridan
DEVILS TOWER
NAT'L MON.

Salmon
LEMHI RANGE
Yellowstone
NATIONAL
PARK
Yellowstone Lake
Cody
Greybull
BIGHORN MOUNTAINS
Buffalo
Sundance
Moorcroft

LOST RIVER RA.
Borah Pk.
12 662
St.
Anthony
Ashton
7733 ft above
sea level
Basin
Cloud Peak
13 167
Gillette

Mackay
Rexburg
Rigby
GRAND TETON
NAT'L PARK
Grand Teton
13 770
Worland
Ten
Sleep
Kaycee

Hyndman Peak
12 009
Arco
Idaho Falls
Shelley
Blackfoot
WIND RIVER
Gebo
Thermopolis
Midwest

CRATERS OF
THE MOON
NAT'L MON.
Garnett Peak
13 804
Fremont
Peak 13 745
IND.
RES.
Shoshoni
Powder River

S N A K E
R I V E R
P L A I N
FORT HALL
Pocatello
WIND RIVER RANGE
Riverton
Lander
Glenrock
Douglas
Orin

AMERICAN FALLS
RES.
Soda Springs
Meade
Peak
9957
Afton
W Y O M I N G
Casper

American Falls
IND. RES.
Rupert
Burley
Laval
Hot Spgs.
Montpelier
GREAT DIVIDE
BASIN
Wheatland

Oakley
Malad
City
Preston
Fontenelle
Res.
Pathfinder
Res.
Seminoe
Res.
Hanna

Lewiston
Richmond
Smithfield
Logan
Providence
Kemmerer
Superior
Rawlins

Garland
Wellsville
Brigham
Granger
Green River
Rock
Springs
Flaming
Gorge
Res.

Lucin
GREAT
SALT LAKE
DESERT
Great
Salt
Lake
Huntsville
Ogden
Morgan
Farmington
Evanston
PARK RANGE
Steamboat
Spgs.

Wendover
Bountiful
Salt Lake City
Park City
Mt. Emmons
13 440
UINTAH AND OURAY
IND. RES.
Kings Peak
13 528
DINOSAUR
NAT'L MON.
COLO.
Craig

Murray
Midvale
U T A H
HUINTA MTS.
Vernal
Oak Creek

Tooele
Heber City
Continued on pages 118-119

Continued on pages 112-113

Relief		
Meters		Feet
3050		10000
1525		5000
610		2000
305		1000
152.5		500
0	Sea Level	0
1525		500

20   40   60   80   100   120 Miles
20   40   60   80   100   120   140   160   180   200 Kilometers

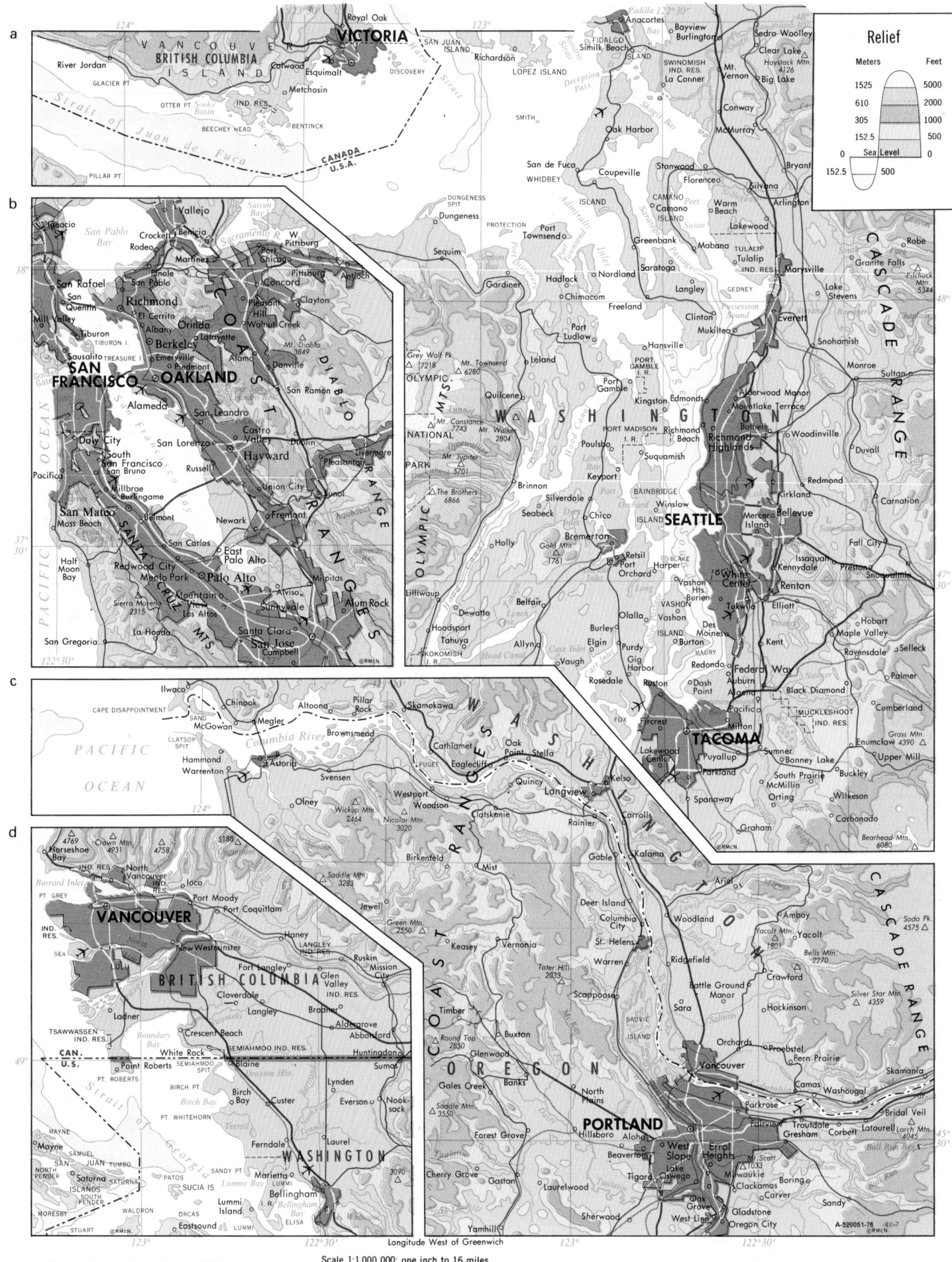

Relief

Meters	Feet
1525	5000
610	2000
305	1000
152.5	500
0	Sea Level	0
152.5	500

a

VANCOUVER
BRITISH COLUMBIA
ISLAND

River Jordan

GLACIER PT.
OTTER PT. Sooke
Basin
IND. RES.

BEECHEY HEAD

PILLAR PT.

Strait of Juan de Fuca

Royal Oak
VICTORIA
Colwood
Esquimalt
Metchosin
Bentinck

DISCOVERY

CANADA
U.S.A.

SAN JUAN
ISLAND
Richardson
LOPEZ ISLAND

SMITH

Anacortes
FIDALGO
Simile Beach
ISLAND
Bayview
Burlington

Sedro Woolley
Clear Lake
Haystack Mtn.
Mt.
Vernon
Big Lake
Conway
McMurray

SWINOMISH
IND. RES.
La Conner

San de Fuca
WHIDBEY
ISLAND

Coupeville
Stanwood
Florence
Silvana
Bryant

CAMANO
Camano
Warm
Beach
Arlington
Lakewood

b

Vallejo
Ignacio
San Pablo
Bay
Crockett Benicia
Rodeo
Martinez
W. Pittsburg
Port
Chicago
Pinole
San Pablo
Pittsburg
Antioch
San Rafael
Concord
Clayton
Pleasant
Hill
Walnut Creek
San
Quentin
Richmond
El Cerrito
Orinda
Mt. Diablo
3849
Mill Valley
Albany
Lafayette
Alamo
Tiburon
Berkeley
Piedmont
Danville
TIBURON I.
Emeryville
San Ramon
Sausalito
TREASURE I.
SAN
FRANCISCO
OAKLAND
Alameda
San Leandro
Golden Gate
Daly City
San Lorenzo
Castro
Valley
Dublin
South
San Francisco
San Bruno
Hayward
Pleasanton
Livermore
Pacifica
Russell
Millbrae
Union City
Burlingame
San Mateo
Newark
Fremont
Moss Beach
Belmont
San Carlos
Half
Moon
Bay
Redwood City
East
Palo Alto
Menlo Park
Palo Alto
Milpitas
Aviso
Mountain
View
Alum
Rock
Sierra Morena
2315
Los Altos
Sunnyvale
San Gregoria
La Honda
SANTA CRUZ MTS.
Santa Clara
San Jose
Campbell

COAST

DIABLO RANGE

RANGES

PACIFIC OCEAN

WASHINGTON

Robe
Granite Falls
CASCADE RANGE
Pilchuck Mtn.
5344
Lake
Stevens

Port
Townsend
PROTECTION

Dungeness

Sequim
Gardiner

DUNGENESS
SPIT

Port
Ludlow

Greenbank
Mabana
TULALIP
Tulalip
IND. RES.
Marysville

Langley
Clinton
Mukilteo
Everett

GEDNEY

Possession
Sound

Snohomish
Monroe
Sultan

Hadlock
Nordland
Saratoga

Chimacum
Freeland

OLYMPIC
MTS.
Grey Wolf Pk.
7218
Mt. Townsend
6280
Quilcene

Mt. Constance
7743
Mt. Walker
2804
Mt. Jupiter
5701
NATIONAL

The Brothers
6866

PARK

Brinnon

Silverdale
Seabeck

Holly

Gold Mtn.
1761

Bremerton
Retsil
Port
Orchard
Harper

Lilliwaup

Hoodsport
Tahuya

Dewatto

Belfair
Allyn
Vaugn

SKOKOMISH
I.R.

Hansville
Port
Gamble
PORT GAMBLE
I.R.
Kingston Edmonds
Poulsbo
Suquamish

PORT MADISON
I.R.
Richmond
Beach
Alderwood Manor
Mountlake
Terrace
Botholl
Richmond
Highlands
Woodinville
Duvall

Keyport
Winslow
Chico
BAINBRIDGE
ISLAND
SEATTLE
Mercer
Island
Bellevue
Kirkland
Redmond
Carnation

BLAKE
I.
White
Center
Burien
Issaquah
Kennydale
Preston
Snoqualmie
Fall City

VASHON
Vashon
HTS.
Des
Moines
Renton
Elliott
Hobart
Maple Valley
Ravensdale
Selleck

Olalla
VASHON
ISLAND
Burton

MAURY
Redondo
Federal
Way
Auburn
Aloma
Black Diamond
Palmer

Purdy
Gig
Harbor
Rosedale
Dash
Point
Pacific
Milton
MUCKLESHOOT
IND. RES.
Cumberland
Grass Mtn.
Enumclaw 4390

c

Ilwaco
CAPE DISAPPOINTMENT
SAND
McGowan
CLATSOP
SPIT
Hammond
Warrenton

PACIFIC
OCEAN

Chinook
Megler
Astoria

Svensen

Olney
Wickup Mtn.
2464

Pillar
Rock
Altoona
Brownsmead
Columbia River
Cathlamet

Skamokawa
Oak
Point Stella
Eaglecliff

Westport
Woodson
Clatskanie
Nicolai Mtn.
3020

Quincy
Longview
Rainier
Carrolls

Fircrest
TACOMA
Lakewood
Center
Parkland
Puyallup
Spanaway
Orting
McMillin
Graham
Sumner
Bonney Lake
South
Prairie
Buckley
Wilkeson
Carbonado

FOX
Rosedale
Ruston

W
A
S
H
I
N
G
T
O
N

COAST RANGES

PUGET

Bearhead Mtn.
6080

d

Horseshoe
Bay
4769
Crown Mtn.
4931
IND. RES.
North
Vancouver
Ioco
4758
5188

Burrard Inlet
PT. GREY
IND.
RES.
VANCOUVER
New Westminster
Port Moody
Port Coquitlam
Haney
LANGLEY
IND. RES.
Ruskin

SEA
LULU
Fort Langley
Glen
Valley
Mission
City

BRITISH COLUMBIA
Cloverdale
Langley
Bradner
Aldergrove
Abbotsford

Ladner
Crescent Beach
Brodner
IND. RES.

TSAWWASSEN
IND. RES.
Boundary
Bay
White Rock
SEMIAHMOO IND. RES.
Huntingdon

CAN.
U.S.
Point Roberts
Blaine
Sumas

PT. ROBERTS
SEMIAHMOO
SPIT
Birch
Bay
Lynden

BIRCH PT.
Birch
Bay
Custer
Everson

PT. WHITEHORN
Nooksack

MAYNE
Ferndale
Laurel

Mayne
SAMUEL
SANDY PT.
Marietta
Terrell

NORTH
PENDER
SATURNA
TUMBO
PATOS
3090
Lummi Bay
Bellingham

ISLANDS
SOUTH
PENDER
SUCIA IS.
LUMMI
IND. RES.
Bellingham
Bay

MORESBY
WALDRON
ORCAS
Eastsound
Lummi
Island
ELISA

STUART

Strait of Georgia

BOUNDARY
BAY
DRAYTON HBR.

O
R
E
G
O
N

Ariel
Woodland
Amboy
Yacolt
Yacolt Mtn.
1801

Deer Island
Columbia
City
St. Helens
Warren
Ridgefield
Battle
Ground
Manor
Crawford
Bells Mtn.
2270
Silver Star Mtn.
4359

Scappoose
Sauvie
Island
Vancouver
Orchards
Proebstel
Fern Prairie

Timber
Round Top
2850
Glenwood
Buxton
Hockinson
Skamania
Camas Washougal

Gales Creek
Banks
North
Plains
Parkrose
Fairview
Troutdale
Gresham
Corbett
Latourell
Larch Mtn.
4045
Bridal Veil
Bull Run Res.

Forest Grove
Cherry Grove
Gaston
Hillsboro
Aloha
PORTLAND
Beaverton
West
Slope
Errol
Heights
Mt. Scott
1033
Fairview

Laurelwood
Tigard
Lake
Oswego
Milwaukie
Boring
Clackamas
Carver
Sandy

Sherwood
Oak
Grove
West Linn
Gladstone
Oregon City

Yamhill

COAST
RANGE
Saddle Mtn.
3283
Jewell
Birkenfeld
Mist
Goble
Kalama
Kelso
Green Mtn.
2550
Keasey
Vernonia
Deer Island
Toter Hill
2033
Saddle Mtn.
3550

CASCADE
RANGE

Soda Pk.
4575

Longitude West of Greenwich

Scale 1:1 000 000; one inch to 16 miles.
Elevations and depressions are given in feet.

0   5   10   15   20 Miles
0 4 8 12 16 20 24 28 32 Kilometers

A-520051-76
48-7

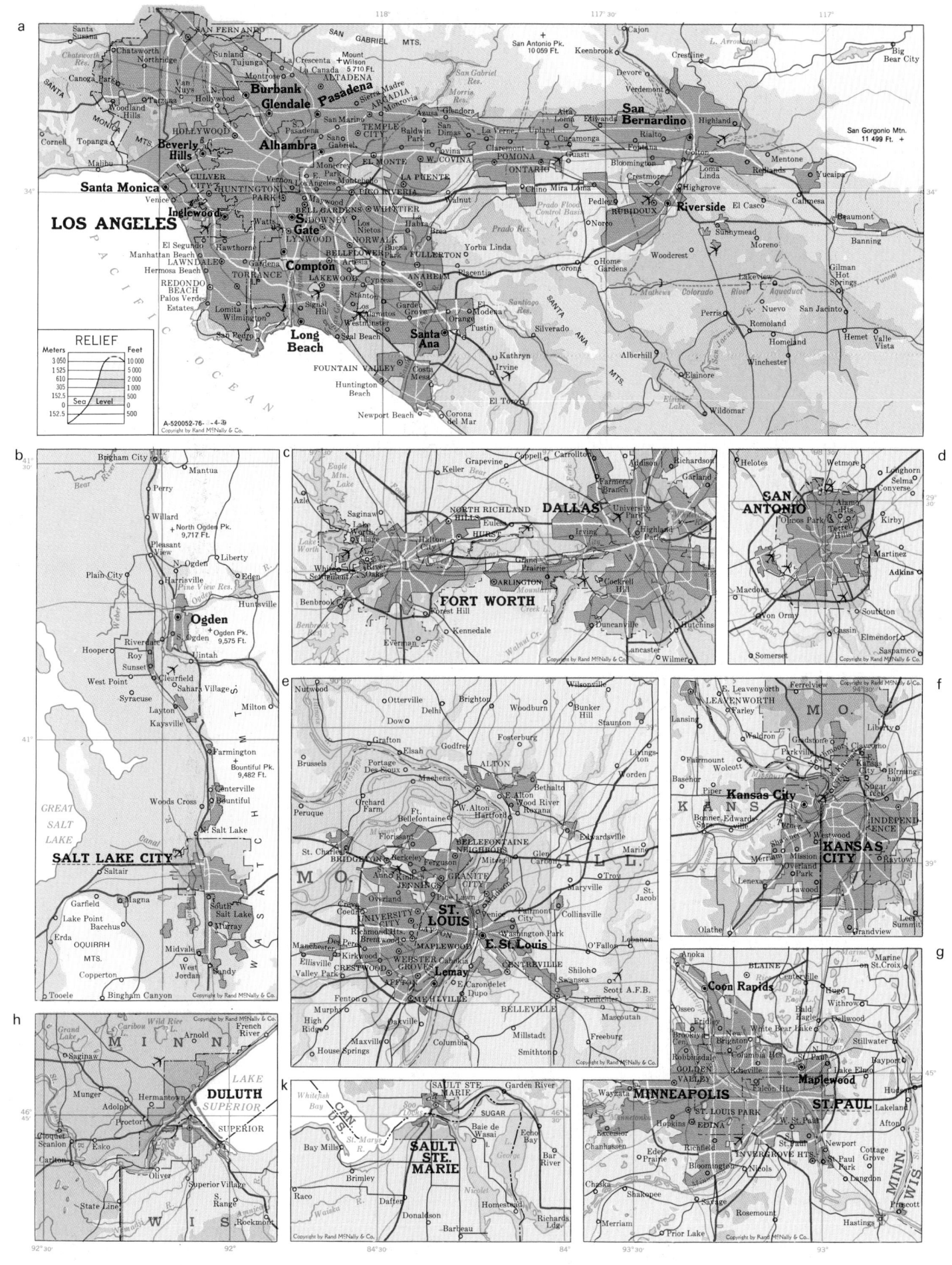

Continued on pages 114-115

Scale 1:4 000 000; one inch to 64 miles. Conic Projection
Elevations and depressions are given in feet

Longitude West of Greenwich

a

San Diego inset map

SAN DIEGO

Scale 1:1 000 000

0   4   10 Miles
0 4 8 12 16 Kilometers

A-520599-76-B-22
COPYRIGHT BY
RAND McNALLY & COMPANY
MADE IN U.S.A.

0   20   40   60   80   100   120 Miles
0 20 40 60 80 100 120 140 160 180 200 Kilometers

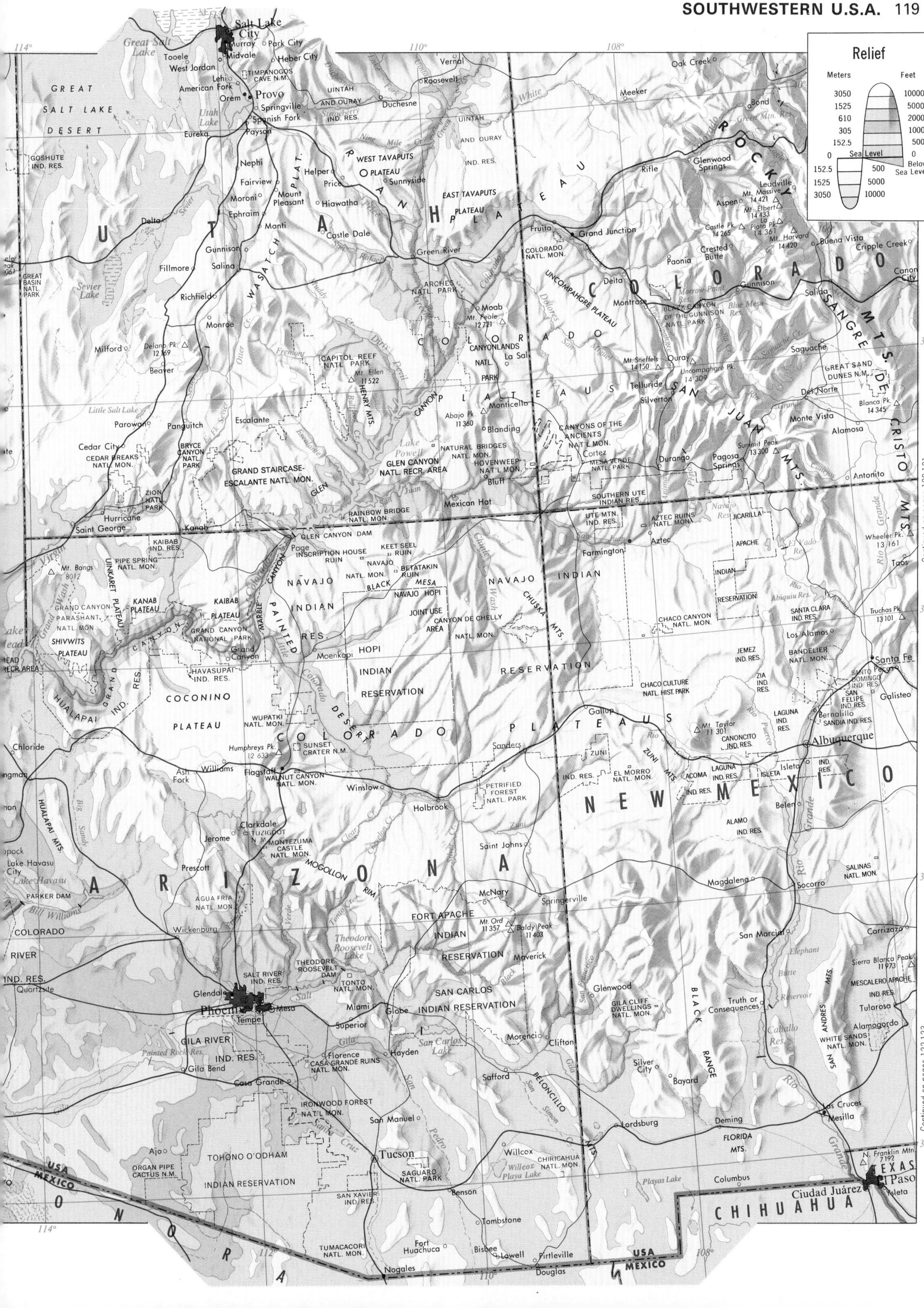

Relief
Meters
Feet
3050
10000
1525
5000
610
2000
305
1000
152.5
500
0
Sea Level
0
152.5
500
Below Sea Level
1525
5000
3050
10000
GREAT SALT LAKE DESERT
Great Salt Lake
Salt Lake City
Murray
Midvale
Park City
Heber City
Tooele
West Jordan
Lehi
American Fork
Orem
Provo
Springville
Spanish Fork
Payson
Eureka
TIMPANOGOS CAVE N.M.
Utah Lake
UINTAH AND OURAY IND. RES.
Duchesne
Roosevelt
Vernal
Oak Creek
Meeker
Bond
GOSHUTE IND. RES.
Nephi
Fairview
Moroni
Mount Pleasant
Ephraim
Manti
Helper
Price
Sunnyside
WEST TAVAPUTS PLATEAU
EAST TAVAPUTS PLATEAU
Hiawatha
Castle Dale
Delta
Sevier
UTAH
WASATCH PLAT.
Gunnison
Salina
Fillmore
Richfield
Monroe
Green River
GREAT BASIN NATL. PARK
Sevier Lake
ARCHES NATL. PARK
Moab
Mt. Peale 12 721
CANYONLANDS NATL. PARK
La Sal
Milford
Delano Pk. 12 169
Beaver
CAPITOL REEF NATL. PARK
Mt. Ellen 11 522
HENRY MTS.
Little Salt Lake
Parowan
Panguitch
Escalante
Cedar City
CEDAR BREAKS NATL. MON.
BRYCE CANYON NATL. PARK
GRAND STAIRCASE-ESCALANTE NATL. MON.
ZION NATL. PARK
Hurricane
Saint George
Kanab
Lake Powell
GLEN CANYON NATL. RECR. AREA
NATURAL BRIDGES NATL. MON.
HOVENWEEP NAT'L MON.
Monticello
Abajo Pk. 11 360
Blanding
Bluff
Mexican Hat
RAINBOW BRIDGE NATL. MON.
CANYONS OF THE ANCIENTS NAT'L MON.
Cortez
MESA VERDE NATL PARK
COLORADO PLATEAUS
Rifle
Glenwood Springs
ROCKY MTS.
Leadville
Mt. Massive 14 421
Mt. Elbert 14 433
Aspen
Castle Pk. 14 265
La Plata Pk. 14 361
Mt. Harvard 14 420
Buena Vista
Cripple Creek
Fruita
Grand Junction
COLORADO NATL. MON.
UNCOMPAHGRE PLATEAU
Paonia
Crested Butte
Delta
Montrose
Gunnison
BLACK CANYON OF THE GUNNISON NATL PARK
Blue Mesa Res.
Salida
Canon City
SANGRE DE CRISTO MTS.
COLORADO
Mt. Sneffels 14 150
Ouray
Uncompahgre Pk. 14 309
Telluride
Silverton
SAN JUAN MTS.
Saguache
GREAT SAND DUNES N.M.
Del Norte
Blanca Pk. 14 345
Monte Vista
Alamosa
Summit Peak 13 300
Durango
Pagosa Springs
Antonito
SOUTHERN UTE INDIAN RES.
UTE MTN. IND. RES.
AZTEC RUINS NATL. MON.
Aztec
Farmington
Navajo Res.
JICARILLA APACHE INDIAN RESERVATION
El Vado Res.
Wheeler Pk. 13 161
Taos
GLEN CANYON DAM
Page
KAIBAB IND. RES.
INSCRIPTION HOUSE RUIN
KEET SEEL RUIN
BETATAKIN RUIN
NAVAJO NATL. MON.
Mt. Bangs 8012
PIPE SPRING NATL. MON.
UINKARET PLATEAU
KANAB PLATEAU
KAIBAB PLATEAU
GRAND CANYON-PARASHANT NATL. MON.
MARBLE CANYON
NAVAJO INDIAN RES.
BLACK MESA
NAVAJO HOPI JOINT USE AREA
CANYON DE CHELLY NATL. MON.
CHUSKA MTS.
NAVAJO INDIAN RESERVATION
Lake Mead
SHIVWITS PLATEAU
GRAND CANYON NATIONAL PARK
Grand Canyon
PAINTED DESERT
Moenkopi
HOPI INDIAN RESERVATION
HAVASUPAI IND. RES.
HUALAPAI IND. RES.
COCONINO PLATEAU
WUPATKI NATL. MON.
SUNSET CRATER N.M.
Humphreys Pk. 12 633
CHACO CANYON NATL. MON.
CHACO CULTURE NATL. HIST. PARK
JEMEZ IND. RES.
ZIA IND. RES.
Abiquiu Res.
SANTA CLARA IND. RES.
Truchas Pk. 13 101
Los Alamos
BANDELIER NATL. MON.
Santa Fe
SANTO DOMINGO IND. RES.
SAN FELIPE IND. RES.
Pecos
Galisteo
Bernalillo
SANDIA IND. RES.
LAGUNA IND. RES.
Gallup
Mt. Taylor 11 301
CANONCITO IND. RES.
Albuquerque
Chloride
Kingman
Williams
Ash Fork
Flagstaff
WALNUT CANYON NATL. MON.
Sanders
ZUNI IND. RES.
ZUNI MTS.
EL MORRO NATL. MON.
ACOMA IND. RES.
LAGUNA IND. RES.
ISLETA IND. RES.
Isleta
Winslow
PETRIFIED FOREST NATL. PARK
Holbrook
NEW MEXICO
Belen
ALAMO IND. RES.
HUALAPAI MTS.
Clarkdale
TUZIGOOT N.M.
Jerome
MONTEZUMA CASTLE NATL. MON.
Saint Johns
Needles
Lake Havasu City
Lake Havasu
Prescott
ARIZONA
MOGOLLON RIM
Magdalena
SALINAS NATL. MON.
Socorro
PARKER DAM
Bill Williams
AGUA FRIA NATL. MON.
McNary
Springerville
COLORADO RIVER IND. RES.
Wickenburg
FORT APACHE INDIAN RESERVATION
Mt. Ord 11 357
Baldy Peak 11 403
San Marcial
Carrizozo
Theodore Roosevelt Lake
THEODORE ROOSEVELT DAM
Maverick
Elephant Butte Reservoir
Sierra Blanca Peak 11 973
MESCALERO APACHE IND. RES.
SALT RIVER IND. RES.
TONTO NATL. MON.
Quartzsite
Glendale
Phoenix
Mesa
Tempe
SAN CARLOS INDIAN RESERVATION
Glenwood
GILA CLIFF DWELLINGS NATL. MON.
BLACK RANGE
Truth or Consequences
Tularosa
Miami
Globe
Superior
Alamogordo
SAN ANDRES MTS.
WHITE SANDS NATL. MON.
GILA RIVER IND. RES.
Painted Rock Res.
Gila Bend
Florence
CASA GRANDE RUINS NATL. MON.
Hayden
San Carlos Lake
Morenci
Clifton
Caballo Res.
Casa Grande
Safford
PELONCILLO MTS.
Silver City
Bayard
IRONWOOD FOREST NAT'L MON.
San Manuel
Lordsburg
Deming
Las Cruces
Mesilla
FLORIDA MTS.
Ajo
ORGAN PIPE CACTUS N.M.
TOHONO O'ODHAM INDIAN RESERVATION
Tucson
SAGUARO NATL. PARK
Willcox
Willcox Playa Lake
CHIRICAHUA NATL. MON.
N. Franklin Mtn. 7 192
TEXAS
El Paso
Playas Lake
Columbus
Ciudad Juárez
Ysleta
USA MEXICO
SAN XAVIER IND. RES.
Benson
CHIHUAHUA
SONORA
Tombstone
Fort Huachuca
TUMACACORI NATL. MON.
Bisbee
Lowell
Pirtleville
Nogales
Douglas
114°
112°
110°
108°
40°
38°
36°
34°
32°

Continued on pages 120-121

Continued on pages 122-123

120

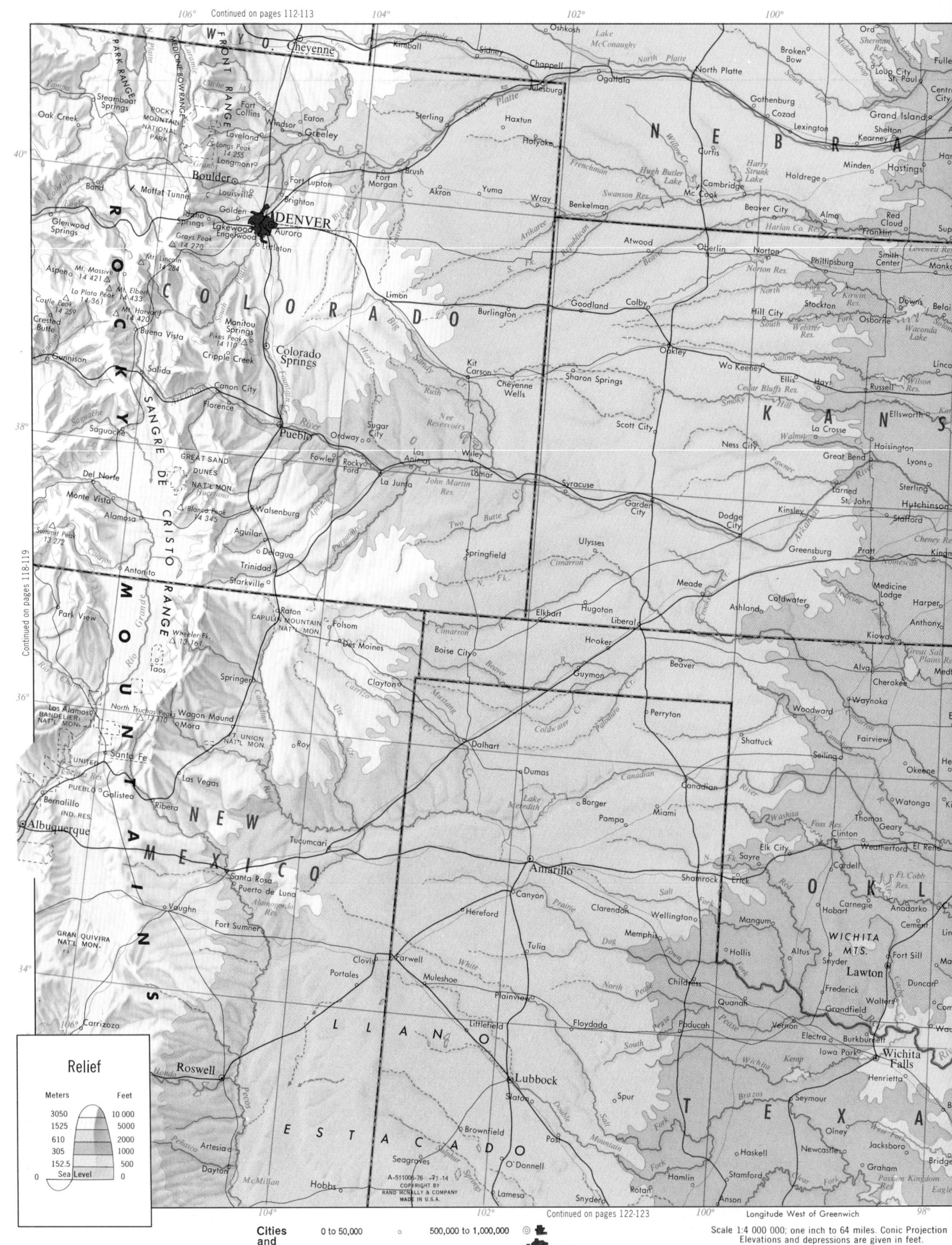

Continued on pages 112-113

Continued on pages 118-119

Continued on pages 122-123

Relief

Meters	Feet
3050	10 000
1525	5000
610	2000
305	1000
152.5	500
0 Sea Level	0

Longitude West of Greenwich

Cities and Towns   0 to 50,000   50,000 to 500,000   500,000 to 1,000,000   1,000,000 and over

Scale 1:4 000 000; one inch to 64 miles. Conic Projection
Elevations and depressions are given in feet.

A-511006-76 77-14
COPYRIGHT BY
RAND M?NALLY & COMPANY
MADE IN U.S.A.

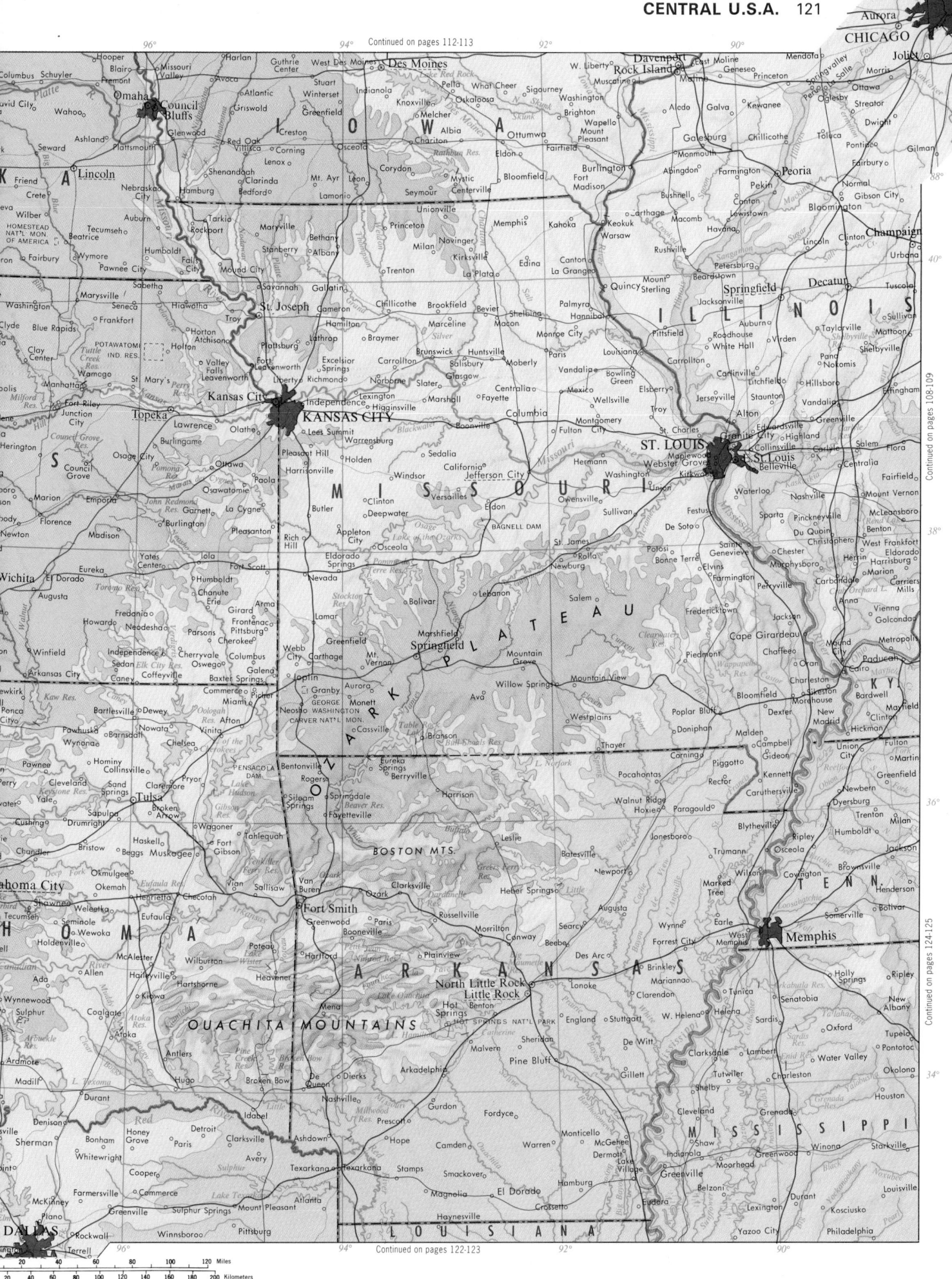

Continued on pages 112-113
Continued on pages 108-109
Continued on pages 124-125
Continued on pages 122-123

Continued on pages 120-121

NEW MEXICO

White Sands Nat'l Mon.
Alamogordo
Alamo Pk. 7820
Penasco
Artesia
Dayton
McMillan
Seagraves
Seminole
O'Donnell
Haskell
Newcastle
Graham
Lamesa
Snyder
Rotan
Hamlin
Stamford
Albany
Breckenridge
Mineral We
Carlsbad
Hobbs
Roscoe
Sweetwater
Merkel
Abilene
Ranger
Eastland
Strawn
32°
N. Franklin Mtn. 7176
Wind Mtn. 7278
Guadalupe Pk. 8749
Red Bluff Res.
Big Spring
Colorado City
Baird
Cisco
Gorman
Desdemo
Dublin
El Paso
Ysleta
Ciudad Juárez
Fabens
Stanton
Midland
Odessa
Wink
Winters
Ballinger
Coleman
Brownwood
Comanche
Ham
Guadalupe
Pecos
Sterling City
Santa Anna
Brownwood
GUADALUPE MTS.
Toyah
North Concha
Concho
Goldthwa
Villa Ahumada
Sierra Blanca
Van Horn
Eagle Pk. 7496
Davis Mts.
Baldy Peak 8382
Marfa
Alpine
Fort Stockton
McCamey
San Angelo
Eden
Menard
Brady
San Saba
Lam
STOCKTON PLATEAU
Big Canyon
Sanderson
Sonora
Junction
Rocksprings
Fredericksburg
Kerrville
EDWARDS PLATEAU
TEXAS
Cathedral Mt 6860
Chinati Pk. 7730
Santiago Mts.
Ojinaga
Presidio
Big Bend Nat'l Park
Emory Pk. 7835
SERRANIAS DEL BURRO
Del Rio
Villa Acuña
Brackettville
Camp Wood
Boerne
New Braunfels
San A
San Antonio
Hondo
Coyame
Cuchillo Parado
Aldama
Chihuahua
Meoqui
Jiménez
Piedras Negras
Fuente
Eagle Pass
Crystal City
Uvalde
Sabinal
Poteet
Floresville
Pleasant
Pearsall
CHIHUAHUA
Naica
San
Gigantes
Jaco
SIERRA
Zaragoza
Morelos
Nava
Allende
Guerrero
Carrizo Springs
Asherton
Cotulla
Fowlerton
George West
28°
San Pedro
Coachis
Ciudad Camargo (Santa Rosalía)
BOLSÓN
Sierra Mojada
Laguna de la Leche
Rosales
Muzquiz
San Juan de Sabinas
Encinal
Toronto
Hidalgo del Parral
Jimenez
Villa Lopez
COAHUILA
Progreso
Presa de V. Martín
Hidalgo
Dolores
San Diego
MADRE
Abasolo
Sacramento
San Buenaventura
Nadadores
Nuevo Laredo
Laredo
Mirando City
Premont
Falfurrias
Santa Barbara
Villa Coronado
Escalón
DE
Rey
Cuatro Ciénegas
ORIENTAL
Monclova
Lampazos
Hebbronville
Rosario
Villa Ocampo
MAPIMI
Bustamante
Villaldama
Sabinas Hidalgo
Mier
Camargo
Riogrande
Mission
26°
Indé
Santa Cruz
Mapimí
San Pedro de las Colonias
Laguna de Mayran
Paredon
Agualeguas
NUEVO
Cerralvo
Los Herreras
Reynosa
DURANGO
MEXICO
Salinas Victoria
Garcia
General Zuazua
China
Gomez Palacio
San Luis del Cordero
Torreón
Lerdo
Matamoros
Laguna de Viesca
Parras
Viesca
General Cepeda
Ramos Arizpe
Santa Catarina
Monterrey
Cadereyta Jimenez
Rodeo
Nazas
San Juan del Rio
Cuencame
San Bartolo
Gomez Farias
Arteaga
Saltillo
Villa de Alfende
Montemorelos
LEON
Canatlán
Pánuco de Coronado
Santa Clara
San Juan de Guadalupe
Mazapil
Concepción del Oro
Galeana
Linares
Burgos
San Fernando
Durango
ZACATECAS
Juan Aldama
Villagrán
San Carlos
Cruillas
TAMAULI

Continued on pages 130-131

Longitude West of Greenwich

Scale 1:4 000 000; one inch to 64 miles. Conic Project
Elevations and depressions are given in feet

Relief

Meters	Feet
1525	5000
610	2000
305	1000
152.5	500
0 Sea Level 0	
152.5	500
1525	5000
3050	10000

Continued on pages 120-121

Continued on pages 124-125

GULF OF MEXICO

a

Scale 1:1 000 000

0   5   10 Miles
0 4 8 12 16 Kilometers

©RMcN.

A-511007-76   5-5-8
COPYRIGHT BY
RAND McNALLY & COMPANY
MADE IN U.S.A.

20   40   60   80   100   120 Miles
20 40 60 80 100 120 140 160 180 200 Kilometers

Cities	0 to 50,000 ∘	500,000 to 1,000,000 ⊚
and		
Towns	50,000 to 500,000 ⊙	1,000,000 and over

Continued on pages 108-109

Continued on pages 120-121

Continued on pages 122-123

GULF OF MEXICO

Longitude West of Greenwich

Scale 1:4 000 000; one inch to 64 miles. Conic Projection
Elevations and depressions are given in feet

A-520598-76   -7-7-14
COPYRIGHT BY
RAND McNALLY & COMPANY
MADE IN U.S.A.

Relief

Meters		Feet
1525		5000
610		2000
305		1000
152.5		500
0	Sea Level	0
152.5		500
1525		5000

a

Same scale as main map

©RMCN.

0 20 40 60 80 100 120 Miles
0 20 40 60 80 100 120 140 160 180 200 Kilometers

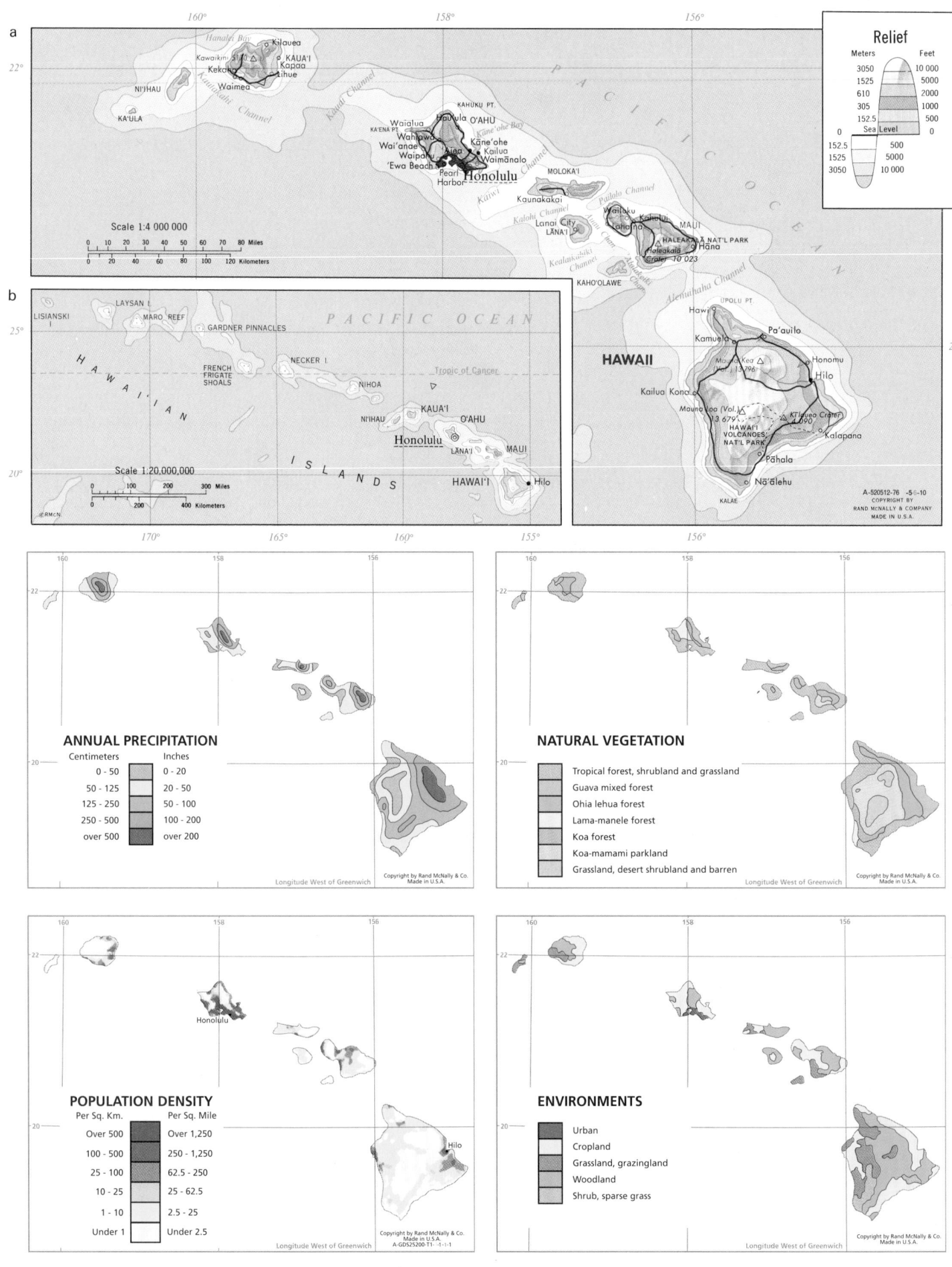

a

Relief

Meters		Feet
3050		10 000
1525		5000
610		2000
305		1000
152.5		500
0	Sea Level	0
152.5		500
1525		5000
3050		10 000

Scale 1:4 000 000

0 10 20 30 40 50 60 70 80 Miles

0 20 40 60 80 100 120 Kilometers

b

Scale 1:20,000,000

0 100 200 300 Miles

0 200 400 Kilometers

©RMCN.

HAWAII

A-520512-76 -5-8-10
COPYRIGHT BY
RAND McNALLY & COMPANY
MADE IN U.S.A.

ANNUAL PRECIPITATION

Centimeters	Inches
0 - 50	0 - 20
50 - 125	20 - 50
125 - 250	50 - 100
250 - 500	100 - 200
over 500	over 200

Longitude West of Greenwich

Copyright by Rand McNally & Co.
Made in U.S.A.

NATURAL VEGETATION

Tropical forest, shrubland and grassland
Guava mixed forest
Ohia lehua forest
Lama-manele forest
Koa forest
Koa-mamami parkland
Grassland, desert shrubland and barren

Longitude West of Greenwich

Copyright by Rand McNally & Co.
Made in U.S.A.

POPULATION DENSITY

Per Sq. Km.	Per Sq. Mile
Over 500	Over 1,250
100 - 500	250 - 1,250
25 - 100	62.5 - 250
10 - 25	25 - 62.5
1 - 10	2.5 - 25
Under 1	Under 2.5

Longitude West of Greenwich

Copyright by Rand McNally & Co.
Made in U.S.A.
A-GDS25200-T1- -1-1-1

ENVIRONMENTS

Urban
Cropland
Grassland, grazingland
Woodland
Shrub, sparse grass

Longitude West of Greenwich

Copyright by Rand McNally & Co.
Made in U.S.A.

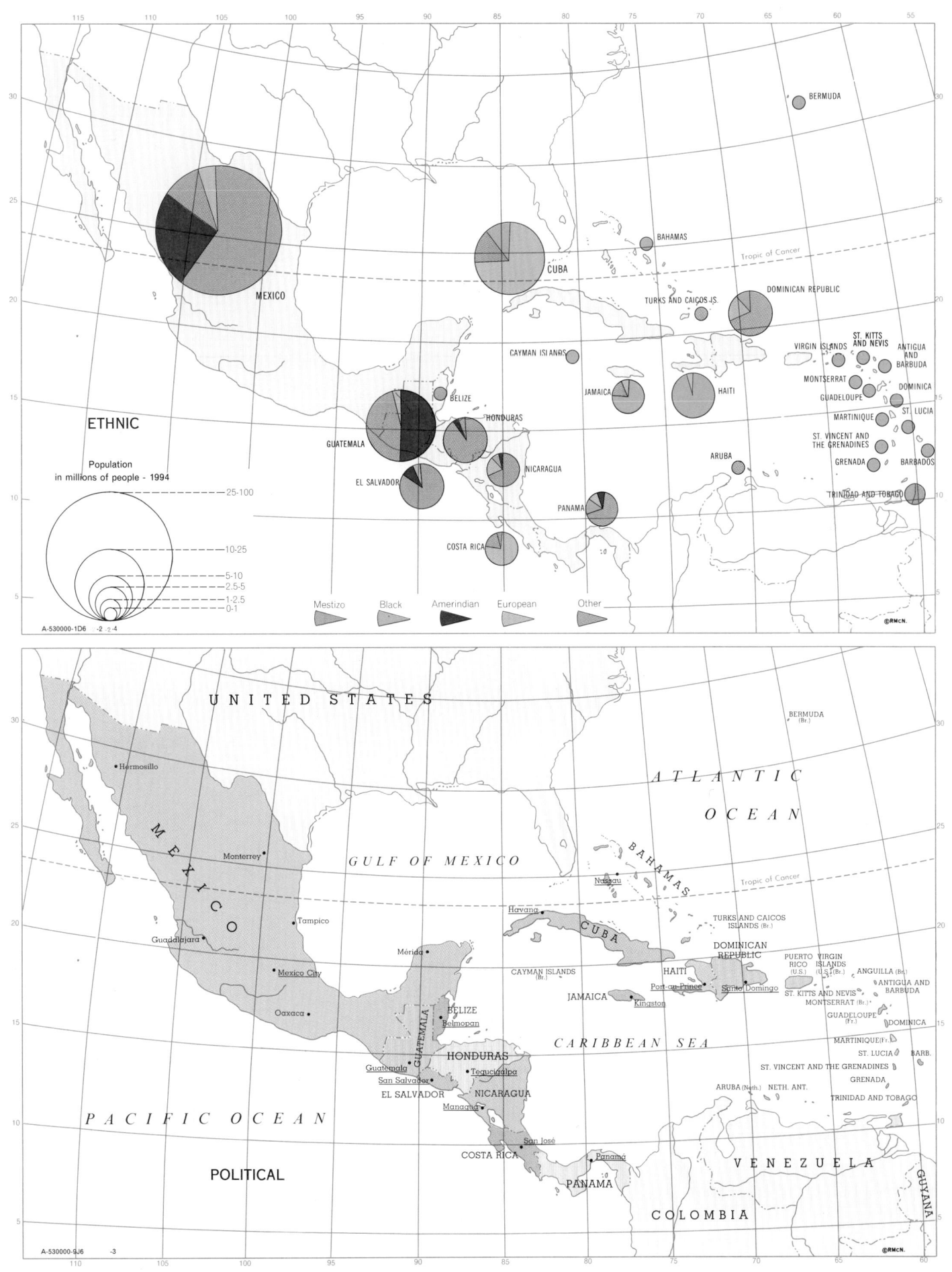

ETHNIC

Population
in millions of people - 1994

25-100

10-25

5-10
2.5-5
1-2.5
0-1

Mestizo   Black   Amerindian   European   Other

MEXICO

CUBA

BAHAMAS

TURKS AND CAICOS IS.

DOMINICAN REPUBLIC

CAYMAN ISLANDS

BELIZE

VIRGIN ISLANDS
ST. KITTS
AND NEVIS
ANTIGUA
AND
BARBUDA
MONTSERRAT
DOMINICA
GUADELOUPE

JAMAICA

HONDURAS

HAITI

MARTINIQUE
ST. LUCIA

GUATEMALA

NICARAGUA

ST. VINCENT AND
THE GRENADINES

ARUBA

GRENADA
BARBADOS

EL SALVADOR

PANAMA

TRINIDAD AND TOBAGO

COSTA RICA

BERMUDA

Tropic of Cancer

POLITICAL

UNITED STATES

ATLANTIC

OCEAN

BERMUDA
(Br.)

Hermosillo

MEXICO

GULF OF MEXICO

BAHAMAS

Nassau

Tropic of Cancer

Monterrey

Tampico

Guadalajara

Havana

CUBA

TURKS AND CAICOS
ISLANDS (Br.)

Mérida

Mexico City

CAYMAN ISLANDS
(Br.)

DOMINICAN
REPUBLIC

HAITI

PUERTO VIRGIN
RICO ISLANDS
(U.S.) (U.S.)(Br.) ANGUILLA (Br.)

ANTIGUA AND
BARBUDA

Oaxaca

BELIZE
Belmopan

Port-au-Prince

JAMAICA

Santo Domingo

ST. KITTS AND NEVIS

MONTSERRAT (Br.)

GUADELOUPE
(Fr.)

GUATEMALA

Kingston

CARIBBEAN SEA

DOMINICA

Guatemala

San Salvador

HONDURAS

Tegucigalpa

MARTINIQUE(Fr.)
ST. LUCIA
BARB.

EL SALVADOR

NICARAGUA

ST. VINCENT AND THE GRENADINES

GRENADA

Managua

ARUBA (Neth.) NETH. ANT.

TRINIDAD AND TOBAGO

PACIFIC OCEAN

San José

COSTA RICA

Panamá

VENEZUELA

GUYANA

PANAMA

COLOMBIA

a

PANAMA

Scale 1:1 000 000

10 Miles

16 Kilometers

©RMCN.

A-530000-76-9 9-27
COPYRIGHT BY
RAND McNALLY & COMPANY
MADE IN U.S.A.

Scale 1:16 000 000; one inch to 250 miles. Polyconic Projectio
Elevations and depressions are given in feet

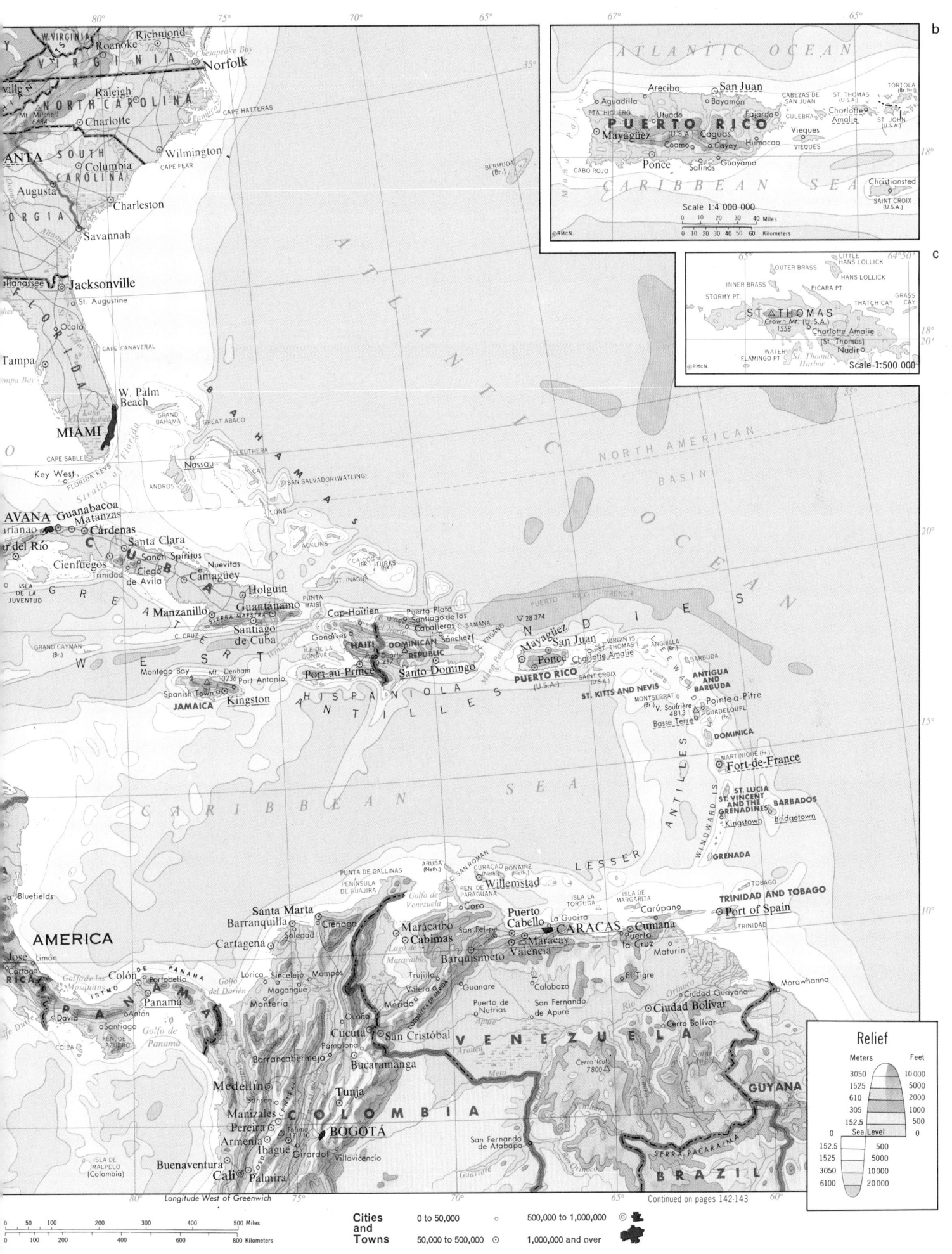

b

ATLANTIC OCEAN

Arecibo   San Juan
Aguadilla   Bayamón   CABEZAS DE   ST. THOMAS   TORTOLA
PTA. HIGUERO   Utuado   SAN JUAN   (U.S.A.)   (Br.)
PUERTO RICO   Fajardo   Charlotte
Mayagüez   (U.S.A.)   Caguas   Amalie   ST. JOHN
Coamo   Cayey   Vieques   (U.S.A.)
Cabo Rojo   Humacao
VIEQUES
Ponce   Salinas   Guayama
Christiansted
CARIBBEAN   SEA   SAINT CROIX
(U.S.A.)

Scale 1:4 000 000

0   10   20   30   40 Miles
0   10 20 30 40 50   60 Kilometers
©RMCN

c

ST. THOMAS

LITTLE   64°50′
HANS LOLLICK
OUTER BRASS   HANS LOLLICK
INNER BRASS   PICARA PT   GRASS
STORMY PT   THATCH CAY   CAY
ST. ◊ THOMAS
Crown Mt.   (U.S.A.)   18°
1558   Charlotte Amalie   20′
(St. Thomas)
WATER   Nadir
FLAMINGO PT   St. Thomas
Harbor   Scale 1:500 000
©RMCN

Continued on pages 142-143

Relief

Meters		Feet
3050		10 000
1525		5000
610		2000
305		1000
152.5		500
0	Sea Level	0
152.5		500
1525		5000
3050		10 000
6100		20 000

Longitude West of Greenwich

0   50   100   200   300   400   500 Miles
0   200   400   600   800 Kilometers

Cities and Towns	0 to 50,000 ○	500,000 to 1,000,000 ◉
	50,000 to 500,000 ⊙	1,000,000 and over

Continued on pages 122-123

PACIFIC OCEAN

Relief

Meters	Feet
3050	10 000
1525	5000
610	2000
305	1000
152.5	500
0 Sea Level	0
152.5	500
1525	5000
3050	10 000

A-531695-76 6. 15
COPYRIGHT BY
RAND McNALLY & COMPANY
MADE IN U.S.A.

Longitude West of Greenwich

Cities and Towns

0 to 50,000 ○	500,000 to 1,000,000 ◉
50,000 to 500,000 ⊙	1,000,000 and over

Scale 1:4 000 000; one inch to 64 miles. Conic Projection
Elevations and depressions are given in feet

a

Inset map (Mexico City area):

MÉXICO

Morelos
Cuautitlán
Tutitlán
Tecamac
Teotihuacán
Otumba
Apan
HIDALGO
Nicolás Romero
Cahuacán
Coacalco
Acolman
Chiconautla
Tepexpan
Pyramids of Teotihuacán
Calpulalpan
San Bartolo
Ixtlahuaca
Atizapán
Tlalnepantla
Tepetlaoxtoc
TLAXCALA
Cerro La Catedral 13 000
Mazatla
Gustavo A. Madero
San Jerónimo
Nanacamilpa
Jiquipilco
Temoaya
Texcoco
Lago de Texcoco (Dry Lake)
Mimiapan
Atzcapotzalco
Naucalpan de Juárez
MEXICO CITY
Chicoloapan
Chimalpa
Cuajimalpa
Ixtacalco
Nezahualcóyotl
Huixquilucan
Ixtapalapa
Los Reyes
Río Frío
HY.
Toluca
Lerma
Villa Obregón Contreras
Coyoacán
Ayotla
INTER - AMERICAN
Ixtapaluca
Texmelucan
Capultitlán
Metepec
Mexicalcingo
San Andrés
Cerro Muneco 12 655
Tláhuac
DISTRITO
Tlalpan
Xochimilco
PUEBLA
Almoloya
Ajusco
Cerro Ajusco 12 850
Topilejo
Tecómitl
Nevado de Toluca 14 409
Tenango
Coatepec
FEDERAL
Oxtotepec
Milpa Alta
Iztaccíhuatl 17 343
Tenango
Amecameca
Tres Cumbres
Ozumba
Volcán Popocatépetl 17 887
Huitzilac
Tepoztlán
Tlalnepantla
MORELOS
Tlayacapan
Cuernavaca

Scale 1:1 000 000
0   5   10 Miles
0 4 8 12 16 Kilometers
©RMcN

Main map:

Tropic of Cancer

Laguna Almagre

PTA. JEREZ

Laguna de
an Andrés

ira
dad Madero
ampico
la Cuauhtémoc
mpico Alto

Laguna
Tamiahua
CABO ROJO
BARRECIFE BLANQUILLA
ISLA DE LOBOS

ma
Tamiahua
Alamo
Túxpan

ARRECIFE TANQUIJO
ARRECIFE TÚXPAN

Tihuatlán
Poza Rica
Tecolutla
Gutiérrez Zamora
lapa
Furbero
Nautla
Coyutla
Coxquihui
Vega de Alatorre
Cuetzalán del Progreso
Tlapacoyan
Misantla
ín
Atempan
Jalacingo
Altotonga
Naolinco
xtla
Teziutlán
Las Vigas
Libres
Perote
14 048 Nauchampatepetl
Xalapa
Coatepec
Teocelo
Antigua Veracruz
Punta Zempoala
cueyetl
Juan
Huatusco
Veracruz
nco
Coscomatepec
ARRECIFE CABEZA
Ciudad Serdán
18 406 Pico de Orizaba (Vol.)
Medellín
atzingo
Hidalgo
atempan
Orizaba
Córdoba
Tlalixcoyan
Nogales
Heroica
Omealca
Cotaxtla
Alvarado
Laguna
Maltrata
Tehuacan
Ajalpan
Zoquitlán
San Martín (Vol.) 6000
PTA. ZAPOTITLÁN
San Gabriel Chilac
Tlacotalpan
Santiago Tuxtla
Chazumba
Zinacatepec
Huatla de Jiménez
Ojitlán (S. Lucas)
San Andrés Tuxtla
Calemaco
S. Miguel
Teotitlán del Camino
Jalapa de Díaz (San Felipe)
Cosamaloápan
Chacaltianguis
Pajapan
Coatzacoalcos (Puerto México)
Tepelmeme
Cuicatlán
Tuxtepec
Tescheacan
Soteapan
de León
Coixtlahuaca
San Juan Evangelista
Jaltipan
Minatitlán
Acayucan
Cosoleacaque
Teposcolula
dro y San Pablo
Nochixtlán (Asunción)
Talea de Castro (San Miguel)
Playa Vicente
Texistepec
Sayula
Tlaxiaco
Sta. María Asunción
Ixtlán de Juárez
Villa Alta (San Ildefonso)
Chalcatongo
Yosonoti
Hidalgo Yalalag
Jesús Carranza
Pueblo Viejo
Sta. Cruz
Zimatlán de Álvarez
Zempoaltepetl 11 142
Zacatepec (Santiago)
Sola de Vega (S. Miguel)
Oaxaca
Mazatlán (San Juan)
Guichicovi (San Juan)
Chapultenango
San Mateo (Etlatongo)
Tlacolula de Matamoros
Tlaxca de Morelos
Ocotlán de Morelos
Táviche
Ejutla de Crespo
Ixtepec
Ixtaltepec (Asunción)
Zanatepec (Sto. Domingo)
ISTMO
DE
TEHUANTEPEC
Miahuatlán
Las Vacas
Jalapa del Marqués
Tehuantepec (Sto. Domingo)
Juchitán de Zaragoza
Unión Hidalgo
Ixhuatán (San Francisco)
Cintalapa
Las Cruces
CHIAPAS
otlán (Sta. María)
Loxicha (Sta. Catarina)
Pluma Hidalgo
Pochutla (San Pedro)
Puerto Ángel
Salina Cruz
Laguna Superior
Laguna Inferior
Mar Muerto
Villa Flores
Arriaga
Tonalá
SIERRA MADRE
CORD. DE CHIAPAS

GULF OF MEXICO

BAHÍA DE CAMPECHE

Sisal
Hunucmá
YUCATÁN
Maxcanú
Halachó
Calkiní
Dzitbalché
Hecelchakán

Lerma
Campeche
Seybaplaya
Champotón
Pustunich
CAMPECHE
Sabancuy
Chicbul
Mamantel

ISLA DEL CARMEN
Laguna de Términos
Ciudad del Carmen
PUNTA FONTERA
San Pedro
Frontera
Paraíso
Allende
Palizada
Comalcalco
TABASCO
Jalpa
Janutla
Cárdenas
Cunduacán
Villahermosa
San Carlos
Balancán
Huimanguillo
Tacotalpa
Emiliano Zapata
Teapa
Palenque
Pichucalco
Tenosique
MEXICO
GUATEMALA
Yajalón
Tecpatán
Pantepec
Simojovel
Bachajón
Compainalá
Jitotol
Ococingo
MESETA DE AGUA ESCONDIDA
Berriozábal
Tuxtla Gutiérrez
9400
Cancuc
Oxchuc
Ozocoautla
Bohom
San Cristóbal de las Casas
Chiapa de Corzo
Teopisca
Amatenango
Venustiano Carranza
Las Rosas
8202
Socoltenango
Comitán
La Concordia
Trinitaria
SA. CUCHUMATANES
GUATEMALA
Cuauhtemoc
Jacatenango
Pijijiapan
San Miguel
Mapastepec

GRAN
BLANCA (coastal labels)
SIERRA DE OAXACA
EL SUR

Golfo de Tehuantepec

Continued on pages 132-133

20 40 60 80 100 120 Miles
20 40 60 80 100 120 140 160 180 200 Kilometers

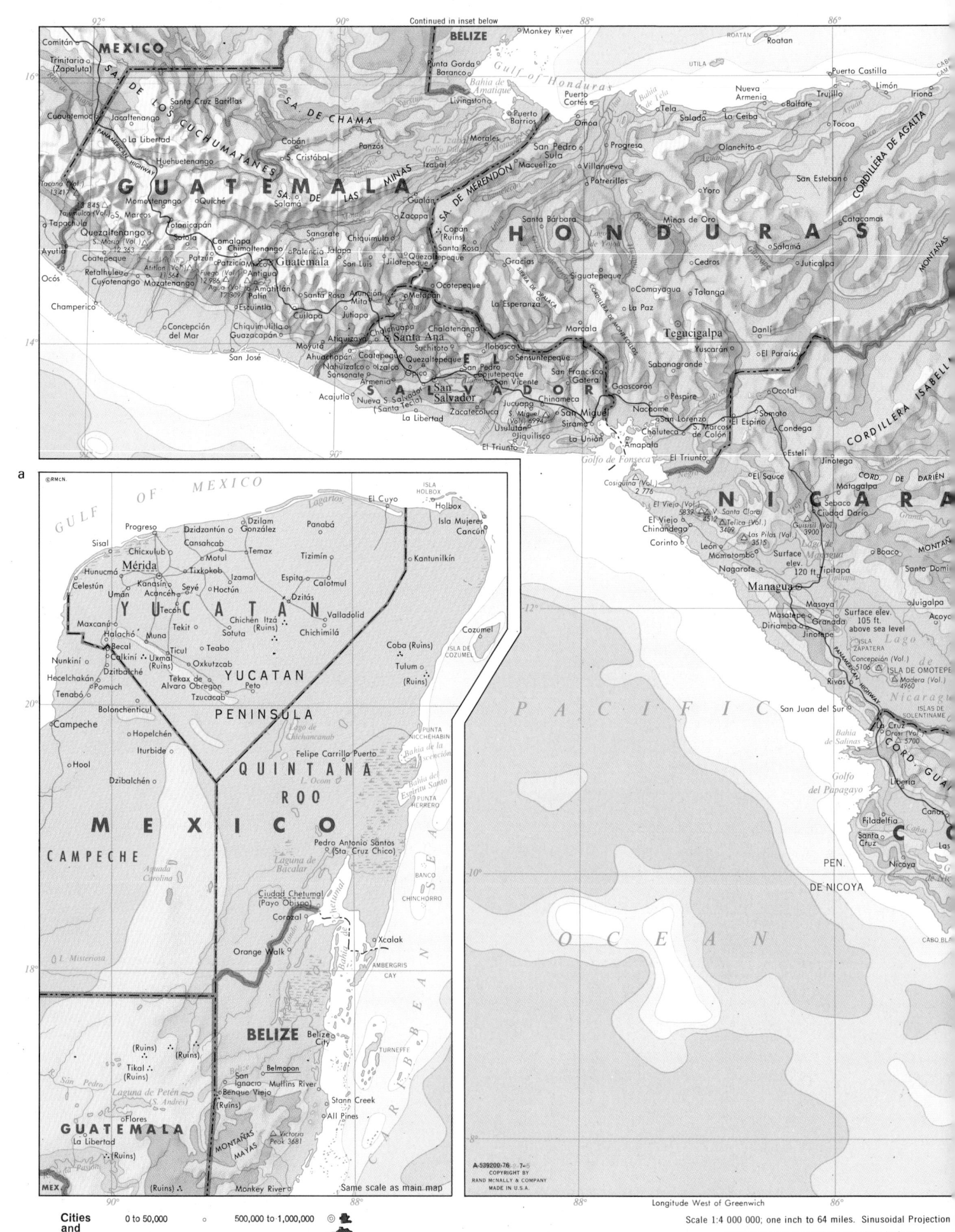

Cities
and
Towns

| 0 to 50,000 | 500,000 to 1,000,000 |
| 50,000 to 500,000 | 1,000,000 and over |

Scale 1:4 000 000; one inch to 64 miles. Sinusoidal Projection

Elevations and depressions are given in feet

Longitude West of Greenwich

Longitude West of Greenwich

Relief

Meters	Feet
3050	10 000
1525	5000
610	2000
305	1000
152.5	500
Sea Level	
152.5	500
1525	5000
3050	10 000

b

ANGUILLA (Br.)
ST. MARTIN (Neth. and Fr.)
ST. BARTHÉLEMY (Fr.)
SABA (Neth.)
ST. EUSTATIUS (Neth.)
Codrington BARBUDA
ST. KITTS
Mt. Misery 3792
Basseterre
ST. KITTS AND NEVIS
Charlestown Nevis Peak 3596
NEVIS
St. Johns
Boggy Peak 1319
ANTIGUA AND BARBUDA
REDONDA

L E E W A R D

MONTSERRAT (Br.)
Plymouth Chances Pk. 3000

POINTE DE LA GRANDE VIGIE
GRANDE TERRE
Ste. Rose Le Moule
Pointe-à-Pitre Ste. Anne DESIRADE (Fr.)
BASSE TERRE PETITE TERRE (Fr.)
Soufrière 4813 **GUADELOUPE** (Fr.)
Basse Terre Capesterre
LES SAINTES IS. MARIE GALANTE (Fr.)
Grand Bourg

Guadeloupe Passage

I S.

Portsmouth Morne Diablotins 4747
St. Joseph **DOMINICA**
Roseau

Dominica Channel

C A R I B B E A N

PUNTA PATUCA

Cabo Gracias a Dios
Coco

CAYOS MISKITO

Lone Star
Puerto Cabezas

Laguna Caratasca

Laguna Huaunta
Huaunta

Prinzapolca

Laguna las Perlas

ISLA DE PROVIDENCIA (Colombia)

SAN ANDRÉS (Colombia)
CAYOS DE ESE

LITTLE CORN

Rama
GREAT CORN
CAYOS DE ALBUQUERQUE (Colombia)

Bluefields
ISLA DE LA CIERVO

PUNTA MICO

Bahía de San Juan del Norte

San Juan del Norte (Greytown)

S E A

Mt. Pelée (Vol.) 4583
St. Pierre Trinité
Pitons du Carbet 3960
Fort-de-France Le François
MARTINIQUE (Fr.)
Le Marin
POINTE D'ENFER

St. Lucia Channel

Castries
Morne Gimie 3117 **ST. LUCIA**
Soufrière

St. Vincent Passage

W I N D W A R D

Soufrière 4048
ST. VINCENT AND THE GRENADINES
Kingstown
BEQUIA
MUSTIQUE
CANOUAN

THE GRENADINES
CARRIACOU

Mt. St. Catherine 2757
St. George's Grenville
GRENADA

NORTH POINT
BARBADOS
Mt. Hillaby 1115
Bathsheba
Bridgetown
SOUTH POINT

A T L A N T I C O C E A N

C A R I B B E A N S E A

Same scale as main map

Carlos

U A

C O S T A

San Ramón Guapiles
Alajuela Heredia Cairo
San José Irazú (Vol.) Turrialba
Cartago Paraíso
Matina Limón

R I C A

Parrita
Quepos
PUNTA QUEPOS San Isidro
Cerro Chirripó 12 530
Cordillera
Cerro Kámuk 11 696
de
PUNTA CAHUITA

Bahía de Coronada

ISLA DE CAÑO
PENÍNSULA
Puerto Jiménez
DE OSA
CABO MATAPALO

Puerto Cortés
Buenos Aires
Cerro Echandi 10 394
Talamanca
Boquete
Volcán Barú 11 401
Golfito
Concepción
La Cuesta David
Puerto Armuelles
PUNTA BURICA

Golfo Dulce

Bahía Charco de Azul

Bocas del Toro Golfo
Bahía de Almirante
Guabito
Almirante
PUNTA CHIRIQUÍ
Chiriquí Grande
Laguna de Chiriquí
ESCUDO DE VERAGUAS

de los Mosquitos

Horconcitos
Remedios
Las Palmas
Santiago
Soná
Río de Jesús

SERRANIA DE TABASARÁ
C. de Santa Catalina 5249
C. Negro 4429

P A N

Nato
Antón
Aguadulce
Río Hato
Penonomé
Bejuco

PUNTA MANZANILLO Nombre de Dios El Porvenir PUNTA SAN BLAS
Portobelo Mandinga Golfo de San Blas
Colón Silver City
Gatún North Gamboa
C. Brewster 3018
Chepo
Balboa Heights
Balboa **Panamá**
Chorrera Bahía de Panamá

A M A

CORD. DE SAN BLAS
SERRANIA DEL DARIEN

Lago Gatún
ISTMO DE PANAMA

PUNTA CHAME
ARCHIPIÉLAGO DE LAS PERLAS
San Miguel
ISLA DEL REY
ISLA DE SAN JOSÉ

Golfo de Parita

Chitré Los Santos
PENÍNSULA
DE AZUERO
Las Tablas
PUNTA MALA

Golfo de Panamá

Bahía San Miguel
La Palma
CABO TIBURON

El Real

C O L O M B I A

Garachiné
PUNTA GARACHINE

ISLA COIBA
ISLA CEBACO
PUNTA MARIATO
ISLA JICARÓN

| 0 | 20 | 40 | 60 | 80 | 100 | 120 Miles |
| 0 | 20 | 40 | 60 | 80 | 100 | 120 | 140 | 160 | 180 | 200 Kilometers |

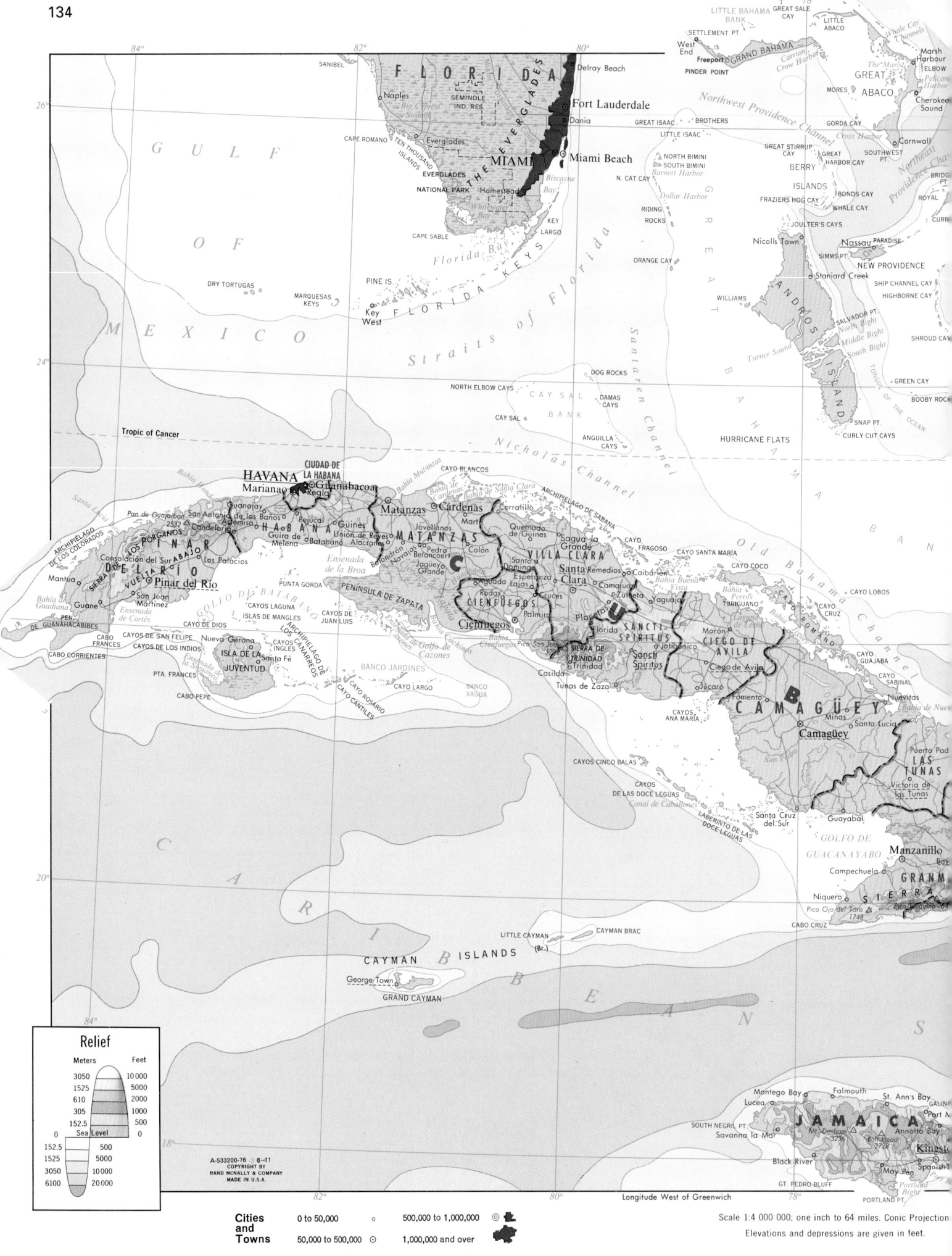

Scale 1:1 000 000

HAVANA
(La Habana)

GULF OF MEXICO

Playa de Guanabo

Cojimar

Guanabacoa

Campo Florido

Regla

San Francisco de Paula

Playa de Santa Fé

Baracoa

Marianao

Cotorro

Cuatro Caminos

Arroya Arena

Calabazar

Bauta

Rancho Boyeros

Managua

Caimito del Guayabal

Santiago de las Vegas

Bejucal

San José de las Lajas

La Sabina

Ceiba del Agua

San Antonio de los Baños

Buenaventura

San Antonio de las Vegas

△ 950

©RMCN.

A T L A N T I C   O C E A N

Tropic of Cancer

ELEUTHERA

Governor's Harbour

PALMETTO PT.

THERA PT.

Rock Sound

Arthur's Town

NORTHEAST PT.

LITTLE SAN SALVADOR

CAT

Old Bight

HAWKS NEST PT.

COLUMBUS PT.

SAN SALVADOR
(WATLING)
(Columbus, Oct. 12, 1492)
SOUTHWEST PT.

GREAT GUANA CAY

CONCEPTION

LEE STOCKING

Rolleville

CAPE STA. MARIA

RUM CAY

GREAT EXUMA

George Town

LITTLE EXUMA

HOG CAY

LONG

Clarence Town

SAMANA OR ATWOOD CAY

JUMENTO CAYS

WATER CAY

FLAMINGO CAY

CAP VERDE

BIRD ROCK

CROOKED

NORTHEAST PT.

JAMAICA CAY

Man of War Channel

SEAL CAYS

FORTUNE

PLANA OR FLAT CAYS

CHINOS BANKS

NURSE CAY

DIANA BANK

FISH CAY

The Bight of Acklins

ACKLINS

Abraham's Bay

MAYAGUANA

RACCOON CAY

SALINA PT.

GREAT RAGGED

MIRA POR VOS ISLETS

CASTLE

CAY VERDE

COLUMBUS BANK

HOGSTY REEF

CAICOS PASSAGE

PROVIDENCIALES

NORTH CAICOS

GRAND CAICOS

CAPE COMETE

EAST CAICOS

CAICOS IS.
(Br.)

WEST CAICOS

GRAND TURK

Grand Turk

CAY STA. DOMINGO

CAICOS BANK

SOUTH CAICOS

TURKS IS. (Br.)

BROWN BANK

LITTLE INAGUA

WEST SAND SPIT

AMBERGRIS CAYS

SALT CAY

PALMETTO PT.

NORTHEAST PT.

Ocean Bight

SEAL CAYS

MOUCHOIR PASSAGE

GREAT INAGUA

The Lake

Matthew Town

Man of War Bay

MOUCHOIR BANK

South Bay

SILVER BANK

CABO LUCRECIA

Banes

Bahía de Nipe

Antilla

Holguín

Mayarí

Sagua de Tánamo

CUCHILLA DE TOA

NAVIDAD BANK

HOLGUÍN

SANTIAGO DE CUBA

GUANTÁNAMO

SA. DE PURIAL

Baracoa

ORIENTAL

Alto Songo

PUNTA MAISÍ

San Luis

Caney

ILE DE LA TORTUE

Bahía de Ovando

CABO ISABELA

CORDILLERA SEPTENTRIONAL

Coumanera

Santiago de Cuba

Guantánamo

Yateras

Naval Station (U.S.A.)

Port de Paix

Cap-Haitien

Monte Cristi

Puerto Plata

Pico Diego

Gaspar Hernández

CABO FRANCÉS VIEJO

Bahía de Guantánamo

CAP ST. NICOLAS

Le Môle

Le Borgne

Limbé

Fort Liberté

Guayubin

Dajabón

Mao

Santiago Rodríguez

Salcedo

San Francisco de Macorís

CABO SAMANÁ

Bahía Escocesa

PTE. PLATEFORME

Grande Rivière du Nord

Ouanaminthe

Vallière

Santiago de los Caballeros

LA VEGA

La Vega

Moca

Nagua

Sánchez

Samaná

Bahía de Samaná

CABO SAN RAFAEL

Windward Passage

GOLFE DES GONAIVES

Gonaïves

St. Michel de l'Atalaye

Pic Beauham

Hinche

Riva

Sabana de la Mar

CORDILLERA ORIENTAL

Miches

St. Marc

DOMINICAN

Pico Duarte

Jarabacoa

Cotui

Hato Mayor

Seibo

Canal de Saint-Marc

HAITI

Mirebalais

Lascahobas

San Juan

Mte. Tina

Bayaguana

Los Llanos

Higüey

POINT OUEST

ILE DE LA GONÂVE

Banica

CORDILLERA CENTRAL

Jérémie

ILE GRANDE CAYEMITE

Canal du Sud

Port-au-Prince

Pétionville

SIERRA DE NEIBA

Neiba

Azua

San Cristóbal

La Romana

CAP DAME MARIE

Anse d'Hainault

Miragoane

Léogâne

Petit Goâve

MASSIF DE LA SELLE

CUL DE SAC

Duvergé

Baoruco

Bani

Santo Domingo

S. Pedro de Macorís

CATALINA

NAVASSA (U.S.A.)

MASSIF DE LA HOTTE

Aquin

Bahía de Neiba

SAONA

Tiburon

Coteaux

SIERRA DE BAHORUCO

Enriquillo

Les Cayes

Jacmel

Belle-Anse

Oviedo

POINTE À GRAVOIS

ILE À VACHE

H I S P A N I O L A

MORANT PT.

CABO FALSO

BEATA

CABO BEATA

ALTO VELO

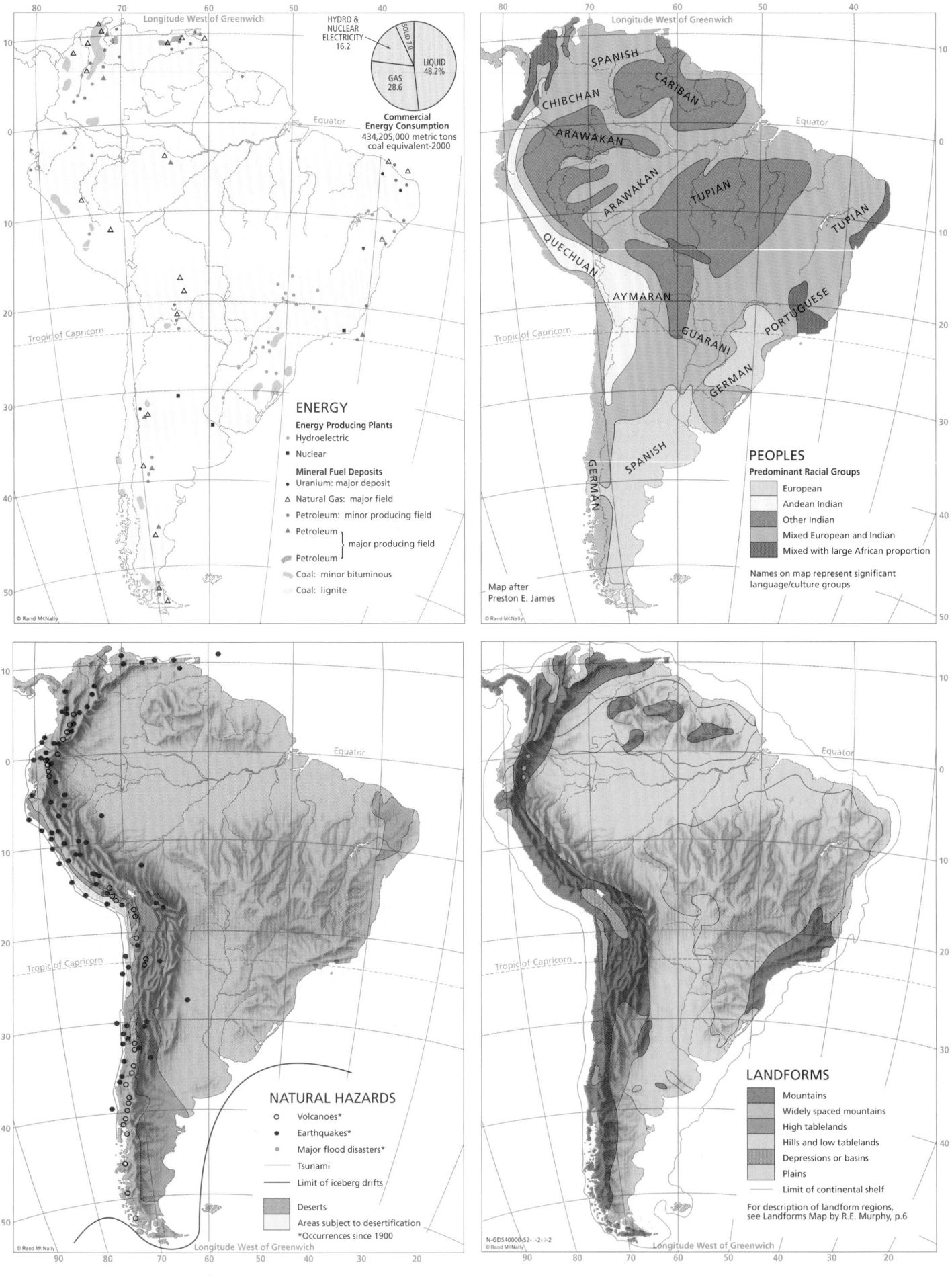

HYDRO & NUCLEAR ELECTRICITY 16.2

SOLID 7.0

LIQUID 48.2%

GAS 28.6

Commercial Energy Consumption 434,205,000 metric tons coal equivalent-2000

ENERGY

Energy Producing Plants
- Hydroelectric
- Nuclear

Mineral Fuel Deposits
- Uranium: major deposit
- Natural Gas: major field
- Petroleum: minor producing field
- Petroleum } major producing field
- Petroleum
- Coal: minor bituminous
- Coal: lignite

© Rand McNally

PEOPLES

Predominant Racial Groups
- European
- Andean Indian
- Other Indian
- Mixed European and Indian
- Mixed with large African proportion

Names on map represent significant language/culture groups

Map after Preston E. James

© Rand McNally

NATURAL HAZARDS

- ○ Volcanoes*
- ● Earthquakes*
- ● Major flood disasters*
- —— Tsunami
- —— Limit of iceberg drifts
- Deserts
- Areas subject to desertification

*Occurrences since 1900

© Rand McNally

LANDFORMS

- Mountains
- Widely spaced mountains
- High tablelands
- Hills and low tablelands
- Depressions or basins
- Plains
- —— Limit of continental shelf

For description of landform regions, see Landforms Map by R.E. Murphy, p.6

N-GDS40000-S2- -2-2-2
© Rand McNally

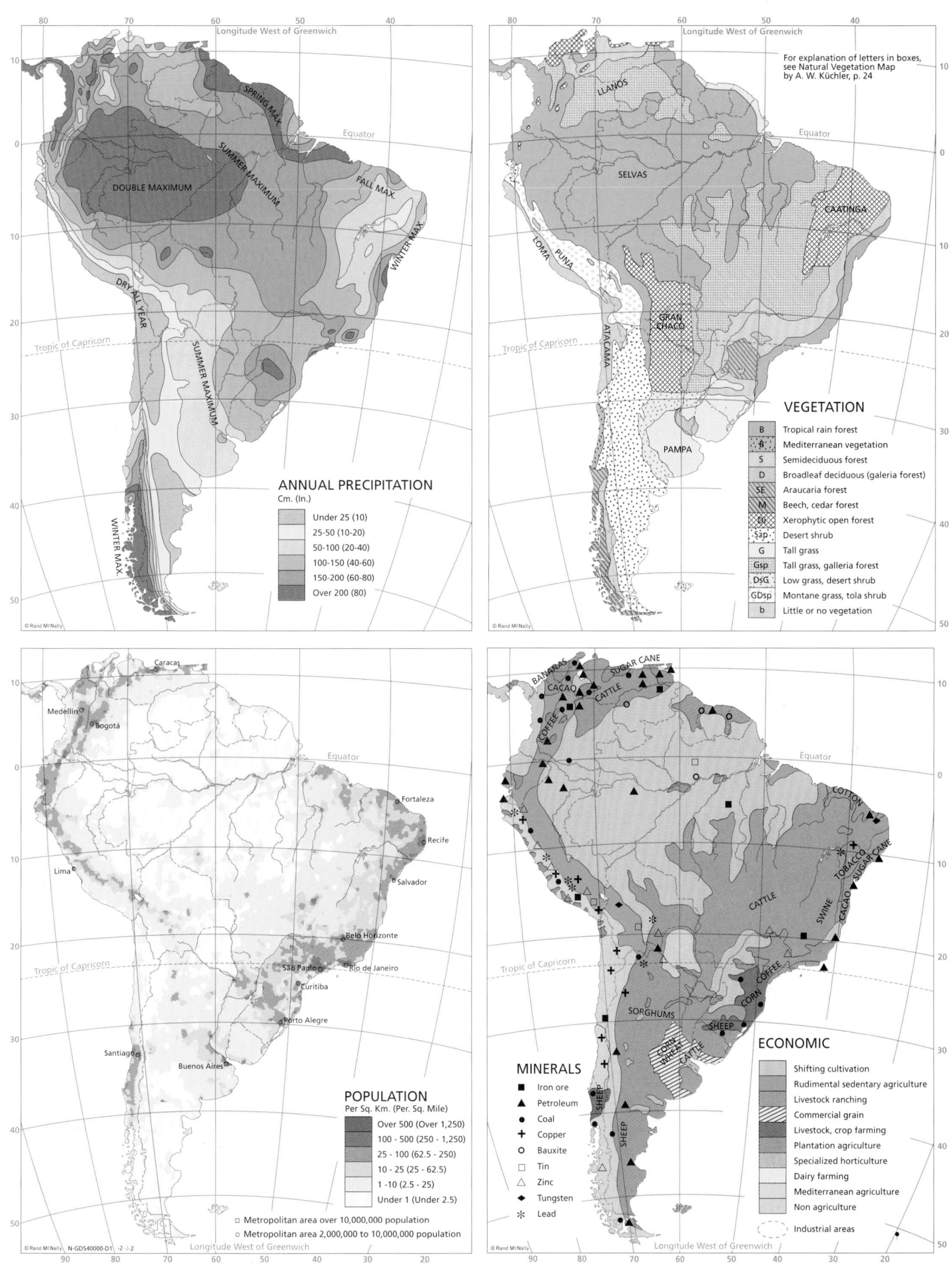

ANNUAL PRECIPITATION

DOUBLE MAXIMUM

SPRING MAX.

SUMMER MAXIMUM

FALL MAX.

WINTER MAX.

DRY ALL YEAR

SUMMER MAXIMUM

WINTER MAX.

Equator

Tropic of Capricorn

Longitude West of Greenwich

© Rand McNally

ANNUAL PRECIPITATION
Cm. (In.)

- Under 25 (10)
- 25-50 (10-20)
- 50-100 (20-40)
- 100-150 (40-60)
- 150-200 (60-80)
- Over 200 (80)

LLANOS

SELVAS

CAATINGA

LOMA

PUNA

ATACAMA

GRAN CHACO

PAMPA

For explanation of letters in boxes, see Natural Vegetation Map by A. W. Küchler, p. 24

Equator

Tropic of Capricorn

© Rand McNally

VEGETATION

B	Tropical rain forest
B	Mediterranean vegetation
S	Semideciduous forest
D	Broadleaf deciduous (galeria forest)
SE	Araucaria forest
M	Beech, cedar forest
Di	Xerophytic open forest
Szp	Desert shrub
G	Tall grass
Gsp	Tall grass, galleria forest
DsG	Low grass, desert shrub
GDsp	Montane grass, tola shrub
b	Little or no vegetation

Caracas

Medellín
Bogotá

Lima

Fortaleza

Recife

Salvador

Belo Horizonte

São Paulo
Rio de Janeiro

Curitiba

Porto Alegre

Santiago

Buenos Aires

Equator

Tropic of Capricorn

© Rand McNally N-GDS40000-D1 -2-2-2

Longitude West of Greenwich

POPULATION
Per Sq. Km. (Per. Sq. Mile)

- Over 500 (Over 1,250)
- 100 - 500 (250 - 1,250)
- 25 - 100 (62.5 - 250)
- 10 - 25 (25 - 62.5)
- 1 -10 (2.5 - 25)
- Under 1 (Under 2.5)

□ Metropolitan area over 10,000,000 population
○ Metropolitan area 2,000,000 to 10,000,000 population

BANANAS
SUGAR CANE
CACAO
CATTLE
COFFEE
COTTON
TOBACCO
SUGAR CANE
CACAO
CATTLE
SWINE
CATTLE
COFFEE
CORN
SORGHUMS
SHEEP
CORN
WHEAT
CATTLE
SHEEP
SHEEP

Equator

Tropic of Capricorn

© Rand McNally

Longitude West of Greenwich

MINERALS

- ■ Iron ore
- ▲ Petroleum
- ● Coal
- + Copper
- ○ Bauxite
- □ Tin
- △ Zinc
- ◆ Tungsten
- ✳ Lead

ECONOMIC

- Shifting cultivation
- Rudimental sedentary agriculture
- Livestock ranching
- Commercial grain
- Livestock, crop farming
- Plantation agriculture
- Specialized horticulture
- Dairy farming
- Mediterranean agriculture
- Non agriculture

◌ Industrial areas

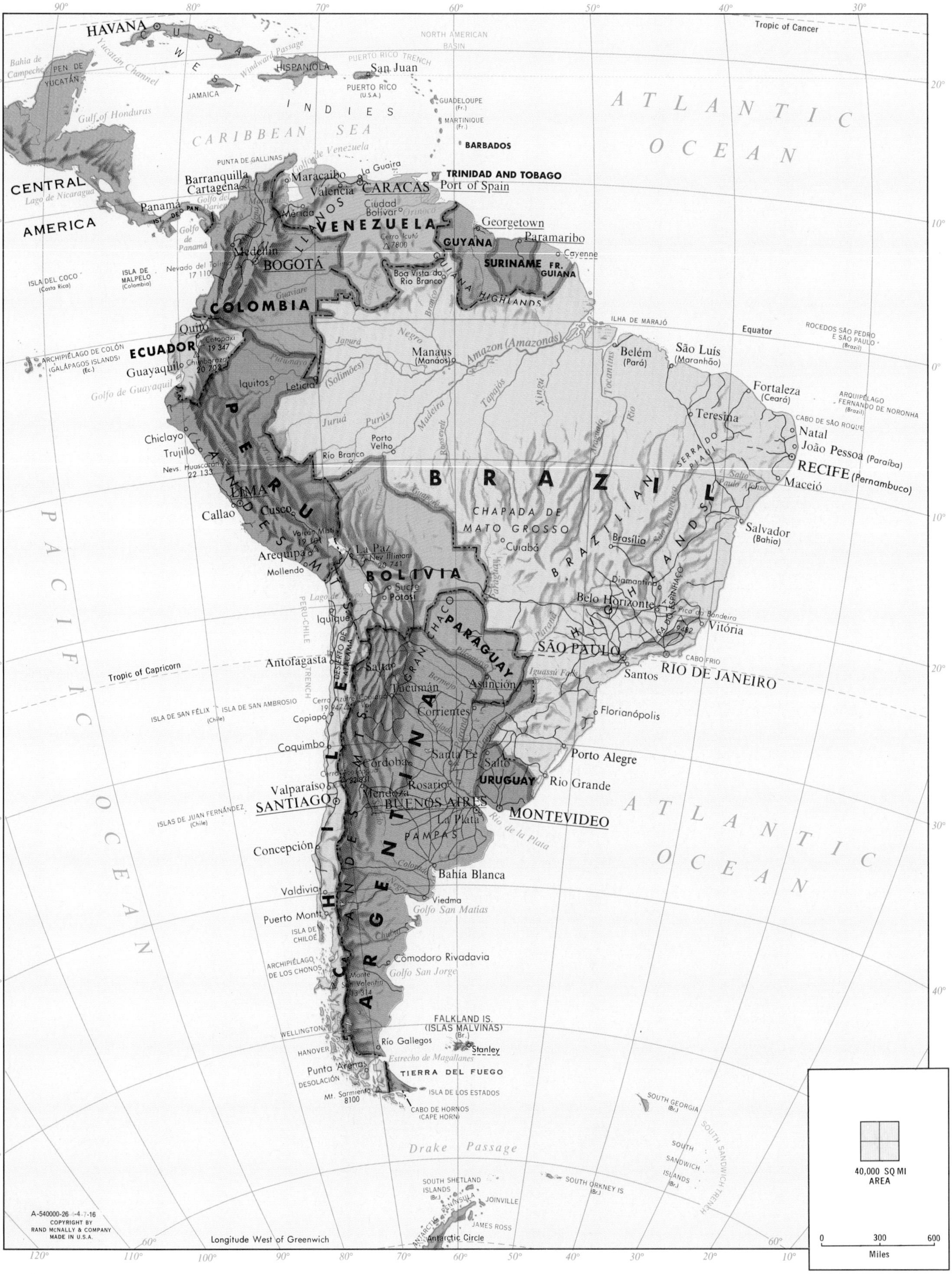

HAVANA
Bahía de Campeche
PEN. DE YUCATÁN
Yucatán Channel
C U B A
W E S T
JAMAICA
HISPANIOLA
San Juan
PUERTO RICO TRENCH
PUERTO RICO (U.S.A.)
NORTH AMERICAN BASIN
Tropic of Cancer

ATLANTIC OCEAN

Gulf of Honduras
CENTRAL
AMERICA
Lago de Nicaragua
Panamá
IST. DE PAN.
Golfo de Panamá
CARIBBEAN SEA
I N D I E S
PUNTA DE GALLINAS
Golfo de Venezuela
GUADELOUPE (Fr.)
MARTINIQUE (Fr.)
BARBADOS
TRINIDAD AND TOBAGO
Port of Spain

ISLA DEL COCO (Costa Rica)
ISLA DE MALPELO (Colombia)
ARCHIPIÉLAGO DE COLÓN (GALÁPAGOS ISLANDS) (Ec.)

Barranquilla
Cartagena
Maracaibo
Valencia
La Guaira
CARACAS
Mérida
Ciudad Bolívar
L L A N O S
VENEZUELA
Cerro Icutú 7800
Georgetown
Paramaribo
Cayenne
GUYANA
SURINAME
FR. GUIANA
Medellín
Golfo del Darién
Nevado del Tolima 17 110
BOGOTÁ
COLOMBIA
Boa Vista do Rio Branco
GUIANA HIGHLANDS

Quito
Cotopaxi 19 347
ECUADOR
Guayaquil
Chimborazo 20 702
Golfo de Guayaquil
Chiclayo
Trujillo
Nevs. Huascarán 22 133
Iquitos
Leticia
Putumayo
Japurá
Negro
Amazon (Amazonas)
Solimões
Juruá
Purús
Manaus (Manáos)
Madeira
Tapajós
Xingú
Belém (Pará)
Equator
São Luís (Maranhão)
ROCEDOS SÃO PEDRO E SÃO PAULO (Brazil)
Fortaleza (Ceará)
ARQUIPÉLAGO FERNANDO DE NORONHA (Brazil)
Teresina
CABO DE SÃO ROQUE
Natal
João Pessoa (Paraíba)
RECIFE (Pernambuco)
Maceió

Callao
LIMA
Cusco
Arequipa
Mollendo
Volcán Misti 19 101
La Paz
Nev. Illimani 20 741
P E R U
A N D E S
M T S.
Río Branco
Porto Velho
B R A Z I L
CHAPADA DE MATO GROSSO
Cuiabá
BOLIVIA
Sucre
Potosí
B R A Z I L I A N
Brasília
Diamantina
Belo Horizonte
Pico da Bandeira 9482
Vitória
Salvador (Bahia)
Salto Paulo Afonso
H I G H L A N D S

PERU-CHILE TRENCH
Iquique
Antofagasta
Tropic of Capricorn
ISLA DE SAN FÉLIX (Chile)
ISLA DE SAN AMBROSIO (Chile)
Copiapó
Cerro Azul 19 947
Salar
GRAN CHACO
Bermejo
Pilcomayo
PARAGUAY
Asunción
Iguassú Falls
SÃO PAULO
Santos
CABO FRIO
RIO DE JANEIRO
Florianópolis

Coquimbo
Valparaíso
SANTIAGO
Concepción
Valdivia
Puerto Montt
ISLAS DE JUAN FERNÁNDEZ (Chile)
Aconcagua 22 835
Mendoza
Tucumán
Córdoba
Rosario
Santa Fe
Corrientes
Salto
Paraná
Santiago
A R G E N T I N A
C H I L E
A N D E S
Salta
PAMPAS
BUENOS AIRES
La Plata
Río de la Plata
URUGUAY
MONTEVIDEO
Rio Grande
Porto Alegre
Bahía Blanca
Colorado
Viedma
Golfo San Matías
ISLA DE CHILOÉ
ARCHIPIÉLAGO DE LOS CHONOS
Chubut
Comodoro Rivadavia
Golfo San Jorge
Monte Valentín 14 314
Mt. Sarmiento 8100
WELLINGTON
HANOVER
DESOLACIÓN
Punta Arenas
Río Gallegos
Estrecho de Magallanes
FALKLAND IS. (ISLAS MALVINAS) (Br.)
Stanley
TIERRA DEL FUEGO
ISLA DE LOS ESTADOS
CABO DE HORNOS (CAPE HORN)

PACIFIC OCEAN

ATLANTIC OCEAN

Drake Passage

SOUTH GEORGIA (Br.)
SOUTH SANDWICH ISLANDS (Br.)
SOUTH ORKNEY IS. (Br.)
SOUTH SHETLAND ISLANDS
JOINVILLE
JAMES ROSS
Antarctic Circle

A-540000-26-4-7-16
COPYRIGHT BY
RAND McNALLY & COMPANY
MADE IN U.S.A.

Longitude West of Greenwich

0 200 400 600 800 1000 Miles
0 400 800 1200 1600 Kilometers

Scale 1:40 000 000; one inch to 630 miles. Lambert's Azimuthal, Equal Area Projection
Elevations and depressions are given in feet

40,000 SQ MI AREA
0 300 600
Miles

Tropic of Cancer

HAVANA

CENTRAL

AMERICA

PACIFIC OCEAN

ATLANTIC OCEAN

CARIBBEAN SEA

WEST INDIES

San Juan

PUERTO RICO (U.S.A.)

GUADELOUPE (Fr.)

MARTINIQUE (Fr.)

BARBADOS

TRINIDAD AND TOBAGO
Port of Spain

Barranquilla
Cartagena
Maracaibo
Valencia
La Guaira
CARACAS

Panama

Medellín
BOGOTÁ

COLOMBIA

VENEZUELA

LLANOS

Ciudad Bolívar
Orinoco

Georgetown
Paramaribo
Cayenne

GUYANA
SURINAME
FR. GUIANA

GUIANA HIGHLANDS

Boa Vista do Rio Branco

Quito
ECUADOR
Guayaquil

Iquitos

Leticia

Manaus (Manáos)

Amazon (Amazonas)

Belém (Pará)

São Luís (Maranhão)

Equator

ROCEDOS SÃO PEDRO E SÃO PAULO (Brazil)

Chiclayo
Trujillo

Río Branco

Porto Velho

B R A Z I L

Fortaleza (Ceará)

Teresina

ARQUIPÉLAGO DE FERNANDO DE NORONHA (Brazil)

CABO DE SÃO ROQUE

Natal
João Pessoa (Paraíba)
RECIFE (Pernambuco)
Maceió

LIMA
Callao

Cusco

Arequipa
Mollendo

CHAPADA DE MATO GROSSO
Cuiabá

BOLIVIA

La Paz
Sucre
Potosí

Brasília

BRAZILIAN HIGHLANDS

Diamantina

Belo Horizonte

Salvador (Bahia)

Vitória

PACIFIC OCEAN

Antofagasta

CHACO

PARAGUAY

Asunción

SÃO PAULO

Santos

CABO FRIO
RIO DE JANEIRO

Tropic of Capricorn

ISLA DE SAN FÉLIX (Chile)
ISLA DE SAN AMBROSIO (Chile)

Copiapó

Coquimbo

Tucumán

Corrientes

Florianópolis

A R G E N T I N A

Valparaíso
SANTIAGO

Concepción

Valdivia

Puerto Montt

ISLA DE CHILOÉ

ARCHIPIÉLAGO DE LOS CHONOS

Córdoba
Rosario
Mendoza
BUENOS AIRES
La Plata

Santa Fe
Salto
URUGUAY

Porto Alegre
Río Grande

MONTEVIDEO

ATLANTIC OCEAN

PAMPAS

Bahía Blanca

Viedma

Golfo San Matías

Comodoro Rivadavia

Golfo San Jorge

FALKLAND IS. (ISLAS MALVINAS) (Br.)

WELLINGTON
HANOVER

Río Gallegos

Stanley

Punta Arenas
DESOLACIÓN

TIERRA DEL FUEGO

ISLA DE LOS ESTADOS

Estrecho de Magallanes

CABO DE HORNOS (CAPE HORN)

Drake Passage

SOUTH GEORGIA (Br.)

SOUTH SANDWICH ISLANDS (Br.)

SOUTH ORKNEY IS. (Br.)

SOUTH SHETLAND ISLANDS (Br.)

Antarctic Circle

Longitude West of Greenwich

Relief	
Meters	Feet
3050	10 000
1525	5000
610	2000
305	1000
0	Sea Level 0
152.5	500
1525	5000
3050	10 000
6100	20 000

0   200   400   600   800   1000 Miles
0   400   800   1200   1600 Kilometers

Scale 1:40 000 000; one inch to 630 miles. Lambert's Azimuthal, Equal Area Projection
Elevations and depressions are given in feet

CUBA
JAMAICA
Kingston   HISPANIOLA
San Juan
PUERTO RICO

Caribbean Sea

ATLANTIC

OCEAN

Barranquilla   Maracaibo   CARACAS   Port of Spain
TRINIDAD

Panamá

L L A N O S   *Orinoco*

Georgetown

BOGOTÁ

Quito   *Negro*   *Equator*

Iquitos   *Amazon*   Manaus   Belém

S E L V A S

Fortaleza

Rio Branco

São Francisco

Recife

LIMA

Salvador

La Paz   Cuiabá
M A T O   Brasília
G R O S S O

Iquique

Belo Horizonte

G R A N   C H A C O   *Paraná*   SÃO
PAULO
Asunción   RIO DE JANEIRO

Tropic of Capricorn

San Miguel
de Tucumán

Porto Alegre

Córdoba

PACIFIC

SANTIAGO   BUENOS AIRES

ATLANTIC

Montevideo

P A M P A   *OCEAN*

OCEAN

Bahía Blanca

P A T A G O N I A

Puerto Montt

Puerto Arenas   TIERRA
DEL FUEGO

FALKLAND
ISLANDS

SOUTH
GEORGIA

Drake   Passage

A-540000-36

■	Urban
■	Cropland
■	Cropland & Woodland
■	Cropland & Grazing Land
■	Grassland, Grazing Land
■	Forest, Woodland
■	Swamp, Marshland
■	Shrub, Sparse Grass, Wasteland
■	Barren Land

Scale 1:36,000,000: one inch to 570 miles   Lambert Azimuthal Equal-Area Projection

0   100   200   400   600   800 Miles
0   150   300   600   900   1200 Kilometers

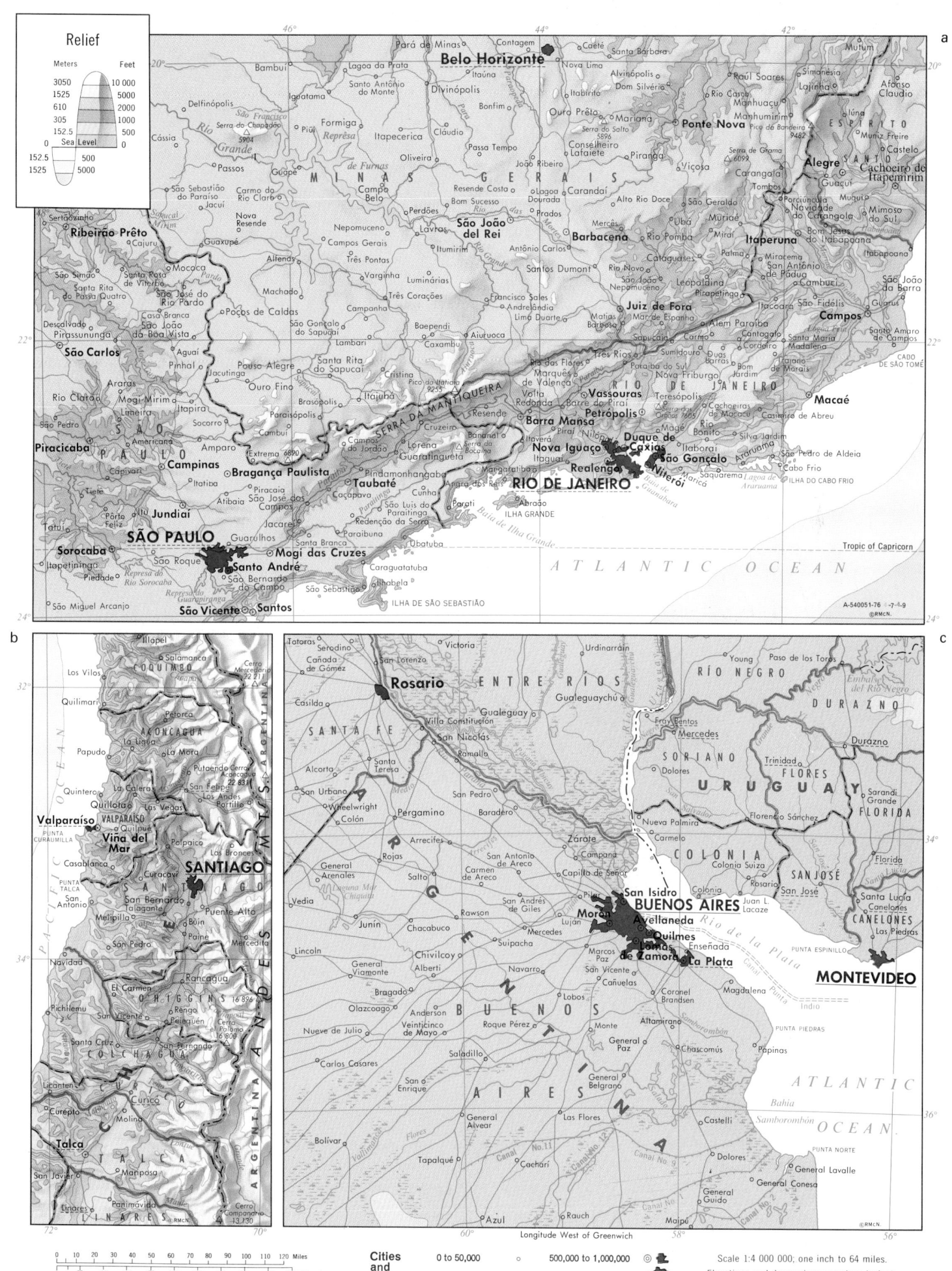

Relief

Meters		Feet
3050		10 000
1525		5000
610		2000
305		1000
152.5		500
0	Sea Level	0
152.5		500
1525		5000

a

b

c

Longitude West of Greenwich

0 10 20 30 40 50 60 70 80 90 100 110 120 Miles
0 20 40 60 80 100 120 140 160 180 200 Kilometers

Cities and Towns

0 to 50,000 o
50,000 to 500,000 ⊙

500,000 to 1,000,000 ◎
1,000,000 and over

Scale 1:4 000 000; one inch to 64 miles.
Elevations and depressions are given in feet.

Continued on pages 128-129

PACIFIC OCEAN

CARIBBEAN SEA

EL SALVADOR

NICARAGUA

COSTA RICA

PANAMA

COLOMBIA

VENEZUELA

ECUADOR

PERU

BOLIVIA

ARGENTINA

AMAZ SELVA

ACRE

RONDO

CARACAS

BOGOTÁ

MEDELLÍN

Quito

LIMA

La Paz

Cities and Towns

| 0 to 50,000 | o | 500,000 to 1,000,000 |
| 50,000 to 500,000 | ⊙ | 1,000,000 and over |

Scale 1:16 000 000; one inch to 250 miles. Sinusoidal Project
Elevations and depressions are given in feet

a

Scale 1:4 000 000

A-549100-76- ●11-10-22
COPYRIGHT BY
RAND McNALLY & COMPANY
MADE IN U.S.A.

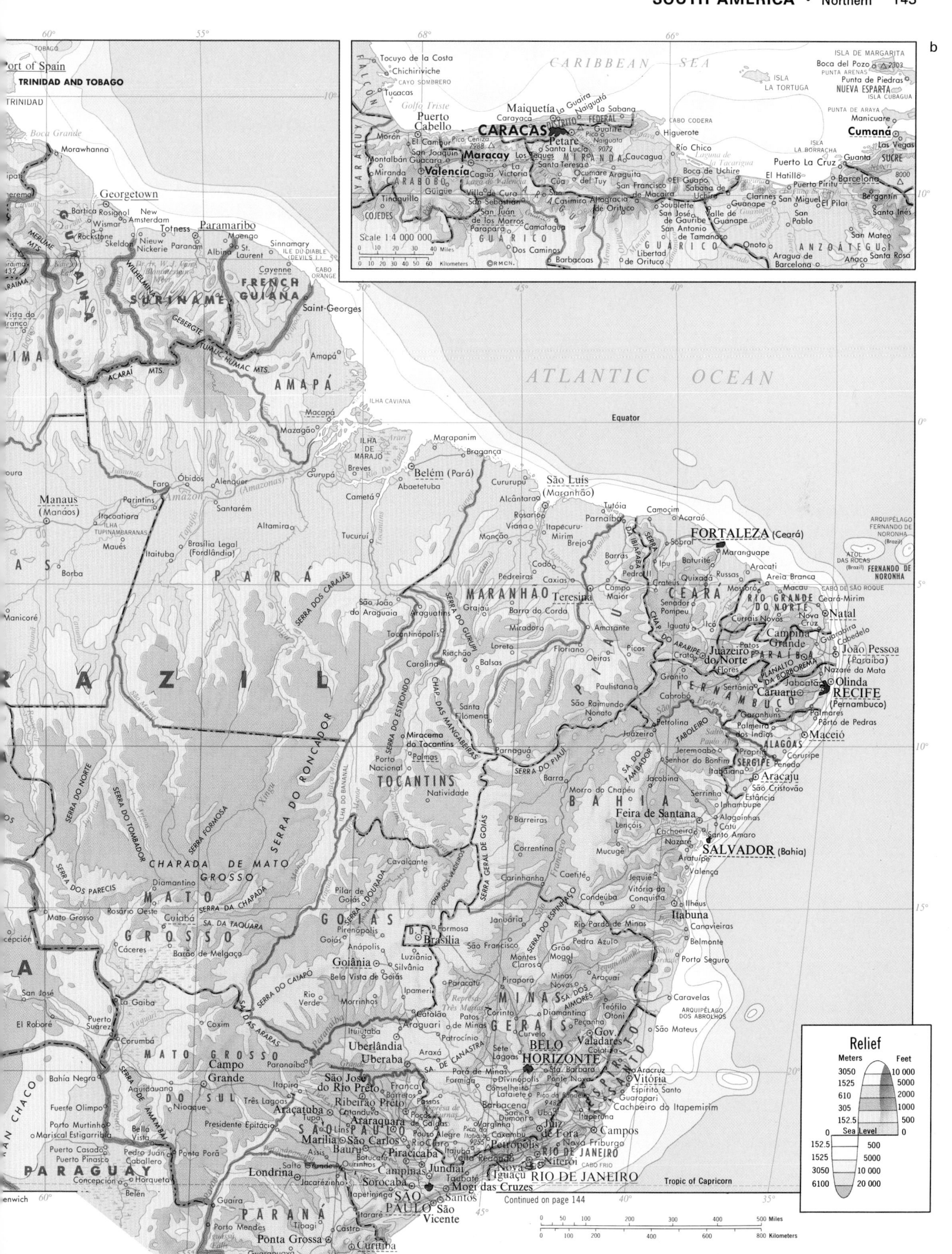

b

Inset map (top right)

CARIBBEAN SEA

ISLA DE MARGARITA
Boca del Pozo △7303
PUNTA ARENAS
Punta de Piedras
NUEVA ESPARTA
ISLA CUBAGUA

Tocuyo de la Costa
Chichiriviche
Cayo Sombrero
Tucacas
ISLA LA TORTUGA

Maiquetía La Guaira Naiguatá
FALCON Carayaca La Sabana
Puerto Cabello Pico Ceniza
7288 CARACAS FEDERAL Guatire
Morón El Cambur Petare Santa Lucía
San Joaquín Los Teques 9072 Caucagua
Montalbán Guacara Maracay Río Chico
Miranda La Santa Teresa
Valencia MIRANDA Higuerote Manicuare
ARABOBO Villa de Cura Ocumare Boca de Uchire Cumaná
Lago de Valencia del Tuy El Guapo Guanta SUCRE 8000
Tinaquillo San Sebastián San Francisco Sabana de Puerto La Cruz Barcelona △
COJEDES de Macaira Uchire El Hatillo Puerto Píritu Bergantín
San Juan Soublette Clarines San Miguel El Pilar
de los Morros San Guanape San Santa Inés
Parapara GUARICO José San Antonio Pablo
de Gauribe de Tamanaco Onoto
Camatagua Guanape
Dos Caminos San Mateo
Barbacoas Memo ANZOÁTEGUI Santa Rosa
Aragua de Anaco
Libertad GUARICO Barcelona
de Orituco Puerto Las Vegas

Scale 1:4 000 000
0 10 20 30 40 Miles
0 10 20 30 40 50 60 Kilometers
©R.M.N.

Main map

Trinidad / Guianas (upper left)

Port of Spain
TOBAGO
TRINIDAD AND TOBAGO
TRINIDAD
Boca Grande

Morawhanna
Georgetown
Bartica New Rosignol Amsterdam
Wismar Totness Paramaribo
Rockstone Nieuw Moengo
Skeldon Nickerie Paranam Albina St. Sinnamary ILE DU DIABLE (DEVIL'S I.)
MERUME MTS. Laurent Cayenne
SURINAME FRENCH GUIANA CABO ORANGE
WILHELMINA GEBERGTE Saint-Georges
TUMAC-HUMAC MTS.
ACARAÍ MTS.
Amapá

Brazil

Vista do
branco
Vista do
Sul

ATLANTIC OCEAN
Equator

RAIMA

Manaus
(Manáos)
Faro Óbidos Alenquer
Parintins
Itacoatiara
ILHA Santarém
TUPINAMBARANAS
Maués
Borba Itaituba
Brasília Legal
(Fordlândia)

Macapá
Mazagão
ILHA DE MARAJO
Breves Gurupá
ILHA CAVIANA
Arari
Marapanim
Bragança
Belém (Pará)
Cururupu São Luís
Abaetetuba (Maranhão)
Cametá Alcântara Tutóia
Tucuruí Rosário Viana Camocim Acaraú
Parnaíba Itapecuru- ARQUIPÉLAGO
Mirim Brejo FERNANDO DE
Manção Barras NORONHA (Brazil)
PARÁ Altamira Codó Sobral FORTALEZA (Ceará)
Maranguape
Pédreiras Caxias Ipu Baturité ATOL DAS ROCAS
Campo Pedro II Quixadá Aracati (Brazil)
Maior MARANHÃO Grateus Russas Areia Branca FERNANDO DE
São João Teresina Senador Macau NORONHA
do Araguaia Araguatins Pompeu Mossoró CABO DE SÃO ROQUE
CEARÁ Ceará-Mirim
Grajaú RIO GRANDE
Barra do Corda Iguatú Icó DO NORTE Natal
Tocantinópolis Currais Novos Nova
Miradorо Amarante Campina Cruz
Riachão Floriano PIAUÍ Crato Patos Grande Guarabira
Loreto Oeiras Picos Juazeiro PARAÍBA João Pessoa
Carolina do Norte (Paraíba)
Balsas Granito Flores Sertânia Nazaré da Mata
BRAZIL Paulistana PLANALTO Olinda
Santa São Raimundo PERNAMBUCO DA BORBOREMA RECIFE
Filomena Nonato Cabrobó Caruaru (Pernambuco)
Miracema Juazeiro Garanhuns
do Tocantins Petrolina Palmeira Pôrto de Pedras
Porto Palmas dos Índios Maceió
Nacional SERRA DO PIAUÍ Jeremoabo ALAGOAS
TOCANTINS Barra Senhor do Bonfim Propriá Penedo
Natividade TABOADO SERGIPE
Jacobina Itabaiana Aracaju
Barreiras BAHIA Serrinha São Cristóvão
Correntina Morro do Chapéu Estância
Inhambupe
Feira de Santana Catu Alagoinhas
Lençóis Santo Amaro
Cachoeiro Nazaré SALVADOR (Bahia)
Mucugê Aratuípe Valença
Cavalcante Caeté Jequié Ilhéus
Pilar de Carinhanha Vitória da Itabuna
Goiás Condeúba Conquista Canavieiras
Barra da Belmonte
Januária Pôrto Seguro

South-central Brazil

Vista
Manicoré

CHAPADA DE MATO GROSSO
Diamantino
SERRA DOS PARECIS
MATO GROSSO
Rosário Oeste Cuiabá
SERRA DA CHAPADA
Mato Grosso SA. DA TAQUARA
Cáceres Batão de Melgaço
GOIÁS
Pirenópolis
Anápolis Formosa
Goiás Luziânia Silvânia
D.F. Brasília
Goiânia Bela Vista de Goiás
Rio Ipameri
Rosário Verde
SERRA DO CAIAPÓ Morrinhos Paracatú
Araguari Patos Três Marias
San José Catalão de Minas Pirapora Grão
El Roboré Rio Patrocínio Montes Mogol
Verde Claros Januária
Coxim Uberlândia Araxá Minas Novas
Puerto Suárez Uberaba SA. DE CANASTRA Diamantina
Corumbá Sete Paracatú Teófilo
MATO GROSSO Lagoas Pará de Minas Otoni
Campo Formiga BELO Pecanha
Bahía Negra Grande Itapira Divinópolis HORIZONTE Gov.
Aquidauana São José MINAS Colatina Valadares
Fuerte Olimpo DO SUL do Rio Preto Cláudio GERAIS Vitória
Porto Murtinho Nioaque Barretos Barbacena Espírito Santo
Mariscal Estigarribia Três Lagoas Ribeirão Prêto Conselheiro Cachoeiro de Itapemirim
Bella Itanhandu Lafaiete
Presidente Epitácio Vista Araçatuba Catanduva Pico da Bandeira Guarapari
Pedro Juan Marília São Carlos 9482 Aracruz
Puerto Casado Caballero SÃO Rio Claro Pouso Alegre Campos
Puerto Pinasco Ponta Porã Assis PAULO Botucatu Taubaté Nova Friburgo
Concepción Bauru Itatiaia 9235 Juiz de Fora
Salto Piracicaba Petrópolis RIO DE JANEIRO
Guaíra Jacarézinho Campinas Jundiaí Nova Niterói CABO FRIO
PARAGUAY Londrina Sorocaba Iguaçu RIO DE JANEIRO
Belén PARANÁ Itapetininga São Mogí das Cruzes Tropic of Capricorn
Guaíra SÃO Santos
Porto Mendes PAULO São
Pedro Juan Vicente
Caballero Ponta Grossa
Concepción Curitiba
Horqueta Castro
Guarapuava

Continued on page 144

0   50   100   200   300   400   500 Miles
0 100 200   400   600   800 Kilometers

Relief legend

Relief		
Meters		Feet
3050		10 000
1525		5000
610		2000
305		1000
152.5		500
0	Sea Level	0
152.5		500
1525		5000
3050		10 000
6100		20 000

ARQUIPÉLAGO DOS ABROLHOS
Caravelas
São Mateus

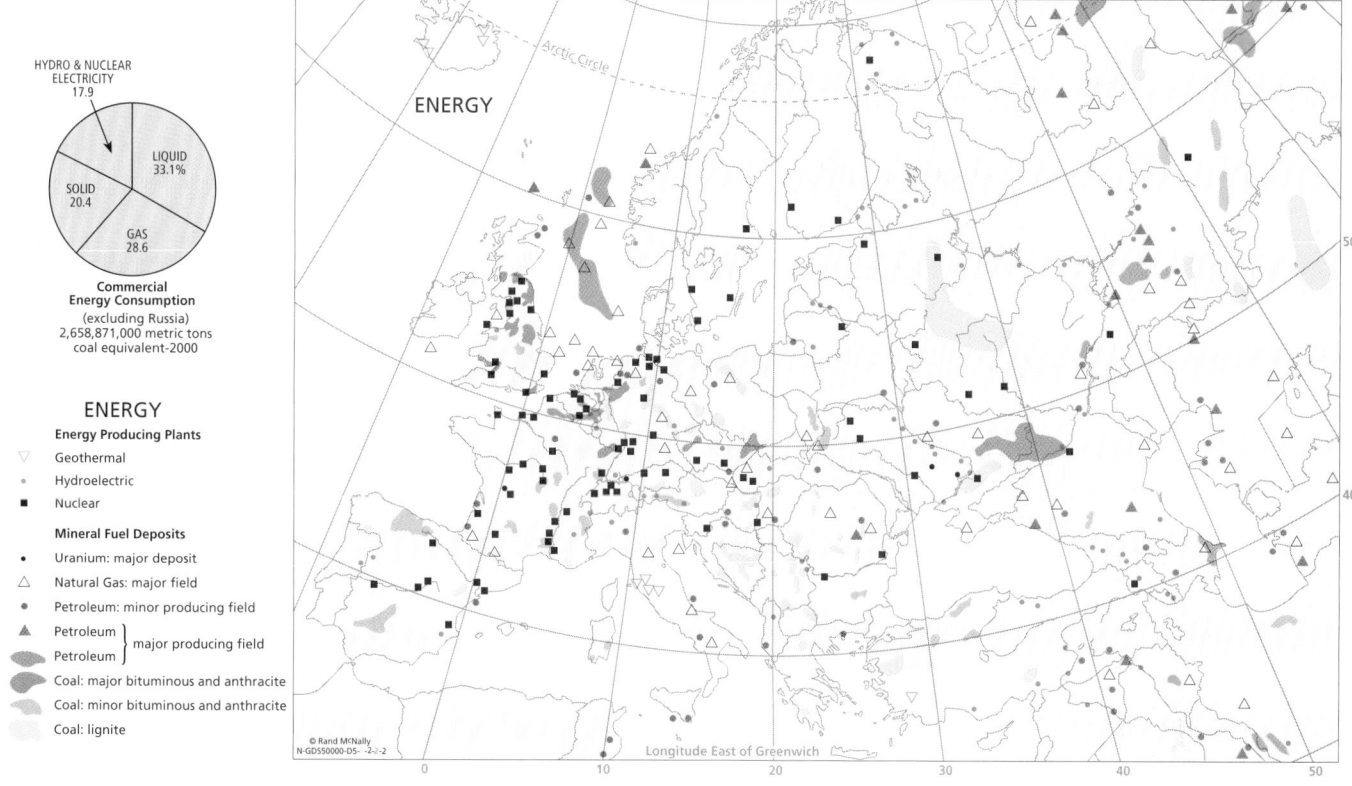

HYDRO & NUCLEAR
ELECTRICITY
17.9

LIQUID
33.1%

SOLID
20.4

GAS
28.6

**Commercial
Energy Consumption**
(excluding Russia)
2,658,871,000 metric tons
coal equivalent-2000

ENERGY

Energy Producing Plants

▽ Geothermal

• Hydroelectric

■ Nuclear

Mineral Fuel Deposits

• Uranium: major deposit

△ Natural Gas: major field

• Petroleum: minor producing field

▲ Petroleum } major producing field
   Petroleum

   Coal: major bituminous and anthracite

   Coal: minor bituminous and anthracite

   Coal: lignite

© Rand McNally
N-GD550000-D5- -2-2-2

ENERGY

Longitude East of Greenwich

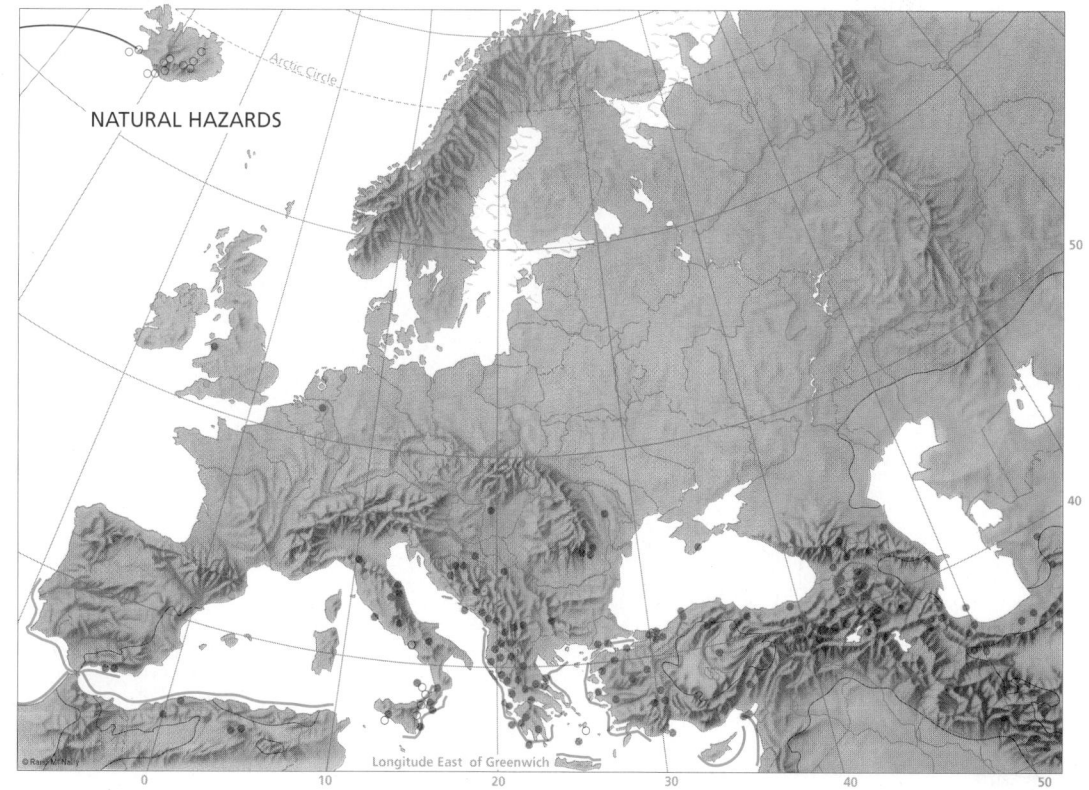

NATURAL HAZARDS

NATURAL HAZARDS

○ Volcanoes*

● Earthquakes*

● Major flood disasters*

——— Tsunamis

——— Limit of iceburg drift

   Temporary pack ice

   Areas subject to desertification

*Occurrences since 1900

Longitude East of Greenwich

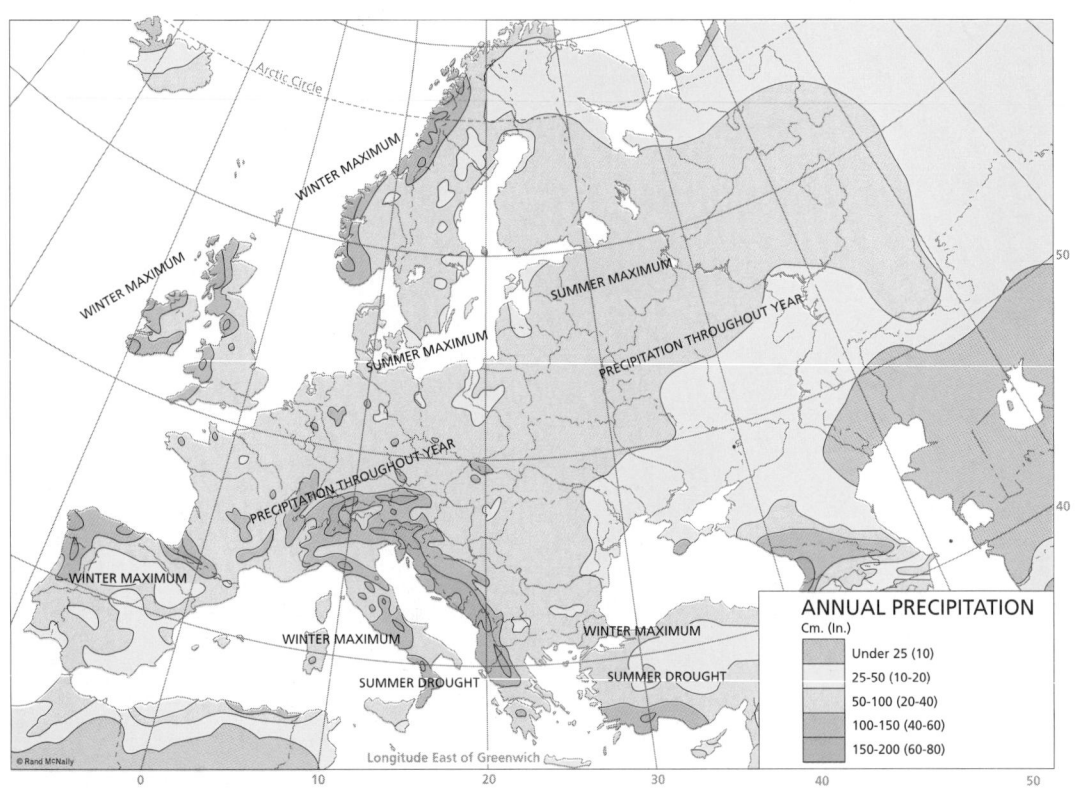

ANNUAL PRECIPITATION
Cm. (In.)

Under 25 (10)
25-50 (10-20)
50-100 (20-40)
100-150 (40-60)
150-200 (60-80)

WINTER MAXIMUM
SUMMER MAXIMUM
SUMMER MAXIMUM
PRECIPITATION THROUGHOUT YEAR
PRECIPITATION THROUGHOUT YEAR
WINTER MAXIMUM
WINTER MAXIMUM
WINTER MAXIMUM
SUMMER DROUGHT
SUMMER DROUGHT

Arctic Circle
Longitude East of Greenwich
© Rand McNally

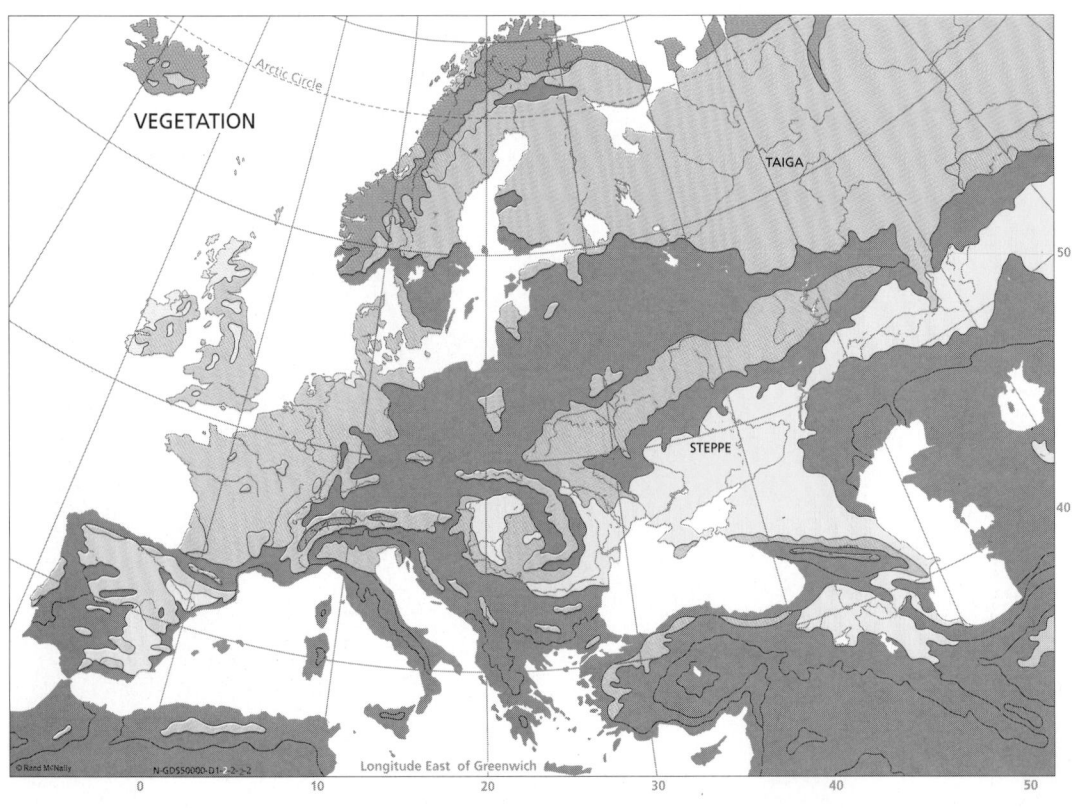

VEGETATION

TAIGA
STEPPE

Arctic Circle
Longitude East of Greenwich
© Rand McNally
N-GDS50000-D1

VEGETATION

E	Coniferous forest
B,Bs	Mediterranean vegetation
M	Mixed forest: coniferous-deciduous
S	Semi-deciduous forest
D	Deciduous forest
DG	Wooded steppe
G	Grass (steppe)
Gp	Short grass
Dsp	Desert shrub
L	Heath and moor
L	Alpine vegetation, tundra
b	Little or no vegetation

For explanation of letters in boxes,
see Natural Vegetation Map
by A. W. Kuchler, p. 24

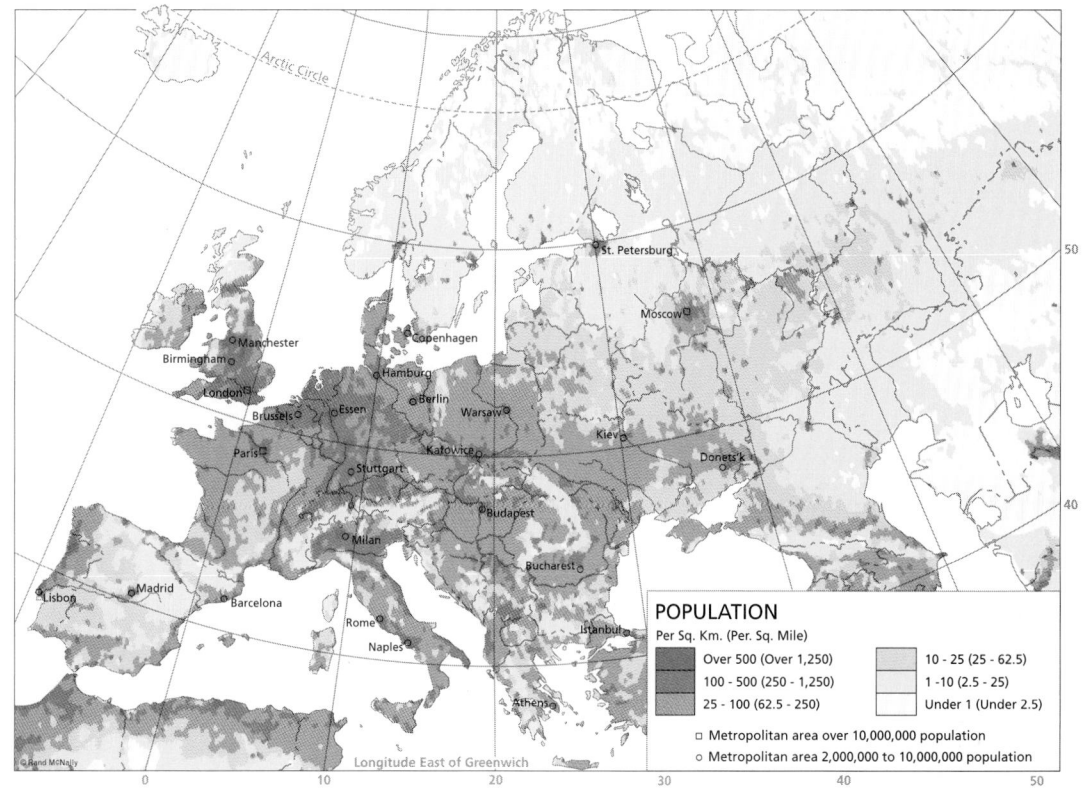

POPULATION

Per Sq. Km. (Per. Sq. Mile)

- Over 500 (Over 1,250)
- 100 - 500 (250 - 1,250)
- 25 - 100 (62.5 - 250)
- 10 - 25 (25 - 62.5)
- 1 -10 (2.5 - 25)
- Under 1 (Under 2.5)

□ Metropolitan area over 10,000,000 population
○ Metropolitan area 2,000,000 to 10,000,000 population

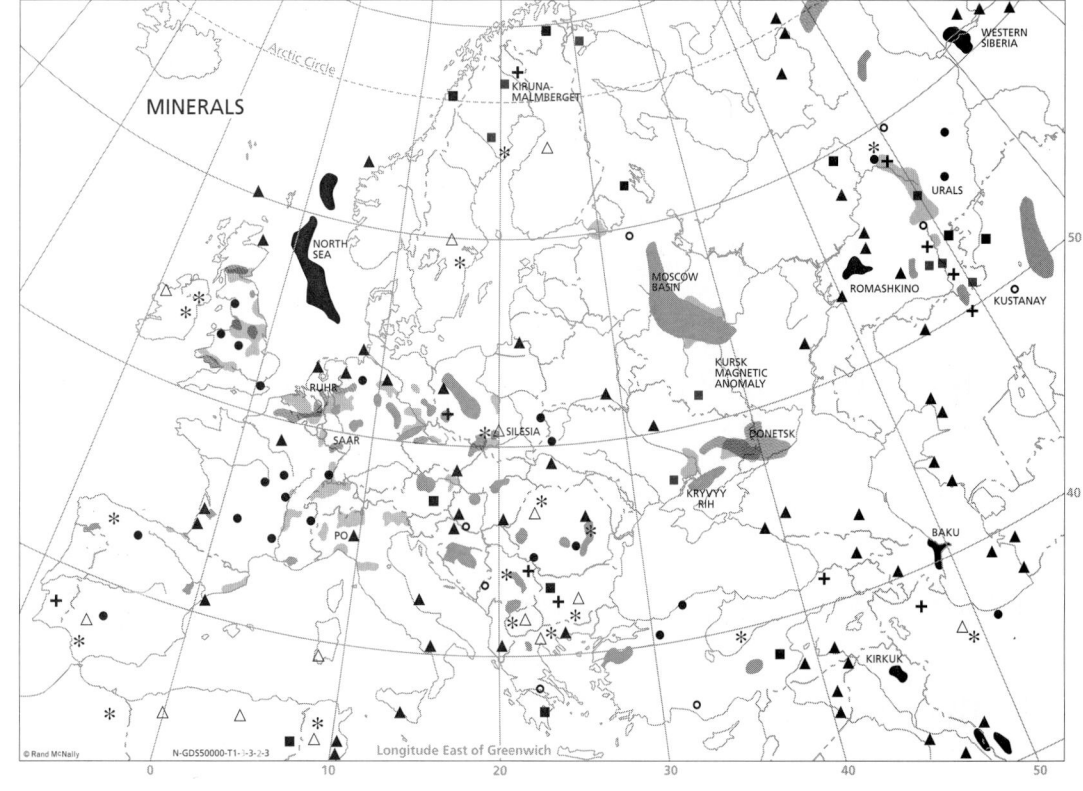

MINERALS

- Industrial areas
- Major coal deposits
- Major petroleum deposits
- Lignite deposits
- ▲ Minor petroleum deposits
- ● Minor coal deposits
- ■ Major iron ore
- ■ Minor iron ore
- ✳ Lead
- ○ Bauxite
- △ Zinc
- ✛ Copper

Urban

Cropland

Cropland & Woodland

Cropland & Grazing Land

Grassland, Grazing Land

Forest, Woodland

Swamp, Marshland

Tundra

Shrub, Sparse Grass, Wasteland (pattern)

Barren Land

Oasis

ATLANTIC OCEAN

Reykjavík

Narvik

Murm

Trondheim

Ume

Gulf of Bothnia

Bergen

Oslo

Helsinki

ST. PETERSBURG

Tallinn

Stockholm

Göteborg

Rīga

North Sea

Copenhagen

Baltic Sea

Kaliningrad

Vilnius

Glasgow

Belfast

MANCHESTER

Dublin

Amsterdam

Hamburg

Elbe

BERLIN

Essen

Oder

Warsaw

Minsk

Pripe

LONDON

Antwerp

Leipzig

Kraków

L'viv

Brest

Frankfurt

Prague

CARPATHIANS

PARIS

Seine

Strasbourg

Rhine

Danube

VIENNA

Loire

Munich

Zürich

BUDAPEST

Tisza

Bay of Biscay

Bordeaux

Garonne

A L P S

Lyon

MILAN

Venice

Sava

Zagreb

A Coruña

Bilbao

PYRENEES

Rhône

Genoa

Belgrade

Bucharest

Duero

MADRID

Ebro

Marseille

Adriatic Sea

Danube

Lisbon

BARCELONA

CORSICA

ROME

Sofia

Sevilla

SARDINIA

Naples

Tiranë

Aegean Sea

Tanger

ISLAS BALEARES

Tyrrhenian Sea

Athens

Oran

Algiers

Palermo

CRETE

Casablanca

ATLAS MOUNTAINS

Tunis

SICILY

Mediterranean Sea

MALTA

Longitude West of Greenwich 0° Longitude East of Greenwich

Scale 1: 16,000,000; one inch to 250 miles. Conic Projection

| 0 | 50 | 100 | 200 | 300 | 400 | 500 Miles |
| 0 | 100 | 200 | 400 | 600 | 800 Kilometers |

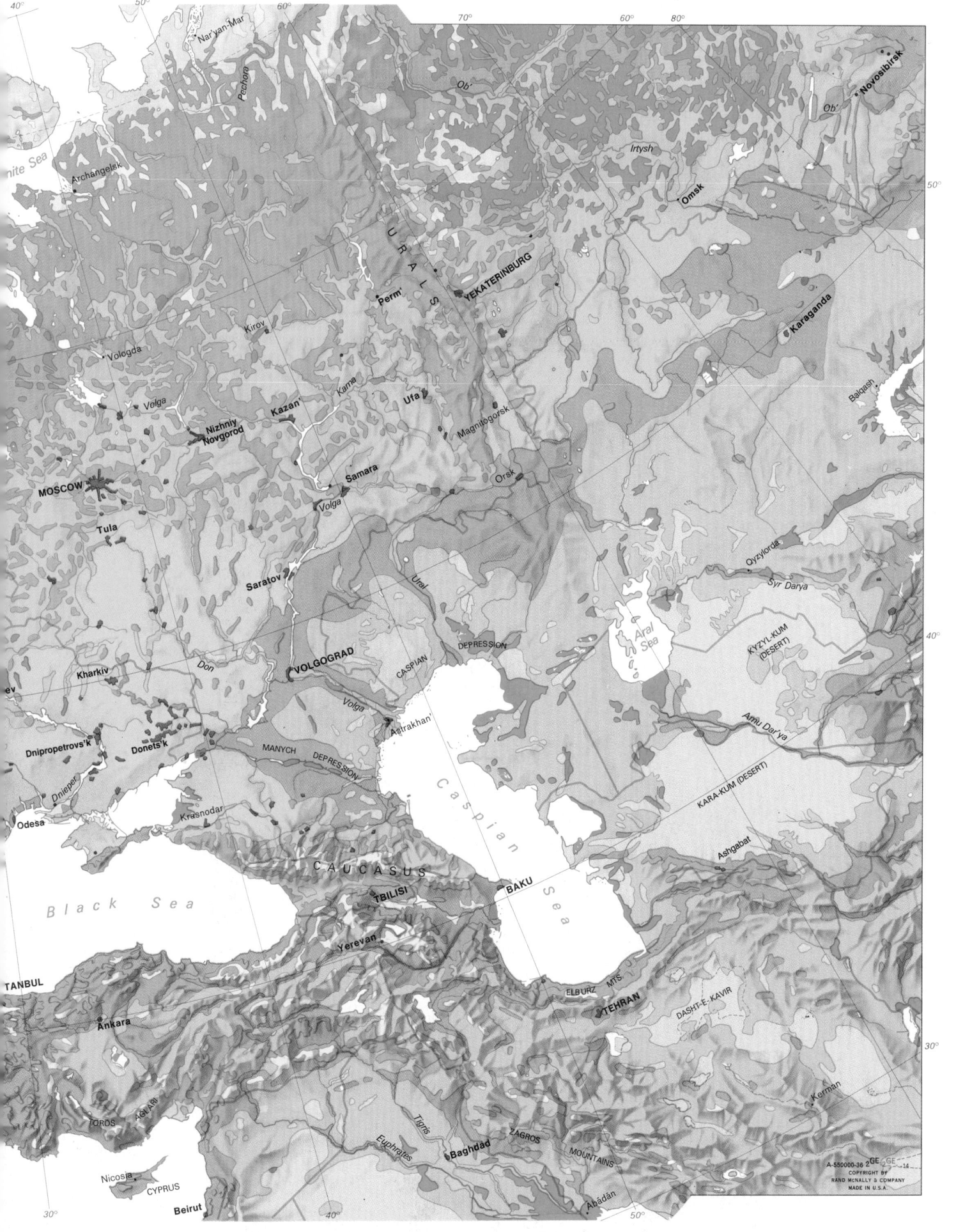

Nar'yan-Mar

Pechora

Ob'

Irtysh

Novosibirsk

Ob'

nite Sea

Archangelsk

Omsk

50°

U R A L S

YEKATERINBURG

Perm'

Karaganda

Kirov

Vologda

Balqash

Kama

Ufa

Volga

Kazan'

Magnitogorsk

Nizhniy
Novgorod

Oyzylorda

MOSCOW

Samara

Orsk

Syr Darya

Volga

Tula

KYZYL-KUM
(DESERT)

Saratov

Ural

40°

Aral
Sea

DEPRESSION

VOLGOGRAD

CASPIAN

Kharkiv

Don

Amu Dar'ya

Volga

Dnipropetrovs'k

Astrakhan'

KARA-KUM (DESERT)

Donets'k

MANYCH   DEPRESSION

Dnieper

C a s p i a n

Ashgabat

Odesa

Krasnodar

C A U C A S U S

BAKU

S e a

B l a c k   S e a

TBILISI

Yerevan

ELBURZ MTS.

DASHT-E-KAVIR

TANBUL

Kerman

Ankara

TEHRAN

30°

TOROS DAĞLARI

Tigris

ZAGROS

Nicosia

Euphrates

Baghdad

MOUNTAINS

CYPRUS

A-550000-36 2
COPYRIGHT 91
RAND MCNALLY & COMPANY
MADE IN U.S.A.

Beirut

Abadan

Scale 1:16 000 000; one inch to 250 miles. Conic Projection
Elevations and depressions are given in feet.

EUROPE LANGUAGES
BY
BOGDAN ZABORSKI

Scale 1:16,500,000; one inch to 260 miles Conic Projection

B-550000-1C6-1-1-1-4
COPYRIGHT BY
RAND McNALLY & COMPANY
MADE IN U.S.A.

| 0 | 100 | 200 | 300 | 400 | 500 | 600 Miles |

| 0 | 200 | 400 | 600 | 800 | 1000 Kilometers |

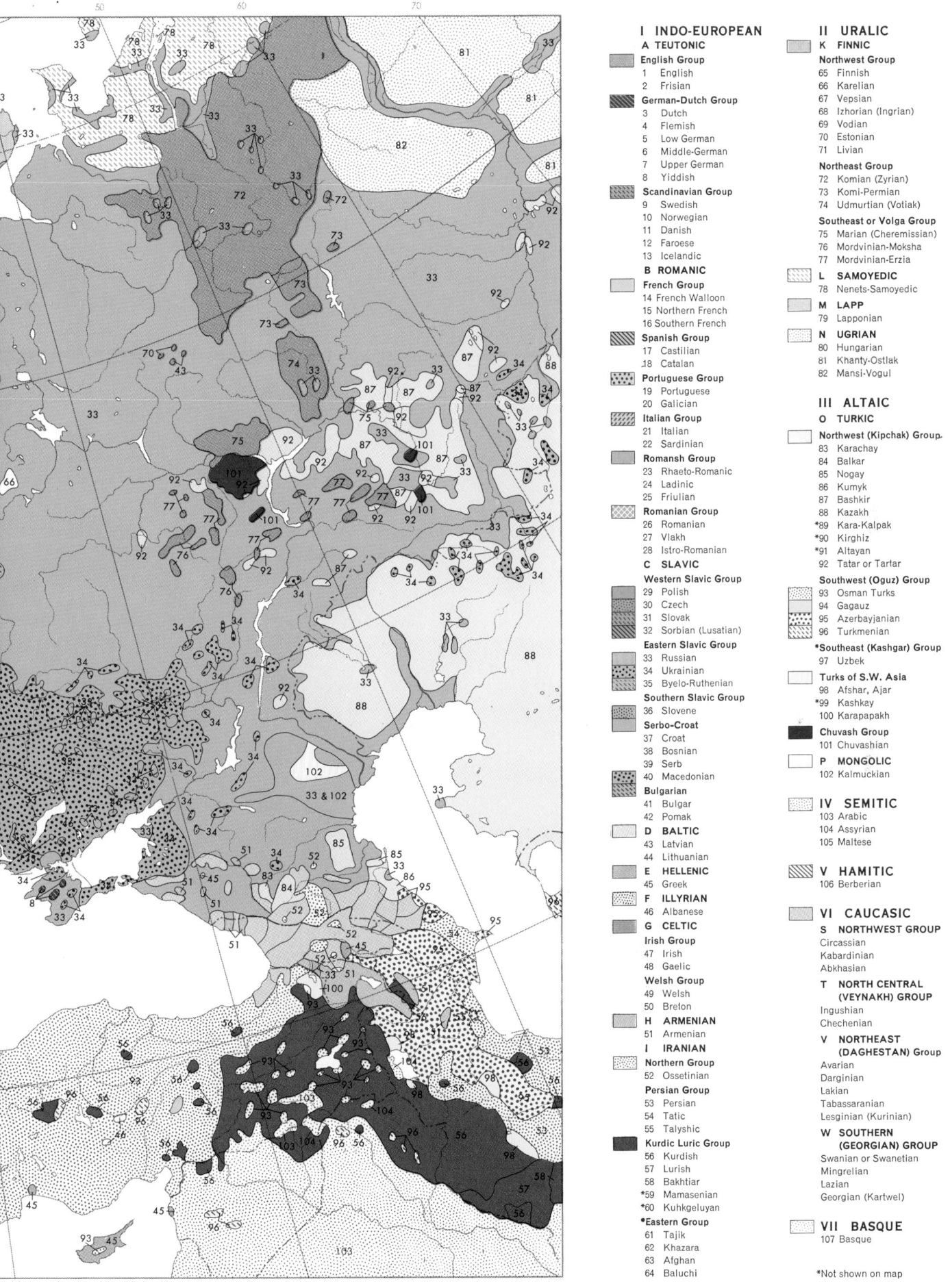

I INDO-EUROPEAN

A TEUTONIC

English Group
1 English
2 Frisian

German-Dutch Group
3 Dutch
4 Flemish
5 Low German
6 Middle-German
7 Upper German
8 Yiddish

Scandinavian Group
9 Swedish
10 Norwegian
11 Danish
12 Faroese
13 Icelandic

B ROMANIC

French Group
14 French Walloon
15 Northern French
16 Southern French

Spanish Group
17 Castilian
18 Catalan

Portuguese Group
19 Portuguese
20 Galician

Italian Group
21 Italian
22 Sardinian

Romansh Group
23 Rhaeto-Romanic
24 Ladinic
25 Friulian

Romanian Group
26 Romanian
27 Vlakh
28 Istro-Romanian

C SLAVIC

Western Slavic Group
29 Polish
30 Czech
31 Slovak
32 Sorbian (Lusatian)

Eastern Slavic Group
33 Russian
34 Ukrainian
35 Byelo-Ruthenian

Southern Slavic Group
36 Slovene
Serbo-Croat
37 Croat
38 Bosnian
39 Serb
40 Macedonian
Bulgarian
41 Bulgar
42 Pomak

D BALTIC
43 Latvian
44 Lithuanian

E HELLENIC
45 Greek

F ILLYRIAN
46 Albanese

G CELTIC

Irish Group
47 Irish
48 Gaelic

Welsh Group
49 Welsh
50 Breton

H ARMENIAN
51 Armenian

I IRANIAN

Northern Group
52 Ossetinian

Persian Group
53 Persian
54 Tatic
55 Talyshic

Kurdic Luric Group
56 Kurdish
57 Lurish
58 Bakhtiar
*59 Mamasenian
*60 Kuhkgeluyan

*Eastern Group
61 Tajik
62 Khazara
63 Afghan
64 Baluchi

II URALIC

K FINNIC

Northwest Group
65 Finnish
66 Karelian
67 Vepsian
68 Izhorian (Ingrian)
69 Vodian
70 Estonian
71 Livian

Northeast Group
72 Komian (Zyrian)
73 Komi-Permian
74 Udmurtian (Votiak)

Southeast or Volga Group
75 Marian (Cheremissian)
76 Mordvinian-Moksha
77 Mordvinian-Erzia

L SAMOYEDIC
78 Nenets-Samoyedic

M LAPP
79 Lapponian

N UGRIAN
80 Hungarian
81 Khanty-Ostlak
82 Mansi-Vogul

III ALTAIC

O TURKIC

Northwest (Kipchak) Group
83 Karachay
84 Balkar
85 Nogay
86 Kumyk
87 Bashkir
88 Kazakh
*89 Kara-Kalpak
*90 Kirghiz
*91 Altayan
92 Tatar or Tartar

Southwest (Oguz) Group
93 Osman Turks
94 Gagauz
95 Azerbayjanian
96 Turkmenian

*Southeast (Kashgar) Group
97 Uzbek

Turks of S.W. Asia
98 Afshar, Ajar
*99 Kashkay
100 Karapapakh

Chuvash Group
101 Chuvashian

P MONGOLIC
102 Kalmuckian

IV SEMITIC
103 Arabic
104 Assyrian
105 Maltese

V HAMITIC
106 Berberian

VI CAUCASIC

S NORTHWEST GROUP
Circassian
Kabardinian
Abkhasian

T NORTH CENTRAL (VEYNAKH) GROUP
Ingushian
Chechenian

V NORTHEAST (DAGHESTAN) Group
Avarian
Darginian
Lakian
Tabassaranian
Lesginian (Kurinian)

W SOUTHERN (GEORGIAN) GROUP
Swanian or Swanetian
Mingrelian
Lazian
Georgian (Kartwel)

VII BASQUE
107 Basque

*Not shown on map

Scale 1: 16 000 000; one inch to 250 miles. Conic Projection
Elevations and depressions are given in feet

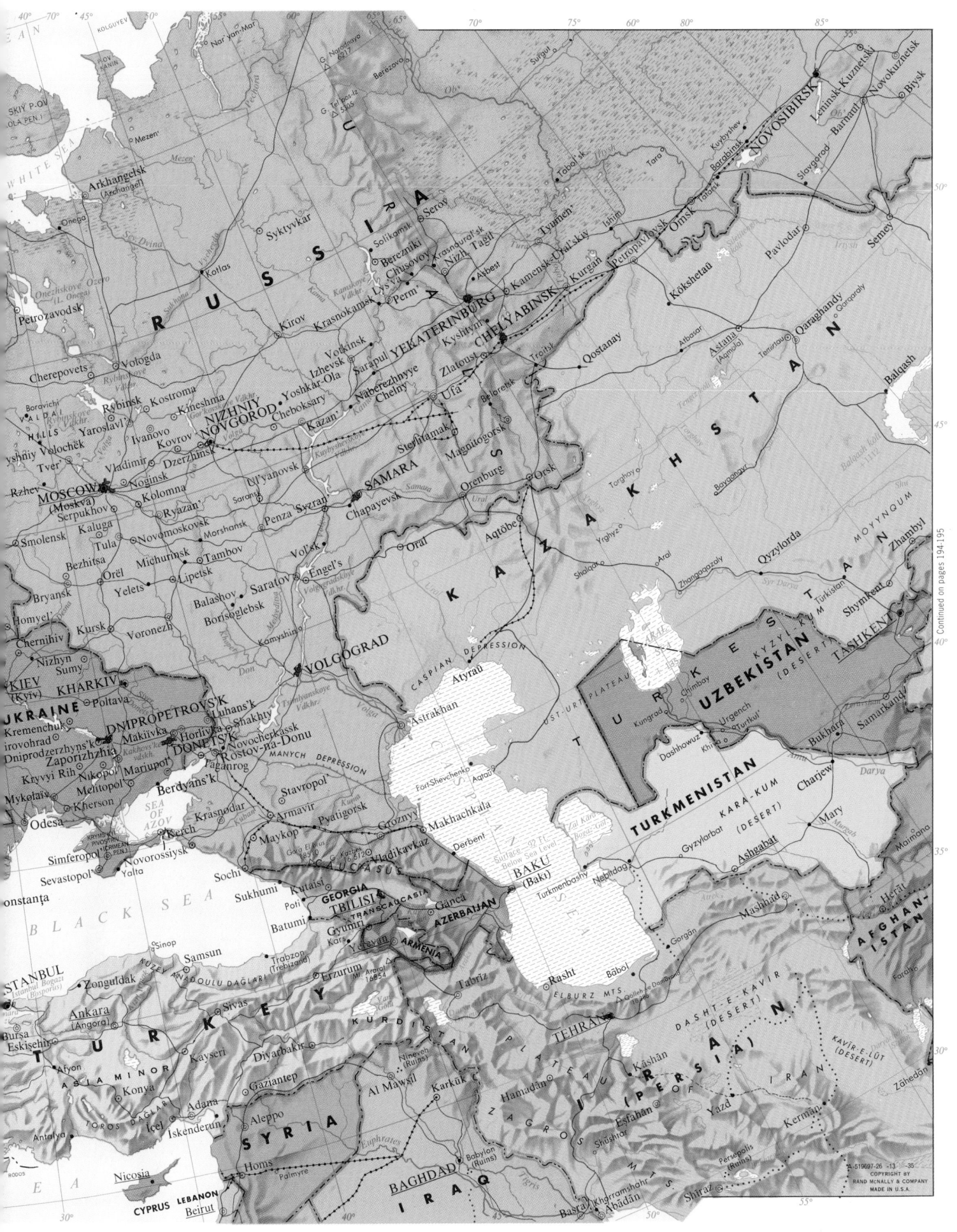

Continued on pages 194-195

Relief

Meters		Feet
3050		10 000
1525		5000
610		2000
305		1000
152.5		500
0	Sea Level	0
152.5		500
1525	Below	5000
3050	Sea Level	10 000

Scale 1: 16 000 000; one inch to 250 miles. Conic Projection

Elevations and depressions are given in feet

Longitude West of Greenwich   Longitude East of Greenwich

Continued on pages 230-231

0 50 100 200 300 400 500 Miles

0 100 200 400 600 800 Kilometers

Continued on pages 184-185

Continued on pages 198-199

a

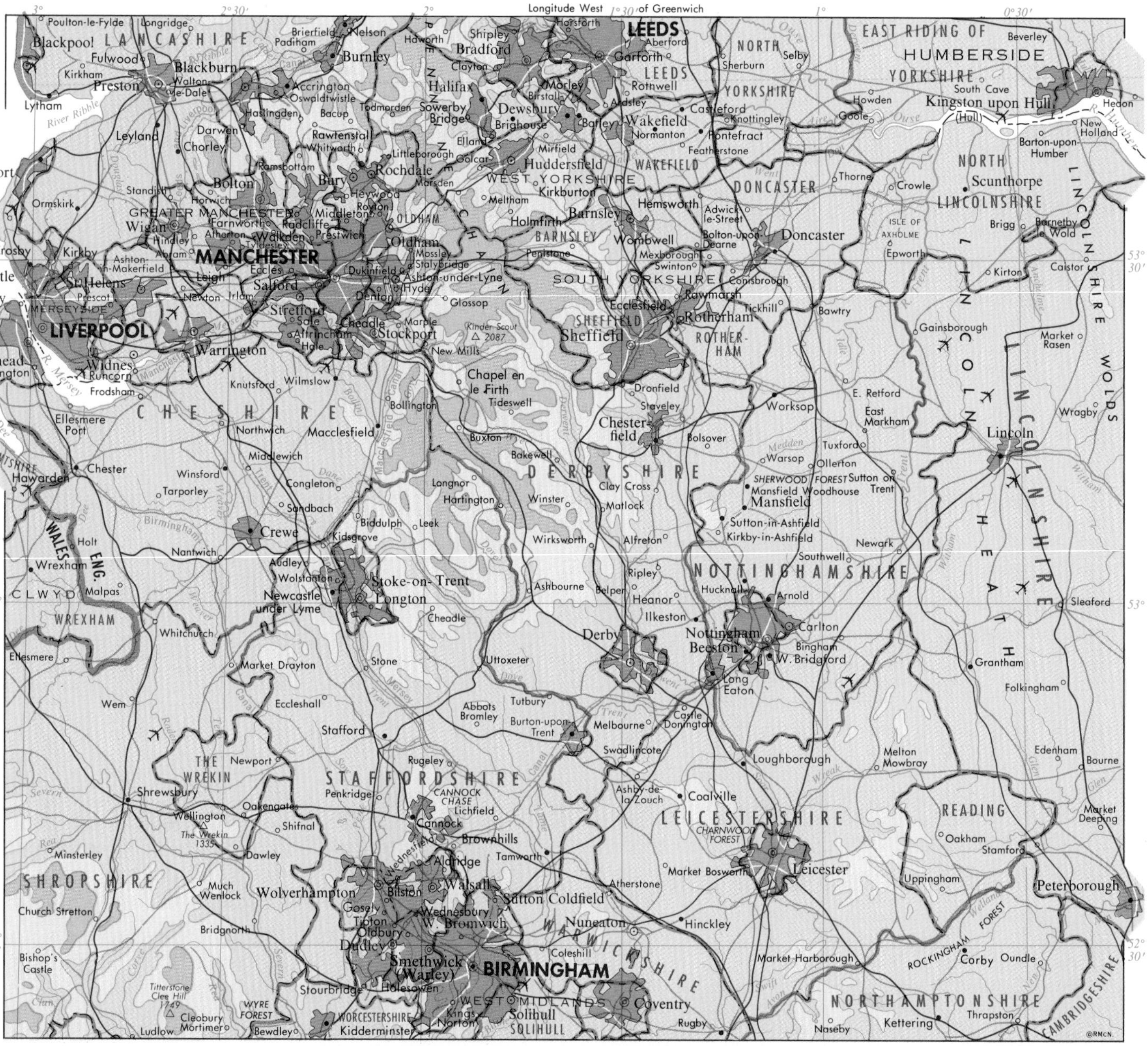

Longitude West of Greenwich

LANCASHIRE
Blackpool
Poulton-le-Fylde
Longridge
Fulwood
Kirkham
Lytham
Preston
Leyland
Chorley
Southport
Formby
FORMBY PT.
Crosby
Bootle
Wallasey
Hoylake
West Kirby
Birkenhead
Bebington
LIVERPOOL
St Helens
Prescot
Kirkby
Widnes
Runcorn
Frodsham
Warrington
Blackburn
Darwen
Accrington
Oswaldtwistle
Haslingden
Rawtenstall
Whitworth
Bacup
Todmorden
Littleborough
Rochdale
Heywood
Bury
Ramsbottom
Bolton
Horwich
Standish
Wigan
Leigh
Atherton
Hindley
Newton
Ashton-in-Makerfield
GREATER MANCHESTER
Farnworth
Radcliffe
Prestwich
Middleton
Eccles
MANCHESTER
Salford
Stretford
Sale
Altrincham
Hale
Cheadle
Stockport
Denton
Ashton-under-Lyne
Hyde
Glossop
Marple
New Mills
Nelson
Burnley
Brierfield
Padiham
Haworth
Clayton
Bradford
Shipley
Halifax
Sowerby Bridge
Elland
Brighouse
Dewsbury
Morley
Batley
Heywood
Huddersfield
Kirkburton
Holmfirth
Meltham
Marsden
LEEDS
Aberford
Garforth
Rothwell
Castleford
Normanton
Wakefield
Featherstone
Pontefract
Knottingley
WEST YORKSHIRE
Penistone
Barnsley
Wombwell
Mexborough
Swinton
Rawmarsh
ROTHERHAM
Tickhill
SHEFFIELD
Dronfield
Staveley
Chesterfield
Bolsover
Clay Cross
Matlock
Bakewell
Buxton
Chapel en le Frith
Tideswell
Longnor
Hartington
Winster
Wirksworth
DERBYSHIRE
CHESHIRE
Ellesmere Port
Chester
Northwich
Middlewich
Winsford
Tarporley
Sandbach
Congleton
Macclesfield
Bollington
Knutsford
Wilmslow
Crewe
Nantwich
Audley
Kidsgrove
Biddulph
Leek
Stoke-on-Trent
Longton
Newcastle under Lyme
Wolstanton
Cheadle
Ashbourne
Belper
Heanor
Ilkeston
Derby
Uttoxeter
Tutbury
Burton-upon-Trent
Abbots Bromley
Melbourne
Swadlincote
Ashby-de-la-Zouch
Coalville
NOTTINGHAMSHIRE
Hucknall
Arnold
Carlton
NOTTINGHAM
Beeston
W. Bridgford
Long Eaton
Castle Donington
Loughborough
Mansfield Woodhouse
Mansfield
Sutton-in-Ashfield
Kirkby-in-Ashfield
Southwell
Newark
SHERWOOD FOREST
Warsop
Ollerton
Tuxford
Sutton on Trent
Worksop
E. Retford
East Markham
LINCOLNSHIRE
Gainsborough
Lincoln
Market Rasen
Wragby
LINCOLN HEATH
Sleaford
Grantham
Folkingham
LINCOLNSHIRE WOLDS
Caistor
Brigg
Barnetby le Wold
Kirton
NORTH LINCOLNSHIRE
Scunthorpe
Crowle
Thorne
ISLE OF AXHOLME
Epworth
DONCASTER
Doncaster
Adwick le Street
Bolton-upon-Dearne
Conisbrough
Bawtry
SOUTH YORKSHIRE
NORTH YORKSHIRE
Selby
Sherburn
Howden
Goole
Ouse
EAST RIDING OF HUMBERSIDE
Beverley
South Cave
Kingston upon Hull (Hull)
Hedon
New Holland
Barton-upon-Humber
WREXHAM
Wrexham
WALES ENG.
CLWYD
Malpas
Whitchurch
Ellesmere
Wem
FLINTSHIRE
Hawarden
Holt
R. Dee
Flint
SHROPSHIRE
Shrewsbury
Wellington
THE WREKIN
The Wrekin 1335
Dawley
Oakengates
Shifnal
Newport
Minsterley
Church Stretton
Ludlow
Cleobury Mortimer
Bishop's Castle
Titterstone Clee Hill 1749
Bridgnorth
Much Wenlock
WYRE FOREST
Bewdley
Kidderminster
WORCESTERSHIRE
Stourbridge
Halesowen
Dudley
Oldbury
Tipton
Wednesbury
W. Bromwich
Bilston
Wolverhampton
Gosley
Cannock
CANNOCK CHASE
Rugeley
Penkridge
Stafford
Eccleshall
Market Drayton
Stone
Cheadle
Lichfield
Brownhills
Aldridge
Walsall
Tamworth
STAFFORDSHIRE
Smethwick (Warley)
Kings Norton
BIRMINGHAM
Solihull
SOLIHULL
WEST MIDLANDS
Coventry
Sutton Coldfield
Coleshill
Atherstone
Nuneaton
Hinckley
Bedworth
Rugby
WARWICKSHIRE
Naseby
Market Bosworth
LEICESTERSHIRE
CHARNWOOD FOREST
Leicester
Market Harborough
Kettering
Corby
Oundle
Thrapston
NORTHAMPTONSHIRE
ROCKINGHAM FOREST
Uppingham
Oakham
Melton Mowbray
Stamford
Market Deeping
Peterborough
Edenham
Bourne
READING
CAMBRIDGESHIRE

®RMcN.

b

Woodstock
Burford
Witney
Bampton
Faringdon
Wantage
OXFORDSHIRE
Oxford
Headington
Cowley
Thame
Abingdon
Didcot
Wallingford
Chalgrove
Watlington
Goring
BUCKINGHAMSHIRE
Aylesbury
Tring
Wendover
Princes Risborough
High Wycombe
Marlow
Henley on Thames
Maidenhead
Gerrards Cross
Berkhamsted
Hemel Hempstead
Chesham
Beaconsfield
Harpenden
HERTFORDSHIRE
St Albans
Welwyn Garden City
Potters Bar
Cheshunt
Hertford
Hatfield Broad Oak
Great Waltham
Witham
Brightlingsea
Tollesbury
Maldon
Danbury
Burnham on Crouch
ESSEX
Chelmsford
Billericay
Rayleigh
Southend-on-Sea
Brentwood
Romford
Basildon
Epping
High Ongar
Harlow
Chigwell
Ilford
Dagenham
Tottenham
Walthamstow
W. Ham
Bulphan
THURROCK
Grays
Thurrock
Tilbury
Gravesend
MEDWAY TOWNS
Sheerness
Rochester
Chatham
Gillingham
Sittingbourne
Faversham
Whitstable
Canterbury
Woolwich
Greenwich
Bexley
Dartford
Farningham
Wrotham
Doddington
Maidstone
Charing
Wye
KENT
Sevenoaks
Westerham
Edenbridge
Tonbridge
Mereworth
Caterham
Oxted
Reigate
Dorking
Leatherhead
Epsom
Banstead
Croydon
Sutton
Esher
Weybridge
Chertsey
Staines
Twickenham
Wandsworth
Bromley
Woolwich
LONDON
Ealing
Willesden
Hendon
Harrow
Slough
Windsor
Egham
Sunninghill
Bracknell
Wokingham
Reading
BERKSHIRE
NEWBURY
Newbury
Tadley
Kingsclere
Basingstoke
Odiham
Hook
Fleet
Aldershot
Farnham
Guildford
Woking
Camberley
Sandhurst
Swallowfield
Hampstead Norris
Bradfield
HAMPSHIRE
Farnborough
SURREY

Longitude West 0°30' of Greenwich
Longitude East 0°30' of Greenwich

®RMcN.

A-553251-76 7-4-11

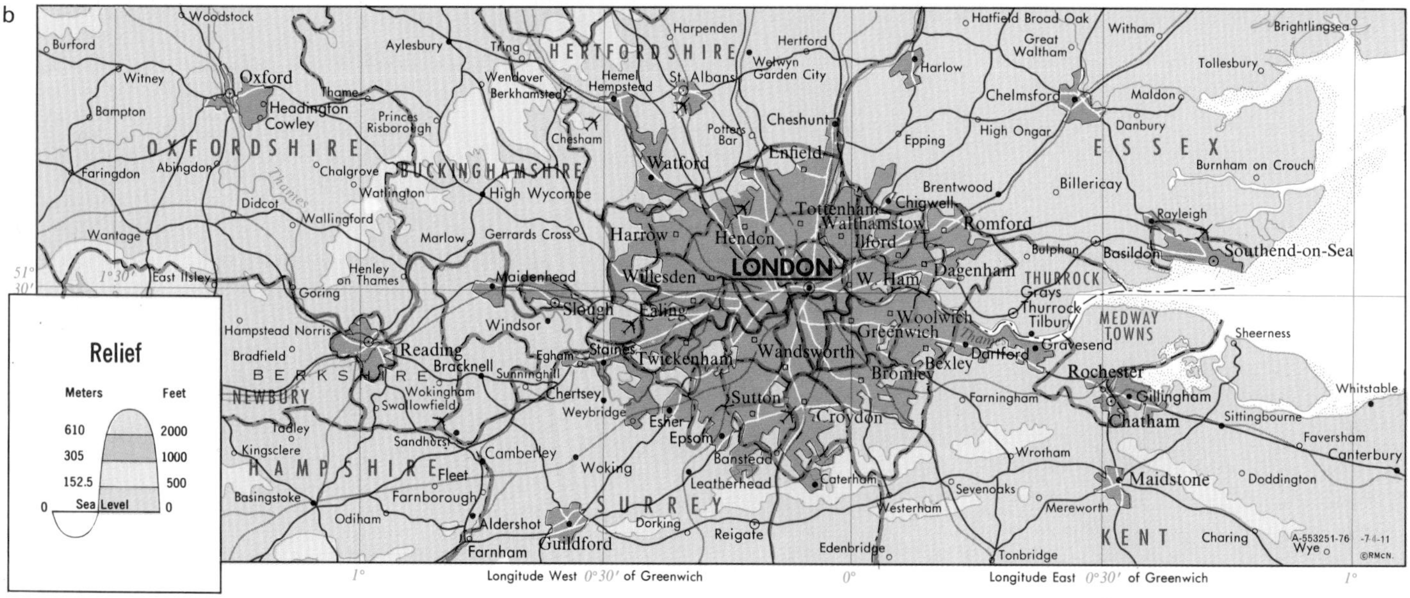

Scale 1:1 000 000; one inch to 16 miles.
Elevations and depressions are given in feet.

Relief

Meters		Feet
610		2000
305		1000
152.5		500
0	Sea Level	0

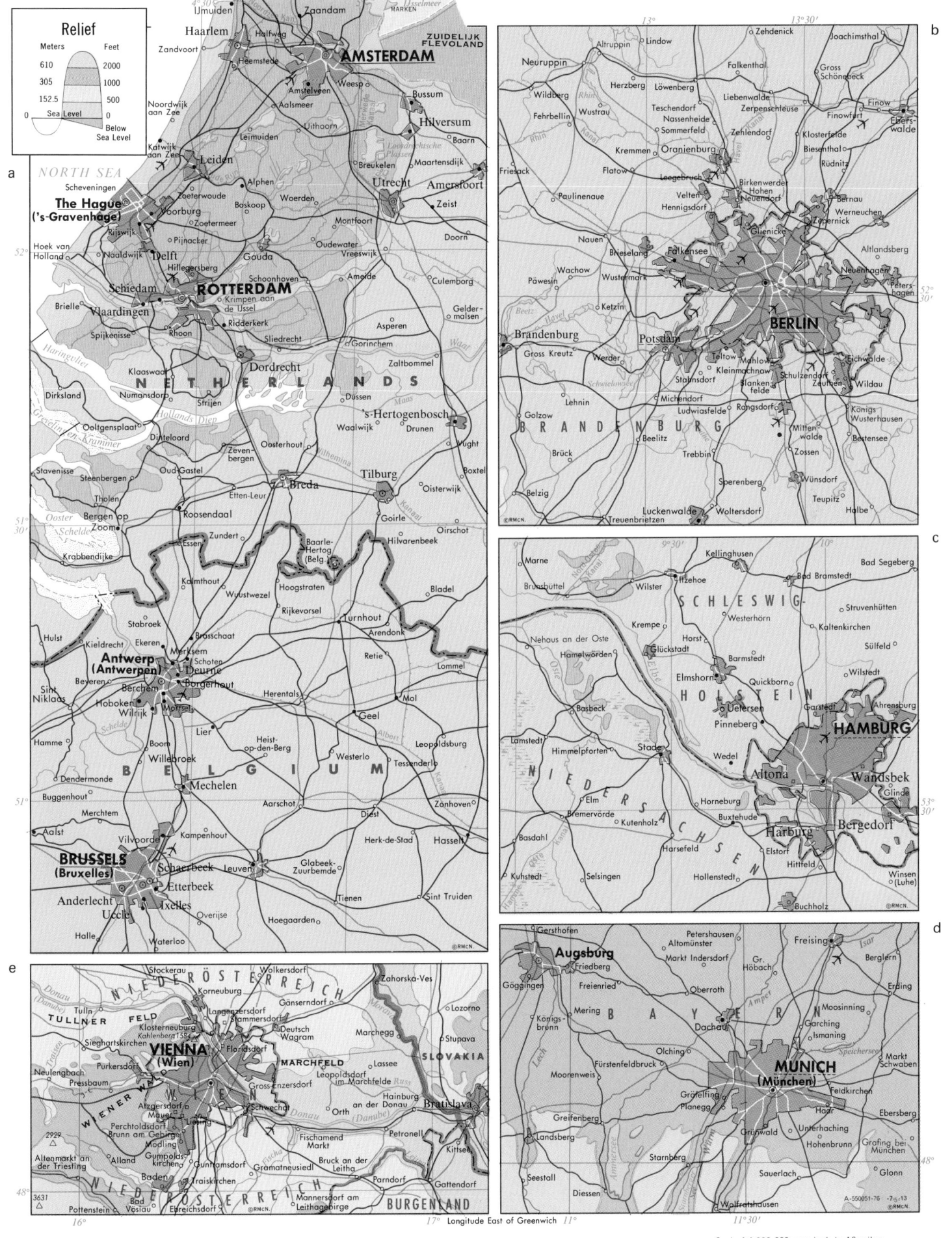

Continued on pages 180-181

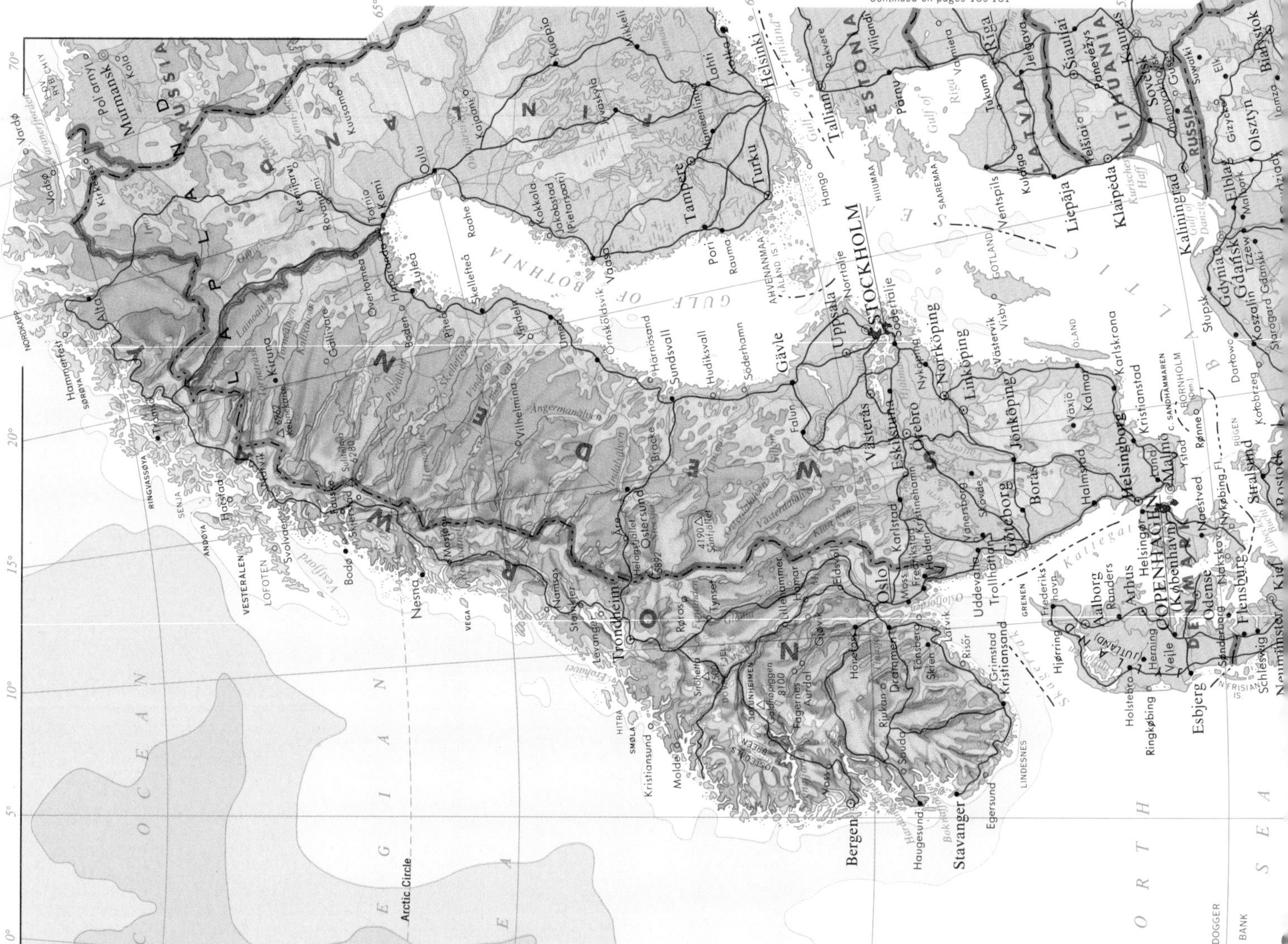

BELARUS

RUSSIA
Murmansk

L A P L A N D

F I N L A N D

ESTONIA
Tallinn
LATVIA
Riga
LITHUANIA
RUSSIA
Kaliningrad

Helsinki
Turku
Tampere
Oulu

GULF OF BOTHNIA

ALAND IS.

STOCKHOLM
Uppsala
Västerås
Örebro
Norrköping
Linköping
Jönköping
Göteborg
Borås
Halmstad
Helsingborg

S W E D E N

N O R W A Y

Oslo
Trondheim
Bergen
Stavanger
Haugesund
Kristiansand
Egersund

Kattegat
Skagerrak

COPENHAGEN
København
Odense
Århus
Ålborg
Esbjerg

D E N M A R K

Gdańsk
Gdynia

N O R W E G I A N   S E A

A R C T I C   O C E A N

Arctic Circle

JAN MAYEN
(Nor.)

FAROE IS.
(Den.)
Tórshavn

SHETLAND IS.
(Br.)
Lerwick
MAINLAND

ORKNEY IS.
(Br.)
Kirkwall

N O R T H   S E A

DOGGER

Aberdeen
Dundee
Edinburgh
GLASGOW
Newcastle
Sunderland
Middlesbrough
Hartlepool
Carlisle
Barrow-in-Furness

S C O T L A N D

U N I T E D   K I N G D O M

B R I T I S H   I S L E S

Belfast
Londonderry
Dublin

IRELAND

HEBRIDES
Stornoway

I C E L A N D
Reykjavik

Relief

Meters	Feet	
3050	10 000	
1525	5000	
610	2000	
305	1000	
152.5	500	
0	0	Below Sea Level
	Sea Level	
152.5	500	
1525	5000	
3050	10 000	

Scale 1: 10 000 000; one inch to 160 miles. Conic Projection

Elevations and depressions are given in feet

Continued on pages 160-161

Scale 1:10 000 000; one inch to 160 miles. Bonne's Projection
Elevations and depressions are given in feet

Continued on pages 180-181

MEDITERRANEAN LANDS

The Turkish Republic of Northern Cyprus
unilaterally declared its independence
on Nov. 15, 1983.

Areas occupied by Israel since 1967.

50 100 150 200 250 300 Miles
100   200   300   400   500 Kilometers

a Same scale as main map

ATLANTIC

SHETLAND
ISLANDS (Br.)
Lerwick
FOULA SUMBURGH HD.

OCEAN

FAIR ISLAND

WESTRAY   N. RONALDSAY
ROUSAY   SANDAY
STRONSAY
Kirkwall ORKNEY
HOY MAINLAND S. RONALDSAY
ISLANDS (Br.)
Thurso Pentland Firth DUNCANSBY HD.
SCOTLAND

©RMCN.

Relief

Meters		Feet
610		2000
305		1000
152.5		500
0	Sea Level	0
152.5		500
1525		5000

A-559700-76--9-7-17
COPYRIGHT BY
RAND McNALLY & COMPANY
MADE IN U.S.A.

Longitude West of Greenwich

Scale 1: 4 000 000; one inch to 64 miles. Conic Projection
Elevations and depressions are given in feet

Continued on pages 166-167

Continued on pages 168-169

Continued on pages 170-171

Longitude East of Greenwich

0 10 20 30 40 50 60 70 80 90 100 110 120 Miles
0 20 40 60 80 100 120 140 160 180 200 Kilometers

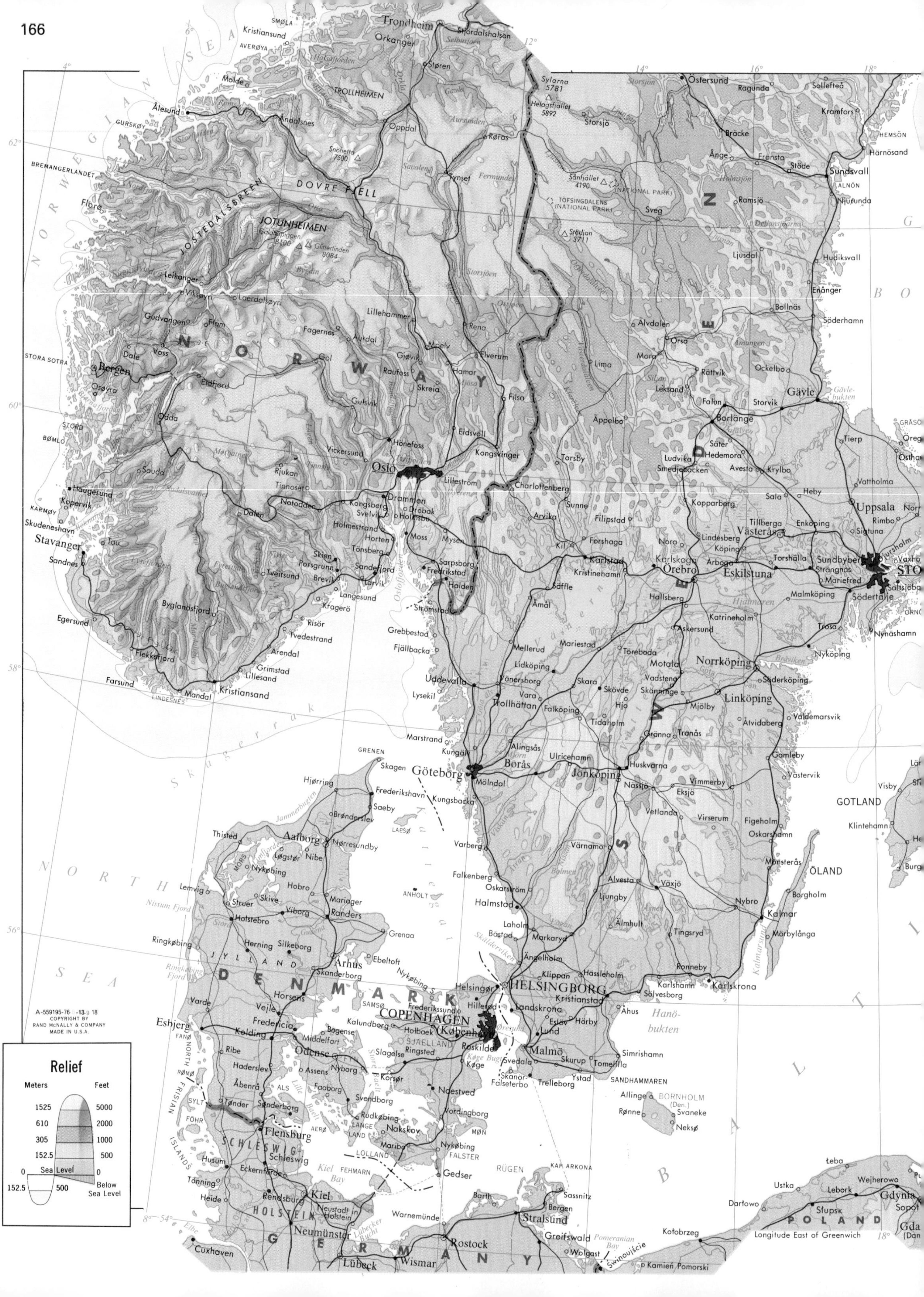

NORWEGIAN SEA

SMØLA
Kristiansund
AVERØYA
Orkanger
Molde
Ålesund
ANDALSNES
Åndalsnes
Oppdal
GURSKØY
TROLLHEIMEN
Trondheim
Stjørdalshalsen
Selbusjøen
Støren
Gaula
Røros
Støren

Sylarna 5781
Helagsfjället 5892
Storsjön
Östersund
Ragunda
Sollefteå
Kramfors
HEMSÖN
Bräcke
Ånge
Fränsta
Stöde
Härnösand

Snøhetta 7500
DOVRE FJELL
Tynset
Fermunden
Sånfjället 4190 (NATIONAL PARK)
TÖFSINGDALENS (NATIONAL PARK)
Sveg
Stödjan 3711
Ljusdal
Hudiksvall
Enånger
Njurunda
Sundsvall
ALNÖN

JOSTEDALSBREEN
JOTUNHEIMEN
Galdhøpiggen 8100
Glittertinden 8084
Savalen
Storsjö
Storsjøen
Bollnäs
Söderhamn

N O R W A Y
Leikanger
Vikøyri
Lærdalsøyri
Bygdin
Lillehammer
Fagernes
Aurdal
Rena
Elverum
Älvdalen
Lima
Mora
Orsa
Rättvik
Ockelbo
Söderhamn
GRÄSÖ

Flore
Gudvangen
Flåm
Dale
Voss
Gol
Gjøvik
Raufoss
Hamar
Filsa
Leksand
Falun
Storvik
Gävle
Gävle-bukten

Bergen
Osøyra
Eldfjord
Odda
Gulsvik
Hønefoss
Eidsvoll
Kongsvinger
Torsby
Sunne
Ludvika
Smedjebacken
Avesta
Krylbo
Heby
Vattholma

STORA SOTRA
STORD
BØMLO
Sauda
Rjukan
Notodden
Kongsberg
Svelvik
Vickersund
Oslo
Drammen
Lillestrøm
Charlottenberg
Arvika
Filipstad
Nora
Kopparberg
Sala
Uppsala
Rimbo
Norr

Haugesund
Kopervik
KARMØY
Skudeneshavn
Tau
Sandnes
Stavanger

Holmestrand
Holmsbu
Dröbak
Moss
Mysen
Kil
Forshaga
Lindesberg
Köping
Torshälla
Sundbyberg
Sigtuna
Enköping
Västerås
STOCKHOLM

Skien
Porsgrunn
Sandefjord
Brevik
Tønsberg
Horten
Sarpsborg
Fredrikstad
Halden
Säffle
Karlstad
Kristinehamn
Örebro
Arboga
Eskilstuna
Strängnäs
Mariefred
Södertälje
Saltsjöba

Egersund
Farsund
Flekkefjord
Mandal
Kristiansand
LINDESNES
Tvedestrand
Arendal
Grimstad
Lillesand
Risør
Kragerø
Langesund
Larvik
Strömstad
Grebbestad
Fjällbacka
Lysekil
Uddevalla
Åmål
Hallsberg
Askersund
Katrineholm
Malmköping
Trosa
Nynäshamn
ORNÖ

Skagerrak
GRENEN
Skagen
Frederikshavn
Sæby
Hjørring
Brønderslev
Nørresundby
Aalborg
Nibe
Løgstør
Mors
Nykøbing
Hobro
Mariager
Randers
Grenaa

Marstrand
Kungälv
Göteborg
Mölndal
Kungsbacka
Varberg
Falkenberg
Oskarström
Halmstad
Laholm
Båstad
Ängelholm
Markaryd
Hässleholm
Klippan
Åstorp
Helsingborg
Landskrona
Lund
Malmö

Alingsås
Borås
Ulricehamn
Huskvarna
Jönköping
Nässjö
Eksjö
Vetlanda
Virserum
Figeholm
Oskarshamn
Mönsterås
Borgholm
ÖLAND
Mörbylånga

Lidköping
Vänersborg
Skara
Skövde
Falköping
Tidaholm
Hjo
Mariestad
Töreboda
Motala
Vadstena
Skänninge
Mjölby
Gränna
Tranås
Linköping
Åtvidaberg
Valdemarsvik
Gamleby
Västervik
GOTLAND
Visby
Klintehamn
Burg

Mjölby
Norrköping
Söderköping
Nyköping

NORTH SEA
Thisted
Lemvig
Struer
Skive
Viborg
Silkeborg
Herning
Ringkøbing
Holstebro
Nissum Fjord
Ringkøbing Fjord
JYLLAND
Århus
Skanderborg
Ebeltoft
SAMSØ
ANHOLT
LÆSØ
Jammerbugten

Varde
Esbjerg
FANØ
Ribe
RØMØ
SYLT
FÖHR
Vejle
Kolding
Fredericia
Middelfart
Assens
Faaborg
ALS
Sønderborg
ÆRØ
Odense
Nyborg
Kalundborg
Slagelse
Korsør
Svendborg
Rudkøbing
LANGE LAND
Nakskov
Maribo
LOLLAND
MØN
Nykøbing FALSTER
Gedser

Haderslev
Åbenrå
Tønder
Flensburg
SCHLESWIG
Husum
Schleswig
Eckernförde
Rendsburg
Kiel
Neumünster
Neustadt in Holstein
Lübeck
HOLSTEIN
Heide
Cuxhaven
Wismar
Rostock
Warnemünde
Lübecker Bucht
Kiel Bay
FEHMARN
GERMANY
Neumünster

DENMARK
Horsens
Bogense
Holbæk
Ringsted
Roskilde
COPENHAGEN
København
Køge
Køge Bugt
SJÆLLAND
Frederikssund
Hillerød
Helsingør
Helsingborg
Øresund
Kristianstad
Sölvesborg
Karlshamn
Karlskrona
Ronneby
Åhus
Hanö-bukten
BORNHOLM (Den.)
Allinge
Rønne
Svaneke
Neksø

Eslöv
Hörby
Svedala
Skurup
Tomelilla
Simrishamn
Ystad
Trelleborg
Skanör
Falsterbo
SANDHAMMAREN

RÜGEN
KAP ARKONA
Bergen
Sassnitz
Stralsund
Greifswald
Wolgast
Świnoujście
Kamień Pomorski

Barth
Pomeranian Bay
Kołobrzeg
Darłowo
Ustka
Słupsk
Lębork
Wejherowo
Gdynia
Sopot
POLAND
Gda
Łeba

BALTIC SEA

A-559195-76
COPYRIGHT BY
RAND MCNALLY & COMPANY
MADE IN U.S.A.

Relief

Meters	Feet
1525	5000
610	2000
305	1000
152.5	500
0	Sea Level 0
152.5	Below Sea Level 500

Longitude East of Greenwich

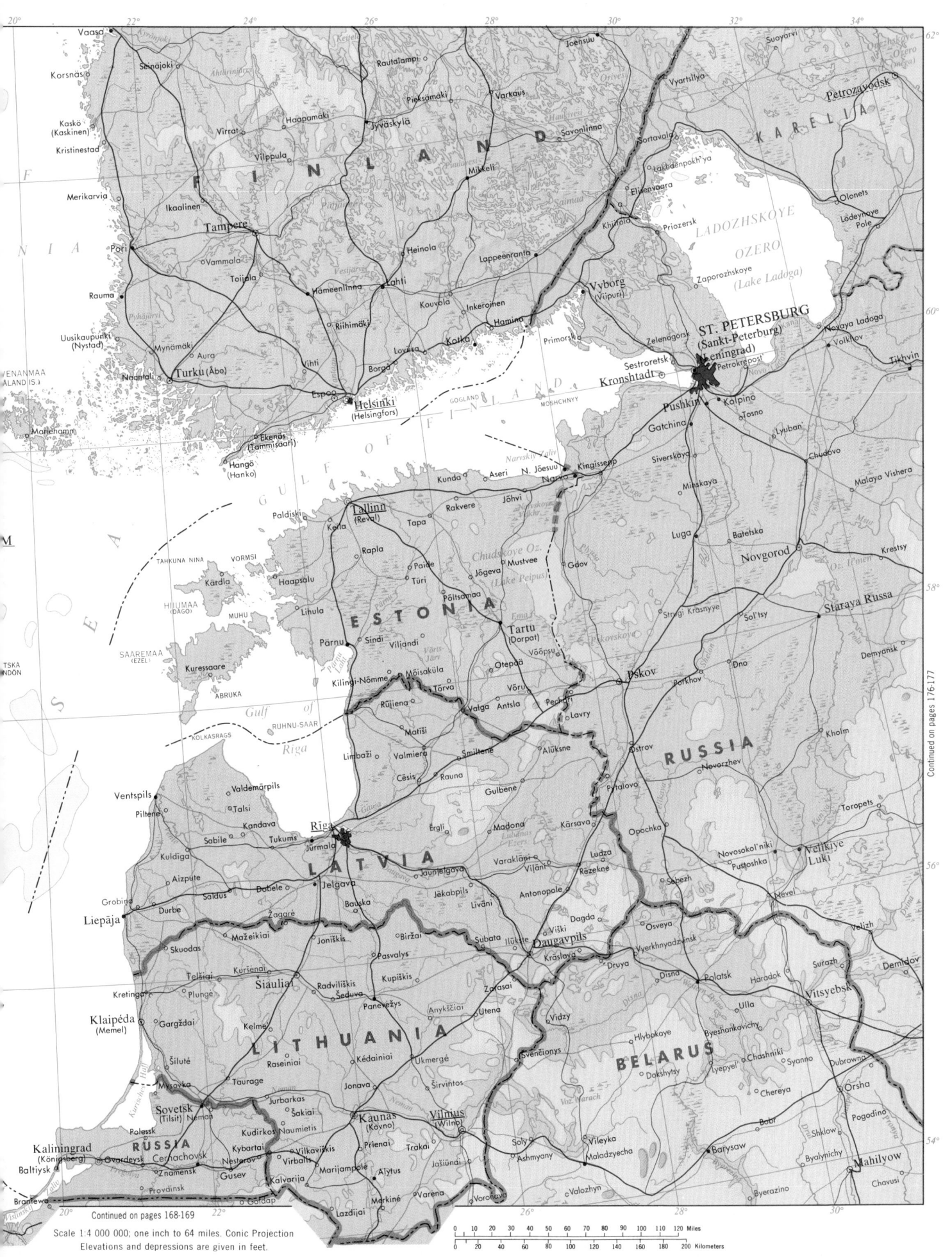

Scale 1:4 000 000; one inch to 64 miles. Conic Projection
Elevations and depressions are given in feet.

Continued on pages 168-169

Continued on pages 176-177

Continued on pages 166-167

Continued on pages 170-171

Continued on pages 174-175

NORTH SEA

DENMARK

Flensburg · Svendborg · Rudkøbing · Nakskov · MØN

Schleswig · Sønderborg · AERØ · Maribo · Nykøbing · FALSTER · Gedser

SCHLESWIG · Husum · Eckernförde · Kiel Bay · LOLLAND

HOLSTEIN · Rendsburg · Kiel · Neustadt in Holstein · Lübecker Bucht

BALTIC

RÜGEN · Sassnitz · Bergen · Stralsund · Barth

Cuxhaven · Stade · HAMBURG · Lübeck · Wismar · Rostock · Greifswald · Wolgast

FRISIAN ISLANDS · NORDERNEY · WANGEROOGE · BORKUM

Wilhelmshaven · Bremerhaven · Bad Oldesloe · Schwerin · Güstrow · Teterow · MECKLENBURG · Anklam · Swinoujście · Kamien Pomorski · Trzebiatów · Koszalin

NETHERLANDS · Emden · Leer · Oldenburg · Bremen · Lüneburg · Parchim · Waren · Neubrandenburg · Pasewalk · Szczecin (Stettin) · Stargard Szczeciński · POMERANIA

Groningen · Delfzijl · Papenburg · Delmenhorst · Verden · LÜNEBURGER HEIDE · Ludwigslust · Neustrelitz · Prenzlau · Gryfino · Pyrzyce · Choszczno · Świdwin

AMSTERDAM · Zwolle · Meppen · Lingen · Nienburg · Celle · Uelzen · Salzwedel · Perleberg · Wittenberge · Neu Ruppin · Eberswalde · Schwedt · Angermünde · Gorzów Wlkp.

Apeldoorn · Deventer · Hengelo · Almelo · Nordhorn · Osnabrück · Minden · Hannover · Wolfsburg · Gardelegen · Stendal · Rathenow · Oranienburg · Bernau · BERLIN · Frankfurt an der Oder

Utrecht · Arnhem · Enschede · Gronau · Rheine · Bielefeld · Herford · Braunschweig · Helmstedt · Haldensleben · Tangermünde · Genthin · Brandenburg · Potsdam · BRANDENBURG · Fürstenwalde · Eisenhüttenstadt

GERMANY

Nijmegen · Kleve · Münster · Detmold · Hameln · Hildesheim · Wolfenbüttel · Magdeburg · Schönebeck · Zerbst · Luckenwalde · Guben · Zielona Góra

's-Hertogenbosch · Gladbeck · Ahlen · Paderborn · Einbeck · Northeim · Halberstadt · Quedlinburg · Staßfurt · Bernburg · Dessau · Wittenberg · Lübben · Cottbus · Forst · Żary · Żagań

Tilburg · Duisburg · Bottrop · Dortmund · Soest · Lippstadt · HARZ · Göttingen · Nordhausen · Eisleben · Aschersleben · Bitterfeld · Delitzsch · Spremberg · Nowa Sól

DÜSSELDORF · ESSEN · Hagen · Kassel · Heiligenstadt · Sangerhausen · Merseburg · Weissenfels · Eilenburg · Senftenberg · Głogów

Mönchengladbach · Wuppertal · Solingen · Gummersbach · Marburg an der Lahn · Eschwege · Mühlhausen · THÜRINGEN · Naumburg · Leipzig · Riesa · Grossenhain · Kamenz · Bautzen · Görlitz

COLOGNE (Köln) · Siegen · Wetzlar · Bad Hersfeld · Eisenach · Gotha · Erfurt · Weimar · Altenburg · Meerane · Glauchau · Freiberg · Dresden · Bischofswerda · Zittau · Liberec · Jelenia Góra · Wałbrzych

Aachen · Bonn · Siegburg · HESSEN · Giessen · Fulda · Schmalkalden · Zella-Mehlis · Suhl · Saalfeld · Gera · Zwickau · Aue · Annaberg · ERZGEBIRGE · Chemnitz · Ústí nad Labem · Česká Lípa · Trutnov · Broumov · Náchod

BELGIUM · Liège · Verviers · Eupen · Malmedy · EIFEL · Andernach · Neuwied · Limburg an der Lahn · Marburg · WESTERWALD · Meiningen · Hildburghausen · Sonneberg · Plauen · Reichenbach · Marienberg · Most · Chomutov · Teplice · Mladá Boleslav · Hradec Králové

LUXEMBOURG · Trier · Koblenz · Bingen · WIESBADEN · FRANKFURT AM MAIN · Hanau · Schweinfurt · Coburg · Neustadt b.C. · Hof · Marktredwitz · Cheb · Karlovy Vary · CZECH REPUBLIC · Kladno · PRAGUE (Praha) · Kolín · Pardubice · Vysoké Mýto

Luxembourg · Mainz · Offenbach · Aschaffenburg · Würzburg · Bamberg · Bayreuth · Weiden · Mariánské Lázně · Plzeň · Beroun · CECHY (BOHEMIA) · Benešov · Havlíčkův Brod

Thionville · Bad Kreuznach · Worms · Darmstadt · Bensheim · ODENWALD · Kitzingen · Erlangen · Forchheim · Rokycany · Příbram · Jihlava

Metz · Saarbrücken · Kaiserslautern · Ludwigshafen · MANNHEIM · Heidelberg · Rothenburg · Fürth · Nürnberg · Schwabach · Amberg · Schwandorf · Domažlice · Klatovy · Strakonice · Písek · Tábor · Pelhřimov

Pirmasens · Speyer · Bruchsal · Heilbronn · Ansbach · BOHEMIAN FOREST · Regensburg · Sušice · České Budějovice · Třeboň · Brno

Nancy · Pont-à-Mousson · Wissembourg · Karlsruhe · Schwäbisch Hall · Ellwangen · Weissenburg · Neumarkt · BÖHMERWALD · Vimperk · Jindřichův Hradec · Znojmo

Saverne · Haguenau · Pforzheim · Ludwigsburg · STUTTGART · Esslingen · Aalen · Schwäbisch Gmünd · Neuburg · Ingolstadt · Straubing · Deggendorf · Passau · Linz · Krems · St. Pölten · VIENNA (Wien)

Strasbourg · Baden-Baden · Tübingen · Reutlingen · Ulm · Heidenheim · Neu Ulm · Augsburg · Freising · Landshut · Mühldorf · Braunau · Ried · Wels · Steyr · Amstetten · Baden

FRANCE · Colmar · Offenburg · Freudenstadt · Rottweil · Villingen · SCHWÄBISCHE ALB · Biberach · Memmingen · Landsberg · Dachau · MUNICH (München) · Rosenheim · Traunstein · Salzburg · Bad Ischl · AUSTRIA

Épinal · St. Dié · Mulhouse · Freiburg · SCHWARZWALD · Ravensburg · Kempten · Kaufbeuren · Weilheim · Bad Tölz · Bad Reichenhall · Gmunden · Judenburg

Belfort · Montbéliard · Basel · Lörrach · Schaffhausen · Konstanz · Friedrichshafen · Bregenz · Garmisch-Partenkirchen · Kufstein · STEIERMARK · Leoben · Bruck · Kapfenberg · Graz

La Chaux-de-Fonds · Neuchâtel · Biel · Bern · Zürich · Winterthur · Sankt Gallen · Dornbirn · LIECHTENSTEIN · Feldkirch · Bludenz · Arlberg Tunnel · Innsbruck · HOHE TAUERN · NIEDERE TAUERN · SEMMERING PASS · Fürstenfeld · Szombathely

SWITZERLAND · Lausanne · Geneva (Genève) · JURA · Fribourg · Thun · Luzern · BERNER ALPEN · Glarus · Chur · Davos · BRENNER PASS · TAUERN TUNNEL · Spittal · St. Veit · Klagenfurt · Maribor

Montreux · Sion · GOTTHARD PASS · RHÄTISCHE ALPEN · ORTLER · Merano · Bolzano · DOLOMITES · Villach · KARAWANKEN · SLOVENIA · CROATIA

Aosta · Bernina · ADIGE · Trento · Belluno · Pieve di Cadore · Udine · Tolmin · Celje

Scale 1:4 000 000; one inch to 64 miles. Conic Projection

Elevations and depressions are given in feet.

Longitude East of Greenwich

COPYRIGHT BY RAND M^cNALLY COMPANY · MADE IN U.S.A.

Continued on pages 166-167

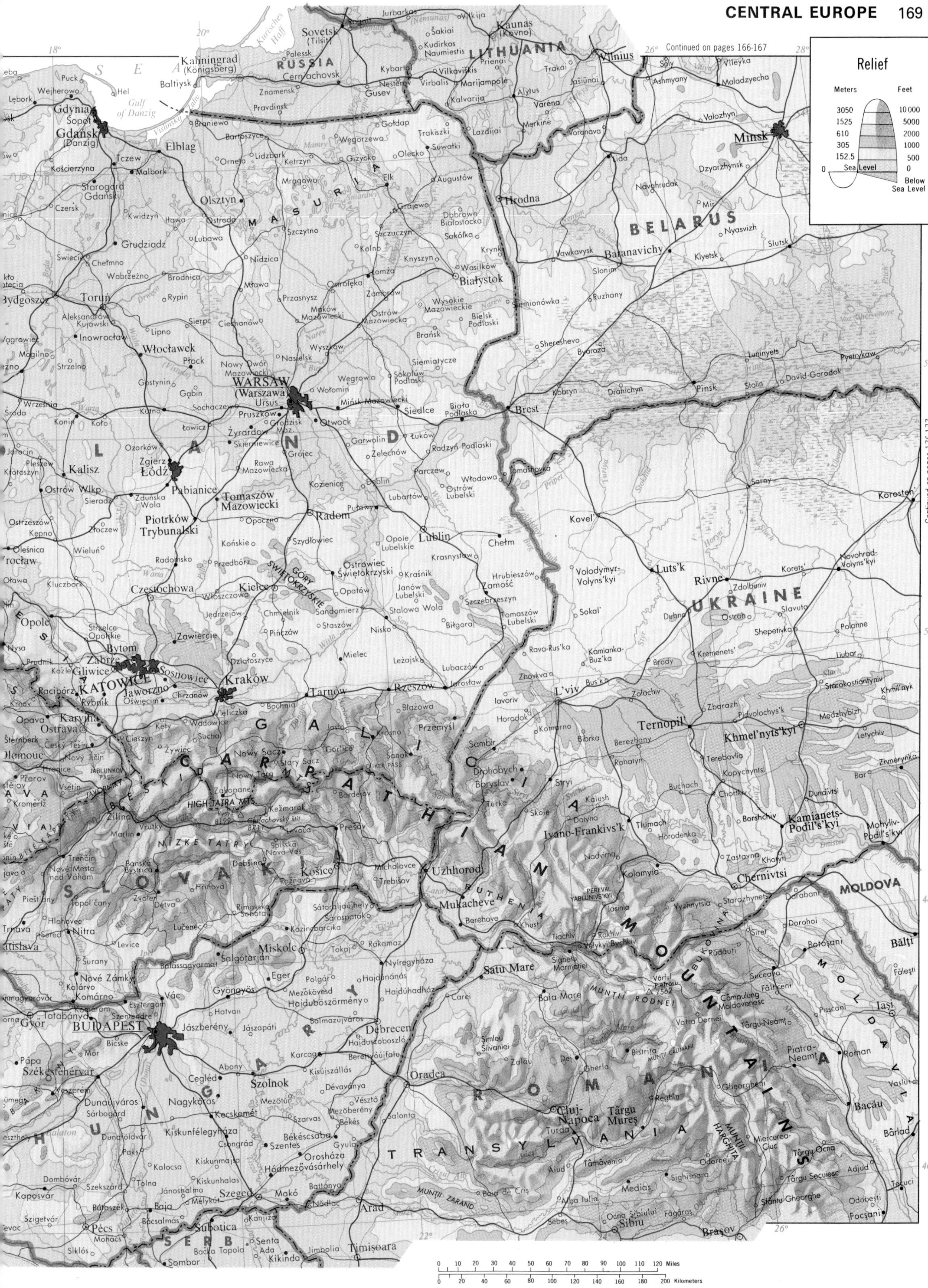

Continued on pages 176-177

Relief

Meters	Feet
3050	10 000
1525	5000
610	2000
305	1000
152.5	500
0 Sea Level	0
Below Sea Level	

Countries / Regions: RUSSIA, LITHUANIA, BELARUS, UKRAINE, MOLDOVA, POLAND, SLOVAKIA, HUNGARY, ROMANIA, SERBIA, GALICIA, MASURIA, TRANSYLVANIA, CARPATHIAN MOUNTAINS, RUTHENIA

Selected place names:

Kaliningrad (Königsberg), Baltiysk, Sovetsk (Tilsit), Kaunas, Vilnius, Minsk, Gdynia, Sopot, Gdańsk (Danzig), Puck, Hel, Wejherowo, Lębork, Elblag, Tczew, Malbork, Braniewo, Bartoszyce, Olsztyn, Kętrzyn, Giżycko, Ełk, Augustów, Suwałki, Hrodna, Białystok, Baranavichy, Navahrudak, Lida, Slonim, Vawkavysk, Slutsk, Klyetsk, Nyasvizh, Mir, Dzyarzhynsk, Kościerzyna, Starogard Gdański, Czersk, Kwidzyń, Iława, Ostróda, Nidzica, Mława, Grudziądz, Chełmno, Brodnica, Rypin, Toruń, Bydgoszcz, Włocławek, Płock, Ciechanów, Przasnysz, Maków Mazowiecki, Ostrołęka, Łomża, Zambrów, Wysokie Mazowieckie, Bielsk Podlaski, Brańsk, Siemiatycze, WARSAW (Warszawa), Ursus, Pruszków, Otwock, Mińsk Mazowiecki, Siedlce, Biała Podlaska, Brest, Kobryn, Pinsk, Stolin, David-Gorodok, Luninyets, Łódź, Zgierz, Pabianice, Tomaszów Mazowiecki, Piotrków Trybunalski, Radom, Lublin, Chełm, Radzyń Podlaski, Łuków, Parczew, Włodawa, Kovel', Luts'k, Rivne, Kalisz, Sieradz, Zduńska Wola, Częstochowa, Kielce, Radom, Opole Lubelskie, Kraśnik, Zamość, Hrubieszów, Volodymyr-Volyns'kyi, Opole, Nysa, Bytom, Zabrze, Gliwice, KATOWICE, Sosnowiec, Jaworzno, Chrzanów, Kraków, Tarnów, Rzeszów, Przemyśl, L'viv, Ternopil', Khmel'nyts'kyi, Nowy Sącz, Krosno, Sanok, Drohobych, Boryslav, Stryi, Ivano-Frankivs'k, Kalush, Chernivtsi, Kamianets-Podil'skyi, ŽILINA, Poprad, Prešov, Košice, Michalovce, Trebišov, Uzhhorod, Mukacheve, Khust, Satu Mare, Baia Mare, Miskolc, Eger, Nyíregyháza, Debrecen, Oradea, Cluj-Napoca, Târgu Mureş, BUDAPEST, Szolnok, Kecskemét, Szeged, Békéscsaba, Arad, Timişoara, Sibiu, Braşov, Piatra-Neamţ, Bacău, Iaşi, Roman, Bârlad, Focşani, Bălţi, Suceava, Győr, Tatabánya, Székesfehérvár, Veszprém, Pécs, Kaposvár, Szekszárd, Baja, Subotica, Sombor, MUNŢII RODNEI, MUNŢII HARGHITA, MUNŢII CĂLIMANI, HIGH TATRA MTS., NÍZKE TATRY, GÓRY ŚWIĘTOKRZYSKIE

Bodies of water / features: SEA (Baltic), Gulf of Danzig, Vistula Lagoon, Nemunas, Pripet, Dnister, Prut, Siret, Wisła, Warta, San, Balaton

Relief

Meters	Feet
3050	10 000
1525	5000
610	2000
305	1000
152.5	500
0 Sea Level	0
152.5	500
1525	5000

Continued on pages 164-165

UNITED KINGDOM

ENGLISH CHANNEL

BAY OF BISCAY

A-550900-76
COPYRIGHT BY
RAND McNALLY & COMPANY
MADE IN U.S.A.

F R A N C E

BRETAGNE

NORMANDIE

PICARDIE

BELGIU

SPAIN

PYRENEES

ANDORRA

a

Marseille

MEDITERRANEAN SEA

Golfe du Lion

Scale 1:1 000 000

Miles
0   4   8   12   16 Kilometers

©rmcn

Continued on pages 172-173

Longitude West of Greenwich | Longitude East of Greenwich

Scale 1:4 000 000; one inch to 64 miles. Conic Projection
Elevations and depressions are given in feet

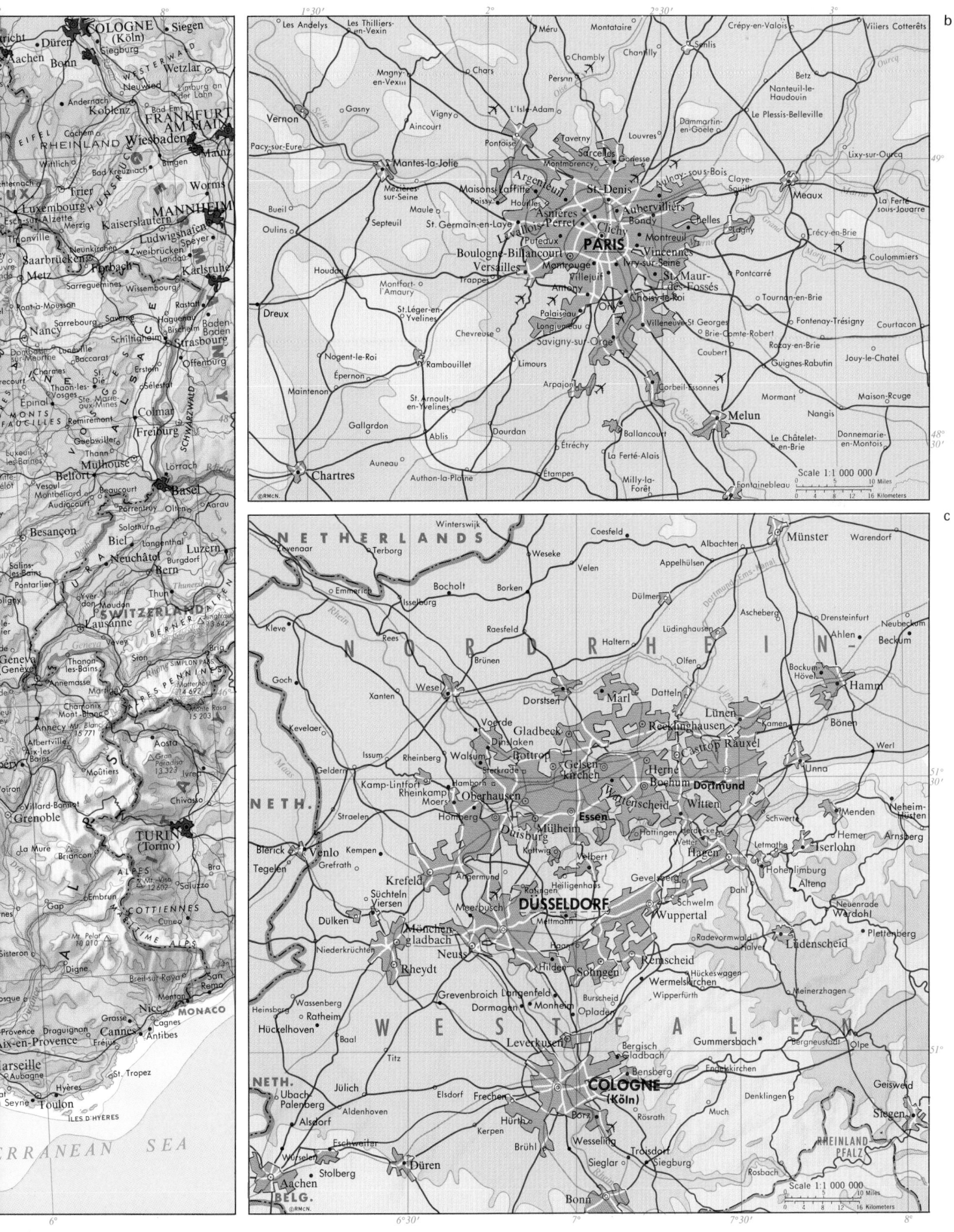

b

COLOGNE (Köln) · Siegen
·Aachen ·Düren ·Bonn ·Siegburg ·Wetzlar
EIFEL ·Andernach ·Koblenz ·Bad Ems ·Limburg an der Lahn
RHEINLAND Wiesbaden FRANKFURT AM MAIN Mainz
Trier ·Bad Kreuznach Bingen Worms
HUNSRÜCK
Luxembourg ·Esch-sur-Alzette ·Merzig MANNHEIM
·Thionville ·Neunkirchen ·Kaiserslautern Ludwigshafen Speyer
Saarbrücken ·Forbach Landau
Metz ·Sarreguemines Wissembourg Karlsruhe
·Sarrebourg ·Saverne ·Haguenau Rastatt
Nancy ·Schiltigheim Baden Baden
Strasbourg Offenburg
·Lunéville ·Baccarat
·Charmes ·Ste. Marie aux Mines
·Épinal ·Remiremont Colmar
MONTS FAUCILLES ·Thann Freiburg
·Vesoul Mulhouse SCHWARZWALD
·Belfort ·Lörrach
·Montbéliard ·Beaucourt Basel
·Besançon ·Porrentruy ·Olten ·Aarau
·Biel Langenthal Luzern
·Neuchâtel ·Burgdorf
·Salins-les-Bains Bern
·Pontarlier SWITZERLAND
·Yverdon ·Moudon ·Thun Thunersee
Lausanne ·Vevey JUNGFRAU
Geneva (Genève) ·Thonon-les-Bains Sion SIMPLON PASS
·Annemasse ·Martigny PENNINES Monte Rosa 15 203
·Chamonix Mt. Blanc 15 771 Aosta
·Albertville ·Aix-les-Bains Gran Paradiso 13 323 ·Ivrea
·Annecy ·Chivasso
·Voiron
·La Mure Grenoble
·Briançon TURIN (Torino)
ALPES ·Bra
·Embrun ·Saluzzo ·Cuneo
·Gap Mt. Viso 12 602 COTTIENNES
·Mt. Pelat 10 010 MARITIME ALPS
·Sisteron ·Digne ·Breil-sur-Roya San Remo
·Draguignan ·Grasse ·Menton MONACO
Aix-en-Provence ·Cannes ·Nice
·Fréjus ·Antibes
Marseille ·St. Tropez
·Hyères
·Toulon ILES D'HYÈRES
RRANEAN SEA

b. Paris region map.

c

NETHERLANDS
·Winterswijk
Zevenaar ·Terborg ·Weseke ·Coesfeld ·Albachten Münster Warendorf
·Bocholt ·Borken ·Velen ·Appelhülsen
·Emmerich ·Isselburg ·Dülmen ·Ascheberg ·Drensteinfurt ·Neubeckum
Kleve ·Raesfeld ·Lüdinghausen ·Ahlen Beckum
·Rees NORDRHEIN- ·Bockum-Hövel
·Goch ·Brünen ·Olfen Hamm
·Kevelaer Wesel ·Haltern
·Xanten Dorstsen Marl Datteln Lünen ·Werl
Issum ·Voerde Gladbeck ·Recklinghausen Kamen Bönen
NETH. ·Geldern Rheinberg Dinslaken Bottrop Castrop-Rauxel Unna
·Straelen Kamp-Lintfort Walsum Gelsenkirchen Herne Dortmund
·Rheinkamp Steckrade Bochum Witten
Blerick Venlo ·Kempen Moers Hamborn Wattenscheid ·Menden
Tegelen ·Grefrath Oberhausen Essen Schwerte Neheim-Hüsten
·Straelen Homberg Mülheim Hattingen Hemer Iserlohn
Krefeld Duisburg Kettwig Wetter Hagen Letmathe Arnsberg
Süchteln Angermund Velbert Heidecke Hohenlimburg
Viersen Heiligenhaus Altena Neuenrade
Dülken Meerbusch Gevelsberg Menden Werdohl
Mönchen- Ratingen DÜSSELDORF Schwelm Plettenberg
gladbach Mettmann Wuppertal
Niederkrüchten Neuss Haan Radevormwald Lüdenscheid
Rheydt Hilden Solingen Remscheid Halver
Grevenbroich Langenfeld Wermelskirchen Hückeswagen Meinerzhagen
Dormagen Monheim Burscheid Wipperfürth
Wassenberg Heinsberg Ratheim Opladen
Hückelhoven Leverkusen Bergisch Gladbach Gummersbach Bergneustadt
Baal WESTFALEN
Titz Bergisch
Gladbach Bensberg Engelskirchen Olpe
NETH. Jülich Elsdorf Frechen COLOGNE Bensberg Denklingen Geisweid
Ubach- (Köln) Much
Palenberg Aldenhoven Börn Rösrath RHEINLAND
Alsdorf Kerpen Hürth Siegen
Eschweiler Brühl Wesseling PFALZ
Würselen Düren Troisdorf Rosbach
Stolberg Sieglar Siegburg
Aachen Wesseling
BELG. Bonn

Scale 1:1 000 000
0 4 8 12 16 Kilometers
0 5 10 Miles

10 20 30 40 50 60 70 80 90 100 110 120 Miles
20 40 60 80 100 120 140 160 180 200 Kilometers

Relief

Meters		Feet
3050		10000
1525		5000
610		2000
305		1000
152.5		500
0	Sea Level	0
152.5		500
1525		5000
3050		10000

A-552900-76   6-12
COPYRIGHT BY
RAND MCNALLY & COMPANY
MADE IN U.S.A.

Scale 1:4 000 000, one inch to 64 miles. Conic Projection
Elevations and depressions are given in feet

Longitude West of Greenwich

Continued on pages 170-171

a

MADRID

Scale 1:1 000 000

b

LISBON (Lisboa)

ATLANTIC OCEAN

Scale 1:1 000 000

c

NAPLES (Napoli)

TYRRHENIAN SEA

Scale 1:1 000 000

d

ROME (Roma)

VATICAN CITY

TYRRHENIAN SEA

Scale 1:1 000 000

Continued on pages 168-169

Continued on pages 170-171

Scale 1:4 000 000; one inch to 64 miles. Conic Projection
Elevations and depressions are given in feet

Relief

Feet					
5000	2000	1000	500	0	
					Sea Level
Meters					500
1525	610	305	152.5	0	
				152.5	

Continued on pages 166-167

Cities and Towns

0 to 50,000	○	500,000 to 1,000,000	◎
50,000 to 500,000	◉	1,000,000 and over	

Scale 1:4 000 000; one inch to 64 miles. Conic Projection
Elevations and depressions are given in feet

A-579900-76 -7-14
COPYRIGHT BY
RAND M^cNALLY & COMPANY
MADE IN U.S.A.

VORONEZH

KURSK

BELGOROD

LUHANS'K

SUMY

KHARKIV

ROSTOV

KRASNODAR

CHERNIHIV

KIEV (Kyiv)

POLTAVA

DNIPROPETROVS'K

DONETS COAL BASIN

ZAPORIZHZHIA

SEA OF AZOV

KHERSON

MYKOLAIV

ODESA

KRYMS'KYI PIVOSTRIV
(CRIMEAN PENINSULA)

REK REPUBLIKA KRYM

BLACK SEA

MOLDOVA

BESSARABIA

ROMANIA

U K R A I N E

Longitude East of Greenwich

0 10 20 30 40 50 60 70 80 90 100 110 120 Miles
0 20 40 60 80 100 120 140 160 180 200 Kilometers

Scale 1:20 000 000; one inch to 315 mi
Lambert's Azimuthal, Equal Area Proje
Elevations and depressions are given in

Relief

Meters		Feet
3050		10 000
1525		5000
610		2000
305		1000
152.5		500
0	Sea Level	
152.5		500 Below
1525		5000 Sea Level
3050		10 000

ARCTIC OCEAN

SEVERNAYA ZEMLYA
(NORTHERN LAND)

DE LONGA

NOVAYA SIBIR

NOVOSIBIRSKIYE O VA
(NEW SIBERIAN ISLANDS)

MALYY LYAKHOVSKIY
LYAKHOVSKIYE

EAST SIBERIAN SEA

VRANGELYA
(WRANGEL)

CHUKOTSKIY P-OV

M. SHELAGSKIY

Arctic Circle

CHUKOTSKOYE NAGOR'YE

Anadyr'

Anadyrskiy Zaliv

KORYAKSKIY KHREBET

LAPTEV SEA

KOTEL'NYY

M. SVYATOY NOS

M. BUOR-KHAYA

Tiksi

M. SVIATOY NOS

KHREBET

MEDVEZH'I

Nizhne-Kolymsk

Sredne-Kolymsk

Ayon

Ambarchik

Markovo

Pevek

Penzhino

TAYMYR
GORY BYRRANGA

P-OV TAYMYR

Nordvik

Khatangskiy Zaliv

M. CHELYUSKIN

Ust'-Olenek

Bulun

Abyy

Verkhoyansk

CHERSKOGO

Gora Chen
3147

KHREBET GYDAN (KOLYMSKIY)

Zashiversk

Zyryanka

Magadan

Gizhiga

M. TAYGONOS

P-OV

Ust'-Kamchatsk

KAMCHATKA

Klyuchevskaya Sopka
15,584

Verkhne-Kamchatsk

Petropavlovsk-
Kamchatskiy

Noril'sk

GORY PUTORANA

Khatanga

Lena

Olenek

Zhigansk

VERKHOYANSKIY KHREBET

Vilyuy

Vilyuysk

Suntar

Yakutsk

Aldan

Aldankaya

Ust'-Maya

Amga

Nel'kan

DZHUGDZHUR KHREBET

Ayan

Okhotsk

Ust'-Bol'sheretsk

SEA OF OKHOTSK

SAKHALIN

Aleksandrovsk

Poronaysk

M. TERPENIYA

M. YELIZAVETY

Okha

Nogliki

Uglegorsk

urukhansk

Tura

Nizhnyaya Tunguska

Olekminsk

Tommot

Udskaya Guba

Chumikan

SHANTAR

Nikolayevsk-na-Amure

Kholmsk

Korsakov

Yuzhno-Sakhalinsk

Tatar Strait

Baykit

Podkamennaya Tunguska

Peleduy

Vitim

G. Golets-Purpula
2577

PATOM PLATEAU

Bodaybo

Golets Skalistyy
9180

Mukhtuya

STANOVOY KHREBET

Zeya

Svobodnyy

KHREBET BUREINSKIY

Komsomol'sk-na-Amure

Sovetskaya Gavan'

Yartsevo

G. Polkan
3543

Kirensk

Ilimsk

Nizhne-Angarsk

Tyndinskiy

Skovorodino

Belogorsk

Ust'-Tyrma

Bureya

Birobidzhan

Khabarovsk

SIKHOTE ALIN

Wakkanai

HOKKAIDŌ

Sapporo

Yeniseysk

TS K Krasnoyarsk

Bogotol

Kansk

Balakhta

etski

Nizhneudinsk

Tulun

G. Piramida
10801

Tayshet

Bratsk

Bratskoye Vdkhr.

Zhigalovo

Kachugo

BAYKAL'SKIY KHREBET

OZ. Baykal
(Lake Baikal)
Surface elev 1535 ft.
above sea level

Barguzin

VITIM KHREBET

Chita

Nerchinsk

Sretensk

NERCHINSKIY KHREBET

Nerchinskiy Zavod

Blagoveshchensk

Zeya

Amur

Nenjiang

Goukou

LESSER KHINGAN RANGE

Hailun

Suihua

Dal'niy

Spassk-Dal'niy

Arsen'yev

Ol'ga

USSURIYSKIY KHREBET

Parlizonsk

Dal'nerechensk

Boli

Molmyzh

HOKKAIDŌ

Otaru

Esashi

Munku Sardyk
11457

Minusinsk

Abakan

SAYAN KHREBET

Cheremkhovo

Angarsk

Kutulik

Irkutsk

Ulan-Ude

YABLONOVYY KHREBET

Aginskoye

Aksha

Borzya

RANGE

GREATER KHINGAN

Qiqihar

Fuyu

Tao an

Jarud Qi

Goukou

Nenjiang

Dunhua

Mudanjiang

Jilin

HARBIN

MANCHURIA

Spassk-Dal'niy

Vladivostok

Nakhodka

Najin

Chŏngjin

SEA OF JAPAN

HONSHŪ

Kyzyl

TANNU-OLA

Uvs Nuur

Har Us Nuur

Uureg Nuur

Hovd

Uliastay

HANGAYN NURUU

KHANGAI MTS.

Tsast Bogd
13 419

Kyren

Goradok

Petrovsk-Zabaykal'skiy

Kyakhta

Selenge

Ulan Bator
(Ulaanbaatar)

Öndörhaan

Kerulen

Wenquan

Tao an

CHANGCHUN

Shuangliao

Dunhua

Hunchun

FUSHUN

SHENYANG

Partizonsk

Artĕm

Vladivostok

NORTH KOREA

P'yŏngyang

Kaesŏng

SEOUL

SOUTH KOREA

Tottori

Matsue

Tsast Bogd
13 419

Sayr Usa

GOBI OR SHAMO
(DESERT)

CHINA

Chifeng

Weichang

Chengde

Zhangjiakou

Fengzhen

BEIJING

TIANJIN

Baoding

Lüshun

Dalian

SHANDONG BANDAO

Bo Hai

YELLOW SEA

Korea Bay

Andong

P'yŏngyang

Taegu

PUSAN

Matsue

Tottori

Hiroshima

KYOTO

KŌBE

OSAKA

Okayama

Kōchi

Kanazawa

HONSHŪ

Longitude East of Greenwich

| 100 | 200 | 300 | 400 | 500 | 600 Miles |
| 200 | 400 | 600 | 800 | 1000 Kilometers |

Cities and Towns

0 to 50,000 ○ 500,000 to 1,000,000 ◉
50,000 to 500,000 ⊙ 1,000,000 and over

Obskaya Guba

WESTERN SIBERIAN LOWLAND

KARA SEA

KHREBET PAY-KHOY

Khabarovo

NOVAYA ZEMLYA

VAYGACH

DOLGIY

Vorkuta

PECHORA BASIN

Arctic Circle

MALOZEMEL'SKAYA TUNDRA

Nar'yan-Mar

Ust'-Tsil'ma

Izhma

Pechora

Ukhta

Sosnogorsk

Ust'-Kulom

U R A L

Krasnotur'insk

Serov

Solikamsk
Berezniki
Kizel
Gubakha
Krasnovishersk
Chusovoy
Perm'
Lys'va
Kungur

YEKATERINBURG

Kamensk-Ural'skiy
Kopeysk
Chelyabinsk

BASHKORTOSTAN
Ufa
Birsk
Sterlitamak
Salavat
Magnitogorsk

Cherdyn'

Troitsko-
Pechorsk

UDMURTIA
Glazov
Votkinsk
Izhevsk

Syktyvkar

Kotlas

Koslas

Nikol'sk

Veliky Ustyug

Sol'vychegodsk

Kirov
Slobodskoy
Kotel'nich

TATARSTAN
Kazan'
Naberezhnyye Chelny
Nizhnekamsk
Chistopol'
Bugul'ma
Al'met'yevsk

R U S S I A

MARI EL
Yoshkar-Ola

CHUVASHIA
Cheboksary

NIZHNIY NOVGOROD
Dzerzhinsk

MORDVINIA
Saransk

KARA SEA

KOLGUYEV

P-OV KANIN

M. KANIN NOS

A R C T I C   O C E A N

B A R E N T S   S E A

P-OV RYBACHIY

Teriberka

Murmansk

Monchegorsk

Kandalaksha

Kirovsk

KOLSKIY P-OV (KOLA PEN.)

Mezen'

Pinega

Arkhangel'sk
(Archangel)

Yemetsk

Shenkursk

Vel'sk

Kargopol'

Onega

Belozersk

Vologda

Gryazovets

Danilov

Kostroma

Galich

Buy

Makar'yev

Ivanovo
Shuya
Kineshma
Vichuga
Teykovo

Vladimir

Murom

Gus'-Khrustal'nyy

Kovrov

MOSCOW (Moskva)

NORWAY

SWEDEN

LAPLAND

FINLAND

Murmansk

KARELIA

Kem'

Belomorsk

Medvezhegorsk

Petrozavodsk

Lake Onega

ST. PETERSBURG
(Sankt-Peterburg) (Leningrad)

Kronshtadt
Pushkin
Kolpino
Gatchina

Vyborg

Helsinki

Tallinn

ESTONIA

LATVIA
Riga

LITHUANIA
Vilnius

Minsk

Novgorod

Pskov

Velikiye Luki

Rzhev

Tver'

Smolensk

V A L D A I

C E N T R A L

Relief

Feet
10000
5000
2000
1000
500
Sea Level
Below Sea Level
500
5000
10000

Meters
3050
1525
610
305
152.5
Sea Level
0
152.5
1525
3050

0   50   100   150   200   250   300 Miles
0   100   200   300   400   500 Kilometers

Continued on pages 160-161

Scale 1:10 000 000; one inch to 160 miles. Conic Projection
Elevations and depressions are given in feet.

Continued on pages 162-163

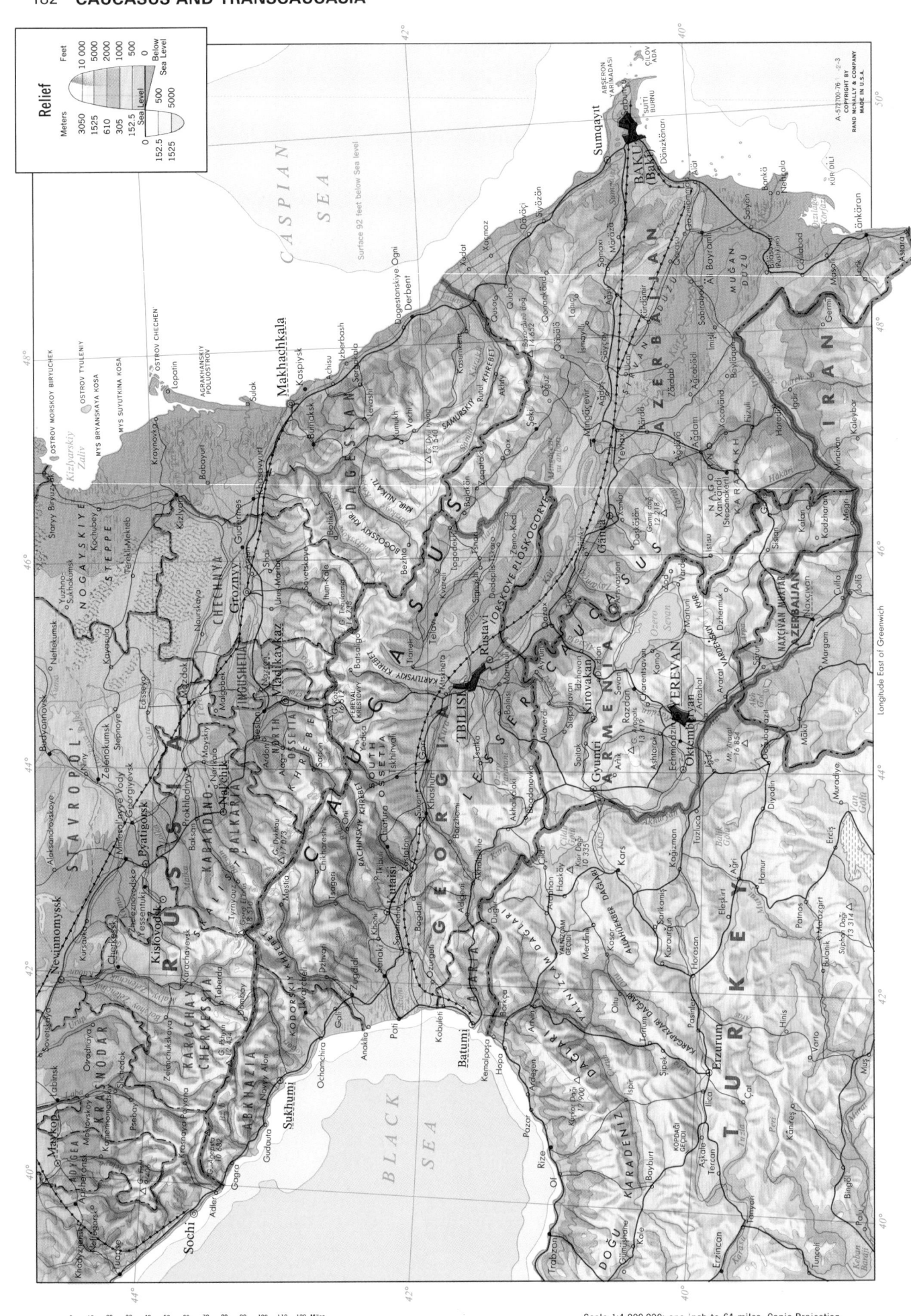

Relief

Meters	Feet	
3050	10 000	
1525	5000	
610	2000	
305	1000	
152.5	500	
0	0	Sea Level
		Below Sea Level
152.5	500	
1525	5000	

Scale 1:4 000 000; one inch to 64 miles. Conic Projection
Elevations and depressions are given in feet

0 10 20 30 40 50 60 70 80 90 100 110 120 Miles
0 20 40 60 80 100 120 140 160 180 200 Kilometers

CASPIAN SEA

BLACK SEA

RUSSIA

GEORGIA

ARMENIA

AZERBAIJAN

IRAN

TURKEY

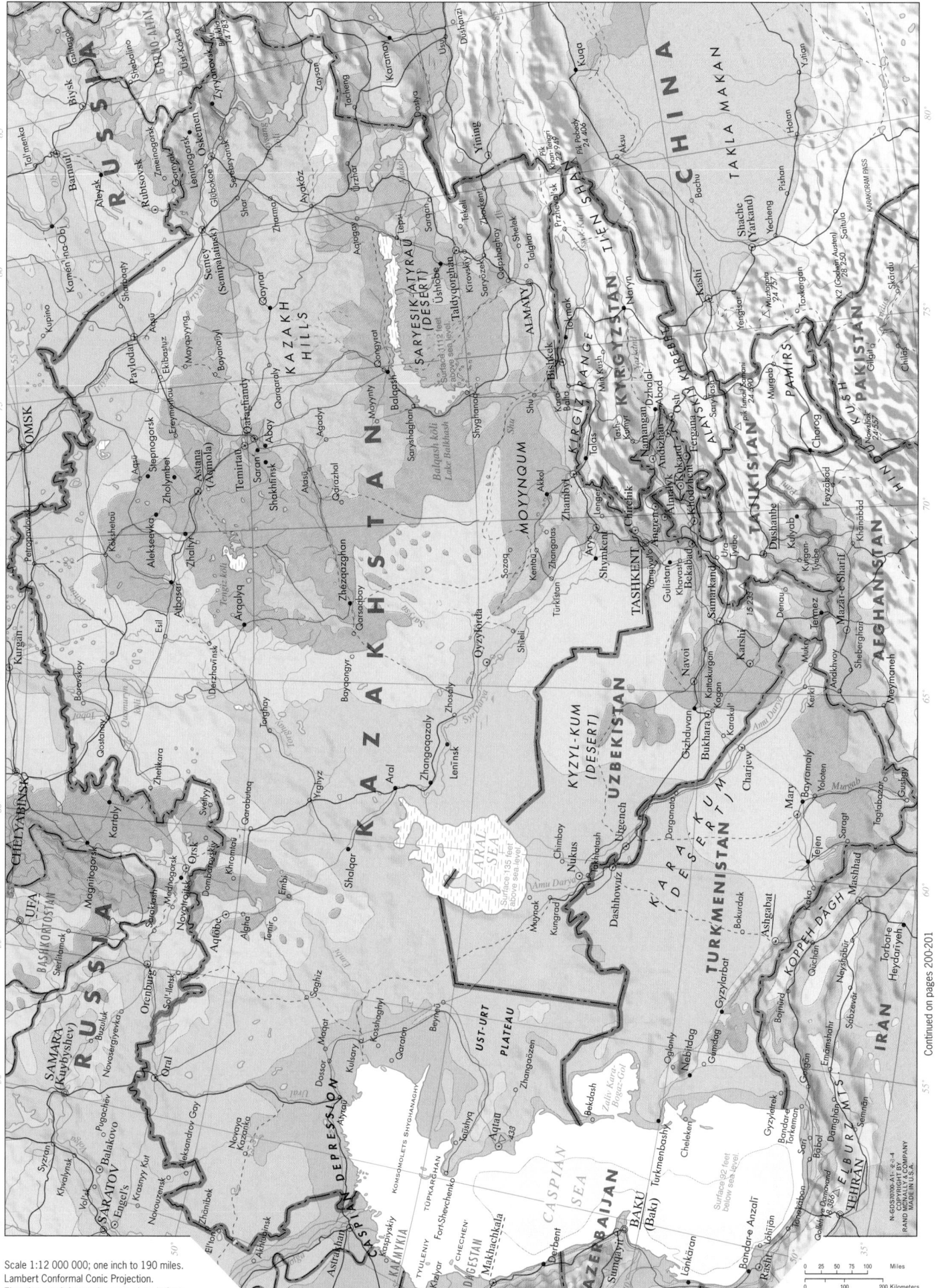

Continued on pages 200-201

Scale 1:12 000 000; one inch to 190 miles.
Lambert Conformal Conic Projection.
Elevations and depressions are given in feet.

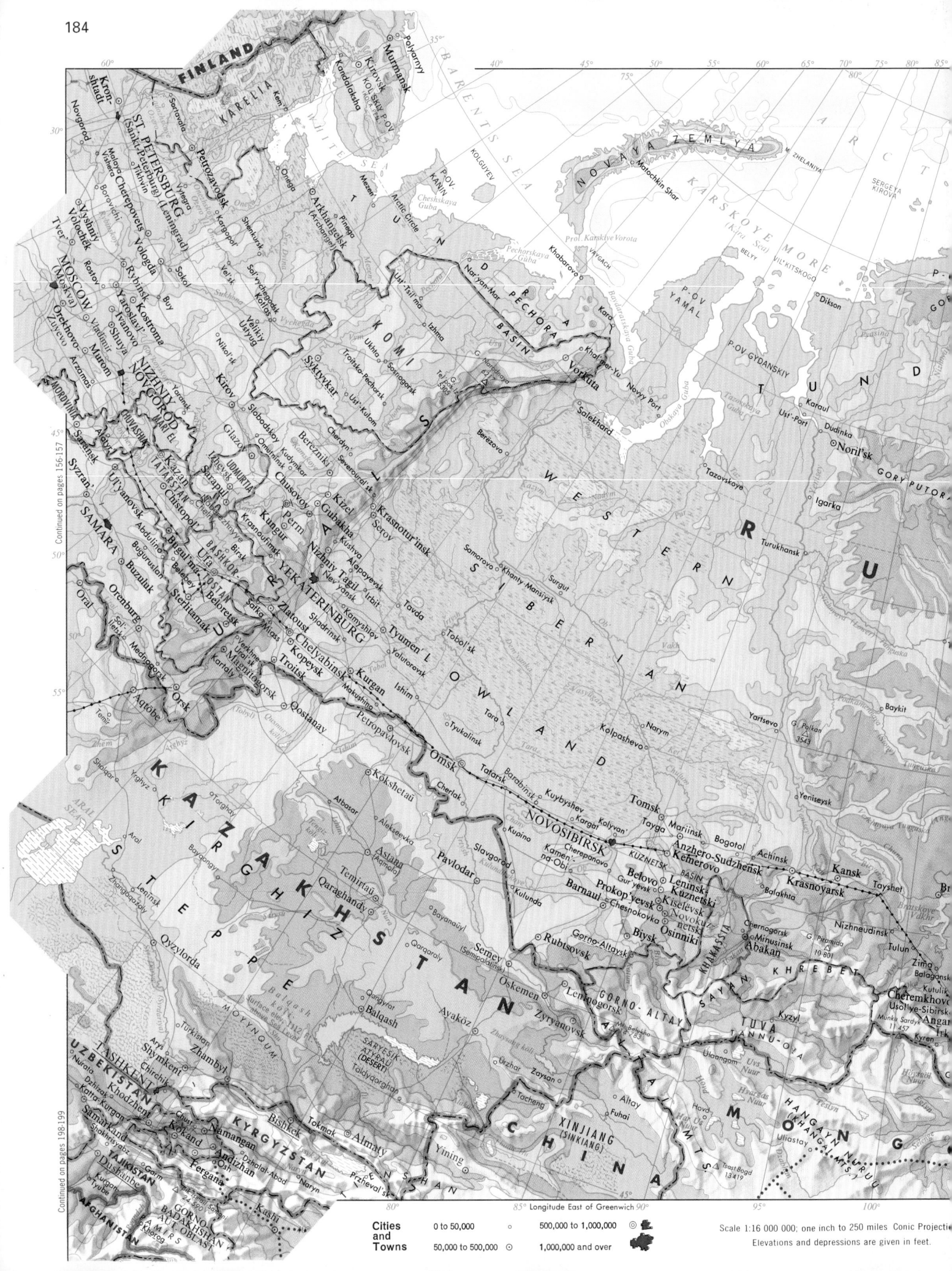

Continued on pages 156-157

Continued on pages 198-199

FINLAND

BARENTS SEA

NOVAYA ZEMLYA

KARSKOYE MORE
(Kara Sea)

KARELIA

WHITE SEA

KOMI

PECHORA BASIN

P-OV YAMAL

P-OV GYDANSKIY

T U N D R A

ST. PETERSBURG
(Sankt-Peterburg) (Leningrad)

MOSCOW
(Moskva)

NIZHNIY NOVGOROD

MORDOVIA

CHUVASHIA

MARI EL

TATARSTAN

UDMURTIA

BASHKOR-TOSTAN

SAMARA

YEKATERINBURG

WESTERN SIBERIAN LOWLAND

R U S

GORY PUTORA

Noril'sk

Vorkuta

KAZAKHSTAN

KIRGIZ STEPPE

MOYNQUM

ARAL SEA

UZBEKISTAN

TASHKENT

KYRGYZSTAN

TAJIKISTAN

AFGHANISTAN

GORNO-BADAKHSHAN AUT. OBLAST

NOVOSIBIRSK

KUZNETSK BASIN

KHAKASSIA

GORNO-ALTAY

TUVA
TANNU-OLA

SAYAN KHREBET

ALTAY MTS

HANGAYN (KHANGAI) NURUU

M O N G

CHINA

XINJIANG
(SINKIANG)

85° Longitude East of Greenwich 90°

| Cities and Towns | 0 to 50,000 | o | 500,000 to 1,000,000 | ⊛ |
| | 50,000 to 500,000 | ⊙ | 1,000,000 and over | |

Scale 1:16 000 000; one inch to 250 miles Conic Projection
Elevations and depressions are given in feet

100° 105° 110° 115° 120° 125° 130° 135° 140° 175° 180° 175° 170°

80°

Bering Strait

CHUKOTSKIY P-OV

WRANGELYA (Wrangel I.)

SEVERNAYA ZEMLYA
(NORTHERN LAND)

MALYY TAMIR

MICHELYUSKIN

NOVOSIBIRSKIYE O-VA
(NEW SIBERIAN ISLANDS)
FADDEYA

NOVAYA SIBIR'

DE-LONGA

SHELAGSKIY

ANADYRSKIY ZALIV

L A P T E V

BEL'KOVSKIY

KOTEL'NYY

STOLBOVOY

MALYY
LYAKHOVSKIYE

LYAKHOVSKIYE

E A S T   S I B E R I A N   S E A

MEDVEZH'I

Anadyr'

180°

BYRRANGA
YMYR

BOLSHOY
BEGICHEV
Zaliv

Nordvik

S E A

M SVYATOY
NOS

Tiksi

Bulun

Kazach'ye

Ambarchik

Arctic Circle

Nizhne-Kolymsk

Markovo

Penzhino

175°

KORYAKSKIY KHREBET

Khatanga

Ust'-Olenëk

G. Sellya Khkana

Guba
Buor
Khaya

M BUOR
KHAYA

U

N

D

R

Srednekolymsk

AYON

Bel'kaya

Gizhiga

CHUKOTSKOYE NAGOR'YE

Tilichiki

M OLYUTORSKIY

170°

Olenëk

Verkhoyansk

Abyy

Zashiversk

Zyryanka

KHREBET GYDAN (KOLYMSKIY)

Ust' Penzhino

60°

Olenëk

KHREBET KULAR

VERKHOYANSKIY KHREBET

KHREBET CHERSKOGO

Kolyma

TAYGONOS

Penzhinskaya Guba

POLUOSTROV

Verkhne-Kamchatsk

165°

Zhigansk

S

A

Gora Chen
10 171

Oymyakon

Magadan

ZALIV

SHELEKHOVA

Palana

KAMCHATKA

Vulk.
Klyuchevskaya
15 584

S

I

A

SAKHA

(YAKUTIA)

Okhotsk

M ALEVINA

Petropavlovsk-
Kamchatskiy

Vilyuysk

Yakutsk

Aldanskaya

Ust'-Bol'sheretsk

Suntar

Amga

Ust'-Maya

Nel'kan

DZHUGDZHUR KHREBET

S E A

O F

O K H O T S K

Mukhtuya

Olëkminsk

A L D A N

Ayan

Chumikan

Ola

Olekma

PATOM
1377

Tommot

Aldan

Uda

Ul'ya

Ul'banskaya G.

SHANTAR

M VELIZAVETY

Okha

Peleduy

Vitim

G. Golets-Purpula
PLATEAU

P L A T E A U

Nel'kan

Ust'-Tuga G.

Nikolayevsk-
na-Amure

SAKHALIN
(Russia)

Kirensk

Badaybo

Golets Skalistyy
9186

STANOVOY   KHREBET

Tyndinskiy

Aleksandrovsk

M TERPENIYA

Nizhne-Angarsk

YABLONOVYY KHREBET

Otekma

Zeya

Skovorodino

Beketova

Zeya

Poronaysk

Uglegorsk

T A T A R   S T R A I T

K U R I L   I S L A N D S   (Russia)

galovo

achuga

BURYATIA

Chita

Komsomol'sk
na-Amure

Nerchinsk

Sretensk

Svobodnyy

KHREBET
BURENSKIY

Malmyzh

Sovetskaya
Gavan'

Dolinsk

Yuzhno-Sakhalinsk

Borzguzin

Lake Baikal
(Ozero Baykal)
Surface elev. 1553 ft.
above Sea Level

Petrovsk-
Zabaykal'skiy

Ulan-Ude

Baley

Belogorsk

Ust'-Tyrma

Zavitinsk

Bureya

Birobidzhan

Khabarovsk

Kholmsk

Korsakov

A-579300-76 -1 -11 -22
COPYRIGHT BY
RAND MCNALLY & COMPANY
MADE IN U.S.A.

NERCHINSKIY KHREBET

Aginskoye

Nerchinskiy
Zavod

Raychikinsk

SIKHOTE ALIN'

Sōya Kaikyō

Kyakhta

Aksha

Borzya

Onon

AMMAN

NEI
MONGGOL

Blagoveshchensk

Aihui

Dalnerechensk

HOKKAIDO

JAPAN

Manzhouli

Hailar

GREATER KHINGAN RANGE

Goukou

Longzhen

LESSER KHINGAN RANGE

Ussuriysk

KHREBET

SEA OF JAPAN

Relief

Meters   Feet

3050   10 000

1525   5000

610   2000

305   1000

152.5   500

Sea Level   0

152.5   500

1525   5000

3050   10 000

Ulan Bator
(Ulaanbaatar)

Undorhaan

C H I N A

H E I L U N G K I A N G

Qiqihar

Hulan

HARBIN

Yilan

Suifenhe

Spassk-Dal'niy

Arsen'yev

Ol'ga

Ussuriysk

Artëm

Nakhodka

Vladivostok

Continued on pages 204-205

115°   120°   125°   130°   135°

50 100   200   300   400   500 Miles

100 200   400   600   800 Kilometers

Relief

Meters	Feet
1525	5000
610	2000
305	1000
152.5	500
0 Sea Level	0

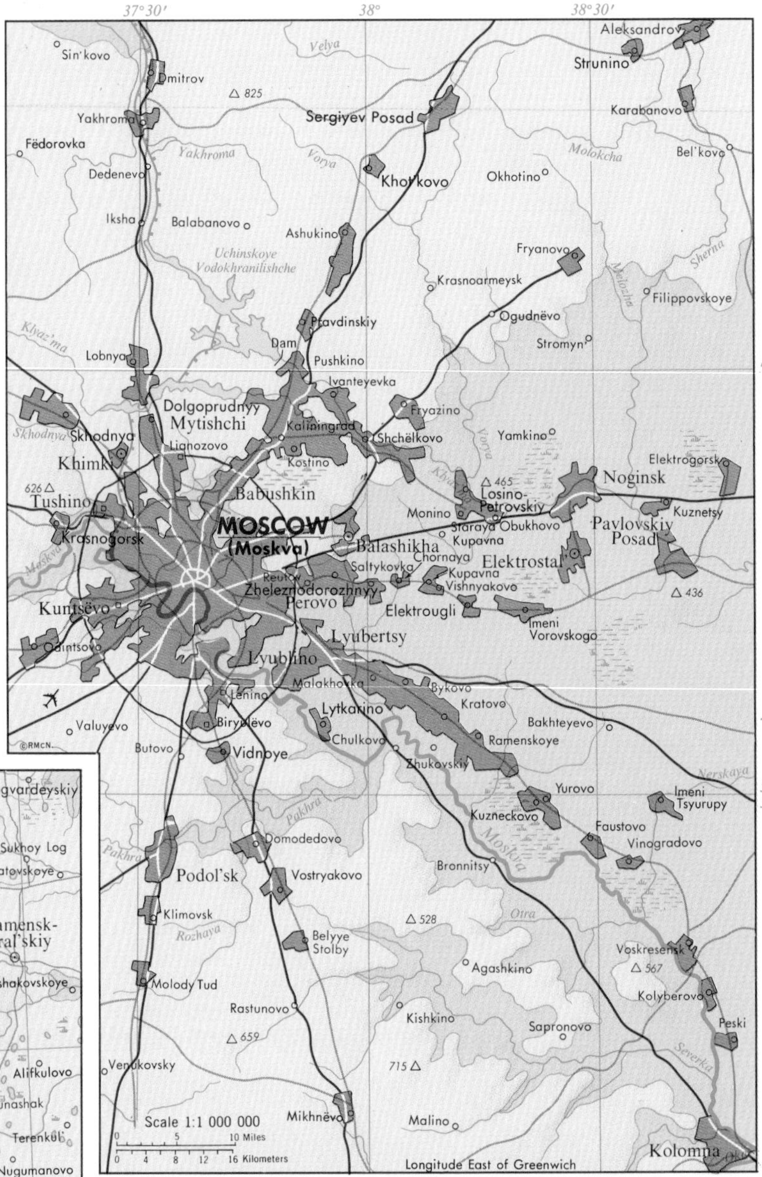

Scale 1:1 000 000
Longitude East of Greenwich

Scale 1:1 000 000
Longitude East of Greenwich

Scale 1:4 000 000
Longitude East of Greenwich

A-570051-76 -7- 3-13
COPYRIGHT BY
RAND M?NALLY & COMPANY
MADE IN U.S.A.

Cities and Towns

0 to 50,000   500,000 to 1,000,000
50,000 to 500,000   1,000,000 and over

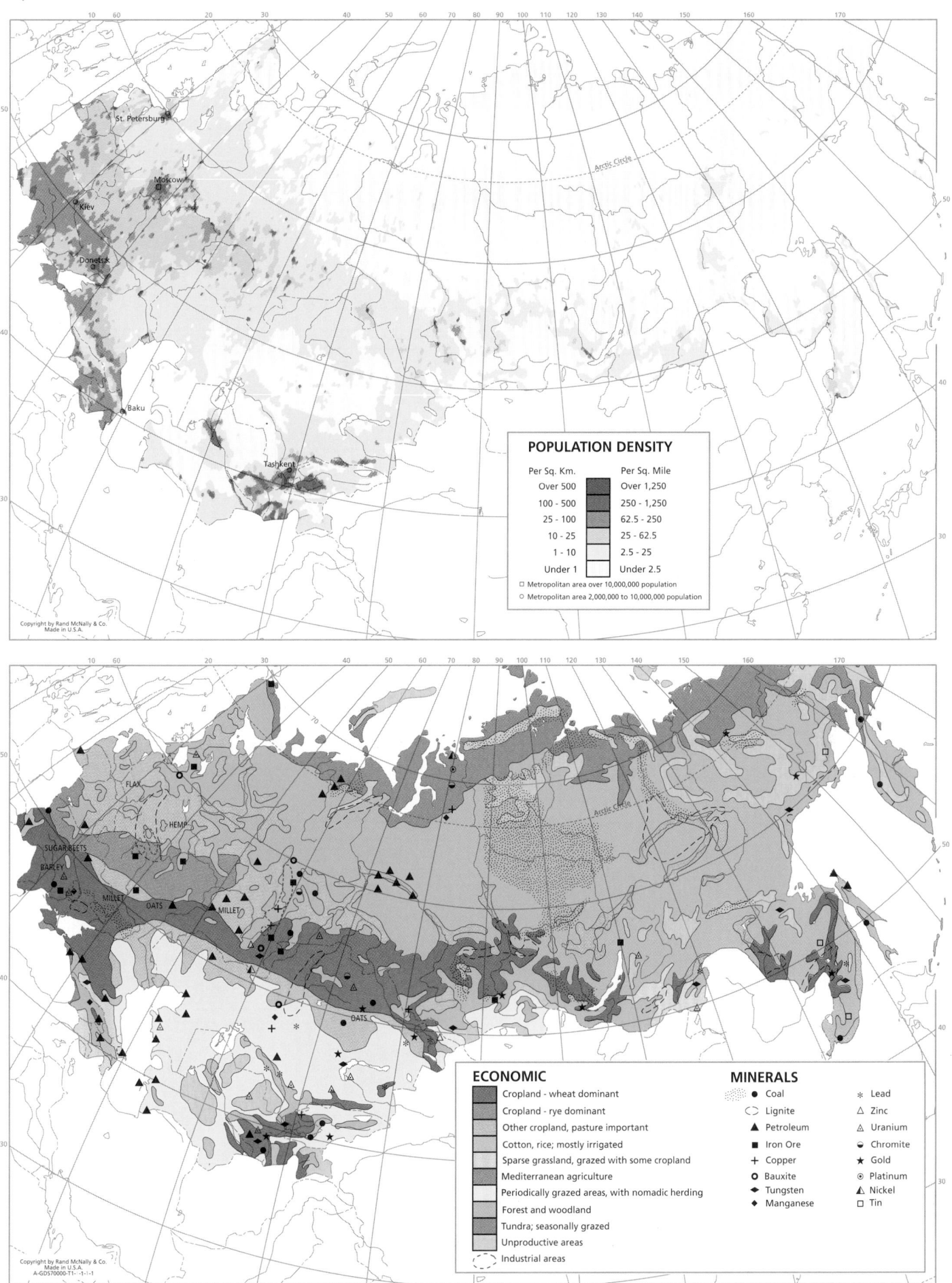

POPULATION DENSITY

Per Sq. Km.	Per Sq. Mile
Over 500	Over 1,250
100 - 500	250 - 1,250
25 - 100	62.5 - 250
10 - 25	25 - 62.5
1 - 10	2.5 - 25
Under 1	Under 2.5

□ Metropolitan area over 10,000,000 population
○ Metropolitan area 2,000,000 to 10,000,000 population

Copyright by Rand McNally & Co.
Made in U.S.A.

ECONOMIC

Cropland - wheat dominant
Cropland - rye dominant
Other cropland, pasture important
Cotton, rice; mostly irrigated
Sparse grassland, grazed with some cropland
Mediterranean agriculture
Periodically grazed areas, with nomadic herding
Forest and woodland
Tundra; seasonally grazed
Unproductive areas
Industrial areas

MINERALS

● Coal   * Lead
◖ Lignite   △ Zinc
▲ Petroleum   ◮ Uranium
■ Iron Ore   ◡ Chromite
+ Copper   ★ Gold
○ Bauxite   ⊙ Platinum
◆ Tungsten   ◭ Nickel
◆ Manganese   □ Tin

Copyright by Rand McNally & Co.
Made in U.S.A.
A-GDS70000-T1--1-1--1

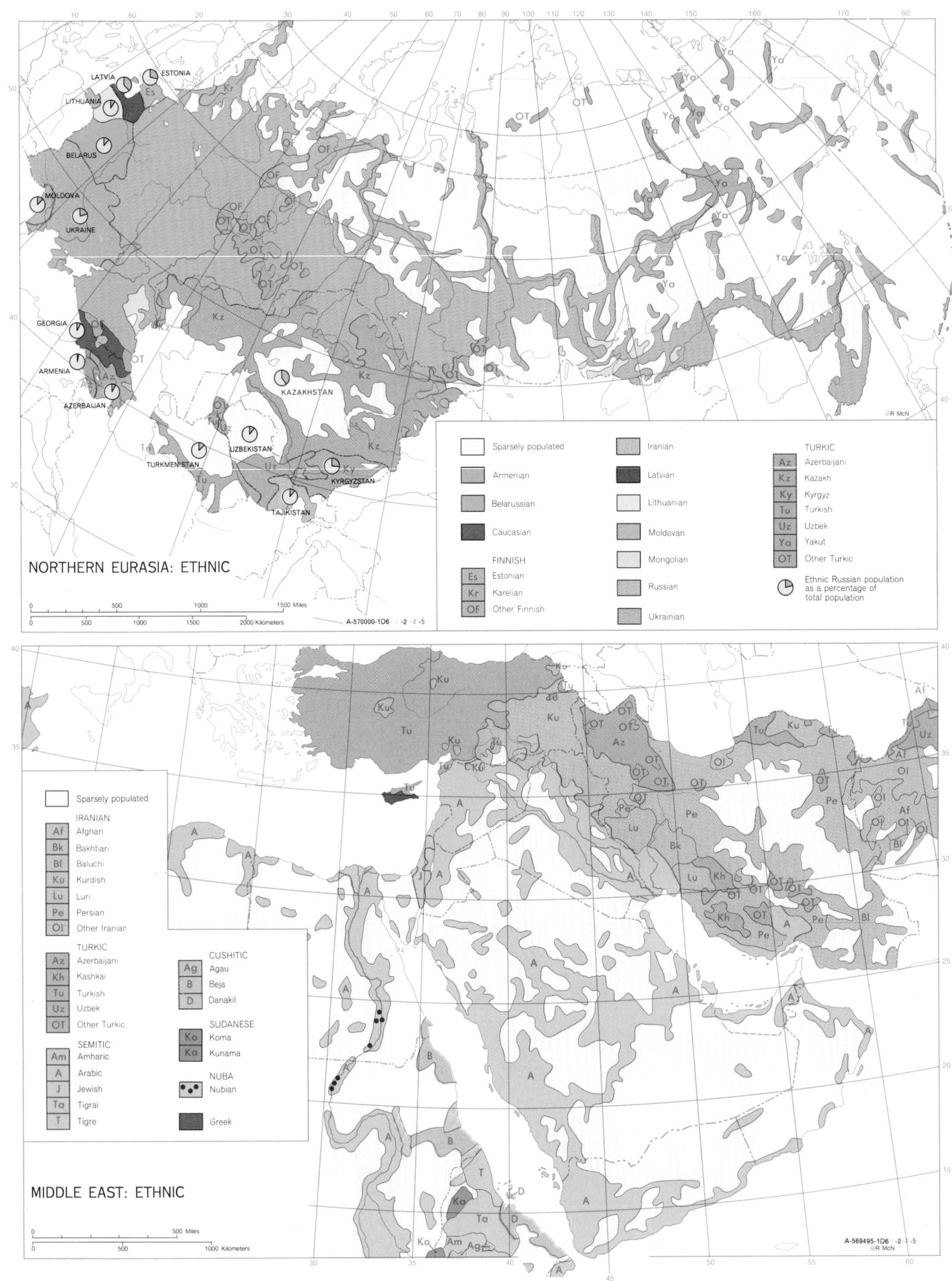

NORTHERN EURASIA: ETHNIC

LATVIA
ESTONIA
LITHUANIA
Es
BELARUS
MOLDOVA
UKRAINE
GEORGIA
ARMENIA
AZERBAIJAN
KAZAKHSTAN
TURKMENISTAN
UZBEKISTAN
KYRGYZSTAN
TAJIKISTAN

Scale bars:
500 1000 1500 Miles
500 1000 1500 2000 Kilometers

A-570000-1D6 -2 -2 -5

Legend (Northern Eurasia)

	Sparsely populated
	Armenian
	Belarussian
	Caucasian

FINNISH
Es	Estonian
Kr	Karelian
OF	Other Finnish

	Iranian
	Latvian
	Lithuanian
	Moldovan
	Mongolian
	Russian
	Ukrainian

TURKIC
Az	Azerbaijani
Kz	Kazakh
Ky	Kyrgyz
Tu	Turkish
Uz	Uzbek
Ya	Yakut
OT	Other Turkic

Ethnic Russian population as a percentage of total population

MIDDLE EAST: ETHNIC

Legend (Middle East)

	Sparsely populated

IRANIAN
Af	Afghan
Bk	Bakhtiari
Bl	Baluchi
Ku	Kurdish
Lu	Luri
Pe	Persian
OI	Other Iranian

TURKIC
Az	Azerbaijani
Kh	Kashkai
Tu	Turkish
Uz	Uzbek
OT	Other Turkic

SEMITIC
Am	Amharic
A	Arabic
J	Jewish
Ta	Tigrai
T	Tigre

CUSHITIC
Ag	Agau
B	Beja
D	Danakil

SUDANESE
Ko	Koma
Ka	Kunama

NUBA
	Nubian

	Greek

Scale bars:
500 Miles
500 1000 Kilometers

A-569495-1D6 -2 -1 -5
©R McN

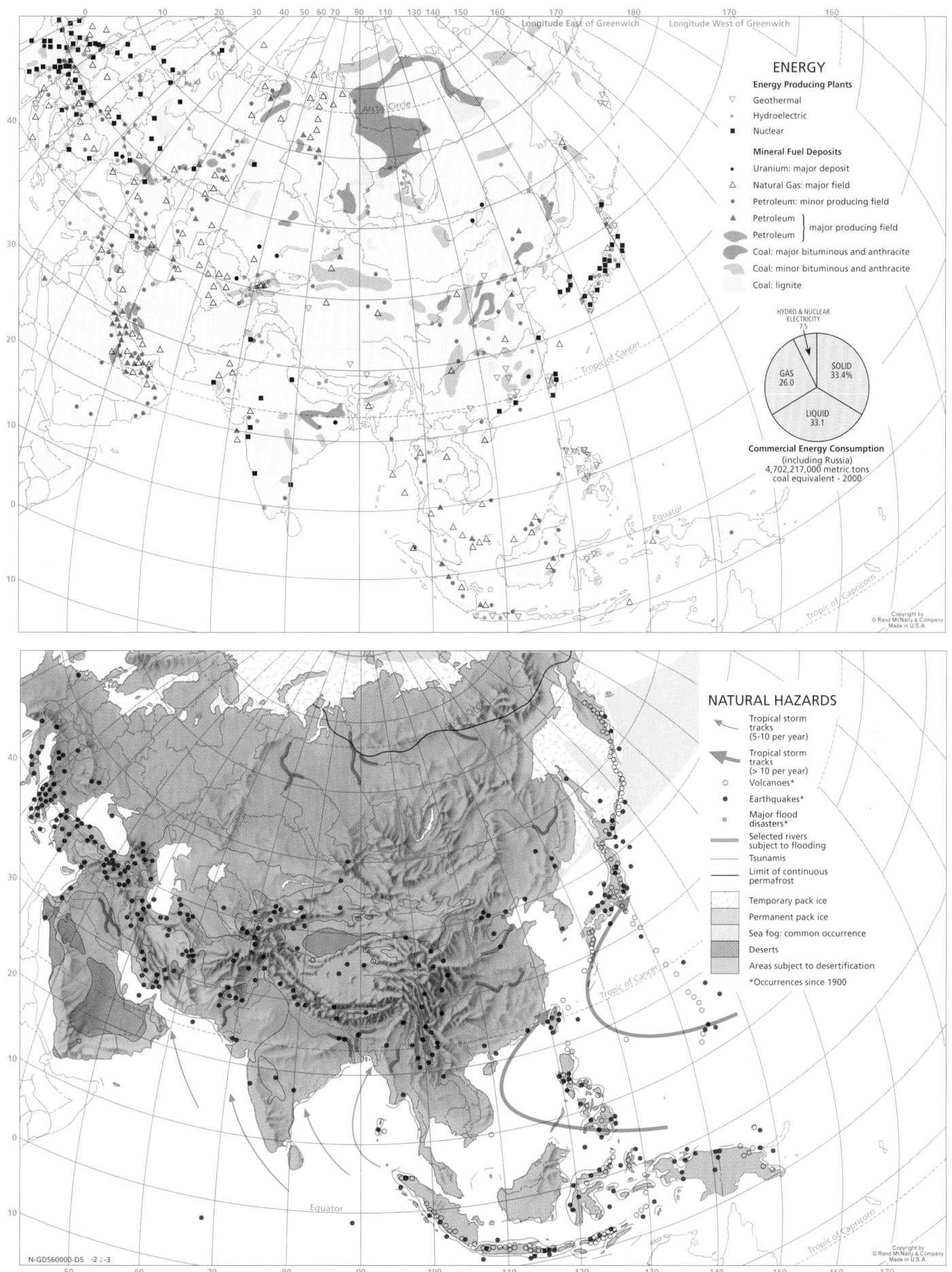

ENERGY

Energy Producing Plants

▽ Geothermal
• Hydroelectric
■ Nuclear

Mineral Fuel Deposits

• Uranium: major deposit
△ Natural Gas: major field
• Petroleum: minor producing field
▲ Petroleum } major producing field
⬛ Petroleum }
Coal: major bituminous and anthracite
Coal: minor bituminous and anthracite
Coal: lignite

HYDRO & NUCLEAR
ELECTRICITY
7.5

GAS
26.0
SOLID
33.4%
LIQUID
33.1

Commercial Energy Consumption
(including Russia)
4,702,217,000 metric tons
coal equivalent - 2000

Copyright by
© Rand McNally & Company
Made in U.S.A.

NATURAL HAZARDS

← Tropical storm tracks (5-10 per year)
← Tropical storm tracks (> 10 per year)
○ Volcanoes*
● Earthquakes*
• Major flood disasters*
Selected rivers subject to flooding
Tsunamis
Limit of continuous permafrost
Temporary pack ice
Permanent pack ice
Sea fog: common occurrence
Deserts
Areas subject to desertification

*Occurrences since 1900

N-GDS60000-D5 -2-2-3

Copyright by
© Rand McNally & Company
Made in U.S.A.

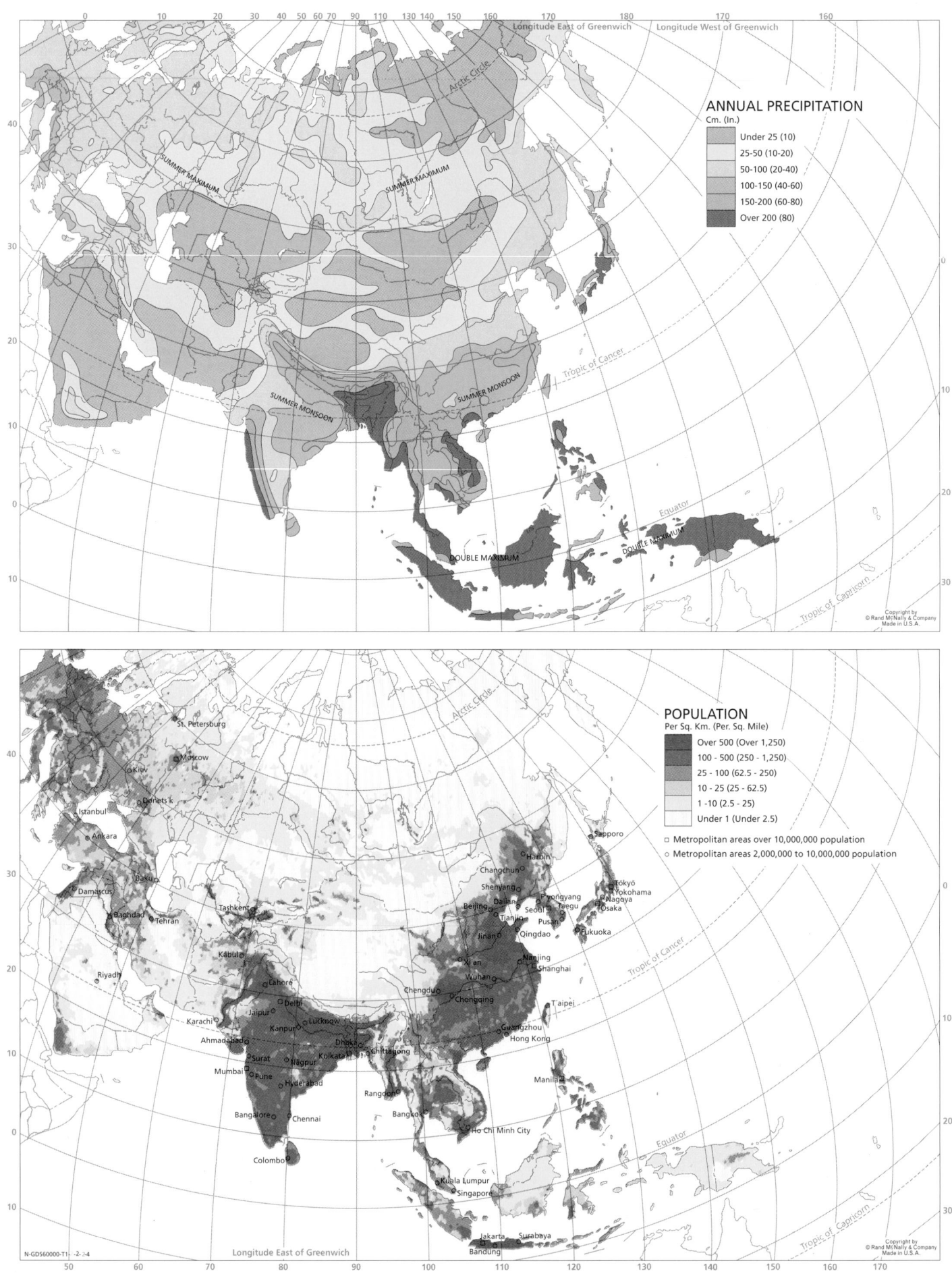

ANNUAL PRECIPITATION
Cm. (In.)

	Under 25 (10)
	25-50 (10-20)
	50-100 (20-40)
	100-150 (40-60)
	150-200 (60-80)
	Over 200 (80)

SUMMER MAXIMUM
SUMMER MAXIMUM
SUMMER MAXIMUM
SUMMER MONSOON
SUMMER MONSOON
SUMMER MONSOON
DOUBLE MAXIMUM
DOUBLE MAXIMUM

Longitude East of Greenwich
Longitude West of Greenwich
Arctic Circle
Tropic of Cancer
Equator
Tropic of Capricorn

POPULATION
Per Sq. Km. (Per. Sq. Mile)

	Over 500 (Over 1,250)
	100 - 500 (250 - 1,250)
	25 - 100 (62.5 - 250)
	10 - 25 (25 - 62.5)
	1 -10 (2.5 - 25)
	Under 1 (Under 2.5)

□ Metropolitan areas over 10,000,000 population
○ Metropolitan areas 2,000,000 to 10,000,000 population

St. Petersburg
Kiev
Moscow
Donets'k
Istanbul
Ankara
Baku
Damascus
Baghdad
Tehran
Tashkent
Riyadh
Kābul
Lahore
Karachi
Jaipur
Delhi
Kanpur
Lucknow
Ahmadabad
Dhaka
Chittagong
Surat
Nagpur
Kolkata
Mumbai
Pune
Hyderabad
Rangoon
Bangalore
Chennai
Bangkok
Colombo
Ho Chi Minh City
Kuala Lumpur
Singapore
Jakarta
Surabaya
Bandung
Sapporo
Harbin
Changchun
Shenyang
Dalian
Pyongyang
Tōkyō
Yokohama
Nagoya
Beijing
Tianjin
Seoul
Taegu
Osaka
Jinan
Pusan
Fukuoka
Qingdao
Xi'an
Nanjing
Shanghai
Wuhan
Chengdu
Chongqing
T'aipei
Guangzhou
Hong Kong
Manila

Arctic Circle
Tropic of Cancer
Equator
Tropic of Capricorn
Longitude East of Greenwich

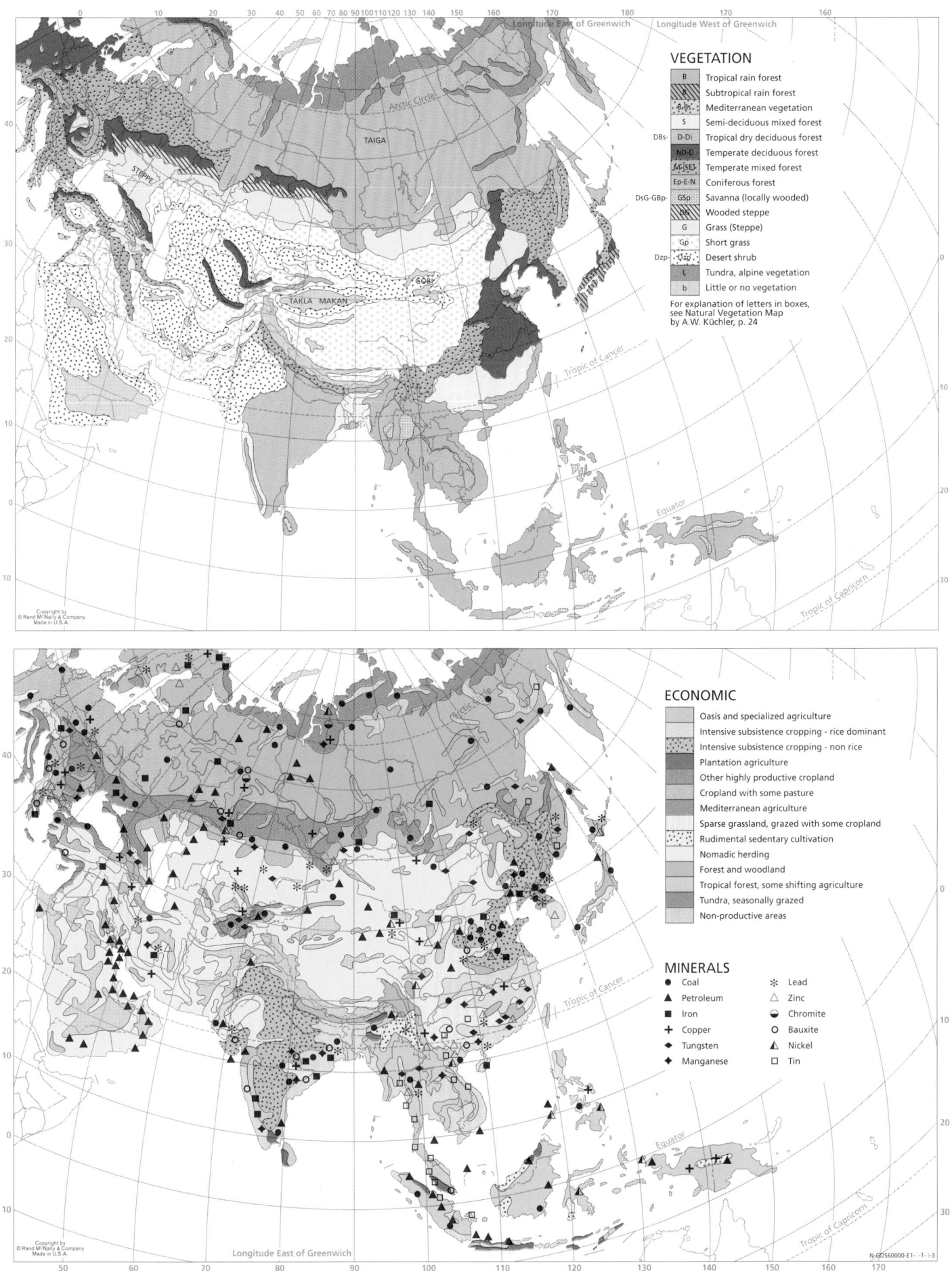

VEGETATION

B	Tropical rain forest
B	Subtropical rain forest
B.Bs.	Mediterranean vegetation
S	Semi-deciduous mixed forest
D-Di	Tropical dry deciduous forest
ND-D	Temperate deciduous forest
M-SE	Temperate mixed forest
Ep-E-N	Coniferous forest
GSp	Savanna (locally wooded)
DS	Wooded steppe
G	Grass (Steppe)
Gp	Short grass
Dzp	Desert shrub
L	Tundra, alpine vegetation
b	Little or no vegetation

DBs-
DsG-GBp-
Dzp-

For explanation of letters in boxes,
see Natural Vegetation Map
by A.W. Küchler, p. 24

TAIGA
STEPPE
GOBI
TAKLA MAKAN

ECONOMIC

	Oasis and specialized agriculture
	Intensive subsistence cropping - rice dominant
	Intensive subsistence cropping - non rice
	Plantation agriculture
	Other highly productive cropland
	Cropland with some pasture
	Mediterranean agriculture
	Sparse grassland, grazed with some cropland
	Rudimental sedentary cultivation
	Nomadic herding
	Forest and woodland
	Tropical forest, some shifting agriculture
	Tundra, seasonally grazed
	Non-productive areas

MINERALS

●	Coal	✳	Lead
▲	Petroleum	△	Zinc
■	Iron	◖	Chromite
✚	Copper	○	Bauxite
◆	Tungsten	◣	Nickel
◆	Manganese	□	Tin

Longitude East of Greenwich

N-GDS60000-E1- -1-1-3

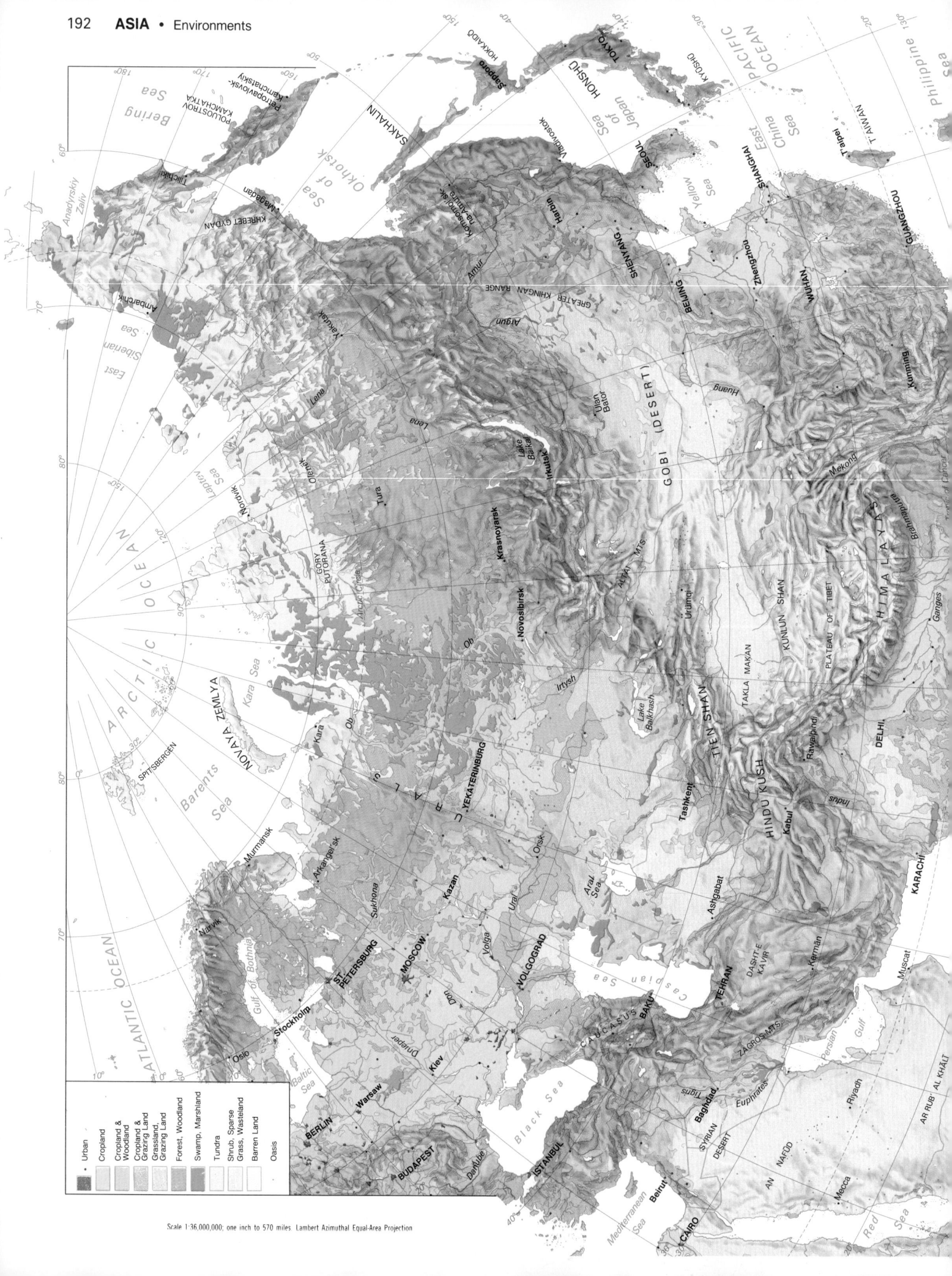

Urban
Cropland
Cropland & Woodland
Cropland & Grazing Land
Grassland, Grazing Land
Forest, Woodland
Swamp, Marshland
Tundra
Shrub, Sparse Grass, Wasteland
Barren Land
Oasis

Scale 1:36,000,000; one inch to 570 miles Lambert Azimuthal Equal-Area Projection

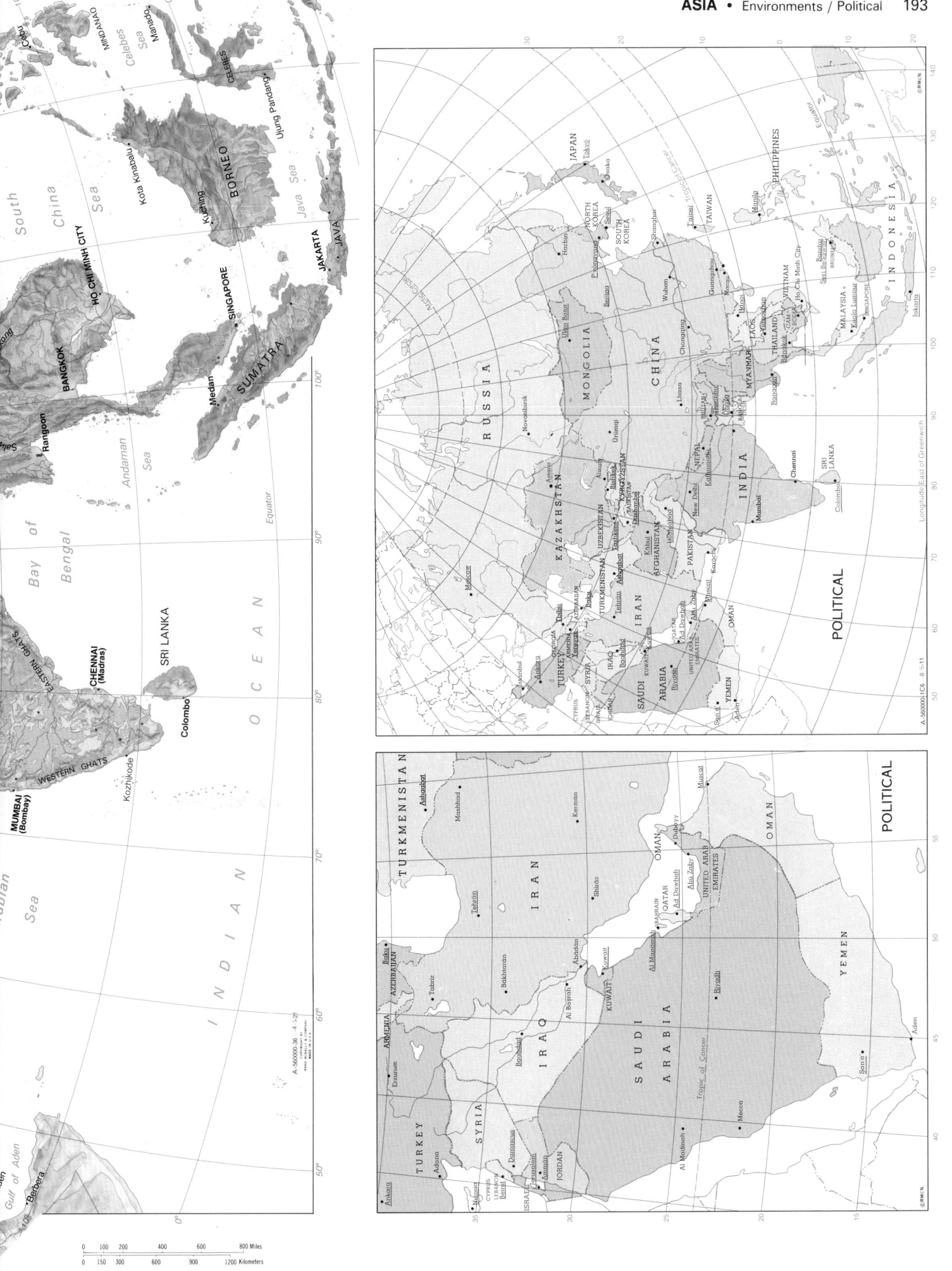

POLITICAL

POLITICAL

Main map labels

RUSSIA
MONGOLIA
CHINA
JAPAN
Tokyo
Osaka
NORTH KOREA
P'yongyang
SOUTH KOREA
Seoul
Shanghai
Harbin
Beijing
Wuhan
Chongqing
Guangzhou
TAIWAN
Taipei
PHILIPPINES
Manila
INDONESIA
Jakarta
Ho Chi Minh City
VIETNAM
LAOS
THAILAND
Bangkok
MYANMAR
Rangoon
Hanoi
MALAYSIA
Kuala Lumpur
SINGAPORE
BRUNEI
Bandar Seri Begawan
Ulan Bator
Lhasa
BHUTAN
Thimphu
NEPAL
Kathmandu
INDIA
New Delhi
Mumbai
Chennai
SRI LANKA
Colombo
BANGLADESH
Dhaka
Kolkata
Ürümqi
Almaty
KAZAKHSTAN
Astana
Novosibirsk
Moscow
UZBEKISTAN
Tashkent
KYRGYZSTAN
Bishkek
TAJIKISTAN
Dushanbe
TURKMENISTAN
Ashgabat
AFGHANISTAN
Kabul
PAKISTAN
Islamabad
Karachi
IRAN
Tehran
Tbilisi
GEORGIA
ARMENIA
Yerevan
AZERBAIJAN
Baku
TURKEY
Ankara
Istanbul
SYRIA
Damascus
IRAQ
Baghdad
LEBANON
ISRAEL
CYPRUS
JORDAN
Amman
KUWAIT
Kuwait
SAUDI ARABIA
Riyadh
QATAR
Ad Dawhah
UNITED ARAB EMIRATES
Abu Zaby
OMAN
Muscat
YEMEN
San'a
Aden
Equator
Tropic of Cancer
Longitude East of Greenwich

Inset map (lower right)

TURKMENISTAN
Ashgabat
IRAN
Mashhad
Tehran
Kerman
Shiraz
AZERBAIJAN
Baku
Tabriz
ARMENIA
Erzurum
Bakhtaran
Abadan
Al Basrah
IRAQ
Baghdad
KUWAIT
Kuwait
SYRIA
Damascus
TURKEY
Ankara
Adana
LEBANON
CYPRUS
Beirut
ISRAEL
Jerusalem
JORDAN
Amman
Al Madinah
Mecca
SAUDI ARABIA
Riyadh
BAHRAIN
QATAR
Ad Dawhah
UNITED ARAB EMIRATES
Abu Zaby
Dubayy
OMAN
Muscat
Al Manamah
YEMEN
San'a
Aden
Tropic of Cancer

Left map labels

MINDANAO
Cebu
Manado
Celebes Sea
CELEBES
Ujung Pandang
BORNEO
Kota Kinabalu
Kuching
Java Sea
JAVA
JAKARTA
SUMATRA
Medan
SINGAPORE
South China Sea
HO CHI MINH CITY
BANGKOK
Mekong
Rangoon
Andaman Sea
SRI LANKA
Colombo
Kozhikode
CHENNAI (Madras)
EASTERN GHATS
WESTERN GHATS
MUMBAI (Bombay)
Bay of Bengal
INDIAN OCEAN
Arabian Sea
Gulf of Aden
Berbera
Equator

A.560000-36 -4 (-5-2)
COPYRIGHT BY
RAND McNALLY & COMPANY
MADE IN U.S.A.

A.5600001C6 -8 (i-11)

©RMCN

0 100 200 400 600 800 Miles
0 150 300 600 900 1200 Kilometers

194

Scale 1:40 000 000; one inch to 630 miles. Lambert's Azimuthal, Equal Area Projection
Elevations and depressions are given in feet

Continued on pages 228

40,000 SQ MI
AREA

0   300   600
Miles

A-519695-26
COPYRIGHT BY
RAND McNALLY & COMPANY
MADE IN U.S.A.

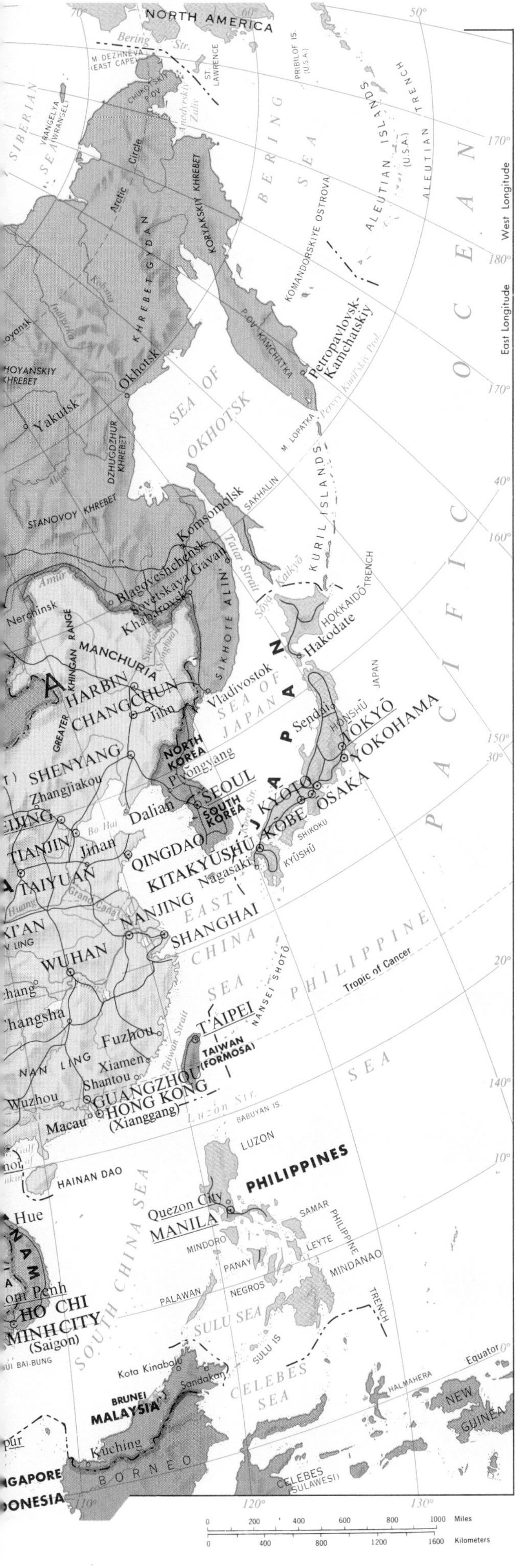

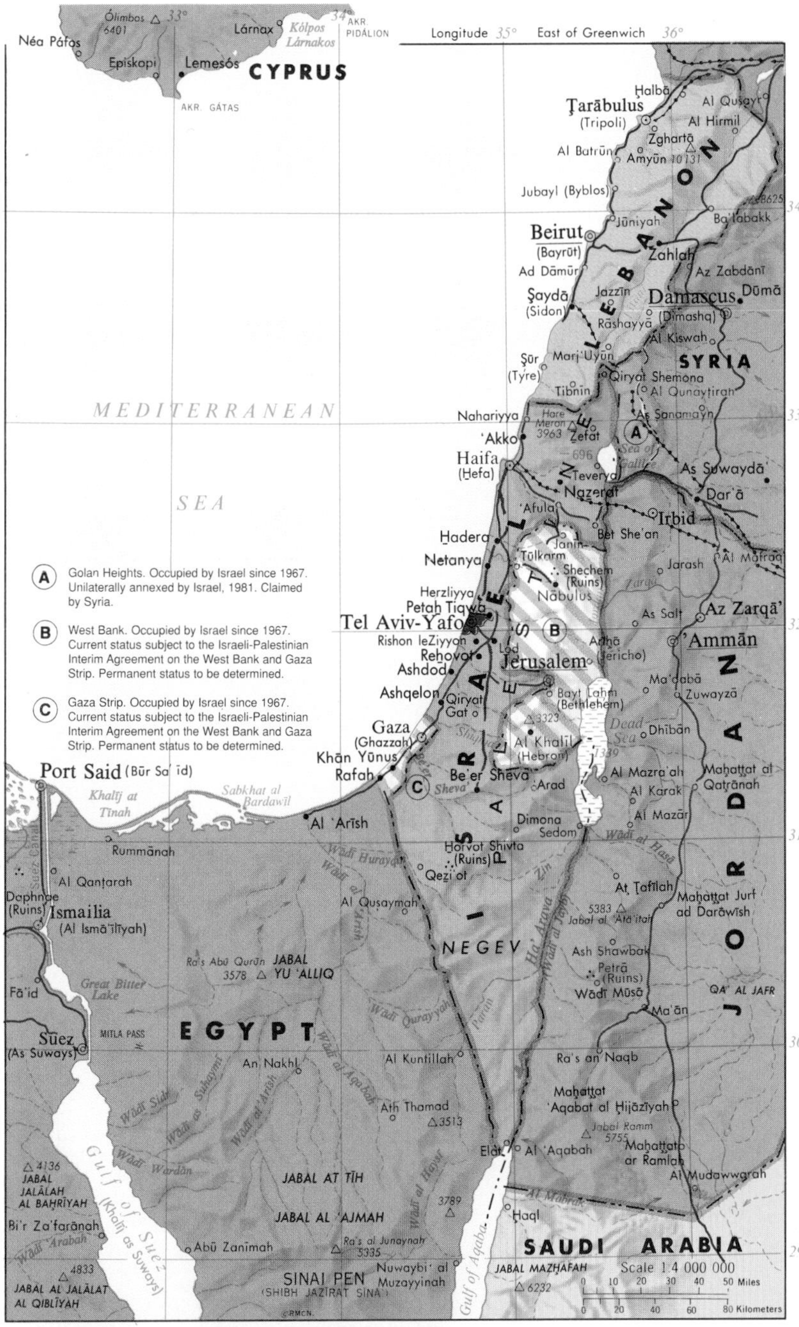

Left map (East Asia)

NORTH AMERICA

Bering Str.
M. DEZHNEVA (EAST CAPE)
ST. LAWRENCE I.
PRIBILOF IS. (USA)
Arctic Circle
KOMANDORSKIYE OSTROVA
ALEUTIAN ISLANDS (USA)
ALEUTIAN TRENCH
West Longitude
East Longitude

SIBERIAN SEA
VRANGELYA (WRANGEL)
CHUKCHI

SEA OF OKHOTSK
Petropavlovsk-Kamchatskiy
M. LOPATKA
KURIL ISLANDS
KURIL TRENCH

KHREBET GYDAN
KORYAKSKIY KHREBET
HOYANSKIY KHREBET
Yakutsk
Nerchinsk
Okhotsk
Komsomolsk
SAKHALIN
Blagoveshchensk
Svobodnyy
Khabarovsk
Vladivostok
SIKHOTE ALIN
Tatar Strait
SOYA STR.
HOKKAIDŌ
Hakodate
HOKKAIDŌ TRENCH

STANOVOY KHREBET
DZHUGDZHUR KHREBET
GREATER KHINGAN RANGE
MANCHURIA
HARBIN
CHANGCHUN
Jilin
SHENYANG
NORTH KOREA
Pyongyang
SEOUL
SOUTH KOREA
Dalian
Bo Hai
QINGDAO
KITAKYUSHU
Nagasaki
KYŪSHŪ
HONSHŪ
Sendai
TŌKYŌ
YOKOHAMA
KYŌTO
KOBE
OSAKA
SHIKOKU
JAPAN
SEA OF JAPAN

Zhangjiakou
TIANJIN
Jinan
TAIYUAN
NANJING
SHANGHAI
XI'AN
WUHAN
Changsha
Fuzhou
Xiamen
Shantou
GUANGZHOU
HONG KONG (Xianggang)
Macau
Wuzhou
HAINAN DAO
NAN LING
LING
EAST CHINA SEA
NANSEI SHOTŌ
Tropic of Cancer

T'AIPEI
TAIWAN (FORMOSA)
Taiwan Str.
PHILIPPINE SEA
PHILIPPINE TRENCH

LUZON
BABUYAN IS.
Luzon Str.
Quezon City
MANILA
MINDORO
SAMAR
LEYTE
PANAY
NEGROS
PALAWAN
MINDANAO
PHILIPPINES

Hue
VIETNAM
Phnom Penh
HO CHI MINH CITY (Saigon)
SOUTH CHINA SEA
SULU SEA
SULU IS.
Kota Kinabalu
Sandakan
BRUNEI
MALAYSIA
Kuching
BORNEO
CELEBES SEA
CELEBES (SULAWESI)
HALMAHERA
NEW GUINEA
Equator
SINGAPORE
INDONESIA

0 200 400 600 800 1000 Miles
0 400 800 1200 1600 Kilometers

Right upper map (Israel / Levant)

CYPRUS
Néa Páfos
Epískopi
Lemesós
Lárnax
Kólpos Lárnakos
Ólimbos 6401
AKR. PIDÁLION
AKR. GÁTAS
Longitude 35° East of Greenwich 36°

MEDITERRANEAN SEA

LEBANON
Ţarābulus (Tripoli)
Al Batrūn
Jubayl (Byblos)
Jūniyah
Beirut (Bayrūt)
Şaydā (Sidon)
Jazzīn
Şūr (Tyre)
Nahariyya
'Akko
Haifa (Hefa)
Teverya
Nazerat
Afula
Hadera
Netanya
Herzliyya
Petah Tiqwa
Tel Aviv-Yafo
Rishon leZiyyon
Rehovot
Ashdod
Ashqelon
Gaza (Ghazzah)
Khān Yūnus
Rafah
Port Said (Būr Sa'īd)
Al 'Arīsh
Rummānah
Al Qanţarah
Ismailia (Al Ismā'īlīyah)
Fā'id
Sūez (As Suways)
MITLA PASS
EGYPT
Great Bitter Lake
Khalīj at Tīnah
Sabkhat al Bardawīl
An Nakhl
SINAI PEN. (SHIBH JAZĪRAT SĪNĀ')
JABAL JALĀLAH AL BAḤRĪYAH 4136
Bi'r Za'farānah
Abū Zanimah
JABAL JALĀLAT AL QIBLĪYAH 4833
JABAL AT TĪH
JABAL AL 'AJMAH
Gulf of Suez (Khalīj as Suways)
Gulf of Aqaba
JABAL YU 'ALLIQ 3578
Ra's Abū Qurūn
Ath Thamad 3513
Al Kuntillah
Ra's an Naqb
JABAL MAZḤAFAH 6232
Nuwaybi' al Muzayyinah 3335
Ḥaql

SYRIA
Halbā
Al Quşayr
Al Hirmil
Zgharta
Amyūn 10131
2625
Ba'labakk
Zaḥlah
Ad Dāmūr
Az Zabdānī
Damascus (Dimashq)
Dūmā
Rashayyā
Al Kiswah
Mari 'Uyūn
Qiryat Shemona
Al Qunayţirah
Tibnin
Hare Meron 3963
Zefat
Al Sanamayn
As Suwaydā
Dar'ā
Irbid
Al Mafraq
Bet She'an
Jarash
Jenin
Shechem (Ruins)
Nābulus
As Salt
Az Zarqā'
'Amman
Ma'dabā
Zuwayzā
Aḍra
Jerusalem
Bayt Laḥm (Bethlehem)
Dhibān
Al Khalīl (Hebron)
Be'er Sheva
Arad
Al Mazra'ah
Al Karak
Al Mazār
Dimona
Sedom
Dead Sea
Wadi al Ḥasā
Aţ Ţafīlah
Maḥaţţat Jurf ad Darāwīsh
Ash Shawbak
Petra (Ruins)
Wādī Mūsā
Ma'ān
QA' AL JAFR
Maḥaţţat 'Aqabat al Hijāziyah
JABAL RAMM 5755
Elāt
Al 'Aqabah
Maḥaţţat ar Ramlah
Al Mudawwarah
SAUDI ARABIA

NEGEV
Horvot Shivta (Ruins)
Qezi ot

JORDAN

Golan Heights. Occupied by Israel since 1967. Unilaterally annexed by Israel, 1981. Claimed by Syria.

West Bank. Occupied by Israel since 1967. Current status subject to the Israeli-Palestinian Interim Agreement on the West Bank and Gaza Strip. Permanent status to be determined.

Gaza Strip. Occupied by Israel since 1967. Current status subject to the Israeli-Palestinian Interim Agreement on the West Bank and Gaza Strip. Permanent status to be determined.

Scale 1:4 000 000
0 10 20 40 60 80 Miles
0 20 40 60 80 Kilometers

Right lower map (Malay Peninsula)

Scale 1:4 000 000
0 10 20 30 40 50 Miles
0 20 40 60 80 Kilometers

Kuala Lumpur
Kelang
SELANGOR
Telok Datok
Sepang
Port Dickson
CAPE RACHADO
Kajang
Kuala Klawang
Gunong Telapa 3915
Rantau
Seremban
NEGERI SEMBILAN
Alor Gajah
MELAKA
Melaka (Malacca)
Jasin
Bandar Maharani
PAHANG
Bahau
Rompin
Rembau
Tampin
Gemas
Segamat
Labis
Mt. Ophir 4187
Gunong Besar 3403
Panchor
MALAYSIA
JOHOR
Paloh
Keluang
Gunong Blumut 3312
Rengam
Ayer Hitam
Batu Pahat
Pontian Kechil
Johor Bahru
SINGAPORE
TANJONG PIAI
STRAIT OF MALACCA
Merging
TIOMAN
Gunong Kajang 3444
Padang Endau
Mersing
PEMANGGIL
AUR
2002
TINGGI
Layang Layang
Kota Tinggi
MALAY PENINSULA
SOUTH CHINA SEA
TANJONG PENYABONG
TANJONG RAMUNIA
TANJONG BERAKIT

SUMATRA
INDONESIA
RIAU
Jumrah
RUPAT
Teluklecak
Batupanjang
Dumai
Bengkalis
BENGKALIS
Ketamputih
Bukitbatu
Telusung
KARIMUN BESAR
KEPULAUAN RIAU
BATAM
BINTAN
Tanjungbalai
Tanjungpinang
Pinggir
Minas 341
Buatan
Siaksriinderapura
KUNDUR
Baranghari
Tanjungbatu
Longitude East of Greenwich 102° 103° 104°

Continued on pages 229

Relief

Meters	Feet
3050	10 000
1525	5000
610	2000
305	1000
0 Sea Level	0 Below Sea Level
152.5	500
1525	5000
3050	10 000
6100	20 000

A-519695-76 24 2 46
COPYRIGHT BY
RAND McNALLY & COMPANY
MADE IN U.S.A.

Scale 1:40 000 000; one inch to 630 miles. Lambert's Azimuthal, Equal Area Projection
Elevations and depressions are given in feet

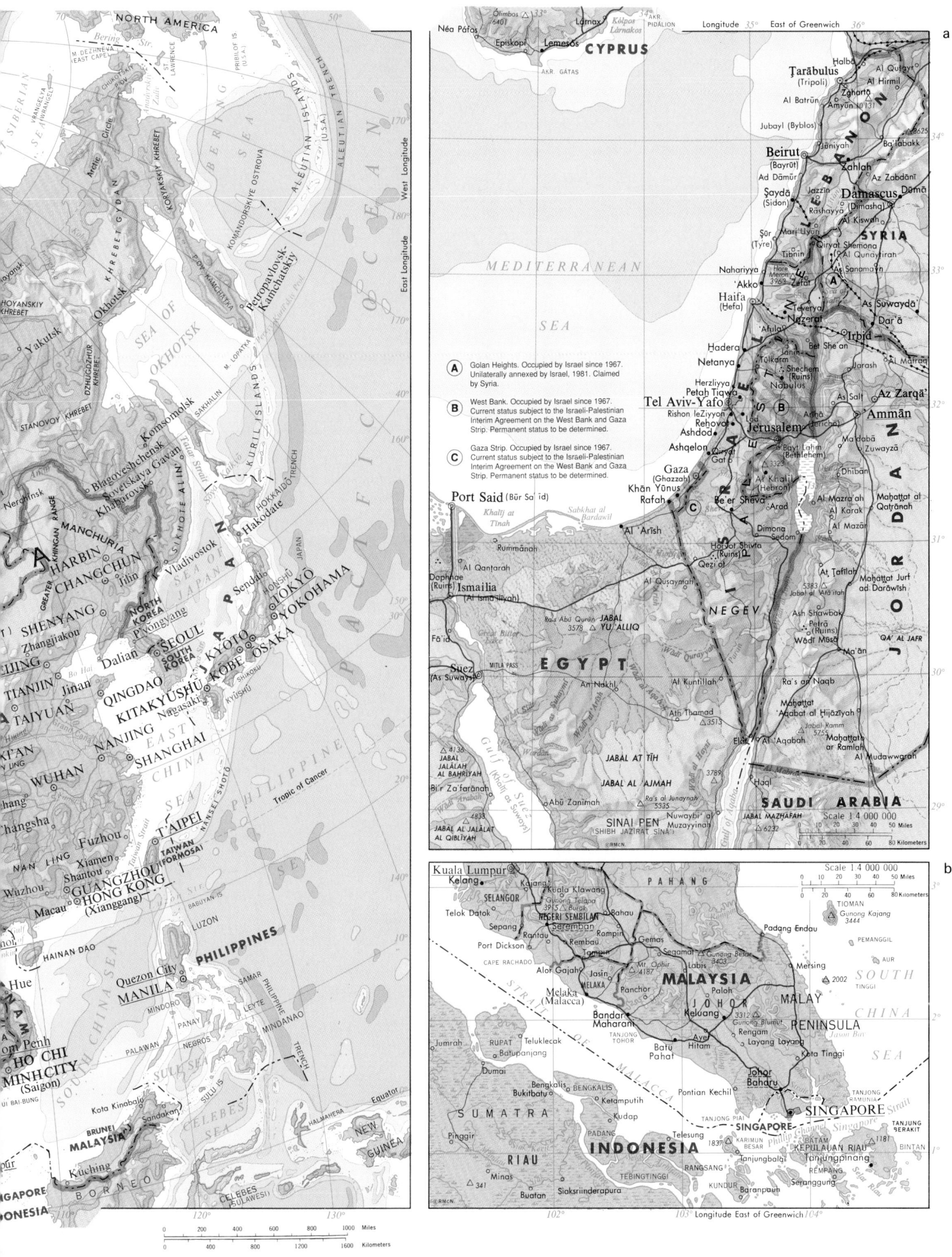

CYPRUS

Néa Páfos
Epískopi
Lemesós
AKR. GÁTAS

Ólimpos △ ☉
Lárnax
Kólpos
Lárnakos
AKR. PIDÁLION

Longitude 35° East of Greenwich 36°

a

Ṭarābulus
(Tripoli)
Al Qusayr
Al Hirmil
Halba
Zgharta
Al Baṭrūn
Amyūn ☉ 131
Ba'labakk

Jubayl (Byblos)
☉ 3625

Beirut
(Bayrūt)
Jūniyah
Zahlah
Ad Dāmūr
Az Zabdānī
Ṣaydā
(Sidon)
Jazzīn
Rashayyā
Damascus
(Dimashq)
Dūmā

Mari 'Uyūn
Al Kiswah
Ṣūr
(Tyre)
Qiryat Shemona
SYRIA
Al Qunayṭirah
Nahariyya
Tibnīn
Ḥore
Meron
3963
Zefat
A
As Sanamayn

Akko
Nazareth
A
As Suwaydā'
Haifa
(Hefa)
Zeveryal
Dar'ā
Afula
Irbid

MEDITERRANEAN

SEA

Ḥadera
Bet She'an
Jarash
Netanya
Ṭūlkarm
Al Maṭran
Herzliyya
Petaḥ Tiqwa
Shechem
Nābulus
As Salt
Az Zarqā'
Tel Aviv-Yafo
B
Rishon leZiyyon
Rehovot
Ariḥa
(Jericho)
Amman
Ashdod
Jerusalem
Lod
Bayt Laḥm
(Bethlehem)
Madaba
Zuwayza
Ashqelon
Qiryat
Gat
Al Khalīl
(Hebron)
Dhībān

Gaza
(Ghazzah)
Al Mazra'ah
Mahaṭṭat at
Qaṭrānah
Khān Yūnus
Be'er Sheva
Arad
Al Karak
C
Rafah
Dimona
Sedom
Al Mazār

Port Said (Būr Sa'īd)
Khalīj at
Tīnah
Sabkhat al
Bardawīl
Al 'Arīsh
Ḥorvot Shivta
(Ruins) Ω
Ат Ṭafīlah

Rummānah
Qezi'ot
5383 △
Jabal al 'Arā'irah
Ash Shawbak
Petra
(Ruins)

Al Qanṭarah
NEGEV
Wādī Mūsā
Ma'ān

Daphnae
(Ruins)
Al Qusaymah
QA' AL JAFR
Fā'id
Ismailia
(Al Ismā'īlīyah)
Mahaṭṭat Jurf
ad Darāwīh

Great Bitter
Lake
Ra's Abū Qurūn
3578 △
JABAL
YU 'ALLIQ

An Nakhl
Al Kuntillah
Ra's an Naqb
Suez
(As Suways)
MITLA PASS
Ath Thamad
'Aqabat al Ḥijāzīyah
3513
Mahaṭṭat
'Aqabat al Ḥijāzīyah

EGYPT

Elat
Al 'Aqabah
Jabal Ramm
575 △
Al Mudawwarah
△ 4138
Abū Zanīmah
Ra's al Junaynah
5335
Mahaṭṭat
ar Ramlah
JABAL AT TĪH
3789 △

JABAL
JALĀLAH
AL BAḤRĪYAH
Bi'r Za'farānah

JABAL AL AJMAH
SAUDI ARABIA

△ 4838
JABAL MAZḤAFAH
Scale 1:4 000 000

SINAI PEN.
(SHIBH JAZĪRAT SĪNĀ')
Nuwaybī' al
Muzayyinah
JABAL AL JALĀLAT
AL QIBLĪYAH
Ḥaql
△ 6232

0 10 20 30 40 50 Miles
0   20   40   60   80 Kilometers

Golan Heights. Occupied by Israel since 1967.
A Unilaterally annexed by Israel, 1981. Claimed
by Syria.

West Bank. Occupied by Israel since 1967.
B Current status subject to the Israeli-Palestinian
Interim Agreement on the West Bank and Gaza
Strip. Permanent status to be determined.

Gaza Strip. Occupied by Israel since 1967.
C Current status subject to the Israeli-Palestinian
Interim Agreement on the West Bank and Gaza
Strip. Permanent status to be determined.

©RMCN

Left map:

NORTH AMERICA
Bering Str.
M. DEZHNEVA
EAST CAPE
ST.
LAWRENCE
PRIBILOF IS.
(U.S.A.)
Arctic Circle
60°
50°

SIBERIAN
VRANGELYA
KHREBET
KOMANDORSKIYE OSTROVA
BERING
SEA
ALEUTIAN ISLANDS (U.S.A.)
170°
West Longitude
180°
East Longitude
170°

M. SHMIDTA

Oloyansk
HOYANSKIY
KHREBET
Yakutsk
KHREBET GYDAN
DZHUGDZHUR
KHREBET
Okhotsk
Petropavlovsk-
Kamchatskiy
M. KAMCHATKA
160°

STANOVOY KHREBET
SEA OF
OKHOTSK
M. LOPATKA
KURIL ISLANDS

Nerchinsk
Komsomolsk
SAKHALIN
150°

Blagoveshchensk
Sovetskaya Gavan
Khabarovsk
Tatar Strait
HOKKAIDO TRENCH

MANCHURIA
GREATER KHINGAN RANGE
SIKHOTE ALIN
Hakodate
Sendai
JAPAN

HARBIN
CHANGCHUN
Jilin
Vladivostok
HONSHŪ
TOKYO
YOKOHAMA
30°

SHENYANG
NORTH
KOREA
Pyongyang
KYŌTO
KOBE OSAKA
Zhangjiakou
SEOUL
SOUTH
KOREA
KITAKYUSHU
SHIKOKU
IJING
Dalian
Nagasaki
KYŪSHŪ

TIANJIN
Jinan
Bo Hai
QINGDAO
NANSEI SHOTŌ
TAIYUAN

'AN
NANJING
SHANGHAI
Y LING
EAST
CHINA
SEA
Tropic of Cancer

WUHAN
SEA
PHILIPPINE
SEA
150°

hangsha
NAN LING
TAIPEI
TAIWAN
(FORMOSA)
Taiwan Strait

hangha
Fuzhou
Xiamen
Shantou
GUANGZHOU
HONG KONG
(Xianggang)
Macau
Wuzhou
LUZON
PHILIPPINES
10°

HAINAN DAO
Quezon City
MANILA
SAMAR
MINDORO
PANAY
LEYTE
PHILIPPINE
TRENCH
Hue

NAM
on Penh
HO CHI
MINH CITY
(Saigon)
UI BAI-BUNG
PALAWAN
NEGROS
MINDANAO
SULU IS.
Equator

Kota Kinabalu
SULU
SEA
HALMAHERA
NEW
GUINEA
Sandakan
CELEBES
SEA
BRUNEI
MALAYSIA
Kuching
BORNEO
CELEBES
(SULAWESI)
PORE
ONESIA

0   200   400   600   800 1000 Miles
0   400   800   1200   1600 Kilometers

120°   130°

Lower right map (b):

Kuala Lumpur
Kelang
PAHANG
Merchang
Scale 1:4 000 000
b
SELANGOR
Kajang
Kuala Klawang
Gunong Telapa
3915 △ Burok
Bahau
0 10 20 30 40 50 Miles
0   20   40   60   80 Kilometers
TIOMAN
Telok Datok
NEGERI SEMBILAN
Seremban
Padang Endau
Gunong Kajang
3444
PEMANGGIL
Sepang
Rantau
Rembau
Rampin
Gemas
Port Dickson
Tampin
Segamat △ Gunung Besar
3403
Mersing
△ 2002
AUR
CAPE RACHADO
Alor Gajah
Jasin
Mt Ophir
△ 4187
Labis
SOUTH
TINGGI
MELAKA
MALAYSIA
Paloh
MALAY
Melaka
(Malacca)
Panchor
JOHOR
CHINA
Bandar
Maharani
Gunung Blumut
3312 △
Kluang
Rengam
Ayer
PENINSULA
Jason Bay
SEA
Jumrah
RUPAT
Teluklecak
Layang Layang
Batu
Pahat
Hitam
Kota Tinggi
Dumai
Pontian Kechil
Johor
Baharu
TANJONG
RAMUNIA
Batupanjang
Bengkalis
BENGKALIS
TANJONG PIAI
SINGAPORE
TANJUNG
BERAKIT
SUMATRA
Kudap
Ketamputih
Bukitbatu
PADANG
BESAR
SINGAPORE
Philip Channel
Singapore Strait
BATAM
Strait
Pinggir
Telesung
1837 △
KEPULAUAN RIAU
Tanjungpinang
△ 1181
BINTAN
RIAU
INDONESIA
Tanjungbalai
KARIMUN
BESAR
REMPANG
RANGSANG
Serangong
Sejor Riau
△ 341
Minas
Siaksriindrapura
Buatan
KUNDUR
Baranpauh
TEBINGTINGGI

©RMCN
102°   103° Longitude East of Greenwich 104°

BLACK SEA

İstanbul Boğazı (Bosporus)

İSTANBUL

T U R K E Y

CAUCASUS RUSSIA KAZA

GEORGIA Tbilisi

ARMENIA Yerevan AZERBAIJAN BAKU (Bakı)

UZBEKISTAN

TURKMENISTAN

KARA-KUM (DESERT)

Ashgabat

Mashhad

CYPRUS

MEDITERRANEAN SEA

LEBANON Beirut

SYRIA Damascus (Dimashq)

Aleppo

ISRAEL Tel Aviv-Yafo Jerusalem

ALEXANDRIA (Al Iskandarīyah)

CAIRO (Al Qāhirah)

JORDAN Ammān

I R A Q BAGHDĀD

TEHRAN

I R A N PLATEAU OF IRAN

DASHT-E KAVĪR DESERT

Esfahān

Shīrāz Kermān

AFGHA

EGYPT

SUDAN

SAUDI ARABIA

Riyadh (Ar Riyāḍ)

AN NAFŪD

Mecca (Makkah)

Jiddah

Al Madīnah (Medina)

KUWAIT Kuwait (Al Kuwayt)

BAHRAIN Al Manāmah

QATAR Ad Dawḥah

UNITED ARAB EMIRATES Abū Ȥaby Dubayy

OMAN Muscat

PERSIAN GULF

GULF OF OMAN

ARABIA

AR RUB' AL KHĀLĪ

HADRAMAWT

YEMEN San'ā'

Aden ('Adan)

GULF OF ADEN

ERITREA Asmera

ETHIOPIA

DJIBOUTI

SOMALIA Berbera

RED SEA

Tropic of Cancer

SUQUTRA (SOCOTRA) (Yemen)

Relief

Meters	Feet
3050	10 000
1525	5000
610	2000
305	1000
152.5	500
0 Sea Level	0
152.5	500 Below Sea Level
1525	5000
3050	10 000

Scale 1:16 000 000; one inch to 250 miles. Polyconic Projection
Elevations and depressions are given in feet

Longitude East of Greenwich

COPYRIGHT BY RAND McNALLY & COMPANY MADE IN U.S.A.

Continued on pages 184-185

Scale 1:40 000 000

Scale 1:4 000 000

0 10 20 30 40 Miles
0 20 40 60 Kilometers

1-TRIPURA
2-MANIPUR
3-LAKSHADWEEP
4-DELHI
5-DĀDRA AND NAGAR HAVELI
6-PONDICHERRY
7-GOA, DAMĀN, AND DIU

INDIA · POLITICAL

Continued on pages 204-205

Ⓐ Area occupied by Pakistan and claimed by India.
Ⓑ Area claimed and occupied by India; status disputed by Pakistan.
Ⓒ Area occupied by China and claimed by India.
Ⓓ Area occupied by India and claimed by China.

SRI LANKA (CEYLON)

Same scale as main map

0 50 100   200   300   400   500 Miles
0 100 200   400   600   800 Kilometers

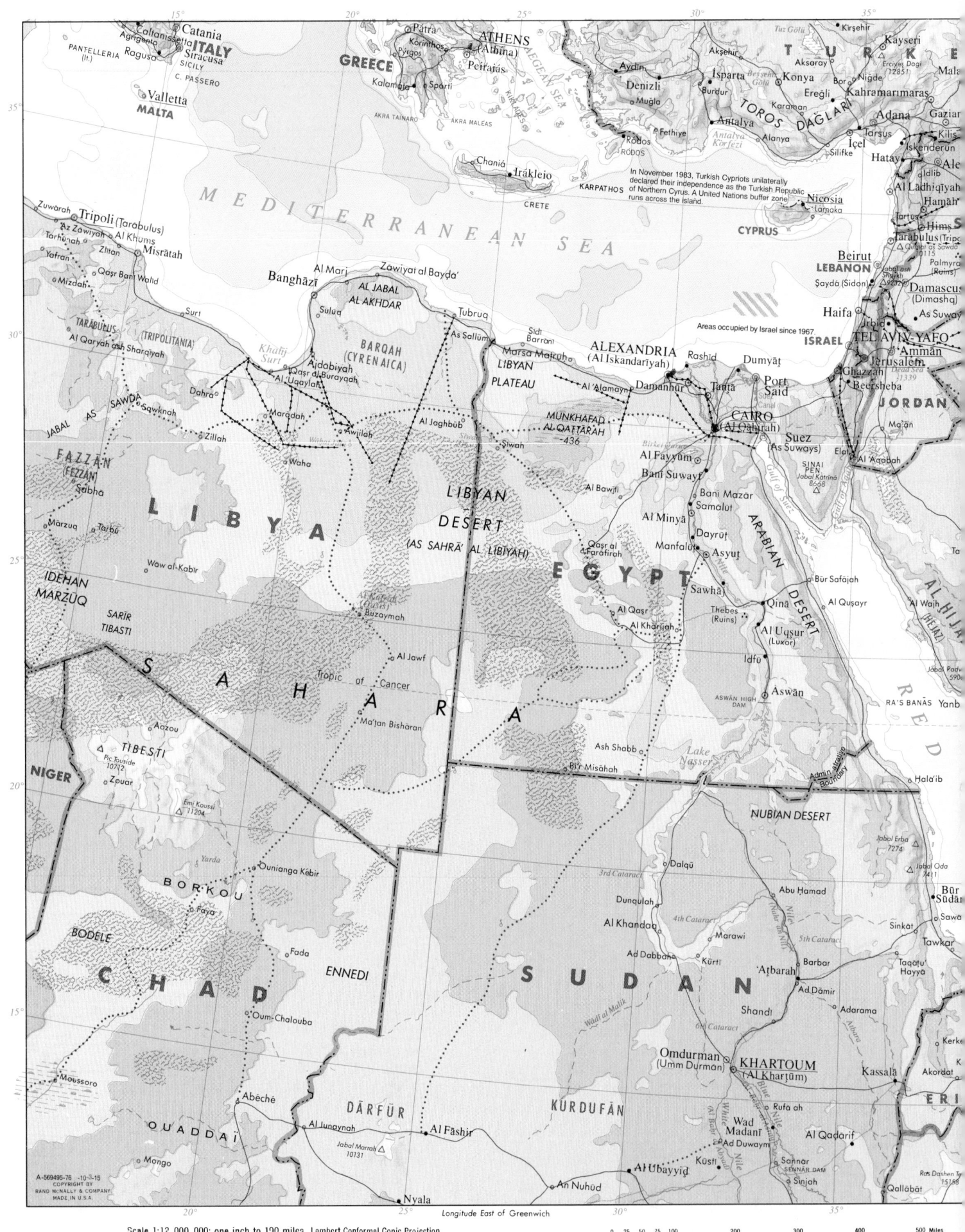

Scale 1:12 000 000; one inch to 190 miles. Lambert Conformal Conic Projection

Elevations and depressions are given in feet

Longitude East of Greenwich

| 0 | 25 | 50 | 75 | 100 | | 200 | | 300 | | 400 | | 500 Miles |

| 0 | 100 | 200 | 300 | 400 | 500 | 600 | | 800 Kilometers |

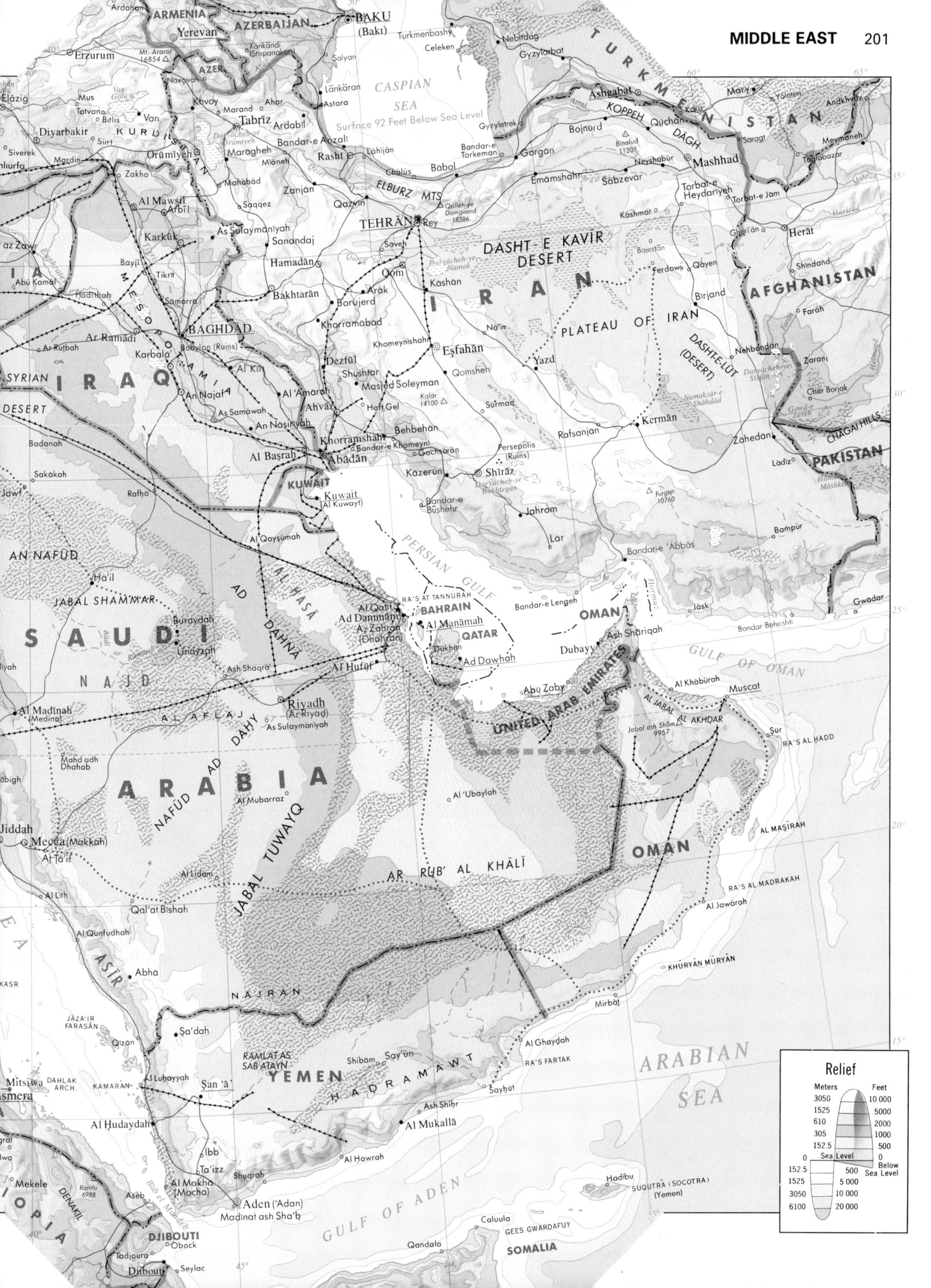

ARMENIA
AZERBAIJAN
Ardahan
Yerevan
Erzurum
Mt. Ararat
16854
Elâzig
Diyarbakir
Mus
Van
Tatvan
Bitlis
Siverek
Mardin
Siirt
urfa
Orūmīyeh
KURD
Zakho
Al Mawsil
Arbil
Karkūk
az Zawr
Abu Kamal
Hadithah
Samarra
Tikrit
Bayji
Ar Ramadi
Ar Rutbah
BAGHDAD
Babylon (Ruins)
Karbala'
Al Kut
SYRIAN
IRAQ
An Najaf
As Samawah
DESERT
Badanah
Sakakah
Jawf
Rafha
Ha'il
AN NAFUD
JABAL SHAMMAR
Buraydah
Unayzah
Iyah
SAUDI
NAJD
AL AFLAJ
Al Madinah
(Medina)
Mahd adh
Dhahab
ARABIA
abigh
Jiddah
Mecca (Makkah)
Al Ta'if
Al Lith
Al Qunfudhah
ASIR
KASR
Abha
Mitsiwa
smera
IOPIA
Mekele
Ramlu
6988
DENAKIL
Tadjoura
DJIBOUTI
Obock
Djibouti
Seylac

BAKU
(Baki)
AZER
Naxcivan
Xankändi
(Stepanakert)
Salyan
Länkäran
Astara
Ardabil
Khvoy
Marand
Ahar
Tabriz
Mahabad
Saqqez
Mianeh
Bandar-e Anzali
Rasht
Lahijan
Zanjan
Qazvin
Sanandaj
Hamadan
Bakhtaran
Borujerd
Arak
Khorramabad
Dezful
Shushtar
Masjed Soleyman
Haft Gel
Kolar
14100
Ahvaz
An Nasiriyah
Khorramshahr
Al Basrah
Abadan
KUWAIT
Kuwait
(Al Kuwayt)
Al Qaysumah
AL HASA
Ad Dahna
Ash Shaqra
Al Hufuf
Ad Dammam
Az Zahran
(Dhahran)
Al Qatif
Dukhan
QATAR
Ad Dawhah
Al Mubarraz
Al Ubaylah
JABAL TUWAYQ
Riyadh
(Ar Riyad)
As Sulaymaniyah
AD DAHY
NAFUD
AR RUB' AL KHALI
NAJRAN
RAMLAT AS
SAB'ATAYN
Najran
Sa'dah
Qizan
JAZA'IR
FARASAN
Al Luhayyah
KAMARAN
San'a
Ibb
YEMEN
HADRAMAWT
Shibam
Say'un
Al Hudaydah
Ta'izz
Al Makha
(Mocha)
Shuqrah
Al Hawrah
Aden ('Adan)
Madinat ash Sha'b
Ash Shihr
Al Mukalla
Sayhut
Ash Shihr

CASPIAN
SEA
Surface 92 Feet Below Sea Level
Turkmenbashy
Celeken
Salyan
Bandar-e
Torkeman
Babol
Chalus
Emamshahr
Gorgan
ELBURZ MTS
TEHRAN
Rey
Saveh
Qom
Kashan
Qolleh-ye
Damgvand
18386
Na'in
Yazd
Esfahan
Qomsheh
Surmaq
Behbehan
Gachsaran
Persepolis
(Ruins)
Shiraz
Kazerun
Bandar-e
Bushehr
Jahrom
Lar
PERSIAN
GULF
RA'S AT TANNURAH
BAHRAIN
Al Manamah
Bandar-e Lengeh
Abu Zaby
UNITED ARAB EMIRATES
Dubayy
Ash Shariqah
Al Khaburah
OMAN

Nebitdag
Gyzylarbat
Ashgabat
KOPPEH
DAGH
Bojnurd
Neyshabur
Sabzevar
Mashhad
Torbat-e
Heydariyeh
Torbat-e Jam
Kashmar
Gonabad
Ferdows
Qayen
Birjand
Nehbandan
PLATEAU OF IRAN
DASHT-E KAVIR
DESERT
IRAN
Rafsanjan
Kerman
Zahedan
Ladiz
Furgun
10760
Bandar-e 'Abbas
Jask
Bandar Beheshti
GULF OF OMAN
OMAN
Jabal ash Sham
9957
AL JABAL
AL AKHDAR
Muscat
Sur
RA'S AL HADD
AL MASIRAH
RA'S AL MADRAKAH
Al Jawarah
KHURYAN MURYAN
Mirbat
Al Ghaydah
RA'S FARTAK
ARABIAN
SEA
Hadibu
SUQUTRA (SOCOTRA)
(Yemen)
Caluula
GEES GWARDAFUY
Qandala
SOMALIA

TURKMENISTAN
Mary
Yoloten
Andkhvoy
Meymaneh
Herat
Shindand
AFGHANISTAN
Farah
DASHT-E LUT
(DESERT)
Zaranj
Char Borjak
CHAGAI HILLS
PAKISTAN
Gwadar

GULF OF ADEN

Relief

Meters	Feet
3050	10 000
1525	5000
610	2000
305	1000
152.5	500
Sea Level	Sea Level
152.5	500
1525	5 000
3050	10 000
6100	20 000

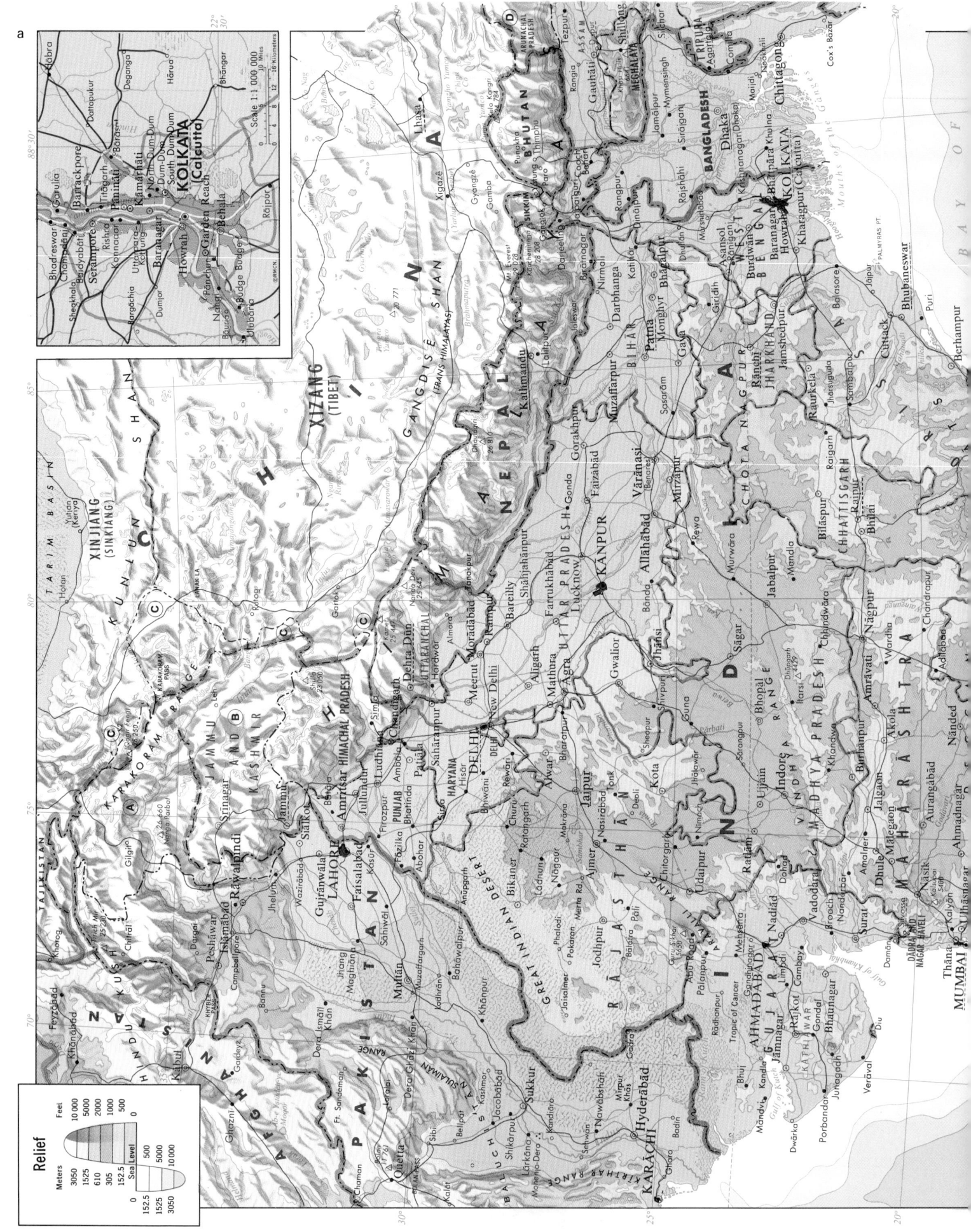

a

Scale 1:1 000 000

KOLKATA
(Calcutta)

Relief

Meters	Feet
3050	10 000
1525	5000
610	2000
305	1000
152.5	500
0	Sea Level 0
152.5	500
1525	5000
3050	10 000

Scale 1:10 000 000; one inch to 160 miles. Lambert Conformal Conic Projection
Elevations and depressions are given in feet

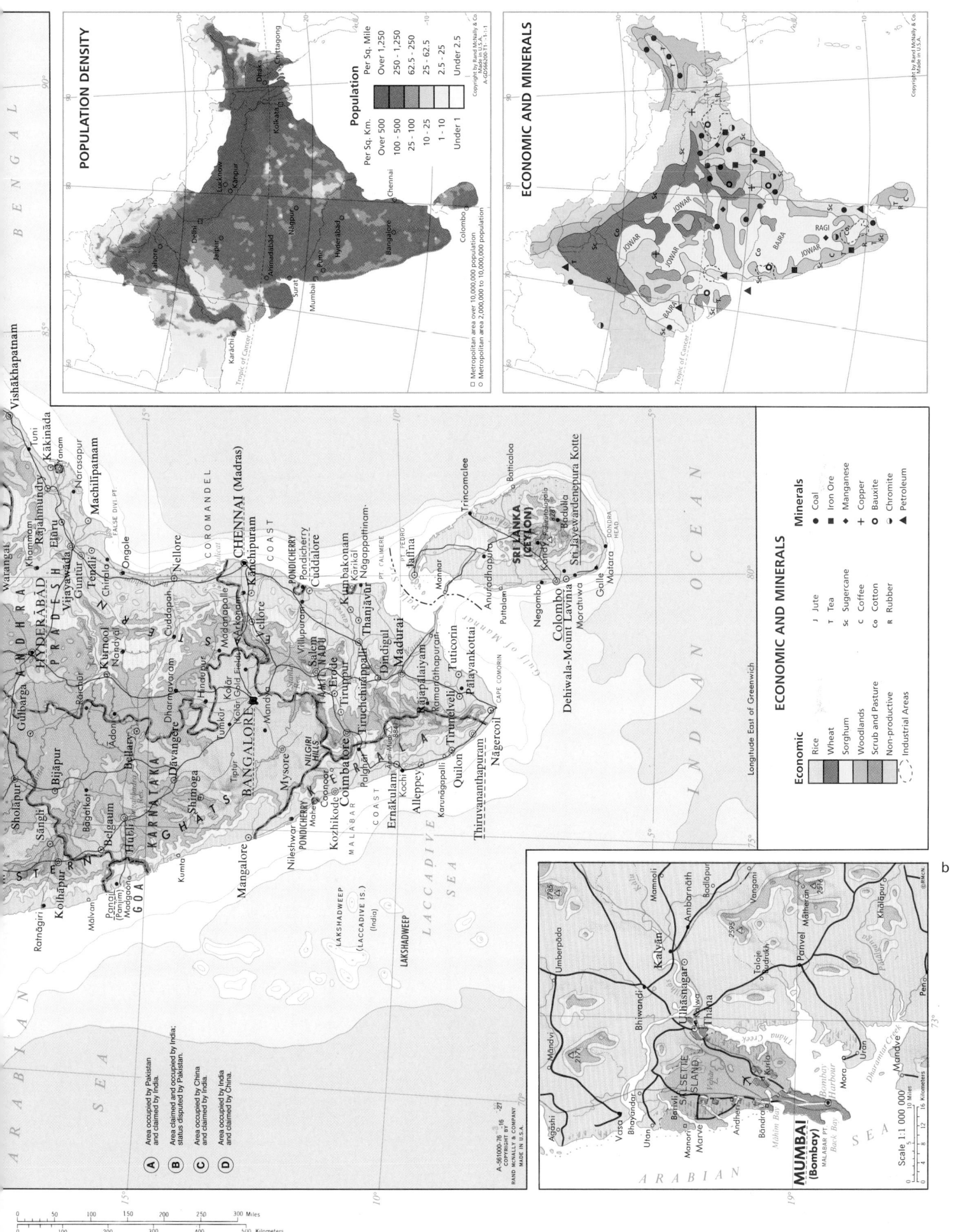

Continued on pages 184-185

Continued on pages 198-199

Scale 1:16 000 000; one inch to 250 miles. Polyconic Projection
Elevations and depressions are given in feet

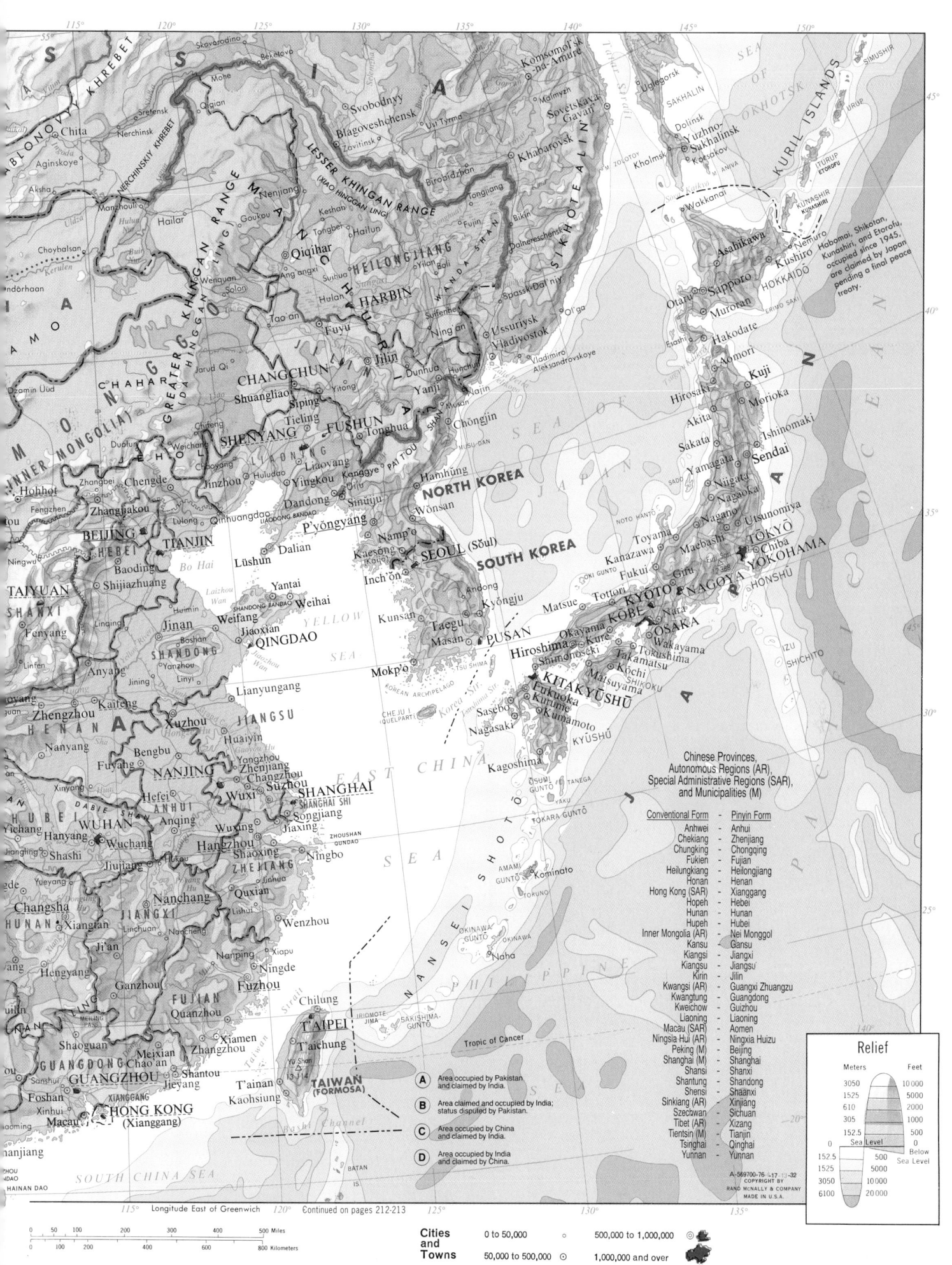

Chinese Provinces,
Autonomous Regions (AR),
Special Administrative Regions (SAR),
and Municipalities (M)

Conventional Form	Pinyin Form
Anhwei	Anhui
Chekiang	Zhenjiang
Chungking	Chongqing
Fükien	Fujian
Heilungkiang	Heilongjiang
Honan	Henan
Hong Kong (SAR)	Xianggang
Hopeh	Hebei
Hunan	Hunan
Hupeh	Hubei
Inner Mongolia (AR)	Nei Monggol
Kansu	Gansu
Kiangsi	Jiangxi
Kiangsu	Jiangsu
Kirin	Jilin
Kwangsi (AR)	Guangxi Zhuangzu
Kwangtung	Guangdong
Kweichow	Guizhou
Liaoning	Liaoning
Macau (SAR)	Aomen
Ningsia Hui (AR)	Ningxia Huizu
Peking (M)	Beijing
Shanghai (M)	Shanghai
Shansi	Shanxi
Shantung	Shandong
Shensi	Shaanxi
Sinkiang (AR)	Xinjiang
Szechwan	Sichuan
Tibet (AR)	Xizang
Tientsin (M)	Tianjin
Tsinghai	Qinghai
Yunnan	Yunnan

Ⓐ Area occupied by Pakistan and claimed by India.

Ⓑ Area claimed and occupied by India; status disputed by Pakistan.

Ⓒ Area occupied by China and claimed by India.

Ⓓ Area occupied by China and claimed by India.

A-569700-76-417-13-32
COPYRIGHT BY
RAND McNALLY & COMPANY
MADE IN U.S.A.

Relief

Meters	Feet
3050	10 000
1525	5000
610	2000
305	1000
152.5	500
0 Sea Level	0
	Below Sea Level
152.5	500
1525	5000
3050	10 000
6100	20 000

Longitude East of Greenwich

Continued on pages 212-213

0   50   100   200   300   400   500 Miles
0   100   200   300   400   500   600   800 Kilometers

Cities
and
Towns

0 to 50,000   ∘
50,000 to 500,000   ⊙
500,000 to 1,000,000   ⊚
1,000,000 and over

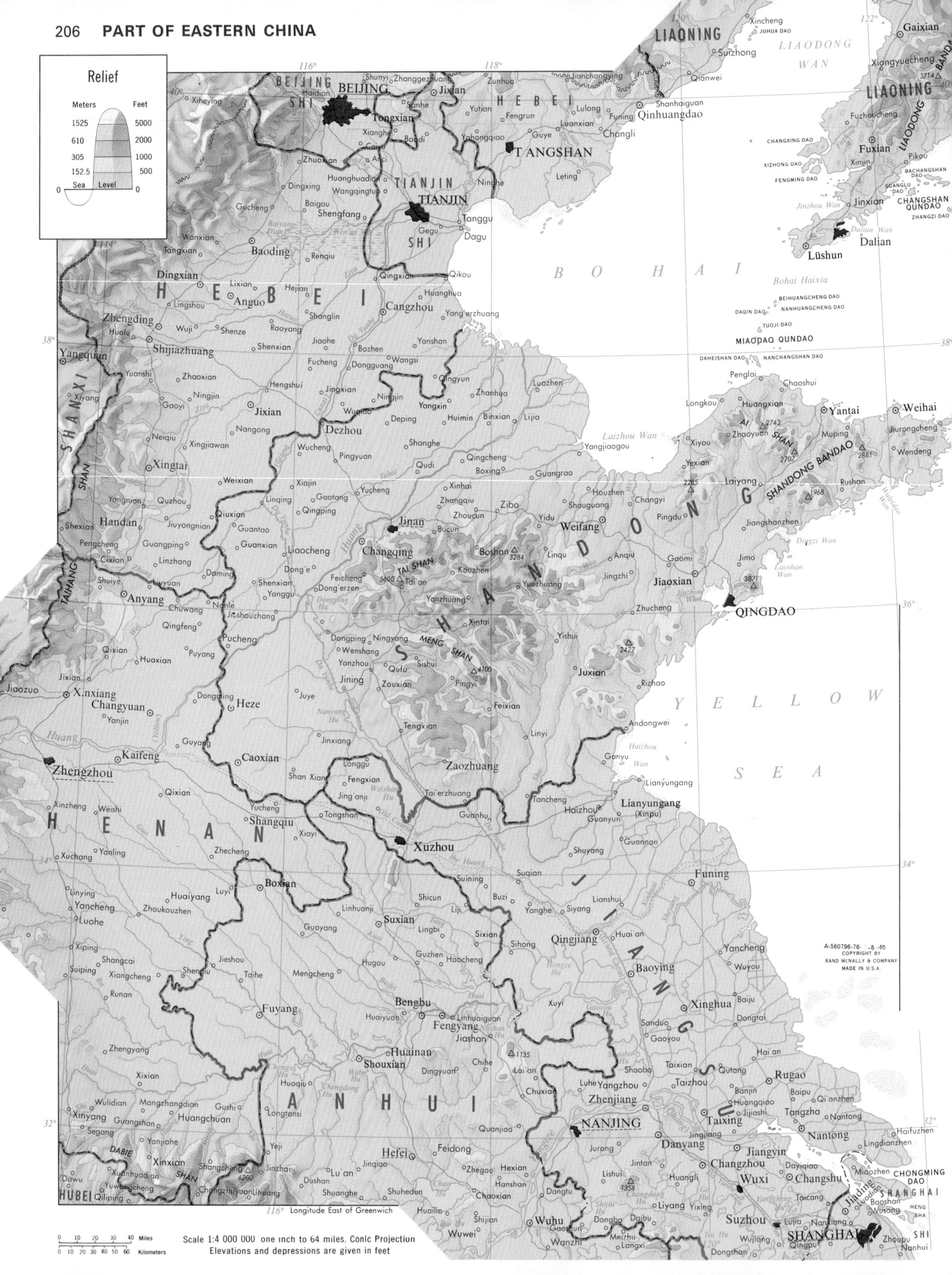

Relief

Meters	Feet
1525	5000
610	2000
305	1000
152.5	500
0 Sea Level	0

LIAONING

Xincheng
JUHUA DAO
Suizhong
Qianwei
Gaixian
Xiongyuecheng
LIAODONG WAN
Xiongyuecheng
Fuzhoucheng
3714
LIAONING
LIAODONG BANDAO
Fuxian
Xinjin
Pikou
CHANGXING DAO
XIZHONG DAO
FENGMING DAO
BACHANGSHAN DAO
GUANGLU DAO
CHANGSHAN QUNDAO
ZHANGZI DAO
Jinxian
Jinzhou Wan
Dalian Wan
Dalian
Lüshun

BEIJING SHI
Shunyi
Zhanggezhuang
Jixian
Zunhua
Jianchangying
HEBEI
Lulong
Qinhuangdao
Shanhaiguan
Xiheying
Haidian
BEIJING
Tongxian
Xiangxe
Caiyu
Anci
Sanhe
Yutian
Fengrun
Fuping
Changli
Guye
Zhuoxian
Huanghuadian
TIANJIN SHI
TIANJIN
Ninghe
Wangqingtuo
Shengfang
Baigou
Dingxing
Tanggu
Dagu
Gucheng
Wanxian
Tangxian
Baoding
Renqiu
Qingxian
Qikou
Huanghua
Yang'erzhuang
Qinhuangdao
TANGSHAN
Leting

BOHAI

CHANGXING DAO

Dingxian
Lixian
Hejian
HEBEI
Cangzhou
Yang'erzhuang
Shanglin
Huimin
Binxian
Lijia
Luozhen
BEIHUANGCHENG DAO
DAQIN DAO
NANHUANGCHENG DAO
TUOJI DAO
MIAODAO QUNDAO
DAHEISHAN DAO
NANCHANGSHAN DAO
Penglai
Chaoshui
Longkou
Huangxian
Yantai
Weihai

HEBEI
Lingshou
Anguo
Zhengding
Wuji
Shenze
Raoyang
Shijiazhuang
Zhaoxian
Ningjin
Jiaohe
Bozhen
Dongguang
Qingyun
Zhanhua
Guangrao
AI
2743
Zhaoyuan
Xiyou
SHAN
Muping
Jiurongcheng
Wendeng
Yangquan
Yuanshi
Gaoyi
Neiqiu
Xingjiawan
Hengshui
Jingxian
Wuqiao
Deping
Pingyuan
Shanghe
Qingcheng
Boxing
2285
Laiyang
SHANDONG BANDAO
1968
Rushan

Xingtai
Yongnian
Quzhou
Weixian
Xiajin
Gaotang
Yucheng
Xinhai
Zhangqiu
Zibo
Yidu
Weifang
Changyi
Pingdu
SHANDONG
Dizigi Wan
Laoshan Wan
Handan
Shexian
Pengcheng
Guangping
Linzhang
Daming
Qiuxian
Guantao
Liaocheng
Dong'e
Shenxian
Yanggu
Feicheng
Changqing
JINAN
Bucun
Zhoucun
Boshan
3284
Linqu
Anqiu
Gaomi
3871
Jiaoxian

TAIHANG
Shuiye
Liuyuan
Anyang
Chuwang
Nanle
Jishouzhuang
TAI SHAN
Tai'an
Kouzhen
Yuezhuang
Yishui
2427
Zhucheng
Jimo

Cixian
Qingfeng
Pucheng
Dongping
Ningyang
MENG SHAN
Xintai
QINGDAO

Jiaozuo
Jixian
Xinxiang
Changyuan
Yanjin
Dongming
Heze
Juye
Wenshang
Yanzhou
Qufu
Sishui
4100
Pingyi
Feixian
Linyi
Juxian
Rizhao

Xinzheng
Weishi
Qixian
Kaifeng
Guyang
Caoxian
Jinxiang
Tengxian
Andongwei

Huang
HENAN
Linying
Xuchang
Xuchang
Yanling
Zhecheng
Xiayi
Yucheng
Longgu
Fengxian
Jing'anji
Tongshan
Shan Xian
Tai'erzhuang
Guanhu
Zaozhuang
Tancheng
Haizhou
Guanyun
Lianyungang (Xinpu)
Lianyungang

Luohe
Yancheng
Zhoukouzhen
Huaiyang
Luyi
Guoyang
Linhuanji
Shicun
Liji
Buzi
Suining
Suiqian
Xuzhou
Yanghe
Siyang
Shuyang
Guannan
JIANGSU
Funing

Xiping
Shangcai
Xiangcheng
Jieshou
Taihe
Mengcheng
Hugou
Guzhen
Haocheng
Sixian
Sihong
Qingjiang
Huai'an
Yancheng
Wuyou

Suiping
Shenqiu
Guoyang
Suixian
Lingbi
Xinghua
Baiju
Dongtai

Runan
Fuyang
ANHUI
Bengbu
Xuyi
Gaoyou
Hai'an

Zhengyang
Huaiyuan
Linhuaiguan
Jiashan
1135
Sanduo
Taixian
Qutang
Rugao
Baipu
Qi'anzhen

Xixian
Zhengzhou
Shouxian
Dingyuan
Lai'an
Shaobo
Taizhou
Banjin
Nantong

DABIE SHAN
Wulidian
Mangzhangdian
Gushi
Huangchuan
Longtansi
Yeji
Huainan
Jiashan
Chuxian
Zhenjiang
Yangzhou
Taixing
Jijiashi
Tangzha

Xinxian
Xinyang
Segang
Yanjiahe
Huoqiu
Shouxian
Chihe
Fengyang
Luhe
Zhenjiang
Jingjiang
Haifuzhen
Lingdaizhen
CHONGMING DAO

HUBEI
Dawu
Yuwangdian
Qiliping
Shangcheng
Jinzhai
Lu'an
Dushan
Feidong
Jiangou
HEFEI
Zhegao
Hexian
Hanshan
Dangtu
Lishui
Jurong
NANJING
Jintan
Huangli
Danyang
Jiangyin
Changzhou
Wuxi
Changshu
Jiading
SHANGHAI SHI

0 Meters
Changzhuyuan Lihuang
6200
Shuanghe
Shuhedun
Shijian
Quanjiao
Wuhu
Chaoxian
Dongshan
Wanzhi
1358
Maanshan
Yixing
Suzhou
SHANGHAI
Zhoupu
Nanhui
Baoshan
Wusong

Scale 1:4 000 000 one inch to 64 miles. Conic Projection
Elevations and depressions are given in feet

0 10 20 30 40 Miles
0 10 20 30 40 50 60 Kilometers

A-560796-76-1-6-40
COPYRIGHT BY
RAND McNALLY & COMPANY
MADE IN U.S.A.

YELLOW SEA

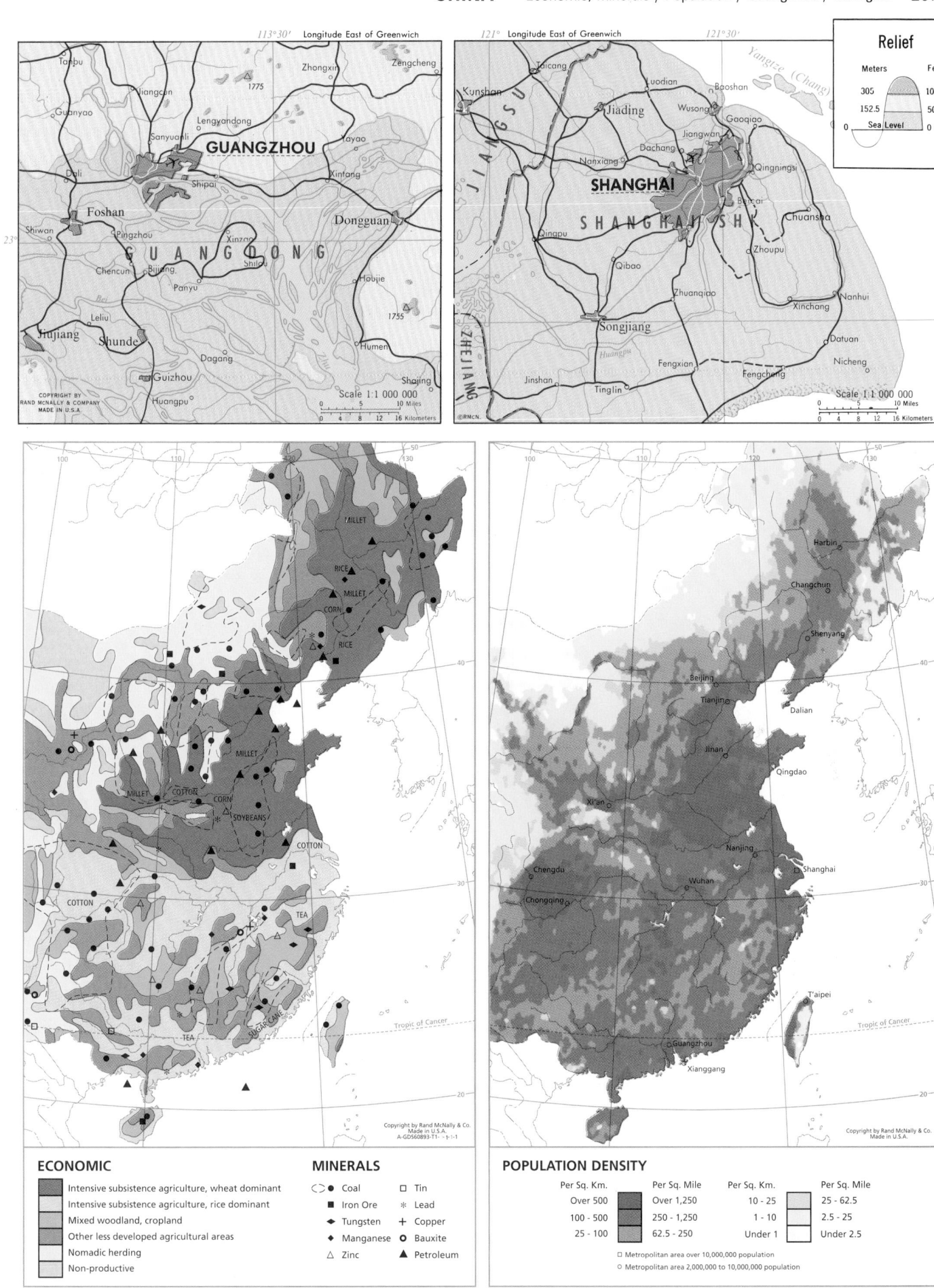

ECONOMIC

- Intensive subsistence agriculture, wheat dominant
- Intensive subsistence agriculture, rice dominant
- Mixed woodland, cropland
- Other less developed agricultural areas
- Nomadic herding
- Non-productive

MINERALS

- ⬭● Coal
- ■ Iron Ore
- ◆ Tungsten
- ◆ Manganese
- △ Zinc
- □ Tin
- ✳ Lead
- + Copper
- ⊙ Bauxite
- ▲ Petroleum

POPULATION DENSITY

Per Sq. Km.	Per Sq. Mile	Per Sq. Km.	Per Sq. Mile
Over 500	Over 1,250	10 - 25	25 - 62.5
100 - 500	250 - 1,250	1 - 10	2.5 - 25
25 - 100	62.5 - 250	Under 1	Under 2.5

□ Metropolitan area over 10,000,000 population
○ Metropolitan area 2,000,000 to 10,000,000 population

Relief

Meters	Feet
305	1000
152.5	500
0 Sea Level	0

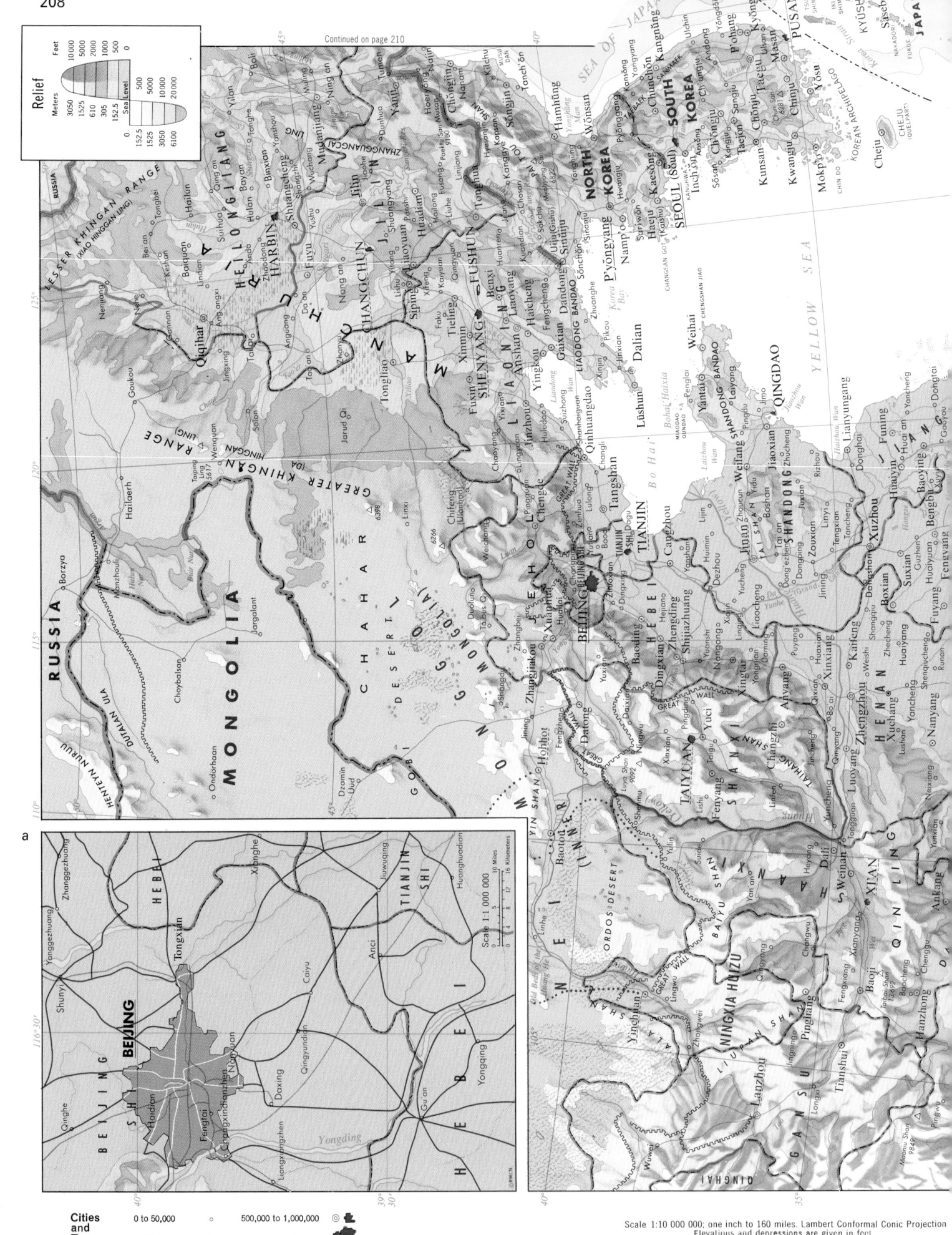

208

Continued on page 210

Relief

Feet
10000
5000
2000
1000
500
0

Meters
3050
1525
610
305
152.5
0

Sea Level
500
5000
10000
20000

152.5
1525
3050
6100

SEA OF JAPAN

JAPAN

KYUSHU

PUSAN

KOREAN ARCHIPELAGO

SOUTH KOREA

NORTH KOREA

SEOUL (Sŏul)

P'yŏngyang

Cheju (QUELPART)

YELLOW SEA

RUSSIA

LESSER KHINGAN RANGE (XIAO HINGGAN LING)

HEILONGJIANG

HARBIN

Qiqihar

JILIN

CHANGCHUN

SHENYANG

LIAONING

FUSHUN

LIAODONG BANDAO

Lüshun

Dalian

DONGBEI

GREATER KHINGAN RANGE (DA HINGGAN LING)

BOHAI HAIXIA

SHANDONG BANDAO

QINGDAO

Yantai

Weihai

CHAHAR

GOBI DESERT

MONGOLIA

RUSSIA

Choybalsan

Borzya

Manzhouli

Ulaanbaatar

DUTALAN ULA

HENTIYN NURUU

Chifeng (Ulanhot)

JEHOL

GREAT WALL

BEIJING SHI

BEIJING

TIANJIN

Tangshan

Qinhuangdao

Bo Hai

HEBEI

Shijiazhuang

Baoding

HENAN

SHANDONG

Jinan

TAI SHAN

Xuzhou

INNER MONGOLIA

YIN SHAN

Hohhot

Baotou

Datong

GREAT WALL

SHANXI

TAIYUAN

Yuci

TAIHANG SHAN

Luoyang

Zhengzhou

Kaifeng

Xian

ORDOS DESERT

Yulin

Yan'an

SHAANXI

QIN LING

NINGXIA HUIZU

Yinchuan

ALA SHAN

Lanzhou

GANSU

Tianshui

QINGHAI

Huang

Hanzhong

Ankang

Inset map (a)

HEBEI

Zhangzhezhuang

Yanggezhuang

Shunyi

TONGXIAN

TIANJIN SHI

Langfang

Wuqing

Huanghuodian

BEIJING SHI

BEIJING

Haidian

Nanyuan

Fengtai

Changxindianzhen

Doxing

Daxing

Qingyundian

Liangxiangzhen

Gu'an

Yongqing

Qinghe

Yongding

Scale 1:1 000 000

Scale 1:10 000 000; one inch to 160 miles. Lambert Conformal Conic Projection
Elevations and depressions are given in feet

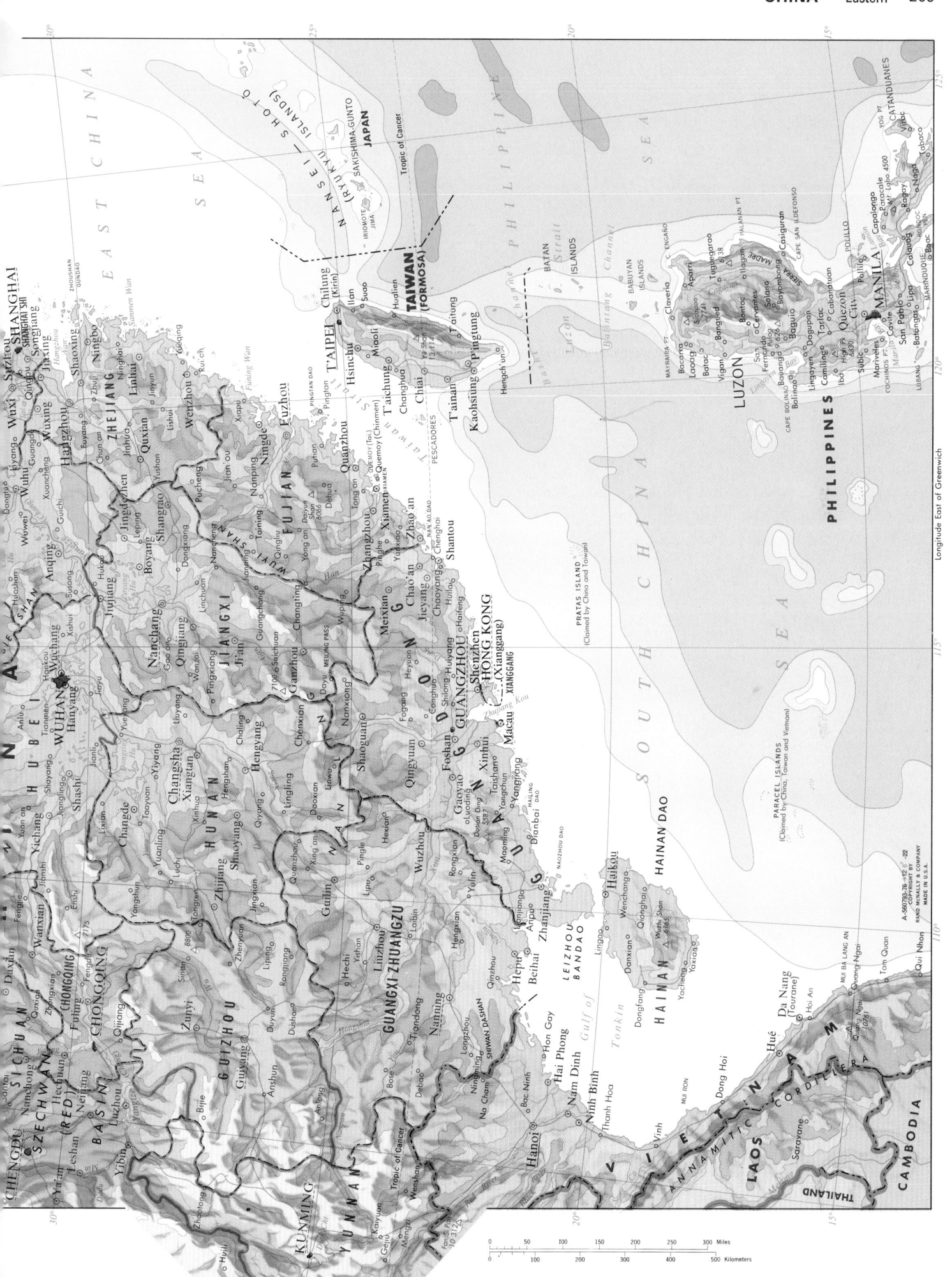

A-560793-76-+12 & -22
COPYRIGHT BY RAND M⊆NALLY
RAND M⊆NALLY & COMPANY
MADE IN U.S.A.

Longitude East of Greenwich

0 50 100 150 200 250 300 Miles
0 100 200 300 400 500 Kilometers

Continued on pages 208-209

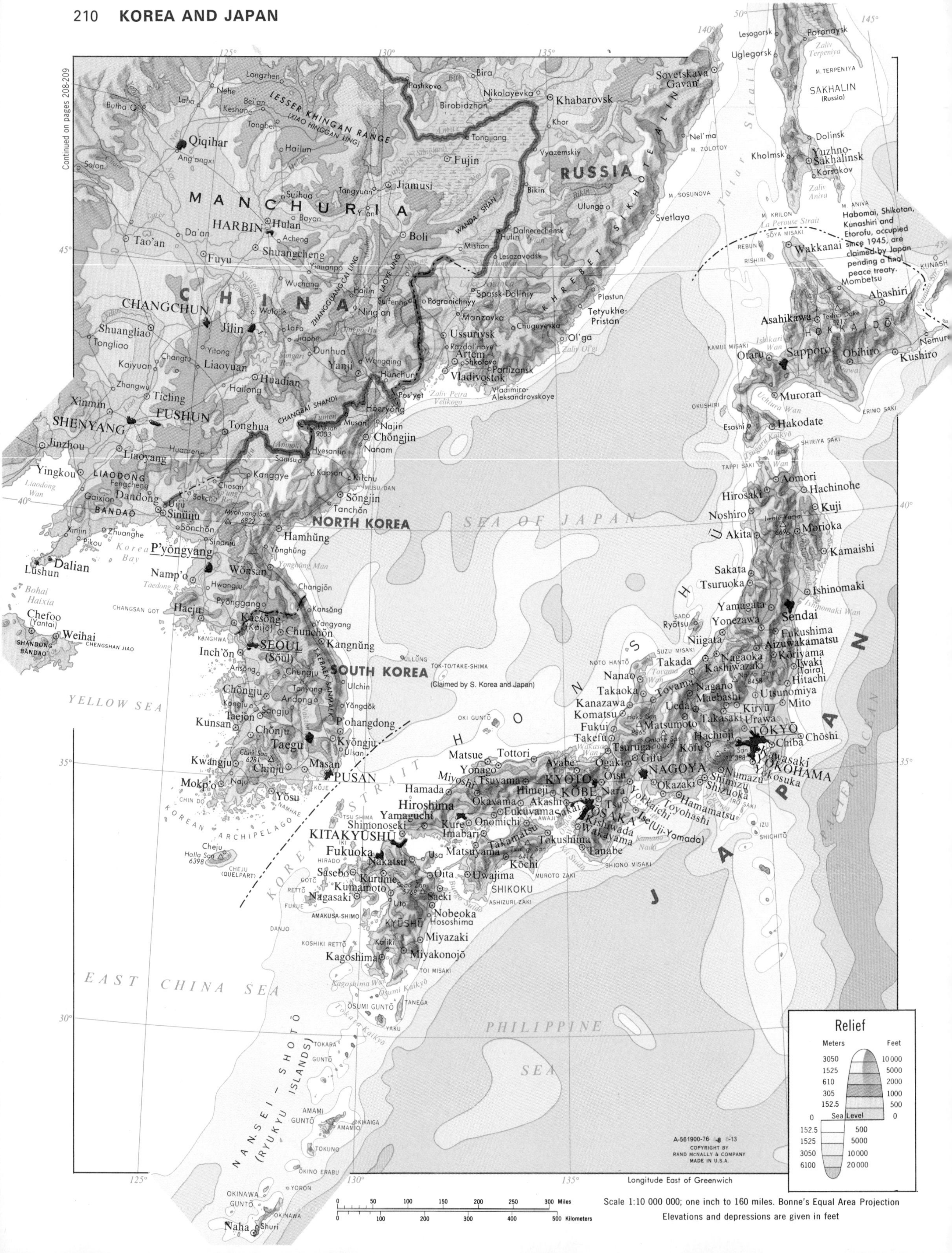

RUSSIA

MANCHURIA

HARBIN

CHINA

CHANGCHUN

SHENYANG

FUSHUN

SAKHALIN (Russia)

Habomai, Shikotan, Kunashiri and Etorofu, occupied since 1945, are claimed by Japan pending a final peace treaty.

HOKKAIDO

Sapporo

NORTH KOREA

P'yŏngyang

SEA OF JAPAN

SEOUL (Sŏul)

SOUTH KOREA

TOK-TO/TAKE-SHIMA (Claimed by S. Korea and Japan)

TOKYO

YOKOHAMA

KYOTO

OSAKA

NAGOYA

KOBE

PUSAN

YELLOW SEA

KITAKYUSHU

FUKUOKA

Nagasaki

KYUSHU

SHIKOKU

HONSHU

JAPAN

PACIFIC OCEAN

EAST CHINA SEA

NAN-SEI-SHOTO (RYUKYU ISLANDS)

PHILIPPINE SEA

KOREAN STRAIT

Longitude East of Greenwich

Relief

Meters		Feet
3050		10 000
1525		5000
610		2000
305		1000
152.5		500
0	Sea Level	0
152.5		500
1525		5000
3050		10 000
6100		20 000

A-561900-76 8-13
COPYRIGHT BY
RAND McNALLY & COMPANY
MADE IN U.S.A.

Scale 1:10 000 000; one inch to 160 miles. Bonne's Equal Area Projection
Elevations and depressions are given in feet

Scale:
0 50 100 150 200 250 300 Miles
0 100 200 300 400 500 Kilometers

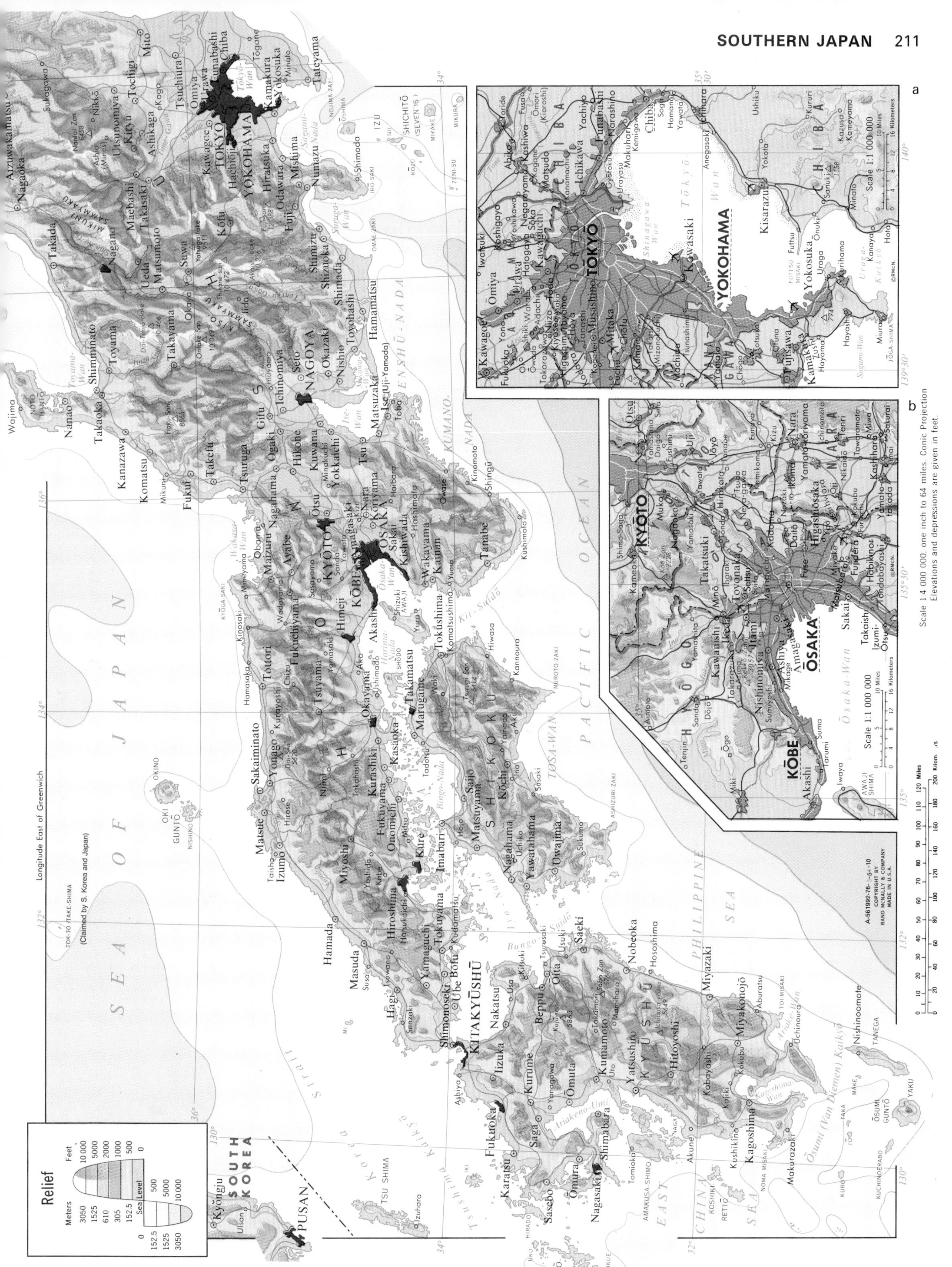

a

b

Scale 1:4 000 000; one inch to 64 miles. Conic Projection
Elevations and depressions are given in feet.

Relief

Meters	Feet	
3050	10 000	
1525	5000	
610	2000	
305	1000	
152.5	500	
0	Sea Level	
152.5	500	
1525	5000	
3050	10 000	

Scale 1:1 000 000

Scale 1:1 000 000

Longitude East of Greenwich

SEA OF JAPAN

PACIFIC OCEAN

PHILIPPINE SEA

EAST CHINA SEA

SOUTH KOREA

KYŪSHŪ

SHIKOKU

TŌKYŌ
YOKOHAMA
NAGOYA
KYŌTO
ŌSAKA
KŌBE
KITAKYŪSHŪ
PUSAN

Cities and Towns

0 to 50,000	○	500,000 to 1,000,000	◎
50,000 to 500,000	⊙	1,000,000 and over	

A-561992-76—5¢—10
COPYRIGHT BY
RAND McNALLY & COMPANY
MADE IN U.S.A.

(Claimed by S. Korea and Japan)

212

CHINA

Wuzhou   Tropic of Cancer   Jieyang   Chao'an
Monywa   Maymyo   Foshan   Sanshui   GUANGZHOU   Shantou   T'ainan   Yu Shan
Pakokku   Mandalay   Xinhui   HONG KONG   Kaohsiung   13 14   TAIWAN
Myingyan   MYANMAR   Lang Son   Beihai   Maoming   Macau   (Xianggang)
Paletwa   (BURMA)   LAOS   Hanoi   Zhanjiang   (Aomen)
Sittwe   Pyinmana   Muong Sing   Hai Phong   LEIZHOU BANDAO
Kyaukpyu   CHEDUBA   Chiang Rai   Louangphrabang   Ninh Binh   Nam Dinh   Haikou   Ballintang Ch.
RAMREE ISLAND   Toungoo   Phou Bia 9249   Thanh Hoa   GULF OF TONKIN   Wuzhi Shan   HAINAN DAO
Sandoway   Prome (Pye)   Chiang Mai   Vianechan   Vinh   6125
Henzada   Bago   Uttaradit   Udon Thani   Dong Hoi   VIETNAM
Rangoon (Yangon)   Tak   Phitsanulok   Khon Kaen   Savannakhet   Hue   Da Nang
Pathein   Mawlamyine   THAILAND   Nakhon Sawan   Ubon Ratchathani   Quang Ngai   PARACEL ISLANDS (Claimed by China, Taiwan and Vietnam)
Mouths of the Irrawaddy   Gulf of Martaban   Ye   Phra Nakhon Si Ayutthaya   Nakhon Ratchasima   An Nhon
Dawei   Prachin Buri   Angkor (Ruins)   Qui Nhon   SOUTH
BANGKOK (Krung Thep)   Siem Reap   Stoeng Treng   Nha Trang
Mergui   Chanthaburi   Batdambang   Kampong Thum   MUI KE GA
CAMBODIA (KAMPUCHEA)   Kracheh   CHINA
Tenasserim   Kampong Saôm   Phnom Penh   Loc Ninh   Phan Thiet
Chau-phu   Bien Hoa   HO CHI MINH CITY (Saigon)
Kampot   Long Xuyen   TIZARD BANK AND REEFS
ISTHMUS OF KRA   Dao Phu Quoc   Bac Lieu   SEA
Surat Thani   Nakhon Si Thammarat   MUI CA MAU   SPRATLY (Claimed by China, Malaysia, Philippines, Taiwan and Vietnam)
CON SON
Phuket   MALAY   Songkhla   Pattani
Hat Yai   PENINSULA   Kota Baharu
Alor Setar   KEDAH   Natuna Besar   Binjai
George Town (Pinang)   KEPULAUAN BUNGURAN UTARA
MALAYSIA   G. Tahan   Kuala Lumpur   Melaka (Malacca)   KEPULAUAN ANAMBAS
Medan   Belawan   Kelang   SINGAPORE   Johor Baharu   SINGAPORE
Pematangsiantar   Batu Pahat   KEPULAUAN RIAU   KEPULAUAN TAMBELAN
SUMATRA   Bengkalis   KEPULAUAN LINGA   Pontianak
Sibolga   Pakanbaru   KEPULAUAN
Equator   Bukittinggi   SUMATERA   INDRAGIRI   Sukadana
Padang   Gunung Kerinci 12 467   Jambi   Muntok   BANGKA
Pangkalpinang   Ketapang
Palembang   Tanjungpandan   BELITUNG
Bengkulu   BARISAN 10 365   GREATER   I N D O N E
Bandar Lampung   KEPULAUAN KARIMUNJAWA   LAUT JAWA (JAVA SEA)
JAKARTA   Serang   Cirebon   Semarang   MADURA   SURABAYA
Sukabumi   Bogor   BANDUNG   Surakarta   Pasuruan
Yogyakarta   JAVA (JAWA)   Malang   Semeru 12 060   BALI 10309   Denpasar

LUZON   Laoag   Aparri
Vigan   Baguio
San Fernando   Lingayen   Tarlac
Olongapo   Quezon City
MANILA   Lipa   Batangas
LUBANG ISLANDS   MINDORO   CALAMIAN GROUP
PALAWAN   Puerto Princesa
CAGAYAN IS.   PANAY
CUYO IS.   SULU SEA
BALABAC ISLAND   PULAU BANGGI   Zamboanga
Kudat   CAGAYAN SULU   JOLO ISLAND   SULU ARCHIPEL
Kota Kinabalu   Gunung Kinabalu 13 455   Sandakan   TAWITAWI GROUP   SIBUTU ISLAND
PULAU LABUAN   SABAH
Bandar Seri Begawan   BRUNEI   Bukit Pagon 6070
Miri   MALAYSIA   Bintulu   Tarakan   TG MANGKALIHAT   CELE SE
SARAWAK   IRAN MTS.   Kuching   UPPER KAPUAS MTS.   Samarinda
BORNEO   KALIMANTAN   Donggala
PEGUNUNGAN MÜLLER   Balikpapan   CELEBES (SULAWESI)
Bukit Raya 7474   SCHWANER   Banjarmasin   Kotabaru   PULAU LAUT
TG PUTING   TG SELATAN   Martapura   Ujungpandang (Makasar)   Parepare
GREATER   SUNDA   Bonthain   PULAU SELAYAR
LAUT JAWA   MASALEMBO-BESAR   Majene
(JAVA SEA)   PULAU BAWEAN   ISLANDS   PULAU KABAENA
Bangkalan   LAUT FLORES   FLORES SEA
G. Agung 12 224   Sumbawa Besar   SUMBAWA   Raba   FLORES
G. Rinjani   Mataram   LOMBOK   LESSER   SUMBA   Waingapu
Banyuwangi   SUNDA   ISLANDS

SOUTH CHINA SEA

INDIAN OCEAN

NORTH ANDAMAN
MIDDLE ANDAMAN (Ind.)
Port Blai
SOUTH ANDAMAN
ANDAMAN IS. (Ind.)
Andaman Sea
MERGUI ARCHIPELAGO
Gulf of Thailand

NICOBAR ISLANDS (India)
GREAT NICOBAR
Sabang
Banda Aceh   Idi   Langsa
Taiping   Ipoh
Dumai   Danau Toba
PULAU SIMEULUE
KEPULAUAN BANYAK
PULAU NIAS
PULAU PINI
PULAU TANAHMASA
PULAU TANAHBALA   KEPULAUAN BATU
KEPULAUAN   PULAU SIBERUT
MENTAWAI   PULAU SIPURA
PULAU PAGAI UTARA
PULAU PAGAI SELATAN
Sawahlunto
PULAU ENGGANO
Selat Sunda
CHRISTMAS ISLAND (Austl.)
JAVA TRENCH
24 440

A-569800-76 -11-11-33
COPYRIGHT BY
RAND McNALLY & COMPANY
MADE IN U.S.A.

Longitude East of Greenwich

Scale 1:16 000 000; one inch to 250 miles. Polyconic Projection
Elevations and depressions are given in feet

Relief

Meters	Feet
3050	10 000
1525	5000
610	2000
305	1000
152.5	500
Sea Level	
152.5	500
1525	5000
3050	10 000
6100	20 000

a

Continued on pages 204-205

PHILIPPINE

PHILIPPINES

SOUTH CHINA SEA

LUZON

PHILIPPINES

SEA

MANILA

Quezon City

MINDORO

SIBUYAN SEA

MASBATE

Scale 1:4 000 000

0 10 20 30 40 Miles

0 10 20 30 40 50 60 Kilometers

©rmcn

PHILIPPINE

PHILIPPINES

Tacloban
SAMAR

LEYTE

PHILIPPINE

SEA

TRENCH

Butuan
Cagayan

MINDANAO
Davao

PALAU

SONSOROL
ISLANDS

KEPULAUAN
TALAUD

Tondano
Ternate
HALMAHERA
MOROTAI

KEPULAUAN
MAPIA

Laut
Maluku
(Moluca Sea)

Halmahera
(Halmahera Sea)

PULAU
WAIGEO

Equator

PULAU BACAN
Labuha

MALUKU
(MOLUCCAS)

SALAWATI
SORONG

JAZIRAH
DOBERAI

Manokwari

BIAK
PULAU NUMFOOR
PULAU YAPEN

TG. PERKAM

NINIGO GROUP

HERMIT IS.

ADMIRALTY ISLANDS

MUSSAU
ISLAND

EMIRA
ISLAND

PULAU TALIBU
PULAU MANGOLE
PULAU SULA

PULAU
OBI

PULAU
MISOOL

Jayapura
(Sukarnapura)

MANUS
ISLAND

NEW HANOVER

Kavieng

CERAM
(SERAM)
Piru
Ambon
PULAU AMBON
Bula

Fakfak

Kaimana

PEGUNUNGAN VAN REES

Aitape

Wewak

Sepik R.

KARKAR ISLAND

BISMARCK

ARCH.

Namatanai
Rabaul
Kakopo

SIA

BURU

KEPULAUAN
BANDA

PEGUNUNGAN MAOKE
Puncak Jaya
16 503
Puncak Trikora
15 584

PULAU ADI

NEW GUINEA

Madang

LONG ISLAND

WITU
ISLANDS

Talasea

The Father
7546

NEW
IRELAND

KEPULAUAN
TUKANGBESI

KEPULAUAN
LUCIPARA

KEPULAUAN KAI
KAI KECIL

Dobo

Mt. Gluwe 14 330

Mt. Wilhelm 14 793

New Britain

LAUT BANDA
(BANDA SEA)

PULAU
DAMAR

KEPULAUAN
ARU
PULAU
TRANGAN

PAPUA

Mt. Bangeta
13 529
Lae

NEW BRITAIN

PULAU WETAR

PULAU BABAR

YAMDENA
KEPULAUAN
TANIMBAR

NEW GUINEA

Huon Gulf

NEW BRITAIN TRENCH

PULAU ALOR
DE ATAURO
Dili
EAST TIMOR

PULAU
MOA
PULAU
SELARU

PULAU
YOS
SUDARSA

TANJUNG VALS

Merauke

Morobe

Mt. Albert Edward
13 090

TROBRIAND IS.

TIMOR

ARAFURA SEA

Buna

OWEN STANLEY RA.

WOODLARK
ISLAND

D'ENTRECASTEAUX IS.

TIMOR
SEA

MELVILLE
ISLAND

COBOURG
PEN.
CROKER ISLAND

WESSEL IS.

Daru

Gulf
of Papua

Port Moresby

Mt. Victoria
13 206

BATHURST
ISLAND

Darwin

Van
Diemen Gulf
C. ARNHEM

Gulf of Carpentaria

CAPE
YORK
PEN.

GREAT
BARRIER
REEF

CORAL SEA

Samarai

AUSTRALIA

Continued on pages 220-221

0 50 100   200   300   400   500 Miles

0 100   200   400   600   800 Kilometers

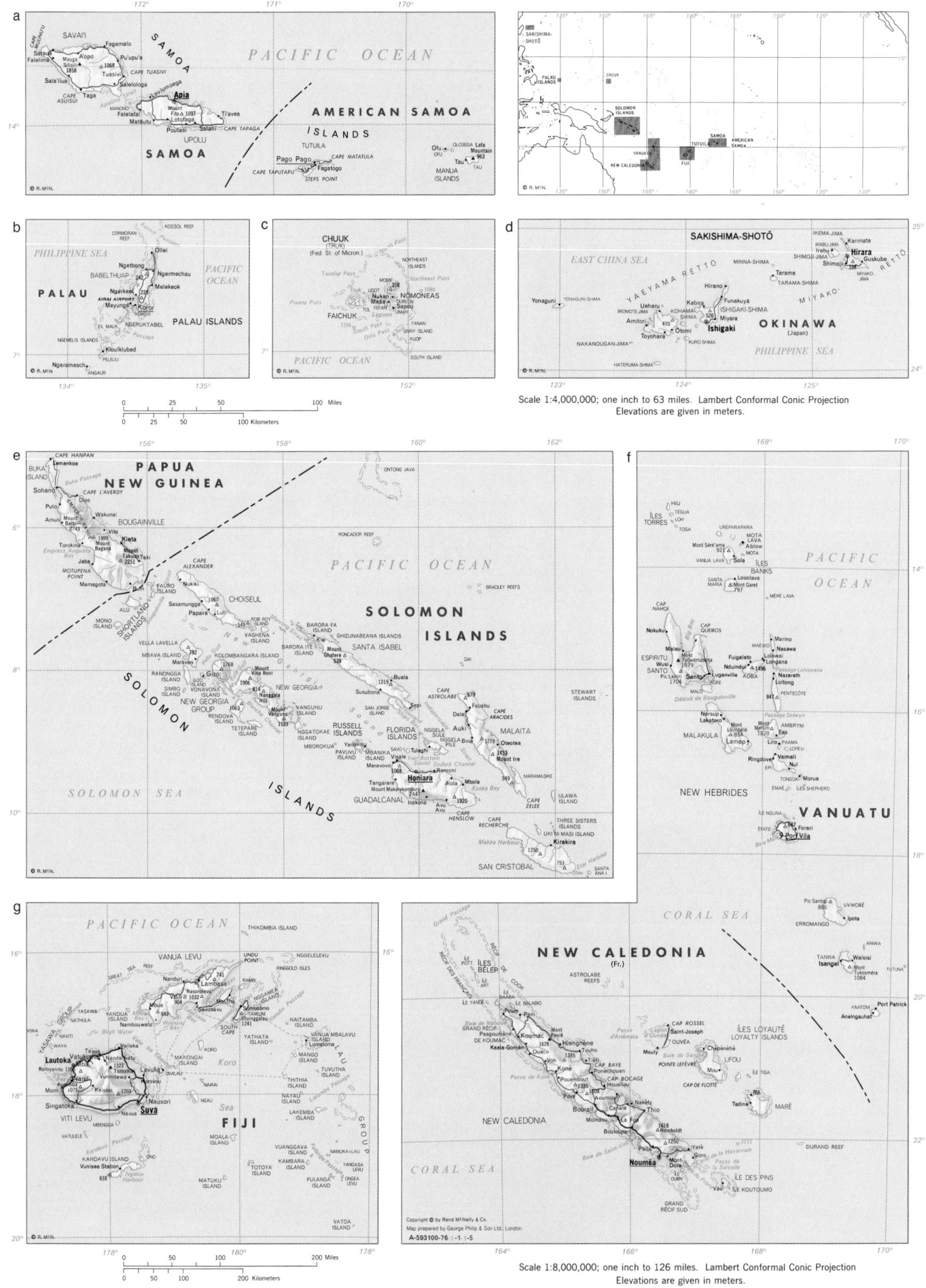

Scale 1:4,000,000; one inch to 63 miles. Lambert Conformal Conic Projection
Elevations are given in meters.

Scale 1:8,000,000; one inch to 126 miles. Lambert Conformal Conic Projection
Elevations are given in meters.

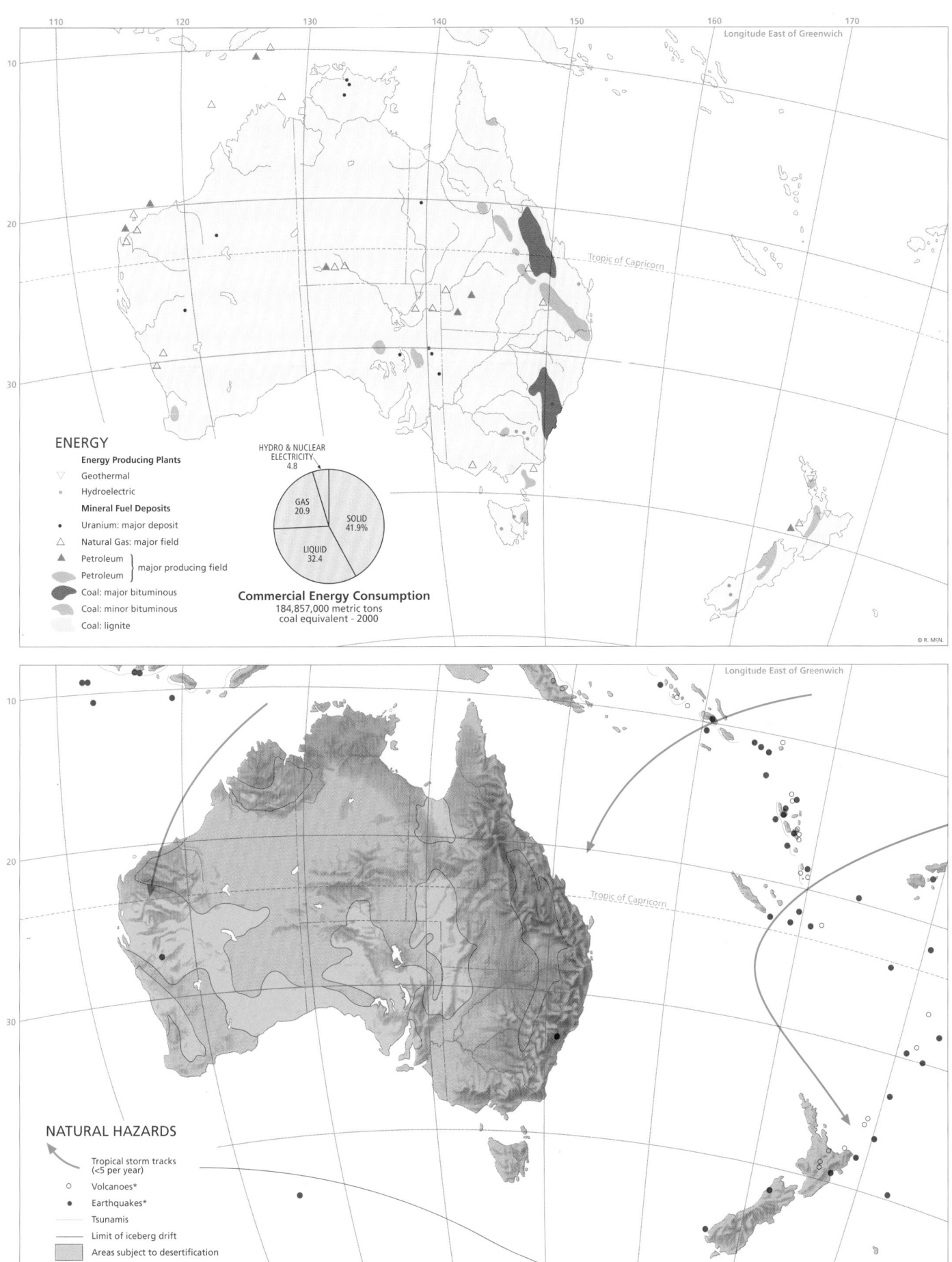

Longitude East of Greenwich

Tropic of Capricorn

ENERGY

Energy Producing Plants

▽ Geothermal

• Hydroelectric

Mineral Fuel Deposits

• Uranium: major deposit

△ Natural Gas: major field

▲ Petroleum } major producing field
  Petroleum

  Coal: major bituminous

  Coal: minor bituminous

  Coal: lignite

HYDRO & NUCLEAR
ELECTRICITY
4.8

GAS
20.9

SOLID
41.9%

LIQUID
32.4

Commercial Energy Consumption
184,857,000 metric tons
coal equivalent - 2000

© R. McN.

Longitude East of Greenwich

Tropic of Capricorn

NATURAL HAZARDS

⤴ Tropical storm tracks
(<5 per year)

○ Volcanoes*

• Earthquakes*

  Tsunamis

  Limit of iceberg drift

  Areas subject to desertification

*Occurrences since 1900

© R. McN.   N-GDS95000-D5 -2-2-2

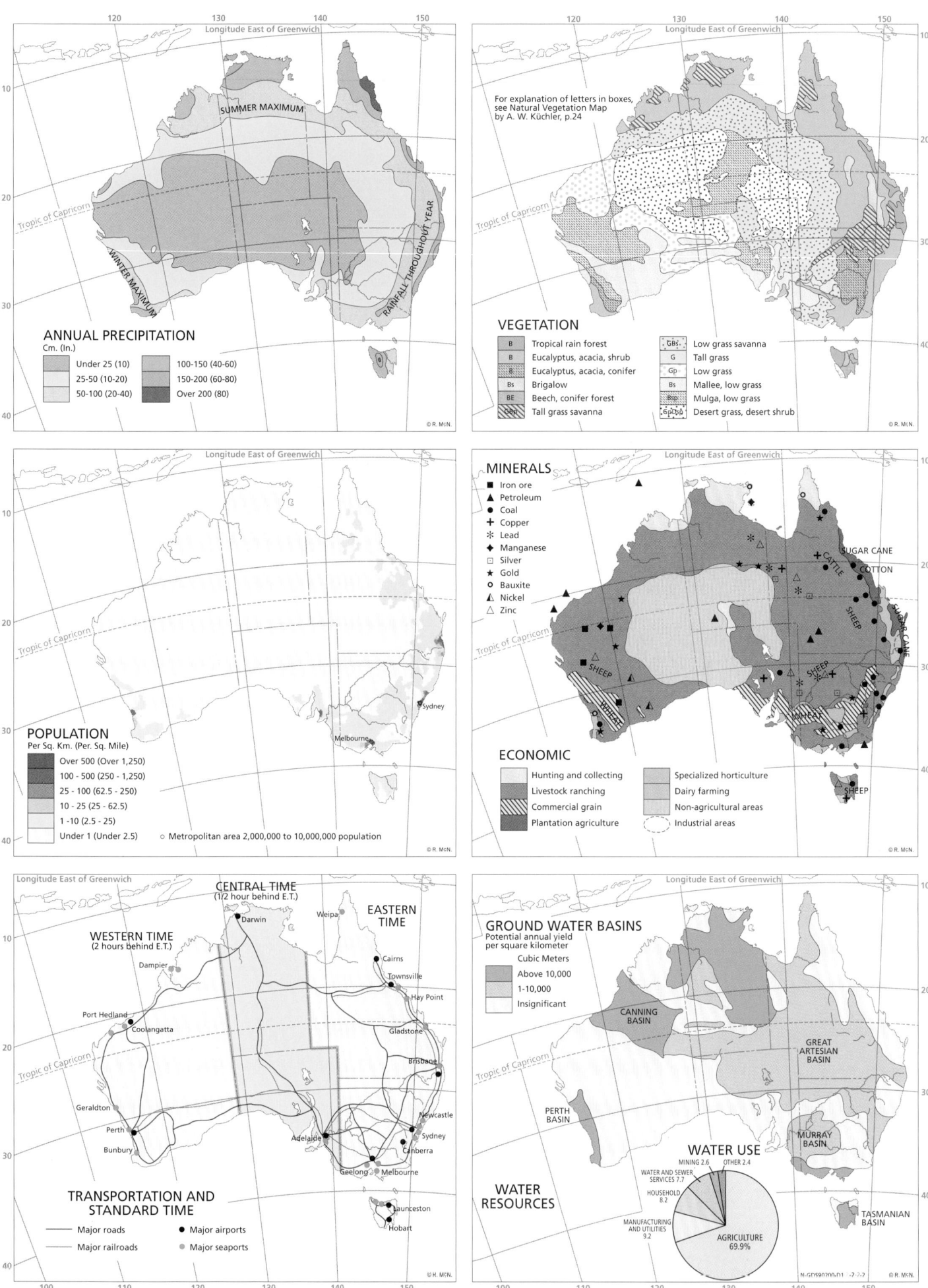

ANNUAL PRECIPITATION
Cm. (In.)

Under 25 (10)	100-150 (40-60)
25-50 (10-20)	150-200 (60-80)
50-100 (20-40)	Over 200 (80)

SUMMER MAXIMUM
WINTER MAXIMUM
RAINFALL THROUGHOUT YEAR
Tropic of Capricorn
Longitude East of Greenwich

VEGETATION

For explanation of letters in boxes, see Natural Vegetation Map by A. W. Küchler, p.24

B	Tropical rain forest	GBs	Low grass savanna
B	Eucalyptus, acacia, shrub	G	Tall grass
B	Eucalyptus, acacia, conifer	Gp	Low grass
Bs	Brigalow	Bs	Mallee, low grass
BE	Beech, conifer forest	Bsp	Mulga, low grass
GBr	Tall grass savanna	GpDsd	Desert grass, desert shrub

POPULATION
Per Sq. Km. (Per. Sq. Mile)

	Over 500 (Over 1,250)
	100 - 500 (250 - 1,250)
	25 - 100 (62.5 - 250)
	10 - 25 (25 - 62.5)
	1 - 10 (2.5 - 25)
	Under 1 (Under 2.5)

○ Metropolitan area 2,000,000 to 10,000,000 population

Sydney
Melbourne

MINERALS

- ■ Iron ore
- ▲ Petroleum
- ● Coal
- ✛ Copper
- ✳ Lead
- ◆ Manganese
- ▢ Silver
- ★ Gold
- ○ Bauxite
- ▲ Nickel
- △ Zinc

SUGAR CANE
COTTON
CATTLE
SHEEP
WHEAT
SHEEP
WHEAT
SHEEP

ECONOMIC

	Hunting and collecting		Specialized horticulture
	Livestock ranching		Dairy farming
	Commercial grain		Non-agricultural areas
	Plantation agriculture		Industrial areas

TRANSPORTATION AND STANDARD TIME

WESTERN TIME (2 hours behind E.T.)
CENTRAL TIME (1/2 hour behind E.T.)
EASTERN TIME

Darwin
Weipa
Cairns
Townsville
Hay Point
Gladstone
Brisbane
Newcastle
Sydney
Canberra
Geelong
Melbourne
Adelaide
Bunbury
Perth
Geraldton
Coolangatta
Port Hedland
Dampier
Launceston
Hobart

——	Major roads	●	Major airports
——	Major railroads	●	Major seaports

GROUND WATER BASINS
Potential annual yield per square kilometer
Cubic Meters

	Above 10,000
	1-10,000
	Insignificant

CANNING BASIN
GREAT ARTESIAN BASIN
PERTH BASIN
MURRAY BASIN
TASMANIAN BASIN

WATER RESOURCES

WATER USE
MINING 2.6 OTHER 2.4
WATER AND SEWER SERVICES 7.7
HOUSEHOLD 8.2
MANUFACTURING AND UTILITIES 9.2
AGRICULTURE 69.9%

Tropic of Capricorn
Longitude East of Greenwich

© R. McN.

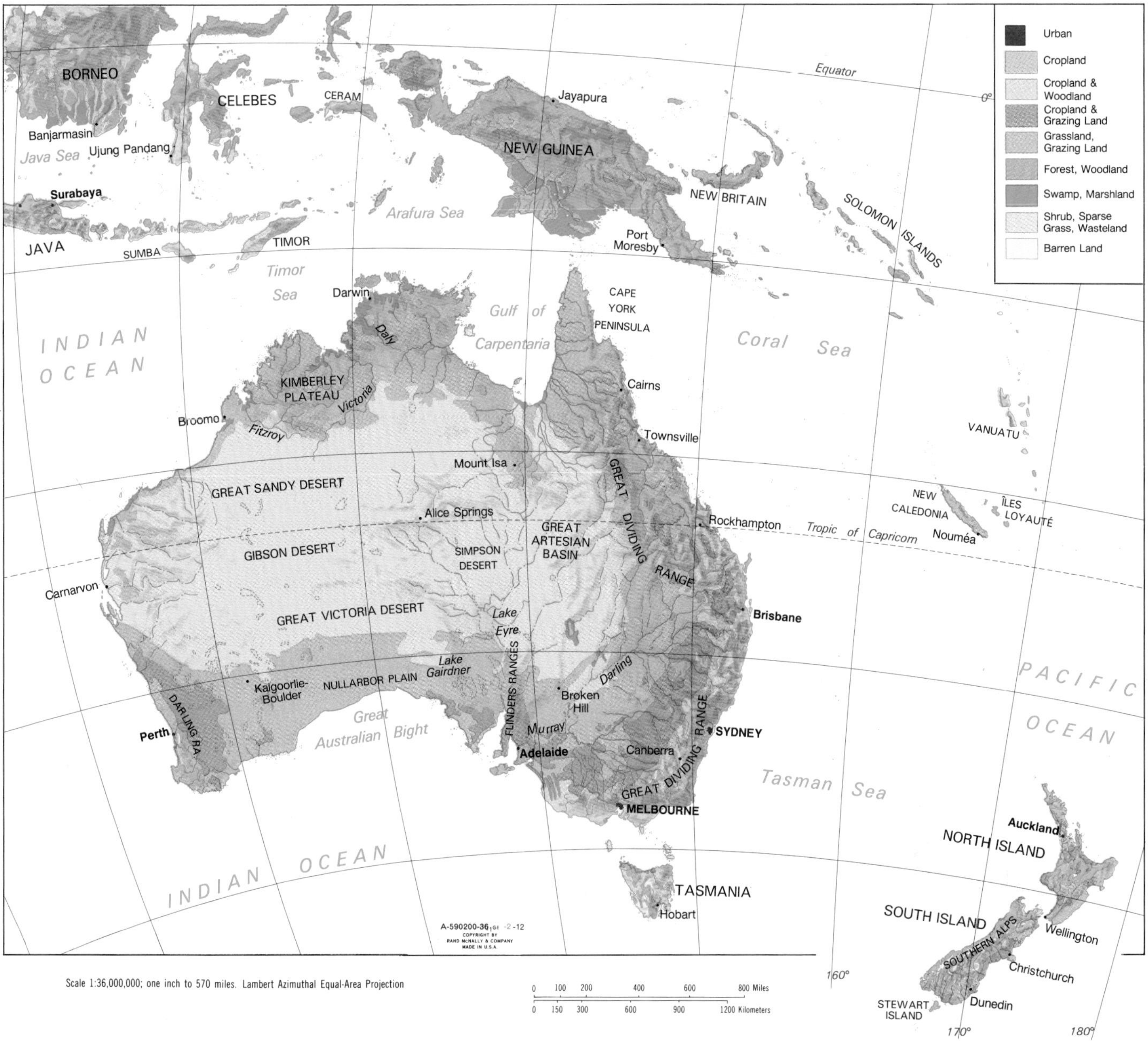

Urban
Cropland
Cropland & Woodland
Cropland & Grazing Land
Grassland, Grazing Land
Forest, Woodland
Swamp, Marshland
Shrub, Sparse Grass, Wasteland
Barren Land

BORNEO
CELEBES
CERAM
Banjarmasin
Java Sea
Ujung Pandang
Surabaya
JAVA
SUMBA
TIMOR
Arafura Sea
NEW GUINEA
Jayapura
NEW BRITAIN
SOLOMON ISLANDS
Port Moresby
Equator
0°

INDIAN OCEAN
Darwin
Timor Sea
Gulf of Carpentaria
CAPE YORK PENINSULA
Coral Sea
Cairns
Townsville
VANUATU
NEW CALEDONIA
ÎLES LOYAUTÉ
Nouméa

KIMBERLEY PLATEAU
Broome
Fitzroy
Victoria
Daly

GREAT SANDY DESERT
Mount Isa
Alice Springs
GIBSON DESERT
SIMPSON DESERT
GREAT ARTESIAN BASIN
GREAT DIVIDING RANGE
Rockhampton
Tropic of Capricorn

Carnarvon
GREAT VICTORIA DESERT
Lake Eyre
Brisbane
PACIFIC OCEAN

Kalgoorlie-Boulder
NULLARBOR PLAIN
Lake Gairdner
FLINDERS RANGES
Broken Hill
Darling
SYDNEY
Perth
DARLING RA.
Great Australian Bight
Murray
Adelaide
Canberra
GREAT DIVIDING RANGE
Tasman Sea
MELBOURNE
Auckland
NORTH ISLAND

INDIAN OCEAN
TASMANIA
Hobart
160°
SOUTH ISLAND
SOUTHERN ALPS
Wellington
Christchurch
STEWART ISLAND
Dunedin
170°
180°

A-590200-36 ,91 -2 -12
COPYRIGHT BY
RAND MCNALLY & COMPANY
MADE IN U.S.A.

Scale 1:36,000,000; one inch to 570 miles. Lambert Azimuthal Equal-Area Projection

0 100 200 400 600 800 Miles
0 150 300 600 900 1200 Kilometers

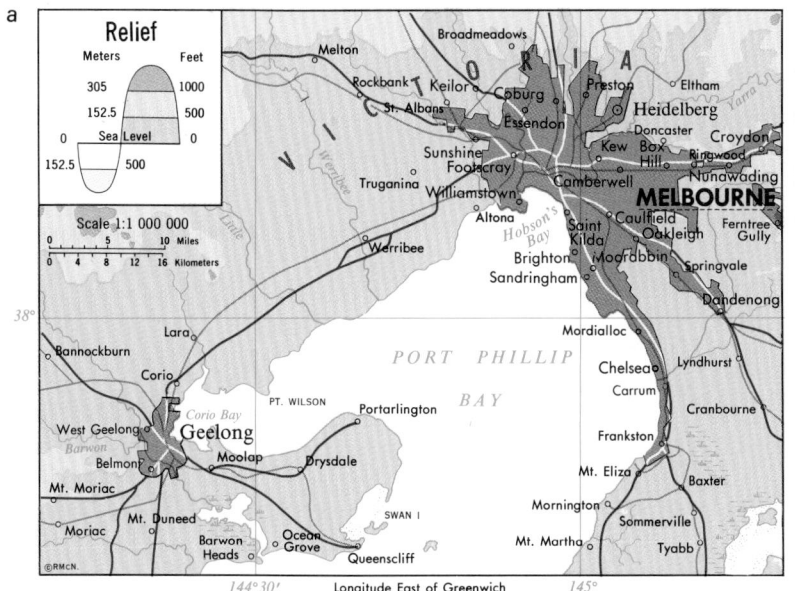

a

Relief

Meters		Feet
305		1000
152.5		500
0	Sea Level	0
152.5		500

Scale 1:1 000 000
0 5 10 Miles
0 4 8 12 16 Kilometers

VICTORIA
Melton
Broadmeadows
Rockbank
Keilor
St. Albans
Coburg
Preston
Eltham
Sunshine
Essendon
Heidelberg
Croydon
Doncaster
Kew
Box Hill
Ringwood
Nunawading
Truganina
Footscray
Camberwell
Williamstown
MELBOURNE
Altona
Caulfield
Oakleigh
Ferntree Gully
Saint Kilda
Springvale
Werribee
Brighton
Moorabbin
Sandringham
Dandenong
Hobson's Bay
Yarra
Werribee
Little

38°
Lara
Bannockburn
Corio
Corio Bay
PT. WILSON
Portarlington
Mordialloc
West Geelong
Geelong
PORT PHILLIP BAY
Chelsea
Lyndhurst
Belmont
Moolap
Drysdale
Carrum
Cranbourne
Mt. Moriac
Barwon
Frankston
Moriac
Mt. Duneed
SWAN I.
Ocean Grove
Mt. Eliza
Baxter
Barwon Heads
Queenscliff
Mornington
Sommerville
Mt. Martha
Tyabb
®RMCN.

144°30'
Longitude East of Greenwich
145°

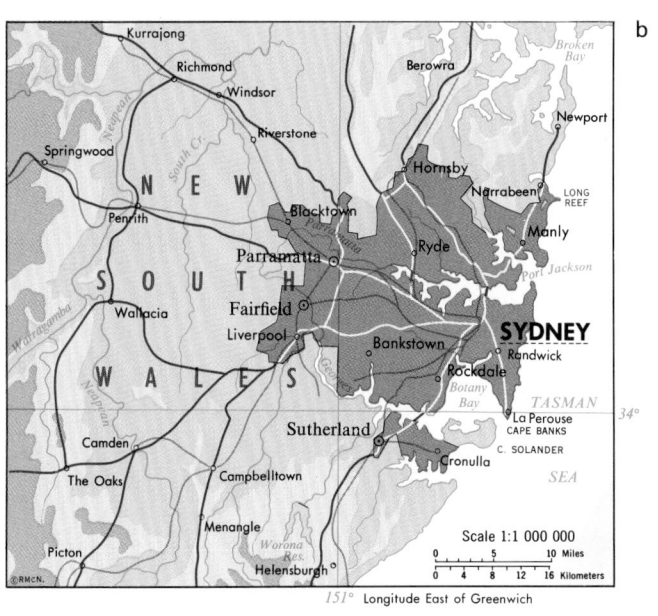

b

Kurrajong
Broken Bay
Richmond
Berowra
Windsor
Newport
Springwood
Riverstone
Hornsby
Narrabeen
LONG REEF
Penrith
Blacktown
Ryde
Manly
Parramatta
NEW
Fairfield
SOUTH
Wallacia
Liverpool
Bankstown
SYDNEY
Randwick
WALES
Rockdale
Botany Bay
La Perouse
CAPE BANKS
Camden
Sutherland
C. SOLANDER
Cronulla
The Oaks
Campbelltown
TASMAN
Menangle
SEA
Picton
Helensburgh
34°

®RMCN.
Scale 1:1 000 000
0 5 10 Miles
0 4 8 12 16 Kilometers

151°
Longitude East of Greenwich

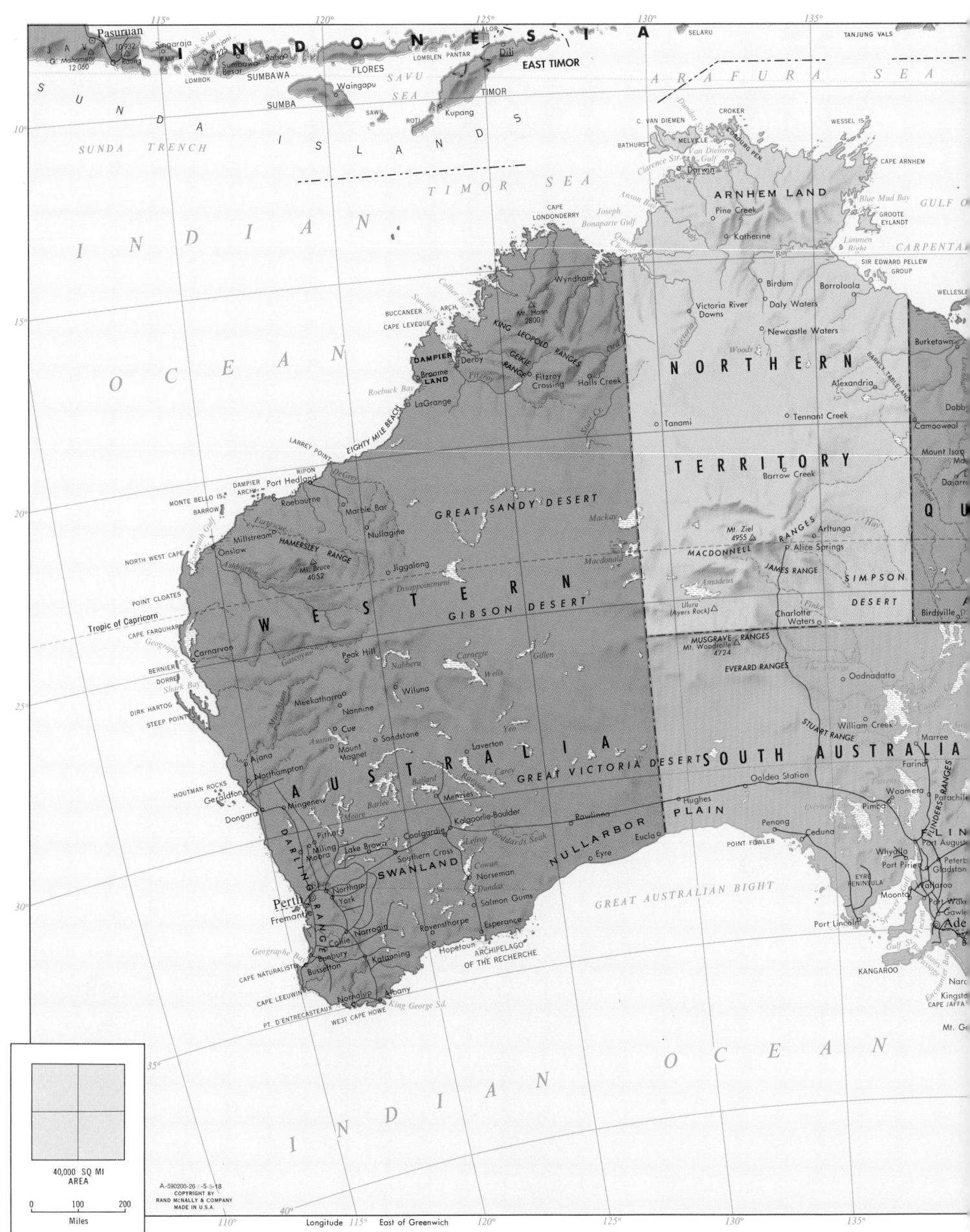

Longitude 115° East of Greenwich

Scale 1:16 000 000; one inch to 250 miles. Lambert's Azimuthal, Equal Area Projection

Elevations and depressions are given in feet

40,000 SQ MI
AREA

0   100   200
Miles

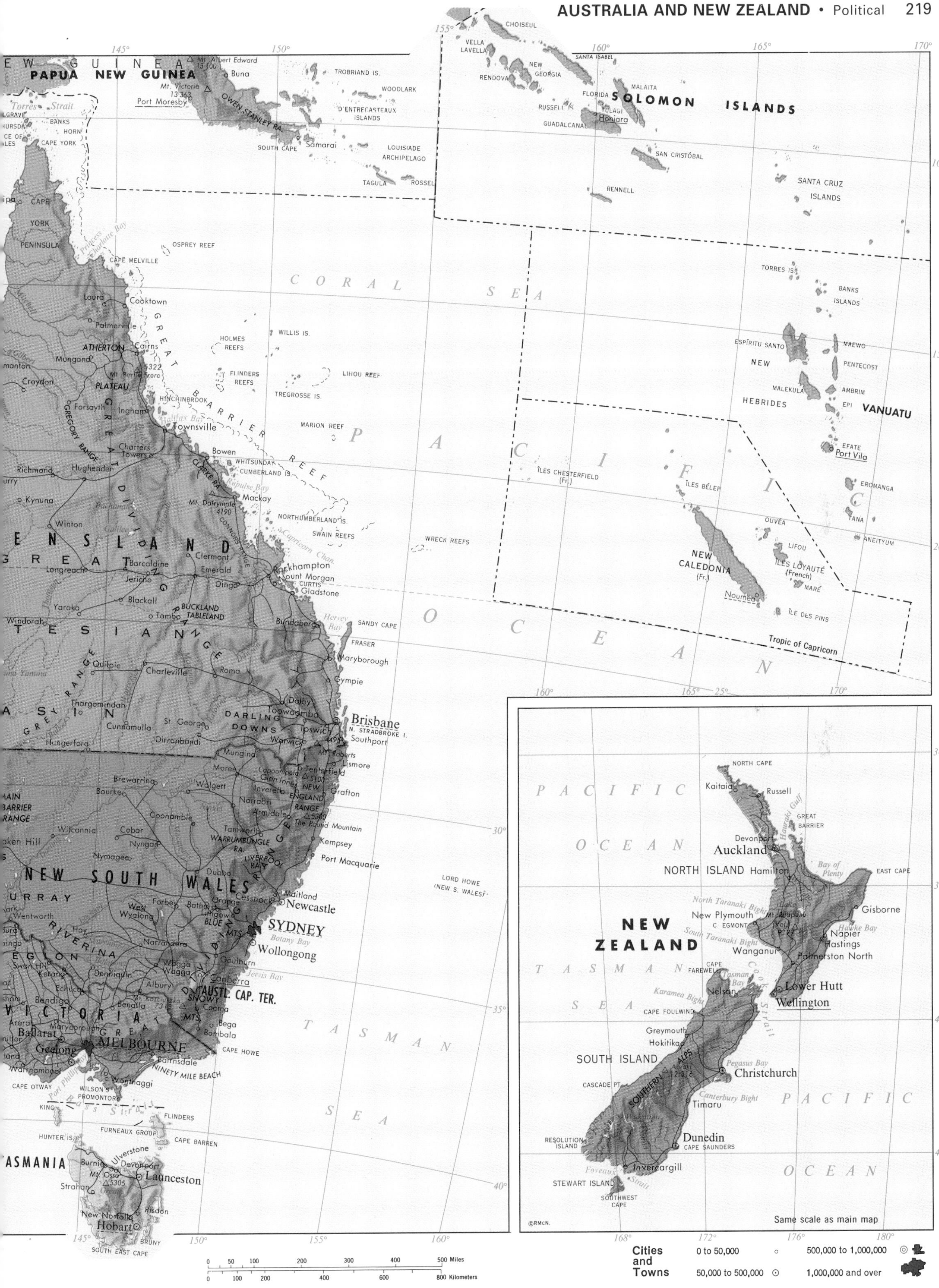

EW GUINEA
PAPUA NEW GUINEA
Mt. Albert Edward 13,100
Mt. Victoria 13,363
Port Moresby
Buna
TROBRIAND IS.
WOODLARK
D'ENTRECASTEAUX ISLANDS
Samarai
SOUTH CAPE
LOUISIADE ARCHIPELAGO
TAGULA
ROSSEL

CHOISEUL
VELLA LAVELLA
NEW GEORGIA
RENDOVA
RUSSELL IS.
SANTA ISABEL
FLORIDA
MALAITA
TULAGI
Honiara
GUADALCANAL
SOLOMON ISLANDS
SAN CRISTÓBAL
RENNELL
SANTA CRUZ ISLANDS

Torres Strait
BANKS
CE OF
THURSDAY
ales
GRAVE
HORN
CAPE YORK

CAPE
YORK
PENINSULA

CORAL SEA
PACIFIC OCEAN

TORRES IS.
BANKS ISLANDS

ESPÍRITU SANTO
MAEWO
NEW
MALEKULA
HEBRIDES
PENTECOST
AMBRIM
EPI
AMBAE
VANUATU
EFATE
Port Vila
EROMANGA
ÎLES CHESTERFIELD (Fr.)
ÎLES BÉLEP
OUVÉA
TANA
LIFOU
NEW CALEDONIA (Fr.)
ILES LOYAUTÉ (French)
MARÉ
ANEITYUM
Nouméa
ÎLE DES PINS

Tropic of Capricorn

OSPREY REEF
CAPE MELVILLE
Laura
Cooktown
Palmerville
ATHERTON
Cairns
Mungana
PLATEAU
Croydon
Forsayth
Ingham
HINCHINBROOK
Townsville
HOLMES REEFS
WILLIS IS.
FLINDERS REEFS
LIHOU REEF
TREGROSSE IS.
MARION REEF
Richmond
Hughenden
GREAT BARRIER REEF
Bowen
WHITSUNDAY
CUMBERLAND IS.
Repulse Bay
Mackay
NORTHUMBERLAND IS.
SWAIN REEFS
Mt. Dalrymple 4190
Winton
Clermont
Emerald
Dingo
Rockhampton
Mount Morgan
CURTIS
Gladstone
WRECK REEFS
Kynuna
ENSLAND
GREAT
Barcaldine
Longreach
Jericho
Blackall
Tambo
BUCKLAND TABLELAND
TESIAN
Bundaberg
Hervey Bay
SANDY CAPE
FRASER
Windorah
Quilpie
Charleville
Roma
Maryborough
Gympie
Thargomindah
Cunnamulla
St. George
Dalby
Toowoomba
DARLING DOWNS
Ipswich
Brisbane
N. STRADBROKE I.
Southport
Hungerford
Dirranbandi
Warwick
Roberts
Lismore
Brewarrina
Moree
Glen Innes
NEW ENGLAND RANGE
Grafton
MAIN BARRIER RANGE
Bourke
Walgett
Narrabri
Inverell
Armidale
The Round Mountain
Wilcannia
Coonamble
Tamworth
WARRUMBUNGLE RA.
Kempsey
Cobar
Nyngan
LIVERPOOL RANGE
Port Macquarie
Broken Hill
Nymagee
Dubbo
NEW SOUTH WALES
Maitland
Cessnock
Newcastle
MURRAY
Forbes
Bathurst
Orange
Lithgow
BLUE MTS.
Wyalong
RIVERINA
Narrandera
SNOWY MTS.
SYDNEY
Botany Bay
Wollongong
Hay
Wagga Wagga
Albury
Canberra
AUSTL. CAP. TER.
Jervis Bay
REGION
Cooma
Bega
Bombala
VICTORIA
Benalla
CAPE HOWE
Ballarat
MELBOURNE
Geelong
NINETY MILE BEACH
WILSON PROMONTORY
KING
FLINDERS
FURNEAUX GROUP
CAPE BARREN
HUNTER IS.
Burnie
Ulverstone
Devonport
Mt. Ossa 5305
Launceston
ASMANIA
Strahan
New Norfolk
Risdon
Hobart
SOUTH EAST CAPE
BRUNY

TASMAN SEA

LORD HOWE (NEW S. WALES)

NEW ZEALAND inset

PACIFIC OCEAN
NORTH CAPE
Kaitaia
Russell
Devonport
Auckland
NORTH ISLAND
Hamilton
Bay of Plenty
GREAT BARRIER
Hauraki Gulf
EAST CAPE
North Taranaki Bight
New Plymouth
C. EGMONT
Gisborne
South Taranaki Bight
Napier
Hastings
Wanganui
Palmerston North
NEW ZEALAND
CAPE FAREWELL
Tasman Bay
Nelson
Cook Strait
Lower Hutt
Wellington
Karamea Bight
CAPE FOULWIND
Greymouth
Hokitika
SOUTH ISLAND
SOUTHERN ALPS
Pegasus Bay
Christchurch
CASCADE PT.
Canterbury Bight
Timaru
RESOLUTION ISLAND
Dunedin
CAPE SAUNDERS
Foveaux Strait
Invercargill
STEWART ISLAND
SOUTHWEST CAPE
PACIFIC OCEAN
TASMAN SEA

Same scale as main map

Cities and Towns
0 to 50,000
50,000 to 500,000
500,000 to 1,000,000
1,000,000 and over

0 50 100 200 300 400 500 Miles
0 200 400 600 800 Kilometers

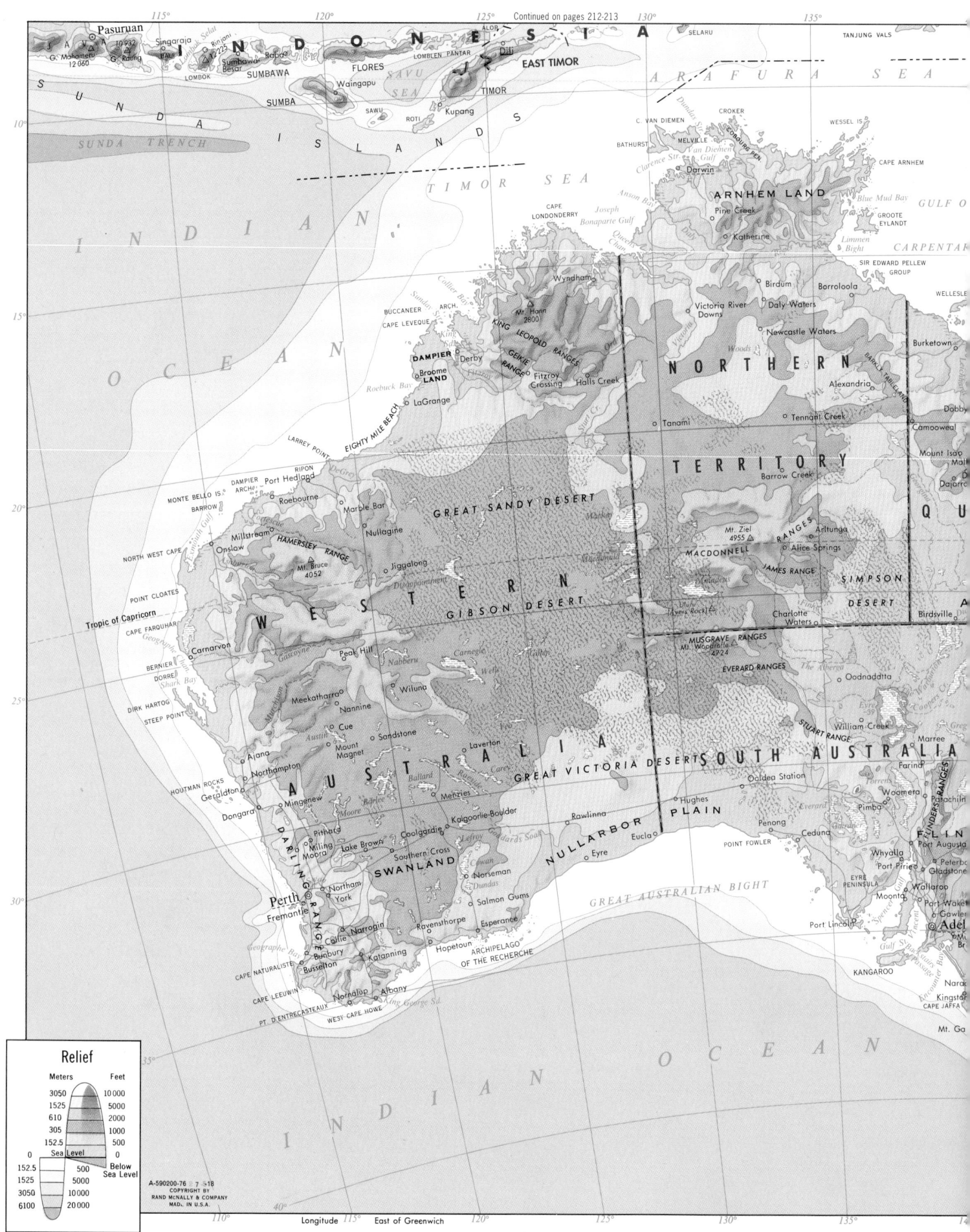

Continued on pages 212-213

I N D O N E S I A

Pasuruan

J A V A

G. Mahameru
12 060

G. Raung

Singaraja
BALI
Rinjani
3726

Sumbawa
Besar

SUMBAWA

Rapa

SUMBAWA

LOMBOK

SUMBA

Waingapu

SAWU

ROTI

SAVU
SEA

FLORES

LOMBLEN PANTAR

TIMOR

Kupang

ALOR

Dili

EAST TIMOR

SELARU

A R A F U R A   S E A

TANJUNG VALS

SUNDA
ISLANDS

S U N D A

I S L A N D S

SUNDA   TRENCH

I N D I A N

O C E A N

T I M O R   S E A

CAPE
LONDONDERRY

Joseph
Bonaparte Gulf

C. VAN DIEMEN

Van Diemen
Gulf

Darwin

BATHURST

MELVILLE

Clarence Str.

CROKER

Anson Bay

Quessy Chan.

Dundas Str.

COBOURG PEN.

WESSEL IS.

CAPE ARNHEM

A R N H E M   L A N D

Pine Creek

Katherine

Blue Mud Bay

GROOTE
EYLANDT

Limmen
Bight

GULF O

CARPENTAR

SIR EDWARD PELLEW
GROUP

WELLESLE

Wyndham

Mt. Hann
2800

KING LEOPOLD RANGES

GEIKIE
RANGE

Fitzroy
Crossing

Halls Creek

Victoria River
Downs

Daly Waters

Newcastle Waters

Birdum

Woods

Borroloola

Burketown

BUCCANEER   ARCH.

CAPE LEVEQUE

Sunday Is.

King
Sd.

Collier Bay

DAMPIER
LAND

Derby

BROOME
LAND

Broome

Roebuck Bay

LaGrange

Ord

Victoria

Spur Cr.

N O R T H E R N

Dobby

Camooweal

Tanami

Tennant Creek

T E R R I T O R Y

BARKLY TABLELAND

Mount Iso

Daiarre

Q U

LARREY POINT

EIGHTY MILE BEACH

DAMPIER
ARCH.

Port Hedland

De Grey

MONTE BELLO IS.

BARROW

NORTH WEST CAPE

Roebourne

Marble Bar

Nullagine

GREAT SANDY DESERT

Barrow Creek

Mt. Ziel
4955

MACDONNELL

RANGES

Arltunga

Alice Springs

JAMES RANGE

SIMPSON

DESERT

Fortescue Gulf

Millstream

Onslow

HAMERSLEY RANGE

Mt. Bruce
4052

Jiggalong

Disappointment

Macumba

Ulura
(Ayers Rock)

Charlotte
Waters

Birdsville

A

POINT CLOATES

W E S T E R N

GIBSON DESERT

Tropic of Capricorn

CAPE FARQUHAR

Geographe

Carnarvon

Gascoyne

Peak Hill

Nabberu

Carnegie

Walton

Oodnadatta

MUSGRAVE RANGES

Mt. Woodroffe
4724

EVERARD RANGES

The Alberga

BERNIER I.

DORRE I.

Shark Bay

DIRK HARTOG

STEEP POINT

Meekatharra

Nannine

Wiluna

Welld

A U S T R A L I A

Laverton

S O U T H   A U S T R A L I A

STUART RANGE

William Creek

Marree

Farina

FLINDERS RANGES

Cue

Sandstone

Austin

Ajana

Mount
Magnet

Northampton

HOUTMAN ROCKS

Geraldton

Ballard

Menzies

Revenue

Carey

GREAT VICTORIA DESERT

Oaldea Station

Woomera

Pimba

F L I N

Patachinka

Dongara

Mingenew

Moore

Kalgoorlie-Boulder

Coolgardie

Rawlinna

Hughes

Penong

Ceduna

Whyalla

Port Pirie

Peterbo

Port Augusta

Pithara

Miling

Moora

Lake Brown

Southern Cross

Lefroy

Cowan

Goddards Soak

Eucla

NULLARBOR   PLAIN

POINT FOWLER

EYRE
PENINSULA

Moonta

Port Wake

Gawler

Adel

Perth

Fremantle

Northam

York

DARLING RANGE

Narrogin

Collie

SWANLAND

Norseman

Dundas

Salmon Gums

Ravensthorpe

Esperance

Hopetoun

Eyre

GREAT AUSTRALIAN BIGHT

Port Lincoln

Spencer Gulf

Gulf St. Vincent

KANGAROO

Nara

Kingsto

CAPE JAFFA

Geographe Bay

Bunbury

Busselton

CAPE NATURALISTE

CAPE LEEUWIN

Nornalup

Albany

King George Sd.

PT. D'ENTRECASTEAUX

WEST CAPE HOWE

ARCHIPELAGO
OF THE RECHERCHE

Mt. Ga

I N D I A N   O C E A N

A-590200-76   7 -18
COPYRIGHT BY
RAND McNALLY & COMPANY
MADE IN U.S.A.

Relief

Meters		Feet
3050		10 000
1525		5000
610		2000
305		1000
152.5		500
0	Sea Level	0
152.5		500	Below
1525		5000	Sea Level
3050		10 000
6100		20 000

Longitude   115°   East of Greenwich

Scale 1:16 000 000; one inch to 250 miles. Lambert's Azimuthal, Equal Area Projection
Elevations and depressions are given in feet

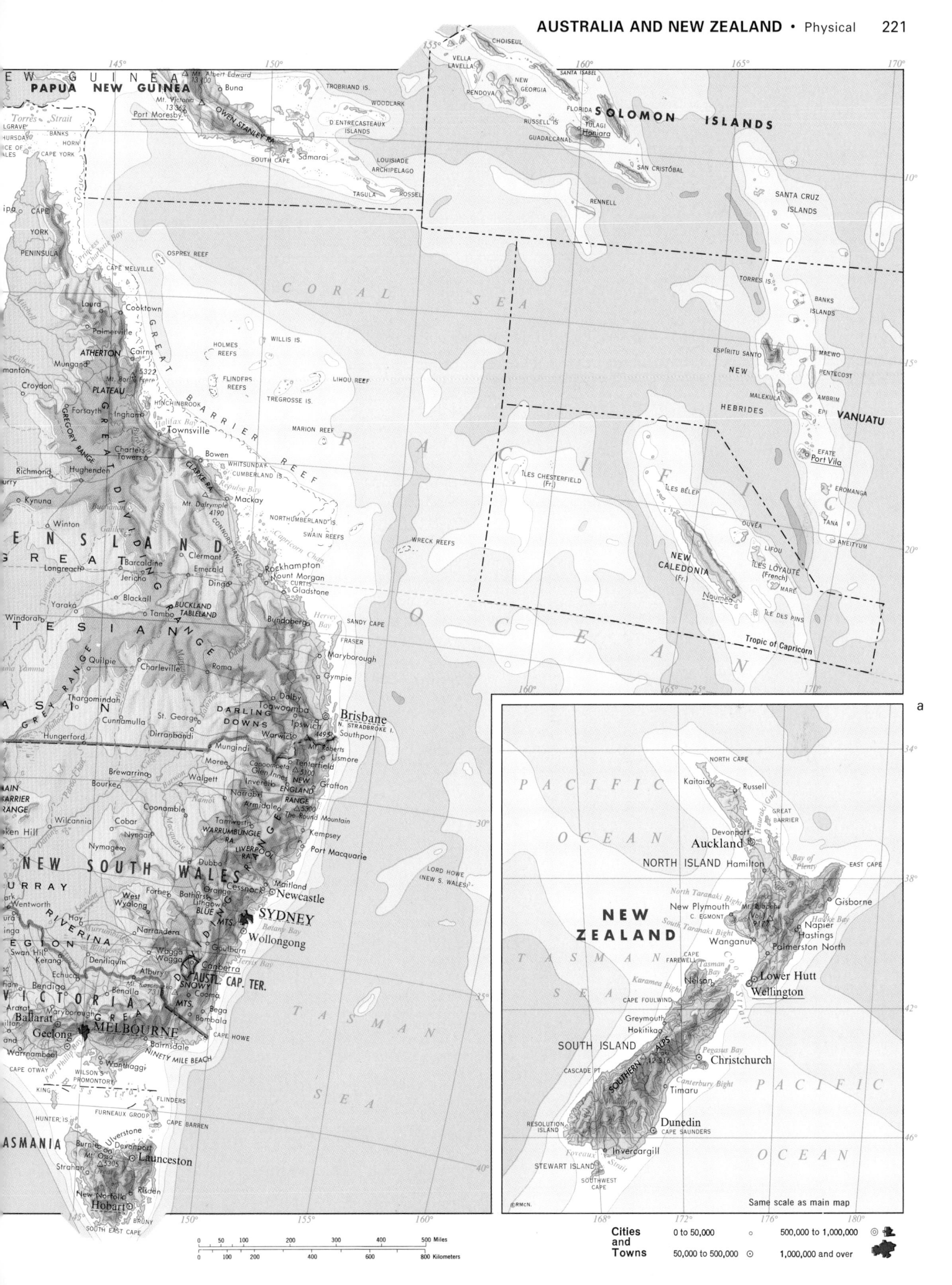

NEW GUINEA
PAPUA NEW GUINEA
Mt. Albert Edward 13,100
Mt. Victoria 13,363
Owen Stanley Ra.
Buna
Port Moresby
TROBRIAND IS.
D'ENTRECASTEAUX ISLANDS
WOODLARK
SOUTH CAPE
Samarai
LOUISIADE ARCHIPELAGO
TAGULA
ROSSEL

Torres Strait
BANKS
HORN
CAPE OF
THURSDAY
ALES
LGRAVE
CAPE YORK

CHOISEUL
VELLA LAVELLA
RENDOVA
NEW GEORGIA
SANTA ISABEL
FLORIDA
RUSSELL IS.
TULAGI
Honiara
GUADALCANAL
SAN CRISTÓBAL
RENNELL
SOLOMON ISLANDS
SANTA CRUZ ISLANDS

CAPE YORK PENINSULA
CAPE MELVILLE
OSPREY REEF
Princess Charlotte Bay

C O R A L   S E A

TORRES IS.
BANKS ISLANDS

Laura
Cooktown
ATHERTON
PLATEAU
Mungana
Croydon
manton
Forsyth
GREGORY RANGE
Mt. Bartle Frere 5322
Cairns
Ingham
Townsville
Halifax Bay
HINCHINBROOK I.
GREAT BARRIER REEF
HOLMES REEFS
FLINDERS REEFS
WILLIS IS.
TREGROSSE IS.
MARION REEF
LIHOU REEF

P A C I F I C

ESPÍRITU SANTO
MAEWO
PENTECOST
NEW
HEBRIDES
MALEKULA
AMBRIM
EPI
EFATE
Port Vila
VANUATU

Richmond
Hughenden
Charters Towers
Bowen
WHITSUNDAY
CUMBERLAND IS.
Repulse Bay
Mackay
NORTHUMBERLAND IS.
SWAIN REEFS
CLARKE RA.

Kynuna
Winton
Buchanan
Galilee
D I V I D I N G
Q U E E N S L A N D
Mt. Dalrymple 4190
CONNORS RANGE
ÎLES CHESTERFIELD (Fr.)

ÎLES BÉLEP
EROMANGA
TANA
ANEITYUM
OUVÉA
LIFOU
ÎLES LOYAUTÉ (French)
NEW CALEDONIA (Fr.)
Nouméa
MARÉ
ÎLE DES PINS

Longreach
Barcaldine
Jericho
Clermont
Emerald
Dingo
Mount Morgan
CURTIS
Gladstone
Rockhampton
Capricorn Chan.

G R E A T
Blackall
BUCKLAND TABLELAND
Tambo
Bundaberg
Hervey Bay
FRASER
SANDY CAPE

WRECK REEFS

Yaraka
Windorah
ma Yamma
Quilpie
Charleville
Roma
Maryborough
Gympie

O C E A N

Thargomindah
Cunnamulla
St. George
Dalby
Toowoomba
Ipswich
DARLING DOWNS
Warwick
Brisbane
N. STRADBROKE I.
Southport

Tropic of Capricorn

160°   165°   170°

Hungerford
Dirranbandi
Mungindi
Mt. Roberts 4495
Tenterfield
NEW ENGLAND RANGE
Casino
Lismore
Grafton

MAIN BARRIER RANGE
Wilcannia
Bourke
Brewarrina
Walgett
Moree
Coonamble
Narrabri
Armidale
The Round Mountain 5300
Cacoombeta 5300
Glen Innes
Inverell
Tamworth
Kempsey
Port Macquarie

ken Hill
Cobar
Nyngan
WARRUMBUNGLE RA.
LIVERPOOL RA.

LORD HOWE I.
(NEW S. WALES)

NEW SOUTH WALES
Nymagee
Dubbo
Coonabarabran
Wellington
Forbes
Bathurst
Orange
Lithgow
Maitland
Cessnock
Newcastle
Narrandera
West Wyalong
BLUE MTS.
SYDNEY
Botany Bay
Wollongong

URRAY
RIVERINA
Wentworth
Hay
Narrandera
Wagga Wagga
Goulburn
Jervis Bay

EGION
Swan Hill
Kerang
Deniliquin
Albury
Canberra
AUSTL. CAP. TER.
Cooma
Bega
Bombala
CAPE HOWE

nga
Echuca
Bendigo
Maryborough
Benalla
SNOWY MTS.
Mt. Kosciusko 7316
GREAT DIVIDING RANGE

VICTORIA
Ararat
hilton
Ballarat
Geelong
MELBOURNE
Bairnsdale
NINETY MILE BEACH
and
Warrnambool
CAPE OTWAY
Wonthaggi
WILSON'S PROMONTORY
Port Phillip
KING
Bass Strait
FLINDERS
FURNEAUX GROUP
HUNTER IS.
CAPE BARREN
CAPE BARREN

T A S M A N

S E A

ASMANIA
Burnie
Ulverstone
Devonport
Mt. Ossa 5305
Strahan
New Norfolk
Hobart
Risdon
BRUNY
SOUTH EAST CAPE
Launceston

145°   150°   155°   160°

0   50 100   200   300   400   500 Miles
0   100   200   400   600   800 Kilometers

Inset — New Zealand:

a

PACIFIC
OCEAN

NORTH CAPE
Kaitaia
Russell
Devonport
Auckland
NORTH ISLAND
Hamilton
Huraki Gulf
GREAT BARRIER
Bay of Plenty
EAST CAPE

North Taranaki Bight
New Plymouth
C. EGMONT
South Taranaki Bight
Mt. Egmont Vol.
Gisborne
Napier
Hastings
Wanganui
Palmerston North

NEW ZEALAND

T A S M A N
CAPE FAREWELL
Tasman Bay
Karamea Bight
Nelson
Lower Hutt
Wellington

S E A
CAPE FOULWIND
Greymouth
Hokitika
SOUTH ISLAND
CASCADE PT.
Pegasus Bay
Christchurch
SOUTHERN ALPS 12,316
Canterbury Bight
Timaru

P A C I F I C

RESOLUTION ISLAND
Dunedin
CAPE SAUNDERS
Foveaux Str.
Invercargill
STEWART ISLAND
SOUTHWEST CAPE
RMCN.

OCEAN

Same scale as main map

34°   38°   42°   46°

168°   172°   176°   180°

Cities and Towns

0 to 50,000 ○	500,000 to 1,000,000 ◎
50,000 to 500,000 ⊙	1,000,000 and over

SIMPSON DESERT

Peera Peera Poolanna L.

L. Machattie

L. Moonda

Lake Yamma Yamma

Cooper

Welford

Yaraka

Windorah

Tambo

GREAT

QUEENSLAND

GREAT

Birdsville

Durham Downs

Innamincka

Lake Eyre

L. Gregory

L. Blanche

Lake Callabonna

Marree

Leigh Creek

Hawker

Quorn

Lake Torrens

Andamooka

Woomera

Pimba

SOUTH

AUSTRALIA

Port Augusta

Wilmington

Peterborough

Whyalla

Iron Knob

Kimba

GAWLER RANGES

Moonta

Wallaroo

Port Pirie

Gladstone

Riverton

Morgan

EYRE PEN

Port Lincoln

Port Wakefield

Gawler

ADELAIDE

YORKE PENINSULA

Yorketown

Murray Bridge

Tailem Bend

THISTLE

Investigator Strait

Victor Harbour

Kingscote

KANGAROO

Encounter Bay

Gulf St. Vincent

Spencer Gulf

Goyder

Coopers

Thargomindah

Naryilco

Hungerford

Bulloo L.

Caryapundy Swamp

Mt. Sturt 1400

White Cliffs

Wilcannia

Broken Hill

Menindee

L. Tandou

MURRAY

Pinnaroo

Peebinga

Ouyen

Kulwin

Tyrrell

REGION

Swan Hill

Kerang

Cohuna

Echuca

Cunnamulla

St. George

Dirranbandi

Mungindi

Brewarrina

Bourke

Narran Lake

Cobar

Nymagee

Tottenham

Ivanhoe

Roto

Hillston

Hay

Balranald

Deniliquin

NEW SOUTH

WALES

RIVERINA

Narrandera

Coolamon

Wagga Wagga

Griffith

West Wyalong

Young

Cootamundra

Cunnamulla

Charleville

Augathella

Quilpie

ARTESIAN

GREAT

BREYAN

BASIN

DARLING DOWNS

Surat

Meandarra

Roma

Miles

Barakula

Chinchilla

Dalby

Toowoomba

Warwick

Goondiwindi

Inglewood

Texas

Moree

Pokataroo

Walgett

Wee Waa

Narrabri

Gwabegar

Coonamble

Gunnedah

Nyngan

Narromine

Dubbo

Wellington

Parkes

Forbes

Orange

Eugowra

Cowra

GREAT DIVIDING RANGE

Mt. Roberts 4495

Lismore

Casino

Ballina

Grafton

Coff's Harbour

Guyra

Armidale

Tamworth

Mt. Banda Banda 4144

Port Macquarie

Kempsey

Taree

WARRUMBUNGLE RANGE

LIVERPOOL

Coolah

Merriwa

Muswellbrook

Maitland

Cessnock

Newcastle

Gosford

Broken Bay

SYDNEY

Botany Bay

Wollongong

Nowra

Goulburn

Canberra

AUSTL. CAP. TER.

SNOWY MTS.

Cooma

Bega

Eden

Bombala

Orbost

CAPE HOWE

GIPPSLAND

Bairnsdale

Lakes Entrance

NINETY MILE BEACH

Sale

Yarram

Corner Inlet

WILSON'S PROMONTORY

Bass Strait

KING

Grassy

FLINDERS

FURNEAUX GROUP

CAPE BARREN

Banks Strait

TASMANIA

Launceston

Deloraine

St. Marys

Campbell Town

Hobart

INDIAN

OCEAN

TASMAN

SEA

A-590298-76 5-10
COPYRIGHT BY
RAND McNALLY & COMPANY
MADE IN U.S.A.

Scale 1:8 000 000; one inch to 126 miles.
Lambert's Azimuthal, Equal Area Projection.
Elevations and depressions are given in feet.

Relief

Meters	Feet
1525	5000
610	2000
305	1000
152.5	500
0 Sea Level	0
152.5	500 Below
1525	5000 Sea Level
3050	10 000

140° Longitude East of Greenwich

0 50 100 150 200 Miles

0 50 100 150 200 250 300 Kilometers

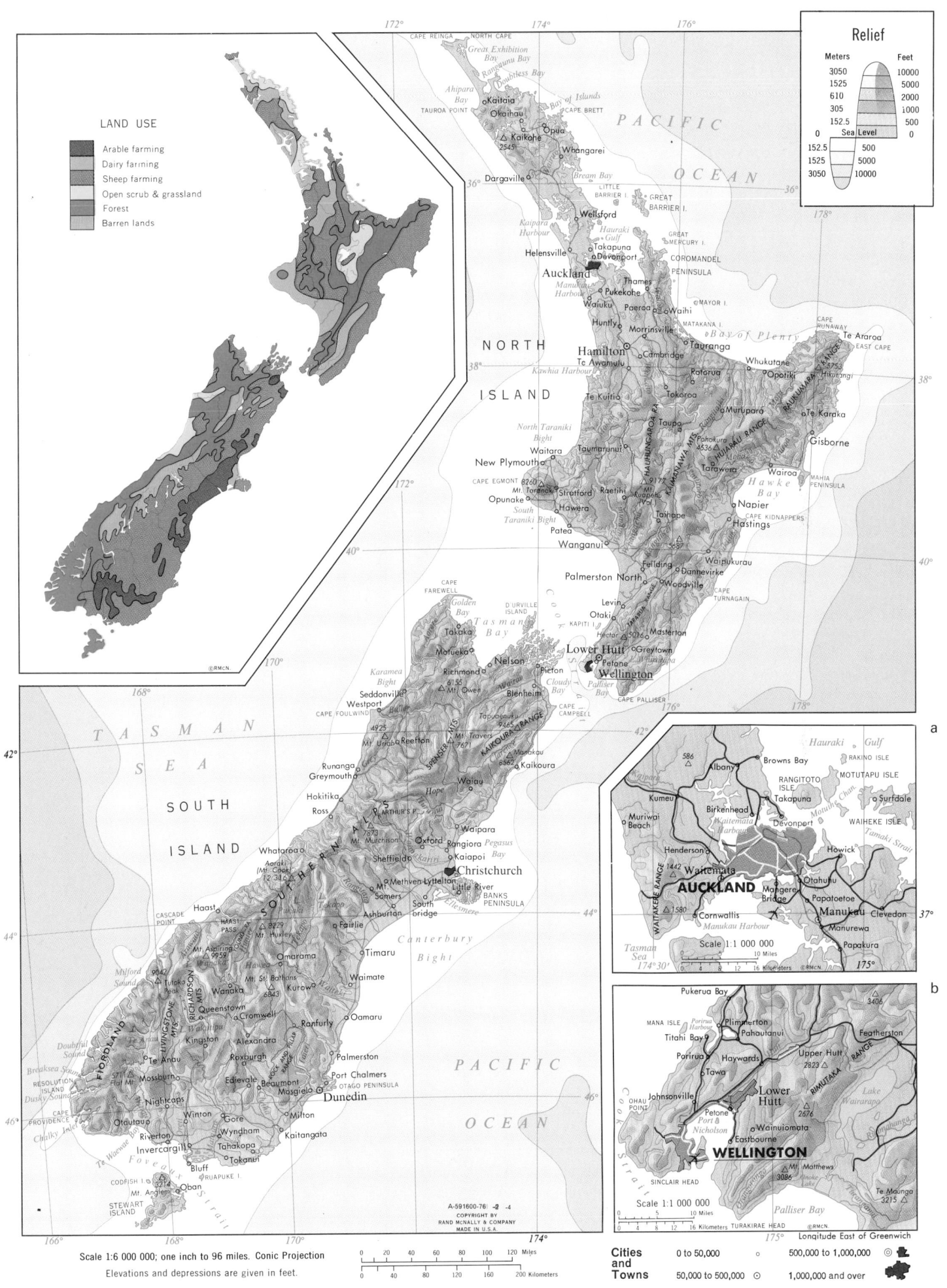

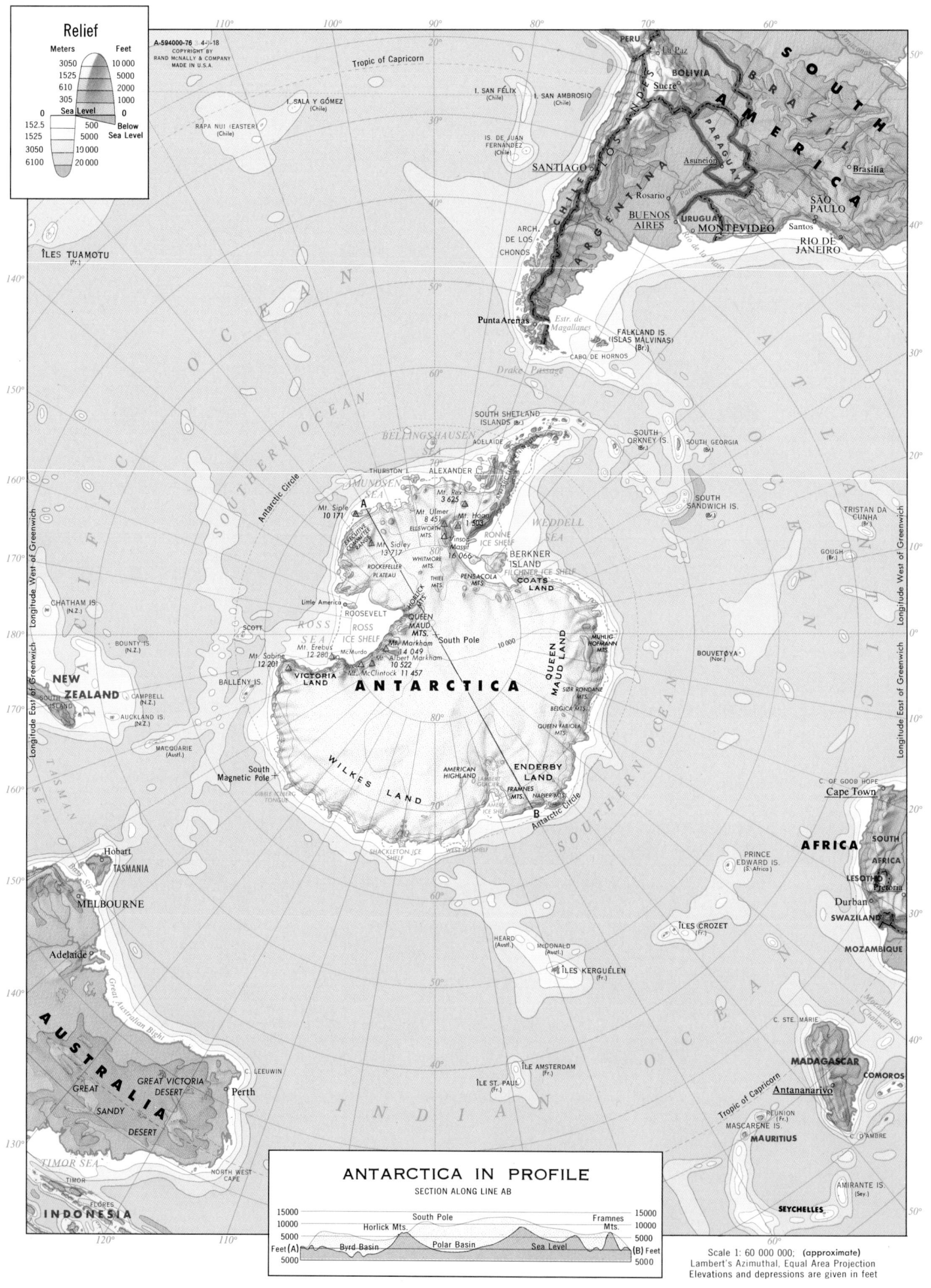

Relief

Meters		Feet
3050		10 000
1525		5000
610		2000
305		1000
0	Sea Level	0
152.5		500
1525		5000
3050	Below	19 000
6100	Sea Level	20 000

A-594000-76 4-7-18
COPYRIGHT BY
RAND McNALLY & COMPANY
MADE IN U.S.A.

Tropic of Capricorn

ANTARCTICA IN PROFILE
SECTION ALONG LINE AB

Scale 1: 60 000 000; (approximate)
Lambert's Azimuthal, Equal Area Projection
Elevations and depressions are given in feet

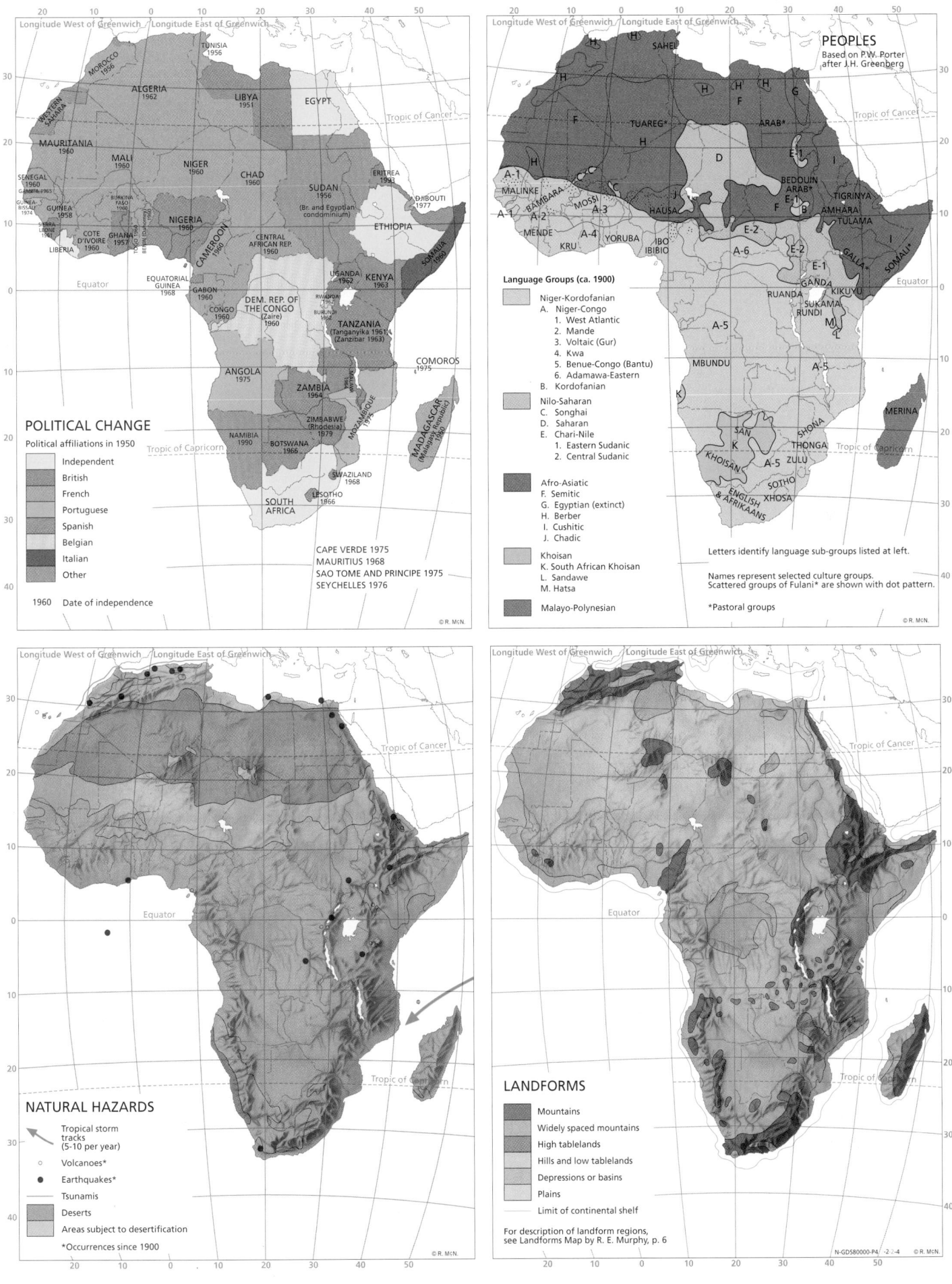

POLITICAL CHANGE

Political affiliations in 1950

- Independent
- British
- French
- Portuguese
- Spanish
- Belgian
- Italian
- Other

1960   Date of independence

CAPE VERDE 1975
MAURITIUS 1968
SAO TOME AND PRINCIPE 1975
SEYCHELLES 1976

© R. McN.

Political Change map labels

MOROCCO 1956
TUNISIA 1956
ALGERIA 1962
LIBYA 1951
EGYPT
WESTERN SAHARA
MAURITANIA 1960
MALI 1960
NIGER 1960
CHAD 1960
SUDAN 1956 (Br. and Egyptian condominium)
ERITREA 1993
DJIBOUTI 1977
SENEGAL 1960
GAMBIA 1965
GUINEA BISSAU 1974
GUINEA 1958
SIERRA LEONE 1961
COTE D'IVOIRE 1960
BURKINA FASO 1960
GHANA 1957
TOGO 1960
BENIN (Dahomey) 1960
NIGERIA 1960
LIBERIA
CAMEROON 1960
CENTRAL AFRICAN REP. 1960
ETHIOPIA
SOMALIA 1960
EQUATORIAL GUINEA 1968
GABON 1960
CONGO 1960
DEM. REP. OF THE CONGO (Zaire) 1960
RWANDA 1962
BURUNDI 1962
UGANDA 1962
KENYA 1963
COMOROS 1975
TANZANIA (Tanganyika 1961/4) (Zanzibar 1963)
ANGOLA 1975
ZAMBIA 1964
MALAWI 1964
MOZAMBIQUE 1975
MADAGASCAR (Malagasy Republic) 1960
NAMIBIA 1990
ZIMBABWE (Rhodesia) 1979
BOTSWANA 1966
SWAZILAND 1968
LESOTHO 1966
SOUTH AFRICA

PEOPLES

Based on P.W. Porter
after J.H. Greenberg

Language Groups (ca. 1900)

Niger-Kordofanian
A. Niger-Congo
1. West Atlantic
2. Mande
3. Voltaic (Gur)
4. Kwa
5. Benue-Congo (Bantu)
6. Adamawa-Eastern
B. Kordofanian

Nilo-Saharan
C. Songhai
D. Saharan
E. Chari-Nile
1. Eastern Sudanic
2. Central Sudanic

Afro-Asiatic
F. Semitic
G. Egyptian (extinct)
H. Berber
I. Cushitic
J. Chadic

Khoisan
K. South African Khoisan
L. Sandawe
M. Hatsa

Malayo-Polynesian

Letters identify language sub-groups listed at left.

Names represent selected culture groups.
Scattered groups of Fulani* are shown with dot pattern.

*Pastoral groups

© R. McN.

Peoples map labels

SAHEL
TUAREG*
ARAB*
BEDOUIN ARAB*
TIGRINYA
AMHARA
TULAMA
GALLA*
SOMALI*
MALINKE
BAMBARA
MOSSI
HAUSA
MENDE
KRU
YORUBA
IBO
IBIBIO
RUANDA
GANDA
KIKUYU
SUKAMA
RUNDI
MBUNDU
SAN
KHOISAN
SHONA
THONGA
ZULU
SOTHO
XHOSA
ENGLISH & AFRIKAANS
MERINA

NATURAL HAZARDS

- Tropical storm tracks (5-10 per year)
- ○ Volcanoes*
- ● Earthquakes*
- Tsunamis
- Deserts
- Areas subject to desertification

*Occurrences since 1900

© R. McN.

LANDFORMS

- Mountains
- Widely spaced mountains
- High tablelands
- Hills and low tablelands
- Depressions or basins
- Plains
- Limit of continental shelf

For description of landform regions,
see Landforms Map by R. E. Murphy, p. 6

N-GDS80000-P4/-2-2-4   © R. McN.

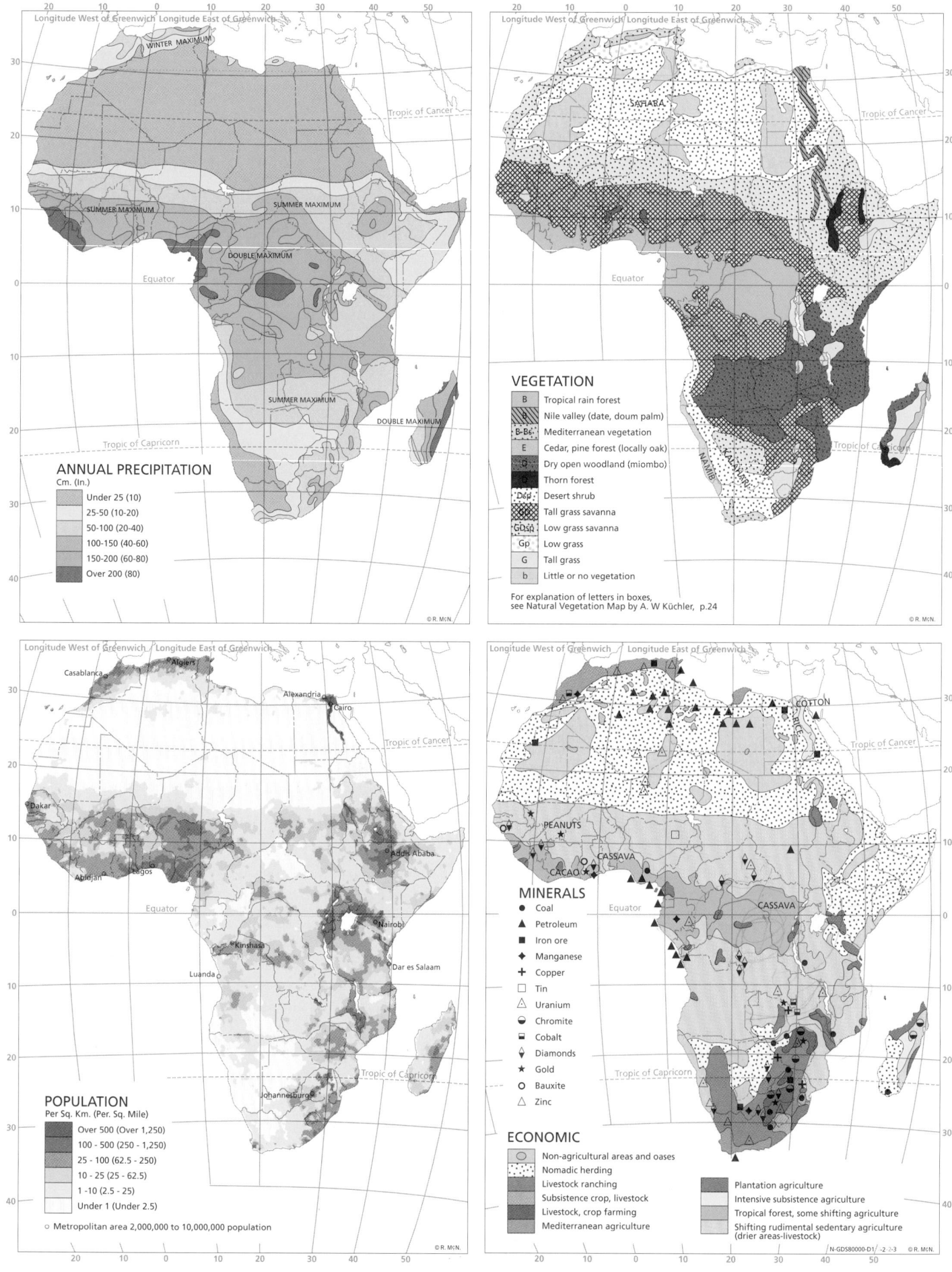

ANNUAL PRECIPITATION
Cm. (In.)

- Under 25 (10)
- 25-50 (10-20)
- 50-100 (20-40)
- 100-150 (40-60)
- 150-200 (60-80)
- Over 200 (80)

VEGETATION

B	Tropical rain forest
	Nile valley (date, doum palm)
B-Bs	Mediterranean vegetation
E	Cedar, pine forest (locally oak)
D	Dry open woodland (miombo)
D	Thorn forest
Dsp	Desert shrub
	Tall grass savanna
GDSp	Low grass savanna
Gp	Low grass
G	Tall grass
b	Little or no vegetation

For explanation of letters in boxes,
see Natural Vegetation Map by A. W Küchler, p.24

POPULATION
Per Sq. Km. (Per. Sq. Mile)

- Over 500 (Over 1,250)
- 100 - 500 (250 - 1,250)
- 25 - 100 (62.5 - 250)
- 10 - 25 (25 - 62.5)
- 1 - 10 (2.5 - 25)
- Under 1 (Under 2.5)

○ Metropolitan area 2,000,000 to 10,000,000 population

MINERALS

- ● Coal
- ▲ Petroleum
- ■ Iron ore
- ◆ Manganese
- ＋ Copper
- □ Tin
- △ Uranium
- ◔ Chromite
- ▱ Cobalt
- ⬦ Diamonds
- ★ Gold
- ○ Bauxite
- △ Zinc

ECONOMIC

- Non-agricultural areas and oases
- Nomadic herding
- Livestock ranching
- Subsistence crop, livestock
- Livestock, crop farming
- Mediterranean agriculture
- Plantation agriculture
- Intensive subsistence agriculture
- Tropical forest, some shifting agriculture
- Shifting rudimental sedentary agriculture (drier areas-livestock)

N-GDS80000-D1 -2 2-3 © R. McN.

ATLANTIC OCEAN

MADRID

CORSICA
ROME
SARDINIA
SICILY
MALTA
CRETE
CYPRUS

Black Sea
İSTANBUL
BAKU
Caspian Sea

Athens

TEHRAN

Algiers
Tunis
Tripoli
Banghāzī
Casablanca

ATLAS MOUNTAINS

CANARY ISLANDS

El Aaiún

Tropic of Cancer

GRAND ERG OCCIDENTAL

GRAND ERG ORIENTAL

AHAGGAR

Beirut
SYRIAN DESERT
Baghdad
Euphrates
Tigris

Alexandria
CAIRO
ARABIAN DESERT
Red Sea

LIBYAN DESERT

Lake Nasser
NUBIAN DESERT

AN NAFŪD

Riyadh

Mecca

Mediterranean Sea

EL DJOUF

S A H A R A

ADRAR DES IFÔGHAS

TIBESTI

ENNEDI

Tamenghest

Tombouctou

S U D A N

Dakar
Bamako
Niger
Kano
Lake Chad
N'Djamena
Al-Fāshir
Khartoum
Asmera
DANAKIL

Aden
Gulf of Aden
Berbera

White Nile
Blue Nile
Addis Ababa

Freetown
Niger
Lake Volta
Lagos
Abidjan

Gulf of Guinea

Equator

Yaoundé

Bangui
Uele
Congo
Ubangi
Kisangani
Mountain Nile

Lake Victoria
Nairobi

Mogadishu

INDIAN OCEAN

Congo
Kinshasa
Kasai

Luanda

ATLANTIC OCEAN

Lake Tanganyika

Dar es Salaam

Lubumbashi
Lake Nyasa

COMORO ISLANDS

Lusaka

Zambezi

Blantyre
Moçambique

Harare

Mozambique Channel

MADAGASCAR

Antananarivo

NAMIB DESERT

Tropic of Capricorn

Windhoek
KALAHARI DESERT
Limpopo

Orange

Johannesburg

Orange

Durban

INDIAN OCEAN

Cape Town

Legend:
- Urban
- Cropland
- Cropland & Woodland
- Cropland & Grazing Land
- Grassland, Grazing Land
- Forest, Woodland
- Swamp, Marshland
- Shrub, Sparse Grass, Wasteland
- Barren Land
- Oasis

A-580000-36 -2 3-13
COPYRIGHT BY
RAND McNALLY & COMPANY
MADE IN U.S.A.

Scale 1:36,000,000; one inch to 570 miles.   Lambert Azimuthal Equal-Area Projection

0 100 200 400 600 800 Miles
0 150 300 600 900 1200 Kilometers

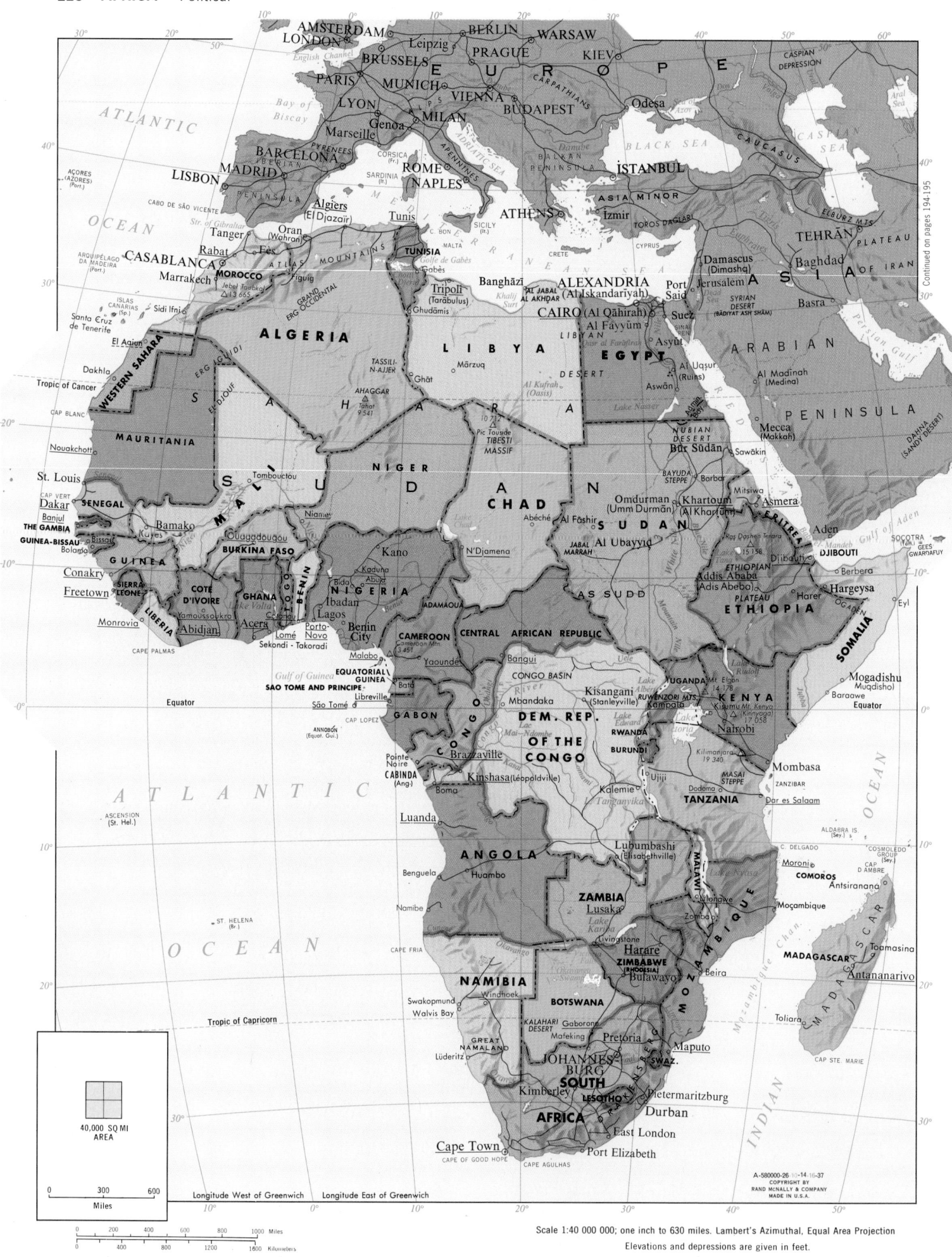

Scale 1:40 000 000; one inch to 630 miles. Lambert's Azimuthal, Equal Area Projection
Elevations and depressions are given in feet.

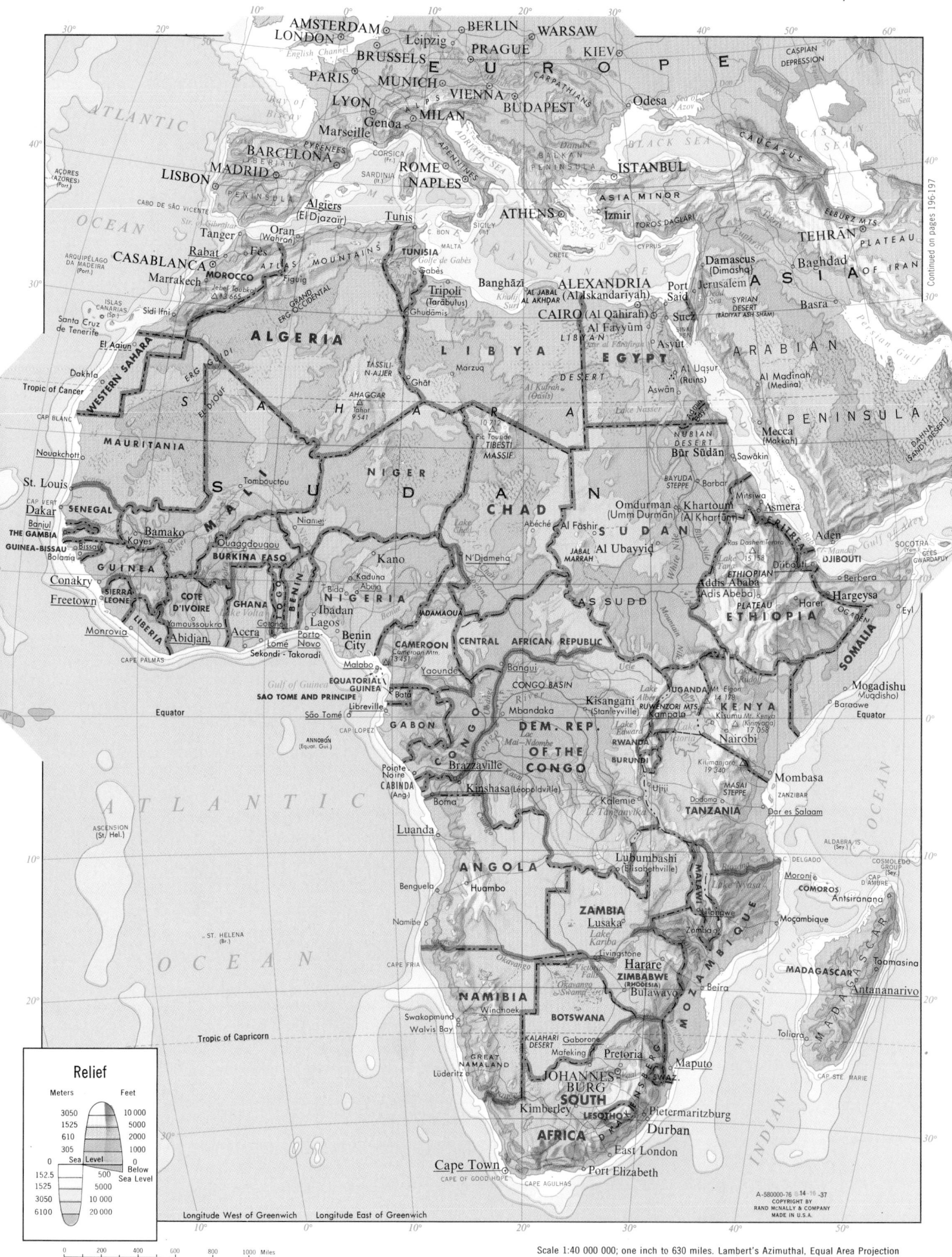

Continued on pages 196-197

Relief

Meters		Feet
3050		10 000
1525		5000
610		2000
305		1000
0	Sea Level	0
152.5		500 Below
1525		5000 Sea Level
3050		10 000
6100		20 000

Longitude West of Greenwich   Longitude East of Greenwich

0   200   400   600   800   1000 Miles
0   400   800   1200   1600 Kilometers

A-580000-76 ⓈⒽ 14-19 -37
COPYRIGHT BY
RAND MCNALLY & COMPANY
MADE IN U.S.A.

Scale 1:40 000 000; one inch to 630 miles. Lambert's Azimuthal, Equal Area Projection
Elevations and depressions are given in feet.

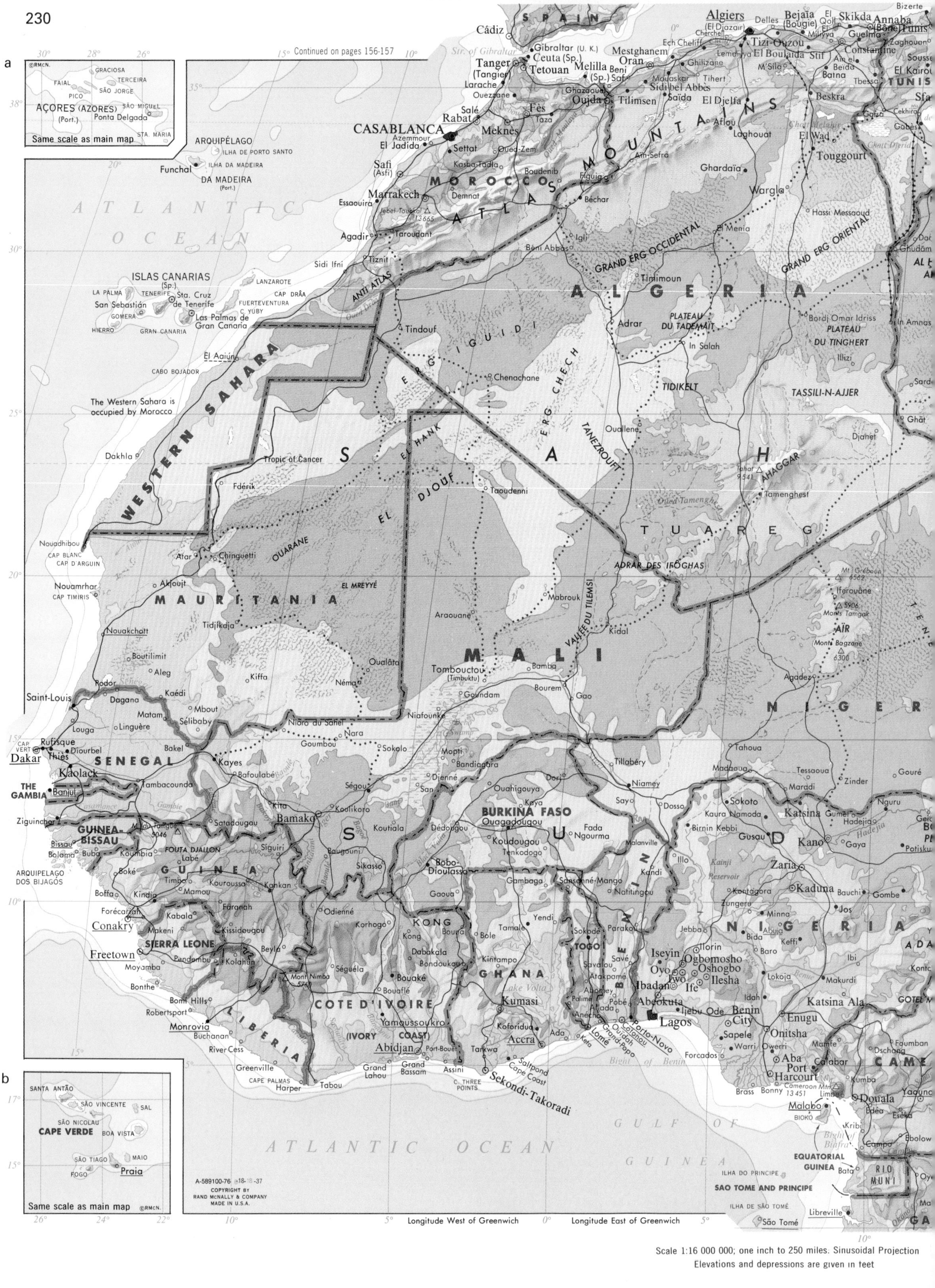

a

Continued on pages 156-157

©RMcN.
FAIAL GRACIOSA
PICO SÃO JORGE TERCEIRA
AÇORES (AZORES) SÃO MIGUEL
(Port.) Ponta Delgada STA. MARIA
Same scale as main map

ARQUIPÉLAGO
ILHA DE PORTO SANTO
ILHA DA MADEIRA
DA MADEIRA
(Port.)
Funchal

SPAIN
Cádiz
Str. of Gibraltar
Gibraltar (U.K.)
Ceuta (Sp.)
Tanger (Tangier) Tetouan Melilla (Sp.)
Larache
Ouezzane Fès Taza
Salé Rabat
Meknès
CASABLANCA
El Jadida Azemmour Settat Oued-Zem
Kasba-Tadla
Safi (Asfi) MOROCCO
Boudenib
Marrakech Demnat Béchar
Essaouira ATLAS Jebel Toubkal 13665 MOUNTAINS
Agadir Taroudant Ain-Sefra
Igli
Tiznit Béni Abbès
Sidi Ifni ANTI ATLAS GRAND ERG OCCIDENTAL
CAP DRÂA
C YUBY Tindouf
El Aaiún Tropic of Cancer
WESTERN SAHARA
The Western Sahara is occupied by Morocco
Dakhla EL HANK
Fdérik Taoudenni
EL DJOUF
Nouadhibou EL HANK
CAP BLANC OUARANE Chinguetti
CAP D'ARGUIN Atar
Nouamrhar EL MREYYÉ
CAP TIMIRIS
MAURITANIA
Nouakchott Tidjikja Mabrouk
Boutilimit Araouane Kidal
Aleg Kiffa
Rosso Néma Oualâta Tombouctou (Timbuktu)
Saint-Louis Kaédi Bamba
Dagana Mbout Goundam Bourem Gao
Matam Sélibaby
Louga Linguère Nioro du Sahel Niafounké
Rufisque Bakel Nara
CAP VERT Thiès Goumbou MALI
Dakar Kayes
Kaolack Bafoulabé
SENEGAL
THE GAMBIA Banjul Kita Bamako
Ziguinchor Tambacounda
GUINEA-BISSAU Satadougou Koolikoro
Bissau FOUTA DJALLON Siguiri
Bolama Mont Tamgué 5046 Kita Koutiala
ARQUIPÉLAGO Boké GUINEA Sikasso Bobo-Dioulasso
DOS BIJAGÓS Kindia Kouroussa
Boffa Mamou Kankan
Forécariah Kabala Farahan Odienné
Conakry Makeni Kissidougou Korhogo
Freetown SIERRA LEONE Beyla KONG Kong
Moyamba Pendembu Kolahun Dabakala
Bonthe Bomi Hills Mont Nimba 5748 Séguéla Bouaké
Robertsport COTE D'IVOIRE Bouaflé
Monrovia LIBERIA Yamoussoukro
Buchanan (IVORY COAST) Abidjan
River Cess Greenville Grand Lahou Grand Bassam
CAPE PALMAS Harper Tabou

ALGERIA
Mestghanem Oran
Saïda El Djelfa
Laghouat
Ghardaïa Wargla
Hassi Messaoud
Adrar In Salah
PLATEAU DU TADEMAÏT
Chenachane TIDIKELT
ERG CHECH TANEZROUFT Ouallene
In Salah
AHAGGAR
ADRAR DES IFÔGHAS
VALLÉE DU TILEMSI
Kidal
NIGER
AÏR
Agadez
Tahoua
Tessaoua Zinder Gouré
Madaoua
Tillabéry Niamey Dosso Sokoto
Say Birnin Kebbi Gusau Katsina
Kaura Namoda Hadejia
BURKINA FASO Fada N'gourma Malanville Gaya Kano
Ouagadougou Illo Zaria
Koudougou Kandi Kaduna
Dédougou Tenkodogo Kainji Kontagora Bauchi Gombe
Gaoua Gambaga Sansanné-Mango Natitingou Zungeru Minna Jos
Bole Yendi NIGERIA Abuja
Tamale Parakou Keffi
Sokodé Jebba Ibi
TOGO Savalou Save Iseyin Ilorin Lokoja Makurdi
GHANA Abomey Oyo Ogbomosho Oshogbo
Kumasi Porto-Novo Ibadan Ife Ilesha Idah Katsina Ala
Koforidua Lagos Abeokuta Benin City Enugu
Accra Ada Ijebu Ode Onitsha
Tarkwa Sapele Warri Aba Calabar
Cape Coast Forcados
Sekondi-Takoradi Port Harcourt
Brass Bonny Cameroon Mtn. 13451
Malabo BIOKO Kumba
EQUATORIAL GUINEA Bata Douala
SÃO TOMÉ AND PRINCIPE RIO MUNI
ILHA DE SÃO TOMÉ Libreville

b
SANTA ANTÃO
SÃO VICENTE SAL
SÃO NICOLAU BOA VISTA
CAPE VERDE
SÃO TIAGO MAIO
FOGO Praia
Same scale as main map

A-589100-76
COPYRIGHT BY
RAND McNALLY & COMPANY
MADE IN U.S.A.

Longitude West of Greenwich 0 Longitude East of Greenwich

ATLANTIC OCEAN

GULF OF GUINEA

Scale 1:16 000 000; one inch to 250 miles. Sinusoidal Projection
Elevations and depressions are given in feet

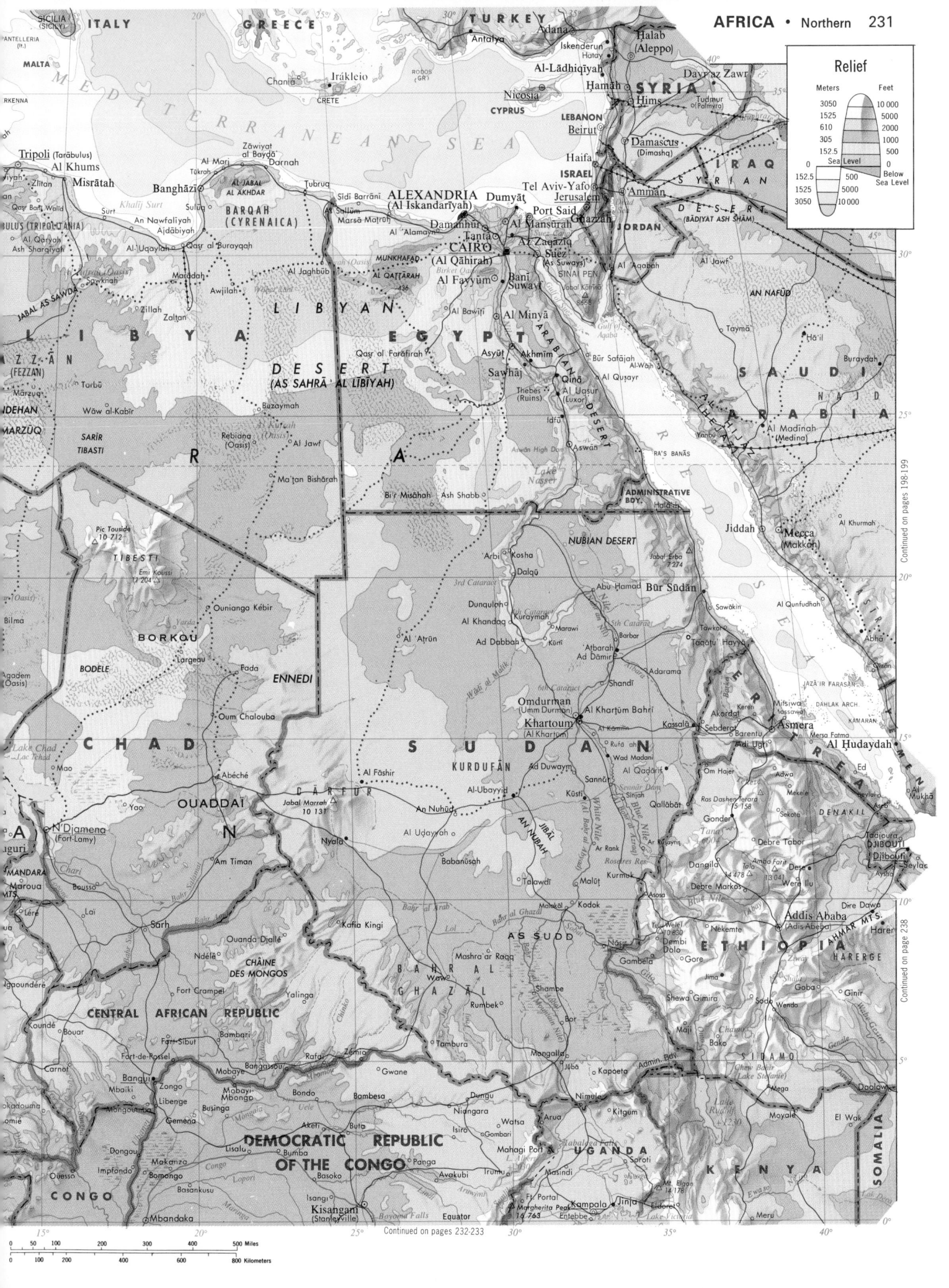

SICILY (SICILIA)
ITALY
GREECE
TURKEY
Antalya
Adana
Halab (Aleppo)
MALTA
ANTELLERIA (It.)
Chania
Irákleio
RODOS (GR.)
Al-Ládhiqiyah
Hamāh
SYRIA
Dayr az Zawr
Nicosia
CRETE
CYPRUS
Hims
Tudmur (Palmyra)
LEBANON
Beirut
Damascus (Dimashq)
RKENNA
MEDITERRANEAN SEA
Haifa
IRAQ
Tripoli (Tarābulus)
Al Khums
Misrātah
Zāwiyat al Baydā'
Darnah
Tel Aviv-Yafo
ISRAEL
Amman
SYRIAN
Al Jawf
Zliten
Banghāzī
AL JABAL AL AKHDAR
Tubruq
Jerusalem
JORDAN
DESERT (BĀDIYAT ASH SHĀM)
Qaşr Banī Walid
Surt
Sulūq
Sīdī Barrānī
ALEXANDRIA (Al Iskandarīyah)
Dumyāţ
Port Said
Al Mansūrah
Ghazzah
Al 'Aqabah
AN NAFŪD
BULUS (TRIPOLITANIA)
Al Qaryah
Ash Shargīyah
An Nawfalīyah
Ajdābiyah
BARQAH (CYRENAICA)
Marsā Maţrūh
Damanhūr
Tanţā
CAIRO (Al Qāhirah)
Az Zaqāzīq
Suez (As Suways)
SINAI PEN.
Taymā'
Ḥā'il
JABAL AS SAWDA'
Marādah
Sawknah
Zillah
Zaltan
Al Jaghbūb
MUNKHAFAD AL QAŢŢĀRAH
Birket Qārūn
Al Fayyūm
Banī Suwayf
Gulf of Aqaba
SAUDI
Buraydah
AZZĀN (FEZZAN)
Mārzuq
Tarbū
Buzaymah
LIBYAN DESERT (AS SAHRĀ' AL LĪBĪYAH)
Qaşr al Farāfirah
Al Bawīţī
Al Minyā
Asyūţ
Akhmīm
Qinā
Al Wajh
ARABIA
NAJD
Al Madīnah (Medina)
IDEHAN MARZŪQ
Wāw al-Kabīr
EGYPT
Sawhāj
Thebes (Ruins)
Al Uqşur (Luxor)
Al Quşayr
Yanbu'
SARĪR TIBASTI
Rebiana (Oasis)
Al Jawf
Idfū
Aswān
RA'S BANĀS
Oasis
Ma'tan Bishārah
Aswān High Dam
Lake Nasser
ADMINISTRATIVE BDY.
Ḥalā'ib
Jiddah
Mecca (Makkah)
Al Khurmah
Pic Touside 10 712
TIBESTI
Emi Koussi 11 204
Bi'r Misāhah
Ash Shabb
NUBIAN DESERT
Arbi
Kosha
Dalqū
Jabal 'Erba 7 274
Būr Sūdān
Al Qunfudhah
Abha
BORKOU
Ounianga Kébir
Dunqulah
Abū Ḥamad
Sawākin
BODÉLE
Largeau
Fada
ENNEDI
Al Khandaq
Kuraymah
Marawi
Kūrtī
Barbar
Tawkar
 Taqāṭu' Ḥayyā
Agadem (Oasis)
Bilma
Oum Chalouba
Ad Dabbah
Atbarah
Ad Dāmir
JAZĀ'IR FARASĀN
DAHLAK ARCH.
Lake Chad
Mao
CHAD
Oum Hadjer
SUDAN
Shandī
6th Cataract
Omdurman (Umm Durmān)
Al Kharţūm Baḥrī
Kassalā
Keren
Mitsiwa (Massawa)
KAMARAN
N'Djamena (Fort-Lamy)
Abéché
Al Fāshir
KURDUFĀN
Khartoum (Al Khartūm)
Ar Rufā'ah
Sebderat
Barentu
Asmera
Al Ḥudaydah
Yao
OUADDAÏ
DĀRFŪR
Jabal Marrah 10 131
Al-Ubayyid
Ad Duwaym
Wad Madanī
Al Qaḍārif
Om Hajer
Adwa
Mekele
DENAKIL
Ed
Am Timan
Nyala
Al Uḍayyah
An Nuhūd
Kūstī
JIBĀL
Sannār
Qallābāt
Ras Dashen Terara 15 158
Gonder
Sekota
Aseb
MANDARA MTS
Maroua
Bousso
Chari
AN NUBA
Sinjah
Sennar Dam
Dangila
Amba Farit 14 478
Dese
Wera Ilu
DJIBOUTI
Djibouti
Lére
Laï
Sarh
Talawdī
Malūţ
Asosa
Debre Markos
AHMAR MTS.
Harer
Am Timan
Ndélé
Kafia Kingi
Lol
Nāsir
Gambēla
Addis Ababa (Ādīs Ābeba)
HARERGE
Dire Dawa
CENTRAL AFRICAN REPUBLIC
CHÀINE DES MONGOS
BAHR AL GHAZĀL
AS SUDD
Malakāl
Kodok
Nekemte
Jima
Shewa Gimira
ETHIOPIA
Bouar
Fort-Sibut
Yalinga
Waw
Rumbek
Bor
Shambe
Mongalla
Bako
Maji
Wenda
SIDAMO
Ginir
Carnot
Bambari
Tambura
Gwane
Kapoeta
Admin. Bdy.
Goba
Banqui
Bangassou
Zémio
Nimule
Chew Bahir Lake Stephanie
Doolow
Zongo
Mobaye
Bondo
Dungu
Arua
Kitgum
Lake Rudolf
Moyale
El Wak
Libenge
Businga
Bambesa
Niangara
Watsa
Gombari
DEMOCRATIC REPUBLIC OF THE CONGO
Isiro
Mt. Elgon 14 178
CONGO
Bumba
Basoko
Mahagi Port
Panga
Avakubi
Masindi
UGANDA
Soroti
KENYA
SOMALIA
Kisangani (Stanleyville)
Equator
Margherita Peak 16 763
Ft. Portal
Kampala
Jinja
Eldoret
Mbandaka
Boyoma Falls
Lake Victoria
Entebbe
Mera

Continued on pages 198-199
Continued on page 238
Continued on pages 232-233

Relief

Meters		Feet
3050		10 000
1525		5000
610		2000
305		1000
152.5		500
0	Sea Level	0
152.5		500
1525	Below	5000
3050	Sea Level	10 000

0 50 100 200 300 400 500 Miles
0 100 200 400 600 800 Kilometers

Continued on pages 230-231

Scale 1:16 000 000; one inch to 250 miles. Sinusoidal Projection
Elevations and depressions are given in feet

WESTERN SAHARA

PUNTILLA NEGRA
CABO BARBAS
ADRAR SOTUF
Fdérik
Kediet Ijill

Taoudenni

TANEZRO N-AHNE

MAKTEÏR

OUARANE

EL DJOUF

S A H A

CAP BLANC
Nouadhibou
Tichla
Atar

MAURITANIA

Akjoujt

Bordj le Prier

Timetrine Monts

ÎLE TIDRA
CAP TIMIRIS
Nouamrhar

ADÂFER EL ABIOD

Araouane

Aguelhok

Nouakchott

Tidjikdja

EL MREYYE

AKLÉ ÄOUÂNA

A Z A O U A D

Moudjéria

AOUKÂR

MALI

TRARZA

Rosso
Dagana

Senegal

Kiffa

Ayoun el Atrous
Néma

IRIGUI
Lac Foguibine
Tombouctou
(Timbuktu)

Taoussa

VALLÉE DU TILEMSI

Niger

Saint-Louis
Louga
Linguère

Kaédi
Matam
Ranérou

Balé

Léré

Lac Débo

Gao

Ansongo

Hombori

CAP VERT Thiès
Rufisque
Dakar
Diourbel

FERLO

Naye
Kayes

Nioro du Sahel
Diéma

Goumbou

Kogoni

Douentza

Aribinda

SENEGAL

Kaolack
Sokone

Tambacounda
Bafoulabé
Goumbou
1 368

Didiéni

Mopti

Karo

Djibo

Dani

THE GAMBIA
Banjul
(Bathurst)
Bignona

Médina Gonasse
PARC NATIONAL DU NIOKOLO-KOBA

Kita

Banamba

Ségou
San

Djibasso

Ouahigouya

Kaya

PARC NATIONAL DE LA BOUCLE DU BAOULÉ

Bla

Tougan

Nyou

Kantch

Niger

CAP ROXO
Ziguinchor
Kolda
Koundara

Koulouguidi

Bamako

Koulikoro

BURKINA FASO

Dédougou

Koudougou

Ouagadougou

Fada Ngo

GUINEA-BISSAU
Bissau

Massif Du Tamgué
5 046

Sadatougou

Sido

Zangasso

Ouarkoye

Boromo

Toécé

Tenkodogo

Madjori

ARQUIPÉLAGO DOS BIJAGÓS
Eticoga

Danané

Labé

Dinguiraye

Siguiri

Badogo

Koyale

Sikasso

Haundé

Bobo Dioulasso

Léo

Bawk

PARC NATIONAL DU Fazao
Dépango

Kabot

Tambadonkéo

Dabola

Kouroussa

Kankan

Tingréla

Bolgatanga

Sarassané Mango

ATLANTIC

Sag Jaca

Danea

Téméléé

GUINEA

Mamou

Fria

Kindia

Faranah

Niélé

Lokosse

Lawra

Wa

Walewale

Gushiago

Niamtougou

PARC NATIONAL DU FAZAO Djebobo 2 873

OCEAN

Boffa

Forécariah
SIERRA
Makeni

Binti
Tingi
5 080
Sankanbinwa

Kissidougou

Kérouané
Pic De Tio
1 934

Odienné

Korhogo

Boundiali

Ferkessédougou

Bouna

Bole

Tamale

Yendi

Conakry

Beyla

Nzérékoré

Touba

Nlakaramandougou

Sio

Gota

Kintampo

Forêt Classée Du Fazao Djebobo 2 873

Freetown

LEONE

Pendembu

Bo

Kenema

COTE D IVOIRE

Séguéla

Katiola

Bondoukou

Wenchi

GHANA

TOGO

Moyamba

Bonthe

NIMBA NAT PARK

Biankouma
Man
Mount Kahoué
1 658

(IVORY COAST)

Daloa

Bouaké

Ouellé

Sunyani

Techiman

Mampong

Ejura

Lake Volta

Atakpamé

Hohoe

SHERBRO ISLAND
TURNERS PENINSULA

Guiglo

Duékoué

Yamoussoukro

Dimbokro

Abengourou

Bibiani

Nkawkaw

Kpandu

Palim

CAPE MOUNT
Robertsport
Brewerville

Gbarnga

Gagnoa

Agboville

Adzopé

Bouaflé

Mampong

Kumasi

Obuasi

Dunkwa

Akwati

Koforidua
Nsawam

Lome

Anloga

Monrovia

LIBERIA

Tchien

Guigla

Mont Niénokoué
2 044

Divo

Abidjan

Prestea

Tarkwa

Nyankom

Winneba

Accra

Tema

Buchanan

Duabo

Aboisso

Grand-Bassam

Esiama

Cape Coast

Greenville

Sassandra

Lagune Tadio

Lagune Ebrié

Sekondi-Takoradi

CAPE THREE POINTS

Harper
Tabou
CAPE PALMAS

GULF OF

Relief

Meters		Feet
3050		10 000
1525		5000
610		2000
305		1000
152.5		500
0	Sea Level	0
152.5		500
1525		5000
3050		10 000

Scale 1:10,000,000; one inch to 160 miles. Lambert Azimuthal Equal Area Projection
Elevations and depressions are given in feet.

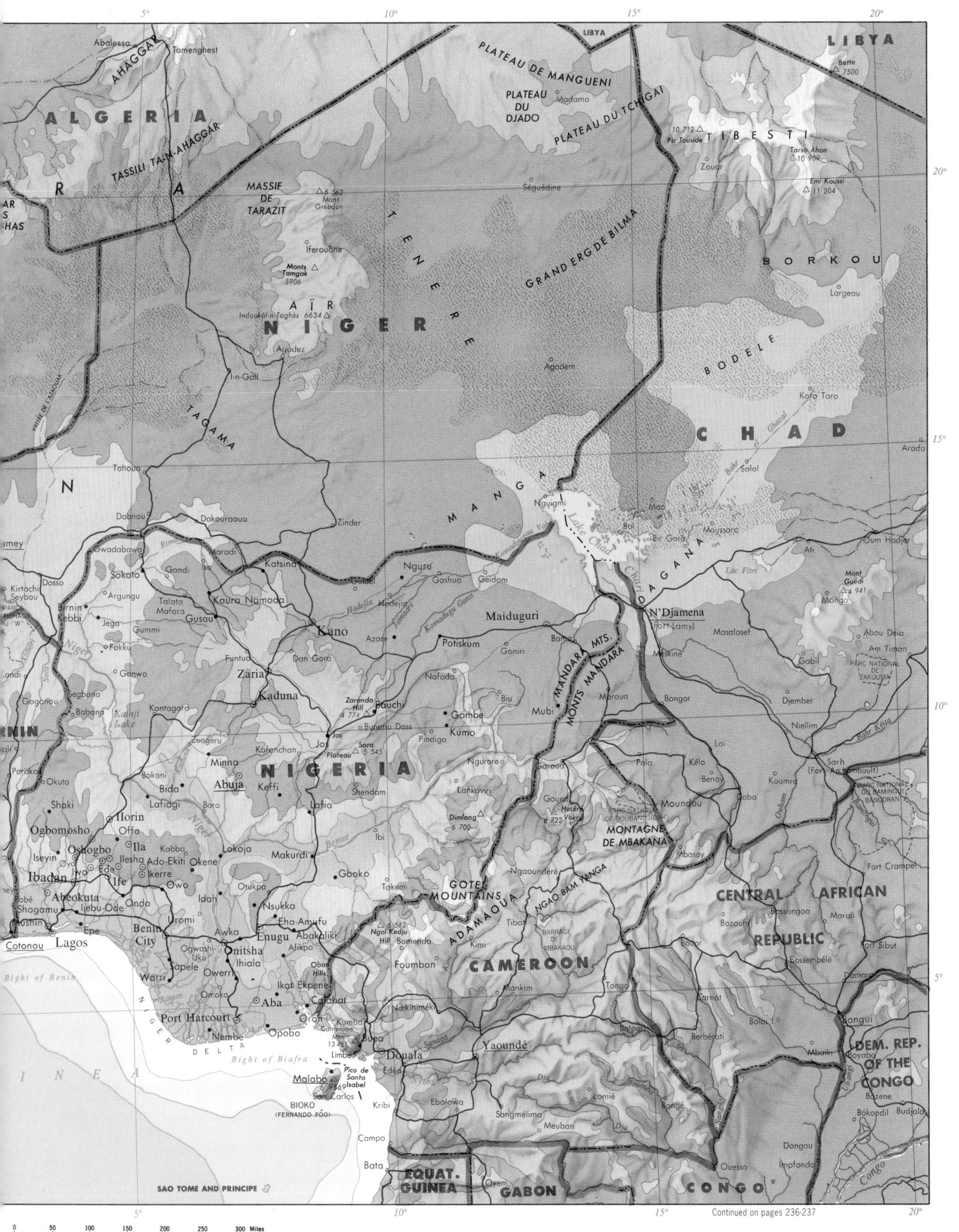

ALGERIA

AHAGGAR
Abalessa
Tamenghest

TASSILI TA-N-AHAGGAR

MASSIF
DE
TARAZIT
△ 6 562
Mont
Grébaun

Iferouâne

Monts
Tamgak
5906

AÏR
Indoukâl-n-Taghès 6634 △

Agadez

I-n-Gall

TAGAMA

Tahoua

Dabnou

Dakouraoua

Zinder

N I G E R

T E N E R E

PLATEAU DE MANGUENI

PLATEAU
DU
DJADO

Madama

PLATEAU DU TCHIGAI

Séguédine

LIBYA

Bette
7500

LIBYA

TIBESTI
Pic Touside 10 712 △
Zouar
Tarso Ahon
△ 10 909
Emi Koussi
△ 11 204

B O R K O U

Largeau

GRAND ERG DE BILMA

Agadem

BODELE

Koro Toro

Arada

C H A D

15°

20°

GRAND ERG DE BILMA

MANGA

Nguigmi

Lake Chad

Bol

Bir Gara

Mao

Moussoro

D A G A N A

Salal
Bahr el Ghazal

Ati

Lac Fitri

Mont
Guédi
△ 4 941
Mongo

Abou Deïa

Am Timan

Gabil

Oum Hadjer

PARC NATIONAL
DE
ZAKOUMA

Niellim

Djember

Bongor

Meskine

Maroua

MONTS MANDARA
MANDARA MTS.

Bama

N'Djamena
(Fort-Lamy)

Maiduguri

Masalasef

Gamey

Gwadabawa

Sokoto

Gandi

Argungu

Talata
Mafara

Jega

Gummi

Fokku

Ganwo

Kcontagora

Maradi

Katsina

Kaura Namoda

Gusau

Dan Gora

Kano

Azare

Potiskum

Nafada

Gumel

Nguru

Gashua

Geidam

Hadejia

Komadugu Gana

Goniri

Biu

Mubi

Garoua

Pala

Kélo

Benoy

Lai

Bongor

Bozoum

Sarh
(Fort-Archambault)

Koumra

Doba

PARC NATIONAL
DU BAMINGUI
BANGORAN

Kirtachi
Seybou

PARC
NATIONAL
DU "W"

Dosso

Birnin
Kebbi

Zuru

Zaria

Kaduna

Zaranda
Hill
4 774

Bauchi

Bununu Dass

Jos
Plateau

Sara
5 545

Pindiga

Gombe

Kumo

Ngororeo

Maroua

Meskine

Mora

MONTAGNE
DE MBAKANA

CENTRAL

AFRICAN

Bossangoa

Marali

Fort Sibut

Bossembélé

Damara

REPUBLIC

Fort Crampel

N I G E R I A

Minna

Abuja

Keffi

Lafia

Shendam

Lankoviri

Dimlang
6 700

Hosere
6 722
Yokra

Goundi

Moundou

Mbasay

Bozoum

Bouar

Baboua

Batouri

Berbérati

Bolai 1°

Garnot

Bangui

DEM. REP.
OF THE
CONGO

Bazene

Bokondji Budjala

Okuta

Bokani

Bida

Lafiagi

Baro

Shaki

Ilorin

Offa

Kabba

Lokoja

Makurdi

Gboko

Takum

GOTEL
MOUNTAINS

ADAMAOUA

Kimi

Tibati

Ngaoundéré

NGAO BAM YANGA

BARRAGE
DE
MBAKAOU

Ogbomosho

Oshogbo

Ila

Ilesha

Kerre

Owo

Ondo

Okene

Otupka

Nsukka

Eha-Amufu

Ngol Kedju
Hill
△ 6 562

Bamenda

Foumban

Mankim

Tongo

Tibo

Iseyin

Oyo

Ede

Ife

Ibadan

Bobé

Abeokuta

Ijebu-Ode

Shagamu

Moshin

Epe

Cotonou

Lagos

Benin
City

Uromi

Awka

Enugu

Abakaliki

Afikpo

Obam
Hills

CAMEROON

Bight of Benin

Ogwashi-
Uku

Onitsha

Ihiala

Ikot Ekpene

Oban
Hills

Ndikinimeki

Batouri

Bélabo

Warri

Sapele

Owerri

Aba

Calabar

Oron

Kumba

Cameroon
Mtn.
13 451
Buea

Douala

Yaoundé

Mbalmayo

Port Harcourt

Nembe

Opobo

DELTA

NIGER

Bight of Biafra

Malabo
Pico de
Santa
Isabel
9869

San Carlos

BIOKO
(FERNANDO POO)

Edéa

Kribi

Nyong

Ebolowa

Sangmélima

Meyomessala

Djoum

Lomié

Bangé

Yokadouma

Dongou

Impfondo

Congo

Campo

Bata

EQUAT.
GUINEA

Oyem

GABON

CONGO

SAO TOME AND PRINCIPE

GUINEA

Ouesso

5°

10°

15°

20°

Continued on pages 236-237

0   50   100   150   200   250   300 Miles

0   100   200   300   400   500 Kilometers

Continued on pages 234-235

10°

15°

NIGERIA

Opobo

Cameroon Mtn. 13 491 △

Bight of Biafra

Douala

Buea

Edéa

Malabo

San Carlos

BIOKO (FERNANDO PÓO)

Kribi

Campo

EQUATORIAL GUINEA

Bata

SAO TOME AND PRINCIPE

PRÍNCIPE

CABO SAN JUAN

ISLA DE CORISCO

São Tomé

SÃO TOMÉ

Libreville

MONTS DE CRISTAL

Acalayong

Kango

Equator

CAMEROON

Yaoundé

Doumé

Yokadouma

Sangmélima

Lomié

Ebolowa

Meuban

Kom

Souanké

Bangé

Moloundou

Dja

Djoum

Oyem

Makokou

Mekambo

Lebango

Djoukoumatombi

CENTRAL

AFRICAN

REPUBLIC

Fort de Passel

Boali

Kongba

Bangassou

Berbérati

Bolai

Mbaiki

Boyabo

Bosobolo

Mbaye

Banguí

Mongoumba

Bozene

Gemena

Yandongi

Budjala

Lisala

Bumba

Buta

Akel

Basoko

Kisangar (Stanleyville)

Impfondo

Bomongo

ILE SUMBA

Loko

Lifanga

Boende

Ekoli

DEMOCRATIC

REP. OF

THE CONGO

(ZAIRE)

Bokungu

Yayama

Litoko

GABON

Bifoum

Booué

3360 △

Koula-Moutou

Franceville

Mbinda

Lambarené

Mouila

CAP LOPEZ

Port-Gentil

Omboué

Petit Loango

Tchibanga

Mossendjo

CONGO

Owando

Gambome

Djambala

St. François de Boundji

Sibiti

Madingou

Kindamba

Bandundu

Makaw

Dekese

Esombo

Lac Tumba

Mbandaka Caquihatville

Lac Mai-Ndombe

Kiri

Monkoto

Lokolama

Ekanga

Ikela

Tiongo

Fimi

Lukenie

Tiebo (Port-Francqui)

Domiongo

Mayumba

Madinga

Loubomo

Brazzaville

Stanley Pool

Kinshasa (Leopoldville)

Chutes De Livingstone (Livingstone Falls)

Tshela

Mari-Manimba

Madimba

Kikwit

Djokupunda

Mbuji-Ma (Bakwang

Pointe-Noire

CABINDA (Ang.)

Cabinda

PONTA DO PADRÃO

Boma

Matadi

Nóqui

Soyo

SERRA DO CONGO

Mbanza-Ngungu

Popokabaka

Kimvula

Kilembe

Kitenda

Kananga (Luluabourg)

Tshikapa

Kanda-Kanda

N'zeto

Mbaia

M'banza Congo

Quimbele

Damba

Uíge

Kahemba

Kibenga

Kapanga

Ambriz

Marimba

Caluango

Sambungo

KATANGA

Luanda

Caxito

Catete

Kalandula

Quela

Quimbonge

Cuilo

Kamowa

PONTA DAS PALMEIRINHAS

Cotete

Malanje

Cacolo

Cambundi-Catembo

Lugo

Lucano

Malanga

N'dalatando

Dondo

PARQUE NACIONAL DE QUIÇAMA

ATLANTIC

CABO DAS TRÉS PONTAS

Porto Amboim

Mussende

PARQUE NACIONAL DA CAMEIA

Calunda

Lwena

Gabela

Waku Kunda

Calucinga

ANGOLA

Saútar

Curunga

Cangamba

Sumbe

Cuvo

Coemba

Covelo

Wama

Kuito

OCEAN

Lobito

SERRA CAMBANDA

Serra do Môco 8596 △

Benguela

Catumbela

Chitembo

Chá Pungana

Huambo (Nova Lisboa)

SERRE DO CHILENGUE

Caconda

Caála

Caluquembe

SERRA DA NEVE

Mussuma

Ninda

KASHIJI PLAIN

Chitokoloki

LIUWA PLAIN

CABO DE SANTA MARTA

Cacula

Bentiaba

Namibe

Lubango

PARQUE NACIONAL DO BIKUAR

Folgares

Cassinga

Menongue

Lungo

Mavinga

BAROTSE PLAIN

Mongu

Nangweshi

PONTA ALBINA

Tômbua

Chiange

Caiundo

Cuando

Catuala

SILOANA PLAINS

PONTA DA MARCA

Baía dos Tigres

Oncocua

PARQUE NACIONAL DO IONA

Cuamato

Foz do Cunene

Ruacana Falls

Melunga

NAMIBIA

Cuangar

Sambusu

CAPRIVI STRIP

BOTS.

CHOBE NAT. P.

20°

Relief

Meters		Feet
3050		10 000
1525		5000
610		2000
305		1000
152.5		500
0	Sea Level	0
152.5		500
1525		5000
3050		10 000

Scale 1:10,000,000; one inch to 160 miles. Lambert Azimuthal Equal Area Projection
Elevations and depressions are given in feet.

SUDAN
ETHIOPIA

Maridi
Juba
Admin
Bdy.
Kapoeta
Didinga
Hills
Keyala
LOTIKIPI
PLAIN
Lakitaung
Lake
Stefanie

Yambio
Goburu
Kinyeti
10 456
Nimule
Padibe
Kaabong
Lodwar
CHALBI
DESERT
Moyale
Baidoa

Bwendi
Bagbele
Aba
ANGIA MOUNTAINS
Gulu
Muruasigar
7 050
Lokichar
Marsabit
Baardheere

Niangara
Watsa
Arua
Moroto
Morato
118
Lakichar

Isiro
(Paulis)
Mungbere
Kabalega
Falls
Lira
Mado Gashi
SOMALIA

Wamba
Nduye
Bunia
Lake
Albert
Nabiswera
Mount Elgon
14 178
CHERANGANY
HILLS
Kitale
Laisamis
Wajir
Baraawe

Panga
Avakubi
Mamba
Fort Portal
Mubende
Mbale
Eldoret
Thomson's
Falls
Nanyuki
Mt. Kenya
(Kirinyaga)
17 058
Alanga Arba
BUN
PLAINS

Balobe
Kasese
Kampala
Entebbe
Jinja
Mumias
Kisumu
Nakuru
Nyeri
Equator
Garissa
Solola
Jamaame

Kamituga
Mwega
Rutshuru
Volcan Karisimbi
14 787
Kabale
Lake
Edward
Masaka
MFANGANO
SSESE
ISLANDS
Kericho
MAU ESCARPMENT
Embu
Thika
Mwingi
Kaningo
Bura
Kolbio
Kiunga

RWANDA
Gisenyi
Kigali
Nyanza
Lake
Victoria
Bukoba
Kagera
Musoma
Subugo
8 668
Lake
Magadi
Nairobi
Machakos
YATTA
PLATEAU
TSAVO
NATIONAL
PARK
LAMU ISLAND
Lamu

BURUNDI
Bujumbura
Biharamulo
Mwanza
UKEREWE
ISLAND
RUBONDO
Ushashi
Loliondo
SERENGETI
NATIONAL
PARK
Magadi
Makindu
Formosa Bay

Kamituga
Uvira
Nyakanazi
Geita
SERENGETI
PLAIN
Loolmalassin
12 969
Longido
Mount
Meru
14 978
Kilimanjaro
19 340
Arusha
Moshi
Kilifi
Mackinnon
Road
Mombasa

Kalima
Elila
Kongolo
Kibondo
Nzega
Shinyanga
Salawe
Lake
Eyasi
Bereku
Hanang
11 215
MASAI
STEPPE
Usa
USAMBARA
MTS.
Tanga
Chake Chake
PEMBA ISLAND

Kabambare
Nyunzu
Kabalo
Kahia
Ankoro
Manono
Kabambo
Kigoma
Ujiji
Uvinza
Kaliua
Tabora
Igalula
Ifigi
Ngowya
Dodoma
Kimamba
Mziha
Morogoro
Zanzibar
ZANZIBAR
Bagamoyo
Dar es Salaam

Kalemie
(Albertville)
MAHALI
MTS.
Masangwe
5 371
Mpanda
Kitunda
Bahi
Swamp
Ugalla
Mpwapwa
RUBEHO MOUNTAINS
NGURU MOUNTAINS
Mvomero
Mikumi
Kibiti
MAFIA ISLAND
Kilindoni

MONTS MITUMBA
MLALA
HILLS
Karema
Kipili
Lusaka
Sumbawanga
Mboga
RUAHA
NATIONAL
PARK
Kipembawe
Iringa
Great Ruaha
Mahenge
Kwangwazi
Somanga

Lukuga
MONTS MALUMBA
Lake
Rukwa
USANGU
FLATS
Chunga
Sao Hill
Mahenge
Ngorimbi

Moliro
Kasanga
Mbeya
Mbala
KIPENGERE RANGE
Njombe
Litoo
Kilwa Kisiwani

MONTS MULUMBE
Kalundwe
PARC
NATIONAL
DE L'UPEMBA
Kialwe
Doba
Lake
Mweru
Mporokoso
Kasama
Nyungwe
NYIKA
PLATEAU
Livingstonia
Masasi
Lindi
Mtwara
Quionga
CABO DELGADO

Lubudi
Kishi
Kasenga
Mwinilunga
Johnston
Falls
Chambeshi
Chinsali
Mbamba Bay
Liuli
Tunduru
Newala
Mocímboa da Praia
Diaca
Ibo

Tenke
Kiubo
Falls
Lake
Bangweulu
Bangweulu
Swamp
MUCHINGA MOUNTAINS
Mpika
Mzuzu
Mzimba
Côbuè
COMOROS
NJAZIDJA
Moroni
Karthala
7 746
NZWANI

Likasi
(Jadotville)
Lubumbashi
(Elisabethville)
Kolwezi
Kipushi
Mansa
Songwe
Kabunda
Chitambo
MWALI

Chililabombwe
(Bancroft)
Mufulira
Sakania
Kabompo
Chamama
Lichinga
Marrupa
Montepuez
Pemba

Chingola
Kitwe
Ndola
Songwe
Kapiri Mposhi
Chipata
Mchinji
MALAWI
Salima
Lilongwe
Monkey Bay
Mucacata
Nampuecha

Luanshya
Busanga
Swamp
Mkushi
Katete
Makataka
Mandimba
Maúa
Malema
Montepuez
Nacala

ZAMBIA
Kabwe
(Broken Hill)
Lake
Nyasa
Nsanje
Cuamba
Serra
Namuli
7 936
Nampula
Mocambique

Lukanga Swamp
Mumbwa
Rutenga
Cabora Bassa
Res.
Fíngoe
Casula
Blantyre
Zomba
Ribauè
Mogincual
António Enes
ILHA ANGOCHE

Lusaka
Chilanga
Zumbo
Cabora
Bassa
Furancungo
Mpimb
Lake
Chilwa
MLANJE
MTS.
Sapitwa
9 849
Alto Molócuè
Erego
Moma
Mucubela
Pebane

Kafue Flats
Mazabuka
UMVUKWE RANGE
MAVURADONA
MTS.
Tete
Vila
Caldas
Xavier
Changara
Nsanje
Mocuba

Munyama
Gwembe
Kariba
Karoi
Kildonan
Bindura
Mtoko
Chemba

Sikalongo
Lake
Kariba
ZIMBABWE
Chinhoyi
Harare
(Salisbury)
Chitungwiza
Marondera
Kadoma
Chegutu

Victoria Falls
Livingstone
Hwange
Tundazi
4 702
(RHODESIA)

INDIAN
OCEAN

0 50 100 150 200 250 300 Miles
0 100 200 300 400 500 Kilometers

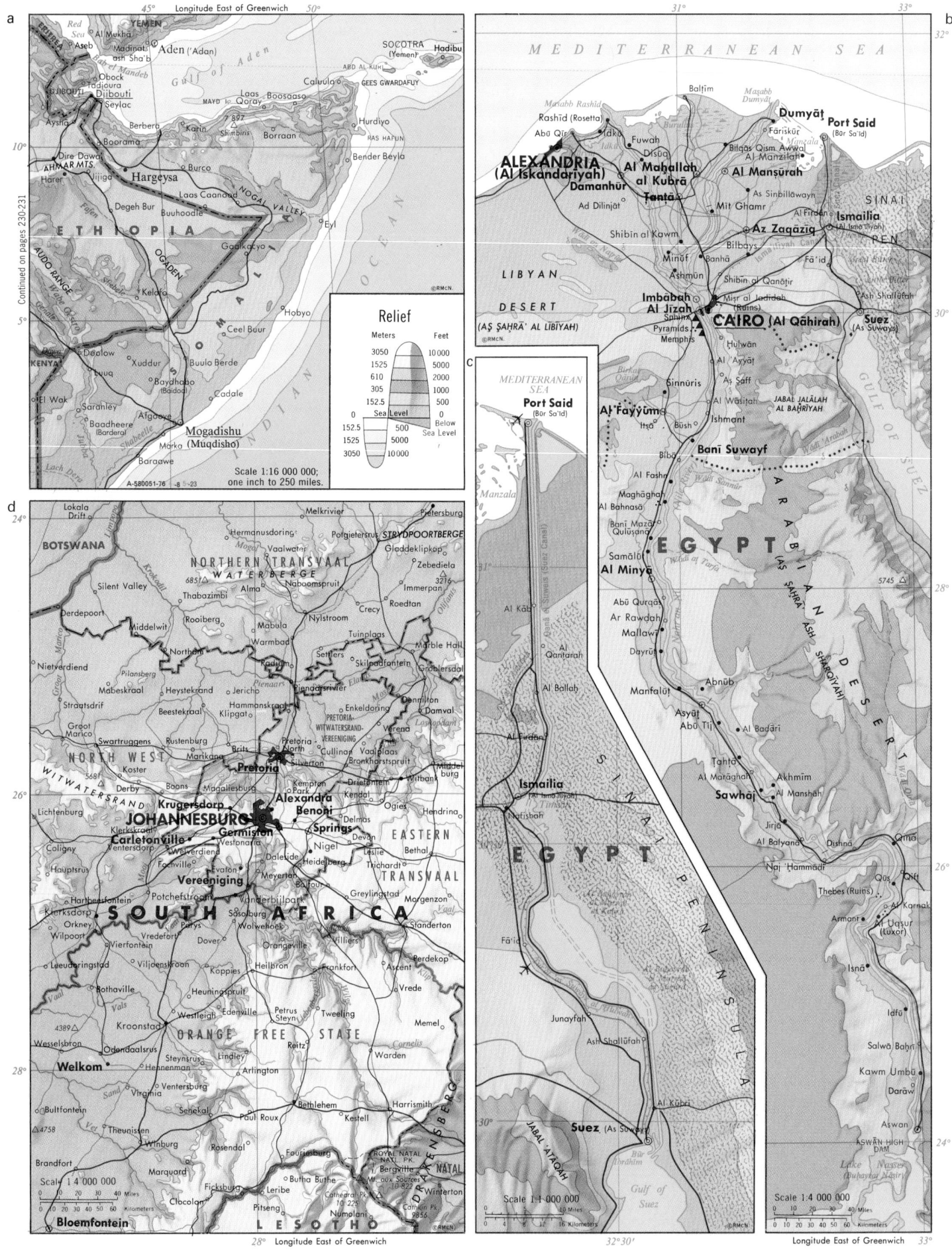

a

Red Sea
YEMEN
Al Mukha
Madinat
ash Sha'b
Aden ('Adan)
Obock
Tadjoura
Aysha
DJIBOUTI Djibouti
Seylac

SOCOTRA (Yemen)
Hadibu
ABD AL KURI

Gulf of Aden

GEES GWARDAFUY

45° Longitude East of Greenwich 50°

AHMAR MTS.
Dire Dawa
Harer
Jijiga Hargeysa

ETHIOPIA
Degeh Bur
Buuhoodle

AUDO RANGE

OGADEN

Keldro

Dooiow

Xuddur

Baydhabo (Baidoa)

KENYA

Sarahley
Baadheere (Bardera)

El Wak

Afgooye

Mogadishu (Muqdisho)

Marka

Baraawe

INDIAN OCEAN

©RMcN.

Berbera
Karin
Boorama
Burco
Degeh Bur

897
Shimbris
Laas Caanood

NOGAL VALLEY

Eyl

Ceel Buur
Buulo Berde
Cadale

Hobyo

Gaalkacyo

RAS HAFUN

Hurdiyo

Bender Beyla

MAYD

Laas Qoray

Caluula

Boosaaso

Hurdiyo

Relief

Meters	Feet
3050	10 000
1525	5000
610	2000
305	1000
152.5	500
0 Sea Level	0 Sea Level
152.5	500 Below Sea Level
1525	5000
3050	10000

Scale 1:16 000 000; one inch to 250 miles.

A-580051-76 -8 5-23

Continued on pages 230-231

b

MEDITERRANEAN SEA

31° 33°
32°

Balṭīm
Maṣabb Rashīd
Rashīd (Rosetta)
Abū Qīr
Idkū
Fuwah
Disūq

Maṣabb Dumyāṭ
Dumyāṭ Port Said (Bōr Sa'īd)
Fāriskūr
Bilqās Qism Awwal
Al Manzilah

ALEXANDRIA (Al Iskandarīyah)
Damanhūr
Al Maḥallah al Kubrā
Ṭanṭā
Ad Dilinjāt
Shibīn al Kawm
Al Manṣūrah
Mīt Ghamr
As Sinbillāwayn

SINAI

Az Zaqāzīq
Ismailia (Al Ismā'īlīyah)
Bilbays
Al Firdān
Banhā

LIBYAN DESERT
(AṢ ṢAḤRĀ' AL LĪBĪYAH)

Minūf
Ashmūn
Shibīn al Qanāṭir
Fā'id

Imbābah
Al Jīzah
Sphinx
Pyramids
Memphis

Misr al Jadīdah
CAIRO (Al Qāhirah)
Ḥulwān
Al 'Ayyāṭ
As Saff

Suez (As Suways)

Sinnūris
Al Wāsiṭah
Ishmant

JABAL JALĀLAH AL BAḤRĪYAH

GULF OF SUEZ

©RMcN.

c

MEDITERRANEAN SEA

Port Said (Bōr Sa'īd)

Manzala

Al Kāb

Al Qantarah

Al Ballah

Al Firdān

Ismailia (Al Ismā'īlīyah)

Nifīshah

Fā'id

SINAI PENINSULA

EGYPT

Junayfah

Ash Shallūfah

Al Kubrī

JABAL 'ATĀQAH

Suez (As Suways)

Bōr Ibrāhīm

Gulf of Suez

Scale 1:1 000 000
0 4 8 10 16 Kilometers

©RMcN.

32°30'

Al Fayyūm
Itsā
Būsh

Banī Suwayf

Al Fashn

Biba

Al Bahnasā

Maghāghah

Banī Mazār
Qulūsana

Samālūṭ

EGYPT

Al Minyā

Abū Qurqāṣ
Ar Rawdah
Mallawī

Al Qantarah

Dayrūṭ

Manfalūṭ

Abnūb

Asyūṭ
Abū Tīj

Al Badārī

ARABIAN DESERT (AṢ ṢAḤRĀ' ASH SHARQĪYAH)

5745

5745

Ṭahṭā
Al Marāghah
Akhmīm

Sawhāj
Al Manshāh

Jirjā
Al Balyanā

Dishnā

Qinā

Naj' Ḥammādī

Thebes (Ruins)
Al Karnak
Armant
Uqsur (Luxor)
Isnā
Idfū

Qūs

28°

Salwā Baḥrī

Kawm Umbū
Darāw

26°

Aswan
ASWĀN HIGH DAM
Lake Nasser (Buḥayrat Nāṣir)

24°

Scale 1:4 000 000
0 10 20 30 40 60 Miles

Longitude East of Greenwich 33°

d

Lokala Drift

BOTSWANA

Silent Valley

Derdepoort

Nietverdiend

Mabeskraal

Straatsdrif

Groot Marico

NORTH WEST

Swartruggens

Lichtenburg

Coligny

Hauptrus

Klerksdorp

Orkney

Wilpoort

Leeudoringstad

Wesselsbron

Bloemfontein

24°

Melkrivier
Hermanusdoring
Potgietersrus STRYDPOORTBERGE

Pietersburg

Vaalwater

WATERBERGE

685¹ 3216

Gladdeklipkop

Zebediela

Thabazimbi

Alma

Naboomspruit

Immerpan

Rooiberg

Mabula

Nylstroom

Crecy
Roedtan

Northam

Warmbad

Tuinplaas

Pilansberg

Settlers

Radium

Jericho

Pienaarsrivier

Skilpadfontein

Groblersdal

Marble Hall

Rustenburg

Beestekraal

Klipgat

Hammanskraal

Enkeldoring
PRETORIA-
WITWATERSRAND-
VEREENIGING

Dennilton

Damval

Loskopdam

Marikana

Koster

Pretoria North

Cullinan

Verena

Brits

Silverton

Bronkhorstspruit

Derby

Magaliesburg

Boons

Kempton Park

Driefontein

Witbank

Middelburg

568¹

Krugersdorp

Pretoria

Alexandra

Kendal

Ogies

Hendrina

WITWATERSRAND

JOHANNESBURG

Germiston

Benoni

Springs

Delmas

Devon

Leslie

Bethal

EASTERN

Carletonville

Klerkskraal

Venterskroon

Westonaria

Nigel

TRANSVAAL

Fochville

Evaton

Daleside

Meyerton

Heidelberg

Trichardt

Greylingstad

Morgenzon

Coligny

Potchefstroom

Vanderbijlpark

Vereeniging

Sasolburg

Wolwehoek

Standerton

SOUTH AFRICA

4389

Kroonstad

Parys

Dover

Heilbron

Frankfort

Villiers

Perdekop

Vrede

Ascent

Memel

ORANGE FREE STATE

Virginia

Viljoenskroon

Koppies

Vredefort

Rothaville

Edenville

Heuningspruit

Lindley

Reitz

Tweeling

Warden

Welkom

Bultfontein

Hennenman

Ventersburg

Steynsrus

Petrus Steyn

Arlington

4758

Theunissen

Winburg

Senekal

Paul Roux

Bethlehem

Kestell

Harrismith

Brandfort

Marquard

Rosendal

Fouriesburg

Winterton

Ficksburg

Leribe

ROYAL NATAL NAT'L PK.
J. Bergville
Mt. aux Sources
10822
Cathedral Pk.
10-225
Cathkin Pk. 9856

DRAKENSBERG

NATAL

Butha Buthe

Clocolan

Numolami

Pitseng

LESOTHO

Bloemfontein

26°

28°

Scale 1:4 000 000
0 10 20 30 40 Miles
0 10 20 30 40 50 60 Kilometers

28° Longitude East of Greenwich

©RMcN.

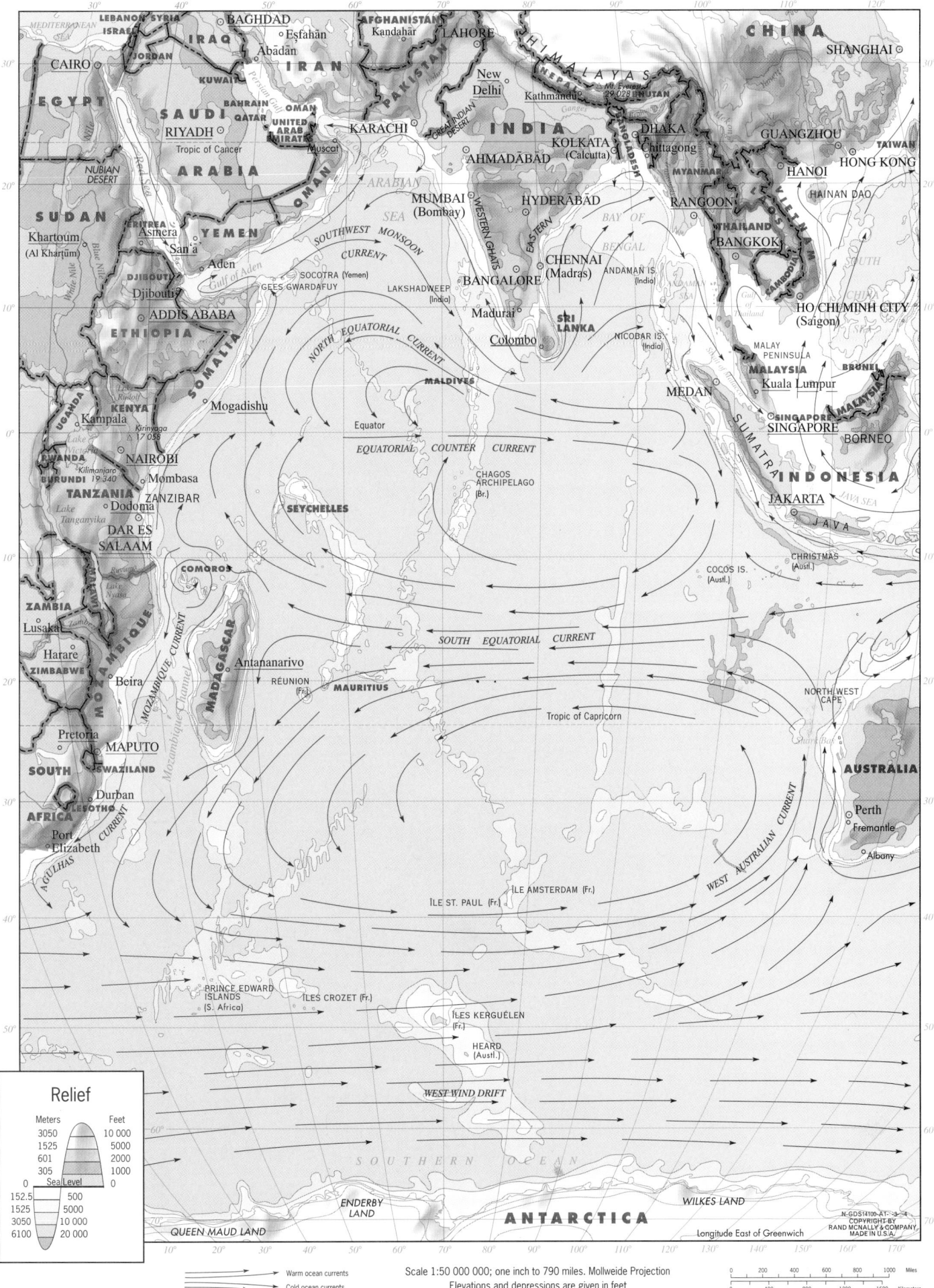

Relief

Meters	Feet
3050	10 000
1525	5000
601	2000
305	1000
0 Sea Level	0
152.5	500
1525	10 000
3050	10 000
6100	20 000

Scale 1:50 000 000; one inch to 790 miles. Mollweide Projection
Elevations and depressions are given in feet

→ Warm ocean currents
→ Cold ocean currents

N-GDS14100-A1--3--4
COPYRIGHT BY
RAND MCNALLY & COMPANY
MADE IN U.S.A.

Relief

Meters	Feet
3050	10 000
1525	5000
610	2000
305	1000
152.5	500
0 Sea Level	0
152.5	500
1525	5000
3050	10 000
6100	20 000

A-598500-76 12-9-30
COPYRIGHT BY
RAND McNALLY & COMPANY
MADE IN U.S.A.

⟶ Warm ocean currents
⟶ Cold ocean currents

Scale 1:50 000 000; one inch to 800 miles. Goode's Homolosine Equal Area Projection
Elevations and depressions are given in feet

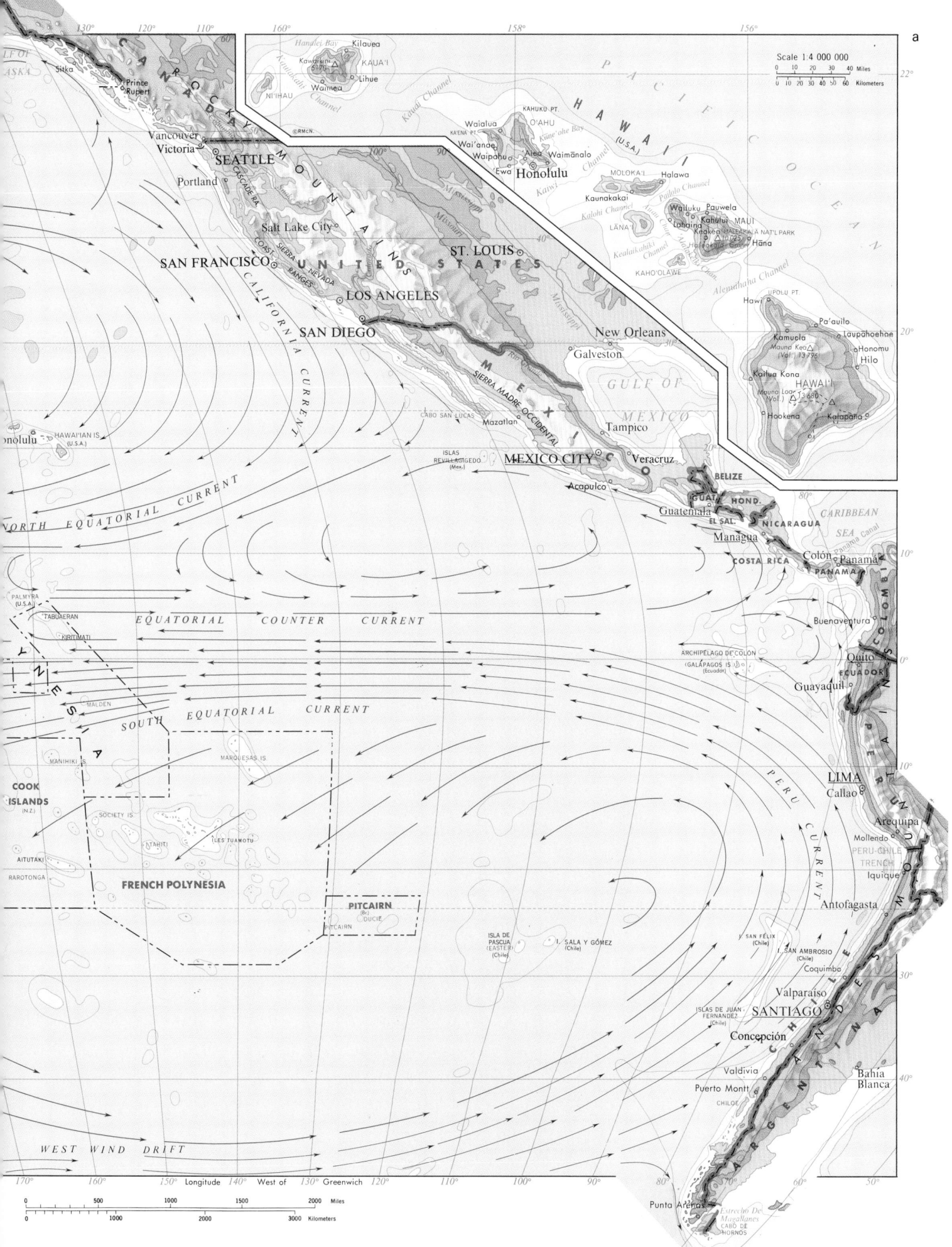

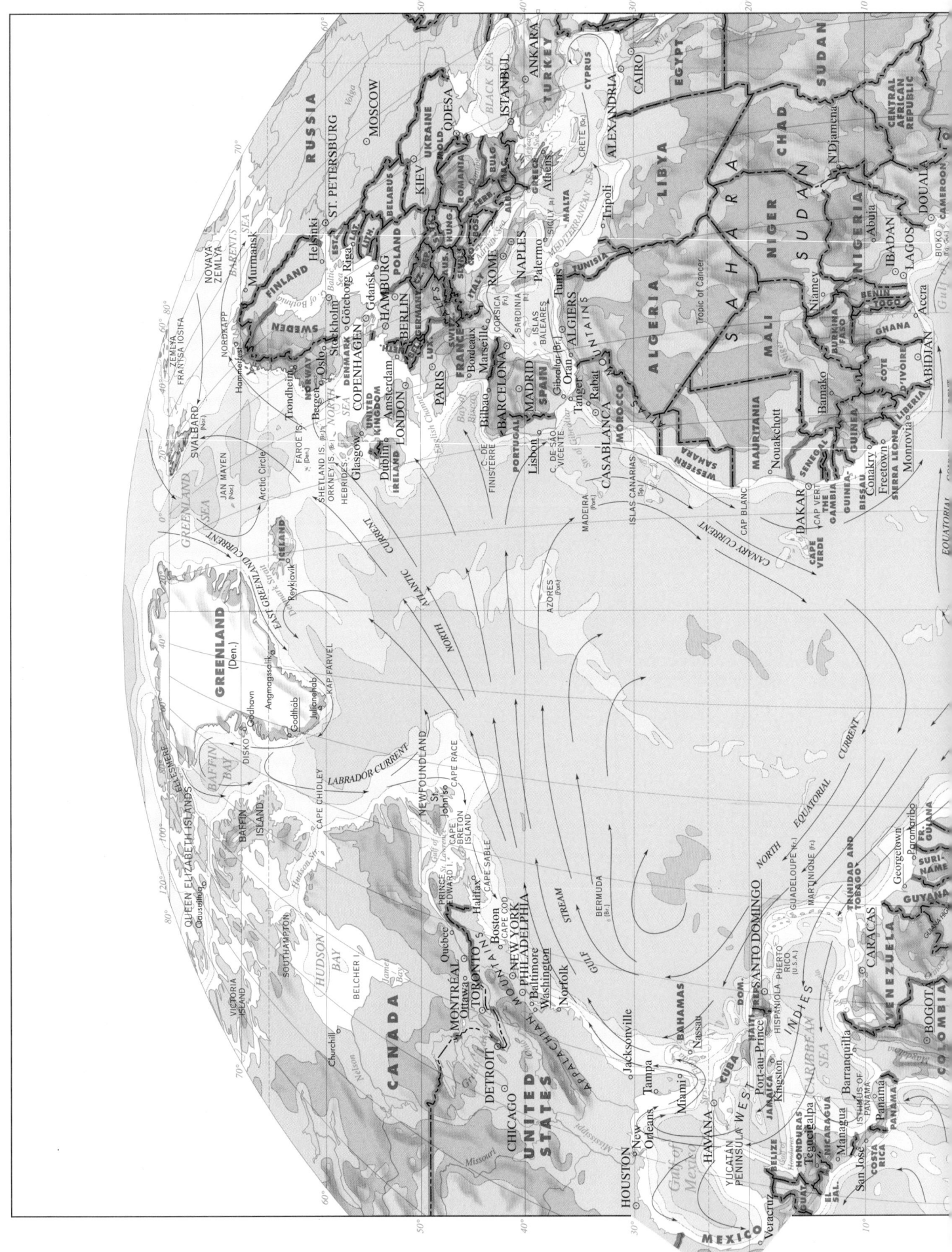

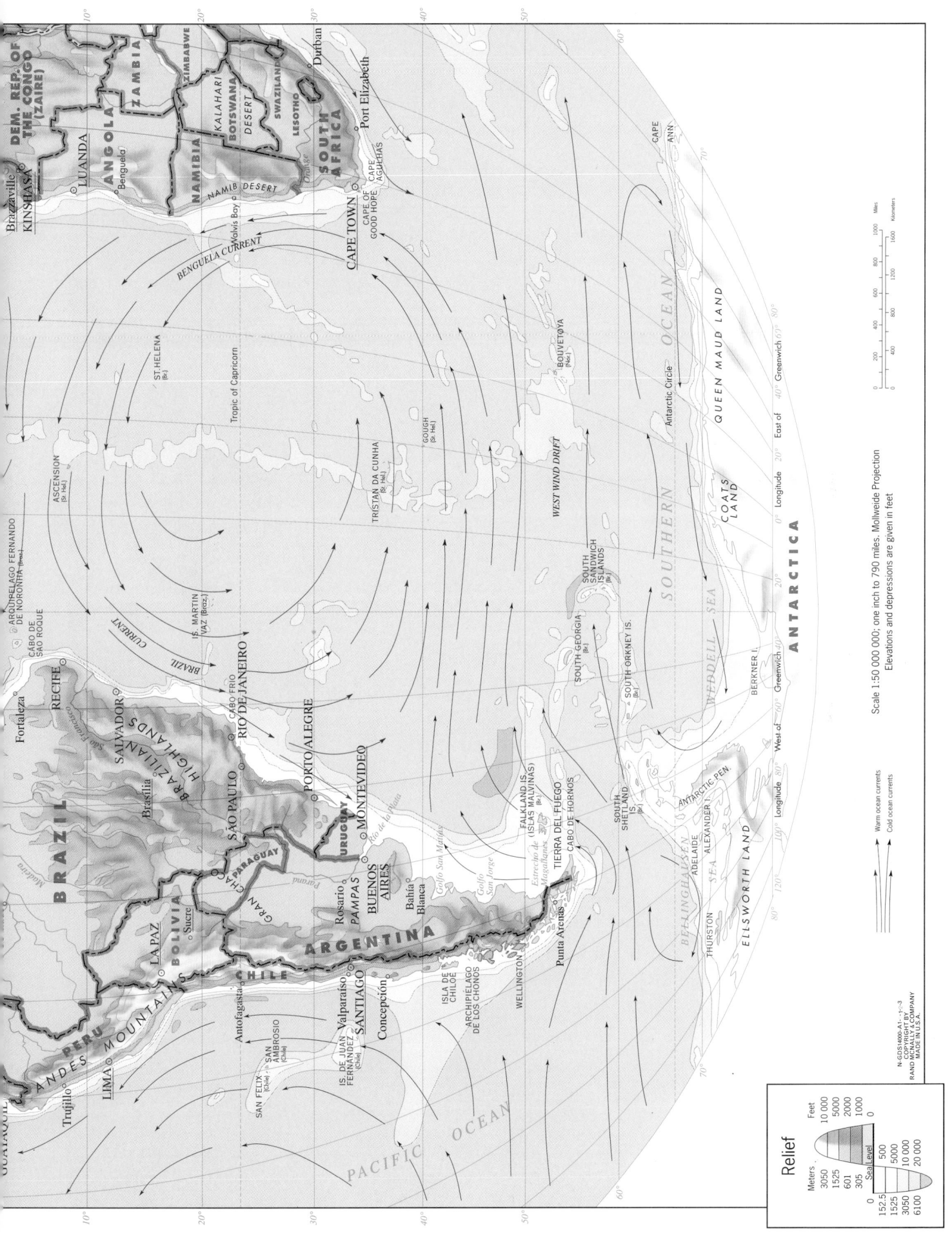

DEM. REP. OF THE CONGO (ZAIRE)
Brazzaville
KINSHASA
ANGOLA
ZAMBIA
ZIMBABWE
LUANDA
Benguela
NAMIBIA
KALAHARI DESERT
BOTSWANA
SWAZILAND
LESOTHO
SOUTH AFRICA
Durban
Port Elizabeth
CAPE ANN
NAMIB DESERT
Walvis Bay
CAPE OF GOOD HOPE
CAPE AGULHAS
CAPE TOWN
BENGUELA CURRENT

QUEEN MAUD LAND
Antarctic Circle
East of Greenwich 40°
COATS LAND
SOUTHERN OCEAN
WEST WIND DRIFT
WEDDELL SEA

ST. HELENA (Br.)
Tropic of Capricorn
GOUGH (St. Hel.)
TRISTAN DA CUNHA (St. Hel.)
BOUVETØYA (Nor.)
ASCENSION (St. Hel.)
ARQUIPÉLAGO FERNANDO DE NORONHA (Braz.)

SOUTH SANDWICH ISLANDS (Br.)
SOUTH GEORGIA (Br.)
SOUTH ORKNEY IS. (Br.)
BERKNER I.
ANTARCTICA

BRAZIL
CABO DE SÃO ROQUE
RECIFE
Fortaleza
SALVADOR
BRAZILIAN HIGHLANDS
Brasília
São Francisco
IS. MARTIM VAZ (Braz.)
BRAZIL CURRENT
CABO FRIO
RIO DE JANEIRO
SÃO PAULO
PORTO ALEGRE
PARAGUAY
Paraná
MONTEVIDEO
URUGUAY
Rosario
PAMPAS
BUENOS AIRES
Río de la Plata
Bahía Blanca
GRAN CHACO
BOLIVIA
LA PAZ
Sucre
PERU
LIMA
Trujillo
ANDES MOUNTAINS
CHILE
Antofagasta
SAN FELIX (Chile)
SAN AMBROSIO (Chile)
IS. DE JUAN FERNÁNDEZ (Chile)
Valparaíso
SANTIAGO
Concepción
ARGENTINA
Golfo San Matías
Golfo San Jorge
FALKLAND IS. (ISLAS MALVINAS) (Br.)
Estrecho de Magallanes
TIERRA DEL FUEGO
CABO DE HORNOS
Punta Arenas
SOUTH SHETLAND IS. (Br.)
ANTARCTIC PEN.
ALEXANDER I.
ADELAIDE
BELLINGHAUSEN SEA
THURSTON
ELLSWORTH LAND
ISLA DE CHILOÉ
ARCHIPIÉLAGO DE LOS CHONOS
WELLINGTON

PACIFIC OCEAN

Scale 1:50 000 000; one inch to 790 miles. Mollweide Projection
Elevations and depressions are given in feet

Warm ocean currents
Cold ocean currents

Miles
Kilometers
0 200 400 600 800 1000
0 400 800 1200 1600

N-GDS14000-A1-⌐7-3
COPYRIGHT BY
RAND McNALLY & COMPANY
MADE IN U.S.A.

Relief

Meters		Feet
3050		10 000
1525		5000
601		2000
305		1000
	Sealevel	0
152.5		500
1525		5000
3050		10 000
6100		20 000

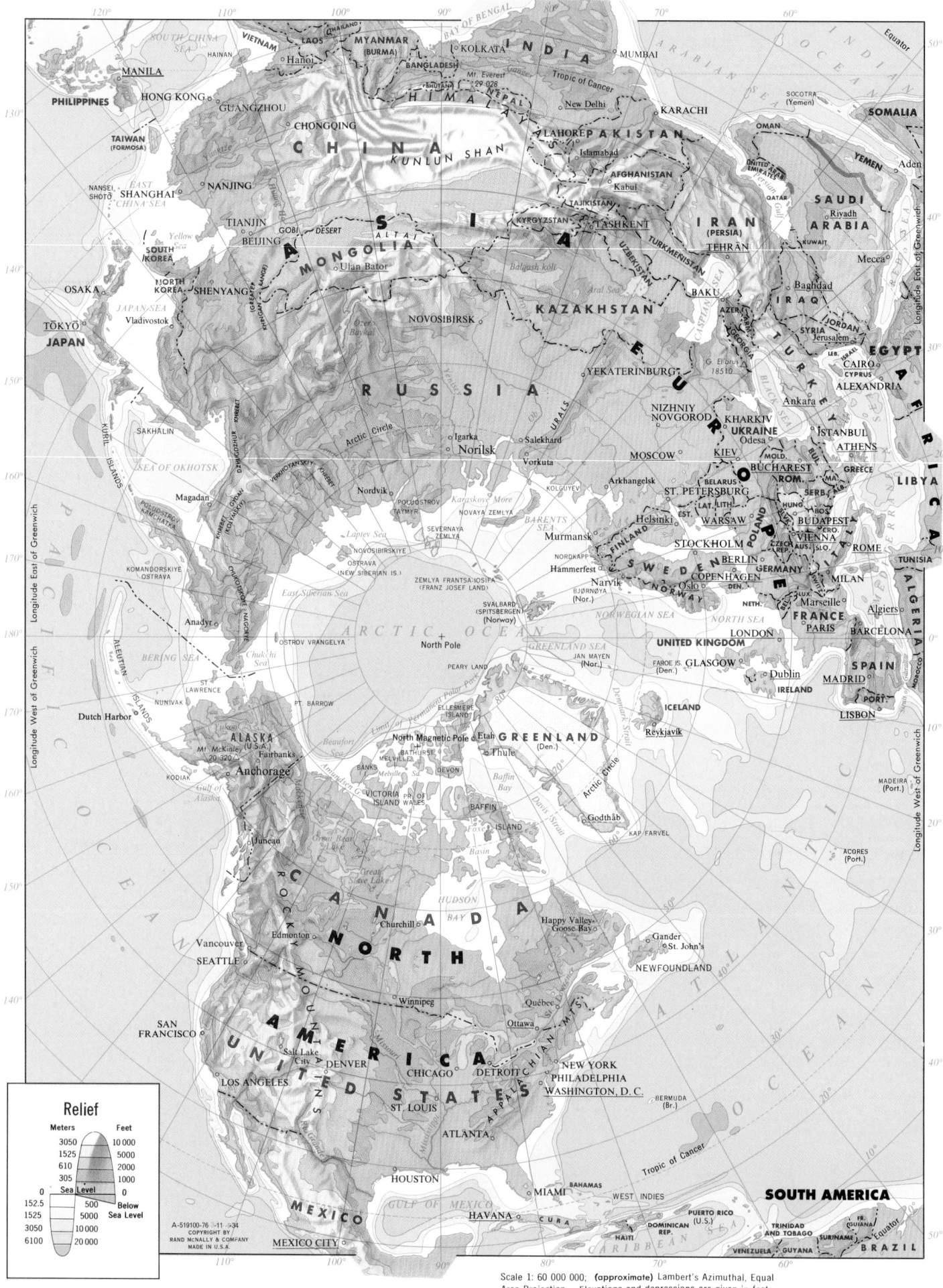

Relief

Meters		Feet
3050		10 000
1525		5000
610		2000
305		1000
0	Sea Level	0
152.5		500
1525		5000 Below
3050		10 000 Sea Level
6100		20 000

A-519100-76 -11- 34
COPYRIGHT BY
RAND McNALLY & COMPANY
MADE IN U.S.A.

Scale 1: 60 000 000; (approximate) Lambert's Azimuthal, Equal
Area Projection   Elevations and depressions are given in feet

WORLD POLITICAL INFORMATION TABLE

This table gives the area, population, population density, political status, capital, and predominant languages for every country in the world. The political units listed are categorized by political status in the form of government column of the table, as follows: A—independent countries; B—internally independent political entities which are under the protection of another country in matters of defense and foreign affairs; C—colonies and other dependent political units; and D—the major administrative subdivisions of Australia, Canada, China, the United Kingdom, and the United States. For comparison, the table also includes the continents and the world. All footnotes appear at the end of the table.

The populations are estimates for January 1, 2004, made by Rand McNally on the basis of official data, United States Census Bureau estimates, and other available information. Area figures include inland water.

REGION OR POLITICAL DIVISION	Area Sq. Mi.	Est. Pop. 1/1/04	Pop. Per Sq. Mi.	Form of Government and Ruling Power	Capital	Predominant Languages	International Organizations
Afars and Issas see Djibouti							
Afghanistan	251,773	29,205,000	116	Transitional ... A	Kābul	Dari, Pashto, Uzbek, Turkmen	UN
Africa	11,700,000	866,305,000	74				
Alabama	52,419	4,515,000	86	State (U.S.) ... D	Montgomery	English	
Alaska	663,267	650,000	1.0	State (U.S.) ... D	Juneau	English, indigenous	
Albania	11,100	3,535,000	318	Republic ... A	Tiranë	Albanian, Greek	NATO/PP, UN
Alberta	255,541	3,215,000	13	Province (Canada) ... D	Edmonton	English	
Algeria	919,595	33,090,000	36	Republic ... A	Algiers (El Djazaïr)	Arabic, Berber dialects, French	AL, AU, OPEC, UN
American Samoa	77	58,000	753	Unincorporated territory (U.S.) ... C	Pago Pago	Samoan, English	
Andorra	181	70,000	387	Parliamentary co-principality (Spanish and French) ... B	Andorra	Catalan, Spanish (Castilian), French, Portuguese	UN
Angola	481,354	10,875,000	23	Republic ... A	Luanda	Portuguese, indigenous	AU, COMESA, UN
Anguilla	37	13,000	351	Overseas territory (U.K.) ... C	The Valley	English	
Anhui	53,668	61,215,000	1,141	Province (China) ... D	Hefei	Chinese (Mandarin)	
Antarctica	5,400,000	(')					
Antigua and Barbuda	171	68,000	398	Parliamentary state ... A	St. John's	English, local dialects	OAS, UN
Aomen (Macau)	6.9	445,000	64,493	Special administrative region (China) ... D	Macau (Aomen)	Chinese (Cantonese), Portuguese	
Argentina	1,073,519	38,945,000	36	Republic ... A	Buenos Aires	Spanish, English, Italian, German, French	MERCOSUR, OAS, UN
Arizona	113,998	5,600,000	49	State (U.S.) ... D	Phoenix	English	
Arkansas	53,179	2,735,000	51	State (U.S.) ... D	Little Rock	English	
Armenia	11,506	3,325,000	289	Republic ... A	Yerevan	Armenian, Russian	CIS, NATO/PP, UN
Aruba	75	71,000	947	Self-governing territory (Netherlands protection) ... B	Oranjestad	Dutch, Papiamento, English, Spanish	
Ascension	34	1,000	29	Dependency (St. Helena) ... C	Georgetown	English	
Asia	17,300,000	3,839,320,000	222				
Australia	2,969,910	19,825,000	6.7	Federal parliamentary state ... A	Canberra	English, indigenous	ANZUS, UN
Australian Capital Territory	911	325,000	357	Territory (Australia) ... D	Canberra	English	
Austria	32,378	8,170,000	252	Federal republic ... A	Vienna (Wien)	German	EU, NATO/PP, UN
Azerbaijan	33,437	7,850,000	235	Republic ... A	Baku (Bakı)	Azeri, Russian, Armenian	CIS, NATO/PP, UN
Bahamas	5,382	300,000	56	Parliamentary state ... A	Nassau	English, Creole	OAS, UN
Bahrain	267	675,000	2,528	Monarchy ... A	Al Manāmah	Arabic, English, Persian, Urdu	AL, UN
Bangladesh	55,598	139,875,000	2,516	Republic ... A	Dkaha (Dacca)	Bangla, English	UN
Barbados	166	280,000	1,687	Parliamentary state ... A	Bridgetown	English	OAS, UN
Beijing (Peking)	6,487	14,135,000	2,179	Autonomous city (China) ... D	Beijing (Peking)	Chinese (Mandarin)	
Belarus	80,155	10,315,000	129	Republic ... A	Minsk	Belarussian, Russian	CIS, NATO/PP, UN
Belau see Palau							
Belgium	11,787	10,340,000	877	Constitutional monarchy ... A	Brussels (Bruxelles)	Dutch (Flemish), French, German	EU, NATO, UN
Belize	8,867	270,000	30	Parliamentary state ... A	Belmopan	English, Spanish, Mayan, Garifuna, Creole	OAS, UN
Benin	43,484	7,145,000	164	Republic ... A	Porto-Novo and Cotonou	French, Fon, Yoruba, indigenous	AU, UN
Bermuda	21	65,000	3,095	Overseas territory (U.K. protection) ... B	Hamilton	English, Portuguese	
Bhutan	17,954	2,160,000	120	Monarchy (Indian protection) ... B	Thimphu	Dzongkha, Tibetan and Nepalese dialects	UN
Bolivia	424,165	8,655,000	20	Republic ... A	La Paz and Sucre	Aymara, Quechua, Spanish	OAS, UN
Bosnia and Herzegovina	19,767	4,000,000	202	Republic ... A	Sarajevo	Bosnian, Serbian, Croatian	UN
Botswana	224,607	1,570,000	7.0	Republic ... A	Gaborone	English, Tswana	AU, UN
Brazil	3,300,172	183,080,000	55	Federal republic ... A	Brasilia	Portuguese, Spanish, English, French	MERCOSUR, OAS, UN
British Columbia	364,764	4,245,000	12	Province (Canada) ... D	Victoria	English	
British Indian Ocean Territory	23	(')		Overseas territory (U.K.) ... C		English	
British Virgin Islands	58	22,000	379	Overseas territory (U.K.) ... C	Road Town	English	
Brunei	2,226	360,000	162	Monarchy ... A	Bandar Seri Begawan	Malay, English, Chinese	ASEAN, UN
Bulgaria	42,855	7,550,000	176	Republic ... A	Sofia (Sofiya)	Bulgarian, Turkish	NATO, UN
Burkina Faso	105,869	13,400,000	127	Republic ... A	Ouagadougou	French, indigenous	AU, UN
Burma see Myanmar							
Burundi	10,745	6,165,000	574	Republic ... A	Bujumbura	French, Kirundi, Swahili	AU, COMESA, UN
California	163,696	35,590,000	217	State (U.S.) ... D	Sacramento	English	
Cambodia	69,898	13,245,000	189	Constitutional monarchy ... A	Phnom Penh (Phnum Pénh)	Khmer, French, English	ASEAN, UN
Cameroon	183,568	15,905,000	87	Republic ... A	Yaoundé	English, French, indigenous	AU, UN
Canada	3,855,103	32,360,000	8.4	Federal parliamentary state ... A	Ottawa	English, French, other	NAFTA, NATO, OAS, UN
Cape Verde	1,557	415,000	267	Republic ... A	Praia	Portuguese, Crioulo	AU, UN
Cayman Islands	102	43,000	422	Overseas territory (U.K.) ... C	George Town	English	
Central African Republic	240,536	3,715,000	15	Republic ... A	Bangui	French, Sango, indigenous	AU, UN
Ceylon see Sri Lanka							
Chad	495,755	9,395,000	19	Republic ... A	N'Djamena	Arabic, French, indigenous	AU, UN
Channel Islands	75	155,000	2,067	Two crown dependencies (U.K. protection)		English, French	
Chile	291,930	15,745,000	54	Republic ... A	Santiago	Spanish	OAS, UN
China (excl. Taiwan)	3,690,045	1,298,720,000	352	Socialist republic ... A	Beijing (Peking)	Chinese dialects	UN
Chongqing	31,815	31,600,000	993	Autonomous city (China) ... D	Chongqing (Chungking)	Chinese (Mandarin)	
Christmas Island	52	400	7.7	External territory (Australia) ... C	Settlement	English, Chinese, Malay	
Cocos (Keeling) Islands	5.4	600	111	External territory (Australia) ... C	West Island	English, Cocos-Malay	
Colombia	439,737	41,985,000	95	Republic ... A	Bogotá	Spanish	OAS, UN
Colorado	104,094	4,565,000	44	State (U.S.) ... D	Denver	English	
Comoros (excl. Mayotte)	863	640,000	742	Republic ... A	Moroni	Arabic, French, Shikomoro	AL, AU, COMESA, UN
Congo	132,047	2,975,000	23	Republic ... A	Brazzaville	French, Lingala, Monokutuba, indigenous	AU, UN
Congo, Democratic Republic of the (Zaire)	905,446	57,445,000	63	Republic ... A	Kinshasa	French, Lingala, indigenous	AU, COMESA, UN
Connecticut	5,543	3,495,000	631	State (U.S.) ... D	Hartford	English	

REGION OR POLITICAL DIVISION	Area Sq. Mi.	Est. Pop. 1/1/04	Pop. Per Sq. Mi.	Form of Government and Ruling Power	Capital	Predominant Languages	International Organizations
Cook Islands	91	21,000	231	Self-governing territory (New Zealand protection) ... B	Avarua	English, Maori	OAS, UN
Costa Rica	19,730	3,925,000	199	Republic ... A	San José	Spanish, English	OAS, UN
Cote d'Ivoire (Ivory Coast)	124,504	17,145,000	138	Republic ... A	Abidjan and Yamoussoukro	French, Dioula and other indigenous	AU, UN
Croatia	21,829	4,430,000	203	Republic ... A	Zagreb	Croatian	NATO/PP, UN
Cuba	42,804	11,290,000	264	Socialist republic ... A	Havana (La Habana)	Spanish	OAS, UN
Cyprus	3,572	775,000	217	Republic ... A	Nicosia	Greek, Turkish, English	EU, UN
Czech Republic	30,450	10,250,000	337	Republic ... A	Prague (Praha)	Czech	EU, NATO, UN
Delaware	2,489	820,000	329	State (U.S.) ... D	Dover	English	
Denmark	16,640	5,405,000	325	Constitutional monarchy ... A	Copenhagen (København)	Danish	EU, NATO, UN
District of Columbia	68	565,000	8,309	Federal district (U.S.) ... D	Washington	English	
Djibouti	8,958	460,000	51	Republic ... A	Djibouti	French, Arabic, Somali, Afar	AL, AU, COMESA, UN
Dominica	290	69,000	238	Republic ... A	Roseau	English, French	OAS, UN
Dominican Republic	18,730	8,775,000	468	Republic ... A	Santo Domingo	Spanish	OAS, UN
East Timor	5,743	1,010,000	176	Republic ... A	Dili	Portuguese, Tetum, Bahasa Indonesia (Malay), English	UN
Ecuador	109,484	13,840,000	126	Republic ... A	Quito	Spanish, Quechua, indigenous	OAS, UN
Egypt	386,662	75,420,000	195	Republic ... A	Cairo (Al Qāhirah)	Arabic	AL, AU, CAEU, COMESA, UN
Ellice Islands see Tuvalu							
El Salvador	8,124	6,530,000	804	Republic ... A	San Salvador	Spanish, Nahua	OAS, UN
England	50,356	50,360,000	1,000	Administrative division (U.K.) ... D	London	English	
Equatorial Guinea	10,831	515,000	48	Republic ... A	Malabo	French, Spanish, indigenous, English	AU, UN
Eritrea	45,406	4,390,000	97	Republic ... A	Asmera	Afar, Arabic, Tigre, Kunama, Tigrinya, other	AU, COMESA, UN
Estonia	17,462	1,405,000	80	Republic ... A	Tallinn	Estonian, Russian, Ukrainian, Finnish, other	EU, NATO, UN
Ethiopia	426,373	67,210,000	158	Federal republic ... A	Addis Ababa (Adis Abeba)	Amharic, Tigrinya, Orominga, Guaraginga, Somali, Arabic	AU, COMESA, UN
Europe	3,800,000	729,330,000	192				
Falkland Islands (²)	4,700	3,000	0.6	Overseas territory (U.K.) ... C	Stanley	English	
Faroe Islands	540	47,000	87	Self-governing territory (Danish protection) ... B	Tórshavn	Danish, Faroese	UN
Fiji	7,056	875,000	124	Republic ... A	Suva	English, Fijian, Hindustani	UN
Finland	130,559	5,210,000	40	Republic ... A	Helsinki (Helsingfors)	Finnish, Swedish, Sami, Russian	EU, NATO/PP, UN
Florida	65,755	17,070,000	260	State (U.S.) ... D	Tallahassee	English	
France (excl. Overseas Departments)	208,482	60,305,000	289	Republic ... A	Paris	French	EU, NATO, UN
French Guiana	32,253	190,000	5.9	Overseas department (France) ... C	Cayenne	French	
French Polynesia	1,544	265,000	172	Overseas territory (France) ... C	Papeete	French, Tahitian	
Fujian	46,332	35,495,000	766	Province (China) ... D	Fuzhou	Chinese dialects	
Gabon	103,347	1,340,000	13	Republic ... A	Libreville	French, Fang, indigenous	AU, UN
Gambia, The	4,127	1,525,000	370	Republic ... A	Banjul	English, Malinke, Wolof, Fula, indigenous	AU, UN
Gansu	173,746	26,200,000	151	Province (China) ... D	Lanzhou	Chinese (Mandarin), Mongolian, Tibetan dialects	
Gaza Strip	139	1,300,000	9,353	Israeli territory with limited self-government		Arabic, Hebrew	(⁴)
Georgia	59,425	8,710,000	147	State (U.S.) ... D	Atlanta	English	
Georgia	26,911	4,920,000	183	Republic ... A	Tbilisi	Georgian, Russian, Armenian, Azeri, other	NATO/PP, UN
Germany	137,847	82,415,000	598	Federal republic ... A	Berlin	German	EU, NATO, UN
Ghana	92,098	20,615,000	224	Republic ... A	Accra	English, Akan and other indigenous	AU, UN
Gibraltar (³)	2.3	28,000	12,174	Overseas territory (U.K.) ... C	Gibraltar	English, Spanish, Italian, Portuguese	
Gilbert Islands see Kiribati							
Golan Heights	454	37,000	81	Occupied by Israel		Arabic, Hebrew	
Great Britain see United Kingdom							
Greece	50,949	10,635,000	209	Republic ... A	Athens (Athina)	Greek, English, French	EU, NATO, UN
Greenland	836,331	56,000	0.07	Self-governing territory (Danish protection) ... B	Godthåb (Nuuk)	Danish, Greenlandic, English	
Grenada	133	89,000	669	Parliamentary state ... A	St. George's	English, French	OAS, UN
Guadeloupe (incl. Dependencies)	687	440,000	640	Overseas department (France) ... C	Basse-Terre	French, Creole	
Guam	212	165,000	778	Unincorporated territory (U.S.) ... C	Hagåtña (Agana)	English, Chamorro, Japanese	
Guangdong	68,649	88,375,000	1,287	Province (China) ... D	Guangzhou (Canton)	Chinese dialects, Miao-Yao	
Guangxi Zhuangzu	91,236	45,905,000	503	Autonomous region (China) ... D	Nanning	Chinese dialects, Thai, Miao-Yao	
Guatemala	42,042	14,095,000	335	Republic ... A	Guatemala	Spanish, indigenous	OAS, UN
Guernsey (incl. Dependencies)	30	65,000	2,167	Crown dependency (U.K. protection) ... B	St. Peter Port	English, French	
Guinea	94,926	9,135,000	96	Republic ... A	Conakry	French, indigenous	AU, UN
Guinea-Bissau	13,948	1,375,000	99	Republic ... A	Bissau	Portuguese, Crioulo, indigenous	AU, UN
Guizhou	65,637	36,045,000	549	Province (China) ... D	Guiyang	Chinese (Mandarin), Thai, Miao-Yao	
Guyana	83,000	705,000	8.5	Republic ... A	Georgetown	English, indigenous, Creole, Hindi, Urdu	OAS, UN
Hainan	13,205	8,050,000	610	Province (China) ... D	Haikou	Chinese, Min, Tai	
Haiti	10,714	7,590,000	708	Republic ... A	Port-au-Prince	Creole, French	OAS, UN
Hawaii	10,931	1,260,000	115	State (U.S.) ... D	Honolulu	English, Hawaiian, Japanese	
Hebei	73,359	68,965,000	940	Province (China) ... D	Shijiazhuang	Chinese (Mandarin)	
Heilongjiang	181,082	37,725,000	208	Province (China) ... D	Harbin	Chinese dialects, Mongolian, Tungus	
Henan	64,479	94,655,000	1,468	Province (China) ... D	Zhengzhou	Chinese (Mandarin)	
Holland see Netherlands							
Honduras	43,277	6,745,000	156	Republic ... A	Tegucigalpa	Spanish, indigenous	OAS, UN
Hubei	72,356	61,645,000	852	Province (China) ... D	Wuhan	Chinese dialects	
Hunan	81,082	65,855,000	812	Province (China) ... D	Changsha	Chinese dialects, Miao-Yao	
Hungary	35,919	10,045,000	280	Republic ... A	Budapest	Hungarian	EU, NATO, UN
Iceland	39,769	280,000	7.0	Republic ... A	Reykjavík	Icelandic, English, other	EFTA, NATO, UN
Idaho	83,570	1,370,000	16	State (U.S.) ... D	Boise	English	
Illinois	57,914	12,690,000	219	State (U.S.) ... D	Springfield	English	
India (incl. part of Jammu and Kashmir)	1,222,510	1,057,415,000	865	Federal republic ... A	New Delhi	English, Hindi, Telugu, Bengali, indigenous	UN
Indiana	36,418	6,215,000	171	State (U.S.) ... D	Indianapolis	English	
Indonesia	735,310	236,680,000	322	Republic ... A	Jakarta	Bahasa Indonesia (Malay), English, Dutch, indigenous	ASEAN, OPEC, UN
Iowa	56,272	2,955,000	53	State (U.S.) ... D	Des Moines	English	
Iran	636,372	68,650,000	108	Islamic republic ... A	Tehrān	Persian, Turkish dialects, Kurdish, other	OPEC, UN
Iraq	169,235	25,025,000	148	Republic ... A	Baghdād	Arabic, Kurdish, Assyrian, Armenian	AL, CAEU, OPEC, UN
Ireland	27,133	3,945,000	145	Republic ... A	Dublin (Baile Átha Cliath)	English, Irish Gaelic	EU, NATO/PP, UN
Isle of Man	221	74,000	335	Crown dependency (U.K. protection) ... B	Douglas	English, Manx Gaelic	

REGION OR POLITICAL DIVISION	Area Sq. Mi.	Est. Pop. 1/1/04	Pop. Per Sq. Mi.	Form of Government and Ruling Power	Capital	Predominant Languages	International Organizations
Israel (excl. Occupied Areas)	8,019	6,160,000	768	Republic A	Jerusalem (Yerushalayim)	Hebrew, Arabic	UN
Italy	116,342	58,030,000	499	Republic A	Rome (Roma)	Italian, German, French, Slovene	EU, NATO, UN
Ivory Coast see Cote d'Ivoire	...	...	...	...	...	...	...
Jamaica	4,244	2,705,000	637	Parliamentary state A	Kingston	English, Creole	OAS, UN
Japan	145,850	127,285,000	873	Constitutional monarchy A	Tōkyō	Japanese	UN
Jersey	45	90,000	2,000	Crown dependency (U.K. protection) B	St. Helier	English, French	...
Jiangsu	39,614	76,065,000	1,920	Province (China) D	Nanjing (Nanking)	Chinese dialects	...
Jiangxi	64,325	42,335,000	658	Province (China) D	Nanchang	Chinese dialects	...
Jilin	72,201	27,895,000	386	Province (China) D	Changchun	Chinese (Mandarin), Mongolian, Korean	...
Jordan	34,495	5,535,000	160	Constitutional monarchy A	'Ammān	Arabic	AL, CAEU, UN
Kansas	82,277	2,730,000	33	State (U.S.) D	Topeka	English	...
Kazakhstan	1,049,156	16,780,000	16	Republic A	Astana (Aqmola)	Kazakh, Russian	CIS, NATO/PP, UN
Kentucky	40,409	4,130,000	102	State (U.S.) D	Frankfort	English	...
Kenya	224,961	31,840,000	142	Republic A	Nairobi	English, Swahili, indigenous	AU, COMESA, UN
Kiribati	313	100,000	319	Republic A	Bairiki	English, I-Kiribati	UN
Korea, North	46,540	22,585,000	485	Socialist republic A	P'yŏngyang	Korean	UN
Korea, South	38,328	48,450,000	1,264	Republic A	Seoul (Sŏul)	Korean	UN
Kuwait	6,880	2,220,000	323	Constitutional monarchy A	Kuwait (Al Kuwayt)	Arabic, English	AL, CAEU, OPEC, UN
Kyrgyzstan	77,182	4,930,000	64	Republic A	Bishkek	Kirghiz, Russian	CIS, NATO/PP, UN
Laos	91,429	5,995,000	66	Socialist republic A	Viangchan (Vientiane)	Lao, French, English	ASEAN, UN
Latvia	24,942	2,340,000	94	Republic A	Rīga	Latvian, Lithuanian, Russian, other	EU, NATO, UN
Lebanon	4,016	3,755,000	935	Republic A	Beirut (Bayrut)	Arabic, French, Armenian, English	AL, UN
Lesotho	11,720	1,865,000	159	Constitutional monarchy A	Maseru	English, Sesotho, Zulu, Xhosa	AU, UN
Liaoning	56,255	43,340,000	770	Province (China) D	Shenyang (Mukden)	Chinese (Mandarin), Mongolian	...
Liberia	43,000	3,345,000	78	Republic A	Monrovia	English, indigenous	AU, UN
Libya	679,362	5,565,000	8.2	Socialist republic A	Tripoli (Ţarābulus)	Arabic	AL, AU, CAEU, OPEC, UN
Liechtenstein	62	33,000	532	Constitutional monarchy A	Vaduz	German	EFTA, UN
Lithuania	25,213	3,590,000	142	Republic A	Vilnius	Lithuanian, Polish, Russian	EU, NATO, UN
Louisiana	51,840	4,510,000	87	State (U.S.) D	Baton Rouge	English	...
Luxembourg	999	460,000	460	Constitutional monarchy A	Luxembourg	French, Luxembourgish, German	EU, NATO, UN
Macedonia	9,928	2,065,000	208	Republic A	Skopje	Macedonian, Albanian, other	NATO/PP, UN
Madagascar	226,658	17,235,000	76	Republic A	Antananarivo	French, Malagasy	AU, COMESA, UN
Maine	35,385	1,310,000	37	State (U.S.) D	Augusta	English	...
Malawi	45,747	11,780,000	258	Republic A	Lilongwe	Chichewa, English, indigenous	AU, COMESA, UN
Malaysia	127,320	23,310,000	183	Federal constitutional monarchy A	Kuala Lumpur and Putrajaya (5)	Bahasa Melayu, Chinese dialects, English, other	ASEAN, UN
Maldives	115	335,000	2,913	Republic A	Male'	Dhivehi	UN
Mali	478,841	11,790,000	25	Republic A	Bamako	French, Bambara, indigenous	AU, UN
Malta	122	400,000	3,279	Republic A	Valletta	English, Maltese	EU, UN
Manitoba	250,116	1,190,000	4.8	Province (Canada) D	Winnipeg	English	...
Marshall Islands	70	57,000	814	Republic (U.S. protection) B	Majuro (island)	English, indigenous, Japanese	UN
Martinique	425	430,000	1,012	Overseas department (France) C	Fort-de-France	French, Creole	...
Maryland	12,407	5,525,000	445	State (U.S.) D	Annapolis	English	...
Massachusetts	10,555	6,455,000	612	State (U.S.) D	Boston	English	...
Mauritania	397,956	2,955,000	7.4	Republic A	Nouakchott	Arabic, Wolof, Pular, Soninke, French	AL, AU, CAEU, UN
Mauritius (incl. Dependencies)	788	1,215,000	1,542	Republic A	Port Louis	English, French, Creole, other	AU, COMESA, UN
Mayotte (6)	144	180,000	1,250	Departmental collectivity (France) C	Mamoutzou	French, Swahili (Mahorian)	...
Mexico	758,452	104,340,000	138	Federal republic A	Mexico City (Ciudad de México)	Spanish, indigenous	NAFTA, OAS, UN
Michigan	96,716	10,110,000	105	State (U.S.) D	Lansing	English	...
Micronesia, Federated States of	271	110,000	406	Republic (U.S. protection) B	Palikir	English, indigenous	UN
Midway Islands	2.0	(1)	...	Unincorporated territory (U.S.) C	...	English	...
Minnesota	86,939	5,075,000	58	State (U.S.) D	St. Paul	English	...
Mississippi	48,430	2,890,000	60	State (U.S.) D	Jackson	English	...
Missouri	69,704	5,720,000	82	State (U.S.) D	Jefferson City	English	...
Moldova	13,070	4,440,000	340	Republic A	Chişinău (Kishinev)	Romanian (Moldovan), Russian, Gagauz	CIS, NATO/PP, UN
Monaco	0.8	32,000	40,000	Constitutional monarchy A	Monaco	French, English, Italian, Monegasque	UN
Mongolia	604,829	2,730,000	4.5	Republic A	Ulan Bator (Ulaanbaatar)	Khalkha Mongol, Turkish dialects, Russian	UN
Montana	147,042	920,000	6.3	State (U.S.) D	Helena	English	...
Montserrat	39	9,000	231	Overseas territory (U.K.) C	Plymouth	English	...
Morocco (excl. Western Sahara)	172,414	31,950,000	185	Constitutional monarchy A	Rabat	Arabic, Berber dialects, French	AL, UN
Mozambique	309,496	18,695,000	60	Republic A	Maputo	Portuguese, indigenous	AU, UN
Myanmar (Burma)	261,228	42,620,000	163	Provisional military government A	Rangoon (Yangon)	Burmese, indigenous	ASEAN, UN
Namibia	317,818	1,940,000	6.1	Republic A	Windhoek	English, Afrikaans, German, indigenous	AU, COMESA, UN
Nauru	8.1	13,000	1,605	Republic A	Yaren District	Nauruan, English	UN
Nebraska	77,354	1,745,000	23	State (U.S.) D	Lincoln	English	...
Nei Mongol (Inner Mongolia)	456,759	24,295,000	53	Autonomous region (China) D	Hohhot	Mongolian	...
Nepal	56,827	26,770,000	471	Constitutional monarchy A	Kathmandu	Nepali, indigenous	UN
Netherlands	16,164	16,270,000	1,007	Constitutional monarchy A	Amsterdam and The Hague ('s-Gravenhage)	Dutch, Frisian	EU, NATO, UN
Netherlands Antilles	309	215,000	696	Self-governing territory (Netherlands protection) B	Willemstad	Dutch, Papiamento, English, Spanish	...
Nevada	110,561	2,250,000	20	State (U.S.) D	Carson City	English	...
New Brunswick	28,150	770,000	27	Province (Canada) D	Fredericton	English, French	...
New Caledonia	7,172	210,000	29	Territorial collectivity (France) C	Nouméa	French, indigenous	...
Newfoundland and Labrador	156,453	535,000	3.4	Province (Canada) D	St. John's	English	...
New Hampshire	9,350	1,290,000	138	State (U.S.) D	Concord	English	...
New Hebrides see Vanuatu	...	...	...	...	...	...	...
New Jersey	8,721	8,665,000	994	State (U.S.) D	Trenton	English	...
New Mexico	121,590	1,880,000	15	State (U.S.) D	Santa Fe	English, Spanish	...
New South Wales	309,129	6,665,000	22	State (Australia) D	Sydney	English	...
New York	54,556	19,245,000	353	State (U.S.) D	Albany	English	...
New Zealand	104,454	3,975,000	38	Parliamentary state A	Wellington	English, Maori	ANZUS, UN
Nicaragua	50,054	5,180,000	103	Republic A	Managua	Spanish, English, indigenous	OAS, UN
Niger	489,192	11,210,000	23	Repubic A	Niamey	French, Hausa, Djerma, indigenous	AU, UN
Nigeria	356,669	135,570,000	380	Transitional military government A	Abuja	English, Hausa, Fulani, Yorbua, Ibo, indigenous	AU, OPEC, UN
Ningxia Huizu	25,637	5,745,000	224	Autonomous region (China) D	Yinchuan	Chinese (Mandarin)	...
Niue	100	2,000	20	Self-governing territory (New Zealand protection) B	Alofi	Niuean, English	...
Norfolk Island	14	2,000	143	External territory (Australia) C	Kingston	English, Norfolk	...

REGION OR POLITICAL DIVISION	Area Sq. Mi.	Est. Pop. 1/1/04	Pop. Per Sq. Mi.	Form of Government and Ruling Power	Capital	Predominant Languages	International Organizations
North America	9,500,000	505,780,000	53				
North Carolina	53,819	8,430,000	157	State (U.S.) D	Raleigh	English	
North Dakota	70,700	635,000	9.0	State (U.S.) D	Bismarck	English	
Northern Ireland	5,242	1,725,000	329	Administrative division (U.K.) D	Belfast	English	
Northern Mariana Islands	179	77,000	430	Commonwealth (U.S. protection) B	Saipan (island)	English, Chamorro, Carolinian	
Northern Territory	520,902	200,000	0.4	Territory (Australia) D	Darwin	English, indigenous	
Northwest Territories	519,735	43,000	0.08	Territory (Canada) D	Yellowknife	English, indigenous	
Norway (incl. Svalbard and Jan Mayen)	125,050	4,565,000	37	Constitutional monarchy A	Oslo	Norwegian, Sami, Finnish	EFTA, NATO, UN
Nova Scotia	21,345	965,000	45	Province (Canada) D	Halifax	English	
Nunavut	808,185	30,000	0.04	Territory (Canada) D	Iqaluit	English, indigenous	
Oceania (incl. Australia)	3,300,000	32,170,000	9.7				
Ohio	44,825	11,470,000	256	State (U.S.) D	Columbus	English	
Oklahoma	69,898	3,520,000	50	State (U.S.) D	Oklahoma City	English	
Oman	119,499	2,855,000	24	Monarchy A	Muscat (Masqat)	Arabic, English, Baluchi, Urdu, Indian dialects	AL, UN
Ontario	415,599	12,495,000	30	Province (Canada) D	Toronto	English	
Oregon	98,381	3,570,000	36	State (U.S.) D	Salem	English	
Pakistan (incl. part of Jammu and Kashmir)	339,732	152,210,000	448	Federal Islamic republic A	Islāmābād	English, Urdu, Punjabi, Sindhi, Pashto, other	UN
Palau (Belau)	188	20,000	106	Republic (U.S. protection) B	Koror and Melekeok (¹)	Angaur, English, Japanese, Palauan, Sonsorolese, Tobi	UN
Panama	29,157	2,980,000	102	Republic A	Panamá	Spanish, English	OAS, UN
Papua New Guinea	178,704	5,360,000	30	Parliamentary state A	Port Moresby	English, Motu, Pidgin, indigenous	UN
Paraguay	157,048	6,115,000	39	Republic A	Asunción	Guarani, Spanish	MERCOSUR, OAS, UN
Pennsylvania	46,055	12,400,000	269	State (U.S.) D	Harrisburg	English	
Peru	496,225	28,640,000	58	Republic A	Lima	Quechua, Spanish, Aymara	OAS, UN
Philippines	115,831	85,430,000	738	Republic A	Manila	English, Filipino, indigenous	ASEAN, UN
Pitcairn Islands (incl. Dependencies)	19	100	5.3	Overseas territory (U.K.) C	Adamstown	English, Pitcairnese	
Poland	120,728	38,625,000	320	Republic A	Warsaw (Warszawa)	Polish	EU, NATO, UN
Portugal	35,516	10,110,000	285	Republic A	Lisbon (Lisboa)	Portuguese, Mirandese	EU, NATO, UN
Prince Edward Island	2,185	140,000	64	Province (Canada) D	Charlottetown	English	
Puerto Rico	3,515	3,890,000	1,107	Commonwealth (U.S. protection) B	San Juan	Spanish, English	
Qatar	4,412	830,000	188	Monarchy A	Ad Dawḥah (Doha)	Arabic	AL, OPEC, UN
Qinghai	277,994	5,295,000	19	Province (China) D	Xining	Tibetan dialects, Mongolian, Turkish dialects, Chinese (Mandarin)	
Quebec	595,391	7,675,000	13	Province (Canada) D	Québec	French, English	
Queensland	668,208	3,785,000	5.7	State (Australia) D	Brisbane	English	
Reunion	969	760,000	784	Overseas department (France) C	Saint-Denis	French, Creole	
Rhode Island	1,545	1,080,000	699	State (U.S.) D	Providence	English	
Rhodesia see Zimbabwe							
Romania	91,699	22,370,000	244	Republic A	Bucharest (București)	Romanian, Hungarian, German	NATO, UN
Russia	6,592,849	144,310,000	22	Federal republic A	Moscow (Moskva)	Russian, other	CIS, NATO/PP, UN
Rwanda	10,169	7,880,000	775	Republic A	Kigali	English, French, Kinyarwanda, Kiswahili	AU, COMESA, UN
St. Helena (incl. Dependencies)	121	7,500	62	Overseas territory (U.K.) C	Jamestown	English	
St. Kitts and Nevis	101	39,000	386	Parliamentary state A	Basseterre	English	OAS, UN
St. Lucia	238	165,000	693	Parliamentary state A	Castries	English, French	OAS, UN
St. Pierre and Miquelon	93	7,000	75	Territorial collectivity (France) C	Saint-Pierre	French	
St. Vincent and the Grenadines	150	115,000	767	Parliamentary state A	Kingstown	English, French	OAS, UN
Samoa	1,093	180,000	165	Constitutional monarchy A	Apia	English, Samoan	UN
San Marino	24	28,000	1,167	Republic A	San Marino	Italian	UN
Sao Tome and Principe	372	180,000	484	Republic A	São Tomé	Portuguese	AU, UN
Saskatchewan	251,366	1,025,000	4.1	Province (Canada) D	Regina	English	
Saudi Arabia	830,000	24,690,000	30	Monarchy A	Riyadh (Ar Riyāḍ)	Arabic	AL, OPEC, UN
Scotland	30,167	5,135,000	170	Administrative division (U.K.) D	Edinburgh	English, Scots Gaelic	
Senegal	75,951	10,715,000	141	Republic A	Dakar	French, Wolof and other indigenous	AU, UN
Serbia and Montenegro (Yugoslavia)	39,449	10,660,000	270	Republic A	Belgrade (Beograd)	Serbian, Albanian	UN
Seychelles	176	81,000	460	Republic A	Victoria	English, French, Creole	AU, COMESA, UN
Shaanxi	79,151	36,865,000	466	Province (China) D	Xi'an (Sian)	Chinese (Mandarin)	
Shandong	59,074	92,845,000	1,572	Province (China) D	Jinan	Chinese (Mandarin)	
Shanghai	2,394	17,120,000	7,151	Autonomous city (China) D	Shanghai	Chinese (Wu)	
Shanxi	60,232	33,715,000	560	Province (China) D	Taiyuan	Chinese (Mandarin)	
Sichuan	188,263	85,175,000	452	Province (China) D	Chengdu	Chinese (Mandarin), Tibetan dialects, Miao-Yao	
Sierra Leone	27,699	5,815,000	210	Republic A	Freetown	English, Krio, Mende, Temne, indigenous	AU, UN
Singapore	264	4,685,000	17,746	Republic A	Singapore	Chinese (Mandarin), English, Malay, Tamil	ASEAN, UN
Slovakia	18,924	5,420,000	286	Republic A	Bratislava	Slovak, Hungarian	EU, NATO, UN
Slovenia	7,821	1,935,000	247	Republic A	Ljubljana	Slovenian, Croatian, Serbian	EU, NATO, UN
Solomon Islands	10,954	515,000	47	Parliamentary state A	Honiara	English, indigenous	UN
Somalia	246,201	8,165,000	33	Transitional A	Mogadishu (Muqdisho)	Arabic, Somali, English, Italian	AL, AU, CAEU, UN
South Africa	470,693	42,770,000	91	Republic A	Pretoria, Cape Town, and Bloemfontein	Afrikaans, English, Xhosa, Zulu, other indigenous	AU, UN
South America	6,900,000	366,600,000	53				
South Australia	379,724	1,525,000	4.0	State (Australia) D	Adelaide	English	
South Carolina	32,020	4,160,000	130	State (U.S.) D	Columbia	English	
South Dakota	77,117	765,000	9.9	State (U.S.) D	Pierre	English	
South Georgia and the South Sandwich Islands (²)	1,450	(¹)		Overseas territory (U.K.) C		English	
South West Africa see Namibia							
Spain	194,885	40,250,000	207	Constitutional monarchy A	Madrid	Spanish (Castilian), Catalan, Galician, Basque	EU, NATO, UN
Spanish North Africa (³)	12	140,000	11,667	Five possessions (Spain) C		Spanish, Arabic, Berber dialects	
Spanish Sahara see Western Sahara							
Sri Lanka	25,332	19,825,000	783	Socialist republic A	Colombo and Sri Jayewardenepura Kotte	English, Sinhala, Tamil	UN
Sudan	967,500	38,630,000	40	Provisional military government A	Khartoum (Al Kharṭūm)	Arabic, Nubian, and other indigenous, English	AL, AU, CAEU, COMESA, UN
Suriname	63,037	435,000	6.9	Republic A	Paramaribo	Dutch, Sranan Tongo, English, Hindustani, Javanese	OAS, UN

REGION OR POLITICAL DIVISION	Area Sq. Mi.	Est. Pop. 1/1/04	Pop. Per Sq. Mi.	Form of Government and Ruling Power	Capital	Predominant Languages	International Organizations
Swaziland	6,704	1,165,000	174	Monarchy ... A	Mbabane and Lobamba	English, siSwati	AU, COMESA, UN
Sweden	173,732	8,980,000	52	Constitutional monarchy ... A	Stockholm	Swedish, Sami, Finnish	EU, NATO/PP, UN
Switzerland	15,943	7,430,000	466	Federal republic ... A	Bern (Berne)	German, French, Italian, Romansch	EFTA, NATO/PP, UN
Syria	71,498	17,800,000	249	Republic ... A	Damascus (Dimashq)	Arabic, Kurdish, Armenian, Aramaic, Circassian	AL, CAEU, UN
Taiwan	13,901	22,675,000	1,631	Republic ... A	T'aipei	Chinese (Mandarin), Taiwanese (Min), Hakka	
Tajikistan	55,251	6,935,000	126	Republic ... A	Dushanbe	Tajik, Russian	CIS, NATO/PP, UN
Tanzania	364,900	36,230,000	99	Republic ... A	Dar es Salaam and Dodoma	English, Swahili, indigenous	AU, UN
Tasmania	26,409	475,000	18	State (Australia) ... D	Hobart	English	
Tennessee	42,143	5,860,000	139	State (U.S.) ... D	Nashville	English	
Texas	268,581	22,185,000	83	State (U.S.) ... D	Austin	English, Spanish	
Thailand	198,115	64,570,000	326	Constitutional monarchy ... A	Bangkok (Krung Thep)	Thai, indigenous	ASEAN, UN
Tianjin (Tientsin)	4,363	10,235,000	2,346	Autonomous city (China) ... D	Tianjin (Tientsin)	Chinese (Mandarin)	
Togo	21,925	5,495,000	251	Republic ... A	Lomé	French, Ewe, Mina, Kabye, Dagomba	AU, UN
Tokelau	4.6	1,500	326	Island territory (New Zealand) ... C		English, Tokelauan	
Tonga	251	110,000	438	Constitutional monarchy ... A	Nuku'alofa	Tongan, English	UN
Trinidad and Tobago	1,980	1,100,000	556	Republic ... A	Port of Spain	English, Hindi, French, Spanish, Chinese	OAS, UN
Tristan da Cunha	40	300	7.5	Dependency (St. Helena) ... C	Edinburgh	English	
Tunisia	63,170	9,980,000	158	Republic ... A	Tunis	Arabic, French	AL, AU, UN
Turkey	302,541	68,505,000	226	Republic ... A	Ankara	Turkish, Kurdish, Arabic, Armenian, Greek	NATO, UN
Turkmenistan	188,457	4,820,000	26	Republic ... A	Ashgabat (Ashkhabad)	Turkmen, Russian, Uzbek	CIS, NATO/PP, UN
Turks and Caicos Islands	166	20,000	120	Overseas territory (U.K.) ... C	Grand Turk	English	
Tuvalu	10	11,000	1,100	Parliamentary state ... A	Funafuti	Tuvaluan, English, Samoan, I-Kiribati	UN
Uganda	93,065	26,010,000	279	Republic ... A	Kampala	English, Luganda, Swahili, indigenous, Arabic	AU, COMESA, UN
Ukraine	233,090	47,890,000	205	Republic ... A	Kiev (Kyïv)	Ukrainian, Russian, Romanian, Polish, Hungarian	CIS, NATO/PP, UN
United Arab Emirates	32,278	2,505,000	78	Federation of monarchs ... A	Abū Ẓaby (Abu Dhabi)	Arabic, Persian, English, Hindi, Urdu	AL, CAEU, OPEC, UN
United Kingdom	93,788	60,185,000	642	Constitutional monarchy ... A	London	English, Welsh, Scots Gaelic	EU, NATO, UN
United States	3,794,083	291,680,000	77	Federal republic ... A	Washington	English, Spanish	ANZUS, NAFTA, NATO, OAS, UN
Upper Volta see Burkina Faso							
Uruguay	67,574	3,425,000	51	Republic ... A	Montevideo	Spanish	MERCOSUR, OAS, UN
Utah	84,899	2,360,000	28	State (U.S.) ... D	Salt Lake City	English	
Uzbekistan	172,742	26,195,000	152	Republic ... A	Tashkent (Toshkent)	Uzbek, Russian, Tajik	CIS, NATO/PP, UN
Vanuatu	4,707	200,000	42	Republic ... A	Port Vila	Bislama, English, French	UN
Vatican City	0.2	900	4,500	Ecclesiastical state ... A	Vatican City	Italian, Latin, French, other	
Venezuela	352,145	24,835,000	71	Federal republic ... A	Caracas	Spanish, indigenous	OAS, OPEC, UN
Vermont	9,614	620,000	64	State (U.S.) ... D	Montpelier	English	
Victoria	87,807	4,905,000	56	State (Australia) ... D	Melbourne	English	
Vietnam	128,066	82,150,000	641	Socialist republic ... A	Hanoi	Vietnamese, English, French, Chinese, Khmer, indigenous	ASEAN, UN
Virginia	42,774	7,410,000	173	State (U.S.) ... D	Richmond	English	
Virgin Islands (U.S.)	134	110,000	821	Unincorporated territory (U.S.) ... C	Charlotte Amalie	English, Spanish, Creole	
Wake Island	3.0	(¹)		Unincorporated territory (U.S.) ... C		English	
Wales	8,023	2,965,000	370	Administrative division (U.K.) ... D	Cardiff	English, Welsh Gaelic	
Wallis and Futuna	99	16,000	162	Overseas territory (France) ... C	Mata-Utu	French, Wallisian	
Washington	71,300	6,150,000	86	State (U.S.) ... D	Olympia	English	
West Bank (incl. Jericho and East Jerusalem)	2,263	2,275,000	1,005	Israeli territory with limited self-government		Arabic, Hebrew	(⁴)
Western Australia	976,792	1,945,000	2.0	State (Australia) ... D	Perth	English	
Western Sahara	102,703	265,000	2.6	Occupied by Morocco ... C		Arabic	
West Virginia	24,230	1,815,000	75	State (U.S.) ... D	Charleston	English	
Wisconsin	65,498	5,490,000	84	State (U.S.) ... D	Madison	English	
Wyoming	97,814	505,000	5.2	State (U.S.) ... D	Cheyenne	English	
Xianggang (Hong Kong)	425	7,440,000	17,506	Special administrative region (China) ... D	Hong Kong (Xianggang)	Chinese (Cantonese), English	
Xinjiang Uygur (Sinkiang)	617,764	19,685,000	32	Autonomous region (China) ... D	Ürümqi	Turkish dialects, Mongolian, Tungus, English	
Xizang (Tibet)	471,045	2,680,000	5.7	Autonomous region (China) ... D	Lhasa	Tibetan dialects	
Yemen	203,850	19,680,000	97	Republic ... A	Şan'ā' (Sanaa)	Arabic	AL, CAEU, UN
Yugoslavia see Serbia and Montenegro							
Yukon Territory	186,272	32,000	0.2	Territory (Canada) ... D	Whitehorse	English, Inuktitut, indigenous	
Yunnan	152,124	43,850,000	288	Province (China) ... D	Kunming	Chinese (Mandarin), Tibetan dialects, Khmer, Miao-Yao	
Zaire see Congo, Democratic Republic of the							
Zambia	290,586	10,385,000	36	Republic ... A	Lusaka	English, indigenous	AU, COMESA, UN
Zhejiang	39,305	47,830,000	1,217	Province (China) ... D	Hangzhou	Chinese dialects	
Zimbabwe	150,873	12,630,000	84	Republic ... A	Harare (Salisbury)	English, indigenous	AU, COMESA, UN
WORLD	57,900,000	6,339,505,000	109				

... None, or not applicable
(1) No permanent population
(2) Claimed by Argentina
(3) Claimed by Spain
(4) The Palestinian Liberation Organization (PLO) is a member of AL and CAEU
(5) Future capital
(6) Claimed by Comoros
(7) Comprises Ceuta, Melilla, and several small islands

AL	Arab League (League of Arab States)
ANZUS	Australia-New Zealand-U.S. Security Treaty
ASEAN	Association of Southeast Asian Nations
AU	African Union
CAEU	Council of Arab Unity
CIS	Commonwealth of Independent States
COMESA	Common Market for Eastern and Southern Africa
EFTA	European Free Trade Association
EU	European Union
MERCOSUR	Southern Common Market
NAFTA	North American Free Trade Agreement
NATO	North Atlantic Treaty Organization
NATO/PP	NATO-Partnership for Peace Program
OAS	Organization of American States
OPEC	Organization of Petroleum Exporting Countries

WORLD DEMOGRAPHIC TABLE

CONTINENT/Country	Population Estimate 2004	Pop. Per Sq. Mile 2004	Percent Urban[1] 2001	Crude Birth Rate per 1,000[2] 2003	Crude Death Rate per 1,000[2] 2003	Natural Increase Percent[2] 2003	Fertility Rate (Children born/Woman)[3] 2003	Infant Mortality Rate per 1,000[3] 2003	Median Age[2] 2002	Life Expectancy Male[2] 2003	Life Expectancy Female[2] 2003
NORTH AMERICA											
Bahamas	300,000	56	64.7	19	9	1.0%	2	26	27	62	69
Belize	270,000	30	48.1	30	6	2.4%	4	27	19	65	70
Canada	32,360,000	8	78.9	11	8	0.3%	2	5	38	76	83
Costa Rica	3,925,000	199	59.5	19	4	1.5%	2	11	25	74	79
Cuba	11,290,000	264	75.5	12	7	0.5%	2	7	35	75	79
Dominica	69,000	238	71.4	17	7	1.0%	2	15	28	71	77
Dominican Republic	8,775,000	468	66.0	24	7	1.7%	3	34	24	66	70
El Salvador	6,530,000	804	61.5	28	6	2.2%	3	27	21	67	74
Guatemala	14,095,000	335	39.9	35	7	2.8%	5	38	18	64	66
Haiti	7,590,000	708	36.3	34	13	2.1%	5	76	18	50	53
Honduras	6,745,000	156	53.7	32	6	2.5%	4	30	19	65	68
Jamaica	2,705,000	637	56.6	17	5	1.2%	2	13	27	74	78
Mexico	104,340,000	138	74.6	22	5	1.7%	3	22	24	72	78
Nicaragua	5,180,000	103	56.5	26	5	2.2%	3	31	20	68	72
Panama	2,980,000	102	56.5	21	5	1.5%	3	21	26	70	75
St. Lucia	165,000	693	38.0	21	5	1.6%	2	14	24	70	77
Trinidad and Tobago	1,100,000	556	74.5	13	9	0.4%	2	25	30	67	72
United States	291,680,000	77	77.4	14	8	0.6%	2	7	36	74	80
SOUTH AMERICA											
Argentina	38,945,000	36	88.3	17	8	1.0%	2	16	29	72	79
Bolivia	8,655,000	20	62.9	26	8	1.8%	3	56	21	62	67
Brazil	183,080,000	55	81.7	18	6	1.2%	2	32	27	67	75
Chile	15,745,000	54	86.1	16	6	1.0%	2	9	30	73	80
Colombia	41,985,000	95	75.5	22	6	1.6%	3	22	26	67	75
Ecuador	13,840,000	126	63.4	25	5	2.0%	3	32	23	69	75
Guyana	705,000	9	36.7	18	9	0.9%	2	38	26	61	66
Paraguay	6,115,000	39	56.7	30	5	2.6%	4	28	21	72	77
Peru	28,640,000	58	73.1	23	6	1.7%	3	37	24	68	73
Suriname	435,000	7	74.8	19	7	1.3%	2	25	26	67	72
Uruguay	3,425,000	51	92.1	17	9	0.8%	2	14	32	73	79
Venezuela	24,835,000	71	87.2	20	5	1.5%	2	24	25	71	77
EUROPE											
Albania	3,535,000	318	42.9	15	5	1.0%	2	23	27	74	80
Austria	8,170,000	252	67.4	9	9	0%	1	5	39	76	82
Belarus	10,315,000	129	69.6	10	14	-0.4%	1	14	37	63	75
Belgium	10,340,000	877	97.4	11	10	0.1%	2	5	40	75	82
Bosnia and Herzegovina	4,000,000	202	43.4	13	8	0.4%	2	23	36	70	75
Bulgaria	7,550,000	176	67.4	10	14	-0.5%	1	22	41	68	75
Croatia	4,430,000	203	58.1	13	11	0.2%	2	7	39	71	78
Czech Republic	10,250,000	337	74.5	9	11	-0.1%	1	4	38	72	79
Denmark	5,405,000	325	85.1	12	11	0.1%	2	5	39	75	80
Estonia	1,405,000	80	69.4	9	13	-0.4%	1	12	38	64	77
Finland	5,210,000	40	58.5	11	10	0.1%	2	4	40	75	82
France	60,305,000	289	75.5	13	9	0.3%	2	4	38	76	83
Germany	82,415,000	598	87.7	9	10	-0.2%	1	4	41	75	82
Greece	10,635,000	209	60.3	10	10	0%	1	6	40	76	81
Hungary	10,045,000	280	64.8	10	13	-0.3%	1	9	38	68	77
Iceland	280,000	7	92.7	14	7	0.7%	2	4	34	78	82
Ireland	3,945,000	145	59.3	14	8	0.6%	2	6	33	75	80
Italy	58,030,000	499	67.1	9	10	-0.1%	1	6	41	76	83
Latvia	2,340,000	94	59.8	9	15	-0.6%	1	15	39	63	75
Lithuania	3,590,000	142	68.6	10	13	-0.2%	1	14	37	64	76
Luxembourg	460,000	460	91.9	12	8	0.4%	2	5	38	75	82
Macedonia	2,065,000	208	59.4	13	8	0.5%	2	12	33	72	77
Moldova	4,440,000	340	41.4	14	13	0.2%	2	42	32	61	69
Netherlands	16,270,000	1,007	89.6	12	9	0.3%	2	5	39	76	81
Norway	4,565,000	37	75.0	12	10	0.3%	2	4	38	77	82
Poland	38,625,000	320	62.5	10	10	0.1%	1	9	36	70	78
Portugal	10,110,000	285	65.8	11	10	0.1%	1	6	38	73	80
Romania	22,370,000	244	55.2	11	12	-0.1%	1	28	35	67	75
Serbia and Montenegro	10,660,000	270	51.7	13	11	0.2%	2	17	36	71	77
Slovakia	5,420,000	286	57.6	10	10	0.1%	1	8	35	70	78
Slovenia	1,935,000	247	49.1	9	10	-0.1%	1	4	39	72	80
Spain	40,250,000	207	77.8	10	9	0.1%	1	5	39	76	83
Sweden	8,980,000	52	83.3	11	10	0%	2	3	40	78	83
Switzerland	7,430,000	466	67.3	10	8	0.1%	1	4	40	77	83
Ukraine	47,890,000	205	68.0	10	16	-0.7%	1	21	38	61	72
United Kingdom	60,185,000	642	89.5	11	10	0.1%	2	5	38	76	81
Russia	144,310,000	22	72.9	10	14	-0.4%	1	20	38	62	73
ASIA											
Afghanistan	29,205,000	116	22.3	41	17	2.3%	6	142	19	48	46
Armenia	3,325,000	289	67.2	13	10	0.2%	2	41	32	62	71
Azerbaijan	7,850,000	235	51.8	19	10	1.0%	2	82	27	59	68
Bahrain	675,000	2,528	92.5	19	4	1.5%	3	19	29	71	76
Bangladesh	139,875,000	2,516	25.6	30	9	2.1%	3	66	21	61	61
Brunei	360,000	162	72.8	20	3	1.6%	2	14	26	72	77
Cambodia	13,245,000	189	17.5	27	9	1.8%	4	76	19	55	60
China	1,298,720,000	352	37.1	13	7	0.6%	2	25	32	70	74
Cyprus	775,000	217	70.2	13	8	0.5%	2	8	34	75	80
East Timor	1,010,000	176	7.5	28	6	2.1%	4	50	20	63	68
Georgia	4,920,000	183	56.5	12	15	-0.3%	2	51	35	61	68
India	1,057,415,000	865	27.9	23	8	1.5%	3	60	24	63	64
Indonesia	236,680,000	322	42.1	21	6	1.5%	3	38	26	67	71
Iran	68,650,000	108	64.7	17	6	1.2%	2	44	23	68	71
Iraq	25,025,000	148	67.4	34	6	2.8%	5	55	19	67	69
Israel	6,160,000	768	91.8	19	6	1.2%	3	7	29	77	81
Japan	127,285,000	873	78.9	10	9	0.1%	1	3	42	78	84
Jordan	5,535,000	160	78.7	24	3	2.1%	3	19	22	75	81
Kazakhstan	16,780,000	16	55.8	18	11	0.8%	2	59	28	58	69
Korea, North	22,585,000	485	60.5	18	7	1.1%	2	26	31	68	74
Korea, South	48,450,000	1,264	82.5	13	6	0.7%	2	7	33	72	79
Kuwait	2,220,000	323	96.1	22	2	1.9%	3	11	26	76	78

CONTINENT/Country	Population Estimate 2004	Pop. Per Sq. Mile 2004	Percent Urban[1] 2001	Crude Birth Rate per 1,000[2] 2003	Crude Death Rate per 1,000[2] 2003	Natural Increase Percent[2] 2003	Fertility Rate (Children born/Woman)[3] 2003	Infant Mortality Rate per 1,000[3] 2003	Median Age[2] 2002	Life Expectancy Male[2] 2003	Life Expectancy Female[2] 2003
Kyrgyzstan	4,930,000	64	34.3	26	9	1.7%	3	75	23	59	68
Laos	5,995,000	66	19.7	37	12	2.5%	5	89	19	52	56
Lebanon	3,755,000	935	90.1	20	6	1.3%	2	26	26	70	75
Malaysia	23,310,000	183	58.1	24	5	1.9%	3	19	24	69	75
Mongolia	2,730,000	5	56.6	21	7	1.4%	2	57	24	62	66
Myanmar	42,620,000	163	28.1	19	12	0.7%	2	70	25	54	58
Nepal	26,770,000	471	12.2	32	10	2.3%	4	71	20	59	59
Oman	2,855,000	24	76.5	37	4	3.4%	6	21	19	70	75
Pakistan	152,210,000	448	33.4	30	9	2.1%	4	77	20	61	63
Philippines	85,430,000	738	59.4	26	6	2.1%	3	25	22	66	72
Qatar	830,000	188	92.9	16	4	1.1%	3	20	31	71	76
Saudi Arabia	24,690,000	30	86.7	37	6	3.1%	6	48	19	67	71
Singapore	4,685,000	17,746	100.0	13	4	0.8%	1	4	35	77	84
Sri Lanka	19,825,000	783	23.1	16	6	1.0%	2	15	29	70	75
Syria	17,800,000	249	51.8	30	5	2.5%	4	32	20	68	71
Taiwan	22,675,000	1,631	(5)	13	6	0.7%	2	7	33	74	80
Tajikistan	6,935,000	126	27.7	33	8	2.4%	4	113	19	61	68
Thailand	64,570,000	326	20.0	16	7	1.0%	2	22	30	69	74
Turkey	68,505,000	226	66.2	18	6	1.2%	2	44	27	69	74
Turkmenistan	4,820,000	26	44.9	28	9	1.9%	4	73	21	58	65
United Arab Emirates	2,505,000	78	87.2	18	4	1.4%	3	16	28	72	77
Uzbekistan	26,195,000	152	36.6	26	8	1.8%	3	72	22	61	68
Vietnam	82,150,000	641	24.5	20	6	1.3%	2	31	25	68	73
Yemen	19,680,000	97	25.0	43	9	3.4%	7	65	16	59	63
AFRICA											
Algeria	33,090,000	36	57.7	22	5	1.7%	3	38	23	69	72
Angola	10,875,000	23	34.9	46	26	2.0%	6	194	18	36	38
Benin	7,145,000	164	43.0	43	14	3.0%	6	87	16	50	52
Botswana	1,570,000	7	49.4	26	31	-0.6%	3	67	19	32	32
Burkina Faso	13,400,000	127	16.9	45	19	2.6%	6	100	17	43	46
Burundi	6,165,000	574	9.3	40	18	2.2%	6	72	16	43	44
Cameroon	15,905,000	87	49.7	35	15	2.0%	5	70	18	47	49
Cape Verde	415,000	267	63.5	27	7	2.0%	4	51	19	67	73
Central African Republic	3,715,000	15	41.7	36	20	1.6%	5	93	18	40	43
Chad	9,395,000	19	24.1	47	16	3.1%	6	96	16	47	50
Comoros	640,000	742	33.8	39	9	3.0%	5	80	19	59	64
Congo	2,975,000	23	66.1	29	14	1.5%	4	95	20	49	51
Congo, Democratic Republic of the	57,445,000	63	30.7	45	15	3.0%	7	97	16	47	51
Cote d'Ivoire	17,145,000	138	44.0	40	18	2.2%	6	98	17	40	45
Djibouti	460,000	51	84.2	41	19	2.1%	6	107	18	42	44
Egypt	75,420,000	195	42.7	24	5	1.9%	3	35	23	68	73
Equatorial Guinea	515,000	48	49.3	37	13	2.4%	5	89	19	53	57
Eritrea	4,390,000	97	19.1	39	13	2.6%	6	76	18	51	55
Ethiopia	67,210,000	158	15.9	40	20	2.0%	6	103	17	40	42
Gabon	1,340,000	13	82.3	37	11	2.5%	5	55	19	55	59
Gambia, The	1,525,000	370	31.3	41	12	2.8%	6	75	17	52	56
Ghana	20,615,000	224	36.4	26	11	1.5%	3	53	20	56	57
Guinea	9,135,000	96	27.9	43	16	2.7%	6	93	18	48	51
Guinea-Bissau	1,375,000	99	32.3	38	17	2.2%	5	110	19	45	49
Kenya	31,840,000	142	34.4	29	16	1.3%	3	63	18	45	45
Lesotho	1,865,000	159	28.8	27	25	0.3%	4	86	20	37	37
Liberia	3,345,000	78	45.5	45	18	2.7%	6	132	18	47	49
Libya	5,565,000	8	88.0	27	3	2.4%	3	27	22	74	78
Madagascar	17,235,000	76	30.1	42	12	3.0%	6	80	17	54	59
Malawi	11,780,000	258	15.1	45	23	2.2%	6	105	16	38	38
Mali	11,790,000	25	30.9	48	19	2.9%	7	119	16	45	46
Mauritania	2,955,000	7	59.1	42	13	2.9%	6	74	17	50	54
Mauritius	1,215,000	1,542	41.6	16	7	0.9%	2	16	30	68	76
Morocco	31,950,000	185	56.1	23	6	1.7%	3	45	23	68	72
Mozambique	18,695,000	60	33.3	37	23	1.4%	5	138	19	39	37
Namibia	1,940,000	6	31.4	34	19	1.5%	5	68	18	44	41
Niger	11,210,000	23	21.1	50	22	2.8%	7	124	16	42	42
Nigeria	135,570,000	380	44.9	39	14	2.5%	5	71	18	51	51
Rwanda	7,880,000	775	6.3	40	22	1.8%	6	103	18	39	40
Sao Tome and Principe	180,000	484	47.7	42	7	3.5%	6	46	16	65	68
Senegal	10,715,000	141	48.2	36	11	2.5%	5	58	18	55	58
Sierra Leone	5,815,000	210	37.3	44	21	2.3%	6	147	18	40	45
Somalia	8,165,000	33	27.9	46	18	2.9%	7	120	18	46	49
South Africa	42,770,000	91	57.7	19	18	0%	2	61	25	47	47
Sudan	38,630,000	40	37.1	36	10	2.7%	5	66	18	57	59
Swaziland	1,165,000	174	26.7	29	21	0.8%	5	67	19	41	38
Tanzania	36,230,000	99	33.3	40	17	2.2%	5	104	18	43	46
Togo	5,495,000	251	33.9	35	12	2.4%	5	69	17	51	55
Tunisia	9,980,000	158	66.2	17	5	1.2%	2	27	26	73	76
Uganda	26,010,000	279	14.5	47	17	3.0%	7	88	15	43	46
Zambia	10,385,000	36	39.8	40	24	1.5%	5	99	17	35	35
Zimbabwe	12,630,000	84	36.0	30	22	0.8%	4	66	19	40	38
OCEANIA											
Australia	19,825,000	7	91.2	13	7	0.5%	2	5	36	77	83
Fiji	875,000	124	50.2	23	6	1.7%	3	13	24	66	71
Kiribati	100,000	319	38.6	31	9	2.3%	4	51	20	58	64
Micronesia, Federated States of	110,000	406	28.6	26	5	2.1%	4	32	19[4]	67	71
New Zealand	3,975,000	38	85.9	14	8	0.7%	2	6	33	75	81
Papua New Guinea	5,360,000	30	17.6	31	8	2.3%	4	55	21	62	66
Samoa	180,000	165	22.3	15	6	0.9%	3	30	24	67	73
Solomon Islands	515,000	47	20.2	32	4	2.8%	4	23	18	70	75
Tonga	110,000	438	33.0	25	6	1.9%	3	13	20	66	71
Vanuatu	200,000	42	22.1	24	8	1.6%	3	58	22	60	63

This table presents data for most independent nations having an area greater than 200 square miles
(1) Source: United Nations World Urbanization Prospects
(2) Source: United States Census Bureau International Database
(3) Source: United States Central Intelligence Agency World Factbook
(4) 2000 Census preliminary count from www.fsmgov.org/info/people.html
(5) Data for Taiwan is included with China

WORLD AGRICULTURE TABLE

CONTINENT/Country	Agricultural Area 2001					Average Production 1999-2001			Average 1999-2001		
	Total Area Sq. Miles	Cropland Area[1] Sq. Miles	Cropland Area[1] %	Pasture Area[1] Sq. Miles	Pasture Area[1] %	Wheat[1] 1,000 metric tons	Rice[1] 1,000 metric tons	Corn[1] 1,000 metric tons	Cattle[1] 1,000	Pigs[1] 1,000	Sheep[1] 1,000
NORTH AMERICA											
Bahamas	5,382	46	0.9%	8	0.1%	-	-	-	1	5	6
Belize	8,867	402	4.5%	193	2.2%	-	12	36	52	25	4
Canada	3,855,103	177,144	4.6%	111,970	2.9%	24,676	-	8,168	13,340	12,970	819
Costa Rica	19,730	2,027	10.3%	9,035	45.8%	-	267	20	1,358	438	3
Cuba	42,804	17,239	40.3%	8,494	19.8%	-	342	207	4,305	2,600	310
Dominica	290	77	26.6%	8	2.7%	-	-	-	13	5	8
Dominican Republic	18,730	6,162	32.9%	8,108	43.3%	-	615	30	2,026	548	106
El Salvador	8,124	3,514	43.2%	3,066	37.7%	-	47	605	1,190	195	5
Guatemala	42,042	7,355	17.5%	10,046	23.9%	9	46	1,057	2,500	1,417	270
Haiti	10,714	4,247	39.6%	1,892	17.7%	-	111	211	1,390	934	147
Honduras	43,277	5,514	12.7%	5,822	13.5%	1	9	509	1,737	474	14
Jamaica	4,244	1,097	25.8%	884	20.8%	-	-	2	400	180	1
Mexico	758,452	105,406	13.9%	308,882	40.7%	3,263	324	18,466	30,428	16,112	6,048
Nicaragua	50,054	8,382	16.7%	18,591	37.1%	-	234	374	2,008	402	4
Panama	29,157	2,683	9.2%	5,927	20.3%	-	237	71	1,348	279	-
St. Lucia	238	69	29.2%	8	3.2%	-	-	-	12	15	13
Trinidad and Tobago	1,980	471	23.8%	42	2.1%	-	13	5	36	41	12
United States	3,794,083	684,401	18.0%	903,479	23.8%	58,862	9,222	244,296	98,197	60,229	7,071
SOUTH AMERICA											
Argentina	1,073,519	135,136	12.6%	548,265	51.1%	15,642	1,140	15,217	49,299	4,200	13,588
Bolivia	424,165	11,973	2.8%	130,618	30.8%	121	281	607	6,715	2,786	8,743
Brazil	3,300,172	256,623	7.8%	760,621	23.0%	2,461	10,998	35,119	170,295	30,608	14,728
Chile	291,930	8,880	3.0%	49,942	17.1%	1,490	113	685	4,117	2,395	4,153
Colombia	439,737	16,405	3.7%	161,391	36.7%	37	2,262	1,128	25,274	2,726	2,247
Ecuador	109,484	11,525	10.5%	19,653	18.0%	19	1,340	483	5,261	2,654	2,214
Guyana	83,000	1,969	2.4%	4,749	5.7%	-	560	3	220	20	130
Paraguay	157,048	12,008	7.6%	83,784	53.3%	256	112	804	9,758	2,633	402
Peru	496,225	16,255	3.3%	104,634	21.1%	180	1,963	1,205	4,936	2,795	14,414
Suriname	63,037	259	0.4%	81	0.1%	-	178	-	128	22	8
Uruguay	67,574	5,174	7.7%	52,290	77.4%	284	1,189	190	10,446	375	13,257
Venezuela	352,145	13,158	3.7%	70,425	20.0%	1	696	1,547	14,620	5,555	780
EUROPE											
Albania	11,100	2,699	24.3%	1,699	15.3%	298	-	203	719	96	1,929
Austria	32,378	5,676	17.5%	7,413	22.9%	1,412	-	1,774	2,166	3,556	357
Belarus	80,155	24,151	30.1%	11,564	14.4%	903	-	13	4,411	3,565	96
Belgium	11,787	3,344[2]	26.2%[2]	2,618[2]	20.5%[2]	1,535	-	420	3,165	7,462	150
Bosnia and Herzegovina	19,767	3,243	16.4%	4,633	23.4%	289	-	656	448	345	645
Bulgaria	42,855	17,900	41.8%	6,236	14.6%	3,071	8	1,137	664	1,459	2,536
Croatia	21,829	6,124	28.1%	6,035	27.6%	852	-	1,958	435	1,276	519
Czech Republic	30,450	12,788	42.0%	3,730	12.2%	4,196	-	324	1,604	3,761	87
Denmark	16,640	8,880	53.4%	1,452	8.7%	4,683	-	-	1,887	12,052	147
Estonia	17,462	2,691	15.4%	745	4.3%	123	-	-	276	304	29
Finland	130,559	8,490	6.5%	77	0.1%	427	-	-	1,060	1,303	101
France	208,482	75,618	36.3%	38,788	18.6%	35,327	110	15,928	20,377	14,693	9,754
Germany	137,847	46,409	33.7%	19,355	14.0%	21,358	-	3,362	14,723	26,021	2,746
Greece	50,949	14,873	29.2%	17,954	35.2%	2,111	153	2,007	584	925	8,977
Hungary	35,919	18,548	51.6%	4,097	11.4%	3,843	9	6,664	845	5,216	991
Iceland	39,769	27	0.1%	8,780	22.1%	-	-	-	72	44	477
Ireland	27,133	4,050	14.9%	12,934	47.7%	688	-	-	6,613	1,765	5,311
Italy	116,342	42,379	36.4%	16,907	14.5%	7,239	1,310	10,222	7,167	8,356	11,000
Latvia	24,942	7,220	28.9%	2,355	9.4%	410	-	-	393	407	28
Lithuania	25,213	11,541	45.8%	1,923	7.6%	1,062	-	-	856	984	14
Luxembourg	999	[3]	[3]	[3]	[3]	-	-	2	134	-	-
Macedonia	9,928	2,363	23.8%	2,432	24.5%	308	20	135	267	209	1,285
Moldova	13,070	8,398	64.3%	1,483	11.3%	902	-	1,096	423	646	929
Netherlands	16,164	3,622	22.4%	3,834	23.7%	995	-	148	4,108	13,253	1,335
Norway	125,050	3,398	2.7%	625	0.5%	265	-	-	1,017	414	2,342
Poland	120,728	55,267	45.8%	15,745	13.0%	8,946	-	962	6,124	17,588	366
Portugal	35,516	10,444	29.4%	5,548	15.6%	295	146	907	1,415	2,346	4,337
Romania	91,699	38,305	41.8%	19,039	20.8%	5,610	3	8,317	3,021	5,946	8,062
Serbia and Montenegro	39,449	14,394	36.5%	7,197	18.2%	2,207	-	5,013	1,550	4,012	1,853
Slovakia	18,924	6,085	32.2%	3,375	17.8%	1,445	-	612	671	1,548	344
Slovenia	7,821	784	10.0%	1,185	15.2%	153	-	283	473	585	80
Spain	194,885	69,298	35.6%	44,209	22.7%	5,785	844	4,208	6,140	22,079	24,185
Sweden	173,732	10,413	6.0%	1,726	1.0%	2,135	-	-	1,683	1,975	440
Switzerland	15,943	1,683	10.6%	4,417	27.7%	535	-	214	1,603	1,499	421
Ukraine	233,090	129,321	55.5%	30,541	13.1%	15,043	74	3,075	10,591	9,270	1,074
United Kingdom	93,788	22,019	23.5%	43,440	46.3%	14,380	-	-	11,052	6,537	41,205
Russia	6,592,849	485,400	7.4%	351,905	5.3%	37,455	509	1,133	27,936	17,076	12,954
ASIA											
Afghanistan	251,773	31,097	12.4%	115,831	46.0%	1,821	205	172	2,600	-	12,762
Armenia	11,506	2,162	18.8%	3,089	26.8%	211	-	9	478	75	515
Azerbaijan	33,437	7,471	22.3%	10,039	30.0%	1,172	19	107	1,965	21	5,321
Bahrain	267	23	8.7%	15	5.8%	-	-	-	12	-	17
Bangladesh	55,598	32,761	58.9%	2,317	4.2%	1,807	36,909	8	23,817	-	1,128
Brunei	2,226	27	1.2%	23	1.0%	-	-	-	2	6	2
Cambodia	69,898	14,699	21.0%	5,792	8.3%	-	4,035	146	2,896	2,079	-
China	3,690,045	599,520[4]	16.2%[4]	1,544,412[4]	41.9%[4]	102,463[4]	189,840[4]	116,240[4]	104,179[4]	440,384[4]	130,536[4]
Cyprus	3,572	436	12.2%	15	0.4%	12	-	-	55	419	240
East Timor	5,743	309	5.4%	579	10.1%	-	33	93	173	300	36
Georgia	26,911	4,104	15.3%	7,490	27.8%	207	-	358	1,117	433	541
India	1,222,510	655,987	53.7%	42,124	3.4%	72,140	132,818	12,285	217,773	17,000	57,900
Indonesia	735,310	129,730	17.6%	43,155	5.9%	-	50,953	9,409	11,370	6,098	7,316
Iran	636,372	63,892	10.0%	169,885	26.7%	8,740	2,103	1,113	8,273	-	53,900
Iraq	169,235	23,514	13.9%	15,444	9.1%	667	110	73	1,342	-	6,700
Israel	8,019	1,637	20.4%	548	6.8%	94	-	73	393	138	373
Japan	145,850	18,510	12.7%	1,564	1.1%	657	11,551	-	4,592	9,823	11
Jordan	34,495	1,544	4.5%	2,865	8.3%	18	-	13	66	-	1,900
Kazakhstan	1,049,156	83,672	8.0%	714,667	68.1%	10,938	225	256	4,021	984	8,785
Korea, North	46,540	10,811	23.2%	193	0.4%	88	2,031	1,253	575	3,076	186
Korea, South	38,328	7,293	19.0%	208	0.5%	4	7,204	67	2,191	8,266	-
Kuwait	6,880	58	0.8%	525	7.6%	-	-	-	19	-	543

CONTINENT/Country	Agricultural Area 2001					Average Production 1999-2001			Average 1999-2001		
	Total Area Sq. Miles	Cropland Area[1] Sq. Miles	Cropland Area[1] %	Pasture Area[1] Sq. Miles	Pasture Area[1] %	Wheat[1] 1,000 metric tons	Rice[1] 1,000 metric tons	Corn[1] 1,000 metric tons	Cattle[1] 1,000	Pigs[1] 1,000	Sheep[1] 1,000
Kyrgyzstan	77,182	5,664	7.3%	35,873	46.5%	1,113	17	363	942	98	3,101
Laos	91,429	3,699	4.0%	3,390	3.7%	-	2,213	108	1,106	1,390	-
Lebanon	4,016	1,208	30.1%	62	1.5%	60	-	4	76	63	354
Malaysia	127,320	29,286	23.0%	1,100	0.9%	-	2,170	63	744	1,943	167
Mongolia	604,829	4,633	0.8%	499,230	82.5%	148	-	-	2,997	17	14,587
Myanmar	261,228	41,023	15.7%	1,212	0.5%	105	20,683	413	10,974	3,923	390
Nepal	56,827	12,324	21.7%	6,784	11.9%	1,143	4,137	1,528	7,012	872	852
Oman	119,499	313	0.3%	3,861	3.2%	1	-	-	299	-	342
Pakistan	339,732	85,560	25.2%	19,305	5.7%	19,319	6,920	1,653	22,007	-	24,067
Philippines	115,831	41,120	35.5%	4,942	4.3%	-	12,377	4,540	2,467	10,724	30
Qatar	4,412	81	1.8%	193	4.4%	-	-	-	15	-	214
Saudi Arabia	830,000	14,649	1.8%	656,373	79.1%	1,871	-	5	304	-	7,848
Singapore	264	4	1.5%	-	0.0%	-	-	-	-	190	-
Sri Lanka	25,332	7,378	29.1%	1,699	6.7%	-	2,804	30	1,580	71	12
Syria	71,498	21,043	29.4%	31,942	44.7%	3,514	-	196	933	-	13,288
Taiwan	13,901	(5)	(5)	(5)	(5)	(5)	(5)	(5)	(5)	(5)	(5)
Tajikistan	55,251	4,093	7.4%	13,514	24.5%	375	67	38	1,045	1	1,481
Thailand	198,115	70,657	35.7%	3,089	1.6%	1	25,578	4,405	4,973	6,539	40
Turkey	302,541	101,757	33.6%	47,792	15.8%	19,341	350	2,266	10,949	4	29,394
Turkmenistan	188,457	7,008	3.7%	118,533	62.9%	1,472	33	9	863	46	5,750
United Arab Emirates	32,278	919	2.8%	1,178	3.6%	-	-	-	94	-	504
Uzbekistan	172,742	18,649	10.8%	88,031	51.0%	3,637	219	133	5,279	83	7,980
Vietnam	128,066	32,579	25.4%	2,479	1.9%	-	31,964	1,961	4,029	20,273	-
Yemen	203,850	6,158	3.0%	62,027	30.4%	145	-	48	1,320	-	4,758
AFRICA											
Algeria	919,595	31,861	3.5%	122,780	13.4%	1,414	-	1	1,667	6	19,000
Angola	481,354	12,741	2.6%	208,495	43.3%	4	16	417	3,995	800	345
Benin	43,484	8,745	20.1%	2,124	4.9%	-	46	740	1,486	463	650
Botswana	224,607	1,440	0.6%	98,842	44.0%	1	-	8	2,035	6	347
Burkina Faso	105,869	15,444	14.6%	23,166	21.9%	-	102	500	4,767	621	6,722
Burundi	10,745	4,865	45.3%	3,610	33.6%	7	57	124	321	67	215
Cameroon	183,568	27,645	15.1%	7,722	4.2%	-	69	759	5,761	1,232	3,734
Cape Verde	1,557	158	10.2%	97	6.2%	-	-	27	22	195	9
Central African Republic	240,536	7,799	3.2%	12,066	5.0%	-	23	101	3,096	669	218
Chad	495,755	14,016	2.8%	173,746	35.0%	3	114	88	5,852	22	2,374
Comoros	863	510	59.1%	58	6.7%	-	17	4	51	-	21
Congo	132,047	849	0.6%	38,610	29.2%	-	1	6	87	46	102
Congo, Democratic Republic of the	905,446	30,425	3.4%	57,915	6.4%	9	338	1,184	823	1,050	925
Cote d'Ivoire	124,504	28,958	23.3%	50,193	40.3%	-	1,217	693	1,398	333	1,439
Djibouti	8,958	4	0.0%	5,019	56.0%	-	-	-	269	-	465
Egypt	386,662	12,888	3.3%	-	0.0%	6,388	5,681	6,487	3,583	29	4,510
Equatorial Guinea	10,831	888	8.2%	402	3.7%	-	-	-	5	6	37
Eritrea	45,406	1,942	4.3%	26,900	59.2%	32	-	13	2,150	-	1,570
Ethiopia	426,373	44,255	10.4%	77,220	18.1%	1,340	-	2,938	35,025	25	22,333
Gabon	103,347	1,911	1.8%	18,012	17.4%	-	1	26	36	213	197
Gambia, The	4,127	985	23.9%	1,772	42.9%	-	28	24	350	12	115
Ghana	92,098	22,780	24.7%	32,240	35.0%	-	244	988	1,297	327	2,715
Guinea	94,926	5,888	6.2%	41,313	43.5%	-	830	96	2,576	93	824
Guinea-Bissau	13,948	2,116	15.2%	4,170	29.9%	-	95	26	509	347	283
Kenya	224,961	19,923	8.9%	82,240	36.6%	184	58	2,419	13,229	311	7,000
Lesotho	11,720	1,290	11.0%	7,722	65.9%	39	-	128	547	63	839
Liberia	43,000	2,317	5.4%	7,722	18.0%	-	188	-	36	127	210
Libya	679,362	8,301	1.2%	51,352	7.6%	128	-	-	207	-	5,100
Madagascar	226,658	13,707	6.0%	92,664	40.9%	9	2,412	175	10,339	1,267	793
Malawi	45,747	9,035	19.7%	7,143	15.6%	2	86	2,190	741	450	110
Mali	478,841	18,147	3.8%	115,831	24.2%	8	801	378	6,594	72	6,282
Mauritania	397,956	1,931	0.5%	151,545	38.1%	-	65	7	1,470	-	7,437
Mauritius	788	409	51.9%	27	3.4%	-	-	-	27	12	10
Morocco	172,414	37,529	21.8%	81,081	47.0%	2,284	33	95	2,629	8	17,059
Mozambique	309,496	16,351	5.3%	169,885	54.9%	1	168	1,136	1,317	179	125
Namibia	317,818	3,166	1.0%	146,719	46.2%	4	-	26	2,436	21	2,330
Niger	489,192	17,375	3.6%	46,332	9.5%	10	66	5	2,217	39	4,386
Nigeria	356,669	120,464	33.8%	151,352	42.4%	75	3,109	4,734	19,677	5,000	20,833
Rwanda	10,169	5,019	49.4%	2,124	20.9%	6	13	66	766	172	264
Sao Tome and Principe	372	205	55.0%	4	1.0%	-	-	-	4	2	3
Senegal	75,951	9,653	12.7%	21,815	28.7%	-	229	84	3,076	263	4,619
Sierra Leone	27,699	2,178	7.9%	8,494	30.7%	-	215	9	413	52	365
Somalia	246,201	4,135	1.7%	166,024	67.4%	1	2	188	5,133	4	13,100
South Africa	470,693	60,664	12.9%	324,048	68.8%	2,200	3	9,147	13,594	1,542	28,677
Sudan	967,500	64,298	6.6%	452,434	46.8%	230	8	48	37,081	-	45,980
Swaziland	6,704	734	10.9%	4,633	69.1%	-	-	94	613	32	27
Tanzania	364,900	19,112	5.2%	135,136	37.0%	87	509	2,567	17,350	449	3,513
Togo	21,925	10,154	46.3%	3,861	17.6%	-	69	480	277	287	1,528
Tunisia	63,170	18,954	30.0%	15,792	25.0%	1,111	-	-	760	6	6,862
Uganda	93,065	27,799	29.9%	19,738	21.2%	12	106	1,108	5,977	1,540	1,065
Zambia	290,586	20,386	7.0%	115,831	39.9%	80	11	768	2,709	324	137
Zimbabwe	150,873	12,934	8.6%	66,410	44.0%	282	-	1,698	5,840	494	602
OCEANIA											
Australia	2,969,910	195,368	6.6%	1,563,327	52.6%	23,654	1,417	363	27,645	2,607	116,736
Fiji	7,056	1,100	15.6%	676	9.6%	-	16	1	335	139	7
Kiribati	313	151	48.1%	-	0.0%	-	-	-	-	10	-
Micronesia, Federated States of	271	139	51.3%	42	15.7%	-	-	-	14	32	-
New Zealand	104,454	13,019	12.5%	53,525	51.2%	337	-	185	9,025	364	45,114
Papua New Guinea	178,704	3,320	1.9%	676	0.4%	-	1	7	87	1,583	6
Samoa	1,093	498	45.6%	8	0.7%	-	-	-	28	179	-
Solomon Islands	10,954	286	2.6%	154	1.4%	-	5	-	11	63	-
Tonga	251	185	73.8%	15	6.2%	-	-	-	11	81	-
Vanuatu	4,707	463	9.8%	162	3.4%	-	-	1	151	62	-

This table presents data for most independent nations having an area greater than 200 square miles
- Zero, insignificant, or not available
(1) Source: United Nations Food and Agriculture Organization
(2) Includes data for Luxembourg
(3) Data for Luxembourg is included with Belgium
(4) Includes data for Taiwan
(5) Data for Taiwan is included with China

WORLD ECONOMIC TABLE

	GDP 2002		Trade		Commercial Energy Production Avg. 2000[2]					Average Production 1999-2001 in Metric Tons			
CONTINENT/Country	Total GDP[1]	GDP Per Capita[1]	Value of Exports[1]	Value of Imports[1]	Total (1,000 Metric Tons of Coal Equiv.)	Solid %	Liquid %	Gas %	Hydro & Nuclear %	Coal[3]	Petroleum[3]	Iron Ore[4]	Bauxite[4]
NORTH AMERICA													
Bahamas	$4,590,000,000	$17,000	$560,700,000	$1,860,000,000	-	-	-	-	-	-	-	-	-
Belize	$1,280,000,000	$4,900	$290,000,000	$430,000,000	12	-	-	-	100%	-	-	-	-
Canada	$934,100,000,000	$29,400	$260,500,000,000	$229,000,000,000	507,218	10%	33%	43%	14%	70,711,084	97,834,913	20,527,000	-
Costa Rica	$32,000,000,000	$8,500	$5,100,000,000	$6,400,000,000	1,937	-	-	-	100%	-	-	-	-
Cuba	$30,690,000,000	$2,300	$1,800,000,000	$4,800,000,000	4,626	-	83%	17%	-	-	2,134,520	-	-
Dominica	$380,000,000	$5,400	$50,000,000	$135,000,000	4	-	-	-	100%	-	-	-	-
Dominican Republic	$53,780,000,000	$6,100	$5,300,000,000	$8,700,000,000	115	-	-	-	100%	-	-	-	-
El Salvador	$29,410,000,000	$4,700	$3,000,000,000	$4,900,000,000	1,110	-	-	-	100%	-	-	-	-
Guatemala	$53,200,000,000	$3,700	$2,700,000,000	$5,600,000,000	1,822	-	81%	1%	18%	-	1,076,526	9,000	-
Haiti	$10,600,000,000	$1,700	$298,000,000	$1,140,000,000	33	-	-	-	100%	-	-	-	-
Honduras	$16,290,000,000	$2,600	$1,300,000,000	$2,700,000,000	347	-	-	-	100%	-	-	-	-
Jamaica	$10,080,000,000	$3,900	$1,400,000,000	$3,100,000,000	18	-	-	-	100%	-	-	-	11,728,000
Mexico	$924,400,000,000	$9,000	$158,400,000,000	$168,400,000,000	340,594	1%	79%	16%	4%	11,097,943	150,165,451	6,860,000	-
Nicaragua	$11,160,000,000	$2,500	$637,000,000	$1,700,000,000	706	-	-	-	100%	-	-	-	-
Panama	$18,060,000,000	$6,000	$5,800,000,000	$6,700,000,000	418	-	-	-	100%	-	-	-	-
St. Lucia	$866,000,000	$5,400	$68,300,000	$319,400,000	-	-	-	-	-	-	-	-	-
Trinidad and Tobago	$11,070,000,000	$9,500	$4,200,000,000	$3,800,000,000	22,768	-	39%	61%	-	-	5,964,991	-	-
United States	$10,450,000,000,000	$37,600	$733,900,000,000	$1,194,100,000,000	2,342,228	33%	22%	30%	14%	996,498,186	289,640,487	35,178,000	-
SOUTH AMERICA													
Argentina	$403,800,000,000	$10,200	$25,300,000,000	$9,000,000,000	118,739	-	50%	45%	5%	260,299	38,783,798	-	-
Bolivia	$21,150,000,000	$2,500	$1,300,000,000	$1,600,000,000	7,732	-	33%	64%	3%	-	1,599,401	-	-
Brazil	$1,376,000,000,000	$7,600	$59,400,000,000	$46,200,000,000	143,640	3%	63%	6%	28%	4,446,477	61,155,586	124,667,000	13,654,000
Chile	$156,100,000,000	$10,000	$17,800,000,000	$15,600,000,000	6,180	6%	11%	45%	38%	475,484	349,201	5,523,000	-
Colombia	$251,600,000,000	$6,500	$12,900,000,000	$12,500,000,000	99,513	36%	52%	9%	4%	38,112,136	34,896,672	348,000	-
Ecuador	$42,650,000,000	$3,100	$4,900,000,000	$6,000,000,000	32,171	-	94%	3%	3%	-	19,520,185	-	-
Guyana	$2,628,000,000	$4,000	$500,000,000	$575,000,000	1	-	-	-	100%	-	-	-	2,272,000
Paraguay	$25,190,000,000	$4,200	$2,000,000,000	$2,400,000,000	6,577	-	-	-	100%	-	-	-	-
Peru	$138,800,000,000	$4,800	$7,600,000,000	$7,300,000,000	10,933	-	73%	9%	18%	52,297	4,932,561	2,701,000	-
Suriname	$1,469,000,000	$3,500	$445,000,000	$300,000,000	1,022	-	84%	-	16%	-	496,400	-	3,946,000
Uruguay	$26,820,000,000	$7,800	$2,100,000,000	$1,870,000,000	867	-	-	-	100%	-	-	-	-
Venezuela	$131,700,000,000	$5,500	$28,600,000,000	$18,800,000,000	311,899	3%	81%	14%	2%	7,482,998	146,621,238	10,497,000	4,309,000
EUROPE													
Albania	$15,690,000,000	$4,500	$340,000,000	$1,500,000,000	1,089	1%	42%	2%	55%	32,666	284,321	-	-
Austria	$227,700,000,000	$27,700	$70,000,000,000	$74,000,000,000	9,611	5%	15%	24%	56%	1,197,660	921,120	525,000	-
Belarus	$90,190,000,000	$8,200	$7,700,000,000	$8,800,000,000	3,644	18%	73%	9%	-	-	1,830,872	-	-
Belgium	$299,700,000,000	$29,000	$162,000,000,000	$152,000,000,000	18,451	2%	-	-	98%	318,998	-	-	-
Bosnia and Herzegovina	$7,300,000,000	$1,900	$1,150,000,000	$2,800,000,000	6,553	90%	-	-	10%	8,414,623	-	50,000	75,000
Bulgaria	$49,230,000,000	$6,600	$5,300,000,000	$6,900,000,000	13,500	46%	-	-	53%	28,841,963	37,048	310,000	-
Croatia	$43,120,000,000	$8,800	$4,900,000,000	$10,700,000,000	4,962	-	42%	43%	15%	5,104	1,191,360	-	-
Czech Republic	$157,100,000,000	$15,300	$40,800,000,000	$43,200,000,000	39,843	85%	1%	1%	14%	63,466,671	283,097	-	-
Denmark	$155,300,000,000	$29,000	$56,300,000,000	$47,900,000,000	36,502	-	70%	29%	2%	-	16,701,163	-	-
Estonia	$15,520,000,000	$10,900	$3,400,000,000	$4,400,000,000	3,892	100%	-	-	-	-	-	-	-
Finland	$133,800,000,000	$26,200	$40,100,000,000	$31,800,000,000	11,933	15%	-	-	85%	-	-	-	-
France	$1,558,000,000,000	$25,700	$307,800,000,000	$303,700,000,000	175,306	2%	4%	1%	93%	3,616,981	1,446,228	12,000	-
Germany	$2,160,000,000,000	$26,600	$608,000,000,000	$487,300,000,000	181,697	47%	2%	13%	38%	204,685,080	3,044,206	5,000	-
Greece	$203,300,000,000	$19,000	$12,600,000,000	$31,400,000,000	12,988	92%	3%	1%	4%	64,503,999	166,807	583,000	1,975,000
Hungary	$134,000,000,000	$13,300	$31,400,000,000	$33,900,000,000	16,319	25%	19%	24%	32%	14,796,257	1,301,710	-	994,000
Iceland	$8,444,000,000	$25,000	$2,300,000,000	$2,100,000,000	1,638	-	-	-	100%	-	-	-	-
Ireland	$113,700,000,000	$30,500	$86,600,000,000	$48,600,000,000	3,232	47%	-	47%	6%	-	-	-	-
Italy	$1,455,000,000,000	$25,000	$259,200,000,000	$238,200,000,000	40,332	-	16%	54%	30%	47,666	4,144,278	-	-
Latvia	$20,990,000,000	$8,300	$2,300,000,000	$3,900,000,000	369	6%	-	-	94%	-	-	-	-
Lithuania	$30,080,000,000	$8,400	$5,400,000,000	$6,800,000,000	3,677	-	12%	-	87%	-	251,824	-	-
Luxembourg	$21,940,000,000	$44,000	$10,100,000,000	$13,250,000,000	113	-	-	-	100%	-	-	-	-
Macedonia	$10,570,000,000	$5,000	$1,100,000,000	$1,900,000,000	3,038	95%	-	-	5%	7,463,628	-	9,000	-
Moldova	$11,510,000,000	$2,500	$590,000,000	$980,000,000	7	-	-	-	100%	-	-	-	-
Netherlands	$437,800,000,000	$26,900	$243,300,000,000	$201,100,000,000	87,974	-	4%	94%	2%	-	1,437,293	-	-
Norway	$149,100,000,000	$31,800	$68,200,000,000	$37,300,000,000	324,396	-	72%	22%	5%	847,996	154,419,533	355,000	-
Poland	$373,200,000,000	$9,500	$32,400,000,000	$43,400,000,000	108,277	94%	1%	5%	-	164,737,813	645,072	-	-
Portugal	$195,200,000,000	$18,000	$25,900,000,000	$39,000,000,000	1,560	-	-	-	100%	-	-	6,000	-
Romania	$169,300,000,000	$7,400	$13,700,000,000	$16,700,000,000	37,598	19%	24%	46%	10%	27,392,191	6,038,110	24,000	-
Serbia and Montenegro	$23,150,000,000	$2,370	$2,400,000,000	$6,300,000,000	14,188	74%	8%	8%	10%	34,480,488	810,787	10,000	580,000
Slovakia	$67,340,000,000	$12,200	$12,900,000,000	$15,400,000,000	8,813	17%	1%	2%	79%	3,606,648	48,134	200,000	-
Slovenia	$37,060,000,000	$18,000	$10,300,000,000	$11,100,000,000	3,644	38%	-	-	62%	4,391,644	991	-	-
Spain	$850,700,000,000	$20,700	$122,200,000,000	$156,600,000,000	40,444	28%	2%	1%	68%	23,479,212	296,665	-	-
Sweden	$230,700,000,000	$25,400	$80,600,000,000	$68,600,000,000	31,413	1%	-	-	99%	-	-	12,114,000	-
Switzerland	$233,400,000,000	$31,700	$100,300,000,000	$94,400,000,000	14,710	-	-	-	100%	-	-	-	-
Ukraine	$218,000,000,000	$4,500	$18,100,000,000	$18,000,000,000	118,973	50%	5%	20%	25%	81,998,575	3,747,936	28,933,000	-
United Kingdom	$1,528,000,000,000	$25,300	$286,300,000,000	$330,100,000,000	397,906	7%	47%	38%	8%	32,758,497	119,820,635	1,000	-
Russia	$1,409,000,000,000	$9,300	$104,600,000,000	$60,700,000,000	1,412,286	10%	33%	52%	5%	253,376,954	324,436,632	48,300,000	3,983,000
ASIA													
Afghanistan	$19,000,000,000	$700	$1,200,000,000	$1,300,000,000	195	1%	-	79%	20%	1,000	-	-	-
Armenia	$12,130,000,000	$3,800	$525,000,000	$991,000,000	901	-	-	-	100%	-	-	-	-
Azerbaijan	$28,610,000,000	$3,500	$2,000,000,000	$1,800,000,000	27,748	-	72%	27%	1%	-	14,183,985	-	-
Bahrain	$9,910,000,000	$14,000	$5,800,000,000	$4,200,000,000	14,442	-	22%	78%	-	-	1,827,397	-	-
Bangladesh	$238,200,000,000	$1,700	$6,200,000,000	$8,500,000,000	11,713	-	-	99%	1%	-	120,476	-	-
Brunei	$6,500,000,000	$18,600	$3,000,000,000	$1,400,000,000	27,922	-	49%	51%	-	-	9,435,323	-	-
Cambodia	$20,420,000,000	$1,500	$1,380,000,000	$1,730,000,000	10	-	-	-	100%	-	-	-	-
China	$5,989,000,000,000	$4,400	$658,260,000,000	$618,930,000,000	1,023,314[5]	70%[5]	23%[5]	4%[5]	3%[5]	1,251,423,183	161,226,848	72,967,000	9,000,000
Cyprus	$9,400,000,000	$15,000	$1,030,000,000	$3,900,000,000	-	-	-	-	-	-	-	-	-
East Timor	$440,000,000	$500	$8,000,000	$237,000,000	-	-	-	-	-	-	-	-	-
Georgia	$16,050,000,000	$3,100	$515,000,000	$750,000,000	963	1%	16%	8%	75%	10,000	102,258	-	-
India	$2,664,000,000,000	$2,540	$44,500,000,000	$53,800,000,000	367,807	73%	14%	8%	4%	304,842,421	32,123,682	48,080,000	7,554,000
Indonesia	$714,200,000,000	$3,100	$52,300,000,000	$32,100,000,000	279,695	27%	45%	26%	2%	79,664,587	70,565,213	282,000	1,168,000
Iran	$458,300,000,000	$7,000	$24,800,000,000	$21,800,000,000	350,729	-	77%	23%	-	1,376,993	181,632,777	5,367,000	136,000
Iraq	$58,000,000,000	$2,400	$13,000,000,000	$7,800,000,000	186,519	-	97%	3%	-	-	124,281,583	-	-
Israel	$117,400,000,000	$19,000	$28,100,000,000	$30,800,000,000	334	94%	2%	4%	1%	-	5,957	-	-
Japan	$3,651,000,000,000	$28,000	$383,800,000,000	$292,100,000,000	142,731	2%	1%	2%	95%	3,286,983	351,650	1,000	-
Jordan	$22,630,000,000	$4,300	$2,500,000,000	$4,400,000,000	316	-	1%	97%	2%	-	1,986	-	-
Kazakhstan	$120,000,000,000	$6,300	$10,300,000,000	$9,600,000,000	113,390	40%	45%	14%	1%	70,311,969	30,508,827	7,467,000	3,668,000
Korea, North	$22,260,000,000	$1,000	$842,000,000	$1,314,000,000	65,932	96%	-	-	4%	94,174,845	-	3,000,000	-
Korea, South	$941,500,000,000	$19,400	$162,600,000,000	$148,400,000,000	43,892	6%	-	-	94%	4,054,646	-	175,000	-
Kuwait	$36,850,000,000	$15,000	$16,000,000,000	$7,300,000,000	161,322	-	92%	8%	-	-	98,844,823	-	-

	GDP 2002		Trade		Commercial Energy Production Avg. 2000[2]					Average Production 1999-2001 in Metric Tons			
CONTINENT/Country	Total GDP[1]	GDP Per Capita[1]	Value of Exports[1]	Value of Imports[1]	Total (1,000 Metric Tons of Coal Equiv.)	Solid %	Liquid %	Gas %	Hydro & Nuclear %	Coal[3]	Petroleum[3]	Iron Ore[4]	Bauxite[4]
Kyrgyzstan	$13,880,000,000	$2,800	$488,000,000	$587,000,000	2,026	9%	5%	2%	83%	423,664	91,503	-	-
Laos	$10,400,000,000	$1,700	$345,000,000	$555,000,000	146	1%	-	-	99%	1,000	-	-	-
Lebanon	$17,610,000,000	$5,400	$1,000,000,000	$6,000,000,000	55	-	-	-	100%	-	-	-	-
Malaysia	$198,400,000,000	$9,300	$95,200,000,000	$76,800,000,000	110,069	-	41%	58%	1%	314,332	33,792,132	208,000	137,000
Mongolia	$5,060,000,000	$1,840	$501,000,000	$659,000,000	2,212	100%	-	-	-	5,099,640	-	-	-
Myanmar	$73,690,000,000	$1,660	$2,700,000,000	$2,500,000,000	9,297	3%	6%	88%	2%	358,331	587,374	-	-
Nepal	$37,320,000,000	$1,400	$720,000,000	$1,600,000,000	172	10%	-	-	90%	9,667	-	-	-
Oman	$22,400,000,000	$8,300	$10,600,000,000	$5,500,000,000	74,376	-	92%	8%	-	-	46,989,489	-	-
Pakistan	$295,300,000,000	$2,100	$9,800,000,000	$11,100,000,000	33,773	6%	12%	74%	7%	3,247,391	2,768,108	-	10,000
Philippines	$379,700,000,000	$4,200	$35,100,000,000	$33,500,000,000	16,244	6%	-	-	94%	1,306,993	173,128	-	-
Qatar	$15,910,000,000	$21,500	$10,900,000,000	$3,900,000,000	92,237	-	57%	43%	-	-	35,018,538	-	-
Saudi Arabia	$268,900,000,000	$10,500	$71,000,000,000	$39,500,000,000	736,996	-	91%	9%	-	-	401,559,222	-	-
Singapore	$112,400,000,000	$24,000	$127,000,000,000	$113,000,000,000									
Sri Lanka	$73,700,000,000	$3,700	$4,600,000,000	$5,400,000,000	394	-	-	-	100%	-	-	-	-
Syria	$63,480,000,000	$3,500	$6,200,000,000	$4,900,000,000	47,898	-	83%	15%	2%	-	26,119,029	-	-
Taiwan	$406,000,000,000	$18,000	$130,000,000,000	$113,000,000,000	(6)	(6)	(6)	(6)	(6)	58,284	38,686	-	-
Tajikistan	$8,476,000,000	$1,250	$710,000,000	$830,000,000	1,790	-	1%	3%	95%	20,667	16,613	-	-
Thailand	$445,800,000,000	$6,900	$67,700,000,000	$58,100,000,000	44,127	25%	24%	50%	2%	18,551,756	5,080,720	20,000	-
Turkey	$489,700,000,000	$7,000	$35,100,000,000	$50,800,000,000	28,167	69%	14%	3%	14%	65,334,995	2,642,106	2,300,000	303,000
Turkmenistan	$31,340,000,000	$5,500	$2,970,000,000	$2,250,000,000	71,764	-	15%	85%	-	-	7,139,688	-	-
United Arab Emirates	$53,970,000,000	$22,000	$44,900,000,000	$30,800,000,000	199,656	-	83%	17%	-	-	112,737,023	-	-
Uzbekistan	$66,060,000,000	$2,500	$2,800,000,000	$2,500,000,000	85,806	1%	13%	85%	1%	2,736,319	4,419,300	-	-
Vietnam	$183,800,000,000	$2,250	$16,500,000,000	$16,800,000,000	39,300	30%	59%	5%	7%	9,688,950	15,926,911	-	-
Yemen	$15,070,000,000	$840	$3,400,000,000	$2,900,000,000	30,622	-	100%	-	-	-	21,304,264	-	-

AFRICA

Algeria	$173,800,000,000	$5,300	$19,500,000,000	$10,600,000,000	222,648	-	47%	53%	-	24,000	61,651,110	757,000	-
Angola	$18,360,000,000	$1,600	$8,600,000,000	$4,100,000,000	53,315	-	98%	1%	-	-	36,961,745	-	-
Benin	$7,380,000,000	$1,070	$207,000,000	$479,000,000	69	-	100%	-	-	-	39,547	-	-
Botswana	$13,480,000,000	$9,500	$2,400,000,000	$1,900,000,000	(7)	(7)	(7)	(7)	(7)	956,767	-	-	-
Burkina Faso	$14,510,000,000	$1,080	$250,000,000	$525,000,000	15	-	-	-	100%	-	-	-	-
Burundi	$3,146,000,000	$600	$26,000,000	$135,000,000	21	29%	-	-	71%	-	-	-	-
Cameroon	$26,840,000,000	$1,700	$1,900,000,000	$1,700,000,000	10,722	-	96%	-	4%	1,000	4,326,440	-	-
Cape Verde	$600,000,000	$1,400	$30,000,000	$220,000,000	-	-	-	-	-	-	-	-	-
Central African Republic	$4,296,000,000	$1,300	$134,000,000	$102,000,000	10	-	-	-	100%	-	-	-	-
Chad	$9,297,000,000	$1,100	$197,000,000	$570,000,000	-	-	-	-	-	-	-	-	-
Comoros	$441,000,000	$720	$16,300,000	$39,800,000	-	-	-	-	-	-	-	-	-
Congo	$2,500,000,000	$900	$2,400,000,000	$73,000,000	19,097	-	99%	1%	-	-	13,651,000	-	-
Congo, Democratic Republic of the	$34,000,000,000	$610	$1,200,000,000	$890,000,000	2,630	4%	71%	-	25%	96,000	1,194,669	-	-
Cote d'Ivoire	$24,030,000,000	$1,500	$4,400,000,000	$2,500,000,000	4,439	-	50%	45%	5%	-	620,450	-	-
Djibouti	$619,000,000	$1,300	$70,000,000	$255,000,000	-	-	-	-	-	-	-	-	-
Egypt	$289,800,000,000	$3,900	$7,000,000,000	$15,200,000,000	86,315	-	65%	32%	2%	-	38,024,058	1,283,000	-
Equatorial Guinea	$1,270,000,000	$2,700	$2,500,000,000	$562,000,000	7,531	-	100%	-	-	-	7,461,521	-	-
Eritrea	$3,300,000,000	$740	$20,000,000	$500,000,000	-	-	-	-	-	-	-	-	-
Ethiopia	$48,530,000,000	$750	$433,000,000	$1,630,000,000	211	-	-	-	100%	-	-	-	-
Gabon	$8,354,000,000	$5,700	$2,600,000,000	$1,100,000,000	23,273	-	95%	5%	-	-	15,674,359	-	-
Gambia, The	$2,582,000,000	$1,800	$138,000,000	$225,000,000	-	-	-	-	-	-	-	-	-
Ghana	$41,250,000,000	$2,100	$2,200,000,000	$2,800,000,000	830	-	2%	-	98%	-	-	330,933	525,000
Guinea	$18,690,000,000	$2,000	$835,000,000	$670,000,000	25	-	-	-	100%	-	-	-	15,663,000
Guinea-Bissau	$901,400,000	$800	$71,000,000	$59,000,000	-	-	-	-	-	-	-	-	-
Kenya	$32,890,000,000	$1,020	$2,100,000,000	$3,000,000,000	642	-	-	-	100%	-	-	-	-
Lesotho	$5,106,000,000	$2,700	$422,000,000	$738,000,000	(7)	(7)	(7)	(7)	(7)				
Liberia	$3,116,000,000	$1,100	$110,000,000	$165,000,000	24	-	-	-	100%	-	-	-	-
Libya	$33,360,000,000	$7,600	$11,800,000,000	$6,300,000,000	103,205	-	92%	8%	-	-	67,767,436	-	-
Madagascar	$12,590,000,000	$760	$700,000,000	$985,000,000	64	-	-	-	100%	-	-	-	-
Malawi	$6,811,000,000	$670	$435,000,000	$505,000,000	107	-	-	-	100%	-	-	-	-
Mali	$9,775,000,000	$860	$680,000,000	$630,000,000	29	-	-	-	100%	-	-	-	-
Mauritania	$4,891,000,000	$1,900	$355,000,000	$360,000,000	4	-	-	-	100%	-	-	7,492,000	-
Mauritius	$12,150,000,000	$11,000	$1,600,000,000	$1,800,000,000	12	-	-	-	100%	-	-	-	-
Morocco	$121,800,000,000	$3,900	$7,500,000,000	$10,400,000,000	201	14%	9%	33%	43%	61,000	15,223	4,000	-
Mozambique	$19,520,000,000	$1,000	$680,000,000	$1,180,000,000	874	2%	-	-	98%	18,667	-	-	8,000
Namibia	$13,150,000,000	$6,900	$1,210,000,000	$1,380,000,000	(7)	(7)	(7)	(7)	(7)				
Niger	$8,713,000,000	$830	$293,000,000	$368,000,000	175	100%	-	-	-	151,666	-	-	-
Nigeria	$112,500,000,000	$875	$17,300,000,000	$13,600,000,000	172,641	-	90%	10%	-	61,000	108,397,478	-	-
Rwanda	$8,920,000,000	$1,200	$68,000,000	$253,000,000	20	-	-	-	100%	-	-	-	-
Sao Tome and Principe	$200,000,000	$1,200	$5,500,000	$24,800,000	1	-	-	-	100%	-	-	-	-
Senegal	$15,640,000,000	$1,500	$1,150,000,000	$1,460,000,000	1	-	-	100%	-	-	-	-	-
Sierra Leone	$2,826,000,000	$580	$35,000,000	$190,000,000	(7)	(7)	(7)	(7)	(7)				
Somalia	$4,270,000,000	$550	$126,000,000	$343,000,000	-	-	-	-	-	-	-	-	-
South Africa	$427,700,000,000	$10,000	$31,800,000,000	$26,600,000,000	245,195(8)	92%(8)	5%(8)	1%(8)	2%(8)	224,286,505	1,277,485	20,751,000	-
Sudan	$52,900,000,000	$1,420	$1,800,000,000	$1,500,000,000	13,436	-	99%	-	1%	-	7,679,837	-	-
Swaziland	$5,542,000,000	$4,400	$820,000,000	$938,000,000	(7)	(7)	(7)	(7)	(7)	288,665	-	-	-
Tanzania	$20,420,000,000	$630	$863,000,000	$1,670,000,000	343	23%	-	-	77%	5,000	-	-	-
Togo	$7,594,000,000	$1,500	$449,000,000	$561,000,000	-	-	-	-	-	-	-	-	-
Tunisia	$67,130,000,000	$6,500	$6,800,000,000	$8,700,000,000	8,065	-	66%	34%	-	-	3,826,400	105,000	-
Uganda	$30,490,000,000	$1,260	$476,000,000	$1,140,000,000	193	-	-	-	100%	-	-	3,000	-
Zambia	$8,240,000,000	$890	$709,000,000	$1,123,000,000	1,117	15%	-	-	85%	192,358	-	-	-
Zimbabwe	$26,070,000,000	$2,400	$1,570,000,000	$1,739,000,000	4,801	92%	-	-	8%	4,508,643	-	237,000	-

OCEANIA

Australia	$525,500,000,000	$27,000	$66,300,000,000	$68,000,000,000	331,923	71%	14%	14%	1%	307,176,075	31,728,994	104,014,000	51,834,000
Fiji	$4,822,000,000	$5,500	$442,000,000	$642,000,000	53	-	-	-	100%	-	-	-	-
Kiribati	$79,000,000	$840	$6,000,000	$44,000,000	-	-	-	-	-	-	-	-	-
Micronesia, Federated States of	$277,000,000	$2,000	$22,000,000	$149,000,000	-	-	-	-	-	-	-	-	-
New Zealand	$78,400,000,000	$20,200	$15,000,000,000	$12,500,000,000	19,812	14%	13%	40%	33%	3,452,315	1,839,394	660,000	-
Papua New Guinea	$10,860,000,000	$2,300	$1,800,000,000	$1,100,000,000	5,864	-	96%	2%	2%	-	3,874,601	-	-
Samoa	$1,000,000,000	$5,600	$15,500,000	$130,100,000	3	-	-	-	100%	-	-	-	-
Solomon Islands	$800,000,000	$1,700	$47,000,000	$82,000,000	-	-	-	-	-	-	-	-	-
Tonga	$236,000,000	$2,200	$8,900,000	$70,000,000	-	-	-	-	-	-	-	-	-
Vanuatu	$563,000,000	$2,900	$22,000,000	$93,000,000	-	-	-	-	-	-	-	-	-

This table presents data for most independent nations having an area greater than 200 square miles
- Zero, insignificant, or not available
(1) Source: United States Central Intelligence Agency World Factbook
(2) Source: United Nations Energy Statistics Yearbook
(3) Source: United States Energy Information Administration International Energy Annual
(4) Source: United States Geological Survey Minerals Yearbook
(5) Includes data for Taiwan
(6) Data for Taiwan is included with China
(7) Data for countries in the South Africa Customs Union are included with South Africa
(8) Includes data for countries in the South Africa Customs Union

WORLD ENVIRONMENT TABLE

CONTINENT/Country	Total Area Sq. Miles	Protected Area 2002[1,2] Sq. Miles	%	Mammal	Bird	Endangered Species 2003[3] Reptile	Amphib.	Fish	Invrt.	Forest Cover[4] Sq. Miles 2000	Percent Change 1990-2000
NORTH AMERICA											
Bahamas	5,382	-	-	5	4	6	0	15	1	3,251	-
Belize	8,867	3,999	45.1%	5	2	4	0	17	1	5,205	-20.9%
Canada	3,855,103	427,916	11.1%	16	8	2	1	25	11	944,294	-
Costa Rica	19,730	4,538	23.0%	13	13	7	1	13	9	7,598	-7.4%
Cuba	42,804	29,578	69.1%	11	18	7	0	23	3	9,066	13.4%
Dominica	290	-	-	1	3	4	0	11	0	178	-8.0%
Dominican Republic	18,730	9,721	51.9%	5	15	10	1	10	2	5,313	-
El Salvador	8,124	33	0.4%	2	0	4	0	5	1	467	-37.3%
Guatemala	42,042	8,408	20.0%	7	6	8	0	14	8	11,004	-15.9%
Haiti	10,714	43	0.4%	4	14	8	1	12	2	340	-44.3%
Honduras	43,277	2,770	6.4%	10	5	6	0	14	2	20,784	-9.9%
Jamaica	4,244	3,590	84.6%	5	12	8	4	12	5	1,255	-14.2%
Mexico	758,452	77,362	10.2%	72	40	18	4	106	41	213,148	-10.3%
Nicaragua	50,054	8,910	17.8%	6	5	7	0	17	2	12,656	-26.3%
Panama	29,157	6,327	21.7%	17	16	7	0	17	2	11,104	-15.3%
St. Lucia	238	-	-	2	5	6	0	10	0	35	-35.7%
Trinidad and Tobago	1,980	119	6.0%	1	1	5	0	15	0	1,000	-7.8%
United States	3,794,083	982,668	25.9%	39	56	27	25	155	557	872,563	1.7%
SOUTH AMERICA											
Argentina	1,073,519	70,852	6.6%	32	39	5	5	9	10	133,777	-7.6%
Bolivia	424,165	56,838	13.4%	25	28	2	1	0	1	204,897	-2.9%
Brazil	3,300,172	221,112	6.7%	74	113	22	6	33	34	2,100,028	-4.1%
Chile	291,930	55,175	18.9%	21	22	0	3	9	0	59,985	-1.3%
Colombia	439,737	44,853	10.2%	39	78	14	0	23	0	191,510	-3.7%
Ecuador	109,484	20,036	18.3%	34	62	10	0	11	48	40,761	-11.5%
Guyana	83,000	249	0.3%	13	2	6	0	13	1	65,170	-2.8%
Paraguay	157,048	5,497	3.5%	10	26	2	0	0	0	90,240	-5.0%
Peru	496,225	30,270	6.1%	46	76	6	1	8	2	251,796	-4.0%
Suriname	63,037	3,089	4.9%	12	1	6	0	12	0	54,491	-
Uruguay	67,574	203	0.3%	6	11	3	0	8	1	4,988	63.3%
Venezuela	352,145	224,669	63.8%	26	24	13	0	19	1	191,144	-4.2%
EUROPE											
Albania	11,100	422	3.8%	3	3	4	0	16	4	3,826	-7.3%
Austria	32,378	10,685	33.0%	7	3	0	0	7	44	15,004	2.0%
Belarus	80,155	5,050	6.3%	7	3	0	0	0	5	36,301	37.5%
Belgium	11,787	-	-	11	2	0	0	7	11	2,811	-1.8%
Bosnia and Herzegovina	19,767	99	0.5%	10	3	1	1	10	10	8,776	-
Bulgaria	42,855	1,928	4.5%	14	10	2	0	10	9	14,247	5.9%
Croatia	21,829	1,637	7.5%	9	4	1	1	26	11	6,884	1.1%
Czech Republic	30,450	4,902	16.1%	8	2	0	0	7	19	10,162	0.2%
Denmark	16,640	5,658	34.0%	5	1	0	0	7	11	1,757	2.2%
Estonia	17,462	2,061	11.8%	5	3	0	0	1	4	7,954	6.5%
Finland	130,559	12,142	9.3%	4	3	0	0	1	10	84,691	0.4%
France	208,482	27,728	13.3%	18	5	3	2	15	65	59,232	4.2%
Germany	137,847	43,973	31.9%	11	5	0	0	12	31	41,467	-
Greece	50,949	1,834	3.6%	13	7	6	1	26	11	13,896	9.1%
Hungary	35,919	2,514	7.0%	9	8	1	0	8	25	7,104	4.1%
Iceland	39,769	3,897	9.8%	7	0	0	0	8	0	120	24.0%
Ireland	27,133	461	1.7%	6	1	0	0	6	3	2,544	34.8%
Italy	116,342	9,191	7.9%	14	5	4	4	16	58	38,622	3.0%
Latvia	24,942	3,342	13.4%	5	3	0	0	3	8	11,286	4.5%
Lithuania	25,213	2,597	10.3%	6	4	0	0	3	5	7,699	2.5%
Luxembourg	999	-	-	3	1	0	0	0	4	-	-
Macedonia	9,928	705	7.1%	11	3	2	0	4	5	3,498	-
Moldova	13,070	183	1.4%	6	5	1	0	9	5	1,255	2.2%
Netherlands	16,164	2,295	14.2%	10	4	0	0	7	7	1,448	2.7%
Norway	125,050	8,503	6.8%	10	2	0	0	7	9	34,240	3.6%
Poland	120,728	14,970	12.4%	14	4	0	0	3	15	34,931	2.0%
Portugal	35,516	2,344	6.6%	17	7	0	1	19	82	14,154	18.4%
Romania	91,699	4,310	4.7%	17	8	2	0	10	22	24,896	2.3%
Serbia and Montenegro	39,449	1,302	3.3%	12	5	1	0	19	19	11,147	-0.5%
Slovakia	18,924	4,315	22.8%	9	4	1	0	8	19	8,405	9.0%
Slovenia	7,821	469	6.0%	9	1	0	1	15	42	4,274	2.0%
Spain	194,885	16,565	8.5%	24	7	7	3	23	63	55,483	6.4%
Sweden	173,732	15,810	9.1%	6	2	0	0	6	13	104,765	-
Switzerland	15,943	4,783	30.0%	5	2	0	0	4	30	4,629	3.7%
Ukraine	233,090	9,091	3.9%	16	8	2	0	11	14	37,004	3.3%
United Kingdom	93,788	19,602	20.9%	12	2	0	0	11	10	10,788	6.5%
Russia	6,592,849	514,242	7.8%	45	38	6	0	18	30	3,287,242	0.2%
ASIA											
Afghanistan	251,773	755	0.3%	13	11	1	1	0	1	5,216	-
Armenia	11,506	874	7.6%	11	4	5	0	1	7	1,355	13.6%
Azerbaijan	33,437	2,040	6.1%	13	8	5	0	5	6	4,224	13.5%
Bahrain	267	-	-	1	6	0	0	6	0	-	-
Bangladesh	55,598	445	0.8%	22	23	20	0	8	0	5,151	14.1%
Brunei	2,226	-	-	11	14	4	0	6	0	1,707	-2.2%
Cambodia	69,898	12,931	18.5%	24	19	10	0	11	0	36,043	-5.7%
China	3,690,045	287,824	7.8%	81	75	31	1	46	4	631,200	12.4%
Cyprus	3,572	-	-	3	3	3	0	6	0	664	44.5%
East Timor	5,743	-	-	0	6	0	0	2	0	1,958	-6.3%
Georgia	26,911	619	2.3%	13	3	7	1	6	10	11,537	-
India	1,222,510	63,571	5.2%	86	72	25	3	27	23	247,542	0.6%
Indonesia	735,310	151,474	20.6%	147	114	28	0	91	31	405,353	-11.1%
Iran	636,372	30,546	4.8%	22	13	8	2	14	3	28,182	-
Iraq	169,235	-	-	11	11	2	0	3	2	3,085	-
Israel	8,019	1,267	15.8%	15	12	4	0	10	10	510	61.0%
Japan	145,850	9,918	6.8%	37	35	11	10	27	45	92,977	0.1%
Jordan	34,495	1,173	3.4%	9	8	1	0	5	3	332	-
Kazakhstan	1,049,156	28,327	2.7%	17	15	2	1	7	4	46,904	24.5%
Korea, North	46,540	1,210	2.6%	13	19	0	0	5	1	31,699	-
Korea, South	38,328	2,645	6.9%	13	25	0	0	7	1	24,124	-0.8%

CONTINENT/Country	Total Area Sq. Miles	Protected Area 2002[1,2] Sq. Miles	%	Endangered Species 2003[3] Mammal	Bird	Reptile	Amphib.	Fish	Invrt.	Forest Cover[4] Sq. Miles 2000	Percent Change 1990-2000
Kuwait	6,880	103	1.5%	1	7	1	0	6	0	19	66.7%
Kyrgyzstan	77,182	2,779	3.6%	7	4	2	0	0	3	3,873	29.4%
Laos	91,429	11,429	12.5%	31	20	11	0	6	· 0	48,498	-4.0%
Lebanon	4,016	20	0.5%	6	7	1	0	8	1	139	-2.7%
Malaysia	127,320	7,257	5.7%	50	37	21	0	34	3	74,487	52.4%
Mongolia	604,829	69,555	11.5%	14	16	0	0	1	3	41,101	-5.3%
Myanmar	261,228	784	0.3%	39	35	20	0	7	2	132,892	-13.1%
Nepal	56,827	5,058	8.9%	29	25	6	0	0	1	15,058	-16.7%
Oman	119,499	16,730	14.0%	11	10	4	0	17	1	4	-
Pakistan	339,732	16,647	4.9%	17	17	9	0	14	0	9,116	-14.3%
Philippines	115,831	6,602	5.7%	50	67	8	23	48	19	22,351	-13.3%
Qatar	4,412	-	-	0	6	1	0	4	0	-	-
Saudi Arabia	830,000	317,890	38.3%	9	15	2	0	8	1	5,807	-
Singapore	264	13	4.9%	3	7	3	0	12	1	8	-
Sri Lanka	25,332	3,420	13.5%	22	14	8	0	22	2	7,490	-15.2%
Syria	71,498	-	-	4	8	3	0	8	3	1,780	-
Taiwan	13,901	-	-	12	21	8	0	23	0	-	-
Tajikistan	55,251	2,321	4.2%	9	7	1	0	3	2	1,544	5.3%
Thailand	198,115	27,538	13.9%	37	37	19	0	35	1	56,996	-7.1%
Turkey	302,541	4,841	1.6%	17	11	12	3	29	13	39,479	2.2%
Turkmenistan	188,457	7,915	4.2%	13	6	2	0	8	5	14,498	-
United Arab Emirates	32,278	-	-	4	8	1	0	6	0	1,239	32.1%
Uzbekistan	172,742	3,455	2.0%	9	9	2	0	4	1	7,602	2.4%
Vietnam	128,066	4,738	3.7%	42	37	24	1	22	0	37,911	5.5%
Yemen	203,850	-	-	6	12	2	0	10	2	1,734	-17.0%
AFRICA											
Algeria	919,595	45,980	5.0%	13	6	2	0	9	12	8,282	14.2%
Angola	481,354	31,769	6.6%	19	15	4	0	8	6	269,329	-1.7%
Benin	43,484	4,957	11.4%	9	2	1	0	7	0	10,232	-20.9%
Botswana	224,607	41,552	18.5%	7	7	0	0	0	0	47,981	-8.7%
Burkina Faso	105,869	12,175	11.5%	7	2	1	0	0	0	27,371	-2.1%
Burundi	10,745	612	5.7%	6	7	0	0	0	3	363	-61.0%
Cameroon	183,568	8,261	4.5%	38	15	1	1	34	4	92,116	-8.5%
Cape Verde	1,557	-	-	3	2	0	0	13	0	328	142.9%
Central African Republic	240,536	20,927	8.7%	14	3	1	0	0	0	88,444	-1.3%
Chad	495,755	45,114	9.1%	15	5	1	0	0	1	49,004	-6.0%
Comoros	863	-	-	2	9	2	0	3	4	31	-33.3%
Congo	132,047	6,602	5.0%	15	3	1	0	9	1	85,174	-0.8%
Congo, Democratic Republic of the	905,446	58,854	6.5%	40	28	2	0	9	45	522,037	-3.8%
Cote d'Ivoire	124,504	7,470	6.0%	19	12	2	1	10	1	27,479	-27.1%
Djibouti	8,958	-	-	5	5	0	0	9	0	23	-
Egypt	386,662	37,506	9.7%	13	7	6	0	13	1	278	38.5%
Equatorial Guinea	10,831	-	-	16	5	2	1	7	2	6,765	-5.7%
Eritrea	45,406	1,952	4.3%	12	7	6	0	8	0	6,120	-3.3%
Ethiopia	426,373	72,057	16.9%	35	16	.1	0	0	4	17,734	-8.1%
Gabon	103,347	723	0.7%	14	5	1	0	11	1	84,271	-0.5%
Gambia, The	4,127	95	2.3%	3	2	1	0	10	0	1,857	10.3%
Ghana	92,098	5,157	5.6%	14	8	2	0	7	0	24,460	-15.9%
Guinea	94,926	664	0.7%	12	10	1	1	7	3	26,753	-4.8%
Guinea-Bissau	13,948	-	-	3	0	1	0	9	1	8,444	-9.0%
Kenya	224,961	17,997	8.0%	50	24	5	0	27	15	66,008	-5.2%
Lesotho	11,720	23	0.2%	6	7	0	0	1	1	54	-
Liberia	43,000	731	1.7%	16	11	2	0	7	2	13,440	-17.9%
Libya	679,362	679	0.1%	8	1	3	0	8	0	1,382	15.1%
Madagascar	226,658	9,746	4.3%	50	27	18	2	25	32	45,278	-9.1%
Malawi	45,747	5,124	11.2%	8	11	0	0	0	8	9,892	-21.6%
Mali	478,841	17,717	3.7%	13	4	1	0	1	0	50,911	-7.0%
Mauritania	397,956	6,765	1.7%	10	2	2	0	10	1	1,224	-23.6%
Mauritius	788	-	-	3	9	4	0	7	32	62	-5.9%
Morocco	172,414	1,207	0.7%	16	9	2	0	10	8	11,680	-0.4%
Mozambique	309,496	25,998	8.4%	15	16	5	0	19	7	118,151	-2.0%
Namibia	317,818	43,223	13.6%	14	11	3	1	11	1	31,043	-8.4%
Niger	489,192	37,668	7.7%	11	3	0	0	0	1	5,127	-31.7%
Nigeria	356,669	11,770	3.3%	27	9	2	0	11	1	52,189	-22.8%
Rwanda	10,169	630	6.2%	8	9	0	0	0	2	1,185	-32.8%
Sao Tome and Principe	372	-	-	3	9	1	0	6	2	104	-
Senegal	75,951	8,810	11.6%	12	4	6	0	17	0	23,958	-6.8%
Sierra Leone	27,699	582	2.1%	12	10	3	0	7	4	4,073	-25.5%
Somalia	246,201	1,970	0.8%	19	10	2	0	16	1	29,016	-9.3%
South Africa	470,693	25,888	5.5%	36	28	19	9	47	113	34,429	-0.9%
Sudan	967,500	50,310	5.2%	22	6	2	0	7	1	237,943	-13.5%
Swaziland	6,704	-	-	5	5	0	0	0	0	2,015	12.5%
Tanzania	364,900	108,740	29.8%	41	33	5	0	26	47	149,850	-2.3%
Togo	21,925	1,732	7.9%	9	0	2	0	7	0	1,969	-29.1%
Tunisia	63,170	190	0.3%	11	5	3	0	8	5	1,969	2.2%
Uganda	93,065	22,894	24.6%	20	13	0	0	27	10	16,178	-17.9%
Zambia	290,586	92,697	31.9%	11	11	0	0	0	6	120,641	-21.4%
Zimbabwe	150,873	18,256	12.1%	11	10	0	0	0	2	73,514	-14.4%
OCEANIA											
Australia	2,969,910	397,968	13.4%	63	35	38	35	74	282	596,678	-1.8%
Fiji	7,056	78	1.1%	5	13	6	1	8	2	3,147	-2.0%
Kiribati	313	-	-	0	4	1	0	4	1	108	-
Micronesia, Federated States of	271	-	-	6	5	2	0	6	4	58	-37.5%
New Zealand	104,454	30,918	29.6%	8	63	11	1	16	13	30,680	5.2%
Papua New Guinea	178,704	4,110	2.3%	58	32	9	0	31	12	118,151	-3.6%
Samoa	1,093	-	-	3	8	1	0	4	1	405	-19.2%
Solomon Islands	10,954	33	0.3%	20	23	4	0	4	6	9,792	-1.7%
Tonga	251	-	-	2	3	2	0	3	2	15	-
Vanuatu	4,707	-	-	5	8	2	0	4	0	1,726	1.4%

This table presents data for most independent nations having an area greater than 200 square miles
- Zero, insignificant, or not available
(1) Source: World Resources Institute, 2003. Earth Trends: The Environmental Information Portal. Available at http://earthtrends.wri.org. Washington D. C. World Resources Institute
(2) Source: United Nations Environment Programme - World Conservation Monitoring Centre (UNEP-WCMC); World Database on Protected Areas
(3) Source: International Union of Conservation of Nature and Natural Resources; IUCN 2003 Red List of Threatened Species <www.redlist.org>
(4) Source: United Nations Food and Agriculture Organization; Global Forest Resources Assessment 2000

WORLD COMPARISONS

General Information

Equatorial diameter of the earth, 7,926.38 miles.
Polar diameter of the earth, 7,899.80 miles.
Mean diameter of the earth, 7,917.52 miles.
Equatorial circumference of the earth, 24,901.46 miles.
Polar circumference of the earth, 24,855.34 miles.
Mean distance from the earth to the sun, 93,020,000 miles.
Mean distance from the earth to the moon, 238,857 miles.
Total area of the earth, 197,000,000 sq. miles.

Highest elevation on the earth's surface, Mt. Everest, Asia, 29,028 ft.
Lowest elevation on the earth's land surface, shores of the Dead Sea, Asia, 1,339 ft. below sea level.
Greatest known depth of the ocean, southwest of Guam, Pacific Ocean, 35,810 ft.
Total land area of the earth (incl. inland water and Antarctica), 57,900,000 sq. miles.

Area of Africa, 11,700,000 sq. miles.
Area of Antarctica, 5,400,000 sq. miles.
Area of Asia, 17,300,000 sq. miles.
Area of Europe, 3,800,000 sq. miles.
Area of North America, 9,500,000 sq. miles.
Area of Oceania (incl. Australia) 3,300,000 sq. miles.
Area of South America, 6,900,000 sq. miles.
Population of the earth (est. 1/1/04), 6,339,505,000.

Principal Islands and Their Areas

ISLAND	Area (Sq. Mi.)
Baffin I., Canada	195,928
Banks I., Canada	27,038
Borneo (Kalimantan), Asia	287,300
Bougainville, Papua New Guinea	3,591
Cape Breton I., Canada	3,981
Celebes (Sulawesi), Indonesia	73,057
Ceram (Seram), Indonesia	7,191
Corsica, France	3,367
Crete, Greece	3,189
Cuba, N. America	42,780
Cyprus, Asia	3,572
Devon I., Canada	21,331
Ellesmere I., Canada	75,767
Flores, Indonesia	5,502
Great Britain, U.K.	88,795
Greenland, N. America	840,000
Guadalcanal, Solomon Is.	2,060
Hainan Dao, China	13,127
Hawaii, U.S.	4,028
Hispaniola, N. America	29,300
Hokkaidō, Japan	32,245
Honshū, Japan	89,176
Iceland, Europe	39,769
Ireland, Europe	32,587
Jamaica, N. America	4,247
Java (Jawa), Indonesia	51,038
Kodiak I., U.S.	3,670
Kyūshū, Japan	17,129
Lyete, Philippines	2,785
Long Island, U.S.	1,377
Luzon, Philippines	40,420
Madagascar, Africa	226,642
Melville I., Canada	16,274
Mindanao, Philippines	36,537
Mindoro, Philippines	3,759
Negros, Philippines	4,907
New Britain, Papua New Guinea	14,093
New Caledonia, Oceania	6,252
Newfoundland, Canada	42,031
New Guinea, Asia-Oceania	308,882
New Ireland, Papua New Guinea	3,475
North East Land, Norway	6,350
North I., New Zealand	44,333
Novaya Zemlya, Russia	31,892
Palawan, Philippines	4,550
Panay, Philippines	4,446
Prince of Wales I., Canada	12,872
Puerto Rico, N. America	3,514
Sakhalin, Russia	29,498
Samar, Philippines	5,050
Sardinia, Italy	9,301
Shikoku, Japan	7,258
Sicily, Italy	9,926
Somerset I., Canada	9,570
Southampton I., Canada	15,913
South I., New Zealand	57,708
Spitsbergen, Norway	15,260
Sri Lanka, Asia	24,942
Sumatra (Sumatera), Indonesia	182,860
Taiwan, Asia	13,900
Tasmania, Australia	26,178
Tierra del Fuego, S. America	18,600
Timor, Asia	5,743
Vancouver I., Canada	12,079
Victoria I., Canada	83,897
Vrangelya (Wrangel), Russia	2,819

Principal Lakes, Oceans, Seas, and Their Areas

LAKE Country	Area (Sq. Mi.)
Arabian Sea	1,492,000
Aral Sea, Kazakhstan-Uzbekistan	13,000
Arctic Ocean	5,400,000
Athabasca, L., Canada	3,064
Atlantic Ocean	29,600,000
Balqash köli (L. Balkhash), Kazakhstan	7,027
Baltic Sea, Europe	163,000
Baykal, Ozero (L. Baikal), Russia	12,162
Bering Sea, Asia-N.A.	876,000
Black Sea, Europe-Asia	178,000
Caribbean Sea, N.A.-S.A.	1,063,000
Caspian Sea, Asia-Europe	144,402
Chad, L., Cameroon-Chad-Nigeria	595
Erie, L., Canada-U.S.	9,910
Eyre, L., Australia	3,668
Gairdner, L., Australia	1,076
Great Bear Lake, Canada	12,096
Great Salt Lake, U.S.	1,700
Great Slave Lake, Canada	11,030
Hudson Bay, Canada	475,000
Huron, L., Canada-U.S.	23,000
Indian Ocean	26,500,000
Japan, Sea of, Asia	389,000
Koko Nor (Qinghai Hu), China	1,722
Ladozhskoye Ozero (L. Ladoga), Russia	7,002
Manitoba, L., Canada	1,785
Mediterranean Sea, Europe-Africa-Asia	967,000
Mexico, Gulf of, N. America	596,000
Michigan, L., U.S.	22,300
Nicaragua, Lago de, Nicaragua	3,147
North Sea, Europe	222,000
Nyasa, L., Malawi-Mozambique-Tanzania	11,120
Onezhskoye Ozero (L. Onega), Russia	3,819
Ontario, L., Canada-U.S.	7,340
Pacific Ocean	60,100,000
Red Sea, Africa-Asia	169,000
Rudolf, L., Ethiopia-Kenya	2,471
Southern Ocean	7,800,000
Superior, L., Canada-U.S.	31,700
Tanganyika. L., Africa	12,355
Titicaca, Lago, Bolivia-Peru	3,232
Torrens, L., Australia	1,076
Vänern (L.), Sweden	2,181
Van Gölü (L.), Turkey	1,434
Victoria, L., Kenya-Tanzania-Uganda	26,564
Winnipeg, L., Canada	9,416
Winnipegosis, L., Canada	2,075
Yellow Sea, China-Korea	480,000

Principal Mountains and Their Heights

MOUNTAIN Country	Elev. (Ft.)
Aconcagua, Cerro, Argentina	22,831
Annapurna, Nepal	26,504
Aoraki, New Zealand	12,316
Api, Nepal	23,399
Apo, Philippines	9,692
Ararat, Mt., Turkey	16,854
Barú, Volcán, Panama	11,401
Bangueta, Mt., Papua New Guinea	13,520
Belukha, Mt., Kazakhstan-Russia	14,783
Bia, Phou, Laos	9,249
Blanc, Mont (Monte Bianco), France-Italy	15,771
Blanca Pk., Colorado, U.S.	14,345
Bolívar, Pico, Venezuela	16,427
Bonete, Cerro, Argentina	22,546
Borah Pk., Idaho, U.S.	12,662
Boundary Pk., Nevada, U.S.	13,140
Cameroon Mtn., Cameroon	13,451
Carrauntoohil, Ireland	3,406
Chaltel, Cerro (Monte Fitzroy), Argentina-Chile	10,958
Chimborazo, Ecuador	20,702
Chirripó, Cerro, Costa Rica	12,530
Colima, Nevado de, Mexico	13,911
Cotopaxi, Ecuador	19,347
Cristóbal Colón, Pico, Colombia	19,029
Damāvand, Qolleh-ye, Iran	18,386
Dhawalāgiri, Nepal	26,810
Duarte, Pico, Dominican Rep.	10,417
Dufourspitze (Monte Rosa), Italy-Switzerland	15,203
Elbert, Mt., Colorado, U.S.	14,433
El'brus, Gora, Russia	18,510
Elgon, Mt., Kenya-Uganda	14,178
Erciyeş, Dağı, Turkey	12,848
Etna, Mt., Italy	10,902
Everest, Mt., China-Nepal	29,028
Fairweather, Mt., Alaska-Canada	15,300
Foladī, Koh-e, Afghanistan	16,847
Foraker, Mt., Alaska, U.S.	17,400
Fuji San, Japan	12,388
Galdhøpiggen, Norway	8,100
Gannett Pk., Wyoming, U.S.	13,804
Gasherbrum, China-Pakistan	26,470
Gerlachovský štít, Slovakia	8,711
Giluwe, Mt., Papua New Guinea	14,331
Gongga Shan, China	24,790
Grand Teton, Wyoming, U.S.	13,770
Grossglockner, Austria	12,457
Hadūr Shu'ayb, Yemen	12,008
Haleakalā Crater, Hawaii, U.S.	10,023
Hekla, Iceland	4,892
Hood, Mt., Oregon, U.S.	11,239
Huascarán, Nevado, Peru	22,133
Huila, Nevado de, Colombia	18,865
Hvannadalshnúkur, Iceland	6,952
Illampu, Nevado, Bolivia	21,066
Illimani, Nevado, Bolivia	20,741
Ismail Samani, pik, Tajikistan	24,590
Iztaccíhuatl, Mexico	17,159
Jaya, Puncak, Indonesia	16,503
Jungfrau, Switzerland	13,642
K2 (Qogir Feng), China-Pakistan	28,250
Kāmet, China-India	25,447
Kānchenjunga, India-Nepal	28,208
Kātrīnā, Jabal, Egypt	8,668
Kebnekaise, Sweden	6,926
Kenya, Mt. (Kirinyaga), Kenya	17,058
Kerinci, Gunung, Indonesia	12,467
Kilimanjaro, Tanzania	19,340
Kinabalu, Gunong, Malaysia	13,455
Klyuchevskaya, Russia	15,584
Kosciuszko, Mt., Australia	7,313
Koussi, Emi, Chad	11,204
Kula Kangri, Bhutan	24,784
La Selle, Massif de, Haiti	8,793
Lassen Pk., California, U.S.	10,457
Llullaillaco, Volcán, Argentina-Chile	22,110
Logan, Mt., Canada	19,551
Longs Pk., Colorado, U.S.	14,255
Makālu, China-Nepal	27,825
Margherita Peak, Dem. Rep. of the Congo-Uganda	16,763
Markham, Mt., Antarctica	14,049
Maromokotro, Madagascar	9,436
Massive, Mt., Colorado, U.S.	14,421
Matterhorn, Italy-Switzerland	14,692
Mauna Kea, Hawaii, U.S.	13,796
Mauna Loa, Hawaii, U.S.	13,679
Mayon Volcano, Philippines	8,077
McKinley, Mt., Alaska, U.S.	20,320
Meron, Hare, Israel	3,963
Meru, Mt., Tanzania	14,978
Misti, Volcán, Peru	19,101
Mitchell, Mt., North Carolina, U.S.	6,684
Môco, Serra do, Angola	8,596
Moldoveanu, Romania	8,346
Mulhacén, Spain	11,424
Musala, Bulgaria	9,596
Muztag, China	25,338
Muztagata, China	24,757
Namjagbarwa Feng, China	25,446
Nanda Devi, India	25,645
Nanga Parbat, Pakistan	26,660
Narodnaya, Gora, Russia	6,217
Nevis, Ben, United Kingdom	4,406
Ojos del Salado, Nevado, Argentina-Chile	22,615
Ólimbos, Cyprus	6,401
Ólympos, Greece	9,570
Olympus, Mt., Washington, U.S.	7,965
Orizaba, Pico de, Mexico	18,406
Paektu San, North Korea-China	9,003
Paricutín, Mexico	9,186
Parnassós, Greece	8,061
Pelée, Montagne, Martinique	4,583
Pidurutalagala, Sri Lanka	8,281
Pikes Pk., Colorado, U.S.	14,110
Pobedy, pik, China-Kyrgyzstan	24,406
Popocatépetl, Volcán, Mexico	17,930
Pulog, Mt., Philippines	9,626
Rainier, Mt., Washington, U.S.	14,410
Ramm, Jabal, Jordan	5,755
Ras Dashen Terara, Ethiopia	15,158
Rinjani, Gunung, Indonesia	12,224
Robson, Mt., Canada	12,972
Roraima, Mt., Brazil-Guyana-Venezuela	9,432
Ruapehu, Mt., New Zealand	9,177
St. Elias, Mt., Alaska, U.S.-Canada	18,008
Sajama, Nevado, Bolivia	21,391
Semeru, Gunung, Indonesia	12,060
Shām, Jabal ash, Oman	9,957
Shasta, Mt., California, U.S.	14,162
Snowdon, United Kingdom	3,560
Tahat, Algeria	9,541
Tajumulco, Guatemala	13,845
Taranaki, Mt., New Zealand	8,260
Tirich Mīr, Pakistan	25,230
Tomanivi (Victoria), Fiji	4,341
Toubkal, Jebel, Morocco	13,665
Triglav, Slovenia	9,396
Trikora, Puncak, Indonesia	15,584
Tupungato, Cerro, Argentina-Chile	21,555
Turquino, Pico, Cuba	6,470
Uluru (Ayers Rock), Australia	2,844
Uncompahgre Pk, Colorado, U.S.	14,309
Vesuvio (Vesuvius), Italy	4,190
Victoria, Mt., Papua New Guinea	13,238
Vinson Massif, Antarctica	16,066
Waddington, Mt., Canada	13,163
Washington, Mt., New Hampshire, U.S.	6,288
Whitney, Mt., California, U.S.	14,494
Wilhelm, Mt., Papua New Guinea	14,793
Wrangell, Mt., Alaska, U.S.	14,163
Xixabangma Feng (Gosainthan), China	26,286
Yü Shan, Taiwan	13,114
Zugspitze, Austria-Germany	9,718

Principal Rivers and Their Lengths

RIVER Continent	Length (Mi.)
Albany, N. America	610
Aldan, Asia	1,412
Amazonas-Ucayali, S. America	4,000
Amu Darya, Asia	1,578
Amur, Asia	1,752
Araguaia, S. America	1,367
Arkansas, N. America	1,460
Atchafalaya, N. America	1,420
Athabasca, N. America	765
Brahmaputra, Asia	1,770
Brazos, N. America	1,280
Canadian, N. America	906
Churchill, N. America	1,000
Colorado, N. America (U.S.-Mexico)	1,450
Colorado, N. America (Texas)	862
Columbia, N. America	1,240
Congo (Zaïre), Africa	2,715
Danube, Europe	1,777
Darling, Australia	864
Dnieper (Dnipro), Europe	1,367
Don, Europe	1,162
Elbe, Europe	690
Essequibo, S. America	603
Euphrates, Asia	1,510
Fraser, N. America	851
Ganges, Asia	1,864
Gila, N. America	649
Godāvari, Asia	932
Huang (Yellow), Asia	2,902
Indigirka, Asia	1,072
Indus, Asia	1,118
Irrawaddy, Asia	1,300
Juruá, S. America	1,250
Kama, Europe	1,122
Kasai, Africa	1,338
Kolyma, Asia	1,323
Lena, Asia	2,734
Limpopo, Africa	1,100
Loire, Europe	690
Mackenzie, N. America	2,635
Madeira, S. America	2,013
Magdalena, S. America	951
Marañón, S. America	1,000
Mekong, Asia	2,796
Meuse, Europe	575
Mississippi, N. America	2,340
Mississippi-Missouri, N. America	3,710
Missouri, N. America	2,540
Murray-Darling, Australia	2,169
Negro, S. America	1,305
Nelson, N. America	1,600
Niger, Africa	2,585
Nile, Africa	4,132
Ob', Asia	2,268
Oder, Europe	565
Ohio, N. America	1,310
Oka, Europe	932
Orange, Africa	1,300
Orinoco, S. America	1,703
Ottawa, N. America	790
Paraguay, S. America	1,610
Parnaíba, S. America	901
Peace, N. America	1,195
Pechora, Europe	1,125
Pecos, N. America	926
Pilcomayo, S. America	1,550
Plata-Paraná, S. America	2,920
Platte, N. America	990
Purús, S. America	1,860
Red, N. America	1,290
Rhine, Europe	820
Rhône, Europe	503
Rio Grande, N. America	1,900
Roosevelt, S. America	950
St. Lawrence, N. America	1,900
Salado, S. America	870
Salween (Nu), Asia	1,750
São Francisco, S. America	1,740
Saskatchewan-Bow, N. America	1,205
Severnaya Dvina (Northern Dvina), Europe	462
Snake, N. America	1,040
Sungari (Songhua), Asia	1,140
Syr Darya, Asia	1,370
Tagus, Europe	625
Tarim, Asia	1,328
Tennessee, N. America	886
Tigris, Asia	1,180
Tisa, Europe	607
Tocantins, S. America	1,640
Ucayali, S. America	1,220
Ural, Asia	1,509
Uruguay, S. America	1,025
Verkhnyaya Tunguska (Angara), Asia	1,105
Vilyuy, Asia	1,647
Volga, Europe	2,082
Volta, Africa	994
Wisła (Vistula), Europe	630
Xiang, Asia	930
Xingu, S. America	1,230
Yangtze (Chang), Asia	3,915
Yellowstone, N. America	692
Yenisey, Asia	2,169
Yukon, N. America	1,980
Zambezi, Africa	1,653

PRINCIPAL CITIES OF THE WORLD

- **Abidjan**, Cote d'Ivoire … 1,929,079
- **Abū Ẓaby (Abu Dhabi)**, United Arab Emirates … 242,975
- **Accra**, Ghana (1,390,000) … 949,113
- **Addis Ababa**, Ethiopia … 2,424,000
- **Ahmadābād**, India (4,519,278) … 3,515,361
- **Aleppo (Ḥalab)**, Syria (1,640,000) … 1,591,400
- **Alexandria (Al Iskandarīyah)**, Egypt (3,350,000) … 3,339,076
- **Algiers (El Djazaïr)**, Algeria (2,547,983) … 1,507,241
- **Al Jīzah (Giza)**, Egypt (*Al Qāhirah) … 2,221,817
- **Almaty**, Kazakhstan (1,190,000) … 1,129,356
- **'Ammān**, Jordan (1,500,000) … 1,147,447
- **Amsterdam**, Netherlands (1,121,303) … 727,053
- **Ankara**, Turkey (3,294,220) … 2,984,099
- **Antananarivo**, Madagascar … 1,250,000
- **Antwerp (Antwerpen)**, Belgium (1,135,000) … 453,030
- **Ashgabat (Ashkhabad)**, Turkmenistan … 557,600
- **Asmera**, Eritrea … 358,100
- **Astana (Aqmola)**, Kazakhstan (319,324) … 312,965
- **Asunción**, Paraguay (700,000) … 546,637
- **Athens (Athína)**, Greece (3,150,000) … 772,072
- **Atlanta**, Georgia, U.S. (4,112,198) … 416,474
- **Auckland**, New Zealand (1,074,510) … 367,737
- **Baghdād**, Iraq … 3,841,268
- **Baku (Bakı)**, Azerbaijan (2,020,000) … 1,792,300
- **Bamako**, Mali … 658,275
- **Bandung**, Indonesia … 5,919,400
- **Bangalore**, India (5,686,844) … 4,292,223
- **Banghāzī**, Libya … 800,000
- **Bangkok (Krung Thep)**, Thailand (7,060,000) … 5,620,591
- **Bangui**, Central African Republic … 451,690
- **Barcelona**, Spain (4,000,000) … 1,496,266
- **Beijing**, China (7,320,000) … 6,690,000
- **Beirut (Bayrūt)**, Lebanon (1,675,000) … 509,000
- **Belfast**, N. Ireland, U.K. (730,000) … 297,300
- **Belgrade (Beograd)**, Serbia and Montenegro … 1,594,483
- **Belo Horizonte**, Brazil (4,055,000) … 1,366,301
- **Berlin**, Germany (4,220,000) … 3,386,667
- **Birmingham**, England, U.K. (2,705,000) … 1,020,589
- **Bishkek**, Kyrgyzstan … 753,400
- **Bogotá**, Colombia … 6,422,198
- **Bonn**, Germany (600,000) … 301,048
- **Boston**, Massachusetts, U.S. (5,819,100) … 589,141
- **Brasília**, Brazil … 1,947,133
- **Bratislava**, Slovakia … 451,395
- **Brazzaville**, Congo … 693,712
- **Brisbane**, Australia (1,627,535) … 888,449
- **Brussels (Bruxelles)**, Belgium (2,390,000) … 133,845
- **Bucharest (București)**, Romania (2,300,000) … 2,016,131
- **Budapest**, Hungary (2,450,000) … 1,825,153
- **Buenos Aires**, Argentina (11,000,000) … 2,960,976
- **Cairo (Al Qāhirah)**, Egypt (9,300,000) … 6,800,992
- **Calgary**, Alberta, Canada (951,395) … 878,866
- **Cali**, Colombia … 2,128,920
- **Canberra**, Australia (342,798) … 311,518
- **Cape Town**, South Africa (1,900,000) … 854,616
- **Caracas**, Venezuela (4,000,000) … 1,822,465
- **Cardiff**, Wales, U.K. (645,000) … 315,040
- **Casablanca**, Morocco (3,400,000) … 3,022,000
- **Changchun**, China … 2,470,000
- **Chelyabinsk**, Russia (1,320,000) … 1,086,300
- **Chengdu**, China … 2,760,000
- **Chennai (Madras)**, India (6,424,624) … 4,216,268
- **Chicago**, Illinois, U.S. (9,157,540) … 2,896,016
- **Chișinău (Kishinev)**, Moldova (746,500) … 658,300
- **Chittagong**, Bangladesh (2,342,662) … 1,566,070
- **Chongqing**, China … 3,870,000
- **Cincinnati**, Ohio, U.S. (1,979,202) … 331,285
- **Cleveland**, Ohio, U.S. (2,945,831) … 478,403
- **Cologne (Köln)**, Germany (1,830,000) … 962,507
- **Colombo**, Sri Lanka (2,050,000) … 615,000
- **Conakry**, Guinea … 950,000
- **Copenhagen (København)**, Denmark (2,030,000) … 499,148
- **Córdoba**, Argentina (1,260,000) … 1,179,067
- **Cotonou**, Benin … 650,660
- **Curitiba**, Brazil (2,595,000) … 1,586,848
- **Dakar**, Senegal (1,976,533) … 879,703
- **Dalian**, China … 2,400,000
- **Dallas**, Texas, U.S. (5,221,801) … 1,188,580
- **Damascus (Dimashq)**, Syria (2,230,000) … 1,549,932
- **Dar es Salaam**, Tanzania … 1,360,850
- **Delhi**, India (12,791,458) … 9,817,439
- **Denver**, Colorado, U.S. (2,581,506) … 554,636
- **Detroit**, Michigan, U.S. (5,456,428) … 951,270
- **Dhaka (Dacca)**, Bangladesh (6,537,308) … 3,637,892
- **Djibouti**, Djibouti … 329,337
- **Dnipropetrovs'k**, Ukraine (1,590,000) … 1,108,682
- **Donets'k**, Ukraine (2,090,000) … 1,050,369
- **Douala**, Cameroon … 712,251
- **Dublin (Baile Átha Cliath)**, Ireland (1,175,000) … 481,854
- **Durban**, South Africa (1,740,000) … 669,242
- **Dushanbe**, Tajikistan (700,000) … 528,600
- **Düsseldorf**, Germany (1,200,000) … 568,855
- **Edinburgh**, Scotland, U.K. (640,000) … 448,850
- **Edmonton**, Alberta, Canada (937,845) … 666,104
- **Eşfahān**, Iran (1,525,000) … 1,266,072
- **Essen**, Germany (5,040,000) … 599,515
- **Fortaleza**, Brazil (2,780,000) … 788,956
- **Frankfurt am Main**, Germany (1,960,000) … 643,821
- **Fukuoka**, Japan (2,000,000) … 1,341,489
- **Geneva (Génève)**, Switzerland (450,592) … 172,598
- **Glasgow**, Scotland, U.K. (1,870,000) … 616,430
- **Goiânia**, Brazil … 1,075,761
- **Guadalajara**, Mexico (3,669,021) … 1,646,183
- **Guangzhou (Canton)**, China … 3,750,000
- **Guatemala**, Guatemala (1,500,000) … 1,006,954
- **Guayaquil**, Ecuador … 2,117,553
- **Halifax**, Nova Scotia, Canada (359,183) … 119,300
- **Hamburg**, Germany (2,460,000) … 1,704,735
- **Hannover**, Germany (1,015,000) … 514,718
- **Hanoi**, Vietnam (1,275,000) … 1,073,760
- **Harare**, Zimbabwe (1,470,000) … 1,189,103
- **Harbin**, China … 3,120,000
- **Havana (La Habana)**, Cuba (2,285,000) … 2,189,716
- **Helsinki**, Finland (939,697) … 548,720
- **Hiroshima**, Japan (1,600,000) … 1,126,282
- **Ho Chi Minh City (Saigon)**, Vietnam (3,300,000) … 3,015,743
- **Hong Kong (Xianggang)**, China (4,770,000) … 1,250,993
- **Honolulu**, Hawaii, U.S. (876,156) … 371,657
- **Houston**, Texas, U.S. (4,669,571) … 1,953,631
- **Hyderābād**, India (5,533,640) … 3,449,878
- **Ibadan**, Nigeria … 1,144,000
- **Islāmābād**, Pakistan (*Rāwalpindi) … 529,180
- **İstanbul**, Turkey (8,506,026) … 8,260,438
- **İzmir**, Turkey (2,554,363) … 2,081,556
- **Jaipur**, India … 2,324,319
- **Jakarta**, Indonesia (10,200,000) … 9,373,900
- **Jerusalem (Yerushalayim)**, Israel (685,000) … 633,700
- **Jiddah**, Saudi Arabia … 1,450,000
- **Jinan**, China … 2,150,000
- **Johannesburg**, South Africa (4,000,000) … 752,349
- **Kābul**, Afghanistan … 1,424,400
- **Kampala**, Uganda … 773,463
- **Kānpur**, India (2,690,486) … 2,540,069
- **Kaohsiung**, Taiwan (1,845,000) … 1,468,586
- **Karāchi**, Pakistan … 9,339,023
- **Katowice**, Poland (2,755,000) … 343,158
- **Kharkiv**, Ukraine (1,950,000) … 1,494,235
- **Khartoum (Al Kharṭūm)**, Sudan (1,450,000) … 947,483
- **Kiev (Kyïv)**, Ukraine (3,250,000) … 2,589,541
- **Kingston**, Jamaica (830,000) … 516,500
- **Kinshasa**, Dem. Rep. of the Congo … 3,000,000
- **Kitakyūshū**, Japan (1,550,000) … 1,011,491
- **Kolkata (Calcutta)**, India (13,216,546) … 4,580,544
- **Kuala Lumpur**, Malaysia (2,500,000) … 1,297,526
- **Kuwait (Al Kuwayt)**, Kuwait (1,126,000) … 28,859
- **Lagos**, Nigeria (3,800,000) … 1,213,000
- **Lahore**, Pakistan … 5,143,495
- **La Paz**, Bolivia (1,487,854) … 792,611
- **Libreville**, Gabon (418,616) … 362,386
- **Lilongwe**, Malawi … 435,964
- **Lima**, Peru (6,321,173) … 340,422
- **Lisbon (Lisboa)**, Portugal (2,350,000) … 563,210
- **Liverpool**, England, U.K. (1,515,000) … 467,995
- **Ljubljana**, Slovenia … 263,832
- **Lomé**, Togo … 450,000
- **London**, England, U.K. (12,000,000) … 7,074,265
- **Los Angeles**, California, U.S. (16,373,645) … 3,694,820
- **Luanda**, Angola … 1,459,900
- **Lucknow**, India (2,266,933) … 2,207,340
- **Lusaka**, Zambia … 1,269,848
- **Lyon**, France (1,648,216) … 445,452
- **Madrid**, Spain (4,690,000) … 2,882,860
- **Managua**, Nicaragua … 864,201
- **Manaus**, Brazil … 1,394,724
- **Manchester**, England, U.K. (2,760,000) … 430,818
- **Manila**, Philippines (11,200,000) … 1,654,761
- **Mannheim**, Germany (1,525,000) … 307,730
- **Maputo**, Mozambique … 966,837
- **Maracaibo**, Venezuela … 1,249,670
- **Marseille**, France (1,516,340) … 798,430
- **Mashhad**, Iran … 1,887,405
- **Mecca (Makkah)**, Saudi Arabia … 630,000
- **Medan**, Indonesia … 1,988,200
- **Medellín**, Colombia (2,290,000) … 1,885,001
- **Melbourne**, Australia (3,366,542) … 67,784
- **Mexico City (Ciudad de México)**, Mexico (17,786,983) … 8,605,239
- **Miami**, Florida, U.S. (3,876,380) … 362,470
- **Milan (Milano)**, Italy (3,790,000) … 1,305,591
- **Milwaukee**, Wisconsin, U.S. (1,689,572) … 596,974
- **Minneapolis**, Minnesota, U.S. (2,968,806) … 382,618
- **Minsk**, Belarus (1,680,567) … 1,677,137
- **Mogadishu (Muqdisho)**, Somalia … 600,000
- **Monrovia**, Liberia … 465,000
- **Monterrey**, Mexico (3,236,604) … 1,110,909
- **Montevideo**, Uruguay (1,650,000) … 1,303,182
- **Montréal**, Quebec, Canada (3,426,350) … 1,039,534
- **Moscow (Moskva)**, Russia (12,850,000) … 8,389,700
- **Mumbai (Bombay)**, India (16,368,084) … 11,914,398
- **Munich (München)**, Germany (1,930,000) … 1,194,560
- **Nagoya**, Japan (5,250,000) … 2,171,378
- **Nāgpur**, India (2,122,965) … 2,051,320
- **Nairobi**, Kenya … 2,143,254
- **Nanjing**, China … 2,490,000
- **Naples (Napoli)**, Italy (3,150,000) … 1,046,987
- **N'Djamena**, Chad … 546,572
- **Newcastle upon Tyne**, England, U.K. (1,350,000) … 282,338
- **New Delhi**, India (*Delhi) … 294,783
- **New York**, New York, U.S. (21,199,865) … 8,008,278
- **Niamey**, Niger … 392,165
- **Nizhniy Novgorod**, Russia (1,950,000) … 1,364,900
- **Nouakchott**, Mauritania … 393,325
- **Novosibirsk**, Russia (1,505,000) … 1,402,400
- **Nürnberg**, Germany (1,065,000) … 486,628
- **Odesa**, Ukraine (1,150,000) … 1,002,246
- **Omsk**, Russia (1,190,000) … 1,157,600
- **Ōsaka**, Japan (17,050,000) … 2,598,589
- **Oslo**, Norway (773,498) … 504,040
- **Ottawa**, Ontario, Canada (1,063,664) … 774,072
- **Ouagadougou**, Burkina Faso … 634,479
- **Palembang**, Indonesia … 1,415,500
- **Panamá**, Panama (995,000) … 415,964
- **Paris**, France (11,174,743) … 2,125,246
- **Patna**, India (1,707,429) … 1,376,950
- **Perm'**, Russia (1,110,000) … 1,017,100
- **Perth**, Australia (1,244,320) … 10,195
- **Philadelphia**, Pennsylvania, U.S. (6,188,463) … 1,517,550
- **Phnom Penh (Phnum Pénh)**, Cambodia … 570,155
- **Phoenix**, Arizona, U.S. (3,251,876) … 1,321,045
- **Port Moresby**, Papua New Guinea … 246,664
- **Port-au-Prince**, Haiti (1,425,594) … 990,558
- **Portland**, Oregon, U.S. (2,265,223) … 529,121
- **Porto**, Portugal (1,230,000) … 273,060
- **Porto Alegre**, Brazil (3,375,000) … 1,304,998
- **Prague (Praha)**, Czech Republic (1,328,000) … 1,193,270
- **Pretoria**, South Africa (1,100,000) … 692,348
- **Pune**, India (3,755,525) … 2,540,069
- **Pusan**, South Korea … 3,814,325
- **P'yŏngyang**, North Korea … 2,741,260
- **Qingdao**, China … 2,300,000
- **Québec**, Quebec, Canada (682,757) … 169,076
- **Quezon City**, Philippines (*Manila) … 1,989,419
- **Quito**, Ecuador … 1,615,809
- **Rabat**, Morocco (1,200,000) … 717,000
- **Rangoon (Yangon)**, Myanmar (2,800,000) … 2,705,039
- **Recife**, Brazil (3,160,000) … 1,421,993
- **Regina**, Saskatchewan, Canada (192,800) … 178,225
- **Reykjavík**, Iceland (166,015) … 107,684
- **Rīga**, Latvia (1,000,000) … 792,508
- **Rio de Janeiro**, Brazil (10,465,000) … 5,851,914
- **Riyadh (Ar Riyāḍ)**, Saudi Arabia … 1,800,000
- **Rome (Roma)**, Italy (3,235,000) … 2,649,765
- **Rosario**, Argentina (1,190,000) … 894,645
- **Rostov-na-Donu**, Russia (1,160,000) … 1,017,300
- **Rotterdam**, Netherlands (1,089,979) … 539,000
- **Sacramento**, California, U.S. (1,796,857) … 407,018
- **St. Louis**, Missouri, U.S. (2,603,607) … 348,189
- **St. Petersburg (Leningrad)**, Russia (6,000,000) … 4,728,200
- **Salvador**, Brazil (2,855,000) … 2,439,823
- **Samara**, Russia (1,450,000) … 1,168,000
- **San Diego**, California, U.S. (2,813,833) … 1,223,400
- **San Francisco**, California, U.S. (7,039,362) … 776,733
- **San José**, Costa Rica (996,194) … 309,672
- **San Juan**, Puerto Rico (1,967,627) … 421,958
- **San Salvador**, El Salvador (1,908,921) … 473,372
- **Santiago**, Chile … 4,788,543
- **Santo Domingo**, Dominican Republic … 2,677,056
- **São Paulo**, Brazil (17,380,000) … 9,713,692
- **Sapporo**, Japan (2,000,000) … 1,822,300
- **Sarajevo**, Bosnia and Herzegovina … 367,703
- **Saratov**, Russia (1,135,000) … 881,000
- **Seattle**, Washington, U.S. (3,554,760) … 563,374
- **Seoul (Sŏul)**, South Korea (15,850,000) … 10,231,217
- **Shanghai**, China (11,010,000) … 8,930,000
- **Shenyang (Mukden)**, China … 4,050,000
- **Singapore**, Singapore (4,400,000) … 4,017,700
- **Skopje**, Macedonia … 440,577
- **Sofia (Sofiya)**, Bulgaria (1,189,794) … 1,138,629
- **Stockholm**, Sweden (1,643,366) … 743,703
- **Stuttgart**, Germany (2,020,000) … 582,443
- **Surabaya**, Indonesia … 2,801,300
- **Sūrat**, India (2,811,466) … 2,433,787
- **Sydney**, Australia (3,741,290) … 11,115
- **T'aipei**, Taiwan (6,200,000) … 2,640,322
- **Tallinn**, Estonia … 403,981
- **Tashkent (Toshkent)**, Uzbekistan (2,325,000) … 2,142,700
- **Tbilisi**, Georgia (1,460,000) … 1,279,000
- **Tegucigalpa**, Honduras … 576,661
- **Tehrān**, Iran (8,800,000) … 6,758,845
- **Tel Aviv-Yafo**, Israel (1,890,000) … 348,100
- **Tianjin (Tientsin)**, China … 5,000,000
- **Tiranë**, Albania … 244,153
- **Tōkyō**, Japan (30,300,000) … 8,130,408
- **Toronto**, Ontario, Canada (4,682,897) … 2,481,494
- **Tripoli (Ṭarābulus)**, Libya … 1,500,000
- **Tunis**, Tunisia (1,300,000) … 702,330
- **Turin (Torino)**, Italy (1,550,000) … 921,485
- **Ufa**, Russia (1,110,000) … 1,088,900
- **Ulan Bator (Ulaanbaatar)**, Mongolia … 672,882
- **Ürümqi**, China … 1,130,000
- **València**, Spain (1,340,000) … 739,014
- **Vancouver**, British Columbia, Canada (1,986,965) … 545,671
- **Viangchan (Vientiane)**, Laos … 464,000
- **Vienna (Wien)**, Austria (1,950,000) … 1,609,631
- **Vilnius**, Lithuania … 578,334
- **Volgograd (Stalingrad)**, Russia (1,358,000) … 1,000,000
- **Warsaw (Warszawa)**, Poland (2,300,000) … 1,615,369
- **Washington**, D.C., U.S. (7,608,070) … 572,059
- **Wellington**, New Zealand (346,500) … 167,400
- **Winnipeg**, Manitoba, Canada (671,274) … 619,544
- **Wuhan**, China … 3,870,000
- **Xi'an**, China … 2,410,000
- **Yekaterinburg**, Russia (1,530,000) … 1,272,900
- **Yerevan**, Armenia (1,315,000) … 1,249,202
- **Yokohama**, Japan (*Tōkyō) … 3,426,506
- **Zagreb**, Croatia … 867,865
- **Zürich**, Switzerland (932,681) … 337,553

Metropolitan area populations are shown in parentheses.
* City is located within the metropolitan area of another city; for example, Yokohama, Japan is located in the Tōkyō metropolitan area.

GLOSSARY OF FOREIGN GEOGRAPHICAL TERMS

Annam	Annamese
Arab	Arabic
Bantu	Bantu
Bur	Burmese
Camb	Cambodian
Celt	Celtic
Chn	Chinese
Czech	Czech
Dan	Danish
Du	Dutch
Fin	Finnish
Fr	French
Ger	German
Gr	Greek
Hung	Hungarian
Ice	Icelandic
India	India
Indian	American Indian
Indon	Indonesian
It	Italian
Jap	Japanese
Kor	Korean
Mal	Malayan
Mong	Mongolian
Nor	Norwegian
Per	Persian
Pol	Polish
Port	Portuguese
Rom	Romanian
Rus	Russian
Siam	Siamese
So. Slav	Southern Slavonic
Sp	Spanish
Swe	Swedish
Tib	Tibetan
Tur	Turkish
Yugo	Yugoslav

å, Nor., Swe	brook, river
aa, Dan., Nor	brook
aas, Dan., Nor	ridge
āb, Per	water, river
abad, India, Per	town, city
ada, Tur	island
adrar, Berber	mountain
air, Indon	stream
akrotírion, Gr	cape
älf, Swe	river
alp, Ger	mountain
altipiano, It	plateau
alto, Sp	height
archipel, Fr	archipelago
archipiélago, Sp	archipelago
arquipélago, Port	archipelago
arroyo, Sp	brook, stream
ås, Nor., Swe	ridge
austral, Sp	southern
baai, Du	bay
bab, Arab	gate, port
bach, Ger	brook, stream
backe, Swe	hill
bad, Ger	bath, spa
bahía, Sp	bay, gulf
bahr, Arab	river, sea, lake
baia, It	bay, gulf
baía, Port	bay
baie, Fr	bay, gulf
bajo, Sp	depression
bak, Indon	stream
bakke, Dan., Nor	hill
balkan, Tur	mountain range
bana, Jap	point, cape
banco, Sp	bank
bandar, Mal., Per.	town, port, harbor
bang, Siam	village
bassin, Fr	basin
batang, Indon., Mal	river
ben, Celt	mountain, summit
bender, Arab	harbor, port
bereg, Rus	coast, shore
berg, Du., Ger., Nor., Swe.	mountain, hill
bir, Arab	well
birkat, Arab	lake, pond, pool
bit, Arab	house
bjaerg, Dan., Nor	mountain
bocche, It	mouth
boğazı, Tur	strait
bois, Fr	forest, wood
boloto, Rus	marsh
bolsón, Sp.	flat-floored desert valley
boreal, Sp	northern
borg, Dan., Nor., Swe	castle, town
borgo, It	town, suburb
bosch, Du	forest, wood
bouche, Fr	river mouth
bourg, Fr	town, borough
bro, Dan., Nor., Swe	bridge
brücke, Ger	bridge
bucht, Ger	bay, bight
bugt, Dan., Nor., Swe	bay, gulf
bulu, Indon	mountain
burg, Du., Ger	castle, town
buri, Siam	town
burun, burnu, Tur	cape
by, Dan., Nor., Swe	village
caatinga, Port. (Brazil)	open brushland
cabezo, Sp	summit
cabo, Port., Sp	cape
campo, It., Port., Sp	plain, field
campos, Port. (Brazil)	plains
cañón, Sp	canyon
cap, Fr	cape
capo, It	cape
casa, It., Port., Sp	house
castello, It., Port	castle, fort
castillo, Sp	castle
càte, Fr	hill
çay, Tur	stream, river
cayo, Sp	rock, shoal, islet
cerro, Sp	mountain, hill
champ, Fr	field
chang, Chn	village, middle
château, Fr	castle
chen, Chn	market town
chiang, Chn	river
chott, Arab	salt lake
chou, Chn.	capital of district; island
chu, Tib	water, stream
cidade, Port	town, city
cima, Sp	summit, peak
città, It	town, city
ciudad, Sp	town, city
cochilha, Port	ridge
col, Fr	pass
colina, Sp	hill
cordillera, Sp	mountain chain
costa, It., Port., Sp	coast
côte, Fr	coast
cuchilla, Sp	mountain ridge
dağ, Tur	mountain(s)
dake, Jap	peak, summit
dal, Dan., Du., Nor., Swe	valley
dan, Kor	point, cape
danau, Indon	lake
dar, Arab	house, abode, country
darya, Per	river, sea
dasht, Per	plain, desert
deniz, Tur	sea
désert, Fr	desert
deserto, It	desert
desierto, Sp	desert
détroit, Fr	strait
dijk, Du	dam, dike
djebel, Arab	mountain
do, Kor	island
dorf, Ger	village
dorp, Du	village
duin, Du	dune
dzong, Tib.	fort, administrative capital
eau, Fr	water
ecuador, Sp	equator
eiland, Du	island
elv, Dan., Nor	river, stream
embalse, Sp	reservoir
erg, Arab	dune, sandy desert
est, Fr., It	east
estado, Sp	state
este, Port., Sp	east
estrecho, Sp	strait
étang, Fr	pond, lake
état, Fr	state
eyjar, Ice	islands
feld, Ger	field, plain
festung, Ger	fortress
fiume, It	river
fjäll, Swe	mountain
fjärd, Swe	bay, inlet
fjeld, Nor	mountain, hill
fjord, Dan., Nor	fiord, inlet
fjördur, Ice	fiord, inlet
fleuve, Fr	river
flod, Dan., Swe	river
flói, Ice	bay, marshland
fluss, Ger	river
foce, It	river mouth
fontein, Du	a spring
forêt, Fr	forest
fors, Swe	waterfall
forst, Ger	forest
fos, Dan., Nor	waterfall
fu, Chn	town, residence
fuente, Sp	spring, fountain
fuerte, Sp	fort
furt, Ger	ford
gang, Kor	stream, river
gangri, Tib	mountain
gat, Dan., Nor	channel
gàve, Fr	stream
gawa, Jap	river
gebergte, Du	mountain range
gebiet, Ger	district, territory
gebirge, Ger	mountains
ghat, India	pass, mountain range
gobi, Mong	desert
gol, Mong	river
göl, gölü, Tur	lake
golf, Du., Ger	gulf, bay
golfe, Fr	gulf, bay
golfo, It., Port., Sp	gulf, bay
gomba, gompa, Tib	monastery
gora, Rus., So. Slav	mountain
góra, Pol	mountain
gorod, Rus	town
grad, Rus., So. Slav	town
guba, Rus	bay, gulf
gundung, Indon	mountain
guntō, Jap	archipelago
gunung, Mal	mountain
haf, Swe	sea, ocean
hafen, Ger	port, harbor
haff, Ger	gulf, inland sea
hai, Chn	sea, lake
hama, Jap	beach, shore
hamada, Arab	rocky plateau
hamn, Swe	harbor
hāmūn, Per	swampy lake, plain
hantō, Jap	peninsula
hassi, Arab	well, spring
haus, Ger	house
haut, Fr	summit, top
hav, Dan., Nor	sea, ocean
havn, Dan., Nor	harbor, port
havre, Fr	harbor, port
háza, Hung	house, dwelling of
heim, Ger	hamlet, home
hem, Swe	hamlet, home
higashi, Jap	east
hisar, Tur	fortress
hissar, Arab	fort
ho, Chn	river
hoek, Du	cape
hof, Ger	court, farmhouse
höfn, Ice	harbor
hoku, Jap	north
holm, Dan., Nor., Swe	island
hora, Czech	mountain
horn, Ger	peak
hoved, Dan., Nor	cape
hsien, Chn	district, district capital
hu, Chn	lake
hügel, Ger	hill
huk, Dan., Swe	point
hus, Dan., Nor., Swe	house
île, Fr	island
ilha, Port	island
indsö, Dan., Nor	lake
insel, Ger	island
insjö, Swe	lake
irmak, irmagi, Tur	river
isla, Sp	island
isola, It	island
istmo, It., Sp	isthmus
järvi, jaur, Fin	lake
jebel, Arab	mountain
jima, Jap	island
jökel, Nor	glacier
joki, Fin	river
jökull, Ice	glacier
kaap, Du	cape
kai, Jap	bay, gulf, sea
kaikyō, Jap	channel, strait
kalat, Per	castle, fortress
kale, Tur	fort
kali, Mal	creek, river
kand, Per	village
kang, Chn	mountain ridge; village
kap, Dan., Ger	cape
kapp, Nor., Swe	cape
kasr, Arab	fort, castle
kawa, Jap	river
kefr, Arab	village
kei, Jap	creek, river
ken, Jap	prefecture
khor, Arab	bay, inlet
khrebet, Rus	mountain range
kiang, Chn	large river
king, Chn	capital city, town
kita, Jap	north
ko, Jap	lake
köbstad, Dan	market-town
kol, Mong	lake
kólpos, Gr	gulf
kong, Chn	river
kopf, Ger	head, summit, peak
köpstad, Swe	market-town
körfezi, Tur	gulf
kosa, Rus	spit
kou, Chn	river mouth
köy, Tur	village
kraal, Du. (Africa)	native village
ksar, Arab	fortified village
kuala, Mal	bay, river mouth
kuh, Per	mountain
kum, Tur	sand
kuppe, Ger	summit
küste, Ger	coast
kyo, Jap	town, capital
la, Tib	mountain pass
labuan, Mal	anchorage, port
lac, Fr	lake
lago, It., Port., Sp	lake
lagoa, Port	lake, marsh
laguna, It., Port., Sp	lagoon, lake
lahti, Fin	bay, gulf
län, Swe	county
landsby, Dan., Nor	village
liehtao, Chn	archipelago
liman, Tur	bay, port
ling, Chn	pass, ridge, mountain
llanos, Sp	plains
loch, Celt. (Scotland)	lake, bay
loma, Sp	long, low hill
lough, Celt. (Ireland)	lake, bay
machi, Jap	town
man, Kor	bay
mar, Port., Sp	sea
mare, It., Rom	sea
marisma, Sp	marsh, swamp
mark, Ger	boundary, limit
massif, Fr	block of mountains
mato, Port	forest, thicket
me, Siam	river
meer, Du., Ger	lake, sea
mer, Fr	sea
mesa, Sp	flat-topped mountain
meseta, Sp	plateau
mina, Port., Sp	mine
minami, Jap	south
minato, Jap	harbor, haven
misaki, Jap	cape, headland
mont, Fr	mount, mountain
montagna, It	mountain
montagne, Fr	mountain
montaña, Sp	mountain
monte, It., Port., Sp.	mount, mountain
more, Rus., So. Slav	sea
morro, Port., Sp	hill, bluff
mühle, Ger	mill
mund, Ger	mouth, opening
mündung, Ger	river mouth
mura, Jap	township
myit, Bur	river
mys, Rus	cape
nada, Jap	sea
nadi, India	river, creek
naes, Dan., Nor	cape
nafud, Arab	desert of sand dunes
nagar, India	town, city
nahr, Arab	river
nam, Siam	river, water
nan, Chn., Jap	south
näs, Nor., Swe	cape
nez, Fr	point, cape
nishi, nisi, Jap	west
njarga, Fin	peninsula
nong, Siam	marsh
noord, Du	north
nor, Mong	lake
nord, Dan., Fr., Ger., It., Nor., Swe	north
norte, Port., Sp	north
nos, Rus	cape
nyasa, Bantu	lake
ö, Dan., Nor., Swe	island
occidental, Sp	western
ocna, Rom	salt mine
odde, Dan., Nor	point, cape
oeste, Port., Sp	west
oka, Jap	hill
oost, Du	east
oriental, Sp	eastern
óros, Gr	mountain
ost, Ger., Swe	east
öster, Dan., Nor., Swe	eastern
ostrov, Rus	island
oued, Arab	river, stream
ouest, Fr	west
ozero, Rus	lake
pää, Fin	mountain
padang, Mal	plain, field
pampas, Sp. (Argentina)	grassy plains
pará, Indian (Brazil)	river
pas, Fr	channel, passage
paso, Sp	mountain pass, passage
passo, It., Port.	mountain pass, passage, strait
patam, India	city, town
pei, Chn	north
pélagos, Gr	open sea
pegunungan, Indon	mountains
peña, Sp	rock
peresheyek, Rus	isthmus
pertuis, Fr	strait
peski, Rus	desert
pic, Fr	mountain peak
pico, Port., Sp	mountain peak
piedra, Sp	stone, rock
ping, Chn	plain, flat
planalto, Port	plateau
planina, Yugo	mountains
playa, Sp	shore, beach
pnom, Camb	mountain
pointe, Fr	point
polder, Du., Ger	reclaimed marsh
polje, So. Slav	plain, field
poluostrov, Rus	peninsula
pont, Fr	bridge
ponta, Port	point, headland
ponte, It., Port	bridge
pore, India	city, town
porthmós, Gr	strait
porto, It., Port	port, harbor
potamós, Gr	river
p'ov, Rus	peninsula
prado, Sp	field, meadow
presqu'île, Fr	peninsula
proliv, Rus	strait
pu, Chn	commercial village
pueblo, Sp	town, village
puerto, Sp	port, harbor
pulau, Indon	island
punkt, Ger	point
punt, Du	point
punta, It., Sp	point
pur, India	city, town
puy, Fr	peak
qal'a, qal'at, Arab	fort, village
qasr, Arab	fort, castle
rann, India	wasteland
ra's, Arab	cape, head
reka, Rus., So. Slav	river
represa, Port	reservoir
rettō, Jap	island chain
ría, Sp	estuary
ribeira, Port	stream
riberão, Port	river
rio, It., Port	stream, river
río, Sp	river
rivière, Fr	river
roca, Sp	rock
rt, Yugo	cape
rūd, Per	river
saari, Fin	island
sable, Fr	sand
sahara, Arab	desert, plain
saki, Jap	cape
sal, Sp	salt
salar, Sp	salt flat, salt lake
salto, Sp	waterfall
san, Jap., Kor	mountain, hill
sat, satul, Rom	village
schloss, Ger	castle
sebkha, Arab	salt marsh
see, Ger	lake, sea
şehir, Tur	town, city
selat, Indon	stream
selvas, Port. (Brazil)	tropical rain forests
seno, Sp	bay
serra, Port	mountain chain
serranía, Sp	mountain ridge
seto, Jap	strait
severnaya, Rus	northern
shahr, Per	town, city
shan, Chn	mountain, hill, island
shatt, Arab	river
shi, Jap	city
shima, Jap	island
shōtō, Jap	archipelago
si, Chn	west, western
sierra, Sp	mountain range
sjö, Nor., Swe	lake, sea
sö, Dan., Nor	lake, sea
söder, södra, Swe	south
song, Annam	river
sopka, Rus	peak, volcano
source, Fr	a spring
spitze, Ger	summit, point
staat, Ger	state
stad, Dan., Du., Nor., Swe.	city, town
stadt, Ger	city, town
stato, It	state
step', Rus	treeless plain, steppe
straat, Du	strait
strand, Dan., Du., Ger., Nor., Swe	shore, beach
stretto, It	strait
strom, Ger	river, stream
ström, Dan., Nor., Swe.	stream, river
stroom, Du	stream, river
su, suyu, Tur	water, river
sud, Fr., Sp	south
süd, Ger	south
suidō, Jap	channel
sul, Port	south
sund, Dan., Nor., Swe	sound
sungai, sungei, Indon., Mal	river
sur, Sp	south
syd, Dan., Nor., Swe	south
tafelland, Ger	plateau
take, Jap	peak, summit
tal, Ger	valley
tanjung, tanjong, Mal	cape
tao, Chn	island
târg, târgul, Rom	market, town
tell, Arab	hill
teluk, Indon	bay, gulf
terra, It	land
terre, Fr	earth, land
thal, Ger	valley
tierra, Sp	earth, land
tō, Jap	east; island
tonle, Camb	river, lake
top, Du	peak
torp, Swe	hamlet, cottage
tsangpo, Tib	river
tsi, Chn	village, borough
tso, Tib	lake
tsu, Jap	harbor, port
tundra, Rus	treeless arctic plains
tung, Chn	east
tuz, Tur	salt
udde, Swe	cape
ufer, Ger	shore, riverbank
ujung, Indon	point, cape
umi, Jap	sea, gulf
ura, Jap	bay, coast, creek
ust'ye, Rus	river mouth
valle, It., Port., Sp	valley
vallée, Fr	valley
valli, It	lake
vár, Hung	fortress
város, Hung	town
varoš, So. Slav	town
veld, Du	open plain, field
verkh, Rus	top, summit
ves, Czech	village
vest, Dan., Nor., Swe	west
vik, Swe	cove, bay
vila, Port	town
villa, Sp	town
villar, Sp	village, hamlet
ville, Fr	town, city
vostok, Rus	east
wad, wādī, Arab.	intermittent stream
wald, Ger	forest, woodland
wan, Chn., Jap	bay, gulf
weiler, Ger	hamlet, village
westersch, Du	western
wüste, Ger	desert
yama, Jap	mountain
yarimada, Tur	peninsula
yug, Rus	south
zaki, Jap	cape
zaliv, Rus	bay, gulf
zapad, Rus	west
zee, Du	sea
zemlya, Rus	land
zuid, Du	south

ABBREVIATIONS OF GEOGRAPHICAL NAMES AND TERMS

Afg.	Afghanistan
Afr.	Africa
Ak., U.S.	Alaska, U.S.
Al., U.S.	Alabama, U.S.
Alb.	Albania
Alg.	Algeria
Am. Sam.	American Samoa
And.	Andorra
Ang.	Angola
Ant.	Antarctica
Antig.	Antigua and Barbuda
aq.	Aqueduct
Ar., U.S.	Arkansas, U.S.
Arg.	Argentina
Arm.	Armenia
arpt.	Airport
Aus.	Austria
Austl.	Australia
Az., U.S.	Arizona, U.S.
Azer.	Azerbaijan
b.	Bay, Gulf, Inlet, Lagoon
Bah.	Bahamas
Bahr.	Bahrain
Barb.	Barbados
Bdi.	Burundi
Bel.	Belgium
Bela.	Belarus
Ber.	Bermuda
Bhu.	Bhutan
bk.	Undersea Bank
bldg.	Building
Blg.	Bulgaria
Bngl.	Bangladesh
Bol.	Bolivia
Bos.	Bosnia and Herzegovina
Bots.	Botswana
Braz.	Brazil
Bru.	Brunei
Br. Vir. Is.	British Virgin Islands
bt.	Bight
Burkina	Burkina Faso
c.	Cape, Point
Ca., U.S.	California, U.S.
Cam.	Cameroon
Camb.	Cambodia
can.	Canal
Can.	Canada
C.A.R.	Central African Republic
Cay. Is.	Cayman Islands
C. Iv.	Cote d'Ivoire
clf.	Cliff, Escarpment
co.	County, Parish
Co., U.S.	Colorado, U.S.
Col.	Colombia
Com.	Comoros
cont.	Continent
Cook Is.	Cook Islands
C.R.	Costa Rica
Cro.	Croatia
cst.	Coast, Beach
Ct., U.S.	Connecticut, U.S.
C.V.	Cape Verde
Cyp.	Cyprus
Czech Rep.	Czech Republic
d.	Delta
D.C., U.S.	District of Columbia, U.S.
De., U.S.	Delaware, U.S.
Den.	Denmark
dep.	Dependency, Colony
depr.	Depression
dept.	Department, District
des.	Desert
Dji.	Djibouti
Dom.	Dominica
Dom. Rep.	Dominican Republic
D.R.C.	Democratic Republic of the Congo
Ec.	Ecuador
educ.	Educational Facility
El Sal.	El Salvador
Eng., U.K.	England, U.K.
Eq. Gui.	Equatorial Guinea
Erit.	Eritrea
Est.	Estonia
est.	Estuary
Eth.	Ethiopia
E. Timor	East Timor
Eur.	Europe
Falk. Is.	Falkland Islands
Far. Is.	Faroe Islands
Fin.	Finland
fj.	Fjord
Fl., U.S.	Florida, U.S.
for.	Forest, Moor
Fr.	France
Fr. Gu.	French Guiana
Fr. Poly.	French Polynesia
Ga., U.S.	Georgia, U.S.
Gam.	The Gambia
Gaza	Gaza Strip
Geor.	Georgia
Ger.	Germany
Grc.	Greece
Gren.	Grenada
Grnld.	Greenland
Guad.	Guadeloupe
Guat.	Guatemala
Guern.	Guernsey
Gui.	Guinea
Gui.-B.	Guinea-Bissau
Guy.	Guyana
Hi., U.S.	Hawaii, U.S.
hist.	Historic Site, Ruins
hist. reg.	Historic Region
Hond.	Honduras
Hung.	Hungary
i.	Island
Ia., U.S.	Iowa, U.S.
ice	Ice Feature, Glacier
Ice.	Iceland
Id., U.S.	Idaho, U.S.
Il., U.S.	Illinois, U.S.
In., U.S.	Indiana, U.S.
Indon.	Indonesia
I. of Man	Isle of Man
I.R.	Indian Reservation
Ire.	Ireland
is.	Islands
Isr.	Israel
isth.	Isthmus
Jam.	Jamaica
Jord.	Jordan
Kaz.	Kazakhstan
Kir.	Kiribati
Kor., N.	Korea, North
Kor., S.	Korea, South
Ks., U.S.	Kansas, U.S.
Kuw.	Kuwait
Ky., U.S.	Kentucky, U.S.
Kyrg.	Kyrgyzstan
l.	Lake, Pond
La., U.S.	Louisiana, U.S.
Lat.	Latvia
Leb.	Lebanon
Leso.	Lesotho
Lib.	Liberia
Liech.	Liechtenstein
Lith.	Lithuania
Lux.	Luxembourg
Ma., U.S.	Massachusetts, U.S.
Mac.	Macedonia
Madag.	Madagascar
Malay.	Malaysia
Mald.	Maldives
Marsh. Is.	Marshall Islands
Mart.	Martinique
Maur.	Mauritania
May.	Mayotte
Md., U.S.	Maryland, U.S.
Me., U.S.	Maine, U.S.
Mex.	Mexico
Mi., U.S.	Michigan, U.S.
Micron.	Micronesia, Federated States of
Mn., U.S.	Minnesota, U.S.
Mo., U.S.	Missouri, U.S.
Mol.	Moldova
Mong.	Mongolia
Monts.	Montserrat
Mor.	Morocco
Moz.	Mozambique
Ms., U.S.	Mississippi, U.S.
Mt., U.S.	Montana, U.S.
mth.	River Mouth or Channel
mtn.	Mountain
mts.	Mountains
Mwi.	Malawi
Mya.	Myanmar
N.A.	North America
N.C., U.S.	North Carolina, U.S.
N. Cal.	New Caledonia
N.D., U.S.	North Dakota, U.S.
Ne., U.S.	Nebraska, U.S.
neigh.	Neighborhood
Neth.	Netherlands
Neth. Ant.	Netherlands Antilles
N.H., U.S.	New Hampshire, U.S.
Nic.	Nicaragua
Nig.	Nigeria
N. Ire., U.K.	Northern Ireland, U.K.
N.J., U.S.	New Jersey, U.S.
N.M., U.S.	New Mexico, U.S.
N. Mar. Is.	Northern Mariana Islands
Nmb.	Namibia
Nor.	Norway
Nv., U.S.	Nevada, U.S.
N.Y., U.S.	New York, U.S.
N.Z.	New Zealand
o.	Ocean
Oc.	Oceania
Oh., U.S.	Ohio, U.S.
Ok., U.S.	Oklahoma, U.S.
Or., U.S.	Oregon, U.S.
p.	Pass
Pa., U.S.	Pennsylvania, U.S.
Pak.	Pakistan
Pan.	Panama
Pap. N. Gui.	Papua New Guinea
Para.	Paraguay
pen.	Peninsula
Phil.	Philippines
Pit.	Pitcairn
pl.	Plain, Flat
plat.	Plateau, Highland
Pol.	Poland
Port.	Portugal
P.R.	Puerto Rico
prov.	Province, Region
pt. of i.	Point of Interest
r.	River, Creek
Reu.	Reunion
rec.	Recreational Site, Park
reg.	Physical Region
rel.	Religious Institution
res.	Reservoir
rf.	Reef, Shoal
R.I., U.S.	Rhode Island, U.S.
Rom.	Romania
Rw.	Rwanda
S.A.	South America
S. Afr.	South Africa
Sau. Ar.	Saudi Arabia
S.C., U.S.	South Carolina, U.S.
sci.	Scientific Station
Scot., U.K.	Scotland, U.K.
S.D., U.S.	South Dakota, U.S.
sea feat.	Undersea Feature
Sen.	Senegal
Serb.	Serbia and Montenegro
Sey.	Seychelles
S. Geor.	South Georgia
Sing.	Singapore
S.L.	Sierra Leone
Slvk.	Slovakia
Slvn.	Slovenia
S. Mar.	San Marino
Sol. Is.	Solomon Islands
Som.	Somalia
Sp. N. Afr.	Spanish North Africa
Sri L	Sri Lanka
St. Hel.	St. Helena
St. K./N.	St. Kitts and Nevis
St. Luc.	St. Lucia
St. P./M.	St. Pierre and Miquelon
strt.	Strait, Channel, Sound
S. Tom./P.	Sao Tome and Principe
St. Vin.	St. Vincent and the Grenadines
Sur.	Suriname
Sval.	Svalbard
sw.	Swamp, Marsh
Swaz.	Swaziland
Swe.	Sweden
Switz.	Switzerland
Tai.	Taiwan
Taj.	Tajikistan
Tan.	Tanzania
T./C. Is.	Turks and Caicos Islands
ter.	Territory
Thai.	Thailand
Tn., U.S.	Tennessee, U.S.
trans.	Transportation Facility
Trin.	Trinidad and Tobago
Tun.	Tunisia
Tur.	Turkey
Turkmen.	Turkmenistan
Tx., U.S.	Texas, U.S.
U.A.E.	United Arab Emirates
Ug.	Uganda
U.K.	United Kingdom
Ukr.	Ukraine
Ur.	Uruguay
U.S.	United States
Ut., U.S.	Utah, U.S.
Uzb.	Uzbekistan
Va., U.S.	Virginia, U.S.
val.	Valley, Watercourse
Ven.	Venezuela
Viet.	Vietnam
V.I.U.S.	Virgin Islands (U.S.)
vol.	Volcano
Vt., U.S.	Vermont, U.S.
Wa., U.S.	Washington, U.S.
W.B.	West Bank
Wi., U.S.	Wisconsin, U.S.
W. Sah.	Western Sahara
wtfl.	Waterfall
W.V., U.S.	West Virginia, U.S.
Wy., U.S.	Wyoming, U.S.
Zam.	Zambia
Zimb.	Zimbabwe

PRONUNCIATION OF GEOGRAPHICAL NAMES

Key to the Sound Values of Letters and Symbols Used in the Index to Indicate Pronunciation

ă-ăt; băttle
a-finăl; appeăl
ā-rāte; elāte
å-senåte; inanimåte
ä-ärm; cälm
à-àsk; bàth
a-sofă; mărine (short neutral or indeterminate sound)
â-fâre; prepâre
ch-choose; church
dh-as th in other; either
ē-bē; ēve
ĕ-ĕvent; crĕate
ĕ-bĕt; ĕnd
ĕ-recĕnt (short neutral or indeterminate sound)
ê-cratêr; cindêr
g-go; gáme
gh-guttural g
ī-bĭt; wĭll
i-(short neutral or indeterminate sound)
ī-rīde; bīte
к-gutteral k as ch in German ich
ng-sing
ŋ-baŋk; liŋger
ɴ-indicates nasalized
ŏ-nŏd; ŏdd
o-cŏmmit; cŏnnect
ō-ōld; bōld
ô-ôbey; hôtel
ô-ôrder; nôrth
oi-boil
ōō-fōōd; rōōt
o̓-as oo in foot; wood
ou-out; thou
s-soft; so; sane
sh-dish; finish
th-thin; thick
ū-pūre; cūre
u̇-ŭnite; u̇sŭrp
û-ûrn; fûr
ŭ-stŭd; ŭp
u-circŭs; sŭbmit
ü-as in French tu
zh-as z in azure
'-indeterminate vowel sound

In many cases the spelling of foreign geographical names does not even remotely indicate the pronunciation to an American, i.e., Słupsk in Poland is pronounced swȯpsk; Jujuy in Argentina is pronounced hōōhwē', La Spezia in Italy is lä-spē'zyä.

This condition is hardly surprising, however, when we consider that in our own language Worcester, Massachusetts, is pronounced wȯs'têr; Sioux City, Iowa, sōō sĭ'tĭ; Schuylkill Haven, Pennsylvania, skōōl'kĭl hā-vĕn; Poughkeepsie, New York, pŏ-kĭp'sĕ.

The indication of pronunciation of geographic names presents several peculiar problems:

1. Many foreign tongues use sounds that are not present in the English language and which an American cannot normally articulate. Thus, though the nearest English equivalent sound has been indicated, only approximate results are possible.

2. There are several dialects in each foreign tongue which cause variation in the local pronunciation of names. This also occurs in identical names in the various divisions of a great language group, as the Slavic or the Latin.

3. Within the United States there are marked differences in pronunciation, not only of local geographic names, but also of common words, indicating that the sound and tone values for letters as well as the placing of the emphasis vary considerably from one part of the country to another.

4. A number of different letters and diacritical combinations could be used to indicate essentially the same or approximate pronunciations.

Some variation in pronunciation other than that indicated in this index may be encountered, but such a difference does not necessarily indicate that either is in error, and in many cases it is a matter of individual choice as to which is preferred. In fact, an exact indication of pronunciation of many foreign names using English letters and diacritical marks is extremely difficult and sometimes impossible.

PRONOUNCING INDEX

This universal index includes in a single alphabetical list approximately 30,000 names of features that appear on the reference maps. Each name is followed by a page reference and geographical coordinates.

Abbreviation and Capitalization Abbreviations of names on the maps have been standardized as much as possible. Names that are abbreviated on the maps are generally spelled out in full in the index. Periods are used after all abbreviations regardless of local practice. The abbreviation "St." is used only for "Saint". "Sankt" and other forms of this term are spelled out.

Most initial letters of names are capitalized, except for a few Dutch names, such as "s-Gravenhage". Capitalization of noninitial words in a name generally follows local practice.

Alphabetization Names are alphabetized in the order of the letters of the English alphabet. Spanish *ll* and *ch*, for example, are not treated as direct letters. Furthermore, diacritical marks are disregarded in alphabetization — German or Scandinavian *ä* or *ö* are treated as *a* or *o*.

The names of physical features may appear inverted, since they are always alphabetized under the proper, not the generic, part of the name, thus: "Gibraltar, Strait of". Otherwise every entry, whether consisting of one word or more, is alphabetized as a single continuous entity. "Lakeland", for example, appears after "La Crosse" and before "La Salle". Names beginning with articles (Le Harve, Den Helder, Al Manāmah, Ad Dawhah) are not inverted.

In the case of identical names, towns are listed first, then political divisions, then physical features.

Generic Terms Except for cities, the names of all features are followed by terms that represent broad classes of features, for example, Mississippi, r. or Alabama, state. A list of all abbreviations used in the index is on page 261.

Country names and the names of features that extend beyond the boundaries of one county are followed by the name of the continent in which each is located. Country designations follow the names of all other places in the index. The locations of places in the United States and the United Kingdom are further defined by abbreviations that include the state or political division in which each is located.

Pronunciations Pronunciations are included for most names listed. An explanation of the pronunciation system used appears on page 261.

Page References and Geographical Coordinates The geographical coordinates and page references are found in the last columns of each entry.

If a page contains several maps or insets, a lowercase letter identifies the specific map or inset.

Latitude and longitude coordinates for point features, such as cities and mountain peaks, indicate the location of the symbols. For extensive areal features, such as countries or mountain ranges, or linear features, such as canals and rivers, locations are given for the position of the type as it appears on the map.

PLACE (Pronunciation)	PAGE	LAT.	LONG.
A			
Aachen, Ger. (ä′kĕn)	161	50°46′N	6°07′E
Aalborg, Den. (ôl′bôr)	154	57°02′N	9°55′E
Aalen, Ger. (ä′lĕn)	168	48°49′N	10°08′E
Aalsmeer, Neth.	159a	52°16′N	4°44′E
Aalst, Bel.	165	50°58′N	4°00′E
Aarau, Switz. (är′ou)	161	47°22′N	8°03′E
Aarschot, Bel.	159a	50°59′N	4°51′E
Aba, D.R.C.	237	3°52′N	30°14′E
Aba, Nig.	230	5°06′N	7°21′E
Ābādān, Iran (ä-bŭ-dän′)	198	30°15′N	48°30′E
Abaetetuba, Braz. (ä′bä̆ĕ-tĕ-tōō′bä)	143	1°44′S	48°45′W
Abajo Peak, mtn., Ut., U.S. (ä-bá′hō)	119	37°51′N	109°28′W
Abakaliki, Nig.	235	6°21′N	8°06′E
Abakan, Russia (ŭ-bá-kän′)	179	53°43′N	91°28′E
Abakan, r., Russia (u-bá-kän′)	184	53°00′N	91°06′E
Abancay, Peru (ä-bän-kä′ē)	142	13°44′S	72°46′W
Abashiri, Japan (ä-bä-shē′rē)	210	44°00′N	144°13′E
Abasolo, Mex. (ä-bä-sō′lō)	130	24°05′N	98°24′W
Abasolo, Mex. (ä-bä-sō′lō)	122	27°13′N	101°25′W
Abaya, Lake, l., Eth. (ä-bä′yä)	231	6°24′N	38°22′E
'Abbāsah, Tur'at al, can., Egypt	238d	30°45′N	32°15′E
Abbeville, Fr. (ȧb-vēl′)	161	50°08′N	1°49′E
Abbeville, Al., U.S. (ăb′ê-vĭl)	124	31°35′N	85°15′W
Abbeville, Ga., U.S. (ăb′ê-vĭl)	124	31°53′N	83°23′W
Abbeville, La., U.S.	123	29°59′N	92°07′W
Abbeville, S.C., U.S.	125	34°09′N	82°25′W
Abbiategrasso, Italy (äb-byä′tä-gräs′sō)	174	45°23′N	8°52′E
Abbots Bromley, Eng., U.K. (ăb′ŭts brŭm′lê)	158a	52°49′N	1°52′W
Abbotsford, Can. (ăb′ŭts-fērd)	116d	49°03′N	122°17′W
'Abd al Kūrī, i., Yemen (äbd-ĕl-kó′rē)	238a	12°12′N	51°00′E
Abdulino, Russia (äb-dò-lē′nô)	180	53°40′N	53°40′E
Abengourou, C. Iv.	234	6°44′N	3°29′W
Abeokuta, Nig. (ä-bâ-ô-kōō′tä)	230	7°10′N	3°26′E
Abercorn see Mbala, Zam.	232	8°50′S	31°22′E
Aberdare, Wales, U.K. (ăb-ēr-dâr′)	164	51°45′N	3°35′W
Aberdeen, Scot., U.K.	154	57°10′N	2°05′W
Aberdeen, Ms., U.S. (ăb-ēr-dēn′)	124	33°49′N	88°33′W
Aberdeen, S.D., U.S. (ăb-ēr-dēn′)	104	45°28′N	98°29′W
Aberdeen, Wa., U.S. (ăb-ēr-dēn′)	104	47°00′N	123°48′W
Aberford, Eng., U.K. (ăb′ēr-fērd)	158a	53°49′N	1°21′W
Abergavenny, Wales, U.K. (ăb′ēr-gá-vĕn′ĭ)	164	51°45′N	3°05′W
Abert, Lake, l., Or., U.S. (ā′bĕrt)	114	42°39′N	120°24′W
Aberystwyth, Wales, U.K. (ă-bĕr-ĭst′wĭth)	164	52°25′N	4°04′W
Abidjan, C. Iv. (ä-bĕd-zhäɴ′)	230	5°19′N	4°02′W
Abiko, Japan (ä-bē-kō).	211a	35°53′N	140°01′E
Abilene, Ks., U.S. (ăb′ĭ-lēn)	121	38°54′N	97°12′W
Abilene, Tx., U.S.	104	32°25′N	99°45′W
Abingdon, Eng., U.K.	158b	51°38′N	1°17′W
Abingdon, Il., U.S. (ăb′ĭng-dŭn)	113	40°48′N	90°21′W
Abingdon, Va., U.S.	125	36°42′N	81°57′W
Abington, Ma., U.S. (ăb′ĭng-tŭn)	101a	42°07′N	70°57′W
Abiquiu Reservoir, res., N.M., U.S.	119	36°26′N	106°42′W
Abitibi, l., Can. (ăb-ĭ-tĭb′ĭ)	93	48°27′N	80°20′W
Abitibi, r., Can.	93	49°30′N	81°10′W
Abkhazia, state, Geor.	181	43°10′N	40°45′E
Ablis, Fr. (ȧ-blē′)	171b	48°31′N	1°50′E
Abnūb, Egypt (ȧb-nōōb′)	238b	27°18′N	31°11′E
Åbo see Turku, Fin.	154	60°28′N	22°12′E
Abohar, India	202	30°12′N	74°13′E
Aboisso, C. Iv.	234	5°28′N	3°12′W
Abomey, Benin (ăb-ô-mā′)	230	7°11′N	1°59′E
Abony, Hung. (ŏ′bô-ny′)	169	47°12′N	20°00′E
Abou Deïa, Chad	235	11°27′N	19°17′E
Abra, r., Phil. (ä′brä)	213a	17°16′N	120°38′E
Abraão, Braz. (ȧbrä-ouɴ′)	141a	23°10′S	44°10′W
Abraham's Bay, b., Bah.	135	22°20′N	73°50′W
Abram, Eng., U.K. (ā′brăm)	158a	53°31′N	2°36′W
Abrantes, Port. (ȧ-brän′tĕs)	172	39°28′N	8°13′W
Abrolhos, Arquipélago dos, is., Braz.	143	17°58′S	38°40′W
Abruka, i., Est. (ȧ-brô′kȧ)	167	58°09′N	22°30′E
Abruzzi e Molise, hist. reg., Italy	174	42°10′N	13°55′E
Absaroka Range, mts., U.S. (ăb-sä-rō-kä̆)	106	44°50′N	109°47′W
Abşeron Yarımadası, pen., Azer.	181	40°20′N	50°30′E
Abū Arīsh, Sau. Ar.	198	16°48′N	43°00′E
Abu Dhabi see Abū Ẓaby, U.A.E.	198	24°15′N	54°28′E
Abū Ḥamad, Sudan (ä′bōō hä′-mĕd)	231	19°37′N	33°21′E
Abuja, Nig.	230	9°12′N	7°11′E
Abū Kamāl, Syria	198	34°45′N	40°46′E
Abunã, r., S.A. (ä-bōō-nä′)	142	10°25′S	67°00′W
Abū Qīr, Egypt (ä′bōō kēr′)	238b	31°18′N	30°06′E
Abū Qurūn, Ra's, mtn., Egypt	197a	29°20′N	33°32′E
Aburatsu, Japan (ä′bò-rät′sōō)	211	31°33′N	131°20′E
Abū Road, India (á′bōō)	199	24°38′N	72°45′E
Abū Tīj, Egypt	238b	27°03′N	31°19′E
Abū Ẓaby, U.A.E.	198	24°15′N	54°28′E
Abū Zanimah, Egypt	197a	29°03′N	33°08′E
Abyy, Russia	179	68°24′N	134°00′E
Acacias, Col. (ä-kä′sēäs)	142a	3°59′N	73°44′W
Acadia National Park, rec., Me., U.S. (ȧ-kā′dī-ȧ)	107	44°19′N	68°01′W
Acajutla, El Sal. (ä-kä-hōōt′lä)	132	13°37′N	89°50′W
Acala, Mex. (ä-kä′lä)	131	16°38′N	92°49′W
Acalayong, Eq. Gui.	236	1°05′N	9°40′E
Acámbaro, Mex. (ä-käm′bä-rō)	130	20°03′N	100°42′W
Acancéh, Mex. (ä-kän-sĕ′)	132a	20°50′N	89°27′W
Acapetlahuaya, Mex. (ä-kä-pĕt′lä-hwä′yä)	130	18°24′N	100°04′W
Acaponeta, Mex. (ä-kä-pô-nā′tä)	130	22°31′N	105°25′W
Acaponeta, r., Mex. (ä-kä-pô-nä′tä)	130	22°47′N	105°23′W
Acapulco, Mex. (ä-kä-pōōl′kō)	128	16°49′N	99°57′W
Acaraí Mountains, mts., S.A.	143	1°30′N	57°40′W
Acarigua, Ven. (äkä-rē′gwä)	142	9°29′N	69°11′W
Acatlán de Osorio, Mex. (ä-kät-län′dā ô-sō′rē-ō)	130	18°11′N	98°04′W
Acatzingo de Hidalgo, Mex.	131	18°58′N	97°47′W
Acayucan, Mex. (ä-kä-yōō′kän)	131	17°56′N	94°55′W
Accoville, W.V., U.S. (ăk′kô-vĭl)	108	37°45′N	81°50′W
Accra, Ghana (ä′krä)	230	5°33′N	0°13′W
Accrington, Eng., U.K. (ăk′rĭng-tŭn)	158a	53°45′N	2°22′W
Acerra, Italy (ä-chĕ′r-rä)	173c	40°42′N	14°22′E
Achacachi, Bol. (ä-chä-kä′chē)	142	16°11′S	68°32′W
Achelóos, r., Grc.	175	38°45′N	21°26′E
Achill Island, i., Ire. (ä-chĭl′)	160	53°55′N	10°05′W
Achinsk, Russia (ä-chênsk′)	184	56°13′N	90°32′E
Acireale, Italy (ä-chē-rä-ä′lä)	174	37°37′N	15°12′E
Acklins, The Bight of, b., Bah. (ăk′lĭns)	135	22°35′N	74°20′W
Acklins, i., Bah. (ăk′lĭns)	129	22°30′N	73°55′W
Acolman, Mex. (ä-kōl-mä′n)	131a	19°38′N	98°56′W
Acoma Indian Reservation, I.R., N.M., U.S.	119	34°52′N	107°40′W
Aconcagua, prov., Chile (ä-kōn-kä′gwä)	141b	32°20′S	71°00′W
Aconcagua, r., Chile (ä-kōn-kä′gwä)	141b	32°43′S	70°53′W
Aconcagua, Cerro, mtn., Arg. (ä-kōn-kä′gwä)	144	32°38′S	70°00′W
Açores (Azores), is., Port.	229	37°44′N	29°25′W
A Coruña, Spain	154	43°20′N	8°20′W
Acoyapa, Nic. (ä-kô-yä′pä)	132	11°54′N	85°11′W
Acqui, Italy (äk′kwē)	174	44°41′N	8°22′E
Acre, state, Braz. (ä′krä)	142	8°40′S	70°45′W
Acre, r., S.A.	142	10°33′S	68°34′W
Acton, Can. (ăk′tŭn)	102d	43°38′N	80°02′W
Acton, Al., U.S. (ăk′tŭn)	110h	33°21′N	86°49′W
Acton, Ma., U.S. (ăk′tŭn)	101a	42°29′N	71°26′W
Actopan, Mex. (äk-tô-pän′)	130	20°16′N	98°57′W
Actópan, r., Mex. (äk-tō′pän)	131	19°25′N	96°31′W
Acuitzio del Canje, Mex. (ä-kwēt′zē-ō dĕl kän′hä)	130	19°28′N	101°21′W
Acul, Baie de l', b., Haiti (ä-kōōl′)	135	19°55′N	72°20′W
Ada, Mn., U.S. (ā′dȧ)	112	47°17′N	96°32′W
Ada, Oh., U.S. (ā′dȧ)	108	40°45′N	83°45′W
Ada, Ok., U.S. (ā′dȧ)	121	34°45′N	96°43′W

PLACE (Pronunciation)	PAGE	LAT.	LONG.
Ada, Serb. (ä′dä)	175	45°48′N	20°06′E
Adachi, Japan	211a	35°50′N	39°36′E
Adak, Ak., U.S. (ă-dăk′)	103a	56°50′N	176°48′W
Adak, i., Ak., U.S. (ă-dăk′)	103a	51°40′N	176°28′W
Adak Strait, strt., Ak., U.S. (ă-dăk′)	103a	51°42′N	177°16′W
Adamaoua, mts., Afr.	230	6°30′N	11°50′E
Adams, Ma., U.S. (ăd′ămz)	109	42°35′N	73°10′W
Adams, Wi., U.S. (ăd′ămz)	113	43°55′N	89°48′W
Adams, r., Can. (ăd′ămz)	95	51°30′N	119°20′W
Adams, Mount, mtn., Wa., U.S. (ăd′ămz)	106	46°15′N	121°19′W
Adamsville, Al., U.S. (ăd′ămz-vĭl)	110h	33°36′N	86°57′W
Adana, Tur. (ä′dä-nä)	198	37°05′N	35°20′E
Adapazarı, Tur. (ä-dä-pä-zä′rē)	163	40°45′N	30°20′E
Adarama, Sudan (ä-dä-rä′mä)	231	17°11′N	34°56′E
Adda, r., Italy (äd′dä)	174	45°43′N	9°31′E
Ad Dabbah, Sudan	231	18°04′N	30°58′E
Ad Dahnā, des., Sau. Ar.	198	26°05′N	47°15′E
Ad-Dāmir, Sudan (ad-dä′mĕr)	231	17°38′N	33°57′E
Ad Dammām, Sau. Ar.	198	26°27′N	49°59′E
Ad Dāmūr, Leb.	197a	33°44′N	35°27′E
Ad Dawhah, Qatar	198	25°02′N	51°28′E
Ad Dilam, Sau. Ar.	198	23°47′N	47°03′E
Ad Dilinjāt, Egypt	238b	30°48′N	30°32′E
Addis Ababa, Eth.	231	9°00′N	38°44′E
Addison, Tx., U.S. (ă′dĭ-sŭn)	117c	32°58′N	96°50′W
Addo, S. Afr. (ădō)	233c	33°33′S	25°43′E
Ad Duwaym, Sudan (ad-dō-ām′)	231	13°56′N	32°22′E
Addyston, Oh., U.S. (ăd′ē-stŭn)	111f	39°09′N	84°42′W
Adel, Ga., U.S. (ā-dĕl′)	124	31°08′N	83°25′W
Adelaide, Austl. (ăd′ē-lād)	218	34°46′S	139°08′E
Adelaide, S. Afr. (ăd-ĕl′ăd)	233c	32°41′S	26°07′E
Adelaide Island, i., Ant. (ăd′ē-lād)	224	67°15′S	68°40′W
Aden ('Adan), Yemen (ä′dĕn)	198	12°48′N	45°00′E
Aden, Gulf of, b.	198	11°45′N	45°45′E
Adi, Pulau, i., Indon. (ä′dē)	213	4°25′S	133°52′E
Adige, r., Italy (ä′dē-jā)	162	46°38′N	10°43′E
Adigrat, Eth.	201	14°17′N	39°28′E
Adilābād, India (ŭ-dĭl-ä-bäd′)	202	19°47′N	78°30′E
Adirondack Mountains, mts., N.Y., U.S. (ăd-ĭ-rŏn′dăk)	107	43°45′N	74°40′W
Adis Abeba *see* Addis Ababa, Eth.	231	9°00′N	38°44′E
Adi Ugri, Erit. (ä-dē ōō′grē)	231	14°54′N	38°52′E
Adjud, Rom. (äd′zhōd)	169	46°05′N	27°12′E
Adkins, Tx., U.S.	117d	29°22′N	98°18′W
Admiralty, i., Ak., U.S. (ăd′mĭ-răl-tē)	103	57°50′N	133°50′W
Admiralty Inlet, Wa., U.S. (ăd′mĭ-răl-tē)	116a	48°10′N	122°45′W
Admiralty Island National Monument, rec., Ak., U.S. (ăd′mĭ-răl-tē)	103	57°50′N	137°30′W
Admiralty Islands, is., Pap. N. Gui. (ăd′mĭ-răl-tē)	213	1°40′S	146°45′E
Ado-Ekiti, Nig.	235	7°38′N	5°12′E
Adolph, Mn., U.S. (ā′dolf)	117h	46°47′N	92°17′W
Ādoni, India	203	15°42′N	77°18′E
Adour, r., Fr. (ä-dōōr′)	161	43°43′N	0°38′W
Adra, Spain (ä′drä)	172	36°45′N	3°02′W
Adrano, Italy (ä-drä′nō)	174	37°42′N	14°52′E
Adrar, Alg.	230	27°53′N	0°15′W
Adria, Italy (ä′drē-ä)	174	45°03′N	12°01′E
Adrian, Mi., U.S. (ā′drĭ-ăn)	108	41°55′N	84°00′W
Adrian, Mn., U.S. (ā′drĭ-ăn)	112	43°39′N	95°56′W
Adrianople *see* Edirne, Tur.	154	41°41′N	26°35′E
Adriatic Sea, sea, Eur.	156	43°30′N	14°27′E
Adwa, Eth.	231	14°02′N	38°58′E
Adwick-le-Street, Eng., U.K. (ăd′wĭk-lē-strēt′)	158a	53°35′N	1°11′W
Adycha, r., Russia (ä′dĭ-chȧ)	185	66°11′N	136°45′E
Adygea, prov., Russia	180	45°00′N	40°00′E
Adz′va, r., Russia (ädz′vȧ)	180	67°00′N	59°20′E
Aegean Sea, sea (ē-jē′ăn)	156	39°04′N	24°56′E
A Estrada, Spain	172	42°42′N	8°29′W
Affton, Mo., U.S.	117e	38°33′N	90°20′W
Afghanistan, nation, Asia (ăf-găn-ĭ-stăn′)	198	33°00′N	63°00′E
Afgooye, Som. (äf-gô′ĭ)	238a	2°08′N	45°08′E
Afikpo, Nig.	235	5°53′N	7°56′E
Aflou, Alg. (ä-flōō′)	230	33°59′N	2°04′E
Afognak, i., Ak., U.S. (ä-fŏg-nàk′)	103	58°28′N	151°35′W
A Fonsagrada, Spain	172	43°08′N	7°07′W
Afonso Claudio, Braz. (äl-fōn′sō-klou′dēō)	141a	20°05′S	41°05′W
Afragola, Italy (ä-frä′gō-lä)	173c	40°40′N	14°19′E
Africa, cont.	229	10°00′N	22°00′E
Afton, Mn., U.S. (ăf′tŭn)	117g	44°54′N	92°47′W
Afton, Ok., U.S. (ăf′tŭn)	121	36°42′N	94°56′W
Afton, Wy., U.S. (ăf′tŭn)	115	42°42′N	110°52′W
'Afula, Isr. (ä-fò′lȧ)	197a	32°36′N	35°17′E
Afyon, Tur. (ä-fē-ōn)	198	38°45′N	30°20′E
Agadem, Niger (ä′gȧ-dĕm)	231	16°50′N	13°17′E
Agadez, Niger (ä′gȧ-dĕs)	230	16°58′N	7°59′E
Agadir, Mor. (ä-gȧ-dēr)	230	30°30′N	9°37′W
Agalta, Cordillera de, mts., Hond. (kôr-dēl-yĕ′rä-dĕ-ä-gä′l-tä)	132	15°15′N	85°42′W
Agapovka, Russia (ä-gä-pôv′kä)	186a	53°18′N	59°10′E
Agartala, India	202	23°53′N	91°22′E
Agāshi, India	203b	19°28′N	72°46′E
Agashkino, Russia (ȧ-gäsh′kĭ-nô)	186b	55°18′N	38°13′E
Agattu, i., Ak., U.S. (ȧ′gä-tōō)	103a	52°14′N	173°40′E
Agboville, C. Iv.	234	5°56′N	4°13′W
Ağdam, Azer. (äg′dăm)	181	40°00′N	47°00′E
Agde, Fr. (ägd)	170	43°19′N	3°30′E
Agen, Fr. (ȧ-zhäN′)	161	44°13′N	0°31′E
Agiásos, Grc.	175	39°06′N	26°25′E
Aginskoye, Russia (ä-hĭn′skô-yĕ)	179	51°15′N	113°15′E

PLACE (Pronunciation)	PAGE	LAT.	LONG.
Ágios Efstrátios, i., Grc.	163	39°30′N	24°58′E
Agíou Órous, Kólpos, b., Grc.	175	40°15′N	24°00′E
Agno, Phil. (äg′nō)	213a	16°07′N	119°49′E
Agno, r., Phil.	213a	15°42′N	120°28′E
Agnone, Italy (än-yō′nä)	174	41°49′N	14°23′E
Agogo, Ghana	234	6°47′N	1°04′W
Agra, India (ä′grä)	199	27°18′N	78°00′E
Ağrı, Tur.	181	39°50′N	43°10′E
Agri, r., Italy (ä′grē)	174	40°15′N	16°21′E
Agrínio, Grc.	163	38°38′N	21°06′E
Agua, vol., Guat. (ä′gwä)	132	14°28′N	90°43′W
Agua Blanca, Río, r., Mex. (rē′ō-ä-gwä-blä′n-kä)	130	21°46′N	102°54′W
Agua Brava, Laguna de, l., Mex.	130	22°04′N	105°40′W
Agua Caliente Indian Reservation, I.R., Ca., U.S. (ä′gwä kal-yĕn′tä)	118	33°50′N	116°24′W
Aguada, Cuba (ä-gwä′dȧ)	134	22°25′N	80°50′W
Aguada, l., Mex. (ä-gwä′dȧ)	132a	18°46′N	89°40′W
Aguadas, Col. (ä-gwä′dȧs)	142	5°37′N	75°27′W
Aguadilla, P.R. (ä-gwä-dēl′yä)	129b	18°27′N	67°10′W
Aguadulce, Pan. (ä-gwä-dōōl′sä)	133	8°15′N	80°33′W
Agua Escondida, Meseta de, plat., Mex.	131	16°54′N	91°35′W
Agua Fria, r., Az., U.S. (ä′gwä frē-ä)	119	33°43′N	112°22′W
Agua Fria National Monument, rec., Az., U.S.	119	34°13′N	112°03′W
Aguai, Braz. (ägwä-ē′)	141a	22°04′S	46°57′W
Agualeguas, Mex. (ä-gwä-lā′gwäs)	122	26°19′N	99°33′W
Aguán, r., Hond. (ä-gwä′n)	132	15°22′N	87°00′W
Aguanaval, r., Mex. (ȧ-guä-nä-väl′)	122	25°12′N	103°28′W
Aguanus, r., Can. (ȧ-gwä′nŭs)	101	50°45′N	62°03′W
Aguascalientes, Mex. (ä′gwäs-käl-yĕn′tās)	128	21°52′N	102°17′W
Aguascalientes, state, Mex. (ä′gwäs-käl-yĕn′tās)	130	22°00′N	102°18′W
Águeda, Port. (ä-gwā′dȧ)	172	40°36′N	8°26′W
Agueda, r., Eur. (ä-gĕ-dä)	172	40°50′N	6°44′W
Aguelhok, Mali	234	19°28′N	0°52′E
Aguilar, Spain	172	37°32′N	4°39′W
Aguilar, Co., U.S. (ä-gē-lär′)	120	37°24′N	104°38′W
Aguilas, Spain (ä-gē-läs)	162	37°26′N	1°35′W
Aguilila, Mex. (ä-gē-lēl-yä)	130	18°44′N	102°44′W
Aguilillla, r., Mex. (ä-gē-lēl-yä)	130	18°30′N	102°48′W
Aguja, Punta, c., Peru (pŭn′tȧ ȧ-gōō′ hä)	142	6°00′S	81°15′W
Agulhas, Cape, c., S. Afr. (ä-gōōl′yäs)	232	34°47′S	20°00′E
Agusan, r., Phil. (ä-gōō′sän)	213	8°12′N	126°07′E
Ahaggar, mts., Alg. (ȧ-hȧ-gär′)	230	23°14′N	6°00′E
Ahar, Iran	201	38°28′N	47°04′E
Ahlen, Ger. (ä′lĕn)	168	51°45′N	7°52′E
Ahmadābād, India (ŭ-mĕd-ä-băd′)	199	23°04′N	72°38′E
Ahmadnagar, India (ä′mûd-nû-gûr)	199	19°09′N	74°45′E
Ahmar Mountains, mts., Eth.	231	9°22′N	42°00′E
Ahoskie, N.C., U.S. (ä-hŏs′kē)	125	36°15′N	77°00′W
Ahrensburg, Ger. (ä′rĕns-bōrg)	159c	53°40′N	10°14′E
Ahrweiler, Ger. (är′vī-lĕr)	168	50°34′N	7°05′E
Ähtärinjärvi, l., Fin.	167	62°46′N	24°25′E
Ahuacatlán, Mex. (ä-wä-kät-län′)	130	21°05′N	104°28′W
Ahuachapán, El Sal. (ä-wä-chä-pän′)	132	13°57′N	89°53′W
Ahualulco, Mex. (ä-wä-lōōl′kō)	130	20°43′N	103°57′W
Ahuatempan, Mex. (ä-wä-tĕm-pän)	130	18°11′N	98°02′W
Åhus, Swe. (ô′hōs)	166	55°56′N	14°19′E
Ahvāz, Iran	198	31°15′N	48°54′E
Ahvenanmaa (Åland), is., Fin. (ä′vĕ-nȧn-mô) (ô′länd)	160	60°36′N	19°55′E
'Aiea, Hi., U.S.	126a	21°18′N	157°52′W
Aígina, Grc.	175	37°43′N	23°35′E
Aígina, i., Grc.	175	37°43′N	23°35′E
Aígio, Grc.	175	38°13′N	22°04′E
Aiken, S.C., U.S. (ā′kĕn)	125	33°32′N	81°43′W
Aimorès, Serra dos, mts., Braz. (sĕ′r-rä-dôs-ī-mō-rĕ′s)	143	17°40′S	42°38′W
Aimoto, Japan (ī-mô-tō)	211b	34°59′N	135°09′E
Aincourt, Fr. (ăN-kōō′r)	171b	49°04′N	1°47′E
Aïn el Beïda, Alg.	230	35°57′N	7°25′E
Ainsworth, Ne., U.S. (ānz′wûrth)	112	42°32′N	99°51′W
Aïn Témouchent, Alg. (ä′ĕntĕ-mōō-shaN′)	162	35°20′N	1°23′W
Aïn Wessara, Alg. (ĕn ōō-sä-rȧ)	173	35°25′N	2°50′E
Aipe, Col. (ī′pĕ)	142a	3°13′N	75°15′W
Aïr, mts., Niger	230	18°00′N	8°30′E
Aire, r., Eng., U.K.	158a	53°42′N	1°00′W
Aire-sur-l'Adour, Fr. (âr)	170	43°42′N	0°17′W
Airhitam, Selat, strt., Indon.	197b	0°58′N	102°38′E
Ai Shan, mts., China (ī′shän)	206	37°27′N	120°35′E
Aisne, r., Fr. (ĕn)	161	49°28′N	3°32′E
Aitape, Pap. N. Gui. (ä-ē-tä′pȧ)	213	3°00′S	142°10′E
Aitkin, Mn., U.S. (āt′kĭn)	113	46°32′N	93°43′W
Aitolikó, Grc.	175	38°27′N	21°21′E
Aitos, Blg. (ä-ē′tōs)	175	42°42′N	27°17′E
Aitutaki, i., Cook Is. (ī-tōō-tä′kē)	241	19°00′S	162°00′W
Aiud, Rom. (ä′ē-ōd)	163	46°19′N	23°40′E
Aiuruoca, Braz. (äē′ōō-rōōō′-kȧ)	141a	21°57′S	44°36′W
Aiuruoca, r., Braz.	141a	22°11′S	44°35′W
Aix-en-Provence, Fr. (ĕks-prō-văNs)	161	43°32′N	5°27′E
Aix-les-Bains, Fr. (ĕks′-lā-băN′)	171	45°42′N	5°56′E
Aizpute, Lat. (ä′ēz-pōō-tĕ)	167	56°44′N	21°37′E
Aizuwakamatsu, Japan	210	37°27′N	139°51′E
Ajaccio, Fr. (ä-yät′chō)	154	41°55′N	8°42′E
Ajalpan, Mex. (ä-häl′pän)	131	18°21′N	97°14′W
Ajana, Austl. (ăj-än′ĕr)	218	28°00′S	114°45′E
Ajaria, state, Geor.	182	41°40′N	42°00′E
Ajdābiyah, Libya	231	30°56′N	20°16′E
Ajjer, Tassili-n-, plat., Alg.	230	25°40′N	6°57′E

PLACE (Pronunciation)	PAGE	LAT.	LONG.
Ajmah, Jabal al, mts., Egypt	197a	29°12′N	34°03′E
Ajman, U.A.E.	198	25°15′N	54°30′E
Ajmer, India (ŭj-mēr′)	199	26°26′N	74°42′E
Ajo, Az., U.S. (ä′hô)	119	32°20′N	112°55′W
Ajuchitlán del Progreso, Mex. (ä-hōō-chet-lån)	130	18°11′N	100°32′W
Ajusco, Mex. (ä-hōō′s-kō)	131a	19°13′N	99°12′W
Ajusco, Cerro, mtn., Mex. (sĕ′r-rô-ä-hōō′s-kō)	131a	19°12′N	99°16′W
Akaishi-dake, mtn., Japan (ä-kī-shē dä′kä)	211	35°30′N	138°00′E
Akashi, Japan (ä′kä-shē)	210	34°38′N	134°59′E
Aketi, D.R.C. (ä-kȧ-tē)	231	2°44′N	23°46′E
Akhaltsikhe, Geor. (äkä′l-tsĭ-kĕ)	181	41°40′N	42°50′E
Akhdar, Al Jabal al, mts., Libya	231	32°00′N	22°00′E
Akhdar, Al Jabal al, mts., Oman	198	23°30′N	56°43′W
Akhisar, Tur. (äk-hĭs-sär′)	163	38°58′N	27°58′E
Akhtarskaya, Bukhta, b., Russia (bōōk′tä äk-tär′skȧ-yȧ)	177	45°53′N	38°22′E
Akhtopol, Blg. (äk′tô-pōl)	175	42°08′N	27°54′E
Akhunovo, Russia (ä-kû′nô-vô)	186a	54°13′N	59°36′E
Aki, Japan (ä′kē)	211	33°31′N	133°51′E
Akiak, Ak., U.S. (äk′yăk)	103	61°00′N	161°02′W
Akimiski, i., Can. (ä-kĭ-mĭ′skĭ)	93	52°54′N	80°22′W
Akita, Japan (ä′kē-tä)	205	39°40′N	140°12′E
Akjoujt, Maur.	230	19°45′N	14°23′W
'Akko, Isr.	197a	32°56′N	35°05′E
Aklavik, Can. (äk′lä-vĭk)	90	68°28′N	135°26′W
'Aklé Âouâna, dunes, Afr.	234	18°07′N	6°00′W
Ako, Japan (ä′kô)	211	34°44′N	134°22′E
Akola, India (ȧ-kō′lä)	199	20°47′N	77°00′E
Akordat, Erit.	231	15°34′N	37°54′E
Akpatok, i., Can. (ȧk′pȧ-tŏk)	93	60°30′N	67°10′W
Akranes, Ice.	160	64°18′N	21°40′W
Akron, Co., U.S. (ăk′rŭn)	120	40°09′N	103°14′W
Akron, Oh., U.S. (ăk′rŭn)	105	41°05′N	81°30′W
Aksaray, Tur. (äk-sȧ-rī′)	163	38°30′N	34°05′E
Akşehır, Tur. (äk′shȧ-hēr)	163	38°20′N	31°20′E
Akşehır Gölü, l., Tur. (äk′shȧ-hēr)	198	38°40′N	31°30′E
Aksha, Russia (äk′shȧ)	179	50°28′N	113°00′E
Aksu, China (ä-kŭ-sōō)	204	41°29′N	80°15′E
Akune, Japan (ä′kò-nȧ)	211	32°03′N	130°16′E
Akureyri, Ice. (ä-kò-rå′rē)	160	65°39′N	18°01′W
Akutan, i., Ak., U.S. (ä-kōō-tän′)	103a	53°58′N	169°54′W
Akwatia, Ghana	234	6°04′N	0°49′W
Alabama, state, U.S. (ăl-ȧ-băm′ȧ)	105	32°50′N	87°30′W
Alabama, r., Al., U.S. (ăl-ȧ-băm′ȧ)	107	31°20′N	87°39′W
Alabat, i., Phil. (ä-lä-bät′)	213a	14°14′N	122°05′E
Alacam, Tur. (ä-lä-chäm′)	181	41°30′N	35°40′E
Alacant, Spain	162	38°20′N	0°30′W
Alacranes, Cuba (ä-lä-krä′nås)	134	22°45′N	81°35′W
Al Aflaj, des., Sau. Ar.	198	24°00′N	44°47′E
Alagôas, state, Braz. (ä-lä-gō′äzh)	143	9°50′S	36°33′W
Alagoinhas, Braz. (ä-lä-gō-ēn′yäzh)	143	12°13′S	38°12′W
Alagón, Spain (ä-lä-gōn′)	172	41°46′N	1°07′W
Alagón, r., Spain (ä-lä-gōn′)	172	39°53′N	6°42′W
Alahuatán, r., Mex. (ä-lä-wä-tä′n)	130	18°30′N	100°00′W
Alajuela, C.R. (ä-lä-hwä′lä)	133	10°01′N	84°14′W
Alajuela, Lago, l., Pan. (ä-lä-hwa′lä)	128a	9°15′N	79°34′W
Alaköl, l., Kaz.	183	45°45′N	81°13′E
'Alalakeiki Channel, strt., Hi., U.S. (ä-lä-lä-kä′kē)	126a	20°40′N	156°30′W
Al 'Alamayn, Egypt	231	30°53′N	28°52′E
Al 'Amārah, Iraq	201	31°50′N	47°09′E
Alameda, Ca., U.S. (ăl-ȧ-mā′dȧ)	104	37°46′N	122°15′W
Alameda, r., Ca., U.S. (ăl-ȧ-mā′dȧ)	116b	37°36′N	122°02′W
Alaminos, Phil. (ä-lä-mē′nôs)	213a	16°09′N	119°58′E
Al 'Amirīyah, Egypt	163	31°01′N	29°52′E
Alamo, Mex. (ä′lä-mô)	131	20°55′N	97°41′W
Alamo, Ca., U.S. (ă′lȧ-mō)	116b	37°51′N	122°02′W
Alamo, Nv., U.S. (ă′lȧ-mō)	118	37°22′N	115°10′W
Alamo, r., Mex. (ä′lä-mô)	122	26°33′N	99°35′W
Alamogordo, N.M., U.S. (ăl-ȧ-mō-gôr′dō)	119	32°55′N	106°00′W
Alamo Heights, Tx., U.S. (ă′lȧ-mō)	117d	29°28′N	98°27′W
Alamo Indian Reservation, I.R., N.M., U.S.	119	34°30′N	107°30′W
Alamo Peak, mtn., N.M., U.S. (ă′lȧ-mō pēk)	122	32°50′N	105°55′W
Alamosa, Co., U.S. (ăl-ȧ-mō′sȧ)	119	37°25′N	105°50′W
Åland *see* Ahvenanmaa, is., Fin.	160	60°36′N	19°55′E
Alandskiy, Russia (ä-länt′skĭ)	186a	52°14′N	59°48′E
Alanga Arba, Kenya	237	0°07′N	40°25′E
Alanya, Tur.	163	36°40′N	32°10′E
Alaotra, l., Madag. (ä-lä-ō′trȧ)	233	17°15′S	48°17′E
Alapayevsk, Russia (ä-lä-pä′yĕfsk)	178	57°50′N	61°35′E
Al 'Aqabah, Jord.	198	29°32′N	35°00′E
Alaquines, Mex. (ä-lȧ-kē′nås)	130	22°07′N	99°35′W
Al 'Arīsh, Egypt (äl-a-rēsh′)	197a	31°08′N	33°48′E
Alaska, state, U.S. (ȧ-lăs′kȧ)	106a	64°00′N	150°00′W
Alaska, Gulf of, b., Ak., U.S. (ȧ-lăs′kȧ)	103	57°42′N	147°40′W
Alaska Highway, Ak., U.S. (ȧ-lăs′kȧ)	103	63°00′N	142°00′W
Alaska Peninsula, pen., Ak., U.S. (ȧ-lăs′kȧ)	103	55°50′N	162°10′W
Alaska Range, mts., Ak., U.S. (ȧ-lăs′kȧ)	103	62°00′N	152°18′W
Al 'Atrūn, Sudan	231	18°13′N	26°44′E
Alatyr′, Russia (ä′lä-tür)	178	54°55′N	46°30′E
Alazani, r., Asia	182	41°05′N	46°40′E
Alba, Italy (äl′bä)	174	44°41′N	8°02′E
Albacete, Spain (äl-bä-thā′tā)	162	39°00′N	1°49′W
Albachten, Ger. (äl-bä′κ-tĕn)	171c	51°55′N	7°31′E
Alba de Tormes, Spain (äl-bȧ dā tôr′mās)	172	40°48′N	5°28′W
Alba Iulia, Rom. (äl-bä yōō′lyȧ)	163	46°05′N	23°32′E

ng-sing; ŋ-baŋk; N-nasalized n; nŏd; cŏmmit; ōld; ôbey; ôrder; oi-boil; fōōd; ò-as oo in foot; ou-out; s-soft; sh-dish; th-thin; pūre; ûnite; ûrn; stŭd; circŭs; ü-as in French tu; ′-indeterminate vowel.

PLACE (Pronunciation)	PAGE	LAT.	LONG.
Albani, Colli, hills, Italy	173d	41°46'N	12°45'E
Albania, nation, Eur. (ăl-bā'nĭ-ȧ)	154	41°45'N	20°00'E
Albano, Lago, l., Italy (lä'-gō äl-bä'nō)	173d	41°45'N	12°44'E
Albano Laziale, Italy (äl-bä'nō lät-zē-ä'lā)	174	41°44'N	12°43'E
Albany, Austl. (ôl'bȧ-nĭ)	218	35°00'S	118°00'E
Albany, Ca., U.S. (ôl'bȧ-nĭ)	116b	37°54'N	122°18'W
Albany, Ga., U.S. (ôl'bȧ-nĭ)	105	31°35'N	84°10'W
Albany, Mo., U.S. (ôl'bȧ-nĭ)	121	40°14'N	94°18'W
Albany, N.Y., U.S. (ôl'bȧ-nĭ)	105	42°40'N	73°50'W
Albany, Or., U.S. (ôl'bȧ-nĭ)	104	44°38'N	123°06'W
Albany, r., Can. (ôl'bȧ-nĭ)	93	51°45'N	83°30'W
Al Başrah, Iraq	198	30°35'N	47°59'E
Al Batrūn, Leb. (äl-bä-trōōn')	197a	34°16'N	35°39'E
Albemarle, N.C., U.S. (ăl'bē-märl)	125	35°24'N	80°36'W
Albemarle Sound, strt., N.C., U.S. (ăl'bē-märl)	107	36°00'N	76°17'W
Albenga, Italy (äl-bĕŋ'gä)	174	44°04'N	8°13'E
Alberche, r., Spain (äl-bĕr'chå)	172	40°08'N	4°19'W
Alberga, The, r., Austl. (ăl-bŭr'gȧ)	220	27°15'S	135°00'E
Albergaria-a-Velha, Port.	172	40°47'N	8°31'W
Alberhill, Ca., U.S. (ăl'bẽr-hĭl)	117a	33°43'N	117°23'W
Albert, Fr. (ål-bâr')	170	50°00'N	2°49'E
Albert, l., Afr. (ăl'bẽrt) (ål-bâr')	231	1°50'N	30°40'E
Albert, Parc National, rec., D.R.C.	237	0°05'N	29°30'E
Alberta, prov., Can. (ăl-bûr'tȧ)	90	54°33'N	117°10'W
Alberta, Mount, mtn., Can. (ăl-bûr'tȧ)	95	52°18'N	117°28'W
Albert Edward, Mount, mtn., Pap. N. Gui. (ăl'bẽrt ĕd'wẽrd)	213	8°25'S	147°25'E
Alberti, Arg. (ål-bĕ'r-tē)	141c	35°01'S	60°16'W
Albert Kanaal, can., Bel.	159a	51°07'N	5°07'E
Albert Lea, Mn., U.S. (ăl'bẽrt lē')	113	43°38'N	93°24'W
Albert Nile, r., Ug.	237	3°25'N	31°35'E
Alberton, Can. (ăl'bẽr-tŭn)	100	46°49'N	64°04'W
Alberton, S. Afr.	233b	26°16'S	28°08'E
Albertville *see* Kalemie, D.R.C.	232	5°56'S	29°12'E
Albertville, Fr. (ål-bêr-vēl')	171	45°42'N	6°25'E
Albertville, Al., U.S. (ăl'bẽrt-vĭl)	124	34°15'N	86°10'W
Albi, Fr. (äl-bē')	161	43°54'N	2°07'E
Albia, Ia., U.S. (ăl-bĭ-ȧ)	113	41°01'N	92°44'W
Albina, Sur. (äl-bē'nä)	143	5°30'N	54°33'W
Albina, Ponta, c., Ang.	236	15°51'S	11°44'E
Albino, Point, c., Can. (äl-bē'nō)	111c	42°50'N	79°05'W
Albion, Mi., U.S. (ăl'bĭ-ŭn)	108	42°15'N	84°50'W
Albion, Ne., U.S. (ăl'bĭ-ŭn)	112	41°42'N	98°00'W
Albion, N.Y., U.S. (ăl'bĭ-ŭn)	109	43°15'N	78°10'W
Alboran, Isla del, i., Spain (ē's-lä-dĕl-äl-bō-rä'n)	156	35°58'N	3°02'W
Albuquerque, N.M., U.S. (ăl-bů-kûr'kē)	104	35°05'N	106°40'W
Albuquerque, Cayos de, is., Col.	133	12°12'N	81°24'W
Alburquerque, Spain (äl-bōōr-kĕr'kā)	172	39°13'N	6°58'W
Albury, Austl. (ôl'bẽr-ē)	219	36°00'S	147°00'E
Alcabideche, Port. (äl-kȧ-bē-dā'chå)	173b	38°43'N	9°24'W
Alcácer do Sal, Port. (äb'ĭ-lĕn)	172	38°24'N	8°33'W
Alcalá de Henares, Spain (äl-kä-lä' dä ā-na'rās)	173a	40°29'N	3°22'W
Alcalá la Real, Spain (äl-kä-lä'lä rā-äl')	172	37°27'N	3°57'W
Alcamo, Italy (äl'kȧ-mō)	174	37°58'N	13°03'E
Alcanadre, r., Spain (äl-kä-nä'drā)	173	41°41'N	0°18'W
Alcanar, Spain (äl-kä-när')	173	40°35'N	0°27'E
Alcañiz, Spain (äl-kän-yēth')	162	41°03'N	0°08'W
Alcântara, Braz. (äl-kän'tȧ-rȧ)	143	2°17'S	44°29'W
Alcaraz, Spain (äl-kä-räth')	172	38°39'N	2°28'W
Alcaudete, Spain (äb'ĭng-dŭn)	172	37°38'N	4°05'W
Alcázar de San Juan, Spain (äl-kä'thär dā sän hwän')	162	39°22'N	3°12'W
Alcira, Spain (ä-thē'rä)	173	39°09'N	0°26'W
Alcoa, Tn., U.S. (ăl-kō'ȧ)	124	35°45'N	84°00'W
Alcobendas, Spain (äl-kō-bĕn'dås)	173a	40°32'N	3°39'W
Alcochete, Port. (äl-kō-chā'ta)	173b	38°45'N	8°58'W
Alcoi, Spain	162	38°42'N	0°30'W
Alcorcón, Spain	173a	40°22'N	3°50'W
Alcorta, Arg. (äl-kôr'tä)	141c	33°32'S	61°08'W
Alcova Reservoir, res., Wy., U.S. (ăl-kō'vȧ)	115	42°31'N	106°33'W
Alcove, Can. (ăl-kōv')	102c	45°41'N	75°55'W
Alcúdia, Badia d', b., Spain	173	39°48'N	3°20'E
Aldabra Islands, is., Sey. (äl-dä'brä)	233	9°16'S	46°17'E
Aldama, Mex. (äl-dä'mä)	130	22°54'N	98°04'W
Aldama, Mex. (äl-dä'mä)	122	28°50'N	105°54'W
Aldan, Russia	179	58°46'N	125°19'E
Aldan, r., Russia	179	63°00'N	134°00'E
Aldan Plateau, plat., Russia	185	57°42'N	130°28'E
Aldanskaya, Russia	179	61°52'N	135°29'E
Aldenhoven, Ger. (äl'dĕn-hō'vĕn)	171c	50°54'N	6°18'E
Aldergrove, Can. (ôl'dẽr-grōv)	116d	49°03'N	122°28'W
Alderney, i., Guern. (ôl'dẽr-nĭ)	170	49°43'N	2°11'W
Aldershot, Eng., U.K. (ôl'dẽr-shŏt)	164	51°14'N	0°46'W
Alderson, W.V., U.S. (ôl-dẽr-sŭn)	108	37°40'N	80°40'W
Alderwood Manor, Wa., U.S. (ôl'dẽr-wŏod măn'ŏr)	116a	47°49'N	122°18'W
Aldridge-Brownhills, Eng., U.K.	158a	52°38'N	1°55'W
Aledo, Il., U.S. (ȧ-le'dō)	121	41°12'N	90°47'W
Aleg, Maur.	230	17°03'N	13°55'W
Alegre, Braz. (ȧlĕ'grĕ)	141a	20°41'S	41°32'W
Alegre, r., Braz. (ȧlĕ'grĕ)	144b	22°22'S	43°34'W
Alegrete, Braz. (ä-lå-grā'tā)	144	29°46'S	55°44'W
Aleksandrov, Russia (ä-lyĕk-sän' drôf)	180	56°24'N	38°45'E
Aleksandrovsk, Russia (ä-lyĕk-sän'drôfsk)	186a	59°11'N	57°36'E
Aleksandrovsk, Russia (ä-lyĕk-sän'drôfsk)	179	51°02'N	142°21'E
Aleksandrów Kujawski, Pol. (ä-lĕk-säh'drōōv kōō-yav'skē)	169	52°54'N	18°45'E
Alekseyevka, Russia (ä-lyĕk-sā-yĕf'kȧ)	177	50°39'N	38°40'E
Aleksin, Russia (äb'ĭng-tŭn)	176	54°31'N	37°07'E
Aleksinac, Serb. (å-lyĕk-sē-nák')	175	43°33'N	21°42'E
Alemán, Presa, res., Mex. (prā'sä-lĕ-mȧ'n)	131	18°20'N	96°35'W
Alem Paraíba, Braz. (ä-lĕ'm-pȧ-rāē'bȧ)	141a	21°54'S	42°40'W
Alençon, Fr. (ȧ-läN-sôN')	161	48°26'N	0°08'E
Alenquer, Braz. (ä-lĕŋ-kĕr')	143	1°58'S	54°44'W
Alenquer, Port. (ä-lĕŋ-kĕr')	172	39°04'N	9°01'W
Alentejo, hist. reg., Port. (ä-lĕŋ-tā'zhō)	172	38°05'N	7°45'W
Alenuihaha Channel, strt., Hi., U.S. (ä'lå-nōō-ê-hä'hä)	126a	20°20'N	156°05'W
Aleppo, Syria (ȧ-lĕp-ō)	198	36°10'N	37°18'E
Alès, Fr. (ä-lĕs')	161	44°07'N	4°06'E
Alessandria, Italy (ä-lĕs-sän'drē-ä)	162	44°53'N	8°35'E
Ålesund, Nor. (ô'lĕ-sōn')	166	62°28'N	6°14'E
Aleutian Islands, is., Ak., U.S. (ȧ-lu'shăn)	106b	52°40'N	177°30'W
Aleutian Trench, deep	103a	50°40'N	177°10'E
Alevina, Mys, c., Russia	179	58°49'N	151°44'E
Alexander Archipelago, is., Ak., U.S. (ăl-ĕg-zăn'dẽr)	103	57°05'N	138°10'W
Alexander City, Al., U.S.	124	32°55'N	85°55'W
Alexander Indian Reserve, I.R., Can.	102g	53°47'N	114°00'W
Alexander Island, i., Ant.	224	71°00'S	71°00'W
Alexandra, S. Afr. (ăl-ex-ăn'drȧ)	238c	26°07'S	28°07'E
Alexandria, Austl. (ăl-ĕg-zăn'drĭ-ȧ)	218	19°00'S	136°56'E
Alexandria, Can. (ăl-ĕg-zăn'drĭ-ȧ)	99	45°50'N	74°35'W
Alexandria, Egypt (ăl-ĕg-zăn'drĭ-ȧ)	231	31°12'N	29°58'E
Alexandria, Rom. (ăl-ĕg-zăn'drĭ-ȧ)	175	43°55'N	25°21'E
Alexandria, S. Afr. (ăl-ex-än-drĭ-ȧ)	233c	33°40'S	26°26'E
Alexandria, In., U.S. (ăl-ĕg-zăn'drĭ-ȧ)	108	40°20'N	85°20'W
Alexandria, La., U.S. (ăl-ĕg-zăn'drĭ-ȧ)	105	31°18'N	92°28'W
Alexandria, Mn., U.S. (ăl-ĕg-zăn'drĭ-ȧ)	112	45°53'N	95°23'W
Alexandria, S.D., U.S. (ăl-ĕg-zăn'drĭ-ȧ)	112	43°39'N	97°45'W
Alexandria, Va., U.S. (ăl-ĕg-zăn'drĭ-ȧ)	105	38°50'N	77°05'W
Alexandria Bay, N.Y., U.S. (ăl-ĕg-zăn'drĭ-ȧ)	109	44°20'N	75°55'W
Alexandroúpoli, Grc.	163	40°41'N	25°51'E
Alfaro, Spain (äl-fär'ō)	172	42°08'N	1°43'W
Al-Fāshir, Sudan (äl-fä'shēr)	231	13°38'N	25°21'E
Al Fashn, Egypt	238b	28°47'N	30°53'E
Al Fayyūm, Egypt	231	29°14'N	30°48'E
Alfeiós, r., Grc.	175	37°33'N	21°50'E
Alfenas, Braz. (äl-fĕ'nȧs)	141a	21°26'S	45°55'W
Al Firdān, Egypt (äl-fēr-dän')	238b	30°43'N	32°20'E
Alfred, Can. (ăl'frĕd)	102c	45°34'N	74°52'W
Alfreton, Eng., U.K. (ăl'fẽr-tŭn)	158a	53°06'N	1°23'W
Algarve, hist. reg., Port. (äl-gär'vĕ)	172	37°15'N	8°12'W
Algeciras, Spain (ăl-hā-thē'rās)	172	36°08'N	5°25'W
Algeria, nation, Afr. (ăl-gē'rĭ-ȧ)	230	28°45'N	1°00'E
Algete, Spain (äl-hā'tā)	173a	40°36'N	3°30'W
Al Ghaydah, Yemen	201	16°12'N	52°15'E
Alghero, Italy (äl-gâ'rō)	162	40°32'N	8°22'E
Algiers, Alg. (ăl-jērs)	230	36°51'N	2°56'E
Algoa, Tx., U.S. (ăl-gō'ȧ)	123a	29°24'N	95°11'W
Algoma, Wa., U.S.	116a	47°17'N	122°15'W
Algoma, Wi., U.S.	113	44°38'N	87°29'W
Algona, Ia., U.S.	113	43°04'N	94°11'W
Algonac, Mi., U.S. (ăl'gō-năk)	108	42°35'N	82°30'W
Algonquin, Il., U.S. (ăl-gŏŋ'kwĭn)	111a	42°10'N	88°17'W
Algonquin Provincial Park, rec., Can.	107	45°50'N	78°20'W
Alhama de Granada, Spain (äl-hä'mä-dĕ-grä-nä'dä)	172	37°00'N	3°59'W
Alhama de Murcia, Spain	172	37°50'N	1°24'W
Alhambra, Ca., U.S. (ăl-hăm'brȧ)	117a	34°05'N	118°08'W
Al Ḩammān, Egypt	163	30°46'N	29°42'E
Alhandra, Port. (äl-yän'drȧ)	173b	38°55'N	9°01'W
Alhaurín, Spain (ä-lou-rēn')	172	36°40'N	4°40'W
Al Ḩawrah, Yemen	201	13°49'N	47°37'E
Al Ḩawṭah, Yemen	198	15°58'N	48°26'E
Al Ḩijāz, reg., Sau. Ar.	198	23°45'N	39°08'E
Al Hirmil, Leb.	197a	34°23'N	36°22'E
Alhos Vedros, Port. (äl'yōs'vā'drōs)	173b	38°39'N	9°02'W
Alhucemas, Baie d', b., Afr.	172	35°18'N	3°50'W
Al Ḩudaydah, Yemen	198	14°43'N	43°03'E
Al Hufūf, Sau. Ar.	198	25°15'N	49°43'E
Al Ḩulwān, Egypt (äl-hĕl'wän)	238b	29°51'N	31°20'E
Aliákmonas, r., Grc.	163	40°26'N	22°17'E
Āli Bayramlı, Azer.	182	39°56'N	48°56'E
Alibori, r., Benin	235	11°40'N	2°55'E
Alice, S. Afr. (ăl-ĭs)	233c	32°47'S	26°51'E
Alice, Tx., U.S. (ăl'ĭs)	122	27°45'N	98°04'W
Alice, Punta, c., Italy (ä-lē'chĕ)	175	39°23'N	17°10'E
Alice Arm, Can.	94	55°29'N	129°29'W
Alicedale, S. Afr. (ăl'ĭs-dāl)	233c	33°18'S	26°04'E
Alice Springs, Austl. (ăl'ĭs)	218	23°38'S	133°56'E
Alicudi, i., Italy (ä-lē-kōō'dē)	174	38°34'N	14°21'E
Alifkulovo, Russia (ä-lĭf-kû'lô-vô)	186a	55°57'N	62°06'E
Alīgarh, India (ä-lē-gŭr')	199	27°58'N	78°08'E
Alingsås, Swe. (ȧ'lĭŋ-sôs)	166	57°57'N	12°30'E
Aliquippa, Pa., U.S. (ăl-ĭ-kwĭp'ȧ)	111e	40°37'N	80°15'W
Al Iskandarīyah *see* Alexandria, Egypt	238b	31°12'N	29°58'E
Aliwal North, S. Afr. (ä-lē-wäl')	232	31°09'S	28°26'E
Al Jafr, Qa'al, pl., Jord.	197a	30°15'N	36°24'E
Al Jaghbūb, Libya	231	29°46'N	24°32'E
Al Jawārah, Oman	201	18°55'N	57°17'E
Al Jawf, Libya	231	24°14'N	23°15'E
Al Jawf, Sau. Ar.	198	29°45'N	39°30'E
Aljezur, Port. (äl-zhä-zōōr')	172	37°18'N	8°52'W
Al Jīzah, Egypt	238b	30°01'N	31°12'E
Al Jubayl, Sau. Ar.	198	27°01'N	49°40'E
Al Jufrah, oasis, Libya	231	29°30'N	15°16'E
Al Junaynah, Sudan	200	13°27'N	22°27'E
Aljustrel, Port. (äl-zhōō-strĕl')	172	37°44'N	8°23'W
Al Kāb, Egypt	238d	30°56'N	32°19'E
Al Kāmilīn, Sudan (käm-lēn')	231	15°09'N	33°06'E
Al Karak, Jord. (kĕ-räk')	197a	31°11'N	35°42'E
Al Karnak, Egypt (kär'nak)	238b	25°42'N	32°43'E
Al Khābūrah, Oman	198	23°45'N	57°30'E
Al Khalīl, W.B.	197a	31°31'N	35°07'E
Al Khandaq, Sudan (kän-däk')	231	18°38'N	30°29'E
Al Khārijah, Egypt	200	25°26'N	30°33'E
Al Khums, Libya	231	32°35'N	14°10'E
Al Khurmah, Sau. Ar.	198	21°37'N	41°44'E
Al Kiswah, Syria	197a	33°31'N	36°13'E
Alkmaar, Neth. (älk-mär')	165	52°39'N	4°42'E
Al Kufrah, oasis, Libya	231	24°45'N	22°45'E
Al Kuntillah, Egypt	197a	29°59'N	34°42'E
Al Kūt, Iraq	201	32°30'N	45°49'E
Al Kuwayt, Kuw. (äl-kōō-wit)	198	29°04'N	47°59'E
Al Lādhiqīyah, Syria	198	35°32'N	35°51'E
Allagash, r., Me., U.S. (ăl'ȧ-găsh)	100	46°50'N	69°24'W
Allāhābād, India (ŭl-ŭ-hä-bäd')	199	25°32'N	81°53'E
All American Canal, can., Ca., U.S. (âl ȧ-mĕr'ĭ-kăn)	118	32°43'N	115°12'W
Alland, Aus.	159e	48°04'N	16°05'E
Allariz, Spain (äl-yä-rēth')	162	42°10'N	7°48'W
Allatoona Lake, res., Ga., U.S. (ăl'ȧ-tōōn'ȧ)	124	34°05'N	84°57'W
Allauch, Fr. (ä-lĕ'ō)	170a	43°21'N	5°30'E
Allaykha, Russia (ä-lī'ĸȧ)	179	70°32'N	148°53'E
Allegan, Mi., U.S. (ăl'ê-găn)	108	42°30'N	85°55'W
Allegany Indian Reservation, I.R., N.Y., U.S. (ăl-ê-gā'nĭ)	109	42°05'N	78°55'W
Allegheny, r., Pa., U.S. (ăl-ê-gā'nĭ)	109	41°10'N	79°20'W
Allegheny Front, mtn., U.S. (ăl-ê-gā'nĭ)	108	38°12'N	80°03'W
Allegheny Mountains, mts., U.S. (ăl-ê-gā'nĭ)	107	37°35'N	81°55'W
Allegheny Plateau, plat., U.S. (ăl-ê-gā'nĭ)	108	39°00'N	81°15'W
Allegheny Reservoir, res., U.S. (ăl-ê-gā'nĭ)	109	41°50'N	78°55'W
Allen, Ok., U.S. (ăl'ĕn)	121	34°51'N	96°26'W
Allen, Lough, l., Ire. (lŏk ăl'ĕn)	164	54°07'N	8°09'W
Allendale, N.J., U.S. (ăl'ĕn-dāl)	110a	41°02'N	74°08'W
Allendale, S.C., U.S. (ăl'ĕn-dāl)	125	33°00'N	81°19'W
Allende, Mex. (äl-yĕn'då)	131	18°23'N	92°49'W
Allende, Mex.	122	28°20'N	100°50'W
Allentown, Pa., U.S. (ălĕn-toun)	105	40°35'N	75°30'W
Alleppey, India (ȧ-lĕp'ē)	203	9°33'N	76°22'E
Aller, r., Ger. (äl'ẽr)	168	52°43'N	9°50'E
Alliance, Ne., U.S. (ȧ-lī'ăns)	104	42°06'N	102°53'W
Alliance, Oh., U.S. (ȧ-lī'ăns)	108	40°55'N	81°10'W
Al Līdām, Sau. Ar.	198	20°45'N	44°12'E
Allier, r., Fr. (ȧ-lyā')	170	46°43'N	3°03'E
Alligator Point, c., La., U.S. (al'ĭ-gā-tẽr)	110d	30°57'N	89°41'W
Allinge, Den. (äl'ĭŋ-ĕ)	166	55°16'N	14°48'E
Al Līth, Sau. Ar.	201	20°09'N	40°16'E
All Pines, Belize (ôl pīnz)	132a	16°55'N	88°15'W
Al Luḩayyah, Yemen	198	15°58'N	42°48'E
Alluvial City, La., U.S.	110d	29°51'N	89°42'W
Allyn, Wa., U.S. (ăl'ĭn)	116a	47°23'N	122°51'W
Alma, Can. (ăl'mȧ)	100	45°36'N	64°59'W
Alma, Can.	91	48°29'N	71°42'W
Alma, S. Afr.	238c	24°30'S	28°05'E
Alma, Ga., U.S.	125	31°33'N	82°31'W
Alma, Mi., U.S.	108	43°25'N	84°40'W
Alma, Ne., U.S.	120	40°08'N	99°21'W
Alma, Wi., U.S.	113	44°21'N	91°57'W
Alma-Ata *see* Almaty, Kaz.	183	43°19'N	77°08'E
Almada, Port. (äl-mä'dä)	173b	38°40'N	9°09'W
Almadén, Spain (äl-mȧ-dhān)	172	38°47'N	4°50'W
Al Madīnah, Sau. Ar.	198	24°26'N	39°42'E
Al Mafraq, Jord.	197a	32°21'N	36°13'E
Almagre, Laguna, l., Mex. (lä-gô'nä-äl-mä'grĕ)	131	23°48'N	97°45'W
Almagro, Spain (äl-mä'grō)	172	38°52'N	3°41'W
Al Maḩallah al Kubrā, Egypt	238b	30°58'N	31°10'E
Al Manāmah, Bahr.	198	26°01'N	50°33'E
Almanor, Lake, l., Ca., U.S. (ăl-măn'ôr)	118	40°11'N	121°20'W
Almansa, Spain (äl-män'sä)	172	38°52'N	1°09'W
Al Manshāh, Egypt	238b	26°31'N	31°46'E
Almansor, r., Port. (äl-män-sôr)	172	38°41'N	8°27'W
Al Manşūrah, Egypt	231	31°02'N	31°25'E
Al Manzilah, Egypt (män'za-la)	238b	31°09'N	32°05'E
Almanzora, r., Spain (äl-män-thō'rä)	172	37°20'N	2°25'W
Al Marāghah, Egypt	238b	26°41'N	31°35'E
Almargem do Bispo, Port. (äl-mär-zhĕN)	173b	38°51'N	9°16'W
Al-Marj, Libya	231	32°44'N	21°08'E
Al Maşīrah, i., Oman	198	20°43'N	58°58'E
Almaty (Alma-Ata), Kaz.	183	43°19'N	77°08'E
Almaty, val., Sau. Ar.	197a	29°16'N	35°12'E
Al Mawşil, Iraq	198	36°00'N	42°53'E
Almazán, Spain (äl-mä-thän')	172	41°30'N	2°33'W
Al Mazār, Jord.	197a	31°04'N	35°41'E
Al Mazra'ah, Jord.	197a	31°17'N	35°33'E
Almeirim, Port. (äl-māĭ-rēN')	172	39°13'N	8°31'W
Almelo, Neth. (äl'mē-lō)	165	52°20'N	6°42'E

ăt; finăl; rāte; senåte; ärm; ȧsk; sofȧ; fâre; ch-choose; dh-as th in other; bē; ėvent; bĕt; recĕnt; cratẽr; g-gō; gh-guttural g; bĭt; ĭ-short neutral; rīde; ĸ-guttural k as ch in German ich;

PRONOUNCING INDEX Almendra – Andrelândia 265

PLACE (Pronunciation)	PAGE	LAT.	LONG.
Almendra, Embalse de, res., Spain	172	41°15'N	6°10'W
Almendralejo, Spain (äl-män-drä-lā'hō)	172	38°43'N	6°24'W
Almería, Spain (äl-mā-rē'ä)	154	36°52'N	2°28'W
Almería, Golfo de, b., Spain (gôl-fô-dĕ-äl-mäī-reɴ')	172	36°45'N	2°26'W
Älmhult, Swe. (älm'hoolt)	166	56°35'N	14°08'E
Almina, Punta, c., Mor. (äl-mē'nä)	172	35°58'N	5°17'W
Al Minyā, Egypt	231	28°06'N	30°45'E
Almirante, Pan. (äl-mē-rän'tā)	133	9°18'N	82°24'W
Almirante, Bahía de, b., Pan.	133	9°22'N	82°07'W
Almodóvar del Campo, Spain (äl-mō-dhō'vär)	172	38°43'N	4°10'W
Almoloya, Mex. (äl-mō-lō'yä)	130	19°32'N	99°44'W
Almoloya, Mex. (äl-mō-lō'yä)	131a	19°11'N	99°28'W
Almonte, Can. (äl-mŏn'tē)	99	45°15'N	76°15'W
Almonte, Spain (äl-mōn'tā)	172	37°16'N	6°32'W
Almonte, r., Spain (äl-mōn'tā)	172	39°35'N	5°50'W
Almora, India	199	29°20'N	79°40'E
Al Mubarraz, Sau. Ar.	198	22°31'N	46°27'E
Al Mudawwarah, Jord.	197a	29°20'N	36°01'E
Al Mukhā (Mocha), Yemen	198	13°11'N	43°20'E
Almuñécar, Spain (äl-moon-yā'kär)	172	36°44'N	3°43'W
Almyrós, Grc.	175	39°13'N	22°47'E
Alnön, i., Swe.	166	62°20'N	17°39'E
Aloha, Or., U.S. (ä'lō-hä)	116c	45°29'N	122°52'W
Alor, Pulau, i., Indon. (ä'lôr)	213	8°07'S	125°00'E
Álora, Spain (ä'lō-rä)	172	36°49'N	4°42'W
Alor Gajah, Malay.	197b	2°23'N	102°13'E
Alor Setar, Malay. (ä'lôr stär)	212	6°10'N	100°16'E
Alouette, r., Can. (ä-loo-ĕt')	116d	49°16'N	122°32'W
Alpena, Mi., U.S. (äl-pē'nȧ)	105	45°05'N	83°30'W
Alpes Cotiennes, mts., Eur.	171	44°46'N	7°02'E
Alphen, Neth.	159a	52°07'N	4°38'E
Alpiarça, Port. (äl-pyär'sȧ)	172	39°38'N	8°37'W
Alpine, Tx., U.S. (ăl'pīn)	122	30°21'N	103°41'W
Alps, mts., Eur. (ălps)	156	46°18'N	8°42'E
Alpujarra, Col. (äl-poo-ká'rä)	142a	3°23'N	74°56'W
Al Qaḍārif, Sudan	231	14°03'N	35°11'E
Al Qāhirah *see* Cairo, Egypt	231	30°00'N	31°17'E
Al Qanṭarah, Egypt	238d	30°51'N	32°20'E
Al Qaryah Ash Sharqīyah, Libya	231	30°36'N	13°13'E
Al Qaṣr, Egypt	200	25°42'N	28°53'E
Al Qaṭīf, Sau. Ar.	198	26°30'N	50°00'E
Al Qayṣūmah, Sau. Ar.	198	28°15'N	46°20'E
Al Qunaytirah, Syria	197a	33°09'N	35°49'E
Al Qunfudhah, Sau. Ar.	198	19°08'N	41°05'E
Al Quṣaymah, Egypt	197a	30°40'N	34°23'E
Al Quṣayr, Egypt	231	26°14'N	34°11'E
Al Qusayr, Syria	197a	34°32'N	36°33'E
Als, i., Den. (äls)	166	55°06'N	9°40'E
Alsace, hist. reg., Fr. (äl-sȧ's)	171	48°25'N	7°24'E
Altadena, Ca., U.S. (ăl-tä-dē'nä)	117a	34°12'N	118°08'W
Alta Gracia, Arg. (äl'tä grä'sē-a)	144	31°41'S	64°19'W
Altagracia, Ven.	142	10°42'N	71°34'W
Altagracia de Orituco, Ven.	143b	9°53'N	66°22'W
Altai Mountains, mts., Asia (äl'tī')	204	49°11'N	87°15'E
Alta Loma, Ca., U.S. (ăl'tă lō'mä)	117a	34°07'N	117°35'W
Alta Loma, Tx., U.S. (ăl'tȧ lō-mȧ)	123a	29°22'N	95°05'W
Altamaha, r., Ga., U.S. (ôl-tȧ-mȧ-hô')	125	31°50'N	82°00'W
Altamira, Braz. (äl-tä-mē'rä)	143	3°13'S	52°14'W
Altamira, Mex.	131	22°25'N	97°55'W
Altamirano, Arg. (äl-tä-mē-rä'nō)	144	35°26'S	58°12'W
Altamura, Italy (äl-tä-moo'rä)	163	40°40'N	16°35'E
Altavista, Va., U.S. (äl-tä-vĭs'tȧ)	125	37°08'N	79°14'W
Altay, China (äl-tä)	204	47°52'N	86°50'E
Altenburg, Ger. (äl-tĕn-boorgh)	168	50°59'N	12°27'E
Altenmarkt an der Triesting, Aus.	159e	48°02'N	16°00'E
Alter do Chão, Port. (äl-tĕr'dò shäɴ'ōɴ)	172	39°13'N	7°38'W
Altiplano, pl., Bol. (äl-tē-plá'nō)	142	18°38'S	68°20'W
Altlandsberg, Ger. (ält länts'bĕrgh)	159b	52°34'N	13°44'E
Alto, La., U.S. (ăl'tō)	123	32°21'N	91°52'W
Alto Marañón, r., Peru (ȧl'tô-mä-rän-yō'n)	142	8°18'S	77°13'W
Altomünster, Ger. (äl'tō-mün'stĕr)	159d	48°24'N	11°16'E
Alton, Can. (ôl'tŭn)	102d	43°52'N	80°05'W
Alton, Il., U.S. (ôl'tŭn)	105	38°53'N	90°11'W
Altona, Austl.	217a	37°52'S	144°50'E
Altona, Can.	97	49°06'N	97°33'W
Altona, Ger. (äl'tō-nȧ)	159c	53°33'N	9°54'E
Altoona, Al., U.S. (ăl-too'nȧ)	124	34°01'N	86°15'W
Altoona, Pa., U.S. (ăl-too'nȧ)	105	40°25'N	78°25'W
Altoona, Wa., U.S. (ăl-too'nȧ)	116c	46°16'N	123°39'W
Alto Rio Doce, Braz. (äl'tô-rē'ô-dō'sĕ)	141a	21°02'S	43°23'W
Alto Songo, Cuba (äl-fō-sôŋ'gō)	135	20°10'N	75°45'W
Altotonga, Mex. (äl-tō-tôŋ'gä)	131	19°44'N	97°13'W
Alto Velo, i., Dom. Rep. (äl-tō-vĕ'lō)	135	17°30'N	71°35'W
Altrincham, Eng., U.K. (ôl'trĭng-ăm)	158a	53°18'N	2°21'W
Altruppin, Ger. (ält roo'ppēn)	159b	52°56'N	12°50'E
Altun Shan, mts., China (äl-tón shän)	204	36°58'N	85°09'E
Alturas, Ca., U.S. (ăl-too'rȧs)	114	41°29'N	120°33'W
Altus, Ok., U.S. (ăl'tŭs)	120	34°38'N	99°20'W
Al 'Ubaylah, Sau. Ar.	201	21°59'N	50°57'E
Al-Uḍayyah, Sudan	231	12°06'N	28°16'E
Alūksne, Lat. (ä'lòks-nĕ)	180	57°24'N	27°04'E
Alumette Island, i., Can. (ȧ-lü-mĕt')	99	45°50'N	77°00'W
Alum Rock, Ca., U.S.	116b	37°23'N	121°50'W
Al 'Uqaylah, Libya	231	30°15'N	19°07'E
Al Uqṣur, Egypt	231	25°38'N	32°59'E
Alushta, Ukr. (ä'lshò-tȧ)	177	44°39'N	34°23'E
Alva, Ok., U.S. (ăl'vȧ)	120	36°46'N	98°41'W

PLACE (Pronunciation)	PAGE	LAT.	LONG.
Alvarado, Mex. (äl-vä-rä'dhō)	131	18°48'N	95°45'W
Alvarado, Luguna de, l., Mex. (lä-gò'nä-dĕ-äl-vä-rá'dò)	131	18°44'N	95°45'W
Älvdalen, Swe. (ĕlv'dä-lĕn)	166	61°14'N	14°04'E
Alverca, Port. (al-vĕr'kȧ)	173b	38°53'N	9°02'W
Alvesta, Swe. (äl-vĕs'tä)	166	56°55'N	14°29'E
Alvin, Tx., U.S. (ăl'vĭn)	123a	29°25'N	95°14'W
Alvinópolis, Braz. (äl-vēnō'pō-lēs)	141a	20°07'S	43°03'W
Alviso, Ca., U.S. (ăl-vī'sō)	116b	37°26'N	121°59'W
Al Wajh, Sau. Ar.	198	26°15'N	36°32'E
Alwar, India (ŭl'wŭr)	199	27°39'N	76°39'E
Al Wāsiṭah, Egypt	238b	29°21'N	31°15'E
Alytus, Lith. (ä'lē-tòs)	167	54°25'N	24°05'E
Amacuzac, r., Mex. (ä-mä-koo-zäk)	130	18°00'N	99°03'W
Amadeus, l., Austl. (ăm-ȧ-dē'ŭs)	220	24°30'S	131°25'E
Amadjuak, l., Can. (ä-mädj'wäk)	93	64°50'N	69°20'W
Amadora, Port.	173b	38°45'N	9°14'W
Amagasaki, Japan (ä'mä-gä-sä'kē)	211	34°43'N	135°25'E
Amakusa-Shimo, i., Japan (ämä-koo'sä shē-mō)	210	32°24'N	129°35'E
Åmål, Swe. (ô'mòl)	166	59°05'N	12°40'E
Amalfi, Col. (ä'má'l-fē)	142a	6°55'N	75°04'W
Amalfi, Italy (ä-mä'l-fē)	173c	40°23'N	14°36'E
Amaliáda, Grc.	175	37°48'N	21°23'E
Amalner, India	202	21°07'N	75°06'E
Amambai, Serra de, mts., S.A.	143	20°06'S	57°08'W
Amami, i., Japan	205	28°10'N	129°55'E
Amapala, Hond. (ä-mä-pä'lä)	132	13°16'N	87°39'W
Amarante, Braz. (ä-mä-rän'tā)	143	6°17'S	42°43'W
Amargosa, r., Ca., U.S. (ȧ'mär-gō'sȧ)	118	35°55'N	116°45'W
Amarillo, Tx., U.S. (ăm-ȧ-rĭl'ō)	104	35°14'N	101°49'W
Amaro, Mount, mtn., Italy (ä-mä'rō)	162	42°07'N	14°07'E
Amasya, Tur. (ä-mä'sē-ȧ)	163	40°40'N	35°50'E
Amatenango, Mex. (ä-mä-tä-naŋ'gō)	131	16°30'N	92°29'W
Amatignak, i., Ak., U.S. (ä-má'tē-näk)	103a	51°12'N	178°30'W
Amatique, Bahía de, b., N.A. (bä-ē'ä-dĕ-ä-mä-tē'kä)	132	15°58'N	88°50'W
Amatitlán, Guat. (ä-mä-tē-tlän')	132	14°27'N	90°39'W
Amatlán de Cañas, Mex. (ä-mät-län'dā kän-yäs)	130	20°50'N	104°22'W
Amazon (Amazonas) (Solimões), r., S.A.	143	2°03'S	53°18'W
Amazonas, state, Braz. (ä-mä-thō'näs)	142	4°15'S	64°30'W
Ambāla, India (ŭm-bä'lŭ)	199	30°31'N	76°48'E
Ambalema, Col. (äm-bä-lā'mä)	142	4°47'N	74°45'W
Ambarchik, Russia (ŭm-bär'chĭk)	179	69°39'N	162°18'E
Ambarnāth, India	203b	19°12'N	73°10'E
Ambato, Ec. (äm-bä'tō)	142	1°15'S	78°30'W
Ambatondrazaka, Madag.	233	17°58'S	48°43'E
Amberg, Ger. (äm'bĕrgh)	168	49°26'N	11°51'E
Ambergris Cay, i., Belize (ăm'bēr-grēs kāz)	132a	18°04'N	87°43'W
Ambergris Cays, is., T./C. Is.	135	21°20'N	71°40'W
Ambérieu-en-Bugey, Fr. (äɴ-bā-rē-u')	171	45°57'N	5°21'E
Ambert, Fr. (äɴ-bĕr')	170	45°32'N	3°41'E
Ambil Island, i., Phil. (äm'bēl)	213a	13°51'N	120°25'E
Ambler, Pa., U.S. (ăm'blẽr)	110f	40°09'N	75°13'W
Amboise, Fr. (äɴ-bwăz')	170	47°25'N	0°56'E
Ambon, Indon.	213	3°45'S	128°17'E
Ambon, Pulau, i., Indon.	213	4°50'S	128°45'E
Ambositra, Madag. (äɴ-bô-sē'trä)	233	20°31'S	47°28'E
Amboy, Il., U.S. (ăm'boi)	108	41°41'N	89°15'W
Amboy, Wa., U.S. (ăm'boi)	116c	45°55'N	122°27'W
Ambre, Cap d', c., Madag.	233	12°06'S	49°15'E
Ambridge, Pa., U.S. (ăm'brĭdj)	111e	40°36'N	80°13'W
Ambrim, i., Vanuatu	221	16°25'S	168°15'E
Ambriz, Ang.	232	7°50'S	13°06'E
Amchitka, i., Ak., U.S. (ăm-chĭt'kȧ)	103a	51°25'N	178°10'E
Amchitka Passage, strt., Ak., U.S. (ăm-chĭt'kȧ)	103a	51°30'N	179°36'W
Amealco, Mex. (ä-mā-äl'kō)	130	20°12'N	100°08'W
Ameca, Mex. (ä-mĕ'kä)	128	20°34'N	104°02'W
Amecameca, Mex. (ä-må-kä-mā'kä)	130	19°06'N	98°46'W
Ameide, Neth.	159a	51°57'N	4°57'E
Ameland, i., Neth.	165	53°29'N	5°54'E
Amelia, Oh., U.S. (ȧ-mēl'yȧ)	111f	39°01'N	84°12'W
American, South Fork, r., Ca., U.S. (ȧ-mĕr'ĭ-kăn)	118	38°43'N	120°45'W
Americana, Braz. (ä-mĕ-rē-kä'nȧ)	141a	22°46'S	47°19'W
American Falls, Id., U.S. (ȧ-mĕr'ĭ-kăn-fôls')	115	42°45'N	112°53'W
American Falls Reservoir, res., Id., U.S. (ȧ-mĕr'ĭ-kăn-fôls')	106	42°56'N	113°18'W
American Fork, Ut., U.S.	119	40°20'N	111°50'W
American Highland, plat., Ant.	224	72°00'S	79°00'E
American Samoa, dep., Oc.	2	14°20'S	170°00'W
Americus, Ga., U.S. (ȧ-mĕr'ĭ-kŭs)	105	32°04'N	84°15'W
Amersfoort, Neth. (ä'mẽrz-fōrt)	159a	52°08'N	5°23'E
Amery, Can. (ā'mẽr-ē)	91	56°34'N	94°03'W
Amery, Wi., U.S.	113	45°19'N	92°24'W
Ames, Ia., U.S. (āmz)	113	42°00'N	93°36'W
Amesbury, Ma., U.S. (āmz'bēr-ē)	101a	42°51'N	70°56'W
Amfissa, Grc. (ȧm-fĭ'sȧ)	175	38°32'N	22°26'E
Amga, Russia (ŭm-gä')	179	61°08'N	132°09'E
Amga, r., Russia	185	61°41'N	133°11'E
Amgun', r., Russia	185	52°30'N	138°00'E
Amherst, Can. (ăm'hẽrst)	91	45°49'N	64°14'W
Amherst, Oh., U.S.	111d	41°24'N	82°13'W
Amherst, i., Can. (ăm'hẽrst)	99	44°08'N	76°45'W
Amiens, Fr. (ä-myăɴ')	161	49°54'N	2°18'E
Amirante Islands, is., Sey.	5	6°02'S	52°30'E
Amisk Lake, l., Can.	97	54°35'N	102°13'W
Amistad Reservoir, res., N.A.	122	29°20'N	101°00'W
Amite, La., U.S. (ă-mēt')	123	30°43'N	90°32'W

PLACE (Pronunciation)	PAGE	LAT.	LONG.
Amite, r., La., U.S.	123	30°45'N	90°48'W
Amity, Pa., U.S. (ăm'ĭ-tĭ)	111e	40°02'N	80°11'W
Amityville, N.Y., U.S. (ăm'ĭ-tĭ-vĭl)	110a	40°41'N	73°24'W
Amlia, i., Ak., U.S. (ȧ'mlēä)	103a	52°00'N	173°28'W
'Ammān, Jord. (äm'mán)	198	31°57'N	35°57'E
Ammersee, l., Ger. (äm'mĕr)	159d	48°00'N	11°08'E
Amnicon, r., Wi., U.S. (ăm'nė-kŏn)	117h	46°35'N	91°56'W
Amorgós, i., Grc. (ä-môr'gōs)	163	36°47'N	25°47'E
Amory, Ms., U.S. (āmô-rē)	124	33°58'N	88°27'W
Amos, Can. (ā'mŭs)	91	48°31'N	78°04'W
Amoy *see* Xiamen, China	205	24°30'N	118°10'E
Amparo, Braz. (äm-pȧ'-rô)	141a	22°43'S	46°44'W
Amper, r., Ger. (äm'pĕr)	159d	48°18'N	11°32'E
Amposta, Spain (äm-pōs'tä)	173	40°42'N	0°34'E
Amqui, Can.	100	48°28'N	67°28'W
Amrāvati, India	199	20°58'N	77°47'E
Amritsar, India (ŭm-rĭt'sŭr)	199	31°43'N	74°52'E
Amstelveen, Neth.	159a	52°18'N	4°51'E
Amsterdam, Neth. (äm-stĕr-däm')	154	52°21'N	4°52'E
Amsterdam, N.Y., U.S. (ăm'stẽr-dăm)	109	42°55'N	74°10'W
Amsterdam, Île, i., Afr.	224	37°52'S	77°32'E
Amstetten, Aus. (äm'stĕt-ĕn)	168	48°09'N	14°53'E
Am Timan, Chad (äm'tē-män')	231	11°18'N	20°30'E
Amu Darya, r., Asia (ä-mó-dä'rēä)	178	38°30'N	64°00'E
Amukta Passage, strt., Ak., U.S. (ä-mook'tȧ)	103a	52°30'N	172°00'W
Amundsen Gulf, b., Can. (ä'mŭn-sĕn-gŭlf)	92	70°17'N	123°28'W
Amundsen Sea, sea, Ant. (ä'mŭn-sĕn-sē')	224	72°00'S	110°00'W
Amungen, l., Swe.	166	61°07'N	16°00'E
Amur, r., Asia	179	49°00'N	136°00'E
Amurskiy, Russia (ä-mûr'skĭ)	186a	52°35'N	59°36'E
Amurskiy, Zaliv, b., Russia (zä'lĭf ä-mòr'skĭ)	210	43°20'N	131°40'E
Amusgos, Mex.	130	16°39'N	98°09'W
Amuyao, Mount, mtn., Phil. (ä-moo-yä'ō)	213a	17°04'N	121°09'E
Amvrakikos Kólpos, b., Grc.	175	39°00'N	21°00'E
Amyun, Leb.	197a	34°18'N	35°48'E
Anabar, r., Russia (ăn-ȧ-băr')	185	71°15'N	113°00'E
Anaco, Ven. (ä-ná'kô)	143b	9°29'N	64°27'W
Anaconda, Mt., U.S. (ăn-ȧ-kŏn'dȧ)	104	46°07'N	112°55'W
Anacortes, Wa., U.S. (ăn-ȧ-kôr'tĕz)	116a	48°30'N	122°37'W
Anadarko, Ok., U.S. (ăn-ȧ-där'kō)	120	35°05'N	98°14'W
Anadyr', Russia (ŭ-nȧ-dĭr')	179	64°47'N	177°01'E
Anadyr, r., Russia	185	65°30'N	172°45'E
Anadyrskiy Zaliv, b., Russia	178	64°10'N	178°00'W
Anaheim, Ca., U.S. (ăn'ȧ-hīm)	117a	33°50'N	117°55'W
Anahuac, Tx., U.S. (ä-nä'wäk)	123a	29°46'N	94°41'W
Ānai Mudi, mtn., India	203	10°10'N	77°00'E
Anama Bay, Can.	97	51°56'N	98°05'W
Ana María, Cayos, is., Cuba	134	21°25'N	78°50'W
Anambas, Kepulauan, is., Indon. (ä-näm-bäs)	212	2°41'N	106°38'E
Anamosa, Ia., U.S. (ăn-ȧ-mō'sȧ)	113	42°06'N	91°18'W
Anan'ïv, Ukr.	181	47°43'N	29°59'E
Anapa, Russia (á-ná'pä)	181	44°54'N	37°19'E
Anápolis, Braz. (ä-ná'pō-lēs)	143	16°17'S	48°47'W
Añatuya, Arg. (ä-nyä-too'yȧ)	144	28°22'S	62°45'W
Anchieta, Braz. (ȧn-chyĕ'tä)	144b	22°49'S	43°24'W
Ancholme, r., Eng., U.K. (ăn'chŭm)	158a	53°28'N	0°27'W
Anchorage, Ak., U.S. (ăŋ'kẽr-āj)	106a	61°12'N	149°48'W
Anchorage, Ky., U.S.	111h	38°16'N	85°32'W
Anci, China (ăn-tsŭ)	206	39°31'N	116°41'E
Ancienne-Lorette, Can. (äɴ-syĕn' lō-rĕt')	102b	46°48'N	71°21'W
Ancon, Pan. (ăŋ-kōn')	128a	8°55'N	79°32'W
Ancona, Italy (än-kō'nä)	154	43°37'N	13°32'E
Ancud, Chile (äŋ-koodh')	144	41°52'S	73°45'W
Ancud, Golfo de, b., Chile (gôl-fô-dĕ-äŋ-koodh')	144	41°15'S	73°00'W
Anda, China	208	46°20'N	125°20'E
Åndalsnes, Nor.	166	62°33'N	7°46'E
Andalucia, hist. reg., Spain (än-dä-loo-sē'ä)	172	37°35'N	5°40'W
Andalusia, Al., U.S. (ăn-dȧ-loo'zhĭȧ)	124	31°19'N	86°19'W
Andaman Islands, is., India (ăn-dȧ-măn')	212	11°38'N	92°17'E
Andaman Sea, sea, Asia	212	12°44'N	95°45'E
Andarax, r., Spain	172	37°00'N	2°40'W
Anderlecht, Bel. (än'dĕr-lĕkt)	159a	50°49'N	4°16'E
Andernach, Ger. (än'dĕr-näk)	168	50°25'N	7°23'E
Anderson, Arg. (ȧ'n-dĕr-sōn)	141c	35°15'S	60°15'W
Anderson, Ca., U.S. (ăn'dẽr-sŭn)	114	40°28'N	122°19'W
Anderson, In., U.S. (ăn'dẽr-sŭn)	108	40°05'N	85°50'W
Anderson, S.C., U.S. (ăn'dẽr-sŭn)	105	34°30'N	82°40'W
Anderson, r., Can. (ăn'dẽr-sŭn)	92	68°32'N	125°12'W
Andes Mountains, mts., S.A. (ăn'dēz) (än'dās)	139	13°00'S	75°00'W
Andheri, neigh., India	203b	19°08'N	72°50'E
Andhra Pradesh, state, India	199	16°00'N	79°00'E
Andikýthira, i., Grc.	163	35°50'N	23°20'E
Andizhan, Uzb. (än-dē-zhän')	183	40°45'N	72°22'E
Andong, Kor., S. (än'dŭng')	205	36°31'N	128°42'E
Andongwei, China (än-dôŋ-wā)	206	35°08'N	119°19'E
Andorra, And. (än-dôr'rä)	173	42°38'N	1°30'E
Andorra, nation, Eur. (än-dôr'rä)	154	42°30'N	2°00'E
Andover, Ma., U.S. (ăn'dô-vẽr)	101a	42°39'N	71°08'W
Andover, N.J., U.S. (ăn'dô-vẽr)	110a	40°59'N	74°45'W
Andøya, i., Nor. (änd-ûê)	160	69°12'N	14°58'E
Andreanof Islands, is., Ak., U.S. (än-drä-ä'nôf-ĭ'ăndz)	106b	51°10'N	177°00'W
Andrelândia, Braz. (än-drĕ-lá'n-dyä)	141a	21°45'S	44°18'W

266 Andrew Johnson National Historic Site – Archidona PRONOUNCING INDEX

PLACE (Pronunciation)	PAGE	LAT.	LONG.
Andrew Johnson National Historic Site, rec., Tn., U.S. (ăn'drōō jŏn'sŭn)	125	36°15'N	82°55'W
Andrews, N.C., U.S. (ăn'drōōz)	124	35°12'N	83°48'W
Andrews, S.C., U.S. (ăn'drōōz)	125	33°25'N	79°32'W
Andria, Italy (än'drē-ä)	163	41°17'N	15°55'E
Andros, Grc. (án'dhrôs)	175	37°50'N	24°54'E
Ándros, i., Grc. (àn'drôs)	163	37°59'N	24°55'E
Androscoggin, r., Me., U.S. (ăn-drŭs-kŏg'ĭn)	100	44°25'N	70°45'W
Andros Island, i., Bah. (ăn'drŏs)	129	24°30'N	78°00'W
Anefis i-n-Darane, Mali	234	18°03'N	0°36'E
Anegasaki, Japan (ä'nå-gä-sä'kê)	211a	35°29'N	140°02'E
Aneityum, i., Vanuatu (ä-nå-ē'tē-ŭm)	221	20°15'S	169°49'E
Aneta, N.D., U.S. (ă-nē'tà)	112	47°41'N	97°57'W
Aneto, Pico de, mtn., Spain (pē'kō-dĕ-ä-nĕ'tô)	156	42°35'N	0°38'E
Angamacutiro, Mex. (än'gä-mä-kōō-tē'rô)	130	20°08'N	101°44'W
Angangueo, Mex. (än-gäŋ'gwå-ō)	130	19°36'N	100°18'W
Ang'angxi, China (äŋ-äŋ-shyē)	205	47°05'N	123°58'E
Angarsk, Russia	179	52°48'N	104°15'E
Ånge, Swe. (ông'ĕ)	166	62°31'N	15°39'E
Angel, Salto, wtfl., Ven. (säl'tō-ä'n-hĕl)	142	5°44'N	62°27'W
Ángel de la Guarda, i., Mex. (á'n-hĕl-dĕ-lä-gwä'r-dä)	128	29°30'N	113°00'W
Angeles, Phil. (än'hå-läs)	213a	15°09'N	120°35'E
Ängelholm, Swe. (ĕng'ĕl-hôlm)	166	56°14'N	12°50'E
Angelina, r., Tx., U.S. (ăn-jê lē'nà)	123	31°30'N	94°53'W
Angels Camp, Ca., U.S. (ān'jĕls kămp')	118	38°03'N	120°33'W
Ångermanälven, r., Swe.	160	64°10'N	17°30'E
Angermund, Ger. (án'ngĕr-mŭnd)	171c	51°20'N	6°47'E
Angermünde, Ger. (äng'ĕr-mûn-dĕ)	168	53°02'N	14°00'E
Angers, Can. (äɴ-zhā')	102c	45°31'N	75°29'W
Angers, Fr.	170	47°29'N	0°36'W
Angkor, hist., Camb. (äng'kôr)	212	13°52'N	103°50'E
Anglesey, i., Wales, U.K. (ăŋ'g'l-sê)	164	53°35'N	4°28'W
Angleton, Tx., U.S. (aŋ'g'l-tŭn)	123a	29°10'N	95°25'W
Angmagssalik, Grnld. (àŋ-má'sá-lĭk)	89	65°40'N	37°40'W
Angoche, Ilha, i., Moz. (ē'lä-ăn-gō'chå)	233	16°20'S	40°00'E
Angol, Chile (aŋ-gōl')	144	37°47'S	72°43'W
Angola, In., U.S. (ăŋ-gō'lå)	108	41°35'S	85°00'W
Angola, nation, Afr. (ăŋ-gō'lå)	232	14°15'S	16°00'E
Angora *see* Ankara, Tur.	198	39°55'N	32°50'E
Angoulême, Fr. (äŋ'gōō-lâm')	170	45°40'N	0°09'E
Angra dos Reis, Braz. (aŋ'grä dōs rā'ēs)	141a	23°01'S	44°17'W
Angri, Italy (ä'n-grē)	173c	40°30'N	14°35'E
Anguang, China (än-gůäŋ)	208	45°28'N	123°42'E
Anguilla, dep., N.A.	129	18°15'N	62°54'W
Anguilla Cays, is., Bah. (ăŋ-gwĭl'á)	134	23°30'N	79°35'W
Anguille, Cape, c., Can. (kāp'-äŋ-gē'yĕ)	101	47°55'N	59°25'W
Anguo, China (än-gwō)	206	38°27'N	115°19'E
Anholt, i., Den. (än'hŏlt)	166	56°43'N	11°34'E
Anhui, prov., China (än-hwā)	205	31°30'N	117°15'E
Aniak, Ak., U.S. (ä-nyà'k)	103	61°32'N	159°35'W
Aniakchak National Monument, rec., Ak., U.S.	104	56°50'N	157°50'W
Animas, r., Co., U.S. (ä'nê-más)	119	37°03'N	107°50'W
Anina, Rom. (ä-nē'nä)	175	45°03'N	21°50'E
Anita, Pa., U.S. (à-nē'á)	109	41°05'N	79°00'W
Aniva, Mys, c., Russia (mĭs à-nē'vå)	210	46°08'N	143°13'E
Aniva, Zaliv, b., Russia (zä'lĭf à-nē'vå)	210	46°30'N	143°00'E
Anjou, Can.	102a	45°37'N	73°33'W
Ankang, China (än-käŋ)	204	32°38'N	109°10'E
Ankara, Tur. (än'ká-rá)	198	39°55'N	32°50'E
Anklam, Ger. (än'kläm)	168	53°52'N	13°43'E
Ankoro, D.R.C. (ăŋ-kō'rō)	232	6°45'S	26°57'E
Anloga, Ghana	234	5°47'N	0°50'E
Anlong, China (än-loŋ)	209	25°01'N	105°32'E
Anlu, China (än'lōō')	209	31°18'N	113°40'E
Ann, Cape, c., Ma., U.S. (kăp'ăn')	109	42°40'N	70°40'W
Anna, Russia (än'ä)	177	51°31'N	40°27'E
Anna, Il., U.S. (ăn'á)	121	37°28'N	89°15'W
Annaba, Alg.	230	36°57'N	7°39'E
Annaberg-Bucholz, Ger. (än'ä-bĕrgh)	168	50°35'N	13°02'E
An Nafūd, des., Sau. Ar.	198	28°30'N	40°30'E
An Najaf, Iraq (än nä-jäf')	198	32°00'N	44°25'E
An Nakhl, Egypt	197a	29°55'N	33°45'E
Annamese Cordillera, mts., Asia	212	17°34'N	105°38'E
Annapolis, Md., U.S. (ă-năp'ô-lĭs)	105	39°00'N	76°25'W
Annapolis Royal, Can.	100	44°45'N	65°31'W
Ann Arbor, Mi., U.S. (ăn är'bēr)	105	42°15'N	83°45'W
An Nāşirīyah, Iraq	198	31°08'N	46°15'E
An Nawfalīyah, Libya	231	30°57'N	17°38'E
Annecy, Fr. (àn sē')	171	45°54'N	6°07'E
Annemasse, Fr. (än'mäs')	171	46°09'N	6°13'E
Annette Island, i., Ak., U.S.	94	55°13'N	131°30'W
An Nhon, Viet.	212	13°55'N	109°00'E
Annieopsquotch Mountains, mts., Can.	101	48°37'N	57°17'W
Anniston, Al., U.S. (ăn'ĭs-tŭn)	105	33°39'N	85°47'W
Annobón, i., Eq. Gui.	229	2°00'S	3°30'E
Annonay, Fr. (àn'ô-nĕ)	170	45°16'N	4°36'E
Annotto Bay, Jam. (än-nō'tō)	134	18°15'N	76°45'W
An Nuhūd, Sudan	231	12°39'N	28°18'E
Anoka, Mn., U.S. (à-nō'ká)	117g	45°12'N	93°24'W
Anori, Col. (à-nō'rē)	142a	7°01'N	75°09'W
Áno Viánnos, Grc.	174a	35°02'N	25°26'E
Anpu, China (än-pōō)	204	21°28'N	110°00'E
Anqiu, China (än-chyō)	206	36°26'N	119°12'E
Ansbach, Ger. (äns'bäk)	168	49°18'N	10°35'E

PLACE (Pronunciation)	PAGE	LAT.	LONG.
Anse à Veau, Haiti (äɴs' ä-vō')	135	18°30'N	73°25'W
Anse d'Hainault, Haiti (äɴs'dĕnō)	135	18°30'N	74°25'W
Anserma, Col. (á'n-sĕ'r-mä)	142a	5°13'N	75°47'W
Ansermanuevo, Col. (á'n-sĕ'r-mä-nwĕ'vō)	142a	4°47'N	75°59'W
Anshan, China	208	41°00'N	123°00'E
Anshun, China (än-shōōn')	204	26°12'N	105°50'E
Anson, Tx., U.S. (ăn'sŭn)	122	32°45'N	99°52'W
Anson Bay, b., Austl.	220	13°10'S	130°00'E
Ansŏng, Kor., S. (än'sŭng')	210	37°00'N	127°12'E
Ansongo, Mali	234	15°40'N	0°30'E
Ansonia, Ct., U.S. (ăn-sō'nĭ-á)	109	41°20'N	73°05'W
Antalya, Tur. (än-tä'lē-ä) (ä-dä'lē-ä)	163	37°00'N	30°50'E
Antalya Körfezi, b., Tur.	163	36°40'N	31°20'E
Antananarivo, Madag.	233	18°51'S	47°40'E
Antarctica, cont.	224	80°15'S	127°00'E
Antarctic Peninsula, pen., Ant.	224	70°00'S	65°00'W
Antelope Creek, r., Wy., U.S. (ăn'tê-lōp)	115	43°29'N	105°42'W
Antequera, Spain (än-tĕ-kĕ'rä)	162	37°01'N	4°34'W
Anthony, Ks., U.S. (ăn'thô-nê)	120	37°08'N	98°01'W
Anthony Peak, mtn., Ca., U.S.	118	39°51'N	122°58'W
Anti Atlas, mts., Mor.	230	28°45'N	9°30'W
Antibes, Fr. (äɴ-tēb')	171	43°36'N	7°12'E
Anticosti, Île d', i., Can. (ăn-tĭ-kŏs'tē)	93	49°30'N	62°00'W
Antigo, Wi., U.S. (ăn'tĭ-gō)	113	45°09'N	89°11'W
Antigonish, Can. (ăn-tĭ-gô-nēsh')	101	45°35'N	61°55'W
Antigua, Guat. (än-tē'gwä)	128	14°32'N	90°43'W
Antigua, r., Mex.	131	19°16'N	96°36'W
Antigua and Barbuda, nation, N.A.	129	17°15'N	61°15'W
Antigua Veracruz, Mex. (än-tē'gwä vā-rä-krōōz')	131	19°18'N	96°17'W
Antilla, Cuba (än-tē'lyä)	135	20°50'N	75°50'W
Antioch, Ca., U.S. (ăn'tĭ-ŏk)	116b	38°00'N	121°48'W
Antioch, Il., U.S.	111a	42°29'N	88°06'W
Antioch, Ne., U.S.	112	42°05'N	102°36'W
Antioquia, Col. (än-tē-ō'kēä)	142	6°34'N	75°49'W
Antioquia, dept., Col.	142a	6°48'N	75°42'W
Antlers, Ok., U.S. (ănt'lērz)	121	34°14'N	95°38'W
Antofagasta, Chile (än-tô-fä-gäs'tä)	144	23°32'S	70°21'W
Antofalla, Salar de, pl., Arg. (sà-lár'de án'tō-fä'lä)	144	26°00'S	67°52'W
Antón, Pan. (än-tōn')	129	8°24'N	80°15'W
Antongila, Helodrano, b., Madag.	233	16°15'S	50°15'E
Antônio Carlos, Braz. (än-tō'nēō-kà'r-lôs)	141a	21°19'S	43°45'W
António Enes, Moz. (ăn-to'nyō ĕn'ēs)	233	16°14'S	39°58'E
Antonito, Co., U.S. (ăn-tô-nē'tō)	120	37°04'N	106°01'W
Antonopole, Lat. (än'tô-nô-pō lyĕ)	167	56°19'N	27°11'E
Antony, Fr.	171b	48°45'N	2°18'E
Antsirabe, Madag. (änt-sê-rä'bā)	233	19°49'S	47°16'E
Antsiranana, Madag.	233	12°18'S	49°16'E
Antsla, Est. (änt'slá)	167	57°49'N	26°29'E
Antuco, vol., S.A. (än-tōō'kō)	144	37°30'S	72°30'W
Antwerp, Bel.	154	51°13'N	4°24'E
Antwerpen *see* Antwerp, Bel.	154	51°13'N	4°24'E
Anūpgarh, India (ŭ-nòp'gŭr)	202	29°22'N	73°20'E
Anuradhapura, Sri L. (ŭ-nōō'rä-dŭ-pōō'rŭ)	203	8°24'N	80°25'E
Anxi, China (än-shyē)	204	40°36'N	95°49'E
Anyang, China (än'yäng)	205	36°05'N	114°22'E
Anykščiai, Lith. (anĭksh-chä'ê)	167	55°34'N	25°04'E
Anzhero-Sudzhensk, Russia (än'zhâ-rô-sòd'zhĕnsk)	178	56°08'N	86°08'E
Anzio, Italy (änt'zê-ō)	174	41°28'N	12°39'E
Anzoátegui, dept., Ven. (àn-zôà'tĕ-gê)	143b	9°38'N	64°45'W
Aoba, i., Vanuatu	214f	15°25'S	167°50'E
Aomori, Japan (äô-mō'rê)	205	40°45'N	140°52'E
Aoraki (Cook, Mount), mtn., N.Z.	221a	43°27'S	170°13'E
Aosta, Italy (ä-ôs'tä)	174	45°45'N	7°20'E
Aouk, Bahr, r., Afr. (ä-ōk')	231	9°30'N	20°45'E
Aoukâr, reg., Maur.	234	18°00'N	9°40'W
Apalachicola, Fl., U.S. (ăp-á-lăch-ĭ-kō'lá)	124	29°43'N	84°59'W
Apan, Mex. (ä-pä'n)	130	19°43'N	98°27'W
Apango, Mex. (ä-päŋ'gō)	130	17°41'N	99°22'W
Apaporis, r., S.A. (ä-pä-pō'rĭs)	142	0°48'N	72°32'W
Aparri, Phil. (ä-pär'rē)	212	18°15'N	121°40'E
Apasco, Mex. (ä-pà's-kō)	130	20°33'N	100°43'W
Apatin, Serb. (ŏ'pŏ-tĭn)	175	45°40'N	19°00'E
Apatzingán de la Constitución, Mex.	130	19°07'N	102°21'W
Apeldoorn, Neth. (ä'pĕl-dōōrn)	161	52°14'N	5°55'E
Apennines *see* Appennino, mts., Italy	156	43°48'N	11°06'E
Apía, Col. (à-pē'ä)	142a	5°07'N	75°58'W
Apia, Samoa	214a	13°50'S	171°44'W
Apipilulco, Mex. (ä-pĭ-pĭ-lōōl'kō)	130	18°09'N	99°40'W
Apishapa, r., Co., U.S. (ăp-ĭ-shä'pá)	120	37°40'N	104°08'W
Apizaco, Mex. (ä-pê-zä'kō)	130	19°18'N	98°11'W
Apo, Mount, mtn., Phil. (ä'pō)	213	6°56'N	125°05'E
Apopka, Fl., U.S. (ä-pŏp'ká)	125a	28°37'N	81°30'W
Apopka, Lake, l., Fl., U.S.	125a	28°38'N	81°50'W
Apostle Islands, is., Wi., U.S. (ă-pŏs'l)	113	47°05'N	90°55'W
Appalachia, Va., U.S. (ăpá-lăch'ĭ-á)	125	36°54'N	82°49'W
Appalachian Mountains, mts., N.A. (ăp-á-lăch'ĭ-án)	107	37°20'N	82°00'W
Appalachicola, r., Fl., U.S. (ăpá-lăch'ĭ-cōlă)	107	30°11'N	85°00'W
Äppelbo, Swe. (ĕp-ĕl-bōō)	166	60°30'N	14°02'E
Appelhülsen, Ger. (ä'pĕl-hül'sĕn)	171c	51°55'N	7°26'E
Appennino, mts., Italy (äp-pĕn-nē'nô)	156	43°48'N	11°06'E
Appleton, Mn., U.S. (ăp'l-tŭn)	112	45°10'N	96°01'W
Appleton, Wi., U.S.	105	44°14'N	88°27'W
Appleton City, Mo., U.S.	121	38°10'N	94°02'W

PLACE (Pronunciation)	PAGE	LAT.	LONG.
Appomattox, r., Va., U.S. (ăp-ô-măt'ŭks)	125	37°22'N	78°09'W
Aprília, Italy (á-prē'lyá)	174	41°36'N	12°40'E
Apsheronsk, Russia	182	44°28'N	39°44'E
Apt, Fr. (äpt)	171	43°54'N	5°19'E
Apure, r., Ven. (ä-pōō'rä)	142	8°08'N	68°46'W
Apurímac, r., Peru (ä-pōō-rē'mäk')	142	11°39'S	73°48'W
Aqaba, Gulf of, b. (ä'kà-bà)	198	28°30'N	34°40'E
Aqabah, Wādī al, r., Egypt	197a	29°48'N	34°05'E
Aqmola *see* Astana, Kaz.	183	51°10'N	71°43'E
Aqtaū, Kaz.	183	43°35'N	51°05'E
Aqtöbe, Kaz.	183	50°20'N	57°00'E
Aquasco, Md., U.S. (á'gwà'scŏ)	110e	38°35'N	76°44'W
Aquidauana, Braz. (ä-kē-däwä'nä)	143	20°24'S	55°46'W
Aquin, Haiti (ä-kăn')	135	18°20'N	73°25'W
Ara, r., Japan (ä-rä)	211a	35°40'N	139°52'E
Arab, Baḥr al, r., Sudan	231	9°46'N	26°52'E
'Arabah, Wādī, val., Egypt	238b	29°02'N	32°10'E
Arabats'ka Strilka (Tongue of Arabat), spit, Ukr.	177	45°50'N	35°05'E
Arabi, La., U.S.	110d	29°58'N	90°01'W
Arabian Desert, des., Egypt (à-rā'bĭ-ăn)	231	27°06'N	32°49'E
Arabian Sea, sea (à-rā'bĭ-ăn)	196	16°00'N	65°15'E
Aracaju, Braz. (ä-rä'kä-zhōō')	143	11°00'S	37°01'W
Aracati, Braz. (ä-rä'kä-tē')	143	4°31'S	37°41'W
Araçatuba, Braz. (ä-rä-sá-tōō'bä)	143	21°14'S	50°19'W
Aracena, Spain	172	37°53'N	6°34'W
Arachthos, r., Grc. (är'äk-thôs)	175	39°10'N	21°05'E
Aracruz, Braz. (ä-rä-krōō's)	143	19°58'S	40°11'W
'Arad, Isr.	197a	31°20'N	35°15'E
Arad, Rom. (ŏ'rŏd)	163	46°10'N	21°18'E
Arafura Sea, sea (ä-rä-fōō'rä)	213	8°40'S	130°00'E
Aragats, Gora, mtn., Arm.	182	40°32'N	44°14'E
Aragon, hist. reg., Spain (ä-rä-gōn')	173	40°55'N	0°45'W
Aragón, r., Spain	172	42°35'N	1°10'W
Aragua, dept., Ven. (ä-rä'gwä)	143b	10°00'N	67°05'W
Aragua de Barcelona, Ven.	142	9°29'N	64°48'W
Araguaía, r., Braz. (ä-rä-gwä'yä)	143	8°37'S	49°43'W
Araguari, Braz. (ä-rä-gwä'rē)	143	18°43'S	48°03'W
Araguatins, Braz. (ä-rä-gwä-tēns)	143	5°41'S	48°04'W
Aragüita, Ven. (ärá-gwē'tá)	143b	10°13'N	66°28'W
Araj, oasis, Egypt (ä-räj')	163	29°05'N	26°51'E
Arāk, Iran	198	34°08'N	49°57'E
Arakan Yoma, mts., Mya. (ŭ-rŭ-kŭn'yō'mà)	199	19°51'N	94°13'E
Aral, Kaz.	183	46°47'N	62°00'E
Aral Sea, sea, Asia	178	45°17'N	60°02'E
Aralsor köli, l., Kaz. (á-räl'sôr')	181	49°00'N	48°20'E
Aramberri, Mex. (ä-râm-bĕr-rē')	130	24°05'N	99°47'W
Arana, Sierra, mts., Spain	172	37°17'N	3°28'W
Aranda de Duero, Spain (ä-rän'dä dā dwā'rō)	172	41°43'N	3°45'W
Arandas, Mex. (ä-rän'däs)	130	20°43'N	102°18'W
Aran Island, i., Ire. (ăr'ăn)	164	54°58'N	8°33'W
Aran Islands, is., Ire.	160	53°04'N	9°59'W
Aranjuez, Spain (ä-rän-hwāth')	162	40°02'N	3°24'W
Aransas Pass, Tx., U.S. (á-răn'sás pás)	123	27°55'N	97°09'W
Araouane, Mali	230	18°54'N	3°33'W
Arapkir, Tur. (ä-räp-kēr')	163	39°00'N	38°10'E
Araraquara, Braz. (ä-rä-rä-kwä'rä)	143	21°47'S	48°08'W
Araras, Braz. (ä-rá'räs)	141a	22°21'S	47°22'W
Araras, Serra das, mts., Braz. (sĕ'r-rä-däs-ä-rá'räs)	143	18°03'S	53°23'W
Araras, Serra das, mts., Braz.	144b	22°24'S	43°15'W
Araras, Serra das, mts., Braz. (sĕ'r-rä-däs-ä-rá'räs)	144	23°30'S	53°00'W
Ararat, Austl. (ăr'ărăt)	219	37°17'S	142°56'E
Ararat, Mount, mtn., Tur.	198	39°50'N	44°20'E
Arari, l., Braz. (ä-rá'rē)	143	0°30'S	48°50'W
Araripe, Chapada do, hills, Braz. (shä-pä'dä-dô-ä-rä-rē'pĕ)	143	5°55'S	40°42'W
Araruama, Braz. (ä-rä-rōō-ä'mä)	141a	22°53'S	42°19'W
Araruama, Lagoa de, l., Braz.	141a	23°00'S	42°15'W
Aras, r., Asia (ä-räs)	198	39°15'N	47°10'E
Aratuípe, Braz. (ä-rä-tōō-ē'pĕ)	143	13°12'S	38°58'W
Arauca, Col. (ä-rou'kä)	142	6°56'N	70°45'W
Arauca, r., S.A.	142	7°13'N	68°43'W
Aravalli Range, mts., India (ä-rä'vŭ-lê)	199	24°15'N	72°40'E
Araya, Punta de, c., Ven. (pŭn'tä-dĕ-ä-rä'yä)	143b	10°40'N	64°15'W
Arayat, Phil. (ä-rä'yät)	213a	15°10'N	120°44'E
'Arbi, Sudan	231	20°36'N	29°57'E
Arbīl, Iraq	198	36°10'N	44°00'E
Arboga, Swe. (är-bō'gä)	166	59°26'N	15°50'E
Arborea, Italy (är-bō-rĕ'ä)	174	39°50'N	8°36'E
Arbroath, Scot., U.K. (är-brōth')	164	56°36'N	2°25'W
Arcachon, Fr. (är-kä-shôn')	161	44°39'N	1°12'W
Arcachon, Bassin d', Fr. (bä-sĕn' där-kä-shôn')	170	44°42'N	1°50'W
Arcadia, Ca., U.S. (är-kā'dĭ-á)	117a	34°08'N	118°02'W
Arcadia, Fl., U.S.	125a	27°12'N	81°51'W
Arcadia, La., U.S.	123	32°33'N	92°56'W
Arcadia, Wi., U.S.	113	44°15'N	91°30'W
Arcata, Ca., U.S. (är-kà'tá)	114	40°54'N	124°05'W
Arc Dome Mountain, mtn., Nv., U.S. (ärk dōm)	118	38°51'N	117°21'W
Arcelia, Mex. (är-sä'lē-ä)	130	18°19'N	100°14'W
Archbald, Pa., U.S. (ärch'bôld)	109	41°30'N	75°35'W
Arches National Park, rec., Ut., U.S. (är'ches)	119	38°45'N	109°35'W
Archidona, Ec. (är-chê-do'nä)	142	1°01'S	77°49'W
Archidona, Spain (är-chē-dô'nä)	172	37°08'N	4°24'W

ăt; fināl; rāte; senåte; ärm; àsk; sofá; fâre; ch-choose; dh-as th in other; bē; ēvent; bĕt; recĕnt; cratēr; g-gō; gh-guttural g; bĭt; ĭ-short neutral; rīde; ĸ-guttural k as ch in German ich;

PRONOUNCING INDEX Arcis-sur-Aube – Atacama 267

PLACE (Pronunciation)	PAGE	LAT.	LONG.
Arcis-sur-Aube, Fr. (är-sēs'sûr-ōb')	170	48°31'N	4°04'E
Arco, Id., U.S. (är'kō)	115	43°39'N	113°15'W
Arcola, Tx., U.S.	123a	29°30'N	95°28'W
Arcola, Va., U.S. (ăr'cōlă)	110e	38°57'N	77°32'W
Arcos de la Frontera, Spain (är'kōs-dĕ-lä-frôn-tĕ'rä)	172	36°44'N	5°48'W
Arctic Ocean, o.	244	85°00'N	170°00'E
Arda, r., Blg. (är'dä)	175	41°36'N	25°18'E
Ardabīl, Iran	198	38°15'N	48°00'E
Ardahan, Tur. (är-dȧ-hän')	181	41°10'N	42°40'E
Ardatov, Russia (är-dȧ-tôf')	180	54°58'N	46°10'E
Ardennes, mts., Eur. (ȧr-dĕn')	161	50°01'N	5°12'E
Ardila, r., Eur. (är-dē'lȧ)	172	38°10'N	7°15'W
Ardmore, Ok., U.S. (ärd'mōr)	104	34°10'N	97°08'W
Ardmore, Pa., U.S.	110f	40°01'N	75°18'W
Ardrossan, Can. (är-dros'ȧn)	102g	53°33'N	113°08'W
Ardsley, Eng., U.K. (ärdz'lē)	158a	53°43'N	1°33'W
Åre, Swe.	160	63°12'N	13°12'E
Arecibo, P.R. (ä-rā-sē'bō)	129b	18°28'N	66°45'W
Areia Branca, Braz. (ä-rĕ'yä-brä'n-kä)	143	4°58'S	37°02'W
Arena, Point, c., Ca., U.S. (ä-rā'nȧ)	118	38°57'N	123°40'W
Arenas, Punta, c., Ven. (pōn'tä-rĕ'näs)	143b	10°57'N	64°24'W
Arenas de San Pedro, Spain	172	40°12'N	5°04'W
Arendal, Nor. (ä'rĕn-däl)	166	58°29'N	8°44'E
Arendonk, Bel.	159a	51°19'N	5°07'E
Arequipa, Peru (ä-rā-kē'pä)	142	16°27'S	71°30'W
Arezzo, Italy (ä-rĕt'sō)	162	43°28'N	11°54'E
Arga, r., Spain (är'gä)	172	42°35'N	1°55'W
Arganda, Spain (är-gän'dä)	173a	40°18'N	3°27'W
Argazi, l., Russia (är'gä-zĭ)	186a	55°24'N	60°37'E
Argazi, r., Russia	186a	55°33'N	57°30'E
Argentan, Fr. (är-zhäN-täN')	170	48°45'N	0°01'W
Argentat, Fr. (ȧr-zhäN-tä')	170	45°07'N	1°57'E
Argenteuil, Fr. (är-zhäN-tû'y')	170	48°56'N	2°15'E
Argentina, nation, S.A. (är-jĕn-tē'nȧ)	144	35°30'S	67°00'W
Argentino, l., Arg. (är-kĕn-tē'nō)	144	50°15'S	72°45'W
Argenton-sur-Creuse, Fr. (är-zhäN'tôN-sür-krôs)	170	46°34'N	1°28'E
Argolikos Kólpos, b., Grc.	175	37°20'N	23°00'E
Argonne, mts., Fr. (ä'r-gôn)	171	49°21'N	5°54'E
Argos, Grc. (är'gŏs)	175	37°38'N	22°45'E
Argostóli, Grc.	175	38°10'N	20°30'E
Arguello, Point, c., Ca., U.S. (är-gwāl'yō)	118	34°35'N	120°40'W
Arguin, Cap d', c., Maur.	230	20°28'N	17°46'W
Argun', r., Asia (ȧr-gōōn')	179	50°00'N	119°00'E
Argungu, Nig.	235	12°45'N	4°31'E
Argyle, Can. (är'gīl)	102f	50°11'N	97°27'W
Argyle, Mn., U.S.	112	48°21'N	96°48'W
Århus, Den. (ôr'hōōs)	160	56°09'N	10°10'E
Ariakeno-Umi, b., Japan (ä-rē'ä-kä-nō ōō'nē)	211	33°03'N	130°18'E
Ariake-Wan, b., Japan (ä'rē-ä'kā wän)	211	31°19'N	131°15'E
Ariano, Italy (ä-rē-ä'nō)	174	41°09'N	15°11'E
Ariari, r., Col. (ä-ryä'rē)	142a	3°34'N	73°42'W
Aribinda, Burkina	234	14°14'N	0°52'W
Arica, Chile (ä-rē'kä)	142	18°34'S	70°14'W
Arichat, Can. (ä-rĭ-shät')	101	45°31'N	61°01'W
Ariège, r., Fr. (ȧ-rē-ĕzh')	170	43°26'N	1°29'E
Ariel, Wa., U.S. (ā'rĭ-ĕl)	116c	45°57'N	122°34'W
Arieş, r., Rom.	169	46°25'N	23°15'E
Ariguanabo, Lago de, l., Cuba (lä'gô-dĕ-ä-rē-gwä-nä'bô)	135a	22°52'N	82°33'W
Arikaree, r., Co., U.S. (ȧ-rĭ-kȧ-rē')	120	39°51'N	102°18'W
Arima, Japan (ä'rē-mä')	211b	34°48'N	135°16'E
Aringay, Phil. (ä-rĭŋ-gä'ē)	213a	16°25'N	120°20'E
Arinos, r., Braz. (ä-rē'nôzsh)	143	12°09'S	56°49'W
Aripuanã, r., Braz. (ȧ-rē-pwän'yȧ)	143	7°06'S	60°29'W
'Arīsh, Wādī al, r., Egypt (ȧ-rēsh')	197a	30°36'N	34°07'E
Aristazabal Island, i., Can.	94	52°30'N	129°20'W
Arizona, state, U.S. (ăr-ĭ-zō'nȧ)	104	34°00'N	113°00'W
Arjona, Spain (är-hō'nä)	172	37°58'N	4°03'W
Arka, r., Russia	185	60°45'N	142°30'E
Arkabutla Lake, res., Ms., U.S. (är-kȧ-bŭt'lȧ)	124	34°48'N	90°00'W
Arkadelphia, Ar., U.S. (är-kȧ-dĕl'fĭ-ȧ)	121	34°06'N	93°05'W
Arkansas, state, U.S. (är'kăn-sô) (är-kăn'sȧs)	105	34°50'N	93°40'W
Arkansas, r., U.S.	106	37°30'N	97°00'W
Arkansas City, Ks., U.S.	121	37°04'N	97°02'W
Arkhangelsk (Archangel), Russia (ȧr-kän'gĕlsk)	178	64°30'N	40°25'E
Arkhangel'skoye, Russia (är-kän-gĕl'skô-yĕ)	186a	54°25'N	56°48'E
Arklow, Ire. (ärk'lō)	164	52°47'N	6°10'W
Arkonam, India (är-kō-näm')	203	13°05'N	79°43'E
Arlanza, r., Spain (är-län-thä')	172	42°08'N	3°45'W
Arlanzón, r., Spain (är-län-thōn')	172	42°12'N	3°58'W
Arlberg Tunnel, trans., Aus. (ärl'bĕrgh)	168	47°05'N	10°15'E
Arles, Fr. (ärl)	170	43°42'N	4°38'E
Arlington, S. Afr.	238c	28°02'S	27°52'E
Arlington, Ga., U.S. (är'lĭng-tun')	124	31°25'N	84°42'W
Arlington, Ma., U.S.	101a	42°26'N	71°13'W
Arlington, S.D., U.S. (är'lēng-tŭn)	112	44°23'N	97°09'W
Arlington, Tx., U.S. (ar'lĭng-tŭn)	117c	32°44'N	97°07'W
Arlington, Va., U.S.	110e	38°55'N	77°10'W
Arlington, Vt., U.S.	109	43°05'N	73°05'W
Arlington, Wa., U.S.	116a	48°11'N	122°08'W
Arlington Heights, Il., U.S. (är'lēng-tŭn-hī'ts)	111a	42°05'N	87°59'W
Arltunga, Austl. (ärl-tôŋ'gȧ)	218	23°19'S	134°45'E
Arma, Ks., U.S. (är'mȧ)	121	37°34'N	94°43'W
Armagh, Can. (är-mä') (är-mäk')	102b	46°45'N	70°36'W
Armagh, N. Ire., U.K.	160	54°21'N	6°25'W
Armant, Egypt (är-mänt')	238b	25°37'N	32°32'E
Armaro, Col. (är-mȧ'rō)	142a	4°58'N	74°54'W
Armavir, Russia (ȧr-mȧ-vĭr')	178	45°00'N	41°00'E
Armenia, Col. (är-mĕ'nē-ȧ)	142	4°33'N	75°40'W
Armenia, El Sal. (är-mā'nē-ä)	132	13°44'N	89°31'W
Armenia, nation, Asia	178	41°00'N	44°39'E
Armentières, Fr. (är-mäN-tyâr')	170	50°43'N	2°53'E
Armeria, Río de, r., Mex. (rē'ō-dĕ-är-mȧ-rē'ä)	130	19°36'N	104°10'W
Armherstburg, Can. (ärm'hĕrst-bōōrgh)	98	42°06'N	83°06'W
Armians'k, Ukr.	177	46°06'N	33°42'E
Armidale, Austl. (är'mĭ-dāl)	219	30°27'S	151°50'E
Armour, S.D., U.S. (är'mĕr)	112	43°18'N	98°21'W
Armstrong Station, Can. (ärm'strŏng)	91	50°21'N	89°00'W
Arnedo, Spain (är-nā'dō)	172	42°12'N	2°03'W
Arnhem, Neth. (ärn'hĕm)	161	51°58'N	5°56'E
Arnhem, Cape, c., Austl.	220	12°15'S	137°00'E
Arnhem Land, reg., Austl. (ärn'hĕm-lănd)	220	13°15'S	133°00'E
Arno, r., Italy (ä'r-nô)	162	43°30'N	11°00'E
Arnold, Eng., U.K. (är'nŭld)	158a	53°00'N	1°08'W
Arnold, Mn., U.S. (är'nŭld)	117h	46°53'N	92°06'W
Arnold, Pa., U.S.	111e	40°35'N	79°45'W
Arnprior, Can. (ärn-prī'ẽr)	99	45°25'N	76°20'W
Arnsberg, Ger. (ärns'bĕrgh)	171c	51°25'N	8°02'E
Arnstadt, Ger. (ärn'shtät)	168	50°51'N	10°57'E
Aroab, Nmb. (är'ō-äb)	232	25°40'S	19°45'E
Aroostook, r., Me., U.S. (ȧ-rōs'tōk)	100	46°44'N	68°15'W
Aroroy, Phil. (ä-rô-rō'ē)	213a	12°30'N	123°24'E
Arpajon, Fr. (ăr-pä-jō'n)	171b	48°35'N	2°15'E
Arpoador, Ponta do, c., Braz. (pô'n-tä-dō-är'pôä-dō'r)	144b	22°59'S	43°11'W
Arraiolos, Port. (är-rī-ō'lōzh)	172	38°47'N	7°59'W
Ar Ramādī, Iraq	198	33°26'N	43°19'E
Arran, Island of, Scot., U.K. (ă'răn)	164	55°25'N	5°25'W
Ar Rank, Sudan	231	11°45'N	32°53'E
Arras, Fr. (ȧ-räs')	161	50°21'N	2°40'E
Ar Rawḑah, Egypt	238b	27°47'N	30°52'E
Arrecifes, Arg. (är-rȧ-sē'fäs)	141c	34°03'S	60°05'W
Arrecifes, r., Arg.	141c	34°07'S	59°50'W
Arrée, Monts d', mts., Fr. (är-rā')	170	48°27'N	4°00'W
Arriaga, Mex. (är-rēä'gä)	131	16°15'N	93°54'W
Arrone, r., Italy	173d	41°57'N	12°17'E
Arrow Creek, r., Mt., U.S. (ăr'ō)	115	47°29'N	109°53'W
Arrowhead, Lake, l., Ca., U.S. (lăk ăr'ōhĕd)	117a	34°17'N	117°13'W
Arrowrock Reservoir, res., Id., U.S. (ăr'ō-rŏk)	114	43°40'N	115°30'W
Arroya Arena, Cuba (är-rô'yä-rĕ'nä)	135a	23°01'N	82°30'W
Arroyo de la Luz, Spain (är-rō'yō-dĕ-lä-lōō'z)	172	39°39'N	6°46'W
Arroyo Seco, Mex. (är-rō'yō sä'kō)	130	21°31'N	99°44'W
Ar Rub' al Khālī, des., Asia	198	20°00'N	51°00'E
Ar Ruṭbah, Iraq	201	33°02'N	40°17'E
Arsen'yev, Russia	179	44°13'N	133°32'E
Arsinskiy, Russia (är-sĭn'skĭ)	186a	53°46'N	59°54'E
Árta, Grc. (är'tä)	163	39°08'N	21°02'E
Arteaga, Mex. (är-tä-ä'gä)	122	25°28'N	100°50'W
Artëm, Russia (ȧr-tyôm')	179	43°28'N	132°29'E
Artemisa, Cuba (är-tȧ-mē'sä)	134	22°50'N	82°45'W
Artemivs'k, Ukr.	181	48°37'N	38°00'E
Artesia, N.M., U.S. (är-tē'sĭ-ȧ)	120	32°44'N	104°23'W
Arthabaska, Can.	99	46°03'N	71°54'W
Arthur's Town, Bah.	135	24°40'N	75°40'W
Arti, Russia (är'tĭ)	186a	56°20'N	58°38'E
Artibonite, r., N.A. (är-tē-bō-nē'tä)	135	19°00'N	72°25'W
Aru, Kepulauan, is., Indon.	213	6°20'S	133°00'E
Arua, Ug. (ä'rōō-ä)	231	3°01'N	30°55'E
Aruba, i., Aruba (ä-rōō'bȧ)	129	12°29'N	70°00'W
Arunachal Pradesh, state, India	199	27°35'N	92°56'E
Arusha, Tan. (ȧ-rōō'shä)	232	3°22'S	36°41'E
Arvida, Can.	91	48°26'N	71°11'W
Arvika, Swe. (är-vē'kȧ)	166	59°41'N	12°35'E
Arzamas, Russia (är-zä-mäs')	180	55°20'N	43°52'E
Arziw, Alg.	162	35°50'N	0°20'W
Arzúa, Spain	172	42°54'N	8°19'W
Aš, Czech Rep. (äsh')	168	50°12'N	12°13'E
Asahi-Gawa, r., Japan (ä-sä'hē-gä'wä)	211	35°01'N	133°40'E
Asahikawa, Japan	205	43°50'N	142°09'E
Asaka, Japan (ä-sä'kä)	211a	35°47'N	139°36'E
Asansol, India	199	23°45'N	86°58'E
Asbest, Russia (äs-bĕst')	180	57°02'N	61°28'E
Asbestos, Can. (ăs-bĕs'tōs)	99	45°49'N	71°52'W
Asbestovskiy, Russia	186a	57°46'N	61°23'E
Asbury Park, N.J., U.S. (ăz'bĕr-ĭ)	110a	40°13'N	74°01'W
Ascención, Bahía de la, b., Mex.	132a	19°39'N	87°30'W
Ascensión, Mex. (äs-sĕn-sē-ōn')	130	24°21'N	99°54'W
Ascension, i., St. Hel. (ȧ-sĕn'shŭn)	229	8°00'S	13°00'W
Ascent, S. Afr. (ă-sĕnt')	238c	27°14'S	29°06'E
Aschaffenburg, Ger. (ä-shäf'ĕn-bōrgh)	168	49°58'N	9°12'E
Ascheberg, Ger. (ä'shĕ-bĕrg)	171c	51°47'N	7°38'E
Aschersleben, Ger. (äsh'ĕrs-lā-bĕn)	168	51°46'N	11°28'E
Ascoli Piceno, Italy (äs'kō-lēpē-chā'nō)	174	42°50'N	13°55'E
Aseb, Erit.	231	12°52'N	43°39'E
Asenovgrad, Blg.	175	42°00'N	24°49'E
Aseri, Est. (á'sĕ-rĭ)	167	59°26'N	26°58'E
Asha, Russia (ä'shä)	186a	55°01'N	57°17'E
Ashabula, l., N.D., U.S. (ăsh'ȧ-bū-lä)	112	47°07'N	97°51'W
Ashan, Russia (ä'shän)	186a	57°08'N	56°25'E
Ashbourne, Eng., U.K. (ăsh'bŭrn)	158a	53°01'N	1°44'W
Ashburn, Ga., U.S. (ăsh'bŭrn)	124	31°42'N	83°42'W
Ashburn, Va., U.S.	110e	39°02'N	77°30'W
Ashburton, r., Austl. (ăsh'bûr-tŭn)	220	22°30'S	115°30'E
Ashby-de-la-Zouch, Eng., U.K. (ăsh'bĭ-dē-lȧ zōōsh')	158a	52°44'N	1°23'W
Ashdod, Isr.	197a	31°46'N	34°39'E
Ashdown, Ar., U.S. (ăsh'doun)	121	33°41'N	94°07'W
Asheboro, N.C., U.S. (ăsh'bŭr-ô)	125	35°41'N	79°50'W
Asherton, Tx., U.S. (ăsh'ẽr-tŭn)	122	28°26'N	99°45'W
Asheville, N.C., U.S. (ăsh'vĭl)	105	35°35'N	82°35'W
Ash Fork, Az., U.S.	119	35°13'N	112°29'W
Ashgabat, Turkmen.	183	37°57'N	58°23'E
Ashikaga, Japan (ä'shē-kä'gȧ)	211	36°22'N	139°26'E
Ashiya, Japan (ä'shē-yä')	211	33°54'N	130°40'E
Ashiya, Japan	211b	34°44'N	135°18'E
Ashizuri-Zaki, c., Japan (ä-shē-zō-rē zä-kē)	210	32°43'N	133°04'E
Ashland, Al., U.S. (ăsh'lănd)	124	33°15'N	85°50'W
Ashland, Ks., U.S.	120	37°11'N	99°46'W
Ashland, Ky., U.S.	108	38°25'N	82°40'W
Ashland, Ma., U.S.	101a	42°16'N	71°28'W
Ashland, Me., U.S.	100	46°37'N	68°26'W
Ashland, Ne., U.S.	112	41°02'N	96°23'W
Ashland, Oh., U.S.	108	40°50'N	82°15'W
Ashland, Or., U.S.	114	42°12'N	122°42'W
Ashland, Pa., U.S.	109	40°45'N	76°20'W
Ashland, Wi., U.S.	105	46°34'N	90°55'W
Ashley, N.D., U.S. (ăsh'lē)	112	46°03'N	99°23'W
Ashley, Pa., U.S.	109	41°15'N	75°55'W
Ashmūn, Egypt (ȧsh-mōōn')	238b	30°19'N	30°57'E
Ashmyany, Bela.	167	54°27'N	25°55'E
Ashqelon, Isr. (äsh'kĕ-lōn)	197a	31°40'N	34°36'E
Ash Shabb, Egypt (shĕb)	231	22°34'N	29°52'E
Ash Shallūfah, Egypt (shäl'lō-fȧ)	238b	30°09'N	32°33'E
Ash Shaqrā', Sau. Ar.	198	25°10'N	45°08'E
Ash Shāriqah, U.A.E.	201	25°22'N	55°23'E
Ash Shawbak, Jord.	197a	30°31'N	35°35'E
Ash Shiḥr, Yemen	198	14°45'N	49°32'E
Ashtabula, Oh., U.S. (ăsh-tȧ-bū'lȧ)	105	41°55'N	80°50'W
Ashton, Id., U.S. (ăsh'tŭn)	115	44°04'N	111°28'W
Ashton-in-Makerfield, Eng., U.K. (ăsh'tŭn-ĭn-māk'ẽr-fēld)	158a	53°29'N	2°39'W
Ashton-under-Lyne, Eng., U.K. (ăsh'tŭn-ŭn-dẽr-līn')	158a	53°29'N	2°04'W
Ashuanipi, l., Can. (ăsh-wȧ-nĭp'ĭ)	93	52°40'N	67°42'W
Ashukino, Russia (ȧ-shōō'kĭnô)	186b	56°10'N	37°57'E
Asia, cont.	196	50°00'N	100°00'E
Asia Minor, reg., Tur. (ā'zhȧ)	157	38°18'N	31°18'E
Asientos, Mex. (ä-sē-ĕn'tōs)	130	22°13'N	102°05'W
Asilah, Mor.	172	35°30'N	6°05'W
Asinara, i., Italy	174	41°02'N	8°22'E
Asinara, Golfo dell', b., Italy (gôl'fô-dĕl-ä-sē-nä'rä)	174	40°58'N	8°28'E
Asīr, reg., Sau. Ar. (ä-sēr')	198	19°30'N	42°00'E
Askarovo, Russia (äs-kä-rō'vō)	186a	53°21'N	58°32'E
Askersund, Swe. (äs'kĕr-sōnd)	166	58°43'N	14°53'E
Askino, Russia (äs'kĭ-nō)	186a	56°06'N	56°29'E
Asmara *see* Asmera, Erit.	230	15°17'N	38°56'E
Asmera, Erit. (äs-mä'rä)	231	15°17'N	38°56'E
Asnieres, Fr. (ä-nyâr')	171b	48°55'N	2°18'E
Asosa, Eth.	231	10°13'N	34°28'E
Asotin, Wa., U.S. (ȧ-sō'tĭn)	114	46°19'N	117°01'W
Aspen, Co., U.S. (ăs'pĕn)	119	39°15'N	106°55'W
Asperen, Neth.	159a	51°52'N	5°07'E
Aspy Bay, b., Can. (ăs'pē)	101	46°55'N	60°25'W
Aş Şaff, Egypt	238b	29°33'N	31°23'E
As Sallūm, Egypt	231	31°35'N	25°05'E
As Salt, Jord.	197a	32°02'N	35°44'E
Assam, state, India (ăs-săm')	199	26°00'N	91°00'E
As Samāwah, Iraq	201	31°18'N	45°17'E
Assens, Den. (äs'sĕns)	166	55°16'N	9°54'E
As Sinbillāwayn, Egypt	238b	30°53'N	31°37'E
Assini, C. Iv. (ȧ-sē-nē')	230	4°52'N	3°16'W
Assiniboia, Can.	90	49°38'N	105°59'W
Assiniboine, r., Can. (ă-sĭn'ĭ-boin)	97	50°03'N	97°57'W
Assiniboine, Mount, mtn., Can.	95	50°52'N	115°39'W
Assis, Braz. (ä-sē's)	143	22°39'S	50°21'W
Assisi, Italy	162	43°04'N	12°37'E
As-Sudd, reg., Sudan	231	8°45'N	30°45'E
As Sulaymānīyah, Iraq	198	35°47'N	45°23'E
As Sulaymānīyah, Sau. Ar.	201	24°09'N	46°19'E
As Suwaydā', Syria	198	32°41'N	36°41'E
Astakós, Grc. (äs'tä-kôs)	175	38°42'N	21°00'E
Astana (Aqmola), Kaz.	183	51°10'N	71°43'E
Astara, Azer.	181	38°30'N	48°50'E
Asti, Italy (äs'tē)	162	44°54'N	8°12'E
Astorga, Spain (äs-tôr'gä)	172	42°28'N	6°03'W
Astoria, Or., U.S. (ăs-tō'rĭ-ȧ)	104	46°11'N	123°51'W
Astrakhan', Russia (äs-trȧ-kän')	178	46°15'N	48°00'E
Astrida, Rw. (äs-trē'dȧ)	232	2°37'S	29°48'E
Asturias, hist. reg., Spain (äs-tōō'ryäs)	172	43°21'N	6°00'W
Astypalaia, i., Grc.	163	36°31'N	26°19'E
Asunción *see* Ixtaltepec, Mex.	131	16°33'N	95°04'W
Asunción *see* Nochistlán, Mex.	130	21°23'N	102°52'W
Asunción, Para. (ä-sōōn-syōn')	144	25°25'S	57°30'W
Asunción Mita, Guat. (ä-sōōn-syō'n-mē'tä)	132	14°19'N	89°43'W
Aswān, Egypt (ä-swän')	231	24°05'N	32°57'E
Aswān High Dam, dam, Egypt	231	23°58'N	32°53'E
Atacama, Desierto de, des., Chile (dĕ-syĕ'r-tô-dĕ-ä-tä-kä'mä)	139	23°50'S	69°00'W

ng-sing; ŋ-baŋk; N-nasalized n; nŏd; cŏmmit; ōld; ôbey; ôrder; oi-boil; fōōd; ŏ-as oo in foot; ou-out; s-soft; sh-dish; th-thin; pūre; ûnite; ûrn; stŭd; circŭs; ü-as in French tu; '-indeterminate vowel.

268 Atacama – Babylon PRONOUNCING INDEX

PLACE (Pronunciation)	PAGE	LAT.	LONG.
Atacama, Puna de, plat., Bol. (pōō'nä-dĕ-ä-tä-kà'mä)	142	21°35'S	66°58'W
Atacama, Puna de, reg., Chile (pōō'nä-dĕ-ätä-kà'mä)	144	23°15'S	68°45'W
Atacama, Salar de, l., Chile (sà-lår'dĕ-ätä-kà'mä)	144	23°38'S	68°15'W
Ataco, Col. (ä-tá'kō)	142a	3°36'N	75°22'W
Atacora, Chaîne de l', mts., Benin	234	10°15'N	1°15'E
Atā 'itah, Jabal al, mtn., Jord.	197a	30°48'N	35°19'E
Atamanovskiy, Russia (ä-tä-mä'nôv-skĭ)	186a	52°15'N	60°47'E
'Ataqah, Jabal, mts., Egypt	238d	29°59'N	32°20'E
Atar, Maur. (ä-tär')	230	20°45'N	13°16'W
Atascadero, Ca., U.S. (ăt-ăs-kà-dâ'rō)	118	35°29'N	120°40'W
Atascosa, r., Tx., U.S. (ăt-ăs-kō'sà)	122	28°50'N	98°17'W
Atauro, Ilha de, i., E. Timor (dĕ-ä-tä'ōō-rō)	213	8°20'S	126°15'E
Atbara, r., Afr.	231	17°14'N	34°27'E
'Aṭbarah, Sudan (ät'bà-rä)	231	17°45'N	33°15'E
Atbasar, Kaz. (ät'bä-sär')	183	51°42'N	68°28'E
Atchafalaya, r., La., U.S.	123	30°53'N	91°51'W
Atchafalaya Bay, b., La., U.S. (ăch-à-fà-lī'à)	123	29°25'N	91°30'W
Atchison, Ks., U.S. (ăch'ĭ-sŭn)	105	39°33'N	95°08'W
Atco, N.J., U.S. (ăt'kō)	110f	39°46'N	74°53'W
Atempan, Mex. (ä-tĕm-pà'n)	131	19°49'N	97°25'W
Atenguillo, r., Mex. (ä-tĕn-gē'l-yô)	130	20°18'N	104°35'W
Athabasca, Can. (ăth-à-băs'kà)	90	54°43'N	113°17'W
Athabasca, l., Can.	92	59°04'N	109°10'W
Athabasca, r., Can.	92	57°30'N	112°00'W
Athens (Athína), Grc.	175	38°00'N	23°38'E
Athens, Al., U.S. (ăth'ĕnz)	124	34°47'N	86°58'W
Athens, Ga., U.S.	105	33°55'N	83°24'W
Athens, Oh., U.S.	108	39°20'N	82°10'W
Athens, Pa., U.S.	109	42°00'N	76°30'W
Athens, Tn., U.S.	124	35°26'N	84°36'W
Athens, Tx., U.S.	123	32°13'N	95°51'W
Atherstone, Eng., U.K. (ăth'ĕr-stŭn)	158a	52°34'N	1°33'W
Atherton, Eng., U.K. (ăth'ĕr-tŭn)	158a	53°32'N	2°29'W
Atherton Plateau, plat., Austl. (ădh-ĕr-tŏn)	221	17°00'S	144°30'E
Athi, r., Kenya (ä'tē)	233	2°43'S	38°30'E
Athína see Athens, Grc.	154	38°00'N	23°38'E
Athlone, Ire. (ăth-lōn')	160	53°24'N	7°30'W
Áthos, mtn., Grc. (ăth'ŏs)	175	40°10'N	24°15'E
Ath Thamad, Egypt	197a	29°41'N	34°17'E
Athy, Ire. (à-thī)	164	52°59'N	7°08'W
Ati, Chad	235	13°13'N	18°20'E
Atibaia, Braz. (ä-tē-bà'yä)	141a	23°08'S	46°32'W
Atikonak, l., Can.	93	52°34'N	63°49'W
Atimonan, Phil. (ä-tē-mō'nän)	213a	13°59'N	121°56'E
Atiquizaya, El Sal. (ä'tē-kē-zä'yä)	132	14°00'N	89°42'W
Atitlan, vol., Guat. (ä-tē-tlän')	132	14°35'N	91°11'W
Atitlan, Lago, l., Guat. (ä-tē-tlän')	132	14°38'N	91°23'W
Atizapán, Mex. (ä'tē-zà-pän')	131a	19°33'N	99°16'W
Atka, Ak., U.S. (ăt'kà)	103a	52°18'N	174°18'W
Atka, i., Ak., U.S.	106b	51°58'N	174°30'W
Atkarsk, Russia (åt-kärsk')	181	51°50'N	45°00'E
Atkinson, Ne., U.S. (ăt'kĭn-sŭn)	112	42°32'N	98°58'W
Atlanta, Ga., U.S. (ăt-lăn'tà)	105	33°45'N	84°23'W
Atlanta, Tx., U.S.	121	33°09'N	94°09'W
Atlantic, Ia., U.S. (ăt-lăn'tĭk)	113	41°23'N	94°58'W
Atlantic, N.C., U.S.	125	34°54'N	76°20'W
Atlantic City, N.J., U.S.	105	39°20'N	74°30'W
Atlantic Highlands, N.J., U.S.	110a	40°25'N	74°04'W
Atlantic Ocean, o.	4	5°00'S	25°00'W
Atlas Mountains, mts., Afr. (ăt'lăs)	230	31°22'N	4°57'W
Atliaca, Mex. (ät-lē-ä'kä)	130	17°38'N	99°24'W
Atlin, l., Can. (ăt'lĭn)	92	59°34'N	133°20'W
Atlixco, Mex. (ät-lēz'kō)	130	18°52'N	98°27'W
Atmore, Al., U.S. (ăt'mōr)	124	31°01'N	87°31'W
Atoka, Ok., U.S. (à-tō'kà)	121	34°23'N	96°07'W
Atoka Reservoir, res., Ok., U.S.	121	34°30'N	96°05'W
Atotonilco el Alto, Mex.	130	20°35'N	102°32'W
Atotonilco el Grande, Mex.	130	20°17'N	98°41'W
Atoui, r., Afr. (à-tōō-ē')	230	21°00'N	15°32'W
Atoyac, Mex. (ä-tō-yäk')	130	20°01'N	103°28'W
Atoyac, r., Mex.	130	18°35'N	98°16'W
Atoyac, r., Mex.	131	16°27'N	97°28'W
Atoyac de Alvarez, Mex. (ä-tō-yäk'dā äl'vä-rāz)	130	17°13'N	100°29'W
Atoyatempan, Mex. (ä-tō'yà-tĕm-pän')	131	18°47'N	97°54'W
Atrak, r., Asia	198	37°45'N	56°30'E
Ätran, r., Swe.	166	57°02'N	12°43'E
Atrato, Río, r., Col. (rē'ō-ä-trä'tō)	142	7°15'N	77°18'W
Aţ Ţafilah, Jord. (tä-fē'la)	197a	30°50'N	35°36'E
Aţ Ţā'if, Sau. Ar.	198	21°03'N	41°00'E
Attalla, Al., U.S. (ă-tăl'yà)	124	34°01'N	86°05'W
Attawapiskat, r., Can. (ăt'à-wà-pĭs'kăt)	93	52°31'N	86°22'W
Attersee, l., Aus.	168	47°57'N	13°25'E
Attica, N.Y., U.S. (ăt'ĭ-kà)	109	42°55'N	78°15'W
Attleboro, Ma., U.S. (ăt''l-bŭr-ō)	110b	41°56'N	71°15'W
Attow, Ben, mtn., Scot., U.K. (bĕn ăt'tō)	164	57°15'N	5°25'W
Attoyac Bay, Tx., U.S. (ă-toi'yăk)	123	31°45'N	94°23'W
Attu, i., Ak., U.S. (ăt-tōō')	106b	53°08'N	173°18'E
Aţ Ţūr, Egypt	163	28°09'N	33°47'E
Aţ Ţurayf, Sau. Ar.	198	31°32'N	38°30'E
Åtvidaberg, Swe. (ôt-vē'dà-bĕrgh)	166	58°12'N	15°55'E
Atwood, Ks., U.S. (ăt'wŏŏd)	120	39°48'N	101°06'W
Atyraū, Kaz.	183	47°10'N	51°50'E
Atzcapotzalco, Mex. (ät'zkä-pô-tzäl'kō)	130	19°29'N	99°11'W
Atzgersdorf, Aus.	159e	48°10'N	16°17'E
Auau Channel, strt., Hi., U.S. (ä'ö-ä'öo)	126a	20°55'N	156°50'W
Aubagne, Fr. (ō-bän'y')	171	43°18'N	5°34'E
Aube, r., Fr. (ōb)	170	48°42'N	3°49'E
Aubenas, Fr. (ōb-nä')	170	44°37'N	4°22'E
Aubervilliers, Fr. (ō-bĕr-vē-yā')	171b	48°54'N	2°23'E
Aubin, Fr. (ō-băN')	170	44°29'N	2°12'E
Aubrey, Can. (ô-brē')	102a	45°08'N	73°47'W
Auburn, Al., U.S. (ô'bŭrn)	124	32°35'N	85°26'W
Auburn, Ca., U.S.	118	38°52'N	121°05'W
Auburn, Il., U.S.	121	39°36'N	89°46'W
Auburn, In., U.S.	108	41°20'N	85°05'W
Auburn, Ma., U.S.	101a	42°11'N	71°51'W
Auburn, Me., U.S.	105	44°04'N	70°24'W
Auburn, Ne., U.S.	121	40°23'N	95°50'W
Auburn, N.Y., U.S.	109	42°55'N	76°35'W
Auburn, Wa., U.S.	116a	47°18'N	122°14'W
Auburn Heights, Mi., U.S.	111b	42°37'N	83°13'W
Aubusson, Fr. (ō-bü-sôN')	170	45°57'N	2°10'E
Auch, Fr. (ōsh)	161	43°38'N	0°35'E
Aucilla, r., Fl., U.S. (ô-sĭl'à)	124	30°15'N	83°55'W
Auckland, N.Z. (ôk'lănd)	221a	36°53'S	174°45'E
Auckland Islands, is., N.Z.	3	50°30'S	166°30'E
Aude, r., Fr. (ōd)	170	42°55'N	2°08'E
Audierne, Fr. (ō-dyĕrn')	170	48°02'N	4°31'W
Audincourt, Fr. (ō-dăn-kōōr')	171	47°30'N	6°49'E
Audley, Eng., U.K. (ôd'lĭ)	158a	53°03'N	2°18'W
Audo Range, mts., Eth.	238a	6°58'N	41°18'E
Audubon, Ia., U.S. (ô'dŏŏ-bŏn)	113	41°43'N	94°57'W
Audubon, N.J., U.S.	110f	39°54'N	75°04'W
Aue, Ger. (ou'ĕ)	168	50°35'N	12°44'E
Augathella, Austl. (ôr'gá'thĕ-là)	222	25°49'S	146°40'E
Augrabiesvalle, wtfl., S. Afr.	232	28°30'S	20°00'E
Augsburg, Ger. (ouks'bŏŏrgh)	161	48°23'N	10°55'E
Augusta, Ar., U.S. (ô-gŭs'tà)	121	35°16'N	91°21'W
Augusta, Ga., U.S.	105	33°26'N	82°00'W
Augusta, Ks., U.S.	121	37°41'N	96°58'W
Augusta, Ky., U.S.	108	38°45'N	84°00'W
Augusta, Me., U.S.	105	44°19'N	69°42'W
Augusta, N.J., U.S.	110a	41°07'N	74°44'W
Augusta, Wi., U.S.	113	44°40'N	91°09'W
Augustow, Pol. (ou-gŏŏs'tôf)	169	53°52'N	23°00'E
Auki, Sol. Is.	214e	8°46'S	160°42'E
Aulnay-sous-Bois, Fr. (ō-nĕ'sōō-bwä')	171b	48°56'N	2°30'E
Aulne, r., Fr. (ōn)	170	48°08'N	3°53'W
Auneau, Fr. (ō-nĕü)	171b	48°28'N	1°45'E
Auob, r., Afr. (ä'wŏb)	232	25°00'S	19°00'E
Aur, i., Malay.	197b	2°27'N	104°51'E
Aura, Fin.	167	60°38'N	22°32'E
Aurangābād, India (ou-rŭŋ-gä-bäd')	199	19°56'N	75°19'E
Aurdal, Nor. (äür-däl)	160	60°54'N	9°24'E
Aurès, Massif de l', mts., Alg.	162	35°16'N	5°53'E
Aurillac, Fr. (ō-rē-yák')	161	44°57'N	2°27'E
Aurora, Can.	99	43°59'N	79°25'W
Aurora, Co., U.S.	120	39°44'N	104°50'W
Aurora, Il., U.S. (ô-rō'rà)	105	41°45'N	88°18'W
Aurora, In., U.S.	111f	39°04'N	84°55'W
Aurora, Mn., U.S.	113	47°31'N	92°17'W
Aurora, Mo., U.S.	121	36°58'N	93°42'W
Aurora, Ne., U.S.	120	40°54'N	98°01'W
Aursunden, l., Nor. (äür-sûndĕn)	166	62°42'N	11°10'E
Au Sable, r., Mi., U.S. (ô-sā'b'l)	108	44°40'N	84°25'W
Ausable, r., N.Y., U.S.	109	44°25'N	73°50'W
Austin, Mn., U.S. (ôs'tĭn)	113	43°40'N	92°58'W
Austin, Nv., U.S.	118	39°30'N	117°05'W
Austin, Tx., U.S.	104	30°15'N	97°42'W
Austin, l., Austl.	220	27°45'S	117°30'E
Austin Bayou, Tx., U.S. (ôs'tĭn bī-ōō')	123a	29°17'N	95°21'W
Australia, nation, Oc.	218	25°00'S	135°00'E
Australian Alps, mts., Austl.	222	37°10'S	147°55'E
Australian Capital Territory, ter., Austl. (ôs-trā'lĭ-ăn)	219	35°30'S	148°40'E
Austria, nation, Eur. (ôs'trĭ-à)	154	47°15'N	11°53'E
Authon-la-Plaine, Fr. (ō-tôN-lä-plĕn')	171b	48°27'N	1°58'E
Autlán, Mex. (ä-ōōt-län')	128	19°47'N	104°24'W
Autun, Fr. (ō-tŭN')	170	46°58'N	4°14'E
Auvergne, mts., Fr. (ō-vĕrn'y')	170	45°12'N	2°31'E
Auxerre, Fr. (ō-sâr')	161	47°48'N	3°32'E
Ava, Mo., U.S. (ā'và)	121	36°56'N	92°40'W
Avakubi, D.R.C. (ä-vá-kōō'bē)	231	1°20'N	27°34'E
Avallon, Fr. (à-và-lôN')	170	47°30'N	3°58'E
Avalon, Ca., U.S.	118	33°21'N	118°22'W
Avalon, Pa., U.S. (ăv'à-lŏn)	111e	40°31'N	80°05'W
Aveiro, Port. (ä-vä'rō)	162	40°38'N	8°38'W
Avelar, Braz. (ä'vĕ-lá'r)	144b	22°20'S	43°25'W
Avellaneda, Arg. (ä-vĕl-yä-nā'dhä)	144	34°40'S	58°23'W
Avellino, Italy (ä-vĕl-lē'nō)	174	40°40'N	14°46'E
Averøya, i., Nor. (ävĕr-ûê)	166	63°40'N	7°16'E
Aversa, Italy (ä-vĕr'sä)	174	40°58'N	14°13'E
Avery, Tx., U.S. (ā'vĕr-ĭ)	121	33°34'N	94°46'W
Avesta, Swe. (ä-vĕs'tä)	166	60°16'N	16°09'E
Aveyron, r., Fr. (ä-vâ-rôN)	170	44°07'N	1°45'E
Avezzano, Italy (ä-vât-sä'nō)	174	42°03'N	13°27'E
Avigliano, Italy (ä-vēl-yä'nō)	174	40°45'N	15°44'E
Avignon, Fr. (à-vē-nyôN')	161	43°55'N	4°50'E
Ávila, Spain (ä-vē-lä)	172	40°39'N	4°42'W
Avilés, Spain (ä-vē-lās')	162	43°33'N	5°55'W
Aviño, Spain	172	43°36'N	8°05'W
Avoca, Ia., U.S. (à-vō'kà)	121	41°29'N	95°16'W
Avon, Ct., U.S. (ā'vŏn)	109	41°40'N	72°50'W
Avon, Ma., U.S. (ā'vŏn)	101a	42°08'N	71°03'W
Avon, Oh., U.S.	111d	41°27'N	82°02'W
Avon, r., Eng., U.K. (ā'vŭn)	164	52°05'N	1°55'W
Avondale, Ga., U.S.	110c	33°47'N	84°16'W
Avon Lake, Oh., U.S.	111d	41°31'N	82°01'W
Avonmore, Can. (ă'vôN-mōr)	102c	45°11'N	74°58'W
Avon Park, Fl., U.S. (ā'vŏn pärk')	125a	27°35'N	81°29'W
Avranches, Fr. (à-vränsh')	170	48°43'N	1°34'W
Awaji-Shima, i., Japan	210	34°32'N	135°02'E
Awe, Loch, l., Scot., U.K. (lŏĸ ôr)	164	56°22'N	5°04'W
Awjilah, Libya	231	29°07'N	21°21'E
Ax-les-Thermes, Fr. (äks'lā tĕrm')	170	42°43'N	1°50'E
Axochiapan, Mex. (äks-ō-chyä'pän)	130	18°29'N	98°49'W
Ay, r., Russia	180	55°55'N	57°55'E
Ayabe, Japan (ä'yä-bĕ)	210	35°16'N	135°17'E
Ayachi, Arin', mtn., Mor.	162	32°29'N	4°57'W
Ayacucho, Arg. (ä-yä-kōō'chō)	144	37°05'S	58°30'W
Ayacucho, Peru	142	13°12'S	74°03'W
Ayaköz, Kaz.	183	48°00'N	80°12'E
Ayamonte, Spain (ä-yä-mô'n-tĕ)	162	37°14'N	7°28'W
Ayan, Russia (à-yän')	179	56°26'N	138°18'E
Ayata, Bol. (ä-yä'tä)	142	15°17'S	68°43'W
Ayaviri, Peru (ä-yä-vē'rē)	142	14°46'S	70°38'W
Aydar, r., Eur. (ī-där')	177	49°15'N	38°48'E
Ayden, N.C., U.S. (ā'dĕn)	125	35°27'N	77°25'W
Aydın, Tur. (āīy-dĕn)	198	37°40'N	27°40'E
Ayer, Ma., U.S. (âr)	101a	42°33'N	71°36'W
Ayer Hitam, Malay.	197b	1°55'N	103°11'E
Ayers Rock *see* Uluru, mtn., Austl.	220	25°23'S	131°05'E
Aylesbury, Eng., U.K. (ālz'bĕr-ĭ)	164	51°47'N	0°49'W
Aylmer, l., Can. (āl'mĕr)	92	64°27'N	108°22'W
Aylmer, Mount, mtn., Can.	95	51°19'N	115°26'W
Aylmer East, Can. (āl'mĕr)	99	45°24'N	75°50'W
Ayo el Chico, Mex. (ä'yô el chē'kō)	130	20°31'N	102°21'W
Ayon, i., Russia (ī-ôn')	179	69°50'N	168°40'E
Ayorou, Niger	234	14°44'N	0°55'E
Ayotla, Mex. (ä-yōt'lä)	131a	19°18'N	98°55'W
Ayoun el Atrous, Maur.	234	16°40'N	9°37'W
Ayr, Scot., U.K. (âr)	164	55°27'N	4°40'W
Aysha, Eth.	231	10°48'N	42°32'E
Ayutla, Guat. (à-yōōt'lä)	132	14°44'N	92°11'W
Ayutla, Mex.	130	16°50'N	99°16'W
Ayutla, Mex.	130	20°09'N	104°20'W
Ayvalık, Tur. (āīy-wä-lĭk)	163	39°19'N	26°40'E
Azaouad, reg., Mali	234	18°00'N	3°20'W
Azaouak, Vallée de l', val., Afr.	235	15°50'N	3°10'E
Azare, Nig.	235	11°40'N	10°11'E
Azemmour, Mor. (à-zē-mōōr')	230	33°20'N	8°21'W
Azerbaijan, nation, Asia	178	40°30'N	47°30'E
Azle, Tx., U.S. (āz'lē)	117c	35°54'N	97°33'W
Azogues, Ec. (ä-sō'gās)	142	2°47'S	78°45'W
Azores *see* Açores, is., Port.	229	37°44'N	29°25'W
Azov, Russia (à-zôf') (ä-zôf)	181	47°07'N	39°19'E
Azov, Sea of, sea, Eur.	178	46°00'N	36°20'E
Aztec, N.M., U.S. (ăz'tĕk)	119	36°40'N	108°00'W
Aztec Ruins National Monument, rec., N.M., U.S.	119	36°50'N	108°00'W
Azua, Dom. Rep. (ä'swä)	135	18°30'N	70°45'W
Azuaga, Spain (ä-thwä'gä)	172	38°15'N	5°42'W
Azucar, Presa de, res., Mex.	122	26°06'N	98°44'W
Azuero, Península de, pen., Pan.	129	7°30'N	80°34'W
Azufre, Cerro (Copiapó), mtn., Chile	144	27°10'S	69°00'W
Azul, Arg. (ä-sōōl')	144	36°46'S	59°51'W
Azul, Cordillera, mts., Peru	142	7°15'S	75°30'W
Azul, Sierra, mts., Mex.	130	23°20'N	98°28'W
Azusa, Ca., U.S. (à-zōō'sà)	117a	34°08'N	117°55'W
Aẓ Ẓahrān (Dhahran), Sau. Ar.	198	26°13'N	50°00'E
Az Zaqāzīq, Egypt	231	30°36'N	31°36'E
Az Zarqā', Jord.	197a	32°03'N	36°07'E
Az Zāwiyah, Libya	230	32°28'N	11°55'E

B

PLACE (Pronunciation)	PAGE	LAT.	LONG.
Baadheere (Bardera), Som.	238a	2°13'N	42°24'E
Baal, Ger. (bäl)	171c	51°02'N	6°17'E
Baao, Phil. (bä'ō)	213a	13°27'N	123°22'E
Baarle-Hertog, Bel.	159a	51°26'N	4°57'E
Baarn, Neth.	159a	52°12'N	5°18'E
Babaeski, Tur. (bä'bä-ĕs'kĭ)	175	41°25'N	27°05'E
Babahoyo, Ec. (bä-bä-ō'yō)	142	1°56'S	79°24'W
Babana, Nig.	235	10°36'N	3°50'E
Babanango, S. Afr.	233c	28°24'S	31°11'E
Babanūsah, Sudan	231	11°30'N	27°55'E
Babar, Pulau, i., Indon. (bä'bär)	213	7°50'S	129°15'E
Bab-el-Mandeb *see* Mandeb, Bab-el-, strt.	198	13°17'N	42°49'E
Babelthuap, i., Palau	214b	7°30'N	134°36'E
Babia, Arroyo de la, r., Mex.	122	28°26'N	101°50'W
Babine, r., Can.	94	55°10'N	127°00'W
Babine Lake, l., Can. (băb'ēn)	92	54°45'N	126°00'W
Bābol, Iran	198	36°30'N	52°48'E
Babruysk, Bela.	180	53°07'N	29°13'E
Babushkin, Russia (bä'bŏŏsh-kĭn)	184	51°47'N	106°08'W
Babushkin, Russia	176	55°52'N	37°42'E
Babuyan Islands, is., Phil. (bä-bōō-yän')	212	19°30'N	122°38'E
Babyak, Blg. (bäb'zhák)	175	41°59'N	23°42'E
Babylon, N.Y., U.S. (băb'ĭ-lŏn)	110a	40°42'N	73°19'W
Babylon, hist., Iraq	198	32°15'N	45°23'E

PRONOUNCING INDEX

Bacalar – Bangor 269

PLACE (Pronunciation)	PAGE	LAT.	LONG.
Bacalar, Laguna de, l., Mex. (lä-gōō-nä-dĕ-bä-kä-lär′)	132a	18°50′N	88°31′W
Bacan, Pulau, i., Indon.	213	0°30′S	127°00′E
Bacarra, Phil. (bä-kär′rä)	209	18°22′N	120°40′E
Bacău, Rom.	163	46°34′N	27°00′E
Baccarat, Fr. (bȧ-kȧ-rȧ′)	171	48°29′N	6°42′E
Bacchus, Ut., U.S. (băk′ŭs)	117b	40°40′N	112°06′W
Bachajón, Mex. (bä-chä-hōn′)	131	17°08′N	92°18′W
Bachu, China (bä-chōō)	204	39°50′N	78°23′E
Back, r., Can.	92	65°30′N	104°15′W
Bačka Palanka, Serb. (băch′kä pälän-kä)	175	45°14′N	19°24′E
Bačka Topola, Serb. (băch′kä tô′pô-lä′)	175	45°48′N	19°38′E
Back Bay, India (băk)	203b	18°55′N	72°45′E
Backstairs Passage, strt., Austl. (băk-stârs′)	220	35°50′S	138°15′E
Bac Lieu, Viet.	212	9°45′N	105°50′E
Bac Ninh, Viet. (bäk′nēn′′)	209	21°10′N	106°02′E
Baco, Mount, mtn., Phil. (bä′kô)	213a	12°50′N	121°11′E
Bacoli, Italy (bä-kō-lē′)	173c	40°33′N	14°05′E
Bacolod, Phil. (bä-kō′lôd)	213	10°42′N	123°03′E
Bácsalmás, Hung. (bäch′ôl-mäs)	169	46°07′N	19°18′E
Bacup, Eng., U.K. (băk′ŭp)	158a	53°42′N	2°12′W
Bad, r., S.D., U.S. (băd)	112	44°04′N	100°58′W
Badajoz, Spain (bȧ-dhä-hōth′)	162	38°52′N	6°56′W
Badalona, Spain (bä-dhä-lō′nä)	173	41°27′N	2°15′E
Badanah, Sau. Ar.	198	30°49′N	40°45′E
Bad Axe, Mi., U.S. (băd′ ăks)	108	43°50′N	82°55′W
Bad Bramstedt, Ger. (bät bräm′shtĕt)	159c	53°55′N	9°53′E
Baden, Aus. (bä′dĕn)	168	48°00′N	16°14′E
Baden, Switz.	168	47°28′N	8°17′E
Baden-Baden, Ger. (bä′dĕn-bä′dĕn)	161	48°46′N	8°11′E
Bad Freienwalde, Ger. (bät frī′ĕn-väl′dĕ)	168	52°47′N	14°00′E
Bad Hersfeld, Ger. (bät hĕrsh′fĕlt)	168	50°53′N	9°43′E
Badīn, Pak.	202	24°47′N	69°51′E
Bad Ischl, Aus. (bät ĭsh′'l)	168	47°46′N	13°37′E
Bad Kissingen, Ger. (bät kĭs′ĭng-ĕn)	168	50°12′N	10°05′E
Bad Kreuznach, Ger. (bät kroits′näk)	168	49°52′N	7°53′E
Badlands, reg., N.D., U.S. (băd′ lănds)	112	46°43′N	103°22′W
Badlands, reg., S.D., U.S.	112	43°43′N	102°36′W
Badlands National Park, rec., S.D., U.S.	112	43°56′N	102°37′W
Badlāpur, India	203b	19°12′N	73°12′E
Badogo, Mali	234	11°02′N	8°13′W
Bad Oldesloe, Ger. (bät ōl′dĕs-lōē)	168	53°48′N	10°21′E
Bad Reichenhall, Ger. (bät rī′kĕn-häl)	168	47°43′N	12°53′E
Bad River Indian Reservation, I.R., Wi., U.S. (băd)	113	46°41′N	90°36′W
Bad Segeberg, Ger. (bät sĕ′gĕ-bōōrgh)	159c	53°56′N	10°18′E
Bad Tölz, Ger. (bät tûltz)	168	47°46′N	11°35′E
Badulla, Sri L.	203	6°55′N	81°07′E
Bad Vöslau, Aus.	159e	47°58′N	16°13′E
Badwater Creek, r., Wy., U.S. (băd′wô-tẽr)	115	43°13′N	107°55′W
Baena, Spain (bä-ā′nä)	162	37°38′N	4°20′W
Baependi, Braz. (bä-å-pĕn′dĭ)	141a	21°57′S	44°51′W
Baffin Bay, b., N.A. (băf′ĭn)	89	72°00′N	65°00′W
Baffin Bay, b., Tx., U.S.	123	27°11′N	97°35′W
Baffin Island, i., Can.	89	67°20′N	71°00′W
Bāfq, Iran (bäfk)	198	31°48′N	55°23′E
Bafra, Tur. (bäf′rä)	163	41°30′N	35°50′E
Bagabag, Phil. (bä-gä-bäg′)	213a	16°38′N	121°16′E
Bāgalkot, India	203	16°14′N	75°40′E
Bagamoyo, Tan. (bä-gä-mō′yō)	233	6°26′S	38°54′E
Bagaryak, Russia (bȧ-gȧr-yäk′)	186a	56°13′N	61°32′E
Bagbele, D.R.C.	237	4°21′N	29°17′E
Bagdad see Baghdād, Iraq	198	33°14′N	44°22′E
Baghdād, Iraq (bȧgh-dȧd′) (băg′dăd)	198	33°14′N	44°22′E
Bagheria, Italy (bä-gå-rē′ä)	174	38°03′N	13°32′E
Bagley, Mn., U.S. (băg′lē)	112	47°31′N	95°24′W
Bagnara, Italy (bän-yä′rä)	174	38°17′N	15°52′E
Bagnell Dam, Mo., U.S. (băg′nĕl)	121	38°13′N	92°40′W
Bagnères-de-Bigorre, Fr. (băn-yâr′dĕ-bē-gor′)	170	43°04′N	0°09′E
Bagnères-de-Luchon, Fr. (băn-yâr′ dĕ-lu chôn′)	170	42°46′N	0°36′E
Bagnols-sur-Ceze, Fr. (bä-nyôl′)	170	44°09′N	4°37′E
Bago, Mya.	212	17°17′N	96°29′E
Bagoé, r., Mali (bȧ-gō′ȧ)	230	12°22′N	6°34′W
Baguio, Phil. (bä-gē-ō′)	212	16°24′N	120°36′E
Bagzane, Monts, mtn., Niger	230	18°40′N	8°40′E
Bahamas, nation, N.A. (bȧ-hä′mȧs)	129	26°15′N	76°00′W
Bahau, Malay.	197b	2°48′N	102°25′E
Bahāwalpur, Pak. (bŭ-hä′wŭl-pōōr)	199	29°29′N	71°41′E
Bahia, state, Braz.	143	11°05′S	43°00′W
Bahía, Islas de la, i., Hond. (ē′s-läs-dĕ-lä-bä-ē′ä)	128	16°15′N	86°30′W
Bahia Blanca, Arg. (bä-ē′ä blän′kä)	144	38°45′S	62°07′W
Bahía de Caráquez, Ec. (bä-e′ä dä kä-rä′kĕz)	142	0°45′S	80°29′W
Bahía Negra, Para. (bä-ē′ä nä′grä)	143	20°11′S	58°05′W
Bahi Swamp, sw., Tan.	237	6°05′S	35°10′E
Bahoruco, Sierra de, mts., Dom. Rep. (sē-ĕ′r-rä-dĕ-bä-ō-rōō′kô)	135	18°10′N	71°25′W
Bahrain, nation, Asia (bä-rān′)	198	26°15′N	51°17′E
Baḥr al Ghazāl, hist. reg., Sudan (bär ĕl ghä-zäl′)	231	7°56′N	27°15′E
Baḥrīyah, oasis, Egypt (bȧ-hȧ-rē′yä)	163	28°34′N	29°01′E
Baía dos Tigres, Ang.	236	16°36′S	11°43′E
Baia Mare, Rom. (bä′yä mä′rä)	163	47°40′N	23°35′E
Baidyabātī, India	202a	22°47′N	88°21′E
Baie-Comeau, Can.	100	49°13′N	68°10′W
Baie de Wasai, Mi., U.S. (bā dē wä-sä′ē)	117k	46°27′N	84°15′W
Baie-Saint Paul, Can. (bā′sănt-pôl′)	91	47°27′N	70°30′W
Baigou, China (bī-gō)	206	39°08′N	116°02′E
Baihe, China (bī-hŭ)	208	32°30′N	110°15′E
Bai Hu, l., China (bī-hōō)	206	31°22′N	117°38′E
Baiju, China (bī-jyōō)	206	33°04′N	120°17′E
Baikal, Lake see Baykal, Ozero, l., Russia	179	53°00′N	109°28′E
Bailén, Spain (bä-ē-lān′)	172	38°05′N	3°48′W
Băileşti, Rom. (bă-ĭ-lĕsh′tē)	175	44°01′N	23°21′E
Bainbridge, Ga., U.S. (bān′brĭj)	124	30°52′N	84°35′W
Bainbridge Island, i., Wa., U.S.	116a	47°39′N	122°32′W
Baipu, China (bī-pōō)	206	32°15′N	120°47′E
Baiquan, China (bī-chyuäŋ)	208	47°22′N	126°00′E
Baird, Tx., U.S. (bârd)	122	32°22′N	99°28′W
Bairdford, Pa., U.S. (bârd′fõrd)	111e	40°37′N	79°53′W
Baird Mountains, mts., Ak., U.S.	103	67°35′N	160°10′W
Bairnsdale, Austl. (bârnz′dāl)	219	37°50′S	147°39′E
Baïse, r., Fr. (bä-ēz′)	170	43°52′N	0°23′E
Baiyang Dian, l., China (bī-yäŋ-dĭĕn)	206	39°00′N	115°45′E
Baiyu Shan, mts., China (bī-yōō shän)	208	37°02′N	108°30′E
Baja, Hung. (bŏ′yŏ)	169	46°11′N	18°55′E
Baja California, state, Mex. (bä-hä)	128	30°15′N	117°25′W
Baja California, pen., Mex.	89	28°00′N	113°30′W
Baja California Sur, state, Mex.	128	26°00′N	113°30′W
Bajo, Canal, can., Spain	173a	40°36′N	3°41′W
Bakal, Russia (bä′kăl)	186a	54°57′N	58°50′E
Baker, Mt., U.S. (bā′kẽr)	115	46°21′N	104°12′W
Baker, Or., U.S.	104	44°46′N	117°52′W
Baker, i., Oc.	2	1°00′N	176°00′W
Baker, l., Can.	92	63°51′N	96°10′W
Baker, Mount, mtn., Wa., U.S.	106	48°46′N	121°52′W
Baker Creek, r., Il., U.S.	111a	41°13′N	87°47′W
Bakersfield, Ca., U.S. (bā′kẽrz-fēld)	104	35°23′N	119°00′W
Bakerstown, Pa., U.S. (bā′kerz-toun)	111e	40°39′N	79°56′W
Bakewell, Eng., U.K. (băk′wĕl)	158a	53°12′N	1°40′W
Bakhchysarai, Ukr.	177	44°46′N	33°54′E
Bakhmach, Ukr. (bȧk-mäch′)	177	51°09′N	32°47′E
Bakhtarān, Iran	198	34°01′N	47°00′E
Bakhtegan, Daryācheh-ye, l., Iran	198	29°29′N	54°31′E
Bakhteyevo, Russia	186b	55°35′N	38°32′E
Bako, Eth. (bä′kō)	231	5°47′N	36°39′E
Bakony, mts., Hung. (bȧ-kōn′y′)	169	46°57′N	17°30′E
Bakoye, r., Afr. (bȧ-kô′ē)	230	12°47′N	9°35′W
Bakr Uzyak, Russia (bȧkr ōōz′yȧk)	186a	52°59′N	58°43′E
Baku (Bakı), Azer. (bȧ-kōō′)	178	40°28′N	49°45′E
Bakwanga see Mbuji-Mayi, D.R.C.	236	6°09′S	23°28′E
Balabac Island, i., Phil. (bä′lä-bäk)	212	8°00′N	116°28′E
Balabac Strait, strt., Asia	212	7°23′N	116°30′E
Ba'labakk, Leb.	197a	34°00′N	36°13′E
Balabanovo, Russia (bȧ-lȧ-bä′nô-vô)	186b	56°10′N	37°44′E
Balagansk, Russia (bä-lä-gänsk′)	184	53°58′N	103°09′E
Balaguer, Spain (bä-lä-gĕr′)	173	41°48′N	0°50′E
Balakhta, Russia (bȧ′lȧk-tȧ′)	179	55°22′N	91°43′E
Balakliia, Ukr.	177	49°28′N	36°51′E
Balakovo, Russia (bȧ′lȧ-kô′vô)	181	52°00′N	47°40′E
Balancán, Mex. (bä-läŋ-kän′)	131	17°47′N	91°32′W
Balanga, Phil. (bä-läŋ′gä)	213a	14°41′N	120°31′E
Ba Lang An, Mui, c., Viet.	209	15°18′N	109°10′E
Balashikha, Russia (bȧ-lä′shĭ-kȧ)	186b	55°48′N	37°58′E
Balashov, Russia (bȧ′lȧ-shôf)	181	51°30′N	43°00′E
Balasore, India (bä-lȧ-sōr′)	199	21°38′N	86°59′E
Balassagyarmat, Hung. (bô′lôsh-shô-dyôr′môt)	169	48°04′N	19°19′E
Balaton Lake, l., Hung. (bô′lô-tôn)	163	46°47′N	17°55′E
Balayan, Phil. (bä-lä-yän′)	213a	13°56′N	120°44′E
Balayan Bay, b., Phil.	213a	13°46′N	120°46′E
Balboa Heights, Pan. (băl-bô′ä)	133	8°59′N	79°33′W
Balboa Mountain, mtn., Pan.	128a	9°05′N	79°44′W
Balcarce, Arg. (bäl-kär′sā)	144	37°49′S	58°17′W
Balchik, Blg.	175	43°24′N	28°13′E
Bald Eagle, Mn., U.S. (bôld ē′g'l)	117g	45°06′N	93°01′W
Bald Eagle Lake, l., Mn., U.S.	117g	45°08′N	93°03′W
Baldock Lake, l., Can.	97	56°33′N	97°57′W
Baldwin Park, Ca., U.S. (bôld′wĭn)	117a	34°05′N	117°58′W
Baldwinsville, N.Y., U.S. (bôld′wĭns-vĭl)	109	43°10′N	76°20′W
Baldy Mountain, mtn., Can.	97	51°28′N	100°44′W
Baldy Peak, mtn., Az., U.S. (bôl′dē)	106	33°55′N	109°35′W
Baldy Peak, mtn., Tx., U.S. (bôl′dē pēk)	122	30°38′N	104°11′W
Balearic Islands see Balears, Illes, is., Spain	156	39°25′N	1°28′E
Balearic Sea, sea, Spain (băl-ē-ăr′ĭk)	173	39°40′N	1°05′E
Balears, Illes, is., Spain	156	39°25′N	1°28′E
Baleine, Grande Rivière de la, r., Can.	93	55°00′N	75°30′W
Baler, Phil. (bä-lar′)	213a	15°46′N	121°33′E
Baler Bay, b., Phil.	213a	15°51′N	121°40′E
Balesin, i., Phil.	213a	14°28′N	122°10′E
Baley, Russia (bȧl-yā′)	185	51°29′N	116°12′E
Balfate, Hond. (băl-fä′tē)	132	15°48′N	86°24′W
Balfour, S. Afr. (băl′fòr)	238c	26°41′S	28°37′E
Bali, i., Indon. (bä′lē)	212	8°00′S	115°22′E
Balıkeşir, Tur. (balĭk′ĭysĭr)	181	39°40′N	27°50′E
Balikpapan, Indon. (bä′lēk-pä′pän)	212	1°13′S	116°52′E
Balintang Channel, strt., Phil. (bä-lĭn-täng′)	212	19°50′N	121°08′E
Balkan Mountains see Stara Planina, mts., Blg.	156	42°50′N	24°45′E
Balkh, Afg. (bälk)	199	36°48′N	66°50′E
Balkhash, Lake see Balqash köli, l., Kaz.	183	45°58′N	72°15′E
Ballancourt, Fr. (bä-läN-kòr′)	171b	48°31′N	2°23′E
Ballarat, Austl. (băl′ȧ-răt)	219	37°37′S	144°00′E
Ballard, l., Austl. (băl′ȧrd)	220	29°15′S	120°45′E
Ballater, Scot., U.K. (bäl′ȧ-tẽr)	164	57°05′N	3°06′W
Balleny Islands, is., Ant. (băl′ĕ nē)	224	67°00′S	164°00′E
Ballina, Austl. (băl-ĭ-nä′)	222	28°50′S	153°35′E
Ballina, Ire.	164	54°06′N	9°05′W
Ballinasloe, Ire. (băl′ĭ-nȧ-slō′)	164	53°20′N	8°09′W
Ballinger, Tx., U.S. (băl′ĭn-jẽr)	122	31°45′N	99°58′W
Ballston Spa, N.Y., U.S. (bôls′tŭn spä′)	109	43°05′N	73°50′W
Balmazújváros, Hung. (bŏl′mŏz-ōō′y′vä′rōsh)	169	47°35′N	21°23′E
Balobe, D.R.C.	237	0°05′N	28°00′E
Balonne, r., Austl. (băl-ōn′)	221	27°00′S	149°10′E
Bālotra, India	202	25°56′N	72°12′E
Balqash, Kaz.	183	46°58′N	75°00′E
Balqash köli, l., Kaz.	183	45°58′N	72°15′E
Balranald, Austl. (băl′-rȧn-ăld)	222	34°42′S	143°30′E
Balsam, l., Can. (bôl′sȧm)	99	44°30′N	78°50′W
Balsas, Braz. (bäl′säs)	143	7°09′S	46°04′W
Balsas, r., Mex.	128	18°00′N	101°00′W
Balta, Ukr. (bäl′tä)	181	47°57′N	29°38′E
Bălţi, Mol.	181	47°47′N	27°57′E
Baltic Sea, sea, Eur. (bôl′tĭk)	156	55°20′N	16°50′E
Baltīm, Egypt (bål-tēm′)	238b	31°33′N	31°04′E
Baltimore, Md., U.S. (bôl′tĭ-môr)	105	39°20′N	76°38′W
Baltiysk, Russia (bäl-tēysk′)	167	54°40′N	19°55′E
Baluarte, Río del, Mex. (rē′ō-dĕl-bä-lōō′r-tĕ)	130	23°09′N	105°42′W
Baluchistān, hist. reg., Asia (bȧ-lò-chĭ-stän′)	199	27°30′N	65°30′E
Balzac, Can. (bôl′zăk)	102e	51°10′N	114°01′W
Bama, Nig.	235	11°30′N	13°41′E
Bamako, Mali (bä-mä-kō′)	230	12°39′N	8°00′W
Bambang, Phil. (bäm-bäng′)	213a	16°24′N	121°08′E
Bambari, C.A.R. (bäm-bȧ-rē)	231	5°44′N	20°40′E
Bamberg, Ger. (bäm′bĕrgh)	161	49°53′N	10°52′E
Bamberg, S.C., U.S. (băm′bûrg)	125	33°17′N	81°04′W
Bamenda, Cam.	235	5°56′N	10°10′E
Bamingui, r., C.A.R.	235	7°35′N	19°45′E
Bampton, Eng., U.K. (băm′tŭn)	158b	51°42′N	1°33′W
Bampūr, Iran (bŭm-pōōr′)	198	27°15′N	60°22′E
Bam Yanga, Ngao, mts., Cam.	235	8°20′N	14°40′E
Banahao, Mount, mtn., Phil. (bä-nä-hä′ô)	213a	14°04′N	121°45′E
Banalia, D.R.C.	237	1°33′N	25°20′E
Banamba, Mali	234	13°33′N	7°27′W
Bananal, Braz. (bä-nä-näl′)	141a	22°42′S	44°17′W
Bananal, Ilha do, i., Braz. (ē′lä-dô-bä-nä-näl′)	143	12°09′S	50°27′W
Banās, r., India (bän-äs′)	199	25°20′N	75°20′E
Banās, Ra's, c., Egypt	231	23°48′N	36°39′E
Banat, reg., Rom. (bä-nät′)	175	45°35′N	21°05′E
Bancroft, Can. (băn′krŏft)	91	45°05′N	77°55′W
Bancroft see Chililabombwe, Zam.	237	12°18′S	27°43′E
Bānda, India (bän′dä)	199	25°36′N	80°21′E
Banda, Kepulauan, is., Indon.	213	4°40′S	129°56′E
Banda, Laut (Banda Sea), sea, Indon.	213	6°05′S	127°28′E
Banda Aceh, Indon.	212	5°10′N	95°10′E
Banda Banda, Mount, mtn., Austl. (băn′dȧ băn′dȧ)	222	31°09′S	152°15′E
Bandama Blanc, r., C. Iv. (bän-dä′mä)	234	6°15′N	5°00′W
Bandar Beheshtī, Iran	198	25°18′N	60°45′E
Bandar-e ʽAbbās, Iran (bän-där′ ȧb-bäs′)	198	27°04′N	56°22′E
Bandar-e Būshehr, Iran	198	28°48′N	50°53′E
Bandar-e Lengeh, Iran	198	26°44′N	54°47′E
Bandar-e Torkeman, Iran	198	37°05′N	54°08′E
Bandar Lampung, Indon.	212	5°16′S	105°06′E
Bandar Maharani, Malay. (bän-där′ mä-hä-rä′nē)	197b	2°02′N	102°34′E
Bandar Seri Begawan, Bru.	212	5°00′N	114°59′E
Bande, Spain (bän′dā)	172	42°02′N	7°58′W
Bandeira, Pico da, mtn., Braz. (pē′kô dä bän-dā′rä)	143	20°27′S	41°47′W
Bandelier National Monument, rec., N.M., U.S. (băn-dĕ-lēr′)	119	35°50′N	106°45′W
Banderas, Bahía de, b., Mex. (bä-ē′ä dĕ bän-dĕ′räs)	130	20°38′N	105°35′W
Bandirma, Tur. (bän-dĭr′mȧ)	163	40°25′N	27°50′E
Bandon, Or., U.S. (băn′dŭn)	114	43°06′N	124°25′W
Bāndra, India	203b	19°04′N	72°49′E
Bandundu, D.R.C.	232	3°18′S	17°20′E
Bandung, Indon.	212	7°00′S	107°22′E
Banes, Cuba (bä′näs)	135	21°00′N	75°45′W
Banff, Can. (bănf)	90	51°10′N	115°34′W
Banff, Scot., U.K.	164	57°39′N	2°37′W
Banff National Park, rec., Can.	92	51°38′N	116°22′W
Bánfield, Arg. (bȧ′n-fyĕ′ld)	144a	34°44′S	58°24′W
Banfora, Burkina	234	10°38′N	4°46′W
Bangalore, India (băŋ′gȧ′lôr)	199	13°03′N	77°39′E
Bangassou, C.A.R. (bän-gȧ-sōō′)	231	4°47′N	22°49′E
Bangeta, Mount, mtn., Pap. N. Gui.	213	6°20′S	147°00′E
Banggai, Kepulauan, is., Indon. (bäng-gī′)	213	1°05′S	123°45′E
Banggi, Pulau, i., Malay.	212	7°12′N	117°10′E
Banghāzī, Libya	231	32°07′N	20°04′E
Bangka, i., Indon. (bäŋ′kȧ)	212	2°24′S	106°55′E
Bangkalan, Indon. (bäng-kȧ-län′)	212	6°07′S	112°50′E
Bangkok, Thai.	212	13°50′N	100°29′E
Bangladesh, nation, Asia	199	24°15′N	90°00′E
Bangong Co, l., Asia (bäŋ-gôŋ tswo)	202	33°40′N	79°30′E
Bangor, Wales, U.K. (băŋ′ôr)	164	53°13′N	4°05′W
Bangor, Me., U.S. (băn′gẽr)	105	44°47′N	68°47′W

PRONOUNCING INDEX Bayard – Bengamisa 271

PLACE (Pronunciation)	PAGE	LAT.	LONG.
Bayard, N.M., U.S.	119	32°45'N	108°07'W
Bayard, W.V., U.S.	109	39°15'N	79°20'W
Bayburt, Tur. (bä'ĭ-bŏort)	181	40°15'N	40°10'E
Bay City, Mi., U.S. (bā)	105	43°35'N	83°55'W
Bay City, Tx., U.S.	123	28°59'N	95°58'W
Baydaratskaya Guba, b., Russia	180	69°20'N	66°10'E
Bay de Verde, Can.	101	48°05'N	52°54'W
Baydhabo (Baidoa), Som.	238a	3°19'N	44°20'E
Baydrag, r., Mong.	204	46°09'N	98°52'E
Bayern, state, Ger.	159d	48°05'N	11°30'E
Bayern (Bavaria), hist. reg., Ger. (bī'ērn) (bȧ-vâ-rĭ-ȧ)	168	49°00'N	11°16'E
Bayeux, Fr. (bȧ-yû')	161	49°19'N	0°41'W
Bayfield, Wi., U.S. (bā'fēld)	113	46°48'N	90°51'W
Baykal, Ozero (Lake Baikal), l., Russia	179	53°00'N	109°28'E
Baykal'skiy Khrebet, mts., Russia	179	53°30'N	107°30'E
Baykit, Russia (bī-kēt')	179	61°43'N	96°39'E
Baymak, Russia (bày'mäk)	186a	52°35'N	58°21'E
Bay Mills, Mi., U.S. (bā mĭlls)	117k	46°27'N	84°36'W
Bay Mills Indian Reservation, I.R., Mi., U.S.	113	46°19'N	85°03'W
Bay Minette, Al., U.S. (bā'mĭn-ĕt')	124	30°52'N	87°44'W
Bayombong, Phil. (bä-yôm-bŏng')	213a	16°28'N	121°09'E
Bayonne, Fr. (bȧ-yôn')	154	43°28'N	1°30'W
Bayonne, N.J., U.S. (bā-yōn')	110a	40°40'N	74°07'W
Bayou Bodcau Reservoir, res., La., U.S. (bī'yōō bŏd'kō)	107	32°49'N	93°22'W
Bayport, Mn., U.S. (bā'pōrt)	117g	45°02'N	92°46'W
Bayqongyr, Kaz.	183	47°46'N	66°11'E
Bayramiç, Tur.	175	39°48'N	26°35'E
Bayreuth, Ger. (bī-roit')	168	49°56'N	11°35'E
Bay Roberts, Can. (bā rŏb'ērts)	101	47°36'N	53°16'W
Bays, Lake of, l., Can. (bās)	99	45°15'N	79°00'W
Bay Saint Louis, Ms., U.S. (bā' sânt lōō'ĭs)	124	30°19'N	89°20'W
Bay Shore, N.Y., U.S. (bā' shôr)	110a	40°44'N	73°15'W
Bayt Lahm, W.B. (bĕth'lē-hĕm)	197a	31°42'N	35°13'E
Baytown, Tx., U.S. (bā'town)	123a	29°44'N	95°01'W
Bayview, Al., U.S. (bā'vū)	110h	33°34'N	86°59'W
Bayview, Wa., U.S.	116a	48°29'N	122°28'W
Bay Village, Oh., U.S. (bā)	111d	41°29'N	81°56'W
Baza, Spain (bä'thä)	162	37°29'N	2°46'W
Baza, Sierra de, mts., Spain	172	37°19'N	2°48'W
Bazar-Dyuzi, mtn., Azer. (bä'zár-dyōōz'ĕ)	181	41°20'N	47°40'E
Bazaruto, Ilha do, i., Moz. (bȧ-zȧ-rōō'tō)	232	21°42'S	36°10'E
Bazièges, Fr.	170	43°25'N	1°41'E
Be, Nosy, i., Madag.	233	13°14'S	47°28'E
Beach, N.D., U.S. (bēch)	112	46°55'N	104°00'W
Beachy Head, c., Eng., U.K. (bēchē hĕd)	165	50°40'N	0°25'E
Beacon, N.Y., U.S. (bē'kŭn)	109	41°30'N	73°55'W
Beaconsfield, Can. (bē'kŭnz-fēld)	102a	45°26'N	73°51'W
Beals Creek, r., Tx., U.S. (bēls)	122	32°10'N	101°14'W
Bear, r., Ut., U.S.	117b	41°28'N	112°10'W
Bear, r., U.S.	115	42°17'N	111°42'W
Bear Brook, r., Can.	102c	45°24'N	75°15'W
Bear Creek, Mt., U.S. (bâr krēk)	115	45°11'N	109°07'W
Bear Creek, r., Al., U.S. (bâr)	124	34°27'N	88°00'W
Bear Creek, r., Tx., U.S.	117c	32°56'N	97°09'W
Beardstown, Il., U.S. (bērds'toun)	121	40°01'N	90°26'W
Bearfort Mountain, mtn., N.J., U.S. (bē'fŏrt)	110a	41°08'N	74°23'W
Bearhead Mountain, mtn., Wa., U.S. (bâr'hĕd)	116a	47°01'N	121°49'W
Bear Lake, l., Can.	97	55°08'N	96°00'W
Bear Lake, l., Id., U.S.	115	41°56'N	111°10'W
Bear River Range, mts., U.S.	115	41°50'N	111°30'W
Beas de Segura, Spain (bā'äs dā sä-gōō'rä)	172	38°16'N	2°53'W
Beata, i., Dom. Rep. (bĕ-ä'tä)	135	17°40'N	71°40'W
Beata, Cabo, c., Dom. Rep. (ká'bô-bĕ-ä'tä)	135	17°40'N	71°20'W
Beatrice, Ne., U.S. (bē'ȧ-trĭs)	104	40°16'N	96°45'W
Beatty, Nv., U.S. (bēt'ē)	118	36°58'N	116°48'W
Beattyville, Ky., U.S. (bēt'ē-vĭl)	108	37°35'N	83°40'W
Beaucaire, Fr. (bō-kâr')	170	43°49'N	4°37'E
Beaucourt, Fr. (bō-kōōr')	171	47°30'N	6°54'E
Beaufort, N.C., U.S. (bō'fŏrt)	125	34°43'N	76°40'W
Beaufort, S.C., U.S.	125	32°25'N	80°40'W
Beaufort Sea, sea, N.A.	103	70°30'N	138°40'W
Beaufort West, S. Afr.	232	32°20'S	22°45'E
Beauharnois, Can. (bō-är-nwä')	99	45°23'N	73°52'W
Beaumont, Can.	102b	46°50'N	71°01'W
Beaumont, Can.	102g	53°22'N	113°18'W
Beaumont, Ca., U.S. (bō'mŏnt)	117a	33°57'N	116°57'W
Beaumont, Tx., U.S.	105	30°05'N	94°06'W
Beaune, Fr. (bōn)	170	47°02'N	4°49'E
Beauport, Can. (bō-pôr')	102b	46°52'N	71°11'W
Beauséjour, Can.	90	50°04'N	96°33'W
Beauvais, Fr. (bō-vĕ')	170	49°25'N	2°05'E
Beaver, Ok., U.S. (bē'vēr)	120	36°46'N	100°31'W
Beaver, Pa., U.S.	111e	40°42'N	80°18'W
Beaver, Ut., U.S.	119	38°15'N	112°40'W
Beaver, i., Mi., U.S.	108	45°40'N	85°30'W
Beaver, r., Can.	92	54°20'N	111°10'W
Beaver City, Ne., U.S.	120	40°08'N	99°52'W
Beaver Creek, r., Co., U.S.	120	39°42'N	103°37'W
Beaver Creek, r., Ks., U.S.	120	39°44'N	101°05'W
Beaver Creek, r., Mt., U.S.	112	46°45'N	104°18'W
Beaver Creek, r., Wy., U.S.	112	43°46'N	104°25'W
Beaver Dam, Wi., U.S.	113	43°29'N	88°50'W
Beaverhead, r., Mt., U.S.	115	45°25'N	112°35'W
Beaverhead Mountains, mts., Mt., U.S. (bē'vēr-hĕd)	115	44°33'N	112°59'W

PLACE (Pronunciation)	PAGE	LAT.	LONG.
Beaver Indian Reservation, I.R., Mi., U.S.	108	45°40'N	85°30'W
Beaverton, Or., U.S. (bē'vēr-tŭn)	116c	45°29'N	122°49'W
Bebington, Eng., U.K. (bē'bĭng-tŭn)	158a	53°20'N	2°59'W
Bečej, Serb. (bĕ'chā)	175	45°36'N	20°03'E
Béchar, Alg.	230	31°39'N	2°14'W
Becharof, l., Ak., U.S. (bĕk-ȧ-rôf)	103	57°58'N	156°58'W
Becher Bay, b., Can. (bēch'ēr)	116a	48°18'N	123°37'W
Beckley, W.V., U.S. (bĕk'lĭ)	108	37°40'N	81°15'W
Bédarieux, Fr. (bā-dȧ-ryû')	170	43°36'N	3°11'E
Beddington Creek, r., Can. (bĕd'ĕng tŭn)	102e	51°14'N	114°13'W
Bedford, Can. (bĕd'fērd)	99	45°10'N	73°00'W
Bedford, S. Afr.	233c	32°43'S	26°19'E
Bedford, Eng., U.K.	161	52°10'N	0°25'W
Bedford, Ia., U.S.	113	40°40'N	94°41'W
Bedford, In., U.S.	108	38°50'N	86°30'W
Bedford, Ma., U.S.	101a	42°30'N	71°17'W
Bedford, N.Y., U.S.	110a	41°12'N	73°38'W
Bedford, Oh., U.S.	111d	41°23'N	81°32'W
Bedford, Pa., U.S.	109	40°05'N	78°20'W
Bedford, Va., U.S.	125	37°19'N	79°27'W
Bedford Hills, N.Y., U.S.	110a	41°14'N	73°41'W
Beebe, Ar., U.S. (bē'bē)	121	35°04'N	91°54'W
Beecher, Il., U.S. (bē'chŭr)	111a	41°20'N	87°38'W
Beechey Head, c., Can. (bē'chĭ hĕd)	116a	48°19'N	123°40'W
Beech Grove, In., U.S. (bēch grōv)	111g	39°43'N	86°05'W
Beecroft Head, c., Austl. (bē'krŏft)	222	35°03'S	151°15'E
Beelitz, Ger. (bĕ'lētz)	159b	52°14'N	12°59'E
Be'er Sheva', Isr. (bēr-shĕ'bȧ)	197a	31°15'N	34°48'E
Be'er Sheva', r., Isr.	197a	31°23'N	34°30'E
Beestekraal, S. Afr.	238c	25°22'S	27°34'E
Beeston, Eng., U.K. (bēs't'n)	158a	52°55'N	1°11'W
Beetz, r., Ger. (bĕtz)	159b	52°28'N	12°37'E
Beeville, Tx., U.S. (bē'vĭl)	123	28°24'N	97°44'W
Bega, Austl. (bā'gȧ)	219	36°50'S	149°49'E
Beggs, Ok., U.S. (bĕgz)	121	35°46'N	96°06'W
Bégles, Fr. (bĕ'gl')	170	44°47'N	0°34'W
Begoro, Ghana	234	6°23'N	0°23'W
Behala, India	202a	22°31'N	88°19'E
Behbehān, Iran	201	30°35'N	50°14'E
Behm Canal, can., Ak., U.S.	94	55°41'N	131°35'W
Bei, r., China (bā)	207a	22°54'N	113°08'E
Bei'an, China (bā-än)	208	48°05'N	126°26'E
Beicai, China (bā-tsī)	207b	31°12'N	121°33'E
Beifei, r., China (bā-fā)	206	33°14'N	117°03'E
Beihai, China (bā-hī)	204	21°30'N	109°10'E
Beihuangcheng Dao, i., China (bā-hûäŋ-chŭŋ dou)	206	38°23'N	120°55'E
Beijing, China	205	39°55'N	116°23'E
Beijing Shi, prov., China (bā-jyĭŋ shr)	208	40°07'N	116°00'E
Beira, Moz. (bā'rȧ)	232	19°45'N	34°58'E
Beira, hist. reg., Port. (bĕ'y-rä)	172	40°38'N	8°00'W
Beirut, Leb. (bā-rōōt')	198	33°53'N	35°30'E
Beja, Port. (bä'zhä)	162	38°03'N	7°53'W
Béja, Tun.	162	36°52'N	9°20'E
Bejaïa (Bougie), Alg.	230	36°46'N	5°00'E
Bejar, Spain	172	40°25'N	5°43'W
Bejestān, Iran	198	34°30'N	58°22'E
Bejucal, Cuba (bā-hōō-käl')	134	22°56'N	82°23'W
Bejuco, Pan. (bĕ-kōō'kō)	133	8°37'N	79°54'W
Békés, Hung. (bā'kāsh)	169	46°45'N	21°08'E
Békéscsaba, Hung. (bā'kāsh-chô'bô)	163	46°39'N	21°06'E
Beketova, Russia (bĕkĕ-to'vȧ)	185	53°23'N	125°21'E
Bela Crkva, Serb. (bĕ'lä tsĕrk'vä)	175	44°53'N	21°25'E
Belalcázar, Spain (bāl-á-kä'thär)	172	38°35'N	5°12'W
Belarus, nation, Eur.	178	53°30'N	25°33'E
Belau *see* Palau, nation, Oc.	3	7°15'N	134°30'E
Bela Vista de Goiás, Braz.	143	16°57'S	48°47'W
Belawan, Indon. (bȧ-lä'wán)	212	3°43'N	98°43'E
Belaya, r., Russia (byĕ'lī-yȧ)	181	52°30'N	56°15'E
Belcher Islands, is., Can. (bĕl'chēr)	93	56°20'N	80°40'W
Belding, Mi., U.S. (bĕl'dĭng)	108	43°05'N	85°25'W
Belebey, Russia (byĕ'lĕ-bā'ĭ)	180	54°00'N	54°10'E
Belém, Braz. (bā-lĕN')	143	1°18'S	48°27'W
Belén, Para. (bā-lān')	144	23°30'S	57°09'W
Belen, N.M., U.S. (bĕ-lân')	119	34°40'N	106°45'W
Bélep, Îles, is., N. Cal.	221	19°30'S	164°00'E
Belëv, Russia (byĕl'yĕf)	180	53°49'N	36°06'E
Belfair, Wa., U.S. (bĕl'far)	116a	47°27'N	122°50'W
Belfast, N. Ire., U.K.	154	54°36'N	5°45'W
Belfast, Me., U.S. (bĕl'fȧst)	100	44°25'N	69°01'W
Belfast, Lough, b., N. Ire., U.K. (lŏk bĕl'fást)	164	54°45'N	6°00'W
Belford Roxo, Braz.	144b	22°46'S	43°24'W
Belfort, Fr. (bā-fôr')	161	47°40'N	7°50'E
Belgaum, India	199	15°57'N	74°32'E
Belgium, nation, Eur. (bĕl'jĭ-ŭm)	154	51°00'N	2°52'E
Belgorod, Russia (byĕl'gŭ-rut)	181	50°36'N	36°32'E
Belgorod, prov., Russia	177	50°40'N	36°42'E
Belgrade (Beograd), Serb.	154	44°48'N	20°32'E
Belhaven, N.C., U.S. (bĕl'hā-vĕn)	125	35°33'N	76°37'W
Belington, W.V., U.S. (bĕl'ĭng-tŭn)	109	39°00'N	79°55'W
Belitung, i., Indon.	212	3°30'S	107°30'E
Belize, nation, N.A.	128	17°00'N	88°40'W
Belize, r., Belize	132a	17°16'N	88°56'W
Belize City, Belize (bĕ-lēz')	128	17°31'N	88°10'W
Bel'kovo, Russia (byĕl'kô-vô)	186b	56°15'N	38°49'E
Bel'kovskiy, i., Russia (byĕl-kôf'skĭ)	185	75°45'N	137°00'E
Bell, i., Can. (bĕl)	101	50°45'N	55°35'W
Bell, r., Can.	99	49°25'N	77°15'W
Bella Bella, Can.	94	52°10'N	128°07'W
Bella Coola, Can.	94	52°22'N	126°46'W
Bellaire, Oh., U.S. (bĕl-âr')	108	40°00'N	80°45'W
Bellaire, Tx., U.S.	123a	29°43'N	95°28'W

PLACE (Pronunciation)	PAGE	LAT.	LONG.
Bellary, India (bĕl-lä'rē)	199	15°15'N	76°56'E
Bella Union, Ur. (bĕ'l-yȧ-ōō-nyô'n)	144	30°18'S	57°26'W
Bella Vista, Arg. (bä'lyȧ vēs'tȧ)	144	27°07'S	65°14'W
Bella Vista, Arg.	144	28°35'S	58°53'W
Bella Vista, Arg.	144a	34°35'S	58°41'W
Bella Vista, Para.	143	22°16'S	56°14'W
Belle-Anse, Haiti	135	18°15'N	72°00'W
Belle Bay, b., Can. (bĕl)	101	47°35'N	55°15'W
Belle Chasse, La., U.S. (bĕl shäs')	110d	29°52'N	90°00'W
Bellefontaine, Oh., U.S. (bel-fŏn'tân)	108	40°25'N	83°50'W
Bellefontaine Neighbors, Mo., U.S.	117e	38°46'N	90°13'W
Belle Fourche, S.D., U.S. (bĕl fōōrsh')	112	44°28'N	103°50'W
Belle Fourche, r., Wy., U.S.	112	44°29'N	104°40'W
Belle Fourche Reservoir, res., S.D., U.S.	112	44°51'N	103°44'W
Bellegarde, Fr. (bĕl-gärd')	171	46°06'N	5°50'E
Belle Glade, Fl., U.S. (bĕl glād)	125a	26°39'N	80°37'W
Belle-Île, i., Fr. (bĕlēl')	161	47°15'N	3°30'W
Belle Isle, Strait of, strt., Can.	93	51°35'N	56°30'W
Belle Mead, N.J., U.S. (bĕl mēd)	110a	40°28'N	74°40'W
Belleoram, Can.	101	47°31'N	55°25'W
Belle Plaine, Ia., U.S. (bĕl plān')	113	41°52'N	92°19'W
Belle Vernon, Pa., U.S. (bĕl vûr'nŭn)	111e	40°08'N	79°52'W
Belleville, Can. (bĕl'vĭl)	99	44°15'N	77°25'W
Belleville, Il., U.S.	117e	38°31'N	89°59'W
Belleville, Ks., U.S.	121	39°49'N	97°37'W
Belleville, Mi., U.S.	111b	42°12'N	83°29'W
Belleville, N.J., U.S.	110a	40°47'N	74°09'W
Bellevue, Ia., U.S. (bĕl'vū)	113	42°14'N	90°26'W
Bellevue, Ky., U.S.	111f	39°06'N	84°29'W
Bellevue, Mi., U.S.	108	42°30'N	85°00'W
Bellevue, Oh., U.S.	108	41°15'N	82°45'W
Bellevue, Pa., U.S.	111e	40°30'N	80°04'W
Bellevue, Wa., U.S.	116a	47°37'N	122°12'W
Belley, Fr. (bĕ-lē')	171	45°46'N	5°41'E
Bellflower, Ca., U.S. (bĕl-flou'ēr)	117a	33°53'N	118°08'W
Bell Gardens, Ca., U.S.	117a	33°59'N	118°11'W
Bellingham, Ma., U.S. (bĕl'ĭng-hăm)	101a	42°05'N	71°28'W
Bellingham, Wa., U.S.	104	48°46'N	122°29'W
Bellingham Bay, b., Wa., U.S.	116d	48°44'N	122°34'W
Bellingshausen Sea, sea, Ant. (bĕl'ĭngz houz'n)	224	72°00'S	80°30'W
Bellinzona, Switz. (bĕl-ĭn-tsō'nä)	168	46°10'N	9°09'E
Bellmore, N.Y., U.S. (bĕl-mōr)	110a	40°40'N	73°31'W
Bello, Col. (bĕ'l-yô)	142	6°20'N	75°33'W
Bellow Falls, Vt., U.S. (bĕl'ōz fôls)	109	43°10'N	72°30'W
Bellpat, Pak.	202	29°08'N	68°00'E
Bell Peninsula, pen., Can.	93	63°50'N	81°16'W
Bells Corners, Can.	102c	45°20'N	75°49'W
Bells Mountain, mtn., Wa., U.S. (bĕls)	116c	45°50'N	122°21'W
Belluno, Italy (bĕl-lōō'nō)	174	46°08'N	12°14'E
Bell Ville, Arg. (bĕl vēl')	144	32°33'S	62°36'W
Bellville, S. Afr.	232a	33°54'S	18°38'E
Bellville, Tx., U.S. (bĕl'vĭl)	123	29°57'N	96°15'W
Bélmez, Spain (bĕl'mĕth)	172	38°17'N	5°17'W
Belmond, Ia., U.S. (bĕl'mŏnd)	113	42°49'N	93°37'W
Belmont, Ca., U.S.	116b	37°34'N	122°18'W
Belmonte, Braz. (bĕl-mōn'tȧ)	143	15°58'S	38°47'W
Belmopan, Belize	128	17°15'N	88°47'W
Belogorsk, Russia	179	51°09'N	128°32'E
Belo Horizonte, Braz. (bĕ'lôre-sô'n-tĕ)	143	19°54'S	43°56'W
Beloit, Ks., U.S. (bē-loit')	120	39°26'N	98°06'W
Beloit, Wi., U.S.	105	42°31'N	89°04'W
Belomorsk, Russia (byĕl-ô-môrsk')	180	64°30'N	34°42'E
Beloretsk, Russia (byĕ'lō-rĕtsk)	180	53°58'N	58°25'E
Belosarayskaya, Kosa, c., Ukr.	177	46°43'N	37°18'E
Belovo, Russia (bvĕ'lŭ-vŭ)	184	54°25'N	86°18'E
Beloye, l., Russia	180	60°10'N	38°05'E
Belozersk, Russia (byĕ-lŭ-zyôrsk')	180	60°00'N	38°00'E
Belper, Eng., U.K. (bĕl'pēr)	158a	53°01'N	1°28'W
Belt, Mt., U.S. (bĕlt)	115	47°11'N	110°58'W
Belt Creek, r., Mt., U.S.	115	47°19'N	110°58'W
Belton, Tx., U.S. (bĕl'tŭn)	123	31°04'N	97°27'W
Belton Lake, l., Tx., U.S.	123	31°15'N	97°35'W
Beltsville, Md., U.S. (belts-vĭl)	110e	39°03'N	76°56'W
Belukha, Mount, mtn., Asia	178	49°47'N	86°23'E
Belvidere, Il., U.S. (bĕl-vĕ-dēr')	113	42°14'N	88°52'W
Belvidere, N.J., U.S.	109	40°50'N	75°05'W
Belyando, r., Austl. (bĕl-yän'dō)	221	22°09'S	146°48'E
Belyanka, Russia (byĕl'yán-kȧ)	186a	56°04'N	59°16'E
Belyy, Russia (byĕ'lē)	180	55°52'N	32°58'E
Belyy, i., Russia	178	73°19'N	72°00'E
Belyye Stolby, Russia (byĕ'lĭ-ye stôl'bĭ)	186b	55°20'N	37°52'E
Belzig, Ger. (bĕl'tsēg)	159b	52°08'N	12°35'E
Belzoni, Ms., U.S. (bĕl-zō'nē)	124	33°09'N	90°30'W
Bembe, Ang. (bĕn'bĕ)	232	7°00'S	14°20'E
Bembézar, r., Spain (bĕm-bā-thär')	172	38°00'N	5°18'W
Bemidji, Mn., U.S. (bē-mĭj'ĭ)	113	47°28'N	94°54'W
Bena Dibele, D.R.C. (bĕn'á dē-bĕ'lĕ)	232	4°00'S	22°49'E
Benalla, Austl. (bĕn-ăl'ȧ)	219	36°30'S	146°00'E
Benares *see* Vārānasi, India	199	25°25'N	83°00'E
Benavente, Spain (bā-nä-vĕn'tä)	162	42°01'N	5°43'W
Benbrook, Tx., U.S. (bĕn'brŏŏk)	117c	32°41'N	97°27'W
Benbrook Reservoir, res., Tx., U.S.	117c	32°35'N	97°30'W
Bend, Or., U.S. (bĕnd)	104	44°04'N	121°17'W
Bendeleben, Mount, mtn., Ak., U.S. (bĕn-dĕl-bĕn)	103	65°18'N	163°45'W
Bender Beyla, Som.	238a	9°40'N	50°45'E
Bendigo, Austl. (bĕn'dĭ-gō)	219	36°39'S	144°20'E
Benedict, Md., U.S. (bĕnĕ'dĭct)	110e	38°31'N	76°41'W
Benešov, Czech Rep. (bĕn'ĕ-shôf)	168	49°48'N	14°40'E
Benevento, Italy (bā-nä-vĕn'tō)	162	41°08'N	14°46'E
Bengal, Bay of, b., Asia (bĕn-gôl')	196	17°30'N	87°00'E
Bengamisa, D.R.C.	237	0°57'N	25°10'E

ăt; final; rāte; senâte; ärm; ásk; sofá; fâre; ch-choose; dh-as th in other; bē; ēvent; bĕt; recĕnt; cratĕr; g-gō; gh-guttural g; bĭt; ī-short neutral; rīde; ᴋ-guttural k as ch in German ich;

PLACE (Pronunciation)	PAGE	LAT.	LONG.
Bīkaner, India (bĭ-kä′nûr)	199	28°07′N	73°19′E
Bikin, Russia (bē-kēn′)	210	46°41′N	134°29′E
Bikin, r., Russia	210	46°37′N	135°55′E
Bikoro, D.R.C. (bē-kō′rō)	232	0°45′S	18°07′E
Bikuar, Parque Nacional do, rec., Ang.	236	15°07′S	14°40′E
Bilāspur, India (bē-läs′po͞or)	199	22°08′N	82°12′E
Bila Tserkva, Ukr.	181	49°48′N	30°09′E
Bilauktaung, mts., Asia	212	14°40′N	98°50′E
Bilbao, Spain (bĭl-bä′ō)	154	43°12′N	2°48′W
Bilbays, Egypt	238b	30°26′N	31°37′E
Bileća, Bos. (bē′lĕ-chä)	175	42°52′N	18°26′E
Bilecik, Tur. (bē-lĕd-zhĕk′)	163	40°10′N	29°58′E
Bilé Karpaty, mts., Eur.	169	48°53′N	17°35′E
Biłgoraj, Pol. (bēw-gō′rī)	169	50°31′N	22°43′E
Bilhorod-Dnistrovs′kyi, Ukr.	181	46°09′N	30°19′E
Bilimbay, Russia (bē′lĭm-báy)	186a	56°59′N	59°53′E
Billabong, r., Austl. (bĭl′ă-bŏng)	221	35°15′S	145°20′E
Billerica, Ma., U.S. (bĭl′rĭk-ȧ)	101a	42°33′N	71°16′W
Billericay, Eng., U.K.	158b	51°38′N	0°25′E
Billings, Mt., U.S. (bĭl′ĭngz)	104	45°47′N	108°29′W
Bill Williams, r., Az., U.S. (bĭl-wĭl′yumz)	119	34°10′N	113°50′W
Bilma, Niger (bēl′mä)	231	18°41′N	13°20′E
Bilopillia, Ukr.	181	51°10′N	34°19′E
Bilovods′k, Ukr.	177	49°12′N	39°36′E
Biloxi, Ms., U.S. (bĭ-lŏk′sĭ)	105	30°24′N	88°50′W
Bilqās Qism Awwal, Egypt	238b	31°14′N	31°25′E
Bimberi Peak, mtn., Austl. (bĭm′bĕrĭ)	222	35°45′S	148°50′E
Binalonan, Phil. (bē-nä-lô′nän)	213a	16°03′N	120°35′E
Bingen, Ger. (bĭn′gĕn)	168	49°57′N	7°54′E
Bingham, Eng., U.K. (bĭng′ăm)	158a	52°57′N	0°57′W
Bingham, Me., U.S.	100	45°03′N	69°51′W
Bingham Canyon, Ut., U.S.	117b	40°33′N	112°09′W
Binghamton, N.Y., U.S. (bĭng′ăm-tŭn)	105	42°05′N	75°55′W
Bingo-Nada, b., Japan (bĭn′gō nä-dä)	211	34°06′N	133°14′E
Binjai, Indon.	212	3°59′N	108°00′E
Binnaway, Austl. (bĭn′ă-wā)	222	31°42′S	149°22′E
Bintan, i., Indon. (bĭn′tän)	197b	1°09′N	104°43′E
Bintimani, mtn., S.L.	234	9°13′N	11°07′W
Bintulu, Malay. (bēn′to͞o-lo͞o)	212	3°07′N	113°06′E
Binxian, China	208	45°40′N	127°20′E
Binxian, China (bĭn-shyän)	206	37°27′N	117°58′E
Bio Gorge, val., Ghana	234	8°30′N	2°05′W
Bioko (Fernando Póo), i., Eq. Gui.	230	3°35′N	7°45′E
Bira, Russia (bē′rȧ)	210	49°00′N	133°18′E
Bira, r., Russia	210	48°55′N	132°25′E
Birātnagar, Nepal (bĭ-rät′nŭ-gŭr)	202	26°35′N	87°18′E
Birbka, Ukr.	169	49°36′N	24°18′E
Birch Bay, Wa., U.S. (bûrch)	116d	48°55′N	122°45′W
Birch Bay, b., Wa., U.S.	116d	48°55′N	122°52′W
Birch Island, i., Can.	97	52°25′N	99°55′W
Birch Mountains, mts., Can.	92	57°36′N	113°10′W
Birch Point, c., Wa., U.S.	116d	48°57′N	122°50′W
Bird Island, i., S. Afr. (bẽrd)	233c	33°51′S	26°21′E
Bird Rock, i., Bah. (bûrd)	135	22°50′N	74°20′W
Birds Hill, Can. (bûrds)	102f	49°58′N	97°00′W
Birdsville, Austl. (bûrdz′vĭl)	218	25°50′S	139°31′E
Birdum, Austl. (bûrd′ŭm)	218	15°45′S	133°25′E
Birecik, Tur. (bē-rĕd-zhĕk′)	163	37°10′N	37°50′E
Bir Gara, Chad	235	13°11′N	15°58′E
Bīrjand, Iran (bēr′jänd)	198	33°07′N	59°16′E
Birkenfeld, Or., U.S.	116c	45°59′N	123°20′W
Birkenhead, Eng., U.K. (bûr′kĕn-hĕd)	164	53°23′N	3°02′W
Birkenwerder, Ger. (bēr′kĕn-vĕr-dĕr)	159b	52°41′N	13°22′E
Birmingham, Eng., U.K.	154	52°29′N	1°53′W
Birmingham, Al., U.S. (bûr′mĭng-häm)	105	33°31′N	86°49′W
Birmingham, Mi., U.S.	111b	42°32′N	83°13′W
Birmingham, Mo., U.S.	117f	39°10′N	94°22′W
Birmingham Canal, can., Eng., U.K.	158a	53°07′N	2°40′W
Bi′r Misāhah, Egypt	231	22°16′N	28°04′E
Birnin Kebbi, Nig.	230	12°32′N	4°12′E
Birobidzhan, Russia (bē′rô-bē-jän′)	179	48°42′N	133°28′E
Birsk, Russia (bĭrsk)	178	55°25′N	55°30′E
Birstall, Eng., U.K. (bûr′stôl)	158a	53°44′N	1°39′W
Biryulëvo, Russia (bēr-yo͞ol′yô-vô)	186b	55°35′N	37°39′E
Biryusa, r., Russia (bēr-yo͞o′sä)	184	56°43′N	97°30′E
Bi′r Za′farānah, Egypt	173a	29°07′N	32°38′E
Biržai, Lith. (bēr-zhä′ē)	167	56°11′N	24°45′E
Bisbee, Az., U.S. (bĭz′bē)	104	31°30′N	109°55′W
Biscay, Bay of, b., Eur. (bĭs′kā′)	156	45°19′N	3°51′W
Biscayne Bay, b., Fl., U.S. (bĭs-kān′)	125a	25°22′N	80°15′W
Bischeim, Fr. (bĭsh′hīm)	171	48°40′N	7°48′E
Biscotasi Lake, l., Can.	98	47°20′N	81°55′W
Biser, Russia (bē′sĕr)	186a	58°24′N	58°54′E
Biševo, is., Serb. (bē′shē-vō)	174	42°58′N	15°50′E
Bishkek, Kyrg.	183	42°49′N	74°42′E
Bisho, S. Afr.	232	32°50′S	27°20′E
Bishop, Ca., U.S. (bĭsh′ŭp)	118	37°22′N	118°25′W
Bishop, Tx., U.S.	123	27°35′N	97°46′W
Bishop's Castle, Eng., U.K. (bĭsh′ŏps kås′l)	158a	52°29′N	2°57′W
Bishopville, S.C., U.S. (bĭsh′ŭp-vĭl)	125	34°11′N	80°13′W
Bismarck, N.D., U.S. (bĭz′märk)	104	46°48′N	100°46′W
Bismarck Archipelago, is., Pap. N. Gui.	213	3°15′S	150°45′E
Bismarck Range, mts., Pap. N. Gui.	213	5°15′S	144°15′E
Bissau, Gui.-B. (bē-sa′o͞o)	234	11°51′N	15°35′W
Bissett, Can.	97	51°01′N	95°45′W
Bistineau, l., La., U.S. (bĭs-tĭ-nō′)	123	32°19′N	93°45′W
Bistrita, Rom. (bĭs-trĭt-sȧ)	163	47°09′N	24°29′E
Bistrita, r., Rom.	169	47°08′N	25°47′E
Bitlis, Tur. (bĭt-lēs′)	198	38°30′N	42°00′E
Bitola, Mac. (bē′tô-lä) (mō′nä-stēr)	174	41°02′N	21°22′E
Bitonto, Italy (bē-tôn′tō)	174	41°08′N	16°42′E

PLACE (Pronunciation)	PAGE	LAT.	LONG.
Bitter Creek, r., Wy., U.S. (bĭt′ẽr)	115	41°36′N	108°29′W
Bitterfeld, Ger. (bĭt′ẽr-fĕlt)	168	51°39′N	12°19′E
Bitterroot, r., Mt., U.S.	115	46°28′N	114°10′W
Bitterroot Range, mts., U.S. (bĭt′ẽr-o͞ot)	106	47°15′N	115°13′W
Bityug, r., Russia (bĭt′yo͞og)	177	51°23′N	40°33′E
Biu, Nig.	235	10°35′N	12°13′E
Biwabik, Mn., U.S. (bē-wä′bĭk)	113	47°32′N	92°24′W
Biwa-ko, l., Japan (bē-wä′kō)	211	35°03′N	135°51′E
Biya, r., Russia (bī′yȧ)	184	52°22′N	87°28′E
Biysk, Russia (bēsk)	178	52°32′N	85°28′E
Bizana, S. Afr. (bĭz-änä)	233c	30°51′S	29°54′E
Bizerte, Tun. (bē-zĕrt′)	230	37°23′N	9°52′E
Bjelovar, Cro. (byĕ-lō′vär)	174	45°54′N	16°53′E
Bjørnafjorden, b., Nor.	166	60°11′N	5°26′E
Bla, Mali	234	12°57′N	5°46′W
Black, l., Mi., U.S. (blăk)	108	45°25′N	84°15′W
Black, l., N.Y., U.S.	109	44°30′N	75°35′W
Black, r., Asia	212	21°00′N	103°30′E
Black, r., Can.	98	49°20′N	81°15′W
Black, r., Az., U.S.	119	33°35′N	109°35′W
Black, r., N.Y., U.S.	109	43°45′N	75°20′W
Black, r., S.C., U.S.	125	33°55′N	80°10′W
Black, r., Wi., U.S.	113	44°07′N	90°56′W
Black, r., U.S.	121	35°47′N	91°22′W
Blackall, Austl. (blăk′ŭl)	219	24°23′S	145°37′E
Black Bay, b., Can. (blăk)	98	48°36′N	88°32′W
Blackburn, Eng., U.K. (blăk′bûrn)	164	53°45′N	2°28′W
Blackburn Mount, mtn., Ak., U.S.	103	61°50′N	143°12′W
Black Butte Lake, res., Ca., U.S.	118	39°45′N	122°20′W
Black Canyon of the Gunnison National Park, rec., Co., U.S.	119	38°34′N	107°43′W
Black Diamond, Wa., U.S. (dī′mŭnd)	116a	47°19′N	122°00′W
Black Down Hills, hills, Eng., U.K. (blăk′doun)	164	50°58′N	3°19′W
Blackduck, Mn., U.S. (blăk′dŭk)	113	47°41′N	94°33′W
Blackfeet Indian Reservation, I.R., Mt., U.S.	115	48°40′N	113°00′W
Blackfoot, Id., U.S. (blăk′fŏt)	115	43°11′N	112°23′W
Blackfoot, r., Mt., U.S.	115	46°53′N	113°33′W
Blackfoot Indian Reservation, I.R., Mt., U.S.	115	48°49′N	112°53′W
Blackfoot Indian Reserve, I.R., Can.	95	50°45′N	113°00′W
Blackfoot Reservoir, res., Id., U.S.	115	42°53′N	111°23′W
Black Forest *see* Schwarzwald, for., Ger.	168	47°54′N	7°57′E
Black Hills, mts., U.S.	106	44°08′N	103°47′W
Black Island, i., Can.	97	51°10′N	96°30′W
Black Lake, Can.	99	46°02′N	71°24′W
Black Mesa, Az., U.S. (blăk māsȧ)	119	36°33′N	110°40′W
Blackmud Creek, r., Can. (blăk′mŭd)	102g	53°28′N	113°34′W
Blackpool, Eng., U.K. (blăk′po͞ol)	164	53°49′N	3°02′W
Black Range, mts., N.M., U.S.	106	33°15′N	107°55′W
Black River, Jam. (blăk′)	134	18°00′N	77°50′W
Black River Falls, Wi., U.S.	113	44°18′N	90°51′W
Black Rock Desert, des., Nv., U.S. (rŏk)	114	40°55′N	119°00′W
Blacksburg, S.C., U.S. (blăks′bûrg)	125	35°09′N	81°30′W
Black Sea, sea	157	43°01′N	32°16′E
Blackshear, Ga., U.S. (blăk′shĭr)	125	31°20′N	82°15′W
Blackstone, Va., U.S. (blăk′stōn)	125	37°04′N	78°00′W
Black Sturgeon, r., Can. (stû′jŭn)	98	49°12′N	88°41′W
Blacktown, Austl. (blăk′toun)	217b	33°47′S	150°55′E
Blackville, Can. (blăk′vĭl)	100	46°44′N	65°50′W
Blackville, S.C., U.S.	125	33°21′N	81°19′W
Black Volta (Volta Noire), r., Afr.	230	11°30′N	4°00′W
Black Warrior, r., Al., U.S. (blăk wŏr′ĭ-ẽr)	124	32°37′N	87°42′W
Blackwater, r., Ire. (blăk-wô′tẽr)	164	52°05′N	9°02′W
Blackwater, r., Mo., U.S.	121	38°53′N	93°22′W
Blackwater, r., Va., U.S.	125	37°07′N	77°10′W
Blackwell, Ok., U.S. (blăk′wĕl)	121	36°47′N	97°19′W
Bladel, Neth.	159a	51°22′N	5°15′E
Blagodarnoye, Russia (blä′gô-där-nō′yĕ)	181	45°00′N	43°30′E
Blagoevgrad, Blg.	175	42°01′N	23°06′E
Blagoveshchensk, Russia (blä′gō-vyĕsh′chĕnsk)	179	50°16′N	127°47′E
Blagoveshchensk, Russia	186a	55°03′N	56°00′E
Blaine, Mn., U.S. (blān)	117g	45°11′N	93°14′W
Blaine, Wa., U.S.	116d	48°59′N	122°49′W
Blaine, W.V., U.S.	109	39°25′N	79°10′W
Blair, Ne., U.S. (blâr)	112	41°33′N	96°09′W
Blairmore, Can.	95	49°38′N	114°25′W
Blairsville, Pa., U.S. (blârs′vĭl)	109	40°30′N	79°40′W
Blake, i., Wa., U.S. (blāk)	116a	47°37′N	122°28′W
Blakely, Ga., U.S. (blāk′lē)	124	31°22′N	84°55′W
Blanc, Cap, c., Afr.	230	20°39′N	18°08′W
Blanc, Mont, mtn., Eur. (môn blän)	156	45°50′N	6°53′E
Blanca, Bahía, b., Arg. (bä-ē′ä-blán′kä)	144	39°30′S	61°00′W
Blanca Peak, mtn., Co., U.S. (blăŋ′kȧ)	106	37°36′N	105°22′W
Blanche, r., Can.	102c	45°34′N	75°38′W
Blanche, Lake, l., Austl. (blănch)	222	29°20′S	139°12′E
Blanchester, Oh., U.S. (blăn′chĕs-tẽr)	111f	39°18′N	83°58′W
Blanco, r., Mex.	130	24°05′N	99°21′W
Blanco, r., Mex.	131	18°42′N	96°03′W
Blanco, Cabo, c., Arg. (bläŋ′kō)	144	47°08′S	65°47′W
Blanco, Cabo, c., C.R. (ká′bô-bläŋ′kō)	132	9°29′N	85°15′W
Blanco, Cape, c., Or., U.S. (blăn′kō)	114	42°53′N	124°38′W
Blancos, Cayo, i., Cuba (kä′yō-bläŋ′kōs)	134	23°15′N	80°55′W

PLACE (Pronunciation)	PAGE	LAT.	LONG.
Blanding, Ut., U.S.	119	37°40′N	109°31′W
Blankenfelde, Ger. (blän′kĕn-fĕl-dĕ)	159b	52°20′N	13°24′E
Blanquefort, Fr.	170	44°53′N	0°38′W
Blanquilla, Arrecife, i., Mex. (är-rĕ-sē′fĕ-blän-kē′l-yä)	131	21°32′N	97°14′W
Blantyre, Mwi. (blăn-tīyr)	232	15°47′S	35°00′E
Blasdell, N.Y., U.S. (blăz′dĕl)	111c	42°48′N	78°51′W
Blato, Cro. (blä′tō)	174	42°55′N	16°47′E
Blaye-et-Sainte Luce, Fr. (blā′ā-săɴt-lüs′)	170	45°08′N	0°40′W
Błażowa, Pol. (bwä-zhō′vȧ)	169	49°51′N	22°05′E
Bleus, Monts, mts., D.R.C.	237	1°10′N	30°10′E
Blind River, Can. (blīnd)	91	46°10′N	83°09′W
Blissfield, Mi., U.S. (blĭs-fēld)	108	41°50′N	83°50′W
Blithe, r., Eng., U.K. (blĭth)	158a	52°22′N	1°49′W
Blitta, Togo	234	8°19′N	0°59′E
Block, i., R.I., U.S. (blŏk)	109	41°05′N	71°35′W
Bloedel, Can.	94	50°07′N	125°23′W
Bloemfontein, S. Afr. (blo͞om′fŏn-tān)	232	29°09′S	26°16′E
Blois, Fr. (blwä)	161	47°36′N	1°21′E
Blood Indian Reserve, I.R., Can.	95	49°30′N	113°10′W
Bloomer, Wi., U.S. (blo͞om′ẽr)	113	45°07′N	91°30′W
Bloomfield, Ia., U.S.	113	40°44′N	92°21′W
Bloomfield, In., U.S. (blo͞om′fēld)	108	39°00′N	86°55′W
Bloomfield, Mo., U.S.	121	36°54′N	89°55′W
Bloomfield, Ne., U.S.	112	42°36′N	97°40′W
Bloomfield, N.J., U.S.	110a	40°48′N	74°12′W
Bloomfield Hills, Mi., U.S.	111b	42°35′N	83°15′W
Blooming Prairie, Mn., U.S. (blo͞om′ĭng prâ′rĭ)	113	43°52′N	93°04′W
Bloomington, Ca., U.S. (blo͞om′ĭng-tŭn)	117a	34°04′N	117°24′W
Bloomington, Il., U.S.	105	40°30′N	89°00′W
Bloomington, In., U.S.	108	39°10′N	86°35′W
Bloomington, Mn., U.S.	117g	44°50′N	93°18′W
Bloomsburg, Pa., U.S. (blo͞omz′bûrg)	109	41°00′N	76°25′W
Blossburg, Al., U.S. (blŏs′bûrg)	110h	33°38′N	86°57′W
Blossburg, Pa., U.S.	109	41°45′N	77°00′W
Bloubergstrand, S. Afr.	232a	33°48′S	18°28′E
Blountstown, Fl., U.S. (blŭnts′tun)	124	30°24′N	85°02′W
Bludenz, Aus. (blo͞o-dĕnts′)	168	47°09′N	9°50′E
Blue Ash, Oh., U.S. (blo͞o ăsh)	111f	39°14′N	84°23′W
Blue Earth, Mn., U.S. (blo͞o ûrth)	113	43°38′N	94°05′W
Blue Earth, r., Mn., U.S.	113	43°55′N	94°16′W
Bluefield, W.V., U.S. (blo͞o′fēld)	125	37°15′N	81°11′W
Bluefields, Nic. (blo͞o′fēldz)	129	12°03′N	83°45′W
Blue Island, Il., U.S.	111a	41°39′N	87°41′W
Blue Mesa Reservoir, res., Co., U.S.	119	38°25′N	107°00′W
Blue Mountain, mtn., Can.	101	50°28′N	57°11′W
Blue Mountains, mts., Austl.	221	33°35′S	149°00′E
Blue Mountains, mts., Jam.	134	18°05′N	76°35′W
Blue Mountains, mts., U.S.	106	45°15′N	118°50′W
Blue Mud Bay, b., Austl. (bo͞o mŭd)	220	13°20′S	136°45′E
Blue Nile, r., Afr.	231	12°30′N	34°00′E
Blue Rapids, Ks., U.S. (blo͞o răp′ĭdz)	121	39°40′N	96°41′W
Blue Ridge, mtn., U.S. (blo͞o rĭj)	107	35°30′N	82°50′W
Blue River, Can.	90	52°05′N	119°17′W
Blue River, r., Mo., U.S.	117f	38°55′N	94°33′W
Bluff, Ut., U.S.	119	37°18′N	109°34′W
Bluff Park, Al., U.S.	110h	33°24′N	86°52′W
Bluffton, In., U.S. (blŭf′tŭn)	108	40°40′N	85°15′W
Bluffton, Oh., U.S.	108	40°50′N	83°55′W
Blumenau, Braz. (blo͞o′mĕn-ou)	144	26°53′S	48°58′W
Blumut, Gunong, mtn., Malay.	197b	2°03′N	103°34′E
Blyth, Eng., U.K. (blĭth)	164	55°03′N	1°34′W
Blythe, Ca., U.S.	119	33°37′N	114°37′W
Blytheville, Ar., U.S. (blīth′vĭl)	121	35°55′N	89°51′W
Bo, S.L.	234	7°56′N	11°21′W
Boac, Phil.	213a	13°26′N	121°50′E
Boaco, Nic. (bô-ä′kō)	132	12°24′N	85°41′W
Bo′ai, China (bwo-ī)	208	35°10′N	113°08′E
Boa Vista, i., C.V. (bō-ä-vēsh′tȧ)	230b	16°01′N	23°52′W
Boa Vista do Rio Branco, Braz.	143	2°46′N	60°45′W
Bobo Dioulasso, Burkina (bō′bô-dyo͞o-lás-sō′)	230	11°12′N	4°18′W
Bobr, Bela. (bō′b′r)	176	54°19′N	29°11′E
Bóbr, r., Pol. (bŭ′br)	168	51°44′N	15°13′E
Bobrov, Russia (bŭb-rôf′)	181	51°07′N	40°01′E
Bobrovyts′a, Ukr.	177	50°43′N	31°27′E
Bobrynets′, Ukr.	177	48°04′N	32°10′E
Boca del Pozo, Ven. (bô-kä-dĕl-pô′zō)	143b	11°00′N	64°21′W
Boca de Uchire, Ven. (bô-kä-dĕ-o͞o-chē′rĕ)	143b	10°09′N	65°27′W
Bocaina, Serra da, mtn., Braz. (sĕ′r-rä-dȧ-bô-kä′ē-nä)	141a	22°47′S	44°39′W
Bocas, Mex. (bō′käs)	130	22°29′N	101°03′W
Bocas del Toro, Pan. (bō′käs dĕl tō′rō)	133	9°24′N	82°15′W
Bochnia, Pol. (bôĸ′nyä)	169	49°58′N	20°28′E
Bocholt, Ger. (bō′kōlt)	171c	51°50′N	6°37′E
Bochum, Ger.	168	51°29′N	7°13′E
Bockum-Hövel, Ger. (bō′kōm-hû′fĕl)	171c	51°41′N	7°45′E
Bodalang, D.R.C.	236	3°14′N	22°14′E
Bodaybo, Russia (bō-dī′bō)	179	57°12′N	114°46′E
Bodele, depr., Chad (bō-dȧ-lā′)	231	16°45′N	17°05′E
Boden, Swe.	160	65°51′N	21°29′E
Bodensee, l., Eur. (bō′dĕn zā)	156	47°48′N	9°22′E
Bodmin, Eng., U.K. (bŏd′mĭn)	164	50°29′N	4°45′W
Bodmin Moor, Eng., U.K. (bŏd′mĭn mŏr)	164	50°36′N	4°43′W
Bodrum, Tur.	181	37°10′N	27°07′E
Boende, D.R.C. (bō-ĕn′dȧ)	232	0°13′S	20°52′E
Boerne, Tx., U.S. (bō′ĕrn)	122	29°49′N	98°44′W
Boesmans, r., S. Afr.	233c	33°29′S	26°09′E
Boeuf, r., U.S. (bĕf)	123	32°23′N	91°57′W

ng-sing; ŋ-baŋk; ɴ-nasalized n; nŏd; cŏmmit; ōld; ôbey; ôrder; oi-boil; fo͞od; ŏ-as oo in foot; ou-out; s-soft; sh-dish; th-thin; pūre; ûnite; ûrn; stŭd; circŭs; ü-as in French tu; ′-indeterminate vowel.

274 Boffa – Bowie PRONOUNCING INDEX

PLACE (Pronunciation)	PAGE	LAT.	LONG.
Boffa, Gui. (bôf'á)	230	10°10'N	14°02'W
Bōfu, Japan (bō'fōō)	211	34°03'N	131°35'E
Bogalusa, La., U.S. (bō-gá-lōō'sá)	123	30°48'N	89°52'W
Bogan, r., Austl. (bŏ'gĕn)	222	32°10'S	147°40'E
Bogense, Den. (bô'gĕn-sĕ)	166	55°34'N	10°09'E
Boggy Peak, mtn., Antig. (bŏg'ĭ-pēk)	133b	17°03'N	61°50'W
Bogong, Mount, mtn., Austl.	222	36°50'S	147°15'E
Bogor, Indon.	212	6°45'S	106°45'E
Bogoroditsk, Russia (bŏ-gŏ'rô-dĭtsk)	176	53°48'N	38°06'E
Bogorodsk, Russia	180	56°02'N	43°40'E
Bogorodskoye, Russia (bô-gô-rôd'skô-yĕ)	186a	56°43'N	56°53'E
Bogotá, Col.	142	4°36'N	74°05'W
Bogotol, Russia (bŏ'gô-tôl)	179	56°15'N	89°45'E
Boguchar, Russia (bō'gò-chär)	181	49°40'N	41°00'E
Bogue Chitto, Ms., U.S. (nôr'fēld)	124	31°26'N	90°25'W
Boguete, Pan. (bô-gĕ'tĕ)	133	8°54'N	82°29'W
Bo Hai, b., China	205	38°30'N	120°00'E
Bohai Haixia, strt., China (bwo-hī hī-shyä)	208	38°05'N	121°40'E
Bohain-en-Vermandois, Fr. (bô-ăN-ŏN-vâr-mäN-dwä')	170	49°58'N	3°22'E
Bohemia see Čechy, hist. reg., Czech Rep.	168	49°51'N	13°55'E
Bohemian Forest, mts., Eur. (bô-hē'mĭ-ăn)	156	49°35'N	12°27'E
Bohodukhiv, Ukr.	181	50°10'N	35°31'E
Bohol, i., Phil. (bô-hôl')	213	9°28'N	124°35'E
Bohom, Mex. (bŏ-ô'm)	131	16°47'N	92°42'W
Bohuslav, Ukr.	177	49°34'N	30°51'W
Boiestown, Can. (boiz'toun)	100	46°27'N	66°25'W
Bois Blanc, i., Mi., U.S. (boi' blăŋk)	108	45°45'N	84°30'W
Boischâtel, Can. (bwä-shä-tĕl')	102b	46°54'N	71°08'W
Bois-des-Filion, Can. (bōō-ä'dĕ-fē-yŏN')	102a	45°40'N	73°46'W
Boise, Id., U.S. (boi'zē)	104	43°38'N	116°12'W
Boise, r., Id., U.S.	114	43°43'N	116°30'W
Boise City, Ok., U.S.	120	36°42'N	102°30'W
Boissevain, Can. (bois'vān)	90	49°14'N	100°03'W
Bojador, Cabo, c., W. Sah.	230	26°21'N	16°08'W
Bojnūrd, Iran	198	37°29'N	57°13'E
Bokani, Nig.	235	9°26'N	5°13'E
Boknafjorden, b., Nor.	160	59°12'N	5°37'E
Boksburg, S. Afr. (bŏks'bûrgh)	233b	26°13'N	28°15'E
Bokungu, D.R.C.	236	0°41'S	22°19'E
Bol, Chad	235	13°28'N	14°43'E
Bolai I, C.A.R.	235	4°20'N	17°21'E
Bolama, Gui.-B. (bô-lä'mä)	230	11°34'S	15°41'W
Bolan, mtn., Pak. (bô-län')	202	30°13'N	67°09'E
Bolaños, Mex. (bō-län'yŏs)	130	21°40'N	103°48'W
Bolaños, r., Mex.	130	21°26'N	103°54'W
Bolan Pass, p., Pak.	199	29°50'N	67°10'E
Bolbec, Fr. (bōl-bĕk')	170	49°37'N	0°26'E
Bole, Ghana (bō'lå)	230	9°02'N	2°29'W
Bolesławiec, Pol. (bō-lĕ-slä'vyĕts)	168	51°15'N	15°35'E
Bolgatanga, Ghana	234	10°46'N	0°52'W
Bolhrad, Ukr.	181	45°41'N	28°38'E
Boli, China (bwo-lē)	205	45°40'N	130°38'E
Bolinao, Phil. (bō-lē-nä'ō)	213a	16°24'N	119°53'E
Bolívar, Arg. (bô-lē'vär)	144	36°15'S	61°05'W
Bolívar, Col.	142	1°46'N	76°58'W
Bolivar, Mo., U.S. (bŏl'ĭ-vȧr)	121	37°37'N	93°22'W
Bolivar, Tn., U.S.	124	35°14'N	88°56'W
Bolívar, Pico, mtn., Ven.	142	8°44'N	70°54'W
Bolivar Peninsula, pen., Tx., U.S. (bŏl'ĭ-vȧr)	123a	29°25'N	94°40'W
Bolivia, nation, S.A. (bô-lĭv'ĭ-ȧ)	142	17°00'S	64°00'W
Bolkhov, Russia (bŏl-Kôf')	180	53°27'N	35°59'E
Bollin, r., Eng., U.K. (bŏl'ĭn)	158a	53°18'N	2°11'W
Bollington, Eng., U.K. (bôl'ĭng-tŭn)	158a	53°18'N	2°06'W
Bollnäs, Swe. (bôl'nĕs)	166	61°22'N	16°20'E
Bolmen, l., Swe. (bôl'mĕn)	166	56°58'N	13°25'E
Bolobo, D.R.C. (bō'lô-bō)	232	2°14'S	16°18'E
Bologna, Italy (bô-lōn'yä)	154	44°30'N	11°18'E
Bologoye, Russia (bŏ-lô-gô'yĕ)	180	57°52'N	34°02'E
Bolonchenticul, Mex. (bô-lôn-chĕn-tē-kōō'l)	132a	20°03'N	89°47'W
Bolondrón, Cuba (bô-lôn-drōn')	134	22°45'N	81°25'W
Bolseno, Lago di, l., Italy (lä'gō-dē-bôl-sä'nō)	174	42°35'N	11°40'E
Bol'shaya Anyuy, r., Russia	185	67°58'N	161°15'E
Bol'shaya Chuya, r., Russia	185	58°15'N	111°40'E
Bol'shaya Kinel', r., Russia	180	53°20'N	52°40'E
Bol'she Ust'ikinskoye, Russia (bôl'she òs-tyĭ-kēn'skô-yĕ)	186a	55°58'N	58°18'E
Bol'shoy Begichëv, i., Russia	179	74°30'N	114°40'E
Bol'shoye Ivonino, Russia (ĭ-vô'nĭ-nô)	186a	59°41'N	61°12'E
Bol'shoy Kuyash, Russia (bôl'-shôy kōō'yásh)	186a	55°52'N	61°07'E
Bolsover, Eng., U.K. (bōl'zō-vĕr)	158a	53°14'N	1°17'W
Boltaña, Spain (bôl-tä'nä)	173	42°28'N	0°03'E
Bolton, Can. (bōl'tŭn)	102d	43°53'N	79°44'W
Bolton, Eng., U.K.	164	53°35'N	2°26'W
Bolton-upon-Dearne, Eng., U.K. (bōl'tŭn-ŭp'ŏn-dûrn)	158a	53°31'N	1°19'W
Bolu, Tur. (bō'lò)	163	40°45'N	31°45'E
Bolva, r., Russia (bôl'vä)	176	53°30'N	34°30'E
Bolvadin, Tur. (bôl-vä-dēn')	163	38°50'N	30°50'E
Bolzano, Italy (bôl-tsä'nō)	162	46°31'N	11°22'E
Boma, D.R.C. (bō'mä)	232	5°51'S	13°03'E
Bombala, Austl. (bŭm-bă'lă)	219	36°55'S	149°07'E
Bombay see Mumbai, India	199	18°58'N	72°50'E
Bombay Harbour, b., India	203b	18°55'N	72°52'E
Bomi Hills, Lib.	230	7°00'N	11°00'W

PLACE (Pronunciation)	PAGE	LAT.	LONG.
Bom Jardim, Braz. (bôn zhär-dēN')	141a	22°10'S	42°25'W
Bom Jesus do Itabapoana, Braz.	141a	21°08'S	41°51'W
Bømlo, i., Nor. (bûmlô)	166	59°47'N	4°57'E
Bomongo, D.R.C.	231	1°22'N	18°21'E
Bom Sucesso, Braz. (bôn-sōō-sĕ'sō)	141a	21°02'S	44°44'W
Bomu see Mbomou, r., Afr.	231	4°50'N	24°00'E
Bon, Cap, c., Tun. (bôN)	162	37°04'N	11°13'E
Bonaire, i., Neth. Ant. (bô-nâr')	142	12°10'N	68°15'W
Bonavista, Can. (bŏ-nȧ-vĭs'tȧ)	93a	48°39'N	53°07'W
Bonavista Bay, b., Can.	93a	48°45'N	53°20'W
Bond, Co., U.S. (bŏnd)	120	39°53'N	106°40'W
Bondo, D.R.C. (bôn'dô)	184	3°49'N	23°40'E
Bondoc Peninsula, pen., Phil. (bôn-dŏk')	213a	13°24'N	122°30'E
Bondoukou, C. Iv. (bŏn-dōō'kōō)	230	8°02'N	2°48'W
Bonds Cay, i., Bah. (bŏnds kē)	134	25°30'N	77°45'W
Bondy, Fr.	171b	48°54'N	2°28'E
Bône see Annaba, Alg.	230	36°57'N	7°39'E
Bone, Teluk, b., Indon.	212	4°09'S	121°00'E
Bonete, Cerro, mtn., Arg. (bô'nĕtĕh çĕrrô)	144	27°50'S	68°35'W
Bonfim, Braz. (bôN-fē'N)	141a	20°20'S	44°15'W
Bongor, Chad	235	10°17'N	15°22'E
Bonham, Tx., U.S. (bŏn'ăm)	121	33°35'N	96°09'W
Bonhomme, Pic, mtn., Haiti	135	19°10'N	72°20'W
Bonifacio, Fr. (bō-nē-fä'chō)	174	41°23'N	9°10'E
Bonifacio, Strait of, strt., Eur.	162	41°14'N	9°02'E
Bonifay, Fl., U.S. (bŏn-ĭ-fā')	124	30°46'N	85°40'W
Bonin Islands, is., Japan (bō'nĭn)	241	26°30'N	141°00'E
Bonn, Ger. (bōn)	154	50°44'N	7°06'E
Bonne Bay, b., Can. (bŏn)	101	49°33'N	57°55'W
Bonners Ferry, Id., U.S. (bonĕrz fĕr'ĭ)	114	48°41'N	116°19'W
Bonner Springs, Ks., U.S. (bŏn'ĕr sprĭngz)	117f	39°04'N	94°52'W
Bonne Terre, Mo., U.S. (bŏn târ')	121	37°55'N	90°32'W
Bonnet Peak, mtn., Can. (bŏn'ĭt)	95	51°26'N	115°53'W
Bonneville Dam, dam, U.S. (bŏn'ĕ-vĭl)	114	45°37'N	121°57'W
Bonny, Nig. (bŏn'ĕ)	230	4°29'N	7°13'E
Bonny Lake, Wa., U.S. (bŏn'ē lăk)	116a	47°11'N	122°11'W
Bonnyville, Can. (bŏnē-vĭl)	95	54°16'N	110°44'W
Bonorva, Italy (bô-nôr'vä)	174	40°26'N	8°46'E
Bonthain, Indon. (bôn-tīn')	212	5°30'S	119°52'E
Bonthe, S.L.	230	7°32'N	12°30'W
Bontoc, Phil. (bôn-tŏk')	213a	17°10'N	121°01'E
Booby Rocks, is., Bah. (bōō'bĭ rŏks)	134	23°55'N	77°00'W
Booker T. Washington National Monument, rec., Va., U.S. (bòk'ĕr tē wŏsh'ĭng-tŭn)	125	37°07'N	79°45'W
Boom, Bel.	159a	51°05'N	4°22'E
Boone, Ia., U.S. (bōōn)	113	42°04'N	93°51'W
Booneville, Ar., U.S. (bōōn'vĭl)	121	35°09'N	93°54'W
Booneville, Ky., U.S.	108	37°25'N	83°40'W
Booneville, Ms., U.S.	124	34°37'N	88°35'W
Boons, S. Afr.	238c	25°59'S	27°15'E
Boonton, N.J., U.S. (bōōn'tŭn)	110a	40°54'N	74°24'W
Boonville, In., U.S.	108	38°00'N	87°15'W
Boonville, Mo., U.S.	121	38°57'N	92°44'W
Boorama, Som.	238a	10°05'N	43°08'E
Boosaaso, Som.	238a	11°19'N	49°10'E
Boothbay Harbor, Me., U.S. (bōōth'bā här'bĕr)	100	43°51'N	69°39'W
Boothia, Gulf of, b., Can. (bōō'thĭ-ȧ)	93	69°04'N	86°04'W
Boothia Peninsula, pen., Can.	89	73°30'N	95°00'W
Bootle, Eng., U.K. (bōōt'l)	158a	53°29'N	3°02'W
Bor, Sudan (bôr)	231	6°13'N	31°35'E
Bor, Tur. (bōr)	181	37°50'N	34°40'E
Boraha, Nosy, i., Madag.	233	16°58'S	50°15'E
Borah Peak, mtn., Id., U.S. (bō'rä)	115	44°12'N	113°47'W
Borås, Swe. (bô'rōs)	160	57°43'N	12°55'E
Borāzjān, Iran (bō-räz-jän')	198	29°13'N	51°13'E
Borba, Braz. (bôr'bä)	143	4°23'S	59°31'W
Borborema, Planalto da, plat., Braz. (plä-näl'tô-dä-bôr-bō-rĕ'mä)	143	7°35'S	36°40'W
Bordeaux, Fr. (bôr-dō')	154	44°50'N	0°37'W
Bordentown, N.J., U.S. (bôr'dĕn-toun)	109	40°05'N	74°40'W
Bordj-bou-Arréridj, Alg. (bôrj-bōō-ȧ-rā-rēj')	162	36°03'N	4°48'E
Bordj Omar Idriss, Alg.	230	28°06'N	6°34'E
Borgarnes, Ice.	160	64°31'N	21°40'W
Borger, Tx., U.S. (bôr'gĕr)	120	35°40'N	101°23'W
Borgholm, Swe. (bôrg-hŏlm')	166	56°52'N	16°40'E
Borgne, l., La., U.S. (bôrn'y')	123	30°03'N	89°36'W
Borgomanero, Italy (bôr'gō-mä-nâ'rō)	174	45°40'N	8°28'E
Borgo Val di Taro, Italy (bô'r-zhō-väl-dē-tä'rō)	174	44°29'N	9°44'E
Börili, Kaz.	186a	53°36'N	61°55'E
Boring, Or., U.S. (bōring)	116c	45°26'N	122°22'W
Borisoglebsk, Russia (bŏ-rē sŏ-glyĕpsk')	178	51°20'N	42°00'E
Borisovka, Russia (bŏ-rē-sôf'kȧ)	181	50°38'N	36°00'E
Borivli, India	203b	19°15'N	72°48'E
Borja, Spain (bôr'hä)	172	41°50'N	1°33'W
Borken, Ger. (bōr'kĕn)	171c	51°50'N	6°51'E
Borkou, reg., Chad (bôr-kōō')	231	18°11'N	18°28'E
Borkum, i., Ger. (bōr'kōōm)	168	53°31'N	6°50'E
Borlänge, Swe. (bôr-lĕng'gĕ)	166	60°30'N	15°24'E
Borneo, i., Asia (bôr'nē-ō)	212	0°25'N	112°39'E
Bornholm, i., Den. (bôrn-hôlm)	156	55°16'N	15°15'E
Boromlia, Ukr.	177	50°36'N	34°58'E
Boromo, Burkina	234	11°45'N	2°56'W
Borovan, Blg. (bô-rô-vän')	175	43°24'N	23°47'E
Borovichi, Russia (bŏ-rō-vē'chē)	178	58°22'N	33°56'E
Borovsk, Russia (bô'rŏvsk)	176	55°13'N	36°26'E
Borraan, Som.	238a	10°38'N	48°30'E

PLACE (Pronunciation)	PAGE	LAT.	LONG.
Borracha, Isla la, i., Ven. (ē's-lä-lä-bôr-rä'chä)	143b	10°18'N	64°44'W
Borriana, Spain	162	39°53'N	0°05'W
Borroloola, Austl. (bŏr-rō-lōō'lȧ)	218	16°15'S	136°19'E
Borshchiv, Ukr.	169	48°47'N	26°04'E
Bort-les-Orgues, Fr. (bôr-lā-zôrg)	170	45°26'N	2°26'E
Borūjerd, Iran	198	33°45'N	48°53'E
Boryslav, Ukr.	169	49°17'N	23°24'E
Boryspil', Ukr.	177	50°17'N	30°54'E
Borzna, Ukr. (bôrz'nȧ)	181	51°15'N	32°26'E
Borzya, Russia (bôrz'yȧ)	179	50°37'N	116°53'E
Bosa, Italy (bō'sä)	174	40°18'N	8°34'E
Bosanska Dubica, Bos. (bō'sän-skä dōō'bĭt-sä)	174	45°10'N	16°49'E
Bosanska Gradiška, Bos. (bō'sän-skä grä-dĭsh'kä)	175	45°08'N	17°15'E
Bosanski Novi, Bos. (bō's än-skĭ nō'vē)	174	45°00'N	16°22'E
Bosanski Petrovac, Bos. (bō'sän-skĭ pĕt'rō-väts)	174	44°33'N	16°23'E
Bosanski Šamac, Bos. (bō'sän-skĭ shä'mȧts)	175	45°03'N	18°30'E
Boscobel, Wi., U.S. (bŏs'kô-bĕl)	113	43°08'N	90°44'W
Bose, China (bwo-sŭ)	209	24°00'N	106°38'E
Boshan, China (bwo-shan)	205	36°32'N	117°51'E
Boskoop, Neth.	159a	52°04'N	4°39'E
Boskovice, Czech Rep. (bŏs'kō-vē-tsĕ)	168	49°26'N	16°37'E
Bosna, r., Serb.	175	44°19'N	17°54'E
Bosnia and Herzegovina, nation, Eur.	175	44°15'N	17°30'E
Bosobolo, D.R.C.	236	4°11'N	19°54'E
Bosporus see İstanbul Boğazı, strt., Tur.	198	41°10'N	29°10'E
Bossangoa, C.A.R.	235	6°29'N	17°27'E
Bossier City, La., U.S. (bŏsh'ĕr)	123	32°31'N	93°42'W
Bosten Hu, l., China (bwo-stŭn hōō)	204	42°06'N	88°01'E
Boston, Ga., U.S. (bôs'tŭn)	124	30°47'N	83°47'W
Boston, Ma., U.S.	105	42°15'N	71°07'W
Boston Heights, Oh., U.S.	111d	41°15'N	81°30'W
Boston Mountains, mts., Ar., U.S.	107	35°46'N	93°32'W
Botany Bay, b., Austl. (bŏt'ȧ-nĭ)	221	33°58'S	151°11'E
Botevgrad, Blg.	175	42°54'N	23°41'E
Bothaville, S. Afr. (bō'tä-vĭl)	238c	27°24'S	26°38'E
Bothell, Wa., U.S. (bŏth'ĕl)	116a	47°46'N	122°12'W
Bothnia, Gulf of, b., Eur. (bŏth'nĭ-ȧ)	156	63°40'N	21°30'E
Botoşani, Rom. (bô-tô-shàn'ĭ)	169	47°46'N	26°40'E
Botswana, nation, Afr. (bŏtswănă)	232	22°10'S	23°13'E
Bottineau, N.D., U.S. (bŏt-ĭ-nō')	112	48°48'N	100°28'W
Bottrop, Ger. (bōt'trōp)	168	51°31'N	6°56'E
Botwood, Can. (bŏt'wòd)	93a	49°08'N	55°21'W
Bouafle, C. Iv. (bò-ȧ-flā')	230	6°59'N	5°45'W
Bouar, C.A.R. (bōō-är)	231	5°57'N	15°36'E
Bou Areg, Sebkha, Mor.	172	35°09'N	3°02'W
Boubandjidah, Parc National de, rec., Cam.	235	8°20'N	14°40'E
Boucherville, Can. (bōō-shā-vēl')	102a	45°37'N	73°27'W
Boudenib, Mor. (bōō-dĕ-nēb')	230	32°14'N	3°04'W
Boudette, Mn., U.S. (bōō-dĕt)	113	48°42'N	94°34'W
Boudouaou, Alg.	173	36°44'N	3°25'E
Boufarik, Alg. (bōō-fä-rēk')	173	36°35'N	2°55'E
Bougainville, i., Pap. N. Gui.	214e	6°00'S	155°00'E
Bougainville Trench, deep (bōō-găN-vĕl')	241	7°00'S	152°00'E
Bougie see Bejaïa, Alg.	230	36°46'N	5°00'E
Bougouni, Mali (bōō-gōō-nē')	230	11°27'N	7°30'W
Bouïra, Alg. (boo-ē'rȧ)	162	36°25'N	3°55'E
Bouïra-Sahary, Alg. (bwē-rȧ sȧ'ȧ-rē)	173	35°16'N	3°23'E
Bouka, r., Gui.	234	11°05'N	10°40'W
Boulder, Co., U.S.	104	40°02'N	105°19'W
Boulder, r., Mt., U.S.	115	46°10'N	112°07'W
Boulder City, Nv., U.S.	104	35°57'N	114°50'W
Boulder Peak, mtn., Id., U.S.	115	43°53'N	114°33'W
Boulogne-Billancourt, Fr. (bōō-lôn'y'-bē-yäN-kōōr')	170	48°50'N	2°14'E
Boulogne-sur-Mer, Fr. (bōō-lôn'y-sür-mâr')	161	50°44'N	1°37'E
Boumba, r., Cam.	235	3°20'N	14°40'E
Bouna, C. Iv. (bōō-nä')	230	9°16'N	3°00'W
Bouna, Parc National de, rec., C. Iv.	234	9°20'N	3°35'W
Boundary Bay, b., N.A. (boun'dȧ-rĭ)	116d	49°03'N	122°59'W
Boundary Peak, mtn., Nv., U.S.	118	37°52'N	118°20'W
Bound Brook, N.J., U.S. (bound bròk)	110a	40°34'N	74°32'W
Bountiful, Ut., U.S. (boun'tĭ-fòl)	117b	40°55'N	111°53'W
Bountiful Peak, mtn., Ut., U.S. (boun'tĭ-fòl)	117b	40°58'N	111°49'W
Bounty Islands, is., N.Z.	5	47°42'S	179°05'E
Bourail, N. Cal.	214f	21°34'S	165°30'E
Bourem, Mali (bōō-rĕm')	230	16°43'N	0°15'W
Bourg-en-Bresse, Fr. (bōōr-gĕN-brĕs')	161	46°12'N	5°13'E
Bourges, Fr. (bōōrzh)	161	47°06'N	2°22'E
Bourget, Can. (bōōr-zhĕ')	102c	45°26'N	75°09'W
Bourgoin, Fr. (bōōr-gwăN')	171	45°46'N	5°17'E
Bourke, Austl. (bŭrk)	219	30°10'S	146°00'E
Bourne, Eng., U.K. (bōrn)	158a	52°46'N	0°22'W
Bournemouth, Eng., U.K. (bôrn'mŭth)	164	50°44'N	1°55'W
Bou Saâda, Alg. (bōō-sä'dä)	162	35°13'N	4°17'E
Bousso, Chad (bōō-sō')	231	10°33'N	16°45'E
Boutilimit, Maur.	230	17°30'N	14°54'W
Bouvetøya, i., Ant.	3	55°00'S	3°00'E
Bow, r., Can. (bō)	92	50°35'N	112°15'W
Bowbells, N.D., U.S. (bō'bĕls)	112	48°50'N	102°16'W
Bowdle, S.D., U.S. (bōd''l)	112	45°28'N	99°42'W
Bowen, Austl. (bō'ĕn)	219	20°02'S	148°14'E
Bowie, Md., U.S. (bōō'ĭ) (bō'ē)	110e	38°59'N	76°47'W
Bowie, Tx., U.S.	121	33°34'N	97°50'W

ăt; finăl; rāte; senāte; ärm; åsk; sofȧ; fâre; ch-choose; dh-as th in other; bē; ēvent; bĕt; recĕnt; cratĕr; g-gō; gh-guttural g; bĭt; ĭ-short neutral; rīde; K-guttural k as ch in German ich;

PRONOUNCING INDEX

Bowling Green – Brownsville 275

PLACE (Pronunciation)	PAGE	LAT.	LONG.
Bowling Green, Ky., U.S. (bōlĭng grēn)	105	37°00'N	86°26'W
Bowling Green, Mo., U.S.	121	39°19'N	91°09'W
Bowling Green, Oh., U.S.	108	41°25'N	83°40'W
Bowman, N.D., U.S. (bō'măn)	112	46°11'N	103°23'W
Bowron, r., Can. (bō'rŭn)	95	53°20'N	121°10'W
Boxelder Creek, r., Mt., U.S. (bŏks'ĕl-dēr)	112	45°35'N	104°28'W
Box Elder Creek, r., Mt., U.S.	115	47°17'N	108°37'W
Box Hill, Austl.	217a	37°49'S	145°08'E
Boxian, China (bwo shyĕn)	208	33°52'N	115°47'E
Boxing, China (bwo-shyĭŋ)	206	37°09'N	118°08'E
Boxtel, Neth.	159a	51°40'N	5°21'E
Boyabo, D.R.C.	236	3°43'N	18°46'E
Boyang, China (bwo-yäŋ)	209	29°00'N	116°42'E
Boyer, r., Can. (boi'ēr)	102b	46°45'N	70°56'W
Boyer, r., Ia., U.S.	112	41°45'N	95°36'W
Boyle, Ire. (boil)	164	53°59'N	8°15'W
Boyne, r., Ire. (boin)	164	53°40'N	6°40'W
Boyne City, Mi., U.S.	108	45°15'N	85°05'W
Boyoma Falls, wtfl., D.R.C.	231	0°30'N	25°12'E
Boysen Reservoir, res., Wy., U.S.	115	43°19'N	108°11'W
Bozcaada, Tur. (bōz-cä'dä)	175	39°50'N	26°05'E
Bozca Ada, i., Tur.	175	39°50'N	26°00'E
Bozeman, Mt., U.S. (bōz'măn)	104	45°41'N	111°00'W
Bozene, D.R.C.	236	2°56'N	19°12'E
Bozhen, China (bwo-jŭn)	206	38°05'N	116°35'E
Bozoum, C.A.R.	235	6°19'N	16°23'E
Bra, Italy (brä)	174	44°41'N	7°52'E
Bracciano, Lago di, l., Italy (lä'gō-dē-brä-chä'nō)	174	42°05'N	12°00'E
Bracebridge, Can. (brās'brĭj)	99	45°05'N	79°20'W
Braceville, Il., U.S. (brās'vĭl)	111a	41°13'N	88°16'W
Bräcke, Swe. (brĕk'kĕ)	160	62°44'N	15°28'E
Brackenridge, Pa., U.S. (brăk'ĕn-rĭj)	111e	40°37'N	79°44'W
Brackettville, Tx., U.S. (brăk'ĕt-vĭl)	122	29°19'N	100°24'W
Braço Maior, mth., Braz.	143	11°00'S	51°00'W
Braço Menor, mth., Braz. (brä'zō-mĕ-nō'r)	143	11°38'S	50°00'W
Bradano, r., Italy (brä-dä'nō)	174	40°43'N	16°22'E
Bradenton, Fl., U.S. (brā'dĕn-tŭn)	125a	27°28'N	82°35'W
Bradfield, Eng., U.K. (brăd'fēld)	158b	51°25'N	1°08'W
Bradford, Eng., U.K. (brăd'fērd)	160	53°47'N	1°44'W
Bradford, Oh., U.S.	108	40°10'N	84°30'W
Bradford, Pa., U.S.	109	42°00'N	78°40'W
Bradley, Il., U.S. (brăd'lĭ)	111a	41°09'N	87°52'W
Bradner, Can. (brăd'nēr)	116d	49°05'N	122°26'W
Brady, Tx., U.S. (brā'dĭ)	122	31°09'N	99°21'W
Braga, Port. (brä'gä)	162	41°20'N	8°25'W
Bragado, Arg. (brä-gä'dō)	144	35°07'S	60°28'W
Bragança, Braz. (brä-gän'sä)	143	1°02'S	46°50'W
Bragança, Port.	172	41°48'N	6°46'W
Bragança Paulista, Braz. (brä-gän'sä-pä'ōō-lē's-tà)	144	22°58'S	46°31'W
Bragg Creek, Can. (brăg)	102e	50°57'N	114°35'W
Brahmaputra, r., Asia (brä'mà-pōō'trà)	199	26°45'N	92°45'E
Brāhui, mts., Pak.	199	28°32'N	66°15'E
Braidwood, Il., U.S. (brād'wŏod)	111a	41°16'N	88°13'W
Brăila, Rom. (brē'ēlà)	154	45°15'N	27°58'E
Brainerd, Mn., U.S. (brān'ērd)	113	46°20'N	94°09'W
Braintree, Ma., U.S. (brān'trē)	101a	42°14'N	71°00'W
Braithwaite, La., U.S. (brīth'wīt)	110d	29°52'N	89°57'W
Brakpan, S. Afr. (brăk'păn)	233b	26°15'S	28°22'E
Bralorne, Can. (brā'lôrn)	95	50°47'N	122°49'W
Bramalea, Can.	102d	43°48'N	79°41'W
Brampton, Can. (brămp'tŭn)	99	43°41'N	79°46'W
Branca, Pedra, mtn., Braz. (pĕ'drä-brà'n-kä)	144b	22°55'S	43°28'W
Branchville, N.J., U.S. (brănch'vĭl)	110a	41°09'S	74°44'W
Branchville, S.C., U.S.	125	33°17'N	80°48'W
Branco, r., Braz. (brăŋ'kō)	143	2°21'N	60°38'W
Brandberg, mtn., Nmb.	232	21°15'S	14°15'E
Brandenburg, Ger. (brän'dĕn-bōrgh)	161	52°25'N	12°33'E
Brandenburg, state, Ger.	159b	52°15'N	13°00'E
Brandenburg, hist. reg., Ger.	168	52°12'N	13°31'E
Brandfort, S. Afr. (brăn'd-fôrt)	238c	28°42'S	26°29'E
Brandon, Can. (brăn'dŭn)	90	49°50'N	99°57'W
Brandon, Vt., U.S.	109	43°45'N	73°05'W
Brandon Mountain, mtn., Ire. (brăn-dŏn)	164	52°15'N	10°12'W
Brandywine, Md., U.S. (brăndĭ'wīn)	110e	38°42'N	76°51'W
Branford, Ct., U.S. (brăn'fērd)	109	41°15'N	72°50'W
Braniewo, Pol. (brä-nyĕ'vô)	169	54°23'N	19°50'E
Brańsk, Pol. (brän' sk)	169	52°44'N	22°51'E
Branson, Mo., U.S.	121	36°39'N	93°13'W
Brantford, Can. (brănt'fērd)	99	43°09'N	80°17'W
Bras d'Or Lake, l., Can. (brä-dôr')	101	45°52'N	60°50'W
Brasília, Braz. (brä-sē'lvä)	143	15°49'S	47°39'W
Brasilia Legal, Braz.	143	3°45'S	55°46'W
Brasópolis, Braz. (brä-sô'pô-lēs)	141a	22°30'S	45°36'W
Braşov, Rom.	163	45°39'N	25°35'E
Brass, Nig. (brăs)	230	4°28'N	6°28'E
Brasschaat, Bel. (bräs'kät)	159a	51°19'N	4°30'E
Bratenahl, Oh., U.S. (brä'tĕn-ôl)	111d	41°34'N	81°36'W
Bratislava, Slvk. (brä'tĭs-lä-vä)	154	48°09'N	17°07'E
Bratsk, Russia (brätsk)	179	56°10'N	102°04'E
Bratskoye Vodokhranilishche, res., Russia	179	56°10'N	102°05'E
Bratslav, Ukr. (brät'släf)	177	48°48'N	28°59'E
Brattleboro, Vt., U.S. (brăt''l-bŭr-ô)	109	42°50'N	72°35'W
Braunau, Aus. (brou'nou)	168	48°15'N	13°05'E
Braunschweig, Ger. (broun'shvīgh)	161	52°16'N	10°32'E
Bråviken, r., Swe.	166	58°40'N	16°40'E
Brawley, Ca., U.S. (brô'lĭ)	104	32°59'N	115°32'W
Bray, Ire. (brā)	164	53°10'N	6°05'W
Braymer, Mo., U.S. (brā'mēr)	121	39°34'N	93°47'W
Brays Bay, Tx., U.S. (brās'bī'yōō)	123a	29°41'N	95°33'W
Brazeau, r., Can.	95	52°55'N	116°10'W
Brazeau, Mount, mtn., Can. (bră-zō')	95	52°33'N	117°21'W
Brazil, In., U.S. (brà-zĭl')	108	39°30'N	87°00'W
Brazil, nation, S.A.	143	9°00'S	53°00'W
Brazilian Highlands, mts., Braz. (brà zĭl yán hī-lăndz)	139	14°00'S	48°00'W
Brazos, r., Tx., U.S. (brä'zōs)	106	33°10'N	98°50'W
Brazos, Clear Fork, r., Tx., U.S.	122	32°56'N	99°14'W
Brazos, Double Mountain Fork, r., Tx., U.S.	120	33°23'N	101°21'W
Brazos, Salt Fork, r., Tx., U.S. (sôlt fôrk)	120	33°20'N	101°57'W
Brazzaville, Congo (brà-zà-vēl')	232	4°16'S	15°17'E
Brčko, Bos. (bĕrch'kô)	175	44°54'N	18°46'E
Brda, r., Pol. (bēr-dä)	169	53°18'N	17°55'E
Brea, Ca., U.S. (brē'à)	117a	33°55'N	117°54'W
Breakeyville, Can.	102b	46°40'N	71°13'W
Breckenridge, Mn., U.S. (brĕk'ĕn-rĭj)	112	46°17'N	96°35'W
Breckenridge, Tx., U.S.	122	32°46'N	98°53'W
Brecksville, Oh., U.S. (brĕks'vĭl)	111d	41°19'N	81°38'W
Břeclav, Czech Rep. (brzhĕl'läf)	168	48°46'N	16°54'E
Breda, Neth. (brā-dä')	165	51°35'N	4°47'E
Bredasdorp, S. Afr. (brā'das-dôrp)	232	34°15'S	20°00'E
Bredy, Russia (brĕ'dĭ)	186a	52°25'N	60°23'E
Bregenz, Aus. (brā'gĕnts)	168	47°30'N	9°46'E
Bregovo, Blg. (brĕ'gō-vō)	175	44°07'N	22°45'E
Breidafjördur, b., Ice.	160	65°15'N	22°50'W
Breidbach, S. Afr. (brēd'băk)	233c	32°54'S	27°26'E
Breil-sur-Roya, Fr. (brê'y')	171	43°57'N	7°36'E
Brejo, Braz. (brå'zhō)	143	3°33'S	42°46'W
Bremangerlandet, i., Nor.	166	61°51'N	4°25'E
Bremen, Ger. (brā-mĕn)	154	53°05'N	8°50'E
Bremen, In., U.S. (brē'mĕn)	108	41°25'N	86°05'W
Bremerhaven, Ger. (brām-ēr-hä'fĕn)	160	53°33'N	8°38'E
Bremerton, Wa., U.S. (brĕm'ēr-tŭn)	114	47°34'N	122°38'W
Bremervörde, Ger. (brĕ'mĕr-fûr-dĕ)	159c	53°29'N	9°09'E
Bremner, Can. (brĕm'nēr)	102g	53°34'N	113°14'W
Bremond, Tx., U.S. (brĕm'ŭnd)	123	31°11'N	96°40'W
Brenham, Tx., U.S. (brĕn'ăm)	123	30°10'N	96°24'W
Brenner Pass, p., Eur. (brĕn'ēr)	161	47°00'N	11°30'E
Brentwood, Eng., U.K. (brĕnt'wŏod)	165	51°37'N	0°18'E
Brentwood, Md., U.S.	109	39°00'N	76°55'W
Brentwood, Mo., U.S.	117e	38°37'N	90°21'W
Brentwood, Pa., U.S.	111e	40°22'N	79°59'W
Brescia, Italy (brā'shä)	162	45°33'N	10°15'E
Bressanone, Italy (brĕs-sä-nō'nā)	174	46°42'N	11°40'E
Bressuire, Fr. (grĕ-swēr')	170	46°49'N	0°14'W
Brest, Bela.	178	52°06'N	23°43'E
Brest, Fr. (brĕst)	154	48°24'N	4°30'W
Brest, prov., Bela.	176	52°30'N	26°50'E
Bretagne, hist. reg., Fr. (brĕ-tän'yĕ)	170	48°00'N	3°00'W
Breton, Pertuis, strt., Fr. (pâr-twē'brĕ-tôn')	170	46°18'N	1°43'W
Breton Sound, strt., La., U.S. (brĕt'ŭn)	124	29°38'N	89°15'W
Breukelen, Neth.	159a	52°09'N	5°00'E
Brevard, N.C., U.S. (brē-värd')	125	35°14'N	82°45'W
Breves, Braz. (brā'vĕzh)	143	1°32'S	50°13'W
Brevik, Nor. (brĕ'vĕk)	166	59°04'N	9°39'E
Brewarrina, Austl. (brōō-ēr-rē'nà)	219	29°54'S	146°50'E
Brewer, Me., U.S. (brōō'ēr)	100	44°46'N	68°46'W
Brewerville, Lib.	234	6°26'N	10°47'W
Brewster, N.Y., U.S. (brōō'stēr)	110a	41°23'N	73°38'W
Brewster, Cerro, mtn., Pan. (sĕ'r-rô-brōō'stēr)	133	9°19'N	79°15'W
Brewton, Al., U.S. (brōō'tŭn)	124	31°06'N	87°04'W
Brežice, Slvn. (brĕ'zhē-tsĕ)	174	45°55'N	15°37'E
Breznik, Blg. (brĕs'nĕk)	175	42°44'N	22°55'E
Briancon, Fr. (brē-äN-sôN')	171	44°54'N	6°39'E
Briare, Fr. (brē-är')	170	47°40'N	2°46'E
Bridal Veil, Or., U.S. (brīd'ăl vāl)	116c	45°33'N	122°10'W
Bridge Point, c., Bah. (brĭj)	134	25°35'N	76°40'W
Bridgeport, Al., U.S. (brĭj'pôrt)	124	34°55'N	85°42'W
Bridgeport, Ct., U.S.	105	41°12'N	73°12'W
Bridgeport, Il., U.S.	108	38°40'N	87°45'W
Bridgeport, Ne., U.S.	112	41°40'N	103°06'W
Bridgeport, Oh., U.S.	108	40°00'N	80°45'W
Bridgeport, Pa., U.S.	110f	40°06'N	75°21'W
Bridgeport, Tx., U.S.	121	33°13'N	97°46'W
Bridgeton, Al., U.S. (brĭj'tŭn)	110h	33°27'N	86°39'W
Bridgeton, Mo., U.S.	117e	38°45'N	90°23'W
Bridgeton, N.J., U.S.	109	39°30'N	75°15'W
Bridgetown, Barb. (brĭj' toun)	129	13°08'N	59°37'W
Bridgetown, Can.	100	44°51'N	65°18'W
Bridgeville, Pa., U.S. (brĭj'vĭl)	111e	40°22'N	80°07'W
Bridgewater, Austl. (brĭj'wô-tēr)	222	42°50'S	147°28'E
Bridgewater, Can.	91	44°23'N	64°31'W
Bridgnorth, Eng., U.K. (brĭj'nôrth)	158a	52°32'N	2°25'W
Bridgton, Me., U.S. (brĭj'tŭn)	100	44°04'N	70°45'W
Bridlington, Eng., U.K. (brĭd'lĭng-tŭn)	164	54°06'N	0°10'W
Brie-Comte-Robert, Fr. (brē-kônt-ĕ-rō-bâr')	171b	48°42'N	2°37'E
Brielle, Neth.	159a	51°54'N	4°08'E
Brierfield, Eng., U.K. (brī'ēr fēld)	158a	53°49'N	2°14'W
Brierfield, Al., U.S. (brī'ēr-fēld)	124	33°01'N	86°55'W
Brier Island, i., Can. (brī'ēr)	100	44°16'N	66°24'W
Brieselang, Ger. (brē'zĕ-läng)	159b	52°36'N	12°59'E
Briey, Fr. (brē-ĕ')	171	49°15'N	5°57'E
Brig, Switz. (brēg)	161	46°17'N	7°59'E
Brigg, Eng., U.K. (brĭg)	158a	53°33'N	0°29'W
Brigham City, Ut., U.S. (brĭg'ăm)	117b	41°31'N	112°01'W
Brighouse, Eng., U.K. (brĭg'hous)	158a	53°42'N	1°47'W
Bright, Austl. (brīt)	222	36°43'S	147°00'E
Bright, In., U.S. (brīt)	111f	39°13'N	84°51'W
Brightlingsea, Eng., U.K. (brī't-lĭng-sē)	158b	51°50'N	1°00'E
Brighton, Austl.	217a	37°55'S	145°00'E
Brighton, Eng., U.K.	161	50°47'N	0°07'W
Brighton, Al., U.S. (brī'tŭn)	110h	33°27'N	86°56'W
Brighton, Co., U.S.	120	39°58'N	104°49'W
Brighton, Ia., U.S.	113	41°11'N	91°47'W
Brighton, Il., U.S.	117e	39°03'N	90°08'W
Brighton Indian Reservation, I.R., Fl., U.S.	125a	27°05'N	81°25'W
Brihuega, Spain (brē-wā'gä)	172	40°32'N	2°52'W
Brimley, Mi., U.S. (brĭm'lē)	117k	46°24'N	84°34'W
Brindisi, Italy (brēn'dē-zē)	154	40°38'N	17°57'E
Brinje, Cro. (brēn'yĕ)	174	45°00'N	15°08'E
Brinkley, Ar., U.S. (brĭŋk'lĭ)	121	34°52'N	91°12'W
Brinnon, Wa., U.S. (brĭn'ŭn)	116a	47°41'N	122°54'W
Brion, i., Can. (brē-ôN')	101	47°47'N	61°29'W
Brioude, Fr. (brē-ōōd')	170	45°18'N	3°22'E
Brisbane, Austl. (brĭz'bān)	222	27°30'S	153°10'E
Bristol, Eng., U.K.	161	51°29'N	2°39'W
Bristol, Ct., U.S. (brĭs'tŭl)	109	41°40'N	72°55'W
Bristol, Pa., U.S.	110f	40°06'N	74°51'W
Bristol, R.I., U.S.	110b	41°41'N	71°14'W
Bristol, Tn., U.S.	105	36°35'N	82°10'W
Bristol, Va., U.S.	105	36°36'N	82°00'W
Bristol, Vt., U.S.	109	44°10'N	73°00'W
Bristol, Wi., U.S.	111a	42°32'N	88°04'W
Bristol Bay, b., Ak., U.S.	103	58°05'N	158°54'W
Bristol Channel, strt., Eng., U.K.	161	51°20'N	3°47'W
Bristow, Ok., U.S. (brĭs'tō)	121	35°50'N	96°25'W
British Columbia, prov., Can. (brĭt'ĭsh kŏl'ŭm-bĭ-à)	90	56°00'N	124°53'W
British Indian Ocean Territory, dep., Afr.	2	7°00'S	72°00'E
British Isles, is., Eur.	156	54°00'N	4°00'W
Brits, S. Afr.	238c	25°39'S	27°47'E
Britstown, S. Afr. (brĭts'toun)	232	30°30'S	23°40'E
Britt, Ia., U.S. (brĭt)	113	43°05'N	93°47'W
Brittany *see* Bretagne, hist. reg., Fr.	170	48°00'N	3°00'W
Britton, S.D., U.S. (brĭt'ŭn)	112	45°47'N	97°44'W
Brive-la-Gaillarde, Fr. (brēv-lä-gī-yärd'ĕ)	161	45°10'N	1°31'E
Briviesca, Spain (brē-vyās'kà)	172	42°34'N	3°21'W
Brno, Czech Rep. (b'r'nô)	154	49°18'N	16°37'E
Broa, Ensenada de la, b., Cuba	134	22°30'N	82°00'W
Broach, India	202	21°47'N	72°58'E
Broad, r., Ga., U.S. (brôd)	124	34°15'N	83°14'W
Broad, r., N.C., U.S.	125	35°38'N	82°40'W
Broadmeadows, Austl. (brôd'mĕd-ōz)	217a	37°40'S	144°53'E
Broadview Heights, Oh., U.S. (brôd'vū)	111d	41°18'N	81°41'W
Brockport, N.Y., U.S. (brŏk'pōrt)	109	43°15'N	77°55'W
Brockton, Ma., U.S. (brŏk'tŭn)	101a	42°04'N	71°01'W
Brockville, Can. (brŏk'vĭl)	91	44°35'N	75°40'W
Brockway, Mt., U.S. (brŏk'wā)	115	47°24'N	105°41'W
Brodnica, Pol. (brôd'nĭt-sà)	169	53°16'N	19°26'E
Brody, Ukr. (brô'dĭ)	181	50°05'N	25°10'E
Broken Arrow, Ok., U.S. (brō'kĕn ăr'ō)	121	36°03'N	95°48'W
Broken Bay, b., Austl.	222	33°34'S	151°20'E
Broken Bow, Ne., U.S. (brō'kĕn bō)	112	41°24'N	99°37'W
Broken Bow, Ok., U.S.	121	34°02'N	94°43'W
Broken Hill, Austl. (brōk'ĕn)	219	31°55'S	141°35'E
Broken Hill *see* Kabwe, Zam.	232	14°27'S	28°27'E
Bromley, Eng., U.K. (brŭm'lĭ)	158b	51°23'N	0°01'E
Bromptonville, Can. (brŭmp'tŭn-vĭl)	99	45°30'N	72°00'W
Brønderslev, Den. (brûn'dēr-slĕv)	166	57°15'N	9°56'E
Bronkhorstspruit, S. Afr.	238c	25°50'S	28°48'E
Bronnitsy, Russia (brô-nyĭ'tsĭ)	176	55°26'N	38°16'E
Bronson, Mi., U.S. (brŏn'sŭn)	108	41°55'N	85°15'W
Bronte Creek, r., Can.	102d	43°25'N	79°53'W
Brood, r., S.C., U.S. (brōōd)	125	34°46'N	81°25'W
Brookfield, Il., U.S. (brŏok'fēld)	111a	41°49'N	87°51'W
Brookfield, Mo., U.S.	121	39°45'N	93°04'W
Brookhaven, Ga., U.S. (brŏok'hāv'n)	110c	33°52'N	84°21'W
Brookhaven, Ms., U.S.	124	31°35'N	90°26'W
Brookings, Or., U.S. (brŏok'ĭngs)	114	42°04'N	124°16'W
Brookings, S.D., U.S.	112	44°18'N	96°47'W
Brookline, Ma., U.S. (brŏok'līn)	101a	42°20'N	71°08'W
Brookline, N.H., U.S.	101a	42°44'N	71°37'W
Brooklyn, Oh., U.S. (brŏok'lĭn)	111d	41°26'N	81°44'W
Brooklyn Center, Mn., U.S.	117g	45°05'N	93°21'W
Brook Park, Oh., U.S. (brŏok)	111d	41°24'N	81°50'W
Brooks, Can.	95	50°35'N	111°53'W
Brooks Range, mts., Ak., U.S. (brŏoks)	106a	68°20'N	159°00'W
Brooksville, Fl., U.S. (brŏoks'vĭl)	125a	28°32'N	82°28'W
Brookville, In., U.S. (brŏok'vĭl)	108	39°20'N	85°00'W
Brookville, Pa., U.S.	109	41°10'N	79°00'W
Brookwood, Al., U.S. (brŏok'wŏod)	124	33°15'N	87°17'W
Broome, Austl. (brōōm)	218	18°00'S	122°15'E
Brossard, Can.	102a	45°26'N	73°28'W
Brothers, is., Bah. (brŭd'hērs)	134	26°05'N	79°00'W
Broumov, Czech Rep. (brōō'môf)	168	50°33'N	15°55'E
Brown Bank, bk.	135	21°30'N	74°35'W
Brownfield, Tx., U.S. (broun'fēld)	120	33°11'N	102°16'W
Browning, Mt., U.S. (broun'ĭng)	115	48°37'N	113°05'W
Brownsboro, Ky., U.S. (brounz'bŏ-rô)	111h	38°22'N	85°30'W
Brownsburg, Can. (brouns'bûrg)	102a	45°40'N	74°24'W
Brownsburg, In., U.S.	111g	39°51'N	86°23'W
Brownsmead, Or., U.S. (brounz'-mēd)	116c	46°13'N	123°33'W
Brownstown, In., U.S. (brounz'toun)	108	38°50'N	86°00'W
Brownsville, Pa., U.S. (brounz'vĭl)	111e	40°01'N	79°53'W
Brownsville, Tn., U.S.	124	35°35'N	89°15'W

ng-sing; ŋ-baŋk; N-nasalized n; nŏd; cŏmmit; ōld; ôbey; ôrder; oi-boil; fōōd; ŏo-as oo in foot; ou-out; s-soft; sh-dish; th-thin; pūre; ûnite; ûrn; stŭd; circŭs; ü-as in French tu; '-indeterminate vowel.

276 Brownsville – Byeshankovichy PRONOUNCING INDEX

PLACE (Pronunciation)	PAGE	LAT.	LONG.
Brownsville, Tx., U.S.	104	25°55'N	97°30'W
Brownville Junction, Me., U.S. (broun'vĭl)	100	45°20'N	69°04'W
Brownwood, Tx., U.S. (broun'wo̤d)	104	31°44'N	98°58'W
Brownwood, l., Tx., U.S.	122	31°55'N	99°15'W
Brozas, Spain (brō'thäs)	172	39°37'N	6°44'W
Bruce, Mount, mtn., Austl. (bro͞os)	220	22°35'S	118°15'E
Bruce Peninsula, pen., Can.	98	44°50'N	81°20'W
Bruceton, Tn., U.S. (bro͞os'tŭn)	124	36°02'N	88°14'W
Bruchsal, Ger. (bro̤k'zäl)	168	49°08'N	8°34'E
Bruck, Aus. (bro̤k)	168	47°25'N	15°14'E
Bruck, Aus.	168	48°01'N	16°47'E
Brück, Ger. (brük)	159b	52°12'N	12°45'E
Bruderheim, Can. (bro͞o'dēr-hīm)	102g	53°47'N	112°56'W
Brugge, Bel.	161	51°13'N	3°05'E
Brühl, Ger. (brül)	171c	50°49'N	6°54'E
Bruneau, r., Id., U.S. (bro͞o-nō')	114	42°47'N	115°43'W
Brunei, nation, Asia (bro̤-nī')	212	4°52'N	113°38'E
Brünen, Ger. (brü'nĕn)	171c	51°43'N	6°41'E
Brunete, Spain (bro͞o-nā'tā)	173a	40°24'N	4°00'W
Brunette, i., Can. (bro̤-nĕt')	101	47°16'N	55°54'W
Brunn am Gebirge, Aus. (bro͞on'äm gĕ-bĭr'gĕ)	159e	48°07'N	16°18'E
Brunsbüttel, Ger. (bro̤ns'büt-tĕl)	159c	53°58'N	9°10'E
Brunswick, Ga., U.S. (brŭnz'wĭk)	105	31°08'N	81°30'W
Brunswick, Md., U.S.	109	39°20'N	77°35'W
Brunswick, Me., U.S.	100	43°54'N	69°57'W
Brunswick, Mo., U.S.	121	39°25'N	93°07'W
Brunswick, Oh., U.S.	111d	41°14'N	81°50'W
Brunswick, Península de, pen., Chile	144	53°25'S	71°15'W
Bruny, i., Austl. (bro͞o'nē)	221	43°30'S	147°50'E
Brush, Co., U.S. (brŭsh)	120	40°14'N	103°40'W
Brusque, Braz. (bro͞o's-ko͞oĕ)	144	27°15'S	48°45'W
Brussels, Bel.	154	50°51'N	4°21'E
Brussels, Il., U.S. (brŭs'ĕls)	117e	38°57'N	90°36'W
Bruxelles see Brussels, Bel.	154	50°51'N	4°21'E
Bryan, Oh., U.S. (brī'ăn)	108	41°25'N	84°30'W
Bryan, Tx., U.S.	123	30°40'N	96°22'W
Bryansk, Russia	178	53°15'N	34°22'E
Bryansk, prov., Russia	176	52°43'N	32°25'E
Bryant, S.D., U.S. (brī'ănt)	112	44°35'N	97°29'W
Bryant, Wa., U.S.	116a	48°14'N	122°10'W
Bryce Canyon National Park, rec., Ut., U.S. (brīs)	106	37°35'N	112°15'W
Bryn Mawr, Pa., U.S. (brĭn mär')	110f	40°02'N	75°20'W
Bryson City, N.C., U.S. (brīs'ŭn)	124	35°25'N	83°25'W
Bryukhovetskaya, Russia (b'ryŭk'ō-vyĕt-skä'yä)	177	45°56'N	38°58'E
Buala, Sol. Is.	214e	8°08'S	159°35'E
Buatan, Indon.	197b	0°45'N	101°49'E
Buba, Gui.-B. (bo͞o'bȧ)	230	11°39'N	14°58'W
Bucaramanga, Col. (bo͞o-kä'rä-mäŋ'gä)	142	7°12'N	73°14'W
Buccaneer Archipelago, is., Austl. (bŭk-ȧ-nēr')	220	16°05'S	122°00'E
Buchach, Ukr. (bo̤'chȧch)	169	49°04'N	25°25'E
Buchanan, Lib. (bu̇-kăn'ăn)	230	5°57'N	10°02'W
Buchanan, Mi., U.S.	108	41°50'N	86°25'W
Buchanan, l., Austl. (bu̇-kân'nŏn)	221	21°40'S	145°00'E
Buchanan, l., Tx., U.S. (bu̇-kăn'ăn)	122	30°55'N	98°40'W
Buchans, Can.	101	48°49'N	56°52'W
Bucharest, Rom.	154	44°23'N	26°10'E
Buchholz, Ger. (bo͝ok'hōltz)	159c	53°19'N	9°53'E
Buck Creek, r., In., U.S. (bŭk)	111g	39°43'N	85°58'W
Buckhannon, W.V., U.S. (bŭk-hăn'ŭn)	108	39°00'N	80°10'W
Buckhaven, Scot., U.K. (bŭk-hā'v'n)	164	56°10'N	3°10'W
Buckie, Scot., U.K. (bŭk'ĭ)	164	57°40'N	2°50'W
Buckingham, Can. (bŭk'ĭng-ăm)	102c	45°35'N	75°25'W
Buckingham, can., India (bŭk'ĭng-ăm)	203	15°18'N	79°50'E
Buckinghamshire, co., Eng., U.K.	158b	51°45'N	0°48'W
Buckland, Can. (bŭk'lănd)	102b	46°37'N	70°33'W
Buckland Tableland, reg., Austl.	221	24°31'S	148°00'E
Buckley, Wa., U.S. (bŭk'lē)	116a	47°10'N	122°02'W
Bucksport, Me., U.S. (bŭks'pôrt)	100	44°35'N	68°47'W
Buctouche, Can. (bük-to͞osh')	100	46°28'N	64°43'W
Bucun, China (bo͞o-tso̤n)	206	36°38'N	117°26'E
București see Bucharest, Rom.	154	44°23'N	26°10'E
Bucyrus, Oh., U.S. (bu̇-sī'rŭs)	108	40°50'N	82°55'W
Budapest, Hung. (bo͞o'dȧ-pĕsht')	154	47°30'N	19°05'E
Budge Budge, India	202a	22°28'N	88°08'E
Budjala, D.R.C.	236	2°39'N	19°42'E
Budyonnovsk, Russia	182	44°46'N	44°09'E
Buea, Cam.	235	4°09'N	9°14'E
Buechel, Ky., U.S. (bē-chŭl')	111h	38°12'N	85°38'W
Bueil, Fr. (bwā')	171b	48°55'N	1°27'E
Buena Park, Ca., U.S. (bwā'nȧ pärk)	117a	33°52'N	118°00'W
Buenaventura, Col. (bwā'nä-vĕn-to͞o'rä)	142	3°46'N	77°09'W
Buenaventura, Cuba	135a	22°53'N	82°22'W
Buenaventura, Bahía de, b., Col.	142	3°45'N	79°23'W
Buena Vista, Co., U.S. (bū'nȧ vĭs'tȧ)	120	38°51'N	106°07'W
Buena Vista, Ga., U.S.	124	32°15'N	84°30'W
Buena Vista, Va., U.S.	109	37°45'N	79°20'W
Buena Vista, Bahía, b., Cuba (bä-ē'ä-bwĕ-nä-vē's-tä)	134	22°30'N	79°10'W
Buena Vista Lake Bed, l., Ca., U.S. (bū'nȧ vĭs'tȧ)	118	35°14'N	119°17'W
Buendia, Embalse de, res., Spain	172	40°30'N	2°45'W
Buenos Aires, Arg. (bwā'nōs ī'rās)	144	34°20'S	58°30'W
Buenos Aires, Col.	142a	3°01'N	76°34'W
Buenos Aires, C.R.	133	9°10'N	83°21'W
Buenos Aires, prov., Arg.	144	36°15'S	61°45'W
Buenos Aires, l., S.A.	144	46°30'S	72°15'W
Buffalo, Mn., U.S. (bŭf'ȧ lō)	113	45°10'N	93°50'W
Buffalo, N.Y., U.S.	105	42°54'N	78°51'W

PLACE (Pronunciation)	PAGE	LAT.	LONG.
Buffalo, Tx., U.S.	123	31°28'N	96°04'W
Buffalo, Wy., U.S.	115	44°19'N	106°42'W
Buffalo, r., S. Afr.	233c	28°35'S	30°27'E
Buffalo, r., Ar., U.S.	121	35°56'N	92°58'W
Buffalo, r., Tn., U.S.	124	35°24'N	87°10'W
Buffalo Bayou, Tx., U.S.	123a	29°46'N	95°32'W
Buffalo Creek, r., Mn., U.S.	113	44°46'N	94°28'W
Buffalo Head Hills, hills, Can.	92	57°16'N	116°18'W
Buford, Can. (bū'fûrd)	102g	53°15'N	113°55'W
Buford, Ga., U.S. (bū'fērd)	124	34°05'N	84°00'W
Bug (Zakhidnyy Buh), r., Eur.	169	52°29'N	21°20'E
Buga, Col. (bo͞o'gä)	142	3°54'N	76°17'W
Buggenhout, Bel.	159a	51°01'N	4°10'E
Buglandsfjorden, l., Nor.	166	58°53'N	7°55'E
Bugojno, Bos. (bo̤-gō'ĭ nō)	175	44°03'N	17°28'E
Bugul'ma, Russia (bo̤-gōl'mȧ)	178	54°40'N	52°40'E
Buguruslan, Russia (bo̤-go̤-ro̤s-lán')	178	53°30'N	52°32'E
Buhi, Phil. (bo͞o'ē)	213a	13°26'N	123°31'E
Buhl, Id., U.S. (būl)	115	42°36'N	114°45'W
Buhl, Mn., U.S.	113	47°28'N	92°49'W
Buin, Chile (bo̤-ēn')	141b	33°44'S	70°44'W
Buinaksk, Russia (bo̤'ē-näksk)	181	42°40'N	47°20'E
Buir Nur, l., Asia (bo͞o-ēr no͞or)	205	47°50'N	117°00'E
Bujalance, Spain (bo͞o-hä-län'thā)	172	37°54'N	4°22'W
Bujumbura, Bdi.	237	3°23'S	29°22'E
Buka Island, i., Pap. N. Gui.	214e	5°15'S	154°35'E
Bukama, D.R.C. (bo͞o-kä'mä)	232	9°08'S	26°00'E
Bukavu, D.R.C.	232	2°30'S	28°52'E
Bukhara, Uzb. (bo̤-kä'rä)	183	39°31'N	64°22'E
Bukitbatu, Indon.	197b	1°25'N	101°58'E
Bukittinggi, Indon.	212	0°25'S	100°28'E
Bukoba, Tan.	232	1°20'S	31°49'E
Bukovina, hist. reg., Eur. (bo̤-kô'vĭ-nȧ)	169	48°06'N	25°20'E
Bula, Indon. (bo͞o'lä)	213	3°00'S	130°30'E
Bulalacao, Phil. (bo͞o-lȧ-lä'kä-ō)	213a	12°30'N	121°20'E
Bulawayo, Zimb. (bo͞o-lȧ-wä'yō)	232	20°12'S	28°43'E
Buldir, i., Ak., U.S. (bŭl dĭr)	103a	52°22'N	175°50'E
Bulgaria, nation, Eur. (bo̤l-gâ'rĭ-ă)	154	42°12'N	24°13'E
Bulkley Ranges, mts., Can. (bŭlk'lē)	94	54°30'N	127°30'W
Bullaque, r., Spain (bo̤-lä'kȧ)	172	39°15'N	4°13'W
Bullas, Spain (bo͞ol'yäs)	172	38°07'N	1°48'W
Bullfrog Creek, r., Ut., U.S.	119	37°45'N	110°55'W
Bull Harbour, Can. (hăr'bēr)	94	50°45'N	127°55'W
Bull Head, mtn., Jam.	134	18°10'N	77°15'W
Bull Run, r., Or., U.S. (bo̤l)	116c	45°26'N	122°11'W
Bull Run Reservoir, res., Or., U.S.	116c	45°29'N	122°11'W
Bull Shoals Reservoir, res., U.S. (bo̤l shōlz)	107	36°35'N	92°57'W
Bulpham, Eng., U.K. (bo͞ol'făn)	158b	51°33'N	0°21'E
Bultfontein, S. Afr. (bo̤lt'fŏn-tān')	238c	28°18'S	26°10'E
Bulun, Russia (bo͞o-lo̤n')	179	70°48'N	127°27'E
Bulungu, D.R.C. (bo͞o-lo̤ŋ'go͞o)	236	6°04'S	21°54'E
Bulwer, S. Afr. (bo̤l-wēr)	233c	29°49'S	29°48'E
Bumba, D.R.C. (bo̤m'bȧ)	231	2°11'N	22°28'E
Bumbire Island, i., Tan.	237	1°40'S	32°05'E
Buna, Pap. N. Gui. (bo͞o'nȧ)	213	8°58'S	148°38'E
Bunbury, Austl. (bŭn'bŭrĭ)	218	33°25'S	115°45'E
Bundaberg, Austl. (bŭn'dȧ-bûrg)	219	24°45'S	152°18'E
Bunguran Utara, Kepulauan, is., Indon.	212	3°22'N	108°00'E
Bunia, D.R.C.	237	1°34'N	30°15'E
Bunker Hill, Il., U.S. (bŭnk'ēr hĭl)	117e	39°03'N	89°57'W
Bunkie, La., U.S. (bŭŋ'kĭ)	123	30°55'N	92°10'W
Bun Plains, pl., Kenya	237	0°55'N	40°35'E
Bununu Dass, Nig.	235	10°00'N	9°31'E
Buor-Khaya, Guba, b., Russia	185	71°45'N	131°00'E
Buor Khaya, Mys, c., Russia	179	71°47'N	133°22'E
Bura, Kenya	237	1°06'S	39°57'E
Buraydah, Sau. Ar.	198	26°23'N	44°14'E
Burbank, Ca., U.S. (bûr'bănk)	117a	34°11'N	118°19'W
Burco, Som.	238a	9°20'N	45°45'E
Burdekin, r., Austl. (bûr'dē-kĭn)	221	19°22'S	145°07'E
Burdur, Tur. (bo͞or-do̤r')	163	37°50'N	30°15'E
Burdwān, India (bo̤d-wän')	199	23°29'N	87°53'E
Bureinskiy, Khrebet, mts., Russia	179	51°15'N	133°30'E
Bureya, Russia (bo̤rā'ȧ)	179	49°55'N	130°00'E
Bureya, r., Russia (bo̤-rā'yä)	185	51°00'N	131°15'E
Burford, Eng., U.K. (bûr-fērd)	158b	51°46'N	1°38'W
Burgas, Blg. (bo̤r-gäs')	163	42°29'N	27°30'E
Burgas, Gulf of, b., Blg.	163	42°30'N	27°40'E
Burgaw, N.C., U.S. (bûr'gô)	125	34°31'N	77°56'W
Burgdorf, Switz. (bo̤rg'dôrf)	168	47°04'N	7°37'E
Burgenland, state, Aus.	159e	47°58'N	16°57'E
Burgeo, Can.	101	47°36'N	57°34'W
Burgess, Va., U.S.	109	37°53'N	76°21'W
Burgo de Osma, Spain	172	41°35'N	3°02'W
Burgos, Mex. (bo̤r'gōs)	122	24°57'N	98°47'W
Burgos, Phil.	213a	16°03'N	119°52'E
Burgos, Spain (bo͞o'r-gôs)	162	42°20'N	3°44'W
Burgsvik, Swe. (bo̤rgs'vĭk)	166	57°04'N	18°18'E
Burhānpur, India (bo̤r'hán-po͞or)	199	21°26'N	76°08'E
Burias Island, i., Phil. (bo͞o'rē-äs)	213a	12°56'N	122°56'E
Burias Pass, strt., Phil. (bo͞o'rē-äs)	213a	13°04'N	123°11'E
Burica, Punta, c., N.A. (po͞o'n-tä-bo͞o'rē-kä)	133	8°02'N	83°12'W
Burien, Wa., U.S. (bū'rĭ-ĕn)	116a	47°28'N	122°20'W
Burin, Can. (bûr'ĭn)	93a	47°02'N	55°10'W
Burin Peninsula, pen., Can.	101	47°00'N	55°40'W
Burkburnett, Tx., U.S. (bûrk-bûr'nĕt)	120	34°04'N	98°35'W
Burke, Vt., U.S. (bûrk)	109	44°40'N	72°00'W
Burke Channel, strt., Can.	94	52°07'N	127°38'W
Burketown, Austl. (bûrk'toun)	218	17°50'S	139°30'E
Burkina Faso, nation, Afr.	230	13°00'N	2°00'W
Burley, Id., U.S. (bûr'lĭ)	115	42°31'N	113°48'W
Burley, Wa., U.S.	116a	47°25'N	122°38'W

PLACE (Pronunciation)	PAGE	LAT.	LONG.
Burlingame, Ca., U.S. (bûr'lĭn-găm)	116b	37°35'N	122°22'W
Burlingame, Ks., U.S.	121	38°45'N	95°49'W
Burlington, Can. (bûr'lĭng-tŭn)	99	43°19'N	79°48'W
Burlington, Co., U.S.	120	39°17'N	102°26'W
Burlington, Ia., U.S.	105	40°48'N	91°05'W
Burlington, Ks., U.S.	121	38°10'N	95°46'W
Burlington, Ky., U.S.	111f	39°01'N	84°44'W
Burlington, Ma., U.S.	101a	42°31'N	71°13'W
Burlington, N.C., U.S.	125	36°05'N	79°26'W
Burlington, N.J., U.S.	110f	40°04'N	74°52'W
Burlington, Vt., U.S.	105	44°30'N	73°15'W
Burlington, Wa., U.S.	116a	48°28'N	122°20'W
Burlington, Wi., U.S.	111a	42°41'N	88°16'W
Burma see Myanmar, nation, Asia	194	21°00'N	95°15'E
Burnaby, Can.	90	49°14'N	122°58'W
Burnet, Tx., U.S. (bûrn'ĕt)	122	30°46'N	98°14'W
Burnham on Crouch, Eng., U.K. (bûrn'ăm-ŏn-krouch)	158b	51°38'N	0°48'E
Burnie, Austl. (bûr'nē)	219	41°15'S	146°05'E
Burnley, Eng., U.K. (bûrn'lē)	164	53°47'N	2°19'W
Burns, Or., U.S. (bûrnz)	114	43°35'N	119°05'W
Burnside, Ky., U.S. (bûrn'sīd)	124	36°57'N	84°33'W
Burns Lake, Can. (bûrnz lăk)	90	54°14'N	125°46'W
Burnsville, Can. (bûrnz'vĭl)	100	47°44'N	65°07'W
Burnt, r., Or., U.S. (bûrnt)	114	44°26'N	117°53'W
Burntwood, r., Can.	97	55°53'N	97°30'W
Burrard Inlet, b., Can. (bûr'ărd)	116d	49°19'N	123°15'W
Burr Gaabo, Som.	233	1°14'N	51°47'E
Burro, Serranías del, mts., Mex. (sĕr-rä-nē'äs dĕl bo͞o'r-rô)	122	29°39'N	102°07'W
Bursa, Tur. (bo͞or'sȧ)	198	40°10'N	28°10'E
Būr Safājah, Egypt	231	26°57'N	33°56'E
Burscheid, Ger. (bo͞or'shīd)	171c	51°05'N	7°07'E
Būr Sūdān, Sudan (so͞o-dán')	231	19°30'N	37°10'E
Burt, N.Y., U.S. (bŭrt)	111c	43°19'N	78°45'W
Burt, l., Mi., U.S. (bŭrt)	108	45°25'N	84°45'W
Burton, Wa., U.S. (bûr'tŭn)	116a	47°24'N	122°28'W
Burton, Lake, res., Ga., U.S.	124	34°46'N	83°40'W
Burtonsville, Md., U.S. (bûrtŏns-vil)	110e	39°07'N	76°57'W
Burton-upon-Trent, Eng., U.K. (bŭr'tŭn-ŭp'-ŏn-trĕnt)	164	52°48'N	1°37'W
Buru, i., Indon.	213	3°30'S	126°30'E
Burullus, l., Egypt	238b	31°20'N	30°58'E
Burundi, nation, Afr.	232	3°00'S	29°30'E
Burwell, Ne., U.S. (bûr'wĕl)	112	41°46'N	99°08'W
Bury, Eng., U.K. (bĕr'ĭ)	158a	53°36'N	2°17'W
Buryatia, prov., Russia	185	55°15'N	112°00'E
Bury Saint Edmunds, Eng., U.K. (bĕr'ĭ-sānt ĕd'mŭndz)	165	52°14'N	0°44'E
Burzaco, Arg. (bo͞or-zá'kô)	144a	34°50'S	58°23'W
Busanga Swamp, sw., Zam.	237	14°10'S	25°50'E
Būsh, Egypt (bo͞osh)	238b	29°13'N	31°08'E
Bushmanland, hist. reg., S. Afr. (bo̤sh-măn lănd)	232	29°15'S	18°45'E
Bushnell, Il., U.S. (bo̤sh'nĕl)	121	40°33'N	90°28'W
Businga, D.R.C. (bo̤-siŋ'gȧ)	231	3°20'N	20°53'E
Busira, r., D.R.C.	236	0°05'S	19°20'E
Bus'k, Ukr.	169	49°58'N	24°39'E
Busselton, Austl. (bŭs'l-tŭn)	218	33°40'S	115°30'E
Bussum, Neth.	159a	52°16'N	5°10'E
Bustamante, Mex. (bo͞os-tȧ-män'tȧ)	122	26°34'N	100°30'W
Busto Arsizio, Italy (bo͞os'tō är-sēd'zē-ō)	174	45°47'N	8°51'E
Busuanga, i., Phil. (bo͞o-swäŋ'gä)	213a	12°20'N	119°43'E
Buta, D.R.C. (bo͞o'tȧ)	231	2°48'N	24°44'E
Butha Buthe, Leso. (bo͞o-thȧ-bo͞o'thȧ)	233c	28°49'S	28°16'E
Butler, Al., U.S. (bŭt'lēr)	124	32°05'N	88°10'W
Butler, In., U.S.	108	41°25'N	84°50'W
Butler, Md., U.S.	110e	39°32'N	76°46'W
Butler, N.J., U.S.	110a	41°00'N	74°20'W
Butler, Pa., U.S.	109	40°50'N	79°55'W
Butovo, Russia (bo̤-tô'vô)	186b	55°33'N	37°36'E
Butsha, D.R.C.	237	0°57'N	29°13'E
Buttahatchee, r., Al., U.S. (bŭt-ȧ-hăch'ē)	124	34°02'N	88°05'W
Butte, Mt., U.S. (būt)	104	46°00'N	112°31'W
Butterworth, S. Afr. (bŭ tĕr'wûrth)	233c	32°20'S	28°09'E
Butt of Lewis, c., Scot., U.K. (bŭt ŏv lū'ĭs)	164	58°34'N	6°15'W
Butuan, Phil. (bo͞o-to͞o'än)	213	8°40'N	125°33'E
Buturlinovka, Russia (bo͞o-to͞o'lē-nôf'ka)	181	50°47'N	40°35'E
Buuhoodle, Som.	238a	8°15'N	46°20'E
Buulo Berde, Som.	238a	3°53'N	45°30'E
Buxtehude, Ger.	159c	53°29'N	9°42'E
Buxton, Eng., U.K. (bŭks't'n)	158a	53°15'N	1°55'W
Buxton, Or., U.S.	116c	45°41'N	123°11'W
Buy, Russia (bwē)	178	58°30'N	41°48'E
Büyükmenderes, r., Tur.	198	37°50'N	28°20'E
Buzău, Rom. (bo͞o-zĕ'o̤)	175	45°09'N	26°51'E
Buzău, r., Rom.	177	45°17'N	27°22'E
Buzaymah, Libya	231	25°14'N	22°13'E
Buzi, China (bo͞o-dz)	206	33°48'N	118°13'E
Buzuluk, Russia (bo̤-zo̤-lo̤k')	178	52°50'N	52°10'E
Bwendi, D.R.C.	237	4°01'N	26°41'E
Byala, Blg.	175	43°26'N	25°44'E
Byala Slatina, Blg. (byä'la slä'tēnä)	175	43°26'N	23°56'E
Byalynichy, Bela. (byĕl-ĭ-nĭ'chĭ)	176	54°02'N	29°42'E
Byarezina, r., Bela. (bĕr-yĕ'zē-nȧ)	176	53°20'N	29°05'E
Byaroza, Bela.	169	52°29'N	24°59'E
Byblos see Jubayl, Leb.	197a	34°07'N	35°38'E
Bydgoszcz, Pol. (bĭd'gôshch)	160	53°07'N	18°00'E
Byelorussia see Belarus, nation, Eur.	178	53°30'N	25°33'E
Byerazino, Bela. (bĕr-yä'zē-nô)	176	53°51'N	28°54'E
Byeshankovichy, Bela.	176	55°04'N	29°29'E

ăt; finăl; rāte; senāte; ärm; ȧsk; sofȧ; fâre; ch-choose; dh-as th in other; bē; ēvent; bĕt; recĕnt; cratēr; g-gō; gh-guttural g; bĭt; ĭ-short neutral; rīde; ĸ-guttural k as ch in German ich;

PRONOUNCING INDEX
Byesville – Camp Indian Reservation 277

PLACE (Pronunciation)	PAGE	LAT.	LONG.
Byesville, Oh., U.S. (bīz-vĭl)	108	39°55'N	81°35'W
Bygdin, l., Nor. (bügh-dēn')	166	61°24'N	8°31'E
Byglandsfjord, Nor. (bügh'länds-fyôr)	166	58°40'N	7°49'E
Bykhaw, Bela.	176	53°32'N	30°15'E
Bykovo, Russia (bĭ-kô'vô)	186b	55°38'N	38°05'E
Byrranga, Gory, mts., Russia	184	74°15'N	94°28'E
Bytantay, r., Russia (byän'tāy)	185	68°15'N	132°15'E
Bytom, Pol. (bĭ'tŭm)	161	50°21'N	18°55'E
Bytosh', Russia (bĭ-tôsh')	176	53°48'N	34°06'E
Bytow, Pol. (bĭ'tŭf)	169	54°10'N	17°30'E
C			
Cabagan, Phil. (kä-bä-gän')	213a	17°27'N	121°50'E
Cabalete, i., Phil. (kä-bä-lā'tå)	213a	14°19'N	122°00'E
Caballones, Canal de, strt., Cuba (kä-nä'l-dĕ-kä-bäl-yô'nĕs)	134	20°45'N	79°20'W
Caballo Reservoir, res., N.M., U.S. (kä-bä-lyō')	119	33°00'N	107°20'W
Cabanatuan, Phil. (kä-bä-nä-twän')	213a	15°30'N	120°56'E
Cabano, Can. (kä-bä-nō')	100	47°41'N	68°54'W
Cabarruyan, i., Phil. (kä-bä-rōō'yän)	213a	16°21'N	120°10'E
Cabedelo, Braz. (kä-bē-dā'lò)	143	6°58'S	34°49'W
Cabeza, Arrecife, i., Mex.	131	19°07'N	95°52'W
Cabeza del Buey, Spain (kä-bā'thä dĕl bwā')	172	38°43'N	5°18'W
Cabimas, Ven. (kä-bē'mäs)	142	10°21'N	71°27'W
Cabinda, Ang.	232	5°33'S	12°12'E
Cabinda, hist. reg., Ang. (kä-bĭn'dä)	232	5°10'S	10°00'E
Cabinet Mountains, mts., Mt., U.S. (kăb'ĭ-nĕt)	114	48°13'N	115°52'W
Cabo Frio, Braz. (kä'bô-frē'ô)	141a	22°53'S	42°02'W
Cabo Frio, Ilha do, Braz. (ē'lä-dô-kä'bô frē'ô)	141a	23°01'S	42°00'W
Cabo Gracias a Dios, Hond. (ká'bô-grä-syäs-ä-dyô's)	133	15°00'N	83°13'W
Cabonga, Réservoir, res., Can.	99	47°25'N	76°35'W
Cabora Bassa Reservoir, res., Moz.	232	15°45'S	32°00'E
Cabot Head, c., Can. (kăb'ŭt)	98	45°15'N	81°20'W
Cabot Strait, strt., Can. (kăb'ŭt)	93a	47°35'N	60°00'W
Cabra, Spain (käb'rä)	172	37°28'N	4°29'W
Cabra, i., Phil.	213a	13°55'N	119°55'E
Cabrera, Illa de, i., Spain	173	39°08'N	2°57'E
Cabrera, Sierra de la, mts., Spain	172	42°15'N	6°45'W
Cabriel, r., Spain (kä-brē-ĕl')	172	39°25'N	1°20'W
Cabrillo National Monument, rec., Ca., U.S. (kä-brēl'yō)	118a	32°41'N	117°03'W
Cabuçu, r., Braz. (kä-bōō'-sōō)	144b	22°57'S	43°36'W
Cabugao, Phil. (kä-bōō'gä-ô)	213a	17°48'N	120°28'E
Čačak, Serb. (chä'chák)	175	43°51'N	20°22'E
Caçapava, Braz. (kä'sä-pá'vä)	141a	23°05'S	45°52'W
Cáceres, Braz. (ká'sĕ-rĕs)	143	16°11'S	57°32'W
Cáceres, Spain (ká'thå-räs)	162	39°28'N	6°20'W
Cachapoal, r., Chile (kä-chä-pô-á'l)	141b	34°23'S	70°19'W
Cache, r., Ar., U.S. (kásh)	121	35°24'N	91°12'W
Cache Creek, Can.	95	50°48'N	121°19'W
Cache Creek, r., Ca., U.S. (kăsh)	118	38°53'N	122°24'W
Cache la Poudre, r., Co., U.S. (kásh lá pōōd'r')	120	40°43'N	105°39'W
Cachi, Nevados de, mtn., Arg. (nĕ-vá'dôs-dĕ-ká'chē)	144	25°05'S	66°40'W
Cachinal, Chile (kä-chē-näl')	144	24°57'S	69°33'W
Cachoeira, Braz. (kä-shô-ā'rä)	143	12°32'S	38°47'W
Cachoeirá do Sul, Braz. (kä-shô-ā'rä-dô-sōō'l)	144	30°02'S	52°49'W
Cachoeiras de Macacu, Braz. (kä-shô-ā'räs-dĕ-mä-ká'kōō)	141a	22°28'S	42°39'W
Cachoeiro de Itapemirim, Braz.	143	20°51'S	41°06'W
Cacólo, Ang.	236	10°07'S	19°17'E
Caconda, Ang. (kä-kōn'dä)	232	13°43'S	15°06'E
Cacouna, Can.	100	47°54'N	69°31'W
Cacula, Ang.	236	14°29'S	14°10'E
Cadale, Som.	238a	2°45'N	46°15'E
Caddo, l., La., U.S. (kăd'ō)	123	32°37'N	94°15'W
Cadereyta, Mex. (kä-då-rā'tä)	130	20°42'N	99°47'W
Cadereyta Jimenez, Mex. (kä-dä-rā'tä hĕ-mā'nāz)	122	25°36'N	99°59'W
Cadi, Sierra de, mts., Spain (sē-ĕ'r-rä-dĕ-kä'dē)	173	42°17'N	1°34'E
Cadillac, Mi., U.S. (kăd'ĭ-lăk)	108	44°15'N	85°25'W
Cádiz, Spain (ká'dēz)	154	36°34'N	6°20'W
Cadiz, Ca., U.S. (kā'dĭz)	118	34°33'N	115°30'W
Cadiz, Oh., U.S.	108	40°15'N	81°00'W
Cádiz, Golfo de, b., Spain (gôl-fô-dĕ-ká'dēz)	162	36°50'N	7°00'W
Caen, Fr. (käN)	161	49°13'N	0°22'W
Caernarfon, Wales, U.K.	160	53°08'N	4°17'W
Caernarfon Bay, b., Wales, U.K.	164	53°09'N	4°56'W
Cagayan, Phil. (kä-gä-yän')	213	8°13'N	124°30'E
Cagayan, r., Phil.	212	16°45'N	121°55'E
Cagayan Islands, is., Phil.	212	9°40'N	120°30'E
Cagayan Sulu, i., Phil. (kä-gä-yän sōō'lōō)	212	7°00'N	118°30'E
Cagli, Italy (käl'yē)	174	43°35'N	12°40'E
Cagliari, Italy (käl'yä-rē)	154	39°16'N	9°08'E
Cagliari, Golfo di, b., Italy (gôl-fô-dē-käl'yä-rē)	162	39°08'N	9°12'E
Cagnes, Fr. (kän'y')	171	43°40'N	7°14'E
Cagua, Ven. (kä'gwä)	143b	10°12'N	67°27'W
Caguas, P.R. (kä'gwäs)	129b	18°12'N	66°01'W
Cahaba, r., Al., U.S. (ká hä-bä)	124	32°50'N	87°15'W
Cahama, Ang. (kä-á'mä)	232	16°17'S	14°19'E
Cahokia, Il., U.S. (ká-hō'kĭ-á)	117e	38°34'N	90°11'W
Cahora-Bassa, wtfl., Moz.	237	15°40'S	32°50'E
Cahors, Fr. (kà-ôr')	161	44°27'N	1°27'E
Cahuacán, Mex. (kä-wä-kä'n)	131a	19°38'N	99°25'W
Cahuita, Punta, c., C.R. (pōō'n-tä-kä-wē'tá)	133	9°47'N	82°41'W
Cahul, Mol.	177	45°49'N	28°17'E
Caibarién, Cuba (kī-bä-rē-ĕn')	134	22°35'N	79°30'W
Caicedonia, Col. (kī-sĕ-dô-nēä)	142a	4°21'N	75°48'W
Caicos Bank, bk. (kī'kōs)	135	21°35'N	72°00'W
Caicos Islands, is., T./C. Is.	129	21°45'N	71°50'W
Caicos Passage, strt., N.A.	135	21°55'N	72°45'W
Caillou Bay, b., La., U.S. (kà-yōō')	123	29°07'N	91°00'W
Caimanera, Cuba (kī-mä-nā'rä)	135	20°00'N	75°10'W
Caiman Point, c., Phil. (kī'mán)	213a	15°56'N	119°33'E
Caimito, r., Pan. (kä-ē-mē'tô)	128a	8°50'N	79°45'W
Caimito del Guayabal, Cuba (kä-ē-mē'tō-dĕl-gwä-yä-bä'l)	135a	22°57'N	82°36'W
Cairns, Austl. (kârnz)	219	17°02'S	145°49'E
Cairo, C.R. (kī'rô)	133	10°06'N	83°47'W
Cairo, Egypt	231	30°00'N	31°17'E
Cairo, Ga., U.S. (kā'rō)	124	30°48'N	84°12'W
Cairo, Il., U.S.	105	36°59'N	89°11'W
Caistor, Eng., U.K. (kâs'tēr)	158a	53°30'N	0°20'W
Caiundo, Ang.	236	15°46'S	17°28'E
Caiyu, China (tsī-yōō)	206	39°39'N	116°36'E
Cajamarca, Col. (kä-ĸä-má'r-kä)	142a	4°25'N	75°25'W
Cajamarca, Peru (kä-hä-mär'kä)	142	7°16'S	78°30'W
Čajniče, Bos. (chī'nĭ-chĕ)	175	43°32'N	19°04'E
Cajon, Ca., U.S. (ká-hōn')	117a	34°18'N	117°28'W
Cajuru, Braz. (ká-zhōō'rōō)	141a	21°17'S	47°17'W
Čakovec, Cro. (chá'kō-vĕts)	174	46°23'N	16°27'E
Cala, S. Afr. (cä-lá)	233c	31°33'S	27°41'E
Calabar, Nig. (kăl-á-bär')	230	4°57'N	8°19'E
Calabazar, Cuba (kä-lä-bä-zä'r)	135a	23°02'N	82°25'W
Calabozo, Ven. (kä-lä-bō'zō)	142	8°48'N	67°27'W
Calabria, hist. reg., Italy (kä-lä'brē-ä)	174	39°26'N	16°23'E
Calafat, Rom. (ká-lá-fát')	175	43°59'N	22°56'E
Calaguas Islands, is., Phil. (kä-läg'wäs)	213a	14°30'N	123°06'E
Calahoo, Can. (kă-là-hōō')	102g	53°42'N	113°58'W
Calahorra, Spain (kä-lä-ôr'rä)	162	42°18'N	1°58'W
Calais, Fr. (ká-lĕ')	154	50°56'N	1°51'E
Calais, Me., U.S.	105	45°11'N	67°15'W
Calama, Chile (kä-lä'mä)	144	22°17'S	68°58'W
Calamar, Col. (kä-lä-mär')	142	10°24'N	75°00'W
Calamar, Col.	142	1°55'N	72°33'W
Calamba, Phil. (kä-läm'bä)	213a	14°12'N	121°10'E
Calamian Group, is., Phil. (kä-lä-myän')	212	12°14'N	118°38'E
Calañas, Spain (kä-län'yäs)	172	37°41'N	6°52'W
Calanda, Spain	173	40°53'N	0°20'W
Calapan, Phil. (kä-lä-pän')	213a	13°25'N	121°11'E
Călăraşi, Rom. (kŭ-lŭ-rásh'ĭ)	163	44°09'N	27°20'E
Calatayud, Spain (kä-lä-tä-yōōdh')	162	41°23'N	1°37'W
Calauag Bay, b., Phil.	213a	14°07'N	122°10'E
Calaveras Reservoir, res., Ca., U.S. (kăl-á-vēr'ăs)	116b	37°29'N	121°47'W
Calavite, Cape, c., Phil. (kä-lä-vē'tä)	213a	13°29'N	120°00'E
Calcasieu, r., La., U.S. (kăl'ká-shū)	123	30°22'N	93°08'W
Calcasieu Lake, l., La., U.S.	123	29°58'N	93°08'W
Calcutta *see* Kolkata, India (kăl-kŭt'á)	199	22°32'N	88°22'E
Caldas, Col. (ká'l-däs)	142a	6°06'N	75°38'W
Caldas, dept., Col.	142a	5°20'N	75°38'W
Caldas da Rainha, Port. (käl'däs dä rīn'yá)	172	39°25'N	9°08'W
Calder, r., Eng., U.K. (kôl'dēr)	158a	53°39'N	1°30'W
Caldera, Chile (käl-dā'rä)	144	27°02'S	70°53'W
Calder Canal, can., Eng., U.K.	158a	53°48'N	2°25'W
Caldwell, Id., U.S. (kôld'wĕl)	114	43°40'N	116°43'W
Caldwell, Ks., U.S.	121	37°04'N	97°36'W
Caldwell, Oh., U.S.	108	39°40'N	81°30'W
Caldwell, Tx., U.S.	123	30°30'N	96°40'W
Caledon, Can. (kăl'ē-dŏn)	102d	43°52'N	79°59'W
Caledonia, Mn., U.S. (kăl-ē-dō'nĭ-á)	113	43°38'N	91°31'W
Calella, Spain (kä-lĕl'yä)	173	41°37'N	2°39'E
Calera Victor Rosales, Mex. (kä-lā'rä-vē'k-tôr-rô-sä'lĕs)	130	22°57'N	102°42'W
Calexico, Ca., U.S. (ká-lĕk'sĭ-kō)	104	32°41'N	115°30'W
Calgary, Can. (kăl'gá-rĭ)	90	51°03'N	114°05'W
Calhoun, Ga., U.S. (kăl-hōōn')	124	34°30'N	84°56'W
Cali, Col. (kä'lē)	142	3°26'N	76°30'W
Caliente, Nv., U.S. (käl-yĕn'tä)	119	37°38'N	114°30'W
California, Mo., U.S. (kăl-ĭ-fôr'nĭ-á)	121	38°38'N	92°38'W
California, Pa., U.S.	111e	40°03'N	79°53'W
California, state, U.S.	104	38°10'N	121°20'W
California, Golfo de, b., Mex. (gôl-fô-dĕ-kä-lē-fôr-nyä)	128	30°30'N	113°45'W
California Aqueduct, aq., Ca., U.S.	118	37°10'N	121°10'W
Călimani, Munţii, mts., Rom.	169	47°05'N	24°47'E
Calimere, Point, c., India	203	10°20'N	80°20'E
Calimesa, Ca., U.S. (kă-lĭ-mā'sá)	117a	34°00'N	117°04'W
Calipatria, Ca., U.S. (kăl-ĭ-pát'rĭ-á)	118	33°03'N	115°30'W
Calkini, Mex. (käl-kē-nē')	131	20°21'N	90°06'W
Callabonna, Lake, l., Austl. (călă'bŏná)	222	29°35'S	140°28'E
Callao, Peru (käl-yä'ô)	142	12°02'S	77°07'W
Calling, l., Can. (kôl'ĭng)	95	55°15'N	113°12'W
Calmar, Can. (kăl'mär)	102g	53°16'N	113°49'W
Calmar, Ia., U.S.	113	43°12'N	91°54'W
Calooshatchee, r., Fl., U.S. (ká-loo-sá-hăch'ē)	125a	26°45'N	81°41'W
Calotmul, Mex. (kä-lôt-mōōl)	132a	20°58'N	88°11'W
Calpulalpan, Mex. (käl-pōō-läl'pän)	130	19°35'N	98°33'W
Caltagirone, Italy (käl-tä-jē-rō'nā)	162	37°14'N	14°32'E
Caltanissetta, Italy (käl-tä-nē-sĕt'tä)	162	37°30'N	14°02'E
Caluango, Ang.	236	8°21'S	19°40'E
Calucinga, Ang.	236	11°18'S	16°12'E
Calumet, Mi., U.S. (kă-lū-mĕt')	113	47°15'N	88°29'W
Calumet, Lake, l., Il., U.S.	111a	41°43'N	87°36'W
Calumet City, Il., U.S.	111a	41°37'N	87°33'W
Calunda, Ang.	236	12°06'S	23°23'E
Caluquembe, Ang.	236	13°47'S	14°44'E
Caluula, Som.	238a	11°53'N	50°40'E
Calvert, Tx., U.S. (kăl'vērt)	123	30°59'N	96°41'W
Calvert Island, i., Can.	92	51°35'N	128°00'W
Calvi, Fr. (käl'vē)	174	42°33'N	8°35'E
Calvillo, Mex. (käl-vēl'yō)	131	21°51'N	102°44'E
Calvinia, S. Afr. (kăl-vĭn'ĭ-á)	232	31°20'S	19°50'E
Cam, r., Eng., U.K. (kăm)	165	52°15'N	0°05'E
Camagüey, Cuba (kä-mä-gwā')	129	21°25'N	78°00'W
Camagüey, prov., Cuba	134	21°30'N	78°10'W
Camajuani, Cuba (kä-mä-hwä'nē)	134	22°25'N	79°50'W
Camano, Wa., U.S. (kä-mä'no)	116a	48°10'N	122°32'W
Camano Island, i., Wa., U.S.	116a	48°11'N	122°29'W
Camargo, Mex. (kä-mär gō)	122	26°19'N	98°49'W
Camarón, Cabo, c., Hond. (ká'bô-kä-mä-rōn')	132	16°06'N	85°05'W
Camas, Wa., U.S. (kăm'ás)	116c	45°36'N	122°24'W
Camas Creek, r., Id., U.S.	115	44°10'N	112°09'W
Camatagua, Ven. (kä-mä-tá'gwä)	143b	9°49'N	66°55'W
Ca Mau, Mui, c., Viet.	212	8°36'N	104°43'E
Cambay, India (kăm-bā')	202	22°22'N	72°39'E
Cambodia, nation, Asia	212	12°15'N	104°00'E
Cambonda, Serra, mts., Ang.	236	12°10'S	14°15'E
Camborne, Eng., U.K. (kăm'bôrn)	164	50°15'N	5°28'W
Cambrai, Fr. (käN-brĕ')	161	50°10'N	3°15'E
Cambrian Mountains, mts., Wales, U.K. (kăm'brĭ-ăn)	164	52°05'N	4°05'W
Cambridge, Can.	99	43°22'N	80°19'W
Cambridge, Eng., U.K. (kām'brĭj)	161	52°12'N	0°11'E
Cambridge, Ma., U.S.	101a	42°23'N	71°07'W
Cambridge, Md., U.S.	109	38°35'N	76°10'W
Cambridge, Mn., U.S.	113	45°35'N	93°14'W
Cambridge, Ne., U.S.	120	40°17'N	100°10'W
Cambridge, Oh., U.S.	108	40°00'N	81°35'W
Cambridge Bay *see* Kaluktutiak, Can.	92	69°15'N	105°00'W
Cambridge City, In., U.S.	108	39°45'N	85°15'W
Cambridgeshire, co., Eng., U.K.	158a	52°26'N	0°19'W
Cambuci, Braz. (käm-bōō'sē)	141a	21°35'S	41°54'W
Cambundi-Catembo, Ang.	236	10°09'S	17°31'E
Camby, In., U.S. (kăm'bē)	111g	39°40'N	86°19'W
Camden, Austl.	217b	34°03'S	150°42'E
Camden, Al., U.S. (kăm'dĕn)	124	31°58'N	87°15'W
Camden, Ar., U.S.	121	33°36'N	92°49'W
Camden, Me., U.S.	100	44°11'N	69°05'W
Camden, N.J., U.S.	105	39°56'N	75°06'W
Camden, S.C., U.S.	125	34°14'N	80°37'W
Cameia, Parque Nacional da, rec., Ang.	236	11°40'S	21°20'E
Camenca, Mol.	177	48°02'N	28°43'E
Cameron, Mo., U.S. (kăm'ēr-ŭn)	121	39°44'N	94°14'W
Cameron, Tx., U.S.	123	30°52'N	96°57'W
Cameron, W.V., U.S.	108	39°40'N	80°35'W
Cameron Hills, hills, Can.	92	60°13'N	120°20'W
Cameroon, nation, Afr.	230	5°48'N	11°00'E
Cameroon Mountain, mtn., Cam.	230	4°12'N	9°11'E
Camiling, Phil. (kä-mē-lĭng')	213a	15°42'N	120°24'E
Camilla, Ga., U.S. (ká-mĭl'á)	124	31°13'N	84°12'W
Caminha, Port. (kä-mĭn'yá)	172	41°52'N	8°44'W
Camoçim, Braz. (kä-mô-sēN')	143	2°56'S	40°55'W
Camooweal, Austl.	218	20°00'S	138°13'E
Campana, Arg. (käm-pä'nä)	141c	34°10'S	58°58'W
Campana, i., Chile (käm-pän'yä)	144	48°20'S	75°15'W
Campanario, Spain (kä-pä-nä'rē-ō)	172	38°51'N	5°36'W
Campanella, Punta, c., Italy (pó'n-tä-käm-pä-nĕ'lä)	173c	40°20'N	14°21'E
Campanha, Braz. (käm-pän-yäN')	141a	21°51'S	45°24'W
Campania, hist. reg., Italy (käm-pän'yä)	174	41°00'N	14°40'E
Campbell, Ca., U.S. (kăm'bĕl)	116b	37°17'N	121°57'W
Campbell, Mo., U.S.	121	36°29'N	90°04'W
Campbell, is., N.Z.	3	52°30'S	169°00'E
Campbellpore, Pak.	202	33°49'N	72°24'E
Campbell River, Can.	90	50°01'N	125°15'W
Campbellsville, Ky., U.S. (kăm'bĕlz-vĭl)	124	37°19'N	85°20'W
Campbellton, Can. (kăm'bĕl-tŭn)	91	48°00'N	66°40'W
Campbelltown, Austl. (kăm'bĕl-toun)	217b	34°04'S	150°49'E
Campbelltown, Scot., U.K. (kăm'b'l-toun)	164	55°25'N	5°50'W
Camp Dennison, Oh., U.S. (dĕ'nĭ-sŏn)	111f	39°12'N	84°17'W
Campeche, Mex. (käm-pā'chå)	128	19°51'N	90°32'W
Campeche, state, Mex.	128	18°55'N	90°20'W
Campeche, Bahía de, b., Mex. (bä-ē'ä-dĕ-käm-pā'chā)	128	19°30'N	93°40'W
Campechuela, Cuba (käm-på-chwā'lä)	134	20°15'N	77°15'W
Camperdown, S. Afr. (kăm'pēr-doun)	233c	29°44'S	30°33'E
Câmpina, Rom.	175	45°08'N	25°47'E
Campina Grande, Braz. (käm-pē'nä grän'dĕ)	143	7°15'S	35°49'W
Campinas, Braz. (käm-pē'näzh)	143	22°53'S	47°03'W
Camp Indian Reservation, I.R., Ca., U.S. (kămp)	118	32°39'N	116°26'W

PLACE (Pronunciation)	PAGE	LAT.	LONG.
Campo, Cam. (käm′pō)	230	2°22′N	9°49′E
Campoalegre, Col. (kä′m-pô-älĕ′grĕ)	142	2°34′N	75°20′W
Campobasso, Italy (käm′pô-bäs′sō)	174	41°35′N	14°39′E
Campo Belo, Braz.	141a	20°52′S	45°15′W
Campo de Criptana, Spain (käm′pō dā krēp-tä′nä)	172	39°24′N	3°09′W
Campo Florido, Cuba (kä′m-pō flô-rē′dō)	135a	23°07′N	82°07′W
Campo Grande, Braz. (käm-pò grän′dĕ)	143	20°28′S	54°32′W
Campo Grande, Braz.	144b	22°54′S	43°33′W
Campo Maior, Braz. (käm-pò mä-yôr′)	143	4°48′S	42°12′W
Campo Maior, Port.	172	39°03′N	7°06′W
Campo Real, Spain (käm′pô râ-äl′)	173a	40°21′N	3°23′W
Campos, Braz. (kä′m-pôs)	143	21°46′S	41°19′W
Campos do Jordão, Braz. (kä′m-pôs-dô-zhôr-dou′n)	141a	22°45′S	45°35′W
Campos Gerais, Braz. (kä′m-pôs-zhĕ-râ′ēs)	141a	21°17′S	45°43′W
Camps Bay, S. Afr. (kămps)	232a	33°57′S	18°22′E
Camp Springs, Md., U.S. (cămp sprĭngz)	110e	38°48′N	76°55′W
Câmpulung, Rom.	163	45°15′N	25°03′E
Câmpulung Moldovenesc, Rom.	169	47°31′N	25°36′E
Camp Wood, Tx., U.S. (kămp wòd)	122	29°39′N	100°02′W
Camrose, Can. (kăm-rōz)	90	53°01′N	112°50′W
Camu, r., Dom. Rep. (kä′mōō)	135	19°05′N	70°15′W
Canada, nation, N.A. (kăn′á-dá)	90	50°00′N	100°00′W
Canada Bay, b., Can.	101	50°43′N	56°10′W
Cañada de Gómez, Arg. (kä-nyä′dä-dĕ-gô′mĕz)	144	32°49′S	61°24′W
Canadian, Tx., U.S. (ká-nā′dĭ-ăn)	120	35°54′N	100°24′W
Canadian, r., U.S.	106	35°30′N	102°30′W
Canajoharie, N.Y., U.S. (kăn-á-jô-hăr′ē)	109	42°55′N	74°35′W
Çanakkale, Tur. (chä-näk-kä′lĕ)	163	40°10′N	26°26′E
Çanakkale Boğazi (Dardanelles), strt., Tur.	163	40°05′N	25°50′E
Canandaigua, N.Y., U.S. (kăn-ăn-dā′gwá)	109	42°55′N	77°20′W
Canandaigua, l., N.Y., U.S.	109	42°45′N	77°20′W
Cananea, Mex. (kä-nä-nĕ′ä)	128	31°00′N	110°20′W
Canarias, Islas (Canary Is.), is., Spain (ē′s-läs-kä-nä′ryäs)	229	29°15′N	16°30′W
Canarreos, Archipiélago de los, is., Cuba	134	21°35′N	82°20′W
Canary Islands *see* Canarias, Islas, is., Spain	229	29°15′N	16°30′W
Cañas, C.R. (kä′-nyäs)	132	10°26′N	85°06′W
Cañas, r., C.R.	132	10°20′N	85°21′W
Cañasgordas, Col. (kä′nyäs-gô′r-däs)	142a	6°44′N	76°01′W
Canastota, N.Y., U.S. (kăn-ăs-tō′tá)	109	43°05′N	75°45′W
Canastra, Serra de, mts., Braz. (sĕ′r-rä-dĕ-kä-nä′s-trä)	143	19°53′S	46°57′W
Canatlán, Mex. (kä-nät-län′)	122	24°30′N	104°45′W
Canaveral, Cape, c., Fl., U.S.	107	28°30′N	80°23′W
Canavieiras, Braz. (kä-nà-vē-ā′räs)	143	15°40′S	38°49′W
Canberra, Austl. (kăn′bĕr-á)	219	35°21′S	149°10′E
Canby, Mn., U.S. (kăn′bĭ)	112	44°43′N	96°15′W
Canchyuaya, Cerros de, mts., Peru (sĕ′r-rôs-dĕ-kän-chōō-ä′ïä)	142	7°30′S	74°30′W
Cancuc, Mex. (kän-kōōk)	131	16°58′N	92°17′W
Cancún, Mex.	132a	21°25′N	86°50′W
Candelaria, Cuba (kän-dĕ-lä′ryä)	134	22°45′N	82°55′W
Candelaria, Phil. (kän-dâ-lä′rē-ä)	213a	15°39′N	119°55′E
Candelaria, r., Mex. (kän-dĕ-lä-ryä)	131	18°25′N	91°21′W
Candeleda, Spain (kän-dhâ-lā′dä)	172	40°09′N	5°18′W
Candia *see* Iráklion, Grc.	154	35°20′N	25°10′E
Candle, Ak., U.S. (kăn′d′l)	103	65°00′N	162°04′W
Cando, N.D., U.S. (kăn′dō)	112	48°27′N	99°13′W
Candon, Phil. (kän-dōn′)	213a	17°13′N	120°26′E
Canelones, Ur. (kä-nĕ-lô-nĕs)	141c	34°32′S	56°19′W
Canelones, dept., Ur.	141c	34°34′S	56°15′W
Cañete, Peru (kän-yā′tâ)	142	13°06′S	76°17′W
Caney, Cuba (kä-nā′) (kā′nĭ)	135	20°05′N	75°45′W
Caney, Ks., U.S. (kā′nĭ)	121	37°00′N	95°57′W
Caney Fork, r., Tn., U.S.	124	36°10′N	85°50′W
Cangamba, Ang.	232	13°40′S	19°54′E
Cangas, Spain (kän′gäs)	172	42°15′N	8°43′W
Cangas de Narcea, Spain (kä′n-gäs-dĕ-när-sĕ-ä)	172	43°08′N	6°36′W
Cangzhou, China (tsäŋ-jō)	208	38°21′N	116°53′E
Caniapiscau, l., Can.	93	54°10′N	71°13′E
Caniapiscau, r., Can.	93	57°00′N	68°45′W
Canicatti, Italy (kä-nē-kät′tē)	174	37°18′N	13°58′E
Cañitas, Mex. (kän-yē′täs)	130	23°38′N	102°44′W
Cannell, Can.	102g	53°35′N	113°38′W
Cannelton, In., U.S. (kăn′ĕl-tŭn)	108	37°55′N	86°45′W
Cannes, Fr. (kán)	161	43°34′N	7°05′E
Canning, Can. (kăn′ĭng)	100	45°09′N	64°25′W
Cannock, Eng., U.K. (kăn′ŭk)	158a	52°41′N	2°02′W
Cannock Chase, reg., Eng., U.K. (kăn′ŭk chās)	158a	52°43′N	1°54′W
Cannon, r., Mn., U.S. (kăn′ŭn)	113	44°18′N	93°24′W
Cannonball, r., N.D., U.S. (kăn′ŭn-bäl)	112	46°17′N	101°35′W
Caño, Isla de, i., C.R. (ē′s-lä-dĕ-kä′nō)	133	8°38′N	84°00′W
Canoga Park, Ca., U.S. (kä-nō′gá)	117a	34°07′N	118°36′W
Canoncito Indian Reservation, I.R., N.M., U.S.	119	35°00′N	107°05′W
Canon City, Co., U.S. (kăn′yŭn)	120	38°27′N	105°16′W
Canonsburg, Pa., U.S. (kăn′ŭnz-bûrg)	111e	40°16′N	80°11′W
Canoochee, r., Ga., U.S. (ká-nōō′chē)	125	32°25′N	82°11′W
Canora, Can. (ká-nōrá)	90	51°37′N	102°26′W
Canosa, Italy (kä-nō′sä)	174	41°14′N	16°03′E
Canouan, i., St. Vin.	133b	12°44′N	61°10′W
Cansahcab, Mex.	132a	21°11′N	89°05′W
Canso, Can. (kăn′sō)	101	45°20′N	61°00′W
Canso, Cape, c., Can.	101	45°21′N	60°46′W
Canso, Strait of, strt., Can.	101	45°37′N	61°25′W
Cantabrica, Cordillera, mts., Spain	156	43°05′N	6°05′W
Cantagalo, Braz. (kän-tä-gá′lo)	141a	21°59′S	42°22′W
Cantanhede, Port. (kän-tän-yā′dâ)	172	40°22′N	8°35′W
Canterbury, Eng., U.K. (kăn′tĕr-bĕr-ē)	165	51°17′N	1°06′E
Canterbury Bight, b., N.Z.	221a	44°15′S	172°08′E
Cantiles, Cayo, i., Cuba (ky-ō-kän-tē′lâs)	134	21°40′N	82°00′W
Canton *see* Guangzhou, China	205	23°07′N	113°15′E
Canton, Ga., U.S.	124	34°13′N	84°29′W
Canton, Il., U.S.	121	40°34′N	90°02′W
Canton, Ma., U.S.	101a	42°09′N	71°09′W
Canton, Mo., U.S.	121	40°08′N	91°33′W
Canton, Ms., U.S.	124	32°36′N	90°01′W
Canton, N.C., U.S.	125	35°32′N	82°50′W
Canton, Oh., U.S.	105	40°50′N	81°25′W
Canton, Pa., U.S.	109	41°50′N	76°45′W
Canton, S.D., U.S.	112	43°17′N	96°37′W
Cantu, Italy (kän-tò′)	174	45°43′N	9°09′E
Cañuelas, Arg. (kä-nyòĕ′-läs)	141c	35°03′S	58°45′W
Canyon, Tx., U.S. (kăn′yŭn)	120	34°59′N	101°57′W
Canyon, r., Wa., U.S.	116a	48°09′N	121°48′W
Canyon de Chelly National Monument, rec., Az., U.S.	119	36°14′N	110°00′W
Canyon Ferry Lake, res., Mt., U.S.	115	46°33′N	111°37′W
Canyonlands National Park, rec., Ut., U.S.	119	38°10′N	110°00′W
Canyons of the Ancients National Monument, rec., Co., U.S.	119	37°30′N	108°50′W
Caoxian, China (tsou shyĕn)	206	34°48′N	115°33′E
Capalonga, Phil. (kä-pä-lôŋ′gä)	213a	14°20′N	122°30′E
Capannori, Italy (kä-pän′nô-rē)	174	43°50′N	10°30′E
Capaya, r., Ven. (kä-pä-ïä)	143b	10°28′N	66°15′W
Cap-Chat, Can. (káp-shä′)	91	48°02′N	65°20′W
Cap-de-la-Madeleine, Can. (káp dĕ lá má-d′lĕn′)	99	46°23′N	72°30′W
Cape Breton, i., Can. (kāp brĕt′ŭn)	101	45°48′N	59°50′W
Cape Breton Highlands National Park, rec., Can.	91	46°45′N	60°45′W
Cape Charles, Va., U.S. (kāp chärlz)	125	37°13′N	76°02′W
Cape Coast, Ghana	230	5°05′N	1°15′W
Cape Fear, r., N.C., U.S. (kāp fēr)	107	35°00′N	79°00′W
Cape Flats, pl., S. Afr. (kăp flăts)	232a	34°01′S	18°37′E
Cape Girardeau, Mo., U.S. (jē-rär-dō′)	105	37°17′N	89°32′W
Cape Krusenstern National Monument, rec., Ak., U.S.	103	67°30′N	163°40′W
Cape May, N.J., U.S. (kāp mā)	109	38°55′N	74°50′W
Cape May Court House, N.J., U.S.	109	39°05′N	75°00′W
Cape Romanzof, Ak., U.S. (rō′ män zôf)	103	61°50′N	165°45′W
Capesterre, Guad.	133b	16°02′N	61°37′W
Cape Tormentine, Can.	100	46°08′N	63°47′W
Cape Town, S. Afr. (kāp toun)	232	33°48′S	18°28′E
Cape Verde, nation, Afr.	230b	15°48′N	26°02′W
Cape York Peninsula, pen., Austl. (kāp yôrk)	221	12°30′S	142°35′E
Cap-Haïtien, Haiti (káp à-ē-syăn′)	129	19°45′N	72°15′W
Capilla de Señor, Arg. (kä-pēl′yä dā sän-yôr′)	141c	34°18′S	59°07′W
Capitachouane, r., Can.	99	47°50′N	76°45′W
Capitol Reef National Park, rec., Ut., U.S. (kăp′ĭ-tŏl)	119	38°15′N	111°10′W
Capivari, Braz. (kä-pē-vá′rē)	141a	22°59′S	47°29′W
Capivari, r., Braz.	144b	22°39′S	43°19′W
Capoompeta, mtn., Austl. (ká-pōōm-pē′tá)	221	29°15′S	152°12′E
Capraia, i., Italy (kä-prä′yä)	162	43°02′N	9°51′E
Caprara Point, c., Italy (kä-prä′rä)	174	41°08′N	8°20′E
Capreol, Can.	99	46°43′N	80°56′W
Caprera, i., Italy (kä-prā′rä)	174	41°12′N	9°28′E
Capri, Italy	173c	40°18′N	14°16′E
Capri, Isola di, i., Italy (ē′-sō-lä-dē-kä′prē)	173c	40°19′N	14°10′E
Capricorn Channel, strt., Austl. (kăp′rĭ-kôrn)	221	22°27′S	151°24′E
Caprivi Strip, hist. reg., Nmb.	232	18°00′S	22°00′E
Cap-Rouge, Can. (káp rōōzh′)	102b	46°45′N	71°21′W
Cap-Saint Ignace, Can. (kĭp săn-tē-nyás′)	102b	47°02′N	70°27′W
Capua, Italy (kä′pwä)	162	41°07′N	14°14′E
Capulhuac, Mex. (kä-pòl-hwäk′)	130	19°33′N	99°43′W
Capulin Mountain National Monument, rec., N.M., U.S. (ká-pū′lĭn)	120	36°15′N	103°58′W
Capultitlán, Mex. (kä-pò′l-tē-tlä′n)	131a	19°15′N	99°40′W
Caquetá (Japurá), r., S.A.	142	0°20′S	73°00′W
Carabaña, Spain (kä-rä-bän′yä)	173a	40°16′N	3°15′W
Carabelle, Fl., U.S. (kăr′á-bĕl)	124	29°50′N	84°40′W
Carabobo, dept., Ven. (kä-rä-bô′-bô)	143b	10°07′N	68°06′W
Caracal, Rom. (ká-rá-kál′)	175	44°06′N	24°22′E
Caracas, Ven. (kä-rä′käs)	142	10°30′N	66°58′W
Carácuaro de Morelos, Mex. (kä-rä′kwä-rō-dĕ-mô-rĕ-lôs)	130	18°44′N	101°04′W
Caraguatatuba, Braz. (kä-rä-gwä-tá-tōō′bä)	141a	23°37′S	45°26′W
Carajás, Serra dos, mts., Braz. (sĕ′r-rä-dôs-kä-rä-zhá′s)	143	5°58′S	51°45′W
Caramanta, Cerro, mtn., Col. (sĕ′r-rô-kä-rä-má′n-tä)	142a	5°29′N	76°01′W
Carangola, Braz. (kä-rán′gō′lä)	141a	20°46′S	42°02′W
Caraquet, Can. (kä-rá-kĕt′)	91	47°48′N	64°57′W
Carata, Laguna, l., Nic. (lä-gò′nä-kä-rä′tä)	133	13°59′N	83°41′W
Caratasca, Laguna, l., Hond. (lä-gò′nä-kä-rä-täs′kä)	133	15°20′N	83°45′W
Caravaca, Spain (kä-rä-vä′kä)	172	38°05′N	1°51′W
Caravelas, Braz. (kä-rä-vĕl′äzh)	143	17°46′S	39°06′W
Carayaca, Ven. (kä-rä-ïá′kä)	143b	10°32′N	67°07′W
Caràzinho, Braz. (kä-rá′zē-nyŏ)	144	28°22′S	52°33′W
Carballiño, Spain	162	42°26′N	8°04′W
Carballo, Spain (kär-bäl′yō)	172	43°13′N	8°40′W
Carbet, Pitons du, mtn., Mart.	133b	14°40′N	61°05′W
Carbon, r., Wa., U.S. (kär′bŏn)	116a	47°06′N	122°08′W
Carbonado, Wa., U.S. (kár-bō-nā′dō)	116a	47°05′N	122°03′W
Carbonara, Cape, c., Italy (kär-bō-nä′rä)	162	39°08′N	9°33′E
Carbondale, Can. (kär′bŏn-dāl)	102g	53°45′N	113°32′W
Carbondale, Il., U.S.	108	37°42′N	89°12′W
Carbondale, Pa., U.S.	109	41°35′N	75°30′W
Carbonear, Can. (kär-bô-nēr′)	101	47°45′N	53°14′W
Carbon Hill, Al., U.S. (kär′bŏn hĭl)	124	33°53′N	87°34′W
Carcaixent, Spain	173	39°09′N	0°29′W
Carcans, Étang de, l., Fr. (ā-taN-dĕ-kär-kän)	170	45°12′N	1°00′W
Carcassonne, Fr. (kár-ká-sôn′)	161	43°12′N	2°23′E
Carcross, Can. (kär′krôs)	90	60°18′N	134°54′W
Cárdenas, Cuba (kär′då-näs)	129	23°00′N	81°10′W
Cárdenas, Mex. (ká′r-dĕ-näs)	131	17°59′N	93°23′W
Cárdenas, Mex.	130	22°01′N	99°38′W
Cárdenas, Bahía de, b., Cuba (bä-ē′ä-dĕ-kär′dĕ-näs)	134	23°10′N	81°10′W
Cardiff, Can. (kär′dĭf)	102g	53°46′N	113°36′W
Cardiff, Wales, U.K.	161	51°30′N	3°18′W
Cardigan, Wales, U.K. (kär′dĭ-găn)	161	52°05′N	4°40′W
Cardigan Bay, b., Wales, U.K.	161	52°35′N	4°40′W
Cardston, Can. (kärds′tŭn)	90	49°12′N	113°18′W
Carei, Rom. (kä-rē′)	169	47°42′N	22°28′E
Carentan, Fr. (kä-rôN-täN′)	170	49°19′N	1°14′W
Carey, Oh., U.S. (kā′rē)	108	40°55′N	83°25′W
Carey, l., Austl. (kâr′ē)	220	29°20′S	123°35′E
Carhaix-Plouguer, Fr. (kär-ĕ′)	170	48°17′N	3°37′W
Caribbean Sea, sea (kăr-ĭ-bē′ăn)	129	14°30′N	75°30′W
Caribe, Arroyo, r., Mex. (är-ro′i-kä-rē′bĕ)	131	18°18′N	90°38′W
Cariboo Mountains, mts., Can. (kă′rĭ-bōō)	92	53°00′N	121°00′W
Caribou, Me., U.S.	100	46°51′N	68°01′W
Caribou, i., Can.	98	47°22′N	85°42′W
Caribou Lake, l., Mn., U.S.	117h	46°54′N	92°16′W
Caribou Mountains, mts., Can.	92	59°20′N	115°30′W
Carinhanha, Braz. (kä-rĭ-nyän′yä)	143	14°14′S	43°44′W
Carini, Italy (kä-rē′nē)	174	38°09′N	13°10′E
Carleton Place, Can. (kärl′tŭn)	99	45°15′N	76°10′W
Carletonville, S. Afr.	238c	26°20′S	27°23′E
Carlinville, Il., U.S. (kär′lĭn-vĭl)	121	39°16′N	89°52′W
Carlisle, Eng., U.K. (kär-līl′)	154	54°54′N	3°03′W
Carlisle, Ky., U.S.	108	38°20′N	84°00′W
Carlisle, Pa., U.S.	109	40°10′N	77°15′W
Carloforte, Italy (kär′lō-fôr-tå)	174	39°11′N	8°28′E
Carlos Casares, Arg. (kär-lôs-kä-sá′rĕs)	144	35°38′S	61°17′W
Carlow, Ire. (kär′lō)	164	52°50′N	7°00′W
Carlsbad, N.M., U.S. (kärlz′băd)	122	32°24′N	104°12′W
Carlsbad Caverns National Park, rec., N.M., U.S.	122	32°08′N	104°30′W
Carlton, Eng., U.K. (kärl′tŭn)	158a	52°58′N	1°05′W
Carlton, Mn., U.S.	117h	46°40′N	92°26′W
Carlton Center, Mi., U.S. (kärl′tŭn sĕn′tēr)	108	42°45′N	85°20′W
Carlyle, Il., U.S. (kärlīl′)	121	38°37′N	89°23′W
Carmagnolo, Italy (kär-mä-nyô′lä)	174	44°52′N	7°48′E
Carman, Can. (kär′mán)	90	49°32′N	98°00′W
Carmarthen, Wales, U.K. (kär-mär′thĕn)	164	51°50′N	4°20′W
Carmaux, Fr. (kár-mō′)	170	44°05′N	2°09′E
Carmel, N.Y., U.S. (kär′mĕl)	110a	41°25′N	73°42′W
Carmelo, Ur. (kär-mĕ′lo)	141c	33°59′S	58°15′W
Carmen, Isla del, i., Mex. (ē′s-lä-dĕl-kä′r-mĕn)	131	18°43′N	91°40′W
Carmen, Laguna del, l., Mex. (lä-gò′nä-dĕl-ká′r-mĕn)	131	18°15′N	93°26′W
Carmen de Areco, Arg. (kär′mĕn′ dā ä-rā′kô)	141c	34°21′S	59°50′W
Carmen de Patagones, Arg. (ká′r-mĕn-dĕ-pä-tä-gô′nĕs)	144	41°00′S	63°00′W
Carmi, Il., U.S. (kär′mī)	108	38°05′N	88°10′W
Carmo, Braz. (ká′r-mô)	141a	21°57′S	42°45′W
Carmo do Rio Clara, Braz. (ká′r-mô-dô-rē′ô-klä′rä)	141a	20°57′S	46°04′W
Carmona, Spain	172	37°28′N	5°38′W
Carnarvon, Austl. (kär-när′vŭn)	218	24°45′S	113°45′E
Carnarvon, S. Afr.	232	31°00′S	22°15′E
Carnation, Wa., U.S. (kär-nā′shŭn)	116a	47°39′N	121°55′W
Carnaxide, Port. (kär-nä-shē′dĕ)	173b	38°44′N	9°15′W
Carndonagh, Ire. (kärn-dō-nä′)	164	55°15′N	7°15′W
Carnegie, Ok., U.S. (kär-nĕg′ĭ)	120	35°06′N	98°38′W
Carnegie, Pa., U.S.	111e	40°24′N	80°06′W
Carneys Point, N.J., U.S. (kär′nĕs)	109	39°45′N	75°25′W
Carnic Alps, mts., Eur.	161	46°43′N	12°38′E
Carnot, Alg. (kär nō′)	173	36°15′N	1°40′E
Carnot, C.A.R.	231	5°00′N	15°52′E
Carnsore Point, c., Ire. (kärn′sôr)	164	52°10′N	6°16′W
Caro, Mi., U.S. (kâ′rō)	108	43°30′N	83°25′W
Carolina, Braz. (kä-rô-lē′nä)	143	7°26′S	47°16′W

PRONOUNCING INDEX

Carolina – Celestún 279

PLACE (Pronunciation)	PAGE	LAT.	LONG.
Carolina, S. Afr. (kăr-ô-lī′nȧ)	232	26°07′S	30°09′E
Carolina, I., Mex. (kä-rō-lē′nä)	132a	18°41′N	89°40′W
Caroline Islands, is., Oc.	5	8°00′N	140°00′E
Caroni, r., Ven. (kä-rō′nē)	142	5°49′N	62°57′W
Carora, Ven. (kä-rô′rä)	142	10°09′N	70°12′W
Carpathians, mts., Eur. (kär-pā′thĭ-ăn)	156	49°23′N	20°14′E
Carpații Meridionali (Transylvanian Alps), mts., Rom.	156	45°30′N	23°30′E
Carpentaria, Gulf of, b., Austl. (kär-pĕn-târ′ĭȧ)	220	14°45′S	138°50′E
Carpentras, Fr. (kär-päɴ-träs′)	171	44°04′N	5°01′E
Carpi, Italy	174	44°48′N	10°54′E
Carrara, Italy (kä-rä′rä)	162	44°05′N	10°05′E
Carrauntoohil, Ire. (kă-răn-tōō′ĭl)	164	52°01′N	9°48′W
Carretas, Punta, c., Peru (pōō′n-tä-kär-rĕ′tĕ′rás)	142	14°15′S	76°25′W
Carriacou, i., Gren.	133b	12°28′N	61°20′W
Carrick-on-Sur, Ire. (kăr′-ĭk)	164	52°20′N	7°35′W
Carrier, Can. (kăr′ĭ-ĕr)	102b	46°43′N	71°05′W
Carriere, Ms., U.S. (kȧ-rēr′)	124	30°37′N	89°37′W
Carriers Mills, Il., U.S. (kăr′ĭ-ĕrs)	108	37°40′N	88°40′W
Carrington, N.D., U.S. (kăr′ĭng-tŭn)	112	47°26′N	99°06′W
Carr Inlet, Wa., U.S. (kăr ĭn′lĕt)	116a	47°20′N	122°42′W
Carrion Crow Harbor, b., Bah. (kăr′ĭŭn krō)	134	26°35′N	77°55′W
Carrión de los Condes, Spain (kär-rê-ōn′ dā los kon′dás)	172	42°20′N	4°35′W
Carrizo Creek, r., N.M., U.S. (kär-rē′zō)	120	36°22′N	103°39′W
Carrizo Springs, Tx., U.S.	122	28°32′N	99°51′W
Carrizozo, N.M., U.S. (kär-rê-zō′zō)	119	33°40′N	105°55′W
Carroll, Ia., U.S. (kăr′ŭl)	113	42°03′N	94°51′W
Carrollton, Ga., U.S. (kăr-ŭl-tŭn)	124	33°35′N	85°05′W
Carrollton, Il., U.S.	121	39°18′N	90°22′W
Carrollton, Ky., U.S.	108	38°45′N	85°15′W
Carrollton, Mi., U.S.	108	43°30′N	83°55′W
Carrollton, Mo., U.S.	121	39°21′N	93°29′W
Carrollton, Oh., U.S.	108	40°35′N	81°10′W
Carrollton, Tx., U.S.	117c	32°58′N	96°53′W
Carrols, Wa., U.S. (kăr′ŭlz)	116c	46°05′N	122°51′W
Carrot, r., Can.	96	53°12′N	103°50′W
Carry-le-Rouet, Fr. (kä-rē′lĕ-rò-ā′)	170a	43°20′N	5°10′E
Carsamba, Tur. (chär-shäm′bä)	163	41°05′N	36°40′E
Carson, r., Nv., U.S. (kär′sŭn)	118	39°15′N	119°25′W
Carson City, Nv., U.S.	104	39°10′N	119°45′W
Carson Sink, Nv., U.S.	118	39°51′N	118°25′W
Cartagena, Col. (kär-tä-hā′nä)	142	10°30′N	75°40′W
Cartagena, Spain (kär-tä-ĸĕ′nä)	154	37°46′N	1°00′W
Cartago, Col. (kär-tä′gō)	142a	4°44′N	75°54′W
Cartago, C.R.	129	9°52′N	83°56′W
Cartaxo, Port. (kär-tä′shō)	172	39°10′N	8°48′W
Carteret, N.J., U.S. (kär′tē-ret)	110a	40°35′N	74°13′W
Cartersville, Ga., U.S. (kär′tĕrs-vĭl)	124	34°09′N	84°47′W
Carthage, Tun.	230	37°04′N	10°18′E
Carthage, Il., U.S. (kär′thāj)	121	40°27′N	91°09′W
Carthage, Mo., U.S.	121	37°10′N	94°18′W
Carthage, N.C., U.S.	125	35°22′N	79°25′W
Carthage, N.Y., U.S.	109	44°00′N	75°45′W
Carthage, Tx., U.S.	123	32°09′N	94°20′W
Carthcart, S. Afr. (cärth-cȧ′t)	233c	32°18′S	27°11′E
Cartwright, Can. (kärt′rīt)	91	53°36′N	57°00′W
Caruaru, Braz. (kä-rò-à-rōō′)	143	8°19′S	35°52′W
Carúpano, Ven. (kä-rōō′pä-nō)	142	10°45′N	63°21′W
Caruthersville, Mo., U.S. (kȧ-rŭdh′ĕrz-vĭl)	121	36°09′N	89°41′W
Carver, Or., U.S. (kärv′ĕr)	116c	45°24′N	122°30′W
Carvoeiro, Cabo, c., Port. (ká′bō-kär-vô-ĕ′y-rō)	172	39°22′N	9°24′W
Cary, Il., U.S. (kā′rê)	111a	42°13′N	88°14′W
Casablanca, Chile (kä-sä-bläŋ′kä)	141b	33°19′S	71°24′W
Casablanca, Mor.	230	33°32′N	7°41′W
Casa Branca, Braz. (ká′sä-brá′ɴ-kä)	141a	21°47′S	47°04′W
Casa Grande, Az., U.S. (kä′sä grän′dā)	119	32°50′N	111°45′W
Casa Grande Ruins National Monument, rec., Az., U.S.	119	33°00′N	111°33′W
Casale Monferrato, Italy (kä-sä′lā)	174	45°08′N	8°26′E
Casalmaggiore, Italy (kä-säl-mäd-jō′rä)	174	45°00′N	10°24′E
Casamance, r., Sen. (kä-sä-mäɴs′)	230	12°30′N	15°00′W
Cascade Mountains, mts., N.A.	95	49°10′N	121°00′W
Cascade Point, c., N.Z. (kăs-kād′)	221a	43°59′S	168°23′E
Cascade Range, mts., N.A.	106	42°50′N	122°20′W
Cascade-Siskiyou National Monument, rec., Or., U.S.	114	42°05′N	122°30′W
Cascade Tunnel, trans., Wa., U.S.	114	47°41′N	120°53′W
Cascais, Port. (käs-kà-ēzh)	172	38°42′N	9°25′W
Case Inlet, Wa., U.S. (kās)	116a	47°22′N	122°47′W
Caseros, Arg. (kä-sā′rôs)	144a	34°35′S	58°34′W
Caserta, Italy (kä-zĕr′tä)	174	41°04′N	14°21′E
Casey, Il., U.S. (kā′sĭ)	108	39°20′N	88°00′W
Cashmere, Wa., U.S. (kăsh′mĭr)	114	47°30′N	120°28′W
Casiguran, Phil. (käs-sē-gōō′rän)	213a	16°15′N	122°10′E
Casiguran Sound, strt., Phil.	213a	16°02′N	121°51′E
Casilda, Arg. (kä-sē′l-dä)	144	33°02′S	61°11′W
Casilda, Cuba	134	21°50′N	80°00′W
Casimiro de Abreu, Braz. (kä′sē-mē′ro-dĕ-á-brĕ′ōō)	141a	22°30′S	42°11′W
Casino, Austl. (kȧ-sē′nō)	222	28°35′S	153°10′E
Casiquiare, r., Ven. (kä-sē-kyä′rä)	142	2°11′N	66°15′W
Caspe, Spain (käs′på)	173	41°18′N	0°02′W
Casper, Wy., U.S. (kăs′pēr)	104	42°51′N	106°18′W
Caspian Depression, depr. (kăs′pĭ-ăn)	178	47°40′N	52°35′E
Caspian Sea, sea	178	40°00′N	52°00′E
Cass, W.V., U.S. (kăs)	109	38°25′N	79°55′W
Cass, I., Mn., U.S.	113	47°23′N	94°28′W
Cassai (Kasai), r., Afr. (kä-sä′ē)	232	11°30′S	21°00′E
Cass City, Mi., U.S. (kăs)	108	43°35′N	83°10′W
Casselman, Can. (kăs′′l-mȧn)	102c	45°18′N	75°05′W
Casselton, N.D., U.S. (kăs′′l-tŭn)	112	46°53′N	97°14′W
Cássia, Braz. (ká′syä)	141a	20°36′S	46°53′W
Cassin, Tx., U.S. (kăs′ĭn)	117d	29°16′N	98°29′W
Cassinga, Ang.	232	15°05′S	16°15′E
Cassino, Italy (käs-sē′nō)	162	41°30′N	13°50′E
Cass Lake, Mn., U.S. (kăs)	113	47°23′N	94°37′W
Cassopolis, Mi., U.S. (kăs-ŏ′pō-lĭs)	108	41°55′N	86°00′W
Cassville, Mo., U.S. (kăs′vĭl)	121	36°41′N	93°52′W
Castanheira de Pêra, Port. (käs-tän-yā′rä-dĕ-pĕ′rä)	172	40°00′N	8°07′W
Castellammare di Stabia, Italy	173c	40°26′N	14°29′E
Castelli, Arg. (kȧs-tĕ′zhē)	141c	36°07′S	57°48′W
Castelló de la Plana, Spain	162	39°59′N	0°05′W
Castelnaudary, Fr. (kȧs′tĕl-nō-dȧ-rē′)	170	43°20′N	1°57′E
Castelo, Braz. (käs-tĕ′lô)	141a	20°37′S	41°13′W
Castelo Branco, Port. (käs-tā′lò bräŋ′kò)	162	39°48′N	7°37′W
Castelo de Vide, Port. (käs-tā′lò dĭ vē′dĭ)	172	39°25′N	7°25′W
Castelsarrasin, Fr. (kȧs′tĕl-sȧ-rȧ-zăɴ′)	170	44°03′N	1°05′E
Castelvetrano, Italy (käs′tĕl-vê-trä′nō)	174	37°43′N	12°50′E
Castilla, Peru (kȧs-tē′l-yä)	142	5°18′S	80°40′W
Castilla La Nueva, hist. reg., Spain (käs-tē′lyä lä nwā′vä)	172	39°15′N	3°55′W
Castilla La Vieja, hist. reg., Spain (käs-tēl′yä lä vyā′hä)	172	40°48′N	4°24′W
Castillo de San Marcos National Monument, rec., Fl., U.S. (käs-tē′lyä de-sän mär-kōs)	125	29°55′N	81°25′W
Castle, i., Bah. (kȧs′′l)	135	22°05′N	74°20′W
Castlebar, Ire. (kȧs′′l-bär)	164	53°55′N	9°15′W
Castle Dale, Ut., U.S. (kȧs′l dāl)	119	39°15′N	111°00′W
Castle Donington, Eng., U.K. (dŏn′ĭng-tŭn)	158a	52°50′N	1°21′W
Castleford, Eng., U.K. (kȧs′l-fẽrd)	158a	53°43′N	1°21′W
Castlegar, Can. (kȧs′′l-gär)	95	49°19′N	117°40′W
Castlemaine, Austl. (kăs′′l-mān)	222	37°05′S	144°10′E
Castle Peak, mtn., Co., U.S.	119	39°00′N	106°50′W
Castle Rock, Wa., U.S. (kȧs′′l-rŏk)	114	46°17′N	122°53′W
Castle Rock Flowage, res., Wi., U.S.	113	44°03′N	89°48′W
Castle Shannon, Pa., U.S. (shăn′ŭn)	111e	40°22′N	80°02′W
Castleton, In., U.S. (kȧs′′l-tŏn)	111g	39°54′N	86°03′W
Castor, r., Can. (kăs′tôr)	102c	45°16′N	75°14′W
Castor, r., Mo., U.S.	121	36°59′N	89°53′W
Castres, Fr. (kȧs′tr′)	170	43°36′N	2°13′E
Castries, St. Luc. (kȧs-trē′)	133b	14°01′N	61°00′W
Castro, Braz. (käs′trò)	143	24°56′S	50°00′W
Castro, Chile (käs′tro)	144	42°27′S	73°48′W
Castro Daire, Port. (käs′trò dīr′ĭ)	172	40°56′N	7°57′W
Castro del Río, Spain (käs-trô-dĕl rē′ō)	172	37°42′N	4°28′W
Castrop Rauxel, Ger. (käs′trōp rou′ksĕl)	171c	51°33′N	7°19′E
Castro-Urdiales, Spain	162	43°23′N	3°11′W
Castro Valley, Ca., U.S.	116b	37°42′N	122°05′W
Castro Verde, Port. (käs-trō vĕr′dĕ)	172	37°43′N	8°05′W
Castrovillari, Italy (käs′trō-vēl-lyä′rē)	174	39°48′N	16°11′E
Castuera, Spain (käs-tò-ā′rä)	172	38°43′N	5°33′W
Casula, Moz.	237	15°25′S	33°40′E
Cat, i., Bah.	135	24°30′N	75°30′W
Catacamas, Hond. (kä-tä-ká′mäs)	132	14°52′N	85°55′W
Cataguases, Braz. (kä-tä-gwá′sĕs)	141a	21°23′S	42°42′W
Catahoula, I., La., U.S. (kăt-ȧ-hò′lȧ)	123	31°35′N	92°20′W
Catalão, Braz. (kä-tä-louɴ′)	143	18°09′S	47°42′W
Catalina, i., Dom. Rep. (kä-tä-lē′nä)	135	18°20′N	69°00′W
Catalunya, hist. reg., Spain	173	41°23′N	0°50′E
Catamarca, Arg. (kä-tä-má′r-kä)	144	28°29′S	65°45′W
Catamarca, prov., Arg. (kä-tä-mär′kä)	144	27°15′S	67°15′W
Catanaun, Phil. (kä-tä-nä′wän)	213a	13°36′N	122°20′E
Catanduanes Island, i., Phil. (kä-tän-dwä′nĕs)	213	13°55′N	125°00′E
Catanduva, Braz. (kä-tàn-dōō′vä)	143	21°12′S	48°47′W
Catania, Italy (kä-tä′nyä)	154	37°30′N	15°09′E
Catania, Golfo di, b., Italy (gôl-fō-dē-kȧ-tä′nyä)	174	37°24′N	15°28′E
Catanzaro, Italy (kä-tän-dzä′rō)	163	38°53′N	16°34′E
Catarroja, Spain (kä-tär-rō′hä)	173	39°24′N	0°25′W
Catawba, r., N.C., U.S. (kȧ-tô′bȧ)	125	35°25′N	80°55′W
Catbalogan, Phil. (kät-bä-lō′gän)	213	11°45′N	124°52′E
Catemaco, Mex. (kä-tä-mä′kō)	131	18°26′N	95°06′W
Catemaco, Lago, I., Mex. (lä′gô-kä-tä-mä′kō)	131	18°23′N	95°04′W
Caterham, Eng., U.K. (kā′tēr-ŭm)	158b	51°16′N	0°04′W
Catete, Ang. (kä-tĕ′tĕ)	232	9°06′S	13°43′E
Cathedral Mountain, mtn., Tx., U.S. (kȧ-thē′drăl)	122	30°09′N	103°46′W
Cathedral Peak, mtn., Afr. (kă-thê′drăl)	233c	28°53′S	29°04′E
Catherine, Lake, I., Ar., U.S. (kă-thēr-ĭn)	121	34°26′N	92°47′W
Cathkin Peak, mtn., Afr. (kăth′kĭn)	232	29°08′S	29°22′E
Cathlamet, Wa., U.S. (kăth-lăm′ĕt)	116c	46°12′N	123°22′W
Catlettsburg, Ky., U.S. (kăt′lĕts-bûrg)	108	38°20′N	82°35′W
Catoche, Cabo, c., Mex. (kä-tô′chĕ)	128	21°30′N	87°15′W
Catonsville, Md., U.S. (kā′tŭnz-vĭl)	110e	39°16′N	76°45′W
Catorce, Mex. (kä-tôr′sȧ)	130	23°41′N	100°51′W
Catskill, N.Y., U.S. (kăts′kĭl)	109	42°15′N	73°50′W
Catskill Mountains, mts., N.Y., U.S.	107	42°20′N	74°35′W
Cattaraugus Indian Reservation, I.R., N.Y., U.S. (kăt′tȧ-rȧ-gŭs)	109	42°30′N	79°05′W
Catu, Braz. (kȧ-tōō)	143	12°26′S	38°12′W
Catuala, Ang.	236	16°29′S	19°03′E
Catumbela, r., Ang. (kă′tŏm-bĕl′ă)	236	12°40′S	14°10′E
Cauayan, Phil. (kou-ä′yän)	213a	16°56′N	121°46′E
Cauca, r., Col. (kou′kä)	142	7°30′N	75°26′W
Caucagua, Ven. (käò-kȧ′gwä)	143b	10°17′N	66°22′W
Caucasus, mts.	178	43°20′N	42°00′E
Cauchon Lake, I., Can. (kô-shŏn′)	97	55°25′N	96°30′W
Caughnawaga, Can.	102a	45°24′N	73°41′W
Caulfield, Austl.	217a	37°53′S	145°03′E
Caulonia, Italy (kou-lō′nyä)	174	38°24′N	16°22′E
Cauquenes, Chile (kou-kā′nās)	144	35°54′S	72°14′W
Caura, r., Ven. (kou′rä)	142	6°48′N	64°40′W
Causapscal, Can.	100	48°22′N	67°14′W
Caution, Cape, c., Can. (kô′shŭn)	94	51°10′N	127°47′W
Cauto, r., Cuba (kou′tō)	134	20°33′N	76°20′W
Cauvery, r., India	199	12°00′N	77°00′E
Cava, Braz. (kȧ′vä)	144b	22°41′S	43°26′W
Cava de′ Tirreni, Italy (kä′vä-dĕ-tēr-rĕ′nē)	173c	40°27′N	14°43′E
Cávado, r., Port. (kä-vä′dō)	172	41°43′N	8°08′W
Cavalcante, Braz. (kä-väl-kän′tä)	143	13°45′S	47°33′W
Cavalier, N.D., U.S. (kăv-ȧ-lēr′)	112	48°45′N	97°39′W
Cavally, r., Afr.	234	4°40′N	7°30′W
Cavan, Ire. (kăv′ăn)	164	54°01′N	7°00′W
Cavarzere, Italy (kä-vär′dzȧ-rā)	174	45°08′N	12°06′E
Cavendish, Vt., U.S. (kăv′ĕn-dĭsh)	109	43°25′N	72°35′W
Caviana, Ilha, i., Braz. (kä-vyä′nä)	143	0°45′N	49°33′W
Cavite, Phil. (kä-vē′tä)	213a	14°30′N	120°54′E
Caxambu, Braz. (kä-shä′m-bōō)	143	22°00′S	44°45′W
Caxias, Braz. (kä′shê-äzh)	143	4°48′S	43°16′W
Caxias do Sul, Braz. (kä′shê-äzh-dò-sōō′l)	144	29°13′S	51°03′W
Caxito, Ang. (kä-shē′tò)	232	8°33′S	13°36′E
Cayambe, Ec. (kȧ-īä′m-bĕ)	142	0°03′N	79°09′W
Cayenne, Fr. Gu. (kā-ĕn′)	143	4°56′N	52°18′W
Cayetano Rubio, Mex. (kä-yĕ-tá-nô-rōō′byô)	130	20°37′N	100°21′W
Cayey, P.R.	129b	18°05′N	66°12′W
Cayman Brac, i., Cay. Is. (kī-män′ brák)	134	19°45′N	79°50′W
Cayman Islands, dep., N.A.	134	19°30′N	80°30′W
Cay Sal Bank, bk. (kē-sál)	134	23°55′N	80°20′W
Cayuga, I., N.Y., U.S. (kā-yōō′gȧ)	109	42°35′N	76°35′W
Cazalla de la Sierra, Spain	172	37°55′N	5°48′W
Cazaux, Étang de, I., Fr. (ā-täɴ′ dĕ kä-zō′)	170	44°32′N	0°59′W
Cazenovia, N.Y., U.S. (kăz-ê-nō′vĭ-ä)	109	42°55′N	75°50′W
Çazenovia Creek, r., N.Y., U.S.	111c	42°49′N	78°45′W
Čazma, Cro. (chäz′mä)	174	45°44′N	16°39′E
Cazombo, Ang. (kä-zô′m-bō)	232	11°54′S	22°52′E
Cazones, r., Mex. (kä-zō′nĕs)	131	20°37′N	97°28′W
Cazones, Ensenada de, b., Cuba (ĕn-sĕ-nä-dä-dĕ-kä-zō′nås)	134	22°05′N	81°30′W
Cazones, Golfo de, b., Cuba (gôl-fô-dĕ-kä-zō′nås)	134	21°55′N	81°15′W
Cazorla, Spain (kä-thôr′lå)	172	37°55′N	2°58′W
Cea, r., Spain (thā′ä)	172	42°18′N	5°10′W
Ceará-Mirim, Braz. (sā-ä-rä′mē-rē′ɴ)	143	6°00′S	35°13′W
Cebaco, Isla, i., Pan. (ē′s-lä-sä-bä′kō)	133	7°27′N	81°08′W
Cebolla Creek, r., Co., U.S. (sē-bōl′yä)	119	38°15′N	107°10′W
Cebreros, Spain (sĕ-brĕ′rôs)	172	40°28′N	4°28′W
Cebu, Phil. (sā-bōō′)	213	10°22′N	123°49′E
Čechy (Bohemia), hist. reg., Czech Rep.	168	49°51′N	13°55′E
Cecil, Pa., U.S. (sē′sĭl)	111e	40°20′N	80°10′W
Cedar, r., Ia., U.S.	113	42°23′N	92°07′W
Cedar, r., Wa., U.S.	116c	45°56′N	122°32′W
Cedar, West Fork, r., Ia., U.S.	113	42°49′N	93°10′W
Cedar Bayou, Tx., U.S.	123a	29°54′N	94°58′W
Cedar Breaks National Monument, rec., Ut., U.S.	119	37°35′N	112°55′W
Cedarburg, Wi., U.S. (sē′dẽr bûrg)	113	43°23′N	88°00′W
Cedar City, Ut., U.S.	119	37°40′N	113°10′W
Cedar Creek, r., N.D., U.S.	112	46°05′N	102°10′W
Cedar Falls, Ia., U.S.	113	42°31′N	92°29′W
Cedar Keys, Fl., U.S.	124	29°06′N	83°03′W
Cedar Lake, In., U.S.	111a	41°22′N	87°27′W
Cedar Lake, I., In., U.S.	111a	41°23′N	87°25′W
Cedar Lake, res., Can.	92	53°10′N	100°00′W
Cedar Rapids, Ia., U.S.	105	42°00′N	91°43′W
Cedar Springs, Mi., U.S.	108	43°15′N	85°40′W
Cedartown, Ga., U.S. (sē′dẽr-toun)	124	34°00′N	85°15′W
Cedarville, S. Afr. (cĕdȧr′vĭl)	233c	30°23′S	29°04′E
Cedral, Mex. (sā-dräl′)	130	23°47′N	100°42′W
Cedros, Hond. (sā′drōs)	132	14°36′N	87°07′W
Cedros, i., Mex.	128	28°10′N	115°10′W
Ceduna, Austl. (sê-dò′nȧ)	218	32°15′S	133°55′E
Ceel Buur, Som.	238a	4°35′N	46°40′E
Cega, r., Spain (thā′gä)	172	41°25′N	4°27′W
Cegléd, Hung. (tsā′glād)	169	47°10′N	19°49′E
Ceglie, Italy (chĕ′lyĕ)	175	40°39′N	17°32′E
Cehegín, Spain (thā-å-hēn′)	172	38°05′N	1°48′W
Ceiba del Agua, Cuba (sā′bä-dĕl-á′gwä)	135a	22°53′N	82°38′W
Cekhira, Tun.	230	34°17′N	10°00′E
Celaya, Mex. (sā-lä′yä)	128	20°33′N	100°49′W
Celebes (Sulawesi), i., Indon.	212	2°15′S	120°30′E
Celebes Sea, sea, Asia	212	3°45′N	121°52′E
Celestún, Mex. (sĕ-lĕs-tōō′n)	132a	20°57′N	90°18′W

ng-sing; ŋ-baŋk; ɴ-nasalized n; nŏd; cŏmmit; ōld; ôbey; ôrder; oi-boil; fōōd; ŏŏ-as oo in foot; ou-out; s-soft; sh-dish; th-thin; pūre; ûnite; ûrn; stŭd; circŭs; ü-as in French tu; ′-indeterminate vowel.

PLACE (Pronunciation)	PAGE	LAT.	LONG.
Celina, Oh., U.S. (sėlī'na)	108	40°30'N	84°35'W
Celje, Slvn. (tsĕl'yĕ)	174	46°13'N	15°17'E
Celle, Ger. (tsĕl'ē)	161	52°37'N	10°05'E
Cement, Ok., U.S. (sė-mĕnt')	120	34°56'N	98°07'W
Cenderawasih, Teluk, b., Indon.	213	2°20'S	135°30'E
Ceniza, Pico, mtn., Ven. (pē'kō-sĕ-nē'zä)	143b	10°24'N	67°26'W
Center, Tx., U.S. (sĕn'tẽr)	123	31°50'N	94°10'W
Center Hill Lake, res., Tn., U.S. (sĕn'tẽr-hĭl)	124	36°02'N	86°00'W
Center Line, Mi., U.S. (sĕn'tẽr līn)	111b	42°29'N	83°01'W
Centerville, Ia., U.S. (sĕn'tẽr-vĭl)	113	40°44'N	92°48'W
Centerville, Mn., U.S.	117g	45°10'N	93°03'W
Centerville, Pa., U.S.	111e	40°02'N	79°58'W
Centerville, S.D., U.S.	112	43°07'N	96°56'W
Centerville, Ut., U.S.	117b	40°55'N	111°53'W
Central, Cordillera, mts., Bol. (kôr-dēl-yĕ'rä-sĕn-trä'l)	142	19°18'S	65°29'W
Central, Cordillera, mts., Col.	142a	3°58'N	75°55'W
Central, Cordillera, mts., Dom. Rep.	135	19°05'N	71°30'W
Central, Cordillera, mts., Phil. (kôr-dēl-yĕ'rä-sĕn'träl)	213a	17°05'N	120°55'E
Central African Republic, nation, Afr.	231	7°50'N	21°00'E
Central America, reg., N.A. (ä-mĕr'ĭ-kȧ)	128	10°45'N	87°15'W
Central City, Ky., U.S. (sĕn'trȧl)	124	37°15'N	87°09'W
Central City, Ne., U.S. (sĕn'trȧl sĭ'tĭ)	112	41°07'N	98°00'W
Central Falls, R.I., U.S. (sĕn'trȧl fôlz)	110b	41°54'N	71°23'W
Centralia, Il., U.S. (sĕn-trā'lĭ-ȧ)	108	38°35'N	89°05'W
Centralia, Mo., U.S.	121	39°11'N	92°07'W
Centralia, Wa., U.S.	114	46°42'N	122°58'W
Central Plateau, plat., Russia	180	55°00'N	33°30'E
Central Valley, N.Y., U.S.	110a	41°19'N	74°07'W
Centreville, Il., U.S. (sĕn'tẽr-vĭl)	117e	38°33'N	90°06'W
Centreville, Md., U.S.	109	39°05'N	76°05'W
Century, Fl., U.S. (sĕn'tů-rĭ)	124	30°57'N	87°15'W
Ceram (Seram), i., Indon.	213	2°45'S	129°30'E
Céret, Fr.	170	42°29'N	2°47'E
Cerignola, Italy (chā-rē-nyō'lä)	174	41°16'N	15°55'E
Cerknica, Slvn. (tsĕr'knē-tsȧ)	174	45°48'N	14°21'E
Cern'achovsk, Russia (chĕr-nyä'kôfsk)	180	54°38'N	21°49'E
Cerralvo, Mex. (sĕr-räl'vō)	122	26°05'N	99°37'W
Cerralvo, i., Mex.	128	24°00'N	109°59'W
Cerrito, Col. (sĕr-rē'-tô)	142a	3°41'N	76°17'W
Cerritos, Mex. (sĕr-rē'tôs)	130	22°26'N	100°16'W
Cerro de Pasco, Peru (sĕr'rō dā päs'kō)	142	10°45'S	76°14'W
Cerro Gordo, Arroyo de, r., Mex. (är-rô-yō-dĕ-sĕ'r-rō-gôr-dō)	122	26°12'N	104°06'W
Certegui, Col. (sĕr-tĕ'gē)	142a	5°21'N	76°35'W
Cervantes, Phil. (sĕr-vän'tās)	213a	16°59'N	120°42'E
Cervera del Río Alhama, Spain	172	42°02'N	1°55'W
Cerveteri, Italy (chĕr-vĕ'tĕ-rē)	173d	42°00'N	12°06'E
Cesena, Italy (chĕ'sĕ-nä)	174	44°08'N	12°16'E
Cēsis, Lat. (sā'sĭs)	167	57°19'N	25°17'E
Česká Lípa, Czech Rep. (chĕs'kä lē'pa)	168	50°41'N	14°31'E
České Budějovice, Czech Rep. (chĕs'kā bōō'dyĕ-yô-vēt-sĕ)	161	49°00'N	14°30'E
Českomoravská Vysočina, hills, Czech Rep.	168	49°21'N	15°40'E
Český Těšín, Czech Rep.	169	49°43'N	18°22'E
Çeşme, Tur. (chĕsh'mĕ)	175	38°20'N	26°20'E
Cessnock, Austl.	219	32°58'S	151°15'E
Cestos, r., Lib.	234	5°40'N	9°25'W
Cetinje, Serb. (tsĕt'in-yĕ)	154	42°23'N	18°55'E
Ceuta, Sp. N. Afr. (thā-ōō'tä)	230	36°04'N	5°36'W
Cévennes, reg., Fr. (sā-vĕn')	161	44°20'N	3°48'E
Ceylon *see* Sri Lanka, nation, Asia	203	8°45'N	82°30'E
Chabot, Lake, l., Ca., U.S. (sha'bŏt)	116b	37°44'N	122°06'W
Chacabuco, Arg. (chä-kä-bōō'kō)	141c	34°37'S	60°27'W
Chacaltianguis, Mex. (chä-käl-tē-äŋ'gwĕs)	131	18°18'N	95°50'W
Chachapoyas, Peru (chä-chä-poi'yäs)	142	6°16'S	77°48'W
Chaco, prov., Arg. (chä'kō)	144	26°00'S	60°45'W
Chaco Culture National Historic Park, rec., N.M., U.S. (chä'kō)	119	36°05'N	108°00'W
Chad, Russia (chäd)	186a	56°33'N	57°11'E
Chad, nation, Afr.	231	17°48'N	19°00'E
Chad, Lake, l., Afr.	231	13°55'N	13°40'E
Chadbourn, N.C., U.S. (chăd'bŭrn)	125	34°19'N	78°55'W
Chadron, Ne., U.S. (chăd'rŭn)	104	42°50'N	103°10'W
Chafarinas, Islas, is., Sp. N. Afr.	172	35°08'N	2°20'W
Chaffee, Mo., U.S. (chăf'ē)	121	37°10'N	89°39'W
Chāgal Hills, hills, Afg.	198	29°15'N	63°28'E
Chagodoshcha, r., Russia (chä-gō-dôsh-chä)	176	59°08'N	35°13'E
Chagres, r., Pan. (chä'grĕs)	133	9°18'N	79°22'W
Chagrin, r., Oh., U.S. (shȧ'grĭn)	111d	41°34'N	81°24'W
Chagrin Falls, Oh., U.S. (shȧ'grĭn fôls)	111d	41°26'N	81°23'W
Chahar, hist. reg., China (chä-här)	205	44°25'N	115°00'E
Chake Chake, Tan.	237	5°15'S	39°46'E
Chalatenango, El Sal. (chäl-ä-tĕ-näŋ'gō)	132	14°04'N	88°54'W
Chalbi Desert, des., Kenya	237	3°40'N	36°50'E
Chalcatongo, Mex. (chäl-kä-tôŋ'gō)	131	17°04'N	97°41'W
Chalchihuites, Mex. (chäl-chê-wē'tås)	130	23°28'N	103°57'W
Chalchuapa, El Sal. (chäl-chwä'pä)	132	14°01'N	89°39'W
Chalco, Mex. (chäl-kō)	131a	19°15'N	98°54'W
Chaleur Bay, b., Can. (shȧ-lûr')	93	47°58'N	65°33'W
Chalgrove, Eng., U.K. (chăl'grôv)	158b	51°38'N	1°05'W
Chaling, China (chä'lĭng)	209	27°00'N	113°31'E
Chalkída, Grc.	163	38°28'N	23°38'E
Chalmette, La., U.S. (shăl-mĕt')	110d	29°57'N	89°57'W
Châlons-sur-Marne, Fr. (shȧ-lôN'sür-märn)	161	48°57'N	4°23'E
Chalon-sur-Saône, Fr.	161	46°47'N	4°54'E
Chaltel, Cerro (Monte Fitzroy), mtn., S.A. (sĕ'r-rô-chäl'tĕl)	144	48°10'S	73°18'W
Chālūs, Iran	201	36°38'N	51°26'E
Chama, Rio, r., N.M., U.S. (chä'mä)	119	36°19'N	106°31'W
Chama, Sierra de, mts., Guat. (sē-ĕ'r-rä-dĕ-chä-mä)	132	15°48'N	90°20'W
Chamama, Mwi.	237	12°55'S	33°43'E
Chaman, Pak. (chŭm-än')	199	30°58'N	66°21'E
Chambal, r., India (chŭm-bäl')	199	24°30'N	75°30'E
Chamberlain, S.D., U.S. (chām'bẽr-lĭn)	112	43°48'N	99°21'W
Chamberlain, l., Me., U.S.	100	46°15'N	69°10'W
Chambersburg, Pa., U.S. (chām'bẽrz-bûrg)	109	40°00'N	77°40'W
Chambéry, Fr. (shäm-bā-rē')	161	45°35'N	5°54'E
Chambeshi, r., Zam.	237	10°35'S	31°20'E
Chamblee, Ga., U.S. (chăm-blē')	110c	33°55'N	84°18'W
Chambly, Can. (shäN-blē')	102a	45°27'N	73°17'W
Chambly, Fr.	171b	49°11'N	2°14'E
Chambord, Can.	91	48°22'N	72°01'W
Chame, Punta, c., Pan. (pō'n-tä-chä'mȧ)	133	8°41'N	79°27'W
Chamelecón, r., Hond. (chä-mĕ-lĕ-kô'n)	132	15°09'N	88°42'W
Chamo, l., Eth.	231	5°58'N	37°00'E
Chamonix-Mont-Blanc, Fr. (shȧ-mô-nē')	171	45°55'N	6°50'E
Champagne, reg., Fr. (shäm-pän'yĕ)	170	48°53'N	4°48'E
Champaign, Il., U.S. (shăm-pān')	105	40°10'N	88°15'W
Champdāni, India	202a	22°48'N	88°21'E
Champerico, Guat. (chăm-pȧ-rē'kō)	132	14°18'N	91°55'W
Champion, Mi., U.S. (chăm'pĭ-ŭn)	113	46°30'N	87°59'W
Champlain, Lake, l., N.A. (shăm-plān')	107	44°45'N	73°20'W
Champlitte-et-le-Prálot, Fr. (shäN-plēt')	171	47°38'N	5°28'E
Champotón, Mex. (chäm-pō-tōn')	131	19°21'N	90°43'W
Champotón, r., Mex.	131	19°19'N	90°15'W
Chañaral, Chile (chän-yä-räl')	144	26°20'S	70°46'W
Chances Peak, vol., Monts.	133b	16°43'N	62°10'W
Chandeleur Islands, is., La., U.S. (shăn-dĕ-lōōr')	124	29°53'N	88°35'W
Chandeleur Sound, strt., La., U.S.	124	29°47'N	89°08'W
Chandīgarh, India	199	30°51'N	77°13'E
Chandler, Can. (chăn'dlẽr)	91	48°21'N	64°41'W
Chandler, Ok., U.S.	121	35°42'N	96°52'W
Chandrapur, India	199	19°58'N	79°21'E
Chang *see* Yangtze, r., China	205	30°30'N	117°25'E
Changane, r., Moz.	232	22°42'S	32°46'E
Changara, Moz.	237	16°54'S	33°14'E
Changchun, China (chäŋ-chòn)	205	43°55'N	125°25'E
Changdang Hu, l., China (chäŋ-däŋ hōō)	206	31°37'N	119°29'E
Changde, China (chäŋ-dŭ)	205	29°00'N	111°38'E
Changhua, Tai. (chäng'hwä')	209	24°02'N	120°32'E
Changjŏn, Kor., N. (chäng'jŭn')	210	38°40'N	128°05'E
Changli, China (chäŋ-lē)	208	39°46'N	119°10'E
Changning, China (chäŋ-nĭŋ)	204	24°34'N	99°49'E
Changping, China (chäŋ-pĭŋ)	208	40°12'N	116°10'E
Changqing, China (chäŋ-chyĭŋ)	206	36°33'N	116°42'E
Changsan Got, c., Kor., N.	210	38°06'N	124°50'E
Changsha, China (chäŋ-shä)	205	28°20'N	113°00'E
Changshan Qundao, is., China (chäŋ-shän chyòn-dou)	206	39°08'N	122°26'E
Changshu, China (chäŋ-shōō)	206	31°40'N	120°45'E
Changting, China	209	25°50'N	116°18'E
Changwu, China (chäng'wōō')	208	35°12'N	107°45'E
Changxindianzhen, China (chäŋ-shyĭn-dĭĕn-jŭn)	208a	39°49'N	116°12'E
Changxing Dao, i., China (chäŋ-shyĭŋ dou)	206	39°38'N	121°10'E
Changyi, China (chäŋ-yē)	206	36°51'N	119°23'E
Changyuan, China (chyäŋ-yuän)	206	35°10'N	114°41'E
Changzhi, China (chäŋ-jr)	208	35°58'N	112°58'E
Changzhou, China (chäŋ-jō)	205	31°47'N	119°56'E
Changzhuyuan, China (chäŋ-jōō-yuän)	206	31°33'N	115°17'E
Chanhassen, Mn., U.S. (shăn'hăs-sĕn)	117g	44°52'N	93°32'W
Chaniá, Grc.	162	35°31'N	24°01'E
Channel Islands, is., Eur. (chăn'ĕl)	156	49°15'N	3°30'W
Channel Islands, is., Ca., U.S.	118	33°30'N	119°15'W
Channel-Port-aux-Basques, Can.	91	47°35'N	59°11'W
Channelview, Tx., U.S. (chănĕlvū)	123a	29°46'N	95°07'W
Chantada, Spain (chän-tä'dä)	172	42°38'N	7°36'W
Chanthaburi, Thai.	212	12°37'N	102°04'E
Chantilly, Fr. (shäN-tē-yē')	171b	49°12'N	2°30'E
Chantilly, Va., U.S. (shăn'tĭlē)	110e	38°53'N	77°26'W
Chantrey Inlet, b., Can. (chăn-trē)	92	67°49'N	95°00'W
Chanute, Ks., U.S. (shȧ-nōōt')	105	37°41'N	95°27'W
Chany, l., Russia (chä'nē)	178	54°15'N	77°31'E
Chao'an, China (chou-än)	205	23°48'N	116°35'E
Chao Hu, l., China	209	31°45'N	116°59'E
Chao Phraya, r., Thai.	212	16°13'N	99°33'E
Chaor, r., China (chou-r)	208	47°20'N	121°40'E
Chaoshui, China (chou-shwā)	206	37°43'N	120°56'E
Chaoxian, China (chou shyĕn)	206	31°37'N	117°50'E
Chaoyang, China	208	41°32'N	120°20'E
Chaoyang, China (chou-yäŋ)	209	23°18'N	116°32'E
Chapada, Serra da, mts., Braz. (sĕ'r-rä-dä-shä-pä'dä)	143	14°57'S	54°34'W
Chapadão, Serra do, mtn., Braz. (sĕ'r-rä-dô-shä-pȧ-dou'N)	141a	20°31'S	46°20'W
Chapala, Mex. (chä-pä'lä)	130	20°18'N	103°10'W
Chapala, Lago de, l., Mex. (lä'gô-dĕ-chä-pä'lä)	128	20°14'N	103°02'W
Chapalagana, r., Mex. (chä-pä-lä-gá'nä)	130	22°11'N	104°09'W
Chaparral, Col. (chä-pär-rá'l)	142	3°44'N	75°28'W
Chapayevsk, Russia (châ-pī'ĕfsk)	180	53°00'N	49°30'E
Chapel Hill, N.C., U.S. (chăp''l hĭl)	125	35°55'N	79°05'W
Chaplain, l., Wa., U.S. (chăp'lĭn)	116a	47°58'N	121°50'W
Chapleau, Can. (chăp-lō')	91	47°43'N	83°28'W
Chapman, Mount, mtn., Can. (chăp'mȧn)	95	51°50'N	118°20'W
Chapman's Bay, b., S. Afr. (chăp'mȧns bă)	232a	34°06'S	18°17'E
Chappell, Ne., U.S. (chă-pĕl')	112	41°06'N	102°29'W
Chapultenango, Mex. (chä-pòl-tē-näŋ'gō)	131	17°19'N	93°08'W
Chá Pungana, Ang.	236	13°44'S	18°39'E
Chār Borjak, Afg.	201	30°17'N	62°03'E
Charcas, Mex. (chär'käs)	130	23°09'N	101°09'W
Charco de Azul, Bahía, b., Pan.	133	8°14'N	82°45'W
Charente, r., Fr. (shȧ-räNt')	170	45°48'N	0°28'W
Chari, r., Afr. (shä-rē')	235	12°45'N	14°55'E
Charing, Eng., U.K. (chă'rĭng)	158b	51°13'N	0°49'E
Chariton, Ia., U.S. (châr'ĭ-tŭn)	113	41°02'N	93°16'W
Chariton, r., Mo., U.S.	121	40°24'N	92°38'W
Charjew, Turkmen.	183	38°52'N	63°37'E
Charlemagne, Can. (shärl-mäny')	102a	45°43'N	73°29'W
Charleroi, Bel. (shȧr-lē-rwä')	161	50°25'N	4°35'E
Charleroi, Pa., U.S. (shär'lē-roi)	111e	40°08'N	79°54'W
Charles, Cape, c., Va., U.S. (chärlz)	109	37°05'N	75°48'W
Charlesbourg, Can. (shȧrl-bōōr')	102b	46°51'N	71°16'W
Charles City, Ia., U.S. (chärlz)	113	43°03'N	92°40'W
Charleston, Il., U.S. (chärlz'tŭn)	108	39°30'N	88°10'W
Charleston, Mo., U.S.	121	36°53'N	89°20'W
Charleston, Ms., U.S.	124	34°00'N	90°02'W
Charleston, S.C., U.S.	105	32°47'N	79°56'W
Charleston, W.V., U.S.	105	38°20'N	81°35'W
Charlestown, St. K./N.	133b	17°10'N	62°32'W
Charlestown, In., U.S. (chärlz'toun)	111h	38°46'N	85°39'W
Charleville, Austl. (chär'lē-vĭl)	219	26°16'S	146°28'E
Charleville Mézières, Fr. (shärl-vēl')	170	49°48'N	4°41'E
Charlevoix, Mi., U.S. (shär'lē-voi)	108	45°20'N	85°15'W
Charlevoix, Lake, l., Mi., U.S.	113	45°17'N	85°43'W
Charlotte, Mi., U.S. (shär'lŏt)	108	42°35'N	84°50'W
Charlotte, N.C., U.S.	105	35°15'N	80°50'W
Charlotte Amalie, V.I.U.S. (shär-lŏt'ĕ ä-mä'lĭ-å)	129	18°21'N	64°54'W
Charlotte Harbor, b., Fl., U.S.	125a	26°49'N	82°00'W
Charlotte Lake, l., Can.	94	52°07'N	125°30'W
Charlottenberg, Swe. (shär-lŭt'ĕn-bĕrg)	166	59°53'N	12°17'E
Charlottesville, Va., U.S. (shär'lŏtz-vĭl)	105	38°00'N	78°25'W
Charlottetown, Can. (shär'lŏt-toun)	91	46°14'N	63°08'W
Charlotte Waters, Austl. (shär'lŏt)	218	26°00'S	134°50'E
Charmes, Fr. (shärm)	171	48°23'N	6°19'E
Charnwood Forest, for., Eng., U.K. (chärn'wòd)	158a	52°42'N	1°15'W
Charny, Can. (shär-nē')	102b	46°43'N	71°16'W
Chars, Fr. (shär)	171b	49°09'N	1°57'E
Chārsadda, Pak. (chŭr-sä'dä)	199a	34°17'N	71°43'E
Charters Towers, Austl. (chär'tẽrz)	219	20°03'S	146°20'E
Chartres, Fr. (shärt'r')	161	48°26'N	1°29'E
Chascomús, Arg. (chäs-kō-mōōs')	144	35°32'S	58°01'W
Chase City, Va., U.S. (chās)	125	36°45'N	78°27'W
Chashniki, Bela. (chäsh'nyē-kē)	176	54°51'N	29°08'E
Chaska, Mn., U.S. (chăs'kȧ)	117g	44°48'N	93°36'W
Châteaudun, Fr. (shä-tō-däN')	170	48°04'N	1°23'E
Château-Gontier, Fr. (chȧ-tō'gôN'tyā')	170	47°48'N	0°43'W
Châteauguay, Can. (shȧ-tō-gā)	102a	45°22'N	73°45'W
Châteauguay, r., N.A.	102a	45°13'N	73°51'W
Châteauneaut, Fr.	170a	43°23'N	5°11'E
Château-Renault, Fr. (shȧ-tō-rĕ-nō')	170	47°36'N	0°57'E
Château-Richer, Can. (shȧ-tō-rē-shā')	102b	47°00'N	71°01'W
Châteauroux, Fr. (shȧ-tō-rōō')	161	46°47'N	1°39'E
Château-Thierry, Fr. (shȧ-tō'ty-ĕr-rē')	170	49°03'N	3°22'E
Châtellerault, Fr. (shä-tĕl-rō')	161	46°48'N	0°31'E
Chatfield, Mn., U.S. (chăt'fēld)	113	43°50'N	92°10'W
Chatham, Can. (chăt'ȧm)	91	42°25'N	82°10'W
Chatham, Can.	91	47°02'N	65°28'W
Chatham, Eng., U.K. (chăt'ŭm)	165	51°23'N	0°32'E
Chatham, N.J., U.S. (chăt'ȧm)	110a	40°44'N	74°23'W
Chatham, Oh., U.S.	111d	41°06'N	82°01'W
Chatham Islands, is., N.Z.	2	44°00'S	178°00'W
Chatham Sound, strt., Can.	94	54°32'N	130°35'W
Chatham Strait, strt., Ak., U.S.	103	57°00'N	134°40'W
Chatsworth, Ca., U.S. (chătz'wûrth)	117a	34°16'N	118°36'W
Chatsworth Reservoir, res., Ca., U.S.	117a	34°15'N	118°41'W
Chattahoochee, Fl., U.S. (chăt-tȧ-hōō'chee)	124	30°42'N	84°47'W
Chattahoochee, r., U.S.	107	32°00'N	85°10'W
Chattanooga, Tn., U.S. (chăt-ȧ-nōō'gȧ)	105	35°01'N	85°15'W
Chattooga, r., Ga., U.S. (chă-tōō'gȧ)	124	34°47'N	83°13'W
Chaudière, r., Can. (shō-dyĕr')	99	46°26'N	71°10'W
Chaumont, Fr. (shō-môN')	161	48°08'N	5°07'E
Chaunskaya Guba, b., Russia	185	69°15'N	170°00'E
Chauny, Fr. (shō-nē')	170	49°40'N	3°09'E
Chau-phu, Viet.	212	10°49'N	104°57'E

ăt; finăl; rāte; senåte; ärm; ȧsk; sofȧ; fâre; ch-choose; dh-as th in other; bē; ėvent; bĕt; recĕnt; cratẽr; g-gō; gh-guttural g; bĭt; ĭ-short neutral; rīde; K-guttural k as ch in German ich;

PRONOUNCING INDEX Chautauqua – Chippewa Lake 281

PLACE (Pronunciation)	PAGE	LAT.	LONG.
Chautauqua, l., N.Y., U.S. (shȧ-tô'kwȧ)	109	42°10'N	79°25'W
Chavaniga, Russia	180	66°02'N	37°50'E
Chaves, Port. (chä'vĕzh)	172	41°44'N	7°30'W
Chavinda, Mex. (chä-vē'n-dä)	130	20°01'N	102°27'W
Chavusi, Bela.	176	53°57'N	30°58'E
Chazumba, Mex. (chä-zòm'bä)	131	18°11'N	97°41'W
Cheadle, Eng., U.K. (chē'd'l)	158a	52°59'N	1°59'W
Cheat, W.V., U.S. (chēt)	109	39°35'N	79°40'W
Cheb, Czech Rep. (κĕb)	168	50°05'N	12°23'E
Chebarkul', Russia (chĕ-bȧr-kûl')	186a	54°59'N	60°22'E
Cheboksary, Russia (chyĕ-bôk-sä'rê)	180	56°00'N	47°20'E
Cheboygan, Mi., U.S. (shê-boi'găn)	108	45°40'N	84°30'W
Chech, Erg, des., Alg.	230	24°45'N	2°07'W
Chechen', i., Russia (chyĕch'ĕn)	181	44°00'N	48°10'E
Chechnya, prov., Russia	182	43°30'N	45°50'E
Checotah, Ok., U.S. (chê-kō'tȧ)	121	35°27'N	95°32'W
Chedabucto Bay, b., Can. (chĕd-ȧ-bŭk-tō)	101	45°23'N	61°10'W
Cheduba Island, i., Mya.	212	18°45'N	93°01'E
Cheecham Hills, hills, Can. (chēē'hăm)	96	56°20'N	111°10'W
Cheektowaga, N.Y., U.S. (chēk-tō-wä'gȧ)	111c	42°54'N	78°46'W
Chefoo *see* Yantai, China	205	37°32'N	121°22'E
Chegutu, Zimb.	232	18°18'S	30°10'E
Chehalis, Wa., U.S. (chê-hā'lĭs)	114	46°39'N	122°58'W
Chehalis, r., Wa., U.S.	114	46°47'N	123°17'W
Cheju, Kor., S. (chĕ'jōō')	210	33°29'N	126°40'E
Cheju (Quelpart), i., Kor., S.	210	33°20'N	126°25'E
Chekalin, Russia (chĕ-kä'lĭn)	176	54°05'N	36°13'E
Chela, Serra da, mts., Ang. (sĕr'rȧ dä shä'lȧ)	232	15°30'S	13°30'E
Chelan, Wa., U.S. (chê-lăn')	114	47°51'N	119°59'W
Chelan, Lake, l., Wa., U.S.	114	48°09'N	120°20'W
Cheleiros, Port. (shĕ-la'rōzh)	173b	38°54'N	9°19'W
Chéliff, r., Alg. (shā-lēf)	230	36°00'N	2°00'E
Chelles, Fr.	171b	48°53'N	2°36'E
Chełm, Pol. (κĕlm)	161	51°08'N	23°30'E
Chełmno, Pol. (κĕlm'nō)	169	53°20'N	18°25'E
Chelmsford, Can.	98	46°35'N	81°12'W
Chelmsford, Eng., U.K. (chĕlm's-fērd)	165	51°44'N	0°28'E
Chelmsford, Ma., U.S.	101a	42°36'N	71°21'W
Chelsea, Austl.	217a	38°05'S	145°08'E
Chelsea, Can.	102c	45°30'N	75°46'W
Chelsea, Al., U.S. (chĕl'sê)	110h	33°20'N	86°38'W
Chelsea, Ma., U.S.	101a	42°23'N	71°02'W
Chelsea, Mi., U.S.	108	42°20'N	84°00'W
Chelsea, Ok., U.S.	121	36°32'N	95°23'W
Cheltenham, Eng., U.K. (chĕlt'nŭm)	164	51°57'N	2°06'W
Cheltenham, Md., U.S. (chĕltĕn-hăm)	110e	38°45'N	76°50'W
Chelyabinsk, Russia (chĕl-yä-bĕnsk')	178	55°10'N	61°25'E
Chelyuskin, Mys, c., Russia (chĕl-yòs'-kĭn)	179	77°45'N	104°45'E
Chemba, Moz.	237	17°08'S	34°52'E
Chemnitz, Ger.	161	50°48'N	12°53'E
Chemung, r., N.Y., U.S. (shê-mŭng)	109	42°20'N	77°25'W
Chën, Gora, mtn., Russia	179	65°13'N	142°12'E
Chenāb, r., Asia (chê-näb)	199	30°30'N	71°30'E
Chenachane, Alg. (shē-ná-shän')	230	26°14'N	4°14'W
Chencun, China (chŭn-tsòn)	207a	22°58'N	113°14'E
Cheney, Wa., U.S. (chē'nȧ)	114	47°29'N	117°34'W
Chengde, China (chŭŋ-dŭ)	205	40°50'N	117°50'E
Chengdong Hu, l., China (chŭŋ-dôŋ hōō)	206	32°22'N	116°32'E
Chengdu, China (chŭŋ-dōō)	204	30°30'N	104°10'E
Chenggu, China (chŭŋ-gōō)	208	33°05'N	107°25'E
Chenghai, China (chŭŋ-hī)	209	23°22'N	116°40'E
Chengshan Jiao, c., China (jyou chŭŋ-shän)	208	37°28'N	122°40'E
Chengxi Hu, l., China (chŭŋ-shyē hōō)	206	32°31'N	116°04'E
Chennai (Madras), India	199	13°08'N	80°15'E
Chenxian, China (chŭn-shyĕn)	209	25°40'N	113°00'E
Chepén, Peru (chĕ-pĕ'n)	142	7°17'S	79°24'W
Chepo, Pan. (chā'pō)	133	9°12'N	79°06'W
Chepo, r., Pan.	133	9°10'N	78°36'W
Cher, r., Fr. (shâr)	161	47°14'N	1°34'E
Cherán, Mex. (chā-rän')	130	19°41'N	101°54'W
Cherangany Hills, hills, Kenya	237	1°25'N	35°20'E
Cheraw, S.C., U.S. (chē'rô)	125	34°40'N	79°52'W
Cherbourg, Fr. (shär-bòr')	154	49°39'N	1°43'W
Cherdyn', Russia (chĕr-dyĕn')	178	60°25'N	56°32'E
Cheremkhovo, Russia (chĕr'yĕm-kô-vō)	179	52°58'N	103°18'E
Cherëmukhovo, Russia (chĕr-yĕ-mû-kô-vô)	186a	60°20'N	60°00'E
Cherepanovo, Russia (chĕr'yĕ pä-nô'vō)	178	54°13'N	83°22'E
Cherepovets, Russia (chĕr-yĕ-pô'vyĕtz)	178	59°08'N	37°59'E
Chereya, Bela. (chĕr-ā'yä)	176	54°38'N	29°16'E
Chergui, i., Tun.	162	34°50'N	11°40'E
Chergui, Chott ech, l., Alg. (chĕr gē)	162	34°12'N	0°10'W
Cherkasy, Ukr.	177	49°26'N	32°03'E
Cherkasy, prov., Ukr.	177	48°58'N	30°55'E
Cherkessk, Russia	182	44°14'N	42°04'E
Cherlak, Russia (chĭr-läk')	178	54°04'N	74°28'E
Chermoz, Russia (chĕr-môz')	180	58°47'N	56°08'E
Chern', Russia (chĕrn)	176	53°28'N	36°49'E
Chërnaya Kalitva, r., Russia (chôr'nȧ yȧ kȧ-lēt'vȧ)	177	50°15'N	39°16'E
Chernihiv, Ukr.	181	51°23'N	31°15'E
Chernihiv, prov., Ukr.	177	51°28'N	31°18'E
Chernihivka, Ukr.	177	47°08'N	36°20'E
Chernivtsi, Ukr.	178	48°18'N	25°56'E
Chernobyl' *see* Chornobai, Ukr.	176	51°17'N	30°14'E
Chernogorsk, Russia (chĕr-nŏ-gôrsk')	184	54°01'N	91°07'E
Chernoistochinsk, Russia (chĕr-nôy-stô'chĭnsk)	186a	57°44'N	59°55'E
Chernyanka, Russia (chĕrn-yäŋ'kä)	177	50°56'N	37°48'E
Cherokee, Ia., U.S. (chĕr-ô-kē')	112	42°43'N	95°33'W
Cherokee, Ks., U.S.	121	37°21'N	94°50'W
Cherokee, Ok., U.S.	120	36°44'N	98°22'W
Cherokee Lake, res., Tn., U.S.	124	36°22'N	83°22'W
Cherokees, Lake of the, res., Ok., U.S. (chĕr-ô-kēz')	107	36°32'N	95°14'W
Cherokee Sound, Bah.	134	26°15'N	76°55'W
Cherryfield, Me., U.S. (chĕr'ĭ-fēld)	100	44°37'N	67°56'W
Cherry Grove, Or., U.S.	116c	45°27'N	123°15'W
Cherryvale, Ks., U.S.	121	37°16'N	95°33'W
Cherryville, N.C., U.S. (chĕr'ĭ-vĭl)	125	35°32'N	81°22'W
Cherskogo, Khrebet, mts., Russia	179	67°15'N	140°00'E
Chertsey, Eng., U.K.	158b	51°24'N	0°30'W
Chervonoye, Vozyera, l., Bela. (chĕr-vô'nô-yĕ)	176	52°24'N	28°00'E
Chervyen', Bela. (chĕr'vyĕn)	176	53°43'N	28°26'E
Cherykaw, Bela.	176	53°34'N	31°22'E
Chesaning, Mi., U.S. (chĕs'ȧ-nĭng)	108	43°10'N	84°10'W
Chesapeake, Va., U.S. (chĕs'ȧ-pēk)	110g	36°48'N	76°16'W
Chesapeake Bay, b., U.S.	107	38°20'N	76°15'W
Chesapeake Beach, Md., U.S.	110e	38°42'N	76°33'W
Chesham, Eng., U.K. (chĕsh'ŭm)	158b	51°41'N	0°37'W
Cheshire, Mi., U.S. (chĕsh'ĭr)	108	42°25'N	86°00'W
Cheshire, co., Eng., U.K.	158a	53°16'N	2°30'W
Chëshskaya Guba, b., Russia	178	67°25'N	46°00'E
Cheshunt, Eng., U.K.	158b	51°43'N	0°02'W
Chesma, Russia (chĕs'mȧ)	186a	53°50'N	60°42'E
Chesnokovka, Russia (chĕs-nŏ-kôf'kȧ)	178	53°28'N	83°41'E
Chester, Eng., U.K. (chĕs'tēr)	164	53°12'N	2°53'W
Chester, Il., U.S.	121	37°54'N	89°48'W
Chester, Pa., U.S.	110f	39°51'N	75°22'W
Chester, S.C., U.S.	125	34°42'N	81°11'W
Chester, Va., U.S.	125	37°20'N	77°24'W
Chester, W.V., U.S.	108	40°35'N	80°30'W
Chesterfield, Eng., U.K. (chĕs'tēr-fēld)	164	53°14'N	1°26'W
Chesterfield, Îles, is., N. Cal.	221	19°38'S	160°08'E
Chesterfield Inlet *see* Igluligaarjuk, Can.	92	63°19'N	91°11'W
Chesterfield Inlet, b., Can.	93	63°59'N	92°09'W
Chestermere Lake, l., Can. (chĕs'tē-mēr)	102e	51°03'N	113°45'W
Chesterton, In., U.S. (chĕs'tēr-tŭn)	108	41°35'N	87°05'W
Chestertown, Md., U.S. (chĕs'tēr-toun)	109	39°15'N	76°05'W
Chesuncook, l., Me., U.S. (chĕs'ŭn-kòk)	100	46°03'N	69°40'W
Chetek, Wi., U.S. (chĕ'tĕk)	113	45°18'N	91°41'W
Chetumal, Bahía de, b., N.A. (bä-ē-ä dĕ chĕt-ōō-mäl')	128	18°07'N	88°05'W
Chevelon Creek, r., Az., U.S. (shĕv'ȧ-lŏn)	119	34°35'N	111°00'W
Cheviot, Oh., U.S. (shĕv'ĭ-ŭt)	111f	39°10'N	84°37'W
Chevreuse, Fr. (shĕ-vrûz')	171b	48°42'N	2°02'E
Chevy Chase, Md., U.S. (shĕvĭ chās)	110e	38°58'N	77°06'W
Chew Bahir, Afr. (stĕf-a-nē)	231	4°46'N	37°31'E
Chewelah, Wa., U.S. (chē-wē'lä)	114	48°17'N	117°42'W
Cheyenne, Wy., U.S. (shī-ĕn')	104	41°10'N	104°49'W
Cheyenne, r., U.S.	106	44°20'N	102°15'W
Cheyenne River Indian Reservation, I.R., S.D., U.S.	112	45°07'N	100°46'W
Cheyenne Wells, Co., U.S.	120	38°46'N	102°21'W
Chhattisgarh, state, India	199	23°00'N	83°00'E
Chhindwāra, India	202	22°08'N	78°57'E
Chiai, Tai. (chī'ī')	209	23°28'N	120°28'E
Chiange, Ang.	236	15°45'S	13°48'E
Chiang Mai, Thai.	212	18°38'N	98°44'E
Chiang Rai, Thai.	212	19°53'N	99°48'E
Chiapa, Río de, r., Mex.	132	16°00'N	92°20'W
Chiapa de Corzo, Mex. (chê-ä'pä dā kôr'zō)	131	16°44'N	93°01'W
Chiapas, state, Mex. (chê-ä'päs)	128	17°10'N	93°00'W
Chiapas, Cordilla de, mts., Mex. (kôr-dēl-yĕ'rä-dĕ-chyä'räs)	131	15°55'N	93°15'W
Chiari, Italy (kyä'rē)	174	45°31'N	9°57'E
Chiasso, Switz.	168	45°50'N	8°57'E
Chiatura, Geor.	182	42°17'N	43°17'E
Chiautla, Mex. (chyä-ōōt'lȧ)	130	18°16'N	98°37'W
Chiavari, Italy (kyä-vä'rē)	174	44°18'N	9°21'E
Chiba, Japan (chē'bȧ)	205	35°37'N	140°08'E
Chiba, dept., Japan	211a	35°47'N	140°02'E
Chibougamau, Can. (chē-bōō'gä-mou)	91	49°57'N	74°23'W
Chibougamau, l., Can.	99	49°53'N	74°21'W
Chicago, Il., U.S. (shĭ-kô-gō) (chĭ-kä'gō)	105	41°49'N	87°37'W
Chicago Heights, Il., U.S.	111a	41°30'N	87°38'W
Chicapa, r., Afr. (chē-kä'pä)	232	7°45'S	20°25'E
Chicbul, Mex. (chēk-bōō'l)	131	18°45'N	90°56'W
Chic-Chocs, Monts, mts., Can.	93	48°38'N	66°37'W
Chichagof, i., Ak., U.S. (chê-chä'gôf)	103	57°50'N	137°00'W
Chichancanab, Lago de, l., Mex. (lä'gô-dĕ-chē-chän-kä-nä'b)	132a	19°50'N	88°28'W
Chichén Itzá, hist., Mex.	132a	20°40'N	88°35'W
Chichester, Eng., U.K. (chĭch'ĕs-tēr)	164	50°50'N	0°55'W
Chichimilá, Mex. (chē-chē-mê'lä)	132a	20°36'N	88°14'W
Chichiriviche, Ven. (chē-chē-rē-vē-chĕ)	143b	10°56'N	68°17'W
Chickamauga, Ga., U.S. (chĭk-ȧ-mô'gȧ)	124	34°50'N	85°15'W
Chickamauga Lake, res., Tn., U.S.	124	35°18'N	85°22'W
Chickasawhay, r., Ms., U.S. (chĭk-ȧ-sô'wā)	124	31°45'N	88°45'W
Chickasha, Ok., U.S. (chĭk'ȧ-shā)	104	35°04'N	97°56'W
Chiclana de la Frontera, Spain (chê-klä'nä)	172	36°25'N	6°09'W
Chiclayo, Peru (chê-klä'yō)	142	6°46'S	79°50'W
Chico, Ca., U.S. (chē'kō)	118	39°43'N	121°51'W
Chico, Wa., U.S.	116a	47°37'N	122°43'W
Chico, r., Arg.	144	44°30'S	66°00'W
Chico, r., Arg.	144	49°15'S	69°30'W
Chico, r., Phil.	213a	17°33'N	121°24'E
Chicoloapan, Mex. (chê-kō-lwä'pän)	131a	19°24'N	98°54'W
Chiconautla, Mex.	131a	19°39'N	99°01'W
Chicontepec, Mex. (chê-kōn'tē-pĕk')	130	20°58'N	98°08'W
Chicopee, Ma., U.S. (chĭk'ô-pē)	109	42°10'N	72°35'W
Chicoutimi, Can. (shē-kōō'tē-mē')	91	48°26'N	71°04'W
Chicxulub, Mex. (chēk-sōō-lōō'b)	132a	21°10'N	89°30'W
Chiefland, Fl., U.S. (chēf'lănd)	125	29°30'N	82°50'W
Chiemsee, l., Ger. (κēm zā)	168	47°58'N	12°20'E
Chieri, Italy (kyâ'rē)	174	45°03'N	7°48'E
Chieti, Italy (kyĕ'tē)	162	42°22'N	14°22'E
Chifeng, China (chr-fŭŋ)	205	42°18'N	118°52'E
Chignanuapan, Mex. (chē'g-nä-nwä-pá'n)	130	19°49'N	98°02'W
Chignecto Bay, b., Can. (shĭg-nĕk'tō)	100	45°33'N	64°50'W
Chignik, Ak., U.S. (chĭg'nĭk)	103	56°14'N	158°12'W
Chignik Bay, b., Ak., U.S.	103	56°18'N	157°22'W
Chigu Co, l., China (chr-gōō tswo)	202	28°55'N	91°47'E
Chigwell, Eng., U.K.	158b	51°38'N	0°05'E
Chihe, China (chr-hŭ)	206	32°32'N	117°57'E
Chihuahua, Mex. (chê-wä'wä)	128	28°37'N	106°06'W
Chihuahua, state, Mex.	128	29°00'N	107°30'W
Chikishlyar, Turkmen. (chê-kêsh-lyär')	183	37°40'N	53°50'E
Chilanga, Zam.	237	15°34'S	28°17'E
Chilapa, Mex. (chê-lä'pä)	130	17°34'N	99°14'W
Chilchota, Mex. (chêl-chō'tä)	130	19°40'N	102°04'W
Chilcotin, r., Can. (chĭl-kō'tĭn)	94	52°20'N	124°15'W
Childress, Tx., U.S. (chĭld'rĕs)	120	34°26'N	100°11'W
Chile, nation, S.A. (chē'lā)	144	35°00'S	72°00'W
Chilecito, Arg. (chê-lā-sē'tō)	144	29°06'S	67°25'W
Chilengue, Serra do, mts., Ang.	236	13°20'S	15°00'E
Chilibre, Pan. (chē-lê'brĕ)	128a	9°09'N	79°37'W
Chililabombwe, Zam.	237	12°18'S	27°43'E
Chilka, l., India	202	19°26'N	85°42'E
Chilko, r., Can. (chĭl'kō)	94	51°53'N	123°53'W
Chilko Lake, l., Can.	94	51°20'N	124°05'W
Chillán, Chile (chēl-yän')	144	36°44'S	72°06'W
Chillicothe, Il., U.S. (chĭl-ĭ-kŏth'ê)	108	41°55'N	89°30'W
Chillicothe, Mo., U.S.	121	39°46'N	93°32'W
Chillicothe, Oh., U.S.	108	39°20'N	83°00'W
Chilliwack, Can. (chĭl'ĭ-wăk)	90	49°10'N	121°57'W
Chiloé, Isla de, i., Chile	144	42°30'S	73°55'W
Chilpancingo de los Bravo, Mex.	128	17°32'N	99°30'W
Chilton, Wi., U.S. (chĭl'tŭn)	113	44°00'N	88°12'W
Chilung, Tai. (chī'lung)	205	25°02'N	121°48'E
Chilwa, Lake, l., Afr.	232	15°12'S	36°30'E
Chimacum, Wa., U.S. (chĭm'ä-kŭm)	116a	48°01'N	122°47'W
Chimalpa, Mex. (chē-mäl'pä)	131a	19°26'N	99°22'W
Chimaltenango, Guat. (chê-mäl-tā-näŋ'gō)	132	14°39'N	90°48'W
Chimaltitan, Mex. (chêmäl-tē-tän')	130	21°36'N	103°50'W
Chimbay, Uzb. (chĭm-bī')	183	43°00'N	59°44'E
Chimborazo, mtn., Ec. (chêm-bô-rä'zō)	142	1°35'S	78°45'W
Chimbote, Peru (chêm-bō'tȧ)	142	9°02'S	78°33'W
China, Mex. (chē'nä)	122	25°43'N	99°13'W
China, nation, Asia (chī'nȧ)	204	36°45'N	93°00'E
Chinameca, El Sal. (Chē-nä-mā'kä)	132	13°31'N	88°18'W
Chinandega, Nic. (chē-nän-dā'gä)	132	12°38'N	87°08'W
Chinati Peak, mtn., Tx., U.S. (chĭ-nä'tē)	122	29°56'N	104°29'W
Chincha Alta, Peru (chĭn'chä äl'tä)	142	13°24'S	76°04'W
Chinchas, Islas, is., Peru (ê's-läs-chē'n-chäs)	142	11°27'S	79°05'W
Chinchilla, Austl. (chĭn-chĭl'ȧ)	222	26°44'S	150°36'E
Chinchorro, Banco, bk., Mex. (bä'n-kô-chēn-chô'r-rō)	132a	18°43'N	87°25'W
Chincilla de Monte Aragon, Spain	172	38°54'N	1°43'W
Chinde, Moz. (shēn'dĕ)	232	17°39'S	36°34'E
Chin Do, i., Kor., S.	210	34°30'N	125°43'E
Chindwin, r., Mya. (chĭn-dwĭn)	199	23°30'N	94°34'E
Chingola, Zam. (chĭng-gōlä)	232	12°32'S	27°52'E
Chinguar, Ang. (chĭng-gär)	232	12°35'S	16°15'E
Chinguetti, Maur. (chēŋ-gĕt'ê)	230	20°34'N	12°34'W
Chinhoyi, Zimb.	232	17°22'S	30°12'E
Chinju, Kor., S. (chĭn'jōō)	210	35°13'N	128°10'E
Chinko, r., C.A.R. (shĭn'kō)	231	6°37'N	24°31'E
Chinmen *see* Quemoy, Tai.	209	24°30'N	118°20'E
Chino, Ca., U.S. (chē'nō)	117a	34°01'N	117°42'W
Chinon, Fr. (shē-nôn')	170	47°09'N	0°13'E
Chinook, Mt., U.S. (shĭn-òk')	115	48°35'N	109°15'W
Chinsali, Zam.	237	10°34'S	32°03'E
Chinteche, Mwi. (chĭn-tĕ'chĕ)	232	11°48'S	34°14'E
Chioggia, Italy (kyôd'jä)	174	45°12'N	12°17'E
Chíos, Grc. (kē'ôs)	163	38°23'N	26°09'E
Chíos, i., Grc.	163	38°20'N	25°45'E
Chipata, Zam.	237	13°39'S	32°40'E
Chipera, Moz. (zhê-pĕ'rä)	232	15°16'S	32°30'E
Chipley, Fl., U.S. (chĭp'lĭ)	124	30°45'N	85°33'W
Chipman, Can. (chĭp'măn)	100	46°11'N	65°53'W
Chipola, r., Fl., U.S. (chĭ-pō'lȧ)	124	30°40'N	85°14'W
Chippawa, Can. (chĭp'ê-wä)	111c	43°03'N	79°03'W
Chippewa, r., Mn., U.S. (chĭp'ê-wä)	112	45°07'N	95°41'W
Chippewa, r., Wi., U.S.	113	45°07'N	91°19'W
Chippewa Falls, Wi., U.S.	113	44°55'N	91°26'W
Chippewa Lake, Oh., U.S.	111d	41°04'N	81°54'W

ng-sing; ŋ-baŋk; ɴ-nasalized n; nŏd; cŏmmit; ōld; ôbey; ôrder; oi-boil; fōōd; ò-as oo in foot; ou-out; s-soft; sh-dish; th-thin; pūre; ûnite; ûrn; stŭd; circŭs; ü-as in French tu; '-indeterminate vowel.

282 Chiputneticook Lakes – Clearwater PRONOUNCING INDEX

PLACE (Pronunciation)	PAGE	LAT.	LONG.
Chiputneticook Lakes, l., N.A. (chĭ-pŏt-nĕt′ĭ-ko̅o̅k)	100	45°47′N	67°45′W
Chiquimula, Guat. (chē-kē-mo̅o̅′lä)	132	14°47′N	89°31′W
Chiquimulilla, Guat. (chē-kē-mo̅o̅-lē′l-yä)	132	14°08′N	90°23′W
Chiquinquira, Col. (chē-kēŋ′kē-rä′)	142	5°33′N	73°49′W
Chirala, India	203	15°52′N	80°22′E
Chirchik, Uzb. (chĭr-chēk′)	183	41°28′N	69°18′E
Chire (Shire), r., Afr.	237	17°15′S	35°25′E
Chiricahua National Monument, rec., Az., U.S. (chĭ-rä-cä′hwä)	119	32°02′N	109°18′W
Chirikof, i., Ak., U.S. (chĭ′rĭ-kôf)	103	55°50′N	155°35′W
Chiriquí, Punta, c., Pan. (po̅′n-tä-chē-rē-kē′)	133	9°13′N	81°39′W
Chiriquí Grande, Pan. (chē-rē-kē′ grän′dā)	133	8°57′N	82°08′W
Chiri San, mtn., Kor., S. (chĭ′rĭ-sän′)	210	35°20′N	127°39′E
Chiromo, Mwi.	232	16°34′S	35°13′E
Chirpan, Blg.	163	42°12′N	25°19′E
Chirripó, Río, r., C.R.	133	9°50′N	83°20′W
Chisasibi, Can.	91	53°40′N	78°58′W
Chisholm, Mn., U.S. (chĭz′ŭm)	113	47°28′N	92°53′W
Chişinău, Mol.	178	47°02′N	28°52′E
Chistopol′, Russia (chĭs-tô′pôl-y′)	178	55°21′N	50°37′E
Chita, Russia (chē-tá′)	179	52°09′N	113°39′E
Chitambo, Zam.	237	12°55′S	30°39′E
Chitato, Ang.	236	7°20′S	20°47′E
Chitembo, Ang.	236	13°34′S	16°40′E
Chitina, Ak., U.S. (chĭ-tē′ná)	103	61°28′N	144°35′W
Chitokoloki, Zam.	236	13°50′S	23°13′E
Chitorgarh, India	202	24°59′N	74°42′E
Chitrāl, Pak. (chē-träl′)	199	35°58′N	71°48′E
Chittagong, Bngl. (chĭt-á-gông′)	199	22°26′N	90°51′E
Chitungwiza, Zimb.	232	17°51′S	31°05′E
Chiumbe, r., Afr. (chē-ŏm′bā)	232	9°45′S	21°00′E
Chivasso, Italy (kē-väs′sō)	174	45°13′N	7°52′E
Chivhu, Zimb.	232	18°59′S	30°58′E
Chivilcoy, Arg. (chē-vēl-koi′)	144	34°51′S	60°03′W
Chixoy, r., Guat. (chē-ĸoi′)	132	15°40′N	90°35′W
Chizu, Japan (chē-zo̅o̅′)	211	35°16′N	134°15′E
Chloride, Az., U.S. (klō′rīd)	119	35°25′N	114°15′W
Chmielnik, Pol. (ĸmyĕl′nēĸ)	169	50°36′N	20°46′E
Choapa, r., Chile (chō-á′pä)	141b	31°56′S	70°48′W
Choctawhatchee, r., Fl., U.S.	124	30°37′N	85°56′W
Choctawhatchee Bay, b., Fl., U.S. (chôk-tô-hăch′ē)	124	30°15′N	86°32′W
Chodziez, Pol. (ĸōj′yĕsh)	168	52°59′N	16°55′E
Choele Choel, Arg. (chō-ĕ′lĕ-chōĕ′l)	144	39°14′S	65°46′W
Chōfu, Japan (chō′fo̅o̅′)	211a	35°39′N	139°33′E
Chōgo, Japan (chō-gō)	211a	35°25′N	139°28′E
Choiseul, i., Sol. Is. (shwä-zûl′)	221	7°30′S	157°30′E
Choisy-le-Roi, Fr.	171b	48°46′N	2°25′E
Chojnice, Pol. (ĸoĭ-nē-tsĕ)	169	53°41′N	17°34′E
Cholet, Fr. (shô-lĕ′)	161	47°06′N	0°54′W
Cholula, Mex. (chō-lo̅o̅′lä)	130	19°04′N	98°19′W
Choluteca, Hond. (chō-lo̅o̅-tā′kä)	132	13°18′N	87°12′W
Choluteco, r., Hond.	132	13°34′N	86°59′W
Chomutov, Czech Rep. (kō′mò-tôf)	168	50°27′N	13°23′E
Chona, r., Russia (chō′nä)	185	60°45′N	109°15′E
Chone, Ec. (chō′nĕ)	142	0°48′S	80°06′W
Chŏngjin, Kor., N. (chŭng-jĭn′)	205	41°48′N	129°46′E
Chŏngju, Kor., S. (chŭng-jo̅o̅′)	210	36°35′N	127°30′E
Chongming Dao, i., China (chôŋ-mĭŋ dou)	209	31°40′N	122°30′E
Chongqing, China (chôŋ-chyĭŋ)	204	29°38′N	107°30′E
Chongqing, prov., China	204	30°00′N	108°00′E
Chŏnju, Kor., S. (chŭn-jo̅o̅′)	210	35°48′N	127°08′E
Chonos, Archipiélago de los, is., Chile	144	44°35′S	76°15′W
Chorley, Eng., U.K. (chôr′lĭ)	158a	53°40′N	2°38′W
Chornaya, neigh., Russia	186b	55°45′N	38°04′E
Chornobai, Ukr.	177	51°17′N	30°14′E
Chornobay, Ukr. (chĕr-nō-bī′)	177	49°41′N	32°24′E
Chornomors′ke, Ukr.	181	45°29′N	32°43′E
Chorrillos, Peru (chôr-rē′l-yōs)	142	12°17′S	76°55′W
Chortkiv, Ukr.	169	49°01′N	25°48′E
Chosan, Kor., N. (chō-sän′)	210	40°44′N	125°48′E
Chosen, Fl., U.S. (chō′z′n)	125a	26°41′N	80°41′W
Chōshi, Japan (chō′shē)	210	35°40′N	140°55′E
Choszczno, Pol. (chôsh′chnô)	168	53°10′N	15°25′E
Chota Nagpur, plat., India	202	23°40′N	82°50′E
Choteau, Mt., U.S. (shō′tō)	115	47°51′N	112°10′W
Chowan, r., N.C., U.S. (chō-wän′)	125	36°13′N	76°46′W
Chowilla Reservoir, res., Austl.	222	34°05′S	141°20′E
Chown, Mount, mtn., Can. (choun)	95	53°24′N	119°22′W
Choybalsan, Mong.	205	47°50′N	114°15′E
Christchurch, N.Z. (krīst′chûrch)	221a	43°30′S	172°38′E
Christian, i., Can. (krĭs′chăn)	99	44°50′N	80°00′W
Christiansburg, Va., U.S. (krĭs′chănz-bûrg)	125	37°08′N	80°25′W
Christiansted, V.I.U.S.	129b	17°45′N	64°44′W
Christmas Island, dep., Oc.	212	10°35′S	105°40′E
Christopher, Il., U.S. (krĭs′tō-fēr)	121	37°58′N	89°04′W
Chrudim, Czech Rep. (ĸro̅o̅′dyĕm)	168	49°57′N	15°46′E
Chrzanów, Pol. (ĸzhä′nòf)	169	50°08′N	19°24′E
Chuansha, China (chuän-shä)	207b	31°12′N	121°41′E
Chubut, prov., Arg. (chò-bo̅o̅t′)	144	44°00′S	69°15′W
Chubut, r., Arg. (chò-bo̅o̅t′)	144	43°05′S	69°00′W
Chuckatuck, Va., U.S. (chŭck á-tŭck)	110g	36°51′N	76°35′W
Chucunaque, r., Pan. (cho̅o̅-ko̅o̅-nä′kä)	133	8°36′N	77°48′W
Chudovo, Russia (chò′dō-vō)	176	59°03′N	31°56′E
Chudskoye Ozero, l., Eur. (chòt′skô-yĕ)	180	58°43′N	26°45′E
Chuguchak, hist. reg., China (cho̅o̅′go̅o̅-chäk′)	204	46°09′N	83°58′E
Chuguyevka, Russia (chò-go̅o̅′yĕf-kå)	210	43°58′N	133°49′E
Chugwater Creek, r., Wy., U.S. (chŭg′wô-tēr)	112	41°43′N	104°54′W
Chuhuiv, Ukr.	181	49°52′N	36°40′E
Chukotskiy Poluostrov, pen., Russia	179	66°12′N	175°00′W
Chukotskoye Nagor′ye, mts., Russia	179	66°00′N	166°00′E
Chula Vista, Ca., U.S. (cho̅o̅′lȧ vĭs′tȧ)	118a	32°38′N	117°05′W
Chulkovo, Russia (cho̅o̅l-kô vô)	186b	55°33′N	38°04′E
Chulucanas, Peru	142	5°13′S	80°13′W
Chulum, r., Russia	184	57°52′N	84°45′E
Chumikan, Russia (cho̅o̅-mē-kän′)	179	54°47′N	135°09′E
Chun′an, China (chòn-än)	209	29°38′N	119°00′E
Chunchŏn, Kor., S. (chòn-chŭn′)	210	37°51′N	127°46′E
Chungju, Kor., S. (chŭng′jo̅o̅′)	210	37°00′N	128°19′E
Chungking *see* Chongqing, China	204	29°38′N	107°30′E
Chunya, Tan.	237	8°32′S	33°25′E
Chunya, r., Russia (chòn′yä′)	184	61°45′N	101°28′E
Chuquicamata, Chile (cho̅o̅-kē-kä-mä′tä)	144	22°08′S	68°57′W
Chur, Switz. (ko̅o̅r)	161	46°51′N	9°32′E
Churchill, Can. (chûrch′ĭl)	91	58°50′N	94°10′W
Churchill, r., Can.	92	58°00′N	95°00′W
Churchill, Cape, c., Can.	93	59°07′N	93°50′W
Churchill Falls, wtfl., Can.	93	53°35′N	64°27′W
Churchill Lake, l., Can.	96	56°12′N	108°40′W
Churchill Peak, mtn., Can.	92	58°10′N	125°14′W
Church Stretton, Eng., U.K. (chûrch strĕt′ŭn)	158a	52°32′N	2°49′W
Churchton, Md., U.S.	110e	38°49′N	76°33′W
Churu, India	202	28°22′N	75°00′E
Churumuco, Mex. (cho̅o̅-ro̅o̅-mo̅o̅′kō)	130	18°39′N	101°40′W
Chuska Mountains, mts., Az., U.S. (chŭs-kȧ)	119	36°21′N	109°11′W
Chusovaya, r., Russia (cho̅o̅-sô-vä′yȧ)	180	58°08′N	58°35′E
Chusovoy, Russia (cho̅o̅-sô-vôy′)	178	58°18′N	57°50′E
Chust, Uzb. (chòst)	183	41°05′N	71°28′E
Chuuk (Truk), is., Micron.	214c	7°25′N	151°47′E
Chuvashia, prov., Russia	180	55°45′N	46°00′E
Chuviscar, r., Mex. (cho̅o̅-vês-kär′)	122	28°34′N	105°36′W
Chuwang, China (cho̅o̅-wäŋ)	206	36°08′N	114°53′E
Chuxian, China (cho̅o̅ shyĕn)	208	32°19′N	118°19′E
Chuxiong, China (cho̅o̅-shyôŋ)	204	25°19′N	101°34′E
Chyhyryn, Ukr.	177	49°02′N	32°39′E
Cicero, Il., U.S. (sĭs′ēr-ō)	111a	41°50′N	87°46′W
Cide, Tur. (jē′dĕ)	163	41°50′N	33°00′E
Ciechanów, Pol. (tsyĕ-kä′nòf)	169	52°52′N	20°39′E
Ciego de Avila, Cuba (syā′gō dā ä′vē-lä)	129	21°50′N	78°45′W
Ciego de Avila, prov., Cuba	134	22°00′N	78°40′W
Ciempozuelos, Spain (thyĕm-pō-thwā′lōs)	172	40°09′N	3°36′W
Ciénaga, Col. (syā′nä-gä)	142	11°01′N	74°15′W
Cienfuegos, Cuba (syĕn-fwā′gōs)	129	22°10′N	80°30′W
Cienfuegos, prov., Cuba	134	22°15′N	80°40′W
Cienfuegos, Bahía, b., Cuba (bä-ē′ä-syĕn-fwā′gōs)	134	22°00′N	80°35′W
Ciervo, Isla de la, i., Nic. (ē′s-lä-dĕ-lä-syĕ′r-vô)	133	11°56′N	83°20′W
Cieszyn, Pol. (tsyĕ′shĕn)	169	49°47′N	18°45′E
Cieza, Spain (thyā′thä)	172	38°13′N	1°25′W
Cigüela, r., Spain	172	39°53′N	2°54′W
Cihuatlán, Mex. (sē-wä-tlá′n)	130	19°13′N	104°36′W
Cihuatlán, r., Mex.	130	19°11′N	104°30′W
Cijara, Embalse de, res., Spain	172	39°25′N	5°00′W
Cilician Gates, p., Tur.	181	37°30′N	35°30′E
Cimarron, r., Co., U.S.	120	37°13′N	102°30′W
Cimarron, r., U.S. (sĭm-ȧ-rōn′)	106	36°26′N	98°27′W
Cinca, r., Spain (thēŋ′kä)	173	42°09′N	0°08′E
Cincinnati, Oh., U.S. (sĭn-sĭ-nát′ĭ)	105	39°08′N	84°30′W
Cinco Balas, Cayos, is., Cuba (kä′yōs-thēŋ′kō bä′läs)	134	21°05′N	79°25′W
Cintalapa, Mex. (sēn-tä-lä′pä)	131	16°41′N	93°44′W
Cinto, Monte, mtn., Fr. (chēn′tō)	161	42°24′N	8°54′E
Circle, Ak., U.S. (sûr′k′l)	106a	65°49′N	144°22′W
Circleville, Oh., U.S. (sûr′k′lvĭl)	108	39°35′N	83°00′W
Cirebon, Indon.	212	6°50′S	108°33′E
Ciri Grande, r., Pan. (sē′rē-grá′n′dĕ)	128a	8°55′N	80°04′W
Cisco, Tx., U.S. (sĭs′kō)	122	32°23′N	98°57′W
Cisneros, Col. (sēs-nĕ′rôs)	142a	6°33′N	75°05′W
Cisterna di Latina, Italy (chēs-tĕ′r-nä-dē-lä-tē′nä)	173d	41°36′N	12°53′E
Cistierna, Spain (thēs-tyĕr′nä)	172	42°48′N	5°08′W
Citronelle, Al., U.S. (cĭt-rō′nĕl)	124	31°05′N	88°15′W
Cittadella, Italy (chēt-tä-dĕl′lä)	174	45°39′N	11°51′E
Città di Castello, Italy (chēt-tä′dē käs-tĕl′lō)	174	43°27′N	12°17′E
Ciudad Altamirano, Mex. (syo̅o̅-dä′d-äl-tä-mē-rä′nô)	130	18°24′N	100°38′W
Ciudad Bolívar, Ven. (syo̅o̅-dhädh′ bō-lē′vär)	142	8°07′N	63°41′W
Ciudad Camargo, Mex.	128	27°42′N	105°10′W
Ciudad Chetumal, Mex.	128	18°30′N	88°17′W
Ciudad Darío, Nic. (syo̅o̅-dhädh′dä′rē-ō)	132	12°44′N	86°08′W
Ciudad de la Habana, prov., Cuba	134	23°20′N	82°10′W
Ciudad del Carmen, Mex. (syo̅o̅-dä′d-dĕl-kà′r-mĕn)	128	18°39′N	91°49′W
Ciudad del Maíz, Mex. (syo̅o̅-dhädh′del mä-ēz′)	130	22°24′N	99°37′W
Ciudad Fernández, Mex. (syo̅o̅-dhädh′fĕr-nän′dĕz)	130	21°56′N	100°03′W
Ciudad García, Mex. (syo̅o̅-dhädh′gär-sē′ä)	128	22°39′N	103°02′W
Ciudad Guayana, Ven.	142	8°30′N	62°45′W
Ciudad Guzmán, Mex. (syo̅o̅-dhädh′gòz-män)	128	19°40′N	103°29′W
Ciudad Hidalgo, Mex. (syo̅o̅-dä′d-ē-dä′l-gô)	130	19°41′N	100°35′W
Ciudad Juárez, Mex. (syo̅o̅-dhädh hwä′rāz)	128	31°44′N	106°28′W
Ciudad Madero, Mex. (syo̅o̅-dä′d-mä-dĕ′rô)	131	22°16′N	97°52′W
Ciudad Mante, Mex. (syo̅o̅-dä′d-màn′tĕ)	128	22°34′N	98°58′W
Ciudad Manual Doblado, Mex. (syo̅o̅-dä′d-män-wāl′dō-blä′dō)	130	20°43′N	101°57′W
Ciudad Obregón, Mex. (syo̅o̅-dhädh-ô-brĕ-gô′n)	128	27°40′N	109°58′W
Ciudad Real, Spain (thyo̅o̅-dhädh′rā-äl′)	172	38°59′N	3°55′W
Ciudad Rodrigo, Spain (thyo̅o̅-dhädh′rô-drē′gō)	162	40°38′N	6°34′W
Ciudad Serdán, Mex. (syo̅o̅-dä′d-sĕr-dá′n)	131	18°58′N	97°26′W
Ciudad Victoria, Mex. (syo̅o̅-dhädh′vēk-tō′rē-ä)	128	23°43′N	99°09′W
Ciutadella, Spain	173	40°00′N	3°52′E
Civitavecchia, Italy (chē′vē-tä-vĕk′kyä)	174	42°06′N	11°49′E
Cixian, China (tsē shyĕn)	206	36°22′N	114°23′E
Clackamas, Or., U.S. (klăc-kȧ′măs)	116c	45°25′N	122°34′W
Claire, l., Can. (klâr)	92	58°33′N	113°16′W
Clair Engle Lake, l., Ca., U.S.	114	40°51′N	122°41′W
Clairton, Pa., U.S. (klârt*ŭ*n)	111e	40°17′N	79°53′W
Clanton, Al., U.S. (klăn′t*ŭ*n)	124	32°50′N	86°38′W
Clare, Mi., U.S. (klâr)	108	43°50′N	84°45′W
Clare Island, i., Ire.	164	53°46′N	10°00′W
Claremont, Ca., U.S. (klâr′mŏnt)	117a	34°06′N	117°43′W
Claremont, N.H., U.S. (klâr′mŏnt)	109	43°20′N	72°20′W
Claremont, W.V., U.S.	108	37°55′N	81°00′W
Claremore, Ok., U.S. (klâr′mōr)	121	36°16′N	95°37′W
Claremorris, Ire. (klâr-mŏr′ĭs)	164	53°46′N	9°05′W
Clarence Strait, strt., Austl. (klăr′*ĕ*ns)	220	12°15′S	130°05′E
Clarence Strait, strt., Ak., U.S.	94	55°25′N	132°00′W
Clarence Town, Bah.	135	23°05′N	75°00′W
Clarendon, Ar., U.S. (klăr′*ĕ*n-d*ŭ*n)	121	34°42′N	91°17′W
Clarendon, Tx., U.S.	120	34°55′N	100°52′W
Clarens, S. Afr. (clâ-rĕns)	233c	28°34′S	28°26′E
Claresholm, Can. (klâr′*ĕ*s-hōlm)	90	50°02′N	113°35′W
Clarinda, Ia., U.S. (klȧ-rĭn′d*ȧ*)	112	40°42′N	95°00′W
Clarines, Ven. (klä-rē′nĕs)	143b	9°57′N	65°10′W
Clarion, Ia., U.S. (klăr′ĭ-*ŭ*n)	113	42°43′N	93°45′W
Clarion, Pa., U.S.	109	41°10′N	79°25′W
Clark, S.D., U.S. (klärk)	112	44°52′N	97°45′W
Clark, Point, c., Can.	98	44°05′N	81°50′W
Clarkdale, Az., U.S. (klärk-dāl)	119	34°45′N	112°05′W
Clarke City, Can.	91	50°12′N	66°38′W
Clarke Range, mts., Austl.	221	20°30′S	148°00′E
Clark Fork, r., Mt., U.S.	114	47°50′N	115°35′W
Clarksburg, W.V., U.S. (klärkz′bûrg)	105	39°15′N	80°20′W
Clarksdale, Ms., U.S. (klärks-dāl)	124	34°10′N	90°31′W
Clark's Harbour, Can. (klärks)	100	43°26′N	65°38′W
Clarks Hill Lake, res., U.S. (klärk-hĭl)	107	33°50′N	82°35′W
Clarkston, Ga., U.S. (klärks′t*ŭ*n)	110c	33°49′N	84°15′W
Clarkston, Wa., U.S.	114	46°24′N	117°01′W
Clarksville, Ar., U.S. (klärks-vĭl)	121	35°28′N	93°26′W
Clarksville, Tn., U.S.	124	36°30′N	87°23′W
Clarksville, Tx., U.S.	121	33°37′N	95°02′W
Clatskanie, Or., U.S.	116c	46°04′N	123°11′W
Clatskanie, r., Or., U.S. (klăt-skā′nē)	116c	46°06′N	123°11′W
Clatsop Spit, Or., U.S. (klăt-sŏp)	116c	46°13′N	124°04′W
Cláudio, Braz. (klou′-dēō)	141a	20°26′S	44°44′W
Claveria, Phil. (klä-vȧ-rē′ä)	209	18°38′N	121°08′E
Clawson, Mi., U.S. (klô′s′n)	111b	42°32′N	83°09′W
Claxton, Ga., U.S. (klăks′t*ŭ*n)	125	32°07′N	81°54′W
Clay, Ky., U.S. (klā)	124	37°28′N	87°50′W
Clay Center, Ks., U.S. (klā sĕn′tēr)	121	39°23′N	97°08′W
Clay City, Ky., U.S. (klā sĭ′t*ĭ*)	108	37°50′N	83°55′W
Claycomo, Mo., U.S. (kla-kō′mo)	117f	39°12′N	94°30′W
Clay Cross, Eng., U.K. (klā krŏs)	158a	53°10′N	1°25′W
Claye-Souilly, Fr. (klĕ-so̅o̅-yē′)	171b	48°56′N	2°43′E
Claymont, De., U.S. (klā-mŏnt)	110f	39°48′N	75°28′W
Clayton, Eng., U.K.	158a	53°47′N	1°49′W
Clayton, Al., U.S. (klā′t*ŭ*n)	124	31°52′N	85°25′W
Clayton, Ca., U.S.	116b	37°56′N	121°56′W
Clayton, Mo., U.S.	117e	38°39′N	90°20′W
Clayton, N.C., U.S.	125	35°40′N	78°27′W
Clayton, N.M., U.S.	120	36°26′N	103°12′W
Clear, l., Ca., U.S.	118	39°05′N	122°50′W
Clear Boggy Creek, r., Ok., U.S. (klēr bŏg′ĭ krēk)	121	34°21′N	96°22′W
Clear Creek, r., Az., U.S.	119	34°40′N	111°05′W
Clear Creek, r., Tx., U.S.	123a	29°34′N	95°13′W
Clear Creek, r., Wy., U.S.	115	44°35′N	106°20′W
Clearfield, Pa., U.S. (klēr-fēld)	109	41°00′N	78°25′W
Clearfield, Ut., U.S.	117b	41°07′N	112°01′W
Clear Hills, Can.	90	57°11′N	119°20′W
Clear Lake, Ia., U.S.	113	43°09′N	93°23′W
Clear Lake, Wa., U.S.	116a	48°27′N	122°14′W
Clear Lake Reservoir, res., Ca., U.S.	114	41°53′N	121°00′W
Clearwater, Fl., U.S. (klēr-wô′tēr)	125a	27°43′N	82°45′W
Clearwater, r., Can.	95	52°00′N	114°50′W
Clearwater, r., Can.	96	56°10′N	110°40′W
Clearwater, r., Can.	95	52°00′N	120°10′W
Clearwater, r., Id., U.S.	114	46°27′N	116°33′W

ăt; finăl; rāte; senāte; ärm; åsk; sofȧ; fâre; ch-choose; dh-as th in other; bē; ēvent; bĕt; recĕnt; cratēr; g-gō; gh-guttural g; bĭt; ĭ-short neutral; rīde; ĸ-guttural k as ch in German ich;

PRONOUNCING INDEX Clearwater – Comacchio 283

PLACE (Pronunciation)	PAGE	LAT.	LONG.
Clearwater, Middle Fork, r., Id., U.S.	114	46°10'N	115°48'W
Clearwater, North Fork, r., Id., U.S.	114	46°34'N	116°08'W
Clearwater, South Fork, r., Id., U.S.	114	45°46'N	115°53'W
Clearwater Mountains, mts., Id., U.S.	114	45°56'N	115°15'W
Cleburne, Tx., U.S. (klē'bŭrn)	104	32°21'N	97°23'W
Cle Elum, Wa., U.S. (klē ĕl'ŭm)	114	47°12'N	120°55'W
Clementon, N.J., U.S. (klē'mĕn-tŭn)	110f	39°49'N	75°00'W
Cleobury Mortimer, Eng., U.K. (klēō-bĕr'ĭ môr'tĭ-mĕr)	158a	52°22'N	2°29'W
Clermont, Austl. (klēr'mŏnt)	219	23°02'S	147°46'E
Clermont, Can.	99	47°45'N	70°20'W
Clermont-Ferrand, Fr. (klĕr-môn'fĕr-räN')	154	45°47'N	3°03'E
Cleveland, Ms., U.S. (klēv'lănd)	124	33°45'N	90°42'W
Cleveland, Oh., U.S.	105	41°30'N	81°42'W
Cleveland, Ok., U.S.	121	36°18'N	96°28'W
Cleveland, Tn., U.S.	124	35°09'N	84°52'W
Cleveland, Tx., U.S.	123	30°18'N	95°05'W
Cleveland Heights, Oh., U.S.	111d	41°30'N	81°35'W
Cleveland Peninsula, pen., Ak., U.S.	94	55°45'N	132°00'W
Cleves, Oh., U.S. (klē'vĕs)	111f	39°10'N	84°45'W
Clew Bay, b., Ire. (klōō)	164	53°47'N	9°45'W
Clewiston, Fl., U.S. (klē'wis-tŭn)	125a	26°44'N	80°55'W
Clichy, Fr. (klē-shē)	170	48°54'N	2°18'E
Clifden, Ire. (klĭf'dĕn)	164	53°31'N	10°04'W
Clifton, Az., U.S. (klĭf'tŭn)	119	33°05'N	109°20'W
Clifton, N.J., U.S.	110a	40°52'N	74°09'W
Clifton, S.C., U.S.	125	35°00'N	81°47'W
Clifton, Tx., U.S.	123	31°45'N	97°31'W
Clifton Forge, Va., U.S.	109	37°50'N	79°50'W
Clinch, r., Tn., U.S. (klĭnch)	124	36°30'N	83°19'W
Clingmans Dome, mtn., U.S. (klĭng'măns dōm)	124	35°37'N	83°26'W
Clinton, Can. (klĭn-'tŭn)	90	51°05'N	121°35'W
Clinton, Ia., U.S.	113	41°50'N	90°13'W
Clinton, Il., U.S.	108	40°10'N	88°55'W
Clinton, In., U.S.	108	39°40'N	87°25'W
Clinton, Ky., U.S.	124	36°39'N	88°56'W
Clinton, Ma., U.S.	101a	42°25'N	71°41'W
Clinton, Md., U.S.	110e	38°46'N	76°54'W
Clinton, Mo., U.S.	121	38°23'N	93°46'W
Clinton, N.C., U.S.	125	34°58'N	78°20'W
Clinton, Ok., U.S.	120	35°31'N	98°56'W
Clinton, S.C., U.S.	125	34°27'N	81°53'W
Clinton, Tn., U.S.	124	36°05'N	84°08'W
Clinton, Wa., U.S.	116a	47°59'N	122°22'W
Clinton, r., Mi., U.S.	111b	42°36'N	83°00'W
Clinton-Colden, l., Can.	92	63°58'N	106°34'W
Clintonville, Wi., U.S. (klĭn'tŭn-vĭl)	113	44°37'N	88°46'W
Clio, Mi., U.S. (klē'ō)	108	43°10'N	83°45'W
Cloates, Point, c., Austl. (klōts)	220	22°47'S	113°45'E
Clocolan, S. Afr.	238c	28°56'S	27°35'E
Clonakilty Bay, b., Ire. (klŏn-á-kĭltē)	164	51°30'N	8°50'W
Cloncurry, Austl. (klŏn-kŭr'ē)	218	20°58'S	140°42'E
Clonmel, Ire. (klŏn-mĕl)	164	52°21'N	7°45'W
Cloquet, Mn., U.S. (klō-kā')	117h	46°42'N	92°28'W
Closter, N.J., U.S. (klōs'tẽr)	110a	40°58'N	73°57'W
Cloud Peak, mtn., Wy., U.S. (kloud)	106	44°23'N	107°11'W
Clover, S.C., U.S. (klō'vẽr)	125	35°08'N	81°08'W
Clover Bar, Can. (klō'vẽr bär)	102g	53°34'N	113°20'W
Cloverdale, Can.	116d	49°06'N	122°44'W
Cloverdale, Ca., U.S. (klō'vẽr-dāl)	118	38°47'N	123°03'W
Cloverport, Ky., U.S. (klō'vẽr pōrt)	108	37°50'N	86°35'W
Clovis, N.M., U.S. (klō'vĭs)	104	34°24'N	103°11'W
Cluj-Napoca, Rom.	154	46°46'N	23°34'E
Clun, r., Eng., U.K. (klŭn)	158a	52°25'N	2°56'W
Cluny, Fr. (klü-nē')	170	46°27'N	4°40'E
Clutha, r., N.Z. (klōō'thà)	221a	45°52'S	169°30'E
Clwyd, hist. reg., Wales, U.K.	158a	53°01'N	2°59'W
Clyde, Ks., U.S.	121	39°34'N	97°23'W
Clyde, Oh., U.S.	108	41°15'N	83°00'W
Clyde, r., Scot., U.K.	164	55°35'N	3°50'W
Clyde, Firth of, b., Scot., U.K. (fûrth ŏv klīd)	164	55°28'N	5°01'W
Côa, r., Port. (kō'ä)	172	40°28'N	6°55'W
Cocalco, Mex. (kō-ä-käl'kō)	131a	19°37'N	99°06'W
Coachella, Canal, can., Ca., U.S. (kō'chĕl-lá)	118	33°15'N	115°25'W
Coahuayana, Río de, r., Mex. (rē'ō-dĕ-kô-ä-wä-yä'nä)	130	19°00'N	103°33'W
Coahuayutla, Mex. (kō'ä-wī-yōōt'lä)	130	18°19'N	101°44'W
Coahuila, state, Mex. (kō-ä-wē'lä)	128	27°30'N	103°00'W
Coal City, Il., U.S. (kōl sĭ'tĭ)	111a	41°17'N	88°17'W
Coalcomán, Río de, r., Mex. (rē'ō-dĕ-kō-äl-kō-män')	130	18°45'N	103°15'W
Coalcomán, Sierra de, mts., Mex.	130	18°30'N	102°45'W
Coalcomán de Matamoros, Mex.	130	18°46'N	103°10'W
Coaldale, Can. (kōl'dāl)	95	49°43'N	112°37'W
Coalgate, Ok., U.S. (kōl'gāt)	121	34°44'N	96°13'W
Coal Grove, Oh., U.S. (kōl grōv)	108	38°20'N	82°40'W
Coalinga, Ca., U.S. (kō-á-lĭŋ'gá)	118	36°09'N	120°23'W
Coalville, Eng., U.K. (kōl'vĭl)	158a	52°43'N	1°21'W
Coamo, P.R. (kō-ä'mō)	129b	18°05'N	66°21'W
Coari, Braz. (kō-är'ē)	142	4°06'S	63°10'W
Coast Mountains, mts., N.A. (kōst)	92	54°10'N	128°00'W
Coast Ranges, mts., U.S.	106	41°28'N	123°30'W
Coatepec, Mex. (kō-ä-tä-pĕk)	130	19°23'N	98°44'W
Coatepec, Mex.	131a	19°08'N	99°25'W
Coatepec, Mex.	131	19°26'N	96°56'W
Coatepeque, El Sal.	132	13°56'N	89°30'W
Coatepeque, Guat. (kō-ä-tà-pā'kå)	132	14°40'N	91°52'W
Coatesville, Pa., U.S. (kōts'vĭl)	109	40°00'N	75°50'W
Coatetelco, Mex. (kō-ä-tà-tĕl'kō)	130	18°43'N	99°17'W
Coaticook, Can. (kō'tĭ-kŏŏk)	99	45°10'N	71°55'W
Coatlinchán, Mex. (kô-ä-tlē'n-chä'n)	131a	19°26'N	98°52'W
Coats, i., Can. (kōts)	93	62°23'N	82°11'W
Coats Land, reg., Ant.	224	74°00'S	30°00'W
Coatzacoalcos, Mex.	128	18°09'N	94°26'W
Coatzacoalcos, r., Mex.	131	17°40'N	94°41'W
Coba, hist., Mex. (kô'bä)	132a	20°23'N	87°23'W
Cobalt, Can. (kō'bôlt)	91	47°21'N	79°40'W
Cobán, Guat. (kō-bän')	128	15°28'N	90°19'W
Cobar, Austl.	219	31°28'S	145°50'E
Cobberas, Mount, mtn., Austl. (cŏ-bēr-ăs)	222	36°45'S	148°15'E
Cobequid Mountains, mts., Can.	100	45°35'N	64°10'W
Cobh, Ire. (kôv)	154	51°52'N	8°09'W
Cobija, Bol. (kô-bē'hä)	142	11°12'S	68°49'W
Cobourg, Can. (kō'bŏŏrg)	91	43°55'N	78°05'W
Cobre, r., Jam. (kō'brā)	134	18°05'N	77°00'W
Coburg, Austl.	217a	37°45'S	144°58'E
Coburg, Ger. (kō'bōōrg)	168	50°16'N	10°57'E
Cocentaina, Spain (kō-thĕn-tä-ē'nä)	173	38°44'N	0°27'W
Cochabamba, Bol.	142	17°24'S	66°09'W
Cochinos, Bahía, b., Cuba (bä-ē'ä-kô-chē'nōs)	134	22°05'N	81°10'W
Cochinos Banks, bk.	134	22°20'N	76°15'W
Cochiti Indian Reservation, I.R., N.M., U.S.	119	35°37'N	106°20'W
Cochran, Ga., U.S. (kŏk'răn)	124	32°23'N	83°23'W
Cochrane, Can. (kŏk'răn)	91	49°01'N	81°06'W
Cochrane, Can.	102e	51°11'N	114°28'W
Cockburn, i., Can. (kŏk-bûrn)	98	45°55'N	83°25'W
Cockeysville, Md., U.S. (kŏk'ĭz-vĭl)	110e	39°30'N	76°40'W
Cockrell Hill, Tx., U.S. (kŏk'rĕl)	117c	32°44'N	96°53'W
Coco, r., N.A.	129	14°55'N	83°45'W
Coco, Cayo, i., Cuba (kä'-yō-kô'kô)	134	22°30'S	78°30'W
Coco, Isla del, i., C.R. (ē's-lä-dĕl-kô-kô)	128	5°33'N	87°02'W
Cocoa, Fl., U.S. (kō'kō)	125a	28°21'N	80°44'W
Cocoa Beach, Fl., U.S.	125a	28°20'N	80°35'W
Cocoli, Pan. (kŏ-kŏ'lē)	128a	8°58'N	79°36'W
Coconino, Plateau, plat., Az., U.S. (kō kō nē'nō)	119	35°45'N	112°28'W
Cocos (Keeling) Islands, is., Oc. (kō'kōs)(kē'lĭng)	3	11°50'S	90°50'E
Coco Solito, Pan. (kō-kō-sō-lē'tō)	128a	9°21'N	79°53'W
Cocula, Mex. (kō-kōō'lä)	130	20°23'N	103°47'W
Cocula, r., Mex.	130	18°17'N	99°45'W
Cod, Cape, pen., Ma., U.S.	107	41°42'N	70°15'W
Codajás, Braz. (kō-dä-häzh')	142	3°44'S	62°09'W
Codera, Cabo, c., Ven. (kä'bô-kō-dĕ'rä)	143b	10°35'N	66°06'W
Codogno, Italy (kô-dō'nyō)	174	45°08'N	9°43'E
Codrington, Antig. (kŏd'rĭng-tŭn)	133b	17°39'N	61°49'W
Cody, Wy., U.S. (kō'dĭ)	115	44°31'N	109°02'W
Coelho da Rocha, Braz.	144b	22°47'S	43°23'W
Coemba, Ang.	236	12°08'S	18°05'E
Coesfeld, Ger. (kûs'fĕld)	171c	51°56'N	7°10'E
Coeur d'Alene, Id., U.S. (kûr dá-lān')	104	47°43'N	116°35'W
Coeur d'Alene, r., Id., U.S.	114	47°26'N	116°35'W
Coeur d'Alene Indian Reservation, I.R., Id., U.S.	114	47°18'N	116°45'W
Coeur d'Alene Lake, l., Id., U.S.	114	47°32'N	116°39'W
Coffeyville, Ks., U.S. (kŏf'ĭ-vĭl)	105	37°01'N	95°38'W
Coff's Harbour, Austl.	222	30°20'S	153°10'E
Cofimvaba, S. Afr. (căfĭm'vä-bá)	233c	32°01'S	27°37'E
Coghinas, r., Italy (kō'gē-nås)	174	40°31'N	9°00'E
Cognac, Fr. (kôn-yak')	161	45°41'N	0°22'W
Cohasset, Ma., U.S. (kô-hăs'ĕt)	101a	42°14'N	70°48'W
Cohoes, N.Y., U.S. (kô-hōz')	109	42°50'N	73°40'W
Coig, r., Arg. (kô'ĕk)	144	51°15'N	71°00'W
Coimbatore, India (kô-ēm-bá-tōr')	199	11°03'N	76°56'E
Coimbra, Port. (kô-ēm'brä)	154	40°14'N	8°23'W
Coín, Spain (kô-ēn')	172	36°40'N	4°45'W
Coina, Port. (kô-ē'ná)	173b	38°35'N	9°03'W
Coina, r., Port. (kô'y-nä)	173b	38°35'N	9°02'W
Coipasa, Salar de, pl., Bol. (sä-lä'r-dĕ-koi-pä'-sä)	142	19°12'S	69°13'W
Coixtlahuaca, Mex. (kō-ēks'tlä-wä'kä)	131	17°42'N	97°17'W
Cojedes, dept., Ven. (kô-kĕ'dĕs)	143b	9°50'N	68°21'W
Cojimar, Cuba (kō-hē-mär')	135a	23°10'N	82°19'W
Cojutepeque, El Sal. (kô-hô-tĕ-pā'kå)	132	13°45'N	88°50'W
Cokato, Mn., U.S. (kō-kā'tō)	113	45°03'N	94°11'W
Cokeburg, Pa., U.S. (kōk bŭgh)	111e	40°06'N	80°03'W
Colac, Austl. (kō'lăc)	222	38°25'S	143°40'E
Colares, Port. (kō-lä'rĕs)	173b	38°47'N	9°27'W
Colatina, Braz. (kō-lä-tē'nä)	143	19°33'S	40°42'W
Colby, Ks., U.S. (kōl'bĭ)	120	39°23'N	101°04'W
Colchagua, prov., Chile (kōl-chá'gwä)	141b	34°42'S	71°24'W
Colchester, Eng., U.K. (kōl'chĕs-tẽr)	165	51°52'N	0°50'E
Cold Lake, l., Can. (kōld)	96	54°33'N	110°05'W
Coldwater, Ks., U.S. (kōld'wô-tẽr)	120	37°14'N	99°21'W
Coldwater, Mi., U.S.	108	41°55'N	85°00'W
Coldwater, r., Ms., U.S.	124	34°25'N	90°12'W
Coldwater Creek, r., Tx., U.S.	120	36°10'N	101°45'W
Coleman, Tx., U.S. (kōl'măn)	122	31°50'N	99°25'W
Colenso, S. Afr. (kŏ-lĕnz'ō)	233c	28°48'S	29°49'E
Coleraine, N. Ire., U.K.	164	55°08'N	6°40'W
Coleraine, Mn., U.S. (kōl-rān')	113	47°16'N	93°29'W
Coleshill, Eng., U.K. (kōlz'hĭl)	158a	52°30'N	1°42'W
Colfax, Ia., U.S. (kōl'făks)	113	41°40'N	93°13'W
Colfax, La., U.S.	123	31°31'N	92°42'W
Colfax, Wa., U.S.	114	46°53'N	117°21'W
Colhué Huapi, l., Arg. (kôl-wā'ōá'pē)	144	45°30'S	68°45'W
Coligny, S. Afr.	238c	26°20'S	26°18'E
Colima, Mex. (kōlē'mä)	128	19°13'N	103°45'W
Colima, state, Mex.	130	19°10'N	104°00'W
Colima, Nevado de, mtn., Mex. (nĕ-vä'dô-dĕ-kô-lē'mä)	128	19°30'N	103°38'W
Coll, i., Scot., U.K. (kŏl)	164	56°42'N	6°23'W
College, Ak., U.S.	103	64°43'N	147°50'W
College Park, Ga., U.S. (kŏl'ĕj)	110c	33°39'N	84°27'W
College Park, Md., U.S.	110e	38°59'N	76°58'W
Collegeville, Pa., U.S. (kŏl'ĕj-vĭl)	110f	40°11'N	75°27'W
Collie, Austl. (kŏl'ē)	218	33°20'S	116°20'E
Collier Bay, b., Austl. (kŏl-yẽr)	220	15°30'S	123°30'E
Collingswood, N.J., U.S. (kŏl'ĭngz-wŏŏd)	110f	39°54'N	75°04'W
Collingwood, Can.	99	44°30'N	80°20'W
Collins, Ms., U.S. (kŏl'ĭns)	124	31°40'N	89°34'W
Collinsville, Il., U.S. (kŏl'ĭnz-vĭl)	117e	38°41'N	89°59'W
Collinsville, Ok., U.S.	121	36°21'N	95°50'W
Colmar, Fr. (kôl'mär)	161	48°03'N	7°25'E
Colmenar de Oreja, Spain (kôl-mā-när'dāōrā'hä)	172	40°06'N	3°25'W
Colmenar Viejo, Spain (kôl-mā-när'vyā'hō)	172	40°40'N	3°46'W
Cologne, Ger.	154	50°56'N	6°57'E
Colombia, Col. (kô-lôm'bē-ä)	142a	3°23'N	74°48'W
Colombia, nation, S.A.	142	3°30'N	72°30'W
Colombo, Sri L. (kō lôm'bō)	203	6°58'N	79°52'E
Colón, Arg. (kō-lōn')	141c	33°55'S	61°08'W
Colón, Cuba (kō-lô'n)	134	22°45'N	80°55'W
Colón, Mex. (kō-lōn')	130	20°46'N	100°02'W
Colón, Pan. (kō-lô'n)	129	9°22'N	79°54'W
Colón, Archipiélago de, is., Ec.	142	0°10'S	87°45'W
Colón, Montañas de, mts., Hond. (môn-tă'n-yäs-dĕ-kō-lô'n)	133	14°58'N	84°39'W
Colonia, Ur. (kō-lō'nē-ä)	144	34°27'S	57°50'W
Colonia, dept., Ur.	141c	34°08'S	57°50'W
Colonia Suiza, Ur. (kō-lō'nēä-sōē'zä)	141c	34°17'S	57°15'W
Colonna, Capo, c., Italy	175	39°02'N	17°15'E
Colonsay, i., Scot., U.K. (kŏl-ôn-sā')	165	56°08'N	6°08'E
Coloradas, Lomas, Arg. (lô'mäs-kō-lō-rä'däs)	144	43°30'S	68°00'W
Colorado, state, U.S.	104	39°30'N	106°55'W
Colorado, r., Arg.	144	38°30'S	66°00'W
Colorado, r., N.A.	106	36°00'N	113°30'W
Colorado, r., Tx., U.S.	106	30°08'N	97°33'W
Colorado City, Tx., U.S. (kŏl-ô-rä'dō sĭ'tĭ)	122	32°24'N	100°50'W
Colorado National Monument, rec., Co., U.S.	119	39°00'N	108°40'W
Colorado Plateau, plat., U.S.	106	36°20'N	109°25'W
Colorado River Aqueduct, aq., Ca., U.S.	118	33°38'N	115°43'W
Colorado River Indian Reservation, I.R., Az., U.S.	119	34°03'N	114°02'W
Colorados, Archipiélago de los, is., Cuba	134	22°25'N	84°25'W
Colorado Springs, Co., U.S. (kŏl-ô-rä'dō)	104	38°49'N	104°48'W
Colotepec, r., Mex. (kô-lô'tĕ-pĕk)	131	15°56'N	96°57'W
Colotlán, Mex. (kô-lô-tlän')	130	22°06'N	103°14'W
Colotlán, r., Mex.	130	22°09'N	103°17'W
Colquechaca, Bol. (kôl-kā-chä'kä)	142	18°47'S	66°02'W
Colstrip, Mt., U.S. (kōl'strip)	115	45°54'N	106°38'W
Colton, Ca., U.S. (kōl'tŭn)	117a	34°04'N	117°20'W
Columbia, Il., U.S. (kô-lŭm'bĭ-á)	117e	38°26'N	90°12'W
Columbia, Ky., U.S.	124	37°06'N	85°15'W
Columbia, Md., U.S.	110e	39°15'N	76°51'W
Columbia, Mo., U.S.	105	38°55'N	92°19'W
Columbia, Ms., U.S.	124	31°15'N	89°49'W
Columbia, Pa., U.S.	109	40°00'N	76°25'W
Columbia, S.C., U.S.	105	34°00'N	81°00'W
Columbia, Tn., U.S.	124	35°36'N	87°02'W
Columbia, r., N.A.	92	46°00'N	120°00'W
Columbia, Mount, mtn., Can.	95	52°09'N	117°25'W
Columbia City, In., U.S.	108	41°10'N	85°30'W
Columbia City, Or., U.S.	116c	45°53'N	112°49'W
Columbia Heights, Mn., U.S.	117g	45°03'N	93°15'W
Columbia Icefield, ice, Can.	95	52°08'N	117°26'W
Columbia Mountains, mts., N.A.	95	51°30'N	118°30'W
Columbiana, Al., U.S. (kô-ŭm-bĭ-ă'ná)	124	33°10'N	86°35'W
Columbretes, is., Spain (kô-lōōm-brĕ'tĕs)	173	39°54'N	0°54'E
Columbus, Ga., U.S. (kô-lŭm'bŭs)	105	32°29'N	84°56'W
Columbus, In., U.S.	108	39°15'N	85°55'W
Columbus, Ks., U.S.	121	37°10'N	94°50'W
Columbus, Ms., U.S.	124	33°30'N	88°25'W
Columbus, Mt., U.S.	115	45°39'N	109°15'W
Columbus, Ne., U.S.	112	41°25'N	97°25'W
Columbus, N.M., U.S.	119	31°50'N	107°40'W
Columbus, Oh., U.S.	105	40°00'N	83°00'W
Columbus, Tx., U.S.	123	29°44'N	96°34'W
Columbus, Wi., U.S.	113	43°20'N	89°01'W
Columbus Bank, bk. (kô-lŭm'bŭs)	135	22°05'N	75°30'W
Columbus Grove, Oh., U.S.	108	40°55'N	84°05'W
Columbus Point, c., Bah.	135	24°10'N	75°15'W
Colusa, Ca., U.S. (kô-lū'sá)	118	39°12'N	122°01'W
Colville, Wa., U.S. (kŏl'vĭl)	114	48°33'N	117°53'W
Colville, r., Ak., U.S.	103	69°00'N	156°25'W
Colville Indian Reservation, I.R., Wa., U.S.	114	48°15'N	119°00'W
Colville R, Wa., U.S.	114	48°25'N	117°58'W
Colvos Passage, strt., Wa., U.S. (kŏl'vōs)	116a	47°24'N	122°32'W
Colwood, Can. (kŏl'wŏŏd)	116a	48°26'N	123°30'W
Comacchio, Italy (kô-mäk'kyō)	174	44°42'N	12°12'E

ng-sing; ŋ-baŋk; N-nasalized n; nŏd; cŏmmit; ōld; ôbey; ôrder; oi-boil; fōōd; ŏŏ-as oo in foot; ou-out; s-soft; sh-dish; th-thin; pūre; ûnite; ûrn; stŭd; circŭs; ü-as in French tu; '-indeterminate vowel.

284 Comala – Cosamaloápan PRONOUNCING INDEX

PLACE (Pronunciation)	PAGE	LAT.	LONG.
Comala, Mex. (kō-mä-lä')	130	19°22'N	103°47'W
Comalapa, Guat. (kō-mä-lä'-pä)	132	14°43'N	90°56'W
Comalcalco, Mex. (kō-mäl-käl'kō)	131	18°16'N	93°13'W
Comanche, Ok., U.S. (kō-màn'chē)	121	34°20'N	97°58'W
Comanche, Tx., U.S.	122	31°54'N	98°37'W
Comanche Creek, r., Tx., U.S.	122	31°02'N	102°47'W
Comayagua, Hond. (kō-mä-yä'gwä)	128	14°24'N	87°36'W
Combahee, r., S.C., U.S. (kŏm-bȧ-hē')	125	32°42'N	80°40'W
Comer, Ga., U.S. (kŭm'ẽr)	124	34°02'N	83°07'W
Comete, Cape, c., T./C. Is. (kō-mā'tȧ)	135	21°45'N	71°25'W
Comilla, Bngl. (kō-mĭl'ä)	199	23°33'N	91°17'E
Comino, Cape, c., Italy (kō-mē'nō)	174	40°30'N	9°48'E
Comitán, Mex. (kō-mē-tän')	128	16°16'N	92°09'W
Commencement Bay, b., Wa., U.S. (kŏ-mĕns'mĕnt bā)	116a	47°17'N	122°21'W
Commentry, Fr. (kō-mäɴ-trē')	170	46°16'N	2°44'E
Commerce, Ga., U.S. (kŏm'ẽrs)	124	34°10'N	83°27'W
Commerce, Ok., U.S.	121	36°57'N	94°54'W
Commerce, Tx., U.S.	121	33°15'N	95°52'W
Como, Italy (kō'mō)	162	45°48'N	9°03'E
Como, Lago di, l., Italy (lä'gō-dē-kō'mō)	162	46°00'N	9°30'E
Comodoro Rivadavia, Arg.	144	45°47'S	67°31'W
Como-Est, Can.	102a	45°27'N	74°08'W
Comonfort, Mex. (kō-mōn-fō'rt)	130	20°43'N	100°47'W
Comorin, Cape, c., India (kŏ'mō-rĭn)	203	8°05'N	78°05'E
Comoros, nation, Afr.	233	12°30'S	42°45'E
Comox, Can. (kō'mŏks)	94	49°40'N	124°55'W
Companario, Cerro, mtn., S.A. (sĕ'r-rō-kôm-pä-nä'ryō)	141b	35°54'S	70°23'W
Compiègne, Fr. (kôɴ-pyĕn'y')	161	49°25'N	2°49'E
Comporta, Port. (kôm-pôr'tȧ)	173b	38°24'N	8°48'W
Compostela, Mex. (kōm-pô-stā'lä)	130	21°14'N	104°54'W
Compton, Ca., U.S. (kŏmpt'tŭn)	117a	33°54'N	118°14'W
Comrat, Mol. (kôm-rät')	181	46°17'N	28°38'E
Conakry, Gui. (kō-nà-krē')	230	9°31'N	13°43'W
Conanicut, i., R.I., U.S. (kŏn'ȧ-nĭ-kŭt)	110b	41°34'N	71°20'W
Conasauga, r., Ga., U.S. (kō-nà)	124	34°40'N	84°51'W
Concarneau, Fr. (kôɴ-kär-nō')	170	47°54'N	3°52'W
Concepción, Bol. (kōn-sĕp'syōn')	143	15°47'S	61°08'W
Concepción, Chile	144	36°51'S	72°59'W
Concepción, Pan.	133	8°31'N	82°38'W
Concepción, Para.	144	23°29'S	57°18'W
Concepcion, Phil.	213a	15°19'N	120°40'E
Concepción, vol., Nic.	132	11°36'N	85°43'W
Concepción, r., Mex.	128	30°25'N	112°20'W
Concepción del Mar, Guat. (kōn-sĕp-syōn'dĕl mär')	132	14°07'N	91°23'W
Concepción del Oro, Mex. (kōn-sĕp-syōn' dĕl ō'rō)	128	24°39'N	101°24'W
Concepción del Uruguay, Arg. (kôn-sĕp-syō'n-dĕl-ōō-rōō-gwī')	144	32°31'S	58°10'W
Conception, i., Bah.	135	23°50'N	75°05'W
Conception, Point, c., Ca., U.S.	106	34°27'N	120°28'W
Conception Bay, b., Can. (kŏn-sĕp'shŭn)	101	47°50'N	52°50'W
Concho, r., Tx., U.S. (kōn'chō)	122	31°34'N	100°00'W
Conchos, r., Mex.	128	29°30'N	105°00'W
Conchos, r., Mex. (kōn'chōs)	122	25°03'N	99°00'W
Concord, Ca., U.S. (kŏŋ'kôrd)	116b	37°58'N	122°02'W
Concord, Ma., U.S.	101a	42°28'N	71°21'W
Concord, N.C., U.S.	125	35°23'N	80°11'W
Concord, N.H., U.S.	105	43°10'N	71°30'W
Concordia, Arg. (kŏn-kôr'dĭ-ȧ)	144	31°18'S	57°59'W
Concordia, Col.	142a	6°04'N	75°54'W
Concordia, Mex. (kôn-kô'r-dyä)	130	23°17'N	106°06'W
Concordia, Ks., U.S.	121	39°32'N	97°39'W
Concrete, Wa., U.S. (kŏn-'krēt)	114	48°33'N	121°44'W
Conde, Fr.	170	48°50'N	0°36'W
Conde, S.D., U.S. (kŏn-dē')	112	45°10'N	98°06'W
Condega, Nic. (kŏn-dĕ'gä)	132	13°20'N	86°27'W
Condeúba, Braz. (kōn-dā-ōō'bä)	143	14°47'S	41°44'W
Condom, Fr.	170	43°58'N	0°22'E
Condon, Or., U.S. (kŏn'dŭn)	114	45°14'N	120°10'W
Conecuh, r., Al., U.S. (kō-nē'kŭ)	124	31°05'N	86°52'W
Conegliano, Italy (kō-nål-yä'nō)	174	45°59'N	12°17'E
Conejos, r., Co., U.S. (kō-nā'hōs)	119	37°07'N	106°19'W
Conemaugh, Pa., U.S. (kŏn'ē-mô)	109	40°25'N	78°50'W
Coney Island, i., N.Y., U.S. (kō'nĭ)	110a	40°34'N	73°27'W
Confolens, Fr. (kôɴ-fā-läɴ')	170	46°01'N	0°41'E
Congaree, r., S.C., U.S. (kŏŋ-gȧ-rē')	125	33°53'N	80°55'W
Conghua, China (tsôŋ-hwä)	209	23°30'N	113°40'E
Congleton, Eng., U.K. (kŏŋ'g'l-tŭn)	158a	53°10'N	2°13'W
Congo, nation, Afr. (kŏn'gō)	232	3°00'S	13°48'E
Congo (Zaire), r., Afr. (kŏn'gō)	229	2°00'S	17°00'E
Congo, Democratic Republic of the (Zaire), nation, Afr.	232	1°00'S	22°15'E
Congo, Serra do, mts., Ang.	236	6°25'S	13°30'E
Congo Basin, basin, D.R.C.	229	2°47'N	20°58'E
Conisbrough, Eng., U.K. (kŏn'ĭs-bŭr-ō)	158a	53°29'N	1°13'W
Coniston, Can.	99	46°29'N	80°51'W
Conklin, Can. (kŏŋk'lĭn)	95	55°38'N	111°05'W
Conley, Ga., U.S. (kŏn'lĭ)	110c	33°38'N	84°19'W
Conn, Lough, l., Ire. (lŏk kŏn)	164	53°56'N	9°25'W
Connacht, hist. reg., Ire. (cŏn'ȧt)	164	53°50'N	8°45'W
Conneaut, Oh., U.S. (kŏn-ē-ôt')	108	41°55'N	80°35'W
Connecticut, state, U.S. (kŏ-nĕt'ĭ-kŭt)	105	41°40'N	73°10'W
Connecticut, r., U.S.	107	43°55'N	72°15'W
Connellsville, Pa., U.S. (kŏn'nĕlz-vĭl)	109	40°00'N	79°40'W
Connemara, mts., Ire. (kŏn-nē-mȧ'rȧ)	164	53°30'N	9°54'W
Connersville, In., U.S. (kŏn'ẽrz-vĭl)	108	39°35'N	85°10'W

PLACE (Pronunciation)	PAGE	LAT.	LONG.
Connors Range, mts., Austl. (kŏn'nŏrs)	221	22°15'S	149°00'E
Conrad, Mt., U.S. (kŏn'răd)	115	48°11'N	111°56'W
Conrich, Can. (kŏn'rĭch)	102e	51°06'N	113°51'W
Conroe, Tx., U.S. (kŏn'rō)	123	30°18'N	95°23'W
Conselheiro Lafaiete, Braz.	143	20°40'S	43°46'W
Conshohocken, Pa., U.S. (kŏn-shō-hŏk'ĕn)	110f	40°04'N	75°18'W
Consolación del Sur, Cuba (kōn-sō-lä-syōn')	134	22°30'N	83°55'W
Con Son, is., Viet.	212	8°30'N	106°28'E
Constance, Mount, mtn., Wa., U.S. (kŏn'stăns)	116a	47°46'N	123°08'W
Constanţa, Rom. (kōn-stán'tsȧ)	154	44°12'N	28°36'E
Constantina, Spain (kōn-stän-tē'nä)	172	37°52'N	5°39'W
Constantine, Alg. (kôɴ-stäɴ'tēn')	230	36°28'N	6°38'E
Constantine, Mi., U.S. (kŏn'stăn-tēn)	108	41°50'N	85°40'W
Constitución, Chile (kōn'stĭ-tōō-syōn')	144	35°24'S	72°25'W
Constitution, Ga., U.S. (kŏn-stĭ-tū'shŭn)	110c	33°41'N	84°20'W
Contagem, Braz. (kōn-tá'zhĕm)	141a	19°54'S	44°05'W
Contepec, Mex. (kōn-tĕ-pĕk')	130	20°04'N	100°07'W
Contreras, Mex. (kôn-trĕ'räs)	131a	19°18'N	99°14'W
Contwoyto, l., Can.	92	65°42'N	110°50'W
Converse, Tx., U.S. (kŏn'vẽrs)	117d	29°31'N	98°17'W
Conway, Ar., U.S. (kŏn'wā)	121	35°06'N	92°27'W
Conway, N.H., U.S.	109	44°00'N	71°10'W
Conway, S.C., U.S.	125	33°49'N	79°01'W
Conway, Wa., U.S.	116a	48°20'N	122°20'W
Conyers, Ga., U.S. (kŏn'yẽrz)	124	33°41'N	84°01'W
Cooch Behār, India (kōōch bē-här')	199	26°25'N	89°34'E
Cook, Cape, c., Can. (kŏŏk)	94	50°08'N	127°55'W
Cook, Mount *see* Aoraki, mtn., N.Z.	221a	43°27'S	170°13'E
Cookeville, Tn., U.S. (kŏŏk'vĭl)	124	36°07'N	85°30'W
Cooking Lake, Can. (kŏŏk'ĭng)	102g	53°25'N	113°08'W
Cooking Lake, l., Can.	102g	53°25'N	113°02'W
Cook Inlet, b., Ak., U.S.	103	60°50'N	151°38'W
Cook Islands, dep., Oc.	2	20°00'S	158°00'W
Cook Strait, str., N.Z.	221a	40°37'S	174°15'E
Cooktown, Austl. (kŏŏk'toun)	219	15°40'S	145°20'E
Cooleemee, N.C., U.S. (kōō-lē'mē)	125	35°50'N	80°32'W
Coolgardie, Austl. (kōōl-gär'dē)	218	31°00'S	121°25'E
Cooma, Austl. (kōō'mȧ)	219	36°22'S	149°10'E
Coonamble, Austl. (kōō-năm'b'l)	219	31°00'S	148°30'E
Coonoor, India	203	10°22'N	76°15'E
Coon Rapids, Mn., U.S. (kōn)	117g	45°09'N	93°17'W
Cooper, Tx., U.S. (kōōp'ẽr)	121	33°23'N	95°40'W
Cooper Center, Ak., U.S.	103	61°54'N	15°30'W
Coopers Creek, r., Austl. (kōō'pẽrz)	221	27°32'N	141°19'E
Cooperstown, N.D., U.S.	112	47°26'N	98°07'W
Cooperstown, N.Y., U.S. (kōōp'ẽrs-toun)	109	42°45'N	74°55'W
Coosa, Al., U.S. (kōō'sȧ)	124	32°43'N	86°25'W
Coosa, r., U.S.	107	34°00'N	86°00'W
Coosawattee, r., Ga., U.S.	124	34°37'N	84°45'W
Coos Bay, Or., U.S. (kōōs)	114	43°21'N	124°12'W
Coos Bay, b., Or., U.S.	114	43°19'N	124°40'W
Cootamundra, Austl. (kŏŏtȧ-mŭnd'rȧ)	222	34°25'S	148°00'E
Copacabana, Braz. (kô'pä-kȧ-bá'nä)	144b	22°57'S	43°11'W
Copalita, r., Mex. (kō-pä-lē'tä)	131	15°55'N	96°06'W
Copán, hist., Hond. (kō-pän')	132	14°50'N	89°10'W
Copano Bay, b., Tx., U.S. (kō-pän'ō)	123	28°08'N	97°25'W
Copenhagen (København), Den.	154	55°43'N	12°27'E
Copiapó, Chile (kō-pyä-pō')	144	27°16'S	70°28'W
Copley, Oh., U.S. (kŏp'lē)	111d	41°06'N	81°38'W
Copparo, Italy (kôp-pä'rō)	174	44°53'N	11°50'E
Coppell, Tx., U.S. (kŏp'pĕl)	117c	32°57'N	97°00'W
Copper, r., Ak., U.S. (kŏp'ẽr)	103	62°38'N	145°00'W
Copper Cliff, Can.	98	46°28'N	81°04'W
Copper Harbor, Mi., U.S.	113	47°27'N	87°53'W
Copperhill, Tn., U.S. (kŏp'ẽr hĭl)	124	35°00'N	84°22'W
Coppermine *see* Kugluktuk, Can.	92	67°46'N	115°19'W
Coppermine, r., Can.	92	66°48'N	114°59'W
Copper Mountain, mtn., Ak., U.S.	94	55°14'N	132°36'W
Copperton, Ut., U.S. (kŏp'ẽr-tŭn)	117b	40°34'N	112°06'W
Coquilee, Or., U.S. (kō-kēl')	114	43°11'N	124°11'W
Coquilhatville *see* Mbandaka, D.R.C.	232	0°04'N	18°16'E
Coquimbo, Chile (kō-kēm'bō)	144	29°58'S	71°31'W
Coquimbo, prov., Chile	141b	31°50'S	71°05'W
Coquitlam Lake, l., Can. (kō-kwĭt-lȧm)	116d	49°23'N	122°44'W
Corabia, Rom. (kō-rä'bĭ-ȧ)	163	43°45'N	24°29'E
Coracora, Peru (kō'rä-kō'rä)	142	15°12'S	73°42'W
Coral Gables, Fl., U.S.	125a	25°43'N	80°14'W
Coral Rapids, Can. (kŏr'ăl)	91	50°18'N	81°49'W
Coral Sea, sea, Oc. (kŏr'ăl)	221	13°30'S	150°00'E
Coralville Reservoir, res., Ia., U.S.	113	41°45'N	91°50'W
Corangamite, Lake, l., Austl. (cŏr-ăŋg'ȧ-mīt)	222	38°05'S	142°55'E
Coraopolis, Pa., U.S. (kō-rä-ŏp'ō-lĭs)	111e	40°30'N	80°09'W
Corato, Italy (kō'rä-tō)	174	41°08'N	16°28'E
Corbeil-Essonnes, Fr. (kôr-bā'yĕ-sōn')	170	48°31'N	2°29'E
Corbett, Or., U.S. (kôr'bĕt)	116c	45°31'N	122°17'W
Corbie, Fr. (kôr-bē')	170	49°55'N	2°27'E
Corbin, Ky., U.S. (kôr'bĭn)	124	36°55'N	84°06'W
Corby, Eng., U.K. (kôr'bĭ)	158a	52°29'N	0°38'W
Corcovado, mtn., Braz. (kôr-kō-vä'dō)	144b	22°57'S	43°13'W
Corcovado, Golfo, b., Chile (kôr-kō-vä'dhō)	144	43°40'S	75°00'W
Cordeiro, Braz. (kôr-dā'rō)	141a	22°03'S	42°22'W
Cordele, Ga., U.S. (kôr-dēl')	124	31°55'N	83°50'W
Cordell, Ok., U.S. (kôr-dĕl')	120	35°19'N	98°58'W

PLACE (Pronunciation)	PAGE	LAT.	LONG.
Córdoba, Arg. (kôr'dō-vä)	144	30°20'S	64°03'W
Córdoba, Mex. (kô'r-dō-bä)	128	18°53'N	96°54'W
Córdoba, Spain (kô'r-dô-bä)	172	37°55'N	4°45'W
Córdoba, prov., Arg. (kôr'dō-vä)	144	32°00'S	64°00'W
Córdoba, Sierra de, mts., Arg.	144	31°15'S	64°30'W
Cordova, Ak., U.S. (kôr'dō-vä)	106a	60°34'N	145°38'W
Cordova, Al., U.S. (kôr'dō-ȧ)	124	33°45'N	86°22'W
Cordova Bay, b., Ak., U.S.	94	54°55'N	132°35'W
Corfu *see* Kérkira, i., Grc.	156	39°33'N	19°36'E
Corigliano, Italy (kō-rē-lyä'nō)	174	39°35'N	16°30'E
Corinth *see* Kórinthos, Grc.	154	37°56'N	22°54'E
Corinth, Ms., U.S. (kŏr'ĭnth)	124	34°55'N	88°30'W
Corinto, Braz. (kō-rē'n-tō)	143	18°20'S	44°16'W
Corinto, Col.	142a	3°09'N	76°12'W
Corinto, Nic. (kōr-ĭn'to)	132	12°30'N	87°12'W
Corio, Austl.	217a	38°05'S	144°22'E
Corio Bay, b., Austl.	217a	38°07'S	144°25'E
Corisco, Isla de, i., Eq. Gui.	236	0°50'N	8°40'E
Cork, Ire. (kôrk)	154	51°54'N	8°25'W
Cork Harbour, b., Ire.	164	51°44'N	8°15'W
Corleone, Italy (kôr-lā-ō'nā)	174	37°48'N	13°18'E
Cormorant Lake, l., Can.	97	54°13'N	100°47'W
Cornelia, Ga., U.S. (kôr-nē'lyȧ)	124	34°31'N	83°30'W
Cornelis, r., S. Afr. (kôr-nē'lĭs)	238c	27°48'S	29°15'E
Cornell, Ca., U.S. (kôr-nĕl')	117a	34°06'N	118°46'W
Cornell, Wi., U.S.	113	45°10'N	91°10'W
Corner Brook, Can. (kôr'nẽr)	91	48°57'N	57°57'W
Corner Inlet, b., Austl.	222	38°55'S	146°45'E
Corning, Ar., U.S. (kôr'nĭng)	121	36°26'N	90°35'W
Corning, Ia., U.S.	113	40°58'N	94°40'W
Corning, N.Y., U.S.	109	42°10'N	77°05'W
Corno, Monte, mtn., Italy (kôr'nō)	162	42°28'N	13°37'E
Cornwall, Bah.	134	25°55'N	77°15'W
Cornwall, Can. (kôrn'wôl)	99	45°05'N	74°35'W
Coro, Ven. (kō'rō)	142	11°22'N	69°43'W
Corocoro, Bol. (kō-rō-kō'rō)	142	17°15'S	68°21'W
Coromandel Coast, cst., India (kŏr-ō-man'dĕl)	199	13°30'N	80°30'E
Coromandel Peninsula, pen., N.Z.	223	36°50'S	176°00'E
Corona, Al., U.S. (kō-rō'nȧ)	124	33°42'N	87°28'W
Corona, Ca., U.S.	117a	33°52'N	117°34'W
Coronada, Bahía de, b., C.R. (bä-ē'ä-dĕ-kō-rō-nä'dō)	133	8°47'N	84°04'W
Corona del Mar, Ca., U.S. (kō-rō'nȧ dĕl mär)	117a	33°36'N	117°53'W
Coronado, Ca., U.S. (kŏr-ō-nä'dō)	118a	32°42'N	117°12'W
Coronation Gulf, b., Can. (kŏr-ō-nā'shŭn)	92	68°07'N	112°50'W
Coronel, Chile (kō-rō-nĕl')	144	37°00'S	73°10'W
Coronel Brandsen, Arg. (kō-rō-nĕl-brá'nd-sĕn)	141c	35°09'S	58°15'W
Coronel Dorrego, Arg. (kō-rō-nĕl-dôr-rĕ'gō)	144	38°43'S	61°16'W
Coronel Oviedo, Para. (kō-rō-nĕl-ō-vē-ĕ'dō)	144	25°28'S	56°22'W
Coronel Pringles, Arg. (kō-rō-nĕl-prēn'glĕs)	144	37°54'S	61°22'W
Coronel Suárez, Arg. (kō-rō-nĕl-swä'rās)	144	37°27'S	61°49'W
Corowa, Austl. (cŏr-ŏwȧ)	222	36°02'S	146°23'E
Corozal, Belize (cŏr-ŏth-äl')	132a	18°25'N	88°23'W
Corpus Christi, Tx., U.S. (kôr'pŭs krĭstē)	104	27°48'N	97°24'W
Corpus Christi Bay, b., Tx., U.S.	123	27°47'N	97°14'W
Corpus Christi Lake, l., Tx., U.S.	122	28°08'N	98°20'W
Corral, Chile (kō-räl')	144	39°57'S	73°15'W
Corral de Almaguer, Spain (kō-räl'dā äl-mä-gâr')	172	39°45'N	3°10'W
Corralillo, Cuba (kō-rä-lē-yō)	134	23°00'N	80°40'W
Corregidor Island, i., Phil. (kō-rā-hē-dōr')	213a	14°21'N	120°25'E
Correntina, Braz. (kō-rĕn-tē-nȧ)	143	13°18'S	44°33'W
Corrib, Lough, l., Ire. (lŏk kŏr'ĭb)	164	53°25'N	9°19'W
Corrientes, Arg. (kō-ryĕn'tās)	144	27°25'S	58°39'W
Corrientes, prov., Arg.	144	28°45'S	58°00'W
Corrientes, Cabo, c., Col. (ká'bō-kō-ryĕn'tās)	142	5°34'N	77°35'W
Corrientes, Cabo, c., Cuba (ká'bō-kôr-rē-ĕn'tĕs)	134	21°50'N	84°25'W
Corrientes, Cabo, c., Mex.	128	20°25'N	105°41'W
Corry, Pa., U.S. (kŏr'ĭ)	109	41°55'N	79°40'W
Corse, Cap, c., Fr. (kôrs)	161	42°59'N	9°19'E
Corsica, i., Fr. (kô'r-sē-kä)	156	42°10'N	8°55'E
Corsicana, Tx., U.S. (kôr-sĭ-kăn'ȧ)	104	32°06'N	96°28'W
Cortazar, Mex. (kôr-tä-zär)	130	20°30'N	100°57'W
Corte, Fr. (kôr'tā)	174	42°18'N	9°10'E
Cortegana, Spain (kôr-tå-gä'nä)	172	37°54'N	6°48'W
Cortés, Ensendada de, b., Cuba (ĕn-sĕ-nä-dä-dĕ-kôr-tās')	134	22°05'N	83°45'W
Cortez, Co., U.S.	119	37°21'N	108°35'W
Cortland, N.Y., U.S. (kôrt'lănd)	109	42°35'N	76°10'W
Cortona, Italy (kôr-tō'nä)	174	43°16'N	12°00'E
Corubal, r., Gui.-B.	234	11°43'N	14°40'W
Coruche, Port. (kō-rōō'she)	172	38°58'N	8°34'W
Çoruh, r., Asia (chō-rōōk')	181	40°30'N	41°10'E
Çorum, Tur. (chō-rōōm')	198	40°34'N	34°45'E
Corunna, Mi., U.S. (kō-rŭn'ȧ)	108	43°00'N	84°05'W
Coruripe, Braz. (kō-rō-rē'pĭ)	143	10°09'S	36°13'W
Corvallis, Or., U.S. (kŏr-văl'ĭs)	104	44°34'N	123°17'W
Corve, r., Eng., U.K. (kôr'vē)	158a	52°28'N	2°43'W
Corydon, Ia., U.S.	113	40°45'N	93°20'W
Corydon, In., U.S. (kŏr'ĭ-dŭn)	108	38°10'N	86°05'W
Corydon, Ky., U.S.	108	37°45'N	87°40'W
Cosamaloápan, Mex. (kō-sä-mä-lwä'pän)	131	18°21'N	95°48'W

PRONOUNCING INDEX Coscomatepec – Cuilo 285

PLACE (Pronunciation)	PAGE	LAT.	LONG.
Coscomatepec, Mex. (kôs′kōmä-tě-pěk′)	131	19°04′N	97°03′W
Cosenza, Italy (kô-zěnt′sä)	163	39°18′N	16°15′E
Coshocton, Oh., U.S. (kô-shŏk′tŭn)	108	40°15′N	81°55′W
Cosigüina, vol., Nic.	132	12°59′N	87°35′W
Cosmoledo Group, is., Sey. (kŏs-mô-lā′dō)	233	9°42′S	47°45′E
Cosmopolis, Wa., U.S. (kŏz-mŏp′ô-lĭs)	114	46°58′N	123°47′W
Cosne-sur-Loire, Fr. (kōn-sür-lwär′)	170	47°25′N	2°57′E
Cosoleacaque, Mex. (kō sō lā-ä-kä′kē)	131	18°01′N	94°38′W
Costa de Caparica, Port.	173b	38°40′N	9°12′W
Costa Mesa, Ca., U.S. (kŏs′tȧ mā′sȧ)	117a	33°39′N	118°54′W
Costa Rica, nation, N.A. (kŏs′tȧ rē′kȧ)	129	10°30′N	84°30′W
Cosumnes, r., Ca., U.S. (kō-sŭm′nĕz)	118	38°21′N	121°17′W
Cotabambas, Peru (kô-tä-bȧm′bäs)	142	13°49′S	72°17′W
Cotabato, Phil. (kō-tä-bä′tō)	213	7°06′N	124°13′E
Cotaxtla, Mex. (kō-täs′tlä)	131	18°49′N	96°22′W
Cotaxtla, r., Mex.	131	18°54′N	96°21′W
Coteau-du-Lac, Can. (cō-tō′dü-läk)	102a	45°17′N	74°11′W
Coteau-Landing, Can.	102a	45°15′N	74°13′W
Coteaux, Haiti	135	18°15′N	74°05′W
Cote d'Ivoire (Ivory Coast), nation, Afr.	230	7°43′N	6°30′W
Côte d'Or, reg., Fr.	170	47°02′N	4°35′E
Cotija de la Paz, Mex. (kô-tē′-кä-dě-lä-pá′z)	130	19°46′N	102°43′W
Cotonou, Benin (kô-tô-nōō′)	230	6°21′N	2°26′E
Cotopaxi, mtn., Ec. (kō-tô-päk′sē)	142	0°40′S	78°26′W
Cotorro, Cuba (kô-tôr-rō)	135a	23°03′N	82°17′W
Cotswold Hills, hills, Eng., U.K. (kŭtz′wōld)	164	51°35′N	2°16′W
Cottage Grove, Mn., U.S. (kŏt′āj grōv)	117g	44°50′N	92°52′W
Cottage Grove, Or., U.S.	114	43°48′N	123°04′W
Cottbus, Ger. (kōtt′bōōs)	161	51°47′N	14°20′E
Cottonwood, r., Mn., U.S. (kŏt′ŭn-wŏŏd)	112	44°25′N	95°35′W
Cotulla, Tx., U.S. (kō-tŭl′lȧ)	122	28°26′N	99°14′W
Coubert, Fr. (kōō-bâr′)	171b	48°40′N	2°43′E
Coudersport, Pa., U.S. (kou′dērz-pōrt)	109	41°45′N	78°00′W
Coudres, Île aux, i., Can.	100	47°17′N	70°12′W
Coulommiers, Fr. (kōō-lô-myā′)	171b	48°49′N	3°05′E
Coulto, Serra do, mts., Braz. (sě′r-rä-dô-kô-ô′tô)	144b	22°33′S	43°27′W
Council Bluffs, Ia., U.S. (koun′sĭl blŭf)	105	41°16′N	95°53′W
Council Grove, Ks., U.S. (koun′sĭl grōv)	121	38°39′N	96°30′W
Coupeville, Wa., U.S. (kōōp′vĭl)	116a	48°13′N	122°41′W
Courantyne, r., S.A. (kôr′ăntīn)	143	4°28′N	57°42′W
Courtenay, Can. (cōōrt-nā′)	90	49°41′N	125°00′W
Coushatta, La., U.S. (kou-shăt′ȧ)	123	32°02′N	93°21′W
Coutras, Fr. (kōō-trá′)	170	45°02′N	0°07′W
Covelo, Ang.	236	12°06′S	13°55′E
Coventry, Eng., U.K. (kŭv′ĕn-trĭ)	164	52°25′N	1°29′W
Covina, Ca., U.S. (kô-vē′nȧ)	117a	34°06′N	117°54′W
Covington, Ga., U.S. (kŭv′ĭng-tŭn)	124	33°36′N	83°50′W
Covington, In., U.S.	108	40°10′N	87°15′W
Covington, Ky., U.S.	105	39°05′N	84°31′W
Covington, La., U.S.	123	30°30′N	90°06′W
Covington, Oh., U.S.	108	40°10′N	84°20′W
Covington, Ok., U.S.	121	36°18′N	97°32′W
Covington, Tn., U.S.	124	35°33′N	89°40′W
Covington, Va., U.S.	108	37°50′N	80°00′W
Cowal, Lake, l., Austl. (kou′ăl)	222	33°30′S	147°10′E
Cowan, l., Austl. (kou′ăn)	220	32°00′S	122°30′E
Cowansville, Can.	99	45°13′N	72°47′W
Cow Creek, r., Or., U.S. (kou)	114	42°45′N	123°35′W
Cowes, Eng., U.K. (kouz)	164	50°43′N	1°25′W
Cowichan Lake, l., Can.	94	48°54′N	124°20′W
Cowlitz, r., Wa., U.S. (kou′lĭts)	114	46°30′N	122°45′W
Cowra, Austl. (kou′rȧ)	222	33°50′S	148°33′E
Coxim, Braz. (kō-shēɴ′)	143	18°32′S	54°43′W
Coxquihui, Mex. (kōz-kē-wē′)	131	20°10′N	97°34′W
Cox's Bāzār, Bngl.	202	21°32′N	92°00′E
Coyaima, Col. (kô-yaè′mä)	142a	3°48′N	75°11′W
Coyame, Mex. (kō-yä′mä)	122	29°26′N	105°05′W
Coyanosa Draw, Tx., U.S. (kô yá-nō′sä)	122	30°55′N	103°07′W
Coyoacán, Mex. (kô-yô-á-kän′)	130	19°21′N	99°10′W
Coyote, r., Ca., U.S. (kī′ōt)	116b	37°37′N	121°57′W
Coyuca de Benítez, Mex. (kō-yōō′kä dā bā-nē′tāz)	130	17°04′N	100°06′W
Coyuca de Catalán, Mex. (kō-yōō′kä dā kä-tä-län′)	130	18°19′N	100°41′W
Coyutla, Mex. (kō-yōō′tlä)	131	20°13′N	97°40′W
Cozad, Ne., U.S. (kō′zăd)	120	40°53′N	99°59′W
Cozaddale, Oh., U.S. (kō-zăd-dāl)	111f	39°16′N	84°09′W
Cozoyoapan, Mex. (kô-zô-yô-ä-pä′n)	130	16°45′N	98°17′W
Cozumel, Mex. (kŏ-zōō-mě′l)	132a	20°31′N	86°55′W
Cozumel, Isla de, i., Mex. (ē′s-lä-dĕ-kŏ-zōō-mĕ′l)	128	20°26′N	87°10′W
Crab Creek, r., Wa., U.S. (krăb)	114	46°47′N	119°43′W
Crab Creek, r., Wa., U.S.	114	47°21′N	119°09′W
Cradock, S. Afr. (kră′dŭk)	232	32°12′S	25°38′E
Crafton, Pa., U.S. (krăf′tŭn)	111e	40°26′N	80°04′W
Craig, Co., U.S. (krāg)	115	40°32′N	107°31′W
Craiova, Rom. (krá-yō′vá)	163	44°18′N	23°50′E
Cranberry, l., N.Y., U.S. (krăn′běr-ĭ)	109	44°10′N	74°50′W
Cranbourne, Austl.	217a	38°07′S	145°16′E
Cranbrook, Can. (krăn′brŏŏk)	90	49°31′N	115°46′W
Cranbury, N.J., U.S. (krăn′bē-rĭ)	110a	40°19′N	74°31′W
Crandon, Wi., U.S. (krăn′dŭn)	113	45°35′N	88°55′W
Crane Prairie Reservoir, res., Or., U.S.	114	43°50′N	121°55′W
Cranston, R.I., U.S. (krăns′tŭn)	110b	41°46′N	71°25′W
Crater Lake, l., Or., U.S. (krā′tēr)	114	43°00′N	122°08′W
Crater Lake National Park, rec., Or., U.S.	114	42°58′N	122°40′W
Craters of the Moon National Monument, rec., Id., U.S. (krā′tēr)	115	43°28′N	113°15′W
Crateús, Braz. (krä-tå-ōōzh′)	143	5°09′S	40°35′W
Crato, Braz. (krä′tò)	143	7°19′S	39°13′W
Crawford, Ne., U.S. (krô′fērd)	112	42°41′N	103°25′W
Crawford, Wa., U.S.	116c	45°49′N	122°24′W
Crawfordsville, In., U.S. (krô′fērdz-vĭl)	108	40°00′N	86°55′W
Crazy Mountains, mts., Mt., U.S. (krā′zĭ)	115	46°11′N	110°25′W
Crazy Woman Creek, r., Wy., U.S.	115	44°08′N	106°40′W
Crecy, S. Afr. (krě-sē)	238c	24°38′S	28°52′E
Crécy-en-Brie, Fr. (krā-sē′-ěɴ-brē′)	171b	48°52′N	2°55′E
Crécy-en-Ponthieu, Fr.	170	50°13′N	1°48′E
Credit, r., Can.	102d	43°41′N	79°55′W
Cree, l., Can. (krē)	92	57°35′N	107°52′W
Creighton, S. Afr. (cre-tŏn)	233c	30°02′S	29°52′E
Creighton, Ne., U.S. (krā′tŭn)	112	42°27′N	97°54′W
Creil, Fr. (krě′y′)	170	49°18′N	2°28′E
Crema, Italy (krā′mä)	174	45°21′N	9°53′E
Cremona, Italy (krā-mō′nä)	162	45°09′N	10°02′E
Crépy-en-Valois, Fr. (krā-pē′ěɴ-vä-lwä′)	171b	49°14′N	2°53′E
Cres, Cro. (tsrěs)	174	44°58′N	14°21′E
Crescent Beach, Can.	116d	49°03′N	122°58′W
Crescent City, Ca., U.S. (krěs′ěnt)	114	41°46′N	124°13′W
Crescent City, Fl., U.S.	125	29°26′N	81°35′W
Crescent Lake, l., Fl., U.S. (krěs′ěnt)	125	29°33′N	81°30′W
Crescent Lake, l., Or., U.S.	114	43°25′N	121°58′W
Cresco, Ia., U.S. (krěs′kō)	113	43°23′N	92°07′W
Crested Butte, Co., U.S. (krěst′ěd būt)	119	38°50′N	107°00′W
Crestline, Ca., U.S. (krěst-līn)	117a	34°15′N	117°17′W
Crestline, Oh., U.S.	108	40°50′N	82°40′W
Crestmore, Ca., U.S. (krěst′môr)	117a	34°02′N	117°23′W
Creston, Can. (krěs′tŭn)	90	49°06′N	116°31′W
Creston, Ia., U.S.	113	41°04′N	94°22′W
Creston, Oh., U.S.	111d	40°59′N	81°54′W
Crestview, Fl., U.S. (krěst′vū)	124	30°44′N	86°35′W
Crestwood, Ky., U.S. (krěst′wŏŏd)	111h	38°20′N	85°28′W
Crestwood, Mo., U.S.	117e	38°33′N	90°23′W
Crete, Il., U.S. (krēt)	111a	41°26′N	87°38′W
Crete, Ne., U.S.	121	40°38′N	96°56′W
Crete, i., Grc.	156	35°15′N	24°30′E
Creus, Cap de, c., Spain	173	42°16′N	3°18′E
Creuse, r., Fr. (krûz)	170	46°51′N	0°49′E
Creve Coeur, Mo., U.S. (krēv kör)	117e	38°40′N	90°27′W
Crevillent, Spain	173	38°12′N	0°48′W
Crewe, Eng., U.K. (krōō)	164	53°06′N	2°27′W
Crewe, Va., U.S.	125	37°09′N	78°08′W
Crimean Peninsula see Kryms'kyi Pivostriv, pen., Ukr.	181	45°18′N	33°30′E
Crimmitschau, Ger. (krĭm′ĭt-shou)	168	50°49′N	12°22′E
Cripple Creek, Co., U.S. (krĭp′′l)	120	38°44′N	105°12′W
Crisfield, Md., U.S. (krĭs-fēld)	109	38°00′N	75°50′W
Cristal, Monts de, mts., Gabon	236	0°50′N	10°30′E
Cristina, Braz. (krēs-tē′-nä)	141a	22°13′S	45°15′W
Cristóbal Colón, Pico, mtn., Col. (pē′kô-krēs-tô′bäl-kō-lôn′)	142	11°00′N	74°00′W
Crişul Alb, r., Rom. (krē′shōōl älb)	169	46°20′N	22°15′E
Crna, r., Serb. (ts′r′nä)	175	41°03′N	21°46′E
Crna Gora (Montenegro), state, Serb.	175	42°55′N	18°52′E
Črnomelj, Slvn. (ch′r′nō-māl′)	174	45°35′N	15°11′E
Croatia, nation, Eur.	174	45°24′N	15°18′E
Crockett, Ca., U.S. (krŏk′ět)	116b	38°03′N	122°14′W
Crockett, Tx., U.S.	123	31°19′N	95°28′W
Crofton, Md., U.S.	110e	39°01′N	76°43′W
Crofton, Ne., U.S.	112	42°44′N	97°32′W
Croix, Lac la, l., N.A. (läk lä krōō-ä′)	113	48°19′N	91°53′W
Croker, i., Austl. (krô′kȧ)	220	10°45′S	132°25′E
Cronulla, Austl. (krō-nŭl′ȧ)	217b	34°03′S	151°09′E
Crooked, i., Bah.	135	22°45′N	74°10′W
Crooked, l., Can.	101	48°25′N	56°05′W
Crooked, r., Can.	95	54°30′N	122°55′W
Crooked, r., Or., U.S.	114	44°07′N	120°30′W
Crooked Creek, r., Il., U.S. (krŏŏk′ěd)	121	40°21′N	90°49′W
Crooked Island Passage, strt., Bah.	135	22°40′N	74°50′W
Crookston, Mn., U.S. (krŏŏks′tŭn)	112	47°44′N	96°35′W
Crooksville, Oh., U.S. (krŏŏks′vĭl)	108	39°45′N	82°05′W
Crosby, Eng., U.K.	158a	53°30′N	3°02′W
Crosby, Mn., U.S. (krôz′bĭ)	113	46°29′N	93°58′W
Crosby, N.D., U.S.	112	48°55′N	103°18′W
Crosby, Tx., U.S.	123a	29°55′N	95°04′W
Cross, l., La., U.S.	123	32°33′N	93°58′W
Cross, r., Nig.	235	5°35′N	8°05′E
Cross City, Fl., U.S.	124	29°55′N	83°25′W
Crossett, Ar., U.S. (krôs′ět)	121	33°08′N	92°00′W
Cross Lake, l., Can.	92	54°45′N	97°30′W
Cross River Reservoir, res., N.Y., U.S. (krôs)	110a	41°14′N	73°34′W
Cross Sound, strt., Ak., U.S. (krŏs)	103	58°12′N	137°20′W
Crosswell, Mi., U.S. (krŏz′wěl)	108	43°15′N	82°35′W
Croswell, i., Serb.	174	44°50′N	14°31′E
Crotch, l., Can.	99	44°55′N	76°55′W
Crotone, Italy (krō-tô′ně)	175	39°05′N	17°08′E
Croton Falls Reservoir, res., N.Y., U.S. (krōtŭn)	110a	41°22′N	73°44′W
Croton-on-Hudson, N.Y., U.S. (krō′tŭn-ŏn hŭd′sŭn)	110a	41°12′N	73°53′W
Crow, l., Can.	113	49°13′N	93°29′W
Crow Agency, Mt., U.S.	115	45°36′N	107°27′W
Crow Creek, r., Co., U.S.	120	41°08′N	104°25′W
Crow Creek Indian Reservation, I.R., S.D., U.S.	112	44°17′N	99°17′W
Crow Indian Reservation, I.R., Mt., U.S. (krō)	115	45°26′N	108°12′W
Crowle, Eng., U.K. (kroul)	158a	53°36′N	0°49′W
Crowley, La., U.S. (krou′lē)	123	30°13′N	92°22′W
Crown Mountain, mtn., Can. (kroun)	116d	49°24′N	123°05′W
Crown Mountain, mtn., V.I.U.S.	129c	18°22′N	64°58′W
Crown Point, In., U.S. (kroun point′)	111a	41°25′N	87°22′W
Crown Point, N.Y., U.S.	109	44°00′N	73°25′W
Crowsnest Pass, p., Can.	95	49°39′N	114°45′W
Crow Wing, r., Mn., U.S. (krō)	113	44°50′N	94°01′W
Crow Wing, r., Mn., U.S.	113	46°42′N	94°48′W
Crow Wing, North Fork, r., Mn., U.S.	113	45°16′N	94°28′W
Crow Wing, South Fork, r., Mn., U.S.	113	44°59′N	94°42′W
Croydon, Austl. (kroi′dŭn)	219	18°15′S	142°15′E
Croydon, Austl.	217a	37°48′S	145°17′E
Croydon, Eng., U.K.	161	51°22′N	0°06′W
Croydon, Pa., U.S.	110f	40°05′N	74°55′W
Crozet, Îles, is., Afr. (krô-zě′)	3	46°20′S	51°30′E
Cruces, Cuba (krōō′sås)	134	22°20′N	80°20′W
Cruces, Arroyo de, r., Mex. (är-rô′yô-dě-krōō′sěs)	122	26°17′N	104°32′W
Cruillas, Mex. (krōō-ēl′yäs)	122	24°45′N	98°31′W
Cruz, Cabo, c., Cuba (ká′-bô-krōōz)	129	19°50′N	77°45′W
Cruz, Cayo, i., Cuba (kä′yō-krōōz)	134	22°15′N	77°50′W
Cruz Alta, Braz. (krōōz äl′tä)	144	28°41′S	54°02′W
Cruz del Eje, Arg. (krōō′s-děl-ě-kě)	144	30°46′S	64°45′W
Cruzeiro, Braz. (krōō-zä′rò)	141a	22°36′S	44°57′W
Cruzeiro do Sul, Braz. (krōō-zä′rò dò sōōl)	142	7°34′S	72°40′W
Crysler, Can.	102c	45°13′N	75°09′W
Crystal City, Tx., U.S. (krĭs′tăl sĭ′tĭ)	122	28°40′N	99°50′W
Crystal Falls, Mi., U.S. (krĭs′tăl fôls)	113	46°06′N	88°21′W
Crystal Lake, Il., U.S. (krĭs′tăl lăk)	111a	42°15′N	88°18′W
Crystal Springs, Ms., U.S. (krĭs′tăl sprĭngz)	124	31°58′N	90°20′W
Crystal Springs, oasis, Ca., U.S.	116b	37°31′N	122°26′W
Csongrád, Hung. (chôn′gräd)	169	46°42′N	20°09′E
Csorna, Hung. (chôr′nä)	169	47°39′N	17°11′E
Cúa, Ven. (kōō′ä)	143b	10°10′N	66°54′W
Cuajimalpa, Mex. (kwä-hē-mäl′pä)	131a	19°21′N	99°18′W
Cuale, Sierra del, mts., Mex. (sē-ě′r-rä-děl-kwä′lě)	130	20°20′N	104°58′W
Cuamato, Ang. (kwä-mä′tō)	236	17°05′S	15°09′E
Cuamba, Moz.	237	14°49′S	36°33′E
Cuando, Ang. (kwän′dō)	236	16°32′S	22°07′E
Cuando, r., Afr.	232	14°30′S	20°00′E
Cuangar, Ang.	236	17°36′S	18°39′E
Cuango, r., Afr.	232	9°00′S	18°00′E
Cuanza, r., Ang. (kwän′zä)	232	9°45′S	15°00′E
Cuarto, r., Arg.	144	33°00′S	63°25′W
Cuatro Caminos, Cuba (kwä′trô-kä-mē′nōs)	135a	23°01′N	82°13′W
Cuatro Ciénegas, Mex. (kwä′trō syā′nå-gäs)	122	26°59′N	102°03′W
Cuauhtemoc, Mex. (kwä-ōō-tě-mŏk′)	131	15°43′N	91°57′W
Cuautepec, Mex. (kwä-ōō-tě-pěk)	130	16°41′N	99°04′W
Cuautepec, Mex.	130	20°01′N	98°19′W
Cuautitlán, Mex. (kwä-ōō-tēt-län′)	131a	19°40′N	99°12′W
Cuautla, Mex. (kwä-ōō′tlȧ)	130	18°47′N	98°57′W
Cuba, Port. (kōō′bȧ)	172	38°10′N	7°55′W
Cuba, nation, N.A. (kū′bȧ)	129	22°00′N	79°00′W
Cubagua, Isla, i., Ven. (ē′s-lä-kōō-bä′gwä)	143b	10°48′N	64°10′W
Cubango (Okavango), r., Afr. (kōō-băŋ′gō)	232	17°10′S	18°20′E
Cub Hills, hills, Can. (kŭb)	96	54°20′N	104°30′W
Cucamonga, Ca., U.S. (kōō-kȧ-mŏŋ′gȧ)	117a	34°05′N	117°35′W
Cuchi, Ang.	232	14°40′S	16°50′E
Cuchillo Parado, Mex. (kōō-chē′lyō pä-rä′dō)	122	29°26′N	104°52′W
Cuchumatanes, Sierra de los, mts., Guat.	132	15°35′N	91°10′W
Cúcuta, Col. (kōō′kōō-tä)	142	7°56′N	72°30′W
Cudahy, Wi., U.S. (kŭd′ȧ-hĭ)	111a	42°57′N	87°52′W
Cuddalore, India (kŭd ȧ-lōr′)	199	11°49′N	79°46′E
Cuddapah, India (kŭd′ȧ-pä)	199	14°31′N	78°52′E
Cue, Austl. (kū)	218	27°30′S	118°10′E
Cuéllar, Spain (kwā′lyär′)	172	41°24′N	4°15′W
Cuenca, Ec. (kwěn′kä)	142	2°52′S	78°54′W
Cuenca, Spain	162	40°05′N	2°07′W
Cuenca, Sierra de, mts., Spain (sē-ě′r-rä-dě-kwě′n-kä)	172	40°02′N	1°50′W
Cuencame, Mex. (kwěn-kä-mā′)	122	24°52′N	103°42′W
Cuerámaro, Mex. (kwā-rä′mä-rô)	130	20°39′N	101°44′W
Cuernavaca, Mex. (kwěr-nä-vä′kä)	128	18°55′N	99°15′W
Cuero, Tx., U.S. (kwā′rō)	123	29°05′N	97°16′W
Cuetzalá del Progreso, Mex. (kwět-zä-lä děl prō-grā′sō)	130	18°07′N	99°51′W
Cuetzalan del Progreso, Mex.	131	20°02′N	97°33′W
Cuevas del Almanzora, Spain (kwě′väs-děl-äl-män-zō-rä)	162	37°19′N	1°54′W
Cuglieri, Italy (kōō-lyâ′rě)	174	40°11′N	8°37′E
Cuicatlán, Mex. (kwē-kä-tlän′)	131	17°46′N	96°57′W
Cuilapa, Guat. (kò-ē-lä′pä)	132	14°16′N	90°20′W
Cuilo (Kwilu), r., Afr.	236	9°15′S	19°30′E

ng-sing; ŋ-baŋk; ɴ-nasalized n; nŏd; cŏmmit; ōld; ôbey; ôrder; oi-boil; fōōd; ŏŏ-as oo in foot; ou-out; s-soft; sh-dish; th-thin; pūre; ûnite; ûrn; stŭd; circŭs; ü-as in French tu; ′-indeterminate vowel.

286 Cuito – Davenport PRONOUNCING INDEX

PLACE (Pronunciation)	PAGE	LAT.	LONG.
Cuito, r., Ang. (kōō-ē-'tō)	232	14°45'S	19°00'E
Cuitzeo, Mex. (kwēt'zā-ō)	130	19°57'N	101°11'W
Cuitzeo, Laguna de, l., Mex. (lä-ō'nä-dĕ-kwēt'zā-ō)	130	19°58'N	101°05'W
Cul de Sac, pl., Haiti (kōō'l-dĕ-sä'k)	135	18°35'N	72°05'W
Culebra, i., P.R. (kōō-lā'brä)	129b	18°19'N	65°32'W
Culebra, Sierra de la, mts., Spain (sē-ĕ'r-rä-dĕ-lä-kōō-lĕ-brä)	172	41°52'N	6°21'W
Culemborg, Neth.	159a	51°57'N	5°14'E
Culfa, Azer.	182	38°58'N	45°38'E
Culgoa, r., Austl. (kŭl-gō'ȧ)	221	29°21'S	147°00'E
Culiacán, Mex. (kōō-lyä-kä'n)	128	24°45'N	107°30'W
Culion, Phil. (kōō-lē-ōn')	212	11°43'N	119°58'E
Cúllar de Baza, Spain (kōō'l-yär-dĕ-bä'zä)	172	37°36'N	2°35'W
Cullera, Spain (kōō-lyā'rä)	162	39°12'N	0°15'W
Cullinan, S. Afr. (kŏ'lĭ-nán)	238c	25°41'S	28°32'E
Cullman, Al., U.S. (kŭl'măn)	124	34°10'N	86°50'W
Culpeper, Va., U.S. (kŭl'pĕp-ẽr)	109	38°30'N	77°55'W
Culross, Can. (kŭl'rôs)	102f	49°43'N	97°54'W
Culver, In., U.S. (kŭl'vẽr)	108	41°15'N	86°25'W
Culver City, Ca., U.S.	117a	34°00'N	118°23'W
Cumaná, Ven.	142	10°28'N	64°10'W
Cumberland, Can. (kŭm'bẽr-lănd)	102c	45°31'N	75°25'W
Cumberland, Md., U.S.	105	39°40'N	78°40'W
Cumberland, Wa., U.S.	116a	47°17'N	121°55'W
Cumberland, Wi., U.S.	113	45°31'N	92°01'W
Cumberland, r., U.S.	124	36°45'N	85°33'W
Cumberland, Lake, res., Ky., U.S.	107	36°55'N	85°20'W
Cumberland Islands, is., Austl.	221	20°20'S	149°46'E
Cumberland Peninsula, pen., Can.	93	65°59'N	64°05'W
Cumberland Plateau, plat., U.S.	124	35°25'N	85°30'W
Cumberland Sound, strt., Can.	93	65°27'N	65°44'W
Cundinamarca, dept., Col. (kōōn-dē-nä-mä'r-kȧ)	142a	4°57'N	74°27'W
Cunduacán, Mex. (kōn-dōō-ȧ-kän')	131	18°04'N	93°23'W
Cunene (Kunene), r., Afr.	232	17°05'S	12°35'E
Cuneo, Italy (kōō'nā-ō)	174	44°24'N	7°31'E
Cunha, Braz. (kōō'nyȧ)	141a	23°05'S	44°56'W
Cunnamulla, Austl. (kŭn-ȧ-mŭl-ȧ)	219	28°00'S	145°55'E
Cupula, Pico, mtn., Mex. (pē'kō-kōō'pōō-lä)	128	24°45'N	111°10'W
Cuquío, Mex. (kōō-kē'ō)	130	20°55'N	103°03'W
Curaçao, i., Neth. Ant. (kōō-rä-sä'ō)	142	12°12'N	68°58'W
Curacautín, Chile (kä-rä-käōō-tē'n)	144	38°25'S	71°53'W
Curaumilla, Punta, c., Chile (kōō-rou-mē'lyä)	141b	33°05'S	71°44'W
Curepto, Chile (kōō-rĕp-tô)	141b	35°06'S	72°02'W
Curitiba, Braz. (kōō-rē-tē'bȧ)	143	25°20'S	49°15'W
Curly Cut Cays, is., Bah.	134	23°40'N	77°40'W
Currais Novos, Braz. (kōōr-rä'ēs nō-vōs)	143	6°02'S	36°39'W
Curran, Can. (kü-räN')	102c	45°30'N	74°59'W
Current, i., Bah. (kŭ-rĕnt)	134	25°20'N	76°50'W
Current, r., Mo., U.S. (kûr'ĕnt)	121	37°18'N	91°21'W
Currie, Mount, mtn., S. Afr. (kŭ-rē)	233c	30°28'S	29°23'E
Currituck Sound, strt., N.C., U.S. (kûr'ĭ-tŭk)	125	36°27'N	75°42'W
Curtis, Ne., U.S. (kûr'tĭs)	120	40°36'N	100°29'W
Curtis, i., Austl.	221	23°38'S	151°43'E
Curtisville, Pa., U.S. (kûr'tĭs-vĭl)	111e	40°38'N	79°50'W
Ćurug, Serb. (chōō'rōg)	175	45°27'N	20°03'E
Curunga, Ang.	236	12°51'S	21°12'E
Curupira, Serra, mts., S.A. (sĕr'rȧ kōō-rōō-pē'rȧ)	142	1°00'N	65°30'W
Cururupu, Braz. (kōō-rō-rō-pōō')	143	1°40'S	44°56'W
Curvelo, Braz. (kōr-vĕl'ō)	143	18°47'S	44°14'W
Cusco, Peru	142	13°36'S	71°52'W
Cushing, Ok., U.S. (kŭsh'ĭng)	121	35°58'N	96°46'W
Custer, S.D., U.S. (kŭs'tẽr)	112	43°46'N	103°36'W
Custer, Wa., U.S.	116d	48°55'N	122°39'W
Cut Bank, Mt., U.S. (kŭt bănk)	115	48°38'N	112°19'W
Cuthbert, Ga., U.S. (kŭth'bẽrt)	124	31°47'N	84°48'W
Cuttack, India (kŭ-tăk')	199	20°38'N	85°53'E
Cutzamala, r., Mex. (kōō-tzä-mä-lä')	130	18°57'N	100°41'W
Cutzamalá de Pinzón, Mex. (kōō-tzä-mä-lä'dĕ-pēn-zō'n)	130	18°28'N	100°36'W
Cuvo, r., Ang. (kōō'vō)	232	11°00'S	14°30'E
Cuxhaven, Ger. (kōks'hä-fĕn)	160	53°51'N	8°43'E
Cuyahoga, r., Oh., U.S. (kī-ȧ-hō'gȧ)	111d	41°22'N	81°38'W
Cuyahoga Falls, Oh., U.S.	111d	41°08'N	81°29'W
Cuyapaire Indian Reservation, I.R., Ca., U.S. (kū-yȧ-pâr)	118	32°46'N	116°20'W
Cuyo Islands, is., Phil. (kōō'yō)	212	10°54'N	120°08'E
Cuyotenango, Guat. (kōō-yō-tĕ-năŋ'gō)	132	14°30'N	91°35'W
Cuyuni, r., S.A. (kōō-yōō'nē)	143	6°40'N	60°44'W
Cuyutlán, Mex. (kōō-yōō-tlän')	130	18°54'N	104°04'W
Cyclades see Kikládhes, is., Grc.	156	37°30'N	24°45'E
Cynthiana, Ky., U.S. (sĭn-thĭ-ăn'ȧ)	108	38°20'N	84°20'W
Cypress, Ca., U.S. (sī'prĕs)	117a	33°50'N	118°03'W
Cypress Hills, hills, Can.	96	49°40'N	110°20'W
Cypress Lake, l., Can.	96	49°28'N	109°43'W
Cyprus, nation, Asia (sī'prŭs)	198	35°00'N	31°00'E
Cyrenaica see Barqah, hist. reg., Libya	231	31°09'N	21°45'E
Czech Republic, nation, Eur.	154	50°00'N	15°00'E
Czersk, Pol. (chĕrsk)	169	53°47'N	17°58'E
Częstochowa, Pol. (chăN-stô'kô'vȧ)	161	50°49'N	19°10'E
D			
Da'an, China (dä-än)	208	45°25'N	124°22'E
Dabakala, C. Iv. (dä-bä-kä'lä)	230	8°16'N	4°36'W
Daba Shan, mts., China (dä-bä shän)	204	32°25'N	108°20'E
Dabeiba, Col. (dȧ-bā'bä)	142a	7°01'N	76°16'W
Dabie Shan, mts., China (dä-bĭĕ shän)	205	31°40'N	114°50'E
Dabnou, Niger	235	14°09'N	5°22'E
Dabob Bay, b., Wa., U.S. (dā'bŏb)	116a	47°50'N	122°50'W
Dabola, Gui.	234	10°45'N	11°07'W
Dąbrowa Białostocka, Pol.	169	53°37'N	23°18'E
Dacca see Dhaka, Bngl.	198	23°45'N	90°29'E
Dachang, China (dä-chäŋ)	207b	31°18'N	121°25'E
Dachangshan Dao, i., China (dä-chäŋ-shän dou)	206	39°21'N	122°31'E
Dachau, Ger. (dä'kou)	168	48°16'N	11°26'E
Dacotah, Can. (dȧ-kō'tȧ)	102f	49°52'N	97°38'W
Dade City, Fl., U.S. (dād)	125a	28°22'N	82°09'W
Dadeville, Al., U.S. (dăd'vĭl)	124	32°48'N	85°44'W
Dādra & Nagar Haveli, India	199	20°00'N	73°00'E
Dadu, r., China (dä-dōō)	209	29°20'N	103°03'E
Daet, mtn., Phil. (dä'ât)	213a	14°07'N	122°59'E
Dafoe, r., Can.	97	55°50'N	95°50'W
Dafter, Mi., U.S. (dăf'tẽr)	117k	46°21'N	84°26'W
Dagana, Sen. (dä-gä'nä)	230	16°31'N	15°30'W
Dagana, reg., Chad	235	12°20'N	15°15'E
Dagang, China (dä-gäŋ)	207a	22°48'N	113°24'E
Dagda, Lat. (dȧg'dȧ)	167	56°04'N	27°30'E
Dagenham, Eng., U.K. (dăg'ĕn-ăm)	158b	51°32'N	0°09'E
Dagestan, prov., Russia (dä-gĕs-tän')	181	43°40'N	46°10'E
Daggett, Ca., U.S. (dăg'ĕt)	118	34°50'N	116°52'W
Dagu, China (dä-gōō)	208	39°00'N	117°42'E
Dagu, r., China	206	36°29'N	120°06'W
Dagupan, Phil. (dä-gōō'pän)	213a	16°02'N	120°20'E
Daheishan Dao, i., China (dä-hā-shän dou)	206	37°57'N	120°37'E
Dahl, Ger. (däl)	171c	51°18'N	7°33'E
Dahlak Archipelago, is., Erit.	231	15°45'N	40°30'E
Dahomey see Benin, nation, Afr.	230	8°00'N	2°00'E
Dahra, Libya	200	29°34'N	17°50'E
Daibu, China (dī-bōō)	206	31°22'N	119°29'E
Daigo, Japan (dī-gō)	211b	34°57'N	135°49'E
Daimiel Manzanares, Spain (dī-myĕl'män-zä-nä'rĕs)	172	39°05'N	3°36'W
Dairen see Dalian, China	204	38°54'N	121°35'E
Dairy, r., Or., U.S. (dâr'ĭ)	116c	45°33'N	123°04'W
Dai-Sen, mtn., Japan (dī'sĕn')	211	35°22'N	133°35'E
Dai-Tenjo-dake, mtn., Japan (dī-tĕn'jō dä-kā)	211	36°21'N	137°38'E
Daiyun Shan, mtn., China (dī-yōn shän)	209	25°40'N	118°08'E
Dajabón, Dom. Rep. (dä-kä-bô'n)	135	19°35'N	71°40'W
Dajarra, Austl. (dȧ-jăr'ȧ)	218	21°45'S	139°30'E
Dakar, Sen. (dȧ-kär')	230	14°40'N	17°26'W
Dakhla, W. Sah.	230	23°45'N	16°04'W
Dakouraoua, Niger	235	13°58'N	6°15'E
Dakovica, Serb.	175	42°33'N	20°28'E
Dalälven, r., Swe.	156	60°26'N	15°50'E
Dalby, Austl. (dôl'bē)	219	27°10'S	151°15'E
Dalcour, La., U.S. (dăl-kour)	110d	29°49'N	89°59'W
Dale, Nor. (dä'lĕ)	166	60°35'N	5°55'E
Dale Hollow Lake, res., Tn., U.S. (dăl hŏl'ō)	107	36°33'N	85°03'W
Dalemead, Can. (dä'lĕ-mēd)	102e	50°53'N	113°38'W
Dalen, Nor. (dä'lĕn)	166	59°28'N	8°01'E
Daleside, S. Afr. (dāl'sīd)	238c	26°30'S	28°03'E
Dalesville, Can. (dālz'vĭl)	102a	45°42'N	74°23'W
Daley Waters, Austl. (dā lē)	218	16°15'N	133°30'E
Dalhart, Tx., U.S. (dăl härt)	120	36°04'N	102°32'W
Dalhousie, Can. (dăl-hōō'zē)	100	48°04'N	66°23'W
Dali, China (dä-lē)	207a	23°07'N	113°06'E
Dali, China	204	26°00'N	100°08'E
Dali, China	204	35°00'N	109°38'E
Dalian, China (lǖ-dä)	205	38°54'N	121°35'E
Dalian Wan, b., China (dä-lĭĕn wän)	206	38°55'N	121°50'E
Dalías, Spain (dä-lē'ȧs)	172	36°49'N	2°50'W
Dall, i., Ak., U.S. (dăl)	103	54°50'N	133°10'W
Dallas, Or., U.S. (dăl'ȧs)	114	44°55'N	123°20'W
Dallas, S.D., U.S.	112	43°13'N	99°34'W
Dallas, Tx., U.S.	104	32°45'N	96°48'W
Dalles Dam, Or., U.S.	114	45°36'N	121°08'W
Dall Island, i., Ak., U.S.	94	54°50'N	132°55'W
Dalmacija, hist. reg., Serb. (däl-mä'tsē-yä)	174	43°25'N	16°37'E
Dalnerechensk, Russia	179	46°07'N	133°21'E
Daloa, C. Iv.	234	6°53'N	6°27'W
Dalroy, Can. (dăl'roi)	102e	51°07'N	113°39'W
Dalrymple, Mount, mtn., Austl. (dăl'rĭm-p'l)	221	21°14'S	148°46'E
Dalton, S. Afr. (dôl'tŏn)	233c	29°21'S	30°41'E
Dalton, Ga., U.S. (dôl'tŭn)	124	34°46'N	84°58'W
Daly, r., Austl. (dā'lĭ)	220	14°15'S	131°15'E
Daly City, Ca., U.S. (dā'lē)	116b	37°42'N	122°27'W
Damān, India	199	20°32'N	72°53'E
Damanhūr, Egypt (dä-män-hōōr')	231	30°59'N	30°31'E
Damar, Pulau, i., Indon.	213	7°15'S	129°15'E
Damara, C.A.R.	235	4°58'N	18°42'E
Damaraland, hist. reg., Nmb. (dă'nȧ-rȧ-lănd)	232	22°15'S	16°15'E
Damas Cays, is., Bah. (dä'mäs)	134	23°50'N	79°50'W
Damascus, Syria	198	33°30'N	36°18'E
Damāvand, Qolleh-ye, mtn., Iran	198	36°05'N	52°05'E
Damba, Ang. (däm'bä)	232	6°41'S	15°08'E
Dâmboviţa, r., Rom.	175	44°43'N	25°41'E
Dame Marie, Cap, c., Haiti (dām mȧrē')	135	18°35'N	74°50'W
Dāmghān, Iran (dām-gān')	198	35°50'N	54°15'E
Daming, China (dä-mĭŋ)	208	36°15'N	115°09'E
Dammartin-en-Goële, Fr. (däN-mär-tăN-äN-gô-ĕl')	171b	49°03'N	2°40'E
Dampier, Selat, strt., Indon. (dăm'pēr)	213	0°40'S	131°15'E
Dampier Archipielago, is., Austl.	220	20°15'S	116°25'E
Dampier Land, reg., Austl.	220	17°30'S	122°25'E
Dan, r., N.C., U.S. (dăn)	125	36°26'N	79°40'W
Dana, Mount, mtn., Ca., U.S.	118	37°54'N	119°13'W
Da Nang, Viet.	212	16°08'N	108°22'E
Danbury, Eng., U.K.	158b	51°42'N	0°34'E
Danbury, Ct., U.S. (dăn'bẽr-ĭ)	110a	41°23'N	73°27'W
Danbury, Tx., U.S.	123a	29°14'N	95°22'W
Dandenong, Austl. (dăn'dē-nông)	222	37°59'S	145°13'E
Dandong, China (dän-dôŋ)	205	40°10'N	124°30'E
Dane, r., Eng., U.K. (dān)	158a	53°11'N	2°14'W
Danea, Gui.	234	11°27'N	13°12'W
Danforth, Me., U.S.	100	45°38'N	67°53'W
Dan Gora, Nig.	235	11°30'N	8°09'E
Dangtu, China (däŋ-tōō)	209	31°35'N	118°28'E
Dani, Burkina	230	13°43'N	0°10'W
Dania, Fl., U.S. (dā'nĭ-ȧ)	125a	26°01'N	80°10'W
Danilov, Russia (dä'nē-lôf)	180	58°12'N	40°08'E
Danissa Hills, hills, Kenya	237	3°20'N	40°55'E
Dänizkänarı, Azer.	182	40°13'N	49°33'E
Dankov, Russia (däŋ'kôf)	180	53°17'N	39°09'E
Dannemora, N.Y., U.S. (dăn-ē-mō'rȧ)	109	44°45'N	73°45'W
Dannhauser, S. Afr. (dän'hou-zẽr)	233c	28°07'S	30°04'E
Dansville, N.Y., U.S. (dănz'vĭl)	109	42°30'N	77°40'W
Danube, r., Eur.	156	43°00'N	24°00'E
Danube, Mouths of the, mth., Rom. (dăn'ub)	177	45°13'N	29°37'E
Danvers, Ma., U.S. (dăn'vẽrz)	101a	42°34'N	70°57'W
Danville, Ca., U.S. (dăn'vĭl)	116b	37°49'N	122°00'W
Danville, Il., U.S.	108	40°10'N	87°35'W
Danville, In., U.S.	108	39°45'N	86°30'W
Danville, Ky., U.S.	108	37°35'N	84°50'W
Danville, Pa., U.S.	109	41°00'N	76°35'W
Danville, Va., U.S.	105	36°35'N	79°24'W
Danxian, China (dän shyĕn)	209	19°30'N	109°38'E
Danyang, China (dän-yäŋ)	206	32°01'N	119°32'E
Danzig see Gdańsk, Pol.	154	54°20'N	18°40'E
Danzig, Gulf of, b., Eur. (dän'tsĭk)	160	54°41'N	19°01'E
Daoxian, China (dou shyĕn)	209	25°35'N	111°27'E
Dapango, Togo	234	10°52'N	0°12'E
Daphnae, hist., Egypt	197a	30°43'N	32°12'E
Daqin Dao, i., China (dä-chyĭn dou)	206	38°18'N	120°50'E
Darabani, Rom. (dă-ră-băn'ĭ)	169	48°13'N	26°38'E
Daraj, Libya	230	30°12'N	10°14'E
Darāw, Egypt (dȧ-rä'ōō)	238b	24°24'N	32°56'E
Darbhanga, India (dŭr-bŭŋ'gä)	199	26°03'N	85°09'E
Darby, Pa., U.S. (där'bĭ)	110f	39°55'N	75°16'W
Darby, i., Bah.	134	23°50'N	76°20'W
Dardanelles see Çanakkale Boğazi, strt., Tur.	163	40°05'N	25°50'E
Dar es Salaam, Tan. (där ĕs sȧ-läm')	233	6°48'S	39°17'E
Dārfūr, hist. reg., Sudan (där-fōōr')	231	13°21'N	23°46'E
Dargai, Pak. (dŭr-gä'ē)	202	34°35'N	72°00'E
Darien, Col. (dā-rĭ-ĕn')	142a	3°56'N	76°30'W
Darien, Ct., U.S. (dâ-rē-ĕn')	110a	41°04'N	73°28'W
Darién, Cordillera de, mts., Nic.	132	13°00'N	85°42'W
Darien, Serranía del, mts.	133	8°13'N	77°28'W
Darjeeling, India (dŭr-jē'lĭng)	199	27°05'N	88°16'E
Darling, r., Austl.	221	31°50'S	143°20'E
Darling Downs, reg., Austl.	221	27°22'S	150°00'E
Darling Range, mts., Austl.	220	30°30'S	115°45'E
Darlington, Eng., U.K. (där'lĭng-tŭn)	164	54°32'N	1°35'W
Darlington, S.C., U.S.	125	34°15'N	79°52'W
Darlington, Wi., U.S.	113	42°41'N	90°06'W
Darłowo, Pol. (där-lô'vô)	168	54°26'N	16°23'E
Darmstadt, Ger. (därm'shtät)	161	49°53'N	8°40'E
Darnah, Libya	231	32°44'N	22°41'E
Darnley Bay, b., Ak., U.S. (därn'lē)	103	70°00'N	124°00'W
Daroca, Spain (dä-rō-kä)	172	41°08'N	1°24'W
Dartford, Eng., U.K.	158b	51°27'N	0°14'E
Dartmoor, for., Eng., U.K. (därt'mōōr)	164	50°35'N	4°05'W
Dartmouth, Can. (därt'mŭth)	91	44°40'N	63°34'W
Dartmouth, Eng., U.K.	164	50°33'N	3°28'W
Daru, Pap. N. Gui. (dä'rōō)	213	9°04'S	143°21'E
Daruvar, Cro. (där'rōō-vär)	175	45°37'N	17°16'E
Darwen, Eng., U.K. (där'wĕn)	158a	53°42'N	2°28'W
Darwin, Austl. (där'wĭn)	218	12°25'S	131°00'E
Darwin, Cordillera, mts., Chile (kôr-dēl-yĕ'rä-där'wēn)	144	54°40'S	69°30'W
Dashhowuz, Turkmen.	183	41°50'N	59°45'E
Dash Point, Wa., U.S. (dăsh)	116a	47°19'N	122°25'W
Dasht, r., Pak. (dŭsht)	198	25°30'N	62°30'E
Dasol Bay, b., Phil. (dä-sōl')	213a	15°53'N	119°40'E
Datian Ding, mtn., China (dä-tĭĕn dĭŋ)	209	22°25'N	111°20'E
Datong, China (dä-tôŋ)	208	40°00'N	113°30'E
Dattapukur, India	202a	22°45'N	88°32'E
Datteln, Ger. (dät'tĕln)	171c	51°39'N	7°20'E
Datu, Tandjung, c., Asia	212	2°08'N	110°15'E
Datuan, China (dä-tůän)	207b	30°57'N	121°43'E
Daugava (Zapadnaya Dvina), r., Eur.	167	56°40'N	24°40'E
Daugavpils, Lat. (dä'ō-gäv-pēls)	180	55°52'N	26°32'E
Dauphin, Can. (dô'fĭn)	90	51°09'N	100°00'W
Dauphin Lake, l., Can.	97	51°17'N	99°48'W
Dāvangere, India	203	14°30'N	75°55'E
Davao, Phil. (dä'vä-ô)	213	7°05'N	125°30'E
Davao Gulf, b., Phil.	213	6°30'N	125°45'E
Davenport, Ia., U.S. (dăv'ĕn-pōrt)	105	41°34'N	90°38'W

ăt; finăl; rāte; senâte; ärm; ȧsk; sofȧ; fâre; ch-choose; dh-as th in other; bē; ēvent; bĕt; recĕnt; cratẽr; g-gō; gh-guttural g; bĭt; ĭ-short neutral; rīde; K-guttural k as ch in German ich;

PRONOUNCING INDEX Davenport – Diablotins 287

PLACE (Pronunciation)	PAGE	LAT.	LONG.
Davenport, Wa., U.S.	114	47°39'N	118°07'W
David, Pan. (dá-vēdh')	129	8°27'N	82°27'W
David City, Ne., U.S. (dā'vĭd)	112	41°15'N	97°10'W
David-Gorodok, Bela. (då-vēt' gô-rō'dôk)	181	52°02'N	27°14'E
Davis, Ok., U.S. (dā'vĭs)	121	34°34'N	97°08'W
Davis, W.V., U.S.	109	39°15'N	79°25'W
Davis Lake, l., Or., U.S.	114	43°38'N	121°43'W
Davis Mountains, mts., Tx., U.S.	122	30°45'N	104°17'W
Davis Strait, strt., N.A.	89	66°00'N	60°00'W
Davlekanovo, Russia	180	54°15'N	55°05'E
Davos, Switz. (dä'vōs)	168	46°47'N	9°50'E
Dawa, r., Afr.	231	4°30'N	40°30'E
Dawāsir, Wādī ad, val., Sau. Ar.	198	20°48'N	44°07'E
Dawei, Mya.	212	14°04'N	98°19'E
Dawen, r., China (dä-wŭn)	206	35°58'N	116°53'E
Dawley, Eng., U.K. (dô'lĭ)	158a	52°38'N	2°28'W
Dawna Range, mts., Mya. (dô'ná)	212	17°02'N	98°01'E
Dawson, Can. (dô'sŭn)	90	64°04'N	139°22'W
Dawson, Ga., U.S.	124	31°45'N	84°29'W
Dawson, Mn., U.S.	112	44°54'N	96°03'W
Dawson, r., Austl.	221	24°20'S	149°45'E
Dawson Bay, b., Can.	97	52°55'N	100°50'W
Dawson Creek, Can.	90	55°46'N	120°14'W
Dawson Range, mts., Can.	103	62°15'N	138°10'W
Dawson Springs, Ky., U.S.	124	37°10'N	87°40'W
Dawu, China (dä-wōō)	206	31°33'N	114°07'E
Dax, Fr. (daks)	161	43°42'N	1°06'W
Daxian, China (dä-shyĕn)	204	31°12'N	107°30'E
Daxing, China (dä-shyĭŋ)	208a	39°44'N	116°19'E
Dayiqiao, China (dä-yē-chyou)	206	31°43'N	120°40'E
Dayr az Zawr, Syria (då-ērēz-zôr')	198	35°15'N	40°01'E
Dayton, Ky., U.S. (dā'tŭn)	111f	39°07'N	84°28'W
Dayton, N.M., U.S.	120	32°44'N	104°23'W
Dayton, Oh., U.S.	105	39°54'N	84°15'W
Dayton, Tn., U.S.	124	35°30'N	85°00'W
Dayton, Tx., U.S.	123	30°03'N	94°53'W
Dayton, Wa., U.S.	114	46°18'N	117°59'W
Daytona Beach, Fl., U.S. (dā-tō'ná)	105	29°11'N	81°02'W
Dayu, China (dä-yōō)	209	25°20'N	114°20'E
Da Yunhe (Grand Canal), can., China (dä yòn-hŭ)	205	35°00'N	117°00'E
Dayville, Ct., U.S. (dā'vĭl)	109	41°50'N	71°55'W
De Aar, S. Afr. (dē-är')	232	30°45'S	24°05'E
Dead, l., Mn., U.S. (dĕd)	112	46°28'N	96°00'W
Dead Sea, l., Asia	198	31°30'N	35°30'E
Deadwood, S.D., U.S. (dĕd'wŏŏd)	104	44°23'N	103°43'W
Deal Island, Md., U.S. (dēl-ī'lănd)	109	38°10'N	75°55'W
Dean, r., Can. (dēn)	94	52°45'N	125°30'W
Dean Channel, strt., Can.	94	52°33'N	127°13'W
Deán Funes, Arg. (dĕ-á'n-fōō-nĕs)	144	30°26'S	64°12'W
Dearborn, Mi., U.S. (dēr'bŭrn)	111b	42°18'N	83°15'W
Dearg, Ben, mtn., Scot., U.K. (bĕn dŭrg)	164	57°48'N	4°59'W
Dease Strait, strt., Can. (dēz)	92	68°50'N	108°20'W
Death Valley, Ca., U.S.	118	36°18'N	116°26'W
Death Valley, val., Ca., U.S.	106	36°30'N	117°00'W
Death Valley National Park, rec., U.S.	118	36°34'N	117°00'W
Debal'tseve, Ukr.	177	48°23'N	38°29'E
Debao, China (dŭ-bou)	204	23°18'N	106°40'E
Debar, Mac. (dĕ'bär) (dā'brä)	175	41°31'N	20°32'E
Dęblin, Pol. (dăN'blĭn)	169	51°34'N	21°49'E
Dębno, Pol. (dĕb-nô')	168	52°47'N	13°43'E
Debo, Lac, l., Mali	234	15°15'N	4°40'W
Debrecen, Hung. (dĕ'brĕ-tsĕn)	154	47°32'N	21°40'E
Debre Markos, Eth.	231	10°15'N	37°45'E
Debre Tabor, Eth.	231	11°57'N	38°09'E
Decatur, Al., U.S. (dē-kā'tŭr)	124	34°35'N	87°00'W
Decatur, Ga., U.S.	110c	33°47'N	84°18'W
Decatur, Il., U.S.	105	39°50'N	88°59'W
Decatur, In., U.S.	108	40°50'N	84°55'W
Decatur, Mi., U.S.	108	42°10'N	86°00'W
Decatur, Tx., U.S.	121	33°14'N	97°33'W
Decazeville, Fr. (dē-käz'vēl')	161	44°33'N	2°16'E
Deccan, plat., India (dĕk'ăn)	199	19°05'N	76°40'E
Deception Lake, l., Can.	96	56°33'N	104°15'W
Deception Pass, p., Wa., U.S. (dē-sĕp'shŭn)	116a	48°24'N	122°44'W
Děčín, Czech Rep. (dyĕ'chēn)	168	50°47'N	14°14'E
Decorah, Ia., U.S. (dē-kō'rá)	113	43°18'N	91°48'W
Dedenevo, Russia (dyĕ-dyĕ'nyĕ-vô)	186b	56°14'N	37°31'E
Dedham, Ma., U.S. (dĕd'ăm)	101a	42°15'N	71°11'W
Dedo do Deus, mtn., Braz. (dĕ-dô-dĕ'ōōs)	144b	22°30'S	43°02'W
Dédougou, Burkina (dā-dò-gōō')	230	12°38'N	3°28'W
Dee, r., Scot., U.K.	164	57°05'N	2°25'W
Dee, r., U.K.	158a	53°15'N	3°05'E
Deep, r., N.C., U.S. (dēp)	125	35°36'N	79°32'W
Deep Fork, r., Ok., U.S.	121	35°35'N	96°42'W
Deep River, Can.	99	46°06'N	77°20'W
Deepwater, Mo., U.S. (dep-wô-tēr)	121	38°15'N	93°46'W
Deer, i., Me., U.S.	100	44°07'N	68°38'W
Deerfield, Il., U.S. (dēr'fēld)	111a	42°10'N	87°51'W
Deer Island, Or., U.S.	116c	45°56'N	122°51'W
Deer Lake, Can.	93a	49°10'N	57°25'W
Deer Lake, l., Can.	97	52°40'N	94°30'W
Deer Lodge, Mt., U.S. (dēr lŏj)	115	46°23'N	112°42'W
Deer Park, Oh., U.S.	111f	39°12'N	84°24'W
Deer Park, Wa., U.S.	114	47°58'N	117°28'W
Deer River, Mn., U.S.	113	47°20'N	93°49'W
Defiance, Oh., U.S. (dē-fī'ăns)	108	41°15'N	84°20'W
DeFuniak Springs, Fl., U.S. (dē fū'nĭ-ăk)	124	30°42'N	86°06'W
Deganga, India	202a	22°41'N	88°41'E
Degeh Bur, Eth.	238a	8°10'N	43°25'E
Deggendorf, Ger. (dĕ'ghĕn-dôrf)	168	48°50'N	12°59'E
Degollado, Mex. (dā-gô-lyä'dō)	130	20°27'N	102°11'W
DeGrey, r., Austl. (dē grā')	220	20°20'S	119°25'E
Degtyarsk, Russia (dĕg-ty'arsk)	186a	56°42'N	60°05'E
Dehiwala-Mount Lavinia, Sri L.	203	6°47'N	79°55'E
Dehra Dūn, India (dā'rŭ)	199	30°09'N	78°07'E
Dehua, China (dŭ-hwä)	209	25°30'N	118°15'E
Dej, Rom. (dāzh)	163	47°09'N	23°53'E
De Kalb, Il., U.S. (dē kălb')	108	41°54'N	88°46'W
Dekese, D.R.C.	236	3°27'S	21°24'E
Delacour, Can. (dĕ-lä-kōōr')	102e	51°09'N	113°45'W
Delagua, Co., U.S. (dĕl-ä'gwä)	120	37°19'N	104°42'W
De Land, Fl., U.S. (dē lănd')	125	29°00'N	81°19'W
Delano, Ca., U.S. (dĕl'á-nō)	118	35°47'N	119°15'W
Delano Peak, mtn., Ut., U.S.	106	38°25'N	112°25'W
Delavan, Wi., U.S. (dĕl'á-văn)	113	42°39'N	88°38'W
Delaware, Oh., U.S. (dĕl'á-wâr)	108	40°15'N	83°05'W
Delaware, state, U.S.	105	38°40'N	75°30'W
Delaware, r., Ks., U.S.	121	39°45'N	95°47'W
Delaware, r., U.S.	109	41°50'N	75°20'W
Delaware Bay, b., U.S.	107	39°05'N	75°10'W
Delaware Reservoir, res., Oh., U.S.	109	40°30'N	83°05'W
Delémont, Switz. (dĕ-lā-môN')	168	47°21'N	7°18'E
De Leon, Tx., U.S. (dē lē-ŏn')	122	32°06'N	98°33'W
Delft, Neth. (dĕlft)	165	52°01'N	4°20'E
Delfzijl, Neth.	165	53°20'N	6°50'E
Delgada, Punta, c., Arg. (pōō'n-tä-dĕl-gä'dä)	144	43°46'S	63°46'W
Delgado, Cabo, c., Moz. (ká'bô-dĕl-gä'dō)	233	10°40'S	40°35'E
Delhi, India	199	28°54'N	77°13'E
Delhi, Il., U.S. (dĕl'hī)	117e	39°03'N	90°16'W
Delhi, La., U.S.	123	32°26'N	91°29'W
Delhi, state, India	199	28°30'N	76°50'E
Delitzsch, Ger. (dā'lĭch)	168	51°32'N	12°18'E
Dellansjöarna, l., Swe.	166	61°57'N	16°25'E
Delles, Alg. (dĕl'ĕs')	230	36°59'N	3°40'E
Dell Rapids, S.D., U.S. (dĕl)	112	43°50'N	96°43'W
Dellwood, Mn., U.S. (dĕl'wŏŏd)	117g	45°05'N	92°58'W
Del Mar, Ca., U.S. (dĕl mär')	118a	32°57'N	117°16'W
Delmas, S. Afr. (dĕl'más)	238c	26°08'S	28°43'E
Delmenhorst, Ger. (dĕl'mĕn-hôrst)	168	53°03'N	8°38'E
Del Norte, Co., U.S. (dĕl nôrt')	119	37°40'N	106°25'W
De-Longa, i., Russia	179	76°21'N	148°56'E
De Long Mountains, mts., Ak., U.S. (dē-lŏng)	103	68°38'N	162°30'W
Deloraine, Austl. (dĕ-lŭ-rān)	222	41°30'S	146°40'E
Delphi, In., U.S. (dĕl'fī)	108	40°35'N	86°40'W
Delphos, Oh., U.S. (dĕl'fōs)	108	40°50'N	84°20'W
Delray Beach, Fl., U.S. (dĕl-rā')	125a	26°27'N	80°05'W
Del Rio, Tx., U.S. (dĕl rē'ō)	104	29°21'N	100°52'W
Delson, Can. (dĕl'sŭn)	102a	45°24'N	73°32'W
Delta, Co., U.S.	119	38°45'N	108°05'W
Delta, Ut., U.S.	119	39°20'N	112°35'W
Delta Beach, Can.	102f	50°10'N	98°20'W
Delvine, Alb. (dĕl'vē-ná)	175	39°58'N	20°10'E
Dëma, r., Russia (dyĕm'ä)	180	53°40'N	54°30'E
Demba, D.R.C.	236	5°30'S	22°16'E
Dembi Dolo, Eth.	231	8°46'N	34°46'E
Demidov, Russia (dzyĕ'mē-dô'f)	176	55°16'N	31°32'E
Deming, N.M., U.S. (dĕm'ĭng)	104	32°15'N	107°45'W
Demmin, Ger. (dĕm'mēn)	168	53°54'N	13°04'E
Demnat, Mor. (dĕm-nät)	230	31°58'N	7°03'W
Demopolis, Al., U.S. (dē-mŏp'ô-lĭs)	124	32°30'N	87°50'W
Demotte, In., U.S. (dē'mŏt)	111a	41°12'N	87°13'W
Dempo, Gunung, mtn., Indon. (dĕm'pô)	212	4°04'S	103°11'E
Dem'yanka, r., Russia (dyĕm-yän'kä)	184	59°07'N	72°58'E
Demyansk, Russia (dyĕm-yänsk')	176	57°39'N	32°26'E
Denain, Fr. (dē-năN')	170	50°23'N	3°21'E
Denakil Plain, pl., Eth.	231	12°45'N	41°01'E
Denali National Park, rec., Ak., U.S.	106a	63°48'N	153°02'W
Denbigh, Wales, U.K. (dĕn'bĭ)	164	53°15'N	3°25'W
Dendermonde, Bel.	159a	51°02'N	4°04'E
Dendron, Va., U.S. (dĕn'drŭn)	125	37°02'N	76°53'W
Denezhkin Kamen, Gora, mtn., Russia (dzyĕ-ŋĕ'zhkĕn kăm'ĭēn)	186a	60°26'N	59°35'E
Denham, Mount, mtn., Jam.	129	18°20'N	77°30'W
Den Helder, Neth. (dĕn hĕl'dĕr)	165	52°55'N	5°45'E
Dénia, Spain	173	38°48'N	0°06'E
Deniliquin, Austl. (dĕ-nĭl'ĭ-kwĭn)	219	35°20'S	144°52'E
Denison, Ia., U.S. (dĕn'ĭ-sŭn)	112	42°01'N	95°22'W
Denison, Tx., U.S.	104	33°45'N	97°02'W
Denizli, Tur. (dĕn-ĭz-lē')	163	37°40'N	29°10'E
Denklingen, Ger. (dĕn'klĕn-gĕn)	171c	50°54'N	7°40'E
Denmark, S.C., U.S. (dĕn'märk)	125	33°18'N	81°09'W
Denmark, nation, Eur.	154	56°14'N	8°30'E
Denmark Strait, strt., Eur.	89	66°30'N	27°00'W
Dennilton, S. Afr. (dĕn-ĭl-tŭn)	238c	25°18'S	29°13'E
Dennison, Oh., U.S. (dĕn'ĭ-sŭn)	108	40°25'N	81°20'W
Denpasar, Indon.	212	8°35'S	115°10'E
Denton, Eng., U.K. (dĕn'tŭn)	158a	53°27'N	2°07'W
Denton, Md., U.S.	109	38°55'N	75°50'W
Denton, Tx., U.S.	121	33°12'N	97°06'W
D'Entrecasteaux, Point, c., Austl. (däN-tr'-kás-tō')	220	34°50'S	114°45'E
D'Entrecasteaux Islands, is., Pap. N. Gui. (däN-tr'-kás-tō')	213	9°45'S	152°00'E
Denver, Co., U.S. (dĕn'vēr)	104	39°44'N	104°59'W
Deoli, India	202	25°52'N	75°23'E
De Pere, Wi., U.S. (dē pēr')	113	44°25'N	88°04'W
Depew, N.Y., U.S. (dē-pū')	111c	42°55'N	78°43'W
Deping, China (dŭ-pĭŋ)	206	37°28'N	116°57'E
Depue, Il., U.S. (dē pū)	108	41°15'N	89°55'W
De Queen, Ar., U.S. (dē kwēn')	121	34°02'N	94°21'W
De Quincy, La., U.S. (dē kwĭn'sĭ)	123	30°27'N	93°27'W
Dera, Lach, r., Afr. (läk dā'rä)	238a	0°45'N	41°26'E
Dera, Lak, r., Afr.	231	0°45'N	41°30'E
Dera Ghāzi Khān, Pak. (dā'rŭ gä-zē' ĸän')	199	30°09'N	70°39'E
Dera Ismāīl Khān, Pak. (dā'rŭ ĭs-mä-ēl' ĸän')	202	31°55'N	70°51'E
Derbent, Russia (dĕr-bĕnt')	181	42°00'N	48°10'E
Derby, Austl. (där'bē) (dûr'bē)	218	17°20'S	123°40'E
Derby, S. Afr. (där'bĭ)	238c	25°55'S	27°02'E
Derby, Eng., U.K. (där'bē)	161	52°55'N	1°29'W
Derby, Ct., U.S. (dûr'bē)	109	41°20'N	73°05'W
Derbyshire, co., Eng., U.K.	158a	53°11'N	1°30'W
Derdepoort, S. Afr.	238c	24°39'S	26°21'E
Derg, Lough, l., Ire. (lŏk dĕrg)	164	53°00'N	8°09'W
De Ridder, La., U.S. (dē rĭd'ēr)	123	30°50'N	93°18'W
Dermott, Ar., U.S. (dûr'mŏt)	121	33°32'N	91°24'W
Derry, N.H., U.S. (dâr'ĭ)	101a	42°53'N	71°22'W
Derventa, Bos. (dĕr'ven-tà)	175	44°58'N	17°58'E
Derwent, r., Austl. (dĕr'wĕnt)	222	42°21'S	146°30'E
Derwent, r., Eng., U.K.	158a	52°54'N	1°24'W
Des Arc, Ar., U.S. (dāz ärk')	121	34°59'N	91°31'W
Descalvado, Braz. (dĕs-käl-vá-dô)	141a	21°55'S	47°37'W
Descartes, Fr.	170	46°58'N	0°42'E
Deschambault Lake, l., Can.	96	54°40'N	103°35'W
Deschênes, Can.	102c	45°23'N	75°47'W
Deschenes, Lake, l., Can.	102c	45°25'N	75°53'W
Deschutes, r., Or., U.S. (dā-shōōt')	114	44°25'N	121°21'W
Desdemona, Tx., U.S. (dĕz-dē-mō'ná)	122	32°16'N	98°33'W
Dese, Eth.	231	11°00'N	39°51'E
Deseado, r., Arg. (dā-sā-ä'dhō)	144	46°50'S	67°45'W
Desirade Island, i., Guad. (dā-zē-rás')	133b	16°21'N	60°51'W
De Smet, S.D., U.S. (dē smĕt')	112	44°23'N	97°33'W
Des Moines, Ia., U.S. (dē moin')	105	41°35'N	93°37'W
Des Moines, N.M., U.S.	120	36°42'N	103°48'W
Des Moines, Wa., U.S.	116a	46°24'N	122°20'W
Des Moines, r., U.S.	107	42°30'N	94°20'W
Desna, r., Eur. (dyĕs-ná')	181	51°55'N	31°45'E
Desolación, i., Chile (dĕ-sô-lä-syô'n)	144	53°05'S	74°00'W
De Soto, Mo., U.S. (dē sō'tō)	121	38°07'N	90°32'W
Des Peres, Mo., U.S. (dĕs pĕr'ĕs)	117e	38°36'N	90°26'W
Des Plaines, Il., U.S. (dĕs plānz')	111a	42°02'N	87°54'W
Des Plaines, r., U.S.	111a	41°39'N	87°56'W
Dessau, Ger. (dĕsou)	161	51°50'N	12°15'E
Detmold, Ger. (dĕt'mōld)	168	51°57'N	8°55'E
Detroit, Mi., U.S. (dē-troit')	105	42°22'N	83°10'W
Detroit, Tx., U.S.	121	33°41'N	95°16'W
Detroit Lake, res., Or., U.S.	114	44°42'N	122°10'W
Detroit Lakes, Mn., U.S. (dē-troit'lăkz)	112	46°48'N	95°51'W
Detva, Slvk. (dyĕt'vá)	169	48°32'N	19°21'E
Deurne, Bel.	159a	51°13'N	4°27'E
Deutsch Wagram, Aus.	159e	48°19'N	16°34'E
Deux-Montagnes, Can.	102a	45°33'N	73°53'W
Deux Montagnes, Lac des, l., Can.	102a	45°28'N	74°00'W
Deva, Rom. (dā'vä)	163	45°52'N	22°52'E
Dévaványa, Hung. (dā'vô-vän-yô)	169	47°01'N	20°58'E
Develi, Tur. (dĕ'vå-lē)	181	38°20'N	35°10'E
Deventer, Neth. (dĕv'ĕn-tēr)	165	52°14'N	6°07'E
Devils, r., Tx., U.S.	122	29°55'N	101°10'W
Devils Island see Diable, Île du, i., Fr. Gu.	143	5°15'N	52°40'W
Devils Lake, N.D., U.S.	104	48°10'N	98°55'W
Devils Lake, l., N.D., U.S. (dĕv''lz)	112	47°57'N	99°04'W
Devils Lake Indian Reservation, I.R., N.D., U.S.	112	48°08'N	99°40'W
Devils Postpile National Monument, rec., Ca., U.S.	118	37°42'N	119°12'W
Devils Tower National Monument, rec., Wy., U.S.	115	44°38'N	105°07'W
Devoll, r., Alb.	175	40°55'N	20°10'E
Devon, Can.	102g	53°23'N	113°43'W
Devon, S. Afr. (dĕv'ŭn)	238c	26°23'S	28°47'E
Devonport, Austl. (dĕv'ŭn-pôrt)	219	41°20'S	146°30'E
Devonport, N.Z.	221a	36°50'S	174°45'E
Devore, Ca., U.S. (dē-vôr')	117a	34°13'N	117°24'W
Dewatto, Wa., U.S. (dē-wät'ō)	116a	47°27'N	123°04'W
Dewey, Ok., U.S. (dū'ĭ)	121	36°48'N	95°55'W
De Witt, Ar., U.S. (dē wĭt')	121	34°17'N	91°22'W
De Witt, Ia., U.S.	113	41°46'N	90°34'W
Dewsbury, Eng., U.K. (dūz'bēr-ĭ)	158a	53°42'N	1°39'W
Dexter, Me., U.S. (dĕks'tēr)	100	45°01'N	69°19'W
Dexter, Mo., U.S.	121	36°46'N	89°56'W
Dezfūl, Iran	198	32°14'N	48°37'E
Dezhnëva, Mys, c., Russia (dyĕzh'nyĭf)	196	68°00'N	172°00'W
Dezhou, China (dŭ-jō)	208	37°28'N	116°17'E
Dhahran see Az̧ Z̧ahrān, Sau. Ar.	198	26°13'N	50°00'E
Dhaka, Bngl. (dä'kä) (dăk'á)	199	23°45'N	90°29'E
Dharamtar Creek, r., India	203b	18°49'N	72°54'E
Dharmavaram, India	203	14°32'N	77°43'E
Dhawalāgiri, mtn., Nepal	199	28°42'N	83°31'E
Dhībān, Jord.	197a	31°30'N	35°46'E
Dhidhimótikhon, Grc.	175	41°20'N	26°27'E
Dhule, India	199	20°58'N	74°43'E
Día, i., Grc. (dē'ä)	174a	35°27'N	25°17'E
Diable, Île du, i., Fr. Gu.	143	5°15'N	52°40'W
Diablo, Mount, mtn., Ca., U.S. (dyä'blō)	116b	37°52'N	121°55'W
Diablo Heights, Pan. (dyá'blō)	128a	8°58'N	79°34'W
Diablo Range, mts., Ca., U.S.	116b	37°47'N	121°50'W
Diablotins, Morne, mtn., Dom.	133b	15°31'N	61°24'W

ng-sing; ŋ-baŋk; N-nasalized n; nŏd; cŏmmit; ōld; ôbey; ôrder; oi-boil; fōōd; ò-as oo in foot; ou-out; s-soft; sh-dish; th-thin; pūre; ûnite; ûrn; stŭd; circŭs; ü-as in French tu; '-indeterminate vowel.

PLACE (Pronunciation)	PAGE	LAT.	LONG.
Diaca, Moz.	237	11°30'S	39°59'E
Diaka, r., Mali	235	14°40'N	5°00'E
Diamantina, Braz.	143	18°14'S	43°32'W
Diamantina, r., Austl. (dī'man-tē'nȧ)	220	25°38'S	139°53'E
Diamantino, Braz. (dē-á-män-tē'no)	143	14°22'S	56°23'W
Diamond Peak, mtn., Or., U.S.	114	43°32'N	122°08'W
Diana Bank, bk. (dī'ăn'á)	135	22°30'N	74°45'W
Dianbai, China (dĭĕn-bī)	209	21°30'N	111°20'E
Dian Chi, l., China (dĭĕn chē)	204	24°58'N	103°18'E
Dickinson, N.D., U.S. (dĭk'ĭn-sŭn)	104	46°52'N	102°49'W
Dickinson, Tx., U.S. (dĭk'ĭn-sŭn)	123a	29°28'N	95°02'W
Dickinson Bayou, Tx., U.S.	123a	29°26'N	95°08'W
Dickson, Tn., U.S. (dĭk'sŭn)	124	36°03'N	87°24'W
Dickson City, Pa., U.S.	109	41°25'N	75°40'W
Didcot, Eng., U.K. (dĭd'cŏt)	158b	51°35'N	1°15'W
Didiéni, Mali	234	13°53'N	8°06'W
Die, Fr. (dē)	171	44°45'N	5°22'E
Diefenbaker, res., Can.	92	51°20'N	108°10'W
Diego de Ocampo, Pico, mtn., Dom. Rep. (pē'-kô-dyĕ'gô-dĕ-ô-kä'm-pô)	135	19°40'N	70°45'W
Diego Ramirez, Islas, is., Chile (dê ā'gō rä-mē'rāz)	144	56°15'S	70°15'W
Diéma, Mali	234	14°32'N	9°12'W
Dien Bien Phu, Viet.	204	21°38'N	102°49'E
Dieppe, Can. (dê-ĕp')	100	46°06'N	64°45'W
Dieppe, Fr.	161	49°54'N	1°05'E
Dierks, Ar., U.S. (dērks)	121	34°06'N	94°02'W
Diessen, Ger. (dēs'sĕn)	159d	47°57'N	11°06'E
Diest, Bel.	159a	50°59'N	5°05'E
Digby, Can. (dĭg'bĭ)	91	44°37'N	65°46'W
Dighton, Ma., U.S. (dī-tŭn)	110b	41°49'N	71°05'W
Digne, Fr. (dēn'y')	171	44°07'N	6°16'E
Digoin, Fr. (dē-gwăn')	170	46°28'N	4°06'E
Digul, r., Indon.	213	7°00'S	140°27'E
Dijohan Point, c., Phil. (dē-kô-än)	213a	16°24'N	122°25'E
Dijon, Fr. (dē-zhôn')	154	47°21'N	5°02'E
Dikson, Russia (dĭk'sŏn)	178	73°30'N	80°35'E
Dikwa, Nig. (dē'kwä)	231	12°06'N	13°53'E
Dili, E. Timor (dĭl'ê)	213	8°35'S	125°35'E
Di Linosa Island, i., Italy (dê-lê-nō'sä)	162	36°01'N	12°43'E
Dilizhan, Arm.	181	40°45'N	45°00'E
Dillingham, Ak., U.S. (dĭl'ĭng-hăm)	106a	59°10'N	158°38'W
Dillon, Mt., U.S. (dĭl'ŭn)	115	45°12'N	112°40'W
Dillon, S.C., U.S.	125	34°24'N	79°28'W
Dillon Reservoir, res., Oh., U.S.	108	40°05'N	82°05'W
Dilolo, D.R.C. (dē-lō'lō)	232	10°19'S	22°23'E
Dimashq *see* Damascus, Syria	198	33°31'N	36°18'E
Dimbokro, C. Iv.	234	6°39'N	4°42'W
Dimitrovo *see* Pernik, Blg.	163	42°36'N	23°04'E
Dimlang, mtn., Nig.	235	8°24'N	11°47'E
Dimona, Isr.	197a	31°03'N	35°01'E
Dinagat Island, i., Phil.	213	10°15'N	126°15'E
Dinājpur, Bngl.	202	25°38'N	87°39'E
Dinan, Fr. (dē-nän')	170	48°27'N	2°03'W
Dinant, Bel. (dē-nän')	165	50°17'N	4°50'E
Dinara, mts., Serb. (dē'nä-rä)	163	43°50'N	16°15'E
Dinard, Fr.	170	48°38'N	2°04'W
Dindigul, India	203	10°25'N	78°03'E
Dingalan Bay, b., Phil. (dĭŋ-gä'län)	213a	15°19'N	121°33'E
Dingle, Ire. (dĭng''l)	164	52°10'N	10°13'W
Dingle Bay, b., Ire.	161	52°02'N	10°15'W
Dingo, Austl. (dĭŋ'gō)	219	23°45'S	149°26'E
Dinguiraye, Gui.	234	11°18'N	10°43'W
Dingwall, Scot., U.K. (dĭng'wôl)	164	57°37'N	4°23'W
Dingxian, China (dĭŋ shyĕn)	208	38°30'N	115°00'E
Dingxing, China (dĭŋ-shyĭŋ)	208	39°18'N	115°50'E
Dingyuan, China (dĭŋ-yüän)	206	32°32'N	117°40'E
Dingzi Wan, b., China	206	36°33'N	121°06'E
Dinosaur National Monument, rec., Co., U.S. (dī'nō-sôr)	115	40°45'N	109°17'W
Dinslaken, Ger. (dēns'lä-kĕn)	171c	51°33'N	6°44'E
Dinteloord, Neth.	159a	51°38'N	4°21'E
Dinuba, Ca., U.S. (dĭ-nū'bȧ)	118	36°33'N	119°29'W
Dios, Cayo de, i., Cuba (kä'yō-dĕ-dē-ōs')	134	22°05'N	83°05'W
Diourbel, Sen. (dê-o͞or-bĕl')	230	14°40'N	16°15'W
Diphu Pass, p., Asia (dĭ-po͞o)	204	28°15'N	96°45'E
Diquis, r., C.R. (dê-kēs')	133	8°59'N	83°24'W
Dire Dawa, Eth.	231	9°40'N	41°47'E
Diriamba, Nic. (dēr-yäm'bä)	132	11°52'N	86°15'W
Dirk Hartog, i., Austl.	220	26°25'S	113°15'E
Dirksland, Neth.	159a	51°45'N	4°04'E
Dirranbandi, Austl. (dĭ-rá-băn'dê)	219	28°24'S	148°29'E
Dirty Devil, r., Ut., U.S. (dûr'tĭ dĕv''l)	119	38°20'N	110°30'W
Disappointment, l., Austl.	220	23°20'S	123°00'E
Disappointment, Cape, c., Wa., U.S. (dĭs'ā-point'ment)	116c	46°16'N	124°11'W
Discovery, S. Afr. (dĭs-kŭv'ēr-ĭ)	233b	26°10'S	27°53'E
Discovery, is., Can. (dĭs-kŭv'ēr-ê)	116a	48°25'N	123°13'W
Disko, i., Grnld. (dĭs'kō)	89	70°00'N	54°00'W
Disna, Bela. (dēs'ná)	180	55°34'N	28°15'E
Dispur, India	202	26°00'N	91°50'E
Disraëli, Can. (dĭs-rā'lĭ)	99	45°53'N	71°23'W
District of Columbia, dept., U.S.	105	38°50'N	77°00'W
Distrito Federal, dept., Braz. (dēs-trē'tô-fĕ-dĕ-rä'l)	143	15°49'S	47°39'W
Distrito Federal, dept., Mex.	130	19°14'N	99°08'W
Disūq, Egypt (dê-so͞ok')	238b	31°07'N	30°41'E
Diu, India (dē'o͞o)	199	20°48'N	70°58'E
Divilacan Bay, b., Phil. (dê-vê-lä'kän)	213a	17°26'N	122°25'E
Divinópolis, Braz. (dē-vē-nō'pō-lēs)	143	20°10'S	44°53'W
Divo, C. Iv.	234	5°50'N	5°22'W
Dixon, Il., U.S. (dĭks'ŭn)	113	41°50'N	89°30'W

PLACE (Pronunciation)	PAGE	LAT.	LONG.
Dixon Entrance, strt., N.A.	92	54°25'N	132°00'W
Diyarbakir, Tur. (dê-yär-bĕk'ĭr)	198	38°00'N	40°10'E
Dja, r., Afr.	231	2°30'N	14°00'E
Djambala, Congo	236	2°33'S	14°45'E
Djanet, Alg.	230	24°29'N	9°26'E
Djebobo, mtn., Ghana	234	8°20'N	0°37'E
Djedi, Oued, r., Alg.	162	34°18'N	4°39'E
Djember, Chad	235	10°25'N	17°50'E
Djerba, Île de, i., Tun.	162	33°53'N	11°26'E
Djerid, Chott, l., Tun. (jĕr'ĭd)	230	33°15'N	8°29'E
Djibasso, Burkina	234	13°07'N	4°10'W
Djibo, Burkina	234	14°06'N	1°38'W
Djibouti, Dji. (jē-bo͞o-tē')	238a	11°34'N	43°00'E
Djibouti, nation, Afr.	238a	11°35'N	48°08'E
Djokoumatombi, Congo	236	0°47'N	15°22'E
Djokupunda, D.R.C.	232	5°27'S	20°58'E
Djoua, r., Afr.	236	1°25'N	13°40'E
Djursholm, Swe. (djo͞ors'hôlm)	166	59°26'N	18°01'E
Dmitriyev-L'govskiy, Russia (d'mē'trĭ-yĕf l'gôf'skĭ)	176	52°07'N	35°05'E
Dmitrov, Russia (d'mē'trôf)	176	56°21'N	37°32'E
Dmitrovsk, Russia (d'mē'trôfsk)	176	52°30'N	35°10'E
Dmytrivka, Ukr.	177	47°57'N	38°56'E
Dnepropetrovsk *see* Dnipropetrovs'k, Ukr.	178	48°15'N	34°08'E
Dnieper (Dnipro), r., Eur.	181	46°45'N	33°40'E
Dniester, r., Eur.	181	48°21'N	28°10'E
Dniprodzerzhyns'k, Ukr.	181	48°32'N	34°38'E
Dniprodzerzhyns'ke vodoskhovyshche, res., Ukr.	178	49°00'N	34°10'E
Dnipropetrovs'k, Ukr.	178	48°15'N	34°08'E
Dnipropetrovs'k, prov., Ukr.	177	48°15'N	34°10'E
Dniprovs'kyi lyman, b., Ukr.	177	46°33'N	31°45'E
Dnistrovs'kyi lyman, l., Ukr.	177	46°13'N	29°50'E
Dno, Russia (d'nô')	176	57°49'N	29°59'E
Do, Lac, l., Mali	234	15°50'N	2°20'W
Doba, Chad	235	8°39'N	16°51'E
Dobbs Ferry, N.Y., U.S. (dŏbz fĕ'rê)	110a	41°01'N	73°53'W
Dobbyn, Austl. (dôb'ĭn)	218	19°45'S	140°02'E
Dobele, Lat. (dô'bĕ-lĕ)	167	56°37'N	23°18'E
Doberai, Jazirah, pen., Indon.	213	1°25'S	133°15'E
Dobo, Indon.	213	6°00'S	134°18'E
Doboj, Bos. (dō'boi)	175	44°42'N	18°04'E
Dobrich, Blg.	163	43°33'N	27°52'E
Dobryanka, Russia (dôb-ryän'kȧ)	186a	58°27'N	56°26'E
Dobšina, Slvk. (dôp'shê-nä)	169	48°48'N	20°25'E
Doce, r., Braz. (dō'sä)	143	19°01'S	42°14'W
Doce, Canal Numero, can., Arg.	141c	36°47'S	59°00'W
Doce Leguas, Cayos de las, is., Cuba	134	20°55'N	79°05'W
Doctor Arroyo, Mex. (dŏk-tōr' är-rō'yō)	130	23°41'N	100°10'W
Doddington, Eng., U.K. (dŏd'dĭng-tŏn)	158b	51°17'N	0°47'E
Dodecanese *see* Dodekanisoy, is., Grc.	175	38°00'N	26°10'E
Dodekanisoy (Dodecanese), is., Grc.	175	38°00'N	26°10'E
Dodge City, Ks., U.S. (dŏj)	104	37°44'N	100°01'W
Dodgeville, Wi., U.S. (dŏj'vĭl)	113	42°58'N	90°07'W
Dodoma, Tan. (dō'dô-má)	232	6°11'S	35°45'E
Dog, l., Can. (dŏg)	98	48°42'N	89°24'W
Dogger Bank, bk. (dŏg'gēr)	165	55°07'N	2°25'E
Dogubayazit, Tur.	181	39°35'N	44°00'E
Doha *see* Ad Dawhah, Qatar	198	25°02'N	51°28'E
Dohad, India	202	22°52'N	74°18'E
Dokshytsy, Bela. (dôk-shētsĕ)	176	54°53'N	27°49'E
Dolbeau, Can.	91	48°52'N	72°16'W
Dole, Fr. (dōl)	161	47°07'N	5°28'E
Dolgaya, Kosa, c., Russia (kô'sȧ dôl-gä'yä)	177	46°42'N	37°42'E
Dolgeville, N.Y., U.S.	109	43°10'N	74°45'W
Dolgiy, i., Russia	180	69°20'N	59°20'E
Dolgoprudnyy, Russia	186b	55°57'N	37°33'E
Dolinsk, Russia (dá-lēnsk')	185	47°29'N	142°31'E
Dollar Harbor, b., Bah.	134	25°30'N	79°15'W
Dolomite, Al., U.S. (dŏl'ô-mīt)	110h	33°28'N	86°57'W
Dolomiti, mts., Italy	174	46°16'N	11°43'E
Dolores, Arg. (dô-lō'rĕs)	144	36°20'S	57°42'W
Dolores, Col.	142a	3°33'N	74°54'W
Dolores, Ur.	141c	33°32'S	58°15'W
Dolores, Tx., U.S. (dô-lō'rĕs)	122	27°42'N	99°47'W
Dolores, r., Co., U.S.	119	38°35'N	108°50'W
Dolores Hidalgo, Mex. (dô-lō'rĕs-ē-däl'gō)	130	21°09'N	100°56'W
Dolphin and Union Strait, strt., Can. (dŏl'fĭn ūn'yŭn)	92	69°22'N	117°10'W
Dolyna, Ukr.	169	48°57'N	24°01'E
Domažlice, Czech Rep. (dō'mäzh-lê-tsĕ)	168	49°27'N	12°55'E
Dombasle-sur-Meurthe, Fr. (dôn-bäl')	171	48°38'N	6°18'E
Dombóvár, Hung. (dŏm'bō-vär)	169	46°22'N	18°08'E
Domeyko, Cordillera, mts., Chile (kôr-dēl-yĕ'rä-dô-mā'kō)	142	20°50'S	69°02'W
Dominica, nation, N.A. (dō-mĭ-nē'kȧ)	129	15°30'N	60°45'W
Dominica Channel, strt., N.A.	133b	15°00'N	61°30'W
Dominican Republic, nation, N.A. (dô-mĭn'ĭ-kăn)	129	19°00'N	70°45'W
Dominion, Can. (dô-mĭn'yŭn)	101	46°13'N	60°01'W
Domiongo, D.R.C.	236	4°37'S	21°15'E
Domodedovo, Russia (dô-mô-dyĕ'do-vô)	186b	55°27'N	37°45'E
Dom Silvério, Braz. (dôn-sĕl-vĕ'ryō)	141a	20°09'S	42°57'W
Don, r., Russia	178	49°50'N	41°30'E
Don, r., Eng., U.K.	158a	53°39'N	0°58'W
Don, r., Scot., U.K.	164	57°19'N	2°39'W
Donaldson, Mi., U.S. (dŏn'ăl-sŭn)	117k	46°19'N	84°22'W

PLACE (Pronunciation)	PAGE	LAT.	LONG.
Donaldsonville, La., U.S. (dŏn'ăld-sŭn-vĭl)	123	30°05'N	90°58'W
Donalsonville, Ga., U.S.	124	31°02'N	84°50'W
Donawitz, Aus. (dō'ná-vĭts)	168	47°23'N	15°05'E
Don Benito, Spain (dōn'bå-nē'tō)	172	38°55'N	5°52'W
Doncaster, Austl. (doŋ'kăs-tēr)	217a	37°47'S	145°08'E
Doncaster, Eng., U.K. (doŋ'kăs-tēr)	164	53°32'N	1°07'W
Doncaster, co., Eng., U.K.	158a	53°35'N	1°10'W
Dondo, Ang. (dōn'dō)	232	9°38'S	14°25'E
Dondo, Moz.	232	19°33'S	34°47'E
Dondra Head, c., Sri L.	203	5°52'N	80°52'E
Donegal, Ire. (dŏn-ê-gôl')	164	54°44'N	8°05'W
Donegal Bay, Ire. (dŏn-ĕ-gôl')	160	54°35'N	8°36'W
Donets Coal Basin, reg., Ukr. (dô-nyĕts')	177	48°15'N	38°50'E
Donets'k, Ukr.	178	48°00'N	37°35'E
Donets'k, prov., Ukr.	177	47°55'N	37°40'E
Dong, r., China (dôŋ)	205	24°13'N	115°08'E
Dongara, Austl. (dôn-gă'rȧ)	218	29°15'S	115°00'E
Dongba, China (dôŋ-bä)	206	31°40'N	119°02'E
Dong'e, China (dôŋ-ŭ)	206	36°21'N	116°14'E
Dong'ezhen, China	208	36°11'N	116°16'E
Dongfang, China (dôŋ-fäŋ)	209	19°08'N	108°42'E
Donggala, Indon. (dōn-gä'lä)	212	0°45'S	119°32'E
Dongguan, China (dôŋ-gůän)	207a	23°03'N	113°46'E
Dongguang, China (dôŋ-gůäŋ)	206	37°54'N	116°33'E
Donghai, China (dôŋ-hī)	208	34°35'N	119°05'E
Dong Hoi, Viet. (dông-hô-ĕ')	212	17°25'N	106°42'E
Dongila, Eth.	231	11°17'N	37°00'E
Dongming, China (dôŋ-mĭŋ)	206	35°16'N	115°06'E
Dongo, Ang. (dôŋ'gō)	232	14°45'S	15°30'E
Dongon Point, c., Phil. (dŏng-ôn')	213a	12°43'N	120°35'E
Dongou, Congo (dôŋ-go͞o')	231	2°02'N	18°04'E
Dongping, China (dôŋ-pĭŋ)	208	35°50'N	116°24'E
Dongping Hu, l., China (dôŋ-pĭŋ ho͞o)	206	36°06'N	116°24'E
Dongshan, China (doŋ-shän)	206	31°05'N	120°24'E
Dongtai, China	206	32°51'N	120°20'E
Dongting Hu, l., China (dôŋ-tĭŋ ho͞o)	205	29°10'N	112°30'E
Dongxiang, China (dôŋ-shyän)	209	28°18'N	116°38'E
Doniphan, Mo., U.S. (dŏn'ĭ-făn)	121	36°37'N	90°50'W
Donji Vakuf, Bos. (dōn'yĭ väk'o͝of)	175	44°08'N	17°25'E
Don Martin, Presa de, res., Mex. (prĕ'sä-dĕ-dôn-mär-tē'n)	122	27°35'N	100°38'W
Donnacona, Can.	99	46°40'N	71°46'W
Donnemarie-en-Montois, Fr. (dôn-mä-rē'ĕn-môn-twä')	171b	48°29'N	3°09'E
Donner und Blitzen, r., Or., U.S. (dŏn'ēr ònt'blĭ'tsĕn)	114	42°45'N	118°57'W
Donnybrook, S. Afr. (dŏ-nĭ-brŏk)	233c	29°56'S	29°54'E
Donora, Pa., U.S. (dŏ-nō'rā)	111e	40°10'N	79°51'W
Donostia-San Sebastián, Spain	154	43°19'N	1°59'W
Donoúsa, i., Grc.	175	37°09'N	25°53'E
Doolow, Som.	238a	4°10'N	42°05'E
Doonerak, Mount, mtn., Ak., U.S. (do͞o'nĕ-răk)	103	68°00'N	150°34'W
Doorn, Neth.	159a	52°02'N	5°21'E
Door Peninsula, pen., Wi., U.S. (dōr)	113	44°40'N	87°36'W
Dora Baltea, r., Italy (dō'rä bäl'tā-ä)	174	45°40'N	7°34'E
Doraville, Ga., U.S. (dō'rá-vĭl)	110c	33°54'N	84°17'W
Dorchester, Eng., U.K. (dôr'chĕs-tēr)	164	50°45'N	2°34'W
Dordogne, r., Fr. (dôr-dôn'yē)	156	44°53'N	0°16'E
Dordrecht, Neth. (dôr'drĕkt)	165	51°48'N	4°39'E
Dordrecht, S. Afr. (dô'drĕkt)	233c	31°24'S	27°06'E
Doré Lake, l., Can.	96	54°31'N	107°06'W
Dorgali, Italy (dôr'gä-lē)	174	40°18'N	9°37'E
Dörgön Nuur, l., Mong.	204	47°47'N	94°01'E
Dorion-Vaudreuil, Can. (dôr-yō)	102a	45°23'N	74°01'W
Dorking, Eng., U.K. (dôr'kĭng)	158b	51°12'N	0°20'W
Dormont, Pa., U.S. (dôr'mŏnt)	111e	40°24'N	80°02'W
Dornbirn, Aus. (dôrn'bērn)	168	47°24'N	9°45'E
Dornoch, Scot., U.K. (dôr'nŏk)	160	57°55'N	4°01'W
Dornoch Firth, b., Scot., U.K. (dôr'nŏk fûrth)	164	57°55'N	3°55'W
Dorogobuzh, Russia (dôrôgô'-bo͞o'zh)	176	54°57'N	33°18'E
Dorohoi, Rom. (dō-rô-hoi')	169	47°57'N	26°28'E
Dorre Island, i., Austl. (dôr)	220	25°19'S	113°10'E
Dorstsen, Ger.	171c	51°40'N	6°58'E
Dortmund, Ger. (dôrt'mŏnt)	161	51°31'N	7°28'E
Dortmund-Ems-Kanal, can., Ger. (dôrt'mo͝ond-ĕms'kä-näl')	171c	51°50'N	7°25'E
Dörtyol, Tur. (dûrt'yôl)	163	36°50'N	36°20'E
Dorval, Can. (dôr-vál')	102a	45°26'N	73°44'W
Dos Bahías, Cabo, c., Arg. (kä'bô-dōs-bä-ē'äs)	144	44°55'S	65°35'W
Dos Caminos, Ven. (dôs-kä-mē'nōs)	143b	9°38'N	67°17'W
Dosewallips, r., Wa., U.S. (dō'sê-wäl'lĭps)	116a	47°45'N	123°04'W
Dos Hermanas, Spain (dôsĕr-mä'näs)	172	37°17'N	5°56'W
Dosso, Niger (dôs-ō')	230	13°03'N	3°12'E
Dothan, Al., U.S. (dō'thăn)	105	31°13'N	85°23'W
Douai, Fr. (do͞o-å')	161	50°23'N	3°04'E
Douala, Cam. (do͞o-ä'lä)	230	4°03'N	9°42'E
Douarnenez, Fr. (do͞o-är nĕ-nĕs')	170	48°06'N	4°18'W
Double Bayou, Tx., U.S. (dŭb''l bī'yo͞o)	123a	29°40'N	94°38'W
Doubs, r., Eur.	171	46°15'N	5°50'E
Douentza, Mali	234	15°00'N	2°57'W
Douglas, I. of Man (dŭg'lȧs)	164	54°10'N	4°24'W
Douglas, Ak., U.S. (dŭg'lȧs)	103	58°18'N	134°35'W
Douglas, Az., U.S.	104	31°20'N	109°30'W
Douglas, Ga., U.S.	125	31°30'N	82°53'W
Douglas, Wy., U.S. (dŭg'lȧs)	115	42°45'N	105°21'W
Douglas, r., Eng., U.K. (dŭg'lȧs)	158a	53°38'N	2°48'W

ăt; finăl; rāte; senåte; ärm; åsk; sofȧ; fâre; ch-choose; dh-as th in other; bē; êvent; bĕt; recĕnt; cratēr; g-gō; gh-guttural g; bĭt; ĭ-short neutral; rīde; ĸ-guttural k as ch in German ich;

PRONOUNCING INDEX

Douglas Channel – East Cleveland 289

PLACE (Pronunciation)	PAGE	LAT.	LONG.
Douglas Channel, strt., Can.	94	53°30'N	129°12'W
Douglas Lake, res., Tn., U.S. (dŭg'lăs)	124	36°00'N	83°35'W
Douglas Lake Indian Reserve, I.R., Can.	95	50°10'N	120°49'W
Douglasville, Ga., U.S. (dŭg'lăs-vĭl)	124	33°45'N	84°47'W
Dourada, Serra, mts., Braz. (sĕ'r-rä-dôōō-rá'dä)	143	15°11'S	49°57'W
Dourdan, Fr. (dōōr-däN')	171b	48°32'N	2°01'E
Douro, r., Port. (dô'ó-rô)	172	41°03'N	8°12'W
Dove, r., Eng., U.K. (dŭv)	158a	52°53'N	1°47'W
Dover, S. Afr.	238c	27°05'S	27°44'E
Dover, Eng., U.K.	154	51°08'N	1°19'E
Dover, De., U.S. (dō vẽr)	105	39°10'N	75°30'W
Dover, N.H., U.S.	109	43°15'N	71°00'W
Dover, N.J., U.S.	110a	40°53'N	74°33'W
Dover, Oh., U.S.	108	40°35'N	81°30'W
Dover, Strait of, strt., Eur.	156	50°50'N	1°15'W
Dover-Foxcroft, Me., U.S. (dō'vẽr fŏks'krôft)	100	45°10'N	69°15'W
Dovre Fjell, mts., Nor. (dŏv'rĕ fyĕl')	156	62°03'N	8°36'E
Dow, Il., U.S. (dou)	117e	39°01'N	90°20'W
Dowagiac, Mi., U.S. (dô-wô'jăk)	108	42°00'N	86°05'W
Downers Grove, Il., U.S. (dou'nẽrz grōv)	111a	41°48'N	88°00'W
Downey, Ca., U.S. (dou'nĭ)	117a	33°56'N	118°08'W
Downieville, Ca., U.S. (dou'nĭ-nĭl)	118	39°35'N	120°48'W
Downs, Ks., U.S. (dounz)	120	39°29'N	98°32'W
Doylestown, Oh., U.S. (doilz'toun)	111d	40°58'N	81°43'W
Drâa, Cap, c., Mor. (drà)	230	28°39'N	12°15'W
Drâa, Oued, r., Afr.	230	28°00'N	9°31'W
Drabiv, Ukr.	177	49°57'N	32°14'E
Drac, r., Fr. (dräk)	171	44°50'N	5°47'E
Dracut, Ma., U.S. (drā'kŭt)	101a	42°40'N	71°19'W
Draganovo, Blg. (drä-gä-nō'vô)	175	43°13'N	25°45'E
Drăgăşani, Rom. (drä-gá-shän'ĭ)	175	44°39'N	24°18'E
Draguignan, Fr. (drä-gēn-yäN')	171	43°35'N	6°28'E
Drahichyn, Bela.	169	52°10'N	25°11'E
Drakensberg, mts., Afr. (drä'kĕnz-bĕrgh)	232	29°15'S	29°07'E
Drake Passage, strt. (drāk păs'ĭj)	139	57°00'S	65°00'W
Dráma, Grc. (drä'mä)	163	41°09'N	24°10'E
Drammen, Nor. (dräm'ĕn)	160	59°45'N	10°15'E
Drau (Drava), r., Eur. (drou)	168	46°44'N	13°45'E
Drava, r., Eur. (drä'vä)	156	45°45'N	17°30'E
Dravograd, Slvn. (drä'vô-gräd')	174	46°37'N	15°01'E
Drawsko Pomorskie, Pol. (dräv'skō pō-mōr'skyĕ)	168	53°31'N	15°50'E
Drayton Harbor, b., Wa., U.S. (drā'tŭn)	116d	48°58'N	122°40'W
Drayton Plains, Mi., U.S.	111b	42°41'N	83°23'W
Drayton Valley, Can.	95	53°13'N	114°59'W
Drensteinfurt, Ger. (drĕn'shtīn-fōōrt)	171c	51°47'N	7°44'E
Dresden, Ger. (drās'dĕn)	154	51°05'N	13°45'E
Dreux, Fr. (drû)	170	48°44'N	1°24'E
Driefontein, S. Afr.	238c	25°53'S	29°10'E
Drin, r., Alb. (drēn)	175	42°13'N	20°13'E
Drina, r., Serb. (drē'nä)	163	44°09'N	19°30'E
Drinit, Pellg i, b., Alb.	175	41°42'N	19°17'E
Dr. Ir. W. J. van Blommestein Meer, res., Sur.	143	4°45'N	55°05'W
Drissa, r., Eur.	176	55°44'N	28°58'E
Driver, Va., U.S.	110g	36°50'N	76°30'W
Dröbak, Nor. (drû'bäk)	166	59°40'N	10°35'E
Drobeta-Turnu Severin, Rom.	163	43°54'N	24°49'E
Drogheda, Ire. (drŏ'hĕ-då)	160	53°43'N	6°15'W
Drohobych, Ukr.	169	49°21'N	23°31'E
Drôme, r., Fr. (drōm)	170	44°42'N	4°53'E
Dronfield, Eng., U.K. (drŏn'fēld)	158a	53°18'N	1°28'W
Drumheller, Can. (drŭm-hĕl-ẽr)	90	51°28'N	112°42'W
Drummond, i., Mi., U.S. (drŭm'ŭnd)	108	46°00'N	83°50'W
Drummondville, Can. (drŭm'ŭnd-vĭl)	91	45°53'N	72°33'W
Drumright, Ok., U.S. (drŭm'rīt)	121	35°59'N	96°37'W
Drunen, Neth.	159a	51°41'N	5°10'E
Drut', r., Bela. (drōōt)	176	53°40'N	29°45'E
Druya, Bela. (drò'yà)	176	55°45'N	27°26'E
Drwęca, r., Pol. (d'r-vĕn'tsà)	169	53°06'N	19°13'E
Dryden, Can. (drī-dĕn)	91	49°47'N	92°50'W
Drysdale, Austl.	217a	38°11'S	144°34'E
Dry Tortugas, is., Fl., U.S. (tôr-tōō'gäz)	125a	24°37'N	82°45'W
Dry Tortugas National Park, rec., Fl., U.S.	125a	24°42'N	83°02'W
Dschang, Cam. (dshäng)	230	5°34'N	10°09'E
Duabo, Lib.	234	5°40'N	8°05'W
Duagh, Can.	102g	53°43'N	113°24'W
Duarte, Pico, mtn., Dom. Rep. (dĭŭ'ărtĕh pēcô)	129	19°00'N	71°00'W
Duas Barras, Braz. (dōō'äs-bá'r-räs)	141a	22°03'S	42°30'W
Dubai see Dubayy, U.A.E.	198	25°18'N	55°26'E
Dubăsari, Mol.	177	47°16'N	29°11'E
Dubawnt, l., Can. (dōō-bônt')	92	63°27'N	103°30'W
Dubawnt, r., Can.	92	61°30'N	103°49'W
Dubayy, U.A.E.	198	25°18'N	55°26'E
Dubbo, Austl. (dŭb'ō)	219	32°20'S	148°42'E
Dubie, D.R.C.	237	8°33'S	28°32'E
Dublin, Ire.	154	53°20'N	6°15'W
Dublin, Ca., U.S. (dŭb'lĭn)	116b	37°42'N	121°56'W
Dublin, Ga., U.S.	125	32°33'N	82°55'W
Dublin, Tx., U.S.	122	32°05'N	98°20'W
Dubna, Russia	176	56°44'N	37°10'E
Dubno, Ukr. (dōō'b-nô)	169	50°24'N	25°44'E
Du Bois, Pa., U.S. (dò-bois')	109	41°10'N	78°45'W
Dubovka, Russia (dōō-bôf'kà)	181	49°00'N	44°50'E
Dubrovka, Russia (dōō-brôf'kà)	186c	59°51'N	30°56'E
Dubrovnik, Cro. (dò'brôv-nĕk) (rä-gōō'sä)	154	42°40'N	18°10'E
Dubrowna, Bela.	176	54°39'N	30°54'E
Dubuque, Ia., U.S. (dò-būk')	105	42°30'N	90°43'W
Duchesne, Ut., U.S. (dò-shān')	119	40°12'N	110°23'W
Duchesne, r., Ut., U.S.	119	40°20'N	110°50'W
Duchess, Austl. (dŭch'ĕs)	218	21°30'S	139°55'E
Ducie Island, i., Pit. (dü-sē')	2	25°30'S	126°20'W
Duck, r., Tn., U.S.	124	35°55'N	87°40'W
Duckabush, r., Wa., U.S. (dŭk'ă-bòsh)	116a	47°41'N	123°09'W
Duck Lake, Can.	96	52°47'N	106°13'W
Duck Mountain, mtn., Can.	97	51°35'N	101°00'W
Ducktown, Tn., U.S. (dŭk'toun)	124	35°03'N	84°20'W
Duck Valley Indian Reservation, I.R., Id., U.S.	114	42°02'N	115°49'W
Duckwater Peak, mtn., Nv., U.S. (dŭk-wô-tẽr)	118	39°00'N	115°31'W
Duda, r., Col. (dōō'dä)	142a	3°25'N	74°23'W
Dudinka, Russia (dōō-dĭn'kà)	178	69°15'N	85°42'E
Dudley, Eng., U.K. (dŭd'lĭ)	161	52°28'N	2°07'E
Duero, r., Eur.	156	41°30'N	4°30'W
Dufourspitze, mtn., Eur.	168	45°55'N	7°52'E
Dugger, In., U.S. (dŭg'ẽr)	108	39°00'N	87°10'W
Dugi Otok, i., Serb. (dōō'gē o'tôk)	174	44°03'N	14°40'E
Duisburg, Ger. (dōō'ĭs-bòrgh)	161	51°26'N	6°46'E
Dukhān, Qatar	201	25°25'N	50°48'E
Dukhovshchina, Russia (dōō-kôfsh-'chēnà)	176	55°13'N	32°26'E
Dukinfield, Eng., U.K. (dŭk'ĭn-fēld)	158a	53°28'N	2°05'W
Dukla Pass, p., Eur. (dò'klä)	161	49°25'N	21°44'E
Dulce, Golfo, b., C.R. (gōl'fô dōōl'sä)	129	8°25'N	83°13'W
Dülken, Ger. (dül'kĕn)	171c	51°15'N	6°21'E
Dülmen, Ger. (dül'mĕn)	171c	51°50'N	7°17'E
Duluth, Mn., U.S. (dò-lōōth')	105	46°50'N	92°07'W
Dumai, Indon.	197b	1°39'N	101°30'E
Dumali Point, c., Phil. (dōō-mä'lē)	213a	13°07'N	121°42'E
Dumas, Tx., U.S.	120	35°52'N	101°58'W
Dumbarton, Scot., U.K. (dŭm'băr-tŭn)	164	56°00'N	4°35'W
Dum-Dum, India	202a	22°37'N	88°25'E
Dumfries, Scot., U.K. (dŭm-frēs')	164	55°05'N	3°40'W
Dumjor, India	202a	22°37'N	88°14'E
Dumont, N.J., U.S. (dōō'mŏnt)	110a	40°56'N	74°00'W
Dumyāt, Egypt	231	31°22'N	31°50'E
Dunaföldvár, Hung. (dò'nô-fûld'vär)	169	46°48'N	18°55'E
Dunaïvtsi, Ukr.	177	48°52'N	26°51'E
Dunajec, r., Pol. (dò-nä'yĕts)	169	49°52'N	20°53'E
Dunaújváros, Hung.	169	46°57'N	18°55'E
Dunay, Russia (dōō'nĭ)	186c	59°59'N	30°57'E
Dunbar, W.V., U.S.	108	38°20'N	81°45'W
Duncan, Can. (dŭŋ'kăn)	90	48°47'N	123°42'W
Duncan, Ok., U.S.	121	34°29'N	97°56'W
Duncan, r., Can.	95	50°30'N	116°45'W
Duncan Dam, dam, Can.	95	50°15'N	116°55'W
Duncan Lake, l., Can.	95	50°20'N	117°00'W
Duncansby Head, c., Scot., U.K. (dŭn'kănz-bĭ)	164	58°40'N	3°01'W
Duncanville, Tx., U.S. (dŭn'kăn-vĭl)	117c	32°39'N	96°55'W
Dundalk, Ire. (dŭn'kôk)	160	54°00'N	6°18'W
Dundalk, Md., U.S.	110e	39°16'N	76°31'W
Dundalk Bay, b., Ire. (dŭn'dôk)	164	53°55'N	6°15'W
Dundas, Can. (dŭn-dăs')	99	43°16'N	79°58'W
Dundas, l., Austl. (dŭn-dás)	220	32°15'S	122°00'E
Dundas Island, i., Can.	94	54°33'N	130°55'W
Dundas Strait, strt., Austl.	220	10°35'S	131°15'E
Dundedin, Fl., U.S. (dŭn-ē'dĭn)	125a	28°00'N	82°43'W
Dundee, S. Afr.	233c	28°14'S	30°16'E
Dundee, Scot., U.K.	154	56°30'N	2°55'W
Dundee, Il., U.S. (dŭn-dē)	111a	42°06'N	88°17'W
Dundrum Bay, b., N. Ire., U.K. (dŭn-drŭm')	164	54°13'N	5°47'W
Dunedin, N.Z.	221a	45°48'S	170°32'E
Dunellen, N.J., U.S. (dŭn-ĕl'l'n)	110a	40°36'N	74°28'W
Dunfermline, Scot., U.K. (dŭn-fĕrm'lĭn)	164	56°05'N	3°30'W
Dungarvan, Ire. (dŭn-gàr'văn)	164	52°06'N	7°50'W
Dungeness, Wa., U.S. (dŭnj-nĕs')	116a	48°09'N	123°07'W
Dungeness, r., Wa., U.S.	116a	48°03'N	123°10'W
Dungeness Spit, Wa., U.S.	116a	48°11'N	123°03'W
Dunhua, China (dòn-hwä)	205	43°18'N	128°10'E
Dunkerque, Fr. (dŭN-kĕrk')	161	51°02'N	2°37'E
Dunkirk, In., U.S. (dŭn'kûrk)	108	40°20'N	85°25'W
Dunkwa, Ghana	234	5°22'N	1°12'W
Dun Laoghaire, Ire. (dŭn-lā'rĕ)	160	53°16'N	6°09'W
Dunlap, Ia., U.S. (dŭn'lăp)	112	41°53'N	95°33'W
Dunlap, Tn., U.S.	124	35°23'N	85°23'W
Dunmore, Pa., U.S. (dŭn'mōr)	109	41°25'N	75°30'W
Dunn, N.C., U.S. (dŭn)	125	35°18'N	78°37'W
Dunnellon, Fl., U.S. (dŭn-ĕl'ŏn)	125	29°02'N	82°28'W
Dunnville, Can. (dŭn'vĭl)	99	42°55'N	79°40'W
Dunqulah, Sudan	231	19°21'N	30°19'E
Dunsmuir, Ca., U.S. (dŭnz'mūr)	114	41°08'N	122°17'W
Dunwoody, Ga., U.S. (dŭn-wòd'ĭ)	110c	33°57'N	84°20'W
Duolun, China (dwô-lōōn)	205	42°12'N	116°15'E
Du Page, r., Il., U.S. (dōō pāj)	111a	41°41'N	88°11'W
Du Page, East Branch, r., Il., U.S.	111a	41°42'N	88°09'W
Du Page, West Branch, r., Il., U.S.	111a	41°42'N	88°09'W
Dupax, Phil. (dōō'päks)	213a	16°16'N	121°06'E
Dupo, Il., U.S. (dū'pō)	117e	38°31'N	90°12'W
Duque de Caxias, Braz. (dōō'kĕ-dĕ-kà'shyás)	141a	22°46'S	43°18'W
Duquesne, Pa., U.S. (dò-kān')	111e	40°22'N	79°51'W
Du Quoin, Il., U.S. (dò-kwoin')	121	38°01'N	89°14'W
Durance, r., Fr. (dü-räNs')	161	43°46'N	5°52'E
Durand, Mi., U.S. (dû-rănd')	108	42°50'N	84°00'W
Durand, Wi., U.S.	113	44°37'N	91°58'W
Durango, Mex. (dōō-rä'n-gô)	128	24°02'N	104°42'W
Durango, Co., U.S. (dò-răŋ'gō)	119	37°15'N	107°55'W
Durango, state, Mex.	128	25°00'N	106°00'W
Durant, Ms., U.S. (dû-rănt')	124	33°05'N	89°50'W
Durant, Ok., U.S.	121	33°59'N	96°23'W
Duratón, r., Spain (dōō-rä-tōn')	172	41°30'N	3°55'W
Durazno, Ur. (dōō-räz'nō)	144	33°21'S	56°31'W
Durazno, dept., Ur.	141c	33°00'S	56°35'W
Durban, S. Afr. (dûr'băn)	232	29°48'S	31°00'E
Durbanville, S. Afr. (dûr-băn'vĭl)	232a	33°50'S	18°39'E
Durbe, Lat. (dōōr'bĕ)	167	56°36'N	21°24'E
Đurđevac, Cro.	163	46°03'N	17°03'E
Düren, Ger. (dü'rĕn)	171c	50°48'N	6°30'E
Durham, Eng., U.K. (dûr'ăm)	164	54°47'N	1°46'W
Durham, N.C., U.S.	105	36°00'N	78°55'W
Durham Downs, Austl.	222	27°30'S	141°55'E
Durrës, Alb. (dòr'ĕs)	154	41°19'N	19°27'E
Duryea, Pa., U.S. (dōōr-yā')	109	41°20'N	75°50'W
Dushan, China	206	31°38'N	116°16'E
Dushan, China (dōō-shän)	209	25°50'N	107°42'E
Dushanbe, Taj.	183	38°30'N	68°45'E
Düsseldorf, Ger. (düs'ĕl-dôrf)	161	51°14'N	6°47'E
Dussen, Neth.	159a	51°43'N	4°58'E
Dutalan Ula, mts., Mong.	208	49°25'N	112°40'E
Dutch Harbor, Ak., U.S. (dŭch här'bẽr)	106a	53°58'N	166°30'W
Duvall, Wa., U.S. (dōō'vâl)	116a	47°44'N	121°59'W
Duwamish, r., Wa., U.S. (dōō-wăm'ĭsh)	116a	47°24'N	122°18'W
Duyun, China (dōō-yòn)	204	26°18'N	107°40'E
Dvinskaya Guba, b., Russia	180	65°10'N	38°40'E
Dwārka, India	202	22°18'N	68°59'E
Dwight, Il., U.S. (dwīt)	108	41°00'N	88°20'W
Dworshak Res, Id., U.S.	114	46°45'N	115°50'W
Dyat'kovo, Russia (dyät'kō-vō)	176	53°36'N	34°19'E
Dyer, In., U.S. (dī'ẽr)	111a	41°30'N	87°31'W
Dyersburg, Tn., U.S. (dī'ẽrz-bûrg)	124	36°02'N	89°23'W
Dyersville, Ia., U.S. (dī'ẽrz-vĭl)	113	42°28'N	91°09'W
Dyes Inlet, Wa., U.S. (dīz)	116a	47°37'N	122°45'W
Dykhtau, Gora, mtn., Russia	182	43°03'N	43°08'E
Dyment, Can. (dī'mĕnt)	97	49°37'N	92°19'W
Dzamïn Üüd, Mong.	205	44°38'N	111°32'E
Dzaoudzi, May. (dzou'dzĭ)	233	12°44'S	45°15'E
Dzavhan, r., Mong.	204	48°19'N	94°08'E
Dzerzhinsk, Russia	180	56°20'N	43°50'E
Dzerzhyns'k, Ukr.	177	48°26'N	37°50'E
Dzhalal-Abad, Kyrg. (já-läl'á-bät')	183	40°56'N	73°00'E
Dzhambul see Zhambyl, Kaz.	183	42°51'N	71°29'E
Dzhankoi, Ukr.	181	45°43'N	34°22'E
Dzhizak, Uzb. (dzhĕ'zäk)	183	40°13'N	67°58'E
Dzhugdzhur Khrebet, mts., Russia (jòg-jōōr')	179	56°15'N	137°00'E
Działoszyce, Pol. (jyä-wō-shē'tsĕ)	169	50°21'N	20°22'E
Dzibalchén, Mex. (zē-bäl-chĕ'n)	132a	19°25'N	89°39'W
Dzidzantún, Mex. (zēd-zän-tōō'n)	132a	21°18'N	89°00'W
Dzierżoniów, Pol. (dzyĕr-zhôn'yŭf)	168	50°44'N	16°38'E
Dzilam González, Mex. (zē-lä'm-gôn-zä'lĕz)	132a	21°21'N	88°53'W
Dzitás, Mex. (zē-tá's)	132a	20°47'N	88°32'W
Dzungaria, reg., China (dzòŋ-gä'rĭ-à)	204	44°39'N	86°13'E
Dzungarian Gate, p., Asia	204	45°00'N	88°00'E
Dzyarzhynsk, Bela.	176	53°41'N	27°14'E

E

PLACE (Pronunciation)	PAGE	LAT.	LONG.
Eagle, W.V., U.S.	108	38°10'N	81°20'W
Eagle, r., Co., U.S.	119	39°32'N	106°28'W
Eaglecliff, Wa., U.S. (ē'gl-klĭf)	116c	46°10'N	123°13'W
Eagle Creek, r., In., U.S.	111g	39°54'N	86°17'W
Eagle Grove, Ia., U.S.	113	42°39'N	93°55'W
Eagle Lake, Me., U.S.	100	47°03'N	68°38'W
Eagle Lake, Tx., U.S.	123	29°37'N	96°20'W
Eagle Lake, l., Ca., U.S.	114	40°45'N	120°52'W
Eagle Mountain, Ca., U.S.	118	33°49'N	115°27'W
Eagle Mountain L, Tx., U.S.	117c	32°56'N	97°27'W
Eagle Pass, Tx., U.S.	104	28°49'N	100°30'W
Eagle Pk, Ca., U.S.	114	41°18'N	120°11'W
Ealing, Eng., U.K. (ē'lĭng)	158b	51°29'N	0°19'W
Earle, Ar., U.S. (ûrl)	121	35°14'N	90°28'W
Earlington, Ky., U.S. (ûr'lĭng-tŭn)	124	37°15'N	87°31'W
Easley, S.C., U.S. (ēz'lĭ)	125	34°48'N	82°37'W
East, Mount, mtn., Pan.	128a	9°09'N	79°46'W
East Alton, Il., U.S. (ôl'tŭn)	117e	38°53'N	90°08'W
East Angus, Can. (ăŋ'gŭs)	99	45°35'N	71°40'W
East Aurora, N.Y., U.S. (ô-rō'rá)	111c	42°46'N	78°38'W
East Bay, b., Tx., U.S.	123a	29°30'N	94°41'W
East Bernstadt, Ky., U.S. (bûrn'stát)	124	37°09'N	84°08'W
Eastbourne, Eng., U.K. (ēst'bôrn)	165	50°48'N	0°16'E
East Caicos, i., T./C. Is. (kī'kōs)	135	21°40'N	71°35'W
East Cape, c., N.Z.	221a	37°37'S	178°33'E
East Cape see Dezhnëva, Mys, c., Russia	196	68°00'N	172°00'W
East Carondelet, Il., U.S. (kå-rŏn'dĕ-lĕt)	117e	38°33'N	90°14'W
East Cherokee Indian Reservation, I.R., N.C., U.S.	124	35°33'N	83°12'W
East Chicago, In., U.S. (shĭ-kô'gō)	111a	41°39'N	87°29'W
East China Sea, sea, Asia	205	30°28'N	125°52'E
East Cleveland, Oh., U.S. (klēv'lănd)	111d	41°33'N	81°35'W

ng-sing; ŋ-baŋk; N-nasalized n; nŏd; cŏmmit; ōld; ōbey; ôrder; oi-boil; fōōd; ò-as oo in foot; ou-out; s-soft; sh-dish; th-thin; pūre; ûnite; ûrn; stŭd; circŭs; ü-as in French tu; '-indeterminate vowel.

ăt; fīnǎl; rāte; senāte; ärm; ȧsk; sofá; fāre; ch-choose; dh-as th in other; bē; ĕvent; bĕt; recĕnt; cratēr; g-gō; gh-guttural g; bĭt; ī-short neutral; rīde; ᴋ-guttural k as ch in German ich;

PRONOUNCING INDEX

Ellicott City – Estarreja 291

PLACE (Pronunciation)	PAGE	LAT.	LONG.
Ellicott City, is., Md., U.S. (ĕl'ĭ-kŏt sĭ'tē)	110e	39°16'N	76°48'W
Ellicott Creek, r., N.Y., U.S.	111c	43°00'N	78°46'W
Elliot, S. Afr.	233c	31°19'S	27°52'E
Elliot, Wa., U.S. (el'ĭ-ŭt)	116a	47°28'N	122°08'W
Elliotdale, S. Afr. (ĕl-ĭ-ōt'dāl)	233c	31°58'S	28°42'E
Elliot Lake, Can.	98	46°23'N	82°39'W
Ellis, Ks., U.S. (ĕl'ĭs)	120	38°56'N	99°34'W
Ellisville, Mo., U.S.	117e	38°35'N	90°35'W
Ellisville, Ms., U.S. (ĕl'ĭs-vĭl)	124	31°37'N	89°10'W
Ellsworth, Ks., U.S. (ĕlz'wûrth)	120	38°43'N	98°14'W
Ellsworth, Me., U.S.	100	44°33'N	68°26'W
Ellsworth Mountains, mts., Ant.	224	77°00'S	90°00'W
Ellwangen, Ger. (ĕl'väŋ-gĕn)	168	48°47'N	10°08'E
Elm, Ger. (ĕlm)	159c	53°31'N	9°13'E
Elm, r., S.D., U.S.	112	45°47'N	98°28'W
Elm, r., W.V., U.S.	108	38°30'N	81°05'W
Elma, Wa., U.S. (ĕl'mȧ)	114	47°02'N	123°20'W
El Mahdia, Tun. (mä-dēȧ)(mä'dē-ȧ)	162	35°30'N	11°09'E
Elmendorf, Tx., U.S. (ĕl'mĕn-dôrf)	117d	29°16'N	98°20'W
El Menia, Alg.	230	30°39'N	2°52'E
Elm Fork, Tx., U.S. (ĕlm fôrk)	117c	32°55'N	96°56'W
Elmhurst, Il., U.S. (ĕlm'hûrst)	111a	41°54'N	87°56'W
El Miliyya, Alg. (mē'ä)	230	36°30'N	6°16'E
Elmira, N.Y., U.S. (ĕl-mī'rȧ)	109	42°05'N	76°50'W
Elmira Heights, N.Y., U.S.	109	42°10'N	76°50'W
El Modena, Ca., U.S. (mô-dē'nō)	117a	33°47'N	117°48'W
El Mohammadia, Alg.	173	35°35'N	0°05'E
El Monte, Ca., U.S. (mōn'tå)	117a	34°04'N	118°02'W
El Morro National Monument, rec., N.M., U.S.	119	35°05'N	108°20'W
Elmshorn, Ger. (ĕlms'hôrn)	168	53°45'N	9°39'E
Elmwood Place, Oh., U.S. (ĕlm'wŏŏd plās)	111f	39°11'N	84°30'W
Elokomin, r., Wa., U.S. (ē-lō'kō-mĭn)	116c	46°16'N	123°16'W
El Oro, Mex. (ô-rô)	130	19°49'N	100°04'W
El Pao, Ven. (ĕl pá'ō)	142	8°08'N	62°37'W
El Paraíso, Hond. (pä-rä-ē'sō)	132	13°55'N	86°35'W
El Pardo, Spain (pä'r-dô)	173a	40°31'N	3°47'W
El Paso, Tx., U.S. (pas'ō)	104	31°47'N	106°27'W
El Pilar, Ven. (pē-lä'r)	143b	9°56'N	64°48'W
El Porvenir, Pan. (pôr-vä-nēr')	133	9°34'N	78°55'W
El Puerto de Santa María, Spain	172	36°36'N	6°18'W
El Qala, Alg.	162	36°52'N	8°23'E
El Qoll, Alg.	230	37°02'N	6°29'E
El Real, Pan. (rā-äl)	133	8°07'N	77°43'W
El Reno, Ok., U.S. (rē'nō)	121	35°31'N	97°57'W
Elroy, Wi., U.S. (ĕl'roi)	113	43°44'N	90°17'W
Elsa, Can.	103	63°55'N	135°25'W
Elsah, Il., U.S. (ĕl'zȧ)	117e	38°57'N	90°22'W
El Salto, Mex. (säl'tō)	130	23°48'N	105°22'W
El Salvador, nation, N.A.	128	14°00'N	89°30'W
El Sauce, Nic. (ĕl-sá'ô-sĕ)	132	13°00'N	86°40'W
Elsberry, Mo., U.S. (ĕlz'bĕr-ĭ)	121	39°09'N	90°44'W
Elsdorf, Ger. (ĕls'dōrf)	171c	50°56'N	6°35'E
El Segundo, Ca., U.S. (sĕgŭn'dō)	117a	33°55'N	118°24'W
Elsinore, Ca., U.S. (ĕl'sĭ-nôr)	117a	33°40'N	117°19'W
Elsinore Lake, l., Ca., U.S.	117a	33°38'N	117°21'W
Elstorf, Ger. (ĕls'tōrf)	159c	53°25'N	9°48'E
Eltham, Austl. (ĕl'thăm)	217a	37°43'S	145°08'E
El Tigre, Ven. (tē'grĕ)	142	8°49'N	64°15'W
El'ton, l., Russia	181	49°10'N	47°00'E
El Toro, Ca., U.S. (tō'rō)	117a	33°37'N	117°42'W
El Triunfo, El Sal.	132	13°17'N	88°32'W
El Triunfo, Hond. (ĕl-trē-ōō'n-fô)	132	13°06'N	87°00'W
Elūru, India	199	16°44'N	80°09'E
El Vado Res, N.M., U.S.	119	36°37'N	106°30'W
Elvas, Port. (ĕl'väzh)	162	38°53'N	7°11'W
Elverum, Nor. (ĕl'vĕ-rom)	166	60°53'N	11°33'E
El Viejo, Nic. (ĕl-vyĕ'κô)	132	12°10'N	87°10'W
El Viejo, vol., Nic.	132	12°44'N	87°03'W
Elvins, Mo., U.S. (ĕl'vĭnz)	121	37°49'N	90°31'W
El Wad, Alg.	230	33°23'N	6°49'E
El Wak, Kenya (wäk')	231	3°00'N	41°00'E
Elwell, Lake, res., Mt., U.S.	115	48°22'N	111°17'W
Elwood, Il., U.S. (ĕ'wŏŏd)	111a	41°24'N	88°07'W
Elwood, In., U.S.	108	40°15'N	85°50'W
Elx, Spain	173	38°15'N	0°42'W
Ely, Eng., U.K. (ē'lĭ)	165	52°25'N	0°17'E
Ely, Mn., U.S.	113	47°54'N	91°53'W
Ely, Nv., U.S.	104	39°16'N	114°53'W
Elyria, Oh., U.S. (ē-lĭr'ĭ-ȧ)	111d	41°22'N	82°07'W
Ema, r., Est. (å'må)	167	58°25'N	27°00'E
Emāmshahr, Iran	198	36°25'N	55°01'E
Emån, r., Swe.	166	57°15'N	15°46'E
Embarrass, r., Il., U.S. (ĕm-băr'ăs)	108	39°15'N	88°05'W
Embrun, Can. (ĕm'brŭn)	102c	45°16'N	75°17'W
Embrun, Fr. (äN-brûN')	171	44°35'N	6°32'E
Embu, Kenya	237	0°32'S	37°27'E
Emden, Ger. (ĕm'dĕn)	168	53°21'N	7°15'E
Emerson, Can. (ĕm'ẽr-sŭn)	90	49°00'N	97°12'W
Emeryville, Ca., U.S. (ĕm'ẽr-ĭ-vĭl)	116b	37°50'N	122°17'W
Emi Koussi, mtn., Chad (ā'mē κōō-sē')	231	19°50'N	18°30'E
Emiliano Zapata, Mex. (ĕ-mē-lyá'nô-zä-pá'tá)	131	17°45'N	91°46'W
Emilia-Romagna, hist. reg., Italy (ē-mēl'yä rô-mä'n-yä)	174	44°35'N	10°48'E
Eminence, Ky., U.S. (ĕm'ĭ-nĕns)	108	38°25'N	85°15'W
Emira Island, i., Pap. N. Gui. (ā-mē-rä')	213	1°40'S	150°28'E
Emmen, Neth. (ĕm'ĕn)	165	52°48'N	6°55'E
Emmerich, Ger. (ĕm'ẽr-ĭk)	171c	51°51'N	6°16'E
Emmetsburg, Ia., U.S. (ĕm'ĕts-bûrg)	113	43°07'N	94°41'W
Emmett, Id., U.S. (ĕm'ĕt)	114	43°53'N	116°30'W
Emmons, Mount, mtn., Ut., U.S. (ĕm'ŭnz)	106	40°43'N	110°20'W
Emory Peak, mtn., Tx., U.S. (ĕ'mō-rē pēk)	122	29°13'N	103°20'W
Empoli, Italy (ām'pô-lē)	174	43°43'N	10°55'E
Emporia, Ks., U.S. (ĕm-pō'rĭ-ȧ)	104	38°24'N	96°11'W
Emporia, Va., U.S.	125	37°40'N	77°34'W
Emporium, Pa., U.S. (ĕm-pō'rĭ-ŭm)	109	41°30'N	78°15'W
Empty Quarter see Ar Rub'al Khālī, des., Asia	198	20°00'N	51°00'E
Ems, r., Ger. (ĕms)	168	52°52'N	7°16'E
Ems-Weser Kanal, can., Ger.	168	52°23'N	8°11'E
Enånger, Swe. (ĕn-ôŋ'gẽr)	166	61°36'N	16°55'E
Encantada, Cerro de la, mtn., Mex. (sĕ'r-rô-dĕ-lä-ĕn-kän-tä'dä)	128	31°58'N	115°15'W
Encanto, Cape, c., Phil. (ĕn-kän'tō)	213a	15°44'N	121°46'E
Encarnación, Para. (ĕn-kär-nä-syōn')	144	27°26'S	55°52'W
Encarnación de Díaz, Mex. (ĕn-kär-nä-syōn dā dē'äz)	130	21°34'N	102°15'W
Encinal, Tx., U.S. (ĕn'sĭ-nôl)	122	28°02'N	99°22'W
Encontrados, Ven. (ĕn-kōn-trä'dōs)	142	9°01'N	72°10'W
Encounter Bay, b., Austl. (ĕn-koun'tẽr)	220	35°50'S	138°45'E
Endako, r., Can.	94	54°05'N	125°30'W
Endau, r., Malay.	197b	2°29'N	103°40'E
Enderbury, i., Kir. (ĕn'dẽr-bûrĭ)	240	2°00'S	171°00'W
Enderby Land, reg., Ant. (ĕn'dẽr bĭ)	224	72°00'S	52°00'E
Enderlin, N.D., U.S. (ĕn'dẽr-lĭn)	112	46°38'N	97°37'W
Endicott, N.Y., U.S. (ĕn'dĭ-kŏt)	109	42°05'N	76°00'W
Endicott Mountains, mts., Ak., U.S.	103	67°30'N	153°45'W
Enez, Tur.	175	40°42'N	26°05'E
Enfer, Pointe d', c., Mart.	133b	14°21'N	60°48'W
Enfield, Eng., U.K.	158b	51°38'N	0°06'W
Enfield, Ct., U.S. (ĕn'fēld)	109	41°55'N	72°35'W
Enfield, N.C., U.S.	125	36°10'N	77°41'W
Engaño, Cabo, c., Dom. Rep. (kå'-bô- ĕn-gä-nô)	129	18°40'N	68°30'W
Engcobo, S. Afr. (ĕŋg-cô-bô)	233c	31°41'S	27°59'E
Engel's, Russia (ĕn'gĕls)	181	51°20'N	45°40'E
Engelskirchen, Ger. (ĕn'gĕls-kẽr'κĕn)	171c	50°59'N	7°25'E
Enggano, Pulau, i., Indon. (ĕng-gä'nō)	212	5°22'S	102°18'E
England, Ar., U.S. (ĭŋ'glȧnd)	121	34°33'N	91°58'W
England, state, U.K. (ĭŋ'glȧnd)	154	51°35'N	1°40'W
Englewood, Co., U.S. (ĕn'g'l-wŏŏd)	120	39°39'N	105°00'W
Englewood, N.J., U.S.	110a	40°54'N	73°59'W
English, In., U.S. (ĭn'glĭsh)	108	38°15'N	86°25'W
English, r., Can.	93	50°31'N	94°12'W
English Channel, strt., Eur.	156	49°45'N	3°06'W
Enguera, Spain (ān'gārä)	173	38°58'N	0°42'W
Enid, Ok., U.S. (ē'nĭd)	104	36°25'N	97°52'W
Enid Lake, res., Ms., U.S.	124	34°13'N	89°47'W
Enkeldoring, S. Afr. (ĕŋ'k'l-dôr-ĭng)	238c	25°24'S	28°43'E
Enköping, Swe. (ĕn'kû-pĭng)	166	59°39'N	17°05'E
Ennedi, mts., Chad (ĕn-nĕd'ē)	231	16°45'N	22°45'E
Ennis, Ire. (ĕn'ĭs)	164	52°54'N	9°05'W
Ennis, Tx., U.S.	123	32°20'N	96°38'W
Enniscorthy, Ire. (ĕn-ĭs-kôr'thĭ)	164	52°33'N	6°27'W
Enniskillen, N. Ire., U.K. (ĕn-ĭs-kĭl'ĕn)	164	54°20'N	7°25'W
Ennis Lake, res., Mt., U.S.	115	45°15'N	111°30'W
Enns, r., Aus. (ĕns)	161	47°37'N	14°35'E
Enoree, S.C., U.S. (ē-nō'rē)	125	34°43'N	81°58'W
Enoree, r., S.C., U.S.	125	34°35'N	81°55'W
Enriquillo, Dom. Rep. (ĕn-rē-kē'l-yō)	135	17°55'N	71°15'W
Enriquillo, Lago, l., Dom. Rep. (lä'gô-ĕn-rē-kē'l-yō)	135	18°35'N	71°35'W
Enschede, Neth. (ĕns'κȧ-dĕ)	161	52°10'N	6°50'E
Enseñada, Arg.	141c	34°50'S	57°55'W
Ensenada, Mex. (ĕn-sĕ-nä'dä)	128	32°00'N	116°30'W
Enshi, China (ŭn-shr)	204	30°18'N	109°25'E
Enshū-Nada, b., Japan (ĕn'shōō nä-dä)	211	34°25'N	137°14'E
Entebbe, Ug.	231	0°04'N	32°28'E
Enterprise, Al., U.S. (ĕn'tẽr-prīz)	124	31°20'N	85°50'W
Enterprise, Or., U.S.	114	45°25'N	117°16'W
Entiat, L, Wa., U.S.	114	45°43'N	120°11'W
Entraygues, Fr. (ĕN-trĕg')	170	44°39'N	2°33'E
Entre Rios, prov., Arg.	144	31°30'S	59°00'W
Enugu, Nig. (ĕ-nōō'gōō)	230	6°27'N	7°27'E
Enumclaw, Wa., U.S. (ĕn'ŭm-klô)	116a	47°12'N	121°59'W
Envigado, Col. (ĕn-vē-gá'dō)	142a	6°10'N	75°34'W
Eolie, Isole, is., Italy (ē'sō-lĕ-ĕ-ô'lyĕ)	162	38°43'N	14°43'E
Epe, Nig.	235	6°37'N	3°59'E
Épernay, Fr. (ā-pĕr-nĕ')	161	49°02'N	3°54'E
Épernon, Fr. (ā-pĕr-nôN')	171b	48°36'N	1°41'E
Ephraim, Ut., U.S. (ē'frā-ĭm)	119	39°20'N	111°40'W
Ephrata, Wa., U.S. (ēfrā'tȧ)	114	47°18'N	119°35'W
Epi, Vanuatu (ā'pē)	219	16°59'S	168°29'E
Épila, Spain (ā'pē-lä)	172	41°38'N	1°15'W
Épinal, Fr. (ā-pē-nàl')	161	48°11'N	6°27'E
Episkopi, Cyp.	197a	34°38'N	32°55'E
Epping, Eng., U.K. (ĕp'ĭng)	158b	51°41'N	0°06'E
Epsom, Eng., U.K.	158b	51°20'N	0°16'W
Epupa Falls, wtfl., Afr.	236	17°00'S	13°05'E
Epworth, Eng., U.K. (ĕp'wûrth)	158a	53°31'N	0°50'W
Equatorial Guinea, nation, Afr.	230	2°00'N	7°15'E
Équilles, Fr.	170a	43°34'N	5°21'E
Eramosa, r., Can. (ĕr-ȧ-mō'sȧ)	102d	43°39'N	80°08'W
Erba, Jabal, mtn., Sudan (ĕr-bȧ)	231	20°53'N	36°45'E
Erciyeş Dağı, mtn., Tur.	163	38°30'N	35°36'E
Erding, Ger. (ĕr'dĕng)	159d	48°19'N	11°54'E
Erechim, Braz. (ĕ-rĕ-shē'N)	144	27°43'S	52°11'W
Ereğli, Tur. (ĕ-rā'ĭ-lē)	163	37°40'N	34°00'E
Ereğli, Tur.	163	41°15'N	31°25'E
Erfurt, Ger. (ĕr'fōrt)	161	50°59'N	11°04'E
Ergene, r., Tur. (ĕr'gĕ-nĕ)	175	41°17'N	26°50'E
Erges, r., Eur. (ĕr'-zhĕs)	172	39°45'N	7°01'W
Ērgļi, Lat.	167	56°54'N	25°38'E
Eria, r., Spain (ā-rē'ä)	172	42°10'N	6°08'W
Erick, Ok., U.S. (âr'ĭk)	120	35°14'N	99°51'W
Erie, Ks., U.S. (ē'rĭ)	121	37°35'N	95°17'W
Erie, Pa., U.S.	105	42°05'N	80°05'W
Erie, Lake, l., N.A.	107	42°15'N	81°25'W
Erimo Saki, c., Japan (ā'rē-mō sä-kē)	205	41°53'N	143°20'E
Erin, Can. (ĕ'rĭn)	102d	43°46'N	80°04'W
Eritrea, nation, Afr. (ā-rē-trā'ȧ)	231	16°15'N	38°30'E
Erlangen, Ger. (ĕr'läng-ĕn)	168	49°36'N	11°03'E
Erlanger, Ky., U.S. (ẽr'lăng-ẽr)	111f	39°01'N	84°36'W
Ermoúpoli, Grc.	175	37°30'N	24°56'E
Ernākulam, India	199	9°58'N	76°23'E
Erne, Lower Lough, l., N. Ire., U.K.	164	54°30'N	7°40'W
Erne, Upper Lough, l., N. Ire., U.K. (lŏk ûrn)	164	54°20'N	7°24'W
Erode, India	203	11°20'N	77°45'E
Eromanga, i., Vanuatu	221	18°58'S	169°18'E
Eros, La., U.S. (ē'rōs)	123	32°23'N	92°22'W
Errego, Moz.	237	16°02'S	37°14'E
Errigal, mtn., Ire. (ĕr-ĭ-gôl')	164	55°02'N	8°07'W
Errol Heights, Or., U.S.	116c	45°29'N	122°38'W
Erstein, Fr. (ĕr'shtīn)	171	48°27'N	7°40'E
Erwin, N.C., U.S. (ûr'wĭn)	125	35°16'N	78°40'W
Erwin, Tn., U.S.	125	36°07'N	82°25'W
Erzgebirge, mts., Eur. (ĕrts'gĕ-bē'gĕ)	156	50°29'N	12°40'E
Erzincan, Tur. (ĕr-zĭn-jän')	198	39°50'N	39°30'E
Erzurum, Tur. (ĕrz'rōōm')	198	39°55'N	41°10'E
Esambo, D.R.C.	236	3°40'S	23°24'E
Esashi, Japan (ĕs'ä-shē)	205	41°50'N	140°10'E
Esbjerg, Den. (ĕs'byĕrgh)	160	55°29'N	8°25'E
Escalante, Ut., U.S. (ĕs-kȧ-lăn'tē)	119	37°50'N	111°40'W
Escalante, r., Ut., U.S.	119	37°40'N	111°20'W
Escalón, Mex.	122	26°45'N	104°20'W
Escambia, r., Fl., U.S. (ĕs-kăm'bĭ-ȧ)	124	30°38'N	87°20'W
Escanaba, Mi., U.S. (ĕs-kȧ-nô'bȧ)	105	45°44'N	87°05'W
Escanaba, r., Mi., U.S.	113	46°10'N	87°22'W
Escarpada Point, Phil.	212	18°40'N	122°45'E
Esch-sur-Alzette, Lux.	171	49°32'N	6°21'E
Eschwege, Ger. (ĕsh'vā-gē)	168	51°11'N	10°02'E
Eschweiler, Ger. (ĕsh'vī-lẽr)	171c	50°49'N	6°15'E
Escondido, Ca., U.S. (ĕs-kŏn-dē'dō)	118	33°07'N	117°00'W
Escondido, r., Nic.	133	12°04'N	84°09'W
Escondido, Río, r., Mex. (rē'ō-ĕs-kōn-dē'dô)	122	28°30'N	100°45'W
Escudo de Veraguas, i., Pan. (ĕs-kōō'dä dā vā-rä'gwäs)	133	9°07'N	81°25'W
Escuinapa, Mex. (ĕs-kwē-nä'pä)	128	22°49'N	105°44'W
Escuintla, Guat. (ĕs-kwēn'tlä)	132	14°16'N	90°47'W
Ese, Cayos de, i., Col.	133	12°24'N	81°07'W
Eşfahān, Iran	198	32°38'N	51°30'E
Esgueva, r., Spain (ĕs-gĕ'vä)	172	41°48'N	4°10'W
Esher, Eng., U.K.	158b	51°23'N	0°22'W
Eshowe, S. Afr. (ĕsh'ô-wē)	233c	28°54'S	31°28'E
Esiama, Ghana	234	4°56'N	2°21'W
Eskdale, W.V., U.S. (ĕsk'dāl)	108	38°05'N	81°25'W
Eskifjördur, Ice. (ĕs'kē-fyŭr'dōōr)	154	65°04'N	14°01'W
Eskilstuna, Swe. (å'shĕl-stü-na)	160	59°23'N	16°28'E
Eskimo Lakes, l., Can. (ĕs'kĭ-mō)	92	69°40'N	130°10'W
Eskişehir, Tur. (ĕs-kē-shĕ'h'r)	198	39°40'N	30°20'E
Esko, Mn., U.S. (ĕs'kō)	117h	46°27'N	92°22'W
Esla, r., Spain (ĕs-lä)	172	41°50'N	5°48'W
Eslöv, Swe. (ĕs'lûv)	166	55°50'N	13°17'E
Esmeraldas, Ec. (ĕs-mā-räl'däs)	142	0°58'N	79°45'W
Espanola, Can. (ĕs-pȧ-nō'lȧ)	91	46°11'N	81°59'W
Esparta, C.R. (ĕs-pär'tä)	133	9°59'N	84°40'W
Esperance, Austl. (ĕs'pē-rāns)	218	33°45'S	122°07'E
Esperanza, Cuba (ĕs-pĕ-rä'n-zä)	134	22°30'N	80°10'W
Espichel, Cabo, c., Port. (kå'bō-ĕs-pē-shĕl')	172	38°25'N	9°13'W
Espinal, Col. (ĕs-pē-näl')	142	4°10'N	74°53'W
Espinhaço, Serra do, mts., Braz. (sĕ'r-rä-dô-ĕs-pē-nä-sô)	143	16°00'S	44°00'W
Espinillo, Punta, c., Ur. (pōō'n-tä-ĕs-pē-nē'l-yô)	141c	34°49'S	56°27'W
Espírito Santo, Braz. (ĕs-pē'rē-tô-sän'tô)	143	20°27'S	40°18'W
Espírito Santo, state, Braz.	143	19°57'S	40°58'W
Espiritu Santo, i., Vanuatu (ĕs-pē'rē-tōō sän'tō)	221	15°45'S	166°50'E
Espíritu Santo, Bahía del, b., Mex.	132a	19°25'N	87°28'W
Espita, Mex. (ĕs-pē'tä)	132a	20°57'N	88°22'W
Espoo, Fin.	167	60°13'N	24°41'E
Es Port de Pollença, Spain	173	39°50'N	3°00'E
Esposende, Port. (ĕs-pô-zĕn'dā)	172	41°33'N	8°45'W
Esquel, Arg. (ĕs-kĕ'l)	144	42°47'S	71°22'W
Esquimalt, Can. (ĕs-kwī'mŏlt)	94	48°26'N	123°24'W
Essaouira, Mor.	230	31°34'N	9°44'W
Essen, Bel.	159a	51°28'N	4°27'E
Essen, Ger. (ĕs'sĕn)	154	51°26'N	6°59'E
Essendon, Austl.	217a	37°46'S	144°55'E
Essequibo, r., Guy. (ĕs-ā-kē'bō)	143	4°26'N	58°17'W
Essex, Il., U.S.	111a	41°11'N	88°11'W
Essex, Ma., U.S.	101a	42°38'N	70°47'W
Essex, Md., U.S.	110e	39°19'N	76°29'W
Essex, Vt., U.S.	109	44°30'N	73°05'W
Essex Fells, N.J., U.S. (ĕs'ĕks fĕlz)	110a	40°50'N	74°16'W
Essexville, Mi., U.S. (ĕs'ĕks-vĭl)	108	43°35'N	83°50'W
Esslingen, Ger. (ĕs'slĕn-gĕn)	168	48°45'N	9°19'E
Estacado, Llano, pl., U.S. (yä-nō ĕs-tȧcȧ-dō')	106	33°50'N	103°20'W
Estância, Braz. (ĕs-tän'sĭ-ä)	143	11°17'S	37°18'W
Estarreja, Port. (ĕ-tär-rā'zhä)	172	40°44'N	8°39'W

ng-sing; ŋ-baŋk; N-nasalized n; nŏd; cŏmmit; ōld; ôbey; ôrder; oi-boil; fōōd; ŏŏ-as oo in foot; ou-out; s-soft; sh-dish; th-thin; pūre; ůnite; ûrn; stŭd; circŭs; ü-as in French tu; '-indeterminate vowel.

292 Estats – Felipe Carrillo Puerto PRONOUNCING INDEX

PLACE (Pronunciation)	PAGE	LAT.	LONG.
Estats, Pique d', mtn., Eur.	173	42°43'N	1°30'E
Estcourt, S. Afr. (ĕst-coort)	233c	29°04'S	29°53'E
Este, Italy (ĕs´tä)	174	45°13'N	11°40'E
Estella, Spain (ĕs-tāl´yä)	172	42°40'N	2°01'W
Estepa, Spain (ĕs-tā´pä)	172	37°18'N	4°54'W
Estepona, Spain (ĕs-tā-pō´nä)	172	36°26'N	5°08'W
Esterhazy, Can. (ĕs´tẽr-hä-zē)	97	50°40'N	102°08'W
Estero Bay, b., Ca., U.S. (ĕs-tā´rōs)	118	35°22'N	121°04'W
Estevan, Can. (ĕ-stē´văn)	90	49°07'N	103°05'W
Estevan Group, is., Can.	94	53°05'N	129°40'W
Estherville, Ia., U.S. (ĕs´tẽr-vĭl)	113	43°24'N	94°49'W
Estill, S.C., U.S. (ĕs´tĭl)	125	32°46'N	81°15'W
Eston, Can.	96	51°10'N	108°45'W
Estonia, nation, Eur.	178	59°10'N	25°00'E
Estoril, Port. (ĕs-tô-rēl´)	173b	38°45'N	9°24'W
Estrêla, mtn., Port. (mäl-you´n-dä-ĕs-trē´lä)	172	40°20'N	7°38'W
Estrêla, r., Braz. (ĕs-trē´lȧ)	144b	22°39'S	43°16'W
Estrêla, Serra da, mts., Port. (sĕr´rȧ dä ĕs-trā´lȧ)	172	40°25'N	7°45'W
Estremadura, hist. reg., Port. (ĕs-trā-mä-dōō´rȧ)	172	39°00'N	8°36'W
Estremoz, Port. (ĕs-trā-mōzh´)	172	38°50'N	7°35'W
Estrondo, Serra do, mts., Braz. (sĕr´-rȧ dò ĕs-trôn´-dò)	143	9°52'S	48°56'W
Esumba, Île, i., D.R.C.	236	2°00'N	21°12'E
Esztergom, Hung. (ĕs´tĕr-gōm)	169	47°46'N	18°45'E
Etah, Grnld. (ē´tȧ)	89	78°20'N	72°42'W
Étampes, Fr. (ā-täɴp´)	170	48°26'N	2°09'E
Étaples, Fr. (ā-täp´l´)	170	50°32'N	1°38'E
Etchemin, r., Can. (ĕch´ĕ-mĭn)	102b	46°39'N	71°03'W
Ethiopia, nation, Afr. (ē-thē-ō´pē-ȧ)	231	7°53'N	37°55'E
Eticoga, Gui.-B.	234	11°09'N	16°08'W
Etiwanda, Ca., U.S. (ĕ-tĭ-wän´dȧ)	117a	34°07'N	117°31'W
Etna, Pa., U.S. (ĕt´nȧ)	111e	40°30'N	79°55'W
Etna, Mount, vol., Italy	156	37°48'N	15°00'E
Etobicoke Creek, r., Can.	102d	43°44'N	79°48'W
Etolin Strait, strt., Ak., U.S. (ĕt ō lĭn)	103	60°35'S	165°40'W
Etoshapan, pl., Nmb. (ĕtō´shä)	232	19°07'S	15°30'E
Etowah, Tn., U.S. (ĕt´ô-wä)	124	35°18'N	84°31'W
Etowah, r., Ga., U.S.	124	34°23'N	84°19'W
Étréchy, Fr. (ā-trā-shē´)	171b	48°29'N	2°12'E
Etten-Leur, Neth.	159a	51°34'N	4°38'E
Etterbeek, Bel. (ĕt´ẽr-bāk)	159a	50°51'N	4°24'E
Etzatlán, Mex. (ĕt-zä-tlän´)	130	20°44'N	104°04'W
Eucla, Austl. (ū´klȧ)	218	31°45'S	128°50'E
Euclid, Oh., U.S. (ū´klĭd)	111d	41°34'N	81°32'W
Eudora, Ar., U.S. (u-dō´rȧ)	121	33°07'N	91°16'W
Eufaula, Al., U.S. (û-fô´lȧ)	124	31°53'N	85°09'W
Eufaula, Ok., U.S.	121	35°16'N	95°35'W
Eufaula Reservoir, res., Ok., U.S.	121	35°00'N	94°45'W
Eugene, Or., U.S. (û-jēn´)	104	44°02'N	123°06'W
Euless, Tx., U.S. (ū´lĕs)	117c	32°50'N	97°05'W
Eunice, La., U.S. (ū´nĭs)	123	30°30'N	92°25'W
Eupen, Bel. (oi´pĕn)	165	50°39'N	6°05'E
Euphrates, r., Asia (û-frā´tēz)	198	36°00'N	40°00'E
Eure, r., Fr. (ûr)	170	49°03'N	1°22'E
Eureka, Ca., U.S. (û-rē´kȧ)	104	40°45'N	124°10'W
Eureka, Ks., U.S.	121	37°48'N	96°17'W
Eureka, Mt., U.S.	114	48°53'N	115°07'W
Eureka, Nv., U.S.	118	39°33'N	115°58'W
Eureka, S.D., U.S.	112	45°46'N	99°38'W
Eureka, Ut., U.S.	119	39°55'N	112°10'W
Eureka Springs, Ar., U.S.	121	36°24'N	93°43'W
Europe, cont. (ū´rŭp)	156	50°00'N	15°00'E
Eustis, Fl., U.S. (ūs´tĭs)	125	28°50'N	81°41'W
Eutaw, Al., U.S. (ū-tȧ)	124	32°48'N	87°50'W
Eutsuk Lake, l., Can. (ōōt´sŭk)	94	53°20'N	126°44'W
Evanston, Il., U.S. (ĕv´ăn-stŭn)	105	42°03'N	87°41'W
Evanston, Wy., U.S.	115	41°17'N	111°02'W
Evansville, In., U.S. (ĕv´ănz-vĭl)	105	38°00'N	87°30'W
Evansville, Wi., U.S.	113	42°46'N	89°19'W
Evart, Mi., U.S. (ĕv´ẽrt)	108	43°55'N	85°10'W
Evaton, S. Afr. (ĕv´ȧ-tŏn)	238c	26°32'S	27°53'E
Eveleth, Mn., U.S. (ĕv´ē-lĕth)	113	47°27'N	92°35'W
Everard, l., Austl. (ĕv´ẽr-ȧrd)	220	31°20'S	134°10'E
Everard Ranges, mts., Austl.	220	27°15'S	132°00'E
Everest, Mount, mtn., Asia (ĕv´ẽr-ĕst)	199	28°00'N	86°57'E
Everett, Ma., U.S. (ĕv´ẽr-ĕt)	101a	42°24'N	71°03'W
Everett, Wa., U.S. (ĕv´ẽr-ĕt)	104	47°59'N	122°11'W
Everett Mountains, mts., Can.	93	62°34'N	68°00'W
Everglades, The, sw., Fl., U.S.	125a	25°35'N	80°55'W
Everglades City, Fl., U.S. (ĕv´ẽr-glādz)	125a	25°50'N	81°25'W
Everglades National Park, rec., Fl., U.S.	107	25°39'N	80°57'W
Evergreen, Al., U.S. (ĕv´ẽr-grēn)	124	31°25'N	87°56'W
Evergreen Park, Il., U.S.	111a	41°44'N	87°42'W
Everman, Tx., U.S. (ĕv´ẽr-măn)	117c	32°38'N	97°17'W
Everson, Wa., U.S. (ĕv´ẽr-sŭn)	116d	48°55'N	122°21'W
Évora, Port. (ĕv´ô-rä)	162	38°35'N	7°54'W
Évreux, Fr. (ā-vrû´)	161	49°02'N	1°11'E
Evrótas, r., Grc. (ĕv-rō´täs)	175	37°15'N	22°17'E
Evvoia, i., Grc.	163	38°38'N	23°45'E
'Ewa Beach, Hi., U.S. (ē´wä)	126a	21°17'N	158°03'W
Ewaso Ng'iro, r., Kenya	231	0°59'N	37°47'E
Excelsior, Mn., U.S. (ĕk-sel´sĭ-ŏr)	117g	44°54'N	93°35'W
Excelsior Springs, Mo., U.S.	121	39°20'N	94°13'W
Exe, r., Eng., U.K. (ĕks)	164	50°57'N	3°37'W
Exeter, Eng., U.K.	161	50°45'N	3°33'W
Exeter, Ca., U.S. (ĕk´sē-tẽr)	118	36°18'N	119°09'W
Exeter, N.H., U.S.	109	43°00'N	71°00'W
Exmoor, for., Eng., U.K. (ĕks´mŏŏr)	164	51°10'N	3°55'W
Exmouth, Eng., U.K. (ĕks´mŭth)	164	50°40'N	3°20'W
Exmouth Gulf, b., Austl.	220	21°45'S	114°30'E
Exploits, r., Can. (ĕks-ploits´)	101	48°50'N	56°15'W
Extórrax, r., Mex. (ĕx-tó´ràx)	130	21°04'N	99°39'W
Extrema, Braz. (ĕsh-trĕ´mä)	141a	22°52'S	46°19'W
Extremadura, hist. reg., Spain (ĕks-trā-mä-doo´rä)	172	38°43'N	6°30'W
Exuma Sound, strt., Bah. (ĕk-sōō´mä)	134	24°20'N	76°20'W
Eyasi, Lake, l., Tan. (ȧ-yä´sē)	232	3°25'S	34°55'E
Eyjafjördur, b., Ice.	160	66°21'N	18°20'W
Eyl, Som.	238a	7°53'N	49°45'E
Eyrarbakki, Ice.	160	63°51'N	20°52'W
Eyre, Austl. (âr)	218	32°15'S	126°20'E
Eyre, l., Austl.	220	28°43'S	137°50'E
Eyre Peninsula, pen., Austl.	220	33°30'S	136°00'E
Ezeiza, Arg. (ĕ-zā´zä)	144a	34°52'S	58°31'W
Ezine, Tur. (ȧ´zĭ-nȧ)	175	39°47'N	26°18'E

F

PLACE (Pronunciation)	PAGE	LAT.	LONG.
Faaborg, Den. (fô´bôrg)	166	55°06'N	10°19'E
Fabens, Tx., U.S. (fā´bĕnz)	122	31°30'N	106°07'W
Fabriano, Italy (fä-brē-ä´nô)	174	43°20'N	12°55'E
Fada, Chad (fä´dä)	231	17°06'N	21°18'E
Fada Ngourma, Burkina (fä´dä´n gōōr´mä)	230	12°04'N	0°21'E
Faddeya, i., Russia (fȧd-yä´)	179	76°12'N	145°00'E
Faenza, Italy (fä-ĕnd´zä)	174	44°16'N	11°53'E
Fafe, Port. (fä´fā)	172	41°30'N	8°10'W
Fafen, r., Eth.	238a	8°15'N	42°40'E
Făgăras, Rom. (fȧ-gä´räsh)	175	45°50'N	24°55'E
Fagerness, Nor. (fä´ghẽr-nĕs)	160	61°00'N	9°10'E
Fagnano, l., S.A. (fäk-nä´nô)	144	54°35'S	68°20'W
Faguibine, Lac, l., Mali	234	16°50'N	4°20'W
Faial, i., Port. (fä-yä´l)	230a	38°40'N	29°19'W
Fā'id, Egypt (fä-yēd´)	238d	30°19'N	32°18'E
Fairbanks, Ak., U.S. (fâr´bănks)	106a	64°50'N	147°48'W
Fairbury, Il., U.S. (fâr´bĕr-ĭ)	108	40°45'N	88°25'W
Fairbury, Ne., U.S.	121	40°09'N	97°11'W
Fairchild Creek, r., Can. (fâr´chīld)	102d	43°18'N	80°10'W
Fairfax, Mn., U.S. (fâr´făks)	113	44°29'N	94°44'W
Fairfax, S.C., U.S.	125	32°29'N	81°13'W
Fairfax, Va., U.S.	110e	38°51'N	77°20'W
Fairfield, Austl.	217b	33°52'S	150°57'E
Fairfield, Al., U.S. (fâr´fēld)	110h	33°30'N	86°50'W
Fairfield, Ct., U.S.	110a	41°08'N	73°22'W
Fairfield, Ia., U.S.	113	41°00'N	91°59'W
Fairfield, Il., U.S.	108	38°25'N	88°20'W
Fairfield, Me., U.S.	100	44°35'N	69°38'W
Fairhaven, Ma., U.S. (fâr-hā´vĕn)	109	41°35'N	70°55'W
Fair Haven, Vt., U.S.	109	43°35'N	73°15'W
Fair Island, i., Scot., U.K. (fâr)	164a	59°34'N	1°41'W
Fairmont, Mn., U.S. (fâr´mŏnt)	113	43°39'N	94°26'W
Fairmont, W.V., U.S.	108	39°30'N	80°10'W
Fairmont City, Il., U.S.	117e	38°39'N	90°05'W
Fairmount, In., U.S.	108	40°25'N	85°45'W
Fairmount, Ks., U.S.	117f	39°12'N	95°55'W
Fair Oaks, Ga., U.S. (fâr ōks)	110c	33°56'N	84°33'W
Fairport, N.Y., U.S. (fâr´pōrt)	109	43°05'N	77°30'W
Fairport Harbor, Oh., U.S.	108	41°45'N	81°15'W
Fairview, Ok., U.S. (fâr´vū)	120	36°16'N	98°28'W
Fairview, Or., U.S.	116c	45°32'N	112°26'W
Fairview, Ut., U.S.	119	39°35'N	111°30'W
Fairview Park, Oh., U.S.	111d	41°27'N	81°52'W
Fairweather, Mount, mtn., N.A. (fâr-wĕdh´ẽr)	103	59°12'N	137°22'W
Faisalabad, Pak.	199	31°29'N	73°06'E
Faith, S.D., U.S. (fāth)	112	45°02'N	120°02'W
Faizābād, India	199	26°50'N	82°17'E
Fajardo, P.R.	129b	18°20'N	65°40'W
Fakfak, Indon.	213	2°56'S	132°25'E
Faku, China (fä-kōō)	208	42°28'N	123°20'E
Falcón, dept., Ven. (fäl-kô´n)	143b	11°00'N	68°28'W
Falconer, N.Y., U.S. (fô´k'n-ẽr)	109	42°10'N	79°10'W
Falcon Heights, Mn., U.S. (fô´k'n)	117g	44°59'N	93°10'W
Falcon Reservoir, res., N.A. (fôk'n)	122	26°47'N	99°03'W
Făleşti, Mol.	177	47°33'N	27°46'E
Falfurrias, Tx., U.S. (făl´fōō-rē´ăs)	122	27°15'N	98°08'W
Falher, Can. (făl´ẽr)	95	55°44'N	117°12'W
Falkenberg, Swe. (fäl´kĕn-bĕrgh)	166	56°54'N	12°25'E
Falkensee, Ger. (fäl´kĕn-zā)	159b	52°34'N	13°05'E
Falkenthal, Ger. (fäl´kĕn-täl)	159b	52°54'N	13°18'E
Falkirk, Scot., U.K. (fôl´kûrk)	164	55°59'N	3°55'W
Falkland Islands, dep., S.A. (fôk´lȧnd)	144	50°45'S	61°00'W
Falköping, Swe. (fäl´chûp-ĭng)	166	58°09'N	13°30'E
Fall City, Wa., U.S.	116a	47°34'N	121°53'W
Fall Creek, r., In., U.S. (fôl)	111g	39°52'N	86°04'W
Fallon, Nv., U.S. (făl´ŭn)	118	39°30'N	118°48'W
Fall River, Ma., U.S.	105	41°42'N	71°07'W
Falls Church, Va., U.S. (fälz chûrch)	110e	38°53'N	77°10'W
Falls City, Ne., U.S.	121	40°04'N	95°37'W
Fallston, Md., U.S. (fâls´ton)	110e	39°32'N	76°26'W
Falmouth, Jam.	134	18°30'N	77°40'W
Falmouth, Eng., U.K. (făl´mŭth)	164	50°08'N	5°04'W
Falmouth, Ky., U.S.	108	38°40'N	84°20'W
False Divi Point, c., India	203	15°45'N	80°50'E
Falster, i., Den. (fäls´tẽr)	166	54°48'N	11°58'E
Fălticeni, Rom. (fŭl-tē-chān´y')	169	47°27'N	26°17'E
Falun, Swe. (fä-lōōn´)	160	60°38'N	15°35'E
Famagusta, Cyp. (fä-mä-gōōs´tä)	163	35°08'N	33°59'E
Famatina, Sierra de, mts., Arg.	144	29°00'S	67°50'W
Fangxian, China (fäŋ-shyĕn)	208	32°05'N	110°45'E
Fanning, i., Can.	102f	49°45'N	97°46'W
Fano, Italy (fä´nō)	174	43°49'N	13°01'E
Fanø, i., Den. (fän´û)	166	55°24'N	8°10'E
Fan Si Pan, mtn., Viet.	209	22°25'N	103°50'E
Farafangana, Madag. (fä-rä-fäŋ-gä´nä)	233	23°18'S	47°59'E
Farāh, Afg. (fä-rä´)	198	32°15'N	62°13'E
Farallón, Punta, c., Mex. (pò´n-tä-fä-rä-lōn)	130	19°21'N	105°03'W
Faranah, Gui. (fä-rä´nä)	230	10°02'N	10°44'W
Farasān, Jaza'ir, is., Sau. Ar.	198	16°45'N	41°08'E
Faregh, Wadi al, r., Libya (wädē ĕl fä-rĕg´)	163	30°10'N	19°34'E
Farewell, Cape, c., N.Z. (fâr-wĕl´)	221a	40°37'S	172°40'E
Fargo, N.D., U.S. (fär´gō)	104	46°53'N	96°48'W
Far Hills, N.J., U.S. (fär hĭlz)	110a	40°41'N	74°38'W
Faribault, Mn., U.S. (fâ´rĭ-bō)	113	44°19'N	93°16'W
Farilhões, is., Port. (fä-rē-lyôɴzh´)	172	39°28'N	9°32'W
Faringdon, Eng., U.K. (fă´rĭng-dŏn)	158b	51°38'N	1°35'W
Fâriskūr, Egypt (fä-rēs-kōōr´)	238b	31°19'N	31°46'E
Farit, Amba, mtn., Eth.	231	10°51'N	37°52'E
Farley, Mo., U.S. (fär´lē)	117f	39°16'N	94°49'W
Farmers Branch, Tx., U.S.	117c	32°56'N	96°53'W
Farmersburg, In., U.S. (fär´mẽrz-bûrg)	108	39°15'N	87°25'W
Farmersville, Tx., U.S. (fär´mẽrz-vĭl)	121	33°11'N	96°22'W
Farmingdale, N.J., U.S. (färm´ĭng-dāl)	110a	40°11'N	74°10'W
Farmingdale, N.Y., U.S.	110a	40°44'N	73°26'W
Farmingham, Ma., U.S. (färm-ĭng-hăm)	101a	42°17'N	71°25'W
Farmington, Il., U.S. (färm-ĭng-tŭn)	121	40°42'N	90°01'W
Farmington, Me., U.S.	100	44°40'N	70°10'W
Farmington, Mi., U.S.	111b	42°28'N	83°23'W
Farmington, Mo., U.S.	121	37°46'N	90°26'W
Farmington, N.M., U.S.	119	36°40'N	108°10'W
Farmington, Ut., U.S.	117b	40°59'N	111°53'W
Farmville, N.C., U.S. (färm-vĭl)	125	35°35'N	77°35'W
Farmville, Va., U.S.	125	37°15'N	78°23'W
Farnborough, Eng., U.K. (färn´bŭr-ô)	158b	51°15'N	0°45'W
Farne Islands, is., Eng., U.K. (färn)	164	55°40'N	1°32'W
Farnham, Can. (fär´năm)	109	45°15'N	72°55'W
Farningham, Eng., U.K. (fär´nĭng-ŭm)	158b	51°22'N	0°14'E
Farnworth, Eng., U.K. (färn´wŭrth)	158a	53°34'N	2°24'W
Faro, Braz. (fä´rò)	143	2°05'S	56°32'W
Faro, Port.	162	37°01'N	7°57'W
Farodofay, Madag.	233	24°59'S	46°58'E
Faroe Islands, is., Eur.	156	62°00'N	5°45'W
Fårön, i., Swe.	167	57°57'N	19°10'E
Farquhar, Cape, c., Austl. (fär´kwȧr)	220	23°50'S	112°55'E
Farrell, Pa., U.S. (făr´ĕl)	108	41°10'N	80°30'W
Farrukhābād, India (fŭ-ròk-hä-bäd´)	199	27°29'N	79°35'E
Fársala, Grc.	175	39°18'N	22°25'E
Farsund, Nor. (fär´sòn)	166	58°05'N	6°47'E
Fartak, Ra's, c., Yemen	198	15°43'N	52°17'E
Fartura, Serra da, mts., Braz. (sĕ´r-rä-dȧ-fär-tōō´rä)	144	26°40'S	53°15'W
Farvel, Kap, c., Grnld.	89	60°00'N	44°00'W
Farwell, Tx., U.S. (fär´wĕl)	120	34°24'N	103°03'W
Fasano, Italy (fä-zä´nō)	175	40°50'N	17°22'E
Fastiv, Ukr.	177	50°04'N	29°57'E
Fatëzh, Russia	176	52°06'N	35°51'E
Fatima, Port.	173	39°36'N	9°36'E
Fatsa, Tur. (fät´sä)	163	40°50'N	37°30'E
Faucilles, Monts, mts., Fr. (môɴ´ fō-sēl´)	171	48°07'N	6°13'E
Fauske, Nor.	160	67°15'N	15°24'E
Faust, Can. (foust)	95	55°19'N	115°38'W
Faustovo, Russia	186b	55°27'N	38°29'E
Faversham, Eng., U.K. (fă´vẽr-sh'm)	158b	51°19'N	0°54'E
Faxaflói, b., Ice.	160	64°33'N	22°40'W
Fayette, Al., U.S. (fā-yĕt´)	124	33°40'N	87°54'W
Fayette, Ia., U.S.	113	42°49'N	91°49'W
Fayette, Mo., U.S.	121	39°09'N	92°41'W
Fayette, Ms., U.S.	124	31°43'N	91°00'W
Fayetteville, Ar., U.S. (fā-yĕt´vĭl)	121	36°03'N	94°08'W
Fayetteville, N.C., U.S.	125	35°02'N	78°54'W
Fayetteville, Tn., U.S.	124	35°10'N	86°33'W
Fazao, Forêt Classée du, for., Togo	234	8°50'N	0°40'E
Fazilka, India	202	30°30'N	74°02'E
Fazzān (Fezzan), hist. reg., Libya	231	26°45'N	13°01'E
Fdérik, Maur.	230	22°45'N	12°38'W
Fear, Cape, c., N.C., U.S. (fēr)	125	33°52'N	77°48'W
Feather, r., Ca., U.S. (fĕth´ẽr)	118	38°56'N	121°41'W
Feather, Middle Fork of, r., Ca., U.S.	118	39°49'N	121°10'W
Feather, North Fork of, r., Ca., U.S.	118	40°00'N	121°20'W
Featherstone, Eng., U.K. (fĕdh´ẽr stŭn)	158a	53°39'N	1°21'W
Fécamp, Fr. (fā-käɴ´)	161	49°45'N	0°20'E
Federal, Distrito, dept., Ven. (dĕs-trē´tô-fĕ-dĕ-rä´l)	143b	10°34'N	66°55'W
Federal Way, Wa., U.S.	116a	47°20'N	122°20'W
Fëdorovka, Russia (fyô´dō-rôf-kȧ)	186b	56°15'N	37°14'E
Fehmarn, i., Ger. (fā´märn)	168	54°28'N	11°15'E
Fehrbellin, Ger. (fĕr´bĕl-lēn)	159b	52°49'N	12°46'E
Feia, Logoa, l., Braz. (lô-gôä-fĕ´yä)	141a	21°54'S	41°15'W
Feicheng, China (fā-chŭŋ)	206	36°18'N	116°45'E
Feidong, China (fā-dôŋ)	206	31°53'N	117°28'E
Feira de Santana, Braz. (fĕ´ê-rä dā sänt-än´ä)	143	12°16'S	38°46'W
Feixian, China (fā-shyĕn)	206	35°17'N	117°59'E
Felanitx, Spain (fā-lä-nēch´)	162	39°29'N	3°09'E
Feldkirch, Aus. (fĕlt´kĭrk)	168	47°15'N	9°36'E
Feldkirchen, Ger. (fĕld´kĕr-ĸĕn)	159d	48°09'N	11°44'E
Felipe Carrillo Puerto, Mex.	132a	19°36'N	88°04'W

ăt; finăl; rāte; senåte; ärm; ȧsk; sofȧ; fâre; ch-choose; dh-as th in other; bē; ēvent; bĕt; recĕnt; cratẽr; g-gō; gh-guttural g; bĭt; ĭ-short neutral; rīde; ĸ-guttural k as ch in German ich;

PRONOUNCING INDEX

Feltre – Fort Bellefontaine 293

PLACE (Pronunciation)	PAGE	LAT.	LONG.
Feltre, Italy (fĕl′trā)	174	46°02′N	11°56′E
Femunden, l., Nor.	160	62°17′N	11°40′E
Fengcheng, China (fŭŋ-chŭŋ)	208	40°28′N	124°03′E
Fengcheng, China	207b	30°55′N	121°38′E
Fengdu, China (fŭŋ-dōō)	204	29°58′N	107°50′E
Fengjie, China (fŭŋ-jyĕ)	204	31°02′N	109°30′E
Fengming Dao, i., China (fŭŋ-mĭŋ dou)	206	39°19′N	121°15′E
Fengrun, China (fŭŋ-ròn)	206	39°51′N	118°06′E
Fengtai, China (fŭŋ-tī)	208a	39°51′N	116°19′E
Fengxian, China (fŭŋ-shyĕn)	207b	30°55′N	121°26′E
Fengxian, China	206	34°41′N	116°36′E
Fengxiang, China (fŭŋ-shyäŋ)	204	34°25′N	107°20′E
Fengyang, China (fûng′yäng′)	208	32°55′N	117°32′E
Fengzhen, China (fŭŋ-jŭn)	205	40°28′N	113°20′E
Fennimore Pass, strt., Ak., U.S. (fĕn-ĭ-mōr)	103a	51°40′N	175°38′W
Fenoarivo Atsinanana, Madag.	233	17°30′S	49°31′E
Fenton, Mi., U.S. (fĕn-tŭn)	108	42°50′N	83°40′W
Fenton, Mo., U.S.	117e	38°31′N	90°27′W
Fenyang, China	205	37°20′N	111°48′E
Feodosiia, Ukr.	181	45°02′N	35°21′E
Ferdows, Iran	198	34°00′N	58°13′E
Ferentino, Italy (fā-rĕn-tē′nō)	174	41°42′N	13°18′E
Fergana, Uzb.	183	40°23′N	71°46′E
Fergus Falls, Mn., U.S. (fûr′gŭs)	104	46°17′N	96°03′W
Ferguson, Mo., U.S. (fûr-gŭ-sŭn)	117e	38°45′N	90°18′W
Ferkéssédougou, C. Iv.	234	9°36′N	5°12′W
Fermo, Italy (fĕr′mō)	174	43°10′N	13°43′E
Fermoselle, Spain (fĕr-mō-säl′yå)	172	41°20′N	6°23′W
Fermoy, Ire. (fûr-moi′)	164	52°05′N	8°06′W
Fernandina Beach, Fl., U.S. (fûr-năn-dē′nȧ)	125	30°38′N	81°29′W
Fernando de Noronha, Arquipélago, is., Braz.	143	3°51′S	32°25′W
Fernando Póo *see* Bioko, i., Eq. Gui.	230	3°35′N	7°45′E
Fernán-Núñez, Spain (fĕr-nän′nōōn′yåth)	172	37°42′N	4°43′W
Fernão Veloso, Baia de, b., Moz.	237	14°20′S	40°55′E
Ferndale, Ca., U.S. (fûrn′dāl)	114	40°34′N	124°18′W
Ferndale, Mi., U.S.	111b	42°27′N	83°08′W
Ferndale, Wa., U.S.	116d	48°51′N	122°36′W
Fernie, Can. (fûr′nĭ)	90	49°30′N	115°03′W
Fern Prairie, Wa., U.S. (fûrn prâr′ĭ)	116c	45°38′N	122°25′W
Ferrara, Italy (fĕr-rä′rä)	162	44°50′N	11°37′E
Ferrat, Cap, c., Alg. (kăp fĕr-rät)	173	35°49′N	0°29′W
Ferreira do Alentejo, Port.	172	38°03′N	8°06′W
Ferreira do Zezere, Port. (fĕr-rĕ′ē-rä dò zå-zā′rĕ)	172	39°49′N	8°17′W
Ferrelview, Mo., U.S. (fĕr′rĕl-vū)	117f	39°18′N	94°40′W
Ferreñafe, Peru (fĕr-rĕn-yä′fĕ)	142	6°38′S	79°48′W
Ferriday, La., U.S. (fĕr′ĭ-dā)	123	31°38′N	91°33′W
Ferrol, Spain	154	43°30′N	8°12′W
Fershampenuaz, Russia (fĕr-shàm′pĕn-wäz)	186a	53°32′N	59°50′E
Fertile, Mn., U.S. (fur′tĭl)	112	47°33′N	96°18′W
Fès, Mor. (fĕs)	230	34°08′N	5°00′W
Fessenden, N.D., U.S. (fĕs′ĕn-dĕn)	112	47°39′N	99°40′W
Festus, Mo., U.S. (fĕst′ŭs)	121	38°12′N	90°22′W
Fethiye, Tur. (fĕt-hē′yĕ)	163	36°40′N	29°05′E
Feuilles, Rivière aux, r., Can.	93	58°30′N	70°50′W
Ffestiniog, Wales, U.K.	164	52°59′N	3°58′W
Fianarantsoa, Madag. (fyȧ-nä′rȧn-tsō′ȧ)	233	21°21′S	47°15′E
Ficksburg, S. Afr. (fĭks′bûrg)	238c	28°53′S	27°53′E
Fidalgo Island, i., Wa., U.S. (fĭ-dăl′gō)	116a	48°28′N	122°39′W
Fieldbrook, Ca., U.S. (fēld′bròk)	114	40°59′N	124°02′W
Fier, Alb. (fyĕr)	175	40°43′N	19°34′E
Fife Ness, c., Scot., U.K. (fĭf′nes′)	164	56°15′N	2°19′W
Fifth Cataract, wtfl., Sudan	231	18°27′N	33°38′E
Figeac, Fr. (fē-zhàk′)	170	44°37′N	2°02′E
Figeholm, Swe. (fē-ghĕ-hōlm)	166	57°24′N	16°33′E
Figueira da Foz, Port. (fē-gwĕy-rä-dȧ-fō′z)	172	40°10′N	8°50′W
Figuig, Mor.	230	32°20′N	1°30′W
Fiji, nation, Oc. (fē′jē)	3	18°40′S	175°00′E
Filadelfia, C.R. (fĭl-ȧ-dĕl′fĭ-ȧ)	132	10°26′N	85°37′W
Filatovskoye, Russia (fĭ-lä′tôf-skô-yĕ)	186a	56°49′N	62°20′E
Filchner Ice Shelf, ice, Ant. (fĭlk′nĕr)	224	80°00′S	35°00′W
Filicudi, i., Italy (fē′le-kōō′dē)	174	38°34′N	14°39′E
Filippovskoye, Russia (fĭ-lĭ-pôf′skô-yĕ)	186b	56°06′N	38°38′E
Filipstad, Swe. (fĭl′ĭps-städh)	166	59°44′N	14°09′E
Fillmore, Ut., U.S. (fĭl′mōr)	119	39°00′N	112°20′W
Filsa, Nor.	166	60°35′N	12°03′E
Fimi, r., D.R.C.	232	2°43′S	17°50′E
Finch, Can. (fĭnch)	102c	45°09′N	75°06′W
Findlay, Oh., U.S. (fĭnd′lå)	108	41°05′N	83°40′W
Fingoe, Moz.	237	15°12′S	31°50′E
Finke, r., Austl. (fĭŋ′kē)	220	25°25′S	134°30′E
Finland, nation, Eur. (fĭn′lănd)	154	62°45′N	26°13′E
Finland, Gulf of, b., Eur. (fĭn′lănd)	156	59°35′N	23°35′E
Finlandia, Col. (fēn-lä′n-dēä)	142a	4°38′N	75°39′W
Finlay, r., Can. (fĭn′lå)	92	57°45′N	125°30′W
Finow, Ger. (fē′nōv)	159b	52°50′N	13°44′E
Finowfurt, Ger. (fē′nō-fōōrt)	159b	52°50′N	13°41′E
Fircrest, Wa., U.S. (fûr′krĕst)	116a	47°14′N	122°31′W
Firenze *see* Florence, Italy	154	43°47′N	11°15′E
Firenzuola, Italy (fē-rĕnt-swô′lä)	174	44°08′N	11°21′E
Firozpur, India	199	30°58′N	74°39′E
Fischa, r., Aus.	159e	48°04′N	16°33′E
Fischamend Markt, Aus.	159e	48°07′N	16°37′E
Fish, r., Nmb. (fĭsh)	232	28°00′S	17°30′E
Fish Cay, i., Bah.	135	22°30′N	74°20′W
Fish Creek, r., Can. (fĭsh)	102e	50°52′N	114°21′W
Fisher, La., U.S. (fĭsh′ĕr)	123	31°28′N	93°30′W
Fisher Bay, b., Can.	97	51°30′N	97°16′W
Fisher Channel, strt., Can.	94	52°10′N	127°42′W
Fisher Strait, strt., Can.	93	62°43′N	84°28′W
Fisterra, Cabo de, c., Spain	156	42°52′N	9°48′W
Fitchburg, Ma., U.S. (fĭch′bûrg)	109	42°35′N	71°48′W
Fitri, Lac, l., Chad	235	12°50′N	17°28′E
Fitzgerald, Ga., U.S. (fĭts-jĕr′ăld)	124	31°42′N	83°17′W
Fitz Hugh Sound, strt., Can. (fĭts hū)	94	51°40′N	127°57′W
Fitzroy, r., Austl. (fĭts-roi′)	220	18°00′S	124°05′E
Fitzroy, r., Austl.	221	23°45′S	150°02′E
Fitzroy, Monte (Cerro Chaltel), mtn., S.A.	144	48°10′S	73°18′W
Fitzroy Crossing, Austl.	218	18°08′S	126°00′E
Fitzwilliam, i., Can. (fĭts-wĭl′yŭm)	98	45°30′N	81°45′W
Fiume *see* Rijeka, Cro.	162	45°22′N	14°24′E
Fiumicino, Italy (fyōō-mē-chē′nô)	173d	41°47′N	12°19′E
Fjällbacka, Swe. (fyĕl′băk-å)	166	58°37′N	11°17′E
Flagstaff, S. Afr. (flăg′stäf)	233c	31°06′S	29°31′E
Flagstaff, Az., U.S. (flăg-stàf)	104	35°15′N	111°40′W
Flagstaff, l., Me., U.S. (flăg-stàf)	109	45°05′N	70°30′W
Flåm, Nor. (flôm)	166	60°50′N	7°00′E
Flambeau, r., Wi., U.S. (flăm-bō′)	113	45°32′N	91°05′W
Flaming Gorge Reservoir, res., U.S.	106	41°13′N	109°30′W
Flamingo, Fl., U.S. (flȧ-mĭŋ′gô)	125	25°10′N	80°55′W
Flamingo Cay, i., Bah. (flȧ-mĭŋ′gô)	135	22°50′N	75°50′W
Flamingo Point, c., V.I.U.S.	129c	18°19′N	65°00′W
Flanders, hist. reg., Fr. (flăn′dĕrz)	165	50°53′N	2°29′E
Flandreau, S.D., U.S. (flăn′drō)	112	44°02′N	96°35′W
Flathead, r., N.A.	95	49°30′N	114°30′W
Flathead, Middle Fork, r., Mt., U.S.	115	48°30′N	113°47′W
Flathead, North Fork, r., N.A.	115	48°45′N	114°20′W
Flathead, South Fork, r., Mt., U.S.	115	48°05′N	113°45′W
Flathead Indian Reservation, I.R., Mt., U.S.	115	47°30′N	114°25′W
Flathead Lake, l., Mt., U.S. (flăt′hĕd)	106	47°57′N	114°20′W
Flatow, Ger.	159b	52°44′N	12°58′E
Flat Rock, Mi., U.S. (flăt rŏk)	111b	42°06′N	83°17′W
Flattery, Cape, c., Wa., U.S. (flăt′ĕr-ĭ)	114	48°22′N	124°45′W
Flatwillow Creek, r., Mt., U.S. (flat wĭl′ô)	115	46°45′N	108°47′W
Flekkefjord, Nor. (flăk′kē-fyôr)	166	58°19′N	6°38′E
Flemingsburg, Ky., U.S. (flĕm′ĭngz-bûrg)	108	38°25′N	83°45′W
Flensburg, Ger. (flĕns′bòrgh)	160	54°48′N	9°27′E
Flers, Fr. (flĕr)	161	48°43′N	0°37′W
Fletcher, N.C., U.S.	125	35°26′N	82°30′W
Flinders, i., Austl.	221	39°35′S	148°10′E
Flinders, r., Austl.	221	18°48′S	141°07′E
Flinders, reg., Austl. (flĭn′dĕrz)	220	32°15′S	138°45′E
Flinders Reefs, rf., Austl.	221	17°30′S	149°02′E
Flin Flon, Can. (flĭn flŏn)	90	54°46′N	101°53′W
Flint, Wales, U.K.	158a	53°15′N	3°07′W
Flint, Mi., U.S.	105	43°00′N	83°45′W
Flint, r., Ga., U.S. (flĭnt)	107	31°25′N	84°15′W
Flintshire, co., Wales, U.K.	158a	53°13′N	3°00′W
Flora, Il., U.S. (flō′rȧ)	108	38°40′N	88°25′W
Flora, In., U.S.	108	40°25′N	86°30′W
Florala, Al., U.S. (flŏr-ăl′ȧ)	124	31°01′N	86°19′W
Floral Park, N.Y., U.S. (flôr′ăl pärk)	110a	40°42′N	73°42′W
Florence, Italy	154	43°47′N	11°15′E
Florence, Al., U.S. (flŏr′ĕns)	105	34°46′N	87°40′W
Florence, Az., U.S.	119	33°00′N	111°25′W
Florence, Co., U.S.	120	38°23′N	105°08′W
Florence, Ks., U.S.	121	38°14′N	96°56′W
Florence, S.C., U.S.	125	34°10′N	79°45′W
Florence, Wa., U.S.	116a	48°13′N	122°21′W
Florencia, Col. (flō-rĕn′sē-ȧ)	142	1°31′N	75°13′W
Florencio Sánchez, Ur. (flō-rĕn-sēō-sà′n-chĕz)	141c	33°52′S	57°24′W
Florencio Varela, Arg. (flō-rĕn′sē-ō vä-rā′lä)	144a	34°50′S	58°16′W
Flores, Braz. (flō′rĕzh)	143	7°57′S	37°48′W
Flores, Guat.	132a	16°53′N	89°54′W
Flores, dept., Ur.	141c	33°33′S	57°00′W
Flores, i., Indon.	212	8°14′S	121°08′E
Flores, r., Arg.	141c	36°13′S	60°28′W
Flores, Laut (Flores Sea), sea, Indon.	212	7°09′S	120°30′E
Floresville, Tx., U.S. (flō′rĕs-vĭl)	122	29°10′N	98°08′W
Floriano, Braz. (flō-rà-ä′nò)	143	6°17′S	42°58′W
Florianópolis, Braz. (flō-rē-ä-nô′pô-lēs)	144	27°30′S	48°30′W
Florida, Col. (flō-rē′dä)	142a	3°20′N	76°12′W
Florida, Cuba	134	22°10′N	79°50′W
Florida, S. Afr.	233b	26°11′S	27°56′E
Florida, Ur. (flô-rê-dhä)	144	34°06′S	56°14′W
Florida, N.Y., U.S. (flŏr′ĭ-dȧ)	110a	41°20′N	74°21′W
Florida, state, U.S. (flŏr′ĭ-dȧ)	105	30°30′N	84°40′W
Florida, dept., Ur. (flô-rē′dhä)	141c	33°48′S	56°15′W
Florida, i., Sol. Is.	221	8°56′S	159°45′E
Florida, Straits of, strt., N.A.	129	24°10′N	81°00′W
Florida Bay, b., Fl., U.S. (flŏr′ĭ-dȧ)	125a	24°55′N	80°55′W
Florida Keys, is., Fl., U.S.	107	24°33′N	81°20′W
Florida Mountains, mts., N.M., U.S.	119	32°10′N	107°35′W
Florido, Río, r., Mex. (flô-rē′dō)	122	27°21′N	104°48′W
Floridsdorf, Aus. (flô′rĭds-dôrf)	159e	48°16′N	16°25′E
Florina, Grc. (flô-rē′nä)	163	40°48′N	21°24′E
Florissant, Mo., U.S. (flŏr′ĭ-sănt)	117e	38°47′N	90°20′W
Floyd, r., Ia., U.S. (floid)	112	42°38′N	96°15′W
Floydada, Tx., U.S. (floi-dā′dȧ)	120	33°59′N	101°19′W
Floyds Fork, r., Ky., U.S. (floi-dz)	111h	38°08′N	85°30′W
Flumendosa, r., Italy	174	39°45′N	9°18′E
Flushing, Mi., U.S. (flûsh′ĭng)	108	43°05′N	83°50′W
Fly, r. (flī)	213	8°00′S	141°45′E
Foča, Bos. (fō′chä)	175	43°29′N	18°48′E
Fochville, S. Afr. (fŏk′vĭl)	238c	26°29′S	27°29′E
Focşani, Rom. (fòk-shä′nê)	169	45°41′N	27°17′E
Fogang, China (fwo-gäŋ)	209	23°50′N	113°35′E
Foggia, Italy (fŏd′jä)	163	41°30′N	15°34′E
Fogo, Can. (fō′gō)	101	49°43′N	54°17′W
Fogo, i., Can.	99	49°40′N	54°13′W
Fogo, i., C.V.	230b	14°46′N	24°51′W
Fohnsdorf, Aus. (fōns′dôrf)	168	47°13′N	14°40′E
Föhr, i., Ger. (fûr)	168	54°47′N	8°30′E
Foix, Fr. (fwä)	170	42°58′N	1°34′E
Fokku, Nig.	235	11°40′N	4°31′E
Foladī, Koh-e, mtn., Afg.	199	34°38′N	67°32′E
Folgares, Ang.	236	14°54′S	15°08′E
Foligno, Italy (fô-lēn′yō)	174	42°58′N	12°41′E
Folkeston, Eng., U.K.	165	51°05′N	1°18′E
Folkingham, Eng., U.K. (fō′kĭng-ăm)	158a	52°53′N	0°24′W
Folkston, Ga., U.S.	125	30°50′N	82°01′W
Folsom, Ca., U.S.	118	38°40′N	121°10′W
Folsom, N.M., U.S. (fŏl′sŭm)	120	36°47′N	103°56′W
Fomento, Cuba (fō-mĕ′n-tō)	134	21°35′N	78°20′W
Fómeque, Col. (fō′mĕ-kĕ)	142a	4°29′N	73°52′W
Fonda, Ia., U.S. (fŏn′dȧ)	113	42°33′N	94°51′W
Fond du Lac, Wi., U.S. (fŏn dū lăk′)	105	43°47′N	88°29′W
Fond du Lac Indian Reservation, I.R., Mn., U.S.	113	46°44′N	93°04′W
Fondi, Italy (fôn′dē)	174	41°23′N	13°25′E
Fonseca, Golfo de, b., N.A. (gôl-fô-dĕ-fôn-sā′kä)	128	13°09′N	87°55′W
Fontainebleau, Fr. (fôɴ-tĕn-blō′)	161	48°24′N	2°42′E
Fontana, Ca., U.S. (fŏn-tă′nȧ)	117a	34°06′N	117°27′W
Fonte Boa, Braz. (fōn′tå bō′ȧ)	142	2°32′S	66°05′W
Fontenay-le-Comte, Fr. (fôɴt-nĕ′lē-kôɴt′)	170	46°28′N	0°53′W
Fontenay-Trésigny, Fr. (fôɴ-te-nā′ tra-sēn-yē′)	171b	48°43′N	2°53′E
Fontenelle Reservoir, res., Wy., U.S.	115	42°05′N	110°05′W
Fontera, Punta, c., Mex. (pōō′n-tä-fôn-tĕ′rä)	131	18°36′N	92°43′W
Fontibón, Col. (fōn-tē-bôn′)	142a	4°42′N	74°09′W
Fontur, c., Ice.	156	66°21′N	14°02′W
Foothills, S. Afr. (fòt-hĭls)	233b	25°55′S	27°36′E
Footscray, Austl.	217a	37°48′S	144°54′E
Foraker, Mount, mtn., Ak., U.S. (fôr′ȧ-kēr)	103	62°40′N	152°40′W
Forbach, Fr. (fôr′bäĸ)	171	49°12′N	6°54′E
Forbes, Austl. (fôrbz)	219	33°24′S	148°05′E
Forbes, Mount, mtn., Can.	95	51°52′N	116°56′W
Forchheim, Ger. (fôrĸ′hīm)	168	49°43′N	11°05′E
Fordyce, Ar., U.S. (fôr′dīs)	121	33°48′N	92°24′W
Forécariah, Gui. (fōr-kà-rē′ä′)	230	9°26′N	13°06′W
Forel, Mont, mtn., Grnld.	89	65°50′N	37°41′W
Forest, Ms., U.S. (fŏr′ĕst)	124	32°22′N	89°29′W
Forest, r., N.D., U.S.	112	48°08′N	97°45′W
Forest City, Ia., U.S.	113	43°14′N	93°40′W
Forest City, N.C., U.S.	125	35°20′N	81°52′W
Forest City, Pa., U.S.	109	41°35′N	75°30′W
Forest Grove, Or., U.S. (grōv)	116c	45°31′N	123°07′W
Forest Hill, Md., U.S.	110e	39°35′N	76°26′W
Forest Hill, Tx., U.S.	117c	32°40′N	97°16′W
Forestville, Can. (fŏr′ĕst-vĭl)	100	48°45′N	69°06′W
Forestville, Md., U.S.	110e	38°51′N	76°55′W
Forez, Monts du, mts., Fr. (môɴ dü fô-rā′)	170	44°55′N	3°43′E
Forfar, Scot., U.K. (fôr′fȧr)	164	57°10′N	2°55′W
Forillon, Parc National, rec., Can.	100	48°50′N	64°05′W
Forio, mtn., Italy (fô′ryō)	173c	40°29′N	13°55′E
Forked Creek, r., Il., U.S. (fôrk′d)	111a	41°16′N	88°01′W
Forked Deer, r., Tn., U.S.	124	35°53′N	89°29′W
Forli, Italy (fôr-lē′)	162	44°13′N	12°03′E
Formby, Eng., U.K. (fôrm′bē)	158a	53°34′N	3°04′W
Formby Point, c., Eng., U.K.	158a	53°33′N	3°06′W
Formentera, Isla de, i., Spain (ē′s-lä-dĕ-fôr-mĕn-tā′rä)	162	38°43′N	1°25′E
Formiga, Braz. (fôr-mē′gȧ)	143	20°27′S	45°25′W
Formigas Bank, bk. (fôr-mē′gäs)	135	18°30′N	75°40′W
Formosa, Arg. (fōr-mō′sä)	144	27°25′S	58°12′W
Formosa, Braz.	143	15°32′S	47°10′W
Formosa, prov., Arg.	144	24°30′S	60°45′W
Formosa, Serra, mts., Braz. (sĕ′r-rä)	143	12°59′S	55°11′W
Formosa Bay, b., Kenya	237	2°45′S	40°30′E
Formosa Strait *see* Taiwan Strait, strt., Asia	205	24°30′N	120°00′E
Fornosovo, Russia (fôr-nô′sô vô)	186c	59°35′N	30°34′E
Forrest City, Ar., U.S. (fŏr′ĕst sĭ′tĭ)	121	35°00′N	90°46′W
Forsayth, Austl. (fôr-sīth′)	219	18°33′S	143°42′E
Forshaga, Swe. (fôrs′hä′gä)	166	59°34′N	13°25′E
Forst, Ger. (fôrst)	161	51°45′N	14°38′E
Forsyth, Ga., U.S. (fôr-sīth′)	124	33°02′N	83°56′W
Forsyth, Mt., U.S.	115	46°15′N	106°41′W
Fort Albany, Can. (fôrt ôl′bȧ nĭ)	91	52°20′N	81°30′W
Fort Alexander Indian Reserve, I.R., Can.	97	50°27′N	96°15′W
Fortaleza, Braz. (fôr′tä-lā′zȧ)	143	3°35′S	38°31′W
Fort Apache Indian Reservation, I.R., Az., U.S. (ȧ-păch′ē)	119	34°02′N	110°27′W
Fort Atkinson, Wi., U.S. (ăt′kĭn-sŭn)	113	42°55′N	88°46′W
Fort Beaufort, S. Afr. (bō′fôrt)	233c	32°47′S	26°39′E
Fort Belknap Indian Reservation, I.R., Mt., U.S.	115	48°16′N	108°38′W
Fort Bellefontaine, Mo., U.S. (bĕl-fōn-tān′)	117f	38°50′N	90°15′W

ng-sing; ŋ-baŋk; ɴ-nasalized n; nŏd; cŏmmit; ōld; ôbey; ôrder; oi-boil; fōōd; ò-as oo in foot; ou-out; s-soft; sh-dish; th-thin; pūre; ûnite; ûrn; stŭd; circŭs; ü-as in French tu; ′-indeterminate vowel.

294 Fort Benton – Fryazino PRONOUNCING INDEX

PLACE (Pronunciation)	PAGE	LAT.	LONG.
Fort Benton, Mt., U.S. (bĕn'tŭn)	115	47°51'N	110°40'W
Fort Berthold Indian Reservation, I.R., N.D., U.S. (bĕrth'ôld)	112	47°47'N	103°28'W
Fort Bragg, Ca., U.S.	118	39°26'N	123°48'W
Fort Branch, In., U.S. (brănch)	108	38°15'N	87°35'W
Fort Chipewyan, Can.	90	58°46'N	111°15'W
Fort Cobb Reservoir, res., Ok., U.S.	120	35°12'N	98°28'W
Fort Collins, Co., U.S. (kŏl'ĭns)	104	40°36'N	105°04'W
Fort Crampel, C.A.R. (kràm-pĕl')	231	6°59'N	19°11'E
Fort-de-France, Mart. (dē fräns)	129	14°37'N	61°06'W
Fort Deposit, Al., U.S. (dē-pŏz'ĭt)	124	31°58'N	86°35'W
Fort-de-Possel, C.A.R. (dē pô-sĕl')	231	5°03'N	19°11'E
Fort Dodge, Ia., U.S. (dŏj)	105	42°31'N	94°10'W
Fort Edward, N.Y., U.S. (wĕrd)	109	43°15'N	73°30'W
Fort Erie, Can. (ē'rĭ)	111c	42°55'N	78°56'W
Fortescue, r., Austl. (fôr'tĕs-kū)	220	21°25'S	116°50'E
Fort Fairfield, Me., U.S. (fâr'fēld)	100	46°46'N	67°53'W
Fort Fitzgerald, Can. (fĭts-jĕr'ăld)	90	59°48'N	111°50'W
Fort Frances, Can. (frăn'sĕs)	91	48°36'N	93°24'W
Fort Frederica National Monument, rec., Ga., U.S. (frĕd'ē-rī-kà)	124	31°13'N	85°25'W
Fort Gaines, Ga., U.S. (gānz)	124	31°35'N	85°03'W
Fort Gibson, Ok., U.S. (gĭb'sŭn)	121	35°50'N	95°13'W
Fort Good Hope, Can. (gŏŏd hōp)	90	66°19'N	128°52'W
Forth, Firth of, b., Scot., U.K. (fûrth ôv fôrth)	156	56°04'N	3°03'W
Fort Hall, Kenya (hôl)	233	0°47'S	37°13'E
Fort Hall Indian Reservation, I.R., Id., U.S.	115	43°02'N	112°21'W
Fort Huachuca, Az., U.S. (wä-chōō'kä)	119	31°30'N	110°25'W
Fortier, Can. (fôr'tyā')	102f	49°56'N	97°55'W
Fort Kent, Me., U.S. (kĕnt)	100	47°14'N	68°37'W
Fort Langley, Can. (lăng'lĭ)	116d	49°10'N	122°35'W
Fort Lauderdale, Fl., U.S. (lô'dĕr-dāl)	125a	26°07'N	80°09'W
Fort Lee, N.J., U.S.	110a	40°50'N	73°58'W
Fort Liard, Can.	90	60°16'N	123°34'W
Fort Loudoun Lake, res., Tn., U.S. (fōrt lou'dĕn)	124	35°52'N	84°10'W
Fort Lupton, Co., U.S. (lŭp'tŭn)	120	40°04'N	104°54'W
Fort Macleod, Can. (má-kloud')	90	49°43'N	113°25'W
Fort Madison, Ia., U.S. (măd'ĭ-sŭn)	113	40°40'N	91°17'W
Fort Matanzas, Fl., U.S. (mä-tän'zäs)	125	29°39'N	81°17'W
Fort McDermitt Indian Reservation, I.R., Or., U.S. (măk dĕr'mĭt)	114	42°04'N	118°07'W
Fort McMurray, Can. (măk-mŭr'ĭ)	90	56°44'N	111°23'W
Fort McPherson, Can. (măk-fŭr's'n)	90	67°37'N	134°59'W
Fort Meade, Fl., U.S. (mēd)	125a	27°45'N	81°48'W
Fort Mill, S.C., U.S. (mĭl)	125	35°03'N	80°57'W
Fort Mojave Indian Reservation, I.R., Ca., U.S. (mō-hä'vâ)	118	34°59'N	115°02'W
Fort Morgan, Co., U.S. (môr'găn)	120	40°14'N	103°49'W
Fort Myers, Fl., U.S. (mī'ĕrz)	125a	26°36'N	81°45'W
Fort Nelson, Can. (nĕl'sŭn)	90	58°57'N	122°30'W
Fort Nelson, r., Can. (nĕl'sŭn)	92	58°44'N	122°20'W
Fort Payne, Al., U.S. (pān)	124	34°26'N	85°41'W
Fort Peck, Mt., U.S. (pĕk)	115	47°58'N	106°30'W
Fort Peck Indian Reservation, I.R., Mt., U.S.	112	48°22'N	105°40'W
Fort Peck Lake, res., Mt., U.S.	106	47°52'N	106°59'W
Fort Pierce, Fl., U.S. (pērs)	125a	27°25'N	80°20'W
Fort Portal, Ug. (pôr'tàl)	231	0°40'N	30°16'E
Fort Providence, Can. (prŏv'ĭ-dĕns)	90	61°27'N	117°59'W
Fort Pulaski National Monument, rec., Ga., U.S. (pu-lăs'kĭ)	125	31°59'N	80°56'W
Fort Qu'Appelle, Can.	96	50°46'N	103°55'W
Fort Randall Dam, dam, S.D., U.S.	112	42°48'N	98°35'W
Fort Resolution, Can. (rĕz'ō-lū'shŭn)	90	61°08'N	113°42'W
Fort Riley, Ks., U.S. (rī'lĭ)	121	39°05'N	96°46'W
Fort Saint James, Can. (fôrt sānt jāmz)	90	54°26'N	124°15'W
Fort Saint John, Can. (sānt jŏn)	90	56°15'N	120°51'W
Fort Sandeman, Pak. (săn'da-măn)	199	31°28'N	69°29'E
Fort Saskatchewan, Can. (săs-kăt'chōō-ån)	102g	53°43'N	113°13'W
Fort Scott, Ks., U.S. (skŏt)	105	37°50'N	94°43'W
Fort Severn, Can. (sĕv'ērn)	91	55°58'N	87°50'W
Fort-Shevchenko, Kaz. (shĕv-chĕn'kô)	183	44°30'N	50°18'E
Fort Sibut, C.A.R. (fôr sē-bü')	231	5°44'N	19°05'E
Fort Sill, Ok., U.S. (fôrt sĭl)	120	34°41'N	98°25'W
Fort Simpson, Can. (sĭmp'sŭn)	90	61°52'N	121°48'W
Fort Smith, Can.	90	60°09'N	112°08'W
Fort Smith, Ar., U.S. (smĭth)	105	35°23'N	94°24'W
Fort Stockton, Tx., U.S. (stŏk'tŭn)	122	30°54'N	102°51'W
Fort Sumner, N.M., U.S. (sŭm'nēr)	120	34°30'N	104°17'W
Fort Sumter National Monument, rec., S.C., U.S. (sŭm'tēr)	125	32°43'N	79°54'W
Fort Thomas, Ky., U.S. (tŏm'ăs)	111f	39°05'N	84°27'W
Fortuna, Ca., U.S. (fôr-tū'ná)	114	40°36'N	124°10'W
Fortune, Can. (fôr'tūn)	101	47°04'N	55°51'W
Fortune, i., Bah.	135	22°35'N	74°20'W
Fortune Bay, b., Can.	93a	47°25'N	55°25'W
Fort Union National Monument, rec., N.M., U.S. (ūn'yŭn)	120	35°51'N	104°57'W
Fort Valley, Ga., U.S. (văl'ĭ)	124	32°33'N	83°53'W
Fort Vermilion, Can. (vēr-mĭl'yŭn)	90	58°23'N	115°50'W
Fort Victoria *see* Masvingo, Zimb.	232	20°07'S	30°47'E
Fort Wayne, In., U.S. (wān)	105	41°00'N	85°10'W
Fort William, Scot., U.K. (wĭl'yăm)	164	56°50'N	3°00'W
Fort William, Mount, mtn., Austl. (wĭ'ĭ-ăm)	222	24°45'S	151°15'E
Fort Worth, Tx., U.S. (wûrth)	104	32°45'N	97°20'W
Fort Yukon, Ak., U.S. (yōō'kŏn)	106a	66°30'N	145°00'W
Fort Yuma Indian Reservation, I.R., Ca., U.S. (yōō'mä)	119	32°54'N	114°47'W
Foshan, China	205	23°02'N	113°07'E
Fossano, Italy (fōs-sä'nō)	174	44°34'N	7°42'E
Fossil Creek, r., Tx., U.S. (fŏs-ĭl)	117c	32°53'N	97°19'W
Fossombrone, Italy (fōs-sôm-brō'nā)	174	43°41'N	12°48'E
Foss Res, Ok., U.S.	120	35°38'N	99°11'W
Fosston, Mn., U.S. (fŏs'tŭn)	112	47°34'N	95°44'W
Fosterburg, Il., U.S. (fŏs'tēr-bûrg)	117e	38°58'N	90°04'W
Fostoria, Oh., U.S. (fŏs-tō'rĭ-á)	108	41°10'N	83°20'W
Fougéres, Fr. (fōō-zhâr')	161	48°23'N	1°14'W
Foula, i., Scot., U.K. (fou'là)	164a	60°08'N	2°04'W
Foulwind, Cape, c., N.Z. (foul'wĭnd)	221a	41°45'S	171°00'E
Foumban, Cam. (fōōm-bän')	230	5°43'N	10°55'E
Fountain Creek, r., Co., U.S. (foun'tĭn)	120	38°36'N	104°37'W
Fountain Valley, Ca., U.S.	117a	33°42'N	117°57'W
Fourche la Fave, r., Ar., U.S. (fōōrsh lä fäv')	121	34°46'N	93°45'W
Fouriesburg, S. Afr. (fō'rēz-bûrg)	238c	28°38'S	28°13'E
Fourmies, Fr. (fōōr-mē')	170	50°01'N	4°01'E
Four Mountains, Islands of the, is., Ak., U.S.	103a	52°58'N	170°40'W
Fourth Cataract, wtfl., Sudan	231	18°52'N	32°07'E
Fouta Djallon, mts., Gui. (fōō'tä jä-lôn)	230	11°37'N	12°29'W
Foveaux Strait, strt., N.Z. (fô-vō')	221a	46°30'S	167°43'E
Fowler, Co., U.S. (foul'ēr)	120	38°04'N	104°02'W
Fowler, In., U.S.	108	40°35'N	87°20'W
Fowler, Point, c., Austl.	220	32°05'S	132°30'E
Fowlerton, Tx., U.S. (foul'ēr-tŭn)	122	28°26'N	98°48'W
Fox, i., Wa., U.S. (fŏks)	116a	47°15'N	122°08'W
Fox, r., Il., U.S.	113	41°35'N	88°43'W
Fox, r., Wi., U.S.	113	44°18'N	88°23'W
Foxboro, Ma., U.S. (fŏks'bŭrō)	101a	42°04'N	71°15'W
Foxe Basin, b., Can. (fŏks)	93	67°35'N	79°21'W
Foxe Channel, strt., Can.	93	64°30'N	79°23'W
Foxe Peninsula, pen., Can.	93	64°57'N	77°26'W
Fox Islands, is., Ak., U.S. (fŏks)	103a	53°04'N	167°30'W
Fox Lake, Il., U.S. (lăk)	111a	42°24'N	88°11'W
Fox Lake, l., Il., U.S.	111a	42°24'N	88°07'W
Fox Point, Wi., U.S.	111a	43°10'N	87°54'W
Foyle, Lough, b., Eur. (lŏk foil')	164	55°07'N	7°08'W
Foz do Cunene, Ang.	236	17°16'S	11°50'E
Fraga, Spain (frä'gä)	173	41°31'N	0°20'E
Fragoso, Cayo, i., Cuba (kä'yō-frä-gō'sō)	134	22°45'N	79°30'W
Framnes Mountains, mts., Ant.	224	67°50'S	62°35'E
Franca, Braz. (frä'n-kä)	143	20°28'S	47°20'W
Francavilla, Italy (fräŋ-kä-vēl'lä)	175	40°32'N	17°37'E
France, nation, Eur. (fråns)	154	46°39'N	0°47'E
Frances, l., Can. (frăn'sĭs)	92	61°27'N	128°28'W
Frances, Cabo, c., Cuba (kä'bô-frän-sĕ's)	134	21°55'N	84°05'W
Frances, Punta, c., Cuba (pōō'n-tä-frän-sĕ's)	134	21°45'N	83°10'W
Francés Viejo, Cabo, c., Dom. Rep. (kà'bô-frän'sås vyā'hô)	135	19°40'N	69°35'W
Franceville, Gabon (fräns-vēl')	232	1°38'S	13°35'E
Francis Case, Lake, res., S.D., U.S. (frăn'sĭs)	106	43°15'N	99°00'W
Francisco Sales, Braz. (frän-sē's-kô-sà'lĕs)	141a	21°42'S	44°26'W
Francistown, Bots. (frăn'sis-toun)	232	21°17'S	27°28'E
Frankfort, S. Afr. (frănk'fŏrt)	233c	32°43'S	27°28'E
Frankfort, S. Afr.	238c	27°17'S	28°30'E
Frankfort, Il., U.S. (frăŋk'fŭrt)	111a	41°30'N	87°51'W
Frankfort, In., U.S.	108	40°15'N	86°30'W
Frankfort, Ks., U.S.	121	39°42'N	96°27'W
Frankfort, Ky., U.S.	105	38°10'N	84°55'W
Frankfort, Mi., U.S.	108	44°40'N	86°15'W
Frankfort, N.Y., U.S.	109	43°05'N	75°05'W
Frankfurt am Main, Ger.	154	50°07'N	8°40'E
Frankfurt an der Oder, Ger.	161	52°20'N	14°31'E
Franklin, S. Afr.	233c	30°19'S	29°28'E
Franklin, In., U.S. (frănk'lĭn)	108	39°25'N	86°00'W
Franklin, Ky., U.S.	124	36°42'N	86°34'W
Franklin, La., U.S.	123	29°47'N	91°31'W
Franklin, Ma., U.S.	101a	42°05'N	71°24'W
Franklin, Ne., U.S.	120	40°06'N	99°01'W
Franklin, N.H., U.S.	109	43°25'N	71°40'W
Franklin, N.J., U.S.	110a	41°08'N	74°35'W
Franklin, Oh., U.S.	108	39°30'N	84°20'W
Franklin, Pa., U.S.	109	41°25'N	79°50'W
Franklin, Tn., U.S.	124	35°54'N	86°54'W
Franklin, Va., U.S.	125	36°41'N	76°57'W
Franklin, l., Nv., U.S.	118	40°23'N	115°10'W
Franklin D. Roosevelt Lake, res., Wa., U.S.	114	48°12'N	118°43'W
Franklin Mountains, mts., Can.	92	65°36'N	125°55'W
Franklin Park, Il., U.S.	111a	41°56'N	87°53'W
Franklin Square, N.Y., U.S.	110a	40°43'N	73°40'W
Franklinton, La., U.S. (frăŋk'lĭn-tŭn)	123	30°49'N	90°09'W
Frankston, Austl.	217a	38°09'S	145°08'E
Franksville, Wi., U.S. (frănkz'vĭl)	111a	42°46'N	87°55'W
Fransta, Swe.	166	62°30'N	16°04'E
Franz Josef Land *see* Zemlya Frantsa-Iosifa, is., Russia	178	81°32'N	40°00'E
Frascati, Italy (fräs-kä'tē)	174	41°49'N	12°45'E
Fraser, Mi., U.S. (frā'zēr)	111b	42°32'N	82°57'W
Fraser, i., Austl.	221	25°12'S	153°00'E
Fraser, r., Can.	92	51°30'N	122°00'W
Fraserburgh, Scot., U.K. (frā'zēr-bûrg)	164	57°40'N	2°01'W
Fraser Plateau, plat., Can.	95	51°30'N	122°00'W
Frattamaggiore, Italy (frät-tä-mäg-zhyô'rĕ)	173c	40°41'N	14°16'E
Fray Bentos, Ur. (frī bĕn'tōs)	144	33°10'S	58°19'W
Frazee, Mn., U.S. (frå-zē')	112	46°42'N	95°43'W
Fraziers Hog Cay, i., Bah.	134	25°25'N	77°55'W
Frechen, Ger. (frĕ'kĕn)	171c	50°54'N	6°49'E
Fredericia, Den. (frĕdh-ĕ-rē'tsē-à)	166	55°35'N	9°45'E
Frederick, Md., U.S. (frĕd'ēr-ĭk)	105	39°25'N	77°25'W
Frederick, Ok., U.S.	120	34°23'N	99°01'W
Frederick House, r., Can.	98	49°05'N	81°20'W
Fredericksburg, Tx., U.S. (frĕd'ēr-ĭkz-bûrg)	122	30°16'N	98°52'W
Fredericksburg, Va., U.S.	109	38°20'N	77°30'W
Fredericktown, Mo., U.S. (frĕd'ēr-ĭk-toun)	121	37°32'N	90°16'W
Fredericton, Can. (frĕd'-ēr-ĭk-tŭn)	91	45°48'N	66°39'W
Frederikshavn, Den. (frĕdh'ĕ-rēks-houn)	160	57°27'N	10°31'E
Frederikssund, Den. (frĕdh'ĕ-rēks-sōn)	166	55°51'N	12°04'E
Fredonia, Col. (frĕ-dō'nyà)	142a	5°55'N	75°40'W
Fredonia, Ks., U.S. (frē-dō'nĭ-á)	121	36°31'N	95°50'W
Fredonia, N.Y., U.S.	109	42°25'N	79°20'W
Fredrikstad, Nor. (frädh'rĕks-städ)	160	59°14'N	10°58'E
Freeburg, Il., U.S. (frē'bûrg)	117e	38°26'N	89°59'W
Freehold, N.J., U.S. (frē'hōld)	110a	40°15'N	74°16'W
Freeland, Pa., U.S. (frē'lănd)	109	41°00'N	75°50'W
Freeland, Wa., U.S.	116a	48°01'N	122°32'W
Freels, Cape, c., Can. (frēlz)	101	46°37'N	53°45'W
Freelton, Can. (frēl'tŭn)	102d	43°24'N	80°02'W
Freeport, Bah.	134	26°30'N	78°45'W
Freeport, Il., U.S. (frē'pōrt)	105	42°19'N	89°30'W
Freeport, N.Y., U.S.	110a	40°39'N	73°35'W
Freeport, Tx., U.S.	123	28°56'N	95°21'W
Freetown, S.L. (frē'toun)	230	8°30'N	13°15'W
Fregenal de la Sierra, Spain (frä-hå-näl' dā lä syĕr'rä)	172	38°09'N	6°40'W
Fregene, Italy (frĕ-zhĕ'-nĕ)	173d	41°52'N	12°12'E
Freiberg, Ger. (frī'bĕrgh)	161	50°54'N	13°18'E
Freiburg, Ger.	161	48°00'N	7°50'E
Freienried, Ger. (frī'ĕn-rēd)	159d	48°20'N	11°08'E
Freirina, Chile (frå-ĭ-rē'nä)	144	28°35'S	71°26'W
Freising, Ger. (frī'zĭng)	168	48°25'N	11°45'E
Fréjus, Fr. (frā-zhüs')	171	43°28'N	6°46'E
Fremantle, Austl. (frē'măn-t'l)	218	32°03'S	116°05'E
Fremont, Ca., U.S. (frē-mŏnt')	116b	37°33'N	122°00'W
Fremont, Mi., U.S.	108	43°25'N	85°55'W
Fremont, Ne., U.S.	112	41°26'N	96°30'W
Fremont, Oh., U.S.	108	41°20'N	83°05'W
Fremont, r., Ut., U.S.	119	38°20'N	111°30'W
Fremont Peak, mtn., Wy., U.S.	115	43°05'N	109°35'W
French Broad, r., Tn., U.S. (frĕnch brôd)	124	35°59'N	83°01'W
French Frigate Shoals, Hi., U.S.	126b	23°30'N	167°10'W
French Guiana, dep., S.A. (gē-ä'nä)	143	4°20'N	53°00'W
French Lick, In., U.S. (frĕnch lĭk)	108	38°35'N	86°35'W
Frenchman, r., N.A.	96	49°25'N	108°30'W
Frenchman Creek, r., Mt., U.S. (frĕnch-măn)	115	48°51'N	107°20'W
Frenchman Creek, r., Ne., U.S.	120	40°24'N	101°50'W
Frenchman Flat, Nv., U.S.	118	36°55'N	116°11'W
French Polynesia, dep., Oc.	2	15°00'S	140°00'W
French River, Mn., U.S.	117h	46°54'N	91°54'W
Freshfield, Mount, mtn., Can. (frĕsh'fēld)	95	51°44'N	116°57'W
Fresnillo, Mex. (frås-nēl'yō)	128	23°10'N	102°52'W
Fresno, Col. (frĕs'nô)	142a	5°10'N	75°01'W
Fresno, Ca., U.S.	104	36°44'N	119°46'W
Fresno, r., Ca., U.S. (frĕz'nō)	118	37°00'N	120°24'W
Fresno Slough, Ca., U.S.	118	36°39'N	120°12'W
Freudenstadt, Ger. (froi'den-shtät)	168	48°28'N	8°26'E
Freycinet Peninsula, pen., Austl. (frā-sē-nĕ')	222	42°13'S	148°56'E
Fria, Gui.	234	10°05'N	13°32'W
Fria, r., Az., U.S. (frē-ä)	119	34°03'N	112°12'W
Fria, Cape, c., Nmb. (frĭá)	232	18°15'S	12°10'E
Friant-Kern Canal, can., Ca., U.S. (kûrn)	118	36°57'N	119°37'W
Frias, Arg. (frē-äs)	144	28°43'S	65°03'W
Fribourg, Switz. (frē-bōōr')	161	46°48'N	7°07'E
Fridley, Mn., U.S. (frĭd'lĭ)	117g	45°05'N	93°16'W
Friedberg, Ger. (frēd'bĕrgh)	159d	48°22'N	11°00'E
Friedland, Ger. (frēt'länt)	168	53°39'N	13°34'E
Friedrichshafen, Ger. (frē-drēks-häf'ĕn)	168	47°39'N	9°28'E
Friend, Ne., U.S. (frĕnd)	121	40°40'N	97°16'W
Friendswood, Tx., U.S. (frĕnds'wŏŏd)	123a	29°31'N	95°11'W
Fries, Va., U.S. (frēz)	125	36°42'N	80°59'W
Friesack, Ger. (frē'säk)	159b	52°44'N	12°35'E
Frio, Cabo, c., Braz. (kä'bō-frē'ō)	143	22°58'S	42°08'W
Frio R, Tx., U.S.	122	29°00'N	99°15'W
Frisian Islands, is., Neth. (frē'zhăn)	160	53°30'N	5°20'E
Friuli-Venezia Giulia, hist. reg., Italy	174	46°20'N	13°20'E
Frobisher Bay, b., Can.	93	62°49'N	66°41'W
Frobisher Lake, l., Can. (frŏb'ĭsh-ēr)	92	56°25'N	108°20'W
Frodsham, Eng., U.K. (frŏdz'ăm)	158a	53°18'N	2°48'W
Frohavet, b., Nor.	160	63°49'N	9°12'E
Frome, Lake, l., Austl. (frōōm)	220	30°40'S	140°13'E
Frontenac, Ks., U.S. (frŏn'tē-năk)	121	37°27'N	94°41'W
Frontera, Mex. (frôn-tā'rä)	131	18°34'N	92°38'W
Front Range, mts., Co., U.S. (frŭnt)	120	40°59'N	105°29'W
Front Royal, Va., U.S. (frŭnt)	109	38°55'N	78°10'W
Frosinone, Italy (frō-zē-nō'nå)	174	41°38'N	13°22'E
Frostburg, Md., U.S. (frôst'bûrg)	109	39°40'N	78°55'W
Fruita, Co., U.S. (frōōt-á)	119	39°10'N	108°45'W
Frunze *see* Bishkek, Kyrg.	183	42°49'N	74°42'E
Fryanovo, Russia (f'ryä'nô-vô)	186b	56°08'N	38°28'E
Fryazino, Russia (f'ryä'zĭ-nô)	186b	55°58'N	38°05'E

ng-sing; ŋ-baŋk; ɴ-nasalized n; nŏd; cǒmmit; ōld; ôbey; ôrder; oi-boil; fōōd; ò-as oo in foot; ou-out; s-soft; sh-dish; th-thin; pūre; ûnite; ûrn; stŭd; circŭs; ü-as in French tu; ´-indeterminate vowel.

PLACE (Pronunciation)	PAGE	LAT.	LONG.
Gatun, Pan. (gä-tōōn′)	133	9°16′N	79°25′W
Gatun, r., Pan.	128a	9°21′N	79°40′W
Gatún, Lago, l., Pan.	133	9°13′N	79°24′W
Gatun Locks, trans., Pan.	128a	9°16′N	79°57′W
Gauhāti, India	199	26°09′N	91°51′E
Gauja, r., Lat. (gå′ò-yå)	167	57°10′N	24°30′E
Gaula, r., Nor.	166	62°55′N	10°45′E
Gávdos, i., Grc. (gäv′dôs)	163	34°48′N	24°08′E
Gavins Point Dam, Ne., U.S. (gă′-vĭns)	112	42°47′N	97°47′W
Gāvkhūnī, Bātlāq-e, l., Iran	198	31°40′N	52°48′E
Gävle, Swe. (yĕv′lĕ)	154	60°40′N	17°07′E
Gävlebukten, b., Swe.	166	60°45′N	17°30′E
Gavrilov Posad, Russia (gá′vrê-lôf′ka po-sát)	176	56°34′N	40°09′E
Gavrilov-Yam, Russia (gá′vrê-lôf yäm′)	176	57°17′N	39°49′E
Gawler, Austl. (gô′lẽr)	218	34°35′S	138°47′E
Gawler Ranges, mts., Austl.	222	32°35′S	136°30′E
Gaya, India (gŭ′yä)(gī′á)	199	24°53′N	85°00′E
Gaya, Nig. (gä′yä)	230	11°58′N	9°05′E
Gaylord, Mi., U.S. (gā′lôrd)	108	45°00′N	84°35′W
Gayndah, Austl. (gān′däh)	222	25°43′S	151°33′E
Gaza, Gaza	198	31°30′N	34°29′E
Gaziantep, Tur. (gä-zē-än′tĕp)	198	37°10′N	37°30′E
Gbarnga, Lib.	234	7°00′N	9°29′W
Gdańsk, Pol. (g′dänsk)	154	54°20′N	18°40′E
Gdov, Russia (g′dôf′)	180	58°44′N	27°51′E
Gdynia, Pol. (g′dēn′yà)	160	54°29′N	18°30′E
Geary, Ok., U.S. (gē′rĭ)	120	35°36′N	98°19′W
Géba, r., Gui.-B.	234	12°25′N	14°35′W
Gebo, Wy., U.S. (gĕb′ō)	115	43°49′N	108°13′W
Ged, La., U.S. (gĕd)	123	30°07′N	93°36′W
Gediz, r., Tur.	163	38°44′N	28°45′E
Gedney, i., Wa., U.S. (gĕd-nê)	116a	48°01′N	122°18′W
Gedser, Den.	166	54°35′N	12°08′E
Geel, Bel.	159a	51°09′N	5°01′E
Geelong, Austl. (jē-lông′)	219	38°06′S	144°13′E
Gegu, China (gŭ-gōō)	206	39°00′N	117°30′E
Ge Hu, l., China (gŭ hōō)	206	31°37′N	119°57′E
Geidam, Nig.	230	12°57′N	11°57′E
Geikie Range, mts., Austl. (gē′kê)	220	17°35′S	125°32′E
Geislingen, Ger. (gīs′lĭng-ĕn)	168	48°37′N	9°52′E
Geist Reservoir, res., In., U.S. (gēst)	111g	39°57′N	85°59′W
Geita, Tan.	237	2°52′S	32°10′E
Gejiu, China (gŭ-jĭo)	209	23°32′N	102°50′E
Geldermalsen, Neth.	159a	51°53′N	5°18′E
Geldern, Ger. (gĕl′dĕrn)	171c	51°31′N	6°20′E
Gelibolu, Tur. (gĕ-lĭb′ŏ-lò)	163	40°25′N	26°40′E
Gelsenkirchen, Ger. (gĕl-zĕn-kĭrk-ĕn)	168	51°31′N	7°05′E
Gemas, Malay. (jĕm′ás)	197b	2°35′N	102°37′E
Gemena, D.R.C.	231	3°15′N	19°46′E
Gemlik, Tur. (gĕm′lĭk)	163	40°30′N	29°10′E
Genale (Jubba), r., Afr.	238a	5°15′N	41°00′E
General Alvear, Arg. (gĕ-nĕ-räl′äl-vĕ-á′r)	141c	36°04′S	60°02′W
General Arenales, Arg. (ä-rĕ-nä′lĕs)	141c	34°19′S	61°16′W
General Belgrano, Arg. (bĕl-grá′nô)	141c	35°45′S	58°32′W
General Cepeda, Mex. (sĕ-pĕ′dä)	122	25°24′N	101°29′W
General Conesa, Arg. (kô-nĕ′sä)	141c	36°30′S	57°19′W
General Guido, Arg. (gē′dô)	141c	36°41′S	57°48′W
General Lavalle, Arg. (là-vá′l-yĕ)	141c	36°25′S	56°55′W
General Madariaga, Arg. (män-dà-rêä′gä)	144	36°59′S	57°14′W
General Paz, Arg. (pá′z)	141c	35°30′S	58°20′W
General Pedro Antonio Santos, Mex.	130	21°37′N	98°58′W
General Pico, Arg. (pē′kô)	144	36°46′S	63°44′W
General Roca, Arg. (rô-kä)	144	39°01′S	67°31′W
General San Martín, Arg. (sän-már-tē′n)	144a	34°35′S	58°32′W
General Sarmiento (San Miguel), Arg.	144a	34°33′S	58°43′W
General Viamonte, Arg. (vēä′môn-tĕ)	141c	35°01′S	60°59′W
General Zuazua, Mex. (zwä′zwä)	122	25°54′N	100°07′W
Genesee, r., N.Y., U.S. (jĕn-ê-sē′)	109	42°25′N	78°10′W
Geneseo, Il., U.S. (jē-nĕsêō)	108	41°28′N	90°11′W
Geneva (Genève), Switz.	154	46°14′N	6°04′E
Geneva, Al., U.S. (jê-nē′vá)	124	31°03′N	85°50′W
Geneva, Il., U.S.	111a	41°53′N	88°18′W
Geneva, Ne., U.S.	121	40°32′N	97°37′W
Geneva, N.Y., U.S.	109	42°50′N	77°00′W
Geneva, Oh., U.S.	108	41°45′N	80°55′W
Geneva, Lake, l., Switz.	161	46°28′N	6°30′E
Genève *see* Geneva, Switz.	154	46°14′N	6°04′E
Genil, r., Spain (hå-nēl′)	172	37°15′N	4°05′W
Genoa, Italy	154	44°23′N	9°52′E
Genoa, Ne., U.S. (jen′ô-á)	121	41°26′N	97°43′W
Genoa City, Wi., U.S.	111a	42°31′N	88°19′W
Genova, Golfo di, b., Italy (gôl-fô-dē-jĕn′ô-vä)	156	44°10′N	8°45′E
Genovesa, i., Ec. (ĕ′s-lä-gĕ-nō-vĕ-sä)	142	0°08′N	90°15′W
Gent, Bel.	161	51°05′N	3°40′E
Genthin, Ger. (gĕn-tēn′)	168	52°24′N	12°10′E
Genzano di Roma, Italy (gzhĕnt-zá′-nô-dē-rô′mä)	173d	41°43′N	12°49′E
Geographe Bay, b., Austl. (jē-ô-graf′)	220	33°00′S	114°00′E
Geographe Channel, strt., Austl. (jēô′gră-fĭk)	220	24°15′S	112°50′E
George, l., N.Y., U.S. (jôrj)	109	43°40′N	73°30′W
George, Lake, l., N.A. (jôrg)	117k	46°26′N	84°09′W
George, Lake, l., Ug.	237	0°02′N	30°25′E
George, Lake, l., Fl., U.S. (jôr-ĭj)	125	29°10′N	81°50′W
George, Lake, l., In., U.S.	111a	41°31′N	87°17′W
Georges, r., Austl.	217b	33°57′S	151°00′E
George Town, Bah.	135	23°30′N	75°50′W
Georgetown, Can. (jôrg-toun)	102d	43°39′N	79°56′W
Georgetown, Can. (jôr-ĭj-toun)	101	46°11′N	62°32′W
George Town, Cay. Is.	134	19°20′N	81°20′W
Georgetown, Guy. (jôrj′toun)	143	7°45′N	58°04′W
George Town, Malay.	212	5°21′N	100°09′E
Georgetown, Ct., U.S.	110a	41°15′N	73°25′W
Georgetown, De., U.S.	109	38°40′N	75°20′W
Georgetown, Il., U.S.	108	40°00′N	87°40′W
Georgetown, Ky., U.S.	108	38°10′N	84°35′W
Georgetown, Ma., U.S. (jôrg-toun)	101a	42°43′N	71°00′W
Georgetown, Md., U.S.	109	39°25′N	75°55′W
Georgetown, S.C., U.S. (jôr-ĭj-toun)	125	33°22′N	79°17′W
Georgetown, Tx., U.S. (jôrg-toun)	123	30°37′N	97°40′W
George Washington Birthplace National Monument, rec., Va., U.S. (jôrj wŏsh′ĭng-tŭn)	109	38°10′N	77°00′W
George Washington Carver National Monument, rec., Mo., U.S. (jôrg wăsh-ĭng-tŭn kär′vẽr)	121	36°58′N	94°21′W
George West, Tx., U.S.	122	28°20′N	98°07′W
Georgia, nation, Asia	178	42°17′N	43°00′E
Georgia, state, U.S. (jôr′jĭ-ă)	105	32°40′N	83°50′W
Georgia, Strait of, strt., N.A.	94	49°20′N	124°00′W
Georgiana, Al., U.S. (jôr-jē-ăn′á)	124	31°39′N	86°44′W
Georgian Bay, b., Can.	93	45°15′N	80°50′W
Georgian Bay Islands National Park, rec., Can.	98	45°20′N	81°40′W
Georgina, r., Austl. (jôr-jē′ná)	220	22°00′S	138°15′E
Georgiyevsk, Russia (gyôr-gyĕfsk′)	181	44°05′N	43°30′E
Gera, Ger. (gā′rä)	161	50°52′N	12°06′E
Geral, Serra, mts., Braz. (sĕr′rá zhå-räl′)	144	28°30′S	51°00′W
Geral de Goiás, Serra, mts., Braz. (zhå-räl′-dĕ-gô-yà′s)	143	14°22′S	45°40′W
Geraldton, Austl. (jĕr′ăld-tŭn)	218	28°40′S	114°35′E
Geraldton, Can.	91	49°43′N	87°00′W
Gérgal, Spain (gĕr′gäl)	172	37°08′N	2°29′W
Gering, Ne., U.S. (gē′rĭng)	112	41°49′N	103°41′W
Gerlachovský štít, mtn., Slvk.	169	49°12′N	20°08′E
Germantown, Oh., U.S. (jûr′măn-toun)	108	39°35′N	84°25′W
Germany, nation, Eur. (jûr′má-nĭ)	154	51°00′N	10°00′E
Germiston, S. Afr. (jûr′mĭs-tŭn)	232	26°19′S	28°11′E
Gerona, Phil. (hā-rō′nä)	213a	15°36′N	120°36′E
Gerrards Cross, Eng., U.K. (jĕrărds krŏs)	158b	51°34′N	0°33′W
Gers, r., Fr. (zhĕr)	173	43°25′N	0°30′E
Gersthofen, Ger. (gĕrst-hō′fĕn)	159d	48°26′N	10°54′E
Getafe, Spain (hā-tä′fā)	172	40°19′N	3°44′W
Gettysburg, Pa., U.S. (gĕt′ĭs-bûrg)	109	39°50′N	77°15′W
Gettysburg, S.D., U.S.	112	45°01′N	99°59′W
Gevelsberg, Ger. (gĕ-fĕls′bĕrgh)	171c	51°18′N	7°20′E
Ghāghra, r., India	199	26°00′N	83°00′E
Ghana, nation, Afr. (gän′ä)	230	8°00′N	2°00′W
Ghanzi, Bots. (gän′zē)	232	21°30′S	22°00′E
Ghardaïa, Alg. (gär-dä′ē-ä)	230	32°29′N	3°38′E
Gharo, Pak.	202	24°50′N	68°35′E
Ghāt, Libya	230	24°52′N	10°16′E
Ghazāl, Bahr al-, r., Sudan	231	9°30′N	30°00′E
Ghazal, Bahr el, r., Chad (bär ĕl ghä-zäl′)	235	14°30′N	17°00′E
Ghazzah *see* Gaza, Gaza	198	31°30′N	34°29′E
Gheorgheni, Rom.	163	46°48′N	25°30′E
Gherla, Rom. (gĕr′lä)	169	47°01′N	23°55′E
Ghilizane, Alg.	230	35°43′N	0°43′E
Ghoriān, Afg.	201	34°21′N	61°30′E
Ghost Lake, Can.	102e	51°15′N	114°46′W
Ghudāmis, Libya	230	30°07′N	9°26′E
Giannitsá, Grc.	175	40°47′N	22°26′E
Giannutri, Isola di, i., Italy (jän-nōō′trē)	174	42°15′N	11°06′E
Giant Sequoia National Monument, rec., Ca., U.S.	118	36°10′N	118°35′W
Gibara, Cuba (hē-bä′rä)	134	21°05′N	76°10′W
Gibeon, Nmb. (gĭb′ē-ŭn)	232	25°15′S	17°30′E
Gibraleón, Spain (hē-brä-lå-ōn′)	172	37°24′N	7°00′W
Gibraltar, dep., Eur. (gĭ-bräl-tă′r)	154	36°08′N	5°22′W
Gibraltar, Strait of, strt.	156	35°55′N	5°45′W
Gibson City, Il., U.S. (gĭb′sŭn)	108	40°25′N	88°20′W
Gibson Desert, des., Austl.	220	24°45′S	123°15′E
Gibson Island, Md., U.S.	110e	39°05′N	76°26′W
Gibson Reservoir, res., Ok., U.S.	121	36°07′N	95°08′W
Giddings, Tx., U.S. (gĭd′ĭngz)	123	30°11′N	96°55′W
Gideon, Mo., U.S. (gĭd′ē-ŭn)	121	36°27′N	89°56′W
Gien, Fr. (zhē-ăN′)	161	47°43′N	2°37′E
Giessen, Ger. (gēs′sĕn)	168	50°35′N	8°40′E
Gifu, Japan (gē′fōō)	205	35°25′N	136°45′E
Gig Harbor, Wa., U.S. (gĭg)	116a	47°20′N	122°36′W
Giglio, Isola del, i., Italy (jēl′yō)	174	42°23′N	10°55′E
Gijón, Spain (hê-hōn′)	154	43°33′N	5°37′W
Gila, r., U.S. (hē′lá)	106	33°00′N	110°00′W
Gila Bend, Az., U.S.	119	32°59′N	112°41′W
Gila Cliff Dwellings National Monument, rec., N.M., U.S.	119	33°15′N	108°20′W
Gila River Indian Reservation, I.R., Az., U.S.	119	33°11′N	112°38′W
Gilbert, Mn., U.S. (gĭl′bĕrt)	113	47°27′N	92°29′W
Gilbert, r., Austl. (gĭl-bĕrt)	221	17°15′S	142°09′E
Gilbert, Mount, mtn., Can.	94	50°51′N	124°20′W
Gilbert Islands, is., Kir.	241	0°30′S	174°00′E
Gilboa, Mount, mtn., S. Afr. (gĭl-bôá)	233c	29°13′N	30°17′W
Gilford Island, i., Can. (gĭl′fĕrd)	94	50°45′N	126°25′W
Gilgit, Pak. (gĭl′gĭt)	199	35°58′N	73°48′E
Gil Island, i., Can. (gĭl)	94	53°13′N	129°15′W
Gillen, l., Austl. (jĭl′ĕn)	220	26°15′S	125°15′E
Gillett, Ar., U.S. (jĭ-lĕt′)	121	34°07′N	91°22′W
Gillette, Wy., U.S.	115	44°17′N	105°30′W
Gillingham, Eng., U.K. (gĭl′ĭng ăm)	165	51°23′N	0°33′E
Gilman, Il., U.S. (gĭl′măn)	108	40°45′N	87°55′W
Gilman Hot Springs, Ca., U.S.	117a	33°49′N	116°57′W
Gilmer, Tx., U.S. (gĭl′mẽr)	123	32°43′N	94°57′W
Gilmore, Ga., U.S. (gĭl′môr)	110c	33°51′N	84°29′W
Gilo, r., Eth.	231	7°40′N	34°17′E
Gilroy, Ca., U.S. (gĭl-roi′)	118	37°00′N	121°34′W
Giluwe, Mount, mtn., Pap. N. Gui.	213	6°04′S	144°00′E
Gimli, Can. (gĭm′lē)	97	50°39′N	97°00′W
Gimone, r., Fr. (zhē-mōn′)	170	43°26′N	0°36′E
Ginir, Eth.	231	7°13′N	40°44′E
Ginosa, Italy (jê-nō′zä)	174	40°35′N	16°48′E
Gioia del Colle, Italy (jô′yä dĕl kôl′lā)	174	40°48′N	16°55′E
Girard, Ks., U.S. (jĭ-rärd′)	121	37°30′N	94°50′W
Girardot, Col. (hē-rär-dôt′)	142	4°19′N	74°47′W
Giresun, Tur. (ghĕr′ĕ-sòn′)	198	40°55′N	38°20′E
Giridih, India (jē-rê-dê)	199	24°12′N	86°18′E
Girona, Spain	162	41°55′N	2°48′E
Gironde, r., Fr. (zhē-rôNd′)	156	45°31′N	1°00′W
Girvan, Scot., U.K. (gûr′văn)	164	55°15′N	5°01′W
Gisborne, N.Z. (gĭz′bŭrn)	221a	38°40′S	178°08′E
Gisenyi, Rw.	232	1°43′S	29°15′E
Gisors, Fr. (zhē-zôr′)	170	49°19′N	1°47′E
Gitambo, D.R.C.	236	4°21′N	24°45′E
Gitega, Bdi.	232	3°39′S	30°05′E
Giurgiu, Rom. (jòr′jò)	175	43°53′N	25°58′E
Givet, Fr. (zhē-vĕ′)	170	50°08′N	4°47′E
Givors, Fr. (zhē-vôr′)	170	45°35′N	4°46′E
Giza *see* Al Jizah, Egypt	238b	30°01′N	31°12′E
Gizhiga, Russia (gē′zhi-gå)	179	61°59′N	160°46′E
Gizo, Sol. Is.	214e	8°06′S	156°51′E
Gizycko, Pol. (gĭ′zhĭ-ko)	160	54°03′N	21°48′E
Gjirokastër, Alb.	163	40°04′N	20°10′E
Gjøvik, Nor. (gyû′vĕk)	160	60°47′N	10°36′E
Glabeek-Zuurbemde, Bel.	159a	50°52′N	4°59′E
Glace Bay, Can. (glās bā)	101	46°12′N	59°57′W
Glacier Bay National Park, rec., Ak., U.S. (glā′shẽr)	106a	58°40′N	136°50′W
Glacier National Park, rec., Can.	92	51°45′N	117°35′W
Glacier Peak, mtn., Wa., U.S.	114	48°07′N	121°10′W
Glacier Point, c., Can.	116a	48°24′N	123°59′W
Gladbeck, Ger. (gläd′bĕk)	168	51°35′N	6°59′E
Gladdeklipkop, S. Afr.	238c	24°17′S	29°36′E
Gladstone, Austl. (glăd′stōn)	219	23°45′S	152°00′E
Gladstone, Austl.	218	33°15′S	138°20′E
Gladstone, Mi., U.S.	113	45°50′N	87°04′W
Gladstone, N.J., U.S.	110a	40°43′N	74°39′W
Gladstone, Or., U.S.	116c	45°23′N	122°36′W
Gladwin, Mi., U.S. (glăd′wĭn)	108	44°00′N	84°25′W
Glåma, r., Nor.	156	61°30′N	10°30′E
Glarus, Switz. (glä′ròs)	168	47°02′N	9°03′E
Glasgow, Scot., U.K. (glàs′gō)	154	55°54′N	4°25′W
Glasgow, Ky., U.S.	124	37°00′N	85°55′W
Glasgow, Mo., U.S.	121	39°14′N	92°48′W
Glasgow, Mt., U.S.	115	48°14′N	106°39′W
Glassport, Pa., U.S. (glàs′pōrt)	111e	40°19′N	79°53′W
Glauchau, Ger. (glou′kou)	168	50°51′N	12°28′E
Glazov, Russia (glä′zôf)	178	58°05′N	52°52′E
Glen, r., Eng., U.K. (glĕn)	158a	52°44′N	0°18′W
Glénan, Îles de, is., Fr. (ĕl-dĕ-glā-näN′)	170	47°43′N	4°42′W
Glen Burnie, Md., U.S. (bûr′nê)	110e	39°10′N	76°38′W
Glen Canyon, p., Ut., U.S.	119	37°10′N	110°50′W
Glen Canyon Dam, dam, Az., U.S. (glĕn kăn′yŭn)	106	36°57′N	111°25′W
Glen Canyon National Recreation Area, rec., U.S.	119	37°00′N	111°20′W
Glen Carbon, Il., U.S. (kär′bŏn)	117e	38°45′N	89°59′W
Glencoe, S. Afr. (glĕn-cô)	233c	28°14′S	30°09′E
Glencoe, Il., U.S.	111a	42°08′N	87°45′W
Glencoe, Mn., U.S. (glĕn′kō)	113	44°44′N	94°07′W
Glen Cove, N.Y., U.S. (kōv)	110a	40°51′N	73°38′W
Glendale, Az., U.S. (glĕn′dāl)	119	33°30′N	112°15′W
Glendale, Ca., U.S.	104	34°09′N	118°15′W
Glendale, Oh., U.S.	111f	31°16′N	84°22′W
Glendive, Mt., U.S. (glĕn′dīv)	104	47°08′N	104°41′W
Glendo, Wy., U.S.	115	42°32′N	104°54′W
Glendora, Ca., U.S. (glĕn-dō′rá)	117a	34°08′N	117°52′W
Glenelg, r., Austl.	222	37°20′S	141°30′E
Glen Ellyn, Il., U.S. (glĕn ĕl′-lĕn)	111a	41°53′N	88°04′W
Glen Innes, Austl. (ĭn′ĕs)	219	29°45′S	152°02′E
Glenns Ferry, Id., U.S. (fĕr′ĭ)	114	42°58′N	115°21′W
Glen Olden, Pa., U.S. (ōl′d′n)	110f	39°54′N	75°17′W
Glenomra, La., U.S. (glĕn-mō′rá)	123	30°58′N	92°36′W
Glenrock, Wy., U.S. (glĕn′rŏk)	115	42°50′N	105°53′W
Glens Falls, N.Y., U.S. (glĕnz fôlz)	109	43°20′N	73°40′W
Glenshaw, Pa., U.S. (glĕn′shô)	111e	40°33′N	79°57′W
Glen Valley, Can.	116d	49°09′N	122°30′W
Glenview, Il., U.S. (glĕn′vū)	111a	42°04′N	87°48′W
Glenville, Ga., U.S. (glĕn′vĭl)	125	31°55′N	81°56′W
Glenwood, Ia., U.S.	112	41°03′N	95°44′W
Glenwood, Mn., U.S.	112	45°39′N	95°23′W
Glenwood, N.M., U.S.	119	33°19′N	108°52′W
Glenwood Springs, Co., U.S.	119	39°35′N	107°20′W
Glienicke, Ger. (glē′nē-kĕ)	159b	52°38′N	13°19′E
Glinde, Ger. (glēn′dĕ)	159c	53°32′N	10°13′E
Glittertinden, mtn., Nor.	166	61°39′N	8°33′E
Gliwice, Pol. (gwĭ-wĭt′sĕ)	161	50°18′N	18°40′E
Globe, Az., U.S. (glōb)	104	33°20′N	110°50′W
Głogów, Pol. (gwō′gōōv)	161	51°40′N	16°04′E
Glommen, r., Nor. (glŏm′ĕn)	166	60°03′N	11°15′E
Glonn, Ger. (glônn)	159d	47°59′N	11°52′E

ăt; finăl; rāte; senåte; ärm; åsk; sofá; fâre; ch-choose; dh-as th in other; bē; êvent; bĕt; recĕnt; cratẽr; g-gō; gh-guttural g; bĭt; ĭ-short neutral; rīde; K-guttural k as ch in German ich;

PRONOUNCING INDEX Glorieuses – Grand Rapids 297

PLACE (Pronunciation)	PAGE	LAT.	LONG.
Glorieuses, Îles, is., Reu.	233	11°28'S	47°50'E
Glossop, Eng., U.K. (glŏs'ŭp)	158a	53°26'N	1°57'W
Gloster, Ms., U.S. (glŏs'tẽr)	124	31°10'N	91°00'W
Gloucester, Eng., U.K. (glŏs'tẽr)	161	51°54'N	2°11'W
Gloucester, Ma., U.S.	101a	42°37'N	70°40'W
Gloucester City, N.J., U.S.	110f	39°53'N	75°08'W
Glouster, Oh., U.S. (glŏs'tẽr)	108	39°35'N	82°05'W
Glover Island, i., Can. (glŭv'ẽr)	101	48°44'N	57°45'W
Gloversville, N.Y., U.S. (glŭv'ẽrz-vĭl)	109	43°05'N	74°20'W
Glovertown, Can. (glŭv'ẽr-toun)	101	48°41'N	54°02'W
Glückstadt, Ger. (glük-shtät)	159c	53°47'N	9°25'E
Glushkovo, Russia (glōsh'kô-vô)	177	51°21'N	34°43'E
Gmünden, Aus. (g'mòn'dĕn)	168	47°57'N	13°47'E
Gniezno, Pol. (g'nyåz'nô)	161	52°32'N	17°34'E
Gnjilane, Serb. (gnyē'lá-nĕ)	175	42°28'N	21°27'E
Goa, state, India (gō'á)	199	15°45'N	74°00'E
Goascorán, Hond. (gō-äs'kō-rän')	132	13°37'N	87°43'W
Goba, Eth. (gō'bä)	231	7°17'N	39°58'E
Gobabis, Nmb. (gō-bä'bĭs)	232	22°25'S	18°50'E
Gobi, des., Asia (gō'be)	204	43°29'N	103°15'E
Goble, Or., U.S. (gō'b'l)	116c	46°01'N	122°53'W
Goch, Ger. (gōk)	171c	51°35'N	6°10'E
Godāvari, r., India (gō-dä'vŭ-rē)	199	19°00'N	78°30'E
Goddards Soak, sw., Austl. (gŏd'árdz)	220	31°20'S	123°30'E
Goderich, Can. (gōd'rĭch)	98	43°45'N	81°45'W
Godfrey, Il., U.S. (gŏd'frē)	117e	38°57'N	90°12'W
Godhavn, Grnld. (gōdh'håvn)	89	69°15'N	53°30'W
Gods, r., Can. (ŏodz)	97	55°17'N	93°35'W
Gods Lake, Can.	91	54°40'N	94°09'W
Godthåb, Grnld. (gŏt'hòb)	89	64°10'N	51°32'W
Goéland, Lac au, l., Can.	99	49°47'N	76°41'W
Goffs, Ca., U.S. (gôfs)	118	34°57'N	115°06'W
Gogebic, l., Mi., U.S. (gō-gē'bĭk)	113	46°24'N	89°25'W
Gogebic Range, mts., Mi., U.S.	113	46°37'N	89°48'W
Göggingen, Ger. (gûg'gĕn-gĕn)	159d	48°21'N	10°53'E
Gogland, i., Russia	167	60°04'N	26°55'E
Gogonou, Benin	235	10°50'N	2°50'E
Gogorrón, Mex. (gō-gō-rōn')	130	21°51'N	100°54'W
Goiânia, Braz. (gô-yá'nyä)	143	16°41'S	48°57'W
Goiás, Braz. (gô-yá's)	143	15°57'S	50°10'W
Goiás, state, Braz.	143	16°00'S	48°00'W
Goirle, Neth.	159a	51°31'N	5°06'E
Gökçeada, i., Tur.	175	40°10'N	25°27'E
Göksu, r., Tur. (gûk'sōō')	181	36°40'N	33°30'E
Gol, Nor. (gûl)	166	60°58'N	8°54'E
Golax, Va., U.S. (gō'lăks)	125	36°41'N	80°56'W
Golcar, Eng., U.K. (gŏl'kár)	158a	53°38'N	1°52'W
Golconda, Il., U.S. (gŏl-kŏn'dá)	121	37°21'N	88°32'W
Gołdap, Pol. (gôl'däp)	169	54°17'N	22°17'E
Golden, Can.	95	51°18'N	116°58'W
Golden, Co., U.S.	120	39°44'N	105°15'W
Goldendale, Wa., U.S. (gōl'dĕn-dāl)	114	45°49'N	120°48'W
Golden Gate, strt., Ca., U.S. (gōl'dĕn gāt)	116b	37°48'N	122°32'W
Golden Hinde, mtn., Can. (hīnd)	94	49°40'N	125°45'W
Golden's Bridge, N.Y., U.S.	110a	41°17'N	73°41'W
Golden Valley, Mn., U.S.	117g	44°58'N	93°23'W
Goldfield, Nv., U.S. (gōld'fēld)	118	37°42'N	117°15'W
Gold Hill, mtn., Pan.	128a	9°03'N	79°08'W
Gold Mountain, mtn., Wa., U.S. (gōld)	116a	47°33'N	122°48'W
Goldsboro, N.C., U.S. (gōldz-bûr'ō)	125	35°23'N	77°59'W
Goldthwaite, Tx., U.S. (gōld'thwāt)	122	31°27'N	98°34'W
Goleniów, Pol. (gō-lĕ-nyŭf')	168	53°33'N	14°51'E
Golets-Purpula, Gora, mtn., Russia	179	59°08'N	115°22'E
Golfito, C.R. (gōl-fē'tō)	133	8°40'N	83°12'W
Goliad, Tx., U.S. (gō-lĭ-ăd')	123	28°40'N	97°12'W
Golo, r., Fr.	174	42°28'N	9°18'E
Golo Island, i., Phil. (gō'lō)	213a	13°38'N	120°17'E
Golovchino, Russia (gō-lôf'chē-nō)	177	50°34'N	35°52'E
Golyamo Konare, Blg. (gō'lā-mō-kō'nä-rĕ)	175	42°16'N	24°33'E
Golzow, Ger. (gōl'tsōv)	159b	52°17'N	12°36'E
Gombe, Nig.	230	10°19'N	11°02'E
Gomera Island, i., Spain (gō-mā'rä)	230	28°00'N	18°01'W
Gomez Farias, Mex. (gō'mäz fä-rē'ás)	122	24°59'N	101°02'W
Gómez Palacio, Mex. (pä-lä'syō)	128	25°35'N	103°30'W
Gonaïves, Haiti (gō-nà-ēv')	129	19°25'N	72°45'W
Gonaïves, Golfe des, b., Haiti (gō-nà-ēv')	135	19°20'N	73°20'W
Gonâve, Île de la, i., Haiti (gô-náv')	129	18°50'N	73°30'W
Gonda, India	202	27°13'N	82°00'E
Gondal, India	202	22°02'N	70°47'E
Gonder, Eth.	231	12°39'N	37°30'E
Gonesse, Fr. (gō-nĕs')	171b	48°59'N	2°28'E
Gongga Shan, mtn., China (gōŋ-gä shän)	204	29°16'N	101°46'E
Goniri, Nig.	235	11°30'N	12°20'E
Gonō, r., Japan (gō'nō)	211	35°00'N	132°25'E
Gonor, Can. (gō'nŏr)	102f	50°04'N	96°57'W
Gonubie, S. Afr. (gŏn'ōō-bē)	233c	32°56'S	28°02'E
Gonzales, Mex. (gôn-zá'lĕs)	130	22°47'N	98°26'W
Gonzales, Tx., U.S. (gŏn-zä'lĕz)	123	29°31'N	97°25'W
González Catán, Arg. (gōn-zá'lĕz-kä-tá'n)	144a	34°47'S	58°39'W
Good Hope, Cape of, c., S. Afr. (kāp ov gŏŏd hōp)	232	34°21'S	18°29'E
Good Hope Mountain, mtn., Can.	94	51°09'N	124°10'W
Gooding, Id., U.S. (gŏd'ĭng)	115	42°55'N	114°43'W
Goodland, In., U.S. (gŏd'lănd)	108	40°50'N	87°15'W
Goodland, Ks., U.S.	120	39°19'N	101°43'W
Goodwood, S. Afr. (gŏd'wŏd)	232a	33°54'S	18°33'E
Goole, Eng., U.K. (gōōl)	158a	53°42'N	0°52'W
Goose, r., N.D., U.S.	112	47°40'N	97°41'W
Gooseberry Creek, r., Wy., U.S. (gōōs-bĕr'ĭ)	115	44°04'N	108°35'W
Goose Creek, r., Id., U.S. (gōōs)	115	42°07'N	113°53'W
Goose Lake, l., Ca., U.S.	114	41°56'N	120°35'W
Gorakhpur, India (gō'rŭk-pōōr)	199	26°45'N	82°39'E
Gorda, Punta, c., Cuba (pōō'n-tä-gôr-dä)	134	22°25'N	82°10'W
Gorda Cay, i., Bah. (gôr'dä)	134	26°05'N	77°30'W
Gordon, Can. (gôr'dŭn)	102f	50°00'N	97°20'W
Gordon, Ne., U.S.	112	42°47'N	102°14'W
Gore, Eth. (gō'rĕ)	231	8°12'N	35°34'E
Gorgān, Iran	198	36°44'N	54°30'E
Gorgona, Isola di, Italy (gôr-gō'nä)	162	43°27'N	9°55'E
Gori, Geor. (gō'rĕ)	181	42°00'N	44°08'E
Gorinchem, Neth. (gō'rĭn-kĕm)	159a	51°50'N	4°59'E
Goring, Eng., U.K. (gôr'ĭng)	158b	51°30'N	1°08'W
Gorizia, Italy (gô-rē'tsē-yä)	174	45°56'N	13°40'E
Gor'kiy see Nizhniy Novgorod, Russia	178	56°15'N	44°05'E
Gor'kovskoye, res., Russia	178	56°38'N	43°40'E
Gorlice, Pol. (gôr-lē'tsĕ)	169	49°38'N	21°11'E
Görlitz, Ger. (gûr'lĭts)	161	51°10'N	15°01'E
Gorman, Tx., U.S. (gôr'măn)	122	32°13'N	98°40'W
Gorna Oryakhovitsa, Blg. (gôr'nä-ôr-yĕk'ô-vē-tsá)	175	43°08'N	25°40'E
Gornji Milanovac, Serb. (gôrn'yē mē'la-nô-väts)	175	44°02'N	20°29'E
Gorno-Altay, prov., Russia	184	51°00'N	86°00'E
Gorno-Altaysk, Russia (gôr'nŭ'ŭl-tĭsk')	178	51°58'N	85°58'E
Gorodishche, Russia (gō-rô'dĭsh-chĕ)	186a	57°57'N	57°03'E
Gorodok, Russia	179	50°30'N	103°58'E
Gorontalo, Indon. (gō-rōn-tä'lo)	213	0°40'N	123°04'E
Gorzów Wielkopolski, Pol. (gō-zhōōv'vyĕl-ko-pōl'skē)	160	53°44'N	15°15'E
Gosely, Eng., U.K.	158a	52°33'N	2°10'W
Goshen, In., U.S. (gō'shĕn)	108	41°35'N	85°50'W
Goshen, Ky., U.S.	111h	38°24'N	85°34'W
Goshen, N.Y., U.S.	110a	41°24'N	74°19'W
Goshen, Oh., U.S.	111f	39°14'N	84°09'W
Goshute Indian Reservation, I.R., Ut., U.S. (gō-shōōt')	119	39°50'N	114°00'W
Goslar, Ger. (gôs'lär)	168	51°55'N	10°25'E
Gospa, r., Ven. (gôs-pä)	143b	9°43'N	64°23'W
Gostivar, Mac. (gos'tē-vär)	175	41°46'N	20°58'E
Gostynin, Pol. (gôs-tē'nĭn)	169	52°24'N	19°30'E
Göta, r., Swe. (gōētä)	166	58°11'N	12°03'E
Göta Kanal, can., Swe. (yû'tá)	166	58°35'N	15°24'E
Göteborg, Swe. (yû'tĕ-bôrgh)	154	57°39'N	11°56'E
Gotel Mountains, mts., Afr.	235	7°05'N	11°20'E
Gotera, El Sal. (gō-tä'rä)	132	13°41'N	88°06'W
Gotha, Ger. (gō'tá)	161	50°47'N	10°43'E
Gothenburg see Göteborg, Swe.	154	57°39'N	11°56'E
Gothenburg, Ne., U.S. (gŏth'ĕn-bûrg)	120	40°57'N	100°08'W
Gotland, i., Swe.	156	57°35'N	17°35'E
Gotska Sandön, i., Swe.	167	58°24'N	19°15'E
Göttingen, Ger. (gût'ĭng-ĕn)	168	51°32'N	9°57'E
Gouda, Neth. (gou'dä)	159a	52°00'N	4°42'E
Gough, i., St. Hel. (gŏf)	2	40°00'S	10°00'W
Gouin, Réservoir, res., Can.	93	48°15'N	74°15'W
Goukou, China (gō-kō)	205	48°45'N	121°42'E
Goulais, r., Can.	98	46°45'N	84°10'W
Goulburn, Austl. (gōl'bŭrn)	219	34°47'S	149°40'E
Goumbati, mtn., Sen.	234	13°08'N	12°06'W
Goumbou, Mali (gōōm-bōō')	230	14°59'N	7°27'W
Gouna, Cam.	235	8°32'N	13°34'E
Goundam, Mali (gōōn-däN')	230	16°29'N	3°37'W
Gouverneur, N.Y., U.S. (gŭv-ẽr-nōōr')	109	44°20'N	75°25'W
Govenlock, Can. (gŭvĕn-lŏk)	90	49°15'N	109°48'W
Governador, Ilha do, i., Braz. (gô-vĕr-nä-dō-'r-ē-lá'dō)	144b	22°48'S	43°13'W
Governador Portela, Braz. (pōr-tĕ'lá)	144b	22°28'S	43°30'W
Governador Valadares, Braz. (vä-lä-dä'rĕs)	143	18°47'S	41°45'W
Governor's Harbour, Bah.	134	25°15'N	76°15'W
Gowanda, N.Y., U.S. (gô-wŏn'dá)	109	42°30'N	78°55'W
Goya, Arg. (gō'yä)	144	29°06'S	59°12'W
Göyçay, Azer. (gĕ-ôk'chī)	181	40°40'N	47°40'E
Goyt, r., Eng., U.K. (goit)	158a	53°19'N	2°03'W
Graaff-Reinet, S. Afr. (gräf'rī'nĕt)	232	32°10'S	24°40'E
Gračac, Cro. (grä'chäts)	174	44°16'N	15°50'E
Gračanica, Bos.	175	44°42'N	18°18'E
Graceville, Fl., U.S. (grās'vĭl)	124	30°57'N	85°30'W
Graceville, Mn., U.S.	112	45°33'N	96°25'W
Gracias, Hond. (grä'sē-äs)	132	14°35'N	88°37'W
Graciosa Island, i., Port. (grä-syō'sä)	230a	39°07'N	27°30'W
Gradačac, Bos. (gra-dä'chats)	163	44°50'N	18°28'E
Grado, Spain (grä'dō)	172	43°24'N	6°04'W
Gräfelfing, Ger. (grä'fĕl-fēng)	159d	48°07'N	11°27'E
Grafing bei München, Ger. (grä'fēng)	159d	48°03'N	11°58'E
Grafton, Austl. (graf'tŭn)	219	29°38'S	153°05'E
Grafton, Il., U.S.	117e	38°58'N	90°26'W
Grafton, Ma., U.S.	101a	42°13'N	71°41'W
Grafton, N.D., U.S.	112	48°24'N	97°25'W
Grafton, Oh., U.S.	111d	41°16'N	82°04'W
Grafton, W.V., U.S.	108	39°20'N	80°00'W
Gragnano, Italy (grän-yä'nô)	173c	40°27'N	14°32'E
Graham, N.C., U.S. (grā'ăm)	125	36°03'N	79°23'W
Graham, Tx., U.S.	120	33°07'N	98°34'W
Graham, Wa., U.S.	116a	47°03'N	122°18'W
Graham, i., Can.	92	53°50'N	132°40'W
Grahamstown, S. Afr. (grā'ăms'toun)	233c	33°19'S	26°33'E
Grajewo, Pol. (grä-yä'vo)	169	53°38'N	22°28'E
Grama, Serra de, mtn., Braz. (sĕ'r-rä-dĕ-grá'mà)	141a	20°42'S	42°28'W
Gramada, Blg. (grä'mä-dä)	175	43°46'N	22°41'E
Gramatneusiedl, Aus.	159e	48°02'N	16°29'E
Grampian Mountains, mts., Scot., U.K. (grăm'pĭ-ăn)	156	56°30'N	4°55'W
Granada, Nic. (grä-nä'dhä)	128	11°55'N	85°58'W
Granada, Spain (grä-nä'dä)	162	37°13'N	3°37'W
Gran Bajo, reg., Arg. (grán'bä'kō)	144	47°35'S	68°45'W
Granbury, Tx., U.S. (grăn'bĕr-ĭ)	123	32°26'N	97°45'W
Granby, Can. (grăn'bĭ)	91	45°30'N	72°40'W
Granby, Mo., U.S.	121	36°54'N	94°15'W
Granby, l., Co., U.S.	120	40°07'N	105°40'W
Gran Canaria Island, i., Spain (grän'kä-nä'rē-ä)	230	27°39'N	15°39'W
Gran Chaco, reg., S.A. (grán'chá'kō)	144	25°30'S	62°15'W
Grand, i., Mi., U.S.	113	46°37'N	86°38'W
Grand, l., Can.	100	45°59'N	66°15'W
Grand, l., Me., U.S.	100	45°17'N	67°42'W
Grand, r., Can.	99	43°45'N	80°20'W
Grand, r., Mi., U.S.	108	42°58'N	85°13'W
Grand, r., Mo., U.S.	121	39°50'N	93°52'W
Grand, r., S.D., U.S.	112	45°40'N	101°55'W
Grand, North Fork, r., U.S.	112	45°52'N	102°49'W
Grand, South Fork, r., S.D., U.S.	112	45°38'N	102°56'W
Grand Bahama, i., Bah.	129	26°35'N	78°30'W
Grand Bank, Can. (grănd băngk)	93a	47°06'N	55°47'W
Grand Bassam, C. Iv. (grän bá-säN')	230	5°12'N	3°44'W
Grand Bourg, Guad. (grän bōōr')	133b	15°54'N	61°20'W
Grand Caicos, i., T./C. Is. (grănd kä-ē'kōs)	135	21°45'N	71°50'W
Grand Canal see Da Yunhe, can., China	205	35°00'N	117°00'E
Grand Canal, can., Ire.	164	53°21'N	7°15'W
Grand Canyon, Az., U.S.	119	36°05'N	112°10'W
Grand Canyon, p., Az., U.S.	106	35°50'N	113°16'W
Grand Canyon National Park, rec., Az., U.S.	106	36°15'N	112°20'W
Grand Canyon-Parashant National Monument, rec., Az., U.S.	119	36°25'N	113°45'W
Grand Cayman, i., Cay. Is. (kā'măn)	129	19°15'N	81°15'W
Grand Coulee Dam, dam, Wa., U.S. (kōō'lē)	106	47°58'N	119°28'W
Grande, r., Arg.	141b	35°25'S	70°14'W
Grande, r., Bol.	142	16°49'S	63°19'W
Grande, r., Braz.	143	19°48'S	49°54'W
Grande, r., Mex.	131	17°37'N	96°41'W
Grande, r., Nic. (grän'dĕ)	133	13°01'N	84°21'W
Grande, r., Ur.	141c	33°19'S	57°15'W
Grande, Arroyo, r., Mex. (är-rō'yō-grä'n-dĕ)	130	23°30'N	98°45'W
Grande, Bahía, b., Arg. (bä-ē'ä-grán'dĕ)	144	50°45'S	68°00'W
Grande, Boca, mth., Ven. (bō'kä-grä'n-dĕ)	143	8°46'N	60°17'W
Grande, Cuchilla, mts., Ur. (kōō-chē'l-yä)	144	33°00'S	55°15'W
Grande, Ilha, i., Braz. (grän'dĕ)	141a	23°11'S	44°14'W
Grande, Rio, r., N.A. (grän'dā)	106	26°50'N	99°10'W
Grande, Salinas, l., Arg. (sä-lē'näs)	144	29°45'S	65°00'W
Grande, Salto, wtfl., Braz. (säl-tô)	143	16°18'S	39°38'W
Grande Cayemite, Île, i., Haiti	135	18°45'N	73°45'W
Grande de Otoro, r., Hond. (grä'dą dā ō-tō'rô)	132	14°42'N	88°21'W
Grande de Santiago, Río, r., Mex. (rêô-grä'n-dĕ-dĕ-sän-tyá'gô)	128	20°30'N	104°00'W
Grande Pointe, Can. (grănd point')	102f	49°47'N	97°03'W
Grande Prairie, Can. (prâr'ĭ)	90	55°10'N	118°48'W
Grand Erg Occidental, des., Alg.	230	30°00'N	1°00'E
Grand Erg Oriental, des., Alg.	230	30°00'N	7°00'E
Grande Rivière du Nord, Haiti (rē-vyâr' dü nôr')	135	19°35'N	72°10'W
Grande Ronde, r., Or., U.S. (rônd')	114	45°32'N	117°52'W
Gran Desierto, des., Mex. (grän-dĕ-syĕ'r-tô)	119	32°14'N	114°28'W
Grande Terre, i., Guad.	133b	16°28'N	61°13'W
Grande Vigie, Pointe de la, c., Guad. (grănd vē-gē')	133b	16°32'N	61°25'W
Grand Falls, Can. (fôlz)	93a	48°56'N	55°40'W
Grandfather Mountain, mtn., N.C., U.S. (grănd-fä-thẽr)	125	36°07'N	81°48'W
Grandfield, Ok., U.S. (grănd'fēld)	120	34°13'N	98°39'W
Grand Forks, Can. (fôrks)	90	49°02'N	118°27'W
Grand Forks, N.D., U.S.	104	47°55'N	97°05'W
Grand Haven, Mi., U.S. (hā'v'n)	108	43°05'N	86°15'W
Grand Island, Ne., U.S. (ī'lănd)	104	40°56'N	98°20'W
Grand Island, i., N.Y., U.S.	111c	43°03'N	78°58'W
Grand Junction, Co., U.S. (jŭngk'shŭn)	104	39°05'N	108°35'W
Grand Lake, l., Can. (lāk)	93a	49°00'N	57°10'W
Grand Lake, l., La., U.S.	123	29°57'N	91°25'W
Grand Lake, l., Mn., U.S.	117h	46°54'N	92°26'W
Grand Ledge, Mi., U.S. (lĕj)	108	42°45'N	84°50'W
Grand Lieu, Lac de, l., Fr. (grän'-lyû)	170	47°00'N	1°45'W
Grand Manan, i., Can. (má-năn)	100	44°40'N	66°50'W
Grand Mère, Can. (grän mâr')	91	46°36'N	72°43'W
Grândola, Port. (grän'dō-lá)	172	38°10'N	8°36'W
Grand Portage Indian Reservation, I.R., Mn., U.S. (pōr'tĭj)	113	47°54'N	89°34'W
Grand Portage National Monument, rec., Mi., U.S.	113	47°59'N	89°47'W
Grand Prairie, Tx., U.S. (prĕ'rē)	117c	32°45'N	97°00'W
Grand Rapids, Can.	97	53°08'N	99°20'W
Grand Rapids, Mi., U.S. (răp'ĭdz)	105	43°00'N	85°45'W
Grand Rapids, Mn., U.S.	113	47°16'N	93°33'W

ng-sing; ŋ-baŋk; N-nasalized n; nŏd; cŏmmit; ōld; ôbey; ôrder; oi-boil; fōōd; ŏ-as oo in foot; ou-out; s-soft; sh-dish; th-thin; pūre; ûnite; ûrn; stŭd; circŭs; ü-as in French tu; '-indeterminate vowel.

298 Grand-Riviere – Guadalajara PRONOUNCING INDEX

PLACE (Pronunciation)	PAGE	LAT.	LONG.
Grand-Riviere, Can.	100	48°26′N	64°30′W
Grand Staircase-Escalante National Monument, rec., Ut., U.S.	119	37°25′N	111°30′W
Grand Teton, mtn., Wy., U.S.	106	43°46′N	110°50′W
Grand Teton National Park, rec., Wy., U.S. (tē′tŏn)	115	43°54′N	110°15′W
Grand Traverse Bay, b., Mi., U.S. (trăv′ērs)	108	45°00′N	85°30′W
Grand Turk, T./C. Is. (tûrk)	135	21°30′N	71°10′W
Grand Turk, i., T./C. Is.	135	21°30′N	71°10′W
Grandview, Mo., U.S. (grănd′vyōō)	117f	38°53′N	94°32′W
Granger, Wy., U.S. (grān′jēr)	115	41°37′N	109°58′W
Grangeville, Id., U.S. (grānj′vĭl)	114	45°56′N	116°08′W
Granite City, Il., U.S. (grăn′ĭt sĭt′ĭ)	117e	38°42′N	90°09′W
Granite Falls, Mn., U.S. (fôlz)	112	44°46′N	95°34′W
Granite Falls, N.C., U.S.	125	35°49′N	81°25′W
Granite Falls, Wa., U.S.	116a	48°05′N	121°59′W
Granite Lake, l., Can.	101	48°01′N	57°00′W
Granite Peak, mtn., Mt., U.S.	106	45°13′N	109°48′W
Graniteville, S.C., U.S. (grăn′ĭt-vĭl)	125	33°35′N	81°50′W
Granito, Braz. (grä-nē′tō)	143	7°39′S	39°34′W
Granma, prov., Cuba	134	20°10′N	76°50′W
Gränna, Swe. (grĕn′à)	166	58°02′N	14°38′E
Granollers, Spain (grä-nôl-yĕrs′)	173	41°36′N	2°19′E
Gran Pajonal, reg., Peru (grä′n-pä-κô-näl′)	142	11°14′S	71°45′W
Gran Paradiso, mtn., Italy	174	45°32′N	7°16′E
Gran Piedra, mtn., Cuba (grän-pyĕ′drä)	135	20°00′N	75°40′W
Grantham, Eng., U.K. (grăn′tăm)	164	52°54′N	0°38′W
Grant Park, Il., U.S. (grănt pärk)	111a	41°14′N	87°39′W
Grants Pass, Or., U.S. (grànts pàs)	114	42°26′N	123°20′W
Granville, Fr. (gräɴ-vēl′)	161	48°52′N	1°35′W
Granville, N.Y., U.S. (grăn′vĭl)	109	43°25′N	73°15′W
Granville, l., Can.	92	56°18′N	100°30′W
Grão Mogol, Braz. (grouɴ′ mȯ-gôl′)	143	16°34′S	42°35′W
Grapevine, Tx., U.S. (grāp′vīn)	117c	32°56′N	97°05′W
Gräso, i., Swe.	166	60°30′N	18°35′E
Grass, r., N.Y., U.S.	109	44°45′N	75°10′W
Grass Cay, i., V.I.U.S.	129c	18°22′N	64°50′W
Grasse, Fr. (gräs)	171	43°39′N	6°57′E
Grass Mountain, mtn., Wa., U.S. (gràs)	116a	47°13′N	121°48′W
Grates Point, c., Can. (grāts)	101	48°09′N	52°57′W
Gravelbourg, Can. (grăv′ĕl-bôrg)	90	49°53′N	106°34′W
Gravesend, Eng., U.K. (grāvz′ĕnd′)	158b	51°26′N	0°22′E
Gravina, Italy (grä-vē′nä)	174	40°48′N	16°27′E
Gravois, Pointe à, c., Haiti (grà-vwä′)	135	18°00′N	74°20′W
Gray, Fr. (grå)	171	47°26′N	5°35′E
Grayling, Mi., U.S. (grā′lĭng)	108	44°40′N	84°40′W
Grays Harbor, b., Wa., U.S. (grās)	106	46°55′N	124°23′W
Grayslake, Il., U.S. (grāz′läk)	111a	42°20′N	88°20′W
Grays Peak, mtn., Co., U.S. (grāz)	120	39°29′N	105°52′W
Grays Thurrock, Eng., U.K. (thŭ′rŏk)	158b	51°28′N	0°19′E
Grayvoron, Russia (grà-ē′vô-rôn)	177	50°28′N	35°41′E
Graz, Aus. (gräts)	154	47°05′N	15°26′E
Great Abaco, i., Bah. (ä′bä-kō)	129	26°30′N	77°05′W
Great Artesian Basin, basin, Austl. (är-tēzh-ăn bā-sĭn)	221	23°16′S	143°37′E
Great Australian Bight, b., Austl. (ôs-trā′lĭ-ăn bĭt)	220	33°30′S	127°00′E
Great Bahama Bank, bk. (bȧ-hā′mȧ)	134	25°00′N	78°50′W
Great Barrier, i., N.Z. (băr′ĭ-ēr)	221a	36°10′S	175°30′E
Great Barrier Reef, rf., Austl. (bȧ-rĭ-ĕr rēf)	221	16°43′S	146°34′E
Great Basin, basin, U.S. (grāt bā′s′n)	106	40°08′N	117°10′W
Great Bear Lake, l., Can. (bâr)	92	66°10′N	119°53′W
Great Bend, Ks., U.S. (bĕnd)	120	38°41′N	98°46′W
Great Bitter Lake, l., Egypt	238b	30°24′N	32°27′E
Great Blasket Island, i., Ire. (blăs′kĕt)	164	52°05′N	10°55′W
Great Corn Island, i., Nic.	133	12°10′N	82°54′W
Great Dismal Swamp, sw., U.S. (dĭz′mȧl)	125	36°35′N	76°34′W
Great Divide Basin, basin, Wy., U.S. (dĭ-vīd′ bā′s′n)	115	42°10′N	108°10′W
Great Dividing Range, mts., Austl. (dĭ-vī-dĭng rānj)	221	35°16′S	146°38′E
Great Duck, i., Can. (dŭk)	98	45°40′N	83°22′W
Greater Antilles, is., N.A.	129	20°30′N	79°15′W
Greater Khingan Range, mts., China (dä hĭŋ-gän lĭŋ)	205	46°30′N	120°00′E
Greater Leech Indian Reservation, I.R., Mn., U.S. (grāt′ēr lēch)	113	47°39′N	94°27′W
Greater Manchester, hist. reg., Eng., U.K.	158a	53°34′N	2°41′W
Greater Sunda Islands, is., Asia	212	4°00′S	108°00′E
Great Exuma, i., Bah. (ĕk-sōō′mä)	134	23°35′N	76°00′W
Great Falls, Mt., U.S. (fôlz)	104	47°30′N	111°15′W
Great Falls, S.C., U.S.	125	34°32′N	80°53′W
Great Guana Cay, i., Bah. (gwä′nä)	134	24°00′N	76°20′W
Great Harbor Cay, i., Bah. (kē)	134	25°45′N	77°50′W
Great Inagua, i., Bah. (ẻ-nä′gwä)	129	21°00′N	73°15′W
Great Indian Desert, des., Asia	199	27°35′N	71°37′E
Great Isaac, i., Bah. (ī′zȧk)	134	26°05′N	79°05′W
Great Karroo, plat., S. Afr. (grāt kȧ′rōō)	232	32°45′S	22°00′E
Great Limpopo Transfrontier Park, rec., Afr.	232	22°00′S	31°30′E
Great Namaland, hist. reg., Nmb.	232	25°45′S	16°15′E
Great Neck, N.Y., U.S. (nĕk)	110a	40°48′N	73°44′W
Great Nicobar Island, i., India (nĭk-ô-bär′)	212	7°00′N	94°18′E
Great Pedro Bluff, c., Jam.	134	17°50′N	78°05′W
Great Pee Dee, r., S.C., U.S. (pē-dē′)	107	34°01′N	79°26′W
Great Plains, pl., N.A. (plāns)	89	45°00′N	104°00′W
Great Ragged, i., Bah.	135	22°10′N	75°45′W
Great Ruaha, r., Tan.	232	7°30′S	37°00′E
Great Salt Lake, l., Ut., U.S. (sôlt lāk)	106	41°19′N	112°48′W
Great Salt Lake Desert, des., Ut., U.S.	106	41°00′N	113°30′W
Great Salt Plains Reservoir, res., Ok., U.S.	120	36°56′N	98°14′W
Great Sand Dunes National Monument, rec., Co., U.S.	120	37°56′N	105°25′W
Great Sand Hills, hills, Can. (sănd)	96	50°35′N	109°05′W
Great Sandy Desert, des., Austl. (săn′dē)	220	21°50′S	123°10′E
Great Sandy Desert, des., Or., U.S. (săn′dĭ)	114	43°43′N	120°44′W
Great Sitkin, i., Ak., U.S. (sĭt-kĭn)	103a	52°18′N	176°22′W
Great Slave Lake, l., Can. (slāv)	92	61°37′N	114°58′W
Great Smoky Mountains National Park, rec., U.S. (smōk-ẻ)	107	35°43′N	83°20′W
Great Stirrup Cay, i., Bah. (stĭr-ŭp)	134	25°50′N	77°55′W
Great Victoria Desert, des., Austl. (vĭk-tō′rĭ-ȧ)	220	29°45′S	124°30′E
Great Wall, hist., China	204	38°00′N	109°00′E
Great Waltham, Eng., U.K. (wôl′thŭm)	158b	51°47′N	0°27′E
Great Yarmouth, Eng., U.K. (yär-mŭth)	161	52°35′N	1°45′E
Grebbestad, Swe. (grĕb-bĕ-städh)	166	58°42′N	11°15′E
Gréboun, Mont, mtn., Niger	230	20°00′N	8°35′E
Gredos, Sierra de, mts., Spain (syĕr′rä dā grā′dōs)	172	40°13′N	5°30′W
Greece, nation, Eur. (grēs)	154	39°00′N	21°30′E
Greeley, Co., U.S. (grē′lĭ)	104	40°25′N	104°41′W
Green, r., Ky., U.S. (grēn)	124	37°13′N	86°30′W
Green, r., N.D., U.S.	112	47°05′N	103°05′W
Green, r., Ut., U.S.	119	38°30′N	110°05′W
Green, r., Wa., U.S.	116a	47°17′N	121°57′W
Green, r., Wy., U.S.	115	41°08′N	110°27′W
Green, r., U.S.	106	38°30′N	110°10′W
Greenbank, Wa., U.S. (grēn′bănk)	116a	48°06′N	122°35′W
Green Bay, Wi., U.S.	105	44°30′N	88°04′W
Green Bay, b., U.S.	107	44°55′N	87°40′W
Green Bayou, Tx., U.S.	123a	29°53′N	95°13′W
Greenbelt, Md., U.S. (grĕn′bĕlt)	110e	38°59′N	76°53′W
Greencastle, In., U.S. (grēn-kȧs′'l)	108	39°40′N	86°50′W
Green Cay, i., Bah.	134	24°05′N	77°10′W
Green Cove Springs, Fl., U.S. (kōv)	125	29°56′N	81°42′W
Greendale, Wi., U.S. (grēn′dāl)	111a	42°56′N	87°59′W
Greenfield, Ia., U.S.	113	41°16′N	94°30′W
Greenfield, In., U.S. (grēn′fēld)	108	39°45′N	85°40′W
Greenfield, Ma., U.S.	109	42°35′N	72°35′W
Greenfield, Mo., U.S.	121	37°23′N	93°48′W
Greenfield, Oh., U.S.	108	39°15′N	83°25′W
Greenfield, Tn., U.S.	124	36°08′N	88°45′W
Greenfield Park, Can.	102a	45°29′N	73°29′W
Greenhills, Oh., U.S. (grēn-hĭls)	111f	39°16′N	84°31′W
Greenland, dep., N.A. (grēn′lănd)	89	74°00′N	40°00′W
Greenland Sea, sea	244	77°00′N	1°00′W
Green Mountain, mtn., Or., U.S.	116c	45°52′N	123°24′W
Green Mountain Reservoir, res., Co., U.S.	119	39°50′N	106°20′W
Green Mountains, mts., N.A.	107	43°10′N	73°05′W
Greenock, Scot., U.K. (grēn′ŭk)	160	55°55′N	4°45′W
Green Peter Lake, res., Or., U.S.	114	44°28′N	122°30′W
Green Pond Mountain, mtn., N.J., U.S. (pŏnd)	110a	41°00′N	74°32′W
Greenport, N.Y., U.S.	109	41°06′N	72°22′W
Green River, Ut., U.S. (grēn rĭv′ēr)	119	39°00′N	110°05′W
Green River, Wy., U.S.	115	41°32′N	109°26′W
Green River Lake, res., Ky., U.S.	124	37°15′N	85°15′W
Greensboro, Al., U.S. (grēnz′bŭro)	124	32°42′N	87°36′W
Greensboro, Ga., U.S. (grēns-bûr′ô)	124	33°34′N	83°11′W
Greensboro, N.C., U.S.	105	36°04′N	79°45′W
Greensburg, In., U.S. (grēnz′bûrg)	108	39°20′N	85°30′W
Greensburg, Ks., U.S. (grēns-bûrg)	120	37°36′N	99°17′W
Greensburg, Pa., U.S.	109	40°20′N	79°30′W
Greenville, Lib.	230	5°01′N	9°03′W
Greenville, Al., U.S. (grēn′vĭl)	124	31°49′N	86°39′W
Greenville, Il., U.S.	121	38°52′N	89°22′W
Greenville, Ky., U.S.	124	37°11′N	87°11′W
Greenville, Me., U.S.	100	45°26′N	69°35′W
Greenville, Mi., U.S.	108	43°10′N	85°25′W
Greenville, Ms., U.S.	105	33°25′N	91°00′W
Greenville, N.C., U.S.	125	35°35′N	77°22′W
Greenville, Oh., U.S.	108	40°05′N	84°35′W
Greenville, Pa., U.S.	108	41°20′N	80°25′W
Greenville, S.C., U.S.	105	34°50′N	82°25′W
Greenville, Tn., U.S.	125	36°08′N	82°50′W
Greenville, Tx., U.S.	123	33°09′N	96°07′W
Greenwich, Eng., U.K.	158b	51°28′N	0°00′
Greenwich, Ct., U.S.	110a	41°01′N	73°37′W
Greenwood, Ar., U.S. (grēn-wȯd)	121	35°13′N	94°15′W
Greenwood, In., U.S.	111g	39°37′N	86°07′W
Greenwood, Ms., U.S.	124	33°30′N	90°09′W
Greenwood, S.C., U.S.	125	34°10′N	82°10′W
Greenwood, Lake, res., S.C., U.S.	125	34°17′N	81°55′W
Greenwood Lake, l., N.Y., U.S.	110a	41°13′N	74°20′W
Greer, S.C., U.S. (grēr)	125	34°55′N	81°56′W
Grefrath, Ger. (grĕf′rät)	171c	51°20′N	6°21′E
Gregory, S.D., U.S. (grĕg′ô-rĭ)	112	43°12′N	99°27′W
Gregory, Lake, l., Austl. (grĕg′ô-rẻ)	220	28°47′S	139°15′E
Gregory Range, mts., Austl.	221	19°23′S	143°45′E
Greifenberg, Ger. (grī′fĕn-bĕrgh)	159d	48°04′N	11°06′E
Greifswald, Ger. (grīfs′vält)	168	54°05′N	13°24′E
Greiz, Ger. (grīts)	168	50°39′N	12°14′E
Gremyachinsk, Russia (grâ′myȧ-chĭnsk)	186a	58°35′N	57°53′E
Grenada, Ms., U.S. (grẻ-nä′da)	124	33°45′N	89°47′W
Grenada, nation, N.A.	129	12°02′N	61°15′W
Grenada Lake, res., Ms., U.S.	124	33°52′N	89°30′W
Grenadines, The, is., N.A. (grĕn′ȧ-dēnz)	133b	12°37′N	61°35′W
Grenen, c., Den.	160	57°43′N	10°31′E
Grenoble, Fr. (grē-nô′bl')	161	45°14′N	5°45′E
Grenora, N.D., U.S. (grẻ-nō′rȧ)	112	48°38′N	103°55′W
Grenville, Can. (grĕn′vĭl)	109	45°40′N	74°35′W
Grenville, Gren.	133b	12°07′N	61°38′W
Gresham, Or., U.S. (grĕsh′ăm)	116c	45°30′N	122°25′W
Gretna, La., U.S. (grĕt′nȧ)	110d	29°56′N	90°03′W
Grevelingen Krammer, r., Neth.	159a	51°42′N	4°03′E
Grevenbroich, Ger. (grĕ′fen-broik)	171c	51°05′N	6°36′E
Grey, r., Can. (grā)	101	47°53′N	57°00′W
Grey, Point, c., Can.	116d	49°22′N	123°16′W
Greybull, Wy., U.S. (grā′bȯl)	115	44°28′N	108°05′W
Greybull, r., Wy., U.S.	115	44°13′N	108°43′W
Greylingstad, S. Afr. (grā-lĭng′shtȧt)	238c	26°40′S	29°13′E
Greymouth, N.Z. (grā′mouth)	221a	42°27′S	171°17′E
Grey Range, mts., Austl.	221	28°40′S	142°05′E
Greytown, S. Afr. (grā′toun)	233c	29°07′S	30°38′E
Grey Wolf Peak, mtn., Wa., U.S. (grā wȯlf)	116a	48°53′N	123°12′W
Gridley, Ca., U.S. (grĭd′lĭ)	118	39°22′N	121°43′W
Griffin, Ga., U.S. (grĭf′ĭn)	124	33°15′N	84°16′W
Griffith, Austl. (grĭf-ĭth)	222	34°16′S	146°10′E
Griffith, In., U.S.	111a	41°31′N	87°26′W
Grigoriopol′, Mol. (grĭ′gor-i-ô′pôl)	177	47°09′N	29°18′E
Grijalva, r., Mex. (grē-häl′vä)	131	17°25′N	93°23′W
Grim, Cape, c., Austl. (grĭm)	222	40°43′S	144°30′E
Grimma, Ger. (grĭm′ä)	168	51°14′N	12°43′E
Grimsby, Can. (grĭmz′bĭ)	102d	43°11′N	79°33′W
Grimsby, Eng., U.K.	160	53°35′N	0°05′W
Grímsey, i., Ice. (grĭms′å)	160	66°30′N	17°50′W
Grimstad, Nor. (grĭm-städh)	160	58°21′N	8°30′E
Grindstone Island, Can.	101	47°25′N	61°51′W
Grinnel, Ia., U.S. (grĭ-nĕl′)	113	41°44′N	92°44′W
Griswold, Ia., U.S. (grĭz′wŭld)	112	41°11′N	95°05′W
Groais Island, i., Can.	101	50°57′N	55°35′W
Grobina, Lat. (grō′bĭŋĭa)	167	56°35′N	21°10′E
Groblersdal, S. Afr.	238c	25°11′S	29°25′E
Grodzisk, Pol. (grō′jēsk)	168	52°14′N	16°22′E
Grodzisk Masowiecki, Pol. (grō′jēsk mä-zō-vyĕts′ke)	169	52°06′N	20°40′E
Groesbeck, Tx., U.S. (grōs′bĕk)	123	31°32′N	96°31′W
Groix, Île de, i., Fr. (ēl dē grwä′)	170	47°39′N	3°28′W
Grójec, Pol. (grȯ′yĕts)	169	51°53′N	20°52′E
Gronau, Ger. (grō′nou)	168	52°12′N	7°05′E
Groningen, Neth. (grō′nĭng-ĕn)	160	53°13′N	6°30′E
Groote Eylandt, i., Austl. (grō′tē ī′länt)	220	13°50′S	137°30′E
Grootfontein, Nmb. (gröt′fōn-tān′)	232	19°30′S	18°15′E
Groot-Kei, r., Afr. (kē)	233c	32°17′S	27°30′E
Grootkop, mtn., S. Afr.	232a	34°11′S	18°23′E
Groot Marico, S. Afr.	238c	25°36′S	26°23′E
Groot Marico, r., Afr.	238c	25°13′S	26°20′E
Groot-Vis, r., S. Afr.	233c	33°04′S	26°08′E
Groot Vloer, pl., S. Afr. (grōt′ vlȯr′)	232	30°00′S	21°00′E
Gros-Mécatina, i., Can.	101	50°50′N	58°33′W
Gros Morne, mtn., Can. (grō môrn′)	101	49°36′N	57°48′W
Gros Morne National Park, rec., Can.	93a	49°45′N	59°15′W
Gros Pate, mtn., Can.	101	50°16′N	57°25′W
Grosse Island, i., Mi., U.S. (grōs)	111b	42°08′N	83°09′W
Grosse Isle, Can. (īl′)	102f	50°04′N	97°27′W
Grossenhain, Ger. (grōs′ĕn-hīn)	168	51°17′N	13°33′E
Gross-Enzersdorf, Aus.	159e	48°13′N	16°33′E
Grosse Pointe, Mi., U.S. (point′)	111b	42°23′N	82°54′W
Grosse Pointe Farms, Mi., U.S. (färm)	111b	42°25′N	82°53′W
Grosse Pointe Park, Mi., U.S. (pärk)	111b	42°23′N	82°55′W
Grosseto, Italy (grôs-sā′tō)	174	42°46′N	11°09′E
Grossglockner, mtn., Aus.	161	47°06′N	12°45′E
Gross Höbach, Ger. (hû′bäk)	159d	48°21′N	11°36′E
Gross Kreutz, Ger. (kroitz)	159b	52°24′N	12°47′E
Gross Schönebeck, Ger. (shō′nĕ-bĕk)	159b	52°54′N	13°32′E
Gros Ventre, r., Wy., U.S. (grōvĕn′t'r)	115	43°38′N	110°34′W
Groton, Ct., U.S. (grŏt′ŭn)	109	41°20′N	72°00′W
Groton, Ma., U.S.	101a	42°37′N	71°34′W
Groton, S.D., U.S.	112	45°25′N	98°04′W
Grottaglie, Italy (grôt-täl′yā)	175	40°32′N	17°26′E
Grouard Mission, Can.	90	55°31′N	116°09′W
Groveland, Ma., U.S. (grōv′land)	101a	42°25′N	71°02′W
Groveton, N.H., U.S. (grōv′tŭn)	109	44°35′N	71°30′W
Groveton, Tx., U.S.	123	31°04′N	95°07′W
Groznyy, Russia (grŏz′nĭ)	178	43°20′N	45°40′E
Grudziądz, Pol. (grȯ′jyŏɴts)	160	53°30′N	18°48′E
Grues, Île aux, i., Can. (ō grü)	102b	47°05′N	70°32′W
Grundy Center, Ia., U.S. (grŭn′dĭ sĕn′tēr)	113	42°22′N	92°45′W
Gruñidora, Mex. (grōō-nyẻ-dô′rō)	130	24°10′N	101°49′W
Grünwald, Ger. (grōōn′väld)	159d	48°04′N	11°34′E
Gryazi, Russia (gryä′zĭ)	176	52°31′N	39°59′E
Gryazovets, Russia (gryä′zô-vĕts)	180	58°52′N	40°14′E
Gryfice, Pol. (grĭ′fĭ-tsĕ)	168	53°55′N	15°11′E
Gryfino, Pol. (grĭ′fẻ-nô)	168	53°16′N	14°30′E
Guabito, Pan. (gwä-bē′tô)	133	9°30′N	82°33′W
Guacanayabo, Golfo de, b., Cuba (gôl-fô-dĕ-gwä-kä-nä-yä′bō)	134	20°30′N	77°40′W
Guacara, Ven. (gwȧ′kä-rä)	143b	10°16′N	67°48′W
Guadalajara, Mex. (gwä-dhä-lä-hä′rä)	128	20°41′N	103°21′W

ăt; finăl; rāte; senåte; ärm; ȧsk; sofȧ; fâre; ch-choose; dh-as th in other; bē; ẻvent; bĕt; recĕnt; cratẽr; g-gō; gh-guttural g; bĭt; ĭ-short neutral; rīde; κ-guttural k as ch in German ich;

PRONOUNCING INDEX

Guadalajara – Haines City 299

PLACE (Pronunciation)	PAGE	LAT.	LONG.
Guadalajara, Spain (gwä-dä-lä-kä'rä)	162	40°37'N	3°10'W
Guadalcanal, Spain (gwä-dhäl-kä-näl')	172	38°05'N	5°48'W
Guadalcanal, i., Sol. Is.	221	9°48'S	158°43'E
Guadalcázar, Mex. (gwä-dhäl-kä'zär)	130	22°38'N	100°24'W
Guadalete, r., Spain (gwä-dhä-lā'tå)	172	36°53'N	5°38'W
Guadalhorce, r., Spain (gwä-dhäl-ôr'thā)	172	37°05'N	4°50'W
Guadalimar, r., Spain (gwä-dhä-lē-mär')	172	38°29'N	2°53'W
Guadalope, r., Spain (gwä-dä-lô-pě)	173	40°48'N	0°10'W
Guadalquivir, Río, r., Spain (rē'ō-gwä-dhäl-kē-vēr')	156	37°30'N	5°00'W
Guadalupe, Mex.	122	31°23'N	106°06'W
Guadalupe, i., Mex.	128	29°00'N	118°45'W
Guadalupe, r., Tx., U.S. (gwä-dhä-lōō'pâ)	122	29°54'N	99°03'W
Guadalupe, Sierra de, mts., Spain (syĕr'rä dā gwä-dhä-lōō'pā)	162	39°30'N	5°25'W
Guadalupe Mountains, mts., N.M., U.S.	122	32°00'N	104°55'W
Guadalupe Peak, mtn., Tx., U.S.	122	31°55'N	104°55'W
Guadarrama, r., Spain (gwä-dhär-rä'mä)	173a	40°34'N	3°58'W
Guadarrama, Sierra de, mts., Spain (gwä-dhär-rä'mä)	156	41°00'N	3°40'W
Guadatentin, r., Spain	172	37°43'N	1°58'W
Guadeloupe, dep., N.A. (gwä-dē-lōōp)	129	16°40'N	61°10'W
Guadeloupe Passage, strt., N.A.	133b	16°26'N	62°00'W
Guadiana, r., Eur. (gwä-dvä'nä)	156	39°00'N	6°00'W
Guadiana, Bahía de, b., Cuba (bä-ē'ä-dě-gwä-dhē-ä'nä)	134	22°10'N	84°35'W
Guadiana Alto, r., Spain (äl'tō)	172	39°02'N	2°52'W
Guadiana Menor, r., Spain (mā'nôr)	172	37°43'N	2°45'W
Guadiaro, r., Spain (gwä-dhē-ä'rō)	172	36°38'N	5°25'W
Guadiela, r., Spain (gwä-dhē-ā'lä)	172	40°27'N	2°05'W
Guadix, Spain (gwä-dēsh')	172	37°18'N	3°09'W
Guaira, Braz. (gwä-ē-rä)	143	24°03'S	54°02'W
Guaire, r., Ven. (gwī'rě)	143b	10°25'N	66°43'W
Guajaba, Cayo, i., Cuba (kä'yō-gwä-hä'bä)	134	21°50'N	77°35'W
Guajará Mirim, Braz. (gwä-zhä-rä'mē-rēn')	142	10°58'S	65°12'W
Guajira, Península de, pen., S.A.	142	12°35'N	73°00'W
Gualán, Guat. (gwä-län')	132	15°08'N	89°21'W
Gualeguay, Arg. (gwä-lě-gwä'y)	144	33°10'S	59°20'W
Gualeguay, r., Arg.	144	32°49'S	59°05'W
Gualicho, Salina, l., Arg. (sä-lē'nä-gwä-lē'chō)	144	40°20'S	65°15'W
Guam, i., Oc. (gwäm)	3	14°00'N	143°20'E
Guamo, Col. (gwä'mō)	142a	4°02'N	74°58'W
Gu'an, China (gōō-än)	208a	39°25'N	116°18'E
Guan, r., China (gůän)	206	31°56'N	115°19'E
Guanabacoa, Cuba (gwä-nä-bä-kō'ä)	129	23°08'N	82°19'W
Guanabara, Baía de, b., Braz.	141a	22°44'S	43°09'W
Guanacaste, Cordillera, mts., C.R.	132	10°54'N	85°27'W
Guanacevi, Mex. (gwä-nä-sě-vē')	128	25°30'N	105°45'W
Guanahacabibes, Península de, pen., Cuba	134	21°55'N	84°35'W
Guanajay, Cuba (gwäṇä-hī')	134	22°55'N	82°40'W
Guanajuato, Mex. (gwä-nä-hwä'tō)	128	21°01'N	101°16'W
Guanajuato, state, Mex.	128	21°00'N	101°00'W
Guanape, Ven. (gwä-nä'pě)	143b	9°55'N	65°32'W
Guanape, r., Ven.	143b	9°52'N	65°20'W
Guanare, Ven. (gwä-nä'rå)	142	8°57'N	69°47'W
Guanduçu, r., Braz. (gwä'n-dōō'sōō)	144b	22°50'S	43°40'W
Guane, Cuba (gwä'nå)	134	22°10'N	84°05'W
Guangchang, China (gůäŋ-chäŋ)	209	26°50'N	116°18'E
Guangde, China (gůäŋ-dŭ)	209	30°40'N	119°20'E
Guangdong, prov., China (gůäŋ-dôŋ)	205	23°45'N	113°15'E
Guanglu Dao, i., China (gůäŋ-lōō dou)	206	39°13'N	122°21'E
Guangping, China (gůäŋ-pĭŋ)	206	36°30'N	114°57'E
Guangrao, China (gůaŋ-rou)	206	37°04'N	118°24'E
Guangshan, China (gůäŋ-shän)	206	32°02'N	114°53'E
Guangxi Zhuangzu, prov., China (gůäŋ-shyē)	204	24°00'N	108°30'E
Guangzhou, China	204	23°07'N	113°15'W
Guanhu, China (gůän-hōō)	206	34°26'N	117°59'E
Guannan, China (gůän-nän)	206	34°17'N	119°17'E
Guanta, Ven. (gwän'tä)	143b	10°15'N	64°35'W
Guantánamo, Cuba (gwän-tä'nä-mō)	135	20°10'N	75°10'W
Guantánamo, prov., Cuba	135	20°10'N	75°05'W
Guantánamo, Bahía de, b., Cuba	135	19°35'N	75°35'W
Guantao, China (gůän-tou)	206	36°39'N	115°25'E
Guanxian, China (gůän-shyĕn)	206	36°30'N	115°28'E
Guanyao, China (gůän-you)	207a	23°13'N	113°04'E
Guanyun, China (gůän-yòn)	206	34°28'N	119°16'E
Guapiles, C.R. (gwä-pē-lěs)	133	10°05'N	83°54'W
Guapimirim, Braz. (gwä-pē-mē-rē'n)	144b	22°31'S	42°59'W
Guaporé, r., S.A. (gwä-pô-rā')	142	12°11'S	63°47'W
Guaqui, Bol. (guä'kē)	142	16°42'S	68°47'W
Guara, Sierra de, mts., Spain (sē-ĕ'r-rä-dě-gwä'rä)	173	42°24'N	0°15'W
Guarabira, Braz. (gwä-rä-bē'rå)	143	6°49'S	35°27'W
Guaranda, Ec. (gwä-rán'dä)	142	1°39'S	78°57'W
Guarapari, Braz. (gwä-rä-pä'rē)	143	20°34'S	40°31'W
Guarapiranga, Represa do, res., Braz.	141a	23°45'S	46°44'W
Guarapuava, Braz. (gwä-rä-pwä'vå)	144	25°29'S	51°26'W
Guarda, Port. (gwär'dä)	172	40°32'N	7°17'W
Guardiato, r., Spain	172	38°10'N	5°05'W
Guarena, Spain (gwä-rā'nyä)	172	38°52'N	6°08'W
Guaribe, r., Ven. (gwä-rē'bě)	143b	9°48'N	65°17'W
Guárico, dept., Ven.	143b	9°42'N	67°25'W
Guarulhos, Braz. (gwå-rô'l-yôs)	141a	23°28'S	46°30'W
Guarus, Braz. (gwå'rōōs)	141a	21°44'S	41°19'W
Guasca, Col. (gwäs'kä)	142a	4°52'N	73°52'W
Guasipati, Ven. (gwä-sē-pä'tē)	143	7°26'N	61°57'W
Guastalla, Italy (gwäs-täl'lä)	174	44°53'N	10°39'E
Guasti, Ca., U.S. (gwäs'tĭ)	117a	34°04'N	117°35'W
Guatemala, Guat. (guä-tå-mä'lä)	128	14°37'N	90°32'W
Guatemala, nation, N.A.	128	15°45'N	91°45'W
Guatire, Ven. (gwä-tē'rě)	143b	10°28'N	66°34'W
Guaviare, r., Col.	142	3°35'N	69°28'W
Guayabal, Cuba (gwä-yä-bä'l)	134	20°40'N	77°40'W
Guayalejo, r., Mex. (gwä-yä-lě'hō)	130	23°24'N	99°09'W
Guayama, P.R. (gwä-yä'mä)	129b	18°00'N	66°08'W
Guayamouc, r., Haiti	135	19°05'N	72°00'W
Guayaquil, Ec. (gwī-ä-kēl')	142	2°16'S	79°53'W
Guayaquil, Golfo de, b., Ec. (gôl-fô-dě)	142	3°03'S	82°12'W
Guaymas, Mex. (gwä'y-mäs)	128	27°49'N	110°58'W
Guayubin, Dom. Rep. (gwå-yōō-bē'n)	135	19°40'N	71°25'W
Guazacapán, Guat. (gwä-zä-kä-pän')	132	14°04'N	90°26'W
Gubakha, Russia (gōō-bä'kå)	178	58°53'N	57°35'E
Gubbio, Italy (gōōb'byô)	174	43°23'N	12°36'E
Guben, Ger.	168	51°57'N	14°43'E
Gucheng, China (gōō-chŭŋ)	206	39°09'N	115°43'E
Gúdar, Sierra de, mts., Spain	173	40°28'N	0°47'W
Gudena, r., Den.	166	56°20'N	9°47'E
Gudermes, Russia	182	43°20'N	46°08'E
Gudvangen, Nor. (gōōdh'väŋ-gěn)	166	60°52'N	6°45'E
Guebwiller, Fr. (gěb-vē-lâr')	171	47°53'N	7°10'E
Guédi, Mont, mtn., Chad	235	12°14'N	18°58'E
Guelma, Alg. (gwěl'mä)	230	36°32'N	7°17'E
Guelph, Can. (gwělf)	99	43°33'N	80°15'W
Güere, r., Ven. (gwě'rě)	143b	9°39'N	65°00'W
Guéret, Fr. (gā-rě')	170	46°09'N	1°52'E
Guernsey, dep., Eur.	170	49°28'N	2°35'W
Guernsey, i., Guern. (gûrn'zĭ)	161	49°27'N	2°36'W
Guerrero, Mex. (gěr-rā'rō)	122	26°47'N	99°20'W
Guerrero, Mex.	122	28°20'N	100°24'W
Guerrero, state, Mex.	128	17°45'N	100°15'W
Gueydan, La., U.S. (gā'dǎn)	123	30°01'N	92°31'W
Guia de Pacobaíba, Braz. (gwē'ä-dě-pä'kō-bī'bä)	144b	22°42'S	43°10'W
Guiana Highlands, mts., S.A.	139	3°20'N	60°00'W
Guichi, China (gwā-chr)	209	30°35'N	117°28'E
Guichicovi, Mex. (gwē-chē-kō'vě)	131	16°58'N	95°10'W
Guidonia, Italy (gwē-dō'nyå)	174	42°00'N	12°45'E
Guiglo, C. Iv.	234	6°33'N	7°29'W
Guignes-Rabutin, Fr. (gēn'yě)	171b	48°38'N	2°48'E
Güigüe, Ven. (gwē'gwě)	143b	10°05'N	67°48'W
Guija, Lago, l., N.A. (gē'hä)	132	14°16'N	89°21'W
Guildford, Eng., U.K. (gĭl'fērd)	164	51°13'N	0°34'W
Guilford, In., U.S. (gĭl'fērd)	111f	39°10'N	84°55'W
Guilin, China (gwā-lĭn)	205	25°18'N	110°22'E
Guimarães, Port. (gē-mä-rănsh')	172	41°27'N	8°22'W
Guinea, nation, Afr. (gĭn'ē)	230	10°48'N	12°28'W
Guinea, Gulf of, b., Afr.	230	2°00'N	1°00'E
Guinea-Bissau, nation, Afr. (gĭn'ē)	230	12°00'N	20°00'W
Guingamp, Fr. (găn-gän')	170	48°35'N	3°10'W
Guir, r., Mor.	162	31°55'N	2°48'W
Güira de Melena, Cuba (gwē'rä dā må-lā'nä)	134	22°45'N	82°30'W
Güiria, Ven. (gwē-rē'ä)	142	10°43'N	62°16'W
Guise, Fr. (guēz)	170	49°54'N	3°37'E
Guisisil, vol., Nic. (gē-sē-sēl')	132	12°40'N	86°11'W
Guiyang, China (gwā-yäŋ)	204	26°45'N	107°00'E
Guizhou, China (gwā-jō)	207a	22°46'N	113°15'E
Guizhou, prov., China	204	27°00'N	106°10'E
Gujānwāla, Pak. (goj-rän'va-lå)	199	32°08'N	74°14'E
Gujarat, India	199	22°54'N	72°00'E
Gulbarga, India (gol-bûr'gå)	199	17°25'N	76°52'E
Gulbene, Lat. (gol-bä'ně)	167	57°09'N	26°49'E
Gulfport, Ms., U.S. (gŭlf'pōrt)	124	30°24'N	89°05'W
Gulja *see* Yining, China	204	43°58'N	80°40'E
Gull Lake, Can.	96	50°10'N	108°25'W
Gull Lake, l., Can.	95	52°35'N	114°00'W
Gulu, Ug.	237	2°47'N	32°18'E
Gumaca, Phil. (gōō-mä-kä')	213a	13°55'N	122°06'E
Gumbeyka, r., Russia (gom-běy'kå)	186a	53°20'N	59°42'E
Gumel, Nig.	230	12°39'N	9°22'E
Gummersbach, Ger. (gom'ěrs-bäk)	168	51°02'N	7°34'E
Gummi, Nig.	235	12°09'N	5°09'E
Gumpoldskirchen, Aus.	159e	48°04'N	16°15'E
Guna, India	202	24°44'N	77°17'E
Gunisao, r., Can. (gŭn-ĭ-sā'ō)	97	53°40'N	97°35'W
Gunisao Lake, l., Can.	97	53°35'N	96°10'W
Gunnedah, Austl. (gŭ'nē-dä)	222	31°00'S	150°10'E
Gunnison, Co., U.S. (gŭn'ĭ-sŭn)	119	38°33'N	106°56'W
Gunnison, Ut., U.S.	119	39°10'N	111°50'W
Gunnison, r., Co., U.S.	119	38°45'N	108°20'W
Guntersville, Al., U.S. (gŭn'tērz-vĭl)	124	34°20'N	86°19'W
Guntersville Lake, res., Al., U.S.	124	34°30'N	86°20'W
Guntramsdorf, Aus.	159e	48°04'N	16°19'E
Guntūr, India (gon'tōōr)	199	16°22'N	80°29'E
Guoyang, China (gwô-yäŋ)	206	33°32'N	116°10'E
Gurdon, Ar., U.S. (gûr'dŭn)	121	33°56'N	93°10'W
Gurgueia, r., Braz.	143	8°12'S	43°49'W
Guri, Embalse, res., Ven.	142	7°30'N	63°00'W
Gurnee, Il., U.S. (gûr'nē)	111a	42°22'N	87°55'W
Gurskøy, i., Nor. (gōōrskûê)	166	62°18'N	5°20'E
Gurupi, Serra do, mts., Braz. (sě'r-rä-dô-gōō-rōō-pē')	143	5°32'S	47°02'W
Guru Sikhar, mtn., India	202	29°42'N	72°50'E
Gur'yevsk, Russia (gōōr-yĭfsk')	178	54°17'N	85°56'E
Gusau, Nig. (gōō-zä'ōō)	230	12°12'N	6°40'E
Gusev, Russia (gōō'sěf)	167	54°35'N	22°15'E
Gushi, China (gōō-shr)	206	32°11'N	115°39'E
Gushiago, Ghana	234	9°55'N	0°12'W
Gusinje, Serb. (gōō-sēn'yě)	175	42°34'N	19°54'E
Gus'-Khrustal'nyy, Russia (gōōs-krōō-stäl'ny')	180	55°39'N	40°41'E
Gustavo A. Madero, Mex. (gōōs-tä'vô-á-mä-dě'rô)	130	19°29'N	99°07'W
Güstrow, Ger. (güs'trō)	168	53°48'N	12°12'E
Gütersloh, Ger. (gü'tērs-lo)	168	51°54'N	8°22'E
Guthrie, Ok., U.S. (gŭth'rĭ)	121	35°52'N	97°26'W
Guthrie Center, Ia., U.S.	113	41°41'N	94°33'W
Gutiérrez Zamora, Mex. (gōō-tī-âr'rāz zä-mō'rä)	131	20°27'N	97°17'W
Guttenberg, Ia., U.S. (gŭt'ěn-bûrg)	113	42°48'N	91°09'W
Guyana, nation, S.A. (gŭy'ănä)	143	7°45'N	59°00'W
Guyang, China (gōō-yäŋ)	206	34°56'N	114°57'E
Guye, China (gōō-yŭ)	206	39°46'N	118°23'E
Guymon, Ok., U.S. (gī'mŏn)	120	36°41'N	101°29'W
Guysborough, Can. (gīz'bŭr-ô)	101	45°23'N	61°30'W
Guzhen, China (gōō-jŭn)	208	33°20'N	117°18'E
Gvardeysk, Russia (gvár-dēysk')	167	54°39'N	21°11'E
Gwadabawa, Nig.	235	13°20'N	5°15'E
Gwādar, Pak. (gwä'dŭr)	198	25°15'N	62°29'E
Gwalior, India	199	26°13'N	78°10'E
Gwane, D.R.C. (gwän)	231	4°43'N	25°50'E
Gwardafuy, Gees, c., Som.	238a	11°55'N	51°30'E
Gwda, r., Pol.	168	53°27'N	16°52'E
Gwembe, Zam.	237	16°30'S	27°35'E
Gweru, Zimb.	232	19°15'S	29°48'E
Gwinn, Mi., U.S. (gwĭn)	113	46°15'N	87°30'W
Gyaring Co, l., China	202	30°37'N	88°33'E
Gydan, Khrebet (Kolymskiy), mts., Russia	179	61°45'N	155°00'E
Gydanskiy Poluostrov, pen., Russia	178	70°42'N	76°03'E
Gympie, Austl. (gĭm'pē)	219	26°20'S	152°50'E
Gyöngyös, Hung. (dyûn'dyûsh)	163	47°47'N	19°55'E
Györ, Hung. (dyûr)	163	47°40'N	17°37'E
Gyōtoku, Japan (gyō'tô-kōō')	211a	35°42'N	139°56'E
Gypsumville, Can. (jĭp'sŭm'vĭl)	90	51°45'N	98°35'W
Gýtheio, Grc.	175	36°50'N	22°37'E
Gyula, Hung. (dyō'lä)	169	46°38'N	21°18'E
Gyumri, Arm.	181	40°40'N	43°50'E
Gyzylarbat, Turkmen.	183	38°55'N	56°33'E

H

PLACE (Pronunciation)	PAGE	LAT.	LONG.
Haan, Ger. (hän)	171c	51°12'N	7°00'E
Haapamäki, Fin. (häp'ä-mě-kě)	167	62°16'N	24°20'E
Haapsalu, Est. (häp'sä-lò)	167	58°56'N	23°33'E
Haar, Ger. (här)	159d	48°06'N	11°44'E
Ha'Arava (Wādī al Jayb), val., Asia	197a	30°33'N	35°10'E
Haarlem, Neth. (här'lěm)	165	52°22'N	4°37'E
Habana, prov., Cuba (hä-vä'nä)	134	22°45'N	82°25'W
Hābra, India	202a	22°49'N	88°38'E
Hachinohe, Japan (hä'chē-nō'hå)	210	40°29'N	141°40'E
Hachiōji, Japan (hä'chē-ō'jē)	210	35°39'N	139°18'E
Hackensack, N.J., U.S. (hăk'ěn-săk)	110a	40°54'N	74°03'W
Ḩadd, Ra's al, c., Oman	198	22°29'N	59°46'E
Haddonfield, N.J., U.S. (hăd'ŭn-fēld)	110f	39°53'N	75°02'W
Haddon Heights, N.J., U.S. (hăd'ŭn hīts)	110f	39°53'N	75°03'W
Hadejia, Nig. (hä-dä'jä)	230	12°30'N	9°59'E
Hadejia, r., Nig.	230	12°15'N	10°00'E
Ḩadera, Isr. (kå-dě'rå)	197a	32°26'N	34°55'E
Haderslev, Den. (hä'dhěrs-lěv)	166	55°17'N	9°28'E
Hadiach, Ukr.	181	50°22'N	33°59'E
Ḩadīdū, Yemen	198	12°40'N	53°50'E
Hadlock, Wa., U.S. (hăd'lŏk)	116a	48°02'N	122°46'W
Ḩaḑramawt, reg., Yemen	198	15°22'N	48°40'E
Hadūr Shu'ayb, mtn., Yemen	198	15°45'N	43°45'E
Haeju, Kor., N. (hä'ĕ-jŭ)	210	38°03'N	125°42'E
Hafnarfjördur, Ice.	160	64°02'N	21°32'W
Haft Gel, Iran	201	31°27'N	49°27'E
Hafun, Ras, c., Som. (hä-fōōn')	238a	10°15'N	51°35'E
Hageland, Mt., U.S. (hăge'lând)	115	48°53'N	108°43'W
Hagen, Ger. (hä'gěn)	168	51°21'N	7°29'E
Hagerstown, In., U.S. (hā'gērz-toun)	108	39°55'N	85°10'W
Hagerstown, Md., U.S.	105	39°40'N	77°45'W
Hagi, Japan (hä'gĭ)	211	34°25'N	131°25'E
Hague, Cap de la, c., Fr. (dē lá ág')	170	49°44'N	1°55'W
Haguenau, Fr. (åg'nō')	171	48°47'N	7°48'E
Hai'an, China (hī-än)	206	32°35'N	120°25'E
Haibara, Japan (hä'ē-bä'rä)	211	34°29'N	135°57'E
Haicheng, China (hī-chŭŋ)	208	40°58'N	122°45'E
Haidian, China (hī-dĭěn)	206	39°59'N	116°17'E
Haifa, Isr. (hä'ē-fà)	198	32°48'N	35°00'E
Haifeng, China (hä'ē-fěng')	209	23°00'N	115°20'E
Haifuzhen, China (hī-fōō-jŭn)	206	31°57'N	121°48'E
Haikou, China (hī-kō)	209	20°00'N	110°20'E
Ḩā'il, Sau. Ar.	198	27°30'N	41°47'E
Hailar, China	205	49°10'N	118°40'E
Hailey, Id., U.S. (hā'lĭ)	115	43°31'N	114°19'W
Haileybury, Can.	99	47°27'N	79°38'W
Haileyville, Ok., U.S. (hā'lĭ-vĭl)	121	34°51'N	95°34'W
Hailing Dao, i., China (hī-lĭŋ dou)	209	21°30'N	112°15'E
Hailong, China (hī-loŋ)	208	42°32'N	125°52'E
Hailun, China (hä'ē-lōōn')	205	47°18'N	126°50'E
Hainan, prov., China	204	19°00'N	109°30'E
Hainan Dao, i., China (hī-nän dou)	205	19°00'N	111°10'E
Hainburg, Aus.	168	48°09'N	16°57'E
Haines, Ak., U.S. (hānz)	103	59°10'N	135°38'W
Haines City, Fl., U.S.	125a	28°05'N	81°38'W

ng-sing; ŋ-baŋk; ɴ-nasalized n; nŏd; cŏmmit; ōld; ōbey; ôrder; oi-boil; fōōd; ò-as oo in foot; ou-out; s-soft; sh-dish; th-thin; pūre; ûnite; ûrn; stŭd; circŭs; ü-as in French tu; '-indeterminate vowel.

PLACE (Pronunciation)	PAGE	LAT.	LONG.
Hai Phong, Viet. (hī'fŏng')(hä'ēp-hŏng)	212	20°52'N	106°40'E
Haisyn, Ukr.	181	48°46'N	29°22'E
Haiti, nation, N.A. (hā'tĭ)	129	19°00'N	72°15'W
Haizhou, China	206	34°34'N	119°11'E
Haizhou Wan, b., China	208	34°49'N	120°35'E
Hajdúböszormény, Hung. (hôl'dŏŏ-bû'sûr-mān')	169	47°41'N	21°30'E
Hajdúhadház, Hung. (hô'ĭ-dŏŏ-hôd'häz)	169	47°32'N	21°32'E
Hajdúnánás, Hung. (hô'ĭ-dŏŏ-nä'näsh)	169	47°52'N	21°27'E
Hakodate, Japan (hä-kō-dä't å)	205	41°46'N	140°42'E
Haku-San, mtn., Japan (hä'kōō-sän')	210	36°11'N	136°45'E
Halā'ib, Egypt (hä-lä'ēb)	231	22°10'N	36°40'E
Halbe, Ger. (häl'bē)	159b	52°07'N	13°43'E
Halberstadt, Ger. (häl'bĕr-shtät)	168	51°54'N	11°07'E
Halcon, Mount, mtn., Phil. (häl-kōn')	213a	13°19'N	120°55'E
Halden, Nor. (häl'dĕn)	160	59°10'N	11°21'E
Haldensleben, Ger.	168	52°18'N	11°23'E
Hale, Eng., U.K. (hāl)	158a	53°22'N	2°20'W
Haleakalā Crater, depr., Hi., U.S. (hä'lä-ä'kä-lä)	126a	20°44'N	156°15'W
Haleakalā National Park, rec., Hi., U.S.	126a	20°46'N	156°00'W
Hales Corners, Wi., U.S. (hālz kŏr'nērz)	111a	42°56'N	88°03'W
Halesowen, Eng., U.K. (hālz'ō-wĕn)	158a	52°26'N	2°03'W
Halethorpe, Md., U.S. (hāl-thôrp)	110e	39°15'N	76°40'W
Haleyville, Al., U.S. (hā'lĭ-vĭl)	124	34°11'N	87°36'W
Half Moon Bay, Ca., U.S. (hăf'mōōn)	116b	37°28'N	122°26'W
Halfway House, S. Afr. (häf-wā hous)	233b	26°00'S	28°08'E
Halfweg, Neth.	159a	52°23'N	4°45'E
Halifax, Can. (hăl'ĭ-făks)	91	44°39'N	63°36'W
Halifax, Eng., U.K.	164	53°44'N	1°52'W
Halifax Bay, b., Austl. (hăl'ĭ-făx)	221	18°56'S	147°07'E
Halifax Harbour, b., Can.	100	44°35'N	63°31'W
Halkett, Cape, c., Ak., U.S.	103	70°50'N	151°15'W
Hallam Peak, mtn., Can.	95	52°11'N	118°46'E
Halla San, mtn., Kor., S. (häl'lä-sän)	210	33°20'N	126°37'E
Halle, Bel. (häl'lē)	159a	50°45'N	4°13'E
Halle, Ger.	161	51°30'N	11°59'E
Hallettsville, Tx., U.S. (hăl'ĕts-vĭl)	123	29°26'N	96°55'W
Hallock, Mn., U.S. (hăl'ŭk)	112	48°46'N	96°57'W
Hall Peninsula, pen., Can. (hôl)	93	63°14'N	65°40'W
Halls Bayou, Tx., U.S.	123a	29°55'N	95°23'W
Hallsberg, Swe. (häls'bĕrgh)	166	59°04'N	15°04'E
Halls Creek, Austl. (hôlz)	218	18°15'S	127°45'E
Halmahera, i., Indon. (häl-mä-hā'rä)	213	0°45'N	128°45'E
Halmahera, Laut, Indon.	213	1°00'S	129°00'E
Halmstad, Swe. (hälm'städ)	160	56°40'N	12°46'E
Halsafjorden, b., Nor. (häl'sĕ fyôrd)	166	63°03'N	8°23'E
Halstead, Ks., U.S. (hôl'stĕd)	121	38°02'N	97°36'W
Haltern, Ger. (häl'tĕrn)	171c	51°45'N	7°10'E
Haltom City, Tx., U.S. (hôl'tŏm)	117c	32°48'N	97°13'W
Halver, Ger.	171c	51°11'N	7°30'E
Hamada, Japan	210	34°53'N	132°05'E
Hamadān, Iran (hŭ-mŭ-dän')	198	34°45'N	48°07'E
Ḩamāh, Syria (hä'mä)	198	35°08'N	36°53'E
Hamamatsu, Japan (hä'mä-mät'sŏŏ)	210	34°41'N	137°43'E
Hamar, Nor. (hä'mär)	160	60°49'N	11°05'E
Hamasaka, Japan (hä'mà-sä'kà)	211	35°57'N	134°27'E
Hamborn, Ger. (häm'bōrn)	171c	51°30'N	6°43'E
Hamburg, Ger. (häm'bŏŏrgh)	154	53°34'N	10°02'E
Hamburg, S. Afr. (hăm'bûrg)	233c	33°18'S	27°28'E
Hamburg, Ar., U.S. (hăm'bûrg)	121	33°15'N	91°49'W
Hamburg, N.J., U.S.	110a	41°09'N	74°35'W
Hamburg, N.Y., U.S.	111c	42°44'N	78°51'W
Hamden, Ct., U.S. (hăm'dĕn)	109	41°20'N	72°55'W
Hämeenlinna, Fin. (hĕ'mån-lĭn-nå)	160	61°00'N	24°29'E
Hameln, Ger. (hä'mĕln)	168	52°06'N	9°23'E
Hamelwörden, Ger. (hä'mĕl-vûr-dĕn)	159c	53°47'N	9°19'E
Hamersley Range, mts., Austl. (hăm'ērz-lē)	220	22°15'S	117°50'E
Hamhŭng, Kor., N. (häm'hŏong')	205	39°57'N	127°35'E
Hami, China (hä-mē)	204	42°58'N	93°14'E
Hamilton, Austl. (hăm'ĭl-tŭn)	219	37°50'S	142°10'E
Hamilton, Can.	91	43°15'N	79°52'W
Hamilton, N.Z.	221a	37°45'S	175°28'E
Hamilton, Al., U.S.	124	34°09'N	88°01'W
Hamilton, Ma., U.S.	101a	42°37'N	70°52'W
Hamilton, Mo., U.S.	121	39°43'N	93°59'W
Hamilton, Mt., U.S.	115	46°15'N	114°09'W
Hamilton, Oh., U.S.	105	39°22'N	84°33'W
Hamilton, Tx., U.S.	122	31°42'N	98°07'W
Hamilton, Lake, l., Ar., U.S.	121	34°25'N	93°32'W
Hamilton Harbour, b., Can.	102d	43°17'N	79°50'W
Hamilton Inlet, b., Can.	93	54°20'N	56°57'W
Hamina, Fin. (hà'mē-nà)	167	60°34'N	27°15'E
Hamlet, N.C., U.S. (hăm'lĕt)	125	34°53'N	79°42'W
Hamlin, Tx., U.S. (hăm'lĭn)	120	32°54'N	100°08'W
Hamm, Ger. (häm)	168	51°40'N	7°48'E
Hammanskraal, S. Afr. (hä-måns-kräl')	238c	25°24'S	28°17'E
Hamme, Bel.	159a	51°06'N	4°07'E
Hamme-Oste Kanal, can., Ger. (hä'mĕ-ōs'tĕ kä-näl)	159c	53°20'N	8°59'E
Hammerfest, Nor. (hä'mĕr-fĕst)	154	70°38'N	23°59'E
Hammond, In., U.S. (hăm'ŭnd)	105	41°37'N	87°31'W
Hammond, La., U.S.	123	30°30'N	90°28'W
Hammond, Or., U.S.	116c	46°12'N	123°57'W
Hammonton, N.J., U.S. (hăm'ŭn-tŭn)	109	39°40'N	74°45'W
Hampden, Me., U.S. (hăm'dĕn)	100	44°44'N	68°51'W
Hampstead, Md., U.S.	110e	39°36'N	76°54'W
Hampstead Norris, Eng., U.K. (hămp-stĕd nŏ'rĭs)	158b	51°27'N	1°14'W
Hampton, Can. (hămp'tŭn)	100	45°32'N	65°51'W

PLACE (Pronunciation)	PAGE	LAT.	LONG.
Hampton, Ia., U.S.	113	42°43'N	93°15'W
Hampton, Va., U.S.	109	37°02'N	76°21'W
Hampton Roads, b., Va., U.S.	110g	36°56'N	76°23'W
Hams Fork, r., Wy., U.S.	115	41°55'N	110°40'W
Hamtramck, Mi., U.S. (hăm-trăm'ĭk)	111b	42°24'N	83°03'W
Han, r., China (hän)	209	25°00'N	116°35'E
Han, r., China	205	31°40'N	112°04'E
Han, r., Kor., S.	210	37°10'N	127°40'E
Hāna, Hi., U.S. (hä'nä)	126a	20°43'N	155°59'W
Hanábana, r., Cuba (hä-nä-bä'nä)	134	22°30'N	80°55'W
Hanalei Bay, b., Hi., U.S. (hä-nä-lä'ē)	126a	22°15'N	159°40'W
Hanang, mtn., Tan.	237	4°26'S	35°24'E
Hanau, Ger. (hä'nou)	168	50°08'N	8°56'E
Hancock, Mi., U.S. (hăn'kŏk)	105	47°08'N	88°37'W
Handan, China (hän-dän)	206	36°37'N	114°30'E
Haney, Can. (hā-nē)	95	49°13'N	122°36'W
Hanford, Ca., U.S. (hăn'fērd)	118	36°20'N	119°38'W
Hangayn Nuruu, mts., Mong.	204	48°03'N	99°45'E
Hango, Fin. (häŋ'gû)	154	59°49'N	22°56'E
Hangzhou, China (hăng'chō')	205	30°17'N	120°12'E
Hangzhou Wan, b., China (häŋ-jō wän)	209	30°20'N	121°25'E
Hankamer, Tx., U.S. (hăn'kà-mẽr)	123a	29°52'N	94°42'W
Hankinson, N.D., U.S. (hăŋ'kĭn-sŭn)	112	46°04'N	96°54'W
Hankou, China (hän-kō)	209	30°42'N	114°22'E
Hann, Mount, mtn., Austl. (hän)	220	16°05'S	126°07'E
Hanna, Can. (hăn'à)	90	51°38'N	111°54'W
Hanna, Wy., U.S.	115	41°51'N	106°34'W
Hannah, N.D., U.S.	112	48°58'N	98°42'W
Hannibal, Mo., U.S. (hăn'ĭ băl)	105	39°42'N	91°22'W
Hannover, Ger. (hän-ō'vẽr)	154	52°22'N	9°45'E
Hannover, hist. reg., Ger.	168	52°52'N	8°27'E
Hanöbukten, b., Swe.	166	55°54'N	14°55'E
Hanoi, Viet. (hä-noi')	212	21°04'N	105°50'E
Hanover, Can. (hăn'ô-vẽr)	98	44°10'N	81°05'W
Hanover, Ma., U.S.	101a	42°07'N	70°49'W
Hanover, N.H., U.S.	109	43°45'N	72°15'W
Hanover, Pa., U.S.	109	39°50'N	77°00'W
Hanover, i., Chile	144	51°00'S	74°45'W
Hanshan, China (hän'shän')	206	31°43'N	118°06'E
Hans Lollick, i., V.I.U.S. (häns'lôl'ĭk)	129c	18°24'N	64°55'W
Hanson, Ma., U.S. (hăn'sŭn)	101a	42°04'N	70°53'W
Hansville, Wa., U.S. (häns'-vĭl)	116a	47°55'N	122°33'W
Hantengri Feng, mtn., Asia (hän-tŭŋ-rē fŭŋ)	204	42°10'N	80°20'E
Hantsport, Can. (hänts'pōrt)	100	45°04'N	64°11'W
Hanyang, China (han'yăng')	205	30°30'N	114°10'E
Hanzhong, China (hän-jôŋ)	208	33°02'N	107°00'E
Haocheng, China (hou-chŭŋ)	206	33°19'N	117°33'E
Haparanda, Swe. (hä-pa-rän'dä)	160	65°54'N	23°57'E
Hapeville, Ga., U.S. (hāp'vĭl)	110c	33°39'N	84°25'W
Happy Camp, Ca., U.S.	114	41°47'N	123°22'W
Happy Valley-Goose Bay, Can.	91	53°19'N	60°33'W
Ḩaql, Sau. Ar.	197a	29°15'N	34°57'E
Har, Laga, r., Kenya	237	2°15'N	39°30'E
Haradok, Bela.	176	55°27'N	29°58'E
Harare, Zimb.	232	17°50'S	31°03'E
Harbin, China	205	45°40'N	126°30'E
Harbor Beach, Mi., U.S. (här'bēr bēch)	108	43°50'N	82°40'W
Harbor Springs, Mi., U.S.	108	45°25'N	85°05'W
Harbour Breton, Can. (brĕt'ŭn) (brē-tôN')	101	47°29'N	55°48'W
Harbour Grace, Can. (grās)	101	47°32'N	53°13'W
Harburg, Ger. (här-bŏŏrgh)	159c	53°28'N	9°58'E
Hardangerfjorden, Nor. (här-däng'ẽr fyôrd)	160	59°58'N	6°30'E
Hardin, Mt., U.S. (här'dĭn)	115	45°44'N	107°36'W
Harding, S. Afr. (här'dĭng)	232	30°34'S	29°54'E
Harding, Lake, res., U.S.	124	32°43'N	85°00'W
Hardwār, India (hŭr'dvär)	199	29°56'N	78°06'E
Hardy, r., Mex. (här'dĭ)	118	32°04'N	115°10'W
Hare Bay, b., Can. (hâr)	101	51°18'N	55°50'W
Harer, Eth.	231	9°43'N	42°10'E
Harerge, hist. reg., Eth.	231	8°15'N	41°00'E
Hargeysa, Som. (här-gā'ē-sà)	238a	9°20'N	43°57'E
Harghita, Munţii, mts., Rom.	169	46°25'N	25°40'E
Harima-Nada, b., Japan (hä'rē-mä nä-dä)	211	34°34'N	134°37'E
Haringvliet, r., Neth.	159a	51°49'N	4°03'E
Harīrūd, r., Asia	198	34°29'N	61°16'E
Harlan, Ia., U.S. (här'lăn)	121	41°40'N	95°10'W
Harlan, Ky., U.S.	124	36°50'N	83°19'W
Harlan County Reservoir, res., Ne., U.S.	120	40°03'N	99°51'W
Harlem, Mt., U.S. (hàr'lĕm)	115	48°33'N	108°50'W
Harlingen, Neth. (här'lĭng-ĕn)	165	53°10'N	5°24'E
Harlingen, Tx., U.S.	104	26°12'N	97°42'W
Harlow, Eng., U.K. (här'lō)	158b	51°46'N	0°08'E
Harlowton, Mt., U.S. (hàr'lō-tun)	115	46°26'N	109°50'W
Harmony, In., U.S. (här'mō-nĭ)	108	39°35'N	87°00'W
Harney Basin, Or., U.S. (här'nĭ)	114	43°26'N	120°19'W
Harney Lake, l., Or., U.S.	114	43°11'N	119°23'W
Harney Peak, mtn., S.D., U.S.	106	43°52'N	103°32'W
Härnosand, Swe. (hĕr-nû-sänd)	160	62°37'N	17°54'E
Haro, Spain (ä'rō)	172	42°35'N	2°49'W
Haro Strait, strt., N.A. (hä'rō)	116a	48°27'N	123°11'W
Harpenden, Eng., U.K. (här'pĕn-d'n)	158b	51°48'N	0°22'W
Harper, Lib.	230	4°25'N	7°43'W
Harper, Ks., U.S. (här'pēr)	120	37°17'N	98°02'W
Harper, Wa., U.S.	116a	47°31'N	122°32'W
Harpers Ferry, W.V., U.S. (här'pērz)	109	39°20'N	77°45'W
Harricana, r., Can.	99	50°10'N	78°50'W
Harriman, Tn., U.S. (hă'ĭ-măn)	124	35°55'N	84°34'W
Harrington, De., U.S. (hăr'ĭng-tŭn)	109	38°55'N	75°35'W
Harris, i., Scot., U.K. (hăr'ĭs)	164	57°55'N	6°40'W

PLACE (Pronunciation)	PAGE	LAT.	LONG.
Harris, Lake, l., Fl., U.S.	125a	28°43'N	81°40'W
Harrisburg, Il., U.S. (hăr'ĭs-bûrg)	108	37°45'N	88°35'W
Harrisburg, Pa., U.S.	105	40°15'N	76°50'W
Harrismith, S. Afr. (hă-rĭs'mĭth)	238c	28°17'S	29°08'E
Harrison, Ar., U.S. (hăr'ĭ-sŭn)	121	36°13'N	93°06'W
Harrison, Oh., U.S.	111f	39°16'N	84°45'W
Harrisonburg, Va., U.S. (hăr'ĭ-sŭn-bûrg)	109	38°30'N	78°50'W
Harrison Lake, l., Can.	95	49°31'N	121°59'W
Harrisonville, Mo., U.S. (hăr-ĭ-sŭn-vĭl)	121	38°39'N	94°21'W
Harrisville, Ut., U.S. (hăr'ĭs-vĭl)	117b	41°17'N	112°00'W
Harrisville, W.V., U.S.	108	39°10'N	81°05'W
Harrodsburg, Ky., U.S. (hăr'ŭdz-bûrg)	108	37°45'N	84°50'W
Harrods Creek, r., Ky., U.S. (hăr'ŭdz)	111h	38°24'N	35°33'W
Harrow, Eng., U.K. (hăr'ō)	158b	51°34'N	0°21'W
Harsefeld, Ger. (här'zĕ-fĕld')	159c	53°27'N	9°30'E
Harstad, Nor. (här'städh)	160	68°49'N	16°10'E
Hart, Mi., U.S. (härt)	108	43°40'N	86°25'W
Hartbeesfontein, S. Afr.	238c	26°46'S	26°25'E
Hartbeespoortdam, res., S. Afr.	233b	25°47'S	27°43'E
Hartford, Al., U.S. (härt'fērd)	124	31°05'N	85°42'W
Hartford, Ar., U.S.	121	35°01'N	94°21'W
Hartford, Ct., U.S.	105	41°45'N	72°40'W
Hartford, Il., U.S.	117e	38°50'N	90°06'W
Hartford, Ky., U.S.	124	37°25'N	86°50'W
Hartford, Mi., U.S.	108	42°15'N	86°15'W
Hartford, Wi., U.S.	113	43°19'N	88°25'W
Hartford City, In., U.S.	108	40°35'N	85°25'W
Hartington, Eng., U.K. (härt'ĭng-tŭn)	158a	53°08'N	1°48'W
Hartington, Ne., U.S.	112	42°37'N	97°18'W
Hartland Point, c., Eng., U.K.	164	51°03'N	4°40'W
Hartlepool, Eng., U.K. (här't'l-pōōl)	160	54°40'N	1°12'W
Hartley, Ia., U.S. (härt'lĭ)	112	43°12'N	95°29'W
Hartley Bay, Can.	94	53°25'N	129°15'W
Hart Mountain, mtn., Can. (härt)	97	52°25'N	101°30'W
Hartsbeespoort, S. Afr.	233b	25°44'S	27°51'E
Hartselle, Al., U.S. (härt'sĕl)	124	34°24'N	86°55'W
Hartshorne, Ok., U.S. (härts'hôrn)	121	34°49'N	95°34'W
Hartsville, S.C., U.S. (härts'vĭl)	125	34°20'N	80°04'W
Hartwell, Ga., U.S. (härt'wĕl)	125	34°21'N	82°56'W
Hartwell Lake, res., U.S.	107	34°30'N	83°00'W
Hārua, India	202a	22°36'N	88°40'E
Harvard, Il., U.S. (här'vàrd)	113	42°25'N	88°39'W
Harvard, Ma., U.S.	101a	42°30'N	71°35'W
Harvard, Ne., U.S.	120	40°36'N	98°08'W
Harvard, Mount, mtn., Co., U.S.	119	38°55'N	106°20'W
Harvey, Can.	100	45°44'N	64°46'W
Harvey, Il., U.S.	111a	41°37'N	87°39'W
Harvey, La., U.S.	110d	29°54'N	90°05'W
Harvey, N.D., U.S.	112	47°46'N	99°55'W
Harwich, Eng., U.K. (här'wĭch)	165	51°53'N	1°13'E
Haryana, state, India	199	29°00'N	75°45'E
Harz Mountains, mts., Ger. (härts)	168	51°42'N	10°50'E
Hashimoto, Japan (hä'shē-mō'tō)	211	34°19'N	135°37'E
Haskell, Ok., U.S. (hăs'kĕl)	121	35°49'N	95°41'W
Haskell, Tx., U.S.	120	33°09'N	99°43'W
Haslingden, Eng., U.K. (hăz'lĭng dĕn)	158a	53°43'N	2°19'W
Hassi Messaoud, Alg.	230	31°17'N	6°13'E
Hässleholm, Swe. (hĕs'lĕ-hōlm)	166	56°10'N	13°44'E
Hastings, N.Z.	221a	39°33'S	176°53'E
Hastings, Eng., U.K. (hās'tĭngz)	161	50°52'N	0°28'E
Hastings, Mi., U.S.	108	42°40'N	85°20'W
Hastings, Mn., U.S.	117g	44°44'N	92°51'W
Hastings, Ne., U.S.	104	40°34'N	98°42'W
Hastings-on-Hudson, N.Y., U.S. (ŏn-hŭd'sŭn)	110a	40°59'N	75°53'W
Hatay, Tur.	198	36°20'N	36°10'E
Hatchie, r., Tn., U.S. (hăch'ē)	124	35°28'N	89°14'W
Haţeg, Rom. (kät-sāg')	175	45°35'N	22°57'E
Hatfield Broad Oak, Eng., U.K. (hăt-fēld brôd ōk)	158b	51°50'N	0°14'E
Hatogaya, Japan (hä'tō-gä-yä)	211a	35°50'N	139°45'E
Hatsukaichi, Japan (hät'sōō-kà'ē-chē)	211	34°22'N	132°19'E
Hatteras, Cape, c., N.C., U.S. (hăt'ẽr-ăs)	107	35°15'N	75°24'W
Hattiesburg, Ms., U.S. (hăt'ĭz-bûrg)	105	31°20'N	89°18'W
Hattingen, Ger. (hä'tĕn-gĕn)	171c	51°24'N	7°11'E
Hatvan, Hung. (hôt'vôn)	169	47°39'N	19°44'E
Hat Yai, Thai.	212	7°01'N	100°29'E
Haugesund, Nor. (hou'gĕ-soon')	160	59°26'N	5°20'E
Haukivesi, l., Fin. (hou'kē-vĕ'sē)	167	62°02'N	29°02'E
Haultain, r., Can.	96	56°15'N	106°35'W
Hauptsrus, S. Afr.	238c	26°35'S	26°16'E
Hauraki Gulf, b., N.Z. (hä-ōō-rä'kē)	221a	36°30'S	175°00'E
Haut, Isle au, Me., U.S. (hō)	100	44°03'N	68°13'W
Haut Atlas, mts., Mor.	162	32°10'N	5°49'W
Hauterive, Can.	100	49°11'N	68°16'W
Hau'ula, Hi., U.S.	126a	21°37'N	157°45'W
Havana, Cuba	129	23°08'N	82°23'W
Havana, Il., U.S. (hà-văn'à)	121	40°17'N	90°02'W
Havasu, Lake, res., U.S. (hăv'â-sōō)	119	34°26'N	114°09'W
Havel, r., Ger. (hä'fĕl)	168	53°09'N	13°10'E
Havel-Kanal, can., Ger.	159b	52°36'N	13°12'E
Haverhill, Ma., U.S. (hā'vēr-hĭl)	101a	42°46'N	71°05'W
Haverhill, N.H., U.S.	109	44°00'N	72°05'W
Haverstraw, N.Y., U.S. (hā'vēr-strô)	110a	41°11'N	73°58'W
Havlíčkův Brod, Czech Rep.	161	49°38'N	15°34'E
Havre, Mt., U.S. (hăv'ēr)	104	48°34'N	109°42'W
Havre-Boucher, Can. (hăv'rà-bōō-shā')	101	45°42'N	61°30'W
Havre de Grace, Md., U.S. (hăv'ēr dē gräs')	109	39°35'N	76°05'W
Havre-Saint Pierre, Can.	100	50°15'N	63°36'W
Haw, r., N.C., U.S. (hô)	125	36°17'N	79°46'W

ăt; finăl; rāte; senåte; ärm; àsk; sofà; fâre; ch-choose; dh-as th in other; bē; ēvent; bĕt; recĕnt; cratẽr; g-gō; gh-guttural g; bĭt; ĭ-short neutral; rīde; κ-guttural k as ch in German ich;

PRONOUNCING INDEX Hawaii – Hindupur 301

PLACE (Pronunciation)	PAGE	LAT.	LONG.
Hawaii, state, U.S.	106c	20°00'N	157°40'W
Hawai'i, i., Hi., U.S. (häw wī'ē)	106c	19°30'N	155°30'W
Hawai'ian Islands, is., Hi., U.S. (hä-wī'än)	106c	22°00'N	158°00'W
Hawai'i Volcanoes National Park, rec., Hi., U.S.	106c	19°30'N	155°25'W
Hawarden, Ia., U.S. (hā'wär-dĕn)	112	43°00'N	96°28'W
Hawi, Hi., U.S. (hä'wē)	126a	20°16'N	155°48'W
Hawick, Scot., U.K. (hô'ĭk)	164	55°25'N	2°55'W
Hawke Bay, b., N.Z. (hôk)	221a	39°17'S	177°20'E
Hawker, Austl. (hô'kēr)	222	31°58'S	138°12'E
Hawkesbury, Can. (hôks'bĕr-ĭ)	99	45°35'N	74°35'W
Hawkinsville, Ga., U.S. (hô'kĭnz-vĭl)	124	32°15'N	83°30'W
Hawks Nest Point, c., Bah.	135	24°05'N	75°30'W
Hawley, Mn., U.S. (hô'lĭ)	112	46°52'N	96°18'W
Haworth, Eng., U.K. (hä'wûrth)	158a	53°50'N	1°57'W
Hawthorne, Ca., U.S. (hô'thôrn)	117a	33°55'N	118°22'W
Hawthorne, Nv., U.S.	118	38°33'N	118°39'W
Haxtun, Co., U.S. (hăks'tŭn)	120	40°39'N	102°38'W
Hay, r., Austl. (hā)	220	23°00'S	136°45'E
Hay, r., Can.	92	60°21'N	117°14'W
Hayama, Japan (hä-yä'mä)	211a	35°16'N	139°35'E
Hayashi, Japan (hä-yä'shē)	211a	35°13'N	139°38'E
Hayden, Az., U.S. (hā'dĕn)	119	33°00'N	110°50'W
Hayes, r., Can.	93	55°25'N	93°55'W
Hayes, Mount, mtn., Ak., U.S. (hāz)	103	63°32'N	146°40'W
Haynesville, La., U.S. (hānz'vĭl)	123	32°55'N	93°08'W
Hayrabolu, Tur.	175	41°14'N	27°05'E
Hay River, Can.	90	60°50'N	115°53'W
Hays, Ks., U.S. (hāz)	120	38°51'N	99°20'W
Haystack Mountain, mtn., Wa., U.S. (hā-stăk')	116a	48°26'N	122°07'W
Hayward, Ca., U.S. (hā'wērd)	116b	37°40'N	122°06'W
Hayward, Wi., U.S.	113	46°01'N	91°31'W
Hazard, Ky., U.S. (hăz'ărd)	124	37°13'N	83°10'W
Hazelhurst, Ga., U.S. (hā'z'l-hûrst)	125	31°50'N	82°36'W
Hazelhurst, Ms., U.S.	124	31°52'N	90°23'W
Hazel Park, Mi., U.S.	111b	42°28'N	83°06'W
Hazelton, Can. (hā'z'l-tŭn)	90	55°15'N	127°40'W
Hazelton Mountains, mts., Can.	94	55°00'N	128°00'W
Hazleton, Pa., U.S.	109	41°00'N	76°00'W
Headland, Al., U.S. (hĕd'lănd)	124	31°22'N	85°20'W
Healdsburg, Ca., U.S. (hēldz'bûrg)	118	38°37'N	122°52'W
Healdton, Ok., U.S. (hēld'tŭn)	121	34°13'N	97°28'W
Heanor, Eng., U.K. (hēn'ŏr)	158a	53°01'N	1°22'W
Heard Island, i., Austl. (hûrd)	3	53°10'S	74°35'E
Hearne, Tx., U.S. (hûrn)	123	30°53'N	96°35'W
Hearst, Can. (hûrst)	91	49°36'N	83°40'W
Heart, r., N.D., U.S. (härt)	112	46°46'N	102°34'W
Heart Lake Indian Reserve, I.R., Can.	95	55°02'N	111°30'W
Heart's Content, Can. (härts kŏn'tĕnt)	101	47°52'N	53°22'W
Heavener, Ok., U.S. (hēv'nēr)	121	34°52'N	94°36'W
Hebbronville, Tx., U.S. (hē'brŭn-vĭl)	122	27°18'N	98°40'W
Hebei, prov., China (hŭ-bā)	205	39°15'N	115°40'E
Heber City, Ut., U.S. (hē'bēr)	119	40°30'N	111°25'W
Heber Springs, Ar., U.S.	121	35°28'N	91°59'W
Hebgen Lake, res., Mt., U.S. (hĕb'gĕn)	115	44°47'N	111°38'W
Hebrides, is., Scot., U.K.	156	57°00'N	6°30'W
Hebrides, Sea of the, sea, Scot., U.K.	164	57°00'N	7°00'W
Hebron, Can. (hĕb'rŭn)	91	58°11'N	62°56'W
Hebron, In., U.S.	111a	41°19'N	87°13'W
Hebron, Ky., U.S.	111f	39°04'N	84°43'W
Hebron, N.D., U.S.	112	46°54'N	102°04'W
Hebron, Ne., U.S.	121	40°11'N	97°36'W
Hebron *see* Al Khalīl, W.B.	197a	31°31'N	35°07'E
Heby, Swe. (hĭ'bü)	166	59°56'N	16°48'E
Hecate Strait, strt., Can. (hĕk'ā-tē)	92	53°00'N	131°00'W
Hecelchakán, Mex. (ā-sĕl-chä-kän')	131	20°10'N	90°09'W
Hechi, China (hŭ-chr)	209	24°50'N	108°18'E
Hechuan, China (hŭ-chyuän)	204	30°00'N	106°20'E
Hecla Island, i., Can.	97	51°08'N	96°45'W
Hedemora, Swe. (hĭ-dĕ-mō'rä)	166	60°16'N	15°55'E
Hedon, Eng., U.K. (hĕ-dŭn)	158a	53°44'N	0°12'W
Heemstede, Neth.	159a	52°20'N	4°36'E
Heerlen, Neth.	165	50°55'N	5°58'E
Hefei, China (hŭ-fā)	205	31°51'N	117°15'E
Heflin, Al., U.S. (hĕf'lĭn)	124	33°40'N	85°33'W
Heide, Ger. (hī'dē)	168	54°13'N	9°06'E
Heidelberg, Austl. (hī'dĕl-bûrg)	217a	37°45'S	145°04'E
Heidelberg, Ger. (hīdĕl-bĕrgh)	161	49°24'N	8°43'E
Heidelberg, S. Afr.	238c	26°32'S	28°22'E
Heidenheim, Ger. (hī'dĕn-hīm)	168	48°41'N	10°09'E
Heilbron, S. Afr. (hīl'brōn)	238c	27°17'S	27°58'E
Heilbronn, Ger. (hīl'brōn)	161	49°09'N	9°16'E
Heiligenhaus, Ger. (hī'lē-gĕn-houz)	171c	51°19'N	6°58'E
Heiligenstadt, Ger. (hī'lē-gĕn-shtät)	168	51°21'N	10°10'E
Heilongjiang, prov., China (hā-lôŋ-jyäŋ)	205	46°36'N	128°07'E
Heinola, Fin. (hå-nō'lå)	167	61°13'N	26°03'E
Heinsberg, Ger. (hīnz'bĕrgh)	171c	51°04'N	6°07'E
Heist-op-den-Berg, Bel.	159a	51°05'N	4°14'E
Hejaz *see* Al Ḩijāz, reg., Sau. Ar.	198	23°45'N	39°08'E
Hejian, China (hŭ-jyĕn)	208	38°28'N	116°05'E
Hekla, vol., Ice.	156	63°53'N	19°37'W
Hel, Pol. (hāl)	169	54°37'N	18°53'E
Helagsfjället, mtn., Swe.	160	62°54'N	12°24'E
Helan Shan, mts., China (hŭ-län shän)	204	38°02'N	105°20'E
Helena, Ar., U.S. (hē-lē'nȧ)	105	34°33'N	90°35'W
Helena, Mt., U.S. (hĕ-lē'nȧ)	104	46°35'N	112°01'W
Helensburgh, Austl. (hĕl'ĕnz-bŭr-ô)	217b	34°11'S	150°59'E
Helensburgh, Scot., U.K.	164	56°01'N	4°53'W
Helgoland, i., Ger. (hĕl'gō-länd)	168	54°13'N	7°30'E
Hellier, Ky., U.S. (hĕl'yēr)	125	37°16'N	82°27'W
Hellín, Spain (ĕl-yén')	162	38°30'N	1°40'W
Hells Canyon, p., U.S.	114	45°20'N	116°45'W
Helmand, r., Afg. (hĕl'mŭnd)	198	31°00'N	63°48'E
Hel'miaziv, Ukr.	177	49°49'N	31°54'E
Helmond, Neth. (hĕl'mŏnt) (ĕl'môN')	165	51°35'N	5°04'E
Helmstedt, Ger. (hĕlm'shtĕt)	168	52°14'N	11°03'E
Helotes, Tx., U.S. (hē'lōts)	117d	29°35'N	98°41'W
Helper, Ut., U.S. (hĕlp'ēr)	119	39°40'N	110°55'W
Helsingborg, Swe. (hĕl'sĭng-bôrgh)	160	56°04'N	12°40'E
Helsingfors *see* Helsinki, Fin.	154	60°10'N	24°53'E
Helsingør, Den. (hĕl-sĭng-ûr')	160	56°03'N	12°33'E
Helsinki, Fin. (hĕl'sēn-kē)	154	60°10'N	24°53'E
Hemel Hempstead, Eng., U.K. (hĕm'ĕl hĕmp'stĕd)	158b	51°43'N	0°29'W
Hemer, Ger.	171c	51°22'N	7°46'E
Hemet, Ca., U.S. (hĕm'ĕt)	117a	33°45'N	116°57'W
Hemingford, Ne., U.S. (hĕm'ĭng-fērd)	112	42°21'N	103°30'W
Hemphill, Tx., U.S. (hĕmp'hĭl)	123	31°20'N	93°48'W
Hempstead, N.Y., U.S. (hĕmp'stĕd)	110a	40°42'N	73°37'W
Hempstead, Tx., U.S.	123	30°07'N	96°05'W
Hemse, Swe. (hĕm'sē)	166	57°15'N	18°25'E
Hemsön, i., Swe.	166	62°43'N	18°22'E
Henan, prov., China (hŭ-nän)	205	33°58'N	112°33'E
Henares, r., Spain (å-nä'rås)	172	40°50'N	2°55'W
Henderson, Ky., U.S. (hĕn'dēr-sŭn)	108	37°50'N	87°30'W
Henderson, N.C., U.S.	125	36°18'N	78°24'W
Henderson, Nv., U.S.	118	36°09'N	115°04'W
Henderson, Tn., U.S.	124	35°25'N	88°40'W
Henderson, Tx., U.S.	123	32°09'N	94°48'W
Hendersonville, N.C., U.S. (hĕn'dēr-sŭn-vĭl)	125	35°17'N	82°28'W
Hendersonville, Tn., U.S.	124	36°18'N	86°37'W
Hendon, Eng., U.K. (hĕn'dŭn)	158b	51°34'N	0°13'W
Hendrina, S. Afr. (hĕn-drē'nȧ)	238c	26°10'S	29°44'E
Hengch'un, Tai. (hĕng'chŭn')	209	22°00'N	120°42'E
Hengelo, Neth. (hĕngĕ-lō)	165	52°20'N	6°45'E
Hengshan, China (hĕng'shän')	209	27°20'N	112°40'E
Hengshui, China (hĕng'shōō-ē')	206	37°43'N	115°42'E
Hengxian, China (hŭŋ shyĕn)	209	22°40'N	109°20'E
Hengyang, China	205	26°58'N	112°30'E
Heniches'k, Ukr.	181	46°11'N	34°47'E
Henley on Thames, Eng., U.K. (hĕn'lē ŏn tĕmz)	158b	51°31'N	0°54'W
Henlopen, Cape, c., De., U.S. (hĕn-lō'pĕn)	109	38°45'N	75°05'W
Hennebont, Fr. (ĕn-bôN')	170	47°47'N	3°16'W
Hennenman, S. Afr.	238c	27°59'S	27°03'E
Hennessey, Ok., U.S. (hĕn'ĕ-sĭ)	121	36°04'N	97°53'W
Hennigsdorf, Ger. (hĕ'nēngz-dōrf)	159b	52°39'N	13°12'E
Hennops, r., S. Afr. (hĕn'ŏps)	233b	25°51'S	27°57'E
Hennopsrivier, S. Afr.	233b	25°50'S	27°59'E
Henrietta, Ok., U.S. (hĕn-rĭ-ĕt'ȧ)	121	35°25'N	95°58'W
Henrietta, Tx., U.S. (hen-rĭ-ĕ'tȧ)	120	33°47'N	98°11'W
Henrietta Maria, Cape, c., Can. (hĕn-rĭ-ĕt'ȧ)	93	55°10'N	82°20'W
Henry Mountains, mts., Ut., U.S. (hĕn'rĭ)	106	37°55'N	110°45'W
Henrys Fork, r., Id., U.S.	115	43°52'N	111°55'W
Henteyn Nuruu, mts., Russia	208	49°40'N	111°00'E
Hentiyn Nuruu, mts., Mong.	204	49°25'N	107°51'E
Henzada, Mya.	199	17°38'N	95°28'E
Heppner, Or., U.S. (hĕp'nēr)	114	45°21'N	119°33'W
Hepu, China (hŭ-pōō)	209	21°28'N	109°10'E
Herāt, Afg. (hĕ-rät')	198	34°28'N	62°13'E
Hercules, Can.	102g	53°27'N	113°20'W
Herdecke, Ger. (hĕr'dĕ-kĕ)	171c	51°24'N	7°26'E
Heredia, C.R. (ā-rā'dhē-ä)	133	10°04'N	84°06'W
Hereford, Eng., U.K. (hĕrĕ'fērd)	164	52°05'N	2°44'W
Hereford, Md., U.S.	110e	39°35'N	76°42'W
Hereford, Tx., U.S. (hĕr'ĕ-fērd)	120	34°47'N	102°25'W
Hereford and Worcester, co., Eng., U.K.	158a	52°24'N	2°15'W
Herencia, Spain (å-rān'thē-ä)	172	39°23'N	3°22'W
Herentals, Bel.	159a	51°10'N	4°51'E
Herford, Ger. (hĕr'fōrt)	168	52°06'N	8°42'E
Herington, Ks., U.S. (hĕr'ĭng-tŭn)	121	38°41'N	96°57'W
Herisau, Switz. (hā'rē-zou)	168	47°23'N	9°18'E
Herk-de-Stad, Bel.	159a	50°56'N	5°13'E
Herkimer, N.Y., U.S. (hûr'kĭ-mēr)	109	43°05'N	75°00'W
Hermansville, Mi., U.S. (hûr'măns-vĭl)	108	45°40'N	87°35'W
Hermantown, Mn., U.S. (hĕr'măn-toun)	117h	46°46'N	92°12'W
Hermanusdorings, S. Afr.	238c	24°08'S	27°46'E
Herminie, Pa., U.S. (hûr-mĭ'nē)	111e	40°16'N	79°45'W
Hermitage Bay, b., Can. (hûr'mĭ-tĕj)	101	47°35'N	56°05'W
Hermit Islands, is., Pap. N. Gui. (hûr'mĭt)	213	1°48'S	144°55'E
Hermosa Beach, Ca., U.S. (hĕr-mō'sȧ)	117a	33°51'N	118°24'W
Hermosillo, Mex. (ĕr-mō-sē'l-yō)	128	29°00'N	110°57'W
Herndon, Va., U.S. (hĕrn'don)	110e	38°58'N	77°22'W
Herne, Ger. (hĕr'nĕ)	171c	51°32'N	7°13'E
Herning, Den. (hĕr'nĭng)	160	56°08'N	8°55'E
Heron, l., Mn., U.S. (hĕr'ŭn)	112	43°42'N	95°23'W
Heron Lake, Mn., U.S.	112	43°48'N	95°20'W
Herrero, Punta, Mex. (pô'n-tä-ĕr-rĕ'rô)	132a	19°18'N	87°24'W
Herrin, Il., U.S. (hĕr'ĭn)	108	37°50'N	89°00'W
Herschel, S. Afr. (hĕr'-shĕl)	233c	30°37'S	27°12'E
Herscher, Il., U.S. (hĕr'shēr)	111a	41°03'N	88°06'W
Herstal, Bel. (hĕr'stäl)	165	50°42'N	5°32'E
Hertford, Eng., U.K.	164	51°48'N	0°05'W
Hertford, N.C., U.S. (hûrt'fērd)	125	36°10'N	76°30'W
Hertfordshire, co., Eng., U.K.	158b	51°46'N	0°05'W
Hertzberg, Ger. (hĕrtz'bĕrgh)	159b	52°54'N	12°58'E
Hervás, Spain	172	40°16'N	5°51'W
Herzliyya, Isr.	197a	32°10'N	34°49'E
Hessen, hist. reg., Ger. (hĕs'ĕn)	168	50°42'N	9°00'E
Hetch Hetchy Aqueduct, Ca., U.S. (hĕtch hĕt'chĭ ăk'wē-dŭkt)	118	37°27'N	120°54'W
Hettinger, N.D., U.S. (hĕt'ĭn-jēr)	112	45°58'N	102°36'W
Heuningspruit, S. Afr.	238c	27°28'S	27°26'E
Hexian, China (hŭ shyĕn)	209	24°20'N	111°28'E
Hexian, China	206	31°44'N	118°20'E
Heyang, China (hŭ-yäŋ)	208	35°18'N	110°18'E
Heystekrand, S. Afr.	238c	25°16'S	27°14'E
Heyuan, China (hŭ-yůän)	209	23°48'N	114°45'E
Heywood, Eng., U.K. (hā'wŏd)	158a	53°36'N	2°12'W
Heze, China (hŭ-dzŭ)	206	35°13'N	115°28'E
Hialeah, Fl., U.S. (hī-ȧ-lē'ăh)	125a	25°49'N	80°18'W
Hiawatha, Ks., U.S. (hī-ȧ-wô'thȧ)	121	39°50'N	95°33'W
Hiawatha, Ut., U.S.	119	39°25'N	111°05'W
Hibbing, Mn., U.S. (hĭb'ĭng)	105	47°26'N	92°58'W
Hickman, Ky., U.S. (hĭk'mȧn)	124	34°33'N	89°10'W
Hickory, N.C., U.S. (hĭk'ô-rĭ)	125	35°43'N	81°21'W
Hicksville, N.Y., U.S.	108	41°15'N	84°45'W
Hicksville, N.Y., U.S. (hĭks'vĭl)	110a	40°47'N	73°25'W
Hico, Tx., U.S. (hī'kō)	122	32°00'N	98°02'W
Hidalgo, Mex. (ē-dhäl'gō)	130	24°14'N	99°25'W
Hidalgo, Mex.	122	27°49'N	99°53'W
Hidalgo, state, Mex.	128	20°45'N	99°30'W
Hidalgo del Parral, Mex. (ē-dä'l-gō-dĕl-pär-rä'l)	128	26°55'N	105°40'W
Hidalgo Yalalag, Mex. (ē-dhäl'gō-yä-lä-läg)	131	17°12'N	96°11'W
Hierro Island, i., Spain (yĕ'r-rô)	230	27°37'N	18°29'W
Higashimurayama, Japan	211a	35°46'N	139°28'E
Higashiōsaka, Japan	211b	34°40'N	135°44'E
Higgins, l., Mi., U.S. (hĭg'ĭnz)	108	44°20'N	84°45'W
Higginsville, Mo., U.S. (hĭg'ĭnz-vĭl)	121	39°05'N	93°44'W
High, i., Mi., U.S.	108	45°45'N	85°45'W
High Bluff, Can.	102f	50°01'N	98°08'W
Highborne Cay, i., Bah. (hībôrn kē)	134	24°45'N	76°50'W
Highgrove, Ca., U.S. (hī'grōv)	117a	34°01'N	117°20'W
High Island, Tx., U.S.	123a	29°34'N	94°24'W
Highland, Ca., U.S. (hī'lănd)	117a	34°08'N	117°13'W
Highland, Il., U.S.	121	38°44'N	89°41'W
Highland, In., U.S.	111a	41°33'N	87°28'W
Highland, Mi., U.S.	111b	42°38'N	83°37'W
Highland Park, Il., U.S.	111a	42°11'N	87°47'W
Highland Park, Mi., U.S.	111b	42°24'N	83°06'W
Highland Park, N.J., U.S.	110a	40°30'N	74°25'W
Highland Park, Tx., U.S.	117c	32°49'N	96°48'W
Highlands, N.J., U.S. (hī-lăndz)	110a	40°24'N	73°59'W
Highlands, Tx., U.S.	123a	29°49'N	95°01'W
Highmore, S.D., U.S. (hī'mōr)	112	44°30'N	99°26'W
High Ongar, Eng., U.K. (on'gēr)	158b	51°43'N	0°15'E
High Peak, mtn., Phil.	213a	15°38'N	120°05'E
High Point, N.C., U.S.	125	35°55'N	80°00'W
High Prairie, Can.	90	55°26'N	116°29'W
High Ridge, Mo., U.S.	117e	38°27'N	90°32'W
High River, Can.	90	50°35'N	113°52'W
High Rock Lake, res., N.C., U.S. (hī'-rŏk)	125	35°40'N	80°15'W
High Springs, Fl., U.S.	125	29°48'N	82°38'W
High Tatra Mountains, mts., Eur.	169	49°15'N	19°40'E
Hightstown, N.J., U.S. (hīts-toun)	110a	40°16'N	74°32'W
High Wycombe, Eng., U.K. (wĭ-kŭm)	164	51°36'N	0°45'W
Higuero, Punta, c., P.R.	129b	18°21'N	67°11'W
Higuerote, Ven. (ē-gĕ-rô'tĕ)	143b	10°29'N	66°06'W
Higüey, Dom. Rep. (ē-gwĕ'y)	135	18°40'N	68°45'W
Hiiumaa, i., Est. (hē'ŏm-ô)	180	58°47'N	22°05'E
Hikone, Japan (hē'kō-nĕ)	211	35°15'N	136°15'E
Hildburghausen, Ger. (hĭld'bôrg hou-zĕn)	168	50°26'N	10°45'E
Hilden, Ger. (hēl'dĕn)	171c	51°10'N	6°56'E
Hildesheim, Ger. (hĭl'dĕs-hīm)	161	52°08'N	9°56'E
Hillaby, Mount, mtn., Barb. (hĭl'ȧ-bĭ)	133b	13°15'N	59°35'W
Hill City, Ks., U.S. (hĭl)	120	39°22'N	99°54'W
Hill City, Mn., U.S.	113	46°58'N	93°38'W
Hillegersberg, Neth.	159a	51°57'N	4°29'E
Hillerød, Den. (hē'lĕ-rûdh)	166	55°56'N	12°17'E
Hillsboro, Il., U.S. (hĭlz'bŭr-ō)	121	39°09'N	89°28'W
Hillsboro, Ks., U.S.	121	38°22'N	97°11'W
Hillsboro, N.D., U.S.	112	47°23'N	97°05'W
Hillsboro, N.H., U.S.	109	43°05'N	71°55'W
Hillsboro, Oh., U.S.	108	39°10'N	83°40'W
Hillsboro, Or., U.S.	116c	45°31'N	122°59'W
Hillsboro, Tx., U.S.	123	32°01'N	97°06'W
Hillsboro, Wi., U.S.	113	43°39'N	90°20'W
Hillsburgh, Can. (hĭlz'bûrg)	102d	43°48'N	80°09'W
Hills Creek Lake, res., Or., U.S.	114	43°41'N	122°26'W
Hillsdale, Mi., U.S. (hĭls-dāl)	119	41°55'N	84°35'W
Hilo, Hi., U.S. (hē'lō)	106c	19°44'N	155°01'W
Hilvarenbeek, Neth.	159a	51°29'N	5°10'E
Hilversum, Neth. (hĭl'vēr-sŭm)	159a	52°13'N	5°10'E
Himachal Pradesh, India	199	32°00'N	77°30'E
Himalayas, mts., Asia	199	29°30'N	85°02'E
Himeji, Japan (hē'mâ-jĕ)	210	34°50'N	134°42'E
Himmelpforten, Ger. (hē'mĕl-pfōr-tĕn)	159c	53°37'N	9°19'E
Ḩimş, Syria	198	34°44'N	36°43'E
Hinche, Haiti (hēn'chå) (ănsh)	135	19°10'N	72°05'W
Hinchinbrook, i., Austl. (hĭn-chĭn-brŏŏk)	220	18°23'S	146°57'W
Hinckley, Eng., U.K. (hĭnk'lĭ)	158a	52°32'N	1°21'W
Hindley, Eng., U.K. (hĭnd'lĭ)	158a	53°32'N	2°35'W
Hindu Kush, mts., Asia (hĭn'dōō kōōsh')	199	35°15'N	68°44'E
Hindupur, India (hĭn'dōō-pōōr)	203	13°52'N	77°34'E

302 Hingham – Hualapai Mountains PRONOUNCING INDEX

PLACE (Pronunciation)	PAGE	LAT.	LONG.
Hingham, Ma., U.S. (hĭng′ăm)	101a	42°14′N	70°53′W
Hinkley, Oh., U.S. (hĭnk′-lĭ)	111d	41°14′N	81°45′W
Hinojosa del Duque, Spain (ē-nō-kô′sä)	172	38°30′N	5°09′W
Hinsdale, Il., U.S. (hĭnz′dāl)	111a	41°48′N	87°56′W
Hinton, Can. (hĭn′tŭn)	95	53°25′N	117°34′W
Hinton, W.V., U.S. (hĭn′tŭn)	108	37°40′N	80°55′W
Hirado, i., Japan (hē′rä-dō)	210	33°19′N	129°18′E
Hirakata, Japan (hē′rä-kä′tä)	211b	34°49′N	135°40′E
Hirara, Japan	214d	24°48′N	125°17′E
Hiratsuka, Japan (hē-rät-sōō′kȧ)	211	35°20′N	139°19′E
Hirosaki, Japan (hē′rô-sä′kê)	205	40°31′N	140°38′E
Hirose, Japan (hē′rô-sä)	211	35°20′N	133°11′E
Hiroshima, Japan (hē-rô-shē′mȧ)	205	34°22′N	132°25′E
Hirson, Fr. (ēr-sôn′)	170	49°54′N	4°00′E
Hisar, India	202	29°15′N	75°47′E
Hispaniola, i., N.A. (hĭ′spăn-ĭ-ō-lȧ)	129	17°30′N	73°15′W
Hitachi, Japan (hē-tä′chē)	210	36°42′N	140°47′E
Hitchcock, Tx., U.S. (hĭch′kŏk)	123a	29°21′N	95°01′W
Hitoyoshi, Japan (hē′tô-yō′shê)	211	32°13′N	130°45′E
Hitra, i., Nor. (hĭträ)	160	63°34′N	7°37′E
Hittefeld, Ger. (hē′tĕ-fĕld)	159c	53°23′N	9°59′E
Hiwasa, Japan (hē′wȧ-sä)	211	33°44′N	134°31′E
Hiwassee, r., Tn., U.S. (hī-wôs′sē)	124	35°10′N	84°35′W
Hjälmaren, l., Swe.	160	59°07′N	16°05′E
Hjo, Swe. (yō)	166	58°19′N	14°11′E
Hjørring, Den. (jûr′ĭng)	160	57°27′N	9°59′E
Hlobyne, Ukr.	177	49°22′N	33°17′E
Hlohovec, Slvk. (hlō′ho-vĕts)	169	48°24′N	17°49′E
Hlukhiv, Ukr.	181	51°42′N	33°52′E
Hlybokaye, Bela.	180	55°08′N	27°44′E
Hobart, Austl. (hō′bȧrt)	219	43°00′S	147°30′E
Hobart, In., U.S.	111a	41°31′N	87°15′W
Hobart, Ok., U.S.	120	35°02′N	99°06′W
Hobart, Wa., U.S.	116a	47°25′N	121°58′W
Hobbs, N.M., U.S. (hŏbs)	120	32°41′N	103°15′W
Hoboken, Bel. (hō′bō-kĕn)	159a	51°11′N	4°20′E
Hoboken, N.J., U.S.	110a	40°43′N	74°03′W
Hobro, Den. (hô-brô′)	166	56°38′N	9°47′E
Hobson, Va., U.S. (hŏb′sŭn)	110g	36°54′N	76°31′W
Hobson's Bay, b., Austl. (hŏb′sŭnz)	217a	37°54′S	144°45′E
Hobyo, Som.	238a	5°24′N	48°28′E
Ho Chi Minh City, Viet.	212	10°46′N	106°34′E
Hockinson, Wa., U.S. (hŏk′ĭn-sŭn)	116c	45°44′N	122°29′W
Hoctún, Mex. (ôk-tōō′n)	132a	20°52′N	89°10′W
Hodgenville, Ky., U.S. (hŏj′ĕn-vĭl)	108	37°35′N	85°45′W
Hodges Hill, mtn., Can. (hŏj′ĕz)	101	49°04′N	55°53′W
Hódmezővásárhely, Hung. (hōd′mĕ-zû-vô′shôr-hĕl-y′)	169	46°24′N	20°21′E
Hodna, Chott el, l., Alg.	162	35°20′N	3°27′E
Hodonin, Czech Rep. (hē′dô-nén)	169	48°50′N	17°06′E
Hoegaarden, Bel.	159a	50°46′N	4°55′E
Hoek van Holland, Neth.	159a	51°59′N	4°05′E
Hoeryŏng, Kor., N. (hwĕr′yŭng)	210	42°28′N	129°39′E
Hof, Ger. (hōf)	168	50°19′N	11°55′E
Hofsjökull, ice, Ice. (hôfs′yü′kōōl)	160	64°55′N	18°40′W
Hog, i., Mi., U.S.	108	45°50′N	85°20′W
Hogansville, Ga., U.S. (hō′gănz-vĭl)	124	33°10′N	84°54′W
Hog Cay, i., Bah.	135	23°35′N	75°30′W
Hogsty Reef, rf., Bah.	135	21°45′N	73°50′W
Hohenbrunn, Ger. (hō′hĕn-brōōn)	159d	48°03′N	11°42′E
Hohenlimburg, Ger. (hō′hĕn lĕm′bōōrg)	171c	51°20′N	7°35′E
Hohen Neuendorf, Ger. (hō′hĕn noi′ĕn-dōrf)	159b	52°40′N	13°22′E
Hohe Tauern, mts., Aus. (hō′ĕ tou′ĕrn)	168	47°11′N	12°12′E
Hohhot, China (hŭ-hōō-tŭ)	205	41°05′N	111°50′E
Hohoe, Ghana	234	7°09′N	0°28′E
Hohokus, N.J., U.S. (hō-hō-kŭs)	110a	41°01′N	74°08′W
Hoi An, Viet.	209	15°48′N	108°30′E
Hoisington, Ks., U.S. (hoi′zĭng-tŭn)	120	38°30′N	98°46′W
Hojo, Japan (hō′jô)	211	33°58′N	132°50′E
Hokitika, N.Z. (hō-kĭ-tē′kä)	221a	42°43′S	170°59′E
Hokkaidō, i., Japan (hôk′kĭ-dō)	210	43°30′N	142°45′E
Holbaek, Den. (hôl′bĕk)	166	55°42′N	11°40′E
Holbox, Mex. (ôl-bŏ′x)	132a	21°33′N	87°19′W
Holbox, Isla, i., Mex. (ē′s-lä-ôl-bŏ′x)	132a	21°40′N	87°21′W
Holbrook, Az., U.S. (hōl′brŏŏk)	119	34°55′N	110°15′W
Holbrook, Ma., U.S.	101a	42°10′N	71°01′W
Holden, Ma., U.S. (hōl′dĕn)	101a	42°21′N	71°51′W
Holden, Mo., U.S.	121	38°42′N	94°00′W
Holden, W.V., U.S.	108	37°45′N	82°05′W
Holdenville, Ok., U.S. (hōl′dĕn-vĭl)	121	35°05′N	96°25′W
Holdrege, Ne., U.S. (hōl′drĕj)	120	40°25′N	99°28′W
Holguín, Cuba (ôl-gēn′)	129	20°55′N	76°15′W
Holguín, prov., Cuba	134	20°40′N	76°15′W
Holidaysburg, Pa., U.S. (hŏl′ĭ-dāz-bûrg)	109	40°30′N	78°30′W
Hollabrunn, Aus.	168	48°33′N	16°04′E
Holland, Mi., U.S. (hŏl′ănd)	108	42°45′N	86°10′W
Hollands Diep, strt., Neth.	159a	51°43′N	4°25′E
Hollenstedt, Ger. (hō′lĕn-shtĕt)	159c	53°22′N	9°43′E
Hollis, N.H., U.S. (hŏl′ĭs)	101a	42°30′N	71°29′W
Hollis, Ok., U.S.	120	34°39′N	99°56′W
Hollister, Ca., U.S. (hŏl′ĭs-tĕr)	118	36°50′N	121°25′W
Holliston, Ma., U.S. (hŏl′ĭs-tŭn)	101a	42°12′N	71°25′W
Holly, Mi., U.S. (hŏl′ĭ)	108	42°45′N	83°30′W
Holly, Wa., U.S.	116a	47°34′N	122°58′W
Holly Springs, Ms., U.S. (hŏl′ĭ sprĭngz)	124	34°45′N	89°28′W
Hollywood, Ca., U.S. (hŏl′ē-wŏŏd)	117a	34°06′N	118°20′W
Hollywood, Fl., U.S.	125a	26°00′N	80°11′W
Holmes Reefs, rf., Austl. (hōmz)	221	16°33′S	148°43′E
Holmestrand, Nor. (hôl′mĕ-strän)	166	59°29′N	10°17′E
Holmsbu, Nor. (hôlms′bōō)	166	59°36′N	10°26′E
Holmsjön, l., Swe.	166	62°23′N	15°43′E
Holstebro, Den. (hôl′stĕ-brô)	160	56°22′N	8°39′E
Holstein, hist. reg., Ger.	168	54°10′N	9°40′E
Holston, r., Tn., U.S. (hōl′stŭn)	124	36°02′N	83°42′W
Holt, Eng., U.K. (hōlt)	158a	53°05′N	2°53′W
Holton, Ks., U.S. (hōl′tŭn)	121	39°27′N	95°43′W
Holy Cross, Ak., U.S. (hō′lĭ krôs)	103	62°10′N	159°40′W
Holyhead, Wales, U.K. (hŏl′ē-hĕd)	164	53°18′N	4°45′W
Holy Island, i., Eng., U.K.	164	55°43′N	1°48′W
Holy Island, i., Wales, U.K. (hō′lĭ)	164	53°15′N	4°45′W
Holyoke, Co., U.S. (hōl′yōk)	120	40°36′N	102°18′W
Holyoke, Ma., U.S.	109	42°10′N	72°40′W
Homano, Japan (hō-mä′nō)	211a	35°33′N	140°08′E
Homberg, Ger. (hōm′bĕrgh)	171c	51°27′N	6°42′E
Hombori, Mali	234	15°17′N	1°42′W
Home Gardens, Ca., U.S. (hōm gär′d′nz)	117a	33°53′N	117°32′W
Homeland, Ca., U.S. (hōm′lănd)	117a	33°44′N	117°07′W
Homer, Ak., U.S. (hō′mẽr)	103	59°42′N	151°30′W
Homer, La., U.S.	123	32°46′N	93°05′W
Homer Youngs Peak, mtn., Mt., U.S.	115	45°19′N	113°41′W
Homestead, Fl., U.S. (hōm′stĕd)	125a	25°27′N	80°28′W
Homestead, Mi., U.S.	117k	46°20′N	84°07′W
Homestead, Pa., U.S.	111e	40°29′N	79°55′W
Homestead National Monument of America, rec., Ne., U.S.	121	40°16′N	96°51′W
Homewood, Al., U.S. (hōm′wŏŏd)	110h	33°28′N	86°48′W
Homewood, Il., U.S.	111a	41°34′N	87°40′W
Hominy, Ok., U.S. (hŏm′ĭ-nĭ)	121	36°25′N	96°24′W
Homochitto, r., Ms., U.S. (hō-mō-chĭt′ō)	124	31°23′N	91°15′W
Homyel′, Bela.	180	52°20′N	31°03′E
Homyel′, prov., Bela.	176	52°18′N	29°00′E
Honda, Col. (hōn′dȧ)	142	5°13′N	74°45′W
Honda, Bahía, b., Cuba (bä-ē′ä-ô′n-dä)	134	23°10′N	83°20′W
Hondo, Tx., U.S.	122	29°20′N	99°08′W
Hondo, r., N.M., U.S.	120	33°22′N	105°06′W
Hondo, Río, r., N.A. (hon-dō′)	132a	18°16′N	88°32′W
Honduras, nation, N.A. (hŏn-dōō′rȧs)	128	14°30′N	88°00′W
Honduras, Gulf of, b., N.A.	128	16°30′N	87°30′W
Honea Path, S.C., U.S. (hŭn′ĭ păth)	125	34°25′N	82°16′W
Hønefoss, Nor. (hē′nĕ-fôs)	160	60°10′N	10°15′E
Honesdale, Pa., U.S. (hōnz′dāl)	109	41°30′N	75°15′W
Honey Grove, Tx., U.S. (hŭn′ĭ grōv)	121	33°35′N	95°54′W
Honey Lake, l., Ca., U.S. (hŭn′ĭ)	118	40°11′N	120°34′W
Honfleur, Can. (ôn-flûr′)	102b	46°39′N	70°53′W
Honfleur, Fr. (ôn-flûr′)	170	49°26′N	0°13′E
Hon Gay, Viet.	209	20°58′N	107°10′E
Hong Kong (Xianggang), China	205	21°45′N	115°00′E
Hongshui, r., China (hôŋ-shwā)	204	24°30′N	105°00′E
Honguedo, Détroit d′, strt., Can.	100	49°08′N	63°45′W
Hongze Hu, l., China	205	33°17′N	118°37′E
Honiara, Sol. Is.	219	9°26′S	159°57′E
Honiton, Eng., U.K. (hŏn′ĭ-tŏn)	164	50°49′N	3°10′W
Honolulu, Hi., U.S. (hŏn-ô-lōō′lōō)	106c	21°18′N	157°50′W
Honomu, Hi., U.S. (hŏn′ô-mōō)	126a	19°50′N	155°04′W
Honshū, i., Japan	205	36°00′N	138°00′E
Hood, Mount, mtn., Or., U.S.	106	45°20′N	121°43′W
Hood Canal, b., Wa., U.S. (hŏŏd)	116a	47°45′N	122°45′W
Hood River, Or., U.S.	104	45°42′N	121°30′W
Hoodsport, Wa., U.S. (hŏŏdz′pōrt)	116a	47°25′N	123°09′W
Hoogly, r., India (hōōg′lĭ)	199	21°35′N	87°50′E
Hoogstraten, Bel.	159a	51°24′N	4°46′E
Hooker, Ok., U.S. (hŏŏk′ẽr)	120	36°49′N	101°13′W
Hool, Mex. (ōō′l)	132a	19°32′N	90°22′W
Hoonah, Ak., U.S. (hōō′nä)	103	58°05′N	135°25′W
Hoopa Valley Indian Reservation, I.R., Ca., U.S.	114	41°18′N	123°35′W
Hooper, Ne., U.S. (hŏŏp′ẽr)	121	41°37′N	96°31′W
Hooper, Ut., U.S.	117b	41°10′N	112°08′W
Hooper Bay, Ak., U.S.	103	61°32′N	166°02′W
Hoopeston, Il., U.S. (hōōps′tŭn)	108	40°35′N	87°40′W
Hoosick Falls, N.Y., U.S. (hōō′sĭk)	109	42°55′N	73°15′W
Hoover Dam, Nv., U.S. (hōō′vẽr)	118	36°00′N	115°06′W
Hoover Dam, dam, U.S.	106	36°00′N	114°27′W
Hopatcong, Lake, l., N.J., U.S. (hō-păt′kong)	110a	40°57′N	74°38′W
Hope, Ak., U.S. (hōp)	103	60°54′N	149°48′W
Hope, Ar., U.S.	121	33°41′N	93°35′W
Hope, N.D., U.S.	112	47°17′N	97°45′W
Hope, Ben, mtn., Scot., U.K. (bĕn hōp)	164	58°25′N	4°25′W
Hopedale, Can. (hōp′dāl)	91	55°26′N	60°11′W
Hopedale, Ma., U.S. (hōp′dāl)	101a	42°08′N	71°33′W
Hopelchén, Mex. (o-pĕl-chĕ′n)	132a	19°47′N	89°51′W
Hopes Advance, Cap, c., Can. (hōps ăd-vans′)	93	61°05′N	69°35′W
Hopetoun, Austl. (hōp′toun)	218	33°50′S	120°15′E
Hopetown, S. Afr. (hōp′toun)	232	29°35′S	24°10′E
Hopewell, Va., U.S. (hōp′wĕl)	125	37°14′N	77°15′W
Hopewell Culture National Historical Park, rec., Oh., U.S.	108	39°25′N	83°00′W
Hopi Indian Reservation, I.R., Az., U.S. (hō′pē)	119	36°20′N	110°30′W
Hopkins, Mn., U.S. (hŏp′kĭns)	117g	44°55′N	93°24′W
Hopkinsville, Ky., U.S. (hŏp′kĭns-vĭl)	105	36°50′N	87°28′W
Hopkinton, Ma., U.S. (hŏp′kĭn-tŭn)	101a	42°14′N	71°31′W
Hoquiam, Wa., U.S. (hō′kwĭ-ăm)	104	47°00′N	123°53′W
Horconcitos, Pan. (ŏr-kôn-sē′-tôs)	133	8°18′N	82°11′W
Horgen, Switz. (hôr′gĕn)	168	47°16′N	8°35′E
Horicon, Wi., U.S. (hŏr′ĭ-kŏn)	113	43°26′N	88°40′W
Horlivka, Ukr.	181	48°17′N	38°03′E
Hormuz, Strait of, strt., Asia (hôr′mŭz′)	198	26°30′N	56°30′E
Horn, i., Austl. (hôrn)	221	10°30′S	143°30′E
Horn, Cape see Hornos, Cabo de, c., Chile	144	56°00′S	67°00′W
Hornavan, l., Swe.	160	65°54′N	16°17′E
Horneburg, Ger. (hŏr′nĕ-bŏrgh)	159c	53°30′N	9°35′E
Hornell, N.Y., U.S. (hŏr-nĕl′)	109	42°20′N	77°40′W
Hornos, Cabo de, c., Chile	144	56°00′S	67°00′W
Horn Plateau, plat., Can.	92	62°12′N	120°29′W
Hornsby, Austl. (hôrnz′bĭ)	217b	33°43′S	151°06′E
Horodenka, Ukr.	169	48°40′N	25°30′E
Horodnia, Ukr.	177	51°54′N	31°31′E
Horodok, Ukr.	169	49°47′N	23°39′E
Horqueta, Para. (ŏr-kē′tä)	144	23°20′S	57°00′W
Horse Creek, r., Co., U.S. (hôrs)	120	38°49′N	103°48′W
Horse Creek, r., Wy., U.S.	112	41°33′N	104°39′W
Horse Islands, is., Can.	101	50°11′N	55°45′W
Horsens, Den. (hôrs′ĕns)	166	55°50′N	9°49′E
Horseshoe Bay, Can. (hôrs-shōō)	116d	49°23′N	123°16′W
Horsforth, Eng., U.K. (hôrs′fŭrth)	158a	53°50′N	1°38′W
Horsham, Austl. (hôr′shăm) (hôrs′ăm)	219	36°42′S	142°17′E
Horst, Ger. (hôrst)	159c	53°49′N	9°37′E
Horten, Nor. (hôr′tĕn)	166	59°26′N	10°27′E
Horton, Ks., U.S. (hôr′tŭn)	121	39°38′N	95°32′W
Horton, r., Ak., U.S. (hôr′tŭn)	103	68°38′N	122°00′W
Horwich, Eng., U.K. (hŏr′ĭch)	158a	53°36′N	2°33′W
Horyn′, r., Eur. (gō′rĕn′)	169	50°55′N	26°07′E
Hososhima, Japan (hō′sô-shē′mä)	210	32°25′N	131°40′E
Hoste, i., Chile (ôs′tā)	144	55°20′S	70°45′W
Hostotipaquillo, Mex. (ôs-tō′tĭ-pä-kēl′yô)	130	21°09′N	104°05′W
Hota, Japan (hō′tä)	211a	35°08′N	139°50′E
Hotan, China (hwô-tän)	204	37°11′N	79°50′E
Hotan, r., China	204	39°09′N	81°08′E
Hoto Mayor, Dom. Rep. (ô-tô-mä-yô′r)	135	18°45′N	69°10′W
Hot Springs, Ak., U.S. (hŏt sprĭngs)	103	65°00′N	150°20′W
Hot Springs, Ar., U.S.	105	34°29′N	93°02′W
Hot Springs, S.D., U.S.	112	43°28′N	103°32′W
Hot Springs, Va., U.S.	109	38°00′N	79°55′W
Hot Springs National Park, rec., Ar., U.S.	107	34°30′N	93°00′W
Hotte, Massif de la, mts., Haiti	135	18°25′N	74°00′W
Hotville, Ca., U.S. (hŏt′vĭl)	118	32°50′N	115°24′W
Houdan, Fr. (ōō-däN′)	171b	48°47′N	1°36′E
Houghton, Mi., U.S. (hō′tŭn)	113	47°06′N	88°36′W
Houghton, l., Mi., U.S.	108	44°20′N	84°45′W
Houilles, Fr. (ōō-yĕs′)	171b	48°55′N	2°11′E
Houjie, China (hwô-jyĕ)	207a	22°58′N	113°39′E
Houlton, Me., U.S. (hōl′tŭn)	100	46°07′N	67°50′W
Houma, La., U.S. (hōō′mȧ)	123	29°36′N	90°43′W
Housatonic, r., U.S. (hōō-sȧ-tŏn′ĭk)	109	41°50′N	73°25′W
House Springs, Mo., U.S. (hous sprĭngs)	117e	38°24′N	90°34′W
Houston, Ms., U.S. (hūs′tŭn)	124	33°53′N	89°00′W
Houston, Tx., U.S.	105	29°46′N	95°21′W
Houston Ship Channel, strt., Tx., U.S.	123a	29°38′N	94°57′W
Houtbaai, S. Afr.	232a	34°03′S	18°22′E
Houtman Rocks, is., Austl. (hout′män)	220	28°15′S	112°45′E
Houzhen, China (hwô-jŭn)	206	36°59′N	118°59′E
Hovd, Mong.	204	48°08′N	91°40′E
Hovd Gol, r., Mong.	204	49°06′N	91°16′E
Hove, Eng., U.K. (hōv)	164	50°50′N	0°09′W
Hövsgöl Nuur, l., Mong.	204	51°11′N	99°11′E
Howard, Ks., U.S. (hou′ȧrd)	121	37°27′N	96°10′W
Howard, S.D., U.S.	112	44°01′N	97°31′W
Howden, Eng., U.K. (hou′dĕn)	158a	53°44′N	0°52′W
Howe, Cape, c., Austl. (hou)	221	37°30′S	150°40′E
Howell, Mi., U.S. (hou′ĕl)	108	42°40′N	84°00′W
Howe Sound, strt., Can.	94	49°22′N	123°18′W
Howick, Can. (hou′ĭk)	102a	45°11′N	73°51′W
Howick, S. Afr.	233c	29°29′S	30°16′E
Howland, i., Oc. (hou′lănd)	2	1°00′N	176°00′W
Howrah, India (hou′rä)	199	22°33′N	88°20′E
Howse Peak, mtn., Can.	95	51°30′N	116°40′W
Howson Peak, mtn., Can.	94	54°25′N	127°45′W
Hoxie, Ar., U.S. (kŏh′sĭ)	121	36°03′N	91°00′W
Hoy, i., Scot., U.K. (hoi)	164a	58°53′N	3°10′W
Hōya, Japan (hō′yä)	211a	35°45′N	139°35′E
Hoylake, Eng., U.K. (hoi-lāk′)	158a	53°23′N	3°11′W
Hoyo, Sierra del, mts., Spain (sē-ĕ′r-rä-dĕl-ô′yô)	173a	40°39′N	3°56′W
Hradec Králové, Czech Rep.	161	50°12′N	15°50′E
Hradyz′k, Ukr.	177	49°12′N	33°06′E
Hranice, Czech Rep. (hrän′yĕ-tsĕ)	169	49°33′N	17°45′E
Hröby, Swe. (hûr′bü)	166	55°50′N	13°41′E
Hrodna, Bela.	180	53°40′N	23°49′E
Hron, r., Slvk.	169	48°22′N	18°42′E
Hrubieszów, Pol. (hrōō-byä′shōōf)	169	50°48′N	23°54′E
Hsawnhsup, Mya.	204	24°29′N	94°45′E
Hsinchu, Tai. (hsĭn′chōō′)	209	24°48′N	121°00′E
Huadian, China (hwä-dĭĕn)	208	42°38′N	126°45′E
Huai, r., China (hwī)	205	32°07′N	114°38′E
Huai′an, China (hwī-än)	208	33°31′N	119°11′E
Huailai, China	208	40°20′N	115°45′E
Huailin, China (hwī-lĭn)	206	31°27′N	117°36′E
Huainan, China	206	32°38′N	117°02′E
Huaiyang, China (hōōäī′yang)	208	33°45′N	114°54′E
Huaiyuan, China (hwī-yůän)	208	32°53′N	117°13′E
Huajicori, Mex. (wä-jē-kō′rē)	130	22°41′N	105°24′W
Huajuapan de León, Mex. (wäj-wä′päm dā lā-ōn′)	131	17°46′N	97°45′W
Hualapai Indian Reservation, I.R., Az., U.S. (wälåpī)	119	35°41′N	113°38′W
Hualapai Mountains, mts., Az., U.S.	119	34°53′N	113°54′W

ăt; finăl; rāte; senâte; ärm; åsk; sofȧ; fâre; ch-choose; dh-as th in other; bē; ēvent; bĕt; recĕnt; cratẽr; g-gō; gh-guttural g; bĭt; ĭ-short neutral; rīde; K-guttural k as ch in German ich;

PLACE (Pronunciation)	PAGE	LAT.	LONG.
Hualien, Tai. (hwä'lyĕn')	209	23°58'N	121°58'E
Huallaga, r., Peru (wäl-yä'gä)	142	8°12'S	76°34'W
Huamachuco, Peru (wä-mä-chōō'kō)	142	7°52'S	78°11'W
Huamantla, Mex. (wä-män'tlȧ)	131	19°18'N	97°54'W
Huambo, Ang.	232	12°44'S	15°47'E
Huamuxtitlán, Mex. (wä-mōōs-tē-tlän')	130	17°49'N	98°38'W
Huancavelica, Peru (wän'kä-vä-lē'kä)	142	12°47'S	75°02'W
Huancayo, Peru (wän-kä'yō)	142	12°09'S	75°04'W
Huanchaca, Bol. (wän-chä'kä)	142	20°09'S	66°40'W
Huang (Yellow), r., China (hůäŋ)	205	35°06'N	113°39'E
Huang, Old Beds of the, mth., China	204	40°28'N	106°34'E
Huang, Old Course of the, r., China	206	34°28'N	116°59'E
Huangchuan, China (hůäŋ-chůän)	208	32°07'N	115°01'E
Huanghua, China (hůäŋ-hwä)	206	38°28'N	117°18'E
Huanghuadian, China (hůäŋ-hwä-dĭĕn)	206	39°22'N	116°53'E
Huangli, China (hōōäng'lē)	206	31°39'N	119°42'E
Huangpu, China (hůäŋ-pōō)	207a	22°44'N	113°20'E
Huangpu, r., China	207b	30°56'N	121°16'E
Huangqiao, China (hůän-chyou)	206	32°15'N	120°13'E
Huangxian, China (hůäŋ shyĕn)	206	37°39'N	120°32'E
Huangyuan, China (hůän-yůän)	204	37°00'N	101°01'E
Huanren, China (hůän-rŭn)	208	41°10'N	125°30'E
Huánuco, Peru (wä-nōō'kō)	142	9°50'S	76°17'W
Huánuni, Bol. (wä-nōō'nē)	142	18°11'S	66°43'W
Huaquechula, Mex. (wä-kĕ-chōō'lä)	130	18°44'N	98°37'W
Huaral, Peru (wä-rä'l)	142	11°28'S	77°11'W
Huarás, Peru (öä'rá's)	142	9°32'S	77°29'W
Huascarán, Nevados, mts., Peru (wäs-kä-rän')	142	9°05'S	77°50'W
Huasco, Chile (wäs'kō)	144	28°32'S	71°16'W
Huatla de Jiménez, Mex. (wá'tlä-dĕ-kĕ-mĕ'nĕz)	131	18°08'N	96°49'W
Huatlatlauch, Mex. (wä'tlä-tlä-ōō'ch)	130	18°40'N	98°04'W
Huatusco, Mex. (wä-tōōs'kō)	131	19°09'N	96°57'W
Huauchinango, Mex. (wä-ōō-chē-näŋ'gō)	130	20°09'N	98°03'W
Huaunta, Nic. (wä-ò'n-tä)	133	13°30'N	83°32'W
Huaunta, Laguna, l., Nic. (lä-gò'nä-wä-ò'n-tä)	133	13°35'N	83°46'W
Huautla, Mex. (wä-ōō'tlä)	130	21°04'N	98°13'W
Huaxian, China (hwä shyĕn)	208	35°34'N	114°32'E
Huaynamota, Río de, r., Mex. (rē'ō-dĕ-wäy-nä-mŏ'tä)	130	22°10'N	104°36'W
Huazolotitlán, Mex. (wäzô-lô-tlē-tlän')	131	16°18'N	97°55'W
Hubbard, N.H., U.S. (hŭb'ẽrd)	101a	42°53'N	71°12'W
Hubbard, Tx., U.S.	123	31°53'N	96°46'W
Hubbard, l., Mi., U.S.	108	44°45'N	83°30'W
Hubbard Creek Reservoir, res., Tx., U.S.	122	32°50'N	98°55'W
Hubei, prov., China (hōō-bā)	205	31°20'N	111°58'E
Hubli, India (hò'blē)	199	15°25'N	75°09'E
Hückeswagen, Ger. (hü'kĕs-vä'gĕn)	171c	51°09'N	7°20'E
Hucknall, Eng., U.K. (hŭk'năl)	158a	53°02'N	1°12'W
Huddersfield, Eng., U.K. (hŭd'ẽrz-fēld)	164	53°39'N	1°47'W
Hudiksvall, Swe. (hōō'dĭks-väl)	160	61°44'N	17°05'E
Hudson, Can. (hŭd'sŭn)	102a	45°26'N	74°08'W
Hudson, Ma., U.S.	101a	42°24'N	71°34'W
Hudson, Mi., U.S.	108	41°50'N	84°15'W
Hudson, N.Y., U.S.	109	42°15'N	73°45'W
Hudson, Oh., U.S.	111d	41°15'N	81°27'W
Hudson, Wi., U.S.	117g	44°59'N	92°45'W
Hudson, r., U.S.	107	42°30'N	73°55'W
Hudson Bay, Can.	97	52°52'N	102°25'W
Hudson Bay, b., Can.	93	60°15'N	85°30'W
Hudson Falls, N.Y., U.S.	109	43°20'N	73°30'W
Hudson Heights, Can.	102a	45°28'N	74°09'W
Hudson Strait, strt., Can.	93	63°25'N	74°05'W
Hue, Viet. (ü-ā')	212	16°28'N	107°42'E
Huebra, r., Spain (wĕ'brä)	172	40°44'N	6°17'W
Huehuetenango, Guat. (wā-wå-tå-näŋ'gō)	132	15°19'N	91°26'W
Huejotzingo, Mex. (wā-hò-tzĭŋ'gō)	130	19°09'N	98°24'W
Huejúcar, Mex. (wā-hōō'kär)	130	22°26'N	103°12'W
Huejuquilla el Alto, Mex. (wā-hōō-kēl'yä ĕl äl'tō)	130	22°42'N	103°54'W
Huejutla, Mex. (wā-hōō'tlä)	130	21°08'N	98°26'W
Huelma, Spain (wĕl'mä)	172	37°39'N	3°36'W
Huelva, Spain (wĕl'vä)	162	37°16'N	6°58'W
Huércal-Overa, Spain (wĕr-käl' ō-vä'rä)	172	37°12'N	1°58'W
Huerfano, r., Co., U.S. (wâr'fȧ-nō)	120	37°41'N	105°13'W
Huésca, Spain (wĕs-kä)	162	42°07'N	0°25'W
Huéscar, Spain (wās'kär)	172	37°50'N	2°34'W
Huetamo de Núñez, Mex.	130	18°34'N	100°53'W
Huete, Spain (wā'tå)	172	40°09'N	2°42'W
Hueycatenango, Mex. (wĕy-kȧ-tĕ-nä'n-gô)	130	17°31'N	99°10'W
Hueytlalpan, Mex. (wā'ĭ-tlăl'păn)	131	20°03'N	97°41'W
Hueytown, Al., U.S.	110h	33°28'N	86°59'W
Huffman, Al., U.S. (hŭf'măn)	110h	33°36'N	86°42'W
Hugh Butler, l., Ne., U.S.	120	40°21'N	100°40'W
Hughenden, Austl. (hū'ĕn-dĕn)	219	20°58'S	144°13'E
Hughes, Austl. (hūz)	218	30°45'S	129°30'E
Hughesville, Md., U.S.	110e	38°32'N	76°48'W
Hugo, Mn., U.S. (hū'gō)	117g	45°10'N	93°00'W
Hugo, Ok., U.S.	121	34°01'N	95°32'W
Hugoton, Ks., U.S. (hū'gō-tŭn)	120	37°10'N	101°28'W
Hugou, China (hōō-gō)	206	33°22'N	117°07'E
Huichapan, Mex. (wē-chä-pän')	130	20°22'N	99°39'W
Huila, dept., Col. (wē'lä)	142a	3°10'N	75°20'W
Huila, Nevado de, mtn., Col. (nĕ-vä-dô-de-wē'lä)	142a	2°59'N	76°01'W

PLACE (Pronunciation)	PAGE	LAT.	LONG.
Huilai, China	209	23°02'N	116°18'E
Huili, China	204	26°48'N	102°20'E
Huimanguillo, Mex. (wē-män-gēl'yō)	131	17°50'N	93°16'W
Huimin, China (hōōĭ mĭn)	205	37°29'N	117°32'E
Huitzilac, Mex. (ōē't-zē-lä'k)	131a	19°01'N	99°16'W
Huitzitzilingo, Mex. (wē-tzē-tzē-lē'n-go)	130	21°11'N	98°42'W
Huitzuco, Mex. (wē-tzōō'kō)	130	18°16'N	99°20'W
Huixquilucan, Mex. (ōē'x-kē-lōō-kä'n)	131a	19°21'N	99°22'W
Huiyang, China	209	23°05'N	114°25'E
Hukou, China (hōō-kō)	205	29°58'N	116°20'E
Hulan, China (hōō'län')	205	45°58'N	126°32'E
Hulan, r., China	208	47°20'N	126°30'E
Huliaipole, Ukr.	177	47°39'N	36°12'E
Hulin, China (hōō'lĭn')	210	45°45'N	133°25'E
Hull, Can. (hŭl)	91	45°26'N	75°43'W
Hull, Ma., U.S.	101a	42°18'N	70°54'W
Hull, r., Eng., U.K.	158a	53°47'N	0°20'W
Hulst, Neth. (hòlst)	159a	51°17'N	4°01'E
Huludao, China (hōō-lōō-dou)	205	40°40'N	120°55'E
Hulun Nur, l., China (hōō-lòn nòr)	205	48°50'N	116°45'E
Humacao, P.R. (ōō-mä-kä'ō)	129b	18°09'N	65°49'W
Humansdorp, S. Afr. (hōō'mäns-dòrp)	232	33°57'S	24°45'E
Humbe, Ang. (hòm'bâ)	232	16°50'S	14°55'E
Humber, r., Can.	102d	43°53'N	79°40'W
Humber, r., Eng., U.K. (hŭm'bẽr)	160	53°30'N	0°30'E
Humbermouth, Can. (hŭm'bẽr-mŭth)	101	48°58'N	57°55'W
Humberside, hist. reg., Eng., U.K.	158a	53°47'N	0°36'W
Humble, Tx., U.S. (hŭm'b'l)	123	29°58'N	95°15'W
Humboldt, Can. (hŭm'bōlt)	90	52°12'N	105°07'W
Humboldt, Ia., U.S.	113	42°43'N	94°11'W
Humboldt, Ks., U.S.	121	37°48'N	95°26'W
Humboldt, Ne., U.S.	121	40°10'N	95°57'W
Humboldt, r., Nv., U.S.	106	40°30'N	116°50'W
Humboldt, East Fork, r., Nv., U.S.	114	40°59'N	115°21'W
Humboldt, North Fork, r., Nv., U.S.	114	41°25'N	115°45'W
Humboldt Bay, b., Ca., U.S.	114	40°48'N	124°25'W
Humboldt Range, mts., Nv., U.S.	118	40°12'N	118°16'W
Humbolt, Tn., U.S.	124	35°47'N	88°55'W
Humbolt Salt Marsh, Nv., U.S.	118	39°49'N	117°41'W
Humbolt Sink, Nv., U.S.	118	39°58'N	118°54'W
Humen, China (hōō-mŭn)	207a	22°49'N	113°39'E
Humphreys Peak, mtn., Az., U.S. (hŭm'frĭs)	106	35°20'N	111°40'W
Humpolec, Czech Rep. (hòm'pō-lĕts)	168	49°33'N	15°21'E
Humuya, r., Hond. (ōō-mōō'yä)	132	14°38'N	87°36'W
Hunaflói, b., Ice. (hōō'nä-flō'ĭ)	160	65°41'N	20°44'W
Hunan, prov., China (hōō'nän')	205	28°08'N	111°25'E
Hunchun, China (hòn-chůn)	205	42°53'N	130°34'E
Hunedoara, Rom. (kōō'nĕd-wä'rȧ)	175	45°45'N	22°54'E
Hungary, nation, Eur. (hŭŋ'gȧ-rĭ)	154	46°44'N	17°55'E
Hungerford, Austl. (hŭn'gẽr-fẽrd)	219	28°50'S	144°32'E
Hungry Horse Reservoir, res., Mt., U.S. (hŭŋ'gȧ-rĭ hôrs)	115	48°11'N	113°30'W
Hunsrück, mts., Ger. (hōōns'rûk)	168	49°43'N	7°12'E
Hunte, r., Ger. (hòn'tĕ)	168	52°45'N	8°26'E
Hunter Islands, is., Austl. (hŭn-tẽr)	221	40°33'S	143°36'E
Huntingburg, In., U.S. (hŭnt'ĭng-bûrg)	108	38°15'N	86°55'W
Huntingdon, Can. (hŭnt'ĭng-dŭn)	99	45°10'N	74°05'W
Huntingdon, Can.	116d	49°00'N	122°16'W
Huntingdon, Tn., U.S.	124	36°00'N	88°23'W
Huntington, In., U.S.	108	40°55'N	85°30'W
Huntington, Pa., U.S.	109	40°30'N	78°00'W
Huntington, W.V., U.S.	105	38°25'N	82°25'W
Huntington Beach, Ca., U.S.	117a	33°39'N	118°00'W
Huntington Park, Ca., U.S.	117a	33°59'N	118°14'W
Huntington Station, N.Y., U.S.	110a	40°51'N	73°25'W
Huntley, Mt., U.S.	115	45°54'N	108°01'W
Huntsville, Can.	91	45°20'N	79°15'W
Huntsville, Al., U.S. (hŭnts'vĭl)	124	34°44'N	86°36'W
Huntsville, Mo., U.S.	121	39°24'N	92°32'W
Huntsville, Tx., U.S.	123	30°44'N	95°34'W
Huntsville, Ut., U.S.	117b	41°16'N	111°46'W
Huolu, China (hwò lōō)	206	38°05'N	114°20'E
Huon Gulf, b., Pap. N. Gui.	213	7°15'S	147°45'E
Huoqiu, China (hwò-chyò)	206	32°19'N	116°17'E
Huoshan, China (hwò-shän)	209	31°30'N	116°25'E
Ḩuraydin, Wādī, r., Egypt	197a	30°55'N	34°12'E
Hurd, Cape, c., Can. (hûrd)	98	45°15'N	81°45'W
Hurdiyo, Som.	238a	10°43'N	51°05'E
Hurley, Wi., U.S. (hûr'lĭ)	113	46°26'N	90°11'W
Hurlingham, Arg. (ōō'r-lēn-gäm)	144a	34°36'S	58°38'W
Huron, Oh., U.S. (hū'rŏn)	108	41°20'N	82°35'W
Huron, S.D., U.S.	104	44°22'N	98°15'W
Huron, r., Mi., U.S.	111b	42°12'N	83°26'W
Huron, Lake, l., N.A. (hū'rŏn)	107	45°15'N	82°40'W
Huron Mountains, mts., Mi., U.S. (hū'rŏn)	113	46°47'N	87°52'W
Hurricane, Ak., U.S. (hûr'ĭ-kān)	103	63°00'N	149°30'W
Hurricane, Ut., U.S.	119	37°10'N	113°20'W
Hurricane Flats, bk. (hŭ-rĭ-kȧn flăts)	134	23°35'N	78°30'W
Hurst, Tx., U.S.	117c	32°48'N	97°12'W
Húsavik, Ice.	160	66°00'N	17°10'W
Huşi, Rom. (kòsh')	177	46°52'N	28°04'E
Huskvarna, Swe. (hòsk-vär'nȧ)	166	57°48'N	14°16'E
Husum, Ger. (hōō'zòm)	168	54°29'N	9°04'E
Hutchins, Tx., U.S. (hŭch'ĭnz)	117c	32°38'N	96°43'W
Hutchinson, Ks., U.S. (hŭch'ĭn-sŭn)	104	38°02'N	97°56'W
Hutchinson, Mn., U.S.	113	44°53'N	94°23'W
Hutuo, r., China	208	38°10'N	114°00'E
Huy, Bel. (û-ē') (hû'ē)	165	50°33'N	5°14'E
Hvannadalshnúkur, mtn., Ice.	160	64°09'N	16°46'W

PLACE (Pronunciation)	PAGE	LAT.	LONG.
Hvar, i., Serb. (khvär)	174	43°08'N	16°28'E
Hwange, Zimb.	232	18°22'S	26°29'E
Hwangju, Kor., N. (hwäng'jōō')	210	38°39'N	125°49'E
Hyargas Nuur, l., Mong.	204	48°00'N	92°32'E
Hyattsville, Md., U.S. (hī'ăt's-vĭl)	110e	38°57'N	76°58'W
Hyco Lake, res., N.C., U.S. (rōks' bŭr-ō)	125	36°22'N	78°58'W
Hydaburg, Ak., U.S. (hī-dă'bûrg)	103	55°12'N	132°49'W
Hyde, Eng., U.K. (hīd)	158a	53°27'N	2°05'W
Hyderābād, India (hī-dẽr-ȧ-băd')	199	17°29'N	78°28'E
Hyderabad, India	199	18°30'N	76°50'E
Hyderābād, Pak.	199	25°29'N	68°28'E
Hyéres, Fr. (ē-âr')	161	43°09'N	6°08'E
Hyéres, Îles d', is., Fr. (ēl'dyâr')	161	42°57'N	6°17'E
Hyesanjin, Kor., N. (hyĕ'sän-jĭn')	210	41°11'N	128°12'E
Hymera, In., U.S. (hī-mē'rȧ)	108	39°10'N	87°20'W
Hyndman Peak, mtn., Id., U.S. (hīnd'măn)	106	43°38'N	114°04'W
Hyōgo, dept., Japan (hĭyō'gō)	211b	34°54'N	135°15'E

I

PLACE (Pronunciation)	PAGE	LAT.	LONG.
Ia, r., Japan (ē'ä)	211b	34°54'N	135°34'E
Iahotyn, Ukr.	177	50°18'N	31°46'E
Ialomiţa, r., Rom.	175	44°37'N	26°42'E
Iaşi, Rom. (yä'shē)	154	47°10'N	27°40'E
Iasinia, Ukr.	169	48°17'N	24°21'E
Iavoriv, Ukr.	169	49°56'N	23°24'E
Iba, Phil. (ē'bä)	213a	15°20'N	119°59'E
Ibadan, Nig. (ē-bä'dän)	230	7°17'N	3°30'E
Ibagué, Col.	142	4°27'N	75°14'W
Ibar, r., Serb. (ē'bär)	175	43°22'N	20°35'E
Ibaraki, Japan (ē-bä'rä-gē)	211b	34°49'N	135°35'E
Ibarra, Ec. (ē-bär'rä)	142	0°19'N	78°08'W
Ibb, Yemen	201	14°01'N	44°10'E
Iberville, Can. (ē-bâr-vēl')(ī'bẽr-vĭl)	99	45°14'N	73°01'W
Ibi, Nig. (ē'bē)	230	8°12'N	9°45'E
Ibiapaba, Serra da, mts., Braz. (sĕ'r-rä-dä-ē-byä-pá'bä)	143	3°30'S	40°55'W
Ibiza *see* Eivissa, i., Spain	156	38°55'N	1°24'E
Ibo, Moz. (ē'bō)	233	12°20'S	40°35'E
Ibrâhīm, Būr, b., Egypt	238d	29°57'N	32°33'E
Ibrahim, Jabal, mtn., Sau. Ar.	198	20°31'N	41°17'E
Ibwe Munyama, Zam.	237	16°09'S	28°34'E
Ica, Peru (ē'kȧ)	142	14°09'S	75°42'W
Icá (Putumayo), r., S.A.	142	3°00'S	69°00'W
Içana, Braz. (ē-sä'nä)	142	0°15'N	67°19'W
Ice Harbor Dam, Wa., U.S.	114	46°15'N	118°54'W
Içel, Tur.	198	37°00'N	34°40'E
Iceland, nation, Eur. (īs'lănd)	154	65°12'N	19°45'W
Ichibusayama, mtn., Japan (ē'chē-bōō'sȧ-yä'mä)	211	32°19'N	131°08'E
Ichihara, Japan	211a	35°31'N	140°05'E
Ichikawa, Japan (ē'chē-kä'wä)	211a	35°44'N	139°54'E
Ichinomiya, Japan (ē'chē-nō-mē'yȧ)	211	35°19'N	136°49'E
Ichinomoto, Japan (ē-chē'nō-mō-tō)	211b	34°37'N	135°50'E
Ichnia, Ukr.	181	50°47'N	32°23'E
Icy Cape, c., Ak., U.S. (ī'sĭ)	103	70°20'N	161°40'W
Idabel, Ok., U.S. (ī'dȧ-bĕl)	121	33°52'N	94°47'W
Idagrove, Ia., U.S. (ī'dȧ-grōv)	112	42°22'N	95°29'W
Idah, Nig. (ē'dä)	230	7°07'N	6°43'E
Idaho, state, U.S. (ī'dȧ-hō)	104	44°00'N	115°10'W
Idaho Falls, Id., U.S.	104	43°30'N	112°01'W
Idaho Springs, Co., U.S.	120	39°43'N	105°32'W
Idanha-a-Nova, Port. (ē-dän'yȧ-ä-nō'vȧ)	172	39°58'N	7°13'W
Ider, r., Mong.	204	48°58'N	98°38'E
Idi, Indon. (ē'dē)	212	4°58'N	97°47'E
Idkū Lake, l., Egypt	238b	31°13'N	30°22'E
Idle, r., Eng., U.K. (īd''l)	158a	53°22'N	0°56'W
Idlib, Syria	200	35°55'N	36°38'E
Idriaj, Slvn. (ē'drē-ä)	174	46°01'N	14°01'E
Idutywa, S. Afr. (ē-dò-tī'wȧ)	233c	32°06'S	28°18'E
Ienakiieve, Ukr.	177	48°14'N	38°12'E
Ieper, Bel.	165	50°50'N	2°53'E
Ierápetra, Grc.	174a	35°01'N	25°48'E
Iesi, Italy (yä'sē)	174	43°37'N	13°20'E
Ievpatoriia, Ukr.	181	45°13'N	33°22'E
Ife, Nig.	230	7°30'N	4°30'E
Iferouâne, Niger (ēf'rōō-än')	230	19°04'N	8°24'E
Ifôghas, Adrar des, plat., Afr.	230	19°55'N	2°00'E
Igalula, Tan.	237	5°14'S	33°00'E
Igarka, Russia (ē-gär'kȧ)	178	67°22'N	86°16'E
Iglesias, Italy (ē-lĕ'syōs)	162	39°20'N	8°34'E
Igli, Alg. (ē-glē')	230	30°32'N	2°15'W
Igluligaarjuk (Chesterfield Inlet), Can.	91	63°19'N	91°11'W
Iglulik, Can.	91	69°33'N	81°18'W
Ignacio, Ca., U.S. (ĭg-nä'cĭ-ō)	116b	38°05'N	122°32'W
Iguaçu, r., Braz. (ē-gwä-sōō')	144b	22°42'S	43°19'W
Iguala, Mex. (ē-gwä'lä)	130	18°18'N	99°34'W
Igualada, Spain (ē-gwä-lä'dä)	173	41°35'N	1°38'E
Iguassu, r., S.A. (ē-gwä-sōō')	144	25°45'S	52°30'W
Iguassu Falls, wtfl., S.A.	143	25°40'S	54°16'W
Iguatama, Braz. (ē-gwä-tá'mä)	141a	20°13'S	45°40'W
Iguatu, Braz. (ē-gwä-tōō')	143	6°22'S	39°17'W
Iguidi, Erg, Afr.	230	26°22'N	6°53'W
Iguig, Phil. (ē-gēg')	213a	17°46'N	121°44'E
Iharana, Madag.	233	13°35'S	50°05'E
Ihiala, Nig.	235	5°51'N	6°51'E
Iida, Japan (ē'ē-dȧ)	211	35°39'N	137°53'E

ng-sing; ŋ-baŋk; ɴ-nasalized n; nŏd; cŏmmit; ōld; ôbey; ôrder; oi-boil; fōōd; ò-as oo in foot; ou-out; s-soft; sh-dish; th-thin; pūre; ůnite; ûrn; stŭd; circŭs; ü-as in French tu; '-indeterminate vowel.

304 Iijoki – Isla-Cristina PRONOUNCING INDEX

PLACE (Pronunciation)	PAGE	LAT.	LONG.
Iijoki, r., Fin. (ē'yō'kĭ)	180	65°28'N	27°00'E
Iizuka, Japan (ē'ė-zȯ-kȧ)	211	33°39'N	130°39'E
Ijebu-Ode, Nig. (ė-jĕ'bōō ōdå)	230	6°50'N	3°56'E
IJmuiden, Neth.	159a	52°27'N	4°36'E
IJsselmeer, l., Neth. (ī'sĕl-mār)	165	52°46'N	5°14'E
Ikaalinen, Fin. (ē'kä-lĭ-nĕn)	167	61°47'N	22°55'E
Ikaría, i., Grc. (ē-kä'ryȧ)	175	37°43'N	26°07'E
Ikeda, Japan (ē'kå-dä)	211b	34°49'N	135°26'E
Ikerre, Nig.	235	7°31'N	5°14'E
Ikhtiman, Blg. (ėk'tė-män)	175	42°26'N	23°49'E
Iki, i., Japan (ē'kė)	210	33°46'N	129°44'E
Ikoma, Japan	211b	34°41'N	135°43'E
Ikoma, Tan. (ė-kō'mä)	232	2°08'S	34°47'E
Iksha, Russia (ĭk'shȧ)	186b	56°10'N	37°30'E
Ila, Nig.	235	8°01'N	4°55'E
Ilagan, Phil.	213a	17°09'N	121°52'E
Ilan, Tai. (ē'län')	209	24°50'N	121°42'E
Iława, Pol. (ė-lä'vȧ)	169	53°35'N	19°36'E
Île-á-la-Crosse, Can.	96	55°34'N	108°00'W
Ilebo, D.R.C.	232	4°19'S	20°35'E
Ilek, Russia (ē'lyĕk)	181	51°30'N	53°10'E
Île-Perrot, Can. (yl-pĕ-rōt')	102a	45°21'N	73°54'W
Ilesha, Nig.	230	7°38'N	4°45'E
Ilford, Eng., U.K. (ĭl'fẽrd)	158b	51°33'N	0°06'E
Ilfracombe, Eng., U.K. (ĭl-frȧ-kōōm')	164	51°13'N	4°08'W
Ilhabela, Braz. (ē'lä-bĕ'lä)	141a	23°47'S	45°21'W
Ilha Grande, Baía de, b., Braz. (ēl'yȧ grän'dĕ)	141a	23°17'S	44°25'W
Ílhavo, Port. (ēl'yȧ-vȯ)	162	40°36'N	8°41'W
Ilhéus, Braz. (ē-lĕ'ōōs)	143	14°52'S	39°00'W
Ili, r., Asia	184	44°30'N	76°45'E
Iliamna, Ak., U.S. (ē-lė-ăm'nȧ)	103	59°45'N	155°05'W
Iliamna, Ak., U.S.	103	60°18'N	153°25'W
Iliamna, l., Ak., U.S.	103	59°25'N	155°30'W
Ilim, r., Russia (ė-lyėm')	184	57°28'N	103°00'E
Ilimsk, Russia (ė-lyêmsk')	179	56°47'N	103°43'E
Ilin Island, i., Phil. (ė-lyēn')	213a	12°16'N	120°57'E
Ilion, N.Y., U.S. (ĭl'ĭ-ŭn)	109	43°00'N	75°05'W
Ilkeston, Eng., U.K. (ĭl'kĕs-tŭn)	158a	52°58'N	1°19'W
Illampu, Nevado, mtn., Bol. (nĕ-vȧ'dȯ-ėl-yäm-pōō')	142	15°50'S	68°15'W
Illapel, Chile (ē-zhä-pĕ'l)	144	31°37'S	71°10'W
Iller, r., Ger. (ĭlẽr)	168	47°52'N	10°06'E
Illimani, Nevado, mtn., Bol. (nĕ-vȧ'dȯ-ēl-yė-mä'nė)	142	16°50'S	67°38'W
Illinois, state, U.S. (ĭl-ĭ-noi') (ĭl-ĭ-noiz')	105	40°25'N	90°40'W
Illinois, r., Il., U.S.	107	39°00'N	90°30'W
Illintsi, Ukr.	177	49°07'N	29°13'E
Illizi, Alg.	230	26°35'N	8°24'E
Il'men, l., Russia (ô'zĕ-rȯ el''men'') (ĭl'mĕn)	180	58°18'N	32°00'E
Ilo, Peru	142	17°46'S	71°13'W
Ilobasco, El Sal. (ė-lȯ-bäs'kȯ)	132	13°57'N	88°46'W
Iloilo, Phil. (ē-lȯ-ē'lō)	212	10°49'N	122°33'E
Ilopango, Lago, l., El Sal. (ē-lȯ-päŋ'gō)	132	13°48'N	88°50'W
Ilorin, Nig. (ē-lȯ-rēn')	230	8°30'N	4°32'E
Ilūkste, Lat.	167	55°59'N	26°20'E
Ilwaco, Wa., U.S. (ĭl-wā'kȯ)	116c	46°19'N	124°02'W
Ilych, r., Russia (ė'l'ĭch)	180	62°30'N	57°30'E
Imabari, Japan (ē'mä-bä'rė)	210	34°05'N	132°58'E
Imai, Japan (ė-mī')	211b	34°30'N	135°47'E
Iman, r., Russia (ė-män')	210	45°40'N	134°31'E
Imandra, l., Russia (ē-män'drȧ)	180	67°40'N	32°30'E
Imbābah, Egypt (ēm-bä'bȧ)	238b	30°06'N	31°09'E
Imeni Morozova, Russia (ĭm-yĕ'nyĭ mô rô'zô vȧ)	186c	59°58'N	31°02'E
Imeni Moskvy, Kanal (Moscow Canal), can., Russia (kȧ-näl'ĭm-yă'nĭ mŏs-kvĭ)	176	56°33'N	37°15'E
Imeni Tsyurupy, Russia	186b	55°30'N	38°39'E
Imeni Vorovskogo, Russia	186b	55°43'N	38°21'E
Imlay City, Mi., U.S. (ĭm'lā)	108	43°00'N	83°15'W
Immenstadt, Ger. (ĭm'ĕn-shtät)	168	47°34'N	10°12'E
Immerpan, S. Afr. (ĭmĕr-pän)	238c	24°29'S	29°14'E
Imola, Italy (ē'mȯ-lä)	174	44°19'N	11°43'E
Imotski, Cro. (ė-môts'kė)	175	43°25'N	17°15'E
Impameri, Braz.	143	17°44'S	48°03'W
Impendle, S. Afr. (ĭm-pĕnd'lå)	233c	29°38'S	29°54'E
Imperia, Italy (ėm-pā'rė-ä)	162	43°52'N	8°00'E
Imperial, Pa., U.S. (ĭm-pē'rĭ-ăl)	111e	40°27'N	80°15'W
Imperial Beach, Ca., U.S.	118a	32°34'N	117°08'W
Imperial Valley, Ca., U.S.	118	33°00'N	115°22'W
Impfondo, Congo (ĭmp-fōn'dȯ)	231	1°37'N	18°04'E
Imphāl, India (ĭmp'hŭl)	199	24°42'N	94°00'E
Ina, r., Japan (ė-nä')	211b	34°56'N	135°21'E
Inaja Indian Reservation, I.R., Ca., U.S. (ė-nä'hä)	118	32°56'N	116°37'W
Inari, l., Fin.	160	69°02'N	26°22'E
Inca, Spain (ėŋ'kä)	173	39°43'N	2°53'E
Ince Burun, c., Tur. (ĭn'jå)	163	42°00'N	35°00'E
Inch'ŏn, Kor., S. (ĭn'chŭn)	205	37°26'N	126°46'E
Incudine, Monte, mtn., Fr. (ēn-kōō-dē'nå) (ăɴ-kü-dēn')	174	41°53'N	9°17'E
Indalsälven, r., Swe.	160	62°50'N	16°50'E
Independence, Ks., U.S. (ĭn-dė-pĕn'dĕns)	121	37°14'N	95°42'W
Independence, Mo., U.S.	117f	39°06'N	94°26'W
Independence, Oh., U.S.	111d	41°23'N	81°39'W
Independence, Or., U.S.	114	44°49'N	123°13'W
Independence Mountains, mts., Nv., U.S.	114	41°15'N	116°02'W
Īnder köli, l., Kaz.	181	48°20'N	52°10'E
India, nation, Asia (ĭn'dĭ-ȧ)	199	23°00'N	77°30'E
Indian, l., Mi., U.S. (ĭn'dĭ-ăn)	113	46°04'N	86°34'W
Indian, r., N.Y., U.S.	109	44°05'N	75°45'W
Indiana, Pa., U.S. (ĭn-dĭ-än'ȧ)	109	40°40'N	79°10'W
Indiana, state, U.S.	105	39°50'N	86°45'W
Indianapolis, In., U.S. (ĭn-dĭ-ăn-ăp'ȯ-lĭs)	105	39°45'N	86°08'W
Indian Arm, b., Can. (ĭn'dĭ-ăn ärm)	116d	49°21'N	122°55'W
Indian Head, Can.	90	50°29'N	103°44'W
Indian Lake, l., Can.	98	47°00'N	82°00'W
Indian Ocean, o.	5	10°00'S	70°00'E
Indianola, Ia., U.S. (ĭn-dĭ-ăn-ō'lȧ)	113	41°22'N	93°33'W
Indianola, Ms., U.S.	124	33°29'N	90°35'W
Indigirka, r., Russia (ėn-dė-gēr'kȧ)	185	67°45'N	145°45'E
Indio, r., Pan. (ē'n-dyô)	128a	9°13'N	79°28'W
Indochina, reg., Asia (ĭn-dȯ-chī'nȧ)	212	17°22'N	105°18'E
Indonesia, nation, Asia (ĭn'dȯ-nė-zhȧ)	212	4°38'S	118°45'E
Indore, India (ĭn-dōr')	199	22°48'N	76°51'E
Indragiri, r., Indon. (ĭn-drȧ-jē'rė)	212	0°27'S	102°05'E
Indrāvati, r., India (ĭn-drŭ-vä'tė)	199	19°00'N	82°00'E
Indre, r., Fr. (ăɴ'dr')	170	47°13'N	0°29'E
Indus, Can. (ĭn'dŭs)	102e	50°55'N	113°45'W
Indus, r., Asia	199	26°43'N	67°41'E
Indwe, S. Afr. (ĭnd'wå)	233c	31°30'S	27°21'E
Inebolu, Tur. (ė-nå-bō'lōō)	163	41°50'N	33°40'E
Inego, Tur. (ė'nå-gŭ)	181	40°05'N	29°20'E
Infanta, Phil. (ėn-fän'tä)	213a	14°44'N	121°39'E
Infanta, Phil.	213a	15°50'N	119°53'E
Inferror, Laguna, l., Mex. (lä-gȯ'nä-ėn-fĕr-rôr)	131	16°18'N	94°40'W
Infiernillo, Presa de, res., Mex.	130	18°50'N	101°50'W
Infiesto, Spain (ēn-fyĕ's-tȯ)	172	43°21'N	5°24'W
I-n-Gall, Niger	235	16°47'N	6°56'E
Ingersoll, Can. (ĭn'gẽr-sŏl)	98	43°05'N	81°00'W
Ingham, Austl. (ĭng'ăm)	219	18°45'S	146°14'E
Ingles, Cayos, is., Cuba (kä-yōs-ė'n-glĕ's)	134	21°55'N	82°35'W
Inglewood, Can.	102d	43°48'N	79°56'W
Inglewood, Ca., U.S. (ĭn'g'l-wȯd)	117a	33°57'N	118°22'W
Ingoda, r., Russia (ėn-gō'dȧ)	185	51°29'N	112°32'E
Ingolstadt, Ger. (ĭŋ'gȯl-shtät)	168	48°46'N	11°27'E
Ingur, r., Geor. (ėn-gȯr')	181	42°30'N	42°00'E
Ingushetia, prov., Russia	182	43°15'N	45°00'E
Inhambane, Moz. (ėn-äm-bä'-nĕ)	232	23°47'S	35°28'E
Inhambupe, Braz. (ėn-yäm-bōō'pä)	143	11°47'S	38°13'W
Inharrime, Moz. (ėn-yär-rē'mä)	232	24°17'S	35°07'E
Inhomirim, Braz. (ē-nô-mė-rē'ɴ)	144b	22°34'S	43°11'W
Inhul, r., Ukr.	177	47°22'N	32°52'E
Inhulets', r., Ukr.	177	47°12'N	33°12'E
Inírida, r., Col. (ē-nė-rē'dä)	142	2°25'N	70°38'W
Injune, Austl. (ĭn'jȯn)	222	25°52'S	148°30'E
Inkeroinem, Fin. (ĭn'kĕr-oi-nĕn)	167	60°42'N	26°50'E
Inkster, Mi., U.S. (ĭngk'stẽr)	111b	42°18'N	83°19'W
Inn, r., Eur. (ĭn)	161	48°00'N	12°00'E
Innamincka, Austl. (ĭnn-ă'mĭn-kă)	222	27°50'S	140°48'E
Inner Brass, i., V.I.U.S. (bräs)	129c	18°23'N	64°58'W
Inner Hebrides, is., Scot., U.K.	164	57°20'N	6°20'W
Inner Mongolia *see* Nei Monggol, prov., China	204	40°15'N	105°00'E
Innisfail, Can.	90	52°02'N	113°57'W
Innsbruck, Aus. (ĭns'brȯk)	161	47°15'N	11°25'E
Ino, Japan (ē'nȯ)	211	33°34'N	133°23'E
Inongo, D.R.C. (ė-nôŋ'gō)	232	1°57'S	18°16'E
Inowrocław, Pol. (ē-nô-vrŏts'läf)	169	52°48'N	18°16'E
In Salah, Alg.	230	27°13'N	2°22'E
Inscription House Ruin, Az., U.S. (ĭn'skrĭp-shŭn hous rōō'ĭn)	119	36°45'N	110°47'W
International Falls, Mn., U.S. (ĭn'tẽr-năsh'ŭn-ăl fôlz)	105	48°34'N	93°26'W
Inuvik, Can.	90	68°40'N	134°10'W
Inuyama, Japan (ē'nōō-yä'mä)	211	35°24'N	137°01'E
Invercargil, N.Z. (ĭn-vẽr-kär'gĭl)	223	46°25'S	168°27'E
Inverel, Austl. (ĭn-vẽr-el')	219	29°50'S	151°32'E
Invergrove Heights, Mn., U.S. (ĭn'vẽr-grōv)	117g	44°51'N	93°01'W
Inverness, Can. (ĭn-vẽr-nĕs')	101	46°14'N	61°18'W
Inverness, Scot., U.K.	160	57°30'N	4°07'W
Inverness, Fl., U.S.	125	28°48'N	82°22'W
Investigator Strait, strt., Austl. (ĭn-vĕst'ĭ'gā-tôr)	222	35°33'S	137°00'E
Inyangani, mtn., Zimb. (ėn-yän-gä'nė)	232	18°06'S	32°37'E
Inyokern, Ca., U.S.	118	35°39'N	117°51'W
Inyo Mountains, mts., Ca., U.S. (ĭn'yō)	106	36°55'N	118°04'W
Inzer, r., Russia (ĭn'zĕr)	186a	54°24'N	57°17'E
Inzia, r., D.R.C.	236	5°55'S	17°50'E
Ioánnina, Grc. (yȯ-ä'nė-nȧ)	163	39°39'N	20°52'E
Ioco, Can.	116d	49°18'N	122°53'W
Iola, Ks., U.S. (ī-ō'lȧ)	121	37°55'N	95°23'W
Iôna, Parque Nacional do, rec., Ang.	236	16°35'S	12°00'E
Ionia, Mi., U.S. (ī-ō'nĭ-ȧ)	108	43°00'N	85°10'W
Ionian Islands, is., Grc. (ī-ō'nĭ-ăn)	163	39°10'N	20°05'E
Ionian Sea, sea, Eur.	156	38°59'N	18°48'E
Iori, r., Asia	182	41°03'N	46°17'E
Íos, i., Grc. (ī'ŏs)	175	36°48'N	25°25'E
Iowa, state, U.S. (ī'ȯ-wȧ)	105	42°05'N	94°20'W
Iowa, r., Ia., U.S.	113	41°55'N	92°20'W
Iowa City, Ia., U.S.	105	41°39'N	91°31'W
Iowa Falls, Ia., U.S.	113	42°32'N	93°16'W
Iowa Park, Tx., U.S.	120	33°57'N	98°39'W
Ipala, Tan.	237	4°30'S	32°53'E
Ípeirus, hist. reg., Grc.	175	39°35'N	20°45'E
Ipel', r., Eur. (ė'pĕl)	169	48°08'N	19°00'E
Ipiales, Col. (ē-pė-ä'lås)	142	0°48'N	77°45'W
Ipoh, Malay.	212	4°45'N	101°05'E
Ipswich, Austl. (ĭps'wĭch)	219	27°40'S	152°50'E
Ipswich, Eng., U.K.	161	52°05'N	1°05'E
Ipswich, Ma., U.S.	101a	42°41'N	70°50'W
Ipswich, S.D., U.S.	112	45°26'N	99°01'W
Ipu, Braz. (ē-pōō)	143	4°11'S	40°45'W
Iput', r., Eur. (ė-pȯt')	181	52°53'N	31°57'E
Iqaluit, Can.	91	63°48'N	68°31'W
Iquique, Chile (ē-kė'kĕ)	142	20°16'S	70°07'W
Iquitos, Peru (ė-kē'tōs)	142	3°39'S	73°18'W
Irákleio, Grc.	154	35°20'N	25°10'E
Iran, nation, Asia (ē-rän')	198	31°15'N	53°30'E
Iran, Plateau of, plat., Iran	198	32°28'N	58°00'E
Iran Mountains, mts., Asia	212	2°30'N	114°30'E
Irapuato, Mex. (ē-rä-pwä'tō)	130	20°41'N	101°24'W
Iraq, nation, Asia (ē-räk')	198	32°00'N	42°30'E
Irazú, vol., C.R. (ē-rä-zōō')	133	9°58'N	83°54'W
Irbid, Jord. (ėr-bēd')	200	32°33'N	35°51'E
Irbit, Russia (ėr-bėt')	178	57°40'N	63°10'E
Irébou, D.R.C. (ē-rā'bōō)	232	0°40'S	17°48'E
Ireland, nation, Eur. (īr-lănd)	154	53°33'N	8°00'W
Iremel', Gora, mtn., Russia (gȧ-rä'ĭ-rĕ'mĕl)	186a	54°32'N	58°52'E
Irene, S. Afr. (ĭ-rē-nē)	233b	25°53'S	28°13'E
Irîgui, reg., Mali	234	16°45'N	5°35'W
Iriklinskoye Vodokhranilishche, res., Russia	181	52°20'N	58°50'E
Iringa, Tan. (ė-rĭŋ'gä)	232	7°46'S	35°42'E
Iriomote Jima, i., Japan (ērē'-ō-mō-tā)	205	24°20'N	123°30'E
Iriona, Hond. (ė-rė-ō'nä)	132	15°53'N	85°12'W
Irish Sea, sea, Eur. (ī'rĭsh)	156	53°55'N	5°25'W
Irkutsk, Russia (ĭr-kȯtsk')	179	52°16'N	104°00'E
Irlam, Eng., U.K. (ûr'lăm)	158a	53°26'N	2°26'W
Irois, Cap des, c., Haiti	135	18°25'N	74°50'W
Iron Bottom Sound, strt., Sol. Is.	214e	9°15'S	160°00'E
Irondale, Al., U.S. (ī'ẽrn-dăl)	110h	33°32'N	86°43'W
Iron Gate, val., Eur.	175	44°43'N	22°32'E
Iron Knob, Austl. (ĭ-ăn nŏb)	222	32°47'S	137°10'E
Iron Mountain, Mi., U.S. (ī'ẽrn)	113	45°49'N	88°04'W
Iron River, Mi., U.S.	113	46°09'N	88°39'W
Ironton, Oh., U.S. (ī'ẽrn-tŭn)	108	38°30'N	82°45'W
Ironwood, Mi., U.S. (ī'ẽrn-wȯd)	113	46°28'N	90°10'W
Ironwood Forest National Monument, rec., Az., U.S.	119	32°30'N	111°25'W
Iroquois, r., Il., U.S. (ĭr'ȯ-kwoi)	108	40°55'N	87°20'W
Iroquois Falls, Can.	91	48°41'N	80°39'W
Irō-Saki, c., Japan (ē'rō sä'kē)	210	34°35'N	138°54'E
Irpin, r., Ukr.	177	50°13'N	29°55'E
Irrawaddy, r., Mya. (ĭr-ȧ-wäd'ė)	199	23°27'N	96°25'E
Irtysh, r., Asia (ĭr-tĭsh')	178	59°00'N	69°00'E
Irumu, D.R.C. (ė-rȯ'mōō)	231	1°30'N	29°52'E
Irun, Spain (ė-rōōn')	172	43°20'N	1°47'W
Irvine, Scot., U.K.	164	55°39'N	4°40'W
Irvine, Ca., U.S. (ûr'vĭn)	117a	33°40'N	117°45'W
Irvine, Ky., U.S.	108	37°40'N	84°00'W
Irving, Tx., U.S. (ûr'vēng)	117c	32°49'N	96°57'W
Irvington, N.J., U.S. (ûr'vēng-tŭn)	110a	40°43'N	74°15'W
Irwin, Pa., U.S. (ûr'wĭn)	111e	40°19'N	79°42'W
Is, Russia (ēs)	186a	58°48'N	59°44'E
Isa, Nig.	235	13°14'N	6°24'E
Isaacs, Mount, mtn., Pan. (ē-sä-ȧ'ks)	128a	9°22'N	79°31'W
Isabela, i., Ec. (ē-sä-bā'lä)	142	0°47'S	91°35'W
Isabela, Cabo, c., Dom. Rep. (kȧ'bȯ-ė-sä-bĕ'lä)	135	20°00'N	71°00'W
Isabella, Cordillera, mts., Nic. (kȯr-dēl-yĕ'rä-ē-sä-bĕlä)	132	13°20'N	85°37'W
Isabella Indian Reservation, I.R., Mi., U.S. (ĭs-ȧ-bĕl'-lå)	108	43°35'N	84°55'W
Isaccea, Rom. (ė-säk'chä)	177	45°16'N	28°26'E
Ísafjördur, Ice. (ēs'ȧ-fŷr-dȯr)	160	66°09'N	22°39'W
Isangi, D.R.C. (ė-säŋ'gē)	204	0°46'N	24°15'E
Isar, r., Ger. (ē'zär)	161	48°30'N	12°30'E
Isarco, r., Italy (ė-sär'kō)	174	46°37'N	11°25'E
Isarog, Mount, mtn., Phil. (ė-sä-rȯ-g)	213a	13°40'N	123°23'E
Ischia, Italy (ēs'kyä)	173c	40°29'N	13°58'E
Ischia, Isola d', i., Italy (dė'sh-kyä)	162	40°26'N	13°55'E
Ise, Japan (ĭs'hĕ) (û'gē-yă'mă'dȧ)	210	34°30'N	136°43'E
Iseo, Lago d', l., Italy (lä-'gō-dē-ė-zĕ'ō)	174	45°50'N	9°55'E
Isére, r., Fr. (ė-zâr')	161	45°15'N	5°15'E
Iserlohn, Ger. (ē'zĕr-lōn)	171c	51°22'N	7°42'E
Isernia, Italy (ė-zĕr'nyä)	174	41°35'N	14°14'E
Ise-Wan, b., Japan (ē'sĕ wän)	210	34°49'N	136°44'E
Iseyin, Nig.	230	7°58'N	3°36'E
Ishigaki, Japan	214d	24°20'N	124°09'E
Ishikari Wan, b., Japan (ē'shē-kä-rē wän)	210	43°30'N	141°05'E
Ishim, Russia (ĭsh-ėm')	178	56°07'N	69°13'E
Ishim, r., Asia	178	53°17'N	67°45'E
Ishimbay, Russia (ē-shēm-bī')	186a	53°28'N	56°02'E
Ishinomaki, Japan (ĭsh-nō-mä'kē)	205	38°22'N	141°22'E
Ishinomaki Wan, b., Japan (ē-shē-nō-mä'kē wän)	210	38°10'N	141°40'E
Ishly, Russia (ĭsh'lĭ)	186a	54°13'N	55°55'E
Ishlya, Russia (ĭsh'lyȧ)	186a	53°54'N	57°48'E
Ishmant, Egypt	238b	29°17'N	31°15'E
Ishpeming, Mi., U.S. (ĭsh'pė-mĭng)	113	46°28'N	87°42'W
Isipingo, S. Afr. (ĭs-ĭ-pĭŋ-gȯ)	233c	29°59'S	30°58'E
Isiro, D.R.C.	231	2°47'N	27°37'E
İskenderun, Tur. (ĭs-kĕn'dĕr-ōōn)	198	36°45'N	36°15'E
İskenderun Körfezi, b., Tur.	163	36°22'N	35°25'E
İskilip, Tur. (ĭs'kĭ-lēp')	163	40°40'N	34°30'E
Iskūr, r., Blg. (ĭs'k'r)	175	43°05'N	23°37'E
Isla-Cristina, Spain (ĭ'lä-krē-stē'nä)	172	37°13'N	7°20'W

ăt; finăl; rāte; senåte; ärm; åsk; sofȧ; fâre; ch-choose; dh-as th in other; bē; ėvent; bĕt; recĕnt; cratẽr; g-gō; gh-guttural g; bĭt; ĭ-short neutral; rīde; ᴋ-guttural k as ch in German ich;

PLACE (Pronunciation)	PAGE	LAT.	LONG.
Islāmābād, Pak.	199	33°55'N	73°05'E
Isla Mujeres, Mex. (ē's-lä-mōō-kĕ'rĕs)	132a	21°25'N	86°53'W
Island Lake, l., Can.	93	53°47'N	94°25'W
Islands, Bay of, b., Can. (ī'lăndz)	101	49°10'N	58°15'W
Islay, i., Scot., U.K. (ī'lā)	160	55°55'N	6°35'W
Isle, r., Fr. (ēl)	170	45°02'N	0°29'E
Isle of Axholme, reg., Eng., U.K. (ăks'-hōm)	158a	53°33'N	0°48'W
Isle of Man, dep., Eur. (măn)	164	54°26'N	4°21'W
Isle Royale National Park, rec., Mi., U.S. (īl'roi-ăl')	107	47°57'N	88°37'W
Isleta, N.M., U.S. (ēs-lā'tă) (ī-lē'tă)	119	34°55'N	106°45'W
Isleta Indian Reservation, I.R., N.M., U.S.	119	34°55'N	106°45'W
Ismailia, Egypt (ēs-mā-ēl'ēā)	238b	30°35'N	32°17'E
Ismā'īlīyah Canal, can., Egypt	238b	30°25'N	31°45'E
Ismail Samani, pik, mtn., Taj.	183	38°57'N	72°01'E
Ismaning, Ger. (ēz'mä-nēng)	159d	48°14'N	11°41'E
Isparta, Tur. (ē-spär'tá)	198	37°50'N	30°40'E
Israel, nation, Asia	198	32°40'N	34°00'E
Issaquah, Wa., U.S. (ĭz'să-kwăh)	116a	47°32'N	122°02'W
Isselburg, Ger. (ē'sĕl-bōōrg)	171c	51°50'N	6°28'E
Issoire, Fr. (ē-swár')	170	45°32'N	3°13'E
Issoudun, Fr. (ē-sōō-dăN')	170	46°56'N	2°00'E
Issum, Ger. (ē'sōōm)	171c	51°32'N	6°24'E
Issyk-Kul, Ozero, l., Kyrg.	183	42°13'N	76°12'E
İstanbul, Tur. (ē-stän-bōōl')	198	41°02'N	29°00'E
İstanbul Boğazı (Bosporus), strt., Tur.	198	41°10'N	29°10'E
Istiaía, Grc. (ĭs-tyī'yä)	175	38°58'N	23°11'E
Istmina, Col. (ēst-mē'nä)	142a	5°10'N	76°40'W
Istokpoga, Lake, l., Fl., U.S. (īs-tŏk-pō'gá)	125a	27°20'N	81°33'W
Istra, pen., Serb. (ē-strä)	174	45°18'N	13°48'E
Istranca Dağlari, mts., Eur. (ĭ-strän'já)	175	41°50'N	27°25'E
Istres, Fr. (ēs'tr')	170a	43°30'N	5°00'E
Itabaiana, Braz. (ē-tä-bä-yä-nä)	143	10°42'S	37°17'W
Itabapoana, Braz. (ē-tä'-bä-pōä'nä)	141a	21°19'S	40°58'W
Itabapoana, r., Braz.	141a	21°11'S	41°18'W
Itabirito, Braz. (ē-tä-bē-rē'tō)	141a	20°15'S	43°46'W
Itabuna, Braz. (ē-tä-bōō'nà)	143	14°47'S	39°17'W
Itacoara, Braz. (ē-tä-kô'ä-rä)	141a	21°41'S	42°04'W
Itacoatiara, Braz. (ē-tá-kwá-tyä'rá)	143	3°03'S	58°18'W
Itagüí, Col. (ē-tä'gwē)	142a	6°11'N	75°36'W
Itagui, r., Braz.	144b	22°53'S	43°43'W
Itaipava, Braz. (ē-tī-pá'-vä)	144b	22°23'S	43°09'W
Itaipu, Braz. (ē-tī'pōō)	144b	22°58'S	43°02'W
Itaituba, Braz. (ē-tä'ī-tōō'bà)	143	4°12'S	56°00'W
Itajái, Braz. (ē-tä-zhī')	144	26°52'S	48°39'W
Italy, Tx., U.S.	123	32°11'N	96°51'W
Italy, nation, Eur. (ĭt'ă-lē)	154	43°58'N	11°14'E
Itambi, Braz. (ē-tä'm-bē)	144b	22°44'S	42°57'W
Itami, Japan (ē'tä'mē')	211b	34°47'N	135°25'E
Itapecerica, Braz. (ē-tä-pĕ-sĕ-rē'kà)	141a	20°29'S	45°08'W
Itapecuru-Mirim, Braz. (ē-tä-pĕ'kōō-rōō-mē-rēN')	143	3°17'S	44°15'W
Itaperuna, Braz. (ē-tá'pâ-rōō'nä)	143	21°12'S	41°53'W
Itapetininga, Braz. (ē-tä-pĕ-tē-nē'N-gä)	143	23°37'S	48°03'W
Itapira, Braz. (ē-tä-pē'rá)	143	20°42'S	51°19'W
Itapira, Braz.	141a	22°27'S	46°47'W
Itarsi, India	202	22°43'N	77°45'E
Itasca, Tx., U.S. (ī-tăs'kă)	123	32°09'N	97°08'W
Itasca, l., Mn., U.S.	112	47°13'N	95°14'W
Itatiaia, Pico da, mtn., Braz. (pē'-kô-dá-ē-tä-tyá'ēä)	143	22°18'S	44°41'W
Itatiba, Braz. (ē-tä-tē'bä)	141a	23°01'S	46°48'W
Itaúna, Braz. (ē-tä-ōō'nä)	141a	20°05'S	44°35'W
Ithaca, Mi., U.S. (ĭth'ă-kă)	108	43°20'N	84°35'W
Ithaca, N.Y., U.S.	105	42°25'N	76°30'W
Itháka, i., Grc. (ē'thä-kē)	175	38°27'N	20°48'E
Itigi, Tan.	237	5°42'S	34°29'E
Itimbiri, r., D.R.C.	236	2°40'N	23°30'E
Itoko, D.R.C. (ē-tō'kō)	232	1°13'S	22°07'E
Itu, Braz. (ē-tōō')	141a	23°16'S	47°16'W
Ituango, Col. (ē-twän'gō)	142	7°07'N	75°44'W
Ituiutaba, Braz. (ē-tōō-ēōō-tä'bä)	143	18°56'S	49°17'W
Itumirim, Braz. (ē-tōō-mē-rē'N)	141a	21°20'S	44°51'W
Itundujia Santa Cruz, Mex. (ē-tōōn-dōō-hē'ä sä'n-tä krōō'z)	131	16°50'N	97°43'W
Iturbide, Mex. (ē'tōōr-bē'dhā)	132a	19°38'N	89°31'W
Iturup, i., Russia (ē-tōō-rōōp')	185	45°35'N	147°15'E
Ituzaingo, Arg. (ē-tōō-zä-ē'n-gō)	144a	34°40'S	58°40'W
Itzehoe, Ger. (ē'tzĕ-hō)	168	53°55'N	9°31'E
Iuka, Ms., U.S. (ī-ū'kă)	124	34°47'N	88°10'W
Iúna, Braz. (ē-ōō'-nä)	141a	20°22'S	41°32'W
Ivanhoe, Austl. (ĭv'ăn-hō)	222	32°53'S	144°10'E
Ivanivka, Ukr.	176	46°43'N	34°33'E
Ivano-Frankivs'k, Ukr.	181	48°53'N	24°46'E
Ivanopil', Ukr.	177	49°51'N	28°11'E
Ivanovo, Russia (ē-vä'nô-vō)	178	57°02'N	41°54'E
Ivanovo, prov., Russia	176	56°55'N	40°30'E
Ivanteyevka, Russia (ē-ván-tyĕ'yĕf-kà)	186b	55°58'N	37°56'E
Ivdel', Russia (ĭv'dyĕl)	186a	60°42'N	60°27'E
Iviza *see* Eivissa, i., Spain	156	38°55'N	1°24'E
Ivohibé, Madag. (ē-vô-hē-bā')	233	22°28'S	46°59'E
Ivory Coast *see* Cote d'Ivoire, nation, Afr.	230	7°43'N	6°30'W
Ivrea, Italy (ē-vrĕ'ä)	162	45°25'N	7°54'E
Ivry-sur-Seine, Fr.	171b	48°49'N	2°23'E
Ivujivik, Can.	91	62°17'N	77°52'W
Ivvavik National Park, rec., Can.	103	69°10'N	139°30'W
Iwaki, Japan	210	37°03'N	140°57'E
Iwate Yama, mtn., Japan (ē-wä-tē-yä'mä)	210	39°50'N	140°56'E
Iwatsuki, Japan	211a	35°48'N	139°43'E
Iwaya, Japan (ē'wá-yá)	211b	34°35'N	135°01'E
Iwo, Nig.	230	7°38'N	4°11'E
Ixcateopán, Mex. (ēs-kä-tä-ō-pän')	130	18°29'N	99°49'W
Ixelles, Bel.	159a	50°49'N	4°23'E
Ixhautlán, Mex. (ēs-wát-län')	130	20°41'N	98°01'W
Ixhuatán, Mex. (ēs-hwä-tän')	131	16°19'N	94°30'W
Ixmiquilpan, Mex. (ēs-mē-kēl'pän)	130	20°30'N	99°12'W
Ixopo, S. Afr.	233c	30°10'S	30°04'E
Ixtacalco, Mex. (ēs-tá-käl'kō)	131a	19°23'N	99°07'W
Ixtaltepec, Mex. (ēs-täl-tĕ-pĕk')	131	16°33'N	95°04'W
Ixtapalapa, Mex. (ēs'tä-pä-lä'pä)	131a	19°21'N	99°06'W
Ixtapaluca, Mex. (ēs'tä-pä-lōō'kä)	131a	19°18'N	98°53'W
Ixtepec, Mex. (ēks-tĕ'pĕk)	131	16°37'N	95°09'W
Ixtlahuaca, Mex. (ēs-tlä-wä'kä)	130	19°34'N	99°46'W
Ixtlán de Juárez, Mex. (ēs-tlän' dā hwä'rāz)	131	17°20'N	96°29'W
Ixtlán del Río, Mex. (ēs-tlän'dĕl rē'ō)	130	21°05'N	104°22'W
Iya, r., Russia	184	53°45'N	99°30'E
Iyo-Nada, b., Japan (ē'yō nä-dä)	211	33°33'N	132°07'E
Izabal, Guat. (ē'zä-bäl')	132	15°23'N	89°10'W
Izabal, Lago, l., Guat.	132	15°30'N	89°04'W
Izalco, El Sal. (ē-zäl'kō)	132	13°50'N	89°40'W
Izamal, Mex. (ē-zä-mä'l)	132a	20°55'N	89°00'W
Izberbash, Russia	182	42°33'N	47°52'E
Izhevsk, Russia (ē-zhyĕfsk')	178	56°50'N	53°15'E
Izhma, Russia (ĭzh'mà)	180	65°00'N	54°05'E
Izhma, r., Russia	180	64°00'N	53°00'E
Izhora, r., Russia (ēz'hô-rá)	186c	59°36'N	30°20'E
Izmail, Ukr.	181	45°00'N	28°49'E
İzmir, Tur. (ĭz-mēr')	198	38°25'N	27°05'E
İzmit, Tur. (ĭz-mēt')	163	40°45'N	29°45'E
Iznajar, Embalse de, res., Spain	172	37°15'N	4°30'W
Iztaccíhuatl, mtn., Mex.	130	19°10'N	98°38'W
Izuhara, Japan (ē'zōō-hä'rä)	211	34°11'N	129°18'E
Izumi-Ōtsu, Japan (ē'zōō-mōō ō'tsōō)	211b	34°30'N	135°24'E
Izumo, Japan (ē'zōō-mō)	211	35°22'N	132°45'E
Izu Shichitō, is., Japan	205	34°32'N	139°25'E

J

PLACE (Pronunciation)	PAGE	LAT.	LONG.
Jabal, Bahr al, r., Sudan	231	7°30'N	31°00'E
Jabalpur, India	199	23°18'N	79°59'E
Jablonec nad Nisou, Czech Rep. (yäb'lô-nyĕts)	168	50°43'N	15°12'E
Jablunkov Pass, p., Eur. (yäb'lōn-kôf)	169	49°31'N	18°35'E
Jaboatão, Braz. (zhä-bô-ä-touN)	143	8°14'S	35°08'W
Jaca, Spain (hä'kä)	173	42°35'N	0°30'W
Jacala, Mex. (hä-kä'lä)	130	21°01'N	99°11'W
Jacaltenango, Guat. (hä-kál-tĕ-nän'gō)	132	15°39'N	91°41'W
Jacarézinho, Braz. (zhä-kä-rĕ'zē-nyō)	143	23°13'S	49°58'W
Jachymov, Czech Rep. (yä'chĭ-môf)	168	50°22'N	12°51'E
Jacinto City, Tx., U.S. (já-sēn'tō) (já-sĭn'tō)	123a	29°45'N	95°14'W
Jacksboro, Tx., U.S. (jăks'bŭr-ō)	120	33°13'N	98°11'W
Jackson, Al., U.S. (jăk'sŭn)	124	31°31'N	87°52'W
Jackson, Ca., U.S.	118	38°22'N	120°47'W
Jackson, Ga., U.S.	124	33°19'N	83°55'W
Jackson, Ky., U.S.	124	37°32'N	83°17'W
Jackson, La., U.S.	123	30°50'N	91°13'W
Jackson, Mi., U.S.	105	42°15'N	84°25'W
Jackson, Mn., U.S.	112	43°37'N	95°00'W
Jackson, Mo., U.S.	121	37°23'N	89°40'W
Jackson, Ms., U.S.	105	32°17'N	90°10'W
Jackson, Oh., U.S.	108	39°00'N	82°40'W
Jackson, Tn., U.S.	105	35°37'N	88°49'W
Jackson, Port, b., Austl.	217b	33°50'S	151°18'E
Jackson Lake, l., Wy., U.S.	115	43°57'N	110°28'W
Jacksonville, Al., U.S. (jăk'sŭn-vĭl)	124	33°52'N	85°45'W
Jacksonville, Fl., U.S.	105	30°20'N	81°40'W
Jacksonville, Il., U.S.	105	39°43'N	90°12'W
Jacksonville, Tx., U.S.	123	31°58'N	95°18'W
Jacksonville Beach, Fl., U.S.	125	30°18'N	81°25'W
Jacmel, Haiti (zhák-mĕl')	135	18°15'N	72°30'W
Jaco, l., Mex. (hä'kō)	122	27°51'N	103°50'W
Jacobābād, Pak.	202	28°22'N	68°30'E
Jacobina, Braz. (zhä-kō-bē'nă)	143	11°13'S	40°30'W
Jacques-Cartier, r., Can.	102b	47°04'N	71°28'W
Jacques Cartier, Détroit de, strt., Can.	100	50°07'S	63°58'W
Jacques-Cartier, Mont, mtn., Can.	100	48°59'N	66°00'W
Jacquet River, Can. (zhá-kĕ') (jăk'ĕt)	100	47°55'N	66°00'W
Jacutinga, Braz. (zhá-kōō-tēn'gä)	141a	22°17'S	46°36'W
Jadebusen, b., Ger.	168	53°28'N	8°17'E
Jadotville *see* Likasi, D.R.C.	232	10°59'S	26°44'E
Jaén, Peru (ĸä-ĕ'n)	142	5°38'S	78°49'W
Jaen, Spain	162	37°45'N	3°48'W
Jaffa, Cape, c., Austl. (jăf'ă)	220	36°58'S	139°29'E
Jaffna, Sri L. (jäf'nă)	203	9°44'N	80°09'E
Jagüey Grande, Cuba (hä'gwā grän'dā)	134	22°35'N	81°05'W
Jahore Strait, strt., Asia	197b	1°22'N	103°37'E
Jahrom, Iran	198	28°30'N	53°28'E
Jaibo, r., Cuba (hä-ē'bō)	135	20°10'N	75°20'W
Jaipur, India	199	27°00'N	75°50'E
Jaisalmer, India	202	27°00'N	70°54'E
Jajce, Bos. (yī'tsĕ)	175	44°20'N	17°19'E
Jajpur, India	199	20°49'N	86°37'E
Jakarta, Indon. (jä-kär'tä)	212	6°17'S	106°45'E
Jakobstad, Fin. (yá'kôb-stádh)	160	63°33'N	22°31'E
Jalacingo, Mex. (hä-lä-sĭn'gō)	131	19°47'N	97°16'W
Jalālābād, Afg. (jŭ-lä-lá-bäd)	199a	34°25'N	70°27'E
Jalālah al Baḩrīyah, Jabal, mts., Egypt	238b	29°20'N	32°00'E
Jalapa, Guat. (hä-lä'pá)	132	14°38'N	89°58'W
Jalapa de Díaz, Mex.	131	18°06'N	96°33'W
Jalapa del Marqués, Mex. (dĕl mär-kās')	131	16°30'N	95°29'W
Jaleswar, Nepal	202	26°50'N	85°55'E
Jalgaon, India	202	21°08'N	75°33'E
Jalisco, Mex. (hä-lēs'kō)	130	21°27'N	104°54'W
Jalisco, state, Mex.	128	20°07'N	104°45'W
Jalón, r., Spain (hä-lōn')	172	41°22'N	1°46'W
Jalostotitlán, Mex. (hä-lōs-tē-tlán')	130	21°09'N	102°30'W
Jalpa, Mex. (häl'pä)	131	18°12'N	93°06'W
Jalpa, Mex. (häl'pä)	130	21°40'N	103°04'W
Jalpan, Mex. (häl'pän)	130	21°13'N	99°31'W
Jaltepec, Mex. (häl-tå-pĕk')	131	17°20'N	95°15'W
Jaltipan, Mex. (häl-tå-pän')	131	17°59'N	94°42'W
Jaltocan, Mex. (häl-tō-kän')	130	21°08'N	98°32'W
Jamaare, r., Nig.	235	11°50'N	10°10'E
Jamaica, nation, N.A.	129	17°45'N	78°00'W
Jamaica Cay, i., Bah.	135	22°45'N	75°55'W
Jamālpur, Bngl.	202	24°56'N	89°58'E
Jamay, Mex. (hä-mī')	130	20°16'N	102°43'W
Jambi, Indon. (mäm'bē)	212	1°45'S	103°28'E
James, r., Mo., U.S.	121	36°51'N	93°22'W
James, r., Va., U.S.	107	37°35'N	77°50'W
James, r., U.S.	106	46°25'N	98°55'W
James, Lake, res., N.C., U.S.	125	36°07'N	81°48'W
James Bay, b., Can. (jāmz)	93	53°53'N	80°40'W
Jamesburg, N.J., U.S. (jāmz'bûrg)	110a	40°21'N	74°26'W
James Point, c., Bah.	134	25°20'N	76°30'W
James Range, mts., Austl.	220	24°15'S	133°30'E
James Ross, i., Ant.	139	64°20'S	58°20'W
Jamestown, S. Afr.	233c	31°07'S	26°49'E
Jamestown, N.D., U.S.	104	46°54'N	98°42'W
Jamestown, N.Y., U.S. (jāmz'toun)	105	42°05'N	79°15'W
Jamestown, R.I., U.S.	110b	41°30'N	71°21'W
Jamestown Reservoir, res., N.D., U.S.	112	47°16'N	98°40'W
Jamiltepec, Mex. (hä-mēl-tå-pĕk)	131	16°16'N	97°54'W
Jammerbugten, b., Den.	166	57°20'N	9°28'E
Jammu, India	199	32°50'N	74°52'E
Jammu and Kashmir, state, India (kåsh-mēr')	199	34°30'N	76°00'E
Jammu and Kashmīr, hist. reg., Asia (kåsh-mēr')	199	39°10'N	75°05'E
Jāmnagar, India (jäm-nŭ'gŭr)	199	22°33'N	70°03'E
Jamshedpur, India (jäm'shĕd-pōōr)	199	22°52'N	86°11'E
Jándula, r., Spain (hän'dōō-lä)	172	38°28'N	3°52'W
Janesville, Wi., U.S. (jānz'vĭl)	113	42°41'N	89°03'W
Janin, W.B.	197a	32°27'N	35°19'E
Jan Mayen, i., Nor. (yän mī'ĕn)	160	70°59'N	8°05'W
Jánoshalma, Hung. (yä'nôsh-hôl-mô)	169	46°17'N	19°18'E
Janów Lubelski, Pol. (yä'nōōf lū-bĕl'skĭ)	169	50°40'N	22°25'E
Januária, Braz. (zhä-nwä'rē-ä)	143	15°31'S	44°17'W
Japan, nation, Asia (jă-păn')	205	36°30'N	133°30'E
Japan, Sea of, sea, Asia (jă-păn')	205	40°08'N	132°55'E
Japeri, Braz. (zhä-pĕ'rē)	144b	22°38'S	43°40'W
Japurá (Caquetá), r., S.A.	142	2°00'S	68°00'W
Jarabacoa, Dom. Rep. (kä-rä-bä-kō'ä)	135	19°05'N	70°40'W
Jaral del Progreso, Mex. (hä-räl dĕl prō-grā'sō)	130	20°21'N	101°05'W
Jarama, r., Spain (hä-rä'mä)	172	40°33'N	3°30'W
Jarash, Jord.	197a	32°17'N	35°53'E
Jardines, Banco, bk., Cuba (bä'n-kō-här-dē'nås)	134	21°45'N	81°40'W
Jargalant, Mong.	208	46°28'N	115°10'E
Jari, r., Braz. (zhä-rē)	143	0°28'N	53°00'W
Jarocin, Pol. (yä-rō'tsyēn)	169	51°58'N	17°31'E
Jarosław, Pol. (yá-rôs-wáf)	161	50°01'N	22°41'E
Jarud Qi, China (jya-lōō-tŭ shyē)	205	44°35'N	120°40'E
Jasin, Malay.	197b	2°19'N	102°26'E
Jašiūnai, Lith. (dzá-shōō-ná'yĕ)	167	54°27'N	25°25'E
Jāsk, Iran (jäsk)	198	25°46'N	57°48'E
Jasło, Pol. (yás'wō)	169	49°44'N	21°28'E
Jason Bay, b., Malay.	197b	1°53'N	104°14'E
Jasonville, In., U.S. (jā'sŭn-vĭl)	108	39°10'N	87°15'W
Jasper, Can.	90	52°53'N	118°05'W
Jasper, Al., U.S. (jăs'pēr)	124	33°50'N	87°17'W
Jasper, Fl., U.S.	125	30°30'N	82°56'W
Jasper, In., U.S.	108	38°20'N	86°55'W
Jasper, Mn., U.S.	112	43°51'N	96°22'W
Jasper, Tx., U.S.	123	30°55'N	93°59'W
Jasper National Park, rec., Can.	92	53°09'N	117°45'W
Jászapáti, Hung. (yäs'ô-pä-tē)	169	47°29'N	20°10'E
Jászberény, Hung.	169	47°30'N	19°56'E
Jatibonico, Cuba (hä-tē-bō-nē'kō)	134	22°00'N	79°15'W
Jauja, Peru (ĸä-ō'ĸ)	142	11°43'S	75°32'W
Jaumave, Mex. (hou-mä'vå)	130	23°23'N	99°24'W
Jaunjelgava, Lat. (youn'yĕl'gá-vá)	180	56°37'N	25°06'E
Java (Jawa), i., Indon.	212	8°35'S	111°11'E
Javari, r., S.A. (ĸä-vä-rē)	142	4°25'S	72°07'W
Java Trench, deep	212	9°45'S	107°30'E
Jawa, Laut (Java Sea), sea, Indon.	212	5°10'S	110°30'E
Jawor, Pol. (yä'vôr)	168	51°04'N	16°12'E
Jaworzno, Pol. (yä-vôzh'nô)	169	50°11'N	19°18'E
Jaya, Puncak, mtn., Indon.	213	4°00'S	137°00'E
Jayapura, Indon.	212	2°30'S	140°45'W
Jayb, Wādī al (Ha'Arava), val., Asia	197a	30°33'N	35°10'E

ng-sing; ŋ-baŋk; N-nasalized n; nŏd; cŏmmit; ōld; ōbey; ôrder; oi-boil; fōōd; ŏ-as oo in foot; ou-out; s-soft; sh-dish; th-thin; pūre; ůnite; ûrn; stŭd; circŭs; ü-as in French tu; '-indeterminate vowel.

ăt; finăl; rāte; senăte; ärm; àsk; sofá; fâre;   ch-choose;   dh-as th in other;   bē; ēvent; bĕt; recĕnt; cratēr;   g-gō; gh-guttural g;   bĭt; ī-short neutral; rīde;   ĸ-guttural k as ch in German ich;

PRONOUNCING INDEX

Jutiapa – Kara-Kum 307

PLACE (Pronunciation)	PAGE	LAT.	LONG.
Jutiapa, Guat. (hōō-tē-ä'pä)	132	14°16'N	89°55'W
Juticalpa, Hond. (hōō-tē-käl'pä)	128	14°35'N	86°17'W
Jutland see Jylland, reg., Den.	160	56°04'N	9°00'E
Juventino Rosas, Mex.	130	20°38'N	101°02'W
Juventud, Isla de la, i., Cuba	129	21°40'N	82°45'W
Juxian, China (jyōō shyĕn)	208	35°35'N	118°50'E
Juxtlahuaca, Mex. (hōōs-tlä-hwä'kä)	130	17°20'N	98°02'W
Juye, China (jyōō-yü)	206	35°25'N	116°05'E
Južna Morava, r., Serb. (ū'zhnä mô'rä-vä)	175	42°30'N	22°00'E
Jylland, reg., Den.	160	56°04'N	9°00'E

K

PLACE (Pronunciation)	PAGE	LAT.	LONG.
K2(Qogir Feng), mtn., Asia	199	36°06'N	76°38'E
Kaabong, Ug.	237	3°31'N	34°08'E
Kaalfontein, S. Afr. (kärl-fŏn-tān)	233b	26°02'S	28°16'E
Kaappunt, c., S. Afr.	232a	34°21'S	18°30'E
Kabaena, Pulau, i., Indon. (kä-bȧ-ā'nȧ)	212	5°35'S	121°07'E
Kabala, S.L. (kȧ-bá'lȧ)	230	9°43'N	11°39'W
Kabale, Ug.	237	1°15'S	29°59'E
Kabalega Falls, wtfl., Ug.	231	2°15'N	31°41'E
Kabalo, D.R.C. (kä-bä'lō)	232	6°03'S	26°55'E
Kabambare, D.R.C. (kä-bäm-bä'rȧ)	232	4°47'S	27°45'E
Kabardino-Balkaria, prov., Russia	180	43°30'N	43°30'E
Kabba, Nig.	235	7°50'N	6°03'E
Kabe, Japan (kä'bā)	211	34°32'N	132°30'E
Kabinakagami, r., Can.	98	49°00'N	84°15'W
Kabinda, D.R.C. (kä-bēN'dä)	232	6°08'S	24°29'E
Kabompo, r., Zam. (kȧ-bôm'pō)	232	14°00'S	23°40'E
Kabongo, D.R.C. (kȧ-bông'ō)	232	7°58'S	25°10'E
Kabot, Gui.	234	10°48'N	14°57'W
Kaboudia, Ra's, c., Tun.	162	35°17'N	11°28'E
Kābul, Afg. (kä'bōōl)	199	34°39'N	69°14'E
Kabul, r., Asia (kä'bōōl)	199	34°44'N	69°43'E
Kabunda, D.R.C.	237	12°25'S	29°22'E
Kabwe, Zam.	232	14°27'S	28°27'E
Kachuga, Russia (kȧ-chōō-gȧ)	179	54°09'N	105°43'E
Kadei, r., Afr.	235	4°00'N	15°10'E
Kadnikov, Russia (käd'nē-kôf)	180	59°30'N	40°10'E
Kadoma, Japan	211b	34°43'N	135°36'E
Kadoma, Zimb.	232	18°21'S	29°55'E
Kaduna, Nig. (kä-dōō'nä)	230	10°33'N	7°27'E
Kaduna, r., Nig.	235	9°30'N	6°00'E
Kaédi, Maur. (kä-ā-dē')	230	16°09'N	13°30'W
Ka'ena Point, c., Hi., U.S. (kä'ā-nä)	106d	21°33'N	158°19'W
Kaesŏng, Kor., N. (kä'ĕ-sŭng) (kī'jō)	205	38°00'N	126°35'E
Kafanchan, Nig.	235	9°36'N	8°17'E
Kafia Kingi, Sudan (kä'fē-ȧ kĭŋ'gē)	231	9°17'N	24°28'E
Kafue, Zam. (kä'fōō)	232	15°45'S	28°17'E
Kafue, r., Zam.	232	15°45'S	26°30'E
Kafue Flats, sw., Zam.	237	16°15'S	26°30'E
Kafue National Park, rec., Zam.	237	15°00'S	25°35'E
Kafwira, D.R.C.	237	12°10'S	27°33'E
Kagal'nik, r., Russia (kä-gäl''nēk)	177	46°58'N	39°25'E
Kagera, r., Afr. (kä-gā'rȧ)	232	1°10'S	31°10'E
Kagoshima, Japan (kä'gō-shē'mȧ)	205	31°35'N	130°31'E
Kagoshima-Wan, b., Japan (kä'gō-shē'mä wän)	210	31°24'N	130°39'E
Kahayan, r., Indon.	212	1°45'S	113°40'E
Kahemba, D.R.C.	236	7°17'S	19°00'E
Kahia, D.R.C.	237	6°21'S	28°24'E
Kahoka, Mo., U.S. (kȧ-hō'kȧ)	121	40°26'N	91°42'W
Kaho'olawe, i., Hi., U.S. (kä-hōō-lä'wē)	106c	20°28'N	156°48'W
Kahramarımaraş, Tur.	198	37°40'N	36°50'W
Kahshahpiwi, r., Can.	113	48°24'N	90°56'W
Kahuku Point, c., Hi., U.S. (kä-hōō'kōō)	106d	21°50'N	157°50'W
Kahului, Hi., U.S.	106c	20°53'N	156°28'W
Kai, Kepulauan, is., Indon.	213	5°35'S	132°45'E
Kaiang, Malay.	197b	3°00'N	101°47'E
Kaiashk, r., Can.	98	49°40'N	89°30'W
Kaibab Indian Reservation, I.R., Az., U.S. (kä'ē-bȧb)	119	36°55'N	112°45'W
Kaibab Plat, Az., U.S.	119	36°30'N	112°10'W
Kaidu, r., China (kī-dōō)	204	42°35'N	84°04'E
Kaieteur Fall, wtfl., Guy. (kī-ĕ-tōōr')	143	4°48'N	59°24'W
Kaifeng, China (kī-fŭŋ)	205	34°48'N	114°22'E
Kai Kecil, i., Indon.	213	5°45'S	132°40'E
Kailua, Hi., U.S. (kä'ē-lōō'ä)	106c	21°18'N	157°43'W
Kailua Kona, Hi., U.S.	126a	19°49'N	155°59'W
Kaimana, Indon.	213	3°32'S	133°47'E
Kaimanawa Mountains, mts., N.Z.	223	39°10'S	176°00'E
Kainan, Japan (kä'ē-nȧn')	211	34°09'N	135°14'E
Kainji Lake, res., Nig.	235	10°25'N	4°50'E
Kaiserslautern, Ger. (kī-zĕrs-lou'tĕrn)	161	49°26'N	7°46'E
Kaitaia, N.Z. (kä-ē-tä'ē-ȧ)	221a	35°30'S	173°28'E
Kaiwi Channel, strt., Hi., U.S. (käē-wē)	106c	21°10'N	157°38'W
Kaiyuan, China (kī-yuän)	209	23°42'N	103°20'E
Kaiyuan, China	208	42°30'N	124°00'E
Kaiyuh Mountains, mts., Ak., U.S. (kī-yōō')	103	64°25'N	157°38'W
Kajaani, Fin. (kä'yȧ-nē)	160	64°15'N	27°16'E
Kajang, Gunong, mtn., Malay.	197b	2°47'N	104°05'E
Kajiki, Japan (kä'jē-kē)	210	31°44'N	130°41'E
Kakhovka, Ukr. (kä-kôf'kȧ)	177	46°46'N	33°32'E
Kakhovs'ke vodoskhovyshche, res., Ukr.	178	47°21'N	33°33'E
Kākināda, India	199	16°58'N	82°18'E
Kaktovik, Ak., U.S. (käk-tō'vĭk)	103	70°08'N	143°51'W
Kakwa, r., Can. (käk'wȧ)	95	54°00'N	118°55'W
Kalach, Russia (kȧ-lȧch')	181	50°15'N	40°55'E
Kaladan, r., Asia	204	21°07'N	93°04'E
Kalae, c., Hi., U.S.	126a	18°55'N	155°41'W
Kalahari Desert, des., Afr. (kä-lä-hä'rē)	232	23°00'S	22°03'E
Kalama, Wa., U.S. (kȧ-lăm'ȧ)	116c	46°01'N	122°50'W
Kalama, r., Wa., U.S.	116c	46°03'N	122°47'W
Kalamáta, Grc.	154	37°04'N	22°08'E
Kalamazoo, Mi., U.S. (kăl-ȧ-mȧ-zōō')	105	42°20'N	85°40'W
Kalamazoo, r., Mi., U.S.	108	42°35'N	86°00'W
Kalanchak, Ukr. (kä-län-chäk')	177	46°17'N	33°14'E
Kalandula, Ang. (dōō'kȧ dȧ brä-gäN'sä)	232	9°06'S	15°57'E
Kalaotoa, Pulau, i., Indon.	212	7°22'S	122°30'E
Kalapana, Hi., U.S. (kä-lä-pá'nä)	126a	19°25'N	155°00'W
Kalar, mtn., Iran	198	31°43'N	51°41'E
Kalāt, Pak. (kŭ-lät')	199	29°05'N	66°36'E
Kalemie, D.R.C.	232	5°56'S	29°12'E
Kalgan see Zhangjiakou, China	205	40°45'N	114°58'E
Kalgoorlie-Boulder, Austl. (kăl-gōōr'lē)	218	30°45'S	121°35'E
Kaliakra, Nos, c., Blg.	163	43°25'N	28°42'E
Kalima, D.R.C.	237	2°34'S	26°37'E
Kaliningrad, Russia	178	54°42'N	20°32'E
Kaliningrad, Russia (kä lē nēn'grät)	186b	55°55'N	37°49'E
Kalinkavichy, Bela.	176	52°07'N	29°19'E
Kalispel Indian Reservation, I.R., Wa., U.S. (kăl-ĭ-spĕl')	114	48°25'N	117°30'W
Kalispell, Mt., U.S. (kăl'ĭ-spĕl)	104	48°12'N	114°18'W
Kalisz, Pol. (kä'lēsh)	161	51°45'N	18°05'E
Kaliua, Tan.	237	5°04'S	31°48'E
Kalixälven, r., Swe.	160	67°12'N	22°00'E
Kalmar, Swe. (käl'mär)	160	56°40'N	16°19'E
Kalmarsund, strt., Swe. (käl'mär)	166	56°30'N	16°17'E
Kal'mius, r., Ukr. (käl''myōōs)	177	47°15'N	37°38'E
Kalmykia, prov., Russia	181	46°56'N	46°00'E
Kalocsa, Hung. (kä'lō-chä)	169	46°32'N	19°00'E
Kalohi Channel, strt., Hi., U.S. (kä-lō'hĭ)	126a	20°55'N	157°15'W
Kaloko, D.R.C.	237	6°47'S	25°48'E
Kalomo, Zam. (kä-lō'mō)	232	17°02'S	26°30'E
Kalsubai Mount, mtn., India	202	19°43'N	73°47'E
Kaltenkirchen, Ger. (käl'tĕn-kēr-kĕn)	159c	53°50'N	9°57'E
Kālu, r., India	203b	19°18'N	73°14'E
Kaluga, Russia (kȧ-lō'gä)	178	54°29'N	36°12'E
Kaluga, prov., Russia	176	54°10'N	35°00'E
Kaluktutiak (Cambridge Bay), Can.	94	69°15'N	105°00'W
Kalundborg, Den. (kȧ-lòn''bôr')	166	55°42'N	11°07'E
Kalush, Ukr. (kä'lòsh)	169	49°02'N	24°24'E
Kalvarija, Lith. (käl-vä-rē'yȧ)	167	54°24'N	23°17'E
Kalwa, India	203b	19°12'N	72°59'E
Kal'ya, Russia (käl'yȧ)	186a	60°17'N	59°58'E
Kalyān, India	202	19°16'N	73°07'E
Kalyazin, Russia (käl-yá'zĕn)	176	57°13'N	37°55'E
Kama, r., Russia (kä'mȧ)	178	56°10'N	53°50'E
Kamaishi, Japan (kä'mä-ē'shē)	210	39°16'N	142°03'E
Kamakura, Japan (kä'mä-kōō'rä)	211	35°19'N	139°33'E
Kamarān, i., Yemen	198	15°19'N	41°47'E
Kāmārhāti, India	202a	22°41'N	88°23'E
Kambove, D.R.C. (käm-bō'vē)	232	10°58'S	26°43'E
Kamchatka, r., Russia	185	54°15'N	158°38'E
Kamchatka, Poluostrov, pen., Russia	185	55°19'N	157°45'E
Kamen, Ger. (kä'mĕn)	171c	51°35'N	7°40'E
Kamenjak, Rt, c., Cro. (kȧ'mĕ-nyäk)	174	44°45'N	13°57'E
Kamen'-na-Obi, Russia (kä-mĭny'nŭ ô'bē)	178	53°43'N	81°28'E
Kamensk-Shakhtinskiy, Russia (kä'mĕnsk shäk'tĭn-skĭ)	177	48°17'N	40°16'E
Kamensk-Ural'skiy, Russia (kä'mĕnsk ōō-räl'skĭ)	180	56°27'N	61°55'E
Kamenz, Ger. (kä'mĕnts)	168	51°16'N	14°05'E
Kameoka, Japan (kä'mā-ōkä)	211b	35°01'N	135°35'E
Kāmet, mtn., Asia	202	30°50'N	79°42'E
Kamianets'-Podil's'kyi, Ukr.	181	48°41'N	26°34'E
Kamianka-Buz'ka, Ukr.	169	50°06'N	24°20'E
Kamień Pomorski, Pol.	168	53°57'N	14°48'E
Kamikoma, Japan (kä'mē-kō'mä)	211b	34°45'N	135°50'E
Kamina, D.R.C.	232	8°44'S	25°00'E
Kaministikwia, r., Can. (kȧ-mĭ-nĭ-stĭk'wĭ-ȧ)	113	48°40'N	89°41'W
Kamituga, D.R.C.	237	3°04'S	28°11'E
Kamloops, Can. (kăm'lōōps)	90	50°40'N	120°20'W
Kamp, r., Aus. (kämp)	168	48°30'N	15°45'E
Kampala, Ug. (käm-pä'lä)	231	0°19'N	32°25'E
Kampar, r., Indon. (käm'pär)	212	0°30'N	101°30'E
Kampene, D.R.C.	237	3°36'S	26°40'E
Kampenhout, Bel.	159a	50°56'N	4°33'E
Kamp-Lintfort, Ger. (kämp-lĕnt'fôrt)	171c	51°30'N	6°34'E
Kâmpóng Saôm, Camb.	212	10°40'N	103°50'E
Kâmpóng Thum, Camb. (kŏm'pŏng-tŏm)	212	12°41'N	104°29'E
Kâmpôt, Camb. (käm'pōt)	212	10°41'N	104°07'E
Kampuchea see Cambodia, nation, Asia	212	12°15'N	104°00'E
Kamsack, Can. (kăm'săk)	90	51°34'N	101°54'W
Kamskoye, res., Russia	178	59°08'N	56°30'E
Kamudilo, D.R.C.	237	7°42'S	27°18'E
Kamuela, Hi., U.S.	126a	20°01'N	155°40'W
Kamui Misaki, c., Japan	210	43°25'N	139°35'E
Kámuk, Cerro, mtn., C.R. (sĕ'r-rô-kä-mōō'k)	133	9°18'N	83°02'W
Kamyshevatskaya, Russia	177	46°24'N	37°58'E
Kamyshin, Russia (kä-mwēsh'ĭn)	178	50°08'N	45°20'E
Kamyshlov, Russia (kä-mēsh'lôf)	178	56°50'N	62°32'E
Kan, r., Russia (kän)	184	56°30'N	94°17'E
Kanab, Ut., U.S. (kăn'ăb)	119	37°00'N	112°30'W
Kanabeki, Russia (kȧ-nä'byĕ-kĭ)	186a	57°48'N	57°16'E
Kanab Plateau, plat., Az., U.S.	119	36°31'N	112°55'W
Kanaga, i., Ak., U.S. (kă-nă'gă)	103a	52°02'N	177°38'W
Kanagawa, dept., Japan (kä'nä-gä'wä)	211a	35°29'N	139°32'E
Kanā'is, Ra's al, c., Egypt	163	31°14'N	28°08'E
Kanamachi, Japan (kä-nä-mä'chē)	211a	35°46'N	139°52'E
Kananga, D.R.C.	232	6°14'S	22°17'E
Kananikol'skoye, Russia	186a	52°48'N	57°29'E
Kanasín, Mex. (kä-nä-sē'n)	132a	20°54'N	89°31'W
Kanatak, Ak., U.S. (kă-nă'tŏk)	103	57°35'N	155°48'W
Kanawha, r., W.V., U.S. (kȧ-nô'wȧ)	107	37°55'N	81°50'W
Kanaya, Japan (kä-nä'yä)	211a	35°10'N	139°49'E
Kanazawa, Japan (kä'nȧ-zä'wȧ)	205	36°34'N	136°38'E
Kānchenjunga, mtn., Asia (kĭn-chĭn-jŏn'gȧ)	199	27°30'N	88°18'E
Kānchipuram, India	199	12°55'N	79°43'E
Kandahār, Afg.	199	31°43'N	65°58'E
Kanda Kanda, D.R.C. (kän'dȧ kän'dȧ)	232	6°56'S	23°36'E
Kandalaksha, Russia (kȧn-dȧ-läk'shȧ)	178	67°10'N	33°05'E
Kandalakshskiy Zaliv, b., Russia	180	66°20'N	35°00'E
Kandava, Lat. (kän'dȧ-vȧ)	167	57°03'N	22°45'E
Kandi, Benin (käN-dē')	230	11°08'N	2°56'E
Kandiāro, Pak.	202	27°09'N	68°12'E
Kandla, India (kŭnd'lŭ)	202	23°00'N	70°20'E
Kandy, Sri L. (kän'dē)	203	7°18'N	80°42'E
Kane, Pa., U.S. (kān)	109	41°40'N	78°50'W
Kāne'ohe, Hi., U.S. (kä-nä-ō'hä)	126a	21°25'N	157°47'W
Kāne'ohe Bay, b., Hi., U.S.	106d	21°32'N	157°40'W
Kanevskaya, Russia (kȧ-nyĕf'skȧ)	177	46°07'N	38°58'E
Kangaroo, i., Austl. (kăŋ-gȧ-rō')	220	36°05'S	137°05'E
Kangāvar, Iran (kŭŋ'gā-vär)	198	34°37'N	46°45'E
Kangean, Kepulauan, is., Indon. (käŋ'gē-än)	212	6°50'S	116°22'E
Kanggye, Kor., N. (käng'gyĕ)	205	40°55'N	126°40'E
Kanghwa, i., Kor., S. (käng'hwä)	210	37°38'N	126°00'E
Kangnŭng, Kor., S. (käng'nò ng)	210	37°42'N	128°50'E
Kango, Gabon (käN-gō)	232	0°09'N	10°08'E
Kangowa, D.R.C.	236	9°55'S	22°48'E
Kanin, Poluostrov, pen., Russia	178	68°00'N	45°00'E
Kaningo, Kenya	237	0°49'S	38°32'E
Kanin Nos, Mys, c., Russia	180	68°40'N	44°00'E
Kaniv, Ukr.	177	49°46'N	31°27'E
Kanivs'ke vodoskhovyshche, res., Ukr.	178	50°10'N	30°40'E
Kanjiža, Serb. (kä'nyē-zhä)	175	46°05'N	20°02'E
Kankakee, Il., U.S. (kăŋ-kȧ-kē')	108	41°07'N	87°53'W
Kankakee, r., Il., U.S.	108	41°15'N	88°15'W
Kankan, Gui. (käN-käN) (kän-kän')	230	10°23'N	9°18'W
Kannapolis, N.C., U.S. (kăn-ăp'ō-lĭs)	125	35°30'N	80°38'W
Kannoura, Japan (kä'nō-ōō'rä)	211	33°34'N	134°18'E
Kano, Nig. (kä'nō)	230	12°00'N	8°30'E
Kanonkop, mtn., S. Afr.	232a	33°49'S	18°37'E
Kanopolis Reservoir, res., Ks., U.S. (kăn-ŏp'ō-lĭs)	120	38°44'N	98°01'W
Kānpur, India (kän'pûr)	202	26°30'N	80°10'E
Kansas, state, U.S. (kăn'zȧs)	104	38°30'N	99°40'W
Kansas, r., Ks., U.S.	121	39°08'N	95°52'W
Kansas City, Ks., U.S.	105	39°06'N	94°39'W
Kansas City, Mo., U.S.	105	39°05'N	94°35'W
Kansk, Russia	179	56°14'N	95°43'E
Kansŏng, Kor., S.	210	38°09'N	128°29'E
Kantang, Thai. (kän'täng')	212	7°26'N	99°28'E
Kantchari, Burkina	234	12°29'N	1°31'E
Kanton, i., Kir.	190	3°50'S	174°00'W
Kantunilkin, Mex. (kän-tōō-nēl-kē'n)	132a	21°07'N	87°30'W
Kanzhakovskiy Kamen, Gora, mtn., Russia (kȧn-zhä'kôvs-kēē kämĭen)	186a	59°38'N	59°12'E
Kaohsiung, Tai. (kä-ō-syŏng')	205	22°35'N	120°25'E
Kaolack, Sen.	230	14°09'N	16°04'W
Kaouar, oasis, Niger	231	19°16'N	13°09'E
Kapaa, Hi., U.S.	126a	22°06'N	159°20'W
Kapanga, D.R.C.	236	8°21'S	22°35'E
Kapfenberg, Aus. (kȧp'fĕn-bĕrgh)	168	47°27'N	15°16'E
Kapiri Mposhi, Zam.	237	13°58'S	28°41'E
Kapoeta, Sudan	231	4°45'N	33°35'E
Kaposvár, Hung. (kô'pôsh-vär)	169	46°21'N	17°45'E
Kapsan, Kor., N. (käp'sän')	210	40°59'N	128°22'E
Kapuskasing, Can.	91	49°28'N	82°22'W
Kapuskasing, r., Can.	98	48°55'N	82°55'W
Kapustin Yar, Russia (kä'pòs-tĕn yär')	181	48°30'N	45°40'E
Kaputar, Mount, mtn., Austl. (kă-pû-tăr)	222	30°11'S	150°11'E
Kapuvár, Hung. (kô'pōō-vär)	169	47°35'N	17°02'E
Kara, Russia (kärȧ)	178	68°42'N	65°30'E
Kara, r., Russia	180	68°30'N	65°20'E
Karabalā', Iraq (kŭr'bȧ-lä)	198	32°31'N	43°58'E
Karabanovo, Russia (kä'rȧ-bȧ-nō-vô)	176	56°19'N	38°43'E
Karabash, Russia (kó-rȧ-bäsh')	186a	55°27'N	60°14'E
Kara-Bogaz-Gol, Zaliv, b., Turkmen. (kȧ-rä' bŭ-gäs')	183	41°30'N	53°40'E
Karachay-Cherkessia, prov., Russia	182	44°00'N	42°00'E
Karachev, Russia (kȧ-rȧ-chôf')	180	53°08'N	34°54'E
Karāchi, Pak.	199	24°59'N	68°56'E
Karaganda see Qaraghandy, Kaz.	183	49°42'N	73°18'E
Karaidel', Russia (kä'rī-dĕl)	186a	55°52'N	56°54'E
Karakoram Pass, p., Asia	199	35°35'N	77°45'E
Karakoram Range, mts., India (kä'rä kō'rŏm)	199	35°24'N	76°38'E
Karakorum, hist., Mong.	204	47°25'N	102°22'E
Kara-Kum, des., Turkmen.	183	40°00'N	57°00'E

ng-sing; ŋ-baŋk; N-nasalized n; nŏd; cŏmmit; ōld; ôbey; ôrder; oi-boil; fōōd; ò-as oo in foot; ou-out; s-soft; sh-dish; th-thin; pūre; ûnite; ûrn; stŭd; circŭs; ü-as in French tu; '-indeterminate vowel.

308 Kara Kum Canal – Keshan

PRONOUNCING INDEX

PLACE (Pronunciation)	PAGE	LAT.	LONG.
Kara Kum Canal, can., Turkmen.	183	37°35'N	61°50'E
Karaman, Tur. (kä-rä-män')	163	37°10'N	33°00'E
Karamay, China (kär-äm-ä)	204	45°37'N	84°53'E
Karamea Bight, b., N.Z. (kȧ-rȧ-mē'ȧ bīt)	221a	41°20'S	171°30'E
Kara Sea *see* Karskoye More, sea, Russia	178	74°00'N	68°00'E
Karashahr (Yanqui), China (kä-rä-shä-är) (yän-chyē)	204	42°14'N	86°28'E
Karatsu, Japan (kä'rȧ-tsōō)	211	33°28'N	129°59'E
Karaul, Russia (kä-rä-ōl')	184	70°13'N	83°46'E
Karawanken, mts., Eur.	168	46°32'N	14°07'E
Karcag, Hung. (kär'tsäg)	169	47°18'N	20°58'E
Kárditsa, Grc.	175	39°23'N	21°57'E
Kärdla, Est. (kĕrd'lȧ)	167	58°59'N	22°44'E
Karelia, prov., Russia	184	62°30'N	32°35'E
Karema, Tan.	232	6°49'S	30°26'E
Kargat, Russia (kär-gät')	178	55°17'N	80°07'E
Karghalik *see* Yecheng, China	204	37°54'N	77°25'E
Kargopol', Russia (kär-gō-pōl'')	178	61°30'N	38°50'E
Kariba, Lake, res., Afr.	232	17°15'S	27°55'E
Karibib, Nmb. (kȧr'ȧ-bĭb)	232	21°55'S	15°50'E
Kārikāl, India (kä-rê-käl')	203	10°58'N	79°49'E
Karimata, Kepulauan, is., Indon. (kä-rê-mä'tȧ)	212	1°08'S	108°10'E
Karimata, Selat, strt., Indon.	212	1°00'S	107°10'E
Karimun Besar, i., Indon.	197b	1°10'N	103°28'E
Karimunjawa, Kepulauan, is., Indon. (kä'rê-mōōn-yä'vä)	212	5°36'S	110°15'E
Karin, Som. (kȧr'ĭn)	238a	10°43'N	45°50'E
Karkar Island, i., Pap. N. Gui. (kär'kär)	213	4°50'S	146°45'E
Karkheh, r., Iran	198	32°45'N	47°50'E
Karkinits'ka zatoka, b., Ukr.	177	45°50'N	32°45'E
Karkūk, Iraq	198	35°28'N	44°22'E
Karlivka, Ukr.	177	49°26'N	35°08'E
Karlobag, Cro. (kär-lō-bäg')	174	44°30'N	15°03'E
Karlovac, Cro. (kär'lô-vȧts)	163	45°29'N	15°16'E
Karlovo, Blg. (kär'lô-vō)	175	42°39'N	24°48'E
Karlovy Vary, Czech Rep. (kär'lô-vê vä'rê)	161	50°13'N	12°53'E
Karlshamn, Swe. (kärls'häm)	166	56°11'N	14°50'E
Karlskrona, Swe. (kärls'krô-nä)	160	56°10'N	15°33'E
Karlsruhe, Ger. (kärls'rōō-ĕ)	161	49°00'N	8°23'E
Karlstad, Swe. (kärl'städ)	154	59°25'N	13°28'E
Karluk, Ak., U.S. (kär'lŭk)	103	57°30'N	154°22'W
Karmøy, i., Nor. (kärm-ûe)	166	59°14'N	5°00'E
Karnataka, state, India	199	14°55'N	75°00'E
Karnobat, Blg. (kär-nô'bät)	175	42°39'N	26°59'E
Karonga, Mwi. (kȧ-rōŋ'gȧ)	232	9°52'S	33°57'E
Kárpathos, i., Grc.	163	35°34'N	27°26'E
Karpinsk, Russia (kär'pĭnsk)	186a	59°46'N	60°00'E
Kars, Tur. (kärs)	198	40°35'N	43°00'E
Kārsava, Lat. (kär'sä-vä)	167	56°46'N	27°39'E
Karshi, Uzb. (kär'shē)	183	38°30'N	66°08'E
Karskiye Vorota, Proliv, strt., Russia	178	70°30'N	58°07'E
Karskoye More (Kara Sea), sea, Russia	178	74°00'N	68°00'E
Kartaly, Russia (kȧr'tȧ lê)	178	53°05'N	60°40'E
Karunagapalli, India	203	9°09'N	76°34'E
Karvina, Czech Rep.	169	49°50'N	18°30'E
Kasai (Cassai), r., Afr.	232	3°45'S	19°10'E
Kasama, Zam. (kȧ-sä'mȧ)	232	10°13'S	31°12'E
Kasanga, Tan. (kȧ-säŋ'gȧ)	232	8°28'S	31°09'E
Kasaoka, Japan (kä'sȧ-ō'kȧ)	211	34°33'N	133°29'E
Kasba-Tadla, Mor. (käs'bȧ-täd'lȧ)	230	32°37'N	5°57'W
Kasempa, Zam. (kȧ-sĕm'pȧ)	232	13°27'S	25°50'E
Kasenga, D.R.C. (kȧ-seŋ'gȧ)	232	10°22'S	28°38'E
Kasese, D.R.C.	237	1°38'S	27°07'E
Kasese, Ug.	237	0°10'N	30°05'E
Kāshān, Iran (kä-shän')	198	33°52'N	51°15'E
Kashgar *see* Kashi, China	204	39°29'N	76°00'E
Kashi (Kashgar), China (kä-shr) (käsh-gär)	204	39°29'N	76°00'E
Kashihara, Japan (kä'shê-hä'rä)	211b	34°31'N	135°48'E
Kashiji Plain, pl., Zam.	236	13°25'S	22°30'E
Kashin, Russia (kä-shēn')	176	57°20'N	37°38'E
Kashira, Russia (kä-shē'rȧ)	176	54°49'N	38°11'E
Kashiwa, Japan (kä'shê-wä)	211a	35°51'N	139°58'E
Kashiwara, Japan	211b	34°35'N	135°38'E
Kashiwazaki, Japan (kä'shē-wä-zä'kê)	210	37°06'N	138°17'E
Kāshmar, Iran	201	35°12'N	58°27'E
Kashmir *see* Jammu and Kashmir, state, India	199	34°30'N	76°00'E
Kashmor, Pak.	202	28°33'N	69°34'E
Kashtak, Russia (käsh'tȧk)	186a	55°18'N	61°25'E
Kasimov, Russia (kȧ-sē'môf)	180	54°56'N	41°23'E
Kaskanak, Ak., U.S. (kăs-kă'năk)	103	60°00'N	158°00'W
Kaskaskia, r., Il., U.S. (kăs-kăs'kĭ-ȧ)	108	39°10'N	88°50'W
Kaskattama, r., Can. (kăs-kă-tä'mȧ)	97	56°28'N	90°55'W
Kaskö (Kaskinen), Fin. (käs'kû) (käs'kē-nĕn)	167	62°24'N	21°18'E
Kasli, Russia (käs'lĭ)	180	55°53'N	60°46'E
Kasongo, D.R.C. (kä-sôŋ'gō)	232	4°31'S	26°42'E
Kásos, i., Grc.	163	35°20'N	26°55'E
Kaspiysk, Russia	182	42°52'N	47°38'E
Kassándras, Kólpos, b., Grc.	175	40°10'N	23°35'E
Kassel, Ger. (käs'ĕl)	161	51°19'N	9°30'E
Kasson, Mn., U.S. (kăs'ŭn)	113	44°01'N	92°45'W
Kastamonu, Tur. (kä-stȧ-mō'nōō)	198	41°20'N	33°50'E
Kastoría, Grc. (kȧs-tō'rĭ-ȧ)	163	40°28'N	21°17'E
Kasūr, Pak.	202	31°10'N	74°29'E
Kataba, Zam.	237	16°05'S	25°10'E
Katahdin, Mount, mtn., Me., U.S. (kȧ-tä'dĭn)	100	45°56'N	68°57'W
Katanga, hist. reg., D.R.C. (kȧ-täŋ'gȧ)	232	8°30'S	25°00'E
Katanning, Austl. (kȧ-tăn'ĭng)	218	33°45'S	117°45'E
Katav-Ivanovsk, Russia (kä'täf ĭ-vä'nôfsk)	186a	54°46'N	58°13'E
Kateninskiy, Russia (kȧtyĕ'nĭs-kĭ)	186a	53°12'N	61°05'E
Kateríni, Grc.	175	40°18'N	22°36'E
Katete, Zam.	237	14°05'S	32°07'E
Katherine, Austl. (kăth'ĕr-ĭn)	218	14°15'S	132°20'E
Kāthiāwār, pen., India (kä'tyȧ-wär')	199	22°10'N	70°20'E
Kathmandu, Nepal (kāt-mān-dōō')	199	27°49'N	85°21'E
Kathryn, Can. (kăth'rĭn)	102e	51°13'N	113°42'W
Kathryn, Ca., U.S.	117a	33°42'N	117°45'W
Katihār, India	202	25°39'N	87°39'E
Katiola, C. Iv.	234	8°08'N	5°06'W
Katmai National Park, rec., Ak., U.S. (kăt'mī)	106a	58°38'N	155°00'W
Katompi, D.R.C.	237	6°11'S	26°20'E
Katopa, D.R.C.	237	2°45'S	25°06'E
Katowice, Pol.	154	50°15'N	19°00'E
Katrineholm, Swe. (kȧ-trē'nĕ-hōlm)	166	59°01'N	16°10'E
Katsbakhskiy, Russia (kȧts-bäk'skĭ)	186a	52°57'N	59°37'E
Katsina, Nig. (kät'sê-nȧ)	230	13°00'N	7°32'E
Katsina Ala, Nig.	230	7°10'N	9°17'E
Katsura, r., Japan (kä'tsō-rä)	211b	34°55'N	135°43'E
Katta-Kurgan, Uzb. (kȧ-tȧ-kōr-gän')	183	39°45'N	66°42'E
Kattegat, strt., Eur. (kăt'ĕ-gät)	156	56°57'N	11°25'E
Katumba, D.R.C.	237	7°45'S	25°18'E
Katun', r., Russia (kȧ-tōn')	184	51°30'N	86°18'E
Katwijk aan Zee, Neth.	159a	52°12'N	4°23'E
Kaua'i, i., Hi., U.S.	106c	22°09'N	159°15'W
Kauai Channel, strt., Hi., U.S. (kä-ōō-ä'ê)	106c	21°35'N	158°52'W
Kaufbeuren, Ger. (kouf'boi-rĕn)	168	47°52'N	10°38'E
Kaufman, Tx., U.S. (kôf'măn)	123	32°36'N	96°18'W
Kaukauna, Wi., U.S. (kô-kô'nȧ)	113	44°17'N	88°15'W
Kaulakahi Channel, strt., Hi., U.S. (kä'ōō-lȧ-kä'hê)	126a	22°00'N	159°55'W
Kaunakakai, Hi., U.S. (kä'ōō-nȧ-kä'kĭ)	126a	21°06'N	156°59'W
Kaunas, Lith. (kou'nȧs) (kôv'nô)	178	54°42'N	23°54'E
Kaura Namoda, Nig.	230	12°35'N	6°35'E
Kavála, Grc. (kä-vä'lä)	163	40°55'N	24°24'E
Kavieng, Pap. N. Gui. (kä-vê-ĕng')	213	2°44'S	151°02'E
Kavīr, Dasht-e, des., Iran (dŭsht-ê-ka-vēr')	198	34°41'N	53°30'E
Kawagoe, Japan (kä-wä-gō'ȧ)	211	35°55'N	139°29'E
Kawaguchi, Japan (kä-wä-gōō-chē)	211a	35°48'N	139°44'E
Kawaikini, mtn., Hi., U.S. (kä-wä'ê-kĭ-nĭ)	126a	22°05'N	159°33'W
Kawanishi, Japan (kä-wä'nê-shē)	211b	34°49'N	135°26'E
Kawasaki, Japan (kä-wä-sä'kê)	210	35°32'N	139°43'E
Kaxgar, r., China	204	39°30'N	75°00'E
Kaya, Burkina (kä'yä)	230	13°05'N	1°05'W
Kayan, r., Indon.	212	1°45'N	115°38'E
Kaycee, Wy., U.S. (kā-sē')	115	43°43'N	106°38'W
Kayes, Mali (kāz)	230	14°27'N	11°26'W
Kayseri, Tur. (kī'sĕ-rē)	198	38°45'N	35°20'E
Kazach'ye, Russia	179	70°46'N	135°47'E
Kazakhstan, nation, Asia	178	48°45'N	59°00'E
Kazan', Russia (kȧ-zän')	178	55°50'N	49°18'E
Kazanka, Ukr. (kȧ-zän'kȧ)	177	47°49'N	32°50'E
Kazanlŭk, Blg. (kä'zȧn-lĕk)	175	42°47'N	25°23'E
Kazbek, Gora, mtn. (kȧz-bĕk')	181	42°42'N	44°31'E
Kāzerūn, Iran	198	29°37'N	51°44'E
Kazincbarcika, Hung. (kô'zĭnts-bôr-tsĭ-ko)	169	48°15'N	20°39'E
Kazungula, Zam.	237	17°45'S	25°20'E
Kazusa Kameyama, Japan (kä-zōō-sä kä-mȧ'yä-mä)	211a	35°14'N	140°06'E
Kazym, r., Russia (kä-zēm')	184	63°30'N	67°41'E
Kéa, i., Grc.	175	37°36'N	24°13'E
Kealaikahiki Channel, strt., Hi., U.S. (kā-ä'lä-ê-kä-hē'kē)	126a	20°38'N	157°00'W
Keansburg, N.J., U.S. (kēnz'bûrg)	110a	40°26'N	74°08'W
Kearney, Ne., U.S. (kär'nĭ)	112	40°42'N	99°05'W
Kearny, N.J., U.S.	110a	40°46'N	74°09'W
Keasey, Or., U.S. (kēz'ĭ)	116c	45°51'N	123°20'W
Kebnekaise, mtn., Swe. (kĕp'nĕ-kä-ēs'ĕ)	156	67°53'N	18°10'E
Kecskemét, Hung. (kĕch'kĕ-māt)	163	46°52'N	19°42'E
Kedah, hist. reg., Malay. (kā'dä)	212	6°00'N	100°31'E
Kédainiai, Lith. (kē-dī'nĭ-ī)	167	55°16'N	23°58'E
Kedgwick, Can. (kĕdj'wĭk)	100	47°39'N	67°21'W
Keenbrook, Ca., U.S. (kēn'brŏk)	117a	34°16'N	117°29'W
Keene, N.H., U.S. (kēn)	109	42°55'N	72°15'W
Keetmanshoop, Nmb. (kāt'mȧns-hōp)	232	26°30'S	18°05'E
Keet Seel Ruin, Az., U.S. (kēt sēl)	119	36°46'N	110°32'W
Keewatin, Mn., U.S. (kē-wä'tĭn)	113	47°24'N	93°03'W
Kefallonía, i., Grc.	163	38°08'N	20°58'E
Keffi, Nig. (kĕf'ê)	230	8°51'N	7°52'E
Ke Ga, Mui, c., Viet.	212	12°58'N	109°50'E
Kei, r., Afr. (kā)	233c	32°57'S	26°50'E
Keila, Est. (kā'lȧ)	167	59°19'N	24°25'E
Keilor, Austl.	217a	37°43'S	144°50'E
Kei Mouth, S. Afr.	233c	32°40'S	28°23'E
Keiskammahoek, S. Afr. (kās'kämä-hōōk')	233c	32°42'S	27°11'E
Kéita, Bahr, r., Chad	235	9°30'N	19°17'E
Keitele, l., Fin. (kā'tĕ-lĕ)	167	62°50'N	25°40'E
Kekaha, Hi., U.S.	126a	21°57'N	159°42'W
Kelafo, Eth.	238a	5°40'N	44°00'E
Kelang, Malay.	212	3°20'N	101°27'E
Kelang, r., Malay.	197b	3°00'N	101°40'E
Kelkit, r., Tur.	163	40°38'N	37°03'E
Keller, Tx., U.S. (kĕl'ēr)	117c	32°56'N	97°15'W
Kellinghusen, Ger. (kĕ'lĕng-hōō-zĕn)	159c	53°57'N	9°43'E
Kellogg, Id., U.S. (kĕl'ŏg)	114	47°32'N	116°07'W
Kelme', Lith. (kĕl-mȧ)	167	55°36'N	22°53'E
Kélo, Chad	235	9°19'N	15°48'E
Kelowna, Can.	90	49°53'N	119°29'W
Kelsey Bay, Can. (kĕl'sê)	94	50°24'N	125°57'W
Kelso, Wa., U.S.	116c	46°09'N	122°54'W
Keluang, Malay.	197b	2°01'N	103°19'E
Kem', Russia (kĕm)	178	65°00'N	34°48'E
Kemah, Tx., U.S. (kē'mȧ)	123a	29°32'N	95°01'W
Kemerovo, Russia	178	55°31'N	86°05'E
Kemi, Fin. (kā'mê)	160	65°48'N	24°38'E
Kemi, r., Fin.	160	67°02'N	27°50'E
Kemigawa, Japan (kĕ'mê-gä'wä)	211a	35°38'N	140°07'E
Kemijarvi, Fin. (kā'mê-yĕr-vē)	160	66°48'N	27°21'E
Kemi-joki, l., Fin.	160	66°37'N	28°13'E
Kemmerer, Wy., U.S. (kĕm'ēr-ēr)	115	41°48'N	110°36'W
Kemp, l., Tx., U.S. (kĕmp)	120	33°55'N	99°22'W
Kempen, Ger. (kĕm'pĕn)	171c	51°22'N	6°25'E
Kempsey, Austl. (kĕmp'sē)	219	30°59'S	152°50'E
Kempt, l., Can. (kĕmpt)	99	47°28'N	74°00'W
Kempten, Ger. (kĕmp'tĕn)	161	47°44'N	10°17'E
Kempton Park, S. Afr. (kĕmp'tŏn pärk)	238c	26°07'S	28°29'E
Ken, r., India	202	25°00'N	79°55'E
Kenai, Ak., U.S. (kĕ-nī')	103	60°38'N	151°18'W
Kenai Fjords National Park, rec., Ak., U.S.	103	59°45'N	150°00'W
Kenai Mountains, mts., Ak., U.S.	103	60°00'N	150°00'W
Kenai Pen, Ak., U.S.	103	64°40'N	150°18'W
Kendal, S. Afr.	238c	26°03'S	28°58'E
Kendal, Eng., U.K. (kĕn'dăl)	164	54°20'N	1°48'W
Kendallville, In., U.S. (kĕn'dăl-vĭl)	108	41°25'N	85°20'W
Kenedy, Tx., U.S. (kĕn'ĕ-dĭ)	123	28°49'N	97°50'W
Kenema, S.L.	234	7°52'N	11°12'W
Kenitra, Mor. (kĕ-nē'trȧ)	162	34°21'N	6°34'W
Kenmare, N.D., U.S. (kĕn-mâr')	112	48°41'N	102°05'W
Kenmore, N.Y., U.S. (kĕn'mōr)	111c	42°58'N	78°53'W
Kennebec, r., Me., U.S. (kĕn-ê-bĕk')	100	44°23'N	69°48'W
Kennebunk, Me., U.S. (kĕn-ê-buŋk')	100	43°24'N	70°33'W
Kennedale, Tx., U.S. (kĕn'-ê-dāl)	117c	32°38'N	97°13'W
Kennedy, Cape *see* Canaveral, Cape, c., Fl., U.S.	107	28°30'N	80°23'W
Kennedy, Mount, mtn., Can.	103	60°25'N	138°50'W
Kenner, La., U.S. (kĕn'ēr)	123	29°58'N	90°15'W
Kennett, Mo., U.S. (kĕn'ĕt)	121	36°14'N	90°01'W
Kennewick, Wa., U.S. (kĕn'ê-wĭk)	114	46°12'N	119°06'W
Kenney Dam, dam, Can.	94	53°37'N	124°58'W
Kennydale, Wa., U.S. (kĕn-nê'dāl)	116a	47°31'N	122°12'W
Kénogami, Can. (kĕn-ō'gä-mê)	91	48°26'N	71°14'W
Kenogamissi Lake, l., Can.	98	48°15'N	81°31'W
Keno Hill, Can.	103	63°58'N	135°18'W
Kenora, Can. (kê-nō'rȧ)	91	49°47'N	94°29'W
Kenosha, Wi., U.S. (kĕ-nō'shȧ)	105	42°34'N	87°50'W
Kenova, W.V., U.S. (kê-nō'vȧ)	108	38°20'N	82°35'W
Kensico Reservoir, res., N.Y., U.S. (kĕn'sĭ-kō)	110a	41°08'N	73°45'W
Kent, Oh., U.S. (kĕnt)	108	41°05'N	81°20'W
Kent, Wa., U.S.	116a	47°23'N	122°14'W
Kentani, S. Afr. (kĕnt-änĭ')	233c	32°31'S	28°19'E
Kentland, In., U.S. (kĕnt'lănd)	108	40°50'N	87°25'W
Kenton, Oh., U.S. (kĕn'tŭn)	108	40°40'N	83°35'W
Kent Peninsula, pen., Can.	92	68°28'N	108°10'W
Kentucky, state, U.S. (kĕn-tŭk'ĭ)	105	37°30'N	87°35'W
Kentucky, res., U.S.	107	36°20'N	88°50'W
Kentucky, r., Ky., U.S.	107	38°15'N	85°01'W
Kentwood, La., U.S. (kĕnt'wŏŏd)	123	30°56'N	90°31'W
Kenya, nation, Afr. (kĕn'yȧ)	232	1°00'N	36°53'E
Kenya, Mount (Kirinyaga), mtn., Kenya	233	0°10'S	37°20'E
Kenyon, Mn., U.S. (kĕn'yŭn)	113	44°15'N	92°58'W
Keokuk, Ia., U.S. (kē'ō-kŭk)	105	40°24'N	91°34'W
Keoma, Can. (kē-ō'mȧ)	102e	51°13'N	113°39'W
Kepenkeck Lake, l., Can.	101	48°13'N	54°45'W
Kępno, Pol. (kàŋ'pnō)	169	51°17'N	17°59'E
Kerala, state, India	199	16°38'N	76°00'E
Kerang, Austl. (kē-răng')	219	35°32'S	143°58'E
Kerch, Ukr.	178	45°20'N	36°26'E
Kerchenskiy Proliv, strt., Eur. (kĕr-chĕn'skĭ prō'lĭf)	177	45°08'N	36°35'E
Kerempe Burun, c., Tur.	163	42°00'N	33°20'E
Keren, Erit.	231	15°46'N	38°28'E
Kerguélen, Îles, is., Afr. (kĕr'gā-lĕn)	3	49°50'S	69°30'E
Kericho, Kenya	237	0°22'S	35°17'E
Kerinci, Gunung, mtn., Indon.	212	1°45'S	101°18'E
Keriya *see* Yutian, China	204	36°55'N	81°39'E
Keriya, r., China (kĕ'rê-yä)	204	37°13'N	81°59'E
Kerkebet, Erit.	200	16°18'N	37°24'E
Kerkenna, Îles, i., Tun. (kĕr'kĕn-nä)	230	34°49'N	11°37'E
Kerki, Turkmen. (kĕr'kê)	183	37°52'N	65°15'E
Kérkyra, Grc.	163	39°36'N	19°56'E
Kérkyra, i., Grc.	162	39°33'N	19°36'E
Kermadec Islands, is., N.Z. (kĕr-mȧd'ĕk)	3	30°30'S	177°00'E
Kermān, Iran (kĕr-män')	198	30°23'N	57°08'E
Kermānshāh *see* Bakhtarān, Iran	198	34°01'N	47°00'E
Kern, r., Ca., U.S.	118	35°31'N	118°37'W
Kern, South Fork, r., Ca., U.S.	118	35°40'N	118°15'W
Kerpen, Ger. (kĕr'pĕn)	171c	50°52'N	6°42'E
Kerrobert, Can.	96	51°53'N	109°13'W
Kerrville, Tx., U.S. (kûr'vĭl)	122	30°02'N	99°07'W
Kerulen, r., Asia (kĕr'ōō-lĕn)	205	47°52'N	113°22'E
Kesagami Lake, l., Can.	99	50°23'N	80°15'W
Keşan, Tur. (kĕ'shȧn)	175	40°50'N	26°37'E
Keshan, China (kŭ-shän)	205	48°00'N	126°30'E

ăt; finăl; rāte; senâte; ärm; åsk; sofȧ; fâre; ch-choose; dh-as th in other; bē; ēvent; bĕt; recĕnt; cratēr; g-gō; gh-guttural g; bĭt; ĭ-short neutral; rīde; ĸ-guttural k as ch in German ich;

PRONOUNCING INDEX Kesour – Kitgum 309

PLACE (Pronunciation)	PAGE	LAT.	LONG.
Kesour, Monts des, mts., Alg.	162	32°51'N	0°30'W
Kestell, S. Afr. (kĕs'tĕl)	238c	28°19'N	28°43'E
Keszthely, Hung. (kĕst'hĕl-lĭ)	169	46°46'N	17°12'E
Ket', r., Russia (kyĕt)	184	58°30'N	84°15'E
Keta, Ghana	230	6°00'N	1°00'E
Ketamputih, Indon.	197b	1°25'N	102°19'E
Ketapang, Indon. (kĕ-tá-päng')	212	2°00'S	109°57'E
Ketchikan, Ak., U.S. (kĕch-ĭ-kăn')	106a	55°21'N	131°35'W
Kętrzyn, Pol. (kăŋ't'r-zĭn)	169	54°04'N	21°24'E
Kettering, Eng., U.K. (kĕt'ĕr-ĭng)	158a	52°23'N	0°43'W
Kettering, Oh., U.S.	108	39°40'N	84°15'W
Kettle, r., Can.	95	49°40'N	119°00'W
Kettle, r., Mn., U.S. (kĕt''l)	113	46°20'N	92°57'W
Kettwig, Ger. (kĕt'vēg)	171c	51°22'N	6°56'E
Kęty, Pol. (kăn tĭ)	169	49°54'N	19°16'E
Ketzin, Ger. (kĕ'tzēn)	159b	52°29'N	12°51'E
Keuka, l., N.Y., U.S. (kē-ū'ká)	109	42°30'N	77°10'W
Kevelaer, Ger. (kĕ'fĕ-lăr)	171c	51°35'N	6°15'E
Kew, Austl.	217a	37°49'S	145°02'E
Kewanee, Il., U.S. (kē-wä'nē)	113	41°15'N	89°55'W
Kewaunee, Wi., U.S. (kē-wô'nē)	113	44°27'N	87°33'W
Keweenaw Bay, b., Mi., U.S. (kē'wē-nô)	113	46°59'N	88°15'W
Keweenaw Peninsula, pen., Mi., U.S.	113	47°28'N	88°12'W
Keya Paha, r., S.D., U.S. (kē-yá pä'hä)	112	43°11'N	100°10'W
Key Largo, i., Fl., U.S.	125a	25°11'N	80°15'W
Keyport, N.J., U.S. (kē'pōrt)	110a	40°26'N	74°12'W
Keyport, Wa., U.S.	116a	47°42'N	122°38'W
Keyser, W.V., U.S. (kī'sĕr)	109	39°25'N	79°00'W
Key West, Fl., U.S. (kē wĕst')	105	24°31'N	81°47'W
Kežmarok, Slvk. (kĕzh'má-rôk)	169	49°10'N	20°27'E
Khabarovo, Russia (kŭ-bár-ôvô)	178	69°31'N	60°41'E
Khabarovsk, Russia (kä-bä'rôfsk)	179	48°35'N	135°12'E
Khakassia, prov., Russia	184	52°32'N	89°33'E
Khālāpur, India	203b	18°48'N	73°17'E
Khalkidhiki, pen., Grc.	175	40°30'N	23°18'E
Khal'mer-Yu, Russia (kŭl-myĕr'-yōō')	178	67°52'N	64°25'E
Khalturin, Russia (käl'tōō-rēn)	180	58°28'N	49°00'E
Khambhāt, Gulf of, b., India	199	21°20'N	72°27'E
Khammam, India	203	17°09'N	80°13'E
Khānābād, Afg.	202	36°43'N	69°11'E
Khandwa, India	202	21°53'N	76°22'E
Khaníon, Kólpos, b., Grc.	174a	35°35'N	23°55'E
Khanka, l., Asia (kän'ká)	179	45°09'N	133°28'E
Khānpur, Pak.	202	28°42'N	70°42'E
Khanty-Mansiysk, Russia (kŭn-te'mŭn-sēsk')	178	61°02'N	69°01'E
Khān Yūnus, Gaza	197a	31°21'N	34°19'E
Kharagpur, India (kŭ-rŭg'pōōr)	199	22°26'N	87°21'E
Kharkiv, Ukr.	178	50°00'N	36°10'E
Kharkiv, prov., Ukr.	177	49°33'N	35°55'E
Kharkov see Kharkiv, Ukr.	178	50°00'N	36°10'E
Kharlovka, Russia	180	68°47'N	37°20'E
Kharmanli, Blg. (kár-män'lē)	175	41°54'N	25°55'E
Khartoum, Sudan	231	15°34'N	32°36'E
Khasavyurt, Russia	182	43°15'N	46°37'E
Khāsh, Iran	198	28°08'N	61°08'E
Khāsh, r., Afg.	198	32°30'N	64°27'E
Khasi Hills, hills, India	199	25°38'N	91°55'E
Khaskovo, Blg. (kás'kō-vō)	163	41°56'N	25°32'E
Khatanga, Russia (ká-tän'gá)	179	71°48'N	101°47'E
Khatangskiy Zaliv, b., Russia (kä-tän'g-skē)	179	73°45'N	108°30'E
Khaybār, Sau. Ar.	198	25°45'N	39°28'E
Kherson, Ukr. (kĕr-sôn')	181	46°38'N	32°34'E
Kherson, prov., Ukr.	177	46°32'N	32°55'E
Khiitola, Russia (khē'tō-lá)	167	61°14'N	29°40'E
Khimki, Russia (kēm'kĭ)	186b	55°54'N	37°27'E
Khmel'nyts'kyi, Ukr.	181	49°29'N	26°54'E
Khmel'nyts'kyy, prov., Ukr.	177	49°27'N	26°30'E
Khmil'nyk, Ukr.	177	49°34'N	27°58'E
Kholm, Russia (kôlm)	176	57°09'N	31°07'E
Kholmsk, Russia (kŭlmsk)	179	47°09'N	142°33'E
Khomeynīshahr, Iran	201	32°41'N	51°31'E
Khon Kaen, Thai.	212	16°37'N	102°41'E
Khopër, r., Russia (kô'pēr)	181	52°00'N	43°00'E
Khor, Russia (kôr')	210	47°50'N	134°52'E
Khor, r., Russia	210	47°23'N	135°20'E
Khóra Sfakión, Grc.	174a	35°12'N	24°10'E
Khorog, Taj.	183	37°30'N	71°36'E
Khorol, Ukr. (kô'rôl)	177	49°48'N	33°17'E
Khorol, r., Ukr.	177	49°50'N	33°21'E
Khorramābād, Iran	201	33°30'N	48°20'E
Khorramshahr, Iran (kô-ram'shär)	198	30°36'N	48°15'E
Khot'kovo, Russia	186b	56°15'N	38°00'E
Khotyn, Ukr.	181	48°29'N	26°32'E
Khoyniki, Bela.	177	51°54'N	30°00'E
Khudzhand, Taj.	183	40°17'N	69°37'E
Khulna, Bngl.	199	22°50'N	89°38'E
Khūryān Mūryān, is., Oman	198	17°27'N	56°02'E
Khust, Ukr. (kôst)	169	48°10'N	23°18'E
Khvalynsk, Russia (kvá-lĭnsk')	181	52°30'N	48°00'E
Khvoy, Iran	198	38°32'N	45°01'E
Khyber Pass, p., Asia (kī'bĕr)	199	34°28'N	71°18'E
Kialwe, D.R.C.	237	9°22'S	27°08'E
Kiambi, D.R.C. (kyäm'bē)	232	7°20'S	28°01'E
Kiamichi, r., Ok., U.S. (kyá-mē'chē)	121	34°31'N	95°34'W
Kianta, l., Fin. (kyán'tá)	180	65°00'N	28°15'E
Kibenga, D.R.C.	236	7°55'S	17°35'E
Kibiti, Tan.	237	7°44'S	38°57'E
Kibombo, D.R.C.	237	3°54'S	25°55'E
Kibondo, Tan.	237	3°35'S	30°42'E
Kičevo, Mac. (kē'chĕ-vô)	175	41°30'N	20°59'E
Kickapoo, r., Wi., U.S. (kĭk'á-pōō)	113	43°20'N	90°55'W

PLACE (Pronunciation)	PAGE	LAT.	LONG.
Kicking Horse Pass, p., Can.	95	51°25'N	116°10'W
Kidal, Mali (kē-dál')	230	18°33'N	1°00'E
Kidderminster, Eng., U.K. (kĭd'ĕr-mĭn-stēr)	158a	52°23'N	2°14'W
Kidd's Beach, S. Afr. (kĭdz)	233c	33°09'S	27°43'E
Kidsgrove, Eng., U.K. (kĭdz'grōv)	158a	53°05'N	2°15'W
Kiel, Ger. (kēl)	154	54°19'N	10°08'E
Kiel, Wi., U.S.	113	43°52'N	88°04'W
Kiel Bay, b., Ger.	168	54°33'N	10°19'E
Kiel Canal see Nord-Ostsee Kanal, can., Ger.	168	54°03'N	9°23'E
Kielce, Pol. (kyĕl'tsĕ)	169	50°50'N	20°41'E
Kieldrecht, Bel. (kēl'drĕkt)	159a	51°17'N	4°09'E
Kiev (Kyïv), Ukr.	178	50°27'N	30°30'E
Kiffa, Maur. (kēf'á)	230	16°37'N	11°24'W
Kigali, Rw. (kē-gä'lē)	232	1°59'S	30°05'E
Kigoma, Tan. (kē-gō'mä)	232	4°57'S	29°38'E
Kii-Suido, strt., Japan (kē sōō-ē'dō)	210	33°53'N	134°55'E
Kikaiga, i., Japan	210	28°25'N	130°10'E
Kikinda, Serb. (kē'kēn-dä)	175	45°49'N	20°30'E
Kikládes, is., Grc.	162	37°30'N	24°45'E
Kikwit, D.R.C. (kē'kwēt)	232	5°02'S	18°49'E
Kil, Swe. (kēl)	166	59°30'N	13°15'E
Kilauea, Hi., U.S. (kē-lä-ōō-ā'ä)	126a	22°12'N	159°25'W
Kīlauea Crater, depr., Hi., U.S.	126a	19°28'N	155°18'W
Kilbuck Mountains, mts., Ak., U.S. (kĭl-bŭk)	103	60°05'N	160°00'W
Kilchu, Kor., N. (kĭl'chō)	210	40°59'N	129°23'E
Kildare, Ire. (kĭl-dār')	164	53°09'N	7°05'W
Kilembe, D.R.C.	236	5°42'S	19°55'E
Kilgore, Tx., U.S.	123	32°23'N	94°53'W
Kilia, Ukr.	177	45°28'N	29°17'E
Kilifi, Kenya	237	3°38'S	39°51'E
Kilimanjaro, mtn., Tan. (kyl-ē-măn-jä'rō)	233	3°09'S	37°19'E
Kilimatinde, Tan. (kĭl-ē-mä-tĭn'dá)	232	5°48'S	34°58'E
Kilindoni, Tan.	237	7°55'S	39°39'E
Kilingi-Nõmme, Est. (kē'lĭn-gē-nôm'mĕ)	167	58°08'N	25°03'E
Kilis, Tur. (kē'lēs)	163	36°50'N	37°20'E
Kilkenny, Ire. (kĭl-kĕn-ĭ)	161	52°40'N	7°30'W
Kilkis, Grc. (kĭl'kĭs)	175	40°59'N	22°51'E
Killala, Ire. (kĭ-lă'lá)	164	54°11'N	9°10'W
Killarney, Ire.	164	52°03'N	9°05'W
Killdeer, N.D., U.S. (kĭl'dēr)	112	47°22'N	102°45'W
Killiniq Island, i., Can.	93	60°32'N	63°56'W
Kilmarnock, Scot., U.K. (kĭl-mär'nŭk)	164	55°38'N	4°25'W
Kilrush, Ire. (kĭl'rŭsh)	164	52°40'N	9°16'W
Kilwa Kisiwani, Tan.	237	8°58'S	39°30'E
Kilwa Kivinje, Tan.	233	8°43'S	39°18'E
Kim, r., Cam.	235	5°40'N	11°17'E
Kimamba, Tan.	237	6°47'S	37°08'E
Kimba, Austl. (kĭm'bá)	222	33°08'S	136°25'E
Kimball, Ne., U.S. (kĭm-bál)	112	41°14'N	103°41'W
Kimball, S.D., U.S.	112	43°44'N	98°58'W
Kimberley, Can. (kĭm'bēr-lĭ)	90	49°41'N	115°59'W
Kimberley, S. Afr.	232	28°40'S	24°50'E
Kimi, Cam.	235	6°05'N	11°30'E
Kimmirut (Lake Harbour), Can.	91	62°43'N	69°40'W
Kímolos, i., Grc. (kē'mô-lôs)	175	36°52'N	24°20'E
Kimry, Russia (kĭm'rē)	180	56°53'N	37°24'E
Kimvula, D.R.C.	236	5°44'S	15°58'E
Kinabalu, Gunong, mtn., Malay.	212	5°45'N	115°26'E
Kincardine, Can. (kĭn-kär'dĭn)	91	44°10'N	81°15'W
Kinda, D.R.C.	237	9°18'S	25°04'E
Kindanba, Congo	236	3°44'S	14°31'E
Kinder, La., U.S. (kĭn'dēr)	123	30°30'N	92°50'W
Kindersley, Can. (kĭn'dērz-lē)	90	51°27'N	109°10'W
Kindia, Gui. (kĭn'dē-á)	230	10°04'N	12°51'W
Kindu, D.R.C.	232	2°57'S	25°56'E
Kinel'-Cherkassy, Russia	180	53°32'N	51°32'E
Kineshma, Russia (kē-nĕsh'má)	180	57°27'N	41°02'E
King, i., Austl. (kĭng)	221	39°35'S	143°40'E
Kingaroy, Austl. (kĭŋ'gă-roi)	222	26°37'S	151°50'E
King City, Can.	102d	43°56'N	79°32'W
King City, Ca., U.S. (kĭng sĭ'tĭ)	118	36°12'N	121°08'W
Kingcome Inlet, b., Can. (kĭng'kŭm)	94	50°50'N	126°10'W
Kingfisher, Ok., U.S. (kĭng'fĭsh-ēr)	121	35°51'N	97°55'W
King George Sound, strt., Austl. (jôrj)	220	35°17'S	118°30'E
Kingisepp, Russia (kĭŋ-gē-sep')	180	59°22'N	28°38'E
King Leopold Ranges, mts., Austl. (lē'ô-pōld)	220	16°25'S	125°00'E
Kingman, Az., U.S. (kĭng'măn)	119	35°10'N	114°05'W
Kingman, Ks., U.S. (kĭng'măn)	120	37°38'N	98°07'W
Kings, r., Ca., U.S.	118	36°28'N	119°43'W
Kings Canyon National Park, rec., Ca., U.S. (kăn'yŭn)	106	36°52'N	118°53'W
Kingsclere, Eng., U.K. (kings-clēr)	158b	51°18'N	1°15'W
Kingscote, Austl. (kĭngz'kŭt)	222	35°45'S	137°32'E
King's Lynn, Eng., U.K. (kĭngz lĭn')	165	52°45'N	0°20'E
Kings Mountain, N.C., U.S.	125	35°13'N	81°30'W
Kings Norton, Eng., U.K. (nôr'tŭn)	158a	52°25'N	1°54'W
King Sound, strt., Austl.	220	16°50'S	123°35'E
Kings Park, N.Y., U.S. (kĭngz pärk)	110a	40°53'N	73°16'W
Kings Peak, mtn., Ut., U.S.	106	40°46'N	110°20'W
Kingsport, Tn., U.S. (kĭngz'pōrt)	125	36°33'N	82°36'W
Kingston, Austl. (kĭngz'tŭn)	218	37°52'S	139°52'E
Kingston, Can.	91	44°15'N	76°30'W
Kingston, Jam.	129	18°00'N	76°45'W
Kingston, N.Y., U.S.	105	42°00'N	74°00'W
Kingston, Pa., U.S.	109	41°15'N	75°50'W
Kingston, Wa., U.S.	116a	47°04'N	122°29'W
Kingston upon Hull, Eng., U.K.	154	53°45'N	0°25'W
Kingstown, St. Vin. (kĭngz'toun)	129	13°10'N	61°14'W

PLACE (Pronunciation)	PAGE	LAT.	LONG.
Kingstree, S.C., U.S. (kĭngz'trē)	125	33°30'N	79°50'W
Kingsville, Tx., U.S. (kĭngz'vĭl)	123	27°32'N	97°52'W
King William Island, i., Can. (kĭng wĭl'yăm)	92	69°25'N	97°00'W
King William's Town, S. Afr. (kĭng-wĭl'-yŭmz-toun)	233c	32°53'S	27°24'E
Kinira, r., S. Afr.	233c	30°37'S	28°52'E
Kinloch, Mo., U.S. (kĭn-lŏk)	117e	38°44'N	90°19'W
Kinnaird, Can. (kĭn-ārd')	95	49°17'N	117°39'W
Kinnairds Head, c., Scot., U.K. (kĭn-ârds'hĕd)	160	57°42'N	3°55'W
Kinomoto, Japan (kē'nō-mōtō)	211	33°53'N	136°07'E
Kinosaki, Japan (kē'nō-sä'kē)	211	35°38'N	134°47'E
Kinshasa, D.R.C.	232	4°18'S	15°18'E
Kinsley, Ks., U.S. (kĭnz'lĭ)	120	37°55'N	99°24'W
Kinston, N.C., U.S. (kĭnz'tŭn)	125	35°15'N	77°35'W
Kintampo, Ghana (kĕn-täm'pō)	230	8°03'N	1°43'W
Kintyre, pen., Scot., U.K.	164	55°50'N	5°40'W
Kiowa, Ks., U.S. (kī'ô-wá)	120	37°01'N	98°30'W
Kiowa, Ok., U.S.	121	34°42'N	95°53'W
Kipawa, Lac, l., Can.	99	46°55'N	79°00'W
Kipembawe, Tan. (kē-pĕm-bä'wá)	232	7°39'S	33°24'E
Kipengere Range, mts., Tan.	237	9°10'S	34°00'E
Kipili, Tan.	237	7°26'S	30°36'E
Kipushi, D.R.C.	237	11°46'S	27°14'E
Kirakira, Sol. Is.	214e	10°27'S	161°55'E
Kirby, Tx., U.S. (kûr'bĭ)	117d	29°29'N	98°23'W
Kirbyville, Tx., U.S. (kûr'bĭ-vĭl)	123	30°39'N	93°54'W
Kirenga, r., Russia (kē-rĕŋ'gá)	185	56°30'N	108°18'E
Kirensk, Russia (kē-rĕnsk')	179	57°47'N	108°22'E
Kirgiz Range, mts., Asia	183	42°30'N	74°00'E
Kiri, D.R.C.	236	1°27'S	19°00'E
Kiribati, nation, Oc.	3	1°30'S	173°00'E
Kirin see Chilung, Tai.	205	25°02'N	121°48'E
Kiritimati, i., Kir.	2	2°20'N	157°40'W
Kirkby, Eng., U.K.	158a	53°29'N	2°54'W
Kirkby-in-Ashfield, Eng., U.K. (kûrk'bē-ĭn-ăsh'fēld)	158a	53°06'N	1°16'W
Kirkcaldy, Scot., U.K. (kĕr-kô'dĭ)	164	56°06'N	3°15'W
Kirkenes, Nor.	160	69°40'N	30°03'E
Kirkham, Eng., U.K. (kûrk'ăm)	158a	53°47'N	2°53'W
Kirkland, Wa., U.S. (kûrk'lănd)	116a	47°41'N	122°12'W
Kirklareli, Tur. (kĕrk'lár-ĕ'lē)	163	41°44'N	27°15'E
Kirksville, Mo., U.S. (kûrks'vĭl)	105	40°12'N	92°35'W
Kirkwall, Scot., U.K. (kûrk'wôl)	160	58°58'N	2°59'W
Kirkwood, S. Afr.	233c	33°26'S	25°24'E
Kirkwood, Mo., U.S. (kûrk'wŏod)	117e	38°35'N	90°24'W
Kirn, Ger. (kĕrn)	168	49°47'N	7°23'E
Kirov, Russia	176	54°04'N	34°19'E
Kirov, Russia	178	58°35'N	49°35'E
Kirovakan, Arm.	182	40°48'N	44°30'E
Kirovgrad, Russia (kē'rŭ-vŭ-grad)	186a	57°26'N	60°03'E
Kirovohrad, Ukr.	181	48°33'N	32°17'E
Kirovohrad, prov., Ukr.	177	48°23'N	31°10'E
Kirovsk, Russia (kē-rôfsk')	186c	59°52'N	30°59'E
Kirovsk, Russia	178	67°40'N	33°58'E
Kirsanov, Russia (kēr-sá'nôf)	181	52°40'N	42°40'E
Kırşehir, Tur. (kēr-shĕ'hēr)	198	39°10'N	34°00'E
Kirtachi Seybou, Niger	235	12°48'N	2°29'E
Kīrthar Range, mts., Pak. (kĭr-tŭr)	199	27°00'N	67°10'E
Kirton, Eng., U.K. (kûr'tŭn)	158a	53°29'N	0°35'W
Kiruna, Swe. (kē-rōō'nä)	160	67°49'N	20°08'E
Kirundu, D.R.C.	237	0°44'S	25°32'E
Kirwin Reservoir, res., Ks., U.S. (kûr'wĭn)	120	39°34'N	99°04'W
Kiryū, Japan	210	36°24'N	139°20'E
Kirzhach, Russia (kēr-zhák')	176	56°08'N	38°53'E
Kisaki, Tan. (kē-sá'kē)	233	7°37'S	37°43'E
Kisangani, D.R.C.	231	0°30'N	25°12'E
Kisarazu, Japan (kē'sá-rá'zōō)	211a	35°23'N	139°55'E
Kiselëvsk, Russia (kē-sĭ-lyôfsk')	178	54°00'N	86°39'E
Kishinev see Chişinău, Mol.	178	47°02'N	28°52'E
Kishiwada, Japan (kē'shē-wä'dä)	210	34°25'N	135°18'E
Kishkino, Russia (kēsh'kĭ-nô)	186b	55°15'N	38°04'E
Kisiwani, Tan.	237	4°08'S	37°57'E
Kiska, i., Ak., U.S. (kĭs'kä)	106b	52°08'N	177°10'E
Kiskatinaw, r., Can.	95	55°10'N	120°20'W
Kiskittogisu Lake, l., Can.	97	54°05'N	99°00'W
Kiskitto Lake, l., Can. (kĭs-kĭ'tō)	97	54°16'N	98°34'W
Kiskunfélegyháza, Hung. (kĭsh'kŏon-fā'lĕd-y'hä'zô)	169	46°42'N	19°52'E
Kiskunhalas, Hung. (kĭsh'kŏon-hô'lôsh)	169	46°24'N	19°26'E
Kiskunmajsa, Hung. (kĭsh'kŏon-mī'shô)	169	46°29'N	19°42'E
Kislovodsk, Russia	182	43°55'N	42°44'E
Kismaayo, Som.	233	0°18'S	42°30'E
Kiso-Gawa, r., Japan (kē'sō-gä'wä)	211	35°29'N	137°12'E
Kiso-Sammyaku, mts., Japan (kē'sō säm'myá-kōō)	211	35°47'N	137°39'E
Kíssamos, Grc.	174a	35°13'N	23°35'E
Kissidougou, Gui. (kē'sē-dōō'gōō)	230	9°11'N	10°06'W
Kissimmee, Fl., U.S. (kĭ-sĭm'ē)	125a	28°17'N	81°25'W
Kissimmee, r., Fl., U.S.	125a	27°45'N	81°07'W
Kissimmee, Lake, l., Fl., U.S.	125a	27°58'N	81°17'W
Kisujszállás, Hung.	169	47°12'N	20°47'E
Kisumu, Kenya (kē'sōō-mōō)	232	0°06'S	34°45'E
Kita, Mali (kē'tá)	230	13°03'N	9°29'W
Kitakami Gawa, r., Japan	210	39°20'N	141°10'E
Kitakyūshū, Japan	205	33°53'N	130°50'E
Kitale, Kenya	237	1°01'N	35°00'E
Kit Carson, Co., U.S.	120	38°46'N	102°48'W
Kitchener, Can. (kĭch'ĕ-nēr)	91	43°25'N	80°35'W
Kitenda, D.R.C.	236	6°53'S	17°21'E
Kitgum, Ug. (kĭt'gōōm)	231	3°29'N	33°04'E

ng-sing; ŋ-baŋk; ɴ-nasalized n; nŏd; cŏmmit; ōld; ôbey; ôrder; oi-boil; fōōd; ŏo-as oo in foot; ou-out; s-soft; sh-dish; th-thin; pūre; ûnite; ûrn; stŭd; circŭs; ü-as in French tu; '-indeterminate vowel.

310 Kitimat – Kozhikode PRONOUNCING INDEX

PLACE (Pronunciation)	PAGE	LAT.	LONG.
Kitimat, Can. (kĭ′tĭ-măt)	90	54°03′N	128°33′W
Kitimat, r., Can.	94	53°50′N	129°00′W
Kitimat Ranges, mts., Can.	94	53°30′N	128°50′W
Kitlope, r., Can. (kĭt′lōp)	94	53°00′N	128°00′W
Kitsuki, Japan (kĕt′sò-kĕ)	211	33°24′N	131°35′E
Kittanning, Pa., U.S. (kĭ-tăn′ĭng)	109	40°50′N	79°30′W
Kittatinny Mountains, mts., N.J., U.S. (kĭ-tŭ-tĭ′nĕ)	110a	41°16′N	74°44′W
Kittery, Me., U.S. (kĭt′ẽr-ĭ)	100	43°07′N	70°45′W
Kittsee, Aus.	159e	48°05′N	17°05′E
Kitty Hawk, N.C., U.S. (kĭt′tĕ hôk)	125	36°04′N	75°42′W
Kitunda, Tan.	237	6°48′S	33°13′E
Kitwe, Zam.	237	12°49′S	28°13′E
Kitzingen, Ger. (kĭt′zĭng-ĕn)	168	49°44′N	10°08′E
Kiunga, Kenya	237	1°45′S	41°29′E
Kivu, Lac, l., Afr.	232	1°45′S	28°55′E
Kīyose, Japan	211a	35°47′N	139°32′E
Kizel, Russia (kē′zĕl)	180	59°05′N	57°42′E
Kızıl, r., Tur.	198	40°00′N	34°00′E
Kizil′skoye, Russia (kĭz′ĭl-skô-yĕ)	186a	52°43′N	58°53′E
Kizlyar, Russia (kĭz-lyär′)	181	44°00′N	46°50′E
Kizlyarskiy Zaliv, b., Russia	182	44°33′N	46°55′E
Kizu, Japan (kē′zōō)	211	34°43′N	135°49′E
Klaas Smits, r., S. Afr.	233c	31°45′S	26°33′E
Klaaswaal, Neth.	159a	51°46′N	4°25′E
Kladno, Czech Rep. (kläd′nō)	168	50°10′N	14°05′E
Klagenfurt, Aus. (klä′gĕn-fōrt)	161	46°38′N	14°19′E
Klaipéda, Lith. (klī′på-då)	180	55°43′N	21°10′E
Klamath, r., U.S.	114	41°40′N	123°25′W
Klamath Falls, Or., U.S.	104	42°13′N	121°49′W
Klamath Mountains, mts., Ca., U.S.	114	42°00′N	123°25′W
Klarälven, r., Swe.	160	60°40′N	13°00′E
Klaskanine, r., Or., U.S. (klăs′kå-nīn)	116c	46°02′N	123°43′W
Klatovy, Czech Rep. (klå′tô-vě)	161	49°23′N	13°18′E
Klawock, Ak., U.S. (klā′wăk)	103	55°32′N	133°10′W
Kleinmachnow, Ger. (klīn-mäκ′nō)	159b	52°22′N	13°12′E
Klerksdorp, S. Afr. (klẽrks′dôrp)	238c	26°52′S	26°40′E
Klerksraal, S. Afr. (klẽrks′kräl)	238c	26°15′N	27°10′E
Kletnya, Russia (klyĕt′nyå)	176	53°19′N	33°14′E
Kleve, Ger. (klĕ′fĕ)	168	51°47′N	6°09′E
Klickitat, r., Wa., U.S.	114	46°01′N	121°07′W
Klimovichi, Bela. (klē-mô-vē′chě)	176	53°37′N	31°21′E
Klimovsk, Russia (klĭ′môfsk)	186b	55°21′N	37°32′E
Klin, Russia (klěn)	176	56°18′N	36°43′E
Klintehamn, Swe. (klēn′tē-häm)	166	57°24′N	18°14′E
Klintsy, Russia (klĭn′tsĭ)	181	52°46′N	32°14′E
Klip, r., S. Afr. (klĭp)	238c	27°18′N	29°25′E
Klipgat, S. Afr.	238c	25°26′S	27°57′E
Klippan, Swe. (klyp′pån)	166	56°08′N	13°09′E
Kłodzko, Pol. (klôd′skô)	168	50°26′N	16°38′E
Klondike Region, hist. reg., N.A. (klŏn′dīk)	90	64°12′N	142°38′W
Klosterfelde, Ger. (klōs′tĕr-fĕl-dĕ)	159b	52°47′N	13°29′E
Klosterneuburg, Aus. (klōs-tẽr-noi′bōōrgh)	159e	48°19′N	16°20′E
Kluane, l., Can.	92	61°15′N	138°40′W
Kluane National Park, rec., Can.	92	60°25′N	137°53′W
Kluczbork, Pol. (klōōch′bōrk)	169	50°59′N	18°15′E
Klyaz′ma, r., Russia (klyäz′må)	176	55°49′N	39°19′E
Klyetsk, Bela. (klĕtsk)	176	53°04′N	26°43′E
Klyuchevskaya, vol., Russia (klyōō-chĕfskä′yä)	179	56°13′N	160°00′E
Klyuchi, Russia (klyōō′chĭ)	186a	57°03′N	57°20′E
Knezha, Blg. (knyā′zhå)	163	43°27′N	24°03′E
Knife, r., N.D., U.S. (nīf)	112	47°06′N	102°33′W
Knight Inlet, b., Can. (nīt)	94	50°41′N	125°40′W
Knightstown, In., U.S. (nīts′toun)	108	39°45′N	85°30′W
Knin, Cro. (knēn)	174	44°02′N	16°14′E
Knittelfeld, Aus.	161	47°13′N	14°50′E
Knob Peak, mtn., Phil. (nŏb)	213a	12°30′N	121°20′E
Knottingley, Eng., U.K. (nŏt′ĭng-lĭ)	158a	53°42′N	1°14′W
Knox, In., U.S. (nŏks)	108	41°15′N	86°40′W
Knox, Cape, c., Can.	94	54°12′N	133°20′W
Knoxville, Ia., U.S. (nŏks′vĭl)	113	41°19′N	93°05′W
Knoxville, Tn., U.S.	105	35°58′N	83°55′W
Knutsford, Eng., U.K. (nŭts′fẽrd)	158a	53°18′N	2°22′W
Knyszyn, Pol. (knĭ′shĭn)	169	53°16′N	22°59′E
Kobayashi, Japan (kō′bå-yä′shē)	211	31°58′N	130°59′E
Kōbe, Japan (kō′bĕ)	205	34°30′N	135°10′E
Kobeliaky, Ukr.	181	49°11′N	34°12′E
København *see* Copenhagen, Den.	154	55°43′N	12°27′E
Koblenz, Ger. (kō′blĕntz)	161	50°18′N	7°36′E
Kobozha, r., Russia (kô-bō′zhå)	176	58°55′N	35°18′E
Kobrinskoye, Russia (kô-brĭn′skô-yĕ)	186c	59°25′N	30°07′E
Kobryn, Bela. (kō′brěn′)	181	52°13′N	24°23′E
Kobuk, r., Ak., U.S. (kō′bŭk)	103	66°58′N	158°48′W
Kobuk Valley National Park, rec., Ak., U.S.	103	67°20′N	159°00′W
Kobuleti, Geor. (kô-bò-lyā′tě)	181	41°50′N	41°40′E
Kočani, Mac. (kô′chä-nĕ)	175	41°54′N	22°25′E
Kočevje, Slvn. (kô′chāv-ye)	174	45°38′N	14°51′E
Kocher, r., Ger. (kôκ′ĕr)	168	49°00′N	9°52′E
Kochi, India	203	9°58′N	76°19′E
Kōchi, Japan (kō′chě)	205	33°35′N	133°32′E
Kodaira, Japan	211a	35°43′N	139°29′E
Kodiak, Ak., U.S. (kō′dyăk)	106a	57°50′N	152°30′W
Kodiak Island, i., Ak., U.S.	103	57°24′N	153°32′W
Kodok, Sudan (ko′dŏk)	231	9°57′N	32°08′E
Koforidua, Ghana (kō fô-rĭ-dōō′å)	230	6°03′N	0°17′W
Kōfu, Japan (kō′fōō′)	210	35°41′N	138°34′E
Koga, Japan (kō′gå)	211	36°13′N	139°40′E
Kogan, r., Gui.	234	11°30′N	14°05′W
Kogane, Japan (kō′gä-nå)	211a	35°50′N	139°56′E
Koganei, Japan (kō′gä-nā)	211a	35°42′N	139°31′E

PLACE (Pronunciation)	PAGE	LAT.	LONG.
Køge, Den. (kû′gĕ)	166	55°27′N	12°09′E
Køge Bugt, b., Den.	166	55°30′N	12°25′E
Kogoni, Mali	234	14°44′N	6°02′W
Kohīma, India (kô-ē′må)	199	25°45′N	94°41′E
Kohyl′nyk, r., Eur.	177	46°08′N	29°10′E
Koito, r., Japan (kô′ě-tō)	211a	35°19′N	139°58′E
Kŏje, i., Kor., S. (kû′jĕ)	210	34°53′N	129°00′E
Kokand, Uzb. (kô-känt′)	183	40°27′N	71°07′E
Kokemäenjoki, r., Fin.	167	61°23′N	22°03′E
Kokhma, Russia (kôκ′må)	176	56°57′N	41°08′E
Kokkola, Fin. (kô′kô-lå)	160	63°47′N	22°58′E
Kokomo, In., U.S. (kō′kô-mô)	108	40°30′N	86°20′W
Koko Nor (Qinghai Hu), l., China (kō′kô nor) (chyĭŋ-hī hōō)	204	37°26′N	98°30′E
Kokopo, Pap. N. Gui. (kô-kô′pō)	213	4°25′S	152°27′E
Kökshetaū, Kaz.	183	53°15′N	69°13′E
Koksoak, r., Can. (kôk′sô-ăk)	93	57°42′N	69°50′W
Kokstad, S. Afr. (kôk′shtät)	233c	30°33′S	29°27′E
Kokubu, Japan (kō′kōō-bōō)	211	31°42′N	130°46′E
Kokuou, Japan (kô′kōō-ô′ōōo)	211b	34°34′N	135°39′E
Kola Peninsula *see* Kol′skiy Poluostrov, pen., Russia	178	67°15′N	37°40′E
Kolār (Kolār Gold Fields), India (kôl-är′)	199	13°39′N	78°33′E
Kolárvo, Slvk. (kōl-árōvō)	169	47°54′N	17°59′E
Kolbio, Kenya	237	1°10′S	41°15′E
Kol′chugino, Russia (kôl-chò′gě-nô)	176	56°19′N	39°29′E
Kolda, Sen.	234	12°53′N	14°57′W
Kolding, Den. (kŭl′dĭng)	166	55°29′N	9°24′E
Kole, D.R.C. (kō′lå)	232	3°19′S	22°46′E
Kolguyev, i., Russia (kôl-gò′yĕf)	178	69°00′N	49°00′E
Kolhāpur, India	203	16°48′N	74°15′E
Kolin, Czech Rep. (kō′lēn)	168	50°01′N	15°11′E
Kolkasrags, c., Lat. (kôl-käs′rágz)	167	57°46′N	22°39′E
Kolkata (Calcutta), India	199	22°32′N	88°22′E
Köln *see* Cologne, Ger.	171c	50°56′N	6°57′E
Kolno, Pol. (kôw′nô)	169	53°23′N	21°56′E
Koło, Pol. (kô′wô)	169	52°11′N	18°37′E
Kołobrzeg, Pol. (kô-lôb′zhĕk)	160	54°10′N	15°35′E
Kolomna, Russia (kál-ôm′nå)	180	55°06′N	38°47′E
Kolomyia, Ukr.	169	48°32′N	25°04′E
Kolp′, r., Russia (kôlp)	176	59°18′N	35°32′E
Kolpashevo, Russia (kŭl på shô′vå)	178	58°16′N	82°43′E
Kolpino, Russia (kôl′pě-nô)	180	59°45′N	30°37′E
Kolpny, Russia (kôlp′nyě)	176	52°14′N	36°54′E
Kol′skiy Poluostrov, pen., Russia	178	67°15′N	37°40′E
Kolva, r., Russia	180	61°00′N	57°00′E
Kolwezi, D.R.C. (kōl-wĕ′zē)	232	10°43′S	25°28′E
Kolyberovo, Russia (kô-lĭ-byâ′rô-vô)	186b	55°16′N	38°45′E
Kolyma, r., Russia	179	66°30′N	151°45′E
Kolymskiy Mountains *see* Gydan, Khrebet, mts., Russia	179	61°45′N	155°00′E
Kom, r., Afr.	236	2°15′N	12°05′E
Komadugu Gana, r., Nig.	235	12°15′N	11°10′E
Komae, Japan	211a	35°37′N	139°35′E
Komandorskiye Ostrova, is., Russia	197	55°40′N	167°13′E
Komárno, Slvk. (kô′mär-nô)	169	47°46′N	18°08′E
Komarno, Ukr.	169	49°38′N	23°42′E
Komárom, Hung. (kô′mä-rôm)	169	47°45′N	18°06′E
Komatipoort, S. Afr. (kō-mä′tě-pōrt)	232	25°21′S	32°00′E
Komatsu, Japan (kō-mät′sōō)	210	36°23′N	136°26′E
Komatsushima, Japan (kō-mät′sōō-shě′mä)	211	34°04′N	134°32′E
Komeshia, D.R.C.	237	8°01′S	27°07′E
Komga, S. Afr. (kōm′gå)	233c	32°36′S	27°54′E
Komi, prov., Russia (kômě)	184	63°00′N	55°00′E
Kommetijie, S. Afr.	232a	34°09′S	18°19′E
Komoé, r., C. Iv.	234	5°40′N	3°40′W
Komsomolets, Kaz.	186a	53°45′N	62°04′E
Komsomol′sk-na-Amure, Russia	179	50°46′N	137°14′E
Kona, Mali	234	14°57′N	3°53′W
Konda, r., Russia (kôn′då)	180	60°50′N	64°00′E
Kondas, r., Russia (kôn′dås)	186a	59°30′N	56°28′E
Kondoa, Tan. (kôn-dō′å)	232	4°52′S	36°00′E
Kondolole, D.R.C.	237	1°20′N	25°58′E
Koné, N. Cal.	214f	21°04′S	164°52′E
Kong, C. Iv. (kông)	230	9°05′N	4°41′W
Kongbo, C.A.R.	236	4°44′N	21°23′E
Kongolo, D.R.C. (kôŋ′gō′lō)	232	5°23′S	27°00′E
Kongsberg, Nor. (kŭngs′bĕrg)	166	59°40′N	9°36′E
Kongsvinger, Nor. (kŭngs′vĭŋ-gẽr)	166	60°12′N	12°00′E
Koni, D.R.C. (kō′nē)	232	10°32′S	27°27′E
Königsberg *see* Kaliningrad, Russia	178	54°42′N	20°32′E
Königsbrunn, Ger. (kû′nēgs-brōōn)	159d	48°16′N	10°53′E
Königs Wusterhausen, Ger. (kû′nēgs vōōs′tĕr-hou-zĕn)	159b	52°18′N	13°38′E
Konin, Pol. (kô′nyĕn)	161	52°11′N	18°17′E
Kónitsa, Grc. (kô′nyē′tså)	175	40°03′N	20°46′E
Konjic, Bos. (kôn′yēts)	175	43°38′N	17°59′E
Konju, Kor., S.	210	36°21′N	127°05′E
Konnagar, India	202a	22°41′N	88°22′E
Konotop, Ukr. (kô-nô-tôp′)	181	51°13′N	33°14′E
Konpienga, r., Burkina	234	11°15′N	0°35′E
Konqi, r., China (kôn-chyē)	204	41°09′N	87°46′E
Końskie, Pol. (koin′′skyĕ)	169	51°12′N	20°26′E
Konstanz, Ger. (kôn′shtänts)	168	47°39′N	9°10′E
Kontagora, Nig. (kōn-tå-gō′rä)	230	10°24′N	5°28′E
Konya, Tur. (kōn′yå)	198	36°55′N	32°25′E
Koocanusa, Lake, res., N.A.	114	49°00′N	115°10′W
Kootenay (Kootenai), r., N.A.	95	49°45′N	117°05′W
Kootenay Lake, l., Can.	95	49°35′N	116°50′W
Kootenay National Park, rec., Can. (kōō′tě-nå)	90	51°06′N	117°02′W
Kōō-zan, mtn., Japan (kōō′zän)	211b	34°53′N	135°32′E
Kopervik, Nor. (kô′pĕr-vĕk)	166	59°18′N	5°20′E

PLACE (Pronunciation)	PAGE	LAT.	LONG.
Kopeysk, Russia (kô-pāsk′)	184	55°07′N	61°37′E
Köping, Swe. (chû′pĭng)	166	59°32′N	15°58′E
Kopparberg, Swe. (kŏp′pår-bĕrgh)	166	59°53′N	15°00′E
Koppeh Dāgh, mts., Asia	198	37°28′N	58°29′E
Koppies, S. Afr.	238c	27°15′S	27°35′E
Koprivnica, Cro. (kô′prēv-nĕ′tså)	174	46°10′N	16°48′E
Kopychyntsi, Ukr.	169	49°06′N	25°55′E
Korčula, i., Serb. (kôr′chōō-lå)	175	42°50′N	17°05′E
Korea, North, nation, Asia	205	40°00′N	127°00′E
Korea, South, nation, Asia	205	36°30′N	128°00′E
Korea Bay, b., Asia	208	39°18′N	123°50′E
Korean Archipelago, is., Kor., S.	205	34°05′N	125°35′E
Korea Strait, strt., Asia	205	33°30′N	128°30′E
Korets′, Ukr.	169	50°35′N	27°13′E
Korhogo, C. Iv. (kôr-hō′gō)	230	9°27′N	5°38′W
Korinthiakós Kólpos, b., Grc.	163	38°15′N	22°33′E
Kórinthos, Grc. (kô-rĕn′thôs) (kŏr′ĭnth)	154	37°56′N	22°54′E
Koriukivka, Ukr.	177	51°44′N	32°24′E
Kōriyama, Japan (kō′rĕ-yä′mä)	210	37°18′N	140°25′E
Korkino, Russia (kôr′kē-nŭ)	186a	54°53′N	61°25′E
Korla, China (kōr-lä)	204	41°37′N	86°03′E
Körmend, Hung. (kûr′mĕnt)	168	47°02′N	16°36′E
Kornat, i., Serb. (kôr-nät′)	174	43°46′N	15°10′E
Korneuburg, Aus. (kôr′noi-bòrgh)	159e	48°22′N	16°21′E
Koro, Mali	234	14°04′N	3°05′W
Korocha, Russia (kô-rō′chå)	177	50°50′N	37°13′E
Korop, Ukr. (kō′rôp)	177	51°33′N	32°54′E
Koro Sea, sea, Fiji	214g	18°00′S	179°50′E
Korosten′, Ukr. (kô′rôs-tĕn)	181	50°51′N	28°39′E
Korostyshiv, Ukr.	177	50°19′N	29°05′E
Koro Toro, Chad	235	16°05′N	18°30′E
Korotoyak, Russia (kô′rô-tô-yåk′)	177	51°00′N	39°06′E
Korsakov, Russia (kôr′så-kôf′)	179	46°42′N	143°16′E
Korsnäs, Fin. (kôrs′nĕs)	167	62°51′N	21°17′E
Korsør, Den. (kôrs′ûr′)	166	55°19′N	11°08′E
Kortrijk, Bel.	165	50°49′N	3°10′E
Koryakskiy Khrebet, mts., Russia	179	62°00′N	168°45′E
Kosa Byriuchyi ostriv, i., Ukr.	177	46°07′N	35°12′E
Kościan, Pol. (kŭsh′tsyån)	168	52°05′N	16°38′E
Kościerzyna, Pol. (kŭsh-tsyĕ-zhē′nå)	169	54°08′N	17°59′E
Kosciusko, Ms., U.S. (kŏs-ĭ-ŭs′kō)	124	33°04′N	89°35′W
Kosciuszko, Mount, mtn., Austl.	221	36°26′S	148°20′E
Kosha, Sudan	231	20°49′N	30°27′E
Koshigaya, Japan (kô′shĕ-gä′yä)	211a	35°53′N	139°48′E
Köshim, r., Kaz.	181	50°30′N	50°40′E
Kosi, r., India (kô′sē)	202	26°00′N	86°20′E
Košice, Slvk. (kō′shĕ-tsĕ′)	161	48°43′N	21°17′E
Kosmos, S. Afr. (kŏz′mŏs)	233b	25°45′S	27°51′E
Kosobrodskiy, Russia (kä-sô′brôd-skĭ)	186a	54°14′N	60°53′E
Kosovo, hist. reg., Serb.	175	42°35′N	21°00′E
Kosovska Mitrovica, Serb. (kô′sôv-skä′ mĕ′trô-vĕ-tsä′)	175	42°51′N	20°50′E
Kostajnica, Cro. (kôs′tä-ĕ-nē′tså)	174	45°14′N	16°32′E
Koster, S. Afr.	238c	25°52′S	26°52′E
Kostiantynivka, Ukr.	177	48°33′N	37°42′E
Kostino, Russia (kôs′tĭ-nô)	186b	55°54′N	37°51′E
Kostroma, Russia (kôs-trô-må′)	178	57°46′N	40°55′E
Kostroma, prov., Russia	176	57°50′N	41°10′E
Kostrzyn, Pol. (kôst′chěn)	161	52°35′N	14°38′E
Kos′va, r., Russia (kôs′vå)	186a	58°44′N	57°08′E
Koszalin, Pol. (kô-shä′lĭn)	160	54°12′N	16°10′E
Köszeg, Hung. (kû′sĕg)	168	47°21′N	16°32′E
Kota, India	199	25°17′N	75°49′E
Kota Baharu, Malay. (kō′tä bä′rōō)	212	6°15′N	102°23′E
Kotabaru, Indon.	212	3°22′S	116°15′E
Kota Kinabalu, Malay.	212	5°55′N	116°05′E
Kota Tinggi, Malay.	197b	1°43′N	103°54′E
Kotel, Blg. (kō-tĕl′)	175	42°54′N	26°28′E
Kotel′nich, Russia (kô-tyĕl′nĕch)	180	58°15′N	48°20′E
Kotel′nyy, i., Russia (kô-tyĕl′nĕ)	179	74°51′N	134°09′E
Kotka, Fin. (kŏt′kå)	160	60°28′N	26°56′E
Kotlas, Russia (kôt′lås)	180	61°10′N	46°50′E
Kotlin, Ostrov, i., Russia (ôs-trôf′ kôt′lĭn)	186c	60°02′N	29°49′E
Kotor, Serb.	175	42°25′N	18°46′E
Kotorosl′, r., Russia (kô-tô′rôsl)	176	57°18′N	39°08′E
Kotovs′k, Ukr.	177	47°49′N	29°31′E
Kotto, r., C.A.R.	231	5°17′N	22°04′E
Kotuy, r., Russia (kô-tōō′)	184	71°00′N	103°15′E
Kotzebue, Ak., U.S. (kôt′sē-bōō)	106a	66°48′N	162°42′W
Kotzebue Sound, strt., Ak., U.S.	103	67°00′N	164°28′W
Kouchibouguac National Park, rec., Can.	100	46°53′N	65°35′W
Koudougou, Burkina (kōō-dōō′gōō)	230	12°15′N	2°22′W
Kouilou, r., Congo	232	4°30′S	12°00′E
Koula-Moutou, Gabon	236	1°08′S	12°29′E
Koulikoro, Mali (kōō-lĕ-kō′rô)	230	12°53′N	7°33′W
Koulouguidi, Mali	235	13°27′N	17°33′E
Koumac, N. Cal.	214f	20°33′S	164°17′E
Koumra, Chad	235	8°55′N	17°33′E
Koundara, Gui.	234	12°29′N	13°18′W
Kouroussa, Gui. (kōō-rōō′sä)	230	10°39′N	9°53′W
Koutiala, Mali (kōō-tĕ-ä′lä)	230	12°29′N	5°29′W
Kouvola, Fin. (kō′ò-vô-lä)	167	60°51′N	26°40′E
Kouzhen, China (kō-jŭn)	206	36°19′N	117°37′E
Kovda, l., Russia (kôv′då)	180	66°45′N	32°00′E
Kovel′, Ukr. (kō′vĕl)	181	51°13′N	24°45′E
Kovno *see* Kaunas, Lith.	178	54°42′N	23°54′E
Kovrov, Russia (kôv-rôf′)	180	56°23′N	41°21′E
Koyuk, Ak., U.S. (kô-yōōk′)	103	65°00′N	161°18′W
Koyukuk, r., Ak., U.S. (kô-yōō′kòk)	103	66°25′N	153°50′W
Kozáni, Grc.	163	40°16′N	21°51′E
Kozelets′, Ukr. (kôzĕ-lyĕts)	177	50°53′N	31°07′E
Kozel′sk, Russia (kô-zĕlsk′)	176	54°01′N	35°49′E
Kozhikode, India	199	11°19′N	75°49′E

ăt; finăl; rāte; senāte; ärm; åsk; sofȧ; fâre; ch-choose; dh-as th in other; bē; ēvent; bĕt; recĕnt; cratẽr; g-gō; gh-guttural g; bĭt; ĭ-short neutral; rīde; κ-guttural k as ch in German ich;

L

ng-sing; ŋ-baŋk; ɴ-nasalized n; nŏd; cŏmmit; ōld; ôbey; ôrder; oi-boil; fōōd; ȯ-as oo in foot; ou-out; s-soft; sh-dish; th-thin; pūre; ûnite; ûrn; stŭd; circǔs; ü-as in French tu; ´-indeterminate vowel.

312 Labuan – L'Anse PRONOUNCING INDEX

PLACE (Pronunciation)	PAGE	LAT.	LONG.
Labuan, Pulau, i., Malay. (lä-bö-än′)	212	5°28′N	115°11′E
Labuha, Indon.	213	0°43′S	127°35′E
L'Acadie, Can. (lȧ-kȧ-dē′)	102a	45°18′N	73°22′W
L'Acadie, r., Can.	102a	45°24′N	73°21′W
La Calera, Chile (lä-kä-lĕ-rä)	141b	32°47′S	71°11′W
La Calera, Col.	142a	4°43′N	73°58′W
Lac Allard, Can.	100	50°38′N	63°28′W
La Canada, Ca., U.S. (lä kän-yä′dä)	117a	34°13′N	118°12′W
Lacantum, r., Mex. (lä-kän-tōō′m)	131	16°13′N	90°52′W
La Carolina, Spain (lä kä-rō-lē′nä)	172	38°16′N	3°48′W
La Catedral, Cerro, mtn., Mex. (sĕ′r-rō-lä-kä-tĕ-drà′l)	131a	19°32′N	99°31′W
Lac-Beauport, Can. (läk-bō-pōr′)	102b	46°58′N	71°17′W
Laccadive Islands *see* Lakshadweep, is., India	199	11°00′N	73°02′E
Laccadive Sea, sea, Asia	203	9°10′N	75°17′E
Lac Court Oreille Indian Reservation, I.R., Wi., U.S.	113	46°04′N	91°18′W
Lac du Flambeau Indian Reservation, I.R., Wi., U.S.	113	46°12′N	89°50′W
La Ceiba, Hond. (lȧ sēbä)	128	15°45′N	86°52′W
La Ceja, Col. (lä-sĕ-κä)	142a	6°02′N	75°25′W
Lac-Frontière, Can.	91	46°42′N	70°00′W
Lacha, l., Russia (là′chä)	180	61°15′N	39°05′E
La Chaux de Fonds, Switz. (lȧ shō dē-fôN′)	168	47°07′N	6°47′E
L'Achigan, r., Can. (lä-shē-gäN)	102a	45°49′N	73°48′W
Lachine, Can. (lȧ-shēn′)	102a	45°26′N	73°40′W
Lachlan, r., Austl. (läk′lăn)	221	34°00′S	145°00′E
La Chorrera, Pan. (làchôr-rā′rä)	133	8°54′N	79°47′W
Lachute, Can. (lȧ-shōōt′)	99	45°39′N	74°20′W
La Ciotat, Fr. (lȧ syô-tȧ′)	171	43°13′N	5°35′E
Lackawanna, N.Y., U.S. (lak-ȧ-wŏn′ȧ)	111c	42°49′N	78°50′W
Lac La Biche, Can.	90	54°46′N	112°58′W
Lacombe, Can.	90	52°28′N	113°44′W
Laconia, N.H., U.S. (lȧ-kō′nĭ-ȧ)	109	43°30′N	71°30′W
La Conner, Wa., U.S. (lȧ kŏn′ẽr)	116a	48°23′N	122°30′W
Lacreek, l., S.D., U.S. (lă′krēk)	112	43°04′N	101°46′W
La Cresenta, Ca., U.S. (lȧ krĕs′ĕnt-ȧ)	117a	34°14′N	118°13′W
La Cross, Ks., U.S. (lȧ-krôs′)	120	38°30′N	99°20′W
La Crosse, Wi., U.S.	105	43°48′N	91°14′W
La Cruz, Col. (lȧ krōōz′)	142	1°37′N	77°00′W
La Cruz, C.R. (lä-krōō′z)	132	11°05′N	85°37′W
Lacs, Riviere des, r., N.D., U.S. (rē-vyĕr′ de läk)	112	48°30′N	101°45′W
La Cuesta, C.R. (lä-kwĕ′s-tä)	133	8°32′N	82°51′W
La Cygne, Ks., U.S. (lȧ-sēn′y′) (lȧ-sēn′)	121	38°20′N	94°45′W
Ladd, Il., U.S. (lăd)	108	41°25′N	89°25′W
Ladíspoli, Italy (lä-dē′s-pô-lē)	173d	41°57′N	12°05′E
Lādīz, Iran	201	28°56′N	61°19′E
Ladner, Can. (lăd′nẽr)	94	49°05′N	123°05′W
Lādnun, India (lăd′nòn)	202	27°45′N	74°20′E
Ladoga, Lake *see* Ladozhskoye Ozero, l., Russia	178	60°59′N	31°30′E
La Dorado, Col. (lä dô-rä′dä)	142	5°28′N	74°42′W
Ladozhskoye Ozero, Russia (lȧ-dôsh′skô-yē ô′zĕ-rô)	178	60°59′N	31°30′E
La Durantaye, Can. (lä dü-räN-tā′)	102b	46°51′N	70°51′W
Lady Frere, S. Afr. (lā-dē frâ′r′)	233c	31°48′S	27°16′E
Lady Grey, S. Afr.	233c	30°44′S	27°17′E
Ladysmith, Can. (lā′dĭ-smĭth)	94	48°58′N	123°49′W
Ladysmith, S. Afr.	232	28°38′S	29°48′E
Ladysmith, Wi., U.S.	113	45°27′N	91°07′W
Lae, Pap. N. Gui. (lä′ā)	213	6°15′S	146°57′E
Laerdalsøyri, Nor.	166	61°08′N	7°26′E
La Esperanza, Hond. (lä ĕs-pā-rän′zä)	132	14°20′N	88°21′W
Lafayette, Al., U.S.	124	32°52′N	85°25′W
Lafayette, Ca., U.S.	116b	37°53′N	122°07′W
Lafayette, Ga., U.S. (lä-fā-yĕt′)	124	34°41′N	85°19′W
Lafayette, In., U.S.	105	40°25′N	86°55′W
Lafayette, La., U.S.	105	30°15′N	92°02′W
La Fayette, R.I., U.S.	110b	41°34′N	71°29′W
La Ferté-Alais, Fr. (lä-fĕr-tā′ā-lā′)	171b	48°29′N	2°19′E
La Ferté-sous-Jouarre, Fr. (lȧ fĕr-tā′sōō-zhōō-är′)	171b	48°56′N	3°07′E
Lafia, Nig.	235	8°30′N	8°30′E
Lafiagi, Nig.	235	8°52′N	5°25′E
La Flèche, Fr. (lȧ flāsh′)	170	47°43′N	0°03′W
La Follete, Tn., U.S. (lä-fŏl′ĕt)	124	36°23′N	84°07′W
Lafourche, Bayou, r., La., U.S. (bă-yōō′lȧ-fōōrsh′)	123	29°25′N	90°15′W
La Gaiba, Braz. (lä-gī′bä)	143	17°54′S	57°32′W
La Galite, i., Tun. (gä-lēt)	162	37°36′N	8°03′E
Lågan, r., Nor. (lô′ghĕn)	156	61°00′N	10°00′E
Lagan, r., Swe.	166	56°34′N	13°25′E
Lagan, r., N. Ire., U.K. (lă′găn)	164	54°30′N	6°00′W
Lagarto, r., Pan. (lä-gä′r-tô)	128a	9°08′N	80°05′W
Lagartos, l., Mex. (lä-gä′r-tôs)	132a	21°32′N	88°15′W
Laghouat, Alg. (lä-gwät′)	230	33°45′N	2°49′E
Lagkadás, Grc.	175	40°44′N	23°10′E
Lagny, Fr. (län-yē′)	171b	48°53′N	2°41′E
Lagoa da Prata, Braz. (lȧ-gô′ȧ-dȧ-prä′tȧ)	141a	20°04′S	45°33′W
Lagoa Dourada, Braz. (lȧ-gô′ȧ-dò-rä′dä)	141a	20°55′S	44°03′W
Lagogne, Fr. (lan-gōn′y′)	170	44°43′N	3°50′E
Lagonay, Phil.	213a	13°44′N	123°31′E
Lagos, Nig. (lä′gōs)	230	6°27′N	3°24′E
Lagos, Port. (lä′gôzh)	172	37°08′N	8°43′W
Lagos de Moreno, Mex. (lä′gōs dā mô-rā′nō)	128	21°21′N	101°55′W
La Grand' Combe, Fr. (lȧ gräN kaNb′)	170	44°12′N	4°03′E
La Grande, Or., U.S. (lȧ grănd′)	104	45°20′N	118°06′W
La Grande, r., Can.	93	53°55′N	77°30′W
La Grange, Austl. (lä grānj)	218	18°40′S	122°00′E
La Grange, Ga., U.S. (lȧ-grānj′)	105	33°01′N	85°00′W
La Grange, Il., U.S.	111a	41°49′N	87°53′W
Lagrange, In., U.S.	108	41°40′N	85°25′W
La Grange, Ky., U.S.	108	38°20′N	85°25′W
La Grange, Mo., U.S.	121	40°04′N	91°30′W
Lagrange, Oh., U.S.	111d	41°14′N	82°07′W
Lagrange, Tx., U.S.	123	29°55′N	96°50′W
La Grita, Ven. (lä grē′tȧ)	142	8°02′N	71°59′W
La Guaira, Ven. (lä gwä′ē-rä)	142	10°36′N	66°54′W
La Guardia, Spain (lä gwär′dē-ȧ)	172	41°55′N	8°48′W
Laguna, Braz. (lä-gōō′nä)	144	28°19′S	48°42′W
Laguna, Cayos, is., Cuba (kä′yōs-lä-gò′nä)	134	22°15′N	82°45′W
Laguna Indian Reservation, I.R., N.M., U.S.	119	35°00′N	107°30′W
Lagunillas, Bol. (lä-gōō-nēl′yäs)	142	19°42′S	63°38′W
Lagunillas, Mex. (lä-gōō-nē′l-yäs)	130	21°34′N	99°41′W
La Habana *see* Havana, Cuba	129	23°08′N	82°23′W
La Habra, Ca., U.S. (lȧ hȧb′rȧ)	117a	34°56′N	117°57′W
Lahaina, Hi., U.S. (lä-hä′ē-nä)	126a	20°52′N	156°39′W
Lāhījān, Iran	201	37°12′N	50°01′E
Laholm, Swe. (lä′hôlm)	166	56°30′N	13°00′E
La Honda, Ca., U.S. (lȧ hôn′dȧ)	116b	37°20′N	122°16′W
Lahore, Pak. (lä-hōr′)	199	32°00′N	74°18′E
Lahr, Ger. (lär)	168	48°19′N	7°52′E
Lahti, Fin. (lä′tē)	160	60°59′N	27°39′E
Lai, Chad	231	9°29′N	16°18′E
Lai'an, China (lī-än)	206	32°27′N	118°25′E
Laibin, China (lī-bĭn)	209	23°42′N	109°20′E
L'Aigle, Fr. (lĕ′gl′)	170	48°45′N	0°37′E
Laisamis, Kenya	237	1°36′N	37°48′E
Laiyang, China (läī′yäng)	208	36°59′N	120°42′E
Laizhou Wan, b., China (lī-jō wän)	205	37°22′N	119°19′E
Laja, Río de la, r., Mex. (rē′ō-dĕ-lä-lä′κä)	130	21°17′N	100°57′W
Lajas, Cuba (lä′häs)	134	22°25′N	80°20′W
Lajeado, Braz. (lä-zhĕä′dô)	144	29°24′S	51°46′W
Lajes, Braz. (lä′zhĕs)	144	27°47′S	50°17′W
Lajinha, Braz. (lä-zhē′nyä)	141a	20°08′S	41°36′W
La Jolla, Ca., U.S. (lȧ hoi′yȧ)	118a	32°51′N	117°16′W
La Jolla Indian Reservation, I.R., Ca., U.S.	118	33°19′N	116°21′W
La Junta, Co., U.S. (lȧ hōōn′tȧ)	120	37°59′N	103°35′W
Lake Arthur, La., U.S. (är′thŭr)	123	30°06′N	92°40′W
Lake Barkley, res., U.S.	124	36°45′N	88°00′W
Lake Benton, Mn., U.S. (bĕn′tŭn)	112	44°15′N	96°17′W
Lake Bluff, Il., U.S. (blŭf)	111a	42°17′N	87°50′W
Lake Brown, Austl. (broun)	218	31°03′S	118°30′E
Lake Charles, La., U.S. (chärlz′)	105	30°15′N	93°14′W
Lake City, Fl., U.S.	125	30°09′N	82°40′W
Lake City, Ia., U.S.	113	42°14′N	94°43′W
Lake City, Mn., U.S.	113	44°28′N	92°19′W
Lake City, S.C., U.S.	125	33°57′N	79°45′W
Lake Clark National Park, rec., Ak., U.S.	103	60°30′N	153°15′W
Lake Cowichan, Can. (kou′ĭ-chăn)	94	48°50′N	124°03′W
Lake Crystal, Mn., U.S. (krĭs′tăl)	113	44°05′N	94°12′W
Lake District, reg., Eng., U.K. (lāk)	164	54°25′N	3°20′W
Lake Elmo, Mn., U.S. (ĕlmō)	117g	45°00′N	92°53′W
Lake Forest, Il., U.S. (fŏr′ĕst)	111a	42°16′N	87°50′W
Lake Fork, r., Ut., U.S.	119	40°30′N	110°25′W
Lake Geneva, Wi., U.S. (jĕ-nē′vȧ)	113	42°36′N	88°28′W
Lake Havasu City, Az., U.S.	119	34°27′N	114°22′W
Lake June, Tx., U.S. (jōōn)	117c	32°43′N	96°45′W
Lakeland, Fl., U.S. (lāk′lănd)	105	28°02′N	81°58′W
Lakeland, Ga., U.S.	124	31°02′N	83°02′W
Lakeland, Mn., U.S.	117g	44°57′N	92°47′W
Lake Linden, Mi., U.S. (lĭn′dĕn)	113	47°11′N	88°26′W
Lake Louise, Can. (lōō-ēz′)	95	51°26′N	116°11′W
Lake Mead National Recreation Area, rec., U.S.	119	36°00′N	114°30′W
Lake Mills, Ia., U.S. (mĭlz′)	113	43°25′N	93°32′W
Lakemore, Oh., U.S. (lāk-mōr)	111d	41°01′N	81°24′W
Lake Odessa, Mi., U.S.	108	42°50′N	85°15′W
Lake Oswego, Or., U.S. (ŏs-wē′go)	116c	45°25′N	122°40′W
Lake Placid, N.Y., U.S.	109	44°17′N	73°59′W
Lake Point, Ut., U.S.	117b	40°41′N	112°16′W
Lakeport, Ca., U.S. (lāk′pōrt)	118	39°03′N	122°54′W
Lake Preston, S.D., U.S. (prēs′tŭn)	112	44°21′N	97°23′W
Lake Providence, La., U.S. (prŏv′ĭ-dĕns)	123	32°48′N	91°12′W
Lake Red Rock, res., Ia., U.S.	113	41°30′N	93°15′W
Lake Sharpe, res., S.D., U.S.	112	44°30′N	100°00′W
Lakeside, Ca., U.S. (lāk′sīd)	118a	32°52′N	116°55′W
Lake Station, In., U.S.	111a	41°34′N	87°15′W
Lake Stevens, Wa., U.S.	116a	48°01′N	122°04′W
Lake Success, N.Y., U.S. (sŭk-sĕs′)	110a	40°46′N	73°43′W
Lakeview, Or., U.S.	114	42°11′N	120°21′W
Lake Village, Ar., U.S.	121	33°20′N	91°17′W
Lake Wales, Fl., U.S. (wālz′)	125a	27°54′N	81°35′W
Lakewood, Ca., U.S. (lāk′wo͝od)	117a	33°50′N	118°09′W
Lakewood, Co., U.S.	120	39°44′N	105°06′W
Lakewood, Oh., U.S.	105	41°29′N	81°48′W
Lakewood, Pa., U.S.	109	40°05′N	74°10′W
Lakewood, Wa., U.S.	116a	48°09′N	122°13′W
Lakewood Center, Wa., U.S.	116a	47°10′N	122°31′W
Lake Worth, Fl., U.S. (wûrth′)	125a	26°37′N	80°04′W
Lake Worth Village, Tx., U.S.	117c	32°49′N	97°26′W
Lake Zurich, Il., U.S. (tsü′rĭk)	111a	42°11′N	88°05′W
Lakhdenpokh'ya, Russia (l′ăk-dīe′npôkyȧ)	167	61°33′N	30°10′E
Lakhtinskiy, Russia (lȧk-tĭn′skĭ)	186c	59°59′N	30°10′E
Lakota, N.D., U.S. (lȧ-kō′tȧ)	112	48°04′N	98°21′W
Lakshadweep, state, India	199	10°10′N	72°50′E
Lakshadweep, is., India	199	11°00′N	73°02′E
La Libertad, El Sal.	132	13°29′N	89°20′W
La Libertad, Guat. (lä lē-bĕr-tädh′)	132	15°31′N	91°44′W
La Libertad, Guat.	132a	16°46′N	90°12′W
La Ligua, Chile (lä lē′gwä)	141b	32°21′S	71°13′W
Lalín, Spain (lä-lē′n)	172	42°40′N	8°05′W
La Línea, Spain (lä lē′nā-ä)	162	36°11′N	5°22′W
Lalitpur, Nepal	199	27°23′N	85°24′E
La Louviere, Bel. (lȧ lōō-vyâr′)	165	50°30′N	4°10′E
La Luz, Mex. (lä lōōz′)	130	21°04′N	101°19′W
Lama-Kara, Togo	234	9°33′N	1°12′E
La Malbaie, Can. (lȧ mäl-bā′)	91	47°39′N	70°10′W
La Mancha, reg., Spain (lä män′chä)	172	38°55′N	4°20′W
Lamar, Co., U.S. (lȧ-mär′)	120	38°04′N	102°44′W
Lamar, Mo., U.S.	121	37°28′N	94°15′W
La Marmora, Punta, mtn., Italy (lä-mä′r-mô-rä)	162	40°00′N	9°28′E
La Marque, Tx., U.S. (lȧ-märk)	123a	29°23′N	94°58′W
Lamas, Peru (lă′màs)	142	6°24′S	76°41′W
Lamballe, Fr. (läN-bäl′)	170	48°29′N	2°36′W
Lambari, Braz. (läm-bá′rē)	141a	21°58′S	45°22′W
Lambasa, Fiji	214g	16°26′S	179°24′E
Lambayeque, Peru (läm-bä-yā′kȧ)	142	6°41′S	79°58′W
Lambert, Ms., U.S. (lăm′bẽrt)	124	34°10′N	90°16′W
Lambertville, N.J., U.S. (lăm′bẽrt-vĭl)	109	40°20′N	75°00′W
Lame Deer, Mt., U.S. (lām dēr′)	115	45°36′N	106°40′W
Lamego, Port. (lä-mā′gō)	172	41°07′N	7°47′W
La Mesa, Col.	142a	4°38′N	74°27′W
La Mesa, Ca., U.S. (lä mā′sä)	118a	32°46′N	117°01′W
Lamesa, Tx., U.S.	120	32°44′N	101°54′W
Lamía, Grc. (lä-mē′ȧ)	163	38°54′N	22°25′E
Lamon Bay, b., Phil. (lä-mōn′)	212	14°35′N	121°52′E
La Mora, Chile (lä-mō′rä)	141b	32°28′S	70°56′W
La Moure, N.D., U.S. (lȧ mōōr′)	112	46°23′N	98°17′W
Lampa, r., Chile (lä′m-pä)	141b	33°15′S	70°55′W
Lampasas, Tx., U.S. (lăm-păs′ȧs)	122	31°06′N	98°10′W
Lampasas, r., Tx., U.S.	122	31°18′N	98°08′W
Lampazos, Mex. (läm-pä′zōs)	128	27°03′N	100°30′W
Lampedusa, i., Italy (läm-pȧ-dōō′sä)	162	35°29′N	12°58′E
Lamstedt, Ger. (läm′shtĕt)	159c	53°38′N	9°06′E
Lamu, Kenya (lä′mōō)	233	2°16′S	40°54′E
Lamu Island, i., Kenya	237	2°25′S	40°50′E
La Mure, Fr. (lȧ mür′)	171	44°55′N	5°50′E
Lan', r., Bela. (làn′)	176	52°38′N	27°05′E
Lāna'i, i., Hi., U.S. (lä-nä′ē)	106c	20°48′N	157°06′W
Lanai City, Hi., U.S.	126a	20°50′N	156°56′W
Lanak La, p., China	204	34°40′N	79°50′E
Lanark, Scot., U.K. (lăn′ȧrk)	164	55°40′N	3°50′W
Lancashire, co., Eng., U.K. (lăŋ′kȧ-shĭr)	158a	53°49′N	2°42′W
Lancaster, Eng., U.K.	160	54°04′N	2°55′W
Lancaster, Ky., U.S.	108	37°35′N	84°30′W
Lancaster, Ma., U.S.	101a	42°28′N	71°40′W
Lancaster, N.H., U.S.	109	44°25′N	71°30′W
Lancaster, N.Y., U.S.	111c	42°54′N	78°42′W
Lancaster, Oh., U.S.	108	39°40′N	82°35′W
Lancaster, Pa., U.S.	105	40°05′N	76°20′W
Lancaster, Tx., U.S.	117c	32°36′N	96°45′W
Lancaster, Wi., U.S.	113	42°51′N	90°44′W
Lândana, Ang. (län-dä′nä)	232	5°15′S	12°07′E
Landau, Ger. (län′dou)	168	49°13′N	8°07′E
Lander, Wy., U.S. (lăn′dẽr)	115	42°49′N	108°24′W
Landerneau, Fr. (läN-dĕr-nō′)	170	48°28′N	4°14′W
Landes, reg., Fr. (läNd)	170	44°22′N	0°52′W
Landsberg, Ger. (länds′bo͝orgh)	168	48°03′N	10°53′E
Lands End, c., Eng., U.K.	156	50°03′N	5°45′W
Landshut, Ger. (länts′ho͝ot)	161	48°32′N	12°09′E
Landskrona, Swe. (làns-krō′nȧ)	166	55°51′N	12°47′E
Lanett, Al., U.S. (lȧ-nĕt′)	124	32°52′N	85°13′W
Langat, r., Malay.	197b	2°46′N	101°33′E
Langdon, Can. (lăng′dŭn)	102e	50°58′N	113°40′W
Langdon, Mn., U.S.	117g	44°49′N	92°56′W
L'Ange-Gardien, Can. (länzh gȧr-dyăN′)	102b	46°55′N	71°06′W
Langeland, i., Den.	166	54°52′N	10°46′E
Langenzersdorf, Aus.	159e	48°30′N	16°22′E
Langesund, Nor. (läng′ĕ-sòn′)	166	58°59′N	9°38′E
Langfjorden, b., Nor.	166	62°40′N	7°45′E
Langhorne, Pa., U.S. (lăng′hôrn)	110f	40°10′N	74°55′W
Langia Mountains, mts., Ug.	237	3°35′N	33°35′E
Langjökoll, ice, Ice. (läng-yû′kōōl)	160	64°40′N	20°31′W
Langla Co, l., China (läŋ-lä tswo)	202	30°42′N	80°40′E
Langley, Can. (lăng′lĭ)	95	49°06′N	122°39′W
Langley, S.C., U.S.	125	33°32′N	81°52′W
Langley, Wa., U.S.	116a	48°02′N	122°25′W
Langley Indian Reserve, I.R., Can.	116d	49°12′N	122°31′W
Langnau, Switz. (läng′nou)	168	46°56′N	7°46′E
Langon, Fr. (läN-gôN′)	170	44°34′N	0°16′W
Langres, Fr. (läN′gr′)	171	47°53′N	5°20′E
Langres, Plateau de, plat., Fr. (plä-tō′dĕ-läN′grĕ)	170	47°39′N	5°00′E
Langsa, Indon. (läng′sȧ)	212	4°33′N	97°52′E
Lang Son, Viet. (läng′sŏn′)	212	21°52′N	106°42′E
L'Anguille, r., Ar., U.S. (läN-gē′y′)	121	35°23′N	90°52′W
Langxi, China (läŋ-shyē)	206	31°10′N	119°09′E
Langzhong, China (läŋ-jôŋ)	204	31°40′N	106°05′E
Lanham, Md., U.S. (lăn′ăm)	110e	38°58′N	76°54′W
Lanigan, Can. (lăn′ĭ-găn)	90	51°52′N	105°02′W
Länkäran, Azer. (lĕn-kô-rän′)	178	38°52′N	48°58′E
Lankoviri, Nig.	235	9°00′N	11°25′E
Lansdale, Pa., U.S. (lănz′dāl)	109	40°20′N	75°15′W
Lansdowne, Pa., U.S.	110f	39°57′N	75°17′W
L'Anse, Mi., U.S. (làns)	113	46°43′N	88°28′W

ăt; fināl; rāte; senâte; ärm; ȧsk; sofȧ; fâre; ch-choose; dh-as th in other; bē; ēvent; bĕt; recĕnt; cratẽr; g-gō; gh-guttural g; bĭt; ĭ-short neutral; rīde; κ-guttural k as ch in German ich;

PRONOUNCING INDEX
L'Anse and Vieux Desert – Leivádia 313

PLACE (Pronunciation)	PAGE	LAT.	LONG.
L'Anse and Vieux Desert Indian Reservation, I.R., Mi., U.S.	113	46°41'N	88°12'W
Lansford, Pa., U.S. (lănz′fērd)	109	40°50'N	75°50'W
Lansing, Ia., U.S.	113	43°22'N	91°16'W
Lansing, Il., U.S.	111a	41°34'N	87°33'W
Lansing, Ks., U.S.	117f	39°15'N	94°53'W
Lansing, Mi., U.S.	105	42°45'N	84°35'W
Lanús, Arg. (lä-nōōs′)	144a	34°42'S	58°24'W
Lanusei, Italy (lä-nōō-sĕ′y)	174	39°51'N	9°34'E
Lanúvio, Italy (lä-nōō′vyô)	173d	41°41'N	12°42'E
Lanzarote Island, i., Spain (län-zá-rō′tā)	230	29°04'N	13°03'W
Lanzhou, China (län-jō)	204	35°55'N	103°55'E
Laoag, Phil. (lä-wäg′)	212	18°13'N	120°38'E
Laon, Fr. (län)	170	49°36'N	3°35'E
La Oroya, Peru (lä-ô-rō′yä)	142	11°30'S	76°00'W
Laos, nation, Asia (lä-ōs) (lá-ōs′)	212	20°15'N	102°00'E
Laoshan Wan, b., China (lou-shän wän)	206	36°21'N	120°48'E
La Palma, Pan. (lä-päl′mä)	133	8°25'N	78°07'W
La Palma, Spain	172	37°24'N	6°36'W
La Palma Island, i., Spain	230	28°42'N	19°03'W
La Pampa, prov., Arg.	144	37°25'S	67°00'W
Lapa Rio Negro, Braz. (lä-pä-rē′ō-nĕ′grô)	144	26°12'S	49°56'W
La Paz, Arg. (lä päz′)	144	30°48'S	59°47'W
La Paz, Bol.	142	16°31'S	68°03'W
La Paz, Hond.	132	14°15'N	87°40'W
La Paz, Mex. (lä-pá′z)	130	23°39'N	100°44'W
La Paz, Mex.	128	24°00'N	110°15'W
Lapeer, Mi., U.S. (lá-pēr′)	108	43°05'N	83°15'W
La-Penne-sur-Huveaune, Fr. (la-pĕn′sür-ü-vōn′)	170a	43°18'N	5°33'E
La Perouse, Austl.	217b	33°59'S	151°14'E
La Piedad Cabadas, Mex. (lä pyå-dhädh′ kä-bä′dhäs)	130	20°20'N	102°04'W
Lapland, hist. reg., Eur. (lăp′lănd)	154	68°20'N	22°00'E
La Plata, Arg. (lä plä′tä)	144	34°54'S	57°57'W
La Plata, Mo., U.S. (lá plā′tá)	121	40°03'N	92°28'W
La Plata Peak, mtn., Co., U.S.	119	39°00'N	106°25'W
La Pocatière, Can. (lá pô-ká-tyår′)	99	47°24'N	70°01'W
La Poile Bay, b., Can. (lá pwäl′)	101	47°38'N	58°20'W
La Porte, In., U.S. (lá pōrt′)	108	41°35'N	86°45'W
Laporte, Oh., U.S.	111d	41°19'N	82°05'W
La Porte, Tx., U.S.	123a	29°40'N	95°01'W
La Porte City, Ia., U.S.	113	42°20'N	92°10'W
Lappeenranta, Fin. (lä′pēn-rän′tä)	167	61°04'N	28°08'E
La Prairie, Can. (lá-prå-rē′)	102a	45°24'N	73°30'W
Lâpseki, Tur. (läp′sá-kē)	175	40°20'N	26°41'E
Laptev Sea, sea, Russia (läp′tyĭf)	179	75°39'N	120°00'E
La Puebla de Montalbán, Spain	172	39°54'N	4°21'W
La Puente, Ca., U.S. (pwĕn′tē)	117a	34°01'N	117°57'W
Lapuşul, r., Rom. (lä′pōō-shōōl)	169	47°29'N	23°46'E
La Quiaca, Arg. (lä kē-ä′kä)	144	22°15'S	65°44'W
L'Aquila, Italy (lá′kē-lä)	162	42°22'N	13°24'E
Lār, Iran (lär)	198	27°31'N	54°12'E
Lara, Austl.	217a	38°02'S	144°24'E
Larache, Mor. (lä-räsh′)	230	35°15'N	6°09'W
Laramie, Wy., U.S. (lăr′á-mĭ)	104	41°20'N	105°40'W
Laramie, r., Co., U.S.	120	40°56'N	105°55'W
Larchmont, N.Y., U.S. (lärch′mŏnt)	110a	40°56'N	73°46'W
Larch Mountain, mtn., Or., U.S. (lärch)	116c	45°32'N	122°06'W
Laredo, Spain (lä-rā′dhō)	172	43°24'N	3°24'W
Laredo, Tx., U.S.	104	27°31'N	99°29'W
La Réole, Fr. (lá rå-ōl′)	170	44°37'N	0°03'W
Largeau, Chad (lär-zhō′)	231	17°55'N	19°07'E
Largo, Cayo, Cuba (kä′yō-lär′gō)	134	21°40'N	81°30'W
Larimore, N.D., U.S. (lăr′ĭ-môr)	112	47°53'N	97°38'W
Larino, Italy (lä-rē′nô)	174	41°48'N	14°54'E
La Rioja, Arg. (lä rê-ōhä)	144	29°18'S	67°42'W
La Rioja, prov., Arg. (lä-rê-ô′kä)	144	28°45'S	68°00'W
Lárisa, Grc. (lä′rē-sä)	163	39°38'N	22°25'E
Lärkāna, Pak.	202	27°40'N	68°12'E
Larnaka, Cyp.	163	34°55'N	33°37'E
Lárnakos, Kólpos, b., Cyp.	197a	36°50'N	33°45'E
Larned, Ks., U.S. (lär′nĕd)	120	38°09'N	99°07'W
La Robla, Spain (lä rōb′lä)	172	42°48'N	5°36'W
La Rochelle, Fr. (lá rô-shĕl′)	154	46°10'N	1°09'W
La Roche-sur-Yon, Fr. (lá rôsh′sûr-yôn′)	161	46°39'N	1°27'W
La Roda, Spain (lä rō′dä)	172	39°13'N	2°08'W
La Romona, Dom. Rep. (lä-rä-mô′nä)	135	18°25'N	69°00'W
Larrey Point, c., Austl. (lăr′ē)	220	19°15'S	118°15'E
Laruns, Fr. (lá-răns′)	170	42°58'N	0°28'W
Larvik, Nor. (lär′vĕk)	160	59°06'N	10°03'E
La Sabana, Ven. (lä-sä-bá′nä)	143b	10°38'N	66°24'W
La Sabina, Cuba (lä-sä-bē′nä)	135a	22°51'N	82°05'W
La Sagra, mtn., Spain (lä sä′grä)	162	37°56'N	2°35'W
La Sal, Ut., U.S. (lá sál′)	119	38°10'N	109°20'W
La Salle, Can. (lá săl′)	111b	42°14'N	83°06'W
La Salle, Can.	102a	45°26'N	73°39'W
La Salle, Can.	102f	49°41'N	97°16'W
La Salle, Il., U.S.	108	41°20'N	89°05'W
Las Animas, Co., U.S. (lás ă′nĭ-más)	120	38°03'N	103°16'W
La Sarre, Can.	91	48°43'N	79°12'W
Lascahobas, Haiti (läs-kä-ō′bás)	135	19°00'N	71°55'W
Las Cruces, Mex. (läs-krōō′sĕs)	131	16°37'N	93°54'W
Las Cruces, N.M., U.S.	104	32°20'N	106°50'W
La Selle, Massif de, mtn., Haiti (lä′sĕl′)	135	18°25'N	72°05'W
La Serena, Chile (lä-sĕ-rĕ′nä)	144	29°55'S	71°24'W
La Seyne, Fr. (lä-sân′)	161	43°07'N	5°52'E
Las Flores, Arg. (läs flo′rĕs)	144	36°01'S	59°07'W
Lashio, Mya. (lăsh′ē-ō)	204	22°58'N	98°03'E
Las Juntas, C.R. (läs-ĸōō′n-täs)	132	10°15'N	85°00'W
Las Maismas, sw., Spain (läs-mī′s-mäs)	172	37°05'N	6°25'W
La Solana, Spain (lä-sô-lä-nä)	172	38°56'N	3°13'W
Las Palmas, Pan.	133	8°08'N	81°30'W
Las Palmas de Gran Canaria, Spain (läs päl′mäs)	230	28°07'N	15°28'W
La Spezia, Italy (lä-spĕ′zyä)	154	44°07'N	9°48'E
Las Piedras, Ur. (läs-pyĕ′dràs)	141c	34°42'S	56°08'W
Las Pilas, vol., Nic. (läs-pē′läs)	132	12°32'N	86°43'W
Las Rosas, Mex. (läs rō thäs)	131	16°24'N	92°23'W
Las Rozas de Madrid, Spain (läs rō′thas dā mä-dhrēd′)	173a	40°29'N	3°53'W
Lassee, Aus.	159e	48°14'N	16°50'E
Lassen Peak, mtn., Ca., U.S. (lăs′ĕn)	106	40°30'N	121°32'W
Lassen Volcanic National Park, rec., Ca., U.S.	106	40°43'N	121°35'W
L'Assomption, Can. (lás-sôm-syôɴ)	102a	45°50'N	73°25'W
Lass Qoray, Som.	238a	11°13'N	48°19'E
Las Tablas, Pan. (läs tä′bläs)	133	7°48'N	80°16'W
Last Mountain, l., Can. (làst moun′tĭn)	92	51°05'N	105°10'W
Lastoursville, Gabon (lás-tōōr-vēl′)	232	1°00'S	12°49'E
Las Tres Vírgenes, Volcán, vol., Mex. (vē′r-hĕ-nĕs)	128	26°00'N	111°45'W
Las Tunas, prov., Cuba	134	21°05'N	77°00'W
Las Vacas, Mex. (läs-vá′käs)	131	16°24'N	95°48'W
Las Vegas, Chile (läs-vĕ′gäs)	141b	32°50'S	70°59'W
Las Vegas, N.M., U.S.	104	35°36'N	105°13'W
Las Vegas, Nv., U.S. (läs vā′gäs)	104	36°12'N	115°10'W
Las Vegas, Ven. (läs-vĕ′gäs)	143b	10°26'N	64°08'W
Las Vigas, Mex.	131	19°38'N	97°03'W
Las Vizcachas, Meseta de, plat., Arg.	144	49°35'S	71°00'W
Latacunga, Ec. (lä-tä-kòŋ′gä)	142	1°02'S	78°33'W
Latakia *see* Al Lādhiqīyah, Syria	198	35°32'N	35°51'E
La Teste-de-Buch, Fr. (lä-tĕst-dĕ-büsh)	170	44°38'N	1°11'W
Lathrop, Mo., U.S. (lā′thrŭp)	121	39°32'N	94°21'W
La Tortuga, Isla, i., Ven. (ē′s-lä-lä-tôr-tōō′gä)	142	10°55'N	65°18'W
Latorytsia, r., Eur.	169	48°27'N	22°30'E
Latourell, Or., U.S. (lá-tou′rĕl)	116c	45°32'N	122°13'W
La Tremblade, Fr. (lä-trĕɴ-bläd′)	170	45°45'N	1°12'W
Latrobe, Pa., U.S. (lá-trōb′)	109	40°25'N	79°15'W
La Tuque, Can. (lá′tük′)	91	47°27'N	72°49'W
Lātūr, India (lä-tōōr′)	202	18°20'N	76°35'E
Latvia, nation, Eur.	178	57°28'N	24°29'E
Lau Group, is., Fiji	214g	18°20'S	178°30'W
Launceston, Austl. (lôn′sĕs-tŭn)	219	41°35'S	147°22'E
Launceston, Eng., U.K. (lôrn′stŏn)	164	50°38'N	4°26'W
La Unión, Chile (lä-ōō-nyô′n)	144	40°15'S	73°04'W
La Unión, El Sal.	132	13°18'N	87°51'W
La Unión, Mex. (lä ōōn-nyōn′)	130	17°59'N	101°48'W
La Unión, Spain	162	37°38'N	0°50'W
Laura, Austl. (lôrá)	219	15°40'S	144°45'E
Laurel, De., U.S. (lô′rĕl)	109	38°30'N	75°40'W
Laurel, Md., U.S.	110e	39°06'N	76°51'W
Laurel, Ms., U.S.	105	31°42'N	89°07'W
Laurel, Mt., U.S.	115	45°41'N	108°45'W
Laurel, Wa., U.S.	116d	48°52'N	122°29'W
Laurelwood, Or., U.S. (lô′rĕl-wòd)	116c	45°25'N	123°05'W
Laurens, S.C., U.S. (lô′rĕnz)	125	34°29'N	82°03'W
Laurentian Highlands, hills, Can. (lô′rĕn-tĭ-án)	89	49°00'N	74°50'W
Laurentides, Can. (lô′rĕn-tīdz)	102a	45°51'N	73°46'W
Lauria, Italy (lou′rē-ä)	163	40°03'N	15°02'E
Laurinburg, N.C., U.S. (lô′rĭn-bûrg)	125	34°45'N	79°27'W
Laurium, Mi., U.S. (lô′rĭ-ŭm)	113	47°13'N	88°28'W
Lausanne, Switz. (lō-zán′)	154	46°32'N	6°35'E
Laut, Pulau, i., Indon.	212	3°39'S	116°07'E
Lautaro, Chile (lou-tä′rô)	144	38°40'S	72°24'W
Laut Kecil, Kepulauan, is., Indon.	212	4°44'S	115°43'E
Lautoka, Fiji	214g	17°37'S	177°27'E
Lauzon, Can. (lō-zōɴ′)	102b	46°50'N	71°10'W
Lava Beds National Monument, rec., Ca., U.S. (lä′vá bĕds)	114	41°38'N	121°44'W
Lavaca, r., Tx., U.S. (lá-vák′á)	123	29°05'N	96°50'W
Lava Hot Springs, Id., U.S.	115	42°37'N	111°58'W
Laval, Can.	91	45°31'N	73°44'W
Laval, Fr. (lä-väl′)	161	48°05'N	0°47'W
La Vecilla de Curueño, Spain	172	42°53'N	5°18'W
La Vega, Dom. Rep. (lä-vĕ′gä)	135	19°15'N	70°35'W
Lavello, Italy (lä-vĕl′lô)	174	41°05'N	15°50'E
La Verne, Ca., U.S. (lá vûrn′)	117a	34°06'N	117°46'W
Laverton, Austl. (lā′vēr-tŭn)	218	28°45'S	122°30'E
La Victoria, Ven. (lä vēk-tō′rē-ä)	142	10°14'N	67°20'W
La Vila Joiosa, Spain	173	38°30'N	0°14'W
Lavonia, Ga., U.S. (lá-vō′nĭ-á)	124	34°26'N	83°05'W
Lavon Reservoir, res., Tx., U.S.	123	33°06'N	96°20'W
Lavras, Braz. (lä′vräzh)	141a	21°15'S	44°59'W
Lávrio, Grc.	175	37°44'N	24°05'E
Lavry, Russia (lou′rá)	176	57°35'N	27°28'E
Lawndale, Ca., U.S. (lôn′dāl)	117a	33°54'N	118°22'W
Lawra, Ghana	234	10°39'N	2°52'W
Lawrence, In., U.S. (lô′rĕns)	111g	39°59'N	86°01'W
Lawrence, Ks., U.S.	105	38°57'N	95°13'W
Lawrence, Ma., U.S.	101a	42°42'N	71°09'W
Lawrence, Pa., U.S.	111e	40°18'N	80°07'W
Lawrenceburg, In., U.S. (lô′rĕns-bûrg)	111f	39°06'N	84°47'W
Lawrenceburg, Ky., U.S.	108	38°00'N	85°00'W
Lawrenceburg, Tn., U.S.	124	35°13'N	87°20'W
Lawrenceville, Ga., U.S. (lô-rĕns-vĭl)	124	33°56'N	83°57'W
Lawrenceville, Il., U.S.	108	38°45'N	87°45'W
Lawrenceville, N.J., U.S.	110a	40°17'N	74°44'W
Lawrenceville, Va., U.S.	125	36°43'N	77°52'W
Lawsonia, Md., U.S. (lô-sō′nĭ-á)	109	38°00'N	75°50'W
Lawton, Ok., U.S. (lô′tŭn)	104	34°36'N	98°25'W
Lawz, Jabal al, mtn., Sau. Ar.	198	28°46'N	35°37'E
Layang Layang, Malay. (lä-yäng′ lä-yäng′)	197b	1°49'N	103°28'E
Laysan, i., Hi., U.S.	126b	26°00'N	171°00'W
Layton, Ut., U.S. (lā′tŭn)	117b	41°04'N	111°58'W
Lazdijai, Lith. (läzh′dē-yī′)	167	54°12'N	23°35'E
Lazio (Latium), hist. reg., Italy	174	42°05'N	12°25'E
Lead, S.D., U.S. (lēd)	104	44°22'N	103°47'W
Leader, Can.	96	50°55'N	109°32'W
Leadville, Co., U.S. (lĕd′vĭl)	120	39°14'N	106°18'W
Leaf, r., Ms., U.S. (lēf)	124	31°43'N	89°20'W
League City, Tx., U.S. (lēg)	123a	29°31'N	95°05'W
Leamington, Can. (lĕm′ĭng-tŭn)	98	42°05'N	82°35'W
Leamington, Eng., U.K. (lĕ′mĭng-tŭn)	164	52°17'N	1°25'W
Leatherhead, Eng., U.K. (lĕdh′ēr-hĕd′)	158b	51°17'N	0°20'W
Leavenworth, Ks., U.S. (lĕv′ĕn-wûrth)	105	39°19'N	94°54'W
Leavenworth, Wa., U.S.	114	47°35'N	120°39'W
Leawood, Ks., U.S. (lē′wòd)	117f	38°58'N	94°37'W
Łeba, Pol. (lă′bä)	169	54°45'N	17°34'E
Lebam, r., Malay.	197b	1°35'N	104°09'E
Lebango, Congo	236	0°22'N	14°49'E
Lebanon, Il., U.S. (lĕb′á-nŭn)	117e	38°36'N	89°49'W
Lebanon, In., U.S.	108	40°00'N	86°30'W
Lebanon, Ky., U.S.	124	37°32'N	85°15'W
Lebanon, Mo., U.S.	121	37°40'N	92°43'W
Lebanon, N.H., U.S.	109	43°40'N	72°15'W
Lebanon, Oh., U.S.	108	39°25'N	84°10'W
Lebanon, Or., U.S.	114	44°31'N	122°53'W
Lebanon, Pa., U.S.	109	40°20'N	76°20'W
Lebanon, Tn., U.S.	124	36°10'N	86°16'W
Lebanon, nation, Asia	198	34°00'N	34°00'E
Lebedyan', Russia (lyĕ′bĕ-dyän′)	180	53°03'N	39°08'E
Lebedyn, Ukr.	181	50°34'N	34°27'E
Le Blanc, Fr. (lĕ-bläɴ′)	170	46°38'N	0°59'E
Le Borgne, Haiti (lĕ bōrn′y′)	135	19°50'N	72°30'W
Lębork, Pol. (lăɴ-bòrk′)	169	54°33'N	17°46'E
Lebrija, Spain (lå-brē′hä)	172	36°55'N	6°06'W
Lecce, Italy (lĕt′chā)	163	40°22'N	18°11'E
Lecco, Italy (lĕk′kō)	174	45°52'N	9°28'E
Lech, r., Ger. (lĕk)	168	47°41'N	10°52'E
Le Châtelet-en-Brie, Fr. (lĕ-shä-tĕ-lā′ĕɴ-brē′)	171b	48°29'N	2°50'E
Leche, Laguna de, l., Cuba (lä-gō′nä-dĕ-lĕ′chĕ)	134	22°10'N	78°30'W
Leche, Laguna de la, l., Mex.	122	27°16'N	102°45'W
Lecompte, La., U.S.	123	31°06'N	92°25'W
Le Creusot, Fr. (lĕkrû-zō)	161	46°48'N	4°23'E
Ledesma, Spain (lå-dĕs′mä)	172	41°05'N	5°59'W
Leduc, Can. (lĕ-dōōk′)	95	53°16'N	113°33'W
Leech, l., Mn., U.S. (lēch)	113	47°06'N	94°16'W
Leeds, Eng., U.K.	154	53°48'N	1°33'W
Leeds, Al., U.S. (lēdz)	110h	33°33'N	86°33'W
Leeds, N.D., U.S.	112	48°18'N	99°24'W
Leeds, co., Eng., U.K.	158a	53°50'N	1°30'W
Leeds and Liverpool Canal, can., Eng., U.K. (lĭv′ēr-pōōl)	158a	53°36'N	2°38'W
Leegebruch, Ger. (lĕh′gĕn-brōōk)	159b	52°43'N	13°12'E
Leek, Eng., U.K. (lēk)	158a	53°06'N	2°01'W
Leer, Ger. (lār)	168	53°14'N	7°27'E
Leesburg, Fl., U.S. (lēz′bûrg)	125	28°49'N	81°53'W
Leesburg, Va., U.S.	109	39°10'N	77°30'W
Lees Summit, Mo., U.S.	117f	38°55'N	94°23'W
Lee Stocking, i., Bah.	134	23°45'N	76°05'W
Leesville, La., U.S. (lēz′vĭl)	123	31°09'N	93°17'W
Leetonia, Oh., U.S. (lē-tō′nĭ-á)	108	40°50'N	80°45'W
Leeuwarden, Neth. (lā′wär-dĕn)	161	52°12'N	5°50'E
Leeuwin, Cape, c., Austl. (lōō′wĭn)	220	34°15'S	114°30'E
Leeward Islands, is., N.A. (lē′wērd)	123	17°00'N	62°15'W
Lefkáda, Grc.	175	38°49'N	20°43'E
Lefkáda, i., Grc.	163	38°42'N	20°22'E
Le François, Mart.	133b	14°37'N	60°55'W
Lefroy, l., Austl. (lē-froi′)	220	31°30'S	122°00'E
Leganés, Spain (lå-gä′nås)	173a	40°20'N	3°46'W
Legazpi, Phil. (lå-gäs′pē)	213	13°09'N	123°44'E
Legge Peak, mtn., Austl. (lĕg)	222	41°33'S	148°10'E
Leggett, Ca., U.S.	118	39°51'N	123°42'W
Leghorn *see* Livorno, Italy	154	43°32'N	11°18'E
Legnano, Italy (lå-nyä′nō)	174	45°35'N	8°53'E
Legnica, Pol. (lĕk-nĭt′sá)	161	51°13'N	16°10'E
Leh, India (lā)	202	34°10'N	77°40'E
Le Havre, Fr. (lē áv′r′)	154	49°31'N	0°07'E
Lehi, Ut., U.S. (lē′hī)	119	40°25'N	111°55'W
Lehman Caves National Monument, rec., Nv., U.S. (lē′măn)	119	38°54'N	114°08'W
Lehnin, Ger. (lĕh′nēn)	159b	52°19'N	12°45'E
Leicester, Eng., U.K. (lĕs′tēr)	154	52°37'N	1°08'W
Leicestershire, co., Eng., U.K.	158a	52°40'N	1°12'W
Leichhardt, r., Austl. (līk′härt)	220	18°30'S	139°45'E
Leiden, Neth. (lī′dĕn)	165	52°09'N	4°29'E
Leigh Creek, Austl. (lē krēk)	222	30°33'S	138°30'E
Leikanger, Nor. (lī′käŋ′gēr)	166	61°11'N	6°51'E
Leimuiden, Neth.	159a	52°13'N	4°40'E
Leine, r., Ger. (lī′nē)	168	51°58'N	9°56'E
Leinster, hist. reg., Ire. (lĕn-stēr)	164	52°45'N	7°19'W
Leipsic, Oh., U.S. (lĭp′sĭk)	108	41°05'N	84°00'W
Leipzig, Ger. (līp′tsĭk)	154	51°20'N	12°24'E
Leiria, Port. (lā-rē′ä)	172	39°45'N	8°50'W
Leitchfield, Ky., U.S. (lēch′fēld)	124	37°28'N	86°20'W
Leitha, r., Aus.	159e	48°04'N	16°57'E
Leitrim, Can.	102c	45°20'N	75°36'W
Leivádia, Grc.	175	38°25'N	22°51'E

ng-sing; ŋ-baŋk; ɴ-nasalized n; nŏd; cŏmmit; ōld; ôbey; ôrder; oi-boil; fōōd; ò-as oo in foot; ou-out; s-soft; sh-dish; th-thin; pūre; ûnite; ûrn; stŭd; circŭs; ü-as in French tu; ′-indeterminate vowel.

314 Leizhou Bandao – Lincoln Park PRONOUNCING INDEX

PLACE (Pronunciation)	PAGE	LAT.	LONG.
Leizhou Bandao, pen., China (lā-jō bän-dou)	204	20°42'N	109°10'E
Leksand, Swe. (lĕk'sänd)	166	60°45'N	14°56'E
Leland, Wa., U.S. (lē'lănd)	116a	47°54'N	122°53'W
Leliu, China (lŭ-lĭō)	207a	22°52'N	113°09'E
Le Locle, Switz. (lẽ lô'kl')	168	47°03'N	6°43'E
Le Maire, Estrecho de, strt., Arg. (ĕs-trĕ'chô-dĕ-lĕ-mī'rĕ)	144	55°15'S	65°30'W
Le Mans, Fr. (lẽ mäN')	161	48°01'N	0°12'E
Le Marin, Mart.	133b	14°28'N	60°55'W
Le Mars, Ia., U.S. (lē märz')	112	42°46'N	96°09'W
Lemay, Mo., U.S.	117e	38°32'N	90°17'W
Lemdiyya, Alg.	230	36°18'N	2°40'E
Lemery, Phil. (lā-mā-rē')	213a	13°51'S	120°55'E
Lemhi, r., Id., U.S.	115	44°40'N	113°27'W
Lemhi Range, mts., Id., U.S. (lĕm'hī)	115	44°35'N	113°33'W
Lemmon, S.D., U.S. (lĕm'ŭn)	112	45°55'N	102°10'W
Le Môle, Haiti (lẽ mōl')	135	19°50'N	73°20'W
Lemon Grove, Ca., U.S. (lĕm'ŭn-grōv)	118a	32°44'N	117°02'W
Le Moule, Guad. (lẽ mōōl')	133b	16°19'N	61°22'W
Lempa, r., N.A. (lĕm'pä)	132	13°20'N	88°46'W
Lemvig, Den. (lĕm'vēgh)	166	56°33'N	8°16'E
Lena, r., Russia	179	68°00'N	123°00'E
Lençóes Paulista, Braz. (lĕN-sôNs' pou-lēs'tä)	144	22°30'S	48°45'W
Lençóis, Braz. (lĕn-sóis)	143	12°38'S	41°28'W
Lenexa, Ks., U.S. (lē'nĕx-ă)	117f	38°58'N	99°44'W
Lengyandong, China (lŭŋ-yän-dôŋ)	207a	23°12'N	113°21'E
Lenik, r., Malay.	197b	1°59'N	102°51'E
Leningrad *see* Saint Petersburg, Russia	178	59°57'N	30°20'E
Leningrad, prov., Russia	176	59°15'N	30°30'E
Leningradskaya, Russia (lyĕ-nĭn-gräd'skȧ-yȧ)	177	46°19'N	39°23'E
Lenino, Russia (lyĕ'nĭ-nô)	186b	55°37'N	37°41'E
Leninogorsk, Kaz.	183	50°29'N	83°25'E
Lenīnsk, Kaz.	183	45°39'N	63°19'E
Leninsk, Russia (lyĕ-nēnsk')	181	48°40'N	45°10'E
Leninsk-Kuznetski, Russia (lyĕ-nēnsk'kōōz-nyĕt'skĭ)	178	54°28'N	86°48'E
Lennox, S.D., U.S. (lĕn'ŭks)	112	43°22'N	96°53'W
Lenoir, N.C., U.S. (lē-nōr')	125	35°54'N	81°35'W
Lenoir City, Tn., U.S.	124	35°47'N	84°16'W
Lenox, Ia., U.S.	113	40°51'N	94°29'W
Léo, Burkina	234	11°06'N	2°06'W
Leoben, Aus. (lå-ō'bĕn)	168	47°22'N	15°09'E
Léogane, Haiti (lā-ô-gȧn')	135	18°30'N	72°35'W
Leola, S.D., U.S. (lē-ō'lȧ)	112	45°43'N	99°55'W
Leominster, Ma., U.S. (lĕm'ĭn-stẽr)	109	42°32'N	71°45'W
León, Mex. (lå-ōn')	128	21°08'N	101°41'W
León, Nic. (lĕ-ô'n)	128	12°28'N	86°53'W
León, Spain (lĕ-ô'n)	162	42°38'N	5°33'W
Leon, Ia., U.S. (lē'ŏn)	113	40°43'N	93°44'W
León, hist. reg., Spain	172	41°18'N	5°50'W
Leon, r., Tx., U.S. (lē'ŏn)	122	31°54'N	98°20'W
Leonforte, Italy (lā-ôn-fôr'tā)	174	37°40'N	14°27'E
Leopold II, Lac *see* Mai-Ndombe, Lac, l., D.R.C.	232	2°16'S	19°00'E
Leopoldina, Braz. (lā-ô-pôl-dē'nä)	141a	21°32'S	42°38'W
Leopoldsburg, Bel.	159a	51°07'N	5°18'E
Leopoldsdorf im Marchfelde, Aus. (lā'ô-pôlts-dôrf')	159e	48°14'N	16°42'E
Léopoldville *see* Kinshasa, D.R.C.	232	4°18'S	15°18'E
Leova, Mol.	177	46°30'N	28°16'E
Lepe, Spain (lā'pā)	172	37°15'N	7°12'W
Leping, China (lŭ-pĭŋ)	209	29°02'N	117°12'E
L'Épiphanie, Can. (lā-pē-fä-nē')	102a	45°51'N	73°29'W
Le Plessis-Belleville, Fr. (lĕ-plĕ-sē'bĕl-vēl')	171b	49°05'N	2°46'E
Lepreau, Can. (lē-prō')	100	45°10'N	66°28'W
Le Puy, Fr. (lẽ pwē')	161	45°02'N	3°54'E
Lercara Friddi, Italy (lĕr-kä'rä)	174	37°47'N	13°36'E
Lerdo, Mex. (lĕr'dō)	128	25°31'N	103°30'W
Leribe, Leso.	233c	28°53'S	28°02'E
Lerma, Mex. (lĕr'mä)	131	19°49'N	90°34'W
Lerma, Mex.	131a	19°17'N	99°30'W
Lerma, Spain (lĕ'r-mä)	172	42°03'N	3°45'W
Lerma, r., Mex.	130	20°14'N	101°50'W
Le Roy, N.Y., U.S. (lē roi')	109	43°00'N	78°00'W
Lerwick, Scot., U.K. (lĕr'ĭk) (lûr'wĭk)	154	60°08'N	1°27'W
Léry, Can. (lā-rī')	102a	45°21'N	73°49'W
Lery, Lake, l., La., U.S. (lē'rē)	110d	29°48'N	89°45'W
Les Andelys, Fr. (lā-zän-dē-lē')	171b	49°15'N	1°25'E
Les Borges Blanques, Spain	173	41°29'N	0°53'E
Lesbos *see* Lésvos, i., Grc.	156	39°15'N	25°40'E
Les Cayes, Haiti	135	18°15'N	73°45'W
Les Cèdres, Can. (lā-sĕdr'')	102a	45°18'N	74°03'W
Lesh, Alb. (lĕshĕ) (ä-lä'sē-ō)	175	41°47'N	19°40'E
Leshan, China (lŭ-shän)	204	29°40'N	103°40'E
Lésina, Lago di, l., Italy (lä'gō dē lā'zē-nä)	174	41°48'N	15°12'E
Leskovac, Serb. (lĕs'kô-väts)	175	43°00'N	21°58'E
Leslie, S. Afr.	238c	26°23'S	28°57'E
Leslie, Ar., U.S. (lĕz'lĭ)	121	35°49'N	92°32'W
Lesnoy, Russia (lĕs'noi)	180	66°45'N	34°45'E
Lesogorsk, Russia (lyĕs'ō-gôrsk)	210	49°28'N	141°59'E
Lesotho, nation, Afr. (lĕsō'thō)	232	29°45'S	28°07'E
Lesozavodsk, Russia (lyĕ-sô-zȧ-vôdsk')	210	45°21'N	133°19'E
Les Sables-d'Olonne, Fr. (lā sȧ'bl'dō-lŭn')	161	46°30'N	1°47'W
Les Saintes Islands, is., Guad. (lā-săNt')	133b	15°50'N	61°40'W
Lesser Antilles, is.	129	12°15'N	65°00'W
Lesser Caucasus, mts., Asia	182	41°00'N	44°35'E
Lesser Khingan Range, mts., China	205	49°50'N	129°26'E
Lesser Slave, r., Can.	95	55°15'N	114°30'W
Lesser Slave Lake, l., Can. (lĕs'ẽr slāv)	92	55°25'N	115°30'W
Lesser Sunda Islands, is., Indon.	212	9°00'S	120°00'E
L'Estaque, Fr. (lĕs-täl)	170a	43°22'N	5°20'E
Les Thilliers-en-Vexin, Fr. (lā-tē-yā'ĕN-vĕ-săN')	171b	49°19'N	1°36'E
Le Sueur, Mn., U.S. (lē sōōr')	113	44°27'N	93°53'W
Lésvos, i., Grc.	156	39°15'N	25°40'E
Leszno, Pol. (lĕsh'nô)	161	51°51'N	16°35'E
Le Teil, Fr. (lẽ tā'y')	170	44°34'N	4°39'E
Lethbridge, Can. (lĕth'brĭj)	90	49°42'N	112°50'W
Leticia, Col. (lĕ-tē'syȧ)	142	4°04'S	69°57'W
Leting, China (lŭ-tĭŋ)	206	39°26'N	118°53'E
Le Tréport, Fr. (lĕ-trā'pôr')	170	50°03'N	1°21'E
Letychiv, Ukr.	177	49°22'N	27°29'E
Leuven, Bel.	165	50°53'N	4°42'E
Levack, Can.	98	46°38'N	81°23'W
Levallois-Perret, Fr. (lē-vȧl-wä'pĕ-rē')	171b	48°53'N	2°17'E
Levanger, Nor. (lĕ-väng'ẽr)	160	63°42'N	11°01'E
Levanna, mtn., Eur. (lå-vä'nä)	174	45°25'N	7°14'E
Leveque, Cape, c., Austl. (lē-vĕk')	220	16°26'S	123°08'E
Leverkusen, Ger. (lĕ'fĕr-kōō-zĕn)	171c	51°01'N	6°59'E
Levice, Slvk. (lā'vē-tsĕ)	169	48°13'N	18°37'E
Levico, Italy (lā'vē-kō)	174	46°02'N	11°20'E
Le Vigan, Fr. (lĕ vē-gäN')	170	43°59'N	3°36'E
Lévis, Can. (lā-vē') (lē'vĭs)	91	46°49'N	71°11'W
Levittown, Pa., U.S. (lĕ'vĭt-toun)	110f	40°08'N	74°50'W
Levoča, Slvk. (lā'vô-chȧ)	169	49°03'N	20°38'E
Levuka, Fiji	214g	17°41'S	178°50'E
Lewes, Eng., U.K.	165	50°51'N	0°01'E
Lewes, De., U.S. (lōō'ĭs)	109	38°45'N	75°10'W
Lewis, r., Wa., U.S.	114	46°05'N	122°09'W
Lewis, East Fork, r., Wa., U.S.	116c	45°52'N	122°40'W
Lewis, Island of, i., Scot., U.K. (lōō'ĭs)	164	58°05'N	6°07'W
Lewisburg, Tn., U.S. (lū'ĭs-bûrg)	124	35°27'N	86°47'W
Lewisburg, W.V., U.S.	108	37°50'N	80°20'W
Lewis Hills, hills, Can.	101	48°48'N	58°30'W
Lewisporte, Can. (lū'ĭs-pōrt)	101	49°15'N	55°04'W
Lewis Range, mts., Mt., U.S. (lū'ĭs)	115	48°15'N	113°20'W
Lewis Smith Lake, res., Al., U.S.	124	34°05'N	87°07'W
Lewiston, Id., U.S. (lū'ĭs-tŭn)	104	46°24'N	116°59'W
Lewiston, Me., U.S.	105	44°05'N	70°14'W
Lewiston, N.Y., U.S.	111c	43°11'N	79°02'W
Lewiston, Ut., U.S.	115	41°58'N	111°51'W
Lewistown, Il., U.S. (lū'ĭs-toun)	121	40°23'N	90°06'W
Lewistown, Mt., U.S.	104	47°05'N	109°25'W
Lewistown, Pa., U.S.	109	40°35'N	77°30'W
Lexington, Ky., U.S. (lĕk'sĭng-tŭn)	105	38°05'N	84°30'W
Lexington, Ma., U.S.	101a	42°27'N	71°14'W
Lexington, Mo., U.S.	121	39°11'N	93°52'W
Lexington, Ms., U.S.	124	33°08'N	90°02'W
Lexington, N.C., U.S.	125	35°47'N	80°15'W
Lexington, Ne., U.S.	120	40°46'N	99°44'W
Lexington, Tn., U.S.	124	35°37'N	88°24'W
Lexington, Va., U.S.	109	37°45'N	79°20'W
Leyte, i., Phil. (lā'tā)	213	10°35'N	125°35'E
Leżajsk, Pol. (lĕ'zhä-ĭsk)	169	50°14'N	22°25'E
Lezha, r., Russia (lĕ-zhä')	176	58°59'N	40°27'E
L'gov, Russia (lgôf)	177	51°42'N	35°15'E
Lhasa, China (läs'ä)	204	29°41'N	91°12'E
Liangxiangzhen, China (lĭäŋ-shyäŋ-jŭn)	208a	39°43'N	116°08'E
Lianjiang, China (lĭĕn-jyäŋ)	209	21°38'N	110°15'E
Lianozovo, Russia (lĭ-a-nô'zô-vô)	186b	55°54'N	37°36'E
Lianshui, China (lĭĕn-shwā)	206	33°46'N	119°15'E
Lianyungang, China (lĭĕn-yòn-gäŋ)	205	34°35'N	119°09'E
Liao, r., China	208	41°40'N	122°40'E
Liao, r., China	205	43°37'N	120°05'E
Liaocheng, China (lĭou-chŭŋ)	208	36°27'N	115°56'E
Liaodong Bandao, pen., China (lĭou-dôŋ bän-dou)	205	39°45'N	122°22'E
Liaodong Wan, b., China (lĭou-dôŋ wän)	208	40°25'N	121°15'E
Liaoning, prov., China	205	41°31'N	122°11'E
Liaoyang, China (lyä'ō-yäng')	205	41°18'N	123°10'E
Liaoyuan, China (lĭou-yůän)	208	43°00'N	124°59'E
Liard, r., Can. (lē-är')	92	59°43'N	126°42'W
Libano, Col. (lē'bȧ-nō)	142a	4°55'N	75°05'W
Libby, Mt., U.S. (lĭb'ē)	114	48°27'N	115°35'W
Libenge, D.R.C. (lē-bĕŋ'gā)	231	3°39'N	18°40'E
Liberal, Ks., U.S. (lĭb'ẽr-ăl)	120	37°01'N	100°56'W
Liberec, Czech Rep. (lē'bĕr-ĕts)	161	50°45'N	15°06'E
Liberia, C.R.	132	10°38'N	85°28'W
Liberia, nation, Afr. (lī-bē'rĭ-ȧ)	230	6°30'N	9°55'W
Libertad, Arg.	144a	34°42'S	58°42'W
Libertad de Orituco, Ven. (lē-bĕr-tä'd-dĕ-ô-rē-tōō'kô)	143b	9°32'N	66°24'W
Liberty, In., U.S. (lĭb'ẽr-tĭ)	108	39°35'N	84°55'W
Liberty, Mo., U.S.	117f	39°15'N	94°25'W
Liberty, S.C., U.S.	125	34°47'N	82°41'W
Liberty, Tx., U.S.	123	30°03'N	94°46'W
Liberty, Ut., U.S.	117b	41°20'N	111°52'W
Liberty Bay, b., Wa., U.S.	116a	47°43'N	122°41'W
Liberty Lake, l., Md., U.S.	110e	39°25'N	76°56'W
Libertyville, Il., U.S. (lĭb'ẽr-tĭ-vĭl)	111a	42°17'N	87°57'W
Libode, S. Afr. (lĭ-bō'dĕ)	233c	31°33'S	29°03'E
Libón, r., N.A.	135	19°30'N	71°45'W
Libourne, Fr. (lē-bōōrn')	161	44°55'N	0°12'W
Libres, Mex. (lē'brās)	131	19°26'N	97°41'W
Libreville, Gabon (lē-br'vēl')	232	0°23'N	9°27'E
Liburn, Ga., U.S. (lĭb'ûrn)	110c	33°53'N	84°09'W
Libya, nation, Afr. (lĭb'ē-ä)	231	27°38'N	15°00'E
Libyan Desert, des., Afr. (lĭb'ē-ăn)	231	28°23'N	23°34'E
Libyan Plateau, plat., Afr.	200	30°58'N	26°20'E
Licancábur, Cerro, mtn., S.A. (sĕ'r-rô-lē-kȧn-kȧ'bōōr)	144	22°45'S	67°45'W
Licanten, Chile (lē-kän-tĕ'n)	141b	34°58'S	72°00'W
Lichfield, Eng., U.K. (lĭch'fēld)	158a	52°41'N	1°49'W
Lichinga, Moz.	237	13°18'S	35°14'E
Lichtenburg, S. Afr. (lĭk'tĕn-bĕrgh)	238c	26°09'S	26°10'E
Lick Creek, r., In., U.S. (lĭk)	111g	39°43'N	86°06'W
Licking, r., Ky., U.S. (lĭk'ĭng)	108	38°30'N	84°10'W
Lida, Bela. (lē'dȧ)	169	53°53'N	25°19'E
Lidgerwood, N.D., U.S. (lĭj'ẽr-wood)	112	46°04'N	97°10'W
Lidköping, Swe. (lĕt'chû-pĭng)	166	58°31'N	13°06'E
Lido di Roma, Italy (lē'dô-dē-rô'mä)	173d	41°19'N	12°17'E
Lidzbark, Pol. (lĭts'bärk)	169	54°07'N	20°36'E
Liebenbergsvlei, r., S. Afr.	238c	27°35'S	28°25'E
Liebenwalde, Ger. (lē'bĕn-väl-dĕ)	159b	52°52'N	13°24'E
Liechtenstein, nation, Eur. (lĕk'tĕn-shtīn)	161	47°10'N	10°00'E
Liège, Bel.	161	50°38'N	5°34'E
Lienz, Aus. (lē-ĕnts')	168	46°49'N	12°45'E
Liepāja, Lat. (le'pä-yä')	180	56°31'N	20°59'E
Lier, Bel.	159a	51°08'N	4°34'E
Liesing, Aus. (lē'sĭng)	159e	48°09'N	16°17'E
Liestal, Switz. (lēs'täl)	168	47°28'N	7°44'E
Lifanga, D.R.C.	236	0°19'N	21°57'E
Lifou, i., N. Cal.	221	21°15'S	167°32'E
Ligao, Phil. (lē-gä'ō)	213a	13°14'N	123°33'E
Lightning Ridge, Austl.	222	29°23'S	147°50'E
Ligonha, r., Moz. (lē-gō'nyȧ)	233	16°14'S	39°00'E
Ligonier, In., U.S. (lĭg-ô-nēr)	108	41°30'N	85°35'W
Ligovo, Russia (lē'gô-vô)	186c	59°51'N	30°13'E
Liguria, hist. reg., Italy (lē-gōō-rē-ä)	174	44°24'N	8°27'E
Ligurian Sea, sea, Eur. (lĭ-gū'rĭ-ăn)	162	43°42'N	8°32'E
Lihou Reef, rf., Austl. (lē-hōō')	221	17°23'S	152°43'E
Lihuang, China (lē'hōōäng)	206	31°32'N	115°46'E
Lihue, Hi., U.S. (lē-hōō'ā)	106c	21°59'N	159°23'W
Lihula, Est. (lē'hò-lȧ)	167	58°41'N	23°50'E
Liji, China (lē-jyē)	206	33°47'N	117°47'E
Lijiang, China (lē-jyäŋ)	204	27°00'N	100°08'E
Lijin, China (lē-jyĭn)	208	37°30'N	118°15'E
Likasi, D.R.C.	232	10°59'S	26°44'E
Likhoslavl', Russia (lyē-kôsläv''l)	176	57°07'N	35°27'E
Likouala, r., Congo	236	0°10'S	16°30'E
Lille, Fr. (lēl)	154	50°38'N	3°01'E
Lille Baelt, strt., Den.	166	55°09'N	9°53'E
Lillehammer, Nor. (lēl'ĕ-häm'mĕr)	160	61°07'N	10°25'E
Lillesand, Nor. (lēl'ĕ-sän')	166	58°16'N	8°19'E
Lilleström, Nor. (lēl'ĕ-strûm)	166	59°56'N	11°04'E
Lilliwaup, Wa., U.S. (lĭl'ĭ-wŏp)	116a	47°28'N	123°07'W
Lillooet, Can. (lĭ'lōō-ĕt)	90	50°30'N	121°55'W
Lillooet, r., Can.	95	49°50'N	122°10'W
Lilongwe, Mwi. (lē-lô-än)	232	13°59'S	33°44'E
Lima, Peru (lē'mä)	142	12°06'S	76°55'W
Lima, Swe.	166	60°54'N	13°24'E
Lima, Oh., U.S. (lī'mȧ)	105	40°40'N	84°05'W
Lima, r., Eur.	172	41°45'N	8°22'W
Lima Duarte, Braz. (dwä'r-tē)	141a	21°52'S	43°47'W
Lima Reservoir, res., Mt., U.S.	115	44°45'N	112°15'W
Limassol, Cyp.	163	34°39'N	33°02'E
Limay, r., Arg. (lē-mä'ē)	144	39°50'S	69°15'W
Limbaži, Lat. (lēm'bä-zĭ)	167	57°32'N	24°44'E
Limbdi, India	202	22°37'N	71°52'E
Limbe, Cam.	230	4°01'N	9°12'E
Limburg an der Lahn, Ger. (lem-bôrg')	168	50°22'N	8°03'E
Limeira, Braz. (lē-mā'rä)	141a	22°34'S	47°24'W
Limerick, Ire. (lĭm'nák)	161	52°39'N	8°35'W
Limestone Bay, b., Can. (lĭm'stōn)	97	53°50'N	98°50'W
Limfjorden, Den.	160	56°55'N	8°56'E
Limmen Bight, b., Austl. (lĭm'ĕn)	220	14°45'S	136°00'E
Limnos, i., Grc.	163	39°58'N	24°48'E
Limoges, Can. (lē-môzh')	102c	45°20'N	75°15'W
Limoges, Fr.	161	45°50'N	1°15'E
Limón, C.R. (lē-mōn')	129	10°01'N	83°02'W
Limón, Hond. (lē-mō'n)	132	15°53'N	85°34'W
Limon, Co., U.S. (lī'mŏn)	120	39°15'N	103°41'W
Limon, r., Dom. Rep.	135	18°20'N	71°40'W
Limón, Bahía, b., Pan.	128a	9°21'N	79°58'W
Limours, Fr. (lē-mōōr')	171b	48°39'N	2°05'E
Limousin, Plateaus du, plat., Fr. (plä-tō' dü lē-mōō-zăN')	170	45°44'N	1°09'E
Limoux, Fr. (lē-mōō')	170	43°03'N	2°14'E
Limpopo, r., Afr. (lĭm-pō'pō)	232	23°15'S	27°46'E
Linares, Chile (lē-nä'rās)	144	35°51'S	71°35'W
Linares, Mex.	128	24°53'N	99°34'W
Linares, Spain (lē-nä'rĕs)	162	38°07'N	3°38'W
Linares, prov., Chile	141b	35°53'S	71°30'W
Linaro, Cape, c., Italy (lē-nä'rä)	174	42°02'N	11°53'E
Linchuan, China (lĭn-chůän)	205	27°58'N	116°18'E
Lincoln, Arg. (lĭŋ'kŭn)	144	34°51'S	61°29'W
Lincoln, Can.	102d	43°10'N	79°29'W
Lincoln, Eng., U.K.	160	53°14'N	0°33'W
Lincoln, Ca., U.S.	118	38°51'N	121°19'W
Lincoln, Il., U.S.	121	40°09'N	89°21'W
Lincoln, Ks., U.S.	120	39°02'N	98°08'W
Lincoln, Ma., U.S.	101a	42°25'N	71°19'W
Lincoln, Me., U.S.	100	45°23'N	68°31'W
Lincoln, Ne., U.S.	104	40°49'N	96°43'W
Lincoln, Mount, mtn., Co., U.S.	120	39°20'N	106°19'W
Lincoln Heath, reg., Eng., U.K.	158a	53°23'N	0°39'W
Lincoln Park, Mi., U.S.	111b	42°14'N	83°11'W
Lincoln Park, N.J., U.S.	110a	40°56'N	74°18'W

ăt; finăl; rāte; senåte; ärm; åsk; sofȧ; fâre; ch-choose; dh-as th in other; bē; ėvent; bĕt; recĕnt; cratẽr; g-gō; gh-guttural g; bĭt; ĭ-short neutral; rīde; K-guttural k as ch in German ich;

PLACE (Pronunciation)	PAGE	LAT.	LONG.
Lincolnshire, co., Eng., U.K.	158a	53°12'N	0°29'W
Lincolnshire Wolds, Eng., U.K. (woldz′)	164	53°25'N	0°23'W
Lincolnton, N.C., U.S. (lĭŋ′kŭn-tŭn)	125	35°27'N	81°15'W
Lindale, Ga., U.S. (lĭn′dāl)	124	34°10'N	85°10'W
Lindau, Ger. (lĭn′dou)	168	47°33'N	9°40'E
Linden, Al., U.S. (lĭn′dĕn)	124	32°16'N	87°47'W
Linden, Mo., U.S.	117f	39°13'N	94°35'W
Linden, N.J., U.S.	110a	40°39'N	74°14'W
Lindenhurst, N.Y., U.S. (lĭn′dĕn-hûrst)	110a	40°41'N	73°23'W
Lindenwold, N.J., U.S. (lĭn′dĕn-wôld)	110f	39°50'N	75°00'W
Lindesberg, Swe. (lĭn′dĕs-bĕrgh)	166	59°37'N	15°14'E
Lindesnes, c., Nor. (lĭn′ĕs-nĕs)	156	58°00'N	7°05'E
Lindi, Tan. (lĭn′dē)	233	10°00'S	39°43'E
Lindi, r., D.R.C.	231	1°00'N	27°13'E
Lindian, China (lĭn-dĭĕn)	208	47°08'N	124°59'E
Lindley, S. Afr. (lĭnd′lē)	238c	27°52'S	27°55'E
Lindow, Ger. (lēn′dōv)	159b	52°58'N	12°59'E
Lindsay, Can. (lĭn′zē)	99	44°20'N	78°45'W
Lindsay, Ok., U.S.	121	34°50'N	97°38'W
Lindsborg, Ks., U.S. (lĭnz′bôrg)	121	38°34'N	97°42'W
Lineville, Al., U.S. (līn′vĭl)	124	33°18'N	85°45'W
Linfen, China	205	36°00'N	111°38'E
Linga, Kepulauan, is., Indon.	212	0°35'S	105°05'E
Lingao, China (lĭn-gou)	209	19°58'N	109°40'E
Lingayen, Phil. (lĭŋ′gä-yän′)	212	16°01'N	120°13'E
Lingayen Gulf, b., Phil.	213a	16°18'N	120°11'E
Lingdianzhen, China	206	31°52'N	121°28'E
Lingen, Ger. (lĭŋ′gĕn)	168	52°32'N	7°20'E
Lingling, China (lĭŋ-lĭŋ)	209	26°10'N	111°40'E
Lingshou, China (lĭŋ-shō)	206	38°21'N	114°41'E
Linguère, Sen. (lĭŋ-gĕr′)	230	15°24'N	15°07'W
Lingwu, China	208	38°05'N	106°18'E
Lingyuan, China (lĭŋ-yůän)	208	41°12'N	119°20'E
Linhai, China	209	28°52'N	121°08'E
Linhe, China (lĭn-hŭ)	208	40°49'N	107°45'E
Linhuaiguan, China (lĭn-hwī-gůän)	206	32°55'N	117°38'E
Linhuanji, China	206	33°42'N	116°33'E
Linjiang, China (lĭn-jyäŋ)	208	41°45'N	127°00'E
Linköping, Swe. (lĭn′chû-pĭng)	160	58°25'N	15°35'E
Linnhe, Loch, b., Scot., U.K. (lĭn′ē)	164	56°35'N	4°30'W
Linqing, China (lĭn-chyĭŋ)	205	36°49'N	115°42'E
Linqu, China (lĭn-chyōō)	206	36°31'N	118°33'E
Lins, Braz. (lĕ′ᴎs)	143	21°42'S	49°41'W
Linthicum Heights, Md., U.S. (lĭn′thĭ-kŭm)	110e	39°12'N	76°39'W
Linton, In., U.S. (lĭn′tŭn)	108	39°05'N	87°15'W
Linton, N.D., U.S.	112	46°16'N	100°15'W
Linwu, China (lĭn′wōō′)	209	25°20'N	112°30'E
Linxi, China (lĭn-shyē)	208	43°30'N	118°02'E
Linyi, China (lĭn-yē)	205	35°04'N	118°21'E
Linying, China (lĭn′yĭng′)	206	33°48'N	113°56'E
Linz, Aus. (lĭnts)	161	48°18'N	14°18'E
Linzhang, China (lĭn-jäŋ)	206	36°19'N	114°40'E
Lion, Golfe du, b., Fin.	156	43°00'N	4°00'E
Lipa, Phil. (lē-pä′)	212	13°55'N	121°10'E
Lipari, Italy (lē′pä-rē)	174	38°29'N	15°00'E
Lipari, i., Italy	174	38°32'N	15°04'E
Lipetsk, Russia (lyē′pĕtsk)	178	52°26'N	39°34'E
Lipetsk, prov., Russia	176	52°18'N	38°30'E
Liping, China (lē-pĭŋ)	204	26°18'N	109°00'E
Lipno, Pol. (lēp′nô)	169	52°50'N	19°12'E
Lippe, r., Ger. (lĭp′ĕ)	171b	51°36'N	6°45'E
Lippstadt, Ger. (lĭp′shtät)	168	51°39'N	8°20'E
Lipscomb, Al., U.S. (lĭp′skŭm)	110h	33°26'N	86°56'W
Lipu, China (lē-pōō)	209	24°38'N	110°35'E
Lira, Ug.	237	2°15'N	32°54'E
Liri, r., Italy (lē′rē)	174	41°49'N	13°30'E
Lisala, D.R.C. (lē-sä′lä)	231	2°09'N	21°31'E
Lisboa *see* Lisbon, Port.	154	38°42'N	9°05'W
Lisbon (Lisboa), Port.	154	38°42'N	9°05'W
Lisbon, N.D., U.S.	112	46°21'N	97°43'W
Lisbon, Oh., U.S.	108	40°45'N	80°50'W
Lisbon Falls, Me., U.S.	100	43°59'N	70°03'W
Lisburn, N. Ire., U.K. (lĭs′bŭrn)	164	54°35'N	6°05'W
Lisburne, Cape, c., Ak., U.S.	106a	68°20'N	165°40'W
Lishi, China (lē-shr)	208	37°32'N	111°12'E
Lishu, China	208	43°12'N	124°18'E
Lishui, China (lĭ′shwĭ′)	206	31°41'N	119°01'E
Lishui, China	205	28°28'N	120°00'E
Lisianski Island, i., Hi., U.S.	126b	25°30'N	174°00'W
Lisieux, Fr. (lē-zyû′)	170	49°10'N	0°13'E
Lisiy Nos, Russia (lĭ′sĭy-nôs)	186c	60°01'N	30°00'E
Liski, Russia (lyēs′kē)	177	50°56'N	39°28'E
Lisle, Il., U.S. (līl)	111a	41°48'N	88°04'W
L'Isle-Adam, Fr. (lēl-ädäᴎ′)	171b	49°05'N	2°13'E
Lismore, Austl. (lĭz′môr)	219	28°48'S	153°18'E
Litani, r., Leb.	197a	33°28'N	35°42'E
Litchfield, Il., U.S. (lĭch′fēld)	121	39°10'N	89°38'W
Litchfield, Mn., U.S.	113	45°08'N	94°34'W
Litchfield, Oh., U.S.	111d	41°10'N	82°01'W
Lithgow, Austl. (lĭth′gō)	219	33°23'S	149°31'E
Lithinon, Akra, c., Grc.	174a	34°59'N	24°35'E
Lithonia, Ga., U.S. (lĭ-thō′nĭ-ȧ)	110c	33°43'N	84°07'W
Lithuania, nation, Eur. (lĭth-ů-ā′nĭ-ȧ)	178	55°42'N	23°30'E
Litóchoro, Grc.	175	40°05'N	22°29'E
Litoko, D.R.C.	236	1°13'S	24°47'E
Litoměřice, Czech Rep. (lē′tô-myĕr′zhĭ-tsĕ)	168	50°33'N	14°10'E
Litomyšl, Czech Rep. (lē′tô-mēsh′l)	168	49°52'N	16°14'E
Litoo, Tan.	237	9°45'S	38°24'E
Little, r., Austl.	217a	37°54'S	144°27'E
Little, r., Tn., U.S.	124	36°28'N	89°39'W
Little, r., Tx., U.S.	123	30°48'N	96°50'W
Little Abaco, i., Bah. (ä′bä-kō)	134	26°55'N	77°45'W
Little Abitibi, r., Can.	98	50°15'N	81°30'W
Little America, sci., Ant.	224	78°30'S	161°30'W
Little Andaman, i., India (ăn-dȧ-măn′)	212	10°39'N	93°08'E
Little Bahama Bank, bk. (bȧ-hā′mȧ)	134	26°55'N	78°40'W
Little Belt Mountains, mts., Mt., U.S. (bĕlt)	106	47°00'N	110°50'W
Little Bighorn, r., Mt., U.S. (bĭg-hôrn)	115	45°08'N	107°30'W
Little Bighorn Battlefield National Monument, rec., Mt., U.S. (bĭg-hôrn băt′′l-fēld)	115	45°44'N	107°15'W
Little Bitter Lake, l., Egypt	238b	30°10'N	32°36'E
Little Bitterroot, r., Mt., U.S. (bĭt′ēr-ōōt)	115	47°45'N	114°45'W
Little Blue, r., Ia., U.S. (blōō)	117f	38°52'N	94°25'W
Little Blue, r., Ne., U.S.	120	40°15'N	98°01'W
Littleborough, Eng., U.K. (lĭt′′l-bŭr-ô)	158a	53°39'N	2°06'W
Little Calumet, r., Il., U.S. (kăl-ů-mĕt′)	111a	41°38'N	87°38'W
Little Cayman, i., Cay. Is. (kā′mȧn)	134	19°40'N	80°05'W
Little Colorado, r., Az., U.S. (kŏl-ô-rä′dō)	106	36°05'N	111°35'W
Little Compton, R.I., U.S. (kŏmp′tŏn)	110b	41°31'N	71°07'W
Little Corn Island, i., Nic.	133	12°19'N	82°50'W
Little Exuma, i., Bah. (ĕk-sōō′mä)	135	23°25'N	75°40'W
Little Falls, Mn., U.S. (fôlz)	113	45°58'N	94°23'W
Little Falls, N.Y., U.S.	109	43°05'N	74°55'W
Littlefield, Tx., U.S. (lĭt′′l-fēld)	120	33°55'N	102°17'W
Little Fork, r., Mn., U.S. (fôrk)	113	48°24'N	93°30'W
Little Goose Dam, dam, Wa., U.S.	114	46°35'N	118°02'W
Little Hans Lollick, i., V.I.U.S. (häns lôl′lĭk)	129c	18°25'N	64°54'W
Little Humboldt, r., Nv., U.S. (hŭm′bōlt)	114	41°10'N	117°40'W
Little Inagua, i., Bah. (ē-nä′gwä)	135	21°30'N	73°00'W
Little Isaac, i., Bah. (ī′zȧk)	134	25°55'N	79°00'W
Little Kanawha, r., W.V., U.S. (kȧ-nô′wȧ)	108	39°05'N	81°30'W
Little Karroo, plat., S. Afr. (kä-rōō)	232	33°50'S	21°02'E
Little Mecatina, r., Can. (mĕ cȧ tĭ nȧ)	93	52°40'N	62°21'W
Little Miami, r., Oh., U.S. (mī-ăm′ĭ)	111f	39°19'N	84°15'W
Little Minch, strt., Scot., U.K.	164	57°35'N	6°45'W
Little Missouri, r., Ar., U.S. (mĭ-sōō′rĭ)	121	34°15'N	93°54'W
Little Missouri, r., U.S.	106	46°00'N	104°00'W
Little Pee Dee, r., S.C., U.S. (pē-dē′)	125	34°35'N	79°21'W
Little Powder, r., Wy., U.S. (pou′dēr)	115	44°51'N	105°20'W
Little Red, r., Ar., U.S. (rĕd)	121	35°25'N	91°55'W
Little Red, r., Ok., U.S.	121	33°53'N	94°38'W
Little Rock, Ar., U.S. (rôk)	105	34°42'N	92°16'W
Little Sachigo Lake, l., Can. (să′chĭ-gō)	97	54°09'N	92°11'W
Little Salt Lake, l., Ut., U.S.	119	37°55'N	112°53'W
Little San Salvador, i., Bah. (săn săl′vȧ-dôr)	135	24°35'N	75°55'W
Little Satilla, r., Ga., U.S. (sȧ-tĭl′ȧ)	125	31°43'N	82°47'W
Little Sioux, r., Ia., U.S. (sōō)	112	42°22'N	95°47'W
Little Smoky, r., Can. (smōk′ĭ)	95	55°10'N	116°55'W
Little Snake, r., Co., U.S. (snāk)	115	40°40'N	108°21'W
Little Tallapoosa, r., Al., U.S. (tăl-ȧ-pōō′sȧ)	124	32°25'N	85°28'W
Little Tennessee, r., Tn., U.S. (tĕn-ĕ-sē′)	124	35°36'N	84°05'W
Littleton, Co., U.S. (lĭt′′l-tŭn)	120	39°34'N	105°01'W
Littleton, Ma., U.S.	101a	42°32'N	71°29'W
Littleton, N.H., U.S.	109	44°15'N	71°45'W
Little Wabash, r., Il., U.S. (wô′băsh)	108	38°50'N	88°30'W
Little Wood, r., Id., U.S. (wŏŏd)	115	43°00'N	114°08'W
Lityn, Ukr.	177	49°16'N	28°11'E
Liubar, Ukr.	177	49°56'N	27°44'E
Liuhe, China	208	42°10'N	125°38'E
Liuli, Tan.	237	11°05'S	34°38'E
Liupan Shan, mts., China	208	36°20'N	105°30'E
Liuwa Plain, pl., Zam.	236	14°30'S	22°40'E
Liuyang, China (lyōō′yäng′)	209	28°10'N	113°35'E
Liuyuan, China (lĭô-yůän)	206	36°09'N	114°37'E
Liuzhou, China (lĭô-jō)	204	24°25'N	109°30'E
Līvāni, Lat. (lē′vȧ-nē)	167	56°24'N	26°12'E
Lively, Can.	98	46°26'N	81°09'W
Livengood, Ak., U.S. (lĭv′ĕn-gŏŏd)	103	65°30'N	148°35'W
Live Oak, Fl., U.S. (lĭv′ōk)	124	30°15'N	83°00'W
Livermore, Ca., U.S. (lĭv′ēr-mōr)	116b	37°41'N	121°46'W
Livermore, Ky., U.S.	108	37°30'N	87°05'W
Liverpool, Austl. (lĭv′ēr-pōōl)	217b	33°55'S	150°56'E
Liverpool, Can.	91	44°02'N	64°41'W
Liverpool, Eng., U.K.	154	53°25'N	2°52'W
Liverpool, Tx., U.S.	123a	29°18'N	95°17'W
Liverpool Bay, b., Can.	103	69°45'N	130°00'W
Liverpool Range, mts., Austl.	221	31°47'S	151°00'E
Livindo, r., Afr.	231	1°09'N	13°30'E
Livingston, Guat.	132	15°50'N	88°45'W
Livingston, Al., U.S. (lĭv′ĭng-stŭn)	124	32°35'N	88°09'W
Livingston, Il., U.S.	117e	38°58'N	89°51'W
Livingston, Mt., U.S.	104	45°40'N	110°35'W
Livingston, N.J., U.S.	110a	40°47'N	74°20'W
Livingston, Tn., U.S.	124	36°23'N	85°20'W
Livingstone, Zam. (lĭv-ĭng-stôn)	232	17°50'S	25°53'E
Livingstone, Chutes de, wtfl., Afr.	236	4°50'S	14°30'E
Livingstonia, Mwi. (lĭv-ĭng-stō′nĭ-ȧ)	232	10°36'S	34°07'E
Livno, Bos. (lēv′nô)	163	43°50'N	17°03'E
Livny, Russia (lēv′nē)	181	52°28'N	37°36'E
Livonia, Mi., U.S. (lĭ-vō-nĭ-ȧ)	111b	42°25'N	83°23'W
Livorno, Italy (lē-vôr′nō) (lĕg′hôrn)	154	43°32'N	11°18'E
Livramento, Braz. (lē-vrȧ-mĕ′n-tô)	144	30°46'S	55°21'W
Lixian, China (lē shyĕn)	209	29°42'N	111°40'E
Lixian, China	206	38°30'N	115°38'E
Liyang, China (lē′yäng′)	209	31°30'N	119°29'E
Lizard Point, c., Eng., U.K. (lĭz′ȧrd)	161	49°55'N	5°09'W
Lizy-sur-Ourcq, Fr. (lēk-sē′sür-ōōrk′)	171b	49°01'N	3°02'E
Ljubljana, Slvn. (lyōō′blyä′na)	154	46°04'N	14°29'E
Ljubuški, Bos. (lyōō′bōsh-kē)	175	43°11'N	17°29'E
Ljungan, r., Swe.	166	62°50'N	13°45'E
Ljungby, Swe. (lyông′bü)	166	56°49'N	13°56'E
Ljusdal, Swe. (lyōōs′däl)	166	61°50'N	16°11'E
Ljusnan, r., Swe.	160	61°55'N	15°33'E
Llandudno, Wales, U.K. (lăn-düd′nō)	164	53°20'N	3°46'W
Llanelli, Wales, U.K. (lȧ-nĕl′ĭ)	161	51°44'N	4°09'W
Llanes, Spain (lyä′nås)	162	43°25'N	4°41'W
Llano, Tx., U.S. (lā′nō) (lyä′nō)	122	30°45'N	98°41'W
Llano, r., Tx., U.S.	122	30°38'N	99°04'W
Llanos, reg., S.A. (lyä′nōs)	142	4°00'N	71°15'W
Lleida, Spain	162	41°38'N	0°37'E
Llera, Mex. (lyā′rä)	130	23°16'N	99°03'W
Llerena, Spain (lyā-rā′nä)	172	38°14'N	6°02'W
Llíria, Spain	173	39°35'N	0°34'W
Llobregat, r., Spain (lyô-brĕ-gät′)	173	41°55'N	1°55'E
Lloyd Lake, l., Can. (loid)	102e	50°52'N	114°13'W
Lloydminster, Can.	90	53°17'N	110°00'W
Llucena, Spain	173	40°08'N	0°18'W
Llucmajor, Spain	173	39°28'N	2°53'E
Llullaillaco, Volcán, vol., S.A. (lyōō-lyī-lyä′kō)	144	24°50'S	68°30'W
Loange, r., Afr. (lô-äŋ′gä)	232	5°00'S	20°15'E
Lobamba, Swaz.	232	26°27'S	31°12'E
Lobatse, Bots. (lō-bä′tsē)	232	25°13'S	25°35'E
Lobería, Arg. (lō-bĕ′rē′ä)	144	38°13'S	58°48'W
Lobito, Ang. (lô-bē′tō)	232	12°30'S	13°34'E
Lobnya, Russia (lôb′nyȧ)	186b	56°01'N	37°29'E
Lobo, Phil.	213a	13°39'N	121°14'E
Lobos, Arg. (lō′bôs)	141c	35°10'S	59°08'W
Lobos, Cayo, i., Bah. (lō′bôs)	134	22°25'N	77°40'W
Lobos, Isla de, i., Mex. (ē′s-lä-dĕ-lô′bōs)	131	21°24'N	97°11'W
Lobos de Tierra, i., Peru (lô′bō-dĕ-tyĕ′r-rä)	142	6°29'S	80°55'W
Lobva, Russia (lôb′vȧ)	186a	59°12'N	60°28'E
Lobva, r., Russia	186a	59°14'N	60°17'E
Locarno, Switz. (lô-kär′nō)	168	46°10'N	8°43'E
Loches, Fr. (lôsh)	170	47°08'N	0°56'E
Loch Raven Reservoir, res., Md., U.S.	110e	39°28'N	76°38'W
Lockeport, Can.	100	43°42'N	65°07'W
Lockhart, S.C., U.S. (lŏk′härt)	125	34°47'N	81°30'W
Lockhart, Tx., U.S.	123	29°54'N	97°40'W
Lock Haven, Pa., U.S. (lŏk′hā-vĕn)	109	41°05'N	77°30'W
Lockland, Oh., U.S. (lŏk′lănd)	111f	39°14'N	84°27'W
Lockport, Il., U.S.	111a	41°35'N	88°04'W
Lockport, N.Y., U.S.	109	43°11'N	78°43'W
Loc Ninh, Viet. (lōk′nĭng′)	212	12°00'N	106°30'E
Lod, Isr. (lôd)	197a	31°57'N	34°55'E
Lodève, Fr. (lô-dĕv′)	170	43°43'N	3°18'E
Lodeynoye Pole, Russia (lô-dĕy-nô′yĕ)	180	60°43'N	33°24'E
Lodge Creek, r., N.A. (lŏj)	115	49°20'N	110°20'W
Lodge Creek, r., Mt., U.S.	115	48°51'N	109°30'W
Lodgepole Creek, r., Wy., U.S. (lŏj′pōl)	112	41°22'N	104°48'W
Lodhran, Pak.	202	29°40'N	71°39'E
Lodi, Italy (lô′dē)	174	45°18'N	9°30'E
Lodi, Ca., U.S. (lō′dī)	118	38°07'N	121°17'W
Lodi, Oh., U.S. (lō′dī)	111d	41°02'N	82°01'W
Lodosa, Spain (lô-dō′sä)	172	42°27'N	2°04'W
Lodwar, Kenya	237	3°07'N	35°36'E
Łódź, Pol.	154	51°46'N	19°30'E
Loeches, Spain (lô-āch′ĕs)	173a	40°22'N	3°25'W
Loffa, r., Afr.	234	7°10'N	10°35'W
Lofoten, is., Nor. (lô′fō-tĕn)	156	68°26'N	13°42'E
Logan, Oh., U.S. (lō′gȧn)	108	39°35'N	82°25'W
Logan, Ut., U.S.	104	41°46'N	111°51'W
Logan, W.V., U.S.	108	37°50'N	82°00'W
Logan, Mount, mtn., Can.	92	60°54'N	140°33'W
Logansport, In., U.S. (lō′gănz-pōrt)	105	40°45'N	86°25'W
Logone, r., Afr. (lō-gō′nā) (lô-gôn′)	231	10°20'N	15°30'E
Logroño, Spain (lô-grō′nyō)	162	42°28'N	2°25'W
Logrosán, Spain (lô-grô-sän′)	172	39°22'N	5°29'W
Løgstør, Den. (lügh-stûr′)	166	56°56'N	9°15'E
Loir, r., Fr. (lwȧr)	170	47°40'N	0°07'E
Loire, r., Fr.	156	47°30'N	2°00'E
Loja, Ec. (lō′hä)	142	3°49'S	79°13'W
Loja, Spain (lô′-kä)	172	37°10'N	4°11'W
Loka, D.R.C.	236	0°20'N	17°57'E
Lokala Drift, Bots. (lō′kä-lȧ drĭft)	238c	24°00'S	26°38'E
Lokandu, D.R.C.	237	2°31'S	25°47'E
Lokhvytsia, Ukr.	181	50°21'N	33°16'E
Lokichar, Kenya	237	2°23'N	35°39'E
Lokitaung, Kenya	237	4°16'N	35°45'E
Lokofa-Bokolongo, D.R.C.	236	0°12'N	19°22'E
Lokoja, Nig. (lô-kō′yä)	230	7°47'N	6°45'E
Lokolama, D.R.C.	236	2°34'S	19°53'E
Lokosso, Burkina	234	10°19'N	3°40'W
Lol, r., Sudan (lōl)	231	9°06'N	28°09'E
Loliondo, Tan.	237	2°03'S	35°37'E
Lolland, i., Den. (lôl′än′)	166	54°41'N	11°00'E
Lolo, Mt., U.S.	115	46°45'N	114°05'W
Lom, Blg. (lōm)	163	43°48'N	23°15'E

ng-sing; ŋ-baŋk; ᴎ-nasalized n; nŏd; cŏmmit; ōld; ôbey; ôrder; oi-boil; fōōd; ŏŏ-as oo in foot; ou-out; s-soft; sh-dish; th-thin; pūre; ûnite; ûrn; stŭd; circŭs; ü-as in French tu; ′-indeterminate vowel.

ăt; finăl; rāte; senāte; ärm; ȧsk; sofȧ; fāre;   ch-choose;   dh-as th in other;   bē; ĕvent; bĕt; recĕnt; cratĕr; g-gō; gh-guttural g;   bĭt; ĭ-short neutral; rīde;   ᴋ-guttural k as ch in German ich;

PRONOUNCING INDEX
Lukuga – Maḩaţţat Jurf ad Darāwīsh 317

PLACE (Pronunciation)	PAGE	LAT.	LONG.
Lukuga, r., D.R.C. (lōō-kōō'gȧ)	232	5°50'S	27°35'E
Lüleburgaz, Tur. (lü'lĕ-bòr-gäs')	175	41°25'N	27°23'E
Luling, Tx., U.S. (lū'lĭng)	123	29°41'N	97°38'W
Lulong, China (lōō-lôŋ)	205	39°54'N	118°53'E
Lulonga, r., D.R.C.	236	1°00'N	18°37'E
Luluabourg *see* Kananga, D.R.C.	232	6°14'S	22°17'E
Lulu Island, i., Can.	116d	49°09'N	123°05'W
Lulu Island, i., Ak., U.S.	94	55°28'N	133°30'W
Lumajangdong Co, l., China	202	34°00'N	81°47'E
Lumber, r., N.C., U.S. (lŭm'bẽr)	125	34°45'N	79°10'W
Lumberton, Ms., U.S. (lŭm'bẽr-tŭn)	124	31°00'N	89°25'W
Lumberton, N.C., U.S.	125	34°47'N	79°00'W
Luminárias, Braz. (lōō-mē-ná'ryäs)	141a	21°32'S	44°53'W
Lummi, i., Wa., U.S.	116d	48°42'N	122°43'W
Lummi Bay, b., Wa., U.S. (lŭm'ĭ)	116d	48°47'N	122°44'W
Lummi Island, Wa., U.S.	116d	48°44'N	122°42'W
Lumwana, Zam.	237	11°50'S	25°10'E
Lün, Mong.	204	47°58'N	104°52'E
Luna, Phil. (lōō'nä)	213a	16°51'N	120°22'E
Lund, Swe. (lŭnd)	160	55°42'N	13°10'E
Lundy, i., Eng., U.K. (lŭn'dē)	164	51°12'N	4°50'W
Lüneburg, Ger. (lü'nē-bòrgh)	168	53°16'N	10°25'E
Lunel, Fr. (lü-nĕl')	170	43°41'N	4°07'E
Lünen, Ger. (lü'nĕn)	171c	51°36'N	7°30'E
Lunenburg, Can. (lōō'nĕn-bûrg)	91	44°23'N	64°19'W
Lunenburg, Ma., U.S.	101a	42°36'N	71°44'W
Lunéville, Fr. (lü-nå-vel')	171	48°37'N	6°29'E
Lunga, Ang.	236	14°42'S	18°32'E
Lungué-Bungo, r., Afr.	232	13°00'S	20°30'E
Lunsar, S.L.	234	8°41'N	12°32'W
Luodian, China (lwô-dĭĕn)	206	31°25'N	121°20'E
Luoding, China (lwô-dĭŋ)	209	23°42'N	111°35'E
Luohe, China (lwô-hŭ)	206	33°35'N	114°02'E
Luoyang, China (lwô-yäŋ)	205	34°45'N	112°32'E
Luozhen, China (lwô-jŭn)	206	37°45'N	118°29'E
Luque, Para. (loo'kā)	144	25°18'S	57°17'W
Luray, Va., U.S. (lū-rā')	109	38°40'N	78°25'W
Lurgan, N. Ire., U.K. (lûr'găn)	160	54°27'N	6°28'W
Lúrio, Moz. (lōō'rē-ô)	233	13°17'S	40°29'E
Lúrio, Moz.	233	14°00'S	38°45'E
Lusaka, D.R.C.	237	7°10'S	29°27'E
Lusaka, Zam. (lò-sä'kå)	232	15°25'S	28°17'E
Lusambo, D.R.C. (lōō-säm'bō)	232	4°58'S	23°27'E
Lusanga, D.R.C.	232	5°13'S	18°43'E
Lusangi, D.R.C.	237	4°37'S	27°08'E
Lushan, China	208	33°45'N	113°00'E
Lushiko, r., Afr.	236	6°35'S	19°45'E
Lushoto, Tan. (lōō-shō'tō)	233	4°47'S	38°17'E
Lüshun, China (lü-shŭn)	205	38°49'N	121°15'E
Lusikisiki, S. Afr. (lōō-sē-kē-sē'kē)	233c	31°22'S	29°37'E
Lusk, Wy., U.S. (lŭsk)	112	42°46'N	104°27'W
Lūt, Dasht-e, des., Iran (dă'sht-ē-lōōt)	198	31°47'N	58°38'E
Lutcher, La., U.S. (lŭch'ẽr)	123	30°03'N	90°43'W
Luton, Eng., U.K. (lū'tŭn)	164	51°55'N	0°28'W
Luts'k, Ukr.	181	50°45'N	25°20'E
Luuq, Som.	238a	3°38'N	42°35'E
Luverne, Al., U.S. (lū-vûn')	124	31°42'N	86°15'W
Luverne, Mn., U.S.	112	43°40'N	96°13'W
Luwingu, Zam.	237	10°15'S	29°55'E
Luxapallila Creek, r., U.S. (lŭk-sȧ-pôl'ĭ-lȧ)	124	33°36'N	88°08'W
Luxembourg, Lux.	154	49°38'N	6°30'E
Luxembourg, nation, Eur.	154	49°30'N	6°22'E
Luxeuil-les-Baines, Fr.	171	47°49'N	6°19'E
Luxomni, Ga., U.S. (lŭx'ôm-nī)	110c	33°54'N	84°07'W
Luxor *see* Al Uqşur, Egypt	231	25°38'N	32°59'E
Luya Shan, mtn., China	208	38°50'N	111°40'E
Luyi, China (lōō-yē)	206	33°52'N	115°32'E
Luzern, Switz. (lò-tsĕrn)	161	47°03'N	8°18'E
Luzhou, China (lōō-jō)	204	28°58'N	105°25'E
Luziânia, Braz. (lōō-zyá'nēä)	143	16°17'S	47°44'W
Luzon, i., Phil. (lōō-zŏn')	212	17°10'N	119°45'E
Luzon Strait, strt., Asia	209	20°40'N	121°00'E
L'viv, Ukr.	178	49°50'N	24°00'E
L'vov *see* L'viv, Ukr.	178	49°50'N	24°00'E
Lyalta, Can.	102e	51°07'N	113°36'W
Lyalya, r., Russia (lyá'lyȧ)	186a	58°58'N	60°17'E
Lyaskovets, Blg.	175	43°07'N	25°41'E
Lydenburg, S. Afr. (lī'dĕn-bûrg)	232	25°06'S	30°21'E
Lyell, Mount, mtn., Ca., U.S. (lī'ĕl)	118	37°44'N	119°22'W
Lyepye', Bela. (lyĕ-pĕl')	176	54°52'N	28°41'E
Lykens, Pa., U.S. (lī'kĕnz)	109	40°35'N	76°45'W
Lykhivka, Ukr.	177	48°52'N	33°57'E
Lyna, r., Eur. (lĭn'á)	169	53°56'N	20°30'E
Lynch, Ky., U.S. (lĭnch)	125	36°56'N	82°55'W
Lynchburg, Va., U.S. (lĭnch'bûrg)	105	37°23'N	79°08'W
Lynch Cove, Wa., U.S. (lĭnch)	116a	47°26'N	122°54'W
Lynden, Can. (lĭn'dĕn)	102d	43°14'N	80°08'W
Lynden, Wa., U.S.	116d	48°56'N	122°27'W
Lyndhurst, Austl.	217a	38°03'S	145°14'E
Lyndon, Ky., U.S. (lĭn'dŭn)	111h	38°15'N	85°36'W
Lyndonville, Vt., U.S. (lĭn'dŭn-vĭl)	109	44°35'N	72°00'W
Lynn, Ma., U.S. (lĭn)	105	42°28'N	70°57'W
Lynn Lake, Can. (lăk)	90	56°51'N	101°05'W
Lynwood, Ca., U.S. (lĭn'wŏd)	117a	33°56'N	118°13'W
Lyon, Fr. (lē-ôn')	154	45°44'N	4°52'E
Lyons, Ga., U.S. (lī'ŭnz)	125	32°08'N	82°19'W
Lyons, Ks., U.S.	120	38°20'N	98°11'W
Lyons, Ne., U.S.	112	41°57'N	96°28'W
Lyons, N.J., U.S.	110a	40°41'N	74°33'W
Lyons, N.Y., U.S.	109	43°05'N	77°00'W
Lyptsi, Ukr.	177	50°11'N	36°25'E
Lysefjorden, b., Nor.	166	58°59'N	6°35'E
Lysekil, Swe. (lü'sĕ-kĕl)	166	58°17'N	11°22'E
Lys'va, Russia (lĭs'vȧ)	180	58°07'N	57°47'E
Lytham, Eng., U.K. (lĭth'ăm)	158a	53°44'N	2°58'W
Lytkarino, Russia	186b	55°35'N	37°55'E
Lyttelton, S. Afr. (lĭt'l'ton)	233b	25°51'S	28°13'E
Lyuban', Russia (lyōō'bȧn)	176	59°21'N	31°15'E
Lyubertsy, Russia (lyōō'bĕr-tsē)	176	55°40'N	37°55'E
Lyubim, Russia (lyōō-bēm')	176	58°24'N	40°39'E
Lyublino, Russia (lyōōb'lĭ-nô)	186b	55°41'N	37°45'E
Lyudinovo, Russia (lū-dē'novō)	176	53°52'N	34°28'E

M

PLACE (Pronunciation)	PAGE	LAT.	LONG.
Ma'ān, Jord. (mä-än')	198	30°12'N	35°45'E
Maartensdijk, Neth.	159a	52°09'N	5°10'E
Maas (Meuse), r., Eur.	165	51°50'N	5°40'E
Maastricht, Neth. (mäs'trĭkt)	165	50°51'N	5°35'E
Mabaia, Ang.	236	7°13'S	14°03'E
Mabana, Wa., U.S. (mä-bä-nä)	116a	48°06'N	122°25'W
Mabank, Tx., U.S. (mā'bănk)	123	32°21'N	96°05'W
Mabeskraal, S. Afr.	238c	25°12'S	26°47'E
Mableton, Ga., U.S. (mā'b'l-tŭn)	110c	33°49'N	84°34'W
Mabrouk, Mali	230	19°27'N	1°16'W
Mabula, S. Afr. (mä'bōō-la)	238c	24°49'S	27°59'E
Macalelon, Phil. (mä-kä-lā-lōn')	213a	13°46'N	122°09'E
Macau, Braz. (mä-kà'ò)	143	5°12'S	36°34'W
Macau, China	205	22°00'N	113°00'E
Macaya, Pico de, mtn., Haiti	135	18°25'N	74°00'W
Macclesfield, Eng., U.K. (măk''lz-fēld)	158a	53°15'N	2°07'W
Macclesfield Canal, can., Eng., U.K. (măk''lz-fēld)	158a	53°14'N	2°07'W
Macdona, Tx., U.S. (măk-dō'nă)	117d	29°20'N	98°42'W
Macdonald, l., Austl. (măk-dŏn'ăld)	220	23°40'S	127°40'E
Macdonnell Ranges, mts., Austl. (măk-dŏn'ĕl)	220	23°40'S	131°30'E
MacDowell Lake, l., Can. (măk-dou ĕl)	97	52°15'N	92°45'W
Macdui, Ben, mtn., Scot., U.K. (bĕn măk-dōō'ē)	160	57°06'N	3°45'W
Macedonia, Oh., U.S. (măs-ē-dō'nĭ-á)	111d	41°19'N	81°30'W
Macedonia, nation, Eur.	175	41°50'N	22°00'E
Macedonia, hist. reg., Eur. (măs-ē-dō'nĭ-á)	163	41°05'N	22°15'E
Maceió, Braz.	143	9°40'S	35°43'W
Macerata, Italy (mä-chå-rä'tä)	174	43°18'N	13°28'E
Macfarlane, Lake, l., Austl. (măc'fär-lān)	222	32°10'S	137°00'E
Machache, mtn., Leso.	233c	29°22'S	27°53'E
Machado, Braz. (mä-shå-dô)	141a	21°42'S	45°55'W
Machakos, Kenya	237	1°31'S	37°16'E
Machala, Ec. (mä-chä'lä)	142	3°18'S	78°54'W
Machens, Mo., U.S. (măk'ĕns)	117e	38°54'N	90°20'W
Machias, Me., U.S. (mȧ-chī'ăs)	100	44°22'N	67°29'W
Machida, Japan (mä-chē'dä)	211a	35°32'N	139°28'E
Machilīpatnam, India	199	16°22'N	81°10'E
Machu Picchu, Peru (mä'chò-pē'k-chò)	142	13°07'S	72°34'W
Măcin, Rom. (mȧ-chēn')	177	45°15'N	28°09'E
Macina, reg., Mali	234	14°50'N	4°40'W
Mackay, Austl. (mă-kī')	219	21°15'S	149°08'E
Mackay, Id., U.S. (măk-kā')	115	43°55'N	113°38'W
Mackay, l., Austl. (mă-kī')	220	22°30'S	127°45'E
MacKay, l., Can. (măk-kā')	92	64°10'N	112°35'W
Mackenzie, r., Can.	92	63°38'N	124°23'W
Mackenzie Bay, b., Can.	103	69°20'N	137°10'W
Mackenzie Mountains, mts., Can. (mȧ-kĕn'zĭ)	92	63°41'N	129°27'W
Mackinaw, r., Il., U.S.	108	40°35'N	89°25'W
Mackinaw City, Mi., U.S. (măk'ĭ-nô)	108	45°45'N	84°45'W
Mackinnon Road, Kenya	237	3°44'S	39°03'E
Macleantown, S. Afr. (măk-lān'toun)	233c	32°48'S	27°48'E
Maclear, S. Afr. (mȧ-klēr')	232	31°06'S	28°23'E
Macomb, Il., U.S. (mȧ-kōōm')	121	40°27'N	90°40'W
Mâcon, Fr. (mä-kôN)	161	46°19'N	4°51'E
Macon, Ga., U.S. (mā'kŏn)	105	32°49'N	83°39'W
Macon, Mo., U.S.	121	39°42'N	92°29'W
Macon, Ms., U.S.	124	32°07'N	88°31'W
Macquarie, r., Austl.	221	31°43'S	148°04'E
Macquarie Islands, is., Austl. (mȧ-kwŏr'ē)	3	54°36'S	158°45'E
Macuelizo, Hond. (mä-kwĕ-lē'zō)	132	15°22'N	88°32'W
Mad, r., Ca., U.S. (măd)	114	40°38'N	123°37'W
Madagascar, nation, Afr. (măd-ȧ-găs'kȧr)	233	18°05'S	43°12'E
Madame, i., Can. (mȧ-dȧm')	101	45°33'N	61°02'W
Madanapalle, India	203	13°06'N	78°09'E
Madang, Pap. N. Gui. (mä-däng')	213	5°15'S	145°45'E
Madaoua, Niger (mȧ-dou'ȧ)	230	14°04'N	6°03'E
Madawaska, r., Can. (măd-ȧ-wôs'kȧ)	99	45°20'N	77°25'W
Madeira, r., S.A.	142	6°48'S	62°43'W
Madeira, Arquipélago da, is., Port.	229	33°26'N	16°44'W
Madeira, Ilha da, i., Port. (mä-dā'rä)	230	32°41'N	16°15'W
Madeleine, Îles de la, is., Can.	93	47°30'N	61°45'W
Madelia, Mn., U.S. (mȧ-dē'lĭ-ȧ)	113	44°03'N	94°23'W
Madeline, i., Wi., U.S. (măd'ĕ-lĭn)	113	46°47'N	91°30'W
Madera, Ca., U.S. (mȧ-dā'rȧ)	118	36°57'N	120°04'W
Madera, vol., Nic.	132	11°27'N	85°30'W
Madgaon, India	203	15°09'N	73°58'E
Madhya Pradesh, state, India (mŭd'vŭ prŭ-dāsh')	199	22°04'N	77°48'E
Madill, Ok., U.S. (mȧ-dĭl')	121	34°04'N	96°45'W
Madīnat ash Sha'b, Yemen	198	12°45'N	44°00'E
Madingo, Congo	236	4°07'S	11°22'E
Madingou, Congo	236	4°09'S	13°34'E
Madison, Fl., U.S. (măd'ĭ-sŭn)	124	30°28'N	83°25'W
Madison, Ga., U.S.	124	33°34'N	83°29'W
Madison, Il., U.S.	117e	38°40'N	90°09'W
Madison, In., U.S.	108	38°45'N	85°25'W
Madison, Ks., U.S.	121	38°08'N	96°07'W
Madison, Me., U.S.	100	44°47'N	69°52'W
Madison, Mn., U.S.	112	44°59'N	96°13'W
Madison, N.C., U.S.	125	36°22'N	79°59'W
Madison, Ne., U.S.	112	41°49'N	97°27'W
Madison, N.J., U.S.	110a	40°46'N	74°25'W
Madison, S.D., U.S.	112	44°01'N	97°08'W
Madison, Wi., U.S.	105	43°05'N	89°23'W
Madison Res, Mt., U.S.	115	45°25'N	111°28'W
Madisonville, Ky., U.S. (măd'ĭ-sŭn-vĭl)	108	37°20'N	87°30'W
Madisonville, La., U.S.	123	30°22'N	90°10'W
Madisonville, Tx., U.S.	123	30°57'N	95°55'W
Madjori, Burkina	234	11°26'N	1°15'E
Mado Gashi, Kenya	237	0°44'N	39°10'E
Madona, Lat. (mȧ'dō'nȧ)	167	56°50'N	26°14'E
Madrakah, Ra's al, c., Oman	198	18°53'N	57°48'E
Madras *see* Chennai, India	199	13°08'N	80°15'E
Madre, Laguna, l., Mex. (lä-gōō'nä mä'drā)	123	25°08'N	97°41'W
Madre, Sierra, mts., N.A. (sē-ĕ'r-rä-mä'drĕ)	131	15°55'N	92°40'W
Madre, Sierra, mts., Phil.	213a	16°40'N	122°10'E
Madre de Dios, r., S.A. (mä'drä dā dē-ōs')	142	12°07'S	68°02'W
Madre de Dios, Archipiélago, is., Chile (mä'drä dā dē-ōs')	144	50°40'S	76°30'W
Madre del Sur, Sierra, mts., Mex. (sē-ĕ'r-rä-mä'drā dĕlsōōr')	128	17°35'N	100°35'W
Madre Occidental, Sierra, mts., Mex.	128	29°30'N	107°30'W
Madre Oriental, Sierra, mts., Mex.	128	25°30'N	100°45'W
Madrid, Spain (mȧ-drĭ'd)	154	40°26'N	3°42'W
Madrid, Ia., U.S. (măd'rĭd)	113	41°51'N	93°48'W
Madridejos, Spain (mä-dhrē-dhä'hōs)	172	39°29'N	3°32'W
Madura, i., Indon. (mȧ-dōō'rä)	212	6°45'S	113°30'E
Madurai, India (mä-dōō'rä)	199	9°57'N	78°04'E
Madureira, Serra do, mtn., Braz. (sĕ'r-rä-dô-mä-dōō-rā'rȧ)	144b	22°49'S	43°30'W
Maebashi, Japan (mä-ĕ-bä'shē)	205	36°26'N	139°04'E
Maestra, Sierra, mts., Cuba (sē-ĕ'r-rȧ-mä-ās'trä)	129	20°05'N	77°05'W
Maewo, i., Vanuatu	221	15°17'S	168°16'E
Mafeking, S. Afr. (mȧf'ê'kĭng)	232	25°46'S	24°45'E
Mafra, Braz. (mä'frä)	144	26°21'N	49°59'W
Mafra, Port. (mäf'rȧ)	173b	38°56'N	9°20'W
Magadan, Russia (mȧ-gȧ-dän')	179	59°39'N	150°43'E
Magadan Oblast, Russia	185	65°00'N	160°00'E
Magadi, Kenya	237	1°54'S	36°17'E
Magalies, r., S. Afr. (mä-gä'lyĕs)	233b	25°51'S	27°42'E
Magaliesberg, mts., S. Afr.	233b	25°45'S	27°43'E
Magaliesburg, S. Afr.	238c	26°01'S	27°32'E
Magallanes, Estrecho de, strt., S.A.	144	52°30'S	68°45'W
Magat, r., Phil. (mä-gät')	213a	16°45'N	121°16'E
Magdalena, Arg. (mäg-dä-lā'nä)	141c	35°05'S	57°32'W
Magdalena, Bol.	142	13°17'S	63°57'W
Magdalena, Mex.	104	30°34'N	110°50'W
Magdalena, N.M., U.S.	119	34°10'N	107°45'W
Magdalena, i., Chile	144	44°45'S	73°15'W
Magdalena, r., Col.	142	7°45'N	74°04'W
Magdalena, Bahía, b., Mex. (bä-ē'ä-mäg-dä-lā'nä)	128	24°30'N	114°00'W
Magdeburg, Ger. (mäg'dĕ-bòrgh)	154	52°07'N	11°39'E
Magellan, Strait of *see* Magallanes, Estrecho de, strt., S.A.	144	52°30'S	68°45'W
Magenta, Italy (mȧ-jĕn'tȧ)	174	45°26'N	8°53'E
Magerøya, i., Nor.	160	71°10'N	24°11'E
Maggiore, Lago, l., Italy	162	46°03'N	8°25'E
Maghāghah, Egypt	238b	28°38'N	30°50'W
Maghniyya, Alg.	162	34°52'N	1°40'W
Magiscatzin, Mex. (mä-kės-kät-zēn')	130	22°48'N	98°42'W
Maglaj, Bos. (mȧ'glä-ē)	175	44°34'N	18°12'E
Maglie, Italy (mäl'yā)	175	40°06'N	18°20'E
Magna, Ut., U.S. (măg'nȧ)	117b	40°43'N	112°06'W
Magnitogorsk, Russia (mȧg-nyē'tô-gôrsk)	178	53°26'N	59°05'E
Magnolia, Ar., U.S. (măg-nō'lĭ-ȧ)	121	33°16'N	93°13'W
Magnolia, Ms., U.S.	124	31°08'N	90°27'W
Magny-en-Vexin, Fr. (mä-nyē'ĕN-vĕ-sȧN')	171b	49°09'N	1°45'E
Magog, Can. (mȧ-gŏg')	99	45°15'N	72°10'W
Magpie, r., Can.	100	50°40'N	64°30'W
Magpie, r., Can.	98	48°13'N	84°50'W
Magpie, Lac, l., Can.	100	50°55'N	64°39'W
Magrath, Can.	90	49°25'N	112°52'W
Magude, Moz. (mä-gōō'då)	232	24°58'S	32°39'E
Magwe, Mya. (mŭg-wā')	199	20°19'N	94°57'E
Mahābād, Iran	201	36°55'N	45°50'E
Mahahi Port, D.R.C. (mä-hä'gē)	231	2°14'N	31°12'E
Mahajanga, Madag.	233	15°12'S	46°26'E
Mahakam, r., Indon.	212	0°30'S	116°15'E
Mahali Mountains, mts., Tan.	237	6°20'S	30°00'E
Mahaly, Madag. (mȧ-hȧl-ē')	233	24°09'S	46°20'E
Mahanoro, Madag. (mȧ-hȧ-nô'rō)	233	19°57'S	48°47'E
Mahanoy City, Pa., U.S. (mä-hȧ-noi')	109	40°50'N	76°10'W
Maḩaţţat al Qaţrānah, Jord.	197a	31°15'N	36°04'E
Maḩaţţat 'Aqabat al Ḩijāzīyah, Jord.	197a	29°45'N	35°55'E
Maḩaţţat ar Ramlah, Jord.	197a	29°31'N	35°57'E
Maḩaţţat Jurf ad Darāwīsh, Jord.	197a	30°41'N	35°51'E

318 Mahd adh-Dhahab – Mansfield PRONOUNCING INDEX

PLACE (Pronunciation)	PAGE	LAT.	LONG.
Mahd adh-Dhahab, Sau. Ar.	201	23°30'N	40°52'E
Mahe, India (mä-ā')	199	11°42'N	75°39'E
Mahenge, Tan. (mä-hĕŋ'gȧ)	232	7°38'S	36°16'E
Mahi, r., India	202	23°16'N	73°20'E
Mahilyow, Bela.	180	53°53'N	30°22'E
Mahilyow, prov., Bela.	176	53°28'N	30°15'E
Māhīm Bay, b., India	203b	19°03'N	72°45'E
Mahlabatini, S. Afr. (mä'lȧ-bȧ-tē'nė)	233c	28°15'S	31°29'E
Mahlow, Ger. (mä'lōv)	159b	52°23'N	13°24'E
Mahnomen, Mn., U.S. (mô-nō'mĕn)	112	47°18'N	95°58'W
Mahone Bay, Can. (mȧ-hōn')	100	44°27'N	64°23'W
Mahone Bay, b., Can.	100	44°30'N	64°15'W
Mahopac, Lake, l., N.Y., U.S. (mā-hō'păk)	110a	41°24'N	73°45'W
Mahwah, N.J., U.S. (mȧ-wä')	110a	41°05'N	74°09'W
Maidenhead, Eng., U.K. (mād'ĕn-hĕd)	158b	51°30'N	0°44'W
Maidstone, Eng., U.K.	165	51°17'N	0°32'E
Maiduguri, Nig. (mä'ē-dȧ-gōō'rē)	231	11°51'N	13°10'E
Maigualida, Sierra, mts., Ven. (sē-ĕ'r-rȧ-mī-gwä'lē-dĕ)	142	6°30'N	65°50'W
Maijdi, Bngl.	202	22°59'N	91°08'E
Maikop *see* Maykop, Russia	178	44°35'N	40°07'E
Main, r., Ger. (mīn)	168	49°49'N	9°20'E
Main Barrier Range, mts., Austl. (băr'ĭ'ēr)	221	31°25'S	141°40'E
Mai-Ndombe, Lac, l., D.R.C.	232	2°16'S	19°00'E
Maine, state, U.S. (mān)	105	45°25'N	69°50'W
Mainland, i., Scot., U.K. (mān-lănd)	160	60°19'N	2°40'W
Maintenon, Fr. (măn-tẽ-nôN')	171b	48°35'N	1°35'E
Maintirano, Madag. (mä'ēn-tē-rä'nō)	233	18°05'S	44°08'E
Mainz, Ger. (mīnts)	154	49°59'N	8°16'E
Maio, i., C.V. (mä'yo)	230b	15°15'N	22°50'W
Maipo, S.A.	144	34°08'S	69°51'W
Maipo, r., Chile (mī'pô)	141b	33°45'S	71°08'W
Maiquetía, Ven. (mī-kĕ-tē'ä)	142	10°37'N	66°56'W
Maison-Rouge, Fr. (mā-zôN-rōōzh')	171b	48°34'N	3°09'E
Maisons-Laffitte, Fr.	171b	48°57'N	2°09'E
Maitland, Austl. (māt'lănd)	219	32°45'S	151°40'E
Maizuru, Japan (mä-ĭ'zōō-rōō)	211	35°26'N	135°15'E
Majene, Indon.	212	3°34'S	119°00'E
Maji, Eth.	231	6°14'N	35°34'E
Majorca *see* Mallorca, i., Spain	156	39°18'N	2°22'E
Makah Indian Reservation, I.R., Wa., U.S.	114	48°17'N	124°52'W
Makanya, Tan. (mä-kän'yä)	233	4°15'S	37°49'E
Makanza, D.R.C.	231	1°42'N	19°08'E
Makarakomburu, Mount, mtn., Sol. Is.	214e	9°43'S	160°02'E
Makarska, Cro. (mȧ'kär-skȧ)	175	43°17'N	17°05'E
Makar'yev, Russia	180	57°50'N	43°48'E
Makasar *see* Ujung Pandang, Indon.	212	5°08'S	119°28'E
Makasar, Selat (Makassar Strait), strt., Indon.	212	2°00'S	118°07'E
Makaw, D.R.C.	236	3°29'S	18°19'E
Make, i., Japan (mä'kȧ)	211	30°43'N	130°49'E
Makeni, S.L.	230	8°53'N	12°03'W
Makgadikgadi Pans, pl., Bots.	232	20°38'S	21°31'E
Makhachkala, Russia (mäκ'äch-kä'lä)	181	43°00'N	47°40'E
Makhaleng, r., Leso.	233c	29°53'S	27°33'E
Makiïvka, Ukr.	181	48°03'N	38°00'E
Makindu, Kenya	237	2°17'S	37°49'E
Makkah *see* Mecca, Sau. Ar.	198	21°27'N	39°45'E
Makkovik, Can.	91	55°01'N	59°10'W
Makokou, Gabon (mȧ-kô-kōō')	230	0°34'N	12°52'E
Maków Mazowiecki, Pol. (mä'kōov mä-zō-vyĕts'kē)	169	52°51'N	21°07'E
Makuhari, Japan (mä-kōō-hä'rē)	211a	35°39'N	140°04'E
Makurazaki, Japan (mä'kò-rä-zä'kė)	211	31°16'N	130°18'E
Makurdi, Nig.	230	7°45'N	8°32'E
Makushin, Ak., U.S. (mȧ-kò'shĭn)	103	53°57'N	166°28'W
Makushino, Russia (mȧ-kò-shēn'ô)	178	55°03'N	67°43'E
Mala, Punta, c., Pan. (pò'n-tä-mä'lä)	133	7°32'N	79°44'W
Malabar Coast, cst., India (măl'ȧ-bär)	203	11°19'N	75°33'E
Malabar Point, c., India	203b	18°57'N	72°47'E
Malabo, Eq. Gui.	230	3°45'N	8°47'E
Malabon, Phil.	213a	14°39'N	120°57'E
Malacca, Strait of, strt., Asia (mȧ-lăk'ȧ)	212	4°15'N	99°44'E
Malad City, Id., U.S. (mȧ-lăd')	115	42°11'N	112°15'W
Maladzyecha, Bela.	180	54°18'N	26°57'E
Málaga, Col. (mä'lä-gȧ)	142	6°41'N	72°46'W
Málaga, Spain	154	36°45'N	4°25'W
Malagón, Spain (mä-lä-gōn')	172	39°12'N	3°52'W
Malaita, i., Sol. Is. (mȧ-lä'ē-tȧ)	221	8°38'S	161°15'E
Malakāl, Sudan (mȧ-lȧ-käl')	231	9°46'N	31°54'E
Malakhovka, Russia (mȧ-läk'ôf-kȧ)	186b	55°38'N	38°01'E
Malang, Indon.	212	8°06'S	112°50'E
Malanje, Ang. (mä-läŋ-gȧ)	232	9°32'S	16°20'E
Malanville, Benin	230	12°04'N	3°09'E
Mälaren, l., Swe.	160	59°38'N	16°55'E
Malartic, Can.	91	48°07'N	78°11'W
Malatya, Tur. (mȧ-lä'tyȧ)	198	38°30'N	38°15'E
Malawi, nation, Afr.	232	11°15'S	33°45'E
Malawi, Lake *see* Nyasa, Lake, l., Afr.	232	10°45'S	34°30'E
Malaya Vishera, Russia (vē-shā'rä)	178	58°51'N	32°13'E
Malay Peninsula, pen., Asia (mȧ-lā') (mā'lā)	212	6°00'N	101°00'E
Malaysia, nation, Asia (mȧ-lā'zhȧ)	212	4°10'N	101°22'E
Malbon, Austl. (măl'bŭn)	218	21°15'S	140°30'E
Malbork, Pol. (mäl'bôrk)	160	54°02'N	19°04'E
Malcabran, r., Port. (mäl-kä-brän')	173b	38°47'N	8°46'W
Malden, Ma., U.S. (môl'dĕn)	101a	42°26'N	71°04'W
Malden, Mo., U.S.	121	36°32'N	89°56'W
Malden, i., Kir.	2	4°20'S	154°30'W
Maldives, nation, Asia	194	4°30'N	71°30'E
Maldon, Eng., U.K. (môrl'dŏn)	158b	51°44'N	0°39'E
Maldonado, Ur. (mäl-dō-nä'dō)	144	34°54'S	54°57'W
Maldonado, Punta, c., Mex. (pōō'n-tä)	130	16°18'N	98°34'W
Maléas, Ákra, c., Grc.	163	36°31'N	23°13'E
Mālegaon, India	202	20°35'N	74°30'E
Malé Karpaty, mts., Slvk.	169	48°31'N	17°15'E
Malekula, i., Vanuatu (mä-lā-kōō'lä)	221	16°44'S	167°45'E
Malema, Moz.	237	14°57'S	37°20'E
Malheur, r., Or., U.S. (mȧ-lōōr')	114	43°45'N	117°41'W
Malheur Lake, l., Or., U.S. (mȧ-lōōr')	114	43°16'N	118°37'W
Mali, nation, Afr.	230	15°45'N	0°15'W
Malibu, Ca., U.S. (mă'lĭ-bōō)	117a	34°03'N	118°38'W
Malik, Wādī al, r., Sudan	231	16°48'N	29°30'E
Malimba, Monts, mts., D.R.C.	237	7°45'S	29°15'E
Malinalco, Mex. (mä-lē-näl'kō)	130	18°54'N	99°31'W
Malinaltepec, Mex. (mä-lē-näl-tå-pĕk')	130	17°01'N	98°41'W
Malindi, Kenya (mä-lēn'dė)	233	3°14'S	40°04'E
Malin Head, c., Ire.	160	55°23'N	7°24'W
Malino, Russia (mä'lĭ-nô)	186b	55°07'N	38°12'E
Malkara, Tur. (mäl'kȧ-rȧ)	175	40°51'N	26°52'E
Malko Tŭrnovo, Blg. (mäl'kō-t'r'nô-vȧ)	175	41°59'N	27°28'E
Mallaig, Scot., U.K.	164	56°59'N	5°55'W
Mallet Creek, Oh., U.S. (măl'ĕt)	111d	41°10'N	81°55'W
Mallorca, i., Spain	156	39°30'N	3°00'E
Mallow, Ire. (măl'ō)	164	52°07'N	9°04'W
Malmédy, Bel. (mȧl-mā-dē')	165	50°25'N	6°01'E
Malmesbury, S. Afr. (mämz'bēr-ĭ)	232	33°30'S	18°35'E
Malmköping, Swe. (mälm'chû'pĭng)	166	59°09'N	16°39'E
Malmö, Swe.	154	55°36'N	13°00'E
Malmyzh, Russia (mȧl-mēzh')	179	49°58'N	137°07'E
Malmyzh, Russia	180	56°30'N	50°48'E
Maloarkhangelsk, Russia (mä'lô-ȧr-κäŋ'gĕlsk)	176	52°26'N	36°29'E
Malolos, Phil. (mä-lô'lôs)	213a	14°51'N	120°49'E
Malomal'sk, Russia (mȧ-lô-mälsk'')	186a	58°47'N	59°55'E
Malone, N.Y., U.S. (mȧ-lōn')	109	44°50'N	74°20'W
Malonga, D.R.C.	236	10°24'S	23°10'E
Maloti Mountains, mts., Leso.	233c	29°00'S	28°29'E
Maloyaroslavets, Russia (mä'lô-yä-rô-slä-vyĕts)	176	55°01'N	36°25'E
Malozemel'skaya Tundra, reg., Russia	180	67°30'N	50°00'E
Malpas, Eng., U.K. (măl'pȧz)	158a	53°01'N	2°46'W
Malpelo, Isla de, i., Col. (mäl-pā'lō)	142	3°55'N	81°30'W
Malpeque Bay, b., Can. (môl-pĕk')	100	46°30'N	63°47'W
Malta, Mt., U.S. (môl'tȧ)	115	48°20'N	107°50'W
Malta, nation, Eur.	154	35°52'N	13°30'E
Maltahöhe, Nmb. (mäl'tä-hō'ē)	232	24°45'S	16°45'E
Maltrata, Mex. (mäl-trä'tä)	131	18°48'N	97°16'W
Maluku (Moluccas), is., Indon.	213	2°22'S	128°25'E
Maluku, Laut (Molucca Sea), sea, Indon.	213	0°15'N	125°41'E
Malūṭ, Sudan	231	10°30'N	32°17'E
Mālvan, India	203	16°08'N	73°32'E
Malvern, Ar., U.S. (măl'vērn)	121	34°21'N	92°47'W
Malyn, Ukr.	177	50°44'N	29°15'E
Malynivka, Ukr.	177	49°50'N	36°43'E
Malyy Anyuy, r., Russia	185	67°52'N	164°30'E
Malyy Tamir, i., Russia	185	78°10'N	107°30'E
Mamantel, Mex. (mä-mȧn-tĕl')	131	18°36'N	91°06'W
Mamaroneck, N.Y., U.S. (măm'ȧ-rō-nĕk)	110a	40°57'N	73°44'W
Mambasa, D.R.C.	237	1°21'N	29°03'E
Mamburao, Phil. (mäm-bōō'rä-ō)	213a	13°14'N	120°35'E
Mamfe, Cam. (mäm'fĕ)	230	5°46'N	9°17'E
Mamihara, Japan (mä'mē-hä-rä)	211	32°41'N	131°12'E
Mammoth Cave, Ky., U.S. (măm'ŏth)	124	37°10'N	86°04'W
Mammoth Cave National Park, rec., Ky., U.S.	107	37°20'N	86°21'W
Mammoth Hot Springs, Wy., U.S. (măm'ŭth hôt sprĭngz)	115	44°55'N	110°50'W
Mamnoli, India	203b	19°17'N	73°15'E
Mamoré, r., S.A.	142	13°00'S	65°20'W
Mamou, Gui.	230	10°26'N	12°07'W
Mampong, Ghana	234	7°04'N	1°24'W
Mamry, Jezioro, l., Pol. (mäm'rĭ)	169	54°10'N	21°28'E
Man, C. Iv.	234	7°24'N	7°33'W
Manacor, Spain (mä-nä-kôr')	173	39°35'N	3°15'E
Manado, Indon.	213	1°29'N	124°50'E
Managua, Cuba (mä-nä'gwä)	135a	22°58'N	82°17'W
Managua, Nic.	128	12°10'N	86°16'W
Managua, Lago de, l., Nic. (lä'gô-dĕ)	132	12°28'N	86°10'W
Manakara, Madag. (mä-nä-kä'rŭ)	233	22°17'S	48°06'E
Manama *see* Al Manāmah, Bahr.	198	26°01'N	50°33'E
Mananara, r., Madag. (mä-nä-nä'rŭ)	233	23°15'S	48°15'E
Mananjary, Madag. (mä-nän-zhä'rė)	233	20°16'S	48°13'E
Manas, China	204	44°30'N	86°00'E
Manassas, Va., U.S. (mȧ-năs'ȧs)	109	38°45'N	77°30'W
Manaus, Braz. (mä-nä'ōōzh)	143	3°01'S	60°00'W
Mancelona, Mi., U.S. (măn-sē-lō'nȧ)	108	44°50'N	85°05'W
Mancha Real, Spain (män'chä rā-äl')	172	37°48'N	3°37'W
Manchazh, Russia (män'chȧsh)	186a	56°30'N	58°10'E
Manchester, Eng., U.K.	154	53°28'N	2°14'W
Manchester, Ct., U.S. (măn'chĕs-tēr)	109	41°45'N	72°30'W
Manchester, Ga., U.S.	124	32°50'N	84°37'W
Manchester, Ia., U.S.	113	42°30'N	91°30'W
Manchester, Ma., U.S.	101a	42°35'N	70°47'W
Manchester, Mo., U.S.	117e	38°36'N	90°31'W
Manchester, N.H., U.S.	105	43°00'N	71°30'W
Manchester, Oh., U.S.	108	38°40'N	83°35'W
Manchester Ship Canal, Eng., U.K.	158a	53°20'N	2°40'W
Manchuria, hist. reg., China (măn-chōō'rē-ȧ)	205	48°00'N	124°58'E
Mandal, Nor. (män'däl)	166	58°03'N	7°28'E
Mandalay, Mya. (măn'dȧ-lā)	199	22°00'N	96°08'E
Mandalselva, r., Nor.	166	58°25'N	7°30'E
Mandan, N.D., U.S. (măn'dăn)	104	46°49'N	100°54'W
Mandara Mountains, mts., Afr. (män-dä'rä)	231	10°15'N	13°23'E
Mandau Siak, r., Indon.	197b	1°03'N	101°25'E
Mandeb, Bab-el-, strt. (băb'ĕl män-dĕb')	198	13°17'N	42°49'E
Mandimba, Moz.	237	14°21'S	35°39'E
Mandinga, Pan. (män-dĭŋ'gä)	133	9°32'N	79°04'W
Mandla, India	202	22°43'N	80°23'E
Mándra, Grc. (män'drä)	175	38°06'N	23°32'E
Mandritsara, Madag. (mȧn-drēt-sä'rȧ)	233	15°49'S	48°47'E
Manduria, Italy (män-dōō'rē-ä)	175	40°23'N	17°41'E
Mandve, India	203b	18°47'N	72°52'E
Māndvi, India (mŭnd'vē)	203b	19°29'N	72°53'E
Māndvi, India (mŭnd'vē)	199	22°54'N	69°23'E
Mandya, India	203	12°40'N	77°00'E
Manfredonia, Italy (män-frȧ-dô'nyä)	174	41°39'N	15°55'E
Manfredónia, Golfo di, b., Italy (gôl-fô-dē)	174	41°34'N	16°05'E
Mangabeiras, Chapada das, pl., Braz.	143	8°05'S	47°32'W
Mangalore, India (mŭŋ-gŭ-lōr')	199	12°53'N	74°52'E
Mangaratiba, Braz. (män-gä-rä-tē'bȧ)	141a	22°56'S	44°03'W
Mangatarem, Phil. (män'gȧ-tä'rĕm)	213a	15°48'N	120°18'E
Mange, D.R.C.	236	0°54'N	20°30'E
Mangkalihat, Tanjung, c., Indon.	212	1°25'N	119°55'E
Mangles, Islas de, Cuba (ĕ's-läs-dĕ-män'glās) (măn'g'lz)	134	22°05'N	82°50'W
Mangoche, Mwi.	232	14°16'S	35°14'E
Mangoky, r., Madag. (män-gō'kē)	233	22°02'S	44°11'E
Mangole, Pulau, i., Indon.	213	1°35'S	126°22'E
Mangualde, Port. (män-gwäl'dĕ)	172	40°38'N	7°44'W
Mangueira, Lagoa da, l., Braz.	144	33°15'S	52°45'W
Mangum, Ok., U.S. (măŋ'gŭm)	120	34°52'N	99°31'W
Mangzhangdian, China (mäŋ-jäŋ-dĭĕn)	206	32°07'N	114°44'E
Manhattan, Il., U.S.	111a	41°25'N	87°29'W
Manhattan, Ks., U.S. (măn-hăt'ăn)	104	39°11'N	96°34'W
Manhattan Beach, Ca., U.S.	117a	33°53'N	118°24'W
Manhuaçu, Braz. (män-ōȧ'sōō)	141a	20°17'S	42°01'W
Manhumirim, Braz. (män-ōō-mē-rē'N)	141a	22°30'S	41°57'W
Manicouagane, r., Can.	93	50°00'N	68°35'W
Manicouagane, Lac, res., Can.	93	51°30'N	68°19'W
Manicuare, Ven. (mä-nē-kwä'rĕ)	143b	10°35'N	64°10'W
Manihiki Islands, is., Cook Is. (mä'nē-hē'kė)	241	9°40'S	158°00'W
Manila, Phil.	212	14°37'N	121°00'E
Manila Bay, b., Phil. (mȧ-nĭl'ȧ)	213a	14°38'N	120°46'E
Manisa, Tur. (mä'nē-sȧ)	163	38°40'N	27°30'E
Manistee, Mi., U.S. (măn-ĭs-tē')	108	44°15'N	86°20'W
Manistee, r., Mi., U.S.	108	44°25'N	85°45'W
Manistique, Mi., U.S. (măn-ĭs-tēk')	113	45°58'N	86°16'W
Manistique, l., Mi., U.S.	113	46°14'N	85°30'W
Manistique, r., Mi., U.S.	113	46°05'N	86°09'W
Manitoba, prov., Can. (măn-ĭ-tō'bȧ)	90	55°12'N	97°29'W
Manitoba, Lake, l., Can.	92	51°00'N	98°45'W
Manito Lake, l., Can. (măn'ĭ-tō)	96	52°45'N	109°45'W
Manitou, i., Mi., U.S. (măn'ĭ-tōō)	113	47°21'N	87°33'W
Manitou, l., Can.	113	49°21'N	93°01'W
Manitou Islands, is., Mi., U.S.	108	45°05'N	86°00'W
Manitoulin Island, i., Can. (măn-ĭ-tōō'lĭn)	93	45°45'N	81°30'W
Manitou Springs, Co., U.S.	120	38°51'N	104°58'W
Manitowoc, Wi., U.S. (măn-ĭ-tô-wŏk')	113	44°05'N	87°42'W
Manitqueira, Serra da, mts., Braz.	141a	22°40'S	45°12'W
Maniwaki, Can.	99	46°23'N	76°00'W
Manizales, Col. (mä-nē-zä'lås)	142	5°05'N	75°31'W
Manjacaze, Moz. (man'yä-kä'zĕ)	232	24°37'S	33°49'E
Mankato, Ks., U.S. (măn-kā'tō)	120	39°45'N	98°12'W
Mankato, Mn., U.S.	105	44°10'N	93°59'W
Mankim, Cam.	235	5°01'N	12°00'E
Manlléu, Spain (män-lyā'ōō)	173	42°00'N	2°16'E
Mannar, Sri L. (mȧ-när')	203	9°48'N	80°03'E
Mannar, Gulf of, b., Asia	199	8°47'N	78°33'E
Mannheim, Ger. (män'hīm)	161	49°30'N	8°31'E
Manning, Ia., U.S. (măn'ĭng)	112	41°53'N	95°04'W
Manning, S.C., U.S.	125	33°41'N	80°12'W
Mannington, W.V., U.S. (măn'ĭng-tŭn)	108	39°30'N	80°55'W
Mano, r., Afr.	234	7°00'N	11°25'W
Man of War Bay, b., Bah.	135	21°05'N	74°05'W
Man of War Channel, strt., Bah.	134	22°45'N	76°10'W
Manokwari, Indon. (mȧ-nŏk-wä'rė)	213	0°56'S	134°10'E
Manono, D.R.C.	237	7°18'S	27°25'E
Manor, Can. (măn'ēr)	97	49°36'N	102°05'W
Manor, Wa., U.S.	116c	45°45'N	122°36'W
Manori, neigh., India	203b	19°13'N	72°43'E
Manosque, Fr. (mȧ-nôsh')	171	43°51'N	5°48'E
Manotick, Can.	102c	45°13'N	75°41'W
Manouane, r., Can.	99	50°15'N	70°30'W
Manouane, Lac, l., Can. (mä-nōō'ȧn)	100	50°36'N	70°50'W
Manresa, Spain (män-rā'sä)	162	41°44'N	1°52'E
Mansa, Zam.	232	11°12'S	28°53'E
Mansel, i., Can. (măn'sĕl)	93	61°56'N	81°10'W
Manseriche, Pongo de, reg., Peru (pŏ'n-gô-dĕ-män-sĕ-rē'chĕ)	142	4°15'S	77°45'W
Mansfield, Eng., U.K. (mănz'fēld)	158a	53°08'N	1°12'W
Mansfield, La., U.S.	123	32°02'N	93°43'W
Mansfield, Oh., U.S.	108	40°45'N	82°30'W
Mansfield, Wa., U.S.	114	47°48'N	119°39'W
Mansfield, Mount, mtn., Vt., U.S.	109	44°30'N	72°45'W

ng-sing; ŋ-baŋk; N-nasalized n; nŏd; cŏmmit; ōld; ȯbey; ôrder; oi-boil; fōͦd; ȯ-as oo in foot; ou-out; s-soft; sh-dish; th-thin; pūre; ûnite; ûrn; stŭd; circŭs; ü-as in French tu; ´-indeterminate vowel.

320 Marysville – Medan PRONOUNCING INDEX

PLACE (Pronunciation)	PAGE	LAT.	LONG.
Marysville, Can.	100	45°59'N	66°35'W
Marysville, Ca., U.S.	118	39°09'N	121°37'W
Marysville, Oh., U.S.	108	40°15'N	83°25'W
Marysville, Wa., U.S.	116a	48°03'N	122°11'W
Maryville, Il., U.S. (mā′rĭ-vĭl)	117e	38°44'N	89°57'W
Maryville, Mo., U.S.	121	40°21'N	94°51'W
Maryville, Tn., U.S.	124	35°44'N	83°59'W
Mārzuq, Libya	231	26°00'N	14°09'E
Marzūq, Idehan, des., Libya	230	24°30'N	13°00'E
Masai Steppe, plat., Tan.	237	4°30'S	36°40'E
Masaka, Ug.	237	0°20'S	31°44'E
Masalasef, Chad	235	11°43'N	17°08'E
Masalembo-Besar, i., Indon.	212	5°40'S	114°28'E
Masan, Kor., S. (mä-sän′)	205	35°10'N	128°31'E
Masangwe, Tan.	237	5°28'S	30°05'E
Masasi, Tan. (mä-sä′sė)	233	10°43'S	38°48'E
Masatepe, Nic. (mä-sä-tĕ′pĕ)	132	11°57'N	86°10'W
Masaya, Nic. (mä-sä′yä)	132	11°58'N	86°05'W
Masbate, Phil. (mäs-bä′tā)	213a	12°21'N	123°38'E
Masbate, i., Phil.	213	12°19'N	123°03'E
Mascarene Islands, is., Afr.	5	20°20'S	56°40'E
Mascot, Tn., U.S. (măs′kŏt)	124	36°04'N	83°45'W
Mascota, Mex. (mäs-kō′tä)	130	20°33'N	104°45'W
Mascota, r., Mex.	130	20°33'N	104°52'W
Mascouche, Can. (mȧs-ko͞osh′)	102a	45°45'N	73°36'W
Mascouche, r., Can.	102a	45°44'N	73°45'W
Mascoutah, Il., U.S. (măs-kū′tā)	117e	38°29'N	89°48'W
Maseru, Leso. (măz′ēr-o͞o)	232	29°09'S	27°11'E
Mashhad, Iran	198	36°17'N	59°30'E
Māshkel, Hāmūn-i-, l., Asia (hā-mo͞on′ē māsh-kĕl′)	198	28°28'N	64°13'E
Mashra'ar Raqq, Sudan	231	8°28'N	29°15'E
Masi-Manimba, D.R.C.	236	4°46'S	17°55'E
Masindi, Ug. (mä-sēn′dė)	231	1°44'N	31°43'E
Masjed Soleymān, Iran	198	31°45'N	49°17'E
Mask, Lough, b., Ire. (lŏk mȧsk)	164	53°35'N	9°23'W
Maslovo, Russia (mäs′lô-vô)	186a	60°08'N	60°28'E
Mason, Mi., U.S. (mā′sŭn)	108	42°35'N	84°25'W
Mason, Oh., U.S.	111f	39°22'N	84°18'W
Mason, Tx., U.S.	122	30°46'N	99°14'W
Mason City, Ia., U.S.	105	43°08'N	93°14'W
Massa, Italy (mäs′sä)	174	44°02'N	10°08'E
Massachusetts, state, U.S. (măs-ȧ-cho͞o′sĕts)	105	42°20'N	72°30'W
Massachusetts Bay, b., Ma., U.S.	100	42°26'N	70°20'W
Massafra, Italy (mäs-sä′frä)	175	40°35'N	17°05'E
Massa Marittima, Italy	174	43°03'N	10°55'E
Massapequa, N.Y., U.S.	110a	40°41'N	73°28'W
Massaua *see* Mitsiwa, Erit.	231	15°40'N	39°19'E
Massena, N.Y., U.S. (mă-sē′nȧ)	109	44°55'N	74°55'W
Masset, Can. (măs′ĕt)	90	54°02'N	132°09'W
Masset Inlet, b., Can.	95	53°42'N	132°20'E
Massif Central, Fr. (mȧ-sēf′ säɴ-trȧl′)	154	45°12'N	3°02'E
Massillon, Oh., U.S. (măs′ĭ-lŏn)	108	40°50'N	81°35'W
Massinga, Moz. (mä-sĭn′gä)	232	23°18'S	35°18'E
Massive, Mount, mtn., Co., U.S. (mȧs′ĭv)	106	39°05'N	106°30'W
Masson, Can. (măs-sŭn)	102c	45°33'N	75°25'W
Masuda, Japan (mä-so͞o′då)	211	34°42'N	131°53'E
Masuria, reg., Pol.	169	53°40'N	21°10'E
Masvingo, Zimb.	232	20°07'S	30°47'E
Matadi, D.R.C. (mȧ-tä′dė)	232	5°49'S	13°27'E
Matagalpa, Nic. (mä-tä-gäl′pä)	128	12°52'N	85°57'W
Matagami, l., Can. (mâ-tä-gä′mė)	93	50°10'N	78°28'W
Matagorda Bay, b., Tx., U.S. (măt-ȧ-gôr′dȧ)	123	28°32'N	96°13'W
Matagorda Island, i., Tx., U.S.	123	28°13'N	96°27'W
Matam, Sen. (mä-täm′)	230	15°40'N	13°15'W
Matamoros, Mex. (mä-tä-mō′rôs)	122	25°32'N	103°13'W
Matamoros, Mex.	128	25°52'N	97°30'W
Matane, Can. (mȧ-tån′)	91	48°51'N	67°32'W
Matanzas, Cuba (mä-tän′zäs)	129	23°05'N	81°35'W
Matanzas, prov., Cuba	134	22°45'N	81°20'W
Matanzas, Bahía, b., Cuba (bä-ē′ä)	134	23°10'N	81°30'W
Matapalo, Cabo, c., C.R. (kȧ′bô-mä-tä-pä′lō)	133	8°22'N	83°25'W
Matapédia, Can. (mă-tȧ-pā′dē-ȧ)	100	47°58'N	66°56'W
Matapédia, l., Can.	100	48°33'N	67°32'W
Matapédia, r., Can.	100	48°10'N	67°10'W
Mataquito, r., Chile (mä-tä-kė′tô)	141b	35°08'S	71°35'W
Matara, Sri L. (mä-tä′rä)	203	5°59'N	80°35'E
Mataram, Indon.	212	8°45'S	116°15'E
Matatiele, S. Afr. (mä-tä-tyā′lā)	233c	30°21'S	28°49'E
Matawan, N.J., U.S.	110a	40°24'N	74°13'W
Matehuala, Mex. (mä-tå-wä′lä)	128	23°38'N	100°39'W
Matera, Italy (mä-tå′rä)	174	40°42'N	16°37'E
Mateur, Tun. (mȧ-tûr′)	162	37°09'N	9°43'E
Mātherān, India	203b	18°58'N	73°16'E
Matheson, Can.	99	48°35'N	80°33'W
Mathews, Lake, l., Ca., U.S. (măth ūz)	117a	33°50'N	117°24'W
Mathura, India (mu-tö′rŭ)	199	27°39'N	77°39'E
Matias Barbosa, Braz. (mä-tē′äs-bȧr-bô-sä)	141a	21°53'S	43°19'W
Matillas, Laguna, l., Mex. (lä-gö′nä-mä-tē̇′l-yäs)	131	18°02'N	92°36'W
Matina, C.R. (mä-tē′nä)	133	10°06'N	83°20'W
Matiši, Lat. (mä′tė-sė)	167	57°43'N	25°09'E
Matlalcueyetl, Cerro, mtn., Mex. (sĕ′r-rä-mä-tläl-kwĕ′yĕtl)	130	19°13'N	98°02'W
Matlock, Eng., U.K. (măt′lŏk)	158a	53°08'N	1°33'W
Matochkin Shar, Russia (mä′tŏch-kĭn)	178	73°57'N	56°16'E
Mato Grosso, Braz. (mät′ö grōs′öo)	143	15°04'S	59°58'W
Mato Grosso, state, Braz.	143	14°38'S	55°36'W
Mato Grosso, Chapada de, hills, Braz. (shä-pä′dä-dĕ)	143	13°39'S	55°42'W
Mato Grosso do Sul, state, Braz.	143	20°00'S	56°00'W
Matosinhos, Port.	172	41°10'N	8°48'W
Maţraḩ, Oman (mȧ-trä′)	198	23°36'N	58°27'E
Matsubara, Japan	211b	34°34'N	135°34'E
Matsudo, Japan (mät′sö-då)	211a	35°48'N	139°55'E
Matsue, Japan (mät′sö-ĕ)	205	35°29'N	133°04'E
Matsumoto, Japan (mät′sö-mō′tå)	210	36°15'N	137°59'E
Matsuyama, Japan (mät′sö-yä′mä)	205	33°48'N	132°45'E
Matsuzaka, Japan (mät′sö-zä′kä)	211	34°35'N	136°34'E
Mattamuskeet, Lake, l., N.C., U.S. (măt-tȧ-mŭs′kēt)	125	35°34'N	76°03'W
Mattaponi, r., Va., U.S. (măt′ȧ-ponī′)	109	37°45'N	77°00'W
Mattawa, Can. (măt′ȧ-wȧ)	91	46°15'N	78°49'W
Matterhorn, mtn., Eur. (mät′ẽr-hôrn)	168	45°57'N	7°36'E
Matteson, Il., U.S. (mătt′ė-sŭn)	111a	41°30'N	87°42'W
Matthew Town, Bah. (măth′ū toun)	135	21°00'N	73°40'W
Mattoon, Il., U.S. (mă-to͞on′)	105	39°30'N	88°20'W
Maturín, Ven. (mä-to͞o-rēn′)	142	9°48'N	63°16'W
Maúa, Moz.	237	13°51'S	37°10'E
Mauban, Phil. (mä′o͞o-bän′)	213a	14°11'N	121°44'E
Maubeuge, Fr. (må-bûzh′)	170	50°18'N	3°57'E
Maud, Oh., U.S. (môd)	111f	39°21'N	84°23'W
Mauer, Aus. (mou′ẽr)	159e	48°09'N	16°16'E
Maués, Braz. (mȧ-wĕ′s)	143	3°34'S	57°30'W
Mau Escarpment, cliff, Kenya	237	0°45'S	35°50'E
Maui, i., Hi., U.S. (mä′o͞o-ē)	106c	20°52'N	156°02'W
Maule, r., Chile (mȧ′ö-lĕ)	141b	35°45'S	70°50'W
Maumee, Oh., U.S. (mô-mē′)	108	41°30'N	83°40'W
Maumee, r., In., U.S.	108	41°10'N	84°50'W
Maumee Bay, b., Oh., U.S.	108	41°50'N	83°20'W
Maun, Bots. (mä-ön′)	232	19°52'S	23°40'E
Mauna Kea, mtn., Hi., U.S. (mä′ö-näkā′ä)	106c	19°52'N	155°30'W
Mauna Loa, mtn., Hi., U.S. (mä′ö-nälō′ä)	106c	19°28'N	155°38'W
Maurepas Lake, l., La., U.S. (mō-rẽ-pä′)	123	30°18'N	90°40'W
Mauricie, Parc National de la, rec., Can.	99	46°46'N	73°00'W
Mauritania, nation, Afr. (mô-rė-tā′nĭ-ȧ)	230	19°38'N	13°30'W
Mauritius, nation, Afr. (mô-rĭsh′ĭ-ŭs)	3	20°18'S	57°36'E
Maury, Wa., U.S. (mô′rĭ)	116a	47°22'N	122°23'W
Mauston, Wi., U.S. (môs′tŭn)	113	43°46'N	90°05'W
Maverick, r., Az., U.S. (mā-vûr′ĭk)	119	33°40'N	109°30'W
Mavinga, Ang.	236	15°50'S	20°21'E
Mawlamyine, Mya.	212	16°30'N	97°39'E
Maxville, Can. (măks′vĭl)	102c	45°17'N	74°52'W
Maxville, Mo., U.S.	117e	38°26'N	90°24'W
Maya, r., Russia (mä′yä)	185	58°00'N	135°45'E
Mayaguana, i., Bah.	135	22°25'N	73°00'W
Mayaguana Passage, strt., Bah.	135	22°20'N	73°25'W
Mayagüez, P.R. (mä-yä-gwāz′)	129	18°12'N	67°10'W
Mayari, r., Cuba	135	20°25'N	75°35'W
Mayas, Montañas, mts., N.A. (mŏntăŋ′ăs mā′ăs)	132a	16°43'N	89°00'W
Mayd, i., Som.	238a	11°24'N	46°38'E
Mayen, Ger. (mī′ĕn)	168	50°19'N	7°14'E
Mayenne, r., Fr. (mȧ-yĕn)	170	48°14'N	0°45'W
Mayfield, Ky., U.S. (mā′fēld)	124	36°44'N	88°19'W
Mayfield Creek, r., Ky., U.S.	124	36°54'N	88°47'W
Mayfield Heights, Oh., U.S.	111d	41°31'N	81°26'W
Mayfield Lake, res., Wa., U.S.	114	46°31'N	122°34'W
Maykop, Russia	178	44°35'N	40°07'E
Maykor, Russia (mī-kôr′)	186a	59°01'N	55°52'E
Maymyo, Mya. (mī′myō)	204	22°14'N	96°32'E
Maynard, Ma., U.S. (mā′nȧrd)	101a	42°25'N	71°27'W
Mayne, Can. (mān)	116d	48°51'N	123°18'W
Mayne, i., Can.	116d	48°52'N	123°14'W
Mayo, Can. (mā-yō′)	90	63°40'N	135°51'W
Mayo, Fl., U.S.	124	30°02'N	83°08'W
Mayo, Md., U.S.	110e	38°54'N	76°31'W
Mayodan, N.C., U.S. (mā-yō′dăn)	125	36°25'N	79°59'W
Mayon Volcano, vol., Phil. (mä-yōn′)	213a	13°21'N	123°43'E
Mayotte, dep., Afr. (mȧ-yåt′)	233	13°07'S	45°32'E
May Pen, Jam.	134	18°00'N	77°25'W
Mayraira Point, c., Phil.	209	18°40'N	120°45'E
Mayran, Laguna de, l., Mex. (lä-ö′nä-dĕ-mī-rän′)	128	25°40'N	102°35'W
Mayskiy, Russia	182	43°38'N	44°04'E
Maysville, Ky., U.S. (māz′vĭl)	108	38°35'N	83°45'W
Mayumba, Gabon	232	3°25'S	10°39'E
Mayville, N.D., U.S.	112	47°30'N	97°20'W
Mayville, N.Y., U.S. (mā′vĭl)	109	42°15'N	79°30'W
Mayville, Wi., U.S.	113	43°30'N	88°45'W
Maywood, Ca., U.S. (mā′wöd)	117a	33°59'N	118°11'W
Maywood, Il., U.S.	111a	41°53'N	87°51'W
Mazabuka, Zam. (mä-zä-bo͞o′kä)	232	15°51'S	27°46'E
Mazagão, Braz. (mä-zȧ-gou′ɴ)	143	0°05'S	51°27'W
Mazapil, Mex. (mä-zä-pēl′)	122	24°40'N	101°30'W
Mazara del Vallo, Italy (mät-sä′rä dĕl väl′lō)	174	37°40'N	12°37'E
Mazār-i-Sharīf, Afg. (mȧ-zär′-ē-shȧ-rēf′)	199	36°48'N	67°12'E
Mazarrón, Spain (mä-zär-rô′n)	172	37°37'N	1°29'W
Mazatenango, Guat. (mä-zä-tå-näŋ′gō)	128	14°30'N	91°30'W
Mazatla, Mex.	131a	19°30'N	99°24'W
Mazatlán, Mex.	128	23°14'N	106°27'W
Mazatlán (San Juan), Mex. (mä-zä-tlän′) (saZ̲ hwän′)	131	17°05'N	95°26'W
Mažeikiai, Lith. (mȧ-zhā′kė-ī)	167	56°19'N	22°24'E
Mazḩafah, Jabal, mtn., Sau. Ar.	197a	28°56'N	35°05'E
Mazyr, Bela.	181	52°03'N	29°14'E
Mbabane, Swaz. (m'bä-bä′nĕ)	232	26°18'S	31°14'E
Mbaiki, C.A.R. (m'bȧ-ē′kė)	231	3°53'N	18°00'E
Mbakana, Montagne de, mts., Cam.	235	7°55'N	14°40'E
Mbakaou, Barrage de, dam, Cam.	235	6°10'N	12°55'E
Mbala, Zam.	232	8°50'S	31°22'E
Mbale, Ug.	237	1°05'N	34°10'E
Mbamba Bay, Tan.	237	11°17'S	34°46'E
Mbandaka, D.R.C.	232	0°04'N	18°16'E
M'banza Congo, Ang.	232	6°30'S	14°10'E
Mbanza-Ngungu, D.R.C.	232	5°20'S	10°55'E
Mbarara, Ug.	237	0°37'S	30°39'E
Mbasay, Chad	235	7°39'N	15°40'E
Mbigou, Gabon (m-bē-go͞o′)	232	2°07'S	11°30'E
Mbinda, Congo	236	2°00'S	12°55'E
Mbogo, Tan.	237	7°26'S	33°26'E
Mbomou (Bomu), r., Afr. (m'bō′mo͞o)	231	4°50'N	24°00'E
Mbout, Maur. (m'bo͞o′)	230	16°03'N	12°31'W
Mbuji-Mayi, D.R.C.	236	6°09'S	23°38'E
McAdam, Can. (măk-ăd′ăm)	100	45°36'N	67°20'W
McAfee, N.J., U.S. (măk-ȧ′fē)	110a	41°10'N	74°32'W
McAlester, Ok., U.S. (măk ăl′ĕs-tēr)	105	34°55'N	95°45'W
McAllen, Tx., U.S. (măk-ăl′ĕn)	122	26°12'N	98°14'W
McBride, Can. (măk-brīd′)	90	53°18'N	120°10'W
McCalla, Al., U.S. (măk-kăl′lā)	110h	33°20'N	87°00'W
McCamey, Tx., U.S. (mă-kā′mĭ)	122	31°08'N	102°13'W
McColl, S.C., U.S. (mȧ-kól′)	125	34°40'N	79°34'W
McComb, Ms., U.S. (mȧ-kōm′)	124	31°14'N	90°27'W
McConaughy, Lake, l., Ne., U.S. (măk kō′nō ĭ′)	112	41°24'N	101°40'W
McCook, Ne., U.S. (mȧ-kök′)	120	40°13'N	100°37'W
McCormick, S.C., U.S. (mȧ-kôr′mĭk)	125	33°56'N	82°20'W
McDonald, Pa., U.S. (măk-dŏn′ăid)	111e	40°22'N	80°13'W
McDonald Island, i., Austl.	224	53°00'S	72°45'E
McDonald Lake, l., Can. (măk-dŏn-ăld)	102e	51°12'N	113°53'W
McGehee, Ar., U.S. (mȧ-gē′)	121	33°39'N	91°22'W
McGill, Nv., U.S. (mȧ-gĭl′)	119	39°25'N	114°47'W
McGowan, Wa., U.S. (măk-gou′ăn)	116c	46°15'N	123°55'W
McGrath, Ak., U.S. (măk′grȧth)	106a	62°58'N	155°20'W
McGregor, Can. (măk-grĕg′ēr)	111b	42°08'N	82°58'W
McGregor, Ia., U.S.	113	42°58'N	91°12'W
McGregor, Tx., U.S.	123	31°26'N	97°23'W
McGregor, r., Can.	95	54°10'N	121°00'W
McGregor Lake, l., Can. (măk-grĕg′ẽr)	102c	45°38'N	75°44'W
McHenry, Il., U.S. (măk-hĕn′rĭ)	111a	42°21'N	88°16'W
Mchinji, Mwi.	232	13°42'S	32°50'E
McIntosh, S.D., U.S. (măk′ĭn-tŏsh)	112	45°54'N	101°22'W
McKay, r., Or., U.S.	116c	45°43'N	123°00'W
McKeesport, Pa., U.S. (mȧ-kez′pōrt)	111e	40°21'N	79°51'W
McKees Rocks, Pa., U.S. (mȧ-kēz′ rŏks)	111e	40°29'N	80°05'W
McKenzie, Tn., U.S. (mȧ-kĕn′zĭ)	124	36°07'N	88°30'W
McKenzie, r., Or., U.S.	114	44°07'N	122°20'W
McKinley, Mount, mtn., Ak., U.S. (mȧ-kĭn′lĭ)	106a	63°00'N	151°02'W
McKinney, Tx., U.S. (mȧ-kĭn′ĭ)	121	33°12'N	96°35'W
McLaughlin, S.D., U.S. (mȧk-lŏf′lĭn)	112	45°48'N	100°45'W
McLean, Va., U.S. (mȧc′lān)	110e	38°56'N	77°11'W
McLeansboro, Il., U.S. (mȧ-klānz′bŭr-å)	108	38°10'N	88°35'W
McLennan, Can. (măk-lĭn′nȧn)	90	55°42'N	116°54'W
McLeod, r., Can.	95	53°45'N	115°55'W
McLeod Lake, Can.	94	54°59'N	123°02'W
McLoughlin, Mount, mtn., Or., U.S. (mȧk-lŏk′lĭn)	114	42°27'N	122°20'W
McMillan Lake, l., Tx., U.S. (măk-mĭl′ȧn)	122	32°40'N	104°09'W
McMillin, Wa., U.S. (mȧk-mĭl′ĭn)	116a	47°08'N	122°14'W
McMinnville, Or., U.S. (măk-mĭn′vĭl)	114	45°13'N	123°13'W
McMinnville, Tn., U.S.	124	35°41'N	85°47'W
McMurray, Wa., U.S. (mȧk-mŭr′ĭ)	116a	48°19'N	122°15'W
McNary, Az., U.S. (mȧk-nâr′ė)	119	34°10'N	109°55'W
McNary, La., U.S.	123	30°58'N	92°32'W
McNary Dam, Or., U.S.	114	45°57'N	119°15'W
McPherson, Ks., U.S. (mȧk-fŭr′s'n)	121	38°21'N	97°41'W
McRae, Ga., U.S. (mȧk-rā′)	125	32°02'N	82°55'W
McRoberts, Ky., U.S. (mȧk-rŏb′ẽrts)	125	37°12'N	82°40'W
Mead, Ks., U.S. (mēd)	120	37°17'N	100°21'W
Mead, Lake, l., U.S.	106	36°20'N	114°14'W
Meade Peak, mtn., Id., U.S.	115	42°19'N	111°16'W
Meadow Lake, Can. (mĕd′ō lāk)	90	54°08'N	108°26'W
Meadows, Can. (mĕd′ōz)	102f	50°02'N	97°35'W
Meadville, Pa., U.S. (mēd′vĭl)	108	41°40'N	80°10'W
Meaford, Can. (mĕ′fẽrd)	99	44°35'N	80°40'W
Mealy Mountains, mts., Can. (mē′lē)	93	53°32'N	57°58'W
Meandarra, Austl. (mē-ȧn-dä′rȧ)	222	27°47'S	149°40'E
Meaux, Fr. (mō)	170	48°58'N	2°53'E
Mecapalapa, Mex. (mă-kä-pä-lä′pä)	131	20°32'N	97°52'W
Mecatina, r., Can. (mā-kȧ-tē′nȧ)	101	50°50'N	59°45'W
Mecca (Makkah), Sau. Ar. (mĕk′ȧ)	198	21°27'N	39°45'E
Mechanic Falls, Me., U.S. (mė-kăn′ĭk)	100	44°05'N	70°23'W
Mechanicsburg, Pa., U.S. (mė-kăn′ĭks-bŭrg)	109	40°15'N	77°00'W
Mechanicsville, Md., U.S. (mė-kăn′ĭks-vĭl)	110e	38°27'N	76°45'W
Mechanicville, N.Y., U.S. (mėkăn′ĭk-vĭl)	109	42°55'N	73°45'W
Mechelen, Bel.	165	51°01'N	4°28'E
Mechriyya, Alg.	162	33°30'N	0°13'W
Mecicine Bow Range, mts., Co., U.S. (mĕd′ĭ-sĭn bō)	120	40°55'N	106°02'W
Mecklenburg, hist. reg., Ger.	168	53°30'N	13°00'E
Medan, Indon. (må-dän′)	212	3°35'N	98°35'E

ăt; finăl; rāte; senåte; ärm; ȧsk; sofȧ; fâre; ch-choose; dh-as th in other; bē; ėvent; bĕt; recĕnt; cratẽr; g-gō; gh-guttural g; bĭt; ĭ-short neutral; rīde; ᴋ-guttural k as ch in German ich;

PRONOUNCING INDEX Medanosa – Mezquitic 321

PLACE (Pronunciation)	PAGE	LAT.	LONG.
Medanosa, Punta, c., Arg. (po͞o'n-tä-mĕ-dä-nō'sä)	144	47°50'S	65°53'W
Medden, r., Eng., U.K. (mĕd'ĕn)	158a	53°14'N	1°05'W
Medellín, Col. (mā-dhĕl-yēn')	142	6°15'N	75°34'W
Medellín, Mex. (mĕ-dĕl-yĕ'n)	131	19°03'N	96°08'W
Medenine, Tun. (mā-dē-nēn')	162	33°22'N	10°33'E
Medfeld, Ma., U.S. (mĕd'fēld)	101a	42°11'N	71°19'W
Medford, Ma., U.S. (mĕd'fērd)	101a	42°25'N	71°07'W
Medford, N.J., U.S.	110f	39°54'N	74°50'W
Medford, Ok., U.S.	121	36°47'N	97°44'W
Medford, Or., U.S.	104	42°19'N	122°52'W
Medford, Wi., U.S.	113	45°09'N	90°22'W
Media, Pa., U.S. (mē'dĭ-à)	110f	39°55'N	75°24'W
Mediaş, Rom. (mĕd-yäsh')	169	46°09'N	24°21'E
Medical Lake, Wa., U.S. (mĕd'ĭ-kăl)	114	47°34'N	117°40'W
Medicine Bow, r., Wy., U.S.	115	41°58'N	106°30'W
Medicine Hat, Can. (mĕd'ĭ-sĭn hăt)	90	50°03'N	110°40'W
Medicine Lake, l., Mt., U.S. (mĕd'ĭ-sĭn)	115	48°24'N	104°15'W
Medicine Lodge, Ks., U.S.	120	37°17'N	98°37'W
Medicine Lodge, r., Ks., U.S.	120	37°20'N	98°57'W
Medina *see* Al Madīnah, Sau. Ar.	198	24°26'N	39°42'E
Medina, N.Y., U.S. (mē-dī'nȧ)	109	43°15'N	78°20'W
Medina, Oh., U.S.	111d	41°08'N	81°52'W
Medina, r., Tx., U.S.	122	29°45'N	99°13'W
Medina del Campo, Spain (mā-dē'nä dĕl käm'pō)	162	41°18'N	4°54'W
Medina de Ríoseco, Spain (mā-dē'nä dā rē-ō-sā'kō)	172	41°53'N	5°05'W
Medina Lake, l., Tx., U.S.	122	29°36'N	98°47'W
Medina Sidonia, Spain	172	36°28'N	5°58'W
Mediterranean Sea, sea (mĕd-ĭ-tēr-ā'nē-ăn)	162	36°22'N	13°25'E
Medjerda, Oued, r., Afr.	162	36°43'N	9°54'E
Mednogorsk, Russia	178	51°27'N	57°22'E
Medveditsa, r., Russia (mĕd-vyĕ'dē tsȧ)	181	50°10'N	43°40'E
Medvezhegorsk, Russia (mĕd-vyĕzh'yĕ-gôrsk')	180	63°00'N	34°20'E
Medway, Ma., U.S. (mĕd'wā)	101a	42°08'N	71°23'W
Medway Towns, co., Eng., U.K.	158b	51°27'N	0°30'E
Medyn', Russia (mĕ-dēn')	176	54°58'N	35°53'E
Medzhybizh, Ukr.	177	49°23'N	27°29'E
Meekatharra, Austl. (mē-kȧ-thăr'ȧ)	218	26°30'S	118°38'E
Meeker, Co., U.S. (mēk'ēr)	119	40°00'N	107°55'W
Meelpaeg Lake, l., Can. (mēl'pȧ-ĕg)	101	48°22'N	56°52'W
Meerane, Ger. (mā-rä'nĕ)	168	50°51'N	12°27'E
Meerbusch, Ger.	171c	51°15'N	6°41'E
Meerut, India (mē'rŭt)	199	28°59'N	77°43'E
Megalópoli, Grc.	175	37°22'N	22°08'E
Mégara, Grc. (mĕg'ȧ-rȧ)	175	37°59'N	23°21'E
Megget, S.C., U.S. (mĕg'ĕt)	125	32°44'N	80°15'W
Megler, Wa., U.S. (mĕg'lēr)	116c	46°15'N	123°52'W
Mehanom, Mys, c., Ukr.	177	44°48'N	35°17'E
Meherrin, r., Va., U.S. (mē-hĕr'ĭn)	125	36°40'N	77°49'W
Mehlville, Mo., U.S.	117e	38°30'N	90°19'W
Mehsāna, India	202	23°42'N	72°23'E
Mehun-sur-Yévre, Fr. (mē-ŭn-sür-yĕvr')	170	47°11'N	2°14'E
Meiling Pass, p., China (mā'lĭng')	205	25°22'N	115°00'E
Meinerzhagen, Ger. (mī'nĕrts-hä-gĕn)	171c	51°06'N	7°39'E
Meiningen, Ger. (mī'nĭng-ĕn)	168	50°35'N	10°25'E
Meiringen, Switz.	168	46°45'N	8°11'E
Meissen, Ger.	168	51°11'N	13°28'E
Meizhu, China (mā-jo͞o)	206	31°17'N	119°12'E
Mejillones, Chile (mā-κē-lyō'nås)	144	23°07'S	70°31'W
Mekambo, Gabon	236	1°01'N	13°56'E
Mekele, Eth.	231	13°31'N	39°19'E
Meknés, Mor. (mĕk'nĕs)(mĕk-nĕs')	230	33°56'N	5°44'W
Mekong, r., Asia	212	18°00'N	104°30'E
Melaka, Malay.	212	2°11'N	102°15'E
Melaka, state, Malay.	197b	2°19'N	102°09'E
Melanesia, is., Oc.	240	13°00'S	164°00'E
Melbourne, Austl. (mĕl'bŭrn)	219	37°52'S	145°08'E
Melbourne, Eng., U.K.	158a	52°49'N	1°26'W
Melbourne, Fl., U.S.	125a	28°05'N	80°37'W
Melbourne, Ky., U.S.	111f	39°02'N	84°22'W
Melcher, Ia., U.S. (mĕl'chēr)	113	41°13'N	93°11'W
Melekess, Russia (mĕl-yĕk-ĕs)	180	54°14'N	49°39'E
Melenki, Russia (mĕ-lyĕŋ'kē)	180	55°25'N	41°34'E
Melfort, Can. (mĕl'fôrt)	90	52°52'N	104°36'W
Melghir, Chott, l., Alg.	230	33°52'N	5°22'E
Melilla, Sp. N. Afr. (mā-lēl'yä)	230	35°24'N	3°30'W
Melipilla, Chile (mā-lē-pē'lyä)	144	33°40'S	71°12'W
Melita, Can.	97	49°11'N	101°09'W
Melitopol', Ukr. (mā-lē-tô'pôl-y')	181	46°49'N	35°19'E
Melívoia, Grc.	175	39°42'N	22°47'E
Melkrivier, S. Afr.	238c	24°01'S	28°23'E
Mellen, Wi., U.S. (mĕl'ĕn)	113	46°20'N	90°40'W
Mellerud, Swe. (mâl'ĕ-ro͞odh)	166	58°43'N	12°25'E
Melmoth, S. Afr.	233c	28°38'S	31°26'E
Melo, Ur. (mā'lō)	144	32°18'S	54°07'W
Melocheville, Can. (mĕ-lôsh-vēl')	102a	45°24'N	73°56'W
Melozha, r., Russia (myĕ'lō-zhȧ)	186b	56°06'N	38°34'E
Melrose, Ma., U.S. (mĕl'rōz)	101a	42°29'N	71°06'W
Melrose, Mn., U.S.	113	45°39'N	94°49'W
Melrose Park, Il., U.S.	111a	41°54'N	87°52'W
Meltham, Eng., U.K. (mĕl'thăm)	158a	53°35'N	1°51'W
Melton, Austl. (mĕl'tŭn)	217a	37°41'S	144°35'E
Melton Mowbray, Eng., U.K. (mō'brā)	158a	52°45'N	0°52'W
Melúli, r., Moz.	237	16°10'S	39°30'E
Melun, Fr. (mē-lŭn')	161	48°32'N	2°40'E
Melunga, Ang.	236	17°16'S	16°24'E
Melville, Can. (mĕl'vĭl)	90	50°55'N	102°48'W
Melville, La., U.S.	123	30°39'N	91°45'W
Melville, i., Austl.	220	11°30'S	131°12'E
Melville, l., Can.	93	53°46'N	59°31'W
Melville, Cape, c., Austl.	221	14°15'S	145°50'E
Melville Hills, hills, Can.	92	69°18'N	124°57'W
Melville Peninsula, pen., Can.	93	67°44'N	84°09'W
Melvindale, Mi., U.S. (mĕl'vĭn-dāl)	111b	42°17'N	83°11'W
Melyana, Alg.	161	36°19'N	1°56'E
Mélykút, Hung. (mā'l'ko͞ot)	169	46°14'N	19°21'E
Memba, Moz. (mĕm'bȧ)	233	14°12'N	40°35'E
Memel *see* Klaipėda, Lith.	180	55°43'N	21°10'E
Memel, S. Afr. (mĕ'mĕl)	238c	27°42'S	29°35'E
Memmingen, Ger. (mĕm'ĭng-ĕn)	168	47°59'N	10°10'E
Memo, r., Ven. (mĕ'mō)	143b	9°32'N	66°30'W
Memphis, Mo., U.S. (mĕm'fĭs)	121	40°27'N	92°11'W
Memphis, Tn., U.S. (mĕm'fĭs)	105	35°07'N	90°03'W
Memphis, Tx., U.S.	120	34°42'N	100°33'W
Memphis, hist., Egypt	238b	29°50'N	31°12'E
Mena, Ukr. (mē-nä')	177	51°31'N	32°14'E
Mena, Ar., U.S. (mē'nȧ)	121	34°35'N	94°09'W
Menangle, Austl.	217b	34°08'S	150°48'E
Menard, Tx., U.S. (mē-närd')	122	30°56'N	99°48'W
Menasha, Wi., U.S. (mē-năsh'ȧ)	113	44°12'N	88°29'W
Mende, Fr. (mäɴd)	170	44°31'N	3°30'E
Menden, Ger. (mĕn'dĕn)	171c	51°26'N	7°47'E
Mendes, Braz. (mĕ'n-dĕs)	144b	22°32'S	43°44'W
Mendocino, Ca., U.S.	118	39°18'N	123°47'W
Mendocino, Cape, c., Ca., U.S. (mĕn'dō-sē'nō)	107	40°25'N	12°42'W
Mendota, Il., U.S. (mĕn-dō'tȧ)	113	41°34'N	89°06'W
Mendota, l., Wi., U.S.	113	43°09'N	89°41'W
Mendoza, Arg. (mĕn-dō'sä)	144	32°48'S	68°45'W
Mendoza, prov., Arg.	144	35°10'S	69°00'W
Mengcheng, China (mŭŋ-chŭŋ)	206	33°15'N	116°34'E
Meng Shan, mts., China (mŭŋ shän)	206	35°47'N	117°23'E
Mengzi, China	204	23°22'N	103°20'E
Menindee, Austl. (mĕ-nĭn-dē)	222	32°23'S	142°30'E
Menlo Park, Ca., U.S. (mĕn'lō pärk)	116b	37°27'N	122°11'W
Menno, S.D., U.S. (mĕn'ō)	112	43°14'N	97°34'W
Menominee, Mi., U.S. (mē-nŏm'ĭ-nē)	113	45°08'N	87°40'W
Menominee, r., Mi., U.S.	113	45°37'N	87°54'W
Menominee Falls, Wi., U.S. (fôls)	111a	43°11'N	88°06'W
Menominee Ra, Mi., U.S.	113	46°07'N	88°53'W
Menomonee, r., Wi., U.S.	111a	43°09'N	88°06'W
Menomonie, Wi., U.S.	113	44°53'N	91°55'W
Menongue, Ang.	236	14°36'S	17°48'E
Menorca (Minorca), i., Spain (mĕ-nō'r-kä)	156	40°05'N	3°58'E
Mentana, Italy (mĕn-tá'nä)	173d	42°02'N	12°40'E
Mentawai, Kepulauan, is., Indon. (mĕn-tä-vī')	212	1°08'S	98°10'E
Menton, Fr. (mäɴ-tôɴ')	171	43°46'N	7°37'E
Mentone, Ca., U.S. (mĕn'tōne)	117a	34°05'N	117°08'W
Mentz, l., S. Afr. (mĕnts)	233c	33°13'S	25°15'E
Menzel Bourguiba, Tun.	162	37°12'N	9°51'E
Menzelinsk, Russia (mĕn'zyĕ-lĕnsk')	180	55°40'N	53°15'E
Menzies, Austl. (mĕn'zēz)	218	29°45'S	122°15'E
Meogui, Mex. (må-ō'gē)	122	28°17'N	105°28'W
Meppel, Neth. (mĕp'ĕl)	165	52°41'N	6°08'E
Meppen, Ger. (mĕp'ĕn)	168	52°40'N	7°18'E
Merabéllou, Kólpos, b., Grc.	174a	35°16'N	25°55'E
Meramec, r., Mo., U.S. (mĕr'ȧ-mĕk)	121	38°06'N	91°06'W
Merano, Italy (må-rä'nō)	162	46°39'N	11°10'E
Merasheen, i., Can. (mē'rȧ-shēn)	101	47°30'N	54°15'W
Merauke, Indon. (må-rou'kä)	213	8°32'S	140°17'E
Meraux, La., U.S. (mē-ro')	110d	29°56'N	89°56'W
Mercato San Severino, Italy	173c	40°34'N	14°38'E
Merced, Ca., U.S. (mĕr-sĕd')	118	37°17'N	120°30'W
Merced, r., Ca., U.S.	118	37°25'N	120°31'W
Mercedario, Cerro, mtn., Arg. (mĕr-så-dhä'rē-ō)	144	31°58'S	70°07'W
Mercedes, Arg.	141c	34°41'S	59°26'W
Mercedes, Arg. (mĕr-sā'dhās)	144	29°04'S	58°01'W
Mercedes, Ur.	144	33°17'S	58°04'W
Mercedes, Tx., U.S.	123	26°09'N	97°55'W
Mercedita, Chile (mĕr-sē-dē'tä)	141b	33°51'S	71°10'W
Mercer Island, Wa., U.S. (mûr'sēr)	116a	47°35'N	122°15'W
Mercês, Braz. (mĕ-sĕ's)	141a	21°13'S	43°20'W
Merchtem, Bel.	159a	50°57'N	4°13'E
Mercier, Can.	102a	45°19'N	73°45'W
Mercy, Cape, c., Can.	93	64°48'N	63°22'W
Meredith, N.H., U.S. (mĕr'ē-dĭth)	109	43°35'N	71°35'W
Merefa, Ukr. (må-rĕ'fȧ)	177	49°49'N	36°04'E
Merendón, Serranía de, mts., Hond.	132	15°01'N	89°05'W
Mereworth, Eng., U.K. (mĕ-rē wûrth)	158b	51°15'N	0°23'E
Mergui, Mya. (mĕr-gē')	212	12°29'N	98°39'E
Mergui Archipelago, is., Mya.	212	12°04'N	97°02'E
Meric (Maritsa), r., Eur.	167	40°43'N	26°19'E
Mérida, Mex.	128	20°58'N	89°37'W
Mérida, Ven.	142	8°30'N	71°15'W
Mérida, Cordillera de, mts., Ven. (mĕ'rē-dhä)	142	8°30'N	70°45'W
Meriden, Ct., U.S. (mĕr'ĭ-dĕn)	109	41°30'N	72°50'W
Meridian, Ms., U.S. (mē-rĭd-ĭ-ăn)	105	32°21'N	88°41'W
Meridian, Tx., U.S.	123	31°56'N	97°37'W
Mérignac, Fr.	170	44°50'N	0°40'W
Merikarvia, Fin. (mā'rē-kär'vē-ä)	167	61°51'N	21°30'E
Mering, Ger. (mē'rĕng)	159d	48°16'N	11°00'E
Merkel, Tx., U.S. (mûr'kĕl)	122	32°26'N	100°02'W
Merkinė, Lith.	167	54°10'N	24°10'E
Merksem, Bel.	159a	51°15'N	4°27'E
Merkys, r., Lith. (măr'kĭs)	169	54°23'N	25°00'E
Merlo, Arg. (mĕr-lō)	144a	34°40'S	58°44'W
Meron, Hare, mtn., Isr.	197a	32°58'N	35°25'E
Merriam, Ks., U.S. (mĕr-rĭ-yăm)	117f	39°01'N	94°42'W
Merriam, Mn., U.S.	117g	44°44'N	93°36'W
Merrick, N.Y., U.S. (mĕr'ĭk)	110a	40°40'N	73°33'W
Merrifield, Va., U.S. (mĕr'ĭ-fēld)	110e	38°50'N	77°12'W
Merrill, Wi., U.S. (mĕr'ĭl)	113	45°11'N	89°42'W
Merrimac, Ma., U.S. (mĕr'ĭ-măk)	101a	45°20'N	71°00'W
Merrimack, N.H., U.S.	101a	42°51'N	71°25'W
Merrimack, r., Ma., U.S. (mĕr'ĭ-măk)	109	43°10'N	71°30'W
Merritt, Can. (mĕr'ĭt)	90	50°07'N	120°47'W
Merryville, La., U.S. (mĕr'ĭ-vĭl)	123	30°46'N	93°34'W
Mersa Fatma, Erit.	231	14°54'N	40°14'E
Merseburg, Ger. (mĕr'zē-bo͞orgh)	168	51°21'N	11°59'E
Mersey, r., Eng., U.K. (mûr'zē)	158a	53°20'N	2°55'W
Merseyside, hist. reg., Eng., U.K.	158a	53°29'N	2°59'W
Mersing, Malay.	197b	2°25'N	103°51'E
Merta Road, India (mär'tŭ rōd)	202	26°50'N	73°54'E
Merthyr Tydfil, Wales, U.K. (mûr'thēr tĭd'vĭl)	164	51°46'N	3°30'W
Mértola Almodóvar, Port. (mĕr-tô-lȧ-äl-mō-dō'vär)	172	37°39'N	8°04'W
Méru, Fr. (mā-rü')	170	49°14'N	2°08'E
Meru, Kenya (mā'ro͞o)	231	0°01'N	37°45'E
Meru, Mount, mtn., Tan.	237	3°15'S	36°43'E
Merume Mountains, mts., Guy. (mĕr-ü'mĕ)	143	5°45'N	60°15'W
Merwede Kanaal, can., Neth.	159a	52°15'N	5°01'E
Merwin, l., Wa., U.S. (mĕr'wĭn)	116c	45°58'N	122°27'W
Merzifon, Tur. (mĕr'ze-fōn)	198	40°50'N	35°30'E
Mesa, Az., U.S. (mā'sȧ)	119	33°25'N	111°50'W
Mesabi Range, mts., Mn., U.S. (mā-sŏb'bē)	113	47°17'N	93°04'W
Mesagne, Italy (mā-sän'yå)	175	40°34'N	17°51'E
Mesa Verde National Park, rec., Co., U.S. (vĕr'dē)	106	37°22'N	108°27'W
Mescalero Apache Indian Reservation, I.R., N.M., U.S. (mĕs-kä-lā'rō)	119	33°10'N	105°45'W
Meshchovsk, Russia (myĕsh'chĕfsk)	176	54°17'N	35°19'E
Mesilla, N.M., U.S. (må-sē'yä)	119	32°15'N	106°45'W
Meskine, Chad	235	11°25'N	15°21'E
Mesolóngi, Grc.	175	38°23'N	21°28'E
Mesopotamia, hist. reg., Asia	201	34°00'N	44°00'E
Mesquita, Braz.	144b	22°48'S	43°26'W
Messina, Italy (mĕ-sē'nȧ)	154	38°11'N	15°34'E
Messina, S. Afr.	232	22°17'S	30°13'E
Messina, Stretto di, strt., Italy (stĕ't-tô dē)	163	38°10'N	15°34'E
Messíni, Grc.	175	37°05'N	22°00'E
Mestaganem, Alg.	230	36°04'N	0°11'E
Mestre, Italy (mĕs'trā)	174	45°29'N	12°15'E
Meta, dept., Col. (mĕ'tä)	142a	3°28'N	74°07'W
Meta, r., S.A.	142	4°33'N	72°09'W
Métabetchouane, r., Can. (mĕ-tá-bĕt-cho͞o-än')	99	47°45'N	72°00'W
Metairie, La., U.S.	123	30°00'N	90°11'W
Metán, Arg. (mĕ-tá'n)	144	25°32'S	64°51'W
Metangula, Moz.	232	12°42'S	34°48'E
Metapán, El Sal. (må-täpän')	132	14°21'N	89°26'W
Metcalfe, Can. (mĕt-käf)	102c	45°14'N	75°27'W
Metchosin, Can.	116a	48°22'N	123°33'W
Metepec, Mex. (må-tĕ-pĕk')	130	18°56'N	98°31'W
Metepec, Mex.	130	19°15'N	99°36'W
Methow, r., Wa., U.S. (mĕt'hou) (mĕt hou')	114	48°26'N	120°15'W
Methuen, Ma., U.S. (mē-thū'ĕn)	101a	42°44'N	71°11'W
Metković, Cro. (mĕt'kō-vĭch)	175	43°02'N	17°40'E
Metlakatla, Ak., U.S. (mĕt-lȧ-kăt'lȧ)	103	55°08'N	131°35'W
Metropolis, Il., U.S. (mē-trŏp'ō-lĭs)	121	37°09'N	88°46'W
Metter, Ga., U.S. (mĕt'ēr)	125	32°21'N	82°05'W
Mettmann, Ger. (mĕt'män)	171c	51°15'N	6°58'E
Metuchen, N.J., U.S. (mē-tŭ'chĕn)	110a	40°32'N	74°21'W
Metz, Fr. (mĕtz)	161	49°08'N	6°10'E
Metztitlán, Mex. (mĕtz-tēt-län)	130	20°36'N	98°45'W
Meuban, Cam.	235	2°27'N	12°41'E
Meuse (Maas), r., Eur. (mûz) (müz)	165	50°32'N	5°22'E
Mexborough, Eng., U.K. (mĕks'bŭr-ō)	158a	53°30'N	1°17'W
Mexia, Tx., U.S. (må-hē'ä)	123	31°32'N	96°29'W
Mexian, China	205	24°20'N	116°10'E
Mexicalcingo, Mex. (mĕ-kē-käl-sēn'go)	131a	19°13'N	99°34'W
Mexicali, Mex. (måk-sē-kä'lē)	128	32°28'N	115°29'W
Mexicana, Altiplanicie, plat., Mex.	130	22°38'N	102°33'W
Mexican Hat, Ut., U.S. (mĕk'sĭ-kăn hăt)	119	37°10'N	109°55'W
Mexico, Me., U.S. (mĕk'sĭ-kō)	100	44°34'N	70°33'W
Mexico, Mo., U.S.	121	39°09'N	91°51'W
Mexico, nation, N.A.	128	23°45'N	104°00'W
Mexico, Gulf of, b., N.A.	128	25°15'N	93°45'W
Mexico City, Mex. (mĕk'sĭ-kō)	128	19°28'N	99°09'W
Mexticacán, Mex. (mĕs'tē-kä-kän')	130	21°12'N	102°43'W
Meyers Chuck, Ak., U.S.	94	55°44'N	132°15'W
Meyersdale, Pa., U.S. (mī'ērz-dāl)	109	39°55'N	79°00'W
Meyerton, S. Afr. (mī'ēr-tŭn)	238c	26°35'S	28°01'E
Meymaneh, Afg.	198	35°53'N	64°38'E
Mezen', Russia	178	65°50'N	44°05'E
Mezen', r., Russia	180	65°20'N	44°45'E
Mézenc, Mont, mtn., Fr. (mōɴ-mā-zĕɴ')	170	44°55'N	4°12'E
Mezha, r., Eur. (myā'zhȧ)	176	55°53'N	31°44'E
Mézieres-sur-Seine, Fr. (mā-zyâr'sür-sån')	171b	48°58'N	1°49'E
Mezökövesd, Hung. (mĕ'zû-kû'vĕsht)	169	47°49'N	20°36'E
Mezötur, Hung. (mĕ'zû-to͞or)	169	47°00'N	20°36'E
Mezquital, Mex. (måz-kē-täl')	130	23°30'N	104°20'W
Mezquitic, Mex. (måz-kē-tēk')	130	22°25'N	103°43'W
Mezquitic, r., Mex.	130	22°25'N	103°45'W

ăt; fināl; rāte; senāte; ärm; ásk; sofá; fâre; ch-choose; dh-as th in other; bē; ĕvent; bĕt; recĕnt; cratēr; g-gō; gh-guttural g; bĭt; ī-short neutral; rīde; ᴋ-guttural k as ch in German ich;

PRONOUNCING INDEX
Mississippi Sound – Monterotondo 323

PLACE (Pronunciation)	PAGE	LAT.	LONG.
Mississippi Sound, strt., Ms., U.S.	124	34°16'N	89°10'W
Missoula, Mt., U.S. (mĭ-zo͞o′lȧ)	104	46°55'N	114°00'W
Missouri, state, U.S. (mĭ-so͞o′rē)	105	38°00'N	93°40'W
Missouri, r., U.S.	106	40°40'N	96°00'W
Missouri City, Tx., U.S.	123a	29°37'N	95°32'W
Missouri Coteau, hills, U.S.	106	47°30'N	101°00'W
Missouri Valley, Ia., U.S.	112	41°35'N	95°53'W
Mist, Or., U.S. (mĭst)	116c	46°00'N	123°15'W
Mistassini, Can. (mĭs-tȧ-sĭ′nē)	99	48°56'N	71°55'W
Mistassini, l., Can. (mĭs-tȧ-sĭ′nē)	93	50°48'N	73°30'W
Mistelbach, Aus. (mĭs′tĕl-bäk)	168	48°34'N	16°33'E
Misteriosa, Lago, l., Mex. (mēs-tĕ-ryô′sä)	132a	18°05'N	90°15'W
Misti, Volcán, vol., Peru	142	16°04'S	71°20'W
Mistretta, Italy (mē-strĕt′tä)	174	37°54'N	14°22'E
Misty Fjords National Monument, rec., Ak., U.S.	103	51°00'N	131°00'W
Mita, Punta de, c., Mex. (po͞o′n-tä-dĕ-mē′tä)	130	20°44'N	105°34'W
Mitaka, Japan (mē′tä-kä)	211a	35°42'N	139°34'E
Mitchell, Il., U.S. (mĭch′ĕl)	117e	38°46'N	90°05'W
Mitchell, In., U.S.	108	38°45'N	86°25'W
Mitchell, Ne., U.S.	112	41°56'N	103°49'W
Mitchell, S.D., U.S.	104	43°42'N	98°01'W
Mitchell, Mount, mtn., N.C., U.S.	107	35°47'N	82°15'W
Mīt Ghamr, Egypt	238b	30°43'N	31°20'E
Mitla Pass, p., Egypt	197a	30°03'N	32°40'E
Mito, Japan (mē′tō)	210	36°20'N	140°23'E
Mitsiwa, Erit.	231	15°40'N	39°19'E
Mitsu, Japan (mēt′sò)	211	34°21'N	132°49'E
Mittelland Kanal, can., Ger. (mĭt′ĕl-länd)	168	52°18'N	10°42'E
Mittenwalde, Ger. (mē′tĕn-väl-dĕ)	159b	52°16'N	13°33'E
Mittweida, Ger. (mĭt-vī′dä)	168	50°59'N	12°58'E
Mitumba, Monts, mts., D.R.C.	237	10°50'S	27°00'E
Mityayevo, Russia (mĭt-yä′yĕ-vô)	186a	60°17'N	61°02'E
Miura, Japan	211a	35°08'N	139°37'E
Miwa, Japan (mē′wä)	211b	34°32'N	135°51'E
Mixico, Guat. (mēs′kô)	132	14°37'N	90°37'W
Mixquiahuala, Mex. (mēs-kē-wä′lä)	130	20°12'N	99°13'W
Mixteco, r., Mex. (mês-tä′kō)	130	17°45'N	98°10'W
Miyake, Japan (mē′yä-kå)	211b	34°35'N	135°34'E
Miyake, i., Japan (mē′yä-kå)	211	34°06'N	139°21'E
Miyakonojō, Japan	210	31°44'N	131°04'E
Miyazaki, Japan (mē′yä-zä′kĕ)	210	31°55'N	131°27'E
Miyoshi, Japan (mê-yō′shē′)	210	34°48'N	132°49'E
Mizdah, Libya (mēz′dä)	200	31°29'N	13°09'E
Mizil, Rom. (mē′zēl)	175	45°01'N	26°30'E
Mizoram, state, India	199	23°25'N	92°45'E
Mjölby, Swe. (myûl′bü)	166	58°20'N	15°09'E
Mjörn, l., Swe.	166	57°55'N	12°22'E
Mjösa, l., Nor. (myûsä)	160	60°41'N	11°25'E
Mkalama, Tan.	232	4°07'S	34°38'E
Mkushi, Zam.	237	13°40'S	29°20'E
Mkwaja, Tan.	237	5°47'S	38°51'E
Mladá Boleslav, Czech Rep. (mlä′dä bô′lĕ-sláf)	168	50°26'N	14°52'E
Mlala Hills, hills, Tan.	237	6°47'S	31°45'E
Mlanje Mountains, mts., Mwi.	237	15°55'S	35°30'E
Mława, Pol. (mwä′vá)	160	53°07'N	20°25'E
Mmabatho, S. Afr.	232	25°42'S	25°43'E
Moa, r., Afr.	234	7°40'N	11°15'W
Moa, Pulau, i., Indon.	213	8°30'S	128°30'E
Moab, Ut., U.S. (mō′ăb)	119	38°35'N	109°35'W
Moanda, Gabon	232	1°37'S	13°09'E
Moar Lake, l., Can. (môr)	97	52°00'N	95°09'W
Moba, D.R.C.	232	7°12'S	29°39'E
Mobaye, C.A.R. (mô-bä′y′)	231	4°19'N	21°11'E
Mobayi-Mbongo, D.R.C.	231	4°14'N	21°11'E
Moberly, Mo., U.S. (mō′bēr-lĭ)	105	39°24'N	92°25'W
Mobile, Al., U.S. (mô-bēl′)	105	30°42'N	88°03'W
Mobile, r., Al., U.S.	124	31°15'N	88°00'W
Mobile Bay, b., Al., U.S.	107	30°26'N	87°56'W
Mobridge, S.D., U.S. (mō′brĭj)	112	45°32'N	100°26'W
Moca, Dom. Rep. (mô′kä)	135	19°25'N	70°35'W
Moçambique, Moz. (mō-säɴ-bē′kĕ)	237	15°03'S	40°42'E
Moçâmedes, Ang. (mô-zá-mĕ-dĕs)	232	15°10'S	12°09'E
Moçâmedes, hist. reg., Ang.	232	16°00'S	12°15'E
Mochitlán, Mex. (mō-chē-tlän′)	130	17°10'N	99°19'W
Mochudi, Bots. (mō-cho͞o′dĕ)	232	24°13'S	26°07'E
Mocímboa da Praia, Moz. (mô-sē′ĕm-bô-á prä′ēá)	233	11°20'S	40°21'E
Moclips, Wa., U.S.	114	47°14'N	124°13'W
Môco, Serra do, mtn., Ang.	236	12°25'S	15°10'E
Mococa, Braz. (mô-kô′kà)	141a	21°29'S	46°58'W
Moctezuma, Mex. (mök′tå-zo͞o′mä)	130	22°44'N	101°06'W
Mocuba, Moz.	237	16°50'S	36°59'E
Modderfontein, S. Afr.	233b	26°06'S	28°10'E
Modena, Italy (mô′dĕ-nä)	162	44°38'N	10°54'E
Modesto, Ca., U.S. (mô-dĕs′tō)	118	37°39'N	121°00'W
Mödling, Aus. (mûd′lĭng)	159e	48°06'N	16°17'E
Moelv, Nor.	166	60°55'N	10°40'E
Moengo, Sur.	143	5°43'N	54°19'W
Moenkopi, Az., U.S.	119	36°07'N	111°13'W
Moers, Ger. (mûrs)	171c	51°27'N	6°38'E
Moffat Tunnel, trans., Co., U.S. (môf′ăt)	120	39°52'N	106°20'W
Mogadishu (Muqdisho), Som.	238a	2°08'N	45°22'E
Mogadore, Oh., U.S. (mŏg-á-dōr′)	111d	41°04'N	81°23'E
Mogaung, Mya. (mō-gä′ông)	199	25°30'N	96°52'E
Mogi das Cruzes, Braz. (mô-gē-däs-kro͞o′sĕs)	143	23°33'S	46°10'W
Mogi-Guaçu, r., Braz. (mô-gē-gwá′so͞o)	141a	22°06'S	47°12'W
Mogilno, Pol. (mô-gēl′nô)	168	52°38'N	17°58'W
Mogi-Mirim, Braz. (mô-gē-mē-rē′ɴ)	141a	22°26'S	46°57'W
Mogok, Mya. (mô-gōk′)	199	23°14'N	96°38'E
Mogol, r., S. Afr. (mô-gŏl)	238c	24°12'S	27°55'E
Mogollon Plateau, plat., Az., U.S.	106	34°15'N	110°45'W
Mogollon Rim, cliff, Az., U.S. (mō-gô-yōn′)	119	34°26'N	111°17'W
Moguer, Spain (mô-gĕr′)	172	37°15'N	6°50'W
Mohács, Hung. (mô′häch)	169	45°59'N	18°38'E
Mohale's Hoek, Leso.	233c	30°09'S	27°28'E
Mohall, N.D., U.S. (mō′hôl)	112	48°46'N	101°29'W
Mohave, l., Nv., U.S. (mô-hä′vä)	119	35°23'N	114°40'W
Mohe, China (mwo-hŭ)	205	53°33'N	122°30'E
Mohenjo-Dero, hist., Pak.	199	27°20'N	68°10'E
Mohyliv-Podil's′kyi, Ukr.	181	48°27'N	27°51'E
Mõisaküla, Est. (mē′ē′sá-kü′lä)	167	58°07'N	25°12'E
Moissac, Fr. (mwä-sák′)	170	44°07'N	1°05'E
Moita, Port. (mô-ē′tȧ)	173b	38°39'N	9°00'W
Mojave, Ca., U.S.	118	35°06'N	118°09'W
Mojave, r., Ca., U.S. (mô-hä′vä)	118	34°46'N	117°24'W
Mojave Desert, Ca., U.S.	118	35°05'N	117°30'W
Mojave Desert, des., Ca., U.S.	106	35°00'N	117°00'W
Mokhotlong, Leso.	233c	29°18'S	29°06'E
Mokp'o, Kor., S. (mŏk′pō′)	205	34°50'N	126°30'E
Mol, Bel.	159a	51°21'N	5°09'E
Moldavia *see* Moldova, nation, Eur.	178	48°00'N	28°00'E
Moldavia, hist. reg., Rom.	169	47°20'N	27°12'E
Molde, Nor. (môl′dĕ)	160	62°44'N	7°15'E
Moldova, nation, Eur.	178	48°00'N	28°00'E
Moldova, r., Rom.	169	47°17'N	26°27'E
Moldoveanu, Vârful, mtn., Rom.	175	45°33'N	24°38'E
Molepolole, Bots. (mō-lå-pô-lō′lå)	232	24°15'S	25°33'W
Molfetta, Italy (môl-fĕt′tä)	163	41°11'N	16°38'E
Molina, Chile (mō-lē′nä)	141b	35°07'S	71°17'W
Molina de Aragón, Spain (mô-lē′nä dĕ ä-rä-gô′n)	172	40°40'N	1°54'W
Molína de Segura, Spain (mô-lē′nä dĕ sĕ-go͞o′rä)	172	38°03'N	1°07'W
Moline, Il., U.S. (mô-lēn′)	121	41°31'N	90°34'W
Moliro, D.R.C.	232	8°13'S	30°34'E
Moliterno, Italy (môl-ē-tĕr′nō)	174	40°13'N	15°54'W
Mollendo, Peru (mô-lyĕn′dō)	142	17°02'S	71°59'W
Moller, Port, Ak., U.S. (pōrt mōl′ēr)	103	56°18'N	161°30'W
Mölndal, Swe. (mûln′däl)	166	57°39'N	12°01'E
Molochna, r., Ukr.	177	47°05'N	35°22'E
Molochnyĭ lyman, l., Ukr.	177	46°35'N	35°32'E
Molody Tud, Russia (mō-lō-dô′ē to͞o′d)	186b	55°17'N	37°31'E
Moloka'i, i., Hi., U.S. (mō-lô kä′ē)	106c	21°15'N	157°05'W
Molokcha, r., Russia (mô′lôk-chä)	186b	56°15'N	38°29'E
Molopo, r., Afr. (mō-lō-pō)	232	27°45'S	20°45'E
Molson Lake, l., Can. (mōl′sŭn)	97	54°12'N	96°45'W
Molteno, S. Afr. (môl-tä′nô)	233c	31°24'S	26°23'E
Moluccas *see* Maluku, is., Indon.	213	2°22'S	128°25'E
Moma, Moz.	237	16°44'S	39°14'E
Mombasa, Kenya (mōm-bä′sä)	233	4°03'S	39°40'E
Mombetsu, Japan (môm′bĕt-so͞o′)	210	44°21'N	142°48'E
Momence, Il., U.S. (mô-mĕns′)	111a	41°09'N	87°40'W
Momostenango, Guat. (mô-môs-tā-näŋ′gô)	132	15°02'N	91°25'W
Momotombo, Nic.	132	12°25'N	86°43'W
Mompog Pass, strt., Phil. (mōm-pōg′)	213a	13°35'N	122°09'E
Mompos, Col. (mōm-pōs′)	142	9°05'N	74°30'W
Momtblanc, Spain	173	41°20'N	1°08'E
Møn, i., Den. (mûn)	166	54°54'N	12°30'E
Monaca, Pa., U.S. (mŏ-nȧ′kō)	111e	40°41'N	80°17'W
Monaco, nation, Eur. (mŏn′ȧ-kō)	154	43°43'N	7°47'E
Monaghan, Ire. (mō′ä-găn)	164	54°16'N	7°20'W
Mona Passage, strt., N.A. (mō′nä)	129	18°00'N	68°10'W
Monarch Mountain, mtn., Can. (mŏn′ērk)	94	51°41'N	125°53'W
Monashee Mountains, mts., Can. (mŏ-nă′shē)	95	50°30'N	118°30'W
Monastir *see* Bitola, Mac.	174	41°02'N	21°22'E
Monastir, Tun. (mōn-ås-tēr′)	162	35°49'N	10°56'E
Monastyrshchina, Russia (mô-nás-tērsh′chĭ-ná)	176	54°19'N	31°49'E
Monastyryshche, Ukr.	177	48°57'N	29°53'E
Monção, Braz. (mon-souɴ′)	143	3°39'S	45°23'W
Moncayo, mtn., Spain (mōn-kä′yō)	172	41°44'N	1°48'W
Monchegorsk, Russia (mōn′chĕ-gôrsk)	180	69°00'N	33°35'E
Mönchengladbach, Ger. (mûn′kĕɴ gläd′bäk)	168	51°12'N	6°28'E
Moncique, Serra de, mts., Port. (sĕr′rä dä mōn-chē′kĕ)	172	37°22'N	8°37'W
Monclova, Mex. (mōn-klō′vä)	128	26°53'N	101°25'W
Moncton, Can. (mŭŋk′tŭn)	91	46°06'N	64°47'W
Mondêgo, r., Port. (mōn-dĕ′gō)	172	40°10'N	8°36'W
Mondego, Cabo, c., Port. (kä′bō mōn-dā′gō)	172	40°12'N	8°55'W
Mondombe, D.R.C. (mōn-dôm′bå)	232	0°45'S	23°06'E
Mondoñedo, Spain (mōn-dō-nyā′dō)	172	43°35'N	7°18'W
Mondovi, Wi., U.S. (mōn-dō′vĭ)	113	44°35'N	91°42'W
Monee, Il., U.S. (mō-nĭ)	111a	41°25'N	87°45'W
Monessen, Pa., U.S. (mŏ-nĕs′sĕn)	111e	40°09'N	79°53'W
Monett, Mo., U.S. (mō-nĕt′)	121	36°55'N	93°55'W
Monfalcone, Italy	174	45°49'N	13°30'E
Monforte de Lemos, Spain (môn-fôr′tä dĕ lĕ′môs)	172	42°30'N	7°30'W
Mongala, r., D.R.C. (mŏn-găl′ȧ)	231	3°20'N	21°30'E
Mongalla, Sudan	231	5°11'N	31°46'E
Monghyr, India (mōn-gēr′)	199	25°23'N	86°34'E
Mongo, r., Afr.	234	9°50'N	11°50'W
Mongolia, nation, Asia (mŏŋ-gō′lĭ-ȧ)	204	46°00'N	100°00'E
Mongos, Chaîne des, mts., C.A.R.	231	8°04'N	21°59'E
Mongoumba, C.A.R. (mŏŋ-go͞om′bȧ)	231	3°38'N	18°36'E
Mongu, Zam. (mŏŋ-go͞o′)	232	15°15'S	23°09'E
Monkey Bay, Mwi.	237	14°05'S	34°55'E
Monkey River, Belize (mŭŋ′kĭ)	132a	16°22'N	88°33'W
Monkland, Can. (mŭngk-lănd)	102c	45°12'N	74°52'W
Monkoto, D.R.C. (môn-kō′tō)	232	1°38'S	20°39'E
Monmouth, Il., U.S. (mŏn′mŭth) (mŏn′mouth)	121	40°54'N	90°38'W
Monmouth Junction, N.J., U.S. (mŏn′mouth jŭngk′shŭn)	110a	40°23'N	74°33'W
Monmouth Mountain, mtn., Can. (mŏn′mŭth)	94	51°00'N	123°47'W
Mono, r., Afr.	234	7°20'N	1°25'E
Mono Lake, l., Ca., U.S. (mō′nō)	118	38°04'N	119°00'W
Monon, In., U.S. (mō′nŏn)	108	40°55'N	86°55'W
Monongah, W.V., U.S. (mô-nŏn′gȧ)	108	39°25'N	80°10'W
Monongahela, Pa., U.S. (mô-nŏn-gȧ-hē′lȧ)	111a	40°11'N	79°55'W
Monongahela, r., W.V., U.S.	108	39°30'N	80°10'W
Monopoli, Italy (mô-nô′pô-lê)	175	40°55'N	17°17'E
Monóvar, Spain (mô-nō′vär)	173	38°26'N	0°50'W
Monreale, Italy (mōn-rå-ä′lä)	174	38°04'N	13°15'E
Monroe, Ga., U.S. (mŭn-rō′)	124	33°47'N	83°43'W
Monroe, La., U.S.	105	32°30'N	92°06'W
Monroe, Mi., U.S.	108	41°55'N	83°25'W
Monroe, N.C., U.S.	125	34°58'N	80°34'W
Monroe, N.Y., U.S.	110a	41°19'N	74°11'W
Monroe, Ut., U.S.	119	38°35'N	112°10'W
Monroe, Wa., U.S.	116a	47°52'N	121°58'W
Monroe, Wi., U.S.	113	42°35'N	89°40'W
Monroe, Lake, l., Fl., U.S.	125	28°50'N	81°15'W
Monroe City, Mo., U.S.	121	39°38'N	91°41'W
Monroeville, Al., U.S. (mŭn-rō′vĭl)	124	31°33'N	87°19'W
Monroeville, Pa., U.S.	111e	40°26'N	79°46'W
Monrovia, Lib.	230	6°18'N	10°47'W
Monrovia, Ca., U.S. (mŏn-rō′vĭ-ȧ)	117a	34°09'N	118°00'W
Mons, Bel. (môɴ′)	161	50°29'N	3°55'E
Monson, Me., U.S. (mŏn′sŭn)	100	45°17'N	69°28'W
Mönsterås, Swe. (mŭn′stĕr-ôs)	166	57°04'N	16°24'E
Montagne Tremblant Provincial Park, rec., Can.	107	46°30'N	75°51'W
Montague, Can. (mŏn′tȧ-gū)	101	46°10'N	62°39'W
Montague, Mi., U.S.	108	43°30'N	86°25'W
Montague, i., Ak., U.S.	103	60°10'N	147°00'W
Montalbán, Ven. (mōnt-äl-bän)	143b	10°14'N	68°19'W
Montalegre, Port. (môn-tä-lā′grĕ)	172	41°49'N	7°48'W
Montana, state, U.S. (mŏn-tăn′ȧ)	104	47°10'N	111°50'W
Montánchez, Spain (mōn-tän′chāth)	172	39°18'N	6°09'W
Montargis, Fr. (môɴ-tár-zhē′)	161	47°59'N	2°42'E
Montataire, Fr. (môɴ-tá-târ)	171b	49°15'N	2°26'E
Montauban, Fr. (môɴ-tô-bäɴ′)	161	44°01'N	1°22'E
Montauk, N.Y., U.S.	109	41°03'N	71°57'W
Montauk Point, c., N.Y., U.S. (mŏn-tôk′)	109	41°05'N	71°55'W
Montbard, Fr. (môɴ-bár′)	170	47°40'N	4°19'E
Montbéliard, Fr. (môɴ-bā-lyár′)	171	47°32'N	6°45'E
Mont Belvieu, Tx., U.S. (mŏnt bĕl′vū)	123a	29°51'N	94°53'W
Montbrison, Fr. (môɴ-brē-zoɴ′)	170	45°38'N	4°06'E
Montceau, Fr. (môɴ-sō′)	170	46°39'N	4°22'E
Montclair, N.J., U.S. (mŏnt-klâr′)	110a	40°49'N	74°13'W
Mont-de-Marsan, Fr. (môɴ-dĕ-mär-säɴ′)	161	43°54'N	0°32'W
Montdidier, Fr. (môɴ-dē-dyā′)	170	49°42'N	2°33'E
Monte, Arg. (mō′n-tĕ)	141c	35°25'S	58°49'W
Monteagudo, Bol. (mōn′tå-ä-go͞o′dhō)	142	19°49'S	63°48'W
Montebello, Can.	102c	45°40'N	74°56'W
Montebello, Ca., U.S. (mŏn-tē-bĕl′ō)	117a	34°01'N	118°06'W
Monte Bello Islands, is., Austl.	220	20°30'S	114°10'E
Monte Caseros, Arg. (mō′n-tĕ-kä-sĕ′rôs)	144	30°16'S	57°39'W
Montecillos, Cordillera de, mts., Hond.	132	14°19'N	87°52'W
Monte Cristi, Dom. Rep. (mô′n-tĕ-krĕ′s-tē)	135	19°50'N	71°40'W
Montecristo, Isola di, i., Italy (mōn-tä-krēs′tō)	174	42°20'N	10°19'E
Monte Escobedo, Mex. (mōn′tå ĕs-kô-bā′dhō)	130	22°18'N	103°34'W
Monteforte Irpino, Italy (môn-tĕ-fô′r-tĕ ē′r-pē′nō)	173c	40°39'N	14°42'E
Montefrío, Spain (mōn-tå-frē′ō)	172	37°20'N	4°02'W
Montego Bay, Jam. (mŏn-tē′gō)	129	18°30'N	77°55'W
Montelavar, Port. (mōn-tĕ-lá-vär′)	173b	38°51'N	9°20'W
Montélimar, Fr. (môɴ-tā-lē-mär′)	161	44°33'N	4°47'E
Montellano, Spain (mōn-tå-lyä′nō)	172	37°00'N	5°34'W
Montello, Wi., U.S. (mŏn-tĕl′ō)	113	43°47'N	89°20'W
Montemorelos, Mex. (mōn′tå-mō-rā′lōs)	128	25°14'N	99°50'W
Montemor-o-Novo, Port. (môn-tĕ-môr′ō-nô′vô)	172	38°39'N	8°11'W
Montenegro *see* Crna Gora, state, Serb.	175	42°55'N	18°52'E
Montenegro, reg., Moz.	237	13°07'S	39°00'E
Montepulciano, Italy (môn′tå-po͞ol-chä′nō)	174	43°05'N	11°48'E
Montereau-faut-Yonne, Fr. (môɴ-t′rō′fō-yōn′)	170	48°24'N	2°57'E
Monterey, Ca., U.S. (mŏn-tĕ-rā′)	104	36°36'N	121°53'W
Monterey, Tn., U.S.	124	36°06'N	85°15'W
Monterey Bay, b., Ca., U.S.	106	36°48'N	122°01'W
Monterey Park, Ca., U.S.	117a	34°04'N	118°08'W
Montería, Col. (mōn-tå-rā′ä)	142	8°47'N	75°57'W
Monteros, Arg. (mōn-tĕ′rôs)	144	27°14'S	65°29'W
Monterotondo, Italy (môn-tĕ-rô-tô′n-dō)	173d	42°03'N	12°39'E

ng-sing; ŋ-baŋk; ɴ-nasalized n; nŏd; cŏmmit; ōld; ôbey; ôrder; oi-boil; fo͞od; ŏ-as oo in foot; ou-out; s-soft; sh-dish; th-thin; pūre; ûnite; ûrn; stŭd; circŭs; ü-as in French tu; ′-indeterminate vowel.

324 Monterrey – Mount Morgan PRONOUNCING INDEX

PLACE (Pronunciation)	PAGE	LAT.	LONG.
Monterrey, Mex. (mōn-tĕr-rā′)	128	25°43′N	100°19′W
Montesano, Wa., U.S. (mŏn-tē-sä′nō)	114	46°59′N	123°35′W
Monte Sant'Angelo, Italy (mô′n-tĕ sän ä′n-gzhĕ-lô)	163	41°43′N	15°59′E
Montes Claros, Braz. (môn-tĕs-klä′rôs)	143	16°44′S	43°41′W
Montevallo, Al., U.S. (mŏn-tē-văl′ō)	124	33°05′N	86°49′W
Montevarchi, Italy (mōn-tå-vär′kē)	174	43°30′N	11°45′E
Montevideo, Ur. (mōn′tå-vē-dhā′ō)	144	34°50′S	56°10′W
Montevideo, Mn., U.S. (mŏn′tå-vē-dhā′ō)	112	44°56′N	95°42′W
Monte Vista, Co., U.S. (mŏn′tē vĭs′tȧ)	119	37°35′N	106°10′W
Montezuma, Ga., U.S. (mŏn-tē-zōō′mȧ)	124	32°17′N	84°00′W
Montezuma Castle National Monument, rec., Az., U.S.	119	34°38′N	111°50′W
Montfoort, Neth.	159a	52°02′N	4°56′E
Montfor-l'Amaury, Fr. (mŏɴ-fŏr′lä-mō-rē′)	171b	48°47′N	1°49′E
Montfort, Fr. (mŏn-fŏr)	170	48°09′N	1°58′W
Montgomery, Al., U.S. (mŏnt-gŭm′ẽr-ĭ)	105	32°23′N	86°17′W
Montgomery, W.V., U.S.	108	38°10′N	81°25′W
Montgomery City, Mo., U.S.	121	38°58′N	91°29′W
Monticello, Ar., U.S. (mŏn-tĭ-sĕl′ō)	121	33°38′N	91°47′W
Monticello, Fl., U.S.	124	30°32′N	83°53′W
Monticello, Ga., U.S.	124	33°00′N	83°11′W
Monticello, Ia., U.S.	113	42°14′N	91°13′W
Monticello, Il., U.S.	108	40°05′N	88°35′W
Monticello, In., U.S.	108	40°40′N	86°50′W
Monticello, Ky., U.S.	124	36°47′N	84°50′W
Monticello, Me., U.S.	100	46°19′N	67°53′W
Monticello, Mn., U.S.	113	45°18′N	93°48′W
Monticello, N.Y., U.S.	109	41°35′N	74°40′W
Monticello, Ut., U.S.	119	37°55′N	109°25′W
Montijo, Port. (môn-tē′zhō)	173b	38°42′N	8°58′W
Montijo, Spain (môn-tē′hō)	172	38°55′N	6°35′W
Montijo, Bahía, b., Pan. (bä-ē′ä môn-tē′hō)	129	7°36′N	81°11′W
Mont-Joli, Can. (môɴ zhô-lē′)	91	48°35′N	68°11′W
Montluçon, Fr. (môɴ-lü-sôɴ′)	161	46°20′N	2°35′E
Montmagny, Can. (môɴ-mán-yē′)	99	46°59′N	70°33′W
Montmorency, Fr. (môɴ′mô-räɴ-sē′)	171b	48°59′N	2°19′E
Montmorency, r., Can. (mŏnt-mô-rĕn′sĭ)	102b	47°03′N	71°10′W
Montmorillon, Fr. (môɴ′mô-rē-yôɴ′)	170	46°26′N	0°50′E
Montone, r., Italy (môn-tō′nĕ)	174	44°03′N	11°45′E
Montoro, Spain (môn-tō′rō)	172	38°01′N	4°22′W
Montpelier, Id., U.S.	115	42°19′N	111°19′W
Montpelier, In., U.S. (mŏnt-pēl′yẽr)	108	40°35′N	85°20′W
Montpelier, Oh., U.S.	108	41°35′N	84°35′W
Montpelier, Vt., U.S.	105	44°20′N	72°35′W
Montpellier, Fr. (môɴ-pĕ-lyā′)	161	43°38′N	3°53′E
Montréal, Can. (mŏn-trē-ôl′)	91	45°30′N	73°35′W
Montreal, r., Can.	99	47°50′N	80°30′W
Montreal, r., Can.	98	47°15′N	84°20′W
Montreal Lake, l., Can.	96	54°20′N	105°40′W
Montréal-Nord, Can.	102a	45°36′N	73°38′W
Montreuil, Fr.	171b	48°52′N	2°27′E
Montreux, Switz. (môn-trû′)	168	46°26′N	6°52′E
Montrose, Scot., U.K.	164	56°45′N	2°25′W
Montrose, Ca., U.S. (mŏnt-rōz)	117a	34°13′N	118°13′W
Montrose, Co., U.S. (mŏn-trōz′)	119	38°30′N	107°55′W
Montrose, Oh., U.S.	111d	41°08′N	81°38′W
Montrose, Pa., U.S. (mŏnt-rōz′)	109	41°50′N	75°50′W
Montrouge, Fr.	171b	48°49′N	2°19′E
Mont-Royal, Can.	102a	47°31′N	73°39′W
Monts, Pointe des, c., Can. (pwăɴt′ dā môɴ′)	100	49°19′N	67°22′W
Mont Saint Martin, Fr. (môɴ săɴ mär-tăɴ′)	171	49°34′N	6°13′E
Montserrat, dep., N.A. (mŏnt-sĕ-răt′)	129	16°48′N	63°15′W
Montvale, N.J., U.S. (mŏnt-vāl′)	110a	41°02′N	74°01′W
Monywa, Mya. (mŏn′yōō-wä)	199	22°02′N	95°16′E
Monza, Italy (mōn′tsä)	174	45°34′N	9°17′E
Monzón, Spain (mōn-thōn′)	173	41°54′N	0°09′E
Moody, Tx., U.S. (mōō′dĭ)	123	31°18′N	97°20′W
Mooi, r., S. Afr. (mōō′ĭ)	238c	26°34′S	27°03′E
Mooi, r., S. Afr.	233c	29°00′S	30°15′E
Mooirivier, S. Afr.	233c	29°14′S	29°59′E
Moolap, Austl.	217a	38°11′S	144°26′E
Moonta, Austl. (mōōn′tȧ)	218	34°05′S	137°42′E
Moora, Austl. (mōr′ȧ)	218	30°35′S	116°12′E
Moorabbin, Austl.	217a	37°56′S	145°02′E
Moore, l., Austl. (mōr)	220	29°50′S	118°12′E
Moorenweis, Ger. (mō′rĕn-vīz)	159d	48°10′N	11°05′E
Moore Reservoir, res., Vt., U.S.	109	44°20′N	72°10′W
Moorestown, N.J., U.S. (mōrz′toun)	110f	39°58′N	74°56′W
Mooresville, In., U.S. (mōrz′vĭl)	111g	39°37′N	86°22′W
Mooresville, N.C., U.S.	125	35°34′N	80°48′W
Moorhead, Mn., U.S. (mōr′hĕd)	112	46°52′N	96°44′W
Moorhead, Ms., U.S.	124	33°25′N	90°30′W
Moose, r., Can.	93	51°01′N	80°42′W
Moose Creek, Can.	102c	45°16′N	74°58′W
Moosehead, Me., U.S. (mōōs′hĕd)	100	45°37′N	69°15′W
Moose Island, i., Can.	97	51°50′N	97°09′W
Moose Jaw, Can. (mōōs jô)	90	50°23′N	105°32′W
Moose Jaw, r., Can.	96	50°34′N	105°17′W
Moose Lake, Can.	97	53°40′N	100°28′W
Moose Mountain, mtn., Can.	97	49°45′N	102°37′W
Moose Mountain Creek, r., Can.	97	49°12′N	102°10′W
Moosilauke, mtn., N.H., U.S. (mōō-sĭ-lȧ′kē)	109	44°00′N	71°50′W
Moosinning, Ger. (mō′zē-nēng)	159d	48°17′N	11°51′E
Moosomin, Can. (mōō′sô-mĭn)	97	50°07′N	101°40′W
Moosonee, Can. (mōō′sô-nē)	91	51°20′N	80°44′W
Mopti, Mali (mŏp′tē)	230	14°30′N	4°12′W
Moquegua, Peru (mô-kā′gwä)	142	17°15′S	70°54′W
Mór, Hung. (mōr)	169	47°25′N	18°14′E
Mora, India	203b	18°54′N	72°56′E
Mora, Spain (mō-rä)	172	39°42′N	3°45′W
Mora, Swe. (mō′rä)	166	61°00′N	14°29′E
Mora, Mn., U.S. (mō′rȧ)	113	45°52′N	93°18′W
Mora, N.M., U.S.	120	35°58′N	105°17′W
Morādābād, India (mô-rä-dä-bäd′)	199	28°57′N	78°48′E
Morales, Guat. (mô-rä′lĕs)	132	15°29′N	88°46′W
Moramanga, Madag. (mō-rä-mäŋ′gä)	233	18°48′S	48°09′E
Morant Point, c., Jam. (mô-rănt′)	134	17°55′N	76°10′W
Morata de Tajuña, Spain (mô-rä′tä dā tä-hōō′nyä)	173a	40°14′N	3°27′W
Moratuwa, Sri L.	203	6°35′N	79°59′E
Morava (Moravia), hist. reg., Czech Rep.	168	49°21′N	16°57′E
Morava, r., Eur.	161	49°00′N	17°30′E
Moravia *see* Morava, hist. reg., Czech Rep.	168	49°21′N	16°57′E
Morawhanna, Guy. (mô-rȧ-hwä′nȧ)	143	8°12′N	59°33′W
Moray Firth, b., Scot., U.K. (mŭr′ȧ)	156	57°41′N	3°55′W
Mörbylånga, Swe. (mûr′bü-lôŋ-gå)	166	56°32′N	16°23′E
Morden, Can. (môr′dĕn)	90	49°11′N	98°05′W
Mordialloc, Austl. (môr-dĭ-ăl′ŏk)	217a	38°00′S	145°05′E
Mordvinia, prov., Russia	180	54°18′N	43°50′E
More, Ben, mtn., Scot., U.K. (bĕn môr)	164	58°09′N	5°01′W
Moreau, r., S.D., U.S. (mô-rō′)	112	45°13′N	102°22′W
Moree, Austl. (mō′rē)	219	29°20′S	149°50′E
Morehead, Ky., U.S.	108	38°10′N	83°25′W
Morehead City, N.C., U.S. (mōr′hĕd)	125	34°43′N	76°43′W
Morehouse, Mo., U.S. (mōr′hous)	121	36°49′N	89°41′W
Morelia, Mex. (mô-rā′lyä)	128	19°43′N	101°12′W
Morella, Spain (mô-rāl′yä)	173	40°38′N	0°07′W
Morelos, Mex. (mô-rā′lōs)	130	22°46′N	102°36′W
Morelos, Mex.	131a	19°41′N	99°29′W
Morelos, Mex.	122	28°24′N	100°51′W
Morelos, r., Mex.	122	25°27′N	99°35′W
Morena, Sierra, mtn., Ca., U.S. (syĕr′rä mô-rā′nä)	116b	37°24′N	122°19′W
Morena, Sierra, mts., Spain (syĕr′rä mô-rā′nä)	156	38°15′N	5°45′W
Morenci, Az., U.S. (mô-rĕn′sĭ)	119	33°05′N	109°25′W
Morenci, Mi., U.S.	108	41°50′N	84°50′W
Moreno, Arg. (mô-rĕ′nō)	144a	34°39′S	58°47′W
Moreno, Ca., U.S.	117a	33°55′N	117°09′W
Mores, i., Bah. (mōrz)	134	26°20′N	77°35′W
Moresby, i., Can. (mōrz′bĭ)	116d	48°43′N	123°15′W
Moresby Island, i., Can.	92	52°50′N	131°55′W
Moreton, i., Austl. (môr′tŭn)	222	26°53′S	152°42′E
Moreton Bay, b., Austl. (môr′tŭn)	222	27°12′S	153°10′E
Morewood, Can. (mōr′wŏŏd)	102c	45°11′N	75°17′W
Morgan, Mt., U.S. (môr′găn)	115	48°55′N	107°56′W
Morgan, Ut., U.S.	115	41°04′N	111°42′W
Morgan City, La., U.S.	123	29°41′N	91°11′W
Morganfield, Ky., U.S. (môr′găn-fēld)	108	37°40′N	87°55′W
Morgan's Bay, S. Afr.	233c	32°42′S	28°19′E
Morganton, N.C., U.S. (môr′găn-tŭn)	125	35°44′N	81°42′W
Morgantown, W.V., U.S. (môr′găn-toun)	109	39°40′N	79°55′W
Morga Range, mts., Afg.	199a	34°02′N	70°38′E
Morgenzon, S. Afr. (môr′gĕnt-sŏn)	238c	26°44′S	29°39′E
Moriac, Austl.	217a	38°15′S	144°20′E
Morice Lake, l., Can.	94	54°00′N	127°37′W
Moriguchi, Japan (mō′rē-gōō′chē)	211b	34°44′N	135°34′E
Morinville, Can. (mō′rĭn-vĭl)	102g	53°48′N	113°39′W
Morioka, Japan (mō′rē-ō′kä)	205	39°40′N	141°21′E
Morkoka, r., Russia (môr-kô′kȧ)	185	65°35′N	111°00′E
Morlaix, Fr. (mōr-lĕ′)	161	48°36′N	3°48′W
Morley, Can. (mŏr′lē)	102e	51°10′N	114°51′W
Mormant, Fr.	171b	48°35′N	2°54′E
Morne Gimie, St. Luc. (môrn′ zhē-mē′)	133b	13°53′N	61°03′W
Mornington, Austl.	217a	38°13′S	145°02′E
Morobe, Pap. N. Gui.	213	8°03′S	147°45′E
Morocco, nation, Afr. (mô-rŏk′ō)	230	32°00′N	7°00′W
Morogoro, Tan. (mō-rô-gō′rō)	233	6°49′S	37°40′E
Moroleón, Mex. (mō-rō-lā-ōn′)	130	20°07′N	101°15′W
Morombe, Madag. (mōō-rōōm′bā)	233	21°39′S	43°34′E
Morón, Arg. (mo-rō′n)	141c	34°39′S	58°37′W
Morón, Cuba (mô-rō′n)	134	22°05′N	78°35′W
Morón, Ven. (mô-rō′n)	143b	10°29′N	68°11′W
Morondava, Madag. (mō-rōn-dä′vȧ)	233	20°17′S	44°18′E
Morón de la Frontera, Spain (mô-rōn′dā läf rôn-tā′rä)	172	37°08′N	5°20′W
Morongo Indian Reservation, I.R., Ca., U.S. (mō-rôŋ′gō)	118	33°54′N	116°47′W
Moroni, Com.	233	11°41′S	43°16′E
Moroni, Ut., U.S. (mō-rō′nī)	119	39°30′N	111°40′W
Morotai, i., Indon. (mō-rō-tä′ē)	213	2°12′N	128°30′E
Moroto, Ug.	237	2°32′N	34°39′E
Morozovsk, Russia	181	48°20′N	41°50′E
Morrill, Ne., U.S. (mŏr′ĭl)	112	41°59′N	103°54′W
Morrilton, Ar., U.S. (mŏr′ĭl-tŭn)	121	35°09′N	92°42′W
Morrinhos, Braz. (mô-rēn′yōzh)	143	17°45′S	48°56′W
Morris, Can. (mŏr′ĭs)	90	49°21′N	97°22′W
Morris, Il., U.S.	108	41°20′N	88°25′W
Morris, Mn., U.S.	112	45°35′N	95°53′W
Morris, r., Can.	97	49°30′N	97°30′W
Morrison, Il., U.S. (mŏr′ĭ-sŭn)	113	41°48′N	89°58′W
Morris Reservoir, res., Ca., U.S.	117a	34°11′N	117°49′W
Morristown, N.J., U.S. (mŏr′rĭs-toun)	110a	40°48′N	74°29′W
Morristown, Tn., U.S.	124	36°10′N	83°18′W
Morrisville, Pa., U.S. (mŏr′ĭs-vĭl)	110f	40°12′N	74°46′W
Morro do Chapéu, Braz. (môr-ō dō-shä-pĕ′ōō)	143	11°34′S	41°03′W
Morrow, Oh., U.S. (mŏr′ō)	111f	39°21′N	84°07′W
Mors, i., Den.	166	56°46′N	8°38′E
Morshansk, Russia (môr-shänsk′)	180	53°25′N	41°35′E
Mortara, Italy (môr-tä′rä)	174	45°13′N	8°47′E
Morteros, Arg. (môr-tĕ′rôs)	144	30°47′S	62°00′W
Mortes, Rio das, r., Braz. (rēō-däs-mô′r-tĕs)	141a	21°04′S	44°29′W
Morton Indian Reservation, I.R., Mn., U.S. (mŏr′tŭn)	113	44°35′N	94°48′W
Mortsel, Bel. (mōr-sĕl′)	159a	51°10′N	4°28′E
Morvan, mts., Fr. (mōr-väɴ′)	170	47°11′N	4°10′E
Morzhovets, i., Russia (môr′zhô-vyĕts′)	180	66°40′N	42°30′E
Mosal'sk, Russia (mō-zálsk′)	176	54°27′N	34°57′E
Moscavide, Port.	173b	38°47′N	9°06′W
Moscow (Moskva), Russia	178	55°45′N	37°37′E
Moscow, Id., U.S. (mŏs′kō)	104	46°44′N	116°57′W
Mosel (Moselle), r., Eur. (mō′sĕl) (mō-zĕl)	168	49°49′N	7°00′E
Moses, r., S. Afr.	238c	25°17′S	29°04′E
Moses Lake, Wa., U.S.	114	47°08′N	119°15′W
Moses Lake, l., Wa., U.S. (mō′zĕz)	114	47°09′N	119°30′W
Moshchnyy, is., Russia (môsh′chnĭ)	167	59°56′N	28°07′E
Moshi, Tan. (mō′shē)	233	3°21′S	37°20′E
Mosjøen, Nor.	160	65°50′N	13°10′E
Moskva *see* Moscow, Russia	178	55°45′N	37°37′E
Moskva, prov., Russia	176	55°38′N	36°48′E
Moskva, r., Russia	180	55°30′N	37°05′E
Mosonmagyaróvár, Hung.	169	47°51′N	17°16′E
Mosquitos, Costa de, cst., Nic. (kôs-tä-dĕ-mŏs-kē′tō)	133	12°05′N	83°49′W
Mosquitos, Gulfo de los, b., Pan. (gōō′l-fō-dĕ-lôs-mŏs-kē′tôs)	129	9°17′N	80°59′W
Moss, Nor. (môs)	160	59°29′N	10°39′E
Moss Beach, Ca., U.S. (môs bēch)	116b	37°32′N	122°31′W
Mosselbaai, S. Afr. (mô′sŭl bā)	232	34°06′S	22°23′E
Mossendjo, Congo	236	2°57′S	12°44′E
Mossley, Eng., U.K. (mŏs′lĭ)	158a	53°31′N	2°02′W
Moss Point, Ms., U.S. (môs)	124	30°25′N	88°32′W
Most, Czech Rep. (môst)	168	50°32′N	13°37′E
Mostar, Bos. (môs′tär)	163	43°20′N	17°51′E
Móstoles, Spain (môs-tō′lās)	173a	40°19′N	3°52′W
Mostoos Hills, hills, Can. (mŏs′tōōs)	96	54°50′N	108°45′W
Mosvatnet, l., Nor.	166	59°55′N	7°50′E
Motagua, r., N.A. (mô-tä′gwä)	132	15°29′N	88°39′W
Motala, Swe. (mô-tō′lä)	166	58°34′N	15°00′E
Motherwell, Scot., U.K. (mŭdh′ẽr-wĕl)	160	55°45′N	4°05′W
Motril, Spain (mô-trēl′)	162	36°44′N	3°32′W
Motul, Mex. (mō-tōō′l)	132a	21°07′N	89°14′W
Mouaskar, Alg.	230	35°25′N	0°08′E
Mouchoir Bank, bk. (mōō-shwär′)	135	21°35′N	70°40′W
Mouchoir Passage, strt., T./C. Is.	135	21°05′N	71°05′W
Moudjéria, Maur.	234	17°53′N	12°20′W
Mouila, Gabon	236	1°52′S	11°01′E
Mouille Point, c., S. Afr.	232a	33°54′S	18°19′E
Moulins, Fr. (mōō-lăɴ′)	161	46°34′N	3°19′E
Moulouya, Oued, r., Mor. (mōō-lōō′yȧ)	230	34°00′N	4°00′W
Moultrie, Ga., U.S. (mōl′trĭ)	124	31°10′N	83°48′W
Moultrie, Lake, l., S.C., U.S.	125	33°12′N	80°00′W
Mound City, Il., U.S.	121	37°06′N	89°13′W
Mound City, Mo., U.S.	121	40°08′N	95°13′W
Moundou, Chad	235	8°34′N	16°05′E
Moundsville, W.V., U.S. (moundz′vĭl)	108	39°50′N	80°50′W
Mount, Cape, c., Lib.	234	6°47′N	11°20′W
Mountain Brook, Al., U.S. (moun′tĭn brŏŏk)	110h	33°30′N	86°45′W
Mountain Creek Lake, l., Tx., U.S.	117c	32°43′N	97°03′W
Mountain Grove, Mo., U.S. (grōv)	121	37°07′N	92°16′W
Mountain Home, Id., U.S. (hōm)	114	43°08′N	115°43′W
Mountain Park, Can. (pärk)	90	52°55′N	117°14′W
Mountain View, Ca., U.S. (moun′tĭn vū)	116b	37°25′N	122°07′W
Mountain View, Mo., U.S.	121	36°59′N	91°46′W
Mount Airy, N.C., U.S. (âr′ĭ)	125	36°28′N	80°37′W
Mount Ayliff, S. Afr. (ā′lĭf)	233c	30°48′S	29°24′E
Mount Ayr, Ia., U.S. (âr)	113	40°43′N	94°06′W
Mount Carmel, Il., U.S. (kär′mĕl)	108	38°25′N	87°45′W
Mount Carmel, Pa., U.S.	109	40°50′N	76°25′W
Mount Carroll, Il., U.S.	113	42°05′N	89°55′W
Mount Clemens, Mi., U.S. (klĕm′ĕnz)	111b	42°36′N	82°52′W
Mount Desert, i., Me., U.S. (dē-zûrt′)	100	44°15′N	68°08′W
Mount Dora, Fl., U.S. (dō′rȧ)	125a	28°45′N	81°38′W
Mount Duneed, Austl.	217a	38°15′S	144°20′E
Mount Eliza, Austl.	217a	38°11′S	145°05′E
Mount Fletcher, S. Afr. (flĕ′chẽr)	233c	30°42′S	28°32′E
Mount Forest, Can. (fŏr′ĕst)	99	44°00′N	80°45′W
Mount Frere, S. Afr. (frâr′)	233c	30°54′S	29°02′E
Mount Gambier, Austl. (găm′bẽr)	218	37°30′S	140°53′E
Mount Gilead, Oh., U.S. (gĭl′ĕăd)	108	40°30′N	82°50′W
Mount Healthy, Oh., U.S. (hĕlth′ē)	111f	39°14′N	84°32′W
Mount Holly, N.J., U.S. (hŏl′ĭ)	110f	39°59′N	74°47′W
Mount Hope, Can.	102d	43°09′N	79°55′W
Mount Hope, N.J., U.S. (hōp)	110a	40°55′N	74°32′W
Mount Hope, W.V., U.S.	108	37°55′N	81°10′W
Mount Isa, Austl. (ī′zȧ)	218	21°00′S	139°45′E
Mount Kisco, N.Y., U.S. (kĭs′kō)	110a	41°12′N	73°44′W
Mountlake Terrace, Wa., U.S. (mount lāk tĕr′ĭs)	116a	47°48′N	122°19′W
Mount Lebanon, Pa., U.S. (lĕb′ȧ-nŭn)	111e	40°22′N	80°03′W
Mount Magnet, Austl. (măg-nĕt)	218	28°00′S	118°00′E
Mount Martha, Austl.	217a	38°17′S	145°01′E
Mount Morgan, Austl. (môr-găn)	219	23°42′S	150°45′E

ăt; finăl; rāte; senåte; ärm; åsk; sofȧ; fâre; ch-choose; dh-as th in other; bē; ēvent; bĕt; recĕnt; cratẽr; g-gō; gh-guttural g; bĭt; ĭ-short neutral; rīde; ĸ-guttural k as ch in German ich;

PRONOUNCING INDEX　　Mount Moriac – Nabberu　　325

PLACE (Pronunciation)	PAGE	LAT.	LONG.
Mount Moriac, Austl.	217a	38°13'S	144°12'E
Mount Morris, Mi., U.S. (mŏr'ĭs)	108	43°10'N	83°45'W
Mount Morris, N.Y., U.S.	109	42°45'N	77°50'W
Mount Nimba National Park, rec., C. Iv.	234	7°35'N	8°10'W
Mount Olive, N.C., U.S. (ŏl'ĭv)	125	35°11'N	78°05'W
Mount Peale, Ut., U.S.	119	38°26'N	109°16'W
Mount Pleasant, Ia., U.S. (plĕz'ănt)	113	40°59'N	91°34'W
Mount Pleasant, Mi., U.S.	108	43°35'N	84°45'W
Mount Pleasant, S.C., U.S.	125	32°46'N	79°51'W
Mount Pleasant, Tn., U.S.	124	35°31'N	87°12'W
Mount Pleasant, Tx., U.S.	123	33°10'N	94°56'W
Mount Pleasant, Ut., U.S.	119	39°35'N	111°20'W
Mount Prospect, Il., U.S. (prŏs'pĕkt)	111a	42°03'N	87°56'W
Mount Rainier National Park, rec., Wa., U.S. (rā-nēr')	106	46°47'N	121°17'W
Mount Revelstoke National Park, rec., Can. (rĕv'ĕl-stōk)	90	51°22'N	120°15'W
Mount Savage, Md., U.S. (săv'āj)	109	39°45'N	78°55'W
Mount Shasta, Ca., U.S. (shăs'tȧ)	114	41°18'N	122°17'W
Mount Sterling, Il., U.S. (stûr'lĭng)	121	39°59'N	90°44'W
Mount Sterling, Ky., U.S.	108	38°05'N	84°00'W
Mount Stewart, Can. (stū'ărt)	101	46°22'N	62°52'W
Mount Union, Pa., U.S. (ūn'yŭn)	109	40°25'N	77°50'W
Mount Vernon, Il., U.S. (vûr'nŭn)	108	38°20'N	88°50'W
Mount Vernon, In., U.S.	108	37°55'N	87°50'W
Mount Vernon, Mo., U.S.	121	37°09'N	93°48'W
Mount Vernon, N.Y., U.S.	110a	40°55'N	73°51'W
Mount Vernon, Oh., U.S.	108	40°25'N	82°30'W
Mount Vernon, Va., U.S.	110e	38°43'N	77°06'W
Mount Vernon, Wa., U.S.	114	48°25'N	122°20'W
Moura, Braz. (mō'rȧ)	143	1°33'S	61°38'W
Moura, Port.	172	38°08'N	7°28'W
Mourne Mountains, mts., N. Ire., U.K. (môrn)	164	54°10'N	6°09'W
Moussoro, Chad	235	13°39'N	16°29'E
Moûtiers, Fr. (mōō-tyâr')	171	45°31'N	6°34'E
Mowbullan, Mount, mtn., Austl.	222	26°50'S	151°34'E
Moyahua, Mex. (mô-yä'wä)	130	21°16'N	103°10'W
Moyale, Kenya (mô-yä'lä)	231	3°28'N	39°04'E
Moyamba, S.L. (mô-yäm'bä)	230	8°10'N	12°26'W
Moyen Atlas, mts., Mor.	162	32°49'N	5°28'W
Moyeuvre-Grande, Fr.	171	49°15'N	6°26'E
Moyie, r., Id., U.S. (moi'yē)	114	38°50'N	116°10'W
Moyobamba, Peru (mō-yō-bäm'bä)	142	6°12'S	76°56'W
Moyuta, Guat. (mô-ē-ōō'tä)	132	14°01'N	90°05'W
Moyyero, r., Russia	184	67°15'N	104°10'E
Moyynqum, des., Kaz.	183	44°30'N	70°00'E
Mozambique, nation, Afr. (mō-zăm-bēk')	232	20°15'S	33°53'E
Mozambique Channel, strt., Afr. (mō-zăm-bek')	233	24°00'S	38°00'E
Mozdok, Russia (môz-dôk')	181	43°45'N	44°35'E
Mozhaysk, Russia (mô-zhäysk')	176	55°31'N	36°02'E
Mozhayskiy, Russia (mô-zhäy'skĭ)	186c	59°42'N	30°08'E
Mpanda, Tan.	237	6°22'S	31°02'E
Mpika, Zam.	237	11°54'S	31°26'E
Mpimbe, Mwi.	237	15°18'S	35°04'E
Mporokoso, Zam. ('m-pō-rō-kō'sō)	232	9°23'S	30°05'E
Mpwapwa, Tan. ('m-pwä'pwä)	232	6°21'S	36°29'E
Mqanduli, S. Afr. ('m-kän'dōō-lē)	233c	31°50'S	28°42'E
Mrągowo, Pol. (mräŋ'gô-vô)	169	53°52'N	21°18'E
M'Sila, Alg. (m'sē'lȧ)	230	35°47'N	4°34'E
Msta, r., Russia (m'stá')	180	58°30'N	33°00'E
Mstsislaw, Bela.	176	54°01'N	31°42'E
Mtakataka, Mwi.	237	14°12'S	34°32'E
Mtamvuna, r., Afr.	233c	30°43'S	29°53'E
Mtata, r., S. Afr.	233c	31°48'S	29°03'E
Mtsensk, Russia (m'tsĕnsk)	180	53°17'N	36°33'E
Mtwara, Tan.	237	10°16'S	40°11'E
Muar, r., Malay.	197b	2°18'N	102°43'E
Mubende, Ug.	237	0°35'N	31°23'E
Mubi, Nig.	235	10°18'N	13°20'E
Mucacata, Moz.	237	13°20'S	39°59'E
Much, Ger. (mōōk)	171c	50°54'N	7°24'E
Muchinga Mountains, mts., Zam.	237	12°40'S	30°50'E
Much Wenlock, Eng., U.K. (mŭch wĕn'lŏk)	158a	52°35'N	2°33'W
Muckalee Creek, r., Ga., U.S. (mŭk'ă lē)	124	31°55'N	84°10'W
Muckleshoot Indian Reservation, I.R., Wa., U.S. (mŭck''l-shōōt)	116a	47°21'N	122°04'W
Mucubela, Moz.	237	16°55'S	37°52'E
Mud, l., Mi., U.S. (mŭd)	113	46°12'N	84°32'W
Mudan, r., China (mōō-dän)	208	45°30'N	129°40'E
Mudanjiang, China (mōō-dän-jyäŋ)	208	44°28'N	129°38'E
Muddy, r., Nv., U.S. (mŭd'ĭ)	119	36°56'N	114°42'W
Muddy Boggy Creek, r., Ok., U.S. (mud'ĭ bôg'ĭ)	121	34°42'N	96°11'W
Muddy Creek, r., Ut., U.S. (mŭd'ĭ)	119	38°45'N	111°10'W
Mudgee, Austl. (mŭ-jē)	222	32°47'S	149°10'E
Mudjatik, r., Can.	96	56°23'N	107°40'W
Mufulira, Zam.	237	12°33'S	28°14'E
Muğla, Tur. (mōōg'lä)	198	37°10'N	28°20'E
Mühldorf, Ger. (mül'dôrf)	168	48°15'N	12°33'E
Mühlhausen, Ger. (mül'hou-zĕn)	168	51°13'N	10°25'E
Muhu, i., Est. (mōō'hōō)	167	58°41'N	22°55'E
Muir Woods National Monument, rec., Ca., U.S. (mūr)	118	37°54'N	123°22'W
Muizenberg, S. Afr. (mwĭz-ĕn-bûrg')	232a	34°07'S	18°28'E
Mukacheve, Ukr.	169	48°25'N	22°43'E
Mukden see Shenyang, China	204	41°45'N	123°22'E
Mukhtuya, Russia (mók-tōō'yȧ)	179	61°00'N	113°00'E
Mukilteo, Wa., U.S. (mū-kĭl-tā'ō)	116a	47°57'N	122°18'W
Muko, Japan (mōō'kō)	211b	34°57'N	135°43'E
Muko, r., Japan (mōō'kō)	211b	34°52'N	135°17'E
Mukutawa, r., Can.	97	53°10'N	97°28'W
Mukwonago, Wi., U.S. (mū-kwō-nȧ'gō)	111a	42°52'N	88°19'W
Mula, Spain (mōō'lä)	172	38°05'N	1°12'W
Mula, Al., U.S. (mŭl'gȧ)	110h	33°33'N	86°59'W
Mulde, r., Ger. (mòl'dĕ)	168	50°30'N	12°30'E
Muleros, Mex. (mōō-lā'rōs)	130	23°44'N	104°00'W
Muleshoe, Tx., U.S.	120	34°13'N	102°43'W
Mulgrave, Can. (mŭl'grāv)	101	45°37'N	61°23'W
Mulhacén, mtn., Spain	162	37°04'N	3°18'W
Mülheim, Ger. (mül'hīm)	171c	51°25'N	6°53'E
Mulhouse, Fr. (mü-lōōz')	161	47°46'N	7°20'E
Muling, China (mōō-lĭŋ)	208	44°32'N	130°18'E
Muling, r., China	208	44°40'N	130°30'E
Mull, Island of, i., Scot., U.K. (mŭl)	164	56°40'N	6°19'W
Mullan, Id., U.S. (mŭl'ăn)	114	47°26'N	115°50'W
Müller, Pegunungan, mts., Indon. (mül'ēr)	212	0°22'N	113°05'E
Mullingar, Ire. (mŭl-ĭn-gär)	164	53°31'N	7°26'W
Mullins, S.C., U.S. (mŭl'ĭnz)	125	34°11'N	79°13'W
Mullins River, Belize	132a	17°08'N	88°18'W
Multān, Pak. (mò-tän')	199	30°17'N	71°13'E
Multnomah Channel, strt., Or., U.S. (mŭl nō mȧ)	116c	45°41'N	122°53'W
Mulumbe, Monts, mts., D.R.C.	237	8°47'S	27°20'E
Mulvane, Ks., U.S. (mŭl-vān')	121	37°30'N	97°13'W
Mumbai (Bombay), India	199	18°58'N	72°50'E
Mumbwa, Zam. (mòm'bwä)	232	14°59'S	27°04'E
Mumias, Kenya	237	0°20'N	34°29'E
Muna, Mex. (mōō'nȧ)	132a	20°28'N	89°42'W
München see Munich, Ger.	154	48°08'N	11°35'E
Muncie, In., U.S. (mŭn'sĭ)	105	40°10'N	85°30'W
Mundelein, Il., U.S. (mŭn-dē-līn')	111a	42°16'N	88°00'W
Mundonueva, Pico de, mtn., Col. (pē'kō-dĕ-mōō'n-dô-nwĕ'vä)	142a	4°18'N	74°12'W
Muneco, Cerro, mtn., Mex. (sĕ'r-rô-mōō-nĕ'kō)	131a	19°13'N	99°20'W
Mungana, Austl. (mŭn-găn'ȧ)	219	17°15'S	144°18'E
Mungbere, D.R.C.	237	2°38'N	28°30'E
Munger, Mn., U.S. (mŭn'gēr)	117h	46°48'N	92°20'W
Mungindi, Austl. (mŭn-gĭn'dē)	219	29°00'S	148°45'E
Munhall, Pa., U.S. (mŭn'hôl)	111e	40°24'N	79°53'W
Munhango, Ang. (mòn-häŋ'gȧ)	232	12°15'S	18°55'E
Munich, Ger.	154	48°08'N	11°35'E
Munising, Mi., U.S. (mū'nĭ-sĭng)	113	46°24'N	86°41'W
Muniz Freire, Braz.	141a	20°29'S	41°25'W
Munku Sardyk, mtn., Asia (mòn'kò sär-dĭk')	179	51°45'N	100°30'E
Muñoz, Phil. (mōōn-nyōth')	213a	15°44'N	120°53'E
Münster, Ger. (mün'stĕr)	161	51°57'N	7°38'E
Munster, In., U.S. (mŭn'stēr)	111a	41°34'N	87°31'W
Munster, hist. reg., Ire. (mŭn-stēr)	164	52°30'N	9°24'W
Muntok, Indon. (mòn-tŏk')	212	2°05'S	105°11'E
Muong Sing, Laos (mōō'ông-sĭng')	212	21°06'N	101°17'E
Muping, China (mōō-pĭŋ)	206	37°23'N	121°36'E
Muqui, Braz. (mōō-kōē)	141a	20°56'S	41°20'W
Mur, r., Eur. (mōōr)	161	47°00'N	15°00'E
Muradiye, Tur. (mōō-rä'dē-yĕ)	181	39°00'N	43°40'E
Murat, Fr. (mü-rä')	170	45°05'N	2°56'E
Murat, r., Tur. (mōō-rät')	198	39°00'N	42°00'E
Murchison, r., Austl. (mûr'chĭ-sŭn)	220	26°45'S	116°15'E
Murcia, Spain (mōōr'thyä)	154	38°00'N	1°10'W
Murcia, hist. reg., Spain	172	38°35'N	1°51'W
Murdo, S.D., U.S. (mûr'dō)	112	43°53'N	100°42'W
Mureş, r., Rom. (mōō'rĕsh)	163	46°02'N	21°50'E
Muret, Fr. (mü-rĕ')	170	43°28'N	1°17'E
Murfreesboro, Tn., U.S. (mûr'frēz-bŭr-ô)	124	35°50'N	86°19'W
Murgab, Taj.	183	38°10'N	73°59'E
Murgab, r., Asia (mōōr-gäb')	198	37°07'N	62°32'E
Muriaé, r., Braz.	141a	21°20'S	41°40'W
Murino, Russia (mōō'rĭ-nô)	186c	60°03'N	30°28'E
Müritz, l., Ger. (mür'ĭts)	168	53°20'N	12°33'E
Murmansk, Russia (mōōr-mänsk')	178	69°00'N	33°20'E
Murom, Russia (mōō'rôm)	178	55°30'N	42°00'W
Muroran, Japan (mōō'rô-rän)	205	42°21'N	141°05'E
Muros, Spain (mōō'rōs)	172	42°48'N	9°00'W
Muroto-Zaki, c., Japan (mōō'rô-tō zä'kē)	210	33°14'N	134°12'E
Murphy, Mo., U.S. (mŭr'fĭ)	117e	38°29'N	90°29'W
Murphy, N.C., U.S.	124	35°05'N	84°00'W
Murphysboro, Il., U.S. (mŭr'fĭz-bŭr-ô)	121	37°46'N	89°21'W
Murray, Ky., U.S. (mŭr'ĭ)	124	36°39'N	88°17'W
Murray, Ut., U.S.	117b	40°40'N	111°53'W
Murray, r., Austl.	220	34°20'S	140°00'E
Murray, r., Can.	95	55°00'N	121°00'W
Murray, Lake, res., S.C., U.S. (mŭr'ĭ)	125	34°07'N	81°18'W
Murray Bridge, Austl.	218	35°10'S	139°35'E
Murray Harbour, Can.	101	46°00'N	62°31'W
Murray Region, reg., Austl. (mŭ'rē)	221	33°20'S	142°30'E
Murrumbidgee, r., Austl. (mŭr-ŭm-bĭd'jē)	221	34°30'S	145°20'E
Murrupula, Moz.	237	15°27'S	38°47'E
Murshidābād, India (mòr'shē-dä-bäd')	202	24°08'N	88°11'E
Murska Sobota, Slvn. (mōōr'skä sô'bô-tä)	174	46°40'N	16°14'E
Muruasigar, mtn., Kenya	237	3°08'N	35°02'E
Murwāra, India	199	23°54'N	80°23'E
Murwillumbah, Austl. (mŭr-wĭl'lŭm-bŭ)	222	28°15'S	153°30'E
Mürz, r., Aus. (mürts)	168	47°30'N	15°21'E
Mürzzuschlag, Aus. (mürts'tsōō-shlägh)	168	47°37'N	15°41'E
Mus, Tur. (mōōsh)	181	38°55'N	41°30'E
Musala, mtn., Blg.	175	42°05'N	23°24'E
Musan, Kor., N. (mò'sän)	205	41°11'N	129°10'E
Musashino, Japan (mōō-sä'shē-nō)	211a	35°43'N	139°35'E
Muscat, Oman (mŭs-kăt')	198	23°23'N	58°30'E
Muscat and Oman see Oman, nation, Asia	198	20°00'N	57°45'E
Muscatine, Ia., U.S. (mŭs-kȧ-tēn)	113	41°26'N	91°00'W
Muscle Shoals, Al., U.S. (mŭs''l shōlz)	124	34°44'N	87°38'W
Musgrave Ranges, mts., Austl. (mŭs'grāv)	220	26°15'S	131°15'E
Mushie, D.R.C. (mŭsh'ē)	232	3°04'S	16°50'E
Mushin, Nig.	235	6°32'N	3°22'E
Musi, r., Indon. (mōō'sē)	212	2°40'S	103°42'E
Musinga, Alto, mtn., Col. (ä'l-tô-mōō-sē'n-gä)	142a	6°40'N	76°13'W
Muskego Lake, l., Wi., U.S. (mŭs-kē'gō)	111a	42°53'N	88°10'W
Muskegon, Mi., U.S. (mŭs-kē'gŭn)	105	43°15'N	86°20'W
Muskegon, r., Mi., U.S.	108	43°20'N	85°55'W
Muskegon Heights, Mi., U.S.	108	43°10'N	86°20'W
Muskingum, r., Oh., U.S. (mŭs-kĭŋ'gŭm)	108	39°45'N	81°55'W
Muskogee, Ok., U.S. (mŭs-kō'gē)	105	35°44'N	95°21'W
Muskoka, l., Can. (mŭs-kō'kȧ)	99	45°00'N	79°30'W
Musoma, Tan.	237	1°30'S	33°48'E
Mussau Island, i., Pap. N. Gui. (mōō-sä'ōō)	213	1°30'S	149°32'E
Musselshell, r., Mt., U.S. (mŭs''l-shĕl)	115	46°25'N	108°20'W
Mussende, Ang.	236	10°32'S	16°05'E
Mussuma, Ang.	236	14°14'S	21°59'E
Mustafakemalpaşa, Tur.	163	40°05'N	28°30'E
Mustang Bayou, Tx., U.S.	123a	29°22'N	95°12'W
Mustang Creek, r., Tx., U.S. (mŭs'tăng)	120	36°22'N	102°46'W
Mustang Island, i., Tx., U.S.	123	27°43'N	97°00'W
Mustique, i., St. Vin. (müs-tēk')	133b	12°53'N	61°03'W
Mustvee, Est. (mōōst'vĕ-ĕ)	167	58°50'N	26°54'E
Musu Dan, c., Kor., N. (mò'sò dän)	205	40°51'N	130°00'E
Muswellbrook, Austl. (mŭs'wŭnl-bròk)	222	32°15'S	150°50'E
Mutare, Zimb.	232	18°49'S	32°39'E
Mutombo Mukulu, D.R.C. (mōō-tôm'bō mōō-kōō'lōō)	232	8°12'S	23°56'E
Mutsu Wan, b., Japan (mōōt'sōō wän)	210	41°20'N	140°55'E
Mutton Bay, Can. (mŭt''n)	101	50°48'N	59°02'W
Mutum, Braz. (mōō-tōō'm)	141a	19°48'S	41°24'W
Muzaffargarh, Pak.	202	30°09'N	71°15'E
Muzaffarpur, India	202	26°13'N	85°20'E
Muzon, Cape, c., Ak., U.S.	94	54°41'N	132°44'W
Muzquiz, Mex. (mōōz'kēz)	122	27°53'N	101°31'W
Muztagata, mtn., China	204	38°20'N	75°28'E
Mvomero, Tan.	237	6°20'S	37°25'E
Mvoti, r., S. Afr.	233c	29°18'S	30°52'E
Mwali, i., Com.	233	12°15'S	43°45'E
Mwanza, Tan. (mwän'zä)	232	2°31'S	32°54'E
Mwaya, Tan. (mwä'yä)	232	9°19'S	33°51'E
Mwenga, D.R.C.	237	3°02'S	28°26'E
Mweru, l., Afr.	232	8°50'S	28°50'E
Mwingi, Kenya	237	0°56'S	38°04'E
Myanmar (Burma), nation, Asia	194	21°00'N	95°15'E
Myingyan, Mya. (myĭng-yŭn')	199	21°37'N	95°26'E
Myitkyina, Mya. (myĭ'chē-nȧ)	199	25°33'N	97°25'E
Myjava, Slvk. (mûê'yȧ-vä)	169	48°45'N	17°33'E
Mykhailivka, Ukr.	177	47°16'N	35°12'E
Mykolaïv, Ukr.	178	46°58'N	32°02'E
Mykolaïv, prov., Ukr.	177	47°27'N	31°25'E
Mýkonos, i., Grc.	175	37°26'N	25°30'E
Mymensingh, Bngl.	199	24°48'N	90°28'E
Mynämäki, Fin.	167	60°41'N	21°58'E
Myohyang San, mtn., Kor., N. (myō'hyang)	210	40°00'N	126°12'E
Mýrdalsjökull, ice, Ice. (mür'däls-yû'kòl)	160	63°34'N	18°04'W
Myrhorod, Ukr.	181	49°56'N	33°36'E
Mýrina, Grc.	175	39°52'N	25°01'E
Myrtle Beach, S.C., U.S. (mûr't'l)	125	33°42'N	78°53'W
Myrtle Point, Or., U.S.	114	43°04'N	124°08'W
Mysen, Nor.	166	59°32'N	11°16'E
Myshikino, Russia (mēsh'kē-nô)	176	57°48'N	38°21'E
Mysore, India (mī-sōr')	199	12°31'N	76°42'E
Mysovka, Russia (mē'sôf-kȧ)	167	55°11'N	21°17'E
Mystic, Ia., U.S. (mĭs'tĭk)	113	40°47'N	92°54'W
Mytilíni, Grc.	163	39°09'N	26°35'E
Mytishchi, Russia (mē-tēsh'chi)	186b	55°55'N	37°46'E
Mziha, Tan.	237	5°54'S	37°47'E
Mzimba, Mwi. ('m-zĭm'bä)	232	11°52'S	33°34'E
Mzimkulu, r., Afr.	233c	30°12'S	29°57'E
Mzimvubu, r., S. Afr.	233c	31°22'S	29°20'E
Mzuzu, Mwi.	237	11°30'S	34°10'E

N

Naab, r., Ger. (näp)	168	49°38'N	12°15'E
Naaldwijk, Neth.	159a	52°00'N	4°11'E
Nā'ālehu, Hi., U.S.	126a	19°00'N	155°35'W
Naantali, Fin. (nän'tȧ-lē)	167	60°29'N	22°03'E
Nabberu, l., Austl. (năb'ēr-ōō)	220	26°05'S	120°35'E

ng-sing; ŋ-baŋk; ɴ-nasalized n; nŏd; cŏmmit; ōld; ôbey; ôrder; oi-boil; fōōd; ò-as oo in foot; ou-out; s-soft; sh-dish; th-thin; pūre; ûnite; ûrn; stŭd; circŭs; ü-as in French tu; '-indeterminate vowel.

326 Naberezhnyye Chelny – Nduye PRONOUNCING INDEX

PLACE (Pronunciation)	PAGE	LAT.	LONG.
Naberezhnyye Chelny, Russia	178	55°42'N	52°19'E
Nabeul, Tun. (nā-bûl')	230	36°34'N	10°45'E
Nabiswera, Ug.	237	1°28'N	32°16'E
Naboomspruit, S. Afr.	238c	24°32'S	28°43'E
Nābulus, W.B.	197a	32°13'N	35°16'E
Nacala, Moz. (nä-kà'là)	233	14°34'S	40°41'E
Nacaome, Hond. (nä-kä-ō'mâ)	132	13°32'N	87°28'W
Na Cham, Viet. (nä chäm')	209	22°02'N	106°30'E
Naches, r., Wa., U.S. (năch'ĕz)	114	46°51'N	121°03'W
Náchod, Czech Rep. (näk'ôt)	168	50°25'N	16°08'E
Nacimiento, Lake, res., Ca., U.S. (ná-sĭ-myĕn'tô)	118	35°50'N	121°00'W
Nacogdoches, Tx., U.S. (năk'ō-dō'chĕz)	123	31°36'N	94°40'W
Nadadores, Mex. (nä-dä-dō'räs)	122	27°04'N	101°36'W
Nadiād, India	202	22°45'N	72°51'E
Nadir, V.I.U.S.	129c	18°19'N	64°53'W
Nădlac, Rom.	175	46°09'N	20°52'E
Nadvirna, Ukr.	169	48°37'N	24°35'E
Nadym, r., Russia (ná'dĭm)	184	64°30'N	72°48'E
Naestved, Den. (nĕst'vĭdh)	160	55°14'N	11°46'E
Nafada, Nig.	235	11°08'N	11°20'E
Nafishah, Egypt	238d	30°34'N	32°15'E
Náfplio, Grc.	175	37°33'N	22°46'E
Nafūd ad Daḩy, des., Sau. Ar.	198	22°15'N	44°15'E
Nag, Co, l., China	202	31°38'N	91°18'E
Naga, Phil. (nä'gä)	213	13°37'N	123°12'E
Naga, i., Japan	211	32°09'N	130°16'E
Nagahama, Japan (nä'gä-hä'mä)	211	33°32'N	132°29'E
Nagahama, Japan	211	35°23'N	136°16'E
Nagaland, India	199	25°47'N	94°15'E
Nagano, Japan (nä'gä-nô)	205	36°42'N	138°12'E
Nagaoka, Japan (nä'gȧ-ō'kȧ)	205	37°22'N	138°49'E
Nagaoka, Japan	211b	34°54'N	135°42'E
Nāgappattinam, India	199	10°48'N	79°51'E
Nagarote, Nic. (nä-gä-rô'tĕ)	132	12°17'N	86°35'W
Nagasaki, Japan (nä'gȧ-sä'kê)	205	32°48'N	129°53'E
Nāgaur, India	202	27°19'N	73°41'E
Nagaybakskiy, Russia (ná-gáy-băk'skĭ)	186a	53°33'N	59°33'E
Nagcarlan, Phil. (näg-kär-län')	213a	14°07'N	121°24'E
Nāgercoil, India	203	8°15'N	77°29'E
Nagorno Karabakh, hist. reg., Azer. (nu-gôr'nŭ-kŭ-rŭ-bäk')	181	40°10'N	46°50'E
Nagoya, Japan	205	35°09'N	136°53'E
Nāgpur, India (näg'po͞or)	199	21°12'N	79°09'E
Nagua, Dom. Rep. (ná'gwä)	135	19°20'N	69°40'W
Nagykanizsa, Hung. (nôd'y'kô'nĕ-shô)	163	46°27'N	17°00'E
Nagykőrös, Hung. (nôd'y'kŭ-rŭsh)	169	47°02'N	19°46'E
Naha, Japan (nä'hä)	205	26°02'N	127°43'E
Nahanni National Park, rec., Can.	92	62°10'N	125°15'W
Nahant, Ma., U.S. (nȧ-hănt)	101a	42°26'N	70°55'W
Nahariyya, Isr.	197a	33°01'N	35°06'E
Nahuel Huapi, l., Arg. (nä'wĕl wä'pê)	144	41°00'S	71°30'W
Nahuizalco, El Sal. (nä-wê-zäl'kō)	132	13°50'N	89°43'W
Naic, Phil. (nä-ēk)	213a	14°20'N	120°46'E
Naica, Mex. (nä-ē'kä)	122	27°53'N	105°30'W
Naiguata, Pico, mtn., Ven. (pē'kô)	143b	10°32'N	66°44'W
Nain, Can. (nīn)	91	56°29'N	61°52'W
Nā'īn, Iran	201	32°52'N	53°05'E
Nairn, Scot., U.K. (nârn)	164	57°35'N	3°54'W
Nairobi, Kenya (nī-rō'bê)	232	1°17'S	36°49'E
Naivasha, Kenya (nī-vä'shȧ)	232	0°47'S	36°29'E
Najd, hist. reg., Sau. Ar.	198	25°18'N	42°38'E
Najin, Kor., N. (nä'jĭn)	205	42°04'N	130°35'E
Najran, des., Sau. Ar. (nŭj-rän')	198	17°29'N	45°30'E
Naju, Kor., S. (nä'jo͞o')	210	35°02'N	126°42'E
Najusa, r., Cuba (nä-ho͞o'sä)	134	20°55'N	77°55'W
Nakatsu, Japan (nä'käts-o͞o)	210	33°34'N	131°10'E
Nakhodka, Russia (nŭ-kôt'kŭ)	179	43°03'N	133°08'E
Nakhon Ratchasima, Thai.	212	14°56'N	102°14'E
Nakhon Sawan, Thai.	212	15°42'N	100°06'E
Nakhon Si Thammarat, Thai.	212	8°27'N	99°58'E
Nakło nad Notecia, Pol.	169	53°10'N	17°35'E
Nakskov, Den. (näk'skou)	160	54°51'N	11°06'E
Naktong, r., Kor., S. (näk'tŭng)	210	36°10'N	128°30'E
Nal'chik, Russia (nál-chĕk')	181	43°30'N	43°35'E
Nalón, r., Spain (nä-lōn')	172	43°15'N	5°38'W
Nālūt, Libya (nä-lo͞ot')	230	31°51'N	10°49'E
Namak, Daryacheh-ye, l., Iran	198	34°58'N	51°33'E
Namakan, l., Mn., U.S. (nă'mȧ-kȧn)	113	48°20'N	92°43'W
Namangan, Uzb. (nȧ-mȧn-gän')	183	41°08'N	71°59'E
Namao, Can.	102g	53°43'N	113°30'W
Namatanai, Pap. N. Gui. (nä'mä-tȧ-nä'ē)	213	3°43'S	152°26'E
Nambour, Austl. (năm'bôr)	222	26°48'S	153°00'E
Nam Co, l., China (näm tswo)	204	30°30'N	91°10'E
Nam Dinh, Viet. (näm dēnк')	212	20°30'N	106°10'E
Nametil, Moz.	237	15°43'S	39°21'E
Namhae, i., Kor., S. (näm'hī')	210	34°23'N	128°05'E
Namib Desert, des., Nmb. (nä-mēb')	232	18°45'S	12°45'E
Namibia, nation, Afr.	232	19°30'S	16°13'E
Namoi, r., Austl. (nămoi)	221	30°10'S	148°43'E
Namous, Oued en, r., Alg. (nȧ-mo͞os')	162	31°48'N	0°19'W
Nampa, Id., U.S. (năm'pȧ)	104	43°35'N	116°35'W
Namp'o, Kor., N.	205	38°47'N	125°28'E
Nampuecha, Moz.	237	13°59'S	40°18'E
Nampula, Moz.	237	15°07'S	39°15'E
Namsos, Nor. (näm'sôs)	160	64°28'N	11°14'E
Namu, Can.	94	51°53'N	127°50'W
Namuli, Serra, mts., Moz.	237	15°05'S	37°05'E
Namur, Bel. (nȧ-mür')	161	50°29'N	4°55'E
Namutoni, Nmb. (nȧ-mo͞o-tō'nê)	232	18°45'S	17°00'E
Nan, r., Thai.	212	18°11'N	100°29'E
Nanacamilpa, Mex. (nä-nä-kä-mē'l-pä)	131a	19°30'N	98°33'W
Nanaimo, Can. (nȧ-nī'mō)	90	49°10'N	123°56'W
Nanam, Kor., N. (nä'nän')	210	41°38'N	129°37'E
Nanao, Japan (nä'nä-ō)	210	37°03'N	136°59'E
Nan'ao Dao, i., China (nän-ou dou)	209	23°30'N	117°30'E
Nanchang, China (nän'chäng')	205	28°38'N	115°48'E
Nanchangshan Dao, i., China (nän-chäŋ-shän dou)	206	37°56'N	120°42'E
Nancheng, China (nän-chäŋ)	205	26°50'N	116°40'E
Nanchong, China (nän-chôŋ)	204	30°45'N	106°05'E
Nancy, Fr. (näɴ-sē')	161	48°42'N	6°11'E
Nancy Creek, r., Ga., U.S. (năn'cē)	110c	33°51'N	84°25'W
Nanda Devi, mtn., India (nän'dä dā'vē)	199	30°30'N	80°25'E
Nānded, India	202	19°13'N	77°21'E
Nandurbār, India	202	21°29'N	74°13'E
Nandyāl, India	203	15°54'N	78°09'E
Nanga Parbat, mtn., Pak.	202	35°20'N	74°35'E
Nangi, India	202a	22°30'N	88°14'E
Nangis, Fr. (näɴ-zhē')	171b	48°33'N	3°01'E
Nangong, China (nän-gôŋ)	208	37°22'N	115°22'E
Nangweshi, Zam.	236	16°26'S	23°17'E
Nanhuangcheng Dao, i., China (nän-hůäŋ-chŭŋ dou)	206	38°22'N	120°54'E
Nanhui, China	206	31°03'N	121°45'E
Nanjing, China (nän-jyĭŋ)	205	32°04'N	118°46'E
Nanjuma, r., China (nän-jyo͞o-mä)	206	39°37'N	115°45'E
Nanking *see* Nanjing, China	204	32°04'N	118°46'E
Nanle, China (nän-lŭ)	206	36°03'N	115°13'E
Nan Ling, mts., China	205	25°15'N	111°40'E
Nanliu, r., China (nän-lĭō)	209	22°00'N	109°18'E
Nannine, Austl. (nă-nēn')	218	25°50'S	118°30'E
Nanning, China (nän'nĭng')	204	22°56'N	108°10'E
Nanpan, r., China (nän-pän)	209	24°50'N	105°30'E
Nanping, China (nän-pĭŋ)	205	26°40'N	118°05'E
Nansei-shotō, is., Japan	205	27°30'N	127°00'E
Nansemond, Va., U.S. (năn'sê-mŭnd)	110g	36°46'N	76°32'W
Nantai Zan, mtn., Japan (nän-tăê zän)	210	36°47'N	139°28'E
Nantes, Fr. (näɴt')	154	47°13'N	1°37'W
Nanteuil-le-Haudouin, Fr. (näɴ-tû-lĕ-ō-dwăɴ')	171b	49°08'N	2°49'E
Nanticoke, Pa., U.S. (năn'tĭ-kōk)	109	41°10'N	76°00'W
Nantong, China (nän-tôŋ)	206	32°02'N	120°51'E
Nantong, China	206	32°08'N	121°06'E
Nantucket, i., Ma., U.S. (năn-tŭk'ĕt)	107	41°15'N	70°05'W
Nantwich, Eng., U.K. (nănt'wĭch)	158a	53°04'N	2°31'W
Nanxiang, China (nän-shyäŋ)	206	31°17'N	121°17'E
Nanxiong, China (nän-shôŋ)	209	25°10'N	114°20'E
Nanyang, China	205	33°00'N	112°42'E
Nanyang Hu, l., China (nän-yäŋ ho͞o)	206	35°14'N	116°24'E
Nanyuan, China (nän-yůän)	208a	39°48'N	116°24'E
Naolinco, Mex. (nä-o-lēŋ'kō)	131	19°39'N	96°50'W
Náousa, Grc. (nä'o͞o-sȧ)	175	40°38'N	22°05'E
Naozhou Dao, i., China (nou-jō dou)	209	20°58'N	110°58'E
Napa, Ca., U.S. (năp'ȧ)	104	38°20'N	122°17'W
Napanee, Can. (năp'ȧ-nē)	99	44°15'N	77°00'W
Naperville, Il., U.S. (nā'pĕr-vĭl)	111a	41°46'N	88°09'W
Napier, N.Z. (nā'pĭ-ēr)	221a	39°30'S	177°00'E
Napierville, Can. (nā'pĭ-ē-vĭl)	102a	45°11'N	73°24'W
Naples (Napoli), Italy	154	40°37'N	14°12'E
Naples, Fl., U.S. (nā'p'lz)	125a	26°07'N	81°46'W
Napo, r., S.A. (nä'pō)	142	1°49'S	74°20'W
Napoleon, Oh., U.S. (nȧ-pō'lē-ŭn)	108	41°20'N	84°10'W
Napoleonville, La., U.S. (nȧ-pō'lē-ŭn-vĭl)	123	29°56'N	91°03'W
Napoli *see* Naples, Italy	154	40°37'N	14°12'E
Napoli, Golfo di, b., Italy	162	40°29'N	14°08'E
Nappanee, In., U.S. (năp'ȧ-nē)	108	41°30'N	86°00'W
Nara, Japan (nä'rä)	205	34°41'N	135°50'E
Nara, Mali	230	15°09'N	7°27'W
Nara, dept., Japan	211b	34°36'N	135°49'E
Nara, r., Russia	176	55°05'N	37°16'E
Narach, Vozyera, l., Bela.	176	54°51'N	27°00'E
Naracoorte, Austl. (nȧ-rȧ-ko͞on'tê)	218	36°50'S	140°50'E
Narashino, Japan	211a	35°41'N	140°01'E
Naraspur, India	203	16°32'N	81°43'E
Narberth, Pa., U.S. (när'bûrth)	110f	40°01'N	75°17'W
Narbonne, Fr. (nȧr-bôn')	161	43°12'N	3°00'E
Nare, Col. (nä'rĕ)	142a	6°12'N	74°37'W
Narew, r., Pol. (nä'rĕf)	169	52°43'N	21°19'E
Narmada, r., India	199	22°30'N	75°30'E
Narodnaya, Gora, mtn., Russia (nȧ-rôd'nȧ-yȧ)	178	65°10'N	60°10'E
Naro-Fominsk, Russia (nä'rô-mênsk')	180	55°23'N	36°43'E
Narrabeen, Austl. (năr-ȧ-bĭn)	217b	33°44'S	151°18'E
Narragansett, R.I., U.S. (năr-ă-găn'sĕt)	110b	41°26'N	71°27'W
Narragansett Bay, b., R.I., U.S.	109	41°20'N	71°15'W
Narrandera, Austl. (nȧ-răn-dē'rȧ)	219	34°40'S	146°40'E
Narrogin, Austl. (năr'ō-gĭn)	218	33°00'S	117°15'E
Narva, Est. (nȧr'vȧ)	180	59°24'N	28°12'E
Narvacan, Phil. (när-vä-kän')	213a	17°27'N	120°29'E
Narva Jõesuu, Est. (nȧr'vȧ ô-ô-ă'so͞o-ô)	167	59°26'N	28°02'E
Narvik, Nor. (när'vêk)	154	68°21'N	17°18'E
Narvskiy Zaliv, b., Eur. (nȧr'vskĭ zä'lĭf)	167	59°35'N	27°25'E
Narvskoye, res., Eur.	167	59°18'N	28°14'E
Nar'yan-Mar, Russia (när'yȧn mär')	178	67°42'N	53°30'E
Naryilco, Austl. (năr-ĭl'kō)	222	28°40'S	141°50'E
Narym, Russia (nä-rēm')	178	58°47'N	82°05'E
Naryn, r., Asia (nŭ-rĭn')	184	41°20'N	76°00'E
Naseby, Eng., U.K. (nāz'bĭ)	158a	52°23'N	0°59'W
Nashua, Mo., U.S. (năsh'ů-ȧ)	117f	39°18'N	94°34'W
Nashua, N.H., U.S.	105	42°47'N	71°23'W
Nashville, Ar., U.S. (năsh'vĭl)	121	33°56'N	93°50'W
Nashville, Ga., U.S.	124	31°12'N	83°15'W
Nashville, Il., U.S.	121	38°21'N	89°42'W
Nashville, Mi., U.S.	108	42°35'N	85°50'W
Nashville, Tn., U.S.	105	36°10'N	86°48'W
Nashwauk, Mn., U.S. (năsh'wôk)	113	47°21'N	93°12'W
Näsi, l., Fin.	160	61°42'N	24°05'E
Našice, Cro. (nä'shĕ-tsĕ)	163	45°29'N	18°06'E
Nasielsk, Pol. (nä'syĕlsk)	169	52°35'N	20°50'E
Nāsik, India (nä'sĭk)	199	20°02'N	73°49'E
Nāşir, Sudan (nä-zēr')	231	8°30'N	33°06'E
Nasirabād, India	202	26°13'N	74°48'E
Naskaupi, r., Can. (năs'kô-pĭ)	93	53°59'N	61°10'W
Nasondoye, D.R.C.	237	10°22'S	25°06'E
Nass, r., Can. (năs)	94	55°00'N	129°30'W
Nassau, Bah. (năs'ô)	129	25°05'N	77°20'W
Nassenheide, Ger. (nä'sĕn-hī-dĕ)	159b	52°49'N	13°13'E
Nasser, Lake, res., Egypt	231	23°50'N	32°50'E
Nasugbu, Phil. (nȧ-sòg-bo͞o')	213a	14°05'N	120°37'E
Nasworthy Lake, l., Tx., U.S. (năz'wûr-thê)	122	31°17'N	100°30'W
Natagaima, Col. (nä-tä-gī'mä)	142a	3°38'N	75°07'W
Natal, Braz. (nä-täl')	143	6°00'S	35°13'W
Natashquan, Can. (nä-tăsh'kwän)	91	50°11'N	61°49'W
Natashquan, r., Can.	101	50°35'N	61°35'W
Natchez, Ms., U.S. (năch'ĕz)	105	31°35'N	91°20'W
Natchitoches, La., U.S. (năk'ĭ-tŏsh) (nȧch-ĭ-tŏsh')	123	31°46'N	93°06'W
Natick, Ma., U.S. (nā'tĭk)	101a	42°17'N	71°21'W
National Bison Range, I.R., Mt., U.S. (năsh'ŭn-ăl bī's'n)	115	47°18'N	113°58'W
National City, Ca., U.S.	118a	32°38'N	117°01'W
Natitingou, Benin	230	10°19'N	1°22'E
Natividade, Braz. (nä-tê-vê-dä'dĕ)	143	11°43'S	47°34'W
Natron, Lake, l., Tan. (nā'trŏn)	232	2°17'S	36°10'E
Natrona Heights, Pa., U.S. (nā'trō nȧ)	111e	40°38'N	79°43'W
Naṭrūn, Wādī an, val., Egypt	238b	30°33'N	30°12'E
Natuna Besar, i., Indon.	212	4°00'N	106°50'E
Natural Bridges National Monument, rec., Ut., U.S. (năt'ů-răl brĭj'ĕs)	119	37°20'N	110°20'W
Naturaliste, Cape, c., Austl. (năt-ů-rȧ-lĭst')	220	33°30'S	115°10'E
Nau, Cap de la, c., Spain	156	38°43'N	0°14'E
Naucalpan de Juárez, Mex.	131a	19°28'N	99°14'W
Nauchampatepetl, mtn., Mex. (näo͞o-chäm-pä-tĕ'pĕtl)	131	19°32'N	97°09'W
Nauen, Ger. (nou'ĕn)	159b	52°36'N	12°53'E
Naugatuck, Ct., U.S. (nô'gȧ-tŭk)	109	41°25'N	73°05'W
Naujan, Phil. (nä-ò-hän')	213a	13°19'N	121°17'E
Naumburg, Ger. (noum'bòrgh)	168	51°10'N	11°50'E
Nauru, nation, Oc.	3	0°30'S	167°00'E
Nautla, Mex. (nä-o͞ot'lä)	128	20°14'N	96°44'W
Nava, Mex. (nä'vä)	122	28°25'N	100°44'W
Nava del Rey, Spain (nä-vä dĕl rā'ê)	172	41°22'N	5°04'W
Navahermosa, Spain (nä-vä-ĕr-mō'sä)	172	39°39'N	4°28'W
Navajas, Cuba (nä-vä-häs')	134	22°40'N	81°20'W
Navajo Hopi Joint Use Area, I.R., Az., U.S.	119	36°15'N	110°30'W
Navajo Indian Reservation, I.R., U.S. (năv'ȧ-hō)	119	36°31'N	109°24'W
Navajo National Monument, rec., Az., U.S.	119	36°43'N	110°39'W
Navajo Reservoir, res., N.M., U.S.	119	36°57'N	107°26'W
Navalcarnero, Spain (nä-väl'kär-nā'rō)	173a	40°17'N	4°05'W
Navalmoral de la Mata, Spain	172	39°53'N	5°32'W
Navan, Can. (nă'vȧn)	102c	45°25'N	75°26'W
Navarino, i., Chile (nä-vä-rē'nô)	144	55°30'S	68°15'W
Navarra, hist. reg., Spain (nä-vär'rä)	172	42°40'N	1°35'W
Navarro, Arg. (nä-vȧ'r-rō)	141c	35°00'S	59°16'W
Navasota, Tx., U.S. (năv-ȧ-sō'tȧ)	123	30°24'N	96°05'W
Navasota, r., Tx., U.S.	123	31°03'N	96°11'W
Navassa, i., N.A. (nȧ-văs'ȧ)	135	18°25'N	75°15'W
Navia, r., Spain (nä-vē'ä)	172	43°10'N	6°45'W
Navidad, Chile (nä-vê-dä'd)	141b	33°57'S	71°51'W
Navidad Bank, bk. (nä-vê-dädh')	135	20°05'N	69°00'W
Navidade do Carangola, Braz. (nȧ-vē-dä'dô-kȧ-rän-gô'la)	141a	21°04'S	41°58'W
Navojoa, Mex. (nä-vô-kô'ä)	128	27°00'N	109°40'W
Nawābshāh, Pak. (nȧ-wäb'shä)	202	26°20'N	68°30'E
Naxçıvan, Azer.	181	39°10'N	45°30'E
Naxçıvan Muxtar, state, Azer.	182	39°20'N	45°30'E
Náxos, i., Grc. (nák'sôs)	163	37°15'N	25°20'E
Nayarit, state, Mex. (nä-yä-rēt')	128	22°00'N	105°15'W
Nayarit, Sierra de, mts., Mex. (sē-ĕ'r-rä-dĕ)	130	23°20'N	105°07'W
Naye, Sen.	234	14°25'N	12°12'W
Naylor, Md., U.S. (nā'lŏr)	110e	38°43'N	76°46'W
Nazaré da Mata, Braz. (dä-mä-tä)	143	7°46'S	35°13'W
Nazas, Mex. (nä'zäs)	122	25°14'N	104°08'W
Nazas, r., Mex.	122	25°30'N	104°40'W
Nazerat, Isr.	197a	32°43'N	35°19'E
Nazilli, Tur. (nȧ-zĭ-lē')	181	37°40'N	28°10'E
Naziya, r., Russia (nȧ-zē'yȧ)	186c	59°48'N	31°18'E
Nazko, r., Can.	94	52°35'N	123°10'W
N'dalatando, Ang.	236	9°18'S	14°54'E
Ndali, Benin	235	9°51'N	2°43'E
Ndikiniméki, Cam.	235	4°46'N	10°50'E
N'Djamena, Chad	231	12°07'N	15°03'E
Ndola, Zam. (n'dō'lä)	232	12°58'S	28°38'E
Ndoto Mountains, mts., Kenya	237	1°55'N	37°05'E
Ndrhamcha, Sebkha de, l., Maur.	234	18°50'N	15°15'W
Nduye, D.R.C.	237	1°50'N	29°01'E

ăt; finăl; rāte; senâte; ärm; àsk; sofȧ; fâre; ch-choose; dh-as th in other; bē; ėvent; bĕt; recĕnt; cratẽr; g-gō; gh-guttural g; bĭt; ĭ-short neutral; rīde; κ-guttural k as ch in German ich;

PRONOUNCING INDEX Neagh – New Providence 327

PLACE (Pronunciation)	PAGE	LAT.	LONG.
Neagh, Lough, l., N. Ire., U.K. (lŏk nā)	160	54°40'N	6°47'W
Néa Páfos, Cyp.	197a	34°46'N	32°27'E
Neapean, r., Austl.	217b	33°40'S	150°39'E
Neápoli, Grc.	175	36°35'N	23°08'E
Neápolis, Grc.	174a	35°17'N	25°37'E
Near Islands, is., Ak., U.S. (nēr)	103a	52°20'N	172°40'E
Neath, Wales, U.K. (nēth)	164	51°41'N	3°50'W
Nebine Creek, r., Austl. (nĕ-bēne')	222	27°50'S	147°00'E
Nebitdag, Turkmen.	183	39°30'N	54°20'E
Nebraska, state, U.S. (nē-brăs'kȧ)	104	41°45'N	101°30'W
Nebraska City, Ne., U.S.	121	40°40'N	95°50'W
Nechako, r., Can.	94	53°45'N	124°55'W
Nechako Plateau, plat., Can. (nĭ-chă'kō)	94	54°00'N	124°30'W
Nechako Range, mts., Can.	94	53°20'N	124°30'W
Nechako Reservoir, res., Can.	94	53°25'N	125°10'W
Neches, r., Tx., U.S. (nĕch'ĕz)	123	31°03'N	94°40'W
Neckar, r., Ger. (nĕk'är)	168	49°16'N	9°06'E
Necker Island, i., Hi., U.S.	126b	24°00'N	164°00'W
Necochea, Arg. (nā-kô-chā'ä)	144	38°30'S	58°45'W
Nedryhailiv, Ukr.	177	50°49'N	33°52'E
Needham, Ma., U.S. (nēd'ăm)	101a	42°17'N	71°14'W
Needles, Ca., U.S. (nē'd'lz)	119	34°51'N	114°39'W
Neenah, Wi., U.S. (nē'nȧ)	113	44°10'N	88°30'W
Neepawa, Can.	90	50°13'N	99°29'W
Nee Reservoir, res., Co., U.S. (nee)	120	38°26'N	102°56'W
Negareyama, Japan (nå'gä-rå-yä'mä)	211a	35°52'N	139°54'E
Negaunee, Mi., U.S. (nē-gô'nē)	113	46°30'N	87°37'W
Negeri Sembilan, state, Malay. (nā'grē-sĕm-bē-län')	197b	2°46'N	101°54'E
Negev, des., Isr. (nĕ'gĕv)	197a	30°34'N	34°43'E
Negombo, Sri L.	203	7°39'N	79°49'E
Negotin, Serb. (nĕ'gô-tĕn)	175	44°13'N	22°33'E
Negro, r., Arg.	144	39°50'S	65°00'W
Negro, r., N.A.	132	13°01'N	87°10'W
Negro, r., S.A.	141c	33°17'S	58°18'W
Negro, r., S.A. (nā'grô)	142	0°18'S	63°21'W
Negro, Cerro, mtn., Pan. (sĕ'-rrô-nā'grô)	133	8°44'N	80°37'W
Negros, i., Phil. (nā'grōs)	212	9°50'N	121°45'E
Nehalem, r., Or., U.S. (nē-hăl'ĕm)	114	45°52'N	123°37'W
Nehaus an der Oste, Ger. (noi'houz) (ōz'tē)	159c	53°48'N	9°02'E
Nehbandān, Iran	201	31°32'N	60°02'E
Nehe, China (nŭ-hŭ)	208	48°23'N	124°58'E
Neheim-Hüsten, Ger. (nĕ'hīm)	171c	51°28'N	7°58'E
Neiba, Dom. Rep. (nå-ē'bä)	135	18°30'N	71°20'W
Neiba, Bahía de, b., Dom. Rep.	135	18°10'N	71°00'W
Neiba, Sierra de, mts., Dom. Rep. (sē-ĕr'rä-dĕ)	135	18°40'N	71°40'W
Neihart, Mt., U.S. (nī'härt)	115	46°54'N	110°39'W
Neijiang, China (nā-jyäŋ)	209	29°38'N	105°01'E
Neillsville, Wi., U.S. (nēlz'vĭl)	113	44°35'N	90°37'W
Nei Monggol (Inner Mongolia), state, China	204	40°15'N	105°00'E
Neiqiu, China (nā-chyō)	206	37°17'N	114°32'E
Neira, Col. (nā'rä)	142a	5°10'N	75°32'W
Neisse, r., Eur. (nēs)	168	51°30'N	15°00'E
Neiva, Col. (nå-ē'vä) (nā'vä)	142	2°55'N	75°16'W
Neixiang, China (nā-shyäŋ)	208	33°00'N	111°38'E
Nekemte, Eth.	231	9°09'N	36°29'E
Nekoosa, Wi., U.S. (nē-kōō'sȧ)	113	44°19'N	89°54'W
Neligh, Ne., U.S. (nē'-lē)	112	42°06'N	98°02'W
Nel'kan, Russia (nĕl-kän')	179	57°45'N	136°36'E
Nellore, India (nĕl-lōr')	199	14°28'N	79°59'E
Nel'ma, Russia (nĕl-mä')	210	47°34'N	139°05'E
Nelson, Can. (nĕl'sŭn)	90	49°29'N	117°17'W
Nelson, N.Z.	221a	41°15'S	173°22'E
Nelson, Eng., U.K.	158a	53°50'N	2°13'W
Nelson, i., Ak., U.S.	103	60°38'N	164°42'W
Nelson, r., Can.	97	56°50'N	93°40'W
Nelson, Cape, c., Austl.	222	38°29'S	141°20'E
Nelsonville, Oh., U.S. (nĕl'sŭn-vĭl)	108	39°30'N	82°15'W
Néma, Maur. (nā'mä)	230	16°37'N	7°15'W
Nemadji, r., Wi., U.S. (nĕ-măd'jē)	117h	46°33'N	92°16'W
Neman, Russia (ŋĕ'-mȧn)	167	55°02'N	22°01'E
Neman, r., Eur.	180	53°28'N	24°45'E
Nembe, Nig.	235	4°35'N	6°26'E
Nemeiben Lake, l., Can. (nĕ-mē'bȧn)	96	55°20'N	105°20'W
Nemours, Fr.	170	48°16'N	2°41'E
Nemuro, Japan (nā'mô-rō)	205	43°13'N	145°10'E
Nemuro Strait, strt., Asia	210	43°07'N	145°10'E
Nemyriv, Ukr.	177	48°56'N	28°51'E
Nen, r., China (nŭn)	205	47°07'N	123°28'E
Nen, r., Eng., U.K. (nĕn)	158a	52°32'N	0°19'W
Nenagh, Ire. (nē'nȧ)	164	52°50'N	8°05'W
Nenana, Ak., U.S. (nå-nä'nȧ)	103	64°28'N	149°18'W
Nenikyul', Russia (nĕ-nyē'kyûl)	186c	59°26'N	30°40'E
Nenjiang, China (nŭn-jyäŋ)	205	49°02'N	125°15'E
Neodesha, Ks., U.S. (nē-ô-dĕ-shô')	121	37°24'N	95°41'W
Neosho, Mo., U.S.	121	36°51'N	94°22'W
Neosho, r., Ks., U.S. (nē-ō'shō)	121	38°07'N	95°40'W
Nepal, nation, Asia (nĕ-pôl')	199	28°45'N	83°00'E
Nephi, Ut., U.S. (nē'fī)	119	39°40'N	111°50'W
Nepomuceno, Braz. (nĕ-pô-mōō-sĕ'no)	141a	21°15'S	45°13'W
Nera, r., Italy (nā'rä)	174	42°45'N	12°54'E
Nérac, Fr. (nā-räk')	170	44°08'N	0°19'E
Nerchinsk, Russia (nyĕr'chēnsk)	179	51°47'N	116°17'E
Nerchinskiy Khrebet, mts., Russia	179	50°30'N	118°30'E
Nerchinskiy Zavod, Russia (nyĕr'chĕn-skĭzȧ-vôt')	179	51°35'N	119°46'E
Nerekhta, Russia (nyĕ-rĕk'tȧ)	176	57°29'N	40°34'E
Neretva, r., Serb. (nĕ'rĕt-vȧ)	175	43°08'N	17°50'E
Nerja, Spain (nĕr'hä)	172	36°45'N	3°53'W
Nerl', r., Russia (nyĕrl)	176	56°59'N	37°57'E
Nerskaya, r., Russia (nyĕr'skȧ-yȧ)	186b	55°31'N	38°46'E
Nerussa, r., Russia (nyå-rōō'sȧ)	176	52°24'N	34°20'E
Ness, Loch, l., Scot., U.K. (lŏk nĕs)	164	57°23'N	4°20'W
Ness City, Ks., U.S. (nĕs)	120	38°27'N	99°55'W
Nesterov, Russia (nyĕs-tā'rôf)	167	54°39'N	22°38'E
Néstos (Mesta), r., Eur. (näs'tōs)	175	41°25'N	24°12'E
Netanya, Isr.	197a	32°19'N	34°52'E
Netcong, N.J., U.S. (nĕt'cŏnj)	110a	40°54'N	74°42'W
Netherlands, nation, Eur. (nĕdh'ĕr-lăndz)	154	53°01'N	3°57'E
Netherlands Guiana *see* Suriname, nation, S.A.	143	4°00'N	56°00'W
Nettilling, l., Can.	93	66°30'N	70°40'W
Nett Lake Indian Reservation, I.R., Mn., U.S. (nĕt lāk)	113	48°23'N	93°19'W
Nettuno, Italy (nĕt-tōō'nô)	173d	41°28'N	12°40'E
Neubeckum, Ger. (noi'bĕ-kōōm)	171c	51°48'N	8°01'E
Neubrandenburg, Ger. (noi-brän'dĕn-bŏorgh)	168	53°33'N	13°16'E
Neuburg, Ger. (noi'bŏorgh)	168	48°43'N	11°12'E
Neuchâtel, Switz. (nû-shȧ-tĕl')	161	47°00'N	6°52'E
Neuchâtel, Lac de, l., Switz.	168	46°48'N	6°53'E
Neuenhagen, Ger. (noi'ĕn-hä-gĕn)	159b	52°31'N	13°41'E
Neuenrade, Ger. (noi'ĕn-rä-dĕ)	171c	51°17'N	7°47'E
Neufchâtel-en-Bray, Fr. (nû-shä-tĕl'ĕɴ-brā')	170	49°43'N	1°25'E
Neulengbach, Aus.	159e	48°13'N	15°55'E
Neumarkt, Ger. (noi'märkt)	168	49°17'N	11°30'E
Neumünster, Ger. (noi'münstĕr)	160	54°04'N	10°00'E
Neunkirchen, Aus. (noin'kĭrk-ĕn)	168	47°43'N	16°05'E
Neuquén, Arg. (nĕ-ô-kān')	144	38°52'S	68°12'W
Neuquén, prov., Arg.	144	39°40'S	70°45'W
Neuquén, r., Arg.	144	38°45'S	69°00'W
Neuruppin, Ger. (noi'rōō-pēn)	168	52°55'N	12°48'E
Neuse, r., N.C., U.S. (nūz)	125	36°12'N	78°50'W
Neusiedler See, l., Eur. (noi-zēd'lĕr)	168	47°54'N	16°31'E
Neuss, Ger. (nois)	171c	51°12'N	6°41'E
Neustadt, Ger. (noi'shtät)	168	49°21'N	8°08'E
Neustadt bei Coburg, Ger. (bī kō'bŏorgh)	168	50°20'N	11°09'E
Neustadt in Holstein, Ger.	168	54°06'N	10°50'E
Neustrelitz, Ger. (noi-strā'lĭts)	168	53°21'N	13°05'E
Neutral Hills, hills, Can. (nū'trăl)	96	52°10'N	110°50'W
Neu Ulm, Ger. (noi ŏŏlm')	168	48°23'N	10°01'E
Neuville, Can. (nū'vĭl)	102b	46°39'N	71°35'W
Neuwied, Ger. (noi'vēdt)	168	50°26'N	7°28'E
Neva, r., Russia (nyĕ-vä')	176	59°49'N	30°54'E
Nevada, Ia., U.S. (nē-vä'dȧ)	113	42°01'N	93°27'W
Nevada, Mo., U.S.	121	37°49'N	94°21'W
Nevada, state, U.S. (nĕ-vȧ'dȧ)	104	39°30'N	117°00'W
Nevada, Sierra, mts., Spain (syĕr'rä nä-vä'dhä)	156	37°01'N	3°28'W
Nevada, Sierra, mts., U.S. (sē-ĕ'r-rä nē-vä'dȧ)	106	39°20'N	120°05'W
Nevado, Cerro el, mtn., Col. (sĕ'r-rô-ĕl-nĕ-vä'dô)	142a	4°02'N	74°08'W
Neva Stantsiya, Russia (nyĕ-vä' stän'tsĭ-yȧ)	186c	59°53'N	30°30'E
Neve, Serra da, mts., Ang.	236	13°40'S	13°20'E
Nevel', Russia (nyĕ'vĕl)	180	56°03'N	29°57'E
Neveri, r., Ven. (nĕ-vĕ-rē)	143b	10°13'N	64°18'W
Nevers, Fr. (nĕ-vår')	161	46°59'N	3°10'E
Neves, Braz.	144b	22°51'S	43°06'W
Nevesinje, Bos. (nĕ-vĕ'sēn-yĕ)	175	43°15'N	18°08'E
Nevinnomyssk, Russia	182	44°38'N	41°56'E
Nevis, i., St. K./N. (nē'vĭs)	129	17°05'N	62°38'W
Nevis, Ben, mtn., Scot., U.K. (bĕn)	160	56°47'N	5°00'W
Nevis Peak, mtn., St. K./N.	133b	17°11'N	62°33'W
Nevşehir, Tur. (nĕv-shĕ'hĕr)	163	38°40'N	34°35'E
Nev'yansk, Russia (nĕv-yänsk')	178	57°29'N	60°14'E
New, r., Va., U.S. (nū)	125	37°20'N	80°35'W
Newala, Tan.	237	10°56'S	39°18'E
New Albany, In., U.S. (nû ôl'bȧ-nĭ)	111h	38°17'N	85°49'W
New Albany, Ms., U.S.	125	34°28'N	39°00'W
New Amsterdam, Guy. (ăm'stĕr-dăm)	143	6°14'N	57°30'W
Newark, Eng., U.K. (nū'ĕrk)	158a	53°04'N	0°49'W
Newark, Ca., U.S. (nū'ĕrk)	116b	37°32'N	122°02'W
Newark, De., U.S. (nōō'ärk)	109	39°40'N	75°45'W
Newark, N.J., U.S. (nōō'ûrk)	105	40°44'N	74°10'W
Newark, N.Y., U.S. (nū'ĕrk)	109	43°05'N	77°10'W
Newark, Oh., U.S.	108	40°05'N	82°25'W
Newaygo, Mi., U.S. (nū'wā-go)	108	43°25'N	85°50'W
New Bedford, Ma., U.S. (bĕd'fērd)	105	41°35'N	70°55'W
Newberg, Or., U.S. (nū'bûrg)	108	45°17'N	122°58'W
New Bern, N.C., U.S. (bûrn)	105	35°05'N	77°05'W
Newbern, Tn., U.S.	124	36°05'N	89°12'W
Newberry, Mi., U.S. (nū'bĕr-ĭ)	113	46°22'N	85°31'W
Newberry, S.C., U.S.	125	34°15'N	81°40'W
New Boston, Mi., U.S. (bôs'tŭn)	111b	42°10'N	83°24'W
New Boston, Oh., U.S.	108	38°45'N	82°55'W
New Braunfels, Tx., U.S. (nū broun'fĕls)	122	29°43'N	98°07'W
New Brighton, Mn., U.S. (brī'tŭn)	117g	45°04'N	93°12'W
New Brighton, Pa., U.S.	111e	40°34'N	80°18'W
New Britain, Ct., U.S. (brĭt''n)	109	41°40'N	72°45'W
New Britain, i., Pap. N. Gui.	213	6°45'S	149°38'E
New Brunswick, N.J., U.S. (brŭnz'wĭk)	110a	40°29'N	74°27'W
New Brunswick, prov., Can.	91	47°14'N	66°30'W
Newburg, In., U.S.	108	38°00'N	87°25'W
Newburg, Mo., U.S.	121	37°54'N	91°53'W
Newburgh, N.Y., U.S.	109	41°30'N	74°00'W
Newburgh Heights, Oh., U.S.	111d	41°27'N	81°40'W
Newbury, Eng., U.K. (nū'bĕr-ĭ)	164	51°24'N	1°26'W
Newbury, Ma., U.S.	101a	42°48'N	70°52'W
Newbury, co., Eng., U.K.	158b	51°25'N	1°15'W
Newburyport, Ma., U.S. (nū'bĕr-ĭ-pōrt)	101a	42°48'N	70°53'W
New Caledonia, dep., Oc.	219	21°28'S	164°40'E
New Canaan, Ct., U.S. (kā-nȧn)	110a	41°06'N	73°30'W
New Carlisle, Can. (kär-līl')	91	48°01'N	65°20'W
Newcastle, Austl. (nū-kȧs''l)	222	33°00'S	151°55'E
Newcastle, Can.	91	47°00'N	65°34'W
New Castle, De., U.S.	109	39°40'N	75°35'W
New Castle, In., U.S.	108	39°55'N	85°25'W
New Castle, Oh., U.S.	108	40°20'N	82°10'W
New Castle, Pa., U.S.	108	41°00'N	80°25'W
Newcastle, Tx., U.S.	120	33°13'N	98°44'W
Newcastle, Wy., U.S.	112	43°51'N	104°11'W
Newcastle under Lyme, Eng., U.K. (nû-kȧs''l) (nū-kȧs''l)	158a	53°01'N	2°14'W
Newcastle upon Tyne, Eng., U.K.	154	55°00'N	1°45'W
Newcastle Waters, Austl. (wô'tĕrz)	218	17°10'S	133°25'E
Newcomerstown, Oh., U.S. (nū'kŭm-ĕrz-toun)	108	40°15'N	81°40'W
New Croton Reservoir, res., N.Y., U.S. (krŏ'tôn)	110a	41°15'N	73°47'W
New Delhi, India (dĕl'hī)	199	28°43'N	77°18'E
Newell, S.D., U.S. (nū'ĕl)	112	44°43'N	103°28'W
New England Range, mts., Austl. (nû ĭŋ'glănd)	221	29°32'S	152°30'E
Newenham, Cape, c., Ak., U.S. (nū-ĕn-hăm)	103	58°40'N	162°32'W
Newfane, N.Y., U.S. (nū-fān)	111c	43°17'N	78°44'W
Newfoundland, i., Can.	93a	48°30'N	56°00'W
Newfoundland and Labrador, prov., Can.	91	48°15'N	56°53'W
Newgate, Can. (nů'gāt)	95	49°01'N	115°10'W
New Georgia, i., Sol. Is. (jôr'jĭ-ȧ)	221	8°08'S	158°00'E
New Georgia Group, is., Sol. Is.	214e	8°30'S	157°20'E
New Georgia Sound, strt., Sol. Is.	214e	8°00'S	158°10'E
New Glasgow, Can. (glȧs'gō)	91	45°35'N	62°36'W
New Guinea, i. (gĭne)	213	5°45'S	140°00'E
Newhalem, Wa., U.S. (nū hā'lŭm)	114	48°44'N	121°11'W
New Hampshire, state, U.S. (hămp'shĭr)	105	43°55'N	71°40'W
New Hampton, Ia., U.S. (hămp'tŭn)	113	43°03'N	92°20'W
New Hanover, S. Afr. (hăn'ôvĕr)	233c	29°23'S	30°32'E
New Hanover, i., Pap. N. Gui.	213	2°37'S	150°15'E
New Harmony, In., U.S. (nū här'mô-nĭ)	108	38°10'N	87°55'W
New Haven, Ct., U.S. (hā'vĕn)	105	41°20'N	72°55'W
New Haven, In., U.S. (nū hāv''n)	108	41°05'N	85°00'W
New Hebrides, is., Vanuatu	221	16°00'S	167°00'E
New Holland, Eng., U.K. (hŏl'ănd)	158a	53°42'N	0°21'W
New Holland, N.C., U.S.	125	35°27'N	76°14'W
New Hope Mountain, mtn., Al., U.S. (hōp)	110h	33°23'N	86°45'W
New Hudson, Mi., U.S. (hŭd'sŭn)	111b	42°30'N	83°36'W
New Iberia, La., U.S. (ī-bē'rĭ-ȧ)	123	30°00'N	91°50'W
Newington, Can. (nū'ĕng-tŏn)	102c	45°07'N	75°00'W
New Ireland, i., Pap. N. Gui. (ĭr'lănd)	213	3°15'S	152°30'E
New Jersey, state, U.S. (jûr'zĭ)	105	40°30'N	74°50'W
New Kensington, Pa., U.S. (kĕn'zĭng-tŭn)	111e	40°34'N	79°35'W
Newkirk, Ok., U.S. (nū'kûrk)	121	36°52'N	97°03'W
New Lenox, Il., U.S. (lĕn'ŭk)	111a	41°31'N	87°58'W
New Lexington, Oh., U.S. (lĕk'sĭng-tŭn)	108	39°40'N	82°10'W
New Lisbon, Wi., U.S. (lĭz'bŭn)	113	43°52'N	90°11'W
New Liskeard, Can.	99	47°30'N	79°40'W
New London, Ct., U.S. (lŭn'dŭn)	109	41°20'N	72°05'W
New London, Wi., U.S.	113	44°24'N	88°45'W
New Madrid, Mo., U.S. (măd'rĭd)	121	36°34'N	89°31'W
Newman's Grove, Ne., U.S. (nū'măn grōv)	112	41°46'N	97°44'W
Newmarket, Can. (nū'mär-kĕt)	99	44°00'N	79°30'W
New Martinsville, W.V., U.S. (mär'tĭnz-vĭl)	108	39°35'N	80°50'W
New Meadows, Id., U.S.	114	44°58'N	116°20'W
New Mexico, state, U.S. (mĕk'sĭ-kō)	104	34°30'N	107°10'W
New Mills, Eng., U.K. (mĭlz)	158a	53°22'N	2°00'W
New Munster, Wi., U.S. (mŭn'stĕr)	111a	42°35'N	88°13'W
Newnan, Ga., U.S. (nū'năn)	124	33°22'N	84°47'W
New Norfolk, Austl. (nôr'fŏk)	219	42°50'S	147°17'E
New Orleans, La., U.S. (ôr'lē-ănz)	105	30°00'N	90°05'W
New Philadelphia, Oh., U.S. (fĭl-ȧ-dĕl'fĭ-ȧ)	108	40°30'N	81°30'W
New Plymouth, N.Z. (plĭm'ŭth)	221a	39°04'S	174°13'E
Newport, Austl.	217b	33°39'S	151°19'E
Newport, Eng., U.K. (nū-pôrt)	164	50°41'N	1°25'W
Newport, Eng., U.K.	158a	52°46'N	2°22'W
Newport, Wales, U.K.	161	51°36'N	3°05'W
Newport, Ar., U.S. (nū'pōrt)	121	35°35'N	91°16'W
Newport, Ky., U.S.	105	39°05'N	84°30'W
Newport, Me., U.S.	100	44°49'N	69°20'W
Newport, Mn., U.S.	117g	44°52'N	92°59'W
Newport, N.H., U.S.	109	43°20'N	72°10'W
Newport, Or., U.S.	114	44°39'N	124°02'W
Newport, R.I., U.S.	109	41°29'N	71°16'W
Newport, Tn., U.S.	124	35°55'N	83°12'W
Newport, Vt., U.S.	109	44°55'N	72°15'W
Newport, Wa., U.S.	114	48°12'N	117°01'W
Newport Beach, Ca., U.S. (bēch)	117a	33°36'N	117°55'W
Newport News, Va., U.S.	105	36°59'N	76°24'W
New Prague, Mn., U.S. (nū prāg)	113	44°33'N	93°35'W
New Providence, i., Bah. (prŏv'ĭ-dĕns)	134	25°00'N	77°25'W

328 New Richmond – Norman PRONOUNCING INDEX

PLACE (Pronunciation)	PAGE	LAT.	LONG.
New Richmond, Oh., U.S. (rĭch′mŭnd)	108	38°55′N	84°15′W
New Richmond, Wi., U.S.	113	45°07′N	92°34′W
New Roads, La., U.S. (rōds)	123	30°42′N	91°26′W
New Rochelle, N.Y., U.S. (rū-shĕl′)	110a	40°55′N	73°47′W
New Rockford, N.D., U.S. (rŏk′fērd)	112	47°40′N	99°08′W
New Ross, Ire. (rôs)	164	52°25′N	6°55′W
New Sarepta, Can.	102g	53°17′N	113°09′W
New Siberian Islands *see* Novosibirskiye Ostrova, is., Russia	179	74°00′N	140°30′E
New Smyrna Beach, Fl., U.S. (smûr′nȧ)	125	29°00′N	80°57′W
New South Wales, state, Austl. (wālz)	219	32°45′S	146°14′E
Newton, Can. (nū′tŭn)	102f	49°56′N	98°04′W
Newton, Eng., U.K.	158a	53°27′N	2°37′W
Newton, Ia., U.S.	113	41°42′N	93°04′W
Newton, Il., U.S.	108	39°00′N	88°10′W
Newton, Ks., U.S.	121	38°03′N	97°22′W
Newton, Ma., U.S.	101a	42°21′N	71°13′W
Newton, Ms., U.S.	124	32°18′N	89°10′W
Newton, N.C., U.S.	125	35°40′N	81°19′W
Newton, N.J., U.S.	110a	41°03′N	74°45′W
Newton, Tx., U.S.	123	30°47′N	93°45′W
Newtonsville, Oh., U.S. (nū′tŭnz-vĭl)	111f	39°11′N	84°04′W
Newtown, N.D., U.S. (nū′toun)	112	47°57′N	102°25′W
Newtown, Oh., U.S.	111f	39°08′N	84°22′W
Newtown, Pa., U.S.	110f	40°13′N	74°56′W
Newtownards, N. Ire., U.K. (nu-t′n-ardz′)	164	54°35′N	5°39′W
New Ulm, Mn., U.S. (ŭlm)	113	44°18′N	94°27′W
New Waterford, Can. (wô′tēr-fērd)	91	46°15′N	60°05′W
New Westminster, Can. (wĕst′mĭn-stēr)	95	49°12′N	122°55′W
New York, N.Y., U.S. (yôrk)	105	40°40′N	73°58′W
New York, state, U.S.	105	42°45′N	78°05′W
New Zealand, nation, Oc. (zē′lȧnd)	221a	42°00′S	175°00′E
Nexapa, r., Mex. (nĕks-ä′pä)	130	18°32′N	98°29′W
Neya-gawa, Japan (nå′yä gä′wä)	211b	34°47′N	135°38′E
Neyshābūr, Iran	198	36°06′N	58°45′E
Neyva, r., Russia (nĕy′vȧ)	186a	57°39′N	60°37′E
Nezahualcóyotl, Mex.	131a	19°27′N	99°03′W
Nez Perce, Id., U.S. (nĕz′ pûrs′)	114	46°16′N	116°15′W
Nez Perce Indian Reservation, I.R., Id., U.S.	114	46°20′N	116°30′W
Ngami, l., Bots. (n′gä′mē)	232	20°56′S	22°31′E
Ngangerabeli Plain, pl., Kenya	237	1°20′S	40°10′E
Ngangla Ringco, l., China (ŋäŋ-lä rĭŋ-tswo)	202	31°42′N	82°53′E
Ngarimbi, Tan.	237	8°28′S	38°36′E
Ngoko, r., Afr.	236	1°55′N	15°53′E
Ngol-Kedju Hill, mtn., Cam.	235	6°20′N	9°45′E
Ngong, Kenya (′n-gông)	232	1°27′S	36°39′E
Ngounié, r., Gabon	236	1°15′S	10°43′E
Ngoywa, Tan.	237	5°56′S	32°48′E
Ngqeleni, S. Afr. (′ng-kĕ-lā′nē)	233c	31°41′S	29°04′E
Nguigmi, Niger (′n-gēg′mē)	231	14°15′N	13°07′E
Ngurore, Nig.	235	9°18′N	12°14′E
Nguru, Nig. (′n-gōō′rōō)	230	12°53′N	10°26′E
Nguru Mountains, mts., Tan.	237	6°10′S	37°35′E
Nha Trang, Viet. (nyä-träng′)	212	12°08′N	108°56′E
Niafounke, Mali	230	16°03′N	4°17′W
Niagara, Wi., U.S. (nī-ăg′ȧ-rȧ)	113	45°45′N	88°05′W
Niagara, r., N.A.	111c	43°12′N	79°03′W
Niagara Falls, Can.	111c	43°05′N	79°05′W
Niagara Falls, N.Y., U.S.	105	43°06′N	79°02′W
Niagara-on-the-Lake, Can.	102d	43°16′N	79°05′W
Niakaramandougou, C. Iv.	234	8°40′N	5°17′W
Niamey, Niger (nē-ä-må′)	230	13°31′N	2°07′E
Niamtougou, Togo	234	9°46′N	1°06′E
Niangara, D.R.C. (nē-äŋ-gä′rȧ)	231	3°42′N	27°52′E
Niangua, r., Mo., U.S. (nī-ăŋ′gwȧ)	121	37°30′N	93°05′W
Nias, Pulau, i., Indon. (nē′äs′)	212	0°58′N	97°43′E
Nibe, Den. (nē′bē)	166	56°57′N	9°36′E
Nicaragua, nation, N.A. (nĭk-ȧ-rä′gwȧ)	128	12°45′N	86°15′W
Nicaragua, Lago de, l., Nic. (lä′gō dĕ)	128	11°45′N	85°28′W
Nicastro, Italy (nē-käs′trō)	163	38°39′N	16°15′E
Nicchehabin, Punta, c., Mex. (pōō′n-tä-nĕk-chĕ-ä-bē′n)	132a	19°50′N	87°20′W
Nice, Fr. (nēs)	154	43°42′N	7°21′E
Nicheng, China (nē-chŭŋ)	207b	30°54′N	121°48′E
Nichicun, l., Can. (nĭch′ĭ-kŭn)	93	53°07′N	72°10′W
Nicholas Channel, strt., N.A. (nĭk′ô-lȧs)	134	23°30′N	80°20′W
Nicholasville, Ky., U.S. (nĭk′ô-lȧs-vĭl)	108	37°55′N	84°35′W
Nicobar Islands, is., India (nĭk-ô-bär′)	212	8°28′N	94°04′E
Nicolai Mountain, mtn., Or., U.S. (nē-cō lī′)	116c	46°05′N	123°27′W
Nicolás Romero, Mex. (nē-kô-lá′s rô-mĕ′rô)	131a	19°38′N	99°20′W
Nicolet, Lake, l., Mi., U.S. (nĭ′kô-lĕt)	117k	46°22′N	84°14′W
Nicolls Town, Bah.	134	25°10′N	78°00′W
Nicols, Mn., U.S. (nĭk′ĕls)	117g	44°50′N	93°12′W
Nicomeki, r., Can.	116d	49°04′N	122°47′W
Nicosia, Cyp. (nē-kô-sē′ȧ)	198	35°10′N	33°22′E
Nicoya, C.R. (nē-kō′yä)	132	10°08′N	85°27′W
Nicoya, Golfo de, b., C.R. (gôl-fô-dĕ)	132	10°03′N	85°04′W
Nicoya, Península de, pen., C.R.	132	10°05′N	86°00′W
Nidzica, Pol. (nē-jēt′sȧ)	169	53°21′N	20°30′E
Niedere Tauern, mts., Aus.	168	47°15′N	13°41′E
Niederkrüchten, Ger. (nē′dĕr-krük-tĕn)	171c	51°12′N	6°14′E
Niederösterreich, state, Aus.	159e	48°24′N	16°20′E
Niedersachsen (Lower Saxony), state, Ger. (nē′dĕr-zäĸ-sĕn)	159c	53°30′N	9°30′E
Niellim, Chad	235	9°42′N	17°49′E
Nienburg, Ger. (nē′ĕn-bŏorgh)	168	52°40′N	9°15′E
Nietverdiend, S. Afr.	238c	25°02′S	26°10′E
Nieuw Nickerie, Sur. (nē-nē′kĕ-rē′)	143	5°51′N	57°00′W
Nieves, Mex. (nyā′vås)	130	24°00′N	102°57′W
Niğde, Tur. (nĭg′dĕ)	163	37°55′N	34°40′E
Nigel, S. Afr. (nī′jĕl)	238c	26°26′S	28°27′E
Niger, nation, Afr. (nī′jēr)	230	18°02′N	8°30′E
Niger, r., Afr.	230	8°00′N	6°00′E
Niger Delta, d., Nig.	235	4°45′N	5°20′E
Nigeria, nation, Afr. (nī-jē′rĭ-ȧ)	230	8°57′N	6°30′E
Nihoa, i., Hi., U.S.	126b	23°15′N	161°30′W
Nii, i., Japan (nē)	211	34°26′N	139°23′E
Niigata, Japan (nē′ē-gä′tȧ)	205	37°47′N	139°04′E
Ni′ihau, i., Hi., U.S. (nē′ē-hä′ōō)	106c	21°50′N	160°05′W
Niimi, Japan (nē′mē)	211	34°59′N	133°28′E
Niiza, Japan	211a	35°48′N	139°34′E
Nijmegen, Neth. (nī′må-gĕn)	165	51°50′N	5°52′E
Nikitinka, Russia (nē-kĭ′tĭn-kȧ)	176	55°33′N	33°19′E
Nikolayevka, Russia (nē-kô-lä′yĕf-kȧ)	186c	59°29′N	29°48′E
Nikolayevka, Russia	210	48°37′N	134°09′E
Nikolayevskiy, Russia	181	50°00′N	45°30′E
Nikolayevsk-na-Amure, Russia	179	53°18′N	140°49′E
Nikol′sk, Russia (nē-kôlsk′)	178	59°30′N	45°40′E
Nikol′skoye, Russia (nē-kôl′skô-yĕ)	186c	59°27′N	30°00′E
Nikopol, Blg. (nē′kô-pŏl′)	163	43°41′N	24°52′E
Nikopol′, Ukr.	181	47°36′N	34°24′E
Nilahue, r., Chile (nē-lȧ′wĕ)	141b	34°36′S	71°50′W
Nile, r., Afr. (nīl)	231	27°30′N	31°00′E
Niles, Mi., U.S. (nīlz)	108	41°50′N	86°15′W
Niles, Oh., U.S.	108	41°15′N	80°45′W
Nileshwar, India	203	12°08′N	74°14′E
Nilgiri Hills, hills, India	203	12°05′N	76°22′E
Nilópolis, Braz. (nē-lô′pō-lēs)	141a	22°48′S	43°25′W
Nīmach, India	202	24°32′N	74°51′E
Nimba, Mont, mtn., Afr. (nĭm′bȧ)	230	7°40′N	8°33′W
Nimba Mountains, mts., Afr.	234	7°30′N	8°35′W
Nîmes, Fr. (nēm)	154	43°49′N	4°22′E
Nimrod Reservoir, res., Ar., U.S. (nĭm′rŏd)	121	34°58′N	93°46′W
Nimule, Sudan (nē-mōō′lå)	231	3°38′N	32°12′E
Ninda, Ang.	236	14°47′S	21°24′E
Nine Mile Creek, r., Ut., U.S. (mīn′īmōd′)	119	39°50′N	110°30′W
Ninety Mile Beach, cst., Austl.	221	38°20′S	147°30′E
Nineveh, Iraq (nĭn′ĕ-vȧ)	198	36°30′N	43°10′E
Ning′an, China (nĭŋ-än)	205	44°20′N	129°20′E
Ningbo, China (nĭŋ-bwo)	205	29°56′N	121°30′E
Ningde, China (nĭŋ-dŭ)	205	26°38′N	119°33′E
Ninghai, China (nĭng′hī′)	209	29°20′N	121°20′E
Ninghe, China (nĭŋ-hŭ)	206	39°20′N	117°50′E
Ningjin, China (nĭŋ-jyĭn)	206	37°39′N	116°47′E
Ningjin, China	206	37°37′N	114°55′E
Ningming, China	209	22°22′N	107°06′E
Ningwu, China (nĭng′wōō′)	205	39°00′N	112°12′E
Ningxia Huizu, prov., China (nĭŋ-shyä)	204	37°10′N	106°00′E
Ningyang, China (nĭng′yäng′)	206	35°46′N	116°48′E
Ninh Binh, Viet. (nĕn bĕnk′)	212	20°22′N	106°00′E
Ninigo Group, is., Pap. N. Gui.	213	1°15′S	143°30′E
Ninnescah, r., Ks., U.S. (nĭn′ĕs-kä)	120	37°37′N	98°31′W
Nioaque, Braz. (nēō-ä′-kĕ)	143	21°14′S	55°41′W
Niobrara, r., U.S. (nī-ô-brâr′ȧ)	106	42°46′N	98°46′W
Niokolo Koba, Parc National du, rec., Sen.	234	13°05′N	13°00′W
Nioro du Sahel, Mali (nē-ō′rō)	230	15°15′N	9°35′W
Nipawin, Can.	90	53°22′N	104°00′W
Nipe, Bahía de, b., Cuba (bä-ē′ä-dĕ-nē′pā)	135	20°50′N	75°30′W
Nipe, Sierra de, mts., Cuba (sē-ĕ′r-rȧ-dĕ)	135	20°20′N	75°50′W
Nipigon, Can. (nĭp′ĭ-gŏn)	91	48°58′N	88°17′W
Nipigon, l., Can.	93	49°37′N	89°55′W
Nipigon Bay, b., Can.	98	48°56′N	88°00′W
Nipisiguit, r., Can. (nĭ-pĭ′sĭ-kwĭt)	100	47°26′N	66°15′W
Nipissing, l., Can. (nĭp′ĭ-sĭng)	93	45°59′N	80°19′W
Niquero, Cuba (nē-kā′rō)	134	20°00′N	77°35′W
Nirmali, India	202	26°30′N	86°43′E
Niš, Serb.	154	43°19′N	21°54′E
Nisa, Port. (nē′sȧ)	172	39°32′N	7°41′W
Nišava, r., Eur. (nē′shȧ-vȧ)	175	43°17′N	22°17′E
Nishino, i., Japan (nēsh′ē-nô)	211	36°06′N	132°49′E
Nishinomiya, Japan (nēsh′ē-nô-mē′yȧ)	211b	34°44′N	135°21′E
Nishio, Japan (nēsh′ē-ô)	211	34°50′N	137°01′E
Niska Lake, l., Can. (nĭs′kȧ)	96	55°35′N	108°38′W
Nisko, Pol. (nēs′kô)	169	50°30′N	22°07′E
Nisku, Can. (nĭs-kū′)	102g	53°21′N	113°33′W
Nisqually, r., Wa., U.S. (nĭs-kwôl′ĭ)	114	46°51′N	122°33′W
Nissan, r., Swe.	166	57°06′N	13°22′E
Nisser, l., Nor. (nĭs′ĕr)	166	59°14′N	8°35′E
Nissum Fjord, b., Den.	166	56°24′N	7°35′E
Niterói, Braz. (nē-tĕ-rô′ĭ)	143	22°53′S	43°07′W
Nith, r., Scot., U.K. (nĭth)	164	55°13′N	3°55′W
Nitra, Slvk. (nē′trȧ)	169	48°18′N	18°04′E
Nitra, r., Slvk.	169	48°13′N	18°14′E
Nitro, W.V., U.S. (nī′trô)	108	38°25′N	81°50′W
Niue, dep., Oc. (nĭ′ô)	241	19°50′S	167°00′W
Nivelles, Bel. (nē′vĕl′)	165	50°33′N	4°17′E
Nixon, Tx., U.S. (nĭk′sŭn)	123	29°16′N	97°48′W
Nizāmābād, India	199	18°48′N	78°07′E
Nizhne-Angarsk, Russia (nyĕzh′nyĭ-ŭngärsk′)	179	55°49′N	108°46′E
Nizhne-Chirskaya, Russia	181	48°20′N	42°50′E
Nizhne-Kolymsk, Russia (kô-lēmsk′)	179	68°32′N	160°56′E
Nizhneudinsk, Russia (nĕzh′nyĭ-ōōdēnsk′)	179	54°58′N	99°15′E
Nizhniye Sergi, Russia (nyēzh′ nyē sĕr′gē)	180	56°41′N	59°19′E
Nizhniy Novgorod (Gor′kiy), Russia	178	56°15′N	44°05′E
Nizhniy Tagil, Russia (tŭgēl′)	178	57°54′N	59°59′E
Nizhnyaya Kur′ya, Russia (nyē′zhnyȧ-yȧ kōōr′yȧ)	186a	58°01′N	56°00′E
Nizhnyaya Salda, Russia (nyē′zhnya′ya säl′da′)	186a	58°05′N	60°43′E
Nizhnyaya Taymyra, r., Russia	184	72°30′N	95°18′E
Nizhnyaya Tunguska, r., Russia	179	64°13′N	91°30′E
Nizhnyaya Tura, Russia (tōō′rȧ)	186a	58°38′N	59°50′E
Nizhnyaya Us′va, Russia (ô′vȧ)	186a	59°05′N	58°53′E
Nizhyn, Ukr.	181	51°03′N	31°52′E
Nízke Tatry, mts., Slvk.	169	48°57′N	19°18′E
Njazidja, i., Com.	233	11°44′S	42°38′E
Njombe, Tan.	237	9°20′S	34°46′E
Njurunda, Swe. (nyōō-rŏon′dȧ)	166	62°15′N	17°24′E
Nkala Mission, Zam.	237	15°55′S	26°00′E
Nkandla, S. Afr. (′n-känd′lä)	233c	28°40′S	31°06′E
Nkawkaw, Ghana	234	6°33′N	0°47′W
Nkhota, Mwi. (kō-tȧ kō-tȧ)	232	12°52′S	34°16′E
Noākhāli, Bngl.	199	22°52′N	91°08′E
Noatak, Ak., U.S. (nō-ȧ′tȧk)	103	67°22′N	163°28′W
Noatak, r., Ak., U.S.	103	67°58′N	162°15′W
Nobeoka, Japan (nō-bå-ō′kȧ)	210	32°36′N	131°41′E
Noblesville, In., U.S. (nō′bl′z-vĭl)	108	40°00′N	86°00′W
Nobleton, Can. (nō′bl′tŭn)	102d	43°54′N	79°39′W
Nocera Inferiore, Italy (ēn-fĕ-ryô′rē)	173c	40°30′N	14°38′E
Nochistlán, Mex. (nô-chēs-tlän′)	130	21°23′N	102°52′W
Nochixtlán, Mex. (ä-sŏn-syōn′)	131	17°28′N	97°12′W
Nogales, Mex. (nō-gä′lĕs)	131	18°49′N	97°09′W
Nogales, Mex.	128	31°15′N	111°00′W
Nogales, Az., U.S. (nô-gä′lĕs)	104	31°20′N	110°55′W
Nogal Valley, val., Som. (nô′gȧl)	238a	8°30′N	47°50′E
Nogent-le-Roi, Fr. (nŏ-zhŏn-lē-rwä′)	171b	48°39′N	1°32′E
Nogent-le-Rotrou, Fr. (rŏ-trōō′)	170	48°22′N	0°47′E
Noginsk, Russia (nô-gēnsk′)	180	55°52′N	38°28′E
Noguera Pallaresa, r., Spain	173	42°18′N	1°03′E
Noia, Spain	172	42°46′N	8°50′W
Noirmoutier, Île de, i., Fr. (nwȧr-mōō-tyā′)	161	47°03′N	3°08′W
Nojima-Zaki, c., Japan (nō′jē-mä zä-kē)	211	34°54′N	139°48′E
Nokomis, Il., U.S. (nô-kō′mĭs)	108	39°15′N	89°10′W
Nola, Italy (nô′lä)	174	40°41′N	14°32′E
Nolinsk, Russia (nô-lēnsk′)	180	57°32′N	49°50′E
Noma Misaki, c., Japan (nō′mä mē′sä-kē)	211	31°25′N	130°09′E
Nombre de Dios, Mex. (nôm-brĕ-dĕ-dyô′s)	130	23°50′N	104°14′W
Nombre de Dios, Pan. (nô′m-brĕ)	133	9°34′N	79°28′W
Nome, Ak., U.S. (nōm)	106a	64°30′N	165°20′W
Nonacho, l., Can.	92	61°48′N	111°20′W
Nong′an, China (nôŋ-än)	208	44°25′N	125°10′E
Nongoma, S. Afr. (nŏn-gō′mȧ)	232	27°48′S	31°45′E
Nooksack, Wa., U.S. (nŏŏk′săk)	116d	48°55′N	122°19′W
Nooksack, r., Wa., U.S.	116d	48°54′N	122°31′W
Noordwijk aan Zee, Neth.	159a	52°14′N	4°25′E
Noordzee Kanaal, can., Neth.	159a	52°27′N	4°42′E
Nootka, i., Can. (nōōt′kȧ)	92	49°32′N	126°42′W
Nootka Sound, strt., Can.	94	49°33′N	126°38′W
Nóqui, Ang. (nô-kē′)	232	5°51′S	13°25′E
Nor, r., China (nou′)	210	46°55′N	132°45′E
Nora, Swe.	166	59°32′N	14°56′E
Nora, In., U.S. (nō′rä)	111g	39°54′N	86°08′W
Noranda, Can.	99	48°15′N	79°01′W
Norbeck, Md., U.S. (nôr′bĕk)	110e	39°06′N	77°05′W
Norborne, Mo., U.S. (nôr′bôrn)	121	39°17′N	93°39′W
Norco, Ca., U.S. (nôr′kô)	117a	33°57′N	117°33′W
Norcross, Ga., U.S. (nôr′krôs)	110c	33°56′N	84°13′W
Nord, Riviere du, Can. (rēv-yĕr′ dü nôr)	102a	45°45′N	74°02′W
Nordegg, Can. (nûr′dĕg)	95	52°28′N	116°04′W
Norden, Ger. (nôr′dĕn)	168	53°35′N	7°14′E
Norderney, i., Ger. (nōr′dĕr-nĕy)	168	53°45′N	6°58′E
Nordfjord, b., Nor. (nô′fyôr)	166	61°50′N	5°35′E
Nordhausen, Ger. (nôrt′hau-zĕn)	161	51°30′N	10°48′E
Nordhorn, Ger. (nôrt′hôrn)	168	52°26′N	7°05′E
Nord Kapp, c., Nor.	180	71°11′N	25°48′E
Nordland, Wa., U.S. (nôrd′lȧnd)	116a	48°03′N	122°41′W
Nördlingen, Ger. (nûrt′lĭng-ĕn)	168	48°51′N	10°30′E
Nord-Ostsee Kanal (Kiel Canal), can., Ger. (nōrd-ōzt-zā) (kēl)	168	54°03′N	9°23′E
Nordrhein-Westfalen (North Rhine-Westphalia), state, Ger. (nôrd′hīn-vĕst-fä-lĕn)	171c	51°40′N	7°00′E
Nordvik, Russia (nôrd′vēk)	179	73°57′N	111°15′E
Nore, r., Ire. (nōr)	164	52°34′N	7°15′W
Norfolk, Ma., U.S. (nôr′fŏk)	101a	42°07′N	71°19′W
Norfolk, Ne., U.S.	104	42°10′N	97°25′W
Norfolk, Va., U.S.	105	36°55′N	76°15′W
Norfolk, i., Oc.	241	27°10′S	166°50′E
Norfork, Lake, l., Ar., U.S.	121	36°25′N	92°09′W
Noril′sk, Russia (nô rēlsk′)	178	69°00′N	87°11′E
Normal, Il., U.S. (nôr′mȧl)	108	40°35′N	89°00′W
Norman, r., Austl.	221	18°27′S	141°29′E
Norman, Lake, res., N.C., U.S.	107	35°30′N	80°53′W

ăt; finăl; rāte; senåte; ärm; åsk; sofȧ; fâre; ch-choose; dh-as th in other; bē; ēvent; bĕt; recĕnt; cratēr; g-gō; gh-guttural g; bĭt; ĭ-short neutral; rīde; ĸ-guttural k as ch in German ich;

PRONOUNCING INDEX Normandie – Nowa Sól 329

PLACE (Pronunciation)	PAGE	LAT.	LONG.
Normandie, hist. reg., Fr. (nŏr-mäɴ-dē´)	170	49°02'N	0°17'E
Normandie, Collines de, hills, Fr. (kō-lēn´dĕ-nōr-män-dē´)	170	48°46'N	0°50'W
Normandy *see* Normandie, hist. reg., Fr.	170	49°02'N	0°17'E
Normanton, Austl. (nôr´măn-tŭn)	219	17°45'S	141°10'E
Normanton, Eng., U.K.	158a	53°40'N	1°21'W
Norman Wells, Can.	90	65°26'N	127°00'W
Nornalup, Austl. (nôr-năl´ŭp)	218	35°00'S	117°00'E
Nørresundby, Den. (nû-rĕ-sòn´bü)	166	57°04'N	9°55'E
Norris, Tn., U.S. (nŏr´ĭs)	124	36°09'N	84°05'W
Norris Lake, res., Tn., U.S.	107	36°17'N	84°10'W
Norristown, Pa., U.S. (nŏr´ĭs-town)	110f	40°07'N	75°21'W
Norrköping, Swe. (nôr´chûp´ĭng)	154	58°37'N	16°10'E
Norrtälje, Swe. (nôr-tĕl´yĕ)	160	59°47'N	18°39'E
Norseman, Austl. (nôrs´măn)	218	32°15'S	122°00'E
Norte, Punta, c., Arg. (pōō´n-tä-nŏr´tĕ)	141c	36°17'S	56°46'W
Norte, Serra do, mts., Braz. (sĕ´r-rä-dô-nôr´te)	143	12°04'S	59°08'W
North, Cape, c., Can.	101	47°02'N	60°25'W
North Adams, Ma., U.S. (ăd´ămz)	109	42°40'N	73°05'W
Northam, Austl. (nôr-dhăm)	218	31°50'S	116°45'E
Northam, S. Afr. (nôr´thăm)	238c	24°52'S	27°16'E
North America, cont.	89	45°00'N	100°00'W
North American Basin, deep (à-mĕr´ĭ-kăn)	4	23°45'N	62°45'W
Northampton, Austl. (nôr-thămp´tŭn)	218	28°22'S	114°45'E
Northampton, Eng., U.K. (nôrth-ămp´tŭn)	161	52°14'N	0°56'W
Northampton, Ma., U.S.	109	42°20'N	72°45'W
Northampton, Pa., U.S.	109	40°45'N	75°30'W
Northamptonshire, co., Eng., U.K.	158a	52°25'N	0°47'W
North Andaman Island, i., India (ăn-dà-măn´)	212	13°15'N	93°30'E
North Andover, Ma., U.S. (ăn´dô-vēr)	101a	42°42'N	71°07'W
North Arm, mth., Can. (ärm)	116d	49°13'N	123°01'W
North Atlanta, Ga., U.S. (ăt-lăn´tà)	110c	33°52'N	84°20'W
North Attleboro, Ma., U.S. (ăt´'l-bŭr-ô)	110b	41°59'N	71°18'W
North Baltimore, Oh., U.S. (bôl´tĭ-môr)	108	41°10'N	83°40'W
North Basque, Tx., U.S. (băsk)	122	31°56'N	98°01'W
North Battleford, Can. (băt´'l-fērd)	90	52°47'N	108°17'W
North Bay, Can.	91	46°13'N	79°26'W
North Bend, Or., U.S. (bĕnd)	114	43°23'N	124°13'W
North Berwick, Me., U.S. (bûr´wĭk)	100	43°18'N	70°46'W
North Bight, b., Bah. (bīt)	134	24°30'N	77°40'W
North Bimini, i., Bah. (bĭ´mĭ-nē)	134	25°45'N	79°20'W
North Borneo *see* Sabah, hist. reg., Malay.	212	5°10'N	116°25'E
Northborough, Ma., U.S.	101a	42°19'N	71°39'W
Northbridge, Ma., U.S. (nôrth´brĭj)	101a	42°09'N	71°39'W
North Caicos, i., T./C. Is. (kī´kōs)	135	21°55'N	72°00'W
North Cape, c., N.Z.	221a	34°31'S	173°02'E
North Carolina, state, U.S. (kăr-ô-lī´nà)	105	35°40'N	81°30'W
North Cascades National Park, rec., Wa., U.S.	114	48°50'N	120°50'W
North Cat Cay, i., Bah.	134	25°35'N	79°20'W
North Channel, strt., Can.	98	46°10'N	83°20'W
North Channel, strt., U.K.	156	55°15'N	7°56'W
North Charleston, S.C., U.S. (chärlz´tŭn)	125	32°49'N	79°57'W
North Chicago, Il., U.S. (shĭ-kô´gō)	111a	42°19'N	87°51'W
North College Hill, Oh., U.S. (kŏl´ĕj hĭl)	111f	39°13'N	84°33'W
North Concho, Tx., U.S. (kŏn´chō)	122	31°40'N	100°48'W
North Cooking Lake, Can. (kòk´ĭng lāk)	102g	53°28'N	112°57'W
North Dakota, state, U.S. (dà-kō´tà)	104	47°20'N	101°55'W
North Downs, Eng., U.K. (dounz)	164	51°11'N	0°01'W
North Dum-Dum, India	202a	22°38'N	88°23'E
Northeast Cape, c., Ak., U.S. (nôrth-ēst)	103	63°15'N	169°04'W
Northeast Point, c., Bah.	135	21°25'N	73°00'W
Northeast Point, c., Bah.	135	22°45'N	73°50'W
Northeast Providence Channel, strt., Bah. (prŏv´ĭ-dĕns)	134	25°45'N	77°00'W
Northeim, Ger. (nôrt´hīm)	168	51°42'N	9°59'E
North Elbow Cays, is., Bah.	134	23°55'N	80°30'W
Northern Cheyenne Indian Reservation, I.R., Mt., U.S.	115	45°32'N	106°43'W
Northern Dvina *see* Severnaya Dvina, r., Russia	178	63°00'N	42°40'E
Northern Ireland, state, U.K. (ĭr´lănd)	154	54°48'N	7°00'W
Northern Land *see* Severnaya Zemlya, is., Russia	179	79°33'N	101°15'E
Northern Mariana Islands, dep., Oc. (mä-rē-ä´nà)	3	17°20'N	145°00'E
Northern Territory, ter., Austl.	218	18°15'S	133°00'E
Northern Yukon National Park, rec., Can.	103	69°00'N	140°00'W
Northfield, Mn., U.S. (nôrth´fēld)	113	44°28'N	93°11'W
North Flinders Ranges, mts., Austl. (flĭn´dērz)	222	31°55'S	138°45'E
North Foreland, Eng., U.K. (nôrth-fōr´lănd)	165	51°20'N	1°30'E
North Franklin Mountain, mtn., Tx., U.S. (frăŋ´klĭn)	122	31°55'N	106°30'W
North Frisian Islands, is., Eur.	160	55°16'N	8°15'E
North Gamboa, Pan. (găm-bô´ä)	133	9°07'N	79°40'W
North Gower, Can. (gŏw´ēr)	102c	45°08'N	75°43'W
North Hollywood, Ca., U.S. (hŏl´ē-wòd)	117a	34°10'N	118°23'W
North Island, i., N.Z.	221a	37°20'S	173°30'E
North Island, i., Ca., U.S.	118a	32°39'N	117°14'W
North Judson, In., U.S. (jŭd´sŭn)	108	41°15'N	86°50'W
North Kansas City, Mo., U.S. (kăn´zàs)	117f	39°08'N	94°34'W
North Kingstown, R.I., U.S.	110b	41°34'N	71°26'W
North Lincolnshire, co., Eng., U.K.	158a	53°40'N	0°35'W
North Little Rock, Ar., U.S. (lĭt´'l rŏk)	121	34°46'N	92°13'W
North Loup, r., Ne., U.S. (lōōp)	112	42°05'N	100°10'W
North Magnetic Pole, pt. of i.	244	77°19'N	101°49'W
North Manchester, In., U.S. (măn´chĕs-tēr)	108	41°00'N	85°45'W
Northmoor, Mo., U.S. (nôth´mōōr)	117f	39°10'N	94°37'W
North Moose Lake, l., Can.	97	54°09'N	100°20'W
North Mount Lofty Ranges, mts., Austl.	222	33°50'S	138°30'E
North Ogden, Ut., U.S. (ŏg´dĕn)	117b	41°18'N	111°58'W
North Ogden Peak, mtn., Ut., U.S.	117b	41°23'N	111°59'W
North Olmsted, Oh., U.S. (ōlm-stĕd)	111d	41°25'N	81°55'W
North Ossetia, prov., Russia	180	43°00'N	44°15'E
North Pease, r., Tx., U.S. (pēz)	120	34°19'N	100°58'W
North Pender, i., Can. (pĕn´dēr)	116d	48°48'N	123°16'W
North Plains, Or., U.S. (plānz)	116c	45°36'N	123°00'W
North Platte, Ne., U.S. (plăt)	104	41°08'N	100°45'W
North Platte, r., U.S.	106	41°20'N	102°40'W
North Point, c., Barb.	133b	13°22'N	59°36'W
North Point, c., Mi., U.S.	108	45°00'N	83°20'W
North Pole, pt. of i.	244	90°00'N	0°00'
Northport, Al., U.S. (nôrth´pōrt)	124	33°12'N	87°35'W
Northport, N.Y., U.S.	110a	40°53'N	73°20'W
Northport, Wa., U.S.	114	48°53'N	117°47'W
North Reading, Ma., U.S. (rĕd´ĭng)	101a	42°34'N	71°04'W
North Richland Hills, Tx., U.S.	117c	32°50'N	97°13'W
Northridge, Ca., U.S. (nôrth´ridj)	117a	34°14'N	118°32'W
North Ridgeville, Oh., U.S. (rĭj-vĭl)	111d	41°23'N	82°01'W
North Ronaldsay, i., Scot., U.K.	164a	59°21'N	2°23'W
North Royalton, Oh., U.S. (roi´ăl-tŭn)	111d	41°19'N	81°44'W
North Saint Paul, Mn., U.S. (sānt pôl´)	113	45°01'N	92°59'W
North Santiam, r., Or., U.S. (săn´tyăm)	114	44°42'N	122°50'W
North Saskatchewan, r., Can. (săn-kăch´ē-wän)	92	54°00'N	111°30'W
North Sea, Eur.	154	56°09'N	3°16'E
North Skunk, r., Ia., U.S. (skŭnk)	113	41°39'N	92°46'W
North Stradbroke Island, i., Austl. (străd´brōk)	221	27°45'S	154°18'E
North Sydney, Can. (sĭd´nē)	101	46°13'N	60°15'W
North Taranaki Bight, N.Z. (tá-rá-nä´kĭ bīt)	221a	38°40'S	174°00'E
North Tarrytown, N.Y., U.S. (tăr´ĭ-toun)	110a	41°05'N	73°52'W
North Thompson, r., Can.	95	50°50'N	120°10'W
North Tonawanda, N.Y., U.S. (tŏn-à-wŏn´dà)	111c	43°02'N	78°53'W
North Truchas Peaks, mtn., N.M., U.S. (trōō´chäs)	106	35°58'N	105°40'W
North Twillingate, i., Can. (twĭl´ĭn-gāt)	100	35°58'N	105°37'W
North Uist, i., Scot., U.K. (ū´ĭst)	164	57°37'N	7°22'W
Northumberland, N.H., U.S.	109	44°30'N	71°30'W
Northumberland Islands, is., Austl.	221	21°42'S	151°30'E
Northumberland Strait, strt., Can. (nôr thŭm´bēr-lănd)	100	46°25'N	64°20'W
North Umpqua, r., Or., U.S. (ŭmp´kwă)	114	43°20'N	122°50'W
North Vancouver, Can. (văn-kōō´vēr)	90	49°19'N	123°04'W
North Vernon, In., U.S. (vûr´nŭn)	108	39°05'N	85°45'W
Northville, Mi., U.S. (nôrth-vĭl)	111b	42°26'N	83°28'W
North Wales, Pa., U.S. (wālz)	110f	40°12'N	75°16'W
North West Cape, c., Austl. (nôrth´wĕst)	220	21°50'S	112°25'E
Northwest Cape Fear, r., N.C., U.S. (căp fēr)	125	34°34'N	79°46'W
North West Gander, r., Can. (găn´dēr)	101	48°40'N	55°15'W
Northwest Providence Channel, strt., Bah. (prŏv´ĭ-dĕns)	134	26°15'N	78°45'W
Northwest Territories, ter., Can. (tĕr´ĭ-tō´rĭs)	90	65°00'N	120°00'W
Northwich, Eng., U.K. (nôrth´wĭch)	158a	53°15'N	2°31'W
North Wilkesboro, N.C., U.S. (wĭlks´bûrô)	125	36°08'N	81°10'W
Northwood, Ia., U.S. (nôrth´wòd)	113	43°26'N	93°13'W
Northwood, N.D., U.S.	112	47°44'N	97°36'W
North Yamhill, r., Or., U.S. (yăm´ hĭl)	116c	45°22'N	123°21'W
North York, Can.	99	43°47'N	79°25'W
North York Moors, for., Eng., U.K. (yôrk mòrz´)	164	54°20'N	0°40'W
North Yorkshire, co., Eng., U.K.	158a	53°50'N	1°10'W
Norton, Ks., U.S. (nôr´tŭn)	120	39°40'N	99°54'W
Norton, Ma., U.S.	110b	41°58'N	71°08'W
Norton, Va., U.S.	125	36°54'N	82°36'W
Norton Bay, b., Ak., U.S.	103	64°22'N	162°18'W
Norton Reservoir, res., Ma., U.S.	110b	42°01'N	71°07'W
Norton Sound, strt., Ak., U.S.	103	63°48'N	164°50'W
Norval, Can. (nôr´vål)	102d	43°39'N	79°52'W
Norwalk, Ca., U.S. (nôr´wôk)	117a	33°54'N	118°05'W
Norwalk, Ct., U.S.	110a	41°06'N	73°25'W
Norwalk, Oh., U.S.	108	41°15'N	82°35'W
Norway, Me., U.S.	100	44°11'N	70°35'W
Norway, Mi., U.S.	113	45°47'N	87°55'W
Norway, nation, Eur. (nôr´wā)	154	63°48'N	11°17'E
Norway House, Can.	90	53°59'N	97°50'W
Norwegian Sea, sea, Eur. (nôr-wē´jăn)	160	66°54'N	1°43'E
Norwell, Ma., U.S. (nôr´wĕl)	101a	42°10'N	70°47'W
Norwich, Eng., U.K.	161	52°40'N	1°15'E
Norwich, Ct., U.S. (nôr´wĭch)	109	41°20'N	72°00'W
Norwich, N.Y., U.S.	109	42°35'N	75°30'W
Norwood, Ma., U.S. (nôr´wōōd)	101a	42°11'N	71°13'W
Norwood, N.C., U.S.	125	35°15'N	80°08'W
Norwood, Oh., U.S.	111f	39°10'N	84°27'W
Nose Creek, r., Can. (nōz)	102e	51°09'N	114°02'W
Noshiro, Japan (nō´shē-rô)	210	40°09'N	140°02'E
Nosivka, Ukr. (nō´sôf-kà)	177	50°54'N	31°35'E
Nossob, r., Afr. (nô´sŏb)	232	24°15'S	19°10'E
Noteć, r., Pol. (nô´tĕcn)	168	52°50'N	16°19'E
Notodden, Nor. (nōt´ôd'n)	166	59°35'N	9°15'E
Notre Dame, Monts, mts., Can.	100	46°35'N	70°35'W
Notre Dame Bay, b., Can. (nō´t'r dàm´)	93a	49°45'N	55°15'W
Notre-Dame-du-Lac, Can.	100	47°37'N	68°51'W
Nottawasaga Bay, b., Can. (nŏt´à-wà-sā´gà)	99	44°45'N	80°35'W
Nottaway, r., Can. (nôt´à-wā)	93	50°58'N	78°02'W
Nottingham, Eng., U.K. (nŏt´ĭng-ăm)	161	52°58'N	1°09'W
Nottingham Island, i., Can.	93	62°58'N	78°53'W
Nottinghamshire, co., Eng., U.K.	158a	53°03'N	1°05'W
Nottoway, r., Va., U.S. (nôt´à-wā)	125	36°53'N	77°47'W
Notukeu Creek, r., Can.	96	49°55'N	106°30'W
Nouadhibou, Maur.	230	21°02'N	17°09'W
Nouakchott, Maur.	230	18°06'N	15°57'W
Nouamrhar, Maur.	230	19°22'N	16°31'W
Nouméa, N. Cal. (nōō-mā´ä)	219	22°16'S	166°27'E
Nouvelle, Can. (nōō-vĕl´)	100	48°09'N	66°22'W
Nouvelle-France, Cap de, c., Can.	93	62°03'N	74°00'W
Nouzonville, Fr. (nōō-zôɴ-vēl´)	170	49°51'N	4°43'E
Nova Cruz, Braz. (nō´và-krōō´z)	143	6°22'S	35°20'W
Nova Friburgo, Braz. (frē-bōōr´gò)	143	22°18'S	42°31'W
Nova Iguaçu, Braz. (nō´vä-ē-gwä-sōō´)	143	22°45'S	43°27'W
Nova Lima, Braz. (lē´mä)	141a	19°59'S	43°51'W
Nova Lisboa *see* Huambo, Ang.	232	12°44'S	15°47'E
Nova Mambone, Moz. (nō´vä-mäm-bō´nĕ)	232	21°04'S	35°13'E
Nova Odesa, Ukr.	177	47°18'N	31°48'E
Nova Praha, Ukr.	177	48°34'N	32°54'E
Novara, Italy (nô-vä´rä)	162	45°24'N	8°38'E
Nova Resende, Braz.	141a	21°12'S	46°25'W
Nova Scotia, prov., Can. (skō´shà)	91	44°28'N	65°00'W
Nova Vodolaha, Ukr.	177	49°43'N	35°51'E
Novaya Ladoga, Russia (nô´vá-ya lá-dô-gá)	167	60°06'N	32°16'E
Novaya Lyalya, Russia (lyá´lyá)	186a	59°03'N	60°36'E
Novaya Sibir, i., Russia (sē-bēr´)	179	75°00'N	149°00'E
Novaya Zemlya, i., Russia (zĕm-lyá´)	178	72°00'N	54°46'E
Nova Zagora, Blg. (zä´gō-rà)	175	42°30'N	26°01'E
Novelda, Spain (nō-vĕl´dà)	173	38°22'N	0°46'W
Nové Mesto nad Váhom, Slvk. (nô´vĕ myĕs´tō)	169	48°44'N	17°47'E
Nové Zámky, Slvk. (zäm´kĕ)	161	47°58'N	18°10'E
Novgorod, Russia (nôv´gô-rŏt)	180	58°32'N	31°16'E
Novgorod, prov., Russia	176	58°27'N	31°55'E
Novhorod-Sivers'kyi, Ukr.	181	52°01'N	33°14'E
Novi, Mi., U.S. (nō´vĭ)	111b	42°29'N	83°28'W
Novigrad, Cro. (nō´vĭ gràd)	174	44°09'N	15°34'E
Novi Ligure, Italy (nô´vē)	174	44°43'N	8°48'E
Novinger, Mo., U.S. (nŏv´ĭn-jēr)	121	40°14'N	92°43'W
Novi Pazar, Blg. (pä-zär´)	175	43°22'N	27°26'E
Novi Pazar, Serb. (pá-zär´)	163	43°08'N	20°30'E
Novi Sad, Serb. (säd´)	154	45°15'N	19°53'E
Novoaidar, Ukr.	177	48°57'N	39°01'E
Novoasbest, Russia (nô-vô-äs-bĕst´)	186a	57°43'N	60°14'E
Novocherkassk, Russia (nô´vô-chĕr-kàsk´)	181	47°25'N	40°04'E
Novokuznetsk, Russia (nō´vô-kô´z-nyĕ´tsk) (stá´lênsk)	178	53°43'N	86°59'E
Novo-Ladozhskiy Kanal, can., Russia (nô-vô-lä´dôzh-skĭ kà-näl´)	167	59°54'N	31°19'E
Novo Mesto, Slvn. (nôvô mäs´tô)	174	45°48'N	15°13'E
Novomoskovsk, Russia (nô´vô-môs-kôfsk´)	178	54°06'N	38°08'E
Novomoskovs'k, Ukr.	181	48°37'N	35°12'E
Novomyrhorod, Ukr.	177	48°46'N	31°44'E
Novonikol'skiy, Russia (nô´vô-nyĭ-kôl´skĭ)	186a	52°28'N	57°12'E
Novorossiysk, Russia (nô´vô-rô-sēsk´)	178	44°43'N	37°48'E
Novorzhev, Russia (nô´vô-rzhêv´)	176	57°01'N	29°17'E
Novo-Selo, Blg. (nô´vô-sĕ´lô)	175	44°09'N	22°46'E
Novosibirsk, Russia (nô´vô-sê-bērsk´)	178	55°09'N	82°58'E
Novosibirskiye Ostrova (New Siberian Islands), is., Russia	179	74°00'N	140°30'E
Novosil', Russia (nô´vô-sĭl)	176	52°58'N	37°03'E
Novosokol'niki, Russia (nô´vô-sô-kôl´nē-kê)	176	56°18'N	30°07'E
Novotatishchevskiy, Russia (nô´vô-tá-tyĭsh´chĕv-skĭ)	186a	53°22'N	60°24'E
Novoukraïnka, Ukr.	181	48°18'N	31°33'E
Novouzensk, Russia (nô-vô-ô-zĕnsk´)	181	50°40'N	48°08'E
Novozybkov, Russia (nô´vô-zĕp´kôf)	181	52°31'N	31°54'E
Novyi Buh, Ukr.	177	47°43'N	32°33'E
Nový Jičín, Czech Rep. (nô´vē yē´chēn)	169	49°36'N	18°02'E
Novyy Oskol, Russia (ôs-kôl´)	177	50°46'N	37°53'E
Novyy Port, Russia (nô´vē)	178	67°19'N	72°28'E
Nowa Sól, Pol. (nô´vá sŭl´)	168	51°49'N	15°41'E

PLACE (Pronunciation)	PAGE	LAT.	LONG.
Nowata, Ok., U.S. (nō-wä'tȧ)	121	36°42'N	95°38'W
Nowood Creek, r., Wy., U.S.	115	44°02'N	107°37'W
Nowra, Austl. (nou'rȧ)	222	34°55'S	150°45'E
Nowy Dwór Mazowiecki, Pol. (nō'vĭ dvōōr mä-zo-vyĕts'ke)	169	52°26'N	20°46'E
Nowy Sącz, Pol. (nō'vĕ sônch')	169	49°36'N	20°42'E
Nowy Targ, Pol. (tärk')	169	49°29'N	20°02'E
Noxon Reservoir, res., Mt., U.S.	114	47°50'N	115°40'W
Noxubee, r., Ms., U.S. (nŏks'û-bē)	124	33°20'N	88°55'W
Noyes Island, i., Ak., U.S. (noiz)	94	55°30'N	133°40'W
Nozaki, Japan (nō'zä-kė)	211b	34°43'N	135°39'E
Nqamakwe, S. Afr. ('n-gä-mä'kwȧ)	233c	32°13'S	27°57'E
Nqutu, S. Afr. ('n-kōō'tōō)	233c	28°17'S	30°41'E
Nsawam, Ghana	234	5°50'N	0°20'W
Ntshoni, mtn., S. Afr.	233c	29°34'S	30°03'E
Ntwetwe Pan, pl., Bots.	232	20°00'S	24°18'E
Nubah, Jibāl an, mts., Sudan	231	12°22'N	30°39'E
Nubian Desert, des., Sudan (nōō'bĭ-ăn)	231	21°13'N	33°09'E
Nudo Coropuna, mtn., Peru (nōō'dô kō-rō-pōō'nä)	142	15°53'S	72°04'W
Nudo de Pasco, mtn., Peru (dĕ pås'kô)	142	10°34'S	76°12'W
Nueces, r., Tx., U.S. (nů-ā'sås)	106	28°20'N	98°08'W
Nueltin, l., Can. (nwĕl'tin)	92	60°14'N	101°00'W
Nueva Armenia, Hond. (nwä'vä är-mā'nė-ȧ)	132	15°47'N	86°32'W
Nueva Esparta, dept., Ven. (nwĕ'vä ĕs-pä'r-tä)	143b	10°50'N	64°35'W
Nueva Gerona, Cuba (kĕ-rô'nä)	134	21°55'N	82°45'W
Nueva Palmira, Ur. (päl-mē'rä)	141c	33°53'S	58°23'W
Nueva Rosita, Mex. (nòĕ'vä rô-sē'tä)	104	27°55'N	101°10'W
Nueva San Salvador, El Sal.	132	13°41'N	89°16'W
Nueve, Canal Numero, can., Arg.	141c	36°22'S	58°19'W
Nueve de Julio, Arg. (nwā'vå dā hōō'lyō)	144	35°26'S	60°51'W
Nuevitas, Cuba (nwā-vē'tås)	129	21°35'N	77°15'W
Nuevitas, Bahía de, b., Cuba (bä-ē'ä dĕ nwā-vē'tås)	134	21°30'N	77°05'W
Nuevo, Ca., U.S. (nwā'vō)	117a	33°48'N	117°09'W
Nuevo Laredo, Mex. (lä-rā'dhō)	128	27°29'N	99°30'W
Nuevo Leon, state, Mex. (lå-ōn')	128	26°00'N	100°00'W
Nuevo San Juan, Pan. (nwĕ'vô sän kōō-ä'n)	128a	9°14'N	79°43'W
Nugumanovo, Russia (nû-gû-mä'nô-vô)	186a	55°28'N	61°50'E
Nulato, Ak., U.S. (nōō-lä'tō)	103	64°40'N	158°18'W
Nullagine, Austl. (nŭ-lă'jēn)	218	22°00'S	120°07'E
Nullarbor Plain, pl., Austl. (nŭ-lär'bôr)	220	31°45'S	126°30'E
Numabin Bay, b., Can. (nōō-mä'bĭn)	96	56°30'N	103°08'W
Numansdorp, Neth.	159a	51°43'N	4°25'E
Numazu, Japan (nōō'mä-zōō)	210	35°06'N	138°55'E
Numfoor, Pulau, i., Indon.	213	1°20'S	134°48'E
Nun, r., Nig.	235	5°05'N	6°10'E
Nunavut, ter., Can.	92	70°00'N	95°00'W
Nunawading, Austl.	217a	37°49'S	145°10'E
Nuneaton, Eng., U.K. (nūn'ē-tŭn)	164	52°31'N	1°28'W
Nunivak, i., Ak., U.S. (nōō'nĭ-văk)	106a	60°25'N	167°42'W
Nunyama, Russia (nûn-yä'mȧ)	103	65°49'N	170°32'W
Nuoro, Italy (nwô'rō)	174	40°29'N	9°20'E
Nura, r., Kaz.	184	49°48'N	73°54'E
Nurata, Uzb. (nōōr'ät'ȧ)	183	40°33'N	65°28'E
Nuremberg *see* Nürnberg, Ger.	154	49°28'N	11°07'E
Nürnberg, Ger. (nürn'bĕrgh)	154	49°28'N	11°07'E
Nurse Cay, i., Bah.	135	22°30'N	75°50'W
Nusabyin, Tur. (nōō'sĭ-bēn)	181	37°05'N	41°10'E
Nushagak, r., Ak., U.S. (nū-shă-găk')	103	59°28'N	157°40'W
Nushan Hu, l., China	206	32°50'N	117°59'E
Nushki, Pak. (nŭsh'kė)	199	29°30'N	66°02'E
Nuthe, r., Ger. (nōō'tĕ)	159b	52°15'N	13°11'E
Nutley, N.J., U.S. (nŭt'lē)	110a	40°49'N	74°09'W
Nutter Fort, W.V., U.S. (nŭt'ēr fôrt)	108	39°15'N	80°15'W
Nutwood, Il., U.S. (nŭt'wŏod)	117e	39°05'N	90°34'W
Nuwaybi 'al Muzayyinah, Egypt	197a	28°59'N	34°40'E
Nuweland, S. Afr.	232a	33°58'S	18°28'E
Nyack, N.Y., U.S. (nī'ăk)	110a	41°05'N	73°55'W
Nyainqêntanglha Shan, mts., China (nyä-ĭn-chyůn-tăŋ-lä shän)	204	29°55'N	88°08'E
Nyakanazi, Tan.	237	3°00'S	31°15'E
Nyala, Sudan	231	12°00'N	24°52'E
Nyanga, r., Gabon	236	2°45'S	10°30'E
Nyanza, Rw.	237	2°21'S	29°45'E
Nyasa, Lake, l., Afr. (nyä'sä)	232	10°45'S	34°30'E
Nyasvizh, Bela. (nyĕs'vēsh)	176	53°13'N	26°44'E
Nyazepetrovsk, Russia (nyä'zĕ-pĕ-trôvsk')	186a	56°04'N	59°38'E
Nyborg, Den. (nü'bôr'')	166	55°20'N	10°45'E
Nybro, Swe. (nü'brô)	166	56°44'N	15°56'E
Nyeri, Kenya	237	0°25'S	36°57'E
Nyika Plateau, plat., Mwi.	237	10°30'S	35°50'E
Nyíregyháza, Hung. (nyē'rĕd-y'hä'zä)	163	47°58'N	21°45'E
Nykøbing, Den. (nü'kû-bĭng)	160	56°46'N	8°47'E
Nykøbing, Den.	166	54°45'N	11°54'E
Nykøbing Sjaelland, Den.	166	55°55'N	11°37'E
Nyköping, Swe. (nü'chû-pĭng)	160	58°46'N	16°58'E
Nylstroom, S. Afr. (nĭl'strōm)	232	24°42'S	28°25'E
Nymagee, Austl. (nī-mȧ-gē')	219	32°17'S	146°18'E
Nymburk, Czech Rep. (nĕm'bòrk)	161	50°12'N	15°03'E
Nynäshamn, Swe. (nü-nĕs-hȧm'n)	166	58°53'N	17°55'E
Nyngan, Austl. (nĭŋ'găn)	219	31°31'S	147°25'E
Nyong, r., Cam. (nyông)	230	4°00'N	12°00'E
Nyou, Burkina	234	12°46'N	1°56'W
Nýřany, Czech Rep. (nēr-zhä'nĕ)	168	49°43'N	13°13'E
Nysa, Pol. (nē'sȧ)	169	50°29'N	17°20'E

PLACE (Pronunciation)	PAGE	LAT.	LONG.
Nytva, Russia	180	58°00'N	55°10'E
Nyungwe, Mwi.	237	10°16'S	34°07'E
Nyunzu, D.R.C.	237	5°57'S	28°01'E
Nyuya, r., Russia (nyōō'yȧ)	185	60°30'N	111°45'E
Nyzhni Sirohozy, Ukr.	177	46°51'N	34°25'E
Nzega, Tan.	237	4°13'S	33°11'E
N'zeto, Ang.	232	7°14'S	12°52'E
Nzi, r., C. Iv.	234	7°00'N	4°27'W
Nzwani, i., Com. (än-zhwän)	233	12°14'S	44°47'E

O

PLACE (Pronunciation)	PAGE	LAT.	LONG.
Oahe, Lake, res., U.S.	106	45°20'N	100°00'W
O'ahu, i., Hi., U.S. (ō-ä'hōō) (ō-ä'hü)	106c	21°38'N	157°48'W
Oak Bay, Can.	94	48°27'N	123°18'W
Oak Bluff, Can. (ōk blŭf)	102f	49°47'N	97°21'W
Oak Creek, Co., U.S. (ōk krēk')	115	40°20'N	106°50'W
Oakdale, Ca., U.S. (ōk'dāl)	118	37°45'N	120°52'W
Oakdale, Ky., U.S.	108	38°15'N	85°50'W
Oakdale, La., U.S.	123	30°49'N	92°40'W
Oakdale, Pa., U.S.	111e	40°24'N	80°11'W
Oakengates, Eng., U.K. (ōk'ĕn-gāts)	158a	52°41'N	2°27'W
Oakes, N.D., U.S. (ōks)	112	46°10'N	98°50'W
Oakfield, Me., U.S. (ōk'fēld)	100	46°08'N	68°10'W
Oakford, Pa., U.S. (ōk'fōrd)	110f	40°08'N	74°58'W
Oak Grove, Or., U.S. (grōv)	116c	45°25'N	122°38'W
Oakham, Eng., U.K. (ōk'ăm)	158a	52°40'N	0°38'W
Oak Harbor, Oh., U.S. (ōk'här'bēr)	108	41°30'N	83°05'W
Oak Harbor, Wa., U.S.	116a	48°18'N	122°39'W
Oakland, Ca., U.S. (ōk'lănd)	104	37°48'N	122°16'W
Oakland, Ne., U.S.	112	41°50'N	96°28'W
Oakland City, In., U.S.	108	38°20'N	87°20'W
Oak Lawn, Il., U.S.	111a	41°43'N	87°45'W
Oakleigh, Austl. (ōk'lå)	217a	37°54'S	145°05'E
Oakley, Id., U.S. (ōk'lĭ)	114	42°15'N	135°53'W
Oakley, Ks., U.S.	120	39°08'N	100°49'W
Oakman, Al., U.S. (ōk'măn)	124	33°42'N	87°20'W
Oakmont, Pa., U.S. (ōk'mōnt)	111e	40°31'N	79°50'W
Oak Mountain, mtn., Al., U.S.	110h	33°22'N	86°42'W
Oak Park, Il., U.S. (pärk)	111a	41°53'N	87°48'W
Oak Point, Wa., U.S.	116c	46°11'N	123°11'W
Oak Ridge, Tn., U.S. (rĭj)	124	36°01'N	84°15'W
Oakville, Can. (ōk'vĭl)	99	43°27'N	79°40'W
Oakville, Can.	102f	49°56'N	97°58'W
Oakville, Mo., U.S.	117e	38°27'N	90°18'W
Oakville Creek, r., Can.	102d	43°34'N	79°54'W
Oakwood, Tx., U.S. (ōk'wŏod)	123	31°36'N	95°48'W
Oatman, Az., U.S. (ōt'măn)	119	34°00'N	114°25'W
Oaxaca, Mex.	128	17°03'N	96°42'W
Oaxaca, state, Mex. (wä-hä'kä)	128	16°45'N	97°00'W
Oaxaca, Sierra de, mts., Mex. (sē-ĕ'r-rä dĕ)	131	16°15'N	97°25'W
Ob', r., Russia	178	62°15'N	67°00'E
Oba, Can. (ō'bȧ)	91	48°58'N	84°09'W
Obama, Japan (ō'bȧ-mä)	211	35°29'N	135°44'E
Oban, Scot., U.K. (ō'băn)	164	56°25'N	5°35'W
Oban Hills, hills, Nig.	235	5°35'N	8°30'E
O'Bannon, Ky., U.S. (ō-băn'nŏn)	111h	38°17'N	85°30'W
O Barco de Valdeorras, Spain	172	42°26'N	6°58'W
Obatogamau, l., Can. (ō-bȧ-tō'găm-ô)	99	49°38'N	74°10'W
Oberhausen, Ger. (ō'bĕr-hou'zĕn)	171c	51°27'N	6°51'E
Oberlin, Ks., U.S. (o'bēr-lĭn)	120	39°49'N	100°30'W
Oberlin, Oh., U.S.	108	41°15'N	82°15'W
Oberroth, Ger. (ō'bĕr-rōt)	159d	48°19'N	11°20'E
Obi, Kepulauan, is., Indon. (ō'bė)	213	1°25'S	128°15'E
Obi, Pulau, i., Indon.	213	1°30'S	127°45'E
Óbidos, Braz. (ō'bė-dòzh)	143	1°57'S	55°32'W
Obihiro, Japan (ō'bē-hē'rō)	210	42°55'N	142°50'E
Obion, r., Tn., U.S.	124	36°10'N	89°25'W
Obion, North Fork, r., Tn., U.S. (ō-bī'ŏn)	124	35°49'N	89°06'W
Obitsu, r., Japan (ō'bēt'sōō)	211a	35°19'N	140°03'E
Obock, Dji. (ō-bŏk')	238a	11°55'N	43°15'E
Obol', r., Bela. (ô-bŏl')	176	55°24'N	29°24'E
Oboyan', Russia (ô-bô-yän')	181	51°14'N	36°16'E
Obskaya Guba, b., Russia	178	67°13'N	73°45'E
Obuasi, Ghana	234	6°14'N	1°39'W
Obukhiv, Ukr.	177	50°07'N	30°36'E
Obukhovo, Russia	186b	55°50'N	38°17'E
Obytichna kosa, spit, Ukr.	177	46°32'N	36°07'E
Ocala, Fl., U.S. (ô-kä'lȧ)	125	29°11'N	82°09'W
Ocampo, Mex. (ô-käm'pō)	130	22°49'N	99°23'W
Ocaña, Col. (ô-kän'yä)	142	8°15'N	73°37'W
Ocaña, Spain (ô-kä'n-yä)	172	39°58'N	3°31'W
Occidental, Cordillera, mts., Col.	142a	5°05'N	76°04'W
Occidental, Cordillera, mts., Peru	142	10°12'S	76°58'W
Ocean Beach, Ca., U.S. (ō'shăn bēch)	118a	32°44'N	117°14'W
Ocean Bight, b., Bah.	135	21°15'N	73°15'W
Ocean City, Md., U.S.	109	38°20'N	75°10'W
Ocean City, N.J., U.S.	109	39°15'N	74°35'W
Ocean Falls, Can. (Fôls)	90	52°21'N	127°40'W
Ocean Grove, Austl.	217a	38°16'S	144°32'E
Ocean Grove, N.J., U.S. (grōv)	109	40°10'N	74°00'W
Oceanside, Ca., U.S. (ō'shăn-sīd)	118	33°11'N	117°22'W
Oceanside, N.Y., U.S.	110a	40°38'N	73°39'W
Ocean Springs, Ms., U.S. (sprĭngs)	124	30°25'N	88°49'W
Ochakiv, Ukr.	177	46°38'N	31°33'E
Ochamchira, Geor.	182	42°44'N	41°28'E

PLACE (Pronunciation)	PAGE	LAT.	LONG.
Ochlockonee, r., Fl., U.S. (ŏk-lô-kō'nē)	124	30°10'N	84°38'W
Ocilla, Ga., U.S. (ô-sĭl'ȧ)	124	31°36'N	83°15'W
Ockelbo, Swe. (ôk'ĕl-bô)	166	60°54'N	16°35'E
Ocklawaha, Lake, res., Fl., U.S.	125	29°30'N	81°50'W
Ocmulgee, r., Ga., U.S.	124	32°25'N	83°30'W
Ocmulgee National Monument, rec., Ga., U.S. (ôk-mŭl'gē)	124	32°45'N	83°28'W
Ocoa, Bahía de, b., Dom. Rep.	135	18°20'N	70°40'W
Ococingo, Mex. (ô-kô-sē'n-gô)	131	17°03'N	92°18'W
Ocom, Lago, l., Mex. (ô-kō'm)	132a	19°26'N	88°18'W
Oconee, r., Ga., U.S. (ô-kō'nē)	107	32°45'N	83°00'W
Oconee, Lake, res., Ga., U.S.	124	33°30'N	83°15'W
Oconomowoc, Wi., U.S. (ô-kŏn'ô-mô-wŏk')	113	43°06'N	88°24'W
Oconto, Wi., U.S. (ô-kŏn'tō)	113	44°54'N	87°55'W
Oconto, r., Wi., U.S.	113	45°08'N	88°24'W
Oconto Falls, Wi., U.S.	113	44°53'N	88°11'W
Ocós, Guat. (ô-kōs')	132	14°31'N	92°12'W
Ocotal, Nic. (ō-kô-täl')	132	13°36'N	86°31'W
Ocotepeque, Hond. (ô-kō-tå-pā'kå)	132	14°25'N	89°13'W
Ocotlán, Mex. (ō-kô-tlän')	130	20°19'N	102°44'W
Ocotlán de Morelos, Mex. (dā mô-rā'lōs)	131	16°46'N	96°41'W
Ocozocoautla, Mex. (ô-kō'zô-kwä-ōō'tlä)	131	16°44'N	93°22'W
Ocumare del Tuy, Ven. (ô-kōō-mä'ra del twē')	142	10°07'N	66°47'W
Oda, Ghana	234	5°55'N	0°59'W
Odawara, Japan (ō'dȧ-wä'rä)	211	35°15'N	139°10'E
Odda, Nor. (ôdh-ȧ)	166	60°04'N	6°30'E
Odebolt, Ia., U.S. (ō'dē-bōlt)	112	42°20'N	95°14'W
Odemira, Port. (ō-då-mē'rȧ)	172	37°35'N	8°40'W
Ödemiş, Tur. (û'dĕ-mēsh)	163	38°12'N	28°00'E
Odendaalsrus, S. Afr. (ō'dĕn-däls-rûs')	238c	27°52'S	26°41'E
Odense, Den. (ō'dhĕn-sĕ)	160	55°24'N	10°20'E
Odenton, Md., U.S. (ō'dĕn-tŭn)	110e	39°05'N	76°43'W
Odenwald, for., Ger. (ō'dĕn-väld)	168	49°39'N	8°55'E
Oder, r., Eur. (ō'dēr)	156	52°40'N	14°19'E
Oderhaff, l., Eur.	168	53°47'N	14°02'E
Odesa, Ukr.	178	46°28'N	30°44'E
Odesa, prov., Ukr.	177	46°05'N	29°48'E
Odessa, Tx., U.S. (ô-dĕs'ȧ)	122	31°52'N	102°21'W
Odessa, Wa., U.S.	114	47°20'N	118°42'W
Odiel, r., Spain (ō-dė-ĕl')	172	37°47'N	6°42'W
Odiham, Eng., U.K. (ŏd'ē-ăm)	158b	51°14'N	0°56'W
Odintsovo, Russia (ô-dēn'tsô-vô)	186b	55°40'N	37°16'E
Odiongan, Phil. (ō-dė-ôŋ'gän)	213a	12°24'N	121°59'E
Odivelas, Port. (ō-dė-vā'lyäs)	173b	38°47'N	9°11'W
Odobeşti, Rom. (ō-dô-bĕsh't')	169	45°46'N	27°08'E
O'Donnell, Tx., U.S. (ō-dŏn'ĕl)	120	32°59'N	101°51'W
Odorhei, Rom. (ō-dôr-hā')	169	46°18'N	25°17'E
Odra *see* Oder, r., Eur. (ô'drȧ)	156	52°40'N	14°19'E
Oeiras, Braz. (wȧ-ē-räzh')	143	7°05'S	42°01'W
Oeirás, Port. (ô-ĕ'y-rȧ's)	173b	38°42'N	9°18'W
Oelwein, Ia., U.S. (ōl'wīn)	113	42°40'N	91°56'W
O'Fallon, Il., U.S. (ō-făl'ŭn)	117e	38°36'N	89°55'W
O'Fallon Creek, r., Mt., U.S.	115	46°25'N	104°47'W
Ofanto, r., Italy (ô-fän'tō)	174	41°08'N	15°33'E
Offa, Nig.	235	8°09'N	4°44'E
Offenbach, Ger. (ôf'ĕn-bäk)	168	50°06'N	8°50'E
Offenburg, Ger. (ôf'ĕn-bòrgh)	168	48°28'N	7°57'E
Ofuna, Japan (ō'fōō-nä)	211a	35°21'N	139°32'E
Ogaden Plateau, plat., Eth.	238a	6°45'N	44°53'E
Ogaki, Japan	210	35°21'N	136°36'E
Ogallala, Ne., U.S. (ō-gä-lä'lä)	112	41°08'N	101°44'W
Ogbomosho, Nig. (ŏg-bô-mō'shō)	230	8°08'N	4°15'E
Ogden, Ia., U.S. (ŏg'dĕn)	113	42°10'N	94°20'W
Ogden, Ut., U.S.	104	41°14'N	111°58'W
Ogden, r., Ut., U.S.	117b	41°16'N	111°54'W
Ogden Peak, mtn., Ut., U.S.	117b	41°11'N	111°51'W
Ogdensburg, N.J., U.S. (ŏg'dĕnz-bûrg)	110a	41°05'N	74°36'W
Ogdensburg, N.Y., U.S.	105	44°40'N	75°30'W
Ogeechee, r., Ga., U.S. (ô-gē'chė)	125	32°35'N	81°50'W
Ogies, S. Afr.	238c	26°03'S	29°04'E
Ogilvie Mountains, mts., Can. (ō'g'l-vĭ)	92	64°45'N	138°10'W
Oglesby, Il., U.S. (ō'g'lz-bĭ)	108	41°20'N	89°00'W
Oglio, r., Italy (ôl'yō)	174	45°15'N	10°19'E
Ōgo, Japan (ō'gô)	211b	34°49'N	135°06'E
Ogou, r., Togo	234	8°05'N	1°30'E
Ogudnëvo, Russia (ôg-òd-nyô'vô)	186b	56°04'N	38°17'E
Ogulin, Cro. (ō-gōō-lēn')	174	45°17'N	15°11'E
Ogwashi-Uku, Nig.	235	6°10'N	6°31'E
O'Higgins, prov., Chile (ô-kē'gēns)	141b	34°17'S	70°52'W
Ohio, state, U.S. (ô'hī'ō)	105	40°30'N	83°15'W
Ohio, r., U.S.	107	37°25'N	88°05'W
Ohoopee, r., Ga., U.S. (ô-hōō'pe-mc)	125	32°32'N	82°38'W
Ohře, r., Eur. (ōr'zhĕ)	168	50°08'N	12°45'E
Ohrid, Mac. (ō'krēd)	175	41°08'N	20°46'E
Ohrid, Lake, l., Eur.	175	40°58'N	20°35'E
Ōi, Japan (oi')	211a	35°51'N	139°31'E
Oi-Gawa, r., Japan (ō'ê-gä'wȧ)	211	35°09'N	138°05'E
Oil City, Pa., U.S. (oil sĭ'tĭ)	109	41°25'N	79°40'W
Oirschot, Neth.	159a	51°30'N	5°20'E
Oise, r., Fr. (wäz)	161	49°30'N	2°56'E
Oisterwijk, Neth.	159a	51°34'N	5°13'E
Oita, Japan (ō'ė-tä)	210	33°14'N	131°38'E
Oji, Japan (ō'jė)	211b	34°36'N	135°43'E
Ojinaga, Mex. (ō-kē-nä'gä)	128	29°34'N	104°26'W
Ojitlán, Mex. (ōkė-tlän') (sän-lōō'käs)	131	18°04'N	96°23'W

PRONOUNCING INDEX Ojo Caliente – Orikhiv 331

PLACE (Pronunciation)	PAGE	LAT.	LONG.
Ojo Caliente, Mex. (ō-kō käl-yĕn′tä)	130	21°50′N	100°43′W
Ojocaliente, Mex. (ō-kō-kä-lyĕ′n-tĕ)	130	22°39′N	102°15′W
Ojo del Toro, Pico, mtn., Cuba (pē′kō-ō-kō-dĕl-tō′rō)	134	19°55′N	77°25′W
Oka, Can. (ō-kä)	102a	45°28′N	74°05′W
Oka, r., Russia (ō-kà′)	180	55°10′N	42°10′E
Oka, r., Russia (ō-kä′)	184	53°28′N	101°09′E
Oka, r., Russia (ō-kä′)	181	52°10′N	35°20′E
Okahandja, Nmb.	232	21°50′S	16°45′E
Okanagan (Okanogan), r., N.A. (ō′kȧ-näg′ăn)	95	49°06′N	119°43′W
Okanagan Lake, l., Can.	92	50°00′N	119°28′W
Okano, r., Gabon (ō′kä′nō)	230	0°15′N	11°08′E
Okanogan, Wa., U.S.	114	48°20′N	119°34′W
Okanogan, r., Wa., U.S.	114	48°36′N	119°33′W
Okatibbee, r., Ms., U.S. (ō′kä-tĭb′ē)	124	32°37′N	88°54′W
Okatoma Creek, r., Ms., U.S. (ō-kȧ-tō′mä)	124	31°43′N	89°34′W
Okavango (Cubango), r., Afr.	232	18°00′S	20°00′E
Okavango Swamp, sw., Bots.	232	19°30′S	23°02′E
Okaya, Japan (ō′kȧ-yȧ)	211	36°04′N	138°01′E
Okayama, Japan (ō′kȧ-yä′mȧ)	205	34°39′N	133°54′E
Okazaki, Japan (ō′kȧ-zä′kē)	210	34°58′N	137°09′E
Okeechobee, Fl., U.S. (ō-kē-chō′bē)	125	27°15′N	80°50′W
Okeechobee, Lake, l., Fl., U.S.	107	27°00′N	80°49′W
Okeene, Ok., U.S. (ō-kēn′)	120	36°06′N	98°19′W
Okefenokee Swamp, sw., U.S. (ō′kē-fē-nō′kē)	125	30°54′N	82°20′W
Okemah, Ok., U.S. (ō-kē′mä)	121	35°26′N	96°18′W
Okene, Nig.	235	7°33′N	6°15′E
Okha, Russia (ŭ-kä′)	179	53°44′N	143°12′E
Okhotino, Russia (ō-kō′tĭ-nō)	186b	56°14′N	38°24′E
Okhotsk, Russia (ō-kôtsk′)	179	59°28′N	143°32′E
Okhotsk, Sea of, sea, Asia (ō-kôtsk′)	179	56°45′N	146°00′E
Okhtyrka, Ukr.	181	50°18′N	34°53′E
Okinawa, i., Japan	205	26°30′N	128°00′E
Okino, i., Japan (ō′kē-nō)	211	36°22′N	133°27′E
Ōkino Erabu, i., Japan (ō-kē′nō-ā-rä′bōō)	210	27°18′N	129°00′E
Oklahoma, state, U.S. (ō-klȧ-hō′mȧ)	104	36°00′N	98°20′W
Oklahoma City, Ok., U.S.	104	35°27′N	97°32′W
Oklawaha, r., Fl., U.S. (ŏk-lȧ-wô′hô)	125	29°13′N	82°00′W
Okmulgee, Ok., U.S. (ōk-mŭl′gē)	121	35°37′N	95°58′W
Okolona, Ky., U.S. (ō-kō-lō′nȧ)	111h	38°08′N	85°41′W
Okolona, Ms., U.S.	124	33°59′N	88°43′W
Oktemberyan, Arm.	182	40°09′N	44°02′E
Okushiri, i., Japan (ō′koo-shē′rē)	210	42°12′N	139°30′E
Okuta, Nig.	235	9°14′N	3°15′E
Olalla, Wa., U.S. (ō-lä′lȧ)	116a	47°26′N	122°33′W
Olanchito, Hond. (ō′län-chē′tō)	132	15°28′N	86°35′W
Öland, i., Swe. (û-länd′)	156	57°03′N	17°15′E
Olathe, Ks., U.S. (ō-lā′thē)	117f	38°53′N	94°49′W
Olavarría, Arg. (ō-lä-vär-rē′ä)	144	36°49′N	60°15′W
Oława, Pol. (ô-lä′vȧ)	169	50°57′N	17°18′E
Olazoago, Arg. (ô-läz-kôä′gō)	141c	35°14′S	60°37′W
Olbia, Italy (ô′l-byä)	174	40°55′N	9°28′E
Olching, Ger. (ōl′kēng)	159d	48°13′N	11°21′E
Old Bahama Channel, strt., N.A. (bȧ-hā′mȧ)	134	22°45′N	78°30′W
Old Bight, Bah.	135	24°15′N	75°20′W
Old Bridge, N.J., U.S. (brĭj)	110a	40°24′N	74°22′W
Old Crow, Can. (crō)	90	67°51′N	139°58′W
Oldenburg, Ger. (ôl′dĕn-bōrgh)	160	53°09′N	8°13′E
Old Forge, Pa., U.S. (fôrj)	109	41°20′N	75°50′W
Oldham, Eng., U.K. (ōld′ăm)	164	53°32′N	2°07′W
Oldham, co., Eng., U.K.	158a	53°35′N	2°05′W
Old Harbor, Ak., U.S. (här′bēr)	103	57°18′N	153°20′W
Old Head of Kinsale, c., Ire. (ōld hĕd ŏv kĭn-sāl)	164	51°35′N	8°35′W
Old R, Tx., U.S.	123a	29°54′N	94°52′W
Olds, Can. (ōldz)	90	51°47′N	114°06′W
Old Tate, Bots.	232	21°18′S	27°43′E
Old Town, Me., U.S. (toun)	100	44°55′N	68°42′W
Old Wives Lake, l., Can. (wīvz)	96	50°05′N	106°00′W
Olean, N.Y., U.S. (ō-lē-ăn′)	105	42°05′N	78°25′W
Olecko, Pol. (ō-lĕt′skō)	169	54°02′N	22°29′E
Olekma, r., Russia (ō-lyĕk-mȧ′)	185	55°41′N	120°33′E
Olëkminsk, Russia (ō-lyĕk-mĕnsk′)	179	60°39′N	120°40′E
Oleksandriia, Ukr.	176	48°40′N	33°07′E
Olenëk, r., Russia (ō-lyĕ-nyôk′)	179	68°00′N	113°00′E
Oléron Île, d′, i., Fr. (ēl′ dō lā-rôn′)	161	45°52′N	1°58′W
Oleśnica, Pol. (ō-lĕsh-nĭ′tsȧ)	161	51°13′N	17°24′E
Olfen, Ger. (ōl′fĕn)	171c	51°43′N	7°22′E
Ol′ga, Russia (ôl′gȧ)	179	43°48′N	135°44′E
Ol′gi, Zaliv, b., Russia (zä′lĭf ôl′gĭ)	210	43°43′N	135°25′E
Olhão, Port. (ôl-youn′)	162	37°02′N	7°54′W
Ol′hopil′, Ukr.	177	48°11′N	29°28′E
Olievenhoutpoort, S. Afr.	233b	25°58′S	27°55′E
Ólimbos, mtn., Cyp.	197a	34°56′N	32°52′E
Olinda, Braz. (ō-lē′n-dä)	143	8°00′S	34°58′W
Olinda, Braz.	144b	22°49′S	43°25′W
Oliva, Spain (ō-lē′vä)	173	38°54′N	0°07′W
Oliva de la Frontera, Spain (ō-lē′vä dā)	172	38°33′N	6°55′W
Olive Hill, Ky., U.S. (ŏl′ĭv)	108	38°15′N	83°10′W
Oliveira, Braz. (ō-lē-vā′rä)	141a	20°42′S	44°49′W
Olivenza, Spain (ō-lē-vĕn′thä)	172	38°42′N	7°06′W
Oliver, Can. (ŏ′lĭ-vēr)	90	49°11′N	119°33′W
Oliver, Can.	102g	53°38′N	113°21′W
Oliver, Wi., U.S. (ŏ′lĭvēr)	117h	46°39′N	92°12′W
Oliver Lake, l., Can.	102g	53°19′N	113°00′W
Olivia, Mn., U.S. (ō-lĭv′ē-ȧ)	112	44°46′N	95°00′W
Olivos, Arg. (ōlē′vōs)	144a	34°30′S	58°29′W
Ollagüe, Chile (ō-lyȧ′gā)	142	21°17′S	68°17′W
Ollerton, Eng., U.K. (ôl′ēr-tŭn)	158a	53°12′N	1°02′W
Olmos Park, Tx., U.S. (ōl′mŭs pärk′)	117d	29°27′N	98°32′W
Olney, Il., U.S. (ŏl′nĭ)	108	38°45′N	88°05′W
Olney, Or., U.S. (ŏl′nē)	116c	46°06′N	123°45′W
Olney, Tx., U.S.	120	33°24′N	98°43′W
Olomane, r., Can. (ō′lō mȧ′nĕ)	101	51°05′N	60°50′W
Olomouc, Czech Rep. (ō′lō-mōts)	161	49°37′N	17°15′E
Olonets, Russia (ō-lō′nĕts)	167	60°58′N	32°54′E
Olongapo, Phil.	212	14°49′S	120°17′E
Oloron, Gave d′, r., Fr. (gäv-dō-lō-rôn′)	170	43°21′N	0°44′W
Oloron-Sainte Marie, Fr. (ō-lō-rônt′sănt mȧ-rē′)	170	43°11′N	1°37′W
Olot, Spain (ō-lōt′)	162	42°09′N	2°30′E
Olpe, Ger. (ōl′pĕ)	171c	51°02′N	7°51′E
Olsnitz, Ger. (ōlz′nētz)	168	50°25′N	12°11′E
Olsztyn, Pol. (ôl′shtĭn)	160	53°47′N	20°28′E
Olt, r., Rom.	163	44°09′N	24°40′E
Olten, Switz. (ōl′tĕn)	168	47°20′N	7°53′E
Oltenița, Rom. (ôl-tä′nĭ-tsȧ)	175	44°05′N	26°39′E
Olvera, Spain (ōl-vĕ′rä)	172	36°55′N	5°16′W
Olympia, Wa., U.S. (ō-lĭm′pĭ-ȧ)	104	47°02′N	122°52′W
Olympic Mountains, mts., Wa., U.S.	114	47°54′N	123°58′W
Olympic National Park, rec., Wa., U.S. (ō-lĭm′pĭk)	106	47°54′N	123°00′W
Ólympos, mtn., Grc.	162	40°05′N	22°21′E
Olympus, Mount, mtn., Wa., U.S. (ō-lĭm′pŭs)	114	47°43′N	123°30′W
Olyphant, Pa., U.S. (ŏl′ĭ-fănt)	109	41°30′N	75°40′W
Olyutorskiy, Mys, c., Russia (ŭl-yōō′tŏr-skē)	179	59°49′N	167°16′E
Omae-Zaki, c., Japan (ō′mä-ā zä′kē)	211	34°37′N	138°15′E
Omagh, N. Ire., U.K. (ō′mä)	164	54°35′N	7°25′W
Omaha, Ne., U.S. (ō′mȧ-hä)	105	41°18′N	95°57′W
Omaha Indian Reservation, I.R., Ne., U.S.	112	42°09′N	96°08′W
Oman, nation, Asia	198	20°00′N	57°45′E
Oman, Gulf of, b., Asia	198	24°24′N	58°58′E
Omaruru, Nmb. (ō-mä-rōō′rōō)	232	21°25′S	16°50′E
Ombrone, r., Italy (ôm-brō′nā)	174	42°48′N	11°18′E
Omdurman, Sudan	231	15°45′N	32°30′E
Omealca, Mex. (ōmā-äl′kō)	131	18°44′N	96°45′W
Ometepec, Mex. (ō-mā-tȧ-pĕk′)	130	16°41′N	98°27′W
Om Hajer, Eth.	231	14°06′N	36°46′E
Omineca, r., Can. (ō-mĭ-nĕk′ȧ)	94	55°50′N	125°45′W
Omineca Mountains, mts., Can.	94	56°00′N	125°00′W
Ōmiya, Japan (ō′mē-yȧ)	211	35°54′N	139°38′E
Omo, r., Eth. (ō′mō)	231	5°54′N	36°09′E
Omoa, Hond. (ō-mō′rä)	132	15°43′N	88°03′W
Omoko, Nig.	235	5°20′N	6°39′E
Omolon, r., Russia (ō′mō)	185	67°43′N	159°15′E
Ōmori, Japan (ō′mō-rē)	211a	35°50′N	140°09′E
Omotepe, Isla de, i., Nic. (ē′s-lä-dĕ-ō-mō-tā′pȧ)	132	11°32′N	85°30′W
Omro, Wi., U.S. (ŏm′rō)	113	44°01′N	89°46′W
Omsk, Russia (ômsk)	178	55°12′N	73°19′E
Ōmura, Japan (ō′mōō-rȧ)	211	32°56′N	129°57′E
Ōmuta, Japan (ō′mō-tȧ)	211	33°02′N	130°28′E
Omutninsk, Russia (ō′mōō-tnēnsk)	180	58°38′N	52°10′E
Onawa, Ia., U.S. (ŏn-ȧ-wȧ)	112	42°02′N	96°05′W
Onaway, Mi., U.S.	108	45°25′N	84°10′W
Oncócua, Ang.	236	16°34′S	13°28′E
Onda, Spain (ōn′dä)	173	39°58′N	0°13′W
Ondava, r., Slvk. (ōn′dȧ-vȧ)	169	48°51′N	21°40′E
Ondo, Nig.	235	7°04′N	4°47′E
Öndörhaan, Mong.	205	47°20′N	110°40′E
Onega, Russia (ō-nyĕ′gȧ)	178	63°50′N	38°08′E
Onega, r., Russia	180	63°20′N	39°20′E
Onega, Lake *see* Onezhskoye Ozero, l., Russia	180	62°02′N	34°35′E
Oneida, N.Y., U.S. (ō-nī′dȧ)	109	43°05′N	75°40′W
Oneida, l., N.Y., U.S.	109	43°10′N	76°00′W
O'Neill, Ne., U.S. (ō-nēl′)	112	42°28′N	98°38′W
Oneonta, N.Y., U.S. (ō-nē-ŏn′tȧ)	109	42°25′N	75°05′W
Onezhskaja Guba, b., Russia	180	64°30′N	36°00′E
Onezhskiy, Poluostrov, pen., Russia	180	64°30′N	37°40′E
Onezhskoye Ozero, Russia (ō-năsh′skō-yĕ ô′zĕ-rō)	180	62°02′N	34°35′E
Ongiin Hiid, Mong.	204	46°00′N	102°46′E
Ongole, India	203	15°36′N	80°03′E
Onilahy, r., Madag.	233	23°41′S	45°00′E
Onitsha, Nig. (ō-nĭt′shȧ)	230	6°09′N	6°47′W
Onomichi, Japan (ō′nō-mē′chē)	210	34°27′N	133°12′E
Onon, r., Asia (ô′nōn)	179	49°00′N	112°00′E
Onoto, Ven. (ô-nŏ′tō)	143b	9°38′N	65°03′W
Onslow, Austl. (ŏnz′lō)	218	21°53′S	115°00′E
Onslow B, N.C., U.S. (ōnz′lō)	125	34°22′N	77°35′W
Ontake San, mtn., Japan (ōn′tä-kå sän)	210	35°55′N	137°29′E
Ontario, Ca., U.S. (ŏn-tā′rĭ-ō)	117a	34°04′N	117°39′E
Ontario, Or., U.S.	114	44°02′N	116°57′W
Ontario, prov., Can.	91	50°47′N	88°50′W
Ontario, Lake, l., N.A.	107	43°35′N	79°05′W
Ontinyent, Spain	173	38°48′N	0°35′W
Ontonagon, Mi., U.S. (ŏn-tō-năg′ŏn)	113	46°50′N	89°20′W
Ōnuki, Japan (ō′nōō-kē)	211a	35°17′N	139°51′E
Oodnadatta, Austl. (ōōd′nȧ-dȧ′tȧ)	218	27°38′S	135°40′E
Ooldea Station, Austl. (ōōl-dā′ȧ)	218	30°35′S	132°08′E
Oologah Reservoir, res., Ok., U.S.	107	36°43′N	95°32′W
Ooltgensplaat, Neth.	159a	51°41′N	4°19′E
Oostanaula, r., Ga., U.S. (ōō-stȧ-nô′lȧ)	124	34°25′N	85°10′W
Oostende, Bel. (ōst-ĕn′dē)	161	51°14′N	2°55′E
Oosterhout, Neth.	159a	51°38′N	4°52′E
Ooster Schelde, r., Neth.	159a	51°40′N	3°40′E
Ootsa Lake, l., Can.	94	53°49′N	126°18′W
Opalaca, Sierra de, mts., Hond. (sē-sĕ′r-rä-dĕ-ō-pä-lä′kä)	132	14°30′N	88°29′W
Opasquia, Can. (ō-păs′kwē-ȧ)	97	53°16′N	93°53′W
Opatów, Pol. (ō-pä′tōf)	169	50°47′N	21°25′E
Opava, Czech Rep. (ō′pä-vä)	169	49°56′N	17°52′E
Opelika, Al., U.S. (ŏp-ē-lī′kȧ)	124	32°39′N	85°23′W
Opelousas, La., U.S. (ŏp-ē-lōō′sȧs)	123	30°33′N	92°04′W
Opeongo, l., Can. (ŏp-ē-ŏŋ′gō)	99	45°40′N	78°20′W
Opheim, Mt., U.S. (ō-fīm′)	115	48°51′N	106°19′W
Ophir, Ak., U.S. (ō′fēr)	103	63°10′N	156°28′W
Ophir, Mount, mtn., Malay.	197b	2°22′N	102°37′E
Opico, El Sal. (ō-pē′kō)	132	13°50′N	89°23′W
Opinaca, r., Can. (ŏp-ĭ-nä′kȧ)	93	52°28′N	77°40′W
Opishnia, Ukr.	177	49°57′N	34°34′E
Opladen, Ger. (ŏp′lä-dĕn)	171c	51°04′N	7°00′E
Opobo, Nig.	235	4°34′N	7°27′E
Opochka, Russia (ō-pôch′kȧ)	180	56°43′N	28°39′E
Opoczno, Pol. (ō-pôch′nō)	169	51°22′N	20°18′E
Opole, Pol. (ō-pôl′ȧ)	161	50°42′N	17°55′E
Opole Lubelskie, Pol. (ō-pō′lā lōō-bĕl′skyĕ)	169	51°09′N	21°58′E
Opp, Al., U.S. (ŏp)	124	31°18′N	86°15′W
Oppdal, Nor. (ôp′däl)	166	62°37′N	9°41′E
Opportunity, Wa., U.S. (ŏp-ŏr tū′nĭ tĭ)	114	47°37′N	117°20′W
Oquirrh Mountains, mts., Ut., U.S. (ō′kwēr)	117b	40°38′N	112°11′W
Oradea, Rom. (ō-räd′yä)	154	47°02′N	21°55′E
Oral, Kaz.	183	51°14′N	51°22′E
Oran, Alg. (ō-rän) (ō-rän′)	230	35°46′N	0°45′W
Orán, Arg. (ō-rä′n)	144	23°13′S	64°17′W
Oran, Mo., U.S. (ôr′ăn)	121	37°05′N	89°39′W
Oran, Sebkha d′, l., Alg.	173	35°28′N	0°28′W
Orange, Austl. (ŏr′ĕnj)	219	33°15′S	149°08′E
Orange, Fr. (ô-ranzh′)	161	44°08′N	4°48′E
Orange, Ca., U.S.	117a	33°48′N	117°51′W
Orange, Ct., U.S.	109	41°15′N	73°00′W
Orange, N.J., U.S.	110a	40°46′N	74°14′W
Orange, Tx., U.S.	121	30°07′N	93°44′W
Orange, r., Afr.	232	29°15′S	17°30′E
Orange, Cabo, c., Braz. (kȧ-bô-rȧ′n-zhĕ)	143	4°25′N	51°30′W
Orangeburg, S.C., U.S. (ŏr′ĕnj-bûrg)	125	33°30′N	80°50′W
Orange Cay, i., Bah. (ŏr-ĕnj kē)	134	24°55′N	79°05′W
Orange City, Ia., U.S.	112	43°01′N	96°06′W
Orange Lake, l., Fl., U.S.	125	29°30′N	82°12′W
Orangeville, Can. (ŏr′ĕnj-vĭl)	99	43°55′N	80°06′W
Orangeville, S. Afr.	238c	27°05′S	28°13′E
Orange Walk, Belize (wôl′′k)	132a	18°09′N	88°32′W
Orani, Phil. (ō-rä′nē)	213a	14°47′N	120°32′E
Oranienburg, Ger. (ō-rä′nē-ĕn-bōrgh)	168	52°45′N	13°14′E
Oranjemund, Nmb.	232	28°33′S	16°20′E
Orăștie, Rom. (ō-rûsh′tyȧ)	175	45°50′N	23°14′E
Orbetello, Italy (ôr-bȧ-tĕl′lō)	174	42°27′N	11°15′E
Orbigo, r., Spain (ôr-bē′gō)	172	42°30′N	5°55′W
Orbost, Austl. (ôr′bŭst)	222	37°43′S	148°20′E
Orcas, i., Wa., U.S. (ôr′kȧs)	116d	48°43′N	122°52′W
Orchard Farm, Mo., U.S. (ôr′chĕrd färm)	117e	38°53′N	90°27′W
Orchard Park, N.Y., U.S.	111c	42°46′N	78°46′W
Orchards, Wa., U.S. (ôr′chĕdz)	116c	45°40′N	122°33′W
Orchila, Isla, i., Ven.	142	11°47′N	66°34′W
Ord, Ne., U.S. (ôrd)	112	41°35′N	98°57′W
Ord, r., Austl.	220	17°30′S	128°40′E
Ord, Mount, mtn., Az., U.S.	119	33°55′N	109°40′W
Orda, Kaz. (ôr′dȧ)	181	48°50′N	47°30′E
Orda, Russia (ôr′dȧ)	186a	57°10′N	57°12′E
Ordes, Spain	172	43°00′N	8°24′W
Ordos Desert, des., China	204	39°12′N	108°10′E
Ordu, Tur. (ôr′dō)	163	41°00′N	37°50′E
Ordway, Co., U.S. (ôrd′wā)	120	38°11′N	103°46′W
Örebro, Swe. (û′rē-brō)	160	59°16′N	15°11′E
Oredezh, r., Russia (ô′rĕ-dĕzh)	186c	59°23′N	30°21′E
Oregon, Il., U.S.	113	42°01′N	89°21′W
Oregon, state, U.S.	104	43°40′N	121°50′W
Oregon Caves National Monument, rec., Or., U.S. (cāvz)	114	42°05′N	123°13′W
Oregon City, Or., U.S.	116c	45°21′N	122°36′W
Öregrund, Swe. (û-rē-grōnd)	166	60°20′N	18°26′E
Orekhovo, Blg.	175	43°43′N	23°59′E
Orekhovo-Zuyevo, Russia (ôr-yĕ′kō-vō zō′yĕ-vō)	178	55°46′N	39°00′E
Orël, Russia (ôr-yôl′)	178	52°59′N	36°05′E
Orël, prov., Russia	176	52°35′N	36°08′E
Orem, Ut., U.S. (ō′rĕm)	119	40°15′N	111°50′W
Ore Mountains *see* Erzgebirge, mts., Eur.	156	50°29′N	12°40′E
Orenburg, Russia (ō′rĕn-bōōrg)	178	51°50′N	55°05′E
Øresund, strt., Eur.	166	55°50′N	12°40′E
Órganos, Sierra de los, mts., Cuba (sē-ĕ′r-rȧ-dĕ-lôs-ŏ′r-gä-nôs)	134	22°20′N	84°10′W
Organ Pipe Cactus National Monument, rec., Az., U.S. (ôr′găn pīp kăk′tŭs)	119	32°14′N	113°05′W
Orgãos, Serra das, mtn., Braz. (sĕ′r-rä-däs-ôr-goun′s)	141a	22°30′S	43°01′W
Orhei, Mol.	181	47°27′N	28°49′E
Orhon, r., Mong.	204	48°33′N	103°07′E
Oriental, Cordillera, mts., Col. (kôr-dēl-yĕ′rä)	142a	3°30′N	74°27′W
Oriental, Cordillera, mts., Dom. Rep. (kôr-dēl-yĕ′rä-ō-ryĕ′n-täl)	135	18°55′N	69°40′W
Oriental, Cordillera, mts., S.A. (kôr-dēl-yĕ′rä ō-rē-ĕn-täl′)	142	14°00′S	68°33′W
Orikhiv, Ukr.	177	47°34′N	35°51′E

ng-sing; ŋ-baŋk; ɴ-nasalized n; nŏd; cŏmmit; ōld; ôbey; ôrder; oi-boil; fōōd; ŏŏ-as oo in foot; ou-out; s-soft; sh-dish; th-thin; pūre; ûnite; ûrn; stŭd; circŭs; ü-as in French tu; ′-indeterminate vowel.

PLACE (Pronunciation)	PAGE	LAT.	LONG.
Oril', r., Ukr.	177	49°08'N	34°55'E
Orillia, Can. (ô-rĭl'ĭ-*a*)	91	44°35'N	79°25'W
Orin, Wy., U.S.	115	42°40'N	105°10'W
Orinda, Ca., U.S.	116b	37°53'N	122°11'W
Orinoco, r., Ven. (ō-rĭ-nō'kō)	142	8°32'N	63°13'W
Oriola, Spain	173	38°04'N	0°55'W
Orion, Phil. (ō-rē-ōn')	213a	14°37'N	120°34'E
Orissa, state, India (ŏ-rĭs'á)	199	25°09'N	83°50'E
Oristano, Italy (ô-rēs-tä'nō)	162	39°53'N	8°38'E
Oristano, Golfo di, b., Italy (gôl-fô-dē-ô-rēs-tä'nō)	174	39°53'N	8°12'E
Orituco, r., Ven. (ô-rē-tōō'kō)	143b	9°37'N	66°25'W
Oriuco, r., Ven. (ô-rēōō'kō)	143b	9°36'N	66°25'W
Orivesi, l., Fin.	167	62°15'N	29°55'E
Orizaba, Mex. (ô-rē-zä'bä)	129	18°52'N	97°05'E
Orizaba, Pico de, vol., Mex.	128	19°04'N	97°14'W
Orkanger, Nor.	166	63°19'N	9°54'W
Orkla, r., Nor. (ôr'klà)	166	62°55'N	9°50'E
Orkney, S. Afr. (ôrk'nĭ)	238c	26°58'S	26°39'E
Orkney Islands, is., Scot., U.K.	156	59°01'N	2°08'W
Orlando, S. Afr. (ôr-lăn-dô)	233b	26°15'S	27°56'E
Orlando, Fl., U.S. (ôr-lăn'dō)	105	28°32'N	81°22'W
Orland Park, Il., U.S. (ôr-lăn')	111a	41°38'N	87°52'W
Orleans, Can. (ôr-lå-äN')	102c	45°28'N	75°31'W
Orléans, Fr. (ôr-lā-äN')	154	47°55'N	1°56'E
Orleans, In., U.S. (ôr-lēnz')	108	38°40'N	86°25'W
Orléans, Île d', i., Can.	99	46°56'N	70°57'W
Orly, Fr.	171b	48°45'N	2°24'E
Ormond Beach, Fl., U.S. (ôr'm*ŏ*nd)	125	29°15'N	81°05'W
Ormskirk, Eng., U.K. (ôrms'kērk)	158a	53°34'N	2°53'W
Ormstown, Can. (ôrms'toun)	102a	45°07'N	74°00'W
Orneta, Pol. (ôr-nyĕ'tä)	169	54°07'N	20°10'E
Örnsköldsvik, Swe. (ûrn'skôlts-vēk)	160	63°10'N	18°32'E
Oro, Río del, r., Mex. (rē'ō dĕl ō'rō)	130	18°04'N	100°59'W
Oro, Río del, r., Mex.	119	26°04'N	105°40'W
Orobie, Alpi, mts., Italy (äl'pē-ô-rō'byĕ)	174	46°05'N	9°47'E
Oron, Nig.	235	4°48'N	8°14'E
Orosei, Golfo di, b., Italy (gôl-fô-dē-ō-rô-sā'ē)	174	40°12'N	9°45'E
Orosháza, Hung. (ô-rôsh-hä'sô)	169	46°33'N	20°31'E
Orosi, vol., C.R. (ō-rō'sē)	132	11°00'N	85°30'W
Oroville, Ca., U.S. (ōr'ô-vĭl)	118	39°29'N	121°34'W
Oroville, Wa., U.S.	114	48°55'N	119°25'W
Oroville, Lake, res., Ca., U.S.	118	39°32'N	121°25'W
Orreagal, Spain	172	43°00'N	1°17'W
Orrville, Oh., U.S. (ôr'vĭl)	108	40°45'N	81°50'W
Orsa, Swe. (ōr'sä)	166	61°08'N	14°35'E
Orsha, Bela. (ôr'shà)	180	54°29'N	30°28'E
Orsk, Russia (ôrsk)	178	51°15'N	58°50'E
Orşova, Rom. (ôr'shô-vä)	175	44°43'N	22°26'E
Ortega, Col. (ôr-tĕ'gä)	142a	3°56'N	75°12'W
Ortegal, Cabo, c., Spain (kà'bô-ôr-tå-gäl')	162	43°46'N	8°15'W
Orth, Aus.	159e	48°09'N	16°42'E
Orthez, Fr. (ôr-tĕz')	171	43°29'N	0°43'W
Órthrys, Óros, mtn., Grc.	175	39°00'N	22°15'E
Ortigueira, Spain (ôr-tē-gā'ē-rä)	162	43°40'N	7°50'W
Orting, Wa., U.S. (ôrt'ĭng)	116a	47°06'N	122°12'W
Ortona, Italy (ôr-tō'nä)	174	42°22'N	14°22'E
Ortonville, Mn., U.S. (ôr-t*ŭ*n-vĭl)	112	45°18'N	96°26'W
Orūmīyeh, Iran	198	37°30'N	45°15'E
Orūmīyeh, Daryacheh-ye, l., Iran	198	38°01'N	45°17'E
Oruro, Bol. (ô-rōō'rō)	142	17°57'S	66°59'W
Orvieto, Italy (ôr-vyâ'tō)	174	42°43'N	12°08'E
Osa, Russia (ō'sà)	180	57°18'N	55°25'E
Osa, Península de, pen., C.R. (ō'sä)	133	8°30'N	83°25'W
Osage, Ia., U.S. (ō'sāj)	113	43°16'N	92°49'W
Osage, r., Mo., U.S.	121	38°10'N	93°12'W
Osage City, Ks., U.S. (ō'sāj sĭ'tĭ)	121	38°28'N	95°53'W
Ōsaka, Japan (ō'sä-kä)	205	34°40'N	135°27'E
Ōsaka, dept., Japan	211b	34°45'N	135°36'E
Ōsaka-Wan, b., Japan (wän)	210	34°34'N	135°16'E
Osakis, Mn., U.S. (ô-sā'kĭs)	112	45°51'N	95°09'W
Osakis, l., Mn., U.S.	113	45°55'N	94°55'W
Osawatomie, Ks., U.S. (ŏs-*a*-wăt'ô-mē)	121	38°29'N	94°57'W
Osborne, Ks., U.S. (ŏz'b*ŭ*rn)	120	39°25'N	98°42'W
Osceola, Ar., U.S. (ŏs-ē-ō'là)	121	35°42'N	89°58'W
Osceola, Ia., U.S.	113	41°04'N	93°45'W
Osceola, Mo., U.S.	121	38°02'N	93°41'W
Osceola, Ne., U.S.	112	41°11'N	97°34'W
Oscoda, Mi., U.S. (ŏs-kō'd*à*)	108	44°25'N	83°20'W
Osëtr, r., Russia (ō'sĕt'r)	176	54°27'N	38°15'E
Osgood, In., U.S. (ŏz'gŏŏd)	108	39°10'N	85°20'W
Osgoode, Can.	102c	45°09'N	75°37'W
Osh, Kyrg. (ôsh)	183	40°33'N	72°48'E
Oshawa, Can. (ŏsh'*à*-w*à*)	91	43°50'N	78°50'W
Ōshima, i., Japan (ō'shē'mä)	211	34°47'N	139°35'E
Oshkosh, Ne., U.S. (ŏsh'kŏsh)	112	41°24'N	102°22'W
Oshkosh, Wi., U.S.	105	44°01'N	88°35'W
Oshogbo, Nig.	230	7°47'N	4°34'E
Osijek, Cro. (ôs'ĭ-yĕk)	163	45°33'N	18°48'E
Osinniki, Russia (ŭ-sē'nyĭ-kē)	184	53°37'N	87°21'E
Oskaloosa, Ia., U.S. (ŏs-k*à*-lōō's*à*)	113	41°16'N	92°40'W
Oskarshamn, Swe. (ôs'kärs-häm'n)	166	57°16'N	16°24'E
Oskarström, Swe. (ôs'kärs-strûm)	166	56°48'N	12°55'E
Öskemen, Kaz.	183	49°58'N	82°38'E
Oskil, r., Eur.	181	51°00'N	37°41'E
Oslo, Nor. (ôs'lō)	154	59°56'N	10°41'E
Oslofjorden, b., Nor.	166	59°03'N	10°35'E
Osmaniye, Tur.	163	37°10'N	36°30'E
Osnabrück, Ger. (ôs-nä-brük')	168	52°16'N	8°05'E
Osorno, Chile (ô-sō'r-nō)	144	40°42'S	73°13'W
Osøyra, Nor.	166	60°24'N	5°22'E
Osprey Reef, rf., Austl. (ŏs'prå)	221	14°00'S	146°45'E
Ossa, Mount, mtn., Austl. (ŏs*á*)	221	41°45'S	146°05'E
Osseo, Mn., U.S. (ŏs'sē-ō)	117g	45°07'N	93°24'W
Ossining, N.Y., U.S. (ŏs'ĭ-nĭng)	110a	41°09'N	73°51'W
Ossipee, N.H., U.S. (ŏs'ĭ-pē)	100	43°42'N	71°08'W
Ossjøen, l., Nor. (ôs-syûĕn)	166	61°20'N	12°00'E
Ostashkov, Russia (ôs-tăsh'kôf)	180	57°07'N	33°04'E
Oster, Ukr. (ōs'tĕr)	177	50°55'N	30°52'E
Osterdalälven, r., Swe.	160	61°40'N	13°00'E
Østerfjord, b., Nor. (ûs'tĕr fyôr')	166	60°40'N	5°25'E
Östersund, Swe. (ûs'tĕr-sōōnd)	160	63°09'N	14°49'E
Östhammar, Swe. (ûst'häm'är)	166	60°16'N	18°21'E
Ostrava, Czech Rep.	154	49°51'N	18°18'E
Ostróda, Pol. (ôs'trōt-à)	169	53°41'N	19°58'E
Ostrogozhsk, Russia (ôs-tr-gôzhk')	181	50°53'N	39°03'E
Ostroh, Ukr.	181	50°21'N	26°40'E
Ostrołęka, Pol. (ôs-trô-wôN'kà)	169	53°04'N	21°35'E
Ostrov, Russia (ôs-trôf')	180	57°21'N	28°22'E
Ostrowiec Świętokrzyski, Pol. (ôs-trō'vyĕts shvyĕN-tō-kzhĭ'ske)	161	50°55'N	21°24'E
Ostrów Lubelski, Pol. (ôs'trôf lōō'bĕl-skĭ)	169	51°32'N	22°49'E
Ostrów Mazowiecka, Pol. (mä-zô-vyĕt'skä)	161	52°47'N	21°54'E
Ostrów Wielkopolski, Pol. (ôs'trōōf vyĕl-kō-pōl'skē)	161	51°38'N	17°49'E
Ostrzeszów, Pol. (ôs-tzhā'shôf)	169	51°26'N	17°56'E
Ostuni, Italy (ôs-tōō'nē)	175	40°44'N	17°35'E
Osum, r., Alb. (ō'sòm)	175	40°37'N	20°00'E
Osuna, Spain (ô-sōō'nä)	172	37°18'N	5°05'W
Osveya, Bela. (ôs'vĕ-yà)	176	56°00'N	28°08'E
Oswaldtwistle, Eng., U.K. (ŏz-w*ă*ld-twĭs''l)	158a	53°44'N	2°23'W
Oswegatchie, r., N.Y., U.S. (ŏs-wē-găch'ĭ)	109	44°15'N	75°20'W
Oswego, Ks., U.S. (ŏs-wē'gō)	121	37°10'N	95°08'W
Oswego, N.Y., U.S.	105	43°25'N	76°30'W
Oświęcim, Pol. (ôsh-vyăN'tsyĭm)	169	50°02'N	19°17'E
Otaru, Japan (ô'tà-rò)	205	43°07'N	141°00'E
Otavalo, Ec. (ōtä-vä'lō)	142	0°14'N	78°16'W
Otavi, Nmb. (ô-tä'vē)	232	19°35'S	17°20'E
Otay, Ca., U.S. (ō'tā)	118a	32°36'N	117°04'W
Otepää, Est.	167	58°03'N	26°30'E
Oti, r., Afr.	234	9°00'N	0°10'E
Otish, Monts, mts., Can. (ô-tĭsh')	93	52°15'N	70°20'W
Otjiwarongo, Nmb. (ŏt-jē-wà-rôn'gō)	232	20°20'S	16°25'E
Otočac, Cro. (ō'tô-chàts)	174	44°53'N	15°15'E
Otra, r., Nor.	166	59°13'N	7°20'E
Otra, r., Russia (ôt'rà)	186b	55°22'N	38°20'E
Otradnoye, Russia (ô-trà'd-nôyĕ)	186c	59°46'N	30°50'E
Otranto, Italy (ô'trän-tô) (ô-trän'tō)	175	40°07'N	18°30'E
Otranto, Strait of, strt., Eur.	156	40°30'N	18°45'E
Otsego, Mi., U.S. (ŏt-sē'gō)	108	42°25'N	85°45'W
Otsu, Japan (ō'tsò)	210	35°00'N	135°54'E
Otta, l., Nor. (ôt'tà)	166	61°53'N	8°40'E
Ottawa, Can. (ŏt'*à*-w*à*)	91	45°25'N	75°43'W
Ottawa, Il., U.S.	108	41°20'N	88°50'W
Ottawa, Ks., U.S.	121	38°37'N	95°16'W
Ottawa, Oh., U.S.	108	41°00'N	84°00'W
Ottawa, r., Can.	93	46°05'N	77°20'W
Otter Creek, r., Ut., U.S. (ŏt'ĕr)	119	38°20'N	111°55'W
Otter Creek, r., Vt., U.S.	109	44°05'N	73°15'W
Otter Point, c., Can.	116a	48°21'N	123°50'W
Otter Tail, l., Mn., U.S.	112	46°21'N	95°52'W
Otterville, Il., U.S. (ŏt'ĕr-vĭl)	117e	39°03'N	90°24'W
Ottery, S. Afr. (ŏt'ĕr-ĭ)	232a	34°02'S	18°31'E
Ottumwa, Ia., U.S. (ô-tŭm'w*à*)	105	41°00'N	92°26'W
Otukpa, Nig.	235	7°09'N	7°41'E
Otumba, Mex. (ô-tŭm'bä)	130	19°41'N	98°46'W
Otway, Cape, c., Austl. (ŏt'wā)	221	38°55'S	153°40'E
Otway, Seno, b., Chile (sĕ'nō-ô't-wä'y)	144	53°00'S	73°00'W
Otwock, Pol. (ôt'vôtsk)	169	52°05'N	21°18'E
Ouachita, r., U.S.	107	33°25'N	92°30'W
Ouachita Mountains, mts., U.S. (wŏsh'ĭ-tô)	107	34°29'N	95°01'W
Ouagadougou, Burkina (wä'gà-dōō'gōō)	230	12°22'N	1°31'W
Ouahigouya, Burkina (wä-ē-gōō'yä)	230	13°35'N	2°25'W
Oualâta, Maur. (wä-lä'tä)	230	17°11'N	6°50'W
Ouallene, Alg. (wäl-lân')	230	24°43'N	1°15'E
Ouanaminthe, Haiti	135	19°35'N	71°45'W
Ouarane, reg., Maur.	230	20°44'N	10°27'W
Ouarkoye, Burkina	234	12°05'N	3°40'W
Ouassel, r., Alg.	173	35°30'N	1°55'E
Oubangui (Ubangi), r., Afr. (ōō-băN-gē')	236	4°30'N	20°35'E
Oude Rijn, r., Neth.	159a	52°09'N	4°33'E
Oudewater, Neth.	159a	52°01'N	4°52'E
Oud-Gastel, Neth.	159a	51°35'N	4°27'E
Oudtshoorn, S. Afr. (outs'hōrn)	232	33°33'S	23°36'E
Oued Rhiou, Alg.	173	35°55'N	0°57'E
Oued Tlelat, Alg.	173	35°33'N	0°28'W
Oued-Zem, Mor. (wĕd-zĕm')	230	33°05'N	5°49'W
Ouessant, Island d', i., Fr. (ēl-dwĕ-säN')	161	48°28'N	5°00'W
Ouesso, Congo	231	1°37'N	16°04'E
Ouest, Point, c., Haiti	135	19°00'N	73°25'W
Ouezzane, Mor. (wĕ-zan')	230	34°48'N	5°40'W
Ouham, r., Afr.	235	8°30'N	17°50'E
Ouidah, Benin (wē-dä')	230	6°25'N	2°05'E
Oujda, Mor.	230	34°41'N	1°45'W
Oulins, Fr. (ōō-lăN')	171b	48°52'N	1°27'E
Oullins, Fr. (ōō-lăN')	170	45°44'N	4°46'E
Oulu, Fin. (ō'lò)	154	64°58'N	25°43'E
Oulujärvi, l., Fin.	160	64°20'N	25°48'E
Oum Chalouba, Chad (ōōm shä-lōō'bä)	231	15°48'N	20°30'E
Oum Hadjer, Chad	235	13°18'N	19°41'E
Ounas, r., Fin. (ō'nàs)	160	67°46'N	24°40'E
Oundle, Eng., U.K. (ôn'd'l)	158a	52°28'N	0°28'W
Ounianga Kébir, Chad (ōō-nē-äŋ'gà kē-bēr')	231	19°04'N	20°22'E
Ouray, Co., U.S. (ōō-rā')	120	38°00'N	107°40'W
Ourense, Spain	172	42°20'N	7°52'W
Ourinhos, Braz. (òò-rē'nyôs)	143	23°04'S	49°45'W
Ourique, Port. (ō-rē'k*ĕ*)	172	37°39'N	8°10'W
Ouro Fino, Braz. (ōŭ-rô-fē'nō)	141a	22°18'S	46°21'W
Ouro Prêto, Braz. (ō'rò prā'tò)	144	20°24'S	43°30'W
Outardes, Rivière aux, r., Can.	93	50°53'N	68°50'W
Outer, i., Wi., U.S. (out'ĕr)	113	47°03'N	90°20'W
Outer Brass, i., V.I.U.S. (bräs)	129c	18°24'N	64°58'W
Outer Hebrides, is., Scot., U.K.	164	57°20'N	7°50'W
Outjo, Nmb. (ōt'yō)	232	20°05'S	17°10'E
Outlook, Can.	96	51°31'N	107°05'W
Outremont, Can. (ōō-trē-môN')	102a	45°31'N	73°36'W
Ouvéa, i., N. Cal.	221	20°43'S	166°48'E
Ouyen, Austl. (ōō-*ĕ*n)	222	35°05'S	142°10'E
Ovalle, Chile (ō-väl'yä)	144	30°43'S	71°16'W
Ovando, Bahía de, b., Cuba (bä-ē'ä-dĕ-ô-vä'n-dō)	135	20°10'N	74°05'W
Ovar, Port. (ô-vär')	172	40°52'N	8°38'W
Overijse, Bel.	159a	50°46'N	4°32'E
Overland, Mo., U.S. (ō-vēr-l*ă*nd)	117e	38°42'N	90°22'W
Overland Park, Ks., U.S.	117f	38°59'N	94°40'W
Overlea, Md., U.S. (ō'vēr-lā)(ō'vēr-lē)	110e	39°21'N	76°31'W
Övertornea, Swe.	160	66°19'N	23°31'E
Ovidiopol', Ukr.	177	46°15'N	30°28'E
Oviedo, Dom. Rep. (ô-vyĕ'dō)	135	17°50'N	71°25'W
Oviedo, Spain (ō-vē-ā'dhō)	154	43°22'N	5°50'W
Ovruch, Ukr.	177	51°19'N	28°51'E
Owada, Japan (ō'wä-dà)	211a	35°49'N	139°33'E
Owambo, hist. reg., Nmb.	232	18°10'S	15°00'E
Owando, Congo	232	0°29'S	15°55'E
Owasco, l., N.Y., U.S. (ō-wăsk'kō)	109	42°50'N	76°30'W
Owase, Japan (ō'wä-shē)	211	34°03'N	136°12'E
Owego, N.Y., U.S. (ō-wē'gō)	109	42°05'N	76°15'W
Owen, Wi., U.S. (ō'ĕn)	113	44°56'N	90°35'W
Owensboro, Ky., U.S. (ō'ĕnz-bŭr-ô)	105	37°45'N	87°05'W
Owens Lake, l., Ca., U.S.	118	37°13'N	118°20'W
Owen Sound, Can. (ō'ĕn)	91	44°30'N	80°55'W
Owen Stanley Range, mts., Pap. N. Gui. (stăn'lē)	213	9°00'S	147°30'E
Owensville, In., U.S. (ō'ĕnz-vĭl)	108	38°15'N	87°40'W
Owensville, Mo., U.S.	121	38°20'N	91°29'W
Owensville, Oh., U.S.	111f	39°08'N	84°07'W
Owenton, Ky., U.S. (ō'ĕn-t*ŭ*n)	108	38°35'N	84°55'W
Owerri, Nig. (ô-wĕr'ē)	230	5°26'N	7°04'E
Owings Mill, Md., U.S. (ōwĭngz mĭl)	110e	39°25'N	76°50'W
Owl Creek, r., Wy., U.S. (oul)	115	43°45'N	108°46'W
Owo, Nig.	235	7°15'N	5°37'E
Owosso, Mi., U.S. (ô-wŏs'ō)	108	43°00'N	84°15'W
Owyhee, r., U.S.	106	43°04'N	117°45'W
Owyhee, Lake, res., Or., U.S.	106	43°27'N	117°30'W
Owyhee, South Fork, r., Id., U.S.	114	42°07'N	116°43'W
Owyhee Mountains, mts., Id., U.S. (ô-wī'hē)	106	43°15'N	116°48'W
Oxbow, Can.	97	49°12'N	102°11'W
Oxchuc, Mex. (ôs-chōōk')	131	16°47'N	92°24'W
Oxford, Can. (ŏks'fērd)	100	45°44'N	63°52'W
Oxford, Eng., U.K.	161	51°43'N	1°16'W
Oxford, Al., U.S. (ŏks'fērd)	125	33°38'N	80°46'W
Oxford, Ma., U.S.	101a	42°07'N	71°52'W
Oxford, Mi., U.S.	108	42°50'N	83°15'W
Oxford, Ms., U.S.	124	34°22'N	89°30'W
Oxford, N.C., U.S.	125	36°17'N	78°35'W
Oxford, Oh., U.S.	108	39°30'N	84°45'W
Oxford Lake, l., Can.	97	54°51'N	95°37'W
Oxfordshire, co., Eng., U.K.	158b	51°36'N	1°30'W
Oxkutzcab, Mex. (ôx-kōō'tz-käb)	132a	20°18'N	89°22'W
Oxmoor, Al., U.S. (ŏks'mŏr)	110h	33°25'N	86°52'W
Oxnard, Ca., U.S. (ŏks'närd)	118	34°08'N	119°12'W
Oxon Hill, Md., U.S. (ŏks'ōn hĭl)	110e	38°48'N	77°00'W
Oyapock, r., S.A. (ō-yà-pŏk')	143	2°45'N	52°15'W
Oyem, Gabon	230	1°37'N	11°35'E
Øyeren, l., Nor. (ûĭĕrĕn)	166	59°50'N	11°25'E
Oymyakon, Russia (oi-myŭ-kôn')	179	63°14'N	142°58'E
Oyo, Nig. (ō'yō)	230	7°51'N	3°56'E
Oyonnax, Fr. (ô-yô-náks')	171	46°16'N	5°40'E
Oyster Bay, N.Y., U.S.	110a	40°52'N	73°32'W
Oyster Bayou, Tx., U.S.	123a	29°41'N	94°33'W
Oyster Creek, r., Tx., U.S. (ois'tēr)	123a	29°13'N	95°29'W
Oyyl, r., Kaz.	181	49°30'N	55°10'E
Ozama, r., Dom. Rep. (ô-zä'mä)	135	18°45'N	69°55'W
Ozamiz, Phil. (ô-zä'mēz)	213	8°06'N	123°43'E
Ozark, Al., U.S. (ō'zärk)	124	31°28'N	85°28'W
Ozark, Ar., U.S.	121	35°29'N	93°49'W
Ozark Plateau, plat., U.S.	107	36°37'N	93°56'W
Ozarks, Lake of the, l., Mo., U.S. (ō'zärksz)	107	38°06'N	93°26'W
Ozëry, Russia (ô-zyô'rē)	176	54°53'N	38°31'E
Ozieri, Italy	162	40°38'N	8°53'E
Ozorków, Pol. (ô-zôr'kôf)	169	51°58'N	19°20'E
Ozuluama, Mex.	131	21°34'N	97°52'W
Ozumba, Mex.	131a	19°02'N	98°48'W
Ozurgeti, Geor.	182	41°56'N	42°00'E

ăt; fin*ă*l; rāte; senåte; ärm; åsk; sof*à*; fâre; ch-choose; dh-as th in other; bē; ēvent; bĕt; recĕnt; cratẽr; g-gō; gh-guttural g; bĭt; *ĭ*-short neutral; rīde; κ-guttural k as ch in German ich;

PRONOUNCING INDEX
Paarl – Paris 333

P

PLACE (Pronunciation)	PAGE	LAT.	LONG.
Paarl, S. Afr. (pärl)	232	33°45'S	18°55'E
Pa'auilo, Hi., U.S. (pä-ä-ōō'ê-lō)	126a	20°03'N	155°25'W
Pabianice, Pol. (pä-byá-nē'tsĕ)	169	51°40'N	19°29'E
Pacaás Novos, Massiço de, mts., Braz.	142	11°03'S	64°02'W
Pacaraima, Serra, mts., S.A. (sĕr'rá pä-kä-rä-ē'mä)	142	3°45'N	62°30'W
Pacasmayo, Peru (pä-käs-mä'yō)	142	7°24'S	79°30'W
Pachuca, Mex. (pä-chōō'kä)	128	20°07'N	98°43'W
Pacific, Wa., U.S. (pá-sĭf'ĭk)	116a	47°16'N	122°15'W
Pacifica, Ca., U.S. (pá-sĭf'ĭ-kä)	116b	37°38'N	122°29'W
Pacific Beach, Ca., U.S.	118a	32°47'N	117°22'W
Pacific Grove, Ca., U.S.	118	36°37'N	121°54'W
Pacific Islands, Trust Territory of the *see* Palau, nation, Oc.	3	7°15'N	134°30'E
Pacific Ocean, o.	2	0°00'	170°00'W
Pacific Ranges, mts., Can.	94	51°00'N	125°30'W
Pacific Rim National Park, rec., Can.	94	49°00'N	126°00'W
Pacolet, r., S.C., U.S. (pă'cō-lĕt)	125	34°55'N	81°49'W
Pacy-sur-Eure, Fr. (pä-sē-sür-ûr')	171b	49°01'N	1°24'E
Padang, Indon. (pä-däng')	212	1°01'S	100°28'E
Padang, i., Indon.	197b	1°12'N	102°21'E
Padang Endau, Malay.	197b	2°39'N	103°38'E
Paden City, W.V., U.S. (pā'dĕn)	108	39°30'N	80°55'W
Paderborn, Ger. (pä-dĕr-bôrn')	168	51°43'N	8°46'E
Padibe, Ug.	237	3°28'N	32°50'E
Padiham, Eng., U.K. (păd'ĭ-hăm)	158a	53°48'N	2°19'W
Padilla, Mex. (pä-dēl'yä)	130	24°00'N	98°45'W
Padilla Bay, b., Wa., U.S. (pä-dēl'lä)	116a	48°31'N	122°34'W
Padova, Italy (pä'dô-vä)(păd'û-á)	162	45°24'N	11°53'E
Padre Island, i., Tx., U.S. (pä'drā)	123	27°09'N	97°15'W
Padua *see* Padova, Italy	162	45°24'N	11°53'E
Paducah, Ky., U.S.	105	37°05'N	88°36'W
Paducah, Tx., U.S.	120	34°01'N	100°18'W
Paektu-san, mtn., Asia (pâk'tōō-sän')	210	42°00'N	128°03'E
Pag, i., Serb. (päg)	174	44°30'N	14°48'E
Pagai Selatan, Pulau, i., Indon.	212	2°48'S	100°22'E
Pagai Utara, Pulau, i., Indon.	212	2°45'S	100°02'E
Pagasitikós Kólpos, b., Grc.	175	39°15'N	23°00'E
Page, Az., U.S.	119	36°57'N	111°27'W
Pago Pago, Am. Sam.	214a	14°16'S	170°42'W
Pagosa Springs, Co., U.S. (pá-gō'sá)	120	37°15'N	107°05'W
Pāhala, Hi., U.S. (pä-hä'lä)	126a	19°11'N	155°28'W
Pahang, state, Malay.	197b	3°02'N	102°57'E
Pahang, r., Malay.	212	3°39'N	102°41'E
Pahokee, Fl., U.S. (pá-hō'kē)	125a	26°45'N	80°40'W
Paide, Est. (pī'dĕ)	167	58°54'N	25°30'E
Päijänne, l., Fin. (pĕ'ē-yĕn-nĕ)	160	61°38'N	25°05'E
Pailolo Channel, strt., Hi., U.S. (pä-ē-lō'lō)	126a	21°05'N	156°41'W
Paine, Chile (pī'nĕ)	141b	33°49'S	70°44'W
Painesville, Oh., U.S. (pānz'vĭl)	108	41°40'N	81°15'W
Painted Desert, des., Az., U.S. (pānt'ĕd)	120	36°15'N	111°35'W
Painted Rock Reservoir, res., Az., U.S.	119	33°00'N	113°05'W
Paintsville, Ky., U.S. (pānts'vĭl)	108	37°50'N	82°50'W
Paisley, Scot., U.K. (pāz'lĭ)	160	55°50'N	4°30'W
Paita, Peru (pä-ē'tä)	142	5°11'S	81°12'W
Pai T'ou Shan, mts., Kor., N.	205	40°30'N	127°20'E
Paiute Indian Reservation, I.R., Ut., U.S.	119	38°17'N	113°50'W
Pajápan, Mex. (pä-hä'pän)	131	18°16'N	94°41'W
Pakanbaru, Indon.	212	0°43'N	101°15'E
Pakhra, r., Russia (päk'rá)	186b	55°29'N	37°51'E
Pakistan, nation, Asia	199	28°00'N	67°30'E
Pakokku, Mya. (pä-kŏk'kò)	204	21°29'N	95°00'E
Paks, Hung. (pôksh)	169	46°38'N	18°53'E
Pala, Chad	235	9°22'N	14°54'E
Palacios, Tx., U.S. (pä-lä'syōs)	123	28°42'N	96°12'W
Palagruža, Otoci, is., Cro.	174	42°20'N	16°23'E
Palaiseau, Fr. (pá-lĕ-zō')	171b	48°44'N	2°16'E
Palana, Russia	179	59°07'N	159°58'E
Palanan Bay, b., Phil. (pä-lä'nän)	213a	17°14'N	122°35'E
Palanan Point, c., Phil.	213a	17°12'N	122°40'E
Pālanpur, India (pä'lŭn-pōōr)	199	24°08'N	73°29'E
Palapye, Bots. (pá-läp'yĕ)	232	22°34'S	27°28'E
Palatine, Il., U.S. (păl'á-tīn)	111a	42°07'N	88°03'W
Palatka, Fl., U.S. (pá-lăt'ká)	125	29°39'N	81°40'W
Palau (Belau), nation, Oc. (pä-lä'ò)	3	7°15'N	134°30'E
Palauig, Phil. (pá-lou'ĕg)	213a	15°27'N	119°54'E
Palawan, i., Phil. (pä-lä'wán)	212	9°50'N	117°38'E
Pālayankottai, India	203	8°50'N	77°50'E
Paldiski, Est. (päl'dĭ-skĭ)	167	59°22'N	24°04'E
Palembang, Indon. (pä-lĕm-bäng')	212	2°57'S	104°40'E
Palencia, Guat. (pä-lĕn'sē-à)	132	14°40'N	90°22'W
Palencia, Spain (pä-lĕ'n-syä)	162	42°02'N	4°32'W
Palenque, Mex. (pä-lĕŋ'kā)	131	17°34'N	91°58'W
Palenque, Punta, c., Dom. Rep. (pōō'n-tä)	135	18°10'N	70°10'W
Palermo, Col. (pä-lĕr'mô)	142a	2°53'N	75°26'W
Palermo, Italy	154	38°08'N	13°24'E
Palestine, Tx., U.S.	105	31°46'N	95°38'W
Palestine, hist. reg., Asia (păl'ĕs-tīn)	197a	31°33'N	35°00'E
Paletwa, Mya. (pŭ-lĕt'wä)	199	21°19'N	92°52'E
Palghāt, India	203	10°49'N	76°40'E
Pāli, India	202	25°53'N	73°18'E
Palín, Guat. (pä-lēn')	132	14°42'N	90°42'W
Palizada, Mex. (pä-lē-zä'dä)	131	18°17'N	92°04'W
Palk Strait, strt., Asia (pôk)	199	10°00'N	79°23'E
Palma, Braz. (päl'mä)	141a	21°23'S	42°18'W
Palma, Spain	154	39°35'N	2°38'E
Palma, Bahía de, b., Spain	173	39°24'N	2°37'E
Palma del Río, Spain	172	37°43'N	5°19'W
Palmares, Braz. (päl-má'rĕs)	143	8°46'S	35°28'W
Palmas, Braz. (päl'mäs)	144	26°20'S	51°56'W
Palmas, Braz.	143	10°08'S	48°18'W
Palmas, Cape, c., Lib.	230	4°22'N	7°44'W
Palma Soriano, Cuba (sô-ré-ä'nō)	134	20°15'N	76°00'W
Palm Beach, Fl., U.S. (päm bēch')	125a	26°43'N	80°03'W
Palmeira dos Índios, Braz. (pä-mä'rä-dôs-ē'n-dyôs)	143	9°26'S	36°33'W
Palmeirinhas, Ponta das, c., Ang.	236	9°05'S	13°00'E
Palmela, Port. (päl-mä'lä)	172	38°34'N	8°54'W
Palmer, Ak., U.S. (päm'ẽr)	103	61°38'N	149°15'W
Palmer, Wa., U.S.	116a	47°19'N	121°53'W
Palmerston North, N.Z. (päm'ẽr-stŭn)	221a	40°20'S	175°35'E
Palmerville, Austl. (päm'ẽr-vĭl)	219	16°08'S	144°15'E
Palmetto, Fl., U.S. (pál-mĕt'ō)	125a	27°32'N	82°34'W
Palmetto Point, c., Bah.	135	21°15'N	73°25'W
Palmi, Italy (päl'mē)	174	38°21'N	15°54'E
Palmira, Col. (päl-mē'rä)	142	3°33'N	76°17'W
Palmira, Cuba	134	22°15'N	80°25'W
Palmyra, Mo., U.S. (păl-mī'rá)	121	39°45'N	91°32'W
Palmyra, N.J., U.S.	110f	40°01'N	75°00'W
Palmyra, i., Oc.	2	6°00'N	162°20'W
Palmyra, hist., Syria	198	34°25'N	38°28'E
Palmyras Point, c., India	202	20°42'N	87°45'E
Palo Alto, Ca., U.S. (pă'lō äl'tō)	116b	37°27'N	122°09'W
Paloduro Creek, r., Tx., U.S. (pă-lō-dōō'rō)	120	36°16'N	101°12'W
Paloh, Malay.	197b	2°11'N	103°12'E
Paloma, l., Mex. (pä-lō'mä)	122	26°53'N	104°02'W
Palomo, Cerro el, mtn., Chile (sĕ'r-rô-ĕl-pä-lô'mô)	141b	34°36'S	70°20'W
Palos, Cabo de, c., Spain (ká'bô-dĕ-pä'lôs)	162	39°38'N	0°43'W
Palos Verdes Estates, Ca., U.S. (pă'lŭs vûr'dĭs)	117a	33°48'N	118°24'W
Palouse, Wa., U.S. (pá-lōōz')	114	46°54'N	117°04'W
Palouse, r., Wa., U.S.	114	47°02'N	117°35'W
Palu, Tur. (pä-lōō')	181	38°55'N	40°10'E
Paluan, Phil. (pä-lōō'än)	213a	13°25'N	120°29'E
Pamiers, Fr. (pá-myā')	161	43°07'N	1°34'E
Pamirs, mts., Asia	199	38°14'N	72°27'E
Pamlico, r., N.C., U.S. (păm'lĭ-kō)	125	35°25'N	76°59'W
Pamlico Sound, strt., N.C., U.S.	107	35°10'N	76°10'W
Pampa, Tx., U.S. (păm'pá)	104	35°32'N	100°56'W
Pampa de Castillo, pl., Arg. (pä'm-pä-dĕ-käs-tē'l-yō)	144	45°30'S	67°30'W
Pampana, r., S.L.	234	8°35'N	11°55'W
Pampanga, r., Phil. (päm-päŋ'gä)	213a	15°20'N	120°48'E
Pampas, reg., Arg. (päm'päs)	144	37°00'S	64°30'W
Pampilhosa do Botão, Port. (päm-pê-lyō'sá-dô-bō-touN)	172	40°21'N	8°32'W
Pamplona, Col. (päm-plō'nä)	142	7°19'N	72°41'W
Pamplona, Spain (päm-plô'nä)	162	42°49'N	1°39'W
Pamunkey, r., Va., U.S. (pá-mŭŋ'kĭ)	109	37°40'N	77°20'W
Pana, Il., U.S. (pā'ná)	108	39°25'N	89°05'W
Panagyurishte, Blg. (pá-ná-gyōō'rēsh-tĕ)	175	42°30'N	24°11'E
Panaji (Panjim), India	199	15°33'N	73°52'E
Panamá, Pan.	129	8°58'N	79°32'W
Panama, nation, N.A.	129	9°00'N	80°00'W
Panamá, Istmo de, isth., Pan.	129	9°00'N	80°00'W
Panama Canal, can., Pan.	128a	9°20'N	79°55'W
Panama City, Fl., U.S. (păn-á mä' sĭ'tĭ)	124	30°08'N	85°39'W
Panamint Range, mts., Ca., U.S. (păn-ă-mĭnt')	118	36°40'N	117°30'W
Panarea, i., Italy (pä-nä'rĕ-a)	174	38°37'N	15°05'E
Panaro, r., Italy (pä-nä'rô)	174	44°47'N	11°06'E
Panay, i., Phil. (pä-nī')	212	11°15'N	121°38'E
Pančevo, Serb. (pán'chĕ-vô)	163	44°52'N	20°42'E
Panchor, Malay.	197b	2°11'N	102°43'E
Pānchur, India	202a	22°31'N	88°17'E
Panda, D.R.C. (pän'dä')	232	10°59'S	27°24'E
Pan de Guajaibon, mtn., Cuba (pän dā gwä-jä-bōn')	134	22°50'N	83°20'W
Panevėžys, Lith. (pä'nyĕ-vāzh'ēs)	180	55°44'N	24°21'E
Panga, D.R.C. (päŋ'gä)	231	1°51'N	26°25'E
Pangani, Tan. (pän-gä'nē)	233	5°28'S	38°58'E
Pangani, r., Tan.	237	4°40'S	37°45'E
Pangkalpinang, Indon. (päng-käl'pē-näng')	212	2°11'S	106°04'E
Pangnirtung, Can.	91	66°08'N	65°26'W
Panguitch, Ut., U.S. (pän'gwĭch)	119	37°50'N	112°30'W
Panié, Mont, mtn., N. Cal.	214f	20°36'S	164°46'E
Pānihāti, India	202a	22°42'N	88°23'E
Panimávida, Chile (pä-nē-má'vē-dä)	141b	35°44'S	71°26'W
Panshi, China (pän-shē)	208	42°50'N	126°48'E
Pantar, Pulau, i., Indon. (pän'tär)	213	8°40'N	123°45'E
Pantelleria, i., Italy (pän-tĕl-lå-rē'ä)	162	36°43'N	11°59'E
Pantepec, Mex. (pän-tå-pĕk')	131	17°11'N	93°04'W
Panuco, Mex. (pä'nōō-kô)	130	22°04'N	98°11'W
Pánuco, Mex. (pä'nōō-kô)	130	23°25'N	105°55'W
Panuco, r., Mex.	128	21°59'N	98°20'W
Pánuco de Coronado, Mex. (pä'nōō-kô dā kō-rô-nä'dhō)	122	24°33'N	104°20'W
Panvel, India	203b	18°59'N	73°06'E
Panyu, China (pä-yōō)	207a	22°56'N	113°22'E
Panzós, Guat. (pä-zós')	132	15°26'N	89°40'W
Pao, r., Ven. (pá'ō)	143b	9°52'N	67°57'W
Paola, Ks., U.S. (på-ō'lá)	121	38°34'N	94°51'W
Paoli, In., U.S. (på-ō'lĭ)	108	38°35'N	86°30'W
Paoli, Pa., U.S.	110f	40°03'N	75°29'W
Paonia, Co., U.S. (pā-ō'nyá)	119	38°50'N	107°40'W
Pápa, Hung. (pä'pô)	163	47°18'N	17°27'E
Papagayo, r., Mex. (pä-pä-gä'yō)	130	16°52'N	99°41'W
Papagayo, Golfo del, b., C.R. (gôl-fô-dĕl-pä-pä-gá'yō)	132	10°44'N	85°56'W
Papagayo, Laguna, l., Mex. (lä-ò-nä)	130	16°44'N	99°44'W
Papantla de Olarte, Mex. (pä-pän'tlä dā-ô-lä'r-tĕ)	128	20°30'N	97°15'W
Papatoapan, r., Mex. (pä-pä-tô-ä-pá'n)	131	18°00'N	96°22'W
Papenburg, Ger. (päp'ĕn-bôrgh)	168	53°05'N	7°23'E
Papinas, Arg. (pä-pē'näs)	141c	35°30'S	57°19'W
Papineauville, Can. (pä-pē-nō'vēl)	102c	45°38'N	75°01'W
Papua, Gulf of, b., Pap. N. Gui. (păp-ōō-á)	213	8°20'S	144°45'E
Papua New Guinea, nation, Oc. (păp-ōō-á)(gĭne)	213	7°00'S	142°15'E
Papudo, Chile (pä-pōō'dô)	141b	32°30'S	71°25'W
Paquequer Pequeno, Braz. (pä-kĕ-kĕ'r-pĕ-kĕ'nô)	144b	22°19'S	43°02'W
Para, r., Russia	176	53°45'N	40°58'E
Paracale, Phil. (pä-rä-kä'lå)	213a	14°17'N	122°47'E
Paracambi, Braz.	144b	22°36'S	43°43'W
Paracatu, Braz. (pä-rä-kä-tōō')	143	17°17'S	46°43'W
Paracel Islands, is., Asia	212	16°40'N	113°00'E
Paraćin, Serb. (pá'rä-chēn)	163	43°51'N	21°26'E
Para de Minas, Braz. (pä-rä-dĕ-mē'näs)	143	19°52'S	44°37'W
Paradise, i., Bah.	134	25°05'N	77°20'W
Paradise Valley, Nv., U.S. (păr'á-dīs)	114	41°28'N	117°32'W
Parados, Cerro de los, mtn., Col. (sĕ'r-rô-dĕ-lôs-pä-rä'dôs)	142a	5°44'N	75°13'W
Paragould, Ar., U.S. (păr'á-gōōld)	121	36°03'N	90°29'W
Paraguaçu, r., Braz. (pä-rä-gwä-zōō')	143	12°25'S	39°46'W
Paraguay, nation, S.A. (păr'á-gwā)	144	24°00'S	57°00'W
Paraguay, r., S.A. (pä-rä-gwä'y)	144	21°12'S	57°31'W
Paraíba, state, Braz. (pä-rä-ē'bä)	143	7°11'S	37°05'W
Paraíba, r., Braz.	141a	23°02'S	45°43'W
Paraíba do Sul, Braz. (dô-sōō'l)	141a	22°10'S	43°18'W
Paraibuna, Braz. (pä-räē-bōō'nä)	141a	23°23'S	45°38'W
Paraíso, C.R.	133	9°50'N	83°53'W
Paraíso, Mex.	131	18°24'N	93°11'W
Paraiso, Pan. (pä-rä-ē'sō)	128a	9°02'N	79°38'W
Paraisópolis, Braz. (pä-räē-sô'pō-lēs)	141a	22°35'S	45°45'W
Paraitinga, r., Braz. (pä-rä-ē-tē'n-gä)	141a	23°15'S	45°24'W
Parakou, Benin (pá-rá-kōō')	230	9°21'N	2°37'E
Paramaribo, Sur. (pá-rá-má'rē-bō)	143	5°50'N	55°15'W
Paramatta, Austl. (păr-á-măt'á)	217b	33°49'S	150°59'E
Paramillo, mtn., Col. (pä-rä-mē'l-yō)	142a	7°06'N	75°55'W
Paramus, N.J., U.S.	110a	40°56'N	74°04'W
Paran, r., Asia	197a	30°05'N	34°50'E
Paraná, Arg.	144	31°44'S	60°32'W
Paraná, r., S.A.	144	24°00'S	54°00'W
Paranaíba, Braz. (pä-rä-ná-ē'bá)	143	19°43'S	51°13'W
Paranaíba, r., Braz.	143	18°58'S	50°44'W
Paraná Ibicuy, r., Arg.	141c	33°27'S	59°26'W
Paranam, Sur.	143	5°39'N	55°13'W
Paranápanema, r., Braz. (pä-rä'ná'pä-nē-mä)	143	22°28'S	52°15'W
Paraopeda, r., Braz. (pä-rä-o-pĕ'dä)	141a	20°09'S	44°14'W
Parapara, Ven. (pä-rä-pä-rä)	143b	9°44'N	67°17'W
Parati, Braz. (pä-rätē)	141a	23°14'S	44°43'W
Paray-le-Monial, Fr. (pá-rĕ'lē-mô-nyäl')	170	46°27'N	4°14'E
Pārbati, r., India	202	24°50'N	76°44'E
Parchim, Ger. (par'kĭm)	168	53°25'N	11°52'E
Parczew, Pol. (pär'chĕf)	169	51°38'N	22°53'E
Pardo, r., Braz. (pär'dō)	143	15°25'S	39°40'W
Pardo, r., Braz.	141a	21°32'S	46°40'W
Pardubice, Czech Rep. (pär'dò-bĭt-sĕ)	168	50°02'N	15°47'E
Parecis, Serra dos, mts., Braz. (sĕr'rá dōs pä-rä-sĕzh')	143	13°45'S	59°28'W
Paredes de Nava, Spain (pä-rā'dās dā nä'vä)	172	42°10'N	4°41'W
Paredón, Mex.	122	25°56'N	100°58'W
Parent, Can.	91	47°59'N	74°30'W
Parent, Lac, l., Can.	99	48°40'N	77°00'W
Parepare, Indon.	212	4°01'S	119°38'E
Pargolovo, Russia (pár-gô'lô vô)	186c	60°04'N	30°18'E
Paria, r., Az., U.S.	119	37°07'N	111°51'W
Paria, Golfo de, b. (gôl-fô-dĕ-br-pä-rē-ä)	142	10°33'N	62°14'W
Paricutín, Volcán, vol., Mex.	130	19°27'N	102°14'W
Parida, Río de la, r., Mex. (rē'ō-dĕ-lä-pä-rē'dä)	122	26°23'N	104°40'W
Parima, Serra, mts., S.A. (sĕr'rá pä-rē'mä)	142	3°45'N	64°00'W
Pariñas, Punta, c., Peru (pōō'n-tä-pä-rē'n-yäs)	142	4°30'S	81°23'W
Parintins, Braz. (pä-rĭn-tĭNzh')	143	2°34'S	56°30'W
Paris, Can.	99	43°15'N	80°23'W
Paris, Fr. (pá-rē')	154	48°51'N	2°20'E
Paris, Ar., U.S. (păr'ĭs)	121	35°17'N	93°43'W
Paris, Il., U.S.	108	39°35'N	87°40'W
Paris, Ky., U.S.	108	38°15'N	84°15'W
Paris, Mo., U.S.	121	39°27'N	91°59'W
Paris, Tn., U.S.	124	36°16'N	88°20'W
Paris, Tx., U.S.	105	33°39'N	95°33'W

PLACE (Pronunciation)	PAGE	LAT.	LONG.
Parita, Golfo de, b., Pan. (gôl-fô-dĕ-pä-rē′tä)	133	8°06′N	80°10′W
Park City, Ut., U.S.	115	40°39′N	111°33′W
Parker, S.D., U.S. (pär′kẽr)	112	43°24′N	97°10′W
Parker Dam, dam, U.S.	106	34°20′N	114°00′W
Parkersburg, W.V., U.S. (pär′kẽrz-bûrg)	105	39°15′N	81°35′W
Parkes, Austl. (pärks)	222	33°10′S	148°10′E
Park Falls, Wi., U.S. (pärk)	113	45°55′N	90°29′W
Park Forest, Il., U.S.	111a	41°29′N	87°41′W
Parkland, Wa., U.S. (pärk′lănd)	116a	47°09′N	122°26′W
Park Range, mts., Co., U.S.	115	40°54′N	106°40′W
Park Rapids, Mn., U.S.	112	46°53′N	95°05′W
Park Ridge, Il., U.S.	111a	42°00′N	87°50′W
Park River, N.D., U.S.	112	48°22′N	97°43′W
Parkrose, Or., U.S. (pärk′rōz)	116c	45°33′N	122°33′W
Park Rynie, S. Afr.	233c	30°22′S	30°43′E
Parkston, S.D., U.S. (pärks′tŭn)	112	43°22′N	97°59′W
Parkville, Md., U.S.	110e	39°22′N	76°32′W
Parkville, Mo., U.S.	117f	39°12′N	94°41′W
Parla, Spain (pär′lä)	173a	40°14′N	3°46′W
Parma, Italy (pär′mä)	162	44°48′N	10°20′E
Parma, Oh., U.S.	111d	41°23′N	81°44′W
Parma Heights, Oh., U.S.	111d	41°23′N	81°36′W
Parnaíba, Braz. (pär-nä-ē′bä)	143	3°00′S	41°42′W
Parnaíba, r., Braz.	143	3°57′S	42°30′W
Parnassós, mtn., Grc.	175	38°36′N	22°35′E
Parndorf, Aus.	159e	48°00′N	16°52′E
Pärnu, Est. (pĕr′nōō)	180	58°24′N	24°29′E
Pärnu, r., Est.	167	58°40′N	25°05′E
Pärnu Laht, b., Est. (läkt)	167	58°15′N	24°17′E
Paro, Bhu. (pä′rô)	202	27°30′N	89°30′E
Paroo, r., Austl. (pä′rōō)	221	30°00′S	144°00′E
Páros, Grc. (pä′rôs) (pā′rŏs)	175	37°05′N	25°14′E
Páros, i., Grc.	163	37°11′N	25°00′E
Parow, S. Afr. (pă′rô)	232a	33°54′S	18°36′E
Parowan, Ut., U.S. (păr′ô-wăn)	119	37°50′N	112°50′W
Parral, Chile (pär-rä′l)	144	36°07′S	71°47′W
Parral, r., Mex.	122	27°25′N	105°08′W
Parramatta, r., Austl. (păr-ȧ-măt′ȧ)	217b	33°42′S	150°58′E
Parras, Mex. (pär-räs′)	122	25°28′N	102°08′W
Parrita, C.R. (pär-rē′tä)	133	9°32′N	84°17′W
Parrsboro, Can. (pärz′bŭr-ô)	100	45°24′N	64°20′W
Parry, i., Can. (păr′ĭ)	99	45°15′N	80°00′W
Parry, Mount, mtn., Can.	94	52°53′N	128°45′W
Parry Islands, is., Can.	89	75°30′N	110°00′W
Parry Sound, Can.	91	45°20′N	80°00′W
Parsnip, r., Can. (pärs′nĭp)	95	54°45′N	122°20′W
Parsons, Ks., U.S. (pär′s′nz)	105	37°20′N	95°16′W
Parsons, W.V., U.S.	109	39°05′N	79°40′W
Parthenay, Fr. (pȧr-t′nĕ′)	170	46°39′N	0°16′W
Partinico, Italy (pär-tē′nê-kô)	174	38°02′N	13°11′E
Partizansk, Russia	179	43°15′N	133°19′E
Parys, S. Afr. (pȧ-rīs′)	238c	26°53′S	27°28′E
Pasadena, Ca., U.S. (păs-ȧ-dē′nȧ)	104	34°09′N	118°09′W
Pasadena, Md., U.S.	110e	39°06′N	76°35′W
Pasadena, Tx., U.S.	123a	29°43′N	95°13′W
Pascagoula, Ms., U.S. (păs-kȧ-gōō′lȧ)	124	30°22′N	88°33′W
Pascagoula, r., Ms., U.S.	124	30°52′N	88°48′W
Paşcani, Rom. (päsh-kän′)	169	47°46′N	26°42′E
Pasco, Wa., U.S. (păs′kō)	114	46°13′N	119°04′W
Pascua, Isla de (Easter Island), i., Chile	241	26°50′S	109°00′W
Pasewalk, Ger. (pä′zē-välk)	168	53°31′N	14°01′E
Pashiya, Russia (pä′shĭ-yȧ)	186a	58°27′N	58°17′E
Pashkovo, Russia (pȧsh-kô′vô)	210	48°52′N	131°09′E
Pashkovskaya, Russia (pȧsh-kôf′skȧ-yȧ)	177	45°00′N	39°04′E
Pasig, Phil.	213a	14°34′N	121°05′E
Pasión, Río de la, r., Guat. (rē′ō-dĕ-lä-pä-syōn′)	132a	16°31′N	90°11′W
Paso de los Libres, Arg. (pä-sô-dĕ-lôs-lē′brĕs)	144	29°33′S	57°05′W
Paso de los Toros, Ur. (tŏ′rôs)	141c	32°43′S	56°33′W
Paso Robles, Ca., U.S. (pă′sō rō′blĕs)	118	35°38′N	120°44′W
Pasquia Hills, hills, Can. (păs′kwê-ȧ)	97	53°13′N	102°37′W
Passaic, N.J., U.S. (pă-sā′ĭk)	110a	40°52′N	74°08′W
Passaic, r., N.J., U.S.	110a	40°42′N	74°26′W
Passamaquoddy Bay, b., N.A. (păs′ȧ-mȧ-kwŏd′ĭ)	100	45°06′N	66°59′W
Passa Tempo, Braz. (pä′s-sä-tĕ′m-pô)	141a	20°40′S	44°29′W
Passau, Ger. (päsŏu)	161	48°34′N	13°27′E
Pass Christian, Ms., U.S. (pȧs krĭs′tyĕn)	124	30°20′N	89°15′W
Passero, Cape, c., Italy (päs-sĕ′rô)	156	36°34′N	15°13′E
Passo Fundo, Braz. (pä′sō fōn′dô)	144	28°16′S	52°13′W
Passos, Braz. (pä′s-sōs)	143	20°45′S	46°37′W
Pastaza, r., S.A. (päs-tä′zä)	142	3°05′S	76°18′W
Pasto, Col. (päs′tô)	142	1°15′N	77°19′W
Pastora, Mex. (päs-tô-rä)	130	22°08′N	100°04′W
Pasuruan, Indon.	212	7°45′S	112°50′E
Pasvalys, Lith. (päs-vä-lēs′)	167	56°04′N	24°23′E
Patagonia, reg., Arg. (păt-ȧ-gō′nĭ-ȧ)	144	46°45′S	69°30′W
Pātālganga, r., India	203b	18°52′N	73°08′E
Patapsco, r., Md., U.S. (pȧ-tăps′kō)	110e	39°12′N	76°30′W
Pateros, Lake, res., Wa., U.S.	114	48°05′N	119°45′W
Paterson, N.J., U.S. (păt′ẽr-sŭn)	110a	40°55′N	74°10′W
Pathein, Mya.	199	16°46′N	94°47′E
Pathfinder Reservoir, res., Wy., U.S. (păth′fīn-dẽr)	115	42°22′N	107°10′W
Patiāla, India (pŭt-ê-ä′lŭ)	199	30°25′N	76°28′E
Pati do Alferes, Braz. (pä-tē-dô-äl-fĕ′rĕs)	144b	22°25′S	43°25′W
Patna, India (pŭt′nŭ)	199	25°33′N	85°18′E

PLACE (Pronunciation)	PAGE	LAT.	LONG.
Patnanongan, i., Phil. (pät-nä-nôŋ′gän)	213a	14°50′N	122°25′E
Patoka, r., In., U.S. (pȧ-tō′kȧ)	108	38°25′N	87°25′W
Patom Plateau, plat., Russia	179	59°30′N	115°00′E
Patos, Braz. (pä′tōzh)	143	7°03′S	37°14′W
Patos, Wa., U.S. (pä′tōs)	116d	48°47′N	122°57′W
Patos, Lagoa dos, l., Braz. (lä′gō-ȧ dozh pä′tōzh)	144	31°15′S	51°30′W
Patos de Minas, Braz. (dĕ-mē′näzh)	143	18°39′S	46°31′W
Pátra, Grc.	163	38°15′N	21°48′E
Patraïkós Kólpos, b., Grc.	175	38°16′N	21°19′E
Patras *see* Pátrai, Grc.	163	38°15′N	21°48′E
Patrocínio, Braz. (pä-trō-sē′nê-ô)	143	18°48′S	46°47′W
Pattani, Thai. (pät′ȧ-nê)	212	6°56′N	101°13′E
Patten, Me., U.S. (păt′′n)	100	45°59′N	68°27′W
Patterson, La., U.S. (păt′ẽr-sŭn)	123	29°41′N	91°20′W
Patterson, i., Can.	98	48°38′N	87°14′W
Patton, Pa., U.S.	109	40°40′N	78°45′W
Patuca, r., Hond.	133	15°22′N	84°31′W
Patuca, Punta, c., Hond. (pōō′n-tä-pä-tōō′kä)	133	15°55′N	84°05′W
Patuxent, r., Md., U.S. (pȧ-tŭk′sĕnt)	109	39°10′N	77°10′W
Pátzcuaro, Mex. (päts′kwä-rô)	130	19°30′N	101°36′W
Pátzcuaro, Lago de, l., Mex. (lä′gô-dĕ)	130	19°36′N	101°38′W
Patzicia, Guat. (pät-zē′syä)	132	14°36′N	90°57′W
Patzún, Guat. (pät-zōōn′)	132	14°40′N	91°00′W
Pau, Fr. (pō)	161	43°18′N	0°23′W
Pau, Gave de, r., Fr. (gäv-dĕ)	170	43°33′N	0°51′W
Paulding, Oh., U.S. (pôl′dĭng)	108	41°05′N	84°35′W
Paulinenaue, Ger. (pou′lē-nĕ-nou-ĕ)	159b	52°40′N	12°43′E
Paulistano, Braz. (pä′ô-lēs-tȧ-nä)	143	8°13′S	41°06′W
Paulo Afonso, Salto, wtfl., Braz. (säl-tô-pou′lô äf-fôn′sô)	143	9°33′S	38°32′W
Paul Roux, S. Afr. (pôrl rōō)	238c	28°18′S	27°57′E
Paulsboro, N.J., U.S. (pôlz′bē-rô)	110f	39°50′N	75°16′W
Pauls Valley, Ok., U.S. (pôlz văl′ē)	121	34°43′N	97°13′W
Pavarandocito, Col. (pä-vä-rän-dô-sē′tô)	142a	7°18′N	76°32′W
Pavda, Russia (päv′da)	186a	59°16′N	59°32′E
Pavia, Italy (pä-vē′ä)	162	45°12′N	9°11′E
Pavlodar, Kaz. (pȧv-lô-dȧr′)	183	52°17′N	77°23′E
Pavlof Bay, b., Ak., U.S. (păv-lŏf)	103	55°20′N	161°20′W
Pavlohrad, Ukr.	181	48°32′N	35°52′E
Pavlovsk, Russia (pȧv-lôfsk′)	177	50°28′N	40°05′E
Pavlovsk, Russia	186c	59°41′N	30°27′E
Pavlovskiy Posad, Russia (pȧv-lôf′skĭ pô-sȧt′)	180	55°47′N	38°39′E
Pavuna, Braz. (pä-vōō′nȧ)	144b	22°48′S	43°21′W
Päwesin, Ger. (pă′vĕ-zēn)	159b	52°31′N	12°44′E
Pawhuska, Ok., U.S. (pô-hŭs′kȧ)	121	36°41′N	96°20′W
Pawnee, Ok., U.S. (pô-nē′)	121	36°20′N	96°47′W
Pawnee, r., Ks., U.S.	120	38°18′N	99°42′W
Pawnee City, Ne., U.S.	121	40°08′N	96°09′W
Paw Paw, Mi., U.S. (pô′pô)	108	42°15′N	85°55′W
Paw Paw, r., Mi., U.S.	113	42°14′N	86°21′W
Pawtucket, R.I., U.S. (pô-tŭk′ĕt)	109	41°53′N	71°23′W
Paxoi, i., Grc.	175	39°14′N	20°15′E
Paxton, Il., U.S. (păks′tŭn)	108	40°35′N	88°00′W
Payette, Id., U.S. (pȧ-ĕt′)	114	44°05′N	116°55′W
Payette, r., Id., U.S.	114	43°57′N	116°26′W
Payette, North Fork, r., Id., U.S.	114	44°10′N	116°10′W
Payette, South Fork, r., Id., U.S.	114	44°07′N	115°43′W
Pay-Khoy, Khrebet, mts., Russia	180	68°08′N	63°04′E
Payne, l., Can. (pān)	93	59°22′N	73°16′W
Paynesville, Mn., U.S. (pānz′vĭl)	113	45°23′N	94°43′W
Paysandú, Ur. (pī-sän-dōō′)	144	32°16′S	57°55′W
Payson, Ut., U.S. (pā′s′n)	119	40°05′N	111°45′W
Pazardzhik, Blg. (pä-zär-dzhek′)	163	42°10′N	24°22′E
Pazin, Cro. (pä′zēn)	174	45°14′N	13°57′E
Peabody, Ks., U.S. (pē′bŏd-ĭ)	121	38°09′N	97°09′W
Peabody, Ma., U.S.	101a	42°32′N	70°56′W
Peace, r., Can.	92	57°30′N	117°30′W
Peace Creek, r., Fl., U.S. (pēs)	125a	27°16′N	81°53′W
Peace Dale, R.I., U.S. (dāl)	110b	41°27′N	71°30′W
Peace River, Can. (rĭv′ẽr)	90	56°14′N	117°17′W
Peacock Hills, hills, Can. (pē-kŏk′ hĭlz)	92	66°08′N	109°55′W
Peak Hill, Austl.	218	25°38′S	118°50′E
Pearl, r., U.S. (pûrl)	107	30°30′N	89°45′W
Pearland, Tx., U.S. (pûrl′ănd)	123a	29°34′N	95°17′W
Pearl Harbor, Hi., U.S.	126a	21°20′N	157°53′W
Pearl Harbor, b., Hi., U.S.	106d	21°22′N	157°58′W
Pearsall, Tx., U.S. (pẽr′sôl)	122	28°53′N	99°06′W
Pearse Island, i., Can. (pērs)	94	54°51′N	130°21′W
Pearston, S. Afr. (pē′ẽrstŏn)	233c	32°36′S	25°09′E
Peary Land, reg., Grnld. (pēr′ĭ)	244	82°00′N	40°00′W
Pease, r., Tx., U.S. (pēz)	120	34°07′N	99°53′W
Peason, La., U.S. (pēz′′n)	123	31°25′N	93°19′W
Pebane, Moz. (pĕ-bá′nĕ)	233	17°10′S	38°08′E
Pecan Bay, Tx., U.S. (pē-kăn′)	122	32°04′N	99°15′W
Peçanha, Braz. (på-kän′yȧ)	143	18°37′S	42°26′W
Pecatonica, r., Il., U.S. (pĕk-ȧ-tŏn-ĭ-kȧ)	113	42°21′N	89°28′W
Pechenga, Russia (pyĕ′chĕŋ-gȧ)	180	69°30′N	31°10′E
Pechora, r., Russia	178	66°00′N	54°00′E
Pechora Basin, Russia (pyĕ-chô′rȧ)	178	67°55′N	58°37′E
Pechori, Russia (pĕt′sĕ-rĕ)	176	57°48′N	27°33′E
Pecos, N.M., U.S. (pā′kōs)	119	35°29′N	105°41′W
Pecos, Tx., U.S.	122	31°26′N	103°30′W
Pecos, r., U.S.	106	31°10′N	103°10′W
Pécs, Hung. (pāch)	163	46°04′N	18°15′E
Peddie, S. Afr.	233c	33°13′S	27°09′E
Pedley, Ca., U.S. (pĕd′lē)	117a	33°59′N	117°29′W

PLACE (Pronunciation)	PAGE	LAT.	LONG.
Pedra Azul, Braz. (pā′drä-zōō′l)	143	16°03′S	41°13′W
Pedreiras, Braz. (pĕ-drā′räs)	143	4°30′S	44°31′W
Pedro, Point, c., Sri L. (pē′drô)	203	9°50′N	80°14′E
Pedro Antonio Santos, Mex.	132a	18°55′N	88°13′W
Pedro Betancourt, Cuba (bā-täŋ-kōrt′)	134	22°40′N	81°15′W
Pedro de Valdivia, Chile (pĕ′drô-dĕ-väl-dē′vê-ä)	144	22°32′S	69°55′W
Pedro do Rio, Braz. (dô-rē′rô)	144b	22°20′S	43°09′W
Pedro II, Braz. (pā′drò sĕ-gòn′dò)	143	4°20′S	41°27′W
Pedro Juan Caballero, Para. (hòá′n-kä-bäl-yĕ′rō)	144	22°40′S	55°42′W
Pedro Miguel, Pan. (mê-gāl′)	128a	9°01′N	79°36′W
Pedro Miguel Locks, trans., Pan. (mê-gāl′)	128a	9°01′N	79°36′W
Peebinga, Austl. (pē-bĭng′ȧ)	218	34°43′S	140°55′E
Peebles, Scot., U.K. (pē′b′lz)	164	55°40′N	3°15′W
Peekskill, N.Y., U.S. (pēks′kĭl)	110a	41°17′N	73°55′W
Pegasus Bay, b., N.Z. (pĕg′ȧ-sŭs)	221a	43°18′S	173°25′E
Pegnitz, r., Ger. (pĕgh-nēts)	168	49°38′N	11°40′E
Pego, Spain (pā′gō)	173	38°50′N	0°09′W
Peguis Indian Reserve, I.R., Can.	97	51°20′N	97°35′W
Pegu Yoma, mts., Mya. (pĕ-gōō′yō′mä)	199	19°16′N	95°59′E
Pehčevo, Mac. (pĕk′chĕ-vô)	175	41°42′N	22°57′E
Peigan Indian Reserve, I.R., Can.	95	49°35′N	113°40′W
Peipus, Lake *see* Chudskoye Ozero, l., Eur.	180	58°43′N	26°45′E
Peiraiás, Grc.	163	37°57′N	23°38′E
Pekin, Il., U.S. (pē′kĭn)	108	40°35′N	89°30′W
Peking *see* Beijing, China	205	39°55′N	116°23′E
Pelagie, Isole, is., Italy	162	35°46′N	12°32′E
Pélagos, i., Grc.	175	39°17′N	24°05′E
Pelahatchie, Ms., U.S. (pĕl-ȧ-hăch′ē)	124	32°17′N	89°48′W
Pelat, Mont, mtn., Fr. (pē-lȧ′)	161	44°16′N	6°43′E
Peleduy, Russia (pyĕl-yĭ-dōō′ē)	179	59°50′N	112°47′E
Pelée, Mont, mtn., Mart. (pē-lā′)	133b	14°49′N	61°10′W
Pelee, Point, c., Can.	98	41°55′N	82°30′W
Pelee Island, i., Can. (pē′lē)	98	41°45′N	82°30′W
Pelequén, Chile (pĕ-lĕ-kĕ′n)	141b	34°26′S	71°52′W
Pelham, Ga., U.S. (pĕl′hăm)	124	31°07′N	84°10′W
Pelham, N.H., U.S.	101a	42°43′N	71°22′W
Pelican, l., Mn., U.S.	113	46°36′N	94°00′W
Pelican Bay, b., Can.	97	52°45′N	100°20′W
Pelican Harbor, b., Bah. (pĕl′ĭ-kăn)	134	26°20′N	76°45′W
Pelican Rapids, Mn., U.S. (pĕl′ĭ-kăn)	112	46°34′N	96°05′W
Pella, Ia., U.S. (pĕl′ȧ)	113	41°25′N	92°50′W
Pellworm, i., Ger. (pĕl′vôrm)	168	54°33′N	8°25′E
Pelly, l., Can.	92	66°08′N	102°57′W
Pelly, r., Can.	92	62°20′N	133°00′W
Pelly Bay, b., Can. (pĕl′ĭ)	93	68°57′N	91°05′W
Pelly Crossing, Can.	103	62°50′N	136°50′W
Pelly Mountains, mts., Can.	92	61°50′N	133°05′W
Peloncillo Mountains, mts., Az., U.S. (pĕl-ôn-sĭl′lō)	119	32°40′N	109°20′W
Peloponnisos, pen., Grc.	175	37°28′N	22°14′E
Pelotas, Braz. (på-lō′tăzh)	144	31°45′S	52°18′W
Pelton, Can. (pĕl′tŭn)	111b	42°15′N	82°57′W
Pelym, r., Russia	180	60°20′N	63°05′E
Pelzer, S.C., U.S. (pĕl′zẽr)	125	34°38′N	82°30′W
Pemanggil, i., Malay.	197b	2°37′N	104°41′E
Pematangsiantar, Indon.	212	2°58′N	99°03′E
Pemba, Moz. (pĕm′bȧ)	233	12°58′S	40°30′E
Pemba, Zam.	232	15°29′S	27°22′E
Pemba Channel, strt., Afr.	237	5°10′S	39°30′E
Pemba Island, i., Tan.	237	5°20′S	39°57′E
Pembina, N.D., U.S. (pĕm′bĭ-nȧ)	112	48°58′N	97°15′W
Pembina, r., Can.	95	53°05′N	114°30′W
Pembina, r., N.A.	97	49°08′N	98°20′W
Pembroke, Can. (pĕm′ brōk)	91	45°50′N	77°00′W
Pembroke, Wales, U.K.	164	51°40′N	5°00′W
Pembroke, Ma., U.S. (pĕm′brōk)	101a	42°05′N	70°49′W
Pen, India	203b	18°44′N	73°06′E
Penafiel, Port. (pā-nȧ-fyĕl′)	172	41°12′N	8°19′W
Peñafiel, Spain (pā-nyȧ-fyĕl′)	172	41°38′N	4°08′W
Peñalara, mtn., Spain (pā-nyä-lä′rä)	162	40°52′N	3°57′W
Pena Nevada, Cerro, Mex.	130	23°47′N	99°52′W
Peñaranda de Bracamonte, Spain	172	40°54′N	5°11′W
Peñarroya-Pueblonuevo, Spain (pĕn-yär-rô′yä-pwĕ′blô-nwĕ′vô)	172	38°18′N	5°18′W
Peñas, Cabo de, c., Spain (kȧ′bô-dĕ-pā′nyäs)	172	43°42′N	6°12′W
Penas, Golfo de, b., Chile (gôl-fô-dĕ-pĕ′n-äs)	144	47°15′S	77°30′W
Penasco, r., Tx., U.S. (pā-nȧs′kō)	122	32°50′N	104°45′W
Pendembu, S.L. (pĕn-dĕm′bōō)	230	8°06′N	10°42′W
Pender, Ne., U.S. (pĕn′dẽr)	112	42°08′N	96°43′W
Penderisco, r., Col. (pĕn-dĕ-rē′s-kô)	142a	6°30′N	76°21′W
Pendjari, Parc National de la, rec., Benin	234	11°25′N	1°30′E
Pendleton, Or., U.S. (pĕn′d′l-tŭn)	104	45°41′N	118°47′W
Pend Oreille, r., Wa., U.S.	114	48°44′N	117°20′W
Pend Oreille, Lake, l., Id., U.S. (pŏn-dô-rā′) (pĕn-dô-rĕl′)	106	48°09′N	116°38′W
Penedo, Braz. (på-nā′dò)	143	10°17′S	36°28′W
Penetanguishene, Can. (pĕn′ê-tăŋ-gĭ-shēn′)	99	44°45′N	79°55′W
Pengcheng, China (pŭŋ-chŭŋ)	206	36°24′N	114°11′E
Penglai, China (pŭŋ-lī)	208	37°49′N	120°45′E
Peniche, Port. (pĕ-nē′chȧ)	172	39°22′N	9°24′W
Peninsula, Oh., U.S. (pĕn-ĭn′sū-lȧ)	111d	41°14′N	81°32′W
Penistone, Eng., U.K. (pĕn′ĭ-stŭn)	158a	53°31′N	1°38′W

ăt; finăl; rāte; senåte; ärm; ȧsk; sofȧ; fâre; ch-choose; dh-as th in other; bē; ēvent; bĕt; recĕnt; cratẽr; g-gō; gh-guttural g; bĭt; ĭ-short neutral; rīde; ĸ-guttural k as ch in German ich;

PRONOUNCING INDEX

Penjamillo – Pillar Rocks 335

PLACE (Pronunciation)	PAGE	LAT.	LONG.
Penjamillo, Mex. (pĕn-hä-mēl'yō)	130	20°06'N	101°56'W
Pénjamo, Mex. (pān'hä-mō)	130	20°27'N	101°43'W
Penk, r., Eng., U.K. (pĕnk)	158a	52°41'N	2°10'W
Penkridge, Eng., U.K. (pĕnk'rĭj)	158a	52°43'N	2°07'W
Penne, Italy (pĕn'nā)	174	42°28'N	13°57'E
Penner, r., India (pĕn'ĕr)	199	14°43'N	79°09'E
Pennines, hills, Eng., U.K. (pĕn-īn')	164	54°30'N	2°10'W
Pennines, Alpes, mts., Eur.	168	46°02'N	7°07'E
Pennsboro, W.V., U.S. (pĕnz'bŭr-ô)	108	39°10'N	81°00'W
Penns Grove, N.J., U.S. (pĕnz grōv)	110f	39°44'N	75°28'W
Pennsylvania, state, U.S. (pĕn-sĭl-vā'nĭ-ȧ)	105	41°00'N	78°10'W
Penn Yan, N.Y., U.S. (pĕn yăn')	109	42°40'N	77°00'W
Pennycutaway, r., Can.	97	56°10'N	93°25'W
Peno, l., Russia (pā'nô)	176	56°55'N	32°28'E
Penobscot, r., Me., U.S.	107	45°00'N	68°36'W
Penobscot Bay, b., Me., U.S. (pē-nŏb'skŏt)	100	44°20'N	69°00'W
Penong, Austl. (pē-nông')	218	32°00'S	133°00'E
Penrith, Austl.	217b	33°45'S	150°42'E
Pensacola, Fl., U.S. (pĕn-sȧ-kō'lȧ)	105	30°25'N	87°13'W
Pensacola Dam, Ok., U.S.	121	36°27'N	95°02'W
Pensilvania, Col. (pĕn-sēl-vä'nyä)	142a	5°31'N	75°05'W
Pentecost, i., Vanuatu (pĕn'tē-kŏst)	221	16°05'S	168°28'E
Penticton, Can.	90	49°30'N	119°35'W
Pentland Firth, strt., Scot., U.K. (pĕnt'lănd)	164	58°44'N	3°25'W
Penza, Russia (pĕn'zȧ)	178	53°10'N	45°00'E
Penzance, Eng., U.K. (pĕn-zăns')	164	50°07'N	5°40'W
Penzberg, Ger. (pĕnts'bĕrgh)	168	47°43'N	11°21'E
Penzhina, r., Russia (pyĭn-zē-nŭ)	185	62°15'N	166°30'E
Penzhino, Russia	179	63°42'N	168°00'E
Penzhinskaya Guba, b., Russia	185	60°30'N	161°30'E
Peoria, Il., U.S. (pē-ō'rĭ-ȧ)	105	40°45'N	89°35'W
Peotillos, Mex. (pā-ō-tel'yōs)	130	22°30'N	100°39'W
Peotone, Il., U.S. (pē'ō-tōn)	111a	41°20'N	87°47'W
Pepacton Reservoir, res., N.Y., U.S. (pĕp-ăc'tŭn)	109	42°05'N	74°40'W
Pepe, Cabo, c., Cuba (kä'bō-pĕ'pĕ)	134	21°30'N	83°10'W
Pepperell, Ma., U.S. (pĕp'ĕr-ĕl)	101a	42°40'N	71°36'W
Peqin, Alb. (pĕ-kēn')	175	41°03'N	19°48'E
Perales, r., Spain (pā-rä'lās)	173a	40°24'N	4°07'W
Perales de Tajuña, Spain (dā tä-hōō'nyä)	173a	40°14'N	3°22'W
Perche, Collines du, hills, Fr.	170	48°25'N	0°40'E
Perchtoldsdorf, Aus. (pĕrk'tōlts-dôrf)	159e	48°07'N	16°17'E
Perdekop, S. Afr.	238c	27°11'S	29°38'E
Perdido, r., Al., U.S. (pĕr-dī'dō)	124	30°45'N	87°38'W
Perdido, Monte, mtn., Spain (pĕr-dē'dō)	173	42°40'N	0°00'
Perdões, Braz. (pĕr-dô'ĕs)	141a	21°05'S	45°05'W
Pereiaslav-Khmel'nyts'kyi, Ukr.	181	50°05'N	31°25'E
Pereira, Col. (pā-rā'rä)	142	4°49'N	75°42'W
Pere Marquette, Mi., U.S.	108	43°55'N	86°10'W
Pereshchepyne, Ukr.	177	49°02'N	35°19'E
Pereslavl'-Zalesskiy, Russia (på-rå-slàv''l zå-lyĕs'kĭ)	180	56°43'N	38°52'E
Pergamino, Arg. (pĕr-gä-mē'nō)	144	33°53'S	60°36'W
Perham, Mn., U.S. (pĕr'hăm)	112	46°37'N	95°35'W
Peribonca, r., Can. (pĕr-ĭ-bŏŋ'kȧ)	93	50°30'N	71°00'W
Périgueux, Fr. (pā-rē-gû')	161	45°12'N	0°43'E
Perija, Sierra de, mts., Col. (sē-ĕ'r-rȧ-dĕ-pĕ-rē'kä)	142	9°25'N	73°30'W
Perkam, Tanjung, c., Indon.	213	1°20'S	138°45'E
Perkins, Can. (pĕr'kĕns)	102c	45°37'N	75°37'W
Perlas, Archipiélago de las, is., Pan.	133	8°29'N	79°15'W
Perlas, Laguna las, l., Nic. (lä-gô'nä-dĕ-läs)	133	12°34'N	83°19'W
Perleberg, Ger. (pĕr'lē-bĕrg)	168	53°06'N	11°51'E
Perm', Russia (pĕrm)	178	58°00'N	56°15'E
Pernambuco *see* Recife, Braz.	143	8°09'S	34°59'W
Pernambuco, state, Braz. (pĕr-näm-bōō'kō)	143	8°08'S	38°54'W
Pernik, Blg. (pĕr-nēk')	163	42°36'N	23°04'E
Péronne, Fr. (pā-rôn')	170	49°57'N	2°49'E
Perote, Mex. (pĕ-rô'tĕ)	131	19°33'N	97°13'W
Perovo, Russia (pâ'rô-vô)	186b	55°43'N	37°47'E
Perpignan, Fr. (pĕr-pē-nyäN')	161	42°42'N	2°48'E
Perris, Ca., U.S. (pĕr'ĭs)	117a	33°46'N	117°14'W
Perros, Bahía, b., Cuba (bä-ē'ä-pā'rōs)	134	22°25'N	78°35'W
Perrot, Île, i., Can.	102a	45°23'N	73°57'W
Perry, Fl., U.S. (pĕr'ĭ)	124	30°06'N	83°35'W
Perry, Ga., U.S.	124	32°27'N	83°44'W
Perry, Ia., U.S.	113	41°49'N	94°40'W
Perry, N.Y., U.S.	109	42°45'N	78°00'W
Perry, Ok., U.S.	121	36°17'N	97°18'W
Perry, Ut., U.S.	117b	41°27'N	112°02'W
Perry Hall, Md., U.S.	110e	39°24'N	76°29'W
Perryopolis, Pa., U.S. (pĕ-rē-ŏ'pō-lĭs)	111e	40°05'N	79°45'W
Perrysburg, Oh., U.S. (pĕr'ĭz-bûrg)	108	41°35'N	83°35'W
Perryton, Tx., U.S. (pĕr'ĭ-tŭn)	120	36°23'N	100°48'W
Perryville, Ak., U.S. (pĕr-ĭ-vĭl)	103	55°58'N	159°28'W
Perryville, Mo., U.S.	121	37°41'N	89°52'W
Persan, Fr. (pĕr-säN')	171b	49°09'N	2°15'E
Persepolis, hist., Iran (pĕr-sĕpô-lĭs)	198	30°15'N	53°08'E
Persian Gulf, b., Asia (pûr'zhăn)	198	27°38'N	50°30'E
Perth, Austl. (pûrth)	218	31°50'S	116°10'E
Perth, Can.	99	44°40'N	76°15'W
Perth, Scot., U.K.	160	56°24'N	3°25'W
Perth Amboy, N.J., U.S. (ăm'boi)	110a	40°31'N	74°16'W
Pertuis, Fr. (pĕr-tüē')	171	43°43'N	5°29'E
Peru, Il., U.S. (pē-rōō')	108	41°20'N	89°10'W
Peru, In., U.S.	108	40°45'N	86°00'W
Peru, nation, S.A.	142	10°00'S	75°00'W
Peru-Chile Trench, deep	139	25°00'S	71°30'W
Perugia, Italy (pā-rōō'jä)	162	43°08'N	12°24'E
Peruque, Mo., U.S. (pĕ rō'kĕ)	117e	38°52'N	90°36'W
Pervomais'k, Ukr.	181	48°04'N	30°52'E
Pervoural'sk, Russia (pĕr-vô-ō-rálsk')	186a	56°54'N	59°58'E
Pesaro, Italy (pā'zä-rō)	162	43°54'N	12°55'E
Pescado, r., Ven. (pĕs-kä'dō)	143b	9°33'N	65°32'W
Pescara, Italy (pās-kä'rä)	174	42°26'N	14°15'E
Pescara, r., Italy	174	42°18'N	13°22'E
Peschanyy müyisi, c., Kaz.	181	43°10'N	51°20'E
Pescia, Italy (pā'shä)	174	43°53'N	11°42'E
Peshāwar, Pak. (pĕ-shä'wŭr)	199	34°01'N	71°34'E
Peshtera, Blg.	175	42°03'N	24°19'E
Peshtigo, Wi., U.S. (pĕsh'tē-gō)	113	45°03'N	87°46'W
Peshtigo, r., Wi., U.S.	113	45°15'N	88°14'W
Peski, Russia (pyâs'kĭ)	186b	55°13'N	38°48'E
Pêso da Régua, Port. (pā-sō-dä-rā'gwä)	172	41°09'N	7°47'W
Pespire, Hond. (pås-pē'rå)	132	13°35'N	87°20'W
Pesqueria, r., Mex. (pås-kå-rē'ȧ)	122	25°55'N	100°25'W
Pessac, Fr.	170	44°48'N	0°38'W
Petacalco, Bahía de, b., Mex. (bä-ē'ä-dĕ-pĕ-tä-käl'kô)	130	17°55'N	102°00'W
Petah Tiqwa, Isr.	197a	32°05'N	34°53'E
Petaluma, Ca., U.S. (pét-ȧ-lō'mȧ)	118	38°15'N	122°38'W
Petare, Ven. (pĕ-tä'rĕ)	143b	10°28'N	66°48'W
Petatlán, Mex. (pā-tä-tlän')	130	17°31'N	101°17'W
Petawawa, Can.	99	45°54'N	77°17'W
Petén, Laguna de, l., Guat. (lä-gô'nä-dĕ-pā-tān')	132a	17°05'N	89°54'W
Petenwell Reservoir, res., Wi., U.S.	113	44°10'N	89°55'W
Peterborough, Austl.	218	32°53'S	138°58'E
Peterborough, Can. (pē'tĕr-bŭr-ô)	91	44°20'N	78°20'W
Peterborough, Eng., U.K.	164	52°35'N	0°14'W
Peterhead, Scot., U.K. (pē-tĕr-hĕd')	164	57°36'N	3°47'W
Peter Pond Lake, l., Can. (pŏnd)	92	55°55'N	108°44'W
Petersburg, Ak., U.S. (pē'tĕrz-bûrg)	103	56°52'N	133°10'W
Petersburg, Il., U.S.	121	40°01'N	89°51'W
Petersburg, In., U.S.	108	38°30'N	87°15'W
Petersburg, Ky., U.S.	111f	39°04'N	84°52'W
Petersburg, Va., U.S.	105	37°12'N	77°30'W
Petershagen, Ger. (pĕ'tĕrs-hä-gĕn)	159b	52°32'N	13°46'E
Petershausen, Ger. (pĕ'tĕrs-hou-zĕn)	159d	48°25'N	11°29'E
Pétionville, Haiti	135	18°30'N	72°20'W
Petitcodiac, Can. (pē-tē-kō-dyák')	100	45°56'N	65°10'W
Petite Terre, i., Guad. (pē-tēt'târ')	133b	16°12'N	61°00'W
Petit Goâve, Haiti (pē-tē' gō-áv')	135	18°25'N	72°50'W
Petit Jean Creek, r., Ar., U.S. (pē-tē'zhäN')	121	35°05'N	93°55'W
Petit Loango, Gabon	236	2°16'S	9°35'E
Petlalcingo, Mex. (pĕ-tläl-sēŋ'gô)	131	18°05'N	97°53'W
Peto, Mex. (pĕ'tô)	132a	20°07'N	88°49'W
Petorca, Chile (pā-tōr'kȧ)	141b	32°14'S	70°55'W
Petoskey, Mi., U.S. (pē-tŏs-kĭ)	108	45°25'N	84°55'W
Petra, hist., Jord.	197a	30°21'N	35°25'E
Petra Velikogo, Zaliv, b., Russia	210	42°40'N	131°50'E
Petre, Point, c., Can.	99	43°50'N	77°00'W
Petrich, Blg. (pā'trĭch)	163	41°24'N	23°13'E
Petrified Forest National Park, rec., Az., U.S. (pĕt'rĭ-fīd fôr'ĕst)	119	34°58'N	109°35'W
Petrinja, Cro. (pā'trēn-yȧ)	174	45°25'N	16°17'E
Petrodvorets, Russia (pyĕ-trô-dvô-ryĕts')	186c	59°53'N	29°55'E
Petrokrepost', Russia (pyĕ'trô-krĕ-pôst)	180	59°56'N	31°03'E
Petrolia, Can. (pē-trō'lĭ-ȧ)	98	42°50'N	82°10'W
Petrolina, Braz. (pĕ-trō-lē'nȧ)	143	9°18'S	40°28'W
Petronell, Aus.	159e	48°07'N	16°52'E
Petropavlivka, Ukr.	177	48°24'N	36°23'E
Petropavlovka, Russia	186a	54°10'N	59°50'E
Petropavlovsk, Kaz.	183	54°44'N	69°07'E
Petropavlovsk-Kamchatskiy, Russia (käm-chät'skĭ)	179	53°13'N	158°56'E
Petrópolis, Braz. (pĕ-trô-pō-lēzh')	143	22°31'S	43°10'W
Petroşani, Rom.	175	45°24'N	23°24'E
Petrovsk, Russia (pyĕ-trôfsk')	181	52°20'N	45°15'E
Petrovskaya, Russia (pyĕ-trôf'skȧ-yȧ)	177	45°25'N	37°50'E
Petrovskoye, Russia	181	45°20'N	43°00'E
Petrovsk-Zabaykal'skiy, Russia (pyĕ-trôfskzä-bī-käl'skĭ)	179	51°13'N	109°08'E
Petrozavodsk, Russia (pyā'trô-zȧ-vôtsk')	178	61°46'N	34°25'E
Petrus Steyn, S. Afr.	238c	27°40'S	28°09'E
Petrykivka, Ukr.	177	48°43'N	34°29'E
Pewaukee, Wi., U.S. (pĭ-wô'kē)	111a	43°05'N	88°15'W
Pewaukee Lake, l., Wi., U.S.	111a	43°03'N	88°18'W
Pewee Valley, Ky., U.S. (pe wē)	111h	38°19'N	85°29'W
Peza, r., Russia (pyâ'zȧ)	180	65°35'N	46°50'E
Pézenas, Fr. (pā-zē-nä')	170	43°26'N	3°24'E
Pforzheim, Ger. (pfôrts'hīm)	161	48°52'N	8°43'E
Phalodi, India	202	27°13'N	72°22'E
Phan Thiet, Viet. (p'hän')	212	11°30'N	108°43'E
Phelps Lake, l., N.C., U.S.	125	35°46'N	76°27'W
Phenix City, Al., U.S. (fē'nĭks)	124	32°29'N	85°00'W
Philadelphia, Ms., U.S. (fĭl-ȧ-dĕl'phĭ-ȧ)	124	32°45'N	89°07'W
Philadelphia, Pa., U.S.	105	40°00'N	75°13'W
Philip, S.D., U.S. (fĭl'ĭp)	112	44°03'N	101°35'W
Philippeville *see* Skikda, Alg.	230	36°58'N	6°51'E
Philippines, nation, Asia (fĭl'ĭ-pēnz)	213	14°25'N	125°00'E
Philippine Sea, sea (fĭl'ĭ-pēn)	241	16°00'N	133°00'E
Philippine Trench, deep	213	10°30'N	127°15'E
Philipsburg, Pa., U.S. (fĭl'lĭps-bĕrg)	109	40°55'N	78°10'W
Philipsburg, Wy., U.S.	115	46°19'N	113°19'W
Phillip, i., Austl. (fĭl'ĭp)	222	38°32'S	145°10'E
Phillip Channel, strt., Indon.	197b	1°04'N	103°40'E
Phillipi, W.V., U.S. (fĭ-lĭp'ĭ)	108	39°10'N	80°00'W
Phillips, Wi., U.S. (fĭl'ĭps)	113	45°41'N	90°24'W
Phillipsburg, Ks., U.S. (fĭl'lĭps-bĕrg)	120	39°44'N	99°19'W
Phillipsburg, N.J., U.S.	109	40°45'N	75°10'W
Phitsanulok, Thai.	212	16°51'N	100°15'E
Phnom Penh (Phnum Pénh), Camb. (nŏm'pĕn')	212	11°39'N	104°53'E
Phnum Pénh *see* Phnom Penh, Camb.	212	11°39'N	104°53'E
Phoenix, Az., U.S. (fē'nĭks)	104	33°30'N	112°00'W
Phoenix, Md., U.S.	110e	39°31'N	76°40'W
Phoenix Islands, is., Kir.	2	4°00'S	174°00'W
Phoenixville, Pa., U.S. (fē'nĭks-vĭl)	110f	40°08'N	75°31'W
Phou Bia, mtn., Laos	212	19°36'N	103°00'E
Phra Nakhon Si Ayutthaya, Thai.	212	14°16'N	100°37'E
Phuket, Thai.	212	7°57'N	98°19'E
Phu Quoc, Dao, i., Viet.	212	10°13'N	104°00'E
Pi, r., China (bē)	206	32°06'N	116°31'E
Piacenza, Italy (pyä-chĕnt'sä)	162	45°02'N	9°42'E
Pianosa, i., Italy (pyä-nō'sä)	174	42°13'N	15°45'E
Piave, r., Italy (pyä'vā)	174	45°45'N	12°15'E
Piazza Armerina, Italy (pyät'sȧ är-mȧ-rē'nä)	174	37°23'N	14°26'E
Pibor, r., Sudan (pē'bôr)	231	7°21'N	32°54'E
Pic, r., Can. (pĕk)	98	48°48'N	86°28'W
Picara Point, c., V.I.U.S. (pē-kä'rä)	129c	18°23'N	64°57'W
Picayune, Ms., U.S. (pĭk'ȧ yōōn)	124	30°32'N	89°41'W
Picher, Ok., U.S. (pĭch'ĕr)	121	36°58'N	94°49'W
Pichilemu, Chile (pē-chē-lĕ'mōō)	141b	34°22'S	72°01'W
Pichucalco, Mex. (pē-chōō-käl'kô)	131	17°34'N	93°06'W
Pickerel, l., Can. (pĭk'ĕr-ĕl)	98	48°35'N	91°10'W
Pickwick Lake, res., U.S. (pĭk'wĭck)	124	35°04'N	88°05'W
Pico, Ca., U.S. (pē'kō)	117a	34°01'N	118°05'W
Pico Island, i., Port. (pē'kò)	230a	38°16'N	28°49'W
Pico Rivera, Ca., U.S.	117a	34°01'N	118°05'W
Picos, Braz. (pē'kōzh)	143	7°13'S	41°23'W
Picton, Austl. (pĭk'tŭn)	217b	34°11'S	150°37'E
Picton, Can.	99	44°00'N	77°15'W
Pictou, Can. (pĭk-tōō')	101	45°41'N	62°43'W
Pidálion, Akrotírion, c., Cyp.	197a	34°50'N	34°05'E
Pidurutalagala, mtn., Sri L. (pē'dō-rō-tä'lá-gä'lȧ)	203	7°00'N	80°46'E
Pidvolochys'k, Ukr.	177	49°32'N	26°16'E
Pie, i., Can. (pī)	98	48°10'N	89°07'W
Piedade, Braz. (pyä-dä'dĕ)	141a	23°42'S	47°25'W
Piedmont, Al., U.S. (pēd'mŏnt)	124	33°54'N	85°36'W
Piedmont, Ca., U.S.	116b	37°50'N	122°14'W
Piedmont, Mo., U.S.	121	37°09'N	90°42'W
Piedmont, S.C., U.S.	125	34°40'N	82°27'W
Piedmont, W.V., U.S.	109	39°30'N	79°05'W
Piedrabuena, Spain (pyā-drä-bwā'nä)	172	39°01'N	4°10'W
Piedras, Punta, c., Arg. (pōō'n-tä-pyĕ'dräs)	141c	35°25'S	57°10'W
Piedras Negras, Mex. (pyā'dräs nā'gräs)	128	28°41'N	100°33'W
Pieksämäki, Fin. (pyĕk'sĕ-mĕ-kē)	167	62°18'N	27°14'E
Piemonte, hist. reg., Italy (pyĕ-mô'n-tĕ)	174	44°30'N	7°42'E
Pienaars, r., S. Afr.	238c	25°13'S	28°05'E
Pienaarsrivier, S. Afr.	238c	25°12'S	28°18'E
Pierce, Ne., U.S. (pērs)	112	42°11'N	97°33'W
Pierce, W.V., U.S.	109	39°15'N	79°30'W
Piermont, N.Y., U.S. (pēr'mŏnt)	110a	41°03'N	73°55'W
Pierre, S.D., U.S. (pēr)	104	44°22'N	100°20'W
Pierrefonds, Can.	102a	45°29'N	73°52'W
Piešt'any, Slvk.	169	48°36'N	17°48'E
Pietermaritzburg, S. Afr. (pē-tēr-mȧ-rĭts-bûrg)	232	29°36'S	30°23'E
Pietersburg, S. Afr. (pē'tĕrz-bûrg)	232	23°56'S	29°30'E
Piet Retief, S. Afr. (pēt rĕ-tēf')	232	27°00'S	30°58'E
Pietrosu, Vârful, mtn., Rom.	169	47°35'N	24°49'E
Pieve di Cadore, Italy (pyā'vå dē kä-dō'rå)	162	46°26'N	12°22'E
Pigeon, r., N.A. (pĭj'ŭn)	113	48°05'N	90°13'W
Pigeon Lake, Can.	102f	49°57'N	97°36'W
Pigeon Lake, l., Can.	95	53°00'N	114°00'W
Piggott, Ar., U.S. (pĭg-ŭt)	121	36°22'N	90°10'W
Pijijiapan, Mex. (pēkē-kē-ä'pän)	131	15°40'N	93°12'W
Pijnacker, Neth.	159a	52°01'N	4°25'E
Pikes Peak, mtn., Co., U.S. (pīks)	106	38°49'N	105°03'W
Pikeville, Ky., U.S. (pīk'vĭl)	108	37°28'N	82°31'W
Pikou, China (pē-kō)	208	39°25'N	122°19'E
Pikwitonei, Can. (pĭk'wĭ-tōn)	97	55°35'N	97°09'W
Piła, Pol. (pē'lȧ)	168	53°09'N	16°44'E
Pilansberg, mtn., S. Afr. (pē'ăns'bûrg)	238c	25°08'S	26°55'E
Pilar, Arg. (pē'lär)	141c	34°27'S	58°55'W
Pilar, Para.	144	27°00'S	58°15'W
Pilar de Goiás, Braz. (dĕ-gô'yá's)	143	14°47'S	49°33'W
Pilchuck, r., Wa., U.S.	116a	48°03'N	121°58'W
Pilchuck Creek, r., Wa., U.S. (pĭl'chŭck)	116a	48°19'N	122°11'W
Pilchuck Mountain, mtn., Wa., U.S.	116a	48°03'N	121°48'W
Pilcomayo, r., S.A. (pēl-cō-mī'ō)	144	24°45'S	59°15'W
Pili, Phil. (pē'lē)	213a	13°34'N	123°17'E
Pilica, r., Pol. (pē-lēt'sä)	169	51°00'N	19°48'E
Pillar Point, c., Wa., U.S. (pĭl'ȧr)	116a	48°14'N	124°06'W
Pillar Rocks, Wa., U.S.	116c	46°16'N	123°35'W

PLACE (Pronunciation)	PAGE	LAT.	LONG.
Pilón, r., Mex. (pē-lōn′)	130	24°13′N	99°03′W
Pilot Point, Tx., U.S. (pī′lŭt)	121	33°24′N	97°00′W
Pilsen *see* Plzeň, Czech Rep.	154	49°46′N	13°25′E
Piltene, Lat. (pĭl′tĕ-nĕ)	167	57°17′N	21°40′E
Pimal, Cerra, mtn., Mex. (sĕ′r-rä-pē-mäl′)	130	22°58′N	104°19′W
Pimba, Austl. (pĭm′bȧ)	218	31°15′S	137°50′E
Pimville, neigh., S. Afr. (pĭm′vĭl)	233b	26°17′S	27°54′E
Pinacate, Cerro, mtn., Mex. (sĕ′r-rô-pē-nä-kä′tĕ)	128	31°45′N	113°30′W
Pinamalayan, Phil. (pē-nä-mä-lä′yän)	213a	13°04′N	121°31′E
Pinang *see* George Town, Malay.	212	5°21′N	100°09′E
Pınarbaşı, Tur. (pē′när-bä′shĭ)	163	38°50′N	36°10′E
Pinar del Río, Cuba (pē-när′ dĕl rē′ô)	129	22°25′N	83°35′W
Pinar del Río, prov., Cuba	134	22°45′N	83°25′W
Pinatubo, mtn., Phil. (pē-nä-tōō′bô)	213a	15°09′N	120°19′E
Pincher Creek, Can. (pĭn′chēr krēk)	95	49°29′N	113°57′W
Pinckneyville, Il., U.S. (pĭnk′nĭ-vĭl)	121	38°06′N	89°22′W
Pińczów, Pol. (pēn′′chôf)	169	50°32′N	20°33′E
Pindamonhangaba, Braz. (pē′n-dä-mōnyȧ′n-gä-bä)	141a	22°56′S	45°26′W
Pinder Point, c., Bah.	134	26°35′N	78°35′W
Pindiga, Nig.	235	9°59′N	10°54′E
Píndos Óros, mts., Grc.	156	39°48′N	21°19′E
Pine, r., Can. (pīn)	95	55°30′N	122°20′W
Pine, r., Wi., U.S.	113	45°50′N	88°37′W
Pine Bluff, Ar., U.S. (pīn blŭf)	105	34°13′N	92°01′W
Pine City, Mn., U.S. (pīn)	113	45°50′N	93°01′W
Pine Creek, Austl.	218	13°45′S	132°00′E
Pine Creek, r., Nv., U.S.	118	40°15′N	116°17′W
Pine Falls, Can.	97	50°35′N	96°15′W
Pine Flat Lake, res., Ca., U.S.	118	36°52′N	119°18′W
Pine Forest Range, mts., Nv., U.S.	114	41°35′N	118°45′W
Pinega, Russia (pē-nyĕ′gȧ)	178	64°40′N	43°30′E
Pinega, r., Russia	180	64°10′N	42°30′E
Pine Hill, N.J., U.S. (pīn hĭl)	110f	39°47′N	74°59′W
Pineiós, r., Grc.	175	39°30′N	21°40′E
Pine Island Sound, strt., Fl., U.S.	125a	26°32′N	82°30′W
Pine Lake Estates, Ga., U.S. (lāk ĕs-tāts′)	110c	33°47′N	84°13′W
Pinelands, S. Afr. (pīn′lănds)	232a	33°57′S	18°30′E
Pine Lawn, Mo., U.S. (lôn)	117e	38°42′N	90°17′W
Pine Pass, p., Can.	95	55°22′N	122°40′W
Pinerolo, Italy (pē-nå-rô′lō)	174	44°47′N	7°18′E
Pines, Lake o′ the, Tx., U.S.	123	32°50′N	94°40′W
Pinetown, S. Afr. (pīn′toun)	233c	29°47′S	30°52′E
Pine View Reservoir, res., Ut., U.S. (vū)	117b	41°17′N	111°54′W
Pineville, Ky., U.S. (pīn′vĭl)	124	36°48′N	83°43′W
Pineville, La., U.S.	123	31°20′N	92°25′W
Ping, r., Thai.	212	17°54′N	98°29′E
Pingding, China (pĭŋ-dĭŋ)	208	37°50′N	113°30′E
Pingdu, China (pĭŋ-dōō)	208	36°46′N	119°57′E
Pinggir, Indon.	197b	1°05′N	101°12′E
Pinghe, China (pĭŋ-hŭ)	209	24°30′N	117°02′E
Pingle, China (pĭŋ-lŭ)	209	24°30′N	110°22′E
Pingliang, China (pĭng′lyäng′)	204	35°12′N	106°50′E
Pingquan, China (pĭŋ-chyůän)	208	40°58′N	118°40′E
Pingtan, China (pĭŋ-tän)	209	25°30′N	119°45′E
Pingtan Dao, i., China (pĭŋ-tän dou)	209	25°40′N	119°45′E
P′ingtung, Tai.	209	22°40′N	120°35′E
Pingwu, China (pĭŋ-wōō)	208	32°20′N	104°40′E
Pingxiang, China (pĭŋ-shyäŋ)	209	27°40′N	113°50′E
Pingyi, China (pĭŋ-yē)	206	35°30′N	117°38′E
Pingyuan, China (pĭŋ-yůän)	206	37°11′N	116°26′E
Pingzhou, China (pĭŋ-jō)	207a	23°01′N	113°11′E
Pinhal, Braz. (pē-nyȧ′l)	141a	22°11′S	46°43′W
Pinhal Novo, Port. (nô vô)	173b	38°38′N	8°54′W
Pinhel, Port. (pēn-yĕl′)	172	40°45′N	7°03′W
Pini, Pulau, i., Indon.	212	0°07′S	98°38′E
Pinnacles National Monument, rec., Ca., U.S. (pĭn′ȧ-k′lz)	118	36°30′N	121°00′W
Pinneberg, Ger. (pĭn′ĕ-bĕrg)	159c	53°40′N	9°48′E
Pinole, Ca., U.S. (pĭ-nō′lē)	116b	38°01′N	122°17′W
Pinos-Puente, Spain (pwān′tå)	172	37°15′N	3°43′W
Pinotepa Nacional, Mex. (pē-nô-tā′pä nä-syô-näl′)	130	16°21′N	98°04′W
Pins, Île des, i., N. Cal.	221	22°44′S	167°44′E
Pinsk, Bela. (pēn′sk)	178	52°07′N	26°05′E
Pinta, i., Ec.	142	0°41′N	90°47′W
Pintendre, Can. (pĕɴ-täɴdr′)	102b	46°45′N	71°07′W
Pinto, Spain (pēn′tō)	173a	40°14′N	3°42′W
Pinto Butte, Can. (pĭn′tō)	96	49°22′N	107°25′W
Pioche, Nv., U.S. (pī-ō′chē)	119	37°56′N	114°28′W
Piombino, Italy (pyôm-bē′nō)	162	42°56′N	10°33′E
Pioneer Mountains, mts., Mt., U.S. (pī′ô-nēr′)	115	45°23′N	112°51′W
Piotrków Trybunalski, Pol. (pyōtr′kōōv trĭ-bōō-nal′skē)	161	51°23′N	19°44′E
Piper, Al., U.S. (pī′pēr)	124	33°04′N	87°00′W
Piper, Ks., U.S.	117f	39°09′N	94°51′W
Pipe Spring National Monument, rec., Az., U.S. (pīp sprĭng)	119	36°50′N	112°45′W
Pipestone, Mn., U.S. (pīp′stōn)	112	44°00′N	96°19′W
Pipestone National Monument, rec., Mn., U.S.	112	44°03′N	96°24′W
Pipmuacan, Réservoir, res., Can. (pĭp-mä-kän′)	99	49°45′N	70°00′W
Piqua, Oh., U.S. (pĭk′wȧ)	108	40°10′N	84°15′W
Piracaia, Braz. (pē-rä-kȧ′yä)	141a	23°04′S	46°20′W
Piracicaba, Braz. (pē-rä-sē-kä′bä)	143	22°43′S	47°39′W
Piraíba, r., Braz. (pä-rä-ē′bȧ)	141a	21°38′S	41°29′W
Piramida, mtn., Russia	179	54°00′N	96°00′E
Piran, Slvn. (pē-rå′n)	174	45°31′N	13°34′E
Piranga, Braz. (pē-rä′n-gä)	141a	20°41′S	43°17′W
Pirapetinga, Braz. (pē-rä-pĕ-tē′n-gä)	141a	21°40′S	42°20′W
Pirapora, Braz. (pē-rȧ-pō′rȧ)	143	17°39′S	44°54′W
Pirassununga, Braz. (pē-rä-sōō-nōō′n-gä)	141a	22°00′S	47°24′W
Pirenópolis, Braz. (pē-rĕ-nô′pō-lēs)	143	15°56′S	48°49′W
Piritu, Laguna de, l., Ven. (lä-gô′nä-dĕ-pē-rē′tōō)	143b	10°00′N	64°57′W
Pirmasens, Ger. (pĭr-mä-zĕns′)	168	49°12′N	7°34′E
Pirna, Ger. (pĭr′nä)	168	50°57′N	13°56′E
Pirot, Serb. (pē′rōt)	163	43°09′N	22°35′E
Pirtleville, Az., U.S. (pûr′t′l-vĭl)	119	31°25′N	109°35′W
Piru, Indon. (pē-rōō′)	213	3°15′S	128°25′E
Pisa, Italy (pē′sä)	162	43°52′N	10°24′E
Pisagua, Chile (pē-sä′gwä)	142	19°43′S	70°12′W
Piscataway, Md., U.S. (pĭs-kă-tă-wā)	110e	38°42′N	76°59′W
Piscataway, N.J., U.S.	110a	40°35′N	74°27′W
Pisco, Peru (pēs′kō)	142	13°43′S	76°07′W
Pisco, Bahía de, b., Peru	142	13°43′S	77°48′W
Piseco, l., N.Y., U.S. (pĭ-sā′kô)	109	43°25′N	74°35′W
Pisek, Czech Rep. (pē′sĕk)	161	49°18′N	14°08′E
Pisticci, Italy (pēs-tē′chē)	174	40°24′N	16°34′E
Pistoia, Italy (pēs-tô′yä)	162	43°57′N	11°54′E
Pisuerga, r., Spain (pē-swĕr′gä)	172	41°48′N	4°28′W
Pit, r., Ca., U.S. (pĭt)	114	40°58′N	121°42′W
Pitalito, Col. (pē-tä-lē′tō)	142	1°45′N	75°09′W
Pitcairn, dep., Oc.	2	25°04′S	130°05′W
Pitealven, r., Swe.	160	66°08′N	18°51′E
Pitești, Rom. (pē-tĕsht′′)	175	44°51′N	24°51′E
Pithara, Austl. (pĭt′ără)	218	30°27′S	116°45′E
Pithiviers, Fr. (pē-tē-vyā′)	170	48°12′N	2°14′E
Pitman, N.J., U.S. (pĭt′măn)	110f	39°44′N	75°08′W
Pitseng, Leso.	233c	29°03′S	28°13′E
Pitt, r., Can.	116d	49°19′N	122°39′W
Pitt Island, i., Can.	94	53°35′N	129°45′W
Pittsburg, Ca., U.S. (pĭts′bûrg)	116b	38°01′N	121°52′W
Pittsburg, Ks., U.S.	105	37°25′N	94°43′W
Pittsburg, Tx., U.S.	121	32°00′N	94°57′W
Pittsburgh, Pa., U.S.	105	40°26′N	80°01′W
Pittsfield, Il., U.S. (pĭts′fēld)	121	39°37′N	90°47′W
Pittsfield, Ma., U.S.	109	42°25′N	73°15′W
Pittsfield, Me., U.S.	100	44°45′N	69°44′W
Pittston, Pa., U.S. (pĭts′tŭn)	109	41°20′N	75°50′W
Piũi, Braz. (pē-ōō′ē)	141a	20°27′S	45°57′W
Piura, Peru (pē-ōō′rä)	142	5°13′S	80°46′W
Pivdennyi Buh, r., Ukr.	181	48°12′N	30°13′E
Piya, Russia (pē′yȧ)	186a	58°34′N	61°12′E
Placentia, Can.	101	47°15′N	53°58′W
Placentia, Ca., U.S. (plă-sĕn′shĭ-ȧ)	117a	33°52′N	117°50′W
Placentia Bay, b., Can.	93a	47°14′N	54°30′W
Placerville, Ca., U.S. (plăs′ēr-vĭl)	118	38°43′N	120°47′W
Placetas, Cuba (plä-thā′täs)	134	22°10′N	79°40′W
Placid, l., N.Y., U.S. (plăs′ĭd)	109	44°20′N	74°00′W
Plain City, Ut., U.S. (plān)	117b	41°18′N	112°06′W
Plainfield, Il., U.S. (plān′fēld)	111a	41°37′N	88°12′W
Plainfield, In., U.S.	111g	39°42′N	86°23′W
Plainfield, N.J., U.S.	110a	40°38′N	74°25′W
Plainview, Ar., U.S. (plān′vū)	121	34°59′N	93°15′W
Plainview, Mn., U.S.	113	44°09′N	93°12′W
Plainview, Ne., U.S.	112	42°20′N	97°47′W
Plainview, Tx., U.S.	120	34°11′N	101°42′W
Plainwell, Mi., U.S. (plan′wĕl)	108	42°25′N	85°40′W
Plaisance, Can. (plĕ-zäɴs′)	102c	45°37′N	75°07′W
Plana or Flat Cays, is., Bah. (plä′nä)	135	22°35′N	73°35′W
Planegg, Ger. (plä′nĕg)	159d	48°06′N	11°27′E
Plano, Tx., U.S. (plā′nō)	121	33°01′N	96°42′W
Plantagenet, Can. (pläɴ-täzh-nĕ′)	102c	45°33′N	75°00′W
Plant City, Fl., U.S. (plȧnt sĭ′tĭ)	125a	28°00′N	82°07′W
Plaquemine, La., U.S. (pläk′mēn′)	123	30°17′N	91°14′W
Plasencia, Spain (plä-sĕn′thē-ä)	172	40°02′N	6°07′W
Plast, Russia (plȧst)	180	54°22′N	60°48′E
Plaster Rock, Can. (plȧs′tēr rŏk)	100	46°54′N	67°24′W
Plastun, Russia (plȧs-tōōn′)	210	44°41′N	136°08′E
Plata, Río de la, est., S.A. (dālä plä′tä)	144	34°35′S	58°15′W
Platani, r., Italy (plä-tä′nē)	174	37°26′N	13°28′E
Plateforme, Pointe, c., Haiti	135	19°35′N	73°50′W
Platinum, Ak., U.S. (plăt′ĭ-nŭm)	103	59°00′N	161°27′W
Plato, Col. (plä′tō)	142	9°49′N	74°48′W
Platón Sánchez, Mex. (plä-tōn′ sän′chĕz)	130	21°14′N	98°20′W
Platte, S.D., U.S. (plăt)	112	43°22′N	98°51′W
Platte, r., Mo., U.S.	121	40°09′N	94°40′W
Platte, r., Ne., U.S.	106	40°50′N	100°40′W
Platteville, Wi., U.S. (plăt′vĭl)	113	42°44′N	90°31′W
Plattsburg, Mo., U.S. (plăts′bûrg)	121	39°33′N	94°26′W
Plattsburg, N.Y., U.S.	109	44°40′N	73°30′W
Plattsmouth, Ne., U.S. (plăts′mŭth)	112	41°00′N	95°53′W
Plauen, Ger. (plou′ĕn)	161	50°30′N	12°08′E
Playa de Guanabo, Cuba (plä-yä-dĕ-gwä-nä′bô)	135a	23°10′N	82°07′W
Playa de Santa Fé, Cuba	135a	23°05′N	82°31′W
Playas Lake, l., N.M., U.S. (plä′yȧs)	119	31°50′N	108°30′W
Playa Vicente, Mex. (vē-sĕn′tå)	131	17°49′N	95°49′W
Playa Vicente, r., Mex.	131	17°36′N	96°13′W
Playgreen Lake, l., Can. (plā′grēn)	97	54°00′N	98°10′W
Pleasant, l., N.Y., U.S. (plĕz′ănt)	109	43°25′N	74°25′W
Pleasant Grove, Al., U.S.	110h	33°29′N	86°57′W
Pleasant Hill, Ca., U.S.	116b	37°57′N	122°04′W
Pleasant Hill, Mo., U.S.	121	38°46′N	94°18′W
Pleasanton, Ca., U.S. (plĕz′ăn-tŭn)	116b	37°40′N	121°53′W
Pleasanton, Ks., U.S.	121	38°10′N	94°41′W
Pleasanton, Tx., U.S.	122	28°58′N	98°30′W
Pleasant Plain, Oh., U.S. (plĕz′ănt)	111f	39°17′N	84°06′W
Pleasant Ridge, Mi., U.S.	111b	42°28′N	83°09′W
Pleasant View, Ut., U.S. (plĕz′ănt vū)	117b	41°20′N	112°02′W
Pleasantville, N.Y., U.S. (plĕz′ănt-vĭl)	110a	41°08′N	73°47′W
Pleasure Ridge Park, Ky., U.S. (plĕzh′ēr rĭj)	111h	38°09′N	85°49′W
Plenty, Bay of, b., N.Z. (plĕn′tē)	221a	37°30′S	177°10′E
Plentywood, Mt., U.S. (plĕn′tē-wo͝od)	115	48°47′N	104°38′W
Ples, Russia (plyĕs)	176	57°26′N	41°29′E
Pleshcheyevo, l., Russia (plĕsh-chă′yĕ-vô)	176	56°50′N	38°22′E
Plessisville, Can. (plĕ-sē′vēl′)	99	46°12′N	71°47′W
Pleszew, Pol. (plĕ′zhĕf)	169	51°54′N	17°48′E
Plettenberg, Ger. (plĕ′tĕn-bĕrgh)	171c	51°13′N	7°53′E
Pleven, Blg. (plĕ′vĕn)	163	43°24′N	24°26′E
Pljevlja, Serb. (plĕv′lyä)	163	43°20′N	19°21′E
Płock, Pol. (pwôtsk)	161	52°32′N	19°44′E
Ploërmel, Fr. (plô-ĕr-mêl′)	170	47°56′N	2°25′W
Ploieşti, Rom. (plô-yĕsht′′)	154	44°56′N	26°01′E
Plomári, Grc.	175	38°51′N	26°24′E
Plomb du Cantal, mtn., Fr. (plôɴ′dükäɴ-täl′)	161	45°30′N	2°49′E
Plonge, Lac la, l., Can. (plōɴzh)	96	55°08′N	107°25′W
Plovdiv, Blg. (plôv′dĭf) (fĭl-ĭp-ŏp′ô-lĭs)	154	42°09′N	24°43′E
Pluma Hidalgo, Mex. (plōō′mä ē-däl′gō)	131	15°54′N	96°23′W
Plunge, Lith. (plo͝on′gā)	167	55°56′N	21°45′E
Plymouth, Monts.	133b	16°43′N	62°12′W
Plymouth, Eng., U.K. (plĭm′ŭth)	161	50°25′N	4°14′W
Plymouth, In., U.S.	108	41°20′N	86°20′W
Plymouth, Ma., U.S.	109	42°00′N	70°45′W
Plymouth, Mi., U.S.	111b	42°23′N	83°27′W
Plymouth, N.C., U.S.	125	35°50′N	76°44′W
Plymouth, N.H., U.S.	109	43°50′N	71°40′W
Plymouth, Pa., U.S.	109	41°15′N	75°55′W
Plymouth, Wi., U.S.	113	43°45′N	87°59′W
Plyussa, r., Russia (plyōō′sȧ)	176	58°33′N	28°30′E
Plzeň, Czech Rep.	154	49°45′N	13°23′E
Po, r., Italy	156	45°10′N	11°00′E
Pocahontas, Ar., U.S. (pō-kȧ-hŏn′tȧs)	121	36°15′N	91°01′W
Pocahontas, Ia., U.S.	113	42°43′N	94°41′W
Pocatello, Id., U.S. (pō-kȧ-tĕl′ō)	104	42°54′N	112°30′W
Pochëp, Russia (pô-chĕp′)	181	52°56′N	33°27′E
Pochinok, Russia (pô-chē′nôk)	176	54°14′N	32°27′E
Pochinski, Russia	180	54°40′N	44°50′E
Pochotitán, Mex. (pô-chô-tē-tȧ′n)	130	21°37′N	104°33′W
Pochutla, Mex.	131	15°46′N	96°28′W
Pocomoke City, Md., U.S. (pō-kō-mōk′)	109	38°05′N	75°35′W
Pocono Mountains, mts., Pa., U.S. (pō-cō′nō)	109	41°10′N	75°30′W
Poços de Caldas, Braz. (pō-sôs-dĕ-käl′dȧs)	143	21°48′S	46°34′W
Poder, Sen. (pô-dôr′)	230	16°35′N	15°04′W
Podgorica, Serb.	175	42°25′N	19°15′E
Podkamennaya Tunguska, r., Russia	179	61°43′N	93°45′E
Podol′sk, Russia (pô-dôl′′sk)	180	55°26′N	37°33′E
Poggibonsi, Italy (pôd-jē-bôn′sē)	174	43°27′N	11°12′E
Pogodino, Bela. (pô-gô′dē-nô)	180	54°17′N	31°00′E
P′ohangdong, Kor., S.	210	35°57′N	129°23′E
Pointe-à-Pitre, Guad. (pwăɴt′ ȧ pē-tr′)	129	16°15′N	61°32′W
Pointe-aux-Trembles, Can. (pōō-äɴt′ ō-träɴbl)	102a	45°39′N	73°30′W
Pointe Claire, Can. (pōō-äɴt′ klĕr)	102a	45°27′N	73°48′W
Pointe-des-Cascades, Can. (kăs-kādz′)	102a	45°19′N	73°58′W
Pointe Fortune, Can. (fôr′tūn)	102a	45°34′N	74°23′W
Pointe-Gatineau, Can. (pōō-äɴt′gä-tē-nō′)	102c	45°28′N	75°42′W
Pointe Noire, Congo	232	4°48′S	11°51′E
Point Hope, Ak., U.S. (hōp)	103	68°18′N	166°38′W
Point Pleasant, W.V., U.S. (plĕz′ănt)	108	38°50′N	82°10′W
Point Roberts, Wa., U.S. (rŏb′ērts)	116d	48°59′N	123°04′W
Poissy, Fr. (pwȧ-sē′)	171b	48°55′N	2°02′E
Poitiers, Fr. (pwȧ-tyā′)	161	46°35′N	0°18′E
Pokaran, India (pō′kŭr-ŭn)	202	27°00′N	72°05′E
Pokrov, Russia (pô-krôf)	176	55°56′N	39°09′E
Pokrovskoye, Russia (pô-krôf′skô-yĕ)	177	47°27′N	38°54′E
Pola, r., Russia (pō′lä)	176	57°44′N	31°53′E
Pola de Laviana, Spain (dĕ-lä-vyä′nä)	172	43°15′N	5°29′W
Pola de Siero, Spain	172	43°24′N	5°39′W
Poland, nation, Eur. (pō′lănd)	154	52°37′N	17°01′E
Polangui, Phil. (pô-läŋ′gē)	213a	13°18′N	123°29′E
Polatsk, Bela.	180	55°30′N	28°48′E
Polazna, Russia (pô′lȧz-nȧ)	186a	58°18′N	56°25′E
Polessk, Russia (pô′lĕsk)	167	54°50′N	21°14′E
Polevskoy, Russia (pô-lĕ′vs-kô′ē)	186a	56°28′N	60°14′E
Polgár, Hung. (pôl′gär)	169	47°54′N	21°10′E
Policastro, Golfo di, b., Italy	174	40°00′N	13°23′E
Polichnítos, Grc.	175	39°05′N	26°11′E
Poligny, Fr. (pō-lē-nyē′)	171	46°48′N	5°42′E
Polillo, Phil. (pô-lēl′yō)	213a	14°42′N	121°56′W
Polillo Islands, is., Phil.	199	15°05′N	122°15′E
Polillo Strait, strt., Phil.	213a	15°02′N	121°40′E
Polist′, r., Russia (pô′lĭst)	176	57°42′N	31°02′E
Polistena, Italy (pō-lēs-tā′nä)	174	38°25′N	16°05′E
Polkan, Gora, mtn., Russia	179	60°18′N	92°08′E
Polochic, r., Guat. (pō-lô-chēk′)	132	15°19′N	89°45′W
Polonne, Ukr.	177	50°07′N	27°31′E
Polpaico, Chile (pôl-pȧ′y-kô)	141b	33°10′S	70°53′W
Polson, Mt., U.S. (pōl′sŭn)	115	47°40′N	114°10′W

ăt; finăl; rāte; senåte; ärm; ȧsk; sofȧ; fâre; ch-choose; dh-as th in other; bē; ēvent; bĕt; recĕnt; cratēr; g-gō; gh-guttural g; bĭt; ĭ-short neutral; rīde; ᴋ-guttural k as ch in German ich;

PRONOUNCING INDEX

Poltava – Pratas Island 337

PLACE (Pronunciation)	PAGE	LAT.	LONG.
Poltava, Ukr. (pôl-tä'vä)	178	49°35'N	34°33'E
Poltava, prov., Ukr.	177	49°53'N	32°58'E
Põltsamaa, Est. (põlt'sá-mä)	167	58°39'N	26°00'E
Polunochnoye, Russia (pô-lōō-nô'ch-nô-yĕ)	186a	60°52'N	60°27'E
Poluy, r., Russia (pôl'wê)	184	65°45'N	68°15'E
Polyakovka, Russia (pŭl-yä'kôv-kå)	186a	54°38'N	59°42'E
Polyarnyy, Russia (pŭl-yär'nē)	178	69°10'N	33°30'E
Polygyros, Grc.	175	40°23'N	23°27'E
Polynesia, is., Oc.	240	4°00'S	156°00'W
Pomba, r., Braz. (pô'm-bä)	141a	21°28'S	42°28'W
Pomerania, hist. reg., Pol. (pŏm-ê-rā'nĭ-å)	168	53°50'N	15°20'E
Pomeroy, S. Afr. (pŏm'ēr-roi)	233c	28°36'S	30°26'E
Pomeroy, Wa., U.S. (pŏm'ēr-oi)	114	46°28'N	117°35'W
Pomezia, Italy (pô-mĕ't-zyä)	173d	41°41'N	12°31'E
Pomigliano d'Arco, Italy (pô-mē-lyä'nô-d-ä'r-kô)	173c	40°39'N	14°23'E
Pomme de Terre, Mn., U.S. (pŏm dē tĕr')	112	45°22'N	95°52'W
Pomona, Ca., U.S. (pô-mō'nå)	104	34°04'N	117°45'W
Pomorie, Blg.	163	42°24'N	27°41'E
Pompano Beach, Fl., U.S. (pŏm'på-nō)	125a	26°12'N	80°07'W
Pompeii Ruins, hist., Italy	173c	40°31'N	14°29'E
Pompton Lakes, N.J., U.S. (pŏmp'tŏn)	110a	41°01'N	74°16'W
Pomuch, Mex. (pô-mōō'ch)	132a	20°12'N	90°10'W
Ponca, Ne., U.S. (pŏn'kå)	112	42°34'N	96°43'W
Ponca City, Ok., U.S.	121	36°42'N	97°07'W
Ponce, P.R. (pōn'sā)	129	18°01'N	66°43'W
Pondicherry, India	199	11°58'N	79°48'E
Pondicherry, state, India	199	11°50'N	74°50'E
Ponferrada, Spain (pôn-fĕr-rä'dhä)	162	42°33'N	6°38'W
Ponoka, Can. (pŏ-nō'kå)	90	52°42'N	113°35'W
Ponoy, Russia	180	66°58'N	41°00'E
Ponoy, r., Russia	180	67°00'N	39°00'E
Ponta Delgada, Port. (pôn'tå dĕl-gä'då)	230a	37°40'N	25°45'W
Ponta Grossa, Braz. (grō'så)	143	25°09'S	50°05'W
Pont-à-Mousson, Fr. (pôN'tá-mōōsôN')	171	48°55'N	6°02'E
Pontarlier, Fr. (pôN'tár-lyā')	171	46°53'N	6°22'E
Pont-Audemer, Fr. (pôN'tōd'mâr')	170	49°23'N	0°28'E
Pontchartrain Lake, l., La., U.S. (pôN-shár-trăn')	123	30°10'N	90°10'W
Ponteareas, Spain	172	42°09'N	8°23'W
Pontedera, Italy (pōn-tå-dā'rä)	174	43°37'N	10°37'E
Ponte de Sor, Port.	172	39°14'N	8°03'W
Pontefract, Eng., U.K. (pŏn'tê-fräkt)	158a	53°41'N	1°18'W
Ponte Nova, Braz. (pô'n-tĕ-nô'vå)	143	20°26'S	42°52'W
Pontevedra, Spain (pôn-tĕ-vĕ-drä)	162	42°28'N	8°38'W
Ponthierville see Ubundi, D.R.C.	232	0°21'S	25°29'E
Pontiac, Il., U.S. (pŏn'tĭ-ăk)	108	40°55'N	88°35'W
Pontiac, Mi., U.S.	105	42°37'N	83°17'W
Pontianak, Indon. (pôn-tê-ä'nák)	212	0°04'S	109°20'E
Pontian Kechil, Malay.	197b	1°29'N	103°24'E
Pontic Mountains, mts., Tur.	181	41°20'N	34°30'E
Pontivy, Fr. (pôN-tē-vē')	170	48°05'N	2°57'W
Pontoise, Fr. (pôN-twáz')	170	49°03'N	2°05'E
Pontonnyy, Russia (pôn'tôn-nyĭ)	186c	59°47'N	30°39'E
Pontotoc, Ms., U.S. (pŏn-tô-tŏk')	124	34°11'N	88°59'W
Pontremoli, Italy (pôn-trĕm'ô-lē)	174	44°21'N	9°50'E
Ponziane, Isole, i., Italy (ē'sō-lĕ)	162	40°55'N	12°58'E
Poole, Eng., U.K. (pōōl)	164	50°43'N	2°00'W
Poolesville, Md., U.S. (poolĕs-vĭl)	110e	39°08'N	77°26'W
Pooley Island, i., Can. (pōō'lē)	94	52°44'N	128°16'W
Poopó, Lago de, l., Bol.	142	18°45'S	67°07'W
Popayán, Col. (pō-pä-yän')	142	2°21'N	76°43'W
Poplar, Mt., U.S. (pŏp'lẽr)	115	48°08'N	105°10'W
Poplar, r., Mt., U.S.	115	48°34'N	105°20'W
Poplar, West Fork, r., Mt., U.S.	115	48°59'N	106°06'W
Poplar Bluff, Mo., U.S. (blŭf)	121	36°43'N	90°22'W
Poplar Plains, Ky., U.S. (plāns)	108	38°20'N	83°40'W
Poplar Point, Can.	102f	50°04'N	97°57'W
Poplarville, Ms., U.S. (pŏp'lẽr-vĭl)	124	30°50'N	89°33'W
Popocatépetl Volcán, Mex. (pô-pô-kä-tā'pĕ't'l)	128	19°01'N	98°38'W
Popokabaka, D.R.C. (pō'pô-kä-bä'kä)	232	5°42'S	16°35'E
Popovo, Blg. (pô'pô-vō)	175	43°23'N	26°17'E
Porbandar, India (pōr-bŭn'dŭr)	199	21°44'N	69°40'E
Porce, r., Col. (pōr-sĕ)	142a	7°11'N	74°55'W
Porcher Island, i., Can. (pôr'kẽr)	94	53°57'N	130°30'W
Porcuna, Spain (pôr-kōō'nä)	172	37°54'N	4°10'W
Porcupine, r., N.A.	103	67°38'N	140°07'W
Porcupine Creek, r., Mt., U.S.	115	48°27'N	106°24'W
Porcupine Hills, hills, Can.	97	52°30'N	101°45'W
Pordenone, Italy (pōr-då-nō'nå)	174	45°58'N	12°38'E
Pori, Fin. (pô'rē)	160	61°29'N	21°45'E
Poriúncula, Braz.	141a	20°58'S	42°02'W
Porkhov, Russia (pôr'kôf)	180	57°46'N	29°33'E
Porlamar, Ven. (pōr-lä-mär')	142	11°00'N	63°55'W
Pornic, Fr. (pôr-nēk')	170	47°08'N	2°07'W
Poronaysk, Russia (pô'rô-nīsk)	179	49°21'N	143°23'E
Porrentruy, Switz. (pô-räN-trüē')	168	47°25'N	7°02'E
Porsgrunn, Nor. (pôrs'grōn')	166	59°09'N	9°36'E
Portachuelo, Bol. (pôrt-ä-chwā'lô)	142	17°20'S	63°12'W
Portage, Pa., U.S. (pôr'tåj)	109	40°25'N	78°35'W
Portage, Wi., U.S.	113	43°33'N	89°29'W
Portage Des Sioux, Mo., U.S. (dē sōō)	117e	38°56'N	90°21'W
Portage la Prairie, Can. (lä-prā'rĭ)	90	49°57'N	98°25'W
Port Alberni, Can. (pōr äl-bĕr-nē')	90	49°14'N	124°48'W
Portalegre, Port. (pôr-tä-lā'grĕ)	162	39°18'N	7°26'W
Portales, N.M., U.S. (pôr-tä'lĕs)	120	34°10'N	103°11'W
Port Alfred, S. Afr.	232	33°36'S	26°55'E
Port Alice, Can. (ăl'ĭs)	90	50°23'N	127°27'W
Port Allegany, Pa., U.S. (ăl-ê-gā'nĭ)	109	41°50'N	78°10'W
Port Angeles, Wa., U.S. (ăn'jê-lĕs)	104	48°07'N	123°26'W
Port Antonio, Jam.	129	18°10'N	76°25'W
Portarlington, Austl.	217a	38°07'S	144°39'E
Port Arthur, Tx., U.S.	105	29°52'N	93°59'W
Port Augusta, Austl. (ô-gŭs'tå)	222	32°28'S	137°50'E
Port au Port Bay, b., Can. (pôr'tō pōr')	101	48°41'N	58°45'W
Port-au-Prince, Haiti (prăNs')	129	18°35'N	72°20'W
Port Austin, Mi., U.S. (ôs'tĭn)	108	44°00'N	83°00'W
Port Blair, India (blâr)	212	12°07'N	92°45'E
Port Bolivar, Tx., U.S. (bŏl'ĭ-vár)	123a	29°22'N	94°46'W
Port Borden, Can. (bôr'dĕn)	100	46°15'N	63°42'W
Port-Bouët, C. Iv.	230	5°24'N	3°56'W
Port-Cartier, Can.	100	50°01'N	66°53'W
Port Chester, N.Y., U.S. (chĕs'tẽr)	110a	40°59'N	73°40'W
Port Chicago, Ca., U.S. (shĭ-kô'gō)	116b	38°03'N	122°01'W
Port Clinton, Oh., U.S. (klĭn'tŭn)	108	41°30'N	83°00'W
Port Colborne, Can.	99	42°53'N	79°13'W
Port Coquitlam, Can. (kô-kwĭt'lăm)	95	49°16'N	122°46'W
Port Credit, Can. (krĕd'ĭt)	102d	43°33'N	79°35'W
Port-de-Bouc, Fr. (pôr-dē-bōōk')	170a	43°24'N	5°00'E
Port de Paix, Haiti (pĕ)	135	19°55'N	72°50'W
Port Dickson, Malay. (dĭk'sŭn)	197b	2°33'N	101°49'E
Port Discovery, b., Wa., U.S. (dĭs-kŭv'ẽr-ĭ)	116a	48°05'N	122°55'W
Port Edward, S. Afr. (ĕd'wẽrd)	233c	31°04'S	30°14'E
Port Elgin, Can. (ĕl'jĭn)	100	46°03'N	64°05'W
Port Elizabeth, S. Afr. (ê-lĭz'å-bĕth)	232	33°57'S	25°37'E
Porterdale, Ga., U.S. (pōr'tẽr-dāl)	124	33°34'N	83°53'W
Porterville, Ca., U.S. (pōr'tẽr-vĭl)	118	36°03'N	119°05'W
Port Francqui see Ilebo, D.R.C.	232	4°19'S	20°35'E
Port Gamble, Wa., U.S. (găm'bŭl)	116a	47°52'N	122°36'W
Port Gamble Indian Reservation, I.R., Wa., U.S.	116a	47°54'N	122°33'W
Port-Gentil, Gabon (zhäN-tē')	232	0°43'S	8°47'E
Port Gibson, Ms., U.S.	124	31°56'N	90°57'W
Port Harcourt, Nig. (här'kŭrt)	230	4°43'N	7°05'E
Port Hardy, Can. (här'dĭ)	94	50°43'N	127°29'W
Port Hawkesbury, Can.	101	45°37'N	61°21'W
Port Hedland, Austl. (hĕd'lănd)	218	20°30'S	118°30'E
Porthill, Id., U.S.	114	49°00'N	116°30'W
Port Hood, Can. (hŏd)	101	46°01'N	61°32'W
Port Hope, Can. (hōp)	99	43°55'N	78°10'W
Port Huron, Mi., U.S. (hū'rŏn)	105	43°00'N	82°30'W
Portici, Italy (pôr'tê-chê)	173c	40°34'N	14°20'E
Portillo, Chile (pôr-tē'l-yô)	141b	32°51'S	70°09'W
Portimão, Port. (pôr-tē-mouN)	172	37°09'N	8°34'W
Port Jervis, N.Y., U.S. (jûr'vĭs)	110a	41°22'N	74°41'W
Portland, Austl. (pōrt'lănd)	219	38°20'S	142°40'E
Portland, In., U.S.	108	40°25'N	85°00'W
Portland, Me., U.S.	105	43°40'N	70°16'W
Portland, Mi., U.S.	108	42°50'N	85°00'W
Portland, Or., U.S.	104	45°31'N	122°41'W
Portland, Tx., U.S.	123	27°53'N	97°20'W
Portland Bight, b., Jam.	134	17°45'N	77°05'W
Portland Canal, can., Ak., U.S.	94	55°10'N	130°08'W
Portland Inlet, b., Can.	94	54°50'N	130°15'W
Portland Point, c., Jam.	134	17°40'N	77°20'W
Port Lavaca, Tx., U.S. (lå-vä'kå)	123	28°36'N	96°38'W
Port Lincoln, Austl. (lĭŋ-kŭn)	218	34°39'S	135°50'E
Port Ludlow, Wa., U.S. (lŭd'lō)	116a	47°26'N	122°41'W
Port Macquarie, Austl. (må-kwŏ'rĭ)	219	31°25'S	152°45'E
Port Madison Indian Reservation, I.R., Wa., U.S. (măd'ĭ-sŭn)	116a	47°46'N	122°38'W
Port Maria, Jam. (må-rī'å)	134	18°20'N	76°55'W
Port Moody, Can. (mōōd'ĭ)	95	49°17'N	122°51'W
Port Moresby, Pap. N. Gui. (mōrz'bê)	213	9°34'S	147°20'E
Port Neches, Tx., U.S. (nĕch'ĕz)	123	29°59'N	93°57'W
Port Nelson, Can. (nĕl'sŭn)	97	57°03'N	92°36'W
Portneuf-Sur-Mer, Can. (pôr-nûf'sür mĕr)	100	48°36'N	69°06'W
Port Nolloth, S. Afr. (nŏl'ŏth)	232	29°10'S	17°00'E
Porto (Oporto), Port. (pōr'tò)	154	41°10'N	8°38'W
Porto Acre, Braz. (ä'krĕ)	142	9°38'S	67°34'W
Porto Alegre, Braz. (ä-lā'grĕ)	144	29°58'S	51°11'W
Porto Amboim, Ang.	232	11°01'S	13°45'E
Portobelo, Pan. (pôr'tô-bā'lô)	129	9°32'N	79°40'W
Pôrto de Pedras, Braz. (pā'dräzh)	143	9°09'S	35°20'W
Pôrto Feliz, Braz. (fĕ-lē's)	141a	23°12'S	47°30'W
Portoferraio, Italy (pōr'tô-fĕr-rä'yō)	174	42°47'N	10°20'E
Port of Spain, Trin. (spān)	143	10°44'N	61°24'W
Portogruaro, Italy (pōr'tô-grô-ä'rō)	174	45°48'N	12°49'E
Portola, Ca., U.S. (pōr'tō-lå)	118	39°47'N	120°29'W
Porto Mendes, Braz. (mĕ'n-dĕs)	143	24°41'S	54°13'W
Porto Murtinho, Braz. (mòr-tēn'yò)	143	21°43'S	57°43'W
Porto Nacional, Braz. (nå-syô-näl')	143	10°43'S	48°14'W
Porto Novo, Benin (pôr'tô-nō'vō)	230	6°29'N	2°37'E
Port Orchard, Wa., U.S. (ôr'chẽrd)	116a	47°32'N	122°38'W
Port Orchard, b., Wa., U.S.	116a	47°40'N	122°39'W
Porto Santo, Ilha de, i., Port. (sän'tò)	230	32°41'N	16°15'W
Porto Seguro, Braz. (sā-gōō'rò)	143	16°26'S	38°59'W
Porto Torres, Italy (tôr'rĕs)	174	40°49'N	8°25'E
Porto-Vecchio, Fr. (vĕk'ê-ô)	174	41°36'N	9°17'E
Porto Velho, Braz. (vāl'yò)	142	8°45'S	63°43'W
Portoviejo, Ec. (pôr-tō-vyā'hō)	142	1°11'S	80°28'W
Port Phillip Bay, b., Austl. (fĭl'ĭp)	221	37°57'S	144°50'E
Port Pirie, Austl. (pĭ'rē)	218	33°10'S	138°00'E
Port Royal, b., Jam. (roi'ăl)	134	17°50'N	76°45'W
Port Said, Egypt	238d	31°15'N	32°19'E
Port Saint Johns, S. Afr. (sånt jŏnz)	232	31°37'S	29°32'E
Port Saint Lucie, Fl., U.S.	125a	27°20'N	80°20'W
Port Shepstone, S. Afr. (shĕps'tŭn)	232	30°45'S	30°23'E
Portsmouth, Dom.	133b	15°33'N	61°28'W
Portsmouth, Eng., U.K. (pôrts'mŭth)	154	50°45'N	1°03'W
Portsmouth, N.H., U.S.	105	43°05'N	70°50'W
Portsmouth, Oh., U.S.	105	38°45'N	83°00'W
Portsmouth, Va., U.S.	105	36°50'N	76°19'W
Port Sulphur, La., U.S. (sŭl'fẽr)	124	29°28'N	89°41'W
Port Susan, b., Wa., U.S. (sū-zăn')	116a	48°11'N	122°25'W
Port Townsend, Wa., U.S. (tounz'ĕnd)	116a	48°07'N	122°46'W
Port Townsend, b., Wa., U.S.	116a	48°05'N	122°47'W
Portugal, nation, Eur. (pōr'tu-găl)	154	38°15'N	8°08'W
Portugalete, Spain (pōr-tōō-gä-lā'tä)	172	43°18'N	3°05'W
Portuguese West Africa see Angola, nation, Ang.	232	14°15'S	16°00'E
Port Vendres, Fr.	170	42°32'N	3°07'E
Port Vila, Vanuatu	219	17°44'S	168°19'E
Port Wakefield, Austl. (wāk'fēld)	218	34°12'S	138°10'E
Port Washington, N.Y., U.S. (wôsh'ĭng-tŭn)	110a	40°49'N	73°42'W
Port Washington, Wi., U.S.	113	43°24'N	87°52'W
Posadas, Arg. (pō-sä'dhäs)	144	27°32'S	55°56'W
Posadas, Spain (pô-sä-däs)	172	37°48'N	5°09'W
Poshekhon'ye Volodarsk, Russia (pô-shyĕ'kôn-yĕ vôl'ô-dårsk)	176	58°31'N	39°07'E
Poso, Danau, l., Indon. (pō'sō)	212	2°00'S	119°40'E
Pospelokova, Russia (pôs-pyĕl'kô-vå)	186a	59°25'N	60°50'E
Possession Sound, strt., Wa., U.S. (pŏ-zĕsh-ŭn)	116a	47°59'N	122°17'W
Possum Kingdom Reservoir, res., Tx., U.S. (pŏs'ŭm kĭng'dŭm)	122	32°58'N	98°12'W
Post, Tx., U.S. (pōst)	120	33°12'N	101°21'W
Postojna, Slvn. (pōs-tōyná)	174	45°45'N	14°13'E
Pos'yet, Russia (pos-yĕt')	210	42°27'N	130°47'E
Potawatomi Indian Reservation, I.R., Ks., U.S. (pŏt-å-wä'tō mē)	121	39°30'N	96°11'W
Potchefstroom, S. Afr. (pŏch'ĕf-strōm)	232	26°42'S	27°06'E
Poteau, Ok., U.S. (pô-tō')	121	35°03'N	94°37'W
Poteet, Tx., U.S. (pô-tēt)	122	29°05'N	98°35'W
Potenza, Italy (pô-tĕnt'sä)	163	40°39'N	15°49'E
Potenza, r., Italy	174	43°09'N	13°00'E
Potgietersrus, S. Afr. (pôt-kē'tērs-rûs)	232	24°09'S	29°04'E
Potholes Reservoir, res., Wa., U.S.	114	47°00'N	119°20'W
Poti, Geor. (pô'tê)	181	42°10'N	41°40'E
Potiskum, Nig.	230	11°43'N	11°05'E
Potomac, Md., U.S. (pô-tō'măk)	110e	39°01'N	77°13'W
Potomac, r., U.S. (pô-tō'măk)	107	38°15'N	76°55'W
Potosí, Bol.	142	19°35'S	65°45'W
Potosi, Mo., U.S. (pō-tō'sĭ)	121	37°56'N	90°46'W
Potosi, r., Mex. (pō-tô-sē')	122	25°04'N	99°36'W
Potrerillos, Hond. (pō-trå-rēl'yôs)	132	15°13'N	87°58'W
Potsdam, Ger. (pôts'däm)	161	52°24'N	13°04'E
Potsdam, N.Y., U.S. (pŏts'dăm)	109	44°40'N	75°00'W
Pottenstein, Aus.	159e	47°58'N	16°06'E
Potters Bar, Eng., U.K. (pŏt'ĕz bär)	158b	51°41'N	0°12'W
Pottstown, Pa., U.S. (pŏts'toun)	109	40°15'N	75°40'W
Pottsville, Pa., U.S. (pŏts'vĭl)	109	40°40'N	76°15'W
Poughkeepsie, N.Y., U.S. (pŏ-kĭp'sē)	105	41°45'N	73°55'W
Poulsbo, Wa., U.S. (pōlz'bō)	116a	47°44'N	122°38'W
Poulton-le-Fylde, Eng., U.K. (pōl'tŭn-lē-fīld')	158a	53°52'N	2°59'W
Pouso Alegre, Braz. (pō'zō ä-lā'grĕ)	143	22°13'S	45°56'W
Póvoa de Varzim, Port. (pō-vō'å dā vär'zēn)	162	41°23'N	8°44'W
Powder, r., Or., U.S.	114	44°55'N	117°35'W
Powder, r., U.S. (pou'dẽr)	106	45°18'N	105°37'W
Powder, South Fork, r., Wy., U.S.	115	43°13'N	106°54'W
Powder River, Wy., U.S.	115	43°06'N	106°55'W
Powell, Wy., U.S. (pou'ĕl)	115	44°44'N	108°44'W
Powell, Lake, res., U.S.	106	37°26'N	110°25'W
Powell Lake, l., Can.	94	50°10'N	124°13'W
Powell Point, c., Bah.	134	24°50'N	76°20'W
Powell Reservoir, res., Ky., U.S.	124	36°30'N	83°35'W
Powell River, Can.	90	49°52'N	124°33'W
Poyang Hu, l., China	205	29°20'N	116°28'E
Poygan, r., Wi., U.S. (poi'găn)	113	44°10'N	89°05'W
Požarevac, Serb. (pô'zhä'rĕ-váts)	175	44°38'N	21°12'E
Poza Rica, Mex. (pô-zô-rē'kä)	131	20°32'N	97°25'W
Poznań, Pol.	154	52°25'N	16°55'E
Pozoblanco, Spain (pô-thō-blän'kō)	172	38°23'N	4°50'W
Pozos, Mex. (pô'zōs)	130	22°05'N	100°50'W
Pozuelo de Alarcón, Spain (pô-thwā'lō dā ä-lär-kōn')	173a	40°27'N	3°49'W
Pozzuoli, Italy (pôt-swô'lē)	174	40°34'N	14°08'E
Pra, r., Ghana (prå)	234	5°45'N	1°35'W
Pra, r., Russia	176	55°00'N	40°13'E
Prachin Buri, Thai. (prä'chĕn)	212	13°59'N	101°15'E
Pradera, Col. (prä-dĕ'rä)	142a	3°24'N	76°13'W
Prades, Fr. (pråd)	170	42°37'N	2°23'E
Prado, Col. (prädô)	142a	3°44'N	74°55'W
Prado Reservoir, res., Ca., U.S. (prä'dō)	117a	33°45'N	117°40'W
Prados, Braz. (prá'dôs)	141a	21°05'S	44°04'W
Prague, Czech Rep.	168	50°05'N	14°26'E
Praha see Prague, Czech Rep.	154	50°05'N	14°26'E
Praia, C.V. (prä'yå)	230b	15°00'N	23°30'W
Praia Funda, Ponta da, c., Braz. (pôn'tä-dá-prä'yá-fōō'n-dä)	144b	23°04'S	43°34'W
Prairie du Chien, Wi., U.S. (prā'rĭ dò shēn')	113	43°02'N	91°10'W
Prairie Grove, Can. (prā'rĭ grōv)	102f	49°48'N	96°57'W
Prairie Island Indian Reservation, I.R., Mn., U.S.	113	44°42'N	92°32'W
Prairies, Rivière des, r., Can. (rē-vyâr' dā prâ-rē')	102a	45°40'N	73°34'W
Pratas Island, i., Asia	209	20°40'N	116°30'E

ng-sing; ŋ-baŋk; N-nasalized n; nŏd; cŏmmit; ōld; ôbey; ôrder; oi-boil; fōōd; ò-as oo in foot; ou-out; s-soft; sh-dish; th-thin; pūre; ûnite; ûrn; stŭd; circŭs; ü-as in French tu; '-indeterminate vowel.

PLACE (Pronunciation)	PAGE	LAT.	LONG.
Prato, Italy (prä'tō)	174	43°53'N	11°03'E
Pratt, Ks., U.S. (prăt)	120	37°37'N	98°43'W
Prattville, Al., U.S. (prăt'vĭl)	124	32°28'N	86°27'W
Pravdinsk, Russia	167	54°26'N	21°00'E
Pravdinskiy, Russia (pràv-dĕn'skĭ)	186b	56°03'N	37°52'E
Pravia, Spain (prä'vē-ä)	172	43°30'N	6°08'W
Pregolya, r., Russia (prĕ-gô'lă)	167	54°37'N	20°50'E
Premont, Tx., U.S. (prē-mŏnt')	122	27°20'N	98°07'W
Prenzlau, Ger. (prĕnts'lou)	168	53°19'N	13°52'E
Přerov, Czech Rep. (przhĕ'rôf)	161	49°28'N	17°28'E
Prescot, Eng., U.K. (prĕs'kŭt)	158a	53°25'N	2°48'W
Prescott, Can. (prĕs'kŭt)	109	44°45'N	75°35'W
Prescott, Ar., U.S.	121	33°47'N	93°23'W
Prescott, Az., U.S. (prĕs'kŏt)	104	34°30'N	112°30'W
Prescott, Wi., U.S. (prĕs'kŏt)	117g	44°45'N	92°48'W
Presho, S.D., U.S. (prĕsh'ō)	112	43°56'N	100°04'W
Presidencia Rogue Sáenz Peña, Arg.	144	26°52'S	60°15'W
Presidente Epitácio, Braz. (prā-sē-dĕn'tĕ å-pē-tä'syō)	143	21°56'S	52°01'W
Presidio, Tx., U.S. (prĕ-sĭ'dĭ-ō)	122	29°33'N	104°23'W
Presidio, Río del, r., Mex. (rē'ō-dĕl-prĕ-sē'dyô)	130	23°54'N	105°44'W
Prešov, Slvk. (prĕ'shôf)	161	49°00'N	21°18'E
Prespa, Lake, l., Eur. (prĕs'pä)	175	40°49'N	20°50'E
Prespuntal, r., Ven.	143b	9°55'N	64°32'W
Presque Isle, Me., U.S. (prĕsk'ēl')	100	46°41'N	68°03'W
Pressbaum, Aus.	159e	48°12'N	16°06'E
Prestea, Ghana	234	5°27'N	2°08'W
Preston, Austl.	217a	37°45'S	145°01'E
Preston, Eng., U.K. (prĕs'tŭn)	164	53°46'N	2°42'W
Preston, Id., U.S. (pres'tŭn)	115	42°05'N	111°54'W
Preston, Mn., U.S. (prĕs'tŭn)	113	43°42'N	92°06'W
Preston, Wa., U.S.	116a	47°31'N	121°56'W
Prestonburg, Ky., U.S. (prĕs'tŭn-bûrg)	108	37°35'N	82°50'W
Prestwich, Eng., U.K. (prĕst'wĭch)	158a	53°32'N	2°17'W
Pretoria, S. Afr. (prē-tō'rĭ-ȧ)	232	25°43'S	28°16'E
Pretoria North, S. Afr. (prē-tō'rĭ-ȧ nōōrd)	238c	25°41'S	28°11'E
Préveza, Grc. (prĕ'vå-zä)	175	38°58'N	20°44'E
Pribilof Islands, is., Ak., U.S. (prĭ'bĭ-lof)	103	57°00'N	169°20'W
Priboj, Serb. (prē'boi)	175	43°33'N	19°33'E
Price, Ut., U.S. (prīs)	119	39°35'N	110°50'W
Price, r., Ut., U.S.	119	39°21'N	110°35'W
Prichard, Al., U.S. (prĭt'chărd)	124	30°44'N	88°04'W
Priddis, Can. (prĭd'dĭs)	102e	50°53'N	114°20'W
Priddis Creek, r., Can.	102e	50°56'N	114°32'W
Priego, Spain (prē-ā'gō)	172	37°27'N	4°13'W
Prienai, Lith. (prē-ĕn'ī)	167	54°38'N	23°56'E
Prieska, S. Afr. (prē-ĕs'kȧ)	232	29°40'S	22°50'E
Priest Lake, l., Id., U.S. (prēst)	114	48°30'N	116°43'W
Priest Rapids Dam, Wa., U.S.	114	46°39'N	119°55'W
Priest Rapids Lake, res., Wa., U.S.	114	46°42'N	119°58'W
Priiskovaya, Russia (prĭ-ēs'kô-va-yȧ)	186a	60°50'N	58°55'E
Prijedor, Bos. (prē'yĕ-dôr)	174	44°58'N	16°43'E
Prijepolje, Serb. (prē'yĕ-pô'lyĕ)	175	43°22'N	19°41'E
Prilep, Mac. (prē'lĕp)	163	41°20'N	21°35'E
Primorsk, Russia (prē-môrsk')	167	60°24'N	28°35'E
Primorsko-Akhtarskaya, Russia (prē-môr'skô äk-tär'skĭ-ê)	181	46°03'N	38°09'E
Primrose, S. Afr.	233b	26°11'S	28°11'E
Primrose Lake, l., Can.	96	54°55'N	109°45'W
Prince Albert, Can. (prĭns ăl'bērt)	90	53°12'N	105°46'W
Prince Albert National Park, rec., Can.	92	54°10'N	105°25'W
Prince Albert Sound, strt., Can.	92	70°23'N	116°57'W
Prince Charles Island, i., Can. (chärlz)	93	67°41'N	74°10'W
Prince Edward Island, prov., Can.	91	46°45'N	63°10'W
Prince Edward Islands, is., S. Afr.	224	46°36'S	37°57'E
Prince Edward National Park, rec., Can. (ĕd'wērd)	93	46°33'N	63°35'W
Prince Edward Peninsula, pen., Can.	109	44°00'N	77°15'W
Prince Frederick, Md., U.S. (prĭnce frĕdĕrĭk)	110e	38°33'N	76°35'W
Prince George, Can. (jôrj)	90	53°51'N	122°57'W
Prince of Wales, i., Austl.	221	10°47'S	142°15'E
Prince of Wales, i., Ak., U.S.	103	55°47'N	132°50'W
Prince of Wales, Cape, c., Ak., U.S. (wālz)	103	65°48'N	169°08'W
Prince Rupert, Can. (roo'pērt)	90	54°19'N	130°19'W
Princes Risborough, Eng., U.K. (prĭns'ĕz rĭz'brŭ)	158b	51°41'N	0°51'W
Princess Charlotte Bay, b., Austl. (shär'lŏt)	221	13°45'S	144°15'E
Princess Royal Channel, strt., Can. (roi'ăl)	94	53°10'N	128°37'W
Princess Royal Island, i., Can.	94	52°57'N	128°49'W
Princeton, Can. (prĭns'tŭn)	90	49°27'N	120°31'W
Princeton, Il., U.S.	108	41°20'N	89°25'W
Princeton, In., U.S.	108	38°20'N	87°35'W
Princeton, Ky., U.S.	124	37°07'N	87°52'W
Princeton, Mi., U.S.	113	46°16'N	87°33'W
Princeton, Mn., U.S.	113	45°34'N	93°36'W
Princeton, Mo., U.S.	121	40°23'N	93°34'W
Princeton, N.J., U.S.	109	40°21'N	74°40'W
Princeton, Wi., U.S.	113	43°50'N	89°09'W
Princeton, W.V., U.S.	125	37°21'N	81°05'W
Prince William Sound, strt., Ak., U.S. (wĭl'yăm)	103	60°40'N	147°10'W
Príncipe, i., S. Tom./P. (prēn'sē-pĕ)	230	1°37'N	7°25'E
Principe Channel, strt., Can. (prĭn'sĭ-pē)	94	53°28'N	129°45'W
Prineville, Or., U.S. (prĭn'vĭl)	114	44°17'N	120°48'W
Prineville Reservoir, res., Or., U.S.	114	44°07'N	120°45'W
Prinzapolca, Nic. (prēn-zä-pōl'kä)	133	13°18'N	83°35'W
Prinzapolca, r., Nic.	133	13°23'N	84°23'W
Prior Lake, Mn., U.S. (prī'ēr)	117g	44°43'N	93°26'W
Priozërsk, Russia (prĭ-ô'zĕrsk)	167	61°03'N	30°08'E
Pripet, r., Eur.	181	51°50'N	29°45'E
Pripet Marshes, sw., Eur.	181	52°10'N	27°30'E
Priština, Serb. (prēsh'tĭ-nä)	163	42°39'N	21°12'E
Pritzwalk, Ger. (prēts'välk)	168	53°09'N	12°12'E
Privas, Fr. (prē-väs')	170	44°44'N	4°37'E
Prizren, Serb. (prē'zrĕn)	163	42°11'N	20°45'E
Procida, Italy (prô'chē-dä)	173c	40°31'N	14°02'E
Procida, Isola di, i., Italy	173c	40°32'N	13°57'E
Proctor, Mn., U.S. (prŏk'tēr)	117h	46°45'N	92°14'W
Proctor, Vt., U.S.	109	43°40'N	73°00'W
Proebstel, Wa., U.S. (prōb'stĕl)	116c	45°40'N	122°29'W
Proenca-a-Nova, Port. (prô-ān'så-ä-nō'vȧ)	172	39°44'N	7°55'W
Progreso, Hond. (prô-grĕ'sô)	132	15°28'N	87°49'W
Progreso, Mex. (prô-grā'sō)	128	21°14'N	89°39'W
Progreso, Mex.	122	27°29'N	101°05'W
Prokhladnyy, Russia	182	43°46'N	44°00'E
Prokop'yevsk, Russia	184	53°53'N	86°45'E
Prokuplje, Serb. (prô'kop'l-yĕ)	175	43°16'N	21°40'E
Prome, Mya.	212	18°46'N	95°15'E
Pronya, r., Bela. (prô'nyä)	176	54°08'N	30°58'E
Pronya, r., Russia	176	54°08'N	39°30'E
Prospect, Ky., U.S. (prŏs'pĕkt)	111h	38°21'N	85°36'W
Prospect Park, Pa., U.S. (prŏs'pĕkt pärk)	110f	39°53'N	75°18'W
Prosser, Wa., U.S. (prŏs'ēr)	114	46°10'N	119°46'W
Prostějov, Czech Rep. (prôs'tyĕ-yôf)	169	49°28'N	17°08'E
Protection, i., Wa., U.S. (prô-tĕk'shŭn)	116a	48°07'N	122°56'W
Protoka, r., Russia (prôt'ô-kȧ)	176	55°00'N	36°42'E
Provadiya, Blg. (prō-väd'ē-yȧ)	175	43°13'N	27°28'E
Providence, Ky., U.S. (prŏv'ĭ-dĕns)	108	37°25'N	87°45'W
Providence, R.I., U.S.	105	41°50'N	71°23'W
Providence, Ut., U.S.	115	41°42'N	111°50'W
Providencia, Isla de, i., Col.	133	13°21'N	80°55'W
Providenciales, i., T./C. Is.	135	21°50'N	72°15'W
Provideniya, Russia (prô-vĭ-dă'nĭ-yȧ)	183	64°30'N	172°54'W
Provincetown, Ma., U.S.	109	42°03'N	70°11'W
Provo, Ut., U.S. (prō'vō)	104	40°15'N	111°40'W
Prozor, Bos. (prō'zôr)	175	43°48'N	17°59'E
Prudence Island, i., R.I., U.S. (prōō'dĕns)	110b	41°38'N	71°20'W
Prudhoe Bay, b., Ak., U.S.	103	70°40'N	147°25'W
Prudnik, Pol. (prôd'nĭk)	169	50°19'N	17°34'E
Prussia, hist. reg., Eur. (prŭsh'ȧ)	168	50°43'N	8°35'E
Pruszków, Pol. (prôsh'kôf)	169	52°09'N	20°50'E
Prut, r., Eur. (prōōt)	156	48°05'N	27°07'E
Pryluky, Ukr.	181	50°36'N	32°21'E
Prymors'k, Ukr.	177	46°43'N	36°21'E
Pryor, Ok., U.S. (prī'ēr)	121	36°16'N	95°19'W
Pryvil'ne, Ukr.	177	47°30'N	32°21'E
Przedbórz, Pol.	169	51°05'N	19°53'E
Przemyśl, Pol. (pzhĕ'mĭsh'l)	154	49°47'N	22°45'E
Przheval'sk, Kyrg. (p'r-zhĭ-välsk')	183	42°29'N	78°24'E
Psel, r., Eur.	181	49°45'N	33°42'E
Pskov, Russia (pskôf)	178	57°48'N	28°19'E
Pskov, prov., Russia	176	57°33'N	29°05'E
Pskovskoye Ozero, l., Eur. (p'skôv'skô'yĕ ôzē-rô)	180	58°05'N	28°15'E
Ptich', r., Bela. (p'têch)	180	53°17'N	28°16'E
Ptuj, Slvn. (ptōō'ē)	174	46°24'N	15°54'E
Pucheng, China (pōō'chĕng')	209	28°02'N	118°25'E
Pucheng, China (pōō-chŭŋ)	206	35°43'N	115°22'E
Puck, Pol. (pòtsk)	169	54°43'N	18°23'E
Pudozh, Russia (pōō'dôzh)	180	61°50'N	36°50'E
Puebla, Mex. (pwā'blä)	128	19°02'N	98°11'W
Puebla, state, Mex.	131	19°00'N	97°45'W
Puebla de Don Fadrique, Spain	172	37°55'N	2°55'W
Pueblo, Co., U.S. (pwā'blō)	104	38°15'N	104°36'W
Pueblo Nuevo, Mex. (nwā'vô)	130	23°23'N	105°21'W
Pueblo Viejo, Mex. (vyā'hô)	131	17°23'N	93°46'W
Puente Alto, Chile (pwĕ'n-tĕ äl'tô)	141b	33°36'S	70°34'W
Puentedeume, Spain (pwĕn-tå-dhå-ōō'mā)	172	43°28'N	8°09'W
Puente-Genil, Spain (pwĕn'tå-hå-nēl')	172	37°25'N	4°18'W
Puerco, Rio, r., N.M., U.S. (pwĕr'kō)	119	35°15'N	107°05'W
Puerto Aisén, Chile (pwĕ'r-tō ä'y-sĕ'n)	144	45°28'S	72°44'W
Puerto Angel, Mex. (pwĕ'r-tō äŋ'hāl)	131	15°42'N	96°32'W
Puerto Armuelles, Pan. (pwe'r-tō är-mōō-ā'lyās)	133	8°18'N	82°52'W
Puerto Barrios, Guat. (pwĕ'r-tō băr'rē-ôs)	128	15°43'N	88°36'W
Puerto Bermúdez, Peru (pwĕ'r-tō bĕr-mōō'dāz)	142	10°17'S	74°57'W
Puerto Berrío, Col. (pwĕ'r-tō bĕr-rē'ō)	142	6°29'N	74°27'W
Puerto Cabello, Ven. (pwĕ'r-tō kä-bĕl'yō)	142	10°28'N	68°01'W
Puerto Cabezas, Nic. (pwĕ'r-tō kä-bā'zäs)	133	14°01'N	83°26'W
Puerto Casado, Para. (pwĕ'r-tō kä-sä'dō)	144	22°16'S	57°57'W
Puerto Castilla, Hond. (pwĕ'r-tō käs-tēl'yō)	132	16°01'N	86°01'W
Puerto Chicama, Peru (pwĕ'r-tō chē-kä'mä)	142	7°46'S	79°18'W
Puerto Colombia, Col. (pwĕr'tō kô-lôm'bē-à)	142	11°08'N	75°09'W
Puerto Cortés, C.R. (pwĕ'r-tō kôr-tās')	133	9°00'N	83°37'W
Puerto Cortés, Hond. (pwĕ'r-tô kôr-tās')	128	15°48'N	87°57'W
Puerto Cumarebo, Ven. (pwĕ'r-tō kōō-mä-rĕ'bô)	142	11°25'N	69°17'W
Puerto de Luna, N.M., U.S. (pwĕr'tô då lōō'nä)	120	34°49'N	104°36'W
Puerto de Nutrias, Ven. (pwĕ'r-tō dĕ nōō-trê-äs')	142	8°02'N	69°19'W
Puerto Deseado, Arg. (pwĕ'r-tō dā-så-ä'dhō)	144	47°38'S	66°00'W
Puerto de Somport, p., Eur.	173	42°51'N	0°25'W
Puerto Eten, Peru (pwĕ'r-tō ĕ-tĕ'n)	142	6°59'S	79°51'W
Puerto Jiménez, C.R. (pwĕ'r-tô kê-mĕ'nĕz)	133	8°35'N	83°23'W
Puerto La Cruz, Ven. (pwĕ'r-tō lä krōō'z)	142	10°14'N	64°38'W
Puertollano, Spain (pwĕ-tôl-yä'nō)	162	38°41'N	4°05'W
Puerto Madryn, Arg. (pwĕ'r-tō mä-drĕn')	144	42°45'S	65°01'W
Puerto Maldonado, Peru (pwĕ'r-tō mäl-dô-nä'dô)	142	12°43'S	69°01'W
Puerto Miniso, Mex. (pwĕ'r-tō mē-nē'sô)	130	16°06'N	98°02'W
Puerto Montt, Chile (pwĕ'r-tō mô'nt)	144	41°29'S	73°00'W
Puerto Natales, Chile (pwĕ'r-tō nä-tá'lĕs)	144	51°48'S	72°01'W
Puerto Niño, Col. (pwĕ'r-tō nē'n-yô)	142a	5°57'N	74°36'W
Puerto Padre, Cuba (pwĕ'r-tō pä'drā)	134	21°10'N	76°40'W
Puerto Peñasco, Mex. (pwĕ'r-tō pĕn-yä's-kô)	128	31°39'N	113°15'W
Puerto Pinasco, Para. (pwĕ'r-tō pē-nä's-kô)	144	22°31'S	57°50'W
Puerto Píritu, Ven. (pwĕ'r-tō pē'rē-tōō)	143b	10°05'N	65°04'W
Puerto Plata, Dom. Rep. (pwĕ'r-tô plä'tä)	129	19°50'N	70°40'W
Puerto Princesa, Phil. (pwĕr-tô prēn-sā'sä)	212	9°45'N	118°41'E
Puerto Rico, dep., N.A. (pwĕr'tô rē'kō)	129	18°16'N	66°50'W
Puerto Rico Trench, deep	129	19°45'N	66°30'W
Puerto Salgar, Col. (pwĕ'r-tō säl-gär')	142a	5°30'N	74°39'W
Puerto Santa Cruz, Arg. (pwĕ'r-tō sän'tä krōōz')	144	50°04'S	68°32'W
Puerto Suárez, Bol. (pwĕ'r-tō swä'räz)	143	18°55'S	57°39'W
Puerto Tejada, Col. (pwĕ'r-tō tĕ-κä'dä)	142	3°13'N	76°23'W
Puerto Vallarta, Mex. (pwĕ'r-tō väl-yär'tä)	130	20°36'N	105°13'W
Puerto Varas, Chile (pwĕ'r-tō vä'räs)	144	41°16'S	73°03'W
Puerto Wilches, Col. (pwĕ'r-tō vēl'c-hĕs)	142	7°19'N	73°54'W
Pugachëv, Russia (pōō'gá-chyôf)	181	52°00'N	48°40'E
Puget, Wa., U.S. (pū'jĕt)	116c	46°10'N	123°23'W
Puget Sound, strt., Wa., U.S.	114	47°49'N	122°26'W
Puglia (Apulia), hist. reg., Italy (pōō'lyä) (ä-pōō'lyä)	174	41°13'N	16°10'E
Pukaskwa National Park, rec., Can.	93	48°22'N	85°55'W
Pukeashun Mountain, mtn., Can.	95	51°12'N	119°14'W
Pukin, r., Malay.	197b	2°53'N	102°54'E
Pula, Cro. (pōō'lä)	162	44°52'N	13°55'E
Pulacayo, Bol. (pōō-lä-kä'yō)	142	20°12'N	66°33'W
Pulaski, Tn., U.S. (pů-lăs'kĭ)	124	35°11'N	87°03'W
Pulaski, Va., U.S.	125	37°00'N	81°45'W
Puławy, Pol. (pò-wä'vê)	169	51°24'N	21°59'E
Pulicat, r., India	203	13°58'N	79°52'E
Pullman, Wa., U.S. (pòl'măn)	114	46°44'N	117°10'W
Pulog, Mount, mtn., Phil. (pōō'lôg)	213a	16°38'N	120°53'E
Puma Yumco, l., China (pōō-mä yōōm-tswo)	202	28°30'N	90°10'E
Pumpkin Creek, r., Mt., U.S. (pŭmp'kĭn)	115	45°47'N	105°35'W
Punakha, Bhu. (pōō-nŭk'ŭ)	199	27°45'N	89°59'E
Punata, Bol. (pōō-nä'tä)	142	17°43'S	65°43'W
Pune, India	199	18°38'N	73°53'E
Punjab, state, India (pŭn'jäb')	199	31°00'N	75°30'E
Puno, Peru (pōō'nô)	142	15°58'S	70°02'W
Punta Arenas, Chile (pōō'n-tä-rĕ'näs)	144	53°09'S	70°48'W
Punta de Piedras, Ven. (pōō'n-tä dĕ pyĕ'dräs)	143b	10°54'N	64°06'W
Punta Gorda, Belize (pòn'tä gôr'dä)	132	16°07'N	88°50'W
Punta Gorda, Fl., U.S. (pŭn'tȧ gôr'dȧ)	125a	26°55'N	82°02'W
Punta Gorda, Río, r., Nic. (pōō'n-tä gô'r-dä)	133	11°34'N	84°13'W
Punta Indio, Canal, strt., Arg. (pōō'n-tä- ē'n-dyô)	141c	34°56'S	57°20'W
Puntarenas, C.R. (pònt-ä-rā'näs)	129	9°59'N	84°49'W
Punto Fijo, Ven. (pōō'n-tô fē'κô)	142	11°48'N	70°14'W
Punxsutawney, Pa., U.S. (pŭnk-sŭ-tô'nē)	109	40°55'N	79°00'W
Puquio, Peru (pōō'kyô)	142	14°43'S	74°02'W
Pur, r., Russia	184	65°30'N	77°30'E
Purcell, Ok., U.S. (pûr-sĕl')	121	35°01'N	97°22'W
Purcell Mountains, mts., N.A. (pûr-sĕl')	95	50°00'N	116°30'W
Purdy, Wa., U.S. (pûr'dē)	116a	47°23'N	122°37'W
Purépero, Mex. (pōō-rā'pā-rō)	130	19°56'N	102°02'W
Purgatoire, r., Co., U.S. (pûr-gȧ-twär')	120	37°25'N	103°53'W
Puri, India (pò'rē)	199	19°52'N	85°51'E
Purial, Sierra de, mts., Cuba (sē-ĕ'r-rȧ-dĕ-pōō-rē-äl')	135	20°15'N	74°40'W
Purificación, Col. (pōō-rē-fē-kä-syōn')	142	3°52'N	74°54'W
Purificación, Mex. (pōō-rē-fē-kä-syō'n)	130	19°44'N	104°38'W
Purificación, r., Mex.	130	19°30'N	104°54'W
Purkersdorf, Aus.	159e	48°13'N	16°11'E

PRONOUNCING INDEX
Puruandiro – Ramanāthapuram 339

PLACE (Pronunciation)	PAGE	LAT.	LONG.
Puruandiro, Mex. (pò-rōō-än'dē-rō)	130	20°04'N	101°33'W
Purús, r., S.A. (pōō-rōō's)	142	6°45'S	64°34'W
Pusan, Kor., S.	205	35°08'N	129°05'E
Pushkin, Russia (pòsh'kĭn)	180	59°43'N	30°25'E
Pushkino, Russia (pōōsh'kē-nô)	176	56°01'N	37°51'E
Pustoshka, Russia (pûs-tôsh'kå)	176	56°20'N	29°33'E
Pustunich, Mex. (pōōs-tōō'nēch)	131	19°10'N	90°29'W
Putaendo, Chile (pōō-tä-ĕn-dô)	141b	32°37'S	70°42'W
Puteaux, Fr. (pü-tō')	171b	48°52'N	2°12'E
Putfontein, S. Afr. (pòt'fŏn-tān)	233b	26°08'S	28°24'E
Putian, China (pōō-tĭĕn)	209	25°40'N	119°02'E
Putla de Guerrero, Mex. (pōō'tlä-dĕ-gĕr-rĕ'rō)	131	17°03'N	97°55'W
Putnam, Ct., U.S. (pŭt'năm)	109	41°55'N	71°55'W
Putorana, Gory, mts., Russia	179	68°45'N	93°15'E
Puttalam, Sri L.	203	8°02'N	79°44'E
Putumayo, r., S.A. (pò-tōō-mä'yō)	142	1°02'S	73°50'W
Putung, Tanjung, c., Indon.	212	3°35'S	111°50'E
Putyvl', Ukr.	177	51°21'N	33°52'E
Puulavesi, l., Fin.	167	61°49'N	27°10'E
Puyallup, Wa., U.S. (pū-ăl'ŭp)	116a	47°12'N	122°18'W
Puyang, China (pōō-yäŋ)	208	35°42'N	114°58'E
Pweto, D.R.C. (pwā'tō)	232	8°29'S	28°58'E
Pyasina, r., Russia (pyä-sē'nå)	184	72°45'N	87°37'E
Pyatigorsk, Russia (pyå-tē-gôrsk')	181	44°00'N	43°00'E
Pyetrykaw, Bela.	176	52°09'N	28°30'E
Pyhäjärvi, l., Fin.	167	60°57'N	21°50'E
Pyinmana, Mya. (pyĕn-ma'nŭ)	199	19°47'N	96°15'E
Pymatuning Reservoir, res., Pa., U.S. (pī-må-tŭn'ĭng)	108	41°40'N	80°30'W
Pyŏnggang, Kor., N. (pyŭng'gäng')	210	38°21'N	127°18'E
P'yŏngyang, Kor., N.	205	39°03'N	125°48'E
Pyramid, l., Nv., U.S. (pĭ'rå-mĭd)	118	40°02'N	119°50'W
Pyramid Lake Indian Reservation, I.R., Nv., U.S.	118	40°17'N	119°52'W
Pyramids, hist., Egypt	238b	29°53'N	31°10'E
Pyrenees, mts., Eur. (pĭr-e-nēz')	156	43°00'N	0°05'E
Pýrgos, Grc.	163	37°51'N	21°28'E
Pyriatyn, Ukr.	181	50°13'N	32°31'E
Pyrzyce, Pol. (pĕzhĭ'tsĕ)	168	53°09'N	14°53'E

Q

PLACE (Pronunciation)	PAGE	LAT.	LONG.
Qal'at Bishah, Sau. Ar.	198	20°01'N	42°30'E
Qamdo, China (chyäm-dwō)	204	31°06'N	96°30'E
Qandala, Som.	201	11°28'N	49°52'E
Qaraghandy (Karaganda), Kaz.	183	49°42'N	73°18'E
Qaraözen, r.	181	49°50'N	49°35'E
Qarqan see Qiemo, China	204	38°02'N	85°16'E
Qarqan, r., China	204	38°55'N	87°15'E
Qarqaraly, Kaz.	183	49°18'N	75°28'E
Qārūn, Birket, l., Egypt	231	29°34'N	30°34'E
Qaşr al Burayqah, Libya	231	30°25'N	19°20'E
Qasr al-Farāfirah, Egypt	231	27°04'N	28°13'E
Qaşr Banī Walīd, Libya	231	31°45'N	14°04'E
Qasr el Boukhari, Alg.	162	35°50'N	2°48'E
Qatar, nation, Asia (kä'tår)	198	25°00'N	52°45'E
Qaţţārah, Munkhafaḑ al, depr., Egypt	231	30°07'N	27°30'E
Qausuittuq (Resolute), Can.	89	74°41'N	95°00'W
Qāyen, Iran	198	33°45'N	59°08'E
Qazvīn, Iran	198	36°10'N	49°59'E
Qeshm, Iran	198	26°51'N	56°10'E
Qeshm, i., Iran	198	26°52'N	56°15'E
Qezel Owzan, r., Iran	198	36°30'N	49°00'E
Qezi'ot, Isr.	197a	30°53'N	34°28'E
Qianwei, China (chyĕn-wā)	206	40°11'N	120°05'E
Qi'anzhen, China (chyē-än-jŭn)	206	32°16'N	120°59'E
Qibao, China (chyē-bou)	207b	31°06'N	121°16'E
Qiblīyah, Jabal al Jalālat al, mts., Egypt	197a	28°49'N	32°21'E
Qijiang, China (chyē-jyäŋ)	209	29°05'N	106°40'E
Qikou, China (chyē-kō)	206	38°37'N	117°33'E
Qilian Shan, mts., China (chyē-lĭĕn shän)	204	38°43'N	98°00'E
Qiliping, China (chyē-lē-pĭŋ)	206	31°28'N	114°41'E
Qindao, China (chyĭn-dou)	205	36°05'N	120°10'E
Qing'an, China (chyĭŋ-än)	208	46°50'N	127°30'E
Qingcheng, China (chyĭŋ-chŭŋ)	206	37°12'N	117°43'E
Qingfeng, China (chyĭŋ-fŭŋ)	206	35°52'N	115°05'E
Qinghai, prov., China (chyĭŋ-hī)	204	36°14'N	95°30'E
Qinghai Hu see Koko Nor, l., China	204	37°26'N	98°30'E
Qinghe, China (chyĭŋ-hŭ)	208a	40°08'N	116°16'E
Qingjiang, China (chyĭŋ-jyäŋ)	209	28°00'N	115°30'E
Qingjiang, China	206	33°34'N	118°58'E
Qingliu, China (chyĭŋ-lĭô)	209	26°15'N	116°50'E
Qingningsi, China (chyĭŋ-nĭŋ-sz)	207b	31°16'N	121°33'E
Qingping, China (chyĭŋ-pĭŋ)	206	36°46'N	116°03'E
Qingpu, China (chyĭŋ-pōō)	209	31°08'N	121°06'E
Qingxian, China (chyĭŋ shyĕn)	206	38°37'N	116°48'E
Qingyang, China (chyĭŋ-yäŋ)	204	36°02'N	107°42'E
Qingyuan, China (chyĭŋ-yòän)	209	23°43'N	113°10'E
Qingyuan, China	208	42°05'N	125°00'E
Qingyun, China (chyĭŋ-yòn)	206	37°52'N	117°26'E
Qingyundian, China (chĭŋ-yòn-dĭĕn)	208a	39°41'N	116°31'E
Qinhuangdao, China (chyĭn-huaŋ-dou)	205	39°57'N	119°34'E
Qin Ling, mts., China (chyĭn lĭŋ)	204	33°25'N	108°58'E
Qinyang, China (chyĭn-yäŋ)	208	35°00'N	112°55'E
Qinzhou, China (chyĭn-jō)	209	22°00'N	108°35'E
Qionghai, China (chyôŋ-hī)	209	19°10'N	110°28'E
Qiqian, China (chyē-chyĕn)	205	52°23'N	121°04'E
Qiqihar, China	205	47°18'N	124°00'E
Qiryat Gat, Isr.	197a	31°38'N	34°36'E
Qiryat Shemona, Isr.	197a	33°12'N	35°34'E
Qitai, China (chyē-tī)	204	44°07'N	89°04'E
Qiuxian, China (chyô shyĕn)	206	36°43'N	115°13'E
Qixian, China (chyē-shyĕn)	206	34°33'N	114°47'E
Qixian, China	208	35°36'N	114°13'E
Qiyang, China (chyē-yäŋ)	209	26°40'N	112°00'E
Qobda, r., Kaz. (kä-rå kôb'dà)	181	50°40'N	55°00'E
Qogir Feng see K2, mtn., Asia	199	36°06'N	76°38'E
Qom, Iran	198	34°28'N	50°53'E
Qongyrat, Kaz.	183	47°25'N	75°10'E
Qostanay, Kaz.	183	53°10'N	63°39'E
Quabbin Reservoir, res., Ma., U.S. (kwā'bĭn)	109	42°20'N	72°10'W
Quachita, Lake, l., Ar., U.S. (kwä shĭ'tô)	121	34°47'N	93°37'W
Quadra Island, i., Can.	94	50°08'N	125°16'W
Quakertown, Pa., U.S. (kwā'kēr-toun)	109	40°30'N	75°20'W
Quanah, Tx., U.S. (kwä'nå)	120	34°19'N	99°43'W
Quang Ngai, Viet. (kwäng n'gä'ē)	212	15°05'N	108°58'E
Quang Ngai, mtn., Viet.	209	15°10'N	108°20'E
Quanjiao, China (chyuän-jyou)	206	32°06'N	118°17'E
Quanzhou, China (chyuän-jō)	205	24°58'N	118°40'E
Quanzhou, China	209	25°58'N	111°02'E
Qu'Appelle, r., Can.	92	50°30'N	104°00'W
Qu'Appelle Dam, dam, Can.	96	51°00'N	106°25'W
Quartu Sant'Elena, Italy (kwär-tōō' sänt ā'lå-nä)	174	39°16'N	9°12'E
Quartzsite, Az., U.S.	119	33°40'N	114°13'W
Quatsino Sound, strt., Can. (kwŏt-sē'nō)	94	50°25'N	128°10'W
Quba, Azer. (kōō'bä)	181	41°05'N	48°30'E
Qūchān, Iran	201	37°06'N	58°30'E
Qudi, China	206	37°06'N	117°15'E
Québec, Can. (kwē-bĕk') (kå-bĕk')	102b	46°49'N	71°13'W
Quebec, prov., Can.	91	51°07'N	70°25'W
Quedlinburg, Ger. (kvĕd'lĕn-bōōrgh)	168	51°45'N	11°10'E
Queen Bess, Can.	94	51°16'N	124°34'W
Queen Charlotte Islands, is., Can. (kwēn shär'lŏt)	92	53°30'N	132°25'W
Queen Charlotte Ranges, mts., Can.	94	53°00'N	132°00'W
Queen Charlotte Sound, strt., Can.	94	51°30'N	129°30'W
Queen Charlotte Strait, strt., Can. (strāt)	92	50°40'N	127°25'W
Queen Elizabeth Islands, is., Can. (ē-lĭz'å-bĕth)	89	78°20'N	110°00'W
Queen Maud Gulf, b., Can. (mäd)	92	68°27'N	102°55'W
Queen Maud Land, reg., Ant.	224	75°00'S	10°00'E
Queen Maud Mountains, mts., Ant.	224	85°00'S	179°00'W
Queens Channel, strt., Austl. (kwēnz)	220	14°25'S	129°10'E
Queenscliff, Austl.	217a	38°16'S	144°39'E
Queensland, state, Austl. (kwēnz'lănd)	219	22°45'S	141°01'E
Queenstown, Austl. (kwēnz'toun)	222	42°00'S	145°40'E
Queenstown, S. Afr.	233c	31°54'S	26°53'E
Queimados, Braz. (kā-må'dòs)	144b	22°42'S	43°34'W
Quela, Ang.	236	9°16'S	17°02'E
Quelimane, Moz. (kā-lē-mä'nĕ)	233	17°48'S	37°05'E
Queluz, Port.	173b	38°45'N	9°15'W
Quemado de Güines, Cuba (kā-mä'dhä-dē-gwē'nĕs)	134	22°45'N	80°20'W
Quemoy, Tai.	209	24°30'N	118°20'E
Quemoy, i., Tai.	209	24°27'N	118°23'E
Quepos, C.R. (kā'pòs)	133	9°26'N	84°10'W
Quepos, Punta, c., C.R. (pōō'n-tä)	133	9°23'N	84°20'W
Querétaro, Mex. (kå-rā'tä-rō)	128	20°37'N	100°25'W
Querétaro, state, Mex.	130	21°00'N	100°00'W
Quesada, Spain (kå-sä'dhä)	172	37°51'N	3°04'W
Quesnel, Can. (kā-nĕl')	90	52°59'N	122°30'W
Quesnel, r., Can.	95	52°15'N	122°00'W
Quesnel Lake, l., Can.	92	52°32'N	121°05'W
Quetame, Col. (kĕ-tä'mĕ)	142a	4°20'N	73°50'W
Quetta, Pak. (kwĕt'ä)	199	30°19'N	67°01'E
Quezaltenango, Guat. (kå-zäl'tå-näŋ'gō)	128	14°50'N	91°30'W
Quezaltepeque, El Sal. (kĕ-zäl'tĕ'pĕ-kĕ)	132	13°50'N	89°17'W
Quezaltepeque, Guat. (kå-zäl'tå-pā'kå)	132	14°39'N	89°26'W
Quezon City, Phil. (kā-zōn)	212	14°40'N	121°02'E
Qufu, China (chyōō-fōō)	206	35°37'N	116°54'E
Quibdo, Col. (kēb'dō)	142	5°42'N	76°41'W
Quiberon, Fr. (kē-bē-rôN')	170	47°29'N	3°08'W
Quiçama, Parque Nacional de, rec., Ang.	236	10°00'S	13°25'E
Quicksborn, Ger. (kvēks'bōrn)	159c	53°44'N	9°54'E
Quilcene, Wa., U.S. (kwĭl-sēn')	116a	47°50'N	122°53'W
Quilimari, Chile (kē-lē-mä'rē)	141b	32°06'S	71°28'W
Quillan, Fr. (kē-yäN')	170	42°53'N	2°13'E
Quillota, Chile (kēl-yō'tä)	144	32°52'S	71°14'W
Quilmes, Arg. (kēl'mās)	141c	34°43'S	58°16'W
Quilon, India (kwē-lōn')	203	8°58'N	76°16'E
Quilpie, Austl. (kwĭl'pē)	219	26°34'S	149°20'E
Quimbaya, Col. (kēm-bä'yä)	142a	4°38'N	75°46'W
Quimbele, Ang.	236	6°28'S	16°13'E
Quimbonge, Ang.	236	8°36'S	18°30'E
Quimper, Fr. (kăN-pĕr')	161	47°59'N	4°04'W
Quinalt, r., Wa., U.S.	114	47°23'N	124°10'W
Quinault Indian Reservation, I.R., Wa., U.S.	114	47°27'N	124°34'W
Quincy, Fl., U.S. (kwĭn'sē)	124	30°35'N	84°35'W
Quincy, Il., U.S.	105	39°55'N	91°23'W
Quincy, Ma., U.S.	101a	42°15'N	71°00'W
Quincy, Mi., U.S.	108	42°00'N	84°50'W
Quincy, Or., U.S.	116c	46°08'N	123°10'W
Qui Nhon, Viet. (kwĭnyŏn)	212	13°51'N	109°03'E
Quinn, r., Nv., U.S. (kwĭn)	114	41°42'N	117°45'W
Quintanar de la Orden, Spain (kēn-tä-när')	172	39°36'N	3°02'W
Quintana Roo, state, Mex. (rō'ô)	128	19°30'N	88°30'W
Quintero, Chile (kēn-tĕ'rô)	141b	32°48'S	71°30'W
Quionga, Moz.	237	10°37'S	40°30'E
Quiroga, Mex. (kē-rō'gä)	130	19°39'N	101°30'W
Quiroga, Spain (kē-rō'gä)	172	42°28'N	7°18'W
Quitman, Ga., U.S. (kwĭt'măn)	124	30°46'N	83°35'W
Quitman, Ms., U.S.	124	33°02'N	88°43'W
Quito, Ec. (kē'tō)	142	0°17'S	78°32'W
Qumbu, S. Afr. (kòm'bōō)	233c	31°10'S	28°48'E
Quorn, Austl. (kwôrn)	222	32°20'S	138°00'E
Qurayyah, Wādī, r., Egypt	197a	30°08'N	34°27'E
Qusmuryn köli, l., Kaz.	183	52°30'N	64°15'E
Qutang, China (chyōō-täŋ)	206	32°33'N	120°07'E
Quthing, Leso.	233c	30°35'S	27°42'E
Quxian, China (chyōō-shyĕn)	205	28°58'N	118°58'E
Quxian, China	209	30°40'N	106°48'E
Quzhou, China (chyoô-jō)	206	36°47'N	114°58'E
Qyzylorda, Kaz.	183	44°58'N	65°45'E

R

PLACE (Pronunciation)	PAGE	LAT.	LONG.
Raab (Raba), r., Eur. (räp)	168	46°55'N	15°55'E
Raahe, Fin. (rä'ĕ)	160	64°39'N	24°22'E
Rab, i., Serb. (räb)	174	44°45'N	14°40'E
Raba, Indon.	212	8°32'S	118°49'E
Raba (Raab), r., Eur.	169	47°28'N	17°12'E
Rabat, Mor. (rà-bät')	230	33°59'N	6°47'W
Rabaul, Pap. N. Gui. (rä'boul)	213	4°15'S	152°19'E
Rābigh, Sau. Ar.	201	22°48'N	39°01'E
Raccoon, r., Ia., U.S. (ră-kōōn')	113	42°07'N	94°45'W
Raccoon Cay, i., Bah.	135	22°25'N	75°50'W
Race, Cape, c., Can. (rās)	101	46°40'N	53°10'W
Rachado, Cape, c., Malay.	197b	2°26'N	101°29'E
Racibórz, Pol. (rä-chē'bōōzh)	169	50°06'N	18°14'E
Racine, Wi., U.S. (rå-sēn')	105	42°43'N	87°49'W
Raco, Mi., U.S. (rá cō)	117k	46°22'N	84°43'W
Rădăuţi, Rom.	163	47°53'N	25°55'E
Radcliffe, Eng., U.K. (răd'klĭf)	158a	53°34'N	2°20'W
Radevormwald, Ger. (rä'dĕ-fōrm-väld)	171c	51°12'N	7°22'E
Radford, Va., U.S. (răd'fērd)	125	37°06'N	81°33'W
Rādhanpur, India	202	23°57'N	71°38'E
Radium, S. Afr. (rā'dĭ-ŭm)	238c	25°06'S	28°18'E
Radom, Pol. (rä'dôm)	161	51°24'N	21°11'E
Radomir, Blg. (rä'dô-mēr)	175	42°33'N	22°58'E
Radomsko, Pol. (rä-dôm'skô)	161	51°04'N	19°27'E
Radomyshl, Ukr. (rä-dô-mēsh''l)	181	50°30'N	29°13'E
Radul', Ukr. (rá'dōōl)	177	51°52'N	30°46'E
Radviliškis, Lith. (ràd'vē-lēsh'kēs)	167	55°49'N	23°31'E
Radwah, Jabal, mtn., Sau. Ar.	198	24°44'N	38°14'E
Radzyń Podlaski, Pol. (räd'zēn-y' pūd-lä'skĭ)	169	51°49'N	22°40'E
Raeford, N.C., U.S. (rā'fērd)	125	34°57'N	79°15'W
Raesfeld, Ger. (răz'fĕld)	171c	51°46'N	6°50'E
Raeside, l., Austl. (rā'sīd)	220	29°20'S	122°30'E
Rae Strait, strt., Can. (rā)	92	68°40'N	95°03'W
Rafaela, Arg. (rä-fä-ā'lä)	144	31°15'S	61°21'W
Rafah, Pak. (rä'fä)	197a	31°14'N	34°12'E
Rafsanjān, Iran	198	30°45'N	56°30'E
Raft, r., Id., U.S. (răft)	115	42°20'N	113°17'W
Ragay, Phil. (rä-gī')	213a	13°49'N	122°45'E
Ragay Gulf, b., Phil.	213a	13°44'N	122°38'E
Ragunda, Swe. (rä-gòn'dä)	166	63°07'N	16°24'E
Ragusa, Italy (rä-gōō'sä)	162	36°58'N	14°41'E
Rahachow, Bela.	180	53°07'N	30°04'E
Rahway, N.J., U.S. (rô'wā)	110a	40°37'N	74°16'W
Rāichūr, India (rä'ē-chōōr')	199	16°23'N	77°18'E
Raigarh, India (rī'gŭr)	199	21°57'N	83°32'E
Rainbow Bridge National Monument, rec., Ut., U.S. (rān'bō)	119	37°05'N	111°00'W
Rainbow City, Pan.	128a	9°20'N	79°53'W
Rainier, Or., U.S.	116c	46°05'N	122°56'W
Rainier, Mount, mtn., Wa., U.S. (rā-nēr')	106	46°52'N	121°46'W
Rainy, r., N.A.	107	48°50'N	94°41'W
Rainy Lake, l., N.A. (rān'ē)	93	48°43'N	94°29'W
Rainy River, Can.	91	48°43'N	94°29'W
Raipur, India (rä'jŭ-bōō-rē')	202	21°25'N	81°37'E
Raisin, r., Mi., U.S. (rā'zĭn)	108	42°00'N	83°35'W
Raitan, N.J., U.S. (rā-tăn)	110a	40°34'N	74°40'W
Rājahmundry, India (räj-ŭ-mŭn'drē)	199	17°03'N	81°51'E
Rajang, r., Malay.	212	2°10'N	113°30'E
Rājapālaiyam, India	203	9°30'N	77°33'E
Rājasthān, state, India (rä'jŭs-tän)	199	26°00'N	72°00'E
Rājkot, India (räj'kōt)	199	22°20'N	70°48'E
Rājpur, India	202a	22°24'N	88°25'E
Rājshāhi, Bngl.	199	24°26'S	88°39'E
Rakhiv, Ukr.	169	48°02'N	24°13'E
Rakh'oya, Russia (räk'yå)	186c	60°06'N	30°50'E
Rakitnoye, Russia (rä-kēt'nô-yĕ)	181	50°51'N	35°53'E
Rakovník, Czech Rep.	168	50°07'N	13°45'E
Rakvere, Est. (räk'vĕ-rĕ)	180	59°22'N	26°14'E
Raleigh, N.C., U.S.	105	35°45'N	78°39'W
Ram, r., Can.	95	52°10'N	115°05'W
Rama, Nic. (rä'mä)	133	12°11'N	84°14'W
Ramallo, Arg. (rä-mä'l-yô)	141c	33°28'S	60°02'W
Ramanāthapuram, India	203	9°13'N	78°52'E

ng-sing; ŋ-baŋk; N-nasalized n; nŏd; cŏmmit; ōld; ôbey; ôrder; oi-boil; fōōd; ò-as oo in foot; ou-out; s-soft; sh-dish; th-thin; pūre; ûnite; ûrn; stŭd; circŭs; ü-as in French tu; '-indeterminate vowel.

340 Rambouillet – Revda PRONOUNCING INDEX

PLACE (Pronunciation)	PAGE	LAT.	LONG.
Rambouillet, Fr. (räɴ-bōō-yĕ´)	170	48°39'N	1°49'E
Rame Head, c., S. Afr.	233c	31°48'S	29°22'E
Ramenskoye, Russia (rá´mĕn-skô-yĕ)	176	55°34'N	38°15'E
Ramlat as Sab'atayn, reg., Asia	198	16°08'N	45°15'E
Ramm, Jabal, mtn., Jord.	197a	29°37'N	35°32'E
Râmnicu Sărat, Rom.	163	45°24'N	27°06'E
Râmnicu Vâlcea, Rom.	175	45°07'N	24°22'E
Ramos, Mex. (rä´mōs)	130	22°46'N	101°52'W
Ramos, r., Nig.	235	5°10'N	5°40'E
Ramos Arizpe, Mex. (ä-rēz´pä)	122	25°33'N	100°57'W
Rampart, Ak., U.S. (răm´pärt)	103	65°28'N	150°18'W
Rampo Mountains, mts., N.J., U.S. (răm´pō)	110a	41°06'N	72°12'W
Rāmpur, India (räm´pōōr)	199	28°53'N	79°03'E
Ramree Island, i., Mya. (räm´rē´)	212	19°01'N	93°23'E
Ramsayville, Can. (răm´zē vĭl)	102c	45°23'N	75°34'W
Ramsbottom, Eng., U.K. (rămz´bŏt-ŭm)	158a	53°39'N	2°20'W
Ramsey, I. of Man (răm´zē)	164	54°20'N	4°25'W
Ramsey, N.J., U.S.	110a	41°03'N	74°09'W
Ramsey Lake, l., Can.	98	47°15'N	82°16'W
Ramsgate, Eng., U.K. (rămz´gāt)	165	51°19'N	1°20'E
Ramu, r., Pap. N. Gui. (rä´mōō)	213	5°35'S	145°16'E
Rancagua, Chile (rän-kä´gwä)	144	34°10'S	70°43'W
Rance, r., Fr. (räɴs)	170	48°17'N	2°30'W
Rānchī, India	199	23°21'N	85°20'E
Rancho Boyeros, Cuba (rä´n-chô-bô-yĕ´rôs)	135a	23°00'N	82°23'W
Randallstown, Md., U.S. (răn´dălz-toun)	110e	39°22'N	76°48'W
Randers, Den. (rän´ĕrs)	160	56°28'N	10°03'E
Randfontein, S. Afr. (rănt´fŏn-tān)	233b	26°10'S	27°42'E
Randleman, N.C., U.S. (răn´d'l-măn)	125	35°49'N	79°50'W
Randolph, Ma., U.S. (răn´dŏlf)	101a	42°10'N	71°03'W
Randolph, Ne., U.S.	112	42°22'N	97°22'W
Randolph, Vt., U.S.	109	43°55'N	72°40'W
Random Island, i., Can. (răn´dŭm)	101	48°12'N	53°25'W
Randsfjorden, Nor.	166	60°35'N	10°10'E
Randwick, Austl.	217b	33°55'S	151°15'E
Ranérou, Sen.	234	15°18'N	13°58'W
Rangeley, Me., U.S. (rānj´lē)	100	44°56'N	70°38'W
Rangeley, l., Me., U.S.	100	45°00'N	70°25'W
Ranger, Tx., U.S. (rān´jĕr)	104	32°26'N	98°41'W
Rangia, India	202	26°32'N	91°39'E
Rangoon (Yangon), Mya. (răŋ-gōōn´)	199	16°46'N	96°09'E
Rangpur, Bngl. (rŭng´pōōr)	199	25°48'N	89°19'E
Rangsang, i., Indon. (räng´säng´)	197b	0°53'N	103°05'E
Rangsdorf, Ger. (rängs´dōrf)	159b	52°17'N	13°25'E
Rāniganj, India (rä-nē-gŭnj´)	202	23°40'N	87°08'E
Rankin Inlet, b., Can. (răŋ´kĕn)	93	62°45'N	94°27'W
Ranova, r., Russia (rä´nô-vá)	176	53°55'N	40°03'E
Rantau, Malay.	197b	2°35'N	101°58'E
Rantekombola, Bulu, mtn., Indon.	212	3°22'S	119°50'E
Rantoul, Il., U.S. (răn-tōōl´)	108	40°25'N	88°05'W
Raoyang, China (rou-yäŋ)	206	38°16'N	115°45'E
Rapallo, Italy (rä-päl´lō)	174	44°21'N	9°14'E
Rapel, r., Chile (rä-pĕl´)	141b	34°05'S	71°30'W
Rapid, r., Mn., U.S. (răp´ĭd)	113	48°21'N	94°50'W
Rapid City, S.D., U.S.	104	44°06'N	103°14'W
Rapla, Est. (räp´lá)	167	59°02'N	24°46'E
Rappahannock, r., Va., U.S. (răp´ȧ-hăn´ŭk)	109	38°20'N	75°25'W
Raquette, l., N.Y., U.S. (răk´ĕt)	109	43°50'N	74°35'W
Raritan, r., N.J., U.S. (răr´ĭ-tăn)	110a	40°32'N	74°27'W
Rarotonga, Cook Is. (rä´rô-tŏŋ´gȧ)	2	20°40'S	163°00'W
Ra's an Naqb, Jord.	197a	30°00'N	35°29'E
Raşcov, Mol.	177	47°55'N	28°51'E
Ras Dashen Terara, mtn., Eth. (räs dä-shän´)	231	12°49'N	38°14'E
Raseiniai, Lith. (rä-syä´nyĭ)	167	55°23'N	23°04'E
Rashayya, Leb.	197a	33°30'N	35°50'E
Rashīd, Egypt (rȧ-shēd´) (rô-zĕt´ȧ)	200	31°22'N	30°25'E
Rashīd, Masabb, mth., Egypt	238b	31°30'N	29°58'E
Rashkina, Russia (rásh´kĭ-ná)	186a	59°57'N	61°30'E
Rasht, Iran	198	37°13'N	49°45'E
Raška, Serb. (räsh´kȧ)	175	43°16'N	20°40'E
Rasskazovo, Russia (räs-kä´sô-vô)	181	52°40'N	41°40'E
Rastatt, Ger. (rä-shtät)	168	48°51'N	8°12'E
Rastes, Russia (rás´tĕs)	186a	59°24'N	58°49'E
Rastunovo, Russia (rás-tōō´nô-vô)	186b	55°15'N	37°50'E
Ratangarh, India (rŭ-tŭn´gŭr)	202	28°10'N	74°30'E
Ratcliff, Tx., U.S. (răt´klĭf)	123	31°22'N	95°09'W
Rathenow, Ger. (rä´tĕ-nō)	168	52°36'N	12°20'E
Rathlin Island, i., N. Ire., U.K. (răth-lĭn)	164	55°18'N	6°13'W
Ratingen, Ger. (rä´tĕn-gĕn)	171c	51°18'N	6°51'E
Rat Islands, is., Ak., U.S. (răt)	103a	51°35'N	176°48'E
Ratlām, India	202	23°19'N	75°05'E
Ratnāgiri, India	203	17°04'N	73°24'E
Raton, N.M., U.S. (rȧ-tōn´)	104	36°52'N	104°26'W
Rattlesnake Creek, r., Or., U.S. (răt´'l snāk)	114	42°38'N	117°39'W
Rättvik, Swe. (rĕt´vĕk)	166	60°54'N	15°07'E
Rauch, Arg. (rá´ōōch)	144	36°47'S	59°05'W
Raufoss, Nor. (rou´fōs)	166	60°44'N	10°30'E
Raúl Soares, Braz. (rä-ōō´l-sôä´rĕs)	141a	20°05'S	42°28'W
Rauma, Fin. (rä´ô-mȧ)	160	61°07'N	21°31'E
Rauna, Lat. (rău´nȧ)	167	57°21'N	25°31'E
Raurkela, India	199	22°15'N	84°53'E
Rautalampi, Fin. (rä´ōō-tĕ-läm´pô)	167	62°39'N	26°25'E
Rava-Rus'ka, Ukr.	169	50°14'N	23°40'E
Ravenna, Italy (rä-vĕn´nä)	162	44°27'N	12°13'E
Ravenna, Ne., U.S. (rȧ-vĕn´ȧ)	112	41°20'N	98°50'W
Ravenna, Oh., U.S.	108	41°10'N	81°20'W
Ravensburg, Ger. (rä´vĕns-bōōrgh)	168	47°48'N	9°35'E
Ravensdale, Wa., U.S. (rā´vĕnz-dāl)	116a	47°22'N	121°58'W
Ravensthorpe, Austl. (rā´vĕns-thôrp)	218	33°30'S	120°20'E
Ravenswood, W.V., U.S. (rā´vĕnz-wŏŏd)	108	38°55'N	81°50'W
Rāwalpindi, Pak. (rä-wŭl-pēn´dē)	199	33°40'N	73°10'E
Rawa Mazowiecka, Pol.	169	51°46'N	20°17'E
Rawandoz, Iraq	181	36°37'N	44°30'E
Rawicz, Pol. (rä´vēch)	168	51°36'N	16°51'E
Rawlina, Austl. (rôr-lēnȧ)	218	31°13'S	125°45'E
Rawlins, Wy., U.S. (rô´lĭnz)	104	41°46'N	107°15'W
Rawson, Arg. (rô´sŭn)	144	43°16'S	65°09'W
Rawson, Arg.	141c	34°36'S	60°03'W
Rawtenstall, Eng., U.K. (rô´tĕn-stôl)	158a	53°42'N	2°17'W
Ray, Cape, c., Can. (rā)	93a	47°40'N	59°18'W
Raya, Bukit, mtn., Indon.	212	0°45'S	112°11'E
Raychikinsk, Russia (rī´chĭ-kēnsk)	185	49°52'N	129°17'E
Rayleigh, Eng., U.K. (rā´lē)	158b	51°35'N	0°36'E
Raymond, Can. (rā´mŭnd)	95	49°27'N	112°39'W
Raymond, Wa., U.S.	114	46°41'N	123°42'W
Raymondville, Tx., U.S. (rā´mŭnd-vĭl)	121	26°30'N	97°46'W
Ray Mountains, mts., Ak., U.S.	103	65°40'N	151°45'W
Rayne, La., U.S. (rān)	123	30°12'N	92°15'W
Rayón, Mex. (rä-yōn´)	130	21°49'N	99°39'W
Rayton, S. Afr. (rā´tŭn)	233b	25°45'S	28°33'E
Raytown, Mo., U.S. (rā´toun)	117f	39°01'N	94°48'W
Rayville, La., U.S. (rā-vĭl)	123	32°28'N	91°46'W
Raz, Pointe du, c., Fr. (pwăɴt dü rä)	161	48°02'N	4°43'W
Razdan, Arm.	182	40°30'N	44°46'E
Razdol'noye, Russia (räz-dôl´nô-yĕ)	210	43°38'N	131°58'E
Razgrad, Blg.	163	43°32'N	26°32'E
Razlog, Blg. (räz´lôk)	175	41°54'N	23°32'E
Razorback Mountain, mtn., Can. (rā´zēr-băk)	94	51°35'N	124°42'W
Rea, r., Eng., U.K. (rē)	158a	52°25'N	2°31'W
Reaburn, Can. (rā´bûrn)	102f	50°06'N	97°53'W
Reading, Eng., U.K. (rĕd´ĭng)	161	51°25'N	0°58'W
Reading, Ma., U.S.	101a	42°32'N	71°07'W
Reading, Mi., U.S.	108	41°45'N	84°45'W
Reading, Oh., U.S.	111f	39°14'N	84°26'W
Reading, Pa., U.S.	105	40°20'N	75°55'W
Reading, co., Eng., U.K.	158a	52°37'N	0°40'W
Realengo, Braz. (rĕ-ä-lān-gô)	141a	23°50'S	43°25'W
Rebiana, Libya	231	24°10'N	22°03'E
Rebun, i., Japan (rē´bōōn)	210	45°25'N	140°54'E
Recanati, Italy (rā-kä-nä´tē)	174	43°25'N	13°35'E
Recherche, Archipelago of the, is., Austl. (rē-shârsh´)	220	34°17'S	122°30'E
Rechytsa, Bela. (ryĕ´chĕt-sȧ)	181	52°22'N	30°24'E
Recife, Braz. (rå-sē´fĕ)	143	8°09'S	34°59'W
Recife, Kapp, c., S. Afr. (rå-sē´fē)	233c	34°03'S	25°43'E
Recklinghausen, Ger. (rĕk´lĭng-hou-zĕn)	171c	51°36'N	7°13'E
Reconquista, Arg. (rā-kôn-kēs´tä)	144	29°01'S	59°41'W
Rector, Ar., U.S. (rĕk´tēr)	121	36°16'N	90°21'W
Red, r., Asia	212	21°00'N	103°00'E
Red, r., N.A. (rĕd)	106	48°00'N	97°00'W
Red, r., Tn., U.S.	124	36°35'N	86°55'W
Red, r., U.S.	107	31°40'N	92°55'W
Red, North Fork, r., U.S.	120	35°20'N	100°08'W
Red, Prairie Dog Town Fork, r., U.S. (prâ´rĭ)	120	34°54'N	101°31'W
Red, Salt Fork, r., U.S.	120	35°04'N	100°31'W
Redan, Ga., U.S. (rē-dăn´) (rĕd´ăn)	110c	33°44'N	84°09'W
Red Bank, N.J., U.S. (băngk)	110a	40°21'N	74°06'W
Red Bluff Reservoir, res., Tx., U.S.	122	32°03'N	103°52'W
Redby, Mn., Mn., U.S. (rĕd´bē)	113	47°52'N	94°55'W
Red Cedar, r., Wi., U.S. (sē´dēr)	113	45°03'N	91°48'W
Redcliff, Can. (rĕd´clĭf)	90	50°05'N	110°47'W
Redcliffe, Austl. (rĕd´clĭf)	222	27°20'S	153°12'E
Red Cliff Indian Reservation, I.R., Wi., U.S.	113	46°48'N	91°22'W
Red Cloud, Ne., U.S. (kloud)	120	40°06'N	98°32'W
Red Deer, Can. (dēr)	90	52°16'N	113°48'W
Red Deer, r., Can.	92	51°00'N	111°00'W
Red Deer, r., Can.	97	52°55'N	102°10'W
Red Deer Lake, l., Can.	97	52°58'N	101°28'W
Reddick, Il., U.S. (rĕd´dĭk)	111a	41°06'N	88°16'W
Redding, Ca., U.S. (rĕd´ĭng)	114	40°36'N	122°25'W
Redenção da Serra, Braz. (rĕ-dĕn-souɴ-dä-sĕ´r-rä)	141a	23°17'S	45°31'W
Redfield, S.D., U.S. (rĕd´fēld)	112	44°53'N	98°30'W
Red Fish Bar, Tx., U.S.	123a	29°29'N	94°53'W
Red Indian Lake, l., Can. (ĭn´dĭ-ăn)	93a	48°40'N	56°50'W
Red Lake, Can. (lāk)	91	51°02'N	93°49'W
Red Lake, r., Mn., U.S.	112	48°02'N	96°04'W
Red Lake Falls, Mn., U.S. (lăk fôls)	112	47°52'N	96°17'W
Red Lake Indian Reservation, I.R., Mn., U.S.	112	48°09'N	95°55'W
Redlands, Ca., U.S. (rĕd´lăndz)	117a	34°04'N	117°11'W
Red Lion, Pa., U.S. (lī´ŭn)	109	39°55'N	76°30'W
Red Lodge, Mt., U.S.	115	45°13'N	107°16'W
Redmond, Wa., U.S. (rĕd´mŭnd)	116a	47°40'N	122°07'W
Rednitz, r., Ger. (rĕd´nētz)	168	49°10'N	11°00'E
Red Oak, Ia., U.S. (ōk)	112	41°00'N	95°12'W
Redon, Fr. (rē-dôɴ´)	170	47°42'N	2°03'W
Redonda, Isla, i., Braz. (ē´s-lä-rē-dô´n-dä)	144b	23°05'S	43°11'W
Redonda Island, i., Antig. (rē-dŏn´dȧ)	133b	16°55'N	62°28'W
Redondela, Spain (rā-dhôn-dā´lä)	172	42°16'N	8°34'W
Redondo, Port. (rå-dôn´dō)	172	38°40'N	7°32'W
Redondo, Wa., U.S. (rē-dŏn´dō)	116a	47°21'N	122°19'W
Redondo Beach, Ca., U.S.	117a	33°50'N	118°23'W
Red Pass, Can. (păs)	95	52°59'N	118°59'W
Red Rock, r., Mt., U.S.	115	44°54'N	112°44'W
Red Sea, sea	198	23°15'N	37°00'E
Redstone, Can. (rĕd´stōn)	94	52°08'N	123°42'W
Red Sucker Lake, l., Can. (sŭk´ēr)	97	54°09'N	93°40'W
Redwater, r., Mt., U.S.	115	47°37'N	105°25'W
Red Willow Creek, r., Ne., U.S.	120	40°34'N	100°48'W
Red Wing, Mn., U.S.	113	44°34'N	92°35'W
Redwood City, Ca., U.S. (rĕd´ wŏŏd)	116b	37°29'N	122°13'W
Redwood Falls, Mn., U.S.	112	44°32'N	95°06'W
Redwood National Park, rec., Ca., U.S.	114	41°20'N	124°00'W
Redwood Valley, Ca., U.S.	118	39°15'N	123°12'W
Ree, Lough, l., Ire. (lŏĸ´rē´)	160	53°30'N	7°45'W
Reed City, Mi., U.S. (rēd)	108	43°50'N	85°35'W
Reed Lake, l., Can.	97	54°37'N	100°30'W
Reedley, Ca., U.S. (rēd´lē)	118	36°37'N	119°27'W
Reedsburg, Wi., U.S. (rēdz´bûrg)	113	43°32'N	90°01'W
Reedsport, Or., U.S. (rēdz´pôrt)	114	43°42'N	124°08'W
Reelfoot Lake, res., Tn., U.S. (rēl´fŏŏt)	124	36°18'N	89°20'W
Rees, Ger. (rĕz)	171c	51°46'N	6°25'E
Reeves, Mount, mtn., Austl. (rēv's)	222	33°50'S	149°56'E
Reform, Al., U.S. (rē-fôrm´)	124	33°23'N	88°00'W
Refugio, Tx., U.S. (rå-fōō´hyô) (rē-fū´jō)	123	28°18'N	97°15'W
Rega, r., Pol. (rĕ-gä)	168	53°48'N	15°30'E
Regen, r., Ger. (rā´ghĕn)	168	49°09'N	12°21'E
Regensburg, Ger. (rā´ghĕns-bôrgh)	161	49°02'N	12°06'E
Reggio, La., U.S. (rĕg´jĭ-ō)	110d	29°50'N	89°46'W
Reggio di Calabria, Italy (rĕ´jô dē kä-lä´brē-ä)	163	38°07'N	15°42'E
Reggio nell' Emilia, Italy	162	44°43'N	10°34'E
Reghin, Rom. (rå-gēn´)	169	46°47'N	24°44'E
Regina, Can. (rē-jī´nȧ)	96	50°25'N	104°39'W
Regla, Cuba (rāg´lä)	134	23°08'N	82°20'W
Regnitz, r., Ger. (rĕg´nētz)	168	49°50'N	10°55'E
Reguengos de Monsaraz, Port.	172	38°26'N	7°30'W
Rehoboth, Nmb.	232	23°10'S	17°15'E
Rehovot, Isr.	197a	31°53'N	34°49'E
Reichenbach, Ger. (rī´ĸĕn-bäĸ)	168	50°36'N	12°18'E
Reidsville, N.C., U.S. (rēdz´vĭl)	125	36°20'N	79°37'W
Reigate, Eng., U.K. (rī´gāt)	164	51°12'N	0°12'W
Reims, Fr. (răɴs)	154	49°16'N	4°00'E
Reina Adelaida, Archipiélago, is., Chile	144	52°00'S	74°15'W
Reinbeck, Ia., U.S. (rīn´bĕk)	113	42°22'N	92°34'W
Reindeer, l., Can. (rān´dēr)	92	57°36'N	101°23'W
Reindeer, r., Can.	96	55°45'N	103°30'W
Reindeer Island, i., Can.	97	52°25'N	98°00'W
Reinosa, Spain (rå-ê-nō´sä)	172	43°01'N	4°08'W
Reistertown, Md., U.S. (rēs´tēr-toun)	110e	39°28'N	76°50'W
Reitz, S. Afr.	238c	27°48'S	28°25'E
Rema, Jabal, mtn., Yemen	198	14°13'N	44°38'E
Rembau, Malay.	197b	2°36'N	102°06'E
Remedios, Col. (rē-mĕ´dyôs)	142a	7°03'N	74°42'W
Remedios, Cuba (rā-mā´dhē-ōs)	134	22°30'N	79°35'W
Remedios, Pan. (rē-mĕ´dyôs)	133	8°14'N	81°46'W
Remiremont, Fr. (rē-mēr-môɴ´)	171	48°01'N	6°35'E
Rempang, i., Indon.	197b	0°51'N	104°04'E
Remscheid, Ger. (rĕm´shīt)	171c	51°10'N	7°11'E
Rena, Nor.	166	61°08'N	11°17'E
Rendova, i., Sol. Is. (rĕn´dô-vȧ)	221	8°38'S	156°26'E
Rendsburg, Ger. (rĕnts´bôrgh)	168	54°19'N	9°39'E
Renfrew, Can. (rĕn´frōō)	91	45°30'N	76°30'W
Rengam, Malay. (rĕn´gäm´)	197b	1°53'N	103°24'E
Rengo, Chile (rĕn´gō)	141b	34°22'S	70°50'W
Reni, Ukr. (rān´)	177	45°26'N	28°18'E
Renmark, Austl. (rĕn´märk)	218	34°10'S	140°50'E
Rennel, i., Sol. Is. (rĕn-nĕl´)	221	11°50'S	160°38'E
Rennes, Fr. (rĕn)	154	48°07'N	1°02'W
Reno, Nv., U.S. (rē´nō)	104	39°32'N	119°49'W
Reno, r., Italy (rā´nō)	174	44°10'N	10°55'E
Renovo, Pa., U.S. (rē-nō´vō)	109	41°20'N	77°50'W
Renqiu, China (rŭn-chyô)	206	38°44'N	116°05'E
Rensselaer, In., U.S. (rĕn´sē-lâr)	108	41°00'N	87°10'W
Rensselaer, N.Y., U.S. (rĕn´sē-lâr)	109	42°40'N	73°45'W
Rentchler, Il., U.S. (rĕnt´chlēr)	117e	38°30'N	89°52'W
Renton, Wa., U.S. (rĕn´tŭn)	116a	47°29'N	122°13'W
Repentigny, Can.	102a	45°47'N	73°26'W
Republic, Al., U.S. (rē-pŭb´lĭk)	110h	33°37'N	86°54'W
Republic, Wa., U.S.	114	48°38'N	118°44'W
Republican, r., U.S.	106	40°15'N	100°00'W
Republican, South Fork, r., Co., U.S. (rē-pŭb´lĭ-kăn)	120	39°35'N	102°28'W
Repulse Bay, b., Austl. (rē-pŭls´)	221	20°56'S	149°22'E
Requena, Spain (rå-kā´nä)	162	39°29'N	1°03'W
Resende, Braz. (rĕ-sĕ´n-dĕ)	141a	22°30'S	44°26'W
Resende Costa, Braz. (kôs-tä)	141a	20°55'S	44°12'W
Reshetylivka, Ukr.	177	49°34'N	34°04'E
Resistencia, Arg. (rā-sēs-tĕn´syä)	144	27°24'S	58°54'W
Reşiţa, Rom. (rā´shē-tȧ)	175	45°18'N	21°56'E
Resolute *see* Qausuittuq, Can.	89	74°41'N	95°00'W
Resolution, i., Can. (rĕz-ô-lū´shŭn)	93	61°30'N	63°58'W
Resolution Island, i., N.Z. (rĕz-ŏl-ûshûn)	221a	45°43'S	166°20'E
Restigouche, r., Can.	100	47°35'N	67°35'W
Restrepo, Col. (rĕs-trĕ´pô)	142a	3°49'N	76°31'W
Restrepo, Col.	142a	4°16'N	73°32'W
Retalhuleu, Guat. (rā-täl-ōō-lān´)	132	14°31'N	91°41'W
Rethel, Fr. (r-tĕl´)	170	49°34'N	4°20'E
Réthimnon, Grc.	174a	35°21'N	24°30'E
Retie, Bel.	159a	51°16'N	5°08'E
Retsil, Wa., U.S. (rĕt´sĭl)	116a	47°33'N	122°37'W
Reunion, dep., Afr. (rā-ü-nyôn´)	3	21°06'S	55°36'E
Reus, Spain (rā´ōōs)	162	41°08'N	1°05'E
Reutlingen, Ger. (roit´lĭng-ĕn)	168	48°29'N	9°14'E
Reutov, Russia (rĕ-ōō´ôf)	186b	55°45'N	37°52'E
Revda, Russia (ryâv´dá)	186a	56°48'N	59°57'E

ăt; finăl; rāte; senâte; ärm; åsk; sofȧ; fâre; ch-choose; dh-as th in other; bē; ēvent; bĕt; recĕnt; cratēr; g-gō; gh-guttural g; bĭt; ĭ-short neutral; rīde; ĸ-guttural k as ch in German ich;

PRONOUNCING INDEX

Revelstoke – Rockingham Forest 341

PLACE (Pronunciation)	PAGE	LAT.	LONG.
Revelstoke, Can. (rĕv´ĕl-stōk)	90	51°00'N	118°12'W
Reventazón, Río, r., C.R. (rā-vĕn-tä-zōn´)	133	10°10'N	83°30'W
Revere, Ma., U.S. (rē-vēr´)	101a	42°24'N	71°01'W
Revillagigedo, Islas, is., Mex. (ė´s-läs-rĕ-vēl-yä-hĕ´gĕ-dô)	128	18°45'N	111°00'W
Revillagigedo Chan, Ak., U.S. (rĕ-vĭl´á-gĭ-gē´dō)	94	55°10'N	131°13'W
Revillagigedo Island, i., Ak., U.S.	94	55°35'N	131°23'W
Revin, Fr. (rĕ-văN)	170	49°56'N	4°34'E
Rewa, India (rā´wä)	199	24°41'N	81°11'E
Rewāri, India	202	28°19'N	76°39'E
Rexburg, Id., U.S. (rĕks´bûrg)	115	43°50'N	111°48'W
Rey, Iran	201	35°35'N	51°25'E
Rey, l., Mex. (rā)	122	27°00'N	103°33'W
Rey, Isla del, i., Pan. (ė´s-lä-dĕl-rā´ė)	133	8°20'N	78°40'W
Reyes, Bol. (rā´yĕs)	142	14°19'S	67°16'W
Reyes, Point, c., Ca., U.S.	118	38°00'N	123°00'W
Reykjanes, c., Ice. (rā´kyá-nĕs)	156	63°37'N	24°33'W
Reykjavík, Ice. (rā´kyá-vĕk)	154	64°09'N	21°39'W
Reynosa, Mex. (rā-ė-nō´sä)	122	26°05'N	98°21'W
Rēzekne, Lat. (rā´zĕk-nĕ)	180	56°31'N	27°19'E
Rezh, Russia (rĕzh´)	186a	57°22'N	61°23'E
Rezina, Mol. (ryĕzh´ĕ-nĭ)	177	47°44'N	28°56'E
Rhaetian Alps, mts., Eur.	168	46°30'N	10°00'E
Rhaetien Alps, mts., Eur.	174	46°22'N	10°33'E
Rheinberg, Ger. (rīn´bĕrgh)	171c	51°33'N	6°37'E
Rheine, Ger. (rī´nĕ)	168	52°16'N	7°26'E
Rheinkamp, Ger.	171c	51°30'N	6°37'E
Rheinland, hist. reg., Ger.	168	50°05'N	6°40'E
Rheydt, Ger. (rĕ´yt)	171c	51°10'N	6°28'E
Rhin, r., Ger. (rēn)	159b	52°52'N	12°49'E
Rhine, r., Eur.	156	50°34'N	7°21'E
Rhinelander, Wi., U.S. (rīn´lăn-dēr)	113	45°39'N	89°25'W
Rhin Kanal, can., Ger. (rēn kä-näl´)	159b	52°47'N	12°40'E
Rhiou, r., Alg.	173	35°45'N	1°18'E
Rhode Island, state, U.S. (rōd ī´lănd)	105	41°35'N	71°40'W
Rhode Island, i., R.I., U.S.	110b	41°31'N	71°14'W
Rhodes, S. Afr. (rōdz)	233c	30°48'S	27°56'E
Rhodes *see* Ródhos, i., Grc.	156	36°00'N	28°29'E
Rhodesia *see* Zimbabwe, nation, Afr.	232	17°50'S	29°30'E
Rhodope Mountains, mts., Eur. (rô´dô-pĕ)	156	42°00'N	24°08'E
Rhondda, Wales, U.K. (rŏn´dhá)	164	51°40'N	3°40'W
Rhône, r., Fr. (rōn)	156	44°30'N	4°45'E
Rhoon, Neth.	159a	51°52'N	4°24'E
Rhum, i., Scot., U.K. (rŭm)	164	57°00'N	6°20'W
Riachão, Braz. (rė-ä-chouN´)	143	7°15'S	46°30'W
Rialto, Ca., U.S. (rē-ăl´tō)	117a	34°06'N	117°23'W
Riau, prov., Indon.	197b	0°56'N	101°25'E
Riau, Kepulauan, i., Indon.	212	0°30'N	104°55'E
Riau, Selat, strt., Indon.	197b	0°40'N	104°27'E
Riaza, r., Spain (rė-ä´thä)	172	41°25'N	3°25'W
Ribadavia, Spain (rē-bä-dhä´vė-ä)	172	42°18'N	8°06'W
Ribadeo, Spain (rė-bä-dhā´ō)	172	43°32'N	7°05'W
Ribadesella, Spain (rē´bä-dā-sāl´yä)	172	43°30'N	5°02'W
Ribe, Den. (rē´bĕ)	166	55°20'N	8°45'E
Ribeirão Prêto, Braz. (rė-bā-rouN-prĕ´tô)	143	21°11'S	47°47'W
Ribera, N.M., U.S. (rē-bĕ´rä)	120	35°23'N	105°27'W
Riberalta, Bol. (rē-bå-räl´tä)	142	11°06'S	66°02'W
Rib Lake, Wi., U.S. (rĭb lāk)	113	45°20'N	90°11'W
Rîbniţa, Mol.	177	47°45'N	29°02'E
Rice, l., Can.	99	44°05'N	78°10'W
Rice Lake, Wi., U.S.	113	45°30'N	91°44'W
Rice Lake, l., Mn., U.S.	117g	45°10'N	93°09'W
Richards Island, i., Can. (rĭch´ĕrds)	103	69°45'N	135°30'W
Richards Landing, Can. (lănd´ĭng)	117k	46°18'N	84°02'W
Richardson, Tx., U.S. (rĭch´ĕrd-sŭn)	117c	32°56'N	96°44'W
Richardson, Wa., U.S.	116a	48°27'N	122°54'W
Richardson Mountains, mts., Can.	92	66°58'N	136°19'W
Richardson Mountains, mts., N.Z.	223	44°50'S	168°30'E
Richardson Park, De., U.S. (pärk)	109	39°45'N	75°35'W
Richelieu, r., Can. (rēsh´lyû´)	99	45°05'N	73°25'W
Richfield, Mn., U.S.	117g	44°53'N	93°17'W
Richfield, Oh., U.S.	111d	41°14'N	81°38'W
Richfield, Ut., U.S.	119	38°45'N	112°05'W
Richford, Vt., U.S. (rĭch´fērd)	109	45°00'N	72°35'W
Rich Hill, Mo., U.S. (rĭch hĭl)	121	38°05'N	94°21'W
Richibucto, Can. (rĭ-chĭ-bŭk´tō)	91	46°41'N	64°52'W
Richland, Ga., U.S. (rĭch´lănd)	124	32°05'N	84°40'W
Richland, Wa., U.S.	114	46°17'N	119°19'W
Richland Center, Wi., U.S. (sĕn´tēr)	113	43°20'N	90°25'W
Richmond, Austl. (rĭch´mŭnd)	219	20°47'S	143°14'E
Richmond, Austl.	217b	33°36'S	150°45'E
Richmond, Can.	102c	45°12'N	75°49'W
Richmond, Can.	99	45°40'N	72°07'W
Richmond, S. Afr.	233c	29°52'S	30°17'E
Richmond, Il., U.S.	111a	42°29'N	88°18'W
Richmond, In., U.S.	108	39°50'N	85°00'W
Richmond, Ky., U.S.	108	37°45'N	84°20'W
Richmond, Mo., U.S.	121	39°16'N	93°58'W
Richmond, Tx., U.S.	123	29°35'N	95°45'W
Richmond, Ut., U.S.	115	41°55'N	111°50'W
Richmond, Va., U.S.	105	37°35'N	77°30'W
Richmond Beach, Wa., U.S.	116a	47°47'N	122°23'W
Richmond Heights, Mo., U.S.	117e	38°38'N	90°20'W
Richmond Highlands, Wa., U.S.	116a	47°46'N	122°22'W
Richmond Hill, Can. (hĭl)	99	43°53'N	79°26'W
Richton, Ms., U.S. (rĭch´tŭn)	124	31°20'N	89°54'W
Richwood, W.V., U.S. (rĭch´wo͝od)	108	38°10'N	80°30'W
Ridderkerk, Neth.	159a	51°52'N	4°35'E
Rideau, r., Can.	102c	45°17'N	75°41'W
Rideau Lake, l., Can. (rė-dō´)	99	44°40'N	76°20'W

PLACE (Pronunciation)	PAGE	LAT.	LONG.
Ridgefield, Ct., U.S. (rĭj´fēld)	110a	41°16'N	73°30'W
Ridgefield, Wa., U.S.	116c	45°49'N	122°40'W
Ridgeway, Can. (rĭj´wā)	111c	42°53'N	79°02'W
Ridgewood, N.J., U.S. (ridj´wo͝od)	110a	40°59'N	74°08'W
Ridgway, Pa., U.S.	109	41°25'N	78°40'W
Riding Mountain, mtn., Can. (rīd´ĭng)	97	50°37'N	99°37'W
Riding Mountain National Park, rec., Can. (rīd´ĭng)	92	50°59'N	99°19'W
Riding Rocks, is., Bah.	134	25°20'N	79°10'W
Riebeek-Oos, S. Afr.	233c	33°14'S	26°09'E
Ried, Aus. (rēd)	168	48°13'N	13°30'E
Riesa, Ger. (rē´zá)	168	51°17'N	13°17'E
Rieti, Italy (rė-ā´tē)	162	42°25'N	12°51'E
Rievleidam, res., S. Afr.	233b	25°52'S	28°18'E
Riffe Lake, res., Wa., U.S.	114	46°20'N	122°10'W
Rifle, Co., U.S. (rī´f'l)	119	39°35'N	107°50'W
Rīga, Lat. (rē´gá)	178	56°55'N	24°05'E
Riga, Gulf of, b., Eur.	180	57°56'N	23°05'E
Rīgān, Iran	198	28°45'N	58°55'E
Rigaud, Can. (rė-gō´)	102a	45°29'N	74°18'W
Rigby, Id., U.S. (rĭg´bė)	115	43°40'N	111°55'W
Rigeley, W.V., U.S. (rĭj´lė)	109	39°40'N	78°45'W
Rīgestān, des., Afg.	198	30°53'N	64°42'E
Rigolet, Can. (rĭg-ō-lā´)	91	54°10'N	58°40'W
Riihimäki, Fin.	167	60°44'N	24°44'E
Rijeka, Cro. (rī-yĕ´kä)	162	45°22'N	14°24'E
Rijkevorsel, Bel.	159a	51°21'N	4°46'E
Rijswijk, Neth.	159a	52°03'N	4°19'E
Rika, r., Ukr. (rē´ká)	169	48°21'N	23°37'E
Rima, r., Nig.	235	13°30'N	5°50'E
Rimavska Sobota, Slvk. (rē´máf-ská sô´bô-tá)	169	48°25'N	20°01'E
Rimbo, Swe. (rēm´bō)	166	59°45'N	18°22'E
Rimini, Italy (rē´mē-nē)	162	44°03'N	12°33'E
Rimouski, Can. (rė-mo͞os´kė)	91	48°27'N	68°32'W
Rincón de Romos, Mex. (rēn-kōn dā rô-mōs´)	130	22°13'N	102°21'W
Ringkøbing, Den. (rĭng´kûb-ĭng)	160	56°06'N	8°14'E
Ringkøbing Fjord, b., Den.	166	55°55'N	8°04'E
Ringsted, Den. (rĭng´stĕdh)	166	55°27'N	11°49'E
Ringvassøya, i., Nor. (rĭng´väs-ûė)	160	69°58'N	16°43'E
Ringwood, Austl.	217a	37°49'S	145°14'E
Rinjani, Gunung, mtn., Indon.	212	8°39'S	116°22'E
Río Abajo, Pan. (rē´ō-ä-bä´kō)	128a	9°01'N	78°30'W
Río Balsas, Mex. (rė´ō-bäl-säs)	130	17°59'N	99°45'W
Riobamba, Ec. (rē´ō-bäm-bä)	142	1°45'S	78°37'W
Rio Bonito, Braz. (rē´ō bō-nē´tō)	141a	22°44'S	42°38'W
Rio Branco, Braz. (rē´ō brän´kō)	142	9°57'S	67°50'W
Río Branco, Ur. (rĭō brănc̄ō)	144	32°33'S	53°29'W
Rio Casca, Braz. (rē´ō-kä´s-kä)	141a	20°15'S	42°39'W
Río Chico, Ven. (rē´ō chē´kŏ)	143b	10°20'N	65°58'W
Rio Claro, Braz. (rē´ō klä´rō)	143	22°25'S	47°33'W
Río Cuarto, Arg. (rē´ō kwär´tō)	144	33°05'S	64°15'W
Rio das Flores, Braz. (rē´ō-däs-flô-rĕs)	141a	22°10'S	43°35'W
Rio de Janeiro, Braz. (rē´ō dā zhä-nā´ė-rō)	144b	22°50'S	43°20'W
Rio de Janeiro, state, Braz.	143	22°27'S	42°43'W
Río de Jesús, Pan.	133	7°54'N	80°59'W
Río Frío, Mex. (rė´ō-frē´ō)	131a	19°21'N	98°40'W
Río Gallegos, Arg. (rē´ō gä-lā´gōs)	144	51°43'S	69°15'W
Rio Grande, Braz. (rē´ō grän´dĕ)	144	31°04'S	52°14'W
Río Grande, Mex. (rē´ō grän´dĕ)	130	23°51'N	102°59'W
Riogrande, Tx., U.S. (rē´ō grán-dā)	122	26°23'N	98°48'W
Rio Grande do Norte, state, Braz.	143	5°26'S	37°20'W
Rio Grande do Sul, state, Braz. (rē´ō grän´dĕ-dō-so͞o´l)	144	29°00'S	54°00'W
Ríohacha, Col. (rē´ō-ä´chä)	142	11°30'N	72°54'W
Río Hato, Pan. (rē´ō-ä´tō)	133	8°19'N	80°11'W
Riom, Fr. (rė-ôN´)	170	45°54'N	3°08'E
Rio Muni, hist. reg., Eq. Gui. (rē´ō mo͞o´nė)	230	1°47'N	8°33'E
Rionegro, Col. (rė´ō-nĕ´grō)	142a	6°09'N	75°22'W
Río Negro, prov., Arg. (rē´ō nā´grō)	144	40°15'S	68°15'W
Río Negro, dept., Ur. (rė´ō-nĕ´grō)	141c	32°48'S	57°45'W
Río Negro, Embalse del, res., Ur.	144	32°45'S	55°50'W
Rionero, Italy (rē-ō-nā´rō)	174	40°55'N	15°42'E
Rioni, r., Geor.	182	42°08'N	41°39'E
Rio Novo, Braz. (rē´ō-nō´vō)	141a	21°30'S	43°08'W
Rio Pardo de Minas, Braz. (rē´ō pär´dō-dĕ-mē´näs)	143	15°43'S	42°24'W
Rio Pombo, Braz. (rē´ō pôm´bä)	141a	21°17'S	43°09'W
Rio Sorocaba, Represa do, res., Braz.	141a	23°37'S	47°19'W
Ríosucio, Col. (rē´ō-so͞o´syō)	142a	5°25'N	75°41'W
Río Tercero, Arg. (rė´ō dĕr-sĕ´rō)	144	32°12'S	63°59'W
Rio Verde, Braz. (vĕr´dĕ)	143	17°47'S	50°49'W
Ríoverde, Mex. (rē´ō-vĕr´då)	128	21°54'N	99°59'W
Ripley, Eng., U.K. (rĭp´lė)	158a	53°03'N	1°24'W
Ripley, Ms., U.S.	124	34°44'N	88°55'W
Ripley, Tn., U.S.	124	35°44'N	89°34'W
Ripoll, Spain (rė-pōl´')	173	42°10'N	2°10'E
Ripon, Wi., U.S. (rĭp´ŏn)	113	43°49'N	88°50'W
Ripon, i., Austl.	220	20°05'S	118°10'E
Ripon Falls, wtfl., Ug.	232	0°38'N	33°02'E
Risaralda, dept., Col.	142a	5°15'N	76°00'W
Risdon, Austl. (rĭz´dŭn)	219	42°37'S	147°32'E
Rishiri, i., Japan (rē-shē´rē)	210	45°10'N	141°08'E
Rishon le Ziyyon, Isr.	197a	31°57'N	34°48'E
Rishra, India	202a	22°42'N	88°22'E
Rising Sun, In., U.S. (rīz´ĭng sŭn)	108	38°55'N	84°55'W
Risor, Nor. (rēs´ûr)	160	58°44'N	9°10'E
Ritacuva, Alto, mtn., Col. (ä´l-tô-rē-tä-ko͞o´vä)	142	6°22'N	72°13'W
Rittman, Oh., U.S. (rĭt´năn)	111d	40°58'N	81°47'W
Ritzville, Wa., U.S. (rĭts´vĭl)	114	47°08'N	118°23'W

PLACE (Pronunciation)	PAGE	LAT.	LONG.
Riva, Dom. Rep. (rē´vä)	135	19°10'N	69°55'W
Riva, Italy (rē´vä)	174	45°54'N	10°49'E
Riva, Md., U.S. (rĭ´vă)	110e	38°57'N	76°36'W
Rivas, Nic. (rē´väs)	132	11°25'N	85°51'W
Rive-de-Gier, Fr. (rēv-dē-zhė-ā´)	170	45°32'N	4°37'E
Rivera, Ur. (rė-vā´rä)	144	30°52'S	55°32'W
River Cess, Lib. (rĭv´ēr sĕs)	230	5°46'N	9°52'W
Riverdale, Il., U.S. (rĭv´ēr dāl)	111a	41°38'N	87°36'W
Riverdale, Ut., U.S.	117b	41°11'N	112°00'W
River Falls, Al., U.S.	124	31°20'N	86°25'W
River Falls, Wi., U.S.	113	44°48'N	92°38'W
Riverhead, N.Y., U.S. (rĭv´ēr hĕd)	109	40°55'N	72°40'W
Riverina, reg., Austl. (rĭv-ēr-ē´nä)	221	34°55'S	144°30'E
River Jordan, Can. (jôr´dăn)	116a	48°25'N	124°03'W
River Oaks, Tx., U.S. (ōkz)	117c	32°47'N	97°24'W
River Rouge, Mi., U.S. (ro͞ozh)	111b	42°16'N	83°09'W
Rivers, Can.	97	50°01'N	100°15'W
Riverside, Ca., U.S. (rĭv´ēr-sīd)	104	33°59'N	117°21'W
Riverside, N.J., U.S.	110f	40°02'N	74°58'W
Rivers Inlet, Can.	94	51°45'N	127°15'W
Riverstone, Austl.	217b	33°41'S	150°52'E
Riverton, Va., U.S.	109	39°00'N	78°15'W
Riverton, Wy., U.S.	115	43°02'N	108°24'W
Rivesaltes, Fr. (rēv´zält´)	170	42°48'N	2°48'E
Riviera Beach, Fl., U.S. (rĭv-ĭ-ĕr´á bēch)	125a	26°46'N	80°04'W
Riviera Beach, Md., U.S.	110e	39°10'N	76°32'W
Rivière-Beaudette, Can.	102a	45°14'N	74°20'W
Rivière-du-Loup, Can. (rė-vyâr´ dü lo͞o´)	91	47°50'N	69°32'W
Rivière Qui Barre, Can. (rēv-yĕr´ kē-bär)	102g	53°47'N	113°51'W
Rivière-Trois-Pistoles, Can. (trwä´pės-tôl´)	100	48°07'N	69°10'W
Rivne, Ukr.	177	48°11'N	31°46'E
Rivne, Ukr.	181	50°37'N	26°17'E
Rivne, prov., Ukr.	177	50°55'N	27°00'E
Riyadh, Sau. Ar.	198	24°31'N	46°47'E
Rize, Tur. (rē´zĕ)	163	41°00'N	40°30'E
Rizhao, China (rē-jou)	208	35°27'N	119°28'E
Rizzuto, Cape, c., Italy (rēt-so͞o´tô)	175	38°53'N	17°05'E
Rjukan, Nor. (ryo͞o´kän)	160	59°53'N	8°30'E
Roanne, Fr. (rō-än´)	161	46°02'N	4°04'E
Roanoke, Al., U.S. (rō´á-nōk)	124	33°08'N	85°21'W
Roanoke, Va., U.S.	105	37°16'N	79°55'W
Roanoke, r., U.S.	107	36°17'N	77°22'W
Roanoke Rapids, N.C., U.S.	125	36°25'N	77°40'W
Roanoke Rapids Lake, res., N.C., U.S.	125	36°28'N	77°37'W
Roan Plateau, plat., Co., U.S. (rōn)	119	39°25'N	110°00'W
Roatan, Hond. (rō-ä-tän´)	132	16°18'N	86°33'W
Roatán, i., Hond.	132	16°19'N	86°46'W
Robbeneiland, i., S. Afr.	232a	33°48'S	18°22'E
Robbins, Il., U.S. (rŏb´ĭnz)	111a	41°39'N	87°42'W
Robbinsdale, Mn., U.S. (rŏb´ĭnz-dāl)	117g	45°03'N	93°22'W
Robe, Wa., U.S. (rōb)	116a	48°06'N	121°50'W
Roberts, Mount, mtn., Austl. (rŏb´ērts)	221	28°05'S	152°30'E
Roberts, Point, c., Wa., U.S. (rŏb´ērts)	116d	48°58'N	123°05'W
Robertson, Lac, l., Can.	101	51°00'N	59°10'W
Robertsport, Lib. (rŏb´ērts-pōrt)	230	6°45'N	11°22'W
Roberval, Can. (rŏb´ēr-văl) (rō-bĕr-vál´)	91	48°32'N	72°15'W
Robinson, Can.	101	48°16'N	58°50'W
Robinson, Il., U.S. (rŏb´ĭn-sŭn)	108	39°00'N	87°45'W
Robinvale, Austl. (rŏb-ĭn´vāl)	222	34°45'S	142°45'E
Roblin, Can.	97	51°15'N	101°25'W
Robson, Mount, mtn., Can. (rŏb´sŭn)	95	53°07'N	119°09'W
Robstown, Tx., U.S. (rŏbz´toun)	123	27°46'N	97°41'W
Roca, Cabo da, c., Port. (ká´bō-dä-rō´kă)	172	38°47'N	9°30'W
Rocas, Atol das, atoll, Braz. (ä-tôl-däs-rō´käs)	143	3°50'S	33°46'W
Rocha, Ur. (rō´chás)	144	34°26'S	54°14'W
Rochdale, Eng., U.K. (rŏch´dāl)	164	53°37'N	2°09'W
Roche à Bateau, Haiti (rôsh á bá-tō´)	135	18°10'N	74°00'W
Rochefort, Fr. (rôsh-fŏr´)	161	45°55'N	0°57'W
Rochelle, Il., U.S. (rō-shĕl´)	113	41°53'N	89°06'W
Rochester, Eng., U.K.	158a	51°24'N	0°30'E
Rochester, In., U.S. (rŏch´ĕs-tēr)	108	41°05'N	86°20'W
Rochester, Mi., U.S.	111b	42°41'N	83°09'W
Rochester, Mn., U.S.	115	44°01'N	92°30'W
Rochester, N.H., U.S.	109	43°20'N	71°00'W
Rochester, N.Y., U.S.	105	43°15'N	77°35'W
Rochester, Pa., U.S.	111e	40°42'N	80°16'W
Rock, r., Ia., U.S.	112	43°17'N	96°13'W
Rock, r., Or., U.S.	116c	45°34'N	122°52'W
Rock, r., Or., U.S.	116c	45°52'N	123°14'W
Rock, r., U.S.	107	41°40'N	90°00'W
Rockaway, N.J., U.S. (rŏck´á-wā)	110a	40°54'N	74°30'W
Rockbank, Austl.	217a	37°44'S	144°40'E
Rockcliffe Park, Can. (rŏk´klĭf pärk)	102c	45°27'N	75°40'W
Rock Creek, r., Can. (rŏk)	115	49°01'N	107°00'W
Rock Creek, r., Il., U.S.	111a	41°16'N	87°54'W
Rock Creek, r., Mt., U.S.	115	46°25'N	113°40'W
Rock Creek, r., Or., U.S.	114	45°30'N	120°06'W
Rock Creek, r., Wa., U.S.	114	47°09'N	117°50'W
Rockdale, Austl.	217b	33°57'S	151°08'E
Rockdale, Md., U.S.	110e	39°22'N	76°49'W
Rockdale, Tx., U.S. (rŏk´dāl)	123	30°39'N	97°00'W
Rock Falls, Il., U.S. (rŏk fôlz)	113	41°45'N	89°42'W
Rockford, Il., U.S. (rŏk´fērd)	105	42°16'N	89°07'W
Rockhampton, Austl. (rŏk-hămp´tŭn)	219	23°26'S	150°29'E
Rock Hill, S.C., U.S. (rŏk´hĭl)	105	34°55'N	81°01'W
Rockingham, N.C., U.S. (rŏk´ĭng-hăm)	125	34°54'N	79°45'W
Rockingham Forest, for., Eng., U.K. (rok´ĭng-hăm)	158a	52°29'N	0°43'W

ăt; fınăl; rāte; senāte; ärm; ásk; sofá; fâre;   ch-choose;   dh-as th in other;   bē; ĕvent; bĕt; recĕnt; cratēr;   g-gō; gh-guttural g;   bĭt; ī-short neutral; rīde; κ-guttural k as ch in German ich;

PRONOUNCING INDEX

Rum Cay – Saint George 343

PLACE (Pronunciation)	PAGE	LAT.	LONG.
Rum Cay, i., Bah.	135	23°40'N	74°50'W
Rumford, Me., U.S. (rŭm'fẽrd)	100	44°32'N	70°35'W
Rummah, Wādī ar, val., Sau. Ar.	198	26°17'N	41°45'E
Rummānah, Egypt	197a	31°01'N	32°39'E
Runan, China (ro͞o-nän)	208	32°59'N	114°22'E
Runcorn, Eng., U.K. (rŭŋ'kôrn)	158a	53°20'N	2°44'W
Ruo, r., China (rwô)	204	41°15'N	100°46'E
Rupat, i., Indon. (ro͞o'pät)	197b	1°55'N	101°35'E
Rupat, Selat, strt., Indon.	197b	1°55'N	101°17'E
Rupert, Id., U.S. (ro͞o'pẽrt)	115	42°36'N	113°41'W
Rupert, Rivière de, r., Can.	93	51°35'N	76°30'W
Ruse, Blg. (ro͞o'sĕ) (rò'sĕ)	154	43°50'N	25°59'E
Rushan, China (ro͞o-shän)	206	36°54'N	121°31'E
Rush City, Mn., U.S.	113	45°40'N	92°59'W
Rushville, Il., U.S. (rŭsh'vĭl)	121	40°08'N	90°34'W
Rushville, In., U.S.	108	39°35'N	85°30'W
Rushville, Ne., U.S.	112	42°43'N	102°27'W
Rusizi, r., Afr.	237	3°00'S	29°05'E
Rusk, Tx., U.S. (rŭsk)	123	31°49'N	95°09'W
Ruskin, Can. (rŭs'kĭn)	116d	49°10'N	122°25'W
Russ, r., Aus.	159e	48°12'N	16°55'E
Russas, Braz. (ro͞o's-säs)	143	4°48'S	37°50'W
Russell, Can. (rŭs'ĕl)	90	50°47'N	101°15'W
Russell, Can.	102c	45°15'N	75°22'W
Russell, Ca., U.S.	116b	37°39'N	122°08'W
Russell, Ks., U.S.	120	38°51'N	98°51'W
Russell, Ky., U.S.	108	38°30'N	82°45'W
Russell Lake, l., Can.	97	56°15'N	101°30'W
Russell Islands, is., Sol. Is.	221	9°16'S	158°30'E
Russellville, Al., U.S. (rŭs'ĕl-vĭl)	124	34°29'N	87°44'W
Russellville, Ar., U.S.	121	35°16'N	93°08'W
Russelville, Ky., U.S.	124	36°48'N	86°51'W
Russia, nation, Russia	178	61°00'N	60°00'E
Russian, r., Ca., U.S. (rŭsh'ăn)	118	38°59'N	123°10'W
Rustavi, Geor.	182	41°33'N	45°02'E
Rustenburg, S. Afr. (rŭs'tĕn-bûrg)	238c	25°40'S	27°15'E
Ruston, La., U.S. (rŭs'tŭn)	123	32°32'N	92°39'W
Ruston, Wa., U.S.	116a	47°18'N	122°30'W
Rute, Spain (ro͞o'tā)	172	38°20'N	4°34'W
Ruth, Nv., U.S. (ro͞oth)	118	39°17'N	115°00'W
Ruthenia, hist. reg., Ukr.	169	48°25'N	23°00'E
Rutherfordton, N.C., U.S. (rŭdh'ẽr-fẽrd-tŭn)	125	35°23'N	81°58'W
Rutland, Vt., U.S.	109	43°35'N	72°55'W
Rutledge, Md., U.S. (rŭt'lĕdj)	110e	39°34'N	76°33'W
Rutog, China	204	33°29'N	79°26'E
Rutshuru, D.R.C. (ro͞ot-sho͞o'ro͞o)	232	1°11'S	29°27'E
Ruvo, Italy (ro͞o'vô)	174	41°07'N	16°32'E
Ruvuma, r., Afr.	232	11°30'S	37°00'E
Ruza, Russia (ro͞o'zȧ)	176	55°42'N	36°12'E
Ruzhany, Bela. (rò-zhän'ĭ)	169	52°49'N	24°54'E
Rwanda, nation, Afr.	232	2°10'S	29°37'E
Ryabovo, Russia (ryä'bô-vô)	186c	59°24'N	31°08'E
Ryazan', Russia (ryä-zän'')	178	54°37'N	39°43'E
Ryazan', prov., Russia	176	54°10'N	39°37'E
Ryazhsk, Russia (ryäzh'sk')	180	53°43'N	40°04'E
Rybachiy, Poluostrov, pen., Russia	180	69°50'N	33°20'E
Rybatskoye, Russia	186c	59°50'N	30°31'E
Rybinsk, Russia	178	58°02'N	38°52'E
Rybinskoye, res., Russia	178	58°23'N	38°15'E
Rybnik, Pol. (rĭb'nĕk)	169	50°06'N	18°37'E
Ryde, Eng., U.K. (rīd)	164	50°43'N	1°16'W
Rye, N.Y., U.S. (rī)	110a	40°58'N	73°42'W
Ryl'sk, Russia (rēl''sk)	181	51°33'N	34°42'E
Ryōtsu, Japan (ryōt'so͞o)	210	38°02'N	138°23'E
Rypin, Pol. (rĭ'pēn)	169	53°04'N	19°25'E
Rysy, mtn., Eur.	169	49°12'N	20°04'E
Ryukyu Islands see Nansei-shotō, is., Japan	205	27°30'N	127°00'E
Rzeszów, Pol. (zhä-shòf)	161	50°02'N	22°00'E
Rzhev, Russia ('r-zhĕf)	178	56°16'N	34°17'E
Rzhyshchiv, Ukr.	177	49°58'N	31°05'E

S

PLACE (Pronunciation)	PAGE	LAT.	LONG.
Saale, r., Ger. (sä-lĕ)	168	51°14'N	11°52'E
Saalfeld, Ger. (säl'fĕlt)	168	50°38'N	11°20'E
Saarbrücken, Ger. (zähr'brü-kĕn)	161	49°15'N	7°01'E
Saaremaa, i., Est.	180	58°25'N	22°30'E
Saavedra, Arg. (sä-ä-vā'drä)	144	37°45'S	62°23'W
Saba, i., Neth. Ant. (sä'bä)	133b	17°39'N	63°20'W
Šabac, Serb. (shä'bàts)	163	44°45'N	19°49'E
Sabadell, Spain (sä-bä-dhâl')	162	41°32'N	2°07'E
Sabah, hist. reg., Malay.	212	5°10'N	116°25'E
Sabana, Archipiélago de, is., Cuba	134	23°05'N	80°00'W
Sabana, Río, r., Pan. (sä-bä'nä)	133	8°40'N	78°02'W
Sabana de la Mar, Dom. Rep. (sä-bä'nä dā lä mär')	135	19°05'N	69°30'W
Sabana de Uchire, Ven. (sä-bà'nä dĕ o͞o-chē'rĕ)	143b	10°02'N	65°32'W
Sabanagrande, Hond. (sä-bä'nä-grä'n-dĕ)	132	13°47'N	87°16'W
Sabanalarga, Col. (sä-bà'nä-lär'gä)	142	10°38'N	75°02'W
Sabanas Páramo, mtn., Col. (sä-bà'näs pà'rä-mô)	142a	6°28'N	76°08'W
Sabancuy, Mex. (sä-bäŋ-kwē')	131	18°58'N	91°09'W
Sabang, Indon. (sä'bäng)	212	5°52'N	95°26'E
Sabaudia, Italy (sà-bou'dē-ä)	174	41°19'N	13°00'E
Sabetha, Ks., U.S. (sȧ-bĕth'ȧ)	121	39°54'N	95°49'W
Sabi (Rio Save), r., Afr. (sä'bē)	232	20°18'S	32°07'E
Sabile, Lat. (sà'bê-lĕ)	167	57°03'N	22°34'E
Sabinal, Tx., U.S. (sȧ-bī'nȧl)	122	29°19'N	99°27'W
Sabinal, Cayo, i., Cuba (kä'yō sä-bē-näl')	134	21°40'N	77°20'W
Sabinas, Mex.	128	28°05'N	101°30'W
Sabinas, r., Mex. (sä-bē'näs)	122	26°37'N	99°52'W
Sabinas, Río, r., Mex. (rē'ō sä-bē'näs)	122	27°25'N	100°33'W
Sabinas Hidalgo, Mex. (ē-däl'gō)	122	26°30'N	100°10'W
Sabine, Tx., U.S. (sȧ-bēn')	123	29°44'N	93°54'W
Sabine, r., U.S.	107	32°00'N	94°30'W
Sabine, Mount, mtn., Ant.	224	72°05'S	169°10'E
Sabine Lake, l., La., U.S.	123	29°53'N	93°41'W
Sablayan, Phil. (säb-lä-yän')	213a	12°49'N	120°47'E
Sable, Cape, c., Can. (sā'b'l)	93	43°25'N	65°24'W
Sable, Cape, c., Fl., U.S.	107	25°12'N	81°10'W
Sables, Rivière aux, r., Can.	99	49°00'N	70°20'W
Sablé-sur-Sarthe, Fr. (säb-lā-sür-särt')	170	47°50'N	0°17'W
Sablya, Gora, mtn., Russia	180	64°50'N	59°00'E
Sàbor, r., Port. (sä-bōr')	172	41°18'N	6°54'W
Sabunchu, Azer.	182	40°26'N	49°56'E
Sabzevār, Iran	201	36°13'N	57°42'E
Sac, r., Mo., U.S. (sôk)	121	38°11'N	93°45'W
Sacandaga Reservoir, res., N.Y., U.S. (să-kăn-dȧ'gȧ)	109	43°10'N	74°15'W
Sacavém, Port. (sä-kä-vĕn')	173b	38°47'N	9°06'W
Sacavém, r., Port.	173b	38°52'N	9°06'W
Sac City, Ia., U.S. (sŏk)	112	42°25'N	95°00'W
Sachigo Lake, l., Can. (săch'ĭ-gō)	97	53°49'N	92°08'W
Sachsen, hist. reg., Ger. (zäk'sĕn)	168	50°45'N	12°17'E
Sacketts Harbor, N.Y., U.S. (săk'ĕts)	109	43°55'N	76°05'W
Sackville, Can. (săk'vĭl)	100	45°54'N	64°22'W
Saco, Me., U.S. (sô'kô)	100	43°30'N	70°28'W
Saco, r., Braz. (sä'kô)	144b	22°20'S	43°26'W
Saco, r., Me., U.S.	100	43°53'N	70°46'W
Sacramento, Mex.	122	25°45'N	103°22'W
Sacramento, Mex.	122	27°05'N	101°45'W
Sacramento, Ca., U.S. (săk-rȧ-mĕn'tō)	104	38°35'N	121°30'W
Sacramento, r., Ca., U.S.	118	40°20'N	122°07'W
Şa'dah, Yemen	198	16°50'N	43°45'E
Saddle Lake Indian Reserve, I.R., Can.	95	54°00'N	111°40'W
Saddle Mountain, mtn., Or., U.S. (săd''l)	116c	45°58'N	123°40'W
Sadiya, India (sŭ-dē'yä)	199	27°53'N	95°35'E
Sado, i., Japan (sä'dō)	205	38°05'N	138°26'E
Sado, r., Port. (sä'dò)	172	38°15'N	8°20'W
Saeby, Den. (sĕ'bü)	166	57°21'N	10°29'E
Saeki, Japan (sä'ā-kĕ)	210	32°56'N	131°51'E
Säffle, Swe.	166	59°10'N	12°55'E
Safford, Az., U.S. (săf'fẽrd)	119	32°50'N	109°45'W
Safi, Mor. (sä'fē) (äs'fē)	230	32°24'N	9°09'W
Safīd Koh, Selseleh-ye, mts., Afg.	198	34°45'N	63°58'E
Saga, Japan (sä'gä)	211	33°15'N	130°18'E
Sagami-Nada, b., Japan (sä'gä'mē nä-dä)	211	35°06'N	139°24'E
Sagamore Hills, Oh., U.S. (săg'ȧ-môr hĭlz)	111d	41°19'N	81°34'W
Saganaga, l., N.A. (să-gȧ-nä'gȧ)	113	48°13'N	91°17'W
Sāgar, India	199	23°55'N	78°45'E
Saghyz, r., Kaz.	181	48°30'N	56°10'E
Saginaw, Mi., U.S. (săg'ĭ-nô)	105	43°25'N	84°00'W
Saginaw, Mn., U.S.	117h	46°51'N	92°26'W
Saginaw, Tx., U.S.	117c	32°52'N	97°22'W
Saginaw Bay, b., Mi., U.S.	107	43°50'N	83°40'W
Saguache, Co., U.S. (sȧ-wăch') (sä-gwä'chê)	119	38°05'N	106°10'W
Saguache Creek, r., Co., U.S.	108	38°05'N	106°40'W
Sagua de Tánamo, Cuba (sä-gwä dĕ tà'nä-mō)	135	20°40'N	75°15'W
Sagua la Grande, Cuba (sä-gwä lä grä'n-dĕ)	134	22°45'N	80°05'W
Saguaro National Park, rec., Az., U.S. (säg-wä'rō)	119	32°12'N	110°40'W
Saguenay, r., Can. (săg-ē-nā')	93	48°20'N	70°15'W
Sagunt, Spain	173	38°58'N	1°29'E
Sagunto, Spain (sä-gòn'tō)	162	39°40'N	0°17'W
Sahara, des., Afr. (sȧ-hä'rȧ)	230	23°44'N	1°40'W
Saharan Atlas, mts., Afr.	162	32°51'N	1°02'W
Sahāranpur, India (sŭ-hä'rŭn-po͞or')	199	29°58'N	77°41'E
Sahara Village, Ut., U.S. (sȧ-hä'rȧ)	117b	41°06'N	111°58'W
Sahel see Sudan, reg., Afr.	230	15°00'N	7°00'E
Sāhīwāl, Pak.	202	30°43'N	73°04'E
Sahuayo de Dias, Mex.	130	20°03'N	102°43'W
Saigon see Ho Chi Minh City, Viet.	212	10°46'N	106°34'E
Saijō, Japan (sä'ē-jō)	211	33°55'N	133°13'E
Saimaa, l., Fin. (sä'ĭ-mä)	160	61°24'N	28°45'E
Sain Alto, Mex. (sä-ēn' äl'tō)	130	23°35'N	103°13'W
Saint Adolphe, Can. (sănt a'dôlf) (săN' tá-dôlf')	102f	49°40'N	97°07'W
Saint Afrique, Fr. (săN' tá-frēk')	170	43°58'N	2°52'E
Saint Albans, Austl. (sănt ôl'bănz)	217a	37°44'S	144°47'E
Saint Albans, Eng., U.K.	164	51°44'N	0°20'W
Saint Albans, Vt., U.S.	109	44°50'N	73°05'W
Saint Albans, W.V., U.S.	108	38°20'N	81°50'W
Saint Albert, Can. (sănt ăl'bẽrt)	95	53°38'N	113°38'W
Saint Amand-Mont Rond, Fr. (săN't à-mäN' môN-rôN')	170	46°44'N	2°28'E
Saint André-Est, Can.	102a	45°33'N	74°19'W
Saint Andrews, Can.	91	45°05'N	67°03'W
Saint Andrews, Scot., U.K.	164	56°20'N	2°40'W
Saint Andrew's Channel, strt., Can.	101	46°06'N	60°28'W
Saint Anicet, Can. (sĕNt ä-nē-sĕ')	102a	45°07'N	74°23'W
Saint Ann, Mo., U.S. (sănt ăn')	117e	38°44'N	90°23'W
Sainte Anne, Guad.	133b	16°15'N	61°23'W
Saint Anne, Il., U.S.	111a	41°01'N	87°44'W
Sainte Anne, r., Can. (sănt ăn') (sănt ăn')	99	46°55'N	71°46'W
Sainte-Anne, r., Can.	102b	47°07'N	70°50'W
Sainte Anne-des-Plaines, Can. (dā plĕN)	102a	45°46'N	73°49'W
Saint Ann's Bay, Jam.	134	18°25'N	77°15'W
Saint Anns Bay, b., Can. (ănz)	101	46°20'N	60°30'W
Saint Anselme, Can. (săN' tän-sĕlm')	102b	46°37'N	70°58'W
Saint Anthony, Can. (sān ăn'thô-nê)	91	51°24'N	55°35'W
Saint Anthony, Id., U.S. (sănt ăn'thô-nê)	115	43°59'N	111°42'W
Saint Antoine-de-Tilly, Can.	102b	46°40'N	71°31'W
Saint Apollinaire, Can. (săN' tá-pôl-ē-nâr')	102b	46°36'N	71°30'W
Saint Arnoult-en-Yvelines, Fr. (sàN-tär-no͞o'ĕN-nēv-lēn')	171b	48°33'N	1°55'E
Saint Augustin-de-Québec, Can. (sĕN tō-güs-tēN')	102b	46°45'N	71°27'W
Saint Augustin-Deux-Montagnes, Can.	102a	45°38'N	73°59'W
Saint Augustine, Fl., U.S. (sănt ô'gŭs-tēn)	105	29°53'N	81°21'W
Sainte Barbe, Can. (sănt bärb')	102a	45°14'N	74°12'W
Saint Barthélemy, i., Guad.	133b	17°55'N	62°32'W
Saint Bees Head, c., Eng., U.K. (sănt bēz' hĕd)	164	54°30'N	3°40'W
Saint Benoit, Can. (sĕN bĕ-no͞o-ä')	102a	45°34'N	74°05'W
Saint Bernard, La., U.S. (bẽr-närd')	110d	29°52'N	89°52'W
Saint Bernard, Oh., U.S.	111f	39°10'N	84°30'W
Saint Bride, Mount, mtn., Can. (sănt brīd)	95	51°30'N	115°57'W
Saint Brieuc, Fr. (săN' brēs')	161	48°32'N	2°47'W
Saint Bruno, Can. (brū'nō)	102a	45°31'N	73°20'W
Saint Canut, Can. (săN' kȧ-nū')	102a	45°43'N	74°04'W
Saint Casimir, Can. (kȧ-zē-mēr')	99	46°45'N	72°34'W
Saint Catharines, Can. (kăth'ȧ-rĭnz)	91	43°10'N	79°14'W
Saint Catherine, Mount, mtn., Gren.	133b	12°10'N	61°42'W
Saint Chamas, Fr. (sàN-shä-mä')	170a	43°32'N	5°03'E
Saint Chamond, Fr. (săN' shȧ-môN')	161	45°30'N	4°17'E
Saint Charles, Can. (săN' shärlz')	102b	46°47'N	70°57'W
Saint Charles, Il., U.S. (sănt chärlz')	111a	41°55'N	88°19'W
Saint Charles, Mi., U.S.	108	43°20'N	84°10'W
Saint Charles, Mn., U.S.	113	43°56'N	92°05'W
Saint Charles, Mo., U.S.	117e	38°47'N	90°29'W
Saint Charles, Lac, l., Can.	102b	46°56'N	71°21'W
Saint Christopher-Nevis see Saint Kitts and Nevis, nation, N.A.	128	17°24'N	63°30'W
Saint Clair, Mi., U.S. (sănt klâr)	108	42°55'N	82°30'W
Saint Clair, l., Can.	107	42°25'N	82°30'W
Saint Clair, r., Can.	98	42°45'N	82°25'W
Sainte Claire, Can.	102b	46°36'N	70°52'W
Saint Clair Shores, Mi., U.S.	111b	42°30'N	82°54'W
Saint Claude, Fr. (săN' klōd')	171	46°24'N	5°53'E
Saint Clet, Can. (săN' klā')	102a	45°22'N	74°21'W
Saint Cloud, Fl., U.S. (sănt kloud')	125a	28°13'N	81°17'W
Saint Cloud, Mn., U.S.	105	45°33'N	94°08'W
Saint Constant, Can. (kŏn'stănt)	102a	45°23'N	73°34'W
Saint Croix, i., V.I.U.S. (sănt kroi')	129	17°40'N	64°43'W
Saint Croix, r., N.A. (kroi')	100	45°28'N	67°32'W
Saint Croix, r., U.S. (sănt kroi')	107	45°45'N	93°00'W
Saint Croix Indian Reservation, I.R., Wi., U.S.	113	45°40'N	92°21'W
Saint Croix Island, i., S. Afr. (săN krwă)	233c	33°48'S	25°45'E
Saint Damien-de-Buckland, Can. (sănt dă'mē-ĕn)	102b	46°37'N	70°39'W
Saint David, Can. (dă'vĭd)	102b	46°47'N	71°11'W
Saint David's Head, c., Wales, U.K.	164	51°54'N	5°25'W
Saint-Denis, Fr. (săN'dē-nē')	161	48°26'N	2°22'E
Saint Dizier, Fr. (dē-zyā')	161	48°49'N	4°55'E
Saint Dominique, Can. (sĕN dō-mē-nēk')	102a	45°19'N	74°09'W
Saint Edouard-de-Napierville, Can. (sĕN-tĕ-do͞o-är')	102a	45°14'N	73°31'W
Saint Elias, Mount, mtn., N.A. (sănt ē-lī'ăs)	92	60°25'N	141°00'W
Saint Étienne, Fr.	161	45°26'N	4°22'E
Saint Etienne-de-Lauzon, Can. (săN' tā-tyĕn')	102b	46°39'N	71°19'W
Sainte Euphémie, Can. (sĕNt û-fĕ-mē')	102b	46°47'N	70°27'W
Saint Eustache, Can. (săN' tû-stàsh')	102a	45°34'N	73°54'W
Saint Eustache, Can.	102f	49°58'N	97°47'W
Sainte Famille, Can. (săN't fà-mē'y')	102b	46°58'N	70°58'W
Saint Félicien, Can. (săN fā-lē-syăN')	91	48°39'N	72°28'W
Sainte Felicite, Can.	100	48°54'N	67°20'W
Saint Féréol, Can. (fa-rā-ôl')	102b	47°07'N	70°52'W
Saint Florent-sur-Cher, Fr. (săN' flô-räN'sür-shâr')	170	46°58'N	2°15'E
Saint Flour, Fr. (săN flo͞or')	170	45°02'N	3°09'E
Sainte Foy, Can. (sănt fwä)	99	46°47'N	71°18'W
Saint Francis, r., Ar., U.S.	121	35°56'N	90°27'W
Saint Francis Lake, l., Can. (săN frăn'sĭs)	99	45°00'N	74°20'W
Saint François, Can. (săN'fräN-swä')	102b	47°01'N	70°49'W
Saint François de Boundji, Congo	236	1°03'S	15°22'E
Saint Francois Xavier, Can.	102f	49°55'N	97°32'W
Saint Gaudens, Fr. (gō-dăNs')	170	43°07'N	0°43'E
Sainte Genevieve, Mo., U.S. (sănt jĕn'ĕ-vēv)	121	37°58'N	90°02'W
Saint George, Austl. (sănt jôrj')	219	28°02'S	148°40'E

344 Saint George - Salem PRONOUNCING INDEX

PLACE (Pronunciation)	PAGE	LAT.	LONG.
Saint George, Can. (săn jôrj')	91	45°08'N	66°49'W
Saint George, Can. (săn' zhôrzh')	102d	43°14'N	80°15'W
Saint George, S.C., U.S. (sånt jôrj')	125	33°11'N	80°35'W
Saint George, Ut., U.S.	119	37°05'N	113°40'W
Saint George, i., Ak., U.S.	103	56°30'N	169°40'W
Saint George, Cape, c., Can.	93a	48°28'N	59°15'W
Saint George, Cape, c., Fl., U.S.	124	29°30'N	85°20'W
Saint George's, Can. (jôrj'ĕs)	91	48°26'N	58°29'W
Saint Georges, Fr. Gu.	143	3°48'N	51°47'W
Saint George's, Gren.	133b	12°02'N	61°57'W
Saint George's Bay, b., Can.	93a	48°20'N	59°00'W
Saint Georges Bay, b., Can.	101	45°49'N	61°45'W
Saint George's Channel, strt., Eur. (jôr-jĕz)	156	51°45'N	6°30'W
Saint Germain-en-Laye, Fr. (săn' zhĕr-măn-än-lā')	170	48°53'N	2°05'E
Saint Gervais, Can. (zhĕr-vĕ')	102b	46°43'N	70°53'W
Saint Girons, Fr. (zhē-rôn')	170	42°58'N	1°08'E
Saint Gotthard Pass, p., Switz.	168	46°33'N	8°34'E
Saint Gregory, Mount, mtn., Can. (sånt grĕg'ẽr-ē)	101	49°19'N	58°13'W
Saint Helena, i., St. Hel.	229	16°01'S	5°16'W
Saint Helenabaai, b., S. Afr.	232	32°25'S	17°15'E
Saint Helens, Eng., U.K. (sånt hĕl'ĕnz)	158a	53°27'N	2°44'W
Saint Helens, Or., U.S. (hĕl'ĕnz)	116c	45°52'N	122°49'W
Saint Helens, Mount, vol., Wa., U.S.	114	46°13'N	122°10'W
Saint Helier, Jersey (hyĕl'yẽr)	170	49°12'N	2°06'W
Saint Henri, Can. (săn' hĕn'rē)	102b	46°41'N	71°04'W
Saint Hubert, Can.	102a	45°29'N	73°24'W
Saint Hyacinthe, Can.	91	45°35'N	72°55'W
Saint Ignace, Mi., U.S. (sånt ĭg'nås)	113	45°51'N	84°39'W
Saint Ignace, i., Can. (săn' ĭg'nås)	98	48°47'N	88°14'W
Saint Irenee, Can. (săn' tē-rå-nā')	99	47°34'N	70°15'W
Saint Isidore-de-Laprairie, Can.	102a	45°18'N	73°41'W
Saint Isidore-de-Prescott, Can. (săn' ĭz'ĭ-dôr-prĕs-kŏt)	102c	45°23'N	74°54'W
Saint Isidore-Dorchester, Can. (dŏr-chĕs'tẽr)	102b	46°35'N	71°05'W
Saint Jacob, Il., U.S. (jā-kŏb)	117e	38°43'N	89°46'W
Saint James, Mn., U.S. (sånt jāmz')	113	43°58'N	94°37'W
Saint James, Mo., U.S.	121	37°59'N	91°37'W
Saint James, Cape, c., Can.	94	51°58'N	131°00'W
Saint Janvier, Can. (săn' zhän-vyā')	102a	45°43'N	73°56'W
Saint Jean, Can. (săn' zhän')	91	45°20'N	73°15'W
Saint Jean, Can.	102b	46°55'N	70°54'W
Saint Jean, Lac, l., Can.	93	48°35'N	72°00'W
Saint Jean-Chrysostome, Can. (krĭ-zŏs-tōm')	102b	46°43'N	71°12'W
Saint Jean-d'Angely, Fr. (dän-zhå-lē')	170	45°56'N	0°33'W
Saint Jean-de-Luz, Fr. (dē lüz')	170	43°23'N	1°40'W
Saint Jérôme, Can. (sånt jĕ-rōm') (săn zhā-rōm')	102a	45°47'N	74°00'W
Saint Joachim-de-Montmorency, Can. (sånt jō'á-kĭm)	102b	47°04'N	70°51'W
Saint John, Can. (sånt jŏn)	91	45°16'N	66°03'W
Saint John, In., U.S.	111a	41°27'N	87°29'W
Saint John, Ks., U.S.	120	37°59'N	98°44'W
Saint John, N.D., U.S.	112	48°57'N	99°42'W
Saint John, i., V.I.U.S.	129b	18°16'N	64°48'W
Saint John, r., N.A.	93	47°00'N	68°00'W
Saint John, Cape, c., Can.	101	50°00'N	55°32'W
Saint Johns, Antig.	133b	17°07'N	61°50'W
Saint John's, Can. (jŏns)	93a	47°34'N	52°43'W
Saint Johns, Az., U.S. (jŏnz)	119	34°30'N	109°25'W
Saint Johns, Mi., U.S.	108	43°05'N	84°35'W
Saint Johns, r., Fl., U.S.	107	29°54'N	81°32'W
Saint Johnsbury, Vt., U.S. (jŏnz'bẽr-ē)	109	44°25'N	72°00'W
Saint Joseph, Dom.	133b	15°25'N	61°26'W
Saint Joseph, Mi., U.S.	108	42°05'N	86°30'W
Saint Joseph, Mo., U.S. (sånt jō-sĕf)	105	39°44'N	94°49'W
Saint Joseph, i., Can.	108	46°15'N	83°55'W
Saint Joseph, l., Can. (jō'zhûf)	93	51°31'N	90°40'W
Saint Joseph, r., Mi., U.S. (sånt jō'sĕf)	108	41°45'N	85°50'W
Saint Joseph Bay, b., Fl., U.S. (jō'zhûf)	124	29°48'N	85°26'W
Saint Joseph-de-Beauce, Can. (sĕn zhō-zĕf' dē bōs)	99	46°18'N	70°52'W
Saint Joseph-du-Lac, Can. (sĕn zhō-zĕf' dü läk)	102a	45°32'N	74°00'W
Saint Joseph Island, i., Tx., U.S. (sånt jō-sĕf)	123	27°58'N	96°50'W
Saint Junien, Fr. (săn'zhü-nyăn')	170	45°53'N	0°54'E
Sainte Justine-de-Newton, Can. (sånt jŭs-tēn')	102a	45°22'N	74°22'W
Saint Kilda, Austl.	217a	37°52'S	144°59'E
Saint Kilda, i., Scot., U.K. (kĭl'dá)	164	57°50'N	8°32'W
Saint Kitts, i., St. K./N. (sānt kĭtts)	129	17°24'N	63°30'W
Saint Kitts and Nevis, nation, N.A.	129	17°24'N	63°30'W
Saint Lambert, Can.	109	45°29'N	73°29'W
Saint Lambert-de-Lévis, Can.	102b	46°35'N	71°12'W
Saint Laurent, Can. (săn'lō-rän)	102a	45°31'N	73°41'W
Saint Laurent, Fr. Gu.	143	5°27'N	53°56'W
Saint Laurent-d'Orleans, Can.	102b	46°52'N	71°00'W
Saint Lawrence, Can. (sånt lô'rĕns)	101	46°55'N	55°23'W
Saint Lawrence, i., Ak., U.S. (sånt lô'rĕns)	106a	63°10'N	172°12'W
Saint Lawrence, r., N.A.	93	48°24'N	69°30'W
Saint Lawrence, Gulf of, b., Can.	93	48°00'N	62°00'W
Saint Lazare, Can. (săn'lá-zár')	102b	46°39'N	70°48'W
Saint Lazare-de-Vaudreuil, Can.	102a	45°24'N	74°08'W
Saint Léger-en-Yvelines, Fr. (săn-lā-zhĕ'ĕn-nēv-lēn')	171b	48°43'N	1°45'E

PLACE (Pronunciation)	PAGE	LAT.	LONG.
Saint Leonard, Can. (sånt lĕn'ård)	100	47°10'N	67°56'W
Saint Léonard, Can.	102a	45°36'N	73°35'W
Saint Leonard, Md., U.S.	110e	38°29'N	76°31'W
Saint Lô, Fr.	161	49°07'N	1°05'W
Saint-Louis, Sen.	230	16°02'N	16°30'W
Saint Louis, Mi., U.S. (sånt lōō'ĭs)	108	43°25'N	84°35'W
Saint Louis, Mo., U.S. (sånt lōō'ĭs) (lōō'ē)	105	38°39'N	90°15'W
Saint Louis, r., Mn., U.S. (sånt lōō'ĭs)	113	46°57'N	92°58'W
Saint Louis, Lac, l., Can. (săn' lōō-ē')	102a	45°24'N	73°51'W
Saint Louis-de-Gonzague, Can. (săn' lōō ē')	102a	45°13'N	74°00'W
Saint Louis Park, Mn., U.S.	117g	44°56'N	93°21'W
Saint Lucia, nation, N.A.	129	13°54'N	60°40'W
Saint Lucia Channel, strt., N.A. (lū'shĭ-á)	133b	14°15'N	61°00'W
Saint Lucie Canal, can., Fl., U.S. (lū'sē)	125a	26°57'N	80°25'W
Saint Magnus Bay, b., Scot., U.K. (măg'nŭs)	164a	60°25'N	2°09'W
Saint Malo, Fr. (săn' må-lō')	161	48°40'N	2°02'W
Saint Malo, Golfe de, b., Fr. (gôlf-dē-săn-mä-lō')	161	48°50'N	2°49'W
Saint Marc, Haiti (săn' mark')	135	19°10'N	72°40'W
Saint-Marc, Canal de, strt., Haiti	135	19°05'N	73°15'W
Saint Marcellin, Fr. (mär-sē-lăn')	171	45°08'N	5°15'E
Saint Margarets, Md., U.S.	110e	39°02'N	76°30'W
Sainte Marie, Cap, c., Madag.	233	25°31'S	45°00'E
Sainte-Marie-aux-Mines, Fr. (săn'tē-mä-rē'ō-mēn')	171	48°14'N	7°08'E
Sainte Marie-Beauce, Can. (sănt'må-rē')	99	46°27'N	71°03'W
Saint Maries, Id., U.S. (sånt mā'rēs)	114	47°18'N	116°34'W
Saint Martin, i., N.A. (mär'tĭn)	133b	18°06'N	62°54'W
Sainte Martine, Can.	102a	45°14'N	73°37'W
Saint Martins, Can. (mär'tĭnz)	100	45°21'N	65°32'W
Saint Martinville, La., U.S. (mär'tĭn-vĭl)	123	30°08'N	91°50'W
Saint Mary, r., Can. (mā'rē)	95	49°25'N	113°00'W
Saint Mary, Cape, c., Gam.	234	13°28'N	16°40'W
Saint Mary Reservoir, res., Can.	95	49°30'N	113°00'W
Saint Marys, Austl. (mā'rēz)	222	41°40'S	148°10'E
Saint Marys, Can.	98	43°15'N	81°10'W
Saint Marys, Ga., U.S.	125	30°43'N	81°35'W
Saint Mary's, Ks., U.S.	121	39°12'N	96°03'W
Saint Mary's, Oh., U.S.	108	40°30'N	84°25'W
Saint Marys, Pa., U.S.	109	41°25'N	78°30'W
Saint Marys, W.V., U.S.	108	39°20'N	81°15'W
Saint Marys, r., N.A.	117k	46°27'N	84°33'W
Saint Marys, r., U.S.	125	30°37'N	82°05'W
Saint Mary's Bay, b., Can.	101	46°50'N	53°47'W
Saint Mary's Bay, b., Can.	100	44°20'N	66°10'W
Saint Mathew, S.C., U.S. (măth'ū)	125	33°40'N	80°46'W
Saint Matthew, i., Ak., U.S.	103	60°25'N	172°10'W
Saint Matthews, Ky., U.S. (măth'ūz)	111h	38°15'N	85°39'W
Saint Maur-des-Fossés, Fr.	171b	48°48'N	2°29'E
Saint Maurice, r., Can. (săn' mō-rēs') (sånt mô'rĭs)	93	47°20'N	72°55'W
Saint Michael, Ak., U.S. (sånt mī'kĕl)	103	63°22'N	162°20'W
Saint Michel, Can. (săn'mē-shĕl')	102b	46°52'N	70°54'W
Saint Michel, Bras, r., Can.	102b	46°47'N	70°51'W
Saint Michel-de-l'Atalaye, Haiti	135	19°25'N	72°20'W
Saint Michel-de-Napierville, Can.	102a	45°14'N	73°34'W
Saint Mihiel, Fr. (săn' mē-yĕl')	171	48°53'N	5°30'E
Saint Nazaire, Fr. (săn'nà-zâr')	154	47°18'N	2°13'W
Saint Nérée, Can. (nā-rā')	102b	46°43'N	70°43'W
Saint Nicolas, Can. (ne-kô-lä')	102b	46°42'N	71°22'W
Saint Nicolas, Cap, c., Haiti	135	19°45'N	73°35'W
Saint Omer, Fr. (săn'tô-mâr')	170	50°44'N	2°16'E
Saint Pascal, Can. (sĕn pä-skäl')	100	47°32'N	69°48'W
Saint Paul, Can. (sånt pôl')	90	53°59'N	111°17'W
Saint Paul, Mn., U.S.	105	44°57'N	93°05'W
Saint Paul, Ne., U.S.	112	41°13'N	98°28'W
Saint Paul, i., Can.	101	47°15'N	60°10'W
Saint Paul, i., Ak., U.S.	103	57°10'N	170°20'W
Saint Paul, r., Lib.	234	7°10'N	10°00'W
Saint Paul, Île, i., Afr.	3	38°43'S	77°31'E
Saint Paul Park, Mn., U.S. (pärk)	117g	44°51'N	93°00'W
Saint Pauls, N.C., U.S. (pôls)	125	34°47'N	78°57'W
Saint Peter, Mn., U.S. (pē tẽr)	113	44°20'N	93°56'W
Saint Peter Port, Guern.	170	49°27'N	2°35'W
Saint Petersburg (Sankt-Peterburg) (Leningrad), Russia	178	59°57'N	30°20'E
Saint Petersburg, Fl., U.S. (pē'tẽrz-bûrg)	105	27°47'N	82°38'W
Sainte Pétronille, Can. (sĕnt pĕt-rō-nēl')	102b	46°51'N	71°08'W
Saint Philémon, Can. (sĕn fēl-mōn')	102b	46°41'N	70°28'W
Saint Philippe-d'Argenteuil, Can. (săn'fe-lēp')	102a	45°38'N	74°25'W
Saint Philippe-de-Lapairie, Can.	102a	45°20'N	73°28'W
Saint Pierre, Mart. (săn'pyâr')	133b	14°45'N	61°12'W
Saint Pierre, St. P./M.	101	46°47'N	56°11'W
Saint Pierre, i., St. P./M.	101	46°47'N	56°11'W
Saint Pierre, Lac, l., Can.	99	46°07'N	72°45'W
Saint Pierre and Miquelon, dep., N.A.	93a	46°53'N	56°40'W
Saint Pierre-d'Orléans, Can.	102b	46°53'N	71°04'W
Saint Pierre-Montmagny, Can.	102b	46°55'N	70°37'W
Saint Placide, Can. (plăs'ĭd)	102a	45°32'N	74°11'W
Saint Pol-de-Léon, Fr. (săn-pô'dē-lā-ôn')	170	48°41'N	4°00'W
Saint Quentin, Fr. (săn'kän-tăn')	161	49°52'N	3°16'E
Saint Raphaël, Can. (rä-fâ-ĕl')	102b	46°48'N	70°46'W

PLACE (Pronunciation)	PAGE	LAT.	LONG.
Saint Raymond, Can.	99	46°50'N	71°51'W
Saint Rédempteur, Can. (săn rā-dänp-tûr')	102b	46°42'N	71°18'W
Saint Rémi, Can. (sĕn rĕ-mē')	102a	45°15'N	73°36'W
Saint Romuald-d'Etchemin, Can. (sĕn rŏ'mōō-äl)	99	46°45'N	71°14'W
Sainte Rose, Guad.	133b	16°19'N	61°45'W
Saintes, Fr.	170	45°44'N	0°41'W
Sainte Scholastique, Can. (skô-lás-tēk')	102a	45°39'N	74°05'W
Saint Siméon, Can.	99	47°51'N	69°55'W
Saint Stanislas-de-Kostka, Can.	102a	45°11'N	74°08'W
Saint Stephen, Can. (stē'vĕn)	91	45°12'N	66°17'W
Saint Sulpice, Can.	102a	45°50'N	73°21'W
Saint Thérèse-de-Blainville, Can. (tē-rĕz' dē blĕn-vēl')	99	45°38'N	73°51'W
Saint Thomas, Can. (tŏm'ás)	91	42°45'N	81°15'W
Saint Thomas, i., V.I.U.S.	129	18°22'N	64°57'W
Saint Thomas Harbor, b., V.I.U.S. (tŏm'ás)	129c	18°19'N	64°56'W
Saint Timothée, Can. (tē-mô-tā')	102a	45°17'N	74°03'W
Saint Tropez, Fr. (trô-pĕ')	171	43°15'N	6°42'E
Saint Valentin, Can. (väl-ĕn-tīn)	102a	45°07'N	73°19'W
Saint Valéry-sur-Somme, Fr. (vá-lā-rē')	170	50°10'N	1°39'E
Saint Vallier, Can. (väl-yā')	102b	46°54'N	70°49'W
Saint Victor, Can. (vĭk'tẽr)	99	46°09'N	70°56'W
Saint Vincent, Gulf, b., Austl. (vĭn'sĕnt)	222	34°55'S	138°00'E
Saint Vincent and the Grenadines, nation, N.A.	129	13°20'N	60°50'W
Saint Vincent Passage, strt., N.A.	133b	13°35'N	61°10'W
Saint Walburg, Can.	90	53°39'N	109°12'W
Saint Yrieix-la-Perche, Fr. (ē-rē-ĕ)	170	45°30'N	1°08'E
Saitama, dept., Japan (sī'tä-mä)	211a	35°52'N	139°40'E
Saitbaba, Russia (sá-ĕt'bá-bá)	186a	54°06'N	56°42'E
Sajama, Nevada, mtn., Bol. (nĕ-vá'dä-sä-há'mä)	142	18°13'S	68°53'W
Sakai, Japan (sä'kä-ē)	210	34°34'N	135°28'E
Sakaiminato, Japan	211	35°33'N	133°15'E
Sakākah, Sau. Ar.	198	29°58'N	40°03'E
Sakakawea, Lake, res., N.D., U.S.	106	47°49'N	101°58'W
Sakania, D.R.C. (sá-kä'nĭ-á)	232	12°45'S	28°34'E
Sakarya, r., Tur. (sá-kär'yá)	198	40°10'N	31°00'E
Sakata, Japan (sä'kä-tä)	205	38°56'N	139°57'E
Sakchu, Kor., N. (säk'chò)	210	40°29'N	125°09'E
Sakha (Yakutia), prov., Russia	185	65°21'N	117°13'E
Sakhalin, i., Russia (sá-ká-lēn')	179	52°00'N	143°00'E
Šakiai, Lith. (shä'kĭ-ī)	167	54°59'N	23°05'E
Sakishima-guntō, is., Japan (sä'kē-shē'ma gòn'tō')	205	24°25'N	125°00'E
Sakmara, r., Russia	181	52°00'N	56°10'E
Sakomet, r., R.I., U.S. (sä-kō'mĕt)	110b	41°32'N	71°11'W
Sakurai, Japan	211b	34°31'N	135°51'E
Sakwaso Lake, l., Can. (sá-kwá'sō)	97	53°01'N	91°55'W
Sal, i., C.V. (säal)	230b	16°45'N	22°39'W
Sal, r., Russia (sál)	181	47°30'N	43°00'E
Sal, Cay, i., Bah. (kē säl)	134	23°45'N	80°25'W
Sala, Swe. (sô'lä)	166	59°56'N	16°34'E
Sala Consilina, Italy (sä'lä kôn-sē-lē'nä)	174	40°24'N	15°38'E
Salada, Laguna, l., Mex. (lä-gò'nä-sä-lä'dä)	118	32°34'N	115°45'W
Saladillo, Arg. (sä-lä-dēl'yō)	144	35°38'S	59°48'W
Salado, Hond. (sä-lä'dhō)	132	15°44'N	87°03'W
Salado, r., Arg.	141c	35°53'S	58°12'W
Salado, r., Arg.	144	37°00'S	67°00'W
Salado, r., Arg. (sä-lä'dô)	144	26°05'S	63°35'W
Salado, r., Mex.	128	28°00'N	102°00'W
Salado, r., Mex. (sä-lä'dô)	131	18°30'N	97°29'W
Salado Creek, r., Tx., U.S.	117d	29°23'N	98°25'W
Salado de los Nadadores, Río, r., Mex. (dĕ-lôs-nä-dä-dô'rĕs)	122	27°26'N	101°35'W
Salal, Chad	235	14°51'N	17°13'E
Salamanca, Chile (sä-lä-mä'n-kä)	141b	31°48'S	70°57'W
Salamanca, Mex.	128	20°36'N	101°10'W
Salamanca, Spain (sä-lä-mä'n-ká)	154	40°54'N	5°42'W
Salamanca, N.Y., U.S. (săl-á-măŋ'ká)	109	42°10'N	78°45'W
Salamat, Bahr, r., Chad (bär sä-lä-mät')	231	10°06'N	19°16'E
Salamina, Col. (sä-lä-mē'-nä)	142a	5°25'N	75°29'W
Salamína, Grc.	175	37°58'N	23°30'E
Salat-la-Canada, Fr.	170	44°52'N	1°13'E
Salaverry, Peru (sä-lä-vā'rē)	142	8°16'S	78°54'W
Salawati, i., Indon. (sä-lä-wä'tē)	213	1°07'S	130°52'E
Salawe, Tan.	237	3°19'S	32°52'E
Sala y Gómez, Isla, i., Chile	241	26°50'S	105°50'W
Salcedo, Dom. Rep. (säl-sä'dō)	135	19°25'N	70°30'W
Saldaña, r., Col. (säl-dá'n-yä)	142a	3°42'N	75°16'W
Saldanha, S. Afr.	232	32°55'S	18°05'E
Saldus, Lat. (sál'dòs)	167	56°39'N	22°30'E
Sale, Austl. (sāl)	222	38°10'S	147°07'E
Sale, Eng., U.K.	158a	53°24'N	2°20'W
Sale, r., Can. (sál'rê-vyâr')	102f	49°44'N	97°11'W
Salekhard, Russia (sŭ-lyĭ-kärt)	180	66°35'N	66°50'E
Salem, India	199	11°39'N	78°11'E
Salem, S. Afr.	233c	33°29'S	26°30'E
Salem, Il., U.S. (sā'lĕm)	108	38°40'N	89°00'W
Salem, In., U.S.	108	38°35'N	86°00'W
Salem, Ma., U.S.	101a	42°31'N	70°54'W
Salem, Mo., U.S.	121	37°36'N	91°33'W
Salem, N.H., U.S.	101a	42°46'N	71°16'W
Salem, N.J., U.S.	109	39°35'N	75°30'W
Salem, Oh., U.S.	108	40°55'N	80°50'W
Salem, Or., U.S.	104	44°55'N	123°03'W

ăt; finăl; rāte; senâte; ärm; åsk; sofá; fâre; ch-choose; dh-as th in other; bē; ēvent; bĕt; recĕnt; cratẽr; g-gō; gh-guttural g; bĭt; ĭ-short neutral; rīde; κ-guttural k as ch in German ich;

PRONOUNCING INDEX Salem – San Felipe 345

PLACE (Pronunciation)	PAGE	LAT.	LONG.
Salem, S.D., U.S.	112	43°43'N	97°23'W
Salem, Va., U.S.	125	37°16'N	80°05'W
Salem, W.V., U.S.	108	39°15'N	80°35'W
Salemi, Italy (sä-lå'mē)	174	37°49'N	12°48'E
Salerno, Italy (sä-lĕr'nō)	162	40°27'N	14°46'E
Salerno, Golfo di, b., Italy (gôl-fô-dē)	162	40°30'N	14°40'E
Salford, Eng., U.K. (săl'fērd)	164	53°26'N	2°19'W
Salgótarján, Hung. (shôl'gō-tôr-yän)	169	48°06'N	19°50'E
Salhyr, r., Ukr.	177	45°25'N	34°22'E
Salida, Co., U.S. (sȧ-lī'dȧ)	120	38°31'N	106°01'W
Salies-de-Béan, Fr.	170	43°27'N	0°58'W
Salima, Mwi.	237	13°47'S	34°26'E
Salina, Ks., U.S. (sȧ-lī'nȧ)	104	38°50'N	97°37'W
Salina, Ut., U.S.	119	39°00'N	111°55'W
Salina, i., Italy (sä-lē'nä)	174	38°35'N	14°48'E
Salina Cruz, Mex. (sä-lē'nä kro͞oz')	128	16°10'N	95°12'W
Salina Point, c., Bah.	135	22°10'N	74°20'W
Salinas, Mex.	128	22°38'N	101°42'W
Salinas, P.R.	129b	17°58'N	66°16'W
Salinas, Ca., U.S. (sȧ-lē'nȧs)	118	36°41'N	121°40'W
Salinas, r., Mex. (sä-lē'näs)	131	16°15'N	90°31'W
Salinas, r., Ca., U.S.	118	36°33'N	121°29'W
Salinas, Bahía de, b., N.A. (bä-ē'ä-dĕ-sȧ-lē'nȧs)	132	11°05'N	85°55'W
Salinas National Monument, rec., N.M., U.S.	119	34°10'N	106°05'W
Salinas Victoria, Mex. (sä-lē'näs vēk-tō'rē-ä)	122	25°59'N	100°19'W
Saline, r., Ar., U.S. (sȧ-lēn')	121	34°06'N	92°30'W
Saline, r., Ks., U.S.	120	39°05'N	99°43'W
Salins-les-Bains, Fr. (sȧ-lăɴ'-lā-băɴ')	171	46°55'N	5°54'E
Salisbury, Can.	100	46°03'N	65°05'W
Salisbury, Eng., U.K. (sôlz'bē-rē)	161	50°35'N	1°51'W
Salisbury, Md., U.S.	109	38°20'N	75°40'W
Salisbury, Mo., U.S.	121	39°24'N	92°47'W
Salisbury, N.C., U.S.	125	35°40'N	80°29'W
Salisbury *see* Harare, Zimb.	232	17°50'S	31°03'E
Salisbury Island, i., Can.	93	63°36'N	76°20'W
Salisbury Plain, pl., Eng., U.K.	164	51°15'N	1°52'W
Salkehatchie, r., S.C., U.S. (sô-kē-hăch'ē)	125	33°09'N	81°10'W
Sallisaw, Ok., U.S. (săl'ĭ-sô)	121	35°27'N	94°48'W
Salmon, Id., U.S. (săm'ŭn)	115	45°11'N	113°54'W
Salmon, r., Can.	94	54°00'N	123°50'W
Salmon, r., Can.	100	46°19'N	65°36'W
Salmon, r., Id., U.S.	106	45°30'N	115°45'W
Salmon, r., N.Y., U.S.	109	44°35'N	74°15'W
Salmon, r., Wa., U.S.	116c	45°44'N	122°36'W
Salmon, Middle Fork, r., Id., U.S.	114	44°50'N	114°52'W
Salmon Arm, Can.	95	50°42'N	119°16'W
Salmon Falls Creek, r., Id., U.S.	115	42°22'N	114°53'W
Salmon Gums, Austl. (gŭmz)	218	33°00'S	122°00'E
Salmon River Mountains, mts., Id., U.S.	106	44°15'N	115°44'W
Salon-de-Provence, Fr. (sȧ-lôɴ-dē-prô-văɴs')	171	43°48'N	5°09'E
Salonika *see* Thessaloníki, Grc.	154	40°38'N	22°59'E
Salonta, Rom. (sä-lôn'tä)	169	46°46'N	21°38'E
Saloum, r., Sen.	234	14°10'N	15°45'W
Salsette Island, i., India	203b	19°12'N	72°52'E
Sal'sk, Russia (sälsk)	181	46°30'N	41°20'E
Salt, r., Az., U.S. (sôlt)	106	33°28'N	111°35'W
Salt, r., Mo., U.S.	121	39°54'N	92°11'W
Salta, Arg. (säl'tä)	144	24°50'S	65°16'W
Salta, prov., Arg.	144	25°15'S	65°00'W
Saltair, Ut., U.S. (sôlt'âr)	117b	40°46'N	112°09'W
Salt Cay, i., T./C. Is.	135	21°20'N	71°15'W
Salt Creek, r., Il., U.S. (sôlt)	111a	42°01'N	88°01'W
Saltillo, Mex. (säl-tēl'yō)	128	25°24'N	100°59'W
Salt Lake City, Ut., U.S. (sôlt lāk sĭ'tĭ)	104	40°45'N	111°52'W
Salto, Arg. (säl'tō)	141c	34°17'S	60°15'W
Salto, Ur.	144	31°18'S	57°45'W
Salto, r., Mex.	130	22°16'N	99°18'W
Salto, Serra do, mtn., Braz. (sĕ'r-rä-dō)	141a	20°26'S	43°28'W
Salto Grande, Braz. (grän'dä)	143	22°57'S	49°58'W
Salton Sea, Ca., U.S. (sôlt'ŭn)	118	33°28'N	115°43'W
Salton Sea, l., Ca., U.S.	106	33°19'N	115°50'W
Saltpond, Ghana	230	5°16'N	1°07'W
Salt River Indian Reservation, I.R., Az., U.S. (sôlt rĭv'ēr)	119	33°40'N	112°01'W
Saltsjöbaden, Swe. (sält'shû-bäd'ĕn)	166	59°15'N	18°20'E
Saltspring Island, i., Can. (sält'spring)	94	48°47'N	123°30'W
Saltville, Va., U.S. (sôlt'vĭl)	125	36°50'N	81°45'W
Saltykovka, Russia (sȧl-tē'kôf-kȧ)	186b	55°45'N	37°56'E
Salud, Mount, mtn., Pan. (sä-lo͞o'th)	128a	9°14'N	79°42'W
Saluda, S.C., U.S. (sȧ-lo͞o'dȧ)	125	34°02'N	81°46'W
Saluda, r., S.C., U.S.	125	34°07'N	81°48'W
Saluzzo, Italy (sä-lo͞ot'sō)	174	44°39'N	7°31'E
Salvador, Braz. (säl-vä-dōr') (bä-ē'ä)	143	12°59'S	38°27'W
Salvador Lake, l., La., U.S.	123	29°45'N	90°20'W
Salvador Point, c., Bah.	134	24°30'N	77°45'W
Salvatierra, Mex. (säl-vä-tyĕr'rä)	130	20°13'N	100°52'W
Salween, r., Asia	196	21°00'N	98°00'E
Salyan, Azer.	181	39°40'N	49°10'E
Salzburg, Aus. (sälts'bŏorgh)	161	47°48'N	13°04'E
Salzwedel, Ger. (sälts-vä'dĕl)	168	52°51'N	11°10'E
Samālūt, Egypt (sä-mä-lo͞ot')	200	28°17'N	30°43'E
Samana, Cabo, c., Dom. Rep.	129	19°20'N	69°00'W
Samana or Atwood Cay, i., Bah.	135	23°05'N	73°45'W
Samar, i., Phil. (sä'mär)	213	11°30'N	126°07'E
Samara (Kuybyshev), Russia	180	53°10'N	50°05'E
Samara, r., Russia	181	52°50'N	50°35'E
Samara, r., Ukr. (sȧ-mä'rȧ)	177	48°47'N	35°30'E
Samarai, Pap. N. Gui. (sä-mä-rä'ē)	213	10°45'S	150°49'E
Samarinda, Indon.	212	0°30'S	117°10'E
Samarkand, Uzb. (sȧ-mȧr-känt')	183	39°42'N	67°00'E
Şamaxı, Azer.	181	40°35'N	48°40'E
Samba, D.R.C.	237	4°38'S	26°22'E
Sambalpur, India (sŭm'bŭl-pŏor)	199	21°30'N	84°05'E
Sāmbhar, r., India	202	27°00'N	74°58'E
Sambir, Ukr.	169	49°31'N	23°12'E
Samborombón, r., Arg.	141c	35°20'S	57°52'W
Samborombón, Bahía, b., Arg. (bä-ē'ä-säm-bô-rôm-bô'n)	141c	35°57'S	57°05'W
Sambre, r., Eur. (säɴ'br')	165	50°20'N	4°15'E
Sambungo, Ang.	236	8°39'S	20°43'E
Sammamish, r., Wa., U.S.	116a	47°43'N	122°08'W
Sammamish, Lake, l., Wa., U.S. (sȧ-măm'ĭsh)	116a	47°35'N	122°02'W
Samoa, nation, Oc.	2	14°30'S	172°00'W
Samoa Islands, is., Oc.	214a	14°00'S	171°00'W
Samokov, Blg. (sä'mô-kôf)	175	42°20'N	23°33'E
Samora Correia, Port. (sä-mô'rä-kôr-rĕ'yä)	173b	38°55'N	8°52'W
Samorovo, Russia (sȧ-mȧ-rô'vô)	184	60°47'N	69°13'E
Sámos, i., Grc. (să'mŏs)	163	37°53'N	26°35'E
Samothráki, i., Grc.	163	40°23'N	25°10'E
Sampaloc Point, c., Phil. (säm-pä'lŏk)	213a	14°43'N	119°56'E
Sam Rayburn Reservoir, res., Tx., U.S.	123	31°10'N	94°15'W
Samson, Al., U.S. (săm'sŭn)	124	31°06'N	86°02'W
Samsu, Kor., N. (säm'so͞o')	210	41°12'N	128°00'E
Samsun, Tur. (sȧm'so͞on')	198	41°20'N	36°05'E
Samtredia, Geor. (sȧm'trĕ-dē)	181	42°18'N	42°25'E
Samuel, i., Can. (sȧm'ū-ĕl)	116d	48°50'N	123°10'W
Samur, r. (sä-mo͞or')	181	41°40'N	47°20'E
San, Mali (sän)	230	13°18'N	4°54'W
San, r., Eur.	161	50°33'N	22°12'E
Şan'ā', Yemen (sän'ä)	198	15°17'N	44°05'E
Sanaga, r., Cam. (sä-nä'gä)	230	4°30'N	12°00'E
San Ambrosio, Isla, i., Chile (ē's-lä-dĕ-sän äm-brō'zē-ō)	139	26°40'S	80°00'W
Sanana, Pulau, i., Indon.	213	2°15'S	126°38'E
Sanandaj, Iran	198	36°44'N	46°43'E
San Andreas, Ca., U.S. (săn ăn'drē-ăs)	118	38°10'N	120°42'W
San Andreas, l., Ca., U.S.	116b	37°36'N	122°26'W
San Andrés, Col. (sän-än-drĕ's)	142a	6°57'N	75°41'W
San Andrés, Mex. (sän än-drās')	131a	19°15'N	99°10'W
San Andrés, i., Col.	133	12°32'N	81°34'W
San Andres, Laguna de, l., Mex.	131	22°40'N	97°50'W
San Andres Mountains, mts., N.M., U.S. (săn ăn'drē-ăs)	106	33°00'N	106°40'W
San Andrés Tuxtla, Mex. (sän-än-drā's-to͞os'tlä)	128	18°27'N	95°12'W
San Angelo, Tx., U.S. (săn ăn-jĕ-lō)	104	31°28'N	100°22'W
San Antioco, Isola di, i., Italy (ē'sō-lä-dē-sän-än-tyō'kō)	174	39°00'N	8°25'E
San Antonio, Chile (sän-ȧn-tô'nyō)	144	33°34'S	71°36'W
San Antonio, Col.	142a	2°57'N	75°06'W
San Antonio, Col.	142a	3°55'N	75°28'W
San Antonio, Phil.	213a	14°57'N	120°05'E
San Antonio, Tx., U.S. (săn ăn-tō'nē-ô)	104	29°25'N	98°30'W
San Antonio, r., Tx., U.S.	123	29°00'N	97°58'W
San Antonio, Cabo, c., Cuba (kȧ'bô-sän-än-tô'nyô)	129	21°55'N	84°55'W
San Antonio, Lake, res., Ca., U.S.	118	36°00'N	121°13'W
San Antonio Bay, b., Tx., U.S.	123	28°20'N	97°08'W
San Antonio de Areco, Arg. (dā ä-rā'kô)	141c	34°16'S	59°30'W
San Antonio de las Vegas, Cuba	135a	22°51'N	82°23'W
San Antonio de los Baños, Cuba (dā lōs bän'yōs)	134	22°54'N	82°30'W
San Antonio de los Cobres, Arg. (dā lōs kō'brās)	144	24°15'S	66°29'W
San Antônio de Pádua, Braz. (dĕ-pä'dwä)	141a	21°32'S	42°09'W
San Antonio de Tamanaco, Ven.	143b	9°42'N	66°03'W
San Antonio Oeste, Arg. (sän-nä-tō'nyô ô-ĕs'tå)	144	40°49'S	64°56'W
San Antonio Peak, mtn., Ca., U.S. (săn ăn-tō'nĭ-ô)	117a	34°17'N	117°39'W
Sanarate, Guat. (sä-nä-rä'tĕ)	132	14°47'N	90°12'W
San Augustine, Tx., U.S. (săn ô'gŭs-tēn)	123	31°33'N	94°08'W
San Bartolo, Mex. (sän bär-tō'lô)	131a	19°36'N	99°43'W
San Bartolo, Mex.	122	24°43'N	103°12'W
San Bartolomeo, Italy (bär-tô-lô-mā'ô)	174	41°25'N	15°04'E
San Benedetto del Tronto, Italy (bā'nå-dĕt'tô dĕl trōn'tō)	174	42°58'N	13°54'E
San Benito, Tx., U.S. (săn bĕ-nē'tô)	123	26°07'N	97°37'W
San Benito, r., Ca., U.S.	118	36°40'N	121°20'W
San Bernardino, Ca., U.S. (bûr-när-dē'nô)	104	34°07'N	117°19'W
San Bernardino Mountains, mts., Ca., U.S.	118	34°05'N	116°23'W
San Bernardo, Chile (sän bĕr-när'dô)	141b	33°35'S	70°42'W
San Blas, Mex. (sän bläs')	128	21°33'N	105°19'W
San Blas, Cape, c., Fl., U.S.	107	29°38'N	85°38'W
San Blas, Cordillera de, mts., Pan.	133	9°17'N	78°20'W
San Blas, Golfo de, b., Pan.	133	9°33'N	78°42'W
San Blas, Punta, c., Pan.	133	9°35'N	78°55'W
San Bruno, Ca., U.S. (săn brū nô)	116b	37°38'N	122°25'W
San Buenaventura, Mex. (bwā'nä-vĕn-to͞o'rä)	122	27°07'N	101°30'W
San Carlos, Chile (sän-kä'r-lôs)	144	36°23'S	71°58'W
San Carlos, Col.	142a	6°11'N	74°58'W
San Carlos, Eq. Gui.	236	3°27'N	8°33'E
San Carlos, Mex. (sän kär'lōs)	131	17°49'N	92°33'W
San Carlos, Mex.	122	24°36'N	98°52'W
San Carlos, Nic. (sän-kä'r-lôs)	133	11°08'N	84°48'W
San Carlos, Phil.	213a	15°56'N	120°20'E
San Carlos, Ca., U.S. (săn kär'lōs)	116b	37°30'N	122°15'W
San Carlos, Ven.	142	9°36'N	68°35'W
San Carlos, r., C.R.	133	10°36'N	84°18'W
San Carlos de Bariloche, Arg.	144	41°15'S	71°26'W
San Carlos Indian Reservation, I.R., Az., U.S. (săn kär'lōs)	119	33°27'N	110°15'W
San Carlos Lake, res., Az., U.S.	119	33°05'N	110°29'W
San Casimiro, Ven. (kä-sē-mē'rô)	143b	10°01'N	67°02'W
San Cataldo, Italy (kä-täl'dō)	174	37°30'N	13°59'E
Sánchez, Dom. Rep. (sän'chĕz)	129	19°15'N	69°40'W
Sanchez, Río de los, r., Mex. (rē'ō-dĕ-lôs)	130	20°31'N	102°29'W
Sánchez Román, Mex. (rô-mä'n)	130	21°48'N	103°20'W
San Clemente, Spain (sän klå-mĕn'tå)	172	39°25'N	2°24'W
San Clemente Island, i., Ca., U.S.	106	32°54'N	118°29'W
San Cristóbal, Dom. Rep. (krēs-tô'bäl)	135	18°25'N	70°05'W
San Cristóbal, Guat.	132	15°22'N	90°26'W
San Cristóbal, Ven.	142	7°43'N	72°15'W
San Cristobal, i., Sol. Is.	221	10°47'S	162°17'E
San Cristóbal de las Casas, Mex.	128	16°44'N	92°39'W
Sancti Spíritus, Cuba (säŋk'tē spē'rē-to͞os)	129	21°55'N	79°25'W
Sancti Spiritus, prov., Cuba	134	22°05'N	79°20'W
Sancy, Puy de, mtn., Fr. (pwē-dĕ-säɴ-sē')	161	45°30'N	2°53'E
Sand, i., Or., U.S. (sănd)	116c	46°16'N	124°01'W
Sand, i., Wi., U.S.	113	46°03'N	91°09'W
Sand, r., S. Afr.	233c	28°30'S	29°30'E
Sand, r., S. Afr.	238c	28°09'S	26°46'E
Sanda, Japan (sän'dä)	211	34°53'N	135°14'E
Sandakan, Malay. (sȧn-dä'kȧn)	212	5°51'N	118°03'E
Sanday, i., Scot., U.K. (sănd'ā)	164a	59°17'N	2°25'W
Sandbach, Eng., U.K. (sănd'băch)	158a	53°08'N	2°22'W
Sandefjord, Nor. (sän'dĕ-fyôr')	166	59°09'N	10°14'E
San de Fuca, Wa., U.S. (de-fo͞o-cä)	116a	48°14'N	122°44'W
Sanders, Az., U.S.	119	35°13'N	109°20'W
Sanderson, Tx., U.S. (săn'dēr-sŭn)	122	30°09'N	102°24'W
Sandersville, Ga., U.S. (săn'dērz-vĭl)	125	32°57'N	82°50'W
Sandhammaren, c., Swe. (sänt'häm-mȧr)	160	55°24'N	14°37'E
Sand Hills, reg., Ne., U.S. (sănd)	112	41°57'N	101°29'W
Sand Hook, N.J., U.S. (sănd hŏŏk)	110a	40°29'N	74°05'W
Sandhurst, Eng., U.K. (sănd'hûrst)	158b	51°20'N	0°48'W
Sandia Indian Reservation, I.R., N.M., U.S.	119	35°15'N	106°30'W
San Diego, Ca., U.S. (săn dē-ā'gô)	104	32°43'N	117°10'W
San Diego, Tx., U.S.	120	27°47'N	98°13'W
San Diego, r., Ca., U.S.	118	32°53'N	116°57'W
San Diego de la Unión, Mex. (sän dē-å-gô dā lä o͞o-nyōn')	130	21°27'N	100°52'W
Sandies Creek, r., Tx., U.S. (sănd'ēz)	123	29°13'N	97°34'W
San Dimas, Mex. (dē-mäs')	130	24°08'N	105°57'W
San Dimas, Ca., U.S. (săn dĕ-mȧs)	117a	34°07'N	117°49'W
Sandnes, Nor. (sänd'nĕs)	166	58°52'N	5°44'E
Sandoa, D.R.C. (sän-dō'ä)	232	9°39'S	23°00'E
Sandomierz, Pol. (sȧn-dô'myĕzh)	169	50°39'N	21°45'E
San Doná di Piave, Italy (sän dô nä' dē pyä'vĕ)	174	45°38'N	12°34'E
Sandoway, Mya. (sän-dô-wī')	199	18°24'N	94°28'E
Sandpoint, Id., U.S. (sănd point)	114	48°17'N	116°34'W
Sandringham, Austl. (săn'drĭng-ăm)	217a	37°57'S	145°01'E
Sandrio, Italy (sä'n-dryô)	174	46°11'N	9°53'E
Sand Springs, Ok., U.S. (sănd sprĭnz)	121	36°08'N	96°06'W
Sandstone, Austl. (sănd'stōn)	218	28°00'S	119°25'E
Sandstone, Mn., U.S.	113	46°08'N	92°53'W
Sanduo, China (sän-dwô)	206	32°49'N	119°39'E
Sandusky, Al., U.S. (săn-dŭs'kē)	110h	33°32'N	86°50'W
Sandusky, Mi., U.S.	108	43°25'N	82°50'W
Sandusky, Oh., U.S.	105	41°25'N	82°45'W
Sandusky, r., Oh., U.S.	108	41°10'N	83°20'W
Sandwich, Il., U.S. (sănd'wĭch)	108	42°35'N	88°53'W
Sandy, Or., U.S. (sănd'ē)	116c	45°24'N	122°16'W
Sandy, Ut., U.S.	117b	40°36'N	111°53'W
Sandy, r., Or., U.S.	116c	45°28'N	122°17'W
Sandy Cape, c., Austl.	221	24°25'S	153°10'E
Sandy Hook, Ct., U.S. (hŏŏk)	110a	41°25'N	73°17'W
Sandy Lake, l., Can.	102g	53°46'N	113°58'W
Sandy Lake, l., Can.	101	49°16'N	57°00'W
Sandy Lake, l., Can.	97	53°00'N	93°07'W
Sandy Point, Tx., U.S.	123a	29°22'N	95°27'W
Sandy Point, c., Wa., U.S.	116d	48°48'N	122°42'W
Sandy Springs, Ga., U.S. (springz)	110c	33°55'N	84°23'W
San Estanislao, Para. (ĕs-tä-nēs-lä'ô)	144	24°38'S	56°20'W
San Esteban, Hond. (ĕs-tĕ'bän)	132	15°13'N	85°53'W
San Fabian, Phil. (fä-byä'n)	213a	16°14'N	120°28'E
San Felipe, Chile (fā-lē'pā)	144	32°45'S	70°43'W
San Felipe, Mex. (fĕ-lē'pĕ)	130	21°29'N	101°13'W
San Felipe, Mex.	130	22°21'N	105°26'W
San Felipe, Ven. (fĕ-lē'pĕ)	142	10°13'N	68°45'W
San Felipe, Cayos de, is., Cuba (kä'yōs-dĕ-sän-fĕ-lē'pĕ)	134	22°00'N	83°30'W

ng-sing; ŋ-baŋk; ɴ-nasalized n; nŏd; cŏmmit; ōld; ôbey; ôrder; oi-boil; fo͞od; ŏŏ-as oo in foot; ou-out; s-soft; sh-dish; th-thin; pūre; ûnite; ûrn; stŭd; circŭs; ü-as in French tu; '-indeterminate vowel.

346 San Felipe Creek – San Sebastian PRONOUNCING INDEX

PLACE (Pronunciation)	PAGE	LAT.	LONG.
San Felipe Creek, r., Ca., U.S. (săn fē-lēp´ā)	118	33°10'N	116°03'W
San Felipe Indian Reservation, I.R., N.M., U.S.	119	35°26'N	106°26'W
San Félix, Isla, i., Chile (ē´s-lä-dĕ-săn fā-lēks´)	139	26°20'S	80°10'W
San Fernanda, Spain (fĕr-nä´n-dä)	172	36°28'N	6°13'W
San Fernando, Arg. (fĕr-nà´n-dô)	144a	34°26'S	58°34'W
San Fernando, Chile	141b	35°36'S	70°58'W
San Fernando, Mex. (fĕr-nän´dô)	122	24°52'N	98°10'W
San Fernando, Phil. (săn fĕr-nä´n-dô)	212	16°38'N	120°19'E
San Fernando, Ca., U.S. (fĕr-nän´dô)	117a	34°17'N	118°27'W
San Fernando, r., Mex. (săn fĕr-nän´dô)	122	25°07'N	98°25'W
San Fernando de Apure, Ven. (săn-fĕr-nä´n-dō-dĕ-ä-pōō´rå)	142	7°46'N	67°29'W
San Fernando de Atabapo, Ven. (dĕ-ä-tä-bä´pō)	142	3°58'N	67°41'W
San Fernando de Henares, Spain (dĕ-ā-nä´rås)	173a	40°23'N	3°31'W
Sånfjället, mtn., Swe.	160	62°19'N	13°30'E
Sanford, Can. (săn´fērd)	102f	49°41'N	97°27'W
Sanford, Fl., U.S. (săn´fôrd)	105	28°46'N	81°18'W
Sanford, Me., U.S. (săn´fērd)	100	43°26'N	70°47'W
Sanford, N.C., U.S.	125	35°26'N	79°10'W
San Francisco, Arg. (săn frăn´sĭs´kô)	144	31°23'S	62°09'W
San Francisco, El Sal.	132	13°48'N	88°11'W
San Francisco, Ca., U.S.	104	37°45'N	122°26'W
San Francisco, r., N.M., U.S.	119	33°35'N	108°55'W
San Francisco Bay, b., Ca., U.S. (săn frăn´sĭs´kô)	118	37°45'N	122°21'W
San Francisco del Oro, Mex. (dĕl ō´rō)	128	27°00'N	106°37'W
San Francisco del Rincón, Mex. (dĕl rēn-kōn´)	130	21°01'N	101°51'W
San Francisco de Macaira, Ven. (dĕ-mä-kī´rä)	143b	9°58'N	66°17'W
San Francisco de Macoris, Dom. Rep. (dā-mä-kō´rēs)	135	19°20'N	70°15'W
San Francisco de Paula, Cuba (dā pou´lá)	135a	23°04'N	82°18'W
San Gabriel, Ca., U.S. (săn gä-brê-ĕl´) (gā´brē-ĕl)	117a	34°06'N	118°06'W
San Gabriel, r., Ca., U.S.	117a	33°47'N	118°06'W
San Gabriel Chilac, Mex. (săn-gä-brē-ĕl-chê-läk´)	131	18°19'N	97°22'W
San Gabriel Mts, Ca., U.S.	117a	34°17'N	118°03'W
San Gabriel Reservoir, res., Ca., U.S.	117a	34°14'N	117°48'W
Sangamon, r., Il., U.S. (săn´gá-msion)	121	40°08'N	90°08'W
Sanger, Ca., U.S. (săng´ēr)	118	36°42'N	119°33'W
Sangerhausen, Ger. (säng´ĕr-hou-zĕn)	168	51°28'N	11°17'E
Sangha, r., Afr.	231	2°40'N	16°10'E
Sangihe, Pulau, i., Indon.	213	3°30'N	125°30'E
San Gil, Col. (săn-кē´l)	142	6°32'N	73°13'W
San Giovanni in Fiore, Italy (săn jô-vän´nê ēn fyō´rā)	174	39°15'N	16°40'E
San Giuseppe Vesuviano, Italy	173c	40°36'N	14°31'E
Sangju, Kor., S. (säng´jōō´)	210	36°20'N	128°07'E
Sāngli, India	199	16°56'N	74°38'E
Sangmélima, Cam.	235	2°56'N	11°59'E
San Gorgonio Mountain, mtn., Ca., U.S. (săn gôr-gō´nĭ-ō)	117a	34°06'N	116°50'W
Sangre de Cristo Mountains, mts., U.S.	106	37°45'N	105°50'W
San Gregoria, Ca., U.S. (săn grĕ-gôr´ā)	116b	37°20'N	122°23'W
Sangro, r., Italy (säŋ´grô)	174	41°38'N	13°56'E
Sangüesa, Spain (sän-gwĕ´sä)	172	42°36'N	1°15'W
Sanhe, China (sän-hŭ)	206	39°59'N	117°06'E
Sanibel Island, i., Fl., U.S. (săn´ĭ-bĕl)	125a	26°26'N	82°15'W
San Ignacio, Belize	132a	17°11'N	89°04'W
San Ildefonso, Cape, c., Phil. (sän-ēl-dĕ-fōn-sô)	213a	16°03'N	122°10'E
San Ildefonso o la Granja, Spain (ō lä grän´khä)	172	40°54'N	4°02'W
San Isidro, Arg. (ē-sē´drô)	141c	34°28'S	58°31'W
San Isidro, C.R.	133	9°24'N	83°43'W
San Jacinto, Phil. (săn hä-sēn´tô)	213a	12°33'N	123°43'E
San Jacinto, Ca., U.S. (săn já-sĭn´tô)	117a	33°47'N	116°57'W
San Jacinto, r., Ca., U.S. (săn já-sĭn´tô)	117a	33°44'N	117°14'W
San Jacinto, r., Tx., U.S.	123	30°25'N	95°05'W
San Jacinto, West Fork, r., Tx., U.S.	123	30°35'N	95°37'W
San Javier, Chile (săn-hà-vĕ´ĕr)	141b	35°35'S	71°43'W
San Jerónimo, Mex.	131a	19°31'N	98°46'W
San Jerónimo de Juárez, Mex. (hå-rō´nê-mô dā hwä´rāz)	130	17°08'N	100°30'W
San Joaquin, Ven.	143b	10°16'N	67°47'W
San Joaquin, r., Ca., U.S. (săn hwä-kēn´)	118	37°10'N	120°51'W
San Joaquin Valley, Ca., U.S.	118	36°45'N	120°30'W
San Jorge, Golfo, b., Arg. (gôl-fô-săn-кô´r-кĕ)	144	46°15'S	66°45'W
San José, C.R. (săn hô-sā´)	129	9°57'N	84°05'W
San Jose, Phil.	213a	12°22'N	121°04'E
San Jose, Phil.	213a	15°49'N	120°57'E
San Jose, Ca., U.S. (săn hô-zā´)	104	37°20'N	121°54'W
San José, i., Mex. (кô-sĕ´)	128	25°00'N	110°35'W
San José, Isla de, i., Pan. (ē´s-lä-dĕ-săn hô-sā´)	133	8°17'N	79°20'W
San Jose, Rio, r., N.M., U.S. (săn hô-zā´)	119	35°15'N	108°10'W
San José de Feliciano, Arg. (dā lä ĕs-kē´nà)	144	30°26'S	58°44'W
San José de Gauribe, Ven. (sän-hô-sĕ´dĕ-gàōō-rē´bĕ)	143b	9°51'N	65°49'W
San José de las Lajas, Cuba (sän-кô-sĕ´dĕ-läs-lä´käs)	135a	22°58'N	82°10'W
San José Iturbide, Mex. (ē-tōōr-bē´dĕ)	130	21°00'N	100°24'W
San Juan, Arg. (hwän´)	144	31°36'S	68°29'W
San Juan, Col. (hòá´n)	142a	3°23'N	73°48'W
San Juan, Dom. Rep. (săn hwän´)	135	18°50'N	71°15'W
San Juan, Phil.	213a	16°41'N	120°20'E
San Juan, P.R. (săn hwän´)	129	18°30'N	66°10'W
San Juan, prov., Arg.	144	31°00'S	69°30'W
San Juan, r., Mex. (sän-hōō-än´)	131	18°10'N	95°23'W
San Juan, r., N.A.	129	10°58'N	84°18'W
San Juan, r., U.S.	106	36°30'N	109°00'W
San Juan, Cabezas de, c., P.R.	129b	18°29'N	65°30'W
San Juan, Cabo, c., Eq. Gui.	236	1°08'N	9°23'E
San Juan, Pico, mtn., Cuba (pē´kô-săn-hòá´n)	134	21°55'N	80°00'W
San Juan, Río, r., Mex. (rē´ō-săn-hwän)	122	25°35'N	99°15'W
San Juan Bautista, Para. (săn hwän´ bou-tēs´tä)	144	26°48'S	57°09'W
San Juan Capistrano, Mex. (sän-hōō-än´ kä-pēs-trä´nō)	130	22°41'N	104°07'W
San Juan Creek, r., Ca., U.S. (săn hwän´)	118	35°24'N	120°12'W
San Juan de Guadalupe, Mex. (săn hwan dā gwä-dhä-lōō´på)	122	24°37'N	102°43'W
San Juan del Norte, Nic.	133	10°55'N	83°44'W
San Juan del Norte, Bahía de, b., Nic.	133	11°12'N	83°40'W
San Juan de los Lagos, Mex. (sän-hōō-än´dā los lä´gōs)	130	21°15'N	102°18'W
San Juan de los Lagos, r., Mex. (dā lōs lä´gōs)	130	21°13'N	102°12'W
San Juan de los Morros, Ven. (dĕ-lôs-mô´r-rôs)	143b	9°54'N	67°22'W
San Juan del Río, Mex.	130	20°21'N	99°59'W
San Juan del Río, Mex. (săn hwän del rē´ō)	122	24°47'N	104°29'W
San Juan del Sur, Nic. (dĕl sōōr)	128	11°15'N	85°53'W
San Juan Evangelista, Mex. (sän-hōō-ä´n-å-väŋ-kå-lĕs´ta´)	131	17°57'N	95°08'W
San Juan Island, i., Wa., U.S.	116a	48°28'N	123°08'W
San Juan Islands, is., Can. (săn hwän)	94	48°49'N	123°14'W
San Juan Islands, is., Wa., U.S.	186a	48°36'N	122°50'W
San Juan Ixtenco, Mex. (ēx-tĕ´n-kô)	131	19°14'N	97°52'W
San Juan Martínez, Cuba	134	22°15'N	83°50'W
San Juan Mountains, mts., Co., U.S. (san hwán´)	106	37°50'N	107°30'W
San Julián, Arg. (săn hōō-lyá´n)	144	49°17'S	68°02'W
San Justo, Arg. (hōōs´tô)	144a	34°40'S	58°33'W
Sankanbiriwa, mtn., S.L.	234	8°56'N	10°48'W
Sankarani, r., Afr. (săn´kä-rä´nê)	230	11°10'N	8°35'W
Sankt Gallen, Switz.	161	47°25'N	9°22'E
Sankt Moritz, Switz. (sånt mō´rĭts) (zäŋkt mō´rēts)	168	46°31'N	9°50'E
Sankt Pölten, Aus. (zäŋkt-pûl´tĕn)	168	48°12'N	15°38'E
Sankt Veit, Aus. (zäŋкt vĭt´)	168	46°46'N	14°20'E
Sankuru, r., D.R.C. (săn-kōō´rōō)	232	4°00'S	22°35'E
San Lázaro, Cabo, c., Mex. (sän-lä´zä-rō)	128	24°58'N	113°30'W
San Leandro, Ca., U.S. (săn lê-ăn´drô)	116b	37°43'N	122°10'W
Şanlıurfa, Tur.	198	37°20'N	38°45'E
San Lorenzo, Arg. (săn lô-rĕn´zô)	144	32°46'S	60°44'W
San Lorenzo, Hond. (săn lô-rĕn´zô)	132	13°24'N	87°24'W
San Lorenzo, Ca., U.S. (săn lô-rĕn´zô)	116b	37°41'N	122°08'W
San Lorenzo de El Escorial, Spain	172	40°36'N	4°09'W
Sanlúcar de Barrameda, Spain (sän-lōō´kär)	162	36°46'N	6°21'W
San Lucas, Bol. (lōō´kás)	142	20°12'S	65°06'W
San Lucas, Cabo, c., Mex.	128	22°45'N	109°45'W
San Luis, Arg. (lò-ēs´)	144	33°16'S	66°15'W
San Luis, Col. (lòē´s)	142a	6°03'N	74°57'W
San Luis, Cuba	135	20°15'N	75°50'W
San Luis, Guat.	132	14°38'N	89°42'W
San Luis, prov., Arg.	144	32°45'S	66°00'W
San Luis de la Paz, Mex. (dā lä päz´)	130	21°17'N	100°32'W
San Luis del Cordero, Mex. (dĕl kôr-dā´rô)	122	25°25'N	104°20'W
San Luis Obispo, Ca., U.S. (ô-bis´pō)	104	35°18'N	120°40'W
San Luis Obispo Bay, b., Ca., U.S.	118	35°07'N	121°05'W
San Luis Potosí, Mex.	128	22°08'N	100°58'W
San Luis Potosí, state, Mex.	128	22°45'N	101°45'W
San Luis Rey, r., Ca., U.S. (rā´ê)	118	33°22'N	117°06'W
San Manuel, Az., U.S. (săn măn´ū-ĕl)	119	32°30'N	110°45'W
San Marcial, N.M., U.S. (săn már-shäl´)	119	33°40'N	107°00'W
San Marco, Italy (săn mär´kô)	174	41°53'N	15°50'E
San Marcos, Guat. (mär´kôs)	132	14°57'N	91°49'W
San Marcos, Mex.	130	16°46'N	99°23'W
San Marcos, Tx., U.S. (săn mär´kôs)	123	29°53'N	97°56'W
San Marcos, r., Tx., U.S.	122	30°08'N	98°15'W
San Marcos de Colón, Hond. (sän-má´r-kōs-dĕ-kô-lô´n)	132	13°17'N	86°50'W
San Maria di Léuca, Cape, c., Italy (dĕ-lĕ´ōō-kä)	163	39°47'N	18°20'E
San Marino, S. Mar. (săn mä-rē´nô)	174	44°55'N	12°26'E
San Marino, Ca., U.S. (săn mĕr-ē´nô)	117a	34°07'N	118°06'W
San Marino, nation, Eur.	154	43°40'N	13°00'E
San Martín, Col. (săn mär-tē´n)	142a	3°42'N	73°44'W
San Martín, vol., Mex. (mär-tē´n)	131	18°36'N	95°11'W
San Martín, l., S.A.	144	48°15'S	72°30'W
San Martín Chalchicuautla, Mex.	130	21°22'N	98°39'W
San Martin de la Vega, Spain (sän mär ten´ dā lä vā´gä)	173a	40°12'N	3°34'W
San Martín Hidalgo, Mex. (sän mär-tē´n-ē-däl´gô)	130	20°27'N	103°55'W
San Mateo, Mex.	131	16°59'N	97°04'W
San Mateo, Ca., U.S. (săn mä-tā´ô)	116b	37°34'N	122°20'W
San Mateo, Ven. (sän mà-tĕ´ô)	143b	9°45'N	64°34'W
San Matías, Golfo, b., Arg. (săn mä-tē´äs)	144	41°30'S	63°45'W
Sanmen Wan, b., China	209	29°00'N	122°15'E
San Miguel, El Sal. (sän mê-gâl´)	128	13°28'N	88°11'W
San Miguel, Mex. (săn mê-gâl´)	131	18°18'N	97°09'W
San Miguel, Pan.	133	8°26'N	78°55'W
San Miguel, Phil. (săn mē-gĕ´l)	213a	15°09'N	120°56'E
San Miguel, Ven. (sän mē-gĕ´l)	143b	9°56'N	64°58'W
San Miguel, vol., El Sal.	132	13°27'N	88°17'W
San Miguel, i., Ca., U.S.	118	34°03'N	120°23'W
San Miguel, r., Bol. (sän-mē-gĕl´)	142	13°34'S	63°58'W
San Miguel, r., N.A. (săn mê-gâl´)	131	15°27'N	92°00'W
San Miguel, r., Co., U.S. (săn mê-gĕl´)	119	38°15'N	108°40'W
San Miguel, Bahía, b., Pan. (bä-ē´ä-săn mê-gâl´)	133	8°17'N	78°26'W
San Miguel Bay, b., Phil.	213a	13°55'N	123°12'E
San Miguel de Allende, Mex. (då ä-lyĕn´då)	130	20°54'N	100°44'W
San Miguel el Alto, Mex. (ĕl äl´tô)	130	21°03'N	102°26'W
Sannār, Sudan	231	14°25'N	33°30'E
San Narcisco, Phil. (sän när-sē´sô)	213a	15°01'N	120°05'E
San Narcisco, Phil.	213a	13°34'N	122°33'E
San Nicolás, Arg. (sän nē-kô-lä´s)	144	33°20'S	60°14'W
San Nicolas, Phil. (nê-kô-läs´)	213a	16°05'N	120°45'E
San Nicolas, i., Ca., U.S. (săn nĭ´kô-lá)	118	33°14'N	119°10'W
San Nicolás, r., Mex.	130	19°40'N	105°08'W
Sanniquellie, Lib.	234	7°22'N	8°43'W
Sannūr, Wādī, Egypt	238b	28°48'N	31°12'E
Sanok, Pol. (sä´nôk)	169	49°31'N	22°13'E
San Pablo, Phil. (sän-pä-blô)	213a	14°05'N	121°20'E
San Pablo, Ca., U.S. (săn păb´lô)	116b	37°58'N	122°21'W
San Pablo, Ven. (sän-pà´blô)	143b	9°46'N	65°04'W
San Pablo, r., Pan. (săn päb´lô)	133	8°12'N	81°12'W
San Pablo Bay, b., Ca., U.S. (săn păb´lô)	116b	38°04'N	122°25'W
San Pablo Res, Ca., U.S.	116b	37°55'N	122°12'W
San Pascual, Phil. (päs-kwäl´)	213a	13°08'N	122°59'E
San Pedro, Arg. (săn pä´drô)	144	24°15'S	64°15'W
San Pedro, Arg.	141c	33°41'S	59°42'W
San Pedro, Chile (săn pĕ´drô)	141b	33°54'S	71°27'W
San Pedro, El Sal. (săn pä´drô)	132	13°49'N	88°58'W
San Pedro, Mex. (săn pä´drô)	131	18°38'N	92°25'W
San Pedro, Para. (sän-pĕ´drô)	144	24°13'S	57°00'W
San Pedro, Ca., U.S. (săn pē´drô)	117a	33°44'N	118°17'W
San Pedro, r., Cuba (sän-pĕ´drô)	134	21°05'N	78°15'W
San Pedro, r., Mex. (săn pä´drô)	130	22°08'N	104°59'W
San Pedro, r., Mex.	122	27°56'N	105°50'W
San Pedro, r., Az., U.S.	119	32°48'N	110°37'W
San Pedro, Río de, r., Mex.	130	21°51'N	102°24'W
San Pedro, Río de, r., N.A.	131	18°23'N	92°13'W
San Pedro Bay, b., Ca., U.S. (săn pē´drô)	117a	33°42'N	118°12'W
San Pedro de las Colonias, Mex. (dĕ-läs-kô-lô´nyäs)	122	25°47'N	102°58'W
San Pedro de Macorís, Dom. Rep. (sän-pĕ´drō-då mä-kō-rēs´)	135	18°30'N	69°30'W
San Pedro Lagunillas, Mex. (săn pä´drô lä-gōō-nēl´yäs)	130	21°12'N	104°47'W
San Pedro Sula, Hond. (săn pä´drô sōō´lä)	132	15°29'N	88°01'W
San Pietro, Isola di, i., Italy (ē´sō-lä-dē-săn pyā´trô)	174	39°09'N	8°15'E
San Quentin, Ca., U.S. (săn kwĕn-tēn´)	116b	37°57'N	122°29'W
San Quintin, Phil. (săn kên-tēn´)	213a	15°59'N	120°47'E
San Rafael, Arg. (sän-rä-fä-ĕl´)	144	34°30'S	68°13'W
San Rafael, Col. (sän-rä-fä-ĕ´l)	142a	6°18'N	75°02'W
San Rafael, Ca., U.S. (săn rá-fĕl)	116b	37°58'N	122°31'W
San Rafael, r., Ut., U.S. (săn rá-fĕl´)	119	39°05'N	110°50'W
San Rafael, Cabo, c., Dom. Rep. (ká´bô)	135	19°00'N	68°50'W
San Ramón, C.R.	133	10°07'N	84°30'W
San Ramon, Ca., U.S. (săn rä-mōn´)	116b	37°47'N	122°59'W
San Remo, Italy (săn rā´mô)	174	43°48'N	7°46'E
San Roque, Col. (sän-rô´kĕ)	142a	6°29'N	75°00'W
San Roque, Spain	172	36°13'N	5°23'W
San Saba, Tx., U.S. (săn sä´bà)	122	31°12'N	98°43'W
San Saba, r., Tx., U.S.	122	30°58'N	99°12'W
San Salvador, El Sal. (săn săl-vä-dōr´)	128	13°45'N	89°11'W
San Salvador (Watling), i., Bah. (săn săl´vá-dôr)	135	24°05'N	74°30'W
San Salvador, i., Ec.	142	0°14'S	90°50'W
San Salvador, r., Ur. (sän-säl-vä-dô´r)	141c	33°42'S	58°04'W
Sansanné-Mango, Togo (sän-sá-nā´ män´gô)	230	10°21'N	0°28'E
San Sebastian, Spain (săn sá-bås-tyän´)	230	28°09'N	17°11'W

ăt; finăl; rāte; senāte; ärm; åsk; sofá; fâre; ch-choose; dh-as th in other; bē; ēvent; bĕt; recĕnt; cratẽr; g-gō; gh-guttural g; bĭt; ĭ-short neutral; rīde; κ-guttural k as ch in German ich;

PRONOUNCING INDEX San Sebastián – Sapitwa 347

PLACE (Pronunciation)	PAGE	LAT.	LONG.
San Sebastián *see* Donostia-San Sebastián, Spain	154	43°19'N	1°59'W
San Sebastián, Ven. (sän-sĕ-bäs-tyä'n)	143b	9°58'N	67°11'W
San Sebastiàn de los Reyes, Spain	173a	40°33'N	3°38'W
San Severo, Italy (sän sĕ-vâ'rō)	163	41°43'N	15°24'E
Sanshui, China (sän-shwā)	205	23°14'N	112°51'E
San Simon Creek, r., Az., U.S. (sàn sī-mōn')	119	32°45'N	109°30'W
Santa Ana, El Sal.	128	14°02'N	89°35'W
Santa Ana, Mex. (sän'tä ä'nä)	130	19°18'N	98°10'W
Santa Ana, Ca., U.S. (săn'tȧ ăn'ȧ)	104	33°45'N	117°52'W
Santa Ana, r., Ca., U.S.	117a	33°41'N	117°57'W
Santa Ana Mountains, mts., Ca., U.S.	117a	33°44'N	117°36'W
Santa Anna, Tx., U.S.	122	31°44'N	99°18'W
Santa Antão, i., C.V. (sä-tä-ä'n-zhĕ-lō)	230b	17°20'N	26°05'W
Santa Bárbara, Braz. (sän-tä-bá'r-bä-rä)	143	19°57'S	43°25'W
Santa Bárbara, Hond.	132	14°52'N	88°20'W
Santa Barbara, Mex.	122	26°48'N	105°50'W
Santa Barbara, Ca., U.S.	104	34°26'N	119°43'W
Santa Barbara, i., Ca., U.S.	118	33°30'N	118°44'W
Santa Barbara Channel, strt., Ca., U.S.	118	34°15'N	120°00'W
Santa Branca, Braz. (sän-tä-brä'ɴ-kä)	141a	23°25'S	45°52'W
Santa Catalina, i., Ca., U.S.	106	33°29'N	118°37'W
Santa Catalina, Cerro de, mtn., Pan.	133	8°39'N	81°36'W
Santa Catalina, Gulf of, b., Ca., U.S. (săn'tȧ kă-tȧ-lē'nȧ)	118	33°00'N	117°58'W
Santa Catarina, Mex. (sän'tä kä-tä-rē'nä)	122	25°41'N	100°27'W
Santa Catarina, state, Braz. (sän-tä-kä-tä-rē'ná)	144	27°15'S	50°30'W
Santa Catarina, r., Mex.	130	16°31'N	98°39'W
Santa Clara, Cuba (sän't klä'rá)	129	22°25'N	80°00'W
Santa Clara, Mex.	122	24°29'N	103°22'W
Santa Clara, Ur.	144	32°46'S	54°51'W
Santa Clara, Ca., U.S. (săn'tȧ klârȧ)	114	37°21'N	121°56'W
Santa Clara, vol., Nic.	132	12°44'N	87°00'W
Santa Clara, r., Ca., U.S. (săn'tȧ klă'rȧ)	118	34°22'N	118°53'W
Santa Clara, Bahía de, b., Cuba (bä-ē'ä-dĕ-sän-tä-klä-rä)	134	23°05'N	80°50'W
Santa Clara, Sierra, mts., Mex. (sē-ĕ'r-rä-sän'tá klä'rà)	128	27°30'N	113°50'W
Santa Clara Indian Reservation, I.R., N.M., U.S.	119	35°59'N	106°10'W
Santa Cruz, Bol. (sän'tä krōōz')	142	17°45'S	63°03'W
Santa Cruz, Braz. (sän-tä-krōō's)	144	29°43'S	52°15'W
Santa Cruz, Braz.	144b	22°55'S	43°41'W
Santa Cruz, Chile	141b	34°38'S	71°21'W
Santa Cruz, C.R.	132	10°16'N	85°37'W
Santa Cruz, Mex.	122	25°50'N	105°25'W
Santa Cruz, Phil.	213a	13°28'N	122°02'E
Santa Cruz, Phil.	213a	15°46'N	119°53'E
Santa Cruz, Phil.	213a	14°17'N	121°25'E
Santa Cruz, Ca., U.S.	104	36°59'N	122°02'W
Santa Cruz, prov., Arg.	144	48°00'S	70°00'W
Santa Cruz, i., Ec. (sän-tä-krōō'z)	142	0°38'S	90°20'W
Santa Cruz, r., Arg. (sän'tá krōōz')	144	50°05'S	71°00'W
Santa Cruz, r., Az., U.S. (săn'tȧ krōōz')	119	32°30'N	111°30'W
Santa Cruz Barillas, Guat. (sän-tä-krōō'z-bä-rē'l-yäs)	132	15°47'N	91°22'W
Santa Cruz del Sur, Cuba (sän-tä-krōō's-dĕl-sōō'r)	134	20°45'N	78°00'W
Santa Cruz de Tenerife, Spain (sän'tä krōōz dā tā-nå-rē'fā)	228	28°07'N	15°27'W
Santa Cruz Islands, is., Sol. Is.	221	10°58'S	166°47'E
Santa Cruz Mountains, mts., Ca., U.S. (săn'tȧ krōōz')	116b	37°30'N	122°19'W
Santa Domingo, Cay, i., Bah.	135	21°50'N	75°45'W
Santa Fe, Arg. (sän'tä fā')	144	31°33'S	60°45'W
Santa Fé, Cuba (sän-tä-fē')	134	21°45'N	82°40'W
Santa Fe, Spain (sän'tä-fā')	172	37°12'N	3°43'W
Santa Fe, N.M., U.S. (săn'tȧ fā')	104	35°40'N	106°00'W
Santa Fe, prov., Arg. (sän'tä fā')	144	32°00'S	61°15'W
Santa Fe de Bogotá *see* Bogotá, Col.	142	4°36'N	74°05'W
Santa Filomena, Braz. (sän-tä-fē-lō-mĕ'nä)	143	9°09'S	44°45'W
Santa Genoveva, mtn., Mex. (sän-tä-hĕ-nō-vĕ'vä)	128	23°30'N	110°00'W
Santai, China (san-tī)	204	31°02'N	105°02'E
Santa Inés, Ven. (sän'tä ē-nĕ's)	143b	9°54'N	64°21'W
Santa Inés, i., Chile (sän'tä ē-näs')	144	53°45'S	74°15'W
Santa Isabel, i., Sol. Is.	221	7°57'S	159°28'E
Santa Isabel, Pico de, mtn., Eq. Gui.	235	3°35'N	8°46'E
Santa Lucia, Cuba (sän'tä lōō-sē'ä)	134	21°15'N	77°30'W
Santa Lucia, Ur. (sän-tä-lōō-sē'ä)	144	34°27'S	56°23'W
Santa Lucia, Ven.	143b	10°18'N	66°40'W
Santa Lucia, r., Ur.	141c	34°19'S	56°13'W
Santa Lucia Bay, b., Cuba (sän'tä lōō-sē'ä)	134	22°55'N	84°20'W
Santa Margarita, i., Mex. (sän'tä mär-gä-rē'tä)	128	24°15'N	112°00'W
Santa Maria, Braz. (sän'tä mä-rē'ä)	144	29°40'S	54°00'W
Santa Maria, Italy (sän-tä mä-rē'ä)	174	41°05'N	14°15'E
Santa Maria, Phil. (sän-tä-mä-rē'ä)	213a	14°48'N	120°57'E
Santa Maria, Ca., U.S. (săn-tȧ mȧ-rē'ȧ)	118	34°57'N	120°28'W
Santa María, vol., Guat.	132	14°45'N	91°33'W
Santa Maria, r., Mex. (sän'tä mä-rē'ä)	130	21°33'N	100°17'W
Santa Maria, Cabo de, c., Port. (kå'bō-dĕ-sän-tä-mä-rē'ä)	172	36°58'N	7°54'W
Santa Maria, Cape, c., Bah.	135	23°45'N	75°30'W
Santa Maria, Cayo, i., Cuba	134	22°40'N	79°00'W
Santa María del Oro, Mex. (sän'tä-mä-rē'ä-dĕl-ô-rō)	130	21°21'N	104°35'W
Santa Maria de los Angeles, Mex. (dĕ-lôs-á'n-hĕ-lĕs)	130	22°10'N	103°34'W
Santa María del Río, Mex.	130	21°46'N	100°43'W
Santa María de Ocotán, Mex.	130	22°56'N	104°30'W
Santa Maria Island, i., Port. (sän-tä-mä-rē'ä)	230a	37°09'N	26°02'W
Santa Maria Madalena, Braz.	141a	22°00'S	42°00'W
Santa Marta, Col. (sän'tä mär'tà)	142	11°15'N	74°13'W
Santa Marta, Cabo de, c., Ang.	236	13°52'S	12°25'E
Santa Monica, Ca., U.S. (săn'tȧ mŏn'ĭ-kȧ)	104	34°01'N	118°29'W
Santa Monica Mountains, mts., Ca., U.S.	117a	34°08'N	118°38'W
Santana, r., Braz. (sän-tä'nä)	144b	22°33'S	43°37'W
Santander, Col. (sän-tän-dĕr')	142a	3°00'N	76°25'W
Santander, Spain (sän-tän-dâr')	154	43°27'N	3°50'W
Sant Antoni de Portmany, Spain	173	38°59'N	1°17'E
Santa Paula, Ca., U.S. (săn'tȧ pô'lȧ)	118	34°24'N	119°05'W
Santarém, Braz. (sän-tä-rĕɴ')	143	2°28'S	54°37'W
Santarém, Port.	172	39°18'N	8°48'W
Santaren Channel, strt., Bah. (săn-tȧ-rĕn')	134	24°15'N	79°30'W
Santa Rita do Sapucai, Braz. (sä-pō-kȧ'ē)	141a	22°15'S	45°41'W
Santa Rosa, Arg. (sän-tä-rô-sä)	144	36°45'S	64°10'W
Santa Rosa, Col. (sän-tä-rô-sä)	142a	6°38'N	75°26'W
Santa Rosa, Ec.	142	3°29'S	79°55'W
Santa Rosa, Guat. (sän'tä rō'sȧ)	132	14°21'N	90°16'W
Santa Rosa, Hond.	132	14°45'N	88°51'W
Santa Rosa, Ca., U.S. (săn'tȧ rō'zȧ)	104	38°27'N	122°42'W
Santa Rosa, N.M., U.S. (săn'tȧ rō'sȧ)	120	34°55'N	104°41'W
Santa Rosa, Ven. (sän-tä-rô-sä)	143b	9°37'N	64°10'W
Santa Rosa de Cabal, Col. (sän-tä-rô-sä-dĕ-kä-bä'l)	142a	4°53'N	75°38'W
Santa Rosa de Viterbo, Braz. (sän-tä-rô-sȧ-dĕ-vē-tĕr'-bō)	141a	21°30'S	47°21'W
Santa Rosa Indian Reservation, I.R., Ca., U.S. (săn'tȧ rō'zȧ')	118	33°28'N	116°50'W
Santa Rosalía, Mex. (sän'tä rō-zä'lē-ȧ)	128	27°13'N	112°15'W
Santa Rosa Range, mts., Nv., U.S. (săn'tȧ rō'zȧ)	114	41°33'N	117°50'W
Santa Susana, Ca., U.S. (săn'tȧ sōō-ză'nȧ)	117a	34°16'N	118°42'W
Santa Teresa, Arg. (sän-tä-tĕ-rĕ'sä)	141c	33°27'S	60°47'W
Santa Teresa, Ven.	143b	10°14'N	66°40'W
Santa Uxia, Spain	172	42°34'N	8°55'W
Santa Vitória do Palmar, Braz. (sän-tä-vē-tô'ryä-dô-päl-már)	144	33°30'S	53°16'W
Santa Ynez, r., Ca., U.S. (săn'tȧ ē-nĕz')	118	34°40'N	120°20'W
Santa Ysabel Indian Reservation, I.R., Ca., U.S. (săn-tȧ ĭ-zȧ-bĕl')	118	33°05'N	116°46'W
Santee, Ca., U.S. (săn tē')	118a	32°50'N	116°58'W
Santee, r., S.C., U.S.	107	33°00'N	79°45'W
Sant' Eufemia, Golfo di, b., Italy (gôl-fô-dē-sän-tĕ'ô-fē'myä)	174	38°53'N	15°53'E
Sant Feliu de Guíxols, Spain	173	41°45'N	3°01'E
Santiago, Braz. (sän-tyá'gô)	144	29°05'S	54°46'W
Santiago, Chile (sän-tē-ä'gô)	144	33°26'S	70°40'W
Santiago, Pan.	129	8°07'N	80°58'W
Santiago, Phil. (sän-tyä'gô)	213a	16°42'N	121°33'E
Santiago, prov., Chile (sän-tyá'gō)	141b	33°28'S	70°55'W
Santiago, i., Phil.	213a	16°29'N	120°03'E
Santiago de Compostela, Spain	162	42°52'N	8°32'W
Santiago de Cuba, Cuba (sän-tyá'gô-dā kōō'bä)	129	20°00'N	75°50'W
Santiago de Cuba, prov., Cuba	134	20°20'N	76°05'W
Santiago de las Vegas, Cuba (sän-tyá'gô-dĕ-läs-vĕ'gäs)	135a	22°58'N	82°23'W
Santiago del Estero, Arg.	144	27°50'S	64°14'W
Santiago del Estero, prov., Arg. (sän-tē-á'gō-dĕl ĕs-tā-rō)	144	27°15'S	63°30'W
Santiago de los Cabelleros, Dom. Rep.	129	19°30'N	70°45'W
Santiago Mountains, mts., Tx., U.S. (sän-tē-ä'gô)	106	30°00'N	103°30'W
Santiago Reservoir, res., Ca., U.S.	117a	33°47'N	117°42'W
Santiago Rodriguez, Dom. Rep. (sän-tyá'gô-rô-drē'gĕz)	135	19°30'N	71°25'W
Santiago Tuxtla, Mex. (sän-tyá'gô-tōō'x-tlä)	131	18°28'N	95°18'W
Santiaguillo, Laguna de, l., Mex. (lä-oō'nä-dĕ-sän-tē-a-gēl'yô)	122	24°51'N	104°43'W
Santisteban del Puerto, Spain (sän'tē stå-bän'dĕl pwĕr'tō)	172	38°15'N	3°12'W
Sant Mateu, Spain	173	40°26'N	0°09'E
Santo Amaro, Braz. (sän'tô ä-mä'rô)	143	12°32'S	38°33'W
Santo Amaro de Campos, Braz.	141a	22°01'S	41°05'W
Santo André, Braz.	141a	23°40'S	46°31'W
Santo Angelo, Braz. (sän-tô-ä'n-zhĕ-lô)	144	28°16'S	53°59'W
Santo Antônio do Monte, Braz. (sän-tô-än-tô'nyô-dô-môn'tĕ)	141a	20°06'S	45°18'W
Santo Domingo, Cuba (sän'tô-dōmĭŋ'gô)	134	22°35'N	80°20'W
Santo Domingo, Dom. Rep. (sän'tô dô-mĭn'gô)	129	18°30'N	69°55'W
Santo Domingo, Nic. (sän-tô-dô-mē'n-gō)	133	12°15'N	84°56'W
Santo Domingo de la Caizada, Spain (dā lä käl-thä'dä)	172	42°27'N	2°55'W
Santoña, Spain (sän-tō'nyä)	172	43°25'N	3°27'W
Santos, Braz. (sän'tozh)	143	23°58'S	46°20'W
Santos Dumont, Braz. (sän'tôs-dō-mô'nt)	143	21°28'S	43°33'W
Sanuki, Japan (sä'nōō-kē)	211a	35°16'N	139°53'E
San Urbano, Arg. (sän-ōr-bä'nô)	141c	33°39'S	61°28'W
San Valentin, Monte, mtn., Chile (sän-vä-lĕn-tē'n)	144	46°41'S	73°30'W
San Vicente, Arg. (sän-vē-sĕn'tĕ)	141c	35°00'S	58°26'W
San Vicente, Chile	141b	34°25'S	71°06'W
San Vicente, El Sal. (sän vê-sĕn'tå)	132	13°41'N	88°43'W
San Vicente de Alcántara, Spain	172	39°24'N	7°08'W
San Vito al Tagliamento, Italy (san vē'tô)	174	45°53'N	12°52'E
San Xavier Indian Reservation, I.R., Az., U.S. (x-ā'vĭēr)	119	32°07'N	111°12'W
San Ysidro, Ca., U.S. (săn ysĭ-drō')	118a	32°33'N	117°02'W
Sanyuanli, China (sän-yůän-lē)	207a	23°11'N	113°16'E
São Bernardo do Campo, Braz. (souɴ-bĕr-nár'dô-dô-ká'm-pô)	141a	23°44'S	46°33'W
São Borja, Braz. (souɴ-bôr-zhä)	144	28°44'S	55°59'W
São Carlos, Braz. (souɴ kär'lōzh)	143	22°02'S	47°54'W
São Cristovão, Braz. (souɴ-krēs-tō vouɴ)	143	11°04'S	37°11'W
São Fidélis, Braz. (souɴ-fē-dĕ'lēs)	141a	21°41'S	41°45'W
São Francisco, Braz. (souɴ frän-sēsh'kô)	143	15°59'S	44°42'W
São Francisco, r., Braz. (sän-frän-sē's-kō)	143	8°56'S	40°20'W
São Francisco do Sul, Braz. (souɴ frän-sēsh'kô-dô-sōō'l)	144	26°15'S	48°42'W
São Gabriel, Braz. (souɴ'gä-brē-ĕl')	144	30°28'S	54°11'W
São Geraldo, Braz. (souɴ-zhĕ-rä'l-dô)	141a	21°01'S	42°49'W
São Gonçalo, Braz. (souɴ'gōŋ-sä'lô)	141a	22°55'S	43°04'W
Sao Hill, Tan.	237	8°20'S	35°12'E
São João, Gui.-B.	234	11°32'N	15°26'W
São João da Barra, Braz. (souɴ-zhôuɴ-dä-bà'rä)	141a	21°40'S	41°03'W
São João da Boa Vista, Braz. (souɴ-zhôuɴ-dä-bôä-vē's-tä)	141a	21°58'S	46°45'W
São João del Rei, Braz. (souɴ zhô-ouɴ'dĕl-rā)	144	21°08'S	44°14'W
São João de Meriti, Braz. (souɴ-zhôuɴ-dĕ-mĕ-rē-tē)	144b	22°47'S	43°22'W
São João do Araguaia, Braz. (souɴ zhô-ouɴ'dô-ä-rä-gwä'yä)	143	5°29'S	48°44'W
São João dos Lampas, Port. (souɴ' zhô-ouɴ' dōzh län-päzh')	173b	38°52'N	9°24'W
São João Nepomuceno, Braz. (souɴ-zhôuɴ-nĕ-pô-mōō-sĕ-nō)	141a	21°33'S	43°00'W
São Jorge Island, i., Port. (souɴ zhôr'zhĕ)	230a	38°28'N	27°34'W
São José do Rio Pardo, Braz. (souɴ-zhô-sĕ'dô-rē'ō-pá'r-dō)	141a	21°36'S	46°50'W
São José do Rio Prêto, Braz. (souɴ zhô-zĕ'dô-re'ō-prĕ-tō)	143	20°57'S	49°12'W
São José dos Campos, Braz. (souɴ zhô-zā'dōzh käɴ pōzh')	141a	23°12'S	45°53'W
São Leopoldo, Braz. (souɴ-lĕ-ô-pôl'dô)	144	29°46'S	51°09'W
São Luis, Braz.	143	2°31'S	43°14'W
São Luis do Paraitinga, Braz. (souɴ-lōōē's-dô-pä-rä-ē-tē'n-gä)	141a	23°15'S	45°18'W
São Manuel, r., Braz.	143	8°28'S	57°07'E
São Mateus, Braz. (souɴ mä-tā'ōzh)	143	18°44'S	39°45'W
São Mateus, Braz.	144b	22°49'S	43°23'W
São Miguel Arcanjo, Braz. (souɴ-mē-gĕ'l-ár-kän-zhō)	141a	23°54'S	47°59'W
São Miguel Island, i., Port.	230a	37°59'N	26°38'W
Saona, i., Dom. Rep. (sä-ō'nä)	135	18°10'N	68°55'W
Saône, r., Fr. (sōn)	156	47°00'N	5°30'E
São Nicolau, i., C.V. (souɴ' nē-kō-louɴ')	230b	16°19'N	25°19'W
São Paulo, Braz. (souɴ' pou'lō)	143	23°34'S	46°38'W
São Paulo, state, Braz. (souɴ pou'lō)	143	21°45'S	50°47'W
São Paulo de Olivença, Braz. (souɴ'pou'lōdå ô-lē-vĕn'sȧ)	142	3°32'S	68°46'W
São Pedro, Braz. (souɴ-pĕ'drô)	141a	22°34'S	47°54'W
São Pedro de Aldeia, Braz. (souɴ-pĕ'drô-dĕ-äl-dĕ'yä)	141a	22°50'S	42°04'W
São Pedro e São Paulo, Rocedos, rocks, Braz.	139	1°50'N	30°00'W
São Raimundo Nonato, Braz. (souɴ' rī-mô'n-do nô-nä'tô)	143	9°09'S	42°32'W
São Roque, Braz. (souɴ' rō'kĕ)	141a	23°32'S	47°08'W
São Roque, Cabo de, c., Braz. (kä'bo-dĕ-souɴ' rō'kĕ)	143	5°06'S	35°11'W
São Sebastião, Braz. (souɴ sĕ-bäs-tē-ouɴ')	141a	23°48'S	45°25'W
São Sebastião, Ilha de, i., Braz.	141a	23°52'S	45°22'W
São Sebastião do Paraíso, Braz.	141a	20°54'S	46°58'W
São Simão, Braz. (souɴ-sē-mouɴ)	141a	21°30'S	47°33'W
São Tiago, i., C.V. (souɴ tē-ä'gô)	230b	15°09'N	24°45'W
São Tomé, S. Tom./P.	230	0°20'N	6°44'E
Sao Tome and Principe, nation, Afr. (prēn'sē-pĕ)	230	1°00'N	6°00'E
Saoura, Oued, r., Alg.	230	29°39'N	1°42'W
São Vicente, Braz. (souɴ ve-se'n-tĕ)	143	23°57'S	46°25'W
São Vicente, i., C.V. (souɴ vē-sĕn'tå)	230b	16°51'N	24°35'W
São Vicente, Cabo de, c., Port. (ká'bō-dĕ-sän-vē-sĕ'n-tĕ)	156	37°03'N	9°31'W
Sapele, Nig. (sä-pā'lā)	230	5°54'N	5°41'E
Sapitwa, mtn., Mwi.	237	15°58'S	35°38'E

348 Sa Pobla – Segura PRONOUNCING INDEX

PLACE (Pronunciation)	PAGE	LAT.	LONG.
Sa Pobla, Spain	173	39°46'N	3°02'E
Sapozhok, Russia (sä-pô-zhôk')	176	53°58'N	40°44'E
Sapporo, Japan (säp-pô'rô)	205	43°02'N	141°29'E
Sapronovo, Russia (såp-rô'nô-vô)	186b	55°13'N	38°25'E
Sapucaí, r., Braz. (sä-pōō-kä-ē')	141a	22°20'S	45°53'W
Sapucaia, Braz. (sä-pōō-kä'yà)	141a	22°01'S	42°54'W
Sapucaí Mirim, r., Braz. (sä-pōō-kä-ē'mē-rēN)	141a	21°06'S	47°03'W
Sapulpa, Ok., U.S. (sȧ-pŭl'pȧ)	121	36°01'N	96°05'W
Saqqez, Iran	201	36°14'N	46°16'E
Saquarema, Braz. (sä-kwä-rĕ-mä)	141a	22°56'S	42°32'W
Sara, Wa., U.S. (sä'rä)	116c	45°45'N	122°42'W
Sara, Bahr, r., Chad (bär)	231	8°19'N	17°44'E
Sarajevo, Bos. (sä-rȧ-yĕv'ô) (så-rä'ya-vô)	154	43°50'N	18°26'E
Sarakhs, Iran	201	36°32'N	61°11'E
Sarana, Russia (så-rä'nȧ)	186a	56°31'N	57°44'E
Saranac Lake, N.Y., U.S.	109	44°20'N	74°05'W
Saranac Lake, l., N.Y., U.S. (săr'ȧ-năk)	109	44°15'N	74°20'W
Sarandi, Arg. (sä-rän'dē)	144a	34°41'S	58°21'W
Sarandi Grande, Ur. (sä-rän'dē-grän'dĕ)	141c	33°42'S	56°21'W
Saranley, Som.	238a	2°28'N	42°15'E
Saransk, Russia (så-ränsk')	178	54°10'N	45°10'E
Sarany, Russia (så-rä'nĭ)	186a	58°33'N	58°48'E
Sara Peak, mtn., Nig.	235	9°37'N	9°25'E
Sarapul, Russia (sä-räpòl')	180	56°28'N	53°50'E
Sarasota, Fl., U.S. (săr-ȧ-sōtȧ)	125a	27°27'N	82°30'W
Saratoga, Tx., U.S. (săr-ȧ-tō'gȧ)	123	30°17'N	94°31'W
Saratoga, Wa., U.S.	116a	48°04'N	122°29'W
Saratoga Pass, Wa., U.S.	116a	48°09'N	122°33'W
Saratoga Springs, N.Y., U.S. (sprĭngz)	109	43°05'N	74°50'W
Saratov, Russia (så rä'tôf)	178	51°30'N	45°30'E
Saravane, Laos	209	15°48'N	106°40'E
Sarawak, hist. reg., Malay. (sȧ-rä'wäk)	212	2°30'N	112°45'E
Sárbogárd, Hung. (shär'bô-gärd)	169	46°53'N	18°38'E
Sarcee Indian Reserve, I.R., Can. (sär'sē)	102e	50°58'N	114°23'W
Sarcelles, Fr.	171b	49°00'N	2°23'E
Sardalas, Libya	230	25°59'N	10°33'E
Sardinia, i., Italy (sär-dĭn'ĭȧ)	156	40°08'N	9°05'E
Sardis, Ms., U.S. (sär'dĭs)	124	34°26'N	89°55'W
Sardis Lake, res., Ms., U.S.	124	34°27'N	89°43'W
Sargent, Ne., U.S. (sär'jĕnt)	112	41°40'N	99°38'W
Sarh, Chad (är-chaN-bô')	231	9°09'N	18°23'E
Sarikamis, Tur.	181	40°30'N	42°40'E
Sariñena, Spain (sä-rēn-yĕ'nä)	173	41°46'N	0°11'W
Sark, i., Guern. (särk)	170	49°28'N	2°22'W
Şarköy, Tur. (shär'kû-ē)	175	40°39'N	27°07'E
Sarmiento, Monte, mtn., Chile (mô'n-tĕ-sär-myĕn'tō)	144	54°28'S	70°40'W
Sarnia, Can. (sär'nē-ȧ)	91	43°00'N	82°25'W
Sarno, Italy (sä'r-nô)	173c	40°35'N	14°38'E
Sarny, Ukr. (sär'nē)	181	51°17'N	26°39'E
Saronikós Kólpos, b., Grc.	175	37°51'N	23°30'E
Saros Körfezi, b., Tur. (sä'rôs)	175	40°30'N	26°20'E
Sárospatak, Hung. (shä'rôsh-pô'tôk)	169	48°19'N	21°35'E
Šar Planina, mts., Serb. (shär plä'nē-na)	175	42°07'N	21°54'E
Sarpsborg, Nor. (särps'bôrg)	166	59°17'N	11°07'E
Sarrebourg, Fr. (sär-bōōr')	171	48°44'N	7°02'E
Sarreguemines, Fr. (sär-gē-mēn')	161	49°06'N	7°05'E
Sarria, Spain (sär'ē-ä)	162	42°14'N	7°17'W
Sarstun, r., N.A. (särs-tōō'n)	132	15°50'N	89°26'W
Sartène, Fr. (sär-tĕn')	174	41°36'N	8°59'E
Sarthe, r., Fr. (särt)	161	47°44'N	0°32'W
Şarur, Azer.	182	39°33'N	44°58'E
Sárvár, Hung. (shär'vär)	168	47°14'N	16°55'E
Sarych, Mys, c., Ukr. (mĭs så-rēch')	181	44°25'N	33°00'E
Saryesik-Atyraū, des., Kaz.	183	45°30'N	76°00'E
Sary-Ishikotrau, Peski, des., Kyrg. (sä'rē ē' shĕk-ō'trou)	183	46°12'N	75°30'E
Sarysū, r., Kaz. (sä'rē-sōō)	183	47°47'N	69°14'E
Sasarām, India (sŭs-ŭ-räm')	199	25°00'N	84°00'E
Sasayama, Japan (sä'sä-yä'mä)	211	35°05'N	135°14'E
Sasebo, Japan (sä'så-bô)	205	33°12'N	129°43'E
Saskatchewan, prov., Can.	90	54°46'N	107°40'W
Saskatchewan, r., Can. (săs-kăch'ē-wän)	92	53°45'N	103°20'W
Saskatoon, Can. (săs-kȧ-tōōn')	90	52°07'N	106°38'W
Sasolburg, S. Afr.	238c	26°52'S	27°47'E
Sasovo, Russia (sås'ô-vô)	180	54°20'N	42°00'E
Saspamco, Tx., U.S. (săs-păm'cō)	117d	29°13'N	98°18'W
Sassandra, C. Iv.	234	4°58'N	6°05'W
Sassandra, r., C. Iv. (sȧs-sän'drȧ)	230	5°35'N	6°25'W
Sassari, Italy (säs'sä-rē)	162	40°44'N	8°33'E
Sassnitz, Ger. (säs'nĕts)	168	54°31'N	13°37'E
Satadougou, Mali (sä-tà-dōō-gōō')	234	12°21'N	12°07'W
Säter, Swe. (sĕ'tĕr)	166	60°21'N	15°50'E
Satilla, r., Ga., U.S. (sȧ-tĭl'ȧ)	125	31°15'N	82°13'W
Satka, Russia (sät'kȧ)	180	55°03'N	59°02'E
Sátoraljaujhely, Hung. (shä'tô-rô-lyô-ōō'yĕl')	169	48°24'N	21°40'E
Satu Mare, Rom. (sȧ'tōō-mȧ'rĕ)	163	47°50'N	22°53'E
Saturna, Can. (să-tûr'nȧ)	116d	48°48'N	123°12'W
Saturna, i., Can.	116d	48°47'N	123°03'W
Sauda, Nor.	160	59°40'N	6°21'E
Saudárkrókur, Ice.	154	65°41'N	19°38'W
Saudi Arabia, nation, Asia (sä-ŏ'dĭ ȧ-rä'bĭ-ȧ)	198	22°40'N	46°00'E
Sauerlach, Ger. (zou'ĕr-läк)	159d	47°58'N	11°39'E
Saugatuck, Mi., U.S. (sô'gȧ-tŭk)	108	42°40'N	86°10'W
Saugeen, r., Can.	98	44°20'N	81°20'W
Saugerties, N.Y., U.S. (sô'gĕr-tēz)	109	42°05'N	73°55'W
Saugus, Ma., U.S. (sô'gŭs)	101a	42°28'N	71°01'W
Sauk, r., Mn., U.S. (sôk)	113	45°30'N	94°45'W
Sauk Centre, Mn., U.S.	113	45°43'N	94°58'W
Sauk City, Wi., U.S.	113	43°16'N	89°45'W
Sauk Rapids, Mn., U.S. (răp'ĭd)	113	45°35'N	94°08'W
Sault Sainte Marie, Can.	91	46°31'N	84°20'W
Sault Sainte Marie, Mi., U.S. (sōō sānt mȧ-rē')	105	46°29'N	84°21'W
Saumatre, Étang, l., Haiti	135	18°40'N	72°10'W
Saunders Lake, l., Can. (săn'dẽrs)	102g	53°18'N	113°25'W
Saurimo, Ang.	232	9°39'S	20°24'E
Sausalito, Ca., U.S. (sô-sȧ-lē'tô)	116b	37°51'N	122°29'W
Sausset-les-Pins, Fr. (sō-sĕ'lā-păN')	170a	43°20'N	5°08'E
Saútar, Ang.	236	11°06'S	18°27'E
Sauvie Island, i., Or., U.S. (sô'vē)	116c	45°43'N	123°49'W
Sava, r., Serb. (sä'vä)	156	44°50'N	18°30'E
Savage, Md., U.S. (să'vĕj)	110e	39°07'N	76°49'W
Savage, Mn., U.S.	117g	44°47'N	93°20'W
Savai'i, i., Samoa	214a	13°35'S	172°25'W
Savalen, l., Nor.	166	62°19'N	10°15'E
Savalou, Benin	230	7°56'N	1°58'E
Savanna, Il., U.S. (sȧ-văn'ȧ)	113	42°05'N	90°09'W
Savannah, Ga., U.S. (sȧ-văn'ȧ)	105	32°04'N	81°07'W
Savannah, Mo., U.S.	121	39°58'N	94°49'W
Savannah, Tn., U.S.	124	35°13'N	88°14'W
Savannah, r., U.S.	107	33°11'N	81°51'W
Savannakhét, Laos	212	16°33'N	104°45'E
Savanna la Mar, Jam. (sȧ-vän'ȧ lȧ mär')	134	18°10'N	78°10'W
Save, r., Fr.	170	43°32'N	0°50'E
Save, Rio (Sabi), r., Afr. (rē'ō-sä'vĕ)	232	21°28'S	34°14'E
Säveh, Iran	201	35°01'N	50°20'E
Saverne, Fr. (så-vĕrn')	171	48°40'N	7°22'E
Savigliano, Italy (sä-vēl-yä'nô)	174	44°38'N	7°42'E
Savigny-sur-Orge, Fr.	171b	48°41'N	2°22'E
Savona, Italy (sä-nō'nä)	162	44°19'N	8°28'E
Savonlinna, Fin. (sá'vôn-lēn'nȧ)	167	61°53'N	28°49'E
Savran', Ukr. (säv-rän')	177	48°07'N	30°09'E
Sawahlunto, Indon.	212	0°37'S	100°50'E
Sawākin, Sudan	231	19°02'N	37°19'E
Sawda, Jabal as, mts., Libya	231	28°14'N	13°46'E
Sawhāj, Egypt	231	26°34'N	31°40'E
Sawknah, Libya	231	29°04'N	15°53'E
Sawu, Laut (Savu Sea), sea, Asia	212	9°15'S	122°15'E
Sawyer, l., Wa., U.S. (sô'yẽr)	116a	47°20'N	122°02'W
Saxony *see* Sachsen, hist. reg., Ger.	168	50°45'N	12°17'E
Say, Niger (sä'ē)	230	13°09'N	2°16'E
Sayan Khrebet, mts., Russia (sŭ-yän')	179	51°30'N	90°00'E
Sayḥūt, Yemen	198	15°23'N	51°28'E
Sayre, Ok., U.S. (sā'ẽr)	120	35°19'N	99°40'W
Sayre, Pa., U.S.	109	41°55'N	76°30'W
Sayreton, Al., U.S. (sā'ẽr-tŭn)	110h	33°34'N	86°51'W
Sayreville, N.J., U.S. (sâr'vĭl)	110a	40°28'N	74°21'W
Sayr Usa, Mong.	204	44°15'N	107°00'E
Sayula, Mex. (sä-yōō'lä)	131	17°51'N	94°56'W
Sayula, Mex.	130	19°50'N	103°33'W
Sayula, Luguna de, l., Mex. (lä-gò'nä-dĕ)	130	20°00'N	103°33'W
Say'un, Yemen	198	16°00'N	48°59'E
Sayville, N.Y., U.S. (sā'vĭl)	109	40°45'N	73°10'W
Sazanit, i., Alb.	163	40°30'N	19°17'E
Sázava, r., Czech Rep.	168	49°36'N	15°24'E
Sazhino, Russia (sȧz-hē'nô)	186a	56°20'N	58°15'E
Scandinavian Peninsula, pen., Eur.	196	62°00'N	14°00'E
Scanlon, Mn., U.S. (skăn'lôn)	117h	46°27'N	92°26'W
Scappoose, Or., U.S. (skă-pōōs')	116c	45°46'N	122°53'W
Scappoose, r., Or., U.S.	116c	45°47'N	122°57'W
Scarborough, Eng., U.K. (skär'bŭr-ô)	164	54°16'N	0°19'W
Scarsdale, N.Y., U.S. (skärz'dāl)	110a	41°01'N	73°47'W
Scatari l, Can. (skăt'ȧ-rē)	101	46°00'N	59°44'W
Schaerbeek, Bel. (skär'bāk)	159a	50°50'N	4°23'E
Schaffhausen, Switz. (shäf'hou-zĕn)	161	47°42'N	8°38'E
Schefferville, Can.	91	54°52'N	67°01'W
Schelde,, r., Eur.	165	51°04'N	3°55'E
Schenectady, N.Y., U.S. (skĕ-nĕk'tȧ-dē)	105	42°50'N	73°55'W
Scheveningen, Neth.	159a	52°06'N	4°15'E
Schiedam, Neth.	159a	51°55'N	4°23'E
Schiltigheim, Fr. (shĕl'tegh-hĭm)	171	48°48'N	7°47'E
Schio, Italy (skē'ô)	174	45°43'N	11°23'E
Schleswig, Ger. (shĕls'vēgh)	160	54°32'N	9°32'E
Schleswig , hist. reg., Ger. (shĕls'vēgh)	168	54°40'N	9°10'E
Schleswig-Holstein, state, Ger. (shlĕs'vēgh-hōl'shtīn)	159c	53°40'N	9°45'E
Schmalkalden, Ger. (shmäl'käl-dĕn)	168	50°41'N	10°25'E
Schneider, In., U.S. (schnīd'ẽr)	111a	41°12'N	87°26'W
Schofield, Wi., U.S. (skō'fēld)	113	44°52'N	89°37'W
Schönebeck, Ger. (shû'nĕ-bergh)	168	52°01'N	11°44'E
Schoonhoven, Neth.	159a	51°56'N	4°51'E
Schramberg, Ger. (shräm'bĕrgh)	168	48°14'N	8°24'E
Schreiber, Can.	98	48°50'N	87°10'W
Schroon, l., N.Y., U.S. (skrōōn)	109	43°50'N	73°50'W
Schultzendorf, Ger. (shōōl'tzĕn-dōrf)	159b	52°21'N	13°55'E
Schumacher, Can.	98	48°30'N	81°30'W
Schuyler, Ne., U.S. (slī'ler)	112	41°28'N	97°05'W
Schuylkill, r., Pa., U.S. (skōōl'kĭl)	110f	40°10'N	75°31'W
Schuylkill-Haven, Pa., U.S. (skōōl'kĭl hā-vĕn)	109	40°35'N	76°10'W
Schwabach, Ger. (shvä'bäk)	168	49°19'N	11°02'E
Schwäbische Alb, mts., Ger. (shvă'bē-shĕ älb)	168	48°11'N	9°09'E
Schwäbisch Gmünd, Ger. (shvă'bēsh gmünd)	168	48°47'N	9°49'E
Schwäbisch Hall, Ger. (häl)	168	49°08'N	9°44'E
Schwandorf, Ger. (shvän'dôrf)	168	49°19'N	12°08'E
Schwaner, Pegunungan, mts., Indon. (skvän'ẽr)	212	1°05'S	112°30'E
Schwarzwald, for., Ger. (shvärts'väld)	168	47°54'N	7°57'E
Schwaz, Aus.	168	47°20'N	11°45'E
Schwechat, Aus. (shvĕk'ät)	168	48°09'N	16°29'E
Schwedt, Ger. (shvĕt)	168	53°04'N	14°17'E
Schweinfurt, Ger. (shvīn'fòrt)	168	50°03'N	10°14'E
Schwelm, Ger. (shvĕlm)	171c	51°17'N	7°18'E
Schwerin, Ger. (shvĕ-rēn')	168	53°36'N	11°25'E
Schweriner See, l., Ger. (shvĕ'rē-nĕr zā)	168	53°40'N	11°06'E
Schwerte, Ger. (shvĕr'tĕ)	171c	51°26'N	7°34'E
Schwielowsee, l., Ger. (shvē'lōv zā)	159b	52°20'N	12°52'E
Schwyz, Switz. (schēts)	168	47°01'N	8°38'E
Sciacca, Italy (shē-äk'kä)	174	37°30'N	13°09'E
Scilly, Isles of, is., Eng., U.K. (sĭl'ē)	156	49°56'N	6°50'W
Scioto, r., Oh., U.S. (sī-ō'tō)	107	39°10'N	82°55'W
Scituate, Ma., U.S. (sĭt'ū-āt)	101a	42°12'N	70°45'W
Scobey, Mt., U.S. (skō'bē)	115	48°48'N	105°29'W
Scoggin, Or., U.S. (skō'gĭn)	116c	45°28'N	123°14'W
Scotch, r., Can. (skŏch)	102c	45°21'N	74°56'W
Scotia, Ca., U.S. (skō'shȧ)	114	40°29'N	124°06'W
Scotland, S.D., U.S.	112	43°08'N	97°43'W
Scotland, state, U.K. (skŏt'lȧnd)	154	57°05'N	5°10'W
Scotland Neck, N.C., U.S. (nĕk)	125	36°06'N	77°25'W
Scotstown, Can. (skŏts'toun)	109	45°35'N	71°15'W
Scott, r., Ca., U.S.	114	41°20'N	122°55'W
Scott, Cape, c., Can. (skŏt)	92	50°47'N	128°26'W
Scott, Mount, mtn., Or., U.S.	116c	45°27'N	122°33'W
Scott, Mount, mtn., Or., U.S.	114	42°55'N	122°00'W
Scott Air Force Base, Il., U.S.	117e	38°33'N	89°52'W
Scottburgh, S. Afr. (skŏt'bŭr-ô)	232	30°18'S	30°42'E
Scott City, Ks., U.S.	120	38°28'N	100°54'W
Scottdale, Ga., U.S. (skŏt'dāl)	110c	33°47'N	84°16'W
Scott Islands, is., Ant.	224	67°00'S	178°00'E
Scottsbluff, Ne., U.S. (skŏts'blŭf)	112	41°52'N	103°40'W
Scottsboro, Al., U.S. (skŏts'bŭro)	124	34°40'N	86°03'W
Scottsburg, In., U.S. (skŏts'bûrg)	108	38°40'N	85°50'W
Scottsdale, Austl. (skŏts'dāl)	222	41°12'S	147°37'E
Scottsville, Ky., U.S. (skŏts'vĭl)	124	36°45'N	86°10'W
Scottville, Mi., U.S.	108	44°00'N	86°20'W
Scranton, Pa., U.S. (skrăn'tŭn)	105	41°15'N	75°45'W
Scugog, l., Can. (skū'gôg)	99	44°05'N	78°55'W
Scunthorpe, Eng., U.K. (skŭn'thôrp)	158a	53°36'N	0°38'W
Scutari *see* Shkodër, Alb.	154	42°04'N	19°30'E
Scutari, Lake, l., Eur. (skōō'tä-rē)	163	42°14'N	19°33'E
Seabeck, Wa., U.S. (sē'bĕck)	116a	47°38'N	122°50'W
Sea Bright, N.J., U.S. (sē brīt)	110a	40°22'N	73°58'W
Seabrook, Tx., U.S. (sē'bròk)	123	29°34'N	95°01'W
Seaford, De., U.S. (sē'fẽrd)	109	38°35'N	75°40'W
Seagraves, Tx., U.S. (sē'grāvs)	120	32°51'N	102°38'W
Sea Islands, is., Ga., U.S. (sē)	125	31°21'N	81°05'W
Seal, r., Can.	92	59°08'N	96°37'W
Seal Beach, Ca., U.S.	117a	33°44'N	118°06'W
Seal Cays, is., Bah.	135	22°40'N	75°55'W
Seal Cays, is., T./C. Is.	135	21°10'N	71°45'W
Seal Island, i., S. Afr. (sēl)	232a	34°07'S	18°36'E
Sealy, Tx., U.S. (sē'lē)	123	29°46'N	96°10'W
Searcy, Ar., U.S. (sûr'sē)	121	35°13'N	91°43'W
Searles, l., Ca., U.S. (sûrl's)	118	35°44'N	117°22'W
Searsport, Me., U.S. (sērz'pōrt)	100	44°28'N	68°55'W
Seaside, Or., U.S. (sē'sīd)	114	45°59'N	123°55'W
Seattle, Wa., U.S. (sē-ăt''l)	104	47°36'N	122°20'W
Sebaco, Nic. (sĕ-bä'kô)	132	12°50'N	86°03'W
Sebago, Me., U.S. (sē-bā'gō)	100	43°52'N	70°20'W
Sebastián Vizcaíno, Bahía, b., Mex.	128	28°45'N	115°15'W
Sebastopol, Ca., U.S. (sē-bȧs'tô-pôl)	118	38°27'N	122°50'W
Sebderat, Erit.	231	15°30'N	36°45'E
Sebewaing, Mi., U.S. (se'bē-wăng)	108	43°45'N	83°25'W
Sebezh, Russia (syĕ'bĕzh)	176	56°16'N	28°29'E
Sebinkarahisar, Tur.	163	40°15'N	38°10'E
Sebnitz, Ger. (zĕb'nĕts)	168	51°01'N	14°16'E
Sebou, Oued, r., Mor.	230	34°23'N	5°18'W
Sebree, Ky., U.S. (sē-brē')	108	37°35'N	87°30'W
Sebring, Fl., U.S. (sē'brĭng)	125a	27°30'N	81°26'W
Sebring, Oh., U.S.	108	40°55'N	81°05'W
Secchia, r., Italy (sĕ'kyä)	174	44°25'N	10°25'E
Seco, r., Mex. (sĕ'kô)	131	18°11'N	93°18'W
Sedalia, Mo., U.S.	105	38°42'N	93°12'W
Sedan, Fr. (sē-däN)	161	49°49'N	4°55'E
Sedan, Ks., U.S. (sē-dăn')	121	37°07'N	96°08'W
Sedom, Isr.	197a	31°04'N	35°24'E
Sedro Woolley, Wa., U.S. (sē'drô-wòl'ē)	116a	48°30'N	122°14'W
Šeduva, Lith. (shĕ'dò-vȧ)	167	55°46'N	23°45'E
Seestall, Ger. (zā'shtäl)	159d	47°58'N	10°52'E
Sefrou, Mor. (sē-frōō')	162	33°49'N	4°46'W
Seg, l., Russia (syĕgh)	180	63°20'N	33°30'E
Segamat, Malay. (sā'gȧ-mát)	197b	2°30'N	102°49'E
Segang, China (sŭ-gäŋ)	206	31°59'N	114°13'E
Segbana, Benin	235	10°56'N	3°42'E
Segorbe, Spain (sĕ-gôr-bĕ)	173	39°50'N	0°30'W
Ségou, Mali (sā-gōō')	230	13°27'N	6°16'W
Segovia, Col. (sĕ-gô'vēä)	142a	7°08'N	74°42'W
Segovia, Spain (sā-gō'vē-ä)	162	40°58'N	4°05'W
Segre, r., Spain (sā'grä)	173	41°54'N	1°10'E
Seguam, i., Ak., U.S. (sē'gwäm)	103a	52°16'N	172°10'W
Seguam Passage, strt., Ak., U.S.	103a	52°20'N	173°00'W
Séguédine, Niger	235	20°12'N	12°59'E
Séguéla, C. Iv. (sā-gā-lä')	230	7°57'N	6°40'W
Seguin, Tx., U.S. (sē-gēn')	123	29°35'N	97°58'W
Segula, i., Ak., U.S. (sē-gū'lá)	103a	52°08'N	178°35'E
Segura, r., Spain	162	38°24'N	2°12'W

ăt; finăl; rāte; senāte; ärm; ȧsk; sofȧ; fâre; ch-choose; dh-as th in other; bē; ēvent; bĕt; recĕnt; cratẽr; g-gō; gh-guttural g; bĭt; ĭ-short neutral; rīde; к-guttural k as ch in German ich;

PRONOUNCING INDEX

Segura – Sheksna 349

PLACE (Pronunciation)	PAGE	LAT.	LONG.
Segura, Sierra de, mts., Spain (sĕ-ĕ'r-rä-dĕ)	172	38°05'N	2°45'W
Sehwān, Pak.	202	26°33'N	67°51'E
Seibo, Dom. Rep. (sĕ'y-bō)	135	18°45'N	69°05'W
Seiling, Ok., U.S.	120	36°09'N	98°56'W
Seim, r., Eur.	181	51°23'N	33°22'E
Seinäjoki, Fin. (sâ'ē-nĕ-yô'kē)	167	62°47'N	22°50'E
Seine, r., Can. (sån)	102f	49°48'N	97°03'W
Seine, r., Can. (sån)	98	49°04'N	91°00'W
Seine, r., Fr.	156	48°00'N	4°30'E
Seine, Baie de la, b., Fr. (bī dĕ lä sån)	170	49°37'N	0°53'W
Seio do Venus, mtn., Braz. (sĕ-yô-dô-vĕ'nōōs)	144b	22°28'S	43°12'W
Seixal, Port. (sä-ê-shäl')	173b	38°38'N	9°06'W
Sekenke, Tan.	237	4°16'S	34°10'E
Şeki, Azer.	182	41°12'N	47°12'E
Sekondi-Takoradi, Ghana (sĕ-kŏn'dē tä-kô-rä'dē)	230	4°59'N	1°43'W
Sekota, Eth.	231	12°47'N	38°59'E
Selangor, state, Malay. (så-län'gōr)	197b	2°53'N	101°29'E
Selanovtsi, Blg. (sål'á-nôv-tsĭ)	175	43°42'N	24°05'E
Selaru, Pulau, i., Indon.	213	8°30'S	130°30'E
Selatan, Tanjung, c., Indon. (så-lä'tän)	212	4°09'S	114°40'E
Selawik, Ak., U.S. (sē-lȧ-wĭk)	103	66°30'N	160°09'W
Selayar, Pulau, i., Indon.	212	6°15'S	121°15'E
Selbusjøen, l., Nor. (sĕl'bōō)	166	63°18'N	11°55'E
Selby, Eng., U.K. (sĕl'bē)	158a	53°47'N	1°03'W
Seldovia, Ak., U.S. (sĕl-dō'vē-ȧ)	103	59°26'N	151°42'W
Selemdzha, r., Russia (sâ-lĕmt-zhä')	185	52°28'N	131°50'E
Selenga (Selenge), r., Asia (sĕ lĕŋ gä')	179	49°00'N	102°00'E
Selenge, r., Asia	204	49°04'N	102°23'E
Selennyakh, r., Russia (sĕl-yĭn-yäk)	185	67°42'N	141°45'E
Sélestat, Fr. (sē-lē-stä')	171	48°16'N	7°27'E
Sélibaby, Maur. (så-lê-bȧ-bē')	230	15°21'N	12°11'W
Seliger, l., Russia (sĕl'lê-gĕr)	180	57°14'N	33°18'E
Selizharovo, Russia (så'lê-zhä'rô-vô)	176	56°51'N	33°28'E
Selkirk, Can. (sĕl'kûrk)	90	50°09'N	96°52'W
Selkirk Mountains, mts., Can.	92	51°00'N	117°40'W
Selleck, Wa., U.S. (sĕl'ĕck)	116a	47°22'N	121°52'W
Sellersburg, In., U.S. (sĕl'ĕrs-bûrg)	111h	38°25'N	85°45'W
Sellya Khskaya, Guba, b., Russia (sĕl-yäk'skȧ-yȧ)	185	72°30'N	136°00'E
Selma, Al., U.S. (sĕl'mȧ)	105	32°25'N	87°00'W
Selma, Ca., U.S.	118	36°34'N	119°37'W
Selma, N.C., U.S.	125	35°33'N	78°16'W
Selma, Tx., U.S.	117d	29°33'N	98°19'W
Selmer, Tn., U.S.	124	35°11'N	88°36'W
Selsingen, Ger. (zĕl'zēn-gĕn)	159c	53°22'N	9°13'E
Selway, r., Id., U.S. (sĕl'wȧ)	114	46°07'N	115°12'W
Selwyn, l., Can. (sĕl'wĭn)	92	59°41'N	104°30'W
Seman, r., Alb.	175	40°48'N	19°53'E
Semarang, Indon. (sĕ-mä'räng)	212	7°03'S	110°27'E
Semenivka, Ukr.	181	52°10'N	32°34'E
Semeru, Gunung, mtn., Indon.	212	8°06'S	112°55'E
Semey (Semipalatinsk), Kaz.	183	50°28'N	80°29'E
Semiahmoo Indian Reserve, I.R., Can.	116d	49°01'N	122°43'W
Semiahmoo Spit, Wa., U.S. (sĕm'ĭ-ȧ-mōō)	116d	48°59'N	122°52'W
Semichi Islands, is., Ak., U.S. (sē-mē'chĭ)	103a	52°40'N	174°50'E
Seminoe Reservoir, res., Wy., U.S. (sĕm'ĭ nō)	115	42°08'N	107°10'W
Seminole, Ok., U.S. (sĕm'ĭ-nōl)	121	35°13'N	96°41'W
Seminole, Tx., U.S.	122	32°43'N	102°39'W
Seminole, Lake, res., U.S.	124	30°57'N	84°46'W
Semipalatinsk *see* Semey, Kaz.	183	50°28'N	80°29'E
Semisopochnoi, i., Ak., U.S. (sĕ-mē-sȧ-pōsh' noi)	103a	51°45'N	179°25'E
Semliki, r., Afr. (sĕm'lê-kē)	231	0°45'N	29°36'E
Semmering Pass, p., Aus. (sĕm'ĕr-ĭng)	168	47°39'N	15°50'E
Senador Pompeu, Braz. (sĕ-nä-dōr-pôm-pĕ'ô)	143	5°34'S	39°18'W
Senaki, Geor.	182	42°17'N	42°04'E
Senatobia, Ms., U.S. (sĕ-nȧ-tō'bē-ȧ)	124	34°36'N	89°56'W
Sendai, Japan (sĕn-dī')	205	38°18'N	141°02'E
Seneca, Ks., U.S. (sĕn'ē-kȧ)	121	39°49'N	96°03'W
Seneca, Md., U.S.	110e	39°04'N	77°20'W
Seneca, S.C., U.S.	125	34°40'N	82°58'W
Seneca, l., N.Y., U.S.	109	42°30'N	76°55'W
Seneca Falls, N.Y., U.S.	109	42°55'N	76°55'W
Senegal, nation, Afr. (sĕn-ĕ-gôl')	230	14°53'N	14°58'W
Sénégal, r., Afr.	230	16°00'N	14°00'W
Senekal, S. Afr. (sĕn'ē-kȧl)	238c	28°20'S	27°37'E
Senftenberg, Ger. (zĕnf'tĕn-bĕrgh)	168	51°32'N	14°00'E
Sengunyane, r., Leso.	233c	29°35'S	28°08'E
Senhor do Bonfim, Braz. (sĕn-yôr dô bôn-fē'n)	143	10°21'S	40°09'W
Senigallia, Italy (så-nē-gäl'lyä)	174	43°42'N	13°16'E
Senj, Cro. (sĕn')	174	44°58'N	14°55'E
Senja, i., Nor. (sĕnyä)	160	69°28'N	16°10'E
Senlis, Fr. (sän-lēs')	171b	49°13'N	2°35'E
Sennar Dam, dam, Sudan	231	13°38'N	33°38'E
Senneterre, Can.	91	48°20'N	77°22'W
Sens, Fr. (säns)	170	48°05'N	3°18'E
Sensuntepeque, El Sal. (sĕn-sōōn-tā-pā'kå)	132	13°53'N	88°34'W
Senta, Serb. (sĕn'tä)	163	45°54'N	20°05'E
Senzaki, Japan (sĕn'zä-kē)	211	34°22'N	131°09'E
Seoul (Sŏul), Kor., S.	205	37°35'N	127°03'E
Sepang, Malay.	197b	2°43'N	101°45'E
Sepetiba, Baía de, b., Braz. (bäē'ä dĕ så-pâ-tē'bȧ)	144b	23°01'S	43°42'W
Sepik, r. (sĕp-ēk')	213	4°07'S	142°40'E
Septentrional, Cordillera, mts., Dom. Rep.	135	19°50'N	71°15'W
Septeuil, Fr. (sĕ-tû')	171b	48°53'N	1°40'E
Sept-Îles, Can. (sĕ-tēl')	100	50°12'N	66°23'W
Sequatchie, r., Tn., U.S. (sē-kwăch'ē)	124	35°33'N	85°14'W
Sequim, Wa., U.S. (sē'kwĭm)	116a	48°05'N	123°07'W
Sequim Bay, b., Wa., U.S.	116a	48°04'N	122°58'W
Sequoia National Park, rec., Ca., U.S. (sē-kwoi'ȧ)	106	36°34'N	118°37'W
Seraing, Bel. (sē-răn')	165	50°38'N	5°28'E
Serāmpore, India	202a	22°44'N	88°21'E
Serang, Indon. (så-räng')	212	6°13'S	106°10'E
Seranggung, Indon.	197b	0°49'N	104°11'E
Serbia and Montenegro (Yugoslavia), nation, Eur.	154	44°00'N	21°00'E
Serbia *see* Srbija, hist. reg., Serb.	175	44°05'N	20°35'E
Serdobsk, Russia (sĕr-dôpsk')	181	52°30'N	44°20'E
Sered', Slvk.	169	48°17'N	17°43'E
Seredyna-Buda, Ukr.	176	52°11'N	34°03'E
Seremban, Malay. (sĕr-ĕm-bän')	197b	2°44'N	101°57'E
Serengeti National Park, rec., Tan.	237	2°20'S	34°50'E
Serengeti Plain, pl., Tan.	237	2°40'S	34°55'E
Serenje, Zam. (sē-rĕn'yē)	232	13°12'S	30°49'E
Seret, r., Ukr. (sĕr'ĕt)	169	49°45'N	25°30'E
Sergeya Kirova, i., Russia (sĕr-gyē'yȧ kē'rô-vȧ)	184	77°30'N	86°10'E
Sergipe, state, Braz. (sĕr-zhē'pĕ)	143	10°27'S	37°04'W
Sergiyev Posad, Russia	186b	56°18'N	38°08'E
Sergiyevsk, Russia	180	53°58'N	51°00'E
Sérifos, Grc.	175	37°10'N	24°32'E
Sérifos, i., Grc.	175	37°42'N	24°17'E
Serodino, Arg. (sĕ-rô-dē'nō)	141c	32°36'S	60°56'W
Seropédica, Braz. (sĕ-rô-pĕ'dē-kä)	144b	22°44'S	43°43'W
Serov, Russia (syĕ-rôf')	184	59°36'N	60°30'E
Serowe, Bots. (sĕ-rō'wĕ)	232	22°18'S	26°39'E
Serpa, Port. (sĕr-pä)	172	37°56'N	7°38'W
Serpukhov, Russia (syĕr'pô-κôf)	178	54°53'N	37°27'E
Sérres, Grc. (sĕr'rĕ) (sĕr'ĕs)	163	41°06'N	23°36'E
Serrinha, Braz. (sĕr-rēn'yȧ)	143	11°43'S	38°49'W
Serta, Port. (sĕr'tȧ)	172	39°48'N	8°01'W
Sertânia, Braz. (sĕr-tȧ'nyä)	143	8°28'S	37°13'W
Sertãozinho, Braz. (sĕr-toun-zē'n-yō)	141a	21°10'S	47°58'W
Serting, r., Malay.	197b	3°01'N	102°32'E
Sese Islands, is., Ug.	237	0°30'S	32°30'E
Sesia, r., Italy (såz'yä)	174	45°33'N	8°25'E
Sesimbra, Port. (sĕ-sē'm-brä)	173b	38°27'N	9°06'W
Sesmyl, r., S. Afr.	233b	25°51'S	28°06'E
Ses Salines, Cap de, c., Spain	173	39°16'N	3°03'E
Sestri Levante, Italy (sĕs'trē lå-vän'tå)	174	44°15'N	9°24'E
Sestroretsk, Russia (sĕs-trô-rĕtsk)	180	60°06'N	29°58'E
Sestroretskiy Razliv, Ozero, l., Russia	186c	60°05'N	30°07'E
Seta, Japan (sĕ'tä)	211b	34°58'N	135°56'W
Séte, Fr. (sĕt)	161	43°24'N	3°42'E
Sete Lagoas, Braz. (sĕ-tĕ lä-gô'äs)	143	19°23'S	43°58'W
Sete Pontes, Braz.	144b	22°51'S	43°05'W
Seto, Japan (sĕ'tō)	211	35°11'N	137°07'E
Seto-Naikai, sea, Japan (sĕ'tô nī'kī)	211	33°50'N	132°25'E
Settat, Mor. (sĕt-ät') (sē-tá')	230	33°02'N	7°30'W
Sette-Cama, Gabon (sĕ-tē-kä-mä')	232	2°29'S	9°40'E
Settlement Point, c., Bah. (sĕt'l-mĕnt)	134	26°40'N	79°00'W
Settlers, S. Afr. (sĕt'lērs)	238c	24°57'S	28°33'E
Settsu, Japan	211b	34°46'N	135°33'E
Setúbal, Port. (så-tōō'bäl)	162	30°32'N	8°54'W
Setúbal, Baía de, b., Port.	172	38°27'N	9°08'W
Seul, Lac, l., Can. (låk sûl)	93	50°20'N	92°30'W
Sevan, l., Arm. (syĭ-vän')	181	40°10'N	45°20'E
Sevastopol', Ukr. (syĕ-väs-tô'pôl'')	178	44°34'N	33°34'E
Sevenoaks, Eng., U.K. (sĕ-vĕn-ōks')	158b	51°16'N	0°12'E
Severka, r., Russia (sâ'vĕr-kȧ)	186b	55°11'N	38°41'E
Severn, r., Can. (sĕv'ērn)	93	55°21'N	88°42'W
Severn, r., U.K.	164	51°50'N	2°25'W
Severna Park, Md., U.S. (sĕv'ērn-ȧ)	110e	39°04'N	76°33'W
Severnaya Dvina, r., Russia	178	63°00'N	42°40'E
Severnaya Zemlya (Northern Land), is., Russia (sĕ-vyĭr-nīū zĭ-m'lyä')	179	79°33'N	101°15'E
Severoural'sk, Russia (sĕ-vyĭ-rŭ-ōō-rälsk')	184	60°08'N	59°53'E
Sevier, r., Ut., U.S.	106	39°25'N	112°20'W
Sevier, East Fork, r., Ut., U.S.	119	37°45'N	112°10'W
Sevier Lake, l., Ut., U.S. (sē-vēr')	119	38°55'N	113°10'W
Sevilla, Col. (sĕ-vē'l-yä)	142a	4°16'N	75°56'W
Sevilla, Spain (så-vēl'yä)	154	37°29'N	5°58'W
Seville, Oh., U.S. (sĕv'ĭl)	111d	41°01'N	81°45'W
Sevlievo, Blg. (sĕv'lyĕ-vô)	163	43°02'N	25°05'E
Sevsk, Russia (syĕfsk)	176	52°08'N	34°28'E
Seward, Ak., U.S. (sū'ård)	106a	60°18'N	149°28'W
Seward, Ne., U.S.	121	40°55'N	97°06'W
Seward Peninsula, pen., Ak., U.S.	103	65°40'N	164°00'W
Sewell, Chile (sĕ'ô-ĕl)	144	34°01'S	70°18'W
Sewickley, Pa., U.S. (sē-wĭk'lē)	111e	40°33'N	80°11'W
Seybaplaya, Mex. (sā-ē-bä-plä'yä)	131	19°38'N	90°40'W
Seychelles, nation, Afr. (sā-shĕl')	3	5°20'S	55°10'E
Seydisfjördur, Ice. (sä'dēs-fyûr-dór)	160	65°21'N	14°08'W
Seyhan, r., Tur.	163	37°28'N	35°40'E
Seylac, Som.	238a	11°19'N	43°20'E
Seymour, S. Afr. (sē'môr)	233c	32°33'S	26°48'E
Seymour, Ia., U.S.	113	40°41'N	93°03'W
Seymour, In., U.S. (sē'mōr)	108	38°55'N	85°55'W
Seymour, Tx., U.S.	120	33°35'N	99°16'W
Sezela, S. Afr.	233c	30°33'S	30°37'W
Sezze, Italy (sĕt'så)	174	41°32'N	13°00'E
Sfântu Gheorghe, Rom.	163	45°53'N	25°49'E
Sfax, Tun. (sfäks)	230	34°51'N	10°45'E
's-Gravenhage *see* The Hague, Neth. ('s κrä'vĕn-hä'κĕ) (hāg)	154	52°05'N	4°16'E
Sha, r., China (shä)	205	33°33'N	114°30'E
Shaanxi, prov., China (shän-shyē)	204	35°30'N	109°10'E
Shabeelle (Shebele), r., Afr.	238a	1°38'N	43°50'E
Shache, China (shä-chŭ)	204	38°15'N	77°15'E
Shackleton Ice Shelf, ice, Ant. (shăk''l-tŭn)	224	65°00'S	100°00'E
Shades Creek, r., Al., U.S. (shādz)	110h	33°20'N	86°55'W
Shades Mountain, mtn., Al., U.S.	110h	33°22'N	86°51'W
Shagamu, Nig.	235	6°51'N	3°39'E
Shāhdād, Namakzār-e, l., Iran (nū-mŭk-zär')	198	31°00'N	58°30'E
Shāhjahānpur, India (shä-jŭ-hän'pōōr)	199	27°58'N	79°58'E
Shajing, China (shä-jyĭŋ)	207a	22°44'N	113°48'E
Shaker Heights, Oh., U.S. (shā'kĕr)	111d	41°28'N	81°34'W
Shakhty, Russia (shäκ'tē)	178	47°41'N	40°11'E
Shaki, Nig.	235	8°39'N	3°25'E
Shakopee, Mn., U.S. (shăk'ô-pe)	117g	44°48'N	93°31'W
Shala Lake, l., Eth. (shä'lȧ)	231	7°34'N	39°00'E
Shalqar, Kaz.	183	47°52'N	59°41'E
Shalqar köli, l., Kaz.	181	50°30'N	51°30'E
Shām, Jabal ash, mtn., Oman	198	23°01'N	57°45'E
Shambe, Sudan (shäm'bå)	231	7°08'N	30°46'E
Shammar, Jabal, mts., Sau. Ar. (jĕb'ĕl shŭm'år)	198	27°13'N	40°16'E
Shamokin, Pa., U.S. (shȧ-mō'kĭn)	109	40°45'N	76°30'W
Shamrock, Tx., U.S. (shăm'rŏk)	120	35°14'N	100°12'W
Shamva, Zimb. (shäm'vȧ)	232	17°18'S	31°35'E
Shandon, Oh., U.S. (shăn-dŭn)	111f	39°20'N	84°13'W
Shandong, prov., China (shän-dôŋ)	205	36°08'N	117°09'E
Shandong Bandao, pen., China (shän-dôŋ bän-dou)	205	37°00'N	120°10'E
Shangcai, China (shäŋ-tsī)	206	33°16'N	114°16'E
Shangcheng, China (shäŋ-chŭŋ)	206	31°47'N	115°22'E
Shangdu, China (shäŋ-dōō)	208	41°38'N	113°22'E
Shanghai, China (shäng'hī')	205	31°14'N	121°27'E
Shanghai Shi, prov., China (shäŋ-hī shr)	205	31°30'N	121°45'E
Shanghe, China (shäŋ-hŭ)	206	37°18'N	117°10'E
Shanglin, China (shäŋ-lĭn)	206	38°20'N	116°05'E
Shangqiu, China (shäŋ-chyō)	208	34°24'N	115°39'E
Shangrao, China (shän-rou)	209	28°25'N	117°58'E
Shangzhi, China (shäŋ-jr)	208	45°18'N	127°52'E
Shanhaiguan, China	208	40°01'N	119°45'E
Shannon, Al., U.S. (shăn'ŭn)	110h	33°23'N	86°52'W
Shannon, r., Ire. (shăn'ŏn)	161	52°30'N	10°15'W
Shanshan, China (shän'shän')	204	42°51'N	89°53'E
Shantar, i., Russia (shän'tär)	185	55°13'N	138°42'E
Shantou, China (shän-tō)	205	23°20'N	116°40'E
Shanxi, prov., China (shän-shyē)	205	37°30'N	112°00'E
Shan Xian, China (shän shyĕn)	206	34°47'N	116°04'E
Shaobo, China (shou-bwo)	208	32°33'N	119°30'E
Shaobo Hu, l., China (shou-bwo hōō)	206	32°47'N	119°13'E
Shaoguan, China (shou-gûän)	205	24°58'N	113°42'E
Shaoxing, China (shou-shyĭŋ)	205	30°00'N	120°40'E
Shaoyang, China	205	27°15'N	111°28'E
Shapki, Russia (shäp'kĭ)	186c	59°36'N	31°11'E
Shark Bay, b., Austl. (shärk)	220	25°30'S	113°00'E
Sharon, Ma., U.S. (shăr'ŏn)	101a	42°07'N	71°11'W
Sharon, Pa., U.S.	108	41°15'N	80°30'W
Sharon Springs, Ks., U.S.	120	38°51'N	101°45'W
Sharonville, Oh., U.S. (shăr'ŏn vĭl)	111f	39°16'N	84°24'W
Sharpsburg, Pa., U.S. (shärps'bûrg)	111e	40°30'N	79°54'W
Sharr, Jabal, mtn., Sau. Ar.	198	28°00'N	36°07'E
Shashi, China (shä-shē)	205	30°20'N	112°18'E
Shasta, Mount, mtn., Ca., U.S.	106	41°35'N	122°12'W
Shasta Lake, res., Ca., U.S. (shăs'tȧ)	106	40°51'N	122°32'W
Shatsk, Russia (shȧtsk)	180	54°00'N	41°40'E
Shattuck, Ok., U.S. (shăt'ŭk)	120	36°16'N	99°53'W
Shaunavon, Can.	90	49°40'N	108°25'W
Shaw, Ms., U.S. (shô)	124	33°36'N	90°44'W
Shawano, Wi., U.S. (shȧ-wô'nō)	113	44°41'N	88°13'W
Shawinigan, Can.	91	46°32'N	72°46'W
Shawnee, Ks., U.S. (shô-nē')	117f	39°01'N	94°43'W
Shawnee, Ok., U.S.	104	35°20'N	96°54'W
Shawneetown, Il., U.S. (shô'nē-toun)	108	37°40'N	88°05'W
Shayang, China	209	31°00'N	112°38'E
Shchara, r., Bela. (sh-chå'rå)	169	53°17'N	25°12'E
Shchëlkovo, Russia (shchĕl'kô-vô)	176	55°55'N	38°00'E
Shchigry, Russia (shchē'grē)	177	51°52'N	36°54'E
Shchors, Ukr. (shchôrs)	177	51°38'N	31°58'E
Shchuch'ye Ozero, Russia (shchōōch'yĕ ô'zĕ-rō)	186a	56°31'N	56°35'E
Sheakhala, India	202a	22°47'N	88°10'E
Shebele (Shabeelle), r., Afr. (shā'bå-lē)	238a	6°07'N	43°10'E
Sheboygan, Wi., U.S. (shē-boi'gȧn)	105	43°45'N	87°44'W
Sheboygan Falls, Wi., U.S.	113	43°43'N	87°51'W
Shechem, hist., W.B.	197a	32°15'N	35°22'E
Shedandoah, Pa., U.S.	109	40°50'N	76°15'W
Shediac, Can. (shĕ'dē-ăk)	100	46°13'N	64°32'W
Shedin Peak, mtn., Can. (shĕd'ĭn)	94	55°55'N	127°32'W
Sheerness, Eng., U.K. (shēr'nĕs)	158b	51°26'N	0°46'E
Sheffield, Can.	102d	43°20'N	80°13'W
Sheffield, Eng., U.K.	160	53°23'N	1°28'W
Sheffield, Al., U.S. (shĕf'fēld)	124	35°42'N	87°42'W
Sheffield, Oh., U.S.	111d	41°26'N	82°05'W
Sheffield, co., Eng., U.K.	158a	53°52'N	1°35'W
Sheffield Lake, Oh., U.S.	111d	41°30'N	82°03'W
Sheksna, r., Russia (shĕks'nȧ)	180	59°50'N	38°40'E

ng-sing; ŋ-baŋk; ɴ-nasalized n; nŏd; cŏmmit; ōld; ôbey; ôrder; oi-boil; fōōd; ŏo-as oo in foot; ou-out; s-soft; sh-dish; th-thin; pūre; ûnite; ûrn; stŭd; circŭs; ü-as in French tu; '-indeterminate vowel.

350 Shelagskiy – Silverdale PRONOUNCING INDEX

PLACE (Pronunciation)	PAGE	LAT.	LONG.
Shelagskiy, Mys, c., Russia (shĭ-läg´skē)	179	70°08'N	170°52'E
Shelbina, Ar., U.S. (shĕl-bī´nȧ)	121	39°41'N	92°03'W
Shelburn, In., U.S. (shĕl´bŭrn)	108	39°10'N	87°30'W
Shelburne, Can.	91	43°46'N	65°19'W
Shelburne, Can.	99	44°04'N	80°12'W
Shelby, In., U.S. (shĕl´bē)	111a	41°12'N	87°21'W
Shelby, Mi., U.S.	108	43°35'N	86°20'W
Shelby, Ms., U.S.	124	33°56'N	90°44'W
Shelby, Mt., U.S.	115	48°35'N	111°55'W
Shelby, N.C., U.S.	125	35°16'N	81°35'W
Shelby, Oh., U.S.	108	40°50'N	82°40'W
Shelbyville, Il., U.S. (shĕl´bē-vĭl)	108	39°20'N	88°45'W
Shelbyville, In., U.S.	108	39°30'N	85°45'W
Shelbyville, Ky., U.S.	108	38°10'N	85°15'W
Shelbyville, Tn., U.S.	124	35°30'N	86°28'W
Shelbyville Reservoir, res., Il., U.S.	108	39°30'N	88°45'W
Sheldon, Ia., U.S. (shĕl´dŭn)	112	43°10'N	95°50'W
Sheldon, Tx., U.S.	123a	29°52'N	95°07'W
Shelekhova, Zaliv, b., Russia	179	60°00'N	156°00'E
Shelikof Strait, strt., Ak., U.S. (shĕ´lē-kôf)	103	57°56'N	154°20'W
Shellbrook, Can.	96	53°15'N	106°22'W
Shelley, Id., U.S. (shĕl´lē)	115	43°24'N	112°06'W
Shellrock, r., Ia., U.S. (shĕl´rŏk)	113	43°25'N	93°19'W
Shelon', r., Russia (shâ´lôn)	176	57°50'N	29°40'E
Shelton, Ct., U.S. (shĕl´tŭn)	109	41°15'N	73°05'W
Shelton, Ne., U.S.	120	40°46'N	98°41'W
Shelton, Wa., U.S.	114	47°14'N	123°05'W
Shemakha, Russia (shĕ-mȧ-kä´)	186a	56°16'N	59°19'E
Shenandoah, Ia., U.S. (shĕn-ăn-dō´ȧ)	121	40°46'N	95°23'W
Shenandoah, Va., U.S.	109	38°30'N	78°30'W
Shenandoah, r., Va., U.S.	109	38°55'N	78°05'W
Shenandoah National Park, rec., Va., U.S.	107	38°35'N	78°25'W
Shendam, Nig.	235	8°53'N	9°32'E
Shengfang, China (shengfäng)	206	39°05'N	116°40'E
Shenkursk, Russia (shĕn-kōōrsk´)	178	62°10'N	43°08'E
Shenmu, China	208	38°55'N	110°35'E
Shenqiu, China	208	33°11'N	115°06'E
Shenxian, China (shŭn shyän)	206	38°02'N	115°33'E
Shenxian, China (shŭn shyĕn)	206	36°14'N	115°38'E
Shenyang, China (shŭn-yäŋ)	205	41°45'N	123°22'E
Shenze, China (shŭn-dzŭ)	206	38°12'N	115°12'E
Shenzhen, China	209	22°32'N	114°08'E
Sheopur, India	199	25°37'N	77°10'E
Shepard, Can. (shĕ´pärd)	102e	50°57'N	113°55'W
Shepetivka, Ukr.	181	50°10'N	27°01'E
Shepparton, Austl. (shĕp´ăr-tŭn)	222	36°15'S	145°25'E
Sherborn, Ma., U.S. (shûr´bŭrn)	101a	42°15'N	71°22'W
Sherbrooke, Can.	91	45°24'N	71°54'W
Sherburn, Eng., U.K. (shûr´bŭrn)	158a	53°47'N	1°15'W
Shereshevo, Bela. (shĕ-rĕ-shĕ-vô)	169	52°31'N	24°08'E
Sheridan, Ar., U.S. (shĕr´ĭ-dăn)	121	34°19'N	92°21'W
Sheridan, Or., U.S.	114	45°06'N	123°22'W
Sheridan, Wy., U.S.	104	44°48'N	106°56'W
Sherman, Tx., U.S. (shĕr´măn)	104	33°39'N	96°37'W
Sherna, r., Russia (shĕr´nȧ)	186b	56°08'N	38°45'E
Sherridon, Can.	97	55°10'N	101°10'W
's Hertogenbosch, Neth. (sĕr-tō´ghĕn-bôs)	165	51°41'N	5°19'E
Sherwood, Or., U.S.	116c	45°21'N	122°50'W
Sherwood Forest, for., Eng., U.K.	158a	53°11'N	1°07'W
Sherwood Park, Can.	95	53°31'N	113°19'W
Shetland Islands, is., Scot., U.K. (shĕt´lănd)	156	60°35'N	2°10'W
Shewa Gimira, Eth.	231	7°13'N	35°49'E
Shexian, China (shŭ shyĕn)	206	36°34'N	113°42'E
Sheyang, r., China (she-yäŋ)	206	33°42'N	119°40'E
Sheyenne, r., N.D., U.S. (shī-ĕn´)	112	46°42'N	97°52'W
Shi, r., China (shr)	206	31°58'N	115°50'E
Shi, r., China	206	32°09'N	114°11'E
Shiawassee, r., Mi., U.S. (shī-ȧ-wôs´ē)	108	43°15'N	84°05'W
Shibām, Yemen (shē´bäm)	198	16°02'N	48°40'E
Shibīn al Kawn, Egypt (shē-bēn´ĕl kōm´)	238b	30°31'N	31°01'E
Shibīn al Qanāṭir, Egypt (kȧ-nä´tēr)	238b	30°18'N	31°21'E
Shicun, China (shr-tsòn)	206	33°47'N	117°18'E
Shields, r., Mt., U.S. (shēldz)	115	45°54'N	110°40'W
Shifnal, Eng., U.K. (shĭf´năl)	158a	52°40'N	2°22'W
Shijian, China (shr-jyĕn)	206	31°27'N	117°51'E
Shijiazhuang, China (shr-jyä-jůäŋ)	205	38°04'N	114°31'E
Shijiu Hu, l., China (shr-jyō hōō)	206	31°29'N	119°07'E
Shikārpur, Pak.	199	27°51'N	68°52'E
Shiki, Japan (shē´kē)	211a	35°50'N	139°35'E
Shikoku, i., Japan (shē´kō´kōō)	205	33°43'N	133°33'E
Shilka, r., Russia (shĭl´kȧ)	185	53°00'N	118°45'E
Shilla, mtn., India	202	32°18'N	78°17'E
Shillong, India (shēl-lông´)	199	25°39'N	91°58'E
Shiloh, Il., U.S. (shī´lō)	117e	38°34'N	89°54'W
Shilong, China (shr-lôŋ)	209	23°05'N	113°58'E
Shilou, China	207a	22°58'N	113°29'E
Shimabara, Japan (shē´mä-bä´rä)	211	32°46'N	130°22'E
Shimada, Japan (shē´mä-dä)	211	34°49'N	138°13'E
Shimbiris, mtn., Som.	238a	10°40'N	47°23'E
Shimizu, Japan (shē´mē-zōō)	210	35°00'N	138°29'E
Shimminato, Japan (shēm´mē´nä-tô)	211	36°47'N	137°05'E
Shimoda, Japan (shē´mô-dȧ)	211	34°41'N	138°58'E
Shimoga, India	203	13°59'N	75°38'E
Shimoni, Kenya	237	4°39'S	39°23'E
Shimonoseki, Japan	205	33°58'N	130°55'E
Shimo-Saga, Japan (shē´mô sä´gä)	211b	35°01'N	135°41'E
Shin, Loch, l., Scot., U.K. (lŏk shĭn)	164	58°08'N	4°02'W
Shinagawa-Wan, b., Japan (shē´nä-gä´wä wän)	211a	35°37'N	139°49'E
Shinano-Gawa, r., Japan (shē-nä´nô gä´wä)	211	36°43'N	138°22'E
Shīndand, Afg.	201	33°18'N	62°08'E
Shinji, l., Japan (shĭn´jē)	211	35°23'N	133°05'E
Shinkolobwe, D.R.C.	237	11°02'S	26°35'E
Shinyanga, Tan. (shĭn-yäŋ´gä)	232	3°40'S	33°26'E
Shiono Misaki, c., Japan (shē-ō´nô mē´sä-kē)	210	33°20'N	136°10'E
Shipai, China (shr-pī)	207a	23°07'N	113°23'E
Ship Channel Cay, i., Bah. (shĭp chă-nĕl kē)	134	24°50'N	76°50'W
Shipley, Eng., U.K. (shĭp´lē)	158a	53°50'N	1°47'W
Shippegan, Can. (shĭ´pē-găn)	100	47°45'N	64°42'W
Shippegan Island, i., Can.	100	47°50'N	64°38'W
Shippenburg, Pa., U.S. (shĭp´ĕn bûrg)	109	40°00'N	77°30'W
Shipshaw, r., Can. (shĭp´shô)	99	48°50'N	71°03'W
Shiqma, r., Isr.	197a	31°31'N	34°40'E
Shirane-san, mtn., Japan (shē´rä´nȧ-sän´)	211	35°44'N	138°14'E
Shirati, Tan. (shē-rä´tē)	232	1°15'S	34°02'E
Shīrāz, Iran (shē-räz´)	198	29°32'N	52°27'E
Shire, r., Afr. (shē´rȧ)	232	15°00'S	35°00'E
Shiriya Saki, c., Japan (shē´rä sä´kē)	210	41°25'N	142°10'E
Shirley, Ma., U.S. (shûr´lē)	101a	42°33'N	71°39'W
Shishaldin Volcano, vol., Ak., U.S. (shī-shăl´dĭn)	103a	54°48'N	164°00'W
Shively, Ky., U.S. (shīv´lē)	111h	38°11'N	85°47'W
Shivpuri, India	199	25°31'N	77°46'E
Shivta, Horvot, hist., Isr.	197a	30°54'N	34°36'E
Shivwits Plateau, plat., Az., U.S.	119	36°13'N	113°42'W
Shiwan, China (shr-wän)	207a	23°01'N	113°04'E
Shiwan Dashan, mts., China (shr-wän dä-shän)	209	22°10'N	107°30'E
Shizuki, Japan (shĭ´zōō-kē)	211	34°29'N	134°51'E
Shizuoka, Japan (shē´zōō´ōkȧ)	210	34°58'N	138°24'E
Shklow, Bela.	176	54°11'N	30°23'E
Shkodër, Alb. (shkô´dûr) (skōō´tarē)	154	42°04'N	19°30'E
Shkotovo, Russia (shkô´tô-vô)	210	43°15'N	132°21'E
Shoal Creek, r., Il., U.S. (shōl)	121	38°37'N	89°25'W
Shoal Lake, l., Can.	97	49°32'N	95°00'W
Shoals, In., U.S. (shōlz)	108	38°40'N	86°45'W
Shōdo, i., Japan (shō´dō)	211	34°27'N	134°27'E
Sholāpur, India (shō´lä-pōōr)	199	17°42'N	75°51'E
Shorewood, Wi., U.S. (shōr´wŏŏd)	111a	43°05'N	87°54'W
Shoshone, Id., U.S. (shô-shōn´tē)	115	42°56'N	114°24'W
Shoshone, r., Wy., U.S.	115	44°35'N	108°50'W
Shoshone Lake, l., Wy., U.S.	115	44°17'N	110°50'W
Shoshoni, Wy., U.S.	115	43°14'N	108°05'W
Shostka, Ukr. (shôst´kȧ)	177	51°51'N	33°31'E
Shouguang, China (shō-gůäŋ)	206	36°53'N	118°45'E
Shouxian, China (shō shyĕn)	206	32°36'N	116°45'E
Shpola, Ukr. (shpô´lȧ)	181	49°01'N	31°36'E
Shreveport, La., U.S. (shrēv´pôrt)	105	32°30'N	93°46'W
Shrewsbury, Eng., U.K. (shrōōz´bēr-ĭ)	164	52°43'N	2°44'W
Shrewsbury, Ma., U.S.	101a	42°18'N	71°43'W
Shropshire, co., Eng., U.K.	158a	52°36'N	2°45'W
Shroud Cay, i., Bah.	134	24°20'N	76°40'W
Shuangcheng, China (shůäŋ-chŭŋ)	208	45°18'N	126°18'E
Shuanghe, China (shůäŋ-hŭ)	206	31°33'N	116°48'E
Shuangliao, China	205	43°37'N	123°30'E
Shuangyang, China	208	43°28'N	125°45'E
Shuhedun, China (shōō-hŭ-dòn)	206	31°33'N	117°01'E
Shuiye, China (shwā-yŭ)	206	36°08'N	114°07'E
Shule, r., China (shōō-lŭ)	204	40°53'N	94°55'E
Shullsburg, Wi., U.S. (shŭlz´bûrg)	113	42°35'N	90°16'W
Shumagin, is., Ak., U.S. (shōō´mȧ-gēn)	103	55°22'N	159°20'W
Shumen, Blg.	163	43°15'N	26°54'E
Shunde, China (shòn-dŭ)	207a	22°50'N	113°15'E
Shungnak, Ak., U.S. (shŭng´nak)	103	66°55'N	157°20'W
Shunut, Gora, mtn., Russia (gȧ-rä shōō´nòt)	186a	56°33'N	59°45'E
Shunyi, China (shòn-yē)	206	40°09'N	116°38'E
Shuqrah, Yemen	198	13°32'N	46°02'E
Shūrāb, r., Iran (shōō räb)	198	31°08'N	55°30'E
Shuri, Japan (shōō´rē)	210	26°10'N	127°48'E
Shurugwi, Zimb.	232	19°34'S	30°03'E
Shūshtar, Iran (shōōsh´tŭr)	198	31°50'N	48°46'E
Shuswap Lake, l., Can. (shōōs´wŏp)	95	50°57'N	119°15'W
Shuya, Russia (shōō´yȧ)	178	56°52'N	41°23'E
Shuyang, China (shōō yäng)	206	34°09'N	118°47'E
Shweba, Mya.	199	22°23'N	96°13'E
Shymkent, Kaz.	183	42°17'N	69°42'E
Shyroke, Ukr.	177	47°40'N	33°18'E
Siak Kecil, r., Indon.	197b	1°01'N	101°45'E
Siaksriinderapura, Indon. (sē-äks´rĭ ēn´drȧ-pōō´rȧ)	197b	0°48'N	102°05'E
Siālkot, Pak. (sē-äl´kōt)	199	32°39'N	74°30'E
Siátista, Grc. (syä´tĭs-ta)	175	40°15'N	21°32'E
Siau, Pulau, i., Indon.	213	2°40'N	126°00'E
Šiauliai, Lith. (shē-ou´lē-ī)	180	55°57'N	23°19'E
Sibay, Russia (sē´báy)	186a	52°41'N	58°40'E
Šibenik, Cro. (shē-bā´nĕk)	163	43°44'N	15°55'E
Siberia, reg., Russia	196	57°00'N	97°00'E
Siberut, Pulau, i., Indon. (sē´bȧ-rōōt)	212	1°22'S	99°45'E
Sibiti, Congo (sē-bē-tē´)	232	3°41'S	13°21'E
Sibiu, Rom. (sē-bĭ-ōō´)	163	45°47'N	24°09'E
Sibley, Ia., U.S. (sĭb´lē)	112	43°24'N	95°33'W
Sibolga, Indon. (sē-bō´gä)	212	1°45'N	98°45'E
Sibsāgar, India (sēb-sŭ´gŭr)	199	26°47'N	94°45'E
Sibutu Island, i., Phil.	212	4°40'N	119°30'E
Sibuyan, i., Phil. (sē-bōō-yän´)	213a	12°19'N	122°25'E
Sibuyan Sea, sea, Phil.	212	12°43'N	122°38'E
Sichuan, prov., China (sz-chůän)	204	31°20'N	103°00'E
Sicily, i., Italy (sĭs´ĭ-lē)	156	37°38'N	13°30'E
Sico, r., Hond. (sē-kô)	132	15°32'N	85°42'W
Sidamo, hist. reg., Eth. (sē-dä´mô)	231	5°08'N	37°45'E
Siderno Marina, Italy (sē-dĕr´nô mä-rē´nä)	174	38°18'N	16°19'E
Sídheros, Ákra, c., Grc.	174a	35°19'N	26°20'E
Sidi Aïssa, Alg.	173	35°53'N	3°44'E
Sidi bel Abbès, Alg. (sē´dē-bĕl á-bĕs´)	230	35°15'N	0°43'W
Sidi Ifni, Mor. (ēf´nē)	230	29°22'N	10°15'W
Sidirókastro, Grc.	175	41°13'N	23°27'E
Sidley, Mount, mtn., Ant. (sĭd´lē)	224	77°25'S	129°00'W
Sidney, Can.	94	48°39'N	123°24'W
Sidney, Mt., U.S. (sĭd´nē)	115	47°43'N	104°07'W
Sidney, Ne., U.S.	112	41°10'N	103°00'W
Sidney, Oh., U.S.	108	40°20'N	84°10'W
Sidney Lanier, Lake, res., Ga., U.S. (lăn´yēr)	107	34°27'N	83°56'W
Sido, Mali	234	11°40'N	7°36'W
Sidon *see* Saydā, Leb.	198	33°34'N	35°23'E
Sidr, Wādī, r., Egypt	197a	29°43'N	32°58'E
Sidra, Gulf of *see* Surt, Khalīj, b., Libya	231	31°30'N	18°28'E
Siedlce, Pol. (syĕd´'l-tsĕ)	169	52°09'N	22°20'E
Siegburg, Ger. (zēg´bōōrgh)	168	50°48'N	7°13'E
Siegen, Ger. (zē´ghĕn)	168	50°52'N	8°01'E
Sieghartskirchen, Aus.	159e	48°16'N	16°00'E
Siemiatycze, Pol. (syĕm´yä´tē-chĕ)	169	52°26'N	22°52'E
Siemionówka, Pol. (sĕĕ-mēō´nôf-kä)	169	52°53'N	23°50'E
Siem Reap, Camb. (syĕm´rā´áp)	212	13°32'N	103°54'E
Siena, Italy (sē-ĕn´ä)	162	43°19'N	11°21'E
Sieradz, Pol. (syĕ´rädz)	169	51°35'N	18°45'E
Sierpc, Pol. (syĕrpts)	169	52°51'N	19°42'E
Sierra Blanca, Tx., U.S. (sē-ĕ´rȧ blaŋ-kä)	122	31°10'N	105°20'W
Sierra Blanca Peak, mtn., N.M., U.S. (blăn´kȧ)	106	33°25'N	105°50'W
Sierra Leone, nation, Afr. (sē-ĕr´rä lā-ō´nȧ)	230	8°48'N	12°30'W
Sierra Madre, Ca., U.S. (mä´drē)	117a	34°10'N	118°03'W
Sierra Mojada, Mex. (sē-ĕ´r-rä-mô-κä´dä)	122	27°22'N	103°42'W
Sífnos, i., Grc.	175	36°58'N	24°30'E
Sigean, Fr. (sē-zhôn´)	170	43°02'N	2°56'E
Sigeurney, Ia., U.S. (sē-gûr-nĭ)	113	41°16'N	92°10'W
Sighetu Marmației, Rom.	169	47°57'N	23°55'E
Sighișoara, Rom. (sē-gē-shwä´rȧ)	169	46°11'N	24°48'E
Siglufjördur, Ice.	160	66°06'N	18°45'W
Signakhi, Geor.	181	41°45'N	45°50'E
Signal Hill, Ca., U.S. (sĭg´năl hĭl)	117a	33°48'N	118°11'W
Sigsig, Ec. (sēg-sēg´)	142	3°04'S	78°44'W
Sigtuna, Swe. (sēgh-tōō´nȧ)	166	59°40'N	17°39'E
Siguanea, Ensenada de la, b., Cuba	134	21°45'N	83°15'W
Siguatepeque, Hond. (sē-gwȧ´tĕ-pĕ-kĕ)	132	14°33'N	87°51'W
Sigüenza, Spain (sē-gwĕ´n-zä)	162	41°03'N	2°38'W
Siguiri, Gui. (sē-gē-rē´)	230	11°25'N	9°10'W
Sihong, China (sz-hôŋ)	206	33°25'N	118°13'E
Siirt, Tur. (sĭ-ērt´)	181	38°00'N	42°00'E
Sikalongo, Zam.	237	16°46'S	27°07'E
Sikasso, Mali (sē-käs´sō)	230	11°19'N	5°40'W
Sikeston, Mo., U.S. (sīks´tŭn)	121	36°50'N	89°35'W
Sikhote Alin', Khrebet, mts., Russia (se-κô´ta a-lēn´)	179	45°00'N	135°45'E
Sikinos, i., Grc. (sĭ´kĭ-nōs)	175	36°45'N	24°55'E
Sikkim, state, India	199	27°42'N	88°25'E
Siklós, Hung. (sĭ´klōsh)	169	45°51'N	18°18'E
Sil, r., Spain (sē´l)	172	42°20'N	7°13'W
Silang, Phil. (sē-läng´)	213a	14°14'N	120°58'E
Silao, Mex. (sē-lä´ō)	130	20°56'N	101°25'W
Silchar, India (sĭl-chär´)	199	24°52'N	92°50'E
Silent Valley, S. Afr. (sī´lĕnt vă´lē)	238c	24°32'S	26°40'E
Siler City, N.C., U.S. (sī´lēr)	125	35°45'N	79°29'W
Silesia, hist. reg., Pol. (sĭ-lē´shȧ)	168	50°58'N	16°53'E
Silifke, Tur.	163	36°20'N	34°00'E
Siling Co, l., China	204	32°05'N	89°10'E
Silistra, Blg. (sē-lēs´trȧ)	163	44°01'N	27°13'E
Siljan, l., Swe. (sēl´yän)	160	60°48'N	14°28'E
Silkeborg, Den. (sĭl´kĕ-bôr´)	166	56°10'N	9°33'E
Sillery, Can. (sēl´-re´)	102b	46°46'N	71°15'W
Siloam Springs, Ar., U.S. (sĭ-lōm)	121	36°10'N	94°32'W
Siloana Plains, pl., Zam.	236	16°55'S	23°10'E
Silocayoápan, Mex. (sē-lô-kä-yô-ä´pän)	130	17°29'N	98°09'W
Silsbee, Tx., U.S. (sĭlz´ bē)	123	30°19'N	94°09'W
Šilutė, Lith.	167	55°21'N	21°29'E
Silva Jardim, Braz. (sĕ´l-vä-zhär-dēɴ)	141a	22°40'N	42°24'W
Silvana, Wa., U.S. (sĭ-văn´ȧ)	116a	48°12'N	122°16'W
Silvânia, Braz. (sēl-vá´nyä)	143	16°43'S	48°33'W
Silvassa, India	202	20°10'N	73°00'E
Silver, l., Mo., U.S.	121	39°38'N	93°12'W
Silverado, Ca., U.S. (sĭl-vēr-ä´dō)	117a	33°45'N	117°40'W
Silver Bank, bk.	135	20°40'N	69°40'W
Silver Bank Passage, strt., N.A.	135	20°40'N	70°20'W
Silver Bay, Mn., U.S.	113	47°24'N	91°07'W
Silver City, Pan.	133	9°20'N	79°54'W
Silver City, N.M., U.S. (sĭl´vēr sĭ´tĭ)	119	32°45'N	108°20'W
Silver Creek, N.Y., U.S. (crēk)	109	42°35'N	79°10'W
Silver Creek, r., Az., U.S.	119	34°30'N	110°05'W
Silver Creek, r., In., U.S.	111h	38°20'N	85°45'W
Silver Creek, Muddy Fork, r., In., U.S.	111h	38°26'N	85°52'W
Silverdale, Wa., U.S. (sĭl´vēr-dāl)	116a	49°39'N	122°42'W

ăt; finăl; rāte; senåte; ärm; åsk; sofȧ; fâre; ch-choose; dh-as th in other; bē; ēvent; bĕt; recĕnt; cratẽr; g-gō; gh-guttural g; bĭt; ĭ-short neutral; rīde; κ-guttural k as ch in German ich;

PRONOUNCING INDEX

Silver Lake – Soest 351

PLACE (Pronunciation)	PAGE	LAT.	LONG.
Silver Lake, Wi., U.S. (lăk)	111a	42°33'N	88°10'W
Silver Lake, l., Wi., U.S.	111a	42°35'N	88°08'W
Silver Spring, Md., U.S. (spring)	110e	39°00'N	77°00'W
Silver Star Mountain, mtn., Wa., U.S.	116c	45°45'N	122°15'W
Silverthrone Mountain, mtn., Can. (sĭl'vẽr-thrōn)	94	51°31'N	126°06'W
Silverton, S. Afr.	238c	25°45'S	28°13'E
Silverton, Co., U.S. (sĭl'vẽr-tŭn)	119	37°50'N	107°40'W
Silverton, Oh., U.S.	111f	39°12'N	84°24'W
Silverton, Or., U.S.	114	45°02'N	122°46'W
Silves, Port. (sĕl'vĕzh)	162	37°15'N	8°24'W
Silvies, r., Or., U.S. (sĭl'vēz)	114	43°44'N	119°15'W
Sim, Russia (sĭm)	186a	55°00'N	57°42'E
Sim, r., Russia	186a	54°50'N	56°50'E
Simao, China (sz-mou)	204	22°56'N	101°07'E
Simard, Lac, l., Can.	99	47°38'N	78°40'W
Simba, D.R.C.	236	0°36'N	22°55'E
Simcoe, Can. (sĭm'kō)	164	42°50'N	80°20'W
Simcoe, l., Can.	93	44°30'N	79°20'W
Simeulue, Pulau, i., Indon.	212	2°27'N	95°30'E
Simferopol', Ukr.	178	44°58'N	34°04'E
Similk Beach, Wa., U.S. (sē'mĭlk)	116a	48°27'N	122°35'W
Simla, India (sĭm'là)	199	31°09'N	77°15'E
Şimleu Silvaniei, Rom.	163	47°14'N	22°46'E
Simms Point, c., Bah.	134	25°00'N	77°40'W
Simojovel, Mex. (sē-mō-hō-vĕl')	131	17°12'N	92°43'W
Simonésia, Braz. (sē-mō-nĕ'syä)	141a	20°04'S	41°53'W
Simonette, r., Can. (sī-mŏn-ĕt')	95	54°15'N	118°00'W
Simonstad, S. Afr.	232a	34°11'S	18°25'E
Simood Sound, Can.	94	50°45'N	126°25'W
Simplon Pass, p., Switz. (sĭm'plŏn) (săn-plôn')	168	46°13'N	7°53'E
Simpson, i., Can.	113	48°43'N	87°44'W
Simpson Desert, des., Austl. (sĭmp-sŭn)	220	24°40'S	136°40'E
Simrishamn, Swe. (sēm'rēs-häm'n)	166	55°35'N	14°19'E
Sims Bayou, Tx., U.S. (sĭmz bī-yōō')	123a	29°37'N	95°23'W
Simushir, i., Russia (se-mōō'shēr)	205	47°15'N	150°47'E
Sinaia, Rom. (sĭ-nä'yȧ)	175	45°20'N	25°30'E
Sinai Peninsula, pen., Egypt (sī'nī)	231	29°24'N	33°29'E
Sinaloa, state, Mex. (sē-nä-lô-ä)	128	25°15'N	107°45'W
Sinan, China (sz-nän)	204	27°50'N	108°30'E
Sinanju, Kor., N. (sĭ'nän-jŏ')	210	39°39'N	125°41'E
Sincelejo, Col. (sēn-sā-lā'hō)	142	9°12'N	75°30'W
Sinclair Inlet, Wa., U.S. (sĭn-klâr')	116a	47°31'N	122°41'W
Sinclair Mills, Can.	95	54°02'N	121°41'W
Sindi, Est. (sēn'dē)	167	58°20'N	24°40'E
Sines, Port. (sē'nȧzh)	172	37°57'N	8°50'W
Singapore, Sing. (sĭn'gȧ-pōr')	212	1°18'N	103°52'E
Singapore, nation, Asia	212	1°22'N	103°45'E
Singapore Strait, strt., Asia	197b	1°14'N	104°20'E
Singu, Mya. (sĭn'gŭ)	204	22°37'N	96°04'E
Siniye Lipyagi, Russia (sēn'ê lēp'yä-gê)	177	51°24'N	38°29'E
Sinj, Cro. (sēn')	174	43°42'N	16°39'E
Sinjah, Sudan	231	13°09'N	33°52'E
Sinkāt, Sudan	200	18°50'N	36°50'E
Sinkiang *see* Xinjiang, prov., China	204	40°15'N	82°15'E
Sin'kovo, Russia (sĭn-kô'vô)	186b	56°23'N	37°19'E
Sinnamary, Fr. Gu.	143	5°15'N	52°52'W
Sinni, r., Italy (sēn'nē)	174	40°05'N	16°15'E
Sinnūris, Egypt	238b	29°25'N	30°52'E
Sino, Pedra de, mtn., Braz. (pĕ'drä-dô-sē'nô)	144b	22°27'S	43°02'W
Sinop, Tur.	198	42°00'N	35°05'E
Sint Eustatius, i., Neth. Ant.	133b	17°32'N	62°45'W
Sint Niklaas, Bel.	159a	51°10'N	4°07'E
Sinton, Tx., U.S. (sĭn'tŭn)	123	28°03'N	97°30'W
Sintra, Port. (sēn'trȧ)	172	38°48'N	9°23'W
Sint Truiden, Bel.	159a	50°49'N	5°14'E
Sinŭiju, Kor., N. (sĭ'nōī-jōō)	205	40°04'N	124°33'E
Sinyavino, Russia (sĭn-yä'vĭ-nô)	186c	59°50'N	31°07'E
Sinyaya, r., Eur. (sēn'yȧ-yȧ)	176	56°40'N	28°20'E
Sion, Switz. (sē'ôn')	168	46°15'N	7°17'E
Sioux City, Ia., U.S. (sōō sĭ'tĭ)	104	42°30'N	96°25'W
Sioux Falls, S.D., U.S. (fôlz)	104	43°33'N	96°43'W
Sioux Lookout, Can.	91	50°06'N	91°55'W
Siping, China (sz-pĭŋ)	205	43°05'N	124°24'E
Sipiwesk, Can.	90	55°27'N	97°24'W
Sipsey, r., Al., U.S. (sĭp'sē)	124	33°26'N	87°42'W
Sipura, Pulau, i., Indon.	212	2°15'S	99°33'E
Siqueros, Mex. (sē-kā'rōs)	130	23°19'N	106°14'W
Siquia, Río, r., Nic. (sē-kē'ä)	133	12°23'N	84°36'W
Siracusa, Italy (sē-rä-koo'sä)	163	37°02'N	15°19'E
Sirājganj, Bngl. (sĭ-räj'gŭnj)	199	24°23'N	89°43'E
Sirama, El Sal. (Sē-rä-mä)	132	13°23'N	87°55'W
Sir Douglas, Mount, mtn., Can. (sûr dŭg'lăs)	95	50°44'N	115°20'W
Sir Edward Pellew Group, is., Austl. (pĕl'ū)	220	15°15'S	137°15'E
Siret, Rom.	169	47°58'N	26°01'E
Siret, r., Eur.	163	47°00'N	27°00'E
Sirhān, Wadi, depr., Sau. Ar.	198	31°02'N	37°16'E
Sirsa, India	202	29°39'N	75°02'E
Sir Sandford, Mount, mtn., Can. (sûr sănd'fẽrd)	95	51°40'N	117°52'W
Sirvintos, Lith. (shēr'vĭn-tôs)	167	55°02'N	24°59'E
Sir Wilfrid Laurier, Mount, mtn., Can. (sûr wĭl'frĭd lôr'yẽr)	95	52°47'N	119°45'W
Sisak, Cro. (sē'sȧk)	163	45°29'N	16°20'E
Sisal, Mex. (sē-säl')	128	21°09'N	90°03'W
Sishui, China (sz-shwā)	206	35°40'N	117°17'E
Sisquoc, r., Ca., U.S. (sĭs'kwŏk)	118	34°47'N	120°13'W
Sisseton, S.D., U.S. (sĭs'tŭn)	112	45°39'N	97°04'W
Sistān, Daryacheh-ye, l., Asia	198	31°45'N	61°15'E
Sisteron, Fr. (sēst'rôn')	171	44°10'N	5°55'E
Sistersville, W.V., U.S. (sĭs'tẽr-vĭl)	108	39°30'N	81°00'W
Sitía, Grc. (sē'tĭ-ȧ)	174a	35°09'N	26°10'E
Sitka, Ak., U.S. (sĭt'kȧ)	106a	57°08'N	135°18'W
Sittingbourne, Eng., U.K. (sĭt-ĭng-bôrn)	158b	51°20'N	0°44'E
Sittwe, Mya.	199	20°09'N	92°54'E
Sivas, Tur. (sē'väs)	198	39°50'N	36°50'E
Siverek, Tur. (sē'vĕ-rĕk)	198	37°50'N	39°20'E
Siverskaya, Russia (sē'vẽr-skȧ-yȧ)	167	59°17'N	30°03'E
Sivers'kyi Donets', r., Eur.	177	48°48'N	38°42'E
Sīwah, Egypt	200	29°12'N	25°31'E
Siwah, oasis, Egypt (sē'wä)	231	29°33'N	25°11'E
Sixaola, r., C.R.	133	9°31'N	83°07'W
Sixian, China (sz shyĕn)	206	33°37'N	117°51'E
Sixth Cataract, wtfl., Sudan	231	16°26'N	32°44'E
Siyang, China (sz-yäŋ)	206	33°43'N	118°42'E
Sjaelland, i., Den. (shĕl'lăn')	166	55°34'N	11°35'E
Sjenica, Serb. (syĕ'nê-tsȧ)	175	43°15'N	20°02'E
Skadovs'k, Ukr.	177	46°08'N	32°54'E
Skagen, Den. (skä'ghĕn)	166	57°43'N	10°32'E
Skagerrak, strt., Eur. (skä-ghĕ-räk')	156	57°43'N	8°28'E
Skagit, r., Wa., U.S.	114	48°29'N	121°52'W
Skagit Bay, b., Wa., U.S. (skăg'ĭt)	116a	48°20'N	122°32'W
Skagway, Ak., U.S. (skăg-wā)	106a	59°30'N	135°28'W
Skälderviken, b., Swe.	166	56°20'N	12°25'E
Skalistyy, Golets, mtn., Russia	179	57°28'N	119°48'E
Skalistyy Khrebet, mts., Russia	182	43°15'N	43°00'E
Skamania, Wa., U.S. (skȧ-mā'nĭ-ȧ)	116c	45°37'N	112°03'W
Skamokawa, Wa., U.S.	116c	46°16'N	123°27'W
Skanderborg, Den. (skän-ẽr-bôr')	166	56°04'N	9°55'E
Skaneateles, N.Y., U.S. (skăn-ĕ-ăt'lĕs)	109	42°55'N	76°25'W
Skaneateles, l., N.Y., U.S.	109	42°50'N	76°20'W
Skänninge, Swe. (shĕn'ĭng-ĕ)	166	58°24'N	15°02'E
Skanör-Falseterbo, Swe. (skän'ûr)	166	55°24'N	12°49'E
Skara, Swe. (skä'rȧ)	166	58°25'N	13°24'E
Skeena, r., Can. (skē'nä)	92	54°30'N	129°00'W
Skeena Mountains, mts., Can.	94	56°00'N	128°00'W
Skeerpoort, S. Afr.	233b	25°49'S	27°45'E
Skeerpoort, r., S. Afr.	233b	25°58'S	27°41'E
Skeldon, Guy. (skĕl'dŭn)	143	5°49'N	57°15'W
Skellefteå, Swe. (shĕl'ĕf-tĕ-a')	160	64°47'N	20°48'E
Skellefteälven, r., Swe.	160	65°15'N	19°30'E
Skhodnya, Russia (skôd'nyȧ)	186b	55°57'N	37°21'E
Skhodnya, r., Russia	186b	55°55'N	37°16'E
Skíathos, i., Grc. (skē'ȧ-thôs)	175	39°15'N	23°25'E
Skibbereen, Ire. (skĭb'ẽr-ēn)	164	51°32'N	9°25'W
Skidegate, b., Can. (skĭ'-dĕ-gāt')	94	53°15'N	132°00'W
Skidmore, Tx., U.S. (skĭd'môr)	123	28°16'N	97°40'W
Skien, Nor. (skē'ĕn)	160	59°13'N	9°35'E
Skierniewice, Pol. (skyẽr-nyĕ-vēt'sĕ)	169	51°58'N	20°13'E
Skihist Mountain, mtn., Can.	95	50°11'N	121°54'W
Skikda, Alg.	230	36°58'N	6°51'E
Skilpadfontein, S. Afr.	238c	25°02'S	28°50'E
Skive, Den. (skē'vĕ)	166	56°34'N	8°56'E
Skjálfandafljót, r., Ice. (skyäl'fănd-ô)	160	65°24'N	16°40'W
Skjerstad, Nor. (skyĕr-städ)	160	67°12'N	15°37'E
Škofja Loka, Slvn. (shkôf'yȧ lō'kȧ)	174	46°10'N	14°20'E
Skokie, Il., U.S. (skō'kê)	111a	42°02'N	87°45'W
Skokomish Indian Reservation, I.R., Wa., U.S. (Skō-kō'mĭsh)	116a	47°22'N	123°07'W
Skole, Ukr. (skô'lĕ)	169	49°03'N	23°32'E
Skópelos, i., Grc. (skô'pȧ-lôs)	175	39°04'N	23°31'E
Skopin, Russia (skô'pĕn)	180	53°49'N	39°35'E
Skopje, Mac. (skôp'yĕ)	174	42°02'N	21°26'E
Skövde, Swe. (shûv'dĕ)	160	58°25'N	13°48'E
Skovorodino, Russia (skô'vô-rô'dĭ-nô)	179	53°53'N	123°56'E
Skowhegan, Me., U.S. (skou-hē'găn)	100	44°45'N	69°27'W
Skradin, Cro. (skrä'dĕn)	175	43°49'N	17°58'E
Skreia, Nor. (skrā'ȧ)	166	60°40'N	10°55'E
Skudeneshavn, Nor. (skōō'dĕ-nes-houn')	166	59°10'N	5°19'E
Skull Valley Indian Reservation, I.R., Ut., U.S. (skŭl)	119	40°25'N	112°50'W
Skuna, r., Ms., U.S. (skû'nȧ)	124	33°57'N	89°36'W
Skunk, r., Ia., U.S. (skŭnk)	113	41°12'N	92°14'W
Skuodas, Lith. (skwô'dȧs)	167	56°16'N	21°32'E
Skurup, Swe. (skû'rŏp)	166	55°29'N	13°27'E
Skvyra, Ukr.	181	49°43'N	29°41'E
Skwierzyna, Pol. (skvē-ẽr'zhĭ-nȧ)	168	52°35'N	15°30'E
Skye, Island of, i., Scot., U.K. (skī)	160	57°25'N	6°17'W
Skykomish, r., Wa., U.S. (skī'kō-mĭsh)	116a	47°50'N	121°55'W
Skyring, Seno de, b., Chile (sĕ'nô-s-krĕ'ng)	144	52°35'S	72°30'W
Skýros, Grc.	175	38°53'N	24°32'E
Skýros, i., Grc.	163	38°50'N	24°43'E
Slagese, Den.	166	55°25'N	11°19'E
Slamet, Gunung, mtn., Indon. (slä'mĕt)	212	7°15'S	109°15'E
Slănic, Rom. (slŭ'nêk)	175	45°13'N	25°56'E
Slater, Mo., U.S. (slāt'ẽr)	121	39°13'N	93°03'W
Slatina, Rom. (slä'tē-nä)	175	44°26'N	24°21'E
Slaton, Tx., U.S. (slā'tŭn)	120	33°26'N	101°38'W
Slave, r., Can. (slāv)	92	59°40'N	111°21'W
Slavgorod, Russia (slàf'gô-rôt)	178	52°58'N	78°43'E
Slavonija, hist. reg., Serb. (slä-vô'nê-yä)	175	45°29'N	17°31'E
Slavonska Požega, Cro. (slä-vôn'skä pô'zhĕ-gä)	175	45°18'N	17°42'E
Slavonski Brod, Cro. (skä-vôn'skê brôd)	163	45°10'N	18°01'E
Slavuta, Ukr. (slȧ-vōō'tȧ)	177	50°18'N	27°01'E
Slavyanskaya, Russia (slȧv-yȧn'skȧ-yȧ)	177	45°14'N	38°09'E
Sławno, Pol. (swav'nō)	168	54°21'N	16°38'E
Slayton, Mn., U.S. (slā'tŭn)	112	44°00'N	95°44'W
Sleaford, Eng., U.K. (slē'fẽrd)	158a	53°00'N	0°25'W
Sleepy Eye, Mn., U.S. (slēp'ĭ ī)	113	44°17'N	94°44'W
Slidell, La., U.S. (slī-dĕl')	123	30°17'N	89°47'W
Sliedrecht, Neth.	159a	51°49'N	4°46'E
Sligo, Ire. (slī'gō)	160	54°17'N	8°19'W
Slite, Swe. (slē'tĕ)	166	57°41'N	18°47'E
Sliven, Blg. (slē'vĕn)	163	42°41'N	26°20'E
Sloatsburg, N.Y., U.S. (slōts'bŭrg)	110a	41°09'N	74°11'W
Slonim, Bela. (swō'nêm)	169	53°05'N	25°19'E
Slough, Eng., U.K. (slou)	158b	51°29'N	0°36'W
Slovakia, nation, Eur.	169	48°50'N	20°00'E
Slovenia, nation, Eur.	174	45°58'N	14°43'E
Slovians'k, Ukr.	181	48°52'N	37°34'E
Sluch, r., Ukr.	181	50°56'N	26°48'E
Slunj, Cro. (slòn')	174	45°08'N	15°46'E
Słupsk, Pol. (swòpsk)	160	54°28'N	17°02'E
Slutsk, Bela. (slòtsk)	180	53°02'N	27°34'E
Slyne Head, c., Ire. (slīn)	160	53°25'N	10°05'W
Smackover, Ar., U.S. (smăk'ô-vẽr)	121	33°22'N	92°42'W
Smederevo, Serb.	175	44°39'N	20°54'E
Smederevska Palanka, Serb. (smĕ-dĕ-rĕv'skä pä-län'kä)	175	44°21'N	21°00'E
Smedjebacken, Swe. (smĭ'tyĕ-bä-kĕn)	166	60°09'N	15°19'E
Smethport, Pa., U.S. (smĕth'pōrt)	109	41°50'N	78°25'W
Smethwick, Eng., U.K.	164	52°31'N	2°04'W
Smila, Ukr.	181	49°14'N	31°52'E
Smile, Ukr.	177	50°55'N	33°36'E
Smiltene, Lat. (smēl'tĕ-nĕ)	167	57°26'N	25°57'E
Smith, Can. (smĭth)	90	55°10'N	114°02'W
Smith, i., Wa., U.S.	116a	48°20'N	122°53'W
Smith, r., Mt., U.S.	115	47°00'N	111°20'W
Smith Center, Ks., U.S. (sĕn'tẽr)	120	39°45'N	98°46'W
Smithers, Can. (smĭth'ẽrs)	90	54°47'N	127°10'W
Smithfield, N.C., U.S. (smĭth'fēld)	125	35°30'N	78°21'W
Smithfield, Ut., U.S.	115	41°50'N	111°49'W
Smithland, Ky., U.S. (smĭth'lănd)	108	37°10'N	88°25'W
Smith Mountain Lake, res., Va., U.S.	125	37°00'N	79°45'W
Smith Point, Tx., U.S.	123a	29°32'N	94°45'W
Smiths Falls, Can. (smĭths)	91	44°55'N	76°05'W
Smithton, Austl. (smĭth'tŭn)	222	40°55'S	145°12'E
Smithton, Il., U.S.	117e	38°24'N	89°59'W
Smithville, Tx., U.S. (smĭth'vĭl)	123	30°00'N	97°08'W
Smitswinkelvlakte, pl., S. Afr.	232a	34°16'S	18°25'E
Smoke Creek Desert, des., Nv., U.S. (smōk crēk)	118	40°28'N	119°40'W
Smoky, r., Can. (smōk'ĭ)	95	55°30'N	117°30'W
Smoky Hill, r., U.S. (smōk'ĭ hĭl)	106	38°40'N	100°00'W
Smøla, i., Nor. (smûlä)	160	63°16'N	7°40'E
Smolensk, Russia (smô-lyĕnsk')	178	54°46'N	32°03'E
Smolensk, prov., Russia	176	55°00'N	32°18'E
Smyadovo, Blg.	175	43°04'N	27°00'E
Smyrna *see* İzmir, Tur.	198	38°25'N	27°05'E
Smyrna, De., U.S. (smûr'nȧ)	109	39°20'N	75°35'W
Smyrna, Ga., U.S.	110c	33°53'N	84°31'W
Snag, Can. (snăg)	103	62°18'N	140°30'W
Snake, r., Mn., U.S. (snāk)	113	45°58'N	93°20'W
Snake, r., U.S.	106	45°30'N	117°00'W
Snake Range, mts., Nv., U.S.	119	39°20'N	114°15'W
Snake River Plain, pl., Id., U.S.	115	43°08'N	114°46'W
Snap Point, c., Bah.	134	23°45'N	77°30'W
Sneffels, Mount, mtn., Co., U.S. (snĕf'ĕlz)	119	38°00'N	107°50'W
Snelgrove, Can. (snĕl'grōv)	102d	43°44'N	79°50'W
Sniardwy, Jezioro, l., Pol. (snyärt'vĭ)	169	53°46'N	21°59'E
Snöhetta, mtn., Nor. (snû-hĕttä)	160	62°18'N	9°12'E
Snohomish, Wa., U.S. (snô-hō'mĭsh)	116a	47°55'N	122°05'W
Snohomish, r., Wa., U.S.	116a	47°53'N	122°04'W
Snoqualmie, Wa., U.S. (snō qwäl'mē)	116a	47°32'N	121°50'W
Snoqualmie, r., Wa., U.S.	114	47°32'N	121°53'W
Snov, r., Eur. (snôf)	177	51°38'N	31°38'E
Snowdon, mtn., Wales, U.K.	164	53°05'N	4°04'W
Snow Hill, Md., U.S. (hĭl)	109	38°15'N	75°20'W
Snow Lake, Can.	97	54°50'N	100°10'W
Snowy Mountains, mts., Austl. (snō'ē)	221	36°17'S	148°30'E
Snyder, Ok., U.S. (snī'dẽr)	120	34°40'N	98°57'W
Snyder, Tx., U.S.	122	32°48'N	100°53'W
Soar, r., Eng., U.K. (sōr)	158a	52°44'N	1°09'W
Sobat, r., Sudan (sō'bȧt)	231	9°04'N	32°02'E
Sobinka, Russia (sô-bĭŋ'kȧ)	176	55°59'N	40°02'E
Sobo Zan, mtn., Japan (sō'bô zän)	210	32°47'N	131°27'E
Sobral, Braz. (sô-brä'l)	143	3°39'S	40°16'W
Sochaczew, Pol. (sô-ĸä'chĕf)	169	52°14'N	20°18'E
Sochi, Russia (sôch'ĭ)	178	43°35'N	39°50'E
Society Islands, is., Fr. Poly. (sô-sī'ĕ-tē)	241	15°00'S	157°30'W
Socoltenango, Mex. (sô-kôl-tĕ-näŋ'gō)	131	16°17'N	92°20'W
Socorro, Braz. (sô-kō'r-rō)	141a	22°35'S	46°32'W
Socorro, Col. (sô-kôr'rō)	142	6°23'N	73°19'W
Socorro, N.M., U.S.	119	34°05'N	106°55'W
Socúellamos, Spain (sô-kōō-āl'yä-môs)	172	39°18'N	2°48'W
Soda, l., Ca., U.S. (sō'dȧ)	118	35°12'N	116°25'W
Soda Peak, mtn., Wa., U.S.	116c	45°53'N	122°04'W
Soda Springs, Id., U.S. (springz)	115	42°39'N	111°37'W
Söderhamn, Swe. (sû-dẽr-häm''n)	166	61°20'N	17°00'E
Söderköping, Swe.	166	58°30'N	16°14'E
Södertälje, Swe. (sû-dẽr-tĕl'yĕ)	160	59°12'N	17°35'E
Sodo, Eth.	231	7°03'N	37°46'E
Soest, Ger. (zōst)	168	51°35'N	8°05'E

352 Sofia – Spas-Klepiki PRONOUNCING INDEX

PLACE (Pronunciation)	PAGE	LAT.	LONG.
Sofia (Sofiya), Blg. (sô'fē-yà) (sô'fē-à)	154	42°43'N	23°20'E
Sofiïvka, Ukr.	177	48°03'N	33°53'E
Sofiya *see* Sofia, Blg.	154	42°43'N	23°20'E
Soga, Japan (sō'gä)	211a	35°35'N	140°08'E
Sogamoso, Col. (sô-gä-mō'sō)	142	5°42'N	72°51'W
Sognafjorden, b., Nor.	156	61°09'N	5°30'E
Sogozha, r., Russia (sô'gô-zhà)	176	58°35'N	39°08'E
Sohano, Pap. N. Gui.	214e	5°27'S	154°40'E
Soissons, Fr. (swä-sôN')	170	49°23'N	3°17'E
Sōka, Japan (sō'kä)	211a	35°50'N	139°49'E
Sokal', Ukr. (sô'käl')	169	50°28'N	24°20'E
Söke, Tur. (sû'kĕ)	163	37°40'N	27°10'E
Sokółka, Pol. (sô-kōl'kà)	169	53°23'N	23°30'E
Sokolo, Mali (sô-kô-lō')	230	14°51'N	6°09'W
Sokołów Podlaski, Pol. (sô-kô-wôf' pŭd-lä'skĭ)	169	52°24'N	22°15'E
Sokone, Sen.	234	13°53'N	16°22'W
Sokoto, Nig. (sō'kô-tō)	230	13°04'N	5°16'E
Sola de Vega, Mex.	131	16°31'N	96°58'W
Solander, Cape, c., Austl.	217b	34°03'S	151°16'E
Solano, Phil. (sō-lä'nō)	213a	16°31'N	121°11'E
Soledad, Col. (sō-lĕ-dä'd)	142	10°47'N	75°00'W
Soledad Díez Gutiérrez, Mex.	130	22°19'N	100°54'W
Soleduck, r., Wa., U.S. (sōl'dŭk)	114	47°59'N	124°28'W
Solentiname, Islas de, is., Nic. (ē's-läs-dĕ-sô-lĕn-tē-nä'mà)	132	11°15'N	85°16'W
Solihull, Eng., U.K. (sō'lĭ-hŭl)	158a	52°25'N	1°46'W
Solihull, co., Eng., U.K.	158a	52°25'N	1°42'W
Solikamsk, Russia (sô-lē-kàmsk')	180	59°38'N	56°48'E
Sol'-Iletsk, Russia	178	51°10'N	55°05'E
Solimões *see* Amazon, r., Braz.	142	2°45'S	67°44'W
Solingen, Ger. (zō'lĭng-ĕn)	168	51°10'N	7°05'E
Söller, Spain (sō'lyĕr)	173	39°45'N	2°40'E
Sologne, reg., Fr. (sō-lôn'yĕ)	170	47°36'N	1°53'E
Solola, Guat. (sô-lō'lä)	132	14°45'N	91°12'W
Solomon, r., Ks., U.S.	120	39°24'N	98°19'W
Solomon, North Fork, r., Ks., U.S.	120	39°34'N	99°52'W
Solomon, South Fork, r., Ks., U.S.	120	39°19'N	99°52'W
Solomon Islands, nation, Oc. (sŏ'lō-mŭn)	3	7°00'S	160°00'E
Solon, China (swo-lōōn)	205	46°32'N	121°18'E
Solon, Oh., U.S. (sō'lŭn)	111d	41°23'N	81°26'W
Solothurn, Switz. (zō'lō-thōōrn)	168	47°13'N	7°30'E
Solovetskiye Ostrova, is., Russia	180	65°10'N	35°40'E
Šolta, i., Serb. (shôl'tä)	174	43°20'N	16°15'E
Soltau, Ger. (sōl'tou)	168	53°00'N	9°50'E
Sol'tsy, Russia (sôl'tsē)	176	58°04'N	30°13'E
Solvay, N.Y., U.S. (sŏl'vā)	109	43°05'N	76°10'W
Sölvesborg, Swe. (sûl'vĕs-bôrg)	166	56°04'N	14°35'E
Sol'vychegodsk, Russia (sôl'vē-chĕ-gôtsk')	180	61°18'N	46°58'E
Solway Firth, b., U.K. (sŏl'wāfûrth')	160	54°42'N	3°55'W
Solwezi, Zam.	237	12°11'S	26°25'E
Soly, Bela.	166	54°31'N	26°11'E
Somalia, nation, Afr. (sō-mä'lē-ă)	238a	3°28'N	44°47'E
Somanga, Tan.	237	8°24'S	39°17'E
Sombor, Serb. (sôm'bôr)	163	45°45'N	19°10'E
Sombrerete, Mex. (sōm-brå-rā'tå)	130	23°38'N	103°37'W
Sombrero, Cayo, i., Ven. (kä-yô-sôm-brĕ'rô)	143b	10°52'N	68°12'W
Somerset, Ky., U.S. (sŭm'ĕr-sĕt)	124	37°05'N	84°35'W
Somerset, Ma., U.S.	110b	41°46'N	71°05'W
Somerset, Pa., U.S.	109	40°00'N	79°05'W
Somerset, Tx., U.S.	117d	29°13'N	98°39'W
Somerset East, S. Afr.	233c	32°44'S	25°36'E
Somersworth, N.H., U.S. (sŭm'ĕrz-wûrth)	100	43°16'N	70°53'W
Somerton, Az., U.S. (sŭm'ĕr-tŭn)	119	32°36'N	114°43'W
Somerville, Ma., U.S. (sŭm'ĕr-vĭl)	101a	42°23'N	71°06'W
Somerville, N.J., U.S.	110a	40°34'N	74°37'W
Somerville, Tn., U.S.	124	35°14'N	89°21'W
Somerville, Tx., U.S.	123	30°21'N	96°31'W
Someș, r., Eur.	169	47°43'N	23°09'E
Somma Vesuviana, Italy (sôm'mä vā-zōō-vē-ä'nä)	173c	40°38'N	14°27'E
Somme, r., Fr. (sŏm)	170	50°02'N	2°04'E
Sommerfeld, Ger. (zō'mĕr-fĕld)	159b	52°48'N	13°02'E
Sommerville, Austl.	217a	38°14'S	145°10'E
Somoto, Nic. (sô-mō'tō)	132	13°28'N	86°37'W
Son, r., India (sōn)	199	24°40'N	82°35'E
Sŏnchŏn, Kor., N. (sŭn'shŭn)	210	39°49'N	124°56'E
Sondags, r., S. Afr.	233c	33°17'S	25°14'E
Sønderborg, Den. (sûn''er-bôrgh)	160	54°55'N	9°47'E
Sondershausen, Ger. (zōn'dĕrz-hou'zĕn)	168	51°17'N	10°45'E
Song Ca, r., Viet.	209	19°15'N	105°00'E
Songea, Tan. (sôn-gā'ä)	232	10°41'S	35°39'E
Songjiang, China	205	31°01'N	121°14'E
Sŏngjin, Kor., N. (sŭng'jĭn')	210	40°38'N	129°10'E
Songkhla, Thai. (sông'klä')	212	7°09'N	100°34'E
Songwe, D.R.C.	237	12°25'S	29°40'E
Sonneberg, Ger. (sôn'ĕ-bĕrgh)	168	50°20'N	11°14'E
Sonora, Ca., U.S. (sô-nō'rá)	118	37°58'N	120°22'W
Sonora, Tx., U.S.	122	30°33'N	100°38'W
Sonora, state, Mex.	128	29°45'N	111°15'W
Sonora, r., Mex.	128	28°45'N	111°35'W
Sonora Peak, mtn., Ca., U.S.	106	38°22'N	119°39'W
Sonseca, Spain (sôn-sā'kä)	172	39°41'N	3°56'W
Sonsón, Col. (sôn-sôn')	142	5°42'N	75°28'W
Sonsonate, El Sal. (sōn-sô-nä'tå)	132	13°46'N	89°43'W
Sonsorol Islands, is., Palau (sŏn-sô-rōl')	213	5°03'N	132°33'E
Sooke Basin, b., Can. (sŏok)	116a	48°21'N	123°47'W
Soo Locks, trans., Mi., U.S. (sōō lŏks)	117a	46°30'N	84°30'W
Sopetrán, Col. (sô-pĕ-trä'n)	142a	6°30'N	75°44'W
Sopot, Pol. (sô'pôt)	169	54°26'N	18°25'E
Sopron, Hung. (shŏp'rôn)	163	47°41'N	16°36'E
Sora, Italy (sō'rä)	174	41°43'N	13°37'E
Sorbas, Spain (sôr'bäs)	172	37°05'N	2°07'W
Sordo, r., Mex. (sô'r-dō)	131	16°39'N	97°33'W
Sorel, Can. (sô-rĕl')	91	46°01'N	73°07'W
Sorell, Cape, c., Austl.	222	42°10'S	144°50'E
Soresina, Italy (sō-rå-zē'nä)	174	45°17'N	9°51'E
Soria, Spain (sō'rē-ä)	162	41°46'N	2°28'W
Soriano, dept., Ur. (sô-rēä'nô)	141c	33°25'S	58°00'W
Soroca, Mol.	181	48°09'N	28°17'E
Sorocaba, Braz. (sô-rô-kä'bá)	143	23°29'S	47°27'W
Sorong, Indon. (sō-rông')	213	1°00'S	131°20'E
Sorot', r., Russia (sō-rō'tzh)	176	57°08'N	29°23'E
Soroti, Ug. (sō-rō'tē)	231	1°43'N	33°37'E
Sørøya, i., Nor.	160	70°37'N	20°58'E
Sorraia, r., Port. (sôr-rī'à)	172	38°55'N	8°42'W
Sorrento, Italy (sôr-rĕn'tō)	174	40°23'N	14°23'E
Sorsogon, Phil. (sôr-sôgōn')	213	12°51'N	124°02'E
Sortavala, Russia (sôr'tä-vä-lä)	178	61°43'N	30°40'E
Sosna, r., Russia (sôs'nà)	177	50°33'N	38°15'E
Sosnogorsk, Russia	178	63°13'N	54°09'E
Sosnowiec, Pol. (sôs-nô'vyĕts)	169	50°17'N	19°10'E
Sosnytsia, Ukr.	177	51°30'N	32°29'E
Sosunova, Mys, c., Russia (mĭs sô'sô-nôf'à)	210	46°28'N	138°06'E
Sos'va, r., Russia (sôs'và)	186a	59°55'N	60°40'E
Sos'va, r., Russia (sôs'và)	180	63°10'N	63°30'E
Sota, r., Benin	235	11°10'N	3°20'E
Sota la Marina, Mex. (sô-tä-lä-mä-rē'nä)	130	23°45'N	98°11'W
Soteapan, Mex. (sō-tå-ä'pän)	131	18°14'N	94°51'W
Soto la Marina, Río, r., Mex. (rē'ō-so'tō lä mä-rē'nä)	130	23°55'N	98°30'W
Sotuta, Mex. (sô-tōō'tä)	132a	20°35'N	89°00'W
Soublette, Ven. (sō-ōō-blĕ'tĕ)	143b	9°55'N	66°06'W
Souflí, Grc.	175	41°12'N	26°17'E
Soufrière, St. Luc. (sōō-frē-âr')	133b	13°50'N	61°03'W
Soufrière, mtn., St. Vin.	133b	13°19'N	61°12'W
Soufrière, vol., Guad. (sōō-frē-âr')	133b	16°06'N	61°42'W
Sŏul *see* Seoul, Kor., S.	205	37°35'N	127°03'E
Sounding Creek, r., Can. (soun'dĭng)	96	51°35'N	111°00'W
Souq Ahras, Alg.	161	36°23'N	8°00'E
Sources, Mount aux, mtn., Afr. (môn'tō sôrs')	232	28°47'S	29°04'E
Soure, Port. (sōr-ĕ)	172	40°04'N	8°37'W
Souris, Can. (sōō'rē')	101	46°20'N	62°17'W
Souris, Can.	90	49°38'N	100°15'W
Souris, r., N.A.	92	48°30'N	101°30'W
Sourlake, Tx., U.S. (sour'lāk)	123	30°09'N	94°24'W
Sousse, Tun. (sōōs)	230	36°00'N	10°39'E
South, r., Ga., U.S.	110c	33°40'N	84°15'W
South, r., N.C., U.S.	125	34°49'N	78°33'W
South Africa, nation, Afr.	232	28°00'S	24°50'E
South Amboy, N.J., U.S. (south'ăm'boi)	110a	40°28'N	74°17'W
South America, cont.	139	15°00'S	60°00'W
Southampton, Eng., U.K. (south-ămp'tŭn)	154	50°54'N	1°30'W
Southampton, N.Y., U.S.	109	40°53'N	72°24'W
Southampton Island, i., Can.	93	64°38'N	84°00'W
South Andaman Island, i., India (ăn-dá-măn')	212	11°57'N	93°24'E
South Australia, state, Austl. (ôs-trā'lĭ-ă)	218	29°45'S	132°00'E
South Bay, b., Bah.	135	20°55'N	73°35'W
South Bend, In., U.S. (bĕnd)	105	41°40'N	86°20'W
South Bend, Wa., U.S. (bĕnd)	114	46°39'N	123°48'W
South Bight, b., Bah.	134	24°20'N	77°35'W
South Bimini, i., Bah. (bē'mē-nē)	134	25°40'N	79°20'W
Southborough, Ma., U.S. (south'bŭr-ō)	101a	42°18'N	71°33'W
South Boston, Va., U.S. (bôs'tŭn)	125	36°41'N	78°55'W
Southbridge, Ma., U.S. (south'brĭj)	109	42°05'N	72°00'W
South Caicos, i., T./C. Is. (kī'kōs)	135	21°30'N	71°35'W
South Carolina, state, U.S. (kăr-ō-lī'ná)	105	34°15'N	81°10'W
South Cave, Eng., U.K. (cāv)	158a	53°45'N	0°35'W
South Charleston, W.V., U.S.	108	38°20'N	81°40'W
South China Sea, sea, Asia (chī'ná)	212	15°23'N	114°12'E
South Creek, r., Austl.	217b	33°43'S	150°50'E
South Dakota, state, U.S. (dá-kō'tá)	104	44°20'N	101°55'W
South Downs, Eng., U.K. (dounz)	164	50°55'N	1°13'W
South Dum-Dum, India	202a	22°36'N	88°25'E
South East Cape, c., Austl.	221	43°47'S	146°03'E
Southend-on-Sea, Eng., U.K. (south-ĕnd')	165	51°33'N	0°41'E
Southern Alps, mts., N.Z. (sŭ-thûrn ălps)	221a	43°35'S	170°00'E
Southern Cross, Austl.	218	31°13'S	119°30'E
Southern Indian, l., Can. (sŭth'ērn ĭn'dĭ-ăn)	92	56°46'N	98°57'W
Southern Pines, N.C., U.S. (sŭth'ērn pīnz)	125	35°10'N	79°23'W
Southern Ute Indian Reservation, I.R., Co., U.S. (ūt)	119	37°05'N	108°23'W
South Euclid, Oh., U.S. (ū'klĭd)	111d	41°30'N	81°34'W
South Fox, i., Mi., U.S. (fŏks)	108	45°25'N	85°55'W
South Gate, Ca., U.S. (gāt)	117a	33°57'N	118°13'W
South Georgia, i., S. Geor. (jôr'jà)	139	54°00'S	37°00'W
South Haven, Mi., U.S. (hāv''n)	108	42°25'N	86°15'W
South Hill, Va., U.S.	125	36°44'N	78°08'W
South Holston Lake, res., U.S.	125	36°35'N	82°00'W
South Indian Lake, Can.	97	56°50'N	99°00'W
Southington, Ct., U.S. (sŭdh'ĭng-tŭn)	109	41°35'N	72°55'W
South Island, i., N.Z.	221a	42°40'S	169°00'E
South Loup, r., Ne., U.S. (lōōp)	112	41°21'N	100°08'W
South Magnetic Pole, pt. of i.	224	65°18'S	139°30'E
South Merrimack, N.H., U.S. (mĕr'ĭ-măk)	101a	42°47'N	71°36'W
South Milwaukee, Wi., U.S. (mĭl-wô'kē)	111a	42°55'N	87°52'W
South Moose Lake, l., Can.	97	53°51'N	100°20'W
South Nation, r., Can.	99	45°00'N	75°25'W
South Negril Point, c., Jam. (nå-grĕl')	134	18°15'N	78°25'W
South Ogden, Ut., U.S. (ŏg'dĕn)	117b	41°12'N	111°58'W
South Orkney Islands, is., Ant.	139	57°00'S	45°00'W
South Ossetia, hist. reg., Geor.	182	42°20'N	44°00'E
South Paris, Me., U.S. (păr'ĭs)	100	44°13'N	70°32'W
South Park, Ky., U.S. (pärk)	111h	38°06'N	85°43'W
South Pasadena, Ca., U.S. (păs-à-dē'ná)	117a	34°06'N	118°08'W
South Pease, r., Tx., U.S. (pēz)	120	33°54'N	100°45'W
South Pender, i., Can. (pĕn'dĕr)	116d	48°45'N	123°09'W
South Pittsburg, Tn., U.S. (pĭs'bûrg)	124	35°00'N	85°42'W
South Platte, r., U.S. (plăt)	106	40°40'N	102°40'W
South Point, c., Barb.	133b	13°00'N	59°43'W
South Point, c., Mi., U.S.	108	44°50'N	83°20'W
South Pole, pt. of i., Ant.	224	90°00'S	0°00'
South Porcupine, Can.	98	48°28'N	81°13'W
Southport, Austl. (south'pōrt)	219	27°57'S	153°27'E
Southport, Eng., U.K. (south'pôrt)	164	53°38'N	3°00'W
Southport, In., U.S.	111g	39°40'N	86°07'W
Southport, N.C., U.S.	125	35°55'N	78°02'W
South Portland, Me., U.S. (pōrt-lănd)	100	43°37'N	70°15'W
South Prairie, Wa., U.S. (prâ'rĭ)	116a	47°08'N	122°06'W
South Range, Wi., U.S. (rānj)	117h	46°37'N	91°59'W
South River, N.J., U.S. (rĭv'ĕr)	110a	40°27'N	74°23'W
South Ronaldsay, i., Scot., U.K. (rŏn'ăld-s'ā)	164a	58°48'N	2°55'W
South Saint Paul, Mn., U.S.	117g	44°54'N	93°02'W
South Salt Lake, Ut., U.S. (sôlt lāk)	117b	40°44'N	111°53'W
South Sandwich Islands, is., S. Geor. (sănd'wĭch)	139	58°00'S	27°00'W
South Sandwich Trench, deep	139	55°00'S	27°00'W
South San Francisco, Ca., U.S. (săn frăn-sĭs'kô)	116b	37°39'N	122°24'W
South Saskatchewan, r., Can. (săs-kach'ĕ-wän)	92	50°30'N	110°30'W
South Shetland Islands, is., Ant.	139	62°00'S	70°00'W
South Shields, Eng., U.K. (shēldz)	160	55°00'N	1°22'W
South Sioux City, Ne., U.S. (sōō sĭt'ē)	112	42°48'N	96°26'W
South Taranaki Bight, b., N.Z. (tä-rä-nä'kē)	221a	39°35'S	173°50'E
South Thompson, r., Can. (tŏmp'sŭn)	95	50°41'N	120°21'W
Southton, Tx., U.S. (south'tŭn)	117d	29°18'N	98°26'W
South Uist, i., Scot., U.K. (ū'ĭst)	164	57°15'N	7°24'W
South Umpqua, r., Or., U.S. (ŭmp'kwâ)	114	43°00'N	122°54'W
Southwell, Eng., U.K. (south'wĕl)	158a	53°04'N	0°56'W
South West Africa *see* Namibia, nation, Afr.	232	19°30'S	16°13'E
Southwest Miramichi, r., Can. (mĭr á-mē'shē)	100	46°35'N	66°17'W
Southwest Point, c., Bah.	134	25°50'N	77°10'W
Southwest Point, c., Bah.	135	23°55'N	74°30'W
South Yorkshire, hist. reg., Eng., U.K.	158a	53°29'N	1°35'W
Sovetsk, Russia (sô-vyĕtsk')	180	55°04'N	21°54'E
Sovetskaya Gavan', Russia (sŭ-vyĕt'skī-u gä'vŭn')	179	48°59'N	140°14'E
Sow, r., Eng., U.K. (sou)	158a	52°45'N	2°12'W
Soya Kaikyō, strt., Asia	210	45°45'N	141°38'E
Sōya Misaki, c., Japan (sō'yä mē'sä-kē)	210	45°35'N	141°25'E
Soyo, Ang.	232	6°10'S	12°25'E
Sozh, r., Eur. (sôzh)	181	52°50'N	31°00'E
Sozopol, Blg. (sôz'ô-pôl')	175	42°18'N	27°50'E
Spa, Bel. (spä)	165	50°30'N	5°50'E
Spain, nation, Eur. (spān)	154	40°15'N	4°30'W
Spalding, Ne., U.S. (spôl'dĭng)	112	41°43'N	98°23'W
Spanaway, Wa., U.S. (spăn'á-wā)	116a	47°06'N	122°26'W
Spangler, Pa., U.S. (spăng'lĕr)	109	40°40'N	78°50'W
Spanish Fork, Ut., U.S. (spăn'ĭsh fôrk)	119	40°10'N	111°40'W
Spanish Town, Jam.	129	18°00'N	76°55'W
Sparks, Nv., U.S. (spärks)	118	39°34'N	119°45'W
Sparrows Point, Md., U.S. (spăr'ōz)	110e	39°13'N	76°29'W
Sparta *see* Spárti, Grc.	175	37°07'N	22°28'E
Sparta, Ga., U.S. (spär'tá)	125	33°16'N	82°59'W
Sparta, Il., U.S.	121	38°07'N	89°42'W
Sparta, Mi., U.S.	108	43°10'N	85°45'W
Sparta, Tn., U.S.	124	35°54'N	85°26'W
Sparta, Wi., U.S.	113	43°56'N	90°50'W
Sparta Mountains, mts., N.J., U.S.	110a	41°00'N	74°38'W
Spartanburg, S.C., U.S. (spär'tăn-bûrg)	105	34°57'N	82°13'W
Spartel, Cap, c., Mor. (spär-tĕl')	172	35°48'N	5°50'W
Spárti (Sparta), Grc.	175	37°07'N	22°28'E
Spartivento, Cape, c., Italy (spär-tē-vĕn'tô)	174	37°55'N	16°09'E
Spartivento, Cape, c., Italy	156	38°54'N	8°52'E
Spas-Demensk, Russia (spás dyĕ-mĕnsk')	176	54°24'N	34°02'E
Spas-Klepiki, Russia (spàs klĕp'ĕ-kē)	176	55°09'N	40°11'E

ăt; finăl; rāte; senâte; ärm; ȧsk; sofȧ; fâre; ch-choose; dh-as th in other; bē; ēvent; bĕt; recĕnt; cratẽr; g-gō; gh-guttural g; bĭt; ĭ-short neutral; rīde; K-guttural k as ch in German ich;

PRONOUNCING INDEX

Spassik-Ryazanskiy – Strängnäs 353

PLACE (Pronunciation)	PAGE	LAT.	LONG.
Spassik-Ryazanskiy, Russia (ryä-zän'skĭ)	176	54°24'N	40°21'E
Spassk-Dal'niy, Russia (spŭsk'däl'nyē)	179	44°30'N	133°00'E
Spátha, Ákra, c., Grc.	174a	35°42'N	23°45'E
Spaulding, Al., U.S. (spôl'dĭng)	110h	33°27'N	86°50'W
Spear, Cape, c., Can. (spēr)	101	47°32'N	52°32'W
Spearfish, S.D., U.S. (spēr'fĭsh)	112	44°28'N	103°52'W
Speed, In., U.S. (spēd)	111h	38°25'N	85°45'W
Speedway, In., U.S. (spēd'wā)	111g	39°47'N	86°14'W
Speichersee, l., Ger.	159d	48°12'N	11°47'E
Spencer, Ia., U.S.	112	43°09'N	95°08'W
Spencer, In., U.S. (spĕn'sẽr)	108	39°15'N	86°45'W
Spencer, N.C., U.S.	125	35°43'N	80°25'W
Spencer, W.V., U.S.	108	38°55'N	81°20'W
Spencer Gulf, b., Austl. (spĕn'sẽr)	220	34°20'S	136°55'E
Sperenberg, Ger. (shpĕ'rĕn-bĕrgh)	159b	52°09'N	13°22'E
Spey, l., Scot., U.K. (spā)	164	57°25'N	3°29'W
Speyer, Ger. (shpī'ẽr)	168	49°18'N	8°26'E
Sphinx, hist., Egypt (sfĭnks)	238b	29°57'N	31°08'E
Spijkenisse, Neth.	159a	51°51'N	4°18'E
Spinazzola, Italy (spē-nät'zô-lä)	174	40°58'N	16°05'E
Spirit Lake, Ia., U.S. (lāk)	112	43°25'N	95°08'W
Spirit Lake, Id., U.S. (spĭr'ĭt)	114	47°58'N	116°51'W
Spišská Nová Ves, Slvk. (spēsh'skä nō'vä vĕs)	161	48°56'N	20°35'E
Spitsbergen see Svalbard, dep., Nor.	178	77°00'N	20°00'E
Split, Cro. (splēt)	154	43°30'N	16°28'E
Split Lake, l., Can.	97	56°08'N	96°15'W
Spokane, Wa., U.S. (spōkăn')	104	47°39'N	117°25'W
Spokane, r., Wa., U.S.	114	47°47'N	118°00'W
Spokane Indian Reservation, I.R., Wa., U.S.	114	47°55'N	118°00'W
Spoleto, Italy (spô-lā'tō)	174	42°44'N	12°44'E
Spoon, r., Il., U.S. (spōōn)	121	40°36'N	90°22'W
Spooner, Wi., U.S. (spōōn'ẽr)	113	45°50'N	91°53'W
Spotswood, N.J., U.S. (spŏtz'wood)	110a	40°23'N	74°22'W
Sprague, r., Or., U.S. (sprāg)	114	42°30'N	121°42'W
Spratly, i., Asia (sprăt'lē)	212	8°38'N	111°54'E
Spray, N.C., U.S. (sprā)	125	36°30'N	79°44'W
Spree, r., Ger. (shprā)	168	51°53'N	14°08'E
Spremberg, Ger. (shprĕm'bĕrgh)	168	51°35'N	14°23'E
Spring, r., Ar., U.S.	121	36°25'N	91°35'W
Springbok, S. Afr. (sprĭng'bŏk)	232	29°35'S	17°55'E
Spring Creek, r., Nv., U.S. (sprĭng)	118	40°18'N	117°45'W
Spring Creek, r., Tx., U.S.	123	30°03'N	95°43'W
Spring Creek, r., Tx., U.S.	122	31°08'N	100°50'W
Springdale, Can.	101	49°30'N	56°05'W
Springdale, Ar., U.S. (sprĭng'dāl)	121	36°10'N	94°07'W
Springdale, Pa., U.S.	111e	40°33'N	79°46'W
Springer, N.M., U.S. (sprĭng'ẽr)	120	36°21'N	104°37'W
Springerville, Az., U.S.	119	34°08'N	109°17'W
Springfield, Co., U.S. (sprĭng'fēld)	120	37°24'N	102°04'W
Springfield, Il., U.S.	105	39°46'N	89°37'W
Springfield, Ky., U.S.	108	37°35'N	85°10'W
Springfield, Ma., U.S.	105	42°05'N	72°35'W
Springfield, Mn., U.S.	113	44°14'N	94°59'W
Springfield, Mo., U.S.	105	37°13'N	93°17'W
Springfield, Oh., U.S.	105	39°55'N	83°50'W
Springfield, Or., U.S.	114	44°01'N	123°02'W
Springfield, Tn., U.S.	124	36°30'N	86°53'W
Springfield, Vt., U.S.	109	43°20'N	72°35'W
Springfontein, S. Afr. (sprĭng'fōn-tīn)	232	30°16'S	25°45'E
Springhill, Can. (sprĭng-hĭl')	91	45°39'N	64°03'W
Spring Mountains, mts., Nv., U.S.	118	36°18'N	115°49'W
Springs, S. Afr. (sprĭngs)	238c	26°16'S	28°27'E
Springstein, Can. (sprĭng'stīn)	102f	49°49'N	97°29'W
Springton Reservoir, res., Pa., U.S. (sprĭng-tŭn)	110f	39°57'N	75°26'W
Springvale, Austl.	217a	37°57'S	145°09'E
Spring Valley, Ca., U.S.	118a	32°46'N	117°01'W
Springvalley, Il., U.S. (sprĭng-văl'ĭ)	108	41°20'N	89°15'W
Spring Valley, Mn., U.S.	113	43°41'N	92°26'W
Spring Valley, N.Y., U.S.	110a	41°07'N	74°03'W
Springville, Ut., U.S. (sprĭng-vĭl)	119	40°10'N	111°40'W
Springwood, Austl.	217b	33°42'S	150°34'E
Spruce Grove, Can. (sprōōs grōv)	102g	53°32'N	113°55'W
Spur, Tx., U.S. (spûr)	120	33°29'N	100°51'W
Squam, l., N.H., U.S. (skwôm)	109	43°45'N	71°30'W
Squamish, Can. (skwŏ'mĭsh)	94	49°42'N	123°09'W
Squamish, r., Can.	94	50°10'N	123°30'W
Squillace, Golfo di, b., Italy (gōō'l-fō-dē skwēl-lä'chā)	174	38°44'N	16°47'E
Srbija (Serbia), hist. reg., Serb. (sr bē-yä) (sĕr'bē-ä)	175	44°05'N	20°35'E
Srbobran, Serb. (s'r'bô-brän')	175	45°32'N	19°50'E
Sredne-Kolymsk, Russia (s'rĕd'nyĕ kô-lêmsk')	179	67°49'N	154°55'E
Sredne Rogatka, Russia (s'red'nà-ya) (rô gär'tkà)	186c	59°49'N	30°20'E
Sredniy Ik, r., Russia (srĕd'nĭ ĭk)	186a	55°46'N	58°50'E
Sredniy Ural, mts., Russia (ŏ'rál)	186a	57°47'N	59°00'E
Śrem, Pol. (shrĕm)	169	52°06'N	17°01'E
Sremska Karlovci, Serb. (srĕm'skē kär'lov-tsē)	175	45°10'N	19°57'E
Sremska Mitrovica, Serb. (srĕm'skä mē'trô-vē-tsä')	175	44°59'N	19°39'E
Sretensk, Russia (s'rĕ'tĕnsk)	179	52°13'N	117°39'E
Sri Jayewardenepura Kotte, Sri L.	203	6°50'N	80°05'E
Sri Lanka, nation, Asia	203	8°45'N	82°30'E
Srīnagar, India (srē-nŭg'ŭr)	199	34°11'N	74°49'E
Środa, Pol. (shrō'dà)	169	52°14'N	17°17'E
Stabroek, Bel.	159a	51°20'N	4°21'E
Stade, Ger. (shtä'dĕ)	168	53°36'N	9°28'E
Städjan, mtn., Swe. (stĕd'yän)	166	61°53'N	12°50'E
Stafford, Eng., U.K. (stăf'fẽrd)	164	52°48'N	2°06'W
Stafford, Ks., U.S.	120	37°58'N	98°37'W
Staffordshire, co., Eng., U.K.	158a	52°45'N	2°00'W
Stahnsdorf, Ger. (shtäns'dôrf)	159b	52°22'N	13°10'E
Staines, Eng., U.K.	158b	51°26'N	0°13'W
Stakhanov, Ukr.	181	48°34'N	38°37'E
Stalingrad see Volgograd, Russia	178	48°40'N	42°20'E
Stalybridge, Eng., U.K.	158a	53°29'N	2°03'W
Stambaugh, Mi., U.S. (stăm'bô)	113	46°03'N	88°38'W
Stamford, Eng., U.K.	158a	52°39'N	0°28'W
Stamford, Ct., U.S. (stăm'fẽrd)	110a	41°03'N	73°32'W
Stamford, Tx., U.S.	120	32°57'N	99°48'W
Stammersdorf, Aus. (shtäm'ĕrs-dôrf)	159e	48°19'N	16°25'E
Stamps, Ar., U.S. (stămps)	121	33°22'N	93°31'W
Stanberry, Mo., U.S. (stan'bĕr-ē)	121	40°12'N	94°34'W
Standerton, S. Afr. (stăn'dẽr-tŭn)	232	26°57'S	29°17'E
Standing Rock Indian Reservation, I.R., N.D., U.S. (stănd'ĭng rŏk)	112	47°07'N	101°05'W
Standish, Eng., U.K. (stăn'dĭsh)	158a	53°36'N	2°39'W
Stanford, Ky., U.S. (stăn'fẽrd)	124	37°29'N	84°40'W
Stanger, S. Afr. (stăŋ-ger)	233c	29°22'S	31°18'E
Staniard Creek, Bah.	134	24°50'N	77°55'W
Stanislaus, r., Ca., U.S. (stăn'ĭs-lô)	118	38°10'N	120°16'W
Stanley, Can. (stăn'lē)	100	46°17'N	66°44'W
Stanley, Falk. Is.	144	51°46'S	57°59'W
Stanley, N.D., U.S.	112	48°20'N	102°25'W
Stanley, Wi., U.S.	113	44°56'N	90°56'W
Stanley Pool, l., Afr.	232	4°07'S	15°40'E
Stanley Reservoir, res., India (stăn'lē)	203	12°07'N	77°27'E
Stanleyville see Kisangani, D.R.C.	231	0°30'S	25°12'E
Stann Creek, Belize (stăn krēk)	132a	17°01'N	88°14'W
Stanovoy Khrebet, mts., Russia (stŭn-à-voi')	179	56°12'N	127°12'E
Stanton, Ca., U.S. (stăn'tŭn)	117a	33°48'N	118°00'W
Stanton, Ne., U.S.	112	41°57'N	97°15'W
Stanton, Tx., U.S.	122	32°08'N	101°46'W
Stanwood, Wa., U.S. (stăn'wŏd)	116a	48°14'N	122°23'W
Staples, Mn., U.S. (stā'p'lz)	113	46°21'N	94°48'W
Stapleton, Al., U.S.	124	30°45'N	87°48'W
Stara Planina, mts., Blg.	156	42°50'N	24°45'E
Staraya Kupavna, Russia (stä'rà-yà kû-päf'nà)	186b	55°48'N	38°10'E
Staraya Russa, Russia (stä'rà-yà rōōsà)	180	57°58'N	31°21'E
Stara Zagora, Blg. (zä'gô-rà)	163	42°26'N	25°37'E
Starbuck, Can. (stär'bŭk)	102f	49°46'N	97°36'W
Stargard Szczeciński, Pol. (shtär'gärt shchĕ-chyn'skē)	160	53°19'N	15°03'E
Staritsa, Russia (stä'rē-tsà)	176	56°29'N	34°58'E
Starke, Fl., U.S. (stärk)	125	29°55'N	82°07'W
Starkville, Co., U.S. (stärk'vĭl)	120	37°06'N	104°34'W
Starkville, Ms., U.S.	124	33°27'N	88°47'W
Starnberg, Ger. (shtärn-bĕrgh)	159d	47°59'N	11°20'E
Starnberger See, l., Ger.	168	47°58'N	11°30'E
Starobil's'k, Ukr.	181	49°19'N	38°57'E
Starodub, Russia (stä-rô-drōp')	176	52°25'N	32°49'E
Starogard Gdański, Pol. (stä'rō-grad gdĕn'skē)	160	53°58'N	18°33'E
Starokostiantyniv, Ukr.	181	49°45'N	27°12'E
Staro-Minskaya, Russia (stä'rô mĭn'skä-yà)	181	46°19'N	38°51'E
Staro-Shcherbinovskaya, Russia	177	46°38'N	38°38'E
Staro-Subkhangulovo, Russia (stăro-sōōb-kan-gōō'lôvô)	186a	53°08'N	57°24'E
Staroutkinsk, Russia (stá-rô-ōōt'kĭnsk)	186a	57°14'N	59°21'E
Starovirivka, Ukr.	177	49°31'N	35°48'E
Start Point, c., Eng., U.K. (stärt)	161	50°14'N	3°34'W
Staryi Ostropil', Ukr.	177	49°48'N	27°32'E
Stary Sącz, Pol. (stä-rē sônch')	169	49°32'N	20°36'E
Staryy Oskol, Russia (stä'rē ôs-kôl')	181	51°18'N	37°51'E
Stassfurt, Ger. (shtäs'fōōrt)	168	51°52'N	11°35'E
Staszów, Pol. (stä'shôf)	169	50°32'N	21°13'E
State College, Pa., U.S. (stāt kŏl'ĕj)	109	40°50'N	77°55'W
State Line, Mn., U.S. (līn)	117h	46°36'N	92°18'W
Staten Island, i., N.Y., U.S. (stăt'ĕn)	110a	40°35'N	74°10'W
Statesboro, Ga., U.S. (stāts'bŭr-ô)	125	32°26'N	81°47'W
Statesville, N.C., U.S. (stāts'vĭl)	125	34°45'N	80°54'W
Staunton, Il., U.S. (stôn'tŭn)	117e	39°01'N	89°47'W
Staunton, Va., U.S.	109	38°10'N	79°05'W
Stavanger, Nor. (stä'väng'ẽr)	154	58°59'N	5°44'E
Stave, r., Can. (stāv)	116d	49°12'N	122°24'W
Staveley, Eng., U.K. (stāv'lē)	158a	53°17'N	1°21'W
Stavenisse, Neth.	159a	51°35'N	3°59'E
Stavropol', Russia	178	45°05'N	41°50'E
Steamboat Springs, Co., U.S. (stēm'bōt')	120	40°30'N	106°48'W
Stebliv, Ukr.	177	49°23'N	31°03'E
Steel, r., Can. (stēl)	98	49°08'N	86°55'W
Steelton, Pa., U.S. (stēl'tŭn)	109	40°15'N	76°45'W
Steenbergen, Neth.	159a	51°35'N	4°18'E
Steens Mountain, mts., Or., U.S. (stēnz)	114	42°15'N	118°52'W
Steep Point, c., Austl. (stēp)	220	26°15'S	112°05'E
Stefanie, Lake see Chew Bahir, l., Afr.	231	4°46'N	37°31'E
Steinbach, Can.	90	49°32'N	96°41'W
Steinkjer, Nor. (stĕĭn-kyẽr)	160	64°00'N	11°19'E
Stella, Wa., U.S. (stĕl'à)	116c	46°11'N	123°12'W
Stellarton, Can. (stĕl'ár-tŭn)	91	45°34'N	62°40'W
Stendal, Ger. (shtĕn'däl)	168	52°37'N	11°51'E
Stepanakert see Xankändi, Azer.	180	39°50'N	46°40'E
Stephens, Port, b., Austl. (stē'fĕns)	222	32°43'S	152°55'E
Stephenville, Can. (stē'vĕn-vĭl)	93a	48°33'N	58°35'W
Stepnogorsk, Kaz.	183	52°20'N	72°05'E
Sterkrade, Ger. (shtĕr'krädĕ)	171c	51°31'N	6°51'E
Sterkstroom, S. Afr.	233c	31°33'S	26°36'E
Sterling, Co., U.S. (stûr'lĭng)	104	40°38'N	103°14'W
Sterling, Il., U.S.	108	41°48'N	89°42'W
Sterling, Ks., U.S.	120	38°11'N	98°11'W
Sterling, Ma., U.S.	101a	42°26'N	71°41'W
Sterling, Tx., U.S.	122	31°53'N	100°58'W
Sterlitamak, Russia (styĕr'lē-ta-mák')	178	53°38'N	55°56'E
Šternberk, Czech Rep. (shtĕrn'bĕrk)	169	49°44'N	17°18'E
Stettin see Szczecin, Pol.	154	53°25'N	14°35'E
Stettler, Can.	90	52°19'N	112°43'W
Steubenville, Oh., U.S. (stū'bĕn-vĭl)	108	40°20'N	80°40'W
Stevens, l., Wa., U.S. (stē'vĕnz)	116a	47°59'N	122°06'W
Stevens Point, Wi., U.S.	113	44°30'N	89°35'W
Stevensville, Mt., U.S. (stē'vĕnz-vĭl)	115	46°31'N	114°03'W
Stewart, r., Can. (stū'ẽrt)	92	63°27'N	138°48'W
Stewart Island, i., N.Z.	221a	46°56'S	167°40'E
Stewiacke, Can. (stū'wē-ăk)	100	45°08'N	63°21'W
Steynsrus, S. Afr. (stīns'rōōs)	238c	27°58'S	27°33'E
Steyr, Aus. (shtīr)	161	48°03'N	14°24'E
Stif, Alg.	230	36°18'N	5°21'E
Stikine, r., Can. (stĭ-kēn')	92	58°17'N	130°10'W
Stikine Ranges, Can.	90	59°05'N	130°00'W
Stillaguamish, r., Wa., U.S.	116a	48°11'N	122°18'W
Stillaguamish, South Fork, r., Wa., U.S. (stĭl-ă-gwä'mĭsh)	116a	48°05'N	121°59'W
Stillwater, Mn., U.S. (stĭl'wô-tẽr)	117g	45°04'N	92°48'W
Stillwater, Mt., U.S.	115	45°23'N	109°45'W
Stillwater, Ok., U.S.	121	36°06'N	97°03'W
Stillwater, r., Mt., U.S.	115	48°47'N	114°40'W
Stillwater Range, mts., Nv., U.S.	118	39°43'N	118°11'W
Štip, Mac. (shtĭp)	175	41°43'N	22°07'E
Stirling, Scot., U.K. (stûr'lĭng)	164	56°05'N	3°59'W
Stittsville, Can. (stĭts'vĭl)	102c	45°15'N	75°54'W
Stizef, Alg. (mĕr-syă' lá-kônb)	173	35°18'N	0°11'W
Stjördalshalsen, Nor. (styûr-däls-hälsĕn)	166	63°26'N	11°00'E
Stockbridge Munsee Indian Reservation, I.R., Wi., U.S. (stŏk'brĭdj mŭn-sē)	113	44°49'N	89°00'W
Stockerau, Aus. (shtô'kĕ-rou)	168	48°24'N	16°13'E
Stockholm, Swe. (stôk'hôlm)	154	59°23'N	18°00'E
Stockholm, Me., U.S. (stŏk'hōlm)	100	47°05'N	68°08'W
Stockport, Eng., U.K. (stŏk'pôrt)	164	53°24'N	2°09'W
Stockton, Eng., U.K.	164	54°35'N	1°25'W
Stockton, Ca., U.S. (stŏk'tŭn)	104	37°56'N	121°16'W
Stockton, Ks., U.S.	120	39°26'N	99°16'W
Stockton, i., Wi., U.S.	113	46°56'N	90°25'W
Stockton Plateau, plat., Tx., U.S.	106	30°34'N	102°35'W
Stockton Reservoir, res., Mo., U.S.	121	37°40'N	93°45'W
Stöde, Swe. (stû'dĕ)	166	62°26'N	16°35'E
Stoeng Trêng, Camb. (stŏng'trĕng')	212	13°36'N	106°00'E
Stoke-on-Trent, Eng., U.K. (stōk-ŏn-trĕnt)	160	53°01'N	2°12'W
Stokhid, r., Ukr.	169	51°24'N	25°20'E
Stolac, Bos. (stô'láts)	175	43°03'N	17°59'E
Stolbovoy, is., Russia (stôl-bô-voi')	185	74°05'N	136°00'E
Stolin, Bela. (stô'lēn)	169	51°54'N	26°52'E
Stömstad, Swe.	166	58°58'N	11°09'E
Stone, Eng., U.K.	158a	52°54'N	2°09'W
Stoneham, Can. (stōn'ám)	102b	46°59'N	71°22'W
Stoneham, Ma., U.S.	101a	42°30'N	71°05'W
Stonehaven, Scot., U.K. (stōn'hā-v'n)	164	56°57'N	2°09'W
Stone Mountain, Ga., U.S. (stōn)	110c	33°49'N	84°10'W
Stonewall, Can. (stōn'wôl)	102f	50°09'N	97°21'W
Stonewall, Ms., U.S.	124	32°08'N	88°44'W
Stoney Creek, Can. (stō'nē)	102d	43°13'N	79°45'W
Stonington, Ct., U.S. (stōn'ĭng-tŭn)	109	41°20'N	71°55'W
Stony Indian Reserve, I.R., Can.	102e	51°10'N	114°45'W
Stony Mountain, Can.	102f	50°05'N	97°13'W
Stony Plain, Can. (stō'nē plān)	102g	53°32'N	114°00'W
Stony Plain Indian Reserve, I.R., Can.	102g	53°29'N	113°48'W
Stony Point, N.Y., U.S.	110a	41°13'N	73°58'W
Stora Sotra, i., Nor.	166	60°24'N	4°35'E
Stord, i., Nor. (stōrd)	166	59°54'N	5°15'E
Store Baelt, strt., Den.	166	55°25'N	10°50'E
Storfjorden, b., Nor.	166	62°17'N	6°19'E
Stormberg, mts., S. Afr. (stôrm'bûrg)	233c	31°28'S	26°35'E
Storm Lake, Ia., U.S.	112	42°39'N	95°12'W
Stormy Point, c., V.I.U.S. (stôr'mē)	129c	18°22'N	65°01'W
Stornoway, Scot., U.K. (stôr'nô-wā)	160	58°13'N	6°21'W
Storozhynets', Ukr.	169	48°10'N	25°44'E
Störsjo, Swe. (stôr'shû)	166	62°49'N	13°08'E
Störsjoen, l., Nor. (stôr-syûĕn)	166	61°32'N	11°30'E
Störsjon, l., Swe.	160	63°06'N	14°00'E
Storvik, Swe.	166	60°37'N	16°31'E
Stoughton, Wi., U.S.	113	42°54'N	89°15'W
Stour, r., Eng., U.K. (stour)	165	52°09'N	0°29'E
Stourbridge, Eng., U.K. (stour'brĭj)	158a	52°27'N	2°08'W
Stow, Ma., U.S. (stō)	101a	42°56'N	71°31'W
Stow, Oh., U.S.	111d	41°09'N	81°26'W
Straatsdrif, S. Afr.	238c	25°19'S	26°22'E
Strabane, N. Ire., U.K. (stră-băn')	164	54°59'N	7°27'W
Straelen, Ger. (shtră'lĕn)	171c	51°26'N	6°16'E
Strahan, Austl. (strā'ăn)	219	42°08'S	145°28'E
Strakonice, Czech Rep. (strä'kô-nyē-tsĕ)	168	49°18'N	13°52'E
Straldzha, Blg. (sträl'dzhà)	175	42°37'N	26°44'E
Stralsund, Ger. (shräl'sŏnt)	160	54°18'N	13°04'E
Strangford Lough, l., N. Ire., U.K.	164	54°30'N	5°34'W
Strängnäs, Swe. (strĕng'nĕs)	166	59°23'N	16°59'E

ng-sing; ŋ-baŋk; ɴ-nasalized n; nŏd; cŏmmit; ōld; ôbey; ôrder; oi-boil; fōōd; ŏŏ-as oo in foot; ou-out; s-soft; sh-dish; th-thin; pūre; ûnite; ûrn; stŭd; circŭs; ü-as in French tu; '-indeterminate vowel.

PLACE (Pronunciation)	PAGE	LAT.	LONG.
Stranraer, Scot., U.K. (străn-rär´)	164	54°55'N	5°05'W
Strasbourg, Fr. (strás-bōōr´)	154	48°36'N	7°49'E
Stratford, Can. (străt´fĕrd)	98	43°20'N	81°05'W
Stratford, Ct., U.S.	109	41°10'N	73°05'W
Stratford, Wi., U.S.	113	44°16'N	90°02'W
Stratford-upon-Avon, Eng., U.K.	164	52°13'N	1°41'W
Straubing, Ger. (strou´bǐng)	168	48°52'N	12°36'E
Strausberg, Ger. (strous´bĕrgh)	168	52°35'N	13°50'E
Strawberry, r., Ut., U.S.	119	40°05'N	110°55'W
Strawn, Tx., U.S. (strôn)	122	32°38'N	98°28'W
Streator, Il., U.S. (strē´tĕr)	108	41°05'N	88°50'W
Streeter, N.D., U.S.	112	46°40'N	99°22'W
Streetsville, Can. (strētz´vĭl)	102d	43°34'N	79°43'W
Strehaia, Rom. (strĕ-kä´yà)	175	44°37'N	23°13'E
Strel'na, Russia (strĕl´ná)	186c	59°52'N	30°01'E
Stretford, Eng., U.K. (strĕt´fĕrd)	158a	53°25'N	2°19'W
Strickland, r., Pap. N. Gui. (strĭk´lǎnd)	213	6°15's	142°00'E
Strijen, Neth.	159a	51°44'N	4°32'E
Stromboli, Italy (strŏm´bô-lē)	163	38°46'N	15°16'E
Stromyn, Russia (strô´mĭn)	186b	56°02'N	38°29'E
Strong, r., Ms., U.S. (strông)	124	32°03'N	89°42'W
Strongsville, Oh., U.S. (strông´vǐl)	111d	41°19'N	81°50'W
Stronsay, i., Scot., U.K. (strŏn´sā)	164a	59°09'N	2°35'W
Stroudsburg, Pa., U.S. (stroudz´bûrg)	109	40°59'N	75°15'W
Struer, Den.	166	56°29'N	8°34'E
Strugi Krasnyye, Russia (strōō´gĭ krä´s-ny´yĕ)	176	58°14'N	29°10'E
Struma, r., Eur. (strōō´má)	175	41°25'N	23°05'E
Strumica, Mac. (strōō´mǐ-tsá)	175	41°26'N	22°38'E
Strunino, Russia	186b	56°23'N	38°34'E
Struthers, Oh., U.S. (strŭdh´ĕrz)	108	41°00'N	80°35'W
Struvenhütten, Ger. (shtrōō´vĕn-hü-tĕn)	159c	53°52'N	10°04'E
Strydpoortberge, mts., S. Afr.	238c	24°08'N	29°18'E
Stryi, Ukr.	169	49°16'N	23°51'E
Strzelce Opolskie, Pol. (stzhĕl´tsĕ o-pôl´skyĕ)	169	50°31'N	18°20'E
Strzelin, Pol. (stzhĕ-lĭn)	169	50°48'N	17°06'E
Strzelno, Pol. (stzhál´nô)	169	52°37'N	18°10'E
Stuart, Fl., U.S. (stū´ĕrt)	125a	27°10'N	80°14'W
Stuart, Ia., U.S.	113	41°31'N	94°20'W
Stuart, i., Ak., U.S.	103	63°25'N	162°45'W
Stuart, i., Wa., U.S.	116d	48°42'N	123°10'W
Stuart Lake, l., Can.	94	54°32'N	124°35'W
Stuart Range, mts., Austl.	220	29°00's	134°30'E
Sturgeon, r., Can.	102g	53°41'N	113°46'W
Sturgeon, r., Mi., U.S.	113	46°43'N	88°43'W
Sturgeon Bay, Wi., U.S.	113	44°50'N	87°22'W
Sturgeon Bay, b., Can.	97	52°00'N	98°00'W
Sturgeon Falls, Can.	91	46°19'N	79°49'W
Sturgis, Ky., U.S.	108	37°35'N	88°00'W
Sturgis, Mi., U.S.	108	41°45'N	85°25'W
Sturgis, S.D., U.S.	112	44°25'N	103°31'W
Sturt Creek, r., Austl.	220	19°40's	127°40'E
Sturtevant, Wi., U.S. (stûr´tĕ-vănt)	111a	42°42'N	87°54'W
Stutterheim, S. Afr. (stŭt´ĕr-hīm)	233c	32°34's	27°27'E
Stuttgart, Ger. (shtŏŏt´gärt)	154	48°48'N	9°15'E
Stuttgart, Ar., U.S. (stŭt´gärt)	121	34°30'N	91°33'W
Stykkishólmur, Ice.	160	65°00'N	21°48'W
Styr', r., Eur. (stĕr)	169	51°44'N	26°07'E
Suao, Tai. (sōōou)	209	24°35'N	121°45'E
Subarnarekha, r., India	202	22°38'N	86°26'E
Subata, Lat. (sô´bä-tä)	167	56°02'N	25°54'E
Subic, Phil. (sōō´bĭk)	213a	14°52'N	120°15'E
Subic Bay, b., Phil.	213a	14°41'N	120°11'E
Subotica, Serb. (sōō´bô´tĕ-tsä)	154	46°06'N	19°41'E
Subugo, mtn., Kenya	237	1°40's	35°49'E
Succasunna, N.J., U.S. (sŭk´ká-sŭn´ná)	110a	40°52'N	74°37'W
Suceava, Rom. (sōō-chä-ä´vä)	169	47°39'N	26°17'E
Suceava, r., Rom.	169	47°45'N	26°10'E
Sucha, Pol. (sōō´ká)	169	49°44'N	19°40'E
Suchiapa, Mex. (sōō-chē-ä´pä)	131	16°38'N	93°08'W
Suchiapa, r., Mex.	131	16°27'N	93°26'W
Suchitoto, El Sal. (sōō-chē-tô´tô)	132	13°58'N	89°03'W
Sucio, r., Col. (sōō´syô)	142	6°55'N	76°15'W
Suck, r., Ire. (sŭk)	164	53°34'N	8°16'W
Sucre, Bol. (sōō´krä)	142	19°06's	65°16'W
Sucre, dept., Ven. (sōō´krĕ)	143b	10°18'N	64°12'W
Sud, Canal du, strt., Haiti	135	18°40'N	73°15'W
Sud, Rivière du, r., Can. (rē-vyär´dü süd´)	102b	46°56'N	70°35'W
Suda, Russia (sōō´dá)	186a	56°58'N	56°45'E
Suda, r., Russia (sōō´dá)	176	59°24'N	36°40'E
Sudair, Sau. Ar. (sū-dä´ĕr)	198	25°48'N	46°28'E
Sudalsvatnet, l., Nor.	166	59°35'N	6°59'E
Sudan, nation, Afr.	231	14°00'N	28°00'E
Sudan, reg., Afr. (sōō-dän´)	230	15°00'N	7°00'E
Sudbury, Can. (sŭd´bĕr-ĕ)	91	46°28'N	81°00'W
Sudbury, r., Ma., U.S.	101a	42°23'N	71°25'W
Sudetes, mts., Eur.	156	50°41'N	15°37'E
Sudogda, Russia (sô´dôk-dá)	176	55°57'N	40°29'E
Sudost', r., Eur. (sô-dôst´)	176	52°43'N	33°13'E
Sudzha, Russia (sōō´zhá)	177	51°14'N	35°11'E
Sueca, Spain (swä´kä)	173	39°12'N	0°18'W
Suez, Egypt	231	29°58'N	32°34'E
Suez, Gulf of, b., Egypt (sōō-ĕz´)	231	29°53'N	32°33'E
Suez Canal, can., Egypt	231	30°53'N	32°21'E
Suffern, N.Y., U.S. (sŭf´fĕrn)	110a	41°07'N	74°09'W
Suffolk, Va., U.S. (sŭf´ŭk)	110g	36°43'N	76°35'W
Sugar City, Co., U.S.	120	38°12'N	103°42'W
Sugar Creek, Mo., U.S.	117f	39°07'N	94°27'W
Sugar Creek, r., Il., U.S.	121	40°14'N	89°28'W
Sugar Creek, r., In., U.S. (shŏg´ĕr)	108	39°55'N	87°10'W

PLACE (Pronunciation)	PAGE	LAT.	LONG.
Sugar Island, i., Mi., U.S.	117k	46°31'N	84°12'W
Sugarloaf Point, c., Austl. (sōgĕr´lôf)	222	32°19's	153°04'E
Suggi Lake, l., Can.	97	54°22'N	102°47'W
Sühbaatar, Mong.	204	50°18'N	106°31'E
Suhl, Ger. (zōōl)	168	50°37'N	10°41'E
Suichuan, mtn., China	209	26°25'N	114°10'E
Suide, China (swä-dǔ)	208	37°32'N	110°12'E
Suifenhe, China (swä-fŭn-hŭ)	205	44°47'N	131°13'E
Suihua, China	205	46°38'N	126°50'E
Suining, China (sōō´ē-nǐng´)	206	33°54'N	117°57'E
Suipacha, Arg. (swĕ-pä´chä)	141c	34°45's	59°43'W
Suiping, China (swä-pǐn)	206	33°09'N	113°58'E
Suir, r., Ire. (sūr)	164	52°20'N	7°32'W
Suisun Bay, b., Ca., U.S. (sōō-soon´)	116b	38°07'N	122°02'W
Suita, Japan (sò´ē-tä)	211b	34°45'N	135°32'E
Suitland, Md., U.S. (sōt´lǎnd)	110e	38°51'N	76°57'W
Suixian, China (swä shyĕn)	209	31°42'N	113°20'E
Suiyüan, hist. reg., China (swä-yüĕn)	204	41°31'N	107°04'E
Suizhong, China (swä-jŏn)	208	40°22'N	120°20'E
Sukabumi, Indon.	212	6°52's	106°56'E
Sukadana, Indon.	212	1°15's	110°30'E
Sukagawa, Japan (sōō´kä-gä´wä)	211	37°08'N	140°07'E
Sukhinichi, Russia (sōō´kē´nē-chē)	180	54°07'N	35°18'E
Sukhona, r., Russia (sōō-kō´ná)	180	59°30'N	42°20'E
Sukhoy Log, Russia (sōō´kôy lôg)	186a	56°55'N	62°03'E
Sukhumi, Geor. (sò-kòm´)	181	43°00'N	41°00'E
Sukkur, Pak. (sŭk´ŭr)	199	27°49'N	68°50'E
Sukkwan Island, i., Ak., U.S.	94	55°05'N	132°45'W
Suksun, Russia (sò-kôn)	186a	57°08'N	57°22'E
Sukumo, Japan (sōō´kò-mò)	211	32°58'N	132°45'E
Sukunka, r., Can.	95	55°00'N	121°50'W
Sula, r., Ukr. (sōō-lá´)	177	50°36'N	33°13'E
Sula, Kepulauan, is., Indon.	213	2°20's	125°20'E
Sulaco, r., Hond. (sōō-lä´kô)	132	14°55'N	87°31'W
Sulaimān Range, mts., Pak. (sò-lä-ē-män´)	199	29°47'N	69°10'E
Sulak, r., Russia (sōō-läk´)	181	43°30'N	47°00'E
Sulfeld, Ger. (zōō´fĕld)	159c	53°48'N	10°13'E
Sulina, Rom. (sōō-lē´ná)	163	45°08'N	29°38'E
Sulitelma, mtn., Eur. (sōō-lē-tyĕl´má)	160	67°03'N	16°35'E
Sullana, Peru (sōō-lyä´ná)	142	4°57's	80°47'W
Sulligent, Al., U.S. (sŭl´ĭ-jĕnt)	124	33°52'N	88°06'W
Sullivan, Il., U.S.	108	41°35'N	88°35'W
Sullivan, In., U.S.	108	39°05'N	87°20'W
Sullivan, Mo., U.S.	121	38°13'N	91°09'W
Sulmona, Italy (sōōl-mō´ná)	174	42°02'N	13°58'E
Sulphur, Ok., U.S. (sŭl´fŭr)	121	34°31'N	96°58'W
Sulphur, r., Tx., U.S.	121	33°26'N	95°06'W
Sulphur Springs, Tx., U.S. (sprĭngz)	121	33°09'N	95°36'W
Sultan, Wa., U.S. (sŭl´tăn)	116a	47°52'N	121°49'W
Sultan, r., Wa., U.S.	116a	47°55'N	121°49'W
Sultepec, Mex. (sōōl-tå-pĕk´)	130	18°50'N	99°51'W
Sulu Archipelago, is., Phil. (sōō´lōō)	212	5°52'N	122°00'E
Suluntah, Libya	163	32°39'N	21°49'E
Sulūq, Libya	231	31°39'N	20°15'E
Sulu Sea, sea, Asia	212	8°25'N	119°00'E
Suma, Japan (sōō´mä)	211b	34°39'N	135°08'E
Sumas, Wa., U.S. (sū´más)	116d	49°00'N	122°16'W
Sumatera, i., Indon. (sò-mä-trä)	212	2°06'N	99°40'E
Sumatra see Sumatera, i., Indon.	212	2°06'N	99°40'E
Sumba, i., Indon. (sŭm´bä)	212	9°52's	119°00'E
Sumba, Île, i., D.R.C.	236	1°44'N	19°32'E
Sumbawa, i., Indon. (sòm-bä´wä)	212	9°00's	118°18'E
Sumbawa-Besar, Indon.	212	8°32's	117°20'E
Sumbawanga, Tan.	237	7°58's	31°37'E
Sumbe, Ang.	232	11°13's	13°50'E
Sümeg, Hung. (shü´mĕg)	169	46°59'N	17°19'E
Sumida, r., Japan (sōō´mĕ-dä)	211	36°01'N	139°24'E
Sumidouro, Braz. (sōō-mĕ-dò´ró)	141a	22°04's	42°41'W
Sumiyoshi, Japan (sōō´mĕ-yō´shĕ)	211b	34°43'N	135°16'E
Summer Lake, l., Or., U.S. (sŭm´ĕr)	114	42°50'N	120°35'W
Summerland, Can. (sŭ´mĕr-lănd)	95	49°39'N	119°40'W
Summerside, Can. (sŭm´ĕr-sīd)	91	46°25'N	63°47'W
Summerton, S.C., U.S. (sŭm´ĕr-tŭn)	125	33°37'N	80°22'W
Summerville, S.C., U.S. (sŭm´ĕr-vĭl)	125	33°00'N	80°10'W
Summit, Il., U.S. (sŭm´mĭt)	111a	41°47'N	87°48'W
Summit, N.J., U.S.	110a	40°43'N	74°21'W
Summit Lake Indian Reservation, I.R., Nv., U.S.	114	41°35'N	119°30'W
Summit Peak, mtn., Co., U.S.	119	37°20'N	106°40'W
Sumner, Wa., U.S. (sŭm´nĕr)	116a	47°12'N	122°14'W
Šumperk, Czech Rep. (shóm´pĕrk)	169	49°57'N	17°02'E
Sumqayıt, Azer.	182	40°36'N	49°38'E
Sumrall, Ms., U.S. (sŭm´rôl)	124	31°25'N	89°34'W
Sumter, S.C., U.S. (sŭm´tĕr)	125	33°55'N	80°21'W
Sumy, Ukr. (sōō´mĭ)	178	50°54'N	34°47'E
Sumy, prov., Ukr.	177	51°02'N	34°05'E
Sun, r., Mt., U.S. (sŭn)	115	47°34'N	111°53'W
Sunburst, Mt., U.S.	115	48°53'N	111°55'W
Sunda, Selat, strt., Indon.	212	5°45's	106°15'E
Sundance, Wy., U.S. (sŭn´dăns)	115	44°24'N	104°27'W
Sundarbans, sw., Asia (sòn´dĕr-bŭns)	199	21°50'N	89°00'E
Sunday Strait, strt., Austl. (sŭn´dä)	220	15°50's	122°45'E
Sundbyberg, Swe. (sòn´bü-bĕrgh)	166	59°24'N	17°56'E
Sunderland, Eng., U.K. (sŭn´dĕr-lǎnd)	160	54°55'N	1°25'W
Sunderland, Md., U.S.	110e	38°41'N	76°36'W
Sundsvall, Swe. (sònds´väl)	154	62°20'N	19°19'E
Sungari (Songhua), r., China	205	46°09'N	127°53'E
Sungari Reservoir, res., China	205	43°20'N	127°50'E
Sungurlu, Tur. (soon´gòr-lò´)	163	40°08'N	34°20'E
Sun Kosi, r., Nepal	202	27°13'N	85°52'E
Sunland, Ca., U.S. (sŭn´lănd)	117a	34°16'N	118°18'W
Sunne, Swe. (sōōn´ĕ)	166	59°51'N	13°07'E
Sunninghill, Eng., U.K. (sŭnĭng´hĭl)	158b	51°23'N	0°40'W

PLACE (Pronunciation)	PAGE	LAT.	LONG.
Sunnymead, Ca., U.S. (sŭn´ĭ-mēd)	117a	33°56'N	117°15'W
Sunnyside, Ut., U.S.	119	39°35'N	110°20'W
Sunnyside, Wa., U.S.	114	46°19'N	120°00'W
Sunnyvale, Ca., U.S. (sŭn-nē-vāl)	116b	37°23'N	122°02'W
Sunol, Ca., U.S. (sōō´nŭl)	116b	37°36'N	122°53'W
Sunset, Ut., U.S. (sŭn-sĕt)	117b	41°08'N	112°02'W
Sunset Crater National Monument, rec., Az., U.S. (krā´tĕr)	119	35°20'N	111°30'W
Sunshine, Austl.	217a	37°47's	144°50'E
Suntar, Russia (sòn-tár´)	179	62°14'N	117°49'E
Sunyani, Ghana	234	7°20'N	2°20'W
Suoyarvi, Russia (sōō´ô-yĕr´vĕ)	180	62°12'N	32°29'E
Superior, Az., U.S. (su-pē´rĭ-ĕr)	119	33°15'N	111°10'W
Superior, Ne., U.S.	120	40°04'N	98°05'W
Superior, Wi., U.S.	105	46°44'N	92°06'W
Superior, Wy., U.S.	115	41°45'N	108°57'W
Superior, Laguna, l., Mex. (lä-gōō´ná sōō-pä-rē-ôr´)	131	16°20'N	94°55'W
Superior, Lake, l., N.A.	107	47°38'N	89°20'W
Superior Village, Wi., U.S.	117h	46°38'N	92°07'W
Sup'ung Reservoir, res., Asia (sōō´pòōng)	210	40°35'N	126°00'E
Suqian, China (sōō-chyĕn)	206	33°57'N	118°17'E
Suquamish, Wa., U.S. (sōō-gwä´mĭsh)	116a	47°44'N	122°34'W
Suquţrā (Socotra), i., Yemen (sô-kō´trá)	198	13°00'N	52°30'E
Şūr, Leb. (sōōr) (tīr)	197a	33°16'N	35°13'E
Şūr, Oman	198	22°23'N	59°28'E
Surabaya, Indon.	212	7°23's	112°45'E
Surakarta, Indon.	212	7°35's	110°45'E
Šurany, Slvk. (shōō´rä-nù´)	169	48°05'N	18°11'E
Surat, Austl. (sū-rät)	222	27°18's	149°00'E
Surat, India (sò´rŭt)	199	21°08'N	73°22'E
Surat Thani, Thai.	212	8°59N	99°14'E
Surazh, Bela.	176	55°24'N	30°46'E
Surazh, Russia (sōō-rázh´)	176	53°02'N	32°27'E
Surgères, Fr. (sür-zhâr´)	170	46°06'N	0°51'W
Surgut, Russia (sòr-gót´)	178	61°18'N	73°38'E
Suriname, nation, S.A. (sōō-rĕ-näm´)	143	4°00'N	56°00'W
Sūrmaq, Iran	201	31°03'N	52°48'E
Surt, Libya	231	31°14'N	16°37'E
Surt, Khalīj, b., Libya	231	31°30'N	18°28'E
Suruga-Wan, b., Japan (sōō´rōō-gä wän)	210	34°52'N	138°36'E
Susa, Japan	211	34°40'N	131°39'E
Sušak, i., Serb.	174	42°45'N	16°30'E
Susak, Otok, i., Serb.	174	44°31'N	14°15'E
Susaki, Japan (sōō´sä-kē)	211	33°23'N	133°16'E
Sušice, Czech Rep.	168	49°14'N	13°31'E
Susitna, Ak., U.S. (sōō-sĭt´ná)	103	61°28'N	150°28'W
Susitna, r., Ak., U.S.	103	62°00'N	150°28'W
Susong, China (sōō-sŏŋ)	209	30°18'N	116°08'E
Susquehanna, Pa., U.S. (sŭs´kwĕ-hăn´á)	109	41°55'N	73°55'W
Susquehanna, r., U.S.	109	39°50'N	76°20'W
Sussex, Can. (sŭs´ĕks)	91	45°43'N	65°31'W
Sussex, N.J., U.S.	110a	41°12'N	74°36'W
Sussex, Wi., U.S.	111a	43°08'N	88°12'W
Sutherland, Austl. (sŭdh´ĕr-lănd)	217b	34°02's	151°04'E
Sutherland, S. Afr. (sū´thĕr-lănd)	232	32°23's	20°40'E
Sutlej, r., Asia (sŭt´lĕj)	199	30°15'N	73°00'E
Sutton, Eng., U.K. (sŭt´n)	158b	51°21'N	0°12'W
Sutton, Ma., U.S.	101a	42°09'N	71°46'W
Sutton Coldfield, Eng., U.K. (kōld´fĕld)	158a	52°34'N	1°49'W
Sutton-in-Ashfield, Eng., U.K. (ĭn-ăsh´fĕld)	158a	53°07'N	1°15'W
Suurberge, mts., S. Afr.	233c	33°15's	25°32'E
Suva, Fiji	214g	18°08's	178°25'E
Suwa, Japan (sōō´wä)	211	36°03'N	138°08'E
Suwałki, Pol. (sò-vou´kĕ)	169	54°05'N	22°58'E
Suwanee Lake, l., Can.	97	52°08'N	100°10'W
Suwannee, r., U.S. (sò-wô´nĕ)	107	29°42'N	83°00'W
Suways al Hulwah, Tur' at as, can., Egypt	238d	30°15'N	32°20'E
Suxian, China (sōō shyĕn)	208	33°29'N	117°51'E
Suzdal', Russia (sōōz´dál)	176	56°26'N	40°29'E
Suzhou, China (sōō-jō)	205	31°19'N	120°37'E
Suzu Misaki, c., Japan (sōō´zōō mĕ´sä-kē)	210	37°30'N	137°35'E
Svalbard (Spitsbergen), dep., Nor. (sväl´bärt) (spĭts´bŭr-gĕn)	178	77°00'N	20°00'E
Svaneke, Den. (svä´nĕ-kĕ)	166	55°08'N	15°07'E
Svatove, Ukr.	181	49°23'N	38°10'E
Svedala, Swe. (svĕ´dä-lä)	166	55°29'N	13°11'E
Sveg, Swe.	166	62°03'N	14°22'E
Svelvik, Nor. (svĕl´vĕk)	166	59°37'N	10°18'E
Svenčionys, Lith.	167	55°09'N	26°09'E
Svendborg, Den. (svĕn-bôrgh)	166	55°05'N	10°35'E
Svensen, Or., U.S. (svĕn´sĕn)	116c	46°10'N	123°39'W
Sverdlovsk see Yekaterinburg, Russia	178	56°51'N	60°36'E
Svetlaya, Russia (svyĕt´lá-yà)	210	46°09'N	137°53'E
Svicha, r., Ukr.	169	49°09'N	24°10'E
Svilajnac, Serb. (svĕ´lä-ĕ-nàts)	175	44°12'N	21°14'E
Svilengrad, Blg. (svĕl´ĕn-grät)	175	41°44'N	26°11'E
Svir', r., Russia	180	60°55'N	33°40'E
Svir Kanal, can., Russia (kä-näl´)	167	60°10'N	32°40'E
Svishtov, Blg. (svēsh´tôf)	163	43°36'N	25°21'E
Svisloch', r., Bela. (svēs´lôk)	168	28°11'N	19°16'E
Svitavy, Czech Rep.	168	49°46'N	16°28'E
Svobodnyy, Russia (svô-bôd´nĭ)	179	51°28'N	128°28'E
Svolvær, Nor. (svôl´vĕr)	160	68°15'N	14°29'E
Svyatoy Nos, Mys, c., Russia (svyü´toi nôs)	179	72°18'N	139°28'E

PRONOUNCING INDEX

Swadlincote – Tamiahua 355

PLACE (Pronunciation)	PAGE	LAT.	LONG.
Swadlincote, Eng., U.K. (swŏd′lĭn-kōt)	158a	52°46′N	1°33′W
Swain Reefs, rf., Austl. (swān)	221	22°12′S	152°08′E
Swainsboro, Ga., U.S. (swānz′bŭr-ô)	125	32°37′N	82°21′W
Swakopmund, Nmb. (svä′kôp-mōnt) (swá′kôp-mònd)	232	22°40′S	14°30′E
Swallowfield, Eng., U.K. (swŏl′ô-fēld)	158b	51°21′N	0°58′W
Swampscott, Ma., U.S. (swômp′skŏt)	101a	42°28′N	70°55′W
Swan, r., Austl.	220	31°30′S	116°30′E
Swan, r., Can.	97	51°58′N	101°45′W
Swan, r., Mt., U.S.	115	47°50′N	113°40′W
Swan Hill, Austl.	219	35°20′S	143°30′E
Swan Hills, Can. (hĭlz)	90	54°52′N	115°45′W
Swan Island, i., Austl. (swŏn)	217a	38°15′S	144°41′E
Swan Lake, l., Can.	97	52°30′N	100°45′W
Swanland, reg., Austl. (swŏn′lănd)	220	31°45′S	119°15′E
Swan Range, mts., Mt., U.S.	115	47°50′N	113°40′W
Swan River, Can. (swŏn rĭv′ẽr)	90	52°06′N	101°16′W
Swansea, Wales, U.K.	161	51°37′N	3°59′W
Swansea, Il., U.S. (swŏn′sē)	117e	38°32′N	89°59′W
Swansea, Ma., U.S.	110b	41°45′N	71°09′W
Swanson Reservoir, res., Ne., U.S. (swŏn′sŭn)	120	40°13′N	101°30′W
Swartberg, mtn., Afr.	233c	30°08′S	29°34′E
Swartkop, mtn., S. Afr.	232a	34°13′S	18°27′E
Swartruggens, S. Afr.	238c	25°40′S	26°40′E
Swartspruit, S. Afr.	233b	25°44′S	28°01′E
Swatow *see* Shantou, China	205	23°20′N	116°40′E
Swaziland, nation, Afr. (Swä′zē-lănd)	232	26°45′S	31°30′E
Sweden, nation, Eur. (swē′dĕn)	154	60°10′N	14°10′E
Swedesboro, N.J., U.S. (swēdz′bē-rô)	110f	39°45′N	75°22′W
Sweetwater, Tn., U.S. (swēt′wô-tẽr)	124	35°36′N	84°29′W
Sweetwater, Tx., U.S.	104	32°28′N	100°25′W
Sweetwater, l., N.D., U.S.	112	48°15′N	98°35′W
Sweetwater, r., Wy., U.S.	115	42°19′N	108°35′W
Sweetwater Reservoir, res., Ca., U.S.	118a	32°42′N	116°54′W
Świdnica, Pol. (shvĭd-nē′tsá)	168	50°50′N	16°30′E
Świdwin, Pol. (shvĭd′vĭn)	168	53°46′N	15°48′E
Świebodzice, Pol.	168	50°51′N	16°17′E
Świebodzin, Pol. (shvyĕɴ-bo′jĕts)	168	52°16′N	15°36′E
Świecie, Pol. (shvyäɴ′tsyĕ)	169	53°23′N	18°26′E
Świętokrzyskie, Góry, mts., Pol. (shvyĕɴ-tō-kzhĭ′skyĕ gōō′rĭ)	169	50°57′N	21°02′E
Swift, r., Eng., U.K.	158a	52°26′N	1°08′W
Swift, r., Me., U.S. (swĭft)	101	44°42′N	70°40′W
Swift Creek Reservoir, res., Wa., U.S.	114	46°03′N	122°10′W
Swift Current, Can. (swĭft kûr′ĕnt)	90	50°17′N	107°50′W
Swindle Island, i., Can.	94	52°32′N	128°35′W
Swindon, Eng., U.K. (swĭn′dŭn)	164	51°35′N	1°55′W
Swinomish Indian Reservation, I.R., Wa., U.S. (swĭ-nō′mĭsh)	116a	48°25′N	122°27′W
Świnoujście, Pol. (shvĭ-nĭ-ô-wēsh′chyĕ)	168	53°56′N	14°14′E
Swinton, Eng., U.K. (swĭn′tŭn)	158a	53°30′N	1°19′W
Swissvale, Pa., U.S. (swĭs′vāl)	111e	40°25′N	79°53′W
Switzerland, nation, Eur. (swĭt′zẽr-lănd)	154	46°30′N	7°43′E
Syanno, Bela. (syĕ′nô)	176	54°48′N	29°43′E
Syas′, r., Russia (syäs)	176	59°28′N	33°24′E
Sycamore, Il., U.S. (sĭk′á-mōr)	113	42°00′N	88°42′W
Sycan, r., Or., U.S.	114	42°45′N	121°00′W
Sychëvka, Russia (sē-chôf′ká)	176	55°52′N	34°18′E
Sydney, Austl. (sĭd′nē)	219	33°55′S	151°17′E
Sydney, Can.	91	46°09′N	60°11′W
Sydney Mines, Can.	91	46°14′N	60°14′W
Syktyvkar, Russia (sük-tüf′kär)	178	61°35′N	50°40′E
Sylacauga, Al., U.S. (sĭl-á-kô′gá)	124	33°10′N	86°15′W
Sylarna, mtn., Eur.	166	63°00′N	12°10′E
Sylt, i., Ger. (sĭlt)	168	54°55′N	8°30′E
Sylvania, Ga., U.S. (sĭl-vā′nĭ-à)	125	32°44′N	81°40′W
Sylvester, Ga., U.S. (sĭl-vĕs′tẽr)	124	31°32′N	83°50′W
Sými, i., Grc.	163	36°27′N	27°41′E
Synel′nykove, Ukr.	181	48°19′N	35°33′E
Syracuse, Ks., U.S. (sĭr′á-kūs)	120	37°59′N	101°44′W
Syracuse, N.Y., U.S.	105	43°05′N	76°10′W
Syracuse, Ut., U.S.	117b	41°06′N	112°04′W
Syr Darya, r., Asia	178	44°15′N	65°45′E
Syria, nation, Asia (sĭr′ĭ-á)	198	35°00′N	37°15′E
Syrian Desert, des., Asia	198	32°00′N	40°00′E
Sýros, i., Grc.	163	37°23′N	24°55′E
Sysert′, Russia (sĕ′sĕrt)	186a	56°30′N	60°48′E
Sysola, r., Russia	180	60°50′N	50°40′E
Syvash, zatoka, b., Ukr.	177	45°55′N	34°42′E
Syzran′, Russia (sĕz-rän′)	178	53°09′N	48°27′E
Szamotuły, Pol. (shá-mô-tōō′wē)	168	52°36′N	16°34′E
Szarvas, Hung. (sôr′vôsh)	169	46°51′N	20°36′E
Szczebrzeszyn, Pol. (shchĕ-bzhä′shĕn)	169	50°41′N	22°58′E
Szczecin, Pol. (shchĕ′tsĭn)	154	53°25′N	14°35′E
Szczecinek, Pol. (shchĕ′tsĭ-nĕk)	160	53°41′N	16°42′E
Szczuczyn, Pol. (shchōō′chĕn)	169	53°32′N	22°17′E
Szczytno, Pol. (shchĭt′nô)	169	53°33′N	21°00′E
Szechwan Basin, basin, China	204	30°45′N	104°40′E
Szeged, Hung. (sĕ′gĕd)	154	46°15′N	20°12′E
Székesfehérvár, Hung. (sā′kĕsh-fĕ′hār-vär)	163	47°12′N	18°26′E
Szekszárd, Hung. (sĕk′särd)	163	46°19′N	18°42′E
Szentendre, Hung. (sĕnt′ĕn-drĕ)	169	47°40′N	19°07′E
Szentes, Hung. (sĕn′tĕsh)	169	46°38′N	20°18′E
Szigetvar, Hung. (sĕ′gĕt-vär)	169	46°05′N	17°50′E
Szolnok, Hung.	169	47°11′N	20°12′E
Szombathely, Hung. (sôm′bôt-hĕl′)	163	47°13′N	16°35′E
Szprotawa, Pol. (shprō-tä′vä)	168	51°34′N	15°29′E
Szydłowiec, Pol. (shid-wô′vyets)	169	51°13′N	20°53′E
T			
Taal, l., Phil. (tä-äl′)	213a	13°58′N	121°06′E
Tabaco, Phil. (tä-bä′kō)	213a	13°27′N	123°40′E
Tabankulu, S. Afr. (tä-bän-kōō′la)	233c	30°56′S	29°19′E
Tabasará, Serranía de, mts., Pan.	133	8°29′N	81°22′W
Tabasco, Mex. (tä-bäs′kō)	130	21°47′N	103°04′W
Tabasco, state, Mex.	128	18°10′N	93°00′W
Taber, Can.	90	49°47′N	112°08′W
Tablas, i., Phil. (tä′bläs)	213a	12°26′N	122°00′E
Tablas Strait, strt., Phil.	213a	12°17′N	121°41′E
Table Bay, b., S. Afr. (tā′b′l)	232a	33°41′S	18°27′E
Table Mountain, mtn., S. Afr.	232a	33°58′S	18°26′E
Table Rock Lake, Mo., U.S.	121	36°37′N	93°29′W
Tabligbo, Togo	234	6°35′N	1°30′E
Taboga, i., Pan. (tä-bō′gä)	128a	8°48′N	79°35′W
Taboguilla, i., Pan. (tä-bô-gē′l-yä)	128a	8°48′N	79°31′W
Tábor, Czech Rep. (tä′bôr)	168	49°25′N	14°40′E
Tabora, Tan. (tä-bō′rä)	232	5°01′S	32°48′E
Tabou, C. Iv. (tá-bōō′)	230	4°25′N	7°21′W
Tabrīz, Iran (tá-brēz′)	198	38°00′N	46°13′E
Tabuaeran, i., Kir.	2	3°52′N	159°20′W
Tabwémasana, Mont, mtn., Vanuatu	214f	15°20′S	166°44′E
Tacámbaro, r., Mex. (tä-käm′bä-rō)	130	18°55′N	101°25′W
Tacámbaro de Codallos, Mex.	130	19°12′N	101°28′W
Tacarigua, Laguna de la, l., Ven.	143b	10°18′N	65°43′W
Tacheng, China (tä-chŭŋ)	204	46°50′N	83°24′E
Tachie, r., Can.	94	54°30′N	125°00′W
Tacloban, Phil. (tä-klō′bän)	213	11°06′N	124°58′E
Tacna, Peru (täk′nä)	142	18°34′S	70°16′W
Tacoma, Wa., U.S. (tá-kō′má)	104	47°14′N	122°27′W
Taconic Range, mts., N.Y., U.S. (tá-kŏn′ĭk)	109	41°55′N	73°40′W
Tacotalpa, Mex. (tä-kô-täl′pä)	131	17°37′N	92°51′W
Tacotalpa, r., Mex.	131	17°24′N	92°38′W
Tademaït, Plateau du, plat., Alg. (tä-dē-mä′ēt)	230	28°00′N	2°15′E
Tadio, Lagune, b., C. Iv.	234	5°20′N	5°25′W
Tadjoura, Dji. (tád-zhōō′rá)	238a	11°48′N	42°54′E
Tadley, Eng., U.K. (tăd′lē)	158b	51°19′N	1°08′W
Tadotsu, Japan (tä′dô-tsò)	211	34°14′N	133°43′E
Tadoussac, Can. (tá-dōō-sák′)	99	48°09′N	69°43′W
Tadzhikistan *see* Tajikistan, nation, Asia	178	39°22′N	69°30′E
Taebaek Sanmaek, mts., Asia (tī-bīk′ sän-mīk′)	210	37°20′N	128°50′E
Taedong, r., Kor., N. (tī-dŏng)	210	38°38′N	124°32′E
Taegu, Kor., S. (tī′gōō′)	205	35°49′N	128°41′E
Taejŏn, Kor., S.	210	36°20′N	127°26′E
Tafalla, Spain (tä-fäl′yä)	172	42°30′N	1°42′W
Tafna, r., Alg. (táf′nä)	172	35°28′N	1°00′W
Taft, Ca., U.S. (táft)	118	35°09′N	119°27′W
Tagama, reg., Niger	235	15°50′N	6°30′E
Taganrog, Russia (tá-gán-rôk′)	181	47°12′N	38°56′E
Taganrogskiy Zaliv, b., Eur. (tá-gán-rôk′skĭ zä′lĭf)	181	46°55′N	38°17′E
Tagula, i., Pap. N. Gui. (tä′gōō-lá)	221	11°45′S	153°46′E
Tagus (Tajo), r., Eur. (tā′gŭs)	156	39°40′N	5°07′W
Tahan, Gunong, mtn., Malay.	212	4°33′N	101°52′E
Tahat, mtn., Alg. (tä-hät′)	230	23°22′N	5°21′E
Tahiti, i., Fr. Poly. (tä-hē′tē) (tä′ē-tē′)	2	17°30′S	149°30′W
Tahkuna Nina, c., Est. (táh-kōō′ná nē′ná)	167	59°08′N	22°03′E
Tahlequah, Ok., U.S. (tă-lĕ-kwä′)	121	35°54′N	94°58′W
Tahoe, l., U.S. (tä′hō)	106	39°09′N	120°18′W
Tahoua, Niger (tä′ōō-ä)	230	14°54′N	5°16′E
Tahtsa Lake, l., Can.	94	53°33′N	127°47′W
Tahuya, Wa., U.S. (tá-hū-yä′)	116a	47°23′N	123°03′W
Tahuya, r., Wa., U.S.	116a	47°28′N	122°55′W
Tai′an, China (tī-än)	208	36°13′N	117°08′E
Taibai Shan, mtn., China (tī-bī shän)	208	33°42′N	107°25′E
Taibus Qi, China (tī-bōō-sz chyē)	208	41°52′N	115°25′E
Taicang, China (tī-tsäŋ)	206	31°26′N	121°06′E
T′aichung, Tai. (tī′chŏng)	205	24°10′N	120°42′E
Tai′erzhuang, China (tī-är-jûäŋ)	206	34°34′N	117°44′E
Taigu, China (tī-gōō)	208	37°25′N	112°35′E
Taihang Shan, mts., China (tī-häŋ shän)	208	35°45′N	112°00′E
Taihe, China (tī-hŭ)	206	33°10′N	115°38′E
Tai Hu, l., China (tī hōō)	205	31°13′N	120°00′E
Tailagoin, reg., Mong. (tī′lá-gän′ kä′rä)	204	43°39′N	105°54′E
Tailai, China (tī-lī)	208	46°20′N	123°10′E
Tailem Bend, Austl. (tā-lĕm)	222	35°15′S	139°30′E
T′ainan, Tai. (tī′nan′)	205	23°08′N	120°18′E
Taínaro, c., Grc.	162	37°45′N	22°00′E
Taining, China (tī′nĭng′)	209	26°58′N	117°15′E
T′aipei, Tai. (tī′pā′)	205	25°02′N	121°38′E
Taiping, pt. of i., Malay.	212	4°56′N	100°39′E
Taiping Ling, mtn., China	208	47°03′N	120°30′E
Taisha, Japan (tī′shä)	211	35°23′N	132°40′E
Taishan, China (tī-shän)	209	22°15′N	112°50′E
Tai Shan, mts., China (tī shän)	208	36°16′N	117°05′E
Taitao, Península de, pen., Chile	144	46°20′S	77°15′W
T′aitung, Tai. (tī′tōōng′)	209	22°45′N	121°02′E
Taiwan, nation, Asia (tī-wän) (fôr-mō′sá)	205	23°30′N	122°20′E
Taiwan Strait, strt., Asia	205	24°30′N	120°00′E
Taixian, China (tī shyĕn)	206	32°31′N	119°54′E
Taixing, China (tī-shyĭŋ)	206	32°12′N	119°58′E
Taiyuan, China (tī-yûän)	205	37°32′N	112°38′E
Taizhou, China (tī-jō)	206	32°23′N	119°41′E
Ta′Izz, Yemen	201	13°38′N	44°04′E
Tajano de Morais, Braz. (tĕ-zhä′nô-dĕ-mô-rä′ēs)	141a	22°05′S	42°04′W
Tajikistan, nation, Asia	178	39°22′N	69°30′E
Tajumulco, vol., Guat. (tä-hōō-mōōl′kô)	132	15°03′N	91°53′W
Tajuña, r., Spain (tä-kōō′n-yä)	172	40°23′N	2°36′W
Tājūrā′, Libya	162	32°56′N	13°24′W
Tak, Thai.	212	16°57′N	99°12′E
Taka, i., Japan (tä′kä)	211	30°47′N	130°23′E
Takada, Japan (tä′ká-dä)	210	37°08′N	138°30′E
Takahashi, Japan (tä′kä′hä-shĭ)	211	34°47′N	133°35′E
Takaishi, Japan	211b	34°32′N	135°27′E
Takamatsu, Japan (tä′kä′mä-tsōō′)	205	34°20′N	134°02′E
Takamori, Japan (tä′kä′mô-rē′)	211	32°50′N	131°08′E
Takaoka, Japan (ta′kä′ô-kä′)	210	36°45′N	136°59′E
Takapuna, N.Z.	223	36°48′S	174°47′E
Takarazuka, Japan (tä′kä-rä-zōō′kä)	211b	34°48′N	135°22′E
Takasaki, Japan (tä′kät′sōō-kē′)	210	36°20′N	139°00′E
Takatsu, Japan (tä-kät′sōō) (mĕ′zō-nô-kò′chĕ)	211a	35°36′N	139°37′E
Takatsuki, Japan (tä′kät′sōō-kē′)	211b	34°51′N	135°38′E
Takayama, Japan (tä′kä′yä′mä)	211	36°11′N	137°16′E
Takefu, Japan (tä′kĕ-fōō)	210	35°57′N	136°09′E
Take-shima, is., Asia	210	37°15′N	131°51′E
Takla Lake, l., Can.	92	55°25′N	125°53′W
Takla Makan, des., China (mä-kán′)	204	39°22′N	82°34′E
Takoma Park, Md., U.S. (tá′kōmă pärk)	110e	38°59′N	77°00′W
Takum, Nig.	235	7°17′N	9°59′E
Tala, Mex. (tä′lä)	130	20°39′N	103°42′W
Talagante, Chile (tä-lä-gá′n-tĕ)	141b	33°39′S	70°54′W
Talamanca, Cordillera de, mts., C.R.	133	9°37′N	83°55′W
Talanga, Hond. (tä-lä′n-gä)	132	14°21′N	87°09′W
Talara, Peru (tä-lä′rä)	142	4°32′S	81°17′W
Talasea, Pap. N. Gui. (tä-lä-sā′ä)	213	5°20′S	150°00′E
Talata Mafara, Nig.	235	12°35′N	6°04′E
Talaud, Kepulauan, is., Indon. (tä-lout′)	213	4°17′N	127°30′E
Talavera de la Reina, Spain	162	39°58′N	4°51′W
Talca, Chile (täl′kä)	144	35°25′S	71°39′W
Talca, prov., Chile	141b	35°23′S	71°15′W
Talca, Punta, c., Chile (pōō′n-tä-täl′kä)	141b	33°25′S	71°42′W
Talcahuano, Chile (täl-kä-wä′nō)	144	36°41′S	73°05′W
Taldom, Russia (täl-dôm)	176	56°44′N	37°33′E
Taldyqorghan, Kaz.	183	45°03′N	77°18′E
Talea de Castro, Mex. (tä′lā-ä dā käs′trō)	131	17°22′N	96°14′W
Talibu, Pulau, i., Indon.	213	1°30′S	125°00′E
Talim, i., Phil. (tä-lēm′)	213a	14°21′N	121°14′E
Talisay, Phil. (tä-lē′sī)	213a	14°08′N	122°56′E
Talkeetna, Ak., U.S. (tál-kēt′ná)	103	62°18′N	150°02′W
Talladega, Al., U.S. (tăl-à-dē′gá)	124	33°25′N	86°06′W
Tallahassee, Fl., U.S. (tăl-á-hăs′ē)	105	30°25′N	84°17′W
Tallahatchie, r., Ms., U.S. (tal-á hăch′ē)	124	34°21′N	90°03′W
Tallapoosa, Ga., U.S. (tăl-á-pōō′sá)	124	33°44′N	85°15′W
Tallapoosa, r., Al., U.S.	124	32°22′N	86°08′W
Tallassee, Al., U.S. (tăl′á-sē)	124	32°30′N	85°54′W
Tallinn, Est. (tál′lĕn) (rä′väl)	178	59°26′N	24°44′E
Tallmadge, Oh., U.S. (tăl′mĭj)	111d	41°06′N	81°26′W
Tallulah, La., U.S. (tă-lōō′lá)	123	32°25′N	91°13′W
Tal′ne, Ukr.	177	48°52′N	30°43′E
Talo, mtn., Eth.	231	10°45′N	37°55′E
Taloje Budrukh, India	203b	19°05′N	73°05′E
Talpa de Allende, Mex. (täl′pä dä äl-yĕn′dā)	130	20°25′N	104°48′W
Talquin, Lake, res., Fl., U.S.	124	30°26′N	84°33′W
Talsi, Lat. (tal′sĭ)	167	57°16′N	22°35′E
Taltal, Chile (täl-täl′)	144	25°26′S	70°32′W
Taly, Russia (täl′ĭ)	177	49°51′N	40°07′E
Tama, Ia., U.S. (tā′mä)	113	41°57′N	92°36′W
Tama, r., Japan	211a	35°38′N	139°35′E
Tamale, Ghana (tä-mä′lā)	230	9°25′N	0°50′W
Taman′, Russia (tá-män′′)	177	45°13′N	36°46′E
Tamanaco, r., Ven. (tä-mä-nä′kō)	143b	9°32′N	66°00′W
Tamaqua, Pa., U.S. (tá-mô′kwá)	109	40°45′N	75°50′W
Tamar, r., Eng., U.K. (tā′mär)	164	50°35′N	4°15′W
Tamarite de Litera, Spain (tä-mä-rē′tā)	173	41°52′N	0°24′E
Tamaulipas, state, Mex. (tä-mä-ōō-lē′päs′)	128	23°45′N	98°30′W
Tamazula de Gordiano, Mex.	130	19°44′N	103°09′W
Tamazulapan del Progreso, Mex.	131	17°41′N	97°34′W
Tamazunchale, Mex. (tä-mä-zón-chä′lå)	130	21°16′N	98°46′W
Tambacounda, Sen. (täm-bä-kōōn′dä)	230	13°47′N	13°40′W
Tambador, Serra do, mts., Braz. (sĕ′r-rä-dô-täm′bä-dōr)	143	10°33′S	41°16′W
Tambelan, Kepulauan, is., Indon. (täm-bå-län′)	212	0°38′N	107°38′E
Tambo, Austl. (tăm′bō)	219	24°50′S	146°15′E
Tambov, Russia (tám-bôf′)	178	52°45′N	41°10′E
Tambov, prov., Russia	176	52°50′N	40°42′E
Tambre, r., Spain (täm′brā)	172	42°59′N	8°33′W
Tambura, Sudan (täm-bōō′rä)	231	5°34′N	27°30′E
Tame, r., Eng., U.K. (tām)	158a	52°41′N	1°42′W
Tâmega, r., Port. (tá-mā′gá)	172	41°30′N	7°45′W
Tamenghest, Alg.	230	22°34′N	5°34′E
Tamenghest, Oued, r., Alg.	230	22°15′N	2°51′E
Tamgak, Monts, mtn., Niger (tam-gäk′)	230	18°40′N	8°40′E
Tamgué, Massif du, mtn., Gui.	230	12°15′N	12°35′W
Tamiahua, Mex. (tä-myä-wä)	131	21°17′N	97°26′W

ng-sing; ŋ-baŋk; ɴ-nasalized n; nŏd; cŏmmit; ōld; ôbey; ôrder; oi-boil; fōōd; ò-as oo in foot; ou-out; s-soft; sh-dish; th-thin; pūre; ûnite; ûrn; stŭd; circŭs; ü-as in French tu; ′-indeterminate vowel.

356 Tamiahua – Temoaya PRONOUNCING INDEX

PLACE (Pronunciation)	PAGE	LAT.	LONG.
Tamiahua, Laguna, l., Mex. (lä-gò′nä-tä-myä-wä)	131	21°38′N	97°33′W
Tamiami Canal, can., Fl., U.S. (tă-mī-ăm′ĭ)	125a	25°52′N	80°08′W
Tamil Nadu, state, India	199	11°30′N	78°00′E
Tampa, Fl., U.S. (tăm′pa)	105	27°57′N	82°25′W
Tampa Bay, b., Fl., U.S.	107	27°35′N	82°38′W
Tampere, Fin. (tám′pĕ-rĕ)	160	61°21′N	23°39′E
Tampico, Mex. (täm-pē′kō)	128	22°14′N	97°51′W
Tampico Alto, Mex. (täm-pē′kō äl′tō)	131	22°07′N	97°48′W
Tampin, Malay.	197b	2°28′N	102°15′E
Tam Quan, Viet.	209	14°20′N	109°10′E
Tamuín, Mex. (tä-mōō-ē′n)	130	22°04′N	98°47′W
Tamworth, Austl. (tăm′wûrth)	219	31°01′S	151°00′E
Tamworth, Eng., U.K.	158a	52°38′N	1°41′W
Tana, i., Vanuatu	221	19°32′S	169°27′E
Tana, r., Kenya (tä′nä)	233	0°30′S	39°30′E
Tanabe, Japan (tä-nä′bā)	210	33°45′N	135°21′E
Tanabe, Japan	211b	34°49′N	135°46′E
Tanacross, Ak., U.S. (tă′nȧ-crōs)	103	63°20′N	143°30′W
Tanaga, i., Ak., U.S. (tä-nä′gä)	103a	51°28′N	178°10′W
Tanahbala, Pulau, i., Indon. (tȧ-nä-bä′lä)	212	0°30′S	98°22′E
Tanahmasa, Pulau, i., Indon. (tȧ-nä-mä′sä)	212	0°03′S	97°30′E
Tanakpur, India (tǎn′ǎk-pòr)	202	29°10′N	80°07′E
Tana Lake, l., Eth.	231	12°09′N	36°41′E
Tanami, Austl. (tȧ-nä′mē)	218	19°45′S	129°50′E
Tanana, Ak., U.S. (tă′nȧ-nô)	103	65°18′N	152°20′W
Tanana, r., Ak., U.S.	103	64°26′N	148°40′W
Tanaro, r., Italy (tä-nä′rô)	174	44°45′N	8°02′E
Tanashi, Japan	211a	35°44′N	139°34′E
Tanbu, China (tän-bōō)	207a	23°20′N	113°06′E
Tancheng, China (tän-chŭŋ)	208	34°37′N	118°22′E
Tanchŏn, Kor., N. (tän′chŭn)	210	40°29′N	128°50′E
Tancítaro, Mex. (tän-sē′tä-rō)	130	19°16′N	102°24′W
Tancítaro, Cerro de, mtn., Mex. (sĕ′r-rô-dĕ)	130	19°24′N	102°19′W
Tancoco, Mex. (tän-kō′kō)	131	21°16′N	97°45′W
Tandil, Arg. (tän-dēl′)	144	36°16′S	59°01′W
Tandil, Sierra del, mts., Arg.	144	38°40′S	59°40′W
Tanega, i., Japan (tä′nȧ-gä′)	205	30°36′N	131°11′E
Tanezrouft, reg., Alg. (tä′nĕz-rōft)	230	24°17′N	0°30′W
Tang, r., China (täŋ)	206	33°38′N	117°29′E
Tang, r., China	206	39°13′N	114°45′E
Tanga, Tan. (tăŋ′gȧ)	233	5°04′S	39°06′E
Tangancícuaro, Mex. (täŋ-gän-sē′kwa-rō)	130	19°52′N	102°13′W
Tanganyika, Lake, l., Afr.	232	5°15′S	29°40′E
Tanger, Mor. (tăn-jēr′)	230	35°52′N	5°55′W
Tangermünde, Ger. (täŋ′ĕr-mün′de)	168	52°33′N	11°58′E
Tanggu, China (täŋ-gōō)	206	39°04′N	117°41′E
Tanggula Shan, mts., China (täŋ-gōō-lä shän)	204	33°15′N	89°07′E
Tanghe, China	208	32°40′N	112°50′E
Tangier *see* Tanger, Mor.	230	35°52′N	5°55′W
Tangipahoa, r., La., U.S. (tăn′jē-pȧ-hō′ȧ)	123	30°48′N	90°28′W
Tangra Yumco, l., China (täŋ-rä yōōm-tswo)	202	30°50′N	85°40′E
T′angshan, China	208	39°38′N	118°11′E
Tangxian, China (täŋ shyĕn)	206	38°49′N	115°00′E
Tangzha, China (täŋ-jä)	206	32°06′N	120°48′E
Tanimbar, Kepulauan, is., Indon.	213	8°00′S	132°00′E
Tanjong Piai, c., Malay.	197b	1°16′N	103°11′E
Tanjong Ramunia, c., Malay.	197b	1°27′N	104°44′E
Tanjungbalai, Indon. (tän′jông-bä′lå)	197b	1°00′N	103°26′E
Tanjungpandan, Indon.	212	2°47′S	107°51′E
Tanjungpinang, Indon. (tän′jông-pē′näng)	197b	0°55′N	104°29′E
Tannu-Ola, mts., Asia	179	51°00′N	94°00′E
Tannūrah, Ra′s at, c., Sau. Ar.	198	26°45′N	49°59′E
Tano, r., Afr.	234	5°40′N	2°30′W
Tanquijo, Arrecife, i., Mex. (är-rĕ-sē′fē-tän-kē′kō)	131	21°07′N	97°16′W
Ṭanṭā, Egypt	231	30°47′N	31°00′E
Tantoyuca, Mex. (tän-tō-yōō′kä)	130	21°22′N	98°13′W
Tanyang, Kor., S.	210	36°53′N	128°20′E
Tanzania, nation, Afr.	232	6°48′S	33°58′E
Tao, r., China (tou)	208	35°30′N	103°40′E
Tao′an, China (tou-än)	205	45°15′N	122°45′E
Tao′er, r., China (tou-är)	205	45°40′N	122°00′E
Taormina, Italy (tä-ôr-mē′nä)	174	37°53′N	15°18′E
Taos, N.M., U.S. (tä′ōs)	119	36°25′N	105°35′W
Taoudenni, Mali (tä′ōō-dĕ-nē′)	230	22°57′N	3°37′W
Taoussa, Mali	234	16°55′N	0°35′W
Taoyuan, China (tou-yüän)	209	29°00′N	111°15′E
Tapa, Est. (tȧ′pȧ)	167	59°16′N	25°56′E
Tapachula, Mex.	132	14°55′N	92°20′W
Tapajós, r., Braz. (tä-pä-zhô′s)	143	3°27′S	55°33′W
Tapalque, Arg. (tä-päl-kĕ′)	141c	36°22′S	60°05′W
Tapanatepec, Mex. (tä-pä-nä-tĕ-pĕk)	131	16°22′N	94°19′W
Tāpi, r., India	199	21°00′N	76°30′E
Tappi Saki, c., Japan (täp′pē sä′kē)	210	41°05′N	139°40′E
Tapps, l., Wa., U.S. (tăpz)	116a	47°20′N	122°12′W
Taquara, Serra de, mts., Braz. (sĕ′r-rä-dĕ-tä-kwä′rä)	143	15°28′S	54°33′W
Taquari, r., Braz. (tä-kwä′rĭ)	143	18°35′S	56°50′W
Tar, r., N.C., U.S. (tär)	125	35°58′N	78°06′W
Tara, Russia (tä′rȧ)	178	56°58′N	74°13′E
Tara, i., Phil. (tä′rä)	213a	12°18′N	120°28′E
Tara, r., Russia (tä′rȧ)	184	56°32′N	76°13′E
Ṭarābulus, Leb. (tȧ-rä′bò-lōōs)	198	34°25′N	35°50′E
Ṭarābulus (Tripolitania), hist. reg., Libya	230	31°00′N	12°26′E

PLACE (Pronunciation)	PAGE	LAT.	LONG.
Tarakan, Indon.	212	3°17′N	118°04′E
Taranaki, Mount, vol., N.Z.	223	39°18′S	174°04′E
Tarancón, Spain (tä-rän-kōn′)	172	40°01′N	3°00′W
Taranto, Italy (tä′rän-tô)	163	40°30′N	17°15′E
Taranto, Golfo di, b., Italy (gôl-fô-dē tä′rän-tô)	156	40°03′N	17°10′E
Tarapoto, Peru (tä-rä-pô′tō)	142	6°29′S	76°26′W
Tarare, Fr. (tȧ-rär′)	170	45°55′N	4°23′E
Tarascon, Fr. (tȧ-rás-kôn′)	170	42°53′N	1°35′E
Tarascon, Fr. (tä-räs-kôn)	170	43°47′N	4°41′E
Tarashcha, Ukr. (tä′rȧsh-chȧ)	177	49°34′N	30°52′E
Tarata, Bol. (tä-rä′tä)	142	17°43′S	66°00′W
Taravo, r., Fr.	174	41°54′N	8°58′E
Tarazit, Massif de, mts., Niger	235	20°05′N	7°35′E
Tarazona, Spain (tä-rä-thō′nä)	172	41°54′N	1°45′W
Tarazona de la Mancha, Spain (tä-rä-zō′nä-dĕ-lä-mä′n-chä)	172	39°13′N	1°50′W
Tarbes, Fr. (tȧrb)	161	43°04′N	0°05′E
Tarboro, N.C., U.S. (tär′bŭr-ô)	125	35°53′N	77°34′W
Taree, Austl. (tȧ-rē′)	222	31°52′S	152°21′E
Tarentum, Pa., U.S. (tȧ-rĕn′tŭm)	111e	40°36′N	79°44′W
Tarfa, Wādī at, val., Egypt	238b	28°14′N	31°00′E
Târgovişte, Rom.	163	44°54′N	25°29′E
Târgu Jiu, Rom.	163	45°02′N	23°17′E
Târgu Mureş, Rom.	163	46°33′N	24°33′E
Târgu Neamţ, Rom.	169	47°14′N	26°23′E
Târgu Ocna, Rom.	169	46°18′N	26°38′E
Târgu Secuiesc, Rom.	169	46°04′N	26°06′E
Tarhūnah, Libya	200	32°26′N	13°38′E
Tarija, Bol. (tär-rē′hä)	142	21°42′S	64°52′W
Tarīm, Yemen (tȧ-rīm′)	198	16°13′N	49°08′E
Tarim, r., China (tȧ-rīm′)	204	40°45′N	85°39′E
Tarim Basin, basin, China (tȧ-rīm′)	204	39°52′N	82°34′E
Tarka, r., S. Afr. (tä′kȧ)	233c	32°15′S	26°00′E
Tarkastad, S. Afr.	233c	32°01′S	26°18′E
Tarkhankut, Mys, c., Ukr. (mĭs tär-ĸän′kòt)	181	45°21′N	32°30′E
Tarkio, Mo., U.S. (tär′kĭ-ō)	121	40°27′N	95°22′W
Tarkwa, Ghana (tärk′wä)	230	5°19′N	1°59′W
Tarlac, Phil. (tär′läk)	212	15°29′N	120°36′E
Tarlton, S. Afr. (tärl′tŭn)	233b	26°05′S	27°38′E
Tarma, Peru (tär′mä)	142	11°26′S	75°40′W
Tarn, r., Fr. (tärn)	161	43°45′N	2°00′E
Târnăveni, Rom.	169	46°19′N	24°18′E
Tarnów, Pol. (tär′nŏf)	161	50°02′N	21°00′E
Taro, r., Italy (tä′rō)	174	44°41′N	10°03′E
Taroudant, Mor. (tȧ-rōō-dänt′)	230	30°39′N	8°52′W
Tarpon Springs, Fl., U.S. (tär′pŏn)	125a	28°07′N	82°44′W
Tarporley, Eng., U.K. (tär′pēr-lē)	158a	53°09′N	2°40′W
Tarpum Bay, b., Bah. (tär′pŭm)	134	25°05′N	76°20′W
Tarquinia, Italy (tär-kwē′nē-ä)	174	42°16′N	11°46′E
Tarragona, Spain (tär-rä-gō′nä)	154	41°05′N	1°15′E
Tarrant, Al., U.S. (tăr′ănt)	110h	33°35′N	86°46′W
Tàrrega, Spain (tä′rȧ-gä)	173	41°40′N	1°09′E
Tarrejón de Ardoz, Spain (tär-rĕ-kô′n-dĕ-är-dōz)	173a	40°28′N	3°29′W
Tarrytown, N.Y., U.S. (tăr′ĭ-toun)	110a	41°04′N	73°52′W
Tarsus, Tur. (tȧr′sòs) (tär′sŭs)	198	37°00′N	34°50′E
Tartagal, Arg. (tär-tä-gȧ′l)	144	23°31′S	63°47′W
Tartu, Est. (tär′tōō) (dôr′pät)	178	58°23′N	26°44′E
Ṭarṭūs, Syria	200	34°54′N	35°59′E
Tarumi, Japan (tä′rōō-mē)	211b	34°38′N	135°04′E
Tarusa, Russia (tä-rōōs′ȧ)	176	54°43′N	37°11′E
Tarzana, Ca., U.S. (tär-ză′ȧ)	117a	34°10′N	118°32′W
Tashkent, Uzb. (tȧsh′kĕnt)	183	41°23′N	69°04′E
Tasman Bay, b., N.Z. (tăz′măn)	221a	40°50′S	173°20′E
Tasmania, state, Austl.	219	41°28′S	142°30′E
Tasman Peninsula, pen., Austl.	222	43°00′S	148°30′E
Tasman Sea, sea, Oc.	241	29°30′S	155°00′E
Tasquillo, Mex. (täs-kē′lyō)	130	20°34′N	99°21′W
Tatarsk, Russia (tȧ-tärsk′)	178	55°13′N	75°58′E
Tatarstan, prov., Russia	180	55°00′N	51°00′E
Tatar Strait, strt., Russia	179	51°00′N	141°45′E
Tater Hill, mtn., Or., U.S. (tāt′ēr hĭl)	116c	45°47′N	123°02′W
Tateyama, Japan (tä′tē-yä′mä)	211	35°04′N	139°52′E
Tatlow, Mount, mtn., Can.	94	51°23′N	123°52′W
Tau, Nor.	166	59°05′N	5°59′E
Tauern Tunnel, trans., Aus.	168	47°12′N	13°17′E
Taung, S. Afr. (tä′ông)	232	27°25′S	24°47′E
Taunton, Ma., U.S. (tän′tŭn)	109	41°54′N	71°03′W
Taunton, r., R.I., U.S.	110b	41°50′N	71°02′W
Taupo, Lake, l., N.Z. (tä′ōō-pō)	221a	38°42′S	175°55′E
Taurage, Lith. (tou′rā-gā)	167	55°15′N	22°18′E
Taurus Mountains *see* Toros Dağları, mts., Tur.	198	37°00′N	32°40′E
Tauste, Spain (tä-ōōs′tå)	172	41°55′N	1°15′W
Tavda, Russia (tȧv-dȧ′)	178	58°00′N	64°44′E
Tavda, r., Russia	184	58°30′N	64°15′E
Taverny, Fr. (tȧ-vĕr-nē′)	171b	49°02′N	2°13′E
Taviche, Mex. (tä-vē′chĕ)	131	16°43′N	96°35′W
Tavira, Port. (tä-vē′rȧ)	172	37°09′N	7°42′W
Tavşanlı, Tur. (táv′shän-lĭ)	181	39°30′N	29°30′E
Tawakoni, l., Tx., U.S.	123	32°51′N	95°59′W
Tawaramoto, Japan (tä′wä-rä-mô-tô)	211b	34°33′N	135°48′E
Tawas City, Mi., U.S.	108	44°15′N	83°30′W
Tawas Point, c., Mi., U.S. (tô′wȧs)	108	44°15′N	83°25′W
Tawitawi Group, is., Phil. (tä′wē-tä′wē)	212	4°52′N	120°35′E
Tawkar, Sudan	231	18°28′N	37°46′E
Taxco de Alarcón, Mex. (täs′kō dĕ ä-lär-kō′n)	130	18°34′N	99°37′W
Tay, r., Scot., U.K.	164	56°35′N	3°37′W
Tay, Loch, l., Scot., U.K.	164	56°25′N	4°07′W
Tayabas Bay, b., Phil. (tä-yä′bäs)	213a	13°44′N	121°40′E
Tayga, Russia (tī′gä)	184	56°12′N	85°47′E

PLACE (Pronunciation)	PAGE	LAT.	LONG.
Taygonos, Mys, c., Russia	179	60°37′N	160°17′E
Taylor, Tx., U.S.	123	30°35′N	97°25′W
Taylor, Mount, mtn., N.M., U.S.	106	35°20′N	107°40′W
Taylorville, Il., U.S. (tā′lēr-vĭl)	108	39°30′N	89°20′W
Taymyr, l., Russia (tī-mĭr′)	179	74°13′N	100°45′E
Taymyr, Poluostrov, pen., Russia	179	75°15′N	95°00′E
Tayshet, Russia (tī-shĕt′)	179	56°09′N	97°49′E
Tayug, Phil.	213a	16°01′N	120°45′E
Taz, r., Russia (tȧz)	184	67°15′N	80°45′E
Taza, Mor. (tä′zä)	230	34°08′N	4°00′W
Tazovskoye, Russia	178	66°58′N	78°28′E
Tbessa, Alg.	230	35°27′N	8°13′E
Tbilisi, Geor. (′tbĭl-yē′sē)	181	41°40′N	44°45′E
Tchentlo Lake, l., Can.	94	55°11′N	125°00′W
Tchibanga, Gabon (chē-bäŋ′gä)	232	2°51′S	11°02′E
Tchien, Lib.	234	6°04′N	8°08′W
Tchigai, Plateau du, plat., Afr.	235	21°20′N	14°50′E
Tczew, Pol. (t′chĕf′)	160	54°06′N	18°48′E
Teabo, Mex. (tĕ-ä′bô)	132a	20°25′N	89°14′W
Teague, Tx., U.S.	123	31°39′N	96°16′W
Teapa, Mex. (tā-ä′pä)	131	17°35′N	92°56′W
Tebing Tinggi, i., Indon. (teb′ĭng-tĭng′gä)	197b	0°54′N	102°39′E
Tecalitlán, Mex. (tā-kä-lē-tlän′)	130	19°28′N	103°17′W
Techiman, Ghana	234	7°35′N	1°56′W
Tecoanapa, Mex. (tāk-wä-nä-pä′)	130	16°33′N	98°46′W
Tecoh, Mex. (tĕ-kô)	132a	20°46′N	89°27′W
Tecolotlán, Mex. (tā-kô-lô-tlän′)	130	20°13′N	103°57′W
Tecolutla, Mex. (tā-kô-lōō′tlä)	131	20°33′N	97°00′W
Tecolutla, r., Mex.	131	20°16′N	97°14′W
Tecomán, Mex. (tā-kô-män′)	130	18°53′N	103°53′W
Tecómitl, Mex. (tĕ-kô′mētl)	131a	19°13′N	98°59′W
Tecozautla, Mex. (tā′kō-zä-ōō′tlä)	130	20°33′N	99°38′W
Tecpan de Galeana, Mex. (tĕk-pän′ dā gä-lā-ä′nä)	130	17°13′N	100°41′W
Tecpatán, Mex. (tĕk-pä-tä′n)	131	17°08′N	93°18′W
Tecuala, Mex. (tĕ-kwä-lä)	130	22°24′N	105°29′W
Tecuci, Rom. (ta-kòch′)	163	45°51′N	27°30′E
Tecumseh, Can. (tē-kŭm′sĕ)	111b	42°19′N	82°53′W
Tecumseh, Mi., U.S.	108	42°00′N	84°00′W
Tecumseh, Ne., U.S.	121	40°21′N	96°09′W
Tecumseh, Ok., U.S.	121	35°18′N	96°55′W
Tees, r., Eng., U.K. (tēz)	164	54°40′N	2°10′W
Teganuna, l., Japan (tā′gä-nōō′nä)	211a	35°50′N	140°02′E
Tegucigalpa, Hond. (tå-gōō-sē-gäl′pä)	128	14°08′N	87°15′W
Tehachapi Mountains, mts., Ca., U.S. (tē-hă-shă′pĭ)	118	34°50′N	118°55′W
Tehrān, Iran (tĕ-hrän′)	198	35°45′N	51°30′E
Tehuacan, Mex. (tā-wä-kän′)	128	18°27′N	97°23′W
Tehuantepec, Mex.	128	16°20′N	95°14′W
Tehuantepec, r., Mex.	131	16°30′N	95°23′W
Tehuantepec, Golfo de, b., Mex. (gôl-fô dĕ)	128	15°45′N	95°00′W
Tehuantepec, Istmo de, isth., Mex. (ē′st-mô dĕ)	131	17°55′N	94°35′W
Tehuehuetla, Arroyo, r., Mex. (tĕ-wĕ-wĕ′tlä är-rô-yô)	130	17°54′N	100°26′W
Tehuitzingo, Mex. (tā-wē-tzĭŋ′gō)	130	18°21′N	98°16′W
Tejeda, Sierra de, mts., Spain (sē-ĕ′r-rä dĕ tĕ-kĕ′dä)	172	36°55′N	4°00′W
Tejúpan, Mex. (tĕ-ĸōō-pä′n) (sän-tyä′gô)	131	17°39′N	97°34′W
Tejúpan, Punta, c., Mex.	130	18°19′N	103°30′W
Tejupilco de Hidalgo, Mex. (tå-hōō-pēl′kō dā ē-dhäl′gō)	130	18°52′N	100°07′W
Tekamah, Ne., U.S. (tē-kā′mȧ)	112	41°46′N	96°13′W
Tekax de Alvaro Obregon, Mex.	132a	20°12′N	89°11′W
Tekeze, r., Afr.	231	13°38′N	38°00′E
Tekit, Mex. (tĕ-kē′t)	132a	20°35′N	89°18′W
Tekoa, Wa., U.S. (tē-kō′ȧ)	114	47°15′N	117°03′W
Tela, Hond. (tā′lä)	128	15°45′N	87°25′W
Tela, Bahía de, b., Hond.	132	15°53′N	87°29′W
Telapa Burok, Gunong, mtn., Malay.	197b	2°51′N	102°04′E
Telavi, Geor.	181	42°00′N	45°20′E
Tel Aviv-Yafo, Isr. (tĕl-ä-vēv′já′fȧ)	198	32°03′N	34°46′E
Telegraph Creek, Can. (tĕl′ē-gráf)	90	57°59′N	131°22′W
Teleneşti, Mol.	177	47°31′N	28°22′E
Telescope Peak, mtn., Ca., U.S. (tĕl′ē skōp)	106	36°12′N	117°05′W
Telesung, Indon.	197b	1°07′N	102°53′E
Telica, vol., Nic. (tå-lē′kä)	132	12°38′N	86°52′W
Tell City, In., U.S. (tĕl)	108	38°00′N	86°45′W
Teller, Ak., U.S. (tĕl′ēr)	103	65°17′N	166°28′W
Tello, Col. (tĕ′l-yô)	142a	3°05′N	75°08′W
Telluride, Co., U.S. (tĕl′ū-rīd)	119	37°55′N	107°50′W
Telok Datok, Malay.	197b	2°51′N	101°33′E
Teloloapan, Mex. (tā′lô-lô-ä′pän)	130	18°19′N	99°54′W
Tel′pos-Iz, Gora, mtn., Russia (tyĕl′pôs-ēz′)	178	63°50′N	59°20′E
Telšiai, Lith. (tĕl′sha′ē)	167	55°59′N	22°17′E
Teltow, Ger. (tĕl′tō)	159b	52°24′N	13°12′E
Teluklecak, Indon.	197b	1°53′N	101°45′E
Tema, Ghana	234	5°38′N	0°01′E
Temascalcingo, Mex. (tā′mäs-käl-sĭŋ′gō)	130	19°55′N	100°00′W
Temascaltepec, Mex. (tā′mäs-käl-tå pĕk)	130	19°00′N	100°03′W
Temax, Mex. (tĕ′mäx)	128	21°10′N	88°51′W
Temir, Kaz.	183	49°10′N	57°15′E
Temirtaū, Kaz.	183	50°08′N	73°13′E
Temiscouata, l., Can. (tĕ′mĭs-kō-ä′tä)	100	47°40′N	68°50′W
Témiskaming, Can. (tē-mĭs′kȧ-mĭng)	91	46°41′N	79°01′W
Temoaya, Mex. (tĕ-mô-a-um-yä)	131a	19°28′N	99°36′W

ăt; finăl; rāte; senåte; ärm; åsk; sofȧ; fâre; ch-choose; dh-as th in other; bē; ēvent; bĕt; recĕnt; cratēr; g-gō; gh-guttural g; bĭt; ĭ-short neutral; rīde; ĸ-guttural k as ch in German ich;

PRONOUNCING INDEX Tempe – Tidjikdja 357

PLACE (Pronunciation)	PAGE	LAT.	LONG.
Tempe, Az., U.S.	119	33°24′N	111°54′W
Temperley, Arg. (tĕ′m-pĕr-lā)	144a	34°47′S	58°24′W
Tempio Pausania, Italy (tĕm′pė-ō pou-sä′nė-ä)	174	40°55′N	9°05′E
Temple, Tx., U.S. (tĕm′p′l)	123	31°06′N	97°20′W
Temple City, Ca., U.S.	117a	34°07′N	118°02′W
Templeton, Can. (tĕm′p′l-tŭn)	102c	45°29′N	75°37′W
Templin, Ger. (tĕm-plēn′)	168	53°08′N	13°30′E
Tempoal, r., Mex. (tĕm-pô-ä′l)	130	21°38′N	98°23′W
Temryuk, Russia (tyĕm-ryök′)	181	45°17′N	37°21′E
Temuco, Chile (tå-mōō′kō)	144	38°46′S	72°38′W
Temyasovo, Russia (tĕm-yä′sô-vô)	186a	53°00′N	58°06′E
Tenāli, India	203	16°10′N	80°32′E
Tenamaxtlán, Mex. (tā′nä-mäs-tlän′)	130	20°13′N	104°06′W
Tenancingo, Mex. (tå-nän-sēŋ′gō)	130	18°54′N	99°36′W
Tenango, Mex. (tå-näŋ′gō)	131a	19°09′N	98°51′W
Tenasserim, Mya. (tĕn-ăs′ẽr-ĭm)	212	12°09′N	99°01′E
Tendrivs'ka Kosa, ostriv, i., Ukr.	177	46°12′N	31°17′E
Tenerife Island, i., Spain (tå-nå-rē′få) (tĕn-ẽr-ĭf′)	230	28°41′N	17°02′W
Tènés, Alg. (tā-nĕs′)	161	36°28′N	1°22′E
Tengiz köli, l., Kaz.	183	50°45′N	68°39′E
Tengxian, China (tŭŋ shyĕn)	208	35°07′N	117°08′E
Tenjin, Japan (tĕn′jĕn)	211b	34°54′N	135°04′E
Tenke, D.R.C. (tĕŋ′kå)	232	11°26′S	26°45′E
Tenkiller Ferry Reservoir, res., Ok., U.S. (tĕn-kĭl′ẽr)	121	35°42′N	94°47′W
Tenkodogo, Burkina (tĕŋ-kō-dō′gō)	230	11°47′N	0°22′W
Tenmile, r., Wa., U.S. (tĕn mīl)	116d	48°52′N	122°32′W
Tennant Creek, Austl. (tĕn′ănt)	218	19°45′S	134°00′E
Tennessee, state, U.S. (tĕn-ĕ-sē′)	105	35°50′N	88°00′W
Tennessee, r., U.S.	107	35°35′N	88°20′W
Tennille, Ga., U.S. (tĕn′ĭl)	124	32°55′N	86°50′W
Teno, r., Chile (tĕ′nō)	141b	34°55′S	71°00′W
Tenora, Austl. (tĕn-ôrȧ)	222	34°23′S	147°33′E
Tenosique, Mex. (tā-nō-sē′kå)	131	17°27′N	91°25′W
Tenri, Japan	211b	34°36′N	135°50′E
Tenryū-Gawa, r., Japan (tĕn′ryōō′gä′wä)	211	35°16′N	137°54′E
Tensas, r., La., U.S. (tĕn′sô)	123	31°54′N	91°30′W
Tensaw, r., Al., U.S. (tĕn′sô)	124	30°45′N	87°52′W
Tenterfield, Austl. (tĕn′tẽr-fēld)	219	29°00′S	152°06′E
Ten Thousand, Islands, is., Fl., U.S. (tĕn thou′zănd)	125a	25°45′N	81°35′W
Teocaltiche, Mex. (tā′ō-käl-tē′chå)	130	21°27′N	102°38′W
Teocelo, Mex. (tā-ō-sā′lō)	131	19°22′N	96°57′W
Teocuitatlán de Corona, Mex.	130	20°06′N	103°22′W
Teófilo Otoni, Braz. (tĕ-ô′fē-lō-tô′nĕ)	143	17°49′S	41°18′W
Teoloyucan, Mex. (tā′ō-lō-yōō′kän)	130	19°43′N	99°12′W
Teopisca, Mex. (tā-ō-pēs′kä)	131	16°30′N	92°33′W
Teotihuacán, Mex. (tĕ-ô-tē-wȧ-kȧ′n)	131a	19°40′N	98°52′W
Teotitlán del Camino, Mex. (tā-ō-tė-tlän′ dĕl kä-mē′nō)	131	18°07′N	97°04′W
Tepalcatepec, Mex. (tā′päl-kä-tå′pĕk)	130	19°11′N	102°51′W
Tepalcatepec, r., Mex.	130	18°54′N	102°25′W
Tepalcingo, Mex. (tā-päl-sēŋ′gō)	130	18°34′N	98°49′W
Tepatitlán de Morelos, Mex. (tā-pä-tė-tlän′ dā mō-rā′los)	128	20°55′N	102°47′W
Tepeaca, Mex. (tā-på-ä′kä)	131	18°57′N	97°54′W
Tepecoacuilco de Trujano, Mex.	130	18°15′N	99°29′W
Tepeji del Río, Mex. (tā-på-ĸe′ dĕl rē′ō)	130	19°55′N	99°22′W
Tepelmeme, Mex. (tā′pĕl-mā′må)	131	17°51′N	97°23′W
Tepetlaoxtoc, Mex. (tā′på-tlä′ōs-tōk′)	130	19°34′N	98°49′W
Tepezala, Mex. (tā-på-zä-lä′)	130	22°12′N	102°12′W
Tepic, Mex. (tā-pēk′)	128	21°32′N	104°53′W
Tëplaya Gora, Russia (tyôp′lȧ-yȧ gô-rȧ)	186a	58°32′N	59°08′W
Teplice, Czech Rep.	161	50°39′N	13°50′E
Teposcolula, Mex.	131	17°33′N	97°29′W
Tequendama, Salto de, wtfl., Col. (sä′l-tō dĕ tĕ-kĕn-dä′mä)	142	4°34′N	74°18′W
Tequila, Mex. (tå-kē′lä)	130	20°53′N	103°48′W
Tequisistlán, r., Mex. (tĕ-kē-sės-tlȧ′n)	131	16°20′N	95°40′W
Tequisquiapan, Mex. (tå-kēs-kė-ä′pän)	130	20°33′N	99°57′W
Ter, r., Spain (tĕr)	173	42°04′N	2°52′E
Téra, Niger	234	14°01′N	0°45′E
Tera, r., Spain (tā′rä)	172	42°05′N	6°24′W
Teramo, Italy (tā′rä-mô)	174	42°40′N	13°41′E
Terborg, Neth. (tĕr-bōrg)	171c	51°55′N	6°23′E
Tercan, Tur. (tĕr′jän)	181	39°40′N	40°12′E
Terceira Island, i., Port. (tĕr-sā′rä)	230a	38°49′N	26°36′W
Terebovlia, Ukr.	169	49°18′N	25°43′E
Terek, r., Russia	181	43°30′N	45°10′E
Terenkul', Russia (tĕ-rĕn′kŏl)	186a	55°38′N	62°18′E
Teresina, Braz. (tĕr-å-sē′nȧ)	143	5°04′S	42°42′W
Teresópolis, Braz. (tĕr-ā-sō′pō-lēzh)	141a	22°25′S	42°59′W
Teriberka, Russia (tyĕr-ė-byôr′kȧ)	180	69°00′N	35°15′E
Terme, Tur. (tĕr′mĕ)	181	41°05′N	37°00′E
Termez, Uzb. (tyĕr′mĕz)	183	37°19′N	67°20′E
Termini, Italy (tĕr′mė-nė)	174	37°58′N	13°39′E
Términos, Laguna de, l., Mex. (lä-gō′nä dĕ ĕ′r-mē-nōs)	128	18°37′N	91°32′W
Termoli, Italy (tĕr′mô-lė)	174	42°00′N	15°01′E
Tern, r., Eng., U.K. (tûrn)	158a	52°49′N	2°31′W
Ternate, Indon. (tĕr-nä′tā)	213	0°52′N	127°25′E
Terni, Italy (tĕr′nė)	162	42°38′N	12°41′E
Ternopil', Ukr.	181	49°32′N	25°36′E
Terpeniya, Mys, c., Russia	179	48°44′N	144°42′E
Terpeniya, Zaliv, b., Russia (zä′lĭf tĕr-pă′nĭ-yȧ)	210	49°10′N	143°05′E
Terrace, Can. (tĕr′ĭs)	90	54°31′N	128°35′W
Terracina, Italy (tĕr-rä-chē′nä)	162	41°18′N	13°14′E
Terra Nova National Park, rec., Can.	93a	48°37′N	54°15′W
Terrassa, Spain	173	41°34′N	2°01′E
Terrebonne, Can. (tĕr-bŏn′)	109	45°42′N	73°38′W
Terrebonne Bay, b., La., U.S.	123	28°55′N	90°30′W
Terre Haute, In., U.S. (tĕr-ė hōt′)	105	39°25′N	87°25′W
Terrell, Tx., U.S. (tĕr′ĕl)	123	32°44′N	96°15′W
Terrell, Wa., U.S.	116d	48°53′N	122°44′W
Terrell Hills, Tx., U.S. (tĕr′ĕl hĭlz)	117d	29°28′N	98°27′W
Terschelling, i., Neth. (tĕr-sĸĕl′ĭng)	165	53°25′N	5°12′E
Teruel, Spain (tå-rōō-ĕl′)	162	40°20′N	1°05′W
Tešanj, Bos. (tĕ′shän’)	175	44°36′N	17°59′E
Teschendorf, Ger. (tĕ′shĕn-dōrf)	159b	52°51′N	13°10′E
Tesecheacan, Mex. (tĕ-sĕ-chĕ-ä-kȧ′n)	131	18°10′N	95°41′W
Teshekpuk, l., Ak., U.S. (tē-shĕk′pŭk)	103	70°18′N	152°36′W
Teshio Dake, mtn., Japan (tĕsh′ė-ō-dä′kā)	210	44°00′N	142°50′E
Teshio Gawa, r., Japan (tĕsh′ė-ō gä′wä)	210	44°53′N	144°55′E
Tesiyn, r., Asia	204	49°45′N	96°00′E
Teslin, Can. (tĕs-lĭn)	103	60°10′N	132°30′W
Teslin, l., Can.	92	60°12′N	132°08′W
Teslin, r., Can.	92	61°18′N	134°14′W
Tessaoua, Niger (tĕs-sä′ō-ä)	230	13°53′N	7°53′E
Tessenderlo, Bel.	159a	51°04′N	5°08′E
Test, r., Eng., U.K. (tĕst)	164	51°10′N	1°30′W
Testa del Gargano, c., Italy (tās′tä dĕl gär-gä′nō)	174	41°48′N	16°13′E
Tetachuck Lake, l., Can.	94	53°20′N	125°50′W
Tete, Moz. (tā′tĕ)	232	16°13′S	33°35′E
Tête Jaune Cache, Can. (tĕt′zhŏn-kăsh)	95	52°57′N	119°26′W
Teteriv, r., Ukr.	181	51°05′N	29°30′E
Teterow, Ger. (tā′tĕ-rō)	168	53°46′N	12°33′E
Teteven, Blg. (tĕt′ĕ-ven’)	175	42°57′N	24°15′E
Teton, r., Mt., U.S. (tē′tŏn)	115	47°54′N	111°37′W
Tétouan, Mor.	230	35°42′N	5°34′W
Tetovo, Mac. (tā′tō-vō)	175	42°01′N	21°00′E
Tetyukhe-Pristan, Russia (tĕt-yōō′ĸĕ prĭ-stän′)	210	44°21′N	135°44′E
Tetyushi, Russia (tÿt-yŏ′shĭ)	180	54°57′N	48°50′E
Teupitz, Ger. (toi′pētz)	159b	42°08′N	13°37′E
Tevere, r., Italy	162	42°30′N	12°14′E
Teverya, Isr.	197a	32°48′N	35°32′E
Tewksbury, Ma., U.S. (tūks′bĕr-ĭ)	101a	42°37′N	71°14′W
Texada Island, i., Can.	94	49°40′N	124°24′W
Texarkana, Ar., U.S. (tĕk-sär-kän′ȧ)	105	33°26′N	94°02′W
Texarkana, Tx., U.S.	105	33°26′N	94°04′W
Texas, state, U.S.	104	31°00′N	101°00′W
Texas City, Tx., U.S.	123	29°23′N	94°54′W
Texcaltitlán, Mex. (tās-käl′tė-tlän′)	130	18°54′N	99°51′W
Texcoco, Mex. (tās-kō′kō)	130	19°31′N	98°53′W
Texcoco, Lago de, l., Mex.	131a	19°30′N	99°00′W
Texel, i., Neth. (tĕk′sĕl)	165	53°10′N	4°45′E
Texistepec, Mex. (tĕk-sēs-tā-pĕk′)	131	17°51′N	94°46′W
Texmelucan, Mex.	130	19°17′N	98°26′W
Texoma, Lake, res., U.S. (tĕk′ō-mă)	106	34°03′N	96°28′W
Texontepec, Mex. (tå-zōn-tå-pĕk′)	130	19°52′N	98°48′W
Texontepec de Aldama, Mex. (dā äl-dä′mä)	130	20°19′N	99°19′W
Teyateyaneng, Leso.	233c	29°11′S	27°43′E
Teykovo, Russia (tĕy-kô-vō)	180	56°52′N	40°34′E
Teziutlán, Mex. (tå-zė-ōō-tlän′)	131	19°48′N	97°21′W
Tezpur, India	202	26°42′N	92°52′E
Tha-anne, r., Can.	92	60°50′N	96°56′W
Thabana Ntlenyana, mtn., Leso.	233c	29°28′S	29°17′E
Thabazimbi, S. Afr.	238c	24°36′S	27°22′E
Thailand, nation, Asia	212	16°30′N	101°00′E
Thailand, Gulf of, b., Asia	212	11°37′N	100°46′E
Thale Luang, l., Thai.	212	7°51′N	99°39′E
Thame, Eng., U.K. (tām)	158b	51°43′N	0°59′W
Thames, r., Can. (tĕmz)	98	42°40′N	81°45′W
Thames, r., Eng., U.K.	156	51°30′N	1°30′W
Thāmit, Wadi, r., Libya	163	30°39′N	16°23′E
Thāna, India (thä′nŭ)	202	19°13′N	72°58′E
Thāna Creek, r., India	203b	19°03′N	72°58′E
Thanh Hoa, Viet. (tän′hō′ȧ)	212	19°46′N	105°42′E
Thanjāvūr, India	199	10°51′N	79°11′E
Thann, Fr. (tän)	171	47°49′N	7°05′E
Thaon-les-Vosges, Fr. (tä-ŏɴ-lā-vōzh′)	171	48°16′N	6°24′E
Thargomindah, Austl. (thär′gō-mĭn′dȧ)	219	27°58′S	143°57′E
Thásos, i., Grc. (thă′sōs)	163	40°41′N	24°53′E
Thatch Cay, i., V.I.U.S. (thăch)	129c	18°22′N	64°53′W
Thaya, r., Eur. (tä′yȧ)	168	48°48′N	15°40′E
Thayer, Mo., U.S. (thâ′ẽr)	121	36°30′N	91°34′W
Thebes *see* Thíva, Grc.	163	38°20′N	23°18′E
Thebes, hist., Egypt (thēbz)	231	25°47′N	32°39′E
The Brothers, mtn., Wa., U.S.	116a	47°39′N	123°08′W
The Coorong, l., Austl. (kŏ′rŏng)	222	36°07′S	139°45′E
The Coteau, hills, Can.	96	51°10′N	107°30′W
The Dalles, Or., U.S. (dălz)	104	45°36′N	121°10′W
The Father, mtn., Pap. N. Gui.	213	5°05′S	151°30′E
The Hague ('s-Gravenhage), Neth.	154	52°05′N	4°16′E
The Oaks, Austl.	217b	34°04′S	150°36′E
Theodore, Austl. (thēō′dôr)	222	24°51′S	150°09′E
Theodore Roosevelt Dam, dam, Az., U.S. (thė-ō-dōr rōō-sȧ-vĕlt)	119	33°46′N	111°25′W
Theodore Roosevelt Lake, res., Az., U.S.	119	33°45′N	111°00′W
Theodore Roosevelt National Park, rec., N.D., U.S.	112	47°20′N	103°42′W
Theológos, Grc.	175	40°37′N	24°41′E
The Pas, Can. (pä)	90	53°50′N	101°15′W
Thermopolis, Wy., U.S. (thẽr-mŏp′ō-lĭs)	115	43°38′N	108°11′W
The Round Mountain, mtn., Austl.	222	30°17′S	152°19′E
Thessalía, hist. reg., Grc.	175	39°50′N	22°09′E
Thessalon, Can.	91	46°11′N	83°37′W
Thessaloníki, Grc. (thĕs-sȧ-lō-nē′kė)	154	40°38′N	22°59′E
Thetford Mines, Can. (thĕt′fẽrd mīns)	99	46°05′N	71°20′W
The Twins, mtn., Afr. (twĭnz)	233c	30°09′S	28°29′E
Theunissen, S. Afr.	238c	28°25′S	26°44′E
The Wrekin, co., Eng., U.K.	158a	53°43′N	2°30′W
Thibaudeau, Can. (tĭ′bŏ-dō′)	97	57°05′N	94°08′W
Thibodaux, La., U.S. (tė-bō-dō′)	123	29°48′N	90°48′W
Thief, l., Mn., U.S. (thēf)	112	48°32′N	95°46′W
Thief, r., Mn., U.S.	113	48°18′N	96°07′E
Thief Rivers Falls, Mn., U.S. (thēf rĭv′ẽr fôlz)	112	48°07′N	96°11′W
Thiers, Fr. (tyâr)	170	45°51′N	3°32′E
Thiès, Sen. (tė-ĕs′)	230	14°48′N	16°56′W
Thika, Kenya	237	1°03′S	37°05′E
Thimphu, Bhu.	199	27°33′N	89°42′E
Thingvallavatn, l., Ice.	160	64°12′N	20°22′W
Thio, N. Cal.	214f	21°37′S	166°14′E
Thionville, Fr. (tyôɴ-vēl′)	161	49°23′N	6°31′E
Third Cataract, wtfl., Sudan	231	19°53′N	30°11′E
Thiruvananthapuram, India	203	8°34′N	76°58′E
Thisted, Den. (tes′tĕdh)	166	56°57′N	8°38′E
Thistilfjördur, b., Ice.	160	66°29′N	14°59′W
Thistle, i., Austl. (thĭs′′l)	222	34°55′S	136°11′E
Thíva (Thebes), Grc.	162	38°20′N	23°18′E
Thjörsá, r., Ice. (tyûr′sȧ)	160	64°23′N	19°18′W
Thohoyandou, S. Afr.	232	23°00′S	30°29′E
Tholen, Neth.	159a	51°32′N	4°11′E
Thomas, Ok., U.S. (tŏm′ăs)	120	35°44′N	98°43′W
Thomas, W.V., U.S.	109	39°15′N	79°30′W
Thomaston, Ga., U.S. (tŏm′ăs-tŭn)	124	32°51′N	84°17′W
Thomasville, Al., U.S. (tŏm′ăs-vĭl)	124	31°55′N	87°43′W
Thomasville, N.C., U.S.	125	35°52′N	80°05′W
Thomlinson, Mount, mtn., Can.	94	55°33′N	127°29′W
Thompson, Can.	90	55°48′N	97°59′W
Thompson, r., Can.	95	50°15′N	121°20′W
Thompson, r., Mo., U.S.	121	40°32′N	93°49′W
Thompson Falls, Mt., U.S.	114	47°35′N	115°20′W
Thomson, r., Austl. (tŏm-sŏn)	221	24°30′S	143°07′E
Thomson's Falls, Kenya	237	0°02′N	36°22′E
Thonon-les-Bains, Fr. (tō-nôɴ′lå-băɴ′)	171	46°22′N	6°27′E
Thorne, Eng., U.K. (thôrn)	158a	53°37′N	0°58′W
Thorntown, In., U.S. (thôrn′tŭn)	108	40°05′N	86°35′W
Thorold, Can. (thō′rōld)	99	43°13′N	79°12′W
Thouars, Fr. (tōō-är′)	170	47°00′N	0°17′W
Thousand Islands, is., N.Y., U.S. (thou′zănd)	109	44°15′N	76°10′W
Thrace, hist. reg. (thrās)	175	41°20′N	26°07′E
Thrapston, Eng., U.K. (thrăp′stŭn)	158a	52°23′N	0°32′W
Three Forks, Mt., U.S. (thrē fôrks)	115	45°56′N	111°35′W
Three Oaks, Mi., U.S. (thrē ōks)	108	41°50′N	86°40′W
Three Points, Cape, c., Ghana	230	4°45′N	2°06′W
Three Rivers, Mi., U.S.	108	42°00′N	83°40′W
Thule, Grnld.	89	76°34′N	68°47′W
Thun, Switz. (tōōn)	168	46°46′N	7°34′E
Thunder Bay, Can.	98	48°28′N	89°12′W
Thunder Bay, b., Can. (thŭn′dẽr)	98	48°29′N	88°52′W
Thunder Hills, hills, Can.	96	54°30′N	106°00′W
Thunersee, l., Switz.	168	46°40′N	7°30′E
Thurber, Tx., U.S. (thûr′bẽr)	122	32°30′N	98°23′W
Thüringen (Thuringia), hist. reg., Ger. (tü′rĭng-ĕn)	168	51°07′N	10°45′E
Thurles, Ire. (thûrlz)	164	52°44′N	7°45′W
Thurrock, co., Eng., U.K.	158b	51°30′N	0°22′E
Thursday, i., Austl. (thûrz-dā)	221	10°17′S	142°23′E
Thurso, Can. (thŭn′sō)	102c	45°36′N	75°15′W
Thurso, Scot., U.K.	164	58°35′N	3°40′W
Thurston Island, i., Ant. (thûrs′tŭn)	224	71°20′S	98°00′W
Tiachiv, Ukr.	169	48°01′N	23°42′E
Tiandong, China (tĭĕn-dōŋ)	209	23°32′N	107°10′E
Tianjin, China	205	39°08′N	117°14′E
Tianjin Shi, prov., China (tĭĕn-jyĭn shr)	208	39°30′N	117°13′E
Tianmen, China (tĭĕn-mŭn)	209	30°40′N	113°10′E
Tianshui, China (tĭĕn-shwā)	208	34°25′N	105°40′E
Tiasmyn, r., Ukr.	177	49°14′N	32°23′E
Tibagi, Braz. (tē′bȧ-zhē)	143	24°40′S	50°35′W
Tibasti, Sarir, des., Libya	231	24°00′N	16°30′E
Tibati, Cam.	235	6°27′N	12°38′E
Tiber *see* Tevere, r., Italy	162	42°30′N	12°14′E
Tibesti, mts., Chad	231	20°40′N	17°48′E
Tibet *see* Xizang, prov., China (tĭ-bĕt′)	204	32°22′N	83°30′E
Tibnīn, Leb.	197a	33°12′N	35°23′E
Tiburon, Haiti	135	18°35′N	74°25′W
Tiburon, Ca., U.S. (tē-bōō-rōn′)	116b	37°53′N	122°27′W
Tiburón, i., Mex.	128	28°45′N	113°10′W
Tiburón, Cabo, c. (kȧ′bō)	133	8°42′N	77°19′W
Tiburon Island, i., Ca., U.S.	116b	37°52′N	122°26′W
Ticao Island, i., Phil. (tė-kä′ō)	213a	12°40′N	123°30′E
Tickhill, Eng., U.K. (tĭk′ĭl)	158a	53°26′N	1°06′W
Ticonderoga, N.Y., U.S. (tī-kŏn-dẽr-ō′gȧ)	109	43°50′N	73°30′W
Ticul, Mex. (tē-kōō′l)	132a	20°22′N	89°32′W
Tidaholm, Swe. (tē′dȧ-hōlm)	166	58°11′N	13°53′E
Tideswell, Eng., U.K. (tīdz′wĕl)	158a	53°17′N	1°47′W
Tidikelt, reg., Alg. (tē-dė-kĕlt′)	230	25°53′N	2°11′E
Tidjikdja, Maur. (tė-jĭk′jä)	230	18°33′N	11°25′W

ng-sing; ŋ-baŋk; ɴ-nasalized n; nŏd; cŏmmit; ōld; ōbey; ôrder; oi-boil; fōōd; ŏ-as oo in foot; ou-out; s-soft; sh-dish; th-thin; pūre; ůnite; ûrn; stŭd; circŭs; ü-as in French tu; ′-indeterminate vowel.

358 Tidra – Topol'čany PRONOUNCING INDEX

PLACE (Pronunciation)	PAGE	LAT.	LONG.
Tidra, Île, i., Maur.	234	19°50'N	16°45'W
Tieling, China (tĭē-lĭŋ)	205	42°18'N	123°50'E
Tielmes, Spain (tyâl-màs')	173a	40°15'N	3°20'W
Tienen, Bel.	159a	50°49'N	4°58'E
Tien Shan, mts., Asia	204	42°00'N	78°46'E
Tientsin *see* Tianjin, China	205	39°08'N	117°14'E
Tierp, Swe. (tyĕrp)	166	60°21'N	17°28'E
Tierpoort, S. Afr.	233b	25°53'N	28°26'E
Tierra Blanca, Mex. (tyĕ'r-rä-blä'n-kä)	131	18°28'N	96°19'W
Tierra del Fuego, i., S.A. (tyĕr'rä dĕl fwā'gō)	144	53°50'S	68°45'W
Tiétar, r., Spain (tê-ā'tär)	172	39°56'N	5°44'W
Tiffin, Oh., U.S. (tĭf'ĭn)	108	41°10'N	83°15'W
Tifton, Ga., U.S. (tĭf'tŭn)	124	31°25'N	83°34'W
Tigard, Or., U.S. (tĭ'gärd)	116c	45°25'N	122°46'W
Tighina, Mol.	181	46°49'N	29°29'E
Tignish, Can. (tĭg'nĭsh)	100	46°57'N	64°02'W
Tigoda, r., Russia (tē'gō-dà)	186c	59°29'N	31°15'E
Tigre, r., Peru	142	2°20'S	75°41'W
Tigres, Península dos, pen., Ang. (pĕ-nê'n-sōō-lä-dôs-tē'grĕs)	232	16°30'S	11°45'E
Tigris, r., Asia	198	34°45'N	44°10'E
Tīh, Jabal at, mts., Egypt	197a	29°23'N	34°05'E
Tihert, Alg.	230	35°28'N	1°15'E
Tihuatlán, Mex. (tê-wä-tlän')	131	20°43'N	97°34'W
Tijuana, Mex. (tê-hwä'nä)	128	32°32'N	117°02'W
Tijuca, Pico da, mtn., Braz. (pē'kō-dä-tē-zhōō'kà)	144b	22°56'S	43°17'W
Tikal, hist., Guat. (tê-käl')	132a	17°16'N	89°49'W
Tikhoretsk, Russia (tê-ĸôr-yĕtsk')	181	45°55'N	40°05'E
Tikhvin, Russia (têĸ-vēn')	178	59°36'N	33°38'E
Tikrīt, Iraq	198	34°36'N	43°31'E
Tiksi, Russia (tĕk-sē')	179	71°42'N	128°32'E
Tilburg, Neth. (tĭl'bûrg)	161	51°33'N	5°05'E
Tilbury, Eng., U.K.	158b	51°28'N	0°23'E
Tilemsi, Vallée du, val., Mali	234	17°50'N	0°25'E
Tilichiki, Russia (tyĭ-le-chĭ-kê)	179	60°49'N	166°14'E
Tilimsen, Alg.	230	34°53'N	1°21'W
Tillabéry, Niger (tē-yà-bā-rē')	230	14°14'N	1°30'E
Tillamook, Or., U.S. (tĭl'á-mŏŏk)	114	45°27'N	123°50'W
Tillamook Bay, b., Or., U.S.	114	45°32'N	124°26'W
Tillberga, Swe. (tēl-bĕr'ghà)	166	59°40'N	16°34'E
Tillsonburg, Can. (tĭl'sŭn-bûrg)	99	42°50'N	80°50'W
Tim, Russia (têm)	177	51°39'N	37°07'E
Timaru, N.Z. (tĭm'á-rōō)	221a	44°26'S	171°17'E
Timashevskaya, Russia (tēmä-shĕfs-kä'yä)	181	45°47'N	38°57'E
Timbalier Bay, b., La., U.S. (tĭm'bá-lēr)	123	28°55'N	90°14'W
Timber, Or., U.S. (tĭm'bēr)	116c	45°43'N	123°17'W
Timbo, Gui. (tĭm'bō)	230	10°41'N	11°51'W
Timbuktu *see* Tombouctou, Mali	230	16°46'N	3°01'W
Timétrine Monts, mts., Mali	234	17°50'N	0°30'W
Timimoun, Alg. (tē-mê-mōōn')	230	29°14'N	0°22'E
Timiris, Cap, c., Maur.	230	19°23'N	16°32'W
Timiş, r., Eur.	175	45°28'N	21°06'E
Timişoara, Rom.	163	45°44'N	21°21'E
Timmins, Can. (tĭm'ĭnz)	91	48°25'N	81°22'W
Timmonsville, S.C., U.S. (tĭm'ŭnz-vĭl)	125	34°09'N	79°55'W
Timok, r., Eur.	175	43°35'N	22°13'E
Timor, i., Asia (tê-mōr')	213	10°08'S	125°00'E
Timor Sea, sea	220	12°40'S	125°00'E
Timpanogos Cave National Monument, rec., Ut., U.S. (tĭ-măn'ō-gŏz)	119	40°25'N	111°45'W
Timpson, Tx., U.S. (tĭmp'sŭn)	123	31°55'N	94°24'W
Timsāh, l., Egypt (tĭm'sä)	238b	30°34'N	32°22'E
Tina, r., S. Afr. (tē'nà)	233c	30°50'S	28°44'E
Tina, Monte, mtn., Dom. Rep. (mô'n-tĕ-tē'nà)	135	18°50'N	70°40'W
Tinaguillo, Ven. (tê-nä-gē'l-yō)	143b	9°55'N	68°18'W
Tīnah, Khalīj at, b., Egypt	197a	31°06'N	32°42'E
Tindouf, Alg. (tên-dōōf')	230	27°43'N	7°44'W
Tinggi, i., Malay.	197b	2°16'N	104°16'E
Tinghert, Plateau du, plat., Alg.	230	27°30'N	7°30'E
Tingi Mountains, mts., S.L.	234	9°00'N	10°50'W
Tinglin, China	207b	30°53'N	121°18'E
Tingo María, Peru (tē'ngô-mä-rē'ä)	142	9°15'S	76°04'W
Tingréla, C. Iv.	234	10°29'N	6°24'W
Tingsryd, Swe. (tĭngs'rüd)	166	56°32'N	14°58'E
Tinguindio, Mex.	130	19°38'N	102°02'W
Tinguiririca, r., Chile (tē'n-gē-rē-rē'kä)	141b	34°48'S	70°45'W
Tinley Park, Il., U.S. (tĭn'lē)	111a	41°34'N	87°47'W
Tinnoset, Nor. (tên'nôs'sĕt)	166	59°44'N	9°00'E
Tinogasta, Arg. (tē-nô-gäs'tä)	144	28°07'S	67°30'W
Tínos, i., Grc.	163	37°45'N	25°12'E
Tinsukia, India (tin-sōō'kĭ-à)	198	27°18'N	95°29'E
Tintic, Ut., U.S. (tĭn'tĭk)	119	39°55'N	112°15'W
Tio, Pic de, mtn., Gui.	234	8°55'N	8°55'W
Tioman, i., Malay.	197b	2°50'N	104°15'E
Tipitapa, Nic. (tē-pê-tä'pä)	132	12°14'N	86°05'W
Tipitapa, r., Nic.	132	12°13'N	85°57'W
Tippah Creek, r., Ms., U.S. (tĭp'pà)	124	34°43'N	88°15'W
Tippecanoe, r., In., U.S. (tĭp-ē-kà-nōō')	108	40°55'N	86°45'W
Tipperary, Ire. (tĭ-pē-râ'rē)	161	52°28'N	8°13'W
Tippo Bay, Ms., U.S. (tĭp'ō bīōō')	121	33°35'N	90°06'W
Tipton, Ia., U.S.	113	41°46'N	91°10'W
Tipton, In., U.S.	108	40°15'N	86°00'W
Tiranë, Alb. (tē-rä'nà)	154	41°48'N	19°50'E
Tirano, Italy (tê-rä'nō)	174	46°12'N	10°09'E
Tiraspol, Mol.	181	46°52'N	29°38'E
Tire, Tur. (tē'rĕ)	163	38°05'N	27°48'E
Tiree, i., Scot., U.K. (tī-rē')	160	56°34'N	6°30'W
Tirlyanskiy, Russia (tĭr-lyän'skĭ)	186a	54°13'N	58°37'E
Tiruchchirāppalli, India (tĭr'ŏ-chĭ-rä'pà-lĭ)	199	10°49'N	78°48'E
Tirunelveli, India	203	8°53'N	77°43'E
Tiruppur, India	203	11°11'N	77°08'E
Tisdale, Can. (tĭz'dāl)	90	52°51'N	104°04'W
Tista, r., Asia	202	26°00'N	89°30'E
Tisza, r., Eur. (tê'sä)	156	47°30'N	21°00'E
Titāgarh, India	202a	22°44'N	88°23'E
Titicaca, Lago, l., S.A. (lä'gô-tē-tē-kä'kä)	142	16°12'S	70°33'W
Titiribi, Col. (tē-tē-rē-bê')	142a	6°05'N	75°47'W
Tito, Lagh, r., Kenya	237	2°25'N	39°05'E
Titov Veles, Mac. (tê'tôv vĕ'lĕs)	175	41°42'N	21°50'E
Titterstone Clee Hill, hill, Eng., U.K. (klē)	158a	52°24'N	2°37'W
Titule, D.R.C.	237	3°17'N	25°32'E
Titusville, Fl., U.S. (tĭ'tŭs-vĭl)	125a	28°37'N	80°44'W
Titusville, Pa., U.S.	109	40°40'N	79°40'W
Titz, Ger. (tētz)	171c	51°00'N	6°26'E
Tiverton, R.I., U.S. (tĭv'ēr-tun)	110b	41°38'N	71°11'W
Tivoli, Italy (tē'vô-lê)	162	41°38'N	12°48'E
Tixkokob, Mex. (tēx-kō-kō'b)	132a	21°01'N	89°23'W
Tixtla de Guerrero, Mex. (tē'x-tlä-dē-gēr-rē'rô)	130	17°36'N	99°24'W
Tizard Bank and Reef, rf., Asia (tĭz'ărd)	212	10°51'N	113°20'E
Tizimín, Mex. (tē-zē-mē'n)	132a	21°08'N	88°10'W
Tizi-Ouzou, Alg. (tē'zê-ōō-zōō')	230	36°44'N	4°04'E
Tiznados, r., Ven. (têz-nä'dôs)	143b	9°53'N	67°49'W
Tiznit, Mor. (têz-nēt)	230	29°52'N	9°39'W
Tkvarcheli, Geor.	182	42°15'N	41°41'E
Tlacolula de Matamoros, Mex.	131	16°56'N	96°29'W
Tlacotálpan, Mex. (tlä-kô-täl'pän)	131	18°39'N	95°40'W
Tlacotepec, Mex. (tlä-kô-tå-pĕ'k)	130	17°46'N	99°57'W
Tlacotepec, Mex.	130	19°11'N	99°41'W
Tlacotepec, Mex.	131	18°41'N	97°40'W
Tláhuac, Mex. (tlä-wäk')	131a	19°16'N	99°00'W
Tlajomulco de Zúñiga, Mex. (tlä-hô-mōō'l-ko-dĕ-zōō'n-yē-gä)	130	20°30'N	103°27'W
Tlalchapa, Mex. (tläl-chä'pä)	130	18°26'N	100°29'W
Tlalixcoyan, Mex. (tlä-lēs'kô-yän')	131	18°53'N	96°04'W
Tlalmanalco, Mex. (tläl-mä-nä'l-kô)	131a	19°12'N	98°48'W
Tlalnepantla, Mex.	131a	19°32'N	99°13'W
Tlalnepantla, Mex. (tläl-nå-pän'tlä)	131a	18°59'N	99°01'W
Tlalpan, Mex. (tläl-pä'n)	131a	19°17'N	99°10'W
Tlalpujahua, Mex. (tläl-pōō-ĸä'wä)	130	19°50'N	100°10'W
Tlapa, Mex. (tlä'pä)	130	17°30'N	98°30'W
Tlapacoyan, Mex. (tlä-pä-kô-yá'n)	131	19°57'N	97°11'W
Tlapehuala, Mex. (tlä-på-wä'lä)	130	18°17'N	100°30'W
Tlaquepaque, Mex. (tlä-kē-pä'kē)	130	20°39'N	103°17'W
Tlatlaya, Mex. (tlä-tlä'yä)	130	18°36'N	100°14'W
Tlaxcala, Mex. (tläs-kä'lä)	128	19°16'N	98°14'W
Tlaxcala, state, Mex.	130	19°30'N	98°15'W
Tlaxco, Mex. (tläs'kō)	130	19°37'N	98°06'W
Tlaxiaco Santa María Asunción, Mex.	131	17°16'N	97°41'W
Tlayacapan, Mex. (tlä-yä-kä-pá'n)	131a	18°57'N	99°00'W
Tlevak Strait, strt., Ak., U.S.	94	53°03'N	132°58'W
Tlumach, Ukr. (t'lû-măch')	169	48°47'N	25°00'E
Toa, r., Cuba (tō'ä)	135	20°25'N	74°35'W
Toamasina, Madag.	233	18°14'S	49°25'E
Toar, Cuchillas de, mts., Cuba (kōō-chē'l-lyäs-dĕ-tō-ä'r)	135	20°20'N	74°50'W
Tobago, i., Trin. (tô-bā'gō)	129	11°15'N	60°30'W
Toba Inlet, b., Can.	94	50°20'N	124°50'W
Tobarra, Spain (tô-bär'rä)	172	38°37'N	1°42'W
Tobol (Tobyl), r., Asia	184	56°00'N	66°30'E
Tobol'sk, Russia (tô-bôlsk')	184	58°09'N	68°28'E
Tobyl *see* Tobol, r., Asia	184	52°00'N	62°00'E
Tocaima, Col. (tô-kā'y-mä)	142a	4°28'N	74°38'W
Tocantinópolis, Braz. (tō-kän-tē-nō'pō-lēs)	143	6°27'S	47°18'W
Tocantins, state, Braz.	143	10°00'S	48°00'W
Tocantins, r., Braz. (tō-kän-tēns')	143	3°28'S	49°22'W
Toccoa, Ga., U.S. (tŏk'ō-à)	124	34°35'N	83°20'W
Toccoa, r., Ga., U.S.	124	34°53'N	84°24'W
Tochigi, Japan (tō'chē-gĭ)	211	36°25'N	139°45'E
Tocoa, Hond. (tô-kō'ä)	132	15°37'N	86°01'W
Tocopilla, Chile (tō-kô-pēl'yä)	144	22°03'S	70°08'W
Tocuyo de la Costa, Ven. (tô-kōō'yō-dĕ-lä-kôs'tä)	143b	11°03'N	68°24'W
Toda, Japan	211a	35°48'N	139°42'E
Todmorden, Eng., U.K. (tŏd'môr-dĕn)	158a	53°43'N	2°05'W
Tofino, Can. (tō-fē'nō)	94	49°09'N	125°54'W
Töfsingdalens National Park, rec., Swe.	166	62°09'N	13°05'E
Tōgane, Japan (tō'gä-nā)	211	35°29'N	140°16'E
Togian, Kepulauan, is., Indon.	212	0°20'S	122°00'E
Togo, nation, Afr. (tō'gō)	230	8°00'N	0°52'E
Toguzak, r., Russia (tō'gō-zák)	186a	53°40'N	61°42'E
Tohono O'odham Indian Reservation, I.R., Az., U.S.	119	32°33'N	112°12'W
Tohopekaliga, Lake, l., Fl., U.S. (tō'hō-pē'kà-lī'gà)	125a	28°16'N	81°09'W
Tohor, Tanjong, c., Malay.	197b	1°53'N	102°29'E
Toijala, Fin. (toi'yà-là)	167	61°11'N	23°46'E
Toi-Misaki, c., Japan (toi mê'sä-kê)	210	31°20'N	131°20'E
Toiyabe, Nv., U.S. (toi'yă-bē)	118	38°59'N	117°22'W
Tokachi Gawa, r., Japan (tō-kä'chē gä'wä)	210	43°10'N	142°30'E
Tokaj, Hung. (tō'kô-ē)	169	48°06'N	21°24'E
Tokat, Tur. (tō-kät')	198	40°20'N	36°30'E
Tokelau, dep., Oc. (tō-kê-lä'ō)	2	8°00'S	176°00'W
Tokmak, Kyrg. (tôk'mák)	183	42°44'N	75°41'E
Tokmak, Ukr.	177	47°17'N	35°48'E
Tokorozawa, Japan (tô'kô-rô-zä'wä)	211a	35°47'N	139°29'E
Tok-to, atoll, Asia	210	37°15'N	131°51'E
Tokuno, i., Japan (tô-kōō'nō)	205	27°42'N	129°25'E
Tokushima, Japan (tō'kò'shē-mä)	205	34°06'N	134°31'E
Tokuyama, Japan (tō'kò'yä-mä)	211	34°04'N	131°49'E
Tōkyō, Japan	205	35°42'N	139°46'E
Tōkyō-Wan, b., Japan (tō'kyō wän)	211	35°56'N	139°56'E
Tolcayuca, Mex. (tôl-kä-yōō'kä)	130	19°55'N	98°54'W
Toledo, Spain (tô-lĕ'dō)	162	39°53'N	4°02'W
Toledo, Ia., U.S. (tō-lē'dō)	113	41°59'N	92°35'W
Toledo, Oh., U.S.	105	41°40'N	83°35'W
Toledo, Or., U.S.	114	44°37'N	123°58'W
Toledo, Montes de, mts., Spain (mô'n-tĕs-dĕ-tô-lĕ'dô)	172	39°33'N	4°40'W
Toledo Bend Reservoir, res., U.S.	107	31°30'N	93°30'W
Toliara, Madag.	233	23°16'S	43°44'E
Tolima, dept., Col. (tô-lē'mä)	142a	4°07'N	75°20'W
Tolima, Nevado del, mtn., Col. (nĕ-vä-dô-dĕl-tô-lē'mä)	142a	4°40'N	75°20'W
Tolimán, Mex. (tô-lê-män')	130	20°54'N	99°54'W
Tollesbury, Eng., U.K. (tōl'z-bĕrĭ)	158b	51°46'N	0°49'E
Tolmezzo, Italy (tôl-mĕt'zō)	174	46°25'N	13°03'E
Tolmin, Slvn. (tôl'mên)	174	46°12'N	13°45'E
Tolna, Hung. (tôl'nô)	169	46°25'N	18°47'E
Tolo, Teluk, b., Indon. (tō'lō)	212	2°00'S	122°06'E
Tolosa, Spain (tô-lō'sä)	162	43°10'N	2°05'W
Tolt, r., Wa., U.S. (tōlt)	116a	47°13'N	121°49'W
Toluca, Mex. (tô-lōō'kà)	128	19°17'N	99°40'W
Toluca, Il., U.S. (tô-lōō'kà)	108	41°00'N	89°10'W
Toluca, Nevado de, mtn., Mex. (nĕ-vä-dô-dĕ-tô-lōō'kä)	128	19°09'N	99°42'W
Tolyatti, Russia	180	53°30'N	49°10'E
Tom', r., Russia	184	55°33'N	85°00'E
Tomah, Wi., U.S. (tō'mà)	113	43°58'N	90°31'W
Tomahawk, Wi., U.S. (tŏm'á-hôk)	113	45°27'N	89°44'W
Tomakivka, Ukr.	177	47°49'N	34°43'E
Tomanivi, mtn., Fiji	214g	17°37'S	178°01'E
Tomar, Port. (tō-mär')	172	39°36'N	8°26'W
Tomashovka, Bela.	169	51°34'N	23°37'E
Tomaszów Lubelski, Pol. (tô-mä'shôf lōō-bĕl'skĭ)	169	50°20'N	23°27'E
Tomaszów Mazowiecki, Pol. (tô-mä'shôf mä-zô'vyĕt-skĭ)	169	51°33'N	20°00'E
Tomatlán, Mex. (tō-mä-tlä'n)	130	19°54'N	105°14'W
Tombadonkéa, Gui.	234	11°00'N	14°23'W
Tombador, Serra do, mts., Braz. (sĕr'rá dò tōm-bä-dôr')	143	11°31'S	57°33'W
Tombigbee, r., U.S. (tŏm-bĭg'bē)	107	33°00'N	88°30'W
Tombos, Braz. (tô'm-bōs)	141a	20°53'S	42°00'W
Tombouctou, Mali	230	16°46'N	3°01'W
Tombstone, Az., U.S. (tōōm'stōn)	119	31°40'N	110°00'W
Tombua, Ang. (á-lĕ-zhän'drĕ)	232	15°49'S	11°53'E
Tomelilla, Swe. (tô'mĕ-lēl-lä)	166	55°34'N	13°55'E
Tomelloso, Spain (tō-mål-lyō'sō)	172	39°09'N	3°02'W
Tommot, Russia (tŏm-mŏt')	179	59°13'N	126°22'E
Tomsk, Russia (tŏmsk)	178	56°29'N	84°57'E
Tonala, Mex.	130	20°38'N	103°14'W
Tonalá, r., Mex.	131	18°05'N	94°08'W
Tonawanda, N.Y., U.S. (tôn-á-wŏn'dá)	111c	43°01'N	78°53'W
Tonawanda Creek, r., N.Y., U.S.	111c	43°05'N	78°43'W
Tonbridge, Eng., U.K. (tŭn-brĭj)	158b	51°11'N	0°17'E
Tonda, Japan (tôn'dä)	211b	34°51'N	135°38'E
Tondabayashi, Japan (tôn-dä-bä'yä-shê)	211b	34°29'N	135°36'E
Tondano, Indon. (tôn-dä'nō)	213	1°15'N	124°50'E
Tønder, Den. (tûn'nĕr)	166	54°47'N	8°49'E
Tone-Gawa, r., Japan (tô'nĕ gä'wa)	211	36°12'N	139°19'E
Tonga, nation, Oc. (tŏŋ'gà)	240	18°50'S	175°20'W
Tong'an, China (tôŋ-än)	209	24°48'N	118°02'E
Tonga Trench, deep	240	23°00'S	172°30'W
Tongbei, China (tôŋ-bā)	205	48°00'N	126°48'E
Tongguan, China (tôŋ-gūän)	205	34°48'N	110°25'E
Tonghe, China (tôŋ-hŭ)	208	45°58'N	128°40'E
Tonghua, China (tôŋ-hwä)	205	41°43'N	125°50'E
Tongjiang, China (tôŋ-jyäŋ)	205	47°38'N	132°54'E
Tongliao, China (tôŋ-lĭou)	208	43°30'N	122°15'E
Tongo, Cam.	235	5°11'N	14°00'E
Tongoy, Chile (tōn-goi')	144	30°16'S	71°29'W
Tongren, China (tôŋ-rŭn)	204	27°45'N	109°12'E
Tongshan, China (tôŋ-shän)	206	34°27'N	116°27'E
Tongtian, r., China (tôŋ-tĭĕn)	204	33°00'N	97°00'E
Tongue, r., Mt., U.S. (tŭng)	115	45°08'N	106°40'W
Tongxian, China (tôŋ shyĕn)	206	39°55'N	116°40'E
Tonj, r., Sudan (tônj)	231	6°18'N	28°33'E
Tonk, India (tŏŋk)	199	26°13'N	75°45'E
Tonkawa, Ok., U.S. (tŏŋ kà-wô)	121	36°42'N	97°19'W
Tonkin, Gulf of, b., Asia (tôn-kăn')	212	20°30'N	108°10'E
Tonle Sap, l., Camb. (tôn'lā säp')	212	13°03'N	102°49'E
Tonneins, Fr. (tō-năn')	170	44°24'N	0°18'E
Tönning, Ger. (tû'nēng)	168	54°20'N	8°55'E
Tonopah, Nv., U.S. (tō-nō-pä')	104	38°04'N	117°15'W
Tönsberg, Nor. (tûns'bĕrgh)	160	59°19'N	10°25'E
Tonto, r., Mex. (tōn'tō)	131	18°15'N	96°13'W
Tonto Creek, r., Az., U.S.	119	34°05'N	111°15'W
Tonto National Monument, rec., Az., U.S. (tôn'tō)	119	33°33'N	111°08'W
Tooele, Ut., U.S. (tò-ĕl ē)	117b	40°33'N	112°17'W
Toowoomba, Austl. (tò wōōm'bá)	219	27°32'S	152°10'E
Topanga, Ca., U.S. (tō'păn-gà)	117a	34°05'N	118°36'W
Topeka, Ks., U.S. (tō-pē'kà)	105	39°02'N	95°41'W
Topilejo, Mex. (tô-pē-lĕ'hô)	131a	19°12'N	99°09'W
Topock, Az., U.S.	119	34°40'N	114°20'W
Topol'čany, Slvk. (tô-pôl'chä-nü)	169	48°38'N	18°10'E

PRONOUNCING INDEX Topolobampo – Tsiafajovona 359

PLACE (Pronunciation)	PAGE	LAT.	LONG.
Topolobampo, Mex. (tō-pō-lô-bä'm-pô)	128	25°45'N	109°00'W
Topolovgrad, Blg.	175	42°05'N	26°19'E
Toppenish, Wa., U.S. (tŏp'ĕn-ĭsh)	114	46°22'N	120°00'W
Torbat-e Ḩeydarīyeh, Iran	201	35°16'N	59°13'E
Torbat-e Jām, Iran	201	35°14'N	60°36'E
Torbay, Can. (tôr-bā')	101	47°40'N	52°43'W
Torbay *see* Torquay, Eng., U.K.	164	50°30'N	3°26'W
Torbreck, Mount, mtn., Austl. (tōr-brĕk)	222	37°05'S	146°55'E
Torch, l., Mi., U.S. (tôrch)	108	45°00'N	85°30'W
Töreboda, Swe. (tü'rĕ-bō'dä)	166	58°44'N	14°04'E
Torhout, Bel.	165	51°01'N	3°04'E
Toribío, Col. (tō-rē-bē'ō)	142a	2°58'N	76°14'W
Toride, Japan (tō'rē-dā)	211a	35°54'N	104°04'E
Torino *see* Turin, Italy	154	45°05'N	7°44'E
Tormes, r., Spain (tōr'mās)	172	41°12'N	6°15'W
Torneälven, r., Eur.	156	67°00'N	22°30'E
Torneträsk, l., Swe. (tôr'nĕ trĕsk)	160	68°10'N	20°36'E
Torngat Mountains, mts., Can.	93	59°18'N	64°35'W
Tornio, Fin. (tôr'nĭ-ô)	154	65°55'N	24°09'E
Toro, Lac, l., Can.	99	46°53'N	73°46'W
Toronto, Can. (tô-rŏn'tō)	91	43°40'N	79°23'W
Toronto, Oh., U.S.	108	40°30'N	80°35'W
Toronto, res., Mex.	122	27°35'N	105°37'W
Toropets, Russia (tô'rô-pyĕts)	180	56°31'N	31°37'E
Toros Dağları, mts., Tur. (tô'rŭs)	198	37°00'N	32°40'E
Torote, r., Spain (tō-rō'tā)	173a	40°36'N	3°24'W
Torquay, Eng., U.K. (tôr-kē')	164	50°30'N	3°26'W
Torra, Cerro, mtn., Col. (sĕ'r-rô-tŏ'r-rä)	142a	4°41'N	76°22'W
Torrance, Ca., U.S. (tŏr'rănc)	117a	33°50'N	118°20'W
Torre Annunziata, Italy (tôr'rä ä-nōōn-tsē-ä'tä)	173c	40°31'N	14°27'E
Torreblanca, Spain	173	40°18'N	0°12'E
Torre del Greco, Italy (tôr'rå dĕl grā'kô)	174	40°32'N	14°23'E
Torrejoncillo, Spain (tôr'rā-hōn-thē'lyō)	172	39°54'N	6°26'W
Torrelavega, Spain (tôr-rā'lä-vā'gä)	172	43°22'N	4°02'W
Torre Maggiore, Italy (tôr'rā mäd-jō'rā)	174	41°41'N	15°18'E
Torrens, Lake, l., Austl. (tŏr-ĕns)	220	30°07'S	137°40'E
Torrent, Spain	173	39°25'N	0°28'W
Torreón, Mex. (tôr-rå-ōn')	128	25°32'N	103°26'W
Torres Islands, is., Vanuatu (tôr'rĕs) (tŏr'ĕz)	221	13°18'N	165°59'E
Torres Martinez Indian Reservation, I.R., Ca., U.S. (tôr'ĕz mär-tē'nĕz)	118	33°33'N	116°21'W
Torres Novas, Port. (tôr'rĕzh nō'väzh)	172	39°28'N	8°37'W
Torres Strait, strt., Austl. (tôr'rĕs)	221	10°30'S	141°30'E
Torres Vedras, Port. (tôr'rĕsh vā'dräzh)	172	39°08'N	9°18'W
Torrevieja, Spain (tôr-rā-vyā'hä)	173	37°58'N	0°40'W
Torrijos, Phil. (tôr-rē'hōs)	213a	13°19'N	122°06'E
Torrington, Ct., U.S. (tŏr'ĭng-tŭn)	109	41°50'N	73°10'W
Torrington, Wy., U.S.	112	42°04'N	104°11'W
Torro, Spain (tô'r-rō)	172	41°27'N	5°23'W
Torsby, Swe. (tôrs'bü)	166	60°07'N	12°56'E
Torshälla, Swe. (tôrs'hĕl-ä)	166	59°26'N	16°21'E
Tórshavn, Far. Is. (tôrs-houn')	154	62°00'N	6°55'W
Tortola, i., Br. Vir. Is. (tôr-tō'lä)	129b	18°34'N	64°40'W
Tortona, Italy (tôr-tō'nä)	174	44°52'N	8°52'W
Tortosa, Spain (tôr-tō'sä)	154	40°59'N	0°33'E
Tortosa, Cap de, c., Spain	173	40°42'N	0°55'E
Tortue, Canal de la, strt., Haiti (tôr-tü')	135	20°05'N	73°20'W
Tortue, Île de la, i., Haiti	135	20°10'N	73°00'W
Tortue, Rivière de la, r., Can. (lä tôr-tü')	102a	45°12'N	73°32'W
Toruń, Pol.	154	53°02'N	18°35'E
Tõrva, Est. (t'r'vȧ)	167	58°02'N	25°56'E
Torzhok, Russia (tôr'zhôk)	180	57°03'N	34°53'E
Toscana, hist. reg., Italy (tôs-kä'nä)	174	43°23'N	11°08'E
Tosna, r., Russia	186c	59°28'N	30°53'E
Tosno, Russia (tôs'nô)	176	59°32'N	30°52'E
Tostado, Arg. (tôs-tä'dō)	144	29°10'S	61°43'W
Tosya, Tur. (tôz'yȧ)	163	41°00'N	34°00'E
Totana, Spain (tō-tä-nä)	172	37°45'N	1°28'W
Tot'ma, Russia (tôt'mȧ)	180	60°00'N	42°20'E
Totness, Sur.	143	5°51'N	56°17'W
Totonicapán, Guat. (tōtō-nē-kä'pän)	128	14°55'N	91°20'W
Totoras, Arg. (tō-tō'räs)	141c	32°33'S	61°13'W
Totsuka, Japan (tōt'sōō-kä)	211a	35°24'N	139°32'E
Tottenham, Eng., U.K. (tŏt'ĕn-ăm)	158b	51°35'N	0°06'W
Tottori, Japan (tō'tō-rē)	205	35°30'N	134°15'E
Touba, C. Iv.	234	8°17'N	7°41'W
Touba, Sen.	234	14°51'N	15°53'W
Toubkal, Jebel, mtn., Mor.	230	31°15'N	7°46'W
Tougan, Burkina	234	13°04'N	3°04'W
Touggourt, Alg. (tō-gōōrt') (tōō-gōōr')	230	33°09'N	6°07'E
Touil, Oued, r., Alg. (tōō-ēl')	162	34°42'N	2°16'E
Toul, Fr. (tōōl)	161	48°39'N	5°51'E
Toulon, Fr. (tōō-lôn')	154	43°09'N	5°54'E
Toulouse, Fr. (tōō-lōōz')	154	43°37'N	1°27'E
Toungoo, Mya. (tō-ŏŋ-gōō')	212	19°00'N	96°29'E
Tourcoing, Fr. (tōr-kwăN')	161	50°44'N	3°06'E
Tournan-en-Brie, Fr. (tōōr-năN-ĕN-brē')	171b	48°45'N	2°47'E
Tours, Fr. (tōōr)	154	47°23'N	0°39'E
Touside, Pic, mtn., Chad (tōō-sē-dā')	231	21°10'N	16°30'E
Tovdalselva, r., Nor. (tôv-däls-ĕlvä)	166	58°23'N	8°16'E
Towanda, Pa., U.S. (tō-wän'dȧ)	109	41°45'N	76°30'W
Town Bluff Lake, l., Tx., U.S.	123	30°52'N	94°30'W
Towner, N.D., U.S. (tou'nẽr)	112	48°21'N	100°24'W
Townsend, Ma., U.S. (toun'zĕnd)	101a	42°41'N	71°42'W
Townsend, Mt., U.S.	115	46°19'N	111°35'W
Townsend, Mount, mtn., Wa., U.S.	116a	47°52'N	123°03'W
Townsville, Austl. (tounz'vĭl)	219	19°18'S	146°50'E
Towson, Md., U.S. (tou'sŭn)	110e	39°24'N	76°36'W
Towuti, Danau, l., Indon. (tō-wōō'tē)	212	3°00'S	121°45'E
Toxkan, r., China	204	40°34'N	77°15'E
Toyah, Tx., U.S. (tô'yȧ)	122	31°19'N	103°46'W
Toyama, Japan (tō'yä-mä)	205	36°42'N	137°14'E
Toyama-Wan, b., Japan	211	36°58'N	137°16'E
Toyohashi, Japan (tō'yō-hä'shē)	210	34°44'N	137°21'E
Toyonaka, Japan (tō'yō-nä'kȧ)	211b	34°47'N	135°28'E
Tozeur, Tun. (tō-zûr')	162	33°59'N	8°11'E
Trabzon, Tur. (tràb'zŏn)	198	41°00'N	39°45'E
Tracy, Can.	99	46°00'N	73°13'W
Tracy, Ca., U.S. (trā'sē)	118	37°45'N	121°27'W
Tracy, Mn., U.S.	112	44°13'N	95°37'W
Tracy City, Tn., U.S.	124	35°15'N	85°44'W
Trafalgar, Cabo, c., Spain (kà'bō-trä-fäl-gä'r)	172	36°10'N	6°02'W
Trafonomby, mtn., Madag.	233	24°32'S	46°35'E
Trail, Can. (trāl)	90	49°06'N	117°42'W
Traisen, r., Aus.	159e	48°15'N	15°55'E
Traiskirchen, Aus.	159e	48°01'N	16°18'E
Trakai, Lith. (trȧ-kāy)	167	54°38'N	24°59'E
Trakiszki, Pol. (trȧ-kē'-sh-kē)	169	54°16'N	23°07'E
Tralee, Ire. (trȧ-lē')	161	52°16'N	9°20'W
Tranås, Swe. (trän'ôs)	166	58°03'N	14°56'E
Trancoso, Port. (träŋ-kō'sō)	172	40°46'N	7°23'W
Trangan, Pulau, i., Indon. (träŋ'gän)	213	6°52'S	133°30'E
Trani, Italy (trä'nē)	174	41°15'N	16°25'E
Transylvania, hist. reg., Rom. (trăn-sĭl-vā'nĭ-ȧ)	169	46°30'N	22°35'E
Trapani, Italy	162	38°01'N	12°31'E
Trappes, Fr. (tràp)	171b	48°47'N	2°01'E
Traralgon, Austl. (trà'răl-gŏn)	222	38°15'S	146°33'E
Trarza, reg., Maur.	234	17°35'N	15°15'W
Trasimeno, Lago, l., Italy (lä'gō trä-sē-mā'nō)	174	43°00'N	12°12'E
Trás-os-Montes, hist. reg., Port. (träzh'ōzh mōn'tāzh)	162	41°33'N	7°13'W
Traun, r., Aus. (troun)	168	48°10'N	14°15'E
Traunstein, Ger. (troun'stīn)	168	47°52'N	12°38'E
Traverse, Lake, l., Mn., U.S. (trăv'ẽrs)	112	45°46'N	96°53'W
Traverse City, Mi., U.S.	108	44°45'N	85°40'W
Travnik, Bos. (träv'nēk)	175	44°13'N	17°43'E
Treasure Island, i., Ca., U.S. (trĕzh'ẽr)	116b	37°49'N	122°22'W
Trebbin, Ger. (trĕ'bēn)	159b	52°13'N	13°13'E
Trebinje, Bos. (trå'bēn-yĕ)	175	42°43'N	18°21'E
Trebišov, Slvk. (trĕ'bē-shôf)	169	48°36'N	21°32'E
Tregrosse Islands, is., Austl. (trē-grōs')	221	18°08'S	150°53'E
Treinta y Tres, Ur. (trå-ĕn'tä ē träs')	144	33°14'S	54°17'W
Trelew, Arg. (trē'lū)	144	43°15'S	65°25'W
Trelleborg, Swe.	166	55°24'N	13°07'E
Tremiti, Isole, is., Italy (ē'sō-lē trā-mē'tē)	174	42°07'N	16°33'E
Trenčín, Czech Rep. (trĕn'chēn)	161	48°52'N	18°02'E
Trenque Lauquén, Arg. (trĕn'kĕ-là'ōō-kĕ'n)	144	35°50'S	62°44'W
Trent, r., Can. (trĕnt)	99	44°15'N	77°55'W
Trent, r., Eng., U.K.	158a	53°25'N	0°45'W
Trent and Mersey Canal, can., Eng., U.K. (trĕnt) (mûr zē)	158a	53°11'N	2°24'W
Trentino-Alto Adige, hist. reg., Italy	174	46°16'N	10°47'E
Trento, Italy (trĕn'tō)	162	46°04'N	11°07'E
Trenton, Can. (trĕn'tŭn)	91	44°05'N	77°35'W
Trenton, Can.	101	45°37'N	62°38'W
Trenton, Mi., U.S.	111b	42°08'N	83°12'W
Trenton, Mo., U.S.	121	40°05'N	93°36'W
Trenton, N.J., U.S.	105	40°13'N	74°46'W
Trenton, Tn., U.S.	124	35°57'N	88°55'W
Trepassey, Can. (trē-păs'ē)	101	46°44'N	53°22'W
Trepassey Bay, b., Can.	101	46°40'N	53°20'W
Tres Arroyos, Arg. (träs'är-rō'yōs)	144	38°18'S	60°16'W
Três Corações, Braz. (trĕ's kō-rä-zō'ĕs)	141a	21°41'S	45°14'W
Tres Cumbres, Mex. (trĕ's kōō'm-brĕs)	131a	19°03'N	99°14'W
Três Lagoas, Braz. (trĕ's lä-gô'ás)	143	20°48'S	51°42'W
Três Marias, Represa, res., Braz.	143	18°15'S	45°30'W
Tres Morros, Alto de, mtn., Col. (à'l-tō dĕ trĕ's mô'r-rôs)	142a	7°08'N	76°10'W
Três Pontas, Braz. (trĕ'pô'n-täs)	141a	21°22'S	45°30'W
Três Pontas, Cabo das, c., Ang.	236	10°23'S	13°32'E
Três Rios, Braz. (trĕ's rē'ōs)	141a	22°07'S	43°13'W
Très-Saint Rédempteur, Can. (săN rā-dăNp-tûr')	102a	45°26'N	74°23'W
Treuenbrietzen, Ger. (troi'ĕn-brē-tzĕn)	159b	52°06'N	12°52'E
Treviglio, Italy (trā-vē'lyô)	174	45°30'N	9°34'E
Treviso, Italy (trĕ-vē'sō)	162	45°39'N	12°15'E
Trichardt, S. Afr. (trĭ-kärt')	238c	26°32'S	29°16'E
Trier, Ger.	161	49°45'N	6°38'E
Trieste, Italy (trē-ĕs'tä)	154	45°39'N	13°48'E
Triglav, mtn., Slvn.	174	46°23'N	13°50'E
Trigueros, Spain (trē-gā'rōs)	172	37°23'N	6°50'W
Tríkala, Grc.	163	39°33'N	21°49'E
Trikora, Puncak, mtn., Indon.	213	4°15'S	138°45'E
Trim Creek, r., Il., U.S. (trĭm)	111a	41°19'N	87°39'W
Trincomalee, Sri L. (trĭŋ-kō-mȧ-lē')	203	8°39'N	81°12'E
Tring, Eng., U.K. (trĭng)	158b	51°46'N	0°40'W
Trinidad, Bol. (trē-nē-dhädh')	142	14°48'S	64°43'W
Trinidad, Cuba (trē-nē-dhädh')	129	21°50'N	80°00'W
Trinidad, Ur.	144	33°29'S	56°55'W
Trinidad, Co., U.S. (trĭn'ĭdăd)	104	37°11'N	104°31'W
Trinidad, i., Trin. (trĭn'ĭ-dăd)	143	10°00'N	61°00'W
Trinidad, r., Pan.	128a	8°55'N	80°01'W
Trinidad, Sierra de, mts., Cuba (sē-ĕ'r-rå dĕ trē-nē-dä'd)	134	21°50'N	79°55'W
Trinidad and Tobago, nation, N.A. (trĭn'ĭ-dăd) (tō-bā'gō)	129	11°00'N	61°00'W
Trinitaria, Mex. (trē-nē-tä'ryä)	131	16°09'N	92°04'W
Trinity, Can. (trĭn'ĭ-tē)	101	48°59'N	53°55'W
Trinity, Tx., U.S.	123	30°52'N	95°27'W
Trinity, is., Ak., U.S.	103	56°25'N	153°15'W
Trinity, r., Ca., U.S.	114	40°50'N	123°20'W
Trinity, r., Tx., U.S.	107	30°50'N	95°09'W
Trinity, East Fork, r., Tx., U.S.	121	33°24'N	96°42'W
Trinity, West Fork, r., Tx., U.S.	120	33°22'N	98°26'W
Trinity Bay, b., Can.	93	48°00'N	53°40'W
Trino, Italy (trē'nô)	174	45°11'N	8°16'E
Trion, Ga., U.S. (trī'ŏn)	124	34°32'N	85°18'W
Trípoli, Grc.	163	37°32'N	22°32'E
Tripoli (Tarābulus), Libya	231	32°50'N	13°13'E
Tripolitania *see* Tarābulus, hist. reg., Libya	230	31°00'N	12°26'E
Tripura, state, India	199	24°00'N	92°00'E
Tristan da Cunha Islands, is., St. Hel. (três-tän'dä kōōn'yȧ)	2	35°30'S	12°15'W
Triste, Golfo, b., Ven. (gôl-fô trē's-tĕ)	143b	10°40'N	68°05'W
Triticus Reservoir, res., N.Y., U.S. (trī tĭ-cŭs)	110a	41°20'N	73°36'W
Trnava, Slvk. (t'r'nȧ-vȧ)	169	48°22'N	17°34'E
Trobriand Islands, is., Pap. N. Gui. (trō-brē-ănd')	213	8°25'S	151°45'E
Trogir, Cro. (trō'gēr)	174	43°32'N	16°17'E
Trois Fourches, Cap des, c., Mor.	172	35°28'N	2°58'W
Trois-Rivières, Can. (trwä'rē-vyâ')	91	46°21'N	72°35'W
Troitsk, Russia (trô'ētsk)	184	54°06'N	61°35'E
Troits'ke, Ukr.	177	47°39'N	30°16'E
Troitsko-Pechorsk, Russia (trô'ĭtsk-ô-pyĕ-chôrsk')	178	62°18'N	56°07'E
Trollhättan, Swe. (trôl'hĕt-ĕn)	160	58°17'N	12°17'E
Trollheimen, mts., Nor. (trôll-hĕĭm)	166	62°48'N	9°05'E
Trona, Ca., U.S. (trō'nȧ)	118	35°49'N	117°20'W
Tronador, Cerro, mtn., S.A. (sĕ'r-rô trō-nä'dôr)	144	41°17'S	71°56'W
Troncoso, Mex. (trôn-kô'sō)	130	22°43'N	102°22'W
Trondheim, Nor. (trôn'hâm)	154	63°25'N	11°35'E
Trosa, Swe. (trô'sä)	166	58°54'N	17°25'E
Trout, l., Can.	93	51°16'N	92°46'W
Trout, l., Can.	92	61°10'N	121°30'W
Trout Creek, r., Or., U.S.	114	42°18'N	118°31'W
Troutdale, Or., U.S. (trout'dāl)	116c	45°32'N	122°23'W
Trout Lake, Mi., U.S.	113	46°20'N	85°02'W
Trouville, Fr. (trōō-vēl')	170	49°23'N	0°05'E
Troy, Al., U.S. (troi)	124	31°47'N	85°46'W
Troy, Il., U.S.	117e	38°44'N	89°53'W
Troy, Ks., U.S.	121	39°46'N	95°07'W
Troy, Mo., U.S.	120	38°56'N	99°57'W
Troy, Mt., U.S.	114	48°28'N	115°56'W
Troy, N.C., U.S.	125	35°21'N	79°58'W
Troy, N.Y., U.S.	105	42°45'N	73°45'W
Troy, Oh., U.S.	108	40°00'N	84°10'W
Troy, hist., Tur.	198	39°59'N	26°14'E
Troyes, Fr. (trwä)	161	48°18'N	4°03'E
Trstenik, Serb. (t'r'stĕ-nēk)	163	43°36'N	21°00'E
Trubchëvsk, Russia (trŏp'chĕfsk)	181	52°36'N	33°46'E
Trucial States *see* United Arab Emirates, nation, Asia	198	24°00'N	54°00'E
Truckee, Ca., U.S. (trŭk'ē)	118	39°20'N	120°12'W
Truckee, r., Ca., U.S.	118	39°25'N	120°07'W
Truganina, Austl.	217a	37°49'N	144°44'E
Trujillo, Col. (trō-ĸĕ'l-yō)	142a	4°10'N	76°20'W
Trujillo, Peru	142	8°08'S	79°00'W
Trujillo, Spain (trōō-ĸĕ'l-yō)	162	39°27'N	5°50'W
Trujillo, Ven.	142	9°15'N	70°28'W
Trujillo, r., Mex.	130	23°12'N	103°10'W
Trujin, Lago, l., Dom. Rep. (trōō-ĸēn')	135	17°45'N	71°25'W
Truk *see* Chuuk, is., Micron.	214c	7°25'N	151°47'E
Trumann, Ar., U.S. (trōō'măn)	121	35°41'N	90°31'W
Trŭn, Blg. (trŭn)	175	42°49'N	22°39'E
Truro, Can. (trōō'rō)	91	45°22'N	63°16'W
Truro, Eng., U.K.	164	50°17'N	5°05'W
Trussville, Al., U.S. (trŭs'vĭl)	110h	33°37'N	86°37'W
Truth or Consequences, N.M., U.S. (trōōth ŏr kŏn'sē-kwĕn-sĭs)	119	33°10'N	107°20'W
Trutnov, Czech Rep. (trŏŏt'nôf)	168	50°36'N	15°36'E
Trzcianka, Pol. (tchyän'kȧ)	168	53°02'N	16°27'E
Trzebiatów, Pol. (tchĕ-byä'tŏ-v)	168	54°03'N	15°16'E
Tsaidam Basin, basin, China (tsī-däm)	204	37°19'N	94°08'E
Tsala Apopka Lake, r., Fl., U.S. (tsä'lȧ ă-pŏp'kȧ)	125	28°57'N	82°11'W
Tsast Bogd, mtn., Mong.	204	46°44'N	92°34'E
Tsavo National Park, rec., Kenya	237	2°35'S	38°45'E
Tsawwassen Indian Reserve, I.R., Can.	116d	49°03'N	123°11'W
Tsentral'nyy-Kospashskiy, Russia (tsĕn-träl'nyĭ-kôs-pàsh'skĭ)	186a	59°03'N	57°48'E
Tshela, D.R.C. (tshā'lȧ)	232	4°59'S	12°56'E
Tshikapa, D.R.C. (tshē-kä'pä)	232	6°25'S	20°48'E
Tshofa, D.R.C.	237	5°14'S	25°15'E
Tshuapa, r., D.R.C.	232	0°30'S	22°00'E
Tsiafajovona, mtn., Madag.	233	19°17'S	47°27'E

ăt; fīnăl; rāte; senåte; ärm; åsk; sofá; fâre; ch-choose; dh-as th in other; bē; ĕvent; bĕt; recĕnt; cratẽr; g-gō; gh-guttural g; bĭt; ĭ-short neutral; rīde; ĸ-guttural k as ch in German ich;

PLACE (Pronunciation)	PAGE	LAT.	LONG.
Ugleural'sk, Russia (ŏg-lĕ-ô-rálsk´)	186a	58°58´N	57°35´E
Uglich, Russia (ōōg-lēch´)	176	57°33´N	38°19´E
Uglitskiy, Russia (ŏg-lĭt´skĭ)	186a	53°50´N	60°18´F
Uglovka, Russia (ōōg-lôf´ká)	176	58°14´N	33°24´E
Ugra, r., Russia (ōōg´rá)	180	54°43´N	34°20´E
Ugŭrchin, Blg.	175	43°06´N	24°23´E
Uhrichsville, Oh., U.S. (ū´riks-vĭl)	108	40°25´N	81°20´W
Uíge, Ang.	232	7°37´S	15°03´E
Uiju, Kor., N. (ó´ējōō)	205	40°09´N	124°33´E
Uinkaret Plateau, plat., Az., U.S. (ů-ĭn´kär-ĕt)	119	36°43´N	113°15´W
Uinskoye, Russia (ó-ĭn´skô-yĕ)	186a	56°53´N	56°25´E
Uinta, r., Ut., U.S. (ů-ĭn´tá)	119	40°25´N	109°55´W
Uintah and Ouray Indian Reservation, I.R., Ut., U.S.	119	40°20´N	110°20´W
Uinta Mountains, mts., Ut., U.S.	106	40°35´N	111°00´W
Uitenhage, S. Afr.	232	33°46´S	25°26´E
Uithoorn, Neth.	159a	52°13´N	4°49´E
Uji, Japan (ōō´jē)	211b	34°53´N	135°49´E
Ujiji, Tan. (ōō-jē´jē)	232	4°55´S	29°41´E
Ujjain, India (ōō-jŭen)	199	23°18´N	75°37´E
Ujungpandang, Indon.	212	5°08´S	119°28´E
Ukerewe Island, i., Tan.	237	2°00´S	32°40´E
Ukhta, Russia (ōōk´tá)	180	65°22´N	31°30´E
Ukhta, Russia	180	63°08´N	53°42´E
Ukiah, Ca., U.S. (ū-kī´á)	118	39°09´N	122°12´W
Ukmerge, Lith. (ŏk´mĕr-ghá)	180	55°16´N	24°45´E
Ukraine, nation, Eur.	178	49°15´N	30°15´E
Uku, i., Japan (ōōk´ōō)	211	33°18´N	129°02´E
Ulaangom, Mong.	204	50°23´N	92°14´E
Ulan Bator (Ulaanbaatar), Mong.	204	47°56´N	107°00´E
Ulan-Ude, Russia (ōō´län ōō´dá)	179	51°59´N	107°41´E
Ulchin, Kor., S. (ōōl´chĕn´)	210	36°57´N	129°26´E
Ulcinj, Serb. (ōōl´tsĕn´)	163	41°56´N	19°15´E
Ulhās, r., India	203b	19°13´N	73°03´E
Ulhāsnagar, India	202	19°10´N	73°07´E
Uliastay, Mong.	204	47°49´N	97°00´E
Ulindi, r., D.R.C. (ōō-lĭn´dĕ)	232	1°55´S	26°17´E
Ulla, Bela.	176	55°14´N	29°15´E
Ulla, r., Bela.	176	54°58´N	29°03´E
Ulla, r., Spain (ōō´lä)	172	42°45´N	8°33´W
Ullŭng, i., Kor., S. (ōōl´lóng´)	210	37°29´N	130°50´E
Ulm, Ger. (ōlm)	161	48°24´N	9°59´E
Ulmer, Mount, mtn., Ant. (ŭl´mûr´)	224	77°30´S	86°00´W
Ulricehamn, Swe. (ól-rē´sĕ-häm)	166	57°49´N	13°23´E
Ulster, hist. reg., Eur. (ŭl´stēr)	164	54°41´N	7°10´W
Ulua, r., Hond. (ōō-lōō´ä)	132	15°49´N	87°45´W
Ulubāria, India	202a	22°27´N	88°09´E
Ulukışla, Tur. (ōō-lōō-kēsh´lá)	163	36°40´N	34°30´E
Ulunga, Russia (ó-lōōn´gà)	210	46°16´N	136°29´E
Ulungur, r., China (ōō-lōōn-gŭr)	204	46°31´N	88°00´E
Uluru (Ayers Rock), mtn., Austl.	220	25°23´S	131°05´E
Ulu-Telyak, Russia (ōō ló´tĕlyāk)	186a	54°54´N	57°01´E
Ulverstone, Austl. (ŭl´vēr-stŭn)	219	41°20´S	146°22´E
Ul'yanovka, Russia	186c	59°38´N	30°47´E
Ul'yanovsk, Russia (ōō-lyä´nôfsk)	178	54°20´N	48°24´E
Ulysses, Ks., U.S. (ū-lĭs´ēz)	120	37°34´N	101°25´W
Umán, Mex. (ōō´mán´)	132a	20°52´N	89°44´W
Uman', Ukr. (ó-mán´)	181	48°44´N	30°13´E
Umatilla Indian Reservation, I.R., Or., U.S. (ū-má-tĭl´á)	114	45°38´N	118°35´W
Umberpāda, India	203b	19°28´N	73°04´E
Umbria, hist. reg., Italy (ŭm´brĭ-á)	174	42°53´N	12°22´E
Umeälven, r., Swe.	156	64°57´N	18°51´E
Umhlatuzi, r., S. Afr. (ôm´hlä-tōō´zī)	233c	28°47´S	31°17´E
Umiat, Ak., U.S. (ōō´mĭ-ăt)	106a	69°20´N	152°28´W
Umkomaas, S. Afr. (ôm-kō´mäs)	233c	30°12´S	30°48´E
Umnak, i., Ak., U.S. (ōōm´nák)	106b	53°10´N	169°08´W
Umnak Pass, Ak., U.S.	103a	53°10´N	168°04´W
Umniati, r., Zimb.	232	17°08´S	29°11´E
Umpqua, r., Or., U.S. (ŭmp´kwá)	114	43°42´N	123°50´W
Umtata, S. Afr. (ōōm-tä´tä)	232	31°36´S	28°47´E
Umtentweni, S. Afr.	233c	30°41´S	30°29´E
Umzimkulu, S. Afr. (ôm-zĕm-kōō´lōō)	233c	30°12´S	29°53´E
Umzinto, S. Afr. (ôm-zīn´tô)	233c	30°19´S	30°41´E
Una, r., Serb. (ōō´nä)	174	44°38´N	16°10´E
Unalakleet, Ak., U.S. (ū-ná-lák´lēt)	103	63°50´N	160°42´W
Unalaska, Ak., U.S. (ū-ná-lás´ka)	103a	53°30´N	166°20´W
Unare, r., Ven.	143b	9°45´N	65°12´W
Unare, Laguna de, l., Ven. (lä-gó´nä-de-ōō-ná´rĕ)	143b	10°07´N	65°23´W
Unayzah, Sau. Ar.	198	25°50´N	44°02´E
Uncas, Can. (ŭŋ´kás)	102g	53°30´N	113°02´W
Uncia, Bol. (ōōn´sē-ä)	142	18°28´S	66°32´W
Uncompahgre, r., Co., U.S.	119	38°20´N	107°45´W
Uncompahgre Peak, mtn., Co., U.S. (ŭn-kŭm-pä´grĕ)	119	38°00´N	107°30´W
Uncompahgre Plateau, plat., Co., U.S.	119	38°40´N	108°40´W
Underberg, S. Afr. (ŭn´dēr-bûrg)	233c	29°51´S	29°32´E
Unecha, Russia (ōō-nĕ´chá)	176	52°51´N	32°44´E
Ungava, Péninsule d', pen., Can.	93	59°55´N	74°00´W
Ungava Bay, b., Can. (ŭŋ-gà´vá)	93	59°46´N	67°18´W
União da Vitória, Braz. (ōō-nĕ´ouⁿ´ dä vē-tó´ryä)	144	26°17´S	51°13´W
Unije, i., Serb. (ōō´nĕ-yĕ)	174	44°39´N	14°10´E
Unimak, i., Ak., U.S. (ōō-nĕ-mák´)	103	54°30´N	163°35´W
Unimak Pass, Ak., U.S.	103a	54°22´N	165°22´W
Union, Mo., U.S.	121	38°28´N	90°59´W
Union, Ms., U.S. (ūn´yŭn)	124	32°35´N	89°07´W
Union, N.C., U.S.	125	34°42´N	81°40´W
Union, or., U.S.	114	45°13´N	117°52´W
Union City, Ca., U.S.	116b	37°36´N	122°01´W
Union City, In., U.S.	108	40°10´N	85°00´W
Union City, Mi., U.S.	108	42°00´N	85°10´W
Union City, Pa., U.S.	109	41°50´N	79°50´W
Union City, Tn., U.S.	124	36°25´N	89°04´W
Unión de Reyes, Cuba	134	22°45´N	81°30´W
Unión de San Antonio, Mex.	130	21°07´N	101°56´W
Unión de Tula, Mex.	130	19°57´N	104°14´W
Union Grove, Wi., U.S. (ūn-yŭn grōv)	111a	42°41´N	88°03´W
Unión Hidalgo, Mex. (ĕ-dä´lgô)	131	16°29´N	94°51´W
Union Point, Ga., U.S.	124	33°37´N	83°08´W
Union Springs, Al., U.S. (sprĭngz)	124	32°08´N	85°43´W
Uniontown, Al., U.S. (ūn´yŭn-toun)	124	32°26´N	87°30´W
Uniontown, Oh., U.S.	111d	40°58´N	81°25´W
Uniontown, Pa., U.S.	109	39°55´N	79°45´W
Unionville, Mo., U.S. (ūn´yŭn-vĭl)	121	40°28´N	92°58´W
Unisan, Phil. (ōō-nē´sän)	213a	13°50´N	121°59´E
United Arab Emirates, nation, Asia	198	24°00´N	54°00´E
United Kingdom, nation, Eur.	154	56°30´N	1°40´W
United States, nation, N.A.	104	38°00´N	110°00´W
Unity, Can.	96	52°27´N	109°10´W
Universal, In., U.S. (ū-nĭ-vûr´sál)	108	39°35´N	87°30´W
University City, Mo., U.S. (ū´nĭ-vûr´sĭ-tĭ)	117e	38°40´N	90°19´W
University Park, Tx., U.S.	117c	32°51´N	96°48´W
Unna, Ger. (ōō´nä)	171c	51°32´N	7°41´E
Uno, Canal Numero, can., Arg.	141c	36°43´S	58°14´W
Unterhaching, Ger. (ōōn´tĕr-hä-kĕng)	159d	48°03´N	11°38´E
Unye, Tur. (ūn´yĕ)	163	41°00´N	37°10´E
Unzha, r., Russia (ón´zhá)	180	57°45´N	44°10´E
Upa, r., Russia (ó´pá)	176	53°54´N	36°48´E
Upata, Ven. (ōō-pä´tä)	142	7°58´N	62°27´W
Upemba, Parc National de l', rec., D.R.C.	237	9°10´S	26°15´E
Upington, S. Afr. (ŭp´ĭng-tŭn)	232	28°25´S	21°15´E
Upland, Ca., U.S. (ŭp´lánd)	119	34°06´N	117°38´W
Upolu, i., Samoa	214a	13°55´S	171°45´W
Upolu Point, c., Hi., U.S. (ōō-pō´lōō)	126a	20°15´N	155°48´W
Upper Arrow Lake, l., Can. (ăr´ō)	95	50°30´N	117°55´W
Upper Darby, Pa., U.S. (där´bĭ)	110f	39°58´N	75°16´W
Upper des Lacs, l., N.A. (dĕ läk)	112	48°58´N	101°55´W
Upper Kapuas Mountains, mts., Asia	212	1°45´N	112°06´E
Upper Klamath Lake, l., Or., U.S.	114	42°23´N	122°55´W
Upper Lake, l., Nv., U.S. (ŭp´ĕr)	114	41°42´N	119°59´W
Upper Marlboro, Md., U.S. (ŭpĕr märl´bŏrō)	110e	38°49´N	76°46´W
Upper Mill, Wa., U.S. (mĭl)	116a	47°11´N	121°55´W
Upper Red Lake, l., Mn., U.S. (rĕd)	113	48°14´N	94°53´W
Upper Sandusky, Oh., U.S. (săn-dŭs´kĕ)	108	40°50´N	83°20´W
Upper San Leandro Reservoir, res., Ca., U.S. (ŭp´ĕr săn lĕ-än´drô)	116b	37°47´N	122°04´W
Upper Volta see Burkina Faso, nation, Afr.	230	13°00´N	2°00´W
Uppingham, Eng., U.K. (ŭp´ĭng-ŭm)	158a	52°35´N	0°43´W
Uppsala, Swe. (ōōp´sá-lá)	154	59°53´N	17°39´E
Uptown, Pa., U.S. (ŭp´toun)	101a	42°10´N	71°36´W
Uraga, Japan (ōō´rä-gá´)	211a	35°15´N	139°43´E
Ural, r. (ū-räl´´) (ū-rôl)	178	48°00´N	51°00´E
Urals, mts., Russia	178	56°28´N	58°13´E
Uran, India (ōō-rän´)	203b	18°53´N	72°46´E
Uranium City, Can.	90	59°34´N	108°59´W
Urawa, Japan (ōō rä-wä´)	210	35°52´N	139°39´E
Urayasu, Japan (ōō´rä-yä´sōō)	211a	35°40´N	139°54´W
Urazovo, Russia (ó-rá´zô-vô)	177	50°08´N	38°03´E
Urbana, Il., U.S. (ûr-băn´á)	108	40°10´N	88°15´W
Urbana, Oh., U.S.	108	40°05´N	83°50´W
Urbino, Italy (ōōr-bē´nô)	174	43°43´N	12°37´E
Urdaneta, Phil. (ōōr-dä-nä´tä)	213a	15°59´N	120°34´E
Urdinarrain, Arg. (ōōr-dē-när-räē´n)	141c	32°43´S	58°53´W
Uritsk, Russia (ōō´rĭtsk)	186c	59°50´N	30°11´E
Urla, Tur. (ór´lä)	175	38°20´N	26°44´E
Urman, Russia (ór´mán)	186a	54°53´N	56°52´E
Urmi, r., Russia (ór´mĕ)	210	48°50´N	134°00´E
Uromi, Nig.	235	6°44´N	6°18´E
Urrao, Col. (ōōr-rá´ô)	142	6°19´N	76°11´W
Urshel'skiy, Russia (ōōr-shĕl´skĕĕ)	176	55°50´N	40°11´E
Ursus, Pol.	169	52°12´N	20°53´E
Urubamba, r., Peru (ōō-rōō-bäm´bä)	142	11°48´S	72°34´W
Uruguaiana, Braz.	144	29°45´S	57°00´W
Uruguay, nation, S.A. (ōō-rōō-gwī´) (ū´rōō-gwā)	144	32°45´S	56°00´W
Uruguay, r., S.A. (ōō-rōō-gwī´)	144	27°05´S	55°15´W
Ürümqi, China (ů-rŭm-chyē)	204	43°49´N	87°43´E
Urup, i., Russia (ó´ròp´)	205	46°00´N	150°00´E
Uryupinsk, Russia (ór´yó-pēn-sk´)	181	50°50´N	42°00´E
Usa, Japan	210	33°31´N	131°22´E
Usa, r., Russia (ó´sá)	180	66°00´N	58°20´E
Uşak, Tur. (ōō-shäk´)	163	38°20´N	29°15´E
Usakos, Nmb. (ōō-sä´kōs)	232	22°00´S	15°40´E
Usambara Mountains, mts., Tan.	237	4°40´S	38°25´E
Usangu Flats, sw., Tan.	237	8°10´S	34°00´E
Ushaki, Russia (ōō´shá-kī)	186c	59°28´N	31°00´E
Ushakovskoye, Russia (ó-shá-kôv´skô-yĕ)	186a	56°18´N	62°23´E
Ushashi, Tan.	237	2°00´S	33°57´E
Ushiku, Japan (ōō´shē-kōō)	211a	35°59´N	140°09´E
Ushimado, Japan (ōō´shĕ-mä´dō)	211	34°37´N	134°09´E
Ushuaia, Arg. (ōō-shōō-ī´ä)	144	54°46´S	68°24´W
Usman', Russia (ōōs-mán´)	181	52°03´N	39°40´E
Usol'ye, Russia (ó-sô´lyĕ)	186a	59°24´N	56°40´E
Usol'ye-Sibirskoye, Russia (ó-sô´lyĕsī´bēr´skô-yĕ)	184	52°44´N	103°46´E
Uspallata Pass, p., S.A. (ōōs-pä-lyä´tä)	144	32°47´S	70°08´W
Uspanapa, r., Mex. (ōōs-pä-nä´pä)	131	17°43´N	94°14´W
Ussel, Fr. (üs´ĕl)	170	45°33´N	2°17´E
Ussuri, r., Asia (ōō-sōō´rĕ)	185	47°30´N	134°00´E
Ussuriysk, Russia	179	43°48´N	132°09´E
Ust'-Bol'sheretsk, Russia	179	52°41´N	157°00´E
Ustica, Isola di, i., Italy	174	38°43´N	12°11´E
Ústí nad Labem, Czech Rep.	168	50°40´N	14°02´E
Ust'-Izhora, Russia (óst-ēz´hô-rà)	186c	59°49´N	30°35´E
Ustka, Pol. (ōōst´ká)	168	54°34´N	16°52´E
Ust'-Kamchatsk, Russia	179	56°13´N	162°18´E
Ust'-Katav, Russia (óst ká´táf)	186a	54°55´N	58°12´E
Ust'-Kishert', Russia (óst kē´shĕrt)	186a	57°21´N	57°13´E
Ust'-Kulom, Russia (kó´lŭm)	178	61°38´N	54°00´E
Ust'-Maya, Russia (má´yá)	179	60°33´N	134°43´E
Ust' Olenëk, Russia	179	72°52´N	120°15´E
Ust-Ordynskiy, Russia (óst-ôr-dyĕnsk´ĭ)	184	52°47´N	104°39´E
Ust' Penzhino, Russia	185	63°00´N	165°10´E
Ust' Port, Russia (óst´pôrt´)	178	69°20´N	83°41´E
Ust'-Tsil'ma, Russia (tsĭl´má)	178	65°25´N	52°10´E
Ust'-Tyrma, Russia (tur´má)	179	50°27´N	131°17´E
Ust' Uls, Russia	186a	60°35´N	58°20´E
Ust-Urt, Plateau, plat., Asia	178	44°03´N	54°58´E
Ustynivka, Ukr.	177	47°59´N	32°31´E
Ustyuzhna, Russia (yōōzh´ná)	180	58°49´N	36°19´E
Usu, China (ů-sōō)	204	44°28´N	84°07´E
Usuki, Japan (ōō´sōō-kĕ´)	211	33°06´N	131°47´E
Usulutan, El Sal. (ōō-sōō-lä-tän´)	132	13°22´N	88°25´W
Usumacinta, r., N.A. (ōō´sōō-mä-sēn´tō)	131	18°24´N	92°30´W
Us'va, Russia (ōōs´vá)	186a	58°41´N	57°38´E
Utah, state, U.S. (ū´tô)	104	39°25´N	112°40´W
Utah Lake, l., Ut., U.S. (ū´tô)	119	40°10´N	111°55´W
Utan, India (ōō-tän´)	203b	19°17´N	72°43´E
Ute Mountain Indian Reservation, I.R., N.M., U.S.	119	36°57´N	108°34´W
Utena, Lith. (ōō-tä´ná)	167	55°32´N	25°40´E
Utete, Tan. (ōō-tä´tä)	233	8°05´S	38°47´E
Utica, In., U.S. (ū´tĭ-ká)	111h	38°25´N	85°39´W
Utica, N.Y., U.S.	105	43°05´N	75°10´W
Utiel, Spain (ōō-tyäl´)	172	39°34´N	1°13´W
Utika, Mi., U.S. (ū´tĭ-ká)	111b	42°37´N	83°02´W
Utik Lake, l., Can.	97	55°16´N	96°00´W
Utikuma Lake, l., Can.	95	55°50´N	115°25´W
Utila, i., Hond. (ōō-tē´lä)	132	16°07´N	87°05´W
Uto, Japan (ōō´tô)	210	32°43´N	130°39´E
Utrecht, Neth. (ü´trĕkt) (ū´trĕkt)	161	52°05´N	5°06´E
Utrera, Spain (ōō-trā´rä)	162	37°12´N	5°48´W
Utsunomiya, Japan (ōōt´sò-nô-mē-yá´)	205	36°35´N	139°52´E
Uttaradit, Thai.	212	17°47´N	100°10´E
Uttaranchal, state, India	199	29°30´N	78°30´E
Uttarpara-Kotrung, India	202a	22°40´N	88°21´E
Uttar Pradesh, state, India (ót-tär-prä-dĕsh)	199	27°00´N	80°00´E
Uttoxeter, Eng., U.K. (ŭt-tŏk´sē-tēr)	158a	52°54´N	1°52´W
Utuado, P.R. (ōō-tōō-ä´dhō)	129b	18°16´N	66°40´W
Uusikaupunki, Fin.	167	60°48´N	21°24´E
Uvalde, Tx., U.S. (ū-väl´dĕ)	122	29°14´N	99°47´W
Uvel'skiy, Russia (ó-vyĕl´skī)	186a	54°27´N	61°22´E
Uvinza, Tan.	237	5°06´S	30°22´E
Uvira, D.R.C. (ōō-vē´rä)	232	3°28´S	29°03´E
Uvod', r., Russia (ó-vôd´)	176	56°40´N	41°10´E
Uvongo Beach, S. Afr.	233c	30°49´S	30°23´E
Uvs Nuur, l., Asia	204	50°29´N	93°32´E
Uwajima, Japan (ōō-wä´jē-mä)	210	33°12´N	132°35´E
Uxbridge, Ma., U.S. (ŭks´brĭj)	101a	42°05´N	71°38´W
Uxmal, hist., Mex. (ōō´x-mä´l)	132a	20°22´N	89°44´W
Uy, r., Russia (ōōy)	186a	54°05´N	62°11´E
Uyskoye, Russia (ōō-īskô-yĕ)	186a	54°22´N	60°01´E
Uyuni, Bol. (ōō-yōō´nĕ)	142	20°28´S	66°45´W
Uyuni, Salar de, pl., Bol. (sä-lär-dĕ)	142	20°58´S	67°09´W
Uzbekistan, nation, Asia	178	42°42´N	60°00´E
Uzh, r., Ukr. (ózh)	177	51°07´N	29°05´E
Uzhhorod, Ukr.	169	48°38´N	22°18´E
Užice, Serb. ōō´zhĕ-tsĕ	175	43°51´N	19°53´E
Uzunköprü, Tur.	175	41°17´N	26°42´E

V

PLACE (Pronunciation)	PAGE	LAT.	LONG.
Vaal, r., S. Afr. (väl)	232	28°15´S	24°30´E
Vaaldam, res., S. Afr.	238c	26°58´S	28°37´E
Vaalplaas, S. Afr.	238c	25°39´S	28°56´E
Vaalwater, S. Afr.	238c	24°17´S	28°08´E
Vaasa, Fin. (vä´sá)	154	63°06´N	21°39´E
Vác, Hung. (väts)	169	47°46´N	19°10´E
Vache, Île à, i., Haiti	135	18°05´N	73°40´W
Vadstena, Swe. (väd´stī´ná)	166	58°27´N	14°53´E
Vaduz, Liech. (vä´dóts)	168	47°10´N	9°32´E
Vaga, r., Russia (vä´gá)	180	61°55´N	42°30´E
Vah, r., Slvk. (väk)	161	48°07´N	17°52´E
Vaigai, r., India	203	10°20´N	78°13´E
Vakh, r., Russia (väk)	184	61°30´N	81°33´E
Valachia, hist. reg., Rom.	175	44°45´N	24°17´E
Valcartier-Village, Can. (väl-kärt-yĕ´vĕ´läzh´)	102b	46°56´N	71°28´W
Valdai Hills, hills, Russia (väl-dī´g´rī)	180	57°50´N	32°35´E
Valday, Russia (väl-dī´)	180	57°58´N	33°13´E
Valdecañas, Embalse de, res., Spain	172	39°45´N	5°30´W

362 Valdemārpils – Vernon PRONOUNCING INDEX

PLACE (Pronunciation)	PAGE	LAT.	LONG.
Valdemārpils, Lat.	167	57°22′N	22°34′E
Valdemorillo, Spain (väl-då-mô-rēl′yō)	173a	40°30′N	4°04′W
Valdepeñas, Spain (väl-då-pān′yäs)	162	38°46′N	3°22′W
Valderaduey, r., Spain (väl-dĕ-rä-dwĕ′y)	172	41°39′N	5°35′W
Valdés, Península, pen., Arg. (vål-dĕ′s)	144	42°15′S	63°15′W
Valdez, Ak., U.S. (văl′dĕz)	103	61°10′N	146°18′W
Valdilecha, Spain (väl-dē-lā′chä)	173a	40°17′N	3°19′W
Valdivia, Chile (väl-dē′vä)	144	39°47′S	73°13′W
Valdivia, Col. (väl-dē′vēä)	142a	7°10′N	75°26′W
Val-d'Or, Can.	91	48°03′N	77°50′W
Valdosta, Ga., U.S. (văl-dŏs′tȧ)	105	30°50′N	83°18′W
Vale, Or., U.S. (vāl)	114	43°59′N	117°14′W
Valença, Braz. (vä-lĕɴ′sȧ)	143	13°43′S	38°58′W
Valença, Port.	172	42°03′N	8°36′W
Valence, Fr. (vä-lĕnɴs)	161	44°56′N	4°54′E
València, Spain	154	39°26′N	0°23′W
Valencia, Ven. (vä-lĕn′syä)	142	10°11′N	68°00′W
València, hist. reg., Spain	173	39°08′N	0°43′W
València, Golf de, b., Spain	173	39°50′N	0°30′E
Valencia, Lago de, l., Ven.	143b	10°11′N	67°45′W
Valencia de Alcántara, Spain	172	39°34′N	7°13′W
Valenciennes, Fr. (vȧ-läɴ-syĕn′)	170	50°24′N	3°36′E
Valentine, Ne., U.S. (vȧ läɴ-tē-nyē′)	104	42°52′N	100°34′W
Valera, Ven. (vä-lĕ′rä)	142	9°12′N	70°45′W
Valerianovsk, Russia (vȧ-lĕ-rĭ-ä′nôvsk)	186a	58°47′N	59°34′E
Valga, Est. (väl′gȧ)	180	57°47′N	26°03′E
Valhalla, S. Afr. (vȧl-hăl-ȧ)	233b	25°49′S	28°09′E
Valier, Mt., U.S. (vă-lēr′)	115	48°17′N	112°14′W
Valjevo, Serb. (väl′yå-vô)	175	44°17′N	19°57′E
Valky, Ukr.	177	49°49′N	35°40′E
Valladolid, Mex. (väl-yä-dhô-lēdh′)	128	20°39′N	88°13′W
Valladolid, Spain (väl-yä-dhô-lēdh′)	154	41°41′N	4°41′W
Valle, Arroyo del, Ca., U.S. (ä-rō′yō dĕl väl′yå)	118	37°36′N	121°43′W
Vallecas, Spain (väl-yā′käs)	173a	40°23′N	3°37′W
Valle de Allende, Mex. (väl′yā dā äl-yĕn′då)	122	26°55′N	105°25′W
Valle de Bravo, Mex. (brä′vô)	130	19°12′N	100°07′W
Valle de Guanape, Ven. (vä′l-yĕ-dĕ-gwä-nä′pĕ)	143b	9°54′N	65°41′W
Valle de la Pascua, Ven. (lä-pä′s-kōōä)	142	9°12′N	65°08′W
Valle del Cauca, dept., Col. (vä′l-yĕ del kou′ĸä)	142a	4°03′N	76°13′W
Valle de Santiago, Mex. (sän-tē-ä′gô)	130	20°23′N	101°11′W
Valledupar, Col. (dōō-pär′)	142	10°13′N	73°39′W
Valle Grande, Bol. (grän′dā)	142	18°27′S	64°03′W
Vallejo, Ca., U.S. (vä-yā′hō) (vă-lā′hō)	104	38°06′N	122°15′W
Vallejo, Sierra de, mts., Mex. (sē-ĕ′r-rä-dĕ-väl-yĕ′ĸô)	130	21°00′N	105°10′W
Vallenar, Chile (väl-yå-när′)	144	28°39′S	70°52′W
Valles, Mex.	128	21°59′N	99°02′W
Valletta, Malta (väl-lĕt′ä)	162	35°50′N	14°29′E
Valle Vista, Ca., U.S. (väl′yā vĭs′tȧ)	117a	33°45′N	116°53′W
Valley City, N.D., U.S.	104	46°55′N	97°59′W
Valley City, Oh., U.S. (văl′ĭ)	111d	41°14′N	81°56′W
Valley Falls, Ks., U.S.	121	39°25′N	95°26′W
Valleyfield, Can. (văl′ē-fēld)	91	45°16′N	74°09′W
Valley Park, Mo., U.S. (văl′ē pärk)	117e	38°33′N	90°30′W
Valley Stream, N.Y., U.S. (văl′ĭ strēm)	110a	40°39′N	73°42′W
Valli di Comácchio, l., Italy (vä′lē-dē-kô-mȧ′chyô)	174	44°38′N	12°15′E
Vallière, Haiti (väl-yâr′)	135	19°30′N	71°55′W
Vallimanca, r., Arg. (väl-yē-mä′n-kä)	141c	36°21′S	60°55′W
Valls, Spain (väls)	162	41°15′N	1°15′E
Valmiera, Lat. (vål′myĕ-rȧ)	180	57°34′N	25°54′E
Valognes, Fr. (vȧ-lôn′y′)	170	49°32′N	1°30′W
Valona *see* Vlorë, Alb.	163	40°28′N	19°31′E
Valozhyn, Bela.	176	54°04′N	26°38′E
Valparaíso, Chile (väl′pä-rä-ē′sô)	144	33°02′S	71°32′W
Valparaíso, Mex.	130	22°49′N	103°33′W
Valparaiso, In., U.S. (văl-pȧ-rā′zô)	108	41°25′N	87°05′W
Valpariso, prov., Chile	141b	32°58′S	71°23′W
Valréas, Fr. (vȧl-rȧ-ä′)	170	44°25′N	4°56′E
Vals, r., S. Afr.	238c	27°32′S	26°51′E
Vals, Tanjung, c., Indon.	213	8°30′S	137°15′E
Valsbaai, b., S. Afr.	232a	34°14′S	18°35′E
Valuyevo, Russia (vȧ-lōō′yĕ-vô)	186b	55°34′N	37°21′E
Valuyki, Russia (vȧ-lò-ē′kē)	181	50°14′N	38°04′E
Valverde del Camino, Spain (väl-vĕr-dĕ-dĕl-kä-mē′nō)	172	37°34′N	6°44′W
Vammala, Fin.	167	61°19′N	22°51′E
Van, Tur. (vȧn)	198	38°04′N	43°10′E
Van Buren, Ar., U.S. (văn bū′rĕn)	121	35°26′N	94°20′W
Van Buren, Me., U.S.	100	47°09′N	67°58′W
Vanceburg, Ky., U.S. (văns′bûrg)	108	38°35′N	83°20′W
Vancouver, Can. (văn-kōō′vẽr)	90	49°16′N	123°06′W
Vancouver, Wa., U.S.	104	45°37′N	122°40′W
Vancouver Island, i., Can.	92	49°50′N	125°05′W
Vancouver Island Ranges, mts., Can.	94	49°25′N	125°25′W
Vandalia, Il., U.S. (văn-dā′lĭ-ȧ)	108	39°00′N	89°00′W
Vandalia, Mo., U.S.	121	39°19′N	91°30′W
Vanderbijlpark, S. Afr.	238c	26°43′S	27°50′E
Vanderhoof, Can.	90	54°01′N	124°01′W
Van Diemen, Cape, c., Austl. (văndē′mĕn)	220	11°05′S	130°15′E
Van Diemen Gulf, b., Austl.	220	11°50′S	131°30′E
Vanegas, Mex. (vä-nĕ′gäs)	128	23°54′N	100°54′W
Vänern, l., Swe.	156	58°52′N	13°17′E
Vänersborg, Swe. (vĕ′nẽrs-bôr′)	160	58°24′N	12°15′E
Vanga, Kenya (väŋ′gä)	233	4°38′S	39°10′E
Vangani, India	203b	19°07′N	73°15′E
Van Gölü, l., Tur.	180	38°33′N	42°46′E
Van Horn, Tx., U.S.	122	31°03′N	104°50′W
Vanier, Can.	102c	45°27′N	75°39′W
Van Lear, Ky., U.S. (văn lēr′)	108	37°45′N	82°50′W
Vannes, Fr. (vȧn)	161	47°42′N	2°46′W
Van Nuys, Ca., U.S. (văn nīz′)	117a	34°11′N	118°27′W
Van Rees, Pegunungan, mts., Indon.	213	2°30′S	138°45′E
Vantaan, r., Fin.	167	60°25′N	24°43′E
Vanua Levu, i., Fiji	214g	16°33′S	179°15′E
Vanuatu, nation, Oc.	219	16°02′S	169°15′E
Van Wert, Oh., U.S. (văn wûrt′)	108	40°50′N	84°35′W
Vara, Swe. (vä′rä)	166	58°17′N	12°55′E
Varaklāni, Lat.	167	56°38′N	26°46′E
Varallo, Italy (vä-räl′lô)	174	45°44′N	8°14′E
Vārānasi (Benares), India	199	25°25′N	83°00′E
Varangerfjorden, b., Nor.	157	70°05′N	30°20′E
Varano, Lago di, l., Italy (lä′gō-dē-vä-rä′nô)	174	41°52′N	15°55′E
Varaždin, Cro. (vä′räzh′dēn)	163	46°17′N	16°20′E
Varazze, Italy (vä-rät′sā)	174	44°23′N	8°34′E
Varberg, Swe. (vär′bĕrg)	166	57°06′N	12°16′E
Vardar, r., Serb. (vär′där)	175	41°40′N	21°50′E
Varėna, Lith. (vä-rā′nȧ)	167	54°16′N	24°35′E
Varennes, Can. (vȧ-rĕn′)	102a	45°41′N	73°27′W
Vareš, Bos. (vä′rĕsh)	175	44°10′N	18°20′E
Varese, Italy (vä-rā′så)	174	45°45′N	8°49′E
Varginha, Braz. (vär-zhē′n-yä)	143	21°33′S	45°25′W
Varkaus, Fin. (vär′kous)	167	62°19′N	27°51′E
Varlamovo, Russia (vár-lá′mô-vô)	186a	54°37′N	60°41′E
Varna, Blg. (vär′nȧ)	154	43°14′N	27°58′E
Varna, Russia	186a	53°22′N	60°59′E
Värnamo, Swe. (vĕr′nȧ-mô)	166	57°11′N	13°45′E
Varnsdorf, Czech Rep. (värns′dôrf)	168	50°54′N	14°36′E
Varnville, S.C., U.S. (värn′vĭl)	125	32°49′N	81°05′W
Vasa, India	203b	19°20′N	72°47′E
Vascongadas *see* Basque Provinces, hist. reg., Spain	172	43°00′N	2°46′W
Vashka, r., Russia	180	64°00′N	48°00′E
Vashon, Wa., U.S. (văsh′ŭn)	116a	47°27′N	122°28′W
Vashon Heights, Wa., U.S. (hītz)	116a	47°30′N	122°28′W
Vashon Island, i., Wa., U.S.	116a	47°27′N	122°27′W
Vaslui, Rom. (vȧs-lōō′ē)	169	46°39′N	27°49′E
Vassar, Mi., U.S. (văs′ẽr)	108	43°25′N	83°35′W
Vassouras, Braz. (väs-sō′räzh)	141a	22°25′S	43°40′W
Västerås, Swe. (vĕs′tẽr-ôs)	160	59°39′N	16°30′E
Västerdalälven, r., Swe.	160	61°06′N	13°10′E
Västervik, Swe. (vĕs′tẽr-vēk)	160	57°45′N	16°35′E
Vasto, Italy (väs′tô)	162	42°06′N	12°42′E
Vasyl'kiv, Ukr.	181	50°10′N	30°22′E
Vasyugan, r., Russia (vȧs-yōō-gȧn′)	184	58°52′N	77°30′E
Vatican City, nation, Eur.	174	41°54′N	12°22′E
Vaticano, Cape, c., Italy (vä-tē-kä′nô)	174	38°38′N	15°52′E
Vatnajökull, ice, Ice. (vät′nȧ-yû-kòl)	160	64°34′N	16°41′W
Vatomandry, Madag.	233	18°53′S	48°13′E
Vatra Dornei, Rom. (vät′rȧ dôr′nå′)	169	47°22′N	25°20′E
Vättern, l., Swe.	156	58°15′N	14°24′E
Vattholma, Swe.	166	60°01′N	17°40′E
Vaudreuil, Can. (vô-drû′y′)	102a	45°24′N	74°02′W
Vaugh, Wa., U.S. (vôn)	116a	47°21′N	122°47′W
Vaughan, Can.	102d	43°47′N	79°36′W
Vaughn, N.M., U.S.	120	34°37′N	105°13′W
Vaupés, r., S.A. (vȧ′ōō-pĕ′s)	142	1°18′N	71°14′W
Vawkavysk, Bela. (vôl-kô-vėsk′)	169	53°11′N	24°29′E
Vaxholm, Swe. (väks′hôlm)	166	59°26′N	18°19′E
Växjo, Swe. (vĕks′shû)	160	56°53′N	14°46′E
Vaygach, i., Russia (vī-gȧch′)	178	70°00′N	59°00′E
Veadeiros, Chapadas dos, hills, Braz. (shä-pä′däs-dôs-vĕ-ȧ-dā′rōs)	143	14°00′S	47°00′W
Vedea, r., Rom. (vå′dyȧ)	175	44°25′N	24°45′E
Vedia, Arg. (vĕ′dyä)	141c	34°29′S	61°30′W
Veedersburg, In., U.S. (vē′dẽrz-bûrg)	108	40°05′N	87°15′W
Vega, i., Nor.	160	65°38′N	10°51′E
Vega de Alatorre, Mex. (vā′gä dā ä-lä-tōr′rå)	131	20°02′N	96°39′W
Vega Real, reg., Dom. Rep. (vĕ′gä-rĕ-ä′l)	135	19°30′N	71°05′W
Vegreville, Can.	90	53°30′N	112°03′W
Vehār Lake, l., India	203b	19°11′N	72°52′E
Veinticinco de Mayo, Arg.	141c	35°26′S	60°09′W
Vejer de la Frontera, Spain	172	36°15′N	5°58′W
Vejle, Den. (vī′lĕ)	160	55°41′N	9°29′E
Velbert, Ger. (fĕl′bĕrt)	171c	51°20′N	7°03′E
Velebit, mts., Serb. (vā′lĕ-bēt)	163	44°25′N	15°23′E
Velen, Ger. (fĕ′lĕn)	171c	51°54′N	7°00′E
Vélez-Málaga, Spain (vā′lāth-mä′lä-gä)	172	36°48′N	4°05′W
Vélez-Rubio, Spain (rōō′bē-ô)	172	37°38′N	2°05′W
Velika Kapela, mts., Serb. (vĕ′lē-kä kä-pĕ′lä)	163	45°03′N	15°20′E
Velika Morava, r., Serb. (mô′rä-vä)	163	44°00′N	21°30′E
Velikaya, r., Russia (vå-lē′kȧ-yȧ)	176	57°25′N	28°07′E
Velikiye Luki, Russia (vyē-lē′-kyē lōō′ke)	178	56°19′N	30°32′E
Velikiy Ustyug, Russia (vå-lē′kĭ ōōs-tyòg′)	178	60°45′N	46°38′E
Veliko Tŭrnovo, Blg.	163	43°06′N	25°38′E
Velikoye, Russia (vå-lē′kô-yĕ)	176	57°21′N	39°45′E
Velikoye, l., Russia	176	57°00′N	36°53′E
Veli Lošinj, Cro. (lô′shēn′)	174	44°30′N	14°29′E
Velizh, Russia (vå′lēzh)	180	55°37′N	31°11′E
Vella Lavella, i., Sol. Is.	221	8°00′S	156°42′E
Velletri, Italy (vĕl-lā′trē)	174	41°42′N	12°48′E
Vellore, India (vĕl-lōr′)	199	12°57′N	79°09′E
Vels, Russia (vĕls)	186a	60°35′N	58°47′E
Vel'sk, Russia (vĕlsk)	178	61°00′N	42°18′E
Velten, Ger. (fel′tĕn)	159b	52°41′N	13°11′E
Velya, r., Russia (vĕl′yȧ)	186b	56°23′N	37°54′E
Velyka Lepetykha, Ukr.	177	47°11′N	33°58′E
Velykyi Bychkiv, Ukr.	169	47°59′N	24°01′E
Venadillo, Col. (vĕ-nä-dē′l-yō)	142a	4°43′N	74°55′W
Venado, Mex. (vå-mä′dō)	130	22°54′N	101°07′W
Venado Tuerto, Arg. (vĕ-nä′dô-tōōĕ′r-tô)	144	33°28′S	61°47′W
Vendôme, Fr. (väɴ-dōm′)	170	47°46′N	1°05′E
Veneto, hist. reg., Italy (vĕ-nĕ′tô)	174	45°58′N	11°24′E
Venëv, Russia (vĕn-ĕf′)	180	54°19′N	38°14′E
Venezia *see* Venice, Italy	154	45°25′N	12°18′E
Venezuela, nation, S.A. (vĕn-ē-zwē′lȧ)	142	8°00′N	65°00′W
Venezuela, Golfo de, b., S.A. (gôl-fô-dĕ)	142	11°34′N	71°02′W
Veniaminof, Mount, mtn., Ak., U.S.	103	56°12′N	159°20′W
Venice, Italy	154	45°25′N	12°18′E
Venice, Ca., U.S. (vĕn′ĭs)	117a	33°59′N	118°28′W
Venice, Il., U.S.	117e	38°40′N	90°10′W
Venice, Gulf of, b., Italy	162	45°23′N	13°00′E
Venlo, Neth.	171c	51°22′N	6°11′E
Venta, r., Eur. (vĕn′tȧ)	167	57°05′N	21°45′E
Ventana, Sierra de la, mts., Arg. (sē-ĕ-rȧ-dĕ-lä-vĕn-tȧ′nä)	144	38°00′S	63°00′W
Ventersburg, S. Afr. (vĕn-tẽrs′bûrg)	238c	28°06′S	27°10′E
Ventersdorp, S. Afr. (vĕn-tẽrs′dôrp)	238c	26°20′S	26°48′E
Ventimiglia, Italy (vĕn-tē-mēl′yä)	174	43°46′N	7°37′E
Ventnor, N.J., U.S. (vĕnt′nẽr)	109	39°20′N	74°25′W
Ventspils, Lat. (vĕnt′spēls)	180	57°24′N	21°41′E
Ventuari, r., Ven. (vĕn-tōōȧ′rē)	142	4°47′N	65°56′W
Ventura, Ca., U.S. (vĕn-tōō′rȧ)	118	34°18′N	119°18′W
Venukovsky, Russia (vĕ-nōō′kôv-skĭ)	186b	55°10′N	37°26′E
Venustiano Carranza, Mex. (vĕ-nōōs-tyä′nō-kär-rä′n-zä)	130	19°44′N	103°48′W
Venustiano Carranzo, Mex. (kär-rä′n-zô)	131	16°21′N	92°36′W
Vera, Arg. (vĕ-rä)	144	29°22′S	60°09′W
Vera, Spain (vā′rä)	172	37°18′N	1°53′W
Veracruz, Mex.	128	19°13′N	96°07′W
Vera Cruz, state, Mex. (vā-rä-krōōz′)	128	20°30′N	97°15′W
Verāval, India (vĕr′vŭ-väl)	199	20°59′N	70°49′E
Vercelli, Italy (vĕr-chĕl′lē)	174	45°18′N	8°27′E
Verchères, Can. (vĕr-shâr′)	102a	45°46′N	73°21′W
Verde, i., Phil. (vĕr′då)	213a	13°34′N	121°11′E
Verde, r., Mex.	130	21°48′N	99°50′W
Verde, r., Mex.	130	20°50′N	103°00′W
Verde, r., Mex.	131	16°05′N	97°44′W
Verde, r., Az., U.S. (vûrd)	119	34°04′N	111°40′W
Verde, Cap, c., Bah.	135	22°50′N	75°00′W
Verde, Cay, i., Bah.	135	22°00′N	75°05′W
Verde Island Passage, strt., Phil. (vĕr′dē)	213a	13°36′N	120°39′E
Verdemont, Ca., U.S. (vûr′dē-mŏnt)	117a	34°12′N	117°22′W
Verden, Ger. (fĕr′dĕn)	168	52°55′N	9°15′E
Verdigris, r., Ok., U.S. (vûr′dē-grēs)	121	36°50′N	95°29′W
Verdun, Can. (vĕr′dŭɴ′)	99	45°27′N	73°34′W
Verdun, Fr. (vâr-dûɴ′)	161	49°09′N	5°21′E
Verdun, Fr.	171	43°48′N	1°10′E
Vereeniging, S. Afr. (vĕ-rā′nĭ-gĭng)	238c	26°40′S	27°56′E
Verena, S. Afr. (vĕr-ēn ȧ)	238c	25°30′S	29°02′E
Vereya, Russia (vĕ-rå′yȧ)	176	55°21′N	36°08′E
Verín, Spain (vå-rēn′)	172	41°56′N	7°26′W
Verkhne-Kamchatsk, Russia (vyĕrk′nyĕ kȧm-chatsk′)	179	54°42′N	158°41′E
Verkhne Neyvinskiy, Russia (nā-vĭn′skĭ)	186a	57°17′N	60°10′E
Verkhne Ural'sk, Russia (ò-ralsk′)	178	53°53′N	59°13′E
Verkhniy Avzyan, Russia (vyĕrk′nyĕ ȧv-zyȧn′)	186a	53°32′N	57°30′E
Verkhniye Kigi, Russia (vyĕrk′nĭ-yĕ kĭ′gĭ)	186a	55°23′N	58°37′E
Verkhniy Ufaley, Russia (ò-fä′lā)	186a	56°04′N	60°15′E
Verkhnyaya Pyshma, Russia (vyĕrk′nyä-yä pōōsh′mȧ)	186a	56°57′N	60°37′E
Verkhnyaya Salda, Russia (säl′dȧ)	186a	58°03′N	60°33′E
Verkhnyaya Tunguska (Angara), r., Russia (tòn-gòs′kȧ)	184	58°13′N	97°00′E
Verkhnyaya Tura, Russia (tò′rȧ)	186a	58°22′N	59°51′E
Verkhnyaya Yayva, Russia (yäy′vȧ)	186a	59°28′N	57°38′E
Verkhotur'ye, Russia (vyĕr-kô-tōōr′yĕ)	186a	58°52′N	60°47′E
Verkhoyansk, Russia (vyĕr-ĸô-yänsk′)	179	67°43′N	133°33′E
Verkhoyanskiy Khrebet, mts., Russia (vyĕr-ĸô-yänskĭ)	179	67°45′N	128°00′E
Vermilion, Can. (vẽr-mĭl′yŭn)	90	53°22′N	110°51′W
Vermilion, l., Mn., U.S.	113	47°49′N	92°35′W
Vermilion, r., Can.	99	47°30′N	73°15′W
Vermilion, r., Can.	96	53°30′N	111°00′W
Vermilion, r., Il., U.S.	108	41°05′N	89°00′W
Vermilion, r., Mn., U.S.	113	48°09′N	92°31′W
Vermilion Hills, hills, Can.	96	50°43′N	106°50′W
Vermilion Range, mts., Mn., U.S.	113	47°55′N	91°59′W
Vermillion, S.D., U.S.	112	42°46′N	96°56′W
Vermillion, r., S.D., U.S.	112	43°54′N	97°14′W
Vermillion Bay, b., La., U.S.	123	29°47′N	92°00′W
Vermont, state, U.S. (vẽr-mŏnt′)	105	43°50′N	72°50′W
Vernal, Ut., U.S. (vûr′nȧl)	115	40°29′N	109°40′W
Verneuk Pan, pl., S. Afr. (vĕr-nŭk′)	232	30°10′S	21°46′E
Vernon, Can. (vĕr-nôɴ′)	90	50°18′N	119°15′W
Vernon, Can.	102c	45°10′N	75°27′W
Vernon, Ca., U.S. (vŭr′nŭn)	117a	34°01′N	118°12′W

ăt; finăl; rāte; senåte; ärm; åsk; sofȧ; fâre; ch-choose; dh-as th in other; bē; ēvent; bĕt; recĕnt; cratẽr; g-gō; gh-guttural g; bĭt; ĭ-short neutral; rīde; ĸ-guttural k as ch in German ich;

PLACE (Pronunciation)	PAGE	LAT.	LONG.
Vernon, In., U.S. (vûr′nŭn)	108	39°00′N	85°40′W
Vernon, N.J., U.S.	110a	39°00′N	85°40′W
Vernon, Tx., U.S.	120	34°09′N	99°16′W
Vernonia, Or., U.S. (vûr-nō′nyȧ)	116c	45°52′N	123°12′W
Vero Beach, Fl., U.S. (vē′rō)	125a	27°36′N	80°25′W
Véroia, Grc.	175	40°30′N	22°13′E
Verona, Italy (vā-rō′nä)	162	45°28′N	11°02′E
Versailles, Fr. (vĕr-sī′y′)	161	48°48′N	2°07′E
Versailles, Ky., U.S. (vẽr-sālz′)	108	38°05′N	84°45′W
Versailles, Mo., U.S.	121	38°27′N	92°52′W
Vert, Cap, c., Sen.	230	14°43′N	17°30′W
Verulam, S. Afr. (vĕ-rōō-lăm)	233c	29°39′S	31°08′E
Verviers, Bel. (vĕr-vyā′)	165	50°35′N	5°57′E
Vesele, Ukr.	177	46°59′N	34°56′E
Vesijärvi, l., Fin.	167	61°09′N	25°10′E
Vesoul, Fr. (vē-sōōl′)	171	47°38′N	6°11′E
Vestavia Hills, Al., U.S.	110h	33°26′N	86°46′W
Vesterålen, is., Nor. (vĕs′tĕr ô′lĕn)	160	68°54′N	14°03′E
Vestfjord, b., Nor.	156	67°33′N	12°59′E
Vestmannaeyjar, Ice. (vĕst′män-ä-ā′yär)	160	63°12′N	20°17′W
Vesuvio, vol., Italy (vĕ-sōō′vyä)	156	40°35′N	14°26′E
Ves′yegonsk, Russia (vĕ-syĕ-gônsk′)	176	58°42′N	37°09′E
Veszprem, Hung. (vĕs′prăm)	169	47°05′N	17°53′E
Vészto, Hung. (vās′tû)	169	46°55′N	21°18′E
Vet, r., S. Afr. (vĕt)	238c	28°25′S	26°37′E
Vetlanda, Swe. (vĕt-län′dä)	166	57°26′N	15°05′E
Vetluga, Russia (vyĕt-lōō′gȧ)	180	57°50′N	45°42′E
Vetluga, r., Russia	180	56°50′N	45°50′E
Vetovo, Blg. (vā′tô-vô)	175	43°42′N	26°18′E
Vetren, Blg. (vĕt′rĕn′)	175	42°16′N	24°04′E
Vevay, In., U.S. (vē′vā)	108	38°45′N	85°05′W
Veynes, Fr. (vān′′)	171	44°31′N	5°47′E
Vézère, r., Fr. (vā-zer′)	170	45°01′N	1°00′E
Viacha, Bol. (vēä′chä)	142	16°43′S	68°16′W
Viadana, Italy (vē-ä-dä′nä)	174	44°55′N	10°30′E
Vian, Ok., U.S. (vī′ăn)	121	35°30′N	95°00′W
Viana, Braz. (vē-ä′nä)	143	3°09′S	44°44′W
Viana do Alentejo, Port. (vē-ä′nȧ dò ä-lĕn-tā′hō)	172	38°20′N	8°02′W
Viana do Bolo, Spain	172	42°10′N	7°07′W
Viana do Castelo, Port. (dò käs-tā′lò)	162	41°41′N	8°45′W
Viangchan, Laos	212	18°07′N	102°33′E
Viar, r., Spain (vē-ä′rä)	172	38°15′N	6°08′W
Viareggio, Italy (vē-ä-rĕd′jô)	174	43°52′N	10°14′E
Viborg, Den. (vē′bôr)	166	56°27′N	9°22′E
Vibo Valentia, Italy (vē′bô-vä-lĕ′n-tyä)	174	38°47′N	16°06′E
Vic, Spain	173	41°55′N	2°14′E
Vicálvaro, Spain	173a	40°25′N	3°37′W
Vicente López, Arg. (vē-sĕ′n-tĕ-lō′pĕz)	144a	34°31′S	58°29′W
Vicenza, Italy (vē-chĕnt′sä)	162	45°33′N	11°33′E
Vichuga, Russia (vē-chōō′gȧ)	180	57°13′N	41°58′E
Vichy, Fr. (vē-shē′)	161	46°06′N	3°28′E
Vickersund, Nor.	166	60°00′N	9°59′E
Vicksburg, Mi., U.S. (vĭks′bûrg)	108	42°10′N	85°30′W
Vicksburg, Ms., U.S.	105	32°20′N	90°50′W
Viçosa, Braz. (vē-sô′sä)	141a	20°46′S	42°51′W
Victoria, Arg. (vēk-tô′rēä)	144	32°36′S	60°09′W
Victoria, Can. (vĭk-tō′rĭ-ȧ)	90	48°26′N	123°23′W
Victoria, Chile (vēk-tô-rēä)	144	38°15′S	72°16′W
Victoria, Col. (vēk-tō′rēä)	142a	5°19′N	74°54′W
Victoria, Phil. (vēk-tô-ryä)	213a	15°34′N	120°41′E
Victoria, Tx., U.S. (vĭk-tō′rĭ-ȧ)	123	28°48′N	97°00′W
Victoria, Va., U.S.	125	36°57′N	78°13′W
Victoria, state, Austl.	219	36°46′S	143°15′E
Victoria, l., Afr.	232	0°50′S	32°50′E
Victoria, r., Austl.	220	17°25′S	130°50′E
Victoria, Mount, mtn., Mya.	199	21°26′N	93°59′E
Victoria, Mount, mtn., Pap. N. Gui.	213	9°35′S	147°45′E
Victoria de las Tunas, Cuba (vēk-tō′rē-ä dā läs tōō′näs)	134	20°55′N	77°05′W
Victoria Falls, wtfl., Afr.	232	17°55′S	25°51′E
Victoria Island, i., Can.	89	70°13′N	107°45′W
Victoria Lake, l., Can.	101	48°20′N	57°40′W
Victoria Land, reg., Ant.	224	75°00′S	160°00′E
Victoria Nile, r., Ug.	237	2°20′N	31°35′E
Victoria Peak, mtn., Belize (vēk-tōrĭ′ȧ)	132a	16°47′N	88°40′W
Victoria Peak, mtn., Can.	94	50°03′N	126°06′W
Victoria River Downs, Austl. (vĭc-tôr′ĭȧ)	218	16°30′S	131°10′E
Victoria Strait, strt., Can. (vĭk-tō′rĭ-ȧ)	92	69°10′N	100°58′W
Victoriaville, Can. (vĭk-tō′rĭ-ȧ-vĭl)	91	46°04′N	71°59′W
Victoria West, S. Afr. (wĕst)	232	31°25′S	23°10′E
Vidalia, Ga., U.S. (vĭ-dā′lĭ-ȧ)	125	32°10′N	82°26′W
Vidalia, La., U.S.	123	31°33′N	91°28′W
Vidin, Blg. (vĭ′dĭn)	163	44°00′N	22°53′E
Vidnoye, Russia	186b	55°33′N	37°41′E
Vidzy, Bela. (vē′dzĭ)	176	55°23′N	26°46′E
Viedma, Arg. (vyād′mä)	144	40°55′S	63°03′W
Viedma, l., Arg.	144	49°40′S	72°35′W
Viejo, r., Nic. (vyā′hō)	132	12°45′N	86°19′W
Vienna (Wien), Aus.	154	48°13′N	16°22′E
Vienna, Ga., U.S. (vē-ĕn′ȧ)	124	32°03′N	83°50′W
Vienna, Il., U.S.	121	37°24′N	88°50′W
Vienna, Va., U.S.	110e	38°54′N	77°16′W
Vienne, Fr. (vyĕn′)	161	45°31′N	4°54′E
Vienne, r., Fr.	170	47°06′N	0°20′E
Vientiane *see* Viangchan, Laos	212	18°07′N	102°33′E
Vieques, P.R. (vyā′kås)	129b	18°09′N	65°27′W
Vieques, i., P.R. (vyā′kås)	129b	18°05′N	65°28′W
Vierfontein, S. Afr. (vẽr′fŏn-tān)	238c	27°06′S	26°45′E
Viersen, Ger. (fēr′zĕn)	171c	51°15′N	6°24′E
Vierwaldstätter See, l., Switz.	168	46°54′N	8°36′E
Vierzon, Fr. (vyâr-zôn′)	161	47°14′N	2°04′E
Viesca, Mex. (vē-ās′kä)	122	25°21′N	102°47′W
Viesca, Laguna de, l., Mex. (lä-ó′nä-dĕ)	122	25°30′N	102°40′W
Vieste, Italy (vyĕs′tå)	174	41°52′N	16°10′E
Vietnam, nation, Asia (vyĕt′näm′)	212	18°00′N	107°00′E
Vigan, Phil. (vēgän)	212	17°36′N	120°22′E
Vigevano, Italy (vē-jå-vä′nô)	174	45°18′N	8°52′E
Vigny, Fr. (vēn-y′ē′)	171b	49°05′N	1°54′E
Vigo, Spain (vē′gō)	154	42°18′N	8°42′W
Vihti, Fin. (vē′tĭ)	167	60°27′N	24°18′E
Vijayawāda, India	199	16°31′N	80°37′E
Viksøyri, Nor.	166	61°06′N	6°35′E
Vila Caldas Xavier, Moz.	237	15°59′S	34°12′E
Vila de Manica, Moz. (vē′lä dā mä-nē′kȧ)	232	18°48′S	32°49′E
Vila de Rei, Port. (vē′lȧ dā rā′ĭ)	172	39°42′N	8°03′W
Vila do Conde, Port. (vē′lȧ dò kôn′dĕ)	172	41°21′N	8°44′W
Vilafranca del Penedès, Spain	173	41°20′N	1°40′E
Vilafranca de Xira, Port. (frän′kȧ dā shē′rȧ)	172	38°58′N	8°59′W
Vilaine, r., Fr. (vē-lân′)	170	47°34′N	2°15′W
Vilalba, Spain	172	43°18′N	7°43′W
Vilanculos, Moz. (vē-län-kōō′lôs)	232	22°03′S	35°13′E
Vilāni, Lat. (vē′lä-nĭ)	167	56°31′N	27°00′E
Vila Nova de Foz Côa, Port. (nō′vȧ dā fôz-kō′ȧ)	172	41°08′N	7°11′W
Vila Nova de Gaia, Port. (vē′lȧ nō′vȧ dā gä′yä)	172	41°08′N	8°40′W
Vila Nova de Milfontes, Port. (nō′vȧ dā mêl-fôn′tāzh)	172	37°44′N	8°48′W
Vila Real, Port. (rā-äl′)	162	41°18′N	7°48′W
Vila-real, Spain	173	39°55′N	0°07′W
Vila Real de Santo Antonio, Port.	172	37°14′N	7°25′W
Vila Viçosa, Port. (vē-sō′zȧ)	172	38°47′N	7°24′W
Vileyka, Bela. (vē-lā′ē-kȧ)	176	54°19′N	26°58′E
Vilhelmina, Swe.	160	64°37′N	16°30′E
Viljandi, Est. (vēl′yän-dē)	180	58°24′N	25°34′E
Viljoenskroon, S. Afr.	238c	27°13′S	26°58′E
Vilkaviškis, Lith. (vêl-kȧ-vēsh′kēs)	167	54°40′N	23°08′E
Vil′kitskogo, i., Russia (vyl-kēts-kōgō)	184	73°25′N	76°00′E
Villa Acuña, Mex. (vēl′yä-kōō′n-yä)	122	29°20′N	100°56′W
Villa Ahumada, Mex. (ä-ōō-mä′dä)	122	30°43′N	106°30′W
Villa Alta, Mex. (äl′tä)(sän ēl-då-fōn′sō)	131	17°20′N	96°08′W
Villa Angela, Arg. (vē′l-yä á′n-kĕ-lä)	144	27°31′S	60°42′W
Villa Ballester, Arg. (vē′l-yä-bäl-yĕs-tĕr)	144a	34°33′S	58°33′W
Villa Bella, Bol. (bĕ′l-yä)	142	10°25′S	65°22′W
Villablino, Spain (vēl-yä-blē′nô)	172	42°58′N	6°18′W
Villacañas, Spain (vēl-yä-kän′yäs)	172	39°39′N	3°20′W
Villacarrillo, Spain (vēl-yä-kä-rēl′yô)	172	38°09′N	3°07′W
Villach, Aus. (fē′läk)	161	46°38′N	13°50′E
Villacidro, Italy (vē-lä-chē′drô)	174	39°28′N	8°41′E
Villa Clara, prov., Cuba	134	22°40′N	80°10′W
Villa Constitución, Arg. (kōn-stē-tōō-syōn′)	141c	33°15′S	60°19′W
Villa Coronado, Mex. (kō-rō-nä′dhō)	122	26°45′N	105°10′W
Villa Cuauhtémoc, Mex. (vēl′yä-kōō-äò-tĕ′môk)	131	22°11′N	97°50′W
Villa de Allende, Mex. (vēl′yä′dä äl-yĕn′då)	122	25°18′N	100°01′W
Villa de Alvarez, Mex. (vēl′yä-dĕ-ä′l-vä-rĕz)	130	19°17′N	103°44′W
Villa de Cura, Ven. (dĕ-kōō′rä)	143b	10°03′N	67°29′W
Villa de Guadalupe, Mex. (dĕ-gwä-dhä-lōō′pȧ)	130	23°22′N	100°44′W
Villa de Mayo, Arg.	144a	34°31′S	58°41′W
Villa Dolores, Arg. (vēl′yä dô-lō′räs)	144	31°50′S	65°05′W
Villa Escalante, Mex. (vēl′yä-ĕs-kä-län′tĕ)	130	19°24′N	101°36′W
Villa Flores, Mex. (vēl′yä-flō′räs)	131	16°13′N	93°17′W
Villafranca, Italy (vēl-lä-fräŋ′kä)	174	45°22′N	10°53′E
Villafranca del Bierzo, Spain	172	42°37′N	6°49′W
Villafranca de los Barros, Spain	172	38°34′N	6°22′W
Villafranche-de-Rouergue, Fr. (dĕ-rōō-ĕrg′)	170	44°21′N	2°02′E
Villa García, Mex. (gär-sē′ä)	130	22°07′N	101°55′W
Villagarcía, Spain	172	42°38′N	8°43′W
Villagrán, Mex.	122	24°28′N	99°30′W
Villa Grove, Il., U.S. (vĭl′ȧ grōv′)	108	39°55′N	88°15′W
Villaguay, Arg. (vē′l-yä-gwī)	144	31°47′S	58°53′W
Villa Hayes, Para. (vēl′yä äyås)(hāz)	144	25°07′S	57°31′W
Villahermosa, Mex. (vēl′yä-ĕr-mō′sä)	128	17°59′N	92°56′W
Villa Hidalgo, Mex. (vēl′yäē-däl′gō)	130	21°39′N	102°41′W
Villaldama, Mex. (vēl-yäl-dä′mä)	128	26°30′N	100°26′W
Villa Lopez, Mex. (vēl′yä lō′pĕz)	122	27°00′N	105°02′W
Villalpando, Spain (vēl-yäl-pän′dō)	172	41°54′N	5°24′W
Villa María, Arg. (vē′l-yä-mä-rē′ä)	144	32°17′S	63°08′W
Villamatín, Spain (vēl-yä-mä-tē′n)	172	36°50′N	5°38′W
Villa Mercedes, Arg. (mĕr-sā′dås)	144	33°38′S	65°16′W
Villa Montes, Bol. (vē′l-yä-mô′n-tĕs)	142	21°13′S	63°26′W
Villa Morelos, Mex. (mô-rĕ′lomcs)	130	20°01′N	101°24′W
Villanueva, Col. (vē′l-yä-nóĕ′vä)	142	10°44′N	73°08′W
Villanueva, Hond. (vēl′yä-nwā′vä)	132	15°19′N	88°02′W
Villanueva, Mex. (vēl′yä-nóĕ′vä)	130	22°25′N	102°53′W
Villanueva de Córdoba, Spain (vēl-yä-nwĕ′vä-dä kôr′dô-bä)	172	38°18′N	4°38′W
Villanueva de la Serena, Spain (lä sä-rā′nä)	172	38°59′N	5°56′W
Villa Obregón, Mex. (vē′l-yä-ô-brĕ-gô′n)	131a	19°21′N	99°11′W
Villa Ocampo, Mex. (ô-käm′pō)	122	26°26′N	105°30′W
Villa Pedro Montoya, Mex. (vēl′yä-pĕ′drô-môn-tô′yȧ)	130	21°38′N	99°51′W
Villard-Bonnot, Fr. (vēl-yär′bôn-nō′)	171	45°15′N	5°53′E
Villarrica, Para. (vēl-yä-rē′kä)	144	25°55′S	56°23′W
Villarrobledo, Spain (vēl-yär-rô-blā′dhō)	162	39°15′N	2°37′W
Villa Unión, Mex. (vēl′yä-ōō-nyōn′)	130	23°10′N	106°14′W
Villavicencio, Col. (vē′l-yä-vē-sĕ′n-syō)	142	4°09′N	73°38′W
Villaviciosa de Odón, Spain	173a	40°22′N	3°38′W
Villavieja, Col. (vē′l-yä-vē-ĕ′kȧ)	142a	3°13′N	75°13′W
Villazón, Bol. (vē′l-yä-zô′n)	142	22°02′S	65°42′W
Villefranche, Fr.	161	45°59′N	4°43′E
Villejuif, Fr. (vēl′zhüst′)	171b	48°48′N	2°22′E
Ville-Marie, Can.	91	47°18′N	79°22′W
Villena, Spain (vē-lyā′nȧ)	162	38°37′N	0°52′W
Villeneuve, Can. (vēl′nûv′)	102g	53°40′N	113°49′W
Villeneuve-Saint Georges, Fr. (sāN-zhôrzh′)	171b	48°43′N	2°27′E
Villeneuve-sur-Lot, Fr. (sür-lō′)	170	44°25′N	0°41′E
Ville Platte, La., U.S. (vēl plát′)	123	30°41′N	92°17′W
Villers Cotterêts, Fr. (vē-âr′kô-trā′)	171b	49°15′N	3°05′E
Villerupt, Fr. (vēl′rüp′)	171	49°28′N	6°16′E
Ville-Saint Georges, Can. (vĭl-sĕN-zhôrzh′)	99	46°07′N	70°40′W
Villeta, Col. (vē′l-yĕ′tȧ)	142a	5°02′N	74°29′W
Villeurbanne, Fr. (vēl-ûr-bän′)	161	45°43′N	4°55′E
Villiers, S. Afr. (vĭl′ĭ-ẽrs)	238c	27°03′S	28°38′E
Villingen-Schwenningen, Ger.	168	48°04′N	8°33′E
Villisca, Ia., U.S. (vĭ′lĭs′kȧ)	113	40°56′N	94°56′W
Villupuram, India	203	11°59′N	79°33′E
Vilnius, Lith. (vĭl′nē-ôs)	178	54°40′N	25°26′E
Vilppula, Fin. (vĭl′pŭ-lȧ)	167	62°01′N	24°24′E
Vil′shanka, Ukr.	177	48°14′N	30°52′E
Vil′shany, Ukr.	177	50°02′N	35°54′E
Vilvoorde, Bel.	159a	50°56′N	4°25′E
Vilyuy, r., Russia (vēl′yĭ)	179	63°00′N	121°00′E
Vilyuysk, Russia (vē-lyōō′ĭsk′)	179	63°41′N	121°47′E
Vimmerby, Swe. (vĭm′ĕr-bü)	166	57°41′N	15°51′E
Vimperk, Czech Rep. (vĭm-pĕrk′)	168	49°04′N	13°41′E
Viña del Mar, Chile (vē′nyä dĕl mär′)	144	33°00′S	71°33′W
Vinalhaven, Me., U.S. (vī-năl-hā′vĕn)	100	44°03′N	68°49′W
Vinaròs, Spain	173	40°29′N	0°27′E
Vincennes, Fr. (văn-sĕn′)	171b	48°51′N	2°27′E
Vincennes, In., U.S. (vĭn-zĕnz′)	105	38°40′N	87°30′W
Vincent, Al., U.S. (vĭn′sĕnt)	124	33°21′N	86°25′W
Vindelälven, r., Swe.	160	65°02′N	18°30′E
Vindeln, Swe. (vĭn′dĕln)	160	64°10′N	19°52′E
Vindhya Range, mts., India (vĭnd′yä)	199	22°30′N	75°50′E
Vineland, N.J., U.S. (vĭn′lănd)	109	39°30′N	75°00′W
Vinh, Viet. (vĕn′y′)	212	18°38′N	105°42′E
Vinhais, Port. (vēn-yä′ēzh)	172	41°51′N	7°00′W
Vinings, Ga., U.S. (vī′nĭngz)	110c	33°52′N	84°28′W
Vinita, Ok., U.S. (vĭ-nē′tȧ)	121	36°38′N	95°09′W
Vinkovci, Cro. (vēn′kôv-tsē)	175	45°17′N	18°47′E
Vinnytsia, Ukr.	178	49°13′N	28°31′E
Vinnytsya, prov., Ukr.	177	48°45′N	28°01′E
Vinogradovo, Russia (vĭ-nô-grä′do-vô)	186b	55°25′N	38°33′E
Vinson Massif, mtn., Ant.	224	77°40′S	87°00′W
Vinton, Ia., U.S. (vĭn′tŭn)	113	42°08′N	92°01′W
Vinton, La., U.S.	123	30°12′N	93°35′W
Violet, La., U.S. (vī′ô-lĕt)	110d	29°54′N	89°54′W
Virac, Phil. (vē-räk′)	209	13°38′N	124°20′E
Virbalis, Lith. (vēr′bá-lēs)	167	54°38′N	22°55′E
Virden, Can. (vûr′dĕn)	90	49°51′N	101°55′W
Virden, Il., U.S.	121	39°28′N	89°46′W
Virgin, r., U.S.	119	36°51′N	113°50′W
Virginia, S. Afr.	238c	28°07′S	26°54′E
Virginia, Mn., U.S. (vẽr-jĭn′yȧ)	105	47°32′N	92°36′W
Virginia, state, U.S.	105	37°00′N	80°45′W
Virginia Beach, Va., U.S.	109	36°50′N	75°58′W
Virginia City, Nv., U.S.	118	39°18′N	119°40′W
Virgin Islands, is., N.A. (vûr′jĭn)	129	18°15′N	64°00′W
Viroqua, Wi., U.S. (vĭ-rō′kwȧ)	113	43°33′N	90°54′W
Virovitica, Cro. (vē-rô-vē′tē-tsȧ)	175	45°50′N	17°24′E
Virpazar, Serb. (vêr′pä-zär′)	175	42°16′N	19°06′E
Virrat, Fin. (vĭr′ăt)	167	62°15′N	23°45′E
Virserum, Swe. (vĭr′sĕ-rôm)	166	57°22′N	15°35′E
Vis, Cro. (vēs)	174	43°03′N	16°11′E
Vis, i., Serb.	163	43°00′N	16°10′E
Visalia, Ca., U.S. (vĭ-sā′lĭ-ȧ)	118	36°20′N	119°18′W
Visby, Swe. (vĭs′bü)	154	57°39′N	18°19′E
Viscount Melville Sound, strt., Can.	89	74°00′N	110°00′W
Višegrad, Bos. (vē′shĕ-gräd)	175	43°48′N	19°17′E
Vishākhapatnam, India	199	17°48′N	83°21′E
Vishera, r., Russia (vĭ′shĕ-rȧ)	186a	60°40′N	58°46′E
Vishnyakovo, Russia	186b	55°44′N	38°10′E
Vishoek, S. Afr.	232a	34°13′S	18°26′E
Visim, Russia (vē′sĭm)	186a	57°38′N	59°32′E
Viskan, r., Swe.	166	57°20′N	12°25′E
Viški, Lat. (vēs′kĭ)	167	56°02′N	26°47′E
Visoko, Bos. (vē′sô-kô)	175	43°59′N	18°10′E
Vistula *see* Wisła, r., Pol.	156	52°30′N	20°00′E
Vitebsk, prov., Bela.	176	55°05′N	29°18′E
Viterbo, Italy (vē-tĕr′bō)	162	42°24′N	12°08′E
Viti Levu, i., Fiji	214g	18°00′S	178°00′E
Vitim, Russia (vē′tēm)	179	59°22′N	112°43′E
Vitim, r., Russia (vē′tēm)	179	54°00′N	115°00′E
Vitino, Russia (vē′tĭ-nô)	186c	59°40′N	29°51′E
Vitória, Braz. (vē-tō′rē-ä)	143	20°09′S	40°17′W
Vitoria, Spain (vē-tô-ryä)	162	42°43′N	2°43′W

ng-sing; ŋ-baŋk; N-nasalized n; nŏd; cŏmmit; ōld; ōbey; ôrder; oi-boil; fōōd; ò-as oo in foot; ou-out; s-soft; sh-dish; th-thin; pūre; ûnite; ûrn; stŭd; circŭs; ü-as in French tu; ′-indeterminate vowel.

364 Vitória de Conquista – Wanzhi PRONOUNCING INDEX

PLACE (Pronunciation)	PAGE	LAT.	LONG.
Vitória de Conquista, Braz. (vē-tō'rē-ä-dä-kōn-kwē's-tä)	143	14°51'S	40°44'W
Vitry-le-François, Fr. (vē-trē'lĕ-fräN-swà')	170	48°44'N	4°34'E
Vitsyebsk, Bela. (vē'tyĕpsk)	180	55°12'N	30°16'E
Vittorio, Italy (vē-tô'rē-ô)	174	45°59'N	12°17'E
Viveiro, Spain	172	43°39'N	7°37'W
Vivian, La., U.S. (vĭv'ĭ-*ă*n)	123	32°51'N	93°59'W
Vizianagaram, India	199	18°10'N	83°29'E
Vlaardingen, Neth. (vlär'dĭng-*ĕ*n)	165	51°54'N	4°20'E
Vladikavkaz, Russia	181	43°05'N	44°35'E
Vladimir, Russia (vlà-dyē'mĭr)	178	56°08'N	40°24'E
Vladimir, prov., Russia (vlä-dyē'mĕr)	176	56°08'N	39°53'E
Vladimiro-Aleksandrovskoye, Russia	210	42°50'N	133°00'E
Vladivostok, Russia (vlà-dē-vôs-tôk')	179	43°06'N	131°47'E
Vlasenica, Bos. (vlä'sĕ-nēt'sà)	175	44°11'N	18°58'E
Vlasotince, Serb. (vlä'sô-tēn-tsĕ)	175	42°58'N	22°08'E
Vlieland, i., Neth. (vlē'länt)	165	53°19'N	4°55'E
Vlissingen, Neth. (vlĭs'sĭng-*ĕ*n)	165	51°30'N	3°34'E
Vlorë, Alb.	163	40°27'N	19°30'E
Vltava, r., Czech Rep.	168	49°24'N	14°18'E
Vodl, l., Russia (vôd''l)	180	62°20'N	37°20'E
Voerde, Ger.	171c	51°35'N	6°41'E
Voghera, Italy (vô-gā'rä)	174	44°58'N	9°02'E
Voight, r., Wa., U.S.	116a	47°03'N	122°08'W
Voinjama, Lib.	234	8°25'N	9°45'W
Voiron, Fr. (vwà-rôN')	171	45°23'N	5°48'E
Voisin, Lac, l., Can. (vwŏ'-zĭn)	96	54°13'N	107°15'W
Volchansk, Ukr. (vôl-chänsk')	181	50°18'N	36°56'E
Volga, r., Russia (vôl'gä)	178	47°30'N	46°20'E
Volga, Mouths of the, mth.	181	46°00'N	49°10'E
Volgograd, Russia (vŏl-gō-grä't)	178	48°40'N	42°20'E
Volgogradskoye, res., Russia (vôl-gô-grad'skô-yĕ)	178	51°10'N	45°10'E
Volkhov, Russia (vôl'kôf)	167	59°54'N	32°21'E
Volkhov, r., Russia	180	58°45'N	31°40'E
Volodarskiy, Russia (vô-lô-där'skĭ)	186c	59°49'N	30°06'E
Volodymyr-Volyns'kyi, Ukr.	169	50°50'N	24°20'E
Vologda, Russia (vô'lôg-dà)	178	59°12'N	39°52'E
Vologda, prov., Russia	176	59°00'N	37°26'E
Volokolamsk, Russia (vô-lô-kôlámsk)	176	56°02'N	35°58'E
Volokonovka, Russia (vô-lô-kô'nôf-kà)	177	50°28'N	37°52'E
Vol'sk, Russia (vôl'sk)	181	52°02'N	47°23'E
Volta, r., Ghana	234	6°05'N	0°30'E
Volta, Lake, res., Ghana (vôl'tà)	230	7°10'N	0°30'W
Volta Blanche (White Volta), r., Afr.	234	11°30'N	0°40'W
Volta Noire *see* Black Volta, r., Afr.	230	11°30'N	4°00'W
Volta Redonda, Braz. (vōl'tä-rā-dôn'dä)	143	22°32'S	44°05'W
Volterra, Italy (vôl-tĕr'rä)	174	43°22'N	10°51'E
Voltri, Italy (vōl'trē)	174	44°25'N	8°45'E
Volturno, r., Italy (vôl-tōōr'nô)	174	41°12'N	14°20'E
Vólvi, Límni, l., Grc.	175	40°41'N	23°23'E
Volzhskoye, l., Russia (vôl'sh-skô-yĕ)	176	56°43'N	36°18'E
Von Ormy, Tx., U.S. (vŏn ôr'mē)	117d	29°18'N	98°36'W
Vōōpsu, Est. (vōōp'sò)	167	58°06'N	27°30'E
Voorburg, Neth.	159a	52°04'N	4°21'E
Voortrekkerhoogte, S. Afr.	233b	25°48'S	28°10'E
Vop', r., Russia (vôp)	176	55°20'N	32°55'E
Vopnafjördur, Ice.	160	65°43'N	14°58'W
Vordingborg, Den. (vôr'dĭng-bôr)	166	55°10'N	11°55'E
Vóreioi Sporades, is., Grc.	175	38°55'N	24°05'E
Vóreios Evvoïkós Kólpos, b., Grc.	175	38°48'N	23°02'E
Vorkuta, Russia (vôr-kōō'tà)	178	67°28'N	63°40'E
Vormsi, i., Est. (vôrm'sĭ)	167	59°06'N	23°05'E
Vorona, r., Russia (vô-rô'na)	181	51°50'N	42°00'E
Voronava, Bela.	169	54°07'N	25°16'E
Voronezh, Russia (vô-rô'nyĕzh)	178	51°39'N	39°11'E
Voronezh, prov., Russia	177	51°10'N	39°13'E
Voronezh, r., Russia	181	52°17'N	39°32'E
Vorontsovka, Russia (vô-rônt'sôv-kà)	186a	59°40'N	60°14'E
Voron'ya, r., Russia (vô-rônyà)	180	68°20'N	35°20'E
Võrts-Järv, l., Est. (vôrts yärv)	167	58°15'N	26°12'E
Võru, Est. (vô'rû)	180	57°50'N	26°58'E
Vorya, r., Russia (vôr'yà)	186b	55°55'N	38°15'E
Vosges, mts., Fr. (vōzh)	161	48°09'N	6°57'E
Voskresensk, Russia (vôs-krĕ-sĕnsk')	186b	55°20'N	38°42'E
Voss, Nor. (vôs)	160	60°40'N	6°24'E
Vostryakovo, Russia	186b	55°23'N	37°49'E
Votkinsk, Russia (vôt-kēnsk')	180	57°00'N	54°00'E
Votkinskoye Vodokhranilishche, res., Russia	180	57°30'N	55°00'E
Vouga, r., Port. (vō'gà)	172	40°43'N	7°51'W
Vouziers, Fr. (vōō-zyā')	170	49°25'N	4°40'E
Voxnan, r., Swe.	166	61°30'N	15°24'E
Voyageurs National Park, rec., Mn., U.S.	113	48°30'N	92°40'W
Vozhe, l., Russia (vôzh'yĕ)	180	60°40'N	39°00'E
Voznesens'k, Ukr.	181	47°34'N	31°22'E
Vradiïvka, Ukr.	177	47°51'N	30°38'E
Vrangelya (Wrangel), i., Russia	178	71°25'N	178°30'W
Vranje, Serb. (vrän'yĕ)	175	42°33'N	21°55'E
Vratsa, Blg. (vrät'tsà)	163	43°12'N	23°31'E
Vrbas, Serb. (v'r'bäs)	175	45°34'N	19°43'E
Vrbas, r., Serb.	175	44°25'N	17°17'E
Vrchlabí, Czech Rep. (v'r'chlä-bē)	168	50°32'N	15°51'E
Vrede, S. Afr. (vrĭ'dĕ)(vrĕd)	238c	27°25'S	29°11'E
Vredefort, S. Afr. (vrĭ'dĕ-fôrt)(vrĕd'fôrt)	238c	27°00'S	27°21'E
Vreeswijk, Neth.	159a	52°00'N	5°06'E
Vršac, Serb. (v'r'shàts)	163	45°08'N	21°18'E
Vrutky, Slvk. (vrōōt'kē)	169	49°09'N	18°55'E
Vryburg, S. Afr. (vrī'bûrg)	232	26°55'S	24°45'E
Vryheid, S. Afr. (vrī'hīt)	232	27°43'S	30°58'E
Vsetín, Czech Rep. (fsĕt'yēn)	169	49°21'N	18°01'E
Vsevolozhskiy, Russia (vsyĕ'vôlô'zh-skĕĕ)	186c	60°01'N	30°41'E
Vuelta Abajo, reg., Cuba (vwĕl'tä ä-bä'hō)	134	22°20'N	83°45'W
Vught, Neth.	159a	51°38'N	5°18'E
Vukovar, Cro. (vò'kô-vär)	175	45°20'N	19°00'E
Vulcan, Mi., U.S. (vŭl'k*ă*n)	108	45°45'N	87°50'W
Vulcano, i., Italy (vōōl-kä'nô)	174	38°23'N	15°00'E
Vŭlchedrŭma, Blg.	175	43°43'N	23°29'E
Vuntut National Park, rec., Can.	92	68°27'N	139°58'W
Vyartsilya, Russia (vyàr-tsē'lyà)	167	62°10'N	30°40'E
Vyatka, r., Russia (vyàt'kà)	180	59°20'N	51°25'E
Vyazemskiy, Russia (vyà-zĕm'skĭ)	210	47°29'N	134°39'E
Vyaz'ma, Russia (vyàz'mà)	180	55°12'N	34°17'E
Vyazniki, Russia (vyàz'nē-kē)	180	56°10'N	42°10'E
Vyborg, Russia (vwē'bôrk)	178	60°43'N	28°46'E
Vychegda, r., Russia (vē'chĕg-d*à*)	180	61°40'N	48°00'E
Vyerkhnyadzvinsk, Bela.	176	55°48'N	27°59'E
Vyetka, Bela. (vyĕt'kà)	176	52°36'N	31°05'E
Vylkove, Ukr.	181	45°24'N	29°36'E
Vym, r., Russia (vwēm)	180	63°15'N	51°20'E
Vyritsa, Russia (vē'rĭ-tsà)	186c	59°24'N	30°20'E
Vyshnevolotskoye, l., Russia (vŭy'sh-ŋĕ'vôlôt's-kô'yĕ)	176	57°30'N	34°27'E
Vyshniy Volochëk, Russia (vĕsh'nyĭ vôl-ô-chĕk')	178	57°34'N	34°35'E
Vyškov, Czech Rep. (vĕsh'kôf)	168	49°17'N	16°58'E
Vysoké Mýto, Czech Rep. (vû'sô-kā mû'tô)	168	49°58'N	16°07'E
Vysokovsk, Russia (vĭ-sô'kôfsk)	176	56°16'N	36°32'E
Vytegra, Russia (vû'tĕg-rà)	178	61°00'N	36°20'E
Vyzhnytsia, Ukr.	169	48°16'N	25°12'E

W

PLACE (Pronunciation)	PAGE	LAT.	LONG.
W, Parcs Nationaux du, rec., Niger	235	12°20'N	2°40'E
Waal, r., Neth. (väl)	165	51°46'N	5°00'E
Waalwijk, Neth.	159a	51°41'N	5°05'E
Wabamun, Grc.	163	39°23'N	22°56'E
Wabamuno, Can. (wŏ'bă-mŭn)	95	53°33'N	114°28'W
Wabasca, Can. (wŏ-bàs'kă)	95	56°00'N	113°53'W
Wabash, In., U.S. (wô'băsh)	108	40°45'N	85°50'W
Wabash, r., U.S.	107	38°00'N	88°00'W
Wabasha, Mn., U.S. (wä'b*à*-shô)	113	44°24'N	92°04'W
Wabe Gestro, r., Eth.	231	6°25'N	41°21'E
Wabowden, Can. (wă-bō'd'n)	97	54°55'N	98°38'W
Wąbrzeźno, Pol. (vôŋ-bzĕzh'nô)	169	53°17'N	18°59'E
Wabu Hu, l., China (wä-bōō hōō)	206	32°25'N	116°35'E
W. A. C. Bennett Dam, dam, Can.	95	56°01'N	122°10'W
Waccamaw, r., S.C., U.S. (wăk'*à*-mô)	125	33°47'N	78°55'W
Waccasassa Bay, b., Fl., U.S. (wă-k*à*-să's*à*)	124	29°02'N	83°10'W
Wachow, Ger. (vä'kōv)	159b	53°32'N	12°46'E
Waco, Tx., U.S. (wā'kō)	104	31°35'N	97°06'W
Waconda Lake, res., Ks., U.S.	120	39°45'N	98°15'W
Wadayama, Japan (wä'dä'yä-mä)	211	35°19'N	134°49'E
Waddenzee, sea, Neth.	165	53°00'N	4°50'E
Waddington, Mount, mtn., Can. (wŏd'dĭng-t*ŭ*n)	92	51°23'N	125°15'W
Wadena, Can.	96	51°57'N	103°50'W
Wadena, Mn., U.S. (wŏ-dē'n*ä*)	112	46°26'N	95°09'W
Wadesboro, N.C., U.S. (wādz'bŭr-ô)	125	34°57'N	80°05'W
Wadley, Ga., U.S. (wŭd'lē)	125	32°54'N	82°25'W
Wad Madani, Sudan (wäd mĕ-dä'nē)	231	14°27'N	33°31'E
Wadowice, Pol. (và-dô'vēt-sĕ)	169	49°53'N	19°31'E
Wadsworth, Oh., U.S. (wŏdz'wûrth)	111d	41°01'N	81°44'W
Wager Bay, b., Can. (wā'jēr)	93	65°48'N	88°19'W
Wagga Wagga, Austl. (wŏg'*ă* wŏg'*ă*)	219	35°10'S	147°30'E
Wagoner, Ok., U.S. (wăg'*ŭ*n-ēr)	121	35°58'N	95°22'W
Wagon Mound, N.M., U.S. (wăg'*ŭ*n mound)	120	35°59'N	104°45'W
Wągrowiec, Pol. (vôŋ-grô'vyĕts)	169	52°47'N	17°14'E
Waha, Libya	200	28°16'N	19°54'E
Wahiawā, Hi., U.S.	106d	21°30'N	158°03'W
Wahoo, Ne., U.S. (wä-hōō')	112	41°14'N	96°39'W
Wahpeton, N.D., U.S. (wô'pē-t*ŭ*n)	112	46°17'N	96°38'W
Waialua, Hi., U.S. (wä'ē-ä-lōō'ä)	126a	21°33'N	158°08'W
Wai'anae, Hi., U.S. (wä'ē-à-nä'ā)	126a	21°25'N	158°11'W
Waidhofen, Aus. (vīd'hôf-ĕn)	168	47°58'N	14°46'E
Waigeo, Pulau, i., Indon. (wä-ē-gä'ô)	213	0°07'N	131°00'E
Waikato, r., N.Z. (wä'ē-kä'to)	221a	38°10'S	175°35'E
Waikerie, Austl. (wā'kēr-ē)	222	34°15'S	140°00'E
Wailuku, Hi., U.S. (wä'ē-lōō'kōō)	106c	20°55'N	156°30'W
Waimānalo, Hi., U.S. (wä-ē-mä'nä-lo)	126a	21°19'N	157°43'W
Waimea, Hi., U.S. (wä-ē-mā'ä)	126a	21°56'N	159°38'W
Wainganga, r., India (wä-ēn-g*ŭ*ŋ'gä)	199	20°30'N	80°15'E
Waingapu, Indon.	212	9°32'S	120°00'E
Wainwright, Can.	90	52°49'N	110°52'W
Wainwright, Ak., U.S. (wān-rīt)	103	74°40'N	159°00'W
Waipahu, Hi., U.S. (wä'ē-pä'hōō)	106d	21°20'N	158°02'W
Waiska, r., Mi., U.S. (w*à*-ĭz-k*à*)	117k	46°20'N	84°38'W
Waitsburg, Wa., U.S. (wāts'bûrg)	114	46°17'N	118°08'W
Wajima, Japan (wä'jē-mà)	211	37°23'N	136°56'E
Wajir, Kenya	237	1°45'N	40°04'E
Wakami, r., Can.	98	47°43'N	82°22'W
Wakasa-Wan, b., Japan (wä'kä-sä wän)	210	35°43'N	135°39'E
Wakatipu, l., N.Z. (wä-kä-tē'pōō)	221a	45°04'S	168°30'E
Wakayama, Japan (wä-kä'yä-mä)	205	34°14'N	135°11'E
Wake, i., Oc. (wāk)	3	19°25'N	167°00'E
Wa Keeney, Ks., U.S. (wô-kē'nē)	120	39°01'N	99°53'W
Wakefield, Can. (wāk-fēld)	102c	45°39'N	75°55'W
Wakefield, Eng., U.K.	164	53°41'N	1°25'W
Wakefield, Ma., U.S.	101a	42°31'N	71°05'W
Wakefield, Mi., U.S.	113	46°28'N	89°55'W
Wakefield, Ne., U.S.	112	42°15'N	96°52'W
Wakefield, R.I., U.S.	110b	41°26'N	71°30'W
Wakefield, co., Eng., U.K.	158a	53°12'N	1°25'W
Wake Forest, N.C., U.S. (wāk fŏr'ĕst)	125	35°58'N	78°31'W
Waki, Japan (wä'kē)	211	34°05'N	134°10'E
Wakkanai, Japan (wä'kä-nä'ē)	205	45°19'N	141°43'E
Wakkerstroom, S. Afr. (vàk'ēr-strōm)(wăk'ēr-strōōm)	232	27°19'S	30°04'E
Wakonassin, r., Can.	98	46°35'N	82°10'W
Waku Kundo, Ang.	232	11°25'S	15°07'E
Wałbrzych, Pol. (väl'bzhûk)	168	50°46'N	16°16'E
Walcott, Lake, res., Id., U.S.	115	42°40'N	113°23'W
Wałcz, Pol. (välch)	168	53°11'N	16°30'E
Waldoboro, Me., U.S. (wôl'dô-bŭr-ô)	100	44°06'N	69°22'W
Waldo Lake, l., Or., U.S. (wôl'dō)	114	43°46'N	122°10'W
Waldorf, Md., U.S. (wäl'dôrf)	110e	38°37'N	76°57'W
Waldron, Mo., U.S.	117f	39°14'N	94°47'W
Waldron, i., Wa., U.S.	116d	48°42'N	123°02'W
Wales, Ak., U.S. (wālz)	103	65°35'N	168°14'W
Wales, state, U.K.	154	52°12'N	3°40'W
Walewale, Ghana	234	10°21'N	0°48'W
Walgett, Austl. (wôl'gĕt)	219	30°00'S	148°10'E
Walhalla, S.C., U.S. (wŭl-hăl'*à*)	124	34°45'N	83°04'W
Walikale, D.R.C.	237	1°25'S	28°03'E
Walkden, Eng., U.K.	158a	53°32'N	2°24'W
Walker, Mn., U.S. (wôk'ēr)	113	47°06'N	94°37'W
Walker, r., Nv., U.S.	118	39°07'N	119°10'W
Walker, Mount, mtn., Wa., U.S.	116a	47°47'N	122°54'W
Walker Lake, l., Can.	97	54°42'N	96°57'W
Walker Lake, l., Nv., U.S.	118	38°46'N	118°30'W
Walker River Indian Reservation, I.R., Nv., U.S.	118	39°06'N	118°20'W
Walkerville, Mt., U.S. (wôk'ēr-vĭl)	115	46°20'N	112°32'W
Wallace, Id., U.S. (wŏl'ás)	114	47°27'N	115°55'W
Wallaceburg, Can.	98	42°39'N	82°25'W
Wallacia, Austl.	217b	33°52'S	150°40'E
Wallaroo, Austl. (wŏl-*à*-rōō)	218	33°52'S	137°45'E
Wallasey, Eng., U.K. (wŏl'*à*-sē)	158a	53°25'N	3°03'W
Walla Walla, Wa., U.S. (wŏl'*à* wŏl'*à*)	104	46°03'N	118°20'W
Walled Lake, Mi., U.S. (wôl'd lāk)	111b	42°32'N	83°29'W
Wallel, Tulu, mtn., Eth.	231	9°00'N	34°52'E
Wallingford, Eng., U.K. (wŏl'ĭng-fērd)	158b	51°34'N	1°08'W
Wallingford, Vt., U.S.	109	43°30'N	72°55'W
Wallis and Futuna Islands, dep., Oc.	241	13°00'S	176°10'E
Wallisville, Tx., U.S. (wŏl'ĭs-vĭl)	123a	29°50'N	94°44'W
Wallowa, Or., U.S. (wôl'ô-w*ă*)	114	45°34'N	117°32'W
Wallowa, r., Or., U.S.	114	45°28'N	117°28'W
Wallowa Mountains, mts., Or., U.S.	114	45°10'N	117°22'W
Wallula, Wa., U.S.	114	46°08'N	118°55'W
Walnut, Ca., U.S. (wôl'nŭt)	117a	34°00'N	117°51'W
Walnut, r., Ks., U.S.	121	37°28'N	97°06'W
Walnut Canyon National Mon, rec., Az., U.S.	119	35°10'N	111°30'W
Walnut Creek, Ca., U.S.	116b	37°54'N	122°04'W
Walnut Creek, r., Tx., U.S.	117c	32°37'N	97°03'W
Walnut Ridge, Ar., U.S. (rĭj)	121	36°04'N	90°56'W
Walpole, Ma., U.S. (wôl'pōl)	101a	42°09'N	71°15'W
Walpole, N.H., U.S.	109	43°05'N	72°25'W
Walsall, Eng., U.K. (wôl-sôl)	164	52°35'N	1°58'W
Walsenburg, Co., U.S. (wôl'sĕn-bûrg)	120	37°38'N	104°46'W
Walsum, Ger.	171c	51°32'N	6°41'E
Walter F. George Reservoir, res., U.S.	124	32°00'N	85°00'W
Walters, Ok., U.S. (wôl'tērz)	120	34°21'N	98°19'W
Waltham, Ma., U.S. (wôl'th*ă*m)	101a	42°22'N	71°14'W
Walthamstow, Eng., U.K. (wôl't*ă*m-stō)	158b	51°34'N	0°01'W
Walton, N.Y., U.S.	109	42°10'N	75°05'W
Walton-le-Dale, Eng., U.K. (lē-dāl')	158a	53°44'N	2°40'W
Walvis Bay, Nmb. (wôl'vĭs)	232	22°50'S	14°30'E
Walworth, Wi., U.S. (wôl'w*ŭ*rth)	113	42°33'N	88°39'W
Wama, Ang.	236	12°14'S	15°33'E
Wamba, r., D.R.C.	232	7°00'S	18°00'E
Wamego, Ks., U.S. (wŏ-mē'gō)	121	39°13'N	96°17'W
Wami, r., Tan. (wä'mē)	233	6°31'S	37°17'E
Wanapitei Lake, l., Can.	99	46°45'N	80°45'W
Wanaque, N.J., U.S. (wŏn'*à*-kū)	110a	41°03'N	74°16'W
Wanaque Reservoir, res., N.J., U.S.	110a	41°06'N	74°20'W
Wanda Shan, mts., China (wän-dä shän)	205	45°54'N	131°45'E
Wandoan, Austl.	222	26°09'S	149°51'E
Wandsbek, Ger. (vänds'bĕk)	159c	53°34'N	10°07'E
Wandsworth, Eng., U.K. (wôndz'wûrth)	158b	51°26'N	0°12'W
Wanganui, N.Z. (wôŋ'gà-nōō'ē)	221a	39°53'N	175°01'E
Wangaratta, Austl. (wŏŋ'gà-răt'*à*)	222	36°23'N	146°18'E
Wangeroog, i., Ger. (vän'gĕ-rōg)	168	53°49'N	7°57'E
Wangqingtuo, China (wäŋ-chyĭŋ-twô)	206	39°14'N	116°56'E
Wangsi, China (wäŋ-sē)	206	37°59'N	116°57'E
Wantage, Eng., U.K. (wŏn't*ā*j)	158b	51°33'N	1°26'W
Wantagh, N.Y., U.S.	110a	40°41'N	73°30'W
Wanxian, China (wän shyĕn)	206	38°51'N	115°10'E
Wanxian, China (wän-shyĕn)	204	30°48'N	108°22'E
Wanzai, China (wän-dzī)	209	28°05'N	114°25'E
Wanzhi, China (wän-jr)	206	31°11'N	118°31'E

ng-sing; ŋ-baŋk; N-nasalized n; nŏd; cŏmmit; ōld; ŏbey; ôrder; oi-boil; fōōd; ȯ-as oo in foot; ou-out; s-soft; sh-dish; th-thin; pūre; ûnite; ûrn; stŭd; circŭs; ü-as in French tu; ′-indeterminate vowel.

366 Wesselsbron – William Creek PRONOUNCING INDEX

PLACE (Pronunciation)	PAGE	LAT.	LONG.
Wesselsbron, S. Afr. (wĕs′ĕl-brŏn)	238c	27°51′S	26°22′E
Wessington Springs, S.D., U.S. (wĕs′ĭng-tŭn)	112	44°06′N	98°35′W
West, Mount, mtn., Pan.	128a	9°10′N	79°52′W
West Allis, Wi., U.S. (wĕst-ăl′ĭs)	111a	43°01′N	88°01′W
West Alton, Mo., U.S. (ôl′tŭn)	117e	38°52′N	90°13′W
West Bay, b., Fl., U.S.	124	30°20′N	85°45′W
West Bay, b., Tx., U.S.	123a	29°11′N	95°03′W
West Bend, Wi., U.S. (wĕst bĕnd)	113	43°25′N	88°13′W
West Bengal, state, India (bĕn-gôl′)	199	23°30′N	87°30′E
West Blocton, Al., U.S. (blŏk′tŭn)	124	33°05′N	87°05′W
Westborough, Ma., U.S. (wĕst′bŭr-ô)	101a	42°17′N	71°37′W
West Boylston, Ma., U.S. (boil′stŭn)	101a	42°22′N	71°46′W
West Branch, Mi., U.S. (wĕst brȧnch)	108	44°15′N	84°10′W
West Bridgford, Eng., U.K. (brĭj′fẽrd)	158a	52°55′N	1°08′W
West Bromwich, Eng., U.K. (wĕst brŭm′ĭj)	158a	52°32′N	1°59′W
Westbrook, Me., U.S. (wĕst′brŏŏk)	100	43°41′N	70°23′W
Westby, Wi., U.S. (wĕst′bē)	113	43°40′N	90°52′W
West Caicos, i., T./C. Is. (käē′kō) (kī′kōs)	135	21°40′N	72°30′W
West Cape Howe, c., Austl.	220	35°15′S	117°30′E
West Chester, Oh., U.S. (chĕs′tẽr)	111f	39°20′N	84°24′W
West Chester, Pa., U.S.	110f	39°57′N	75°36′W
West Chicago, Il., U.S. (chĭ-kå′gō)	111a	41°53′N	88°12′W
West Columbia, S.C., U.S. (cōl′ŭm-bē-ȧ)	125	33°58′N	81°05′W
West Columbia, Tx., U.S.	123	29°08′N	95°39′W
West Cote Blanche Bay, b., La., U.S.	123	29°30′N	92°17′W
West Covina, Ca., U.S. (wĕst kô-vē′nȧ)	117a	34°04′N	117°55′W
West Des Moines, Ia., U.S. (dē moin′)	113	41°35′N	93°42′W
West Des Moines, r., Ia., U.S.	113	42°52′N	94°32′W
West End, Bah.	134	26°40′N	78°55′W
Westerham, Eng., U.K. (wĕ′stẽr′ŭm)	158b	51°15′N	0°05′E
Westerhörn, Ger. (vĕs′tĕr-hōrn)	159c	53°52′N	9°41′E
Westerlo, Bel.	159a	51°05′N	4°57′E
Westerly, R.I., U.S. (wĕs′tẽr-lē)	109	41°25′N	71°50′W
Western Australia, state, Austl. (ôs-trā′lĭ-ȧ)	218	24°15′S	121°30′E
Western Dvina, r., Eur.	167	55°30′N	28°27′E
Western Ghāts, mts., India	199	17°35′N	74°00′E
Western Port, Md., U.S. (wĕs′tẽrn pōrt)	109	39°30′N	79°00′W
Western Sahara, dep., Afr. (sá-hä′rȧ)	230	23°05′N	15°33′W
Western Samoa see Samoa, nation, Oc.	2	14°30′S	172°00′W
Western Siberian Lowland, depr., Russia	178	63°37′N	72°45′E
Westerville, Oh., U.S. (wĕs′tẽr-vĭl)	108	40°10′N	83°00′W
Westerwald, for., Ger. (vĕs′tĕr-väld)	168	50°35′N	7°45′E
Westfalen, hist. reg., Ger. (vĕst-fä-lĕn)	168	51°20′N	8°30′E
Westfield, Ma., U.S. (wĕst′fēld)	109	42°05′N	72°45′W
Westfield, N.J., U.S.	110a	40°39′N	74°21′W
Westfield, N.Y., U.S. (wĕst′fēld)	110	42°20′N	79°40′W
Westford, Ma., U.S. (wĕst′fẽrd)	101a	42°35′N	71°26′W
West Frankfort, Il., U.S. (frănk′fŭrt)	108	37°55′N	88°55′W
West Ham, Eng., U.K.	158b	51°30′N	0°00′W
West Hartford, Ct., U.S. (härt′fẽrd)	109	41°45′N	72°45′W
West Helena, Ar., U.S. (hĕl′ĕn-ȧ)	121	34°32′N	90°39′W
West Indies, is. (ĭn′dēz)	129	19°00′N	78°30′W
West Jordon, Ut., U.S. (jôr′dăn)	117b	40°37′N	111°56′W
West Kirby, Eng., U.K. (kûr′bē)	158a	53°22′N	3°11′W
West Lafayette, In., U.S. (lä-fā-yĕt′)	108	40°25′N	86°55′W
Westlake, Oh., U.S.	111d	41°27′N	81°55′W
Westleigh, S. Afr. (wĕst-lē)	238c	27°39′S	27°18′E
West Liberty, Ia., U.S. (wĕst lĭb′ẽr-tĭ)	113	41°34′N	91°15′W
West Linn, Or., U.S. (lĭn)	116c	45°22′N	122°37′W
Westlock, Can. (wĕst′lŏk)	95	54°09′N	113°52′W
West Memphis, Ar., U.S.	121	35°08′N	90°11′W
West Midlands, hist. reg., Eng., U.K.	158a	52°26′N	1°50′W
Westminster, Ca., U.S. (wĕst′mĭn-stẽr)	117a	33°45′N	117°59′W
Westminster, Md., U.S.	109	39°40′N	76°55′W
Westminster, S.C., U.S.	124	34°38′N	83°10′W
Westmount, Can. (wĕst′mount)	102a	45°29′N	73°36′W
West Newbury, Ma., U.S. (nū′bẽr-ē)	101a	42°47′N	70°57′W
West Newton, Pa., U.S. (nū′tŭn)	111e	40°12′N	79°45′W
West New York, N.J., U.S. (nů yŏrk)	110a	40°47′N	74°01′W
West Nishnabotna, r., Ia., U.S. (nĭsh-nȧ-bŏt′nȧ)	112	40°56′N	95°37′W
Weston, Ma., U.S. (wĕs′tŭn)	101a	42°22′N	71°18′W
Weston, W.V., U.S.	108	39°00′N	80°30′W
Westonaria, S. Afr.	238c	26°19′S	27°38′E
Weston-super-Mare, Eng., U.K. (wĕs′tŭn sū′pẽr-mā′rē)	164	51°23′N	3°00′W
West Orange, N.J., U.S. (wĕst ŏr′ĕnj)	110a	40°46′N	74°14′W
West Palm Beach, Fl., U.S. (päm bēch)	105	26°44′N	80°04′W
West Pensacola, Fl., U.S. (pĕn-sȧ-kō′lȧ)	124	30°24′N	87°18′W
West Pittsburg, Ca., U.S. (pĭts′bûrg)	116b	38°02′N	121°56′W
Westplains, Mo., U.S. (wĕst-plānz′)	121	36°42′N	91°51′W
West Point, Ga., U.S.	124	32°52′N	85°10′W
West Point, Ms., U.S.	124	33°36′N	88°39′W
Westpoint, Ne., U.S.	112	41°50′N	96°00′W
West Point, N.Y., U.S.	110a	41°23′N	73°58′W
West Point, Ut., U.S.	117b	41°07′N	112°05′W
West Point, Va., U.S.	109	37°25′N	76°50′W
West Point Lake, res., U.S.	124	33°00′N	85°10′W
Westport, Ire.	164	53°44′N	9°36′W
Westport, Ct., U.S. (wĕst′pōrt)	110a	41°07′N	73°22′W
Westport, Or., U.S. (wĕst′pôrt)	116c	46°08′N	123°22′W
Westray, i., Scot., U.K. (wĕs′trā)	164a	59°19′N	3°05′W
West Road, r., Can. (rōd)	94	53°00′N	124°00′W
West Saint Paul, Mn., U.S. (sānt pôl′)	117g	44°55′N	93°05′W
West Sand Spit, i., T./C. Is.	135	21°25′N	72°10′W
West Slope, Or., U.S.	116c	45°30′N	122°46′W
West Tavaputs Plateau, plat., Ut., U.S. (wĕst tăv′á-pòts)	119	39°45′N	110°35′W
West Terre Haute, In., U.S. (tĕr-ē hōt′)	108	39°30′N	87°30′W
West Union, Ia., U.S. (ūn′yŭn)	113	42°58′N	91°48′W
West University Place, Tx., U.S.	123a	29°43′N	95°26′W
Westview, Oh., U.S. (wĕst′vů)	111d	41°21′N	81°54′W
West View, Pa., U.S.	111e	40°31′N	80°02′W
Westville, Can. (wĕst′vĭl)	101	45°35′N	62°43′W
Westville, Il., U.S.	108	40°00′N	87°40′W
West Virginia, state, U.S. (wĕst vẽr-jĭn′ĭ-ȧ)	105	39°00′N	80°50′W
West Walker, r., Ca., U.S. (wôk′ẽr)	118	38°25′N	119°25′W
West Warwick, R.I., U.S. (wŏr′ĭk)	110b	41°42′N	71°31′W
Westwego, La., U.S. (wĕst-wē′gō)	110d	29°55′N	90°09′W
Westwood, Ca., U.S. (wĕst′wŏŏd)	118	40°18′N	121°00′W
Westwood, Ks., U.S.	117f	39°03′N	94°37′W
Westwood, Ma., U.S.	101a	42°13′N	71°14′W
Westwood, N.J., U.S.	110a	40°59′N	74°02′W
West Wyalong, Austl. (wīălông)	219	34°00′S	147°20′E
West Yorkshire, hist. reg., Eng., U.K.	158a	53°37′N	1°48′W
Wetar, Pulau, i., Indon. (wĕt′ár)	213	7°34′S	126°00′E
Wetaskiwin, Can. (wĕ-tăs′kē-wŏn)	90	52°58′N	113°22′W
Wetmore, Tx., U.S. (wĕt′mōr)	117d	29°34′N	98°25′W
Wetter, Ger.	171c	51°23′N	7°23′E
Wetumpka, Al., U.S. (wē-tŭmp′kȧ)	124	32°33′N	86°12′W
Wetzlar, Ger. (vĕts′lär)	168	50°35′N	8°30′E
Wewak, Pap. N. Gui. (wā-wäk′)	213	3°19′S	143°30′E
Wewoka, Ok., U.S. (wē-wō′kȧ)	121	35°09′N	96°30′W
Wexford, Ire. (wĕks′fẽrd)	161	52°20′N	6°30′W
Weybridge, Eng., U.K. (wā′brĭj)	158b	51°20′N	0°26′W
Weyburn, Can. (wā′bûrn)	90	49°41′N	103°52′W
Weymouth, Eng., U.K. (wā′mŭth)	164	50°37′N	2°34′W
Weymouth, Ma., U.S.	101a	42°44′N	70°57′W
Weymouth, Oh., U.S.	111d	41°11′N	81°48′W
Whale Cay, i., Bah.	134	25°20′N	77°45′W
Whale Cay Channels, strt., Bah.	134	26°45′N	77°10′W
Wharton, N.J., U.S. (hwôr′tŭn)	110a	40°54′N	74°35′W
Wharton, Tx., U.S.	123	29°19′N	96°06′W
What Cheer, Ia., U.S. (hwŏt chēr)	113	41°23′N	92°24′W
Whatcom, Lake, l., Wa., U.S. (hwät′kŭm)	116c	48°44′N	123°34′W
Whatshan Lake, l., Can. (wŏt′shăn)	95	50°00′N	118°03′W
Wheatland, Wy., U.S. (hwēt′lănd)	115	42°04′N	104°52′W
Wheatland Reservoir Number 2, res., Wy., U.S.	115	41°52′N	105°36′W
Wheaton, Il., U.S. (hwē′tŭn)	111a	41°52′N	88°06′W
Wheaton, Md., U.S.	110e	39°05′N	77°05′W
Wheaton, Mn., U.S.	112	45°48′N	96°29′W
Wheeler Peak, mtn., N.M., U.S.	120	36°34′N	105°25′W
Wheeler Peak, mtn., Nv., U.S.	106	38°58′N	114°15′W
Wheeling, Il., U.S. (hwēl′ĭng)	111a	42°08′N	87°54′W
Wheeling, W.V., U.S.	108	40°05′N	80°45′W
Wheelwright, Arg. (ōē′l-rē′gt)	141c	33°46′S	61°14′W
Whidbey Island, i., Wa., U.S. (hwĭd′bē)	116a	48°13′N	122°50′W
Whippany, N.J., U.S. (hwĭp′á-nē)	110a	40°49′N	74°25′W
Whitby, Can. (hwĭt′bē)	91	43°50′N	79°00′W
Whitchurch, Eng., U.K. (hwĭt′chûrch)	158a	52°58′N	2°49′W
White, l., Can.	98	48°47′N	85°50′W
White, l., Can.	99	45°15′N	76°35′W
White, r., Can.	98	48°34′N	85°46′W
White, r., In., U.S.	108	39°15′N	86°45′W
White, r., S.D., U.S.	112	43°13′N	101°04′W
White, r., Tx., U.S.	120	36°25′N	102°20′W
White, r., Vt., U.S.	109	43°45′N	72°35′W
White, r., Wa., U.S.	114	47°07′N	121°48′W
White, r., U.S.	107	35°30′N	92°00′W
White, r., U.S.	112	43°41′N	99°48′W
White, r., U.S.	119	40°10′N	108°55′W
White, East Fork, r., In., U.S.	108	38°45′N	86°20′W
White Bay, b., Can.	93a	50°00′N	56°30′W
White Bear Indian Reserve, I.R., Can.	97	49°50′N	102°15′W
White Bear Lake, l., Mn., U.S.	117g	45°04′N	92°58′W
White Castle, La., U.S.	123	30°10′N	91°09′W
White Center, Wa., U.S.	116a	47°31′N	122°21′W
White Cloud, Mi., U.S.	108	43°35′N	85°45′W
Whitecourt, Can. (wĭt′côrt)	90	54°09′N	115°41′W
White Earth, r., N.D., U.S.	112	48°30′N	102°44′W
White Earth Indian Reservation, I.R., Mn., U.S.	112	47°18′N	95°42′W
Whiteface, r., Mn., U.S. (whĭt′fās)	113	47°12′N	92°13′W
Whitefield, N.H., U.S. (hwĭt′fēld)	109	44°20′N	71°35′W
Whitefish Bay, Wi., U.S.	111a	43°07′N	77°54′W
Whitefish Bay, b., Can.	97	49°26′N	94°14′W
Whitefish Bay, b., N.A.	113	46°36′N	84°50′W
White Hall, Il., U.S.	121	39°26′N	90°23′W
Whitehall, Mi., U.S. (hwĭt′hôl)	108	43°20′N	86°20′W
Whitehall, N.Y., U.S.	109	43°30′N	73°25′W
Whitehaven, Eng., U.K. (hwĭt′hā-vĕn)	164	54°35′N	3°30′W
Whitehorn, Point, c., Wa., U.S. (hwĭt′hôrn)	116d	48°54′N	122°48′W
Whitehorse, Can. (whĭt′hôrs)	90	60°39′N	135°01′W
White Lake, l., La., U.S.	123	29°40′N	92°35′W
White Mountain Peak, mtn., Ca., U.S.	118	37°38′N	118°13′W
White Mountains, mts., Me., U.S.	100	44°22′N	71°15′W
White Mountains, mts., N.H., U.S.	109	42°20′N	71°05′W
Whitemouth, l., Can.	97	49°14′N	95°40′W
White Nile (Al Bahr al Abyad), r., Sudan	231	12°30′N	32°30′E
White Otter, l., Can.	98	49°15′N	91°48′W
White Pass, p., N.A.	103	59°35′N	135°03′W
White Plains, N.Y., U.S.	110a	41°02′N	73°47′W
White River, Can.	98	48°38′N	85°23′W
White Rock, Can.	95	49°01′N	122°49′W
Whiterock Reservoir, res., Tx., U.S. (hwĭt′rŏk)	117c	32°51′N	96°40′W
White Russia see Belarus, nation, Eur.	178	53°30′N	25°33′E
Whitesail Lake, l., Can. (whĭt′sāl)	94	53°30′N	127°00′W
White Sands National Monument, rec., N.M., U.S.	119	32°50′N	106°20′W
White Sea, sea, Russia	178	66°00′N	40°00′E
White Settlement, Tx., U.S.	117c	32°45′N	97°28′W
White Sulphur Springs, Mt., U.S.	115	46°32′N	110°49′W
White Umfolzi, r., S. Afr. (ŭm-fô-lō′zē)	233c	28°12′S	30°55′E
Whiteville, N.C., U.S. (hwĭt′vĭl)	125	34°18′N	78°45′W
White Volta (Volta Blanche), r., Afr.	234	9°40′N	1°10′W
Whitewater, Wi., U.S. (whĭt-wŏt′ẽr)	113	42°49′N	88°40′W
Whitewater, l., Can.	97	49°14′N	100°39′W
Whitewater, r., In., U.S.	111f	39°19′N	84°55′W
Whitewater Bay, b., Fl., U.S.	125a	25°16′N	80°21′W
Whitewater Creek, r., Mt., U.S.	115	48°50′N	107°50′W
Whitewell, Tn., U.S. (hwĭt′wĕl)	124	35°11′N	85°31′W
Whitewright, Tx., U.S. (hwĭt′rĭt)	121	33°33′N	96°25′W
Whitham, r., Eng., U.K. (wĭth′ŭm)	158a	53°08′N	0°15′W
Whiting, In., U.S. (hwĭt′ĭng)	111a	41°41′N	87°30′W
Whitinsville, Ma., U.S. (hwĭt′ĕns-vĭl)	101a	42°06′N	71°40′W
Whitman, Ma., U.S. (hwĭt′măn)	101a	42°05′N	70°57′W
Whitmire, S.C., U.S. (hwĭt′mīr)	125	34°30′N	81°40′W
Whitney, Mount, mtn., Ca., U.S.	106	36°34′N	118°18′W
Whitney Lake, l., Tx., U.S. (hwĭt′nē)	123	32°02′N	97°36′W
Whitstable, Eng., U.K. (wĭt′stȧb′l)	158b	51°22′N	1°03′E
Whitsunday, i., Austl. (hwĭt′s′n-dā)	221	20°16′S	149°00′E
Whittier, Ca., U.S. (hwĭt′ĭ-ẽr)	117a	33°58′N	118°02′W
Whittlesea, S. Afr. (wĭt′l′sē)	233c	32°11′S	26°51′E
Whitworth, Eng., U.K. (hwĭt′wŭrth)	158a	53°40′N	2°10′W
Whyalla, Austl. (hwī-ăl′ȧ)	218	33°00′S	137°32′E
Whymper, Mount, mtn., Can. (wĭm′pẽr)	94	48°57′N	124°10′W
Wiarton, Can. (wī′ăr-tŭn)	91	44°45′N	80°45′W
Wichita, Ks., U.S. (wĭch′ĭ-tô)	104	37°42′N	97°21′W
Wichita, r., Tx., U.S.	120	33°50′N	99°38′W
Wichita Falls, Tx., U.S. (fôls)	104	33°54′N	98°29′W
Wichita Mountains, mts., Ok., U.S.	106	34°48′N	98°43′W
Wick, Scot., U.K. (wĭk)	160	58°25′N	3°05′W
Wickatunk, N.J., U.S. (wĭk′á-tŭnk)	110a	40°21′N	74°15′W
Wickenburg, Az., U.S.	119	33°58′N	112°44′W
Wickiup Reservoir, res., Or., U.S.	114	43°40′N	121°43′W
Wickliffe, Oh., U.S. (wĭk′klĭf)	111d	41°37′N	81°29′W
Wicklow, Ire.	164	52°59′N	6°06′W
Wicklow Mountains, mts., Ire. (wĭk′lō)	164	52°49′N	6°20′W
Wickup Mountain, mtn., Or., U.S. (wĭk′ŭp)	116c	46°06′N	123°35′W
Wiconisco, Pa., U.S. (wĭ-kŏn′ĭs-kō)	109	43°35′N	76°45′W
Widen, W.V., U.S. (wī′dĕn)	108	38°25′N	80°55′W
Widnes, Eng., U.K. (wĭd′nĕs)	158a	53°21′N	2°44′W
Wieliczka, Pol. (vyĕ-lēch′kȧ)	169	49°58′N	20°06′E
Wien see Vienna, Aus.	154	48°13′N	16°22′E
Wien, state, Aus.	159e	48°11′N	16°23′E
Wiener Neustadt, Aus. (vē′nẽr noi′shtät)	161	47°48′N	16°15′E
Wiener Wald, for., Aus.	159e	48°09′N	16°05′E
Wieprz, r., Pol. (vyĕpzh)	169	51°25′N	22°45′E
Wiergate, Tx., U.S. (wẽr′gāt)	123	31°00′N	93°42′W
Wiesbaden, Ger. (vēs′bä-dĕn)	161	50°05′N	8°15′E
Wigan, Eng., U.K. (wĭg′ăn)	164	53°33′N	2°37′W
Wiggins, Ms., U.S. (wĭg′ĭnz)	124	30°51′N	89°05′W
Wight, Isle of, i., Eng., U.K. (wīt)	164	50°44′N	1°17′W
Wilber, Ne., U.S. (wĭl′bẽr)	121	40°29′N	96°57′W
Wilburton, Ok., U.S. (wĭl′bẽr-tŭn)	121	34°54′N	95°18′W
Wilcannia, Austl. (wĭl-cān-ĭȧ)	219	31°30′S	143°30′E
Wildau, Ger. (vēl′dou)	159b	52°20′N	13°39′E
Wildberg, Ger. (vēl′bĕrgh)	159b	52°52′N	12°39′E
Wildcat Hill, hill, Can. (wīld′kăt)	97	53°17′N	102°30′W
Wildhay, r., Can. (wīld′hā)	95	53°15′N	117°20′W
Wildomar, Ca., U.S. (wĭl′dô-mär)	117a	33°35′N	117°17′W
Wild Rice, r., Mn., U.S.	112	47°10′N	96°40′W
Wild Rice, r., N.D., U.S.	112	46°10′N	97°12′W
Wild Rice Lake, l., Mn., U.S.	117h	46°54′N	92°10′W
Wildspitze, mtn., Aus.	168	46°55′N	10°50′E
Wildwood, N.J., U.S.	109	39°00′N	74°50′W
Wiley, Co., U.S. (wī′lē)	120	38°08′N	102°41′W
Wilge, r., S. Afr. (wĭl′jĕ)	238c	25°38′S	29°09′E
Wilge, r., S. Afr.	238c	27°27′S	28°46′E
Wilhelm, Mount, mtn., Pap. N. Gui.	213	5°58′S	144°58′E
Wilhelmina Gebergte, mts., Sur.	143	4°30′N	57°00′W
Wilhelmina Kanaal, can., Neth.	159a	51°37′N	4°55′E
Wilhelmshaven, Ger. (vēl-hĕlms-hä′fĕn)	160	53°30′N	8°10′E
Wilkes-Barre, Pa., U.S. (wĭlks′băr-ē)	105	41°15′N	75°50′W
Wilkes Land, reg., Ant.	224	71°00′S	126°00′E
Wilkeson, Wa., U.S. (wĭl-kē′sŭn)	116a	47°06′N	122°03′W
Wilkie, Can. (wĭlk′ē)	90	52°25′N	108°43′W
Wilkinsburg, Pa., U.S. (wĭl′kĭnz-bûrg)	111e	40°26′N	79°53′W
Willamette, r., Or., U.S.	106	45°00′N	123°00′W
Willapa Bay, b., Wa., U.S.	114	46°37′N	124°00′W
Willard, Oh., U.S. (wĭl′ȧrd)	108	41°00′N	82°50′W
Willard, Ut., U.S.	117b	41°24′N	112°02′W
Willcox, Az., U.S. (wĭl′kŏks)	119	32°15′N	109°50′W
Willcox Playa, l., Az., U.S.	119	32°08′N	109°51′W
Willemstad, Neth. Ant.	142	12°12′N	68°58′W
Willesden, Eng., U.K. (wĭlz′dĕn)	158b	51°31′N	0°17′W
William "Bill" Dannelly Reservoir, res., Al., U.S.	124	32°10′N	87°15′W
William Creek, Austl. (wĭl′yăm)	218	28°45′S	136°20′E

PLACE (Pronunciation)	PAGE	LAT.	LONG.
Williams, Az., U.S. (wĭl'yămz)	119	35°15'N	112°15'W
Williams, i., Bah.	134	24°30'N	78°30'W
Williamsburg, Ky., U.S. (wĭl'yămz-bûrg)	124	36°42'N	84°09'W
Williamsburg, Oh., U.S.	111f	39°04'N	84°02'W
Williamsburg, Va., U.S.	125	37°15'N	76°41'W
Williams Lake, Can.	95	52°08'N	122°09'W
Williamson, W.V., U.S. (wĭl'yăm-sŭn)	108	37°40'N	82°15'W
Williamsport, Md., U.S.	109	39°35'N	77°45'W
Williamsport, Pa., U.S.	109	41°15'N	77°05'W
Williamston, N.C., U.S. (wĭl'yămz-tŭn)	125	35°50'N	77°04'W
Williamston, S.C., U.S.	125	34°36'N	82°30'W
Williamstown, Austl.	217a	37°52'S	144°54'E
Williamstown, W.V., U.S. (wĭl'yămz-toun)	108	39°20'N	81°30'W
Williamsville, N.Y., U.S. (wĭl'yăm-vĭl)	111c	42°58'N	78°46'W
Willimantic, Ct., U.S. (wĭl-ĭ-măn'tĭk)	109	41°40'N	72°10'W
Willis, Tx., U.S. (wĭl'ĭs)	123	30°24'N	95°29'W
Willis Islands, is., Austl.	221	16°15'S	150°30'E
Williston, N.D., U.S. (wĭl'ĭs-tŭn)	104	48°08'N	103°38'W
Williston, Lake, l., Can.	92	55°40'N	123°40'W
Willmar, Mn., U.S. (wĭl'mär)	112	45°07'N	95°05'W
Willoughby, Oh., U.S. (wĭl'ô-bē)	111d	41°39'N	81°25'W
Willow, Ak., U.S.	103	61°50'N	150°00'W
Willow Creek, r., Or., U.S.	114	44°21'N	117°34'W
Willow Grove, Pa., U.S.	110f	40°07'N	75°07'W
Willowick, Oh., U.S. (wĭl'ô-wĭk)	111d	41°39'N	81°28'W
Willowmore, S. Afr. (wĭl'ô-môr)	232	33°15'S	23°37'E
Willow Run, Mi., U.S. (wĭl'ô rŭn)	111b	42°16'N	83°34'W
Willows, Ca., U.S. (wĭl'ōz)	118	39°32'N	122°11'W
Willow Springs, Mo., U.S. (sprĭngz)	121	36°59'N	91°56'W
Willowvale, S. Afr. (wĭ-lô'vāl)	233c	32°17'S	28°32'E
Wills Point, Tx., U.S. (wĭlz point)	123	32°42'N	96°02'W
Wilmer, Tx., U.S. (wĭl'mēr)	117c	32°35'N	96°40'W
Wilmette, Il., U.S. (wĭl-mĕt')	111a	42°04'N	87°42'W
Wilmington, Austl.	222	32°39'S	138°07'E
Wilmington, Ca., U.S. (wĭl'mĭng-tŭn)	117a	33°46'N	118°16'W
Wilmington, De., U.S.	105	39°45'N	75°33'W
Wilmington, Il., U.S.	111a	41°19'N	88°09'W
Wilmington, Ma., U.S.	101a	42°34'N	71°10'W
Wilmington, N.C., U.S.	105	34°12'N	77°56'W
Wilmington, Oh., U.S.	108	39°20'N	83°50'W
Wilmore, Ky., U.S. (wĭl'môr)	108	37°50'N	84°35'W
Wilmslow, Eng., U.K. (wĭlmz'lō)	158a	53°19'N	2°14'W
Wilno *see* Vilnius, Lith.	178	54°40'N	25°26'E
Wilpoort, S. Afr.	238c	26°57'S	26°17'E
Wilson, Ar., U.S. (wĭl'sŭn)	121	35°35'N	90°02'W
Wilson, N.C., U.S.	125	35°42'N	77°55'W
Wilson, Ok., U.S.	121	34°09'N	97°27'W
Wilson, r., Al., U.S.	124	34°53'N	87°28'W
Wilson, Mount, mtn., Ca., U.S.	117a	34°15'N	118°06'W
Wilson, Point, c., Austl.	217a	38°05'S	144°31'E
Wilson Lake, res., Al., U.S.	107	34°45'N	87°30'W
Wilson's Promontory, pen., Austl. (wĭl'sŭnz)	221	39°05'S	146°50'E
Wilsonville, Il., U.S. (wĭl'sŭn-vĭl)	117e	39°04'N	89°52'W
Wilstedt, Ger. (vēl'shtĕt)	159c	53°45'N	10°04'E
Wilster, Ger. (vēl'stĕr)	159c	53°55'N	9°23'E
Wilton, Ct., U.S. (wĭl'tŭn)	110a	41°11'N	73°25'W
Wilton, N.D., U.S.	112	47°09'N	100°47'W
Wiluna, Austl. (wĭ-lōō'nȧ)	218	26°35'S	120°25'E
Winamac, In., U.S. (wĭn'ȧ măk)	108	41°05'N	86°40'W
Winburg, S. Afr. (wĭm-bûrg)	238c	28°31'S	27°02'E
Winchester, Eng., U.K.	164	51°04'N	1°20'W
Winchester, Ca., U.S. (wĭn'chĕs-tēr)	117a	33°41'N	117°06'W
Winchester, Id., U.S.	114	46°14'N	116°39'W
Winchester, In., U.S.	108	40°10'N	84°50'W
Winchester, Ky., U.S.	108	38°00'N	84°15'W
Winchester, Ma., U.S.	101a	42°28'N	71°09'W
Winchester, N.H., U.S.	109	42°45'N	72°25'W
Winchester, Tn., U.S.	124	35°11'N	86°06'W
Winchester, Va., U.S.	109	39°10'N	78°10'W
Wind, r., Wy., U.S.	115	43°17'N	109°02'W
Windber, Pa., U.S. (wĭnd'bēr)	109	40°15'N	78°45'W
Wind Cave National Park, rec., S.D., U.S.	112	43°36'N	103°53'W
Winder, Ga., U.S. (wīn'dēr)	124	33°58'N	83°43'W
Windermere, Eng., U.K. (wĭn'dēr-mēr)	164	54°25'N	2°59'W
Windham, Ct., U.S. (wĭnd'ăm)	109	41°45'N	72°05'W
Windham, N.H., U.S.	101a	42°49'N	71°21'W
Windhoek, Nmb. (vĭnt'hòk)	232	22°05'S	17°10'E
Wind Lake, l., Wi., U.S.	111a	42°49'N	88°06'W
Wind Mountain, mtn., N.M., U.S.	122	32°02'N	105°30'W
Windom, Mn., U.S. (wĭn'dŭm)	112	43°50'N	95°04'W
Windora, Austl. (wĭn-dō'rȧ)	219	25°15'S	142°50'E
Wind River Indian Reservation, I.R., Wy., U.S.	115	43°26'N	109°00'W
Wind River Range, mts., Wy., U.S.	106	43°19'N	109°47'W
Windsor, Austl. (wĭn'zēr)	217b	33°37'S	150°49'E
Windsor, Can.	91	42°19'N	83°00'W
Windsor, Can.	93a	48°57'N	55°40'W
Windsor, Can.	91	44°59'N	64°08'W
Windsor, Eng., U.K.	164	51°27'N	0°37'W
Windsor, Co., U.S.	120	40°27'N	104°51'W
Windsor, Mo., U.S.	121	38°32'N	93°31'W
Windsor, N.C., U.S.	125	35°58'N	76°57'W
Windsor, Vt., U.S.	109	43°30'N	72°25'W
Windward Islands, is., N.A. (wĭnd'wērd)	129	12°45'N	61°40'W
Windward Passage, strt., N.A.	129	19°30'N	74°20'W
Winefred Lake, l., Can.	96	55°30'N	110°35'W
Winfield, Ks., U.S.	121	37°14'N	97°00'W
Winifred, Mt., U.S. (wĭn ĭ frĕd)	115	47°35'N	109°20'W
Winisk, r., Can.	93	54°30'N	86°30'W
Wink, Tx., U.S. (wĭŋk)	122	31°48'N	103°06'W
Winkler, Can. (wĭnk'lēr)	97	49°11'N	97°56'W
Winneba, Ghana (wĭn'ê-bȧ)	234	5°25'N	0°36'W
Winnebago, Mn., U.S. (wĭn'ê-bā'gō)	113	43°45'N	94°08'W
Winnebago, Lake, l., Wi., U.S.	113	44°09'N	88°10'W
Winnebago Indian Reservation, I.R., Ne., U.S.	112	42°15'N	96°06'W
Winnemucca, Nv., U.S. (wĭn-ê-mŭk'ȧ)	104	40°59'N	117°43'W
Winnemucca, l., Nv., U.S.	118	40°06'N	119°07'W
Winner, S.D., U.S. (wĭn'ēr)	112	43°22'N	99°50'W
Winnetka, Il., U.S. (wĭ-nĕt'kȧ)	111a	42°07'N	87°44'W
Winnett, Mt., U.S. (wĭn'ĕt)	115	47°01'N	108°20'W
Winnfield, La., U.S. (wĭn'fēld)	123	31°56'N	92°39'W
Winnibigoshish, l., Mn., U.S. (wĭn'ĭ-bĭ-gō'shĭsh)	113	47°30'N	93°45'W
Winnipeg, Can. (wĭn'ĭ-pĕg)	90	49°53'N	97°09'W
Winnipeg, r., Can.	92	50°30'N	95°00'W
Winnipeg, Lake, l., Can.	92	52°00'N	97°00'W
Winnipegosis, Can. (wĭn'ĭ-pê-gō'sĭs)	90	51°39'N	99°56'W
Winnipegosis, l., Can.	92	52°30'N	100°00'W
Winnipesaukee, l., N.H., U.S. (wĭn'ê-pê-sô'kê)	109	43°40'N	71°20'W
Winnsboro, La., U.S. (wĭnz'bŭr'ô)	123	32°09'N	91°42'W
Winnsboro, S.C., U.S.	125	34°29'N	81°05'W
Winnsboro, Tx., U.S.	121	32°56'N	95°15'W
Winona, Can. (wĭ-nō'nȧ)	102d	43°13'N	79°39'W
Winona, Mn., U.S.	105	44°03'N	91°40'W
Winona, Ms., U.S.	124	33°29'N	89°43'W
Winooski, Vt., U.S. (wĭ-nōōs'kê)	109	44°30'N	73°10'W
Winsen, Ger. (vĕn'zĕn)	159c	53°22'N	10°13'E
Winsford, Eng., U.K. (wĭnz'fērd)	158a	53°11'N	2°30'W
Winslow, Az., U.S. (wĭnz'lō)	119	35°00'N	110°45'W
Winslow, Wa., U.S.	116a	47°38'N	122°31'W
Winsted, Ct., U.S. (wĭn'stĕd)	109	41°55'N	73°05'W
Winster, Eng., U.K. (wĭn'stēr)	158a	53°08'N	1°38'W
Winston-Salem, N.C., U.S. (wĭn stŭn-sā'lĕm)	105	36°05'N	80°15'W
Winterberge, mts., Afr.	233c	32°18'S	26°25'E
Winter Garden, Fl., U.S. (wĭn'tēr gär'd'n)	125a	28°32'N	81°35'W
Winter Haven, Fl., U.S. (hā'vĕn)	125a	28°01'N	81°38'W
Winter Park, Fl., U.S. (pärk)	125a	28°35'N	81°21'W
Winters, Tx., U.S. (wĭn'tērz)	122	31°59'N	99°58'W
Winterset, Ia., U.S. (wĭn'tēr-sĕt)	113	41°19'N	94°03'W
Winterswijk, Neth.	171c	51°58'N	6°44'E
Winterthur, Switz. (vĭn'tĕr-tōōr)	168	47°30'N	8°32'E
Winterton, S. Afr.	233c	28°51'S	29°33'E
Winthrop, Ma., U.S.	101a	42°23'N	70°59'W
Winthrop, Me., U.S. (wĭn'thrŭp)	100	44°19'N	70°00'W
Winthrop, Mn., U.S.	113	44°31'N	94°20'W
Winton, Austl. (wĭn-tŭn)	219	22°17'S	143°08'E
Wipperfürth, Ger. (vĕ'pĕr-fürt)	171c	51°07'N	7°23'E
Wirksworth, Eng., U.K. (wûrks'wûrth)	158a	53°05'N	1°35'W
Wisconsin, state, U.S. (wĭs-kŏn'sĭn)	105	44°30'N	91°00'W
Wisconsin, r., Wi., U.S.	107	43°14'N	90°34'W
Wisconsin Dells, Wi., U.S.	113	43°38'N	89°46'W
Wisconsin Rapids, Wi., U.S.	113	44°24'N	89°50'W
Wishek, N.D., U.S. (wĭsh'ĕk)	112	46°15'N	99°34'W
Wisła, r., Pol. (vēs'wȧ)	156	52°30'N	20°00'E
Wisłoka, r., Pol. (vēs-wô'kȧ)	169	49°55'N	21°26'E
Wismar, Ger. (vĭs'mär)	160	53°53'N	11°28'E
Wismar, Guy. (wĭs'mȧr)	143	5°58'N	58°15'W
Wisner, Ne., U.S. (wĭz'nēr)	112	42°00'N	96°55'W
Wissembourg, Fr. (vē-săn-bōōr')	171	49°03'N	7°58'E
Wister, Lake, l., Ok., U.S. (vĭs'tēr)	121	35°02'N	94°52'W
Witbank, S. Afr. (wĭt-băŋk)	238c	25°53'S	29°14'E
Witberg, mtn., Afr.	233c	30°32'S	27°18'E
Witham, Eng., U.K. (wĭdh'ăm)	158b	51°48'N	0°37'E
Witham, r., Eng., U.K.	158a	53°11'N	0°20'W
Withamsville, Oh., U.S. (wĭdh'ămz-vĭl)	111f	39°04'N	84°16'W
Withlacoochee, r., Fl., U.S. (wĭth-lȧ-kōō'chê)	125a	28°58'N	82°30'W
Withlacoochee, r., Ga., U.S.	124	31°15'N	83°30'W
Withrow, Mn., U.S. (wĭdh'rō)	117g	45°08'N	92°54'W
Witney, Eng., U.K. (wĭt'nê)	158b	51°45'N	1°30'W
Witt, Il., U.S. (vĭt)	108	39°10'N	89°15'W
Witten, Ger. (vē'tĕn)	171c	51°26'N	7°19'E
Wittenberg, Ger. (vē'tĕn-bĕrgh)	168	51°53'N	12°40'E
Wittenberge, Ger. (vĭt-ĕn-bĕr'gĕ)	168	52°59'N	11°45'E
Wittlich, Ger. (vĭt'lĭk)	168	49°58'N	6°54'E
Witu, Kenya (wē'tōō)	233	2°18'S	40°28'E
Witu Islands, is., Pap. N. Gui.	213	4°45'S	149°50'E
Witwatersberg, mts., S. Afr. (wĭt-wôr-tĕrz-bûrg)	233b	25°58'S	27°53'E
Witwatersrand, mts., S. Afr. (wĭt-wôr'tĕrs-rănd)	238c	25°55'S	26°27'E
Wkra, r., Pol. (f'krȧ)	169	52°40'N	20°35'E
Włocławek, Pol. (vwô-tswä'vĕk)	169	52°38'N	19°08'E
Włodawa, Pol. (vwô-dä'vä)	169	51°33'N	23°33'E
Włoszczowa, Pol. (vwôsh-chô'vä)	169	50°51'N	19°58'E
Woburn, Ma., U.S. (wō'bŭrn) (wō'bûrn)	101a	42°29'N	71°10'W
Woerden, Neth.	159a	52°05'N	4°52'E
Woking, Eng., U.K.	158b	51°18'N	0°33'W
Wokingham, Eng., U.K. (wô'kĭng-hăm)	158b	51°23'N	0°50'W
Wolcott, Ks., U.S. (wōl'kŏt)	117f	39°12'N	94°47'W
Wolf, i., Can. (wòlf)	99	44°10'N	76°25'W
Wolf, r., Ms., U.S.	124	30°45'N	89°36'W
Wolf, r., Wi., U.S.	113	45°14'N	88°45'W
Wolfenbüttel, Ger. (vòl'fĕn-büt-ĕl)	168	52°10'N	10°32'E
Wolf Lake, l., Il., U.S.	111a	41°39'N	87°33'W
Wolf Point, Mt., U.S. (wòlf point)	115	48°07'N	105°40'W
Wolfratshausen, Ger. (vōlf'räts-hou-zĕn)	159d	47°55'N	11°25'E
Wolfsburg, Ger. (vōlfs'bōōrgh)	168	52°30'N	10°37'E
Wolfville, Can. (wòlf'vĭl)	100	45°05'N	64°22'W
Wolgast, Ger. (vôl'gäst)	168	54°04'N	13°46'E
Wolhuterskop, S. Afr.	233b	25°41'S	27°40'E
Wolkersdorf, Aus.	159e	48°24'N	16°31'E
Wollaston, l., Can. (wòl'ăs-tŭn)	92	58°15'N	103°20'W
Wollaston Peninsula, pen., Can.	92	70°00'N	115°00'W
Wollongong, Austl. (wòl'ŭn-gŏng)	219	34°26'S	151°05'E
Wołomin, Pol. (vô-wō'mēn)	169	52°19'N	21°17'E
Wolseley, Can.	96	50°25'N	103°15'W
Woltersdorf, Ger. (vōl'tĕs-dōrf)	159b	52°07'N	13°13'E
Wolverhampton, Eng., U.K. (wòl'vēr-hămp-tŭn)	161	52°35'N	2°07'W
Wolwehoek, S. Afr.	238c	26°55'S	27°50'E
Wŏnsan, Kor., N. (wŭn'sän')	205	39°08'N	127°24'E
Wonthaggi, Austl. (wônt-hăg'ê)	219	38°45'S	145°42'E
Wood, S.D., U.S. (wòd)	112	43°26'N	100°25'W
Woodbine, Ia., U.S. (wòd'bīn)	112	41°44'N	95°42'W
Woodbridge, N.J., U.S. (wòd'brĭj')	110a	40°33'N	74°18'W
Wood Buffalo National Park, rec., Can.	92	59°50'N	118°53'W
Woodburn, Il., U.S. (wòd'bûrn)	117e	39°03'N	90°01'W
Woodburn, Or., U.S.	114	45°10'N	122°51'W
Woodbury, N.J., U.S. (wòd'bĕr-ê)	110f	39°50'N	75°14'W
Woodcrest, Ca., U.S. (wòd'krĕst)	117a	33°53'N	117°18'W
Woodinville, Wa., U.S. (wòd'ĭn-vĭl)	116a	47°46'N	122°09'W
Woodland, Ca., U.S. (wòd'lănd)	118	38°41'N	121°47'W
Woodland, Wa., U.S.	116c	45°54'N	122°45'W
Woodland Hills, Ca., U.S.	117a	34°10'N	118°36'W
Woodlark Island, i., Pap. N. Gui. (wòd'lärk)	213	9°07'S	152°00'E
Woodlawn Beach, N.Y., U.S. (wòd'lôn bēch)	111c	42°48'N	78°51'W
Wood Mountain, mtn., Can.	96	49°14'N	106°20'W
Wood River, Il., U.S.	117e	38°52'N	90°06'W
Woodroffe, Mount, mtn., Austl. (wòd'rŭf)	220	26°05'S	132°00'E
Woodruff, S.C., U.S. (wòd'rŭf)	125	34°43'N	82°03'W
Woods, l., Austl. (wòdz)	220	18°00'S	133°18'E
Woods, Lake of the, l., N.A.	93	49°25'N	93°25'W
Woods Cross, Ut., U.S. (krôs)	117b	40°53'N	111°54'W
Woodsfield, Oh., U.S. (wòdz-fēld)	108	39°45'N	81°10'W
Woodson, Or., U.S. (wòdsŭn)	116c	46°07'N	123°20'W
Woodstock, Can. (wòd'stŏk)	99	43°10'N	80°50'W
Woodstock, Can.	91	46°09'N	67°34'W
Woodstock, Eng., U.K.	158b	51°48'N	1°22'W
Woodstock, Il., U.S.	113	42°20'N	88°29'W
Woodstock, Va., U.S.	109	38°55'N	78°25'W
Woodsville, N.H., U.S. (wòdz'vĭl)	109	44°10'N	72°00'W
Woodville, Ms., U.S. (wòd'vĭl)	124	31°06'N	91°11'W
Woodville, Tx., U.S.	123	30°48'N	94°25'W
Woodward, Ok., U.S. (wòd'wôrd)	120	36°25'N	99°24'W
Woolwich, Eng., U.K. (wòl'ĭj)	158b	51°28'N	0°05'E
Woomera, Austl. (wōōm'ērȧ)	218	31°15'S	136°43'E
Woonsocket, R.I., U.S. (wōōn-sŏk'ĕt)	110b	42°00'N	71°30'W
Woonsocket, S.D., U.S.	112	44°03'N	98°17'W
Wooster, Oh., U.S. (wòs'tēr)	108	40°50'N	81°55'W
Worcester, S. Afr. (wōōs'tēr)	232	33°35'S	19°31'E
Worcester, Eng., U.K. (wò'stēr)	161	52°09'N	2°14'W
Worcester, Ma., U.S. (wòs'tēr)	105	42°16'N	71°49'W
Worcestershire, co., Eng., U.K.	158a	52°25'N	2°10'W
Worden, Il., U.S. (wôr'dĕn)	117e	38°56'N	89°50'W
Workington, Eng., U.K. (wûr'kĭng-tŭn)	164	54°40'N	3°30'W
Worksop, Eng., U.K. (wûrk'sŏp) (wûr'sŭp)	158a	53°18'N	1°07'W
Worland, Wy., U.S. (wûr'lănd)	115	44°02'N	107°56'W
Worms, Ger. (vōrms)	161	49°37'N	8°22'E
Worona Reservoir, res., Austl.	217b	34°12'S	150°55'E
Worth, Il., U.S. (wûrth)	111a	41°42'N	87°47'W
Wortham, Tx., U.S. (wûr'dhăm)	123	31°46'N	96°22'W
Worthing, Eng., U.K. (wûr'dhĭng)	164	50°48'N	0°29'W
Worthington, In., U.S. (wûr'dhĭng-tŭn)	108	39°05'N	87°00'W
Worthington, Mn., U.S.	112	43°38'N	95°36'W
Worth Lake, l., Tx., U.S.	117c	32°48'N	97°32'W
Wowoni, Pulau, i., Indon. (wō-wō'nê)	213	4°05'S	123°45'E
Wragby, Eng., U.K. (răg'bê)	158a	53°17'N	0°19'W
Wrangell, Ak., U.S. (răn'gĕl)	106a	56°28'N	132°25'W
Wrangell, Cape, c., Ak., U.S.	103a	52°55'N	172°30'E
Wrangell, Mount, mtn., Ak., U.S.	103	61°58'N	143°50'W
Wrangell Mountains, mts., Ak., U.S.	103	62°28'N	142°40'W
Wrangell-Saint Elias National Park, rec., Ak., U.S.	103	61°00'N	142°00'W
Wrath, Cape, c., Scot., U.K. (răth)	164	58°34'N	5°01'W
Wray, Co., U.S. (rā)	120	40°06'N	102°14'W
Wreak, r., Eng., U.K. (rēk)	158a	52°45'N	0°59'W
Wreck Reefs, rf., Austl. (rĕk)	221	22°00'S	155°52'E
Wrekin, The, mtn., Eng., U.K. (rĕk'ĭn)	158a	52°40'N	2°33'W
Wrens, Ga., U.S. (rĕnz)	125	33°15'N	82°25'W
Wrentham, Ma., U.S.	101a	42°04'N	71°20'W
Wrexham, Wales, U.K. (rĕk'săm)	164	53°03'N	3°00'W
Wrexham, co., Wales, U.K.	158a	53°00'N	2°57'W
Wrights Corners, N.Y., U.S. (rīts kôr'nērz)	111c	43°14'N	78°42'W
Wrightsville, Ga., U.S. (rīts'vĭl)	125	32°44'N	82°44'W
Wrocław, Pol. (vrôtsläv) (brĕs'lou)	169	51°07'N	17°10'E
Wrotham, Eng., U.K. (rōōt'ŭm)	158b	51°18'N	0°19'E
Września, Pol. (vzhăsh'nyȧ)	169	52°19'N	17°33'E
Wu, r., China (wōō')	204	27°30'N	107°00'E
Wuchang, China	208	44°59'N	127°00'E
Wuchang, China (wōō-chäŋ)	205	30°32'N	114°25'E
Wucheng, China (wōō-chŭŋ)	206	37°14'N	116°03'E
Wuhan, China	205	30°30'N	114°15'E

ng-sing; ŋ-baŋk; N-nasalized n; nŏd; cŏmmit; ōld; ōbey; ôrder; oi-boil; fōōd; ò-as oo in foot; ou-out; s-soft; sh-dish; th-thin; pūre; ûnite; ûrn; stŭd; circŭs; ü-as in French tu; '-indeterminate vowel.

368 Wuhu – Yellowstone Lake PRONOUNCING INDEX

PLACE (Pronunciation)	PAGE	LAT.	LONG.
Wuhu, China (wo͞o'ho͞o)	209	31°22'N	118°22'E
Wuji, China (wo͞o-jyī)	206	38°12'N	114°57'E
Wujiang, China (wo͞o-jyäŋ)	206	31°10'N	120°38'E
Wuleidao Wan, b., China (wo͞o-lā-dou wän)	206	36°55'N	122°00'E
Wulidian, China (wo͞o-lē-dǐĕn)	206	32°09'N	114°17'E
Wünsdorf, Ger. (vüns'dorf)	159b	52°10'N	13°29'E
Wupatki National Monument, rec., Az., U.S.	119	35°35'N	111°45'W
Wuping, China (wo͞o-pĭŋ)	209	25°05'N	116°01'E
Wuppertal, Ger. (vŏp'ĕr-täl)	161	51°16'N	7°14'E
Wuqiao, China (wo͞o-chyou)	206	37°37'N	116°29'E
Würm, r., Ger. (vürm)	159d	48°07'N	11°20'E
Würselen, Ger. (vür'zĕ-lĕn)	171c	50°49'N	6°09'E
Würzburg, Ger. (vürts'bŏrgh)	161	49°48'N	9°57'E
Wurzen, Ger. (vŏrt'sĕn)	161	51°22'N	12°45'E
Wushi, China (wo͞o-shr)	204	41°13'N	79°08'E
Wusong, China (wo͞o-sôŋ)	206	31°23'N	121°29'E
Wustermark, Ger. (vo͞os'tĕr-märk)	159b	52°33'N	12°57'E
Wustrau, Ger. (vo͞ost'rou)	159b	52°40'N	12°51'E
Wuustwezel, Bel.	159a	51°23'N	4°36'E
Wuwei, China (wo͞o'wā')	209	31°19'N	117°53'E
Wuxi, China (wo͞o-shyē)	205	31°36'N	120°17'E
Wuxing, China (wo͞o-shyĭŋ)	205	30°38'N	120°10'E
Wuyi Shan, mts., China (wo͞o-yē shän)	209	26°38'N	116°35'E
Wuyou, China (wo͞o-yō)	206	33°18'N	120°15'E
Wuzhi Shan, mtn., China (wo͞o-jr shän)	209	18°48'N	109°30'E
Wuzhou, China (wo͞o-jō)	205	23°32'N	111°25'E
Wyandotte, Mi., U.S. (wī'ăn-dŏt)	111b	42°12'N	83°10'W
Wye, Eng., U.K. (wī)	158b	51°12'N	0°57'E
Wye, r., Eng., U.K.	158a	53°14'N	1°46'W
Wylie, Lake, res., S.C., U.S.	125	35°02'N	81°21'W
Wymore, Ne., U.S. (wī'mōr)	121	40°09'N	96°41'W
Wynberg, S. Afr. (wĭn'bĕrg)	232a	34°00'S	18°28'E
Wyndham, Austl. (wĭnd'ăm)	218	15°30'S	128°15'E
Wynne, Ar., U.S. (wĭn)	121	35°12'N	90°46'W
Wynnewood, Ok., U.S. (wĭn'wŏd)	121	34°39'N	97°10'W
Wynona, Ok., U.S. (wī-nō'nȧ)	121	36°33'N	96°19'W
Wynyard, Can. (wĭn'yĕrd)	90	51°47'N	104°10'W
Wyoming, Oh., U.S. (wī-ō'mĭng)	111f	39°14'N	84°28'W
Wyoming, state, U.S.	104	42°50'N	108°30'W
Wyoming Range, mts., Wy., U.S.	106	42°43'N	110°35'W
Wyre Forest, for., Eng., U.K. (wīr)	158a	52°24'N	2°24'W
Wysokie Mazowieckie, Pol. (vē-sô'kyĕ mä-zô-vyĕts'kyĕ)	169	52°55'N	22°42'E
Wyszków, Pol. (vēsh'kŏf)	169	52°35'N	21°29'E
Wytheville, Va., U.S. (wĭth'vĭl)	125	36°55'N	81°06'W

X

PLACE (Pronunciation)	PAGE	LAT.	LONG.
Xàbia, Spain	173	38°45'N	0°07'E
Xagua, Banco, bk., Cuba (bä'n-kō-sä'gwä)	134	21°35'N	80°50'W
Xai Xai, Moz.	232	25°00'S	33°45'E
Xalapa, Mex.	128	19°32'N	96°53'W
Xangongo, Ang.	232	16°50'S	15°05'E
Xankändi (Stepanakert), Azer. (styĕ'pän-á-kĕrt)	181	39°50'N	46°40'E
Xanten, Ger. (ksän'tĕn)	171c	51°40'N	6°28'E
Xánthi, Grc.	163	41°08'N	24°53'E
Xàtiva, Spain	162	38°58'N	0°31'W
Xau, Lake, l., Bots.	232	21°15'S	24°38'E
Xcalak, Mex. (sä-lä'k)	132a	18°15'N	87°50'W
Xelva, Spain	172	39°43'N	1°00'W
Xenia, Oh., U.S. (zē'nĭ-ȧ)	108	39°40'N	83°55'W
Xi, r., China (shyē)	209	23°15'N	112°10'E
Xiajin, China (shyä-jyĭn)	208	36°58'N	115°59'E
Xiamen, China	205	24°30'N	118°10'E
Xiamen, i., Tai. (shyä-mŭn)	209	24°28'N	118°20'E
Xi'an, China (shyē-än)	204	34°20'N	109°00'E
Xiang, r., China (shyäŋ)	205	27°30'N	112°30'E
Xianghe, China (shyäŋ-hŭ)	206	39°46'N	116°59'E
Xiangtan, China (shyäŋ-tän)	205	27°55'N	112°45'E
Xianyang, China (shyĕn-yäŋ)	208	34°20'N	108°40'E
Xiaoxingkai Hu, l., China (shyou-shyĭŋ-kī ho͞o)	210	42°25'N	132°45'E
Xiapu, China (shyä-po͞o)	205	27°00'N	120°00'E
Xiayi, China (shyä-yē)	206	34°15'N	116°07'E
Xicotencatl, Mex. (sē-kō-tĕn-kät'l)	130	23°00'N	98°58'W
Xifeng, China (shyē-fŭŋ)	208	42°40'N	124°40'E
Xiheying, China (shyē-hŭ-yĭŋ)	206	39°58'N	114°50'E
Xiliao, r., China (shyē-lĭou)	208	43°23'N	121°40'E
Xilitla, Mex. (sē-lē'tlä)	130	21°24'N	98°59'W
Xinchang, China (shyĭn-chäŋ)	207b	31°02'N	121°38'E
Xing'an, China (shyĭŋ-än)	209	25°44'N	110°32'E
Xingcheng, China (shyĭŋ-chŭŋ)	206	40°38'N	120°41'E
Xinghua, China (shyĭŋ-hwä)	206	32°58'N	119°48'E
Xingjiawan, China (shyĭŋ-jyä-wän)	206	37°16'N	114°54'E
Xingtai, China (shyĭŋ-tī)	208	37°04'N	114°33'E
Xingu, r., Braz. (zhĕŋ-gō')	143	6°20'S	52°34'W
Xinhai, China (shyĭn-hī)	206	36°59'N	117°33'E
Xinhua, China (shyĭn-hwä)	209	27°45'N	111°20'E
Xinhuai, r., China (shyĭn-hwī)	206	33°48'N	119°39'E
Xinhui, China (shyn-hwā)	209	22°40'N	113°08'E
Xining, China (shyē-nĭŋ)	204	36°52'N	101°36'E
Xinjiang (Sinkiang), prov., China (shyĭn-jyäŋ)	204	40°15'N	82°15'E
Xinjin, China (shyĭn-jyĭn)	208	39°23'N	121°57'E
Xinmin, China (shyĭn-mĭn)	208	42°00'N	122°42'E
Xintai, China (shyĭn-tī)	206	35°55'N	117°44'E
Xintang, China (shyĭn-täŋ)	207a	23°08'N	113°36'E
Xinxian, China (shyĭn shyĕn)	206	31°47'N	114°50'E
Xinxian, China	208	38°20'N	112°45'E
Xinxiang, China (shyĭn-shyäŋ)	208	35°17'N	113°49'E
Xinyang, China (shyĭn-yäŋ)	205	32°08'N	114°04'E
Xinye, China (shyĭn-yŭ)	208	32°40'N	112°20'E
Xinzao, China (shyĭn-dzou)	207a	23°01'N	113°25'E
Xinzheng, China (shyĭn-jŭŋ)	206	34°24'N	113°43'E
Xinzo de Limia, Spain	172	42°03'N	7°43'W
Xiongyuecheng, China (shyôŋ-yûĕ-chŭŋ)	206	40°10'N	122°08'E
Xiping, China (shyē-pĭŋ)	206	33°21'N	114°01'E
Xishui, China (shyē-shwā)	209	30°30'N	115°10'E
Xixian, China (shyē shyĕn)	206	32°20'N	114°42'E
Xixona, Spain	173	38°31'N	0°29'W
Xiyang, China (shyē-yäŋ)	206	37°37'N	113°42'E
Xiyou, China (shyē-yō)	206	37°21'N	119°59'E
Xizang (Tibet), prov., China (shyē-dzäŋ)	204	31°15'N	87°30'E
Xizhong Dao, i., China (shyē-jôŋ dou)	206	39°27'N	121°06'E
Xochihuehuetlán, Mex. (sō-chē-wĕ-wĕ-tlà'n)	131	17°53'N	98°29'E
Xochimilco, Mex. (sō-chê-mēl'kô)	131a	19°15'N	99°06'W
Xuancheng, China (shyůän-chŭŋ)	209	30°52'N	118°48'E
Xuanhua, China (shyůän-hwä)	208	40°35'N	115°05'E
Xuanhuadian, China (shyůän-hwä-dĭĕn)	206	31°42'N	114°29'E
Xuchang, China (shyo͞o-chäŋ)	208	34°02'N	113°49'E
Xudat, Azer.	182	41°38'N	48°42'E
Xuddur, Som.	238a	3°55'N	43°45'E
Xun, r., China (shyòn)	209	23°28'N	110°30'E
Xuzhou, China	205	34°17'N	117°10'E

Y

PLACE (Pronunciation)	PAGE	LAT.	LONG.
Ya'an, China (yä-än)	204	30°00'N	103°20'E
Yablonovyy Khrebet, mts., Russia (yȧ-blô-nô-vē')	179	51°15'N	111°30'E
Yablunivskyi, Pereval, p., Ukr.	169	48°20'N	24°25'E
Yacheng, China (yä-chŭŋ)	209	18°20'N	109°10'E
Yachiyo, Japan	211a	35°43'N	140°07'E
Yacolt, Wa., U.S. (yă'kŏlt)	116c	45°52'N	122°24'W
Yacolt Mountain, mtn., Wa., U.S.	116c	45°52'N	122°27'W
Yacona, r., Ms., U.S. (yȧ'cō nä)	124	34°13'N	89°30'W
Yacuiba, Bol. (yȧ-ko͞o-ē'bä)	142	22°02'S	63°44'W
Yadkin, r., N.C., U.S. (yăd'kĭn)	125	36°12'N	80°40'W
Yafran, Libya	230	31°57'N	12°04'E
Yaguajay, Cuba (yä-guä-hä'ê)	134	22°20'N	79°20'W
Yahagi-Gawa, r., Japan (yä'hä-gē gä'wä)	211	35°16'N	137°22'E
Yahongqiao, China (yä-hôŋ-chyou)	206	39°45'N	117°52'E
Yahualica, Mex. (yä-wä-lē'kä)	130	21°08'N	102°53'W
Yajalón, Mex. (yä-hä-lōn')	131	17°16'N	92°20'W
Yakhroma, Russia (yäl'rô-ma)	186b	56°17'N	37°30'E
Yakhroma, r., Russia	186b	56°15'N	37°38'E
Yakima, Wa., U.S. (yăk'ĭmȧ)	104	46°35'N	120°30'W
Yakima, r., Wa., U.S. (yăk'ĭ-mȧ)	114	46°48'N	120°22'W
Yakima Indian Reservation, I.R., Wa., U.S.	114	46°16'N	121°03'W
Yakoma, D.R.C.	236	4°05'N	22°27'E
Yaku, i., Japan (yä'ko͞o)	205	30°15'N	130°41'E
Yakutat, Ak., U.S. (yăk'ō-tăt)	103	59°32'N	139°35'W
Yakutsk, Russia (yá-kŏtsk')	179	62°13'N	129°49'E
Yale, Mi., U.S.	108	43°05'N	82°45'W
Yale, Ok., U.S.	121	36°07'N	96°42'W
Yale Lake, res., Wa., U.S.	114	46°00'N	122°20'W
Yalinga, C.A.R. (yá-lĭŋ'gá)	231	6°56'N	23°22'E
Yalobusha, r., Ms., U.S. (yȧ-lô-bŏsh'ȧ)	124	33°48'N	90°02'W
Yalong, r., China (yä-lôŋ)	204	32°29'N	98°41'E
Yalta, Ukr. (yäl'tá)	181	44°29'N	34°12'E
Yalu, r., Asia	205	41°20'N	126°35'E
Yalutorovsk, Russia (yä-lo͞o-tô'rôfsk)	178	56°42'N	66°32'E
Yamada, Japan (yä'má-dä)	211	33°37'N	133°39'E
Yamagata, Japan (yä-má'gä-tá)	205	38°12'N	140°24'E
Yamaguchi, Japan (yä-má'go͞o-chê)	210	34°10'N	131°30'E
Yamal, Poluostrov, pen., Russia (yä-mäl')	178	71°15'N	70°00'E
Yamantau, Gora, mtn., Russia (gȧ-rä' yä'man-tȧw)	186a	54°16'N	58°08'E
Yamasaki, Japan (yä'má'sä-kê)	211	35°01'N	134°33'E
Yamasaki, Japan	211b	34°53'N	135°41'E
Yamashina, Japan (yä'mä-shē'nä)	211b	34°59'N	135°50'E
Yamashita, Japan (yä'mä-shē'tä)	211b	34°53'N	135°25'E
Yamato, Japan	211a	35°28'N	139°28'E
Yamato-Kōriyama, Japan	211b	34°39'N	135°48'E
Yamato-takada, Japan (yä'mä-tô tä'kä-dä)	211b	34°31'N	135°45'E
Yambi, Mesa de, mtn., Col. (mĕ'sä-dĕ-yá'm-bē)	142	1°55'N	71°45'W
Yambol, Blg. (yàm'bŏl)	163	42°28'N	26°31'E
Yamdena, i., Indon.	213	7°23'S	130°30'E
Yamethin, Mya. (yŭ-mē'thĕn)	199	20°14'N	96°27'E
Yamhill, Or., U.S. (yăm'hĭl)	116c	45°20'N	123°11'W
Yamkino, Russia (yäm'kĭ-nô)	186b	55°56'N	38°25'E
Yamma Yamma, Lake, l., Austl. (yăm'á yăm'á)	221	26°15'S	141°30'E
Yamoussoukro, C. Iv.	230	6°49'N	5°17'W
Yamsk, Russia (yämsk)	179	59°41'N	154°09'E
Yamuna, r., India	199	25°30'N	80°30'E
Yamzho Yumco, l., China (yäm-jwo yo͞om-tswo)	204	29°11'N	91°26'E
Yana, r., Russia (yä'ná)	179	71°00'N	136°00'E
Yanac, Austl. (yăn'ăk)	219	36°10'S	141°30'E
Yanagawa, Japan (yä-nä'gä-wä)	211	33°11'N	130°24'E
Yanam, India (yŭnŭm')	199	16°48'N	82°15'E
Yan'an, China (yän-än)	204	36°46'N	109°15'E
Yanbu', Sau. Ar.	198	23°57'N	38°02'E
Yancheng, China (yän-chŭŋ)	208	33°23'N	120°11'E
Yancheng, China	208	33°38'N	113°59'E
Yandongi, D.R.C.	236	2°51'N	22°16'E
Yangcheng Hu, l., China (yäŋ-chŭŋ ho͞o)	206	31°30'N	120°31'E
Yangchun, China (yäŋ-chòn)	209	22°08'N	111°48'E
Yang'erzhuang, China (yäŋ-är-jůäŋ)	206	38°18'N	117°31'E
Yanggezhuang, China (yäŋ-gŭ-jůäŋ)	208a	40°10'N	116°48'E
Yanggu, China (yäŋ-go͞o)	206	36°06'N	115°46'E
Yanghe, China (yäŋ-hŭ)	206	33°48'N	118°23'E
Yangjiang, China (yäŋ-jyäŋ)	209	21°52'N	111°58'E
Yangjiaogou, China (yäŋ-jyou-gō)	206	37°17'N	118°53'E
Yangon see Rangoon, Mya.	199	16°46'N	96°09'E
Yangquan, China (yäŋ-chyůän)	206	37°52'N	113°36'E
Yangtze (Chang), r., China (yăng'tse) (chäŋ)	205	30°30'N	117°25'E
Yangxin, China (yäŋ-shyĭn)	206	37°39'N	117°34'E
Yangyang, Kor., S. (yäng'yäng')	210	38°02'N	128°38'E
Yangzhou, China (yäŋ-jō)	205	32°24'N	119°24'E
Yanji, China (yän-jyē)	205	42°55'N	129°35'E
Yanjiahe, China (yän-jyä-hŭ)	206	31°55'N	114°47'E
Yanjin, China (yän-jyĭn)	206	35°09'N	114°13'E
Yankton, S.D., U.S. (yănk'tŭn)	104	42°51'N	97°24'W
Yanling, China (yän-lĭŋ)	206	34°07'N	114°12'E
Yanshan, China (yän-shän)	208	38°05'N	117°15'E
Yanshou, China (yän-shō)	208	45°25'N	128°43'E
Yantai, China	205	37°32'N	121°22'E
Yanychi, Russia (yä'nĭ-chĭ)	186a	57°42'N	56°24'E
Yanzhou, China (yäŋ-jō)	205	35°35'N	116°50'E
Yanzhuang, China (yän-jůäŋ)	206	36°08'N	117°47'E
Yao, Chad (yä'ō)	218	13°00'N	17°38'E
Yao, Japan	211b	34°37'N	135°37'E
Yaoundé, Cam.	230	3°52'N	11°31'E
Yap, i., Micron. (yăp)	3	11°00'N	138°00'E
Yapen, Pulau, i., Indon.	213	1°30'S	136°15'E
Yaque del Norte, r., Dom. Rep. (yä'kå dĕl nôr'tä)	129	19°40'N	71°25'W
Yaque del Sur, r., Dom. Rep. (yä-kĕ-dĕl-so͞o'r)	135	18°35'N	71°05'W
Yaqui, r., Mex. (yä'kē)	128	28°15'N	109°40'W
Yaracuy, dept., Ven. (yä-rä-ko͞o'ē)	143b	10°10'N	68°31'W
Yaraka, Austl. (yȧ-răk'ȧ)	219	24°50'S	144°08'E
Yaransk, Russia (yä-ränsk')	178	57°18'N	48°05'E
Yarda, oasis, Chad (yär'dȧ)	231	18°29'N	19°13'E
Yare, r., Eng., U.K.	165	52°40'N	1°32'E
Yarkand see Shache, China	204	38°15'N	77°15'E
Yarmouth, Can. (yär'mŭth)	100	43°50'N	66°07'W
Yaroslavka, Russia (yá-rô-släv'ká)	186a	55°52'N	57°59'E
Yaroslavl', Russia (yá-rô-släv''l)	178	57°37'N	39°54'E
Yaroslavl', prov., Russia	176	58°05'N	38°05'E
Yarra, r., Austl.	217a	37°51'S	144°54'E
Yarro-to, l., Russia (yá'rô-tô')	180	67°55'N	71°35'E
Yartsevo, Russia (yär'tsyê-vô)	180	55°04'N	32°38'E
Yartsevo, Russia	179	60°13'N	89°52'E
Yarumal, Col. (yä-ro͞o-mäl')	142	6°57'N	75°24'W
Yasawa Group, is., Fiji	214g	17°00'S	177°23'E
Yasel'da, r., Bela. (yä-syŭl'dá)	169	52°13'N	25°53'E
Yateras, Cuba (yä-tā'räs)	135	20°00'N	75°00'W
Yates Center, Ks., U.S. (yāts)	121	37°53'N	95°44'W
Yathkyed, l., Can. (yáth-kī-ĕd')	92	62°41'N	98°00'W
Yatsuga-take, mtn., Japan (yät'so͞o-gä dä'kä)	211	36°01'N	138°21'W
Yatsushiro, Japan (yät'so͞o'shê-rô)	211	32°30'N	130°35'E
Yatta Plateau, plat., Kenya	237	1°55'S	38°10'E
Yautepec, Mex. (yä-o͞o-tå-pĕk')	130	18°53'N	99°04'W
Yawata, Japan (yä'wä-tä)	211	34°52'N	135°43'E
Yawatahama, Japan (yä'wä'tä'hä-mä)	211	33°24'N	132°25'E
Yaxian, China (yä shyĕn)	209	18°10'N	109°32'E
Yayama, D.R.C.	236	1°16'S	23°07'E
Yayao, China (yä-you)	207a	23°10'N	113°40'E
Yazd, Iran	198	31°59'N	54°03'E
Yazoo, r., Ms., U.S. (yă'zo͞o)	107	32°32'N	90°40'W
Yazoo City, Ms., U.S.	124	32°50'N	90°18'W
Ýdra, i., Grc.	175	37°20'N	23°30'E
Ye, Mya. (yā)	212	15°13'N	97°52'E
Yeadon, Pa., U.S. (yē'dŭn)	110f	39°56'N	75°16'W
Yecla, Spain (yā'klä)	172	38°35'N	1°09'W
Yefremov, Russia (yĕ-frā'môf)	176	53°08'N	38°04'E
Yegor'yevsk, Russia (yĕ-gôr'yĕfsk)	180	55°23'N	38°59'E
Yeji, China (yŭ-jyē)	206	31°52'N	115°57'E
Yekaterinburg, Russia	178	56°51'N	60°36'E
Yelabuga, Russia (yĕ-lä'bŏ-gá)	180	55°50'N	52°18'E
Yelan, Russia	181	50°50'N	44°00'E
Yelets, Russia (yĕ-lyĕts')	178	52°35'N	38°28'E
Yelizavetpol'skiy, Russia (yĕ'lĭ-za-vĕt-pôl-skĭ)	186a	52°51'N	60°38'E
Yelizavety, Mys, c., Russia (yĕ-lyĕ-sá-vyĕ'tĭ)	179	54°28'N	142°59'E
Yell, i., Scot., U.K. (yĕl)	164a	60°35'N	1°27'W
Yellow see Huang, r., China	205	35°06'N	113°39'E
Yellow, r., Fl., U.S. (yĕl'ō)	124	30°33'N	86°53'W
Yellowhead Pass, p., Can. (yĕl'ō-hĕd)	95	52°52'N	118°35'W
Yellowknife, Can. (yĕl'ō-nīf)	90	62°29'N	114°38'W
Yellow Sea, sea, Asia	205	35°20'N	122°15'E
Yellowstone, r., U.S.	106	46°00'N	108°00'W
Yellowstone, Clarks Fork, r., U.S.	115	44°55'N	109°05'W
Yellowstone Lake, l., Wy., U.S.	106	44°27'N	110°03'W

ăt; finăl; rāte; senåte; ärm; åsk; sofȧ; fâre; ch-choose; dh-as th in other; bē; ėvent; bĕt; recĕnt; cratẽr; g-gō; gh-guttural g; bĭt; ĭ-short neutral; rīde; ĸ-guttural k as ch in German ich;

PRONOUNCING INDEX Yellowstone National Park – Zeya 369

PLACE (Pronunciation)	PAGE	LAT.	LONG.
Yellowstone National Park, rec., U.S. (yĕl'ô-stōn)	106	44°45'N	110°35'W
Yel'nya, Russia (yĕl'nya)	176	54°34'N	33°12'E
Yemanzhelinsk, Russia (yĕ-màn-zhâ'lĭnsk)	186a	54°47'N	61°24'E
Yemen, nation, Asia (yĕm'ĕn)	198	15°00'N	47°00'E
Yemetsk, Russia	180	63°28'N	41°28'E
Yenangyaung, Mya. (yä'nän-d oung)	199	20°27'N	94°59'E
Yencheng, China	204	37°30'N	79°26'E
Yendi, Ghana (yĕn'dê)	230	9°26'N	0°01'W
Yengisar, China (yŭn-gē-sär)	204	39°01'N	75°29'E
Yenice, r., Tur.	181	41°10'N	33°00'E
Yenisey, r., Russia (yĕ-nê-sĕ'ê)	178	71°00'N	82°00'E
Yeniseysk, Russia (yĕ-nĭĕsā'ĭsk)	179	58°27'N	90°28'E
Yeo, I., Austl. (yō)	220	28°15'S	124°00'E
Yerevan, Arm. (yĕ-rĕ-vän')	181	40°10'N	44°30'E
Yerington, Nv., U.S. (yē'rĭng-tŭn)	118	38°59'N	119°10'W
Yermak, i., Russia	180	66°45'N	71°30'E
Yeste, Spain (yĕs'tå)	172	38°23'N	2°19'W
Yeu, Île d', i., Fr. (ēl dyû)	161	46°43'N	2°45'W
Yevlax, Azer.	182	40°36'N	47°09'E
Yexian, China (yŭ-shyĕn)	206	37°09'N	119°57'E
Yeya, r., Russia (yă'yà)	177	46°25'N	39°17'E
Yeysk, Russia (yĕysk)	181	46°41'N	38°13'E
Yi, r., China	206	34°38'N	118°07'E
Yibin, China (yē-bĭn)	204	28°50'N	104°40'E
Yichang, China (yē-chăŋ)	205	30°38'N	111°22'E
Yidu, China (yē-dōō)	208	36°42'N	118°30'E
Yilan, China (yē-län)	205	46°10'N	129°40'E
Yinchuan, China (yĭn-chůän)	204	38°22'N	106°22'E
Yingkou, China (yĭŋ-kō)	205	40°35'N	122°10'E
Yining, China (yē-nĭŋ)	204	43°58'N	80°40'E
Yin Shan, mts., China (yĭng'shän')	208	40°50'N	110°30'E
Yishan, China (yē-shän)	204	24°32'N	108°42'E
Yishui, China (yē-shwā)	206	35°49'N	118°40'E
Yitong, China (yē-tôŋ)	205	43°15'N	125°10'E
Yixian, China (yē shyĕn)	208	41°30'N	121°15'E
Yixing, China	206	31°26'N	119°57'E
Yiyang, China (yē-yäŋ)	209	28°52'N	112°12'E
Yoakum, Tx., U.S. (yō'kŭm)	123	29°18'N	97°09'W
Yockanookany, r., Ms., U.S. (yŏk'à-nōō-kă-nĭ)	124	32°47'N	89°38'W
Yodo-Gawa, strt., Japan (yō'dō'gä-wä)	211b	34°46'N	135°35'E
Yog Point, c., Phil. (yōg)	209	14°00'N	124°30'E
Yogyakarta, Indon. (yŏg-yȧ-kär'tȧ)	212	7°50'S	110°20'E
Yoho National Park, rec., Can. (yō'hō)	90	51°26'N	116°30'W
Yojoa, Lago de, l., Hond. (lä'gô dĕ yô-hō'ä)	132	14°49'N	87°53'W
Yokkaichi, Japan (yō'kä'ê-chê)	210	34°58'N	136°35'E
Yokohama, Japan (yō'kô-hä'mạ)	205	35°37'N	139°40'E
Yokosuka, Japan (yô-kō'sò-kä)	210	35°17'N	139°40'E
Yokota, Japan (yō-kō'tä)	211a	35°23'N	140°02'E
Yola, Nig. (yō'lä)	230	9°13'N	12°27'E
Yolaina, Cordillera de, mts., Nic.	133	11°34'N	84°34'W
Yomou, Gui.	234	7°34'N	9°16'W
Yonago, Japan (yō'nä-gō)	210	35°27'N	133°19'E
Yonezawa, Japan (yō'nĕ'zȧ-wä)	210	37°50'N	140°07'E
Yong'an, China (yôŋ-än)	209	26°00'N	117°22'E
Yongding, r., China (yôŋ-dĭŋ)	208	40°25'N	115°00'E
Yŏngdŏk, Kor., S. (yŭng'dŭk')	210	36°28'N	129°25'E
Yŏnghŭng, Kor., N. (yŭng'hòng')	210	39°31'N	127°11'E
Yonghŭng Man, b., Kor., N.	210	39°10'N	128°00'E
Yongnian, China (yôŋ-nĭĕn)	208	36°47'N	114°32'E
Yongqing, China (yôŋ-chyĭŋ)	208a	39°18'N	116°27'E
Yongshun, China (yôŋ-shòn)	204	29°05'N	109°58'E
Yonkers, N.Y., U.S. (yŏŋ'kẽrz)	110a	40°57'N	73°54'W
Yonne, r., Fr. (yôn)	170	48°18'N	3°15'E
Yono, Japan (yō'nō)	211a	35°53'N	139°36'E
Yorba Linda, Ca., U.S. (yôr'bă lĭn'dȧ)	117a	33°55'N	117°51'W
York, Austl.	218	32°00'S	117°00'E
York, Eng., U.K.	160	53°58'N	1°10'W
York, Al., U.S. (yôrk)	124	32°33'N	88°16'W
York, Ne., U.S.	121	40°52'N	97°36'W
York, Pa., U.S.	105	40°00'N	76°40'W
York, S.C., U.S.	125	34°59'N	81°14'W
York, Cape, c., Austl.	221	10°45'S	142°35'E
York, Kap, c., Grnld.	89	75°30'N	73°00'W
Yorke Peninsula, pen., Austl.	222	34°24'S	137°20'E
Yorketown, Austl.	222	35°00'S	137°28'E
York Factory, Can.	97	57°05'N	92°18'W
Yorkshire Wolds, Eng., U.K. (yôrk'shĭr)	164	54°00'N	0°35'W
Yorkton, Can. (yôrk'tŭn)	90	51°13'N	102°28'W
Yorktown, Tx., U.S. (yôrk'toun)	123	28°57'N	97°30'W
Yorktown, Va., U.S.	125	37°12'N	76°31'W
Yoro, Hond. (yō'rō)	132	15°09'N	87°05'W
Yoron, i., Japan	210	26°48'N	128°40'E
Yosemite National Park, rec., Ca., U.S. (yô-sĕm'ĭ-tê)	106	38°03'N	119°36'W
Yoshida, Japan (yō'shê-dà)	211	34°39'N	132°41'E
Yoshikawa, Japan (yō-shê'kä'wä')	211a	35°53'N	139°51'E
Yoshino, r., Japan (yō'shē-nō)	211	34°04'N	133°57'E
Yoshkar-Ola, Russia (yôsh-kär'ô-lä')	180	56°35'N	48°05'E
Yos Sudarsa, Pulau, i., Indon.	213	7°20'S	138°30'E
Yŏsu, Kor., S. (yŭ'sōō')	210	34°42'N	127°42'W
You, r., China (yō)	209	23°55'N	106°50'E
Youghal, Ire. (yōō'ôl) (yôl)	165	51°58'N	7°57'E
Youghal Bay, b., Ire.	164	51°52'N	7°46'W
Young, Austl. (yŭng)	222	34°15'S	148°18'E
Young, Ur. (yô-ōō'ng)	141c	32°42'S	57°38'W
Youngs, l., Wa., U.S. (yŭngz)	116a	47°25'N	122°08'W
Youngstown, N.Y., U.S.	111c	43°15'N	79°02'W
Youngstown, Oh., U.S.	108	41°05'N	80°40'W
Yozgat, Tur. (yôz'gȧd)	198	39°50'N	34°50'E
Ypsilanti, Mi., U.S. (ĭp-sĭ-lăn'tĭ)	111b	42°15'N	83°37'W
Yreka, Ca., U.S. (wī-rē'kȧ)	114	41°43'N	122°36'W
Yrghyz, Kaz.	183	48°30'N	61°17'E
Yrghyz, r., Kaz.	156	49°30'N	60°32'E
Ysleta, Tx., U.S. (ēz-lĕ'tȧ)	122	31°42'N	106°18'W
Yssingeaux, Fr. (ē-säN-zhō)	170	45°09'N	4°08'E
Ystad, Swe.	160	55°25'N	13°49'E
Ystādeh-ye Moqor, Āb-e, l., Afg.	202	32°35'N	68°00'E
Yu'alliq, Jabal, mts., Egypt	197a	30°12'N	33°42'E
Yuan, r., China (yůän)	205	28°50'N	110°50'E
Yuan'an, China (yůän-än)	209	31°08'N	111°28'E
Yuanling, China (yůän-lĭŋ)	209	28°30'N	110°18'E
Yuanshi, China (yůän-shr)	208	37°45'N	114°32'E
Yuasa, Japan	211	34°02'N	135°10'E
Yuba City, Ca., U.S. (yōō'bȧ)	118	39°08'N	121°38'W
Yucaipa, Ca., U.S. (yū-kȧ-ē'pȧ)	117a	34°02'N	117°02'W
Yucatán, state, Mex. (yōō-kä-tän')	128	20°45'N	89°00'W
Yucatan Channel, strt., N.A.	128	22°30'N	87°00'W
Yucatan Peninsula, pen., N.A.	132	19°30'N	89°00'W
Yucheng, China (yōō-chŭŋ)	206	34°31'N	115°54'E
Yucheng, China	208	36°55'N	116°39'E
Yuci, China (yōō-tsz)	208	37°32'N	112°40'E
Yudoma, r., Russia (yōō-dō'mȧ)	185	59°13'N	137°00'E
Yueqing, China (yûĕ-chyĭn)	209	28°02'N	120°40'E
Yueyang, China (yůĕ-yäŋ)	205	29°25'N	113°05'E
Yuezhuang, China (yůĕ-jůäŋ)	206	36°13'N	118°17'E
Yug, r., Russia (yòg)	180	59°50'N	45°55'E
Yugoslavia, *see* Serbia and Montenegro, nation, Eur. (yōō-gô-slä-vĭ-ȧ)	154	44°00'N	21°00'E
Yukhnov, Russia (yòk'nof)	176	54°44'N	35°15'E
Yukon, ter., Can. (yōō'kŏn)	90	63°16'N	135°30'W
Yukon, r., N.A.	106a	64°00'N	159°30'W
Yukutat Bay, b., Ak., U.S. (yōō-kū tăt')	103	59°34'N	140°50'W
Yuldybayevo, Russia (yòld'bä'yĕ-vô)	186a	52°20'N	57°52'E
Yulin, China (yōō-lĭn)	209	22°38'N	110°10'E
Yulin, China	204	38°18'N	109°45'E
Yuma, Az., U.S. (yōō'mä)	104	32°40'N	114°40'W
Yuma, Co., U.S.	120	40°08'N	102°50'W
Yuma, r., Dom. Rep.	135	19°05'N	70°05'W
Yumbi, D.R.C.	237	1°14'S	26°14'E
Yumen, China (yōō-mŭn)	204	40°14'N	96°56'E
Yuncheng, China (yòn-chŭŋ)	208	35°00'N	110°40'E
Yunnan, prov., China (yun'nän')	204	24°23'N	101°03'E
Yunnan Plat, plat., China (yò-nän)	204	26°03'N	101°26'E
Yunxian, China (yòn shyĕn)	205	32°50'N	110°55'E
Yunxiao, China (yòn-shyou)	209	24°00'N	117°20'E
Yura, Japan (yōō'rä)	211	34°18'N	134°54'E
Yurécuaro, Mex. (yōō-rā'kwä-rô)	130	20°21'N	102°16'W
Yurimaguas, Peru (yōō-rê-mä'gwäs)	142	5°59'S	76°12'W
Yuriria, Mex. (yōō'rê-rē'ä)	130	20°11'N	101°08'W
Yurovo, Russia	186b	55°30'N	38°24'E
Yur'yevets, Russia	180	57°15'N	43°08'E
Yuscarán, Hond. (yōōs-kä-rän')	132	13°57'N	86°48'W
Yushan, China (yōō-shän)	209	28°42'N	118°20'E
Yü Shan, mtn., Tai.	205	23°38'N	121°05'E
Yushu, China (yōō-shōō)	208	44°58'N	126°32'E
Yutian, China (yōō-tĭĕn)	208	39°54'N	117°45'E
Yutian, China (yōō-tĭĕn) (kū-r-yä)	204	36°55'N	81°39'E
Yuty, Para. (yōō-tē')	144	26°45'S	56°13'W
Yuwangcheng, China (yü'wäng'chĕng)	206	31°32'N	114°26'E
Yuxian, China (yōō shyĕn)	208	39°40'N	114°38'E
Yuzha, Russia (yōō'zhȧ)	180	56°38'N	42°20'E
Yuzhno-Sakhalinsk, Russia (yōōzh'nô-sä-кä-lĭnsk')	179	47°11'N	143°04'E
Yuzhnoural'skiy, Russia (yōōzh-nô-ò-rál'skĭ)	186a	54°26'N	61°17'E
Yuzhnyy Ural, mts., Russia (yōō'zhnĭ ò-räl')	186a	52°51'N	57°48'E
Yverdon, Switz. (ê-vĕr-dôn)	168	46°46'N	6°35'E
Yvetot, Fr. (ēv-tō')	170	49°39'N	0°45'E

Z

PLACE (Pronunciation)	PAGE	LAT.	LONG.
Za, r., Mor.	162	34°19'N	2°23'W
Zaachila, Mex. (sä-ä-chē'lȧ)	131	16°56'N	96°45'W
Zaandam, Neth. (zän'dàm)	165	52°25'N	4°49'E
Ząbkowice Śląskie, Pol.	168	50°35'N	16°48'E
Zabrze, Pol. (zäb'zhĕ)	161	50°18'N	18°48'E
Zacapa, Guat. (sä-kä'pä)	132	14°56'N	89°30'W
Zacapoaxtla, Mex. (sä-kä-pō-äs'tlä)	131	19°51'N	97°34'W
Zacatecas, Mex. (sä-kä-tā'käs)	128	22°44'N	102°32'W
Zacatecas, state, Mex.	128	24°00'N	102°45'W
Zacatecoluca, El Sal. (sä-kä-tå-kô-lōō'kä)	132	13°31'N	88°50'W
Zacatelco, Mex.	130	19°12'N	98°12'W
Zacatepec, Mex. (sä-kä-tå-pĕk') (sän-tê-ä'gô)	131	17°10'N	95°53'W
Zacatlán, Mex. (sä-kä-tlän')	131	19°55'N	97°57'W
Zacoalco de Torres, Mex. (sä-kô-äl'kō dā tōr'rĕs)	130	20°12'N	103°33'W
Zacualpan, Mex. (sä-kô-äl-pän')	130	18°43'N	99°46'W
Zacualtipan, Mex. (sȧ-kô-äl-tē-pän')	130	20°38'N	98°39'W
Zadar, Cro. (zä'där)	154	44°08'N	15°16'E
Zadonsk, Russia (zä-dônsk')	176	52°22'N	38°55'E
Žagare, Lat. (zhȧgärĕ)	167	56°21'N	23°14'E
Zagarolo, Italy (tzä-gä-rō'lō)	173d	41°51'N	12°53'E
Zaghouan, Tun. (zȧ-gwän')	230	36°30'N	10°04'E
Zagreb, Cro. (zä'grĕb)	154	45°50'N	15°50'E
Zagros Mountains, mts., Iran	198	33°30'N	46°30'E
Zāhedān, Iran (zä'hȧ-dän)	198	29°37'N	60°31'E
Zahlah, Leb. (zä'lä')	197a	33°50'N	35°54'E
Zaire *see* Congo, Democratic Republic of the, nation, Afr.	232	1°00'S	22°15'E
Zaječar, Serb. (zä'yĕ-chär')	175	43°54'N	22°16'E
Zakhidnyi Buh (Bug), r., Eur.	168	52°29'N	21°20'E
Zakopane, Pol. (zȧ-kô-pä'nĕ)	169	49°18'N	19°57'E
Zakouma, Parc National de, rec., Chad	235	10°50'N	19°20'E
Zákynthos, Grc.	175	37°48'N	20°55'E
Zákynthos, i., Grc.	163	37°45'N	20°32'E
Zalaegerszeg, Hung. (zŏ'lô-ĕ'gĕr-sĕg)	168	46°50'N	16°50'E
Zalău, Rom. (zȧ-lŭ'ò)	169	47°11'N	23°06'E
Zaltan, Libya	231	28°20'N	19°40'E
Zaltbommel, Neth.	159a	51°48'N	5°15'E
Zambezi, r., Afr. (zȧm-bā'zê)	232	16°00'S	29°45'E
Zambia, nation, Afr. (zăm'bê-ȧ)	232	14°23'S	24°15'E
Zamboanga, Phil. (säm-bô-aŋ'gä)	212	6°58'N	122°02'E
Zambrów, Pol. (zäm'bròf)	169	52°29'N	22°17'E
Zamora, Mex. (sä-mō'rä)	128	19°59'N	102°16'W
Zamora, Spain (thä-mō'rä)	162	41°32'N	5°43'W
Zanatepec, Mex.	131	16°30'N	94°22'W
Zandvoort, Neth.	159a	52°22'N	4°30'E
Zanesville, Oh., U.S. (zānz'vĭl)	108	39°55'N	82°00'W
Zangasso, Mali	234	12°09'N	5°37'W
Zanjān, Iran	198	36°26'N	48°24'E
Zanzibar, Tan. (zăn'zĭ-bär)	233	6°10'S	39°11'E
Zanzibar, i., Tan.	233	6°20'S	39°37'E
Zanzibar Channel, strt., Tan.	237	6°05'S	39°00'E
Zaozhuang, China (dzou-jůäŋ)	206	34°51'N	117°34'E
Zapadnaya Dvina *see* Western Dvina, r., Eur.	167	55°30'N	28°27'E
Zapala, Arg. (zä-pä'lä)	144	38°53'S	70°02'W
Zapata, Tx., U.S. (sä-pä'tä)	122	26°52'N	99°18'W
Zapata, Ciénaga de, sw., Cuba (syĕ'nä-gä-dĕ-zä-pȧ'tä)	134	22°30'N	81°20'W
Zapata, Península de, pen., Cuba (pĕ-nĕ'n-sōō-lä-dĕ-zä-pȧ'tä)	134	22°20'N	81°30'W
Zapatera, Isla, i., Nic. (ê's-lä-sä-pä-tā'rō)	132	11°45'N	85°45'W
Zapopan, Mex. (sä-pō'pän)	130	20°42'N	103°23'W
Zaporizhzhia, Ukr.	178	47°50'N	35°10'E
Zaporizhzhia, prov., Ukr.	177	47°20'N	35°05'E
Zaporoshskoye, Russia (zȧ-pô-rôsh'skô-yĕ)	167	60°36'N	30°31'E
Zapotiltic, Mex. (sä-pô-tĕl-tēk')	130	19°37'N	103°25'W
Zapotitlán, Mex. (sä-pô-tê-tlän')	130	17°13'N	98°58'W
Zapotitlán, Punta, c., Mex.	131	18°34'N	94°48'W
Zapotlanejo, Mex. (sä-pô-tlä-nā'hô)	130	20°38'N	103°05'W
Zaragoza, Mex. (sä-rä-gō'sä)	130	23°59'N	99°45'W
Zaragoza, Mex.	130	22°02'N	100°45'W
Zaragoza, Spain (thä-rä-gō'thä)	154	41°39'N	0°53'W
Zarand, Munții, mts., Rom.	169	46°07'N	22°21'E
Zaranda Hill, mtn., Nig.	235	10°15'N	9°35'E
Zaranj, Afg.	201	31°06'N	61°53'E
Zarasai, Lith. (zä-rä-sī')	167	55°45'N	26°18'E
Zárate, Arg. (zä-rä'tā)	144	34°05'S	59°05'W
Zaraysk, Russia (zä-rä'ēsk)	180	54°46'N	38°53'E
Zaria, Nig. (zä'rê-ä)	230	11°07'N	7°44'E
Zarqā', r., Jord.	197a	32°13'N	35°43'E
Zarzal, Col. (zär-zá'l)	142a	4°23'N	76°04'W
Zashiversk, Russia (zá'shĭ-vĕrsk')	179	67°08'N	144°02'E
Zastavna, Ukr. (zȧs-täf'nȧ)	169	48°32'N	25°50'E
Zastron, S. Afr. (zȧs'trŭn)	233c	30°19'S	27°07'E
Žatec, Czech Rep. (zhä'tĕts)	168	50°19'N	13°32'E
Zavitinsk, Russia	185	50°12'N	129°44'E
Zawiercie, Pol. (zȧ-vyĕr'tsyĕ)	169	50°28'N	19°25'E
Zāwiyat al-Baydā', Libya	231	32°49'N	21°46'E
Zāyandeh, r., Iran	198	32°15'N	51°00'E
Zaysan, Kaz. (zī'sȧn)	183	47°43'N	84°44'E
Zaza, r., Cuba (zá'zá)	134	21°40'N	79°25'W
Zbarazh, Ukr. (zbä-räzh')	169	49°39'N	25°48'E
Zbruch, r., Ukr. (zbròch)	169	48°56'N	26°18'E
Zdolbuniv, Ukr.	169	50°31'N	26°17'E
Zduńska Wola, Pol. (zdōōn''skä vō'lä)	169	51°36'N	18°27'E
Zebediela, S. Afr.	238c	24°19'S	29°21'E
Zeeland, Mi., U.S. (zē'lȧnd)	108	42°50'N	86°00'W
Ẕefat, Isr.	197a	32°58'N	35°30'E
Zehdenick, Ger. (tsā'dĕ-nĕk)	168	52°59'N	13°20'E
Zehlendorf, Ger. (tsā'lĕn-dôrf)	159b	52°47'N	13°23'E
Zeist, Neth.	159a	52°05'N	5°14'E
Zelenogorsk, Russia (zĕ-lä'nô-gôrsk)	167	60°13'N	29°39'E
Zella-Mehlis, Ger. (tsâl'á-mā'lĕs)	168	50°40'N	10°38'E
Zémio, C.A.R. (za-myō')	231	5°03'N	25°11'E
Zemlya Frantsa-Iosifa (Franz Josef Land), is., Russia	178	81°32'N	40°00'E
Zempoala, Punta, c., Mex. (pōō'n-tä-sĕm-pô-ä'lä)	131	19°30'N	96°18'W
Zempoatlépetl, mtn., Mex. (sĕm-pô-ä-tlā'pĕt'l)	131	17°13'N	95°59'W
Zemun, Serb. (zĕ'mōōn) (sĕm'lĭn)	163	44°50'N	20°25'E
Zengcheng, China (dzŭŋ-chŭŋ)	207a	23°18'N	113°49'E
Zenica, Bos. (zĕ'nēt-sä)	175	44°10'N	17°54'E
Zeni-Su, is., Japan (zĕ'nē sōō)	211	33°55'N	138°55'E
Žepče, Bos. (zhĕp'chĕ)	177	44°26'N	18°01'E
Zepernick, Ger. (tsĕ'pĕr-nĕk)	159b	52°39'N	13°32'E
Zerbst, Ger. (tsĕrbst)	168	51°58'N	12°03'E
Zerpenschleuse, Ger. (tsĕr'pĕn-shloi-zĕ)	159b	52°51'N	13°30'E
Zeuthen, Ger. (tsoi'tĕn)	159b	52°21'N	13°38'E
Zevenaar, Neth.	171c	51°56'N	6°06'E
Zevenbergen, Neth.	159a	51°38'N	4°36'E
Zeya, Russia (zâ'yȧ)	179	53°43'N	127°29'E

ng-sing; ŋ-baŋk; N-nasalized n; nŏd; cŏmmit; ōld; ôbey; ôrder; oi-boil; fōōd; ò-as oo in foot; ou-out; s-soft; sh-dish; th-thin; pūre; ûnite; ûrn; stŭd; circŭs; ü-as in French tu; '-indeterminate vowel.

ăt; fin*ă*l; rāte; senâte; ärm; ásk; sof*á*; fãre;   ch-choose;   dh-as th in other;   bē; ĕvent; bĕt; recĕnt; cratĕr;   g-gō; gh-guttural g;   bĭt; *ĭ*-short neutral; rīde;   к-guttural k as ch in German ich;

SUBJECT INDEX

Listed below are major topics covered by the thematic maps, graphs and/or statistics.
Page citations are for world, continent and country maps and for world tables.

SOURCES

The following sources have been consulted during the process of creating and updating the thematic maps and statistics for the 21st Edition.

Air Carrier Traffic at Canadian Airports, Statistics Canada
Annual Coal Report, U.S. Dept. of Energy, Energy Information Administration
Armed Conflicts Report, Project Ploughshares
Atlas of Canada, Natural Resources Canada
Canadian Minerals Yearbook, Statistics Canada
Census of Canada, Statistics Canada
Census of Population, U.S. Census Bureau
Chromium Industry Directory, International Chromium Development Association
Coal Fields of the Conterminous United States, U.S. Geological Survey
Coal Quality and Resources of the Former Soviet Union, U.S. Geological Survey
Coal-Bearing Regions and Structural Sedimentary Basins of China and Adjacent Seas, U.S. Geological Survey
Commercial Service Airports in the United States with Percent Boardings Change, Federal Aviation Administration (FAA)
Completed Peacekeeping Operations, Center for Defense Information
Conventional Arms Transfers to Developing Nations, Library of Congress, Congressional Research Service
Current Status of the World's Major Episodes of Political Violence: Hot Wars and Hot Spots, Center for Systemic Peace
Dependencies and Areas of Special Sovereignty, U.S. Dept. of State, Bureau of Intelligence and Research
Earth's Seasons - Equinoxes, Solstices, Perihelion, and Aphelion, U.S. Naval Observatory
EarthTrends: The Environmental Information Portal, World Resources Institute and World Conservation Monitoring Centre 2003. Available at http://earthtrends.wri.org. Washington, D.C.: World Resources Institute
Economic Census, U.S. Census Bureau
Employment, Hours, and Earnings from the Current Employment Statistics Survey, U.S. Dept. of Labor, Bureau of Labor Statistics
Energy Statistics Yearbook, United Nations Dept. of Economic and Social Affairs
Epidemiological Fact Sheets by Country, Joint United Nations Program on HIV/AIDS (UNAIDS), World Health Organization, United Nations Children's Fund (UNICEF)
Estimated Water Use in the United States, U.S. Geological Survey
Estimates of Health Personnel, World Health Organization
FAO Food Balance Sheet, Food and Agriculture Organization of the United Nations (FAO)
FAO Statistical Databases (FAOSTAT), Food and Agriculture Organization of the United Nations (FAO)
Fishstat Plus, Food and Agriculture Organization of the United Nations (FAO)
Geothermal Resources Council Bulletin, Geothermal Resources Bulletin
Geothermal Resources in China, Bob Lawrence and Associates, Inc.
Global Alcohol Database, World Health Organization
Global Forest Resources Assessment, Food and Agriculture Organization of the United Nations (FAO), Forest Resources Assessment Programme
Great Lakes Factsheet Number 1, U.S. Environmental Protection Agency
The Hop Atlas, Joh. Barth & Sohn GmbH & Co. KG
Human Development Report 2003, United Nations Development Programme, © 2003 by United Nations Development Programme. Used by permission of Oxford University Press, Inc.
Installed Generating Capacity, International Geothermal Association
International Database, U.S. Census Bureau
International Energy Annual, U.S. Dept. of Energy, Energy Information Administration
International Journal on Hydropower and Dams , International Commission on Large Dams
International Petroleum Encyclopedia, PennWell Publishing Co.
International Sugar and Sweetener Report, F.O. Licht, Licht Interactive Data
International Trade Statistics, World Trade Organization
International Water Power and Dam Construction Yearbook, Wilmington Publishing
Iron and Steel Statistics, U.S. Geological Survey, Thomas D. Kelly and Michael D. Fenton
Lakes at a Glance, LakeNet
Land Scan Global Population Database, U.S. Dept. of Energy, Oak Ridge National Laboratory (© 2003 UT-Battelle, LLC. All rights reserved. Notice: These data were produced by UT-Battelle, LLC under Contract No. DE-AC05-00OR22725 with the Department of Energy. The Government has certain rights in this data. Neither UT-Battelle, LLC nor the United States Department of Energy, nor any of their employees, makes any warranty, express or implied, or assumes any legal liability or responsibility for the accuracy, completeness, or usefulness of any data, apparatus, product, or process disclosed, or represents that its use would not infringe privately owned rights.)
Largest Rivers in the United States, U.S. Geological Survey
Lengths of the Major Rivers, U.S. Geological Survey
Likely Nuclear Arsenals Under the Strategic Offensive Reductions Treaty, Center for Defense Information
Major Episodes of Political Violence, Center for Systemic Peace
Maps of Nuclear Power Reactors, International Nuclear Safety Center
Mineral Commodity Summaries, U.S. Geological Survey, Bureau of Mines
Mineral Industry Surveys, U.S. Geological Survey, Bureau of Mines
Minerals Yearbook, U.S. Geological Survey, Bureau of Mines
National Priorities List, U.S. Environmental Protection Agency
National Tobacco Information Online System (NATIONS), U.S. Dept. of Health and Human Services, Centers for Disease Control and Prevention (CDC)
Natural Gas Annual, U.S. Dept. of Energy, Energy Information Administration
New and Recent Conflicts of the World, The History Guy
Nuclear Power Reactors in the World, International Atomic Energy Agency
Oil and Gas Journal DataBook, PennWell Publishing Co.
Oil and Gas Resources of the World, Oilfield Publications, Ltd.
Petroleum Supply Annual, U.S. Dept. of Energy, Energy Information Administration
Population of Capital Cities and Cities of 100,000 and More Inhabitants, United Nations Dept. of Economic and Social Affairs
Preliminary Estimate of the Mineral Production of Canada, Natural Resources Canada
Red List of Threatened Species, International Union for Conservation and Natural Resources
Significant Earthquakes of the World, U.S. Geological Survey
State of Food Insecurity in the World, Food and Agriculture Organization of the United Nations (FAO)
State of the World's Children, United Nations Children's Fund (UNICEF)
Statistical Abstract of the United States, U.S. Census Bureau
Statistics on Asylum-Seekers, Refugees and Others of Concern to UNHCR, United Nations High Commissioner for Refugees (UNHCR)
Survey of Energy Resources, World Energy Council
Tables of Nuclear Weapons Stockpiles, Natural Resources Defense Council
TeleGeography Research, PriMetrica, Inc. (www.primetrica.com)
Tobacco Atlas, World Health Organization
Tobacco Control Country Profiles, World Health Organization
Transportation in Canada, Minister of Public Works and Government Services, Transport Canada
UNESCO Statistical Tables, United Nations Educational, Scientific and Cultural Organization (UNESCO)
United Nations Commodity Trade Statistics (COMTRADE), United Nations Dept. of Economic and Social Affairs
United Nations Peacekeeping in the Service of Peace, United Nations Dept. of Peacekeeping Operations
United Nations Peacekeeping Operations, United Nations Dept. of Peacekeeping Operations
Uranium: Resources, Production and Demand, United Nations Organization for Economic Co-operation and Development (OECD)
Volcanoes of the World, Smithsonian National Museum of Natural History
Water Account for Australia, Australian Bureau of Statistics
Women in National Parliaments, Inter-Parliamentary Union
Women's Suffrage, Inter-Parliamentary Union
The World at War, Center for Defense Information, The Defense Monitor
The World at War, Federation of American Scientists, Military Analysis Network
World Conflict List, National Defense Council Foundation
World Contraceptive Use, United Nations Dept. of Economic and Social Affairs
The World Factbook, U.S. Dept. of State, Central Intelligence Agency (CIA)
World Facts and Maps, Rand McNally
World Lakes Database, International Lake Environment Committee
World Population Prospects, United Nations Dept. of Economic and Social Affairs
World Urbanization Prospects, United Nations Dept. of Economic and Social Affairs
World Water Resources and Their Use, State Hydrological Institute of Russia/UNESCO
The World's Nuclear Arsenal, Center for Defense Information

Special Acknowledgements
The American Geographical Society, for permission to use the Miller cylindrical projection.
The Association of American Geographers, for permission to use R. Murphy's landforms map.
The McGraw-Hill Book Company, for permission to use G. Trewartha's climatic regions map.
The University of Chicago Press, for permission to use Goode's Homolosine equal-area projection.